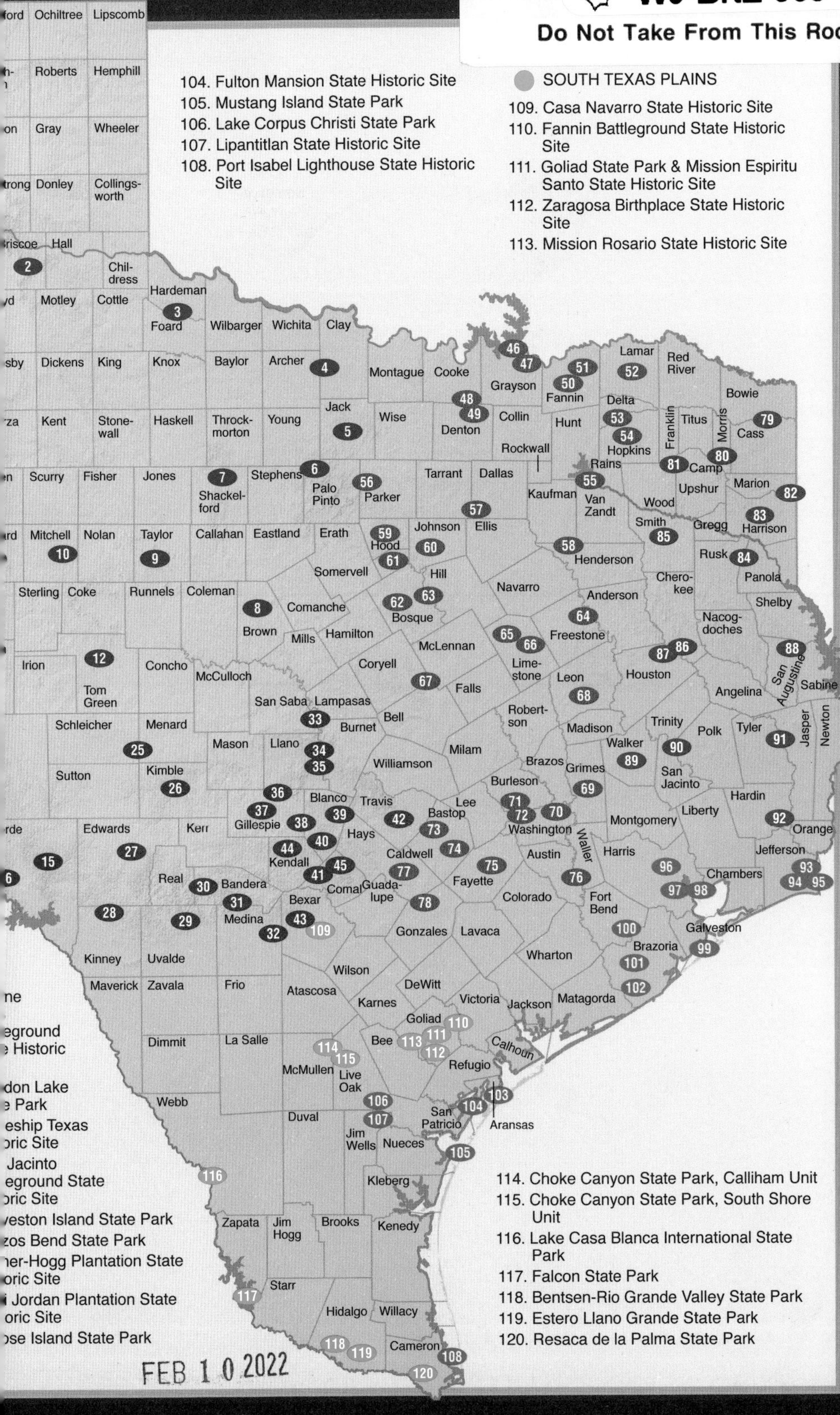

104. Fulton Mansion State Historic Site
105. Mustang Island State Park
106. Lake Corpus Christi State Park
107. Lipantitlan State Historic Site
108. Port Isabel Lighthouse State Historic Site

SOUTH TEXAS PLAINS

109. Casa Navarro State Historic Site
110. Fannin Battleground State Historic Site
111. Goliad State Park & Mission Espiritu Santo State Historic Site
112. Zaragosa Birthplace State Historic Site
113. Mission Rosario State Historic Site

ne
eground
Historic
don Lake
Park
eship Texas
oric Site
Jacinto
eground State
oric Site
veston Island State Park
zos Bend State Park
ner-Hogg Plantation State
oric Site
Jordan Plantation State
oric Site
ose Island State Park

114. Choke Canyon State Park, Calliham Unit
115. Choke Canyon State Park, South Shore Unit
116. Lake Casa Blanca International State Park
117. Falcon State Park
118. Bentsen-Rio Grande Valley State Park
119. Estero Llano Grande State Park
120. Resaca de la Palma State Park

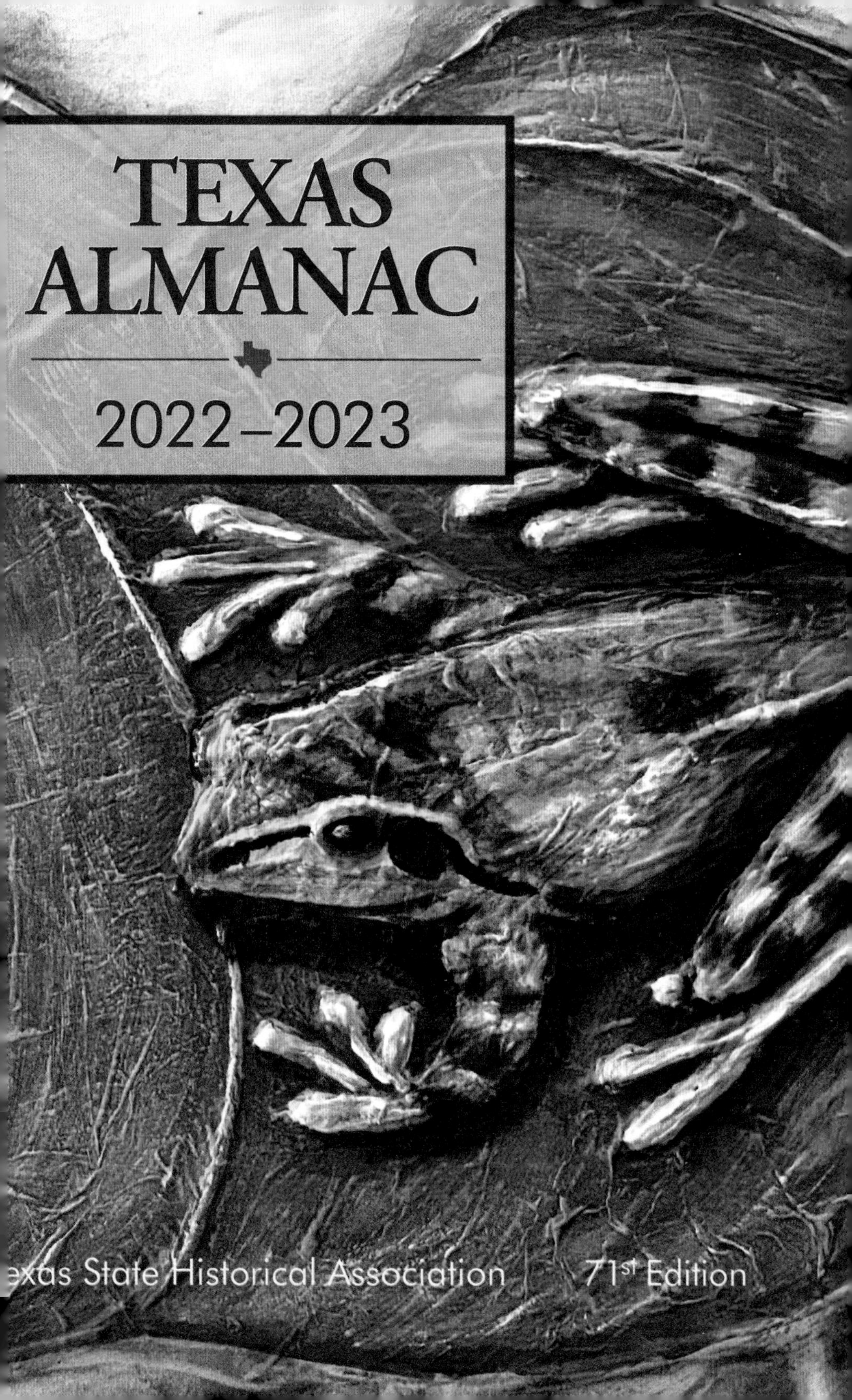

TEXAS ALMANAC

2022–2023

exas State Historical Association

71st Edition

TEXAS ALMANAC
2022–2023

MANAGING EDITOR
Rosie Hatch

ASSOCIATE EDITOR
Rachel Kaelin

ASSISTANT EDITOR
John Willis

COVER DESIGN
Joel Phillips

PAINTING ON COVER
Michele Newton

ISBN (hardcover) 978-1-62511-066-4
ISBN (flexbound) 978-1-62511-067-1
ISBN (ebook) 978-1-62511-068-8

Library of Congress ISSN: 2378-2188 (Print)
Library of Congress ISSN: 2378-2234 (Digital)

TEXAS STATE HISTORICAL ASSOCIATION

The University of Texas at Austin
3001 Lake Austin Blvd., Suite 3.116, Austin, TX 78703; (512) 471-2600
TSHAonline.org and LegacyofTexas.com

Printed in Dallas, Texas, by Taylor Specialty Books
Bound in San Antonio by Universal Bindery
For permission requests, contact **Rosie.Hatch@TSHAonline.org**.

Distributed by Texas A&M University Press and the Texas Book Consortium
4354 TAMU, College Station, Texas, 77843-4354

Order hardcover or flexbound editions at **(800) 826-8911**
or online at www.tamupress.com

TexasAlmanac.com

PREFACE

Welcome to the *Texas Almanac 2022–2023*. I hope the past two years have treated you kindly.

We've got three terrific new features this year. You'll find the first one, "Texas Wildlife," on page 75. Dr. Travis LaDuc and Dr. Drew Davis expand on our usual list of mammals with descriptions and lists of many of the fishes, reptiles, amphibians, and birds you'll see in Texas. The second feature is "African American Texans" by Dr. Merline Pitre on page 536. It covers the long history of Black Texans and their many contributions to our culture.

Our last feature was a late addition to the book, but one we couldn't ignore. "COVID-19 Pandemic in Texas 2020–2021" by Dr. Ana Martinez-Catsum will give you the details of how the virus hit our state and the impact it had on our economy, society, and politics. There's also a table that compares our current pandemic to the last one: the Spanish influenza that hit the world hard in 1918. Read all about it, starting on page 563.

Thanks as always to everyone at the TSHA, the board of directors, our members, and my amazing team: Rachel Kaelin and John Willis.

I hope you enjoy the book!

Rosie Hatch

Managing Editor, Texas Almanac

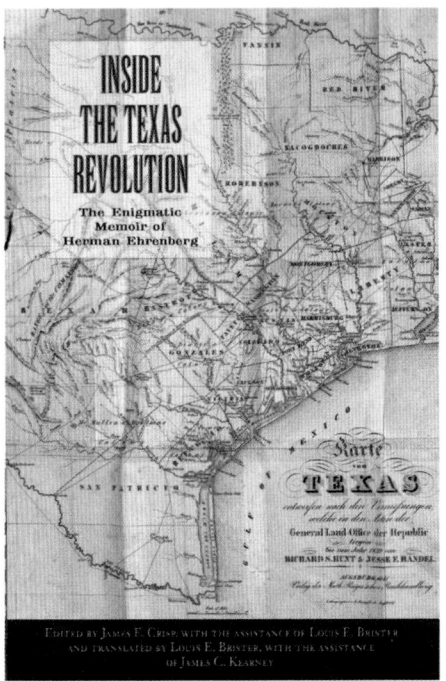

Patrick Cox

Published by the Texas State Historical Association (TSHA), the *Texas Almanac* is a wealth of information on the state's people, culture, history, landmarks, government, business, science, education, and much more. Since 1857, the *Texas Almanac* has served as an invaluable, engaging, and popular publication. A full history of the *Texas Almanac* and many early editions can be found in the *Handbook of Texas Online*; www.tshaonline.org.

TSHA focuses our efforts on two important areas: historical publications and education programs. TSHA is the oldest learned society in our state. Organized in Austin on March 2, 1897, the founders of TSHA brought lay and professional historians together to document and celebrate our state's multifaceted history.

Today, TSHA follows the path laid out by its founders, sharing our rich Texas history with stories of events and people from all walks of life. People and organizations across the state, nation, and globe rely on TSHA for accurate and substantive information. The *Texas Almanac*, the *Southwestern Historical Quarterly*, the *Handbook of Texas* and all TSHA's publications follow the tenets, methods and practices advocated by the professional historical community.

Importantly, we are involved with educators and students throughout the state who are enthusiastically engaged in these initiatives: Texas History Day, Texas History Challenge, Teaching Texas, Junior Historians of Texas, and the Walter Prescott Webb Historical Society.

I have many vintage volumes of the *Texas Almanac* in my personal library. Combined with the modern editions, this historic publication provides a wealth of information about Texas and how we have evolved over the years. On behalf of the TSHA members and staff, we invite everyone to know more about this special place we call Texas.

We proudly present the latest edition of the *Texas Almanac 2022-2023.*

Patrick Cox, Ph.D.
Texas State Historical Association President, 2021–2022

TSHA

Texas State Historical Association

An Independent Nonprofit Since 1897

Organized in Austin on March 2, 1897, the Texas State Historical Association is the oldest learned society in the state. Its mission is to "foster the appreciation, understanding, and teaching of the rich and unique history of Texas and, by example and through programs and activities, encourage and promote research, preservation, and publication of historical material affecting the state of Texas." The association's publications include the *Southwestern Historical Quarterly*, more than 150 scholarly books, the *Texas Almanac*, and the well-known *Handbook of Texas Online*. The online Handbook, the nation's preeminent state history encyclopedia, attracts 400,000 visitors per month from more than 200 countries and territories around the world. Through its varied education programs, the Association directly serves more than 50,000 elementary through college-aged students each year, while indirectly reaching an additional 86,000 through its teacher training opportunities.

GREG ABBOTT
Governor of Texas

Greetings,

As the 48th Governor of the great state of Texas, it is my honor to welcome you to the 2022-2023 edition of the *Texas Almanac*, the premier reference for everything Texas.

Texas is the Lone Star State for a reason: We stand apart as a model for the nation. Jobs are growing here, businesses are growing here, and families are growing here. In fact, Texas is growing faster than the nation, and more than eight in 10 who are born here stay here.

Now the 9th-largest economy when compared to the nations of the world, the Texas of today was built on the bold ideas of those who came before us. Men and women who dared to explore the vast new frontier pulled themselves up by their own bootstraps and made a living from the bounty of the land. They innovated, invested, and persevered. And they built an even bigger Texas of tomorrow for the generations yet to come.

I invite you to explore the pages that follow to learn more about the rich and storied history of the Lone Star State and its people, government, economics, natural resources, holidays, diverse cultures, education, recreation, the arts and so much more. Texas is big, and each of our 254 counties has something unique to offer – as do the featured articles in this edition.

If you're not in Texas right now, we invite you to come visit for a while. We're making history every day.

First Lady Cecilia Abbott joins me in thanking the Texas State Historical Association for their dedication to sharing the history and blessings of Texas and for producing this invaluable Almanac preserving the past and present for the future of this great state.

Greg Abbott
Governor of Texas

DAN PATRICK
Lt. Governor of Texas

People from all over the world envy Texas; our natural beauty, bustling economy, vibrant culture and rich history are second to none.

The Texas story is one of liberty, perseverance and determination to succeed, and our independence was bought with the blood of our forefathers. Texas history is filled with stories of settlers, immigrants, native peoples, freedmen, outlaws and carpetbaggers, forging their own way forward. Each Texan has contributed to building a better Texas for all of posterity.

Our commitment to God-given freedoms, liberty and the right to self-determination has presented generations of Texans the opportunity to prosper.

The *Texas Almanac* remains a premier resource to learn about Texas' beautiful history and culture that make our state the light of the United States and the world. Please join me in honoring it as you learn about the greatest state that God ever made: Texas.

Dan Patrick
Lt. Governor of Texas

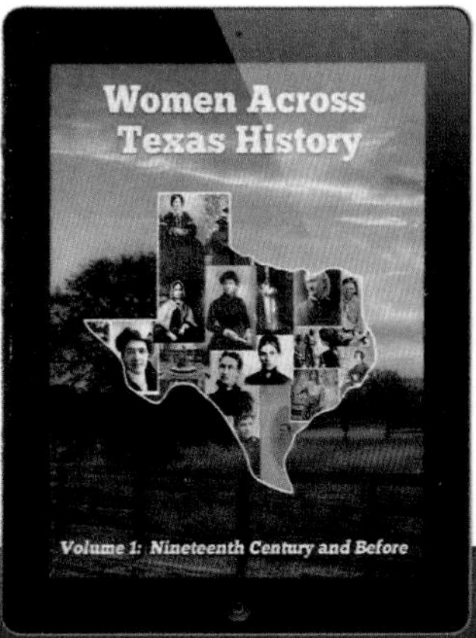
Women Across
Texas History
Volume 1: Nineteenth Century and Before

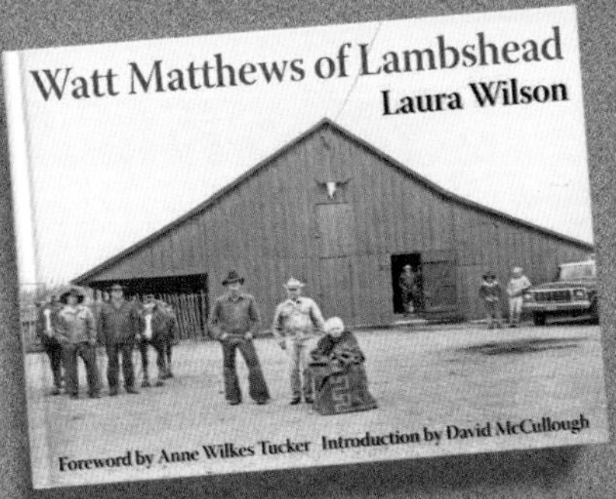
Watt Matthews of Lambshead
Laura Wilson
Foreword by Anne Wilkes Tucker Introduction by David McCullough

THE HOGGS OF TEXAS
SAN ANTONIO
A Tricentennial History
Char Miller
CHRONICLES of the BIG BEND

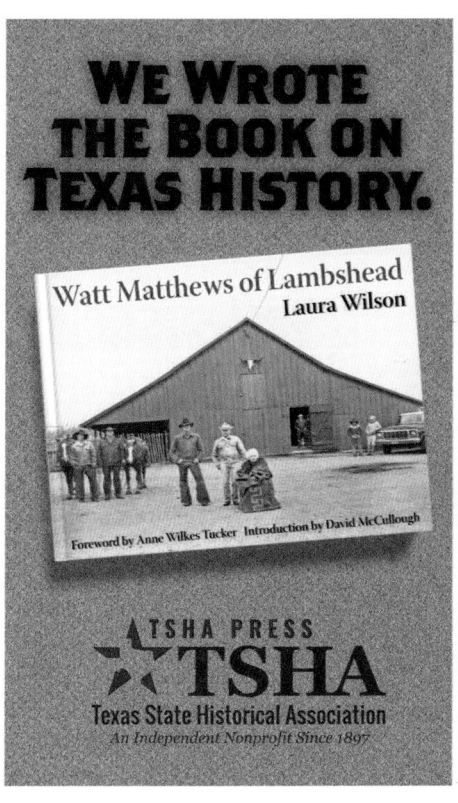

EPIC
A Wild and Vivid Land
Julian Onderdonk in New York

TABLE OF CONTENTS

INDEX OF TABLES

STATE PROFILE

ENVIRONMENT

WEATHER

CALENDAR

RECREATION

SPORTS

COUNTIES

POPULATION

ELECTIONS

GOVERNMENT

LAW ENFORCEMENT

CULTURE & THE ARTS

HEALTH & SCIENCE

EDUCATION

BUSINESS

TRANSPORTATION

AGRICULTURE

A common slider taking in some sun. Photo by Shiva Shenoy, CC by 2.0/Flickr

INDEX OF MAPS

ENVIRONMENT

WEATHER

CALENDAR

RECREATION

COUNTIES

POPULATION

ELECTIONS

GOVERNMENT

RELIGION

BUSINESS

Transportation

TEXAS

The Lone Star State

This section offers a demographic and geographic profile of the second-largest, second-most-populous state in the United States. Check the ***Table of Contents*** and the ***Index*** for more-detailed information about each subject.

GOVERNMENT

Capital: Austin
Government: Bicameral Legislature
28th State to enter the Union: Dec. 29, 1845
Present Constitution adopted: 1876
State Senators: 31
State Representatives: 150
Legislative sessions are held for a maximum of 140 days, every 2 years

State motto: Friendship (1930)
Origin of name: Texas, or Tejas, was the Spanish pronunciation of a Caddo Indian word meaning "friends" or "allies."

BUSINESS

Per Capita Personal Income (2019)	$52,813
Per Capita Consumption (2019)	$40,552
Top spending categories:	
Housing and utilities	$6,885
Health care	$6,279
Non-Farm Employment (2020)	12,087,300
Employment by industry:	
Trade, transportation, utilities	2,418,300
Government	1,887,400
Goods producing	1,808,300
Professional and business services	1,730,200
Education and health services	1,667,200
Leisure and hospitality	1,168,800
Manufacturing	873,400
Construction	743,600

(Per capita income/consumption: U.S. Bureau of Economic Analysis. Employment: Texas Workforce Commission.)

POPULATION

Population, 2019	**28,995,881**
Population, 2010 U.S. Census	25,145,561
Population increase, 2010–2019	15.3%
Population, 2000 U.S. Census	20,851,820
Population increase, 2000–2019	39.1%

Ethnicity, 2019

Group	Percent
White, NH	41.5%
Hispanic	39.5%
Black	11.9%
Asian	4.9%
Other	2.2%

Ten Largest Cities

Houston (Harris Co.)	2,325,489
San Antonio (Bexar Co.)	1,555,370
Dallas (Dallas Co.)	1,358,328
Austin (Travis Co.)	993,129
Fort Worth (Tarrant Co.)	899,597
El Paso (El Paso Co.)	687,690
Arlington (Tarrant Co.)	391,443
Corpus Christi (Nueces Co.)	328,390
Plano (Collin Co.)	291,791
Laredo (Webb Co.)	267,001

Number of counties	254
Largest by pop: Harris Co.	4,713,325
Smallest by pop: Loving Co.	169
Number of incorporated cities	**1,229**
Number of cities of 100,000 pop. or more	41
Number of cities of 50,000 pop. or more	68
Number of cities of 10,000 pop. or more	239

(Texas Demographic Center estimates for Jan. 1, 2019.)

NATURAL ENVIRONMENT

Area (total) . . . . 268,596 sq. miles
. . . . (171,901,440 acres)

Land Area . . . . 261,232 sq. miles
. . . . (167,188,480 acres)

Water Area . . . . 7,365 sq. miles
. . . .(4,713,600 acres)

Geographic Center:
About 15 miles northeast of Brady in northern McCulloch County.

Highest Point:
Guadalupe Peak (8,749 ft.) in Culberson County in far West Texas.

Lowest Point:
Gulf of Mexico (sea level).

Normal Average Annual Precipitation Range:
From 60.57 inches at Jasper County in far East Texas to 9.43 inches at El Paso, in far West Texas.

Record Highest Temperature:
Seymour, Baylor Co., ... Aug. 12, 1936, 120°F
Monahans, Ward Co.,. . . . . June 28, 1994, 120°F

Record Lowest Temperature:
Tulia, Swisher Co., ... Feb. 12, 1899, -23°F
Seminole, Gaines Co.,. . . . . Feb. 8, 1933, -23°F

PRINCIPAL PRODUCTS

Manufactures: Chemicals and allied products, petroleum and coal products, food and kindred products, transportation equipment.

Farm Products: Cattle, cotton, vegetables, fruits, nursery and greenhouse, dairy products.

Minerals: Petroleum, natural gas, and natural gas liquids.

Finance (as of 12/31/2018):
Number of banks. 409
Total deposits. $328,907,699,000
Number of savings & loan associations. 5
Total deposits. $73,570,292,000
Number of savings banks 24
Total deposits. $17,635,204,000

(Banks: Federal Reserve Bank of Dallas; savings and loans and savings banks: Texas Dept. of Savings and Mortgage Lending.)

Agriculture (2019):
Total cash receipts. $21.25 billion
Animals & products. . . . . $14.36 billion
All Crops . . . . $6.89 billion
Total exports . . . . $6.30 billion
Land in farms in acres, ...130.0 million

(U.S. Department of Agriculture, National Agricultural Statistics Service Farm Numbers.)

The Texas State Fair. Photo by Nicholas Henderson, CC by 2.0/Flickr

Texas' Rank Among the States

GDP by State, FYE 2020

	State	In Millions
1.	California	$3,091,871.5
2.	**Texas**	**$1,759,734.4**
3.	New York	$1,699,044.7
4.	Florida	$1,095,888.2
5.	Illinois	$863,516.7
6.	Pennsylvania	$780,176.1
7.	Ohio	$675,037.3
8.	Georgia	$619,240.0
9.	New Jersey	$619,061.1
10.	Washington	$618,704.9
		United States: $20,936,558.0

Number of Births, 2019

	State	Total
1.	California	446,479
2.	**Texas**	**377,599**
3.	New York	221,539
4.	Florida	220,002
5.	Illinois	140,128
6.	Ohio	134,461
7.	Pennsylvania	134,230
8.	Georgia	126,371
9.	North Carolina	118,725
10.	Michigan	107,886
		United States: 3,747,540

Crude Oil Production, April 2021

	State	1,000's of Barrels
1.	**Texas**	**4,741**
2.	New Mexico	1,222
3.	North Dakota	1,061
4.	Alaska	443
5.	Colorado	408
6.	Oklahoma	400
7.	California	362
8.	Wyoming	228
9.	Louisiana	97
10.	Utah	90

Energy Consumption, 2019

	State	Million BTU, per capita
1.	Wyoming	932
2.	Louisiana	922
3.	North Dakota	875
4.	Alaska	839
5.	Iowa	517
6.	**Texas**	**491**
7.	Nebraska	466
8.	West Virginia	461
9.	South Dakota	453
10.	Oklahoma	432

Agriculture, All Commodities, 2019

	State	Income
1.	California	$49,938,076
2.	Iowa	$27,487,829
3.	Nebraska	$21,436,242
4.	**Texas**	**$21,249,024**
5.	Minnesota	$16,632,782
6.	Illinois	$16,318,156
7.	Kansas	$16,301,222
8.	Wisconsin	$11,246,602
9.	North Carolina	$10,603,108
10.	Indiana	$10,587,053

Energy Production, 2019

	State	Percent of Total
1.	**Texas**	**23.1%**
2.	Pennsylvania	9.5%
3.	Wyoming	7.0%
4.	Oklahoma	5.2%
5.	West Virginia	5.1%
6.	North Dakota	4.6%
7.	New Mexico	4.3%
8.	Louisiana	3.9%
9.	Colorado	3.8%
10.	Ohio	3.6%

Sources for these tables are: the Bureau of Economic Analysis, U.S. Census Bureau, U.S. Dept. of Agriculture, and the U.S. Energy Information Administration.

FLAGS OF TEXAS

Texas is called the **Lone Star State** because of its state flag with a single star. The state flag was also the **flag of the Republic of Texas**.

The following information about historic Texas flags, the current flag, and other Texas symbols is from the **Texas State Library & Archives** in Austin. More information is at:

www.tsl.texas.gov/ref/abouttx/index.html#flags

Six Flags of Texas

Six different flags have flown over Texas during eight changes of sovereignty. The accepted sequence of these flags follows:

Spanish: 1519–1821

French: 1685–1690

Mexican: 1821–1836

Republic of Texas: 1836–1845

Confederate States of America: 1861–1865

United States: 1845 to the present.

Evolution of the Lone Star Flag

The Convention at Washington-on-the-Brazos in March 1836 allegedly adopted a flag for the Republic that was designed by **Lorenzo de Zavala.** The design of de Zavala's flag is unknown, but the convention journals state that a "Rainbow and star of five points above the western horizon; and a star of six points sinking below" was added to de Zavala's flag.

There was a suggestion the letters "T E X A S" be placed around the star in the flag, but there is no evidence that the Convention ever approved a final flag design. Probably because of the hasty dispersion of the Convention and the loss of part of the Convention notes, nothing further was done with the Convention's proposals for a national flag.

A **so-called "Zavala flag"** is sometimes flown in Texas today that consists of a blue field with a white five-pointed star in the center and the letters "T E X A S" between the star points, but there is no historical evidence to support this flag's design.

The **first official flag of the Republic,** known as the **National Standard of Texas** or **David G. Burnet's flag,** was adopted by the Texas Congress and approved by President Sam Houston on Dec. 10, 1836. The design "**shall be an azure ground with a large golden star central.**"

The Lone Star Flag

On Jan. 25, 1839, President Mirabeau B. Lamar approved the adoption by Congress of a new national flag. This flag consisted of "a blue perpendicular stripe of the width of one third of the whole length of the flag, with a white star of five points in the centre thereof, and two horizontal stripes of equal breadth, the upper stripe white, the lower red, of the length of two thirds of the length of the whole flag." This is the **Lone Star Flag,** which later became the state flag.

Although Senator William H. Wharton proposed the adoption of the Lone Star Flag in 1838, no one knows who actually designed the flag. The legislature in 1879 inadvertently repealed the law establishing the state flag, but the legislature adopted a new law in 1933 that legally re-established the flag's design.

The red, white, and blue of the state flag stand, respectively, for bravery, purity, and loyalty. The proper **finial** for use with the state flag is either **a star or a spearhead.** Texas is one of only two states that has a flag that formerly served as the flag of an independent nation. The other is Hawaii.

Displaying the State Flag

The Texas Flag Code was first adopted in 1933 and completely revised in 1993. Laws governing display of the state flag are found in sections 3100.002 through 3100.152 of the Texas Government Code: **www.tsl.state.tx.us/ref/abouttx/flagcode.html**.

Here is a summary of those rules:

★ The Texas flag should be **displayed on state and national holidays** and on special occasions of historical significance, and it should be displayed at every school on regular school days. **When flown out of doors,** the Texas flag should not be flown earlier than sunrise nor later than sunset unless properly illuminated. It should not be left out in inclement weather unless a weather-proof flag is used. It should be flown with the white stripe uppermost **except in case of distress.**

★ **No flag other than the United States flag should be placed above or, if on the same level,** to the state flag's right (observer's left). The state flag should be underneath the national flag when the two are flown from the same halyard. **When flown from adjacent flagpoles,** the national flag and the state flag should be of approximately the same size and on flagpoles of equal height; the national flag should be on the flag's own right (observer's left).

★ **If the state flag is displayed with the flag of another U.S. state, a nation other than the United States, or an international organization,** the state flag should be, from an observer's perspective, to the left of the other flag on a separate flagpole or flagstaff, and the state flag should not be above the other flag on the same flagpole or flagstaff or on a taller flagpole or flagstaff. If the state flag and the U.S. flag are **displayed from crossed flagstaffs,** the state flag should be, from an observer's perspective, to the right of the U.S. flag and the state flag's flagstaff should be behind the U.S. flag's flagstaff.

★ **When the flag is displayed horizontally,** the white stripe should be above the red stripe and, from an observer's perspective, to the right of the blue stripe. **When the flag is displayed vertically,** the blue stripe should be uppermost and the white stripe should be to the state flag's right (observer's left).

★ If the state and national flags are both **carried in a procession,** the national flag should be on the marching right and state flag should be on the national flag's left (observer's right).

★ **On Memorial Day,** the state flag should be displayed at half-staff until noon and then completely raised. **On Peace Officers Memorial Day** (May 15), the state flag should be displayed at half-staff all day, unless that day is also Armed Forces Day.

★ The state flag should not touch anything beneath it or be dipped to any person or thing except the U.S. flag. Advertising should not be fastened to a flagpole, flagstaff, or halyard on which the state flag is displayed.

★ If a state flag is no longer used or useful as an emblem for display, it should be destroyed, preferably by burning. A **flag retirement ceremony** is set out in the Texas Government Code mentioned earlier.

Honor the Texas flag;
I pledge allegiance
to thee, Texas,
one state under God,
one and indivisible.

Pledge to the Texas Flag

A pledge to the Texas flag was adopted in 1933 by the 43rd Legislature. It contained a phrase, "Flag of 1836," which inadvertently referred to the **David G. Burnet flag** instead of the Lone Star Flag adopted in 1839. In 2007, the 80th Legislature changed the pledge to its current form:

A person reciting the pledge to the state flag should face the flag, place the right hand over the heart, and remove any easily removable hat.

The pledge to the Texas flag may be recited at all public and private meetings at which the Pledge of Allegiance to the national flag is recited and at state historical events and celebrations.

The pledge to the Texas flag should be recited after the pledge of allegiance to the United States flag, if both are recited. ☆

TEXAS STATE SYMBOLS

Photo by nagaraju gajula/Pexels

State Song

The state song of Texas is "Texas, Our Texas." The music was written by the late William J. Marsh (who died Feb. 1, 1971, in Fort Worth at age 90), and the words by Marsh and Gladys Yoakum Wright, also of Fort Worth. It was the winner of a state song contest sponsored by the 41st Legislature and was adopted in 1929. The wording has been changed once: Shortly after Alaska became a state in January 1959, the word "Largest" in the third line was changed by Mr. Marsh to "Boldest." The text follows:

TEXAS, OUR TEXAS

Texas, our Texas! All hail the mighty State!
Texas, our Texas! So wonderful, so great!
Boldest and grandest, Withstanding ev'ry test;
O Empire wide and glorious, You stand supremely blest.

CHORUS

God bless you Texas!
And keep you brave and strong,
That you may grow in power and worth,
Thro'out the ages long.

REFRAIN

Texas, O Texas! Your freeborn single star,
Sends out its radiance to nations near and far.
Emblem of freedom! It sets our hearts aglow,
With thoughts of San Jacinto and glorious Alamo.
Texas, dear Texas! From tyrant grip now free,
Shines forth in splendor your star of destiny!
Mother of heroes! We come your children true,
Proclaiming our allegiance, our faith, our love for you.

State Motto

The state motto is "Friendship." The word Texas, or Tejas, was the Spanish pronunciation of a Caddo Indian word meaning "friends" or "allies." It was designated by the 41st Legislature in 1930.

State Citizenship Designation

The people of Texas usually call themselves Texans. However, Texian was generally used in the early period of the state's history.

State Seal

The design of the obverse (front) of the State Seal consists of "a star of five points encircled by olive and live oak branches, and the words, 'The State of Texas.' " (State Constitution, Art. IV, Sec. 19.) This design is a slight modification of the Great Seal of the Republic of Texas, adopted by the Congress of the Republic, Dec. 10, 1836, and readopted with modifications in 1839.

Front of Seal

An official design for the reverse (back) of the seal was adopted by the 57th Legislature in 1961, but there were discrepancies between the written description and the artistic rendering that was adopted at the same time. To resolve the problems, the 72nd Legislature in 1991 adopted an official design.

Back of Seal

The 73rd Legislature in 1993 finally adopted the reverse by law. The current description is in the Texas Government Code, section 3101.001:

"(b) The reverse side of the state seal contains a shield displaying a depiction of:

(1) the Alamo; (2) the cannon of the Battle of Gonzales; and (3) Vince's Bridge.

(c) The shield on the reverse side of the state seal is encircled by:

(1) live oak and olive branches; and (2) the unfurled flags of: (A) the Kingdom of France; (B) the Kingdom of Spain; (C) the United Mexican States; (D) the Republic of Texas; (E) the Confederate States of America; and (F) the United States of America.

(d) Above the shield is emblazoned the motto, 'REMEMBER THE ALAMO,' and beneath are the words, 'TEXAS ONE AND INDIVISIBLE.'

(e) A white five-pointed star hangs over the shield, centered between the flags."

Texas State Symbols

State Bird: The mockingbird (*Mimus polyglottos*) is the state bird of Texas, adopted by the 40th Legislature of 1927 at the request of the Texas Federation of Women's Clubs.

State Flower: The state flower of Texas is the bluebonnet, also called buffalo clover, wolf flower, and el conejo (the rabbit). The bluebonnet was adopted as the state flower, at the request of the Society of Colonial Dames in Texas, by the 27th Legislature in 1901. The original resolution made Lupinus subcarnosus the state flower, but a resolution by the 62nd Legislature in 1971 provided legal status as the state flower of Texas for "Lupinus Texensis and any other variety of bluebonnet."

State Tree: The pecan tree (*Carya illinoinensis*) was adopted as the state tree of Texas by the 36th Legislature in 1919. The sentiment that led to its adoption probably grew out of the request of Gov. James Stephen Hogg that a pecan tree be planted at his grave.

Other State Symbols

(In 2001, the Texas Legislature placed restrictions on the adoption of future symbols by requiring that a joint resolution to designate a symbol must specify the item's historical or cultural significance to the state.)

State Air Force: The Commemorative Air Force (formerly known as the Confederate Air Force), based in Midland at Midland International Airport, was proclaimed the state air force of Texas by the 71st Legislature in 1989.

State Amphibian: The Texas toad was named the state amphibian by the 81st Legislature in 2009.

State Aquarium: The Texas State Aquarium in Corpus Christi was designated the state aquarium of Texas by the 69th Legislature in 1985.

State Bison Herd: The bison herd at Caprock Canyons State Park was named the official Texas State Bison Herd by the 82nd Legislature in 2011.

State Bluebonnet City: The city of Ennis in Ellis County was designated the state bluebonnet city by the 75th Legislature in 1997.

State Bluebonnet Festival: The Chappell Hill Bluebonnet Festival, held in April, was named state bluebonnet festival by the 75th Legislature in 1997.

State Bluebonnet Trail: The city of Ennis was proclaimed the official state bluebonnet trail by the 75th Legislature in 1997.

State Bread: Pan de campo, translated "camp bread" and often called cowboy bread, was named the state bread by the 79th Legislature in 2005. It is a simple baking-powder bread that was a staple of early Texans and often baked in a Dutch oven.

State Cobbler: Peach cobbler was named the state cobbler of Texas by the 83rd Legislature in 2013.

State Cooking Implement: The cast iron Dutch oven was named the cooking implement of Texas by the 79th Legislature in 2005.

State Crustacean: Texas Gulf Shrimp was designated the state crustacean by the 84th Legislature in 2015.

State Dinosaur: *Paluxysaurus jonesi* was proclaimed the state dinosaur by the 81st Legislature in 2009, after it was discovered that the previous state dinosaur, the Brachiosaur Sauropod, Pleurocoelus, (75th Legislature in 1997) had been a misidentification.

State Dish: Chili was proclaimed the Texas state dish by the 65th Legislature in 1977.

State Dog Breed: The Blue Lacy was designated the state dog breed by the 79th Legislature in 2005. The Blue Lacy is a herding and hunting breed descended from greyhound, scent-hound, and coyote stock and developed by the Lacy brothers, who left Kentucky and settled near Marble Falls in 1858.

State Domino Game: 42 was named the state domino game by the 82nd Legislature in 2011.

State Epic Poem: "The Legend of Old Stone Ranch," written by John Worth Cloud, was named the epic poem of Texas by the 61st Legislature in 1969. The work is a 400-page history of the Albany–Fort Griffin area written in verse form.

State Fiber and Fabric: Cotton was designated the state fiber and fabric of Texas by the 75th Legislature in 1997.

State Fish: The Guadalupe bass, a member of the genus *Micropterus* within the sunfish family, was named the state fish of Texas by the 71st Legislature in 1989. It is one of a group of fish collectively known as black bass.

State Flower Song: "Bluebonnets," written by Julia D. Booth and Lora C. Crockett, was named the state flower song by the 43rd Legislature in 1933.

State Folk Dance: The square dance was designated the state folk dance by the 72nd Legislature in 1991.

State Footwear: The cowboy boot was named the state footwear by the 80th Legislature in 2007.

State Fruit: Texas red grapefruit was designated the state fruit by the 73rd Legislature in 1993.

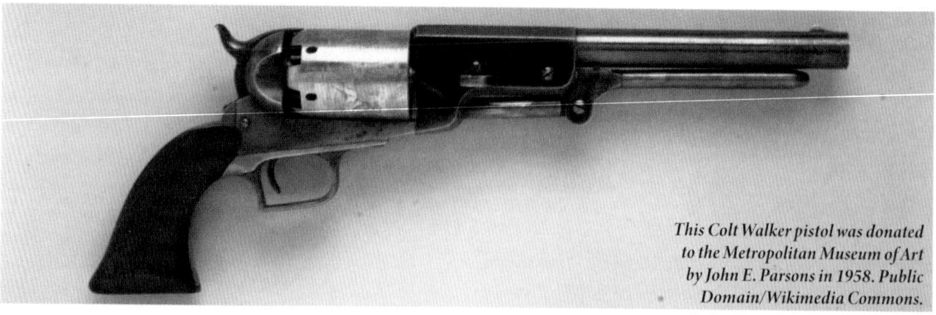

This Colt Walker pistol was donated to the Metropolitan Museum of Art by John E. Parsons in 1958. Public Domain/Wikimedia Commons.

State Gem: Texas blue topaz, the state gem of Texas, is found in the Llano uplift area in Central Texas, especially west to northwest of Mason. It was designated by the 61st Legislature in 1969.

State Gemstone Cut: The Lone Star Cut was named the state gemstone cut by the 65th Legislature in 1977.

State Grass: Sideoats grama (Bouteloua curtipendula), a native grass found on many different Texas soils, was designated the state grass of Texas by the 62nd Legislature in 1971.

State Handgun: The 1847 Colt Walker pistol was named the state handgun by the 87th Legislature in 2021.

State Hashtags: #Texas (state), #TexasToDo (tourism), and #txlege (legislature) were all proclaimed state hashtags by the 84th Legislature in 2015.

State Hat: The cowboy hat was named the state hat of Texas by the 84th Legislature in 2015.

State Health Nut: The pecan was designated the state health nut by the 77th Legislature in 2001.

State Horse: The American Quarter Horse was named state horse by the 81st Legislature in 2009.

State Insect: The Monarch butterfly (*Danaus plexippus*) was designated the state insect by the 74th Legislature in 1995.

State Knife: The 87th Legislature designated the Bowie knife our official state knife in 2021.

State Longhorn Herd: The longhorn herd at Fort Griffin State Historic Site was named the state longhorn herd by the 61st Legislature in 1969.

State Mammals: The state mammals were all designated by the 74th Legislature in 1995:

- **Flying:** Mexican free-tailed bat (*Tadarida brasiliensis*);
- **Large:** Longhorn (*Bos Texanus*);
- **Small:** Armadillo (*Dasypus novemcinctus*).

State Maritime Museum: The Texas Maritime Museum in Rockport was named the state maritime museum by the 70th Legislature in 1987.

State Mushroom: The Texas Star Mushroom (*Chorioactis geaster*) was recognized as the official state mushroom by the 87th Legislature in 2021.

State Music: Western swing was named the state's official music by the 82nd Legislature in 2011.

State Musical Instrument: The guitar was designated the state musical instrument by the 75th Legislature in 1997.

State Native Pepper: The chiltepin (*Capsicum annuum* var. *glabriusculum*) was named the native pepper of Texas by the 75th Legislature in 1997.

State Native Shrub: Texas purple sage (*Leucophyllum frutescens*) was designated the state native shrub by the 79th Legislature in 2005.

State Nickname: "The Lone Star State" was designated the state nickname of Texas by the 84th Legislature in 2015.

State Pastries: Both the sopaipilla and strudel were named the state pastries of Texas by the 78th Legislature in 2003.

State Pepper: The jalapeño pepper (*Capsicum annuum*) was designated the state pepper by the 74th Legislature in 1995.

The Texas Star mushroom, also known as the Devil's Cigar mushroom, first resembles a dark cigar before splitting and unfurling into rays while releasing spores. Photo by Tim Jones, CC 3.0/Wikipedia Commons.

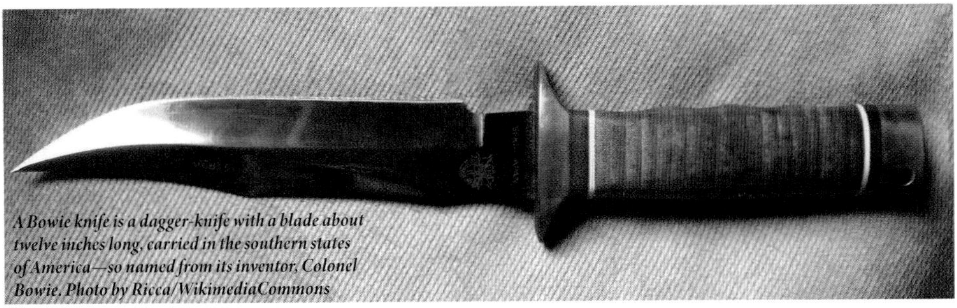

A Bowie knife is a dagger-knife with a blade about twelve inches long, carried in the southern states of America—so named from its inventor, Colonel Bowie. Photo by Ricca/WikimediaCommons

State Pie: Pecan pie was named the state pie by the 83rd Legislature in 2013.

State Plant: The prickly pear cactus (*Genus Opuntia*) was named the state plant by the 74th Legislature in 1995.

State Plays: There are four official state plays that were designated by the 66th Legislature in 1979:

1. **The Lone Star**
2. **Texas**
3. **Beyond the Sundown**
4. **Fandangle**

State Pollinator: The Western Honey Bee (*Apis mellifera*) was designated the official pollinator of Texas by the 84th Legislature in 2015.

State Precious Metal: Silver was named the official precious metal by the 80th Legislature in 2007.

State Railroad: The Texas State Railroad was designated the state railroad by the 78th Legislature in 2003. It is a steam-powered tourist excursion train that runs between the towns of Rusk and Palestine.

State Reptile: The Texas horned lizard (*Phrynosoma cornutum*) was named the state reptile by the 73rd Legislature in 1993.

State Rodeo Drill Team: Ghostriders were named the official rodeo drill team of Texas by the 80th Legislature in 2007.

State Saltwater Fish: Red Drum (*Sciaenops ocellatus*) was named the state's saltwater fish by the 82nd Legislature in 2011.

State Sea Turtle: Kemp's Ridley Sea Turtle was named the state sea turtle of Texas by the 83rd Legislature in 2013.

State Seashell: The lightning whelk (*Busycon perversum pulleyi*) was named the state seashell by the 70th Legislature in 1987. One of the few shells that open on the left side, the lightning whelk is named for its colored stripes and is found only on the Gulf Coast.

State Ship: The battleship USS Texas was designated the state ship by the 74th Legislature in 1995. The USS Texas was launched on May 18, 1912, from Newport News, Virginia, and commissioned on March 12, 1914. In 1919, it became the first U.S. battleship to launch an aircraft, and in 1939, it received the first commercial radar in the U.S. Navy. In 1940, the Texas was designated flagship of the U.S. Atlantic Fleet and was the last of the battleships to participate in both World Wars I and II. It was decommissioned on April 21, 1948, and is a National Historic Landmark and a National Mechanical Engineering Landmark. It is docked along the Houston Ship Channel.

State Shrub: The crape myrtle (*Lagerstroemia indica*) was designated the official state shrub by the 75th Legislature in 1997.

State Snack: Tortilla chips and salsa was named the state snack by the 78th Legislature in 2003.

State Sport: Rodeo was named the state sport of Texas by the 75th Legislature in 1997.

State Squash: Pumpkin was designated the state squash of Texas by the 83rd Legislature in 2013.

State Stone: Petrified palmwood, found in Texas principally near the Gulf Coast, was designated the state stone by the 61st Legislature in 1969.

State Tall Ship: The Elissa was named the state tall ship by the 79th Legislature in 2005. The 1877 ship makes its home at the Texas Seaport Museum at the port of Galveston.

State Tartan: The Texas Bluebonnet Tartan was named the official state tartan by the 71st Texas Legislature in 1989.

State 10K: The Texas Roundup 10K was named the official state 10K by the 79th Legislature in 2005 to encourage Texans to exercise and incorporate physical activity into their daily lives.

State Tie: The bolo tie was designated the state tie by the 80th Legislature in 2007.

State Vegetable: The Texas sweet onion was designated the state vegetable by the 75th Legislature in 1997.

State Vehicle: The chuck wagon was named the state vehicle by the 79th Legislature in 2005. Texas rancher Charles Goodnight is credited with inventing the chuck wagon to carry food and supplies for the cowboys on trail drives.

State Waterlily: The Nymphaea "Texas Dawn" was named the state waterlily by the 82nd Legislature in 2011. ☆

Explore Texas History

Texas State Historical Association HANDBOOK OF TEXAS

The *Texas Almanac* has long published feature articles about various aspects of Texas history, all of which are still available on our website, **TexasAlmanac.com**. In recent years, many of those articles were edited and combined to create a single article, "A Brief Sketch of Texas History," which was featured in several editions of the book. That article served its purpose, but a brief look has obvious limitations. After all, the history of Texas is anything but brief.

For this edition we are calling upon our colleagues at the *Handbook of Texas* to present an introductory selection of entries you can read online to learn about the history of Texas. Every entry offers a piece of the fabric of Texas past and present, and just as originally envisioned, the goal of those who write, revise, and edit entries remains ensuring that the *Handbook* is accurate, inclusive, accessible, and reflective of current scholarly standards.

Consider this list a starting point in your further study of Texas history, and explore our chronological overview entries and a few examples of our entries on cities and regions, specific topics, and biographies of deceased individuals. Dig in to these interesting samples of Texas history, and then go on to discover more at the *Handbook of Texas Online*,

https://www.tshaonline.org/handbook.

Chronological Overview

Prehistory: www.tshaonline.org/handbook/entries/prehistory

Spanish Texas: www.tshaonline.org/handbook/entries/spanish-texas

Texas in the Age of Mexican Independence:: www.tshaonline.org/handbook/entries/texas-in-the-age-of-mexican-independence

Mexican Texas: www.tshaonline.org/handbook/entries/mexican-texas

Texas Revolution: tshaonline.org/handbook/online/articles/qdt01

Republic of Texas: www.tshaonline.org/handbook/entries/texas-revolution

Antebellum Texas: www.tshaonline.org/handbook/entries/antebellum-texas

Civil War: www.tshaonline.org/handbook/entries/civil-war

Reconstruction: www.tshaonline.org/handbook/entries/reconstruction

Late-Nineteenth Century Texas: www.tshaonline.org/handbook/entries/late-nineteenth-century-texas

Progressive Era: www.tshaonline.org/handbook/entries/progressive-era

Texas in the 1920s: www.tshaonline.org/handbook/entries/texas-in-the-1920s

Great Depression: www.tshaonline.org/handbook/entries/great-depression

World War II: www.tshaonline.org/handbook/entries/world-war-ii

Texas Post World War II: www.tshaonline.org/handbook/entries/texas-post-world-war-ii

Biographical

Athanase de Mézières: www.tshaonline.org/handbook/entries/mezieres-athanase-de

Sam Houston: www.tshaonline.org/handbook/entries/houston-sam

Stephen F. Austin: www.tshaonline.org/handbook/entries/austin-stephen-fuller

Mary Eleanor Brackenridge: www.tshaonline.org/handbook/entries/brackenridge-mary-eleanor

Lyndon B. Johnson: www.tshaonline.org/handbook/entries/johnson-lyndon-baines

Minnie Fisher Cunningham: www.tshaonline.org/handbook/entries/cunningham-minnie-fisher

Jesse H. Jones: www.tshaonline.org/handbook/entries/jones-jesse-holman

Ernie Banks: www.tshaonline.org/handbook/entries/banks-ernest-ernie-mr-cub

José Francisco Ruiz: www.tshaonline.org/handbook/entries/ruiz-jose-francisco

Barbara Jordan: www.tshaonline.org/handbook/entries/jordan-barbara-charline

George T. Ruby: www.tshaonline.org/handbook/entries/ruby-george-thompson

Jovita Idar: www.tshaonline.org/handbook/entries/idar-jovita

Lady Bird Johnson: www.tshaonline.org/handbook/entries/johnson-claudia-alta-taylor-lady-bird

Henry B. González: www.tshaonline.org/handbook/entries/gonzalez henry-barbosa

Katherine Stinson: www.tshaonline.org/handbook/entries/stinson-katherine

Babe Didrikson Zaharias: www.tshaonline.org/handbook/entries/zaharias-mildred-ella-didrikson-babe

Topical

Spanish Missions: www.tshaonline.org/handbook/entries/spanish-missions

Slavery: www.tshaonline.org/handbook/entries/slavery

Battle of the Alamo: www.tshaonline.org/handbook/entries/alamo-battle-of-the

Civil Rights in Texas: www.tshaonline.org/handbook/entries/civil-rights

Music: www.tshaonline.org/handbook/entries/music

Woman Suffrage: www.tshaonline.org/handbook/entries/woman-suffrage

Germans: www.tshaonline.org/handbook/entries/germans

African Americans: www.tshaonline.org/handbook/entries/african-americans

Anglo American Colonization: www.tshaonline.org/handbook/entries/anglo-american-colonization

LULAC: www.tshaonline.org/handbook/entries/league-of-united-latin-american-citizens

Kerrville Folk Festival: www.tshaonline.org/handbook/entries/kerrville-folk-festival

Surface Water: www.tshaonline.org/handbook/entries/surface-water

Comanche: www.tshaonline.org/handbook/entries/comanche-indians

People's Party: www.tshaonline.org/handbook/entries/peoples-party

Houston Astros: www.tshaonline.org/handbook/entries/houston-astros

San Antonio Spurs: www.tshaonline.org/handbook/entries/san-antonio-spurs

Witte Museum: www.tshaonline.org/handbook/entries/witte-museum

Railroads: www.tshaonline.org/handbook/entries/railroads

Vietnamese: www.tshaonline.org/handbook/entries/vietnamese

Mexican Americans: www.tshaonline.org/handbook/entries/mexican-americans

Segregation: www.tshaonline.org/handbook/entries/segregation

Porvenir Massacre: www.tshaonline.org/handbook/entries/porvenir-massacre

Armadillo: www.tshaonline.org/handbook/entries/armadillo

Visual Arts: www.tshaonline.org/handbook/entries/visual-arts

Cities and Regions

Dallas: www.tshaonline.org/handbook/entries/dallas-tx

Fort Worth: www.tshaonline.org/handbook/entries/fort-worth-tx

Houston: www.tshaonline.org/handbook/entries/houston-tx

Panhandle: www.tshaonline.org/handbook/entries/panhandle

Trans-Pecos: www.tshaonline.org/handbook/entries/trans-pecos

Hill Country: www.tshaonline.org/handbook/entries/hill-country

El Paso: www.tshaonline.org/handbook/entries/el-paso-tx

Austin: www.tshaonline.org/handbook/entries/austin-tx-travis-

San Antonio: www.tshaonline.org/handbook/entries/san-antonio-tx

Rio Grande Valley: www.tshaonline.org/handbook/entries/rio-grande-valley

East Texas: www.tshaonline.org/handbook/entries/east-texas

Permian Basin: www.tshaonline.org/handbook/entries/permian-basin

The *Handbook of Texas* is a collaborative scholarly project of the Texas State Historical Association (TSHA) that began in 1939 under the direction of Professor Walter Prescott Webb at the University of Texas at Austin to create, "the most useful book that has ever been published in Texas."

- FREE and Accessible on computers, phones, and tablets
- Nearly 27,000 entries by 6,000+ authors
- 10 million page views annually
- 4.5 million users annually

Lady Bird Johnson at the groundbreaking of the wildflower center that bears her name. Photo by Frank Wolfe/Wikimedia Commons

Environment

PHYSICAL REGIONS, GEOLOGY, SOILS

AQUIFERS, RIVERS, LAKES, ESTUARIES

PLANT LIFE, FORESTS, GRASSLANDS

TEXAS WILDLIFE: FISH, AMPHIBIANS, REPTILES, BIRDS, MAMMALS

The Red-tailed Hawk (Buteo jamaicensis) is found statewide, often seen soaring or perched on telephone poles and fence posts. Photo by Jill D. Miller.

The Physical State of Texas

The Area of Texas

Texas occupies about 7 percent of the total water and land area of the United States. Second in size among the states, Texas has a land and water area of 268,596 square miles, as compared with Alaska's 665,384 square miles, according to the United States Bureau of the Census. California, the third-largest state, has 163,695 square miles. Texas is as large as all of New England, New York, Delaware, Pennsylvania, Ohio, and Virginia combined.

The state's total area consists of 261,232 square miles of land and 7,365 square miles of water.

Length and Breadth

The longest straight-line distance in a general north-south direction is 801 miles from the northwest corner of the Panhandle to the extreme southern tip of Texas on the Rio Grande southeast of Brownsville. The greatest east-west distance is 773 miles from the extreme eastward bend in the Sabine River in Newton County to the extreme western bulge of the Rio Grande just northwest of El Paso.

Texas' Boundary Lines

The boundary of Texas by segments, including only larger river bends and only the great arc of the coastline, is as follows:

Boundary	Length (miles)
Rio Grande	889.0
Coastline	367.0
Sabine River, Lake, and Pass	180.0
Sabine River to Red River	106.5
Red River	480.0
East Panhandle line	133.6
North Panhandle line	167.0
West Panhandle line	310.2
Along 32nd parallel	209.0
TOTAL	**2,842.3**

Following the smaller meanderings of the rivers and the tidewater coastline, the following are the boundary measurements:

Boundary	Length (miles)
Rio Grande	1,254.0
Coastline (tidewater)	624.0
Sabine River, Lake, and Pass	292.0
Sabine River to Red River	106.5
Red River	726.0
East Panhandle line	133.6
North Panhandle line	167.0
West Panhandle line	310.2
Along 32nd parallel	209.0
TOTAL	**3,822.3**

Latitude and Longitude

The extremes of latitude and longitude in Texas are as follows:

★ From 25° 50' North latitude at the extreme southern turn of the Rio Grande on the south line of Cameron County to 36° 30' North latitude along the north line of the Panhandle, and

★ From 93° 31' West longitude at the extreme eastern point of the Sabine River on the east line of Newton County to 106° 38' West longitude at the extreme westward point of the Rio Grande on the western edge of El Paso.

Named Mountain Peaks in Texas Above 8,000 Feet

The highest point in the state is Guadalupe Peak at 8,749 feet above sea level. Its twin, El Capitan, stands at 8,085 feet and also is located in Culberson County near the New Mexico state line. Both are in Guadalupe Mountains National Park, which includes the scenic McKittrick Canyon.

The elevations used on this page are from various sources, including the U.S. Geological Survey, the National Park Service, and the Texas Department of Transportation. The named peaks above 8,000 feet and the counties in which they are located are listed below.

Name	County	Height (Ft.)
Guadalupe Peak	Culberson	8,749
Bush Mountain	Culberson	8,631
Shumard Peak	Culberson	8,615
Bartlett Peak	Culberson	8,508
Mount Livermore (Baldy Peak)	Jeff Davis	8,378
Hunter Peak (Pine Top Mtn.)	Culberson	8,368
El Capitan	Culberson	8,085

Elevation Highs and Lows

Highest Town: Fort Davis in Jeff Davis County is the highest town of any size in Texas at 5,050 feet above sea level, and the county has the highest average elevation.

Highest Highway: The highest state highway point also is in Jeff Davis County at McDonald Observatory on Mount Locke, where the road reaches 6,781 feet above sea level, as determined by the Texas Department of Transportation.

Highest Railway: The highest railway point is Paisano Pass, 14 miles east of Marfa in Presidio County, which is 5,074 above sea level.

Lowest Point: Sea level is the lowest elevation determined in Texas, and it can be found in all the coastal counties. No point in the state has been found by the geological survey to be below sea level. ☆

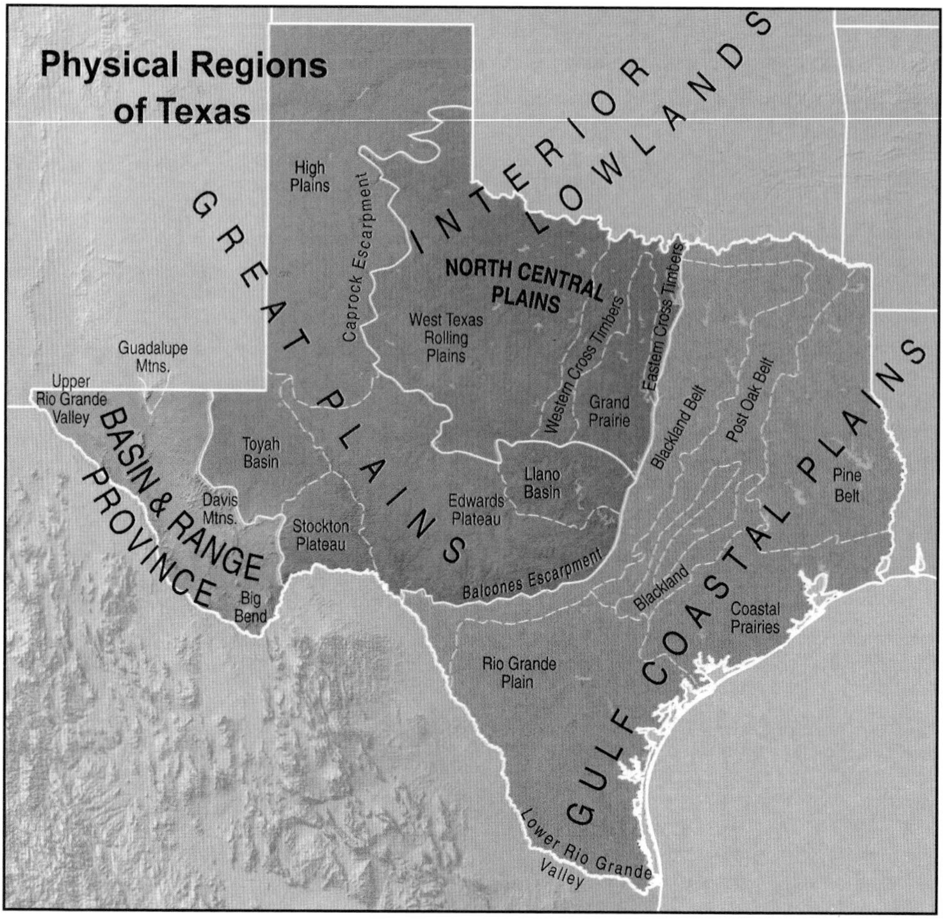

Physical Regions

This section was reviewed by Dr. David R. Butler, Texas State University System Regents' Professor of Geography

The principal physical regions of Texas are usually listed as follows:

I. Gulf Coastal Plains

Texas' Gulf Coastal Plains are the western extension of the coastal plain extending from the Atlantic Ocean to beyond the Rio Grande. Its characteristic rolling to hilly surface covered with a heavy growth of pine and hardwoods extends into East Texas. In the increasingly arid west, however, its forests become secondary in nature, consisting largely of post oaks and, farther west, prairies and brushlands.

The interior limit of the Gulf Coastal Plains in Texas is the line of the Balcones Fault and Escarpment. This geologic fault or shearing of underground strata extends eastward from a point on the Rio Grande near Del Rio. It extends to the northwestern part of Bexar County, where it turns northeastward and extends through Comal, Hays, and Travis counties, intersecting the Colorado River immediately north of Austin. The fault line is a single, definite geologic feature, accompanied by a line of southward- and eastward-facing hills.

The resemblance of the hills to balconies when viewed from the plain below accounts for the Spanish name for this area: balcones.

North of Waco, features of the fault zone are sufficiently inconspicuous that the interior boundary of the Coastal Plain follows the traditional geologic contact between upper and lower Cretaceous rocks. This contact is along the eastern edge of the Eastern Cross Timbers.

This fault line is usually accepted as the boundary between lowland and upland Texas. Below the fault line, the surface is characteristically coastal plains. Above the Balcones Fault, the surface is characteristically interior rolling plains.

A. Pine Belt or "Piney Woods"

The Pine Belt, called the "Piney Woods," extends 75 to 125 miles into Texas from the east. From north to south, it extends from the Red River to within about 25 miles of the Gulf Coast. Interspersed among the pines are hardwood timbers, usually in valleys of rivers and creeks. This area is the source of practically all of Texas' commercial timber production (see Texas Forest Resources, page 115). It was settled early in Texas' history and is one of the oldest farming areas in the state.

This area's soils and climate are adaptable to the production of a variety of fruit and vegetable crops. Cattle raising is widespread, along with the development of pastures planted to improved grasses. Lumber production is the principal industry. There is a large iron-and-steel industry near Daingerfield in Morris County based on nearby iron deposits. Iron deposits are also worked in Rusk and one or two other counties.

A great oil field discovered in Gregg, Rusk, and Smith counties in 1931 has done more than anything else to contribute to the economic growth of the area. This area has a variety of clays, lignite, and other minerals as potentials for development.

B. Post Oak Belt

The main Post Oak Belt of Texas is wedged between the Pine Belt on the east, Blacklands on the west, and the Coastal Prairies on the south, covering a considerable area in East-Central Texas. The principal industry is diversified farming and livestock raising.

It is spotty in character, with some insular areas of blackland soil and some that closely resemble those of the Pine Belt. There is a small, isolated area of loblolly pines in Bastrop, Caldwell, Fayette, and Lee counties known as the "Lost Pines," the westernmost southern pines in the United States. The Post Oak Belt has lignite, commercial clays, and some other minerals.

C. Blackland Belt

The Blackland Belt stretches from the Rio Grande to the Red River, lying just below the line of the Balcones Fault and varying in width from 15 to 70 miles. It is narrowest below the segment of the Balcones Fault from the Rio Grande to Bexar County and gradually widens as it runs northeast to the Red River.

Its rolling prairie, easily turned by the plow, developed rapidly as a farming area until the 1930s and was the principal cotton-producing area of Texas. Now, however, other Texas areas that are irrigated and mechanized lead in farming.

Because of the early growth, the Blackland Belt is still the most thickly populated area in the state and contains within it and along its border more of the state's large and middle-sized cities than any other area. Primarily because of this concentration of population, this belt has the most diversified manufacturing industry of the state.

D. Coastal Prairies

The Texas Coastal Prairies extend westward along the coast from the Sabine River, reaching inland 30 to 60 miles. Between the Sabine and Galveston Bay, the line of demarcation between the prairies and the Pine Belt forests to the north is very distinct. The Coastal Prairies extend along the Gulf of Mexico from the Sabine to the Lower Rio Grande Valley.

The eastern half is covered with a heavy growth of grass; the western half, which is more arid, is covered with short grass and, in some places, with small timber and brush. The soil is heavy clay. Grass supports the densest cattle population in Texas, and cattle ranching is the principal agricultural industry. Rice is a major crop, grown under irrigation from wells and rivers. Cotton, grain sorghum, and truck crops also are grown.

Coastal Prairie areas have seen the greatest industrial development in Texas history since World War II. Chief concentration has been from Orange and Beaumont to Houston, and much of the development has been in petrochemicals and the aerospace industry.

Corpus Christi, in the Coastal Bend, and Brownsville, in the Lower Rio Grande Valley, have seaports and agricultural and industrial sections. Cotton, grain, vegetables, and citrus fruits are the principal crops. Cattle production is significant, with the famed King Ranch and other large ranches located here.

E. Lower Rio Grande Valley

The deep alluvial soils and distinctive economy cause the Lower Rio Grande Valley to be classified as a subregion of the Gulf Coastal Plains. "The Valley," as it is called locally, is Texas' greatest citrus and winter vegetable growing region because of the normal absence of freezing weather and the rich delta soils of the Rio Grande. Despite occasional damaging freezes, the Lower Valley ranks high among the nation's fruit and truck-farming regions. Much of the acreage is irrigated, although dry-land farming also is practiced.

F. Rio Grande Plain

This area may be roughly defined as lying south of San Antonio between the Rio Grande and the Gulf Coast. The Rio Grande Plain shows characteristics of both the Gulf Coastal Plains and the North Mexico Plains because there is similarity of topography, climate, and plant life all the way from the Balcones Escarpment in Texas to the Sierra Madre Oriental in Mexico, which runs past Monterrey about 160 miles south of Laredo.

The Rio Grande Plain is partly prairie, but much of it is covered with a dense growth of prickly pear, mesquite, dwarf oak, catclaw, guajillo, huisache, blackbrush, cenizo, and other cactus and wild shrubs. It is devoted primarily to raising cattle, sheep, and goats. The Texas Angora goat and mohair industry centers in this area and on the Edwards Plateau, which borders it on the north. San Antonio and Laredo are its chief commercial centers, with San Antonio dominating trade.

There is some farming, and the Winter Garden, centering in Dimmit and Zavala counties north of Laredo, is irrigated from wells and streams to produce vegetables in late winter and early spring. Primarily, however, the central and western part of the Rio Grande Plain is devoted to livestock raising.

The rainfall is less than 25 inches annually, and the hot summers cause heavy evaporation, so that cultivation without irrigation is limited.

Over a large area in the central and western parts of the Rio Grande Plain, the growth of small oaks, mesquite, prickly pear (Opuntia) cactus, and a variety of wild shrubs is very dense, and it is often called the Brush Country. It is also referred to as the chaparral and the monte, from a Spanish word that can mean dense brush.)

II. Interior Lowlands

North Central Plains

The North Central Plains of Texas are a southwestern extension into Texas of the interior, or central, lowlands that extend northward to the Canadian border, paralleling the Great Plains to the West. The North Central Plains of Texas extend from the Blackland Belt on the east to the Caprock Escarpment on the west. From north to south, they extend from the Red River to the Colorado River.

A. West Texas Rolling Plains

The West Texas Rolling Plains, approximately the western two-thirds of the North Central Plains in Texas, rise from east to west in altitude from about 750 feet to 2,000 feet at the base of the Caprock Escarpment. Annual rainfall ranges from about 30 inches on the east to 20 inches on the west. In general, as one progresses westward in Texas, the precipitation not only declines but also becomes more variable from year to year. Temperature varies rather widely between summer's heat and winter's cold.

This area still has a large cattle-raising industry with many of the state's largest ranches. However, there is much level, cultivable land.

B. Grand Prairie

Near the eastern edge of the North Central Plains is the Grand Prairie, extending south from the Red River in an irregular band through Cooke, Montague, Wise, Denton, Tarrant, Parker, Hood, Johnson, Bosque, Coryell, and some adjacent counties.

It is a limestone-based area, usually treeless except along the numerous streams, and adapted primarily to raising livestock and growing staple crops. Sometimes called the Fort Worth Prairie, it has an agricultural economy and largely rural population, with no large cities, except Fort Worth on its eastern boundary.

C. Eastern and Western Cross Timbers

Hanging over the top of the Grand Prairie and dropping down on each side are the Eastern and Western Cross Timbers. The two southward-extending bands are connected by a narrow strip along the Red River.

The Eastern Cross Timbers extend southward from the Red River through eastern Denton County and along the boundary between Dallas and Tarrant counties. It then stretches through Johnson County to the Brazos River and into Hill County.

The much larger Western Cross Timbers extend from the Red River south through Clay, Montague, Jack, Wise, Parker, Palo Pinto, Hood, Erath, Eastland, Comanche, Brown, and Mills counties to the Colorado River, where they meet the Llano Basin.

Their soils are adapted to fruit and vegetable crops, which reach considerable commercial production in some areas in Parker, Erath, Eastland, and Comanche counties.

III. Great Plains

A. High Plains

The Great Plains, which lie to the east of the base of the Rocky Mountains, extend into northwestern Texas. This area, commonly known as the High Plains, is a vast, flat, high plain covered with thick layers of alluvial material. It is also known as the Staked Plains or Llano Estacado.

Historians differ as to the origin of this name. Some say it came from the fact that the explorer Coronado's expedition used stakes to mark its route across the trackless sea of grass so that it would be guided on its return trip. Others think that the estacado refers to the palisaded appearance of the Caprock in many places, especially the west-facing escarpment in New Mexico.

The Caprock Escarpment is the dividing line between the High Plains and the lower West Texas Rolling Plains. Like the Balcones Escarpment, the Caprock Escarpment is a striking physical feature, rising abruptly 200 feet, 500 feet, and in some places almost 1,000 feet above the plains. Unlike the Balcones Escarpment, the Caprock was caused by surface erosion.

Where rivers issue from the eastern face of the Caprock, there frequently are notable canyons, such as Palo Duro Canyon on the Prairie Dog Town Fork of the Red River, Blanco Canyon on the White River, as well as the breaks along the Canadian River as it crosses the Panhandle north of Amarillo.

Along the eastern edge of the Panhandle, there is a gradual descent of the land's surface from high to low plains; but at the Red River, the Caprock Escarpment becomes a striking surface feature.

It continues as an east-facing wall south through Briscoe, Floyd, Motley, Dickens, Crosby, Garza, and Borden counties, gradually decreasing in elevation. South of Borden County, the escarpment is less obvious, and the boundary between the High Plains and the Edwards Plateau occurs where the alluvial cover of the High Plains disappears.

Stretching over the largest level plain of its kind in the United States, the High Plains rise gradually from about 2,700 feet on the east to more than 4,000 in spots along the New Mexico border.

Chiefly because of climate and the resultant agriculture, subdivisions are called the North Plains and South Plains. The North Plains, from Hale County north, has primarily wheat and grain sorghum farming, but with significant ranching and petroleum developments. Amarillo is the largest city, with Plainview on the south and Borger on the north as important commercial centers.

The South Plains, also a leading grain sorghum region, leads Texas in cotton production. Lubbock is the principal city, and Lubbock County is one of the state's largest cotton producers. Irrigation from underground reservoirs, centered around Lubbock and Plainview, waters much of the crop acreage.

B. Edwards Plateau

Geographers usually consider that the Great Plains at the foot of the Rocky Mountains actually continue southward from the High Plains of Texas to the Rio Grande and the Balcones Escarpment. This southern and lower extension of the Great Plains in Texas is known as the Edwards Plateau.

It lies between the Rio Grande and the Colorado River. Its southeastern border is the Balcones Escarpment from the Rio Grande at Del Rio eastward to San Antonio and thence

A view of Palo Duro Canyon from the sky. Palo Duro Canyon is part of the Caprock Escarpment, and the second largest canyon in the U.S. Photo by Ken Lund, CC by 2.0/Flickr

to Austin on the Colorado River. Its upper boundary is the Pecos River, though the Stockton Plateau is geologically and topographically classed with the Edwards Plateau.

The Edwards Plateau varies from about 750 feet high at its southern and eastern borders to about 2,700 feet in places. Almost the entire surface is a thin, limestone-based soil covered with a medium to thick growth of cedar, small oak, and mesquite and a varying growth of prickly pear. Grass for cattle, weeds for sheep, and tree foliage for the browsing goats support three industries — cattle, goat, and sheep raising — upon which the area's economy depends. It is the nation's leading Angora goat and mohair producing region and one of the nation's leading sheep and wool areas. A few crops are grown.

Hill Country

The Hill Country is a popular name for the eastern portion of the Edwards Plateau south of the Llano Basin. Its notable large springs include Barton Springs at Austin, San Marcos Springs at San Marcos, Comal Springs at New Braunfels, several springs at San Antonio, and a number of others.

The Hill Country is characterized by rugged hills with relatively steep slopes and thin soils overlying limestone bedrock. High gradient streams combine with these steep hillslopes and occasionally heavy precipitation to produce an area with a significant flash-flood hazard.

C. Toyah Basin

To the northwest of the Edwards and Stockton plateaus is the Toyah Basin, a broad, flat remnant of an old sea floor that occupied the region as recently as Quaternary time.

Located in the Pecos River Valley, this region, in relatively recent time, has become important for many agricultural products as a result of irrigation. Additional economic activity is afforded by local oil fields.

D. Llano Basin

The Llano Basin lies at the junction of the Colorado and Llano rivers in Burnet and Llano counties. Earlier, this was known as the "Central Mineral Region" because of evidence there of a large number of minerals.

On the Colorado River in this area, a succession of dams impounds two large and five small reservoirs. Uppermost is Lake Buchanan, one of the large reservoirs, between Burnet and Llano counties. Below it in the western part of Travis County is Lake Travis.

Between these two large reservoirs are three smaller ones, Inks, Lyndon B. Johnson (formerly Granite Shoals), and Marble Falls reservoirs, used primarily to produce electric power from the overflow from Lake Buchanan. Lake Austin is along the western part of the city of Austin. Still another small lake, Lady Bird Lake (formerly Town Lake), is formed by a low-water dam in Austin.

The recreational area around these lakes has been called the Highland Lakes Country. This is an interesting area with Precambrian and Paleozoic rocks found on the surface. Granitic domes, exemplified by Enchanted Rock north of Fredericksburg, form the core of this area of ancient rocks.

IV. Basin and Range Province

The Basin and Range Province, with its center in Nevada, surrounds the Colorado Plateau on the west and south and enters far West Texas from southern New Mexico on the east. It consists of broad interior drainage basins interspersed with scattered fault-block mountain ranges.

Although this is the only part of Texas regarded as mountainous, these should not be confused with the Rocky

Mountains. Of all the independent ranges in West Texas, only the Davis Mountains resemble the Rockies, and there is much debate about this.

Texas west of the Edwards Plateau, bounded on the north by New Mexico and on the south by the Rio Grande, is distinctive in its physical and economic conditions. Traversed from north to south by fault-block mountains, it contains all of Texas' true mountains and also is very interesting geologically.

A. Guadalupe Mountains

Highest of the Trans-Pecos Mountains is the Guadalupe Range, which enters Texas from New Mexico. It abruptly ends about 20 miles south of the boundary line, where Guadalupe Peak, (8,749 feet, highest in Texas) and El Capitan (8,085 feet) are situated. El Capitan, because of perspective, appears to the observer on the plain below to be higher than Guadalupe.

Lying just west of the Guadalupe Range and extending to the Hueco Mountains a short distance east of El Paso is the Diablo Plateau or basin. It has no drainage outlet to the sea. The runoff from the scant rain that falls on its surface drains into a series of salt lakes that lie just west of the Guadalupe Mountains. These lakes are dry during periods of low rainfall, exposing bottoms of solid salt; for years they were a source of commercial salt. West of the Hueco Mountains are the Franklin Mountains in El Paso, with the Hueco Bolson (a down-dropped area approximately 4,000 feet above sea level) separating the two fault-block ranges.

B. Davis Mountains

The Davis Mountains are principally in Jeff Davis County. The highest peak, Mount Livermore (8,378 feet), is one of the highest in Texas; there are several others more than 7,000 feet high. These mountains intercept the moisture-bearing winds and receive more precipitation than elsewhere in the Trans-Pecos, so they have more vegetation than the other Trans-Pecos mountains. Noteworthy are the San Solomon Springs at the northern base of these mountains.

C. Big Bend

South of the Davis Mountains lies the Big Bend country, so called because it is encompassed on three sides by a great southward swing of the Rio Grande. It is a mountainous country of scant rainfall and sparse population. Its principal mountains, the Chisos, rise to 7,825 feet in Mount Emory.

Along the Rio Grande are the Santa Elena, Mariscal, and Boquillas canyons with rim elevations of 3,500 to 3,775 feet. They are among the noteworthy canyons of the North American continent.

Because of its remarkable topography and plant and animal life, the southern part of this region along the Rio Grande is home to Big Bend National Park, with headquarters in the Chisos Basin, a deep valley in the Chisos Mountains. It is a favorite recreation area.

D. Upper Rio Grande Valley

The Upper Rio Grande Valley, or El Paso Valley, is a narrow strip of irrigated land running down the river from El Paso for a distance of 75 miles or more.

In this area are the historic towns and missions of Ysleta, Socorro, and San Elizario, some of the oldest in Texas. Cotton is the chief product of this valley, much of it the long-staple variety. This limited area has a dense urban and rural population, in marked contrast to the territory surrounding it. ☆

Hikers enjoying a vista in the Guadalupe Mountains. Photo by Jonathan Cutrer/jcutrer.com

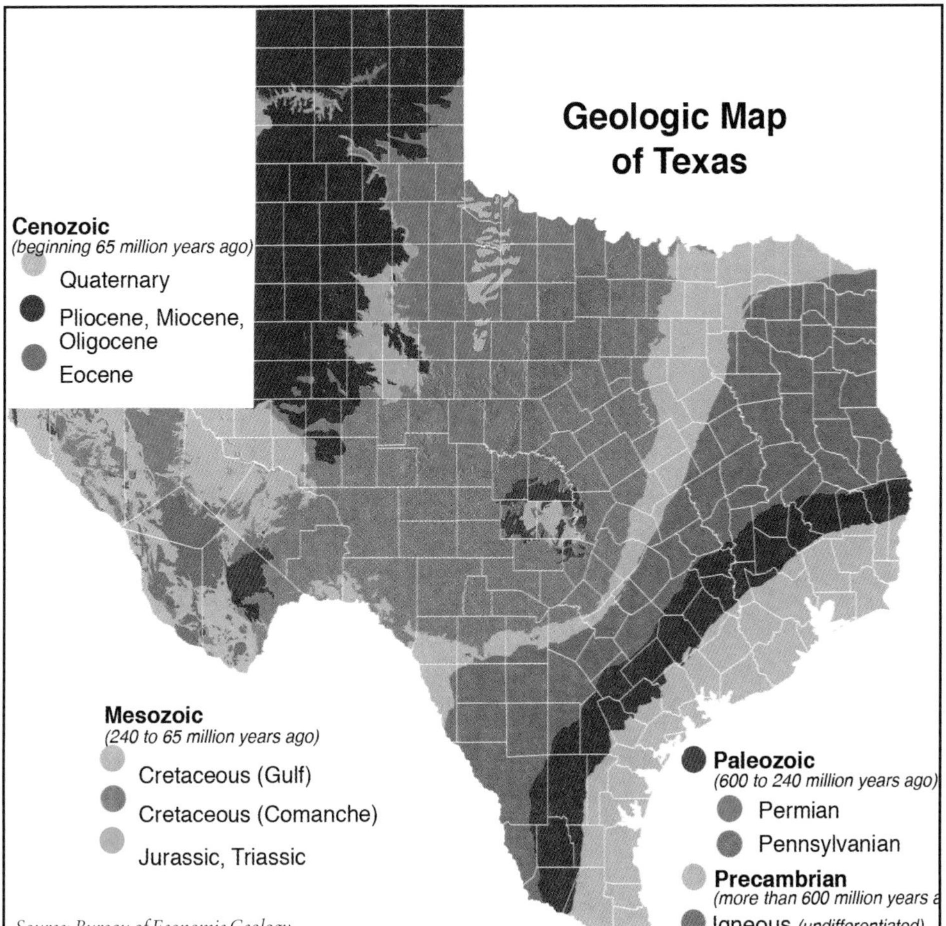

Source: Bureau of Economic Geology

Geology of Texas

Source: Bureau of Economic Geology, The University of Texas at Austin; www.beg.utexas.edu

Mountains, seas, coastal plains, rocky plateaus, high plains, forests — all of this physiographic variety in Texas is controlled by the varied rocks and structures that underlie and crop out across the state. The fascinating geologic history of Texas is recorded in the rocks — both those exposed at the surface and those penetrated by holes drilled in search of oil and natural gas.

The rocks reveal a dynamic, ever-changing earth: ancient mountains, seas, volcanoes, earthquake belts, rivers, hurricanes, and winds. Today, the volcanoes and great earthquake belts are no longer active, but rivers and streams, wind and rain, and the slow, inexorable alterations of rocks at or near the surface continue to change the face of Texas.

The geologic history of Texas, as documented by the rocks, began more than a billion years ago. Its legacy is the mineral wealth and varied land forms of modern Texas.

Geologic Time Travel

The story preserved in rocks requires an understanding of the origin of strata and how they have been deformed. **Stratigraphy is the study of the composition, sequence, and origin of rocks**: what rocks are made of, how they were formed, and the order in which the layers were formed.

Structural geology reveals the architecture of rocks: the locations of the mountains, volcanoes, sedimentary basins, and earthquake belts.

The map above shows where rocks of various geologic ages are visible on the surface of Texas today. History concerns events through time, but geologic time is such a grandiose concept, most find it difficult to comprehend. So geologists have **named the various chapters of earth history.**

Precambrian Eon

Precambrian rocks, more than 600 million years old, are exposed at the surface in the Llano Uplift of Central Texas and in scattered outcrops in West Texas, around and north of Van Horn and near El Paso.

These rocks, some more than a billion years old, include complexly deformed rocks that were originally formed by cooling from a liquid state, as well as rocks that were altered from pre-existing rocks.

Precambrian rocks, often called the "basement complex," are thought to form the foundation of continental masses. They underlie all of Texas. The outcrop in Central Texas is only the exposed part of the Texas Craton, which is primarily buried by younger rocks. (A craton is a stable, almost immovable portion of the earth's crust that forms the nuclear mass of a continent.)

Paleozoic Era

During the early part of the Paleozoic Era (approximately 600 million to 350 million years ago), **broad, relatively shallow seas repeatedly inundated the Texas Craton and much of North and West Texas.** The evidence for these events is found exposed around the Llano Uplift and in far West Texas near Van Horn and El Paso, and also in the subsurface throughout most of West and North Texas.

The evidence includes early Paleozoic rocks, sandstones, shales, and limestones, similar to sediments that form in seas today, and the fossils of animals, similar to modern crustaceans: the brachiopods, clams, snails, and related organisms that live in modern marine environments.

By late Paleozoic (approximately 350 million to 240 million years ago), the Texas Craton was bordered on the east and south by a long, deep marine basin called the Ouachita Trough. Sediments slowly accumulated in this trough until late in the Paleozoic Era.

Plate-tectonic theory postulates that the collision of the North American Plate (upon which the Texas Craton is located) with the European and African–South American plates uplifted the thick sediments that had accumulated in the trough **to form the Ouachita Mountains**.

At that time, the Ouachitas extended across Texas. Today, the Texas portion of the old mountain range is mostly buried by younger rocks. Ancient remnants can be seen in the Marathon Basin of West Texas due to uplift and erosion of younger sediments.

The public can see the remains of this once-majestic Ouachita Mountain range at Post Park, just south of Marathon in Brewster County. Other remnants at the surface are exposed in southeastern Oklahoma and southwestern Arkansas.

During the **Pennsylvanian** Period, however, the Ouachita Mountains bordered the eastern margin of shallow inland seas that covered most of West Texas. Rivers flowed westward from the mountains to the seas bringing sediment to form deltas along an ever-changing coastline.

The sediments were then reworked by the waves and currents of the inland sea. Today, these fluvial, delta, and shallow marine deposits compose the late Paleozoic rocks that crop out and underlie the surface of North-Central Texas.

Broad marine shelves divided the West Texas seas into several sub-basins, or deeper areas, that received more sediments than accumulated on the limestone shelves. Limestone reefs rimmed the deeper basins. **Today, these limestone reefs are important oil reservoirs in West Texas.**

These seas gradually withdrew from Texas, and by the late **Permian** Period, all that was left in West Texas were shallow basins and wide tidal flats in which salt, gypsum, and red muds accumulated in a hot, arid land. Strata deposited during the Permian Period are exposed today along the edge of the Panhandle, as far east as Wichita Falls and south to Concho County, and in the Trans-Pecos.

Mesozoic Era

Approximately 240 million years ago, the major geologic events in Texas shifted from West Texas to East and Southeast Texas. The European and African–South American plates, which had collided with the North American plate to form the Ouachita Mountains, began to separate from North America.

A series of faulted basins, or rifts, extending from Mexico to Nova Scotia were formed. These rifted basins received sediments from adjacent uplifts. As Europe and the southern continents continued to drift away from North America, **the Texas basins were eventually buried beneath thick deposits of marine salt within the newly formed East Texas and Gulf Coast basins.**

Jurassic and Cretaceous rocks in East and Southeast Texas document a sequence of broad limestone shelves at the edge of the developing Gulf of Mexico. From time to time, the shelves were buried beneath deltaic sandstones and shales, which built the northwestern margin of the widening Gulf of Mexico to the south and southeast.

As the underlying salt was buried more deeply by dense sediments, the salt became unstable and moved toward areas of least pressure. As the salt moved, it arched or pierced overlying sediments forming, in some cases, columns known as "salt domes." In some cases, these salt domes moved to the surface; others remain beneath a sedimentary overburden. This mobile salt formed numerous structures that would later serve to trap oil and natural gas.

By the early **Cretaceous** (approximately 140 million years ago), the shallow Mesozoic seas covered a large part of Texas, eventually extending west to the Trans-Pecos area and north almost to present-day state boundaries.

Today, the **limestone deposited in those seas is exposed in the walls of the magnificent canyons of the Rio Grande in the Big Bend National Park area** and in the canyons and headwaters of streams that drain the Edwards Plateau, as well as in Central Texas from San Antonio to Dallas.

Animals of many types lived in the shallow Mesozoic seas, tidal pools, and coastal swamps. Today, these lower Cretaceous rocks are some of the most fossiliferous in the state. **Tracks of dinosaurs occur in several places**, and remains of terrestrial, aquatic, and flying reptiles have been collected from Cretaceous rocks in many areas.

During most of the late Cretaceous, much of Texas lay beneath marine waters that were deeper than those of the early Cretaceous seas, except where rivers, deltas, and shallow marine shelves existed.

River delta and strandline sandstones are the reservoir rocks for the most prolific oil field in Texas. When discovered in 1930, this East Texas oil field contained recoverable reserves estimated at 5.6 billion barrels.

The chalky rock that we now call the "Austin Chalk" was deposited when the Texas seas became deeper. Today, the chalk and other Upper Cretaceous rocks crop out in a wide band that extends from near Eagle Pass on the Rio Grande, east to San Antonio, north to Dallas, and east to the Texarkana area. The Austin Chalk and other upper Cretaceous rocks dip southeastward beneath the East Texas and Gulf Coast basins.

The late Cretaceous was the time of the last major seaway across Texas, because mountains were forming in the western United States that influenced areas as far away as Texas.

A chain of volcanoes formed beneath the late Cretaceous seas in an area roughly parallel to and south and east of the old, buried Ouachita Mountains. The eruptions of these volcanoes were primarily on the sea floor and great clouds of steam and ash likely accompanied them.

Between eruptions, invertebrate marine animals built reefs on the shallow volcanic cones. Pilot Knob, located southeast of Austin, is one of these old volcanoes that is now exposed at the surface.

Cenozoic Era

At the dawn of the Cenozoic Era, approximately 65 million years ago, deltas fed by rivers were in the northern and northwestern margins of the East Texas Basin. These streams flowed eastward, draining areas to the north and west. Although there were minor incursions of the seas, the Cenozoic rocks principally document extensive seaward building by broad deltas, marshy lagoons, sandy barrier islands, and embayments.

Thick vegetation covered the levees and areas between the streams. Coastal plains were taking shape under the same processes still at work today.

The Mesozoic marine salt became buried by thick sediments in the coastal plain area. The salt began to form ridges and domes in the Houston and Rio Grande areas. The heavy load of sand, silt, and mud deposited by the deltas eventually caused some areas of the coast to subside and form large fault systems, essentially parallel to the coast.

Many of these coastal faults moved slowly and probably generated little earthquake activity. However, movement along the Balcones and Luling-Mexia-Talco zones, a complex system of faults along the western and northern edge of the basins, likely generated large earthquakes millions of years ago.

Predecessors of modern animals roamed the Texas Cenozoic coastal plains and woodlands. Bones and teeth of horses, camels, sloths, giant armadillos, mammoths, mastodons, bats, rats, large cats, and other modern or extinct mammals have been excavated from coastal plain deposits.

Vegetation in the area included varieties of plants and trees both similar and dissimilar to modern ones. Fossil palmwood, the Texas "state stone," is found in sediments of early Cenozoic age.

The Cenozoic Era in Trans-Pecos Texas was entirely different. There, extensive volcanic eruptions formed great calderas and produced copious lava flows. These eruptions ejected great clouds of volcanic ash and rock particles into the air — many times the amount of material ejected by the 1980 eruption of Mount St. Helens.

Photo by April Andreas

Want to Visit the Late Cenozoic Era?

Check out the **Waco Mammoth National Monument**. The park was opened in 2015 around the site where, in 1978, Paul Barron and Eddie Bufkin discovered large bones sticking out of a ravine.

Researchers found the remains of 19 mammoths, "an unidentified animal associated with a juvenile sabertooth cat", and other animals that had been buried there by floods some 65,000 years ago.

Visit **www.nps.gov/waco/index.htm** for more information. (And read more on page 165 of this book.)

Ash from the eruptions drifted eastward and is found in many of the sand-and-siltstones of the Gulf Coastal Plains. Lava flowed over older Paleozoic and Mesozoic rocks, and igneous intrusions melted their way upward into crustal rocks. These volcanic and intrusive igneous rocks are well exposed in arid areas of the Trans-Pecos today.

In the Texas Panhandle, streams originating in the recently elevated southern Rocky Mountains brought floods of gravel and sand into Texas. As the braided streams crisscrossed the area, they formed great alluvial fans.

These fans, which were deposited on the older Paleozoic and Mesozoic rocks, occur from northwestern Texas into Nebraska. Between 1 million and 2 million years ago, the streams of the Panhandle were isolated from their Rocky Mountain source, and the eastern edge of this sheet of alluvial material began to retreat westward, forming the Caprock of the modern High Plains.

Late in the Cenozoic Era, a great Ice Age descended on the northern North American continent. For more than 2 million years, there were successive advances and retreats of the thick sheets of glacial ice. Four periods of extensive glaciation were separated by warmer interglacial periods. Although the glaciers never reached as far south as Texas, the state's climate and sea level underwent major changes with each period of glacial advance and retreat.

Sea level during times of glacial advance was 300 to 450 feet lower than during the warmer interglacial periods because so much sea water was captured in the ice sheets. The climate was both more humid and cooler than today, and the major Texas rivers carried more water and more sand and gravel to the sea. These deposits underlie the outer 50 miles or more of the Gulf Coastal Plain.

Approximately 3,000 years ago, sea level reached its modern position. The rivers, deltas, lagoons, beaches, and barrier islands that we know as coastal Texas today have formed since that time. ☆

Soils of Texas

Source: Natural Resources Conservation Service, U.S. Department of Agriculture, www.tx.nrcs.usda.gov

One of Texas' most important natural resources is its soil. Texas soils are complex because of the wide diversity of climate, vegetation, geology, and landscape. More than 1,300 different kinds of soil are recognized in Texas. Each has a specific set of properties that affect its use.

Soils information that was once available only through paper maps or books is now easily accessed online through the Web Soil Survey, found here: **http://websoilsurvey.nrcs.usda.gov.**

As the state's population continues to move from rural to urban areas, the Web Soil Survey is a tool landowners can use to make land-use and management decisions. This free tool allows landowners to analyze soil data and maps. It is used by farmers and ranchers to find information about soil properties and qualities to optimize agricultural production.

The soil survey is also used by homeowners and commercial builders looking for information on the suitability or the limitations of a building site.

For more information, contact the Natural Resources Conservation Service at 101 S. Main, Temple 76501-7602; (254) 742-9800; or visit www.tx.nrcs.usda.gov; find the "Topic" menu and choose the "Soils" option.

Major Soil Areas

Texas can be divided into **21 Major Land Resource Areas** that have similar or related soils, vegetation, topography, climate, and land uses. Following are brief descriptions of these 21 areas:

Trans-Pecos Soils

The 18.7 million acres of the Trans-Pecos, mostly west of the Pecos River, are diverse plains and valleys intermixed with mountains. Surface drainage is slow to rapid. This arid region is used mainly as rangeland. A small amount of irrigated cropland lies on the more fertile soils along the Rio Grande and the Pecos River. Vineyards are a more recent use of these soils, as is the disposal of large volumes of municipal wastes.

Upland soils are mostly well-drained, light reddish-brown to brown clay loams, clays, and sands. Some have a large amount of gypsum or other salts. Many areas have shallow soils and rock outcrops, and sizable areas have deep sands.

Bottomland soils are deep, well-drained, dark grayish-brown to reddish-brown silt loams, loams, clay loams, and clays. The lack of soil moisture and wind erosion are the major soil-management problems. Only irrigated crops can be grown on these soils, and most areas lack an adequate source of good water.

Upper Pecos, Canadian Valleys and Plains Soils

The Upper Pecos, Canadian Valleys, and Plains area occupies a little over a half-million acres and is in the northwest part of Texas near the Texas–New Mexico border. It is characterized by broad rolling plains and tablelands broken by drainageways and tributaries of the Canadian River. It includes the Canadian Breaks, which are rough, steep lands below the adjacent High Plains. The average annual precipitation is about 15 inches, but it fluctuates widely from year to year. Surface drainage is slow to rapid.

The soils are well drained and alkaline. The mostly reddish-brown clay loams and sandy loams were formed mostly in material weathered from sandstone and shale. Depths range from shallow to very deep.

The area is used mainly as rangeland and wildlife habitat. Native vegetation is mid- to short-grass prairie species, such as hairy grama, sideoats grama, little bluestem, alkali sacaton, vine-mesquite, and galleta in the plains and tablelands. Juniper and mesquite grow on the relatively higher breaks. Soil management problems include low soil moisture and brush control.

High Plains Soils

The High Plains area comprises a vast high plateau of more than 19.4 million acres in northwestern Texas. It lies in the southern part of the Great Plains province that includes large, similar areas in Oklahoma and New Mexico. The flat, nearly level treeless plain has few streams to cause local relief. However, several major rivers originate in the High Plains or cross the area. The largest is the Canadian River, which has cut a deep valley across the Panhandle section.

Playas, small intermittent lakes scattered through the area, lie up to 20 feet below the surrounding plains. A 1965 survey counted more than 19,000 playas in 44 counties occupying some 340,000 acres. Most runoff from rainfall is collected in the playas, but only 10 to 40% of this water percolates back to the Ogallala Aquifer. The aquifer is virtually the exclusive water source in this area.

Upland soils are mostly well-drained, deep, neutral to alkaline clay loams and sandy loams in shades of brown or red. Sandy soils are in the southern part. Many soils have large amounts of lime at various depths and some are shallow over caliche. Soils of bottomlands are minor in extent.

The area is used mostly for cropland, but significant areas of rangeland are in the southwestern and extreme northern parts. Millions of cattle populate the many large feedlots in the area. The soils are moderately productive, and the flat surface encourages irrigation and mechanization. Limited soil moisture, constant danger of wind erosion, and irrigation water management are the major soil-management problems, but the region is Texas' leading producer of three important crops: cotton, grain sorghums, and wheat.

Rolling Plains Soils

The Rolling Plains include 21.7 million acres east of the High Plains in northwestern Texas. The area lies west of the North Central Prairies and extends from the edge of the Edwards Plateau in Tom Green County northward into Oklahoma. The landscape is nearly level to strongly rolling, and surface drainage is moderate to rapid. Outcrops of red beds, geologic materials, and associated reddish soils have led some scientists to use the name "Red Plains." Limestone underlies the soils in the southeastern part. The eastern part contains large areas of badlands (dry terrain with extensive erosion).

Upland soils are mostly deep, pale-brown through reddish-brown to dark grayish-brown, neutral to alkaline sandy loams, clay loams, and clays; some are deep sands.

Many soils have a large amount of lime in the lower part, and a few others are saline; some are shallow and stony. Bottomland soils are mostly reddish-brown and sandy to clayey; some are saline.

This area is used mostly for rangeland, but cotton, grain sorghums, and wheat are important crops. The major soil-management problems are brush control, wind erosion, low fertility, and lack of soil moisture. Salt spots are a concern in some areas.

North Central Prairie Soils

The North Central Prairie occupies about 7 million acres in North Central Texas. Adjacent to this area on the north is the rather small area (less than 1 million acres) called Rolling Red Prairies, which extends into Oklahoma and is included here because the soils and land use are similar.

This area lies between the Western Cross Timbers and the Rolling Plains. It is predominantly grassland intermixed with small wooded areas. The landscape is undulating with slow to rapid surface drainage.

Upland soils are mostly deep, well-drained, brown or reddish-brown, slightly acid loams over neutral to alkaline, clayey subsoils. Some soils are shallow or moderately deep to shale. Bottomland soils are mostly well-drained, dark-brown or gray loams and clays.

This area is used mostly as rangeland, but wheat, grain sorghums, and other crops are grown on the better soils. Brush control, wind and water erosion, and limited soil moisture are the major management concerns.

Edwards Plateau Soils

The 22.7 million acres of the Edwards Plateau are in South Central Texas east of the Trans-Pecos and west of the Blackland Prairie. Uplands are nearly level to undulating except near large stream valleys, where the landscape is hilly with deep canyons and steep slopes. There are many cedar brakes in this area. Surface drainage is rapid.

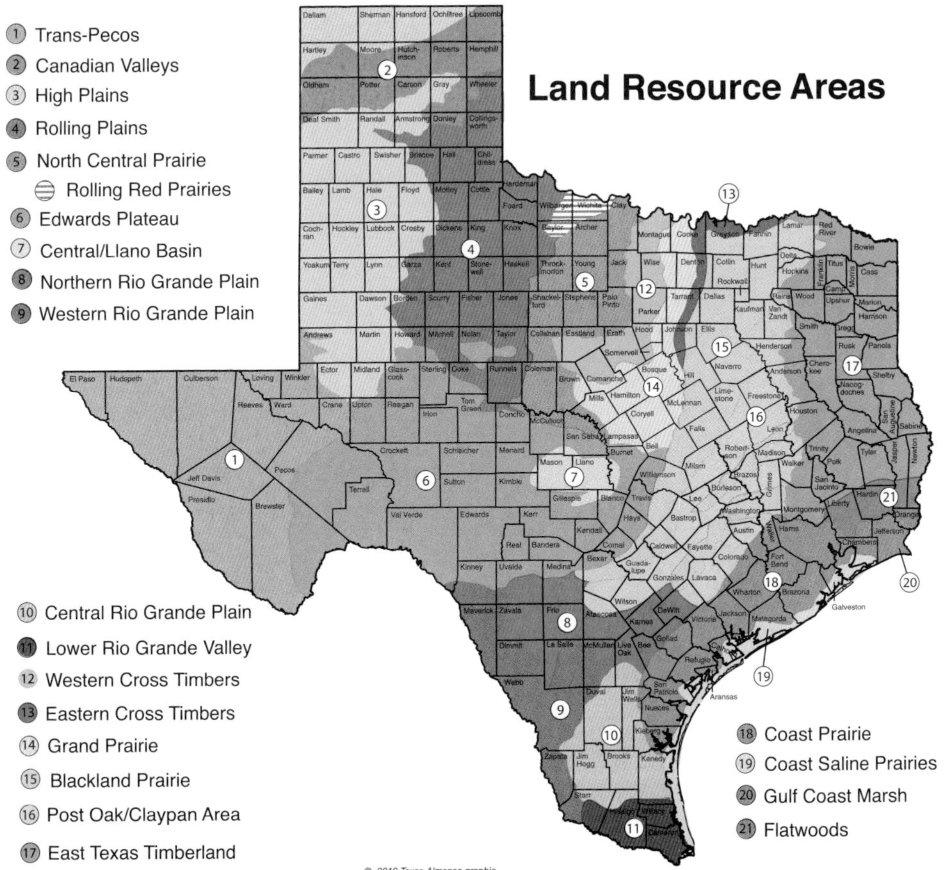

© 2010 Texas Almanac graphic.
Source: Natural Resources Conservation Service of the U.S. Department of Agriculture.

The map above shows the land resource areas of Texas, as defined by the Natural Resources Conservation Service at the U.S. Department of Agriculture. A land resource area is defined as "a geographic area, usually several thousand acres in extent, that is characterized by a particular pattern of soils, climate, water resources, land uses, and type of farming."

Mesquite trees and prickly pear cacti are common in most parts of the state, and are often cleared from pastureland as part of regular land management. Photo by USDA NRCS Texas/Flickr.

Upland soils are mostly shallow, stony, or gravelly, dark alkaline clays and clay loams underlain by limestone. Lighter-colored soils are on steep sideslopes and deep, less-stony soils are in the valleys. Bottomland soils are mostly deep, dark-gray or brown, alkaline loams and clays.

Raising beef cattle is the main enterprise in this region, but it is also the center of Texas' and the nation's mohair and wool production. The area is a major deer habitat, and hunting leases produce income. Cropland is mostly in the valleys on the deeper soils and is used mainly for growing forage crops and hay. The major soil-management concerns are brush control, large stones, low fertility, excess lime, and limited soil moisture.

Central or Llano Basin Soils

The Central Basin, also known as the Llano Basin, occupies a relatively small area in Central Texas. It includes parts or all of Llano, Mason, Gillespie, and adjoining counties. The total area is about 1.6 million acres of undulating to hilly landscape.

Upland soils are mostly shallow, reddish-brown to brown, mostly gravelly and stony, neutral to slightly acid sandy loams over granite, limestone, gneiss, and schist bedrock. Large boulders are on the soil surface in some areas. Deeper, less stony sandy-loam soils are in the valleys. Bottomland soils are minor areas of deep, dark-gray or brown loams and clays.

Ranching is the main enterprise, with some farms producing peaches, grain sorghum, and wheat. The area provides excellent deer habitat, and hunting leases are a major source of income. Brush control, large stones, and limited soil moisture are soil-management concerns.

Northern Rio Grande Plain Soils

The Northern Rio Grande Plain comprises about 6.3 million acres in South Texas extending from Uvalde to Beeville. The landscape is nearly level to rolling, mostly brush-covered plains with slow to rapid surface drainage.

The major upland soils are deep, reddish-brown or dark grayish-brown, neutral to alkaline loams and clays. Bottomland soils are mostly dark-colored loams.

The area is mostly rangeland with significant areas of cropland. Grain sorghums, cotton, corn, and small grains are the major crops. Crops are irrigated in the western part, especially in the Winter Garden area, where vegetables such as spinach, carrots, and cabbage are grown. Much of the area is good deer and dove habitat; hunting leases are a major source of income. Brush control, soil fertility, and irrigation-water management are the major soil-management concerns.

Western Rio Grande Plain Soils

The Western Rio Grande Plain comprises about 5.3 million acres in an area of southwestern Texas from Del Rio to Rio Grande City. The landscape is nearly level to undulating except near the Rio Grande where it is hilly. Surface drainage is slow to rapid.

The major soils are mostly deep, brown or gray alkaline clays and loams. Some are saline.

Most of the soils are used for rangeland. Irrigated grain sorghums and vegetables are grown along the Rio Grande. Hunting leases are a major source of income. Brush control and limited soil moisture are the major soil-management problems.

Central Rio Grande Plain Soils

The Central Rio Grande Plain comprises about 5.9 million acres in an area of South Texas from Live Oak County to Hidalgo County. It includes the South Texas Sand Sheet, an area of deep, sandy soils and active sand dunes. The landscape is nearly level to gently undulating. Surface drainage is slow to rapid. Upland soils are mostly deep, light-colored, neutral to alkaline sands and loams. Many are saline or sodic. Bottomland soils are of minor extent.

Most of the area is used for raising beef cattle. A few areas, mostly in the northeast part, are used for growing grain sorghums, cotton, and small grains. Hunting leases are a major source of income. Brush control is the major soil-management problem on rangeland; wind erosion and limited soil moisture are major concerns on cropland.

Lower Rio Grande Valley Soils

The Lower Rio Grande Valley comprises about 2.1 million acres in extreme southern Texas. The landscape is level to gently sloping with slow surface drainage.

Upland soils are mostly deep, grayish-brown, neutral to alkaline loams; coastal areas are mostly gray, silty clay loam and silty clay; some are saline. Bottomland soils are minor in extent.

Most of the soils are used for growing irrigated vegetables and citrus, along with cotton, grain sorghums, and sugar cane. Some areas are used for growing beef cattle. Irrigation water management and wind erosion are the major soil-management problems on cropland; brush control is the major problem on rangeland.

Western Cross Timbers Soils

The Western Cross Timbers area comprises about 2.6 million acres. It includes the wooded section west of the Grand Prairie and extends from the Red River southward to the north edge of Brown County. The landscape is undulating and is dissected by many drainageways including the Brazos and Red rivers. Surface drainage is rapid.

Upland soils are mostly deep, grayish-brown, slightly acid loams with loamy and clayey subsoils. Bottomland soils along the major rivers are deep, reddish-brown, neutral to alkaline silt loams and clays.

The area is used mostly for grazing beef and dairy cattle on native range and improved pastures. Crops are peanuts, grain sorghums, small grains, peaches, pecans, and vegetables. The major soil-management problem on grazing lands is brush control. Waste management on dairy farms is a more recent concern. Wind and water erosion are the major problems on cropland.

Eastern Cross Timbers Soils

The Eastern Cross Timbers area comprises about 1 million acres in a long narrow strip of wooded land that separates the northern parts of the Blackland Prairie and Grand Prairie and extends from the Red River southward to Hill County. The landscape is gently undulating to rolling and is dissected by many streams, including the Red and Trinity rivers. Sandstone-capped hills are prominent in some areas. Surface runoff is moderate to rapid.

The upland soils are mostly deep, light-colored, slightly acid sandy loams and loamy sands with reddish loamy or clayey subsoils. Bottomland soils are reddish-brown to dark gray, slightly acid to alkaline loams or gray clays.

Grassland consisting of native range and improved pastures is the major land use. Peanuts, grain sorghums, small grains, peaches, pecans, and vegetables are grown in some areas. Brush control, water erosion, and low fertility are the major soil concerns in management.

Grand Prairie Soils

The Grand Prairie comprises about 6.3 million acres in North Central Texas. It extends from the Red River to about the Colorado River. It lies between the Eastern and Western Cross Timbers in the northern part and just west of the Blackland Prairie in the southern part. The landscape is undulating to hilly and is dissected by many streams including the Red, Trinity, and Brazos rivers. Surface drainage is rapid.

Upland soils are mostly dark-gray, alkaline clays; some are shallow over limestone and some are stony. Some areas have light-colored loamy soils over chalky limestone. Bottomland soils along the Red and Brazos rivers are reddish silt loams and clays. Other bottomlands have dark-gray loams and clays.

Land use is a mixture of rangeland, pastureland, and cropland. The area is mainly used for growing beef cattle. Some small grain, grain sorghums, corn, and hay are grown. Brush control and water erosion are the major management concerns.

Blackland Prairie Soils

The Blackland Prairies consist of about 12.6 million acres of east-central Texas extending southwesterly from the Red River to Bexar County. There are smaller areas to the southeast. The landscape is undulating with few scattered wooded areas that are mostly in the bottomlands. Surface drainage is moderate to rapid.

Both upland and bottomland soils are deep, dark-gray to black alkaline clays. Some soils in the western part are shallow to moderately deep over chalk. Some soils on the eastern edge are neutral to slightly acid, grayish clays and loams over mottled clay subsoils (sometimes called graylands).

Blackland soils are known as "cracking clays" because of the large, deep cracks that form in dry weather. This high shrink-swell property can cause serious damage to foundations, highways, and other structures and is a safety hazard in pits and trenches.

Land use is divided about equally between cropland and grassland. Cotton, grain sorghums, corn, wheat, oats, and hay are grown. Grassland is mostly improved pastures, with native range on the shallower and steeper soils. Water erosion, cotton root rot, soil tilth, and brush control are the major management problems.

Claypan Area Soils

The Claypan Area consists of about 6.1 million acres in east-central Texas just east of the Blackland Prairie. The landscape is a gently undulating to rolling, moderately dissected woodland also known as the Post Oak Belt or Post Oak Savannah. Surface drainage is moderate.

Upland soils commonly have a thin, light-colored, acid sandy loam surface layer over dense, mottled red, yellow, and gray claypan subsoils. Some deep, sandy soils with less clayey subsoils exist. Bottomlands are deep, highly fertile, reddish-brown to dark-gray loamy to clayey soils.

Land use is mainly rangeland. Some areas are in improved pastures. Most cropland is in bottomlands that are protected from flooding. Major crops are cotton, grain sorghums, corn, hay, and forage crops, most of which are irrigated. Brush control on rangeland and irrigation water management on cropland are the major soil-management problems. Water erosion is a serious problem on the highly erosive claypan soils, especially where they are overgrazed.

East Texas Timberland Soils

The East Texas Timberlands area comprises about 16.1 million acres of the forested eastern part of the state. The land is gently undulating to hilly and well dissected by many streams. Surface drainage is moderate to rapid.

This area has many kinds of upland soils but most are deep, light-colored, acid sands and loams over loamy and clayey subsoils. Deep sands are in scattered areas, and red clays are in areas of "redlands." Bottomland soils are mostly brown to dark-gray, acid loams and some clays.

The land is used mostly for growing commercial pine timber and for woodland grazing. Improved pastures are scattered throughout and are used for grazing beef and dairy cattle and for hay production. Some commercial hardwoods are in the bottomlands. Woodland management problems include seedling survival, invasion of hardwoods in pine stands, effects of logging on water quality, and control of the southern pine beetle. Lime and fertilizers are necessary for productive cropland and pastures.

Coast Prairie Soils

The Coast Prairie includes about 8.7 million acres near the Gulf Coast. It ranges from 30 miles to 80 miles in width and parallels the coast from the Sabine River in Orange County in Southeast Texas to Baffin Bay in Kleberg County in South Texas. The landscape is level to gently undulating with slow surface drainage.

Upland soils are mostly deep, dark-gray, neutral to slightly acid clay loams and clays. Lighter-colored and more-sandy soils are in a strip on the northwestern edge. Some soils in the southern part are alkaline; some are saline and sodic. Bottomland soils are mostly deep, dark-colored clays and loams along small streams but are greatly varied along the rivers.

Land use is mainly grazing lands and cropland. Some hardwood timber is in the bottomlands. Many areas are also managed for wetland wildlife habitat. The nearly level topography and productive soils encourage farming. Rice, grain sorghums, cotton, corn, and hay are the main crops. Brush management on grasslands and removal of excess water on cropland are the major management concerns.

Coast Saline Prairies Soils

The Coast Saline Prairies area includes about 3.2 million acres along a narrow strip of wet lowlands adjacent to the coast; it includes the barrier islands that extend from Mexico to Louisiana. The surface is at or only a few feet above sea level with many areas of salt-water marsh. Surface drainage is very slow.

The soils are mostly deep, dark-colored clays and loams; many are saline and sodic. Light-colored sandy soils are on the barrier islands. The water table is at or near the surface of most soils.

Cattle grazing is the chief economic use of the various salt-tolerant cordgrasses and sedges. Many areas are managed for wetland wildlife. Recreation is popular on the barrier islands. Providing fresh water and access to grazing areas are the major management concerns.

Gulf Coast Marsh Soils

This 150,000-acre area lies in the extreme southeastern corner of Texas. The area can be subdivided into four parts: freshwater, intermediate, brackish, and saline (saltwater) marsh. The degree of salinity of this system grades landward from saltwater marshes along the coast to freshwater marshes inland. Surface drainage is very slow.

This area contains many lakes, bayous, tidal channels, and man-made canals. About one-half of the marsh is fresh; one-half is salty. Most of it is susceptible to flooding either by fresh water drained from lands adjacent to the marsh or by saltwater from the Gulf of Mexico.

Most of the soils are poorly drained, continuously saturated, soft, and can carry little weight. In general, the organic soils have a thick layer of dark gray, relatively undecomposed organic material over a gray, clayey subsoil. The mineral soils have a surface of dark gray, highly decomposed organic material over a gray, clayey subsoil.

Most of the almost treeless and uninhabited area is in marsh vegetation, such as grasses, sedges, and rushes. It is used mainly for wildlife habitat. Part of the fertile and productive estuarine complex supports marine life of the Gulf of Mexico. It also provides wintering ground for waterfowl and habitat for many fur-bearing animals and alligators. A significant acreage is firm enough to support livestock and is used for winter grazing of cattle. The major management problems are providing fresh water and access to grazing areas.

Flatwoods Soils

The Flatwoods area includes about 2.5 million acres of woodland in humid Southeast Texas just north of the Coast Prairie and extending into Louisiana. The landscape is level to gently undulating. Surface drainage is slow.

Upland soils are mostly deep, light-colored, acid loams with gray, loamy, or clayey subsoils. Bottomland soils are deep, dark-colored, acid clays and loams. The water table is near the surface at least part of the year.

The land is mainly used for forest, although cattle are grazed in some areas. Woodland management problems include seedling survival, invasion of hardwoods in pine stands, effects of logging on water quality, and control of the southern pine beetle. ☆

A footbridge over the Concho River. Photo by Jonathan Cutrer, jcutrer.com.

Texas Water Resources

Contributed by Dr. Andrew Sansom, leading conservationist and executive director of the Meadows Center for Water and the Environment.

Water shortage is the **most serious** natural resource issue facing Texas today.

Here, as elsewhere in the world, the struggle over the uses to which water should be put — and who has the right to decide on those uses — is **intense and escalating**, particularly as the cyclical occurrence of severe flooding and drought increase. The bottom line is that Texas' population is going to double in the next fifty years (for more about this, see our feature article on page 373) and if all the water rights we have issued in our major rivers since Texas was a colony of Spain were fully exercised, many of them would be dry today. Thus, **many of our most iconic rivers**, which are vital to both our economy and the environment, **are at risk**.

Due in part to increasing stress on our rivers and lakes in Texas, we are also increasingly dependent on groundwater from the State's diverse major and minor aquifers. Unfortunately, **we do not recognize in law or policy the hydrologic linkage of our groundwater resources to surface water** — this failure will complicate sound water management of both in the future.

Texas' sensational system of bays and estuaries are arguably the finest such system of any state in the union. These coastal systems provide billions of dollars of economic benefit to the State and constitute some of the most prolific marine ecosystems in the world. What is less understood is that this spectacular natural resource is entirely dependent on continued supplies of freshwater flowing down our rivers and streams to mix with saltwater to **create the unique conditions vital to the existence of so many species of fish and wildlife**. Despite the enormous economic and environmental benefits we receive from these freshwater inflows, we have done a very inadequate job of insuring their continuation.

Historically, we have been reluctant to make difficult choices and decisions relating to water but when faced with crisis we have reacted. Following the drought of the 1950's, which we formally consider the worst on record, we built over 200 major reservoirs for flood control, water supply, and hydropower and they have served us well. However, since the 1970's there has been a dramatic decline in reservoir construction, due to a number of reasons.

More and more communities are creating underground reservoirs in a process called aquifer storage and retrieval, which captures water in times of high flows and stores it to avoid evaporation. We also have millions of acre feet of **brackish groundwater** in Texas **which has been largely untapped** and is less saline than water from the Gulf and closer to the consumer, making it less costly to produce and deliver.

But will that be enough to ensure our future? Despite much progress in water conservation, particularly in cities like San Antonio and El Paso, we still waste far too much water. **It is likely that the key to having a healthy water supply in the future will be increased efficiency.**

Our rivers and streams, our bays, estuaries, and our aquifers not only help define us as a state but are essential components of the one resource that no plant and animal can live without: water. We must do everything we can to make sure it is there for our economy, our environment, and our children. ☆

Major Aquifers of Texas

Sources: Texas Water Development Board, www.twdb.texas.gov; U.S. Geological Survey, https://www.usgs.gov/centers/tx-water

Aquifers are water-bearing rock formations beneath the earth's surface. Texas has a wealth of fresh to slightly saline groundwater in **nine major and 22 minor aquifers** that underlie more than 81 percent of the state.

Each year, groundwater provides approximately 60 percent of the water used in the state. Annual water use ranged from 14.23 million acre-feet in 2016 to 18.18 million acre-feet in 2011. The median annual water use between the years 2007 and 2016 was 14.6 million acre-feet.

Groundwater is an important resource to every industry in Texas, from farming, ranching, and manufacturing to energy exploration and refining.

Groundwater also provides water for municipal and environmental needs. Approximately 55 percent of the groundwater produced in 2016 was used for agriculture (mostly for irrigation). About half of this amount is used in the Panhandle region of the state. In 2016, groundwater supplied approximately 31 percent of the state's municipal water needs.

For more information about the aquifers of Texas and groundwater management, watch these videos created by the Texas Water Development Board:

www.twdb.texas.gov/groundwater/video/index.asp

Ogallala

The Ogallala Aquifer underlies most of the Texas Panhandle. It is the southernmost extension of the largest aquifer (High Plains Aquifer) in North America. The Ogallala Formation of late Miocene to early Pliocene age consists of heterogeneous sequences of coarse-grained sand and gravel in the lower part, grading upward into clay, silt, and fine sand.

The formation reaches a maximum thickness of 800 feet, and its freshwater saturated thickness averages 95 feet. In Texas, the Panhandle is the most extensive region irrigated with groundwater. About 95 percent of the water pumped from the Ogallala Aquifer is used for irrigation.

Extensive pumping that exceeds the amount of recharge has resulted in consistently declining water levels throughout much of the aquifer. Water conservation measures promoted by agricultural and municipal users have slowed the rate of decline, and water levels have risen in a few areas. Several agencies are investigating playa recharge and agricultural reuse projects in the aquifer area.

Gulf Coast

The Gulf Coast Aquifer system forms a broad belt parallel to the Texas coastline, extending through 54 counties from the Rio Grande northeastward to the Louisiana border. The aquifer system is composed of Quaternary- and Tertiary-age layers including the Catahoula, Oakville, Fleming, Goliad, Willis, Lissie, Bentley, Montgomery, and Beaumont formations.

The Gulf Coast Aquifer system has been divided into three major water-producing components referred to as the Chicot, Evangeline, and Jasper aquifers. These aquifers are composed of discontinuous layers of sand, silt, clay, and gravel.

The maximum total sand thickness of the Gulf Coast Aquifer system ranges from 700 feet in the south to 1,300 feet in the north. Freshwater saturated thickness averages 1,000 feet. The Gulf Coast Aquifer system is used primarily for municipal, industrial, and agricultural purposes.

Water quality is generally good in the central and northeastern parts of the aquifer but deteriorates to the southwest. Years of heavy pumping have caused significant water-level declines in portions of the aquifer. Some of these declines have resulted in land subsidence, particularly in the Houston-Galveston area.

Edwards Balcones Fault Zone

The Edwards Balcones Fault Zone (BFZ) Aquifer forms a narrow belt extending through the south-central part of the state from a groundwater divide in Kinney County through the San Antonio area northeastward to the Leon River in Bell County. A groundwater divide in Hays County hydrologically separates the aquifer into the San Antonio and Austin regions.

The aquifer is highly permeable, with water occurring in fractures, honeycomb-like zones (or intergranular pores), and solution channels that characterize the Edwards and associated limestone formations of Cretaceous age. Because the aquifer is highly permeable, water levels and spring flows respond quickly to rainfall, drought, and pumping. Aquifer thickness ranges from 200 to 600 feet, and freshwater saturated thickness averages 560 feet in the southern part of the aquifer.

Water from the Edwards BFZ is used primarily for municipal, irrigation, and recreational purposes. The City of San Antonio meets the majority of its water needs with Edwards BFZ water. The aquifer also feeds several well-known recreational springs and underlies some of Texas's most environmentally sensitive areas.

In 1993, the Texas Legislature created the Edwards Aquifer Authority (EAA) to regulate pumping from the aquifer to benefit all users within EAA's jurisdiction. The Barton Springs/Edwards Aquifer Conservation District and the Kinney County Groundwater Conservation District also provide aquifer management in the areas of the aquifer that are not within the EAA boundaries.

The EAA has an active outreach program used to educate the public on water conservation. It also operates several active groundwater recharge sites. The San Antonio River Authority also has a number of flood-control structures that effectively recharge the aquifer.

Carrizo-Wilcox

The Carrizo-Wilcox Aquifer extends from south of the Rio Grande in Mexico through Texas northeastward into Arkansas and Louisiana in a wide band parallel to and northwest of the Gulf Coast Aquifer.

The aquifer consists of the Tertiary-age Wilcox Group and overlying Carrizo Sand Formation of the Claiborne Group. The aquifer is composed of a hydrologically connected system of sand locally interbedded with clay, silt, lignite, and gravel. Although the Carrizo-Wilcox Aquifer reaches 3,000 feet in thickness, the freshwater saturated thickness of the sands averages 670 feet.

Throughout most of its extent in Texas, the aquifer yields fresh to slightly saline water. A little more than half of the water pumped from the aquifer is used for irrigation; the remaining amount pumped is used for municipal, industrial, domestic, and livestock purposes.

Recently, the Carrizo-Wilcox Aquifer has been considered as an alternative water supply for growing central Texas communities that have traditionally used the Edwards BFZ Aquifer to meet municipal needs.

Trinity

The Trinity Aquifer consists of Cretaceous-age Trinity Group formations that extend from the Red River in North Texas southward to the Hill Country of Central Texas. It is composed of several smaller aquifers contained within the Trinity Group. Depending on where they occur in the state, they are referred to as the Antlers, Glen Rose, Paluxy, Twin Mountains, Travis Peak, Hensell, and Hosston aquifers.

These aquifers consist of limestones, sands, clays, gravels, and conglomerates. Their combined freshwater saturated thickness averages about 600 feet in North Texas, and about 1,900 feet in Central Texas. The aquifer discharges to many small springs, with most flowing less than 10 cubic feet per second.

The Trinity Aquifer is primarily used to meet municipal water demands, but also provides water for irrigation, livestock, and other domestic purposes. Extensive development of the Trinity Aquifer in the Dallas–Fort Worth and Waco areas has resulted in water-level declines of 350 feet to more than 1,000 feet, though these declines have slowed with more reliance on surface water and reductions in groundwater pumping.

Edwards-Trinity Plateau

The Edwards-Trinity Plateau Aquifer extends from the Hill Country of Central Texas westward and southwestward to the Trans-Pecos region, covering much of the southwestern part of the state. The aquifer consists of early Cretaceous limestone and dolomites of the Edwards Group and sands of the Trinity Group. Although the maximum saturated thickness of the aquifer is greater than 800 feet, freshwater saturated thickness averages 433 feet.

The aquifer lies beneath the Edwards Plateau. Near the plateau's edge, along the northern, eastern, and southern

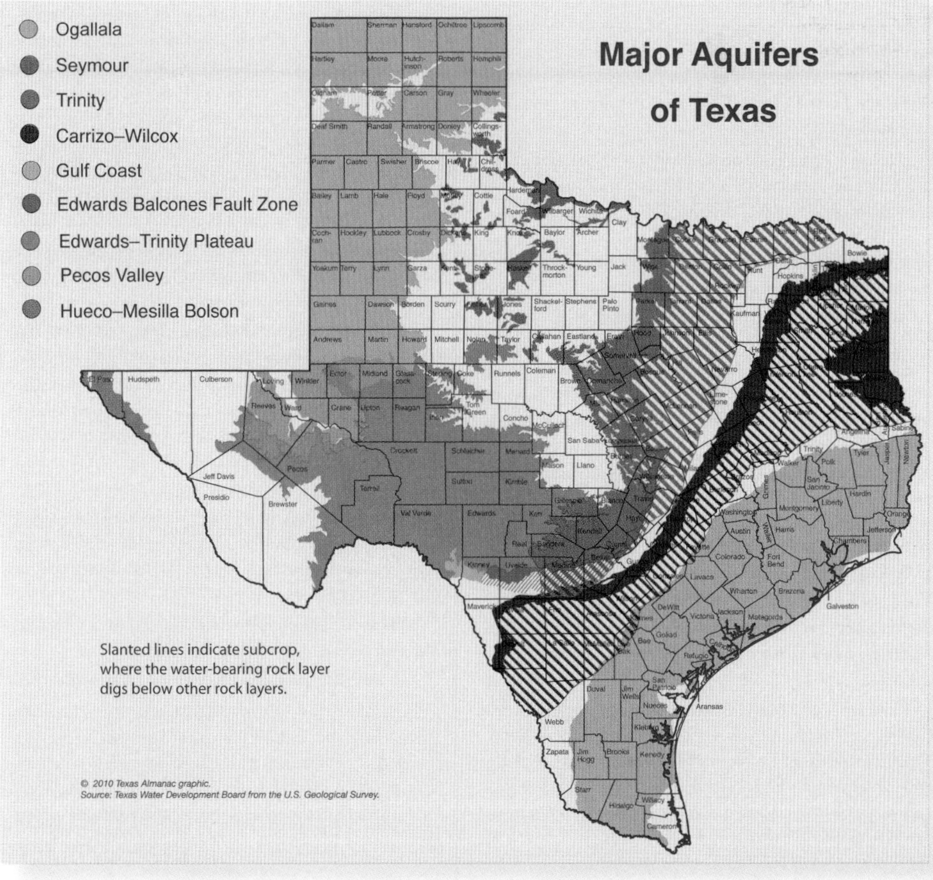

margins of the aquifer, groundwater flows towards streams, where water discharges from springs. Irrigation, mainly in the northwestern portion of the region, accounts for more than two-thirds of aquifer use.

Seymour

The Seymour Aquifer extends across north-central Texas. It consists of Quaternary-age, alluvial sediments unconformably overlying Permian-age rocks. Water is contained within isolated patches of discontinuous beds of poorly sorted gravel, conglomerate, sand, and silty clay. These deposits may reach 360 feet in thickness, but most of the Seymour is less than 100 feet thick.

About 90 percent of the water pumped from the Seymour is used for irrigation. Water quality generally ranges from fresh to slightly saline; however, some areas have moderately to very saline water quality. Nitrate concentrations occur above primary drinking water standards throughout much of the aquifer.

Hueco-Mesilla Bolsons

The Hueco-Mesilla Bolsons Aquifer is located in El Paso and Hudspeth counties in far West Texas. The aquifer consists of Tertiary and Quaternary basin-fill deposits of silt, sand, gravel, and clay that extend northward into New Mexico and westward into Mexico in two basins. The Hueco Bolson, located on the eastern side of the Franklin Mountains, has a maximum thickness of 9,000 feet and is an important source of drinking water for both El Paso and Juárez, Mexico. The Mesilla Bolson, located on the western side of the Franklin Mountains, has a maximum thickness of 2,000 feet.

Historical large-scale groundwater withdrawals, especially for the municipal uses of El Paso and Juárez, have caused major water-level declines. This pumping has also caused a deterioration of the chemical quality of the groundwater in the aquifer, according to El Paso Water Utilities and the United States Geological Survey.

Nearly 90 percent of the water pumped from the aquifer in the Texas extent of the bolsons is used for public supply. The City of El Paso has reduced its use of groundwater from the Hueco Bolson since 1989, and observation wells indicate that water levels have stabilized from a previously declining trend. El Paso and Fort Bliss also have built the world's largest inland desalination plant in El Paso County, which uses brackish groundwater from the Hueco Bolson.

Pecos Valley

The Pecos Valley Aquifer is located in the upper Pecos River Valley of West Texas. This aquifer, formerly called the Cenozoic Pecos Alluvium, consists of up to 1,500 feet of Tertiary and Quaternary alluvial fill and windblown deposits.

The aquifer occupies two hydrologically separate basins: the Pecos Trough in the west and the Monument Draw Trough in the east. The alluvial fill reaches 1,500 feet thick, and freshwater saturated thickness averages about 250 feet. Naturally occurring arsenic and radionuclides occur in excess of primary drinking water standards.

More than 80 percent of groundwater pumped from the aquifer is used for irrigation, and the remainder is withdrawn for industrial, power supply, and municipal uses. Water-level declines in excess of 200 feet have occurred in Reeves and Pecos counties but have slowed since the mid-1970s as irrigation pumping has decreased. Declines continue in Ward County due to increased municipal and industrial pumping. ☆

Water Regulation in Texas

In Texas, water law historically has been different for surface water and groundwater. **Surface water belongs to the state** and, except for limited amounts of water for household and on-farm livestock use, requires a permit for use.

The **Texas Commission on Environmental Quality (TCEQ)** is responsible for permitting and adjudicating surface water rights. The TCEQ is the primary regulator of surface water and polices contamination and pollution of both surface and groundwater.

In general, groundwater is considered the private property of the surface landowner by "rule of capture," meaning the landowner may pump as much water as he wishes from beneath his land for any beneficial use and that does not harm neighboring property.

This right may be limited only by groundwater conservation districts, which are the state's preferred method of groundwater management and provide for the conservation, preservation, protection, recharging, and prevention of waste of groundwater resources within their jurisdictions.

As of August 2021, there are 98 **groundwater conservation districts** in Texas, covering nearly 70 percent of the state. In addition, two subsidence districts cover Harris, Galveston, and Fort Bend counties. Subsidence districts regulate groundwater production to prevent land subsidence: the gradual caving in or sinking of an area of land.

The **Texas Water Development Board (TWDB)** collects data on water quality and availability within the state, plans for future supply and use, and administers the state's funds for grants and loans to finance future water development and supply. See the current members of the TWDB on page 481.

On July 7, 2021, the TWDB voted to adopt the 2022 State Water Plan. It outlines water conservation strategies for meeting projected water supply needs in 2070. The board has also adopted 16 regional water plans focusing on specific parts of the state.

You can see an interactive version of the current state water plan here:

2022.texasstatewaterplan.org/statewide

In addition, Texas has a Water Conservation Advisory Council, created in 2007. The council provides reports to the Texas Legislature to make recommendations about funding for water-related programs and suggest legislation to extend the lives of our water resources. Learn more at:

savetexaswater.org

Diners sit along the San Antonio River Walk. Photo by Pedro Szekely, CC by 2.0/Flickr.

Major Rivers of Texas

Sources: Texas Water Development Board, www.twdb.texas.gov; U.S. Geological Survey, https://www.usgs.gov/centers/tx-water

There are 11,247 named Texas streams identified in the U.S. Geological Survey Geographic Names Information System. Their combined length is about 80,000 miles, and they drain 263,513 square miles within Texas. Fourteen major rivers are described in this section, starting with the southernmost and moving northward.

Rio Grande

The Pueblo Indians called this river P'osoge, which means the "river of great water." In 1582, Antonio de Espejo of Nueva Vizcaya, Mexico, followed the course of the Río Conchos to its confluence with a great river, which he named Río del Norte (River of the North). The name Rio Grande was first used, apparently by the explorer Juan de Oñate, who arrived on its banks near present-day El Paso in 1598.

Thereafter the names were often consolidated as Río Grande del Norte. It was shown also on early Spanish maps as Río San Buenaventura and Río Ganapetuán. In its lower course, it early acquired the name Río Bravo, which is its name on most Mexican maps. At times it has also been known as Río Turbio, probably because of its muddy appearance during its frequent rises. Some people erroneously call this watercourse the Rio Grande River.

This river forms the boundary of Texas and the international U.S.-Mexican border for 889 or 1,254 river miles, depending upon method of measurement. (See Texas Boundary Lines, page 27.)

The U.S. Geological Survey figure for the total length from its headwaters to its mouth on the Gulf of Mexico is 1,900 miles.

According to the USGS, the Rio Grande is tied with the St. Lawrence River (also 1,900 miles) as the fourth-longest North American river, exceeded only by the Missouri-Mississippi, Mackenzie-Peace, and Yukon rivers. Since all of these except the Missouri-Mississippi are partly in Canada, the Rio Grande is the second-longest river entirely within or bordering the United States. It is Texas' longest river.

The snow-fed flow of the Rio Grande is used for irrigation in Colorado below the San Juan Mountains, where the river rises at the Continental Divide. Turning south, it flows through a canyon in northern New Mexico and again irrigates a broad valley of central New Mexico. Southern

Average Annual Flow

	River	Acre-Feet*
1.	Brazos	6,074,000
2.	Sabine	5,864,000
3.	Trinity	5,727,000
4.	Neches	4,323,000
5.	Red	3,464,000
6.	Colorado	1,904,000

* One acre-foot equals 325,851 gallons of water.
Source: Texas Water Development Board, 2017 State Water Plan.

Lengths Of Major Rivers

	River	Length (Miles)
1.	Rio Grande	1,900
2.	Red	1,290
3.	Brazos	1,280
4.	Pecos	926
5.	Canadian	906
6.	Colorado	865

Source: U.S. Geological Survey, 2008.

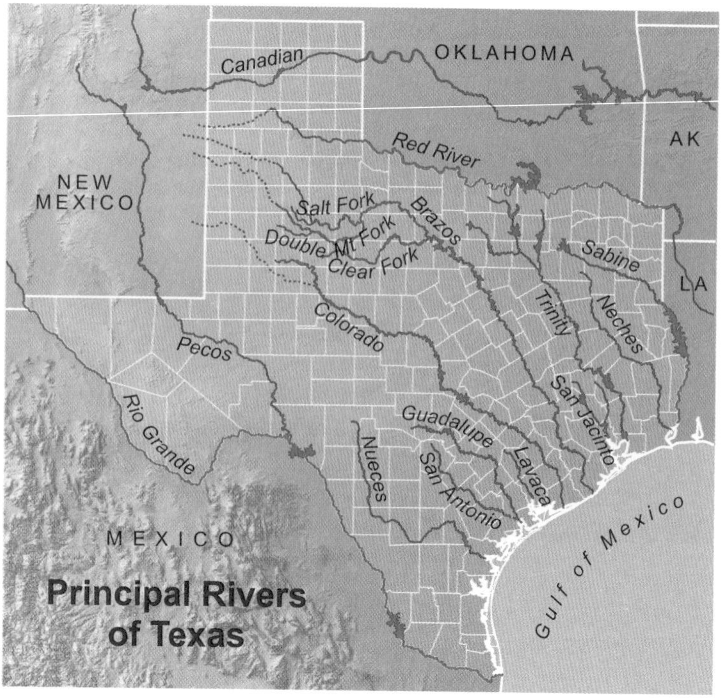

New Mexico impounds Rio Grande waters in Elephant Butte Reservoir for irrigation of the valley above and below El Paso.

The valley near El Paso is thought to be the oldest irrigated area in Texas because Indians were irrigating crops here when Spanish explorers arrived in the early 1500s.

From source to mouth, the Rio Grande drops 12,000 feet to sea level as a mountain torrent, desert stream, and meandering coastal river. Along its banks and in its valley, Europeans established some of their first North American settlements. Here are situated three of the oldest towns in Texas: Ysleta, Socorro, and San Elizario.

Because of the extensive irrigation, the Rio Grande virtually ends at the lower end of the El Paso valley, except in seasons of above-normal flow.

The river starts again as a perennially flowing stream where the Río Conchos of Mexico flows into it at Presidio-Ojinaga. Through the Big Bend, the Rio Grande flows through three successive canyons, the Santa Elena, the Mariscal, and the Boquillas. The Santa Elena has a river bed elevation of 2,145 feet and a canyon-rim elevation of 3,661. Corresponding figures for Mariscal are 1,925 and 3,625, and for Boquillas, 1,850 and 3,490. The river here flows for about 100 miles around the base of the Chisos Mountains as the southern boundary of Big Bend National Park.

Below the Big Bend, the Rio Grande gradually emerges from mountains onto the Coastal Plains. A 191.2-mile strip on the U.S. side from Big Bend National Park downstream to the Terrell–Val Verde county line has federal designation as the Rio Grande Wild and Scenic River.

At the confluence of the Rio Grande and Devils River, the United States and Mexico have built Amistad Dam, to impound 3,275,532 acre-feet of water, of which Texas' share is 56.2 percent. Falcon Reservoir, also an international project in Zapata and Starr counties, impounds 2,646,813 acre-feet of water, of which Texas' share in Zapata and Starr counties is 58.6 percent.

The Rio Grande, where it joins the Gulf of Mexico, has created a fertile delta called the Lower Rio Grande Valley, a major vegetable- and fruit-growing area. The river drains 49,387 square miles of Texas and has an average annual flow of 1,064,613 acre-feet.

Principal tributaries flowing from the Texas side are the Pecos and Devils rivers. On the Mexican side are Río Conchos, Río Salado, and Río San Juan. About three-fourths of the water running into the Rio Grande below El Paso comes from the Mexican side.

Pecos River

The Pecos, one of the major tributaries of the Rio Grande, rises on the western slope of the Santa Fe Mountains in the Sangre de Cristo Range of northern New Mexico. It enters Texas as the boundary between Loving and Reeves counties and flows 350 miles southeast as the boundary for several other counties, entering Val Verde County at its northwestern corner and angles across that county to its mouth on the Rio Grande, northwest of Del Rio.

According to the Handbook of Texas, the origins of the river's several names began with Antonio de Espejo, who called the river the Río de las Vacas ("river of the cows") because of the number of buffalo in the vicinity. Gaspar Castaño de Sosa, who followed the Pecos northward, called it the Río Salado because of its salty taste, which caused it to be shunned by men and animals alike.

It is believed that the name "Pecos" first appears in Juan de Oñate's reports concerning the Indian pueblo of Cicuye, now known as the Pecos Pueblo in New Mexico, and is of unknown origin.

Through most of its 926-mile-long course from its headwaters, the Pecos River parallels the Rio Grande. The total drainage area of the Pecos in New Mexico and Texas is about 44,000 square miles. Most of its tributaries flow from the west; these include the Delaware River and Toyah Creek.

The topography of the river valley in Texas ranges from semi-arid irrigated farmlands, desert with sparse vegetation, and, in the lowermost reaches of the river, deep canyons.

Nueces River

The Nueces River rises in two forks in Edwards and Real counties and flows 315 miles to Nueces Bay on the Gulf near Corpus Christi. Draining 16,700 square miles, it is a beautiful, spring-fed stream flowing through canyons until it issues from the Balcones Escarpment onto the Coastal Plains in northern Uvalde County.

Alonso de León, in 1689, gave it its name. Nueces, plural of nuez, means nuts in Spanish. (More than a century earlier, Cabeza de Vaca had referred to a Río de las Nueces in this region, but that is now thought to have been the Guadalupe.)

The original Indian name for this river seems to have been Chotilapacquen. Crossing Texas in 1691, Terán de los Ríos named the river San Diego.

The Nueces was the boundary line between the Spanish provinces of Texas and Nuevo Santander. After the Texas Revolution of 1836, both Texas and Mexico claimed the territory between the Nueces and the Rio Grande, a dispute that was settled in 1848 by the Treaty of Guadalupe Hidalgo, which fixed the international boundary at the Rio Grande.

Average runoff of the Nueces is about 539,700 acre-feet a year. Principal water supply projects are Lake Corpus Christi and Choke Canyon Reservoir. Principal tributaries of the Nueces are the Frio and the Atascosa rivers. The river terminates in Nueces and Corpus Christi bays along the Coastal Bend.

San Antonio River

The San Antonio River has at its source large springs within and near the city limits of San Antonio. It flows 180 miles across the Coastal Plains to a junction with the Guadalupe River to enter San Antonio Bay along the Gulf Coast. Its channel through San Antonio has been developed into a parkway known as the River Walk.

Its principal tributaries are the Medina River and Cibolo Creek, both spring-fed streams, and this, with its own spring origin, gives it remarkably clear water and makes it one of the steadiest of Texas rivers. Including the Medina River headwaters, it is 238 miles in length.

The river was first named the León by Alonso de León in 1689; the name was not for himself, but he called it "lion" because its channel was filled with a rampaging flood.

Because of its limited and arid drainage area (4,180 square miles) the average runoff of the San Antonio River is relatively small, about 562,700 acre-feet annually.

Guadalupe River

The Guadalupe rises in its North and South forks in western Kerr County. A spring-fed stream, it flows eastward through the Hill Country until it issues from the Balcones Escarpment near New Braunfels. It then crosses the Coastal Plains to San Antonio Bay. Its total length is 409 miles, and its drainage area is 5,953 square miles. Its principal tributaries are the Comal, which joins it at New Braunfels; the San Marcos, another spring-fed stream, which joins it in Gonzales County; and the San Antonio, which joins it just above its mouth on San Antonio Bay.

There has been power development on the Guadalupe near Gonzales and Cuero for many years, and there is also power generation at Canyon Lake. Because of its springs and its considerable drainage area, the Guadalupe has an average annual runoff of more than 1.42 million acre-feet.

The name Guadalupe is derived from Nuestra Señora de Guadalupe, the name given the stream by Alonso de León.

Lavaca River

The Lavaca rises in extreme southwestern Fayette County and flows 117 miles to terminate in Lavaca Bay. Without a spring-fed water source and with only a small watershed, including that of its principal tributary, the Navidad, its flow is intermittent. Runoff averages about 277,000 acre-feet yearly.

The Spanish called it the Lavaca (the cow) because of the numerous bison found near it. It is the principal stream flowing to the Texas Coast between the Guadalupe and the Colorado, and drains 2,309 square miles. The principal lake on the Navidad is Lake Texana.

Colorado River

The Colorado River rises in east-central Dawson County and flows 600 miles to Matagorda Bay. Its drainage area, which extends into New Mexico, is 42,318 square miles. The U.S. Geological Survey puts is total length from source at 865 miles.

Its average annual runoff reaches a volume of 1.9 million acre-feet near the coast. Its name is a Spanish word meaning "reddish." There is evidence that Spanish explorers originally named the muddy Brazos "Colorado," but Spanish mapmakers later transposed the two names.

The river flows through a rolling, mostly prairie terrain to the vicinity of San Saba County, where it enters the rugged Hill Country and Llano Basin. It passes through a picturesque series of canyons until it issues from the Balcones Escarpment at Austin and flows across the Coastal Plains.

In the Hill Country, a remarkable series of reservoirs has been built to provide hydoelectric power, flood control, and water supply. The largest of these are Lake Buchanan in Burnet and Llano counties and Lake Travis in Travis County. Between the two in Burnet County are three smaller reservoirs: Inks, Lyndon B. Johnson (formerly Granite Shoals), and Marble Falls. Below Lake Travis is the older Lake Austin, largely filled with silt, whose dam is used to produce power from waters flowing down from the lakes above. Lady Bird Lake (formerly Town Lake) is in the city of Austin. This entire area is known as the Highland Lakes Country.

As early as the 1820s, Anglo-Americans settled on the banks of the lower Colorado, and in 1839, the Capital Commission of the Republic of Texas chose the picturesque area where the river flows from the Balcones Escarpment as the site of a new capital of the Republic — now Austin, capital of the state.

The early colonists encouraged navigation along the lower channel with some success. However, a natural log raft that formed 10 miles from the Gulf blocked river traffic after 1839, although shallow-draught vessels occasionally ventured as far upstream as Austin.

Conservation and utilization of the waters of the Colorado are under the jurisdiction of two agencies created

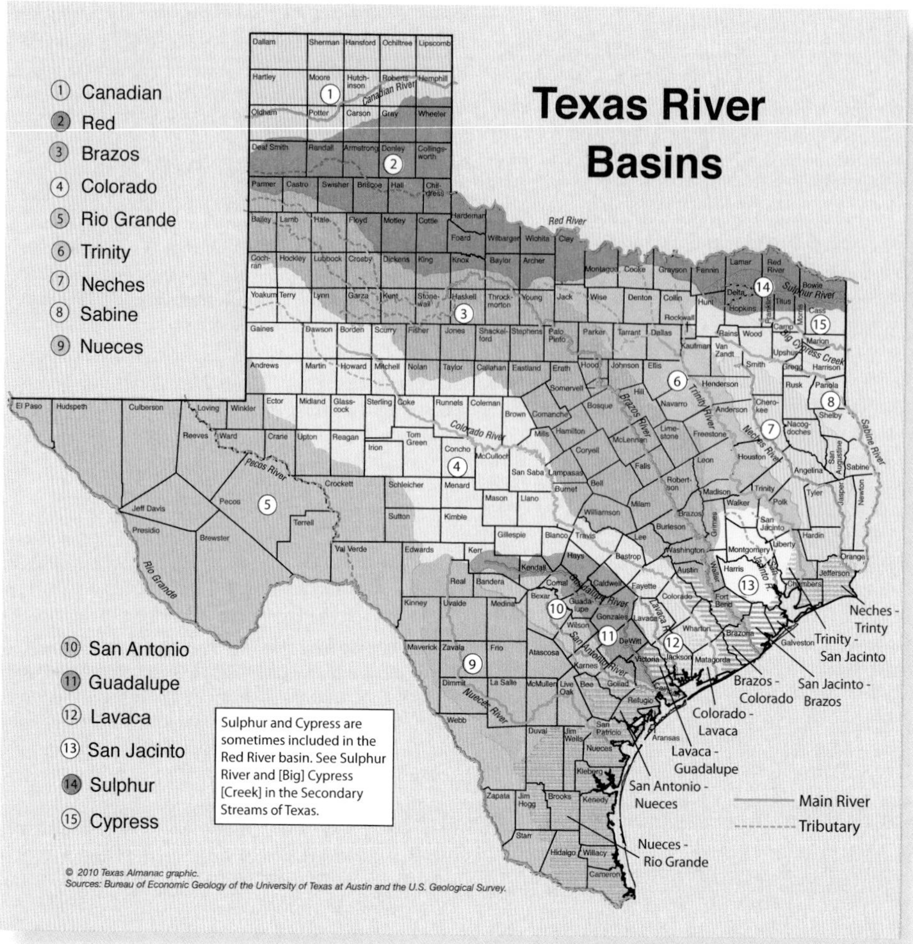

by the Legislature — the Lower and Upper Colorado River authorities.

The principal tributaries of the Colorado River are the several prongs of the Concho River on its upper course, Pecan Bayou (farthest west "bayou" in the United States), and the Llano, San Saba, and Pedernales rivers. All except Pecan Bayou flow into the Colorado from the Edwards Plateau and are spring-fed, perennially flowing rivers. In the numerous mussels found along these streams, pearls occasionally have been found. On early Spanish maps, the Middle Concho was called Río de las Perlas.

Brazos River

The Brazos River proper is considered to begin where the Double Mountain and Salt Forks flow together in northeastern Stonewall County; it then flows 840 miles across Texas. The U.S. Geological Survey puts the total length from the New Mexico source of its longest upper prong at 1,280 miles.

With a drainage area of about 42,865 square miles, it is the second-largest river basin in Texas, after the Rio Grande. It flows directly into the Gulf southwest of Freeport in Brazoria County. Its average annual flow approaches 6.1 million acre-feet, the largest volume of any river in the state.

The Brazos' third upper fork is the Clear Fork, which joins the main stream in Young County, just above Possum Kingdom Lake. The Brazos crosses most of the main physiographic regions of Texas: High Plains, West Texas Rolling Plains, Western Cross Timbers, Grand Prairie, and Gulf Coastal Plains.

The original name of this river was Brazos de Dios, meaning "Arms of God." There are several legends as to why. One story is that the Coronado expedition, wandering on the trackless Llano Estacado, exhausted its water and was threatened with death from thirst. Arriving at the bank of the river, they gave it the name "Brazos de Dios" in thankfulness. Another legend is that a ship exhausted its water supply, and its crew was saved when they found the mouth of the Brazos. Still another story is that miners on the San Saba were forced by drought to seek water near present-day Waco and in gratitude called it Brazos de Dios.

Much early Anglo-American colonization of Texas took place in the Brazos Valley. Along its channel were San Felipe de Austin, capital of Austin's colony;

Washington-on-the-Brazos, where Texans declared independence from Mexico; and other historic settlements. There was some navigation of the lower channel of the Brazos in this period. Near its mouth, it intersects the Gulf Intracoastal Waterway, which provides connection with commerce throughout Texas and the Gulf Coast.

Most of the Brazos Valley lies within the boundaries of the Brazos River Authority, which conducts a multipurpose program for development. A large reservoir on the main channel of the Brazos is Lake Whitney (554,203 acre-feet capacity), where it is the boundary line between Hill and Bosque counties. Lake Waco on the Bosque and Belton Lake on the Leon are among the principal reservoirs on its tributaries. In addition to its three upper forks, other chief tributaries are the Paluxy, Little, and Navasota rivers.

San Jacinto River

The San Jacinto is a short river with a drainage basin of 3,936 square miles and an average annual runoff of about 1.36 million acre-feet. It is formed by the junction of its East and West forks in northeastern Harris County and runs to the Gulf through Galveston Bay. Its total length, including the East Fork, is about 85 miles.

Lake Conroe is on the West Fork, and Lake Houston is at the junction of the West Fork and the East Fork. The Houston Ship Channel runs through the lower course of the San Jacinto and its tributary, Buffalo Bayou, connecting the Port of Houston to the Gulf.

There are two stories concerning the origin of its name. One is that when early explorers discovered it, its channel was choked with hyacinth ("jacinto" is the Spanish word for hyacinth). The other is that it was discovered on Aug. 17, St. Hyacinth's Day.

The Battle of San Jacinto was fought on the bank of this river on April 21, 1836, when Texas won its independence from Mexico. San Jacinto Battleground State Historic Site and monument commemorate the battle.

Trinity River

The Trinity rises in its East Fork, Elm Fork, West Fork, and Clear Fork in Grayson, Montague, Archer, and Parker counties, respectively. The main stream begins with the junction of the Elm and West forks at Dallas. Its length is 550 miles, and its drainage area is 17,913 square miles. Because of moderate to heavy rainfall over its drainage area, it has an average annual flow of 5.7 million acre-feet near its mouth on Trinity Bay in the Galveston Bay system.

The Trinity derives its name from the Spanish "Trinidad." Alonso de León named it La Santísima Trinidad (the Most Holy Trinity).

Navigation was developed along its lower course with several riverport towns, such as Sebastopol in Trinity County. For many years, there has been a basin-wide movement for navigation, conservation, and utilization of its water. The Trinity River Authority is a state agency and the Trinity Improvement Association is a publicly supported nonprofit organization that has advocated its development.

The Trinity has in its valley more large cities, greater population, and more industrial development than any other river basin in Texas. On the Coastal Plains, there is large use of its waters for rice irrigation. Large reservoirs on the Elm Fork are Lewisville Lake and Ray Roberts Lake. There are four reservoirs above Fort Worth: Lake Worth, Eagle Mountain Lake, and Lake Bridgeport on the West Fork and Benbrook Lake on the Clear Fork.

Lake Lavon in southeast Collin County and Lake Ray Hubbard in Collin, Dallas, Kaufman, and Rockwall counties are on the East Fork. Lake Livingston is in Polk, San Jacinto, Trinity, and Walker counties.Two other reservoirs in the Trinity basin below the Dallas–Fort Worth area are Cedar Creek Reservoir and Richland-Chambers Reservoir.

Neches River

The Neches rises in Van Zandt County in East Texas and flows 416 miles to Sabine Lake near Port Arthur. It has a drainage area of 9,937 square miles. Abundant rainfall over its entire basin gives it an average annual flow near the Gulf of about 4.3 million acre-feet a year. The river takes its name from the Neches Indians, who the early Spanish explorers found living along its banks. Principal tributary of the Neches, and comparable with the Neches in length and flow above their confluence, is the Angelina River, so named for Angelina (Little Angel), a Hainai Indian girl who converted to Christianity and played an important role in the early development of this region.

Both the Neches and the Angelina run most of their courses in the Piney Woods, and there was much settlement along them as early as the 1820s.

Sam Rayburn Reservoir, near Jasper on the Angelina River, was completed and dedicated in 1965. With a storage capacity of 2.88 million acre-feet, it is the fourth-largest reservoir in Texas. Reservoirs located on the Neches River include Lake Palestine in the upper basin and B. A. Steinhagen Lake located at the junction of the Neches and the Angelina rivers.

Sabine River

The Sabine River is formed by three forks rising in Collin and Hunt counties. From its sources to its mouth on Sabine Lake, it flows approximately 360 miles and drains 7,570 square miles.

Sabine comes from the Spanish word for cypress, as does the name of the Sabinal River, which flows into the Frio River in Southwest Texas. The Sabine has an average annual flow volume of 5.8 million acre-feet.

Throughout most of Texas history, the lower Sabine has been the eastern Texas boundary line, although for a while there was doubt as to whether the Sabine or the Arroyo Hondo, east of the Sabine in Louisiana, was the boundary. For a number of years, the outlaw-infested neutral ground lay between them. There was also a boundary dispute in which it was alleged that the Neches River was really the Sabine and, therefore, the boundary.

Travelers over the part of the Camino Real known as the Old San Antonio Road crossed the Sabine at the Gaines Ferry in Sabine County, and there were crossings for the Atascosito Road and other travel and trade routes of that day.

Toledo Bend Reservoir is the largest lake lying wholly or partly in Texas. The reservoir impounds 4.47 million acre-feet of water on the Sabine River in Newton, Panola, Sabine, and Shelby counties. It is the 16th-largest reservoir (in capacity by volume) in the United States. This is a joint project of Texas and Louisiana, through the Sabine River Authority.

Red River

The Red River, with a length of 1,290 miles from its headwaters, is exceeded in length only by the Rio Grande among rivers associated with Texas. Its original source is water in Curry County, New Mexico, near the Texas boundary, forming a definite channel as it crosses Deaf Smith County, Texas, in tributaries that flow into the Prairie Dog Town Fork of the Red River. These waters carve the spectacular Palo Duro Canyon of the High Plains before the Red River leaves the Caprock Escarpment, flowing eastward.

Where the Red River crosses the 100th meridian at the bottom of the Panhandle, the river becomes the Texas-Oklahoma boundary and is soon joined by Buck Creek to form the main channel, according to the U.S. Geological Survey. Its length in Texas is 695 miles, before it flows into Arkansas, where it swings south to flow through Louisiana.

The Red River, which drains 24,297 square miles in Texas, is a part of the Mississippi drainage basin, and at one time it emptied all of its water into the Mississippi. In recent years, however, part of its water, especially at flood stage, has flowed to the Gulf via the Atchafalaya River in Louisiana.

The Red River takes its name from the red color of the water. This caused every explorer who came to its banks to call it "red" regardless of the language he spoke — Río Rojo or Río Roxo in Spanish, Rivière Rouge in French. At an early date, the river became the axis for French advance from Louisiana northwestward as far as present-day Montague County. There was consistent early navigation of the river from its mouth on the Mississippi to Shreveport, above which navigation was blocked by a natural log raft.

A number of important gateways into Texas from the north were established along the stream, such as Pecan Point and Jonesborough in Red River County, Colbert's Ferry and Preston in Grayson County, and later, Doan's Store Crossing in Wilbarger County. The river was a menace to the early traveler because of both its variable current and its quicksands, which brought disaster to many a trail-herd cow, as well as ox team and covered wagon.

The largest water conservation project on the Red River is Lake Texoma, with a conservation storage capacity of 2.5 million acre-feet.

The Red River's high content of salt and other minerals limits the usefulness of its water along its upper reaches. Ten salt springs and tributaries in Texas and Oklahoma contribute most of these minerals.

The uppermost tributaries of the Red River in Texas are Tierra Blanca Creek, which rises in Curry County, N.M., and flows easterly across Deaf Smith and Randall counties to meet Palo Duro Creek and form the Prairie Dog Town Fork a few miles east of Canyon.

Other principal tributaries in Texas are the Pease and the Wichita in North Central Texas and the Sulphur in Northeast Texas, which flows through Wright Patman Lake, then into the Red River after it has crossed the boundary line into Arkansas.

The last major tributary in Northeast Texas is the Cypress Creek system, which flows into Louisiana before joining with the Red River. Major reservoirs in this basin are Lake O' The Pines and Caddo Lake.

From Oklahoma, the principal tributary is the Washita, which has its headwaters in Roberts County, Texas. The Ouachita, a river with the same pronunciation though spelled differently, is the principal tributary to the Red River's lower course in Arkansas.

The Red River boundary dispute, a long-standing feud between Oklahoma and Texas, was finally settled in 2000 when the boundary was set at the vegetation line on the south bank, except for Lake Texoma, where the boundary was set within the channel of the lake.

Canadian River

The Canadian River heads near Raton Pass in northern New Mexico near the Colorado boundary line and flows into Texas on the west line of Oldham County. It crosses the Texas Panhandle into Oklahoma and there flows into the Arkansas River, a total distance of 906 miles. It drains 12,865 square miles in Texas, and much of its 213-mile course across the Panhandle is in a deep gorge.

A tributary, the North Canadian River, dips briefly into the Texas Panhandle in Sherman County before it joins the main channel in Oklahoma.

One of several theories as to how the Canadian got its name is that some early explorers thought it flowed into Canada. Lake Meredith, formed by Sanford Dam, provides water for several Panhandle cities.

Because of the deep gorge and the quicksand that occurs in many places, the Canadian River has been a particularly difficult stream to bridge. It is known, especially in its lower course in Oklahoma, as outstanding among the streams of the country for the great amount of quicksand in its channel. ☆

The Hunt Crossing Dam across the Guadalupe River. Photo by Jonathan Cutrer, jcutrer.com.

Secondary Streams of Texas

In addition to the principal rivers, Texas has many other streams of various size. The following list gives a few of these streams as designated by the U.S. Geological Survey, with additional information from the new Handbook of Texas and previous Texas Almanacs.

Alamito Creek: Formed by confluence of North, South forks 3 mi. N Marfa in Presidio County. Flows SE 82 mi. to Rio Grande 5 mi. S Presidio.

Angelina River: Rises in central Rusk County; flows SE 120 mi. through Cherokee, Nacogdoches, Angelina, San Augustine counties into Sam Rayburn Reservoir, then into Jasper County to the Neches River 12 mi. west of Jasper. A meandering stream through forested country.

Aransas River: Formed 2 mi. N Skidmore in SC Bee County by union of Poesta and Aransas creeks; flows SE 40 mi. forming boundary between San Patricio and Refugio counties; then briefly into Aransas County where it empties into Copano Bay.

Atascosa River: Formed NW Atascosa County by confluence of North, West prongs, flows SE 92 mi. through Atascosa and Live Oak counties into Frio River 2 mi. NW Three Rivers.

Attoyac Bayou: Rises 2.8 mi. NE Mount Enterprise in SE Rusk County; flows SE 67 mi. through Shelby, San Augustine and Nacogdoches counties into Angelina River at Sam Rayburn Reservoir.

Barton Creek: Rises NE of Henly in NW Hays County; flows E 40 mi. through Travis County to Colorado River at Lady Bird Lake in Austin.

Beals Creek: Formed by confluence of Sulphur Springs and Mustang draws 4 mi. W Big Spring SW Howard County; flows E 55 mi. into Mitchell County to mouth on Colorado River.

Big Cypress Creek: Forms in SE Hopkins County E of Pickton; flows SE 60 mi. to mouth on Big Cypress Bayou 3 mi. E Jefferson in Marion County and just before the bayou flows into Caddo Lake. The creek forms the boundary lines between Camp and Titus, Camp and Morris, and Morris and Upshur counties. It passes through Lake Cypress Springs, Lake Bob Sandlin, and Lake O' The Pines, and is part of the Red River drainage basin.

Blackwater Draw: Rises in Curry County, N.M.; flows into Texas in extreme NW Bailey County; flows SE through Lamb, Hale, and Lubbock counties to junction with Yellow House Draw to form North Fork of the Double Mountain Fork Brazos River. Length, 100 mi.

Blanco Creek: Rises near the intersection of Bee, Goliad and Karnes county lines in extreme S Karnes County; flows SE 45 mi. forming boundary of Bee and Goliad counties. Joins Medio Creek in Refugio County to form Mission River.

Blanco Creek: Rises E of Concan in Uvalde County; flows S 44 mi. to Frio River.

Blanco River: Rises W Lindendale in NE Kendall County; flows SE 64 mi. through Blanco and Hays counties; joins San Marcos River, a tributary of the Guadalupe; fed by many springs.

Bosque River: Flows from Lake Waco in McLennan County 5 mi. into Brazos River.

Bosque River, North: Formed at Stephenville by the union of North, South forks in Erath County; flows generally SE 96 mi. through Hamilton, Bosque and McLennan counties into Lake Waco.

Bosque River, South: Rises near Coryell-McLennan county line; flows NE 24 mi. into Lake Waco.

Brady Creek: Rises 14 mi. SW Eden in SW Concho County; flows 90 mi. through McCulloch and San Saba counties into San Saba River 10 mi. SW of Richland Springs.

Brazos River, Clear Fork: Rises 8 mi. E Snyder in Scurry County; flows NE 180 mi. through Fisher, Jones, Haskell, Throckmorton, Shackelford and Stephens counties into Brazos River in S Young County; drainage area 5,728 sq. mi.

Brazos River, Double Mountain Fork: Rises 12 mi. SE Tahoka, Lynn County; flows E 175 mi. through Garza, Kent, Fisher and Haskell counties to confluence with Salt Fork of the Brazos, north of Old Glory in Stonewall County.

Brazos River, North Fork: DOUBLE MOUNTAIN FORK: Formed by union of Yellow House and Blackwater draws in Lubbock; flows SE 75 miles through Crosby, Garza and Kent counties to junction with Double Mountain Fork Brazos River.

Brazos River, Salt Fork: Rises in SE Crosby County; flows 150 mi. through Garza and Kent counties to confluence

Boykin Creek runs through Angelina National Forest. Photo by William L. Farr, CC by SA 4.0/Flickr.

with Double Mountain Fork in NE Stonewall County to form the main stream of Brazos River.

Buck Creek: Also called Spiller Creek. Rises SE Donley County; flows SE 49 mi. through Collingsworth and Childress counties to Texas-Oklahoma boundary; then 3 mi. through Oklahoma to junction with Prairie Dog Town Fork of Red River NW Hardeman County to form main stream of the Red River.

Buffalo Bayou: Rises in extreme N Fort Bend County; flows E 46 mi. through Houston into San Jacinto River in Harris County. Part of Houston Ship Channel.

California Creek: Rises 10 mi. NE Roby in Fisher County; flows NE 70 mi. through Jones County into Paint Creek in E Haskell County.

Caney Creek: Rises near Wharton in Wharton County; flows 75 mi. through Matagorda County into east end of Matagorda Bay. Centuries ago, the current Caney Creek channel was the channel for the Colorado River.

Capote/Wildhorse Draw: Rises N of Van Horn in Culberson County; runs 86 mi. S through Jeff Davis County to SW of Marfa in Presidio County. One of a number of streams in this area with no outlet to the sea.

Cedar Bayou: Rises 11 mi. NW Liberty in Liberty County; flows 46 mi. S as boundary between Harris County and Liberty and Chambers counties, and into Trinity Bay.

Chambers Creek: Formed SW Waxahachie in Ellis County by union North, South forks; flows SE 45 mi. through Navarro County into Richland Creek at Richland-Chambers Reservoir.

Cibolo Creek: Rises 7 mi. W Boerne in Kendall County; flows SE through Bexar, Comal, Guadalupe and Wilson counties into San Antonio River in Karnes County; 96 mi. in length. Spring-fed, perennially flowing stream.

Coleto Creek: Formed SW of Mission Valley in NW Victoria County by union of Twelve Mile and Fifteen Mile creeks forming boundary between Victoria and Goliad counties. From Coleto Creek Reservoir flows to Guadalupe River in Victoria County.

Comal River: Rises in Comal Springs in City of New Braunfels and flows SE about 2.5 miles to Guadalupe River. Shortest river in Texas by name.

Concho River: Formed at San Angelo by conjunction North, South Concho rivers; flows E 24 mi. through Tom Green County, then 29 mi. through Concho County into Colorado River 12 m. NE Paint Rock. Drainage basin, including North and South Concho, 6,613 sq. mi. A spring-fed stream.

Concho River, Middle: Rises SW Sterling County; flows S, then E 66 mi. through Tom Green panhandle, Irion and Reagan counties into South Concho River at Lake Nasworthy near Tankersley in Tom Green County.

Concho River, North: Rises in S Howard County; flows 137 mi. through Glasscock, Sterling and Coke counties to confluence with South Concho to form Concho River in Tom Green County. Drainage basin, 1,510 sq. mi.

Concho River, South: Rises in C Schleicher County; flows N through Lake Nasworthy to confluence with North Concho River in Tom Green County; length, 41 mi.; drainage basin area 3, 866 sq. mi. Perennial flow from springs.

Cowleech Fork Sabine River: Rises 2 mi. NW Celeste NW Hunt County; flows SE 40 mi. to Lake Tawakoni.

Deep Creek: Rises SE Baird, Callahan County; flows N 55 mi. into Hubbard Creek in Shackelford County near McCatherine Mountain.

Deep Creek: Rises 4 mi. N Fluvanna NW Scurry County; flows SSE 70 mi. to mouth on Colorado River in extreme N Mitchell County.

Delaware River: Rises eastern slope Delaware Mountains in N Culberson County; flows in NE course; crosses

Texas-New Mexico state line and enters Pecos River; length, 50 mi.

Devils River: Formed SW Sutton County by union Dry Devils River and Granger Draw; flows SE 95 mi. through Val Verde County into Rio Grande at Amistad Reservoir. Spring-fed, perennially flowing stream throughout most of its course.

Elm Creek: Rises 3 mi. SE Nolan in Nolan County; flows NE 60 mi., passes through Lake Abilene, Buffalo Gap and Abilene in Taylor County and through Lake Fort Phantom Hill into Clear Fork Brazos River near Nugent, SE Jones County.

Frio River: Formed at Leakey in Real County by union of West and East Frio rivers; flows S 190 mi. through Uvalde, Medina, Frio, La Salle, McMullen counties (Choke Canyon Reservoir); joins Nueces River S of Three Rivers in Live Oak County. Drainage area, 7,310 sq. mi. Fed by springs in northern part, where it flows through picturesque canyon.

Greens Bayou: Rises 9 mi. W Aldine, C Harris County; flows ESE into Houston Ship Channel; 42 mi. long.

Hondo Creek: Rises 7.5 mi. NW Tarpley C Bandera County; flows SSE 67 mi. through Medina and Frio counties to Frio River 5 mi. NW Pearsall.

Howard Draw: Rises at Crockett-Reagan county line; flows SSW 45 mi. through Val Verde County to Pecos River near Pandale.

Hubbard Creek: Rises 3 mi. NW Baird N Callahan County; flows NE 62 mi. through Shackelford County; then into Stephens County (Hubbard Creek Reservoir) and joins Clear Fork of the Brazos River 10 mi. NW Breckenridge.

James River: Rises SE Kimble County; flows NE 37 mi. to join Llano River in Mason County.

Jim Ned Creek: Rises 10 mi. NW Tuscola SC Taylor County; flows SE 71 mi. through Callahan and Coleman counties to Brown County to join Pecan Bayou, a tributary of Colorado River.

Johnson Draw: Rises NE Crockett County; runs SSE 66 miles to mouth on Devils River in Val Verde County.

Lampasas River: Rises NW Mills County; flows SE 100 miles through Hamilton, Lampasas, Burnet and Bell counties (Stillhouse Hollow Lake); unites with Leon River to form Little River.

Leon River: Formed by confluence North, Middle and South Forks in NC Eastland County; flows SE 185 mi. through Comanche, Hamilton and Coryell counties to junction with Lampasas River to form Little River in Bell County.

Leona River: Rises N Uvalde in central Uvalde County; flows SE 83 mi. through Zavala County into Frio River in Frio County.

Limpia Creek: Heads in the Davis Mountains on the NE slope of Mount Livermore in Jeff Davis County and flows 52 mi. E, NE and E through Limpia Canyon to disappear at the head of Barrilla Draw in Pecos County. Part of course through Limpia Canyon noted for its scenic beauty.

Little Brazos River: Rises 5 mi. SW Thornton, SW Limestone County; flows 72 mi. SE through Falls and Robertson counties into Brazos River in Brazos County.

Little River: Formed central Bell County by union Leon, Lampasas rivers; flows 75 mi. SE through Milam County into Brazos River.

Llano River: Formed C Kimble County by union North, South Llano rivers; flows E 100 mi. through Mason, Llano counties to Colorado River. Drainage area, including North, South Llano rivers, 4,460 sq. mi. A spring-fed stream of the Edwards Plateau, known for scenic beauty.

Llano River, North: Rises C Sutton County; flows E 40 mi. to union with South Llano River at Junction in Kimble County.

Llano River, South: Rises in NC Edwards County; flows 55 mi. NE to confluence with North Llano River at Junction in Kimble County.

Los Olmos Creek: Rises central Duval County; flows SE 71 mi. through Jim Wells and Brooks counties; forms boundary between Kenedy and Kleberg counties; into Baffin Bay.

Madera Canyon: Rises N slope Mount Livermore, Jeff Davis County, at altitude of 7,500 ft.; flows 40 mi. NE to join Aguja Creek at Reeves County line to form Toyah Creek, tributary through Pecos River to Rio Grande. Intermittent stream. Noteworthy for its beauty.

Medina River: Rises in North, West prongs in W Bandera County; flows SE 116 mi. through Medina and Bexar counties to San Antonio River. A spring-fed stream. Scenically beautiful along upper course.

Medio Creek: Rises S Karnes County; flows SE 2 mi. through Karnes County, then 7 mi. along boundary Karnes and Bee counties, then SE 37 mi. through Bee County, SE 7 mi. through Refugio County to junction with Blanco Creek to form Mission River.

Mission River: Formed by confluence of Blanco and Medio creeks in C Refugio County; flows SE 24 mi. to mouth on Mission Bay, an inlet of Copano Bay.

Mulberry Creek: Rises NW Armstrong County at Fairview; flows SE 58 mi. through Donley and Briscoe counties into Prairie Dog Town Fork Red River in NW Hall County.

Navasota River: Rises SE Hill County; flows SE 125 mi. through Limestone County and along boundary Leon, Madison, Robertson, Brazos and Grimes counties to Brazos River near Navasota.

Navidad River: Forms at juncture of East and West Navidad rivers in NE Lavaca County; flows 74 mi. through Lavaca and Jackson counties into Lake Texana near Ganado; then joins Lavaca River.

Nolan River: Rises in NW Johnson County; flows S 30 mi. through Lake Pat Cleburne and into Hill County, where it empties into Brazos River at Lake Whitney.

Onion Creek: Rises 1 mi. W of Hays-Blanco county line SE Blanco County; flows SE 37 mi. through N Hays County; then 22 mi. through S Travis County into Colorado River near Garfield.

Paint Creek: Rises in extreme NW Jones County near Tuxedo; flows NE, then SE 53 mi. through SE corner of Stonewall County; then across S Haskell County (Lake Stamford) and into W Throckmorton County to mouth on Clear Fork Brazos River.

Palo Blanco Creek: Rises SE Hebbronville in N Jim Hogg County; flows SE 59 mi. through Duval and Brooks, where it passes through Laguna Salada; then into NW Kenedy County.

Palo Duro Creek: Rises in W Deaf Smith County; flows E 45 mi. into C Randall County to junction with Tierra Blanca Creek near Canyon to form the Prairie Dog Town Fork of the Red River. Lends its name to the notable canyon.

Paluxy River: Formed in E Erath County by convergence of North and South branches at Bluff Dale; flows SE 29 mi. through Hood and Somervell counties to mouth on Brazos River. Dinosaur Valley State Park at a large bend of the river in Somervell County is site of 100-million-year-old dinosaur tracks.

Pease River: Formed by union of North and Middle Pease rivers in NE Cottle County; flows E 100 mi. through Hardeman, Foard and Wilbarger counties into Red River 8 mi. NE of Vernon.

Pease River, Middle: Rises 8 mi. NW Matador in WC Motley County; flows E 63 miles into North Pease River to form the Pease River in NE Cottle County.

Pease River, North: Rises 9 mi. SE Cedar Hill in E Floyd County; flows E 60 mi. through Motley, Hall and Cottle counties. Joins Middle Pease to form Pease River.

Pease River, South: Also called Tongue River. Rises 11 mi. SW Roaring Springs in SW Motley County; flows ENE 40 mi. to mouth on Middle Pease River in W Cottle County.

Pecan Bayou: Formed by union of South, North prongs in SC Callahan County; flows SE 90 mi. through Coleman, Brown (Lake Brownwood) and Mills counties into Colorado River SW Goldthwaite. Westernmost bayou.

Pedernales River: Rises NE corner of Kerr County; flows E 106 mi. through Kimble, Gillespie, Blanco, Hays and Travis counties into Colorado River at Lake Travis. Spring-fed; a beautiful stream.

Pine Island Bayou: Rises near Rye, NE Liberty County; flows 76 mi. SE through Hardin and Jefferson counties into Neches River.

Red River, Prairie Dog Town Fork: Formed by union of Palo Duro and Tierra Blanca creeks in Randall County; flows E 160 mi. through Armstrong, Briscoe, Hall, and Childress counties to junction with Buck Creek to form Red River in NW corner of Hardeman County. Palo Duro Canyon is along course of this stream as it descends from Great Plains.

Red River, North Fork: Rises W Gray County; flows SE 180 mi. through Wheeler County into Oklahoma to junction with the Red River NE Vernon in Wilbarger County.

Red River, Salt Fork: Rises N Armstrong County; flows SE 155 mi. through Donley and Collingsworth counties and into Oklahoma. It joins the Red River opposite the northernmost point of Wilbarger County.

Richland Creek: Rises 3.5 mi. E Itasca N Hill County; flows E 50 mi. through Ellis and Navarro counties, through Navarro Mills Lake and Richland-Chambers Reservoir; then into the Trinity River in Freestone County.

Running Water Draw: Rises 24 mi. WNW Clovis, N.M.; flows ESE into Texas in C Parmer County; then through Castro, Lamb, Hale and Floyd counties to join Callahan Draw 8 mi. W Floydada at head of White River, a tributary of the Brazos River.

Sabana River: Rises at Callahan-Eastland county line; flows SE 50 mi. through Comanche County into Leon River at Proctor Lake.

Sabinal River: Rises 7 mi. N Vanderpool in NW Bandera County; flows S 60 mi. to junction with Frio River in SE Uvalde County. The West Sabinal River, which rises in Real County, joins the main stream at the Bandera-Uvalde county line.

San Bernard River: Rises 1 mi. S New Ulm in W Austin County; flows SE, forming boundary Austin and Colorado counties, 31 mi.; Austin and Wharton counties, 8 mi.; Wharton and Fort Bend counties, 28 mi.; approaches Gulf of Mexico in Brazoria County. Total length, 120 mi. (For more than 100 years locals have reported hearing the wail of a violin from the river. The mystery has never been solved, although some say the musical sounds are caused by escaping gas. The phenomenon has caused the stream to be called the Singing River: Handbook of Texas.)

San Gabriel River: Formed at Georgetown in C Williamson County by union of North and South forks; flows NE 50 mi. into Milam County to join Little River. Originally called San Xavier River.

San Jacinto River, East: Rises E Walker County; flows SE and S 69 mi. through San Jacinto, Liberty, Montgomery and Harris counties into Lake Houston and San Jacinto River.

San Jacinto River, West: Rises E Grimes County NE Shiro; flows SE 90 mi. through Walker County; into Lake Conroe in Montgomery County; then through Montgomery County to Lake Houston in Harris County.

San Marcos River: Formed near N limits City of San Marcos, Hays County, by several large springs, although watershed extends about 10 mi. NE of springs; Blanco River joins the San Marcos River 4 mi. downstream; flows SE 59 mi. as boundary between Guadalupe and Caldwell counties; then through Gonzales County to join Guadalupe River 2 mi. W Gonzales.

Sandy Creek: Rises SW Colorado County; flows SSE 42 mi. through Lavaca, Wharton and Jackson counties into Lake Texana.

San Saba River: Formed W Fort McKavett at Schleicher-Menard county line by union of North Valley and Middle Valley prongs; flows NE 140 mi. through Menard, Mason, McCulloch and San Saba counties into Colorado River 8 mi. NE San Saba. One of the picturesque streams of the Edwards Plateau.

Spring Creek: Rises NE Waller County near Fields Store; flows E 64 mi. forming boundary between Waller and Harris counties, and Montgomery and Harris counties to junction with West Fork San Jacinto River and Lake Houston.

Sulphur River: Formed E Delta County by junction North, South branches; flows E 183 miles forming boundary between Franklin and Red River counties; Titus and Red River counties; Morris and Red River and Bowie counties; then between Bowie and Cass counties, where it flows into Wright Patman Lake; continues on into Red River in S Miller County, Ark.

Sulphur River, North: Rises 1 mi. SW Gober S Fannin County; flows SE, E 54 mi. as boundary between Delta and Lamar counties and to union with South Sulphur River to form Sulphur River.

Sulphur River, South: Rises N Leonard S Fannin County; flows ESE 50 mi. through Hunt County; then as boundary between Hopkins and Delta counties (through Cooper Lake) to union with North Sulphur to form Sulphur River.

Sulphur Springs Draw: Rises in E Lea County, N.M.; enters Texas W Yoakum County at Bronco; flows SE 100 mi. through Terry, Gaines, Dawson, Martin, and Howard counties to confluence with Mustang Creek to form Beals Creek, a tributary of Colorado River.

Sweetwater Creek: Rises 2 mi. W Maryneal, C Nolan County; flows NE 45 mi. through Fisher and Jones counties into Clear Fork Brazos River.

Terlingua Creek: Rises WC Brewster County; flows S 83 mi. into Rio Grande just E Santa Elena Canyon.

Tierra Blanca Creek: Rises N Curry County, N.M.; flows E across Texas state line in SW Deaf Smith County and 75 mi. through Deaf Smith, Parmer and Randall counties to junction with Palo Duro Creek where it forms Prairie Dog Town Fork Red River.

Toyah Creek: Forms near boundary Jeff Davis-Reeves counties; flows NE 50 mi. into Pecos River NC Reeves County.

Trinity River, Clear Fork: Rises NW Poolville in NW Parker County; flows SE 56 mi. through Tarrant County into West Fork Trinity River at Fort Worth.

Trinity River, East Fork: Rises 1.5 mi. NW Dorchester in SC Grayson County; flows S 85 mi. through Collin County (Lake Lavon and Lake Ray Hubbard); then Rockwall and Dallas counties into Trinity River in SE Kaufman County.

Trinity River, Elm Fork: Rises 1 mi. NW Saint Jo in E Montague County; flows 85 mi. SE through Cooke, Denton counties (Ray Roberts Lake and Lewisville Lake) to junction with West Fork to form Trinity River proper at Irving in WC Dallas County.

Trinity River, West Fork: Rises in SC Archer County; flows SE 145 mi. through Jack, Wise (Lake Bridgeport) and Tarrant (Eagle Mountain Lake and Lake Worth) counties to conjunction with Elm Fork to form Trinity River proper in WC Dallas County.

Tule Creek: Formed in Swisher County by union of North, Middle and South Tule draws; flows E 40 mi. through Mackenzie Reservoir and Briscoe County into Prairie Dog Town Fork Red River. Remarkably beautiful Tule Canyon along lower course.

Turkey Creek: Rises near Turkey Mountain EC Kinney County; flows SE 54 mi. through Uvalde, Zavala, Dimmit counties to Nueces River.

Washita River: Rises SE Roberts County; flows E 35 mi. through Hemphill County to Oklahoma state line, then SE to Red River at Lake Texoma. Total length, 295 mi.

West Caney Creek: Rises 1 mi. SW Normangee in SW Leon County; flows SW 11 mi. through NW Madison County to junction with Navasota River on Brazos county line. The historic Old San Antonio Road, a thoroughfare for early Spanish and French explorers, crossed the headwaters of the stream.

White River: Formed 8 mi. W Floydada in WC Floyd County by union of Running Water and Callahan draws; flows SE 62 mi. through Blanco Canyon and White River Lake in Crosby County; then through Garza and Kent counties into Salt Fork Brazos River; principal tributary to Salt Fork.

Wichita River: Formed NE Knox County by union North, South Wichita rivers; flows NE 90 mi. through Baylor (Lake Kemp and Lake Diversion), Archer, Wichita and Clay counties to Red River N Byers.

Wichita River, Little: Formed in C Archer County by union of its North, Middle and South forks; flows NE 62 mi. through Clay County (Lake Arrowhead) into Red River.

Wichita River, North: Rises 6 mi. E East Afton in NE Dickens County; flows E through King, Cottle, Foard counties; then as boundary for Foard and Knox counties; then briefly into Baylor County to junction with South Wichita River to form Wichita River proper NE Vera in Knox County. Length, 100 mi.

Wichita River, South: Rises 10 mi. E Dickens in EC Dickens County; flows E 85 mi. through King and Knox counties to junction with North Wichita to form Wichita River.

Yellow House Draw: Rises in SE Bailey County; flows SE 80 mi. through Cochran, Hockley and Lubbock counties to confluence with Blackwater Draw at Lubbock to form the North Fork of Double Mountain Fork Brazos River. ☆

Fishermen on Cooper Lake. Photo by Texas Parks and Wildlife/Flickr

Artificial Lakes and Reservoirs

Sources: U.S. Geological Survey; Texas Water Development Board; New Handbook of Texas; Texas Parks & Wildlife; U.S. Army Corps of Engineers; various river basin authorities; reservoir websites.

The large increase in the number of reservoirs in Texas during the past half-century has greatly improved water conservation and supplies.

As late as 1917, Texas had only four major reservoirs with a total storage capacity of 288,340 acre-feet. (One acre-foot is the amount of water necessary to cover an acre of surface area with water one foot deep, about 325,851 gallons of water.) Most of this capacity was in Medina Lake in southwest Texas, with 254,000 acre-feet capacity, created by a dam completed in May 1913.

By January 2012, Texas had 188 major water supply reservoirs (those with a normal capacity of 5,000 acre-feet or larger) and 21 major non-water supply reservoirs (those that do not have a water supply function). The 188 water supply reservoirs have a total conservation surface area of 1.67 million acres and an original conservation storage capacity of 35 million acre-feet (only Texas' share is counted in border reservoirs). The 21 non-water supply reservoirs have a total normal surface area of 62,079 acres and an original normal storage capacity of 760,000 acre-feet.

According to the U.S. Census Bureau's Master Address File (last updated August 2010), Texas has 5,616 square miles of inland water, ranking it first in the 48 contiguous states, followed by Florida, with 5,027 sq. mi. The only state with more inland water is Alaska, with 19,304 sq. mi.

There are 6,976 reservoirs in Texas with a normal storage capacity of 10 acre-feet or larger.

Natural Lakes in Texas

There are many natural lakes in Texas, though none is of great size. The largest designated natural lake touching the border of Texas is **Sabine Lake**, into which the Sabine and Neches rivers discharge. It is more properly called the **Sabine-Neches Estuary** of the Gulf of Mexico. (Find more information about this estuary on page 64.)

Also near the coast, in Calhoun County, is **Green Lake**, which has about 10,000 acre-feet of storage capacity. It is one of the state's largest natural freshwater lakes.

Caddo Lake, on the Texas-Louisiana border, was a natural lake originally, but its present capacity and surface area are largely due to dams built to raise the surface of the original body of water.

Natural Dam Lake, in Howard County, has a similar history to Caddo Lake.

In East Texas, there are many small natural lakes formed by "horse-shoe" bends that have been eliminated from the main channel of a river. There are also a number of these "horse-shoe" lakes along the Rio Grande in the Lower Valley, where they are called resacas.

On the South Plains and west of San Angelo there are lakes, such as **Big Lake** in Reagan County, that are usually dry.

List of Lakes and Reservoirs

The table that begins below lists the lakes and reservoirs in Texas that have **more than 5,000 acre-feet of storage capacity**. Some industrial cooling reservoirs are not included in this table.

The surface area listed in the table is the **area at conservation elevation** as calculated by the Texas Water Development Board (TWDB). Because sediment deposition constantly changes reservoir volumes over time, storage capacity figures are from the most recent surveys available.

Various methods of computing capacity area are used, and detailed information may be obtained from the TWDB, from the U.S. Army Corps of Engineers, or from local sources. Boundary reservoir capacities include water designated for Texas and non-Texas water. Texas' share will be included in the description.

Information is in the following order: (1) Name of lake or reservoir; (2) year of first impounding of water; (3) county or counties in which it is located; (4) river or creek on which it is located; (5) location with respect to some city or town; (6) purpose of reservoir; (7) owner of reservoir.

Some of these items, when not listed, are not available. For the larger lakes and reservoirs, the dam impounding water to form the lake bears the same name, unless otherwise indicated. The years in the table refer to first impounding of water. Double years refer to later, larger dams.

Lakes and Reservoirs, Date of Origin	Surface Area (acres)	Storage Capacity (acre-ft.)
Abilene, L.: (1919) Taylor Co.; Elm Cr.; 6 mi. NW Tuscola; (M-In.-R); City of Abilene	588	7,900
Addicks Reservoir: (1948) Harris Co.; South Mayde Cr.; 1 mi. E of Addicks; (FC only); USAE; Addicks only has water during times of flood and is dry most of the year	16,780	202,128
Alan Henry, L.: (1993) Garza Co.; Double Mountain Fork Brazos River; 10 mi. E Justiceburg; (M-In.-Ir.); City of Lubbock	2,395	96,207
Alcoa L.: (1952) Milam Co.; Sandy Cr.; 7 mi. SW Rockdale; (In.-R); Alcoa Aluminum (also called Sandow L.)	914	15,650
Amistad Reservoir, International: (1969) Val Verde Co.; Rio Grande; an international project of the U.S. and Mexico; 12 mi. NW Del Rio; (C-R-Ir.-P-FC); International Boundary and Water Commission (Texas' share of conservation capacity is 56.2 percent.) (Formerly Diablo Reservoir)	65,597	3,275,532
Amon G. Carter, L.: (1961) Montague Co.; Big Sandy Cr.; 6 mi. S Bowie; (M-In.); City of Bowie	1,524	19,266
Anahuac, L.: (1936, 1954) Chambers Co.; Turtle Bayou; near Anahuac; (Ir.-In.-Mi.); Chambers-Liberty Counties Navigation District. (also called Turtle Bayou Reservoir)	5,035	33,348
Anzalduas Channel Dam: Hidalgo Co.; Rio Grande; 11 mi. upstream from Hidalgo; (Ir.-FC); United States and Mexico	1,472	13,910
Aquilla L.: (1983) Hill Co.; Aquilla Cr.; 10.2 mi. W of Hillsboro; (FC-M-Ir.-In.-R); USAE–Brazos R. Auth.	3,119	43,243
Arlington, L.: (1957) Tarrant Co.; Village Cr.; 7 mi. W Arlington; (M-In.); City of Arlington	1,908	40,188
Arrowhead, L.: (1966) Clay-Archer counties.; Little Wichita R.; 13 mi. SE Wichita Falls; (M); City of Wichita Falls	14,372	230,359
Athens, L.: (1962) Henderson Co.; 8 mi. E Athens; (M-FC-R); Athens Municipal Water Authority (formerly Flat Creek Reservoir)	1,799	29,503
Austin, L.: (1893, 1915, 1939) Travis Co.; Colorado R.; W Austin city limits; (M-In.-P); City of Austin, leased to LCRA (Imp. by Tom Miller Dam) (In 1893, the first dam was completed. It broke in 1900. In 1915, a second dam was partially built but not completed. In 1939, the present Tom Miller Dam was completed.)	1,589	23,972
Ballinger L.: (1947) Runnels Co.; Valley Creek; 5 mi. W Ballinger; (M); City of Ballinger (also known as Lake Moonen)	500	8,215
Balmorhea L.: (1917) Reeves Co.; Sandia Cr.; 3 mi. SE Balmorhea; (Ir.-R); Reeves Co. WID No. 1	573	6,350
Bardwell L.: (1965) Ellis Co.; Waxahachie Cr.; 3 mi. SE Bardwell; (FC-C-R); USAE	3,138	46,122
Barker Reservoir: (1945) Harris Co.; above Buffalo Bayou; (FC only); USAE; Barker only has water during times of flood and is dry most of the year	17,225	206,860
B. A. Steinhagen L.: (1951) Tyler-Jasper counties; Neches R.; 1/2 mi. N Town Bluff; (FC-R-C); USAE; (also called Town Bluff Reservoir and Dam B. Reservoir); (Imp. by Town Bluff Dam)	10,421	66,961
Bastrop, L.: (1964) Bastrop Co.; Spicer Cr.; 3 mi. NE Bastrop; (In.-R); LCRA	906	16,590
Baylor L.: (1950) Childress Co.; 10 mi. NW Childress; (M-R); City of Childress (also called Baylor Creek Reservoir)	610	9,220
Belton L.: (1954) Bell-Coryell counties; Leon R.; 3 mi. N. Belton; (M-FC-R); USAE–Brazos R. Auth.	12,135	435,225
Benbrook L.: (1952) Tarrant Co.; Clear Fk. Trinity R.; 10 mi. SW Fort Worth; (FC-R); USAE	3,635	85,648
Bivins L.: (1927) Randall Co.; Palo Duro Cr.; 8 mi. NW Canyon; (M); Amarillo; City of Amarillo (also called Amarillo City Lake)	379	5,122
Bob Sandlin, L.: (1977) Titus-Wood-Camp-Franklin counties; Big Cypress Cr.; 5 mi. SW Mount Pleasant; (In.-M-R); Titus Co. FWSD No. 1 (Imp. by Fort Sherman Dam)	8,888	203,148

Abbreviations used in this table: L., lake; R., river; Co., county; Cr., creek; (C) conservation; (FC) flood control; (R) recreation; (P) power; (M) municipal; (D) domestic; (Ir.) irrigation; (In.) industry; (Mi.) mining, including oil production; (FH) fish hatchery; USAE, United States Army Corps of Engineers; WC&ID, Water Control and Improvement District; WID, Water Improvement District; USBR, United States Bureau of Reclamation; Auth., Authority; LCRA, Lower Colorado River Authority; TPWD, Texas Parks & Wildlife Dept.; USDA, United States Department of Agriculture; Imp., impounded.

Lakes and Reservoirs, Date of Origin	Surface Area (acres)	Storage Capacity (acre-ft.)
Bonham, L.: (1969) Fannin Co.; Timber Cr.; 5 mi. NE Bonham; (M); Bonham Municipal Water Auth.	1,056	11,027
Brady Creek Reservoir: (1963) McCulloch Co.; Brady Cr.; 3 mi. W Brady; (M-In.-R); City of Brady	2,020	30,430
Brandy Branch Reservoir: (1983) Harrison Co.; Brandy Br.; 10 mi. SW Marshall; (In.); AEP-Southwestern Electric Power Co.	1,242	29,513
Brazoria Reservoir: (1954) Brazoria Co.; off-channel reservoir; 1 mi. NE Brazoria; (In.); Dow Chemical Co.	1,865	21,970
Bridgeport, L.: (1932) Wise-Jack counties; W. Fk. of Trinity R.; 4 mi. W Bridgeport; (M-FC-R); Tarrant Regional Water District	11,712	366,236
Brownwood, L.: (1933) Brown Co.; Pecan Bayou; 8 mi. N Brownwood; (M-R); Brown Co. WID No. 1	6,460	128,839
Bryan Utilities L.: (1977) Brazos Co.; unnamed stream; 6 mi. NW Bryan; (In.); City of Bryan (also called Lake Bryan)	818	14,163
Buchanan, L.: (1937) Burnet-Llano-San Saba counties; Colorado R.; 13 mi. W Burnet; (M-FC-R-P); LCRA	21,618	860,607
Buffalo L.: (1938) Randall Co.; Tierra Blanca Cr.; 2 mi. S. Umbarger; (C-FC); U.S. Fish and Wildlife Service; Imp. by Umbarger Dam; See Buffalo Lake entry in Wildlife Refuge section for more info. Buffalo Lake is dry most of the year.	1,900	18,150
Caddo L.: (1873, 1914, 1971) Harrison-Marion counties, Texas, and Caddo Parish, La.; Cypress Bayou; 29 mi. NE Marshall; (C-R-M); Northeast Texas Municipal Water District; An original natural lake, whose surface and capacity were increased by construction of dams.	26,138	129,000
Calaveras L.: (1969) Bexar Co.; Calaveras Cr.; 15 mi. SE San Antonio; (In.-R); CPS Energy of San Antonio	3,624	63,200
Camp Creek L.: (1949) Robertson Co.; 13 mi. E Franklin; (R); Camp Creek Water Co.	750	8,550
Canyon L.: (1964) Comal Co.; Guadalupe R.; 12 mi. NW New Braunfels; (M-R-P-FC); Guadalupe-Blanco R. Authority & USAE	8,308	378,781
Casa Blanca, L.: (1951) Webb Co.; Chacon Cr.; 3 mi. NE Laredo; (R); Webb Co.; (Imp. by Country Club Dam)	1,680	20,000
Cedar Creek Reservoir: (1965) Henderson-Kaufman counties; Cedar Cr.; 3 mi. NE Trinidad; (M-R);Tarrant Regional Water District; (also called Lake Joe B. Hogsett)	32,796	644,686
Champion Creek Reservoir: (1959) Mitchell Co.; 7 mi. S. Colorado City; (M-In.); City of Colorado City	1,196	41,580
Cherokee, L.: (1948) Gregg-Rusk counties; Cherokee Bayou; 12 mi. SE Longview; (M-In.-R); Cherokee Water Co.	3,889	40,094
Choke Canyon Reservoir: (1982) Live Oak-McMullen counties; Frio R.; 4 mi. W Three Rivers; (M-In.-R-FC); City of Corpus Christi-USBR	17,660	662,820
Cisco, L.: (1923) Eastland Co.; Sandy Cr.; 4 mi. N. Cisco; (M); City of Cisco (Imp. by Williamson Dam)	985	29,003
Clyde, L.: (1970) Callahan Co.; N. Prong Pecan Bayou; 6 mi. S. Clyde; (M-R); City of Clyde and USDA Soil Conservation Service	449	5,748
Coffee Mill L.: (1939, 1967) Fannin Co.; Coffee Mill Cr.; 12 mi. NW Honey Grove; (R); U.S. Forest Service	650	8,000
Coleman L.: (1966) Coleman Co.; Jim Ned Cr.; 14 mi. N. Coleman; (M-In.); City of Coleman	1,811	38,094
Coleto Creek Reservoir: (1980) Goliad–Victoria counties; Coleto Cr.; 12 mi. SW Victoria; (In); Guadalupe-Blanco River Auth.	3,100	31,040
Colorado City, L.: (1949) Mitchell Co.; Morgan Cr.; 4 mi. SW Colorado City; (M-In.-P); TXU	1,612	30,758
Conroe, L.: (1973) Montgomery-Walker counties; W. Fork San Jacinto R.; 7 mi. NW Conroe; (M-In.); San Jacinto River Authority, City of Houston and Texas Water Development Board	19,590	410,988
Cooper, L./Olney: (1935) Archer Co.; Mesquite Crk; 8 mi. E Megargel; (M-R); City of Olney; (see L. Olney)	446	6,650
Cooper L.: (1991) Delta-Hopkins counties; Sulphur R.; 3 mi.SE Cooper; (FC-M-R); USAE; (also called Jim Chapman Lake)	17,958	260,332
Corpus Christi, L.: (1930) Live Oak-San Patricio-Jim Wells counties; Nueces R.; 4 mi. SW Mathis; (M-R); City of Corpus Christi (Imp. by Wesley E. Seale Dam)	18,700	256,062
Cox Creek Reservoir: Calhoun Co.; Cox Creek; 2 mi. E Point Comfort; (In); Alcoa Alumninum; (Also called Raw Water Lake and Recycle Lake)	541	5,034
Crook, L.: (1923) Lamar Co.; Pine Cr.; 5 Mi. N. Paris; (M); City of Paris	1,051	9,195
Cypress Springs, L.: (1970) Franklin Co.; Big Cypress Cr.; 8 mi. SE Mount Vernon; (In-M); Franklin Co. Water Development and Texas Water Development Board (formerly Franklin Co. L.); (Imp. by Franklin Co. Dam)	3,252	66,756
Daniel, L.: (1948) Stephens Co.; Gunsolus Cr.; 7 mi. S Breckenridge; (M-In.); City of Breckenridge; (Imp. by Gunsolus Creek Dam)	924	9,515
Davis, L.: Knox Co.; Double Dutchman Cr.; 5 mi. SE Benjamin; (Ir); League Ranch	585	5,454
Delta Lake Res. Units 1 and 2: (1939) Hidalgo Co.; Rio Grande (off channel); 4 mi. N. Monte Alto; (Ir.); Hidalgo-Willacy counties WC&ID No. 1 (formerly Monte Alto Reservoir)	2,371	14,000

Abbreviations used in this table: L., lake; R., river; Co., county; Cr., creek; (C) conservation; (FC) flood control; (R) recreation, (P) power; (M) municipal; (D) domestic; (Ir.) irrigation; (In.) industry; (Mi.) mining, including oil production; (FH) fish hatchery; USAE, United States Army Corps of Engineers; WC&ID, Water Control and Improvement District; WID, Water Improvement District; USBR, United States Bureau of Reclamation; Auth., Authority; LCRA, Lower Colorado River Authority; TPWD, Texas Parks & Wildlife Dept.; USDA, United States Department of Agriculture; Imp., impounded.

Lakes and Reservoirs, Date of Origin	Surface Area (acres)	Storage Capacity (acre-ft.)
Diversion, L.: (1924) Archer-Baylor counties; Wichita R.; 14 mi. W Holliday; (M-In.); City of Wichita Falls and Wichita Co. WID No. 2	3,397	35,324
Dunlap, L.: (1928) Guadalupe Co.; Guadalupe R.; 9 mi. NW Seguin; (P); Guadalupe-Blanco R. Auth.; (Imp. by TP-1 Dam)	410	5,900
Eagle L.: (1900) Colorado Co.; Colorado R. (off channel); in Eagle Lake; (Ir.); Lakeside Irrigation Co.	1,200	9,600
Eagle Mountain L.: (1934) Tarrant-Wise counties; West Fork Trinity R.; 14 mi. NW Fort Worth; (M-In.-Ir.); Tarrant Regional Water District	8,666	179,880
Eagle Nest L.: (1951) Brazoria Co.; off-channel Brazos R.; 12 mi. WNW Angleton; (Ir.); T.M. Smith, et al. (also called Manor Lake)	N/A	18,000
Eastman Lakes: 8 lakes; Harrison Co.; Sabine R. basin; NW of Longview; Texas Eastman Co.	N/A	8,135
Electra, L.: (1950) Wilbarger Co.; Camp Cr. and Beaver Cr.; 7 mi. SW Electra; (In.-M); City of Electra	731	5,626
Ellison Creek Reservoir: (1943) Morris Co.; Ellison Cr.; 8 mi. S. Daingerfield; (P-In.); Lone Star Steel	1,516	24,700
E. V. Spence Reservoir: (1969) Coke Co.; Colorado R.; 2 mi. W. Robert Lee; (M-In.-Mi); Colorado R. Municipal Water District; (Imp. by Robert Lee Dam)	6,372	517,272
Fairfield L.: (1970) Freestone Co.; Big Brown Cr.; 11 mi. NE Fairfield; (In.); TXU; (formerly Big Brown Creek Reservoir)	2,159	44,169
Falcon International Reservoir: (1954) Starr-Zapata counties; Rio Grande; (International U.S.-Mexico); 3 mi. W Falcon Heights; (M-In.-Ir.-FC-P-R); International Boundary and Water Commission; (Texas' share of total conservation capacity is 58.6 percent)	85,195	2,646,765
Fayette County Reservoir: (1978) Fayette Co.; Cedar Cr.; 8.5 mi. E. La Grange; (P-R); LCRA (also called Cedar Creek Reservoir)	2,400	71,400
Forest Grove Reservoir: (1982) Henderson Co.; Caney Cr.; 7 mi. NW Athens; (In.); TXU, Agent	1,502	20,038
Fort Phantom Hill, L.: (1938) Jones Co.; Elm Cr.; 5 mi. S. Nugent; (M-R); City of Abilene	4,213	70,030
Georgetown, L.: (1980) Williamson Co.; N. Fk. San Gabriel R.; 3.5 mi. W Georgetown; (FC-M-In.); USAE	1,287	36,823
Gibbons Creek Reservoir: (1981) Grimes Co.; Gibbons Cr.; 9.5 mi NW Anderson; (In.); Texas Municipal Power Agency	2,576	27,603
Gilmer Reservoir: (2001) Upshur Co.; Kelsey Creek; 15 mi. N of Longview; 4 mi. W of Gilmer; (M); City of Gilmer	895	12,720
Gladewater, L.: (1952) Upshur Co.; Glade Cr.; in Gladewater; (M-R); City of Gladewater	481	4,637
Gonzales, L.: (1931) Gonzales Co.; Guadalupe R.; 4.5 mi. SE Belmont; (P); Guadalupe-Blanco R. Auth.(also called H-4 Reservoir)	696	6,500
Graham, L.: (1929) Young Co.; Flint and Salt creeks; 2 mi. NW Graham; (M-In.); City of Graham	2,436	45,288
Granbury, L.: (1969) Hood Co.; Brazos R.; 8 mi. SE Granbury; (M-In.-Ir.-P); Brazos River Authority (Imp. by DeCordova Bend Dam)	8,139	132,949
Granger L.: (1980) Williamson Co.; San Gabriel R.; 10 mi. NE Taylor; (FC-M-In.); USAE (formerly Laneport L.)	4,159	51,822
Grapevine L.: (1952) Tarrant-Denton counties; Denton Cr.; 2 mi. NE Grapevine; (M-FC-In.-R.); USAE	6,978	164,703
Greenbelt L.: (1967) Donley Co.; Salt Fork of Red R.; 5 mi. N Clarendon; (M-In.); Greenbelt Municipal and Industrial Water Auth.	668	59,968
Greenville City Lakes: 6 lakes; Hunt Co.; Cowleech Fork, Sabine R.; 2 mi. Greenville; (M-Other); City of Greenville	N/A	6,864
Halbert, L.: (1921) Navarro Co.; Elm Cr.; 4 mi. SE Corsicana; (M-In-R); City of Corsicana	549	6,033
Hawkins, L.: (1962) Wood Co.; Little Sandy Cr.; 3 mi. NW Hawkins; (FC-R); Wood County; (Imp. by Wood Co. Dam No. 3)	776	11,690
Holbrook, L.: (1962) Wood Co.; Keys Cr.; 4 mi. NW Mineola; (FC-R); Wood County; (Imp. by Wood Co. Dam No. 2)	653	7,790
Hords Creek L.: (1948) Coleman Co.; Hords Cr.; 5 mi. NW Valera; (M-FC); City of Coleman and USAE	364	8,443
Houston, L.: (1954) Harris Co.; San Jacinto R.; 4 mi. N Sheldon; (M-In.-Ir.-Mi.-R); City of Houston	10,023	120,686
Houston County L.: (1966) Houston Co.; Little Elkhart Cr.; 10 mi. NW Crockett; (M-In.); Houston Co. WC&ID No. 1	1,330	17,113
Hubbard Creek Reservoir: (1962) Stephens Co.; 6 mi. NW Breckenridge; (M-In.-Mi.); West Central Texas Municipal Water Authority	15,687	313,174
Hubert H. Moss L.: (1960) Cooke Co.; Fish Cr.; 10 mi. NW Gainesville; (M-In.); City of Gainesville	1,121	24,058
Imperial Reservoir: (1912) Reeves-Pecos counties; Pecos R.; 35 mi. N Fort Stockton; (Ir.); Pecos County WC&ID No. 2	1,530	6,000
Inks L.: (1938) Burnet-Llano counties; Colorado R.; 12 mi. W Burnet; (M-Ir.-Mi.-P); LCRA	757	13,962

Abbreviations used in this table: L., lake; R., river; Co., county; Cr., creek; (C) conservation; (FC) flood control; (R) recreation; (P) power; (M) municipal; (D) domestic; (Ir.) irrigation; (In.) industry; (Mi.) mining, including oil production; (FH) fish hatchery; USAE, United States Army Corps of Engineers; WC&ID, Water Control and Improvement District; WID, Water Improvement District; USBR, United States Bureau of Reclamation; Auth., Authority; LCRA, Lower Colorado River Authority; TPWD, Texas Parks & Wildlife Dept.; USDA, United States Department of Agriculture; Imp., impounded.

The Austin skyline over Lady Bird Lake. Photo by Jonathan Cutrer, jcutrer.com.

Lakes and Reservoirs, Date of Origin	Surface Area (acres)	Storage Capacity (acre-ft.)
Jacksonville, L.: (1959) Cherokee Co.; Gum Cr.; 5 mi. SW Jacksonville; (M-R); City of Jacksonville; (Imp. by Buckner Dam)	1,164	25,670
J. B. Thomas, L.: (1952) Scurry-Borden counties; Colorado R.; 16 mi. SW Snyder; (M- In.-R); Colorado River Municipal Water District; (Imp. by Colorado R. Dam)	4,060	199,931
J. D. Murphree Wildlife Management Area Impoundments: Jefferson Co.; off-channel reservoirs between Big Hill and Taylor bayous; at Port Acres; (FH-R); TPWD (formerly Big Hill Reservoir)	6,881	32,000
Joe Pool L.: (1986) Dallas-Tarrant-Ellis counties; Mountain Cr.; 14 mi. SW Dallas; (FC-M-R); USAE–Trinity River Auth. (formerly Lakeview Lake)	7,470	175,358
Johnson Creek Reservoir: (1961) Marion Co.; 13 mi. NW Jefferson; (In.); AEP-Southwestern Electric Power Co.	650	10,100
Kemp, L.: (1923) Baylor Co.; Wichita R.; 6 mi. N Mabelle; (M-P-Ir.); City of Wichita Falls; Wichita Co. WID 2	15,357	245,307
Kickapoo, L.: (1945) Archer Co.; N. Fk. Little Wichita R.; 10 mi. NW Archer City; (M); City of Wichita Falls	5,861	86,345
Kiowa, L.: (1967) Cooke Co.; Indian Cr.; 8 mi. SE Gainesville; (R); Lake Kiowa, Inc.	560	7,000
Kirby, L.: (1928) Taylor Co.; Cedar Cr.; 5 mi. S. Abilene; (M); City of Abilene	740	7,620
Kurth, L.: (1950) Angelina Co.; off-channel reservoir; 8 mi. N Lufkin; (In.); Abitibi Consolidated Industries	726	14,769
Lady Bird L.: (1960) Travis Co.; Colorado R.; within Austin city limits; (R); City of Austin (formerly Town Lake)	468	6,409
Lake Creek L.: (1952) McLennan Co.; Manos Cr.; 4 mi. SW Riesel; (In.); TXU	550	8,400
Lake Fork Reservoir: (1980) Wood-Rains counties; Lake Fork Cr.; 5 mi. W Quitman; (M-In.); Sabine River Authority	26,889	605,061
Lake O' the Pines: (1959) Marion-Upshur-Morris counties; Cypress Cr.; 9 mi. W Jefferson; (FC-C-R-In.-M); USAE; (Imp. by Ferrell's Bridge Dam)	17,638	241,363
Lavon, L.: (1953) Collin Co.; East Fk. Trinity R.; 2 mi. W Lavon; (M-FC-In.); USAE	20,650	406,388
Leon, Lake: (1954) Eastland Co.; Leon R.; 7 mi. S Ranger; (M-In.); Eastland Co. Water Supply District	1,738	27,762
Lewis Creek Reservoir: (1969) Montgomery Co.; Lewis Cr.; 10 mi. NW Conroe; (In.); Entergy	1,010	16,400
Lewisville L.: (1929, 1954) Denton Co.; Elm Fork of Trinity R.; 2 mi. NE Lewisville; (M-FC-In.-R); USAE; (also called Lake Dallas and Garza-Little Elm)	27,175	563,228
Limestone, L.: (1978) Leon-Limestone-Robertson counties; Navasota R.; 7 mi. NW Marquez; (M-In.-Ir.); Brazos River Authority	12,486	203,780

Abbreviations used in this table: L., lake; R., river; Co., county; Cr., creek; (C) conservation; (FC) flood control; (R) recreation; (P) power; (M) municipal; (D) domestic; (Ir.) irrigation; (In.) industry; (Mi.) mining, including oil production; (FH) fish hatchery; USAE, United States Army Corps of Engineers; WC&ID, Water Control and Improvement District; WID, Water Improvement District; USBR, United States Bureau of Reclamation; Auth., Authority; LCRA, Lower Colorado River Authority; TPWD, Texas Parks & Wildlife Dept.; USDA, United States Department of Agriculture; Imp., impounded.

Lakes and Reservoirs, Date of Origin	Surface Area (acres)	Storage Capacity (acre-ft.)
Livingston, L.: (1969) Polk-San Jacinto-Trinity-Walker counties; Trinity R.; 6 mi. SW Livingston; (M-In.-Ir.); City of Houston and Trinity River Authority	83,730	1,785,348
Loma Alta Lake: (1963) Cameron Co.; off-channel Rio Grande; 8 mi. NE Brownsville; (M-In.); Brownsville Navigation District	2,490	26,500
Lost Creek Reservoir: (1990) Jack Co.; Lost Cr.; 4 mi. NE Jacksboro; (M); City of Jacksboro	413	11,950
Lyndon B. Johnson, L.: (1951) Burnet-Llano counties; Colorado R.; 5 mi. SW Marble Falls; (P); LCRA; (Imp. by Alvin Wirtz Dam); (formerly Granite Shoals L.)	6,110	115,249
Mackenzie Reservoir: (1974) Briscoe Co.; Tule Cr.; 9 mi. NW Silverton; (M); Mackenzie Mun. Water Auth.	253	46,450
Marble Falls, L.: (1951) Burnet Co.; Colorado R.; 1.25 mi. SE Marble Falls; (P); LCRA; (Imp. by Max Starcke Dam)	347	6,901
Martin Creek L.: (1974) Rusk-Panola counties; Martin Cr.; 17 mi. NE Henderson; (P); TXU.	4,954	75,726
Medina L.: (1913) Medina-Bandera counties; Medina R.; 8 mi. W Rio Medina; (Ir.); Bexar-Medina-Atascosa Co. WID No. 1	6,059	254,823
Meredith, L.: (1965) Moore-Potter-Hutchinson counties; Canadian R.; 10 mi. NW Borger; (M-In.-FC-R); cooperative project for municipal water supply by Amarillo, Lubbock and other High Plains cities. Canadian R. Municipal Water Authority–USBR; (Imp. by Sanford Dam); Governed by the Canadian R. Compact (1950), Lake Meredith can only hold 500,000 acre-ft. before it must release water to flow to Oklahoma.	7,097	500,000
Millers Creek Reservoir: (1990) Baylor-Throckmorton counties.; Millers Cr.; 9 mi. SE Goree; (M); North Central Texas Municipal Water Auth. and Texas Water Development Board	2,212	26,768
Mineral Wells, L.: (1920) Parker Co.; Rock Cr.; 4 mi. E Mineral Wells; (M); Palo Pinto Co. Municipal Water District No. 1	473	5,273
Mitchell County Reservoir: (1993) Mitchell Co.; branch of Beals Creek; (Mi.-In.); Colorado River Municipal Water District	1,463	27,266
Monticello Reservoir: (1972) Titus Co.; Blundell Cr.; 2.5 mi. E. Monticello; (In.); TXU	1,795	34,740
Mountain Creek L.: (1937) Dallas Co.; Mountain Cr.; 4 mi. SE Grand Prairie; (In.); TXU.	2,710	22,840
Murvaul, L.: (1958) Panola Co.; Murvaul Bayou; 10 mi. W Carthage; (M-In.-R); Panola Co. Fresh Water Supply District No. 1	3,507	38,285
Mustang Lake East/West: Brazoria Co.; Mustang Bayou; 6 mi. S Alvin; (Ir.-In.-R); Chocolate Bayou Land & Water Co.	N/A	6,451
Nacogdoches, L.: (1976) Nacogdoches Co.; Bayou Loco Cr.; 10 mi. W Nacogdoches; (M); City of Nacogdoches	2,180	39,522
Naconiche, L.: (2009) Nacogdoches Co.; Naconishe Cr. and Telesco Cr.; 14 mi. NE Nacogdoches; (R); Nacogdoches Co.	692	15,031
Nasworthy, L.: (1930) Tom Green Co.; S Concho R.; 6 mi. SW San Angelo; (M-In.-Ir); City of San Angelo	1,249	9,615
Natural Dam L.: (1957, 1989) Howard Co.; Sulphur Springs Draw; 8 mi. W Big Spring; An original natural lake, whose surface and capacity were increased by construction of dams; (FC); Wilkinson Ranch & Colorado River Municipal Water District. Natural Dam Lake only has water during times of flood and is dry most of the year	2,272	54,560
Navarro Mills L.: (1963) Navarro-Hill counties; Richland Cr.; 16 mi. SW Corsicana; (M-FC); USAE	4,736	49,827
Nocona, L.: (1960) Montague Co.; 8 mi. NE Nocona; (M-In.-Mi.); North Montague County Water Supply District (also known as Farmers Creek Reservoir)	1,362	21,444
North Fork Buffalo Creek Reservoir: (1964) Wichita Co.; 5 mi. NW Iowa Park; (M); Wichita Co. WC&ID No.3	1,489	15,400
North L.: (1957) Dallas Co.; S. Fork Grapevine Cr.; 2 mi. SE Coppell; (In.); TXU	800	9,400
Oak Creek Reservoir: (1952) Coke Co.; 5 mi. SE Blackwell; (M-In.); City of Sweetwater	2,389	39,210
O. C. Fisher L.: (1952) Tom Green Co.; N Concho R.; 3 mi. NW San Angelo; (M-FC-C- Ir.-R-In.-Mi.); USAE; Upper Colorado River Auth. (formerly San Angelo L.)	1,265	119,445
O. H. Ivie Reservoir: (1990) Coleman-Concho-Runnels counties; 24 mi. SE Ballinger; (M-In.), Colorado R. Municipal Water District (formerly Stacy Reservoir)	19,149	554,340
Olney, L./Cooper: (1935) Archer Co.; Mesquite Crk; 8 mi. E Megargel; (M-R); City of Olney; (see L. Cooper)	432	4,546
Palestine, L.: (1962) Anderson-Cherokee-Henderson-Smith counties; Neches R.; 4 mi. E Frankston; (M-In.-R); Upper Neches R. Municipal Water Auth.; (Imp. by Blackburn Crossing Dam)	23,112	367,303
Palo Duro Reservoir: (1991) Hansford Co.; Palo Duro Cr.; 12 mi. N Spearman; (M-R); Palo Duro River Auth.	2,407	61,066
Palo Pinto, L.: (1964) Palo Pinto Co.; 15 mi. SW Mineral Wells; (M-In.); Palo Pinto Co. Municipal Water District 1	2,173	26,766

Abbreviations used in this table: L., lake; R., river; Co., county; Cr., creek; (C) conservation; (FC) flood control; (R) recreation; (P) power; (M) municipal; (D) domestic; (Ir.) irrigation; (In.) industry; (Mi.) mining, including oil production; (FH) fish hatchery; USAE, United States Army Corps of Engineers; WC&ID, Water Control and Improvement District; WID, Water Improvement District; USBR, United States Bureau of Reclamation; Auth., Authority; LCRA, Lower Colorado River Authority; TPWD, Texas Parks & Wildlife Dept.; USDA, United States Department of Agriculture; Imp., impounded.

Lakes and Reservoirs, Date of Origin	Surface Area (acres)	Storage Capacity (acre-ft.)
Pat Cleburne, L.: (1964) Johnson Co.; Nolan R.; 4 mi. S. Cleburne; (M-FC-In.-Ir.); City of Cleburne	1,568	26,008
Pat Mayse L.: (1967) Lamar Co.; Sanders Cr.; 2 mi. SW Arthur City; (M-In.-FC); USAE	5,638	113,683
Pinkston Reservoir: (1976) Shelby Co.; Sandy Cr.; 12.5 mi. SW Center; (M); City of Center; (formerly Sandy Creek Reservoir)	523	7,380
Possum Kingdom L.: (1941) Palo Pinto-Young-Stephens-Jack counties; Brazos R.; 11 mi. SW Graford; (M-In.-Ir.-Mi.-P-R); Brazos R. Auth.; (Imp. by Morris Sheppard Dam)	17,970	538,139
Proctor L.: (1963) Comanche Co.; Leon R.; 9 mi. NE Comanche; (M-In.-Ir.-FC); USAE–Brazos River Auth.	4,715	54,762
Quitman, L.: (1962) Wood Co.; Dry Cr.; 4 mi. N Quitman; (FC-R); Wood County; (Imp. by Wood Co. Dam No.1)	814	7,440
Randell L.: (1909) Grayson Co.; Shawnee Cr.; 4 mi. NW Denison; (M); City of Denison	311	5,900
Ray Hubbard, L.: (1968) Collin-Dallas-Kaufman-Rockwall counties; (formerly Forney Reservoir); E. Fork of Trinity R.; 15 mi. E Dallas; (M); City of Dallas	20,739	439,559
Ray Roberts, L.: (1987) Denton-Cooke-Grayson counties; Elm Fk. Trinity R.; 11 mi. NE Denton; (FC-M-D); City of Denton, Dallas, USAE; (also known as Aubrey Reservoir)	28,612	788,167
Red Bluff Reservoir: (1937) Loving-Reeves counties, Texas; and Eddy Co.; N.M.; Pecos R.; 5 mi. N Orla; (Ir.-P); Red Bluff Water Power Control District	7,495	151,110
Red Draw Reservoir: (1985) Howard Co.; Red Draw; 5 mi. E Bi Spring; (Mi.-In.); Colorado River Municipal Water District	374	8,538
Richland-Chambers Reservoir: (1987) Freestone-Navarro counties; Richland Cr.; 20 mi. SE Corsicana; (M); Tarrant Regional Water District.	43,384	1,087,839
Rita Blanca, L.: (1940) Hartley Co.; Rita Blanca Cr.; 2 mi. S Dalhart; (R) City of Dalhart	524	12,050
River Crest L.: (1953) Red River Co.; off-channel reservoir; 7 mi. SE Bogata; (In.); TXU	555	7,000
Sam Rayburn Reservoir: (1965) Jasper-Angelina-Sabine-Nacogdoches-San Augustine counties; Angelina R.; (FC-P-M-In.-Ir.-R); USAE; (formerly McGee Bend Reservoir)	112,590	2,857,077
San Bernard Reservoirs #1, #2, #3: Brazoria Co.; Off-Channel San Bernard R.; 3 mi. N Sweeney; (In.); ConocoPhillips	N/A	8,610
Santa Rosa L.: (1929) Wilbarger Co.; Beaver Cr.; 15 mi. S Vernon; (Mi.); W. T. Waggoner Estate	1,500	11,570
Sheldon Reservoir: (1943) Harris Co.; Carpenters Bayou; 2 mi. SW Sheldon; (R-FH); TPWD	1,244	4,224
Smithers L.: (1957) Fort Bend Co.; Dry Creek; 10 mi. SE Richmond; (In.); Texas Genco	2,480	18,700
Somerville L.: (1967) Burleson-Washington-Lee counties; Yegua Cr.; 2 mi. S Somerville; (M-In.-Ir.- FC); USAE–Brazos River Authority	10,928	147,104
South Texas Project Reservoir: (1983) Matagorda Co.; off-channel Colorado R.; 16 mi. S Bay City; (In.); STP Nuclear Operating Co.	7,000	202,600
Squaw Creek Reservoir: (1983) Somervell-Hood counties; Squaw Cr.; 4.5 mi. N Glen Rose; (In.); TXU	3,163	151,250
Stamford, L.: (1953) Haskell Co.; Paint Cr.; 10 mi. SE Haskell; (M-In.); City of Stamford	5,316	51,570
Stillhouse Hollow L.: (1968) Bell Co.; Lampasas R.; 5 mi. SW Belton; (M-In.-Ir.-FC); USAE–Brazos River Authority; (also called Lampasas Reservoir)	6,484	227,825
Striker Creek Reservoir: (1957) Rusk-Cherokee counties; Striker Cr.; 18 mi. SW Henderson; (M-In.); Angelina-Nacogdoches WC&ID No. 1	1,920	16,934
Sulphur Springs, L.: (1950) Hopkins Co.; White Oak Cr.; 2 mi. N Sulphur Springs; (M); Sulphur Springs Water District; (formerly called White Oak Creek Reservoir)	1,340	17,747
Sulphur Springs Draw Reservoir: (1992) Martin Co.; Sulphur Springs Draw; 12 mi. NE Stanton; (FC); Colorado River Municipal Water District	970	7,997
Sweetwater, L.: (1930) Nolan Co.; Bitter Creek; 6 mi. SE Sweetwater (M-R); City of Sweetwater	652	12,267
Tawakoni, L.: (1960) Rains-Van Zandt-Hunt counties; Sabine R.; 9 mi. NE Wills Point; (M-In.-Ir-R); Sabine River Authority; (Imp. by Iron Bridge Dam)	37,325	871,695
Terrell City L.: (1955) Kaufman Co.; Muddy Cedar Cr.; 6 mi. E Terrell; (M-R); City of Terrell	849	8,594
Texana, L.: (1980) Jackson Co.; Navidad R. and Sandy Cr.; 6.8 mi. SE Edna; (M-Ir); USBR, Lavaca-Navidad R. Auth., Texas Water Dev. Bd.; (formerly Palmetto Bend Reservoir)	9,154	159,566
Texoma, L.: (1943) Grayson-Cooke counties, Texas; Bryan-Marshall-Love counties, Okla.; (Imp. by Denison Dam) on Red R. below confluence of Red and Washita rivers; (P-FC-C-R); USAE; Texas and Oklahoma each have the right to 50 percent of capacity	71,975	2,516,226
Toledo Bend Reservoir: (1967) Newton-Panola-Sabine-Shelby counties; Sabine R.; 14 mi. NE Burkeville; (M-In.-Ir.-PR); Sabine River Authority; Texas and Louisiana each have rights to 50 percent capacity	178,553	4,472,900
Tradinghouse Creek Reservoir: (1968) McLennan Co.; Tradinghouse Cr.; 9 mi. E Waco; (In.); TXU	2,010	35,124
Travis, L.: (1942) Travis-Burnet counties; Colorado R.; 13 mi. NW Austin; (M-In.-Ir.- Mi.-P-FC-R); LCRA; (Imp. by Mansfield Dam)	19,533	1,113,348

Abbreviations used in this table: L., lake; R., river; Co., county; Cr., creek; (C) conservation; (FC) flood control; (R) recreation; (P) power; (M) municipal; (D) domestic; (Ir.) irrigation; (In.) industry; (Mi.) mining, including oil production; (FH) fish hatchery; USAE, United States Army Corps of Engineers; WC&ID, Water Control and Improvement District; WID, Water Improvement District; USBR, United States Bureau of Reclamation; Auth., Authority; LCRA, Lower Colorado River Authority; TPWD, Texas Parks & Wildlife Dept.; USDA, United States Department of Agriculture; Imp., impounded.

A boatramp at O.H. Ivie Reservoir. Photo by Jonathan Cutrer, jcutrer.com.

Lakes and Reservoirs, Date of Origin	Surface Area (acres)	Storage Capacity (acre-ft.)
Trinidad L.: (1923) Henderson Co.; off-channel reservoir Trinity R.; 2 mi. S. Trinidad; (P); TXU	690	6,200
Truscott Brine L.: (1987) Knox Co.; Bluff Cr.; 26 mi. NNW Knox City; (Chlorine Control); Red River Auth.	3,146	111,147
Twin Buttes Reservoir: (1963) Tom Green Co.; Concho R.; 8 mi. SW San Angelo; (M-In. -FC-Ir.-R.); City of San Angelo, USBR, Tom Green Co. WC&ID No. 1	6,320	182,454
Twin Oaks Reservoir: (1982) Robertson Co.; Duck Cr.; 12 mi. N. Franklin; (In); TXU	2,330	30,319
Tyler, L. /Lake Tyler East: (1949/1967) Smith Co.; Prairie and Mud creeks.; 12 mi. SE Tyler; (M-In); City of Tyler; (Imp. by Whitehouse and Mud Creek dams)	4,714	72,073
Upper Nueces L.: (1926, 1948) Zavala Co.; Nueces R.; 6 mi. N Crystal City; (Ir.); Zavala-Dimmit Co. WID No. 1	316	5,200
Valley Acres Reservoir: (1956) Hidalgo Co.; off-channel Rio Grande; 7 mi. N Mercedes; (Ir-M-FC); Valley Acres Water District.	325	1,950
Valley L.: (1961) Fannin-Grayson counties; 2.5 mi. N Savoy; (P); TXU; (formerly Brushy Creek Reservoir)	1,080	16,400
Victor Braunig LAKE: (1962) Bexar Co.; Arroyo Seco; 15 mi. SE San Antonio; (In.-R); CPS Energy of San Antonio	1,350	26,500
Waco, L.: (1929) McLennan Co.; Bosque R.; 2 mi. W Waco; (M-FC-C-R); City of Waco, USAE, Brazos River Authority	8,161	189,418
Walter E. Long, L.: (1967) Travis Co.; Decker Cr.; 9 mi. E Austin; (M-In.-R); City of Austin; (formerly Decker Lake)	1,269	33,940
Waxahachie, L.: (1956) Ellis Co.; S Prong Waxahachie Cr.; 4 mi. SE Waxahachie; (M-In); Ellis County WC&ID No. 1; (Imp. by S. Prong Dam)	656	10,780
Weatherford, L.: (1956) Parker Co.; Clear Fork Trinity River; 7 mi. E Weatherford; (M-In.); City of Weatherford	1,083	17,812
Welsh Reservoir: (1976) Titus Co.; Swauano Cr.; 11 mi. SE Mount Pleasant; (R-In.); AEP- Southwestern Electric Power Co.; (formerly Swauano Creek Reservoir)	1,269	18,431
White River L.: (1963) Crosby Co.; 16 mi. SE Crosbyton; (M-In.-Mi.); White River Municipal Water District	653	29,880
White Rock L.: (1911) Dallas Co.; White Rock Cr.; within NE Dallas city limits; (R); City of Dallas	1,088	9,004
Whitney, L.: (1951) Hill-Bosque-Johnson counties; Brazos R.; 5.5 mi. SW Whitney; (FC-P); USAE	21,442	553,344
Wichita, L.: (1901) Wichita Co.; Holliday Cr.; 6 mi. SW Wichita Falls; (M-P-R); City of Wichita Falls	2,200	14,000
William Harris Reservoir: (1947) Brazoria Co.; off-channel between Brazos R. and Oyster Cr.; 8 mi. NW Angleton; (In.); Dow Chemical Co.	1,663	9,200
Winnsboro, L.: (1962) Wood Co.; Big Sandy Cr.; 6 mi. SW Winnsboro; (FC-R); Wood County; (Imp. by Wood Co. Dam No. 4)	806	8,100
Winters, L.: (1983) Runnels Co.; Elm Cr.; 4.5 mi. E Winters; (M); City of Winters (also known as Elm Creek Lake and New Lake Winters)	638	7,779
Worth, L.: (1914) Tarrant Co.; West Fork of Trinity R.; in NW Fort Worth; (M); City of Fort Worth	3,377	33,495
Wright Patman L.: (1957) Bowie-Cass-Morris-Titus-Red River counties; Sulphur R.; 8 mi. SW Texarkana; (FC-M); USAE; (formerly Lake Texarkana)	18,247	97,927

Abbreviations used in this table: L., lake; R., river; Co., county; Cr., creek; (C) conservation; (FC) flood control; (R) recreation; (P) power; (M) municipal; (D) domestic; (Ir.) irrigation; (In.) industry; (Mi.) mining, including oil production; (FH) fish hatchery; USAE, United States Army Corps of Engineers; WC&ID, Water Control and Improvement District; WID, Water Improvement District; USBR, United States Bureau of Reclamation; Auth., Authority; LCRA, Lower Colorado River Authority; TPWD, Texas Parks & Wildlife Dept.; USDA, United States Department of Agriculture; Imp., impounded.

Estuaries and Bays on the Texas Coast

Source: Texas Water Development Board; www.twdb.texas.gov

Texas has 367 miles of coastline along which 11 major river basins and eight coastal basins terminate, bringing fresh water from rivers, streams, and surface runoff to the coast to mix with the Gulf of Mexico seawater. These unique zones, known as estuaries, are a significant feature of the Texas coast.

Texas has seven major estuaries, which are formed by a complex of individual bays separated from the Gulf by barrier islands, and five minor, riverine estuaries, which occur near the mouths of major rivers that flow directly into the Gulf.

Texas estuaries range from the nearly fresh-water Sabine-Neches, which borders Louisiana, to the frequently hypersaline Laguna Madre along the southern coast.

Most Texas bays are shallow, ranging in average depth from two feet to ten feet.

Although each estuary differs in size and hydrological and ecological characteristics, together they support a diverse array of species that serve as the raw materials for a variety of economic activities associated with commercial and recreational fishing, hunting, and birding.

In addition, estuaries provide many other ecological services, such as:

- Water filtration and nutrient regulation through nutrient cycling
- Storm surge protection
- Shoreline stabilization through trapping sediments that support the growth of wetlands

The major estuaries, in order from east to west, include:

Sabine-Neches Estuary (Sabine Lake)

The Sabine-Neches Estuary, commonly known as Sabine Lake, is located along the Texas-Louisiana border and is the smallest of Texas' seven major estuaries with an area of 45,320 acres.

This estuary receives around 14 million acre-feet of fresh water inflow per year from the Sabine and Neches rivers and surrounding coastal watersheds, making it the freshest estuary along the Texas coast. Average bay salinity is eight parts per thousand.

The Sabine-Neches Waterway and Gulf Intracoastal Waterway are important shipping channels in this system.

The estuary is connected to the Gulf by Sabine Pass and lies within Orange and Jefferson counties on the Texas side.

Trinity-San Jacinto Estuary (Galveston Bay)

The Trinity-San Jacinto Estuary, also known as Galveston Bay, is located on the upper Texas coast. It is the largest estuary in Texas, with an area of 345,280 acres, and is the seventh largest in the United States.

Key features include Trinity Bay, Galveston Bay, East Bay, West Bay, and connections with the Gulf at Bolivar Roads, San Luis Pass, and Rollover Pass.

The Houston Ship Channel and the Gulf Intracoastal Waterway are notable man-made features of the system.

This estuary receives on average 11 million acre-feet of fresh water inflow annually from the Trinity and San Jacinto rivers and surrounding coastal watersheds. It is bounded by Bolivar Peninsula and Galveston Island and lies within Chambers, Harris, Galveston, and Brazoria counties.

Colorado-Lavaca Estuary (Matagorda Bay System)

The Colorado-Lavaca Estuary, or Matagorda Bay system, is located along the mid-Texas coast and covers an area of 244,490 acres. The estuary is bounded by Matagorda Island and consists of Matagorda Bay, Lavaca Bay, and several smaller bays, including Carancahua Bay, Tres Palacios Bay, Keller Bay, Cox Bay, and Turtle Bay.

Other key features include Pass Cavallo, the Matagorda Ship Channel, and the Gulf Intracoastal Waterway.

The estuary averages 3.5 million acre-feet of fresh water inflow annually from the Colorado, Lavaca, and Tres Palacios rivers and surrounding coastal watersheds. It is bordered by Matagorda, Jackson, Victoria, and Calhoun counties.

Guadalupe Estuary

The Guadalupe Estuary is located on the mid-Texas coast and covers 148,703 acres. The estuary includes San Antonio Bay, Mission Lake, Hynes Bay, Espiritu Santo Bay, and Mesquite Bay.

This estuary is largely protected from the Gulf by Matagorda Island and typically does not have a direct connection to the Gulf except through Cedar Bayou.

The other closest connection with the Gulf is through Pass Cavallo to the northeast in the Colorado-Lavaca Estuary.

The Guadalupe Estuary typically receives an average of 2.5 million acre-feet of fresh water inflow per year from the Guadalupe and San Antonio rivers and from surrounding coastal watersheds. The estuary lies adjacent to Calhoun, Aransas, and Refugio counties.

Mission-Aransas Estuary

The Mission-Aransas Estuary, located in the Coastal Bend, covers 111,780 acres and consists of Aransas Bay, Copano Bay, and several smaller bays, including Saint Charles Bay, Mission Bay, and Redfish Bay.

The estuary has a direct connection to the Gulf through Aransas Pass but is largely protected by a barrier island, San Jose Island.

Typically, the estuary receives 490,000 acre-feet of freshwater inflow per year from the Aransas and Mission rivers and surrounding coastal basins. The estuary is bordered by Aransas, Refugio, and San Patricio counties.

Nueces Estuary

The Nueces Estuary, located in the Coastal Bend, consists of Nueces Bay, Corpus Christi Bay, and Oso Bay. It spans 106,990 acres and is separated from the Gulf by Mustang Island, except for a direct connection through Aransas Pass.

The Corpus Christi Ship Channel and the Gulf Intracoastal Waterway are notable man-made features of the system.

This estuary typically receives 587,000 acre-feet of fresh water inflow per year from the Nueces River, Oso Creek, and surrounding coastal watersheds. The estuary is bordered by San Patricio and Nueces counties.

Laguna Madre Estuary

The Laguna Madre Estuary is the southernmost major estuary in Texas and extends almost to the Texas-Mexico border.

The Laguna Madre is a unique hypersaline lagoon with an average salinity between 32 and 38 parts per thousand. It is the only hypersaline estuary in the nation and one of only a handful that exist worldwide.

The estuary spans 280,910 acres but is divided by a coastal land mass known as Saltillo Flats, though more commonly referred to as the Landcut, and separated from the Gulf by Padre Island.

The Upper Laguna Madre has one major bay, Baffin Bay, and is hydrologically connected to the Nueces Estuary on its northern end and to the Gulf via the Packery Channel.

San Fernando Creek is the principal source of fresh- water inflow to this arid estuary, where freshwater inflows typically are 326,000 acre-feet per year.

The Lower Laguna Madre has one major bay, South Bay, and is connected to the Gulf via the Port Mansfield Channel and Brazos-Santiago Pass.

The Arroyo Colorado and surrounding coastal watersheds are principal sources of freshwater inflow to the Lower Laguna Madre, providing on average 425,000 acre-feet of inflows per year.

The estuary is bordered by Nueces, Kleberg, Kenedy, Willacy, and Cameron counties.

Minor Estuaries and Bays

Christmas Bay

Southwest of Galveston Bay, this system includes both Bastrop Bay and Drum Bay, and it is protected from the Gulf of Mexico by Follet's Island. It has two connections to the gulf, through Cold Pass and San Luis Pass.

It receives fresh water from runoff and through Bastrop Bayou.

Brazos River Estuary

The Brazos River Estuary, located on the upper Texas coast, is a riverine estuary that flows directly into the Gulf rather than into a system of bays. The estuarine portion of the river occurs near the mouth where tidal water from the Gulf mixes with river water.

Typically, this estuary receives 6.3 million acre-feet of fresh water inflow per year. It is located in Brazoria county.

San Bernard Estuary

The San Bernard Estuary is a minor estuary located along the mid-Texas coast, covering an area of 3,760 acres.

While the San Bernard River flows directly into the Gulf, creating a riverine estuary, neighboring Cowtrap Lake and Cedar Lake are small bays that connect with the Gulf through small tidal inlets.

On average, this estuary receives 683,753 acre-feet of fresh water inflow per year from the San Bernard River and surrounding coastal watersheds. It is located in Brazoria and Matagorda counties.

East Matagorda Bay

East Matagorda Bay is a small bay covering an area of 37,810 acres and is separated from the larger estuary by the Colorado River delta. There are no direct sources of river inflow into this bay, which receives an average of 536,165 acre-feet of fresh water per yearfrom runoff of surrounding coastal watersheds.

Rio Grande Estuary

The Rio Grande Estuary forms a natural border between the United States and Mexico and is a riverine estuary, which flows directly into the Gulf with no associated bay system.

The estuarine portion of the river occurs where tides from the Gulf mix with fresh water from the river. Annual average inflow from the Rio Grande is 370,722 acre-feet per year. The estuary is bordered by Cameron County on the north, and Mexico on the south. ☆

Water Conservation Tips

- Check all faucets, pipes, and toilets for leaks.
- Install water-saving showerheads and ultra-low-flush toilets.
- Take shorter showers.
- Never use the toilet as a wastebasket.
- Turn off the water while brushing teeth or shaving.
- Wash full loads of clothes.
- Fully load the dishwasher.
- Rinse dishes and vegetables in a full sink or pot of water and not under running water.
- Defrost frozen food in the refrigerator and not under running water.
- Do not over-water landscaping.
- Water the lawn or garden early in the morning or late in evening.
- Adjust sprinklers so they do not water the sidewalk or street.
- Do not water on cool, rainy, or windy days.
- Equip all hoses with shut-off nozzles.
- Use drip irrigation systems.
- Plant drought-tolerant or low-water-use plants and grasses.
- Place mulch around plants to reduce evaporation and discourage weeds.

Texas Plant Life

Source: This article was updated for the Texas Almanac by Stephan L. Hatch, Director, S.M. Tracy Herbarium and professor, Department of Ecosystem Science and Management, Texas A&M University

The types of plants found in Texas vary widely from one region to the next. This is due to the amount and frequency of rainfall, diversity of soils, and the number of frost-free days. From the forests of East Texas to the deserts of West Texas, from the grassy plains of North Texas to the semi-arid brushlands of South Texas, plant species change continuously.

More than 100 million acres of Texas are devoted to grazing, both for domestic and wild animals. This is the largest single use of land in the state. More than 80 percent of the acreage is devoted to range in the Edwards Plateau, Cross Timbers and Prairies, South Texas Plains, and Trans-Pecos Mountains and Basins.

Sideoats grama, which occurs on more different soils in Texas than any other native grass, was officially designated as the state grass of Texas by the Texas Legislature in 1971.

The 10 principal plant life areas of Texas, starting in the east, are:

1. Piney Woods

Most of this area of some 16 million acres ranges from about 50 to 700 feet above sea level and receives 40 to 56 inches of rain yearly. Many rivers, creeks, and bayous drain the region. Nearly all of Texas' commercial timber comes from this area. There are three native species of pine, the principal timber: longleaf, shortleaf, and loblolly. An introduced species, the slash pine, also is widely grown. Hardwoods include oaks, elm, hickory, magnolia, sweet and black gum, tupelo, and others.

The area is interspersed with native and improved grasslands. Cattle are the primary grazing animals. Deer and quail are abundant in properly managed habitats. Primary forage plants, under proper grazing management, include species of bluestems, rossettegrass, panicums, paspalums, blackseed needlegrass, Canada and Virginia wildryes, purpletop, broadleaf and spike woodoats, switchcane, lovegrasses, indiangrass, and numerous legume species.

Highly disturbed areas have understory and overstory of undesirable woody plants that suppress growth of pine and desirable grasses. The primary forage grasses have been reduced, and the grasslands have been invaded by threeawns, annual grasses, weeds, broomsedge bluestem, red lovegrass, and shrubby woody species.

2. Gulf Prairies and Marshes

The Gulf Prairies and Marshes cover approximately 10 million acres. There are two subunits: (a) the marsh and salt grasses immediately at tidewater, and (b) a little farther inland, a strip of bluestems and tall grasses, with some gramas in the western part. Many of these grasses make excellent grazing.

Oaks, elm, and other hardwoods grow to some extent, especially along streams, and the area has some post oak and brushy extensions along its borders. Much of the Gulf Prairies is fertile farmland, and the area is well suited for cattle.

Principal grasses of the Gulf Prairies are tall bunchgrasses, including big bluestem, little bluestem, seacoast bluestem, indiangrass, eastern gamagrass, Texas wintergrass, switchgrass, and gulf cordgrass. Saltgrass occurs on moist saline sites.

Heavy grazing has changed the native vegetation in many cases so the predominant grasses are the less desirable broomsedge bluestem, smutgrass, threeawns, tumblegrass, and many other less desirable grasses. Other plants that have invaded the productive grasslands include oak underbrush, Macartney rose, huisache, mesquite, prickly pear, ragweed, bitter sneezeweed, broomweed, and others.

Vegetation of the Gulf Marshes consists primarily of sedges, bullrush, flat-sedges, beakrush and other rushes, smooth cordgrass, marshhay cordgrass, marshmillet, and maidencane. The marshes are grazed best during winter.

3. Post Oak Savannah

This secondary forest area, also called the Post Oak Belt, covers some 7 million acres. It is immediately west of the primary forest region, with less annual rainfall and a little higher elevation. Principal trees are post oak, blackjack oak, and elm. Pecans, walnuts, and other kinds of water-demanding trees grow along streams. The southwestern extension of this belt is often poorly defined, with large areas of prairie.

The upland soils are sandy and sandy loam, while the bottomlands are sandy loams and clays.

The original vegetation consisted mainly of little bluestem, big bluestem, indiangrass, switchgrass, purpletop, silver bluestem, Texas wintergrass, woodoats, narrowleaf, post oak, and blackjack oak. The area is still largely native or improved grasslands, with small farms located throughout. Intensive grazing has contributed to dense stands of a woody understory of yaupon, greenbriar, and oak brush.

Mesquite has become a serious problem. Good forage plants have been replaced by such plants as split-beard bluestem, red lovegrass, broomsedge bluestem, broomweed, bullnettle, and western ragweed.

4. Blackland Prairies

This area of about 12 million acres, while called a "prairie," has much timber along the streams, including a variety of oaks, pecan, elm, bois d'arc, and mesquite. In its native state, it was largely a grassy plain — the first native grassland in the westward extension of the Southern Forest Region.

Most of this fertile area has been cultivated, and only small acreages of grassland remain in original vegetation. In heavily grazed pastures, the tall bunchgrass has been replaced by buffalograss, Texas grama, and other less productive grasses. Mesquite, lotebush, and other woody plants have invaded the grasslands.

The original grass vegetation includes big and little bluestem, indiangrass, switchgrass, sideoats grama, hairy grama, tall dropseed, Texas wintergrass, and buffalograss. Non-grass vegetation is largely legumes and composites.

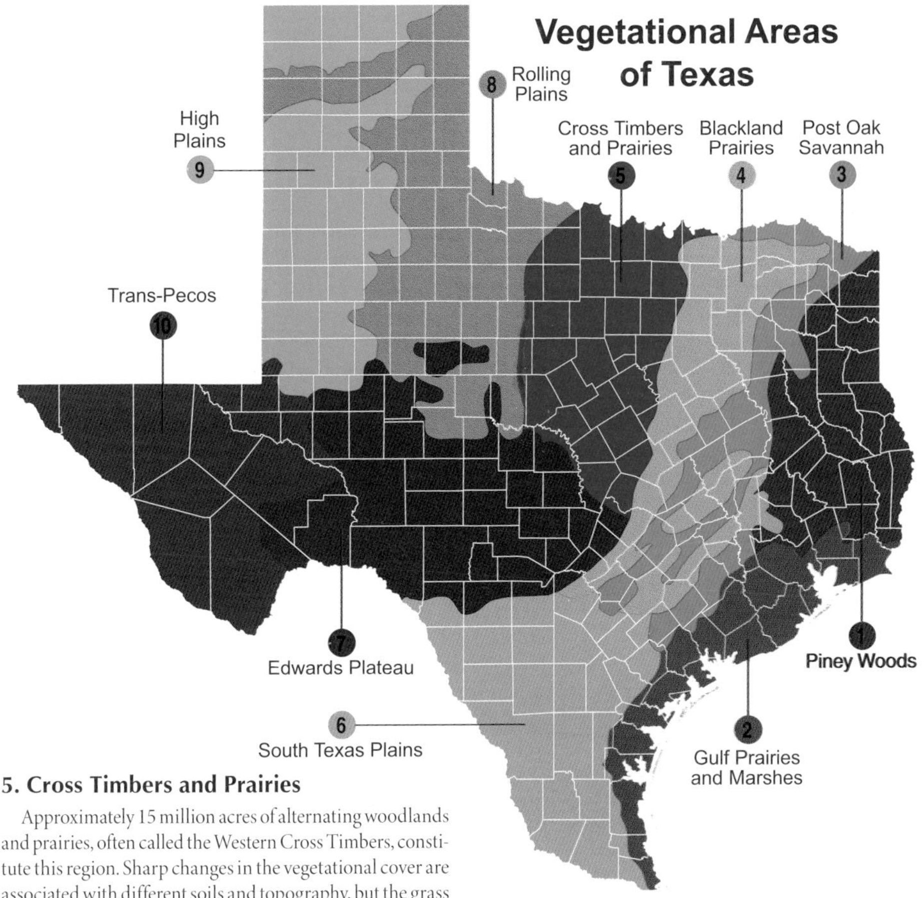

5. Cross Timbers and Prairies

Approximately 15 million acres of alternating woodlands and prairies, often called the Western Cross Timbers, constitute this region. Sharp changes in the vegetational cover are associated with different soils and topography, but the grass composition is rather uniform.

The prairie grasses are big bluestem, little bluestem, indiangrass, switchgrass, Canada wildrye, sideoats grama, hairy grama, tall grama, tall dropseed, Texas wintergrass, blue grama, and buffalograss.

On Cross Timbers soils, the vegetation is composed of big bluestem, little bluestem, hooded windmillgrass, sand lovegrass, indiangrass, switchgrass, and many species of legumes. The woody vegetation includes shinnery, blackjack, post, and live oaks.

The entire area has been invaded heavily by woody brush plants of oaks, mesquite, juniper, and other unpalatable plants that furnish little forage for livestock.

6. South Texas Plains

South of San Antonio, between the coast and the Rio Grande, are some 21 million acres of subtropical dryland vegetation, consisting of small trees, shrubs, cactus, weeds, and grasses. The area is noteworthy for extensive brushlands and is known as the Brush Country, or the Spanish equivalents of chaparral or monte. Principal plants are mesquite, small live oak, post oak, prickly pear (Opuntia) cactus, catclaw, blackbrush, whitebrush, guajillo, huisache, cenizo, and others that often grow very densely.

The original vegetation was mainly perennial warm-season bunchgrasses in savannahs of post oak, live oak, and mesquite. Other brush species form dense thickets on the ridges and along streams. Long-continued grazing has contributed to the dense cover of brush. Most of the desirable grasses have only persisted under the protection of brush and cacti.

There are distinct differences in the original plant communities on various soils. Dominant grasses on the sandy loam soils are seacoast bluestem, bristlegrass, paspalum, windmillgrass, silver bluestem, big sandbur, and tanglehead. Dominant grasses on the clay and clay loams are silver bluestem, Arizona cottontop, buffalograss, common curlymesquite, bristlegrass, pappusgrass, gramas, plains lovegrass, Texas cupgrass, vinemesquite, other panicums, and Texas wintergrass.

Low saline areas are characterized by gulf cordgrass, saltgrass, alkali sacaton, and switchgrass. In the post oak and live oak savannahs, the grasses are mainly seacoast bluestem, indiangrass, switchgrass, crinkleawn, paspalums, and panicums. Today much of the area has been reseeded to buffelgrass.

7. Edwards Plateau

These 25 million acres are rolling to mountainous, with woodlands in the eastern part and grassy prairies in the west. There is a good deal of brushy growth in the central and eastern areas. The combination of grasses, weeds, and small trees is ideal for cattle, sheep, goats, deer, and wild turkey.

This limestone-based area is characterized by the large number of springfed, perennially flowing streams that originate in its interior and flow across the Balcones Escarpment, which bounds it on the south and east. The soils are shallow, ranging from sands to clays, and are calcareous in reaction. This area is predominantly rangeland, with cultivation confined to the deeper soils.

In the east-central portion is the well-marked Central or Llano Basin, centering in Mason, Llano, and Burnet counties, with a mixture of granitic and sandy soils. The western portion of the area comprises the semi-arid Stockton Plateau.

Noteworthy is the growth of cypress along the perennially flowing streams. Separated by many miles from the cypress growth of the moist Southern Forest Belt, they constitute one of Texas' several "islands" of vegetation. These trees, which grow to stately proportions, were commercialized in the past.

The principal grasses of the clay soils are cane bluestem, silver bluestem, little bluestem, sideoats grama, hairy grama, indiangrass, curly-mesquite, buffalograss, fall witchgrass, plains lovegrass, wildryes, and Texas wintergrass.

The rocky areas support tall or mid-grasses with an overstory of live oak, shinnery oak, juniper, and mesquite. The heavy clay soils have a mixture of tobosagrass, buffalograss, sideoats grama, and mesquite.

Throughout the Edwards Plateau, live oak, shinnery oak, mesquite, and juniper dominate the woody vegetation. Woody plants have invaded to the degree that they must be controlled before range forage plants can re-establish.

8. Rolling Plains

This is a region of approximately 24 million acres of alternating woodlands and prairies. The area is half mesquite woodland and half prairie. Mesquite trees have steadily invaded and increased in the grasslands for many years, despite constant control efforts.

Soils range from coarse sands along outwash terraces adjacent to streams to tight or compact clays on redbed clays and shales. Rough broken lands on steep slopes are found in the western portion. About two-thirds of the area is rangeland, but cultivation is important in certain localities.

The original vegetation includes big, little, sand and silver bluestems, Texas wintergrass, indiangrass, switchgrass, sideoats and blue gramas, wildryes, tobosagrass, and buffalograss on the clay soils.

The sandy soils support tall bunchgrasses, mainly sand bluestem. Sand shinnery oak, sand sagebrush, and mesquite are the dominant woody plants.

Continued heavy grazing contributes to the increase in woody plants, low-value grasses such as red grama, red lovegrass, tumblegrass, gummy lovegrass, Texas grama, sand dropseed, and sandbur, with western ragweed, croton, and many other weedy forbs. Yucca is a problem plant on certain rangelands.

9. High Plains

The High Plains, some 19 million treeless acres, are an extension of the Great Plains to the north. Its level nature and porous soils prevent drainage over wide areas.

The relatively light rainfall flows into the numerous shallow "playa" lakes or sinks into the ground to feed the great underground aquifer that is the source of water for the countless wells that irrigate the surface of the plains. A large part of this area is under irrigated farming, but native grassland remains in about one-half of the High Plains.

Blue grama and buffalograss comprise the principal vegetation on the clay and clay loam "hardland" soils. Important grasses on the sandy loam "sandy land" soils are little bluestem, western wheatgrass, indiangrass, switchgrass, and sand reedgrass. Sand shinnery oak, sand sagebrush, mesquite, and yucca are conspicuous invading brushy plants.

10. Trans-Pecos Mountains and Basins

With as little as eight inches of annual rainfall, long hot summers, and usually cloudless skies to encourage evaporation, this 18-million-acre area produces only drought-resistant vegetation without irrigation. Grass is usually short and sparse.

The principal vegetation consists of lechuguilla, ocotillo, yucca, cenizo, prickly pear, and other arid land plants. In the more arid areas, gyp and chino grama, and tobosagrass prevail. There is some mesquite. The vegetation includes creosote-tarbush, desert shrub, grama grassland, yucca and juniper savannahs, pine oak forest, and saline flats.

The mountains are 3,000 to 8,749 feet in elevation and support piñon pine, juniper, and some ponderosa pine and other forest vegetation on a few of the higher slopes. The grass vegetation, especially on the higher mountain slopes, includes many southwestern and Rocky Mountain species not present elsewhere in Texas. On the desert flats, black grama, burrograss, and fluffgrass are frequent.

More productive sites have numerous species of grama, muhly, Arizona cottontop, dropseed, and perennial three-awn grasses. At the higher elevations, plains bristlegrass, little bluestem, Texas bluestem, sideoats grama, chino grama, blue grama, piñon ricegrass, wolftail, and several species of needlegrass are frequent.

The common invaders on all depleted ranges are woody plants, burrograss, fluffgrass, hairy erioneuron, ear muhly, sand muhly, red grama, broom snakeweed, croton, cacti, and several poisonous plants. ☆

Public Forests and Grasslands in Texas

Sources: U.S. Forest Service, www.fs.usda.gov/texas/ and the Texas A&M Forest Service, tfsweb.tamu.edu

There are **four national forests and five national grasslands in Texas**. These federally owned lands are administered by the U.S. Department of Agriculture Forest Service and by district rangers. The **five state forests** in Texas are I.D. Fairchild State Forest, **W. Goodrich Jones State Forest, John Henry Kirby Memorial State Forest, Paul N. Masterson Memorial Forest, and E.O. Siecke State Forest.**

The national forests are managed to achieve sustainable conditions and provide wildlife habitat, outdoor recreation, water, wood, minerals, and forage for public use while retaining the aesthetic, historic, and spiritual qualities of the land.

In 1960, the Multiple Use–Sustained Yield Act put into law what had been practiced in Texas for almost 30 years: that resources on public lands will be managed so that they are used in ways that best meet the needs of the people, that the benefits obtained will exist indefinitely, and that each natural resource will be managed in balance with other resources.

However, even the most carefully planned system of management cannot foresee factors that can cause drastic changes in a forest. Fire, storms, insects, and disease, for example, can prompt managers to deviate from land management plans and can alter the way a forest is managed.

A tree in Sam Houston National Forest. Photo by Adrian Delgado2012 CC by 2.0/Flickr..

1. Timber Production

About 486,000 acres of the national forests in Texas are suitable for timber production. Sales of sawtimber, pulpwood, and other forest products are initiated to implement forest plans and objectives. The estimated net growth is more than 200 million board feet per year and is valued at $40 million. A portion of this growth is normally removed by cutting.

2. Cattle Grazing

Permits to graze cattle on national grasslands are granted to the public for an annual fee. About 600 head of cattle are grazed on the Caddo–Lyndon B. Johnson National Grasslands annually. On the Rita Blanca National Grasslands, 5,425 head of cattle are grazed each year, most of them in Texas.

3. Hunting and Fishing

State hunting and fishing laws and regulations apply to all national forest land. Game law enforcement is carried out by the Texas Parks and Wildlife Department.

A wide variety of fishing opportunities are available on the Angelina, Sabine, Neches, and San Jacinto rivers; the Sam Rayburn and Toledo Bend reservoirs; Lake Conroe; and many small streams. Hunting is not permitted on the McClellan Creek National Grassland nor at the Lake Marvin Unit of the Black Kettle National Grassland.

4. Recreational Facilities

An estimated 3 million people visit the recreational areas in the national forests and grasslands in Texas each year, primarily for picnicking, swimming, fishing, camping, boating, and nature enjoyment.

The Sabine and Angelina National Forests are on the shores of Toledo Bend and Sam Rayburn Reservoirs, two large East Texas lakes featuring fishing and other water sports. Lake Conroe and Lake Livingston offer water-related outdoor recreation opportunities on and near the Sam Houston National Forest.

National Forests

National forests in Texas were established by invitation of the Texas Legislature by an Act of 1933, authorizing the purchase of lands in Texas for the establishment of national forests. President Franklin D. Roosevelt proclaimed these purchases on Oct. 15, 1936.

The national forests cover 639,959 acres in parts of 12 Texas counties.

The four East Texas forests and two North Texas grasslands are under the supervision of the National Forests and Grasslands in Lufkin. The three West Texas grasslands (Black Kettle, McClellan Creek, and Rita Blanca) are administered by the Forest Supervisor in Albuquerque, N.M., as units of the Cibola National Forest.

Each of Texas' National Forests contain wilderness areas, made possible by the Texas Wilderness Act of 1984, introduced by Representative John W. Bryant of Texas' 5th Congressional district, and signed into law by President Ronald Regan. These areas are allowed to return to a completely natural state with limited intervention, and visitors mush follow strict guidelines while within those areas.

(Recreational activities offered in National Forests and Grasslands are listed in the Recreation chapter on page **211**.)

Angelina National Forest (154,474 acres) is spread across five East Texas counties: San Augustine (64,906 acres), Angelina (57,471), Jasper (21,867) Nacogdoches (10,222) and Tyler (8). The southern portion of the forest is predominantly covered by the longleaf pine. Loblolly and shortleaf pine cover much of the rest of the forest. Angelina NF is home to two wilderness areas: Upland Island (13,331 acres), found south of the Sam Rayburn Reservoir, and Turkey Hill (5,473), north of the reservoir.

Davy Crockett National Forest (161,141 acres) is found in Houston and Trinity counties (93,746 acres and 67,395 acres, respectively). This is a diverse forest, with both hardwoods (including white oak, red oak, hickory, chestnut oak, cherry-bark oak, sweetgum, nutall oak, and willow) and pines (loblolly and shortleaf). In the northern part of Davy Crockett NF you'll find the Big Slough Wilderness Area (3,639 acres). The forest also contains the Alabama Creek Wildlife Management Area, 14,500 acres.

Sabine National Forest (161,087 acres) is another wide ranging forest that touches 5 different counties, Sabine (95,195 acres), Shelby (59,897), San Augustine (4,184), Newton (1,754), and Jasper (57), and even forms part of the border between Texas and Louisiana. The forest contains both hardwoods (American beech, southern red oak) and pines (loblolly, shortleaf, and longleaf). The Toledo Bend Reservoir runs along the eastern edge of much of the forest, including the Indian Mounds Wilderness Area (12,369 acres) near the middle.

Sam Houston National Forest (163,257 acres) is about 50 miles north of Houston, with parts found in San Jacinto (60,970 acres), Walker (55,115), and Montgomery (47,172) counties. It contains a variety of pines and hardwoods, and features redbuds and dogwoods, which are said to create a spectacular show of flowers in mid-February (redbud) and March (dogwood). Part of the forest stretches around the northern end of Lake Conroe, including the Little Lake Creek Wilderness (3,855 acres). Big Creek Scenic Area is near the eastern-most part of the forest.

Forests and Grasslands in Texas

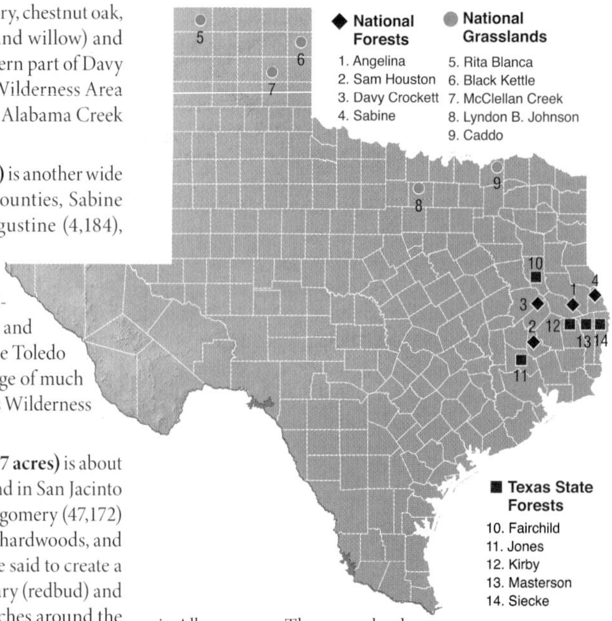

National Grasslands

The national grasslands were originally submarginal Dust Bowl project lands, purchased by the federal government primarily under the Bankhead-Jones Farm Tenant Act (1937). Today they are well covered with grasses and native shrubs.

The national grasslands cover 117,077 acres in six Texas counties. Two of these grasslands extend into Oklahoma, as well.

Lyndon B. Johnson National Grassland (20,102 acres) and Caddo National Grassland (17,630 acres) are located northeast and northwest of DFW, with a district ranger office at Decatur.These grasslands provide grazing land for cattle, but also habitat for native wildlife, including white-tailed deer, bobcats, red foxes, and several game birds. Lyndon B. Johnson NG is found mostly in Wise county (20,042 acres). The remaining 60 acres are in Montague county. Caddo NG is only in Fannin county. The Bois d' Arc unit of Caddo contains Lake Fannin, Coffee Mill Lake, and Lake Crockett, which are popular for fishing.

Black Kettle National Grassland (31,264 acres) and McClellan Creek National Grassland (1,402 acres) are both administered by the Cibola National Forest & National Grasslands in Albuquerque, New Mexico. Black Kettle NG lies mostly in Oklahoma, with a mere 577 acres in Texas' Hemphill county; McClellan Creek NG is found near Pampa, TX (in Gray county) and includes the Lake McClellan Recreation area. Both grasslands have active oil and gas wells installed, and lie within the Anadarko Basin.

Rita Blanca National Grassland (117,077 acres) is also managed by Cibola National Forest & National Grasslands, in Albuqueuque. These grasslands also stretch across the Texas border, from Dallam county (77,366 acres) into Oklahoma (15,653).

State Forests

Texas has **five state forests**, all of which are used primarily for demonstration and research. They are all game sanctuaries with no firearms or hunting allowed.

Recreational opportunities, such as horseback riding, hiking, bird watching, and picnicking, are available in all but the Masterson Forest.

I.D. Fairchild State Forest: Texas' largest forest is located west of Rusk in Cherokee County. This forest was transferred from the state prison system in 1925. Additional land was obtained in 1963 from the Texas State Hospitals and Special Schools for a total acreage of 2,740.

W. Goodrich Jones State Forest: Located south of Conroe in Montgomery County, it comprises 1,733 acres. It was purchased in 1926 and named for the founder of the Texas Forestry Association.

John Henry Kirby Memorial State Forest: This 600-acre forest in Tyler County was donated by lumberman John Henry Kirby in 1929, as well as later donors. Revenue from this forest is given to the Association of Former Students of Texas A&M University for student-loan purposes.

Paul N. Masterson Memorial Forest: Mrs. Leonora O'Neal Masterson of Beaumont donated this 519 acres in Jasper County in 1984 in honor of her husband, who was a tree farmer and an active member of the Texas Forestry Association.

E.O. Siecke State Forest: The first state forest, it was purchased by the state in 1924. It contains 1,722 acres of pine land in Newton County. An additional 100 acres was obtained by a 99-year lease in 1946. ☆

Angelina National Forest in East Texas. Photo by William L. Farr, CC by SA 4.0/Wikimedia Commons.

Texas Forest Resources

Source: Texas A&M Forest Service, Texas A&M University System; http://tfsweb.tamu.edu.

Forests resources in Texas are abundant and diverse. Forest land covers roughly 38 percent of the state's land area. According to the Forest Inventory and Analysis (FIA), there are over 63 million acres of forests and woodlands in Texas.

The principal forest region in Texas is called the **East Texas Piney Woods**, due to the abundance of pine-hardwood in the region. The 43-county region forms the western edge of the southern pine region, extending from Bowie and Red River counties in Northeast Texas to Jefferson, Harris, and Waller counties in Southeast Texas. The counties contain 12.0 million acres of forestland and 9.4 million acres of non-forest land.

Family forest ownership (non-industrial, private) in East Texas accounts for 6.0 million acres (50%). Forest industry owns 4.6 million acres (3.7%). The rest of the timberland in the east is owned by national forests (580,000 acres; 5%) and other public entities (427,000, 4%).

Forest Types

Five major forest types are found in the East Texas Piney Woods. Two are pine-forest types: loblolly-shortleaf and longleaf-slash. These are dominated by the four species of southern yellow pine. In these forests, the various pine trees make up at least 50 percent of the trees. Loblolly-shortleaf forest is the predominate forest type in the area.

Oak-hickory is the next most common forest type. These are upland hardwood forests in which oaks or hickories make up at least 50 percent of the trees, and pine species are less than 25 percent. Oak-pine is a mixed-forest type in which more than 50 percent of the trees are hardwoods, but pines make up 25–49 percent of the trees.

Bottomland hardwood forests can include a variety of trees, including oak, gum, cypress, elm, and ash, and are commonly found along creeks, river bottoms, swamps, and other wet areas.

Other forest types found in East Texas include small acreages of mesquite, exotic hardwoods, red cedar, and unproductive lands that are considered forested but do not meet stocking requirements.

Forest Types in East Texas

Forest Type Group	Area
Loblolly-shortleaf pine	5.5 million acres (46%)
Oak-hickory	2.6 million acres (22%)
Bottomland hardwood	2.2 million acres (19%)
Oak-pine	1.3 million acres (11%)
Longleaf-slash	0.1 million acres (1%)

Southern pine plantations, established by tree planting and usually managed intensively to maximize timber production, are an important source of wood fiber. Texas forests include 3.2 million acres of pine plantations, 63 percent of which are on industrially managed land, 34 percent on non-industrial private land, and 3 percent on public land. Genetically superior tree seedlings are usually planted to improve survival and growth.

Growth and Removals

Keeping track of growth and removals on timberland is extremely important as a measure of sustainability. On average, timberland annual net growth in East Texas is about 590.8 cubic feet. Removals of live trees in East Texas timberland is estimated to average 561.3 million cubic feet. Softwood represents 73 percent of that total. Annual growth exceeds removals by an average of 29.5 million cubic feet.

The 2019 Timber Harvest

Total volume of growing stock removed in 2019 was 542.9 million cubic feet, a 4.5 percent increase over the 519.7 million cubic feet removed the year before. The 2019 figure is comprised of 462.2 milion cubic feet of pine and 80.8 million cubic feet of hardwood.

Industrial roundwood harvest in Texas in 2019, utilized in the manufacture of wood products, totaled 484.8 million cubic feet for pine and 81.3 million cubic feet for hardwood. The combined harvest of 566.2 million cubic feet was an increase of 4.8 percent over 2018. Top producing counties included Cass, Cherokee, Newton, Polk, and San Augustine.

Total Harvest Value

Stumpage value of the East Texas timber harvest in 2019 was $331.2 million, a 19.1-percent increase from 2018. The delivered value of timber was up 10.2 percent to $695.4 million. Pine timber accounted for 86 percent of the total stumpage value.

Compared with 2018, the harvest of sawlogs for production of lumber increased 1.4 percent in 2018 to 1.1 billion board feet. The pine sawlog cut totaled 1.0 billion board feet, and the hardwood sawlog harvest was 73.1 million board feet. Angelina, Cherokee, Jasper Newton, and Polk counties were the top producers of sawlogs.

Timber cut for the production of structural panels, including both plywood and OSB (oriented strand board) and hardwood veneer, totaled 169.2 million cubic feet, a 15.4 percent increase from the prior year. Cherokee, Harrison, Houston, Polk, and Trinity counties were the top producers of veneer and panel roundwood.

Harvest of timber for manufacture of pulp and paper products increased 0.3 percent from 2018 to 2019 to 2.6 million cords. Cass, Hardin, Jasper, Newton and San Augustine counties were the top producers of pulpwood.

Other roundwood harvest, including posts, poles, and pilings, totaled 3.9 million cubic feet in 2019.

Import–Export Trends

Texas was a net importer of timber products in 2019. Total imports from other states was 109.4 million cubic feet, while the total export was 52.4 million cubic feet. Texas mills utilized 90.7 percent of the timber harvested in the state in 2017. The remainder was processed mainly by mills in Arkansas, Louisiana, and Oklahoma.

Production of Forest Products

Lumber: Texas sawmill production of 1.5 billion board feet of lumber in 2019 represents a decrease of 3.5 percent from 2018. Production of pine lumber decreased 2.7 percent to 1.4 billion board feet in 2019, and hardwood lumber production decreased 16.1 percent to 76.0 million board feet.

Structural Panel Products: Production of structural panels, including plywood and OSB, increased 14.3 percent to 3.1 billion square feet in 2019.

Paper Products: Production of pulp and paperboard products (includes fiberboard, paperboard, market pulp and miscellaneous products) totaled 2.4 million tons in 2019, down 9.6 percent from the previous year. There has not been any major paper production in Texas since 2003.

Treated Wood: There was a 13.4 percent decrease in the volume of wood processed by Texas wood treaters in 2019 from 2018. The total volume treated in 2019 was 33.7 million cubic feet. Among major treated products, lumber accounted for 58.5 percent of the total volume; crossties accounted for 12.5 percent; utility poles and pilings accounted for 11.3 percent.

Primary Mill Residue: Total mill residue, including chips, sawdust, shavings, and bark in primary mills, such as sawmills, panel mills, and chip mills, was 5.7 million tons in 2019. Pine residue was 88 percent of the total and the rest was from hardwood. Mill residue was a combination of chips (48.9 percent), bark (31.7 percent), sawdust (13.3 percent), and shavings (6.1 percent).

Texas Industrial Roundwood Products 2005–2019

	Lumber* (thousand board feet)		Paper Products (short tons)	Structural Panel (thousand square feet*)
Year	Pine	Hardwood	Paperboard	Pine
2005	1,733,314	230,090	2,512,262	3,249,558
2006	1,676,461	240,214	2,781,865	2,935,637
2007	1,550,716	180,713	2,788,308	2,503,941
2008	1,406,103	213,191	2,329,347	2,204,544
2009	1,237,801	171,514	2,007,054	1,958,794
2010	1,188,294	139,389	2,089,521	1,881,763
2011	1,308,427	154,593	2,029,405	1,915,605
2012	1,291,578	118,823	2,081,521	2,049,084
2013	1,385,043	140,427	2,168,403	2,017,406
2014	1,444,203	104,089	2,213,026	2,348,023
2015	1,410,472	107,029	2,106,412	2,444,464
2016	1,357,409	88,001	2,317,537	2,729,569
2017	1,399,502	79,090	2,384,711	2,443,043
2018	1,451,042	90,568	1,541,610	2,303,996
2019	1,411,440	76,026	1,487,466	3,106,076
	* Includes tie volumes.			* 3/8-inch basis

Sources: Annual Harvest Trends *reports by Texas A&M Forest Service*

Issues Facing Texas Forests

Reforestation

A total of 75,983 acres were planted during the winter 2018 and spring 2019 planting season. Industrial landowners planted 37,667 acres, a decrease of 49.7 percent from the previous season.

Family forest owners planted 37,744 acres, and public landowners planted 572 acres. Family forest owners received $3.3 million in cost-share assistance for reforestation through federal cost-share programs.

Texas Primary Mill Residue, 2019*

Residue Type	Pine	Hardwood	Total
Chips[1]	2,555,737	143,038	2,698,775
Sawdust	643,846	87,221	731,067
Shavings	319,412	16,827	336,238
Bark[2]	1,561,114	417,194	1,978,308
Total	5,080,108	664,280	5,744,388

* Primary mills include sawmills, structural panel mills, and chip mills.
[1] Does not include chips produced in chip mills.
[2] Includes bark from sawmills, panel mills, and chip mills.
Source: Harvest Trends 2019, *Texas A&M Forest Service*

Total Industrial Timber Production and Value by County in Texas, 2019

County	Pine	Hardwood	Total	Stumpage Value	Total Value
	– – – – cubic feet – – – –			– – thousand dollars – –	
Anderson	8,093,193	1,046,588	9,139,781	5,799	11,704
Angelina	20,961,922	2,691,691	23,653,613	16,947	32,252
Bowie	9,021,627	2,730,855	11,752,482	6,912	14,553
Camp	1,100,898	46,844	1,147,742	733	1,467
Cass	29,839,327	9,858,130	39,697,457	21,850	47,578
Chambers	182,203	2,348	184,551	71	186
Cherokee	26,299,155	5,373,447	31,672,602	21,331	41,952
Franklin	18,641	67,268	85,909	85	148
Gregg	1,004,104	527,603	1,531,707	1,151	2,181
Grimes	746,830	2,348	749,178	671	1,159
Hardin	19,297,500	1,960,332	21,257,832	10,807	24,316
Harris	1,685,565	153,211	1,838,776	1,691	2,908
Harrison	19,252,202	2,439,665	21,691,867	13,668	27,622
Henderson	1,093,361	288,720	1,382,081	935	1,835
Houston	16,723,679	204,902	16,928,581	9,353	20,057
Jasper	28,834,773	1,694,974	30,529,747	15,971	35,311
Jefferson	195,889	3,628	199,517	170	300
Leon	879,481	1,858,591	2,738,072	1,426	3,272
Liberty	10,552,899	3,899,135	14,452,034	9,070	18,572
Madison	63,096	0	63,096	60	101
Marion	7,463,596	746,854	8,210,450	4,052	9,254
Montgomery	4,160,922	213,161	4,374,083	3,124	5,945
Morris	1,288,661	757,371	2,046,032	1,145	2,490
Nacogdoches	22,165,332	2,909,835	25,075,167	15,625	31,763
Newton	42,348,936	1,687,853	44,036,789	23,336	51,187
Orange	426,522	76,988	503,510	309	634
Panola	14,125,761	1,483,546	15,609,307	9,348	19,340
Polk	40,547,445	1,751,405	42,298,850	25,474	52,483
Red River	7,013,180	3,433,757	10,446,937	5,533	12,361
Rusk	17,682,723	2,718,349	20,401,072	14,306	27,579
Sabine	16,932,598	2,195,200	19,127,798	10,234	22,425
San Augustine	18,752,325	14,147,868	32,900,193	16,569	38,137
San Jacinto	7,057,158	134,185	7,191,343	5,031	9,640
Shelby	16,819,312	2,512,634	19,331,946	11,779	24,203
Smith	4,422,030	3,147,871	7,569,901	3,963	8,929
Titus	132,621	182,502	315,123	321	548
Trinity	22,234,058	410,378	22,644,436	13,113	27,492
Tyler	23,932,092	1,540,267	25,472,359	14,282	30,522
Upshur	7,969,784	2,865,425	10,835,209	5,688	12,710
Van Zandt	285,190	800	285,990	173	354
Walker	7,716,037	226,133	7,942,170	4,651	9,693
Waller	685,221	2,348	687,569	629	1,078
Wood	3,904,479	1,765,601	5,670,080	2,459	6,111
Other Counties	933,943	1,567,875	2,501,818	1,324	3,014
Total Production	**484,846,271**	**81,328,486**	**566,174,757**	**$ 331,169**	**$ 695,367**

Source: Harvest Trends 2019, *Texas A&M Forest Service*

Beyond the Piney Woods: Texas' Other Tree Regions

In addition to the 12 million acres of timberland in East Texas, there are an additional 51.1 million acres of land in the remainder of Texas that are considered forestland. These forests consist of mesquite woodlands, oak-hickory forests, juniper woodlands, and other western forest types. These forests do not have the commercial timber value of the East Texas Piney Woods but are environmentally important with benefits of wildlife habitat, improved water quality, recreation, and aesthetics.

- **Post Oak Belt**: The Post Oak Belt forms a band of wooded savannah mixed with pasture and cropland immediately west of the Piney Woods. It extends from Lamar and Red River counties southwest as far as Bee and Atascosa counties. Predominant species include post oak, blackjack oak, and elm. An interesting area called the "Lost Pines" forms an isolated island of southern-pine forest in Bastrop, Caldwell, Fayette, and Lee counties just a few miles southeast of Austin.
- **Eastern and Western Cross Timbers:** The Eastern and Western Cross Timbers cover an area of about 3 million acres in North-Central Texas. The term "cross timbers" originated with the early settlers who, in their travels from east to west, crossed alternating patches of oak forest and prairies and so affixed the name "cross timbers" to these forests.
- **Cedar Brakes:** Farther south in the Edwards Plateau region are the cedar brakes, which extend over 3.7 million acres. Cedar, live oak, and mesquite dominate these steep slopes and rolling hills. Mesquite is harvested for cooking wood, knick-knacks, and woodworking. Live oak in this region is declining because of the oak wilt disease.
- **Mountain Forests:** The mountain forests of the Trans-Pecos region, including Jeff Davis County and the Big Bend, are rugged and picturesque. Several western tree species, including piñon pine, ponderosa pine, southwestern white pine, and even Douglas fir are found there, along with aspen and several species of oak.
- **Coastal Forests:** The coastal forests of the southern Gulf Coast are characterized by a mix of brush and short, scrubby trees. Common species include mesquite, live oak, and acacia. Some of these scrub forests are particularly important as migratory bird habitat.

Do you have forests in your region of Texas? Go explore!

Wildfires

Once a primarily rural concern, wildfires are now a threat statewide. Texas has seen significant fire seasons since 1996, some of which threatened or burned through small towns and cities and destroyed homes. The December 2020 Forest Action Plan, published by Texas A&M Forest Service, cites three factors that are intensifying the threat: population growth, changing land use, and increasing drought frequency.

Information on state wildfire response, wildfire risk assessments, fire department assistance programs, and how homeowners and communities can reduce their wildfire risk is online at: (http://tfsweb.tamu.edu and http://ticc.tamu.edu).

Sustainability

Although East Texas forests have provided jobs and economic growth for more than a century, the resource is coming under increasing pressure with changes in management and use of the piney woods. The forests are being impacted by residential development, ownership changes and parcelization, and population growth.

The woodlands in Central and West Texas are facing similar pressures, along with additional challenges such as wildfires, invasive plants, oak wilt, and other pests.

It will require partnerships and cooperation to protect these resources so that the high quality of life in these regions can continue.

Urban Forest Sustainability

An estimated 86 percent of Texans live in urban areas, making urban trees and forests important. Trees reduce urban heat island effect with shade and evaporative cooling; purify the air by absorbing pollutants, slowing chemical reactions that produce harmful ozone, and filter dust; reduce storm water runoff, and soil erosion; buffer against noise, glare, and strong winds; and provide habitat for urban wildlife.

Texas has seen an increase of 4 million residents since 2010, resulting in rapid urbanization in some areas. That in turn has increased the pressure on the sustainability of trees and forests in urban areas.

Water Resource Protection

Did you know that almost half of Texas' freshwater resources originate on forests? Covering about one-third of the state's land area, those forests and woodlands are integral to keeping a stable supply of clean drinking water for Texans. When those lands are cleared for other uses, our water supply is adversely affected.

Learn more about our state's water resources on page 41. ☆

TEXAS WILDLIFE

By Drew R. Davis and Travis J. LaDuc

The wide variation in soils, climate, and vegetation in Texas has resulted in a rich diversity of animal life. There are over 1,600 species of vertebrates (animals with backbones) found in Texas, categorized into five groups or classes: fishes, amphibians, reptiles, birds, and mammals. A summary of each class is listed, followed by annotated lists of the species diversity in each of the five groups.

These annotated lists are not intended to be exhaustive, but rather to provide a review of both the common and uncommon species in our state. Those marked by an asterisk (*) are non-native species.

For more information about Texas wildlife, we recommend the following references: The Fishes of Texas database (fishesoftexas.org); the *Texas Natural History Guide* series for reptiles and amphibians (2005–2020, University of Texas Press); *The Texas Ornithological Society Handbook of Texas Birds*, 2nd edition (2014, Texas A&M University Press), *The Mammals of Texas*, 3rd edition (2016, University of Texas Press and https://www.depts.ttu.edu/nsrl/mammals-of-texas-online-edition); and David Schmidly's *Texas Natural History: A Century of Change* (2002, Texas Tech University Press).

There are, of course, numerous other regional print and online guides. We encourage you to visit online citizen science platforms such as iNaturalist.org, eBird.org, and HerpMapper.org to learn more about the natural world around you as well and contribute your observations. Go explore!

Group Descriptions

Lists of Wildlife Found in Texas

Phrynosoma cornutum (aka Texas Horned Lizard, or Horny Toad) taking in the sun. Photo by Travis LaDuc.

Fishes

Fishes are a large group of gilled aquatic vertebrates, which include jawless fish, cartilaginous fish, and bony fish. Jawless fish include both hagfish and lampreys, the latter of which only two species are known from Texas. Cartilaginous fish are a class of fish that have skeletons primarily composed of cartilage (rather than bone) and include sharks, skates, and rays.

The final group, the bony fish, is the most diverse and abundant class of fish and is named due to their skeletons being primarily composed of bone (rather than cartilage). Over 34,000 species of bony fish are recognized and include species that range widely in size, shape, and behaviors, making them the most diverse group of vertebrates.

Despite there being over 560 species of fish from 117 different families in freshwater and marine environments in Texas, fishes are only the second most diverse group of vertebrates in Texas, after birds. In addition to native species, many non-native species of fish have become established in Texas.

Fish are all aquatic, gilled animals that lack limbs with digits. Like amphibians and reptiles, most fish are cold-blooded (or ectothermic), meaning that their body temperatures vary as environmental temperatures change and they cannot self-regulate their temperature. Most fish are covered in scales, which help protect them from predators and pathogens and can help serve as camouflage, but some species like catfish and eels lack scales altogether.

Fish are an important source of food for humans worldwide. Species of carp, anchovy, pollock, tilapia, salmon, and tuna all top lists of commercially important fishes.

Recreational fishing has been recognized as an important economic activity for the state. Popular freshwater sport fishes include Largemouth Bass, several species of sunfish, crappie, Blue Catfish, Channel Catfish, Flathead Catfish, Striped Bass, and Rainbow Trout. Popular saltwater sport fish include Red Drum, Black Drum, Spotted Sea Trout, flounder, mackerel, Sheepshead, and Red Snapper. (Read more about fishing in the state on page 175.)

The Rio Grande Cichlid is the only species of cichlid that is native to the United States. Photo by Clinton & Charles Robertson, CC by SA 4.0.

Amphibians

Amphibians include frogs, toads, salamanders, newts, and caecilians. Approximately 8,100 amphibian species are found worldwide, and new species are described each year. Texas is home to 70 native species of amphibians, comprising 13 different families and two orders. These species include frogs, toads, salamanders, and newts, but no caecilians. Texas is also home to one introduced species, the Greenhouse Frog.

Amphibians lack claws, although arboreal frogs often have toe pads that assist in climbing and burrowing toads may have spades on the hind feet for digging. Amphibians typically have moist, smooth skin, although species like toads have dry, warty skin. The skin of aquatic frogs is highly permeable to allow gas exchange in aquatic environments. Toads have parotid glands just behind the head. These glands release a toxin to deter predators by irritating their mouths.

All amphibians play important roles in ecosystems. Frogs and toads are primarily herbivorous as larvae and carnivorous as adults, eating insects and other invertebrate pests. Larval salamanders are known to consume mosquito larvae. Further, amphibians

You'll find Squirrel Tree frogs in East Texas and along the coast. Photo by Dr. Drew R. Davis

are an essential food source for many animals and help to move nutrients from aquatic habitats into upland, terrestrial food webs.

Most of the amphibian diversity in Texas is in the eastern and central regions. A large number of aquatic blind and spring salamanders occur in springs and karst environments along the Edwards Plateau, many of which are only found in a handful of localities and are classified as threatened or endangered. Outside of blind salamanders and spring salamanders and a few other species, most other species of salamanders occur in the eastern third of Texas.

Despite fewer species of amphibians occurring in South Texas, several species that do occur there exist nowhere else in the United States and occupy very limited distributions, such as the Mexican Burrowing Toad, Mexican Treefrog (featured on this year's cover), and Mexican White-lipped Frog.

Several of our native amphibians have been accidentally spread and introduced to areas of Texas where they do not naturally occur. For example, the Rio Grande Chirping Frog was widely introduced across the state due to the horticultural trade, and the Green Treefrog became established at Big Bend National Park due to individuals likely hitchhiking on RVs or other camping equipment from areas where this species is native.

Reptiles

The order Reptilia consists of over 1,200 genera and 11,000 species and includes lizards, snakes, turtles, and crocodilians. Texas is home to 153 native species of reptiles and ten introduced species: Florida Red-bellied Cooter, Bent-toed Gecko, Common House Gecko, Indo-Pacific House Gecko, Tropical House Gecko, Sri Lankan Spotted House Gecko, Mediterranean Gecko, Mexican Spiny-tailed Iguana, Brown Anole, and the Brahminy Blindsnake.

Unlike amphibians, all reptiles have skin that is covered in scales. These scales serve as protection, but also help to prevent water loss, allowing reptiles to tolerate more arid habitats than amphibians.

Most species of reptiles lay eggs, but some species will give birth to live young, such as rattlesnakes. For egg-laying species, young develop in hard or leathery-shelled eggs, which are often laid in a nest and abandoned by the female.

The sex of many juveniles that are developing in eggs is often determined by the temperature at which the eggs develop, and for species like turtles, warmer temperatures produce higher proportions of female individuals. Species that give birth to live young are better able to regulate the temperature at which offspring develop and can avoid predation of unguarded nests.

Most reptiles have a well-developed sense of smell and use their tongue to collect chemical compounds from the air and move the compounds to the Jacobson's organ. This chemosensory organ is located on the roof of the mouth and provides sensory feedback for detecting airborne chemicals.

Reptiles also have relatively good vision. Snakes often detect movement with their eyes, and visual cues help them locate prey or attract mates.

Like amphibians, reptiles play an important role in nature as part of the food chain. Within Texas, the highest reptile diversity is located in South and West Texas. The Chihuahuan Desert of West Texas is home to most of the diversity of venomous snakes found in the state, including six species of rattlesnakes. Species like the Pond Slider, Texas Spiny Lizard, and Coachwhip are found across almost the entire state, while species like the Rough-footed Mud Turtle, Reticulate Banded Gecko, and Speckled Racer have extremely limited occurrences in the state.

Anolis carolinensis, or Green Anole. Photo by Drew R. Davis.

Most of the introduced species of reptiles cannot tolerate harsh winter temperatures, and as such many of these species are only known in South Texas due to its milder winters. For several introduced species, individuals are only known from few populations, but species like the Brown Anole and Mediterranean Gecko have been documented from large regions across the state.

Birds

The order Aves consists of over 2,000 genera and over 10,000 species. Texas is home to 639 species of birds, including purposefully introduced species (e.g., House Sparrow, European Starling) and accidental releases (e.g., Monk Parakeet), as well as recent introductions or range expansions (e.g., Cattle Egret, Red-crowned Parrot). Because many species migrate long distances flying between spring breeding grounds and overwintering sites, some individuals find themselves off-course and are recorded as accidental visitors in our state each year.

All birds in Texas can fly, though modes of flight can range from soaring to actively flapping to preferring not to fly unless threatened. All birds have feathers that provide lightweight insulation and an increased surface area to help generate power and lift, as well as aerodynamics for flight. Bright colors and feather patterns are frequently seen in those species where there may be limited resources and/or mating occurs between a single male and multiple females.

A male Peregrine Falcon. Photo by Roy W. Lowe, CC by 2.0/Flickr.

Birds are well-known for their vocalizations, which are unique to each species. Calls include courtship songs, alarm calls, and threat displays. Both males and females will vocalize, but the males typically have elaborate songs used to attract mates. Song attractiveness may be enhanced by behavioral displays in some species that include bright colorations and elaborate dances or flight patterns. Some bird species will form single pair bonds (some for life), while other species may breed with more than one partner.

All birds lay eggs; some species may construct elaborate nests from vegetation or build nests in cavities, while some species like Killdeer and nighthawks lay camouflaged eggs directly on the ground. A few species are nest parasites, laying eggs in the nests of other species.

When chicks hatch, they may be altricial (naked, helpless, blind; e.g., songbirds), semi-precocial (downy, dependent, eyes open; e.g., gulls), or precocial (downy, independent, eyes open; e.g., ducklings).

Bird diets vary from scavenging and eating carrion to hunting small and medium-sized vertebrates; other diet items can include invertebrates from grasshoppers to spiders, snails to worms, and many other bird species eat a variety of seeds, fruit, and even nectar. Birds also serve as important diet items for many species.

The areas of highest bird diversity in Texas are South Texas and along the Gulf Coast, particularly during spring migration. Species like the Northern Mockingbird and Red-tailed Hawk are found across almost the entire state, while species like the Altamira Oriole and Colima Warbler have extremely limited occurrences in the state. Some species, like the Greater Prairie Chicken and the Whooping Crane, only exist in Texas because of active federal and state management programs.

Several species are game species (e.g., doves, ducks, geese, quail, Sandhill Crane, Wild Turkey) harvested annually by permit holders. Many introduced bird species have proven to be resilient generalists and have spread statewide; the persistence and establishment of additional introduced bird species have yet to be documented (e.g., Red-vented Bulbul, Nutmeg Mannikin, and Orange Bishop, all observed in Harris County).

Mammals

Mammals, with a few notable exceptions (the egg-laying monotremes: four species of echidna and the Platypus), are a large group of vertebrates with hair that give birth to live young. There are over 6,400 species worldwide (~1,200 genera), including species-rich groups like rodents, bats, and shrews.

A total of 145 species of native terrestrial mammals occur in Texas, a number exceeded in the United States only by California and New Mexico. Also, 28 species of marine mammals have been reported from the Texas coast or are expected to occur there. A single species of marsupial, the Virginia Opossum, is found in the state.

Mammals are found in every ecoregion across the state, with species diversity highest in the Trans-Pecos. Mammals occupy many different habitats, such as species that live almost entirely underground (moles and gophers), are primarily aquatic (American Beaver, Nutria, River Otter), or can fly (bats) or glide (Flying Squirrel).

A badger and a skunk having a confrontation. Photo by Jill D. Miller.

Recreational hunting is an important economic activity for the state, with the breeding and hunting of deer impacting the Texas economy by over $1 billion each year. Game animals include White-tailed Deer, Mule Deer, Pronghorn, Javelina, and squirrels. There are also 18 exotics or non-native species that have been introduced by man either accidentally (e.g., Japanese Macaque, House Mouse, Black Rat, Norway Rat) or intentionally (e.g., Nutria, Red Fox, Feral Pig, Axis Deer, Fallow Deer, Sika Deer, Nilgai, Greater Kudu, Eastern Thomson's Gazelle, Sable Antelope, Scimitar-horned Oryx, Common Eland, Aoudad, Blackbuck) and have become established.

Threats and Successes

The distribution and abundance of Texas wildlife have changed dramatically over the last 100 years. While a few native species have increased their numbers and expanded their ranges during this period (e.g., White-tailed Deer, Coyote, White-winged Dove), these species are the exceptions. Many species have declined and face continued threats across their shrinking distributions in Texas.

In general, these threats are not focused on individual species, but are widespread risks to ecoregions as a whole, impacting both plant and animal communities. Habitat loss is the primary threat and can include land lost to urbanization and agriculture. The development of land for resource extraction activities contributes to habitat loss and fragmentation. Some technologies, such as wind turbines, have led to the direct mortality of some groups of animals (e.g., birds and bats).

The loss of riparian habitats is often linked to the reallocation or reprioritization of water resources. The suppression of wildfire across many habitats has removed the natural cycle of vegetative change important for maintaining species diversity. Modifications to rainfall patterns and temperatures due to climate change affect the distribution of plant and animal communities as well as the timing of processes and behaviors (e.g., dates for plants to flower and birds to begin migration).

The introduction of invasive grasses (e.g., King Ranch Bluestem, Bufflegrass), aquatic plants (e.g., Hydrilla, Giant Reed), trees (e.g., Chinaberry, Tamarisk), and animals (e.g., Red Imported Fire Ant, Zebra Mussel) has allowed non-native species to outcompete and replace populations of native species across the state. Historical instances of overhunting led to the demise of native Bighorn Sheep, Bison, and Elk; predator control efforts removed the Jaguar and Gray Wolf from the state as well.

All hope is not lost; success stories do exist. Focused conservation efforts have removed species such as the Black-capped Vireo, Concho Watersnake, and American Alligator from the Federal Threatened and Endangered Species List. However, many species still require thoughtful and intensive management plans at local, state, and federal levels to help them remain a part of our state's natural heritage.

To learn more about threats to Texas wildlife and what steps you can do to help conserve native species and their habitats, visit the websites of Texas Parks and Wildlife Department (tpwd.texas.gov), U.S. Fish and Wildlife Service (fws.gov/offices), Natural Resources Conservation Center (nrcs.usda.gov), the Texas Master Naturalist Program (txmn.tamu.edu), private conservation groups like The Nature Conservancy (nature.org/texas), Texas Conservation Alliance (tcatexas.org), and Texas Land Conservancy (texaslandconservancy.org), and species- or location-specific conservation groups, like Audubon Texas (tx.audubon.org) and the Coastal Bend Bays and Estuaries Program (cbbep.org). ☆

Meet the Authors

Drew R. Davis

Drew is an Associate Research Scientist at the University of Texas Rio Grande Valley in Brownsville where he studies several threatened species of amphibians and reptiles, including the Black-spotted Newt and Rio Grande Cooter. Much of his current research involves using novel survey methods to generate occurrence and distribution data in order to better conserve imperiled species and their habitats. He received a Ph.D. from the University of South Dakota, an M.S. from Texas State University, and a B.S. from the University of Texas at Austin. His past research has utilized field-based and laboratory studies to better understand how natural and anthropogenic stressors affect the behavior and physiology of amphibians and reptiles.

Travis J. LaDuc

Travis, a native of Tucson, Arizona, has been interested in reptiles since a young age, with a particular affinity for snakes. He received degrees from the University of Arizona, The University of Texas at El Paso, and the University of Texas at Austin. As the Curator of Herpetology at the Biodiversity Center at the University of Texas at Austin, his job includes working with the preserved collection of 115,000 amphibian and reptile specimens, teaching natural history field courses, and continuing his own research program. His research focuses on the biodiversity and natural history of Texas reptiles and amphibians, with current projects centered on the Spot-tailed Earless Lizard and the Yellow Mud Turtle.

The scalloped hammerhead is one of the sharks found in Texas coastal waters. Photo by Barry Peters; CC by 2.0.

Fishes

amberjack: see jack

American sole: see flatfish

anchovy: Three species of anchovy occur in Texas, including the Striped Anchovy (*Anchoa hepsetus*) and Bay Anchovy (*Anchoa mitchilli*). All anchovies occur along the Texas Gulf Coast, inhabiting bays and estuaries and reaching lengths up to 4". These fish are somewhat translucent, with a silver head and broad lateral streak, and a large, rounded head.

barracuda: Three species of barracuda are known from Texas, including the Great Barracuda (*Sphyraena barracuda*), Northern Sennet (*Sphyraena borealis*), and the Guaguanche (*Sphyraena guachancho*). Barracudas are large, predatory fishes that occur in marine waters along the Texas coast, and have large jaws with fang-like teeth, and two dorsal fins that are widely separated.

bass: see sunfish or sea bass

bowfin: The Bowfin (*Amia calva*) can be found across East Texas. These fish have a long, robust body, a conical head, short barbels, a single long dorsal fin, a large bony gular plate, and are patterned with dark reticulations.

buffalo: see sucker

bullhead: see catfish

butterfly ray: see ray

carp: see cyprinid

carpsucker: see sucker

catfish: Two families of native catfish are known in Texas. North American catfish consist of at least 11 freshwater species, including the Yellow Bullhead (*Ameiurus natalis*), Channel Catfish (*Ictalurus punctatus*), and Tadpole Madtom (*Noturus gyrinus*). Most species have relatively widespread distributions across the state and vary in their body size and shape, but all species have four pairs of barbels (whiskers). Additionally, three species of blind, aquifer-dwelling species are part of this group: the Toothless Blindcat (*Trogloglanis pattersoni*), Widemouth Blindcat (*Satan eurystomus*), and Mexican Blindcat (*Prietella phreatophila*), which was only discovered in 2016. The second group, sea catfish, is marine, and only two species are known: Hardhead Catfish (*Ariopsis felis*) and Gafftopsail Catfish (*Bagre marinus*). Sea catfish are large fish that lack scales, typically are gray in coloration, and have two or three pairs of barbels. A third, non-native family of catfish called suckermouth armored catfish have been introduced in Texas from Central and South America, and are covered in tough, bony plates, and have a sucker-like mouth.

chub: see cyprinid

cichlid: One native species of cichlid, the Rio Grande Cichlid (*Herichthys cyanoguttatus*) can be found in South Texas but has been introduced throughout central Texas. The Rio Grande Cichlid typically has gray background coloration covered in small cream or turquoise-colored spots. Additional species of non-native cichlids also occur in Texas, such as the Blue Tilapia* (*Oreochromis aureus*).

combtooth blenny: Six species of combtooth blennies are known to occur along the Texas coast, including the Molly Miller (*Scartella cristata*) and the Featherduster Blenny (*Hypleurochilus multifilis*). Combtooth blennies have large heads, large eyes, fleshy flaps called cirri between the eyes, compressed and elongated bodies, long and continuous dorsal fins, and rounded caudal fins.

cownose ray: see ray

crappie: see sunfish

croaker: see drum

cusk-eel: see eel

cutlassfish: One species, the Atlantic Cutlassfish (*Trichiurus lepturus*) occurs along the Texas coast. These elongated silver fish have a thin, tapering tail, and a large mouth with fang-like teeth.

cyprinid: This group of fishes is the most diverse in Texas, with over 75 recognized species. This group includes species such as the Central Stoneroller (*Campostoma anomalum*), Blacktail Shiner (*Cyprinella venusta*), Common Carp (*Cyprinus carpio*), Shoal Chub (*Macrhybopsis hyostoma*), and Bullhead Minnow (*Pimephales vigilax*). These fish vary greatly in size and specific habitats used, but all occupy freshwater habitats.

damselfish: Four species of damselfish occur in marine habitats off the Texas coast, including the Sergeant Major (*Abudefduf saxatilis*). The Sergeant Major has a deep, laterally compressed body that is silvery-blue and five dark vertical bars.

darter: see perch

dolphinfish: The Dolphinfish (*Coryphaena hippurus*) is an elongate, laterally compressed marine fish that has is often metallic blue or green in coloration. Their dorsal fin is long, extending from the head to its deeply forked tail.

drum: Eighteen species of drum occur along the Texas Gulf Coast, many of which are popular sport fish, and include Red Drum (*Sciaenops ocellatus*), Black Drum (*Pogonias cromis*), Freshwater Drum (*Aplodinotus grunniens*), Spotted Seatrout (*Cynoscion nebulosus*), and Atlantic Croaker (*Micropogonias undulatus*). These fish vary greatly in their shape, but all can be relatively large fish, and all have a deep notch separating the dorsal fin into two parts. The Red Drum is the state saltwater fish.

eel: At least six different families of eels are known to occur in marine habitats along the Texas coast. There are seven species of cusk-eel, including the Crested Cusk-eel (*Ophidion josephi*). Cusk-eels have long dorsal and anal fins and their pelvic fins are modified into barbel-like structures occurring below the mouth. There are seven species of snake eels, including the Speckled Worm Eel (*Myrophis punctatus*) and Shrimp Eel (*Ophichthus gomesii*). Snake eels have long, snake-like bodies and often bury among sand or mud substrates. Additional eels, like the Conger Eel (*Conger oceanicus*), Ridged Eel (*Neoconger mucronatus*), Blackedge Moray (*Gymnothorax nigromarginatus*), and Freckled Pikeconger (*Hoplunnis macrura*) also occur along the Texas coast, but are less abundant. In addition to marine species, one native species of freshwater eel occurs in Texas, the American Eel (*Anguilla rostrata*). This eel has small scales embedded in the skin giving it a smooth appearance, a long snake-like body, and a single continuous dorsal, caudal, and anal fin.

flatfish: Four families of flatfish inhabit coastal waters. Flatfish are flat, laterally compressed fishes, with two eyes on one side of their head, and often bury down into the mud. Flatfish consist of American soles, lefteye flounders, sand flounders, and tonguefish. American soles, including the Lined Sole (*Achirus lineatus*), Fringed Sole (*Gymnachirus texae*), and Hogchoker (*Trinectes maculatus*), have eyes on their right side, fleshy lips, and a distinct caudal fin. Lefteye flounders, including the Twospot Flounder (*Bothus robinsi*), have an oval-shaped, flattened body with eyes on their left side and elongated dorsal and anal fins that are separate from the caudal fin. There are at least 14 different species of sand flounders, including the Southern Flounder (*Paralichthys lethostigma*) and Bay Whiff (*Citharichthys spilopterus*), which are football-shaped, have eyes on the left side of their body, and have both a distinct snout and tail. Tonguefish, such as the Blackcheek Tonguefish (*Symphurus plagiusa*), can be distinguished from other flatfish by having a single continuous dorsal, caudal, and anal fin.

flounder: see flatfish

frogfish: Three species of frogfish occur along the Texas coast, including the Sargassumfish (*Histrio histrio*). The Sargassumfish has a short, rounded body with many fleshy extensions, that aid in its camouflage among sargassum (marine algae), and angled limb-like pectoral fins.

gar: Four species of gars are native to Texas, including the Alligator Gar (*Atractosteus spatula*), Spotted Gar (*Lepisosteus oculatus*), Longnose Gar (*Lepisosteus osseus*), and Shortnose Gar (*Lepisosteus platostomus*). All gars have elongated, cylindrical bodies, elongate slender snouts, and bony scales. The Alligator Gar can reach lengths up to 9' and up to 275 pounds.

goby: Fourteen species of gobies are found along the Texas coast, including the Naked Goby (*Gobiosoma bosc*) and Darter Goby (*Ctenogobius boleosoma*). Gobies are small, elongated, bottom-dwelling fishes that have rounded heads with eyes that are positioned close together and on top of the head. Additionally, gobies have pelvic fins that are fused together to form a suctioning disk. Gobies are the most diverse group of marine fishes.

grinnel: see bowfin

grouper: see sea bass

grunt: Six species of grunts occur in marine habitats along the Texas coast, including the Pigfish (*Orthopristis chrysoptera*), Tomtate (*Haemulon aurolineatum*), and Barred Grunt (*Conodon nobilis*). Grunts are variable in appearance, but all are moderately-sized fishes with mouths that have thick lips. The pharyngeal teeth in these species make a grunting noise when rubbed together, which is how this group was named.

halfbeak: Two species occur along the Texas coast, including the False Silverstripe Halfbeak (*Hyporhamphus meeki*). These unusual-looking fish have round, elongated bodies with a very short upper jaw and an elongated, needle-like lower jaw.

hammerhead shark: see shark

herring: Ten species of herrings are found in both marine and freshwater habitats in Texas. Four of the more common species include the Gizzard Shad (*Dorosoma cepedianum*), Threadfin Shad (*Dorosoma petenense*), Gulf Menhaden (*Brevoortia patronus*), and Skipjack Herring (*Alosa chrysochloris*). These silvery fish are important as food for many other fishes and can reach lengths up to 2'. Herrings are variable in their body shape and typically have forked caudal fins.

hind: see sea bass

jack: Twenty species of jacks have been recorded along the Texas Gulf Coast, including the Greater Amberjack (*Seriola dumerili*), Crevalle Jack (*Caranx hippos*), and Florida Pompano (*Trachinotus carolinus*). Jacks vary widely in their shape and size but are generally large fish that form schools and are important for commercial fisheries. All jacks have a narrow base of the tail and a deeply forked tail.

killifish: see topminnow

kingfish: see drum

lamprey: Both the Chestnut Lamprey (*Ichthyomyzon castaneus*) and Southern Brook Lamprey (*Ichthyomyzon gagei*) occur in streams and rivers in East Texas. These eel-like fish have a characteristic circular disk-like mouth. The Chestnut Lamprey parasitizes fish as an adult, but adult Southern Brook Lamprey do not feed and rely on previously accumulated energy stores from its filter-feeding larval stage.

lefteye flounder: see flatfish

livebearer: There are at least 17 species of livebearers in Texas, including the Western Mosquitofish (*Gambusia affinis*) and Sailfin Molly (*Poecilia latipinna*). These small freshwater fish are widespread across most of Texas and species like the Western Mosquitofish have been widely introduced around the world. As the name suggests, all Texas species are live-bearing, and males have a modified anal fin called a gonopodium.

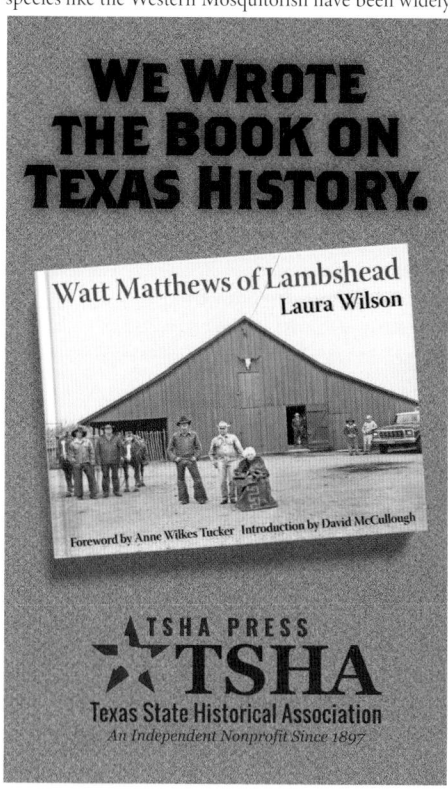

lizardfish: Three species of marine lizardfish occur along the Texas coast, including the Inshore Lizardfish (*Synodus foetens*). Lizardfish have elongated cylindrical bodies, large mouths with needle-like teeth, and a large eye.

mackerel: Five species of mackerels are known from the Texas Gulf Coast, with the most abundant being the Spanish Mackerel (*Scomberomorus maculatus*) and King Mackerel (*Scomberomorus cavalla*). Mackerels have elongated, laterally compressed bodies, with a pointed snout. A defining characteristic of these fish is that there is a series of small fins behind both the dorsal and anal fin.

madtom: see catfish

menhaden: see herring

minnow: see cyprinid

mojarra: Nine species of mojarra occur in coastal waters along Texas, including the Spotfin Mojarra (*Eucinostomus argenteus*). Mojarras are silvery fish that are 8–12" in length, with arched backs, deeply forked tails, and a downward-facing mouth to accommodate feeding on bottom-dwelling organisms.

molly: see livebearer

mosquitofish: see livebearer

mullet: Four species of mullet occur in Texas, including the Striped Mullet (*Mugil cephalus*) and White Mullet (*Mugil curema*). Most mullets are marine, but individuals can also be found in freshwater rivers much further inland. Mullets are silvery in appearance and have an elongated, cylindrical body, a flat head, and a large eye relative to their head size.

needlefish: Four species of needlefish occur along the Texas coast, including the Atlantic Needlefish (*Strongylura marina*), which on occasion move up rivers into freshwater habitats. All needlefish have an elongated, round body with their upper and lower jaws extended into long, narrow beaks that are filled with small teeth.

New World silverside: Five species of New World silversides occur in Texas, including the Brook Silverside (*Labidesthes sicculus*), Rough Silverside (*Membras martinica*), Inland Silverside (*Menidia beryllina*), Texas Silverside (*Menidia clarkhubbsi*), and Tidewater Silverside (*Menidia peninsulae*). Silversides are long slender fish, often with translucent bodies and a silver streak running down the sides of the body. Most species are freshwater, but some also are found in brackish waters.

perch: Over 25 species of perch can be found in freshwater habitats in Texas, including the Plains Orangethroat Darter (*Etheostoma pulchellum*) and the Dusky Darter (*Percina sciera*). These fish are often found in riverine systems and often rest on the substrates or woody debris on the bottom of these habitats. All perch have a dorsal fin that is split into two large lobes or has a narrow connection, and some species have bright colors, especially in breeding males. They get their name due to their darting movements through the water.

pickerel: see pike

pike: Two species of pike, the Redfin Pickerel (*Esox americanus*) and Chain Pickerel (*Esox niger*), occur in East Texas. The much more widespread and larger Redfin Pickerel has a long, cylindrical body, with a broad, short, flat snout, and a body coloration that is often green with dark wavy vertical bars and a vertical stripe through the eye. The Chain Pickerel is similar in appearance but is considerably larger than the Redfin Pickerel.

pipefish: This group of seven species includes the Gulf Pipefish (*Syngnathus scovelli*) and the Lined Seahorse (*Hippocampus erectus*). Pipefish have elongate bodies covered in armored plates or spines and tubular snouts, and males possess a brood pouch where they store fertilized eggs from the female until they hatch.

pirate perch: One species of Pirate Perch (*Aphredoderus sayanus*) can be found throughout freshwater habitats in East Texas. Pirate Perch superficially resemble sunfishes but are often quite dark in body coloration with black speckles on a light underside.

pompano: see jack

porcupinefish: see puffer

porgy: Six species of porgies are known from marine habitats in Texas, including the Pinfish (*Lagodon rhomboides*) and Sheepshead (*Archosargus probatocephalus*). Porgies have laterally compressed, deep bodies and most have teeth that are flattened for grinding.

puffer: Two families of puffers are known from marine habitats along the Texas coastline: puffers and porcupinefish. Puffers, including the Least Putter (*Sphoeroides parvus*), have elongated, globular-shaped bodies covered in small spines (*sometimes unnoticeable*), loose skin on the underside, a beaklike mouth with two teeth in the upper and lower jaw. Porcupinefish, such as the Striped Burrfish (*Chilomycterus schoepfii*), have globular bodies covered in short spines and a beaklike mouth with one upper and lower tooth. Both families can swallow water to expand their bodies when threatened.

pupfish: Six species of pupfish are native to Texas, including the federally endangered Leon Springs Pupfish (*Cyprinodon bovinus*) and Comanche Springs Pupfish (*Cyprinodon elegans*) and the state threatened Conchos Pupfish (*Cyprinodon eximius*), Pecos Pupfish (*Cyprinodon pecosensis*), and Red River Pupfish (*Cyprinodon rubrofluviatilis*). Several of these imperiled species have extremely limited distributions or have suffered widespread declines. Unlike the other species of pupfish, the Sheepshead Minnow (*Cyprinodon variegatus*) remains common and has a widespread distribution across coastal Texas and the Rio Grande drainage, and has been widely introduced into freshwater habitats in Texas.

pygmy sunfish: The Banded Pygmy Sunfish (*Elassoma zonatum*) occurs in freshwater habitats in East Texas. These small (<2" long) fish have a shallow body shape, are laterally compressed, have 9–12 dark bands, and are covered in small dark spots.

ray: Two families of rays occur in shallow estuaries and lagoons along the Texas coast. Butterfly rays, such as the Smooth Butterfly Ray (*Gymnura micrura*), are diamond-shaped and have a short tail with dark lines on it that lacks a dorsal spine. The other family is cownose rays, which is represented by a single species, the Cownose Ray (*Rhinoptera bonasus*). Cownose Rays reach 2–3' in width, are brown on top and white underneath, have a long tail with a venomous barb and get their name from their squared, indented snout and wide-set eyes.

redfish: see drum

redhorse: see sucker

remora: Four species occur in Texas, including the Remora (*Remora remora*) and the Sharksucker (*Echeneis naucrates*). These marine fish have heavily modified dorsal fins that form an oval-shaped sucker-like organ that allows them to attach to larger marine animals like whales, sea turtles, and sharks.

sand flounder: see flatfish

sardine: see herring

scorpionfish: Six species of scorpionfish, including the Spotted Scorpionfish (*Scorpaena plumieri*), can be found along the Texas coast. Scorpionfish are large, robust fish with large heads and venomous spines.

sea bass: This group of fish are popular saltwater sport fishes and include hind and grouper. At least 25 species occur along the Texas coast, including the Rock Sea Bass (*Centropristis philadelphica*) and Warsaw Grouper (*Epinephelus nigritus*). Species in this diverse group range in size and shape, but many species are brightly colored, have robust bodies, and large teeth.

seahorse: see pipefish

searobin: Nine species of searobins, including the Bighead Searobin (*Prionotus tribulus*), occur along the Gulf Coast of Texas. All searobins have a large, bony head that has numerous spines and ridges and modified pectoral fins that allow the fish to "walk" along the substrate.

seatrout: see drum

shad: see herring

shark: Sharks include both the requiem and hammerhead sharks, with 13 species found in marine habitats along the Texas coast. Species include the Atlantic Sharpnose Shark (*Rhizoprionodon terraenovae*), which is relatively small, only reaching lengths up to 4', has a pointed snout, and is typically gray in coloration with lighter undersides. The Scalloped Hammerhead (*Sphyrna lewini*) and the Bonnethead (*Sphyrna tiburo*) are easily differentiated from other sharks by their flattened heads that resemble a hammer or shovel and eyes on the outer edges.

shiner: see cyprinid

skate: The Roundel Skate (*Raja texana*) occurs along the Texas coastline and can be differentiated from other skates by a dark rounded spot on each pectoral wing. In addition, Roundel Skates have a slightly pointed snout, two dorsal fins at the base of the tail, and lack a serrated spine on their tails.

sleepers: Four species of sleepers can be found in Texas, including the Fat Sleeper (*Dormitator maculatus*), Spinycheek Sleeper (*Eleotris pisonis*), Emerald Sleeper (*Erotelis smaragdus*), and Bigmouth Sleeper (*Gobiomorus dormitor*). All species occur along the Texas Gulf Coast and use both freshwater and brackish habitats. Of these four species, the most abundant appears to be the Fat Sleeper, which has a small, rounded body, two distinct dorsal fins, and black lines along the sides of its face.

snake eel: see eel

snapper: Ten species of snappers are known from Texas, including the Red Snapper (*Lutjanus campechanus*) and Gray Snapper (*Lutjanus griseus*), and all are popular sport and commercial fish. Snappers are diverse in their size, pattern, and coloration, but are generally oblong, heavy-bodied, and have pointed snouts with large teeth.

snook: Two species of snook, the Smallscale Fat Snook (*Centropomus parallelus*) and the Common Snook (*Centropomus undecimalis*), occur in coastal waters along South Texas. Snook reach 2–4' in length, have elongate, laterally compressed bodies covered in silvery scales, and a thin dark line running down the length of the body.

stargazer: Stargazers are marine fish that have eyes on the top of their heads and upward-pointing mouths. Species like the Southern Stargazer (*Astroscopus y-graecum*) typically bury in the mud and ambush prey as they pass overhead.

stingray: Four species of whiptail stingrays occur in Texas, and the most common is the Atlantic Stingray (*Dasyatis sabina*). The Atlantic Stingray has a pointed snout and a long, whip-like tail with a serrated spine.

stoneroller: see cyprinid

sucker: At least 16 species of suckers can be found across Texas, including the River Carpsucker (*Carpiodes carpio*), Smallmouth Buffalo (*Ictiobus bubalus*), Spotted Sucker (*Minytrema melanops*), and the Gray Redhorse (*Moxostoma congestum*). All suckers have their mouth located on the underside of their head, have thick, fleshy lips, and primarily inhabit freshwater river systems.

suckermouth armored catfish: see catfish

sunfish: This group (sometimes also called "perch") includes bass and crappie, all of which are popular freshwater sport fishes. Eighteen species are known from Texas, including the Bluegill (*Lepomis macrochirus*), Green Sunfish (*Lepomis cyanellus*), Longear Sunfish (*Lepomis megalotis*), Largemouth Bass (*Micropterus salmoides*), and White Crappie (*Pomoxis annularis*). Most sunfish species are deep-bodied and laterally compressed, with a series of vertical bars. Crappie are similar in shape to sunfish, but reach larger sizes. Basses are more elongated and with spotting or a large dark stripe down the sides. The Guadalupe Bass (*Micropterus treculii*) is the state fish of Texas.

tarpon: The Tarpon (*Megalops atlanticus*) is a large marine fish that is present along the Gulf Coast of Texas. It can reach lengths of up to 8' in length and weigh more than 350 pounds. The mouth is turned upwards, the last ray of the dorsal fin is elongated, the caudal fin is deeply forked, and it is covered in shiny silver scales.

temperate bass: There are three species of temperate basses in Texas: the native White Bass (*Morone chrysops*) and Yellow Bass (*Morone mississippiensis*) and the non-native Striped Bass* (*Morone saxatilis*). Temperate basses are somewhat deep-bodied, laterally compressed, and have a pointed snout. Species are typically white or silver in appearance with 6–10 dark stripes running the length of the body.

tenpounder: One species, the Ladyfish (*Elops saurus*), occurs along the Texas coastline in bays and estuarine habitats. The Ladyfish has a long, rounded body, silvery scales, a deeply forked caudal fin, and can be up 2–3' in length.

tetra: The Mexican Tetra (*Astyanax mexicanus*) is a small (<4" long) freshwater fish found throughout flowing river systems in south, central and West Texas, and has an oblong, laterally compressed body shape. It is silver in body coloration but has a small black band at the base of the caudal fin. Adult males will have red coloration on the anal fins.

threadfin: The Atlantic Threadfin (*Polydactylus octonemus*) is a marine fish occurring along the Texas coastline and reaches lengths up to 12". These fish have two, widely separated dorsal fins, a deeply forked caudal fin, and 8 soft and flexible pectoral filaments giving it its name.

tilapia: see cichlid

toadfish: Two species of toadfish occur in marine habitats along the Texas coast and include the Gulf Toadfish (*Opsanus beta*) and the Atlantic Midshipman (*Porichthys plectrodon*). Both species are ambush predators that wait among muddy substrates. They are scaleless and have numerous barbels or skin flaps that help provide camouflage.

tonguefish: see flatfish

topminnow: Thirteen species of freshwater topminnows occur in Texas, including the Blackstripe Topminnow (*Fundulus notatus*) and Plains Killifish (*Fundulus zebrinus*). Topminnows can be found throughout the state, are up to approximately 4" in length, and can be variable in their patterning, with some species having a single horizontal strip down the body, while others have numerous vertical bands.

wahoo: see mackerel

The black spotted newt in South Texas is on the state endangered list. Photo by Clinton J. Guadiana.

Amphibians

amphiuma: There is one species of amphiuma found in Texas, the Three-toed Amphiuma (*Amphiuma tridactylum*). These aquatic salamanders look similar to sirens in that they are elongate and eel-like, but lack external gills, and have four small, frail limbs (sirens have external gills and lack hindlimbs). In aquatic environments, amphiumas can be voracious predators, consuming a wide variety of prey items.

barking frog: The Barking Frog (*Craugastor augusti*) is a secretive species found on the Edwards Plateau in rocky outcrops, though they are also known to inhabit mammal burrows. This species gets its name from the bark-like call it makes. Juveniles have a gray background coloration with numerous black spots covering the body and a light band across the midsection of the body. As adults, this light band darks and becomes less noticeable. Like some other species of frogs, Barking Frogs have skin secretions that can be noxious which serve as an anti-predator defense.

blind salamander: Five species of blind salamanders occur in Texas, all occurring along the Edwards Plateau and Balcones Faultline in central Texas. These five species include the Texas Blind Salamander (*Eurycea rathbuni*), Blanco Blind Salamander (*Eurycea robusta*), Comal Blind Salamander (*Eurycea tridentifera*), Valdina Farms Salamander (*Eurycea troglodytes*), and Austin Blind Salamander (*Eurycea waterlooensis*). Like the closely related spring salamanders, these species are fully aquatic but have reduced or absent vision, as these species occur in aquifers, spring outflows, or within karst habitats where there is little visible light. Several species, such as the Texas Blind Salamander, have lost skin pigmentation and appear white, with elongated limbs.

bullfrog: The American Bullfrog (*Rana catesbeiana*) occurs statewide and is the largest species of frog in North America, having a body length up to 7", and is capable of jumping 3–6'. This large frog lives in large, permanent lakes and wetlands and breeds throughout the summer on warm, humid nights. This species has been widely introduced around the world where it is often farmed for human consumption.

burrowing toad: The Mexican Burrowing Toad (*Rhinophrynus dorsalis*) is an odd-looking, secretive frog that only occurs in extreme South Texas. These frogs are dark gray with small white spots with a red or orange line running down their back. Mexican Burrowing Toads spend the majority of their lives underground and only emerge after heavy rains, often associated with hurricanes or tropical storms. The larval development of Mexican Burrowing Toads is extremely rapid, as the ponds they frequently use dry quickly after filling up after rains.

chirping frog: Texas is home to three species of native chirping frog and one introduced species. The Spotted Chirping Frog (*Eleutherodactylus guttilatus*) can be found in montane regions of West Texas such as Big Bend and the Cliff Chirping Frog (*Eleutherodactylus marnockii*) can be found in the Edwards Plateau. The third native species is the Rio Grande Chirping Frog (*Eleutherodactylus cystignathoides*) which is native to the Rio Grande Valley in South Texas but has great spread throughout much of central and East Texas through the horticultural trade. The non-native Greenhouse Frog* (*Eleutherodactylus planirostris*), originally from the Caribbean Islands, has established populations in Houston, Corpus Christi, and South Padre Island. All chirping frogs are small, mostly leaf-litter-dwelling frogs that get their name from the sound of their call. Additionally, all chirping frogs have direct development, meaning that there is no aquatic swimming tadpole stage and small juvenile frogs hatch from eggs.

chorus frog: Four species of chorus frog occur in Texas. Chorus frogs are closely related to treefrogs and have expanded toe pads on the ends of their digits that allow them to climb up vegetation. The Spotted Chorus Frog (*Pseudacris clarkii*) has a gray background color with irregular green markings and ranges from the panhandle South through central and North Texas into South Texas. Both the Spring Peeper (*Pseudacris crucifer*) and the Cajun Chorus Frog (*Pseudacris fouquettei*) occur in wooded habitats in East Texas. The Strecker's Chorus Frog (*Pseudacris streckeri*) occurs throughout central, east, and North Texas. Most chorus frogs are considerably smaller than treefrogs, except the Strecker's Chorus Frog. Chorus frogs primarily use temporary wetlands that fill up after heavy rains for reproduction. Despite their small size, their call can be surprisingly loud.

congo eel: see amphiuma

cricket frog: The Blanchard's Cricket Frog (*Acris blanchardi*) occurs throughout much of Texas except the western panhandle, far West Texas, and South Texas. This small frog is variable in its appearance and can range from grey to green to brown in background coloration with darker markings that can be black, green, or rust-colored. Typically, a dark-colored triangle occurs between the eyes on the top of the head. Blanchard's Cricket Frogs occur along flowing and non-flowing aquatic habitats. Though closely related to treefrogs and chorus frogs, this species has diminished toe pads resulting in more terrestrial behaviors.

dusky salamander: One species of dusky salamander, Spotted Dusky Salamander (*Desmognathus conanti*) has a limited distribution in East Texas. Apparent declines in this species have occurred throughout much of their historic range in the state.

dwarf salamander: One species of dwarf salamander occurs in Texas, the Western Dwarf Salamander (*Eurycea paludicola*). This small, slender species of salamander can be found among leaf litter and logs on forest floors in East Texas. Until recently, this species was part of a single species that ranged from East Texas along the Gulf Coast to North Carolina, that has since been separated into four separate species.

greenhouse frog: see chirping frog

leopard frog: Four species of leopard frogs occur in Texas: the Plains Leopard Frog (*Rana blairi*), Rio Grande Leopard Frog (*Rana berlandieri*), Southern Leopard Frog (*Rana sphenocephala*), and Northern Leopard Frog (*Rana pipiens*). All four species look similar to one another and are olive-green to brown in coloration, with dark spots and dorsolateral stripes from the eye to the hindlimb. These large frogs use permanent water bodies and rivers and have powerful hindlimbs that allow them to jump large distances.

mole salamander: Six species of mole salamanders are found in Texas, including the Spotted Salamander (*Ambystoma maculatum*), Eastern Tiger Salamander (*Ambystoma tigrinum*), Western Tiger Salamander (*Ambystoma mavortium*), Marbled Salamander (*Ambystoma opacum*), Small-mouthed Salamander (*Ambystoma texanum*), and Mole Salamander (*Ambystoma talpoideum*). All species are found throughout East Texas, except the Western Tiger Salamander, which occurs in south, west, and North Texas. All species are largely terrestrial and spend much of their time in upland habitats after breeding in wetland habitats. As aquatic larvae, these salamanders are sometimes colloquially called waterdogs or mudpuppies.

mudpuppy: see waterdog

narrow-mouthed toad: Two species of narrow-mouthed toads are found in Texas. The Eastern Narrow-mouthed Toad (*Gastrophryne carolinensis*) is restricted to eastern and coastal Texas, the Western Narrow-mouthed Toad (*Gastrophryne olivacea*) occurs throughout much of the state. The Eastern Narrow-mouth Toad is small (>1.5" in length) and is typically brown or gray in coloration with dark flecks and a heavily mottled underside. The Western Narrow-mouthed Toad is similar in size but is typically light gray with small black flecks and an unpatterned underside. Both species spend a large amount of time underground and use ephemeral habitats that fill up after rains for breeding.

newt: Two species of newts occur in Texas: the Eastern Newt (*Notophthalmus viridescens*) and the Black-spotted Newt (*Notophthalmus meridionalis*). The Eastern Newt occurs throughout East Texas and parts of coastal Texas while the Black-spotted Newt is restricted to South Texas, where it experienced widespread population declines in recent decades. As a result, the Black-spotted Newt is listed as state-threatened and is a proposed species for federal protection. The Eastern Newt is known to have a terrestrial immature stage called an eft, which is typically bright orange with orange spots outlined in black. As efts mature into adults, they often return to aquatic habitats.

sheep frog: The Sheep Frog (*Hypopachus variolosus*) is closely related to narrow-mouthed toads and is restricted to South Texas. The Sheep Frog is larger than narrow-mouthed toads (2" in length), has a brown background coloration, gray sides with irregular black markings, and a yellow or orange thin stripe down the middle of the back. This species is typically active only after rains where it uses temporary wetlands for reproduction.

siren: Sirens are elongate, slender aquatic salamanders that have external gills behind the head, reduced forelimbs, and no hindlimbs. One species of siren, the Lesser Siren (*Siren intermedia*) is native to Texas and occurs from South Texas up the Gulf Coast and throughout East Texas. These salamanders are sometimes confused as eels due to their body shape and can bury down into the mud at the bottom of wetlands as they dry for prolonged periods and wait for these habitats to fill again after rains.

slimy salamander: The Western Slimy Salamander (*Plethodon albagula*) occurs along the Edwards Plateau and Balcones Faultline in central Texas. These salamanders are black with white speckling along their bodies and can be found under rocks and logs in moist areas in the winter and early spring. As it becomes warm and dry, these salamanders often move deeper underground. Western Slimy Salamanders can secrete a white, sticky substance if disturbed which deters would-be predators.

spadefoot: Spadefoots are toad-like amphibians, which have elliptical (vertical) pupils, smooth skin, and large keratinized spades on their hind feet. Four species occur in Texas: Couch's Spadefoot (*Scaphiopus couchii*), Hurter's Spadefoot (*Scaphiopus hurterii*), Plains Spadefoot (*Spea bombifrons*), and the New Mexico Spadefoot (*Spea multiplicata*). All species spend large amounts of time underground and emerge on warm, wet, rainy nights to forage and reproduce. Like some other species of amphibians, spadefoots are often considered explosive breeders, as reproduction often takes place over a few days following heavy rains when breeding sites (temporary pools) form. Like the Barking Frog and toads, spadefoots can secrete a noxious substance from their skin that is irritating to the eyes and skin of potential predators.

spring peeper: see chorus frog

spring salamander: Eight species of spring salamanders occur in central Texas, all occurring in spring outflows and associated stream runs. Most of these species occur in a limited number of localities and have very small ranges. These species include the Salado Salamander (*Eurycea chisholmensis*), Cascade Caverns Salamander (*Eurycea latitans*), San Marcos Salamander (*Eurycea nana*), Georgetown Salamander (*Eurycea naufragia*), Texas Salamander (*Eurycea neotenes*), Fern Bank Salamander (*Eurycea pterophila*), Barton Springs Salamander (*Eurycea sosorum*), and Jollyville Plateau Salamander (*Eurycea tonkawae*). Most species are federally and state-protected due to their limited occurrence in Texas and the threats these species face.

tiger salamander: see mole salamander

treefrog: Six species of treefrogs occur in Texas. The Canyon Treefrog (*Hyla arenicolor*) occurs in rocky, montane habitats in West Texas, and the Squirrel Treefrog (*Hyla squirella*) is restricted to the Texas coast and parts of East Texas. The Green Treefrog (*Hyla cinerea*) occurs throughout East and coastal Texas, West to the Edwards Plateau, and South towards Corpus Christi and an introduced population is present in Big Bend National Park. Two additional species of treefrogs, the Cope's Gray Treefrog (*Hyla chrysoscelis*) and the Gray Treefrog (*Hyla versicolor*) are indistinguishable from one another and only able to be differentiated by the number of chromosomes they have and by their call. Both Cope's Gray Treefrogs and Gray Treefrogs overlap in much of their range throughout east, central, and North Texas. The Mexican Treefrog (*Smilisca baudinii*) is restricted to South Texas and is listed as threatened by TPWD. All treefrogs have expanded toe pads on the tips of their digits which allow them to climb well. Treefrogs are primarily arboreal and can be found near permanent aquatic habitats during the spring breeding season.

true frog: True frogs are a group of large frogs which also include leopard frogs and bullfrogs. Species of true frogs that occur in Texas include the Pickerel Frog (*Rana palustris*) and Green Frog (*Rana clamitans*), which both have relatively large distributions throughout East Texas. The Pickerel Frog looks similar to leopard frogs but has squarish blotches instead of round blotches and yellow or orange coloration on the inside of its hind legs. Despite their name, Green Frogs can also be tan or bronze in coloration and can look similar to American Bullfrogs. These two species can be differentiated by looking at the dorsolateral fold (a fold of skin occurring from behind the eye). In Green Frogs, the dorsolateral fold extends to the hind limb, but in American Bullfrogs, the dorsolateral fold curves around the tympanum (eardrum) and never reaches the hind limb. Both the Pig Frog (*Rana grylio*) and Crawfish Frog (*Rana areolata*) also occur in East Texas but have a much more limited distribution in the state.

true toad: Ten species of toads occur throughout Texas, all varying in size, distribution, and preferred habitats. The largest toad that occurs in Texas is the Mesoamerican Cane Toad (*Rhinella horribilis*) that occurs in extreme South Texas, which can exceed 7" in length. The smallest toad in Texas is the Green Toad (*Anaxyrus debilis*), rarely exceeding 2" in length, which is found across much of the state except East Texas. All other species of toads are similar in size. Likely the rarest toad in Texas is the Houston Toad (*Anaxyrus houstonensis*). The Houston Toad only occurs in a handful of counties in the east-central portion of the state, has suffered widespread population declines, and is both federally- and state-protected. Two of the most widespread and abundant toads in Texas are the Texas Toad (*Anaxyrus speciosus*), which occurs throughout much of Texas except the eastern portion of the state and is also the state amphibian, and the Gulf Coast Toad (*Incilius nebulifer*), which occurs throughout south, central, and East Texas. The American Toad (*Anaxyrus americanus*) occurs in the extreme northeast corner of the state and is similar in appearance to the Fowler's Toad (*Anaxyrus fowleri*), which occupies a larger distribution throughout East Texas. The Great Plains Toad (*Anaxyrus cognatus*) primarily occurs in the Texas panhandle and the Trans-Pecos region. Widespread across west, north, and central Texas, the Red-spotted Toad (*Anaxyrus punctatus*) can be found in rocky, limestone habitats. The Woodhouse's Toad (*Anaxyrus woodhousii*) historically ranged from the Texas panhandle down the Gulf Coast but has experienced declines across much of its range in central Texas. Despite these declines, there remain areas where populations are still robust. Toads typically have dry, warty skin, bony ridges on the top of their head, and large poison glands called parotoid glands behind their eyes. These parotoid glands can secrete noxious compounds which are distasteful and irritating to potential predators.

waterdog: These salamanders are also occasionally called mudpuppy and one species occurs in Texas: the Gulf Coast Waterdog (*Necturus beyeri*). The Gulf Coast Waterdog occurs in small creek systems in the Big Thicket of East Texas. This species is fully aquatic, has four limbs, and bushy external gills on the sides of its head.

white-lipped frog: The Mexican White-lipped Frog (*Leptodactylus fragilis*) barely makes it into Texas along the Rio Grande in extreme South Texas. In Texas, this species is rare and can only be found after rains, but it is much more common throughout Central America. These frogs appear similar to other true frogs in body shape but have rougher skin, a more pointed snout, and a prominent white stripe along the upper lip. The Mexican White-lipped Frog has a unique nesting habitat unlike other species of frogs in Texas. During reproduction, a foam nest is created from skin secretions and surrounds the eggs. This foam nest helps to prevent the eggs from drying out until the eggs hatch and tadpoles emerge.

The Rio Grande Cooter is found in the Rio Grande and Pecos rivers of West Texas. Photo by Drew R. Davis.

Reptiles

alligator: The American Alligator (*Alligator mississippiensis*) is the largest reptile in North America and is found across the eastern third of Texas.

alligator lizard: The Texas Alligator Lizard (*Gerrhonotus infernalis*) can be found on rocky hillsides and wooded canyons in central and West Texas. With a long and somewhat prehensile tail, this species can measure over 17" in total length.

anole: The Green Anole (*Anolis carolinensis*) is a frequent visitor seen on fences and trees in the eastern two-thirds of Texas. Sometimes called chameleons because of their ability to change color between brown and green, but they are not related to true chameleons. The Brown Anole* (*Anolis sagrei*) is found along the coast from Brownsville to Galveston and is displacing the native Green Anole in parts of its range.

black-headed snake: Four species of black-headed snakes in Texas reach lengths of 6–8 inches, and a fifth species that lives in West Texas, the Trans-Pecos Black-headed Snake (*Tantilla cucullata*), can grow to 2' in length. The Flat-headed Snake (*Tantilla gracilis*) has a salmon-colored belly and lives in the eastern half of the state. The Plains Black-headed Snake (*Tantilla nigriceps*) is found in West and South Texas as well as the Panhandle.

blindsnake: see threadsnake

box turtle: Box turtles have a domed shell with a single hinge on the underside that allows the turtles to completely withdraw their limbs and head into the shell when threatened. These turtles have a generalist diet, consuming worms, insects, and vegetation. The Eastern Box Turtle (*Terrapene carolina*) is primarily found in eastern Texas, while the Ornate Box Turtle (*Terrapene ornata*) is found across most of the remainder of the state.

brownsnake: The Dekay's Brownsnake (*Storeria dekayi*) is one of several small (6–8") snakes found under rocks and logs in both urban backyards and rural settings. Other small snakes that are similar include the Rough Earthsnake (*Haldea striatula*), Smooth Earthsnake (*Virginia valeriae*), Lined Snake (*Tropidoclonion lineatum*), and Western Groundsnake (*Sonora semiannulata*). This group of snakes feeds on a variety of invertebrates, from worms and slugs to centipedes, scorpions, and spiders. Most are brown or tan, though Dekay's Brownsnakes and Lined Snakes are striped, and Western Groundsnakes may be either striped or banded.

bullsnake: see gophersnake

chicken snake: see ratsnake

chicken turtle: The Chicken Turtle (*Deirochelys reticularia*) is an uncommon species of turtle found in East Texas that looks similar to some sliders in shape and size. This turtle was once widely consumed, and its name refers to the taste of its meat.

coachwhip: see whipsnake

collared lizard: The Eastern Collared Lizard (*Crotaphytus collaris*), or Mountain Boomer, is found in rocky areas of central, north, and West Texas. This species has a dark collar around its neck with overall green body color. The Reticulate Collared Lizard (*Crotaphytus reticulatus*) is mostly brown or gray with a network of light lines and dark spots on its back. This species is found in South Texas from Maverick to Hidalgo counties.

cooter: Cooters are large, aquatic turtles that inhabit river systems throughout Texas. Four species of cooters are found in Texas, including one non-native species. The River Cooter (*Pseudemys concinna*) is found throughout East Texas, the Texas Cooter (*Pseudemys texana*) is found throughout central Texas, and the Rio Grande Cooter (*Pseudemys gorzugi*) is found in the Rio Grande and Pecos Rivers of West Texas. The Florida Red-bellied Cooter* (*Pseudemys nelsoni*) is not native to Texas and has been introduced to the headwaters of the San Marcos River and Houston.

copperhead: VENOMOUS. The Copperhead (*Agkistrodon contortrix*) is found in most of the state, except South Texas and the Panhandle. Its copper-colored body with rusty orange or grayish bands help camouflage the snake in leaf litter. They feed on small mammals and insects, particularly, freshly-molted cicadas in the summer.

coralsnake: VENOMOUS. The Texas Coralsnake (*Micrurus tener*) is a common species across south, central, and East Texas. It is infrequently seen because it spends the majority of its life underground, and it feeds almost exclusively on other snakes. Because of variability in color intensity and pattern in Texas Coralsnakes, the commonly used rhyme "red next to yellow, kill a fellow; red next to black, venom lack" is not a reliable method to distinguish venomous coralsnakes from look-a-likes, such as the non-venomous Milksnake (*Lampropeltis triangulum*).

cottonmouth: VENOMOUS. The Cottonmouth (*Agkistrodon piscivorus*), or Water Moccasin, is more commonly encountered in East Texas though populations persist as far West as San Angelo and Junction. Not an aggressive animal, however, it will vigorously defend itself against would-be predators. Defensive behavior includes vibrating its tail and gaping open its mouth, showing off the white lining.

earless lizard: All five species of earless lizards have ears, but they have skin covering the ear opening. The largest species, the Greater Earless Lizard (*Cophosaurus texanus*) is a conspicuous and fast-moving species identified by the black-and-white bands on the bottom of its tail. The Common Lesser Earless Lizard (*Holbrookia maculata*) is found across the west, north, and central portions of Texas. The Keeled Earless Lizard (*Holbrookia propinqua*) is restricted to the sand sheets and dunes of South Texas. The Plateau Earless Lizard (*Holbrookia lacerata*) is found patchily across central Texas, South of the Colorado River and East of the Pecos River. The Tamaulipan Spot-tailed Lizard (*Holbrookia subcaudalis*) is restricted to populations near Del Rio and Kingsville.

earthsnake: see brownsnake

gartersnake: Four species occur in the state, primarily feeding on amphibians and fish, but also earthworms. All species have light-colored lines running the length of their dark-colored bodies. The Checkered Gartersnake (*Thamnophis marcianus*) is found everywhere except East Texas. The Black-necked Gartersnake (*Thamnophis cyrtopsis*), found in central and West Texas, is one of the most beautiful snakes in the state with a brilliant orange stripe. Both the Plains Gartersnake (*Thamnophis radix*) and Common Gartersnake (*Thamnophis sirtalis*), though widely found across the north-central and eastern portions of the United States, only have limited ranges in Texas.

gecko: The Texas Banded Gecko (*Coleonyx brevis*) is the smaller of the two native geckos in the state and is found in West and South Texas. The Reticulate Banded Gecko (*Coleonyx reticulatus*) is native to the Big Bend. Six species of geckos have been introduced to Texas. The Mediterranean Gecko* (*Hemidactylus turcicus*) first arrived in Brownsville in the 1950s and is now found as far North as Lubbock and the Red River. Other species like the Tropical House Gecko* (*Hemidactylus mabouia*) and the Sri Lankan Spotted Gecko* (*Hemidactylus parvimaculatus*) are recent arrivals to the state.

glass lizard: The legless Slender Glass Lizard (*Ophisaurus attenuatus*) is restricted to sandy habitats across the eastern half of the state. This species has eyelids and ear openings, distinguishing them from snakes. They can be seen among the coastal dunes on Mustang Island and Padre Island National Seashore where they feed on insects and small vertebrates.

gophersnake: The Gophersnake (*Pituophis catenifer*), sometimes called Bullsnake, can grow to be the longest snake in the U.S., reaching over 9' in length. Found across the western three-quarters of the state, this non-venomous species may hiss and vibrate its tail when threatened. The related Louisiana Pinesnake (*Pituophis ruthveni*) is a federally-listed species historically found in longleaf pine-oak sandhills habitats in East Texas.

greensnake: The Rough Greensnake (*Opheodrys aestivus*) feeds on spiders and insects, growing to 2' in length in the eastern third of Texas. The Smooth Greensnake (*Opheodrys vernalis*) is thought to be extirpated from the state and is only known from six specimens collected in the 1960s and 1970s.

groundsnake: see brownsnake

hog-nosed snake: Hog-nosed snakes are known for their defensive displays towards predators, ending with the snake playing dead. The Eastern Hog-nosed Snake (*Heterodon platirhinos*) prefers to eat toads and is found in the eastern half of the state. The Plains Hog-nosed Snake (*Heterodon nasicus*) is more commonly found in sandy and gravely habitats in West Texas and the Panhandle.

horned lizard: The Texas Horned Lizard (*Phrynosoma cornutum*), or Horny Toad, is the state reptile. Originally found across the majority of the state, it is now restricted to pockets in west, south, and North Texas due to habitat loss and the introduction of invasive grasses and insects. The Greater Short-horned Lizard (*Phrynosoma hernandesi*) is found at higher elevations in the Davis, Guadalupe, and Hueco mountains. The Round-tailed Horned Lizard (*Phrynosoma modestum*) is found mostly in West Texas and the Panhandle and blends into its arid habitats as a rock mimic.

horny toad: see horned lizard

iguana: The Mexican Spiny-tailed Iguana* (*Ctenosaura pectinata*) is the only species of iguana found in the state. It was introduced in Brownsville in the 1960s but has not expanded its range outside of Cameron County.

indigo snake: Famed for their ability to eat rattlesnakes, the Central American Indigo Snake (*Drymarchon melanurus*) also eats a variety of mammals, birds, turtles, amphibians, and other snakes. Found in South Texas, this heavy-bodied snake is colored dark black and can grow over 8' long.

kingsnake: The Prairie Kingsnake (*Lampropeltis calligaster*) is found in the grasslands and woodlands of East Texas, with some populations in the Panhandle and South Texas. The Gray-banded Kingsnake (*Lampropeltis alterna*) lives in the drier regions of West Texas and is prized by collectors for its beautiful banding patterns of orange or dark grey. The Common Kingsnake (*Lampropeltis getula*) is found throughout the state, though its pattern is more speckled in East Texas and more dark-blotched in West Texas.

lined snake: see brownsnake

loggerhead: see snapping turtle

map turtle: Map turtles, sometimes called sawback turtles, are characterized by a keeled ridge down the middle of the shell and numerous yellow lines on their head and limbs and inhabit river systems across the state. The Texas Map Turtle (*Graptemys versa*) is found in the Colorado and Concho rivers and the Cagle's Map Turtle (*Graptemys caglei*) is restricted to the Guadalupe River. Both the False Map Turtle (*Graptemys pseudogeographica*) and the Ouachita Map Turtle (*Graptemys ouachitensis*) are found in river systems in East and North Texas.

milksnake: The Milksnake (*Lampropeltis triangulum*) is a close relative of the kingsnakes. Its bright red, black, and yellow colors help confuse would-be predators that might instead think this snake to be the venomous Texas Coralsnake (*Micrurus tener*). Because of variability in color intensity and pattern in Texas coralsnakes, the commonly used rhyme "red next to yellow, kill a fellow; red next to black, venom lack" is not a reliable method to distinguish coralsnakes from look-a-likes, such as the Milksnake, the Scarletsnake (*Cemophora coccinea*), the Texas Scarletsnake (*Cemophora lineri*), or the Long-nosed Snake (*Rhinocheilus lecontei*).

moccasin: see cottonmouth

mountain boomer: see collared lizard

mudsnake: The Red-bellied Mudsnake (*Farancia abacura*) is a boldly patterned snake, with dark glossy scales on its back with a bright red belly. It will defend itself when captured by pressing the hard and pointed tip of its tail into the attacker's skin. Occasionally, this species is called a Hoop Snake because of the false myth that it can roll down a hill like a wheel with its tail in its mouth!

mud turtle: Three species of mud turtles are found in Texas, all of which are small (4–6" shell length), secretive species rarely encountered. The Yellow Mud Turtle (*Kinosternon flavescens*) is found throughout most of Texas, except the Piney Woods, and spend a large amount of time in rodent burrows on land, waiting for rains to move into temporary wetlands. The Rough-footed Mud Turtle (*Kinosternon hirtipes*) can only be found in the Alamito Creek drainage of West Texas. The Eastern Mud Turtle (*Kinosternon subrubrum*) occurs across East Texas, often in slow-moving water bodies, including bayous and flooded forests.

musk turtle: These turtles are similar in appearance and ecology to mud turtles, with only two species known in the state. Like mud turtles, musk turtles can discharge a foul-smelling substance from specialized glands on their undersides to deter predators. The Razor-backed Musk Turtle (*Sternotherus carinatus*) gets its name from its shell having small, raised ridges along the midline, and is restricted to aquatic habitats in East Texas. The Eastern Musk Turtle (*Sternotherus odoratus*) is more widespread across eastern and central Texas and has a smooth top of its shell.

painted turtle: Two species of painted turtles can be found in Texas, both extremely uncommon and limited in their range. The Southern Painted Turtle (*Chrysemys dorsalis*) can be found in extreme northeast Texas and only a few records of the Painted Turtle (*Chrysemys picta*) are known from along the Red River and in far West Texas.

pinesnake: see gophersnake

racer: Often a dull green and around 3' in length, the North American Racer (*Coluber constrictor*) is found across the majority of the state, typically in open areas with large amounts of undergrowth. Racers feed on small mammals, birds, reptiles, amphibians, and insects. In East Texas, North American Racers can be brown or tan with some populations being steel-blue or olive intermixed with light white or yellow scales (buttermilk phase).

racerunner: see whiptail lizard

ratsnake: Five species of ratsnake occur in Texas. The Western Ratsnake (*Pantherophis obsoletus*), also Chicken Snake, is frequently encountered in the eastern half of the state. It can reach lengths over 5' and spends much of its time in trees, eating squirrels, birds, and bird eggs. The Baird's Ratsnake (*Pantherophis bairdi*) is found only in the Trans-Pecos. This species changes its pattern from blotches (juvenile) to stripes (adult). A mostly gray snake with dark brown blotches, the Great Plains Ratsnake (*Pantherophis emoryi*) is found across most of the state. The Trans-Pecos Ratsnake (*Bogertophis subocularis*) is found in rocky areas of West Texas where it eats mammals, including bats.

rattlesnake: VENOMOUS. Rattlesnakes are seen in every habitat in Texas, with 11 species represented in the state. The largest, the Western Diamond-backed Rattlesnake (*Crotalus atrox*), can reach lengths over 7' and is found everywhere except far East Texas. The Timber Rattlesnake (*Crotalus horridus*) is a heavy-bodied snake found in the hardwood bottomlands of East and North Texas. The Rock Rattlesnake (*Crotalus lepidus*) can reach 2.5' in length and is restricted to the Trans-Pecos. The smallest rattlesnake species in Texas, the Pygmy Rattlesnake (*Sistrurus miliarius*) is found in East Texas, rarely growing longer than 20".

ribbonsnake: The Western Ribbonsnake (*Thamnophis proximus*) is found almost everywhere in the state, except West Texas. It has a series of three stripes down its olive-colored back and is closely related to the gartersnakes.

sea turtle: Five species of sea turtles can be found in saltwater habitats along the Texas coastline. The largest of all sea turtles, the Leatherback Sea Turtle (*Dermochelys coriacea*), has a shell length that exceeds 7' in length and can weigh almost a ton. The Kemp's Ridley Sea Turtle (*Lepidochelys *kempii*) is among the rarest and smallest of the sea turtles, which primarily nest along South Padre Island and into coastal Mexico and is designated as the state sea turtle. Other sea turtles include the Green Sea Turtle (*Chelonia mydas*), Hawksbill Sea Turtle (*Eretmochelys imbricata*), and Loggerhead Sea Turtle (*Caretta caretta*). All species of sea turtle are federally- and state-protected and any observed nesting or stranded along the coastline should be reported to appropriate individuals, such as TPWD.

skink: Eight species of skinks in Texas, all with smooth and shiny scales. The smallest species is the Ground Skink (*Scincella lateralis*) is often seen scurrying off dirt paths or sidewalks to hide from predators across the eastern three-quarters of Texas. The largest species is the Great Plains Skink (*Plestiodon obsoletus*) and is found in the western half of the state. This species can measure over 1' in total length.

slider: Two species of sliders are found in Texas. One species, the Pond Slider (*Trachemys scripta*) is among the most common turtle found throughout Texas, occurring in most aquatic habitats. The second species, the Mexican Plateau Slider (*Trachemys gaigeae*) only occurs in the Rio Grande of West Texas.

snapping turtle: Snapping turtles are among the largest freshwater turtles in North America and have a generalist diet, consuming almost anything in the water it encounters, including carrion. Two species of snapping turtles are found in Texas. The Snapping Turtle (*Chelydra serpentina*) is found throughout the central and eastern regions while the Alligator Snapping Turtle (*Macrochelys temminckii*) is restricted to East Texas.

softshell: Softshells get their name from the reduced bony elements in their shell, which gives them a leathery, flexible shell, unlike most other turtles. Having this modified shape gives the turtles the ability to be extremely agile and fast swimmers. These species also have a snorkel-like snout and long necks that allow individuals to raise their heads up and breathe while they are submerged in the sandy bottoms of rivers and streams. Two species of softshells occur in Texas, including the Smooth Softshell (*Apalone mutica*) that is uncommon throughout parts of northern, central, and eastern Texas, and the Spiny Softshell (*Apalone spinifera*) that is much more abundant in suitable habitats across most of Texas.

spiny lizard: Over 10 species of spiny lizards are found in Texas, so-called 'spiny' because of their large, keeled scales that give them a rough appearance. The Crevice Spiny Lizard (*Sceloporus poinsettii*) is unique among Texas spiny lizards as it does not lay eggs but instead gives birth to live young. The Texas Spiny Lizard (*Sceloporus olivaceus*), or Rusty Lizard, prefers to spend their time in trees, often on the opposite side of the trunk from any observers! The Dunes Sagebrush Lizard (*Sceloporus arenicolus*) is restricted to the shinnery-oak dunes of West Texas near Kermit and Andrews. The Rose-bellied Lizard (*Sceloporus variabilis*) is found in rocky and drier environments in South Texas. The Tree Lizard (*Urosaurus ornatus*) is found on trees and rocks from El Paso to central Texas. The Side-blotched Lizard (*Uta stansburiana*) is found in the western deserts and southern portions of the Panhandle.

terrapin: The Diamond-backed Terrapin (*Malaclemys terrapin*) inhabits brackish waters along the Texas coast from the Louisiana border to Corpus Christi. Throughout the 1800s, this turtle was widely consumed, and population declines were widespread.

threadsnake: The three native species of threadsnakes can initially look like earthworms; however, their tiny tongues and scaled bodies give them away as snakes. Threadsnakes feed on ant and termite larvae. The Texas Threadsnake (*Rena dulcis*) is found in the middle third of Texas; two other species, the New Mexico Threadsnake (*Rena dissecta*) and Western Threadsnake (*Rena humilis*), are found in West Texas. The Brahminy Blindsnake* (*Indotyphlops braminus*) has been introduced to Texas as it hitchhikes around the world, hiding in the soil of plants in the nursery trade.

tortoise: One species of tortoise occurs in Texas, the Berlandier's Tortoise (*Gopherus berlandieri*). This tortoise occurs throughout South Texas and into Mexico and has a domed shell and elephant-like feet. Unlike most other turtles, tortoises spend the majority of their time on land foraging on vegetation.

watersnake: Seven species are known in the state and all are non-venomous. Often, these species are confused with the venomous Cottonmouth (*Agkistrodon piscivorous*). The Diamond-backed Watersnake (*Nerodia rhombifer*), is the largest in the state, often reaching 4', and is found in the eastern two-thirds of Texas. The Plain-bellied Watersnake (*Nerodia erythrogaster*) feeds on amphibians and fish. Both the Brazos River Watersnake (*Nerodia harteri*) and Concho Watersnake (*Nerodia paucimaculata*) are found only in Texas (endemic species).

whipsnake: Whipsnakes are long and slender snakes with large eyes that hunt almost exclusively during the day. The Coachwhip (*Masticophis flagellum*) is found across the entire state and can be found with a variety of body colors: brown, tan, black, and red. Schott's Whipsnake (*Masticophis schotti*) is found in the thornscrub of South Texas and the Striped Whipsnake (*Masticophis taeniatus*) is found in the drier regions of central and West Texas.

whiptail lizard: There are 10 species of whiptail lizards found across the state, with the majority of species found in West Texas. Two species are widely distributed in Texas, except portions of West Texas: the Six-lined Racerunner (*Aspidoscelis sexlineata*), which has six light stripes across its dark back, and the Common Spotted Whiptail (*Aspidoscelis gularis*), which also has light stripes but with additional small light spots between the stripes and across its dark back. The Laredo Striped Whiptail (*Aspidoscelis laredoensis*) is the only species restricted to South Texas, found along the Rio Grande from Val Verde to Cameron counties. The Chihuahuan Spotted Whiptail (*Aspidoscelis exsanguis*) is an all-female species and can reproduce without fertilization from males.

A Golden-Fronted Woodpecker. Photo by Andy Morffew, CC by 2.0/Flickr.

Birds

blackbird: To protect their nests from predators, the Red-winged Blackbird (*Agelaius phoeniceus*) build their nests in dense reeds surrounded by water. A single male will defend a quality patch of nesting area, mating with multiple females that build nests within his territory. Additional species are found in the state, primarily as winter visitors, including the Yellow-headed Blackbird (*Xanthocephalus xanthocephalus*) and the Brewer's Blackbird (*Euphagus cyanocephalus*).

bluebird: Three species. The Eastern Bluebird (*Sialia sialis*) is a welcomed summer resident in the eastern half of the state and a winter resident and migrant across the western half. Bright blue above with a rusty red chest, this species has faced declines across its range, likely due to introduced bird species such as House Sparrow and European Starling.

bunting: Once seen, a male Painted Bunting (*Passerina ciris*) is a bird not soon forgotten: a deep blue head with a distinct red eye ring, a yellow back, and red breast; almost a 'color-by-numbers' assortment of brilliant colors. A summer resident across much of the state. The male Varied Bunting (*Passerina versicolor*), found along the Rio Grande in West Texas, is equally stunning with its combination of purple, deep blue, and a small amount of red. A male Indigo Bunting (*Passerina cyanea*) is bright blue. Female buntings are inconspicuously colored with a wash of tan or pale yellow covering their body.

caracara: see falcon.

cardinal: The Northern Cardinal (*Cardinalis cardinalis*) is a frequent and loud visitor to both backyards and mixed forests. A conspicuous bird due to its bright red color (though females are not as bright), this species is monogamous, and the pair remains together throughout the year. Its thick, stout bill is used to feed on seeds.

chachalaca: The Plain Chachalaca (*Ortalis vetula*) is a native species found in the Lower Rio Grande Valley. Also called a Mexican Pheasant, this species can be found on the ground as well as in trees. Eats fruit, leaves, and insects. When multiple animals call at the same time, the loud chorus of 'cha-cha-lac' can be deafening.

chickadee: The Carolina Chickadee (*Poecile carolinensis*) is found across the eastern half of the state. Often seen in a mixed flock with titmice. Feeds on insects as well as seeds and berries. Call is 'chick-a-dee-dee-dee'.

coot: The American Coot, or Mud Hen (*Fulica americana*), is found in ponds and waterways across the state. A dark-gray and black bird with widened toes that aid in swimming. A memorable characteristic of these birds is their ungraceful method of flapping and running across the water's surface to fly.

cormorant: Two species are commonly seen. Great at catching fish, their outer feathers lack waterproofing, an adaptation that enables them to stay underwater rather than float. Often seen along bodies of water as they hold their wings out to dry. The Neotropical Cormorant (*Phalacrocorax brasilianus*) is a common resident across the South and East portions of the state. The Double-crested Cormorant (*Phalacrocorax auritus*) is a winter migrant and visitor.

cowbird: Cowbirds are obligate brood parasites, meaning they do not build their own nests, and instead they lay their eggs in the nests of other species. The baby cowbirds hatch earlier than the other chicks and grow larger, often the only chick to survive and successfully leave the nest. The Brown-headed Cowbird (*Molothrus ater*) and Bronzed Cowbird (*Molothrus aeneus*) are the two most common species in Texas.

crane: Cranes are among the tallest birds in North America, standing over 4' high, but are only winter visitors to Texas. The Sandhill Crane (*Grus canadensis*) is often found in large flocks in open fields where they feed on spent grain.

The Whooping Crane (*Grus americana*) is found in coastal marshes where they feed on blue crabs. The Whooping Crane is a critically endangered species with recent surveys estimating the Texas population size to be around 500 individuals.

crow: The American Crow (*Corvus brachyrhynchos*) is a common resident of the Panhandle and eastern half of the state. An omnivorous species with a wide diet, it has been the focus of efforts to control populations because of damage to agricultural areas. The Fish Crow (*Corvus ossifragus*) is found in extreme East Texas; in Texas, the Tamaulipan Crow (*Corvus imparatus*) is known only from a handful of localities in Cameron County.

dove: Many species occur in Texas. Several species are game species, including Mourning Dove (*Zenaida macroura*), White-winged Dove (*Zenaida asiatica*), and White-tipped Dove (*Leptotila verreauxi*). The Rock Dove (*Columba livia*), or Pigeon, can be found in large numbers in urban areas. The Eurasian Collared-dove* (*Steptopelia decaocto*) first arrived in the state in 1995 and can now be found in every county.

duck: Over 20 species occur in Texas, though most are primarily winter visitors. The Wood Duck (*Aix sponsa*) is an exception, a summer resident across three-quarters of the state. The Northern Shoveler (*Anas clypeata*) uses its remarkably long spatulate bill to filter water, eating plankton and invertebrates. The winter aggregations of Redhead (*Aythya americana*) in the Laguna Madre are the largest in the world. The Muscovy Duck* (*Cairina moschata*) is restricted to counties in the Lower Rio Grande Valley.

eagle: The Bald Eagle (*Haliaeetus leucocephalus*) is the largest raptor in Texas, feeding on fish and ducks primarily in the eastern third of the state. It can be seen in most of Texas during migration. The Golden Eagle (*Aquila chrysaetos*), with its 7' wingspan, is often associated with mountainous regions where it feeds on mammals, birds, and reptiles.

egret: see heron.

falcon: Eight species, belonging to two groups, are found in Texas. The larger group possesses long tails and long, narrow wings which enable them to dive at incredible speeds when hunting. Common falcons include the American Kestrel (*Falco sparevius*) and Merlin (*Falco columbarius*), and uncommon falcons include the Peregrine Falcon (*Falco peregrinus*) and the Aplomado Falcon (*Falco femoralis*). Alone in the second group, the Crested Caracara (*Caracara cheriway*) is more like a vulture than a true falcon, with its weak claws but long wings.

finch: Finches are small birds with short, stout bills that primarily feed on seeds and some insects, and often move in flocks. The Lesser Goldfinch (*Spinus psaltria*) is a summer resident of the Trans-Pecos and Lower Rio Grande Valley. The male House Finch (*Haemorhous mexicanus*), with its orange-red head and chest, is found throughout most of the state. The Purple Finch (*Haemorhous purpureus*) is a winter migrant seen in North and East Texas.

flycatcher: Flycatchers have a hunting strategy of catching insects in flight, first spotting them while sitting in the top of a tree or fence post and then flying up to catch the insect and returning to their original spot. With its extremely long tail, the Scissor-tailed Flycatcher (*Tyrannus forficatus*) is a conspicuous resident across much of the state; the Vermillion Flycatcher (*Pyrocephalus rubinus*) is also conspicuous with its brilliantly crimson-colored males. Brown above, yellow below, and with a black mask over its eyes, the Great Kiskadee (*Pitangus sulphuratus*) is well known in South Texas. The Eastern Phoebe (*Sayornis phoebe*) is found in backyards as well as open woodlands. The White-eyed Vireo (*Vireo griseus*) is found across the eastern half of the state, sometimes combining the calls of other species into their own. The Western Kingbird (*Tyrannus verticalis*) is seen in open habitats, often on fence posts or utility lines.

goose: Several species occur as winter migrants, and most can occur in huge populations in the Panhandle and along the coast. Species include the Snow Goose (*Chen caerulescens*), the Ross's Goose (*Chen rossii*), and the Canada Goose (*Branta canadensis*).

grackle: Sociable and eye-catching in many urban areas across the state, these shiny black birds have a showy courtship display and nest in large colonies. Three species occur in Texas: the Common Grackle (*Quiscalus quiscula*) and Great-tailed Grackle (*Quiscalus mexicanus*) are found across much of the state and the Boat-tailed Grackle (*Quiscalus major*) is restricted to a narrow band of habitat close to the ocean along the upper Gulf Coast.

gull: Although gulls are frequently associated with the coast, many species can be found along lakes and marshes far inland from the coast. Gulls rely on their skills as scavengers, grabbing floating items from the water, as well as unattended or abandoned food items from the ground. The Franklin's Gull (*Larus pipixcan*) and the Ring-billed Gull (*Larus delawarensis*) are among the most common gulls seen across the state. With its distinctive "laughing" call, the Laughing Gull (*Leucophaeus atricilla*) is primarily found along the coast.

harrier: see hawks.

hawk: Hawks are birds of prey in the same family as eagles, kites, and harriers. The Cooper's Hawk (*Accipiter cooperii*) feeds on birds and is often seen in wooded urban backyards. The Northern Harrier (*Circus cyaneus*) can be found gliding low across prairies searching for small vertebrates. The Harris's Hawk (*Parabuteo unicinctus*) is known for cooperatively hunting in social groups. The Red-tailed Hawk (*Buteo jamaicensis*) is found statewide, often seen soaring or perched on telephone poles and fence posts.

heron: Herons and egrets are long-legged and long-billed birds. The Great Blue Heron (*Ardea herodias*) and the Great Egret (*Ardea alba*) are frequently seen around the edges of lakes, marshes, and even in roadside drainage ditches where they feed on fish and other small vertebrates like snakes. The nocturnal Black-crowned Night-heron (*Nycticorax nycticorax*) can be found along urban streams. The Cattle Egret (*Bubulcus ibis*) was unknown in Texas until 1955 as this species spread from Africa to South America in the 1880s (blown across the Atlantic Ocean in giant storms), and then to Florida and Texas in the 1940s and 1950s.

hummingbird: Texas is home to at least 18 species, some species being residents, others only brief migratory visitors. The Ruby-throated Hummingbird (*Archilochus colubris*) is a summer resident in the eastern third of the state; the Black-chinned Hummingbird (*Archilochus alexandri*) is commonly seen in the western two-thirds of the state. The

Lucifer Hummingbird (*Calothorax lucifer*) can be found in the Christmas and Chisos mountains in the Big Bend during the summer; the Green-breasted Mango (*Anthracothorax prevostii*) has been seen sporadically in the Lower Rio Grande Valley, primarily in the fall.

jay: Seven species are recorded from Texas. The Blue Jay (*Cyanocitta cristata*) is the most wide-ranging species, inhabiting rural and urban areas across the state, except West Texas. Eating insects and large amounts of nuts and fruit, this species will also hoard surplus food. The spectacular and distinctive Green Jay (*Cyanocorax yncas*) has slowly been expanding its South Texas range northward towards San Antonio. The Brown Jay (*Psilorhinus morio*) is known only from Starr and Zapata counties.

kestrel: see falcon.

killdeer: The Killdeer (*Charadrius vociferus*) is a type of plover found throughout Texas, often seen along open fields and grassy lots. They lay their eggs directly on the ground, camouflaged among rocks and pebbles. Well-known for their distraction displays leading predators away from their nests, they will often pretend to have a broken wing.

kingbird: see flycatcher.

kingfisher: Three resident species in Texas. They hover and dive into the water to catch fish. The Belted Kingfisher (*Megaceryle alcyon*) is found throughout the state. Both the Ringed Kingfisher (*Megaceryle torquata*) and the Green Kingfisher (*Chloroceryle americana*) are restricted to central and South Texas.

kiskadee: see flycatcher.

kite: Kites are small raptors that feed insects and small vertebrates, but some species, like the Hook-billed Kite (*Chondrohierax uncinatus*) specialize in snails. Kites can catch and eat insects while in flight or can hover, then swoop down to grab prey off the ground. The Mississippi Kite Actiniaa mississippiensis) can be seen across the state; the White-tailed Kite (*Elanus leucurus*), and the Swallow-tailed Kite (*Elanoides forficatus*) are found inEastt Texas and along the coast.

meadowlark: Meadowlarks are conspicuous birds found perched on fences along open prairie or grassy habitats. The call of the Western Meadowlark (*Sturnella neglecta*) is a bit more complex than that of the Eastern Meadowlark (*Sternella magna*), but subtle differences in their markings can make the species difficult to tell apart without the aid of their calls.

mockingbird: The Northern Mockingbird (*Mimus polyglottos*) is the state bird of Texas. Known for mimicking songs of other birds to attract mates and intimidate other males; unmated males will sing at night in the spring. Both males and females may vigorously attack would-be predators to defend their eggs and young.

nighthawk: These are nocturnal birds, with large mouths edged with large bristles that act as flytraps, feed at night to catch flying insects. They are also called goatsuckers. They do not build nests, but instead lay camouflaged eggs on bare ground. The Common Nighthawk (*Chordeiles minor*) is seen across the state, whereas the Common Pauraque (*Nyctidromus albicollis*) is restricted to South Texas.

oriole: Orioles are somewhat conspicuous with their bright yellow, orange, or rusty red colors, particularly the males in spring breeding plumage. Nine species reported in the state. The Orchard Oriole (*Icterus spurius*) can be a common resident in East Texas. The Altamira Oriole (*Icterus gularis*) is an orange and black species found only along the Rio Grande in extreme South Texas. The Scott's Oriole (*Icterus parisorum*) is a yellow and black species found across the drier Trans-Pecos region.

osprey: The Osprey (*Pandion haliaetus*) feeds on fish, hovering above the water before plunging in feet first to grab its prey. When flying, they are sometimes confused with gulls, but their sharply hooked beak and dark eye stripe help in their identification.

owl: Seventeen species are observed in the state. With large eyes, incredible hearing, and wings adapted to maintain silence in flight, owls are amazing nocturnal predators. More frequently seen owls include the Barn Owl (*Tyto alba*), Great Horned Owl (*Bufo virginianus*), Eastern Screech Owl (*Megascops asio*), Burrowing Owl (*Athene cunicularia*), and Barred Owl (*Strix varia*). In the summer, the small Elf Owl (*Micrathene whitneyi*) can be seen in West Texas.

parakeet: Following several accidental and at least one intentional introduction, the Monk Parakeet* (*Myiopsitta monachus*), or Quaker Parakeet*, is established in several urban areas from Dallas to Austin, San Antonio to Kingsville. The presence of another species found in South Texas along the Rio Grande, the Green Parakeet (*Aratinga holochlora*), may be linked to habitat loss further South in its native range of Mexico.

parrot: A single species, the Red-crowned Parrot (*Amazona viridigenalis*) is found in Texas, common in the metropolitan areas of Cameron, Hidalgo, and Starr counties along the lower Rio Grande border.

pelican: The Brown Pelican (*Pelecanus occidentalis*) is a resident along the Texas coast and may range inland up to 150 miles. The White Pelican (*Pelecanus erythrorhynchos*) is a common winter resident in the eastern half of the state.

phoebe: see flycatcher.

pigeon: see dove.

plover: see shorebird.

prairie chicken: Both the Greater Prairie-chicken (*Tympanuchus cupido*) and the Lesser Prairie-chicken (*Tympanuchus pallidicinctus*) are famed for their elaborate courtship displays: the males gather in tall-grass prairie clearings to dance in a competition for females. The males inflate their large orange neck pouches with air, then force air out with a "boom" that can be heard for over half a mile.

purple martin: see swallow.

quail: The Northern Bobwhite (*Colinus virginianus*) is the most widespread quail species in Texas, found across all but West Texas. The Gambel's Quail (*Callipepla gambelii*) and the Montezuma Quail (*Cyrtonyx montezumae*) are restricted to the Trans-Pecos; the Scaled Quail (*Callipepla squamata*), or Blue Quail, is found in the Panhandle as well as West and South Texas. All but the Montezuma Quail are legal game species in the state.

rail: Found in both freshwater and brackish marshes, rails are typically heard rather than seen. The Sora (*Porzana* *carolina*) may be the most conspicuous of the rails, hunting along the open margins in search of seeds and insects. Other species, like the Yellow Rail (*Coturnicops noveboracensis*) and Black Rail (*Laterallus jamaicensis*) are elusive winter migrants to brackish marshes along the coast.

raven: The Common Raven (*Corvus corax*) is a large black bird found in central and West Texas; the Chihuahuan Raven (*Corvus cryptoleucus*) is slightly smaller in size but with a wider distribution in the Panhandle and both West and South Texas. The larger body size, stouter bill, and longer wings distinguish ravens from the crow. Ravens are omnivorous, eating vertebrates, insects, seeds, and fruit.

roadrunner: The Greater Roadrunner (*Geococcyx californicus*) is found across the state, though uncommon in East Texas. They feed on a variety of prey, including insects, spiders, small mammals, small birds, lizards, and snakes, including rattlesnakes, but will also eat fruit and seeds. Other names include Paisano and Chaparral Cock.

robin: The American Robin (*Turdus migratorius*) is known across the state as either a winter visitor (west and South Texas) or as a summer resident (north, central, and East Texas), although its summer range in Texas continues to expand. With its red breast and brown or black back, this species can form large flocks that feed on insects and fruit.

sandpiper: see shorebird.

shorebird: A large group of wading birds commonly found along the water's edge, whether ocean or freshwater. Shorebirds' long bills are used to probe moist sand and sediment for invertebrates and featherless legs adapted for wading. The Willet (*Tringa semipalmata*) breeds along the Gulf Coast, identified by its black-and-white wing pattern visible during flight. The Spotted Sandpiper (*Actitis macularius*) can be identified by the exaggerated bobbing of its longish tail when walking. The Mountain Plover (*Charadrius montanus*) is a summer resident in open grasslands of the northern Panhandle with some populations wintering in central and South Texas. The secretive and solitary Wilson's Snipe (*Callinago delicata*), the focus of many invented hunts, is an actual game bird found along grassy marshes and meadows.

shrike: The Loggerhead Shrike (*Lanius ludovicianus*), or Butcher Bird, is known for impaling its prey (insects and small vertebrates) on barbed wire fences or sharp-thorned plants. The food items are eaten quickly or saved for future use. Its gray, black, and white body makes this species look similar to a Northern Mockingbird, but its black eye mask and sharp, hooked bill instead help identify it as a shrike.

snipe: see shorebird.

sparrow: Many of the 30 species of sparrows found in Texas are small brown or gray birds that may be difficult to identify from one another. Identification relies on noting the presence (or absence), number, and color of stripes on their head and bars on their wings. The Chipping Sparrow (*Spizella passerina*) can be found throughout the state, breeding in pockets of the west, central, and East Texas. The Black-throated Sparrow (*Amphispiza bilineata*) is a common

A pair of Scaled Quail. Photo by Jill D. Miller.

species in drier habitats of central, west, and South Texas. The Seaside Sparrow (*Ammodramus maritimus*) is restricted to coastal marshes on the coast. The White-collared Seedeater (*Sporophila torqueola*) is restricted to habitat along the Rio Grande from Val Verde to Starr counties. The ubiquitous House Sparrow* (*Passer domesticus*), distantly related to the New World sparrows, was intentionally released in Galveston in 1867 and spread throughout the state by 1905.

starling: The European Starling* (*Sturnus vulgaris*) was first introduced to North America in New York in 1890. It reached East Texas by 1925 and El Paso in 1939. This aggressive species will often take over cavities and nest boxes, often out-competing native species such as bluebirds and Purple Martins. A visually striking bird in its breeding plumage with a brilliant yellow bill and iridescent black feathers.

swallow: Nine species of small, swift fliers that feed on insects while in flight are found in Texas. The arrival of the first Purple Martin (*Progne subis*) is a harbinger of spring; fall migratory roosts can number in the hundreds of thousands. The Cliff Swallow (*Poetrochelidon pyrrhonota*) has a short, squared tail and builds mud nests in groups on cliffs or bridges. The Barn Swallow (*Hirundo rustica*) has a longer, forked tail and builds small mud nests under the eaves of buildings.

swift: With their long wings and slender bodies, swifts have been called "flying cigars." They are fast fliers, catching and feeding on insects in flight. The Chimney Swift (*Chaetura pelagica*) uses hollow trees and crevices for nesting sites, using saliva to glue together a nest of twigs on the inside of the structure. This species has gained its name because it can utilize man-made structures such as abandoned buildings, silos, and chimneys for nesting sites.

tern: Related to gulls, terns can be found along the coast and inland near lakes and marshes. Terms form large breeding colonies to provide protection in numbers, more experienced adults occupying the center of the colony. The Caspian Tern (*Hydroprogne caspia*) is the largest species in the world. The Royal Tern (*Thalasseus maximus*) and the Sandwich Tern (*Thalasseus sanvicensis*) are restricted to coastal habitats; the Forester's Tern (*Sterna forsteri*) is common along the coast and inland lakes.

thrush: Related to bluebirds and the robin, thrushes are medium-sized birds with melodious calls. Many species are secretive winter migrants, their inconspicuous brown coloration helping hide them in woody brush. The Hermit Thrush (*Catharus guttatus*) is a common winter visitor across the state, with a breeding population in the Davis Mountains. The Wood Thrush (*Hylocichla mustelina*) is a summer resident of East Texas.

titmouse: Titmice in Texas are conspicuous and talkative birds with a noticeable tuft or crest on their head. Often in mixed-species flocks with chickadees and small woodpeckers. The Tufted Titmouse (*Baeolophus bicolor*) is found in the eastern third of the state; the Black-crested Titmouse (*Baeolophus atricristatus*), with a prominent black patch on its crest, is found in the western two-thirds of the state.

turkey: The Wild Turkey (*Maleagris gallopavo*) has a patchwork distribution across Texas, commonly seen in the middle third of state, but in more isolated pockets in West and East Texas. Males with conspicuous display to attract females: they will strut and gobble, while extending their wings, tail and body feathers. Turkeys often roost in trees at night.

vireo: see flycatcher.

vulture: With their long wings, both species of vultures are experts at soaring, generally only flapping their wings when they take off from feeding or roosting. Featherless heads and curved bills are adaptations to feeding on carrion. The Black Vulture (*Coragyps atratus*) has a black head and white wingtips when viewed from below; the Turkey Vulture (*Cathartes aura*) has a red head and two-toned (black and white) wings from below: black on the leading edge, gray or white on the trailing edge. Turkey Vultures use both sight and smell to find food, Black Vultures rely more on sight.

warbler: Almost 50 species of warblers, more properly called "wood-warblers," are known from Texas. Many are migrants passing through, while others are breeding summer residents. Many bird watchers anxiously await the last two weeks of April for the peak of spring migration, when birds return from their winter locations in spectacular full breeding plumage. If birds flying from the Yucatan across the Gulf of Mexico encounter strong winds or storms, they will be exhausted from their non-stop flight and "fallout" once they finally reach land. The Golden-cheeked Warbler (*Setophaga chrysoparia*) breeds only in the steep, wooded canyons of central Texas. The population of Colima Warblers (*Oreothlypis crissalis*) found in the Chisos Mountains (Big Bend) is the only U.S. population. The Tropical Parula (*Setophaga pitiayumi*) is a large warbler found in South Texas. The Yellow-rumped Warbler (*Setophaga coronata*) is a common winter visitor to most of Texas.

waxwing: A conspicuous winter visitor, the Cedar Waxwing (*Bombycilla cedrorum*) moves around in large flocks feeding on berries and fruits. It has a black mask, head crest, and a row of feathers on the wings are tipped with a bright red waxy substance.

woodpecker: Over a dozen species of woodpeckers occur in Texas, all with sharp, stout bills used to probe wood for insects or used to excavate cavities to nest. At 16" long, the Pileated Woodpecker (*Dryocopus pileatus*) is the largest species in Texas and is found in East Texas; at just under 7", the Downy Woodpecker (*Picoides pubescens*) is one of the smallest and is found across all but West and South Texas. The Acorn Woodpecker (*Melanerpes formicivorus*) is known for storing (and defending) large amounts of acorns wedged into small holes in dead limbs and trees.

wren: Wrens are small brown birds that can be quite vocal when advertising for mates or in defense of their nests. Many species have a white eye-stripe and often hold their tails up at an angle over their backs and are insectivorous. The Carolina Wren (*Thyrothorus ludovicianus*), House Wren (*Troglodytes aedon*), and the Bewick's Wren (*Thryomanes bewickii*) build nests in cavities, often close to human dwellings. The slowly cascading call of the Canyon Wren (*Catherpes mexicanus*) is often heard in rocky areas of West and central Texas.

Mule Deer are commonly found in the Panhandle and Trans-Pecos regions of the state. Photo by Jill D. Miller.

Mammals

armadillo: The Nine-banded Armadillo (*Dasypus novemcinctus*) is one of Texas' most iconic mammals and is the state small mammal. It is found in most of the state except the western Trans-Pecos. It is now common as far North and East as Kansas and Mississippi.

badger: The American Badger (*Taxidea taxus*) is most common in parts of West and South Texas and is occasionally spotted in the eastern part of the state. It is a fierce fighter and is valuable in helping control the rodent population.

bat: Thirty-two species of these winged mammals have been found in Texas, more than in any other state in the United States. Of these, 27 species are known residents, though they are seldom seen by the casual observer. The Mexican Free-tailed Bat (*Tadarida brasiliensis*) and the Cave Myotis (*Myotis velifer*) constitute most of the cave-dwelling bats of central and West Texas. They have some economic value for their deposits of nitrogen-rich guano. Some commercial guano has been produced from Beaver Creek Cavern (Burnet County) and James River Bat Cave (Mason County), and from large deposits in other caves, including Bandera Bat Cave (Bandera County), Blowout Cave (Blanco County), and Devil's Sinkhole (Edwards County). The largest concentration of bats in the world is found at Bracken Cave in Comal County, which is thought to hold between 20 and 40 million bats. The Big Brown Bat (*Eptesicus fuscus*), the Eastern Red Bat (*Lasiurus borealis*), and the Evening Bat (*Nycticeius humeralis*) are found in East and southeast Texas. The Evening Bat and Big Brown Bat are forest and woodland dwelling mammals. The rarer species of Texas bats have been found along the Rio Grande and in the Trans-Pecos. Bats can be observed at dusk near a water source, and many species may also be found foraging on insects attracted to streetlights. Everywhere bats occur, they are the main predators of night-flying insects, including mosquitoes and many crop pests. The state flying mammal of Texas is the Mexican Free-tailed Bat.

bear: The American Black Bear (*Ursus americanus*), formerly common throughout most of the state, is now surviving in remnant populations in mountainous areas of the Trans-Pecos from Big Bend to Del Rio.

beaver: The American Beaver (*Castor canadensis*) is found over most of the state except for the Llano Estacado and parts of the Trans-Pecos.

bighorn: see sheep

bison: The largest of native terrestrial wild mammals of North America, the American Bison (*Bos bison*), commonly called buffalo, was formerly found in the western two-thirds of the state. Today, it is extirpated or confined on ranches. Deliberate slaughter of this majestic animal for hides and to eliminate the Plains Indians' main food source reached a peak about 1877–1878, and the American Bison was almost eradicated by 1885. Estimates of the number of buffalo killed vary, but as many as 200,000 hides were sold in Fort Worth at a single two-day sale. Except for the interest of the late Col. Charles Goodnight and a few other foresighted men, the American Bison might be extinct.

buffalo: see bison

cat: The Jaguar (*Felis onca*) is probably now extinct in Texas (last recorded in 1948 near Kingsville), along with the Jaguarundi (*Puma yagouaroundi*) and Margay (*Felis wiedii*). The Bobcat (*Lynx rufus*) is found throughout the state in large numbers. The Mountain Lion (*Felis concolor*), also known as the cougar or puma, was once found statewide and is now found in the mountainous areas of the Trans-Pecos and the dense Rio Grande brushland. The Ocelot (*Felis pardalis*) is now restricted to extreme South Texas. The last documented report of a Jaguarundi, was reported from Brownsville in 1986, although unverified reports continue to be described along the length of the Rio Grande. The Margay was last reported before 1852 near Eagle Pass.

chipmunk: The Gray-footed Chipmunk (*Tamias canipes*) is found at high altitudes in the Guadalupe and Sierra Diablo ranges of the Trans-Pecos. See also ground squirrel, with which the chipmunk is often confused in public reference.

coati: The White-nosed coati (*Nasua narica*), a relative of the raccoon, historically ranged from Brownsville to the Big Bend, but today its distribution is mostly restricted to the Trans-Pecos and it is listed as a threatened species in the state. It inhabits woodland areas and feeds both on the ground and in trees. In Texas, the Whit-nosed Coati is most commonly seen in Big Bend National Park.

coyote: The Coyote (*Canis latrans*) exists in great numbers in Texas, including in and around urban areas. While a significant predator of Texas livestock, it is also a valuable predator in the balance of nature, providing a layer of protection to crops and range lands by its control of rodents and rabbits. In terms of economic importance, it is second only to the raccoon in being the most important fur-bearing animal in the state.

deer: The White-tailed Deer (*Odocoileus virginianus*), found throughout the state in brushy or wooded areas, is the most important Texas game animal. Its numbers in Texas are estimated at more than 3 million. The Mule Deer (*Odocoileus heminous*) is found principally in the Trans-Pecos and Panhandle areas and has increased in number in recent years. In Texas, the only native species of Elk (*Cervus canadensis merriami*) was found in the southern Guadalupe Mountains and became extinct about the turn of the 20th century. A separate subspecies of Elk (*Cervus c. canadensis*) was introduced into the same area from South Dakota around 1928. There are currently several herds totaling several thousand individuals. Several exotic deer species have been introduced, mostly for hunting purposes. The Axis Deer* (*Axis axis*) is the most numerous of the exotics. Native to India, it is found mostly in central and South Texas, both free-ranging and confined on ranches. Blackbuck* (*Antilope cervicapra*), also native to India, is the second-most numerous exotic deer in the state and is found on ranches in 86 counties. Fallow Deer* (*Dama dama*), native to the Mediterranean, have been introduced to 93 counties, while the Nilgai* (*Boselaphus tragocamelus*), native of India and Pakistan, is found mostly in Kenedy, Willacy, and Cameron counties. The Sika Deer* (*Cervus nippon*), native of southern Siberia, Japan, and China, has been introduced in 77 counties in central and South Texas.

dolphin: The Atlantic Spotted Dolphin (*Stenella frontalis*) is rather small, long snouted, and spotted; it is purplish gray, appearing blackish at a distance, usually with numerous small white or gray spots on its sides and back. In the Gulf of Mexico, this dolphin is second in abundance only to the Common Bottlenose Dolphin. The Common Bottlenose Dolphin (*Tursiops truncatus*) is stout and short-beaked with sloping forehead, projecting lower jaw, and high dorsal fin. Other species, such as the Clymene Dolphin, Pantropical Spotted Dolphin, Risso's Dolphin, Rough-toothed Dolphin, Spinner Dolphin, and Striped Dolphin are unusual and known in Texas only through strandings along gulf beaches.

ferret: The Black-footed Ferret (*Mustela nigripes*) was formerly found widely ranging through the West Texas country where its main prey, the prairie dog, was formerly plentiful. Related to the mink and weasel, it is now considered extinct in Texas.

fox: The Common Gray Fox (*Urocyon cinereoargenteus*) is found throughout most of the state, primarily in the woods of East Texas, in broken parts of the Edwards Plateau, and in the rough country at the foot of the High Plains. The Swift Fox (*Vulpes velox*) is found in the western third of the state. A second species of Kit Fox (*Vulpes macrotis*) is found in the Trans-Pecos and is fairly numerous in some localities. The Red Fox* (*Vulpes vulpes*), which ranges across central Texas, was introduced for sport.

gopher: Eleven species of pocket gopher occur in Texas. The Botta's Pocket Gopher (*Thomomys bottae*) is found from the Trans-Pecos eastward across the Edwards Plateau. The Plains Pocket Gopher (*Geomys bursarius*) is found from Midland and Tom Green counties East and North to McLennan, Dallas, and Grayson counties. The Desert Pocket Gopher (*Geomys arenarius*) is found only in the Trans-Pecos, while the Yellow-faced Pocket Gopher (*Cratogeomys castanops*) is found in the western third of the state, with occasional sightings along the Rio Grande in Maverick and Cameron counties. The Texas Pocket Gopher (*Geomys personatus*) is found in South Texas from San Patricio County to Val Verde County. Attwater's Pocket Gopher (*Geomys attwateri*) and Baird's Pocket Gopher (*Geomys breviceps*) are both found generally in south-central and coastal Texas from the Brazos River to the San Antonio River and South to Matagorda and San Patricio counties. Jones' Pocket Gopher (*Geomys knoxjonesi*) is found only in far West Texas, while the Llano Pocket Gopher (*Geomys texensis*) is found only in two isolated areas of the Hill Country. Hall's Pocket Gopher (*Geomys jugossicularis*) is restricted to Dallam and Hartley counties in the far northwest Panhandle and Strecker's Pocket Gopher (*Geomys streckeri*) is found only in Dimmit and Zavala counties in South Texas.

ground squirrel: Five species of ground squirrel live in Texas, mostly in the western part of the state. The Rock Squirrel (*Otopermophilus variegatus*) is found throughout the Edwards Plateau and Trans-Pecos. The Rio Grande Ground Squirrel (*Ictidomys parvidens*) occurs throughout much of South Texas, the Trans-Pecos, and almost to the Red River just East of the Panhandle. The Spotted Ground Squirrel (*Xermospermophilus spilosoma*) is found generally in the western half of the state. The Thirteen-lined Ground Squirrel (*Ictidomys tridecemlineatus*) is found in a narrow strip from Dallas and Tarrant counties to the gulf. The Texas Antelope Squirrel (*Ammospermophilus interpres*) is found along the Rio Grande from El Paso to Val Verde County.

hog: Feral Hogs (*Sus scrofa*) are found in almost every county in Texas but especially in areas of the Rio Grande and Coastal Plains, as well as in the woods of East Texas. They are descendants of escaped domestic hogs or of European wild hogs that were imported for sport. Their rooting habits can extensively destroy vegetation and soil and their ever-expanding populations threaten many native mammal populations through competition and disease.

javelina: The Javelina or Collared Peccary (*Pecari tajacu*) is found in brushy semidesert areas where Prickly Pear, a favorite food, is found. The Javelina was hunted commercially for its hide until 1939. They are harmless to livestock and to people, though they can defend themselves ferociously when attacked by hunting dogs.

mink: The American Mink (*Vison vison*) is found in the eastern half of the state, always near streams, lakes, or other water sources. Although it is an economically important fur-bearing animal in the eastern United States, it ranked only 13th in both numbers and economic value to trappers in Texas in 2001–2002 trapping season.

mole: The Eastern Mole (*Scalopus aquaticus*) is found in the eastern two-thirds of Texas. Moles cannot see and spend most of their life in underground burrows they excavate for themselves or usurp from other mammals, such as pocket gophers. The burrowing of moles can damage lawns, row crops, and the greens of golf courses. Benefits, however, are aerating soil and eating larval insects that destroy roots of grass and crops.

muskrat: The Common Muskrat (*Ondatra zibethicus*) occurs in aquatic habitats in the northern and southeastern parts of the state as well as along the Pecos River in West Texas. Although the muskrat was once economically valuable for its fur, its numbers have declined, mostly because of the loss of habitat.

nutria: The Nutria* (*Myocastor coypus*) is an introduced species of rodent originally native to South America. It is found primarily in the eastern two-thirds of the state, but they have expanded their range into the Big Bend region. The fur is not highly valued and, because Nutrias are in competition with muskrats, their spread is discouraged. They have been used widely in Texas as a cure-all for ponds choked with vegetation, with spotty results.

opossum: A marsupial, the Virginia Opossum (*Didelphis virginiana*) is found in nearly all parts of the state. The opossum has economic value for its pelt, and its meat is considered a delicacy by some.

otter: Northern River Otters (*Lontra canadensis*) are found in the eastern third of the state. This species has probably been extirpated from the Panhandle and some north-central locations but over the past 20 years, it has been expanding its range back into remaining suitable habitat in East and South Texas.

peccary: see javelina

pig: see hog

porcupine: The North American Porcupine (*Erethizon dorsatum*) is found from the western half of the state east to Bosque County. It is adapted to a variety of habitats and, in recent years, has expanded into South Texas. Porcupines are expert at climbing trees but are as much at home in rocks as on the ground or in trees. They have a relatively long lifespan; one marked female lived more than 10 years under natural conditions.

prairie dog: Until recent years, probably no sight was so universal in West Texas as the Black-tailed Prairie Dog (*Cynomys ludovicianus*). Naturalists estimated its population in the hundreds of millions, and prairie dog towns often covered many acres with thickly spaced burrows. However, this species has been replaced by livestock and cultivated crops across most of its range, a loss of over 98% of the original population in the state. It is being propagated in several public zoos, notably in the prairie dog town in Mackenzie Park at Lubbock. It has been honored in Texas by the naming of the Prairie Dog Town Fork of the Red River, in one segment of which is located the beautiful Palo Duro Canyon.

pronghorn: The Pronghorn (*Antilocapra americana*) formerly was found in the western two-thirds of the state. It is currently found only in limited areas from the Panhandle to the Trans-Pecos. Despite management efforts, its numbers have been decreasing in recent years.

rabbit: The Black-tailed Jackrabbit (*Lepus californicus*) is found throughout Texas except the Big Thicket area of East Texas. It breeds rapidly, and its long hind legs make it one of the world's faster-running animals. The Eastern Cottontail (*Sylvilagus floridanus*) is found mostly in the eastern three-quarters of the state. The Desert Cottontail (*Sylvilagus audubonii*) is found in the western half of the state, usually on the open range. The Swamp Rabbit (*Sylvilagus aquaticus*) is found in East Texas and the coastal area. The Davis Mountains Cottontail (*Sylvilagus robustus*) is restricted to Jeff Davis County.

raccoon: The Northern Raccoon (*Procyon lotor*) is found throughout Texas, especially in woodlands and near water. It is strictly nocturnal. A raccoon makes its den in a large hollow tree or hollow log, in which it spends the daylight hours sleeping and in which it also rears its young. In western areas, dens usually are in crevices of rocky bluffs.

rats, mice, and voles: There are 40 to 50 species of rats, mice, and voles in Texas of varying characteristics, habitats, and economic destructiveness. The Norway Rat* (*Rattus norvegicus*) and the Roof Rat* (*Rattus rattus*), both non-native species, are probably the most common and most destructive. They also are instrumental in the transmission of several dread diseases, including bubonic plague and typhus. Populations of the Common House Mouse* (*Mus musculus*) are estimated in the hundreds of millions annually. The Mogollon Vole (*Microtus mogolollonensis*) is found only in the higher elevations of Guadalupe Mountains National Park. With its long tail tipped with a white tuft of fur, the state-threatened Texas Kangaroo Rat (*Dipodomys elator*) is restricted to less than a dozen Texas counties near the Red River.

ringtail: The Ringtail (*Bassariscus astutus*) is a cat-sized carnivore resembling a small fox with a long raccoon-like tail. It found statewide but is rare in the extreme South Texas and the Panhandle. Ringtails are nocturnal and live in a variety of habitats, preferring rocky areas, such as rock piles, stone fences, and canyon walls.

sheep: The Mountain or Bighorn Sheep (*Ovis canadensis*), formerly was found in isolated areas of the mountainous Trans-Pecos, but the last native sheep were seen in 1959. Recently, they have been introduced into the same areas with success. The Barbary Sheep* (*Ammotragus lervia*), also called Aoudad, were first introduced to the Palo Duro Canyon area in 1957–1958 and have become firmly established. A multi-partner wildlife restoration project has brought the Bighorn Sheep into the Edwards Plateau, Trans-Pecos, South Texas, Rolling Plains, and Post Oak Savannah regions, including Big Bend Ranch State Park.

shrew: The shrew is one of the smallest mammals. Four species are found in Texas: the Southern Short-tailed Shrew (*Blarina carolinensis*), found in the eastern fourth of the state; the Least Shrew (*Cryptotis parva*), in all but western areas; Elliot's Short-tailed Shrew (*Blarina hylophaga*), known to live in Aransas, Montague, and Bastrop counties; and the Desert Shrew (*Notiosorex crawfordi*), found in the western two-thirds of the state.

skunk: There are five species of skunk in Texas. The Eastern Spotted Skunk (*Spilogale putorius*) is found in the eastern half of the state, the Gulf Coast, and across north-central Texas to the Panhandle. A small skunk, it is often erroneously called civet cat. The Western Spotted Skunk (*Spilogale gracilis*) is found in the southwestern part of the state North to Garza and Howard counties and East to Bexar and Duval counties. The Striped Skunk (*Mephitis mephitis*) is found statewide, mostly in brush or wooded areas. The Hooded Skunk (*Mephitis macroura*) was found in limited numbers in the Big Bend and adjacent parts of the Trans-Pecos but may be extirpated from the state. The Hog-nosed Skunk (*Conepatus leuconotus*) is found in across the western, central, and southern portion of the state, as well as the upper Gulf Coast.

squirrel: The Eastern Fox Squirrel (*Sciurus niger*) is found in the eastern two-thirds of the state. The Eastern Gray Squirrel (*Sciurus carolinensis*) is found generally in the eastern third of the state. The Southern Flying Squirrel (*Glaucomys volans*) is found in wooded areas of East Texas. The fox and gray squirrels are important small game animals. See also ground squirrel.

weasel: The Long-tailed Weasel (*Mustela frenata*), akin to the mink, is found statewide but is scarce in West Texas and the far North Panhandle. In general, their predation on mice, ground squirrels, and pocket gophers benefits agricultural interests, though they are known to enter poultry houses and kill chickens.

whale: Some species that are found in the Gulf of Mexico include: Dwarf Sperm Whale (*Kogia sima*); Pygmy Sperm Whale (*Kogia breviceps*), found near the Texas coast where strandings occur relatively frequently; Short-finned Pilot Whale (*Globicephala macrorhynchus*), common in the gulf, where there are numerous strandings and sightings; Sperm Whale (*Physeter macrocephalus*), an endangered species and the most numerous and frequently sighted of the great whales in the gulf. Other species are known in Texas only through strandings on gulf beaches.

wolf: The Red Wolf (*Canis rufus*) was once found throughout the eastern half of the state. It has now been extirpated from the wild, with the only known remnants of the population now in captive propagation. The Gray Wolf (*Canis lupus*) once had a wide range over the western two-thirds of the state. It is now considered extinct in Texas. Both species of wolf are on the federal and state endangered species lists. ☆

*A herd of Pronghorn (*Antilocapra americana*) moving across a plain. Photo by Jill D. Miller*

Texas' Threatened and Endangered Species

Endangered species are those the TPWD has named as being at risk of statewide extinction. Threatened species are likely to become endangered in the future. The following lists include species that are listed by TPWD as either threatened or endangered as of March 2020 (the most recent list available). The species on these lists vary from those on the federal list of threatened and endangered species managed by the United States Fish and Wildlife Service. Learn more and see the TPWD Conservation Action Plan at: https://tpwd.texas.gov/landwater/land/tcap/.

Threatened Species

Plants: Cacti: Bunched Cory Cactus, Chisos Mountains Hedgehog Cactus, Lloyd's Mariposa Cactus; Grasses: Dune Umbrella-sedge, Small-headed Pipewort; Trees, Shrubs, Sub-shrubs: Gypsum Scalebroom, Hinckley's Oak; Quillworts: Rock Quillwort; Wildflowers: Brush-pea, Earth Fruit, Houston Daisy, Leoncita False Foxglove, Livermore Sweet-cicely, Neches River Rose-mallow, Pecos Sunflower

Invertebrates: Bivalves: Brazos Heelsplitter, False Spike, Guadalupe Fatmucket, Guadalupe Orb, Louisiana Pigtoe, Mexican Fawnsfoot, Salina Mucket, Sandbank Pocketbook, Southern Hickorynut, Texas Fatmucket, Texas Fawnsfoot, Texas Heelsplitter, Texas Pigtoe, Texas Pimpleback, Trinity Pigtoe; Crustaceans: Clear Creek Amphipod, Texas Troglobitic Water Slater; Snails: Carolinae Tryonia, Caroline's Springs Pyrg, Crowned Cave Snail, Limpia Creek Springsnail, Metcalf's Tryonia, Presidio County Springsnail

Fishes: Catfish: Headwater Catfish, Toothless Blindcat, Widemouth Blindcat; Coastal Fishes: Mexican Goby, Opossum Pipefish, River Goby; Large River Fish: Paddlefish, Shovelnose Sturgeon; Livebearers: Blotched Gambusia, San Felipe Gambusia; Minnows: Arkansas River Shiner, Bluehead Shiner, Bluntnose Shiner, Chihuahua Shiner, Chub Shiner, Devils River Minnow, Medina Roundnose Minnow, Mexican Stoneroller, Nueces Roundnose Minnow, Peppered Chub, Plateau Shiner, Prairie Chub, Proserpine Shiner, Rio Grande Chub, Rio Grande Shiner, Roundnose Minnow, Speckled Chub, Tamaulipas Shiner; Perches: Blackside Darter, Guadalupe Darter, Rio Grande Darter; Pupfish: Conchos Pupfish, Pecos Pupfish, Red River Pupfish; Sharks: Great Hammerhead, Oceanic Whitetip, Shortfin Mako; Suckers: Blue Sucker, Creek Chubsucker

Amphibians: Mexican Burrowing Toad, Mexican Treefrog, Mexican White-Lipped Frog, Sheep Frog; Black-Spotted Newt, Blanco Blind Salamander, Cascade Caverns Salamander, Comal Blind Salamander, Georgetown Salamander, Jollyville Plateau Salamander, Salado Springs Salamander, San Marcos Salamander, South Texas Siren (*Large Form*), Texas Salamander

Reptiles: Lizards: Mountain Short-Horned Lizard, Texas Horned Lizard; Snakes: Black-Striped Snake, Brazos Watersnake, Louisiana Pine Snake, Northern Cat-Eyed Snake, Northern Scarlet Snake, Speckled Racer, Texas Scarlet Snake, Trans-Pecos Black-Headed Snake; Turtles: Alligator Snapping Turtle, Cagle's Map Turtle, Chihuahuan Mud Turtle, Green Sea Turtle, Loggerhead Sea Turtle, Texas Tortoise

Birds: Parrots: Red-Crowned Parrot; Raptors: Cactus Ferruginous Pygmy-Owl, Common Black Hawk, Gray Hawk, Mexican Spotted Owl, Peregrine Falcon, Swallow-Tailed Kite, White-Tailed Hawk, Zone-Tailed Hawk; Shorebirds: Black Rail, Piping Plover, Rufa Red Knot, Sooty Tern; Songbirds: Arizona Botteri's Sparrow, Bachman's Sparrow, Northern Beardless-Tyrannulet, Rose-Throated Becard, Texas Botteri's Sparrow, Tropical Parula; Waterbirds: Reddish Egret, White-Faced Ibis, Wood Stork

Mammals: Bats: Rafinesque's Big-Eared Bat, Spotted Bat; Carnivores: American Black Bear, Louisiana Black Bear, White-Nosed Coati; Marine Mammals: Atlantic Spotted Dolphin, Dwarf Sperm Whale, False Killer Whale, Killer Whale, Gervais' Beaked Whale, Goose-beaked Whale, Pygmy Killer Whale, Pygmy Sperm Whale, Rough-toothed Dolphin, Short-finned Pilot Whale, West Indian Manatee; Rodents: Coues' Rice Rat, Palo Duro Mouse, Tawny-bellied Cotton Rat, Texas Kangaroo Rat

Endangered Species

Plants: Cacti: Black Lace Cactus, Davis' Green Pitaya, Nellie's Cory Cactus, Sneed's Pincushion Cactus, Star Cactus, Tobusch fishhook Cactus; Grasses: Guadalupe Fescue, Little Aguja Pondweed, Texas Wild Rice; Orchids: Navasota Ladies'-tresses; Trees, Shrubs, Sub-shrubs: Texas Ayenia, Texas Snowbells, Walker's Manioc; Wildflowers: Ashy Dogweed, Large-fruited Sand-verbena, Slender Rushpea, South Texas Ambrosia, Terlingua Creek Cat's-eye, Texas Golden Gladecress, Texas Poppy-mallow, Texas Prairie Dawn, Texas Trailing Phlox, White Bladderpod, Zapata Bladderpod

Invertebrates: Beetles: Comal Springs Dryopid Beetle, Comal Springs Riffle Beetle; Bivalves: Texas Hornshell; Crustaceans: Diminutive Amphipod, Peck's Cave Amphipod, Pecos Amphipod; Snails: Pecos Assiminea, Diamond Y Spring Snail, Phantom Cave Snail, Phantom Spring Snail, Gonzales Springsnail

Fishes: Catfish: Mexican Blindcat; Coastal Fishes: Smalltooth Sawfish; Livebearers: Big Bend Gambusia, Clear Creek Gambusia, Pecos Gambusia, San Marcos Gambusia; Minnows: Rio Grande Silvery Minnow, Sharpnose Shiner, Smalleye Shiner; Perches: Fountain Darter; Pupfish: Comanche Springs Pupfish, Leon Springs Pupfish

Amphibians: Houston Toad; Austin Blind Salamander, Barton Springs Salamander, Texas Blind Salamander

Reptiles: Turtles: Hawksbill Sea Turtle, Kemp's Ridley Sea Turtle, Leatherback Sea Turtle

Birds: Raptors: Northern Aplomado Falcon; Shorebirds: Eskimo Curlew, Interior Least Tern; Songbirds: Golden-Cheeked Warbler, Southwestern Willow Flycatcher; Upland Birds: Attwater's Greater Prairie Chicken; Waterbirds: Whooping Crane; Woodpeckers: Red-Cockaded Woodpecker

Mammals: Bats: Mexican Long-nosed Bat; Carnivores: Jaguar, Jaguarundi, Ocelot, Gray Wolf, Red Wolf; Marine Mammals: Blue Whale, Finback Whale, Gulf of Mexico Bryde's Whale, North Atlantic Right Whale, Sei Whale, Sperm Whale ☆

Texas Wildlife Management Areas

Source: Texas Parks and Wildlife Department; http://tpwd.texas.gov/huntwild/hunt/wma/

Texas Parks and Wildlife Department is responsible for managing 47 wildlife management areas (WMAs) in the state totaling more than 710,000 acres. Every vegetational area in the state has at least one WMA, with the exception of the Cross Timbers and Prairies area, in north central Texas. (See page 69 for more information about the Vegetational Areas of Texas.)

Wildlife management areas are used principally for hunting, but many are also used for research, fishing, wildlife viewing, hiking, camping, bicycling, and horseback riding, when those activities are compatible with the primary goals for which the WMA was established. See the table below for activities available in Texas' WMAs.

Access to WMAs at times designated for public use is provided through various permits, depending on the activity.

A Limited Public Use Permit ($12) allows access for such activities as birdwatching, hiking, camping, or picnicking.

On most WMAs, restrooms and drinking water are not provided, but **check with the TPWD about facilities before visiting a WMA**.

For further information, contact the Texas Parks and Wildlife Department, 4200 Smith School Rd., Austin 78744; or call 1-800-792-1112 and choose menu #5, selection #1. ☆

Texas Wildlife Management Areas

Name (Acreage)	County	Hunting	Fishing	Camping	Wildlife Viewing	Hiking	Driving	Bicycling	Equestrian	Comments
Alabama Creek (14,561)	Trinity	★	★	★	★	★	★	★	★	In Davy Crockett NF
Alazan Bayou (2,063)	Nacogdoches	★	★	★	★				★	
Angelina-Neches/Dam B (12,636)	Jasper/Tyler	★	★	★	★	★		★		
Atkinson Island (150)	Harris		★		★					Boat access only
Bannister (25,695)	San Augustine	★	★	★	★	★		★	★	In Angelina NF
Big Lake Bottom (3,894)	Anderson	★	★		★					
Black Gap (103,000)	Brewster	★	★	★	★	★	★	★	★	NW of Big Bend NP
Caddo Lake (8,124)	Marion/Harrison	★	★	★	★				★	
Caddo Nat. Grasslands (16,140)	Fannin	★	★	★	★	★		★	★	Separated into two units
Candy Cain Abshier (207)	Chambers				★					Excellent birding spring and fall
Cedar Creek Islands (160)	Henderson		★		★					Wildlife viewing from boat or bank of reservoir only
Chaparral (15,200)	La Salle/Dimmit	★		★	★	★	★	★		
Cooper (14,480)	Delta/Hopkins	★	★		★	★		★		Camping: Cooper Lake SP
D.R. Wintermann (246)	Wharton				★					Restricted access; bird refuge
East Texas Conservation Center (223)	Jasper									By appointment only
Elephant Mountain (23,147)	Brewster	★		★	★	★	★			
Gene Howe (5,886)	Hemphill	★	★	★	★	★		★	★	Riding March–August only
Gene Howe: W.A. "Pat" Murphy (889)	Hemphill	★	★		★	★				
Guadalupe Delta (7,411)	Calhoun/Refugio	★	★		★	★		★		Freshwater marsh
Gus Engeling (10,958)	Anderson	★	★	★	★	★	★	★	★	
J.D. Murphree (24,498)	Jefferson	★	★		★					Access by boat only
James E. Daughtrey (34,000)	Live Oak/McMullen	★			★					Primitive camping requires special permit
Justin Hurst (15,612)	Brazoria	★	★		★	★		★		On Texas Coastal Birding Trail
Keechi Creek (1,500)	Leon	★								
Kerr (6,493)	Kerr	★	★		★		★	★		On Guadalupe River
Las Palomas: Anacua (222)	Cameron	★			★					
Las Palomas: Lower Rio Grande Valley (3,311)	Cameron/Hidalgo	★			★	★				Also Presidio County
Lower Neches (7,998)	Orange	★	★		★	★				Coastal marsh
M.O. Neasloney (100)	Gonzales				★	★				Primarily for school groups
Mad Island (7,200)	Matagorda	★			★					Reservations needed for wildlife tours
Mason Mountain (5,300)	Mason	★								Restricted access
Matador (28,183)	Cottle	★	★	★	★	★	★		★	Primitive camping; tours
Matagorda Island (56,688)	Calhoun	★	★	★	★	★		★		
Moore Plantation (26,772)	Sabine/Jasper	★	★	★	★	★		★	★	In Sabine National Forest
Muse (1,972)	Brown	★			★					
Nannie M. Stringfellow (3,666)	Brazoria	★			★					Open for special hunts only

National Wildlife Refuges in Texas

Source: U.S. Fish and Wildlife Service, U.S. Department of the Interior.

Texas has more than 470,000 acres in 17 national wildlife refuges. Their descriptions, with date of acquisition in parentheses, follow.

Included in this acreage are two conservation easement refuges, which may be visited at different times of the year for bird watching and wildlife viewing, as well as hunting and fishing. Write or call before visiting to check on facilities and days and hours of operation. On the web: **www.fws.gov/southwest/**.

Anahuac (1963): The more than 37,000 acres of this refuge are located along the upper Gulf Coast in Chambers County. Fresh and saltwater marshes and miles of beautiful, sweeping coastal prairie provide wintering habitat for large flocks of waterfowl, including geese, 27 species of ducks, and six species of rails. Roseate spoonbills, great and snowy egrets, and white-faced ibis are among the other birds frequenting the refuge. Other species include alligator, muskrat, and bobcat. Fishing, bird watching, auto tours, and hunting are available. Office: Box 278, Anahuac 77514; (409) 267-3337.

Aransas (1937): This refuge complex comprises 115,000 acres including Blackjack Peninsula, Matagorda Island, and three satellite units in Aransas and Refugio counties. Besides providing wintering grounds for the largest wild flock of endangered whooping cranes, the refuge is home to more than 390 species of waterfowl and other migratory birds. Refuge Tour Loop is open daily, sunrise to sunset. Claude F. Lard Visitor Center is open daily, 6:45 a.m. to 7:30 p.m. Other facilities include a 40-foot observation tower and walking trails. Office: Box 100, Austwell 77950; (361) 349-1181.

Attwater Prairie Chicken (1972): Established in Colorado County to preserve habitat for the endangered Attwater's prairie chicken (a ground-dwelling grouse), the refuge comprises 10,528 acres of native tallgrass prairie, sandy knolls, and wooded areas. A 5-mile auto tour loop is available year-round. There are two hiking trails — the Sycamore and the Pipit trails — that traverse the prairie, potholes, and riparian areas. The auto tour loop can also serve as a hiking trail. Refuge open sunrise to sunset. Office: Box 519, Eagle Lake 77434; (979) 234-3021.

Balcones Canyonlands (1992): This 25,000-acre refuge is located in Burnet, Travis, and Williamson counties northwest of Austin. It was established to protect the nesting habitat of two endangered birds: black-capped vireo and golden-cheeked warbler. The Shin Oak Observation Deck is open almost year around (excluding a few weekends in the fall). Hunting available. Open Monday–Friday, 8:00 a.m.–4:30 p.m Office: 24518 FM-1431, Marble Falls, 78654; (512) 339-9432.

Big Boggy (1983): This refuge occupies 5,000 acres of coastal prairie and salt marsh along East Matagorda Bay for the benefit of wintering waterfowl. The refuge is only open to waterfowl hunting in season. Office: 6801 County Road 306, Brazoria, 77422; (979) 964-4011.

Brazoria (1966): The 43,388 acres of this refuge, located along the Gulf Coast in Brazoria County, serve as haven for wintering waterfowl and a wide variety of other migratory birds. The refuge also supports many marsh and water birds, from

Texas Wildlife Management Areas

Name (Acreage)	County	Hunting	Fishing	Camping	Wildlife Viewing	Hiking	Driving	Bicycling	Equestrian	Comments
Nature Center (82)	Smith				★	★				Primarily for school groups
North Toldeo Bend (3,650)	Shelby	★	★	★	★	★			★	
Old Sabine Bottom (5,158)	Smith	★	★	★	★	★		★	★	
Pat Mayse (8,925)	Lamar	★	★	★	★	★			★	
Playa Lakes: Armstrong (160)	Castro				★					Registration req., must stay on the roads
Playa Lakes: Dimmitt (422)	Cottle	★								Limited access
Playa Lakes: Taylor Lakes (530)	Donley	★			★	★				
Powderhorn (15,069)	Calhoun	★			★					Birding tours in Spring
Redhead Pond (37)	Nueces				★					Freshwater wetland; part of Great Texas Birding Trail
Richland Creek (13,783)	Freestone/Navarro	★	★	★	★	★		★	★	
Roger R. Fawcett (5,459)	Palo Pinto	★	★							Restricted access
Sam Houston National Forest (161,508)	San Jacinto/Walker	★	★	★	★	★	★	★	★	Also Montgomery County
Sierra Diablo (11,624)	Hudspeth/ Culberson	★								Restricted access
Tawakoni (2,335)	Hunt/Van Zandt	★	★	★	★	★			★	Primitive camping
Tony Houseman (3,985)	Orange	★	★	★	★	★				Canoeing
Welder Flats (1,480)	Calhoun		★		★					Boat access only
White Oak Creek (25,777)	Bowie/Cass/Morris/ Titus	★	★		★	★			★	Camp in Atlanta and Daingerfield SPs
Yoakum Dunes (14,037)	Cochran/Terry/ Yoakum	*In development, not yet open to the public. Commissioned and authorized in 2014, this site will preserve the breeding and nesting habitats of the lesser prairie-chicken, as well as many other native wildlife, including quail, mule deer, and Texas horned lizards.*								

roseate spoonbills and great blue herons to white-faced ibis and sandhill cranes. Brazoria Refuge is within the Freeport Christmas Bird Count circle, which frequently achieves the highest number of species seen in a 24-hour period. Open daily sunrise to sunset. Hunting and fishing also available. Office: 24907 FM 2004, Angleton, 77515; (979) 922-1037.

Buffalo Lake (1958): Comprising 7,664 acres in the Central Flyway in Randall County in the Panhandle, this refuge contains some of the best remaining shortgrass prairie in the United States. Buffalo Lake is now dry; a marsh area is artificially maintained for the numerous birds, reptiles, and mammals. Available activities include picnicking, auto tour, birding, photography, and hiking. Office: Box 179, Umbarger 79091; (806) 499-3382.

Caddo Lake (2000): Established on portions of the 8,5000-acre Longhorn Army Ammunition Plant in Harrison County, this refuge contains a mature flooded bald cypress forest, with some trees nearly 400 years old. The wetlands support a diverse plant community. The bottomland hardwood forest ecosystem provides essential habitat for migratory and resident wildlife. The wetlands of Caddo Lake are important to migratory birds within the Central Flyway. The area supports one of the highest breeding populations of wood ducks and prothonotary warblers. Bird watching, hunting, equestrian use, auto tour, hiking, and biking are available. Office: (903) 679-9144.

Hagerman (1946): Hagerman National Wildlife Refuge lies on the Big Mineral arm of Lake Texoma in Grayson County. The 4,500 acres of marsh and water and 6,900 acres of upland and farmland provide a feeding and resting place for migrating waterfowl. Bird watching, fishing, and hunting are available. Office: 6465 Refuge Road, Sherman, 75092-5817; (903) 786-2826.

Laguna Atascosa: (1946): This refuge is the southernmost waterfowl refuge in the Central Flyway and contains more than 45,000 acres fronting on the Laguna Madre in the Lower Rio Grande Valley in Cameron and Willacy counties. Open lagoons, coastal prairies, salt flats, and brushlands support a wide diversity of wildlife. The United States' largest concentration of redhead ducks winters here, along with many other species of waterfowl and shorebirds. White-tailed deer, javelina, and armadillo can be found, along with endangered ocelot. Bird watching and nature study are popular; auto-tour roads and nature trails are available. Camping and fishing are permitted within Adolph Thomae Jr. County Park. Hunting also available. Office: 22817 Ocelot Road, Los Fresnos, 78566; (956) 748-3607.

Lower Rio Grande Valley (1979): Part of the 180,000 acre South Texas Refuge Complex, this refuge lies within Cameron, Hidalgo, Starr, and Willacy counties. It comprises more than 100 separate tracts of land, some fallow farm fields connecting healthy habitat that can become travel corridors for wildlife. The refuge includes 11 different habitat types, including sabal palm forest, tidal flats, coastal brushland, mid-delta thorn forest, woodland potholes and basins, upland thorn scrub, flood forest, barretal, riparian woodland, and Chihuahuan thorn forest. Nearly 500 species of birds and over 300 butterfly species have been found there, as well as four of the five cats that occur within the United States: jaguarundi, ocelot, bobcat, and mountain lion. Seasonal hunting and canoe tours are available. Office: 3325 Green Jay Road, Alamo, 78516; (956) 784-7500.

McFaddin (1980): This refuge's 55,000 acres in Jefferson and Chambers counties are of great importance to wintering populations of migratory waterfowl. One of the densest populations of alligators in Texas is found here. Activities on the refuge include wildlife observation, hunting, fishing, and crabbing. Seven boat ramps provide access to inland lakes and waterways; limited roadways. Open daily from sunrise until sunset. Office: Box 358, Sabine Pass, 77655; (409) 971-2909.

Muleshoe (1935): Oldest of the national refuges in Texas, Muleshoe provides winter habitat for waterfowl and the continent's largest wintering population of sandhill cranes. Comprising 5,809 acres in the High Plains of Bailey County, the refuge contains playa lakes, marsh areas, caliche outcroppings, and native grasslands. A nature trail, campground, and picnic area are available. Office: Box 549, Muleshoe 79347; (806) 946-3341.

Neches River (2013): Anderson and Cherokee counties.It was established to protect wintering and nesting habitat for migratory birds of the Central Flyway and the bottomland hardwoods for their diverse biological value. Office: 262 West Highway 79, Jacksonville 75766; (956) 245-9426.

San Bernard (1968): Located in Brazoria and Matagorda counties on the Gulf Coast near Freeport, this refuge's 27,414 acres attract migrating waterfowl, including thousands of white-fronted and Canada geese and several duck species, which spend the winter on the refuge. Habitats, consisting of coastal prairies, salt-mud flats, and saltwater and freshwater ponds and potholes, also attract yellow rails, roseate spoonbills, reddish egrets, and American bitterns. Visitors enjoy auto and hiking trails, photography, bird watching, fishing, and waterfowl hunting in season. Office: 6801 County Road 306, Brazoria, 77422; (979) 964-4011.

Santa Ana (1943): Santa Ana is located on the north bank of the Rio Grande in Hidalgo County. Santa Ana's 2,088 acres of subtropical forest and native brushland are at an ecological crossroads of subtropical, Gulf Coast, Great Plains, and Chihuahuan desert habitats. Santa Ana attracts birders from across the United States who can view many species of Mexican birds as they reach the northern edge of their ranges in South Texas. Also found at Santa Ana are ocelot and jaguarundi, endangered members of the cat family. Visitors enjoy a tram or auto drive, bicycling and hiking trails, and a tower overlook. Office: 3325 Green Jay Road, Alamo, 78516; (956) 784-7500.

Texas Point (1980): Texas Point's 8,900 acres are located in Jefferson County on the upper Gulf Coast, 12 miles east of McFaddin NWR, where they serve a large wintering population of waterfowl and migratory birds. The endangered southern bald eagle and peregrine falcon may occasionally be seen during peak fall and spring migrations. Alligators are commonly observed during the spring, summer, and fall months. Activities include wildlife observation, hunting, fishing, and crabbing. Access to the refuge is by boat and on foot only. Open daily from sunrise until sunset. Office: Box 358, Sabine Pass, 77655; (409) 971-2909.

Trinity River (1994): Established to protect remnant bottomland hardwood forests and associated wetlands, this refuge, located in northern Liberty County off State Highway 787 about 15 miles east of Cleveland, provides habitat for wintering, migrating, and breeding waterfowl and a variety of other wetland-dependent wildlife. A tract south of Liberty includes Champion Lake. Office: Box 10015, Liberty 77575; (936) 336-9786. ☆

Weather

HIGHLIGHTS & SUMMARIES, 2029 & 2020

TEMPERATURES, PRECIPITATION

TORNADOS, DROUGHTS

DESTRUCTIVE WEATHER

RECORDS BY COUNTY

A thunderstorm rolls over the Lubbock/Shallowater skyline April 2016 in Hockley County. Photo by Ashley K. Saed/www.livingtreedesignsphoto.com.

Weather

All temperatures are given in Fahrenheit. CDT stands for "Central Daylight Time."

Sources: Unless otherwise noted, this information is provided by Texas State Climatologist John W. Nielsen-Gammon and graduate research assistants Christopher Larson and Hayden Dove at Texas A&M University. Monthly summaries are supplemented by the National Centers for Environmental Information, State of the Climate: National Climate Report.

Weather Highlights 2019

March 12–13, 2019: An intense, slow-moving storm system brought showers and thunderstorms into western Texas. As moisture content improved, the storms organized into an intense line of thunderstorms. These storms produced gusty winds; some became severe and produced a brief EF-1 tornado near Anton. Widespread rain totals ranged from 0.75 to 1.25 inches, with some areas receiving almost 1.5 inches. The storms produced straight-line winds up to 72 mph. Near O'Donnell, the wind damaged large buildings, flipped a semitruck, and knocked over trees and power lines.

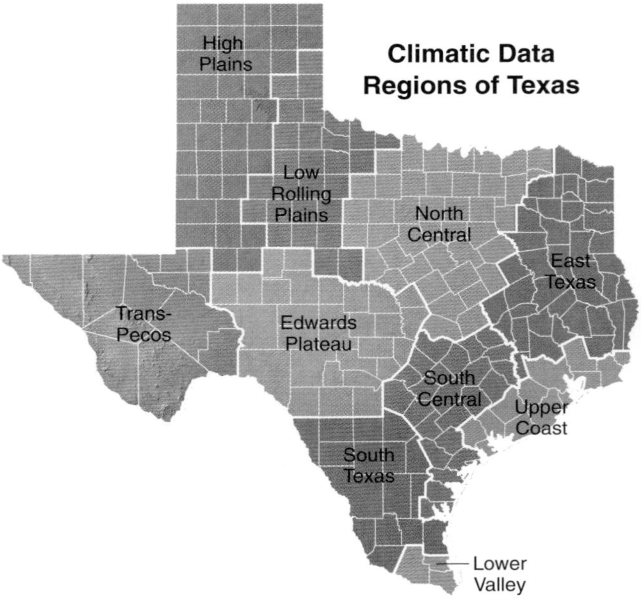

March 22, 2019: A strong upper-level low moved across the Four Corners region, gradually shifting from east to northeast throughout the day. Mid-level lift and convergence along a weak moisture gradient supported the development of thunderstorms. Hail from the sizes of quarters to baseballs was reported. Two tornadoes were confirmed, one near Wilco and one near Cactus.

March 24, 2019: The storm system explained above continued moving across the southern Plains, bringing large hail to the Dallas area. Grapefruit-size hail was reported near McKinney.

April 7, 2019: In April, an unusually severe storm system brought gusty winds and three reported tornadoes to the coastal regions of Texas. Baseball-size hail was reported near Grapeland. An EF-1 tornado touched down in Pasadena, causing moderate damage to power lines and ripping the back wall off a vacant business. Strong winds up to 70 mph also caused considerable damage around Houston. Downed power lines caused more than 175,000 homes to lose power.

April 17, 2019: A cold front came through the Texas Panhandle and stalled as a low-pressure system moved into the area from New Mexico. These two components enhanced the already high instability in the region. Severe storms soon developed, producing one to two inches of hail and

Average Temperatures 2019

	High Plains	Low Plains	North Central	East Texas	Trans-Pecos	Edwards Plateau	South Central	Upper Coast	South Texas	Lower Valley
Jan.	40.4	43.6	45.3	47.4	46.5	48.4	52.6	53.7	55.1	60.1
Feb.	42.4	46.4	50.1	53.1	52	53.5	58.1	59.8	61	65.3
Mar.	47.5	50.8	53.7	56.2	56.5	56.7	61.2	62.1	65.1	67.6
April	59.3	62.9	64.2	64.6	65.4	65.9	68.5	68.6	70.8	73.5
May	64.7	69.1	72.1	74.4	71.6	72.6	77.4	78.1	80.3	82.9
June	74.5	77.4	78.3	78.7	78.8	79.1	82.4	82.4	85.8	86.5
July	80.4	83	82.7	81.7	82.4	82.5	84.6	84.2	86.7	86.7
Aug.	82.5	86.5	86.2	85	85.1	86.5	87.8	86.1	89.4	89.5
Sep.	76.9	81.3	83.3	82.1	78.6	82	84.7	83.7	85.2	84.6
Oct.	55.1	61	64.5	66.5	64.3	66.4	71.4	72.3	75	77.4
Nov.	45.5	48.8	52	53.5	53.6	53.9	58.4	59.8	61.3	66.1
Dec.	43.3	47.2	49.3	51.5	49	51.6	56.2	57.6	59.2	63.6
Ann.	59.4	63.2	65.1	66.2	65.3	66.6	70.3	70.7	72.9	75.3

Precipitation in Inches 2019

	High Plains	Low Plains	North Central	East Texas	Trans-Pecos	Edwards Plateau	South Central	Upper Coast	South Texas	Lower Valley
Jan.	0.14	0.44	1.79	4.69	0.23	0.64	2.42	4.29	0.81	1.22
Feb.	0.24	0.17	1.29	3.12	0.08	0.27	1.1	2.72	0.29	0.42
Mar.	1.45	1.4	1.81	2.08	0.46	0.88	0.53	0.75	0.68	2.42
April	1.78	4.41	5.93	6.56	1.07	3.32	4.10	2.67	1.95	1.13
May	4	5.71	8.05	9.87	1.23	4.16	4.69	7.60	2.81	1.52
June	2.46	3.18	5.21	7.42	1.94	4.22	4.7	9.35	2.45	7.26
July	1.71	1.04	0.99	2.02	1.36	0.85	1.08	2.15	0.61	1.09
Aug.	1.58	1.03	2.04	2.05	1	1	0.53	3.55	0.64	0.94
Sep.	2.53	2.69	0.92	3.46	2.18	0.71	1.63	11.06	1.97	3.65
Oct.	2.53	0.48	3.49	6.06	0.82	1.35	3.44	5.32	2.21	2.44
Nov.	1.23	2.16	2.20	1.22	1.11	0.95	1.41	1.84	0.81	1.81
Dec.	0.76	0.59	0.96	1.59	0.69	0.68	0.91	1.13	0.71	0.65
Ann.	20.41	23.30	34.68	50.14	12.17	19.03	26.54	52.43	15.94	24.55

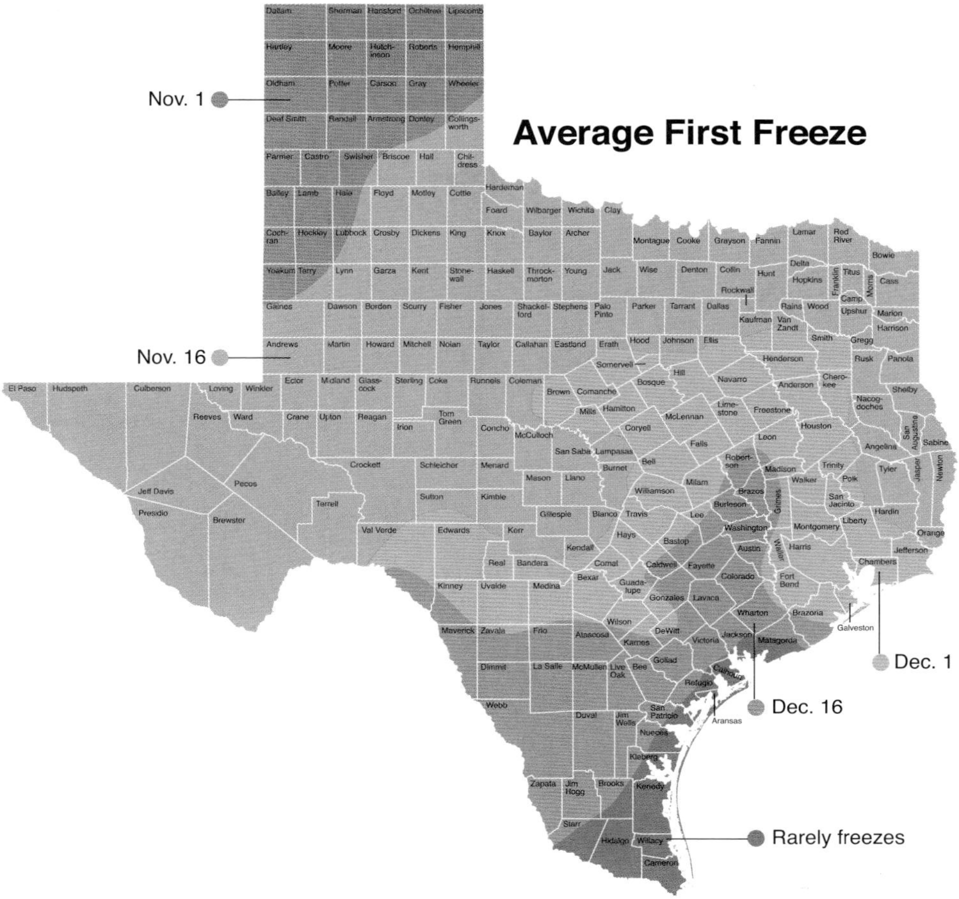

numerous small rope tornadoes, with four confirmed to have touched down.

April 24, 2019: Strong storms moved from central to southeast Texas, bringing locally heavy rain, hail up to 1.75 inches, and an EF-2 tornado to Bryan. The tornado damaged one house and four commercial buildings and warehouses, injuring one person inside the warehouse.

May 5, 2019: Persistent southwesterly flow aloft, upper-level disturbances, and plenty of moisture and instability east of a dryline passing through the Panhandle brought multiple rounds of severe weather to northwest Texas. May 5 was a particularly active day: an EF-2 tornado caused damage near Tahoka and was on the ground for 17 miles. There were no injuries or deaths, but high winds caused damage to several homes, buildings, trees, and power poles. Tennis ball-size hail was also reported with this storm. This same supercell also dropped torrential rain in Lynn County—as much as two inches—inundating some roads.

May 7, 2019: Moisture advected from the Gulf of Mexico and an upper-level low moved into the Four Corners region, bringing surface low pressure to New Mexico and severe weather conditions for the Panhandle. Hail up to the size of baseballs fell near Lake Meredith and Fritch. Wind shear increased throughout the afternoon, allowing the storms to drop seven tornadoes around the Panhandle, all rated EF-0, with the longest path being 11.6 miles. In southeast Texas, heavy rains battered the Houston area, with as much as ten inches of rainfall in some areas. In Sugar Land, more than seven inches of rain fell in four hours, causing major flash flooding in the city. Some children had to spend the night at their school as buses couldn't drive in the flooded roadways.

May 23, 2019: An upper-level low had set itself up over southern Nevada with a frontal boundary settled across the Panhandle. Significant wind shear and instability increased in magnitude as moisture was advected into the region. Severe thunderstorms quickly popped up in the Panhandle,

2019 Weather Extremes

Lowest Temp.: Lipscomb, Lipscomb Co., February 7	–1°
Highest Temp.: Rio Grande Village, Brewster Co., August 27	116°
24-Hour Precip.: Beaumont, Jefferson Co., September 19	19.80″
Monthly Precip.: Roman Forest, Montgomery Co., September	33.47″
Least Annual Precip.: El Paso, El Paso Co.	6.92″
Greatest Annual Precip.: Beaumont, Jefferson Co	93.67″

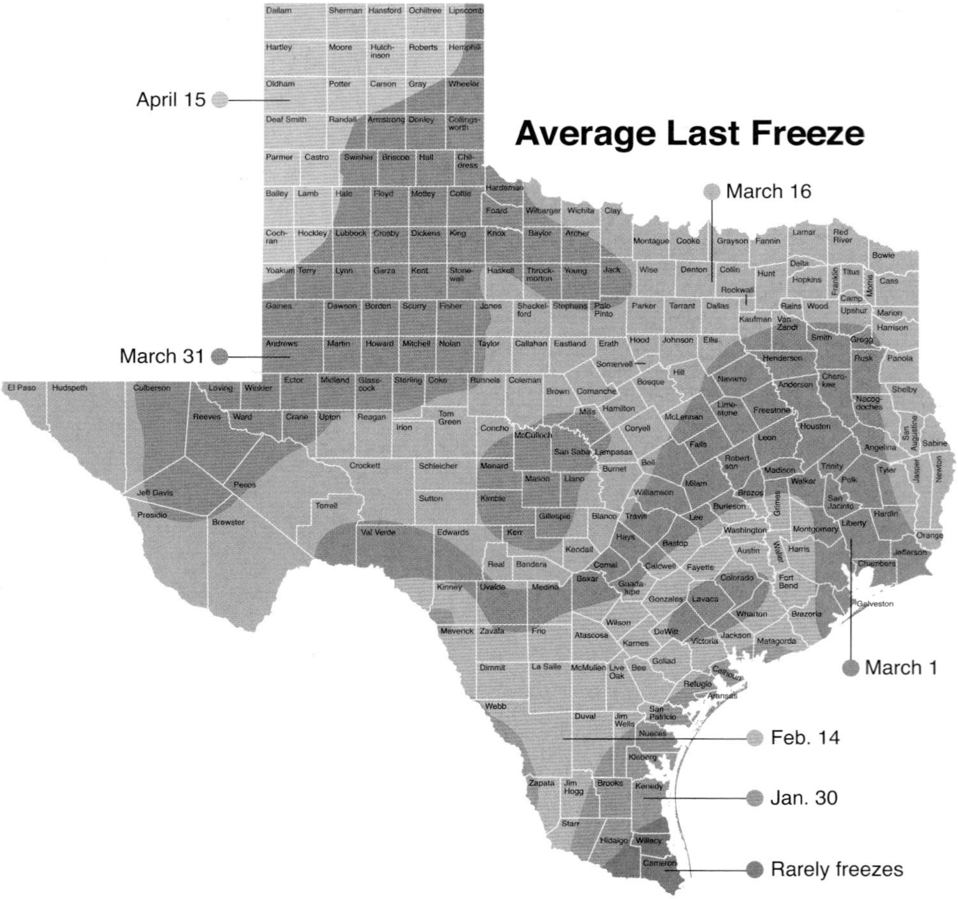

producing baseball-size hail and tornadoes. Two tornadoes were very large, reaching over a half-mile wide at some point, both in Lipscomb County. These were both rated EF-2. These tornadoes only destroyed a single home and damaged trees and power lines. Four more tornadoes were reported in the Panhandle, all EF-1 or less.

June 18, 2019: An upper-level disturbance and weak frontal boundary initiated storm development in the Texas Panhandle. This event produced hail larger than baseballs, strong winds, a few funnels, and an EF-0 tornado near Pampa.

June 24, 2019: A returning warm front brought strong instability to the Panhandle, fueling intense thunderstorms. Softball-size hail fell near Wilson and Slaton, strong winds blew over a wind turbine near Petersburg, and 2.08 inches of rain fell near Lubbock, causing street flooding.

Monthly Summaries 2019

Texas experienced mostly above-normal temperatures in **January.** Parts of southern and eastern Texas experienced temperatures two to four degrees below normal. Parts of western, southern, central, and eastern Texas experienced temperatures zero to two degrees below normal. Parts of western, southern, central, eastern, and northern Texas experienced temperatures two to four degrees above normal. Parts of northern and eastern Texas experienced temperatures four to six degrees above normal. The average temperature in Texas during January was 47 degrees. Parts of southwestern, western, northwestern, and northern Texas received 50 percent or less of normal precipitation. Far southern, eastern, and northeastern Texas received 150 percent or more of normal precipitation. Texas received 1.47 inches of precipitation in January.

Some parts of northern Texas experienced temperatures three to six degrees below normal in **February.** Other parts of northern Texas experienced temperatures zero to three degrees below normal. Western, central, and eastern Texas experienced temperatures three to six degrees above normal. The average temperature for February in Texas was 51.9 degrees. Parts of northern, western, southern, central, and eastern Texas received 50 percent or less of normal precipitation. Other parts of northern, central, southern, and western Texas received 25 percent or less of normal precipitation. Parts of northern and western Texas received five percent or less of normal precipitation. Texas received 0.88 inches of precipitation in February.

During **March,** parts of central, north-central, and western Texas experienced temperatures four to six degrees below normal. Parts of southern, central, western, eastern, and northern Texas experienced temperatures two to four degrees below normal. In extreme western Texas, there were temperatures zero to four degrees above normal. Texas

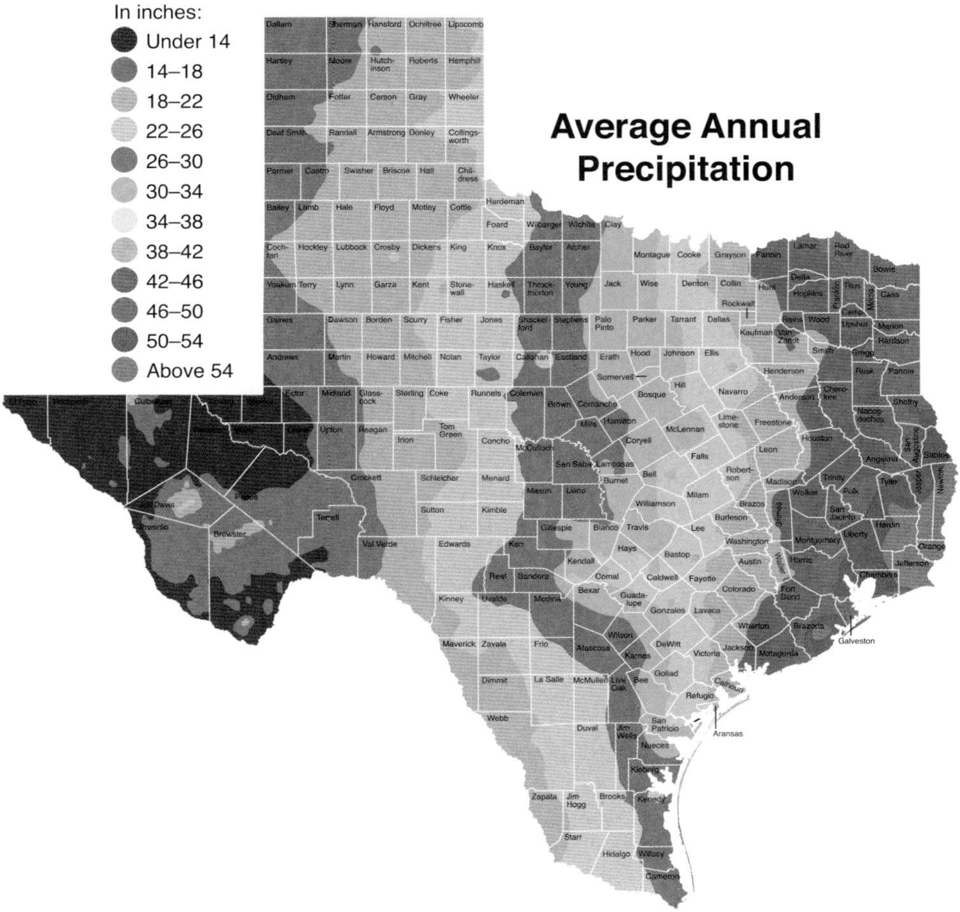

experienced an average temperature of 56 degrees. Eastern, central, southern, and western Texas received 50 percent or less of normal precipitation. Parts of south-central and extreme western Texas received five percent or less of normal precipitation. In northern, extreme western, and extreme southern Texas, 110 percent or more of normal precipitation fell. Texas received 1.13 inches of precipitation in March.

Parts of southern and eastern Texas experienced temperatures two to three degrees below normal in **April.** Parts of southern, eastern, and central Texas experienced temperatures one to two degrees below normal. Parts of western and northern Texas experienced temperatures one to two degrees above normal. Parts of far western Texas experienced temperatures two to three degrees above normal. The average temperature in Texas was 64.1 degrees. Far northern, far western, and southeastern Texas received 25 percent or less of normal precipitation. Parts of western, central, southern, northern, and eastern Texas received 150 percent or more of normal precipitation. Parts of western, central, northern, and eastern Texas received 200 percent or more of normal precipitation. Parts of western and central Texas received as much as 300 percent or more of normal precipitation. Texas received 3.52 inches of precipitation during April.

In **May,** parts of northern Texas experienced temperatures four to six degrees below normal. Parts of western and northern Texas experienced temperatures two to four degrees below normal. Parts of southern and eastern Texas experienced temperatures two to four degrees above normal. The average temperature experienced in Texas was 72.5 degrees. Parts of western and southern Texas received 50 percent or less of normal precipitation. Parts of southern and western Texas received 25 percent or less of normal precipitation. Parts of central, southern, northern, and eastern Texas received 150 percent or more of normal precipitation. Parts of central, northern, and eastern Texas received 200 percent or more of normal precipitation. Parts of eastern Texas received 300 percent or more of normal precipitation. Texas received 5.08 inches of precipitation in May.

Parts of northern, central, and southwestern Texas experienced temperatures two to three degrees below normal in **June.** Parts of northern, central, western, and eastern Texas experienced temperatures one to two degrees below normal. Parts of central, southern, and southeastern Texas experienced temperatures one to two degrees above normal. The average temperature in Texas was 78.9 degrees. Parts of western and southern Texas received 25 percent or less of normal precipitation. Parts of southwestern, southern, northern, and eastern Texas received 150 percent or more of normal precipitation. Parts of southwestern, southern, southeastern, and eastern Texas received 200 percent or more of

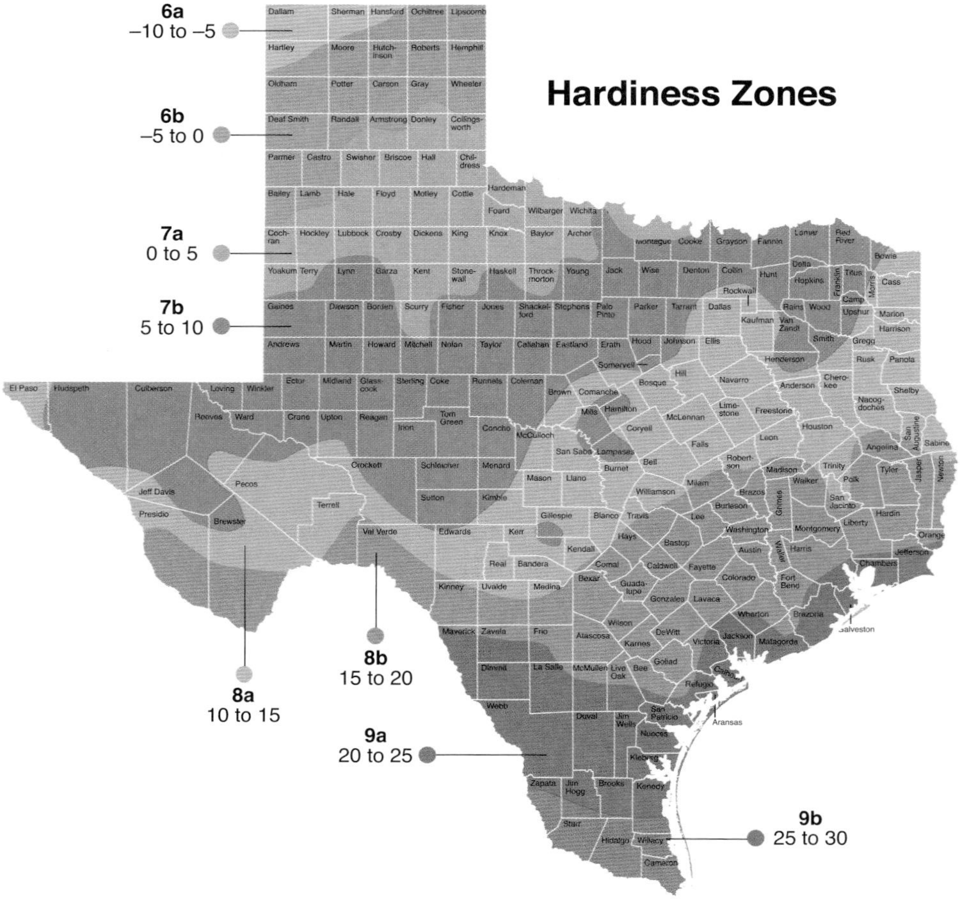

normal precipitation. Texas received 4.01 inches of precipitation during June.

In **July**, parts of north-central and eastern Texas experienced temperatures one to two degrees below normal, while some isolated parts experienced temperatures two to three degrees below normal. Parts of northern, western, southern, and southeastern Texas experienced temperatures one to two degrees above normal. Parts of southern and western Texas experienced temperatures two to three degrees above normal. Parts of far western Texas experienced temperatures three to five degrees above normal. Texas experienced an average of 82.8 degrees. Parts of central, eastern, southern, and western Texas received 50 percent or less of normal precipitation. Parts of central, western, southern, and eastern Texas received 25 percent or less of normal precipitation. Parts of southern and central Texas received five percent or less of normal precipitation. Texas received 1.27 inches of precipitation in July.

Most of Texas experienced temperatures two to four degrees above normal during **August.** Parts of northern and western Texas experienced temperatures four to six degrees above normal. Parts of far western Texas experienced temperatures six to eight degrees above normal. The average temperature in Texas during August was 86 degrees. Parts of northern, western, southern, central, and eastern Texas received 50 percent or less of normal precipitation. Parts of northern, western, and southern Texas received 25 percent or less of normal precipitation. Parts of southern and western Texas received five percent or less of normal precipitation. Parts of northeastern Texas received 150 percent or more of normal precipitation. Parts of northeastern Texas received 200 percent or more of normal precipitation. Texas received 1.35 inches of precipitation during August.

In **September,** Texas experienced above-normal temperatures, putting this month in the top-three warmest Septembers on record. Parts of southeastern, southern, and western Texas experienced temperatures four to six

2020 Weather Extremes

Lowest Temp.: Big Spring McMahon-Wrinkle Airport, Howard Co., February 6 . . . . 0°

Highest Temp.: Turkey, Hall Co., July 15 . . . . .117°

24-hour Precip.: Santa Rosa, Hidalgo Co., July 28 . . . . 15.49″

Monthly Precip.: Houston, Harris Co., September . . . . 15.89″

Least Annual Precip.: Kermit, Winkler Co. . . . . 3.65″

Greatest Annual Precip.: Douglasville, Cass Co. . . . . 74.16″

degrees above normal. Parts of northern, eastern, central, and southern Texas experienced temperatures six to eight degrees above normal. Parts of central, northern, and eastern Texas experienced temperatures eight to ten degrees above normal. The average temperature during September in Texas was 81.4 degrees. Parts of central, eastern, and northern Texas received 50 percent or less of normal precipitation. Parts of central, eastern, and southwestern Texas received 25 percent or less of normal precipitation. Parts of central and eastern Texas received five percent or less of normal precipitation. Parts of northern, western, and southeastern Texas received 150 percent or more of normal precipitation. Parts of southeastern Texas received 200 percent or more of normal precipitation. Parts of southeastern Texas received 300 percent or more of normal precipitation, due in part to Tropical Storm Imelda. Texas received 2.48 inches of precipitation in September.

Parts of northern Texas experienced temperatures zero to eight degrees below normal in **October.** Parts of southern Texas experienced temperatures two to four degrees above normal. The average temperature in Texas during this month was 65.6 degrees. Parts of northern, western, central, and southern Texas received 50 percent or less of normal precipitation. Parts of north-central, southern, and western Texas received 25 percent or less of normal precipitation. Parts of north-central and western Texas received 5 percent or less of normal precipitation. Parts of northern and eastern Texas received 150 percent or more of normal precipitation. Parts of northern Texas received 200 percent or more of normal precipitation. Other parts of northern Texas received 300 percent or more of normal precipitation. Texas received 2.56 inches of precipitation during October.

In **November,** parts of central, eastern, and southern Texas experienced temperatures four to six degrees below normal. Most of Texas experienced temperatures two to four degrees below normal. Parts of western Texas experienced temperatures zero to two degrees above normal. Texas experienced an average temperature of 53.2 degrees during this month. Parts of eastern, central, and southern Texas received 50 percent or less of normal precipitation. Other parts of eastern, central, and southern Texas received 25 percent or less of normal precipitation. Parts of north-central, western, and southern Texas received 150 percent or more of normal precipitation. Other parts of north-central, western, and southern Texas received 200 percent or more of normal precipitation. Texas received 1.33 inches of precipitation in November.

Parts of eastern, southern, and western Texas experienced temperatures zero to two degrees above normal during **December.** Parts of eastern, central, southern, western, and northern Texas experienced temperatures two to four degrees above normal. Parts of western, southwestern, central, eastern, and northern Texas experienced temperatures four to six degrees above normal. Parts of northern Texas experienced temperatures six to eight degrees above normal. The average temperature during this month in Texas was 50.6 degrees. Parts of eastern, northern, western, central, and southern Texas received 50 percent or less of normal precipitation. Parts of northern, eastern, western, and southern Texas received 25 percent or less of normal precipitation. Parts of western and southwestern Texas received five percent or less of normal precipitation. Parts of southern, western, and northern Texas received 150 percent or more of normal precipitation. Parts of southern and western Texas received 200 percent or more of normal precipitation. Texas received 0.85 inches of precipitation during December.

Weather Highlights 2020

April 11–14, 2020: Severe storms developed in the western Panhandle as a result of Gulf moisture, a dryline, and an upper-level disturbance. Hail as large as golf balls was reported near Aspermont. Aspermont also received 1.43 inches of rain on the 11th. A cold front then advected in from the north, bringing temperatures to the 20s for most of the Panhandle. Another storm system then developed across the region and brought snow. Friona accumulated the most snow, with five inches reported.

May 7–13, 2020: Strong instability and moderate wind shear led to strong storms in the Panhandle region, producing large hail and heavy rainfall. Hail up to the size of baseballs was reported. The next few days, an upper-level disturbance combining with increasing moisture brought strong storms back to the region. Hail up to the size of golf balls was reported on May 11. Strong winds caused damage around Woodrow and New Home. Rainfall amounts measured around half an inch to an inch throughout the region that day. On the 13th,

Average Temperatures 2020

	High Plains	Low Plains	North Central	East Texas	Trans-Pecos	Edwards Plateau	South Central	Upper Coast	South Texas	Lower Valley
Jan.	42.1	46.9	49.7	51.4	48.3	51.7	57.7	58.4	60.9	66.1
Feb.	40.3	44.4	48.4	51.2	48.5	50.2	55.6	57.1	59.1	63.5
Mar.	54.2	58.4	62.3	65.2	61.1	64.1	69.9	70.8	72.8	76.2
April	57.9	61.1	62.9	64.6	66.5	66.2	69.7	70.5	73.8	78.6
May	70.1	73.3	72.8	72.3	76.1	75.7	77.5	77	80.3	81.7
June	78.8	80.6	79.9	79.5	81.6	80.9	81.6	81.6	83.1	83.6
July	83.1	86.4	85.2	83.3	85.3	86.2	86.5	85	87.2	86.9
Aug.	81.1	84.7	84.8	83	84.6	85.5	86.3	85.3	86.5	86.1
Sep.	68.6	71.7	73.4	75.8	72.5	73.9	78.3	80.3	79.8	81.4
Oct.	58.4	61.7	64.1	66	66	67.4	71.5	71.9	73.8	76.4
Nov.	52.9	57.2	59.4	60.7	59.7	61.4	66.3	66.9	69.4	73.2
Dec.	40.4	45.2	47.9	49.8	45.5	49.1	54.7	55.6	57.2	61.7
Ann.	60.7	64.3	65.9	66.9	66.3	67.7	71.3	71.7	73.7	76.3

Precipitation in Inches 2020

	High Plains	Low Plains	North Central	East Texas	Trans-Pecos	Edwards Plateau	South Central	Upper Coast	South Texas	Lower Valley
Jan.	0.56	1.55	2.95	4.79	0.46	1.65	2	4.37	0.57	0.46
Feb.	0.63	1.51	3.51	5.31	0.64	1.61	1.21	1.29	0.33	0.11
Mar.	2.08	3.63	6.44	5.37	1.21	3.24	2.07	1.01	1.18	0.47
April	0.27	0.54	2.20	5.37	0.06	1.61	3.03	3.40	2.04	0.96
May	0.79	2.76	5.47	5.28	0.70	3.44	6.09	5.84	4.55	4.81
June	1.21	2.22	3.07	2.88	0.79	0.92	2.80	5.30	2.35	5.17
July	2.22	1.84	2.13	4.22	0.72	0.95	1.88	5.38	2.24	6.62
Aug.	1.08	1.19	1.51	3.37	0.19	0.69	1.29	2.10	1.07	0.67
Sep.	0.88	3.68	7.05	6.72	1.31	3.96	5.40	7.08	3.75	4.44
Oct.	1.07	1.34	1.72	1.95	0.03	0.25	0.51	1.83	0.63	0.66
Nov.	0.27	0.66	0.98	1.81	0.01	0.45	1.76	4.04	0.98	0.32
Dec.	0.30	0.74	2.26	5.65	0.57	0.97	2.02	5.34	0.66	0.85
Ann.	11.36	21.66	39.29	52.72	6.69	19.74	30.06	46.98	20.35	25.54

Winter Storm Uri left a frozen landscape behind in Orient on February 15, 2021. Photo by Jonathan Cutrer, jcutrer.com.

similar weather conditions reoccurred, bringing ping pong ball-size hail, strong winds, and heavy rainfall.

May 20, 2020: A dryline moved into the western Panhandle region, combining with warm temperatures, significant moisture, strong instability, and moderate wind shear, thus bringing large hail. Tennis ball-size hail was reported near Post and baseball-size hail was reported near Lubbock. The hail destroyed many plants, vehicles, and roofs. Rainfall of 0.42 inches fell in Lubbock while 0.96 inches of rain fell in Childress.

May 23, 2020: Increasing moisture, warm temperatures, and instability in the Panhandle region produced severe thunderstorms. One supercell in Garza County remained stationary for a few hours and dropped large hail, heavy rain, and a couple of tornadoes. Other storms produced baseball-size hail, strong winds, and heavy rain. Three to five inches fell in a couple of hours in Garza County, with 6.6 inches measured in Graham. Flash flooding occurred in the area near the Brazos River.

June 18, 2020: Severe storms in Hidalgo County produced straight-line winds up to 70 mph that ripped the roofs off of nine homes, flipped three vehicles, and damaged three dozen trees. Hail up to 1.75 inches was also reported.

June 19, 2020: A cold front moved south of the Panhandle region, stalled, and lifted northward, developing strong storms. Storms near Amarillo produced three to five inches of rain over three rounds of thunderstorms. A brief landspout was also reported near Groom.

June 22, 2020: An upper-level disturbance, along with abundant moisture and instability, brought severe storms to the Panhandle region. Hail with a diameter of 2.5 inches was reported near Cactus, 1.5 to 3 inches of rain fell near Dumas and caused flash flooding, 3.25-inch hail was reported near Vega, a brief EF-0 tornado occurred near Dawn, and strong winds flipped over multiple semitrucks near Vega.

August 13–14, 2020: Record heat was measured in Lubbock, where the temperature hit 107 degrees on the 13th and 14th. Record high minimum temperatures were also reached, dropping to only 75 and 80 degrees. Childress recorded a high of 109 degrees, while Paducah, Guthrie, and Aspermont reached 112 degrees, although none of these were new records.

August 16, 2020: Warm temperatures and mid-level moisture in the Panhandle region generated strong storms. Strong winds up to 86 mph and heavy rain battered the region. A record daily rainfall of 2.38 inches fell in Childress.

December 30, 2020: Severe storms swept across north Texas, bringing an EF-0 tornado to Corsicana. The tornado damaged roofs and 13 manufactured homes, and several trees were downed. Wind speeds were estimated to have peaked at 85 mph. There were no deaths or injuries.

Monthly Summaries 2020

Texas experienced above-normal temperatures in **January.** Parts of western Texas experienced temperatures zero to two degrees above normal. Parts of northern, western, and eastern Texas experienced temperatures two to four degrees above normal. Parts of northern, central, southern, and eastern Texas experienced temperatures four to six degrees above normal. Parts of southern and southeastern Texas experienced temperatures six to eight degrees above normal. The average temperature in Texas during January was 50.8 degrees. Precipitation in January was also mostly above normal in Texas. Parts of southern, northern, and western Texas received 50 percent or less of normal precipitation. Parts of southern and western Texas received 25 percent or less of normal precipitation. Parts of far southern and far western Texas received two percent or less of normal precipitation. Parts of central, northern, and eastern Texas received 150 percent or more of normal precipitation. Parts of central and eastern Texas received 200 percent or more of normal precipitation. Parts of northern Texas received 400 percent or more of normal precipitation. Texas received 1.89 inches of precipitation in January.

Texas experienced varied temperatures across the state in **February.** Parts of northern and western Texas experienced temperatures two to four degrees below normal. Parts of northern, western, central, southern, and eastern Texas experienced temperatures zero to two degrees below normal. Parts of eastern and southern Texas experienced temperatures zero to two degrees above normal. Parts of eastern Texas experienced temperatures two to four degrees above normal. The average temperature in Texas during February was 49.4 degrees. Precipitation was mostly above normal in February in Texas. Parts of northern, western, and southern Texas received 50 percent or less of normal precipitation. Parts of southern Texas received 25 percent or less of normal precipitation. Parts of southern Texas received two percent or less of normal precipitation. Parts of western, central, and eastern Texas received 150 percent or more of normal precipitation. Parts of eastern Texas received 200 percent or more of normal precipitation. Texas received 1.83 inches of precipitation in February.

Texas experienced above normal temperatures during **March.** Parts of northern and western Texas experienced temperatures two to four degrees above normal. Parts of northern, central, eastern, and western Texas experienced temperatures four to six degrees above normal. Parts of eastern, central, and southern Texas experienced temperatures six to eight degrees above normal. Parts of eastern and southern Texas experienced temperatures eight to ten degrees above normal. The average temperature in Texas in March was 63.2 degrees. Parts of northern, southern, southeastern, and eastern Texas received 50 percent or less of normal precipitation. Parts of coastal Texas received 25 percent or less of normal precipitation. Other parts of coastal Texas received two percent or less of normal precipitation. Parts of northern, central, eastern, and western Texas received 150 percent or more of normal precipitation. Parts of central, eastern, and western Texas received 200 percent or more of normal precipitation. Parts of western Texas received 400 percent or more of normal precipitation. Texas received 3.12 inches of precipitation in March.

Temperatures were mostly below normal across Texas in **April**. Parts of north-central Texas experienced temperatures two to four degrees below normal. Parts of central, eastern, and northern Texas experienced temperatures zero to two degrees below normal. Parts of northern, western, southern, and southeastern Texas experienced temperatures zero to two degrees above normal. Parts of western and southern Texas experienced temperatures two to four degrees above normal. The average temperature in Texas during April was 65.0 degrees. Parts of north-central, southern, and western Texas received 50 percent or less of normal precipitation. Parts of northern, western, and southern Texas received 25 percent or less of normal precipitation. Parts of western and southern Texas received 5 percent or less of normal precipitation. Parts of southern and eastern Texas received 150 percent or more of normal precipitation. Parts of eastern Texas received 200 percent or more of normal precipitation. Texas received 1.78 inches of precipitation in April.

Temperatures during **May** were above normal in Texas. Parts of eastern Texas experienced temperatures zero to two degrees below normal. Parts of southern, southeastern, central, western, and northern Texas experienced temperatures zero to two degrees above normal. Parts of northern and western Texas experienced temperatures two to four degrees above normal. The average temperature in Texas was 74.4 degrees. Precipitation varied across Texas in May. Parts of northern and western Texas received 25 percent or less of normal precipitation. Other parts of western Texas received five percent or less of normal precipitation. Parts of southern, north-central, and eastern Texas received 150 percent or more of normal precipitation. Parts of southern Texas received 200 percent or more of normal precipitation. Other parts of southern Texas received 300 percent or more of normal precipitation. Texas received 3.5 inches of precipitation in May.

Temperatures during **June** were mostly below normal across Texas. Parts of southern Texas experienced temperatures one to two degrees below normal. Parts of eastern and southern Texas experienced temperatures zero to one degrees below normal. Parts of eastern and central Texas experienced temperatures zero to one degrees above

Flowers freeze after Winter Storm Uri on February 11, 2021. Photo by Thomas Park/ Unsplash (CC).

normal. Parts of northern and western Texas experienced temperatures one to two degrees above normal. Other parts of northern and western Texas experienced temperatures two to three degrees above normal. Parts of northern Texas experienced temperatures four to five degrees above normal. Texas experienced an average temperature of 80.6 degrees in June. Precipitation varied across Texas. Parts of northern, western, central, and eastern Texas received 50 percent or less of normal precipitation. Parts of northern, central, and western Texas received 25 percent or less of normal precipitation. Parts of western and central Texas received five percent or less of normal precipitation. Parts of southern Texas received 150 percent or more of normal precipitation. Parts of southern Texas received 200 percent or more of normal precipitation. Texas received 2.16 inches of precipitation during June.

Temperatures were primarily above normal across Texas in **July.** Parts of eastern Texas experienced temperatures zero to two degrees below normal. Parts of eastern and southern Texas experienced temperatures zero to two degrees above normal. Parts of central, northern, and western Texas experienced temperatures two to four degrees above normal. Other parts of northern, central, and western Texas experienced temperatures four to six degrees above normal. Parts of western Texas experienced temperatures six to eight degrees above normal. Texas experienced an average temperature of 85.1 degrees during July. Precipitation varied across Texas. Parts of northern, southern, central, and western Texas received 50 percent or less of normal precipitation. Parts of northern, central, and western Texas received 25 percent or less of normal precipitation. Parts of western Texas received five percent or less of normal precipitation. Parts of eastern and southern Texas received 150 percent or more of normal precipitation. Parts of eastern and southern Texas received 200 percent or more of normal precipitation. Other parts of eastern and southern Texas received 300 percent or more of normal precipitation. Texas received 2.22 inches of precipitation in July.

Temperatures varied across Texas during **August.** Parts of northeastern Texas experienced temperatures two to four degrees below normal. Parts of southern and eastern Texas experienced temperatures zero to two degrees below normal. Parts of northern, eastern, and southern Texas experienced temperatures zero to two degrees above normal. Parts of southeastern, central, northern, and western Texas experienced temperatures two to four degrees above normal. Parts of central, northern, and western Texas experienced temperatures four to six degrees above normal. Parts of western Texas experienced temperatures six to eight degrees above normal. The average temperature during August in Texas was 84.3 degrees. Precipitation also varied across Texas. Parts of northern, eastern, central, southern, and western Texas received 50 percent or less of normal precipitation. Parts of northern, central, southern, and western Texas received 25 percent or less of normal precipitation. Parts of eastern and northeastern Texas received 150 percent or more of normal precipitation. Other parts of eastern and northeastern Texas received 200 percent or more of normal precipitation. Texas received 1.25 inches of precipitation during August.

Temperatures were mainly below normal across Texas during **September.** Parts of northern, central, western, and eastern Texas experienced temperatures two to four degrees below normal. A large portion of Texas experienced temperatures zero to two degrees below normal. Parts of eastern and southern Texas experienced temperatures zero to two degrees above normal. Parts of southeastern Texas experienced temperatures two to four degrees above normal. The average temperature during September in Texas was 74.1 degrees. Precipitation varied across Texas. Parts of northern and western Texas received 25 percent or less of normal precipitation. Parts of northern and western Texas received 50 percent or less of normal precipitation. Parts of western Texas received two percent or less of normal precipitation. Parts of central, eastern, and southern Texas received 150 percent or more of normal precipitation. Parts of central and eastern Texas received 200 percent or more of normal precipitation. Texas received 3.97 inches of precipitation during September.

Temperatures during **October** in Texas were mainly above normal. Parts of northern, north-central, and northeastern Texas experienced temperatures two to four degrees below normal. Parts of northern, eastern, and southern Texas experienced temperatures zero to two degrees below normal. Parts of western, southern, and eastern Texas experienced temperatures zero to two degrees above normal. Parts of western Texas experienced temperatures two to four degrees above normal. Texas experienced an average of 65.9 degrees during October. Precipitation during October varied across Texas. Parts of northern, central, eastern, western, and southern Texas received 50 percent or less of normal precipitation. Parts of eastern, central, western, and southern Texas received 25 percent or less of normal precipitation. Parts of western and southern Texas received two percent or less of normal precipitation. Parts of northern Texas received 150 percent or more of normal precipitation. Texas received 0.96 inches of precipitation in October.

Temperatures during **November** were above normal in Texas. Parts of eastern and central Texas experienced temperatures two to four degrees above normal. Parts of northern, western, southern, southeastern, and eastern Texas experienced temperatures four to six degrees above normal. Parts of central, southern, and western Texas experienced temperatures six to eight degrees above normal. Texas experienced an average temperature of 60.5 degrees during November. Precipitation during November in Texas was mainly below normal. Parts of northern, eastern, central, southern, and western Texas received 50 percent or less of normal precipitation. Parts of northern, eastern, southern, and western Texas received 25 percent or less of normal precipitation. Parts of western and southern Texas received five percent or less of normal precipitation. Parts of southern Texas received 110 percent or more of normal precipitation. Texas received 0.90 inches of precipitation in November.

Temperatures during **December** varied in Texas. Parts of western Texas experienced temperatures zero to two degrees below normal. Parts of northern, central, western, southern, and eastern Texas experienced temperatures zero to two degrees above normal. Parts of northern, central, and southern Texas experienced temperatures two to four degrees above normal. The average temperature in Texas in December was 48.3 degrees. Precipitation also varied across Texas. Parts of northern, central, western, and southern Texas received 50 percent or less of normal precipitation. Parts of northern and western Texas received five percent or less of normal precipitation. Parts of eastern and western Texas received 130 percent or more of normal precipitation. Other parts of eastern and western Texas received 150 percent or more of normal precipitation. Parts of western Texas received 200 percent or more of normal precipitation. Texas received 1.76 inches of precipitation in December.☆

Meteorological Data

Source: National Climatic Data Center. Additional data for these locations are listed by county in the table of Texas Climatological Normals for 1981–2010 and Extreme Weather Records by County, beginning on page 126.

City	Temperature		Precipitation					Relative Humidity		Wind			Sun
	No. Days Max. 100° and Above	No. Days Min. 32° and Below	Maximum in 24 Hours	Month & Year	Snowfall (Mean Annual)	Max. Snowfall in 24 Hours	Month & Year	6:00 a.m., CT	Noon, CT	Speed, MPH (Mean Annual)	Highest MPH	Month & Year	Percent Possible Sunshine
Abilene	90	48	6.70	9/1961	3.7	9.3	4/1996	75	50	10.9	55	4/1998	70
Amarillo	61	108	7.25	7/2010	17.2	20.6	3/1934	75	46	12.8	68	6/2008	74
Austin	111	12	15.00	9/1931	1.0	9.7	11/1937	84	57	7.0	52	5/1997	60
Brownsville	123	1	12.19	9/1967	0.0	**	3/1993	90	61	10.4	51	7/2008	59
Corpus Christi	106	4	11.52	6/2006	0.2	2.3	12/2004	90	62	11.7	56	5/1999	60
Dallas-Fort Worth	95	29	5.91	10/1959	1.2	12.1	1/1964	82	56	10.5	73	8/1959	61
Del Rio	131	15	17.03	8/1998	0.9	8.6	1/1985	73	65	8.8	60	8/1970	84
El Paso	99	44	6.50	7/1881	6.9	16.8	12/1987	58	35	8.1	64	1/1996	84
Galveston	30	5	13.91	10/1901	0.2	15.4	2/1895	91	64	11.0	*100	9/1900	62
Houston †	102	10	11.02	6/2001	0.1	2.0	1/1973	90	60	7.5	51	8/1983	59
Lubbock	78	84	7.80	9/2008	8.2	16.3	1/1983	75	46	12.0	70	3/1952	72
Midland-Odessa	101	58	5.99	7/1961	5.1	10.6	1/2012	74	43	10.9	67	2/1960	74
Port Arthur-Beaumont	80	9	17.16	9/1980	0.0	4.4	2/1960	91	64	8.6	105	8/2005	58
San Angelo	102	46	6.25	9/1980	2.4	7.4	1/1978	80	49	9.7	75	4/1969	70
San Antonio	111	15	13.35	10/1998	0.7	13.2	1/1985	84	56	8.2	51	6/2010	60
Victoria	107	11	9.87	4/1991	0.1	2.1	1/1985	91	60	9.5	99	7/1963	49
Waco	104	31	7.98	12/1997	1.2	7.0	1/1949	86	57	10.1	69	6/1961	59
Wichita Falls	98	59	6.22	9/1980	4.2	9.7	3/1989	82	52	11.2	69	6/2002	60
Shreveport, LA §	88	32	10.76	5/2008	1.0	5.6	1/1982	89	59	7.3	63	5/2000	64

*100 mph recorded at 6:15 p.m., Sept. 8, 1900, just before the anemometer blew away. Maximum velocity was estimated to be 120 mph from the northeast between 7:30 p.m. and 8:30 p.m.

†The official Houston station was moved from near downtown to Intercontinental Airport, 12 miles north of the old station.

§Shreveport is included because it is near the boundary line and its data can be considered representative of Texas' east border.

**Trace is an amount too small to measure.

Storms rumble over the plains outside Smyer on May 11, 2020. Photo by Ashley K. Saed/www.livingtreedesignsphoto.com.

Texas Droughts

Drought is difficult to define, and there is no universally accepted definition. The most commonly used drought definitions are based on meteorological, agricultural, hydrological, and socioeconomic effects.

Meteorological drought is often defined as a period when precipitation is diminished in duration and/or intensity. The commonly used definition of meteorological drought is an interval of time, generally on the order of months or years, during which the moisture supply at a given place consistently falls below the climatically appropriate moisture supply.

Agricultural drought occurs when there is inadequate soil moisture to meet the needs of a particular crop at a particular time. Agricultural drought usually occurs after or during meteorological drought but before hydrological drought and can also affect livestock and other dryland agricultural operations.

Hydrological drought refers to deficiencies in surface and subsurface water supplies. It is measured as streamflow and as lake, reservoir, and groundwater levels. There is usually a delay between lack of rain and less measurable water in streams, lakes, and reservoirs. Therefore, hydrological measurements tend to lag other drought indicators.

Socioeconomic drought occurs when physical water shortages start to affect the health, well-being, and quality of life of the people, or when the drought starts to affect the supply and demand of an economic product.

The table on this page uses the **Palmer drought severity index (PDSI)**, the index preferred by the Texas State Climatologist's Office, the National Weather Service, and NOAA. It was developed by meteorologist Wayne Palmer, who first published this method in 1965.

The PDSI is based on a **supply-and-demand model of soil moisture** that factors in temperature, the amount of moisture in the soil, evapotranspiration, and recharge rates. It is most effective in determining long-term drought. Years were included in the table if at least one climate division had a PDSI of -4 or below, and the past 10 years, even when no periods of drought occurred. ☆

Source: Texas State Climatologist and the New Mexico Drought Planning Team

PDSI Table Indicators

- Moderate drought, PDSI between –2 and –4
- Severe drought, PDSI between –4 and –6
- Extreme drought, PDSI below –6

Palmer Drought Severity Index

	High Plains	Low Rolling Plains	North Central	East Texas	Trans–Pecos	Edwards Plateau	South Central	Upper Coast	South Texas	Lower Valley
Frequency	27	28	27	25	28	28	26	26	25	25
1901	-2.01	-2.55	-4.58	-2.39	-2.28	-3.14	-3.84	-2.78	-3.21	-5.05
1902	-2.54	-3.73	-5.64	-3.23	-3.23	-4.05	-4.99	-3.45	-4.97	-5.70
1910	-3.47	-3.89	-5.04	-3.99	-4.21	-4.48	-3.63	-2.51	-3.26	-3.43
1911	-3.69	-4.10	-5.97	-5.02	-4.02	-4.03	-4.21	-4.31	-4.39	-3.03
1916	-2.60	-2.79	-2.49	-3.23	-3.53	-2.37	-4.19	-3.26	-4.71	-4.51
1917	-3.90	-4.66	-4.53	-4.90	-4.58	-4.88	-6.00	-6.03	-4.56	-3.91
1918	-3.88	-5.97	-6.11	-6.42	-3.75	-5.61	-6.13	-7.00	-4.50	-4.09
1925	-2.96	-3.26	-6.41	-6.20	-3.09	-3.95	-6.09	-5.20	-3.79	-2.51
1934	-4.66	-4.42	-4.84	-3.55	-4.88	-4.51	-2.82	-2.27	-1.54	-1.33
1935	-4.57	-3.83	-0.58	0.19	-4.68	-3.99	0.66	-0.39	0.10	-1.76
1951	-1.65	-3.36	-4.26	-3.84	-4.15	-4.66	-4.64	-4.37	-3.91	-4.10
1952	-4.23	-5.38	-5.53	-3.72	-4.28	-5.10	-4.53	-4.47	-4.45	-3.71
1953	-5.33	-5.41	-3.12	-1.27	-5.67	-4.64	-2.58	-2.21	-5.26	-4.45
1954	-4.46	-4.24	-4.29	-4.27	-4.59	-5.09	-4.87	-3.89	-3.59	-3.38
1955	-4.13	-3.76	-3.81	-3.18	-3.35	-4.78	-4.95	-3.75	-4.59	-3.60
1956	-5.62	-6.25	-6.82	-5.09	-5.47	-6.16	-6.68	-5.72	-4.77	-3.81
1957	-4.94	-5.02	-5.08	-4.92	-4.85	-5.10	-5.82	-5.64	-4.29	-4.12
1963	-2.38	-2.91	-3.95	-3.77	-2.07	-4.29	-4.80	-4.15	-3.71	-3.57
1967	-3.31	-3.42	-4.61	-3.34	-2.55	-4.12	-4.73	-2.99	-3.62	-2.44
1971	-3.33	-4.18	-4.41	-3.11	-2.80	-3.46	-5.01	-3.28	-3.68	-2.70
1974	-4.43	-4.20	-2.44	1.60	-3.44	-3.09	1.26	1.95	-1.29	-1.97
1996	-3.83	-3.57	-4.28	-3.63	-3.76	-3.88	-4.51	-2.59	-3.64	-3.04
2000	-3.88	-3.97	-3.76	-4.34	-4.93	-4.78	-4.39	-5.17	-4.12	-3.73
2006	-4.58	-4.80	-4.93	-4.16	-3.72	-4.14	-5.23	-4.32	-4.73	-4.77
2009	-2.24	-2.97	-3.88	-2.43	-2.35	-3.82	-6.36	-4.23	-5.19	-4.09
2010	-1.13	-1.20	-1.27	-3.67	-2.08	-2.02	-1.49	-1.19	-1.59	-1.68
2011	-6.98	-6.99	-5.99	-6.86	-6.52	-6.39	-6.21	-5.70	-5.45	-4.87
2012	-5.12	-4.75	-3.70	-4.36	-4.93	-3.75	-4.37	-4.72	-4.17	-4.69
2013	-4.16	-4.26	-3.43	-2.94	-3.02	-3.40	-4.47	-3.47	-4.33	-4.94
2014	-3.45	-3.29	-2.56	-1.34	-2.85	-2.93	-3.29	-2.49	-2.72	-1.23
2015	0.69	0.39	0.38	0.84	1.74	0.33	0.41	-0.59	-1.14	-0.56
2016	1.30	2.57	2.85	-2.04	-1.15	1.98	-0.47	-1.63	-1.50	-2.86
2017	-1.15	-1.43	-1.31	-2.40	-1.82	-1.47	-1.72	0.59	-1.97	-3.72
2018	-3.84	-4.35	-3.30	-2.16	-3.18	-3.67	-2.31	0.79	-2.72	-4.09
2020	-3.57	-0.58	1.41	1.63	-4.94	-3.17	-3.74	-0.40	-3.05	-3.22

Normal Annual Rainfall in Inches by Texas Climatic Region

Listed below is the normal annual rainfall in inches for three 30-year periods in each geographical region (see map, p. 106).

Region	HP	LRP	NC	ET	TP	EP	SC	UC	ST	LV
1961–1990	18.88	23.77	33.99	45.67	13.01	24.00	34.49	47.63	23.47	25.31
1971–2000	19.64	24.51	35.23	48.08	13.19	24.73	36.21	50.31	24.08	25.43
1981–2010	20.02	24.85	36.17	48.21	13.16	24.86	35.54	51.14	24.17	24.67

Texas Is Tornado Capital

Source: The Office of the State Climatologist.

An average of 130 tornadoes touch Texas soil each year. The annual total varies considerably, and certain areas are struck more often than others. Tornadoes occur with greatest frequency in the Red River Valley.

Tornadoes may occur in any month and at any hour of the day, but they occur with greatest frequency during the late spring and early summer months, and between the hours of 4:00 p.m. and 8:00 p.m. In the period 1951–2020, 63 percent of all Texas tornadoes occurred within the three-month period of April, May, and June, with almost one-third of the total tornadoes occurring in May.

More tornadoes have been recorded in Texas than in any other state, which is partly due to the state's size. Between 1951–2020, 9,166 funnel clouds are known to have reached the ground, thus becoming tornadoes. Texas ranks 11th among the 50 states in the density of tornadoes, experiencing an annual average of 4.85 tornadoes per 10,000 square miles.

The greatest outbreak of tornadoes on record in Texas was associated with Hurricane Beulah in September 1967. Within a five-day period (Sept. 19–23) 115 known tornadoes, all in Texas, were spawned by this great hurricane. Sixty-seven occurred on Sept. 20, a Texas record for a single day.

In May 2015, there were 130 tornadoes, which is a Texas record for a single month. The greatest number of tornadoes in Texas in a single year was 248, which was also in 2015. The second-highest number in a single year was in 1967, when 232 tornadoes occurred in Texas.

On average, May has the highest number of tornadoes with 40. January has the lowest average number of tornadoes with 3.

The accompanying table, compiled by the National Climatic Data Center, Environmental Data Service, and the National Oceanic and Atmospheric Administration, lists tornado occurrences in Texas, by months, for the period 1951–2020. Additional years are available at texasalmanac.org.☆

Tornadoes by Year and Month

Year	Jan.	Feb.	March	April	May	June	July	Aug.	Sept.	Oct.	Nov.	Dec.	TOTAL
1951-56	0	9	19	49	93	61	16	16	8	16	3	7	**297**
1957	0	1	21	69	33	5	0	3	2	6	5	0	**145**
1958-66	8	16	61	107	224	201	66	59	41	29	33	4	**849**
1967	0	2	11	17	34	22	10	5	124	2	0	5	**232**
1968-72	4	25	38	89	205	91	41	68	35	61	23	42	**722**
1973	14	1	29	25	21	24	4	8	5	3	9	4	**147**
1974	2	1	8	19	18	26	3	9	6	22	2	0	**116**
1975	5	2	9	12	50	18	10	3	3	3	1	1	**117**
1976	1	1	8	53	63	11	16	6	13	4	0	0	**176**
1977	0	0	3	34	50	4	5	5	12	0	6	4	**123**
1978	0	0	0	34	65	10	13	6	6	1	2	0	**137**
1979	1	2	24	33	39	14	12	10	4	15	3	0	**157**
1980	0	2	7	26	44	21	2	34	10	5	0	2	**153**
1981	0	7	7	9	71	26	5	20	5	23	3	0	**176**
1982	0	0	6	27	123	36	4	0	3	0	3	1	**203**
1983	5	7	24	1	62	35	4	22	5	0	7	14	**186**
1984	0	13	9	18	19	19	0	4	1	5	2	5	**95**
1985	0	0	5	41	28	5	3	1	1	3	1	2	**90**
1986	0	12	4	21	50	24	3	5	4	7	1	0	**131**
1987	1	1	7	0	54	19	11	3	8	0	16	4	**124**
1988	0	0	0	11	7	7	6	2	42	4	10	0	**89**
1989	3	0	5	3	70	63	0	6	3	6	1	0	**160**
1990	3	3	4	56	62	20	5	2	3	0	0	0	**158**
1991	20	5	2	39	72	36	1	2	3	8	4	0	**192**
1992	0	5	13	22	43	66	4	4	4	7	21	0	**189**
1993	1	4	5	17	39	4	4	0	12	23	8	0	**117**
1994	0	1	1	48	88	2	1	4	3	9	8	0	**165**
1995	6	0	13	36	66	75	11	3	2	1	0	10	**223**
1996	7	1	2	21	33	9	3	8	33	8	4	1	**130**
1997	0	6	7	31	59	50	2	2	1	16	3	0	**177**
1998	24	15	4	9	11	6	3	5	3	28	1	0	**109**
1999	22	0	22	23	70	26	3	8	0	0	0	4	**178**
2000	0	7	49	33	23	8	3	0	0	10	20	1	**154**
2001	0	0	4	12	36	12	0	7	15	24	27	5	**142**
2002	0	0	44	25	61	5	1	4	13	8	0	22	**183**
2003	0	0	4	31	50	29	6	1	4	12	29	0	**166**
2004	1	1	27	25	29	34	1	5	0	4	55	2	**184**
2005	0	0	6	7	27	46	15	4	2	0	0	2	**109**
2006	0	1	4	20	43	7	3	3	0	9	0	27	**117**
2007	2	1	56	61	43	21	8	4	14	2	1	3	**216**
2008	0	3	15	48	33	9	5	1	2	3	1	3	**123**
2009	0	5	4	48	18	32	2	4	1	4	1	12	**131**
2010	10	0	0	19	34	23	3	1	12	10	0	0	**112**
2011	1	1	3	57	20	6	1	4	1	2	8	0	**104**
2012	22	3	9	36	31	3	0	1	2	3	0	5	**115**
2013	1	16	0	8	41	3	0	6	0	6	0	3	**84**
2014	0	0	0	6	15	15	5	0	0	2	0	3	**46**
2015	0	0	0	48	130	3	0	0	2	20	23	22	**248**
2016	0	1	14	33	43	4	1	1	5	0	0	0	**102**
2017	22	17	36	29	43	3	3	25	1	1	0	3	**183**
2018	5	0	9	4	6	3	3	2	1	22	1	2	**58**
2019	**0**	**0**	**12**	**39**	**104**	**13**	**1**	**0**	**2**	**13**	**0**	**0**	**184**
2020	**14**	**0**	**18**	**17**	**24**	**3**	**8**	**2**	**1**	**0**	**2**	**3**	**92**
Total	**205**	**198**	**692**	**1,606**	**2,820**	**1,318**	**340**	**408**	**483**	**470**	**348**	**228**	**9,116**
Avg.	3	3	10	23	40	19	5	6	7	7	5	3	**130**
Max	24	20	56	69	130	75	19	34	124	28	55	27	**248**

Extreme Weather Records in Texas

Sources: Office of the State Climatologist and the National Weather Service, Dallas–Fort Worth.

Temperature

Lowest	-23°F	Tulia	Feb. 12, 1899
	-23°F	Seminole	Feb. 8, 1933
Highest	120°F	Seymour	Aug. 12, 1936
	120°F	Monahans	June 28, 1994
Coldest Winter	41.3°F average		1898–1899
Hottest Summer	86.8°F average		2011

Wind Velocity

Highest sustained wind		
145 mph SE	Matagorda	Sept. 11, 1961
145 mph NE	Port Lavaca	Sept. 11, 1961
Highest peak gust		
180 mph SW	Aransas Pass	Aug. 3, 1970
180 mph WSW	Robstown	Aug. 3, 1970

These winds occurred during Hurricane Carla in 1961 and Hurricane Celia in 1970.

Tornadoes

Since 1950, there have been six tornadoes of the F-5 category, that is, with winds between 261–318 mph.

Waco	McLennan County	May 11, 1953
Wichita Falls	Wichita County	April 3, 1964
Lubbock	Lubbock County	May 11, 1970
Valley Mills	McLennan County	May 6, 1973
Brownwood	Brown County	April 19, 1976
Jarrell	Williamson County	May 27, 1997

Rainfall

Wettest year statewide		2015	41.23 in.
Driest year statewide		1917	14.06 in.
Most annual	Bridge City	2017	109.42 in.
Least annual	Terlingua	2011	1.30 in.
Most in 24 hours†	Alvin	July 25–26, 1979	43.00 in.
Most in 18 hours	Thrall	Sept. 9, 1921	36.40 in.

†Unofficial estimate of rainfall during Tropical Storm Claudette. Greatest 24-hour rainfall at an official site occurred at Albany, Shackelford County, on Aug. 4, 1978: 29.05 inches.

Hail

Hailstones six inches or greater, since 1950

7.50 in.	Young County	April 14, 1965
7.05 in.	Burleson County	Dec. 17, 1995
7.00 in.	Winkler County	May 31, 1960
6.42 in.	Medina County	April 28, 2021
6.00 in.	Ward County	May 10, 1991
6.00 in.	Moore County	June 12, 2010

Snowfall

65.0 in.	Season	Romero*	1923–1924
61.0 in.	Month	Vega	Feb. 1956
61.0 in.	Single storm	Vega	Feb. 1–8, 1956
26.0 in.	24 hours	Cleburne	Dec. 21–22, 1929
24.2 in	Annual avg.	Vega, Oldham County	

*Romero was in southwestern Hartley County.

A thunderstorm rolls over the Texas prairie. Photo by Raychel Sanner/Unsplash (CC).

Hurricane Hanna hits the southern coast of Texas on July 25, 2020. Photo by International Space Station, courtesy of NASA Johnson Space Center/Flickr (CC).

Significant and Destructive Weather

This list of significant weather events in Texas since 1980 was compiled from ESSA–Weather Bureau information, previous Texas Almanacs, the Handbook of Texas, The Dallas Morning News, and the Office of the State Climatologist. For historical significant weather dating back to 1766, see texasalmanac.com!

2020

March 18, 2020: Tornadoes, North Central & High Plains. Severe storms rolled through North Texas and brought a couple of significant tornadoes. Eight were confirmed, with two as strong as EF-2. An EF-1 tornado was confirmed in Graham, and there was widespread damage throughout the area, including damaged buildings, downed power lines, and uprooted trees. Two EF-2 tornadoes, with winds estimated up to 135 mph, were confirmed near Abilene, where several wind turbines were damaged, a small home was destroyed, and at least 75 vehicles were tossed around the area. Hail as large as 2.25 inches was also reported. There were no injuries.

April 22, 2020: Tornado, Upper Coast. A line of severe storms moved through southeastern Texas, bringing an EF-3 tornado in Onalaska and hail up to two inches in diameter. The tornado had peak winds of 140 mph and was on the ground for 32 miles. Many homes were destroyed and trees were uprooted. Thirty-three people were injured and three were killed.

May 22, 2020: Hail, North Central. Strong instability and moisture brought severe storms through far northern Texas, producing significant hail in Burkburnett. The largest hail reported had a diameter of 5.33 inches. Widespread damage in the area was also reported.

July 25–27, 2020: Hurricane, Lower Valley. Hurricane Hanna, the 2020 Atlantic season's first hurricane, made landfall near Padre Island on July 25th. Winds at this time were around 90 mph with gusts over 100 mph. Eight to 15 inches of rain fell throughout the Valley, 250,000 people lost power, hundreds of homes were damaged, tens of thousands of tree limbs were blown down, hundreds of trees were uprooted, and there was an estimated $366 million in damage.

September 21–23, 2020: Tropical Storm, South Central. Tropical Storm Beta formed on the 18th in the Gulf of Mexico, slowed considerably, and moved towards the Texas coast. Beta made landfall at Matagorda Bay on the 21st and weakened significantly shortly after. Torrential rainfall caused major flooding in streets, highways, and interstates in Houston, as rainfall surpassed nine inches, forcing road closures. There was one death. Total damage from Beta was estimated at $225 million.

November 24, 2020: Tornado, North Central. Severe storms moved through North Texas, bringing heavy rain and an EF-2 tornado to Arlington. The tornado had wind speeds estimated at 115 mph, stayed on the ground for 5.04 miles, and had a width of 150 yards. Buildings were destroyed, power lines were downed, roads were impassable because of debris, and five people were injured.

2019

April 13, 2019: Tornadoes, East Texas. A large, upper-level storm system moved across the southern Plains states. Severe thunderstorms impacted southeast Texas, producing two EF-3 tornadoes. One of the EF-3 tornadoes hit Franklin with peak winds estimated at 140 mph, injuring 14 people and damaging upwards of 20 buildings. Mobile homes were damaged, cars were overturned, and power lines were downed; about 4,000 people lost power. The other EF-3 tornado touched down near Weches, killing the occupant of a double-wide trailer.

May 20, 2019: Tornadoes/Hail, High Plains. All the ingredients were present for a severe weather outbreak. NWS offices called for a strong chance of long-track, destructive tornadoes, and schools and businesses closed in preparation. Although the outbreak wasn't as significant as expected, tornadoes and hail pummeled northwest Texas. There were seven tornado reports that day, with the strongest being an EF-3 near West Odessa. Hail 5.5 inches in diameter was reported near Wellington, and now holds a record for one of the largest hailstones to fall in the state.

June 9, 2019: Strong Winds, North-Central. Severe thunderstorms moved through northern Texas, bringing heavy rain and strong winds to the Dallas area. Wind damage to power lines caused 350,000 to lose power and collapsed a large construction crane on an apartment building in downtown Dallas. The wind was measured around 70 mph at Love Field. The crane collapse killed one person and injured five others.

June 24, 2019: Flooding, Lower Valley. The Rio Grande Valley experienced the "Great June Flood II" on this day. Over a foot of rain fell in 6 hours, reaching 15 inches near Santa Rosa. Streets all over the area were flooded, 1,188 homes were destroyed or incurred major damage, more than 100 people had to be evacuated, 45,000 people lost power, 75 mph winds damaged five mobile homes beyond repair, and many rainfall records were broken.

September 17–19, 2019: Tropical Storm, East Texas and Upper Coast. A tropical disturbance formed near Florida on September 14 and reached the Texas coast on the 17th, becoming Tropical Storm Imelda at 12:45 PM CDT. The tropical storm made landfall near Freeport at 1:30 PM CDT with maximum sustained winds of 40 mph and weakened to a tropical depression by 7 PM that evening. Imelda stalled between Houston and Lufkin from the 17th to the 19th. There was significant flooding in Galveston, Houston, Fannett, Beaumont, Vidor, and Orange, accumulating 30 to 44 inches of rainfall. Vehicles were flooded or stuck on I-10 for 2½ days. Rainfall was measured at 44.29 inches near Fannett, making Imelda the seventh wettest tropical cyclone to impact the United States, the fifth wettest in the contiguous United States, and the fourth wettest in Texas. The flooding killed two people and inundated about 10,000 homes.

October 20, 2019: Tornado, North Central. An upper-level disturbance combining with an unstable atmosphere across northeastern Texas brought severe thunderstorms to the Dallas area. These storms produced golf ball-size hail, strong winds, and seven confirmed tornadoes. The strongest of these was an EF-3, which hit northern Dallas. The tornado was on the ground for 15.76 miles, had maximum winds of 140 mph, remained on the ground for 32 minutes, and caused $1.55 billion in damage, becoming the costliest tornado event in Texas history. In addition to this EF-3, there were two EF-2, two EF-1, and two EF-0 tornadoes in northern Texas.

October 24, 2019: Winter Weather, High Plains. A strong, closed low moved across the Panhandle while a cold front provided significantly colder air across the area. Heavy bands of snow and thundersnow occurred from 9 AM CDT on the 24th to 2 AM CDT the next day. As much as 11 inches of snow fell in Booker and Miami.

2018

Jan. 16–17, 2018: Winter Weather, North Central Texas. North Texas citizens experienced a frigid Martin Luther King Jr. Day as a strong Arctic cold front pushed through the region. The air mass brought freezing temperatures, snow, sleet, and freezing rain. Two homeless citizens in Dallas lost their lives from the extreme cold conditions.

Jan. 21, 2018: Tornado, East Texas. Unstable atmospheric conditions produced supercell thunderstorms in the Ark-La-Tex midwinter season. Moderately-sized hail and strong winds were products of the intense storms. Reports of an EF-2 tornado on the ground for 7 miles in Bowie County reached an estimated maximum wind speed of 125 mph. Many homes were damaged, as well as injuries sustained by local residents and farm animals with an estimated loss of $2.5 million.

April, 3, 2018: Strong Winds, Upper Coast. Strong storms along the Texas coast produced damaging winds and gusts in Harris County. The most damaging winds were short-lived as a phenomenon known as a, "microburst", a powerful downward rush of air from a thunderstorm. Sustained winds from this event reached an estimated maximum of 80 mph, causing $2 million in damages to a hangar at Houston Hobby Airport.

May 19–20, 2018: Hail, High Plains. Slow moving supercell thunderstorms caused a great deal of damage to residents of West Texas during the evening hours and in to the night. The storms produced heavy rainfall that led to flash flooding and large size hail. The magnitude of hail produced had the greatest toll on residents. Several observations of tennis- to baseball-sized hail were reported during the event which caused an estimated $30 million in damages to property.

June 7, 2018: Severe Weather, High Plains and Low Rolling Plains. A late-spring storm produced heavy rains and destructive winds in West Texas. Estimated winds during this event reached hurricane force, peaking near 115 mph. One family in Scurry County reported an overturned manufactured home that resulted in one injury. Total damages by flash flooding and strong winds were estimated to over $600 thousand.

June 19–22, 2018: Flooding/Tropical Weather, Lower Valley and South Texas. A low pressure system originating from the Caribbean made landfall in South Texas in the early days of summer. The system interacted with other atmospheric features to create strong, heavy rain producing storms. For nearly four days, the region was drenched with continual precipitation that caused widespread flooding. Locally flooded areas saw water depths of 2 to 4 feet. Disaster responders in the region reported more than 2,000 rescues during the event. With at least 20,000 residents and businesses considered affected by the storms a preliminary estimate of $115 million in property damage was reported.

Oct. 16–17, 2018: Flooding, Central Texas. Strong thunderstorms slowly rolled through Central Texas during the early morning hours bringing torrential downpours to the region. Flash flooding was extensive in the western areas of the region where rainfall totals between 6 to 9 inches caused overfilling of the Llano River, Lake LBJ, Lake Marble Falls, and Lake Travis. One loss of life was reported in Llano County. The combined property damage in Llano, Burnet, and Travis counties exceeded $100 million.

2017

Jan. 14–15, 2017: Ice Storm, High Plains. A strong winter storm made its way from the western US into the Texas Panhandle in the second weekend of January, bringing frigid temperatures, strong winds, ice, and snow. Ice and snow accumulations were measured to be 1-3 inches across the region. Many residents lost power during this event, along with damages to some infrastructure and economic losses to businesses. Total damages were estimated to be nearly $50 million for both Texas and Oklahoma Panhandles.

Jan. 21, 2017: Tornadoes, East Texas. An advancing cold front from the Southern High Plains made its way into East Texas where it interacted with unstable and unseasonably warm air developing into strong thunderstorms and supercells. Twelve tornadoes touched down across the Ark-La-Tex region, with two destructive EF-2s pushing through East Texas. The severe storms were responsible for over $4 million in damages to vehicles, local infrastructure, and resident homes.

March 7, 2017: Fire Weather, High Plains. Hot, dry, and windy conditions lead to the ignition of a wildfire in the Texas Panhandle along with other fires within the Great Plains. The Gray County fire took the lives of three who were attempting to save livestock. After more than 521,000 acres of land burned, damages and losses of land, livestock, and infrastructure were estimated to be over $25.1 million.

April 14, 2017: Tornado, High Plains. Strong thunderstorms firing in the Texas Panhandle produced a significant tornadic supercell in the southern High Plains. A post-storm survey conducted by the National Weather Service (NWS) determined that the tornado that tore through Castro County during the early evening hours was an EF-3 with a massive diameter of 1.1 miles. Reports by the NWS affirm no deaths or injuries, though damages were estimated to be nearly $2 million.

April 29, 2017: Tornadoes, East Texas. 4 deaths and over 50 injuries were the result of a devastating tornado outbreak in East Texas. There was a total of 7 confirmed tornadoes passing through Henderson, Hopkins, Rains and Van Zandt counties. Post-storm surveys confirmed the strongest storm was an EF-4 that had estimated wind speeds near 180 mph in Van Zant County.

June 4, 2017: Hail, West Texas. The development of a strong line of thunderstorms produced strong winds and large hail in Odessa, Texas. 5-inch hail and 100 mph winds were recorded when the storm was at its peak. These conditions significantly damaged vehicles and infrastructure, uprooted trees, and caused power outages across the area. $208 million in damages was sustained from these storms.

August 25–29, 2017: Hurricane, Southeast. Hurricane Harvey made landfall in Southeast Texas, the first Category 4 landfall in the state since 1961. Strong winds and torrential downpours were the most destructive impacts to the region; maximum wind speeds reached 130 mph and the largest observed rainfall total was 60 inches. There were 68 deaths directly related to the storm and an estimate of $125 billion in damage.

2016

March 9–10, 2016: Flood, East Texas. Multiple days of heavy rain fell across the Sabine River Valley causing massive flooding in the basin. More than 1,500 homes received flood damage, and damage in Texas and Louisiana was estimated at $2.4 billion.

March 17, 2016: Hail, North Central. Intense, warm advection led to thunderstorm development over the western counties of North Texas. Damage from hail as large as tennis balls was estimated at $600 million.

March 23, 2016: Hail, North Central. Severe thunderstorms developed along a dry line as it surged east to the Interstate 35 corridor. Damaging winds, hail, and one tornado caused $2.3 billion in damage.

April 11–12, 2016: Hail, South Central. Severe thunderstorms produced 4.25-inch hail that damaged an estimated 136,000 vehicles and 125,000 homes. Combined damage of $3.5 billion made this the costliest hail storm ever in Texas.

April 17, 2016: Flood, Southeast. Ten to 15 inches of rain in less than 12 hours produced devastating flooding in west Houston in an event called the "Tax Day Flood." There were eight deaths and $2.7 billion in property damage.

May 21–26, 2016: Widespread Severe Weather. Five-inch hail and tornadoes were reported in the Panhandle. Rainfall totals of 6 to 10 inches occurred there and in Southeast Texas. The storms caused four deaths and a combined $1.2 billion in damage.

2015

May 4, 2015: Flood, Lubbock. Dozens of motorists from Lubbock to Tahoka needed to be rescued from their vehicles after driving into deep floodwaters. Combined damage to vehicles, homes, and thousands of acres of wheat crops exceeded $300 million.

May 8, 2015: Hail, Lubbock. Widespread hail damage to homes, businesses, vehicles, and wheat crops. Nearly $500 million of combined property damage and $100 million in crop damage.

May 23–30, 2015: Flash Flood, Central Texas. More than 25 deaths from flash floods and tornadoes from North-Central to South-Central Texas. Flood waters inundated at least 2,585 homes and 73 commercial buildings. Property damage exceeded $1 billion.

October 23–24, 2015: Flash Flood, North Central. Heavy rain led to flash flooding across portions of North-Central Texas. Rainfall totals in flood-damaged areas ranged from 5 inches to 21-plus inches within a 36-hour period. Property damage estimated at $1 billion.

December 26–27, 2015: Tornado, North. A potent storm system brought blizzard conditions to Lubbock and 12 deadly tornadoes to North Texas, followed by significant flooding across parts of North and Central Texas. In total, 15 people died, more than 600 were injured, and tens of thousands of dairy cows in West Texas were killed.

2014

April 3, 2014: Hailstorm, Denton. A severe thunderstorm moving through the Denton area dropped hail as big as softballs, which caused more than $500 million in damages to homes, businesses, and vehicles.

May 11, 2014: Wildfire, Hutchinson County. A wildfire in Hutchinson County destroyed about 100 homes and caused the evacuation of more than 700 residents. The fire burned more than 1,000 acres and caused at least $10 million in damages.

June 12, 2014: Hailstorm, Abilene. A severe hailstorm moving through Abilene dropped hail up to 4.5 inches in diameter across the city. There were 12 injuries and $400 million in property damage.

2013

May 15, 2013: Tornado Outbreak, North Texas. A deadly tornado outbreak in North Texas claimed the lives of six people and injured more than 100 others. $250 million in damages were a result of an EF4 tornado in Mambrino and an EF3 tornado in Cleburne.

May 28, 2013: Hailstorm, Amarillo. A massive hailstorm moving through the Amarillo area dropped hail as big as baseballs and caused $200 million in damages. An estimated 35,000 vehicles and thousands of homes in Amarillo were damaged.

June 5, 2013: Hailstorm, Lubbock. Baseball-sized hail along with winds in excess of 90 mph caused more than $400 million in property damage in Lubbock. There were numerous reports of damage to homes, vehicles, as well as downed trees and power lines.

October 30–31, 2013: Flash Flooding, Travis County. Six to ten inches of rain fell in Travis County and more than a foot of rain fell near Wimberley and Driftwood. Near Oak Hill, four people died and the flooding caused $100 million in property damage.

2012

Jan. 9, 2012: Supercells, South Texas. Squall-line thunderstorms, hail, and an EF-1 tornado hit southeast of Alice International Airport and parts of Robstown, causing an estimated $5 million in damage. Other straight-line winds and hail caused total damage of $8.66 million.

March 29, 2012: Hail, McAllen. Strong thunderstorms, with wind gusts over 70 mph at Edinburg Airport, and severe hail up to 2.75 inches caused $50 million in property damage to homes and $1 million to crops. Rainfall between 4–6 inches fell in less than two hours, causing $5 million in flood damage.

April 16, 2012: Tornadoes, Flash Floods. Gregory. Thunderstorms along the Coastal Bend caused four tornadoes, including an EF-1 in Portland, two EF-0 tornadoes in Gregory, and another in Kleberg County. The Portland tornado caused $2 million in damage to homes and property. Around 80 percent of all homes in Gregory were flooded when storms dumped 2–6 inches of rain; some locations received up to 15 inches over several hours. Total damages topped $8.3 million.

April 29, 2012: Hail, Doud. Several severe storms blew up in West Texas near Lubbock with damaging hail and winds. Hailstones up to 4.5 inches fell in Whitharral, and winds gusts up to 95 mph near Wolfforth tore apart homes and cars. Damage estimates were $20 million from hail in Doud and more than $5 million from wind.

Nov. 22, 2012: Fog, Winnie, Chambers County. Dense fog early Thanksgiving morning caused a massive 150-car pileup on both sides of Interstate-10, causing two deaths and 80 injuries, 12 serious. Vehicular damage was $6 million.

Dec. 19, 2012: Dust Storm, Lubbock. A strong Pacific front kicked up winds up to 70 mph, reducing visibility below 1/2 mile for more than 5 hours, the longest such event since 1977; property damage, $1 million.

Dec. 25, 2012: Heavy Snow, Plano. A moderate cold front and minor storms in North Texas produced wrap-around snow between 3–6 inches that caused 89 traffic accidents and costing $1.2 million.

2011

Jan. 8, 2011: Heavy Snow, Sherman. Between 3–7 inches of snow fell across Northeast Texas, causing hundreds of vehicle accidents, including more than 40 in Sherman and one fatality. Total damage, $1 million.

Feb. 27, 2011: Wildfire, West Texas. High winds and temperatures produced a series of wildfire complexes. The costliest was in Tanglewood, burning 1,659 acres and destroying 26 homes at a cost of $25 million. The biggest was in Willow Creek, burning 24,310 acres and 29 homes at a cost of $10 million. A combination of fires near Lubbock, Matador, Post, and Levelland burned 60,500 acres and several urban dwellings, costing $3.45 million.

March 11, 2011: Wildfire, Aransas. High heat, dry air, and high winds produced several fires in North-Central Texas. More than 10,000 acres burned, including fields of hay bales in Aransas worth $4 million. Three injuries were reported; other property losses were around $1 million.

April 6, 2011: Wildfire, Swenson. A wildfire near Swenson was spawned during critical fire conditions due to a cutting torch. The fire burned for 15 days, burning 122,500 acres of grass and ranchland; damage, $2.54 million.

April 9, 2011: Wildfire, West Texas. Dry conditions near the Pecos River spawned two fires near Midland and Marfa. The former burned 16,500 acres and 34 homes, causing 500 evacuations; the latter was caused by an electrical problem and burned 314,444 acres, 41 homes, and hundreds of cattle and utility poles. Total property damage was estimated at $7.7 million.

April 9–13, 2011: Wildfire, Possum Kingdom Lake. Drought and high winds helped spark a massive fire complex that burned for 16 days, destroying 167 homes, 126 other buildings, and 90 percent of Possum Kingdom State Park — about 126,734 acres total. Damage was $120 million, not including the estimated $11 million needed to combat the fire, nor the loss of cattle.

April 15, 2011: Wildfire, Cisco. Dry conditions caused several wildfires in North Texas. The largest was near Cisco, burning around 2,000 acres and destroying five homes. The fires burned 18,000 acres, costing $1.01 million.

April 17, 2011: Wildfire, Oak Hill. Dry conditions and human negligence combined to cause a wildfire in Travis County. Although it covered only 100 acres, it destroyed 11 homes and damage estimates reached $2 million.

April 19, 2011: Hail, North Texas. A series of supercells brought widespread hail ranging from 0.75 inches to 3.5 inches over the course of the 5-hour storm. Damage was around $1 million.

April 25–26, 2011: Supercells, East Texas. An upper level trough brought severe storms to East Texas for two days. On the 25th, 3 tornadoes touched down in Cherokee and Angelina counties, including two EF-1s; moderate hail was seen and downburst winds of 90-plus mph were reported. The next day, 10 tornadoes were reported, two of which were EF-1s near Ben Wheeler and Groesbeck, causing injuries. Total damage, $2.718 million.

May 1, 2011: Thunderstorm Wind, Clyde. Isolated thunderstorms popped up in the Big Country, bringing hail and strong winds. In Clyde, straight-line winds were reported in excess of 100 mph; damage, $2 million.

May 11, 2011: Thunderstorm Wind, Interstate-20 Corridor. Scattered thunderstorms from Killeen to Burns caused strong winds, hail, flash flooding, and an EF-0 tornado near Lake Kiowa; damage, $1 million.

June 18, 2011: Thunderstorm Wind, Meunster. Thunderstorms followed by a strong microburst in the early evening and straight-line winds greater than 80 mph caused widespread damage in excess of $1.36 million.

June 20–21, 2011: Thunderstorm Wind, East Texas. Severe thunderstorms culminated in strong downburst winds, hail, and an EF-0 tornado. Winds greater than 80 mph occurred in Nacogdoches and San Augustine, a tornado in Shelby County, and moderate hail; damage, $1.04 million.

June 28, 2011: Thunderstorm Wind, Titus County. Thunderstorms with 65 mph winds caused widespread damage at a cost of $1.6 million.

Aug. 11, 2011: Flash Flood, Lubbock. Scattered thunderstorms brought heavy rain, wind, and hail to the Lubbock area. Some area received 1–4 inches of rain in an hour, causing high water damage to homes and vehicles. Farm and weather equipment in Dimmit were damaged by 90 mph winds. Total damage, $1.175 million.

September–October 2011: Wildfires, Bastrop County. Three separate fires that began Sept. 4 merged into a single blaze east of the city of Bastrop and became known as the Bastrop County Complex fire. The fire destroyed 1,691 homes and much of Bastrop State Park was burned. Declared the most destructive wildfire in Texas history, it was finally extinguished on Oct. 29.

Oct. 9, 2011: Tornado, San Antonio. An EF-1 tornado with winds up to 90–100 mph tore apart roofs, utility poles, and vehicles; damage, $1 million.

2010

June 9, 2010: Flash Flood. New Braunfels. Storms produced rains in excess of 11 inches, which caused the Guadalupe River to rise over 20 feet in just two hours. Campers, vehicles, boats, homes, and businesses suffered extensive damages along the riverbanks. The flash flood resulted in one death; damage, more than $10 million.

July 2, 2010: Tornado. Hebbronville. An EF-1 tornado that developed following Hurricane Alex caused considerable damage in Hebbronville. Over half of the town's population lost power, and the tornado was reported to be as wide as a football field. Estimated damage, $1.5 million.

July 4, 2010: Flood. Terry, Lubbock, Garza, and Lynn Counties. A series of thunderstorms erupted in the early morning of the Fourth of July over the west South Texas Plains. Local flooding caused roadway closures and damage to more 100 vehicles. More than 300 homes and businesses were affected; economic losses were around $16.5 million.

July 8, 2010: Flood. Starr County. Another storm that formed in the aftermath of Hurricane Alex, dumped an estimated 50 inches or more of rain on the lower Rio Grande Valley over 10 days leading up to the 8th. Falcon Reservoir rose during days of rain and finally spilled over on the 8th. The Rio Grande was nearly 2 miles wide at some points. Estimated damage was around $37 million.

Oct. 24, 2010: Tornado. Rice, Navarro County. An intense EF-2 tornado struck with maximum winds of 135 mph. Vehicles were overturned on Interstate 45 and 11 train cars were derailed when the tornado hit the tracks. The football, baseball, and softball fields of the local high school were damaged; the intermediate school lost the gymnasium roof and suffered a caved-in wall; damage was $1 million.

2009

Jan. 19, 2009: Wildfire. Hidalgo County. Aided by strong gusts, low humidity, lack of rain, and warm temperatures, a wildfire spread across 2,560 acres in Hidalgo County and consumed four buildings at Moore Air Force Base. Damage at the base was $10 million.

March 30, 2009: Hail. Northeast Tarrant County. A strong line of severe storms dumped ping-pong- to baseball-sized hail on numerous cities in northeast Tarrant County. Much of the damage was to automobiles; overall damage was $95 million.

April 11, 2009: Hail. Midland. Up to golf-ball-sized hail caused tremendous damage to homes and vehicles during a severe storm, with an estimated $160 million in roof damage. A woman was pelted in the stomach by a hailstone that broke through the window in her dining room.

May 2, 2009: Thunderstorm Wind. Irving. The National Weather Service determined that a microburst caused the Dallas Cowboys' bubble practice facility to collapse from winds estimated at 70 mph. Twelve people were injured, including one coach who was paralyzed from the waist down. The damage was estimated at $5 million.

June 11, 2009: Thunderstorm Wind. Burnet. A peak wind of 67 mph was measured at the Burnet Airport and numerous planes were flipped or blown across the tarmac. Damage in the city was $5 million.

Sept. 16, 2009: Hail. El Paso. A series of supercell storms produced golf-ball- to tennis-ball-sized hail and the most costly hailstorm in recorded history for the El Paso area. Estimated damage was $150 million.

Dec. 23, 2009: Tornado. Lufkin. An EF-3 tornado touched down in Lufkin, damaging structures, homes, and vehicles. The twister and heavy rains caused damage estimated at $10 million.

2008

March 31, 2008: Hail. Northeast Texas. Severe thunderstorms developed across the Red River valley, many producing large hail that damaged car windows, skylights, and roofs in Texarkana and elsewhere in Bowie County. Damage was estimated at $120 million.

April 10, 2008: Tornadoes. Johnson County. A lone supercell thunderstorm evolved in the afternoon of the 9th, producing tornadoes and large hail. A tornado touched down near Happy Hill and traveled northeast 3 miles to Pleasant Point, where it dissipated. The F-1 tornado, with maximum wind speeds of 90–95 mph, destroyed three homes and damaged more than 30 homes and other buildings. Damage was $25 million.

May 14, 2008: Hail. Austin. A severe thunderstorm southwest of Austin moved northeast across downtown, causing extensive damage from winds and large hail. Large trees and branches were knocked down, and baseball-sized hail and 70–80 mph winds blew out windows in apartments and office buildings, including the State Capitol. Total damage was estimated at $50 million.

August 18, 2008: Floods. Wichita Falls. An unseasonably strong upper-level storm system moved over North Texas, and several waves of heavy thunderstorms caused heavy rain and widespread flooding in the Iowa Park, Burkburnett, and Wichita Falls areas. In Wichita Falls, at least 118 homes were flooded, 19 of which were destroyed, and residents were evacuated by boat. Burkburnett and Iowa Park were isolated for a few hours because of street flooding. Damage was estimated at $25 million, and Gov. Rick Perry declared Wichita County a disaster area.

Sept. 12, 2008: Hurricane Ike. Galveston. The eye of the hurricane moved ashore near the Galveston with central pressure of 951.6 millibars and maximum sustained winds around 110 mph, which made Hurricane Ike a strong category-2 storm. There were 12 deaths directly related to Ike (11 occurring in Galveston County from drowning due to storm surge) and at least another 25 fatalities either due to carbon monoxide poisoning from generators, accidents while clearing debris, or house fires from candles. Storm tide and storm surge caused the majority of property damage at the coast. Damage in Harris, Chambers, Galveston, Liberty, Polk, Matagorda, Brazoria, Fort Bend, San Jacinto, and Montgomery counties totaled $14 billion.

2007

March 29, 2007: Floods. Corsicana. Flash flooding along Interstate 45 submerged two cars in Navarro County, north of Corsicana, and 2 feet of water was reported on I-45 and Texas 31, east of town; damage to businesses, roads, and bridges, $19 million.

April 13, 2007: Hail. Colleyville. Teacup-size hail was reported as strong storms developed in Tarrant County. Hail damage to 5,500 cars and 3,500 homes and businesses was estimated at $10 million.

April 24, 2007: Tornado. Eagle Pass. A large tornado crossed the Rio Grande from Mexico around 6 p.m., striking Rosita Valley, near Eagle Pass. Ten deaths were reported, including a family of five in a mobile home. Golf-ball-sized hail and the tornado struck Rosita Valley Elementary School, leaving only the interior walls standing. Damage indicated wind speeds near 140 mph and an F-3 level, with a path 1/4-mile wide and 4 miles long. The tornado also destroyed 59 manufactured homes and 57 houses. Total damage was estimated at $80 million.

June 17–18, 2007: Floods. North Texas. Torrential rain fell as an upper-level low lingered for several days. In Tarrant County, one person drowned after her rescue boat capsized. Hundreds of people were rescued from high water. In Grayson County, a woman died in floodwaters as she drove under an overpass, and another death occurred in a flooded truck. Three people in Cooke County died when a mobile home was carried away by floodwaters. Damage was estimated at $30 million in Tarrant County, $20 million in Grayson County, and $28 million in Cooke County.

June 27, 2007: Floods. Marble Falls. Two lines of thunderstorms produced 10–19 inches of rain in southern Burnet County. Hardest hit was Marble Falls, where two young men died in the early morning when their jeep was swept into high water east of town. Damage to more than 315 homes and businesses was $130 million.

Sept. 13, 2007: Hurricane Humberto. Jefferson County. The hurricane made landfall around 1 a.m. in rural southwestern Jefferson County near McFaddin National Wildlife Refuge. Minimum pressure was around 985 millibars, with maximum winds at 90 mph. Flash flooding occurred in urban areas between Beaumont and Orange, as 11 inches of rain fell. Coastal storm tides were 3–5 feet, with the highest storm surge occurring at Texas Point. Humberto caused one death, 12 injuries, and $25 million in damage.

2006

Jan. 1, 2006: Wildfires. North Texas. Several wildfires exploded across North Texas due to low humidity, strong winds, and the ongoing drought. Fires were reported in Montague, Eastland, and Palo Pinto counties. Five injuries were reported, as well as $10.8 million in property damage.

March 12–18, 2006: Wildfires. Borger. A wildfire now known as the Borger wildfire started four miles southwest of Borger, Hutchinson County. It killed seven people and burned 479,500 acres and 28 structures; total property damage, $49.9 million; crop damage, $45.4 million. A second wildfire known as the Interstate-40 wildfire burned 427,696 acres. The Texas Forest Service named the two wildfires the East Amarillo Complex. In all, 12 people were killed; total property damage, $49.9 million; crop damage, $45.4 million.

March 19, 2006: Tornado. Uvalde. An F-2 tornado moved through the Uvalde area causing $1.5 million in property damage. It was the strongest tornado in South- Central Texas since Oct. 12, 2001.

April 11–13, 2006: Wildfire. Canadian. A wildfire 10 miles north of Canadian, Hemphill County, injured two; burned 18,000 acres; and destroyed $90 million of crops.

April 18, 2006: Hail. Gillespie County. Hailstones as large as 2.5 inches in diameter destroyed windows in homes and car windshields between Harper and Doss in Gillespie County. The hail also damaged 70 percent of the area's peach crop, an estimated loss of $5 million.

April 20, 2006: Hail. San Marcos. Hailstones as large at 4.25 inches in diameter (grapefruit-size) were reported south of San Marcos, damaging 10,000 vehicles on the road and another 7,000 vehicles at homes; total damage was estimated at $100 million.

May 4, 2006: Hail. Snyder. Lime-to-baseball-size hail fell across Snyder in Scurry County for a least 15 minutes. The hail was blown sideways at times by 60-to-70-mph winds. Total damage was estimated at $15 million.

May 5, 2006: Tornado. Waco. A tornado with peak intensity estimated at low F-2 caused damage of $3 million.

May 9, 2006: Tornado. Childress. An F-2 tornado caused significant damage along a 1-1/2-mile path through the north side of Childress in the evening. An instrument at Childress High School measured a wind gust of 109 mph. Property damage was estimated at $5.7 million.

Aug. 1, 2006: Thunderstorms. El Paso. Storms in a saturated atmosphere repeatedly developed and moved over the northwest third of El Paso County, concentrating near the Franklin Mountains. Rainfall reports varied from 4–6 inches within 15 hours, with an isolated report of about 8 inches on the western slope of the mountain range. Four days of heavy rains, combined with the mountains' terrain, led to excessive runoff and flooding not seen on such a large scale in the El Paso area in more than 100 years. Property damage was estimated at $180 million.

2005

March 25, 2005: Hail. Austin. In the evening, the most destructive hailstorm in 10 years struck the greater Austin area. The storm knocked out power to 5,000 homes in northwest Austin. Hail 2 inches in diameter was reported near the Travis County Exposition Center. Total damage was estimated at $100 million.

May 2005–December 2006: Drought. North-Central Texas. In May, portions of the area were upgraded from moderate to severe drought. By month's end, the drought had made significant agricultural and hydrological impacts on the region. In November, many Central Texas counties were added to the drought. The Texas Cooperative Extension estimated statewide drought losses at $4.1 billion, $1.9 billion in North Texas alone.

June 9, 2005: Tornado. Petersburg. An F-3 tornado affected an area from Petersburg in southeast Hale County to portions of southwest and south-central Floyd County. Total damage was estimated at $70 million.

Sept. 23, 2005: Hurrican Rita. Southeast Texas. The eye of Hurricane Rita moved ashore in extreme southwest Louisiana between Sabine Pass and Johnson's Bayou in Cameron Parish with maximum sustained winds of 120 mph, category-3 strength. On the 22nd, Rita had strengthened to a peak intensity of 175 mph winds. In Southeast Texas, Rita caused 3 fatalities, 3 injuries, and $159.5 million in property and crop damage. Total property damage, $2.1 billion.

Dec. 27, 2005: Wildfire. Cross Plains, Callahan County. The fire started just west of Cross Plains and, fanned by winds gusting near 40 mph, quickly moved east into town. Two elderly people were unable to escape the flames; 16 firefighters were also injured; property damage, $11 million.

2004

June 1–9, 2004: Floods. North-Central Texas. Flash flooding due to an upper air disturbance and a cold front caused damage to more than 1,000 homes. This was the first of many days in which heavy rains fell throughout the state. Estimated damage was more $7.5 million.

June 21, 2004: Tornadoes. Panhandle. Severe weather kicked up just ahead of a frontal boundary causing damage to Amarillo and the surrounding area. Eight tornadoes were reported around the Panhandle, and there were many reports of hail, topping out at 4.25 inches in diameter in Potter County. Thousands of homes were damaged, and the total damage was estimated at more than $150 million.

July 28–29, 2004: Rainstorm. North-Central Texas. A stationary front lead to torrential rainfall in Dallas and Waco. Hundreds of homes were damaged by flash flooding, as 24-hour rainfall totals for the two cities approached 5 inches. Outlying areas of the cities reported as much as 7 inches of rain in a 12-hour period on the 29th. Damage estimates topped $20 million.

Sept. 14, 2004: Storm. Grapeland. A lightning strike during football practice at Grapeland High School, Houston County, caused one death and injuries to 40 players and coaches.

Dec. 24–26, 2004: Snow. Coastal Texas. Large portions of Southeast and South Texas saw their first white Christmas in recorded history. A cold front past over the state a few days prior to Christmas Eve dropping temperatures below freezing. Another cold front brought snow, which accumulated Christmas Eve night and into Christmas day. Galveston and Houston recorded 4 inches of snow, while areas further south, such as Victoria, had 12 inches. Brownsville recorded 1.5 inches of snow.

2003

Feb. 24–26, 2003: Snow. Ice. North-Central Texas. A severe cold front brought freezing rain, sleet, and snow to the region. Snow accumulations were as high as 5 inches, resulting in $15 million in damages. Most schools and businesses were closed for this period.

April 8, 2003: Rainstorm. Brownsville. A severe thunderstorm caused one of the most destructive hail events in the history of Brownsville. Hail exceeded 2.75 inches in diameter and caused $50 million in damage to the city. At least 5 injuries were reported.

July 14–16, 2003: Hurricane Claudette. Port O'Connor. The hurricane made landfall near Port O'Connor in the late morning hours of the 14th. At landfall, wind speeds were more than 90 mph. The system then moved westward toward Big Bend and northern Mexico; 1 death; 2 injuries; damage, more than $100 million.

September 2003: Floods. Upper Coast, South Texas. Persistent flooding caused more than $2 million in damage. The remnants of Tropical Storm Grace caused flash flooding along the Upper Coast region near Galveston early in September, with rainfall estimates in Matagorda County ranging from 6–12 inches. During the second half of the month, South Texas was hit with a deluge of rain caused by a tropical wave combined with cold fronts. Monthly rainfall totals ranged from 7–15 inches in the deep south.

2002

March 2002: Storms. Central Texas. Several violent storms occurred, which produced hail, tornadoes, and strong winds. Hail 1-3/4 inches in diameter caused $16 million in damage to San Angelo on the 19th, while 30 people where injured on the same day by an F-2 tornado in Somerset, Bexar County, that caused $2 million in damage. For the month: 3 fatalities; 64 injuries; damage, $37.5 million.

June 30–July 7, 2002: Rainstorm. Central Texas. Excessive rainfall occurred in the South-Central and Edwards Plateau regions, with some areas reporting more than 30 inches of rain. Damage in the South-Central region alone was nearly $250 million. In Central Texas, 29 counties were devastated by flooding and declared federal disaster areas by President George W. Bush. Total event damage, $2 billion.

Sept. 5–7, 2002: Tropical Storm Fay. Coastal Plains. The storm made landfall along the coast on the 6th. This system produced extremely heavy rainfall, strong damaging wind gusts, and tornadoes. Ten to 20 inches of rain fell in eastern Wharton County. Brazoria County was hit the hardest with about 1,500 homes flooded. The storm produced five tornadoes, flooded many areas, and caused significant wind damage; total damage, $4.5 million.

Oct. 24, 2002: Rainstorms. South Texas. Severe thunderstorms in South Texas produced heavy rain, causing flooding and two tornadoes in Corpus Christi. The most extensive damage occurred across Del Mar College. The storm caused one death and 26 injuries; total damages, more then $85 million.

2001

Jan. 1–31, 2001: Drought. South Texas. The USDA's Farm Service Agency received a Presidential Disaster Declaration in December 2000 because of persistent drought conditions in South Texas; $125 million in damage was reported in the region.

May 2001: Storms. San Antonio, High Plains. Numerous storms caused excessive damage. Four-inch hail caused nearly $150 million in damage in San Antonio on the 6th. On the 30th, supercell thunderstorms in the High Plains produced winds over 100 mph, and golf-ball-sized hail caused more than $186 million in damage. In all, 36 injuried; property and agriculture damage, $358 million.

June–December 2001: Drought. Significant drought-like conditions occurred in Texas from early summer through December. After the yearly drought report was filed, it was determined that total crop damage across the South Plains was about $420 million. Losses occurred to crops such as cotton, wheat, grain sorghum, and corn.

June 5–10, 2001: Tropical Storm Allison. Houston area. The storm dumped large amounts of rain on the city and made landfall on the western end of Galveston Island. Over the next five days, it produced record rainfall, which led to devastating flooding across southeastern Texas. Some weather stations in the Houston area reported more than 40 inches of rain total and more than 18 inches in a 24-hour period. Twenty-two deaths; damage, $5.2 billion.

July–August 2001: Heat. Excessive heat plagued Texas, resulting in 17 deaths in the Houston area.

Oct. 12, 2001: Tornado. Hondo. An F-2 tornado caused $20 million in damage. The tornado injured 25 people and damaged the National Guard Armory, a large hangar at the Hondo Airport, and nearly two dozen aircraft. Also damaged, were some 150 homes in Hondo, 50 on its outskirts, and nearly 100 mobile homes.

Nov. 15, 2001: Rainstorms. Central Texas. Storms caused flash flooding and weak tornadoes in the Edwards Plateau, South-Central, and southern portions of North-Central Texas. Flash flooding caused 8 deaths and 198 injuries.

2000

January–October 2000: Drought. A severe drought plagued most of Texas. Some regions experienced little to no rain for several months during the summer. Abilene saw no rain for 72 consecutive days, while Dallas had no rain for 84 consecutive days during the summer. During July, aquifers hit all-time lows, and lakes and streams fell to critical levels. Most regions had to cut back or stop agricultural activities, which resulted in $515 million in agricultural loss, according to USDA figures.

March 28, 2000: Tornado. Fort Worth. A supercell over Fort Worth produced an F-3 tornado, which injured 80 people and caused significant damage. Flooding killed two people.

May 20, 2000: Rainstorm. Southeast Texas. A flash flood in the Liberty and Dayton area was caused by 18.3 inches of rain falling in five hours. Up to 80 people were rescued from flood waters; property damage, $10 million.

July 2000: Heat. Dallas–Fort Worth. Excessive heat resulted from a high-pressure ridge, particularly from the 12th–21st. DFW Airport reported a 10-day average of 103.3 degrees. College Station had 12 consecutive days of 100 degrees or greater. The heat caused 34 deaths in North and Southeast Texas, primarily among the elderly.

Aug. 2, 2000: Storm. Houston. Lightning struck a tree at Astroworld in Houston injuring 17 teens.

Sept. 5, 2000: Heat. Excessive heat resulted in at least eight all-time high temperature records around the state, one of which was Possum Kingdom Lake, which reached 114 degrees. This day is regarded as the hottest day ever in Texas, considering the state as a whole.

Dec. 13 and 24–25, 2000: Ice. Snow. Northeast Texas. Two major winter storms blanketed the area with up to 6 inches of ice from each storm. Eight inches of snow fell in the Panhandle, while areas in North Texas received 12 inches. Thousands of motorists were stranded on Interstate 20 and had to be rescued by the National Guard; 235,000 people lost electric service from the first storm alone. Roads were treacherous, driving was halted in several counties; total cost of damages from both storms, more than $156 million.

1999

Jan. 22, 1999: Hail. Brazos County. Golfball- and softball-sized hail fell in the Bryan–College Station area; damage, $10 million to cars, homes, and offices.

May 1999: Storms. Tornadoes. East, Central, West Texas. Numerous severe weather outbreaks caused damaging winds, large hail, dangerous lightning, and numerous tornadoes. An F-3 tornado moved through downtown area and high school of De Kalb, Bowie County, on the 4th, injuring 22 people and causing $125 million in damage to the community. On the same day, two F-2 tornadoes roared through Kilgore simultaneously. On the 11th, an F-4 tornado moved through parts of Loyal Valley, Mason County, and Castell, Llano County, killing one and injuring six. The 25th saw storms produce 2.5-inch hail in Levelland and Amarillo. Total damages, more than $157 million.

August 1999: Heat. Dallas–Fort Worth. Excessive heat throughout the month resulted in 16 fatalities. The airport reported 26 consecutive days of 100 degrees or greater.

1998

March–May, 1998: Drought. According to the Climate Prediction Center, this three-month period ranks as the seventh driest for a region including Texas, Oklahoma, Arkansas, Louisiana, and Mississippi. May 1998 has been ranked as both the warmest and the driest May in this region.

Aug. 22–25, 1998: Tropical Storm Charley. Hill Country. The storm dumped torrential rains in the area that caused flash floods; 13 killed; more than 200 were injured.

Oct. 17–19, 1998: Rainstorm. Hill Country. A massive, devastating flood set all-time records for rainfall and river levels; 25 killed; more than 2,000 injured; damage, more than $500 million from the Hill Country to counties south and east of San Antonio.

1997

May 27, 1997: Tornado. Jarrell. A half-mile-wide F-5 tornado struck Jarrell, Williamson County, leveling the Double Creek subdisivion, claiming 27 lives, injuring 12 others, and causing more than $40 million in damage.

1996

Feb. 21, 1996: Heat. Anomalously high temperatures were reported over the entire state, breaking records in nearly every region. Temperatures near 100 degrees shattered previous records by as many as 10 degrees, and Texans experienced heat more characteristic of mid-summer than winter.

May 10, 1996: Hail. Howard County. Hail up to 5 inches in diameter fell; 48 injuries; property damage, $30 million.

1995

May 5, 1995: Thunderstorm. Hail. Dallas–Fort Worth. A thunderstorm moved across the area with 70 mph wind gusts and rainfall rates of almost 3 inches in 30 minutes (5 inches in one hour); 20 people killed; 109 injured by large hail, many at Fort Worth's outdoor Mayfest near the Trinity River. With more than $2 billion in damage, NOAA dubbed it the "costliest thunderstorm event in history."

May 28, 1995: Supercell Thunderstorm. San Angelo. The storm produced extreme winds and giant hail, injuring at least 80 people and causing about $120 million in damage. Sixty-one homes were destroyed; more than 9,000 were slightly damaged. In some areas, hail was 6 inches deep, with drifts to 2 feet.

1994

Oct. 15–19, 1994: Rain. Southest Texas. Extreme amounts of rainfall, up to 28.90 inches over a 4-day period, fell throughout southeastern Texas; 17 killed, mostly in flash flooding. Many rivers reached record flood levels. Houston was cut off as numerous roads, including Interstate 10, were under water. Damage was estimated at $700 million; 26 counties were declared disaster areas.

1983

Aug. 15–21, 1983: Hurricane Alicia. This was the first hurricane to make landfall in the continental U.S. in three years (Aug. 18) and one of the costliest in Texas history ($3 billion). Alicia caused widespread damage to a large section of Southeast Texas, including coastal areas near Galveston and the entire Houston area. Alicia spawned 22 tornadoes; highest winds were estimated near 130 mph. In all, 18 people were killed and 1,800 injured.

1982

April 2, 1982: Tornadoes. Northeast Texas. A tornado outbreak with the most severe striking Paris; 10 people killed; 170 injured; 1,000 left homeless; damage, $50 million. In all, seven tornadoes that day left 11 dead and 174 injured.

May 1982: Tornadoes. Texas recorded 123 tornadoes, the most ever in May and one less than the most recorded in any single month in the state; 1 death; 23 injuries.

Dec. 1982: Heavy Snow. El Paso. Snowfall recorded at 18.2 inches was the most to fall there in any month.

1981

May 24–25, 1981: Severe Flooding. Austin. Thirteen killed; 100 injured; damage, $40 million. Up to 5.5 inches of rain fell in one hour west of the city.

Oct. 11–14, 1981: Rain. North-Central Texas. Record rain caused by the remains of Pacific Hurricane Norma reached more than 20 inches in some locations.

1980

Aug. 9–11, 1980: Hurricane Allen. South Texas. Three persons killed; property and crop damage, $650 million to $750 million; more than 250,000 coastal residents evacuated. The worst damage was along Padre Island and in Corpus Christi; 20 inches of rain fell on extreme South Texas; 29 tornadoes, one of the worst hurricane-related outbreaks.

Summer 1980: Heat. One of the hottest summers in the history of the Lone Star State.

Sept. 5–8, 1980: Hurricane Danielle. The storm brought rain and flooding to southeast and Central Texas; 17 inches of rain fell at Port Arthur; 25 inches near Junction.

Texas Climatological Normals for 1981–2010 and Extreme Weather Records by County through 2020

Explanations and Sources

Data in this table are provided by the Office of the Texas State Climatologist, Texas A&M University, College Station, Texas.

The Climatological Normals include Mean Maximum July Temperature, Mean Minimum January Temperature, Average Freeze Dates, Growing Season, and Mean Precipitation. They are calculated every 10 years and are based on the previous 30-year period, which is 1981–2010. Data in italics are from the period 1971–2000.

Data for counties where a weather station has not been maintained long enough to establish a reliable mean are interpolated from isoline charts prepared from mean values from stations with long-established records.

Mean Maximum for July is computed from the sum of the daily maxima. Mean Minimum for January is computed from the sum of the daily minima.

Extreme Weather Records include Record High Temperature, Record Low Temperature, and Record Rainfall; they are compiled yearly and are current through 2018.

The far left column lists Texas' 254 counties and identifies the town or landmark nearest to the National Weather Service station used to calculate Climatological Normals. If that weather station is outside the county, the town or landmark is in italics. Extreme Weather Records may have occurred at any weather station in that county and are identified only for Record Rainfall.

An asterisk (*) preceding an Extreme Weather Record means it also occurred on a previous date.

County, Town or Landmark Closest to Station for Normals	Temperature								Average Freeze Dates			
	Mean Max. July	No. At or Above 100°	Mean Min. January	No. At or Below 32°	Record Highest	Record High Date	Record Lowest	Record Low Date	Last in Spring		First in Fall	
	F.	Days	F.	Days	F.	M-D-Y	F.	M-D-Y	Mo.	Day	Mo.	Day
Anderson, Palestine	92.8	4	36.9	38	114	7-26-1954	–6	2-12-1899	Mar.	24	Nov.	12
Andrews, Andrews	95.2	15	33.0	59	113	6-27-1994	–1	2-2-1985	Mar.	31	Nov.	10
Angelina, County Airport	92.4	5	39.4	28	*110	8-19-1909	–2	2-2-1951	Mar.	10	Nov.	20
Aransas, Rockport	91.6	0	48.3	4	107	9-5-2000	9	12-23-1989	Feb.	6	Dec.	20
Archer, Archer City	95.5	22	32.6	57	114	6-28-1980	*–10	12-23-1989	Mar.	27	Nov.	8
Armstrong, Claude	91.2	3	26.0	108	*108	6-28-1980	–16	2-13-1905	Apr.	16	Oct.	24
Atascosa, Pleasanton	96.0	15	42.1	19	*113	8-22-1917	–1	1-31-1949	Feb.	27	Nov.	29
Austin, Sealy	94.0	7	43.5	13	*111	9-4-2000	0	12-23-1989	Feb.	22	Dec.	5
Bailey, Muleshoe NWR	91.6	9	22.1	123	*112	6-28-1994	–21	2-8-1933	Apr.	20	Oct.	23
Bandera, Medina	93.9	4	37.0	44	*110	7-9-1939	*–5	2-2-1951	Mar.	24	Nov.	13
Bastrop, Elgin	94.3	13	41.0	18	*111	9-5-2000	–3	12-23-1989	Mar.	5	Nov.	28
Baylor, Seymour	95.5	24	29.7	69	120	8-12-1936	–14	1-4-1947	Mar.	28	Nov.	7
Bee, Beeville	93.8	7	45.5	9	114	6-22-1990	5	2-12-1899	Feb.	18	Dec.	10
Bell, Stillhouse Hollow Dam	94.1	13	37.7	33	*112	8-11-1947	–5	12-23-1989	Mar.	10	Nov.	27
Bexar, San Antonio Intl. Airport	94.4	8	42.8	14	*113	8-28-2011	*0	1-31-1949	Mar.	1	Dec.	1
Blanco, Blanco	92.4	5	37.2	44	110	9-6-2000	*–6	1-31-1949	Mar.	22	Nov.	13
Borden, Gail	92.6	15	33.7	56	116	6-27-1994	–1	12-23-1989	Mar.	24	Nov.	12
Bosque, Lake Whitney Dam	94.1	20	36.3	43	113	9-5-2000	*–3	12-23-1989	Mar.	13	Nov.	18
Bowie, Texarkana	92.0	7	35.2	46	*112	8-5-2011	–9	2-12-1899	Mar.	16	Nov.	19
Brazoria, Angleton	91.1	0	48.3	4	109	9-4-2000	6	2-12-1899	Feb.	6	Dec.	17
Brazos, College Station	94.7	12	43.1	16	112	9-4-2000	–3	1-31-1949	Feb.	26	Dec.	2
Brewster, Alpine	90.9	2	32.5	56	*117	6-17-1992	*–6	1-12-1962	Apr.	4	Nov.	2
Briscoe, Silverton	90.6	4	25.2	111	112	07-15-2020	–10	12-25-2004	Apr.	13	Oct.	27
Brooks, Falfurrias	97.2	28	45.3	10	116	7-13-2016	9	1-12-1962	Feb.	23	Dec.	5
Brown, Brownwood	95.4	18	33.9	55	113	7-19-1925	–6	12-23-1989	Mar.	29	Nov.	7
Burleson, Somerville Dam	95.9	13	36.8	37	114	9-5-2000	3	12-23-1989	Mar.	8	Nov.	24
Burnet, Burnet Muni. Airport	94.1	6	39.7	26	*114	7-11-1917	*–4	12-23-1989	Mar.	6	Nov.	24
Caldwell, Luling	96.2	13	41.2	29	111	8-28-2011	–3	1-31-1949	Mar.	9	Nov.	23
Calhoun, Port O'Connor	88.8	1	48.6	4	*109	8-29-2011	9	12-23-1989	Jan.	29	Dec.	22
Callahan, Putnam	94.0	15	33.6	53	*110	5-28-2011	–8	12-23-1989	Mar.	31	Nov.	8
Cameron, Brownsville	95.1	1	54.9	1	108	8-18-1915	12	2-13-1899	Dec.	25	Jan.	24
Camp, *Daingerfield*	91.4	9	36.8	34	111	8-3-2011	*10	12-9-2005	Mar.	8	Nov.	23
Carson, Panhandle	91.3	7	25.2	122	112	6-27-2011	*–10	1-12-1963	Apr.	22	Oct.	19

Table Highlights

Record Highs in 2011

Thirty-five new record highs were set in 2011 from the Gulf Coast to West Texas and the Panhandle. The highest records were 118 degrees set in Knox County on June 20 and in Cottle county on June 27. That year began a severe drought that lasted through part of 2015. This period is now considered a "drought of record" by some water suppliers.

The years 1951–1957, however, are still considered the drought of record for other officials and agencies. On a statewide basis, the most intense drought, as measured by the Palmer Drought Severity Index, was in 2011; but the most severe drought, as measured by combined intensity and duration, was 1951–1957.

Rain Records in 2015

Eleven rainfall records were set in 2015, including six records during Oct. 24–25. Most records were set in Central and East Texas and ranged from 9.5 inches in Mineola in Wood County to 18.95 inches in Corsicana in Navarro County.

Rain Records in 2017

Twenty one rainfall records were set in 2017, 17 of which occurred between August 26 and August 30, during Hurricane Harvey. Six counties recorded more than 20 inches of rain: Galveston, Harris, Jefferson, Lavaca, Liberty, and Orange. The highest rainfall total, 26.03 inches, fell on Port Arthur in Jefferson County.

Rain Records in 2018

Eight rain records were set in 2018. Six of those occurred in the months of September (the third wettest month in Texas history) and October (the second wettest month in Texas history).

Combined, September–October 2018 are the wettest consecutive months ever. ☆

Growing Season	Mean Precipitation												Record Rainfall Highest Daily Total		
	January	February	March	April	May	June	July	August	September	October	November	December	Annual		
Days	In.	In.	In.	In.	In.	In.	In.	In.	In.	In.	In.	In.	In.	Location	In.	M-D-Y
234	3.66	3.90	3.89	3.29	4.21	4.97	2.65	3.31	3.21	5.07	4.24	4.20	46.60	Palestine	9.10	8-14-1991
240	0.56	0.69	0.86	0.66	1.63	2.03	1.83	1.65	1.85	1.58	0.71	0.69	14.74	Andrews	7.60	7-2-1914
247	4.18	3.87	3.78	3.05	4.64	4.68	3.05	3.34	4.08	4.83	5.01	4.44	48.95	Lufkin	10.65	10-17-1994
328	2.42	2.20	2.40	1.76	3.10	3.17	3.46	2.57	5.08	4.22	3.02	1.78	35.18	Aransas NWR	14.25	11-1-1974
231	1.36	2.07	2.24	2.53	4.09	3.81	1.92	2.61	2.62	3.81	1.82	1.84	30.72	Olney	8.45	5-15-1989
195	0.72	0.56	1.39	1.40	2.29	3.16	2.84	2.91	1.92	1.66	0.80	0.71	20.36	Claude	6.42	5-16-1951
274	1.94	1.95	2.19	2.06	4.05	4.19	2.78	2.36	3.22	3.03	2.43	1.87	32.07	Rossville	9.09	9-15-1919
276	3.25	2.72	2.84	3.56	4.57	3.62	2.65	3.56	3.91	4.84	4.51	2.89	42.92	San Felipe	12.25	4-18-2016
177	0.54	0.48	0.86	0.81	2.32	2.50	2.18	2.88	2.50	1.73	0.71	0.73	18.24	Muleshoe	5.25	5-16-1951
244	2.00	1.92	3.28	2.37	4.74	4.17	3.96	2.14	3.58	4.36	2.61	2.24	37.37	Vanderpool	11.53	8-1-1978
264	2.41	2.30	2.81	2.13	4.29	4.03	2.00	2.05	2.74	4.07	3.13	2.47	34.43	Smithville	16.05	6-30-1940
222	1.21	1.89	1.94	1.95	4.11	4.00	2.38	2.76	2.91	2.71	1.66	1.43	28.95	Lake Kemp	6.25	9-1-1986
299	1.96	1.74	2.28	2.55	2.88	3.86	3.39	2.30	3.74	3.45	2.14	1.68	31.97	Chase Field	11.55	7-16-1990
251	2.13	2.59	3.19	2.59	4.51	4.23	1.93	2.25	3.70	3.97	2.94	2.75	36.78	Killeen	11.43	9-8-2010
277	1.76	1.79	2.31	2.10	4.01	4.14	2.74	2.09	3.03	4.11	2.28	1.91	32.27	San Antonio	14.33	10-18-1998
236	2.11	2.04	2.92	2.29	4.16	4.23	2.41	1.90	3.33	4.26	2.88	2.34	34.87	Hye	20.70	9-11-1952
226	0.66	0.77	1.06	1.44	2.68	2.62	1.73	2.30	2.32	1.78	0.97	0.73	19.06	Gail	10.79	9-20-2014
243	2.16	2.42	3.50	2.81	4.16	4.58	1.76	2.04	3.28	3.98	2.75	2.75	36.19	Kopperl	11.87	6-23-2014
249	3.90	4.32	4.65	4.16	5.13	4.79	3.78	2.17	3.59	5.25	4.99	5.23	51.96	New Boston	8.15	5-10-2009
338	4.12	2.79	3.08	2.80	3.30	4.91	4.68	4.02	6.73	4.81	4.83	3.50	49.57	Alvin	25.75	7-26-1979
278	3.24	2.85	3.17	2.66	4.33	4.45	2.14	2.68	3.18	4.91	3.22	3.23	40.06	College Station	13.39	10-16-1994
216	0.54	0.57	0.46	0.60	1.48	2.62	2.74	2.93	2.60	1.40	0.47	0.59	17.00	O2 Ranch	7.80	8-6-1920
197	0.72	0.82	1.32	1.60	2.86	4.15	2.34	2.78	2.18	1.87	0.92	0.85	22.41	Quitaque	8.58	6-1-1957
285	1.13	1.53	1.14	1.46	3.10	2.85	3.08	2.49	4.07	3.23	1.12	1.27	26.47	Falfurrias	10.00	9-20-1967
233	1.35	2.38	2.68	2.31	3.75	4.49	2.01	2.24	2.93	3.07	1.68	1.54	30.43	Winchell	8.20	9-23-1955
238	2.98	2.91	3.05	2.73	3.96	4.35	1.89	2.50	3.19	4.47	3.53	3.11	38.67	Somerville Dam	15.25	10-17-1994
262	1.84	2.03	2.98	2.15	4.03	4.25	2.04	1.82	3.10	3.40	2.76	2.01	32.41	Marble Falls	11.00	9-10-1921
263	2.30	2.30	2.56	2.66	4.30	4.28	2.04	2.14	3.34	4.56	2.89	2.56	35.93	Lockhart	13.38	10-18-1998
323	3.90	1.88	2.09	1.39	2.94	3.87	5.32	1.84	3.47	3.13	2.52	3.58	35.93	Point Comfort	14.65	6-26-1960
225	1.10	1.78	2.35	1.77	3.32	4.01	2.12	2.05	2.58	3.06	1.93	1.35	27.42	Baird	10.29	8-3-1978
365	1.27	1.08	1.23	1.54	2.64	2.57	2.04	2.44	5.92	3.74	1.82	1.15	27.44	San Benito	12.67	9-5-1933
259	3.24	3.85	4.55	3.56	4.75	4.16	3.29	2.72	3.22	4.58	4.45	4.42	46.79	Pittsburg	8.11	4-27-1958
196	0.61	0.61	1.35	1.68	2.74	3.53	2.57	2.94	2.19	1.87	0.93	0.76	21.78	Panhandle	8.05	5-16-1951

County, Town or Landmark Closest to Station for Normals	Temperature								Average Freeze Dates			
	Mean Max. July	No. At or Above 100°	Mean Min. January	No. At or Below 32°	Record Highest	Record High Date	Record Lowest	Record Low Date	Last in Spring		First in Fall	
	F.	Days	F.	Days	F.	M-D-Y	F.	M-D-Y	Mo.	Day	Mo.	Day
Cass, Wright Patman Dam	90.9	4	37.1	44	*111	8-5-2011	–1	12-23-1989	Mar.	5	Nov.	21
Castro, Dimmitt	90.6	4	23.5	131	111	7-4-1983	–11	12-25-2004	Apr.	23	Oct.	20
Chambers, Anahuac	90.3	1	44.8	11	106	7-9-1939	8	12-23-1989	Feb.	15	Dec.	7
Cherokee, Rusk	89.8	3	39.2	27	*111	8-20-1925	*–5	2-13-1899	Mar.	11	Nov.	24
Childress, Childress	94.3	20	28.8	76	*117	6-26-2011	–13	1-17-1930	Apr.	1	Nov.	7
Clay, Henrietta	94.7	23	30.8	70	*116	8-7-1951	*–8	12-24-1989	Mar.	27	Nov.	9
Cochran, Morton	92.2	6	25.8	102	111	6-26-2011	–12	1-13-1963	Apr.	8	Oct.	31
Coke, Robert Lee	94.4	27	31.9	63	114	5-25-2000	–2	12-24-1989	Mar.	31	Nov.	6
Coleman, Coleman	95.4	20	36.4	42	114	8-3-1943	–9	12-23-1989	Mar.	19	Nov.	17
Collin, McKinney	93.1	3	35.5	45	115	8-4-2001	–11	12-23-1989	Mar.	28	Nov.	7
Collingsworth, Wellington	96.9	30	29.7	79	117	6-26-2011	–6	12-23-1989	Apr.	1	Nov.	5
Colorado, Columbus	95.7	15	40.7	30	116	9-4-2000	*4	12-24-1989	Feb.	25	Dec.	2
Comal, Canyon Dam	93.6	4	41.6	18	*112	8-4-2011	*2	12-23-1989	Mar.	1	Dec.	3
Comanche, Proctor Reservoir	95.1	19	36.2	56	113	8-3-2000	–8	12-23-1989	Mar.	20	Nov.	14
Concho, Paint Rock	95.1	17	32.1	61	*111	5-29-2011	–8	2-2-1985	Apr.	1	Nov.	5
Cooke, Gainesville	92.1	14	33.8	50	114	8-10-1936	–12	2-12-1899	Mar.	20	Nov.	17
Coryell, Gatesville	94.1	8	37.1	43	*112	9-5-2000	–6	1-31-1949	Mar.	29	Nov.	6
Cottle, Paducah	95.5	31	29.0	71	*118	6-27-2011	*–7	12-24-1989	Mar.	27	Nov.	8
Crane, Crane	95.1	7	33.6	49	115	6-27-1994	–6	2-2-1985	Mar.	24	Nov.	11
Crockett, Ozona	93.7	8	31.9	67	113	8-3-2015	–8	2-2-1951	Mar.	29	Nov.	7
Crosby, Crosbyton	91.5	8	27.6	89	113	6-28-1994	–14	2-12-1899	Apr.	4	Nov.	3
Culberson, Van Horn	93.1	8	31.6	70	112	6-25-1969	–14	2-3-2011	Mar.	31	Nov.	7
Dallam, Dalhart *(6 mi. SW)*	91.6	2	22.4	131	110	6-26-2011	–21	1-4-1959	Apr.	28	Oct.	12
Dallas, Dallas Love Field	95.5	17	39.9	23	115	8-18-1909	–10	2-12-1899	Mar.	4	Nov.	30
Dawson, Lamesa	93.3	10	27.6	93	114	6-28-1994	–12	2-8-1933	Apr.	3	Nov.	5
Deaf Smith, Hereford	91.1	4	23.9	118	111	6-8-1910	–17	2-1-1951	Apr.	14	Oct.	26
Delta, Cooper Dam	92.5		36.1	45	110		–1		Mar.	25	Nov.	13
Denton, Denton	94.3	15	35.9	38	*113	7-25-1954	–3	1-31-1949	Mar.	19	Nov.	17
DeWitt, Cuero	96.4	20	43.7	21	114	8-29-2011	2	1-31-1949	Mar.	13	Nov.	18
Dickens, Spur	93.5	17	28.0	89	117	6-28-1994	*–17	2-8-1933	Apr.	4	Nov.	4
Dimmit, Carrizo Springs	98.9	40	39.4	25	*114	6-11-1942	8	12-24-1989	Feb.	22	Dec.	3
Donley, Clarendon	92.8	17	25.3	105	117	8-12-1936	*–13	1-19-1984	Apr.	10	Oct.	26
Duval, Freer	96.8	32	45.5	9	116	6-15-1998	*12	1-24-1963	Feb.	13	Dec.	8
Eastland, Eastland	94.4	13	31.6	68	*115	8-11-1936	–8	12-24-1989	Mar.	31	Nov.	5
Ector, Penwell	93.6	20	33.9	44	116	6-28-1994	–12	2-2-1985	Mar.	31	Nov.	7
Edwards, Rocksprings	90.1	1	38.8	31	110	6-9-1988	0	12-22-1929	Mar.	16	Nov.	22
Ellis, Waxahachie	92.5	7	33.3	59	115	8-18-1909	–9	2-12-1899	Mar.	19	Nov.	17
El Paso, El Paso Intl. Airport	93.5	14	35.8	33	*115	8-18-2002	*–13	2-5-2011	Mar.	17	Nov.	14
Erath, Stephenville	96.0	11	32.9	54	114	8-11-1936	–9	2-12-1899	Mar.	27	Nov.	11
Falls, Marlin	93.6	8	35.3	38	*112	8-11-1969	*–7	1-31-1949	Mar.	16	Nov.	15
Fannin, Bonham	92.1	6	34.5	55	115	8-10-1936	–5	1-19-1930	Mar.	26	Nov.	8
Fayette, La Grange	95.4	15	41.8	19	111	8-23-1917	3	12-23-1989	Mar.	8	Nov.	23
Fisher, Rotan	94.4	13	35.4	55	116	6-27-1994	–12	2-12-1899	Mar.	30	Nov.	8
Floyd, Floydada	91.0	7	26.8	97	111	6-28-1994	–9	1-13-1963	Apr.	5	Nov.	3
Foard, *Truscott*	95.6	29	31.0	66	114		–7		Mar.	28	Nov.	9
Fort Bend, Sugar Land	93.4	7	45.3	7	*108	8-27-2011	8	12-23-1989	Feb.	6	Dec.	16
Franklin, Mount Vernon	93.0	6	36.0	41	112	8-3-2011	*–5	12-23-1989	Mar.	24	Nov.	12
Freestone, Fairfield	92.5	9	37.9	32	*110	9-4-2000	–2	12-23-1989	Mar.	19	Nov.	17
Frio, Dilley	96.7	27	43.4	10	113	9-6-2000	7	12-23-1989	Feb.	18	Dec.	6
Gaines, Seminole	93.4	11	29.1	82	114	6-28-1994	*–23	2-8-1933	Mar.	31	Nov.	7
Galveston, Galveston	89.4	0	49.9	3	106	9-4-2000	7	2-12-1899	Feb.	3	Dec.	28
Garza, Lake Alan Henry	93.6	9	31.6	65	116	6-28-1994	–1	12-22-1989	Mar.	28	Nov.	11
Gillespie, Fredericksburg	92.6	4	36.2	42	*109	9-5-2000	–5	1-31-1949	Mar.	26	Nov.	9
Glasscock, Garden City	93.7	6	30.6	73	114	6-27-1994	*–3	12-22-1989	Mar.	31	Nov.	5
Goliad, Goliad	94.1	7	45.0	13	*112	6-14-1998	7	1-12-1962	Mar.	2	Nov.	26

Growing Season	Mean Precipitation													Record Rainfall Highest Daily Total		
	January	February	March	April	May	June	July	August	September	October	November	December	Annual			
Days	In.	In.	In.	In.	In.	In.	In.	In.	In.	In.	In.	In.	In.	Location	In.	M-D-Y
261	3.75	4.04	4.52	3.79	4.74	4.58	3.29	2.53	3.14	4.92	4.87	5.00	49.17	Linden	8.45	3-28-1989
182	0.62	0.56	1.04	1.05	2.83	3.72	2.21	3.21	2.59	1.86	0.75	0.78	21.22	Hart	5.17	6-11-1965
302	4.47	3.21	3.40	3.59	5.20	6.50	5.45	5.09	6.39	5.06	4.21	4.54	57.11	Anahuac	15.87	8-28-1945
263	4.08	4.35	4.44	3.34	4.36	4.73	3.25	3.07	3.55	5.27	4.57	4.53	49.54	Jacksonville	11.00	11-22-1940
217	0.85	1.16	1.74	2.28	3.95	4.33	2.23	2.50	3.21	2.04	1.18	0.96	26.43	Childress Airport	5.32	10-20-1983
221	1.56	2.17	2.70	2.74	4.57	4.28	1.89	2.59	2.73	3.31	2.01	2.13	32.68	Henrietta	6.07	6-23-1959
199	0.64	0.67	1.11	0.89	2.09	2.50	2.55	2.57	2.35	1.78	0.92	0.86	18.93	Morton	4.69	7-7-1960
226	0.88	1.35	1.41	1.55	2.94	3.11	1.51	2.52	2.55	2.76	1.21	0.96	22.75	Robert Lee	8.40	10-13-1957
249	1.11	2.07	2.45	1.92	3.62	4.43	1.99	2.38	2.57	3.00	1.85	1.35	28.74	Burkett	9.47	7-5-2002
241	2.63	3.17	4.06	3.69	5.72	4.48	2.43	1.90	3.03	4.31	3.85	3.05	42.32	Gunter	11.03	5-13-1982
215	0.79	0.73	1.44	1.86	3.02	3.45	2.25	1.86	2.32	2.45	1.18	0.91	22.26	Wellington	9.50	10-3-1986
255	3.57	2.88	3.18	3.12	4.77	4.98	3.24	2.87	3.06	4.68	4.42	3.16	43.93	New Ulm	12.13	4-18-2016
276	2.24	2.10	2.91	2.48	4.20	5.14	2.93	2.24	3.39	4.30	3.22	2.29	37.44	New Braunfels	18.35	10-18-1998
249	1.38	2.23	2.70	2.42	4.36	4.90	1.89	2.46	3.02	3.27	2.13	1.62	32.38	Comanche	8.86	8-19-2004
222	1.00	1.64	1.92	1.33	3.26	3.92	1.98	2.13	2.31	2.68	1.60	1.19	24.96	Paint Rock	8.25	9-9-1980
242	1.96	2.70	3.63	3.87	5.34	5.69	2.58	2.39	4.02	4.64	2.98	2.90	42.70	Gainesville	10.07	7-2-1903
236	0.00	0.00	0.00	0.00	0.00	0.00	0.00	0.00	0.00	0.00	0.00	0.00	0.00	Gatesville	8.67	9-8-2010
223	0.88	1.09	1.58	2.17	3.47	4.05	1.96	2.05	2.73	2.38	1.47	1.11	24.94	Paducah	7.00	6-2-1991
243	0.77	0.69	0.59	0.87	1.47	1.79	1.60	2.17	2.11	1.89	0.81	0.84	15.60	Crane	5.55	8-11-1986
227	0.93	1.04	1.63	1.74	2.20	2.04	1.39	1.97	2.00	2.36	0.90	0.66	18.86	Ozona (22 mi. SE)	8.02	8-18-2007
213	0.82	0.99	1.41	2.05	2.75	3.17	2.36	2.52	2.99	2.22	1.10	0.96	23.34	Crosbyton	5.78	6-30-1913
234	0.45	0.49	0.20	0.32	0.53	1.22	2.37	2.15	1.50	1.31	0.49	0.55	11.58	Pine Springs	9.42	9-12-2014
181	0.52	0.40	1.17	1.08	2.24	2.30	2.79	2.85	1.65	1.47	0.58	0.54	17.59	Bunker Hill	5.25	7-11-1959
272	2.06	2.59	3.49	3.07	4.92	4.11	2.21	1.87	2.84	4.79	2.88	2.74	37.57	Joe Pool Lake	12.05	7-29-2004
212	0.58	0.86	1.11	0.90	2.30	2.96	1.83	1.73	3.19	1.93	0.93	0.82	19.14	Lamesa	6.24	10-10-1985
189	0.72	0.56	1.27	1.01	2.03	3.53	2.17	3.43	2.07	1.68	0.74	0.84	20.05	Hereford	*5.30	8-3-1976
241	3.00	3.61	4.37	3.41	5.11	4.11	3.29	2.46	2.92	4.06	4.35	4.11	44.80	Cooper	8.46	5-13-1982
251	2.06	2.81	3.23	3.25	5.11	3.59	2.39	2.14	3.09	4.96	2.90	2.56	38.09	Isle Du Bois SP	13.00	5-13-1982
270	2.23	1.88	2.64	3.05	4.02	4.58	2.93	2.41	3.33	3.60	2.80	2.20	35.67	Cuero	12.40	6-30-1940
209	0.78	0.95	1.26	1.87	2.95	3.40	2.11	2.52	2.26	2.50	1.15	1.00	22.75	Pitchfork Ranch	7.60	9-18-1996
265	1.10	1.12	1.16	1.59	2.82	2.06	1.96	1.53	2.42	2.12	1.12	0.77	19.77	Carrizo Springs	11.48	10-14-2013
194	0.76	0.81	1.48	2.27	3.31	3.53	2.13	3.02	2.54	2.20	1.02	0.95	24.02	Clarendon	9.25	5-4-2001
304	1.43	1.56	2.26	2.08	3.16	3.68	2.24	2.11	2.49	2.47	1.47	1.04	25.99	Benavides	9.60	9-12-1971
222	1.17	2.05	2.57	1.98	3.45	4.21	1.77	2.43	2.56	3.44	1.74	1.65	29.02	Eastland	7.00	10-13-1957
243	0.53	0.64	0.68	0.65	1.79	1.22	1.55	1.70	1.82	1.63	0.65	0.59	13.45	Pleasant Farms	4.57	8-01-2017
258	0.99	1.16	1.80	1.97	3.37	3.22	2.07	2.74	2.83	3.62	1.58	1.21	26.56	Carta Valley	10.75	8-24-1998
230	0.50	0.54	0.38	0.35	0.47	0.98	2.52	2.46	1.53	1.03	0.52	0.76	12.04	Waxahachie	10.80	9-19-1958
245	2.27	2.93	3.84	3.34	3.99	4.12	2.66	2.34	3.05	4.45	3.03	3.10	39.12	El Paso	6.50	7-9-1881
226	1.45	2.25	2.86	2.52	4.39	4.01	1.56	2.38	3.02	3.11	2.09	1.90	31.54	Huckabay	10.21	4-26-1990
234	2.63	2.78	3.52	2.72	4.76	3.91	2.07	2.57	2.77	4.25	3.15	3.33	38.46	Marlin	11.90	7-31-1903
242	2.69	3.60	4.37	3.87	5.57	5.30	3.15	2.17	3.41	5.06	3.37	3.57	46.13	Bonham	13.30	7-3-1903
267	3.07	3.08	2.99	2.58	4.25	4.16	2.48	2.57	3.61	4.91	3.55	3.21	40.46	La Grange	14.69	8-27-2017
243	0.89	1.59	1.70	1.96	3.68	2.93	2.22	2.44	2.71	2.19	1.33	1.12	24.76	Rotan	6.85	8-13-1972
208	0.61	0.75	1.28	1.65	2.82	3.96	2.11	2.23	2.82	1.73	0.82	0.82	21.60	Floydada	7.75	9-12-2008
227	1.12	1.52	1.78	2.19	4.33	3.63	2.08	2.15	2.85	2.85	1.63	1.10	27.23	Crowell	8.25	9-19-1965
305	3.55	3.07	3.43	3.36	4.30	5.65	3.97	4.43	5.10	5.28	4.84	3.37	50.35	Katy	16.43	8-28-2017
245	2.77	3.62	4.47	3.34	5.13	4.61	3.68	2.43	3.25	5.22	4.57	4.33	47.42	Winfield	10.44	9-15-1913
243	2.96	3.64	3.84	3.12	5.14	4.29	2.08	2.58	3.02	4.37	4.30	3.78	43.12	Fairfield	7.90	1-29-1999
296	1.36	1.33	1.85	1.86	2.85	2.92	2.71	2.01	2.46	3.00	1.46	1.13	24.94	Derby	12.80	5-16-1980
219	0.71	0.84	0.98	0.96	2.46	2.37	2.51	1.85	2.47	1.48	0.91	0.82	18.36	Loop	6.35	10-19-1983
348	3.69	2.99	2.85	2.19	3.01	4.83	3.85	3.35	5.36	4.15	3.42	3.36	43.05	Bacliff	21.62	8-27-2017
225	0.72	1.15	1.34	1.57	2.29	3.00	2.40	2.30	2.16	2.12	1.07	0.77	20.89	Polar	9.00	9-25-1955
235	1.60	2.01	2.45	2.34	3.90	3.80	2.40	2.20	2.91	3.71	2.20	2.01	31.53	Gold	13.80	9-10-1952
215	0.87	0.92	1.18	1.17	2.31	1.82	1.53	1.97	2.48	1.68	0.94	0.70	17.57	Garden City	8.75	7-7-1945
280	2.41	1.98	2.44	2.52	4.06	4.14	3.71	2.94	4.26	3.85	2.56	1.91	36.78	Goliad	12.15	7-16-1990

County, Town or Landmark Closest to Station for Normals	Temperature								Average Freeze Dates			
	Mean Max. July	No. At or Above 100°	Mean Min. January	No. At or Below 32°	Record Highest	Record High Date	Record Lowest	Record Low Date	Last in Spring		First in Fall	
	F.	Days	F.	Days	F.	M-D-Y	F.	M-D-Y	Mo.	Day	Mo.	Day
Gonzales, Gonzales	93.9	10	41.8	19	*114	8-10-1962	1	1-31-1949	Feb.	28	Dec.	1
Gray, Pampa	90.8	5	24.5	110	113	6-27-2011	–12	1-11-1962	Apr.	14	Oct.	27
Grayson, Sherman	91.1	5	35.7	43	113	8-10-1936	–3	12-23-1989	Mar.	17	Nov.	19
Gregg, Longview	92.7	6	36.1	44	113	8-10-1936	–7	2-12-1899	Mar.	17	Nov.	18
Grimes, *Washington St. Park*	94.1	17	40.3	31	108	8-11-1969	14	1-7-1970	Mar.	14	Nov.	19
Guadalupe, *New Braunfels*	92.8	3	39.1	32	112	9-5-2000	0	1-30-1949	Mar.	9	Nov.	25
Hale, Plainview	91.2	4	27.5	92	112	6-27-2011	–8	2-8-1933	Apr.	5	Nov.	1
Hall, Memphis	94.3	21	27.0	89	*117	8-3-1944	–11	1-18-1930	Apr.	1	Nov.	4
Hamilton, Hico	93.6	9	33.2	54	113	8-11-1936	–11	1-31-1949	Mar.	31	Nov.	6
Hansford, Spearman	94.2	19	26.2	102	111	8-13-1936	–22	1-4-1959	Apr.	11	Oct.	28
Hardeman, Quanah	94.9	20	28.3	78	*119	6-27-1994	–15	12-23-1989	Apr.	3	Nov.	1
Hardin, Evadale	92.1		41.3	24	110	9-1-2000	15	12-22-2000	Mar.	31	Nov.	14
Harris, Houston Hobby Airport	92.5	1	48.1	4	111	9-4-2000	5	1-18-1930	Feb.	3	Dec.	20
Harrison, Marshall	92.8	5	34.9	39	*112	8-18-1909	*–9	2-12-1899	Mar.	11	Nov.	22
Hartley, Channing	90.2	5	22.8	121	110	9-7-1907	*–20	2-8-1933	Apr.	17	Oct.	24
Haskell, Haskell	93.8	15	30.8	63	115	6-27-1994	*–6	12-23-1989	Mar.	28	Nov.	9
Hays, Dripping Springs	93.5	6	40.8	29	111	9-5-2000	–2	1-31-1949	Mar.	19	Nov.	17
Hemphill, Canadian	92.3	10	19.1	136	*112	6-26-1994	–14	1-5-1942	Apr.	16	Oct.	20
Henderson, Athens	93.1	5	36.5	41	*109	9-5-2000	–6	2-2-1985	Mar.	19	Nov.	14
Hidalgo, McAllen Intl. Airport	98.5	26	54.6	1	113	6-16-1998	10	1-12-1962	Jan.	13	Dec.	31
Hill, Hillsboro	94.9	10	35.9	37	113	7-10-1917	–6	12-23-1989	Mar.	23	Nov.	13
Hockley, Levelland	91.4	7	26.7	98	115	6-28-1994	–16	1-13-1963	Apr.	4	Nov.	3
Hood, Cresson	94.7		33.1	58	*111	8-10-1947	–6	1-31-1949	Mar.	26	Nov.	13
Hopkins, Sulphur Springs	93.0	5	36.0	49	*115	8-10-1969	–10	2-12-1899	Mar.	21	Nov.	13
Houston, Crockett	93.6	9	38.0	31	114	8-18-1909	0	2-1-1951	Mar.	9	Nov.	24
Howard, Big Spring	94.8	14	32.9	54	114	6-28-1994	–7	1-11-1962	Mar.	22	Nov.	16
Hudspeth, Sierra Blanca	93.1	7	31.6	70	115	6-28-1994	–10	2-2-1985	Apr.	12	Oct.	29
Hunt, Greenville	96.0	23	35.3	50	116	8-10-1936	*–4	1-18-1930	Mar.	19	Nov.	18
Hutchinson, Borger	93.7	12	27.6	93	116	7-11-2020	–19	1-8-1912	Apr.	13	Oct.	27
Irion, Cope Ranch	95.3	15	29.8	79	*108	6-9-1985	4	2-1-1985	Apr.	8	Oct.	31
Jack, Jacksboro	94.2	13	31.8	56	*113	8-29-2011	–8	12-22-1989	Mar.	25	Nov.	9
Jackson, *Point Comfort*	91.0	0	47.7	5	107	7-27-1954	8	1-31-1949	Feb.	8	Dec.	16
Jasper, Sam Rayburn Dam	93.2	2	42.9	30	109	9-5-2000	*2	2-2-1951	Mar.	6	Nov.	27
Jeff Davis, Fort Davis	90.2	1	32.4	72	*108	6-27-1994	*–10	1-11-1962	Apr.	8	Oct.	30
Jefferson, Port Arthur / Airport	92.2	1	45.8	8	*108	8-31-2000	4	2-12-1899	Feb.	16	Dec.	8
Jim Hogg, Hebbronville	98.5	25	47.9	8	118	7-9-2009	12	12-23-1989	Feb.	14	Dec.	12
Jim Wells, Alice	96.7	18	49.5	4	*114	7-6-1997	11	12-25-1989	Feb.	5	Dec.	17
Johnson, Cleburne	93.5	15	35.3	41	114	9-2-1939	–6	12-23-1989	Mar.	24	Nov.	11
Jones, Anson	94.5	23	31.2	56	118	6-28-1994	*–12	12-23-1989	Mar.	27	Nov.	11
Karnes, Karnes City	95.2	14	44.2	11	112	7-27-1954	6	2-12-1899	Feb.	24	Dec.	5
Kaufman, Kaufman	93.0	11	35.2	46	113	8-10-1936	–3	12-23-1989	Mar.	20	Nov.	16
Kendall, Boerne	92.1	4	38.4	40	112	8-23-1925	–4	1-31-1949	Mar.	20	Nov.	14
Kenedy, *Port Mansfield*	97.2	0	45.3	10	110	6-16-1963	14	1-13-1975	Jan.	22	Dec.	30
Kent, Jayton	95.1	16	29.4	82	116	6-28-1994	–6	2-3-1985	Apr.	1	Nov.	6
Kerr, Kerrville	91.0	5	35.8	46	110	7-27-1954	–7	1-31-1949	Mar.	29	Nov.	8
Kimble, Junction / Co. Airport	94.5	12	35.5	52	112	8-2-2011	–11	12-22-1929	Mar.	25	Nov.	7
King, Guthrie	96.2	23	28.8	87	119	6-28-1994	–10	12-23-1989	Apr.	2	Nov.	4
Kinney, Brackettville	93.2	17	37.9	31	111	6-10-1988	4	1-12-1962	Mar.	6	Nov.	27
Kleberg, Kingsville Air Station	95.7	8	48.4	5	115	6-15-1998	10	12-24-1989	Feb.	5	Dec.	13
Knox, Munday	95.8	21	33.1	56	*118	6-20-2011	–11	1-4-1947	Mar.	27	Nov.	9
Lamar, Paris	98.3	20	41.1	25	115	8-10-1936	–13	2-12-1899	Mar.	18	Nov.	17
Lamb, Littlefield	94.4	6	35.4	46	112	6-28-1994	*–14	1-13-1963	Apr.	8	Oct.	31
Lampasas, Lampasas	91.4	17	24.3	109	*112	7-11-1917	–12	1-31-1949	Mar.	22	Nov.	15
La Salle, Fowlerton	94.9	33	35.5	55	*116	9-8-1893	9	1-12-1962	Mar.	3	Nov.	26
Lavaca, Hallettsville	95.7	4	46.4	13	112	8-29-2011	5	12-23-1989	Mar.	2	Nov.	30

Growing Season	Mean Precipitation													Record Rainfall Highest Daily Total		
	January	February	March	April	May	June	July	August	September	October	November	December	Annual			
Days	In.	In.	In.	In.	In.	In.	In.	In.	In.	In.	In.	In.	In.	Location	In.	M-D-Y
272	2.39	2.15	2.44	2.51	4.23	4.17	2.23	2.27	3.07	3.92	2.99	2.54	34.91	Gonzales	16.31	8-31-1981
194	0.70	0.69	1.64	2.04	2.98	3.65	2.71	2.77	2.12	1.95	1.06	0.88	23.19	McLean	7.60	4-3-1997
250	2.47	2.94	3.92	3.55	5.32	5.00	2.62	2.06	3.59	5.29	3.70	3.14	43.60	Van Alstyne	9.30	9-22-2018
244	3.69	4.26	4.28	3.73	4.79	4.44	2.95	2.87	3.46	4.46	4.47	4.69	48.09	Longview	12.03	3-9-2016
259	3.54	2.83	3.52	2.80	3.90	4.76	2.37	2.79	3.36	4.63	3.80	3.38	41.68	Richards	11.98	10-16-1994
253	1.95	1.98	2.58	2.03	3.95	4.78	2.93	2.11	3.04	3.80	2.46	2.36	33.97	Kingsbury	9.25	10-9-2002
209	0.72	0.63	1.16	1.64	2.80	3.20	2.42	2.25	2.17	1.74	0.92	0.80	20.45	Plainview	7.00	7-8-1960
215	0.69	0.94	1.47	2.05	3.07	3.32	2.05	2.56	2.49	1.89	1.12	0.94	22.59	Memphis	8.80	6-7-1960
229	2.00	2.58	3.16	2.63	4.91	4.86	1.97	2.48	3.02	3.44	2.20	2.03	35.28	Hamilton	8.20	10-4-1959
209	0.47	0.63	1.62	1.68	2.50	3.89	2.69	2.62	1.97	1.55	0.83	0.74	21.19	Gruver	9.72	6-13-2010
210	1.00	1.19	1.90	2.13	3.29	3.95	2.42	2.79	2.83	2.56	1.64	1.15	26.85	Quanah	8.03	8-2-1995
281	4.87	4.38	3.30	3.86	4.80	6.63	5.32	4.65	5.02	5.79	6.37	6.07	61.06	Kountze	15.50	8-30-2017
330	3.87	3.21	3.20	3.25	4.75	7.10	4.66	5.06	5.21	5.99	4.32	4.03	54.65	Houston-South	20.84	8-27-2017
233	3.72	4.33	4.49	3.64	4.85	5.18	3.49	2.61	3.32	4.93	4.58	5.04	50.18	Harleton	10.50	3-29-1989
190	2.70	0.61	1.58	0.80	1.91	2.02	2.64	3.85	1.68	1.52	0.79	0.92	21.02	Romero	8.27	5-17-1914
225	1.04	1.75	1.80	2.20	3.43	3.95	1.92	2.20	2.63	2.54	1.48	1.46	26.40	Haskell	14.29	8-4-1978
242	2.36	2.24	3.00	2.20	4.13	5.02	2.09	1.76	3.08	4.08	3.17	2.61	35.74	San Marcos	15.78	10-17-1998
170	0.56	0.74	1.79	1.76	2.91	3.92	2.35	2.68	1.84	1.77	1.02	0.91	22.25	Canadian	7.00	6-8-2008
242	2.98	3.87	4.04	3.21	4.77	4.35	2.11	2.37	2.56	4.96	3.74	3.98	42.94	Payne Springs	11.28	10-25-2015
365	1.05	1.11	1.03	1.34	2.25	2.58	2.00	2.21	4.47	2.08	0.89	1.19	22.20	Santa Rosa	15.49	7-28-2020
235	2.39	2.92	3.78	2.95	4.37	4.34	1.59	2.10	3.03	4.53	2.84	3.09	37.93	Aquilla	11.49	10-24-2015
205	0.72	0.68	1.02	1.02	2.48	2.84	2.17	2.63	2.74	1.68	0.99	0.87	19.84	Ropesville	5.06	9-12-2008
228	0.00	0.00	0.00	0.00	0.00	0.00	0.00	0.00	0.00	0.00	0.00	0.00	0.00	Cresson	11.08	6-4-2000
245	3.07	3.66	4.41	3.83	4.79	4.36	3.38	2.44	2.99	5.39	4.54	4.32	47.18	Cumby	8.64	4-11-2017
251	3.77	3.62	3.66	3.16	4.41	4.64	3.02	3.03	3.02	4.76	4.09	4.00	45.18	Crockett	9.11	6-8-2001
239	0.71	0.90	1.02	1.36	2.41	2.69	1.64	2.55	2.65	1.88	1.09	0.60	19.50	Ackerly	6.40	6-9-1993
234	0.45	0.49	0.20	0.32	0.53	1.22	2.37	2.15	1.50	1.31	0.49	0.55	11.58	Dell City	7.10	9-12-2013
244	2.75	3.44	4.22	3.48	5.52	4.18	3.16	1.88	3.34	5.09	4.01	3.58	44.65	Commerce	12.00	8-13-2017
198	0.71	0.69	1.54	1.79	2.68	3.28	2.68	3.56	2.09	1.94	1.03	0.86	22.85	Borger	6.27	9-22-2004
202	0.79	1.04	1.08	1.14	2.19	2.78	1.76	2.22	2.58	2.06	0.90	0.95	19.49	Mertzon	8.35	8-12-1971
225	1.31	2.19	2.82	2.67	4.80	4.19	1.91	1.54	3.36	3.86	2.29	1.98	32.92	Antelope	11.18	5-16-1989
321	3.06	2.46	3.10	2.30	4.27	4.72	4.06	2.66	4.42	4.78	3.93	2.63	42.39	Maurbro	14.80	6-26-1960
280	5.27	4.70	4.95	3.94	4.50	6.18	3.89	4.01	4.29	5.54	6.33	6.15	59.75	Evadale	14.52	9-18-1963
209	0.48	0.51	0.46	0.67	1.50	2.46	3.26	3.28	2.23	1.45	0.52	0.65	17.47	Jasper	8.05	3-29-2018
301	5.26	3.58	3.53	3.21	5.23	7.09	5.95	5.38	5.97	5.58	4.40	5.29	60.47	Port Arthur Reg AP	26.03	8-29-2017
320	1.25	1.45	1.19	1.46	3.10	2.57	2.67	1.69	3.30	2.36	1.35	1.40	23.79	Kaffie Ranch	21.02	9-12-1971
337	0.00	0.00	0.00	0.00	0.00	0.00	0.00	0.00	0.00	0.00	0.00	0.00	0.00	Alice Intl. Airport	13.21	9-13-1951
240	2.24	2.59	3.64	2.91	4.85	4.27	2.10	2.59	3.15	3.89	2.80	2.58	37.61	Lillian	9.30	5-17-1989
221	1.12	1.55	1.69	2.10	3.32	3.66	2.32	2.42	2.35	2.66	1.51	1.36	26.06	Stamford	8.22	8-4-1978
300	1.63	1.68	2.20	2.20	3.03	3.47	2.97	2.35	3.06	3.33	2.30	1.92	30.14	Cibolo Creek	13.75	9-21-1967
243	2.85	3.03	3.89	2.68	4.50	3.51	2.20	2.50	2.83	5.07	3.56	3.30	39.92	Crandall	10.22	4-19-1976
243	2.08	2.39	2.95	2.26	4.64	4.63	3.27	2.73	3.41	4.38	3.12	2.24	38.10	Kendalia	12.32	5-24-2015
285	1.13	1.53	1.14	1.46	3.10	2.85	3.08	2.49	4.07	3.23	1.12	1.27	26.47	Sarita	9.30	10-12-1973
220	0.96	1.22	1.42	1.83	3.39	3.45	2.40	2.21	2.25	2.36	1.17	0.84	23.51	Jayton	*6.50	7-29-2004
226	1.58	1.81	2.48	2.10	4.00	3.97	2.82	1.69	3.65	3.66	2.43	1.86	32.05	Lynxhaven Ranch	15.20	8-2-1978
229	0.86	1.57	2.41	2.12	3.29	3.61	1.95	2.34	2.76	2.96	1.89	1.22	26.98	Junction	8.56	10-08-2018
213	1.03	1.42	1.53	2.06	3.42	3.66	2.27	2.69	2.58	2.50	1.30	1.07	25.53	Guthrie	8.85	7-4-1986
255	0.73	0.92	1.61	1.56	3.16	2.81	1.92	2.52	3.15	2.88	1.29	1.01	23.56	Fort Clark	18.00	6-15-1899
314	1.55	1.79	1.45	1.64	3.59	3.49	2.46	2.67	5.15	3.39	1.75	1.45	30.38	Ricardo	11.30	6-21-1924
232	1.12	1.67	2.08	2.11	3.49	4.16	1.83	2.24	2.48	2.72	1.33	1.20	26.43	Munday	8.00	6-14-1930
266	1.15	1.16	1.85	1.96	2.95	2.75	2.61	1.83	2.96	2.76	1.44	1.28	24.70	Arthur City	10.50	5-12-1920
247	2.70	3.28	4.44	3.41	5.56	4.17	3.68	2.22	3.84	5.10	4.68	3.99	47.07	Olton	6.30	6-4-1985
192	0.65	0.63	1.08	1.10	2.05	3.08	2.30	2.53	2.20	1.55	0.86	0.84	18.87	Lometa	9.50	10-4-1959
238	1.88	2.23	2.79	2.25	4.20	3.96	2.05	2.28	2.62	3.49	2.31	2.17	32.23	Fowlerton	12.80	9-9-2002
297	3.01	2.50	2.72	3.14	4.66	4.73	2.81	2.80	3.87	4.44	3.74	2.64	41.06	Halletsville	20.60	8-27-2017

County, Town or Landmark Closest to Station for Normals	Temperature								Average Freeze Dates			
	Mean Max. July	No. At or Above 100°	Mean Min. January	No. At or Below 32°	Record Highest	Record High Date	Record Lowest	Record Low Date	Last in Spring		First in Fall	
	F.	Days	F.	Days	F.	M-D-Y	F.	M-D-Y	Mo.	Day	Mo.	Day
Lee, Lexington	94.2	7	40.5	27	111	9-6-2000	*2	12-23-1989	Mar.	7	Nov.	24
Leon, Centerville	93.1	7	36.9	46	113	8-18-1909	0	2-1-1951	Mar.	21	Nov.	16
Liberty, Liberty	92.9	1	43.0	14	112	8-9-1962	5	12-24-1989	Feb.	24	Dec.	4
Limestone, Mexia	94.6	10	38.0	34	112	8-18-1909	–5	12-23-1989	Mar.	10	Nov.	24
Lipscomb, Lipscomb	92.3	16	19.1	136	*114	6-27-2011	–19	1-19-1984	Apr.	23	Oct.	14
Live Oak, Choke Canyon Dam	95.0	20	44.7	9	112	9-6-2000	11	12-26-1983	Feb.	17	Dec.	9
Llano, Llano	95.3	34	35.9	50	115	7-14-1933	–7	12-22-1929	Mar.	24	Nov.	10
Loving, *Red Bluff Dam*	97.7	52	31.5	69	*112	7-30-1944	0	1-5-1947	Mar.	29	Nov.	9
Lubbock, Lubbock	92.4	7	28.7	84	114	6-27-1994	–17	2-8-1933	Apr.	4	Nov.	2
Lynn, Tahoka	92.2	6	29.8	80	111	6-28-1994	–15	2-8-1933	Apr.	1	Nov.	8
Madison, Madisonville	94.1	9	38.4	35	112	9-5-2000	*–2	1-31-1949	Mar.	17	Nov.	14
Marion, Jefferson	93.0	6	35.5	55	*112	8-5-2011	*–5	12-23-1989	Mar.	21	Nov.	10
Martin, Lenorah	94.8		32.7	54	109		*–8		Apr.	5	Nov.	6
Mason, Mason	94.6	4	35.6	51	110	7-13-2020	*3	2-2-1985	Mar.	27	Nov.	10
Matagorda, Bay City	90.2	1	45.0	7	109	9-4-2000	7	12-23-1989	Feb.	10	Dec.	18
Maverick, Eagle Pass	97.4	42	41.0	13	*115	7-25-1944	7	2-12-1899	Feb.	14	Dec.	8
McCulloch, Brady	92.3	11	37.0	43	110	6-29-1980	*–2	1-18-1930	Mar.	26	Nov.	11
McLennan, Waco Reg. Airport	95.5	17	37.9	34	*114	7-23-2018	*–7	1-31-1949	Mar.	13	Nov.	21
McMullen, Tilden	97.2	26	45.3	12	119	7-2-1910	5	12-22-1989	Feb.	16	Dec.	6
Medina, Hondo Muni. Airport	96.1	12	40.7	25	*112	9-5-2000	4	2-1-1949	Mar.	6	Nov.	24
Menard, Menard	93.8	6	31.2	64	114	5-29-1927	–6	1-9-1879	Apr.	9	Oct.	30
Midland, Midland	95.2	15	34.3	58	*116	6-27-1994	*–12	1-11-1962	Mar.	29	Nov.	10
Milam, Cameron	93.1	0	41.0	28	114	7-10-1917	–7	1-17-1930	Mar.	25	Nov.	10
Mills, Goldthwaite	91.8	2	35.3	37	110	8-6-1964	–7	12-23-1989	Mar.	21	Nov.	13
Mitchell, Lake Colorado City	93.1	12	32.7	57	115	6-30-1907	*–7	1-4-1947	Mar.	25	Nov.	15
Montague, Bowie	92.0	9	32.0	64	115	6-28-1980	–12	2-12-1899	Mar.	30	Nov.	9
Montgomery, Conroe	94.4	5	43.8	17	113	9-4-2000	2	2-12-1899	Feb.	28	Dec.	1
Moore, Dumas	90.5	5	23.1	124	*109	6-28-1980	–18	1-5-1959	Apr.	17	Oct.	24
Morris, Daingerfield	91.4	9	36.8	34	112	8-4-1998	4	1-10-1962	Mar.	8	Nov.	23
Motley, Matador	91.9	13	29.6	72	116	6-28-1994	*–5	12-23-1989	Apr.	1	Nov.	7
Nacogdoches, Nacogdoches	91.7	7	37.9	41	*113	9-3-2000	–4	1-18-1930	Mar.	19	Nov.	16
Navarro, Corsicana	93.5	10	36.8	38	*113	7-26-1954	–7	2-12-1899	Mar.	13	Nov.	21
Newton, Toledo Bend Dam	92.9	4	39.0	39	110	6-5-2011	4	1-19-1930	Mar.	14	Nov.	20
Nolan, Roscoe	93.1	11	32.7	57	113	6-27-1994	–11	1-5-1947	Apr.	2	Nov.	6
Nueces, Corpus Christi	93.4	2	49.9	4	113	8-31-1983	*7	2-12-1899	Feb.	2	Dec.	19
Ochiltree, Perryton	93.2	9	24.9	131	*113	6-10-1981	–17	1-7-1988	Apr.	25	Oct.	18
Oldham, Vega	89.4	3	22.1	128	110	7-27-1982	*–17	2-1-1951	Apr.	22	Oct.	19
Orange, Orange	89.4	1	42.1	19	107	9-1-2000	10	12-25-1989	Feb.	28	Nov.	26
Palo Pinto, Mineral Wells	94.6	16	34.8	48	115	8-14-1999	–8	12-23-1989	Mar.	23	Nov.	11
Panola, Carthage	91.6	5	37.9	39	109	9-5-2000	1	12-24-1989	Mar.	14	Nov.	19
Parker, Weatherford	93.1	8	33.7	61	119	6-26-1980	*–11	2-12-1899	Mar.	31	Nov.	5
Parmer, Friona	90.2	3	23.7	118	109	6-19-2017	–15	1-13-1963	Apr.	20	Oct.	23
Pecos, Fort Stockton	94.4	15	37.3	40	117	6-29-1994	–7	1-3-1911	Mar.	17	Nov.	18
Polk, Livingston	93.9	5	41.7	36	116	8-3-2016	*3	12-24-1989	Mar.	4	Nov.	26
Potter, Amarillo	91.2	5	26.0	108	111	6-26-2011	–16	2-12-1899	Apr.	15	Oct.	24
Presidio, Presidio	101.4	73	36.4	25	*117	6-18-1960	–2	1-5-1972	Feb.	27	Nov.	28
Rains, Emory	90.6	4	34.4	54	112	9-5-2000	–5	12-25-1989	Mar.	25	Nov.	10
Randall, Canyon	91.4	4	23.7	107	*109	6-27-2011	–14	2-1-1951	Apr.	16	Oct.	22
Reagan, Big Lake	94.0	9	35.1	56	115	6-28-1994	–9	2-2-1985	Mar.	27	Nov.	10
Real, Camp Wood	93.3	5	36.7	48	*109	9-6-2000	0	11-29-1976	Mar.	22	Nov.	12
Red River, *DeKalb*	92.1	7	33.3	49	115	8-10-1936	*–7	1-18-1930	Mar.	27	Nov.	7
Reeves, Balmorhea	93.8	15	32.1	65	118	6-29-1968	–14	1-11-1962	Mar.	29	Nov.	10
Refugio, Refugio	93.3	2	46.2	11	112	9-5-2000	8	1-12-1962	Feb.	24	Dec.	5
Roberts, Miami	90.5	7	23.3	116	114	6-11-1917	–15	1-5-1942	Apr.	16	Oct.	21
Robertson, Franklin	94.3	12	41.3	24	112	9-4-2000	–1	12-23-1989	Mar.	8	Nov.	22
Rockwall, *Lavon Dam*	91.3	10	36.1	44	*109	7-25-1954	4	2-2-1951	Mar.	10	Nov.	24

Growing Season	Mean Precipitation													Record Rainfall Highest Daily Total		
	January	February	March	April	May	June	July	August	September	October	November	December	Annual			
Days	In.	In.	In.	In.	In.	In.	In.	In.	In.	In.	In.	In.	In.	Location	In.	M-D-Y
262	2.58	2.43	2.84	2.05	4.20	3.74	2.11	2.17	2.98	5.04	3.52	2.95	36.61	Fedor	13.00	10-17-1994
239	3.16	3.45	3.82	2.73	4.61	4.18	2.49	2.65	2.79	4.96	3.80	3.65	42.29	Buffalo	9.19	10-14-1957
286	4.42	4.18	3.90	3.88	5.58	7.35	5.20	4.24	5.49	6.51	5.25	5.25	61.25	Dayton	25.00	8-27-2017
251	2.46	3.34	3.82	2.91	4.39	3.92	1.93	2.35	3.46	4.35	3.64	3.77	40.34	Mexia	8.63	2-4-1986
170	0.56	0.74	1.79	1.76	2.91	3.92	2.35	2.68	1.84	1.77	1.02	0.91	22.25	Booker	7.76	6-9-1997
302	1.45	1.47	1.88	2.16	2.62	3.16	3.38	1.53	3.07	2.45	1.70	1.49	26.36	Whitsett	15.69	9-22-1967
235	1.43	1.83	2.51	1.92	3.64	3.57	2.00	1.55	2.21	2.97	2.22	1.85	27.70	Moss Ranch	13.53	9-11-1952
239	0.53	0.53	0.48	0.56	1.45	1.98	2.17	2.06	1.96	1.26	0.59	0.63	14.20	Mentone	3.79	9-24-1955
210	0.65	0.75	1.10	1.41	2.30	3.04	1.91	1.91	2.51	1.93	0.85	0.76	19.12	Lubbock	7.81	9-12-2008
220	0.76	0.85	1.07	1.44	2.82	3.16	2.63	2.25	2.28	2.07	1.00	0.88	21.21	Tahoka	9.10	5-5-2015
240	3.86	3.28	3.26	2.82	4.49	4.10	3.84	2.91	3.42	4.84	4.38	3.92	45.12	Madisonville	8.89	10-16-2018
236	3.96	4.45	4.48	3.50	4.61	5.17	2.88	2.25	3.43	5.01	4.51	4.71	48.96	Jefferson	9.10	4-26-1921
226	0.67	0.58	0.69	0.71	2.00	1.56	1.50	2.14	1.99	1.52	0.90	0.54	14.80	Tarzan	6.54	9-20-2014
241	1.13	1.97	2.30	2.16	3.58	4.31	2.47	1.95	2.73	3.12	2.08	1.39	29.19	Mason	7.80	10-16-2018
290	3.86	2.69	3.07	2.98	4.45	5.30	4.78	3.75	5.11	5.06	4.25	3.59	48.89	Matagorda	12.20	5-7-1951
287	0.90	0.96	1.01	1.88	2.55	2.73	2.08	1.46	3.11	2.07	0.95	0.71	20.41	Eagle Pass	15.60	6-29-1936
244	1.18	1.81	2.24	1.94	3.61	3.40	2.23	2.21	2.83	2.75	1.84	1.56	27.60	Brady	9.13	7-8-2015
245	2.12	2.63	3.15	2.69	4.30	3.43	1.79	2.05	3.06	3.90	2.82	2.75	34.69	McGregor	13.08	6-16-1964
299	1.11	1.30	1.64	2.05	3.15	3.24	1.74	1.95	3.16	2.11	1.24	1.30	23.99	Calliham	12.00	4-17-2010
263	1.38	1.49	2.13	1.98	3.38	3.49	2.09	1.67	2.60	3.31	1.58	1.14	26.24	Natalia	11.47	9-27-1973
204	1.17	1.52	2.01	1.47	2.97	3.17	1.86	1.90	2.10	2.43	1.56	1.16	23.32	Callan	7.67	10-10-1961
239	0.56	0.71	0.60	0.65	1.74	1.80	1.82	1.84	1.86	1.73	0.69	0.60	14.60	Midland	7.20	5-9-1968
261	2.29	2.66	2.74	2.53	4.94	3.69	2.17	2.15	3.44	4.14	3.33	2.89	36.97	Cameron	12.45	9-10-1921
234	1.43	2.34	2.57	2.15	3.87	4.79	1.89	2.16	2.60	3.15	2.05	1.61	30.61	Goldthwaite	7.20	10-5-1969
223	0.98	1.21	1.23	1.62	2.86	3.38	2.17	2.16	2.38	2.45	0.93	1.05	22.42	Colorado City	8.65	4-6-1900
228	1.45	2.44	3.08	2.99	5.00	4.34	1.98	2.07	3.41	4.02	2.21	2.07	35.06	Bonita	12.47	4-30-2009
285	3.85	3.47	3.25	2.91	4.94	5.26	3.07	3.61	3.75	5.73	5.09	3.84	48.77	Roman Forest	18.88	2019-9-19
183	0.62	0.52	1.26	1.28	2.17	2.41	2.43	2.89	1.87	1.37	0.73	0.82	18.37	Sunray	4.49	10-16-1968
259	3.24	3.85	4.55	3.56	4.75	4.16	3.29	2.72	3.22	4.58	4.45	4.42	46.79	Daingerfield	7.50	7-28-2009
213	0.80	0.90	1.49	1.92	2.91	3.67	2.19	2.44	2.90	2.15	1.14	0.92	23.43	Flomot	7.08	7-9-1994
248	4.13	4.42	4.20	3.73	4.38	4.42	3.01	3.25	3.64	4.70	4.56	4.84	49.28	Nacogdoches	14.22	6-28-1902
246	2.64	3.39	3.91	3.02	4.70	3.52	2.25	2.14	2.96	4.50	3.30	3.45	39.78	Corsicana	18.95	10-24-2015
253	4.74	4.94	4.47	3.57	4.62	5.50	4.00	3.11	3.38	5.07	5.53	5.99	54.92	Deweyville	20.60	9-18-1963
223	0.98	1.21	1.23	1.62	2.86	3.38	2.17	2.16	2.38	2.45	0.93	1.05	22.42	Roscoe	8.28	9-9-1980
331	1.54	1.93	1.89	1.84	3.07	3.36	2.79	2.92	4.98	3.64	1.97	1.83	31.76	Port Aransas	13.89	8-22-1999
197	0.47	0.62	1.75	1.82	2.96	3.32	3.12	2.63	1.86	1.83	0.88	0.84	22.10	Perryton	7.11	5-17-1989
182	0.63	0.60	1.36	1.44	2.28	3.58	2.75	3.37	1.99	1.63	0.72	0.79	21.14	Vega	6.07	5-16-1951
273	5.40	4.63	3.67	3.50	5.45	7.32	5.77	5.69	6.23	6.04	4.99	5.52	64.21	Bridge City	23.82	8-30-2017
231	1.45	2.14	3.19	2.38	3.95	4.16	1.99	2.24	2.82	3.73	2.16	1.84	32.05	Gordon	8.20	5-8-1997
255	4.38	4.46	4.22	3.78	4.53	4.73	3.31	2.92	3.64	5.15	4.94	5.37	51.43	Carthage	9.25	4-14-1991
230	1.57	2.82	3.27	2.54	4.59	4.56	2.14	2.07	3.10	4.00	2.95	2.16	35.77	Weatherford	8.57	8-20-2016
182	0.72	0.63	1.20	1.03	2.20	2.65	2.48	3.33	2.40	1.81	0.83	0.86	20.14	Bovina	4.73	7-21-1918
254	0.61	0.59	0.53	0.84	1.40	2.23	1.75	2.29	2.08	1.76	0.53	0.54	15.15	Bakersfield	7.10	4-30-2007
269	4.24	3.92	3.87	3.26	4.88	5.70	3.56	3.34	4.06	4.85	5.15	4.70	51.53	Corrigan	14.69	10-17-1994
195	0.72	0.56	1.39	1.40	2.29	3.16	2.84	2.91	1.92	1.66	0.80	0.71	20.36	Amarillo	5.89	10-08-2018
275	0.51	0.47	0.22	0.28	0.65	1.27	1.66	1.73	1.20	0.94	0.34	0.39	9.66	Bunton Rch	5.50	8-23-1944
238	2.87	3.82	4.60	3.30	4.91	4.20	2.99	2.22	2.97	4.87	3.95	3.77	44.47	Lake Tawakoni	10.05	10-25-2015
192	0.60	0.48	1.12	1.10	2.55	3.33	2.24	3.43	2.13	1.81	0.76	0.60	20.15	Canyon	7.87	8-29-1968
238	0.95	1.11	1.29	1.48	2.19	2.14	2.77	1.96	2.00	1.69	0.91	0.80	19.29	Big Lake	5.87	8-15-2005
248	1.21	1.30	1.96	1.99	2.91	3.40	2.35	2.41	3.22	3.14	2.14	1.35	27.38	Leakey	11.95	9-26-2016
225	3.54	4.19	5.19	4.17	5.67	4.35	4.10	2.70	3.60	6.01	5.33	5.26	54.11	Avery	9.29	12-28-2015
228	0.58	0.00	0.00	0.00	0.00	0.00	0.00	0.00	0.00	0.00	0.00	0.00	0.58	Red Bluff Dam	7.24	6-19-1984
283	2.15	2.39	3.01	2.27	3.17	3.52	3.64	3.15	4.39	4.31	2.82	2.07	36.89	Austwell	15.96	8-26-2017
192	0.91	0.76	2.04	1.97	3.42	3.36	2.33	2.65	2.30	2.30	1.02	1.02	24.08	Miami	5.58	10-10-1985
277	2.92	2.99	3.22	2.58	4.54	3.52	1.84	2.90	3.08	4.71	3.57	3.63	39.50	Bremond	8.49	8-19-2008
254	2.45	2.97	3.67	3.44	5.17	4.47	2.02	1.85	3.17	4.55	3.55	3.22	40.53	Rockwall	7.08	9-22-2018

County, Town or Landmark Closest to Station for Normals	Temperature								Average Freeze Dates			
	Mean Max. July	No. At or Above 100°	Mean Min. January	No. At or Below 32°	Record Highest	Record High Date	Record Lowest	Record Low Date	Last in Spring		First in Fall	
	F.	Days	F.	Days	F.	M-D-Y	F.	M-D-Y	Mo.	Day	Mo.	Day
Runnels, Ballinger	94.2	11	33.1	52	116	6-30-1907	–6	1-31-1949	Mar.	25	Nov.	10
Rusk, Henderson	93.0	6	37.3	41	*111	9-2-2000	*–1	12-23-1989	Mar.	19	Nov.	18
Sabine, *Toledo Bend Dam*	92.9	4	39.0	39	114	8-9-1947	6	2-2-1951	Mar.	14	Nov.	20
San Augustine, Broaddus	92.7		37.0	37	112	8-18-1909	7	1-17-2018	Mar.	19	Nov.	12
San Jacinto, Coldspring	94.4	6	43.8	17	110	8-2-1998	3	12-24-1989	Mar.	8	Nov.	27
San Patricio, Sinton	92.8	4	46.9	7	111	9-6-2000	10	12-23-1989	Feb.	9	Dec.	13
San Saba, San Saba	94.1	16	34.8	51	113	8-30-2020	–1	12-23-1989	Mar.	13	Nov.	18
Schleicher, *Fort McKavett*	92.1	8	34.0	56	*107	6-26-1972	–7	2-2-1985	Mar.	29	Nov.	6
Scurry, Snyder	94.1	10	30.5	71	115	8-12-1936	–11	2-2-1985	Mar.	30	Nov.	10
Shackelford, Albany	93.4	16	33.3	57	115	6-27-1972	–8	1-4-1947	Apr.	1	Nov.	6
Shelby, Center	92.9	10	37.3	42	112	9-2-2000	0	2-2-1951	Mar.	16	Nov.	16
Sherman, Stratford	91.3	4	22.0	137	108	6-24-1953	–20	2-9-1933	Apr.	25	Oct.	17
Smith, Tyler	92.2	4	40.3	29	*110	8-3-2011	–8	2-12-1899	Mar.	14	Nov.	19
Somervell, Glen Rose	94.7	24	33.4	63	115	8-19-1984	–15	12-23-1989	Apr.	8	Oct.	22
Starr, Rio Grande City	98.9	44	47.2	6	*116	6-14-1998	7	2-13-1899	Jan.	30	Dec.	19
Stephens, Breckenridge	94.5	19	30.4	70	114	8-12-1936	–7	12-22-1989	Mar.	29	Nov.	9
Sterling, Sterling City	92.5	8	31.5	72	112	6-27-1994	–13	2-2-1985	Apr.	4	Nov.	2
Stonewall, Aspermont	95.2	29	31.0	73	117	6-28-1994	–10	12-23-1989	Mar.	30	Nov.	8
Sutton, Sonora	95.0	10	32.6	70	109	6-28-1980	–8	2-2-1951	Apr.	4	Nov.	3
Swisher, Tulia	89.7	6	24.2	119	111	6-27-2011	*–23	2-12-1899	Apr.	16	Oct.	23
Tarrant, Benbrook Dam	95.8	16	35.4	43	115	8-18-1909	*–12	2-12-1899	Mar.	16	Nov.	18
Taylor, Abilene Reg. Airport	95.1	10	35.5	48	*111	8-3-1943	–9	1-4-1947	Mar.	24	Nov.	12
Terrell, Sanderson	94.2	7	34.1	49	120	6-14-2008	1	12-22-1989	Mar.	18	Nov.	11
Terry, Brownfield	92.8	7	28.1	89	111	6-28-1994	–8	1-14-1963	Apr.	1	Nov.	6
Throckmorton, Throckmorton	95.2	22	31.4	71	119	8-30-1947	–11	12-23-1989	Mar.	31	Nov.	7
Titus, Mount Pleasant	92.3	6	33.9	61	109	8-5-2011	–12	2-2-1951	Mar.	28	Nov.	7
Tom Green, San Angelo	96.1	15	35.4	49	113	6-30-1907	–6	1-18-1930	Mar.	26	Nov.	11
Travis, Austin-Camp Mabry	95.9	16	43.7	12	112	9-5-2000	*–5	1-31-1949	Feb.	19	Dec.	6
Trinity, Groveton	94.9	5	40.3	26	111	9-4-2000	1	12-23-1989	Mar.	19	Nov.	14
Tyler, Town Bluff Dam	90.6	2	39.9	28	*111	9-4-2000	*2	1-31-1949	Mar.	9	Nov.	24
Upshur, Gilmer	91.1	7	34.0	54	114	8-10-1936	*–4	12-24-1989	Mar.	31	Nov.	7
Upton, McCamey	95.9	18	34.7	46	*113	6-27-1994	*–2	1-11-1962	Mar.	20	Nov.	14
Uvalde, Uvalde	96.1	23	40.7	25	114	6-9-1910	*6	2-3-1951	Mar.	1	Nov.	28
Val Verde, Del Rio Intl. Airport	97.9	25	42.6	12	*114	7-30-1995	*2	2-3-1985	Feb.	19	Dec.	4
Van Zandt, Wills Point	93.2	10	36.7	41	115	8-18-1909	–2	12-24-1989	Mar.	16	Nov.	21
Victoria, Victoria Reg. Airport	94.1	4	45.5	9	*111	9-5-2000	*9	1-18-1930	Feb.	22	Dec.	6
Walker, Huntsville	91.3	4	41.0	17	110	9-4-2000	*–2	2-12-1899	Feb.	28	Dec.	3
Waller, *Sealy*	94.0	7	43.5	13	107	8-12-1969	13	1-30-1966	Feb.	22	Dec.	5
Ward, Monahans	97.3	33	28.8	74	120	6-28-1994	–9	1-11-1962	Mar.	31	Nov.	7
Washington, Brenham	93.2	8	41.3	18	113	9-5-2000	–2	1-19-1930	Mar.	2	Dec.	1
Webb, Laredo	100.1	54	48.8	5	116	6-17-1998	5	2-12-1899	Feb.	3	Dec.	14
Wharton, Pierce	94.5	2	44.5	11	112	9-5-2000	3	2-12-1899	Feb.	21	Dec.	8
Wheeler, Shamrock	91.9	11	25.3	97	117	7-12-2011	*–13	1-19-1984	Apr.	6	Oct.	29
Wichita, Wichita Falls Airport	95.3	25	31.8	59	117	6-28-1980	–15	1-4-1947	Mar.	28	Nov.	10
Wilbarger, *Lake Kemp*	95.4	26	30.2	71	119	8-3-1943	–9	12-23-1989	Mar.	21	Nov.	14
Willacy, Raymondville	96.8	18	49.9	3	109	6-6-1916	14	1-13-1962	Jan.	31	Dec.	22
Williamson, Taylor	94.9	9	38.1	28	113	7-11-1917	*–5	1-31-1949	Mar.	7	Nov.	24
Wilson, Floresville	95.7	15	40.9	27	*114	7-6-1984	5	1-21-1985	Mar.	12	Nov.	22
Winkler, County Airport	97.1	32	31.5	65	117	6-27-1994	*–14	1-11-1962	Mar.	31	Nov.	5
Wise, Bridgeport	94.1	13	32.8	61	*115	6-29-1980	*–8	12-23-1989	Apr.	2	Nov.	5
Wood, Mineola	91.9	8	35.3	52	114	6-18-1996	1	12-30-1983	Mar.	29	Nov.	8
Yoakum, Plains	91.9	7	26.2	99	113	6-27-1994	–12	2-1-1951	Apr.	6	Nov.	2
Young, Olney	95.4	22	31.8	56	*120	6-3-1998	–8	12-23-1989	Apr.	1	Nov.	6
Zapata, Zapata	98.5	39	48.6	4	116	6-16-1998	13	1-4-1911	Jan.	27	Dec.	23
Zavala, Crystal City	97.6	29	45.9	8	115	9-5-2000	6	1-12-1962	Feb.	13	Dec.	7

Growing Season	Mean Precipitation													Record Rainfall Highest Daily Total		
	January	February	March	April	May	June	July	August	September	October	November	December	Annual			
Days	In.	In.	In.	In.	In.	In.	In.	In.	In.	In.	In.	In.	In.	Location	In.	M-D-Y
233	0.99	0.00	0.00	0.00	0.00	0.00	0.00	0.00	0.00	0.00	0.00	0.00	0.99	Wingate	7.68	6-19-1982
247	3.68	4.22	4.40	3.65	4.70	5.22	3.06	2.86	3.48	4.84	4.78	4.47	49.36	Henderson	11.05	3-29-1989
253	4.74	4.94	4.47	3.57	4.62	5.50	4.00	3.11	3.38	5.07	5.53	5.99	54.92	Hemphill	11.70	3-10-2018
240	4.47	4.96	4.50	3.69	5.25	5.32	3.39	3.59	4.07	4.87	5.02	5.44	54.57	San Augustine	10.60	8-18-1915
285	3.85	3.47	3.25	2.91	4.94	5.26	3.07	3.61	3.75	5.73	5.09	3.84	48.77	Oakhurst	16.50	8-28-2017
324	1.75	2.15	2.25	1.85	3.26	3.28	3.52	2.36	5.29	4.75	2.27	1.55	34.28	Welder Wildlife	14.40	9-13-1974
239	1.38	1.97	2.60	2.11	3.62	4.55	1.99	2.47	2.51	3.03	2.04	1.71	29.98	San Saba	11.20	10-5-1969
234	0.86	1.51	1.68	1.54	2.90	3.06	2.06	2.34	2.01	2.83	1.50	0.92	23.21	D. Wilson Ranch	9.51	7-16-1990
227	0.82	1.14	1.55	1.74	2.96	3.37	2.22	2.28	2.28	2.22	1.06	1.04	22.68	Knapp	5.93	5-15-1980
225	1.12	1.92	2.35	2.47	3.64	4.07	2.11	2.01	2.40	3.00	1.70	1.57	28.36	Albany	29.05	8-4-1978
248	4.45	4.95	4.60	4.16	4.47	5.30	3.31	3.52	3.65	5.32	5.04	5.43	54.20	Neuville	10.20	10-30-1941
181	0.54	0.45	1.27	1.26	2.41	2.37	2.25	2.75	1.74	1.35	0.70	0.68	17.77	Stratford	5.60	8-17-1992
257	3.42	4.12	4.19	3.10	4.41	5.15	2.75	2.66	3.05	4.91	4.38	4.49	46.63	Eads	8.24	6-7-1943
225	1.71	2.26	2.95	2.58	4.28	4.09	1.56	2.57	2.88	3.15	2.18	1.97	32.18	Glen Rose	10.73	6-22-2014
321	1.00	1.25	0.89	1.14	2.22	3.07	2.26	1.89	4.46	2.48	1.14	0.85	22.65	Rio Grande City	12.51	9-22-1967
213	1.44	1.89	2.58	2.12	4.01	4.09	2.23	2.36	2.65	3.48	1.56	1.57	29.98	Breckenridge	15.70	10-13-1981
219	0.89	1.12	1.21	1.33	2.59	2.37	1.72	2.57	2.48	2.20	0.98	1.00	20.46	Case Ranch	6.79	9-21-1972
223	1.00	1.36	1.64	1.88	3.22	3.56	1.86	2.75	2.10	2.16	1.14	1.10	23.77	Aspermont	6.92	4-28-1930
221	0.97	1.31	1.57	1.71	2.60	2.59	1.92	2.62	2.96	2.54	1.30	0.94	23.03	Humble Pump Stn	8.60	7-11-1988
189	0.77	0.75	1.38	1.54	2.79	3.32	2.26	2.91	2.13	1.95	0.95	0.82	21.57	Tulia	6.01	10-21-1918
245	1.90	2.42	3.33	2.86	4.69	3.98	1.91	2.16	3.26	3.98	2.66	2.35	35.50	Arlington	9.70	5-17-1949
236	1.02	1.36	1.74	1.64	3.18	3.56	1.87	2.59	2.24	2.98	1.41	1.23	24.82	Lawn	9.19	8-4-1978
243	0.55	0.65	0.65	0.73	1.68	2.25	2.04	1.60	1.70	1.74	0.63	0.50	14.72	Dryden	6.30	9-23-1990
215	0.68	0.75	1.03	1.18	2.75	3.01	2.41	1.95	2.38	1.77	0.90	0.77	19.58	Brownfield	7.85	9-21-1936
223	1.20	1.93	2.26	2.18	4.49	3.99	2.22	2.12	2.71	3.38	1.70	1.60	29.78	Throckmorton	6.53	8-4-1978
230	3.17	4.12	4.30	3.49	5.54	4.63	3.51	2.21	3.03	5.09	4.19	4.42	47.70	Mount Pleasant	8.06	11-5-1994
232	0.93	1.35	1.50	1.42	2.82	2.59	1.20	2.26	2.46	2.73	1.14	0.85	21.25	Mathis Field	11.75	9-15-1936
291	2.22	2.02	2.76	2.09	4.44	4.33	1.88	2.35	2.99	3.88	2.96	2.40	34.32	Hill's Ranch	16.02	9-10-1921
267	3.90	3.71	3.96	2.82	4.81	5.23	3.16	3.20	3.81	5.57	4.90	4.24	49.31	Groveton	12.10	10-17-1994
258	4.57	4.58	4.12	3.89	4.94	5.97	3.85	3.90	4.66	4.85	5.29	5.56	56.18	Spurger	11.50	8-30-2017
229	3.46	4.16	4.37	3.38	4.55	3.90	3.08	2.79	3.40	4.98	4.31	4.46	46.84	Gilmer	7.88	4-23-1966
247	0.68	0.64	0.48	1.02	1.31	2.11	1.32	2.14	1.85	2.23	0.70	0.66	15.14	McCamey	9.13	10-4-1986
263	1.38	1.49	2.13	1.98	3.38	3.49	2.09	1.67	2.60	3.31	1.58	1.14	26.24	Montell	20.05	6-29-1913
293	0.72	0.88	1.14	1.65	2.81	2.35	1.78	2.18	2.20	2.23	0.93	0.65	19.52	Del Rio Intl. AP	17.03	8-23-1998
252	3.18	3.58	4.30	3.01	4.73	4.47	2.19	2.25	3.23	4.96	4.41	3.84	44.15	S. County Line	11.55	10-24-2015
291	2.52	2.08	2.77	2.82	5.19	4.46	4.18	2.85	4.16	4.64	3.24	2.31	41.22	Inez	10.45	8-26-2017
272	4.25	3.33	3.70	3.26	4.45	5.45	2.80	3.67	4.16	4.68	5.19	4.14	49.08	Huntsville	14.75	8-28-2017
276	3.25	2.72	2.84	3.56	4.57	3.52	2.65	3.56	3.91	4.84	4.51	2.89	42.92	Brookshire	16.75	8-28-2017
216	0.58	0.70	0.59	0.64	1.44	1.37	1.94	1.68	2.16	1.66	0.60	0.79	14.15	Grandfalls	5.87	9-4-1986
273	3.46	3.09	3.42	2.89	4.66	4.38	2.56	2.93	4.46	5.09	4.28	3.42	45.14	Brenham	21.46	5-27-2016
329	0.90	0.94	1.12	1.42	2.49	2.23	2.01	1.88	2.93	2.21	1.19	0.88	20.20	Laredo	9.70	5-10-1972
287	3.16	2.68	3.52	2.92	4.52	4.70	4.67	4.30	4.75	4.98	5.20	3.47	48.87	New Gulf	14.00	6-26-1960
202	0.76	0.88	1.96	2.13	3.56	3.99	2.25	2.45	2.59	2.27	1.35	0.97	25.16	Shamrock	8.24	6-4-1995
228	1.14	1.75	2.20	2.61	3.79	4.15	1.59	2.50	2.81	3.11	1.65	1.62	28.92	Wichita V. Farm	8.00	8-15-1971
225	1.17	1.40	2.21	2.25	3.34	4.24	2.09	2.43	3.15	2.79	1.66	1.21	27.94	Vernon	14.82	8-2-1995
340	1.14	1.55	1.24	1.46	3.03	2.31	2.27	2.31	5.51	3.12	0.99	1.15	26.08	Port Mansfield	14.50	7-26-2020
259	2.18	2.54	3.12	2.73	4.38	4.66	2.07	2.19	3.75	4.19	3.00	2.51	37.32	Taylor	16.11	9-10-1921
261	1.59	1.76	2.01	2.14	3.39	3.05	2.48	2.11	3.08	3.36	2.20	1.90	29.07	Falls City	8.83	9-15-1968
222	0.43	0.56	0.75	0.59	1.62	1.60	1.99	1.49	1.35	1.56	0.59	0.56	13.09	NE of Kermit	3.80	9-20-2014
222	1.55	2.38	3.09	2.88	5.23	4.22	2.04	1.98	3.06	4.01	2.20	2.07	34.71	Boyd	9.15	10-31-1981
235	3.07	3.74	3.99	3.41	4.24	3.86	2.40	1.88	2.94	4.86	4.17	4.46	43.02	Mineola	9.50	10-24-2015
200	0.46	0.70	0.90	0.82	1.89	2.78	2.58	2.32	2.63	1.35	0.84	0.93	18.20	Plains	6.11	7-5-1960
222	1.40	1.86	2.56	2.70	5.00	4.03	2.41	1.98	2.43	3.56	1.89	1.64	31.46	Olney	8.74	7-28-2004
341	0.95	0.99	0.80	1.33	2.50	2.11	2.71	1.50	3.53	1.38	1.22	0.75	19.77	Zapata	6.10	4-14-1966
307	1.06	1.06	1.43	1.52	2.15	2.54	2.25	1.54	2.08	2.08	1.11	0.76	19.58	Crystal City	13.88	10-14-2013

Astronomical Calendar

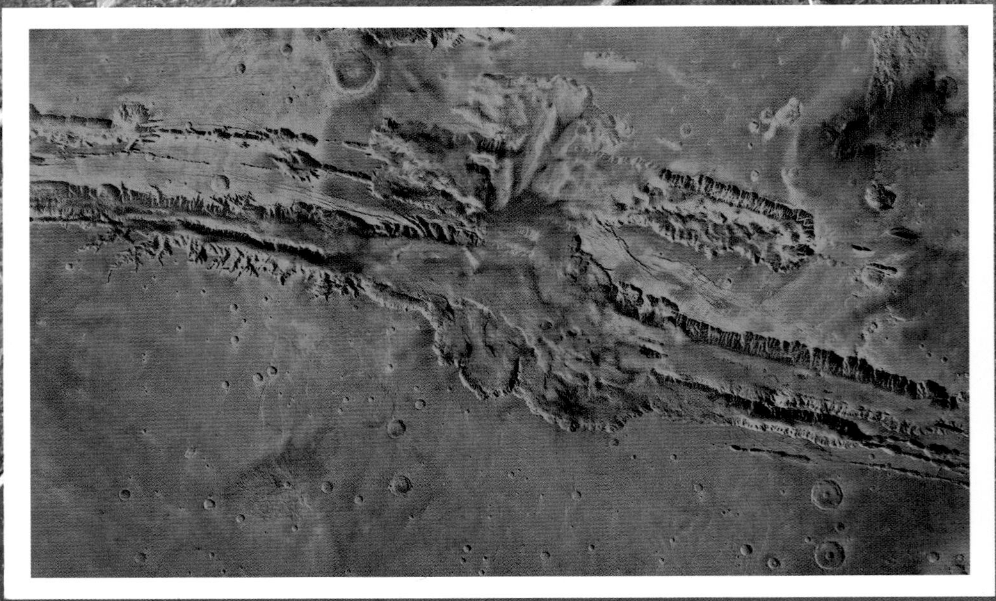

MORNING AND EVENING STARS

SEASONS, ECLIPSES, METEOR SHOWERS

CHRONOLOGIAL ERAS AND CYCLES

CALENDARS FOR 2022 AND 2023

One small section of the Valles Marineris canyon system that runs along the Martian equator. Photo courtesy of NASA/JPL-Caltech.

Astronomical Calendars for 2022 & 2023

Sources: McDonald Observatory; U.S. Naval Observatory's website (https://aa.usno.navy.mil/index.php) and publications, Astronomical Phenomena For The Year 2022 *and* Astronomical Phenomena For The Year 2023; *In-The-Sky.org*

The Year 2022

The year 2022 CE comprises the latter part of the 246th and the beginning of the 247th year of the independence of the United States of America. All dates in this book are given in terms of the Gregorian calendar.

The Seasons

Spring begins on Sunday, March 20, at 10:33 a.m. (CDT)

Summer begins on Tuesday, June 21, at 4:13 a.m. (CDT)

Autumn begins on Thursday, Sept. 22, at 8:03 p.m. (CDT)

Winter begins on Wednesday, Dec. 21, at 3:48 p.m. (CST)

Chronological Eras, 2022

Era	Year	Begins
Julian	6735	Jan. 14
Byzantine	7531	Sept. 14
Jewish (A.M.)*	5783	Sept. 25
Chinese (rén yín)	—	Feb. 1
Roman (A.U.C.)	2775	Jan. 14
Nabonassar	2771	April 18
Japanese	2682	Jan. 1
Seleucidæ (Grecian)	2334	Sept. 14 or Oct. 14
Saka (Indian)	1944	March 21
Diocletian (Coptic)	1739	Sept. 11
Islamic (Hegira)*	1444	Aug. 19

**Year begins at sunset.*

Chronological Cycles, 2022

Dominical Letter	B	Golden Number (Lunar Cycle)	IX
Epact	27		
Roman Indiction	15	Solar Cycle	15

Morning & Evening Stars, 2022

Morning Stars	
Venus ♀	January 15 through September 15
Mars ♂	January 1 through December 8
Jupiter ♃	March 19 through September 26
Saturn ♄	February 22 through August 14
Evening Stars	
Venus ♀	Jan. 1–Jan. 3; Dec. 3–Dec. 8
Mars ♂	December 8 through December 31
Jupiter ♃	Jan. 1–Feb. 20; Sept. 26–Dec. 31
Saturn ♄	Jan. 1–Jan. 19; Aug. 14–Dec. 31

Eclipses 2022

April 30: Solar, partial. Visible in S.E Pacific Ocean, Antarctic Peninsula, Ellsworth Land, and S. South America.

May 16: Lunar, total. Visible in most of Africa, W. Europe, Iceland, Americas except N.W. part, Polynesia except W. part.

Oct. 25: Solar, partial. Visible in Iceland, Europe, N.E. Africa, Middle East, W. Asia, India, W. China.

Nov. 8: Lunar, total. Visible in N.W. South America, North America, Pacific Ocean, Australasia, S.E. Asia, Japan, China, E. Russia.

The Year 2023

The year 2023 CE comprises the latter part of the 247th and the beginning of the 248th year of the independence of the United States of America.

The Seasons

Spring begins on Monday, March 20, at 4:24 p.m. (CDT)

Summer begins on Wednesday, June 21, at 9:57 a.m. (CDT)

Autumn begins on Friday, Sept. 22, at 1:50 a.m. (CDT)

Winter begins on Thursday, Dec. 21, at 9:27 p.m. (CST)

Chronological Eras, 2023

Era	Year	Begins
Julian	6736	Jan. 14
Byzantine	7532	Sept. 14
Jewish (A.M.)*	5784	Sept. 6
Chinese (gui mao)	—	Jan. 22
Roman (A.U.C.)	2776	Jan. 14
Nabonassar	2772	April 18
Japanese	2683	Jan. 1
Seleucidæ (Grecian)	2335	Sept. 14 or Oct. 14
Saka (Indian)	1945	March 22
Diocletian (Coptic)	1740	Sept. 12
Islamic (Hegira)*	1445	July 18

**Year begins at sunset.*

Chronological Cycles, 2023

Dominical Letter	A	Golden Number (Lunar Cycle)	X
Epact	8		
Roman Indiction	1	Solar Cycle	16

Morning & Evening Stars, 2023

Morning Stars	
Venus ♀	August 18 through December 31
Jupiter ♃	April 26 through November 3
Saturn ♄	March 6 through August 27
Evening Stars	
Venus ♀	January 1 through August 8
Mars ♂	January 1 through September 30
Jupiter ♃	Jan. 1–March 29, Nov. 3–Dec. 31
Saturn ♄	Jan. 1–Jan. 30, Aug. 27–Dec. 31

Eclipses 2023

April 20: Solar, annular-total. Visible to Southern Indian Ocean, parts of Antarctica, most of Australasia, Indonesia, Philippines, most of Oceania, Western Pacific Ocean.

May 5: Lunar, penumbral. Visible to Antarctica, Oceania, Australasia, Asia, Europe (except British Isles and Norway), Africa, S. Georgia, and S. Sandwich Island.

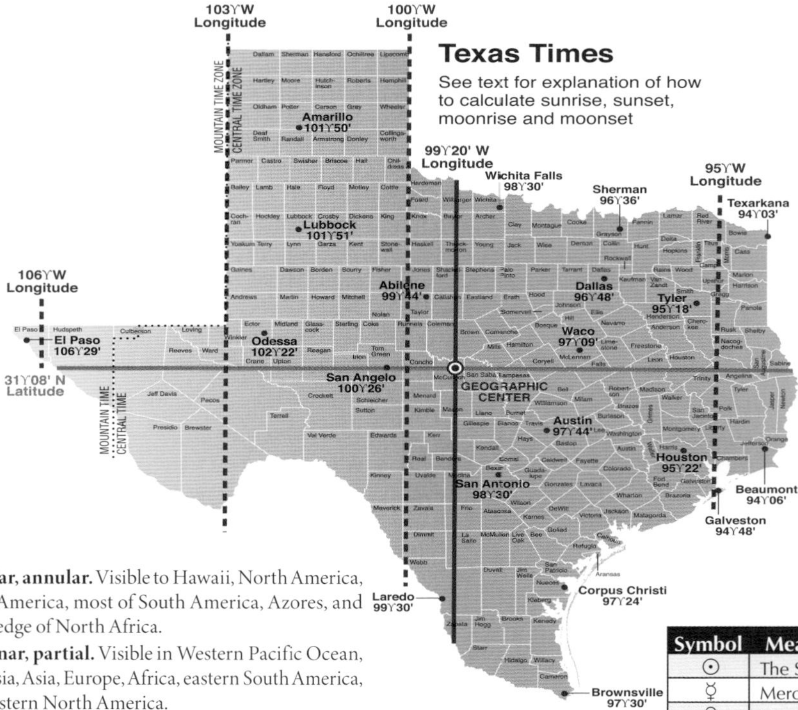

Oct. 14: Solar, annular. Visible to Hawaii, North America, Central America, most of South America, Azores, and western edge of North Africa.

Oct. 28: Lunar, partial. Visible in Western Pacific Ocean, Australasia, Asia, Europe, Africa, eastern South America, north-eastern North America.

An Explanation of Texas Time

Times listed here are **Central Standard Time**, except for the period from 2:00 a.m. on the second Sunday in March until 2:00 a.m. on the first Sunday in November, when **Daylight Saving Time**, which is one hour later than Central Standard Time, is in effect.

All of Texas is in the Central Time Zone, except El Paso and Hudspeth counties and the northwest corner of Culberson County, which observe **Mountain Time**. Mountain Time is one hour earlier than Central Time.

All times are calculated for the intersection of 99° 20' west longitude and 31° 08' north latitude, which is **closest to the town of Mercury and** about 15 miles northeast of Brady, McCulloch County. This point is the **approximate geographical center of the state.**

How to Adjust Rise & Set Times

To adjust the time of sunrise or sunset, moonrise or moonset for any point in Texas, apply the following rules:

- For each degree of longitude that the place lies **west** of the 99th meridian, **add four minutes** to the times given in the calendar.
- For each degree of longitude the place lies **east** of the 99th meridian, **subtract four minutes**.

At times there will be considerable variation for distances north and south of the line of 31° 08' north latitude, but this formula will give sufficiently close results.

The map above shows the intersection for which all times given in this chapter are calculated, with some major cities and longitudes to aid in calculating times.

Astronomical Calendars

The calendars on the following pages feature phenomena and planetary configurations of the heavens for 2022 and 2023 in the center columns. The table to the right is a key to those symbols. You'll find find additional keys below the calendars.

Symbol	Meaning
☉	The Sun
☿	Mercury
♀	Venus
●	The Earth
☾	The Moon
♂	Mars
♃	Jupiter
♄	Saturn
⛢	Uranus
♆	Neptune
☌	conjunction
☍	opposition

Aspects: Conjunction & Opposition

☌ This symbol, appearing between symbols for heavenly bodies, means they are "in conjunction," that is, having the same longitude in the sky and appearing near each other. For example, ♀ ☌ ☾ means Venus is north or south of the moon by a few degrees. Conjunctions listed in this calendar are separated by 10 degrees or less. Inferior and superior conjuctions mean an inner planet, Venus or Mercury, is in line with the Sun, either between the Earth and the Sun (inferior) or on the opposite side of the Sun (superior).

☍ This symbol means that the heavenly body listed is in "opposition" to the Sun, or that they differ by 180 degrees of longitude.

Common Astronomical Terms

Aphelion: Point at which a planet's orbit is farthest from the sun.

Perihelion: Point at which a planet's orbit is nearest the sun.

Apogee: Point of the moon's orbit farthest from the earth.

Perigee: Point of the moon's orbit nearest the earth.

2022

Times are **Central Standard Time**, except from **Sunday, March 13 to Sunday, Nov. 6**, during which **Daylight Saving Time** is observed. **Boldface times for moonrise and moonset indicate p.m.** Times are figured for the point **31° 08' N 99° 20' W**, the approximate geographical center of the state. **See page 138 for explanation of how to get the approximate time at any other Texas point.**

1st Month — January 2022 — 31 Days

Moon Phases — New Moon Jan. 2, 12:33 pm; First Qtr. Jan 9, 12:11 pm; Full Moon Jan. 17, 5:48 pm; Last Qtr. Jan. 25, 7:41 am; New Moon Jan 31, 11:46 pm

Day of Year	Day of Month	Day of Week	Planetary Configurations and Phenomena	Sunrise	Sunset	Moonrise	Moonset
1	1	Sat	☾ at perigee (5 pm)	7:35	5:46	6:30	**4:40**
2	2	Sun	New ☾	7:36	5:46	7:40	**5:46**
3	3	Mon	☿ ☌ ☾ (7 pm)	7:36	5:47	8:42	**6:57**
4	4	Tue	● at perihelion (1 am)	7:36	5:48	9:35	**8:09**
5	5	Wed	♃ ☌ ☾ (6 pm)	7:36	5:49	10:19	**9:17**
6	6	Thu		7:36	5:50	10:56	**10:22**
7	7	Fri	☿ gr. elongation E (5 am)	7:36	5:50	11:29	**11:22**
8	8	Sat	♀ in inferior ☌ (7 pm)	7:36	5:51	11:58	
9	9	Sun	First qtr. ☾	7:36	5:52	**12:27**	12:20
10	10	Mon		7:36	5:53	**12:55**	1:17
11	11	Tue	♅ ☌ ☾ (5 am)	7:36	5:54	**1:25**	2:12
12	12	Wed		7:36	5:55	**1:57**	3:08
13	13	Thu	☿ stationary (7 pm)	7:36	5:55	**2:33**	4:04
14	14	Fri	☾ at apogee (3 am)	7:36	5:56	**3:14**	5:00
15	15	Sat		7:36	5:57	**4:00**	5:55
16	16	Sun		7:36	5:58	**4:51**	6:48
17	17	Mon	Full ☾	7:35	5:59	**5:46**	7:36
18	18	Tue		7:35	6:00	**6:45**	8:20
19	19	Wed		7:35	6:01	**7:44**	9:00
20	20	Thu		7:35	6:02	**8:43**	9:35
21	21	Fri		7:34	6:02	**9:42**	10:07
22	22	Sat		7:34	6:03	**10:42**	10:37
23	23	Sun	☿ in inferior ☌ (4 am)	7:33	6:04	**11:42**	11:07
24	24	Mon		7:33	6:05		11:38
25	25	Tue	Last qtr. ☾	7:33	6:06	12:44	**12:11**
26	26	Wed		7:32	6:07	1:50	**12:48**
27	27	Thu		7:32	6:08	2:58	**1:32**
28	28	Fri		7:31	6:09	4:08	**2:23**
29	29	Sat	♀ ♂ ☌ ☾	7:31	6:10	5:18	**3:23**
30	30	Sun	☿ ☌ ☾ (6 pm)	7:30	6:11	6:23	**4:31**
31	31	Mon	New ☾	7:29	6:11	7:20	**5:42**

2nd Month — February 2022 — 28 Days

Moon Phases — First Qtr. Feb. 8, 6:50 am; Full Moon Feb. 16, 10:56 am; Last Qtr. Feb. 23, 4:32 pm

Day of Year	Day of Month	Day of Week	Planetary Configurations and Phenomena	Sunrise	Sunset	Moonrise	Moonset
32	1	Tue		7:29	6:12	8:08	**6:53**
33	2	Wed	♃ ☌ ☾ (3 pm)	7:28	6:13	8:49	**8:01**
34	3	Thu	☿ stationary (4 pm)	7:28	6:14	9:24	**9:05**
35	4	Fri	♄ ☌ ⊙ (1 pm)	7:27	6:15	9:56	**10:06**
36	5	Sat		7:26	6:16	10:26	**11:05**
37	6	Sun		7:25	6:17	10:54	
38	7	Mon	♅ ☌ ☾ (2 pm)	7:25	6:18	11:24	12:02
39	8	Tue	First qtr. ☾	7:24	6:18	11:56	12:59
40	9	Wed		7:23	6:19	**12:31**	1:56
41	10	Thu	☾ at apogee (9 pm)	7:22	6:20	**1:10**	2:52
42	11	Fri		7:21	6:21	**1:54**	3:48
43	12	Sat	♀ gr. illumination (4 pm)	7:21	6:22	**2:43**	4:41
44	13	Sun		7:20	6:23	**3:37**	5:31
45	14	Mon		7:19	6:24	**4:35**	6:17
46	15	Tue		7:18	6:24	**5:35**	6:58
47	16	Wed	Full ☾	7:17	6:25	**6:35**	7:35
48	17	Thu		7:16	6:26	**7:35**	8:08
49	18	Fri		7:15	6:27	**8:35**	8:40
50	19	Sat		7:14	6:28	**9:36**	9:10
51	20	Sun		7:13	6:28	**10:38**	9:40
52	21	Mon		7:12	6:29	**11:42**	10:12
53	22	Tue		7:11	6:30		10:48
54	23	Wed	Last qtr. ☾	7:10	6:31	12:49	11:28
55	24	Thu		7:09	6:31	1:57	**12:16**
56	25	Fri		7:08	6:32	3:05	**1:11**
57	26	Sat	☾ at perigee (4 pm)	7:07	6:33	4:10	**2:14**
58	27	Sun	♀ ♂ ☌ ☾	7:06	6:34	5:08	**3:22**
59	28	Mon	☿ ♄ ☌ ☾	7:04	6:35	5:59	**4:32**

3rd Month — March 2022 — 31 Days

Moon Phases — New Moon Mar. 2, 11:35 am; First Qtr. Mar. 10, 4:45 am; Full Moon Mar. 18, 2:18 am; Last Qtr. Mar. 25, 12:37 am

Day of Year	Day of Month	Day of Week	Planetary Configurations and Phenomena	Sunrise	Sunset	Moonrise	Moonset
60	1	Tue		7:03	6:35	6:42	**5:40**
61	2	Wed	New ☾; ☿ ☌ ♄ (7 am)	7:02	6:36	7:19	**6:46**
62	3	Thu		7:01	6:37	7:52	**7:49**
63	4	Fri		7:00	6:37	8:23	**8:49**
64	5	Sat	♃ ☌ ⊙ (8 am)	6:59	6:38	8:52	**9:48**
65	6	Sun		6:58	6:39	9:22	**10:46**
66	7	Mon	♅ ☌ ☾ (12 am)	6:56	6:40	9:53	**11:44**
67	8	Tue		6:55	6:40	10:27	
68	9	Wed		6:54	6:41	11:04	12:42
69	10	Thu	First qtr. ☾ at apogee	6:53	6:42	11:46	1:38
70	11	Fri		6:52	6:42	**12:34**	2:33
71	12	Sat	♀ ☌ ♂ (8 am)	6:50	6:43	**1:26**	3:24
72	13	Sun	**DST begins (2 am)**	7:49	7:44	**3:22**	5:11
73	14	Mon		7:48	7:44	**4:21**	5:54
74	15	Tue		7:47	7:45	**5:22**	6:32
75	16	Wed		7:45	7:46	**6:22**	7:07
76	17	Thu		7:44	7:46	**7:24**	7:39
77	18	Fri	Full ☾	7:43	7:47	**8:26**	8:10
78	19	Sat		7:42	7:48	**9:29**	8:41
79	20	Sun	Equinox (10:33 am)	7:41	7:48	**10:34**	9:13
80	21	Mon		7:39	7:49	**11:41**	9:48
81	22	Tue		7:38	7:50		10:27
82	23	Wed	☾ at perigee (7 pm)	7:37	7:50	12:50	11:13
83	24	Thu		7:36	7:51	1:59	**12:05**
84	25	Fri	Last qtr. ☾	7:34	7:52	3:04	**1:06**
85	26	Sat		7:33	7:52	4:04	**2:11**
86	27	Sun	♂ ☌ ☾ (10 pm)	7:32	7:53	4:55	**3:19**
87	28	Mon	♀ ♄ ☌ ☾ (6 am)	7:31	7:54	5:40	**4:27**
88	29	Tue	♀ ☌ ♄ (8 am)	7:29	7:54	6:18	**5:32**
89	30	Wed	♃ ♆ ☌ ☾	7:28	7:55	6:51	**6:34**
90	31	Thu		7:27	7:56	7:22	**7:35**

Astronomical Calendar for 2022

4th Month — April 2022 — 30 Days

Moon Phases — New Moon Apr. 1, 1:24 am; First Qtr. Apr. 9, 1:48 am; Full Moon Apr 16, 1:55 pm; Last Qtr. Apr 23, 6:56 am; New Moon Apr. 30, 3:28 pm

Day of Year	Day of Month	Day of Week	Planetary Configurations and Phenomena	Sunrise	Sunset	Moonrise	Moonset
91	1	Fri	New ☾	7:26	7:56	7:51	**8:34**
92	2	Sat	☿ in superior ☌ (6 pm)	7:24	7:57	8:20	**9:33**
93	3	Sun	♅ ☌ ☾ (12 pm)	7:23	7:57	8:51	**10:31**
94	4	Mon	♂ ☌ ♄ (5 pm)	7:22	7:58	9:23	**11:30**
95	5	Tue		7:21	7:59	9:59	
96	6	Wed		7:19	7:59	10:40	12:27
97	7	Thu	☾ at apogee (2 pm)	7:18	8:00	11:25	1:23
98	8	Fri		7:17	8:01	**12:15**	2:16
99	9	Sat	First qtr. ☾	7:16	8:01	**1:10**	3:05
100	10	Sun		7:15	8:02	**2:07**	3:49
101	11	Mon		7:13	8:03	**3:06**	4:29
102	12	Tue	♃ ☌ ♆ (3 pm)	7:12	8:03	**4:06**	5:04
103	13	Wed		7:11	8:04	**5:07**	5:37
104	14	Thu		7:10	8:05	**6:09**	6:08
105	15	Fri		7:09	8:05	**7:12**	6:39
106	16	Sat	Full ☾	7:08	8:06	**8:17**	7:10
107	17	Sun		7:07	8:07	**9:26**	7:44
108	18	Mon		7:05	8:07	**10:37**	8:23
109	19	Tue	☾ at perigee (10 am)	7:04	8:08	**11:48**	9:07
110	20	Wed		7:03	8:09		9:59
111	21	Thu		7:02	8:09	12:57	10:58
112	22	Fri		7:01	8:10	2:00	**12:03**
113	23	Sat	Last qtr. ☾	7:00	8:11	2:54	**1:11**
114	24	Sun	♄ ☌ ☾ (4 pm)	6:59	8:11	3:40	**2:19**
115	25	Mon	♂ ☌ ☾ (5 pm)	6:58	8:12	4:19	**3:24**
116	26	Tue	♀ ♆ ☌ ☾ (9 pm)	6:57	8:13	4:53	**4:26**
117	27	Wed	♃ ☌ ☾; ♀ ☌ ♆	6:56	8:13	5:24	**5:26**
118	28	Thu		6:55	8:14	5:53	**6:25**
119	29	Fri	☿ gr. elongation E (3 am)	6:54	8:15	6:21	**7:23**
120	30	Sat	New ☾; ☉ eclipse (5 pm)	6:53	8:15	6:51	**8:21**

5th Month — May 2022 — 31 Days

Moon Phases — First Qtr. May 8, 7:21 pm; Full Moon May 15, 11:14 pm; Last Qtr. May 22, 1:43 pm; New Moon May 30, 6:30 am

Day of Year	Day of Month	Day of Week	Planetary Configurations and Phenomena	Sunrise	Sunset	Moonrise	Moonset
121	1	Sun	☿ ☌ ☾ (9 am)	6:52	8:16	7:22	**9:19**
122	2	Mon		6:51	8:17	7:57	**10:17**
123	3	Tue		6:50	8:17	8:35	**11:14**
124	4	Wed		6:50	8:18	9:19	
125	5	Thu	☾ at apogee (8 am)	6:49	8:19	10:07	12:09
126	6	Fri		6:48	8:19	11:00	12:59
127	7	Sat		6:47	8:20	11:56	1:45
128	8	Sun	First qtr. ☾	6:46	8:21	**12:54**	2:26
129	9	Mon		6:45	8:22	**1:52**	3:02
130	10	Tue	☿ stationary (6 pm)	6:45	8:22	**2:51**	3:35
131	11	Wed		6:44	8:23	**3:51**	4:06
132	12	Thu		6:43	8:24	**4:53**	4:36
133	13	Fri		6:43	8:24	**5:56**	5:06
134	14	Sat		6:42	8:25	**7:03**	5:39
135	15	Sun	Full ☾; eclipse (11 pm)	6:41	8:26	**8:14**	6:15
136	16	Mon		6:41	8:26	**9:27**	6:57
137	17	Tue	☾ at perigee (10 am)	6:40	8:27	**10:40**	7:47
138	18	Wed		6:39	8:28	**11:49**	8:45
139	19	Thu		6:39	8:28		9:51
140	20	Fri		6:38	8:29	12:48	11:00
141	21	Sat	☿ in inferior ☌ (2 pm)	6:38	8:30	1:39	**12:10**
142	22	Sun	♄ ☌ last qtr. ☾ (12 am)	6:37	8:30	2:21	**1:17**
143	23	Mon		6:37	8:31	2:56	**2:20**
144	24	Tue	♂ ♃ ♆ ☌ ☾	6:36	8:31	3:28	**3:21**
145	25	Wed		6:36	8:32	3:57	**4:19**
146	26	Thu	♀ ☌ ☾ (10 pm)	6:36	8:33	4:25	**5:17**
147	27	Fri		6:35	8:33	4:54	**6:14**
148	28	Sat	♅ ☌ ☾; ♂ ☌ ♃	6:35	8:34	5:24	**7:11**
149	29	Sun		6:34	8:34	5:57	**8:09**
150	30	Mon	New ☾	6:34	8:35	6:34	**9:07**
151	31	Tue		6:34	8:36	7:15	**10:02**

6th Month — June 2022 — 30 Days

Moon Phases — First Qtr. Jun. 8, 7:21; Full Moon Jun. 14, 6:52 am; Last Qtr. Jun. 20, 10:11; New Moon Jun. 28, 9:52 pm

Day of Year	Day of Month	Day of Week	Planetary Configurations and Phenomena	Sunrise	Sunset	Moonrise	Moonset
152	1	Wed	☾ at apogee (8 pm)	6:34	8:36	8:02	**10:54**
153	2	Thu	☿ stationary (7 pm)	6:33	8:37	8:53	**11:41**
154	3	Fri		6:33	8:37	9:48	
155	4	Sat		6:33	8:38	10:45	12:24
156	5	Sun	♄ stationary (9 am)	6:33	8:38	11:42	1:01
157	6	Mon		6:33	8:39	**12:40**	1:35
158	7	Tue	First qtr. ☾	6:33	8:39	**1:38**	2:06
159	8	Wed		6:33	8:40	**2:37**	2:35
160	9	Thu		6:32	8:40	**3:38**	3:04
161	10	Fri		6:32	8:40	**4:41**	3:34
162	11	Sat	♀ ☌ ♅ (8 am)	6:32	8:41	**5:49**	4:08
163	12	Sun		6:32	8:41	**7:01**	4:46
164	13	Mon		6:32	8:42	**8:15**	5:32
165	14	Tue	Full ☾ at perigee (6 pm)	6:33	8:42	**9:27**	6:26
166	15	Wed		6:33	8:42	**10:33**	7:30
167	16	Thu	☿ gr. elongation W (10 am)	6:33	8:43	**11:30**	8:40
168	17	Fri		6:33	8:43		9:53
169	18	Sat	♄ ☌ ☾ (7 am)	6:33	8:43	12:17	11:04
170	19	Sun		6:33	8:43	12:56	**12:11**
171	20	Mon	Last qtr. ☾	6:33	8:44	1:30	**1:14**
172	21	Tue	Solstice (4:14 am)	6:34	8:44	2:00	**2:14**
173	22	Wed	♂ ☌ ☾ (1 pm)	6:34	8:44	2:28	**3:12**
174	23	Thu	☿ ☌ Aldebaran (9 am)	6:34	8:44	2:57	**4:09**
175	24	Fri	♅ ☌ ☾ (5 pm)	6:34	8:44	3:26	**5:06**
176	25	Sat		6:35	8:45	3:58	**6:04**
177	26	Sun	♀ ☌ ☾ (3 am)	6:35	8:45	4:34	**7:01**
178	27	Mon	☿ ☌ ☾ (3 am)	6:35	8:45	5:14	**7:57**
179	28	Tue	New ☾	6:36	8:45	5:59	**8:50**
180	29	Wed	☾ at apogee (1 am)	6:36	8:45	6:49	**9:39**
181	30	Thu		6:36	8:45	7:43	**10:23**

☉ The Sun ● The Earth ☾ The Moon ☿ Mercury ♀ Venus ♂ Mars ♃ Jupiter ♄ Saturn ♆ Neptune ♅ Uranus ☌ = in conjunction ☍ = opposition to the ☉

Astronomical Calendar for 2022

7th Month — July 2022 — 31 Days

Moon Phases — First Qtr. Jul. 6, 9:14 pm; Full Moon Jul. 13, 1:38 pm; Last Qtr. Jul 20, 9:19 am; New Moon Jul. 28, 12:55 pm

Day of Year	Day of Month	Day of Week	Planetary Configurations and Phenomena	Sunrise	Sunset	Moon-rise	Moon-set
182	1	Fri	♀ ☌ Aldebaran (7 pm)	6:37	8:45	8:39	**11:02**
183	2	Sat		6:37	8:45	9:36	**11:36**
184	3	Sun		6:38	8:15	10:34	
185	4	Mon	● aphelion (2 am)	6:38	8:45	11:31	12:07
186	5	Tue		6:38	8:44	**12:28**	12:36
187	6	Wed	First qtr. ☾	6:39	8:44	**1:26**	1:05
188	7	Thu		6:39	8:44	**2:27**	1:34
189	8	Fri		6:40	8:44	**3:30**	2:04
190	9	Sat		6:40	8:44	**4:38**	2:39
191	10	Sun		6:41	8:44	**5:49**	3:20
192	11	Mon		6:41	8:43	**7:02**	4:09
193	12	Tue		6:42	8:43	**8:12**	5:07
194	13	Wed	Full ☾ at perigee (4 am)	6:42	8:43	**9:13**	6:15
195	14	Thu		6:43	8:42	**10:06**	7:28
196	15	Fri	♄ ☌ ☾ (3 pm)	6:44	8:42	**10:50**	8:42
197	16	Sat	☿ in superior ☌ (3 pm)	6:44	8:42	**11:27**	9:53
198	17	Sun	♆ ☌ ☾ (8 pm)	6:45	8:41	**11:59**	11:00
199	18	Mon	♃ ☌ ☾ (8 pm)	6:45	8:41		**12:03**
200	19	Tue	Pluto ☍ (9 pm)	6:46	8:40	12:29	**1:03**
201	20	Wed	Last qtr. ☾	6:46	8:40	12:59	**2:02**
202	21	Thu	♂ ☌ ☾ (12 pm)	6:47	8:39	1:28	**3:00**
203	22	Fri	⛢ ☌ ☾ (1 am)	6:48	8:39	2:00	**3:58**
204	23	Sat		6:48	8:38	2:34	**4:55**
205	24	Sun		6:49	8:38	3:13	**5:52**
206	25	Mon		6:50	8:37	3:56	**6:46**
207	26	Tue	♀ ☌ ☾ (9 am)	6:50	8:36	4:44	**7:36**
208	27	Wed		6:51	8:36	5:37	**8:22**
209	28	Thu	New ☾	6:51	8:35	6:33	**9:02**
210	29	Fri	♃ stationary (7 am)	6:52	8:34	7:31	**9:38**
211	30	Sat		6:53	8:34	8:29	**10:10**
212	31	Sun		6:53	8:33	9:26	**10:40**

8th Month — August 2022 — 31 Days

Moon Phases — First Qtr. Aug. 5, 6:07 am; Full Moon Aug. 11, 8:36 pm; Last Qtr. Aug. 18, 11:36 pm; New Moon Aug. 27, 3:17 am

Day of Year	Day of Month	Day of Week	Planetary Configurations and Phenomena	Sunrise	Sunset	Moon-rise	Moon-set
213	1	Mon	♂ ☌ ⛢ (4 am)	6:54	8:32	10:23	**11:08**
214	2	Tue		6:55	8:31	11:20	**11:36**
215	3	Wed		6:55	8:30	**12:19**	
216	4	Thu	☿ ☌ Regulus (12 am)	6:56	8:30	**1:20**	12:05
217	5	Fri	First qtr. ☾	6:56	8:29	**2:24**	12:37
218	6	Sat		6:57	8:28	**3:32**	1:14
219	7	Sun	♀ ☌ Pollux (5 am)	6:58	8:27	**4:42**	1:58
220	8	Mon		6:58	8:26	**5:51**	2:50
221	9	Tue		6:59	8:25	**6:55**	3:52
222	10	Wed	☾ at perigee (12 pm)	7:00	8:24	**7:52**	5:02
223	11	Thu	♄ ☌ Full ☾ (11 pm)	7:00	8:23	**8:40**	6:16
224	12	Fri		7:01	8:22	**9:20**	7:29
225	13	Sat		7:02	8:21	**9:55**	8:39
226	14	Sun	♆ ☌ ☾ (5 am); ♄ ☍ (12 pm)	7:02	8:20	**10:27**	9:46
227	15	Mon	♃ ☌ ☾ (5 am)	7:03	8:19	**10:57**	10:49
228	16	Tue		7:03	8:18	**11:27**	11:50
229	17	Wed		7:04	8:17	**11:59**	**12:50**
230	18	Thu	Last qtr. ☾	7:05	8:16		**1:49**
231	19	Fri	♂ ☌ ☾ (7 am)	7:05	8:15	12:32	**2:48**
232	20	Sat		7:06	8:14	1:10	**3:45**
233	21	Sun		7:06	8:13	1:52	**4:40**
234	22	Mon	☾ at apogee (5 pm)	7:07	8:12	2:39	**5:32**
235	23	Tue		7:08	8:11	3:31	**6:19**
236	24	Wed		7:08	8:10	4:26	**7:01**
237	25	Thu	♀ ☌ ☾ (4 pm)	7:09	8:08	5:23	**7:39**
238	26	Fri		7:09	8:07	6:22	**8:12**
239	27	Sat	New ☾; ☿ gr. elongation E	7:10	8:06	7:20	**8:42**
240	28	Sun		7:11	8:05	8:17	**9:11**
241	29	Mon	☿ ☌ ☾ (6 am)	7:11	8:04	9:15	**9:39**
242	30	Tue		7:12	8:02	10:14	**10:08**
243	31	Wed		7:12	8:01	11:14	**10:39**

9th Month — September 2022 — 30 Days

Moon Phases — First Qtr. Sep 3, 1:08 pm; Full Moon Sep. 10, 4:59 am; Last Qtr. Sep. 17, 4:52 pm; New Moon Sep. 25, 4:55 pm

Day of Year	Day of Month	Day of Week	Planetary Configurations and Phenomena	Sunrise	Sunset	Moon-rise	Moon-set
244	1	Thu		7:13	8:00	**12:17**	**11:14**
245	2	Fri		7:14	7:59	**1:23**	**11:54**
246	3	Sat	First qtr. ☾	7:14	7:58	**2:31**	
247	4	Sun	☿ ☌ Regulus (8 pm)	7:15	7:56	**3:38**	12:42
248	5	Mon		7:15	7:55	**4:43**	1:39
249	6	Tue		7:16	7:54	**5:41**	2:44
250	7	Wed	☾ at perigee (1 pm)	7:17	7:53	**6:31**	3:54
251	8	Thu	♄ ☌ ☾ (6 am)	7:17	7:51	**7:13**	5:06
252	9	Fri	☿ stationary (3 pm)	7:18	7:50	**7:50**	6:17
253	10	Sat	Full ☾	7:18	7:49	**8:23**	7:25
254	11	Sun	♃ ☌ ☾ (10 am)	7:19	7:47	**8:54**	8:30
255	12	Mon		7:19	7:46	**9:24**	9:33
256	13	Tue		7:20	7:45	**9:56**	10:35
257	14	Wed	⛢ ☌ ☾ (6 pm)	7:21	7:44	**10:29**	11:36
258	15	Thu		7:21	7:42	**11:05**	**12:36**
259	16	Fri	♆ ☍ (5 pm); ♂ ☌ ☾ (9 pm)	7:22	7:41	**11:46**	**1:35**
260	17	Sat	Last qtr. ☾	7:22	7:40		**2:32**
261	18	Sun		7:23	7:38	12:32	**3:26**
262	19	Mon	☾ at apogee (12 pm)	7:23	7:37	1:22	**4:15**
263	20	Tue		7:24	7:36	2:16	**4:59**
264	21	Wed		7:25	7:35	3:13	**5:37**
265	22	Thu	Equinox (8:04 pm)	7:25	7:33	4:11	**6:12**
266	23	Fri	☿ in inferior ☌ (2 am)	7:26	7:32	5:10	**6:43**
267	24	Sat		7:26	7:31	6:08	**7:13**
268	25	Sun	New ☾	7:27	7:29	7:06	**7:41**
269	26	Mon	♃ ☍ (3 pm)	7:28	7:28	8:06	**8:10**
270	27	Tue		7:28	7:27	9:07	**8:41**
271	28	Wed		7:29	7:26	10:10	**9:14**
272	29	Thu		7:29	7:24	11:16	**9:53**
273	30	Fri		7:30	7:23	12:23	**10:39**

Bright stars: Aldebaran, Antares, Spica, Pollux, Regulus. **Minor planets or asteroids:** Pluto, Ceres, Pallas, Juno, Vesta. ☌ = in conjunction by 10° or < ☍ = opposition to the ☉

Astronomical Calendar for 2022

10th Month October 2022 31 Days

Moon Phases — First Qtr. Oct. 2, 7:14 pm; Full Moon Oct. 9, 3:55 pm; Last Qtr. Oct. 17, 12:15 pm; New Moon Oct. 25, 5:49 am

Day of Year	Day of Month	Day of Week	Planetary Configurations and Phenomena	Sunrise	Sunset	Moon-rise	Moon-set
274	1	Sat	☿ stationary (10 am)	7:31	7:22	**1:31**	11:32
275	2	Sun	First qtr. ☾	7:31	7:21	**2:36**	
276	3	Mon		7:32	7:19	**3:35**	12:34
277	4	Tue	☾ at perigee (12 pm)	7:32	7:18	**4:26**	1:41
278	5	Wed	♄ ☌ ☾ (11 am)	7:33	7:17	**5:10**	2:51
279	6	Thu		7:34	7:16	**5:48**	4:01
280	7	Fri	♆ ☌ ☾ (10 pm)	7:34	7:14	**6:21**	5:08
281	8	Sat	♃ ☌ ☾ (1 pm)	7:35	7:13	**6:52**	6:13
282	9	Sun	Full ☾	7:36	7:12	**7:22**	7:16
283	10	Mon		7:36	7:11	**7:53**	8:18
284	11	Tue		7:37	7:10	**8:25**	9:20
285	12	Wed	♅ ☌ ☾ (2 am)	7:38	7:08	**9:00**	10:21
286	13	Thu		7:38	7:07	**9:40**	11:22
287	14	Fri		7:39	7:06	**10:24**	**12:21**
288	15	Sat	♂ ☌ ☾ (12 am)	7:40	7:05	**11:12**	**1:17**
289	16	Sun		7:40	7:04		**2:08**
290	17	Mon	Last qtr. ☾ at apogee	7:41	7:03	12:05	**2:54**
291	18	Tue		7:42	7:02	1:01	**3:35**
292	19	Wed		7:42	7:01	1:59	**4:10**
293	20	Thu		7:43	7:00	2:57	**4:43**
294	21	Fri		7:44	6:58	3:55	**5:13**
295	22	Sat	♀ in superior ☌ (4 pm)	7:45	6:57	4:53	**5:41**
296	23	Sun	♄ stationary (4 am)	7:45	6:56	5:52	**6:10**
297	24	Mon		7:46	6:55	6:53	**6:40**
298	25	Tue	New ☾; ☉ eclipse (6 am)	7:47	6:54	7:56	**7:13**
299	26	Wed		7:48	6:53	9:02	**7:50**
300	27	Thu		7:48	6:53	10:12	**8:34**
301	28	Fri		7:49	6:52	11:22	**9:27**
302	29	Sat	☾ at perigee (10 am)	7:50	6:51	**12:30**	**10:27**
303	30	Sun	♂ stationary (6 am)	7:51	6:50	**1:31**	**11:33**
304	31	Mon		7:52	6:49	**2:25**	

11th Month November 2022 30 Days

Moon Phases — First Qtr. Nov. 1, 1:37 am; Full Moon Nov. 8, 6:02 am; Last Qtr. Nov. 16, 7:27 am; New Moon Nov. 23, 4:57 pm; First Qtr. Nov. 30, 8:37 am

Day of Year	Day of Month	Day of Week	Planetary Configurations and Phenomena	Sunrise	Sunset	Moon-rise	Moon-set
305	1	Tue	♄ ☌ first qtr. ☾ (4 pm)	7:52	6:48	**3:10**	12:43
306	2	Wed		7:53	6:47	**3:49**	1:51
307	3	Thu	Juno ☌ ☾ (3 am)	7:54	6:46	**4:22**	2:58
308	4	Fri	♃ ♆ ☌ ☾	7:55	6:46	**4:53**	4:02
309	5	Sat		7:56	6:45	**5:23**	5:04
310	6	Sun	**DST ends (2 am)**	6:56	5:44	**4:52**	5:05
311	7	Mon		6:57	5:43	**5:23**	6:06
312	8	Tue	Full ☾; eclipse (5 am)	6:58	5:43	**5:57**	7:07
313	9	Wed	♅ ☍ (2 am)	6:59	5:42	**6:34**	8:08
314	10	Thu		7:00	5:41	**7:16**	9:08
315	11	Fri	♂ ☌ ☾ (8 am)	7:01	5:41	**8:04**	10:06
316	12	Sat		7:01	5:40	**8:55**	11:00
317	13	Sun		7:02	5:40	**9:50**	11:48
318	14	Mon	☾ at apogee (1 am)	7:03	5:39	**10:47**	**12:31**
319	15	Tue		7:04	5:39	**11:44**	**1:08**
320	16	Wed	Last qtr. ☾	7:05	5:38		**1:41**
321	17	Thu		7:06	5:38	12:41	**2:12**
322	18	Fri		7:07	5:37	1:38	**2:40**
323	19	Sat		7:07	5:37	2:36	**3:08**
324	20	Sun		7:08	5:36	3:35	**3:37**
325	21	Mon		7:09	5:36	4:37	**4:08**
326	22	Tue		7:10	5:36	5:42	**4:43**
327	23	Wed	New ☾	7:11	5:35	6:51	**5:25**
328	24	Thu	♃ stationary (7 am)	7:12	5:35	8:03	**6:15**
329	25	Fri	☾ at perigee (8 pm)	7:13	5:35	9:14	**7:14**
330	26	Sat		7:13	5:35	10:21	**8:21**
331	27	Sun		7:14	5:35	11:20	**9:32**
332	28	Mon	♄ ☌ ☾ (11 pm)	7:15	5:34	**12:09**	**10:43**
333	29	Tue		7:16	5:34	**12:50**	**11:51**
334	30	Wed	Juno ☌ first qtr. ☾	7:17	5:34	**1:25**	

12th Month December 2022 31 Days

Moon Phases — Full Moon Dec. 7, 10:08 pm; Last Qtr. Dec. 16, 2:56 am; New Moon Dec. 23, 4:17 am; First Qtr. Dec. 29, 7:21 pm

Day of Year	Day of Month	Day of Week	Planetary Configurations and Phenomena	Sunrise	Sunset	Moon-rise	Moon-set
335	1	Thu.	♃ ♆ ☌ ☾	7:18	5:34	**1:56**	12:56
336	2	Fri		7:18	5:34	**2:26**	1:58
337	3	Sat		7:19	5:34	**2:55**	2:58
338	4	Sun	♆ stationary (4 am)	7:20	5:34	**3:24**	3:58
339	5	Mon	♅ ☌ ☾ (12 pm)	7:21	5:34	**3:56**	4:58
340	6	Tue		7:22	5:34	**4:32**	5:58
341	7	Wed	♂ ☌ full ☾ (10 pm)	7:22	5:34	**5:12**	6:58
342	8	Thu	♂ ☍ (12 am)	7:23	5:34	**5:57**	7:56
343	9	Fri		7:24	5:35	**6:48**	8:52
344	10	Sat		7:24	5:35	**7:42**	9:42
345	11	Sun	☾ at apogee (6 pm)	7:25	5:35	**8:38**	10:27
346	12	Mon		7:26	5:35	**9:35**	11:06
347	13	Tue		7:27	5:36	**10:31**	11:41
348	14	Wed		7:27	5:36	**11:27**	**12:12**
349	15	Thu		7:28	5:36		**12:40**
350	16	Fri	Last qtr. ☾	7:28	5:37	12:23	**1:07**
351	17	Sat		7:29	5:37	1:20	**1:35**
352	18	Sun		7:30	5:37	2:18	**2:04**
353	19	Mon		7:30	5:38	3:20	**2:36**
354	20	Tue		7:31	5:38	4:26	**3:14**
355	21	Wed	Solstice (3:48 pm)	7:31	5:39	5:36	**3:59**
356	22	Thu		7:32	5:39	6:49	**4:54**
357	23	Fri	New ☾	7:32	5:40	8:00	**5:59**
358	24	Sat	☿ ♀ ☌ ☾ at perigee	7:33	5:40	9:05	**7:11**
359	25	Sun		7:33	5:41	10:00	**8:25**
360	26	Mon	♄ ☌ ☾ (10 am)	7:33	5:42	10:46	**9:38**
361	27	Tue		7:34	5:42	11:25	**10:46**
362	28	Wed	♆ ☌ ☾; ☿ stationary	7:34	5:43	11:58	**11:51**
363	29	Thu	☿ ☌ ♀; ♄ ☌ first qtr. ☾	7:35	5:43	**12:29**	
364	30	Fri		7:35	5:44	**12:58**	12:52
365	31	Sat		7:35	5:45	**1:27**	1:53

☉ The Sun ● The Earth ☾ The Moon ☿ Mercury ♀ Venus ♂ Mars ♃ Jupiter ♄ Saturn ♆ Neptune ♅ Uranus ☌ = in conjunction ☍ = opposition to the ☉

2023

Times are **Central Standard Time**, except from **Sunday, March 12 to Sunday, Nov. 5**, during which **Daylight Saving Time** is observed. **Boldface times for moonrise and moonset indicate p.m**. Times are figured for the point **31° 08' N 99° 20' W**, the approximate geographical center of the state. **See page 138 for explanation of how to get the approximate time at any other Texas point.**

1st Month — January 2023 — 31 Days

Moon Phases — Full Moon Jan. 6, 5:08 pm; Last Qtr. Jan. 14, 8:10 pm; New Moon Jan. 21, 2:53 pm; First Qtr. Jan. 28, 9:19 am

Day of Year	Day of Month	Day of Week	Planetary Configurations and Phenomena	Sunrise	Sunset	Moon-rise	Moon-set
1	1	Sun	♅ ☌ ☾ (4 pm)	7:35	5:46	**1:58**	2:52
2	2	Mon		7:36	5:46	**2:32**	3:52
3	3	Tue	♂ ☌ ☾ (2 pm)	7:36	5:47	**3:11**	4:51
4	4	Wed	● at perihelion (10 am)	7:36	5:48	**3:54**	5:50
5	5	Thu		7:36	5:49	**4:42**	6:46
6	6	Fri	Full ☾	7:36	5:49	**5:35**	7:38
7	7	Sat	☿ in inferior ☌ (7 am)	7:36	5:50	**6:31**	8:24
8	8	Sun	☾ at apogee (3 am)	7:36	5:51	**7:28**	9:05
9	9	Mon		7:36	5:52	**8:24**	9:41
10	10	Tue		7:36	5:53	**9:20**	10:13
11	11	Wed		7:36	5:53	**10:16**	10:42
12	12	Thu	♂ stationary (2 pm)	7:36	5:54	**11:11**	11:09
13	13	Fri		7:36	5:55		11:35
14	14	Sat	Last qtr. ☾	7:36	5:56	12:07	**12:03**
15	15	Sun		7:36	5:57	1:06	**12:32**
16	16	Mon		7:36	5:58	2:07	**1:06**
17	17	Tue		7:35	5:59	3:13	**1:46**
18	18	Wed	☿ stationary (6 am)	7:35	6:00	4:23	**2:35**
19	19	Thu		7:35	6:00	5:34	**3:34**
20	20	Fri	☿ ☌ ☾ (2 am)	7:35	6:01	6:42	**4:42**
21	21	Sat	New ☾ at perigee (3 pm)	7:34	6:02	7:42	**5:57**
22	22	Sun	♀ ☌ ♄ (2 pm)	7:34	6:03	8:34	**7:13**
23	23	Mon	♀ ♄ ☌ ☾ (2 am)	7:34	6:04	9:17	**8:26**
24	24	Tue		7:33	6:05	9:54	**9:35**
25	25	Wed	♄ ♆ ☌ ☾	7:33	6:06	10:27	**10:40**
26	26	Thu		7:32	6:07	10:58	**11:43**
27	27	Fri		7:32	6:08	11:28	
28	28	Sat	First qtr. ☾	7:31	6:09	11:59	12:45
29	29	Sun		7:31	6:09	**12:33**	1:45
30	30	Mon	♂ ☌ ☾ (10 pm)	7:30	6:10	**1:10**	2:45
31	31	Tue		7:30	6:11	**1:52**	3:44

2nd Month — February 2023 — 28 Days

Moon Phases — Full Moon Feb. 5, 12:29 pm; Last Qtr. Feb. 13, 10:01 am; New Moon Feb 20, 1:06 am; First Qtr. Feb 27, 2:06 am

Day of Year	Day of Month	Day of Week	Planetary Configurations and Phenomena	Sunrise	Sunset	Moon-rise	Moon-set
32	1	Wed		7:29	6:12	**2:38**	4:41
33	2	Thu		7:28	6:13	**3:30**	5:34
34	3	Fri		7:28	6:14	**4:25**	6:22
35	4	Sat	☾ at apogee (3 am)	7:27	6:15	**5:22**	7:05
36	5	Sun	♂ ☌ Aldebaran; full ☾	7:26	6:16	**6:19**	7:42
37	6	Mon		7:26	6:17	**7:15**	8:15
38	7	Tue		7:25	6:17	**8:11**	8:45
39	8	Wed		7:24	6:18	**9:06**	9:12
40	9	Thu		7:23	6:19	**10:02**	9:39
41	10	Fri		7:22	6:20	**10:58**	10:05
42	11	Sat		7:22	6:21	**11:58**	10:33
43	12	Sun		7:21	6:22		11:05
44	13	Mon	Last qtr. ☾	7:20	6:22	1:00	11:41
45	14	Tue		7:19	6:23	2:06	**12:24**
46	15	Wed	♀ ☌ ♆ (6 am)	7:18	6:24	3:14	**1:16**
47	16	Thu	♄ ☌ ☉ (11 am)	7:17	6:25	4:21	**2:18**
48	17	Fri		7:16	6:26	5:24	**3:28**
49	18	Sat	☿ ☌ ☾ (3 pm)	7:15	6:27	6:19	**4:43**
50	19	Sun	☾ at perigee (3 am)	7:14	6:27	7:06	**5:58**
51	20	Mon	New ☾	7:13	6:28	7:46	**7:10**
52	21	Tue	♆ ☌ ☾ (12 pm)	7:12	6:29	8:22	**8:19**
53	22	Wed	♀ ♃ ☌ ☾	7:11	6:30	8:54	**9:25**
54	23	Thu		7:10	6:31	9:25	**10:30**
55	24	Fri		7:09	6:31	9:57	**11:33**
56	25	Sat	♅ ☌ ☾ (7 am)	7:08	6:32	10:30	
57	26	Sun		7:07	6:33	11:07	12:35
58	27	Mon	♂ ☌ first qtr. ☾ (11 pm)	7:06	6:34	11:48	1:36
59	28	Tue		7:05	6:34	**12:33**	2:35

3rd Month — March 2023 — 31 Days

Moon Phases — Full Moon Mar. 7, 6:40 am; Last Qtr. Mar. 14, 9:08 pm; New Moon Mar. 21, 12:23 pm; First Qtr. Mar. 28, 9:32 pm

Day of Year	Day of Month	Day of Week	Planetary Configurations and Phenomena	Sunrise	Sunset	Moon-rise	Moon-set
60	1	Wed		7:04	6:35	**1:24**	3:30
61	2	Thu	♀ ☌ ♃ (5 am)	7:03	6:36	**2:18**	4:20
62	3	Fri	☾ at apogee (12 pm)	7:01	6:37	**3:14**	5:04
63	4	Sat		7:00	6:37	**4:11**	5:43
64	5	Sun		6:59	6:38	**5:08**	6:17
65	6	Mon		6:58	6:39	**6:05**	6:47
66	7	Tue	Full ☾	6:57	6:39	**7:01**	7:15
67	8	Wed		6:56	6:40	**7:57**	7:42
68	9	Thu		6:54	6:41	**8:53**	8:09
69	10	Fri		6:53	6:41	**9:52**	8:36
70	11	Sat		6:52	6:42	**10:54**	9:07
71	12	Sun	**DST begins (2 am)**	7:51	7:43		10:41
72	13	Mon		7:49	7:44	12:58	11:21
73	14	Tue	Last qtr. ☾	7:48	7:44	2:04	**12:08**
74	15	Wed	♆ ☌ ☉ (7 pm)	7:47	7:45	3:10	**1:05**
75	16	Thu		7:46	7:46	4:13	**2:10**
76	17	Fri	☿ in superior ☌ (6 am)	7:45	7:46	5:09	**3:21**
77	18	Sat		7:43	7:47	5:57	**4:34**
78	19	Sun	♄ ☌ ☾ at perigee (10 am)	7:42	7:48	6:39	**5:45**
79	20	Mon	Equinox (4:24 pm)	7:41	7:48	7:16	**6:55**
80	21	Tue	New ☾	7:40	7:49	7:49	**8:03**
81	22	Wed	♃ ☌ ☾ (3 pm)	7:38	7:50	8:21	**9:09**
82	23	Thu		7:37	7:50	8:52	**10:14**
83	24	Fri	♀ ♅ ☌ ☾	7:36	7:51	9:25	**11:18**
84	25	Sat		7:35	7:52	10:01	
85	26	Sun		7:33	7:52	10:41	12:22
86	27	Mon		7:32	7:53	11:26	1:24
87	28	Tue	♂ ☌ first qtr. ☾; ☿ ☌ ♃	7:31	7:53	**12:15**	2:21
88	29	Wed		7:30	7:54	**1:09**	3:14
89	30	Thu		7:28	7:55	**2:05**	4:01
90	31	Fri	♀ ☌ ♅; ☾ at apogee	7:27	7:55	**3:02**	4:42

Astronomical Calendar for 2023

4th Month — April 2023 — 30 Days

Moon Phases — Full Moon Apr. 5, 11:35 pm; Last Qtr. Apr. 13, 4:11 am; New Moon Apr. 19, 11:13 pm; First Qtr. Apr. 27, 4:20 pm

Day of Year	Day of Month	Day of Week	Planetary Configurations and Phenomena	Sunrise	Sunset	Moon-rise	Moon-set
91	1	Sat		7:26	7:56	**3:59**	5:17
92	2	Sun		7:25	7:57	**4:56**	5:49
93	3	Mon		7:23	7:57	**5:52**	6:18
94	4	Tue		7:22	7:58	**6:48**	6:45
95	5	Wed	Full ☾	7:21	7:59	**7:45**	7:11
96	6	Thu		7:20	7:59	**8:44**	7:39
97	7	Fri		7:18	8:00	**9:46**	8:08
98	8	Sat		7:17	8:01	**10:50**	8:41
99	9	Sun		7:16	8:01	**11:57**	9:20
100	10	Mon		7:15	8:02		10:05
101	11	Tue	☿ gr. elongation E (5 pm)	7:14	8:03	1:04	10:59
102	12	Wed		7:13	8:03	2:07	**12:01**
103	13	Thu	Last qtr. ☾	7:11	8:04	3:04	**1:09**
104	14	Fri		7:10	8:04	3:54	**2:20**
105	15	Sat	♄ ☌ ☾ at perigee (10 pm)	7:09	8:05	4:37	**3:30**
106	16	Sun		7:08	8:06	5:14	**4:38**
107	17	Mon	♆ ☌ ☾ (12 pm)	7:07	8:06	5:47	**5:44**
108	18	Tue		7:06	8:07	6:18	**6:50**
109	19	Wed	New ☾; ☉ eclipse	7:05	8:08	6:49	**7:54**
110	20	Thu		7:04	8:08	7:21	**8:59**
111	21	Fri	⛢ ☌ ☾; ☿ stationary	7:02	8:09	7:55	**10:04**
112	22	Sat		7:01	8:10	8:34	**11:08**
113	23	Sun	♀ ☌ ☾ (8 am)	7:00	8:10	9:17	
114	24	Mon		6:59	8:11	10:05	12:09
115	25	Tue	♂ ☌ ☾ (9 pm)	6:58	8:12	10:58	1:05
116	26	Wed		6:57	8:13	11:54	1:55
117	27	Thu	First qtr. ☾	6:56	8:13	**12:51**	2:38
118	28	Fri	☾ at apogee (2 am)	6:55	8:14	**1:48**	3:16
119	29	Sat		6:54	8:15	**2:45**	3:49
120	30	Sun		6:53	8:15	**3:41**	4:18

5th Month — May 2023 — 31 Days

Moon Phases — Full Moon May 5, 12:34 pm; Last Qtr. May 12, 9:28 am; New Moon May 19, 10:53 am; First Qtr. May 27 10:22 am

Day of Year	Day of Month	Day of Week	Planetary Configurations and Phenomena	Sunrise	Sunset	Moon-rise	Moon-set
121	1	Mon	☿ in inferior ☌ (6 pm)	6:52	8:16	**4:37**	4:46
122	2	Tue		6:52	8:17	**5:33**	5:12
123	3	Wed		6:51	8:17	**6:32**	5:39
124	4	Thu		6:50	8:18	**7:33**	6:08
125	5	Fri	Full ☾; eclipse	6:49	8:19	**8:37**	6:40
126	6	Sat		6:48	8:19	**9:45**	7:17
127	7	Sun		6:47	8:20	**10:54**	8:01
128	8	Mon		6:46	8:21		8:53
129	9	Tue	⛢ ☌ ☉ (3 pm)	6:46	8:21	12:00	9:54
130	10	Wed	♂ ☌ Pollux (3 pm)	6:45	8:22	1:00	11:01
131	11	Thu	☾ at perigee (12 am)	6:44	8:23	1:53	**12:11**
132	12	Fri	Last qtr. ☾	6:43	8:23	2:37	**1:21**
133	13	Sat	♄ ☌ ☾ (8 am)	6:43	8:24	3:15	**2:29**
134	14	Sun	☿ stationary; ♆ ☌ ☾	6:42	8:25	3:48	**3:34**
135	15	Mon		6:41	8:25	4:19	**4:38**
136	16	Tue		6:41	8:26	4:49	**5:41**
137	17	Wed	☿ ♃ ☌ ☾	6:40	8:27	5:20	**6:44**
138	18	Thu		6:40	8:27	5:53	**7:48**
139	19	Fri	New ☾	6:39	8:28	6:29	**8:52**
140	20	Sat		6:38	8:29	7:10	**9:55**
141	21	Sun		6:38	8:29	7:56	**10:53**
142	22	Mon		6:37	8:30	8:47	**11:46**
143	23	Tue	♀ ☌ ☾ (7 am)	6:37	8:31	9:42	
144	24	Wed	♂ ☌ ☾ (1 pm)	6:36	8:31	10:40	12:33
145	25	Thu	☾ at apogee (9 pm)	6:36	8:32	11:37	1:13
146	26	Fri		6:36	8:32	**12:34**	1:48
147	27	Sat	First qtr. ☾	6:35	8:33	**1:30**	2:18
148	28	Sun		6:35	8:34	**2:25**	2:46
149	29	Mon	☿ gr. elongation W (1 am)	6:35	8:34	**3:20**	3:13
150	30	Tue	♀ ☌ Pollux (11 am)	6:34	8:35	**4:17**	3:39
151	31	Wed		6:34	8:35	**5:16**	4:07

6th Month — June 2023 — 30 Days

Moon Phases — Full Moon Jun. 3, 10:42 pm; Last Qtr. Jun. 10, 2:31 pm; New Moon Jun 17, 11:37 pm; First Qtr. Jun. 26, 2:50 am

Day of Year	Day of Month	Day of Week	Planetary Configurations and Phenomena	Sunrise	Sunset	Moon-rise	Moon-set
152	1	Thu		6:34	8:36	**6:19**	4:37
153	2	Fri		6:33	8:36	**7:26**	5:11
154	3	Sat	Full ☾	6:33	8:37	**8:36**	5:52
155	4	Sun	☿ ☌ ⛢ (12 am)	6:33	8:38	**9:45**	6:42
156	5	Mon		6:33	8:38	**10:50**	7:41
157	6	Tue	☾ at perigee (6 pm)	6:33	8:39	**11:47**	8:48
158	7	Wed		6:33	8:39		10:00
159	8	Thu		6:33	8:39	12:35	11:12
160	9	Fri	♄ ☌ ☾ (3 pm)	6:32	8:40	1:16	**12:21**
161	10	Sat	Last qtr. ☾	6:32	8:40	1:51	**1:28**
162	11	Sun	♆ ☌ ☾ (3 am)	6:32	8:41	2:22	**2:32**
163	12	Mon		6:32	8:41	2:52	**3:34**
164	13	Tue		6:32	8:42	3:22	**4:36**
165	14	Wed	♃ ☌ ☾ (2 am)	6:33	8:42	3:53	**5:39**
166	15	Thu	⛢ ☌ ☾ (5 am)	6:33	8:42	4:28	**6:42**
167	16	Fri	☿ ☌ ☾ (4 pm)	6:33	8:43	5:06	**7:44**
168	17	Sat	New ☾	6:33	8:43	5:50	**8:44**
169	18	Sun	♄ stationary	6:33	8:43	6:39	**9:39**
170	19	Mon		6:33	8:43	7:33	**10:28**
171	20	Tue		6:33	8:44	8:30	**11:10**
172	21	Wed	Solstice (9:58 am); ♀ ☌ ☾	6:34	8:44	9:28	**11:47**
173	22	Thu	♂ ☌ ☾ at apogee	6:34	8:44	10:25	
174	23	Fri		6:34	8:44	11:21	12:19
175	24	Sat		6:34	8:44	**12:15**	12:47
176	25	Sun		6:35	8:44	**1:10**	1:14
177	26	Mon	First qtr. ☾	6:35	8:45	**2:05**	1:39
178	27	Tue		6:35	8:45	**3:02**	2:06
179	28	Wed		6:35	8:45	**4:02**	2:34
180	29	Thu		6:36	8:45	**5:06**	3:06
181	30	Fri		6:36	8:45	**6:13**	3:43

☉ The Sun ● The Earth ☾ The Moon ☿ Mercury ♀ Venus ♂ Mars ♃ Jupiter ♄ Saturn ♆ Neptune ⛢ Uranus ☌ = in conjunction ☍ = opposition to the ☉

Astronomical Calendar for 2023

7th Month — July 2023 — 31 Days

Moon Phases — Full Moon Jul. 3, 6:39 am; Last Qtr. Jul. 9, 8:48 pm; New Moon Jul. 17, 1:32 pm; First Qtr. Jul. 25, 5:07 pm

Day of Year	Day of Month	Day of Week	Planetary Configurations and Phenomena	Sunrise	Sunset	Moon-rise	Moon-set
182	1	Sat	☿ in superior ☌ (12 am)	6:37	8:45	**7:23**	4:28
183	2	Sun		6:37	8:45	**8:32**	5:23
184	3	Mon	Full ☾	6:37	8:45	**9:34**	6:28
185	4	Tue	☾ at perigee	6:38	8:45	**10:27**	7:40
186	5	Wed		6:38	8:44	**11:12**	8:54
187	6	Thu	● at aphelion (3 pm)	6:39	8:44	**11:50**	10:07
188	7	Fri	♀ gr. illumination (3 pm)	6:39	8:44		11:17
189	8	Sat	♆ ☌ ☾ (9 am)	6:40	8:44	12:24	**12:24**
190	9	Sun	Last qtr. ☾	6:40	8:44	12:55	**1:28**
191	10	Mon	♂ ☌ Regulus (3 am)	6:41	8:44	1:25	**2:30**
192	11	Tue	♃ ☌ ☾ (4 pm)	6:41	8:43	1:56	**3:33**
193	12	Wed	⛢ ☌ ☾ (1 pm)	6:42	8:43	2:29	**4:35**
194	13	Thu		6:42	8:43	3:06	**5:37**
195	14	Fri		6:43	8:42	3:47	**6:37**
196	15	Sat		6:43	8:42	4:35	**7:33**
197	16	Sun		6:44	8:42	5:27	**8:24**
198	17	Mon	New ☾	6:45	8:41	6:22	**9:08**
199	18	Tue		6:45	8:41	7:20	**9:46**
200	19	Wed	☿ ☌ ☾ (4 am)	6:46	8:40	8:17	**10:20**
201	20	Thu	♀ ☌ ☾ at apogee	6:46	8:40	9:14	**10:49**
202	21	Fri	Pluto ☍ (11 pm)	6:47	8:39	10:09	**11:16**
203	22	Sat		6:48	8:39	11:03	**11:42**
204	23	Sun		6:48	8:38	11:57	
205	24	Mon		6:49	8:38	**12:52**	12:07
206	25	Tue	First qtr. ☾	6:49	8:37	**1:49**	12:34
207	26	Wed	☿ ☌ ♀ (8 am)	6:50	8:36	**2:50**	1:03
208	27	Thu		6:51	8:36	**3:54**	1:37
209	28	Fri	☿ ☌ Regulus (8 pm)	6:51	8:35	**5:02**	2:17
210	29	Sat		6:52	8:34	**6:10**	3:06
211	30	Sun		6:53	8:34	**7:15**	4:05
212	31	Mon		6:53	8:33	**8:13**	5:14

8th Month — August 2023 — 31 Days

Moon Phases —Full Moon Aug. 1, 1:32 pm; Last Qtr. Aug. 8, 5:28 am; New Moon Aug. 16, 4:38 am; First Qtr. Aug. 24, 4:57 am; Full Moon Aug. 30, 8:36 pm

Day of Year	Day of Month	Day of Week	Planetary Configurations and Phenomena	Sunrise	Sunset	Moon-rise	Moon-set
213	1	Tue	Full ☾	6:54	8:32	**9:02**	6:28
214	2	Wed	☾ at perigee (1 am)	6:54	8:31	**9:44**	7:44
215	3	Thu	♄ ☌ ☾ (5 am)	6:55	8:31	**10:21**	8:58
216	4	Fri	♆ ☌ ☾ (5 pm)	6:56	8:30	**10:54**	10:08
217	5	Sat		6:56	8:29	**11:25**	11:15
218	6	Sun		6:57	8:28	**11:56**	**12:21**
219	7	Mon		6:58	8:27		**1:25**
220	8	Tue	♃ ⛢ ☌ last qtr. ☾	6:58	8:26	12:29	**2:28**
221	9	Wed	☿ gr. elongation E (9 pm)	6:59	8:25	1:05	**3:31**
222	10	Thu		6:59	8:25	1:46	**4:32**
223	11	Fri		7:00	8:24	2:31	**5:30**
224	12	Sat		7:01	8:23	3:22	**6:22**
225	13	Sun	♀ in inferior ☌ (6 am)	7:01	8:22	4:17	**7:07**
226	14	Mon		7:02	8:21	5:14	**7:47**
227	15	Tue		7:03	8:20	6:11	**8:22**
228	16	Wed	New ☾ at apogee (7 am)	7:03	8:19	7:08	**8:52**
229	17	Thu		7:04	8:18	8:04	**9:20**
230	18	Fri	☿ ♂ Pallas ☌ ☾	7:04	8:16	8:58	**9:45**
231	19	Sat		7:05	8:15	9:52	**10:11**
232	20	Sun		7:06	8:14	10:46	**10:36**
233	21	Mon		7:06	8:13	11:42	**11:04**
234	22	Tue		7:07	8:12	**12:40**	**11:35**
235	23	Wed	☿ stationary (12 am)	7:08	8:11	**1:42**	
236	24	Thu	Antares ☌ first qtr. ☾	7:08	8:10	**2:46**	12:12
237	25	Fri		7:09	8:09	**3:52**	12:55
238	26	Sat		7:09	8:08	**4:57**	1:48
239	27	Sun	♄ ☍ (3 am)	7:10	8:06	**5:57**	2:51
240	28	Mon	⛢ stationary (10 pm)	7:11	8:05	**6:50**	4:01
241	29	Tue		7:11	8:04	**7:35**	5:16
242	30	Wed	♄ ☌ full ☾ at perigee	7:12	8:03	**8:14**	6:31
243	31	Thu		7:12	8:02	**8:49**	7:44

9th Month — September 2023 — 30 Days

Moon Phases — Last Qtr. Sep. 6, 5:21 pm; New Moon Sep. 14, 8:40 pm; First Qtr. Sep. 22, 2:32 pm; Full Moon Sep. 29, 4:58 am

Day of Year	Day of Month	Day of Week	Planetary Configurations and Phenomena	Sunrise	Sunset	Moon-rise	Moon-set
244	1	Fri	♆ ☌ ☾ (2 am)	7:13	8:00	**9:21**	8:54
245	2	Sat	♀ stationary (11 pm)	7:13	7:59	**9:53**	10:02
246	3	Sun		7:14	7:58	**10:27**	11:09
247	4	Mon	♃ stationary ☌ ☾ (4 pm)	7:15	7:57	**11:03**	**12:16**
248	5	Tue	⛢ ☌ ☾ (4 am)	7:15	7:55	**11:42**	**1:21**
249	6	Wed	Last qtr. ☾	7:16	7:54		**2:24**
250	7	Thu		7:16	7:53	12:27	**3:24**
251	8	Fri		7:17	7:52	1:17	**4:18**
252	9	Sat		7:18	7:50	2:11	**5:06**
253	10	Sun		7:18	7:49	3:08	**5:48**
254	11	Mon	♀ ☌ ☾ (8 am)	7:19	7:48	4:05	**6:24**
255	12	Tue	☾ at apogee (11 am)	7:19	7:46	5:02	**6:55**
256	13	Wed		7:20	7:45	5:58	**7:23**
257	14	Thu	☿ stationary; new ☾	7:20	7:44	6:53	**7:50**
258	15	Fri		7:21	7:43	7:47	**8:15**
259	16	Sat	♂ ☌ ☾ (2 pm)	7:22	7:41	8:42	**8:40**
260	17	Sun		7:22	7:40	9:37	**9:07**
261	18	Mon		7:23	7:39	10:35	**9:37**
262	19	Tue	♀ gr. illumination (2 am)	7:23	7:37	11:35	**10:11**
263	20	Wed		7:24	7:36	**12:38**	**10:52**
264	21	Thu	Antares ☌ ☾ (3 am)	7:24	7:35	**1:42**	**11:40**
265	22	Fri	First qtr. ☾	7:25	7:34	**2:46**	
266	23	Sat	Equinox (1:50 am)	7:26	7:32	**3:46**	12:37
267	24	Sun		7:26	7:31	**4:40**	1:42
268	25	Mon		7:27	7:30	**5:26**	2:53
269	26	Tue	♄ ☌ ☾ (8 pm)	7:27	7:28	**6:07**	4:06
270	27	Wed	☾ at perigee (8 pm)	7:28	7:27	**6:43**	5:18
271	28	Thu	♆ ☌ ☾ (12 pm)	7:29	7:26	**7:16**	6:29
272	29	Fri	Full ☾	7:29	7:25	**7:48**	7:39
273	30	Sat		7:30	7:23	**8:21**	8:47

Bright stars: Aldebaran, Antares, Spica, Pollux, Regulus. **Minor planets or asteroids:** Pluto, Ceres, Pallas, Juno, Vesta ☌ = in conjunction by 10° or < ☍ = opposition to the ☉

Astronomical Calendar for 2023

10th Month October 2023 31 Days

Moon Phases —Last Qtr. Oct. 6, 8:48 am; New Moon Oct. 14, 12:55 pm; First Qtr. Oct. 21, 10:29 pm; Full Moon Oct. 28, 3:24 pm

Day of Year	Day of Month	Day of Week	Planetary Configurations and Phenomena	Sunrise	Sunset	Moon-rise	Moon-set
274	1	Sun	♃ ☌ ☾ (10 pm)	7:30	7:22	**8:57**	9:55
275	2	Mon	♅ ☌ ☾ (12 pm)	7:31	7:21	**9:36**	11:03
276	3	Tue		7:32	7:20	**10:19**	**12:10**
277	4	Wed		7:32	7:18	**11:08**	**1:13**
278	5	Thu		7:33	7:17		**2:11**
279	6	Fri	Last qtr. ☾	7:34	7:16	12:02	**3:02**
280	7	Sat		7:34	7:15	12:59	**3:47**
281	8	Sun		7:35	7:13	1:57	**4:24**
282	9	Mon		7:35	7:12	2:54	**4:57**
283	10	Tue	♀ ☌ ☾ at apogee	7:36	7:11	3:51	**5:26**
284	11	Wed		7:37	7:10	4:46	**5:53**
285	12	Thu		7:37	7:09	5:41	**6:19**
286	13	Fri		7:38	7:08	6:35	**6:44**
287	14	Sat	New ☾; ☉ eclipse (12:36 pm)	7:39	7:06	7:31	**7:11**
288	15	Sun		7:40	7:05	8:28	**7:40**
289	16	Mon		7:40	7:04	9:28	**8:13**
290	17	Tue		7:41	7:03	10:31	**8:51**
291	18	Wed	Antares ☌ ☾ (9 am)	7:42	7:02	11:36	**9:37**
292	19	Thu		7:42	7:01	**12:40**	**10:31**
293	20	Fri	☿ in superior ☌ (1 am)	7:43	7:00	**1:40**	**11:33**
294	21	Sat	First qtr. ☾	7:44	6:59	**2:35**	
295	22	Sun		7:45	6:58	**3:22**	12:41
296	23	Mon	♀ gr. elongation W (6 pm)	7:45	6:57	**4:04**	1:51
297	24	Tue	♄ ☌ ☾ (3 am)	7:46	6:56	**4:40**	3:01
298	25	Wed	♆ ☌ ☾ at perigee (9 pm)	7:47	6:55	**5:13**	4:10
299	26	Thu		7:47	6:54	**5:44**	5:17
300	27	Fri		7:48	6:53	**6:16**	6:25
301	28	Sat	Full ☾; eclipse (3 pm)	7:49	6:52	**6:50**	7:32
302	29	Sun	♃ ☌ ☾ (3 am)	7:50	6:51	**7:27**	8:41
303	30	Mon		7:51	6:50	**8:09**	9:49
304	31	Tue		7:51	6:49	**8:57**	10:55

11th Month November 2023 30 Days

Moon Phases — Last Qtr. Nov. 5, 2:37 am; New Moon Nov. 13, 3:27 am; First Qtr. Nov. 20, 4:50 am; Full Moon Nov. 27, 3:16 am

Day of Year	Day of Month	Day of Week	Planetary Configurations and Phenomena	Sunrise	Sunset	Moon-rise	Moon-set
305	1	Wed		7:52	6:48	**9:50**	11:58
306	2	Thu		7:53	6:47	**10:47**	**12:53**
307	3	Fri	♃ ☍ (12 am)	7:54	6:47	**11:46**	**1:41**
308	4	Sat	♄ stationary (12 pm)	7:55	6:46		**2:22**
309	5	Sun	**DST ends (2 am)**; last qtr. ☾	6:55	5:45	12:44	**1:57**
310	6	Mon	☾ at apogee (4 pm)	6:56	5:44	12:41	**2:27**
311	7	Tue		6:57	5:44	1:37	**2:55**
312	8	Wed		6:58	5:43	2:31	**3:21**
313	9	Thu	♀ ☌ ☾ (3 am)	6:59	5:42	3:26	**3:46**
314	10	Fri		7:00	5:42	4:21	**4:12**
315	11	Sat		7:00	5:41	5:18	**4:40**
316	12	Sun		7:01	5:40	6:17	**5:12**
317	13	Mon	New ☾; ♅ ☍ (11 am)	7:02	5:40	7:20	**5:49**
318	14	Tue	Antares ☌ ☾ (2 pm)	7:03	5:39	8:26	**6:33**
319	15	Wed		7:04	5:39	9:31	**7:26**
320	16	Thu	☿ ☌ Antares (12 pm)	7:05	5:38	10:34	**8:26**
321	17	Fri		7:06	5:38	11:32	**9:33**
322	18	Sat	♂ ☌ ☉ (12 am)	7:06	5:37	**12:21**	**10:42**
323	19	Sun		7:07	5:37	**1:04**	**11:51**
324	20	Mon	♄ ☌ first qtr. ☾ (8 am)	7:08	5:36	**1:41**	
325	21	Tue	☾ at perigee (3 pm)	7:09	5:36	**2:13**	12:59
326	22	Wed	♆ ☌ ☾ (2 am)	7:10	5:36	**2:44**	2:05
327	23	Thu		7:11	5:36	**3:15**	3:10
328	24	Fri		7:12	5:35	**3:47**	4:15
329	25	Sat	♃ ☌ ☾ (5 am)	7:12	5:35	**4:22**	5:22
330	26	Sun	♅ ☌ ☾ (3 am)	7:13	5:35	**5:01**	6:29
331	27	Mon	Full ☾	7:14	5:35	**5:46**	7:36
332	28	Tue	♀ ☌ Spica (3 am)	7:15	5:34	**6:37**	8:41
333	29	Wed		7:16	5:34	**7:33**	9:40
334	30	Thu		7:17	5:34	**8:32**	10:32

12th Month December 2023 31 Days

Moon Phases — Last Qtr. Dec. 4, 11:49 pm; New Moon Dec. 12, 5:32 pm; First Qtr. Dec. 19, 12:39 pm; Full Moon Dec. 26, 6:33 pm

Day of Year	Day of Month	Day of Week	Planetary Configurations and Phenomena	Sunrise	Sunset	Moon-rise	Moon-set
335	1	Fri		7:17	5:34	**9:31**	11:17
336	2	Sat		7:18	5:34	**10:30**	11:54
337	3	Sun		7:19	5:34	**11:26**	**12:27**
338	4	Mon	☿ gr. elong. E (8 am); Last qtr. ☾	7:20	5:34		**12:55**
339	5	Tue		7:21	5:34	12:21	**1:22**
340	6	Wed	♆ stationary (6 pm)	7:21	5:34	1:15	**1:47**
341	7	Thu		7:22	5:34	2:09	**2:12**
342	8	Fri		7:23	5:34	3:05	**2:39**
343	9	Sat	♀ ☌ ☾ (11 am)	7:24	5:35	4:03	**3:09**
344	10	Sun		7:24	5:35	5:04	**3:44**
345	11	Mon		7:25	5:35	6:09	**4:25**
346	12	Tue	New ☾; ☿ stationary	7:26	5:35	7:16	**5:15**
347	13	Wed	☿ ☌ ☾ (11 pm)	7:26	5:36	8:22	**6:14**
348	14	Thu		7:27	5:36	9:23	**7:21**
349	15	Fri		7:28	5:36	10:17	**8:32**
350	16	Sat	☾ at perigee (1 pm)	7:28	5:37	11:03	**9:43**
351	17	Sun	♄ ☌ ☾ (4 pm)	7:29	5:37	11:42	**10:52**
352	18	Mon		7:30	5:37	**12:16**	**11:58**
353	19	Tue	First qtr. ☾	7:30	5:38	**12:47**	
354	20	Wed		7:31	5:38	**1:17**	1:03
355	21	Thu	Solstice (9:27 pm)	7:31	5:39	**1:48**	2:07
356	22	Fri	♃ ☌ ☾; ☿ in inferior ☌	7:32	5:39	**2:21**	3:11
357	23	Sat	♅ ☌ ☾ (9 am)	7:32	5:40	**2:57**	4:17
358	24	Sun		7:33	5:40	**3:39**	5:22
359	25	Mon		7:33	5:41	**4:27**	6:27
360	26	Tue	Full ☾	7:33	5:41	**5:21**	7:28
361	27	Wed		7:34	5:42	**6:19**	8:23
362	28	Thu		7:34	5:43	**7:19**	9:10
363	29	Fri		7:34	5:43	**8:18**	9:51
364	30	Sat		7:35	5:44	**9:16**	10:25
365	31	Sun	♃ stationary (9 am)	7:35	5:45	**10:11**	10:55

☉ The Sun ● The Earth ☾ The Moon ☿ Mercury ♀ Venus ♂ Mars ♃ Jupiter ♄ Saturn ♆ Neptune ♅ Uranus ☌ = in conjunction ☍ = opposition to the ☉

Recreation

STATE PARKS & HISTORIC SITES

STATE FORESTS

NATIONAL PARKS & LANDMARKS

BIRDING

FAIRS & FESTIVALS

HUNTING & FISHING

People enjoying the day at South Padre Island.
Photo by Vince Smith, CC by 2.0/Flickr

Texas State Parks and Historic Sites

Sources: Texas Parks and Wildlife, https://tpwd.texas.gov; and the Texas Historical Commission, www.thc.texas.gov

Texas' diverse system of state parks and historic sites offers contrasting attractions: mountains and canyons, arid deserts and lush forests, spring-fed streams, sandy dunes, saltwater surf and fascinating historic sites.

The Texas Parks and Wildlife's (TPWD) **Central Reservation Center** can take reservations for almost all state parks. Exceptions are the facilities not operated by the TPW. Call the center during usual business hours at 512-389-8900. The TDD line is 512-389-8915.

The following information is a brief glimpse of what each park has to offer. Refer to the chart on pages 152–153 for a more complete list of available activities and facilities. Entrance fees to state parks range from $1 to $5 per person. There are also fees for tours and some activities. For up-to-date information, call the information number listed above before you go.

Road abbreviations used in this list are:

- IH: interstate highway
- US: U.S. highway
- TX: state highway
- FM: farm-to-market road
- PR: park road

Ready to Plan Your Trip?

The **Texas Department of Transportation** publishes the **Texas State Travel Guide**, a full-color publication with information about attractions, activities, history and historic sites, and the official **Texas state highway map**. You can get both sent to you for free by calling the toll-free number, **1-800-888-8TEX**, or download a free digital version at the site:

www.traveltex.com

The TPWD sells discount passes for youth groups, qualifying seniors, veterans and disabled persons, and families. For further information, call the TPW at 512-389-8900 or visit:

https://tpwd.texas.gov/state-parks/park-information/passes/park-passes

List of State Parks and Historic Sites

Abilene State Park, 16 miles southwest of Abilene on FM 89 and PR 32 in Taylor County, consists of 529.4 acres that were deeded by the City of Abilene in 1933. A part of the official Texas longhorn herd and bison are located in the park. Large groves of pecan trees that once shaded bands of Comanches now shade visitors at picnic tables. Activities include camping, hiking, picnicking, nature study, biking, and swimming and fishing on Lake Abilene. Nearby is Buffalo Gap, the original Taylor County seat (1878) and one of the early frontier settlements. Buffalo Gap was on the Western, or Goodnight-Loving Trail, over which pioneer Texas cattlemen drove herds to railheads in Kansas.

Acton State Historic Site is a 0.006-acre cemetery plot in Hood County where Davy Crockett's second wife, Elizabeth, was buried in 1860. It is 4.5 miles east of Granbury on US 377 to FM 167 south, then 2.4 miles south to Acton. Nearby attractions include Cleburne, Dinosaur Valley and Lake Whitney state parks.

Atlanta State Park is 1,475 acres located 11 miles northwest of Atlanta on FM 1154 in Cass County; adjacent to Wright Patman Dam and Reservoir. Land acquired from the U.S. Army in 1954 by license to 2004 with option to renew to 2054. Camping, biking and hiking in pine forests, as well as water activities, such as boating, fishing, and lake swimming. Nearby are the historic town of Jefferson and the Caddo Lake and Daingerfield state parks.

Balmorhea State Park is 45.9 acres four miles southwest of Balmorhea on TX 17 between Balmorhea and Toyahvale in Reeves County. Deeded in 1934-35 by private owners and Reeves Co. Water Imp. Dist. No. 1 and built by the Civilian Conservation Corps (CCC). Swimming pool (1-3/4 acres) fed by artesian San Solomon Springs; also provides water to aquatic refuge in park. Activities include swimming, picnicking, camping, scuba and skin diving. Motel rooms available at San Solomon Springs Courts. Nearby are city of Pecos, Fort Davis National Historic Site, Davis Mountains State Park and McDonald Observatory.

Barton Warnock Environmental Education Center consists of 99.9 acres in Brewster County on FM 170, one mile east of Lajitas. Originally built by the Lajitas Foundation in 1982 as the Lajitas Museum Desert Gardens, the TPW purchased it in 1990 and renamed it for Texas botanist Dr. Barton Warnock. The center is also the eastern entrance station to Big Bend Ranch State Park. Self-guiding museum and botanical tours in the Trans-Pecos Vegetation Area.

Bastrop State Park is 6,600 acres, found one mile east of Bastrop on TX 21 or from TX 71. The park was acquired by deeds from the City of Bastrop and private owners in 1933-35. Site of famous "Lost Pines," an isolated region of loblolly pines and hardwoods. Swimming pool, cabins and lodge are among facilities. The park offers fishing at Lake Bastrop, geocahcing, picnicking, canoeing, bicycling, and hiking. A golf course lies adjacent to the park. The state capitol at Austin is 32 miles away; a 13-mile drive through forest leads to Buescher State Park.

Battleship Texas State Historic Site sits within the San Jacinto Battleground State Historic Site in LaPorte. Battle Ship *Texas* once took part in naval battles during both world wars. She is now docked along the Houston Ship Channel after being acquired by the State of Texas in 1948. Today the ship serves as a memorial to the servicemen who fought both world wars and as an engineering landmark.

Bentsen-Rio Grande Valley State Park, a scenic park, is along the Rio Grande five miles southwest of Mission off FM 2062 in Hidalgo County. Originally acquired from private owners in 1944, the park's subtropical resaca woodlands and brushlands has grown to 797 acres. Hiking trails provide chance to study unique plants and animals of park. Many birds unique to southern United States found here, including pauraque, groove-billed ani, green kingfisher, rose-throated becard and tropical parula. Birdwatching tours guided by park naturalists offered daily December–March. The park is one of last natural refuges in Texas for ocelot and jaguarundi. Trees include cedar elm, anaqua, ebony and Mexican ash. Camping, hiking, picnicking, boating, fishing also available. Nearby are Santa Ana National Wildlife Refuge, Falcon State Park and Sabal Palm Sanctuary.

Big Bend Ranch State Park, more than 300,000 acres of Chihuahuan Desert wilderness in Brewster and Presidio counties along the Rio Grande, was purchased from private owners in 1988. The purchase more than doubled the size of the state park system, which comprised at that time 220,000 acres. Eastern entrance at Barton Warnock Environmental Education Center one mile east of Lajitas on FM 170; western entrance is at Fort Leaton State Historic Park four miles east of Presidio on FM 170. The area includes extinct volcanoes, several waterfalls, two mountain ranges, at least 11 rare species of plants and animals, and 90 major archaeological sites. There is little development. Vehicular access limited; wilderness backpacking, hiking, scenic drive, picnicking, fishing and swimming. There are longhorns in the park, although they are not part of the official state longhorn herd.

Big Spring State Park is 382 acres located on FM 700 within the city limits of Big Spring in Howard County. Both city and park were named for a natural spring that was replaced by an artificial one. The park was deeded by the City of Big Spring in 1934 and 1935. Drive to top of Scenic Mountain provides panoramic view of surrounding country and look at prairie dog colony. The "big spring," nearby in a city park, provided watering place for herds of bison, antelope and wild horses. Used extensively also as campsite for early Indians, explorers and settlers.

Blanco State Park is 104.6 acres along the Blanco River four blocks south of Blanco's town square in Blanco County. The land was deeded by private owners in 1933. Park area was used as campsite by early explorers and settlers. The park offers fishing, camping, swimming, picnicking, and boating. LBJ Ranch and LBJ State Historic Site, Pedernales Falls and Guadalupe River state parks are nearby.

Bonham State Park is a 261-acre park located two miles southeast of Bonham on TX 78, then two miles southeast on FM 271 in Fannin County. It includes a 65-acre lake, rolling prairies and woodlands. The land was acquired in 1933 from the City of Bonham. Swimming, camping, mountain-bike trail, lighted fishing pier, boating. Sam Rayburn Memorial Library in Bonham. Sam Rayburn Home and Valley Lake nearby.

Brazos Bend State Park in Fort Bend County, eight miles east of Damon off FM 1462 on FM 762, approximately 28 miles southwest of Houston. The 4,897-acre park was purchased from private owners in 1976–77. George Observatory in park. Observation platform for spotting and photographing the 270 species of birds, 23 species of mammals, and 21 species of reptiles and amphibians, including American alligator, that frequent the park. Interpretive and educational programs every weekend. Backpacking, camping, hiking, biking, fishing. Creekfield Lake Nature Trail.

Buescher State Park, a scenic area, is 1,017 acres, found two miles northwest of Smithville off TX 71 to FM 153 in Bastrop County. Acquired between 1933 and 1936, about one-third deeded by private owner; heirs donated a third; balance from City of Smithville. El Camino Real once ran near park, connecting San Antonio de Béxar with Spanish missions in East Texas. Park land was part of Stephen F. Austin's colonial grant. Some 250 species of birds can be seen. Camping, fishing, hiking, boating. Scenic park road connects with Bastrop State Park through Lost Pines area.

Caddo Lake State Park, north of Karnack one mile off TX 43 to FM 2198 in Harrison County, consists of 483.9 acres along Cypress Bayou, which runs into Caddo Lake. A scenic area, it was acquired from private owners in 1933. Nearby Karnack is childhood home of Lady Bird Johnson. Close by is old city of Jefferson, famous as commercial center of Northeast Texas during last half of 19th century. Caddo Indian legend attributes formation of Caddo Lake to a huge flood. Cypress trees, American lotus and lily pads, as well as 71 species of fish, predominate in lake. Nutria, beaver, mink, squirrel, armadillo, alligator and turtle abound. Activities include camping, hiking, swimming, fishing, canoeing. Screened shelters, cabins.

Caddo Mounds State Historic Site in Cherokee County six miles southwest of Alto on TX 21. Total of 93.8 acres acquired in 1975. Open for day visits only, park offers exhibits and interpretive trails through reconstructed Caddo dwellings and ceremonial areas, including two temple mounds, a burial mound and a village area typical of people who lived in region for 500 years beginning about A.D. 800. Open Tuesday–Sunday. Nearby are Jim Hogg and Mission Tejas State historic sites and Texas State Railroad.

Caprock Canyons State Park and Trailway, 100 miles southeast of Amarillo and 3.5 miles north of Quitaque off FM 1065 and TX 86 in Briscoe, Floyd, and Hall counties, has 15,313 acres. Purchased in 1975. Scenic escarpment's canyons provided camping areas for Indians of Folsom culture more than 10,000 years ago. Mesquite and cacti in the badlands give way to tall grasses, cottonwood and plum thickets in the bottomlands. Wildlife includes aoudad sheep, coyote, bobcat, porcupine and fox. Activities include scenic drive, camping, hiking, mountain-bike riding, horse riding and horse camping. A 64.3-mile trailway (hike, bike, and equestrian trail) extends from South Plains to Estelline.

Casa Navarro State Historic Site, on 0.7 acres at corner of S. Laredo and W. Nueva streets in downtown San Antonio, was acquired by donation from San Antonio Conservation Society Foundation in 1975. The furnished Navarro House three-building complex, built about 1848, was home of statesman, rancher and Texas patriot José Antonio Navarro. Guided tours; exhibits. Open Wednesday through Sunday.

Cedar Hill State Park, an urban park on 1,826 acres ten miles southwest of Dallas via US 67 and FM 1382 on Joe Pool Lake, was acquired by long-term lease from the Army Corp of Engineers in 1982. Camping mostly in wooded areas. Fishing from two lighted jetties and a perch pond for children. Swimming, boating, bicycling, birdwatching and picnicking. Vegetation includes several sections of tall-grass prairie. Penn Farm Agricultural History Center includes reconstructed buildings of the 19th-century Penn Farm and exhibits; self-guided tours.

Choke Canyon State Park consists of two units, South Shore and Calliham, located on 26,000-acre Choke Canyon Reservoir. Park acquired in 1981 in a 50-year agreement among Bureau of Reclamation, City of Corpus Christi and Nueces River Authority. Thickets of mesquite and blackbrush acacia predominate, supporting populations of javelina, coyote, skunk and alligator, as well as the crested caracara. The 385-acre South Shore Unit is located 3.5 miles west of Three Rivers on TX 72 in Live Oak County; the 1,100-acre Calliham Unit is located 12 miles west of Three Rivers, on TX 72, in McMullen County. Both units offer camping, picnicking, boating, fishing, lake swimming, and baseball and volleyball areas. The Calliham Unit also has a hiking trail, wildlife educational center, screened shelters, rentable gym and kitchen. Sports complex includes swimming pool and tennis, volleyball, shuffleboard and basketball courts. Across dam from South Shore is North Shore Equestrian and Camping Area; 18 miles of horseback riding trails.

Cleburne State Park is a 528-acre park located 10 miles southwest of Cleburne via US 67 and PR 21 in Johnson County with 116-acre spring-fed lake; acquired from the City of Cleburne and private owners in 1935 and 1936. Oak, elm, mesquite, cedar and redbud cover white rocky hills. Bluebonnets in spring. Activities include camping, picnicking, hiking, bicycling, canoeing, swimming, boating, fishing. Nearby are Fossil Rim Wildlife Center and dinosaur tracks in Paluxy River at Dinosaur Valley State Park.

Colorado Bend State Park, a 5,328.3-acre facility, is 28 miles west of Lampasas in Lampasas and San Saba counties. Access is from Lampasas to Bend on FM 580 west, then follow signs (access road subject to flooding). Park site was purchased partly in 1984, with balance acquired in 1987. Primitive camping, fishing, swimming, hiking, biking and picnicking; guided tours to Gorman Falls; crawling cave tours require reservations. Rare and endangered species here include golden-cheeked warbler, black-capped vireo and bald eagle.

Confederate Reunion Grounds State Historic Site, located in Limestone County on the Navasota River, is 77.1 acres in size. Acquired 1983 by deed from Joseph E. Johnston Camp No. 94 CSA. Entrance is 6 miles south of Mexia on TX 14, then 2.5 miles west on FM 2705. Historic buildings, two scenic footbridges span creek; hiking trail. Nearby are Fort Parker State Park and Old Fort Parker.

Cooper Lake State Park comprises 3,026 acres and just three miles southeast of Cooper in Delta and Hopkins counties. The park was acquired in 1991 from Army Corps of Engineers. Two units, Doctors Creek and South Sulphur, adjoin 19,300-surface-acre Cooper Lake. Fishing, boating, camping, picnicking, swimming. Screened shelters and cabins South Sulphur offers equestrian camping and horseback riding trails.

Hikers at sunset in Choke Canyon State Park. Photo by Stuart Seeger, CC by 2.0/Flickr.

Copper Breaks State Park, 12 miles south of Quanah on TX 6 in Hardeman County, was acquired by purchase from private owner in 1970. Park features rugged scenic beauty on 1,898.8 acres, two lakes, grass-covered mesas and juniper breaks. Nearby medicine mounds were important ceremonial sites of Comanche Indians. Nearby Pease River was site of 1860 battle in which Cynthia Ann Parker was recovered from Comanches. Part of state longhorn herd lives at park. Abundant wildlife. Nature, hiking and equestrian trails; natural and historical exhibits; summer programs; horseback riding; camping, equestrian camping.

Daingerfield State Park, off TX 49 and PR 17 southeast of Daingerfield in Morris County, is a 550.9-acre recreational area that includes an 80-surface-acre lake; deeded in 1935 by private owners. This area is center of iron industry in Texas; nearby is Lone Star Steel Co. In spring, dogwood, redbuds and wisteria bloom; in fall, brilliant foliage of sweetgum, oaks and maples contrast with dark green pines. Campsites, lodge and cabins.

Davis Mountains State Park is 2,709 acres in Jeff Davis County, four miles northwest of Fort Davis via TX 118 and PR 3. The scenic area was deeded in 1933-1937 by private owners. First European, Antonio de Espejo, came to area in 1583. Extremes of altitude produce both plains grasslands and piñon-juniper-oak woodlands. Montezuma quail, rare in Texas, visit park. Scenic drives, camping and hiking. Indian Lodge, built by the Civilian Conservation Corps during the early 1930s, has 39 rooms, restaurant and swimming pool (reservations: 432-426-3254). Four-mile hiking trail leads to Fort Davis National Historic Site. Other nearby points of interest include McDonald Observatory and 74-mile scenic loop through Davis Mountains. Nearby are scenic Limpia, Madera, Musquiz and Keesey canyons; Camino del Rio; ghost town of Shafter; Big Bend National Park; Big Bend Ranch State Park; Fort Davis National Historic Site; and Fort Leaton State Historic Site.

Devils River State Natural Area comprises 37,000 acres in Val Verde County, 22 miles off US 277, about 65 miles north of Del Rio on graded road. It is an ecological and archaeological crossroads. Ecologically, it is in a transitional area between the Edwards Plateau, the Trans-Pecos desert and the South Texas brush country. Archaeological studies suggest occupation and use by cultures from both east and west. Camping, hiking, and mountain biking. All camping, facility stays, canyon, and pictograph-site tours are by reservation only. Dolan Falls is nearby and is accessible only through The Nature Conservancy of Texas.

Devil's Sinkhole State Natural Area, comprising 1,859.7 acres about six miles northeast of Rocksprings on US 377 in Edwards County, is a vertical cavern. The sinkhole, discovered by Anglo settlers in 1867, is a registered National Natural Landmark; it was purchased in 1985 from private owners. The cavern opening is about 40 by 60 feet, with a vertical drop of about 140 feet. Access by prearranged tour with Devil's Sinkhole Society (830-683-BATS). Bats can be viewed in summer leaving cave at dusk; no access to cave itself. Contact Kickapoo Cavern State Park to arrange a tour.

Dinosaur Valley State Park, located off US 67 four miles west of Glen Rose in Somervell County, is a 1,524.72-acre scenic park. Land was acquired from private owners in 1968. Features dinosaur tracks in bed of Paluxy River and two full-scale dinosaur models, originally created for New York World's Fair in 1964–65, on display. Part of state longhorn herd is in park. Camping, picnicking, hiking, mountain biking, swimming, fishing. The riverbed featuring the dinosaur tracks was designated a national landmark in 1968. See page 154 for more.

Eisenhower Birthplace State Historic Site is six acres off US 75 at 609 S. Lamar, Denison, Grayson County. The property was acquired in 1958 from the Eisenhower Birthplace Foundation. Restoration of home of President Dwight Eisenhower includes furnishings of period and some personal effects of Gen. Eisenhower. Guided tour; call for schedule. Park open daily, except Christmas Day and New Year's Day; call for hours. Town of Denison established on Butterfield Overland Mail Route in 1858.

Eisenhower State Park, 423.1 acres five miles northwest of Denison via US 75 to TX 91N to FM 1310 on the shores of Lake Texoma in Grayson County, was acquired by an Army lease in 1954. Named for the 34th U.S. president, Dwight D. Eisenhower. First Anglo settlers came to area in 1835; Fort Johnson was established in area in 1840; Colbert's Ferry established on Red River in 1853 and operated until 1931. Areas of tall-grass prairie exist. Hiking, camping, picnicking, fishing, swimming.

Enchanted Rock State Natural Area is 1,643.5 acres on Big Sandy Creek 18 miles north of Fredericksburg on FM 965 on the line between Gillespie and Llano counties. Acquired in 1978 by The Nature Conservancy of Texas; state acquired from TNCT in 1984. Enchanted Rock is huge pink granite boulder rising 425 feet above ground and covering 640 acres. It is second-largest batholith (underground rock formation uncovered by erosion) in the United States. Indians believed ghost fires flickered at top and were awed by weird creaking and groaning, which geologists say resulted from rock's heating and expanding by day, cooling and contracting at night. Enchanted Rock is a National Natural Landmark and is on the National Register of Historic Places. Activities include hiking, geological study, camping, rock climbing and star gazing.

Estero Llano Grande State Park, part of the World Birding Center network, is a 176-acre wetlands refuge 3.2 miles southeast of Weslaco off FM 1015. Birds seen here include waders, shorebirds and migrating waterfowl, as well as coastal species such as Roseate spoonbill and Ibis. Rare spottings include red-crowned parrots and green parakeets. Opened daily. Guided tours offered.

Fairfield Lake State Park is 1,460 acres adjacent to Lake Fairfield, six miles northeast of the city of Fairfield off FM 2570 and FM 3285 in Freestone County. It was leased from Texas Utilities in 1971-72. Surrounding woods offer sanctuary for many species of birds and wildlife. Camping, hiking, backpacking, nature study, water-related activities available. Extensive schedule of tours, seminars and other activities.

Parks text continues on page 154.

Texas State Parks & State Historic Sites

Park †Type of Park	(Special Features)	NEAREST TOWN	Day Use Only	Historic Site/ Museum	Exhibit/Interpretive Cntr	Restrooms	Showers	Trailer Dump Station	Camping	Screened Shelters	Cabins	Group Facilities	Nature Trail	Hiking Trail	Picnicking	Boat Ramp	Fishing	Swimming	Canoe Rentals	Activities/Amenities
Abilene SP		BUFFALO GAP				★	★	★	★	★	★	BG	★		★		☆	★	★	
Acton SHS ▲	(Grave of Davy Crockett's Wife)	GRANBURY	★	★																
Atlanta SP		ATLANTA				★	★	★	★			DG	★	★	★	★	★	☆	★	
Balmorhea SP	(San Solomon Springs Courts)	BALMORHEA			★	★	★	★	★		★	DG	★		★			★		L
Barton Warnock Environmental Ed. Center		LAJITAS	★		★	★							★							
Bastrop SP		BASTROP				★	★	★	★		★	BG		★	★		★	★	★	G
Battleship Texas SHS	(San Jacinto Battleground)	DEER PARK	★	★	★							DG								
Bentsen–Rio Grande Valley SP		MISSION			★	★	★		★			BG	★	★	★					H
Big Bend Ranch SP		LAJITAS			★	★	★		★			NG	★	★	★		☆	☆		B1, E
Big Spring SP		BIG SPRING				★						DG	★	★	★					B1, H
Blanco SP		BLANCO				★	★	★	★	★		DG		★	★		★	★	★	
Bonham SP		BONHAM				★	★	★	★		★	BG		★	★	★	★	☆	★	B1
Brazos Bend SP	(George Observatory)	RICHMOND			★	★	★	★	★	★	★	BG	★	★	★		★			B1/2,E,H
Buescher SP		SMITHVILLE				★	★	★	★	★	★	BG		★	★		★	☆	★	B2
Caddo Lake SP		KARNACK			★	★	★	★	★	★	★	BG	★	★	★	★	★		★	
Caddo Mounds SHS ▲		ALTO	★	★	★	★							★							
Caprock Canyons SP & TW		QUITAQUE			★	★	★	★	★			BG	★	★	★	★	☆	☆		B1, E
Casa Navarro SHS ▲		SAN ANTONIO	★	★	★	★														
Cedar Hill SP		CEDAR HILL				★	★	★	★			DG	★	★	★	★	★	☆		B1, H
Choke Canyon SP, Calliham Unit		THREE RIVERS				★	★	★	★		★	BG	★	★	★	★	☆	☆		
South Shore Unit		THREE RIVERS	★			★						DG			★	★	★	☆		B1
Cleburne SP		CLEBURNE				★	★	★	★	★	★	BG	★	★	★	★	★	☆		H
Colorado Bend SP	(Cave Tours)	BEND				★	★		★			NG		★	★	★	★	☆	★	B1
Confederate Reunion Grounds SHS ▲		MEXIA	★	★	★	★								★	★					
Cooper Lake SP, Doctors Creek Unit		COOPER				★	★	★	★	★		DG	★	★	★	★	★	★		
South Sulphur Unit		SULPHUR SPRINGS				★	★	★	★	★	★	DG		★	★	★	★	★	★	B1, E
Copper Breaks SP		QUANAH			★	★	★	★	★			BG	★	★	★	★	★	☆		B1, E, C
Daingerfield SP		DAINGERFIELD			★	★	★	★	★		★	BG		★	★	★	★	☆	★	
Davis Mountains SP	(Indian Lodge)	FORT DAVIS			★	★	★	★	★			DG		★	★					B1, L, E
Devils River SNA	(Reservations Required)	DEL RIO							★			BG					☆	★		B1
Devil's Sinkhole SNA		ROCKSPRINGS	No access to cavern. Tours of SNA by special request only.																	
Dinosaur Valley SP	(Dinosaur Footprints)	GLEN ROSE			★	★	★	★	★			DG	★	★	★		☆	☆		B1, E
Eisenhower SP	(Marina)	DENISON				★	★	★	★	★	★	BG	★	★	★	★	★	☆		B1, R
Eisenhower Birthplace SHS ▲		DENISON	★	★	★	★						DG								
Enchanted Rock SNA		FREDERICKSBURG			★	★	★		★			DG	★	★	★					R
Estero Llano Grande SP		WESLACO										BG	★							
Fairfield Lake SP		FAIRFIELD				★	★	★	★			DG		★	★	★	★	☆	★	B1, E
Falcon SP (Airstrip)		ZAPATA				★	★	★	★	★	★	DG	★	★	★	★	★	☆		
Fannin Battleground SHS ▲		GOLIAD	★	★	★	★						DG			★					
Fanthorp Inn SHS		ANDERSON	★	★	★	★									★					
Fort Boggy SP		CENTERVILLE	★			★	★		★		★	DG		★	★	★	★	☆		B1
Fort Griffin SHS ▲		ALBANY		★	★	★	★	★	★			BG	★	★	★		☆			C, E
Fort Lancaster SHS ▲		OZONA	★	★	★	★									☆					
Fort Leaton SHS		PRESIDIO	★	★	★	★							★		★					
Fort McKavett SHS, ▲		FORT McKAVETT	★	★	★	★							★		★					
Fort Parker SP		MEXIA				★	★	★	★	★	★	BG		★	★	★	★	☆	★	B1
Fort Richardson SP, HS & Lost Creek Res. TW		JACKSBORO		★	★	★	★	★	★		★	DG	★	★	★		★	★		B1, E
Franklin Mountains SP	(Wyler Aerial Tramway)	EL PASO	★			★			★			BG		★	★					B1, R
Fulton Mansion SHS ▲		FULTON	★	★	★															
Galveston Island SP	(Summer Theater)	GALVESTON			★	★	★	★	★			NG		★	★		☆	☆		B1
Garner SP		CONCAN				★	★	★	★	★	★	BG		★	★		☆	☆	★	B1
Goliad SP & Mission Espíritu Santo HS		GOLIAD		★	★	★	★	★	★	★		DG	★	★	★		☆	★		
Goose Island SP		ROCKPORT				★	★	★	★			BG		★	★	★	★			
Government Canyon SNA		SAN ANTONIO				★			★			DG		★	★					B1
Guadalupe River SP & Honey Creek SNA		BOERNE			★	★	★	★	★			DG		★	★		☆	☆		B1, E
Hill Country SNA		BANDERA				★			★			NG		★			☆	☆		B1, E
Hueco Tanks SP & HS	(Indian Pictographs)	EL PASO		★	★	★	★	★	★			DG	★	★	★					R
Huntsville SP		HUNTSVILLE			★	★	★	★	★	★	★	DG	★	★	★	★	★	☆	★	G

ACTIVITIES/AMENITIES CODES

B1	Mountain biking	**E**	Equestrian facilities and/or trails	**DG**	Day-use group facilities
B2	Surfaced bike trail	**G**	Golf	**NG**	Overnight group facilities
H	Some handicap accessible facilities	**L**	Hotel-type facilities	**BG**	Both day and night group facilities
R	Rock climbing	**C**	Texas Longhorn herd		

FACILITIES CODES	★ Facilities or services available for activity	☆	Permitted, but facilities not provided

Texas State Parks & State Historic Sites

Park †Type of Park	(Special Features)	NEAREST TOWN	Day Use Only	Historic Site/ Museum	Exhibit/Interpretive Cntr	Restrooms	Showers	Trailer Dump Station	Camping	Screened Shelters	Cabins	Group Facilities	Nature Trail	Hiking Trail	Picnicking	Boat Ramp	Fishing	Swimming	Canoe Rentals	Activities/Amenities
Inks Lake SP		BURNET				★	★	★	★		★	DG		★	★	★	★	☆	★	
Kickapoo Cavern SP	(Reservations Required)	BRACKETTVILLE				★	★	★	★				★	★	★					B1
Lake Arrowhead SP		WICHITA FALLS				★	★	★	★			DG	★	★	★	★	★	☆		E
Lake Bob Sandlin SP		MOUNT PLEASANT				★	★	★	★	★	★	DG		★	★	★	★	☆		B1
Lake Brownwood SP		BROWNWOOD				★	★	★	★	★	★	BG	★	★	★	★	★	☆		
Lake Casa Blanca International SP		LAREDO				★	★	★	★			DG			★	★	☆	☆		B1
Lake Colorado City SP		COLORADO CITY				★	★	★	★		★	DG	★	★	★	★	★	☆		
Lake Corpus Christi SP		MATHIS				★	★	★	★	★	★	DG			★	★	★	☆	★	
Lake Livingston SP		LIVINGSTON			★	★	★	★	★	★		DG	★	★	★	★	★	☆		B1, B2, E
Lake Mineral Wells SP & TW		MINERAL WELLS				★	★	★	★	★		DG	★	★	★	★	★	☆	★	B1, E, R
Lake Somerville SP & TW, Birch Creek Unit		SOMERVILLE			★	★	★	★	★			BG	★	★	★	★	★	☆	★	B1, E
Nails Creek Unit		LEDBETTER			★	★	★	★	★			DG	★	★	★	★	★	☆	★	B1, E
Lake Tawakoni SP		WILLS POINT				★	★	★	★			BG		★	★	★	☆	☆		
Lake Whitney SP	(Airstrip)	WHITNEY				★	★	★	★	★		BG		★	★	★	☆	☆		B1
Landmark Inn SHS ▲	(Hotel Rooms)	CASTROVILLE		★	★	★						DG	★		★		☆			L
Lipantitlan SHS		SAN PATRICIO	★												★					
Lockhart SP		LOCKHART				★	★	★	★			DG			★		★	★		G
Longhorn Cavern SP ▲	(Cavern Tours)	BURNET	★	★	★	★							★	★	★					
Lost Maples SNA		VANDERPOOL			★	★	★	★	★				★	★	★		☆	☆		
Lyndon B. Johnson SP & HS		STONEWALL	★	★	★	★						DG	★		★			★		C
Magoffin Home SHS ▲		EL PASO	★	★	★	★														
Martin Creek Lake SP		TATUM				★	★	★	★	★	★	DG		★	★	★	★	☆		B1
Martin Dies Jr. SP		JASPER			★	★	★	★	★	★	★	BG	★	★	★	★	★	☆	★	B1
McKinney Falls SP		AUSTIN		★	★	★	★	★	★		★	BG	★	★	★		☆	☆		B1, B2
Meridian SP		MERIDIAN				★	★	★	★	★		BG	★		★	★	☆	☆	★	
Mission Dolores SHS ▲	(El Camino Real Trail)	SAN AUGUSTINE		★	★	★	★		★			DG		★	★					
Mission Rosario SHS		GOLIAD		★	★	★	★	★	★	★		DG		★	★		★	★		
Mission Tejas SP		WECHES		★		★	★	★	★			BG		★	★		☆			
Monahans Sandhills SP		MONAHANS			★	★	★	★	★			DG	★		★					E
Monument Hill & Kreische Brewery SHS		LA GRANGE	★	★	★	★						DG	★		★					
Mother Neff SP		MOODY				★	★		★			BG		★	★		☆			
Mustang Island SP		PORT ARANSAS				★	★	★	★						★		☆	☆		
National Museum of the Pacific War ▲		FREDERICKSBURG	★	★	★	★							★							
Old Tunnel SP	(Bat viewing, May – Oct.)	FREDERICKSBURG	★			★							★							
Palmetto SP		LULING				★	★	★	★		★	BC	★	★	★		★	☆	★	
Palo Duro Canyon SP	(Summer Drama: "Texas")	CANYON			★	★	★	★	★		★			★	★		★			B1,E, C
Pedernales Falls SP		JOHNSON CITY				★	★	★	★			NG	★	★	★		☆	☆		B1, E
Port Isabel Lighthouse SHS ▲		PORT ISABEL	★	★		★														
Possum Kingdom SP		CADDO				★	★	★	★		★			★	★	★	★	☆	★	
Purtis Creek SP		EUSTACE				★	★	★	★			DG	★	★	★	★	★	☆	★	
Ray Roberts Lake SP, Isle du Bois Unit		PILOT POINT			★	★	★	★	★			DG		★	★	★	★	☆	★	B1, B2, E
Johnson Branch Unit		VALLEY VIEW				★	★	★	★			DG		★	★	★	★	☆	★	B1, B2
Jordan Unit	(Lantana Resort)	PILOT POINT																		L
Resaca de la Palma SP		BROWNSVILLE				★						DG								
Sabine Pass Battleground SHS ▲		SABINE PASS		★	★	★		★	★						★	★	☆			
Sam Bell Maxey House SHS ▲		PARIS	★	★	★	★														
Sam Rayburn House SHS ▲		BONHAM																		
San Angelo SP		SAN ANGELO				★	★	★	★		★	BG		★	★	★	★	☆		B1, E, C
San Felipe de Austin SHS ▲		SAN FELIPE																		
San Jacinto Battleground SHS	(Battleship Texas)	HOUSTON	★	★	★	★						DG	★		★		☆			
Sea Rim SP		PORT ARTHUR				★	★	★	★		★		★		★	★	☆	★	★	B1
Sebastopol House SHS ▲		SEGUIN	★	★	★										★					
Seminole Canyon SP & HS	(Indian Pictographs)	LANGTRY		★	★	★	★	★	★				★	★	★					B1
Sheldon Lake SP	(Environmental Learning Center)	HOUSTON	★		★	★								★	☆	★	★			
South Llano River SP		JUNCTION		★		★	★	★	★				★	★	★		☆	☆		B1
Starr Family Home SHS ▲		MARSHALL	★	★	★	★														
Stephen F. Austin SP		SAN FELIPE			★	★	★	★	★	★	★	BG	★	★	★		☆			G
Tyler SP		TYLER				★	★	★	★	★		BG	★	★	★	★	★	☆	★	B1
Varner-Hogg Plantation SHS ▲		WEST COLUMBIA	★	★	★	★							★		★		☆			
Village Creek SP		LUMBERTON				★	★	★	★			BG	★	★	★		☆	☆		B1
Walter Umphrey SP ▲		PORT ARTHUR	(Managed by Jefferson County)																	
Washington-on-the-Brazos SHS Barrington Living History Farm (Anson Jones Home)		WASHINGTON	★	★	★	★						DG		★	★					
Zaragoza Birthplace SHS		GOLIAD	★	★	★															

Falcon State Park is 572.6 acres located 15 miles north of Roma off US 83 and FM 2098 at southern end of Falcon Reservoir in Starr and Zapata counties. Park leased from International Boundary and Water Commission in 1949. Gently rolling hills covered by mesquite, huisache, wild olive, ebony, cactus. Excellent birding and fishing. Camping and water activities also. Nearby are Mexico, Fort Ringgold in Rio Grande City and historic city of Roma. Bentsen-Rio Grande Valley State Park is 65 miles away.

Fannin Battleground State Historic Site, nine miles east of Goliad in Goliad County off US 59 to PR 27. The 13.6-acre park site was acquired by the state in 1914; transferred to TPW by legislative enactment in 1965. At this site on March 20, 1836, Col. James Fannin surrendered to Mexican Gen. José Urrea after Battle of Coleto; 342 massacred and 28 escaped near what is now Goliad SP.

Fanthorp Inn State Historic Site includes a historic double-pen cedar-log dogtrot house and 1.4 acres in Anderson, county seat of Grimes County, south of TX 90. Acquired by purchase in 1977 from a Fanthorp descendant and opened to the public in 1987. Inn records report visits from many prominent civic and military leaders, including Sam Houston, Anson Jones, and generals Ulysses S. Grant, Robert E. Lee and Stonewall Jackson. Originally built in 1834, it has been restored to its 1850 use as a family home and travelers' hotel. Tours available Friday, Saturday, Sunday. Call TPW for stagecoach-ride schedule. No dining or overnight facilities.

Fort Boggy State Park is 1,847 acres of wooded, rolling hills in Leon County near Boggy Creek, about four miles south of Centerville on TX 75. Land donated to TPWD in 1985 by Eileen Crain Sullivan. Area once home to Keechi and Kickapoo tribes. Log fort was built by settlers in 1840s; first settlement north of the Old San Antonio Road and between the Navasota and Trinity rivers. Swimming beach, fishing, picnicking, nature trails for hiking and mountain biking. Fifteen-acre lake open to small craft. Open-air group pavilion overlooking lake can be reserved ($50 per day). Nearby attractions include Rusk/Palestine, Fort Parker, and Texas State Railroad state parks, and Old Fort Parker Historic Site. Open Wed.–Sun. for day use only; entrance fee. For reservations, call 512-389-8900.

Fort Griffin State Historic Site is 506.2 acres 15 miles north of Albany off US 283 in Shackelford County. The state was deeded the land by the county in 1935. Portion of state longhorn herd resides in park. On bluff overlooking townsite of Fort Griffin and Clear Fork of Brazos River valley are partially restored ruins of Old Fort Griffin, restored bakery, replicas of enlisted men's huts. Fort constructed in 1867, deactivated 1881. Camping, equestrian camping, hiking. Nearby are Albany with restored courthouse square, Abilene and Possum Kingdom state parks. Albany annually holds "Fandangle" musical show in commemoration of frontier times.

Fort Lancaster State Historic Site, 81.6-acres located about eight miles east of Sheffield on TX 290 in Crockett County. Acquired in 1968 by deed from Crockett County; Henry Meadows donated 41 acres in 1975. Fort Lancaster established Aug. 20, 1855, to guard San Antonio-El Paso Road and protect movement of supplies and immigrants from Indian hostilities. Site of part of Camel Corps experiment. Fort abandoned March 19, 1861, after Texas seceded from Union. Exhibits on history, natural history and archaeology; nature trail, picnicking. Open daily; day use only.

Fort Leaton State Historic Site, four miles southeast of Presidio in Presidio County on FM 170, was acquired in 1967 from private owners. Consists of 23.4 acres, 5 of which are on site of trading post. In 1848, Ben Leaton built fortified adobe trading post known as Fort Leaton near present Presidio. Ben Leaton died in 1851. Guided tours; exhibits trace history, natural history and archaeological history of area. Serves as western entrance to Big Bend Ranch State Park. Day use only.

Fort McKavett State Historic Site, 79.5 acres acquired from 1967 through the mid-1970s from Fort McKavett Restoration, Inc., Menard County and private individuals, is located 23 miles west of Menard off US 190 and FM 864. Originally called Camp San Saba, the fort was built by War Department in 1852 to protect frontier settlers and travelers on Upper El Paso Road from Indians. Camp later renamed for Capt. Henry McKavett, killed at Battle of Monterrey, Sept. 21, 1846. Fort abandoned March 1859; reoccupied April 1868. A Buffalo Soldier post. Abandoned again June 30, 1883. Once called by Gen. Wm. T. Sherman, "the prettiest post in Texas." More than 25 restored buildings, ruins of many others. Interpretive exhibits. Day use only.

Fort Parker State Park includes 1,458.8 acres, including 758.78 land acres and 700-acre lake between Mexia and Groesbeck off TX 14 in Limestone County. Named for the former private fort built near present park in 1836, the site was acquired from private owners and the City of Mexia 1935-1937. Camping, fishing, swimming, canoeing, picnicking. Nearby is Old Fort Parker Historic Site, which is operated by the City of Groesbeck.

Fort Richardson State Park, Historic Site, and Lost Creek Reservoir Trailway, located one-half mile south of Jacksboro off US 281 in Jack County, contains 454 acres. Acquired in 1968 from City of Jacksboro. Fort founded in 1867, northernmost of line of federal forts established after Civil War for protection from Indians; originally named Fort Jacksboro. In April 1867, fort was moved to its present location from 20 miles farther south; on Nov. 19, 1867, made permanent post at Jacksboro and named for Israel Richardson, who was fatally wounded at Battle of Antietam. Expeditions sent from Fort Richardson arrested Indians responsible for Warren Wagon Train Massacre in 1871 and fought Comanches in Palo Duro Canyon. Fort abandoned in May 1878. Park contains seven restored buildings and two replicas. Interpretive center, picnicking, camping, fishing; ten-mile trailway.

Franklin Mountains State Park, created by an act of the legislature in 1979 to protect the mountain range as a wilderness preserve and acquired by TPW in 1981, comprises 24,247.56 acres, all within El Paso city limits. Largest urban park in the nation. It includes virtually an entire Chihuahuan Desert mountain range, with an elevation of 7,192 feet at the summit. The park is habitat for

A Ringed Kingfisher at Estero Llano Grande State Park. This park is a popular site for birders and other wildlife photographers. Photo by Andy Reago and Chrissy McClarren, CC by 2.0/Flickr

many Chihuahuan Desert plants including sotol, lechuguilla, ocotillo, cholla and barrel cactus, and such animals as mule deer, fox and an occasional cougar. Camping, mountain biking, nature study, hiking, picnicking, rock-climbing. Wyler Aerial Tramway, an aerial cable-car tramway on 195 acres of rugged mountain on east side of Franklin Mountains. Purchase tickets at tramway station on McKinley Ave. Check with park for fees and hours; 915-566-6622. Other area attractions include Hueco Tanks State Historic Site and Magoffin Home State Historic Site.

French Legation State Historic Site was built in 1841 as a private home for Alphones Dubois, French chargé d'affaires to the Republic of Texas. In 1848 it was purchased by Dr. Joseph W. Robertson, who lived there with his large family and nine enslaved workers. Daughter Lillie Robertson lived in the house her entire life. The state acquired the house after her death, and appointed the Daughters of the Republic as custodian. In 2017, HB 3810 transferred the French Legation to the THC. The site is currently closed for restoration.

Fulton Mansion State Historic Site in Fulton is 3.5 miles north of Rockport off TX Business 35 on South Fulton Beach Rd. in Aransas County. The 2.3 acre-property was acquired by purchase from private owner in 1976. Three-story wooden structure, built in 1874-1877, was home of George W. Fulton, prominent in South Texas for economic and commercial influence; mansion derives significance from its innovative construction and Victorian design. Call ahead for days and hours of guided tours; open Wednesday–Sunday; 800-792-1112.

Galveston Island State Park, on the west end of Galveston Island on FM 3005, is a 2,013.1-acre site acquired in 1969 from private owners. Camping, birding, nature study, swimming, bicycling and fishing amid **sand dunes and grassland**. Musical productions in amphitheater during summer.

Garner State Park is 1,419.8 acres of recreational facilities on US 83 on the Frio River in Uvalde County 9 miles south of Leakey. Named for John Nance Garner, U.S. Vice President, 1933-1941, the park was deeded in 1934-36 by private owners. Camping, hiking, picnicking, river recreation, miniature golf, biking, boat rentals. Cabins available. Nearby is John Nance "Cactus Jack" Garner Museum in Uvalde. Nearby also are ruins of historic Mission Nuestra Señora de la Candelaria del Cañon, founded in 1749; Camp Sabinal (a U.S. Cavalry post and later Texas Ranger camp) established 1856; Fort Inge, established 1849.

Goliad State Park and Mission Espíritu Santo Historic Site are 188.3 acres one-fourth mile south of Goliad on US 183 and 77A, along the San Antonio River in Goliad County. The land was deeded to the state in 1931 by the City and County of Goliad; transferred to TPW 1949. Nearby are the sites of several battles in the Texas fight for independence from Mexico. The park includes a replica of Mission Nuestra Señora del Espíritu Santo de Zúñiga, originally established 1722 and settled at its present site in 1749. At Goliad State Park are camping, picnicking, historical exhibits, nature trail. (See also Fannin Battleground State Historic Site.)

Goose Island State Park, 321.4 acres 10 miles northeast of Rockport on TX 35 and PR 13 on St. Charles and Aransas bays in Aransas County, was deeded by private owners in 1931-1935 plus an additional seven acres donated in the early 1990s by Sun Oil Co. Located here is "Big Tree"

Tall trees at Huntsville State Park. Photo by Roy Luck, CC by 2.0/Flickr.

estimated to be a 1,000-year-old live oak. Fishing, picnicking and camping, plus excellent birding; no swimming. Rare and endangered whooping cranes can be viewed during winter just across St. Charles Bay in Aransas National Wildlife Refuge.

Government Canyon State Natural Area is an 8,622-acre area in Bexar County, northwest of San Antonio, 3.5 miles northwest of Loop 1604 and FM 471, then 1.6 miles north on Galm Road. Day use only. No camping. Open Friday–Monday. Trees such as mounatin laurel, Ashe juniper, Mexican buckeye and Escarpment black cherry.

Guadalupe River State Park comprises 1,938.7 acres on cypress-shaded Guadalupe River in Kendall and Comal counties, 13 miles east of Boerne on TX 46. Acquired by deed from private owners in 1974. Park has four miles of river frontage with several white-water rapids and is located in a stretch of Guadalupe River noted for canoeing, tubing. Picnicking, camping, hiking, nature study. Trees include sycamore, elm, basswood, pecan, walnut, persimmon, willow and hackberry (see also Honey Creek State Natural Area).

Hill Country State Natural Area in Bandera and Medina counties, 9 miles west of Bandera on FM 1077. The 5,369.8-acre site acquired by gift from Merrick Bar-O-Ranch and purchased in 1976. Park is located in typical Texas Hill Country on West Verde Creek and contains several spring-fed streams. Primitive and equestrian camping, hiking, horseback riding, mountain biking, fishing. Group lodge.

Hueco Tanks State Park and Historic Site, located 32 miles northeast of El Paso in El Paso County on FM 2775 just north of US 62-180, was obtained from the county in 1969, with additional 121 acres purchased in 1970. Featured in this 860.3-acre park are large natural rock basins that provided water for archaic hunters, Plains Indians, Butterfield Overland Mail coach horses and passengers, and other travelers in this arid region. In park are Indian pictographs, old ranch house and relocated ruins of stage station. Rock climbing, picnicking, camping, hiking. Wildlife includes gray fox, bobcat, prairie falcons, golden eagles. Visitation is limited. Pictograph tours are by advanced request. Call 1-800-792-112, (Option 3).

Huntsville State Park is 2,083.2-acre recreational area off IH 45 and PR 40 six miles south of Huntsville in Walker County, acquired by deeds from private owners in 1937. Heavily wooded park adjoins Sam Houston National Forest and encloses Lake Raven. Hiking, camping, fishing, biking, paddle boats, canoeing. At nearby Huntsville are Sam Houston's old homestead (Steamboat House), containing some of his personal effects, and his grave. Approximately 50 miles away is Alabama-Coushatta Indian Reservation in Polk County.

Inks Lake State Park is 1,201 acres of recreational facilities along Inks Lake, 9 miles west of Burnet on the Colorado River off TX 29 on PR 4 in Burnet County. Acquired by deeds from the Lower Colorado River Authority and private owners in 1940. Camping, hiking, fishing, swimming, boating, golf. Deer, turkey and other wildlife abundant. Nearby are Longhorn Cavern State Park, LBJ Ranch, LBJ State Historic Site, Pedernales Falls State Park and Enchanted Rock State Natural Area. Granite Mountain quarry at nearby Marble Falls furnished red granite for Texas state capitol. Buchanan Dam, considered the largest multi-arch dam in the nation, located 4 miles from park.

Kickapoo Cavern State Park is located about 22 miles north of Brackettville on RM 674 on the Kinney/Edwards county line in the southern Edwards Plateau. The park (6,368.4 acres) contains 20 known caves, two of which are large enough to be significant: Kickapoo Cavern, about 1/4 mile in length, has impressive formations, and Stuart Bat Cave (formally Green Cave), slightly shorter, supports a nursery colony of Mexican freetail bats in summer. Public observations of bat flights are available with an entrance permit. Birds include rare species such as black-capped vireo, varied bunting and Montezuma quail. Reptiles and amphibians include barking frog, mottled rock rattlesnake and Texas alligator lizard. Open Friday–Monday. Cavern tours on Saturday by reservation. Group lodge; primitive camping; hiking and mountain-biking trails.

Lake Arrowhead State Park consists of 524 acres in Clay County, about 14 miles south of Wichita Falls on US 281 to FM 1954, then 8 miles to park. Acquired in 1970 from the City of Wichita Falls. Lake Arrowhead is a reservoir on the Little Wichita River with 106 miles of shoreline. The land surrounding the lake is generally semiarid, gently rolling prairie, much of which has been invaded by mesquite in recent decades. Fishing, camping, lake swimming, picnicking, horseback-riding area.

Lake Bob Sandlin State Park, on the wooded shoreline of 9,400-acre Lake Bob Sandlin, is located 12 miles southwest of Mount Pleasant off FM 21 in Titus County. Activities in the 639.8-acre park include picnicking, camping, mountain biking, hiking, swimming, fishing and boating. Oak, hickory, dogwood, redbud, maple and pine produce spectacular fall color. Eagles can sometimes be spotted in winter months.

Lake Brownwood State Park in Brown County is 537.5 acres acquired from Brown County Water Improvement District No. 1 in 1934. Park reached from TX 279 to PR 15, 16 miles northwest of Brownwood on Lake Brownwood near geographical center of Texas. Water sports, hiking, camping. Cabins available.

Lake Casa Blanca International State Park, located one mile east of Laredo off US 59 on Loop 20, was formerly operated by the City of Laredo and Webb County and was acquired by TPW in 1990. Park includes 371 acres on Lake Casa Blanca. Recreation hall can be reserved. Camping, picnicking, fishing, ball fields, playgrounds, amphitheater, and tennis courts. County-operated golf course nearby.

Lake Colorado City State Park, 500 acres leased for 99 years from a utility company. It is located in Mitchell County 11 miles southwest of Colorado City off IH 20 on FM 2836. Water sports, picnicking, camping, hiking. Part of state longhorn herd can be seen in park.

Lake Corpus Christi State Park, a 14,112-acre park in San Patricio, Jim Wells and Live Oak counties. Located 35 miles northwest of Corpus Christi and four miles southwest of Mathis off TX 359 and Park Road 25. Was leased from City of Corpus Christi in 1934. Camping, picnicking, birding, water sports. Nearby are Padre Island National Seashore; Mustang Island, Choke Canyon, Goliad and Goose Island state parks; Aransas National Wildlife Refuge, and Fulton Mansion State Historic Site.

Lake Livingston State Park, in Polk County, about one mile southwest of Livingston on FM 3126 and PR 65, contains 635.5 acres along Lake Livingston. Acquired by deed from private landowners in 1971. Near ghost town of Swartwout, steamboat landing on Trinity River in 1830s and 1850s. Camping, picnicking, swimming pool, fishing, mountain biking and stables.

Lake Mineral Wells State Park and Trailway, located four miles east of Mineral Wells on US 180 in Parker County, consists of 3,282.5 acres encompassing Lake Mineral Wells. In 1975, the City of Mineral Wells donated 1,095 land acres and the lake to TPW; the federal government transferred additional land from Fort Wolters army post. Popular for rock-climbing/rappelling. Swimming, fishing, boating, camping; the 20-mile Lake Mineral Wells State Trailway avaiable for hiking, bicycling, equestrian use.

Lake Somerville State Park, northwest of Brenham in Lee and Burleson counties, was leased from the federal government in 1969. Birch Creek Unit (2,365 acres reached from TX 60 and PR 57) and Nails Creek Unit (3,155 acres reached from US 290 and FM 180), are connected by a 13-mile trailway system, with equestrian and primitive camp sites, rest benches, shelters and drinking water. Also camping, birding, picnicking, volleyball and water sports. Somerville Wildlife Management Area, 3,180 acres is nearby.

Lake Tawakoni State Park is a 376.3-acre park in Hunt County along the shore of its namesake reservoir. It was acquired in 1984 through a 50-year lease agreement with the Sabine River Authority and opened in 2001. Includes a swimming beach, half-mile trail, picnic sites, boat ramp and campsites. A 40-acre tallgrass prairie managed in the post-oak woodlands. The park is reached from IH 20 on TX 47 north to FM 2475 about 20 miles past Wills Point.

Lake Whitney State Park is 1,280.7 acres along the east shore of Lake Whitney west of Hillsboro via TX 22 and FM 1244 in Hill County. Acquired in 1954 by a Department of the Army lease. Located near ruins of Towash, early Texas settlement inundated by the lake. Towash Village named for chief of Hainai Indians. Park noted for bluebonnets in spring. Camping, hiking, birding, picnicking, water activities.

Landmark Inn State Historic Site, 4.7 acres in Castroville, Medina County, about 15 miles west of San Antonio, was acquired through donation by Miss Ruth Lawler in 1974. Castroville, settled in the 1840s by Alsatian farmers, is called Little Alsace of Texas. Landmark Inn built about 1844 as residence and store for Cesar Monod, mayor of Castroville 1851-1864. Special workshops, tours and events held at inn; grounds may be rented for receptions, family reunions and weddings. Overnight lodging; all rooms air-conditioned and nonsmoking.

Levi Jordan Plantation State Historic Site was a sugar and cotton plantation, established in the 1850s. The site is currently under development and is not open to the public.

Lipantitlan State Historic Site is five acres, found nine miles east of Orange Grove in Nueces County off Texas 359, FM 624 and FM 70. The property was deeded by private owners in 1937. Fort constructed here in 1833 by Mexican government fell to Texas forces in 1835. Only facilities are picnic tables. Lake Corpus Christi State Park is nearby.

Lockhart State Park is 263.7 acres, found four miles south of Lockhart via US 183, FM 20 and PR 10 in Caldwell County. The land was deeded by private owners between 1934 and 1937. Camping, picnicking, hiking, fishing, 9-hole golf course. After Comanche raid at Linnville, the Battle of Plum Creek (1840) was fought in area.

Longhorn Cavern State Park, off US 281 and PR 4 about six miles west and six miles south of Burnet in Burnet County, is 645.62 acres dedicated as a natural landmark in 1971. It was acquired in 1932-1937 from private owners. The cave has been used as a shelter since prehistoric times. Among legends about the cave is that the outlaw Sam Bass hid stolen money there. Confederates made gunpowder in the cave during the Civil War. Nature trail; guided tours of cave; picnicking, hiking. Cavern operated by concession agreement. Inks Lake State Park and Lyndon B. Johnson Ranch located nearby.

Lost Maples State Natural Area consists of 2,174.2 scenic acres on the Sabinal River in Bandera and Real counties, five miles north of Vanderpool on FM 187. Acquired by purchase from private owners in 1973-1974. Outstanding example of Edwards Plateau flora and fauna, features isolated stand of uncommon Uvalde bigtooth maple. Rare golden-cheeked warbler, black-capped vireo and green kingfisher nest and feed in park. Fall foliage can be spectacular (late Oct. through early Nov.). Hiking trails, camping, fishing, picnicking, birding.

Lyndon B. Johnson State Park & Historic Site, off US 290 in Gillespie County 14 miles west of Johnson City near Stonewall, contains 717.9 acres. Acquired in 1965 with private donations. Home of Lyndon B. Johnson located north bank of Pedernales River across Ranch Road 1 from park; portion of official Texas longhorn herd maintained at park. Wildlife exhibit includes turkey, deer and bison. Living-history demonstrations at restored Sauer-Beckmann house. Reconstruction of Johnson birthplace is open to public. Historic structures, swimming pool, tennis courts, baseball field, picnicking. Day use only. Nearby is family cemetery where former president and relatives are buried. In Johnson City is boyhood home of President Johnson. (See National Parks.)

Magoffin Home State Historic Site, in El Paso, is a 19-room territorial-style adobe on a 1.5-acre site. Purchased by the state and City of El Paso in 1976, it is operated by TPW. Home was built in 1875 by El Pasoan Joseph Magoffin. Furnished with original family artifacts. Guided tours; call for schedule. Day use only.

Martin Creek Lake State Park, 286.9 acres, is located four miles south of Tatum off TX 43 and CR 2183 in Rusk County. It was deeded to the TPW by Texas Utilities in 1976. Water activities; also cabins, camping, picnicking. Roadbed of Trammel's Trace, old Indian trail that became major route for settlers moving to Texas from Arkansas, can be seen. Hardwood and pine forest shelters abundant wildlife including swamp rabbits, gophers, nutria and numerous species of land birds and waterfowl. Annual perch fishing contest for children ages 4–12 the first Saturday in September.

Martin Dies Jr. State Park is 705 acres in Jasper and Tyler counties on the B. A. Steinhagen Reservoir between Woodville and Jasper via US 190. Land leased for 50 years from Corps of Engineers in 1964. Located at edge of Big Thicket. Plant and animal life varied and abundant. Winter bald eagle census conducted at nearby Sam Rayburn Reservoir Camping, hiking, mountain biking, water activities. Wildscape herb garden. Park is about 30 miles from Alabama and Coushatta Indian Reservation.

McKinney Falls State Park is 744.4 acres, located about 13 miles southeast of the state Capitol in Austin, off US 183. Acquired in 1970 by gift from private owners. Named for Thomas F. McKinney, one of Stephen F. Austin's first 300 colonists, who built his home here in the mid-1800s on Onion Creek. Ruins of his homestead can be viewed. Swimming, hiking, biking, camping, picnicking, fishing, guided tours.

Meridian State Park in Bosque County is a 505.4-acre park. The heavily wooded land, on TX 22 three miles southwest of Meridian, was acquired from private owners in 1933-1935. Texas-Santa Fe expedition of 1841 passed through Bosque County near present site of park on Bee Creek. Endangered golden-cheeked warbler nests here. Camping, picnicking, hiking, fishing, lake swimming, birding, bicycling.

Mission Dolores State Historic Site was once a Spanish mission built in 1721 just 20 miles west of the Texas-Louisiana border. There are no longer any above ground remains of the mission. Visitors can camp, view the museum and explore its rich history.

Mission Rosario State Historic Site is located four miles west of Goliad on US 59. It contains the ruins of Nuestra Señora del Rosario mission, established 1754.

Mission Tejas State Park is a 363.5-acre park in Houston County. Situated 12 miles west of Alto via TX 21 and PR 44, the park was acquired from the Texas Forest Service in 1957. In the park is a representation of Mission San Francisco de los Tejas, the first mission in East Texas (1690). It was abandoned, then re-established 1716; abandoned again 1719; re-established again 1721; abandoned for last time in 1730 when the mission was moved to San Antonio. Also in park is restored Rice Family Log Home, built about 1828. Camping, hiking, fishing, picnicking.

Monahans Sandhills State Park consists of 3,840 acres of sand dunes, some up to 70 feet high, in Ward and Winkler counties 5 miles northeast of Monahans on IH 20 to PR 41. Land leased by state from private foundation until 2056. Dunes used as meeting place by raiding Indians. Camping, hiking, picnicking, sand-surfing. Scheduled tours. Odessa meteor crater is nearby, as is Balmorhea State Park.

Monument Hill State Historic Site and Kreische Brewery State Historic Site are operated as one park unit. Monument Hill consists of 40.4 acres one mile south of La Grange on US 77 to Spur Road 92 in Fayette County. Monument and tomb area acquired by state in 1907; additional acreage acquired from the Archdiocese of San Antonio in 1956. Brewery and home purchased from private owners in 1977. Monument is dedicated to Capt. Nicholas Dawson and his men, who fought at Salado Creek in 1842, in Mexican Gen. Adrián Woll's invasion of Texas, and to the men of the "black bean lottery" (1843) of the Mier Expedition. Remains were brought to Monument Hill for reburial in 1848. Kreische Complex, on 36 acres, is linked to Monument Hill through interpretive trail. Kreische Brewery State Historic Site includes the brewery and stone-and-wood house built between 1850–1855 on Colorado River. One of first commercial breweries in state, it closed in 1884. Smokehouse and barn also in complex. Guided tours of brewery and house; call for schedule. Also picknicking, nature study.

Mother Neff State Park was the first official state park in Texas. It originated with six acres donated by Mrs. I. E. Neff, mother of Pat M. Neff, governor of Texas from 1921 to 1925. Gov. Neff and Frank Smith donated remainder in 1934. The park, located eight miles west of Moody on FM 107 and TX 236, now contains 259 acres along the Leon River in Coryell County. Heavily wooded. Camping, picnicking, fishing, hiking.

Mustang Island State Park, 3,954 acres on Gulf of Mexico in Nueces County, 14 miles south of Port Aransas on TX 361, was acquired from private owners in 1972. Mustang Island is a barrier island with a complicated ecosystem, dependent upon the sand dune. The foundation plants of the dunes are sea oats, beach panic grass and soilbind morning glory. Beach camping, picknicking; sun, sand and water activities. Excellent birding. Padre Island National Seashore 14 miles south.

National Museum of the Pacific War and Admiral Nimitz State Historic Site is on seven acres in downtown Fredericksburg. First established as a state agency in 1969 by Texas Legislature; transferred to TPW in 1981. George Bush Gallery opened in 1999. Named for Adm. Chester W. Nimitz of World War II fame, it includes the Pacific War Museum in the Nimitz Steamboat Hotel; the Japanese Garden of Peace, donated by the people of Japan; the History Walk of the Pacific War, featuring planes, boats and other equipment from World War II; and other special exhibits. Nearby is Kerrville State Park.

Old Tunnel State Park sits on 16.1 acres of land, making it the smallest state park in Texas. Located at 10619 Old San Antonio Road, 13.6 miles south of Fredericksburg, the park is great for wildlife-viewing opportunites. The abandoned railroad tunnel provides a home to over 3 million Mexican free-tailed bats and 3,000 cave myotis from May to October, and the park provides nightly bat viewing access. An upper viewing area, open seven days a week, is limited to 250 visitors. Thursday through Sunday, a secondary viewing area opens. Call (866) 978-2287 for viewing time information. The park also has a half-mile trail open year-round for bird-watching or for a short hike.

Palmetto State Park, a scenic park of 270.3 acres, is eight miles southeast of Luling on US 183 and PR 11 along the San Marcos River in Gonzales County. Land deeded in 1934-1936 by private owners and City of Gonzales. Named for tropical dwarf palmetto found there. Diverse plant and animal life; excellent birding. Also picnicking, fishing, hiking, pedal boats, swimming. Nearby Gonzales and Ottine important in early Texas history. Gonzales settled 1825 as center of Green DeWitt's colonies.

Palo Duro Canyon State Park consists of 16,402 acres found 12 miles east of Canyon on TX 217 in Armstrong and Randall counties. The land was deeded by private owners in 1933 and is the scene of the annual summer production of the musical drama, "Texas." Spectacular one-million-year-old scenic canyon exposes rocks spanning about 200 million years of geological time. Coronado may have visited canyon in 1541. Canyon officially discovered by Capt. R. B. Marcy in 1852. Scene of decisive battle in 1874 between Comanche and Kiowa Indians and U.S. Army troops under Gen. Ranald Mackenzie. Also scene of ranching enterprise started by Charles Goodnight in 1876. Part of state longhorn herd is kept here. Camping, mountain biking, scenic drives, horseback and hiking trails, horse rentals.

Pedernales Falls State Park, 5,211.7 acres in Blanco County about nine miles east of Johnson City on FM 2766 along Pedernales River, was acquired from private owners in 1970. Typical Edwards Plateau terrain, with live oaks, deer, turkey and stone hills. Camping, picnicking, hiking, swimming, tubing. Falls main scenic attraction.

Port Isabel Lighthouse State Historic Site consists of 0.9 acres in Port Isabel, Cameron County. Acquired by purchase from private owners in 1950, site includes lighthouse constructed in 1852; visitors can climb to top. Park is near sites of Civil War battle of Palmito Ranch (1865), and Mexican War battles of Palo Alto and Resaca de la Palma (1846). Operated by City of Port Isabel.

Monahans Sandhills State Park near Odessa. Photo by Plum Pine, CC by 2.0/Flickr.

Possum Kingdom State Park, west of Mineral Wells via US 180 and PR 33 in Palo Pinto County, is 1,529 acres adjacent to Possum Kingdom Lake, in Palo Pinto Mountains and Brazos River Valley. Rugged canyons home to deer, other wildlife. Acquired from the Brazos River Authority in 1940. Camping, picnicking, swimming, fishing, boating. Cabins available.

Purtis Creek State Park is 1,582 acres in Henderson and Van Zandt counties 3.5 miles north of Eustace on FM 316. Acquired in 1977 from private owners. Fishing, camping, hiking, picnicking, paddle boats and canoes.

Ray Roberts Lake State Park (Isle du Bois Unit) consists of 2,263 acres on the south side of Ray Roberts Lake on FM 455 in Denton County. Johnson Branch Unit contains 1,514 acres on north side of the lake in Denton and Cooke counties, seven miles east of IH 30 on FM 3002. There are also six satellite parks. Land acquired in 1984 by lease from Department of the Army. Abundant and varied plant and animal life. Fishing, camping, picnicking, swimming, hiking, biking; tours of 19th-century farm buildings at Johnson Branch. Includes Lantana Ridge Lodge on the east side of the lake. It is a full-service lodging facility with restaurant.

Resaca de la Palma State Park, part of the World Birding Center network, is 1,700 semi-tropical acres off US 281, four miles west of Brownsville in Cameron County. Park grounds are open seven days a week year-round from sunrise to sunset. Birding and natural history tours offered. Colorful Neotropical and Neartic migrant birds have been seen.

Sabine Pass Battleground State Historic Site in Jefferson County 1.5 miles south of Sabine Pass on Dick Dowling Road, contains 57.6 acres acquired from Kountze and Couch Trust in 1972. Lt. Richard W. Dowling, with small Confederate force, repelled an attempted 1863 invasion of Texas by Union gunboats. Monument, World War II ammunition bunkers. Fishing, picnicking, camping.

Sam Bell Maxey House State Historic Site, at the corner of South Church and Washington streets in Paris, Lamar County, was donated by City of Paris in 1976. Consists of 0.4 acres with 1868 Victorian Italianate-style frame house, plus outbuildings. Most of furnishings accumulated by Maxey family. Maxey served in Mexican and Civil wars and was two-term U.S. Senator. House is on the National Register of Historic Places. Open for tours Friday through Sunday.

Sam Rayburn House State Historic Site preserves personal belongings, original furniture, and photos just as they were when Sam Rayburn lived here. Visitors can explore the home and grounds to the once powerful and influential Texas politician.

San Angelo State Park, on O.C. Fisher Reservoir adjacent to the city of San Angelo in Tom Green County, contains 7,677 acres of land, most of which will remain undeveloped. Leased from U.S. Corps of Engineers in 1995. Access is from US 87 or US 67, then FM 2288. Highly diversified plant and animal life. Activities include boating, water activities, hiking, mountain biking, horseback riding, camping, picnicking. Part of state longhorn herd in park. Nearby is Fort Concho.

San Felipe de Austin State Historic Site was once the location of Stephen F. Austin's headquarters for his colony in Mexican Texas. Visitors are able to walk the grounds of the former political and economic center of American immigration to Texas before its fall in the war of Texas independence.

San Jacinto Battleground State Historic Site and Battleship Texas State Historic Site are located 20 miles east of downtown Houston off TX 225 east to TX 134 to PR 1836 in east Harris County. The park is 1,200 acres with a 570-foot-tall monument erected in 1936-1939 in honor of Texans who defeated Mexican Gen. Antonio López de Santa Anna on April 21, 1836, to win Texas' independence from Mexico. The park is original site of Texans' camp acquired in 1883. Subsequent acquisitions made in 1897, 1899 and 1985. Park transferred to TPW in 1965. Park registered as National Historic Landmark. Elevator ride to observation tower near top of monument; museum. Monument known as tallest free-standing concrete structure in the world at the time it was erected. Interpretive trail around battleground. Adjacent to park is the *U.S.S. Texas*, commissioned in 1914. The battleship, the only survivor of the dreadnought class and the only surviving veteran of two world wars, was donated to people of Texas by U.S. Navy. Ship was moored in the Houston Ship Channel at the San Jacinto Battleground on San Jacinto Day, 1948. Extensive repairs were done 1988-1990. Some renovation is on-going, but ship is open for tours. Ship closed Christmas Eve and Christmas Day.

Sea Rim State Park in Jefferson County, 20 miles south of Port Arthur, off TX 87, contains 4,141 acres of marshland and 5.2 miles of Gulf beach shoreline, acquired from private owners in 1972. It is prime wintering area for waterfowl. Wetlands also shelter such wildlife as river otter, nutria, alligator, mink, muskrat. Camping, fishing, swimming; wildlife observation; nature trail; boating. Airboat tours of marsh. Near McFaddin National Wildlife Refuge.

Sebastopol House State Historic Site at 704 Zorn Street in Seguin, Guadalupe County, was acquired by purchase in 1976 from Seguin Conservation Society; approximately 2.2 acres. Built about 1856 by Col. Joshua W. Young of limecrete, concrete made from local gravel and lime, the Greek Revival-style house, which was restored to its 1880 appearance by the TPW, is on National Register of Historic Places. Tours available Friday and Sunday. Also of interest in the area is historic Seguin, founded 1838.

Seminole Canyon State Historic Site in Val Verde County, nine miles west of Comstock off US 90, contains 2,17 acres; acquired by purchase from private owners 1973-1977. Fate Bell Shelter in canyon contains several important prehistoric Indian pictographs. Historic interpretive center. Tours of rock-art sites Wednesday-Sunday; also hiking, mountain biking, camping.

Sheldon Lake State Park and Environmental Learning Center, 2,800 acres in Harris County on Garrett Road two miles east of Beltway 8. Acquired by purchase in

Sebastopol House State Historic Site in Seguin. Photo by Larry D. Moore, CC by SA 3.0./Wikimedia Commons.

1952 from the City of Houston. Freshwater marsh habitat. Activities include nature study, birding, fishing. Wildscape gardens of native plants.

South Llano River State Park, five miles south of Junction in Kimble County off US 377, is a 524-acre site donated to the TPW by a private owner in 1977. Wooded bottomland along the winding South Llano River is the largest and oldest winter roosting site for the Rio Grande turkey in Central Texas. Roosting area closed to visitors October-March. Other animals include wood ducks, javelina, fox, beaver, bobcat and armadillo. Camping, picnicking, tubing, swimming and fishing, hiking, mountain biking.

Starr Family Home State Historic Site, 3.1 acres at 407 W. Travis in Marshall, Harrison County. Greek Revival-style mansion, Maplecroft, built 1870-1871, was home to four generations of Starr family, powerful and economically influential Texans. Two other family homes also in park. Acquired by gift in 1976; additional land donated in 1982. Maplecroft is on National Register of Historic Places. Tours Friday–Sunday or by appointment. Special events during year.

Stephen F. Austin State Park is 663.3 acres along the Brazos River in San Felipe, Austin County, named for the "Father of Texas." The area was deeded by the San Felipe de Austin Corporation and the San Felipe Park Association in 1940. Site of township of San Felipe was seat of government where conventions of 1832 and 1833 and Consultation of 1835 held. These led to Texas Declaration of Independence. San Felipe was home of Stephen F. Austin and other famous early Texans; home of Texas' first Anglo newspaper (the Texas Gazette) founded in 1829; postal system of Texas originated here. Area called "Cradle of Texas Liberty." Museum. Camping, picnicking, golf, fishing, hiking.

Tyler State Park is 985.5 acres found two miles north of IH 20 on FM 14 north of Tyler in Smith County. Includes 64-acre lake. The land was deeded by private owners in 1934–1935. Heavily wooded. Camping, hiking, fishing, boating, lake swimming. Nearby Tyler called Rose Capital of Nation, with Tyler Rose Garden and annual Tyler Rose Festival. Also in Tyler are Caldwell Children's Zoo and Goodman Museum.

Varner-Hogg Plantation State Historic Site is 66 acres in Brazoria County, two miles north of West Columbia on FM 2852. Land originally owned by Martin Varner, a member of Stephen F. Austin's "Old Three Hundred" colony; later was home of Texas governor James Stephen Hogg. Property was deeded to the state in 1957 by Miss Ima Hogg, Gov. Hogg's daughter. First rum distillery in Texas established in 1829 by Varner. Mansion tours Tuesday through Saturday. Also picnicking, fishing.

Village Creek State Park, comprising 1,004 heavily forested acres, is located in Lumberton, Hardin County, ten miles north of Beaumont off US 69 and FM 3513. Purchased in 1979 from private owner, the park contains abundant flora and fauna typical of the Big Thicket area. The 200 species of birds found here include wood ducks, egrets and herons. Activities include fishing, camping, canoeing, swimming, hiking and picnicking. Nearby is the Big Thicket National Preserve.

Walter Umphrey State Park is operated by Jefferson County on the south end of Pleasure Island off TX 82. For RV site reservations, contact SGS Causeway Bait & Tackle, 409-985-4811.

Washington-on-the-Brazos State Historic Site consists of 293.1 acres found seven miles southwest of Navasota in Washington County on TX 105 and FM 1155. Land acquired by deed from private owners in 1916, 1976 and 1996. Park includes the site of the signing on March 2, 1836, of the Texas Declaration of Independence from Mexico, as well as the site of the later signing of the Constitution of the Republic of Texas. In 1842 and 1845, the land included the capitol of the Republic. Star of the Republic Museum. Activities include picnicking and birding. Barrington Living History Farm is the home of Anson Jones, the last president of the Republic of Texas. Activities are guided by entries that Jones made in his daybook while living there. For more information: call 916-878-2214 or email office@wheretexasbecametexas.org.

Zaragoza Birthplace State Historic Site is located across the river from Goliad SP. Gen. Ignacio Zaragoza was the Mexican national hero who led troops in the fight for Mexican independence against the French at historic Battle of Puebla on May 5, 1862. The nearby Zaragoza statue was donated by the people of Puebla, Mexico. Also found nearby is Presidio la Bahía, which was originally constructed in 1721 near Matagorda Bay and moved to the present site in 1749. Adjacent is a memorial monument, marking the common burial site of Col. Fannin and his men, victims of Goliad massacre (1836).

Recreation in State Forests

All Texas State Forests are game sanctuaries with no firearms or hunting allowed. For general information about the Texas State Forests, see page 70 in the Environment chapter.

I.D. Fairchild State Forest

Located in Cherokee County, recreation includes hiking, horseback riding, picnicking, wildlife viewing and biking. Special attractions are a historical fire tower site with plaque, Red Cockaded Woodpecker Management Area and a pond with picnic area. Forest management demonstration sites throughout the forest. There are no restroom facilities in this forest.

Open year-round during daylight hours. Obtain information and maps at the Jacksonville District Office, 1015 SE Looop 456 or call (903) 586-7545 weekdays.

W. Goodrich Jones State Forest

Recreational opportunities in this forest, located in Montgomery County, include bird watching, hiking, horseback riding, picnicking, wildlife viewing and biking.

Special attractions include Sweetleaf Nature Trail with State Champion Sweetleaf Tree, Red Cockaded Woodpecker Management Area, two small lakes with limited fishing and picnicking. Forest management demonstration sites throughout the forest.

Open year-round during daylight hours. Information, maps, permits and restrooms available at the Conroe District Office on FM 1488, 1.5 miles west of I-45. Call (936) 273-2261 for information.

John Henry Kirby Memorial State Forest

Located in Tyler County, forest resource educational opportunities at this forest include demonstrations and nature study. Group education tours available by appointment. Recreational opportunities include hiking, picnicking, bird and wildlife watching. Special attractions are forest management demonstration sites, small picnic area and John Henry Kirby Monument.

Open year-round to foot traffic during daylight hours. Contact the district office prior to entry. Special arrangements are needed for vehicle access. Information and maps can be obtained at the Olive District Office on Hwy. 69 north of Kountze or by calling (409) 246-2484 weekdays. No restroom facilities are available in this forest.

Masterson State Forest

All use of this forest in Jasper County is by reservation only. Group resource education tours are available by appointment. No public facilities are available. Information and maps can be obtained at the Kirbyville District Office, FM 82, 4.5 miles southeast of Kirbyville; call weekdays at (409) 423-2890.

E.O. Siecke State Forest

Recreational opportunities in this Newton County forest include hiking, bird watching, nature study, horseback riding, picnicking and wildlife viewing.

Special attractions are a historic fire tower, the oldest slash pine stand in Texas and a trout creek. Forest management demonstration sites throughout.

Open year-round during daylight hours. Limited access by vehicle. Information, maps and restrooms are available at the Kirbyville District Office, located at the state forest on FM 82, 4.5 miles southeast of Kirbyville. Call (409) 423-2890 weekdays for information. ☆

Recreational Facilities, Corps of Engineers Lakes, 2021

Reservoir	Swim Beaches	Boat Ramps	Picnic Sites	Camp Sites	Group Camping	Rental Cabins
Aquilla		★				
Bardwell	★	★	★	★	★	
Belton	★	★	★	★	★	★
Benbrook	★	★	★	★	★	★
Buffalo Bayou	★		★	★		★
Canyon	★	★	★	★	★	★
Cooper	★	★	★	★	★	★
Georgetown	★	★	★	★	★	
Granger	★	★	★	★	★	
Grapevine	★	★	★	★	★	★
Hords Creek	★	★	★	★	★	
Joe Pool	★	★	★	★		★
Lake O' the Pines	★	★	★	★	★	
Lavon	★	★	★	★	★	
Lewisville	★	★	★	★		★
Navarro Mills	★	★	★	★		
O.C. Fisher		★	★	★		
Pat Mayse		★	★	★		★
Proctor	★	★	★	★	★	
Ray Roberts	★	★	★	★	★	
Sam Rayburn	★	★	★	★	★	★
Somerville	★	★	★	★	★	★
Stillhouse Hollow	★	★	★	★		
Texoma	★	★	★	★	★	★
Town Bluff	★	★	★	★		
Waco	★	★	★	★	★	★
Wallisville		★	★			
Whitney	★	★	★	★	★	★
Wright Patman	★	★	★	★	★	

Source: U.S. Army Corps of Engineers

National Parks, Historic Sites, Recreation Areas

Source: U.S. Dept of Interior, https://www.nps.gov/state/tx/index.htm

Below is a list of facilities and activities that can be enjoyed at Texas' two national parks, a national seashore, a biological preserve, a marine sanctuary, and several historic sites, memorials, and recreation areas in Texas. Most are under supervision of the **U.S. Department of Interior**. Recreational opportunities in the state and national forests and national grasslands in Texas are under the jurisdiction of the **U.S. Department of Agriculture**.

Alibates Flint Quarries National Monument consists of 1,371 acres in Potter County. For more than 10,000 years, pre-Columbian Indians dug agatized limestone from the quarries to make projectile points, knives, scrapers and other tools. The area is presently undeveloped. You may visit the flint quarries on guided walking tours with a park ranger. Tours are at 10:00 a.m. and 2:00 p.m. from Memorial Day to Labor Day. Off-season tours can be arranged by writing to Lake Meredith National Recreation Area, Box 1460, Fritch 79036, or by calling 806-857-3151.

Amistad National Recreation Area is located on the U.S. side of Amistad Reservoir, an international reservoir on the Texas-Mexico border. The 57,292-acre park's attractions include boating, water skiing, swimming, fishing, camping and archaeological sites. If lake level is normal, visitors can see 4000-year-old prehistoric pictographs in Panther and Parida caves, which are accessible only by boat. Check with park before visiting. The area is one of the densest concentrations of Archaic rock art in North America — more than 300 sites. Commercial campgrounds, motels and restaurants nearby. Marinas located at Diablo East and Rough Canyon. Open year round. NPS Administration, 4121 Hwy. 90 W, Del Rio 78840; 830-775-7491.

Big Bend National Park, established in 1944, has spectacular mountain and desert scenery and a variety of unusual geological structures. It is the nation's largest protected area of Chihuahuan Desert. Located in the great bend of the Rio Grande, the 801,000-acre park, which is part of the international boundary between the United States and Mexico, was designated a U.S. Biosphere Reserve in 1976. Hiking, birding and float trips are popular. Numerous campsites are located in park, and the Chisos Mountain Lodge has accommodations for approximately 345 guests. Write for reservations to National Park Concessions, Inc., Big Bend National Park, Texas 79834; 915-477-2291; www.chisosmountainslodge.com. Park open year round; facilities most crowded during spring break. PO Box 129, Big Bend National Park 79834; 915-477-2251.

Big Thicket National Preserve, established in 1974, consists of 15 separate units totalling 97,000 acres of diverse flora and fauna, often nicknamed the "biological crossroads of North America." The preserve, which includes parts of seven East Texas counties, has been designated an "International Biosphere Reserve" by the United Nations Educational, Scientific and Cultural Organization (UNESCO). The preserve includes four different ecological systems: Southeastern swamps, Eastern forests, Central Plains and Southwestern deserts. The visitor information station is located on FM 420, seven miles north of Kountze; phone 409-951-6725. Open daily from 9 a.m. to 5 p.m. Naturalist activities are available by reservation only; reservations are made through the station. Eight trails, ranging in length from one-half mile to 18 miles, visit a variety of forest communities. The two shortest trails are handicapped accessible. Trails are open year round, but flooding may occur after heavy rains. Horses permitted on the Big Sandy Horse Trail only. Boating and canoeing are popular on preserve corridor units. Park headquarters are at 3785 Milam, Beaumont 77701; 409-246-2337.

Chamizal National Memorial, established in 1963 and opened to the public in 1973, stands as a monument to Mexican-American friendship and goodwill. The memorial, on 52 acres in El Paso, commemorates the peaceful settlement on Aug. 29, 1963, of a 99-year-old boundary dispute between the United States and Mexico. Chamizal uses the visual and performing arts as a medium of interchange, helping people better understand not only other cultures but their own, as well. It hosts a variety of programs throughout the year, including: the fall Chamizal Festival musical event; the Siglo de Oro drama festival (early March); the Oñate Historical Festival celebrating the First Thanksgiving (April); and Music Under the Stars (Sundays, June-August). The park has a 1.8-mile walking trail and picnic areas. Phone: 915-532-7273.

El Camino Real de los Tejas was designated a National Historic Trail in 2004. It traces the "royal road" from Mexico to the Red River Valley, established when the area was under Spanish rule. The full route stretched over 2,500 miles, down to Mexico City, and connected to Spanish missions and posts along the way to Los Adaes, the first capital of the Texas province. Today's trail travels many roads, the longest straight route being TX 21 to Hwy 6 in Louisiana, connecting parks, historic sites, and museums along the way. The website, **https://www.nps.gov/elte/index.htm**, has tools to help you plan your trip, and photos and videos to learn more about travelers in the past.

El Camino Real De Tierra Adentro became a National Historic Trail in 2000. This royal road brought travelers from Mexico City through what is now El Paso and north into New Mexico, ending near Santa Fe, which was one of the capitals of New Mexico under Spanish rule. This path takes travelers to historic sites and museums along Interstate 25. Learn more and plan your trip at **https://www.nps.gov/elca/index.htm**.

Flower Garden Banks National Marine Sanctuary was named after the brightly colored sponges, plants, and other marine life found in the area. The reefs were discovered by snapper and grouper fishermen in the early 1900s. Situated 70–115 miles offshore, the sanctuary is only accessible by boat, so divers interested in visiting

Flower Garden Banks National Marine Sanctuary is home to many varieties of coral and other marine life. Photo by NOAA

can book dive charters that depart from numerous Texas ports, including: Galveston, Freeport, Sabine Pass, and Surfside. The sanctuary protects three separate areas: East Flower Garden Bank and West Flower Garden Bank were designed as a sanctuary under the National Marine Sanctuary Act in 1992, and the algal-sponge communities of Stetson Bank were added to the sanctuary in 1996. Exceptional underwater visibility allows divers to experience spectacular sights, such as giant coral heads, schools of fish, eagle and manta rays, and even majestic whale sharks during summer visits to the area. The banks of the sanctuary include more than a dozen moored dive sites, with typical dive profiles of 70–130 feet. Several ports that offer dive trips are also home to commercial fishing charters for anglers wanting to fish the Flower Garden and Stetson banks. Snappers, jacks, barracuda, and wahoo are just a few of the fish commonly caught by sportfishing enthusiasts. On the web: flowergarden.noaa.gov.

Fort Davis National Historic Site in Jeff Davis County was a key post in the West Texas defense system, guarding immigrants and tradesmen on the San Antonio-El Paso road from 1854 to 1891. At one time, Fort Davis was manned by black troops, called "Buffalo Soldiers" (because of their curly hair) who fought with great distinction in the Indian Wars. Henry O. Flipper, the first black graduate of West Point, served at Fort Davis in the early 1880s. The 474-acre historic site is located on the north edge of the town of Fort Davis in the Davis Mountains, the second-highest mountain range in the state. The site includes a museum, an auditorium with daily audio-visual programs, restored and refurnished buildings, picnic area and hiking trails. Open year round except Christmas Day. PO Box 1379, Fort Davis 79734; 915-426-3224.

Guadalupe Mountains National Park, established in 1972, includes 86,416 acres in Hudspeth and Culberson counties. The Park contains one of the most extensive fossil reefs on record. Deep canyons cut through this reef and provide a rare opportunity for geological study. Special points of interest are McKittrick Canyon, a fragile riparian environment, and Guadalupe Peak, the highest in Texas. Camping, hiking on 80 miles of trails, Frijole Ranch Museum, summer amphitheater programs. Orientation, free information and natural history exhibits available at Visitor Center. Open year round. Lodging at Van Horn, Texas, and White's City or Carlsbad, NM. HC 60, Box 400, Salt Flat 79847; 915-828-3251.

Lake Meredith National Recreation Area, 30 miles northeast of Amarillo, centers on a reservoir on the Canadian River, in Moore, Hutchinson and Potter counties. The 50,000-acre recreational area is popular for water-based activities. Boat ramps, picnic areas, unimproved campsites. Commercial lodging and trailer hookups available in nearby towns. Open year round. PO Box 1460, Fritch 79036; 806-857-3151.

Lyndon B. Johnson National Historic Park includes two separate districts 14 miles apart. The Johnson City District comprises the boyhood home of the 36th President of United States and the Johnson Settlement, where his grandparents resided during the late 1800s. The LBJ Ranch District can be visited only by taking the National Park Service bus tour starting at the LBJ State Historic Site. The tour includes the reconstructed LBJ Birthplace, old school, family cemetery, show barn and a view of the Texas White House. Site in Blanco and Gillespie counties was established in 1969, and contains 1,570 acres, 674 of which are federal. Open year round except Thanksgiving, Christmas Day, and New Year's Day. No camping on site; commercial campgrounds, motels in area. PO Box 329, Johnson City 78636; 830-868-7128.

Padre Island National Seashore consists of a 67.5-mile stretch of a barrier island along the Gulf Coast; noted for white-sand beaches, excellent fishing and abundant bird and marine life. Contains 133,000 acres in Kleberg, Willacy and Kenedy counties. Open year round. One paved campground (fee charged) located north of Malaquite Beach; unpaved (primitive) campground area south on beach. Five miles of beach are accessible by regular vehicles; 55 miles are accessible only by 4x4 vehicles. Off-road vehicles prohibited. Camping permitted in two designated areas. Commercial lodging available on the island outside the National Seashore boundaries. PO Box 181300, Corpus Christi 78480; 361-949-8068.

Palo Alto Battlefield National Historic Park preserves the site of the first major battle in the Mexican-American War. Fought on May 8, 1846, near Brownsville, it is recognized for the innovative use of light or "flying" artillery. Participating in the battle were three future presidents: General Zachary Taylor and Ulysses S. Grant on the U.S. side, and Gen. Mariano Arista on the Mexican. Historical markers are located at the junction of Farm-to-Market roads 1847 and 511. Access to the 3,400-acre site is currently limited. Exhibits at the visitors center interpret the battle as well as the causes and consequences of the war. Phone 956-541-2785.

Rio Grande Wild and Scenic River is a 196-mile strip on the U.S. shore of the Rio Grande in the Chihuahuan Desert, beginning in Big Bend National Park and continuing downstream to the Terrell-Val Verde County line. There are federal facilities in Big Bend National Park only. Contact Big Bend National Park for more information.

San Antonio Missions National Historical Park preserves four Spanish Colonial Missions — Concepción, San José, San Juan and Espada — as well as the Espada dam and aqueduct, which are two of the best-preserved remains in the United States of the Spanish Colonial irrigation system, and Rancho de las Cabras, the colonial ranch of Mission Espada. All were crucial elements to Spanish settlement on the Texas frontier. When Franciscan attempts to establish a chain of missions in East Texas in the late 1600s failed, the Spanish Crown ordered three missions transferred to the San Antonio River valley in 1731. The missions are located within the city limits of San Antonio, while Rancho de las Cabras is located 25 miles south in Wilson County near Floresville. The four missions, which are still in use as active parishes, are open to the public from 9 a.m. to 5 p.m. daily except Thanksgiving, Christmas and New Year's. Public roadways connect the sites; a hike-bike trail is being developed. The visitor center for the mission complex is at San José. For more information, write to 2202 Roosevelt Ave., San Antonio 78210; 210-932-1001.

Waco Mammoth National Monument was designated in 2015 and is the newest Texas unit of the National Park System. This paleontological site represents the nation's only recorded discovery of a nursery herd of Columbian mammoths. Visitors can view "in situ" fossils including female mammoths, a bull mammoth, and a camel that lived approximately 67,000 years ago.The park is managed in partnership by the National Park Service, the City of Waco, and Baylor University. Welcome Center located at 6220 Steinbeck Bend Road. It is open Tuesday through Saturday, except Thanksgiving, Christmas Day, and New Year's Day. ☆

National Forests

For general information about the National Forests and National Grasslands, see page 69 in the Environment chapter.

An estimated three million people visit the National Forests in Texas for recreation annually. These visitors use established recreation areas primarily for hiking, picnicking, swimming, fishing, camping, boating and nature enjoyment. In the following list of some of these areas, Forest Service Road is abbreviated FSR:

Angelina National Forest

Boykin Springs, 14 miles southeast of Zavalla, has a 6-acre lake and facilities for hiking, swimming, picnicking, fishing, and camping. Bouton Lake, 14 miles southeast of Zavalla off Texas 63 and FSR 303, has a 9-acre natural lake with primitive facilities for camping, picnicking, and fishing.

Caney Creek on Sam Rayburn Reservoir, ten miles southeast of Zavalla off FM 2743, offers fishing, boating, and camping. Sandy Creek, 15.5 miles east of Zavalla on Sam Rayburn, offers fishing, boating, and camping.

The Sawmill Hiking Trail is 2.5 miles long and winds from Aldridge Sawmill trail head to Boykin Springs Recreation Area.

Davy Crockett National Forest

Ratcliff Lake, 25 miles west of Lufkin on TX 7, is a 45-acre lake with facilities for picnicking, hiking, swimming, boating, fishing, and camping. There is also an amphitheater.

The 20-mile-long 4C National Recreation Trail connects Ratcliff Recreation Area to the Neches Bluff overlook. The Piney Creek Horse Trail is 54 miles long and can be entered approximately 5.5 miles south of Kennard off County Road 4625. There are two horse camps along this trail system.

Sabine National Forest

Indian Mounds Recreation Area, located 12 miles southeast of Hemphill off FM 83, has camping facilities and a boat ramp. Lakeview, on Toledo Bend Reservoir, 21 miles from Pineland, offers camping, hiking, and fishing and can be reached via Texas 87, FM 2928, and FSR 120.

Ragtown, 26 miles southeast of Center and accessible by Texas 87 and Texas 139, County Road 3184, and FSR 132, is also on Toledo Bend and has facilities for hiking, camping, and boating. Red Hill Lake, three miles north of Milam on Texas 87, has facilities for fishing, swimming, camping, and picnicking. Willow Oak Recreation Area on Toledo Bend, 13 miles south of Hemphill off Texas 87, offers fishing, picnicking, camping, and boating. Trail Between the Lakes is 28 miles long from Lakeview Recreation Area on Toledo Bend to U.S. 96 near Sam Rayburn Reservoir.

Sam Houston National Forest

Cagle Recreation Area is located on the shores of Lake Conroe, 50 miles north of Houston and five miles west of I-45 at FM 1375. Cagle offers camping, fishing, hiking, birding, and other recreational opportunities in a forested lakeside setting.

Double Lake, three miles south of Coldspring on FM 2025, has facilities for picnicking, hiking, camping, swimming, and fishing.

Stubblefield Lake, 15 miles west-northwest of New Waverly off Texas 1375 on the shores of Lake Conroe, has facilities for camping, hiking, picnicking, and fishing.

The Lone Star Hiking Trail, approximately 128 miles long, is located in Sam Houston National Forest in Montgomery, Walker, and San Jacinto counties.

National Grasslands

North Texas

Lake Davy Crockett Recreation Area (**Caddo National Grassland**), 12 miles north of Honey Grove (Fannin County) on FM 409, just off FM 100, has a boat-launch ramp and camping sites on a 450-acre lake.

Coffee Mill Lake Recreation Area has camping and picnicking facilities on a 650-acre lake. This area is four miles west of Lake Davy Crockett Recreation Area.

The Caddo Multi-Use Trail system, also four miles west of Lake Crockett, offers camping, hiking, and horseback riding on 35 miles of trails.

Black Creek Lake Recreation Area (**Lyndon B. Johnson National Grassland**) is eight miles north of Decatur (Wise County) and has camping, picnic facilities, and a boat-launch ramp on a 35-acre lake.

Cottonwood Lake, 13 miles north of Decatur, is around 40 acres and offers hiking, boating, and fishing.

The Cottonwood-Black Creek Hiking Trail is four miles long and connects the two lakes. It is rated moderately difficult. There are nearly 75 miles of multipurpose trails that run in the Cottonwood Lake vicinity.

TADRA Horse Trail, ten miles north of Decatur, has camping and 75 miles of horse trails. Restrooms and and parking facilities are available.

West Texas

Lake McClellan (**McClellan Creek National Grassland**) in Gray County and Lake Marvin, which is part of the Black Kettle National Grassland in Hemphill County, receive more than 28,000 recreation visitors annually.

These areas provide camping, picnicking, fishing, birdwatching, and boating facilities. Concessionaires operate facilities at Lake McClellan, and a nominal fee is charged for use of the areas.

At the **Rita Blanca National Grassland** (Dallam County), about 4,500 visitors a year enjoy picnicking and hunting. Thompson Grove Picnic Area is 14 miles northeast of Texline. ☆

The Boykin Springs Recreation Area in Angelina National Forest. Photo by U.S. Forest Service – Southern Region.

A panorama of Palo Duro Canyon State Park. Photo by Jonathan Cutrer, jcutrer.com.

National Natural Landmarks in Texas

Source: National Natural Landmarks Directory, https://www.nps.gov/subjects/nnlandmarks/nation.htm

Twenty Texas natural areas have been listed on the **National Registry of Natural Landmarks**.

The registry was established by the Secretary of the Interior in 1962 to identify and encourage the preservation of geological and ecological features that represent nationally significant examples of the nation's natural heritage.

The registry currently lists a total of 599 national natural landmarks. Below is the list of those landmarks found in Texas, as of August 2019, and their characteristics (year of listing in parentheses).

Attwater Prairie Chicken Preserve: Colorado County, 55 miles west of Houston in the national wildlife refuge, is rejuvenated Gulf Coastal Prairie, which is habitat for Attwater's prairie chickens. (1968)

Bayside Resaca Area: Cameron County, Laguna Atascosa National Wildlife Refuge, 28 miles north of Brownsville. Excellent example of a resaca, supporting coastal salt-marsh vegetation and rare birds. (1980)

Catfish Creek: Anderson County, 20 miles northwest of Palestine, is undisturbed riparian habitat. (1983)

Cave Without a Name: Kendall County, 12 miles northeast of Boerne, is a cave of several rooms that are filled with spectacular formations. (2009)

Caverns of Sonora: Sutton County, 16 miles southwest of Sonora, has unusual geological formations. (1965)

Devil's Sink Hole: Edwards County, 9 miles northeast of Rocksprings, is a deep, bell-shaped, collapsed limestone sink with cave passages extending below the regional water table. (1972)

Dinosaur Valley: Somervell County, in Dinosaur Valley State Park, four miles west of Glen Rose, contains fossil footprints exposed in bed of Paluxy River. (1968)

Enchanted Rock: Gillespie and Llano counties, 12 miles southwest of Oxford, is a classic batholith, composed of coarse-grained pink granite. (1971)

Ezell's Cave: Hays County, within the city limits of San Marcos, houses at least 36 species of cave creatures. (1971)

Fort Worth Nature Center and Refuge: Tarrant County, within the Fort Worth city limits. Contains remnants of the Grand Prairie and a portion of the Cross Timbers, with limestone ledges and marshes. Refuge for migratory birds and other wildlife, and home to 11 buffalo raised by the center's staff. Educational programs offered for youth and adults. Self-guided hiking. (1980)

Greenwood Canyon: Montague County, along a tributary of Braden Branch, is a rich source of Cretaceous fossils. (1975)

High Plains Natural Area: Randall County, Buffalo Lake National Wildlife Refuge, 26 miles southwest of Amarillo, is a grama-buffalo shortgrass area. (1980)

Little Blanco River Bluff: Blanco County, comprises an Edwards Plateau limestone-bluff plant community. (1982)

Longhorn Cavern, Burnet County: 11 miles southwest of Burnet. Formed at least 450 million years ago, cave contains several unusual geologic features. (1971)

Lost Maples State Natural Area: Bandera and Real counties, 61 miles northwest of San Antonio, contains Edwards Plateau fauna and flora, including unusual bigtooth maple. Largest known nesting population of golden-cheeked warbler. (1980)

Muleshoe National Wildlife Refuge: Bailey County, 59 miles northwest of Lubbock, contains playa lakes and typical High Plains shortgrass grama grasslands. (1980)

Natural Bridge Caverns: Comal County, 16 miles west of New Braunfels, is a multilevel cavern system, with beautiful and unusual geological formations. (1971)

Odessa Meteor Crater: Ector County, 10 miles southwest of Odessa, is one of only two known meteor sites in the country. (1965)

Palo Duro Canyon State Park: Armstrong and Randall counties, 22 miles south-southwest of Amarillo. Cut by waters of the Red River, it contains cross-sectional views of sedimentary rocks representing four geological periods. (1976)

Santa Ana National Wildlife Refuge: Hidalgo County, 7 miles south of Alamo, is a lowland forested area with jungle-like vegetation. It is habitat for more than 300 species of birds and some rare mammals. (1966) ☆

The hacienda at Quinta Mazatlan, near McAllen. Photo by Alan Schmierer.

Birding in Texas

World Birding Center

The World Birding Center comprises nine birding education centers and observation sites in the Lower Rio Grande Valley designed to protect wildlife habitat and offer visitors a view of more than 500 species of birds. The center has partnered with the Texas Parks and Wildlife Department, the U.S. Fish and Wildlife Service and nine communities to turn 10,000 acres back into natural areas for birds, butterflies and other wildlife.

This area in Cameron, Hidalgo and Starr counties is a natural migratory path for millions of birds that move between the Americas. The nine WBC sites listed here are situated along the border with Mexico. Learn more at **http://www.theworldbirdingcenter.com/**.

Bentsen–Rio Grande Valley State Park

This is the World Birding Center Headquarters and comprises the 760-acre Bentsen-RGV State Park and 1,700 acres of adjoining federal refuge land near Mission.

The site offers: daily tram service; four nature trails ranging in length from one quarter mile to two miles; 2-story high Hawk Observation Tower with a 210-foot-long handicapped access ramp; 2 observation decks; 2 accessible bird blinds; primitive camping sites (by reservation); rest areas; picnic sites with tables; exhibit hall; park store; coffee bar; meeting room (available for rental); catering kitchen; bike rentals (1 and 2 seat bikes). Access within the park is by foot, bike and tram only; (956) 585-1107.

Hours: 6 a.m. to 10 p.m., seven days a week.

Edinburg Scenic Wetlands

This 40-acre wetlands in Edinburg is an oasis for water-loving birds, butterflies and other wildlife. The site is currently offering:walking trails, nature tours and classes; (956) 381-9922.

Hours: 8 a.m.–5 p.m., Monday through Wednesday; 8 a.m.–6 p.m., Thursday through Saturday. Closed Sunday.

Estero Llano Grande State Park

This 176-acre refuge in Weslaco attracts a wide array of South Texas wildlife with its varied landscape of shallow lake, woodlands and thorn forest; (956) 565-3919.

Hours: 8 a.m.–5 p.m., Monday through Friday; 8 a.m.–7:30 p.m., Saturday and Sunday through August.

Harlingen Arroyo Colorado

This site in Harlingen is connected by an arroyo waterway, as well as hike-and-bike trails meandering through the city, Hugh Ramsey Nature Park to the east and the Harlingen Thicket to the west; (956) 427-8873.

Hours: Office, 8 a.m.–5:00 p.m., Monday through Friday. Nature trails are open seven days a week, sunrise to sunset.

Old Hidalgo Pumphouse

Visitors to this museum in Hidalgo on the Rio Grande can learn about the steam-driven irrigation pumps that transformed Hidalgo County into a year-round farming area. The museum's grounds feature hummingbird gardens, walking trails and historic tours; (956) 843-8686.

Hours: 10 a.m.–5 p.m., Monday through Friday; 1 p.m.–5 p.m., Sunday. Closed Saturday.

Quinta Mazatlan

This 1930s country estate in McAllen is a historic Spanish Revival adobe hacienda surrounded by lush tropical landscaping and native woodland. It is also an urban oasis, where quiet trails wind through more than 15 acres of birding habitat; (956) 688-3370.

Hours: 8 a.m.–5 p.m., Tuesday through Saturday. Open until sunset on Thursdays. Closed Mondays and holidays.

Resaca de la Palma State Park

More than 1,700 acres of newly opened wilderness near Brownsville, this site comprises the largest tract of native habitat in the World Birding Center network. The park offers birding tours and natural history tours. Admission is by appointment and reservation only; (956) 565-3919.

Roma Bluffs

History and nature meet on scenic bluffs above the Rio Grande, where the World Birding Center in Roma is located on the old plaza of a once-thriving steamboat port. Part of a national historic district, the WBC Roma Bluffs includes a riverside nature area of three acres in Starr County. The site offers: walking trails, canoe trips, birding tours, natural history tours and classes; (956) 849-4930.

Hours: 8 a.m.–4 p.m. Tuesday through Saturday, although trails are open seven days a week and are free to the public.

South Padre Island Birding and Nature Center

At the southern tip of the world's longest barrier island, South Padre Island Birding and Nature Center is a slender thread of land between the shallow Laguna Madre and the Gulf of Mexico. This site offers: a nature trail boardwalk and birding tours; 1-800-SOPADRE. Hours: 9 a.m.–5 p.m., seven days a week.

A Tropical Parula found at Quinta Mazatlan. Photo by Alan Schmierer

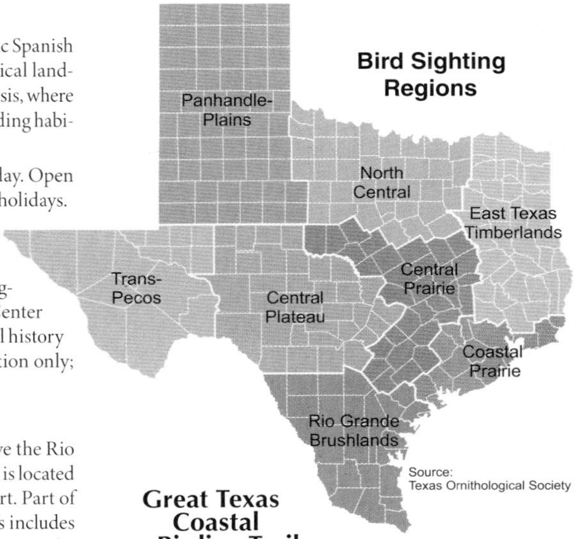

Great Texas Coastal Birding Trail

This trail winds its way through 43 Texas counties along the entire Texas coastal region. The trail was completed in April 2000 and is divided into upper, central, and lower coastal regions. It includes 308 wildlife-viewing sites and such amenities as boardwalks, parking pullouts, kiosks, observation platforms, and landscaping to attract native wildlife.

Color-coded maps are available, and signs mark each site. Trail maps contain information about the birds and habitats likely to be found at each site, the best season to visit, and food and lodging.

For information, contact: Nature Tourism Coordinator, Texas Parks and Wildlife Department, 4200 Smith School Road, Austin, TX 78744; (512) 389-4396.

On the web: **http://tpwd.texas.gov/huntwild/wildlife/wildlife-trails/coastal.**

I-20 Wildlife Preserve and Jenna Welch Nature Study Center

The I-20 Wildlife Preserve is an 87-acre urban playa lake in its natural state in southwest Midland that opened in 2013. It was maintained for many years by the Midland Naturalists and other volunteers, including Jenna Welch, a birding enthusiast and a member of the group. It comprises 3.4 miles of hiking trails, including 1.5 miles of ADA-accessible trails, seven bird observation blinds, four teaching platforms, the 24-foot tall Hawk Observation Platform, and the Merritt Pavilion.

Jenna Welch Nature Study Center operates an educational outreach program to local schools and area colleges and universities. Land was acquired to build a facility to house the nature study center.

The preserve, at 2201 S. Midland Dr., Midland, TX 79701, is open to the public daily from dawn until dusk. For more information, call (432) 853-9453. On the web: **www.i20wildlifepreserve.org**. ☆

A pair of jellyfish drift by at the Texas State Aquarium. Photo by Trac Vu on Unsplash.

Texas State Aquarium

Sources: New Handbook of Texas Online; Texas State Aquarium, https://www.texasstateaquarium.org/

The Texas State Aquarium, 7.3 acres on the southernmost tip of Corpus Christi Beach in Corpus Christi, is operated by the Texas State Aquarium Association, a nonprofit, self-supporting organization established in 1978. Efforts to fund a public aquarium in South Texas began in 1952, and several nonprofit organizations founded over the years eventually grew into the Texas State Aquarium Association.

Since 1978, the association has raised more than $28 million in private and public funding to build and operate of the aquarium. Corpus Christi provided $14.5 million, including $4 million from a bond issue.

In 1985, the 69th Texas Legislature declared the project the "Official Aquarium of the State of Texas."

The Jesse H. and Mary Gibbs Jones Gulf of Mexico Exhibit Building was completed in July 1990. In 2003, Dolphin Bay opened for Atlantic bottlenose dolphins and the Environmental Discovery Center opened, featuring a library, a Family Learning Center, and the Flint Hills Resources Distance Learning Studio.

The aquarium's exhibits and research focus on the plants and animals of the Gulf of Mexico and the Caribbean. It is the first U.S. facility to do so.

The aquarium is open daily 9 a.m. to 5 p.m., Labor Day through March 1, and until 6 p.m. March 1 through Labor Day. There are admission and parking fees.

For more information, call 1-800-477-GULF. ☆

Sea Center Texas

Source: Texas Parks and Wildlife Department, https://tpwd.texas.gov/fishing/sea-center-texas/

The Texas Parks and Wildlife Department operates Sea Center Texas: a marine aquarium, fish hatchery, and nature center that educates and entertains visitors. It is located in Lake Jackson, 50 miles south of Houston, off of Texas 288.

The visitor center opened in 1996 and has interpretive displays, a "touch tank," and native Texas habitat exhibits depicting a salt marsh, bay, jetty, reef, and open Gulf waters. The Gulf aquarium features "Cooper," a 50-pound grouper; a green moray eel; a nurse shark; and other offshore species.

Sea Center is said to be the world's largest redfish hatchery and is one of three marine hatcheries on the Texas coast that produces juvenile red drum and spotted seatrout for enhancing natural populations in Texas bays. The hatchery can produce 15 million juvenile fish yearly and is a testing ground for production of other marine species, such as flounder. Hatchery tours and educational programs are available by reservation.

A half-acre youth fishing pond introduces youngsters to saltwater fishing through scheduled activities. The pond is handicap accessible, and stocked with a variety of marine fish.

The center's wetland area is part of the Great Texas Coastal Birding Trail, where more than 150 species of birds have been identified. They include one acre of salt marsh and three acres of freshwater marsh. Damselflies, dragonflies, butterflies, turtles, and frogs can be sighted off the boardwalk, and an outdoor pavilion is adjacent to butterfly and hummingbird gardens.

Sea Center Texas is operated in partnership with The Dow Chemical Company and the Coastal Conservation Association. Admission and parking are free. Hours are 9 a.m. to 4 p.m. Tuesday through Saturday, and 1 p.m. to 4 p.m. Sunday, except some holidays. Reservations are required for group tours, nature tours, and hatchery tours. For more information; (979) 292-0100 or email: Seacenter@tpwd.texas.gov. ☆

Fairs, Festivals, and Special Events

Fairs, festivals, and other special events provide year-round recreation in Texas. Some are of national interest, while many attract visitors from across the state. Each county profile in the Counties section also lists events in the Recreation paragraph and following town names. Information here was furnished by event coordinators.

To have your town's event included here, submit your information in the form at:

www.TexasAlmanac.com/ListOurEvent

Abilene: West Texas Fair & Rodeo; September; 1700 Hwy. 36, 79602; www.taylorcountyexpocenter.com. Since 1897. rjohnson@expoctc.com. (325) 677-4376.

Albany: Fort Griffin Fandangle; June; PO Box 155, 76430; www.fortgriffinfandangle.org. Since 1938. info@fandangle.org. (325) 762-3838.

Alvarado: Johnson County Pioneers & Old Settlers Reunion; August; PO Box 217, 76009. Since 1893.

Amarillo: Tri-State Fair; September; 3301 SE 10th Ave.,79104; www.tristatefair.com. (806) 376-7767.

Anderson: Grimes County Fair; June; PO Box 435, 77830; www.grimescountyfair.com. (936)825-5995.

Angleton: Brazoria County Fair; October; PO Box 818, 77516; www.bcfa.org. Since 1939. (979) 849-6416.

Aransas Pass: Shrimporee; June, 130 W. Goodnight, 78336; www.aransaspass.org. Since 1949.

Athens: Texas Fiddlers' Asso. Reunion; May; Since 1932.

Austin: Rodeo Austin; March; 9100 Decker Lake Rd. 78724; www.rodeoaustin.com. Since 1937. Info@rodeoaustin.com. (512) 919-3000.

Austin: Art City Austin; April; PO Box 5705, 78763; www.artcityaustin.org. info@artcityaustin.org. (512) 609.8587.

Bay City: Matagorda County Fair & Livestock Show; February; PO Box 1803, 77404; www.matagordacountyfair.com. Since 1945. mcfa@matagordacountyfair.com. (979) 245-2454.

Bay City: Bay City Rice Festival; September; PO Box 867; 77404; www.baycitylions.org. info@baycitylions.com.

Beaumont: South Texas State Fair; October; 7250 Wespark Cr., 77705; www.ymbl.org. Since 1943. info@ymbl.org. (409) 832-9991.

Bellville: Austin County Fair; October; PO Box 141, 77418; www.austincountyfair.com. ACFair@austincountyfair.com. (979) 865-5995.

Belton: 4th of July Celebration & PRCA Rodeo; July; PO Box 659, 76513; www.rodeobelton.com. (254) 939.3551.

Belton: Central Texas State Fair; Aug.-Sept.; PO Box 206, 76513; www.centraltexasstatefair.com. (254) 933-5353.

Big Spring: Howard County Fair; September; PO Box 2356, 79721; www.hcfair.org. Since 1973. howardcountyfairtx@gmail.com.

Boerne: Boerne Berges Fest; June; PO Box 748, 78006; www.bergesfest.com.

Boerne: Kendall County Fair; September (Labor Day Wknd.); PO Box 954, 78006; www.kcfa.org. Since 1906. info@kfca.org. (830) 249-2839.

Brenham: Washington County Fair; September; 1305 E. Blue Bell Rd., 77833; www.washingtoncofair.com. Since 1870. washingtoncofair@sbcglobal.net. (979) 836.4112.

Brownsville: Charro Days Fiesta; February; PO Box 3247, 78523; www.charrodaysfiesta.com. Since 1938. charrodaysfiesta@sbcglobal.net. (956) 542-4245.

Burnet: Burnet Bluebonnet Festival; April; 101 N Pierce St, 78611; bluebonnetfestival.org. Since 1986. (512) 756-4297.

Burton: Cotton Gin Festival; April (3rd wknd.); PO Box 98; 77835; www.cottonginmuseum.org. Since 1990. texascottongin@gmail.com. (979) 289-3378.

Caldwell: Kolache Festival; September; 301 N. Main Street; www.burlesoncountytx.com. 77836; (979) 567-0000.

Caldwell: Burleson County Fair; September; PO Box 634, 77836; www.burlesoncountytx.com. (979) 567-3938.

Canyon: TEXAS! Outdoor Musical; June–August; 1514 5th Ave., 79015; www.texas-show.com. Since 1966. info@texas-show.com. (806) 655-2181.

Chappell Hill: Bluebonnet Festival; April; PO Box 547, 77426; chappellhillhistoricalsociety.com. chappellhillfestivals@gmail.com. (979) 203-1242

Clifton: Norse Smorgasbord; November; 152 County Rd. 4145, 76634; www.oursaviorsnorse.org. oslcnorse1869@gmail.com. (254) 675-3962.

Clute: Great Texas Mosquito Festival; July; 100 Parkview Dr., 77531; www.mosquitofestival.com. Since 1981. (979) 265-8392.

Columbus: Colorado County Fair; September; PO Box 506, 78933; www.coloradocountyfair.org. info@coloradocountyfair.org. (979) 732-9266

Conroe: Montgomery County Fair; March; PO Box 869, 77305; www.mcfa.org. Since 1957. (936) 760-3631.

Corpus Christi: Buc Days; April–May; PO Box 30404, 78463; www.bucdays.com. info@bucdays.com. (361) 882.3242.

Corsicana: Derrick Days; April; 301 S Beaton St., 75110; www.derrickdays.com. Since 1976. (903) 654-4850

Dalhart: XIT Rodeo & Reunion; August (1st full wknd.); www.xitrodeoreunion.com. Since 1937.

Dallas: State Fair of Texas; September–October; PO Box 150009, 75315; www.bigtex.com. Since 1886. info@bigtex.com. (214) 565-9931.

Decatur: Wise County Old Settlers Reunion; July (last full week).

De Leon: De Leon Peach & Melon Festival; August; PO Box 44, 76444; peachandmelonfestival.net. Since 1917. pmdeleon@cctc.net.

The carnival at the San Angelo Rodeo. Photo by Jonathan Cutrer, jcutrer.com.

Denton: North Texas State Fair & Rodeo; August; 2217 N. Carroll Blvd., 76201; www.ntfair.com. Since 1929. info@ntfair.com. (940) 391-3452.

Edna: Jackson County Youth Fair; October; 284 Brackenridge Parkway, 77957; www.jcyf.org. Since 1949.

Ennis: National Polka Festival; May; PO Box 1177, 75120-1237; www.nationalpolkafestival.com. ennis4u@swbell.net.

Fairfield: Freestone County Fair; June; www.freestone-countyfairandrodeo.com.

Flatonia: Czhilispiel; October (4th full wknd.); PO Box 610, 78941; www.flatoniachamber.com. Since 1973. flatonia-cofc@sbcglobal.net. (361) 865-3920.

Fort Worth: Pioneer Days; September; 131 E. Exchange Ave., Ste 100B, 76106; www.fortworthstockyards.org.

Fort Worth: Southwestern Exposition & Livestock Show; January-February; PO Box 150, 76101; www.fwssr.com. Since 1896. contact@fwssr.com. (817) 877-2400.

Fredericksburg: Food and Wine Fest; October (4th Sat.); 703 North Llano Street, 78624; www.fbgfoodandwine-fest.com. Since 1990. creativemarketing1975@gmail.com. (830) 997-8515.

Fredericksburg: Night in Old Fredericksburg; July; 302 E. Austin, 78624; www.gillespiefair.net. Since 1963. info@gillespiefair.com. (830) 997-2359.

Fredericksburg: Oktoberfest; October (1st wknd.); PO Box 222, 78624; www.oktoberfestinfbg.com. Since 1980. creativemarketing1975@gmail.com. (830) 997-4810.

Freer: Freer Rattlesnake Roundup; May; PO Box 717, 78357; www.therattlesnakeroundup.com. Since 1966. freercofc@yahoo.com. (361) 394-6891.

Galveston: Dickens on The Strand; December; 502 20th St., 77550; www.dickensonthestrand.org. Since 1973.

Galveston: Galveston Historic Homes Tour; May; 502 20th St., 77550-2014; www.galvestonhistory.org. Since 1974.

Gilmer: East Texas Yamboree; October; PO Box 854, 75644; www.yamboree.com. Since 1937. gilmerareachamber@gmail.com. (903) 843-2413.

Glen Flora: Wharton County Youth Fair; April; PO Box 167, 77443; www.whartoncountyyouthfair.org. Since 1976. wcyf@whartoncountyyouthfair.org. (979) 677-3350.

Graham: Art Splash on the Square; May.

Graham: Red, White & You Parade & Festivities; July; 608 Elm St.; 76450; www.visitgrahamtexas.com. (940) 549-0401.

Granbury: Annual July 4th Celebration; July; 116 W. Bridge St., 76048; www.granburychamber.com.

Granbury: Harvest Moon Festival; October; PO Box 2011 201 E. Pearl St., 76048; www.granburysquare.com. Since 1977. granburyhgma@gmail.com. (682) 936-4550.

Grand Prairie: National Championship Pow-Wow; September; 2602 Mayfield Rd, 75052; www.tradersvil-lage.com. Since 1963. dfwinfo@tradersvillage.com. (972) 647-2331.

Grapevine: GrapeFest; September; 636 S. Main St., 76051; www.grapevinetexasusa.com. Since 1986. (800) 457-6338

Greenville: Hunt County Fair; June; PO Box 1403, 75403; www.huntcountyfair.com. Since 1970. info@huntcoun-tyfair.net. (903) 454.1503.

Groesbeck: Limestone County Fair; March–April; PO Box 965, 76642. limestonefair.org.

Hallettsville: Hallettsville Kolache Fest; September; PO Box 313, 77964; www.hallettsville.com. Since 1995.

Helotes: Helotes Cornyval; May (1st wknd.); PO Box 376, 78023; www.cornyval.com. Since 1967. cornyval@sbcglobal.net. (210) 695-2103.

Hempstead: Waller County Fair; September–October; PO Box 911, 77445. www.wallercountyfair.com. Since 1946. (979) 826-2825.

Hico: Hico Old Settler Reunion; July; PO Box 93, 76457; www.hico-tx.com. Since 1887.

Hidalgo: BorderFest; March; PO Box 722; 78557; www.hidalgoborderfest.com.

Hondo: Medina County Fair; September (3rd wknd.); PO Box 4, 78861; www.medinacountyfair.net. Since 1980. havefun@medinacountyfair.net. (830) 426-5406.

Houston: Houston Livestock Show and Rodeo; March; PO Box 20070, 77225; www.rodeohouston.com. questions@rodeohouston.com. (832) 667-1134

Hughes Springs: Wildflower Trails of Texas; April; PO Box 805, 75656; www.hughesspringstxusa.com Since 1970. (903) 639-7519

Huntsville: Walker County Fair & Rodeo; March–April; PO Box 1817, 77342; www.walkercountyfair.com. Since 1979. wcfa@walkercountyfair.com. (936) 291-8763

Ingram: The Official Texas State Arts & Crafts Fair; September; PO Box 489, 78025; txartsandcraftsfair.com. wgcash@hcaf.com. (830) 367-5121.

Jefferson: Historical Pilgrimage and Spring Festival; May (1st wknd.); PO Box 301, 75657-0301; www.jeffersonpilgrimage.com. Since 1947.

Johnson City: Blanco County Fair; August; PO Box 1257, 78636; www.bcfra.org. info@bcfra.org.

Kenedy: Bluebonnet Days; April; 205 South 2nd St., 78119. kenedychamber.org. (830) 583-3223.

Kerrville: Kerr County Fair; October; PO Box 290842, 78029; www.kerrcountyfair.com. Since 1980. kcfa@kerrcountyfair.com. (830) 257-6833.

Kerrville: Kerrville Folk Festival; May–June; PO Box 291466, 78029; www.kerrvillefolkfestival.com. Since 1972. info@kerrville-music.com. (830) 257-3600.

Killeen: Take 190 WestArts Festival; 3601 S. WS Young Dr., 76542; www.take190west.com. info@take190west.com. (254) 501-3888

LaGrange: Fayette County Fair; September; PO Box 544, 78945; www.fayettecountyfairnet. Since 1926. info@fayettecountyfair.org. (979) 968-3911.

Laredo: Border Olympics; January–March; PO Box 450037, 78044; borderolympics.net. Since 1947.

Laredo: Laredo International Fair & Expo; March; PO Box 1770, 78043; www.laredofair.com. Since 1963. laredofair@att.net. (956) 722-9948

Laredo: Washington's Birthday Celebration; January–February; 1819 E. Hillside Rd., 78041; www.wbcalaredo.com. Since 1898. wbca@wbcalaredo.org. (956) 722-0589

Longview: Gregg County Fair & Exposition; September; 1511 Judson Rd., Ste. F, 75601; www.greggcountyfair.com. Since 1951. ayohe3184@gmail.com. (903) 753-4478.

Lubbock: 4th on Broadway Festival; July; PO Box 1643, 79408; www.broadwayfestivals.com. Since 1991. (806) 749.2929.

Lubbock: Lights on Broadway Celebration; December; PO Box 1643, 79408; www.broadwayfestivals.com.

Lubbock: Panhandle-South Plains Fair; September; PO Box 208, 79408; www.southplainsfair.com. Since 1914. info@southplainsfair.com. (806) 763-2833.

Lufkin: Texas Forest Festival; September; 1200 Ellen Trout Dr., 75904; www.texasforestfestival.com. (936) 634.6644.

Luling: Luling Watermelon Thump; June (last full wknd); PO Box 710, 78648; www.watermelonthump.com. Since 1953.

McKinney: Texas Scottish Festival & Highland Games; May; 1705 West University Drive, Suite 108 - 110, 75069; www.texasscots.com.com. Since 1986. postmaster@texas-scottishfestival.com. (469) 424.1930

Marshall: Fire Ant Festival; October; PO Box 520, 75671; www.marshalltexas.com. Since 1984.

Marshall: Stagecoach Days Festival; May; PO Box 520, 75671; www.marshalltexas.com. Since 1973.

Marshall: Wonderland of Lights; November–December; PO Box 520, 75671; www.marshalltxchamber.com.

Mercedes: Rio Grande Valley Livestock Show; March; 1000 N. Texas; www.rgvls.com. Since 1940. info@rgvls.com. (956) 565-2456.

Mesquite: Mesquite Championship Rodeo; April–September (each Fri. & Sat.); 1818 Rodeo Dr, 75149-3800; www.mesquiterodeo.com. Since 1957. info@ mesquiterodeo.com. (972) 285-8777.

Monahans: Butterfield-Overland Stage Coach and Wagon Festival; July; 401 S. Dwight Ave., 79756; www.monahans.org. Since 1994. chamber@monahans.org.

Mount Pleasant: Titus County Fair; September; PO Box 1232, 75456; www.tituscountyfair.com. Since 1975. info@tituscountyfair.com.

Nacogdoches: Piney Woods Fair; October; 3805 NW Stallings Dr., 75964; www.nacexpo.net. Since 1978. nacexpo@co.nacogdoches.tx.us. (936) 564-0849.

Nederland: Nederland Heritage Festival; March; PO Box 1176, 77627; www.nederlandhf.org. Since 1973. (409) 724-2269.

New Braunfels: Comal County Fair; September; PO Box 310223, 78131; www.comalcountyfair.org. Since 1894. ccfa.nbtx@sbcglobal.net. (830) 625.1505.

New Braunfels: Wurstfest; October–November; PO Box 310309, 78131; www.wurstfest.com. info@ wurstfest.com. (830) 625-9167.

Odessa: Permian Basin Fair & Expo; September; 218 W. 46th St., 79764; www.pbfair.com.

Palestine: Dogwood Trails Festival; March–April; PO Box 2828, 75802-2828; www.visitpalestine.com.

Paris: Red River Valley Fair; August–September; 570 E. Center St., 75460; www.paristx-rrvfair.com. Since 1911. rrvfair@suddenlinkmail.com. (903) 785-7971.

Pasadena: Pasadena Livestock Show & Rodeo; September–October; 7601 Red Bluff Rd., 77507-1035; www.pasadenarodeo.com. contactus@ pasadenarodeo.com. (281) 487-0240.

Port Aransas: Whooping Crane Festival; February (last weekend); 403 West Cotter, 78373; www.whoopingcranefestival.org. Since 1996. (361) 749-5919.

Port Arthur: cavOILcade; October; PO Box 2336, 77643; www.cavoilcade.portarthur.com. Since 1953. cavoilcade@portarthur.com. (409) 983-1009.

Port Lavaca: Calhoun County Fair; October (3rd wknd.); PO Box 42, 77979; http://www.calcofair.com Since 1963. calcofair77979@gmail.com. (361) 250-0930.

Poteet: Poteet Strawberry Festival; April; PO Box 227, 78065; www.strawberryfestival.com. Since 1948. info@strawberryfestival.com. (830) 742-8144.

Refugio: Refugio County Fair & Rodeo & Livestock Show; March; PO Box 88, 78377. Since 1961.

Rio Grande City: Starr County Fair; March (1st full wknd.); PO Box 841, 78582; www.starrcountyfair.com. Since 1961. starrcountyfair@aol.com. (956) 488-0122.

Rosenberg: Fort Bend County Fair; September–October; PO Box 428, 77471; www.fortbendcountyfair.com. Since 1937. info@fbcfa.org. (281) 342-6171.

Salado: Salado Scottish Games and Competitions; November (2nd wknd); 423 S. Main St.; www.saladomuseum.org. office@saladomuseum.org. (254) 947-5232.

San Angelo: San Angelo Stock Show & Rodeo; February; 200 W 43rd St., 76903; www.sanangelorodeo.com. Since 1932. (325)653-7785.

San Antonio: Fiesta San Antonio; April; 2611 Broadway St.; 78215; www.fiesta-sa.org. Since 1891. info@fiesta-sa.org. (210) 227-5191.

San Antonio: Texas Folklife Festival; June; 801 E. Cesar E. Chavez Blvd., 78205; www.texasfolklifefestival.org. Since 1972. itcweb@utsa.edu. (210) 458-2300.

Sanderson: Cinco de Mayo Celebration; May; PO Box 598, 79848; www.sandersonchamber.com. sandersonchamber@yahoo.com. (432) 345-3331.

Sanderson: 4th of July Celebration; July; PO Box 598, 79848; www.sandersonchamber.com. Since 1908. sandersonchamber@yahoo.com. (432) 345-3331.

Sanderson: Pachanga!; November; July; PO Box 598, 79848; www.sandersonchamber.com. Since 2001. sandersonchamber@yahoo.com. (432) 345-3331.

Santa Fe: Galveston County Fair & Rodeo; April; PO Box 889, 77510; www.galvestoncountyfair.com. (409) 986-6010

Schulenburg: Schulenburg Festival; August (1st full wknd.); PO Box 115; 78956; www.schulenburgfestival.com. Since 1976.

Shamrock: St. Patrick's Day Celebration; March; 207 N. Main St., 79079. www.shamrocktexas.net. Since 1947. shamrockedc@gmail.com. (806) 256-2516.

Stamford: Texas Cowboy Reunion; July; PO Box 928, 79553; www.texascowboyreunion.com. Since 1933. tcrrodeo@gmail.com

Sulphur Springs: Hopkins County Fall Festival; September; 125 S. Davis St., 75482. www.sulphurspringstx.org. hopkinscountyfallfestival@gmail. (903) 243-1925.

Sweetwater: Rattlesnake Roundup; March; PO Box 416, 79556; www.rattlesnakeroundup.net. Since 1958.

Terlingua: Terlingua International Chili Championship; November; PO Box 39, 79852; www.casichili.net. Since 1947.

Texarkana: Four States Fair; September; 3700 E. 50th St., Texarkana AR, 75504; www.fourstatesfair.com. (870) 773-2941.

Todd Mission: Texas Renaissance Festival; October–November (8 weekends); 21778 FM 1774, 77363; www.texrenfest.com. Since 1975. info@texasrenfest.com. (800) 458-3435.

Tyler: East Texas State Fair; September; 2112 W. Front St., 75702; www.etstatefair.com. Since 1914. info@etstatefair.com. (903) 597-2501.

Tyler: Texas Rose Festival; Ocober (3rd wknd.); PO Box 8224, 75711; www.texasrosefestival.com. Since 1933. (903) 597-3130.

Waco: Heart O' Texas Fair & Rodeo; October; 4601 Bosque Blvd.; 76710; www.hotfair.com. Since 1954. (254) 776-1660.

Waxahachie: Gingerbread Trail Tour of Homes; June (1st full wknd); PO Box 706, 75168; www.-rootsweb.com/~txecm/ginger. Since 1969.

Waxahachie: Scarborough Renaissance Festival; April–May; PO Box 538, 75168; www.srfestival.com. Since 1980. (972) 938-3247.

Weatherford: Parker County Peach Festival; July (2nd Sat.); PO Box 310, 76086; www.parkercountypeachfestival.org. Since 1985. info@weatherford-chamber.com. (817) 596-3801.

Weatherford: Christmas on the Square; December; PO Box 310, 76086; www.weatherford-chamber.com. Since 1988.

West: Westfest; September (Labor Day wknd.); PO Box 65, 76691; www.westfest.com. Since 1976. (254) 826-5058

Winnsboro: Autumn Trails Festival; October (every wkend.); PO Box 464, 75494; www.winnsboroautumntrails.com. winnsboroautumntrails@gmail.com. (903) 342-1958.

Woodville: Tyler County Dogwood Festival; March–April; PO Box 2151, 75979-2151; www.tylercountydogwoodfestival.org. Since 1944. dogwood_festival@yahoo.com. (409) 283-2632.

Yorktown: Yorktown's Annual Western Days Celebration; October (3rd full wknd.); PO Box 488, 78164; www.yorktowntx.com. Since 1959. westerndays@yorktowntx.com. (361)564.2611. ☆

A kayak angler caught this Guadalupe Bass as part of the Habitat and Angler Access Program with Texas Parks and Wildlife. Photo by Texas Parks and Wildlife.

Hunting and Fishing

Source: Texas Parks and Wildlife Department; http://tpwd.texas.gov

The popularity of hunting and fishing in Texas cannot be denied. Just ask the Texas Parks and Wildlife Department — which should probably be the place you start, because that's where you can find all of the current hunting and fishing regulations for the state.

According to the 2018 State of Texas Annual Cash Report, public hunting, fishing and other participation fees (including sales of hunting and fishing licenses) brought in revenues of $106,511,841.49 in 2017 and $103,447,864.28 in 2018.

Hunting Licenses

A **hunting license** is required of Texas residents and non-residents who hunt any legal bird or animal. Hunting licenses and endorsements are valid during the period Sept. 1 through the following Aug. 31 of each year, except licenses issued for a specific number of days or time periods.

A hunting license (except the non-resident special hunting license and non-resident 5-day special hunting license) is valid for taking all legal species of wildlife in Texas including deer, turkey, javelina, antelope, aoudad (sheep), alligator, and all small game and migratory game birds. Endorsement and tag requirements apply.

A trapper's license is required for all persons to hunt, shoot, or take for sale those species classified as fur-bearing animals or their pelts.

In addition to a valid hunting license:

- An **Archery Endorsement** is required to hunt deer or turkey during Archery-Only open season.
- An **Upland Game Bird Endorsement** is required to hunt turkey, pheasant, quail, or chachalaca. Non-residents who purchase the non-resident spring turkey license are exempt from this endorsement requirement.
- A **Migratory Game Bird Endorsement** and **HIP (Harvest Information Program) Certification** is required to hunt any migratory game birds, including waterfowl, coot, rail, gallinule, snipe, dove, sandhill crane, and woodcock.
- A valid **Federal Duck Stamp** is required of waterfowl hunters age 16 or older.

On the web, information from TPWD on hunting can be found at:**tpwd.texas.gov/huntwild/hunt/**

Hunting and Fishing Licenses Sold

2019	**Volume**
Hunting Licenses	477,399
Fishing Licenses	1,276,384
Combined Licenses	614,877
TOTALS	**2,368,660**
2020*	**Volume**
Hunting Licenses	465,331
Fishing Licenses	1,539,576
Combined Licenses	624,196
TOTALS	**2,629,103**

* Volumes for 2020 are estimated.

Source: 2022–23 Legislative Appropriation Request, TPWD

Game Harvest Estimates

The TPWD conducts random surveys of hunters every year to create estimates of hunter and harvest trends in two categories: small game (23 species total, birds and small mammals), and big game (white-tailed deer, mule deer, and javelina). They collect data not just on what animals were hunted, but also where, and how. You can learn about the methodology and see the full results of these surveys on the web at: **https://tpwd.texas.gov/publications/huntwild/hunt**

2019–2020 Wildlife Game Harvest

Game	Hunters	Harvest Estimates
Dove, combined*	292,346	6,881,986
Duck	82,134	1,085,509
Gallinule	0	0
Goose	11,994	51,891
Pheasant	9,329	20,065
Quail, combined**	39,669	383,829
Rabbit	35,209	168,156
Rail	491	4,339
Snipe	1,948	4,424
Squirrel	44,870	333,094
Teal	23,584	212,392
Turkey (fall and spring)	57,844	27,979
Woodcock	1,144	2,354
White-tailed Deer	791,619	846,330
Mule Deer	36,250	15,201
Javalina	40,632	35,505

*Dove, combined includes the following species: Eurasian, mourning, white-tipped, and white-winged.
**Quail, combined includes the following species: bobwhite and scaled.
Source: TPWD Game Harvest Surveys

Fishing Licenses

All fishing licenses and endorsements are valid only from Sept. 1 through the following Aug. 31, except licenses issued for a specific number of days or time periods. If you own any valid freshwater fishing package, you will be able to purchase a saltwater stamp and also fish saltwater.

If you own any valid saltwater fishing package, you will be able to purchase a freshwater stamp and also fish freshwater. An all-water fishing package is available that enables anglers to fish both fresh- and saltwater.

Detailed information concerning licenses, endorsements, seasons, and regulations can be obtained from Texas Parks and Wildlife Department, 4200 Smith School Road, Austin 78744, (800) 792-1112 or (512) 389-4820; or on the web at: **tpwd.texas.gov/business/licenses**

Freshwater Fishing

Freshwater fishing in Texas is an activity enjoyed by an estimated 1.21 million recreational anglers. In 2015, these anglers contributed an economic output of approximately $96 million to the Texas economy.

Among the 268 species of freshwater fish in Texas, the most popular fish for recreational fishing are: **largemouth bass, catfish, crappie, and striped, white, and hybrid striped bass**.

Texas anglers can fish in approximately 1,100 public reservoirs and about 191,000 miles of rivers and streams, together totaling 1.7 million acres.

The Texas Parks and Wildlife Department operates field stations, fish hatcheries, and research facilities to support the conservation and management of fishery resources. The hatcheries operated by TPWD raise largemouth and smallmouth bass, as well as catfish, striped and hybrid striped bass, and sunfish.

TPWD has continued its programs of stocking fish in public waters to increase angling opportunities. Many conservation-minded anglers who desire continued quality fishing practice catch-and-release fishing.

Texas Freshwater Fisheries Center

The Texas Freshwater Fisheries Center in Athens, about 75 miles southeast of Dallas, is an $18-million hatchery and educational center, where visitors can learn about underwater life.

The interactive Visitors Center includes aquarium displays of fish in their natural environment. Visitors get an "eye-to-eye" view of three authentically designed Texas freshwater habitats: a Hill Country stream, an East Texas pond, and a reservoir. A marsh exhibit features live American alligators.

A casting pond stocked with rainbow trout in the winter and catfish year-around provides a place for visitors to learn how to bait a hook, cast a line, and land a fish. The center has conference facilities and hosts groups by appointment.

The Texas Freshwater Fisheries Center is open Tuesday through Saturday, 9 a.m. to 4 p.m., and Sunday, 1 p.m. to 4 p.m. It is closed on Monday. Admission is charged. The center is located 4.5 miles east of Athens on FM 2495 at Lake Athens. Address: 5550 FM 2495, Athens 75752, or call (903) 676-2277. For more information, visit: **https://tpwd.texas.gov/spdest/visitorcenters/tffc/.**

Saltwater Fishing

According to the most recent report available, Texas has about 672,000 saltwater anglers (16 years old and older) who spend an estimated $1.1 billion annually on fishing-related expenditures. In 2013, anglers harvested 1.74 million fish from both Texas bays and the Gulf of Mexico off Texas.

The most popular saltwater sport fish in Texas bays are **spotted seatrout, sand seatrout, Atlantic croaker, red drum, southern flounder, black drum, sheepshead, and gafftopsail catfish**.

Offshore, some of the fish that anglers target are **red snapper, king mackerel, Spanish mackerel, dolphinfish, cobia, tarpon, and yellowfin tuna.** ☆

Learn more about the fish found in Texas in our expanded wildlife section, starting on page 75.

For information about commercial fishing, see page 621 in the Business chapter.

Sports

HIGH SCHOOL CHAMPIONS

COLLEGE CHAMPIONS

PROFESSIONAL SPORTS TEAMS

HALL OF FAME & OLYMPIC MEDALISTS

Westlake Chaparrals face off against the Steele Knights at the UIL quarterfinals for high school football at Kelly Reeves Athletic Complex in Round Rock on January 2, 2021. Photo by Ralph Arvesen/Flickr (CC)

Liberty Hill Panthers face the Rouse Raiders in the 5A Division II regional semifinals at Kelly Reeves Athletic Complex in Round Rock, Texas, on December 26, 2020. Photographer/ Photo by Ralph Arvesen/ Flickr (CC).

Texas Sports and the COVID-19 Pandemic

Reporting by A.J. Smuskiewicz

The COVID-19 pandemic, caused by the SARS-CoV-2 coronavirus, had a major impact on sports in Texas through 2020 and 2021. Texas, under the leadership of Republican governor Greg Abbott, maintained looser restrictions on sports, schools, and other public gatherings compared with most other states, and lifted those restrictions sooner.

Many public health experts disagreed with Governor Abbott's policies, maintaining that they would worsen the crisis. [1] Abbott defended his efforts to "reopen Texas," citing the importance of school activities to the social and emotional health of students, as well as the economic and social importance of sports and other businesses. He also argued that the state maintained sufficient safety protocols to keep the spread of the virus under control. [2]

Pandemic-Related Closings

As the pandemic spread in early 2020, most professional, amateur, and school sports throughout the United States were shut down, closed to in-person spectators, or otherwise altered to slow the spread of the virus. In Texas, most school sports were shut down by the schools themselves in early 2020. [3] If school games were played, no fans were allowed. [4] For the first time ever, the high school football season was delayed in fall 2020. [5] Many professional sports, including baseball and football, played shortened preseasons and seasons in 2020 throughout the nation, including in Texas, with few or no fans allowed in attendance. [6]

Reopenings Begin

Texas sports were reopened to fans ahead of those in most other states. By the summer of 2020, some fans began to be allowed into sporting events, from high school through professional. [7]

By late 2020 to early 2021, most high school sports, even those played indoors, were being played in Texas. [3] To mitigate risks, students wore face masks while sitting on the bench. If not participating in the game, they used hand sanitizer, and the playing ball was frequently sanitized. [3, 8] Student athletes were tested multiple times each week for the virus. [9] Spectators, if allowed to attend the game, were required to wear masks. [3] As high school football was being played throughout Texas in January 2021, Brandon Smith, coach of the Prosper High School team, reflected the famous Texas love of the game when he said, "It's Friday night in Texas. It's what we do." [8]

Fan attendance at sporting events generally remained limited from late 2020 to early 2021. The state initially limited attendance at university games for football, basketball, and other sports to 25% capacity in 2020; this figure was later raised to 50%. [4, 9] Despite the 50% maximum capacity, most universities chose to keep the 25% limit through early 2021. [4, 10]

Moves to Texas

In late 2020, some university teams from other states played their home games in Texas to escape their own states' restrictions banning "nonessential businesses." [9] Such teams included the University of New Mexico men's and women's basketball teams.

In February 2021, the National Collegiate Athletic Association (NCAA) announced that all games of the current season's women's Division I national tournament would be held in Texas—in San Antonio, Austin, and San Marcos. [11] The games had originally been scheduled for San Antonio; Austin; Albany, New York; Cincinnati, Ohio; and Spokane, Washington. The latter three cities maintained tougher restrictions on sports than those in Texas. The consolidation of the tournament in the San Antonio area made it easy to manage the event in terms of hotel accommodations and other safety considerations. In the 2020 season, the NCAA cancelled both the women's and the men's tournaments because of the pandemic. All of the 2021 men's games were scheduled for Indiana, which also had looser restrictions than most other states.

The USA Olympic wrestling team announced in February 2021 that it would relocate its team trials to Texas. The usual location was in Pennsylvania, where pandemic restrictions prevented the trials. [12]

"Reopen Texas 100%"

In March 2021, Governor Abbott issued a number of executive orders to reopen businesses and other activities back to normal levels in Texas. [2, 4, 13] He said, "It's time to reopen Texas 100%," [4] adding that this move was possible because of "advancements of vaccines and antibody therapeutic drugs." [13] Businesses in the state could operate at full capacity with "no COVID-19-related operating limits."

[2, 7] His orders ended the mask-wearing mandate and the crowd-capacity limits at sporting events. [14]

Despite Abbott's orders, individual leagues and teams could each set their own policies. For example, Mark Cuban, owner of the Dallas Mavericks National Basketball Association franchise, said that the team's mask mandate and other COVID-related safety protocols would remain in place. [4]

On April 5, 2021, the season home opener for the Texas Rangers Major League Baseball team had a full-capacity crowd at the new 40,518-seat Globe Life Field in Arlington, Texas. It was the largest crowd at any sporting event in the United States since the start of the pandemic. [7, 14] The stadium had opened in 2020, but no fans had been allowed at the regular-season games. [7] The 2020 National League Championship Series and the World Series had both been played there, but at only 28% capacity. [7] For the 2021 opening day, fans were encouraged to wear masks at their seats and to practice social distancing at concession stands and on concourses. Among the fans in attendance was former President George W. Bush, who had once been an owner of the Rangers. [14]

Allowing the sell-out crowd at the Rangers game was criticized by some public health authorities and Democrat politicians, including President Joe Biden, who said that it was "not responsible." [15] Texas officials responded by pointing out that the number of COVID-19 infections was declining in Texas, while numbers were still increasing in much of the rest of the country. [14] They argued that these figures showed that the pandemic policies in Texas were working.

Evaluation of Impact

As of June 2021, about 40% of Texans had been fully vaccinated against the coronavirus that causes COVID-19. [16] The vaccines allowed the public to advance further to normal conditions regarding sports and other public events. As 2021 progressed, an increasing number of universities allowed full-capacity crowds at sporting events. [10]

While Texas sports returned to normal in 2021, many teams evaluated the financial impact of the pandemic. In May 2021, Ross Bjork, athletic director at Texas A&M University, announced that the university's athletics programs had lost $48 million as a result of the pandemic-related restrictions. [17, 18]

Officials at the University of Texas had previously announced that revenue from its athletics programs had declined more than $23 million in the 2019-2020 fiscal year compared with 2018-2019. [19] The university expected to have a much more profitable 2021 for its athletics department, especially with the unveiling of a stadium expansion and renovation that included additional premium seating and amenities. [19]

References

1. Beauvais, Sally, Lexi Churchill, Kiah Collier, Vianna Davilla, and Ren Larson. Gov. Greg Abbott is limiting enforcement of COVID-19 orders, but many cities already took a lax approach. *The Texas Tribune*. May 14, 2020. https://www.texastribune.org/2020/05/14/texas-coronavirus-enforcement/
2. Opening the state of Texas. Texas Health and Human Services. Updated June 8, 2021. https://www.dshs.state.tx.us/coronavirus/opentexas.aspx
3. Taboada, Melissa B. Texas school sports moved indoors for the winter. So did the coronavirus. *The Texas Tribune*. January 4, 2021. https://www.texastribune.org/2021/01/04/texas-high-school-sports-coronavirus-pandemic/
4. Schnitker, Andrew. What does Gov. Abbott's mandate mean for Texas Longhorns sports? KXAN. March 3, 2021. https://www.kxan.com/sports/what-does-gov-abbotts-mandate-mean-for-texas-longhorns-sports/
5. Marquez, RJ, and Valerie Gomez. COVID-19 pandemic puts Texas high school football, fall sports in jeopardy. KSAT. July 31, 2020. https://www.ksat.com/news/local/2020/07/31/covid-19-pandemic-puts-texas-high-school-football-fall-sports-in-jeopardy/
6. Walker, Andrew. NFL cancels all 2020 preseason games. Colts.com. July 27, 2020. https://www.colts.com/news/preseason-canceled-roger-goodell-2020-covid-19
7. Hawkins, Stephen. MLB's Rangers in line to be first team back to full capacity. AP News. March 10, 2021. https://apnews.com/article/mlb-baseball-coronavirus-pandemic-greg-abbott-texas-rangers-dcd4d8bf0c62904f8c392522304b1bf6
8. Jackson, Austin. Inside the battle between COVID-19 & the 2020 Texas high school football season. Local Profile. January 18, 2021. https://localprofile.com/2021/01/18/hospitals-are-filling-covid-19-lingers-but-for-better-or-worse-texas-high-school-football-finds-a-way/
9. Rosenzweig-Ziff, Dan. Fleeing their home state's strict restrictions on sports, New Mexico basketball teams seek refuge in two of Texas' worst hot spots. *The Texas Tribune*. November 19, 2020. https://www.texastribune.org/2020/11/19/new-mexico-basketball-texas-lubbock-coronavirus/
10. Straka, Dean. Report: Sarkisian calls for Texas fans to mirror intensity from NCAA Super Regional at home football games. 247 Sports. June 17, 2021. https://247sports.com/LongFormArticle/The-best-of-the-best-Highest-ranked-recruits-on-each-MaxPreps-Top-25-team-166682367/
11. Blinder, Alan. N.C.A.A. women's basketball tournament will be held in Texas. *The New York Times*. February 5, 2021. https://www.nytimes.com/2021/02/05/sports/ncaabasketball/ncaa-womens-basketball-tournament-texas.html
12. Radnofsky, Louise, and Rachel Bachman. Moving sports events to Texas was easy, maybe too easy. *The Wall Street Journal*. March 14, 2021. https://www.wsj.com/articles/texas-mask-rules-sports-events-11615685393
13. Governor Abbott lifts mask mandate, opens Texas 100 percent [press release]. Office of the Texas Governor. March 2, 2021. https://gov.texas.gov/news/post/governor-abbott-lifts-mask-mandate-opens-texas-100-percent
14. Boren, Cindy. Here's what the largest crowd at a U.S. sports event since the pandemic looked like. *The Washington Post*. April 6, 2021. https://www.washingtonpost.com/sports/2021/04/06/texas-rangers-sports-crowd-coronavirus/
15. Scribner, Herb. The Texas Rangers have no crowd limit for opening day. President Joe Biden says that's 'not responsible'. *Deseret News*. April 1, 2021. https://www.deseret.com/sports/2021/4/1/22362180/texas-rangers-no-crowd-limit-opening-day-president-joe-biden
16. Texas coronavirus vaccination progress. USA Facts. Updated June 2021. https://usafacts.org/visualizations/covid-vaccine-tracker-states/state/texas
17. Paterik, Brice. AD Ross Bjork says Texas A&M athletics suffered $48 million loss due to COVID-19 pandemic. *The Dallas Morning News*. May 23, 2021. https://www.dallasnews.com/sports/texas-am-aggies/2021/05/23/texas-am-athletic-director-ross-bjork-says-aggies-athletics-suffered-48-million-loss-due-to-covid-19-pandemic/
18. Zwerneman, Brent. Texas A&M lost $48 million between department, 12th Man Foundation during pandemic, say AD. *Houston Chronicle*. May 23, 2021. https://www.houstonchronicle.com/texas-sports-nation/college/article/A-M-AD-84-million-in-losses-between-department-16196627.php
19. Davis, Brian. Texas athletics generates $200.7 million in revenue, $22.1 million profit in 2019-20 fiscal year. *Hook'Em*. January 29, 2021. https://www.hookem.com/story/sports/football/2021/01/29/texas-football-longhorns-turn-22-1-million-profit-2020/4301655001/

The Llano Yellow Jackets play against the Hallettsville Brahmas in the UIL 3A Division I varsity high school football semifinals at Birkelbach Field in Georgetown, Texas, on December 10, 2020. Photo by Ralph Arvesen/ Flickr (CC)..

STATE: High School Championships

The University Interscholastic League (UIL), which governs literary and athletic competition among public schools in Texas, was organized in 1910 as a division of the University of Texas extension service.

Initially, it sponsored forensic competition. By 1920, the UIL organized the structure of the high school football game in response to the growing popularity of the sport in Texas.

The Texas Association of Private and Parochial Schools (TAPPS) is the largest group of private schools in the state with more than 225 member institutions. The interscholastic competition began in 1978 and was significantly expanded when the Texas Christian Interscholastic League ceased to exist in 2000 and many of those schools moved into TAPPS.

The Southwest Preparatory Conference (SPC), established in 1952, is an athletic conference of certain private schools in Oklahoma and Texas.

Listed are state champions and the game scores.

Sources: The University Interscholastic League at uil.utexas.edu; the Texas Association of Private and Parochial Schools.

Football

Year	Division	Champion	Runner Up
UIL 2020	1A Division I	Sterling City 68	May 22
	1A Division II	Balmorhea 74	Richland Springs 38
	2A Division I	Shiner 42	Post 20
	2A Division II	Windthorst 22	Mart 21
	3A Division I	Tuscola Jim Ned 29	Hallettsville 28
	3A Division II	Canadian 35	Franklin 34
	4A Division I	Argyle 49	Lindale 21
	4A Division II	Carthage 70	Gilmer 14
	5A Division I	Denton Ryan 59	Cedar Park 14
	5A Division II	Aledo 56	Crosby 21
	6A Division I	Austin Westlake 52	Southlake Carroll 34
	6A Division II	Katy 51	Cedar Hill 14
TAPPS 2020	Division I	Dallas Parish Episcopal 42	Fort Worth Nolan Catholic 28
	Division II	Austin Regents 26	Dallas Christian 20
	Division III	Colleyville Covenant 40	Houston Cypress Christian 30
	Division IV	Shiner St. Paul 63	Waco Reicher Catholic 13

Year	Division	Champion	Runner Up
UIL 2019	1A Division I	Blum 58	McLean 52
	1A Division II	Richland Springs 62	Matador Motley County 16
	2A Division I	Refugio 28	Post 7
	2A Division II	Mart 25	Hamlin 20
	3A Division I	Grandview 42	Pottsboro 35
	3A Division II	Gunter 43	Omaha Pewitt 22
	4A Division I	Carthage 42	Waco La Vega 28
	4A Division II	Texarkana Pleasant Grove 35	Wimberley 21
	5A Division I	Alvin Shadow Creek 28	Denton Ryan 22
	5A Division II	Aledo 45	Fort Bend Marshall 42
	6A Division I	Galena Park North Shore 31	Duncanville 17
	6A Division II	Austin Westlake 24	Denton Guyer 0
TAPPS 2019	Division I	Dallas Parish Episcopal 42	Plano John Paul II 14
	Division II	Cedar Hill Trinity 48	Austin Regents 19
	Division III	Boerne Geneva 49	Lubbock Christian 21
	Division IV	Shiner St. Paul 20	Hallettsville Sacred Heart 16
SPC 2019	3A Division	Fort Worth Country Day 41	The Woodlands John Cooper 0
	4A Division	Bellaire Episcopal 42	Houston Kinkaid 21

Volleyball

Year	Division	Champion	Runner Up
UIL 2020	1A	Neches 3	Blum 0
	2A	Iola 3	Crawford 1
	3A	Bushland 3	Goliad 0
	4A	Decatur 3	Wimberley 0
	5A	Lucas Lovejoy 3	Lamar Fulshear 0
	6A	Katy Seven Lakes 3	Klein 1
TAPPS 2020	1A	Wichita Falls Christ Academy 3	San Antonio The Atonement 0
	2A	Red Oak Ovilla Christian 3	Bulverde Bracken Christian 0
	3A	New Braunfels Christian 3	Midland Classical 0
	4A	Houston Northland Christian 3	Fort Worth Lake Country Christian 1
	5A	Victoria St. Joseph 3	Carrollton Prince of Peace 0
	6A	Argyle Liberty Christian 3	Houston St. Agnes 2
UIL 2019	1A	Neches 3	Round Top-Carmine 0
	2A	Crawford 3	Jewett Leon 0
	3A	Vanderbilt Industrial 3	Van Alstyne 0
	4A	Lamar Fulshear 3	Hereford 0
	5A	Lucas Lovejoy 3	Canyon Randall 0
	6A	Northwest Nelson 3	Plano West 2
TAPPS 2019	1A	Wichita Falls Notre Dame 3	San Antonio Legacy Christian 0
	2A	Red Oak Ovilla Christian 3	Austin Waldorf 0
	3A	New Braunfels Christian 3	Round Rock Christian 0
	4A	Lubbock Trinity Christian 3	Boerne Geneva School 1
	5A	Carrollton Prince of Peace 3	San Antonio Christian 0
	6A	Houston St. Agnes 3	Plano Prestonwood Christian 2

Boys Basketball

Year	Division	Champion	Runner Up
UIL 2021	1A	Texline 54	Slidell 53
	2A	Clarendon 64	Grapeland 60
	3A	San Antonio Cole 77	Tatum 60
	4A	Argyle 49	Huffman Hargrave 30
	5A	Beaumont United 71 (OT)	Dallas Kimball 70
	6A	Duncanville 66	Austin Westlake 53
TAPPS 2021	1A	Cypress Covenant 50	Irving Faustina Academy 37
	2A	Houston Grace Christian 59	Lubbock Kingdom Prep 48
	3A	Huntsville Alpha Omega 31	Midland Classical 26
	4A	Houston Westbury Christian 97	Lubbock Trinity 93
	5A	The Woodlands Christian 60	Fort Worth Christian 47
	6A	San Antonio Antonian 73	Dallas Bishop Lynch 57
UIL 2020	Canceled due to COVID-19 pandemic.		
TAPPS 2020	1A	Longview Trinity School of Texas 50	Houston Robert M. Beren 33
	2A	Huntsville Alpha Omega 43	Lubbock All Saints Episcopal 38
	3A	Dallas Yavneh 50	Tomball Rosehill Christian 35
	4A	The Woodlands Christian 68	Colleyville Covenant Christian 50
	5A	Frisco Legacy Christian 62	Houston Westbury Christian 59
	6A	Plano John Paul II 51	San Antonio Antonian College Prep 48
UIL 2019	1A	Slidell 49	Jayton 36
	2A	Shelbyville 67	Gruver 48
	3A	Dallas Madison 49	Brock 48
	4A	Oak Cliff Faith Family Academy 53	Liberty Hill 51
	5A	Mansfield Timberview 77	San Antonio Wagner 64
	6A	Duncanville 73	Klein Forest 69
TAPPS 2019	1A	Baytown Christian 63	Dallas Tyler Street 39
	2A	Bryan Allen Academy 68	Abilene Christian 47
	3A	Kerrville Our Lady of the Hills 50	Midland Classical 47
	4A	Arlington Grace Prep 58	The Woodlands Christian 54
	5A	Frisco Legacy Christian 66	Houston Lutheran South 51
	6A	San Antonio Antonian 70	Plano Prestonwood Christian 67

Girls Basketball

Year	Division	Champion	Runner Up
UIL 2021	1A	Dodd City 30	Nazareth 21
	2A	Lipan 44	Martin's Mill 39
	3A	Brownfield 68 (OT)	Fairfield 64
	4A	Canyon 56	Hardin-Jefferson 55
	5A	Cedar Park 46	Frisco Liberty 39
	6A	DeSoto 53	S. Grand Prairie 37

Year	Division	Champion	Runner Up
TAPPS 2021	1A	San Angelo Cornerstone Christian 35	Wichita Falls Christ Academy 27
	2A	Lubbock Southcrest Christian 58	Shiner St. Paul 33
	3A	Houston Lutheran High North 62	McKinney Cornerstone 34
	4A	Lubbock Christian 75	The Woodlands Legacy Prep 39
	5A	Fort Worth Southwest 54	Houston Second Baptist 40
	6A	Dallas Bishop Lynch 56	Houston The Village 46
UIL 2020	1A	Nazareth 44	Lipan 31
	2A	Gruver 42	Muenster 39
	3A	Shallowater 61	Woodville 43
	4A	Fairfield 40	Argyle 39 (OT)
	5A	Frisco Liberty 35	SA Veterans Memorial 26
	6A	Duncanville 63	Cypress Creek 47
TAPPS 2020	1A	San Antonio Legacy Christian 58	Lubbock Kingdom Preparatory Academy 32
	2A	Lubbock Southcrest Christian 46	Austin Waldorf 28
	3A	Midland Classical 72	Beaumont Legacy Christian 37
	4A	Lubbock Trinity Christian 50	Austin Texas School for the Deaf 25
	5A	Fort Worth Southwest Christian 73	Houston Second Baptist 63
	6A	Houston The Village 75	Plano Prestonwood Christian 48
UIL 2019	1A	Nazareth 54	Dodd City 33
	2A	Martins Mill 60	Grapeland 56
	3A	Chapel Hill (Tyler) 55	Woodville 46
	4A	Argyle 49	Hardin-Jefferson 41
	5A	Amarillo 47	Frisco Liberty 42
	6A	Converse Judson 49	DeSoto 46
TAPPS 2019	1A	San Antonio Legacy Christian 50	Wichita Falls Notre Dame 39
	2A	Lubbock Southcrest Christian 41	Shiner St. Paul 34
	3A	Midland Classical 72	Beaumont Legacy Christian 47
	4A	Lubbock Trinity Christian 72	Houston Lutheran North 34
	5A	Cedar Hill Trinity Christian 76	San Antonio Christian 33
	6A	Dallas Bishop Lynch 81	Houston Village 62

Boys Soccer

Year	Division	Champion	Runner Up
UIL 2021	4A	Boerne 3	Fort Worth Diamond Hill-Jarvis 1
	5A	Frisco Wakeland 3	Humble Kingwood Park 2
	6A	San Antonio LEE 2	Rockwall Heath 0
TAPPS 2021	Fall 2020	Dallas International 2	San Antonio Lutheran 0
	Division I	Monsignor Kelly Catholic 2	Plano John Paul II 1
	Division II	San Antonio TMI Episcopal 5	Frisco Legacy 0
	Division III	Dallas Covenant 1	Schertz John Paul II 0
UIL 2020	Canceled due to COVID-19 pandemic.		

For track, tennis, and other high school sports champions, see page 589 in the Education section.

Year	Division	Champion	Runner Up
TAPPS 2020	Fall 2019	Dallas International 2	Brownsville First Baptist 1
	Division I	San Antonio Central Catholic 2	El Paso Cathedral 1
	Division II	San Antonio TMI Episcopal 3	Bullard Brook Hill 2
	Division III	Houston St. Thomas Episcopal 1	Dallas Covenant 0
UIL 2019	4A	San Elizario 1	Midlothian Heritage 0 (OT)
	5A	El Paso Bel Air 2	Frisco Wakeland 1
	6A	Flower Mound 1	San Antonio Lee 0 (SO 4-1)
TAPPS 2019	Fall 2018	Nacogdoches Regents 2	Pflugerville Concordia 1
	Division III	Dallas Covenant 2	Houston St. Thomas Episcopal 1
	Division II	San Antonio TMI Episcopal 3	Carrollton Prince of Peace 2
	Division I	San Antonio Central Catholic 4	Dallas Bishop Lynch 0

Girls Soccer

Year	Division	Champion	Runner Up
UIL 2021	4A	Midlothian Heritage 6	Corpus Christi Calallen 0
	5A	Dripping Springs 2	Frisco Wakeland 1
	6A	Lewisville Flower Mound 2	Austin Vandegrift 1
TAPPS 2021	Division I	Ursuline Academy 5	St. Agnes 0
	Division II	Grapevine Faith 7	St. Michael's 1
	Division III	Dallas Covenant 3	Schertz John Paul II 1
UIL 2020	Canceled due to COVID-19 pandemic.		
TAPPS 2020	Division I	Houston St. Agnes 6	Fort Worth Nolan Catholic 0
	Division II	Grapevine Faith Christian 2	San Antonio Christian 0
	Division III	Schertz John Paul II 4	Dallas Covenant 1
UIL 2019	4A	Stephenville 2	Liberty Hill 0
	5A	Highland Park (Dallas) 2	Mansfield Legacy 0
	6A	Southlake Carroll 5	Katy Tompkins 0
TAPPS 2019	Division III	Houston St. Thomas Episcopal 6	Austin Veritas 0
	Division II	Grapevine Faith 7	Houston Second Baptist 0
	Division I	Dallas Bishop Lynch 1	Houston St. Agnes 0

Baseball

Year	Division	Champion	Runner Up
UIL 2021	1A	Fayetteville 6	Kennard 4
	2A	New Deal 7	Garrison 2
	3A	Malakoff 8	Corpus Christi London 7
	4A	Texarkana Pleasant Grove 2	Rusk 1
	5A	Mont Belvieu Barbers Hill 2	Hallsville 1
	6A	Rockwall Heath 4	Keller 3
TAPPS 2021	Division I	Midland Christian 1	Concordia Lutheran 0
	Division II	Lutheran South Academy 16	Southwest Christian 0
	Division III	Bay Area Christian 3	Lubbock Trinity Christian 1
	Division IV	Midland Classical 5	Rosehill Christian 4
	Division V	Weatherford Christian 14	Sacred Heart Hallettsville 2

Year	Division	Champion	Runner Up
UIL 2020	Canceled due to COVID-19 pandemic.		
TAPPS 2020	Canceled due to COVID-19 pandemic.		
UIL 2019	1A	D'Hanis 4	New Home 0
	2A	Dallardsville Big Sandy 7	Linden-Kildare 1
	3A	Wall 2	Blanco 1
	4A	Argyle 6	Sweeny 3
	5A	Colleyville Heritage 14	Georgetown 2 (6 innings)
	6A	Southlake Carroll 17	Ft. Bend Ridge Point 0 (5 innings)
TAPPS 2019	Division V	Weatherford Christian 7	Brazosport Christian 6
	Division IV	Amarillo San Jacinto Christian 5	New Braunfels Chrisitan 3
	Division III	Houston Northland Christian 3	Willow Park Trinity Christian 2
	Division II	Houston Lutheran South 11	Fort Worth Christian 1
	Division I	Argyle Liberty Christian 3	Fort Worth All Saints Episcopal 5

Softball

Year	Division	Champion	Runner Up
UIL 2021	1A	Dodd City 8	D'Hanis 4
	2A	Stamford 5	Crawford 4
	3A	Rains 11	Diboll 5
	4A	Liberty 10	Calallen 3
	5A	Mont Belvieu Barbers Hill 4	Aledo 1
	6A	Deer Park 1	Converse Judson 0
TAPPS 2021	Division I	John Paul II Plano 4	Antonian College Prep 2
	Division II	Second Baptist 13	Faith Christian Grapevine 0
	Division III	Holy Cross of San Antonio 10	Bay Area Christian 0
	Division IV	Sacred Heart Hallettsville 13	Temple Christian 3
UIL 2020	Canceled due to COVID-19 pandemic.		
TAPPS 2020	Canceled due to COVID-19 pandemic.		
UIL 2019	1A	D'Hanis 9	Chireno 7
	2A	Crawford 8	Thorndale 7 (8 innings)
	3A	Rains 6	Hallettsville 2
	4A	Huffman Hargrave 12	Anna 0 (6 innings)
	5A	Angleton 8	Calallen 1
	6A	Katy 8	Klein Collins 2
TAPPS 2019	Division IV	Shiner St. Paul 15	Round Rock Concordia 0
	Division III	Waco Reicher 10	The Woodlands Christian 2
	Division II	Houston Lutheran South 6	Bullard Brook Hill 2
	Division I	Houston St. Agnes 3	Dallas Bishop Lynch 2

Texas College Sports NCAA Champions

The National Collegiate Athletic Association is a member-led organization dedicated to college athletes. NCAA schools award nearly $3.5 billion in athletic scholarships every year and provide support to help student-athletes graduate at a rate higher than their general student peers.

The employees at the NCAA's national office manage all championships, oversee programs that benefit student-athletes, and support member committees that make rules and policies for college sports. Member schools and conferences ultimately decide which rules to adopt for their division — everything from recruiting and compliance to academics and championships.

There are three divisions in the NCAA, all of which are represented in Texas colleges: Division I, Division II, and Division III. Here, we touch on all Division I conferences and one conference in Division II.

Source: National Collegiate Athletic Association website.

Displayed are season champions, conference tournament champions, and the entrants in national championships.

NCAA Division I

Big 12 Conference Champions

In 2021, the Texas schools in the Big 12 were:

- University of Texas at Austin
- Texas Tech University
- Texas Christian University
- Baylor University

Other schools in the Big 12 are the University of Kansas, Kansas State University, the University of Oklahoma, Oklahoma State University, Iowa State University, and West Virginia University.

Football

Year	Season	College Football Playoff
2020	University of Oklahoma	No Big 12 Texas teams advanced to the College Football Playoff.
2019	University of Oklahoma	No Big 12 Texas teams advanced to the College Football Playoff.

Men's Basketball

Year	Season	Tournament	Postseason
2021	Baylor	University of Texas	• Baylor beat Gonzaga 86-70 to win national championship. • University of Texas lost to Abilene Christian 53-52 in first round. • Texas Tech lost to University of Arkansas 68-66 in second round.
2020	Kansas	Canceled	Canceled due to COVID-19 pandemic.

Women's Basketball

Year	Season	Tournament	Postseason
2021	Baylor	Baylor	• Baylor lost to University of Connecticut 69-67 in Elite Eight. • University of Texas lost to South Carolina 62-34 in Elite Eight.
2020	Baylor	Canceled	Canceled due to COVID-19 pandemic.

Baseball

Year	Season	Championship	NCAA Division I Baseball Tournament
2021	Texas, TCU	Texas Christian	• Texas lost to Mississippi State 4-3 in the College World Series. • Texas Tech lost to Stanford 9-0 in Super Regional. • Texas Christian University lost to Oregon State 3-2 in Regional.
2020	Texas Tech	Canceled	Canceled due to COVID-19 pandemic.

Softball

Year	Season	Championship	NCAA Division I Softball Tournament
2021	University of Oklahoma	University of Oklahoma	University of Texas lost to Oklahoma State 2-0 in Super Regional.
2020	University of Oklahoma	Canceled	Canceled due to COVID-19 pandemic.

Southeastern Conference Champions

Texas A&M University joined the Southeastern Conference in 2012 and competes in the West Division against Louisiana State University, the University of Arkansas, the University of Mississippi, Mississippi State University, the University of Alabama, and Auburn University.

Schools in the East Division are the University of Missouri, the University of Kentucky, Vanderbilt University, the University of Tennessee, the University of Georgia, the University of South Carolina, and the University of Florida.

Football

Year	Season	College Football Playoff
2020	University of Alabama	Texas A&M did not advance to postseason.
2019	Louisiana State University	Texas A&M did not advance to postseason.

Men's Basketball

Year	Season	Tournament	Postseason
2021	Alabama	Alabama	Texas A&M did not advance to postseason.
2020	Kentucky	Canceled	Canceled due to COVID-19 pandemic.

Women's Basketball

Year	Season	Tournament	Postseason
2021	Texas A&M	South Carolina	Texas A&M lost to Arizona 74-59 in Sweet Sixteen of NCAA Division 1 Basketball Championship.
2020	South Carolina	South Carolina	Canceled due to COVID-19 pandemic.

Baseball

Year	Season	Championship	NCAA Division I Baseball Tournament
2021	East: Tennessee West: Arkansas	Arkansas	Texas A&M did not advance to postseason.
2020	East: Florida West: Alabama, Ole Miss	Canceled	Canceled due to COVID-19 pandemic.

Softball

Year	Season	Championship	NCAA Division I Softball Tournament
2021	Florida, Arkansas	Alabama	Texas A&M lost to Wichita State 9-6 in Regional.
2020	Florida	Canceled	Canceled due to COVID-19 pandemic.

Did you know

When it comes to football, each conference tackles the national championship in a different way. Schools in the American Athletic, Big 12, Conference-USA, Southeastern, and Sun Belt conferences play in the NCAA Division I Football Bowl Division. A 13-member committee votes on which four teams enter the College Football Playoff semifinals.

The Southland Conference plays in the NCAA Division I Football Championship Subdivision, a single-elimination bracket tournament.

Southwestern Athletic Conference schools are eligible for the Football Championship Subdivision championship playoffs, but opt out in favor of the Celebration Bowl.

American Athletic Conference Champions

The 2013-14 season was the first for the AAC after the breakup of the Big East Conference. Texas schools in the AAC are:

- Southern Methodist University
- University of Houston

Other schools in the conference are the University of Memphis, University of Cincinnati, University of Central Florida, East Carolina University, Temple University, University of South Florida, Tulane University, University of Tulsa, the University of Connecticut, and Wichita State University.

Football

Year	Season	Championship	College Football Playoff
2020	Cincinnati, Tulsa	Cincinnati	Neither AAC Texas team entered the College Football Playoff.
2019	East: Cincinnati West: Memphis	Memphis	Neither AAC Texas team entered the College Football Playoff.
2018	East: UCF West: Memphis	UCF	Neither AAC Texas team entered the College Football Playoff.

Men's Basketball

Year	Season	Tournament	Postseason
2021	Wichita State	Houston	Houston lost to Baylor 78-59 in Elite Eight.
2020	Cincinnati, Houston, Tulsa	Canceled	Canceled due to COVID-19 pandemic.
2019	Houston	Cincinnati	Houston lost to Kentucky 62-58 in Sweet Sixteen.

Women's Basketball

Year	Season	Tournament	Postseason
2021	South Florida	South Florida	Houston beat Arizona State 50-48 in the Women's National Invitational Tournament Fort Worth Region Consolation Final.
2020	University of Connecticut	University of Connecticut	Canceled due to COVID-19 pandemic.
2019	University of Connecticut	University of Connecticut	Neither AAC Texas team entered the NCAA Division I Championship nor Women's National Invitational Tournament.

Baseball

Year	Season	Championship	NCAA Division I Baseball Tournament
2021	East Carolina	South Florida	Neither AAC Texas team advanced to the NCAA Division I Baseball Tournament.
2020	Alabama, University of Mississippi, Florida	Canceled	Canceled due to COVID-19 pandemic.
2019	East Carolina	Cincinnati	Neither AAC Texas team advanced to the NCAA Division I Baseball Tournament.

Softball

Year	Season	Championship	NCAA Division I Softball Tournament
2021	Wichita State	Wichita State	Neither AAC Texas team advanced to the NCAA Division I Softball Tournament.
2020	Florida	Canceled	Canceled due to COVID-19 pandemic.
2019	South Florida	Championship canceled; no champion declared	Houston lost to Texas 7-0 in NCAA Division I Softball Championship's Austin Regional Final.

C-USA Champions

Texas schools in the West Division of Conference USA in 2021 were:

- Rice University
- University of Texas at San Antonio
- University of Texas at El Paso
- University of North Texas

Rice and UTEP joined in 2005. In 2013, the University of North Texas and the University of Texas at San Antonio joined the conference. The University of Houston joined in 1996 and left in 2013.

Other teams in the West Division of Conference USA are University of Alabama-Birmingham, Louisiana Tech University, and University of Southern Mississippi.

Teams in the East Division include Florida Atlantic University, Florida International University, Marshall University, Middle Tennessee State University, University of North Carolina at Charlotte, Old Dominion University (in Virginia), and Western Kentucky University.

Football

Year	Season	Championship	College Football Playoff
2020	East: Marshall West: UAB	UAB	No C-USA Texas teams advanced to the College Football Playoff.
2019	East: Florida Atlantic West: UAB	Florida Atlantic	No C-USA Texas teams advanced to the College Football Playoff.

Men's Basketball

Year	Season	Tournament	Postseason
2021	East: WKU West: Louisiana Tech	North Texas	North Texas lost to Villanova 84-61 in second round.
2020	North Texas	Canceled	Canceled due to COVID-19 pandemic.

Women's Basketball

Year	Season	Tournament	Postseason
2021	East: Middle Tennessee West: Rice	Middle Tennessee	Rice beat University of Mississippi 71-58 in Women's National Invitation Tournament championship game.
2020	Rice	Canceled	Canceled due to COVID-19 pandemic.

Baseball

Year	Season	Championship	NCAA Division I Baseball Tournament
2021	East: Charlotte West: LA Tech	Old Dominion	No C-USA Texas teams advanced to the postseason.
2020	Old Dominion, Southern Miss	Canceled	Canceled due to COVID-19 pandemic.

Softball

Year	Season	Championship	NCAA Division I Softball Tournament
2021	East: Charlotte West: North Texas	University of Texas-San Antonio	No C-USA Texas teams advanced to the postseason.
2020	Canceled	Canceled	Canceled due to COVID-19 pandemic.

Did you know

More than one team from a conference can advance to the NCAA tournament.

Sometimes, if a team just misses an NCAA playoff berth, they might be chosen for an invitational tournament. The two most prominent are in basketball: the National Invitational Tournament (NIT, for men's teams), and the Women's National Invitational Tournament (WNIT).

Southwestern Athletic Conference Champions

Texas schools in the Western Division of the Southwestern Athletic Conference in 2019 were:

- Prairie View A&M University
- Texas Southern University

The Prairie View A&M Panthers have been in the conference since its founding in 1920 and the Texas Southern Tigers joined the conference in 1954. Other teams in the SWAC Western Division are Grambling State University (Louisiana), Southern University (Louisiana), and University of Arkansas at Pine Bluff.

Schools in the Eastern Division are Jackson State University (in Mississippi), Mississippi Valley State University, Alcorn State University (in Mississippi), Alabama State University, and Alabama A&M University.

SWAC schools opt to play the Celebration Bowl as opposed to the NCAA Division I Football Championships.

Football

Year	Season	Championship	Celebration Bowl
Spring 2021	East: Alabama A&M West: University of Arkansas-Pine Bluff	Alabama A&M	Not applicable.
2020	Canceled	Canceled	Canceled due to COVID-19 pandemic.
2019	East: Alcorn State West: Southern (Louisiana)	Alcorn State	North Carolina A&T 64, Alcorn State 44

Men's Basketball

Year	Season	Tournament	Postseason
2021	Prairie View A&M, Jackson State	Texas Southern	Texas Southern lost to Michigan 82-66 in first round.
2020	Prairie View A&M	Canceled	Canceled due to COVID-19 pandemic.
2019	Prairie View A&M	Prairie View A&M	• Prairie View A&M lost to 82-76 in the First Four of the NCAA Division I Basketball Championship. • Texas Southern lost to Green Bay 87-86 OT in the semifinals at the CollegeInsider.com Postseason Tournament.

Women's Basketball

Year	Season	Tournament	Postseason
2021	Jackson State	Jackson State	Jackson State lost to Baylor 101-52 in first round.
2020	Jackson State	Canceled	Canceled due to COVID-19 pandemic.
2019	Jackson State	Southern (Louisiana)	Prairie View A&M lost to Texas Christian University 72-41 in the first round of the Women's National Invitational Tournament.

Baseball

Year	Season	Championship	NCAA Division I Baseball Tournament
2021	East: Jackson State West: Prairie View	Texas Southern	Texas Southern lost to Fairfield 6-2 in Austin Regional of the NCAA Division I Baseball Tournament.
2020	Canceled	Canceled	Canceled due to COVID-19 pandemic.
2019	East: Alabama West: Southern (Louisiana)	Southern (Louisiana)	Neither SWAC Texas team advanced to the NCAA Division I Baseball Tournament.

Softball

Year	Season	Championship	NCAA Division I Softball Tournament
2021	East: Jackson State West: Texas Southern	Alabama State	No SWAC Texas team advanced to the postseason.
2020	Canceled	Canceled	Canceled due to COVID-19 pandemic.

Sun Belt Conference Champions

In 2013, Texas State University and the University of Texas at Arlington joined the Sun Belt Conference.

Other schools in the conference are the University of Louisiana-Monroe, the University of Louisiana-Lafayette, the University of Arkansas-Little Rock, Arkansas State University, Coastal Carolina University (South Carolina), Troy University (Alabama), the University of South Alabama, Middle Tennessee State University, Appalachian State University (in North Carolina), Georgia Southern University, and Georgia State University.

Football

Year	Season	Championship	College Football Playoff
2020	East: Coastal Carolina West: Louisiana-Lafayette	Coastal Carolina, Louisiana-Lafayette	No SBC teams advanced to the College Football Playoff.
2019	East: App State West: Louisiana-Lafayette	Appalachian State	No SBC teams advanced to the College Football Playoff.
2018	East: Appalachian State West: Louisiana-Lafayette	Appalachian State	No SBC teams advanced to the College Football Playoff.

Men's Basketball

Year	Season	Tournament	Postseason
2021	East: Georgia State West: Texas State	Appalachian State	No SBC Texas teams advanced to the postseason.
2020	Little Rock	Canceled	Canceled due to COVID-19 pandemic.
2019	Georgia State	Georgia State	Texas State lost to Florida International University 87-81 in the first round of the CollegeInsider.com Postseason Tournament.

Women's Basketball

Year	Season	Tournament	Postseason
2021	East: Troy West: Louisiana-Lafayette	Troy	No SBC Texas teams advanced to the postseason.
2020	Troy	Canceled	Canceled due to COVID-19 pandemic.
2019	Little Rock, University of Texas-Arlington	Little Rock	University of Texas-Arlington lost to Texas Christian University 71-54 in the second round of the Women's National Invitational Tournament.

Baseball

Year	Season	Championship	NCAA Division I Baseball Tournament
2021	East: South Alabama West: Louisiana-Lafayette	South Alabama	No SBC Texas teams advanced to the postseason.
2020	Canceled	Canceled	Canceled due to COVID-19 pandemic.
2019	East: Georgia Southern West: Texas State	Coastal Carolina	Neither SBC Texas team advanced to the postseason.

Softball

Year	Season	Championship	Postseason
2021	Louisiana-Lafayette	Louisiana-Lafayette	Texas State lost to University of Texas 6-0 at Austin in the Austin Regional of the NCAA Division I Softball Tournament.
2020	Canceled	Canceled	Canceled due to COVID-19 pandemic.
2019	Louisiana-Lafayette	Louisiana-Lafayette	University of Texas-Arlington beat Iowa State 4-3 to win the Postseason National Invitational Softball Championship.

Southland Conference Champions

Texas schools in the Southland Conference in 2019:

- Abilene Christian University
- Houston Baptist University
- Texas A&M University–Corpus Christi
- Stephen F. Austin State University
- Sam Houston State University
- Lamar University
- University of the Incarnate Word

Other schools are Central Arkansas University, McNeese State University, the University of New Orleans, Nicholls State University, Northwestern State University, and Southeastern Louisiana University.

McNeese, Nicholls, and Northwestern are all in Louisiana

Football

Year	Season	NCAA Division I Football Championship
2020	Sam Houston	Sam Houston beat South Dakota State 23-21 to win Football Championship.
2019	Central Arkansas	Central Arkansas lost to Illinois State 24-14 in Football Championship first round.
2018	Nicholls, Incarnate Word	Incarnate Word lost to Montana State 35-14 in Football Championship first round.

Men's Basketball

Year	Season	Tournament	Postseason
2021	Nicholls	Abilene Christian	Abilene Christian loses to UCLA 67-47 in second round.
2020	Stephen F. Austin	Canceled	Canceled due to COVID-19 pandemic.
2019	Sam Houston	Abilene Christian	• Abilene Christian lost to Kentucky 75-44 in NCAA Division I Basketball Championship first round. • Sam Houston lost to Texas Christian University 82-69 in National Invitation Tournament first round.

Women's Basketball

Year	Season	Tournament	Postseason
2021	Stephen F. Austin	Stephen F. Austin	Stephen F. Austin loses to Georgia Tech 54-52 in first round.
2020	Texas A&M-Corpus Christi	Canceled	Canceled due to COVID-19 pandemic.
2019	Lamar	Abilene Christian	• Abilene Christian lost to Baylor 95-38 in NCAA Division 1 Basketball Championship first round. • Stephen F. Austin lost to University of Texas-Arlington 60-54 in Women's National Invitation Tournament first round. • Lamar lost to South Alabama 73-71 in Women's National Invitation Tournament first round.

Baseball

Year	Season	Championship	NCAA Division I Baseball Tournament
2021	Abilene Christian	McNeese	McNeese lost to Texas Christian University 12-4 in Fort Worth Regional of the NCAA Division I Baseball Tournament.
2020	Canceled	Canceled	Canceled due to COVID-19 pandemic.
2019	Sam Houston	McNeese	McNeese lost to Ohio State 9-8 in single-elimination game in NCAA Division I Baseball Nashville Regional.

Softball

Year	Season	Championship	Postseason
2021	Stephen F. Austin	McNeese	McNeese lost to LSU 10-2 in Baton Rouge Regional.
2020	Canceled	Canceled	Canceled due to COVID-19 pandemic.
2019	Sam Houston	Sam Houston	• Sam Houston lost to University of Texas-Austin 3-0 in NCAA Division I Softball Austin Regional. • Stephen F. Austin lost to McNeese 3-1 in Postseason National Invitational Softball Championship, Stephen F. Austin Regional.

NCAA Division II

Lone Star Conference Champions

The Lone Star Conference, founded in 1931, has long been the athletic conference for Texas schools in the NCAA second tier of schools, Division II.

Texas schools in the conference in 2021 were:

- Angelo State University
- Dallas Baptist University
- Lubbock Christian University
- Midwestern State University
- St. Mary's University
- St. Edward's University
- Tarleton State University
- Texas A&M International University
- Texas A&M University—Commerce
- Texas A&M University—Kingsville
- Texas Woman's University
- West Texas A&M University
- University of Texas at Tyler
- University of Texas of the Permian Basin

Other teams in the conference are Cameron University (Oklahoma), Eastern New Mexico State University, Oklahoma Christian University, Rogers State University (in Oklahoma), University of Arkansas-Fort Smith, and Western New Mexico University.

Football

Year	Season	NCAA Division II Football Championship
2020	Canceled	Canceled due to the COVID-19 pandemic.
2019	Tarleton	No Lone Star Conference teams advanced to the Division II FCS.

Men's Basketball

Year	Season	Tournament	NCAA Division II Championship
2021	Lubbock Christian	West Texas A&M	• West Texas A&M loses to Northwest Missouri State 80-54 in national championship game. • Lubbock Christian lost to West Texas A&M 101-92 in third round. • Dallas Baptist lost to West Texas A&M 82-65 in second round.
2020	West Texas A&M	Canceled	Canceled due to COVID-19 pandemic.

Women's Basketball

Year	Season	Tournament	NCAA Division II Championship
2021	Lubbock Christian	Lubbock Christian	• Lubbock Christian beat Drury 69-59 to win national championship. • Texas A&M-Commerce lost to Southwestern Oklahoma 97-79 in regional.
2020	Lubbock Christian	Canceled	Canceled due to COVID-19 pandemic.

Baseball

Year	Season	Championship	NCAA Division II Baseball Tournament
2021	West Texas A&M	Angelo State	• Angelo State lost to Wingate 8-7 in semifinals. • West Texas A&M lost to Angelo State 10-2 in regional.
2020	Canceled	Canceled	Canceled due to COVID-19 pandemic.

Softball

Year	Season	Championship	NCAA Division II Softball Tournament
2021	UT Tyler	West Texas A&M	• West Texas A&M beat Biola 4-1 to win national championship. • Texas A&M Commerce lost to West Texas A&M 4-0 in regional championship. • Texas A&M-Kingsville lost to West Texas A&M 9-1 in regional second round. • Angelo State lost to A&M Kingsville 7-3 in regional first round.
2020	Canceled	Canceled	Canceled due to COVID-19 pandemic.

Texas A&M football players cheer teammates December 27, 2019, at the Texas Bowl. Photo by Jackson Lavarnway/Flickr (CC).

Football Bowl Games

Following are the college football bowl games involving Texas schools, as well as bowl and national championship games held in the state.

2020-2021

Bowl	Winner	Opponent	Date, Place
Myrtle Beach Bowl	Appalachian St. 56	North Texas 28	Dec. 21, Conway, Brooks Stadium
New Mexico Bowl	Hawaii 28	Houston 14	Dec. 24, Frisco, Toyota Stadium
First Responder Bowl	Louisiana-Lafayette 31	University of Texas-San Antonio 24	Dec. 26, Dallas, Gerald J. Ford St.
Alamo Bowl	Texas 55	Colorado 23	Dec. 29, San Antonio, Alamodome
Cotton Bowl	Oklahoma 55	Florida 20	Dec. 30, Arlington, AT&T Stadium
Armed Forces Bowl	Mississippi St. 28	Tulsa 26	Dec. 31, Ft. Worth, Amon Carter St.
Rose Bowl	Alabama 31	Notre Dame 14	Jan. 1, Arlington, AT&T Stadium
Orange Bowl	Texas A&M 41	North Carolina 27	Jan. 2, Miami, Hard Rock Stadium

2019-2020

Bowl	Winner	Opponent	Date, Place
Frisco Bowl	Kent State 51	Utah State 41	Dec. 21, Frisco, Toyota Stadium
Boca Raton Bowl	FAU 52	SMU 28	Dec. 21, Boca Raton, FAU Stadium
Texas Bowl	Texas A&M 24	Oklahoma State 21	Dec. 27, Houston, NRG Stadium
First Responder Bowl	W. Kentucky 23	W. Michigan 20	Dec. 30, Dallas, Gerald J. Ford Sta.
Sun Bowl	Arizona St. 20	Florida St. 14	Dec. 31, El Paso, Sun Bowl
Alamo Bowl	Texas 38	Utah 10	Dec. 31, San Antonio, Alamodome
Sugar Bowl	Georgia 26	Baylor 14	Jan. 1, New Orleans, Superdome
Armed Forces Bowl	Tulane 30	S. Mississippi 13	Jan. 4, Fort Worth, Amon G. Carter

Major Professional Sports

Major League Baseball

Houston Astros (American League West)

Year	Win	Loss	%	Finish
2013	51	111	.315	5th in division.
2014	70	92	.432	4th in division.
2015	86	76	.531	2nd in division; lost division series to Kansas City Royals 3-2.
2016	84	78	.519	3rd in division.
*2017	101	61	.623	**World Series champions**; defeated LA Dodgers 4-3.
2018	103	59	.636	1st in division; lost ALCS to Boston Red Sox 4-1.
2019	107	55	.660	1st in division; lost to Washington Nationals in World Series, 4-3.
**2020	29	31	.483	2nd in division.

*Astros used cameras to steal signals during 2018 and 2019 seasons, notably the 2017 postseason.
**COVID-19 pandemic-shortened season

Texas Rangers (American League West)

Year	Win	Loss	%	Finish
2013	91	72	.562	2nd in division.
2014	67	95	.414	5th in division.
2015	88	74	.543	1st in division; lost division series to Toronto Blue Jays 3-2.
2016	95	67	.586	1st in division; lost division series to Toronto Blue Jays 3-0.
2017	78	84	.481	Tied for 3rd in division.
2018	67	95	.414	5th in division.
2019	78	84	.481	3rd in division.
2020	22	38	.414	5th in division.

National Football League (NFL)

Houston Texans (AFC South)

Year	Win	Loss	Finish
2013	2	14	4th in division.
2014	9	7	2nd in division.
2015	9	7	1st in division; lost wild-card round to Kansas City Chiefs 30-0.
2016	9	7	1st in division; lost division playoff to New England Patriots 34-16.
2017	4	12	4th in division.
2018	11	5	1st in division; lost wild-card playoff to Indianapolis Colts 21-7.
2019	10	6	1st in division; lost divisional round to Kansas City Chiefs 51-31.
2020	4	12	3rd in division.

Dallas Cowboys (NFC East)

Year	Win	Loss	Finish
2013	8	8	2nd in division.
2014	12	4	1st in division; lost divisional playoff to Green Bay Packers 26-21.
2015	4	12	4th in division.
2016	13	3	1st in division; lost divisional playoff to Green Bay Packers 34-31.
2017	9	7	2nd in division.
2018	10	6	2nd in division; lost divisional playoff to Los Angeles Rams 30-22.
2019	8	8	2nd in division.
2020	6	10	3rd in division.

National Basketball Association (NBA)

San Antonio Spurs (Southwest)

Year	Win	Loss	%	Finish
2013–14	62	20	.756	Won NBA championship over Miami Heat 4–1.
2014–15	55	27	.671	Lost first round to Los Angeles Clippers 4–3.
2015–16	67	15	.817	Lost conference semifinals to Oklahoma City Thunder 4-2.
2016–17	61	21	.744	Lost conference finals to Golden State Warriors 4–0.
2017–18	47	35	.573	Lost first round to Golden State Warriors 4–1.
2018–19	48	34	.582	Lost first round to Denver Nuggets 4-3.
2019–20	32	39	.451	Run of 22 consecutive postseason appearances ends.
2020–21	33	39	.458	Lost to Memphis Grizzlies 100-96 in play-in tournament.

Houston Rockets (Southwest)

Year	Win	Loss	%	Finish
2013–14	54	28	.659	Lost first round to Portland Trail Blazers 4-2.
2014–15	56	26	.683	Lost conference finals to Golden State Warriors 4–1.
2015–16	41	41	.500	Lost first round to Golden State Warriors 4-1.
2016–17	55	27	.671	Lost conference semifinals to San Antonio Spurs 4–2.
2017–18	65	17	.793	Lost Western Conference finals to Golden State Warriors 4–3.
2018–19	53	29	.646	Lost conference semifinals to Golden State Warriors 4–2.
2019–20	44	28	.611	Lost conference semifinals to Los Angeles Lakers 4-1.
2020–21	17	55	.236	Did not advance to playoffs.

Dallas Mavericks (Southwest)

Year	Win	Loss	%	Finish
2013–14	49	33	.598	Lost first round to San Antonio Spurs 4-3.
2014–15	50	32	.610	Lost first round to Houston Rockets 4–1.
2015–16	42	40	.512	Lost first round to Oklahoma City Thunder 4-1.
2016–17	33	49	.402	Did not advance to playoffs.
2017–18	24	58	.293	Did not advance to playoffs.
2018–19	33	49	.402	Did not advance to playoffs.
2019–20	43	32	.573	Lost first round to Clippers 4-2.
2020–21	42	30	.583	Clinched division; lost to LA Clippers 4-3.

Women's National Basketball Association (WNBA)

Dallas Wings (Western Conference)

The franchise was founded in 1998 as the Detroit Shock, where it played until 2010. In 2015, it moved to Dallas-Fort Worth from Tulsa.

The Wings play in College Park Center at the University of Texas at Arlington.

The majority owner is Bill Cameron, who is an Oklahoma City businessman. He also owns part of the Oklahoma City Thunder in the NBA.

The WNBA has 12 teams, and its season is played from May to September. The other WNBA team in Texas was the Houston Comets, who were an original franchise when the league was formed in 1997. The team folded in 2008 when no new owners could be found.

Year	Win	Loss	%	Finish
2016	11	23	.324	Did not advance to playoffs.
2017	16	18	.470	Lost first-round game to Washington Mystics 86-76
2018	15	19	.441	Lost first-round game to Phoenix Mercury 101-83
2019	10	24	.294	Did not advance to playoffs.
2020	8	14	.364	Did not advance to playoffs.

Clockwise: The Dallas Stars face off against the Los Angeles Kings in Los Angeles on January 5, 2020; February 28, 2019; and January 5, 2020. Photos by Dinur/Flickr (CC).

National Hockey League (NHL)

Dallas Stars (Central Division)

Year	Win	Loss	Overtime loss	Finish
2013–14	40	30	11	Lost conference quarterfinals to Anaheim 4-2.
2014–15	41	31	10	Did not advance to playoffs.
2015–16	50	23	9	Lost second round to St. Louis Blues 4–3.
2016–17	34	37	11	Did not advance to playoffs.
2017–18	42	32	8	Did not advance to playoffs.
2018–19	43	32	7	Lost second round to St. Louis Blues 4–3.
2019–20	37	24	8	Lost to Tampa Bay Lightning 4-2 in Stanley Cup Finals.
2020–21	23	19	14	Did not advance to playoffs.

Did you know

Blake Coleman, a Plano native, helped the Tampa Bay Lightning win the Stanley Cup in 2020 and 2021. He scored two goals against the Dallas Stars in Game 6 of the Stanley Cup Final in 2020.

Major League Soccer (MLS)

Austin FC (Western Conference)

On January 15, 2019, Major League Soccer announced the addition of its 27th member, the Austin Football Club. A new stadium, dubbed Q2 Stadium, was built at McKalla Place in north Austin specifically to house the team.

Austin FC is the first major professional sports team to play in the Texas capital; prior to 2021, Austin was the largest city in the United States without any kind of major league presence.

Austin FC's first eight games were played on the road. The inaugural match was played on April 17, 2021, against the Los Angeles FC, where Austin FC lost 2-0. The first win was also on the road, this against the Colorado Rapids, 3-1, on April 24, 2021. Diego Fagundez scored the team's first official goal during this match.

The first home match was played on June 19, 2021, to a scoreless draw, and the first home win was on July 1, 2021, against the Portland Timbers, 4-1. Jon Gallagher scored Q2 Stadium's inaugural goal during the Timbers match.

Choosing a Logo

Austin FC's logo features four intertwined live oaks, their roots representing the four cardinal directions. This represents the four quarters of Austin: north, south, east, and west. It was designed by a local studio known as "The Butler Bros." Following the theme of "growth," the team's rallying cry is, "Grow the legend."

Sources: Major League Soccer, Austin FC, Forbes, Austin Statesman.

FC Dallas (Western Conference)

Year	Win	Loss	Draw	Finish
2013	11	12	11	8th in conference
2014	16	12	6	4th in conference; lost semifinals to Seattle Sounders
2015	18	10	6	1st in conference; lost finals to Portland Timbers 5-3
2016	17	8	9	1st in conference; lost semifinals to Seattle Sounders 4-2
2017	11	10	13	7th in conference
2018	16	9	9	4th in conference; lost knockout round to Portland Timbers 2-1
2019	13	12	9	7th in conference; lost round one to Seattle Sounders 4-3
2020	9	6	7	6th in conference; lost semifinals to Seattle Sounders 1-0

Houston Dynamo (Western Conference)

Year	Win	Loss	Draw	Finish
Eastern Conference				
2013	14	11	9	4th in conference; lost final to Kansas City 2-1
2014	11	17	6	8th in conference
Western Conference				
2015	11	14	9	8th in conference
2016	7	14	13	8th in conference
2017	13	10	11	4th in conference
2018	10	16	8	9th in conference
2019	12	18	4	10th in conference
2020	23	4	10	12th in conference

National Women's Soccer League (NWSL)

Houston Dash

Year	Win	Loss	Draw	Finish
2016	6	10	4	8th in league
2017	7	14	3	8th in league
2018	9	10	5	6th in league
2019	7	12	5	7th in league
2020	3	1	0	Season cancelled due to COVID-19 pandemic.

Texas Sports Hall of Fame

The Texas Sports Hall of Fame was organized in 1951 by the Texas Sports Writers Association. Each year the honorees are inducted into the Hall of Fame at a gala dinner.

The second such fete in 1952 was headlined by, "That filmland athlete, Ronald Reagan, and his actress wife, Nancy Davis," according to *The Dallas Morning News* on June 9, 1952.

The hall was originally in Grand Prairie in the Dallas-Fort Worth area. The Hall of Fame was closed in 1986 for financial reasons, but in 1991 it was reopened in Waco. In addition to memorabilia, the new location also houses archives.

Under the current selection process, dues-paying members of the Texas Sports Hall of Fame can nominate any number of individuals. (Anyone can become a member.)

The selection committee, chaired by Dave Campbell, founder of *Texas Football Magazine*, reviews all nominees and creates the "Official Voting Membership" ballot.

Ballots are then mailed to the voting membership, former Texas Sports Hall of Fame inductees, and the media selection committee.

The results of the balloting are announced in the autumn with the induction banquet following in the winter.

The hall of fame website is at tshof.org.

Year	Inductee	Sport	Texas connection, career
2020	Adrian Beltre	Baseball	Texas Ranger baseman; 4-time All-Star, 5-time Golden Glove
	Paul Cass	Tennis	Developed State Team Tournament; coached winning teams
	Michelle Carter	Track and Field	US record-holder in shot with throw of 67′8″ in 2016 Olympics
	Clint Dempsey	Soccer	Scored in 3 World Cups; 5th-fastest score in Cup history
	Robert Griffin III	Football	Led Baylor to 10-3 record; Heisman winner; AP Player of Year
	Shane Lechler	Football	Houston Texan punter; records for career punting average
	Chuck Sanchelli	Tennis	Founder, volunteer, and member of multiple tennis programs
	Francie Larrieu Smith	Track & Field	Olympian; established 36 US records, 12 world bests
	Kathy Vick	Tennis	Ranked first in Texas in singles, doubles consistently, ages 40-60
	Teresa Weatherspoon	Basketball	Led LA Tech to title, 1988; won gold medal in 1988 Olympics
	Carol Weyman	Tennis	Founded circuit for junior players, "Road to Little Mo Nationals"
2019	Maureen Connolly-Brinker	Tennis	Dallas, 9 Grand Slam singles titles 1950s
	Tony Franklin	Football	Big Spring, FW Arlington Heights, A&M, NFL kicker 1979–88
	Andre Johnson	Football	Wide receiver 14 years mostly with Houston Texans
	Nancy Liebermann	Basketball	First woman coach of men's professionals, for Texas Legends
	Loyd Phillips	Football	Longview, 1967–69 Chicago Bears, Outland Trophy
	Greg Swindell	Baseball	Houston Sharpstown High, UT, MLB pitcher 1986–2002
	Jason Witten	Football	All-Pro tight end, Dallas Cowboys 2003–17
2018	Johnny Bailey	Football	Running back, Houston Yates, Texas A&I, NFL 1990-95
	Nell Fortner	Basketball	New Braunfels, UT, Olympics 2000, coach 1983-2012
	Pete Fredenburg	Football	Player SWT 1966-70, coach Mary Hardin-Baylor 1998–present
	Gary Kubiak	Football	QB Houston St. Pius, A&M 1983, coach Texans, Broncos
	Cathy Self-Morgan	Basketball	Jourdanton, coach Duncanville, 8 girls state champs 2003–19
	Gerald Myers	Basketball	Borger, player, coach, AD, Houston Baptist, Texas Tech – 2011
	Michael Young	Baseball	All-star infielder, Texas Rangers 2000-12
	Vince Young	Football	Houston Madison, QB UT national champs 2005, NFL
	Jill Sterkel	Swimming	UT 1980–83, Olympic medialist 1976, 1980, 1984

Go to **texasalmanac.com/topics/sports/texas-sports-hall-fame** for a complete list of inductees beginning with 1951.

Year	Inductee	Sport	Texas connection, career
2017	Rita Buck-Crockett	Volleyball	San Antonio, U of H All-American 1977, Olympics 1980, 1984
	Dave Elmendorf	Football/Baseball	Houston, All-American at A&M 1970, LA Rams
	Pat Henry	Track	Blinn 1988–2004, A&M coach 2007–11, 35 team national titles
	Flo Hyman	Volleyball	U of H All-American 1970s, Olympics 1984
	Nastia Liukin	Gymnastics	Parker, 5 medals at Olympics 2008
	Eric Metcalf	Football/Track	UT 1980s All-American, NFL
	Wade Phillips	Football	Orange, U of H, coach Cowboys, Houston Oilers, Texans
	Darren Woodson	Football	Cowboys tackle 1992–2004
2016	Fred Akers	Football	Coach, Edinburg, Lubbock 1960s, UT 1977–86
	Larry Allen	Football	Dallas Cowboys All-Pro lineman 1994–2005
	Trevor Brazile	Rodeo	Amarillo, 13-time cowboy world champion 2006–15
	T.J. Ford	Basketball	Houston Willowridge, UT All-American, NBA 2003–12
	Ken Gray	Football	San Saba, Howard Payne, Cardinals, Oilers lineman 1958–70
	Jacob Green	Football	Pasadena, A&M, Seattle, 49ers lineman 1980–92
	Andy Pettitte	Baseball	Deer Park, Yankees, Astros pitcher 1995–2013
	"Smokey" Joe Williams	Baseball	Seguin, San Antonio, Negro Leagues pitcher 1907–32
2015	Zelmo Beaty	Basketball	Hillister, Woodville. Prairie View A&M, NBA-ABA 1962–75
	Gil Brandt	Football	Dallas Cowboys personnel executive 1960–88
	Ty Detmer	Football	Laredo, SA Southwest quarterback, 1990 Heisman at BYU
	Cliff Harris	Football	Dallas Cowboys safety 1970–79
	Richard Quick	Swimming	Highland Park, SMU, UT coach, Olympics coach 1984–2004
	Nolan Richardson	Basketball	El Paso, Texas Western 1961–64, Western Texas coach
	Everson Walls	Football	Richardson Berkner. Cowboys defensive back 1981–89
	Jeremy Wariner	Track	Arlington Lamar, Baylor, Olympic medalist 2004–08
2014*	Doug English	Football	Dallas Adams, UT tackle, Detroit Lions 1975–85
	Larry Johnson	Basketball	Dallas Skyline, Odessa College, UNLV, NBA 1991–2001
	Charlie Krueger	Football	Caldwell, A&M All-American under Bear Bryant, 49ers 1959–73
	Dat Nguyen	Football	Rockport-Fulton, A&M linebacker 1995-98, Dallas 1999–2005
	Pudge Rodriguez	Baseball	Texas Ranger starting in 1991, All-Star catcher 14 times
	Thurman Thomas	Football	Houston, Oklahoma State, NFL running back 1988–2000
	Sanya Richards-Ross	Track	Austin, UT track, Olympic medalist 2004, 2008, 2012
	Don Trull	Football	All-American quarterback Baylor 1960s, AFL-NFL 1963–74
2012*	Drew Brees	Football	Austin Westlake quarterback 1993–96, New Orleans Saints
	Walt Garrison	Football	Lewisville, fullback Dallas Cowboys 1966–74
	Eddie Mathews	Baseball	Texarkana, Boston/Milwaukee/Atlanta Braves 1952–66
	Bobby Moegle	Baseball	Winningest high school coach, Lubbock Monterey 1960–99
	Shaquille O'Neal	Basketball	San Antonio Cole, 19 years NBA, Lakers, Heat
	Cat Osterman	Softball	Houston, Cypress Springs, UT pitcher, Olympics
	Ricky Williams	Football	UT running back 1995–98, Heisman, NFL 1999–2011

*Designation changed in 2013 from year the inductees were selected to the year the award was presented.

Sources: Texas Sports Hall of Fame, The Handbook of Texas, The Dallas Morning News and other sources.

Texas Olympic Medalists

This is a list of athletes with Texas connections who have won medals in the Olympics including the 2016 games in Rio de Janeiro. This list includes those born here or have lived in Texas, as well as U.S. team members who spent their collegiate careers at Texas universities.

Information included is: the athlete's name, the sport and the year, as well as the types of medals (G-Gold, S-Silver, B-Bronze).

If the athlete won more than one of the same kind of medal in any one year, the number is noted before the letter code; i.e., 2G indicates that the athlete won two gold medals in the games that year.

The symbol (†) following the medal code indicates that the athlete participated in preliminary contests only; the medal was awarded because of membership on a winning team.

Years in which the athlete participated but did not win a medal are not included. Track indicates all track and field events except those noted separately.

More results can be seen at tshaonline.org.

Source: United States Olympic Committee.

Olympian	Sport	Year	Medal
Abdallah, Nia Nicole	Taekwondo	2004	S
Adams, Rachel	Volleyball	2016	B
Allen, Chad	Baseball	1996	B
Armstrong, Lance	*Cycling*	*2000*	*B**
Arnette, Jay Hoyland	Basketball	1960	G
Austin, Charles	Track	1996	G
Baker, Walter Thane	Track	1956	G,S,B
		1952	S
Baptiste, Kirk	Track	1984	S
Barr, Beth	Swimming	1988	S
Bassham, Lanny Robert	Shooting	1976	G
		1972	S
Bates, Michael D.	Track	1992	B
Beck, Robert Lee	Pentathlon	1960	2B
Beckie, Janine	Soccer	2016	B
Bedforth, B.J.	Swimming	2000	G
Berens, Ricky	Swimming	2012	G, S
		2008	G
Berube, Ryan Thomas	Swimming	1996	G
Biles, Simone	Gymnastics	2016	4G, B
Boudia, David	Diving	2016	S, B
		2012	G, B
Brew, Derrick K.	Track	2004	G, B
Brown, Earlene Dennis	Track	1960	B
Browning, David (Skippy)	Diving	1952	G
Buckner, William Quinn	Basketball	1976	G
Buford-Bailey, Tonja	Track	1996	B
Burrell, Leroy Russel	Track	1992	G
Butler, Jimmy	Basketball	2016	G
Carey, Rick	Swimming	1984	3G
Carlisle, Daniel T.	Shooting	1984	B
Carter, Michael D.	Shotput	1984	S
Carter, Michelle	Shotput	2016	G

* In January 2013, the International Olympic Committee disqualified Lance Armstrong from the 2000 events he competed in after he was found to have used drugs to enhance his performance.

Olympian	Sport	Year	Medal
Catchings, Tamika	Basketball	2016	G
		2012	G
Clay, Bryan E.	Decathlon	2008	G
		2004	S
Clement, Kerron	Track	2016	G
Cline, Nancy Lieberman	Basketball	1976	S
Cohen, Tiffany	Swimming	1984	G
Conger, Jack	Swimming	2016	G
Corbelli, Laurie Flachmeier	Volleyball	1984	S
Cotton, John	Baseball	2000	G
Crocker, Ian	Swimming	2008	G
		2004	G,S,B
		2000	G
Cross-Battle, Tara	Volleyball	1992	B
Crouser, Ryan	Shotput	2016	G
Davis, Clarissa G.	Basketball	1992	B
Davis, Jack Wells	Track	1956	S
		1952	S
Davis, Josh C.	Swimming	2000	2S
		1996	3G
Davis, W.F. (Buddy)	High Jump	1952	G
DeLoach, Joseph N. Jr.	Track	1988	G
Dersch, Hans	Swimming	1992	G
Didrikson, Mildred (Babe)	Track	1932	2G, S
Donie, Scott R.	Diving	1992	S
Drexler, Clyde	Basketball	1992	G
Dumais, Troy	Diving	2012	B
Durant, Kevin	Basketball	2016	G
		2012	G
Dusing, Nate	Swimming	2004	B
		2000	S
Eller, Glenn	Shooting	2008	G
Ethridge, Mary (Kamie)	Basketball	1988	G
Farmer-Patrick, Sandra	Track	1992	S
Feigen, Jimmy	Swimming	2016	G
		2012	S†

Olympian	Sport	Year	Medal
Fields, Connor	Cycling	2016	G
Finn-Burrell, Michelle Bonae	Track	1992	G
Foerster, Paul	Sailing	1992	S
		2000	S
		2004	G
Forbes, James Ricardo	Basketball	1972	S
Ford, Gilbert (Gib)	Basketball	1956	G
Foreman, George	Boxing	1968	G
Fortenberry, Joe Cephis	Basketball	1936	G
Francis, Phyllis	Track	2016	G
Galloway, Jackie	Taekwondo	2016	B
Garrison, Zina	Tennis	1988	G, B
George, Chris	Baseball	2000	G
Gjertson, Doug	Swimming	1992	G, B
		1988	G
Glenesk, Dean William	Pentathlon	1984	S
Goldblatt, Scott	Swimming	2004	G
		2000	B
Gonzáles, Paul G. Jr.	Boxing	1984	G
Gordon, Chris-Ann	Track	2016	S
Griner, Brittney	Basketball	2016	G
Guidry, Carlette D.	Track	1996	G†
		1992	G
Haas, Townley	Swimming	2016	G
Hall, Gary Jr.	Swimming	2004	G, B
		2000	2G,S,B
		1996	2G, 2S
Hamm, Mia	Soccer	2004	G
		2000	S
		1996	G
Hannan, Tommy	Swimming	2000	G
Hansen, Brendan	Swimming	2012	G, B
		2008	G
		2004	G,S,B
Hansen, Fred Morgan	Track	1964	G
Hardee, Trey	Track	2012	S
Harkrider, Kiplan P.	Baseball	1996	B
Hartwell, Erin Wesley	Cycling	1996	S
		1992	B
Hays, Todd	Bobsled	2002	S
Heath, Michael Steward	Swimming	1984	2G, S
Hedgepeth, Whitney L.	Swimming	1996	G, 2S
Hedrick, Chad	Speed Skating	2010	S,B
		2006	G,S,B
Heidenreich, Jerry	Swimming	1972	2G,S,B
Henry, James Edward	Diving	1968	B

Olympian	Sport	Year	Medal
Hill, Denean E.	Track	1992	S
		1988	S
		1984	G
Hill, Grant Henry	Basketball	1996	G
Homfeld, Conrad E.	Equestrian	1984	G, S
Hooker, Destinee	Volleyball	2012	S
Hooper, Darrow	Shotput	1952	S
Horton, Jonathan	Gymnastics	2008	S
Howard, Sherri Francis	Track	1988	S
		1984	G
Jackson, Lucious Brown	Basketball	1964	G
Jacobs, Chris	Swimming	1988	2G, S
Johnson, Michael	Track	2000	2G
		1996	2G
		1992	G
Johnson, Rafer L.	Decathlon	1960	G
		1956	S
Jones, John Wesley (Lam)	Track	1976	G
Jordan, DeAndre	Basketball	2016	G
Jordan, Shaun	Swimming	1992	G
		1988	G
Juarez, Ricardo Rocky	Boxing	2000	S
Julich, Robert William	Cycling	2004	B
Keeler, Kathryn Elliott	Rowing	1984	G
Kern, Douglas James	Sailing	1992	S
Kiefer, Adolph	Swimming	1936	G
Kimmons, Trell	Track	2012	S
King, Judith Brown	Track	1984	S
Kleine, Megan	Swimming	1992	G†
Knight, Bianca	Track	2012	G
Kocian, Madison	Gymnastics	2016	G, S
Kolius, John Waldrip	Sailing	1976	S
Lane, Colleen	Swimming	2004	S
Langkop, Dorothy Franey	Speed Skating	1932	B
Leetch, Brian Joseph	Ice Hockey	2002	S
Lewis, F. (Carl) Carlton	Track	1996	G
		1992	2G
		1988	2G, S
		1984	4G
Lienhard, William Barner	Basketball	1952	G
Lipinski, Tara K.	Figure Skating	1998	G
Liukin, Nastia	Gymnastics	2008	G,3S,B
Lloyd, Andrea	Basketball	1988	G
Losey, Robert G. (Greg)	Pentathlon	1984	S
Lopez, Diana	Taekwondo	2008	B
Lopez, Mark	Taekwondo	2008	S

Counties

HISTORY

MAPS

VITAL STATISTICS

CITIES & TOWNS

CLIMATE

This bridge, where State Highway 53 bridge crosses Leon River in Bell County, is on the National Register of Historic Places. Photo by Larry D. Moore, CC by 3/Wikimedia Commons

Counties of Texas

These pages describe Texas' 254 counties and hundreds of towns. Descriptions are based on reports from chambers of commerce, the Texas AgriLife Extension agents, federal and state agencies, the Handbook of Texas, and other sources. Consult the index for other county information.

County maps are based on those of the Texas Department of Transportation and are copyrighted, 2019, as are the entire contents.

Physical Features: Descriptions are from U.S. Geological Survey and local sources.

Economy: From information provided by local chambers of commerce and county extension agents.

History: From Texas statutes, Fulmore's History and Geography of Texas as Told in County Names, WPA Historical Records Survey, Texas Centennial Commission Report, and the Handbook of Texas.

Race/Ethnicity: Percentage estimates from the 2017 American Community Survey conducted by the U.S. Bureau of the Census. "Anglo" refers to non-Hispanic whites; "Asian" refers to persons having origins in the Far East, Southeast Asia, or the Indian subcontinent. "Other" includes those of American Indian origin, Pacific Islanders, and those who identify with two or more races. People may choose to report more than one race to indicate their racial mixture, such as "American Indian" and "White." People who identify their origin as Hispanic may be of any race. Thus, the totals may add up to more than 100 percent.

Vital Statistics: From the Texas Department of State Health Services Annual Report 2015, the most recent report available.

Recreation: From information provided by local chambers of commerce and county extension agents. Attempts were made to note activities unique to the area or that point to ethnic or cultural heritage.

Minerals: From county extension agents.

Agriculture: Condensed from information provided to the Texas Almanac by county extension agents in 2019. Market value (total cash receipts) of agricultural products sold is from the Census of Agriculture of the U.S. Department of Agriculture that was conducted in 2017, the most recent report available.

Cities: Towns listed include the county seat, incorporated cities, and towns with post offices, as well as certain census designated places (CDP). Population figures for incorporated towns and CDPs are estimates for July 1, 2019, from the Texas Demographic Center. Population estimates for other towns are from local officials received through a Texas Almanac survey. When figures for small portions of major cities are given, they are in brackets, such as **part [46,885] of Dallas** in Collin County.

Sources Of Data Lists

Population (of county): The county population estimate of July 1, 2019, U.S. Census Bureau. The line following gives the percentage of increase or decrease from the 2010 U.S. census count.

Area: Total area in square miles, including water surfaces, as determined in the 2010 U.S. census.

Land Area: The land area in square miles as determined by the U.S. Census Bureau in 2010.

Altitude (ft.): Principally from U.S. Geological Survey topographic maps, including revisions available in 2008. Not all of the surface of Texas has been precisely surveyed for elevation; in some cases data are from the Texas Railroad Commission or the Texas Department of Transportation.

Climate: Provided by the National Oceanic and Atmospheric Administration state climatologist, College Station. Data are revised at 10-year intervals to cover the previous three decades. Listed are the latest compilations, as of Feb. 1, 2013, and pertain to a particular site within the county (usually the county seat). The data include: Rainfall (annual mean in inches); Temperature (in degrees Fahrenheit); January mean minimum and July mean maximum.

Workforce/Wages: Prepared by the Texas Workforce Commission, Austin, in cooperation with the Bureau of Labor Statistics of the U.S. Department of Labor. The data are computed from reports by all establishments subject to the Texas Unemployment Compensation Act.

(Agricultural employers are subject to the act if they employ as many as three workers for 20 weeks or pay cash wages of $6,250 in a quarter. Employers who pay $1,000 in wages in a quarter for domestic services are subject also. Still not mandatorily covered are self-employed, unpaid family workers, and those employed by churches and some small nonprofit organizations.)

The work/wage data include (state total, lowest county and highest county included here):

Civ. Labor: Civilian labor force as of April 1, 2021. Texas, 14,043,919; Kenedy County, 175; Harris County, 2,280,347.

Unemployed: The unemployment rate (percentage of workforce) as of April 1, 2021. Texas, 6.3; Loving County, 1.3; Starr County, 17.7.

Wages: Total Wages paid in the fourth quarter of 2020. Texas, $205,148,778,233; King County, $2,218,449; Harris County, $ 43,242,163,732.

Per Capita Income: Per capita personal income for 2019, as reported by the U.S. Bureau of Economic Analysis. Texas, $52,813; Hudspeth County, $23,569; Midland County, $130,983.

Property Values: Appraised gross market value of real and personal property from the Comptroller's Property Tax Assistance Division 2020 report.

Retail Sales: Figures for 2020 as reported to the state Comptroller of Public Accounts.

County Facts Elsewhere In Volume

Anderson County

Physical Features: Forested, hilly East Texas county, slopes to Trinity and Neches rivers; Lake Palestine; sandy, clay, black soils; pines, hardwoods.

Economy: Manufacturing, distribution, agribusiness, tourism; hunting and fishing leases; prison units.

History: Comanche, Waco, other tribes. Anglo-American settlers arrived in the 1830s. Antebellum slaveholding area. County created and organized from Houston County in 1846; named for K.L. Anderson, last vice president of the Republic of Texas.

Race/Ethnicity: Anglo, 57.8%; Black, 21.2%; Hispanic, 18.1%; Asian, 0.5%; Other, 2.3%.

Vital Statistics, annual: Births, 636; deaths, 655; marriages, 352; divorces, 102.

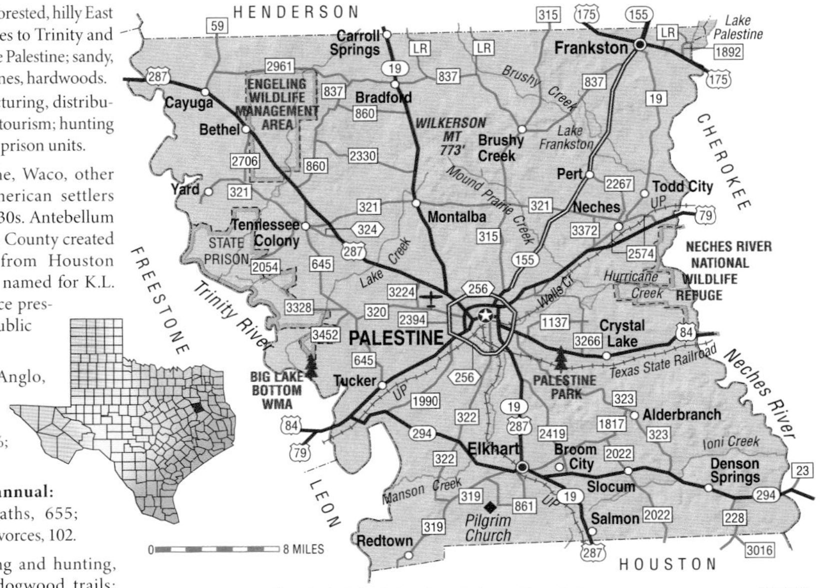

Recreation: Fishing and hunting, streams, lakes; dogwood trails; national wildlife refuge; historic sites; Texas State Railroad depot, park; museums.

Minerals: Oil and gas.

Agriculture: Beef cattle, hay, truck vegetables, melons, pecans, peaches. Market value $92.9 million. Timber sold.

PALESTINE (19,115) county seat; medical services, education, transportation; clothing, metal, wood products; scientific balloon station; historic bakery; library; vocational-technical facilities; hospital; UT-Tyler extension, community college; Museum of East Texas Culture; hot pepper festival in October.

Other towns include: **Cayuga** (137); **Elkhart** (1,299); **Frankston** (1,216), tourism, packaging industry, oil and gas, commuters to Tyler; depot museum, Square Fair in October; **Montalba** (110); **Neches** (175); and **Tennessee Colony** (300) site of state prisons.

Population	**59,025**
Change from 2010 (%)	1.0
Area (sq. mi.)	1,078.0
Land Area (sq. mi.)	1,062.6
Altitude (ft.)	174–773
Rainfall (in.)	46.6
Jan. mean min (°F)	34.5
July mean max (°F)	92.3
Civ. Labor	22,818
Unemployed (%)	5.4
Wages	$255,017,241
Per Capita Income	$36,027
Prop. Value	$4,623,249,054
Retail Sales	$558,575,224

Railroad Abbreviations

AAT	Austin Area Terminal Railroad
AGC	Alamo Gulf Coast Railway
ATK	AMTRAK
ANR	Angelina & Neches River Railroad
ATCX	Austin & Texas Central Railroad
BLR	Blacklands Railroad
BNSF	BNSF Railroad
BOP	Border Pacific Railroad
BRG	Brownsville & Rio Grande Int'l Railroad
CMC	CMC Railroad
DART	Dallas Area Rapid Transit
DGNO	Dallas, Garland & Northeastern Railroad
FWWR	Fort Worth & Western Railroad/Tarantula
GCSR	Gulf, Colorado & San Saba RailwayCorp.
GRR	Georgetown Railroad
GVSR	Galveston Railroad
KCS	Kansas City Southern Railway
KRR	Kiamichi Railroad Company
MCSA	Moscow, Camden & San Augustine RR
PCN	Point Comfort & Northern Railway
PNR	Panhandle Northern Railroad Company
PTRA	Port Terminal Railroad Association
PVS	Pecos Valley Southern Railway
RC	Rusk County Rural Rail Transportation District
RSS	Rockdale, Sandow & Southern Railroad
RVSC	Rio Valley Switching
SAW	South Plains Switching LTD
SRN	Sabine River & Northern Railroad Company
SSC	Southern Switching (Lone Star Railroad)
SW	Southwestern Shortline Railroad
TCT	Texas City Terminal Railway
TIBR	Timber Rock Railroad
TM	The Texas Mexican Railway Company
TN	Texas & Northern Railway
TNER	Texas Northeastern Railroad
TNMR	Texas & New Mexico Railroad
TNW	Texas North Western Railway
TP	Texas Pacifico Transportation
TSE	Texas South-Eastern Railroad Company
TXGN	Texas, Gonzales & Northern Railway
TXR	Texas Rock Crusher Railway
TSSR	Texas State Railroad
UP	Union Pacific Railroad Company
WTJR	Wichita, Tillman & Jackson Railway
WTLR	West Texas & Lubbock Railroad

Andrews County

Physical Features: South Plains, drain to playas; grass, mesquite, shin oak; red clay, sandy soils.

Economy: Natural resources/mining; manufacturing; construction; government/services; agribusiness.

History: Apache, Comanche area until U.S. Army campaigns of 1875. Ranching developed around 1900. Oil boom in 1940s. County created 1876 from Bexar Territory; organized 1910; named for Texas Revolutionary soldier Richard Andrews.

Race/Ethnicity: Anglo, 35.1%; Black, 1.1%; Hispanic, 62.1%; Asian, 0.4%; Other, 1.1%.

Vital Statistics, annual: Births, 323; deaths, 137; marriages, 119; divorces, 67.

Recreation: Prairie dog town, wetlands, bird viewing; museum; camper facilities; Fall Fiesta in September.

Minerals: Oil and gas.

Agriculture: Beef, cotton, sorghums, grains, corn, hay; significant irrigation. Market value $10.6 million.

ANDREWS (14,704) county seat; trade center, amphitheatre, hospital.

Other towns include, **McKinney Acres** (1,079).

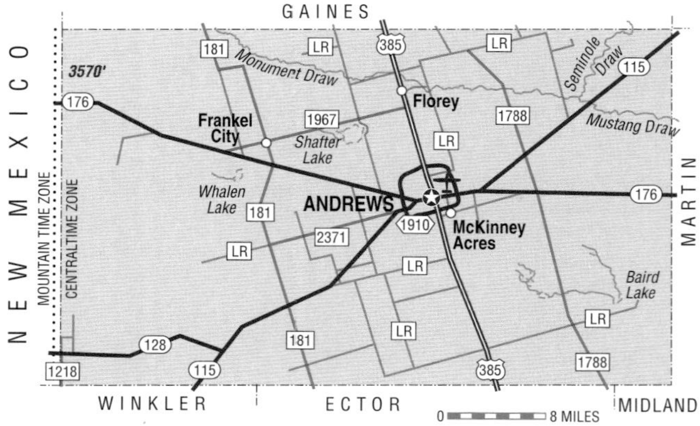

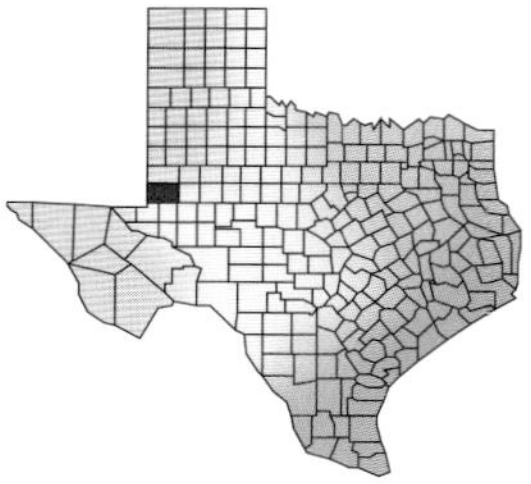

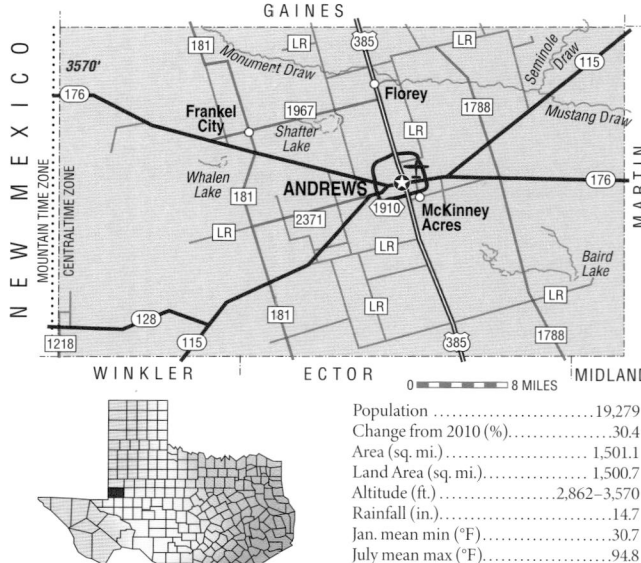

Population	19,279
Change from 2010 (%)	30.4
Area (sq. mi.)	1,501.1
Land Area (sq. mi.)	1,500.7
Altitude (ft.)	2,862–3,570
Rainfall (in.)	14.7
Jan. mean min (°F)	30.7
July mean max (°F)	94.8
Civ. Labor	8,703
Unemployed (%)	6.7
Wages	$122,230,195
Per Capita Income	$51,769
Prop. Value	$5,717,766,952
Retail Sales	$205,278,799

Angelina County

Physical Features: Rolling, hilly East Texas county; black, red, gray soils; Angelina National Forest.

Economy: Timber; manufacturers of iron and steel castings, truck trailers, mobile homes; government/services; wood and paper products.

History: Caddoan area. First land deed to Vicente Micheli 1801. Anglo-American setters arrived in 1820s. County created and organized in 1846 from Nacogdoches County; named for legendary Indian maiden Angelina.

Race/Ethnicity: Anglo, 59.7%; Black, 15%; Hispanic, 22.6%; Asian, 1%; Other, 1.6%.

Vital Statistics, annual: Births, 1,215; deaths, 871; marriages, 672; divorces, 327.

Recreation: Sam Rayburn Reservoir; national, state forests, parks; locomotive exhibit; Forest Festival, bike ride in fall.

Minerals: Limited output of natural gas and oil.

Agriculture: Poultry, beef, horticulture, limited fruits and vegetables. Market value $61.4 million. A leading timber-producing county.

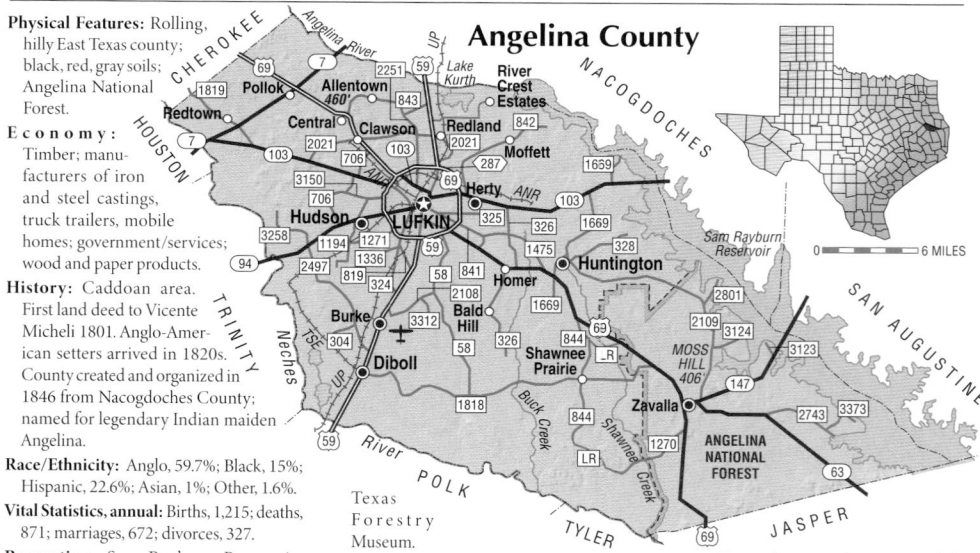

LUFKIN (36,423) county seat; manufacturing; Angelina College; hospitals; U.S., Texas Forest centers; zoo; Expo Center and Texas Forestry Museum.

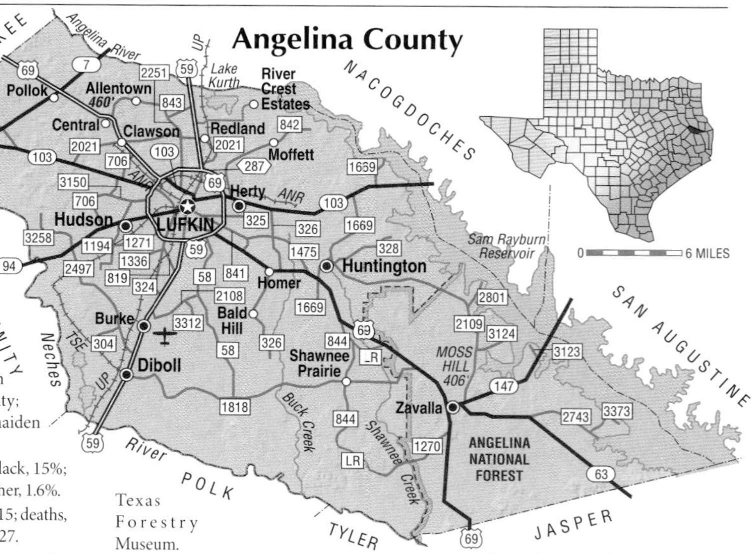

Other towns include: **Burke** (727); **Diboll** (5,279); **Hudson** (4,979); **Huntington** (2,149); **Pollok** (430); **Redland** (1,118); **Zavalla** (730).

For explanation of sources, symbols and abbreviations, see p. 204, and foldout map.

Population	**90,989**
Change from 2010 (%)	4.9
Area (sq. mi.)	864.7
Land Area (sq. mi.)	797.8
Altitude (ft.)	102–460
Rainfall (in.)	49.0
Jan. mean min (°F)	38.3
July mean max (°F)	93.3
Civ. Labor	35,055
Unemployed (%)	7.2
Wages	$397,384,176
Per Capita Income	$39,644
Prop. Value	$6,508,462,256
Retail Sales	$1,356,419,538

The Aransas National Wildlife Refuge, which spans through Aransas, Refugio, and Calhoun counties, sees a lot of Whooping Cranes in the wintertime. Photo by Klaus Nigge, CC 2/Wikimedia Commons

Aransas County

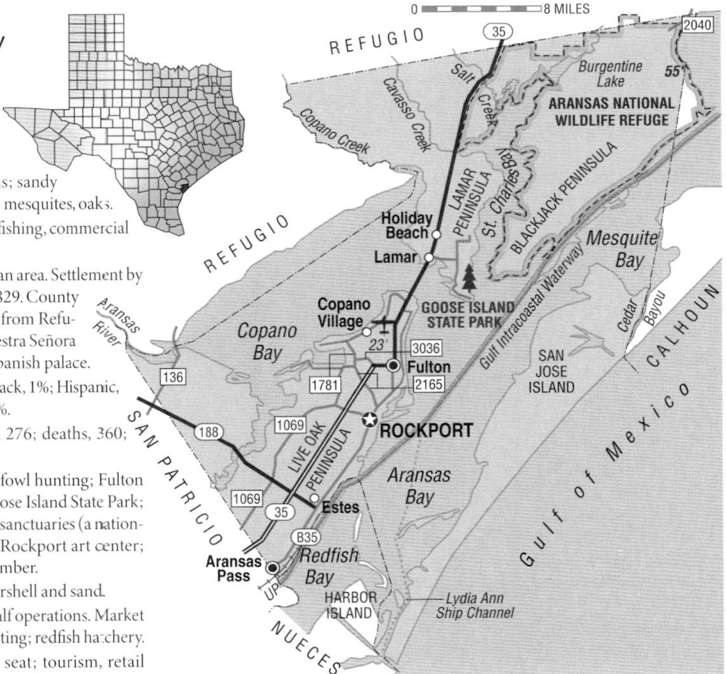

Physical Features: Coastal plains; sandy loam, coastal clays; bays, inlets; mesquites, oaks.

Economy: Tourism, recreational fishing, commercial shrimping, hunting.

History: Karankawa, Coahuiltecan area. Settlement by Irish and Mexicans began in 1829. County created and organized in 1871 from Refugio County; named for Rio Nuestra Señora de Aranzazu, derived from a Spanish palace.

Race/Ethnicity: Anglo, 65.6%; Black, 1%; Hispanic, 29.6%; Asian, 1.7%; Other, 1.9%.

Vital Statistics, annual: Births, 276; deaths, 360; marriages, 256; divorces, 100.

Recreation: Sport fishing, waterfowl hunting; Fulton Mansion; state marine lab; Goose Island State Park; Texas Maritime Museum; bird sanctuaries (a nationally known birding hotspot); Rockport art center; Hummer Bird festival in September.

Minerals: Oil and gas, also oystershell and sand.

Agriculture: Cotton, hay, cow-calf operations. Market value $1.9 million. Fishing, hunting; redfish hatchery.

ROCKPORT (10,449) county seat; tourism, retail trade, health care, construction/real estate; Festival of Wines Memorial Day weekend.

Fulton (1,437) tourism, retail trade, oyster and shrimp harvesting, museums, Oysterfest in March; **Holiday Beach** (507); and **Lamar** (618).

Also, part [808] of **Aransas Pass**.

Population	**23,710**
Change from 2010 (%)	2.4
Area (sq. mi.)	528.0
Land Area (sq. mi.)	252.1
Altitude (ft.)	sea level–55
Rainfall (in.)	34.6
Jan. mean min (°F)	47.9
July mean max (°F)	91.5
Civ. Labor	9,167
Unemployed (%)	7.9
Wages	$57,195,777
Per Capita Income	$51,614
Prop. Value	$4,237,577,962
Retail Sales	$303,206,949

Archer County

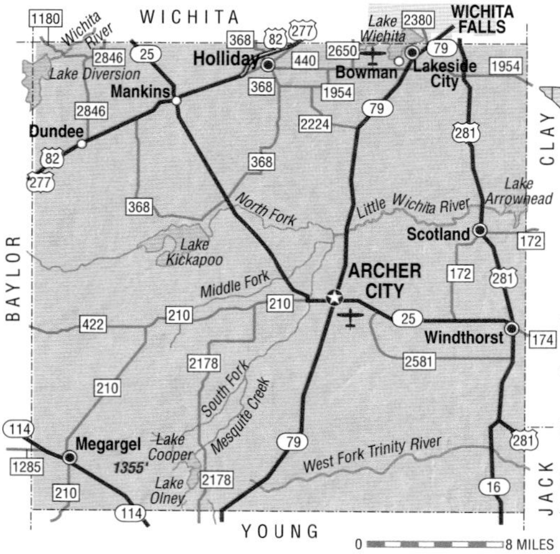

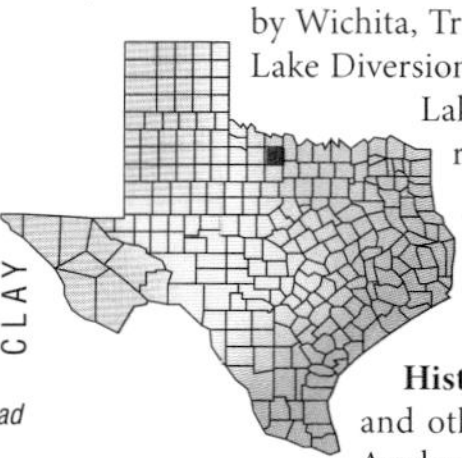

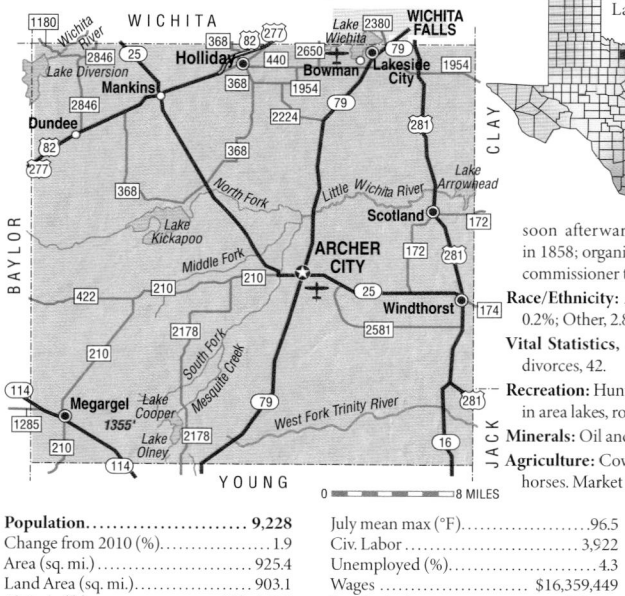

Physical Features: Northwestern county, rolling to hilly, drained by Wichita, Trinity River forks; Lake Kickapoo, Lake Diversion, Lake Wichita, Lake Arrowhead, Lake Cooper and Lake Olney; black, red loams, sandy soils; mesquites, post oaks.

Economy: Cattle, milk production, oil, hunting leases. Part of Wichita Falls metropolitan area.

History: Caddo, Comanche, Kiowas and other tribes in the area until 1875; Anglo-American settlement developed soon afterward. County created from Fannin Land District in 1858; organized in 1880. Named for Dr. B.T. Archer, Republic commissioner to United States.

Race/Ethnicity: Anglo, 85.7%; Black, 0.6%; Hispanic, 10.4%; Asian, 0.2%; Other, 2.8%.

Vital Statistics, annual: Births, 78; deaths, 91; marriages, 33; divorces, 42.

Recreation: Hunting of deer, turkey, dove, feral hog, coyote; fishing in area lakes, rodeo in June.

Minerals: Oil and natural gas.

Agriculture: Cow/calf, stocker cattle, dairy, wheat, hay, silage and horses. Market value $72.4 million.

Population	**9,228**	July mean max (°F)	96.5
Change from 2010 (%)	1.9	Civ. Labor	3,922
Area (sq. mi.)	925.4	Unemployed (%)	4.3
Land Area (sq. mi.)	903.1	Wages	$16,359,449
Altitude (ft.)	900–1,355	Per Capita Income	$52,335
Rainfall (in.)	30.7	Prop. Value	$2,043,858,534
Jan. mean min (°F)	29.0	Retail Sales	$50,170,110

ARCHER CITY (1,920) county seat; cattle, oil field service center; museum; book center; Royal Theatre productions; some manufacturing.

Other towns include: **Holliday** (1,774) Mayfest in spring; **Lakeside City** (1,047); **Megargel** (196); **Scotland** (512); **Windthorst** (395), biannual German sausage festival (also in Scotland).

For explanation of sources, symbols and abbreviations, see p. 204, and foldout map.

Armstrong County

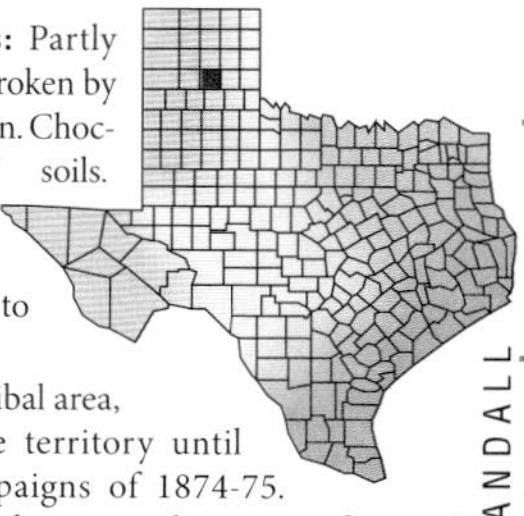

Physical Features: Partly on High Plains, broken by Palo Duro Canyon. Chocolate loam, gray soils.

Economy: Agribusiness, tourism, commuting to Amarillo.

History: Apache tribal area, then Comanche territory until U.S. Army campaigns of 1874-75. Anglo-Americans began ranching soon afterward. County created from Bexar District, 1876; organized in 1890; name honors pioneer Texas family.

Race/Ethnicity: Anglo, 90.7%; Black, 0.5%; Hispanic, 6.6%; Asian, 0%; Other, 2%.

Vital Statistics, annual: Births, 21; deaths, 38; marriages, 11; divorces, 3.

Recreation: Palo Duro Canyon State Park; Goodnight Ranch Home.

Minerals: Sand, gravel.

Agriculture: Stocker cattle, cow-calf operations; wheat, sorghum, cotton and hay; some irrigation. Market value $49.3 million.

CLAUDE (1,210) county seat; farm, ranch supplies; glass company; medical center; Caprock Roundup in July.

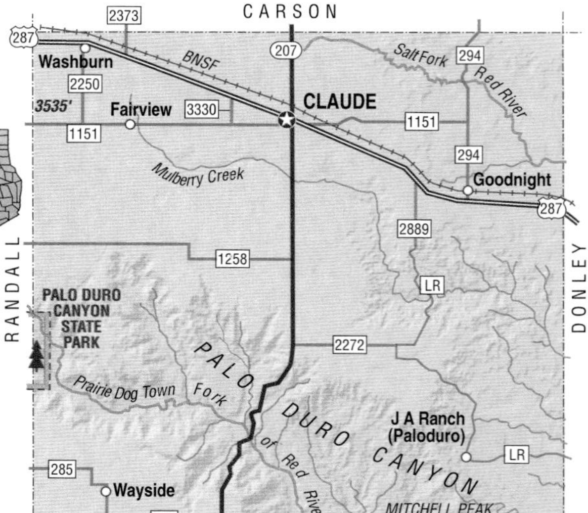

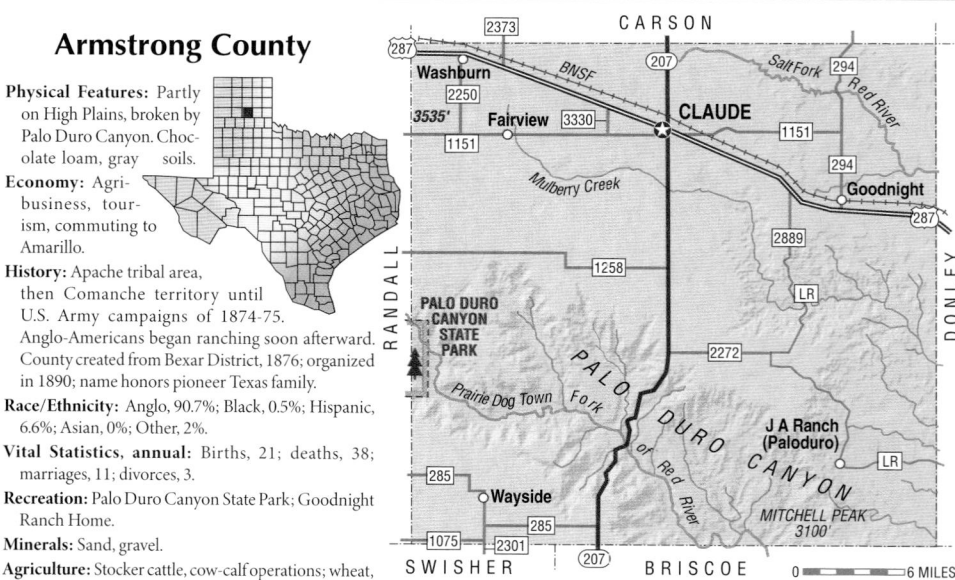

Population	**2,001**	July mean max (°F)	90.6
Change from 2010 (%)	5.3	Civ. Labor	943
Area (sq. mi.)	913.8	Unemployed (%)	3.8
Land Area (sq. mi.)	909.1	Wages	$4,710,368
Altitude (ft.)	2,300–3,535	Per Capita Income	$53,422
Rainfall (in.)	22.3	Prop. Value	$835,057,181
Jan. mean min (°F)	22.4	Retail Sales	$15,735,412

Atascosa County

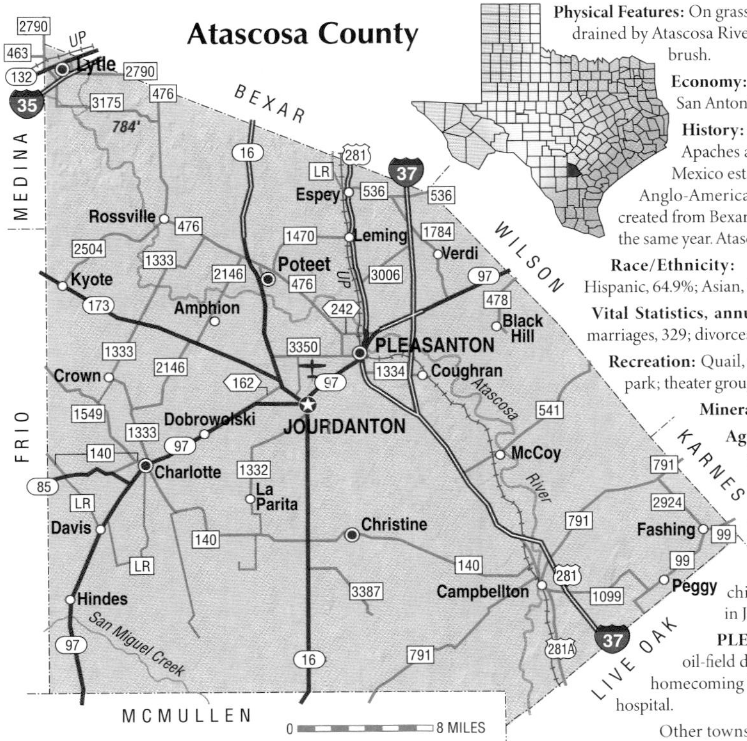

Physical Features: On grassy prairie south of San Antonio, drained by Atascosa River, tributaries; mesquites, other brush.

Economy: Coal plant, oil, commuters to San Antonio.

History: Coahuiltecan tribal area; later Apaches and Comanches. Families from Mexico established ranches in mid-1700s. Anglo-Americans arrived in 1840s. County created from Bexar District in 1856 and organized the same year. Atascosa means boggy in Spanish.

Race/Ethnicity: Anglo, 33.1%; Black, 0.5%; Hispanic, 64.9%; Asian, 0.2%; Other, 1%.

Vital Statistics, annual: Births, 689; deaths, 408; marriages, 329; divorces, 100.

Recreation: Quail, deer hunting; museums; river park; theater group.

Minerals: Lignite, oil, gas.

Agriculture: Beef cattle, peanuts, vegetable farming. Some 25,000 acres irrigated. Market value $74.3 million.

JOURDANTON (4,522) county seat; coal mining; hospital; park, walking trail; chili cookoff in May, Czech Day in July.

PLEASANTON (10,912) farming, oil-field drilling, health services; cowboy homecoming in August, Longhorn museum; hospital.

Other towns include: **Campbellton** (350); **Charlotte** (1,865); **Christine** (439); **Leming** (1,028); **Lytle** (3,069) greenhouse, peanuts processed; **Peggy** (22); **Poteet** (3,554) government/services, library, strawberry festival in April.

Population	**50,898**	July mean max.	95.4
Change from 2010 (%)	13.3	Civ. Labor	22,206
Area (sq. mi.)	1,221.5	Unemployed (%)	6.6
Land Area (sq. mi.)	1,219.5	Wages	$163,005,213
Altitude (ft.)	180–784	Per Capita Income	$37,644
Rainfall (in.)	32.1	Prop. Value	$6,487,746,450
Jan. mean min (°F)	39.3	Retail Sales	$670,593,391

Palo Duro Canyon takes up a lot of the land in Armstrong County. It is the second largest canyon in the United States. Photo by Peter Fitzgerald, CC 3/Wikimedia Commons

Austin County

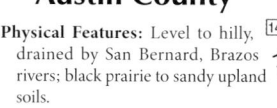

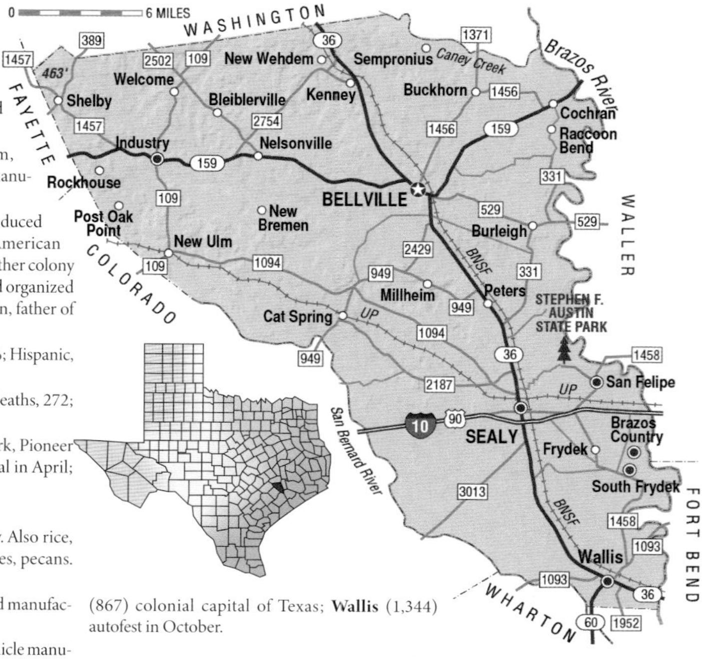

Physical Features: Level to hilly, drained by San Bernard, Brazos rivers; black prairie to sandy upland soils.

Economy: Agribusiness; tourism, government/services; metal, other manufacturing; commuting to Houston.

History: Tonkawa Indian tribal area; reduced by diseases. Birthplace of Anglo-American colonization, 1821, and German mother colony at Industry, 1831. County created and organized in 1837; named for Stephen F. Austin, father of Texas.

Race/Ethnicity: Anglo, 61%; Black, 9%; Hispanic, 27.5%; Asian, 0.4%; Other, 1.8%.

Vital Statistics, annual: Births, 347; deaths, 272; marriages, 182; divorces, 125.

Recreation: Fishing, hunting; state park, Pioneer Trail; Bellville Country Livin' festival in April; Lone Star Raceway Park.

Minerals: Oil and natural gas.

Agriculture: Beef production and hay. Also rice, corn, sorghum, nursery crops, grapes, pecans. Market value $33.1 million.

BELLVILLE (4,602) county seat; varied manufacturing; hospital; oil.

SEALY (6,805) oil-field and military vehicle manufacturing, varied industries; Blinn College branch; polka fest in March.

Other towns include: **Bleiblerville** (125); **Brazos Country** (488); **Cat Spring** (200); **Frydek** (900) Grotto celebration in April; **Industry** (331); **Kenney** (957); **New Ulm** (974) retail, art festival in April; **San Felipe** (867) colonial capital of Texas; **Wallis** (1,344) autofest in October.

Population	**32,067**
Change from 2010 (%)	12.8
Area (sq. mi.)	656.4
Land Area (sq. mi.)	646.5
Altitude (ft.)	70–463
Rainfall (in.)	41.8
Jan. mean min (°F)	39.7
July mean max (°F)	93.2
Civ. Labor	13,820
Unemployed (%)	5.9
Wages	$162,535,288
Per Capita Income	$51,118
Prop. Value	$6,961,592,737
Retail Sales	$370,248,025

Bailey County

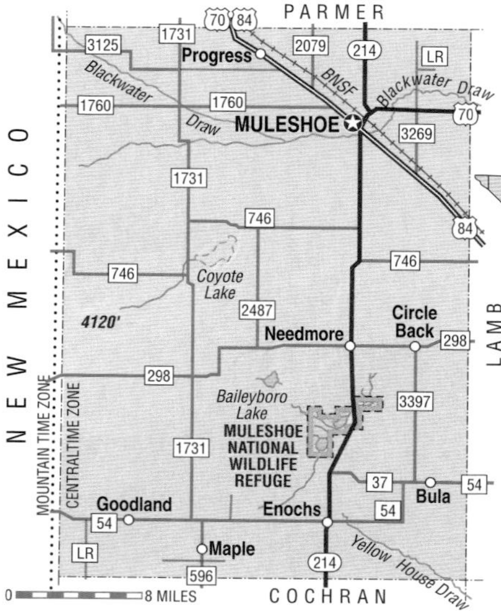

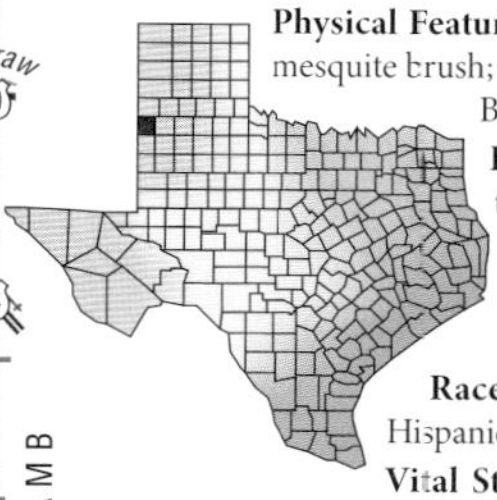

Physical Features: High Plains county, sandy loam soils; mesquite brush; drains to draws forming upper watershed of Brazos River, playas.

Economy: Farm supply manufacturing; electric generating plant; food-processing plants.

History: Settlement began after 1900. County created from Bexar District 1876, organized 1917. Named for Alamo hero Peter J. Bailey.

Race/Ethnicity: Anglo, 31.2%; Black, 0.8%; Hispanic, 65.4%; Asian, 0.3%; Other, 2%.

Vital Statistics, annual: Births, 137; deaths, 50; marriages, 58; divorces, 13..

Recreation: Muleshoe National Wildlife Refuge; "Old Pete," the national mule memorial; historical building park; museum; motorcycle rally; mule deer, sandhill crane, pheasant hunting.

Minerals: Insignificant.

Agriculture: Feedlot, dairy cattle; cotton, wheat, sorghum, corn, vegetables; some 50,000 acres irrigated. Market value $357.0 million.

MULESHOE (5,159) county seat; agribusiness center; feed-corn milling; hospital; livestock show.

Other towns include: **Enochs** (80); **Maple** (40).

Population	**7,113**
Change from 2010 (%)	-0.7
Area (sq. mi.)	827.5
Land Area (sq. mi.)	826.8
Altitude (ft.)	3,660–4,120
Rainfall (in.)	18.4
Jan. mean min (°F)	19.4
July mean max (°F)	92.0
Civ. Labor	2,499
Unemployed (%)	4.6
Wages	$29,271,987
Per Capita Income	$44,665
Prop. Value	$682,599,141
Retail Sales	$57,568,612

Bandera County

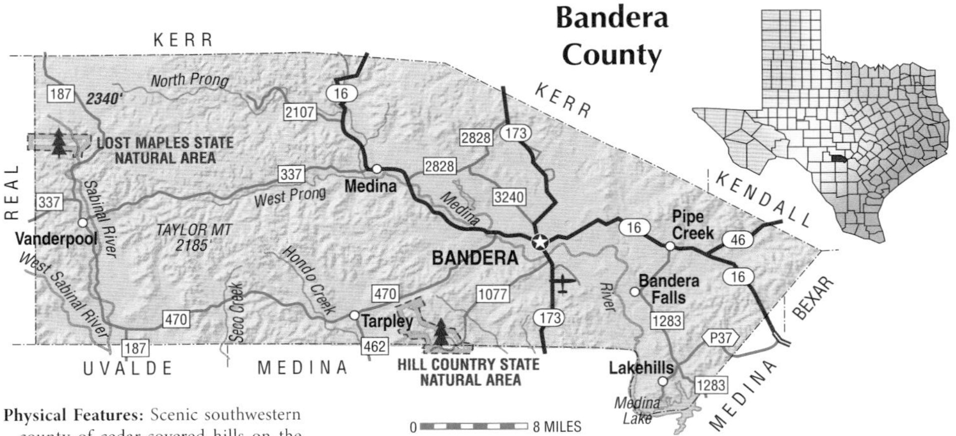

Physical Features: Scenic southwestern county of cedar-covered hills on the Edwards Plateau; Medina, Sabinal Rivers; limestone, sandy soils; species of oaks, walnuts, native cherry and Uvalde maple.

Economy: Tourism, hunting, fishing, ranching supplies, forest products.

History: Apache tribal area, then Comanche territory. White settlement began in the early 1850s, including Mormons and Poles. County created, organized from Bexar, Uvalde counties in 1856; named for Bandera (flag) Mountains.

Race/Ethnicity: Anglo, 77.1%; Black, 0.4%; Hispanic, 19.8%; Asian, 0.2%; Other, 2.2%.

Vital Statistics, annual: Births, 154; deaths, 221; marriages, 131; divorces, 94.

Recreation: RV parks, resort ranches; Lost Maples and Hill Country State Natural Areas; rodeo, parade on Memorial Day weekend; Medina Lake.

Minerals: Not significant.

Agriculture: Beef cattle, sheep, goats, horses, deer (first in numbers in captivity), apples. Market value $6.9 million. Hunting and nature tourism important.

BANDERA (941) county seat; tourism, ranching, service industries; historic sites, Frontier Times Museum.

Other towns include: **Medina** (850) apple growing; **Pipe Creek** (130); **Tarpley** (30); **Vanderpool** (20). Also, the community of **Lakehills** (5,912) on Medina Lake, Cajun Fest in September, and **Lake Medina Shores** (1,375)

Population	**23,129**
Change from 2010 (%)	12.9
Area (sq. mi.)	797.6
Land Area (sq. mi.)	791.0
Altitude (ft.)	1,064–2,340
Rainfall (in.)	37.4
Jan. mean min (°F)	34.5
July mean max (°F)	93.0
Civ. Labor	10,111
Unemployed (%)	4.9
Wages	$37,734,338
Per Capita Income	$44,925
Prop. Value	$4,391,467,607
Retail Sales	$134,100,585

For explanation of sources, symbols and abbreviations, see p. 204, and foldout map.

The city hall in Muleshoe, county seat of Bailey County. Photo by Larry D. Moore, CC 4/Wikipedia Commons

Bastrop County

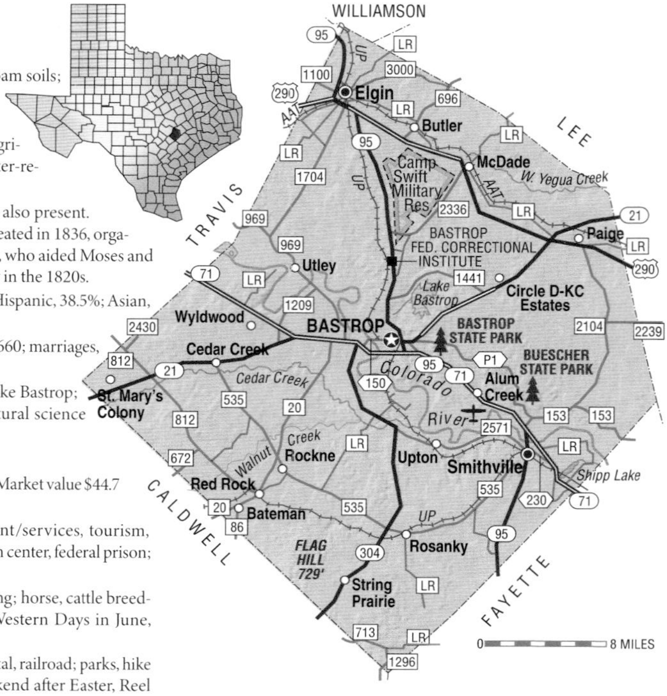

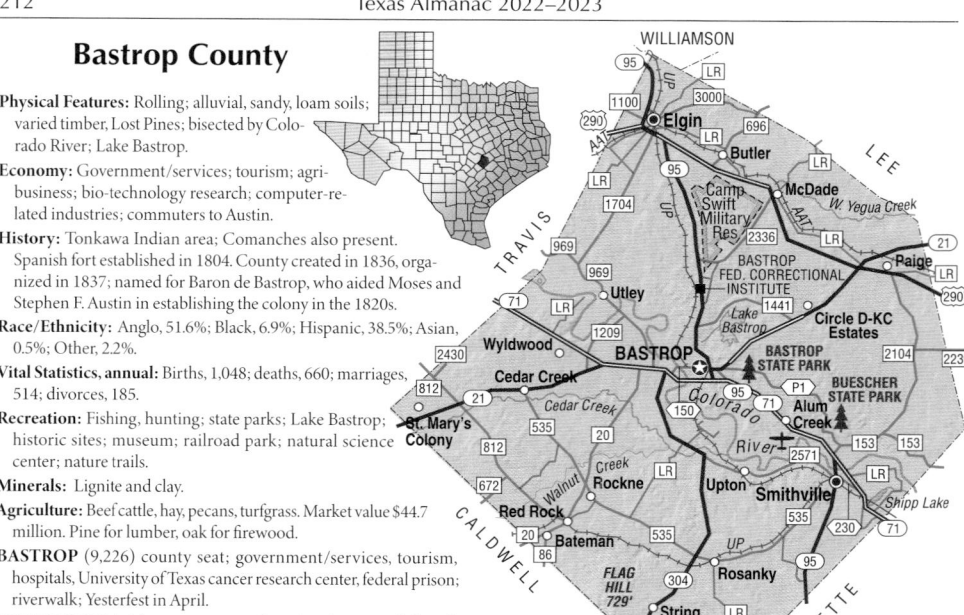

Physical Features: Rolling; alluvial, sandy, loam soils; varied timber, Lost Pines; bisected by Colorado River; Lake Bastrop.

Economy: Government/services; tourism; agribusiness; bio-technology research; computer-related industries; commuters to Austin.

History: Tonkawa Indian area; Comanches also present. Spanish fort established in 1804. County created in 1836, organized in 1837; named for Baron de Bastrop, who aided Moses and Stephen F. Austin in establishing the colony in the 1820s.

Race/Ethnicity: Anglo, 51.6%; Black, 6.9%; Hispanic, 38.5%; Asian, 0.5%; Other, 2.2%.

Vital Statistics, annual: Births, 1,048; deaths, 660; marriages, 514; divorces, 185.

Recreation: Fishing, hunting; state parks; Lake Bastrop; historic sites; museum; railroad park; natural science center; nature trails.

Minerals: Lignite and clay.

Agriculture: Beef cattle, hay, pecans, turfgrass. Market value $44.7 million. Pine for lumber, oak for firewood.

BASTROP (9,226) county seat; government/services, tourism, hospitals, University of Texas cancer research center, federal prison; riverwalk; Yesterfest in April.

ELGIN (10,262) bricks, sausage manufacturing; horse, cattle breeding; medical research; depot museum; Western Days in June, Hogeye festival in October.

Smithville (4,461) government/services, hospital, railroad; parks, hike & bike trails, museums; jamboree on weekend after Easter, Reel Film Expo in May.

Other towns: **Cedar Creek** (145); **Circle D-KC Estates** (2,730); **McDade** (746) watermelon festival in July; **Paige** (275); **Red Rock** (40); **Rosanky** (210) automotive museum; **Wyldwood** (2,756). Also, **Camp Swift** (7,908).

Population	**89,564**
Change from 2010 (%)	20.8
Area (sq. mi.)	895.6
Land Area (sq. mi.)	888.2
Altitude (ft.)	300–729
Rainfall (in.)	37.6
Jan. mean min (°F)	37.6
July mean max (°F)	95.4
Civ. Labor	43,750
Unemployed (%)	4.8
Wages	$217,283,698
Per Capita Income	$38,289
Prop. Value	$11,472,929,435
Retail Sales	$1,394,732,326

A member of AmeriCorps pauses to pose for a picture. The group cleaned up a community garden in Beeville on MLK Jr. Day in 2021. Photo by AmeriCorps, PD/Wikimedia Commons

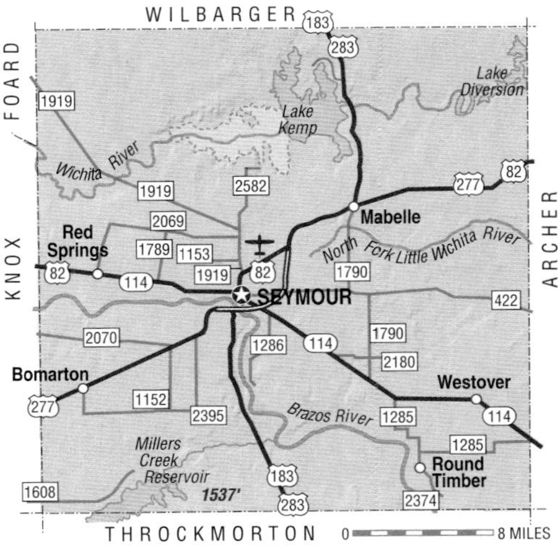

Baylor County

Physical Features: Northwest county; level to hilly; drains to Brazos, Wichita rivers; Lake Kemp, Lake Diversion, Millers Creek Reservoir; sandy, loam, red soils; grassy, mesquites, cedars.

Economy: Agribusiness; retail/service; health services.

History: Comanches, with Wichitas and other tribes also in the area; U.S. Army removed tribes in 1874-75. Anglo-Americans settled in the 1870s. County created from Fannin County in 1858; organized in 1879. Named for H.W. Baylor, Texas Ranger surgeon.

Race/Ethnicity: Anglo, 82.1%; Black, 1.8%; Hispanic, 13.2%; Asian, 0.1%; Other, 2.6%.

Vital Statistics, annual: Births, 41; deaths, 61; marriages, 19; divorces, 7.

Recreation: Lakes; hunting; settlers reunion, rodeo, go-cart races in July.

Population	**3,751**
Change from 2010 (%)	0.7
Area (sq. mi.)	901.1
Land Area (sq. mi.)	867.5
Altitude (ft.)	1,053–1,537
Rainfall (in.)	29.0
Jan. mean min (°F)	28.1
July mean max (°F)	96.5
Civ. Labor	1,811
Unemployed (%)	3.4
Wages	$15,593,175
Per Capita Income	$46,615
Prop. Value	$1,148,838,793
Retail Sales	$29,607,145

Minerals: Oil, gas produced.

Agriculture: Wheat, cattle, cow-calf operations, grain sorghum, cotton, hay. Market value $53.7 million.

SEYMOUR (2,740) county seat; agribusiness; hospital; dove hunters' breakfast in September.

Bee County

Population	**33,471**
Change from 2010 (%)	5.1
Area (sq. mi.)	880.3
Land Area (sq. mi.)	880.2
Altitude (ft.)	39–540
Rainfall (in.)	32.0
Jan. mean min (°F)	43.7
July mean max (°F)	93.9
Civ. Labor	9,486
Unemployed (%)	9.4
Wages	$81,842,152
Per Capita Income	$29,792
Prop. Value	$3,564,090,581
Retail Sales	$333,098,236

Physical Features: South Coastal Plain, level to rolling; black clay, sandy, loam soils; brushy.

Economy: Agriculture, government/services; hunting leases; oil and gas business.

History: Karankawa, Apache, Pawnee territory. First Spanish land grant, 1789. Irish settlers arrived 1826-29. County created from Karnes, Live Oak, Goliad, Refugio, San Patricio, 1857; organized 1858; named for Barnard Bee Sr., secretary of state and diplomat for the Republic.

Race/Ethnicity: Anglo, 30.4%; Black, 8%; Hispanic, 59.9%; Asian, 0.4%; Other, 1%.

Vital Statistics, annual: Births, 412; deaths, 271; marriages, 167; divorces, 61.

Recreation: Hunting, birding, camping; historical sites, antiques; rodeo/roping events.

Minerals: Oil, gas produced.

Agriculture: Beef cattle, corn, cotton and grain sorghum. Market value $37.7 million. Hunting leases.

BEEVILLE (13,554) county seat; aircraft maintenance, waste-bind manufacturing, retail center; Coastal Bend College; hospital; art museum; Diez y Seis festival in September.

Other towns and places include: **Blueberry Hill** (863); **Mineral** (65); **Normanna** (112); **Pawnee** (155); **Pettus** (559); **Skidmore** (932); **Tuleta** (306); **Tynan** (283).

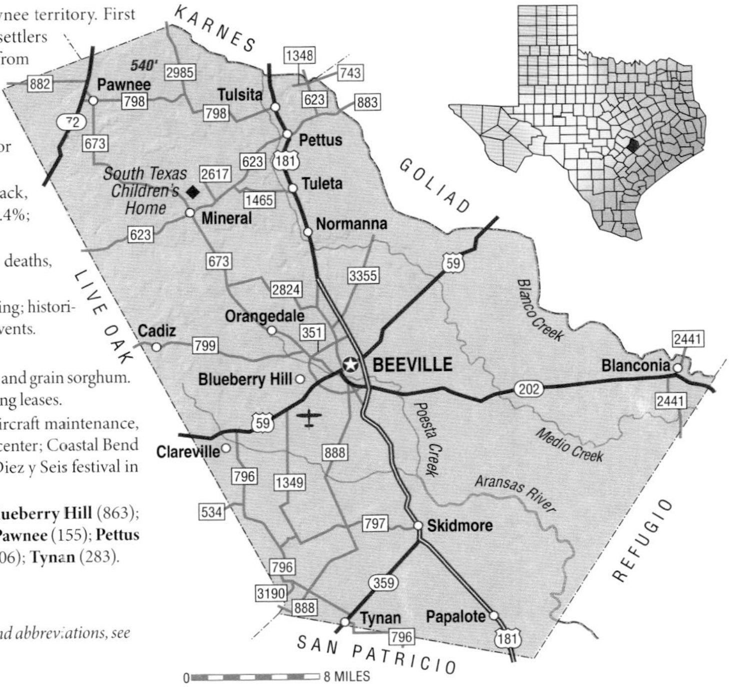

For explanation of sources, symbols and abbreviations, see p. 204, and foldout map.

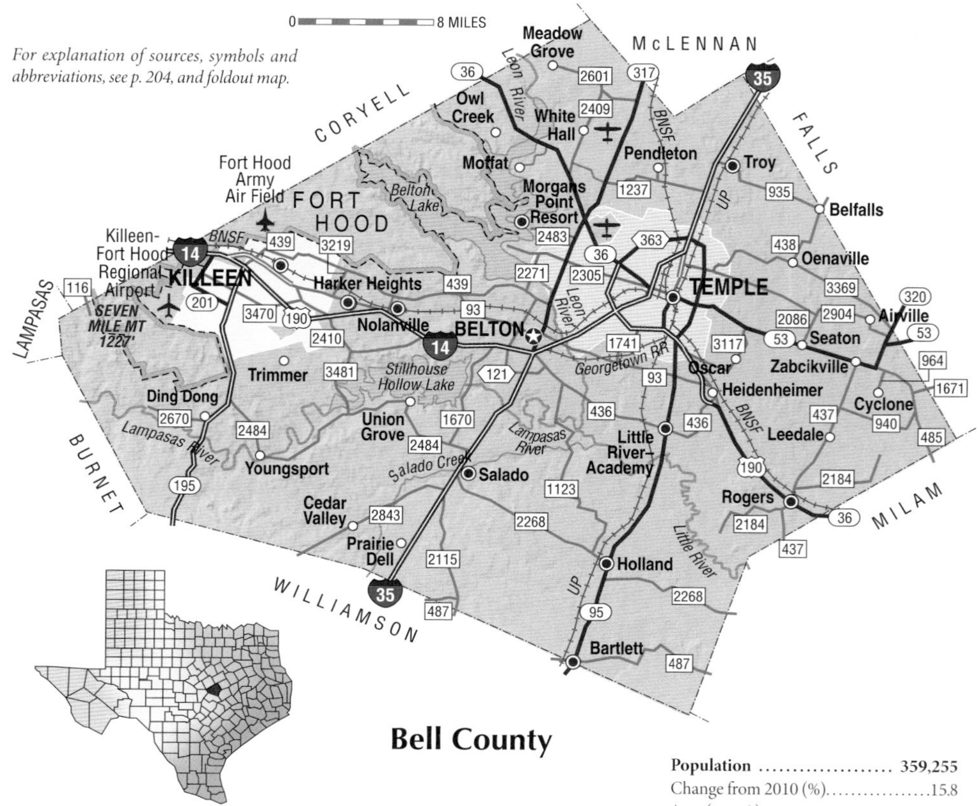

Bell County

Physical Features: Central Texas Blackland, level to hilly; black to light soils in west; mixed timber; Belton Lake, Stillhouse Hollow Lake.

Economy: Fort Hood; manufacturing includes computers, plastic goods, furniture, clothing; agribusiness; distribution center; tourism.

History: Tonkawas, Lipan Apaches; reduced by disease and advancing frontier by 1840s. Comanches raided into 1870s.

Settled in 1830s as part of Robertson's colony. A few slaveholders in 1850s. County created from Milam County in 1850; named for Gov. P.H. Bell.

Race/Ethnicity: Anglo, 44.4%; Black, 21.2%; Hispanic, 26.2%; Asian, 3%; Other, 5%.

Vital Statistics, annual: Births, 6,496; deaths, 2,274; marriages, 3,865; divorces, 2,198.

Recreation: Fishing, hunting; lakes; historic sites; exposition center; Salado gathering of Scottish clans in November.

Minerals: Gravel.

Agriculture: Beef, corn, sorghum, wheat, cotton. Market value $77.0 million.

BELTON (22,695) county seat; University of Mary Hardin-Baylor; government/services; manufacturing; museum, nature center.

KILLEEN (151,463) Fort Hood; Texas A&M University–Central Texas and Central Texas College; regional airport; retail center, varied manufacturing; hospital; museums, planetarium; Four Winds Powwow in September.

TEMPLE (78,267) Major medical center with two hospitals and VA hospital; diversified industries; rail and wholesale distribution center; retail center; Temple College, Texas A&M College of Medicine; Azalee Marshall Cultural Activities Center; Czech museum; early-day tractor, engine show in October.

Other towns include: Harker Heights (32,665) Founder's Day in October; **Heidenheimer** (224); **Holland** (1,170) corn festival in June; **Little River-Academy** (2,098).

Population	**359,255**
Change from 2010 (%)	15.8
Area (sq. mi.)	1,087.8
Land Area (sq. mi.)	1,051.0
Altitude (ft.)	390–1,227
Rainfall (in.)	36.1
Jan. mean min (°F)	35.6
July mean max (°F)	94.6
Civ. Labor	145,714
Unemployed (%)	6
Wages	$1,675,289,061
Per Capita Income	$43,919
Prop. Value	$30,136,088,721
Retail Sales	$5,299,888,552

Also, **Morgan's Point Resort** (4,736); **Nolanville** (5,533); **Pendleton** (369); **Rogers** (1,247); **Salado** (2,380) tourism, civic center, amphitheatre, art fair in August; **Troy** (1,982).

Also, part [714] of **Bartlett.**

Fort Hood has a population of 26,245.

Physical Features: On edge of Balcones Escarpment, Coastal Plain; heavy black to thin limestone soils; spring-fed streams; underground water; mesquite, other brush; Braunig Lake, Calaveras Lake.

Economy: Medical/biomedical research and services; government center with large federal payroll, military bases; tourism; education center.

History: Coahuiltecan Indian area; also Lipan Apache and Tonkawa tribes present. Mission San Antonio de Valero (Alamo) founded in 1718. Canary Islanders arrived in 1731. Anglo-American settlers began arriving in the late 1820s. County created and organized in 1836 from Spanish municipality named to honor the duke of Bexar; a colonial capital of Texas.

Race/Ethnicity: Anglo, 27%; Black, 7.3%; Hispanic, 60.4%; Asian, 2.8%; Other, 2.2%.

Vital Statistics, annual: Births, 28,172; deaths, 12,982; marriages, 13,456; divorces, 3,067.

Recreation: Historic sites include the Alamo, other missions, Casa Navarro, La Villita; River Walk, El Mercado (market), Tower of the Americas, Brackenridge Park, zoo, SeaWorld, HemisFair Park, Institute of Texan Cultures; museums, symphony orchestra; hunting, fishing; NBA Spurs; Fiesta in April, Folklife Festival in June.

Minerals: Gravel, sand, limestone.

Agriculture: Nursery crops, beef cattle, grain sorghum, hay, corn. Market value $67.9 million.

Education: Fourteen colleges including Our Lady of the Lake, St. Mary's University, Texas A&M University–San Antonio, Trinity University, the University of Texas at San Antonio.

SAN ANTONIO (1,548,248) county seat; Texas' second largest city; healthcare/biosciences, government/services, manufacturing, tourism, information technology, aerospace, education, energy; Alamodome. Leon Springs is now part of San Antonio.

Other towns include: **Alamo Heights** (8,614); **Balcones Heights** (3,362); **Castle Hills** (4,509); **China Grove** (1,321); **Converse** (29,210); **Elmendorf** (2,112); **Fair Oaks Ranch** (9,434); **Grey Forest** (566); **Helotes** (10,297) government/services, retail trade, Cornyval Festival in May, Highland games in April, John T. Floore Country Store, Gugger Homestead; **Hill Country Village** (1,102); **Hollywood Park** (3,367).

Also, **Kirby** (8,743); **Leon Valley** (11,799); **Live Oak** (16,451); **Macdona** (603); **Olmos Park** (2,508); **St. Hedwig** (2,488); **Selma** (11,795, parts in Guadalupe and Comal counties); **Shavano Park** (4,007); **Somerset** (1,996); **Terrell Hills** (5,344); **Universal City** (21,927); **Von Ormy** (1,320); **Windcrest** (5,933).

Part [1,157] of **Schertz** (38,084).

Lackland Air Force Base (9,124); **Randolph Air Force Base** (1,386).

Population	**1,997,417**
Change from 2010 (%)	16.5
Area (sq. mi.)	1,256.1
Land Area (sq. mi.)	1,239.8
Altitude (ft.)	400–1,896
Rainfall (in.)	32.3
Jan. mean min (°F)	40.7
July mean max (°F)	94.6
Civ. Labor	954,802
Unemployed (%)	5.8
Wages	$12,823,018,353
Per Capita Income	$47,830
Prop. Value	$212,733,203,664
Retail Sales	$31,711,528,500

Bexar County

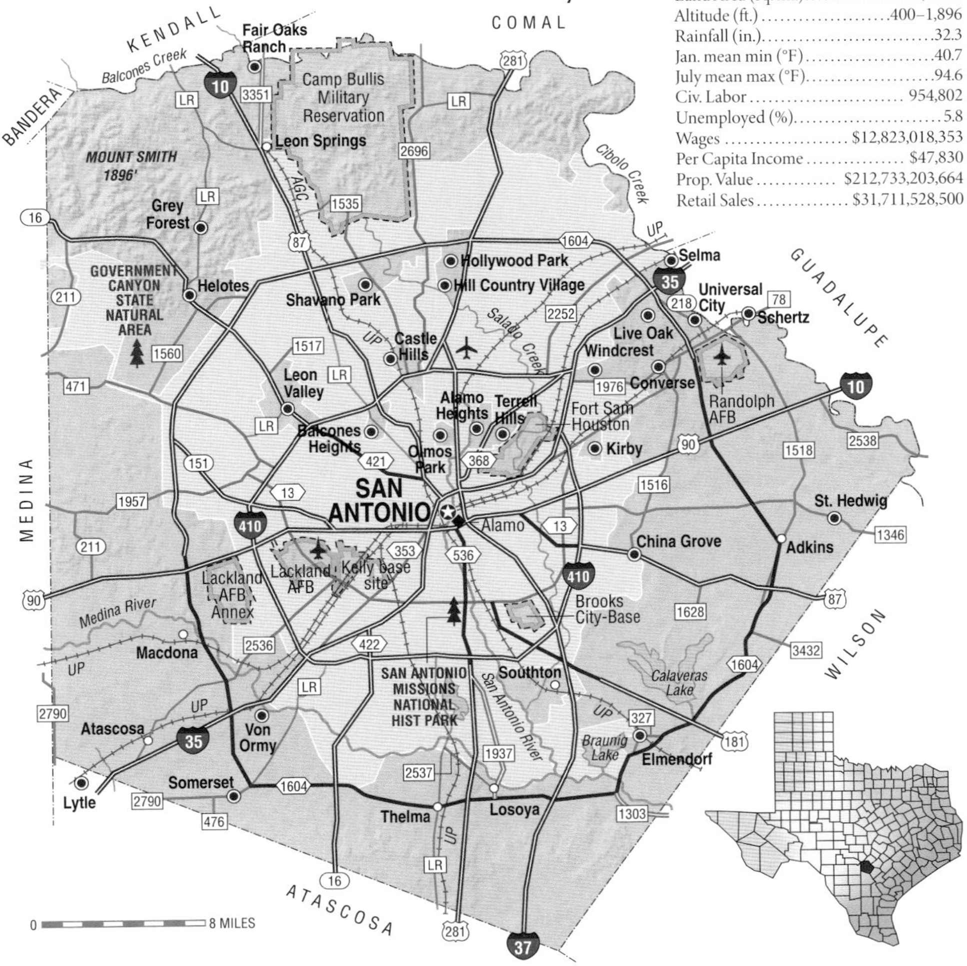

Blanco County

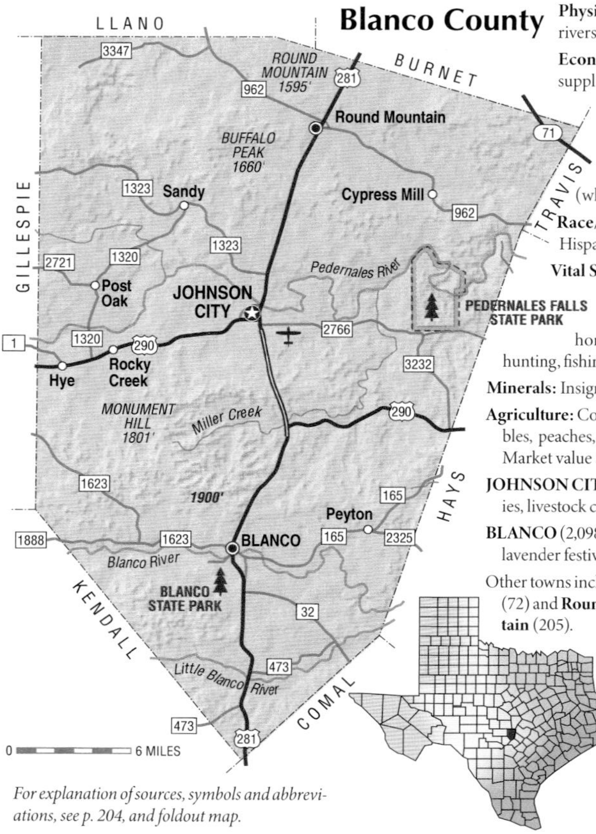

For explanation of sources, symbols and abbreviations, see p. 204, and foldout map.

Physical Features: Hill Country county; Blanco, Pedernales rivers; cedars, pecans, live oaks, other trees.

Economy: Tourism, agribusiness/wholesale nursery, ranch supplies, hunting/fishing.

History: Lipan Apache area. Comanches were present when Anglo-Americans settled in the 1850s. County created in 1858 from Burnet, Comal, Gillespie, Hays counties, organized the same year; named for the Blanco (white) River.

Race/Ethnicity: (In percent), Anglo, 77.8%; Black, 0.5%; Hispanic, 19.5%; Asian, 0.4%; Other, 1.6%.

Vital Statistics, annual: Births, 96; deaths, 122; marriages, 96; divorces, 39.

Recreation: President Lyndon B. Johnson's boyhood home, state parks, Saur-Beckmann living history farm; hunting, fishing; bike ride in March; scenic drives, wineries/vineyards.

Minerals: Insignificant.

Agriculture: Cow-calf operation, stocker cattle; sheep, goats; hay, vegetables, peaches, grapes, pecans, greenhouse nurseries; limited irrigation. Market value $17.0 million.

JOHNSON CITY (2,167) county seat; tourism, electric co-op; art galleries, livestock center.

BLANCO (2,098) tourism, old courthouse, Pioneer museum, nature trail; lavender festival in June.

Other towns include: **Hye** (72) and **Round Mountain** (205).

Population	**12,159**
Change from 2010 (%)	15.8
Area (sq. mi.)	713.4
Land Area (sq. mi.)	709.3
Altitude (ft.)	741–1,900
Rainfall (in.)	34.9
Jan. mean min (°F)	34.8
July mean max (°F)	92.8
Civ. Labor	6,648
Unemployed (%)	3.6
Wages	$52,080,901
Per Capita Income	$54,814
Prop. Value	$6,124,140,263
Retail Sales	$88,958,807

Borden County

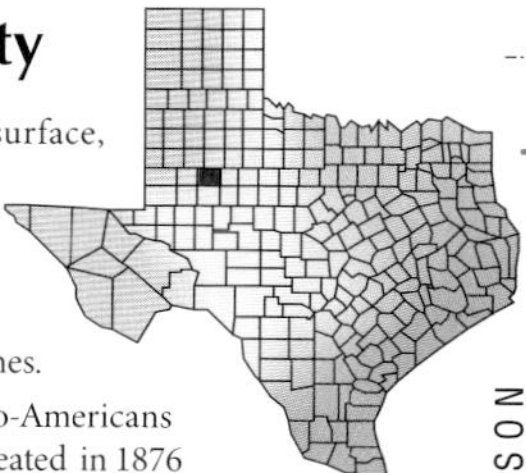

Physical Features: Rolling surface, broken by Caprock Escarpment; drains to Colorado River; sandy loam, clay soils.

Economy: Agriculture and hunting leases; oil; wind turbines.

History: Comanche area. Anglo-Americans settled in the 1870s. County created in 1876 from Bexar District, organized in 1891; named for Gail Borden, patriot, inventor, editor.

Race/Ethnicity: Anglo, 83.6%; Black, 0%; Hispanic, 15.1%; Asian, 0%; Other, 1.1%.

Vital Statistics, annual: Births, 0; deaths, 10; marriages, 2; divorces, 1.

Recreation: Fishing; quail and deer hunting; Lake J.B. Thomas; museum; Coyote Opry in September; junior livestock show in January, ranch horse competition in September.

Minerals: Oil, gas, caliche, sand, gravel.

Agriculture: Beef cattle, cotton, wheat, hay, pecans, oats; some irrigation. Market value $28.8 million.

GAIL (284) county seat; museum, antique shop, ambulance service; "star" construction atop Gail Mountain.

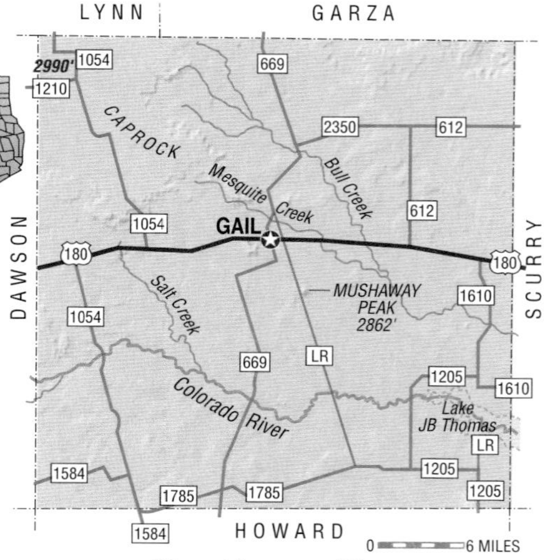

Population	**680**
Change from 2010 (%)	6.1
Area (sq. mi.)	906.1
Land Area (sq. mi.)	897.4
Altitude (ft.)	2,258–2,990
Rainfall (in.)	19.1
Jan. mean min (°F)	33.1
July mean max (°F)	94.8
Civ. Labor	490
Unemployed (%)	2.7
Wages	$3,758,302
Per Capita Income	$61,287
Prop. Value	$1,143,463,782
Retail Sales	$17,906

Bosque County

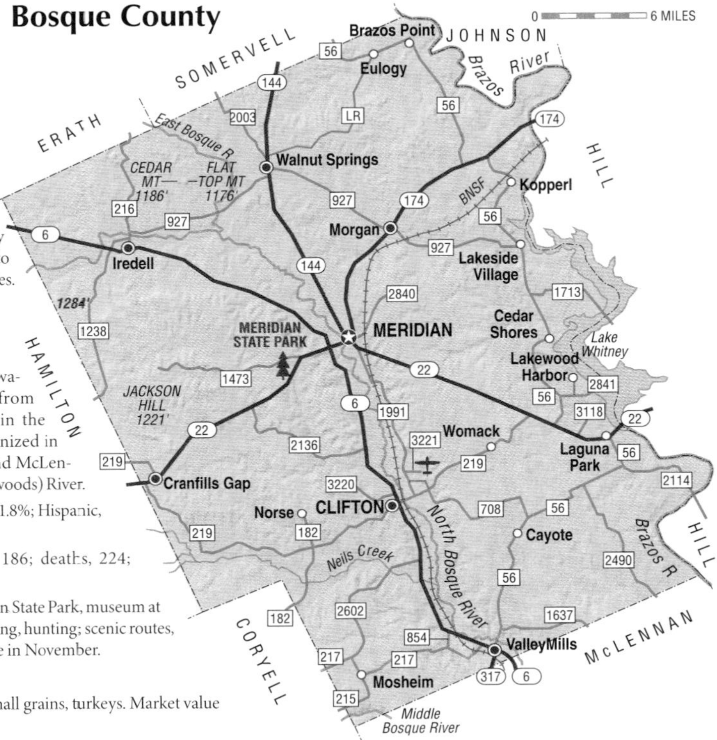

Physical Features: Hilly, broken by Brazos, Bosque rivers; limestone to alluvial soils; cedars, oaks, mesquites.

Economy: Agribusiness, government/services, small industries, tourism.

History: Tonkawa, Waco, and Tawakoni Indian tribes. Settlers from England and Norway arrived in the 1850s. County created and organized in 1854 from the Milam District and McLennan County; named for Bosque (woods) River.

Race/Ethnicity: Anglo, 76%; Black, 1.8%; Hispanic, 19.1%; Asian, 0.2%; Other, 2.6%.

Vital Statistics, annual: Births, 186; deaths, 224; marriages, 104; divorces, 44.

Recreation: Lake Whitney, Meridian State Park, museum at Clifton, fine art conservatory; fishing, hunting; scenic routes, Norwegian smorgasbord at Norse in November.

Minerals: Limestone, gas & oil.

Agriculture: Beef cattle, forages, small grains, turkeys. Market value $45.1 million. Hunting leases.

MERIDIAN (1,515) county seat; food processing, government/services, tourism; retirement home, community college; national championship barbecue cookoff in October.

CLIFTON (3,594) retirement/health care; hospital, nursing school; library; Norwegian historic district; Norwegian Country Christmas.

Other towns include: **Cranfills Gap** (286) Lutefisk dinner in December, Old Rock Church.

Iredell (343); **Kopperl** (225); **Laguna Park** (1,261); **Morgan** (518); **Valley Mills** (1,253); **Walnut Springs** (911).

Population	**19,062**	July mean max (°F)	96.4
Change from 2010 (%)	4.7	Civ. Labor	8,356
Area (sq. mi.)	1,002.5	Unemployed (%)	4.7
Land Area (sq. mi.)	983.0	Wages	$44,111,050
Altitude (ft.)	410–1,284	Per Capita Income	$42,366
Rainfall (in.)	36.0	Prop. Value	$4,209,438,455
Jan. mean min (°F)	34.8	Retail Sales	$101,740,364

A view of the shops in downtown Meridian, the county seat of Bosque County. Photo by Renelibrary, CC 4/Wikimedia Commons

Bowie County

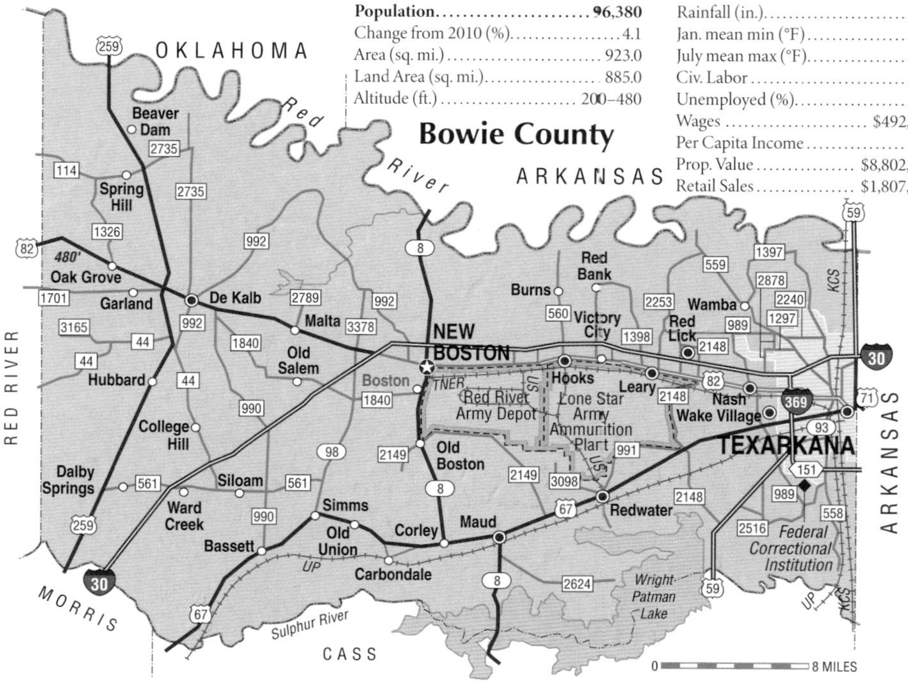

Population	**96,380**
Change from 2010 (%)	4.1
Area (sq. mi.)	923.0
Land Area (sq. mi.)	885.0
Altitude (ft.)	200–480
Rainfall (in.)	52.0
Jan. mean min (°F)	33.1
July mean max (°F)	92.9
Civ. Labor	38,841
Unemployed (%)	6.2
Wages	$492,974,024
Per Capita Income	$41,172
Prop. Value	$8,802,773,070
Retail Sales	$1,807,983,759

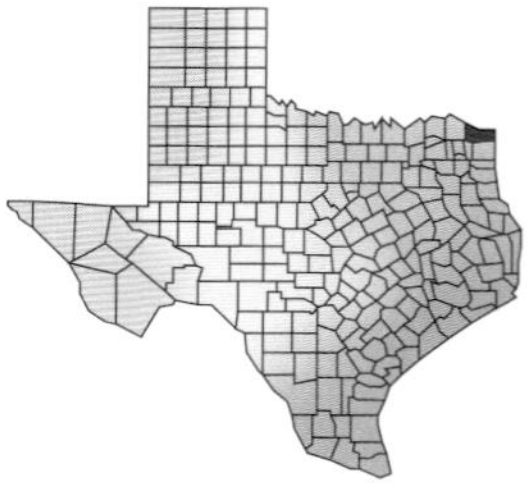

Physical Features: Forested hills at northeast corner of the state; clay, sandy, alluvial soils; drained by Red and Sulphur rivers; Wright Patman Lake.

Economy: Government/services, lumber, manufacturing, agribusiness.

History: Caddo tribal area, abandoned in the 1790s after trouble with the Osage tribe. Anglo-Americans began arriving 1815-20. County created and organized in 1840 from Red River County; named for the Alamo hero James Bowie.

Race/Ethnicity: Anglo, 63.4%; Black, 24.5%; Hispanic, 7.4%; Asian, 1%; Other, 3.5%.

Vital Statistics, annual: Births, 1,259; deaths, 1,076; marriages, 572; divorces, 377.

Recreation: Lake activities, Crystal Springs beach; hunting, fishing; historic sites; Four-States Fair in September, Octoberfest.

Minerals: Oil, gas, sand, gravel.

Agriculture: Beef cattle, pecans, hay, corn, poultry, soybeans, dairy, nurseries, wheat, rice, horses, milo. Market value $60.1 million. Pine timber, hardwoods, pulpwood harvested.

NEW BOSTON (4,556) site of county courthouse; army depot, lumber mill, steel manufacture, agribusiness, state prison; Pioneer Days in August. The area of Boston, officially designated as the county seat, has been annexed by New Boston.

TEXARKANA (39,059 in Texas, 29,901 in Arkansas) rubber company, paper manufacturing, distribution; hospitals; tourism; colleges; federal prison; Perot Theatre; Quadrangle Festival in September.

Other towns include: **De Kalb** (1,673) agriculture, government/services, commuting to Texarkana, Oktoberfest; **Hooks** (2,720); **Leary** (515); **Maud** (1,095); **Nash** (3,825); **Red Lick** (1,027); **Redwater** (1,109); **Simms** (300); **Wake Village** (5,669).

The public library in Brazoria is part of a county-wide library system. Photo by Djmaschek, CC 4/ Wikimedia Commons

Physical Features: Flat Coastal Plain, coastal soils, drained by Brazos and San Bernard rivers; Brazoria Reservoir, Eagle Nest Lake, Harris Reservoir, Mustang Lake East/West, San Bernard Reservoirs.

Economy: Petroleum and chemical industry, fishing, tourism, agribusiness. Part of Houston metropolitan area.

History: Karankawa area. Part of Austin's "Old Three Hundred" colony of families arriving in early 1820s. County created 1836 from Municipality of Brazoria, organized in 1837; name derived from Brazos River.

Race/Ethnicity: Anglo, 46.4%; Black, 13.6%; Hispanic, 30.7%; Asian, 6.8%; Other, 2.2%.

Vital Statistics, annual: Births, 4,939; deaths, 2,155; marriages, 2,205; divorces, 1,235.

Recreation: Beaches, water sports; fishing, hunting; wildlife refuges, historic sites, plantations; state and county parks; replica of the first capitol of the Republic of Texas at West Columbia.

Minerals: Oil, gas, sand, gravel.

Agriculture: Cattle, hay, rice, soybeans, sorghum, nurseries, corn, cotton, aquaculture, bees. Some 20,000 acres of rice irrigated. Market value $79.5 million.

ANGLETON (21,483) county seat; banking and distribution center for oil, chemical, agricultural area; fish-processing plant; hospital.

BRAZOSPORT (61,590) is a community of eight cities; chemical complex, deepwater seaport, commercial fishing, tourism; college; hospital; **Brazosport cities include: Clute** (11,919) mosquito festival in July, **Freeport** (12,990) museum, Riverfest in late April, **Jones Creek** (2,158), **Lake Jackson** (28,421) research & development, museum, sea center, Gulf Coast Bird Observatory, **Oyster Creek** (1,170), **Quintana** (20); Neotropical Bird Sanctuary, **Richwood** (4,341), **Surfside Beach** (571) tourism, St. Patrick's Day parade.

PEARLAND (122,331, parts in Harris, Fort Bend counties) trucking, metal fabrication, oilfield, chemical production; commuting to Houston, NASA; community college; Hindu temple; Winter Fest in January.

Other towns include: **Alvin** (29,391) petrochemical processing, agribusiness, rail, trucking; junior college; hospital; Crawfest and Shrimp Boil in April. **Bailey's Prairie** (789); **Bonney** (358); **Brazoria** (3,531) government/services, retail, manufacturing; library; No-Name Festival in June, Santa Anna Ball in July; **Brookside Village** (1,632).

Also, Damon (614); **Danbury** (1,883); **Danciger** (90); **Hillcrest Village** (758); **Holiday Lakes** (1,242); **Iowa Colony** (6,107); **Liverpool** (561); **Manvel** (12,671); **Old Ocean** (150); **Rosharon** (1,384); **Sandy Point** (237); **Sweeny** (4,047) petrochemicals, government/services, hospital, library, Pride Day in May, Levi Jordan Plantation; **West Columbia** (4,160) chemical industry, retail, cattle, rice farming, museum, historic sites, plantation, San Jacinto Festival in April, Stephen F. Austin funeral procession re-enactment in October.

Population	**380,439**
Change from 2010 (%)	21.5
Area (sq. mi.)	1,608.6
Land Area (sq. mi.)	1,357.7
Altitude (ft.)	sea level–146
Rainfall (in.)	56.5
Jan. mean min (°F)	45.6
July mean max (°F)	90.3
Civ. Labor	178,148
Unemployed (%)	7.6
Wages	$1,720,529,383
Per Capita Income	$48,374
Prop. Value	$62,464,812,811
Retail Sales	$4,889,945,756

Brazoria County

For explanation of sources, symbols and abbreviations, see p. 204, and foldout map.

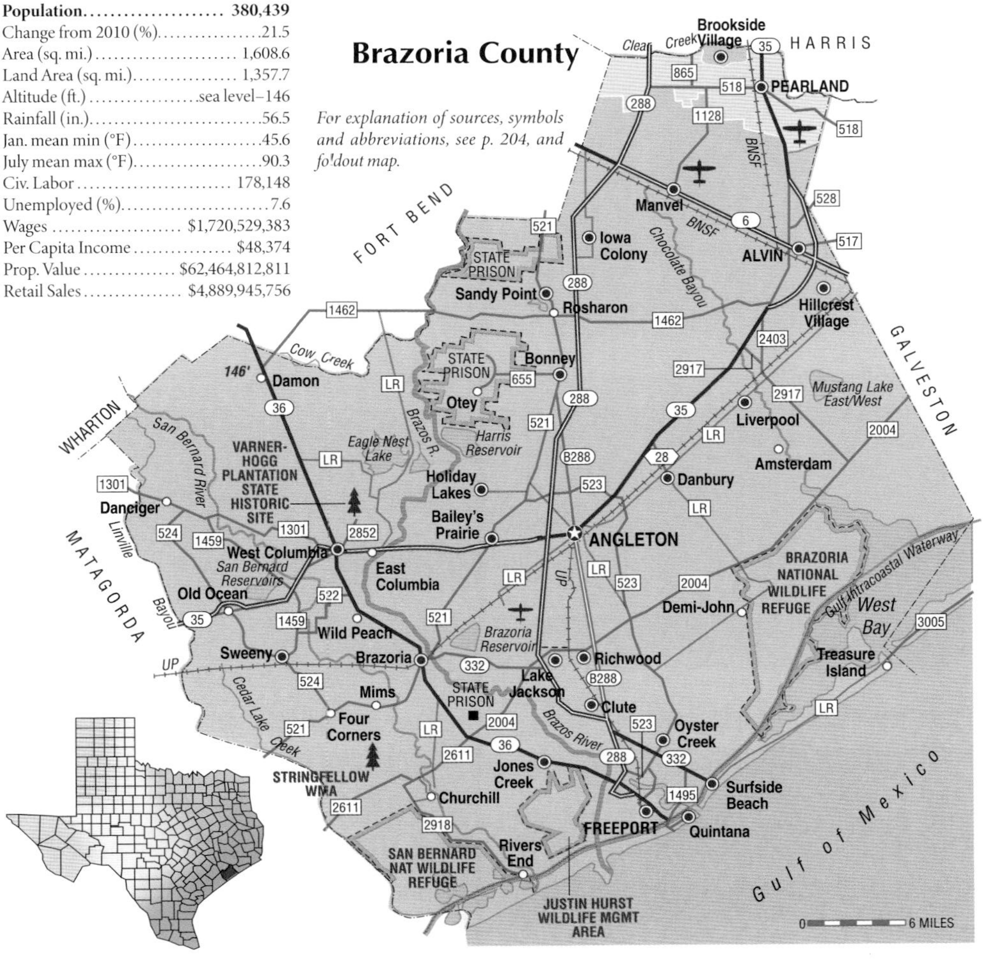

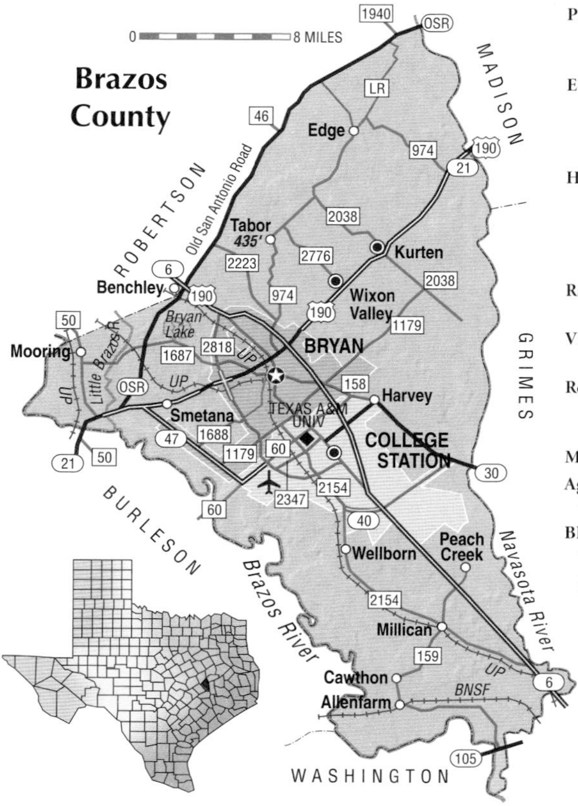

Physical Features: South central county between Brazos, Navasota rivers; Bryan Lake; rich bottom soils, sandy, clays on rolling uplands; oak trees.

Economy: Texas A&M University; market and medical center; agribusiness; computers, research and development; government/services; winery; industrial parks; tourism.

History: Bidais and Tonkawas; Comanches hunted in the area. Part of Stephen F. Austin's second colony of the late 1820s. County created in 1841 from Robertson, Washington counties and named Navasota; renamed for Brazos River in 1842, organized in 1843.

Race/Ethnicity: Anglo, 54.7%; Black, 11%; Hispanic, 26.1%; Asian, 5.8%; Other, 2.2%.

Vital Statistics, annual: Births, 2,903; deaths, 1,064; marriages, 1,498; divorces, 258.

Recreation: Fishing, hunting; raceway; many events related to Texas A&M activities; George Bush Presidential Library and Museum; winery harvest weekends in August.

Minerals: Sand and gravel, lignite, gas, oil.

Agriculture: Cattle, poultry, cotton, hay, horses and horticulture. Market value $91.6 million.

BRYAN (86,202) county seat; defense electronics, other varied manufacturing, agribusiness center; hospitals, psychiatric facilities; Blinn College extension; Brazos Valley African American Museum; steak & grape festival in June, Fiestas Patrias in September.

COLLEGE STATION (118,410) home of Texas A&M University, varied high-tech manufacturing, research; hospital.

Other towns include: **Kurten** (409); **Lake Bryan** (1,977); **Millican** (245); **Wellborn** (400); **Wixon Valley** (255).

Population	**230,789**	Rainfall (in.)	40.1	Wages	$1,299,595,756
Change from 2010 (%)	18.4	Jan. mean min (°F)	41.2	Per Capita Income	$41,348
Area (sq. mi.)	591.2	July mean max (°F)	94.8	Prop. Value	$27,070,353,454
Land Area (sq. mi.)	585.5	Civ. Labor	116,569	Retail Sales	$3,156,412,407
Altitude (ft.)	157–435	Unemployed (%)	4.5		

The Brazos Valley African American Museum in Bryan was opened in July 2006. Photo by Larry D. Moore, CC 3/Wikimedia Commons

Brewster County

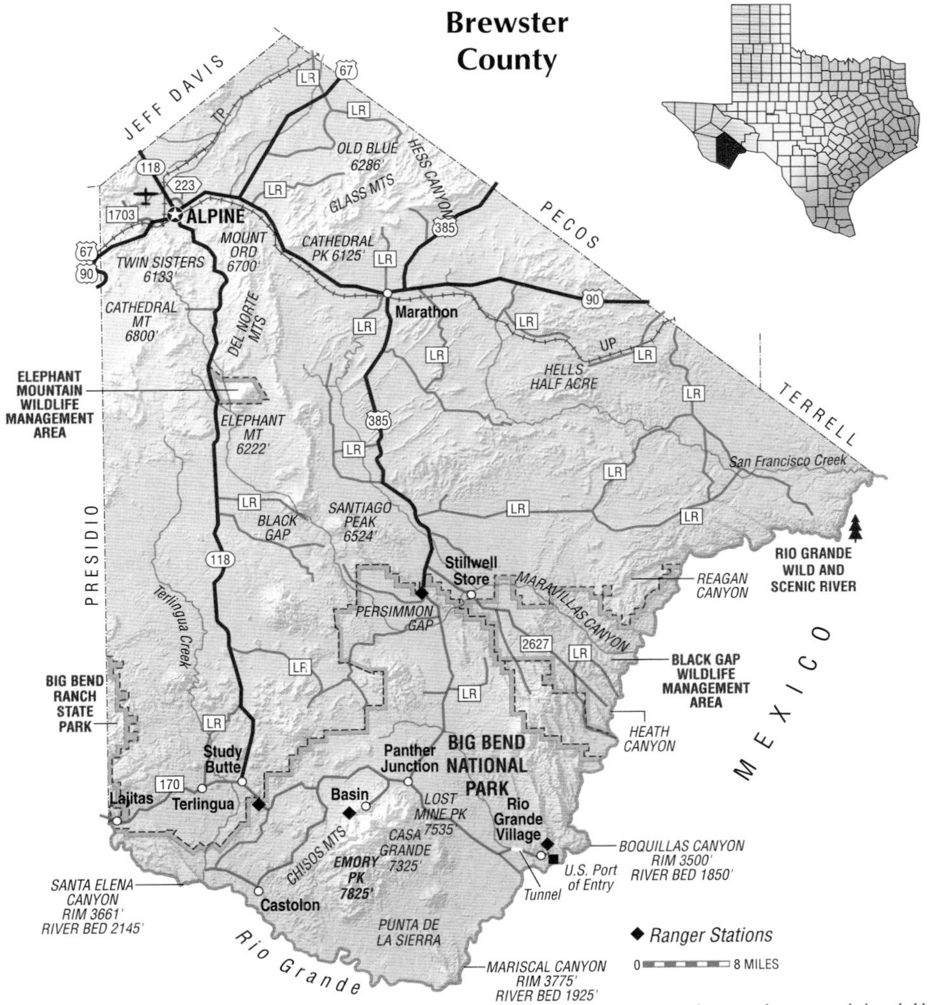

For explanation of sources, symbols and abbreviations, see p. 204, and foldout map.

Physical Features: Largest county, with area slightly less than that of Connecticut plus Rhode Island; mountains, canyons, distinctive geology, plant life, animals.

Economy: Agriculture, tourism, government/services, Sul Ross State University, mining.

History: Pueblo culture had begun when Spanish explored in the 1500s. Mescalero Apaches in Chisos Mountains; Comanches raided in area. Ranching developed in northern part in the 1880s, with Mexican agricultural communities along river. County created, organized, 1887 from Presidio County; named for Henry P. Brewster, Republic secretary of war.

Race/Ethnicity: Anglo, 51.2%; Black, 0.9%; Hispanic, 43.8%; Asian, 0.9%; Other, 2.9%.

Vital Statistics, annual: Births, 96; deaths, 81; marriages, 83; divorces, 0.

Recreation: Big Bend National Park, Big Bend Ranch State Park, Rio Grande Wild and Scenic River; ghost towns, scenic drives; hunting; museum; rockhound areas; cavalry post.

Also, Barton Warnock Environmental Education Center at Lajitas; cowboy poetry and Western art show in Feburary; Terlingua chili cookoff in November.

Minerals: Bentonite.

Agriculture: Beef cattle, meat goats, horses. Market value $16.3 million. Hunting leases important.

ALPINE (5,928) county seat; ranch trade center, tourism, varied manufacturing; Sul Ross State University; hospital.

Marathon (399) tourism, ranching center, Gage Hotel, Marathon Basin quilt show in October.

Also, **Basin** (30); **Study Butte** (247), and **Terlingua** (50).

Population	**9,092**
Change from 2010 (%)	-1.5
Area (sq. mi.)	6,192.3
Land Area (sq. mi.)	6,183.7
Altitude (ft.)	1,400–7,825
Rainfall (in.)	17.0
Jan. mean min (°F)	30.3
July mean max (°F)	88.5
Civ. Labor	3,967
Unemployed (%)	4.9
Wages	$48,141,900
Per Capita Income	$48,422
Prop. Value	$1,825,748,262
Retail Sales	$108,269,802

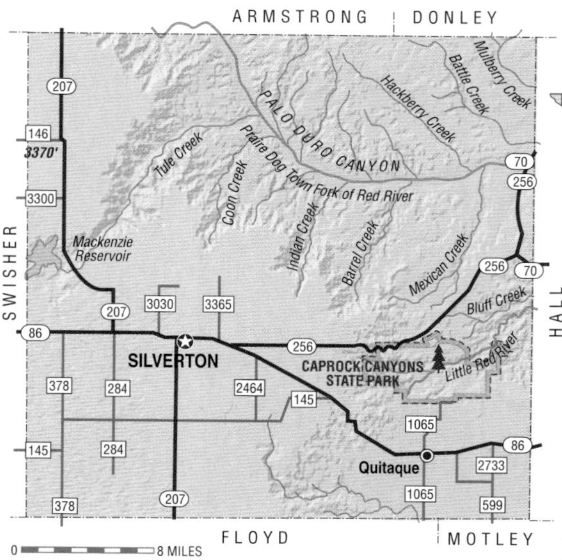

Briscoe County

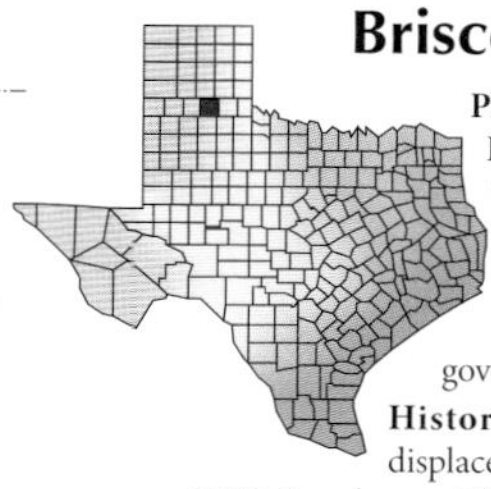

Physical Features: Partly on High Plains, broken by Caprock Escarpment, fork of Red River; sandy, loam soils.

Economy: Agriculture, government/services.

History: Apaches in area, displaced by Comanches around 1700. Ranchers settled in the 1880s. County created from the Bexar District in 1876 and organized in 1892; named for Andrew Briscoe, Republic of Texas soldier.

Race/Ethnicity: Anglo, 66.5%; Black, 2.6%; Hispanic, 29.5%; Asian, 0%; Other, 1.3%.

Vital Statistics, annual: Births, 13; deaths, 20;marriages, 10; divorces, 7.

Recreation: Hunting, fishing; scenic drives; museum at Quitaque; Caprock Canyons State Park, trailway, bison herd, Clarity tunnel with bats, Mackenzie Reservoir; Briscoe County Celebration in August, Bison Music Festival in September.

Minerals: Insignificant.

Agriculture: Cotton, beef, grain sorghum, wheat, hay. Some 23,000 acres irrigated. Market value $36.6 million.

SILVERTON (687) county seat; agribusiness center, irrigation supplies manufactured; clinics.

Quitaque (392) agribusiness, nature tourism, government/services.

Population	**1,572**
Change from 2010 (%)	-4.0
Area (sq. mi.)	901.6
Land Area (sq. mi.)	900.0
Altitude (ft.)	2,064–3,370
Rainfall (in.)	22.4
Jan. mean min (°F)	23.2
July mean max (°F)	90.9
Civ. Labor	576
Unemployed (%)	4.3
Wages	$3,850,918
Per Capita Income	$44,413
Prop. Value	$779,526,540
Retail Sales	$8,624,697

Brooks County

Physical Features: On Rio Grande plain; level to rolling; brushy; light to dark sandy loam soils.

Economy: Oil, gas, hunting leases, cattle, watermelons and hay.

History: Coahuiltecan Indians. Spanish land grants date to around 1800. County created from Hidalgo, Starr, Zapata counties, 1911; organized in 1912. Named for J.A. Brooks, Texas Ranger and legislator.

Race/Ethnicity: Anglo, 8.5%; Black, 0.2%; Hispanic, 90.6%; Asian, 0.2%; Other, 0.2%.

Vital Statistics, annual: Births, 117; deaths, 90; marriages, 65; divorces, 10.

Recreation: Hunting, fishing; Heritage Museum, Don Pedrito shrine; Fiesta del Campo in October.

Minerals: Oil, gas production; uranium.

Agriculture: Beef cow-calf operations, stocker; crops include hay, squash, watermelons, habanero peppers. Market value $26.2 million.

FALFURRIAS (4,916) county seat; oil and gas, agricultural, government/services.

Other towns include: **Encino** (145).

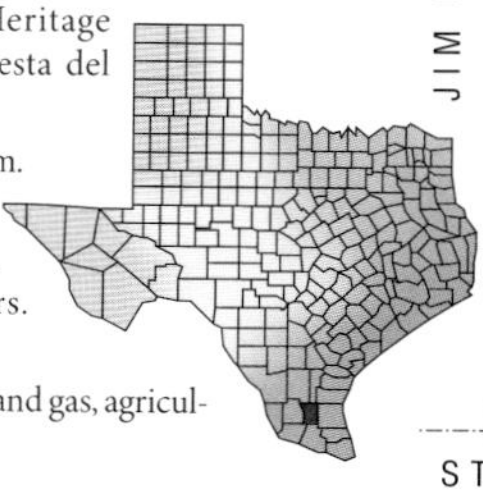

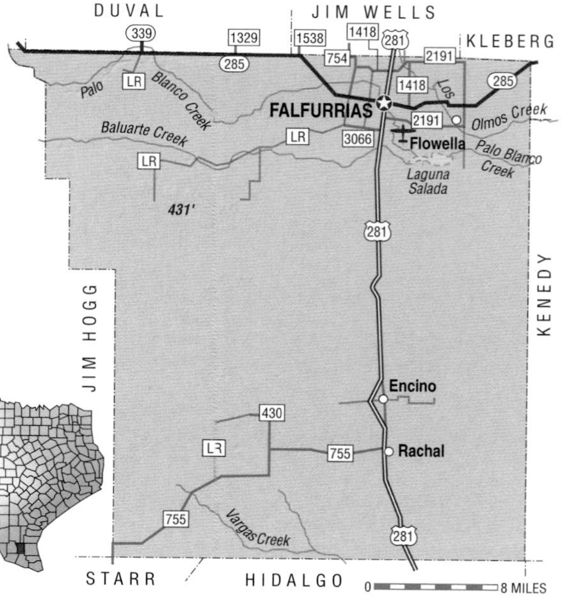

For explanation of sources, symbols and abbreviations, see p. 204, and foldout map.

Population	**7,115**
Change from 2010 (%)	-1.5
Area (sq. mi.)	943.7
Land Area (sq. mi.)	943.4
Altitude (ft.)	46–431
Rainfall (in.)	26.5
Jan. mean min (°F)	42.5
July mean max (°F)	97.0
Civ. Labor	2,471
Unemployed (%)	10.2
Wages	$31,530,351
Per Capita Income	$36,558
Prop. Value	$1,305,570,827
Retail Sales	$96,518,447

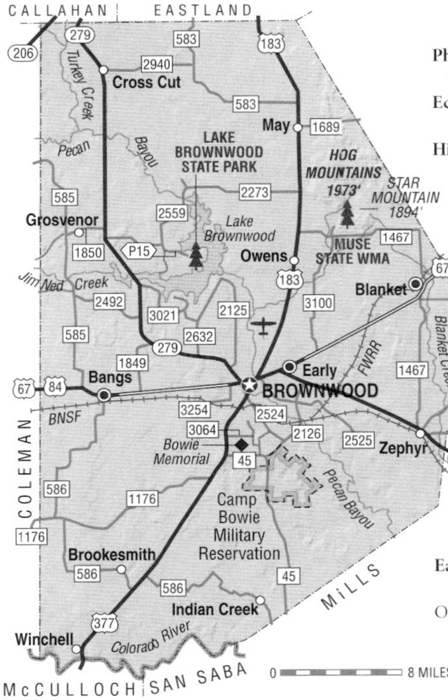

Brown County

Physical Features: Rolling, hilly; drains to Colorado River; Lake Brownwood; varied soils, timber.

Economy: Manufacturing plants, distribution centers, government/services, agribusiness, medical, education.

History: Apaches; displaced by Comanches who were removed by U.S. Army in 1874-75. Anglo-Americans first settled in mid-1850s. County created 1856 from Comanche, Travis counties, organized in 1857. Named for frontiersman Henry S. Brown.

Race/Ethnicity: Anglo, 70.1%; Black, 3.8%; Hispanic, 23.3%; Asian, 0.4%; Other, 2.1%.

Vital Statistics, annual: Births, 410; deaths, 515; marriages, 303; divorces, 44.

Recreation: State park; museums; fishing, hunting; wildflowers, walking trails.

Minerals: Oil, gas, paving materials, gravel, clays.

Agriculture: Cattle, hay, peanuts, pecans, meat goats, wheat, hogs. Market value $46.0 million.

BROWNWOOD (19,556) county seat; manufacturing, retail trade, distribution center; Howard Payne University, MacArthur Academy of Freedom; state substance abuse treatment center; state 4-H Club center; hospital; train museum, aquatic park; Reunion Celebration in September.

Early (3,049) retail, light manufacturing, government/services, agribusiness; motorcycle rally in October.

Other towns include: **Bangs** (1,588); **Blanket** (377); **Brookesmith** (61); **May** (270); **Zephyr** (201). **Lake Brownwood** area (1,450).

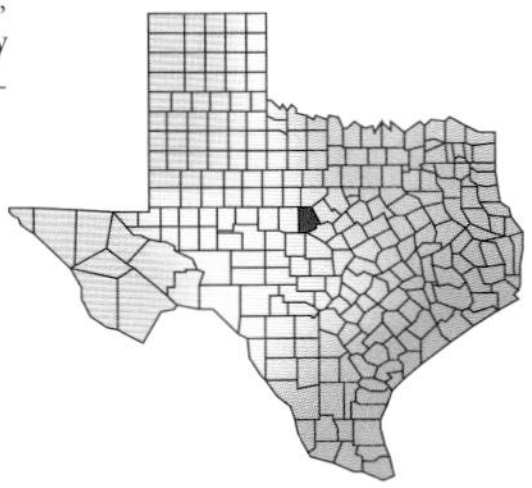

Population	**38,993**	July mean max (°F)	95.7
Change from 2010 (%)	2.3	Civ. Labor	14,786
Area (sq. mi.)	957.0	Unemployed (%)	5.5
Land Area (sq. mi.)	944.4	Wages	$157,782,399
Altitude (ft.)	1,230–1,973	Per Capita Income	$39,661
Rainfall (in.)	30.4	Prop. Value	$5,055,612,244
Jan. mean min (°F)	30.1	Retail Sales	$528,378,906

The coliseum in Brownwood is home to the Howard Payne University Yellow Jackets basketball and volleyball teams. It was built in 1963 and has 4,000 seats. Photo by Larry D. Moore, CC by SA 4/ Wikimedia Commons

Burleson County

Physical Features: Rolling to hilly; drains to Brazos, Yegua Creek, Somerville Lake; loam and heavy bottom soils; oaks, other trees.

Economy: Oil and gas, tourism, commuters to Texas A&M University, agribusiness.

History: Tonkawa and Caddo tribes roamed the area. Mexicans and Anglo-Americans settled around Fort Tenoxtitlan in 1830. Black freedmen migration increased until 1910. Germans, Czechs, Italians migrated in the 1870s-80s. County created and organized in 1846 from Milam, Washington counties; named for Edward Burleson, a hero of the Texas Revolution.

Race/Ethnicity: Anglo, 62.5%; Black, 12.1%; Hispanic, 23.4%; Asian, 0.1%; Other, 1.6%..

Vital Statistics, annual: Births, 215; deaths, 214; marriages, 99; divorces, 2.

Recreation: Fishing, hunting; lake recreation; historic sites; Czech heritage museum.

Minerals: Oil, gas, sand, gravel.

Agriculture: Cattle, cotton, corn, hay, sorghum, broiler production, soybeans; some irrigation. Market value $58.6 million.

CALDWELL (4,515) county seat; agribusiness, oil and gas, manufacturing, distribution center, tourism; hospital; civic center, museum; Kolache Festival in September.

Somerville (1,502) tourism, railroad center, some manufacturing; museum; Country Cajun festival in March.

Other towns include: **Chriesman** (30); **Deanville** (130); **Lyons** (360); **Snook** (535) Snookfest in June.

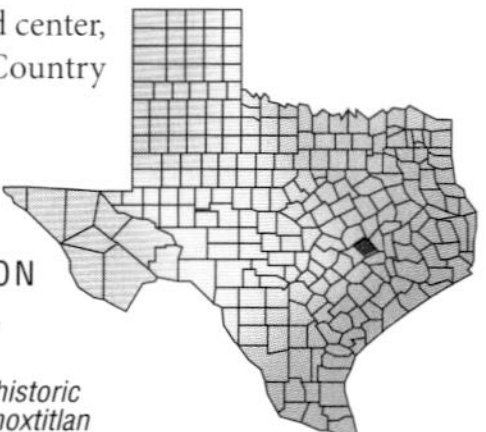

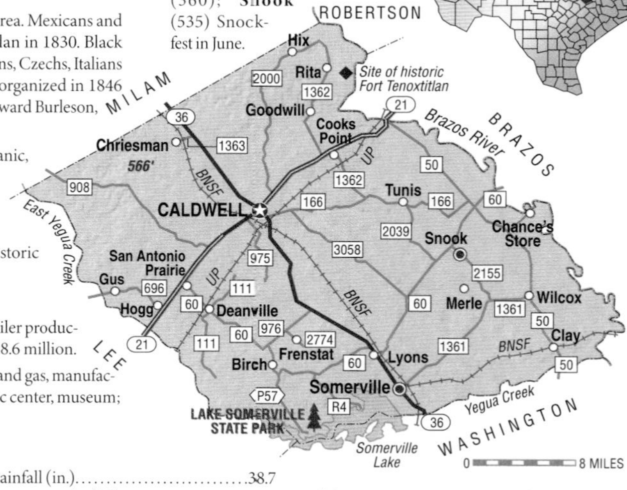

Population	**18,373**
Change from 2010 (%)	6.9
Area (sq. mi.)	676.8
Land Area (sq. mi.)	659.0
Altitude (ft.)	177–566
Rainfall (in.)	38.7
Jan. mean min (°F)	36.8
July mean max (°F)	95.2
Civ. Labor	8,229
Unemployed (%)	5.5
Wages	$56,948,342
Per Capita Income	$45,970
Prop. Value	$4,796,149,557
Retail Sales	$188,056,525

Burnet County

Physical Features: Scenic Hill Country county with Lake Buchanan, Inks Lake, Lake Lyndon B. Johnson, Lake Travis, Lake Marble Falls; caves; sandy, red, black waxy soils; cedars, other trees.

Economy: Tourism, stone processing, hunting leases.

History: Tonkawas, Lipan Apaches. Comanches raided in area. Frontier settlers arrived in the late 1840s. County created from Bell, Travis, Williamson counties, 1852; organized 1854; named for David G. Burnet, provisional president of the Republic.

Race/Ethnicity: Anglo, 72.4%; Black, 1.5%; Hispanic, 23.8%; Asian, 0.4%; Other, 1.6%.

Vital Statistics, annual: Births, 526; deaths, 528; marriages, 310; divorces, 210.

Recreation: Water sports on lakes; sites of historic forts; hunting; state parks, wildlife refuge; wildflowers; birding, scenic train ride.

Minerals: Granite, limestone.

Agriculture: Cattle, goats, grapes, hay. Market value $14.1 million. Deer, wild hog, and turkey hunting leases.

BURNET (7,025) county seat; tourism, government/services, varied industries, ranching; hospital; museums; vineyards; bluebonnet festival in April.

MARBLE FALLS (7,098) tourism, retail, manufacturing; granite, limestone quarries; August drag boat race.

Other towns include: **Bertram** (1,576) Oatmeal festival on Labor Day; **Briggs** (172); **Cottonwood Shores** (1,359); **Granite Shoals** (5,337); **Highland Haven** (442); **Meadowlakes** (1,816); **Spicewood** (4,000). Also, part of **Horseshoe Bay** (3,192).

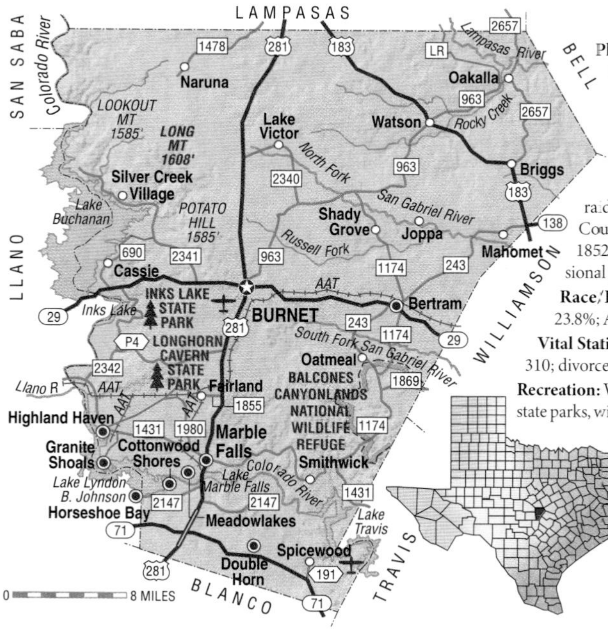

Population	**48,716**
Change from 2010 (%)	14.0
Area (sq. mi.)	1,021.3
Land Area (sq. mi.)	944.3
Altitude (ft.)	682–1,608
Rainfall (in.)	32.9
Jan. mean min (°F)	34.7
July mean max (°F)	93.0
Civ. Labor	23,785
Unemployed (%)	4
Wages	$196,378,144
Per Capita Income	$49,731
Prop. Value	$11,251,898,623
Retail Sales	$901,271,102

A lovely view of Marble Falls from a roadside park on U.S. Highway 281. Photo by Larry D. Moore, CC 3/Wikimedia Commons

Caldwell County

Population	**43,199**	July mean max (°F)	94.8
Change from 2010 (%)	13.5	Civ. Labor	19,884
Area (sq. mi.)	547.2	Unemployed (%)	5.3
Land Area (sq. mi.)	545.3	Wages	$95,409,285
Altitude (ft.)	315–736	Per Capita Income	$34,617
Rainfall (in.)	35.9	Prop. Value	$5,007,638,506
Jan. mean min (°F)	37.8	Retail Sales	$390,566,181

For explanation of sources, symbols and abbreviations, see p. 204, and foldout map.

Physical Features: Varied soils ranging from black clay to waxy; level, draining to San Marcos River.

Economy: Petroleum, varied manufacturing, government/services; part of Austin metro area, also near San Antonio.

History: Tonkawa area. Part of the DeWitt colony, Anglo-Americans settled in the 1830s. Mexican migration increased after 1890. County created from Bastrop and Gonzales counties and organized in 1848; named for frontiersman Mathew Caldwell.

Race/Ethnicity: Anglo, 38.9%; Black, 5.5%; Hispanic, 53.2%; Asian, 0.8%; Other, 1.4%.

Vital Statistics, annual: Births, 542; deaths, 320; marriages, 188; divorces, 125.

Recreation: Fishing, state park, nature trails, museums, barbecue havens; Luling Watermelon Thump and Lockhart Chisholm Trail roundup in June.

Minerals: Oil, gas, sand, gravel.

Agriculture: Eggs, beef cattle, hay, broilers. Market value $53.6 million.

LOCKHART (14,410) county seat; agribusiness center, government/services, tourism, light manufacturing, prison; renowned barbecue at Kreuz, Smitty's, Black's.

Luling (5,835) oil, tourism, agriculture; oil museum; hospital, barbecue cook-off in April.

Other towns include: **Dale** (300); **Fentress** (380); **Martindale** (1,262); **Maxwell** (500); part of **Mustang Ridge** (941, mostly in Travis County), and **Prairie Lea** (320).

Also, part of **Niederwald** (625), part of **Uhland** (1,331), and a small part of **San Marcos** (61,480), mostly in Hays County.

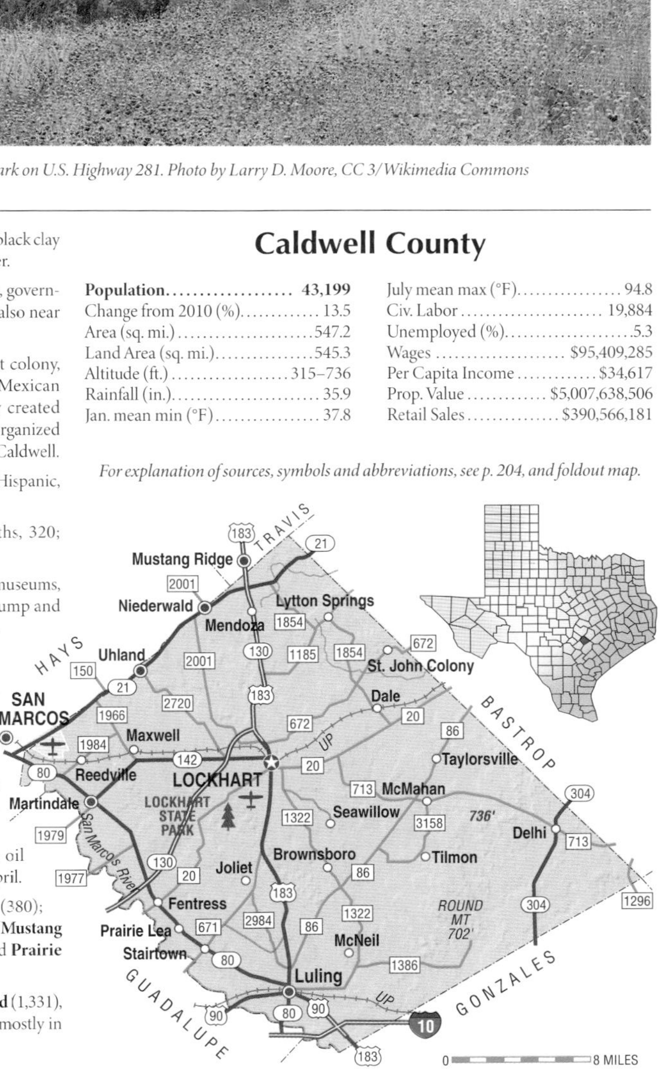

Calhoun County

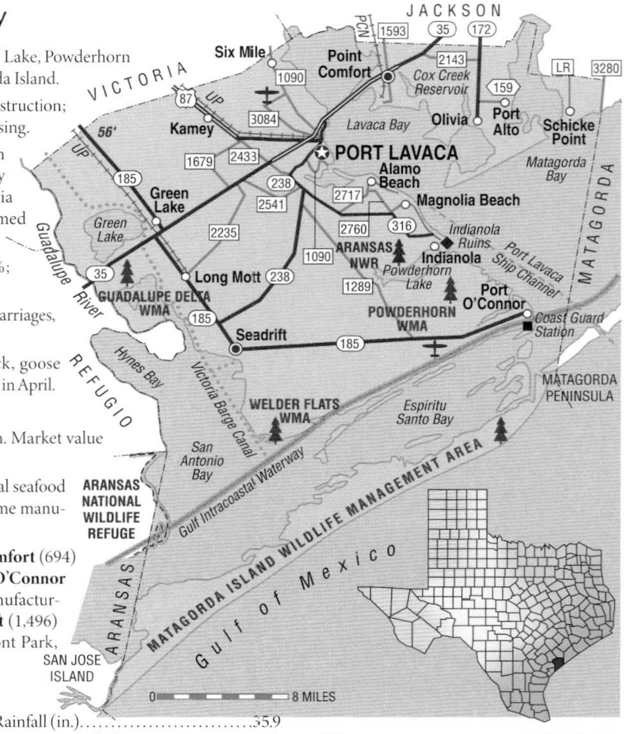

Physical Features: Sandy, broken by bays; Green Lake, Powderhorn Lake, Cox Creek Reservoir; partly on Matagorda Island.

Economy: Aluminum, plastics plants; marine construction; agribusinesses; petroleum; tourism; fish processing.

History: Karankawa tribal area. Empresario Martín De León brought 41 families in 1825. County created from Jackson, Matagorda, and Victoria counties in 1846; organized the same year. Named for John C. Calhoun, U.S. statesman.

Race/Ethnicity: Anglo, 41.8%; Black, 2.4%; Hispanic, 49.6%; Asian, 4.9%; Other, 1.1%.

Vital Statistics, annual: Births, 319; deaths, 198; marriages, 155; divorces, 20.

Recreation: Beaches, fishing, water sports, duck, goose hunting; historic sites, county park; La Salle Days in April.

Minerals: Oil, gas.

Agriculture: Cotton, cattle, corn, grain sorghum. Market value $32.1 million. Commercial fishing.

PORT LAVACA (12,641) county seat; commercial seafood operations, offshore drilling, tourist center; some manufacturing; convention center; hospital.

Other towns include: **Long Mott** (76); **Point Comfort** (694) aluminum, plastic plants, deepwater port; **Port O'Connor** (1,139) tourist center, seafood processing, manufacturing, lighted boat parade in December; **Seadrift** (1,496) commercial fishing, processing plants, Bayfront Park, Shrimpfest in June.

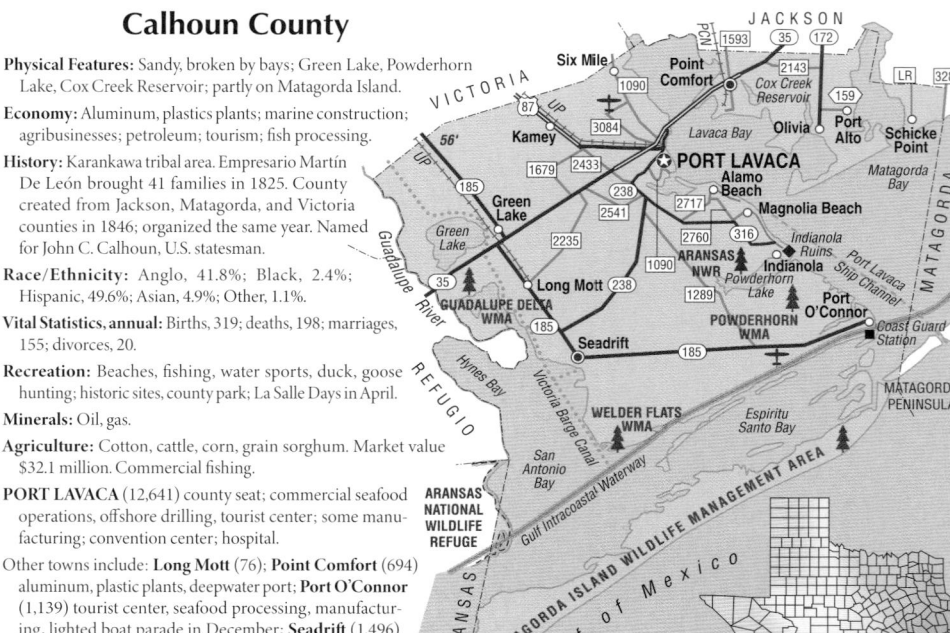

Population	**22,028**
Change from 2010 (%)	3.0
Area (sq. mi.)	1,032.7
Land Area (sq. mi.)	506.8
Altitude (ft.)	sea level–56
Rainfall (in.)	35.9
Jan. mean min (°F)	46.5
July mean max (°F)	89.0
Civ. Labor	12,338
Unemployed (%)	5.3
Wages	$259,895,848
Per Capita Income	$46,208
Prop. Value	$6,183,538,209
Retail Sales	$258,287,918

Callahan County

Population	**14,070**
Change from 2010 (%)	3.9
Area (sq. mi.)	901.3
Land Area (sq. mi.)	899.4
Altitude (ft.)	1,350–2,204
Rainfall (in.)	27.4
Jan. mean min (°F)	31.4
July mean max (°F)	94.8
Civ. Labor	6,070
Unemployed (%)	4.8
Wages	$32,332,312
Per Capita Income	$41,962
Prop. Value	$2,042,572,399
Retail Sales	$176,551,968

Physical Features: On divide between Brazos, Colorado rivers; Lake Clyde, Lake Baird; level to rolling.

Economy: Ranching; feed and fertilizer business; many residents commute to Abilene; 200,000 acres in hunting leases.

History: Comanche territory until the 1870s. Anglo-American settlement began around 1860. County created in 1858 from Bexar, Bosque, and Travis counties; organized in 1877. Named for Texas Ranger J.H. Callahan.

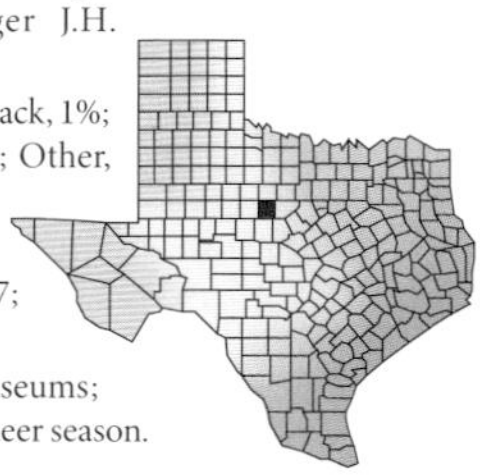

Race/Ethnicity: Anglo, 85.5%; Black, 1%; Hispanic, 10.4%; Asian, 0.5%; Other, 2.3%.

Vital Statistics, annual: Births, 147; deaths, 179; marriages, 57; divorces, 34.

Recreation: Hunting, lakes; museums; Cross Plains Hunters' Feed at deer season.

Minerals: Oil and gas.

Agriculture: Cattle, wheat, sorghum, oats. Market value $31.2 million. Hunting leases important.

BAIRD (1,496) county seat; ranching/agricultural trade center, some manufacturing, shipping; historic sites; Railhead Day in May, depot museum.

Clyde (3,956) steel water systems manufacturing, government/services; library; Pecan Festival in October.

Other towns include: **Cross Plains** (1,014) oil and gas, agriculture, government/services, home of creator of Conan the Barbarian, museum, Barbarian Festival in June; **Putnam** (96).

Physical Features: Southernmost county in rich Rio Grande Valley soils; flat landscape; semitropical climate; Loma Alta Lake.

Economy: Agribusiness, tourism, seafood processing, shipping, manufacturing, government/services.

History: Coahuiltecan tribal area. Spanish land grants date to 1781. County created from Nueces County, 1848; named for Capt. Ewen Cameron of Mier Expedition.

Race/Ethnicity: Anglo, 8.7%; Black, 0.3%; Hispanic, 89.8%; Asian, 0.6%; Other, 0.3%.

Vital Statistics, annual: Births, 7,238; deaths, 2,684; marriages, 2,305; divorces, 651.

Recreation: South Padre Island: year-round resort; fishing, hunting, water sports; historical sites, Palo Alto visitors center; gateway to Mexico, state parks; wildlife refuge; recreational vehicle center.

Minerals: Natural gas, oil.

Agriculture: Cotton, grain sorghums, vegetables, corn, citrus. Ranked second in sugar cane acreage. Wholesale nursery plants raised. Small feedlot and cow-calf operations. Some 112,000 acres irrigated, mostly cotton and grain sorghums. Market value $122.6 million. Ranked third in value of aquaculture.

BROWNSVILLE (184,500) county seat; international trade, varied industries, shipping, tourism; college, hospitals, crippled children health center; Gladys Porter

Cameron County

Zoo, historic Fort Brown; University of Texas–Rio Grande Valley, Texas Southmost College.

HARLINGEN (68,835) health care, government/services, tourism; hospitals; college extension campuses; nature center; birding festival in November.

SAN BENITO (24,581) retail center, tourism, agriculture; hospital; museums, arts center, historic buildings; recreation facilities, including walking/jogging trail; ResacaFest on July 4.

SOUTH PADRE ISLAND (2,766) beaches, tourism/convention center, real estate and construction; birding/nature center, Sandcastle Days in October, Spring Break in March.

Other towns include: **Bayview** (408); **Bluetown** (351); **Cameron Park** (7,417); **Combes** (3,094); **Encantada-Ranchito El Calaboz** (2,201); **Indian Lake** (833); **La Feria** (7,703); **Laguna Heights** (4,219); **Laguna Vista** (3,348); **Laureles** (3,670); **Los Fresnos** (7,937) Little Graceland Museum, Butterfly Farm, library; **Los Indios** (1,075); **Olmito** (1,074); **Palm Valley** (1,241).

Also, **Port Isabel** (5,288) tourist center, fishing, museums, old lighthouse, Shrimp Cook-Off in November; **Primera** (4,905); **Rancho Viejo** (2,531); **Rangerville** (350); **Rio Hondo** (2,729); **Santa Maria** (651); **Santa Rosa** (2,766).

Population	**426,210**
Change from 2010 (%)	4.9
Area (sq. mi.)	1,276.5
Land Area (sq. mi.)	890.9
Altitude (ft.)	sea level–67
Rainfall (in.)	27.4
Jan. mean min (°F)	51.6
July mean max (°F)	93.6
Civ. Labor	169,777
Unemployed (%)	9.1
Wages	$1,379,306,529
Per Capita Income	$29,928
Prop. Value	$25,473,967,448
Retail Sales	$5,066,926,858

For explanation of sources, symbols and abbreviations, see p. 204, and foldout map.

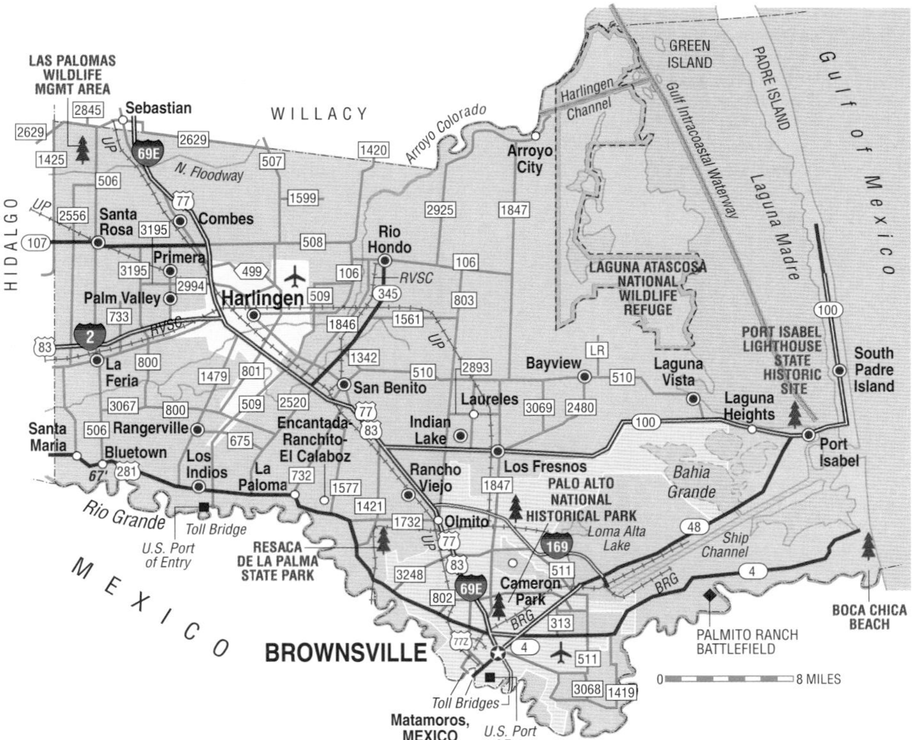

Physical Features: East Texas county with forested hills; drains to Big Cypress Creek on the north; Lake Bob Sandlin; third smallest county in Texas.

Economy: Agribusiness, chicken processing, timber industries, light manufacturing, retirement center.

History: Caddo area. Anglo-American settlers arrived in late 1830s. Antebellum slaveholding area. County created, organized from Upshur County 1874; named for jurist J.L. Camp.

Race/Ethnicity: Anglo, 55.5%; Black, 16.2%; Hispanic, 24.4%; Asian, 0.5%; Other, 3.1%.

Vital Statistics, annual: Births, 172; deaths, 132; marriages, 90; divorces, 22.

Recreation: Water sports, fishing on lakes; farmstead and airship museum; Pittsburg hot links; Chickfest in September.

Minerals: Oil, gas, clays, coal.

Agriculture: Poultry and products important; beef, dairy cattle, horses; peaches, hay, blueberries, vegetables. Market value $114.2 million. Forestry.

PITTSBURG (4,760) county seat; agribusiness, timber, tourism, food processing, light manufacturing, commuting to Longview, Tyler; hospital; community college; Prayer Tower.

Other towns include: **Leesburg** (128) and **Rocky Mound** (71).

Population	**12,914**
Change from 2010 (%)	4.1
Area (sq. mi.)	203.2
Land Area (sq. mi.)	195.8
Altitude (ft.)	236–538
Rainfall (in.)	45.1
Jan. mean min (°F)	33.1
July mean max (°F)	95.2
Civ. Labor	4,956
Unemployed (%)	6.5
Wages	$41,435,738
Per Capita Income	$37,111
Prop. Value	$1,506,904,810
Retail Sales	$121,104,756

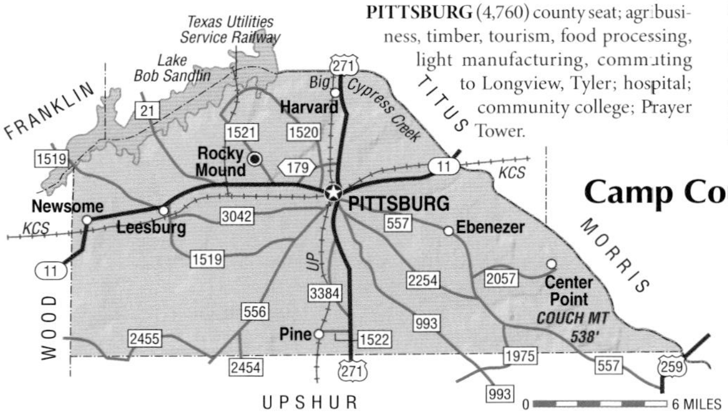

Camp County

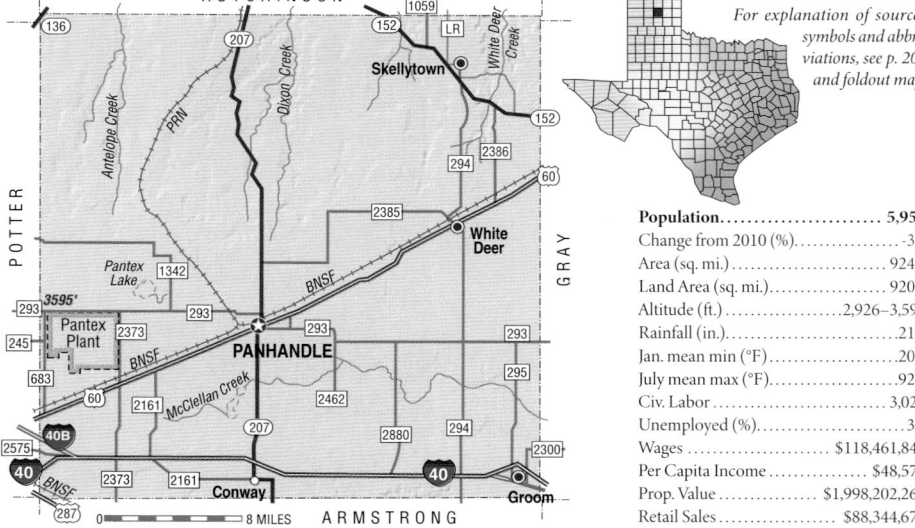

Carson County

Physical Features: In center of Panhandle on level, some broken land; loam soils.

Economy: Pantex nuclear weapons assembly/disassembly facility (U.S. Department of Energy), commuting to Amarillo, petrochemical plants, agribusiness.

History: Apaches, displaced by Comanches. Anglo-American ranchers settled in the 1880s. German, Polish farmers arrived around 1910. County created from Bexar District, 1876; organized 1888. Named for Republic secretary of state S.P. Carson.

Race/Ethnicity: Anglo, 85.9%; Black, 0.7%; Hispanic, 10.6%; Asian, 0.3%; Other, 2.3%.

Vital Statistics, annual: Births, 55; deaths, 58; marriages, 44; divorces, 6.

Recreation: Museum, The Cross at Groom; Square House Barbecue in fall.

Minerals: Oil, gas production.

Agriculture: Cattle, cotton, wheat, sorghum, corn, hay, soybeans. Market value $91.8 million.

PANHANDLE (2,315) county seat; government/services, agribusiness, petroleum center, commuters to Amarillo; Veterans Day celebration, car show in June.

Other towns include: **Groom** (542) farming center, government/services, Groom Day festival in August; **Skellytown** (436); **White Deer** (963) Polish sausage festival in November.

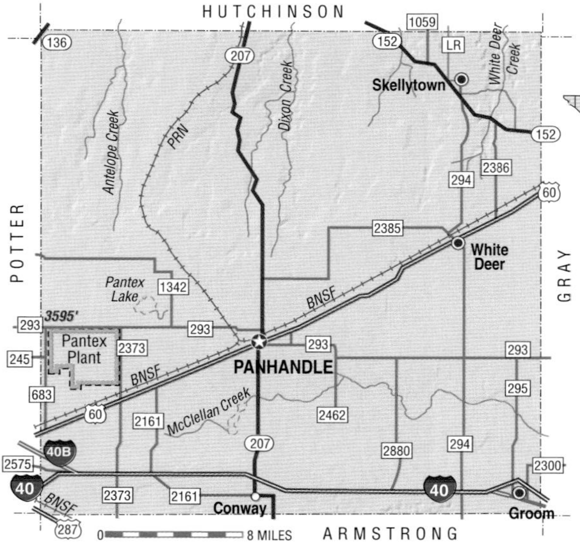

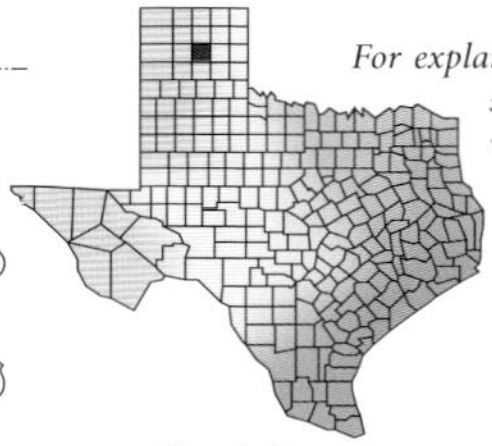

For explanation of sources, symbols and abbreviations, see p. 204, and foldout map.

Population	**5,951**
Change from 2010 (%)	-3.7
Area (sq. mi.)	924.1
Land Area (sq. mi.)	920.2
Altitude (ft.)	2,926–3,595
Rainfall (in.)	21.8
Jan. mean min (°F)	20.3
July mean max (°F)	92.2
Civ. Labor	3,020
Unemployed (%)	3.7
Wages	$118,461,840
Per Capita Income	$48,571
Prop. Value	$1,998,202,269
Retail Sales	$88,344,673

Cass County

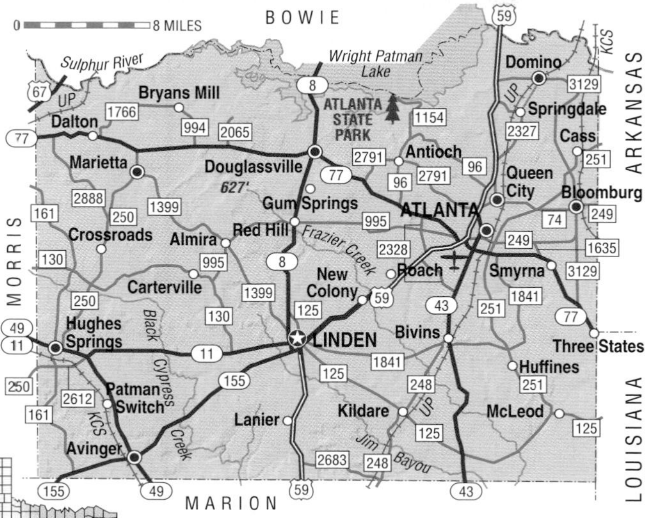

Physical Features: Forested Northeast county rolling to hilly; drained by Cypress Bayou, Sulphur River; Wright Patman Lake.

Economy: Timber and paper industries, government/services.

History: Caddoes, who were displaced by other tribes in the 1790s. Anglo-Americans arrived in the 1830s. Antebellum slaveholding area. County created and organized in 1846 from Bowie County; named for U.S. Sen. Lewis Cass.

Race/Ethnicity: Anglo, 76.2%; Black, 16.6%; Hispanic, 4.3%; Asian, 0.3%; Other, 2.3%.

Vital Statistics, annual: Births, 386; deaths, 414; marriages, 168; divorces, 152.

Recreation: Fishing, hunting, water sports; state park, county park; lake, wildflower trails.

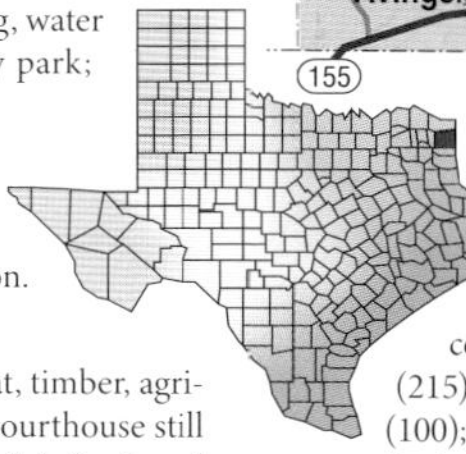

Minerals: Oil, iron ore.

Agriculture: Cattle, poultry. Market value $53.4 million. Timber important.

LINDEN (2,034) county seat, timber, agribusiness, tourism; oldest courthouse still in use as courthouse, hospital; Rock and Roll Hall of Fame.

ATLANTA (5,610) Paper and timber industries, government/services, varied manufacturing, hospital, library; Forest Festival in August.

Other towns include: **Avinger** (431) timber, paper industry, steel plant, early cemetery, Glory Days celebration in October; **Bivins** (215); **Bloomburg** (406); **Domino** (100); **Douglassville** (225); **Hughes Springs** (1,733) varied manufacturing, warehousing, trucking school, Pumpkin Glow in October; **Kildare** (104); **Marietta** (129); **McLeod** (600); **Queen City** (1,477) paper industry, commuters to Texarkana, government/services, historic sites.

Population	**30,451**
Change from 2010 (%)	0.0
Area (sq. mi.)	960.3
Land Area (sq. mi.)	937.0
Altitude (ft.)	167–627
Rainfall (in.)	49.2
Jan. mean min (°F)	34.6
July mean max (°F)	92.1
Civ. Labor	12,169
Unemployed (%)	7.4
Wages	$80,481,168
Per Capita Income	$37,566
Prop. Value	$3,161,122,671
Retail Sales	$264,010,650

The public library in Atlanta, Texas. the largest town in Cass County. Photo by Michael Barera, CC by SA 4/Wikimedia Commons

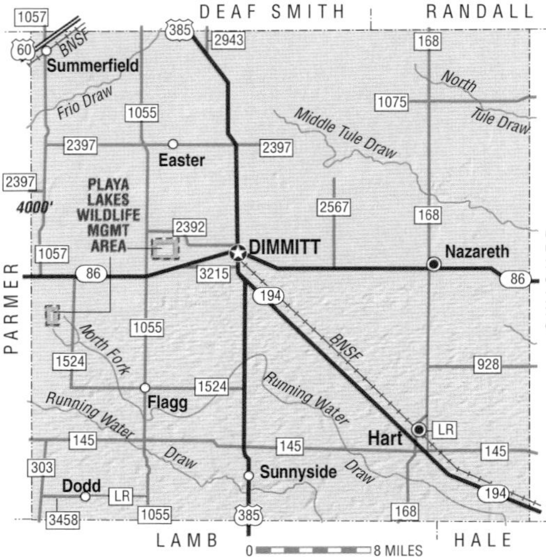

Castro County

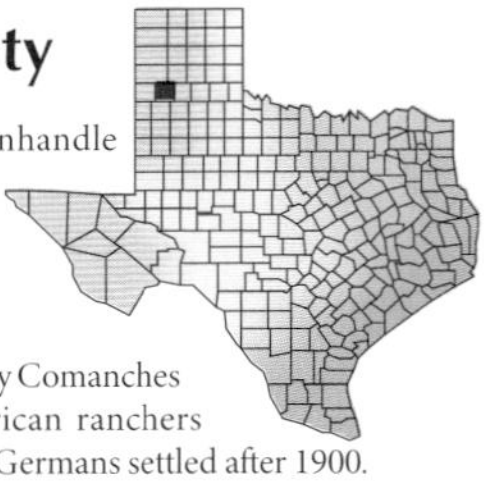

Physical Features: Flat Panhandle county, drains to creeks, draws and playas; underground water.

Economy: Agribusiness.

History: Apaches, displaced by Comanches in the 1720s. Anglo-American ranchers began settling in the 1880s. Germans settled after 1900. Mexican migration increased after 1950. County created, 1876 from Bexar District, organized 1891. Named for Henri Castro, Texas colonizer.

Race/Ethnicity: Anglo, 32%; Black, 2.3%; Hispanic, 64.3%; Asian, 0.5%; Other, 0.8%.

Vital Statistics, annual: Births, 125; deaths, 65; marriages, 44; divorces, 16.

Recreation: Pheasant hunting; Italian POW camp site; Dimmitt Harvest Days celebrated in August.

Minerals: Insignificant.

Agriculture: Beef cattle, dairies (first in number of milk cows), corn, cotton, wheat, sheep. Market value $1.1 billion; third in state.

DIMMITT (4,063) county seat; agribusiness center; library, hospital; quilt festival in April.

Other towns include: **Hart** (1,014) and **Nazareth** (291) German festival/Suds & Sounds in July.

Population	**7,380**
Change from 2010 (%)	-8.5
Area (sq. mi.)	899.3
Land Area (sq. mi.)	894.4
Altitude (ft.)	3,565–4,000
Rainfall (in.)	21.2
Jan. mean min (°F)	21.3
July mean max (°F)	91.0
Civ. Labor	3,458
Unemployed (%)	3.5
Wages	$26,693,020
Per Capita Income	$64,427
Prop. Value	$1,783,703,439
Retail Sales	$63,788,201

Chambers County

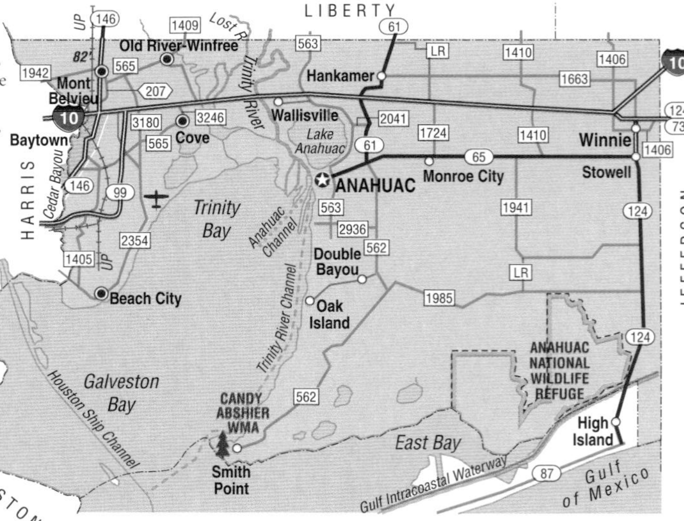

Physical Features: Gulf coastal plain, coastal soils; Lake Anahuac; some forests.

Economy: Water suppliers, banking, chemical distribution facilities, air services, carbon dioxide disposal.

History: Karankawa and other coastal tribes. Nuestra Señora de la Luz Mission established near present Wallisville in 1756. County created and organized in 1858 from Liberty, Jefferson counties. Named for Gen. T. J. Chambers, surveyor.

Race/Ethnicity: Anglo, 65.1%; Black, 8.2%; Hispanic, 23.9%; Asian, 0.9%; Other, 1.6%.

Vital Statistics, annual: Births, 512; deaths, 290; marriages, 216; divorces, 189.

Recreation: Fishing, hunting; water sports; camping; county parks; wildlife refuge; historic sites; Wallisville Heritage Museum; Texas Gatorfest at Anahuac in September.

Minerals: Oil, gas.

Agriculture: Beef cattle, rice, hay, aquaculture; significant irrigation. Market value $19.3 million. Hunting, fishing important.

ANAHUAC (2,491) county seat; canal connects with Houston Ship Channel; agribusiness; hospital, library.

WINNIE (3,606) ecotourism; commuting to Beaumont, Houston; rice farming; antiques market; hospital; library, museum; Texas Rice Festival in early October.

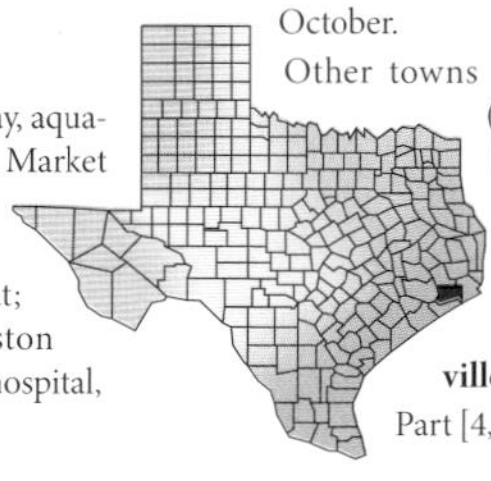

Other towns include: **Beach City** (2,856), **Cove** (567), **Hankamer** (226), **Mont Belvieu** (6,666), **Old River-Winfree** (1,475), **Stowell** (2,096), and **Wallisville** (300).

Part [4,180] of **Baytown.**

Population	**44,298**
Change from 2010 (%)	26.2
Area (sq. mi.)	871.2
Land Area (sq. mi.)	597.1
Altitude (ft.)	sea level–82
Rainfall (in.)	57.1
Jan. mean min (°F)	42.2
July mean max (°F)	90.6
Civ. Labor	20,031
Unemployed (%)	9.2
Wages	$272,257,418
Per Capita Income	$56,610
Prop. Value	$21,350,895,447
Retail Sales	$539,773,084

Shops in downtown Jacksonville, in Cherokee County. Photo by Renelibrary, CC by SA 4.0/Wikimedia Commons

Cherokee County

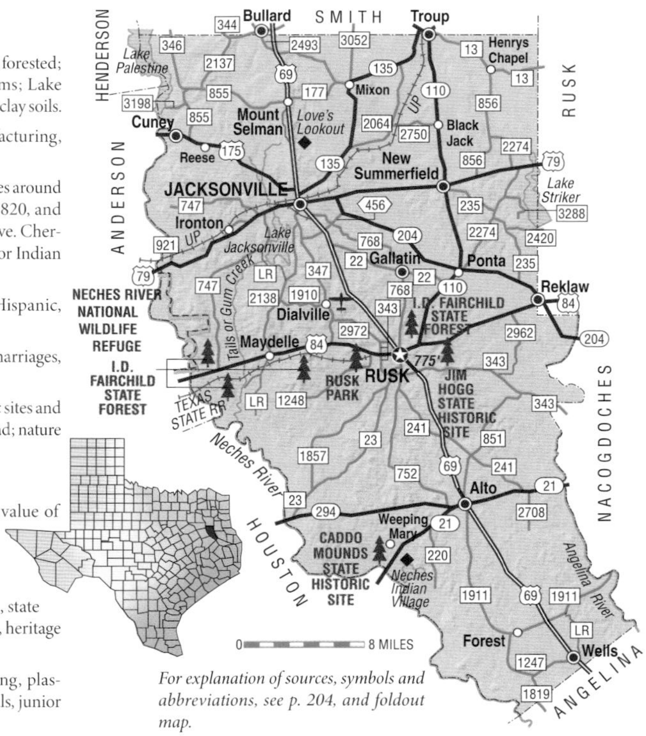

For explanation of sources, symbols and abbreviations, see p. 204, and foldout map.

Physical Features: East Texas county; hilly, partly forested; drains to Angelina, Neches rivers; many streams; Lake Palestine, Lake Striker, Lake Jacksonville; sandy, clay soils.

Economy: Government/services, varied manufacturing, agribusiness.

History: Caddo tribes attracted Spanish missionaries around 1720. Cherokees began settling area around 1820, and soon afterward Anglo-Americans began to arrive. Cherokees forced to Indian Territory 1839. Named for Indian tribe; created 1846 from Nacogdoches County.

Race/Ethnicity: Anglo, 60.3%; Black, 13.7%; Hispanic, 23.3%; Asian, 0.4%; Other, 2.1%..

Vital Statistics, annual: Births, 827; deaths, 557; marriages, 319; divorces, 152.

Recreation: Water sports; fishing, hunting; historic sites and parks, national wildlife refuge; Texas State Railroad; nature trails through forests; lakes.

Minerals: Gas, oil.

Agriculture: Nurseries (second in the state in value of sales), hay, beef cattle, dairies, poultry. Market value $115.7 million. Timber, hunting income significant.

RUSK (5,796) county seat; agribusiness, tourism, state mental hospital, prison unit; historic footbridge, heritage festival in October.

JACKSONVILLE (15,152) varied manufacturing, plastics, agribusiness, tourism, retail center; hospitals, junior colleges; Love's Lookout; Tomato Fest in June.

Other towns include: **Alto** (1,306) farming, timber, light manufacturing, pecan festival in November; **Cuney** (140); **Gallatin** (447); **Maydelle** (250); **New Summerfield** (1,227); **Reklaw** (395, partly in Rusk County); **Wells** (813). Part [68] of **Bullard** and part [66] of **Troup**.

Population	**53,539**
Change from 2010 (%)	5.3
Area (sq. mi.)	1,062.2
Land Area (sq. mi.)	1,052.9
Altitude (ft.)	187–775
Rainfall (in.)	49.5
Jan. mean min (°F)	36.3
July mean max (°F)	91.2
Civ. Labor	21,243
Unemployed (%)	6.8
Wages	$148,998,494
Per Capita Income	$35,245
Prop. Value	$4,907,715,917
Retail Sales	$478,740,093

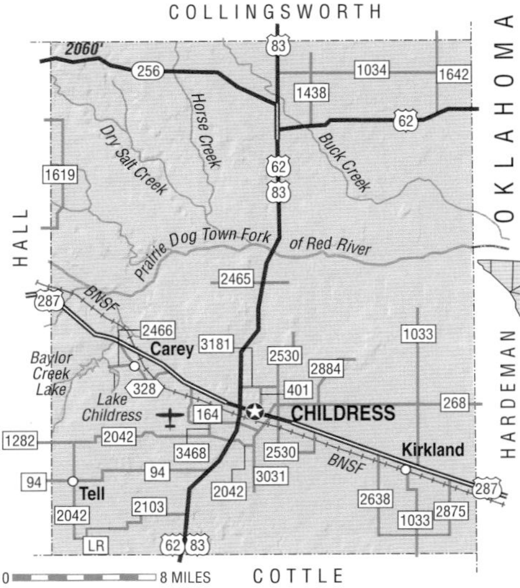

Childress County

Physical Features: Rolling prairie, at corner of Panhandle, draining to fork of Red River; Baylor Creek Lake, Lake Childress; mixed soils.

Economy: Government/services, retail trade, tourism, agriculture.

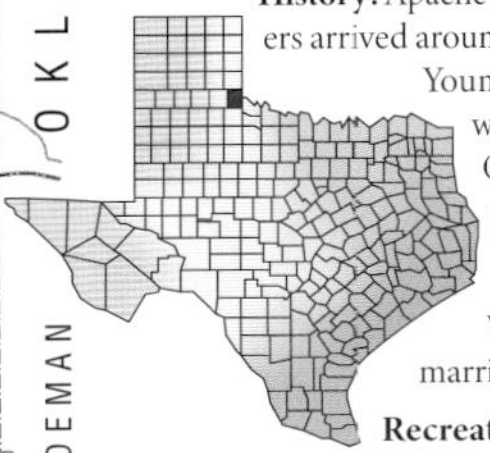

History: Apache tribal area, displaced by Comanches. Ranchers arrived around 1880. County created in 1876 from Bexar, Young districts; organized in 1887; named for writer of Texas Declaration of Independence, George C. Childress.

Race/Ethnicity: Anglo, 57.3%; Black, 9.9%; Hispanic, 29.9%; Asian, 0.8%; Other, 1.8%.

Vital Statistics, annual: Births, 62; deaths, 75; marriages, 45; divorces, 16.

Recreation: Recreation on lakes and creeks, fishing; hunting of deer, turkey, wild hog, quail, dove; parks; county museum.

Minerals: Insignificant.

Agriculture: Cotton, beef cattle, wheat, hay, sorghum, peanuts; some 9,000 acres irrigated. Market value $27.2 million. Hunting leases.

CHILDRESS (6,289) county seat; agribusiness, hospital, prison unit; settlers reunion and rodeo in July.

Other towns include: **Tell** (20).

Population	**7,038**	Rainfall (in.)	26.4		
Change from 2010 (%)	0.0	Jan. mean min (°F)	26.8	Wages	$29,353,367
Area (sq. mi.)	713.7	July mean max (°F)	95.7	Per Capita Income	$30,731
Land Area (sq. mi.)	696.4	Civ. Labor	3,168	Prop. Value	$1,146,283,645
Altitude (ft.)	1,560–2,060	Unemployed (%)	3.6	Retail Sales	$118,586,882

Clay County

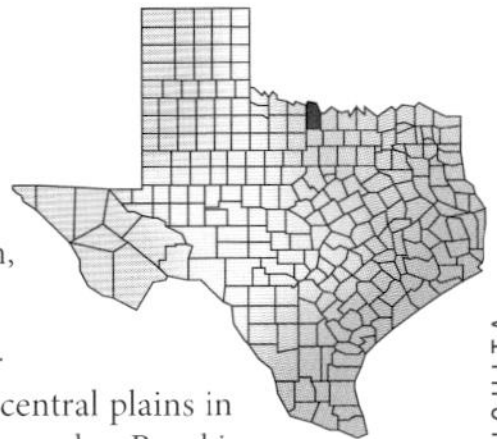

Physical Features: Hilly, rolling; Northwest county drains to Red, Trinity rivers; Lake Arrowhead; sandy loam, chocolate soils; mesquites, post oaks.

Economy: Oil, agribusiness, commuting.

History: Wichitas arrived from north-central plains in mid-1700s, followed by Apaches and Comanches. Ranching attempts began in 1850s. County created from Cooke County, 1857; Indians forced disorganization, 1862; reorganized, 1873; named for Henry Clay, U.S. statesman.

Race/Ethnicity: Anglo, 90.6%; Black, 0.5%; Hispanic, 5.4%; Asian, 0.3%; Other, 2.9%.

Vital Statistics, annual: Births, 84; deaths, 131; marriages, 68; divorces, 20.

Recreation: Fishing, hunting, horses, water sports; state park; pioneer reunion in September.

Minerals: Oil and gas, stone.

Agriculture: Beef cattle, wheat, pecans, peaches, dairy cattle. Market value $55.7 million. Oaks, cedar, elms sold to nurseries, mesquite cut for firewood.

HENRIETTA (3,104) county seat; agribusiness, government/services, manufacturing; hospital; museum; Turkey Fest in April.

Other towns include: **Bellevue** (347), **Bluegrove** (135), **Byers** (474), **Dean** (463), **Jolly** (159), **Petrolia** (672).

For explanation of sources, symbols and abbreviations, see p. 204, and foldout map.

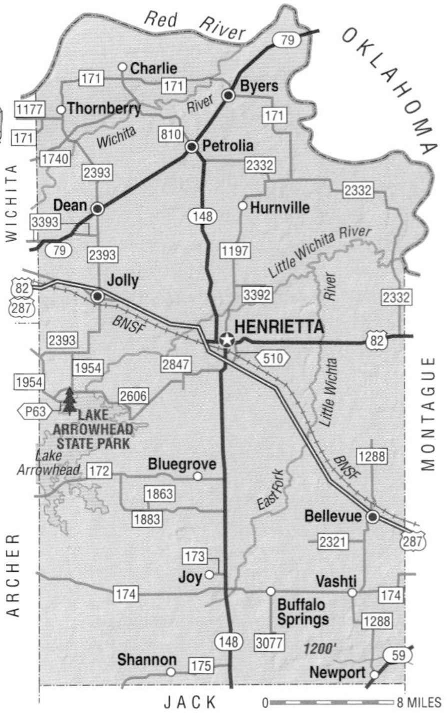

Population	**10,351**	Rainfall (in.)	32.7		
Change from 2010 (%)	-3.7	Jan. mean min (°F)	28.7	Wages	$15,804,739
Area (sq. mi.)	1,116.8	July mean max (°F)	96.6	Per Capita Income	$44,295
Land Area (sq. mi.)	1,088.7	Civ. Labor	4,852	Prop. Value	$2,270,799,249
Altitude (ft.)	791–1,200	Unemployed (%)	5.2	Retail Sales	$67,009,797

Cochran County

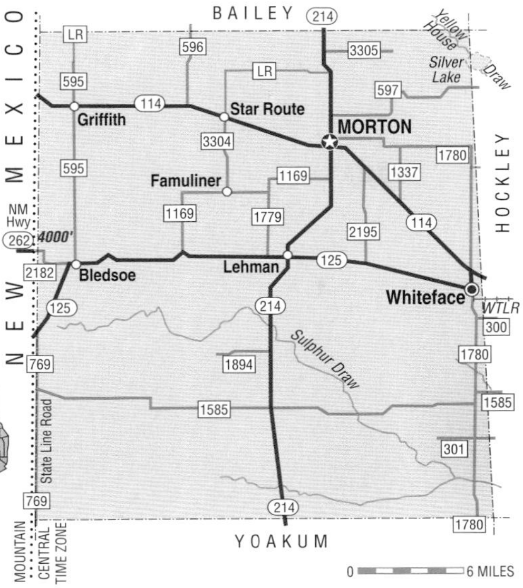

Physical Features: South Plains bordering New Mexico with small lakes (playas); underground water; loam, sandy loam soils.

Economy: Farming, government/services, retail.

History: Hunting area for various Indian tribes. Ranches operated in the 1880s but population in 1900 was still only 25. Farming began in the 1920s. County created from Bexar and Young districts in 1876; organized in 1924; named for Robert Cochran, who died at the Alamo.

Race/Ethnicity: Anglo, 35.9%; Black, 3.4%; Hispanic, 58.9%; Asian, 0%; Other, 1.6%.

Vital Statistics, annual: Births, 39; deaths, 31; marriages, 9; divorces, 5.

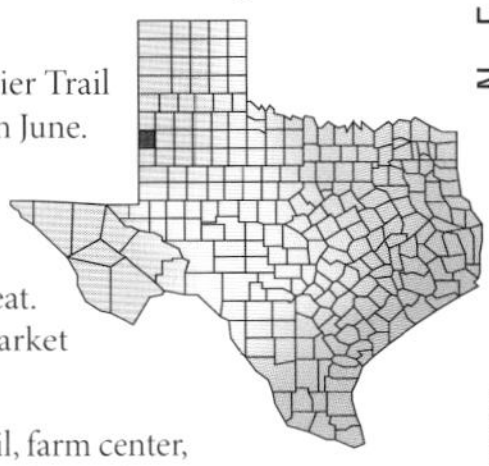

Recreation: Museum; Last Frontier Trail Drive and Buffalo Soldier Day in June.

Minerals: Insignificant.

Agriculture: Cotton, peanuts, sorghum, peas, sunflowers, wheat. Crops 60 percent irrigated. Market value $87.6 million.

MORTON (1,846) county seat; oil, farm center, meat packing, light manufacture; hospital.

Other towns include: **Bledsoe** (126), **Whiteface** (432).

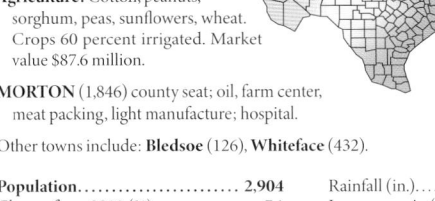

Population	**2,904**
Change from 2010 (%)	-7.1
Area (sq. mi.)	775.2
Land Area (sq. mi.)	775.2
Altitude (ft.)	3,565–4,000

Rainfall (in.)	18.9
Jan. mean min (°F)	24.4
July mean max (°F)	91.5
Civ. Labor	1,145
Unemployed (%)	5.6

Wages	$8,110,083
Per Capita Income	$39,333
Prop. Value	$766,027,380
Retail Sales	$26,421,176

Coke County

Physical Features: West Texas prairie, hills, Colorado River valley; sandy loam, red soils; E.V. Spence Reservoir, Oak Creek Reservoir.

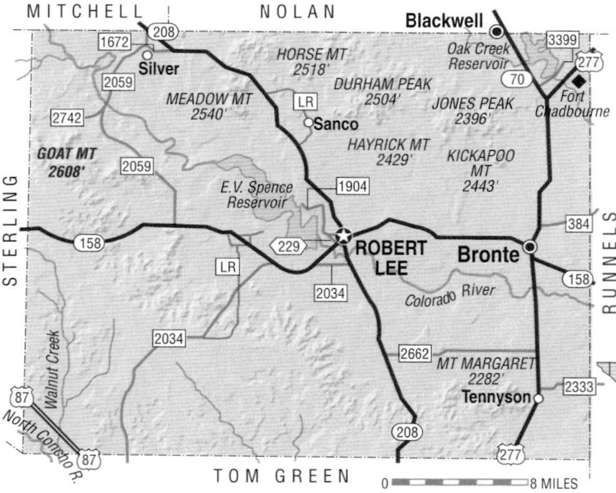

Economy: Oil and gas, government/services, agriculture.

History: From around 1700 to 1870s, Comanche bands roamed through the area. Ranches began operating after the Civil War. County was created and organized in 1889 from Tom Green County; named for Gov. Richard Coke.

Race/Ethnicity: Anglo, 78%; Black, 0.1%; Hispanic, 19.5%; Asian, 0.1%; Other, 2%.

Vital Statistics, annual: Births, 39; deaths, 53;marriages, 11; divorces, 12.

Recreation: Hunting, fishing, Caliche Loop birdwatching trail; lakes; Sumac hiking trail; historic sites, Fort Chadbourne, county museum, Fort Chadbourne Days in May; amphitheater.

Minerals: Oil, gas.

Agriculture: Beef cattle, small grains, sheep and goats, hay. Market value $7.8 million.

ROBERT LEE (1,092) county seat; oil and gas, wind farms, ranching, government/services; old jail museum.

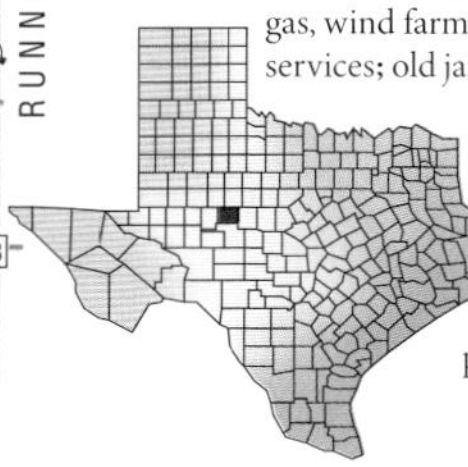

BRONTE (1,025) ranching, oil.

Other towns include: **Silver** (34) and **Tennyson** (46). Also, a small part of **Blackwell** (295).

Population	**3,390**
Change from 2010 (%)	2.1
Area (sq. mi.)	928.0
Land Area (sq. mi.)	911.5
Altitude (ft.)	1,700–2,608
Rainfall (in.)	22.8
Jan. mean min (°F)	28.4
July mean max (°F)	96.7
Civ. Labor	1,349
Unemployed (%)	5.3
Wages	$8,254,808
Per Capita Income	$41,669
Prop. Value	$1,023,620,554
Retail Sales	$22,155,760

Coleman County

Physical Features: Hilly, rolling; drains to Colorado River, Pecan Bayou; O.H. Ivie Reservoir, Hords Creek Lake, Lake Coleman; mesquite, oaks.

Economy: Agribusiness, petroleum, ecotourism, varied manufacturing.

History: Presence of Apaches and Comanches brought military outpost, Camp Colorado, before the Civil War. Settlers arrived after organization. County created in 1858 from Brown, Travis counties; organized in 1864; named for Houston's aide, R.M. Coleman.

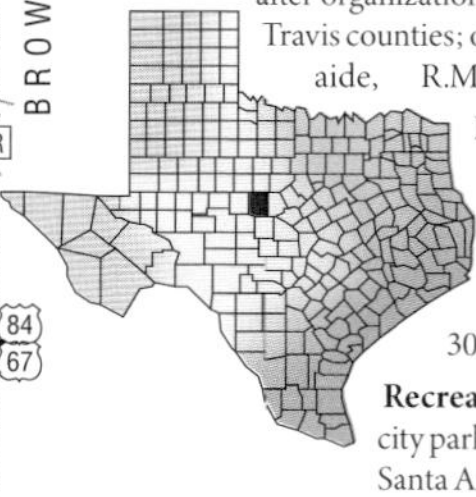

Race/Ethnicity: Anglo, 74.8%; Black, 2.7%; Hispanic, 19.4%; Asian, 0.3%; Other, 2.5%.

Vital Statistics, annual: Births, 72; deaths, 131; marriages, 45; divorces, 30.

Recreation: Fishing, hunting; water sports; city park, historic sites; lakes; Santa Anna Peak; Santa Anna bison cook-off in May.

Minerals: Oil, gas, stone, clays.

Agriculture: Cattle, wheat, sheep, hay, grain sorghum, goats, oats, cotton. Market value $41.2 million. Mesquite for firewood and furniture.

COLEMAN (4,305) county seat; varied manufacturing; hospital, library, museums: Fiesta de la Paloma in October.

SANTA ANNA (1,010) agribusiness, oil, tourism; museum; Funtier days in May.

Other towns include: **Burkett** (90), **Goldsboro** (15), **Gouldbusk** (70), **Novice** (126), **Rockwood** (53), **Talpa** (127), and **Valera** (80).

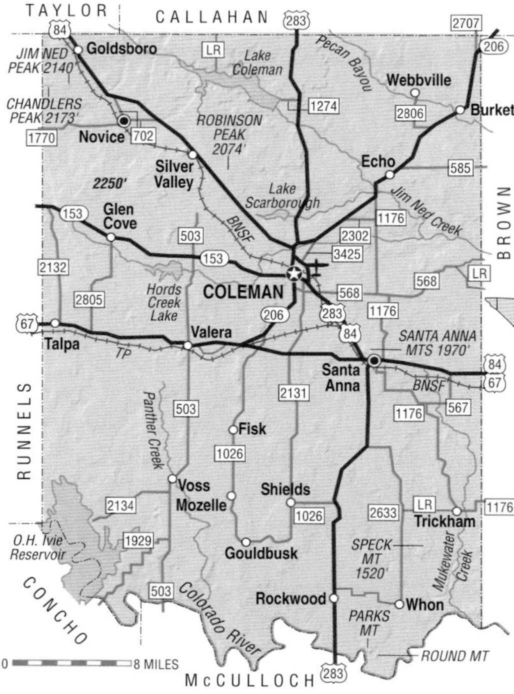

Population	**8,191**
Change from 2010 (%)	-7.9
Area (sq. mi.)	1,281.4
Land Area (sq. mi.)	1,262.0
Altitude (ft.)	1,289–2,250
Rainfall (in.)	28.7
Jan. mean min (°F)	33.7
July mean max (°F)	95.7
Civ. Labor	2,845
Unemployed (%)	6.4
Wages	$19,039,698
Per Capita Income	$42,683
Prop. Value	$1,806,985,326
Retail Sales	$67,723,793

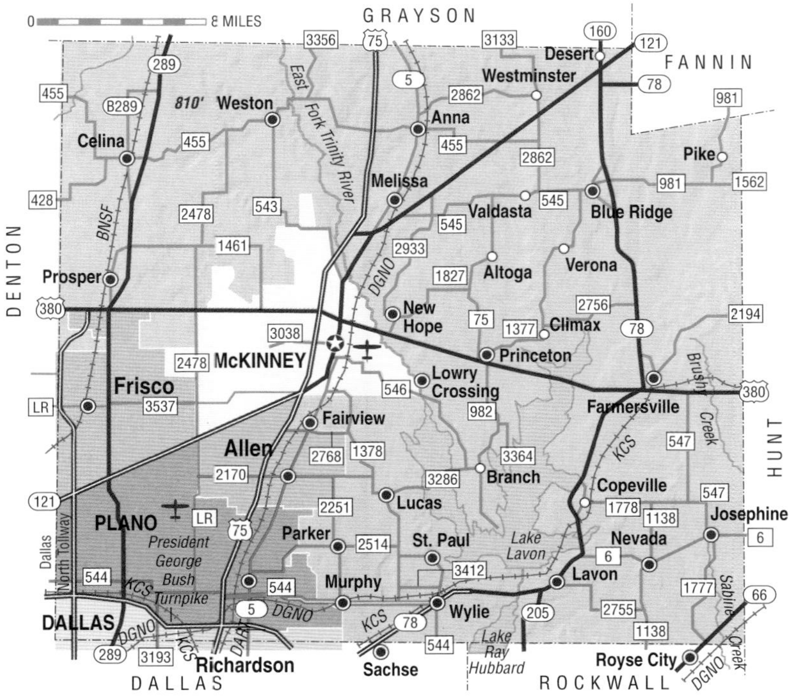

Collin County

Physical Features: Heavy, black clay soil; level to rolling; drains to Trinity; Lake Lavon, Lake Ray Hubbard.

Economy: Government/services, manufacturing plants, retail and wholesale center, many residents work in Dallas.

History: Caddo tribal area until 1850s. Settlers of Peters colony arrived in the early 1840s. County created, organized, from Fannin County in 1846. Named for pioneer settler Collin McKinney.

Race/Ethnicity: Anglo, 56.5%; Black, 9.8%; Hispanic, 15.4%; Asian, 14.7%; Other, 3.3%.

Vital Statistics, annual: Births, 10,921; deaths, 4,005; marriages, 5,554; divorces, 2,374.

Recreation: Fishing, water sports; historic sites; old homes restoration, tours; natural science museum.

Minerals: Insignificant.

Agriculture: Landscape nurseries, corn, wheat, cattle, hay, grain sorghum. Market value $66.8 million.

McKINNEY (197,391) county seat; agribusiness, trade center, varied industry; hospital, community college; museums.

PLANO (290,855) professional services, banking, finance, insurance, health care/hospitals; community college, university extensions; museums, fine arts organizations, nature preserves, hiking trails; balloon festival in September, AsiaFest in April.

FRISCO (190,974) technical, aerospace industry, hospital, community college.

Other towns include: **Allen** (105,524) retail, manufacturing, wholesale trade, hospital, community college, nature conservatory, natatorium, historic stone dam, Stampede rodeo in October; **Anna** (14,708); **Blue Ridge** (957); **Celina** (13,399) museum, historic town square, Fun Day in September.

Also, **Copeville** (243); **Fairview** (9,021) government/services, retail center, commuters, museum, old mill site, wildlife sanctuary, veterans celebration in November; **Farmersville** (4,534) agriculture, light industries, Audie Murphy Day in June.

Also, **Josephine** (1,750); **Lavon** (3,839); **Lowry Crossing** (1,753); **Lucas** (8,183); **Melissa** (13,461) industrial plants, library, old town; **Murphy** (20,595); **Nevada** (1,098); **New Hope** (635); **Parker** (5,216); **Princeton** (15,222) manufacturing, commuters, Spring Onion festival in April.

Also, **Prosper** (24,579); **St. Paul** (1,105); **Westminster** (1,155); **Weston** (580); **Wylie** (53,514) manufacturing, retail, hospital, historic sites, big cat sanctuary, July Jubilee.

Also, part [52,147] of **Dallas**, part [34,920] of **Richardson** and part [8,172] of **Sachse**.

For explanation of sources, symbols and abbreviations, see p. 204, and foldout map.

Population	**1,033,046**
Change from 2010 (%)	32.0
Area (sq. mi.)	886.1
Land Area (sq. mi.)	841.2
Altitude (ft.)	434–810
Rainfall (in.)	42.3
Jan. mean min (°F)	30.1
July mean max (°F)	91.5
Civ. Labor	576,083
Unemployed (%)	4.8
Wages	$8,485,909,167
Per Capita Income	$68,474
Prop. Value	$189,257,810,623
Retail Sales	$20,897,295,384

Collingsworth County

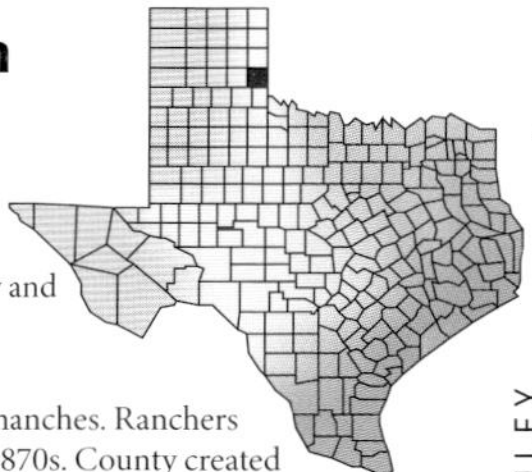

Physical Features: Panhandle county of rolling, broken terrain, draining to Red River forks; sandy and loam soils.

Economy: Agribusiness.

History: Apaches, displaced by Comanches. Ranchers from England arrived in the late 1870s. County created in 1876, from Bexar and Young districts, organized in 1890. Named for Republic of Texas' first chief justice, James Collinsworth (name misspelled in law).

Race/Ethnicity: Anglo, 58.4%; Black, 4.1%; Hispanic, 34.5%; Asian, 0.1%; Other, 2.7%.

Vital Statistics, annual: Births, 26; deaths, 39; marriages, 15; divorces, 2.

Recreation: Deer, quail hunting; children's camp, county museum, pioneer park; county fair/parade in September.

Minerals: Gas, oil production.

Agriculture: Cotton, peanuts, cow-calf operations, wheat, stocker cattle; 22,000 acres irrigated. Market value $39.7 million.

WELLINGTON (2,002) county seat; peanut-processing plants, varied manufacturing, agriculture; hospital, library; restored Ritz Theatre.

Other towns include: **Dodson** (104), **Quail** (18), **Samnorwood** (56).

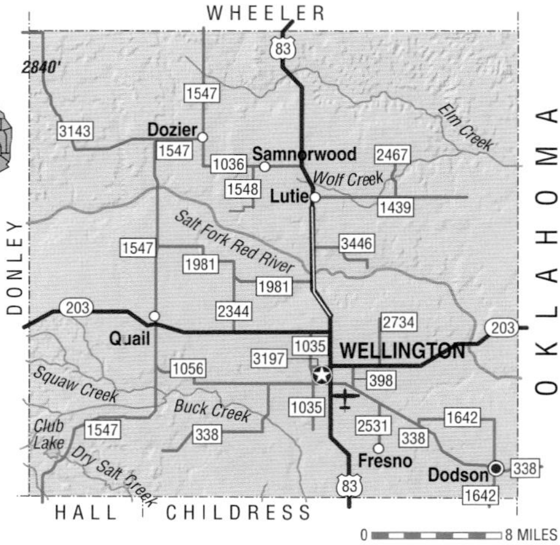

Population	**2,853**
Change from 2010 (%)	-6.7
Area (sq. mi.)	919.3
Land Area (sq. mi.)	918.4
Altitude (ft.)	1,750–2,840
Rainfall (in.)	22.6
Jan. mean min (°F)	27.4
July mean max (°F)	97.6
Civ. Labor	1,082
Unemployed (%)	5.1
Wages	$9,825,687
Per Capita Income	$42,026
Prop. Value	$748,191,080
Retail Sales	$15,608,737

Colorado County

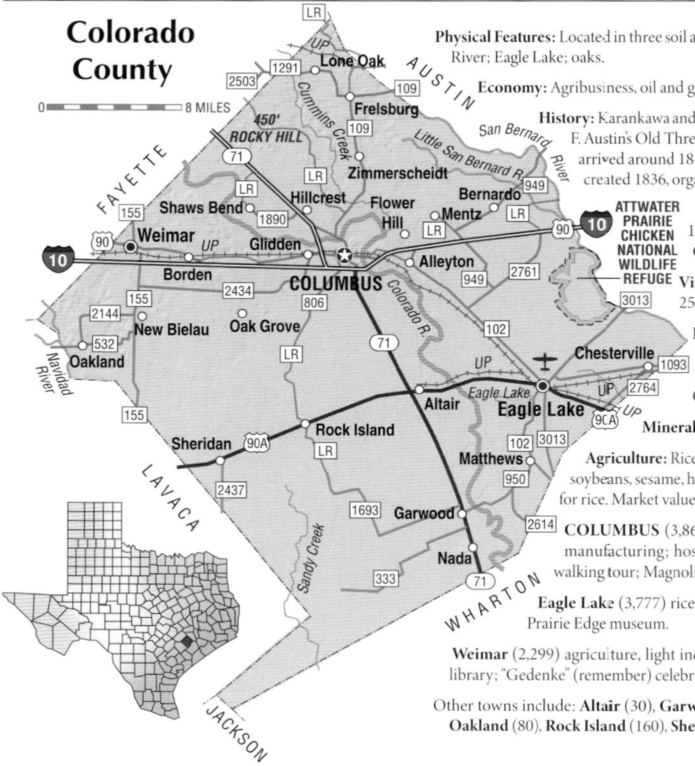

Physical Features: Located in three soil areas; level to rolling; bisected by Colorado River; Eagle Lake; oaks.

Economy: Agribusiness, oil and gas services, gravel mining.

History: Karankawa and other tribes. Anglo settlers among Stephen F. Austin's Old Three Hundred families. First German settlers arrived around 1840. Antebellum slaveholding area. County created 1836, organized 1837; named for river.

Race/Ethnicity: Anglo, 53.6%; Black, 12.8%; Hispanic, 31.4%; Asian, 0.3%; Other, 1.6%.

Vital Statistics, annual: Births, 265; deaths, 256; marriages, 113; divorces, 44.

Recreation: Hunting of duck, geese, deer, exotics; canoeing, bicycling; historic sites; prairie chicken refuge; opera house in Columbus, water park in Sheridan.

Minerals: Gas, oil, gravel.

Agriculture: Rice (third in state in acres), cattle, corn, cotton, soybeans, sesame, hay, pecans, nurseries; significant irrigation for rice. Market value $71.0 million.

COLUMBUS (3,868) county seat; agriculture, quarrying, manufacturing; hospital; historical sites, homes, museums, walking tour; Magnolia Days festival in May.

Eagle Lake (3,777) rice drying center; hospital; goose hunting; Prairie Edge museum.

Weimar (2,299) agriculture, light industry, meat processing, retail; hospital, library; "Gedenke" (remember) celebration on Mother's Day weekend.

Other towns include: **Altair** (30), **Garwood** (600), **Glidden** (762), **Nada** (165), **Oakland** (80), **Rock Island** (160), **Sheridan** (300).

Population	**22,283**
Change from 2010 (%)	6.8
Area (sq. mi.)	973.7
Land Area (sq. mi.)	960.3
Altitude (ft.)	125–450
Rainfall (in.)	43 9
Jan. mean min (°F)	40.8
July mean max (°F)	94.3
Civ. Labor	9,647
Unemployed (%)	5.1
Wages	$87,034,303
Per Capita Income	$46,909
Prop. Value	$5,910,988,837
Retail Sales	$386,611,198

Comal County

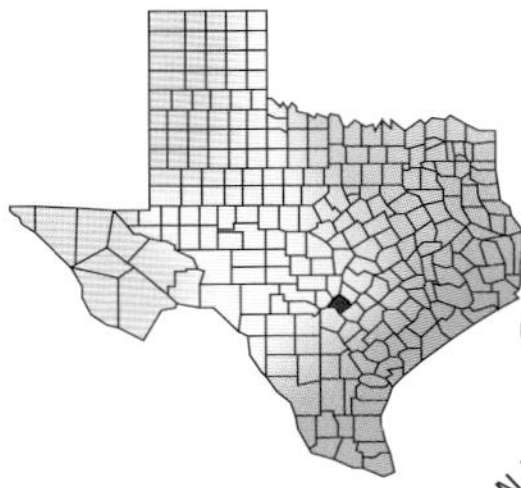

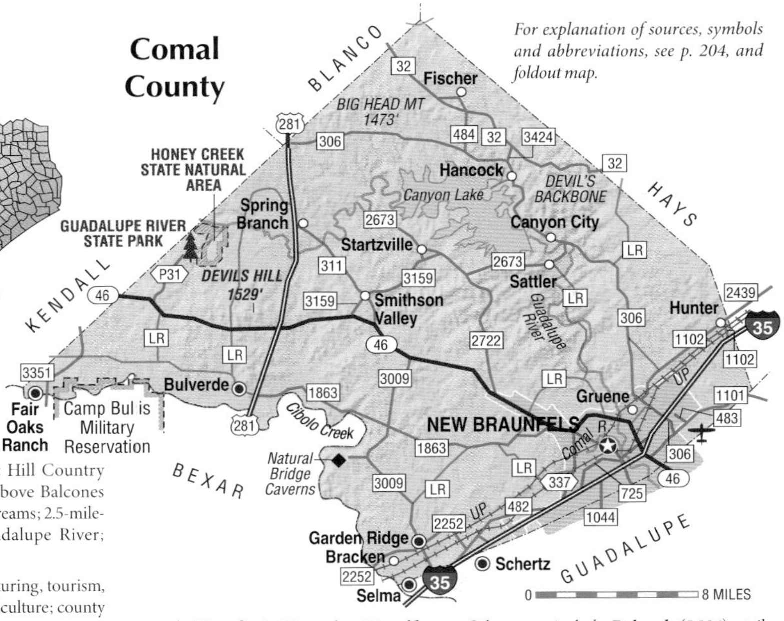

For explanation of sources, symbols and abbreviations, see p. 204, and foldout map.

Physical Features: Scenic Hill Country county. Eighty percent above Balcones Escarpment. Spring-fed streams; 2.5-mile-long Comal River, Guadalupe River; Canyon Lake.

Economy: Varied manufacturing, tourism, government/services, agriculture; county in San Antonio metropolitan area.

History: Tonkawa, Waco Indians. A pioneer German settlement 1845. Mexican migration peaked during Mexican Revolution. County created from Bexar, Gonzales, Travis counties and organized in 1846; named for river, a name for Spanish earthenware or metal pan used for cooking tortillas.

Race/Ethnicity: Anglo, 66.6%; Black, 2.1%; Hispanic, 28.8%; Asian, 0.7%; Other, 1.5%.

Vital Statistics, annual: Births, 1,632; deaths, 1,108; marriages, 1,186; divorces, 197.

Recreation: Fishing, hunting; historic sites; scenic drives, Devil's Backbone; lake facilities; Prince Solms Park, other county parks; Landa Park with 76 species of trees; Gruene historic area; caverns; river resorts; river tubing; Schlitterbahn water park; Wurstfest in November, Wasselfest in December.

Minerals: Stone, lime, sand and gravel.

Agriculture: Cattle, goats, sheep, hogs, horses; nursery, hay, corn, sorghum, wheat. Market value $9.6 million.

NEW BRAUNFELS (87,388) county seat; manufacturing, retail, distribution center; picturesque city, making it a tourist center; Conservation Plaza; rose garden; hospital; library; mental health and retardation center. Gruene is now part of New Braunfels.

Canyon Lake (27,978), which includes Startzville, Sattler, Smithson Valley, Canyon City, Fischer, Hancock, and Spring Branch, retirement and recreation area, tourism, barbecue cook-off in April.

Other towns include: **Bulverde** (5,806) retail center; **Garden Ridge** (4,187);

Also in the county, parts of **Fair Oaks Ranch** [7,204], **Selma** [8,493], and **Schertz** [38,784].

Population	**156,317**
Change from 2010 (%)	44.1
Area (sq. mi.)	574.9
Land Area (sq. mi.)	559.5
Altitude (ft.)	560–1,529
Rainfall (in.)	34.0
Jan. mean min (°F)	38.1
July mean max (°F)	93.3
Civ. Labor	76,409
Unemployed (%)	4.8
Wages	$805,783,518
Per Capita Income	$60,056
Prop. Value	$30,269,959,001
Retail Sales	$2,410,863,876

A view of Canyon Lake and the dam from above. Photo by U.S. Army Corps of Engineers, PD/Wikimedia Commons

Comanche County

Physical Features: Rolling, hilly terrain; sandy, loam, waxy soils; drains to Leon River, Proctor Lake; pecans, oaks, mesquites, cedars.

Economy: Dairies, peanut-, pecan-shelling plants, manufacturing.

History: Comanche area. Anglo-American settlers arrived in 1854 on land granted earlier to Stephen F. Austin and Samuel May Williams. County created and organized in 1856 from Bosque and Coryell counties; named for the Indian tribe.

Race/Ethnicity: Anglo, 68.6%; Black, 0.2%; Hispanic, 29.2%; Asian, 0.2%; Other, 1.5%.

Vital Statistics, annual: Births, 174; deaths, 188; marriages, 93; divorces, 47.

Recreation: Hunting, fishing, water sports, nature tourism; parks, community center, museums; Comanche Pow-Wow in September, rodeo in July.

Minerals: Limited gas, oil, stone, clay.

Agriculture: Dairies, beef cattle, pecans (first in state in acreage), hay, wildlife, melons. Market value $173.3 million.

COMANCHE (4,336) county seat; plants process feed, food; varied manufacturing; agribusiness; winery; hospital; Ranger College branch; library; state's oldest courthouse, "Old Cora," on display on town square.

De Leon (2,233) pecans, light manufacturing; hospital; car museum, Peach and Melon Festival in August.

Other towns include: **Energy** (70), **Gustine** (484), **Proctor** (228), and **Sidney** (148).

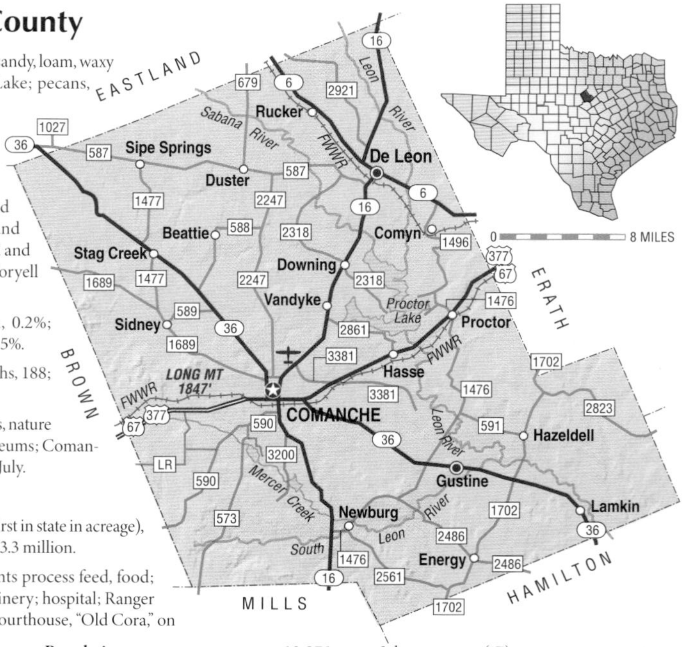

Population	**13,878**
Change from 2010 (%)	-0.7
Area (sq. mi.)	947.7
Land Area (sq. mi.)	937.8
Altitude (ft.)	1,020–1,847
Rainfall (in.)	32.4
Jan. mean min (°F)	31.4
July mean max (°F)	95.7
Civ. Labor	5,729
Unemployed (%)	5.1
Wages	$41,547,100
Per Capita Income	$43,242
Prop. Value	$2,984,617,487
Retail Sales	$159,464,081

Concho County

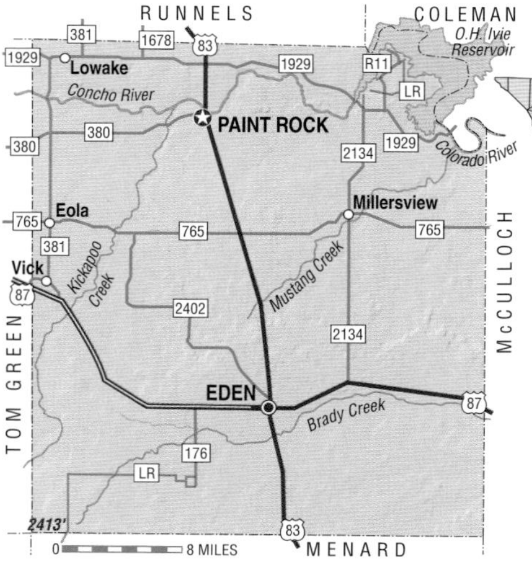

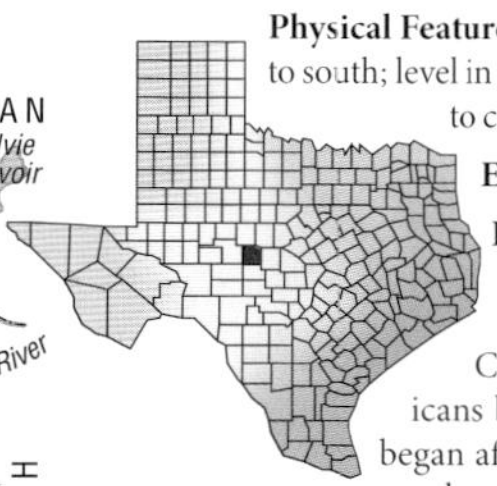

Physical Features: On Edwards Plateau; rough, broken to south; level in north; sandy, loam and dark soils; drains to creeks and Colorado and Concho rivers.

Economy: Agribusiness, manufacturing.

History: Athabascan-speaking Plains Indians, then Jumanos in the 1600s, absorbed by Lipan Apaches in the 1700s. Comanches raided after 1800. Anglo-Americans began ranching around 1850; farming began after the Civil War. Mexican-Americans employed on sheep ranches in 1920s-30s. County created from Bexar District in 1858, organized in 1879; named for the river.

Race/Ethnicity: Anglo, 42.4%; Black, 1.3%; Hispanic, 55%; Asian, 0.2%; Other, 0.8%.

Vital Statistics, annual: Births, 33; deaths, 33; marriages, 12; divorces, 3.

Recreation: Famed for 1,500 Indian pictographs; O.H. Ivie Reservoir.

Minerals: Oil, gas, stone.

Agriculture: Sheep, cattle, goats; wheat, feed grains; 2,000 acres irrigated for cotton. Market value $28.1 million.

PAINT ROCK (275) county seat; named for Indian pictographs nearby; farming, ranching center.

EDEN (1,297) steel fabrication; hospital; fall fest.

Other towns include: **Eola** (215), **Lowake** (40), and **Millersview** (80).

Population	**2,716**
Change from 2010 (%)	-33.5
Area (sq. mi.)	993.7
Land Area (sq. mi.)	983.8
Altitude (ft.)	1,421–2,413
Rainfall (in.)	25.0
Jan. mean min (°F)	29.5
July mean max (°F)	95.2
Civ. Labor	1,364
Unemployed (%)	4.5
Wages	$10,751,392
Per Capita Income	$35,758
Prop. Value	$1,242,955,512
Retail Sales	$16,673,501

Cooke County

Physical Features: North Texas county; drains to Red, Trinity rivers; Ray Roberts Lake, Lake Texoma, Lake Kiowa, Hubert H. Moss Lake; sandy, red, loam soils.

Economy: Oil and gas, varied manufacturing, commuting to Dallas and Fort Worth.

History: Frontier between Caddoes and Comanches. Anglo-Americans arrived in the late 1840s. Germans settled western part around 1890. County created and organized in 1848 from Fannin County; named for Capt. W.G. Cooke of the Texas Revolution.

Race/Ethnicity: Anglo, 74.2%; Black, 2.9%; Hispanic, 19.3%; Asian, 0.7%; Other, 2.7%.

Vital Statistics, annual: Births, 545; deaths, 413; marriages, 442; divorces, 123.

Recreation: Water sports; hunting, fishing; zoo; museum; park, Gainesville Depot Day/car show in October.

Minerals: Oil, natural gas, sand, gravel.

Agriculture: Beef cattle, horses, forages, wheat. Market value $53.8 million. Hunting leases important.

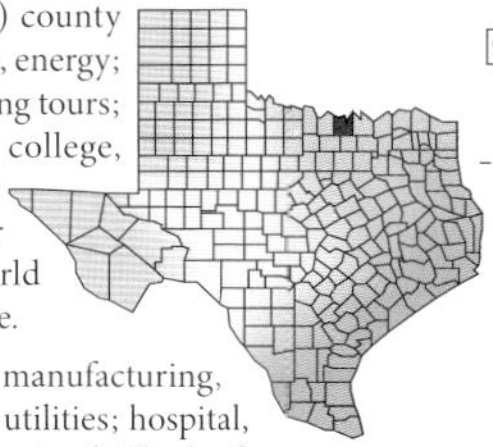

GAINESVILLE (16,373) county seat; aerospace, plastics, energy; Victorian homes, walking tours; hospital; community college, juvenile correction unit; Camp Sweeney for diabetic children; World War II Camp Howze site.

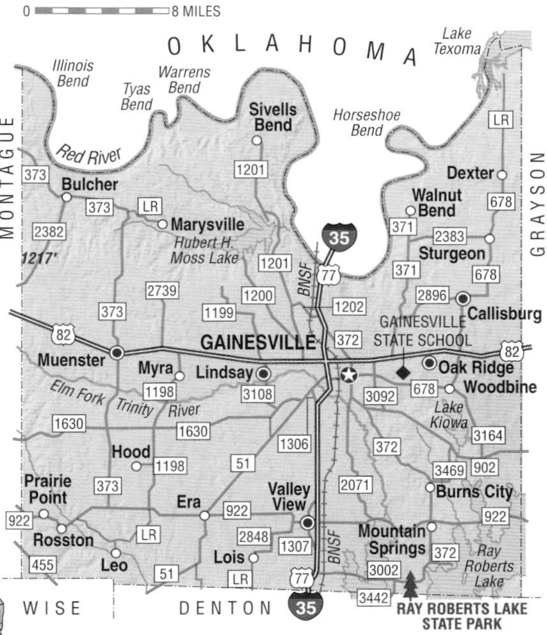

For explanation of sources, symbols and abbreviations, see p. 204, and foldout map.

Muenster (1,603) varied manufacturing, food processing, water utilities; hospital, museum, Germanfest late April, Oktoberfest.

Other towns include: **Callisburg** (365), **Era** (150), **Lindsay** (1,081) 1919 Romanesque-style church, **Myra** (150), **Oak Ridge** (190), **Rosston** (75), **Valley View** (785), and the residential community around **Lake Kiowa** (1,970).

Population	**40,477**	July mean max (°F)	93.4
Change from 2010 (%)	5.3	Civ. Labor	18,774
Area (sq. mi.)	898.4	Unemployed (%)	5.4
Land Area (sq. mi.)	874.8	Wages	$175,008,435
Altitude (ft.)	617–1,217	Per Capita Income	$52,875
Rainfall (in.)	42.7	Prop. Value	$7,421,351,087
Jan. mean min (°F)	31.3	Retail Sales	$695,300,612

The headquarters of The Comanche Chief newspaper. The local paper is family-owned and published weekly. Photo by Leaflet, PD/Wikimedia Commons

Coryell County

Physical Features: Leon Valley in center, remainder rolling, hilly; Belton Lake.

Economy: Fort Hood, prisons, agribusiness, manufacturing.

History: Tonkawa area, later various other tribes. Anglo-Americans settled around Fort Gates in late 1840s. Permanent establishment of Fort Hood in 1950 changed cultural geography. County created from Bell County, organized 1854; named for local pioneer James Coryell.

Race/Ethnicity: (Anglo, 55.9%; Black, 15.7%; Hispanic, 19.4%; Asian, 1.7%; Other, 7.1%.

Vital Statistics, annual: Births, 1,045; deaths, 526; marriages, 466; divorces, 288.

Recreation: State park; deer hunting; fishing; lake, Leon River; bluebonnet area; historic homes; log jail; Shivaree in June.

Minerals: Oil and gas.

Agriculture: Beef, forages, oats, wildlife, row crops. Market value $36.3 million. Hunting leases, timber.

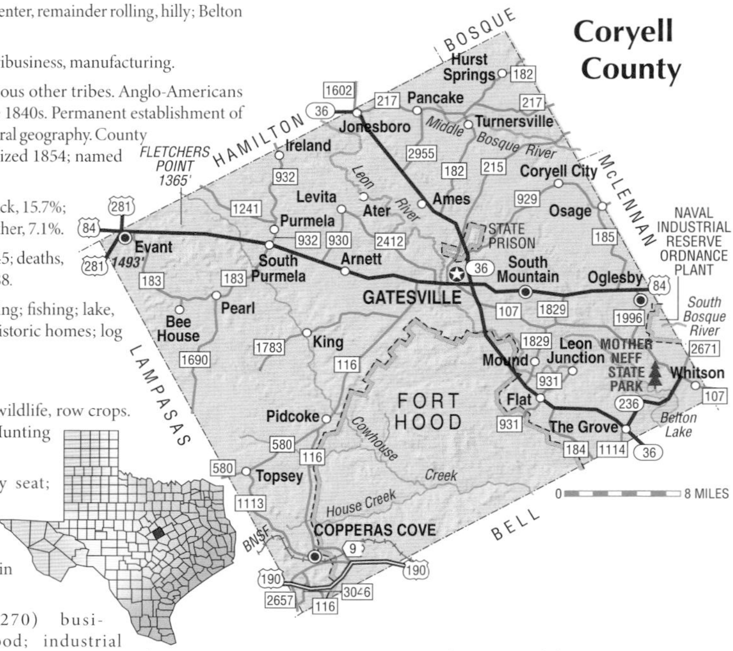

GATESVILLE (15,997) county seat; prisons, varied manufacturing; hospital; refurbished courthouse; museum; branch Central Texas College; Spurfest in September.

COPPERAS COVE (35,270) business center for Fort Hood; industrial filters, other manufacturing; hospital, library; Central Texas College; Rabbit Fest in May.

Other towns include: **Evant** (405, partly in Hamilton County), **Flat** (210), **Jonesboro** (125), **Mound** (125), **Oglesby** (466), **Purmela** (50), **South Mountain** (365). Part [14,415] of **Fort Hood**.

Population	**75,137**	July mean max (°F)	94.2
Change from 2010 (%)	-0.3	Civ. Labor	24,233
Area (sq. mi.)	1,056.8	Unemployed (%)	5.8
Land Area (sq. mi.)	1,052.1	Wages	$197,708,631
Altitude (ft.)	600–1,493	Per Capita Income	$35,570
Rainfall (in.)	33.7	Prop. Value	$5,080,751,637
Jan. mean min (°F)	31.9	Retail Sales	$563,571,745

The bell at Mother Neff State Park in Coryell County. It was used by the Civilian Conservation Corps, who built the park between 1934 and 1938. Photo by Larry D. Moore, CC 3/Wikimedia Commons

Cottle County

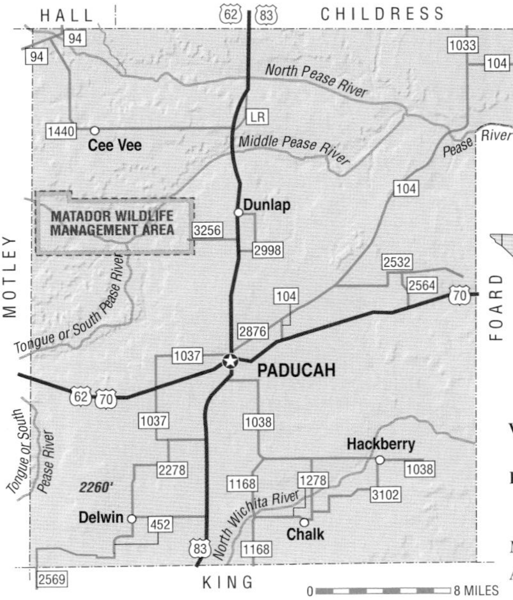

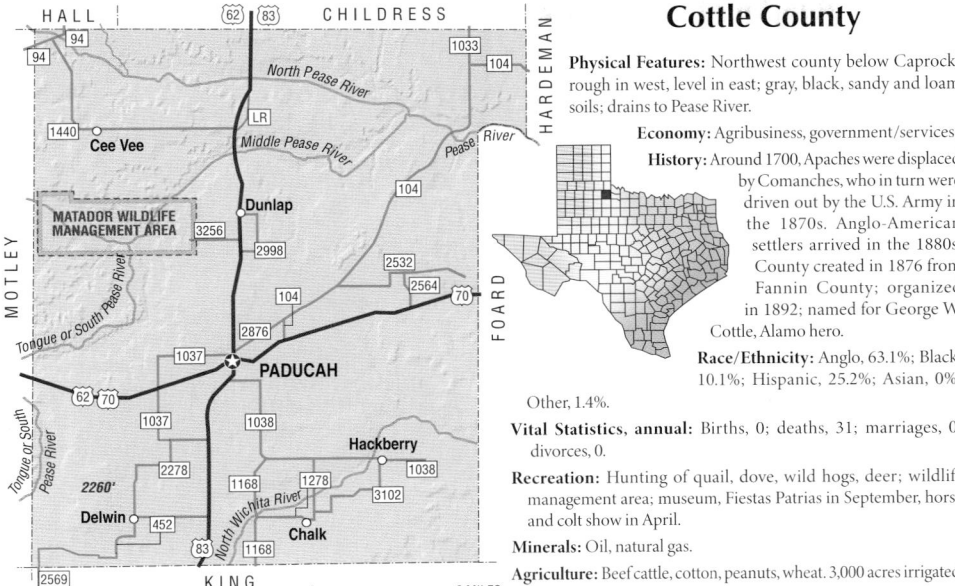

Physical Features: Northwest county below Caprock, rough in west, level in east; gray, black, sandy and loam soils; drains to Pease River.

Economy: Agribusiness, government/services.

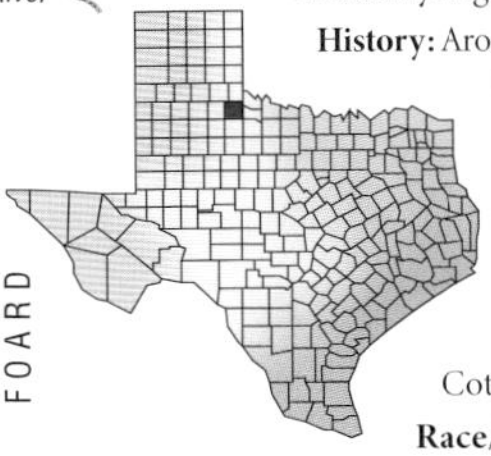

History: Around 1700, Apaches were displaced by Comanches, who in turn were driven out by the U.S. Army in the 1870s. Anglo-American settlers arrived in the 1880s. County created in 1876 from Fannin County; organized in 1892; named for George W. Cottle, Alamo hero.

Race/Ethnicity: Anglo, 63.1%; Black, 10.1%; Hispanic, 25.2%; Asian, 0%; Other, 1.4%.

Vital Statistics, annual: Births, 0; deaths, 31; marriages, 0; divorces, 0.

Recreation: Hunting of quail, dove, wild hogs, deer; wildlife management area; museum, Fiestas Patrias in September, horse and colt show in April.

Minerals: Oil, natural gas.

Agriculture: Beef cattle, cotton, peanuts, wheat. 3,000 acres irrigated. Market value $27.7 million.

Population	**1,354**
Change from 2010 (%)	-10.0
Area (sq. mi.)	901.6
Land Area (sq. mi.)	900.6
Altitude (ft.)	1,470–2,260
Rainfall (in.)	24.9
Jan. mean min (°F)	27.9
July mean max (°F)	97.2
Civ. Labor	630
Unemployed (%)	4.6
Wages	$6,685,283
Per Capita Income	$60,260
Prop. Value	$686,745,401
Retail Sales	$6,653,507

PADUCAH (1,085) county seat; government/services, library.

Other towns include: **Cee Vee** (45).

For explanation of sources, symbols and abbreviations, see p. 204, and foldout map.

Crane County

Physical Features: Rolling prairie, Pecos Valley, some hills; sandy, loam soils; Juan Cordona Lake (intermittent).

Economy: Oil and gas; agriculture; government/services.

History: Lipan Apache area. Ranching developed in the 1890s. Oil discovered in 1926. County created from Tom Green County in 1887, organized in 1927; named for Baylor University president W. C. Crane.

Race/Ethnicity: (Anglo, 29.8%; Black, 2.3%; Hispanic, 66.4%; Asian, 0.2%; Other, 1.1%.

Vital Statistics, annual: Births, 79; deaths, 36; marriages, 19; divorces, 4.

Recreation: Museum of the Desert Southwest; sites of pioneer trails and historic Horsehead Crossing on Pecos River; hunting of mule deer, quail; camping park; rodeo in May.

Minerals: Oil, gas production.

Agriculture: Beef cattle, goats. Market value $1.9 million.

CRANE (3,582) county seat; oil-well servicing and production, foundry, steel, surfboard manufacturing; hospital.

Population	**4,678**
Change from 2010 (%)	6.9
Area (sq. mi.)	785.7
Land Area (sq. mi.)	785.1
Altitude (ft.)	2,290–2,945
Rainfall (in.)	15.6
Jan. mean min (°F)	31.9
July mean max (°F)	93.3
Civ. Labor	1,525
Unemployed (%)	11.4
Wages	$17,294,941
Per Capita Income	$51,025
Prop. Value	$1,609,435,199
Retail Sales	$46,794,681

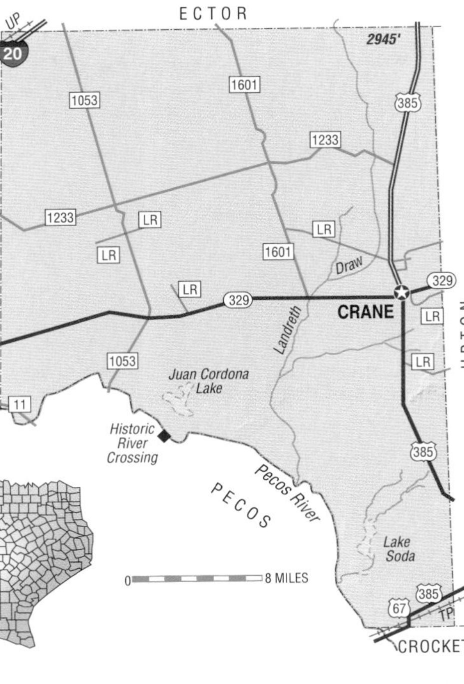

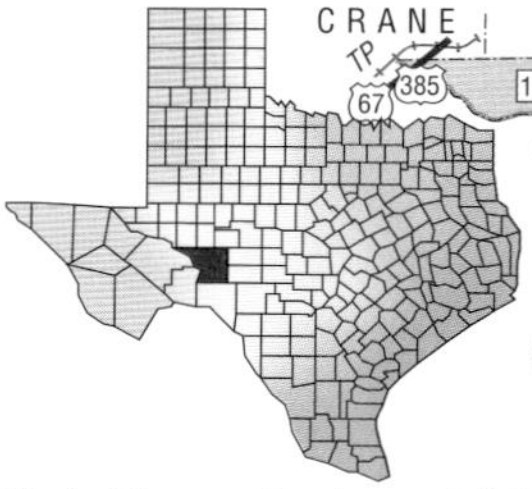

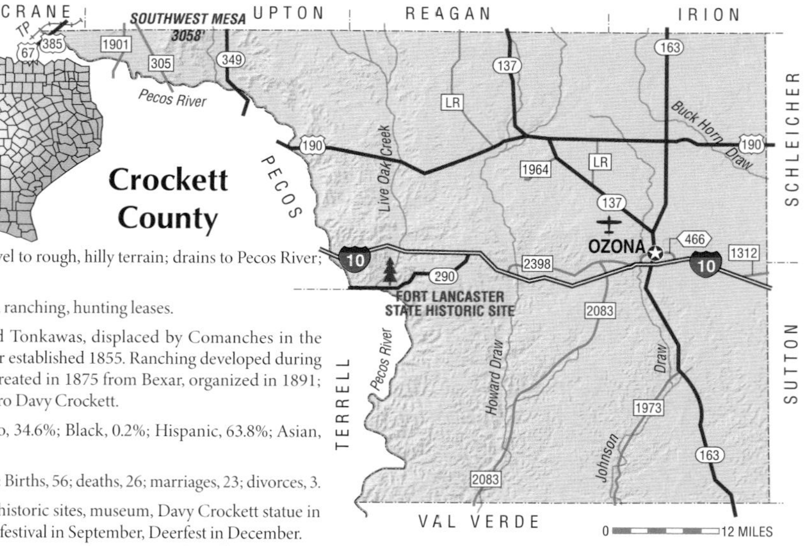

Crockett County

Physical Features: Level to rough, hilly terrain; drains to Pecos River; rocky soils.

Economy: Oil and gas, ranching, hunting leases.

History: Apaches and Tonkawas, displaced by Comanches in the 1700s. Fort Lancaster established 1855. Ranching developed during the 1880s. County created in 1875 from Bexar, organized in 1891; named for Alamo hero Davy Crockett.

Race/Ethnicity: Anglo, 34.6%; Black, 0.2%; Hispanic, 63.8%; Asian, 0.3%; Other, 0.8%.

Vital Statistics, annual: Births, 56; deaths, 26; marriages, 23; divorces, 3.

Recreation: Hunting, historic sites, museum, Davy Crockett statue in park; Davy Crockett festival in September, Deerfest in December.

Minerals: Oil, gas production.

Agriculture: Sheep (first in numbers), goats; beef cattle. Market value $15.4 million.

OZONA (2,912) county seat; ranching, oil & gas, hunting, tourism; health care clinics.

Population	**3,461**
Change from 2010 (%)	-6.9
Area (sq. mi.)	2,807.4
Land Area (sq. mi.)	2,807.3
Altitude (ft.)	1,720–3,058
Rainfall (in.)	18.9
Jan. mean min (°F)	30.2
July mean max (°F)	93.4
Civ. Labor	1,465
Unemployed (%)	7.5
Wages	$15,453,626
Per Capita Income	$44,458
Prop. Value	$2,531,974,282
Retail Sales	$37,370,638

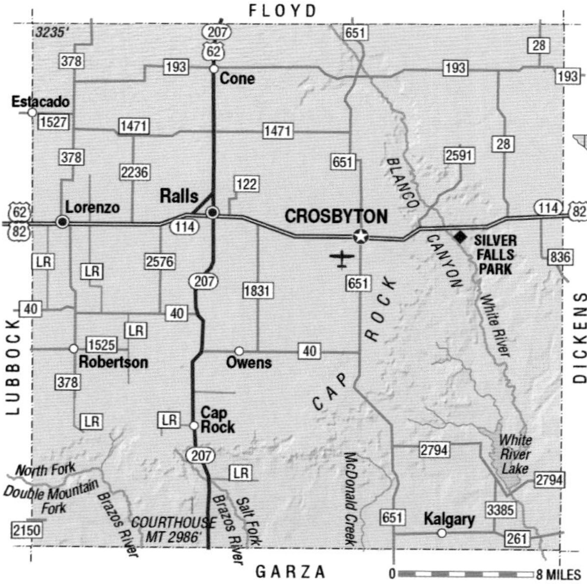

For explanation of sources, symbols and abbreviations, see p. 204, and foldout map.

Crosby County

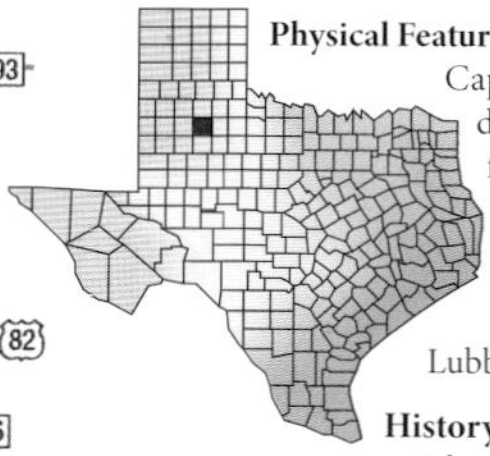

Physical Features: Flat, rich soil above Caprock, broken below; drains into Brazos River forks and playas.

Economy: Agribusiness, tourism, commuters to Lubbock.

History: Comanches, driven out by U.S. Army in 1870s; ranching developed soon afterward. Quaker colony founded in 1879. County created from Bexar District 1876, organized 1886; named for Texas Land Commissioner Stephen Crosby.

Race/Ethnicity: Anglo, 36.5%; Black, 3.2%; Hispanic, 58.9%; Asian, 0%; Other, 1.1%.

Vital Statistics, annual: Births, 90; deaths, 77; marriages, 35; divorces, 16.

Recreation: White River Lake; Silver Falls Park; hunting.

Minerals: Sand, gravel, oil, gas.

Agriculture: Cotton, beef cattle, sorghum; about 112,000 acres irrigated. Market value $86.9 million.

CROSBYTON (1,602) county seat; agribusiness center; hospital, Pioneer Museum, Prairie Ladies Multi-Cultural Center, library; Cowboy Gathering in October.

Other towns include: **Lorenzo** (1,142); **Ralls** (1,824) government/services, agribusiness, museums, Cotton Boll Fest in September.

Population	**5,702**
Change from 2010 (%)	-5.9
Area (sq. mi.)	901.7
Land Area (sq. mi.)	900.2
Altitude (ft.)	2,250–3,235
Rainfall (in.)	23.3
Jan. mean min (°F)	25.9
July mean max (°F)	92.3
Civ. Labor	2,520
Unemployed (%)	5.4
Wages	$13,629,379
Per Capita Income	$37,580
Prop. Value	$1,007,060,081
Retail Sales	$35,372,963

The east side of Blanco Canyon in Crosby County. The red area is the Ogallala formation and the white area is the Blanco formation. Photo by Leaflet, CC 3/Wikimedia Commons

Culberson County

Physical Features: Contains Texas' highest mountain; slopes toward Pecos Valley on east, Diablo Bolson on west; salt lakes; unique vegetation in canyons.

Economy: Tourism, government/services, talc mining and processing, agribusiness, sulfur mining.

History: Apaches arrived about 600 years ago. U.S. military frontier after Civil War. Ranching developed after 1880. Mexican migration increased after 1920. County created from El Paso County 1911, organized 1912; named for D.B. Culberson, Texas congressman.

Race/Ethnicity: Anglo, 23.6%; Black, 0.3%; Hispanic, 73.1%; Asian, 0.9%; Other, 1.9%..

Vital Statistics, annual: Births, 36; deaths, 14; marriages, 1; divorces, 1.

Recreation: National park; Guadalupe and El Capitan, twin peaks; scenic canyons and mountains; classic car museum, antique saloon bar; frontier days in June, big buck tournament.

Minerals: Sulfur, talc, marble, oil.

Agriculture: Beef cattle; crops include cotton, vegetables, melons, pecans; 6,000 acres in irrigation. Market value $15.9 million.

VAN HORN (1,913) county seat; agribusiness, tourism, rock crushing, government/services; hospital.

Other towns: **Kent** (30).

Population	**2,211**
Change from 2010 (%)	-7.8
Area (sq. mi.)	3,813.0
Land Area (sq. mi.)	3,812.8
Altitude (ft.)	2,900–8,749
Rainfall (in.)	11.6
Jan. mean min (°F)	28.3
July mean max (°F)	92.3
Civ. Labor	1,196
Unemployed (%)	4.5
Wages	$20,272,589
Per Capita Income	$59,506
Prop. Value	$3,417,603,577
Retail Sales	$100,308,865

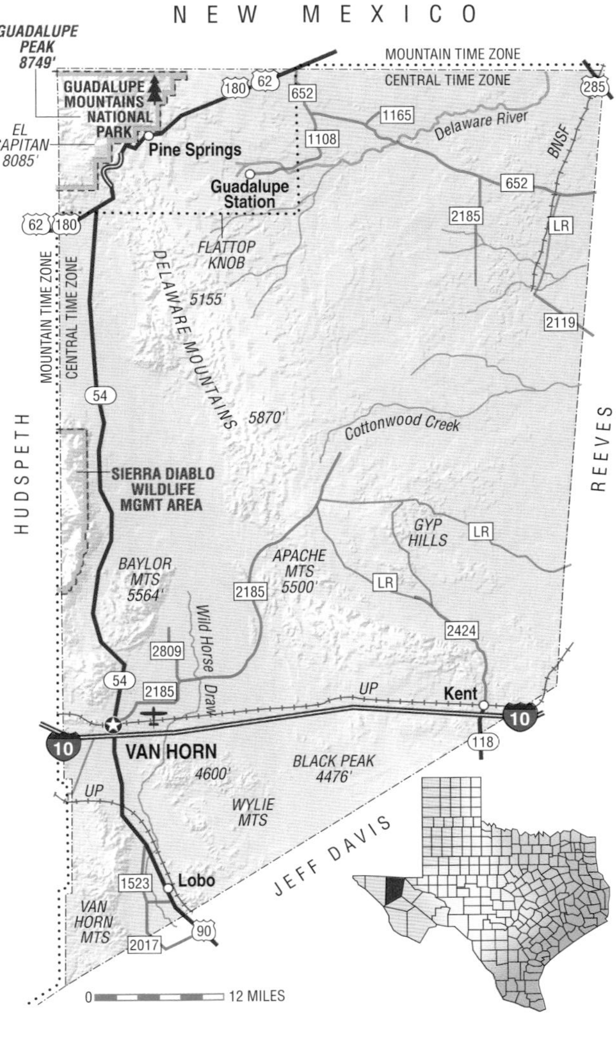

Dallam County

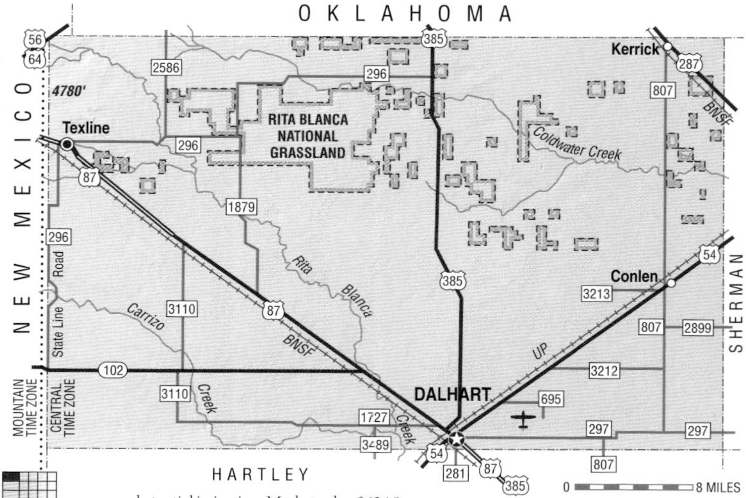

Physical Features: Prairie, broken by creeks; playas; sandy, loam soils; Rita Blanca National Grassland.

Economy: Agribusiness, dairies, cheese manufacturing, tourism.

History: Earliest Plains Apaches; displaced by Comanches and Kiowas. Ranching developed in late 19th century. Farming began after 1900. County created from Bexar District, 1876, organized 1891. Named for lawyer-editor James W. Dallam.

Race/Ethnicity: Anglo, 48%; Black, 1.2%; Hispanic, 46.2%; Asian, 0.4%; Other, 3.9%.

Vital Statistics, annual: Births, 157; deaths, 38; marriages, 304; divorces, 25.

Recreation: XIT museum, XIT rodeo in August, pheasant hunting, wildlife, grasslands.

Minerals: Petroleum.

Agriculture: A leader in production of grain (corn, wheat, sorghum). Cattle, hogs, dairies, potatoes, sunflowers, beans; substantial irrigation. Market value $634.9 million.

DALHART (8,097, partly in Hartley County) county seat; government/services; agribusiness center for parts of Texas, New Mexico, Oklahoma; railroad; cheese plant; grain operations; junior college branch; hospital; prison.

Other towns include: **Kerrick** (35) and **Texline** (519).

Population	**7,053**
Change from 2010 (%)	5.2
Area (sq. mi.)	1,505.3
Land Area (sq. mi.)	1,503.3
Altitude (ft.)	3,655–4,780
Rainfall (in.)	17.6
Jan. mean min (°F)	18.3
July mean max (°F)	91.1
Civ. Labor	3,704
Unemployed (%)	2.6
Wages	$67,337,865
Per Capita Income	$64,756
Prop. Value	$1,851,197,600
Retail Sales	$130,804,819

Dallas County

Physical Features: Mostly flat, heavy blackland soils, sandy clays in west; drains to Trinity River; Joe Pool Lake, White Rock Lake, Mountain Creek Lake, Lake Ray Hubbard, North Lake.

Economy: A national center for telecommunications, transportation, electronics manufacturing, data processing, conventions and trade shows; foreign-trade zone located at D/FW International Airport, U.S. Customs port of entry; government/services.

History: Caddoan area. Anglo-Americans began arriving in 1840. Antebellum slaveholding area. County created and organized in 1846 from Nacogdoches, Robertson counties; named for U.S. Vice President George Mifflin Dallas.

Race/Ethnicity: Anglo, 28.3%; Black, 22.6%; Hispanic, 40.2%; Asian, 6.6%; Other, 2%.

Vital Statistics, annual: Births, 40,112; deaths, 15,727; marriages, 17,207; divorces, 7,365.

Recreation: One of the state's top tourist destinations and one of the nation's most popular convention centers; State Fair, museums, zoo, West End shopping and tourist district, historical sites, including Sixth Floor museum in the old Texas School Book Depository, site of the assassination of President Kennedy.

Also, the Morton H. Meyerson Symphony Center; performing arts; professional sports; Texas broadcast museum; lakes, state park, Audubon center; theme and amusement parks.

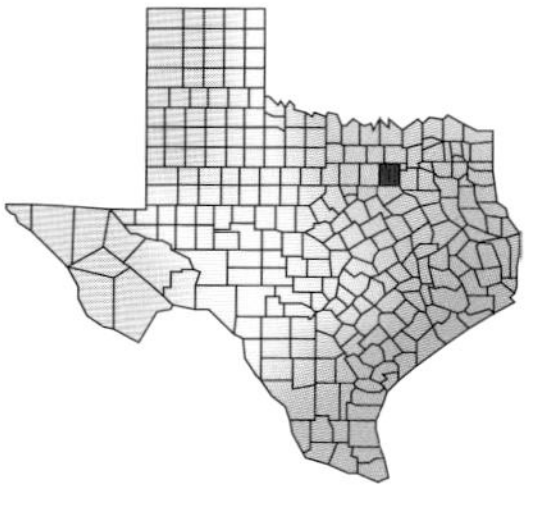

Population	**2,647,576**
Change from 2010 (%)	11.8
Area (sq. mi.)	908.6
Land Area (sq. mi.)	871.3
Altitude (ft.)	350–870
Rainfall (in.)	37.6
Jan. mean min (°F)	37.3
July mean max (°F)	96.0
Civ. Labor	1,368,473
Unemployed (%)	6.2
Wages	$34,155,175,879
Per Capita Income	$62,782
Prop. Value	$374,526,283,216
Retail Sales	$46,609,884,668

Minerals: Sand, gravel, oil and gas.

Agriculture: Horticultural crops, wheat, hay, corn, soybeans, horses. Market value $29.8 million.

Education: Southern Methodist University, University of Dallas, Dallas Baptist University, University of Texas at Dallas, University of North Texas at Dallas, University of Texas Southwestern Medical Center and many other education centers.

DALLAS (1,357,986) county seat; center of state's largest consolidated metropolitan area and third-largest city in Texas; D/FW International Airport is one of the world's busiest; headquarters for the U.S. Army and Air Force Exchange Service; Federal Reserve Bank; a leader in fashions and in computer operations; hospitals; many hotels in downtown area offer adequate accommodations for most conventions.

GARLAND (242,493) varied manufacturing, community college branch, hospitals, performing arts center.

IRVING (245,941) finance, technology, tourism, distribution center; Boy Scout headquarters and museum; North Lake College; hospitals; parks; Dragon Boat Festival in May.

Other cities include: **Addison** (16,450) general aviation airport, theater center; **Balch Springs** (26,426); part [56,834] of **Carrollton** (139,248) residential community, distribution center, hospital; **Cedar Hill** (48,836) residential, light manufacturing, retail, distribution center, Northwood University, community college, state park, Penn Farm, Country Day on the Hill in October; **Cockrell Hill** (4,412); **Coppell** (41,250) distribution, varied manufacturing, office center, hike and bike trails; **DeSoto** (52,631) residential community, light industry and distribution, hospitals; Toad Holler Creekfest in June.

Also: **Duncanville** (39,782) construction, health care, manufacturing; library, museums; Juneteenth celebration; **Farmers Branch** (41,093) distribution center, varied manufacturing, Brookhaven College, hospital; **Glenn Heights** (13,325, partly in Ellis County); most [133,445] of **Grand Prairie** (195,756) wholesale trade, aerospace, entertainment, hospital, library, Joe Pool Reservoir, Indian pow-wow in September, Lone Star horse-racing track; **Highland Park** (8,666); **Hutchins** (6,240) varied manufacturing; **Lancaster** (39,508) residential, industrial, distribution center, Cedar Valley College, Commemorative Air Force museum, Cold War air museum, Bear Creek nature preserve, depot, historic town square, Oktoberfest.

Also: **Mesquite** (142,030) shipping, rail port hub, retail, hospitals, arts center, championship rodeo July – September, rodeo parade in spring, Summer Sizzle festival in June, community college, historical parks; most [86,403] of **Richardson** (124,695) telecommunications, software development, financial services, hospital, library, Wildflower Music Festival in May; **Rowlett** (67,818) residential, manufacturing, government/services, hospital, library, park, hike and bike trails; **Sachse** (26,126, partly in Collin County) commuting to Dallas, government/services, Fallfest in October; **Seagoville** (17,107) rural/suburban setting, federal prison, Seagofest in October; **Sunnyvale** (6,795) tile manufacturing, hospital, Samuell Farm, Sunnyfest on July 4; **University Park** (25,017); **Wilmer** (4,478).

Part of **Combine** (2,442) and part of **Ovilla** (4,167).

For explanation of sources, symbols and abbreviations, see p. 204, and foldout map.

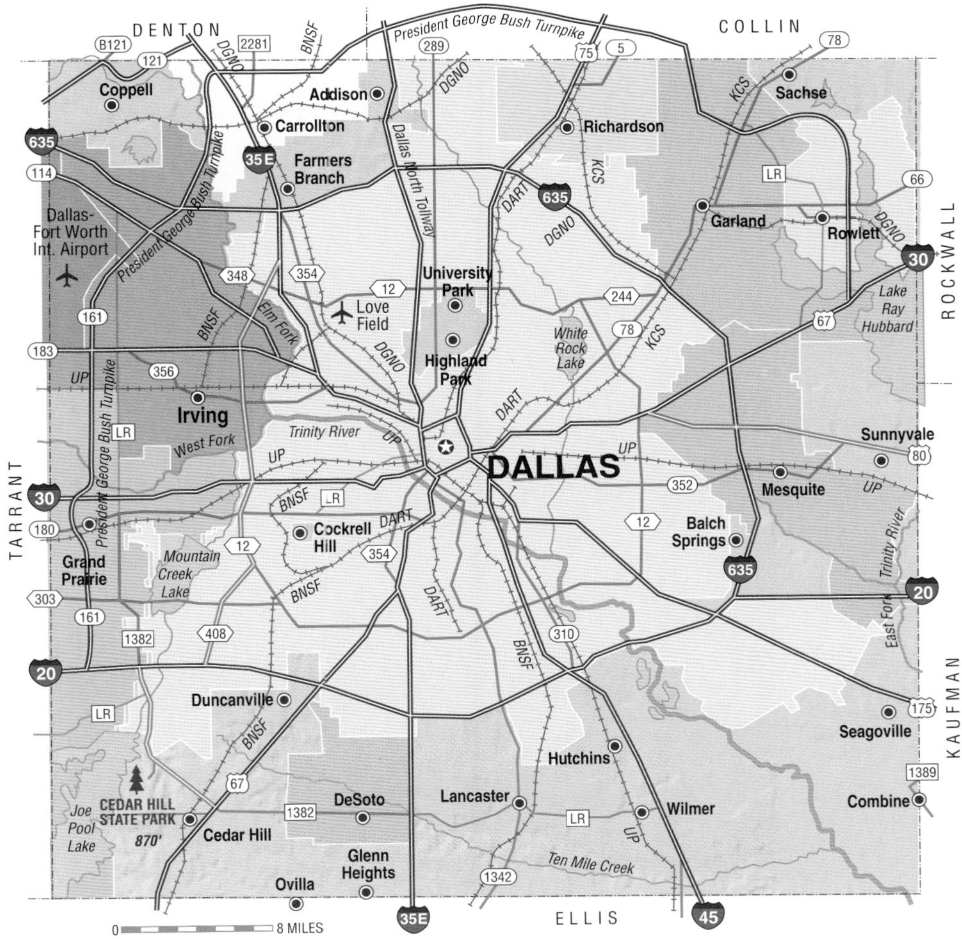

Dawson County

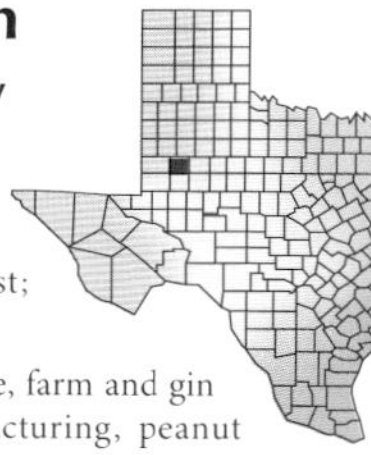

Physical Features: South Plains county, broken on the east; loam and sandy soils.

Economy: Agriculture, farm and gin equipment manufacturing, peanut plant, government/services.

History: Comanche, Kiowa area. Ranching developed in 1880s. Farming began after 1900. Hispanic population increased after 1940. County created from Bexar District, 1876, organized 1905; named for Nicholas M. Dawson, San Jacinto veteran.

Race/Ethnicity: Anglo, 34.7%; Black, 6.7%; Hispanic, 56.4%; Asian, 0.3%; Other, 1.6%.

Vital Statistics, annual: Births, 205; deaths, 129; marriages, 72; divorces, 37.

Recreation: Parks, museum, campground, part of Quanah Parker Trail; Lamesa poetry and music fest in May.

Minerals: Oil, natural gas.

Agriculture: Cotton, peanuts, sorghums, watermelons, alfalfa, grapes. 60,000 acres irrigated. Market value $121.3 million.

LAMESA (8,857) county seat; agribusiness, food processing, oil-field services, some manufacturing, computerized cotton-classing office; hospital, library; Howard College branch; prison unit; chicken-fried steak festival last weekend in April.

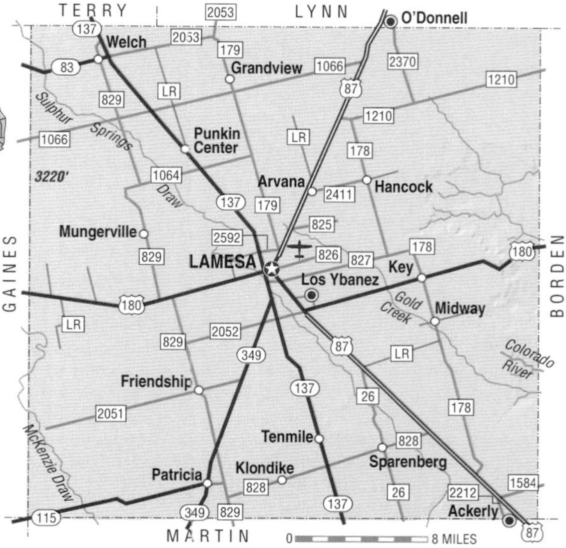

Other towns include: **Ackerly** (227, partly in Martin County), **Los Ybanez** (18) and **Welch** (230).

Also, **O'Donnell** (837, mostly in Lynn County) bust of Dan Blocker.

For explanation of sources, symbols and abbreviations, see p. 204, and foldout map.

Population	**12,720**
Change from 2010 (%)	-8.0
Area (sq. mi.)	902.1
Land Area (sq. mi.)	900.3
Altitude (ft.)	2,580–3,220
Rainfall (in.)	19.1
Jan. mean min (°F)	26.0
July mean max (°F)	93.1
Civ. Labor	4,522
Unemployed (%)	7.7
Wages	$45,374,444
Per Capita Income	$40,131
Prop. Value	$1,299,120,900
Retail Sales	$211,886,234

Shops in the Erath County Courthouse Historic District. Photo by Renelibrary, CC by SA 4.0/Wikimedia Commons

Deaf Smith County

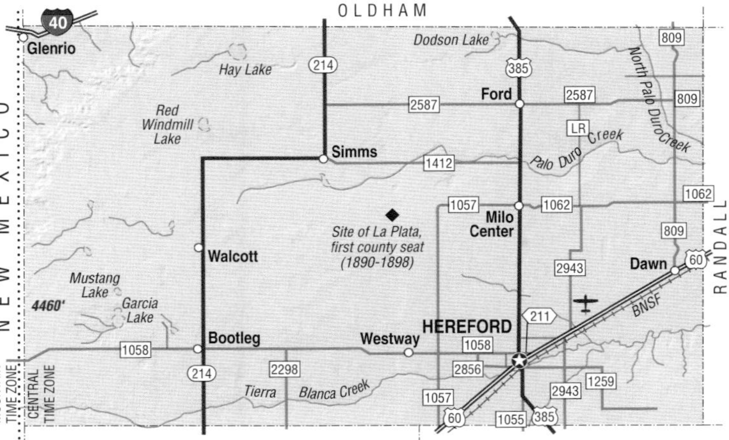

Physical Features: High Plains county, partly broken; chocolate and sandy loam soils; drains to Palo Duro and Tierra Blanca creeks.

Economy: Agriculture, varied industries, meat packing, offset printing.

History: Apache Indians, were displaced by Comanches and Kiowas. Ranching developed after the U.S. Army drove out the Indian tribes 1874-1875. Farming began after 1900. Hispanic settlement increased after 1950. County created in 1876 from the Bexar District; organized in 1890. Named for famed scout in Texas Revolution, Erastus "Deaf" Smith.

Race/Ethnicity: Anglo, 22.8%; Black, 0.9%; Hispanic, 74.7%; Asian, 0.3%; Other, 1%.

Vital Statistics, annual: Births, 348; deaths, 143; marriages, 139; divorces, 16.

Recreation: Museum, tours, POW camp chapel; Cinco de Mayo, Pioneer Days in May.

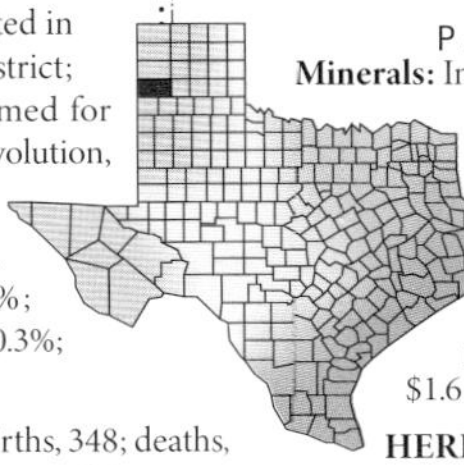

Minerals: Insignificant.

Agriculture: Leading agricultural county, dairies (second in number of milk cows), feedlot operations, cotton, wheat, sorghum, corn; 50 percent irrigated. Market value $1.6 billion, first in state.

HEREFORD (15,635) county seat; cattle feeding, agriculture, trucking; hospital; Amarillo College branch; aquatic center.

Other towns include: **Dawn** (52).

Population	**19,572**
Change from 2010 (%)	1.0
Area (sq. mi.)	1,498.4
Land Area (sq. mi.)	1,496.9
Altitude (ft.)	3,650–4,460
Rainfall (in.)	20.1
Jan. mean min (°F)	22.5
July mean max (°F)	91.4
Civ. Labor	8,892
Unemployed (%)	3.8
Wages	$98,459,221
Per Capita Income	$52,368
Prop. Value	$3,032,275,134
Retail Sales	$399,396,687

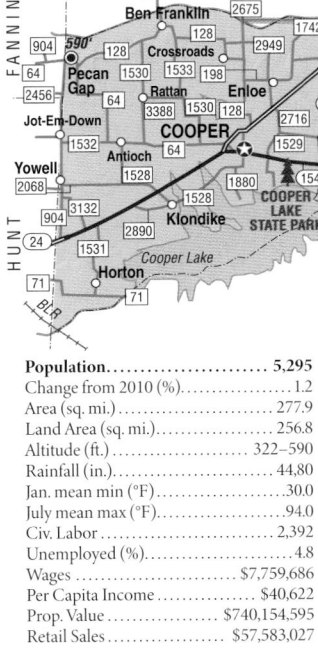

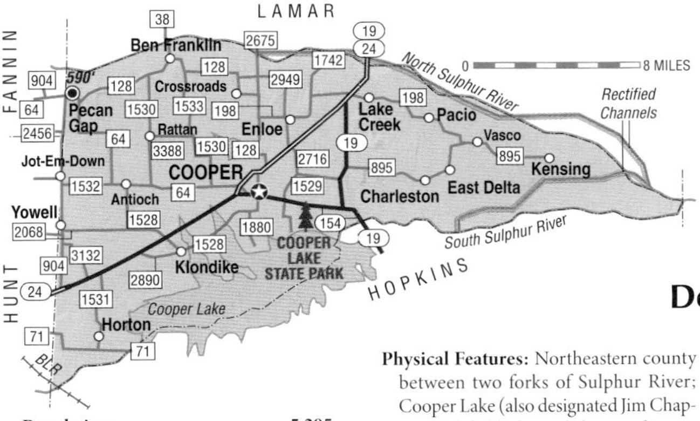

Delta County

Population	**5,295**
Change from 2010 (%)	1.2
Area (sq. mi.)	277.9
Land Area (sq. mi.)	256.8
Altitude (ft.)	322–590
Rainfall (in.)	44,80
Jan. mean min (°F)	30.0
July mean max (°F)	94.0
Civ. Labor	2,392
Unemployed (%)	4.8
Wages	$7,759,686
Per Capita Income	$40,622
Prop. Value	$740,154,595
Retail Sales	$57,583,027

Physical Features: Northeastern county between two forks of Sulphur River; Cooper Lake (also designated Jim Chapman Lake); black, sandy loam soils.

Economy: Agriculture, government/services, retirement location.

History: Caddo area, but disease, other tribes caused displacement around 1790. Anglo-Americans arrived in 1820s. County created from Lamar, Hopkins counties 1870. Greek letter delta origin of name, because of shape of the county.

Race/Ethnicity: Anglo, 79.5%; Black, 8%; Hispanic, 7.6%; Asian, 0.6%; Other, 4%.

Vital Statistics, annual: Births, 60; deaths, 73; marriages, 30; divorces, 23.

Recreation: Fishing, hunting; lake, state park; Cooper Chiggerfest in October.

Minerals: Insignificant.

Agriculture: Beef, hay, soybeans, wheat, corn, sorghum, cotton. Market value $36.3 million.

COOPER (1,933) county seat; commuters, industrial park, some manufacturing, agribusiness; museum, library; post office mural.

Other towns include: **Ben Franklin** (60), **Enloe** (90), **Klondike** (175), **Lake Creek** (55), and **Pecan Gap** (204).

For explanation of sources, symbols and abbreviations, see p. 204, and foldout map.

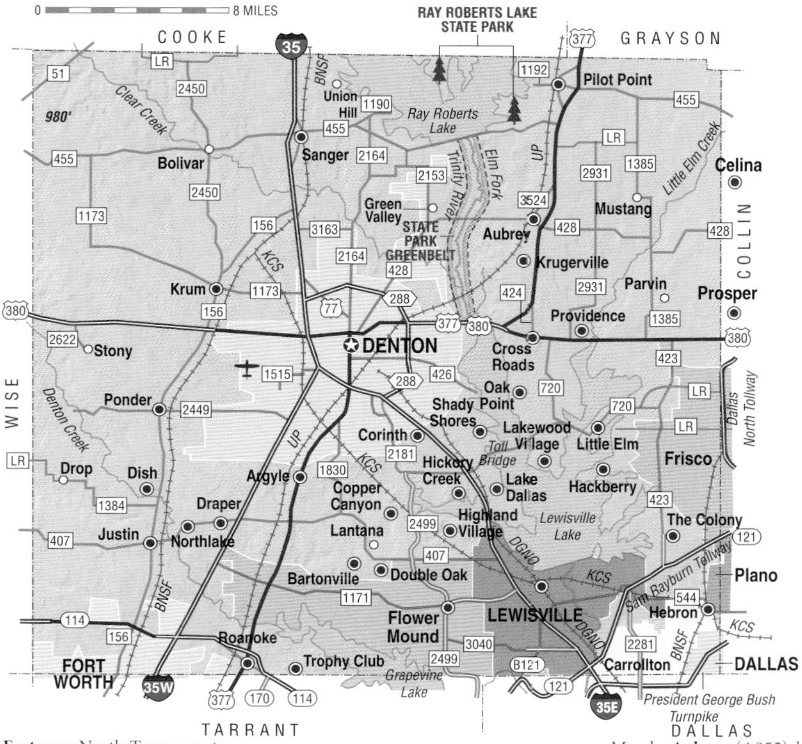

Denton County

Physical Features: North Texas county; partly hilly, draining to Elm Fork of Trinity River, Lewisville Lake, Ray Roberts Lake, Grapevine Lake; Blackland and Grand Prairie soils and terrain.

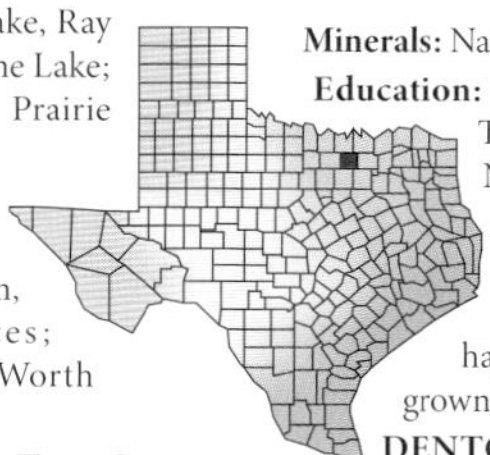

Economy: Varied industries, colleges, horse industry, tourism, government/services; part of Dallas-Fort Worth metropolitan area.

History: Land grant from Texas Congress 1841 for Peters colony. County created, organized, out of Fannin County in 1846; named for John B. Denton, pioneer Methodist minister.

Race/Ethnicity: Anglo, 58%; Black, 10.5%; Hispanic, 19.4%; Asian, 8.8%; Other, 3%.

Vital Statistics, annual: Births, 10,040; deaths, 3,374; marriages, 4,698; divorces, 2,763.

Recreation: Lake activities, parks; universities' cultural, athletic activities, including "Texas Women; A Celebration of History"; "First Ladies of Texas" collection of memorabilia; Little Chapel in the Woods; Texas Motor Speedway; Denton Jazz Festival in April.

Population	**886,563**
Change from 2010 (%)	33.8
Area (sq. mi.)	953.0
Land Area (sq. mi.)	878.4
Altitude (ft.)	433–980
Rainfall (in.)	38.1
Jan. mean min (°F)	33.0

Minerals: Natural gas.

Education: University of North Texas, Texas Woman's University, and North Central Texas College.

Agriculture: Second in number of horses. Eggs, nurseries, turf, cattle; also, hay, sorghum, wheat, peanuts grown. Market value $123.2 million.

DENTON (142,944) county seat; universities, manufacturers of trucks (Peterbilt), medical, aviation; hospitals; historic courthouse square; storytelling festival in March.

LEWISVILLE (114,262) commuting to Dallas-Fort Worth, retail center, electronics and varied industries; hospital, library; Celtic Feis & Scottish Highland Games in March.

FLOWER MOUND (79,640) residential community, library, mound of native grasses, bike classic in spring.

Carrollton (139,248, also in Dallas County), hospital.

Other towns include: **Argyle** (4,555) horse farms/training, bluegrass festival in March; **Aubrey** (4,855) horse farms/training, cabinet construction, museum, peanut festival early October; **Bartonville** (1,814); **Copper Canyon** (1,515); **Corinth** (23,304); **Cross Roads** (1,618); **Draper** (33); **Dish** (467); **Double Oak** (3,234); **Hackberry** (1,128); **Hebron** (449); **Hickory Creek** (4,425); **Highland Village** (17,300); **Justin** (4,320); **Krugerville** (2,013); **Krum** (5,589) commuters, old grain mill, heritage museum, North Pole Days in December; **Lake Dallas** (8,399) light manufacturing, marina, historic downtown, Mardi Gras.

Also: **Lakewood Village** (731); **Lantana** (8,473); **Little Elm** (53,126) real estate, retail, lake activities/beach area, summer concert series; **Northlake** (3,435); **Oak Point** (4,487); **Pilot Point** (4,590) light manufacturing, horse ranches, Fireman's Fest in April; **Ponder** (2,280); **Providence** (6,414); **Roanoke** (9,012); **Sanger** (9,388) distribution center, commuters, government/services, lakes, Sellabration in September; **Shady Shores** (3,200); **The Colony** (46,686) retail, business offices, industrial firms; parks, nature trails, salute to veterans on Veterans Day; and **Trophy Club** (13,947) commuters, retail.

Part [31,056] of **Dallas**, part [9,502] **Fort Worth**, part [77,073] **Frisco**, part [6,090] **Plano**, and small parts of **Coppell, Celina, Prosper, Southlake, Westlake.**

July mean max (°F)	95.3
Civ. Labor	507,813
Unemployed (%)	4.9
Wages	$3,980,186,216
Per Capita Income	$59,414
Prop. Value	$134,731,479,596
Retail Sales	$12,121,926,016

DeWitt County

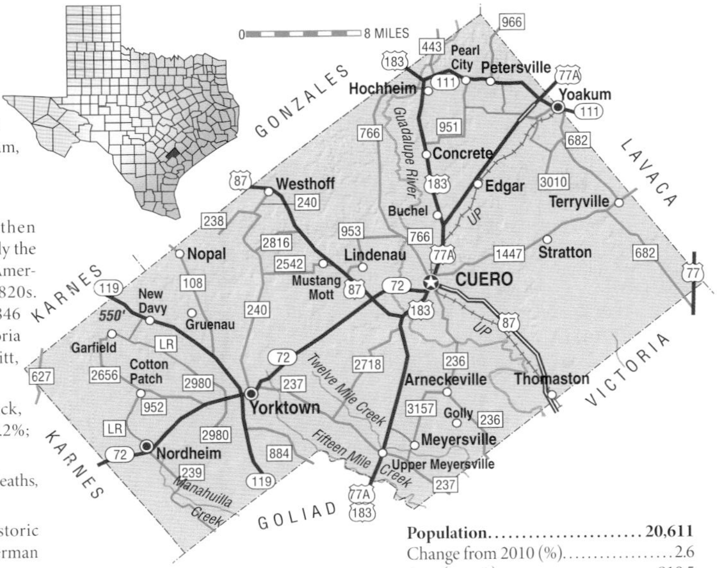

Physical Features: Gulf Coastal Plain county drained by Guadalupe and tributaries; rolling to level; waxy, loam, sandy soils.

Economy: Oil, tourism.

History: Coahuiltecan area, then Karankawas and other tribes, finally the Comanches. Mexican and Anglo-American settlers arrived in the 1820s. County created, organized, in 1846 from Gonzales, Goliad, and Victoria counties; named for Green DeWitt, colonizer.

Race/Ethnicity: Anglo, 53.8%; Black, 8.1%; Hispanic, 35.8%; Asian, 0.2%; Other, 1.9%.

Vital Statistics, annual: Births, 270; deaths, 253; marriages, 136; divorces, 86.

Recreation: Hunting, fishing, historic homes, museums, wildflowers, German dance halls.

Minerals: Oil and natural gas, gravel.

Agriculture: Cattle, pecans, row crops. Market value $38.7 million.

CUERO (7,482) county seat; medical/hospital, government/services, retail, ranching, oil and gas; Turkeyfest in October.

YORKTOWN (2,112) oil and gas, agriculture; library, museum, park, hike/bike trail; Western Days in October.

Other towns include: **Hochheim** (70), **Meyersville** (110), **Nordheim** (304), **Thomaston** (45), **Westhoff** (410).

Part [2,118] of **Yoakum** (5,940 total) cattle, leather, meat processing, hospital, museum, Tom Tom festival in June.

For explanation of sources, symbols and abbreviations, see p. 204, and foldout map.

Population	**20,611**
Change from 2010 (%)	2.6
Area (sq. mi.)	910.5
Land Area (sq. mi.)	909.0
Altitude (ft.)	100–550
Rainfall (in.)	35.7
Jan. mean min (°F)	39.1
July mean max (°F)	96.5
Civ. Labor	8,933
Unemployed (%)	5.8
Wages	$83,731,638
Per Capita Income	$59,389
Prop. Value	$7,642,246,639
Retail Sales	$224,281,170

The Hurley Administration building on the campus of the University of North Texas in Denton. The school has historically been known for its jazz music department. Photo by Michael Barera, CC by SA 4.0/Wikimedia Commons

Dickens County

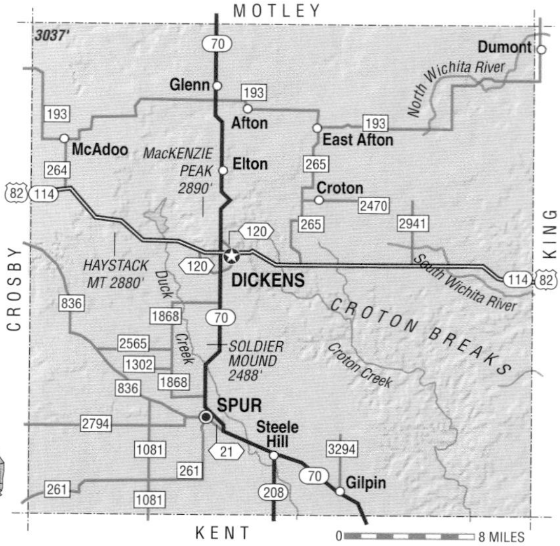

Physical Features: West Texas county; broken land, Caprock in northwest; sandy, chocolate, red soils; drains to Croton, Duck creeks.

Economy: Agriculture, government services/prison unit, hunting leases, wind farms.

History: Comanches driven out by U.S. Army 1874-75. Ranching and some farming began in late 1880s. County created 1876, from Bexar District; organized 1891; named for Alamo hero who is variously listed as James R. Demkins or Dimpkins and J. Dickens.

Race/Ethnicity: Anglo, 61.4%; Black, 4.4%; Hispanic, 31.7%; Asian, 0.7%; Other, 1.6%.

Vital Statistics, annual: Births, 25; deaths, 26; marriages, 10; divorces, 7.

Recreation: Hunting, fishing; Soldiers Mound site, Dickens Springs; downtown Spur.

Minerals: Oil, gas.

Agriculture: Cattle, horses, cotton, hay, small grains. Some irrigation. Market value $26.9 million. Hunting leases important.

DICKENS (253) county seat, market for ranching country.

SPUR (1,173) farming, ranching, hunting, government/services; museum; homecoming in October.

Other towns include: **Afton** (15) and **McAdoo** (75).

Population	**2,119**
Change from 2010 (%)	-13.3
Area (sq. mi.)	905.2
Land Area (sq. mi.)	901.7
Altitude (ft.)	1,800–3,037
Rainfall (in.)	22.8
Jan. mean min (°F)	26.6
July mean max (°F)	94.7
Civ. Labor	676
Unemployed (%)	6.1
Wages	$4,232,504
Per Capita Income	$33,843
Prop. Value	$738,611,052
Retail Sales	$16,012,258

Dimmit County

Physical Features: Southwest county; level to rolling; much brush; sandy, loam, red soils; drained by Nueces River.

Economy: Government/services, agribusiness, petroleum products, tourism.

History: Coahuiltecan area, later Comanches. John Townsend, a black man from Nacogdoches, led the first attempt at settlement before the Civil War. Texas Rangers forced out the Comanches in 1877. Mexican migration increased after 1910. County created 1858 from Bexar, Maverick, Uvalde, Webb counties; organized 1880. Named for Philip Dimmitt of the Texas Revolution; law misspelled name.

Race/Ethnicity: Anglo, 12.4%; Black, 0.6%; Hispanic, 85.8%; Asian, 0.4%; Other, 0.5%.

Vital Statistics, annual: Births, 173; deaths, 109; marriages, 62; divorces, 3.

Recreation: Hunting, fishing, campsites, wildlife area; winter haven for tourists; old jailhouse museum.

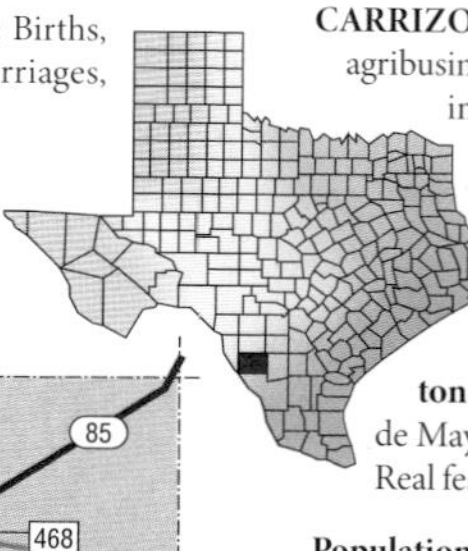

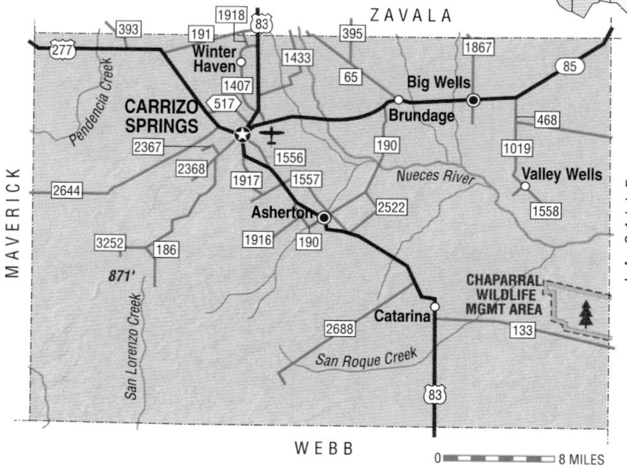

Minerals: Oil, natural gas.

Agriculture: Onions, pecans, cantaloupes, olives, tomatoes, tangerines, cattle, goats, horses, hay. Market value $28.5 million.

CARRIZO SPRINGS (5,567) county seat; agribusiness center, feedlot, food processing, oil, gas processing, hunting center; hospital; historic Baptist church; Mt. Hope cemetery with 17 Texas Rangers buried; bull riding event in April.

Other towns include: **Asherton** (1,018), **Big Wells** (694) Cinco de Mayo, and **Catarina** (100) Camino Real festival in April.

Population	**9,709**
Change from 2010 (%)	-2.9
Area (sq. mi.)	1,334.5
Land Area (sq. mi.)	1,328.9
Altitude (ft.)	410–871
Rainfall (in.)	19.8
Jan. mean min (°F)	40.5
July mean max (°F)	97.8
Civ. Labor	6,017
Unemployed (%)	6.2
Wages	$76,251,324
Per Capita Income	$38,800
Prop. Value	$8,032,398,170
Retail Sales	$125,796,131

For explanation of sources, symbols and abbreviations, see p. 204, and foldout map.

Donley County

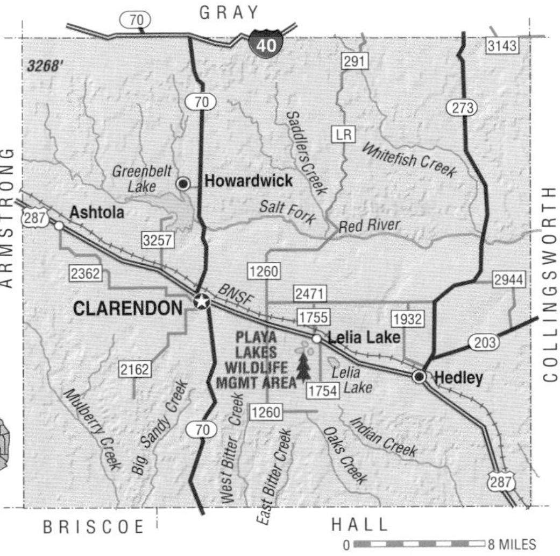

Physical Features: Panhandle county bisected by Red River Salt Fork; Greenbelt Lake, Lelia Lake; rolling to level; clay, loam, sandy soils.

Economy: Agribusiness, government/services, tourism.

History: Apaches displaced by Kiowas and Comanches, who were driven out in 1874-75 by U.S. Army. Methodist colony from New York settled in 1878. County created in 1876, organized 1882, out of Bexar District; named for Texas Supreme Court Justice S.P. Donley.

Race/Ethnicity: Anglo, 81.1%; Black, 6.4%; Hispanic, 10.1%; Asian, 0.3%; Other, 1.8%.

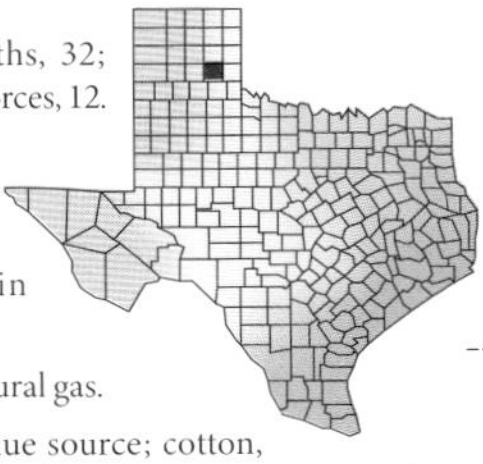

Vital Statistics, annual: Births, 32; deaths, 51; marriages, 24; divorces, 12.

Recreation: Lake, hunting, fishing, camping, water sports; Col. Goodnight Chuckwagon cook-off in September.

Minerals: Small amount of natural gas.

Agriculture: Cattle top revenue source; cotton, peanuts, alfalfa, wheat, hay, melons; 15,000 acres irrigated. Market value $94.2 million.

CLARENDON (1,772) county seat; higher education, agribusiness, tourism, medical center clinic; Saints Roost museum, library, junior college; restored historic buildings.

Other towns include: **Hedley** (287) cotton festival in October, **Howardwick** (368), and **Lelia Lake** (70).

Population	**3,228**	July mean max (°F)	94.7
Change from 2010 (%)	-12.2	Civ. Labor	1,426
Area (sq. mi.)	933.1	Unemployed (%)	4.3
Land Area (sq. mi.)	929.9	Wages	$8,065,758
Altitude (ft.)	2,080–3,268	Per Capita Income	$45,531
Rainfall (in.)	24.0	Prop. Value	$899,367,510
Jan. mean min (°F)	23.8	Retail Sales	$44,330,694

The county courthouse for Donley, in downtown Clarendon. Photo by Avalliso, CC by SA 4.0/Wikimedia Commons

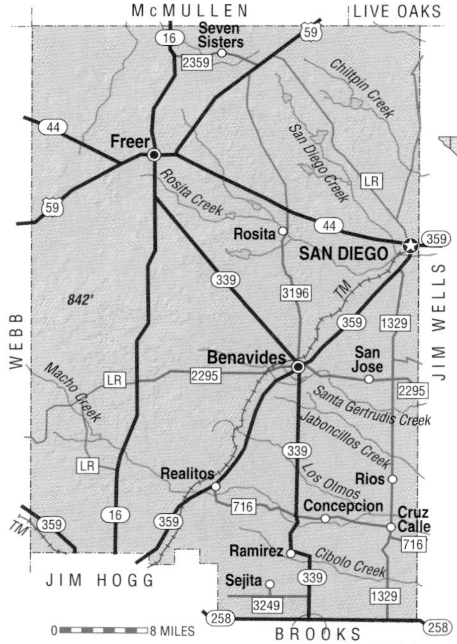

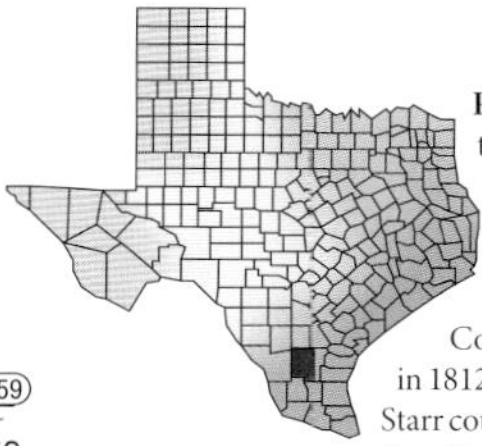

Duval County

Physical Features: South Texas county; level to hilly, brushy in most areas; varied soils.

Economy: Ranching, petroleum, tourism, government/services.

History: Coahuiltecans, displaced by Comanche bands. Mexican settlement began in 1812. County created from Live Oak, Nueces, and Starr counties in 1858, organized in 1876; named for Burr H. Duval, a victim of Goliad massacre.

Race/Ethnicity: Anglo, 10.4%; Black, 0.6%; Hispanic, 88.2%; Asian, 0.1%; Other, 0.4%

Vital Statistics, annual: Births, 181; deaths, 149; marriages, 68; divorces, 4.

Recreation: Hunting, tourist crossroads.

Minerals: Oil, gas, salt, sand, gravel, uranium.

Agriculture: Most income from beef cattle; grains, cotton, vegetables, hay, dairy. Market value $11.0 million.

SAN DIEGO (4,217, part [879] in Jim Wells County) county seat; ranching, oil field, tourist center; hospital.

FREER (2,632) oil and gas, construction, ranching and hunting; rattlesnake roundup in May.

BENAVIDES (1,239) serves truck-farming area.

Other towns include: **Concepcion** (57) and **Realitos** (167).

Population	**10,907**
Change from 2010 (%)	-7.4
Area (sq. mi.)	1,795.6
Land Area (sq. mi.)	1,793.5
Altitude (ft.)	180–842
Rainfall (in.)	26.0
Jan. mean min (°F)	43.1
July mean max (°F)	97.0
Civ. Labor	4,622
Unemployed (%)	11.4
Wages	$31,617,872
Per Capita Income	$39,029
Prop. Value	$2,995,898,064
Retail Sales	$46,351,098

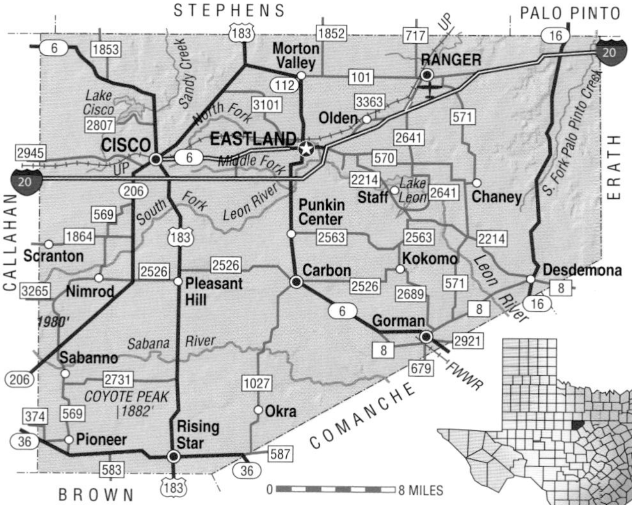

Eastland County

Population	**18,307**
Change from 2010 (%)	-1.5
Area (sq. mi.)	931.9
Land Area (sq. mi.)	926.5
Altitude (ft.)	960–1,980
Rainfall (in.)	29.0
Jan. mean min (°F)	28.8
July mean max (°F)	94.6
Civ. Labor	6,975
Unemployed (%)	6.6
Wages	$79,249,434
Per Capita Income	$78,826
Prop. Value	$3,102,327,320
Retail Sales	$325,525,149

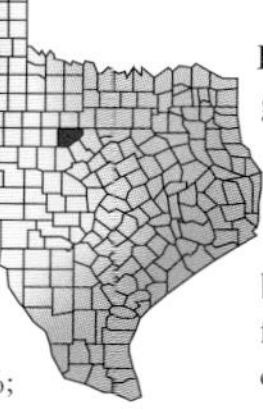

Physical Features: Hilly, rolling; sandy, loam soils; drains to Leon River forks; Lake Cisco, Lake Leon.

Economy: Agribusiness, education, petroleum industries.

History: Plains Indian area. Frank Sánchez among first settlers in 1850s. County created from Bosque, Coryell, Travis counties, 1858, organized 1873; named for W.M. Eastland, Mier Expedition casualty.

Race/Ethnicity: Anglo, 78.7%; Black, 1.8%; Hispanic, 17.2%; Asian, 0.4%; Other, 1.7%.

Vital Statistics, annual: Births, 200; deaths, 265; marriages, 147; divorces, 53.

Recreation: Hunting, water sports; museums; historic sites and displays.

Minerals: Oil, natural gas.

Agriculture: Beef cattle, hay, cotton. Some 9,000 acres irrigated. Market value $23.5 million.

EASTLAND (4,010) county seat; tourism, government/services, petroleum industries, varied manufacturing; hospital, library; Old Ripfest in September.

CISCO (3,834) manufacturing, distribution, oilfield services; Conrad Hilton's first hotel restored, museums; community college; folklife festival in April.

RANGER (2,444) oil center, varied manufacturing, junior college.

Other towns include: **Carbon** (270) livestock equipment manufacturing; **Desdemona** (180); **Gorman** (1,034) peanut processing, agribusiness, hospital; **Olden** (113), and **Rising Star** (820) cap manufacturing, plant nursery; Octoberfest.

Ector County

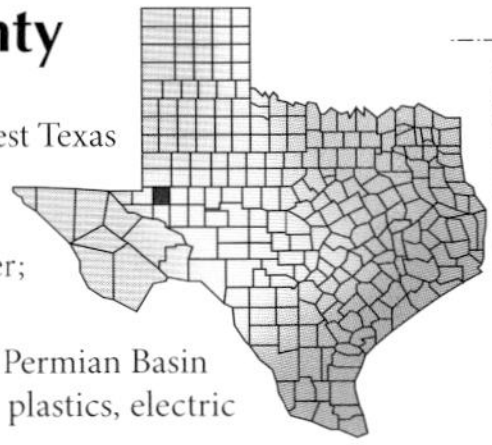

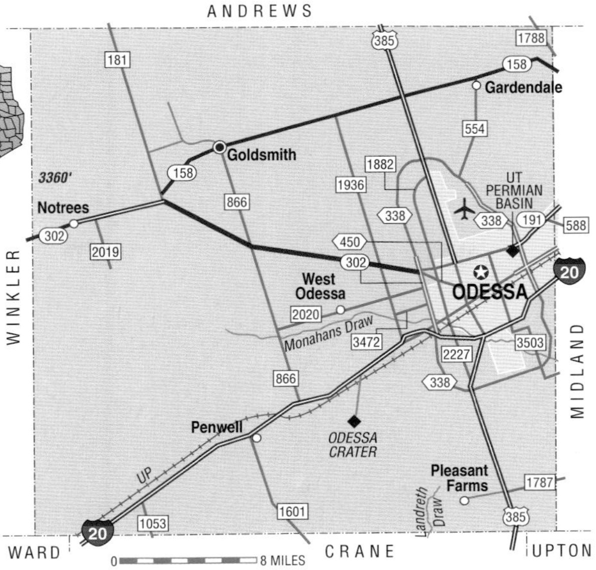

Physical Features: West Texas county; level to rolling, some sand dunes; meteor crater; desert vegetation.

Economy: Center for Permian Basin oil field operations, plastics, electric generation plants.

History: First settlers in late 1880s. Oil boom in 1926. County created from Tom Green County, 1887; organized 1891; named for jurist M.D. Ector.

Race/Ethnicity: Anglo, 30.7%; Black, 4.4%; Hispanic, 62.2%; Asian, 1%; Other, 1.5%.

Vital Statistics, annual: Births, 2,991; deaths, 1,196; marriages, 1262; divorces, 327.

Recreation: Globe Theatre replica; presidential museum and Bush childhood home; ranching museum, art institute; second-largest U.S. meteor crater, museum; Stonehenge replica.

Minerals: More than 3 billion barrels of oil produced since 1926; gas, cement, stone.

Agriculture: Beef cattle, horses are chief producers; pecans, hay, poultry; minor irrigation. Market value $3.4 million.

Education: University of Texas of Permian Basin, Texas Tech University Health Sciences Center, Odessa (junior) College.

ODESSA (126,729, part [2,166] in Midland County) county seat; oil and gas, manufacturing, ranching; hospitals; cultural center; Permian Basin Fair and Expo in September.

Other towns include: **Gardendale** (1,959), **Goldsmith** (286), **Notrees** (20), **Penwell** (41), and **West Odessa** (29,224).

For explanation of sources, symbols and abbreviations, see p. 204, and foldout map.

Population	**167,383**
Change from 2010 (%)	22.1
Area (sq. mi.)	901.8
Land Area (sq. mi.)	897.7
Altitude (ft.)	2,780–3,360
Rainfall (in.)	13.5
Jan. mean min (°F)	31.8
July mean max (°F)	94.8
Civ. Labor	78,715
Unemployed (%)	9.9
Wages	$1,010,325,242
Per Capita Income	$50,161
Prop. Value	$18,856,673,701
Retail Sales	$3,409,649,399

Edwards County

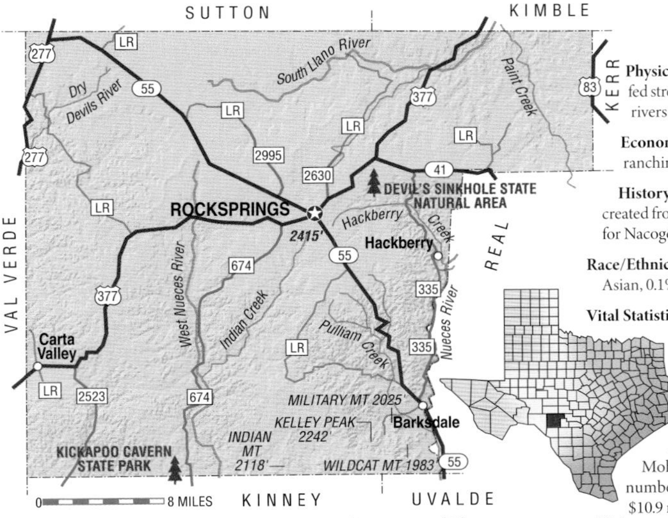

Physical Features: Rolling, hilly, with caves and spring-fed streams; rocky, thin soils; drained by Llano, Nueces rivers; varied timber.

Economy: Hunting leases, tourism, oil, gas production, ranching.

History: Apache area. First land sold in 1876. County created from Bexar District, 1858; organized 1883; named for Nacogdoches empresario Hayden Edwards.

Race/Ethnicity: Anglo, 43.3%; Black, 0.6%; Hispanic, 55.1%; Asian, 0.1%; Other, 0.7%.

Vital Statistics, annual: Births, 22; deaths, 33; mmarriages, 7; divorces, 1.

Recreation: Hunting, fishing; scenic drives; Devil's Sinkhole, Kickapoo Cavern state parks.

Minerals: Gas.

Agriculture: Second in number of goats. Mohair-wool production, Angora goats (first in numbers), sheep, cattle, some pecans. Market value $10.9 million. Cedar for oil.

ROCKSPRINGS (1,149) county seat; government/services, hunting, ranching, oil and gas, hunters' barbecue in November.

Other towns include: **Barksdale** (100).

Population	**1,959**
Change from 2010 (%)	-2.1
Area (sq. mi.)	2,119.9
Land Area (sq. mi.)	2,117.9
Altitude (ft.)	1,480–2,415
Rainfall (in.)	26.6
Jan. mean min (°F)	36.6
July mean max (°F)	90.4
Civ. Labor	1,357
Unemployed (%)	4.2
Wages	$8,299,913
Per Capita Income	$45,429
Prop. Value	$2,318,827,959
Retail Sales	$24,104,267

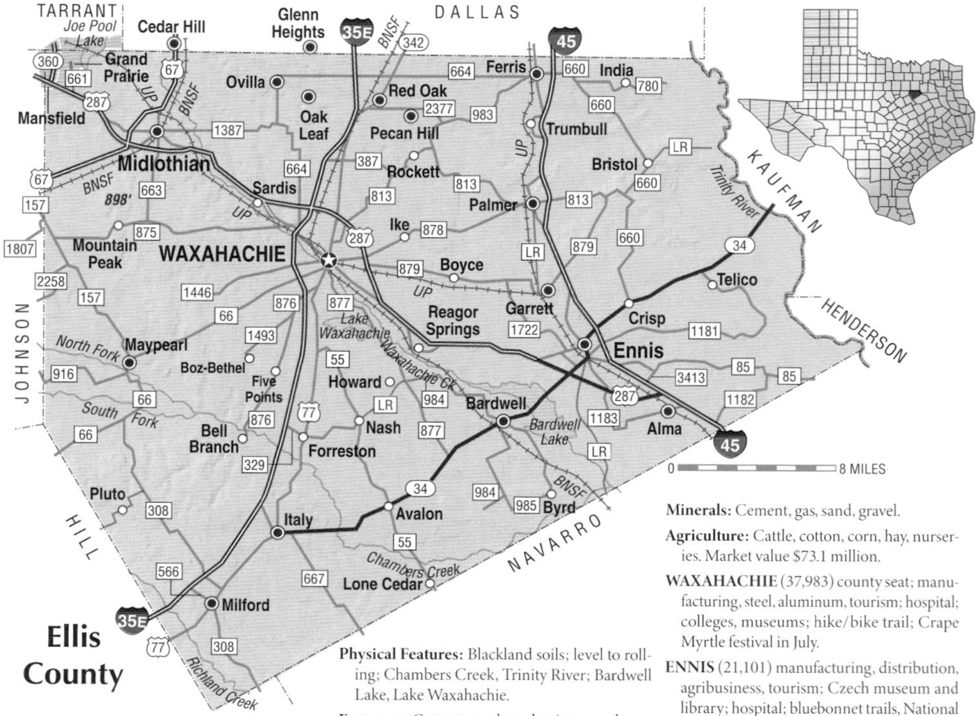

Ellis County

Population	**188,464**
Change from 2010 (%)	26.0
Area (sq. mi.)	951.8
Land Area (sq. mi.)	935.5
Altitude (ft.)	300–898
Rainfall (in.)	39.1
Jan. mean min (°F)	33.8
July mean max (°F)	93.9
Civ. Labor	364,592
Unemployed (%)	6.9
Wages	$3,495,606,899
Per Capita Income	$37,715
Prop. Value	$24,935,423,576
Retail Sales	$2,354,874,161

Physical Features: Blackland soils; level to rolling; Chambers Creek, Trinity River; Bardwell Lake, Lake Waxahachie.

Economy: Cement, steel production, warehousing and distribution, government/services; many residents work in Dallas.

History: Tonkawa area. Part of Peters colony settled in 1843. County created 1849, organized 1850, from Navarro County. Named for Richard Ellis, president of convention that declared Texas' independence.

Race/Ethnicity: Anglo, 61%; Black, 9.8%; Hispanic, 26.6%; Asian, 0.4%; Other, 1.9%.

Vital Statistics, annual: Births, 2,126; deaths, 1,209; marriages, 1,140; divorces, 337.

Recreation: Lakes, fishing, hunting; bluebonnet trails, historic homes, courthouse; Medieval-theme Scarborough Faire in spring.

Minerals: Cement, gas, sand, gravel.

Agriculture: Cattle, cotton, corn, hay, nurseries. Market value $73.1 million.

WAXAHACHIE (37,983) county seat; manufacturing, steel, aluminum, tourism; hospital; colleges, museums; hike/bike trail; Crape Myrtle festival in July.

ENNIS (21,101) manufacturing, distribution, agribusiness, tourism; Czech museum and library; hospital; bluebonnet trails, National Polka Festival in May.

MIDLOTHIAN (34,164) cement plants, steel plant, distribution center, manufacturing; heritage park, cabin; spring fling in April.

Other towns include: **Alma** (402); **Avalon** (400); **Bardwell** (726); **Bristol** (736); **Ferris** (2,987); **Forreston** (400); **Garrett** (900); **Howard** (60); **Italy** (1,957); **Maypearl** (1,116); **Milford** (767); **Oak Leaf** (1,442); **Ovilla** (4,320); **Palmer** (2,203); **Pecan Hill** (706); and **Red Oak** (13,648) manufacturing, Founders Day in September.

Also, **Glenn Heights** (13,377, mostly in Dallas County). Part of **Grand Prairie** and **Mansfield.**

A tank at the Fort Bliss Main Post Historic District in El Paso. Photo by ForgottenColorado, CC by SA 4.0/Wikipedia Commons

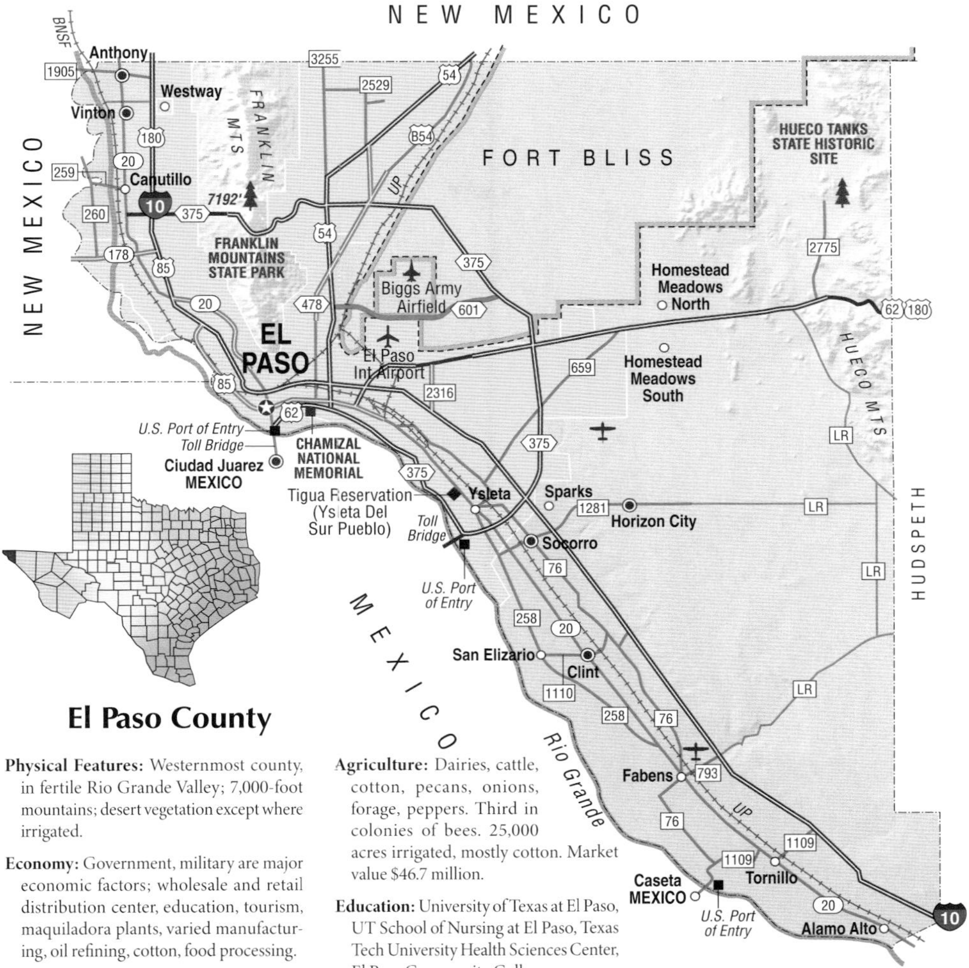

El Paso County

Physical Features: Westernmost county, in fertile Rio Grande Valley; 7,000-foot mountains; desert vegetation except where irrigated.

Economy: Government, military are major economic factors; wholesale and retail distribution center, education, tourism, maquiladora plants, varied manufacturing, oil refining, cotton, food processing.

History: Various Indian tribes inhabited the valley before Spanish civilization arrived in the late 1650s. Agriculture in area dates to at least 100 A.D. Spanish along with Tigua and Piro tribes fleeing Santa Fe uprising of 1680 sought refuge in the area. County created from the Bexar District in 1849; organized in 1850; named for historic pass (Paso del Norte), lowest all-weather pass through the southern Rocky Mountains.

Race/Ethnicity: Anglo, 13%; Black, 3.4%; Hispanic, 80.5%; Asian, 1.2%; Other, 1.7%.

Vital Statistics, annual: Births, 13,521; deaths, 5,296; marriages, 6,809; divorces, 98.

Recreation: Gateway to Mexico; Chamizal Museum; major tourist center; December Sun Carnival with football game; state parks, mountain tramway, missions and other historic sites.

Minerals: Production of cement, stone, sand and gravel.

Agriculture: Dairies, cattle, cotton, pecans, onions, forage, peppers. Third in colonies of bees. 25,000 acres irrigated, mostly cotton. Market value $46.7 million.

Education: University of Texas at El Paso, UT School of Nursing at El Paso, Texas Tech University Health Sciences Center, El Paso Community College.

EL PASO (686,265) county seat; Texas' sixth-largest city and metro area, largest U.S. city on Mexican border. A center for government operations. Federal installations include Fort Bliss, home of the U.S. Army 1st Armored Division, William Beaumont General Hospital, and La Tuna federal prison.

Manufactured products include clothing, electronics, auto equipment, plastics; trade and distribution; refining; processing oil, food, cotton, and other farm products. Hospitals; museums; convention center; theater, symphony orchestra.

Other towns include: **Anthony** (5,640 in Texas, 9,310 in New Mexico); **Canutillo** (7,073); **Clint** (1,163); **Fabens** (8,500); **Homestead Meadows North** (5,571); **Homestead Meadows South** (7,600); **Horizon City** (19,733); **Prado Verde** (266); **San Elizario** (14,313), red & green chile war festival in September; **Socorro** (34,740) settled in 1680; **Sparks** (5,501); **Tornillo** (1,540); **Vinton** (2,042); **Westway** (4,297), and **Ysleta** (now within El Paso) settled in 1680, called the oldest town in Texas.

And, **Fort Bliss** (9,137).

For explanation of sources, symbols and abbreviations, see p. 204, and foldout map.

Population	**852,224**
Change from 2010 (%)	6.4
Area (sq. mi.)	1,015.0
Land Area (sq. mi.)	1,012.7
Altitude (ft.)	3,520–7,192
Rainfall (in.)	9.7
Jan. mean min (°F)	32.5
July mean max (°F)	94.7
Civ. Labor	94,893
Unemployed (%)	4.9
Wages	$714,885,134
Per Capita Income	$45,968
Prop. Value	$57,122,910,826
Retail Sales	$11,436,167,636

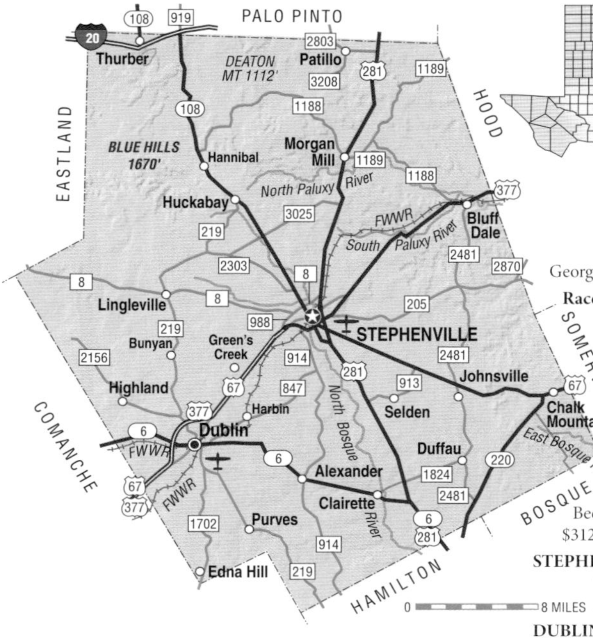

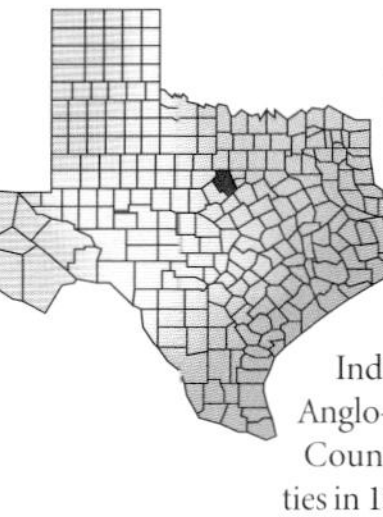

Erath County

Physical Features: On Rolling Plains; clay loam, sandy soils; drains to Bosque, Paluxy rivers.

Economy: Agricultural, industrial, and educational enterprises.

History: Caddo and Anadarko Indians were moved to Oklahoma in 1860. Anglo-American settlement began 1854-1855. County created from Bosque, Coryell counties in 1856, organized the same year; named for George B. Erath, Texas Revolution figure.

Race/Ethnicity: Anglo, 73.8%; Black, 1.2%; Hispanic, 22.5%; Asian, 0.6%; Other, 1.5%.

Vital Statistics, annual: Births, 448; deaths, 323; marriages, 285; divorces, 140.

Recreation: Old courthouse, log cabins, museums; nearby lakes, hunting, Bosque River Park; university fine arts center; Dairy Fest in June.

Minerals: Gas, oil.

Agriculture: Dairies (first in number of milk cows). Beef cattle, horticulture industry, horses raised. Market value $312.3 million.

STEPHENVILLE (21,245) county seat; Tarleton State University, varied manufacturing; hospital, mental health center; Texas A&M research and extension center.

DUBLIN (3,562) dairies, food processing, varied manufacturing, tourism; library; old Dr Pepper plant; grist mill; St. Patrick's Day celebration.

Other towns include: **Bluff Dale** (400); **Lingleville** (100); **Morgan Mill** (206); **Thurber** (48) former coal-mining town; Gordon Center for Industrial History of Texas.

Population	**43,042**	July mean max (°F)	94.2
Change from 2010 (%)	13.6	Civ. Labor	19,430
Area (sq. mi.)	1,089.8	Unemployed (%)	4.9
Land Area (sq. mi.)	1,083.1	Wages	$177,453,265
Altitude (ft.)	820–1,670	Per Capita Income	$40,462
Rainfall (in.)	31.5	Prop. Value	$6,910,048,560
Jan. mean min (°F)	31.0	Retail Sales	$630,238,007

Falls County

Physical Features: On rolling prairie; bisected by Brazos; blackland, red, sandy loam soils; mineral springs.

Economy: Government/services, agribusiness, varied manufacturing.

History: Wacos, Tawokanis, Anadarkos in conflict with Comanches. Cherokees alone in area 1830 until 1835 when Anglo-American settlement began. Antebellum slave-holding area. County created, organized, 1850 from Limestone, Milam counties; named for Brazos River falls.

Race/Ethnicity: Anglo, 50.6%; Black, 22.7%; Hispanic, 23.9%; Asian, 0.3%; Other, 2.3%.

Vital Statistics, annual: Births, 207; deaths, 178; marriages, 85; divorces, 16.

Recreation: Fishing, hunting, camping; Highland Mansion and Falls on the Brazos.

Minerals: Gravel, sand, oil.

Agriculture: Stocker cattle, cow-calf operations, corn, grain sorghum, soybeans, cotton, wheat, oats (first in acreage), goats, sheep, horses. Some cotton irrigated. Market value $157.9 million.

MARLIN (5,577) county seat; agriculture, prison; hospital; museum.

Other towns include: **Chilton** (958); **Golinda** (592); **Lott** (773); **Reagan** (300); **Rosebud** (1,345) feed, fertilizer processing, clothing manufactured; **Satin** (86). Part of **Bruceville-Eddy** (1,693).

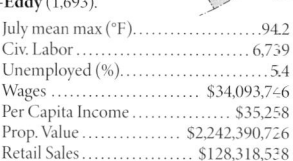

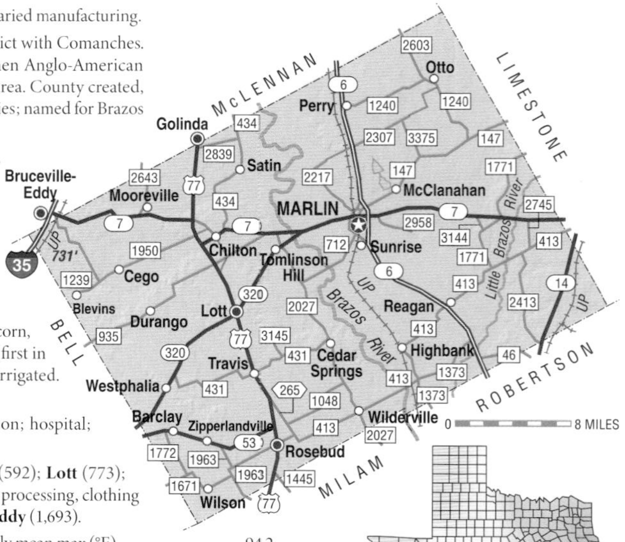

Population	17,401	July mean max (°F)	94.2
Change from 2010 (%)	-2.6	Civ. Labor	6,739
Area (sq. mi.)	773.8	Unemployed (%)	5.4
Land Area (sq. mi.)	765.5	Wages	$34,093,746
Altitude (ft.)	282–731	Per Capita Income	$35,258
Rainfall (in.)	38.5	Prop. Value	$2,242,390,726
Jan. mean min (°F)	35.4	Retail Sales	$128,318,528

Fannin County

Physical Features: North Texas county of rolling prairie, drained by Red River, Bois d'Arc Creek; Coffee Mill Lake, Lake Bonham, Valley Lake; mostly blackland soils; national grasslands.

Economy: Commuting to DFW metroplex, agribusiness.

History: Caddoes who later joined with Cherokees. Anglo-American settlement began in 1836. County created from Red River County in 1837 and organized in 1838; named for James W. Fannin, a victim of the Goliad massacre.

Race/Ethnicity: Anglo, 77.7%; Black, 6.8%; Hispanic, 11.9%; Asian, 0.4%; Other, 3%.

Vital Statistics, annual: Births, 353; deaths, 458; marriages, 211; divorces, 127.

Recreation: Water activities on lakes; hunting; state park, fossil beds; winery; Sam Rayburn home, library; Bois D'Arc festival in May.

Minerals: Sand.

Agriculture: Beef cattle, wheat, corn. Market value $86.3 million. Hunting leases important.

BONHAM (10,786) county seat; varied manufacturing, veterans hospital/private hospital, state jail; Sam Rayburn birthday celebration in January.

Other towns include: **Bailey** (315); **Dodd City** (395); **Ector** (740); **Gober** (146); **Honey Grove** (1,732) agribusiness center, varied manufacturing, tourism, historic buildings, library, Davy Crockett Festival in October; **Ivanhoe** (110).

Also: **Ladonia** (632) restored historical downtown, tourism, varied manufacturing, commuters, rodeo; **Leonard** (2,092) government/services, power plant, retail, light industry, museums, community picnic in July; **Randolph** (600); **Ravenna** (221); **Savoy** (860); **Telephone** (210); **Trenton** (684); **Windom** (206).

Also, part of **Pecan Gap** (197) and part of **Whitewright** (1,713).

For explanation of sources, symbols and abbreviations, see p. 204, and foldout map.

Population	**36,230**
Change from 2010 (%)	6.8
Area (sq. mi.)	898.9
Land Area (sq. mi.)	890.8
Altitude (ft.)	450–800
Rainfall (in.)	46.1
Jan. mean min (°F)	30.9
July mean max (°F)	92.3
Civ. Labor	16,763
Unemployed (%)	4.3
Wages	$93,639,841
Per Capita Income	$39,830
Prop. Value	$5,014,592,019
Retail Sales	$355,967,365

Fayette County

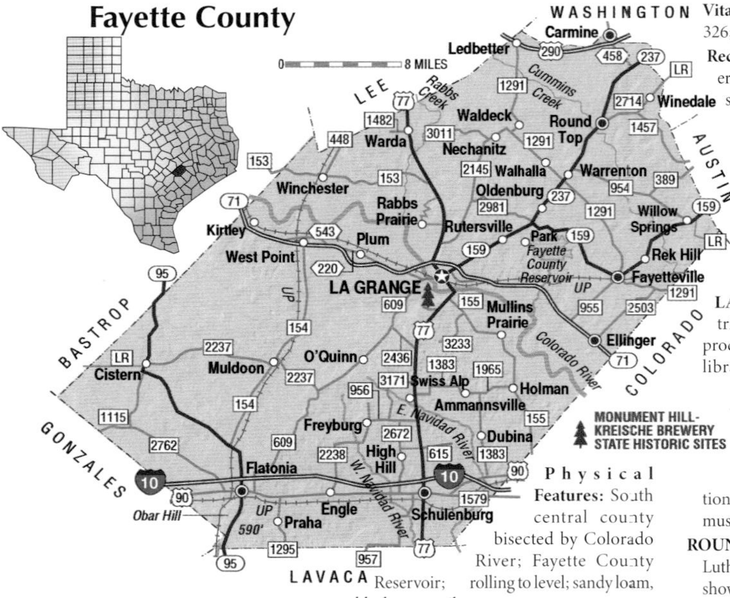

Physical Features: South central county bisected by Colorado River; Fayette County Reservoir; rolling to level; sandy loam, black waxy soils.

Population	**26,328**
Change from 2010 (%)	7.2
Area (sq. mi.)	959.8
Land Area (sq. mi.)	950.0
Altitude (ft.)	200–590
Rainfall (in.)	40.5
Jan. mean min (°F)	39.2
July mean max (°F)	95.5
Civ. Labor	11,368
Unemployed (%)	4.8
Wages	$108,002,539
Per Capita Income	$54,552
Prop. Value	$7,605,240,234
Retail Sales	$467,737,178

Economy: Agribusiness, production of electricity, mineral production, government/services, small manufacturing, tourism.

History: Lipan Apaches and Tonkawas. Austin's colonists arrived in 1822. Germans and Czechs began arriving in 1840s. County created from Bastrop, Colorado counties in 1837; organized in 1838; named for hero of American Revolution, Marquis de Lafayette.

Race/Ethnicity: Anglo, 70.1%; Black, 6.8%; Hispanic, 21.1%; Asian, 0.2%; Other, 1.4%.

Vital Statistics, annual: Births, 282; deaths, 326; marriages, 125; divorces, 81.

Recreation: Monument Hill, Kreische brewery, Faison Home Museum, other historic sites including "Painted Churches"; hunting, fishing, lake; German and Czech ethnic foods; Prazska Pout in August, Octoberfests.

Minerals: Oil, gas, sand, gravel, bentonite clay.

Agriculture: Beef cattle, corn, hay, sorghum, pecans, dairies. Market value $47.4 million. Firewood sold.

LA GRANGE (4,759) county seat; electricity generation, manufacturing, food processing, retail trade, tourism; hospital, library, quilt museum, polka museum, archives; Czech heritage center; Best Little Cowboy Gathering in March.

SCHULENBURG (3,006) varied manufacturing, food processing; Blinn College extension; aircraft, International Festival Institute, July-August; polka music museums; sausagefest in April.

ROUND TOP (90) music center, tourism; old Lutheran church, heritage museum; antiques shows, April/October; Shakespeare festival in April, Schuetzenfest in September, and **Winedale** (67), historic restorations including Winedale Inn.

Other towns include: **Carmine** (262); **Ellinger** (386) Tomato Festival in May; **Fayetteville** (262) tourism, antiques, old precinct courthouse, Lickskillet festival in October; **Flatonia** (1,507) food production, manufacturing, government/services; rail history museum, parks, Czhilispiel in October; **Ledbetter** (83); **Muldoon** (95); **Plum** (145); **Warda** (121); **Warrenton** (186) antique Cadillac museum; **West Point** (213), and **Winchester** (232).

Fisher County

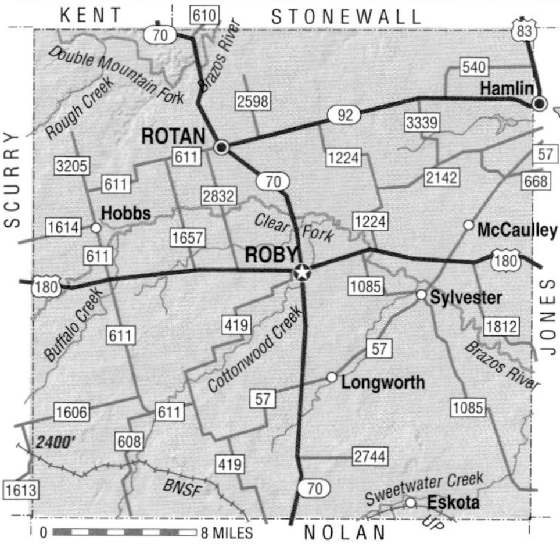

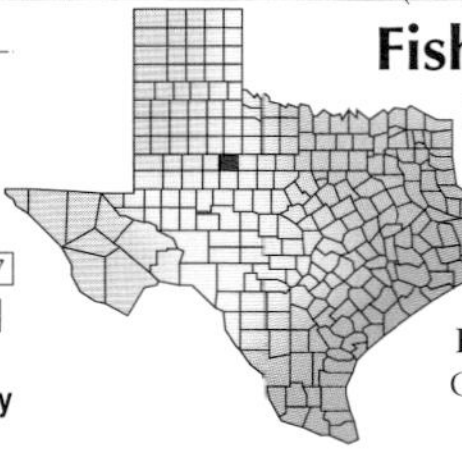

Physical Features: On rolling prairie; mesquite; red, sandy loam soils; drains to forks of Brazos River.

Economy: Agribusiness, hunting, gypsum.

History: Lipan Apaches, disrupted by Comanches and other tribes around 1700. Ranching began in 1876. County created from the Bexar District in 1876 and organized in 1886; named for S.R. Fisher, Republic of Texas secretary of navy.

Race/Ethnicity: Anglo, 65.4%; Black, 3.3%; Hispanic, 29.8%; Asian, 0.2%; Other, 1.1%.

Vital Statistics, annual: Births, 50; deaths, 52; marriages, 13; divorces, 4.

Recreation: Quail, dove, turkey hunting; wildlife viewing; county fair, rodeo in August in Roby.

Minerals: Gypsum, oil.

Population	**3,859**
Change from 2010 (%)	-2.9
Area (sq. mi.)	901.8
Land Area (sq. mi.)	898.9
Altitude (ft.)	1,720–2,405
Rainfall (in.)	24.8
Jan. mean min (°F)	30.5
July mean max (°F)	94.6
Civ. Labor	1,643
Unemployed (%)	4.6
Wages	$10,263,820
Per Capita Income	$44,630
Prop. Value	$1,488,462,493
Retail Sales	$15,847,143

Agriculture: Cattle, cotton, hay, wheat, sorghum, horses, sheep, goats. Irrigation for cotton and alfalfa. Market value $35.7 million.

ROBY (624) county seat; agribusiness, cotton gin; hospital between Roby and Rotan.

ROTAN (1,470) gypsum plant, oil mill, agribusiness.

Other towns include: **McCaulley** (96) and **Sylvester** (79). Part of **Hamlin** (2,021).

Floyd County

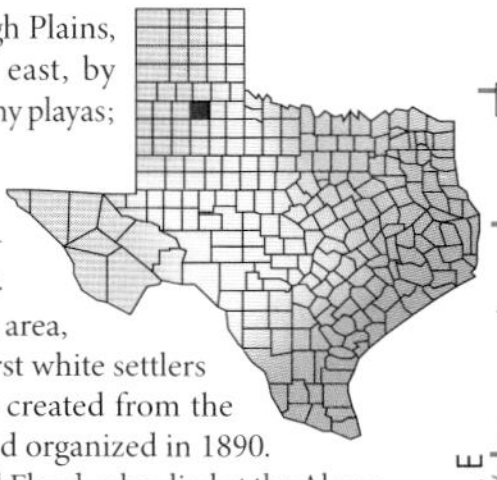

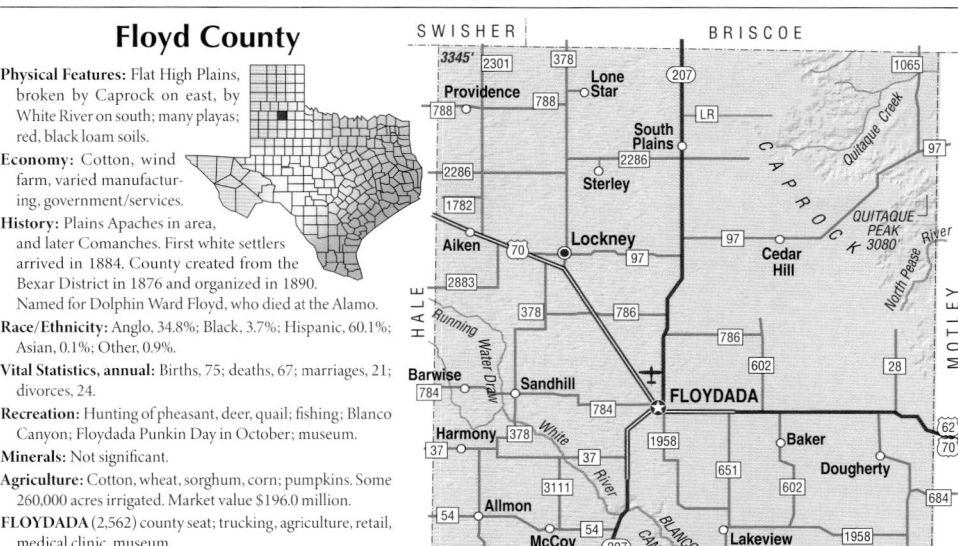

Physical Features: Flat High Plains, broken by Caprock on east, by White River on south; many playas; red, black loam soils.

Economy: Cotton, wind farm, varied manufacturing, government/services.

History: Plains Apaches in area, and later Comanches. First white settlers arrived in 1884. County created from the Bexar District in 1876 and organized in 1890. Named for Dolphin Ward Floyd, who died at the Alamo.

Race/Ethnicity: Anglo, 34.8%; Black, 3.7%; Hispanic, 60.1%; Asian, 0.1%; Other, 0.9%.

Vital Statistics, annual: Births, 75; deaths, 67; marriages, 21; divorces, 24.

Recreation: Hunting of pheasant, deer, quail; fishing; Blanco Canyon; Floydada Punkin Day in October; museum.

Minerals: Not significant.

Agriculture: Cotton, wheat, sorghum, corn; pumpkins. Some 260,000 acres irrigated. Market value $196.0 million.

FLOYDADA (2,562) county seat; trucking, agriculture, retail, medical clinic, museum.

LOCKNEY (1,637) agriculture center; manufacturing; hospital.

Other towns include: **Aiken** (52), **Dougherty** (91), and **South Plains** (67).

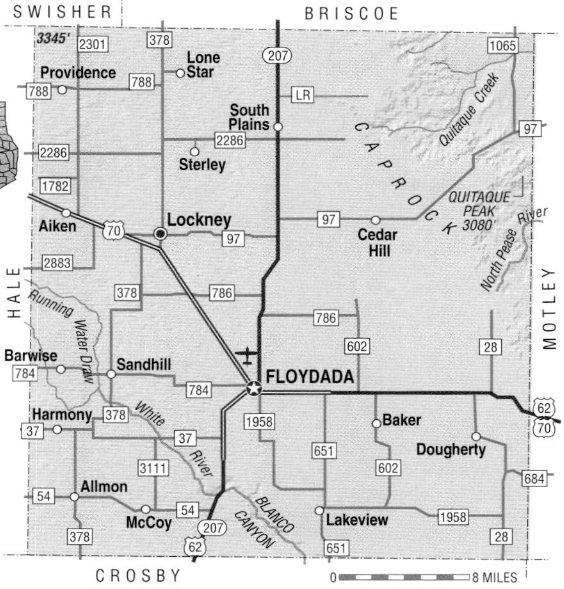

Population	**5,535**
Change from 2010 (%)	-14.1
Area (sq. mi.)	992.5
Land Area (sq. mi.)	992.1
Altitude (ft.)	2,440–3,345
Rainfall (in.)	21.6
Jan. mean min (°F)	25.1
July mean max (°F)	92.4
Civ. Labor	2,545
Unemployed (%)	5.9
Wages	$17,251,660
Per Capita Income	$44,646
Prop. Value	$1,408,049,053
Retail Sales	$42,100,168

Foard County

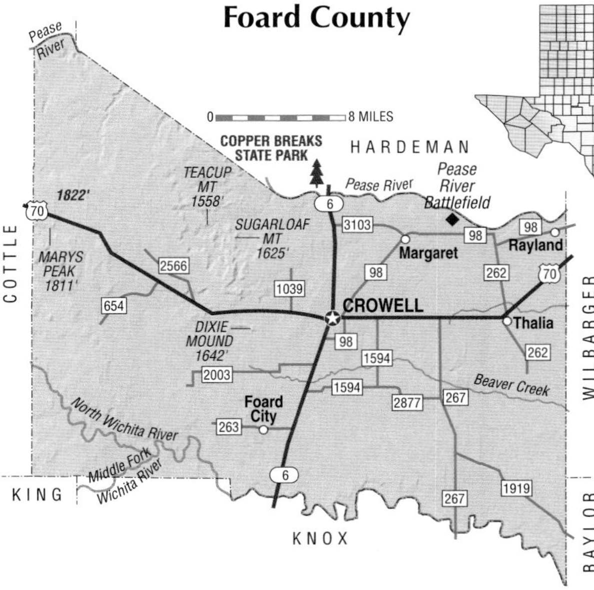

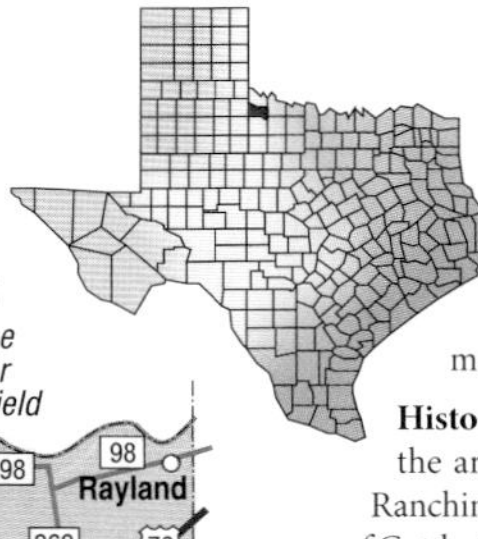

Physical Features: Northwest county drains to North Wichita, Pease rivers; sandy, loam soils, rolling surface.

Economy: Agribusiness, clothes manufacturing, government/service.

History: Comanches and Kiowas ranged the area until driven away in the 1870s. Ranching began in 1880. County created out of Cottle, Hardeman, King, and Knox counties in 1891, organized the same year; named for Maj. Robert L. Foard of the Confederate army.

Race/Ethnicity: Anglo, 76.2%; Black, 5%; Hispanic, 17.7%; Asian, 0.4%; Other, 0.4%.

Vital Statistics, annual: Births, 10; deaths, 16; marriages, 0; divorces, 1.

Recreation: Three museums; hunting; astronomy and ecotourism foundation; wild hog cook-off in November.

Minerals: Natural gas, some oil.

Agriculture: Wheat, cattle, alfalfa, cotton, sorghum, dairies. Market value $14.9 million. Hunting leases important.

CROWELL (813) county seat; retail center, clothing manufacturing; library, Fire Hall museum.

Population	**1,139**
Change from 2010 (%)	-14.7
Area (sq. mi.)	707.7
Land Area (sq. mi.)	704.4
Altitude (ft.)	1,210–1,822
Rainfall (in.)	27.3
Jan. mean min (°F)	26.0
July mean max (°F)	98.0
Civ. Labor	574
Unemployed (%)	3
Wages	$3,125,283
Per Capita Income	$44,895
Prop. Value	$1,019,925,798
Retail Sales	$7,147,802

For explanation of sources, symbols and abbreviations, see p. 204, and foldout map.

Fort Bend County

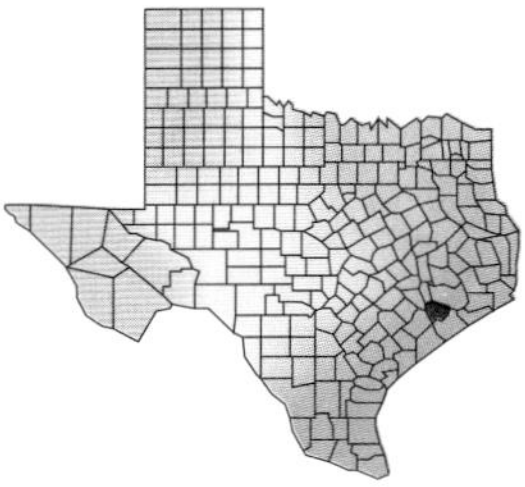

Physical Features: On Gulf Coastal Plain; drained by Brazos, San Bernard rivers; Smithers Lake; level to rolling; rich alluvial soils.

Economy: Agribusiness, petrochemicals, technology, government/services; many residents work in Houston.

History: Karankawa groups in area, who retreated to Mexico by the 1850s. Named for river bend where some of Austin's colonists settled in 1824 and built a blockhouse for protection against the Indians. Antebellum plantations made it one of six Texas counties with black majority in 1850. County created in 1837 from Austin County and organized in 1838.

Race/Ethnicity: Anglo, 33.2%; Black, 19.3%; Hispanic, 24.2%; Asian, 20.4%; Other, 2.7%.

Vital Statistics, annual: Births, 9,887; deaths, 2,984; marriages, 3,321; divorces, 1,871.

Recreation: Many historic sites, museums, memorials, parks; George Ranch historical park; Brazos Bend State Park with George Observatory; fishing, waterfowl hunting.

Minerals: Oil, gas, sulfur, salt, clays, sand and gravel.

Agriculture: Nursery crops, cotton, sorghum, corn, hay, cattle, horses; irrigation for rice. Market value $85.0 million.

RICHMOND (13,598) county seat; foundry; University of Houston branch, Wharton County Junior College branch; Richmond State supported-living center, hospital.

SUGAR LAND (131,448) government/services, prisons, commuting to Houston; hospitals; University of Houston branch; Museum of Southern History. New Territory and Greatwood are now part of Sugar Land.

MISSOURI CITY (80,681, part [6,276] in Harris County) hospital.

ROSENBERG (37,823) varied industry, railroad museum.

Other towns include: **Arcola** (2,360); **Beasley** (804); **Cinco Ranch** (24,176); **Fairchilds** (1,068); **Fresno** (28,243); **Fulshear** (13,914); **Guy** (239); **Katy** (21,729, mostly in Harris County) hospital; **Kendleton** (461); **Meadows Place** (4,591); **Mission Bend** (46,172).

Also: **Needville** (3,522) agriculture, commuting, historic Schendel house, historic cemetery, Czech soup supper in January; **Orchard** (434); **Pecan Grove** (20,569); **Pleak** (1,517); **Simonton** (965); **Stafford** (19,501, partly in Harris County); **Thompsons** (331); **Weston Lakes** (4,699).

Also, part [42,242] of **Houston.**

Population	**805,788**
Change from 2010 (%)	37.7
Area (sq. mi.)	885.3
Land Area (sq. mi.)	861.5
Altitude (ft.)	46–158
Rainfall (in.)	50.4
Jan. mean min (°F)	44.1
July mean max (°F)	94.9
Civ. Labor	395,859
Unemployed (%)	6.7
Wages	$2,743,891,540
Per Capita Income	$59,653
Prop. Value	$103,143,863,651
Retail Sales	$9,340,038,608

For explanation of sources, symbols and abbreviations, see p. 204, and foldout map.

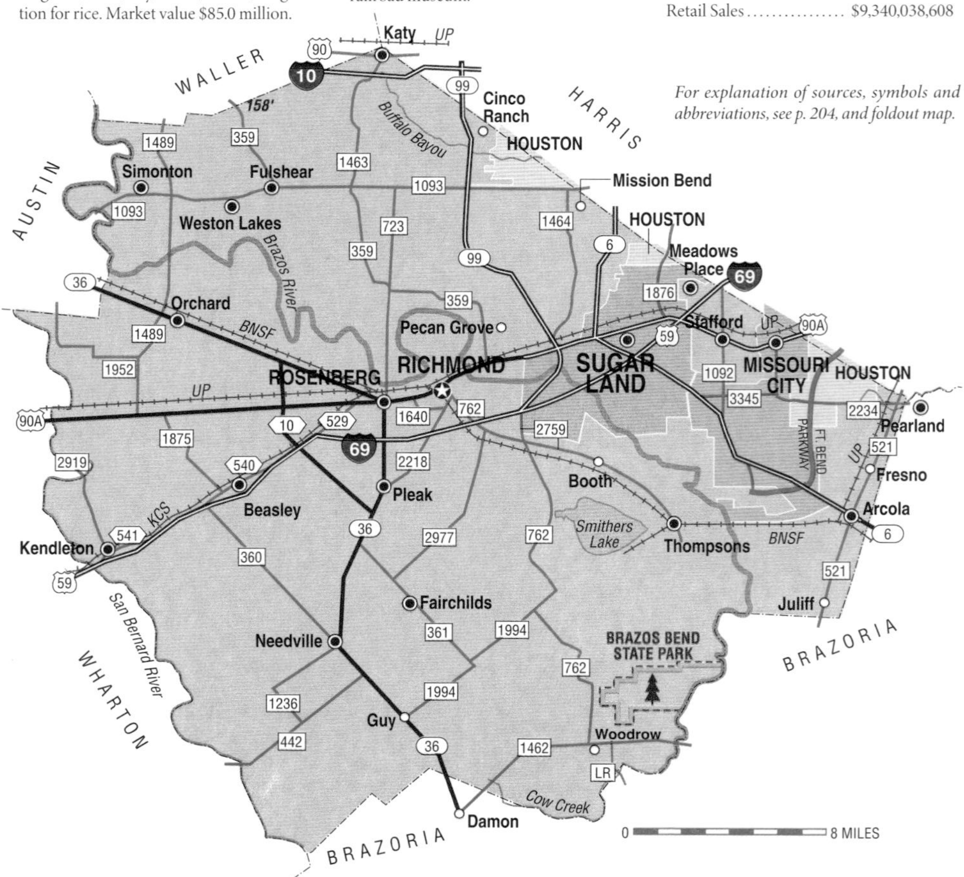

Franklin County

Physical Features: Small Northeast county with many wooded hills; drained by numerous streams; alluvial to sandy clay soils; Lake Bob Sandlin, Lake Cypress Springs.

Economy: Agribusiness, government/services, retirement area, distribution.

History: Caddoes abandoned the area in the 1790s because of disease and other tribes. First white settlers arrived around 1818. County created in 1875 from Titus County, organized the same year; named for jurist B.C. Franklin.

Race/Ethnicity: Anglo, 77.3%; Black, 4.5%; Hispanic, 15.2%; Asian, 0.5%; Other, 2.3%.

Population	**10,791**
Change from 2010 (%)	1.8
Area (sq. mi.)	294.8
Land Area (sq. mi.)	284.4
Altitude (ft.)	300–600
Rainfall (in.)	47.4
Jan. mean min (°F)	47.4
July mean max (°F)	92.0
Civ. Labor	5,004
Unemployed (%)	5.1
Wages	$42,085,288
Per Capita Income	$41,307
Prop. Value	$1,910,721,168
Retail Sales	$109,279,360

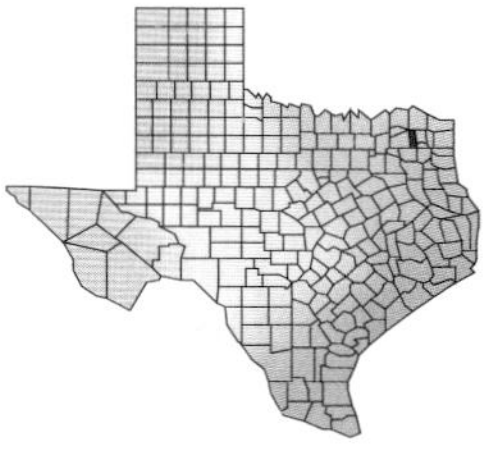

Vital Statistics, annual: Births, 123; deaths, 122; marriages, 62; divorces, 33.

Recreation: Fishing, water sports; historic homes; wild hog hunting, horse stables; stew cook-off in October.

Minerals: Lignite coal, oil and gas.

Agriculture: Beef cattle, milk production, poultry, hay. Market value $134.1 million. Timber marketed.

MOUNT VERNON (2,789) county seat; distribution center, manufacturing, tourism, antiques; hospital; nature preserves, museum with Don Meredith exhibit; wine festivals in May and October.

Other towns include: **Scroggins** (150), and **Winnsboro** (3,299, mostly in Wood County) commercial center, Autumn Trails.

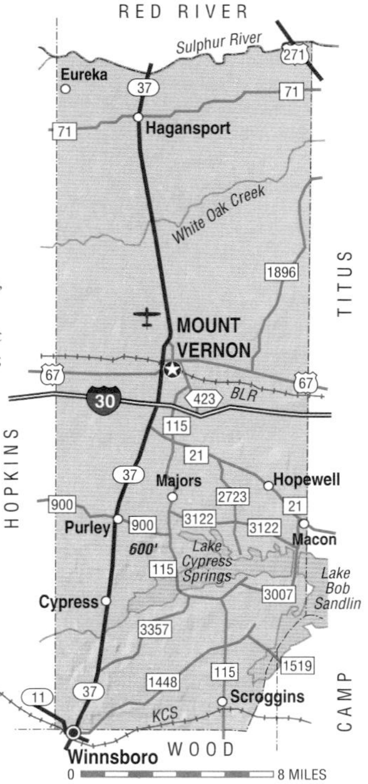

Freestone County

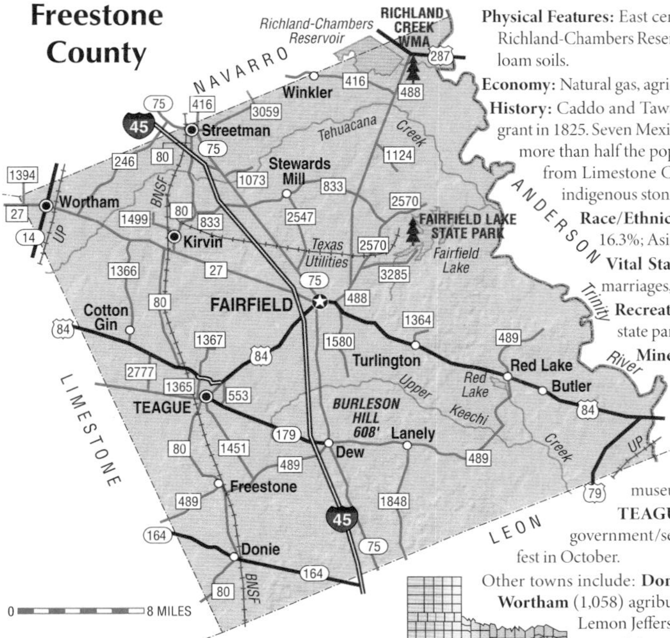

Physical Features: East central county bounded by the Trinity River; Richland-Chambers Reservoir, Fairfield Lake; rolling Blackland, sandy, loam soils.

Economy: Natural gas, agriculture.

History: Caddo and Tawakoni area. David G. Burnet received land grant in 1825. Seven Mexican citizens received grants in 1833. In 1860, more than half the population was black. County created in 1850 from Limestone County; organized in 1851. Named for the indigenous stone.

Race/Ethnicity: Anglo, 65.8%; Black, 15.9%; Hispanic, 16.3%; Asian, 0.2%; Other, 1.5%.

Vital Statistics, annual: Births, 215; deaths, 202; marriages, 166; divorces, 33.

Recreation: Fishing, hunting; lakes; historic sites; state park; Teague amateur rodeo in July.

Minerals: Natural gas, oil.

Agriculture: Beef cattle, peaches (second in acreage), hay, blueberries, horticulture. Market value $68.1 million. Hunting leases.

FAIRFIELD (2,984) county seat; government/services, trade center; hospital, museum; wild game supper in July.

TEAGUE (3,495) railroad terminal, oil and gas, government/services, agriculture; library, museum; Parkfest in October.

Other towns include: **Donie** (250), **Kirvin** (136), **Streetman** (259), **Wortham** (1,058) agribusiness, blues festivals in September, Blind Lemon Jefferson gravesite.

Population	**20,621**
Change from 2010 (%)	4.1
Area (sq. mi.)	892.0
Land Area (sq. mi.)	877.7
Altitude (ft.)	200–608
Rainfall (in.)	43.1
Jan. mean min (°F)	35.3

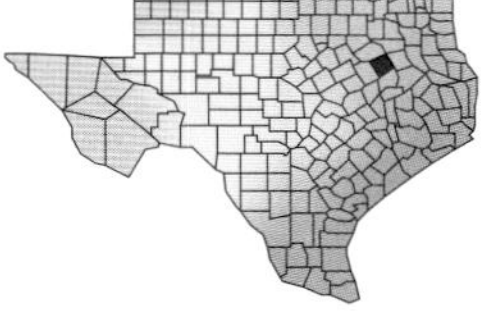

July mean max (°F)	93.5
Civ. Labor	6,244
Unemployed (%)	8
Wages	$49,296,705
Per Capita Income	$38,182
Prop. Value	$4,034,441,610
Retail Sales	$166,245,570

Frio County

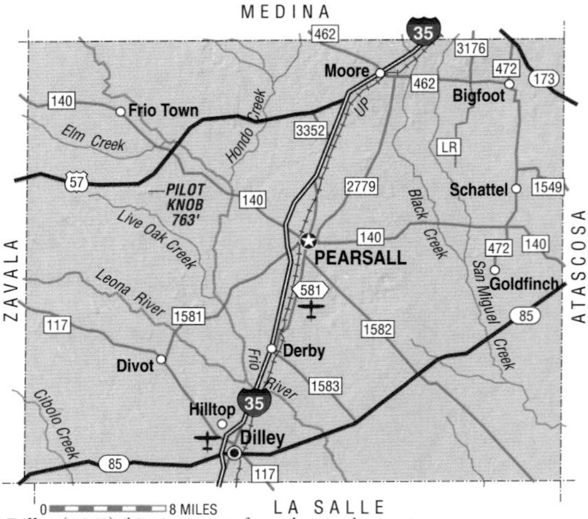

Physical Features: South Texas county of rolling terrain with much brush; bisected by Frio River; sandy, red sandy loam soils.

Economy: Agribusiness, oil-field services, hunting leases.

History: Coahuiltecans; many taken into San Antonio missions. Comanches kept settlers out until after Civil War. Mexican citizens recruited for labor after 1900. County created in 1858 from Atascosa, Bexar, Uvalde counties, organized in 1871; named for the Frio (cold) River.

Race/Ethnicity: Anglo, 14.5%; Black, 2.7%; Hispanic, 80%; Asian, 1.9%; Other, 0.8%.

Vital Statistics, annual: Births, 242; deaths, 155; marriages, 96; divorces, 27.

Recreation: Hunting, Big Foot Wallace Museum, Winter Garden area, splash pad/skate parks.

Minerals: Oil, natural gas, stone.

Agriculture: Peanuts, potatoes, sorghum, cotton, corn, spinach, cucumbers, watermelons, bees (second in number of colonies). Second in vegetables harvested. Market value $124.4 million. Hunting leases.

PEARSALL (10,577) county seat; agriculture center, oil and gas, food processing, shipping, government/services; old jail museum; hospital, junior college extension; Cinco de Mayo celebration.

Dilley (4,269) shipping center for melons and peanuts; hospital.

Other towns include: **Bigfoot** (537), **Hilltop** (282); **Moore** (441), and **North Pearsall** (657).

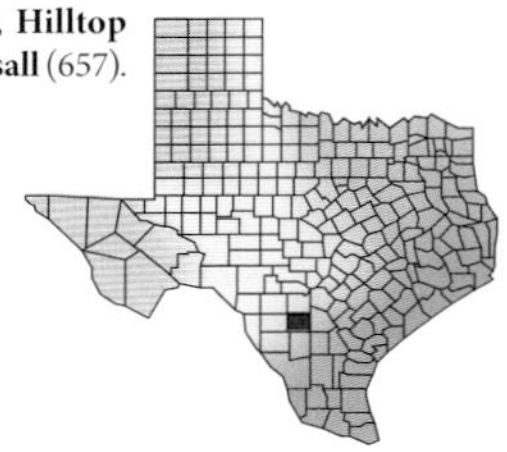

Population	**19,103**
Change from 2010 (%)	11.0
Area (sq. mi.)	1,134.4
Land Area (sq. mi.)	1,133.5
Altitude (ft.)	400–763
Rainfall (in.)	24.7
Jan. mean min (°F)	35.0
July mean max (°F)	97.4
Civ. Labor	9,238
Unemployed (%)	5.4
Wages	$90,709,167
Per Capita Income	$30,223
Prop. Value	$3,808,188,908
Retail Sales	$167,656,307

Gaines County

Physical Features: On South Plains, drains to draws; playas; underground water.

Economy: Oil, gas, cotton, peanuts.

History: Comanche country until the U.S. Army campaigns of 1875. Ranchers arrived in the 1880s; farming began around 1900. County created from Bexar District in 1876; organized in 1905; named for James Gaines, signer of the Texas Declaration of Independence.

Race/Ethnicity: Anglo, 54.8%; Black, 1.4%; Hispanic, 42.5%; Asian, 0.3%; Other, 0.8%.

Vital Statistics, annual: Births, 460; deaths, 128; marriages, 231; divorces, 49.

Recreation: Cedar Lake one of largest alkali lakes on Texas plains.

Minerals: Oil, gas.

Agriculture: Cotton (first in bales produced), peanuts (first in acreage), small grains, pecans, paprika, rosemary; cattle, sheep, hogs; substantial irrigation. Market value $188.8 million.

SEMINOLE (7,660) county seat; manufacturing, oil and gas, agriculture; hospital, library, museum; Ag & Oil Day celebration in September.

SEAGRAVES (2,946) market for three-county area; cotton, peanut farming; library, museum; Celebrate Seagraves in July.

Other towns include: **Loop** (243). Also, part of **Denver City** (4,911).

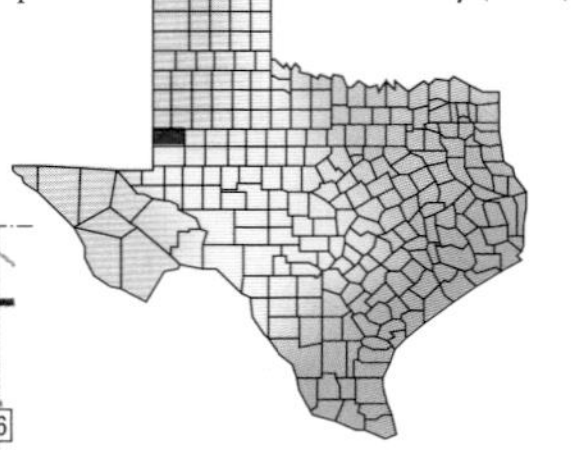

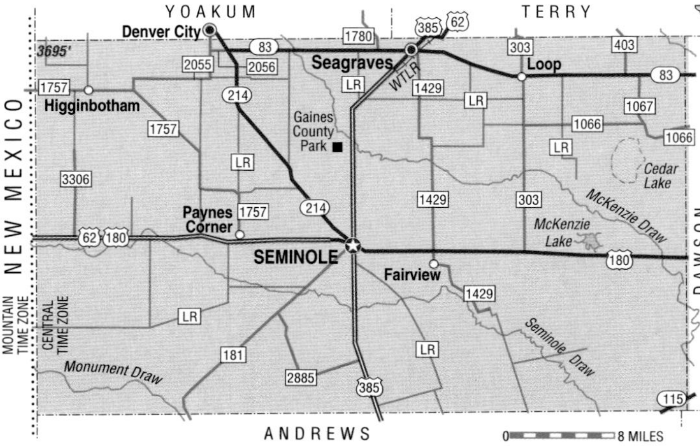

Population	**21,170**
Change from 2010 (%)	20.8
Area (sq. mi.)	1,502.9
Land Area (sq. mi.)	1,502.4
Altitude (ft.)	2,935–3,695
Rainfall (in.)	18.4
Jan. mean min (°F)	27.7
July mean max (°F)	93.4
Civ. Labor	9,731
Unemployed (%)	5.3
Wages	$89,556,983
Per Capita Income	$44,405
Prop. Value	$4,661,042,737
Retail Sales	$300,682,571

Galveston County

Physical Features: Partly island, partly coastal; flat, artificial drainage; sandy, loam, clay soils; broken by bays.

Economy: Port activities dominate economy; insurance and finance center, petrochemical plants, varied manufacturing, tourism, medical education, oceanographic research, ship building, commercial fishing.

History: Karankawa and other tribes roamed the area until 1850. French, Spanish, and American settlement began in 1815 and reached 1,000 by 1817.

County created from Brazoria County in 1838; organized in 1839; named for the Spanish governor of Louisiana Count Bernardo de Gálvez.

Race/Ethnicity: Anglo, 56.1%; Black, 12.7%; Hispanic, 25%; Asian, 3.6%; Other, 2.3%.

Vital Statistics, annual: Births, 4,219; deaths, 2,675; marriages, 1,770; divorces, 1,185.

Recreation: One of Texas' most historic cities; popular tourist and convention center; fishing, surfing, boating, sailing and other water sports; state park; historic homes tour in spring, Moody Gardens.

Also, Mardi Gras celebration; Rosenberg Library; museums; restored sailing ship, "Elissa," railroad museum; Dickens on the Strand in early December.

Minerals: Oil, gas, clays, sand and gravel.

Agriculture: Cattle, aquaculture, nursery crops, rice, hay, horses, soybeans, grain sorghum. Market value $9.2 million.

GALVESTON (50,372) county seat; tourist center, shipyard, other industries, insurance, port container facility; University of Texas Medical Branch; National Maritime Research Center; Texas A&M University at Galveston; Galveston College; hospitals.

LEAGUE CITY (108,604, part [1,987] in Harris County) residential community, commuters to Houston, hospital.

TEXAS CITY (51,178) refining, petrochemical plants, port, rail shipping; College of the Mainland; hospital, library; dike; Cinco de Mayo, Shrimp Boil in August.

Bolivar Peninsula (2,800) includes: **Port Bolivar** (700) lighthouse, free ferry; **Crystal Beach** (800) seafood industry, sport fishing, tourism, Fort Travis Seashore Park, shorebird sanctuary, Crab Festival in May; **Gilchrist** (400), and **High Island** (300).

Other towns include: **Bacliff** (10,073); **Bayou Vista** (1,645); **Clear Lake Shores** (1,190).

Also: **Dickinson** (21,576) manufacturing, commuters, strawberry festival in May; **Friendswood** (40,659, part [11,499] in Harris County); **Hitchcock** (7,895) residential community, tourism, fishing and shrimping, Good Ole Days in August, WWII blimp base, museum.

Also: **Jamaica Beach** (1,088); **Kemah** (2,006) tourism, boating, commuters, museum, Blessing of Fleet in August; **La Marque** (17,326) refining, greyhound racing, farming, hospital, library, Gulf Coast Grill-off in October; **San Leon** (5,439); **Santa Fe** (13,645); **Tiki Island** (1,083).

Population	**339,931**
Change from 2010 (%)	16.7
Area (sq. mi.)	873.8
Land Area (sq. mi.)	378.4
Altitude (ft.)	sea level–40
Rainfall (in.)	50.8
Jan. mean min (°F)	48.6
July mean max (°F)	89.6
Civ. Labor	164,318
Unemployed (%)	7.3
Wages	$1,542,972,986
Per Capita Income	$54,250
Prop. Value	$46,645,264,094
Retail Sales	$4,531,612,556

For explanation of sources, symbols and abbreviations, see p. 204, and foldout map.

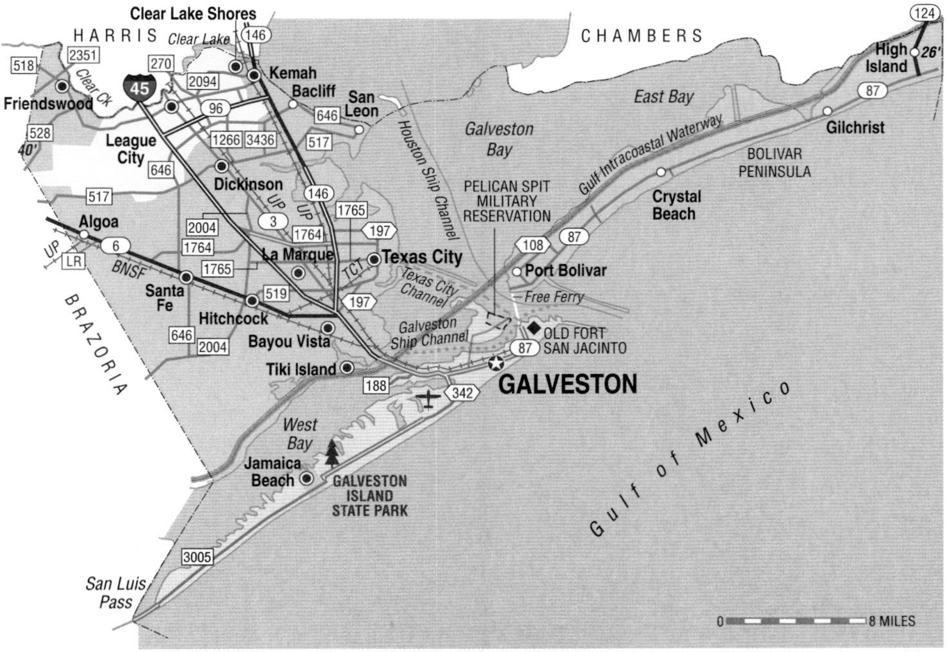

Garza County

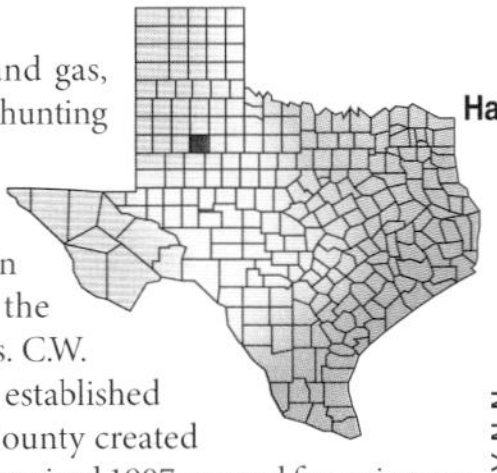

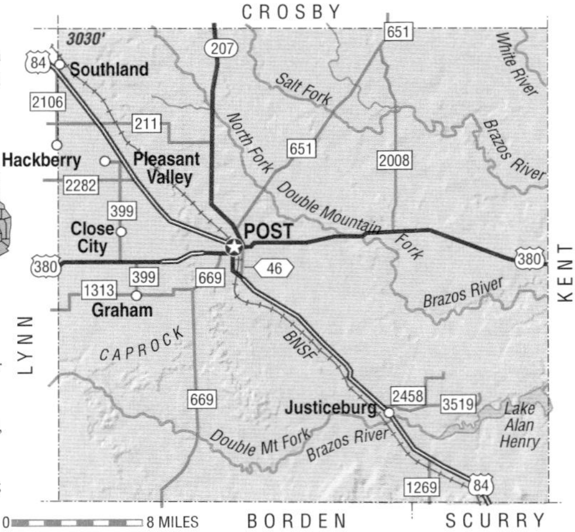

For explanation of sources, symbols and abbreviations, see p. 204, and foldout map.

Physical Features: On edge of Caprock; rough, broken land, with playas, gullies, canyons, Brazos River forks, Lake Alan Henry; sandy, loam, clay soils.

Economy: Agriculture, oil and gas, trade, government/services, hunting leases.

History: Kiowas and Comanches yielded to U.S. Army in 1875. Ranching began in the 1870s, farming in the 1890s. C.W. Post, the cereal millionaire, established enterprises here in 1906. County created from Bexar District 1876; organized 1907; named for a pioneer Bexar County family.

Race/Ethnicity: Anglo, 42.5%; Black, 6.2%; Hispanic, 50%; Asian, 0.1%; Other, 0.9%.

Vital Statistics, annual: Births, 71; deaths, 56; marriages, 29; divorces, 10.

Recreation: Scenic areas, lake activities, Post-Garza Museum, trade days monthly.

Minerals: Oil, gas, sand, gravel.

Agriculture: Cotton, beef cattle, hay. Some 8,000 acres irrigated. Market value $22.1 million. Hunting leases.

POST (5,138) county seat; founded by C.W. Post; agriculture, tourism, government/services, prisons; museums, theater.

Population	**6,115**
Change from 2010 (%)	-5.4
Area (sq. mi.)	896.2
Land Area (sq. mi.)	893.4
Altitude (ft.)	2,140–3,030
Rainfall (in.)	22.0
Jan. mean min (°F)	29.0
July mean max (°F)	94.4
Civ. Labor	1,939
Unemployed (%)	5.5
Wages	$18,112,470
Per Capita Income	$32,601
Prop. Value	$1,139,614,447
Retail Sales	$30,557,378

A beautiful drive in Garza County, down FM 669. Photo by Leaflet, CC 3/Wikimedia Commons

Gillespie County

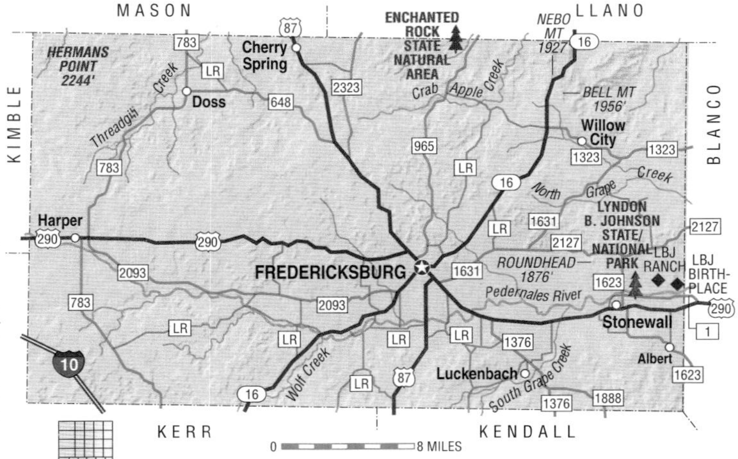

Physical Features: Picturesque Edwards Plateau area with hills, broken by spring-fed streams.

Economy: Tourism, government/services, agriculture, wine and specialty foods, hunting leases.

History: German settlement founded in 1846 in heart of Comanche country. County created in 1848 from Bexar and Travis counties, organized the same year; named for Texas Ranger Capt. R.A. Gillespie.

The birthplace of President Lyndon B. Johnson and Fleet Admiral Chester W. Nimitz.

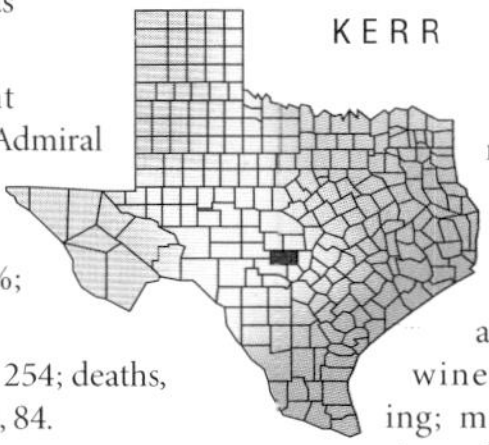

Race/Ethnicity: Anglo, 72.9%; Black, 0.4%; Hispanic, 24.9%; Asian, 0.3%; Other, 1.2%.

Vital Statistics, annual: Births, 254; deaths, 318; marriages, 220; divorces, 84.

Recreation: Among leading deer-hunting areas; numerous historic sites and tourist attractions include LBJ Ranch, Nimitz Hotel and Pacific war museum; Pioneer Museum Complex, Enchanted Rock, wineries, produce stands.

Minerals: Sand, gravel.

Agriculture: Beef cattle, wine, hay, peaches (first in acreage). Market value $31.2 million. Hunting leases important.

FREDERICKSBURG (11,482) county seat; agribusiness, tourism, wineries, food processing; museum; tourist attractions; hospital; Easter Fires, Oktoberfest.

Other towns include: **Doss** (100); **Harper** (1,388) ranching, deer hunting, Dachshund Hounds Downs race and Trades Day in October; **Luckenbach** (25) saloon, general store and dance hall; **Stonewall** (543) agribusiness, wineries, tourism, hunting, Peach Jamboree in June, and **Willow City** (22) scenic drive.

Population	**27,375**
Change from 2010 (%)	10.2
Area (sq. mi.)	1,061.7
Land Area (sq. mi.)	1,058.2
Altitude (ft.)	1,040–2,244
Rainfall (in.)	31.5
Jan. mean min (°F)	34.3
July mean max (°F)	92.7
Civ. Labor	12,821
Unemployed (%)	3.7
Wages	$128,867,213
Per Capita Income	$63,291
Prop. Value	$10,071,369,340
Retail Sales	$577,736,080

Glasscock County

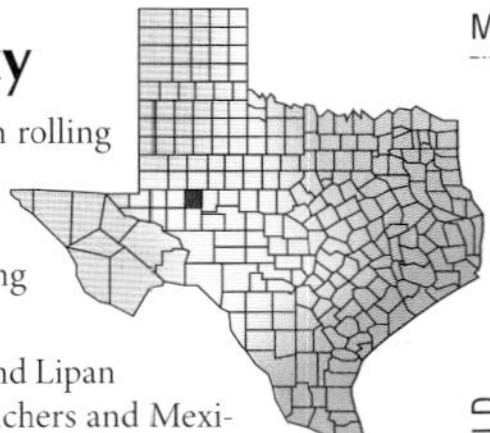

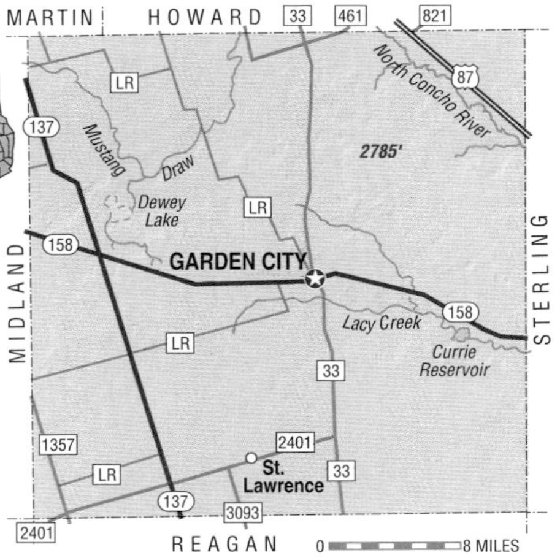

Physical Features: Western county on rolling plains, broken by small streams; sandy, loam soils.

Economy: Farming, ranching, hunting leases, oil and gas.

History: Hunting area for Kickapoos and Lipan Apaches. Anglo-American sheep ranchers and Mexican-American shepherds or pastores moved into the area in the 1880s. County created in 1887 from Tom Green County; organized in 1893; named for Texas pioneer George W. Glasscock.

Race/Ethnicity: Anglo, 65.3%; Black, 1%; Hispanic, 32.7%; Asian, 0.1%; Other, 0.7%.

Vital Statistics, annual: Births, 16; deaths, 3; marriages, 10; divorces, 0.

Recreation: Hunting of deer, quail, turkey, fox, bobcat, coyote; St. Lawrence Fall Festival in October.

Minerals: Oil, gas, stone/rock.

Agriculture: Cotton, watermelons, wheat, sorghum, hay; 25,000 acres irrigated. Cattle, goats, sheep, hogs raised. Market value $50.6 million.

GARDEN CITY (427) county seat; serves sparsely settled ranching, oil area.

Also, **St. Lawrence** (90) farming.

Population	**1,369**
Change from 2010 (%)	11.7
Area (sq. mi.)	901.1
Land Area (sq. mi.)	900.2
Altitude (ft.)	2,470–2,785
Rainfall (in.)	17.6
Jan. mean min (°F)	28.3
July mean max (°F)	92.6
Civ. Labor	824
Unemployed (%)	3
Wages	$9,646,690
Per Capita Income	$84,623
Prop. Value	$4,899,719,498
Retail Sales	$23,674,618

Goliad County

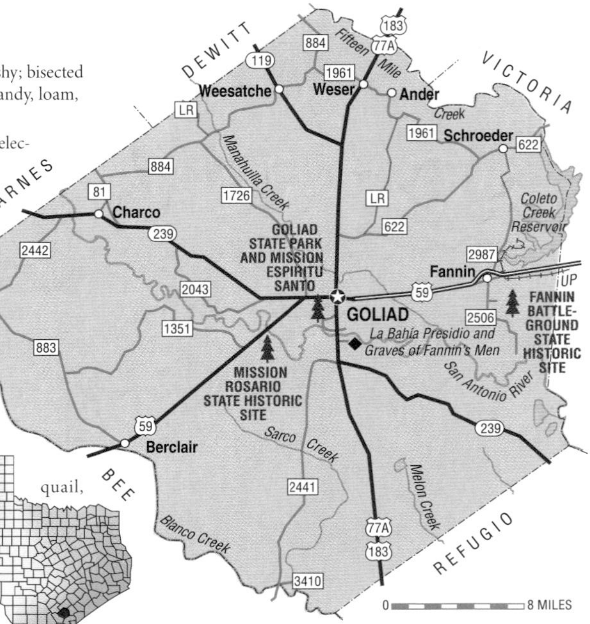

For explanation of sources, symbols and abbreviations, see p. 204, and foldout map.

Physical Features: Coastal Plain county; rolling, brushy; bisected by San Antonio River; Coleto Creek Reservoir; sandy, loam, alluvial soils.

Economy: Government/services, oil/gas, agriculture, electricity-generating plant, tourism.

History: Karankawas, Comanches, other tribes in area in historic period. La Bahía presidio/mission established, 1749. County created, 1836, from Spanish municipality; organized, 1837; name is anagram of (H)idalgo. Birthplace of Gen. Ignacio Zaragoza, hero of Battle of Puebla.

Race/Ethnicity: Anglo, 55.1%; Black, 4.5%; Hispanic, 38.5%; Asian, 0.1%; Other, 1.5%.

Vital Statistics, annual: Births, 78; deaths, 87; marriages, 34; divorces, 4.

Recreation: Missions, restored Presidio La Bahía, Fannin Battleground; Old Market House museum; lake, fishing, hunting (deer, quail, dove, hogs), camping, canoeing, birding.

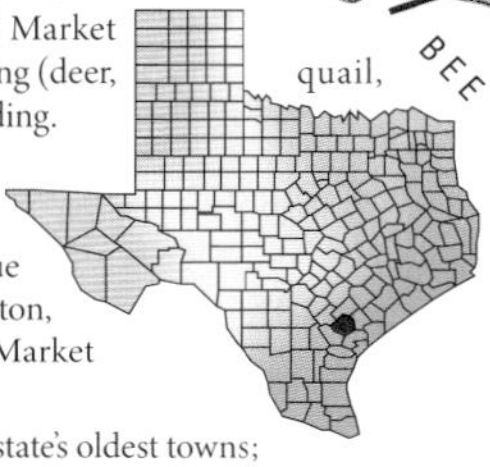

Minerals: Production of oil, gas.

Agriculture: Beef cattle, stocker operations and fed cattle are top revenue producers; corn, grain sorghum, cotton, hay; minor irrigation for pasture. Market value $17.7 million. Hunting leases.

GOLIAD (2,089) county seat; one of state's oldest towns; power plant; tourism; library; Zaragoza Birthplace State Historic Site, statue; Goliad Massacre re-enactment in March, Diez y Seis celebration in September.

Other towns include: **Berclair** (253), **Fannin** (359), and **Weesatche** (411).

Population	**8,007**	July mean max (°F)	93.8
Change from 2010 (%)	11.1	Civ. Labor	3,176
Area (sq. mi.)	859.4	Unemployed (%)	7.4
Land Area (sq. mi.)	852.0	Wages	$13,455,766
Altitude (ft.)	50–420	Per Capita Income	$45,589
Rainfall (in.)	36.8	Prop. Value	$2,984,681,304
Jan. mean min (°F)	42.5	Retail Sales	$45,043,367

Shops on a street in Pampa, the county seat of Gray County. Photo by Charles Henry, CC 2/Wikimedia Commons

Gonzales County

Physical Features: South central county; rolling, rich bottom soils along Guadalupe River and its tributaries; Lake Gonzales; some sandy areas; many oaks, pecans.

Economy: Agribusiness, hunting leases.

History: Coahuiltecan tribal area. Among the first Anglo-American settlements was the DeWitt colony in the late 1820s. County created in 1836; organized in 1837; named for Coahuila y Texas Gov. Rafael Gonzales.

Race/Ethnicity: Anglo, 40.2%; Black, 6.4%; Hispanic, 51.8%; Asian, 0.3%; Other, 1.1%.

Vital Statistics, annual: Births, 342; deaths, 187; marriages, 109; divorces, 56.

Recreation: Historic sites, homes, Pioneer Village Living History Center, Palmetto State Park, museums, Independence Park.

Minerals: Gas, oil, clay, gravel.

Agriculture: Second in poultry and egg production, cattle; hay, corn, sorghum, pecans, mushrooms. Market value $560.8 million.

GONZALES (7,576) county seat; first shot in Texas Revolution fired here; cattle ranching, chicken farming; hospital, college extensions; pioneer village; "Come and Take It" festival in October.

Other towns include: **Belmont** (55); **Cost** (84) First Shot monument; **Harwood** (118); **Leesville** (152); **Nixon** (2,505) poultry-processing plant, Feather Fest in September; **Ottine** (80); **Smiley** (571); **Waelder** (1,144) Guacamole Fest in September; **Wrightsboro** (10).

For explanation of sources, symbols and abbreviations, see p. 204, and foldout map.

Population	**20,769**	July mean max (°F)	94.2
Change from 2010 (%)	4.9	Civ. Labor	9,701
Area (sq. mi.)	1,069.9	Unemployed (%)	4.6
Land Area (sq. mi.)	1,066.7	Wages	$88,120,341
Altitude (ft.)	200–562	Per Capita Income	$44,789
Rainfall (in.)	34.9	Prop. Value	$6,595,404,327
Jan. mean min (°F)	39.9	Retail Sales	$259,124,002

Gray County

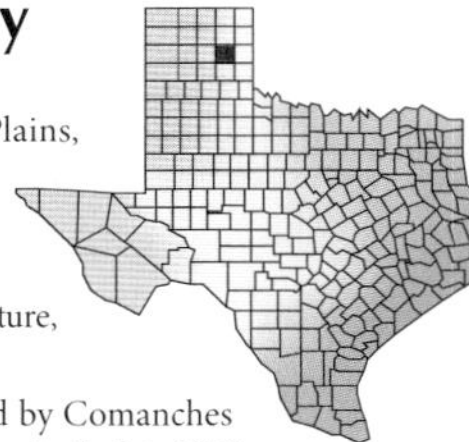

Physical Features: High Plains, broken by Red River forks, tributaries; sandy loam, waxy soils.

Economy: Petroleum, agriculture, government/services.

History: Apaches, displaced by Comanches and Kiowas. Ranching began in the late 1870s. Farmers arrived around 1900. Oil discovered in 1926. County created in 1876 from Bexar District; organized in 1902; named for Peter W. Gray, member of first Legislature.

Race/Ethnicity: Anglo, 60.7%; Black, 4.6%; Hispanic, 31.8%; Asian, 0.4%; Other, 2.3%.

Vital Statistics, annual: Births, 338; deaths, 267; marriages, 150; divorces, 72.

Recreation: Water sports, Lake McClellan and grassland; White Deer Land Museum, barbed-wire museum; Top of Texas livestock show in January.

Minerals: Natural gas, oil.

Agriculture: Cattle, hogs, wheat, cotton, corn, sorghum, hay, milk. Market value $154.6 million.

PAMPA (17,277) county seat; petroleum, agriculture; hospital; college; prison; Woody Guthrie museum; Mud Bog car show in June.

Other towns include: **Alanreed** (48); **Lefors** (474); **McLean** (747) commercial center for southern part of county.

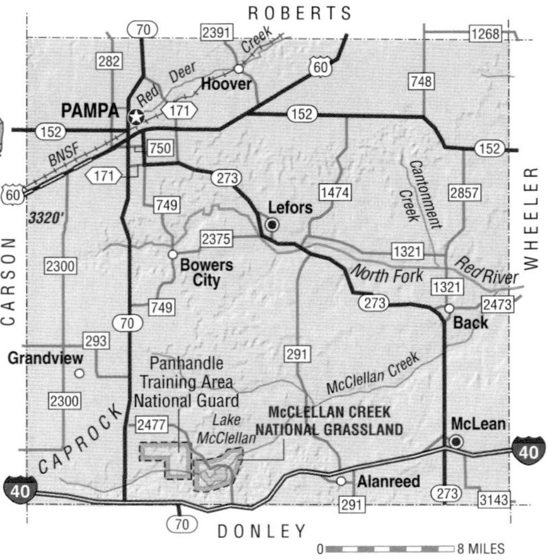

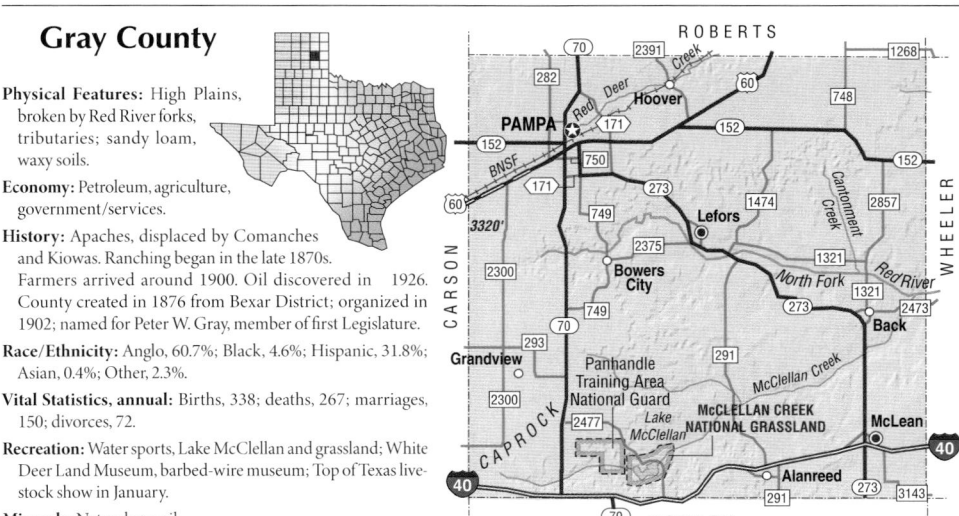

Population	**21,930**	July mean max (°F)	91.4
Change from 2010 (%)	-2.7	Civ. Labor	7,454
Area (sq. mi.)	929.3	Unemployed (%)	7.6
Land Area (sq. mi.)	926.0	Wages	$92,193,428
Altitude (ft.)	2,450–3,320	Per Capita Income	$44,127
Rainfall (in.)	23.2	Prop. Value	$2,317,377,470
Jan. mean min (°F)	23.3	Retail Sales	$352,409,801

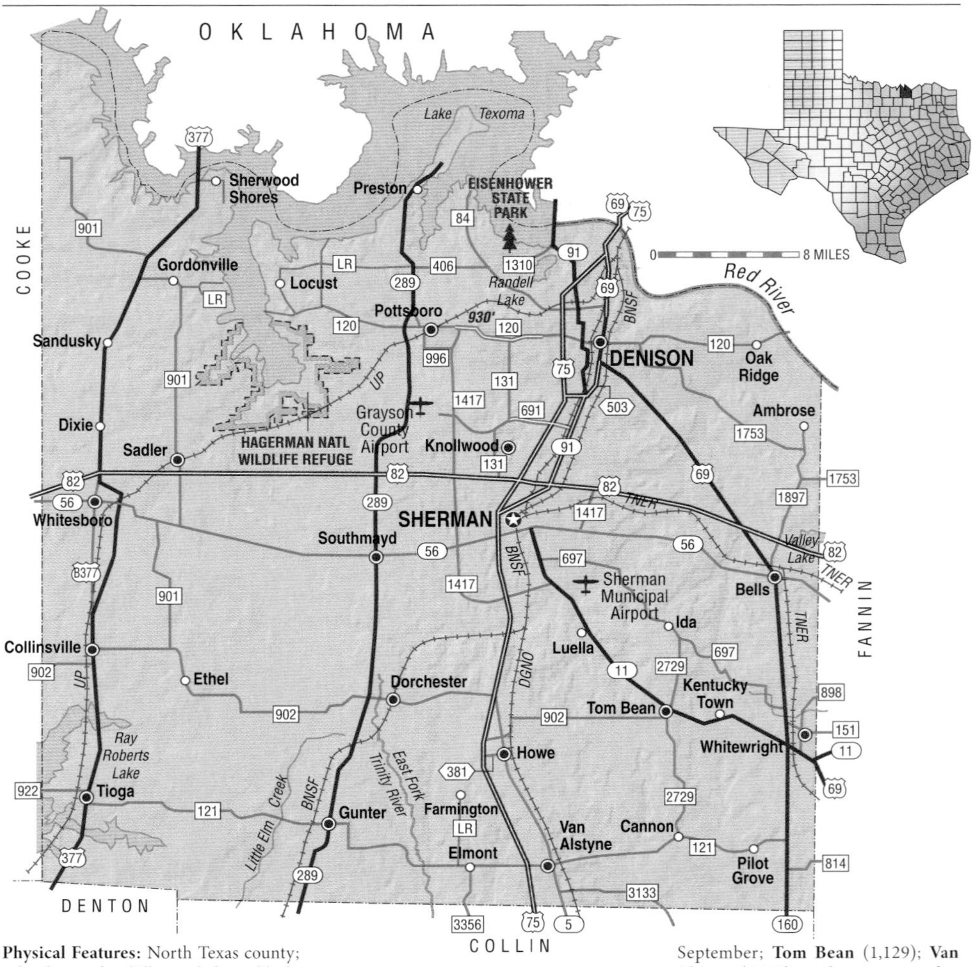

Grayson County

Physical Features: North Texas county; level, some low hills; sandy loam, blackland soils; drains to Red River and tributaries of Trinity River; Lake Texoma, Ray Roberts Lake, Valley Lake, Randell Lake.

Economy: A manufacturing, distribution and trade center for northern Texas and southern Oklahoma; nature tourism, mineral production.

History: Caddo and Tonkawa area. Preston Bend trading post established 1836-1837. Peters colony settlers arrived in the 1840s. County created in 1846 from Fannin County, organized the same year; named for Republic Attorney General Peter W. Grayson.

Race/Ethnicity: Anglo, 75%; Black, 5.7%; Hispanic, 13.8%; Asian, 1%; Other, 4.3%.

Vital Statistics, annual: Births, 1,579; deaths, 1,461; marriages, 919; divorces, 178.

Recreation: Lakes, fishing, hunting, water sports, state park, cultural activities, Hagerman National Wildlife Refuge, Pioneer Village, railroad museum.

Minerals: Oil, gas, gravel, sand.

Agriculture: Wheat, corn, hay, beef cattle, horses. Market value $66.2 million.

Education: Austin College in Sherman and Grayson County College located between Sherman and Denison.

SHERMAN (44,113) county seat; varied manufacturing, processors and distributors for major companies; Austin College; hospital.

DENISON (25,402) health care, manufacturing, retail center; hospital; Eisenhower birthplace, air force base museum; Main Street Fall festival in October.

Other towns include: **Bells** (1,542); **Collinsville** (1,934); **Dorchester** (167); **Gordonville** (165); **Gunter** (1,660); **Howe** (3,391) manufacturing, agriculture, trucking services, library, Founders' Day in May; **Knollwood** (591); **Pottsboro** (2,479) lake activities, marinas, education, Frontier Days in September; **Sadler** (341).

Also: **Southmayd** (1,122); **Tioga** (1,141) Gene Autry museum, festival in September; **Tom Bean** (1,129); **Van Alstyne** (4,449) retail center, manufacturing, government/services, museum, Grayson County College-South Campus, Fall Der All in October; **Whitesboro** (4,075) agribusiness, tourism, manufacturing, library, Peanut Festival in October; **Whitewright** (1,721) government/services, retail, manufacturing, museum, truck & tractor pull in June.

Population	**135,612**
Change from 2010 (%)	12.2
Area (sq. mi.)	979.2
Land Area (sq. mi.)	932,8
Altitude (ft.)	500–930
Rainfall (in.)	43.6
Jan. mean min (°F)	33.1
July mean max (°F)	92.1
Civ. Labor	64,881
Unemployed (%)	4.8
Wages	$614,290,578
Per Capita Income	$43,987
Prop. Value	$18,607,634,688
Retail Sales	$2,194,234,733

Gregg County

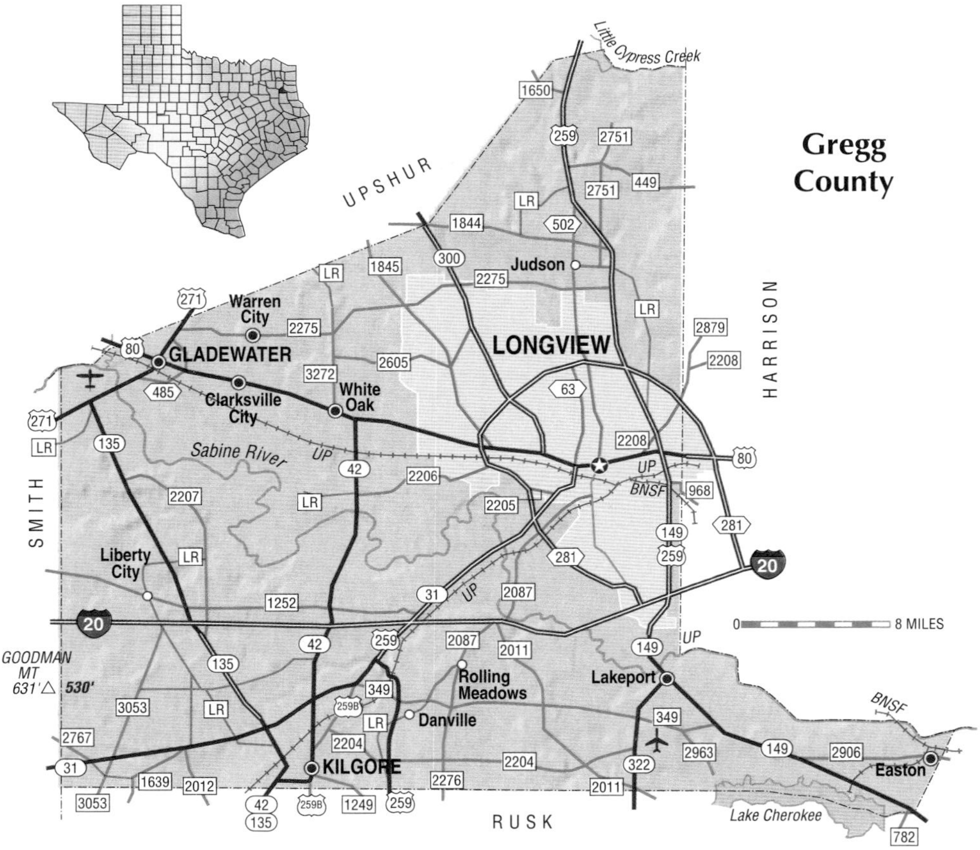

Physical Features: A populous, leading petroleum county, heart of the famed East Texas oil field; bisected by the Sabine River; hilly, timbered; with sandy, clay, alluvial soils.

Economy: Oil but with significant other manufacturing; tourism, conventions, agribusiness, and lignite coal production.

History: Caddoes; later Cherokees, who were driven out in 1838 by President Lamar. First land grants issued in 1835 by Republic of Mexico. County created and organized in 1873 from Rusk, Upshur counties; named for Confederate Gen. John Gregg. In U.S. censuses 1880-1910, blacks were more numerous than whites. Oil discovered in 1931.

Race/Ethnicity: Anglo, 56.6%; Black, 20.1%; Hispanic, 19.4%; Asian, 1.1%; Other, 2.5%.

Vital Statistics, annual: Births, 1,858; deaths, 1,274; marriages, 1,240; divorces, 416.

Recreation: Water activities on Lake Cherokee, hunting, varied cultural events, East Texas Oil Museum in Kilgore.

Minerals: Leading oil-producing county with more than 3 billion barrels produced since 1931; also, sand, gravel and natural gas.

Agriculture: Cattle, horses, hay, nursery crops. Market value $4.1 million. Timber sales.

LONGVIEW (83,749, small part [1,958] in Harrison County) county seat; chemical manufacturing, oil industry, distribution and retail center; hospitals; LeTourneau University, University of Texas-Tyler Longview center; convention center; balloon race in July.

Kilgore (14,329, part [3,515] in Rusk County), oil, distribution center; Kilgore College, Rangerette museum; Shakespeare festival in summer.

Gladewater (6,788, part [2,496] in Upshur County) oil, manufacturing, tourism, antiques; library, airport, skydiving; Gusher Days in April; daffodils in February-March.

Other towns include: **Clarksville City** (932); **Easton** (639, partly in Rusk County); **Judson** (1,057); **Lakeport** (1,051); **Liberty City** (2,624) oil, tourism, government/services, Honor America Night in November.

Also: **Warren City** (277); **White Oak** (6,570) oil and gas, commuting to Longview, Tyler; park, Roughneck Days in spring every three years.

Population	**126,116**
Change from 2010 (%)	3.6
Area (sq. mi.)	275.8
Land Area (sq. mi.)	273.3
Altitude (ft.)	240–530
Rainfall (in.)	48.1
Jan. mean min (°F)	34.2
July mean max (°F)	93.8
Civ. Labor	56,141
Unemployed (%)	7
Wages	$909,383,161
Per Capita Income	$47,109
Prop. Value	$11,982,080,454
Retail Sales	$3,205,849,271

For explanation of sources, symbols and abbreviations, see p. 204, and foldout map.

Grimes County

Physical Features: Rich bottom soils along Brazos, Navasota rivers; remainder hilly, partly forested; Gibbons Creek Reservoir.

Economy: Varied manufacturing, agribusiness, tourism.

History: Bidais (customs similar to the Caddoes) lived peacefully with Anglo-American settlers who arrived in 1820s, but tribe was removed to Indian Territory. Planter agriculture reflected in 1860 census, which listed 77 persons owning 20 or more slaves. County created from Montgomery County in 1846, organized the same year; named for Jesse Grimes, who signed Texas Declaration of Independence.

Race/Ethnicity: Anglo, 57.5%; Black, 15.2%; Hispanic, 24.5%; Asian, 0.2%; Other, 2.4%.

Vital Statistics, annual: Births, 328; deaths, 279; marriages, 139; divorces, 71.

Recreation: Hunting, fishing; Gibbons Creek Reservoir; historic sites; fall Renaissance Festival at Plantersville.

Minerals: Lignite coal, natural gas.

Agriculture: Cattle, forage, horses, poultry; berries, pecans, honey sales significant. Market value $47.5million. Some timber sold, Christmas tree farms.

ANDERSON (243) county seat; rural center; Fanthorp Inn historic site; Go-Texan weekend in February.

NAVASOTA (7,867) agribusiness center for parts of three counties; varied manufacturing; food, wood processing; hospital; prisons; La Salle statue; Blues Fest in August.

Other towns include: **Bedias** (474); **Iola** (435); **Plantersville** (869); **Richards** (300); **Roans Prairie** (64); **Shiro** (210); **Todd Mission** (117).

Population	**29,466**	July mean max (°F)	96.0
Change from 2010 (%)	10.8	Civ. Labor	10,978
Area (sq. mi.)	801.6	Unemployed (%)	7.1
Land Area (sq. mi.)	787.5	Wages	$96,278,105
Altitude (ft.)	150–470	Per Capita Income	$36,909
Rainfall (in.)	43.5	Prop. Value	$6,883,799,586
Jan. mean min (°F)	40.0	Retail Sales	$216,825,003

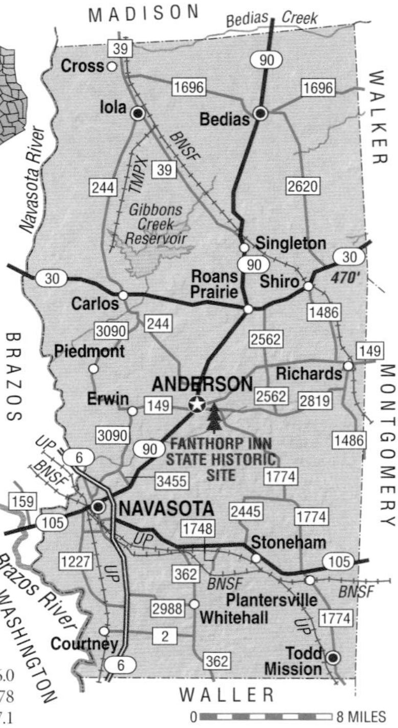

For explanation of sources, symbols and abbreviations, see p. 204, and foldout map.

The City Hall building in Navasota in Grimes County. Photo by Larry D. Moore, CC by SA 4.0/Wikimedia Commons

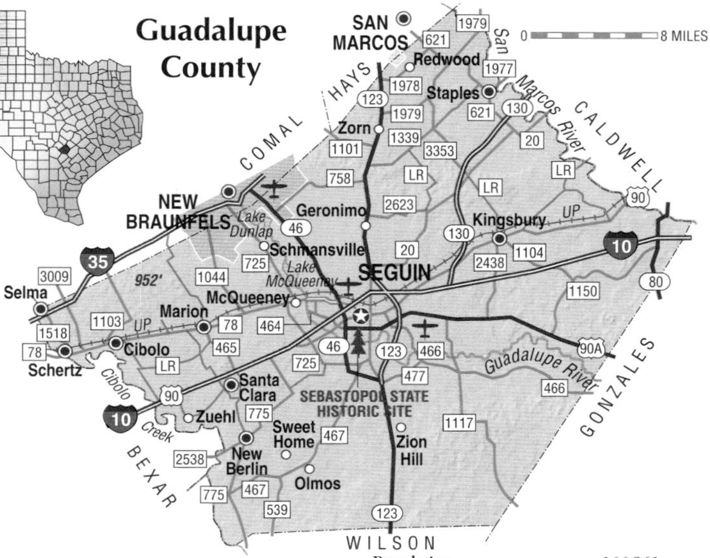

Physical Features: South central county bisected by Guadalupe River, Lake Dunlap, Lake McQueeney; level to rolling surface; sandy, loam, blackland soils.

Economy: Varied manufacturing, commuting to San Antonio, agribusiness.

History: Karankawas, Comanches, and other tribes until the 1850s. The first Spanish land grant was in 1806 to José de la Baume. DeWitt colonists arrived in 1827. County created, organized, in 1846 from Bexar, Gonzales counties; named for the river.

Race/Ethnicity: Anglo, 49.5%; Black, 7.8%; Hispanic, 38.8%; Asian, 1.4%; Other, 2.3%.

Vital Statistics, annual: Births, 1,838; deaths, 1,043; marriages, 578; divorces, 471.

Recreation: Fishing, hunting, river floating; Sebastopol House, other historic sites; river drive; Fiestas Juan Seguin in June, Diez y Seis in September in Seguin.

Minerals: Oil, gas, gravel, clays.

Agriculture: Cattle, corn, milo, wheat, cotton, hay, nursery crops, pecans. Market value $73.6 million.

SEGUIN (31,884) county seat; varied manufacturing/logistics, health care, government/services; hospital, museums, heritage village; Texas Lutheran University; Pecan Fest in late October.

Other towns include: **Cibolo** (31,951), **Geronimo** (1,374), **Kingsbury** (874), **Marion** (1,243), **McQueeney** (2,793), **New Berlin** (621), **Redwood** (4,219), **Santa Clara** (725), **Schertz** (42,709, parts in Bexar and Comal counties), **Staples** (272).

Also, part [15,408] of **New Braunfels**, part [2,612] of **Selma**, and a small part of **San Marcos**.

Population	**166,961**
Change from 2010 (%)	26.9
Area (sq. mi.)	714.8
Land Area (sq. mi.)	711.3
Altitude (ft.)	350–952
Rainfall (in.)	34.6
Jan. mean min (°F)	40.5
July mean max (°F)	95.2
Civ. Labor	82,056
Unemployed (%)	4.7
Wages	$543,634,031
Per Capita Income	$45,797
Prop. Value	$20,354,569,687
Retail Sales	$1,948,275,256

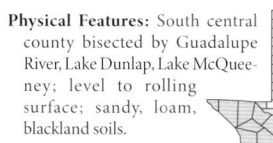

The Seguin Gazette building in Guadalupe County. The Gazette has been around since 1888 and publishes 5 days a week. Photo by Larry D. Moore, CC by SA 4.0/Wikimedia Commons

Hale County

Physical Features: High Plains; fertile sandy, loam soils; playas; large underground water supply.

Economy: Agribusiness, food processing/distribution, manufacturing, government/services.

History: Comanche hunters driven out by U.S. Army in 1875. Ranching began in 1880s. First motor-driven irrigation well drilled in 1911. County created from Bexar District in 1876; organized in 1888; named for Lt. J.C. Hale, who died at San Jacinto.

Race/Ethnicity: Anglo, 33%; Black, 5.4%; Hispanic, 59.3%; Asian, 0.4%; Other, 1.6%.

Vital Statistics, annual: Births, 483; deaths, 322; marriages, 223; divorces, 35.

Recreation: Llano Estacado Museum; art gallery, antiques stores; pheasant hunting; Cowboy Days in September at Plainview.

Minerals: Some oil.

Agriculture: Cotton, fed beef, sorghum, dairies, corn, vegetables, wheat. Market value $411.7 million. Irrigation of 200,000 acres.

PLAINVIEW (20,124) county seat; agriculture, distribution, corn milling; Wayland Baptist University, South Plains College branch; hospital, library, mental health center; prisons.

Hale Center (2,059) trade center; farm museum, library, parks, murals, cacti gardens.

Abernathy (2,699, part [752] in Lubbock County) government/services, farm supplies, textile plant, gins.

Other towns include: **Cotton Center** (300), **Edmonson** (101), **Petersburg** (1,108), **Seth Ward** (1,899).

Population	**33,165**	July mean max (°F)	91.0
Change from 2010 (%)	-8.6	Civ. Labor	11,818
Area (sq. mi.)	1,004.8	Unemployed (%)	6.4
Land Area (sq. mi.)	1,004.7	Wages	$125,039,648
Altitude (ft.)	3,180–3,620	Per Capita Income	$35,633
Rainfall (in.)	20.5	Prop. Value	$3,497,861,510
Jan. mean min (°F)	25.8	Retail Sales	$368,154,160

Hall County

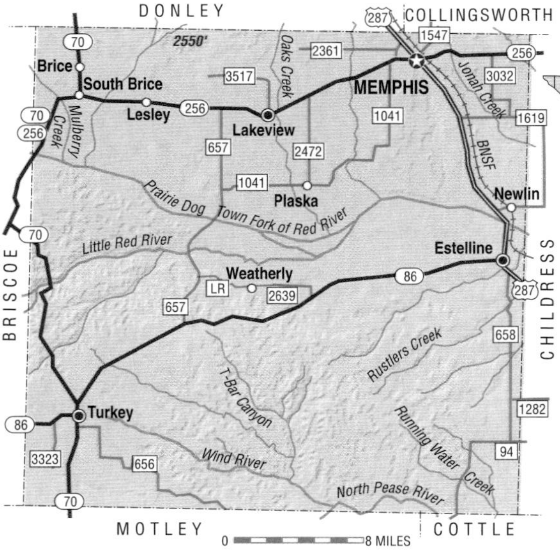

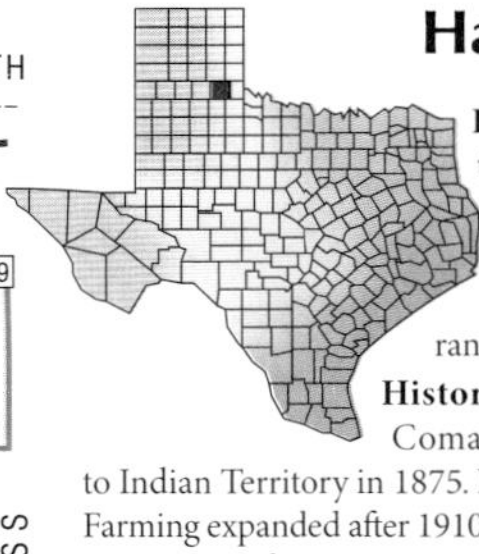

Physical Features: Rolling to hilly, broken by Red River forks, tributaries; red and black sandy loam.

Economy: Agriculture, farm/ranch supplies.

History: Apaches displaced by Comanches, who were removed to Indian Territory in 1875. Ranching began in the 1880s. Farming expanded after 1910. County created in 1876 from Bexar, Young districts; organized in 1890; named for Republic of Texas secretary of war W.D.C. Hall.

Race/Ethnicity: Anglo, 53.3%; Black, 9%; Hispanic, 36.4%; Asian, 0%; Other, 1%.

Vital Statistics, annual: Births, 22; deaths, 57;marriages, 0; divorces, 8.

Recreation: Hunting of deer, wild hog, dove; Rails to Trails system; Bob Wills museum; Memphis Picnic festival in September.

Minerals: None.

Agriculture: Cotton (lint and seed), beef cattle, hay, alfalfa, peanuts. Market value $56.4 million. Hunting leases important.

MEMPHIS (2,063) county seat; agriculture, foundry, trucking; historic buildings including Presbyterian church (1911); amphitheater built by WPA.

Other towns include: **Estelline** (131), motorcycle rally/chili cookoff in August, **Lakeview** (92), **Turkey** (375) Bob Wills Day in April.

Population	**3,017**	July mean max (°F)	95.7
Change from 2010 (%)	-10.0	Civ. Labor	1,110
Area (sq. mi.)	904.1	Unemployed (%)	5.8
Land Area (sq. mi.)	883.5	Wages	$6,856,184
Altitude (ft.)	1,750–2,550	Per Capita Income	$33,095
Rainfall (in.)	22.6	Prop. Value	$726,721,041
Jan. mean min (°F)	26.0	Retail Sales	$39,172,687

Hamilton County

Physical Features: Hilly north central county broken by scenic valleys; loam soils.

Economy: Varied manufacturing, agribusiness, hunting leases, tourism.

History: Waco and Tawakoni Indian area. Anglo-American settlers arrived in the mid-1850s. County created and organized in 1858, from Bosque, Comanche, Lampasas counties; named for South Carolina Gov. James Hamilton, who aided the Texas Revolution and Republic.

Race/Ethnicity: Anglo, 84.5%; Black, 0.4%; Hispanic, 13.3%; Asian, 0.3%; Other, 1.2%.

Vital Statistics, annual: Births, 92; deaths, 154; marriages, 50; divorces, 30.

Recreation: Deer, quail, dove hunting; Linear Pecan Creek park in Hamilton; old Bulman (bowstring) bridge over Leon River; Hamilton dove festival in October.

Minerals: Natural gas.

Agriculture: Beef, milk, hay. Market value $62.0 million. Hunting leases important.

HAMILTON (3,108) county seat; manufacturing, agribusiness; hospital and medical clinics; museum, historical homes.

Hico (1,428) tourism, agriculture, varied manufacturing; antiques shops, Billy the Kid museum; steak cookoff in May.

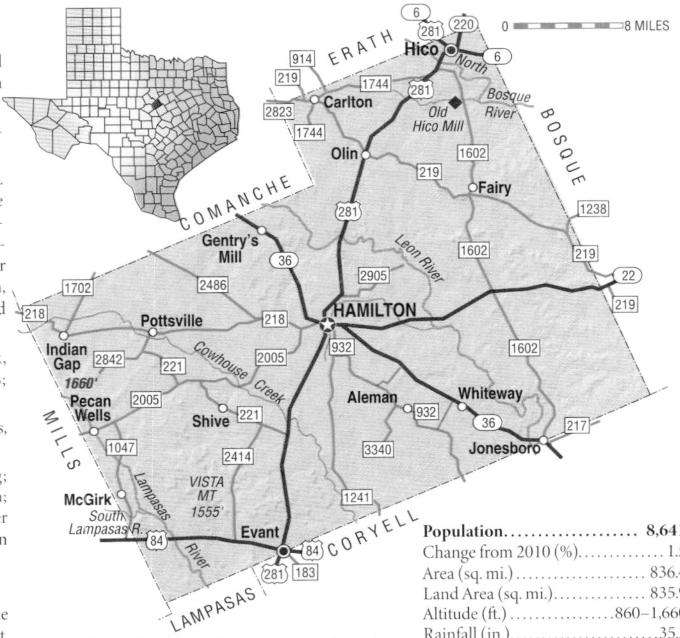

For explanation of sources, symbols and abbreviations, see p. 204, and foldout map.

Other towns include: **Carlton** (75), **Evant** (388, partly in Coryell County), **Jonesboro** (125, partly in Coryell County); **Pottsville** (105).

Population	**8,641**
Change from 2010 (%)	1.5
Area (sq. mi.)	836.4
Land Area (sq. mi.)	835.9
Altitude (ft.)	860–1,660
Rainfall (in.)	35.3
Jan. mean min (°F)	30.8
July mean max (°F)	94.0
Civ. Labor	3,743
Unemployed (%)	4.1
Wages	$29,356,682
Per Capita Income	$60,584
Prop. Value	$2,102,802,245
Retail Sales	$87,546,967

A scenic drive down State Highway 70 in Hall County. Photo by Leaflet, CC by SA 4.0/Wikimedia Commons

Hansford County

Physical Features: High Plains, many playas, creeks, draws; sandy, loam, black soils; underground water; Palo Duro Reservoir.

Economy: Agribusinesses; oil, gas operations; wind energy.

History: Apaches in area, later pushed out by Comanches around 1700. The U.S. Army removed the Comanches to the Indian Territory in 1874-1875, and ranching began soon afterward. Farmers, including Norwegians, moved in around 1900. County created in 1876, from the Bexar, Young districts and organized in 1889; named for jurist J.M. Hansford.

Race/Ethnicity: Anglo, 49%; Black, 0.5%; Hispanic, 48.7%; Asian, 0.3%; Other, 1.2%.

Vital Statistics, annual: Births, 75; deaths, 53; marriages, 45; divorces, 8.

Recreation: Stationmasters House Museum, hunting, lake activities, ecotourism, Lindbergh landing site.

Minerals: Production of gas, oil.

Agriculture: Large cattle-feeding operations; corn, wheat (first in acreage), sorghum; hogs. Substantial irrigation. Market value $737.4 million.

SPEARMAN (3,245) county seat; farming, cattle production, oil and gas, wind energy, biofuels; hospital, library, windmill collection; Heritage Days in May with rib cookoff.

Other towns include: **Gruver** (1,133) farm-ranch market, natural gas production, Fourth of July barbecue; **Morse** (112).

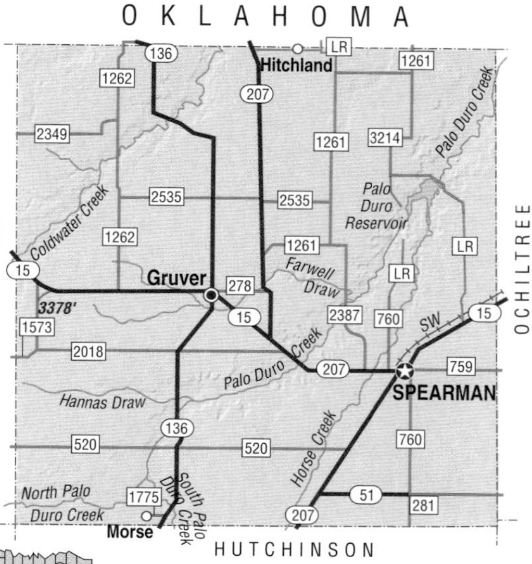

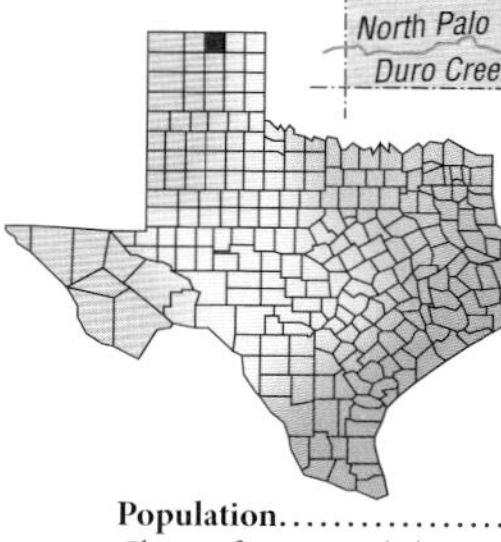

Population	**5,327**
Change from 2010 (%)	-5.1
Area (sq. mi.)	920.4
Land Area (sq. mi.)	919.8
Altitude (ft.)	2,750–3,378
Rainfall (in.)	21.2
Jan. mean min (°F)	24.8
July mean max (°F)	95.6
Civ. Labor	2,450
Unemployed (%)	3.1
Wages	$25,187,117
Per Capita Income	$65,330
Prop. Value	$1,198,317,431
Retail Sales	$63,123,741

Hardeman County

Physical Features: Rolling, broken area on divide between the Pease and Red rivers; Lake Pauline; sandy, loam soils.

Economy: Agriculture, gypsum production, oil and natural gas.

History: Apaches, later the semi-sedentary Wichitas and Comanche hunters. Ranching began in the late 1870s. Farming expanded after 1900. County created in 1858 from Fannin County; re-created in 1876, organized in 1884; named for pioneer brothers Bailey and T.J. Hardeman.

Race/Ethnicity: Anglo, 62.3%; Black, 6.3%; Hispanic, 28%; Asian, 0.3%; Other, 2.9%.

Vital Statistics, annual: Births, 52; deaths, 49; marriages, 165; divorces, 18.

Recreation: State park; lake activities; Medicine Mound aborigine gathering site; Quanah Parker monument; hunting of deer, quail, wild hogs.

Minerals: Oil, natural gas, gypsum.

Agriculture: Wheat, cattle, cotton. Market value $18.0 million. Hunting leases.

QUANAH (2,480) county seat; manufacturing, farming, ranching, oil and gas; state hospital, general hospital; historical sites; Fall Festival in September.

Other towns include: **Chillicothe** (665) farm market center, hospital.

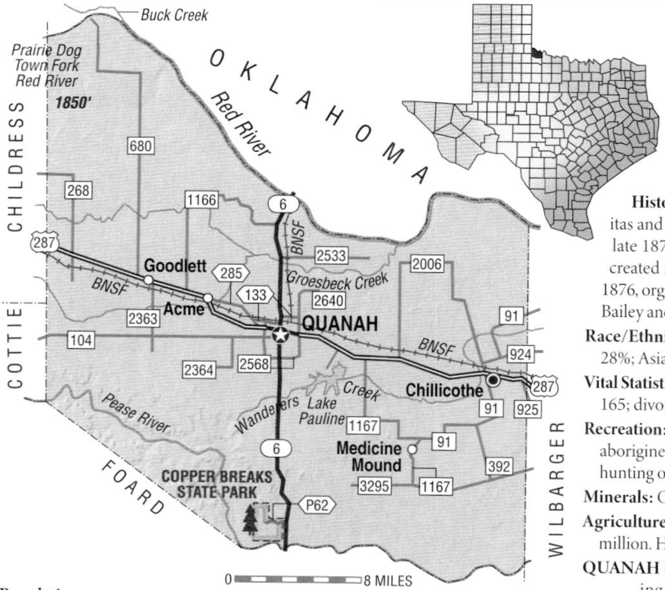

Population	**3,856**
Change from 2010 (%)	-6.8
Area (sq. mi.)	696.9
Land Area (sq. mi.)	695.1
Altitude (ft.)	1,250–1,850
Rainfall (in.)	26.9
Jan. mean min (°F)	26.2
July mean max (°F)	95.7
Civ. Labor	1,727
Unemployed (%)	4.2
Wages	$13,757,614
Per Capita Income	$42,023
Prop. Value	$1,122,416,897
Retail Sales	$57,513,675

Hardin County

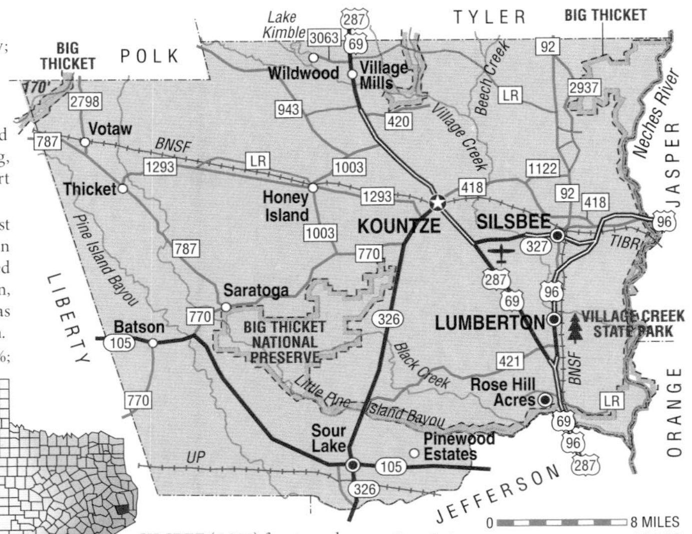

Physical Features: Southeast county; timbered; many streams; sandy, loam soils; Big Thicket covers much of area.

Economy: Paper manufacturing, wood processing, minerals, food processing, oil and gas; county in Beaumont-Port Arthur-Orange metropolitan area.

History: Lorenzo de Zavala received first land grant in 1829. Anglo-American settlers arrived in 1830. County created and organized in 1858 from Jefferson, Liberty counties. Named for Texas Revolutionary leader William Hardin.

Race/Ethnicity: Anglo, 87%; Black, 5.1%; Hispanic, 5.6%; Asian, 0.5%; Other, 1.6%.

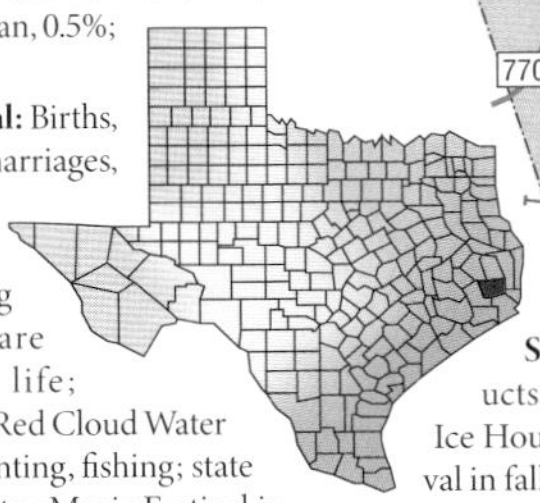

Vital Statistics, annual: Births, 696; deaths, 536; marriages, 390; divorces, 304.

Recreation: Big Thicket with rare plant, animal life; national preserve; Red Cloud Water Park in Silsbee; hunting, fishing; state park; Cajun Country Music Festival in October in Kountze.

Minerals: Oil, gas, sand, gravel.

Agriculture: Beef cattle, hay, blueberries, bees and rice. Market value 4.7 million. Timber provides most income; more than 85 percent of county forested. Hunting leases.

KOUNTZE (2,217) county seat; government/services, retail center, commuting to Beaumont; library, museum.

SILSBEE (6,805) forest products, rail center, oil, gas; library, Ice House museum; Dulcimer Festival in fall.

LUMBERTON (12,816) construction, government/services, tourism; library; Village Creek Festival in October.

Other towns and places include: **Batson** (140); **Pinewood Estates** (1,698); **Rose Hill Acres** (441); **Saratoga** (1,000) Big Thicket Museum; **Sour Lake** (1,944) oil, lumbering; Old Timer's Day in September; **Thicket** (306); **Village Mills** (200); **Votaw** (160), and **Wildwood** (1,173).

Population	**59,178**
Change from 2010 (%)	8.3
Area (sq. mi.)	897.6
Land Area (sq. mi.)	890.6
Altitude (ft.)	7–170
Rainfall (in.)	61.1
Jan. mean min (°F)	37.5
July mean max (°F)	93.6
Civ. Labor	25,218
Unemployed (%)	8
Wages	$159,016,943
Per Capita Income	$47,221
Prop. Value	$5,124,601,721
Retail Sales	$834,282,655

For explanation of sources, symbols and abbreviations, see p. 204, and foldout map.

A monument to Quanah Parker, who was appointed by the U.S. federal government as the chief of the Comanche nation. It stands on the grounds of the Hardeman County Courthouse. Photo by Billy Hathorn, CC 3/Wikimedia Commons

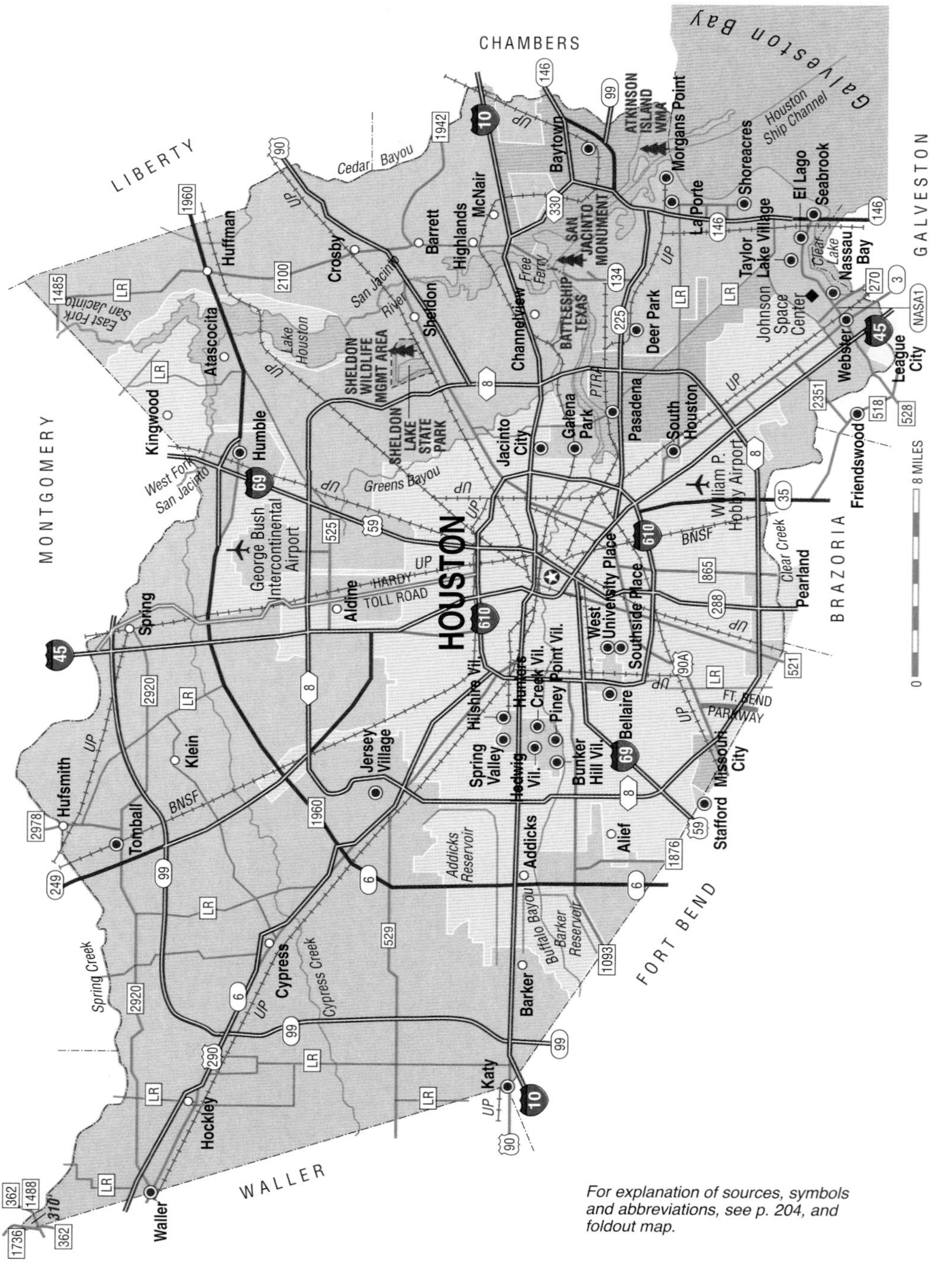

For explanation of sources, symbols and abbreviations, see p. 204, and foldout map.

Harris County

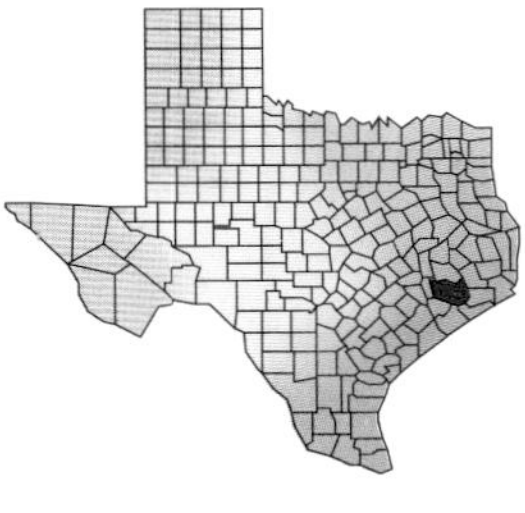

Physical Features: Largest county in eastern half of state; level; typically coastal surface and soils; many bayous, canals for artificial drainage; Lake Houston, Sheldon Reservoir; partly forested.

Economy: Highly industrialized county with largest population; more than 92 foreign governments maintain offices in Houston; corporate management center; nation's largest concentration of petrochemical plants; largest U.S. wheat-exporting port, among top U.S. ports in the value of foreign trade and total tonnage.

Petroleum refining, chemicals, food, fabricated metal products, non-electrical machinery, primary metals, scientific instruments; paper and allied products, printing and publishing; center for energy, space and medical research; center of international business.

History: Orcoquiza villages were visited by Spanish authorities in 1746. Pioneer settlers arrived by boat from Louisiana in 1822. Antebellum planters brought black slaves. Mexican migration increased after the Mexican Revolution. County created in 1836 and organized in 1837; named for John R. Harris, founder of Harrisburg (now part of Houston).

Race/Ethnicity: Anglo, 29.1%; Black, 18.5%; Hispanic, 42.6%; Asian, 7.4%; Other, 2.1%.

Vital Statistics, annual: Births, 73,427; deaths, 25,342; marriages, 29,882; divorces, 12,463.

Recreation: Professional baseball, basketball, football, soccer; rodeo and livestock show; Jones Hall for the Performing Arts; Nina Vance Alley Theatre; Convention Center; Toyota Center, a 19,000-seat sports and entertainment center; Reliant Stadium and downtown ballpark.

Sam Houston Park, with restored early Houston homes, church, stores; Museum of Fine Arts, Contemporary Arts Museum, Rice Museum; Wortham Theater; Hobby Center for Performing Arts; museum of natural science, planetarium, zoo in Hermann Park.

San Jacinto Battleground, Battleship Texas; Johnson Space Center.

Fishing, boating, other freshwater and saltwater activities.

Minerals: Among leading oil, gas, petrochemical areas; production of petroleum, cement, natural gas, salt, lime, sulfur, sand and gravel, clays, stone.

Agriculture: Nursery crops, grass (third in acreage of sod), cattle, hay, horses, vegetables, Christmas trees (first in acreage), goats, rice, corn. Market value $50.6 million. Substantial income from forest products.

Education: Houston is a major center of higher education, with more than 300,000 students enrolled in 28 colleges and universities in the county. Among these are Rice University, the University of Houston, Texas Southern University, University of St. Thomas, Houston Baptist University.

Medical schools include Houston Baptist University School of Nursing, University of Texas Health Science Center, Baylor College of Medicine, Institute of Religion and Human Development, Texas Chiropractic College, Texas Woman's University-Houston Center.

HOUSTON (2,325,298, small parts in Fort Bend and Montgomery counties) county seat; largest Texas city; fourth-largest in nation.

A leading center for manufacture of petroleum equipment, agricultural chemicals, fertilizers, pesticides, oil and gas pipeline transmission; a leading scientific center; manufacture of machinery, fabricated metals; a major distribution, shipping center; engineering and research center; food processing; 85 hospitals.

Plants make apparel, lumber and wood products; furniture, paper, chemical, petroleum and coal products; publishing center; one of the nation's largest public school systems; prominent corporate center; Go Texan Days (rodeo) in February/March, international festival in March/April.

PASADENA (156,841) residential city with large industrial area manufacturing petrochemicals and other petroleum-related products; civic center; San Jacinto College, Texas Chiropractic College; hospitals; historical museum; Strawberry Festival in May.

BAYTOWN (81,725, part [4,180] in Chambers County) refining, petrochemical center; commuters to Houston; Lee College; hospital, museum, library; historical homes; Chili When It's Chilly cookoff and the Great Bull Run in January.

The Clear Lake Area: which includes **El Lago** (2,680); **Nassau Bay** (4,095); **Seabrook** (14,059); **Taylor Lake Village** (3,594); **Webster** (11,989) — tourism, Johnson Space Center, University of Houston-Clear Lake, commuting to Houston; Bayport Industrial Complex includes Port of Bayport; 12 major marinas; hospitals; Christmas lighted boat parade.

Other towns include: **Aldine** (17,792); **Atascocita** (78,165); **Barrett** (3,483); **Bellaire** (18,283) residential city with several major office buildings; **Bunker Hill Village** (3,865); **Channelview** (46,373) hospital; **Crosby** (2,875) government/services, chemical plant, Czech Fest in October; **Cypress** (120,000); **Deer Park** (34,050) ship-channel industries, Totally Texas celebration in April; **Galena Park** (11,022); **Hedwig Village** (2,601); **Highlands** (7,793) commuters, heritage museum, Jamboree in October; **Hilshire Village** (793); **Hockley** (400); **Huffman** (15,000); **Humble** (15,704) oil-field equipment manufactured, retail center, hospital; **Hunters Creek Village** (4,738); **Jacinto City** (10,499); **Jersey Village** (7,907).

Also: **Katy** (21,912, partly in Fort Bend and Waller counties) corporate headquarters, distribution center, hospitals; museums, park; Rice Harvest festival in October; **Klein** (45,000); **La Porte** (34,757) petrochemical industry; depot museum; Sylvan Beach Festival in April; Galveston Bay; **Morgan's Point** (358); **Piney Point Village** (3,338); **Sheldon** (2,157); **Shoreacres** (1,580); **South Houston** (17,674).

Also: **Southside Place** (1,867); **Spring** (68,450); **Spring Valley** (4,248); **Tomball** (11,754) health care, oil and gas, retail, hospital, museum, junior college, parks and nature preserve, German festival in March; **West University Place** (15,699).

Parts of **Friendswood, League City, Missouri City, Pearland, Stafford,** and **Waller.**

Addicks, Alief, and Kingwood are now within the city limits of Houston.

Population	**4,698,655**
Change from 2010 (%)	14.8
Area (sq. mi.)	1,777.5
Land Area (sq. mi.)	1,703.5
Altitude (ft.)	sea level–310
Rainfall (in.)	56.8
Jan. mean min (°F)	43.4
July mean max (°F)	90.7
Civ. Labor	2,280,347
Unemployed (%)	7.1
Wages	$43,242,163,732
Per Capita Income	$60,002
Prop. Value	$720,163,806,322
Retail Sales	$90,436,159,789

Harrison County

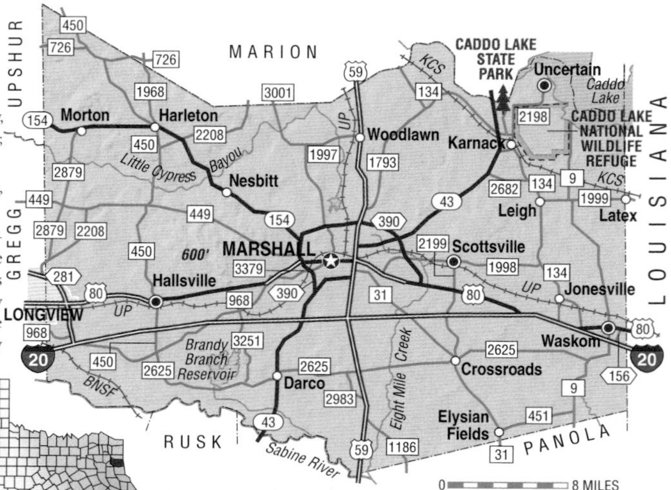

Physical Features: East Texas county; hilly, rolling; over half forested; Sabine River; Caddo Lake, Brandy Branch Reservoir.

Economy: Oil, gas processing, lumbering, pottery, other varied manufacturing.

History: Area was populated by agriculturist Caddo Indians whose numbers were reduced by disease. Anglo-Americans arrived in the 1830s. In 1850, the county had more slaves than any other in the state. County created in 1839 from Shelby County; organized in 1842. Named for eloquent advocate of the Texas Revolution, Jonas Harrison.

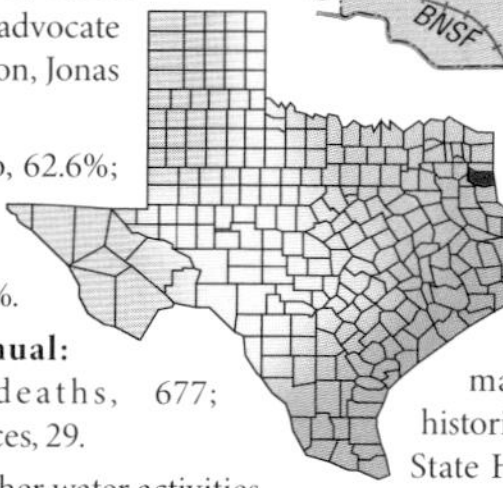

Race/Ethnicity: Anglo, 62.6%; Black, 20.8%; Hispanic, 13.9%; Asian, 0.5%; Other, 2%.

Vital Statistics, annual: Births, 826; deaths, 677; marriages, 420; divorces, 29.

Recreation: Fishing, other water activities on Caddo and other lakes; hunting; plantation homes, historic sites; Stagecoach Days in May; Old Courthouse Museum; Old World Store; state park, performing arts; Fire Ant festival in October.

Minerals: Oil, gas, lignite coal, clays, sand and gravel.

Agriculture: Cattle, hay. Also, poultry, nursery plants, horses, vegetables, watermelons. Market value $15.8 million. Hunting leases important. Substantial timber industry.

MARSHALL (23,950) county seat; petroleum and lumber processing, varied manufacturing; civic center; historic sites, including Starr Family State Historic Site; hospital; Wiley College, East Texas Baptist University; Wonderland of Lights in December.

Other towns include: **Elysian Fields** (500); **Hallsville** (4,344) government/services, utilities, Western Days in October, museum; **Harleton** (390); **Jonesville** (70); **Karnack** (350); **Nesbitt** (262); **Scottsville** (391); **Uncertain** (97) tourism, fishing, hunting, Mayhaw Festival in May; **Waskom** (2,263) oil, gas, ranching, Armadillo Daze in April; **Woodlawn** (550).

Also, part [1,958] of **Longview.**

For explanation of sources, symbols and abbreviations, see p. 204, and foldout map.

Population	**68,559**
Change from 2010 (%)	4.5
Area (sq. mi.)	915.8
Land Area (sq. mi.)	900.0
Altitude (ft.)	168–600
Rainfall (in.)	50.2
Jan. mean min (°F)	35.3
July mean max (°F)	92.3
Civ. Labor	28,683
Unemployed (%)	7.2
Wages	$308,223,278
Per Capita Income	$42,891
Prop. Value	$8,759,938,099
Retail Sales	$682,662,605

A group of pronghorn in the Rita Blanca National Grassland, which dips into Hartley County. Photo by Larry Lamsa, CC 2/Wikimedia Commons

Hartley County

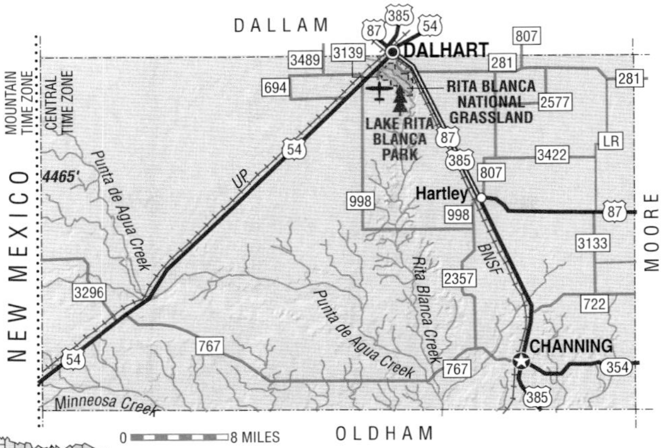

Physical Features: Panhandle High Plains; drains to Canadian River tributaries, playas; sandy, loam, chocolate soils; lake.

Economy: Agriculture, dairies, gas production.

History: Apaches in area, pushed out by Comanches around 1700. The U.S. Army removed the Indians in 1875. Pastores (sheepmen) were in area until the 1880s when cattle ranching began. Farming expanded after 1900. County created in 1876 from the Bexar, Young districts; organized in 1891; named for Texas pioneers O.C. and R.K. Hartley.

Race/Ethnicity: Anglo, 63.6%; Black, 7%; Hispanic, 27.6%; Asian, 0.5%; Other, 1.1%.

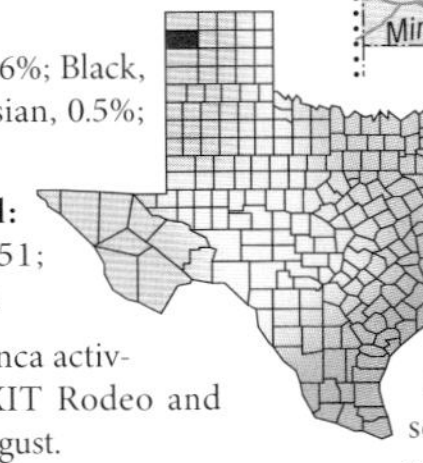

Vital Statistics, annual: Births, 54; deaths, 51; marriages, 1; divorces, 12.

Recreation: Lake Rita Blanca activities; ranch museum; XIT Rodeo and Reunion at Dalhart in August.

Minerals: Sand, gravel, natural gas.

Agriculture: Cattle, corn (second in acreage), wheat, hay, dairy cows, vegetables. 155,000 acres irrigated. Market value $1.2 billion. Hunting leases.

CHANNING (346) county seat, old XIT Ranch headquarters, Roundup in July.

DALHART (8,310, mostly in Dallam County), government/services; agribusiness center for parts of Texas, New Mexico, Oklahoma; railroad; cheese plant; grain operations; junior college branch; hospital; prison.

Also, **Hartley** (595).

Population	**5,861**
Change from 2010 (%)	-3.3
Area (sq. mi.)	1,463.2
Land Area (sq. mi.)	1,462.0
Altitude (ft.)	3,340–4,465
Rainfall (in.)	21.0
Jan. mean min (°F)	21.4
July mean max (°F)	91.6
Civ. Labor	2,620
Unemployed (%)	2.2
Wages	$31,957,981
Per Capita Income	$81,238
Prop. Value	$1,539,230,664
Retail Sales	$58,815,571

Haskell County

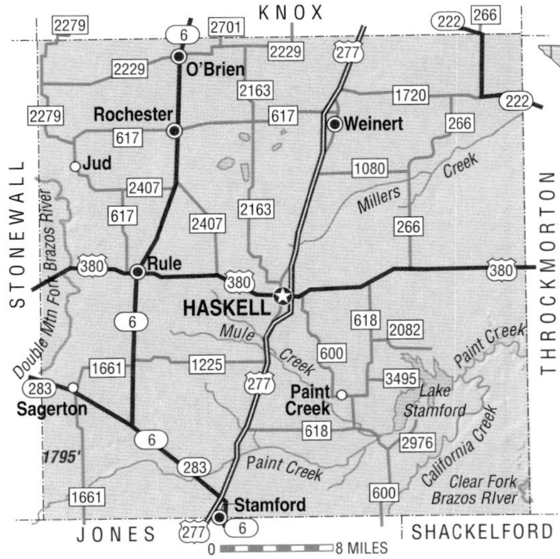

For explanation of sources, symbols and abbreviations, see p. 204, and foldout map.

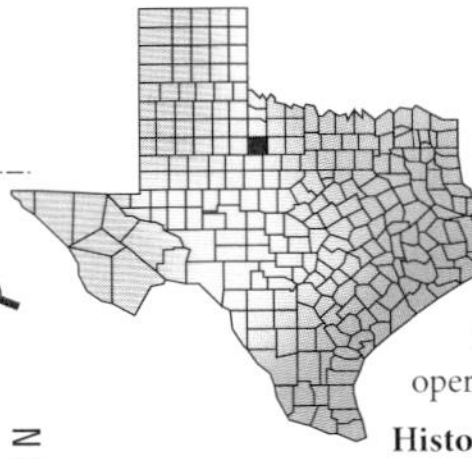

Physical Features: Northwest county; rolling; broken areas; drained by Brazos tributaries; lake; sandy loam, gray, black soils.

Economy: Agribusiness, oil-field operations.

History: Apaches until 1700, then a Comanche area. Ranching began in the late 1870s after the Indians were removed. Farming expanded after 1900. County created in 1858, from Milam and Fannin counties; re-created in 1876 and organized in 1885; named for Goliad victim C.R. Haskell.

Race/Ethnicity: Anglo, 63.3%; Black, 3.8%; Hispanic, 30.3%; Asian, 0.5%; Other, 1.8%

Vital Statistics, annual: Births, 57, deaths, 62; marriages, 42; divorces, 26.

Recreation: Lake Stamford activities, bass tournament in August; Haskell arts & crafts show in November; hunting of deer, geese, wild hogs.

Minerals: Oil and gas.

Agriculture: Wheat, cotton, peanuts; 28,000 acres irrigated. Beef cattle raised. Market value $54.3 million.

HASKELL (3,169) county seat; farming center; hospital; city park; Wild Horse Prairie Days in June.

Other towns include: **O'Brien** (101), **Rochester** (310), **Rule** (600) farming, cotton gins/warehouses, oil, mural, park, Trunk or Treat in October, **Weinert** (161).

Population	**5,628**
Change from 2010 (%)	-4.6
Area (sq. mi.)	910.3
Land Area (sq. mi.)	903.1
Altitude (ft.)	1,340–1,795
Rainfall (in.)	26.4
Jan. mean min (°F)	29.1
July mean max (°F)	94.9
Civ. Labor	2,795
Unemployed (%)	3.9
Wages	$20,983,594
Per Capita Income	$39,899
Prop. Value	$1,504,490,280
Retail Sales	$116,936,845

Physical Features: Hilly in west, blackland in east; bisected by Blanco River; on edge of Balcones Escarpment.

Economy: Education, tourism, retirement area, some manufacturing; part of Austin metropolitan area.

History: Tonkawa area, also some Apache and Comanche presence. Spanish authorities attempted the first permanent settlement in 1807. Mexican land grants in early 1830s to Juan Martín Veramendi, Juan Vicente Campos and Thomas Jefferson Chambers. County created in 1843 from Travis County, organized the same year; named for Capt. Jack Hays, a famous Texas Ranger.

Race/Ethnicity: Anglo, 53.7%; Black, 2.5%; Hispanic, 39.6%; Asian, 1.5%; Other, 2.3%.

Vital Statistics, annual: Births, 2,467; deaths, 1,007; marriages, 1,056; divorces, 527.

Recreation: Fishing, hunting; college cultural, athletic events; African-American museum, LBJ museum; Cypress Creek and Blanco River resorts, guest ranches, Wonder World park.

Minerals: Sand, gravel, cement produced.

Agriculture: Beef cattle, goats, exotic wildlife; greenhouse nurseries; hay, corn, sorghum, wheat and cotton. Market value $21.8 million.

SAN MARCOS (69,731) county seat; Texas State University, outlet center, tourism, distribution center, commuting; hospital; San Marcos, Blanco rivers; jazz festival in February, Mermaid Fest in September.

KYLE (47,899) medical, education, retail center, Claiborne Kyle Log House, Katherine Anne Porter House, 5k Kyle-O-Meter in October.

Other towns include: **Bear Creek** (466); **Buda** (17,862) construction, manufacturing, retail, government/services, Stagecoach park, Weiner Dog races in April; **Driftwood** (193); **Dripping Springs** (5,918); **Hays** (263); **Mountain City** (785); **Niederwald** (665, partly in Caldwell County); **Uhland** (1,355, partly in Caldwell County); **Wimberley** (3,170) tourism, retirement community, artists, historic homes, museum, Blue Hole park/swimming, Jacob's Well spring/natural area, art festival in April; **Woodcreek** (1,755).

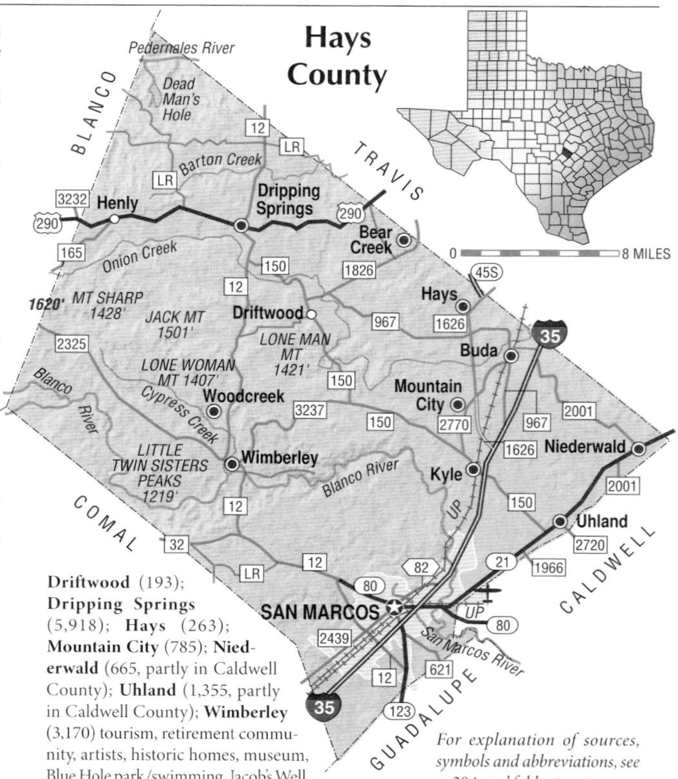

For explanation of sources, symbols and abbreviations, see p. 204, and foldout map.

Population	**228,364**	July mean max (°F)	94.3
Change from 2010 (%)	45.4	Civ. Labor	123,618
Area (sq. mi.)	679.9	Unemployed (%)	4.5
Land Area (sq. mi.)	678.0	Wages	$892,570,489
Altitude (ft.)	550–1,620	Per Capita Income	$45,332
Rainfall (in.)	35.7	Prop. Value	$33,283,505,777
Jan. mean min (°F)	38.7	Retail Sales	$5,134,061,990

An airplane at the Commemorative Air Force, Central Texas Wing hangar and museum, in San Marcos. Photo by Larry D. Moore, CC 3/ Wikimedia Commons

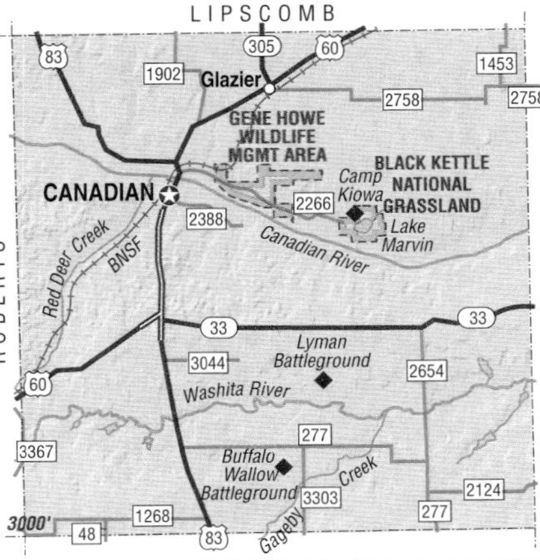

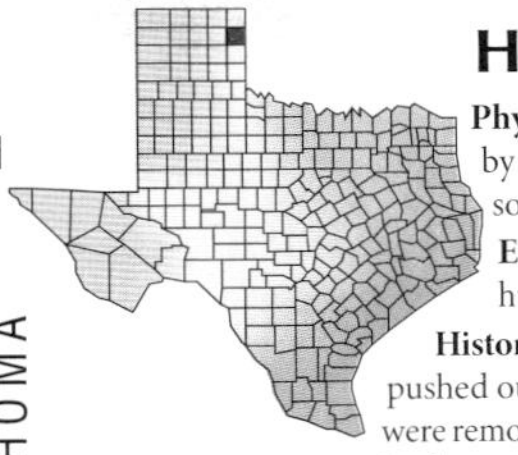

Hemphill County

Physical Features: Sloping surface, broken by Canadian, Washita rivers; sandy, red, dark soils.

Economy: Oil, gas, agriculture, tourism, hunting, government/services.

History: Apaches who were in the area were later pushed out by Comanches and Kiowas. The tribes were removed to the Indian Territory in 1875. Ranching began in the late 1870s. Farmers began to arrive after 1900. County created from the Bexar and Young districts in 1876 and organized in 1887; named for Republic of Texas Justice John Hemphill.

Race/Ethnicity: Anglo, 62%; Black, 0.1%; Hispanic, 36.4%; Asian, 0.3%; Other, 1%.

Vital Statistics, annual: Births, 76; deaths, 34; marriages, 47; divorces, 12.

Recreation: Lake Marvin; fall foliage tour; hunting, fishing; Indian Battleground, wildlife management area; museum; 4th of July rodeo; prairie chicken viewing in April.

Population	**3,838**
Change from 2010 (%)	0.8
Area (sq. mi.)	912.2
Land Area (sq. mi.)	906.3
Altitude (ft.)	2,170–3,000
Rainfall (in.)	21.8
Jan. mean min (°F)	21.2
July mean max (°F)	93.2
Civ. Labor	1,631
Unemployed (%)	4.5
Wages	$22,366,755
Per Capita Income	$57,053
Prop. Value	$1,466,667,565
Retail Sales	$29,647,534

Minerals: Oil, natural gas, caliche.

Agriculture: Cattle, wheat, horses, hay, alfalfa; some irrigation. Market value $138.9 million. Hunting, nature tourism.

CANADIAN (2,717) county seat; oil, gas production; hospital; art foundation.

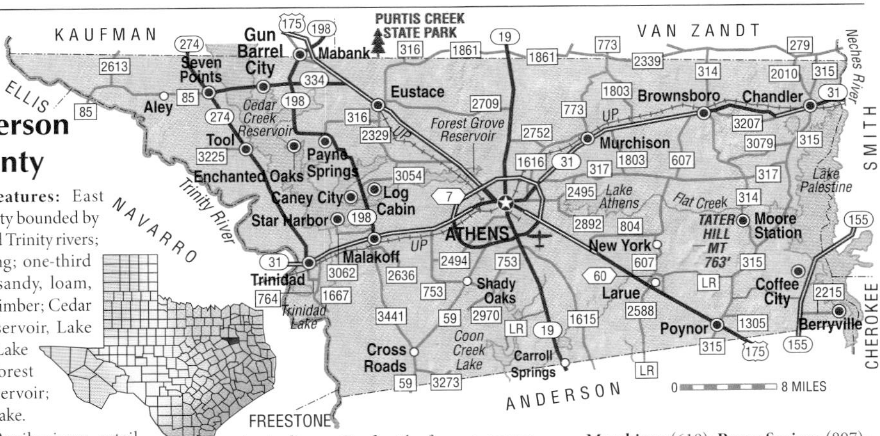

Henderson County

Physical Features: East Texas county bounded by Neches and Trinity rivers; hilly, rolling; one-third forested; sandy, loam, clay soils; timber; Cedar Creek Reservoir, Lake Palestine, Lake Athens, Forest Grove Reservoir; Trinidad Lake.

Economy: Agribusiness, retail trade, varied manufacturing, minerals, recreation, tourism.

History: Caddo tribal area. Cherokees and other tribes migrated into the area in 1819-1820 ahead of white settlement. Cherokees were forced into Indian Territory in 1839. Anglo-American settlers arrived in the 1840s. County created in 1846 from Nacogdoches and Houston counties; organized the same year. County named for Gov. J. Pinckney Henderson.

Race/Ethnicity: Anglo, 77.5%; Black, 6.6%; Hispanic, 13%; Asian, 0.4%; Other, 2.3%.

Vital Statistics, annual: Births, 897; deaths, 1,084; marriages, 503; divorces, 38.

Recreation: Cedar Creek Reservoir, Lake Palestine, other lakes; Purtis Creek State Park; hunting, fishing, bird-watching; aerial ropeslide at New York; East Texas Arboretum.

Minerals: Oil, gas, clays, lignite, sulfur, sand and gravel.

Agriculture: Beef cattle, forages, nurseries/horticulture, rodeo stock. Market value $40.2 million. Hunting leases and fishing. Timber important.

ATHENS (13,649) county seat; agribusiness center, varied manufacturing, tourism, state fish hatchery and museum, hospital, mental health center; Trinity Valley Community College; Texas Fiddlers' Contest in May.

GUN BARREL CITY (6,222) recreation, retirement, retail center.

MALAKOFF (2,434) brick factory, varied industry, tourism, library, Cornbread Festival in April.

Other towns include: **Berryville** (1,075); **Brownsboro** (1,286); **Caney City** (230); **Chandler** (3,259) commuting to Tyler, retail trade, tourism, Pow Wow Festival in October; **Coffee City** (1,504); **Enchanted Oaks** (344); **Eustace** (1,007); **Larue** (250); **Log Cabin** (780); **Moore Station** (214); **Murchison** (618); **Payne Springs** (807); **Poynor** (315); **Seven Points** (1,558) agribusiness, retail trade, recreation, Monte Carlo celebration in November; **Star Harbor** (495); **Tool** (2,374), and **Trinidad** (882).

Also, **Mabank** (3,995, mostly in Kaufman County).

Population	**82,989**
Change from 2010 (%)	5.7
Area (sq. mi.)	949.3
Land Area (sq. mi.)	873.8
Altitude (ft.)	256–763
Rainfall (in.)	42.9
Jan. mean min (°F)	34.5
July mean max (°F)	92.6
Civ. Labor	37,256
Unemployed (%)	5.6
Wages	$196,421,634
Per Capita Income	$40,135
Prop. Value	$10,514,070,328
Retail Sales	$938,607,129

Hidalgo County

Population	**886,294**
Change from 2010 (%)	14.4
Area (sq. mi.)	1,582.9
Land Area (sq. mi.)	1,570.9
Altitude (ft.)	28–376
Rainfall (in.)	22.2
Jan. mean min (°F)	49.3
July mean max (°F)	96.2
Civ. Labor	364,476
Unemployed (%)	10.3
Wages	$2,608,704,301
Per Capita Income	$27,415
Prop. Value	$51,843,534,647
Retail Sales	$11,054,150,664

Physical Features: Rich alluvial soils along Rio Grande; sandy, loam soils in north; semitropical vegetation; Anzalduas Channel Dam, Delta Lake, Valley Acres Reservoir.

Economy: Food processing and shipping, other agribusinesses, tourism, mineral operations; Texas' fifth-largest metro area.

History: Coahuiltecan and Karankawa area. Comanches forced Apaches southward into valley in the 1700s; Comanches arrived in valley in the 1800s. Spanish settlement occurred 1750-1800. County created in 1852 from Cameron and Starr counties, organized the same year; named for leader of Mexico's independence movement of 1810, Father Miguel Hidalgo y Costillo.

Race/Ethnicity: Anglo, 6.2%; Black, 0.3%; Hispanic, 92%; Asian, 1%; Other, 0.2%.

Vital Statistics, annual: Births, 16,325; deaths, 4,179; marriages, 4,783; divorces, 0.

Recreation: Winter resort, retirement area; fishing, hunting; gateway to Mexico; historical sites; Bentsen-Rio Grande Valley State Park; museums; All-Valley Winter Vegetable Show at Pharr.

Minerals: Oil, gas, stone, sand and gravel.

Agriculture: Ninety percent of farm cash receipts from crops (ranked first in state), principally from sugar cane (first in acreage), grain sorghum (first in acreage), vegetables (first in acreage), citrus, cotton; livestock includes cattle; 184,000 acres irrigated. Market value $311.0 million.

EDINBURG (99,454) county seat; vegetable processing and packing, petroleum operations, tourism, clothing; planetarium; the University of Texas-Rio Grande Valley; hospitals; behavioral, health center; museum; Texas Cook'em High Steaks July 4 weekend, Fiesta Edinburg in February.

McALLEN (144,785) retail center, medical care/hospitals, government/services; community college; birding center, Mxlan arts/music celebration of Mexican culture in late July.

MISSION (86,214) citrus groves, agricultural processing/distribution; hospital; community college; international butterfly park; Citrus Fiesta in January.

PHARR (81,473) agriculture, trading center; trucking; tourism; old clock, juke box museums; folklife festival in February.

Other towns include: **Abram** (2,461); **Alamo** (20,208) live steam museum; **Alton** (17,165); **Doffing** (5,722); **Donna** (17,235) citrus center, varied manufacturing; **Edcouch** (3,368); **Elsa** (7,174); **Granjeno** (320); **Hargill** (919); **Hidalgo** (13,984) trade zone, shipping, winter resort, agribusiness, historical sites, library, Borderfest in March; **La Blanca** (2,652); **La Homa** (12,102); **La Joya** (4,409); **La Villa** (2,544); **Los Ebanos** (313).

Also: Mercedes (17,096) "boot capital," citrus, and vegetable center, food processing, tourism, recreation vehicle show in January, Hispanic Fest July 4; **Mila Doce** (6,778); **Monte Alto** (1,976); **North Alamo** (3,926); **Murillo** (9,095); **Palmhurst** (2,737); **Palmview** (10,829); **Palmview South** (6,064); **Peñitas** (4,721); **Perezville** (6,022); **Progreso** (6,073); **Progreso Lakes** (268); **San Carlos** (3,486); **San Juan** (38,033) retirement area, trucking, Shrine of Our Lady of San Juan, Spring Fiesta in February; **San Manuel-Linn** (787); **South Alamo** (3,589); **Sullivan City** (4,273); **Weslaco** (42,047) agriculture, nature tourism, South Texas College, hospital, Dragonfly Days in May.

For explanation of sources, symbols and abbreviations, see p. 204, and foldout map.

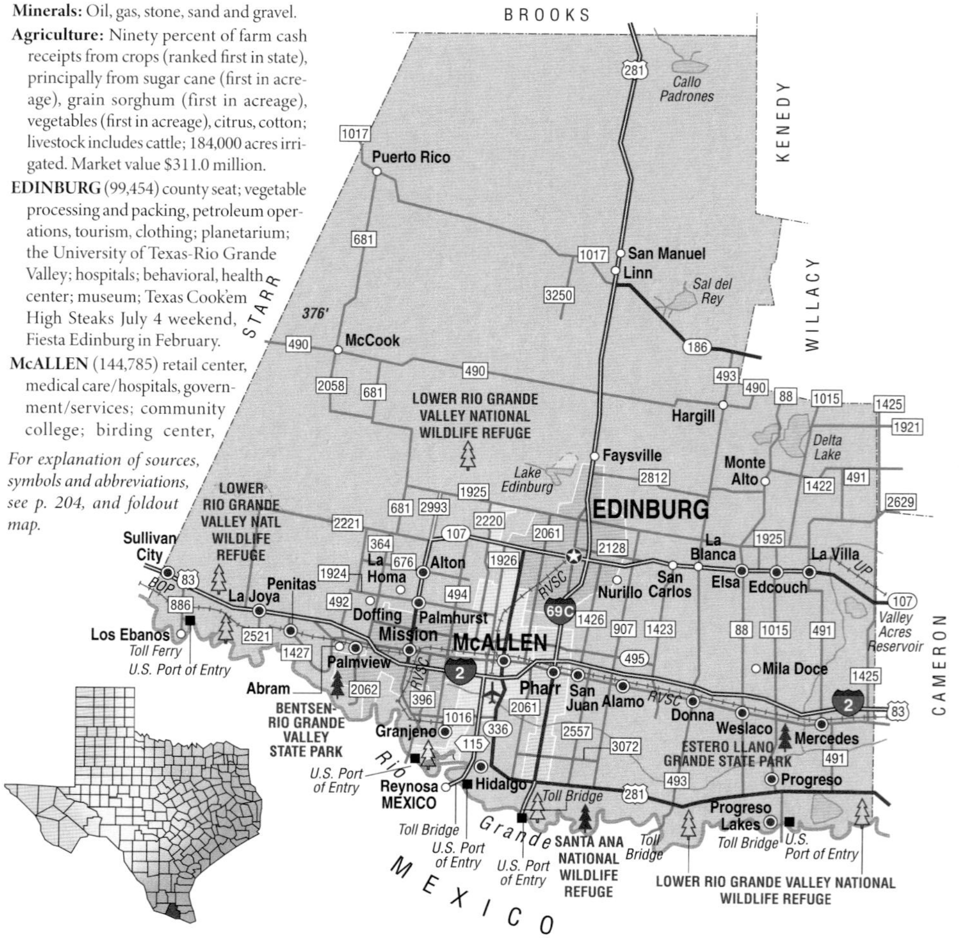

The old Hidalgo County jail in Edinburg. Photo by Larry D. Moore, CC by 4.0/Wikimedia Commons

Hill County

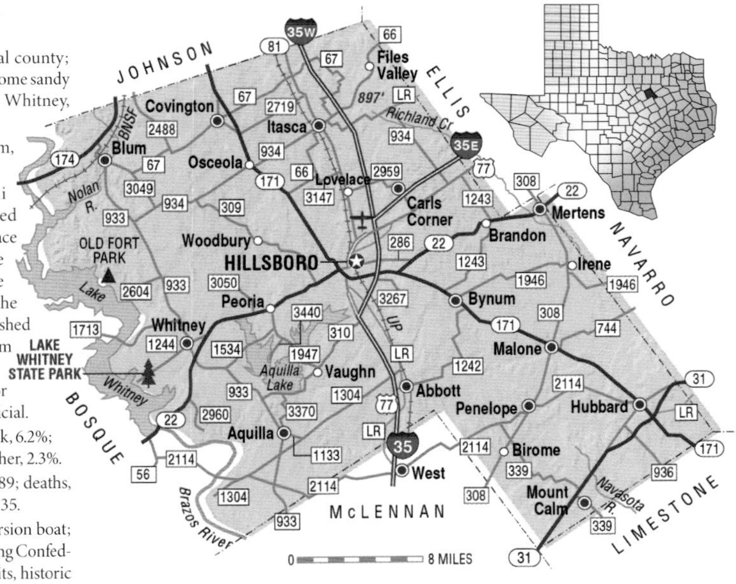

Physical Features: North central county; level to rolling; blackland soils, some sandy loams; drains to Brazos; Lake Whitney, Aquilla Lake.

Economy: Agribusiness, tourism, varied manufacturing.

History: Waco and Tawakoni area, later Comanches. Believed to be Indian "council spot," a place of safe passage without evidence of raids. Anglo-Americans of the Robertson colony arrived in the early 1830s. Fort Graham established in 1849. County created from Navarro County in 1853, organized the same year; named for G.W. Hill, Republic of Texas official.

Race/Ethnicity: Anglo, 69%; Black, 6.2%; Hispanic, 22%; Asian, 0.3%; Other, 2.3%.

Vital Statistics, annual: Births, 389; deaths, 455; marriages, 233; divorces, 135.

Recreation: Lake activities; excursion boat; Texas Heritage Museum including Confederate and Audie Murphy exhibits, historic structures, rebuilt frontier fort barracks; motorcycle track.

Minerals: Gas, limestone.

Agriculture: Corn, cattle, sorghum, wheat, cotton, dairies, turkeys. Market value $114.0 million. Some firewood marketed.

HILLSBORO (8,767) county seat; agribusiness, varied manufacturing, retail, outlet center, tourism, antiques malls; Hill College; hospital; Cell Block museum, restored courthouse; Cotton Pickin Fair in September.

WHITNEY (2,202) manufacturing, stone works, government/services; hospital; museum; Pioneer Days in October.

Other towns include: **Abbott** (375); **Aquilla** (114); **Blum** (471); **Brandon** (75); **Bynum** (210); **Carl's Corner** (187); **Covington** (276); **Hubbard** (1,405) agriculture, machine shop, antiques, museum, library, Magnolias & Mistletoe Victorian Christmas celebration; **Irene** (170); **Itasca** (1,761); **Malone** (279); **Mertens** (131); **Mount Calm** (336); **Penelope** (207).

Population	**37,069**
Change from 2010 (%)	5.6
Area (sq. mi.)	985.7
Land Area (sq. mi.)	958.9
Altitude (ft.)	417–897
Rainfall (in.)	37.9
Jan. mean min (°F)	34.8
July mean max (°F)	95.0
Civ. Labor	16,143
Unemployed (%)	5.6
Wages	$122,380,429
Per Capita Income	$41,240
Prop. Value	$5,017,877,080
Retail Sales	$404,487,424

Hockley County

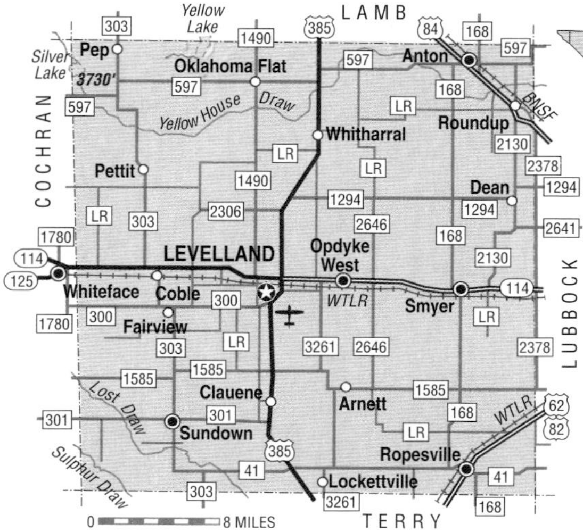

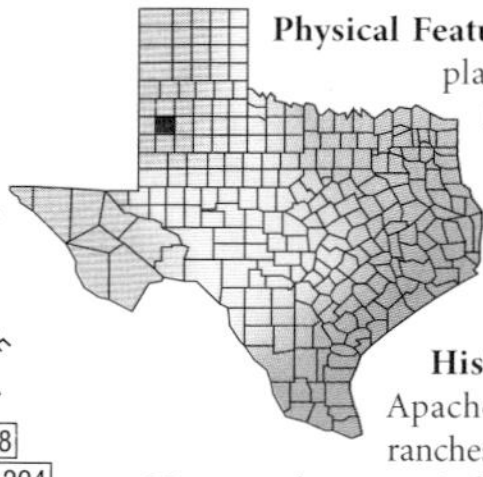

Physical Features: South Plains, numerous playas, drains to Yellow House Draw; loam, sandy loam soils.

Economy: Extensive oil, gas production and services; manufacturing; varied agribusiness.

History: Comanches displaced Apaches in the early 1700s. Large ranches of 1880s brought few residents. Homesteaders arrived after 1900. County created in 1876 from Bexar, Young districts; organized in 1921. Named for the Republic of Texas secretary of war Gen. G.W. Hockley.

Race/Ethnicity: Anglo, 44.4%; Black, 3.9%; Hispanic, 49.7%; Asian, 0.3%; Other, 1.5%.

Vital Statistics, annual: Births, 335; deaths, 224; marriages, 129; divorces, 79.

Recreation: Early Settlers' Day in July; Marigolds Arts, Crafts Festival in November.

Minerals: Oil, gas, stone; one of leading oil counties with more than 1 billion barrels produced.

Agriculture: Cotton, grain sorghum; cattle, hogs raised; substantial irrigation. Market value $92.0 million.

LEVELLAND (13,555) county seat; oil, cotton, cattle center; government/services; hospital; South Plains College; Hot Burrito & Bluegrass Music Festival in July.

Other towns include: **Anton** (1,100); **Opdyke West** (196); **Pep** (30); **Ropesville** (430); **Smyer** (477); **Sundown** (1,422); **Whitharral** (158).

Population	**22,862**
Change from 2010 (%)	-0.3
Area (sq. mi.)	908.6
Land Area (sq. mi.)	908.4
Altitude (ft.)	3,300–3,730
Rainfall (in.)	19.8
Jan. mean min (°F)	26.1
July mean max (°F)	91.6
Civ. Labor	10,275
Unemployed (%)	7.0
Wages	$118,438,810
Per Capita Income	$42,162
Prop. Value	$3,298,901,811
Retail Sales	$249,333,994

Hood County

Physical Features: Hilly; broken by Paluxy, Brazos rivers; sandy loam soils; Lake Granbury, Squaw Creek Reservoir.

Economy: Tourism, commuting to Fort Worth and Dallas, nuclear power plant, agriculture.

History: Lipan Apache and Comanche area. Anglo-American settlers arrived in the late 1840s. County created in 1866 from Johnson and Erath counties, organized the same year; named for Confederate Gen. John B. Hood.

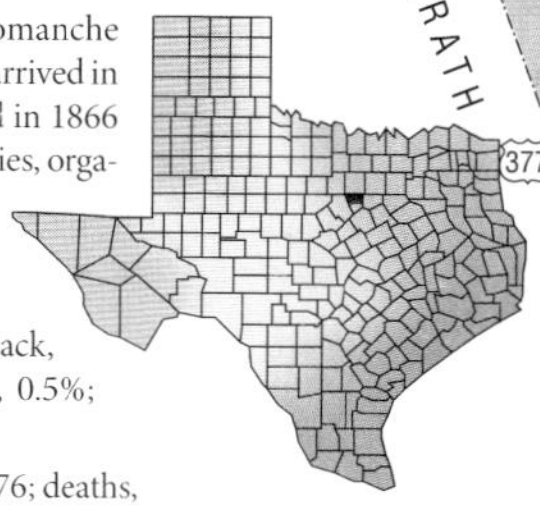

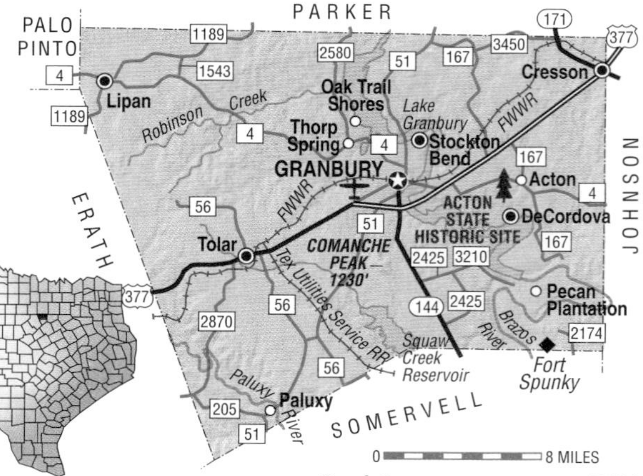

Race/Ethnicity: Anglo, 84.3%; Black, 0.4%; Hispanic, 13%; Asian, 0.5%; Other, 1.6%.

Vital Statistics, annual: Births, 676; deaths, 751; marriages, 389; divorces, 193.

Recreation: Lakes, fishing, scenic areas; summer theater; Gen. Granbury's Bean & Rib cookoff in March; Acton historic site; hike & bike trail.

Minerals: Oil, gas, stone.

Agriculture: Hay, turfgrass, beef cattle, nursery crops, pecans, peaches; some irrigation. Market value $18.9 million.

For explanation of sources, symbols and abbreviations, see p. 204, and foldout map.

GRANBURY (10,454) county seat; retail, tourism, medical services; historic downtown area, opera house, museums; hospital, library, college extensions; Harvest Moon festival in October.

Other towns include: **Acton** (1,129) grave of Elizabeth Crockett, wife of Davy; **Cresson** (1,123); **DeCordova** (2,998); **Lipan** (500); **Oak Trail Shores** (3,411); **Pecan Plantation** (5,719); **Stockton Bend** (334); **Tolar** (983).

Population	**60,984**
Change from 2010 (%)	19.2
Area (sq. mi.)	436.8
Land Area (sq. mi.)	420.6
Altitude (ft.)	600–1,230
Rainfall (in.)	35.1
Jan. mean min (°F)	30.1
July mean max (°F)	95.1
Civ. Labor	27,911
Unemployed (%)	5.5
Wages	$185,348,660
Per Capita Income	$51,384
Prop. Value	$9,887,101,845
Retail Sales	$1,131,428,240

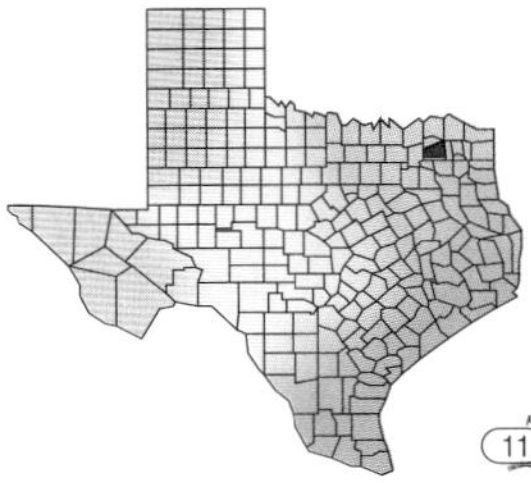

Hopkins County

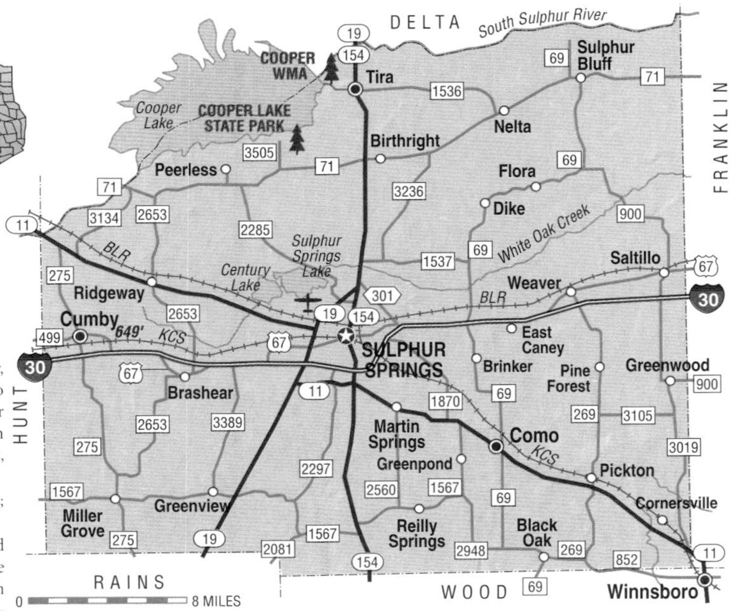

Physical Features: Varied timber, including pines; drains north to South Sulphur River; Cooper Lake (also known as Jim Chapman Lake), Sulphur Springs Lake; light, sandy to heavier black soils.

Economy: Agribusiness, feed mills; varied manufacturing.

History: Caddo area, displaced by Cherokees, who in turn were forced out by President Lamar in 1839. First Anglo-American settlement in 1837. County created in 1846 from Lamar and Nacogdoches counties, organized the same year; named for pioneer Hopkins family.

Race/Ethnicity: Anglo, 72.9%; Black, 7%; Hispanic, 16.9%; Asian, 0.5%; Other, 2.4%.

Vital Statistics, annual: Births, 444; deaths, 398; marriages, 276; divorces, 183.

Recreation: Fishing, hunting; state park, lake activities; dairy museum; dairy festival in June; stew contest in September.

Minerals: Lignite coal.

Agriculture: Dairies, beef cattle, hay (first in acreage). Market value $253.7 million. Firewood and hardwood lumber marketed.

SULPHUR SPRINGS (16,279) county seat; dairy farming, equine center, food processing and distribution, varied manufacturing, tourism; hospital; library, heritage park, music box gallery, civic center.

Other towns include: **Brashear** (280), **Como** (746), **Cumby** (826), **Dike** (170), **Pickton** (300), **Saltillo** (200), **Sulphur Bluff** (280), **Tira** (316).

Population	**37,312**
Change from 2010 (%)	6.1
Area (sq. mi.)	792.8
Land Area (sq. mi.)	767.2
Altitude (ft.)	340–649
Rainfall (in.)	47.2
Jan. mean min (°F)	32.9
July mean max (°F)	93.1
Civ. Labor	17,519
Unemployed (%)	4.7
Wages	$144,505,785
Per Capita Income	$41,562
Prop. Value	$3,592,266,686
Retail Sales	$632,933,308

The Granbury Square Plaza in Hood County. Photo by Michael Barera, CC by SA 4.0/Wikimedia Commons

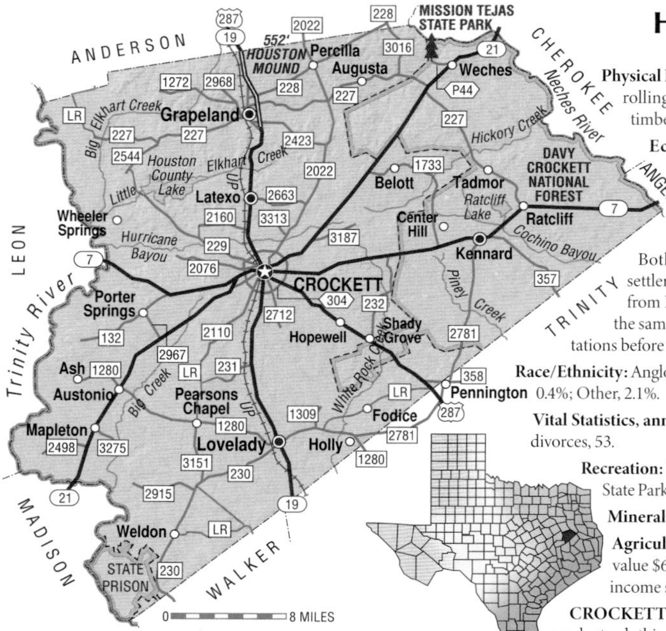

Houston County

Physical Features: East Texas county over half forested; rolling terrain, draining to Neches, Trinity rivers; timber production.

Economy: Livestock, timber, government/services, manufacturing, tourism.

History: Caddo group attracted mission San Francisco de los Tejas in 1690. Spanish town of Bucareli established in 1774. Both lasted only a few years. Anglo-American settlers arrived in the 1820s. County created in 1837 from Nacogdoches County by Republic, organized the same year; named for Sam Houston. Cotton plantations before the Civil War had many slaves.

Race/Ethnicity: Anglo, 60.9%; Black, 24.2%; Hispanic, 12.1%; Asian, 0.4%; Other, 2.1%.

Vital Statistics, annual: Births, 231; deaths, 268; marriages, 124; divorces, 53.

Recreation: Fishing, hunting; national forest; Mission Tejas State Park; 75 historical markers; Houston County Lake.

Minerals: Oil, gas, gravel.

Agriculture: Cattle, hay, watermelons, cotton. Market value $64.5 million. Hunting leases. Timber principal income source.

CROCKETT (6,741) county seat; timber, steel and plastic products, clothing manufacturing, hospital; historic sites; Black Expo in February; fiddlers festival in June.

Other towns include: **Grapeland** (1,456) steel, agribusiness, oil and gas, Peanut Festival in October; **Kennard** (329); **Latexo** (338); **Lovelady** (639) Lovefest in February; **Ratcliff** (106).

Population	**23,381**
Change from 2010 (%)	-1.5
Area (sq. mi.)	1,236.6
Land Area (sq. mi.)	1,230.9
Altitude (ft.)	150–552
Rainfall (in.)	45.2
Jan. mean min (°F)	36.8

July mean max (°F)	93.4
Civ. Labor	9,771
Unemployed (%)	5.5
Wages	$110,956,318
Per Capita Income	$39,609
Prop. Value	$3,756,325,697
Retail Sales	$172,885,814

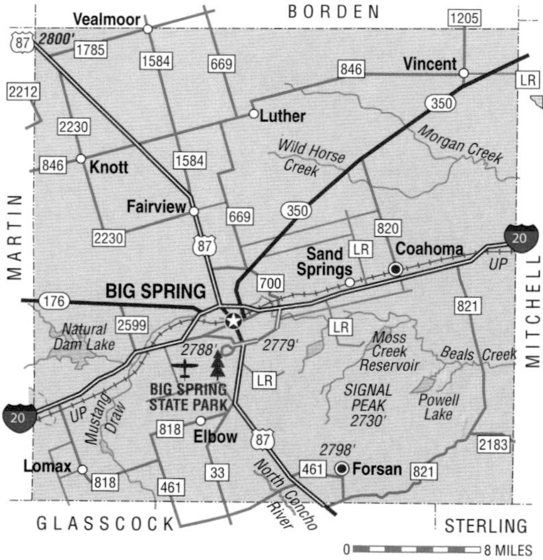

Howard County

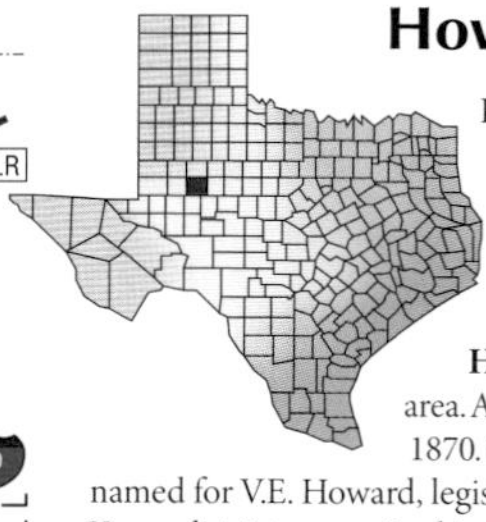

Physical Features: On edge of Llano Estacado; sandy loam soils; Natural Dam Lake.

Economy: Agriculture, petrochemicals, government/services.

History: Pawnee and Comanche area. Anglo-American settlement began in 1870. Oil boom in the mid-1920s. County named for V.E. Howard, legislator; created in 1876 from Bexar, Young districts; organized in 1882.

Race/Ethnicity: Anglo, 47.3%; Black, 6.2%; Hispanic, 43.9%; Asian, 0.6%; Other, 1.7%.

Vital Statistics, annual: Births, 484; deaths, 416; marriages, 247; divorces, 18.

Recreation: Lakes, state park; campground in Comanche Trail Park, Native Plant Trail, museum, historical sites, Pow Wow in April, Pops in the Park in July.

Minerals: Oil, gas, sand, gravel, and stone.

Agriculture: Cotton, beef, hay. Market value $26.9 million.

BIG SPRING (28,349) county seat; agriculture, petrochemicals, varied manufacturing; hospitals including a state institution and Veterans Administration hospital; federal prison; Howard College; railroad plaza.

Other towns include: **Coahoma** (948), **Forsan** (215), **Knott** (200), and **Sand Springs** (859).

Population	**36,294**
Change from 2010 (%)	3.7
Area (sq. mi.)	904.2
Land Area (sq. mi.)	900.8
Altitude (ft.)	2,180–2,800
Rainfall (in.)	19.5
Jan. mean min (°F)	31.3

July mean max (°F)	94.6
Civ. Labor	13,138
Unemployed (%)	7.0
Wages	$167,859,752
Per Capita Income	$43,348
Prop. Value	$6,861,060,684
Retail Sales	$569,307,386

Hudspeth County

Physical Features: Plateau, basin terrain, draining to salt lakes; Rio Grande; mostly rocky, alkaline, clay soils and sandy loam soils, except alluvial along Rio Grande; desert, mountain vegetation. Fertile agricultural valley.

Economy: Agribusiness, mining, tourism, hunting leases.

History: Mescalero Apache area. Fort Quitman established in 1858 to protect routes to west. Railroad in 1881 brought Anglo-American settlers. Political turmoil in Mexico (1912–1929) brought more settlers from Mexico. County named for Texas political leader Claude B. Hudspeth; created in 1917 from El Paso County, organized the same year.

Race/Ethnicity: Anglo, 19.8%; Black, 0.9%; Hispanic, 77.7%; Asian, 0.3%; Other, 1%.

Vital Statistics, annual: Births, 45; deaths, 12; marriages, 1; divorces, 0.

Recreation: Scenic drives; fort sites; hot springs; salt basin; white sands; hunting; birding; part of Guadalupe Mountains National Park, containing unique plant life, canyons.

Minerals: Talc, stone, gypsum.

Agriculture: Most income from cotton, vegetables, hay, alfalfa; beef cattle raised; 18,000 acres irrigated. Market value $17.4 million.

SIERRA BLANCA (574) county seat; ranching center, tourist stop on interstate highway; adobe courthouse; 4th of July fair, livestock show in January.

Other towns include: **Dell City** (948) agriculture, government/services, telephone co-op; some of largest water wells in state, Dell Valley Hudspeth fair in September, and **Fort Hancock** (1,832).

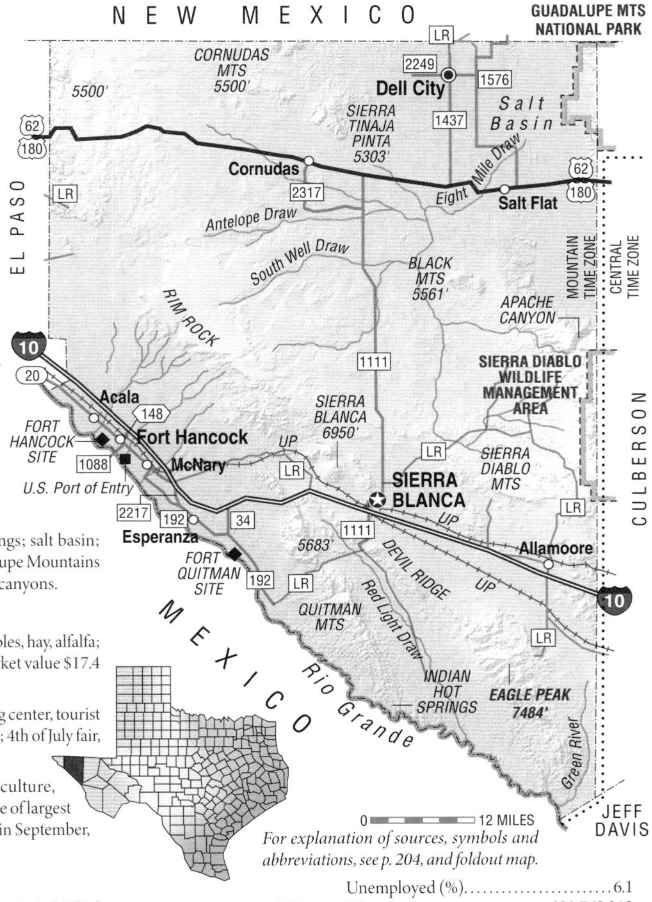

For explanation of sources, symbols and abbreviations, see p. 204, and foldout map.

Population	**3,680**			Unemployed (%)	6.1
Change from 2010 (%)	5.9	Rainfall (in.)	11.2	Wages	$23,762,212
Area (sq. mi.)	4,571.8	Jan. mean min (°F)	25.7	Per Capita Income	$23,569
Land Area (sq. mi.)	4,571.0	July mean max (°F)	92.5	Prop. Value	$934,208,395
Altitude (ft.)	3,117–7,484	Civ. Labor	1,894	Retail Sales	$10,734,143

Forever view down Texas Ranch Road 1111 in Hudspeth County. Photo by Carol M. Highsmith, courtesy of the Library of Congress

Hunt County

Population	**97,842**
Change from 2010 (%)	13.6
Area (sq. mi.)	882.0
Land Area (sq. mi.)	840.3
Altitude (ft.)	437–730
Rainfall (in.)	44.7
Jan. mean min (°F)	32.7
July mean max (°F)	96.4
Civ. Labor	44,223
Unemployed (%)	5.6
Wages	$371,650,829
Per Capita Income	$38,892
Prop. Value	$12,145,491,435
Retail Sales	$1,550,355,394

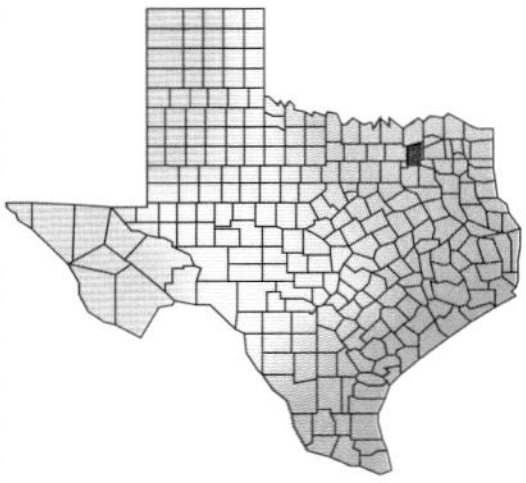

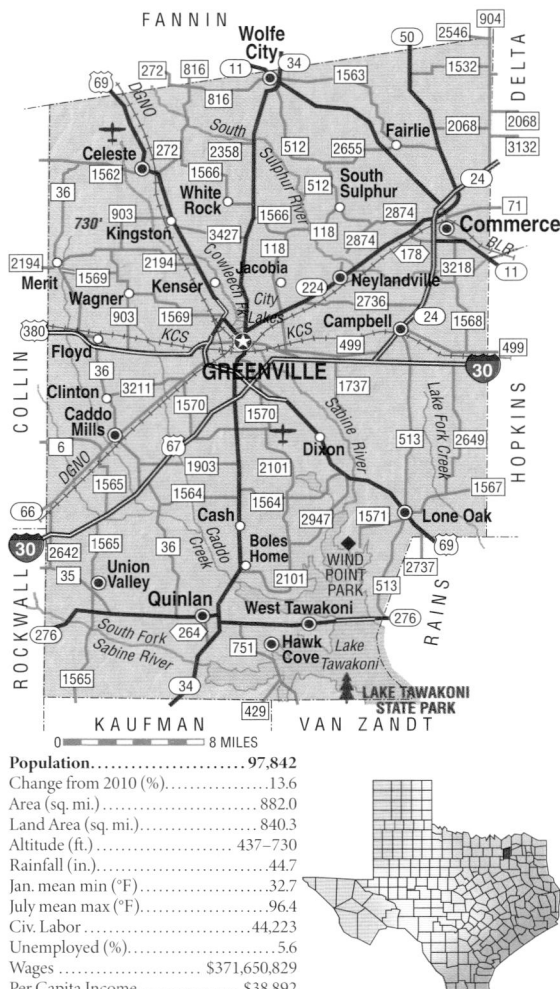

Physical Features: Level to rolling surface; Sabine, Sulphur rivers; Lake Tawakoni, Greenville City Lakes; mostly heavy Blackland soil, some loam, sandy loams.

Economy: Education, varied manufacturing, agribusiness; several Fortune 500 companies in county; many residents employed in Dallas area.

History: Caddo Indians gone by 1790s. Kiowa bands in the area when Anglo-American settlers arrived in 1839. County named for Memucan Hunt, Republic secretary of navy; created in 1846 from Fannin, Nacogdoches counties, organized the same year.

Race/Ethnicity: Anglo, 70.4%; Black, 8.7%; Hispanic, 17%; Asian, 1.1%; Other, 2.5%.

Vital Statistics, annual: Births, 1,097; deaths, 958; marriages, 531; divorces, 216.

Recreation: Lake Tawakoni sports, catfish tournament in August; Texas A&M University–Commerce events.

Minerals: Sand and white rock, gas, oil.

Agriculture: Cattle, forage, greenhouse crops, top revenue sources; horses, wheat, oats, cotton, grain sorghum. Market value $55.3 million. Some firewood sold.

GREENVILLE (28,992) county seat; varied manufacturing, retail trade, health and government services, commuters to Dallas; hospital; branch of Paris Junior College; cotton museum, Audie Murphy exhibit; fiddle festival in October.

COMMERCE (9,696) Texas A&M University–Commerce, government/services, varied manufacturing; emergency medical center; planetarium, children's museum; Bois d'Arc Bash in September.

Other towns include: **Caddo Mills** (1,698); **Campbell** (675); **Celeste** (907); **Hawk Cove** (559); **Lone Oak** (696); **Merit** (225); **Neylandville** (105); **Quinlan** (1,541); **Union Valley** (425); **West Tawakoni** (1,844) tourist center, light industry, Lakefest in October; **Wolfe City** (1,543) manufacturing, antiques shops, commuters to Dallas, museum, library, car and truck show in October.

For explanation of sources, symbols and abbreviations, see p. 204, and foldout map.

This ditch was built in Irion County in the early 1900's as a source of water for plants, and it is still in use today. Photo by USDA NRCS Texas

Hutchinson County

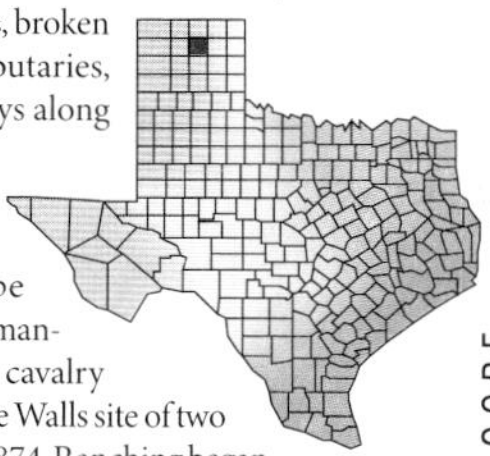

Physical Features: High Plains, broken by Canadian River and tributaries, Lake Meredith; fertile valleys along streams.

Economy: Oil and gas, petrochemicals, carbon black plants. History: Antelope Creek Indian area. Later, Comanches were driven out in U.S. cavalry campaigns of 1874-75. Adobe Walls site of two Indian attacks, in 1864 and 1874. Ranching began in the late 1870s. Oil boom in the early 1920s. County created in 1876 from Bexar Territory; organized in 1901; named for pioneer jurist Anderson Hutchinson.

Race/Ethnicity: Anglo, 68.3%; Black, 2.6%; Hispanic, 24.5%; Asian, 0.5%; Other, 3.9%.

Vital Statistics, annual: Births, 287; deaths, 239; marriages, 133; divorces, 92.

Recreation: Lake Meredith activities, fishing, camping; Adobe Walls, historic Indian battle site; Alibates Flint Quarries.

Minerals: Oil and gas.

Agriculture: Beef cattle, corn, wheat; about 35,000 acres irrigated. Market value $44.9 million. Hunting important.

STINNETT (1,460) county seat; petroleum refining, farm center.

BORGER (12,331) petroleum refining, petrochemicals, nitrogen plant, carbon-black production, oil-field servicing, retail center; Frank Phillips College; museum; hospital; Downtown Merchants Beach Bash in June.

Other cities include: **Fritch** (1,961), **Sanford** (151).

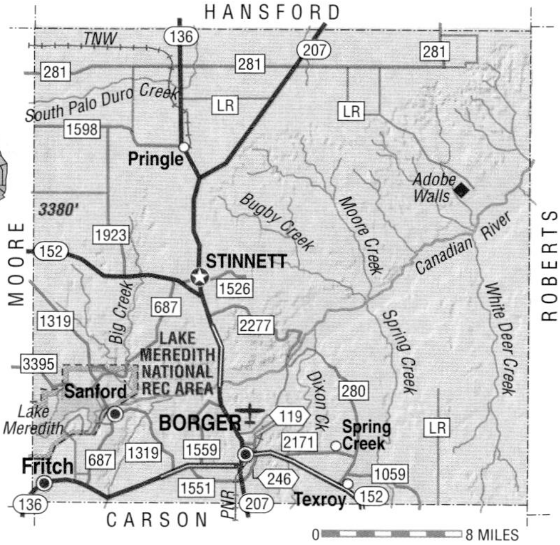

Population	**20,550**
Change from 2010 (%)	-7.2
Area (sq. mi.)	895.0
Land Area (sq. mi.)	887.4
Altitude (ft.)	2,600–3,380
Rainfall (in.)	21.7
Jan. mean min (°F)	25.2
July mean max (°F)	93.8
Civ. Labor	8,181
Unemployed (%)	6.8
Wages	$126,611,146
Per Capita Income	$43,981
Prop. Value	$3,556,872,718
Retail Sales	$231,490,884

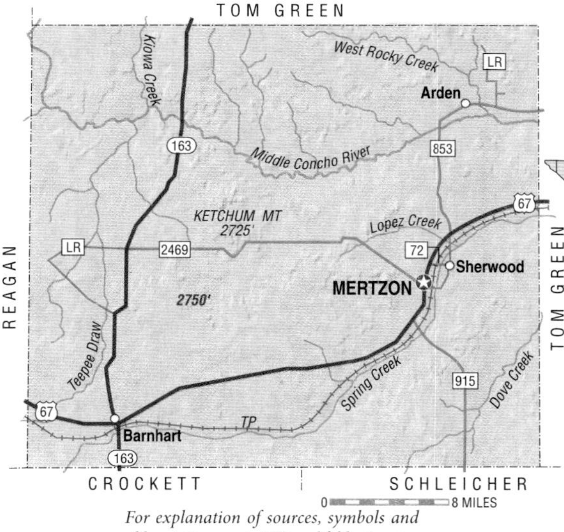

For explanation of sources, symbols and abbreviations, see p. 204, and foldout map.

Population	1,592
Change from 2010 (%)	-0.4
Area (sq. mi.)	1,051.6
Land Area (sq. mi.)	1,051.6
Altitude (ft.)	2,000–2,750
Rainfall (in.)	20.2
Jan. mean min (°F)	32.0
July mean max (°F)	95.0
Civ. Labor	774
Unemployed (%)	5.4
Wages	$12,597,469
Per Capita Income	$72,177
Prop. Value	$2,383,411,679
Retail Sales	$5,246,586

Irion County

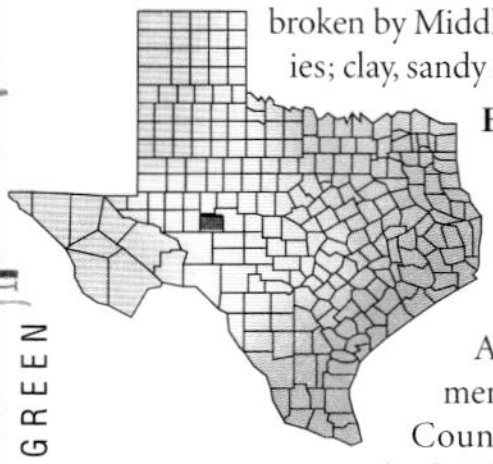

Physical Features: West Texas county with hilly surface, broken by Middle Concho River, tributaries; clay, sandy soils.

Economy: Ranching, oil, gas production, wildlife recreation.

History: Tonkawa Indian area. Anglo-American settlement began in the late 1870s. County named for Republic leader R.A. Irion; created in 1889 from Tom Green County, organized the same year.

Race/Ethnicity: Anglo, 70.4%; Black, 0.6%; Hispanic, 27%; Asian, 0.2%; Other, 1.5%.

Vital Statistics, annual: Births 12; deaths, 20; marriages, 10; divorces, 2.

Recreation: Hunting; historic sites, including Dove Creek battlefield and stagecoach stops, old Sherwood courthouse built 1900; hunters appreciation dinner in November.

Minerals: Oil, gas.

Agriculture: Beef cattle, sheep, goats; hay, wheat. Market value $9.3 million.

MERTZON (797) county seat; farm center, wool warehousing.

Other towns include: **Barnhart** (110).

Jack County

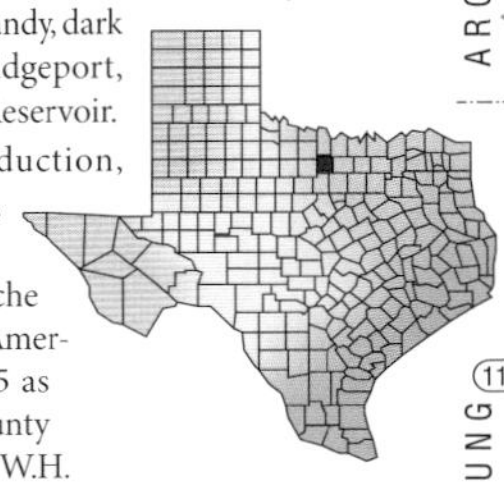

Physical Features: Rolling Cross Timbers, broken by West Fork of the Trinity, other streams; sandy, dark brown, loam soils; Lake Bridgeport, Lake Jacksboro, Lost Creek Reservoir.

Economy: Petroleum production, oil-field services, livestock, manufacturing, tourism.

History: A Caddo and Comanche borderland. The first Anglo-American settlers arrived in 1855 as part of the Peters Colony. County named for brothers P.C. and W.H. Jack, who were leaders in Texas' independence effort; created in 1856 from Cooke County; organized in 1857 with Mesquiteville (original name of Jacksboro) as the county seat.

Race/Ethnicity: Anglo, 75.4%; Black, 3.9%; Hispanic, 18.8%; Asian, 0.3%; Other, 1.4%.

Vital Statistics, annual: Births, 104; deaths, 96; marriages, 54; divorces, 31.

Recreation: Hunting, wildlife leases; fishing; lake activities; Fort Richardson, Texas 4-H Museum (county is birthplace of 4-H clubs in Texas), other historic sites; Lost Creek Reservoir State Trailway.

Minerals: Oil, gas.

Agriculture: Cattle, hay, wheat, goats, sheep. Market value $23.2 million. Firewood sold.

JACKSBORO (4,648) county seat; agribusiness, petroleum production and services, tourism; hospital; library; Fort Richardson Living History Days in April.

Other towns include: **Bryson** (572), **Jermyn** (75), **Perrin** (443127).

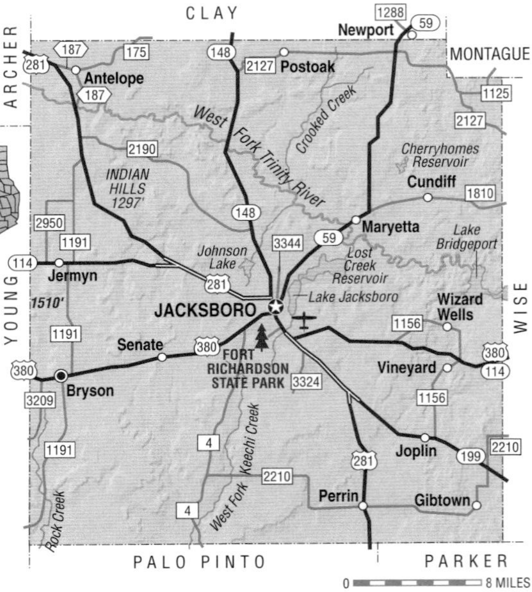

Population	**9,265**
Change from 2010 (%)	2.4
Area (sq. mi.)	920.1
Land Area (sq. mi.)	910.7
Altitude (ft.)	836–1,510
Rainfall (in.)	32.9
Jan. mean min (°F)	29.7
July mean max (°F)	94.4
Civ. Labor	3,273
Unemployed (%)	6
Wages	$33,513,008
Per Capita Income	$40,827
Prop. Value	$2,628,453,317
Retail Sales	$43,483,479

Jackson County

Physical Features: South coastal county of prairie and motts of trees; loam, clay, black soils; drains to creeks, rivers, bays.

Economy: Plastics manufacturing, agribusinesses.

History: Karankawa area. Lipan Apaches and Tonkawas arrived later. Six of Austin's Old Three Hundred families settled in the 1820s. Mexican municipality, created in 1835, became an original county the following year; named for U.S. President Andrew Jackson. Oil discovered in 1934.

Race/Ethnicity: Anglo, 56%; Black, 6.7%; Hispanic, 35.3%; Asian, 0.3%; Other, 1.4%.

Vital Statistics, annual: Births, 211; deaths, 146; marriages, 105; divorces, 41.

Recreation: Hunting, fishing, birding (southern bald eagle in area); historic sites; Texana Museum; Lake Texana, Brackenridge Plantation campground, state park; Chili Spill in November at Lake Texana, county fair, rodeo in April.

Minerals: Oil and natural gas.

Agriculture: Cotton, cattle, corn, rice; 13,000 acres of rice irrigated. Market value $85.0 million.

EDNA (5,690) county seat; oil and gas, chemical plants, agriculture; hospital, library, museums.

Other towns include: **Francitas** (125); **Ganado** (2,115) oil and gas, agriculture, historic movie theater, Crawfish Festival in May; **LaSalle** (110); **La Ward** (221); **Lolita** (606); **Vanderbilt** (418).

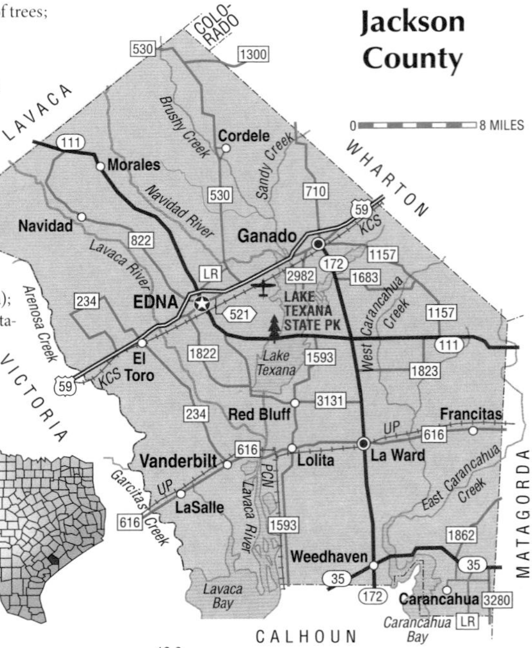

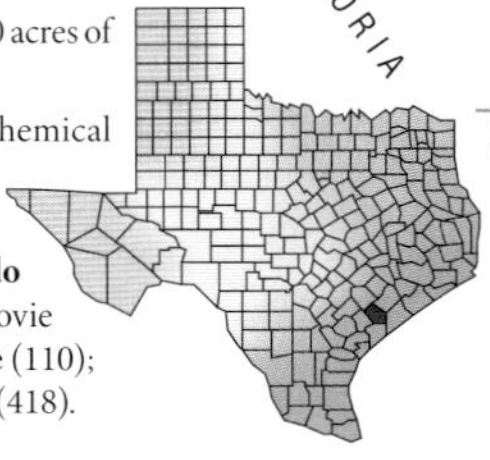

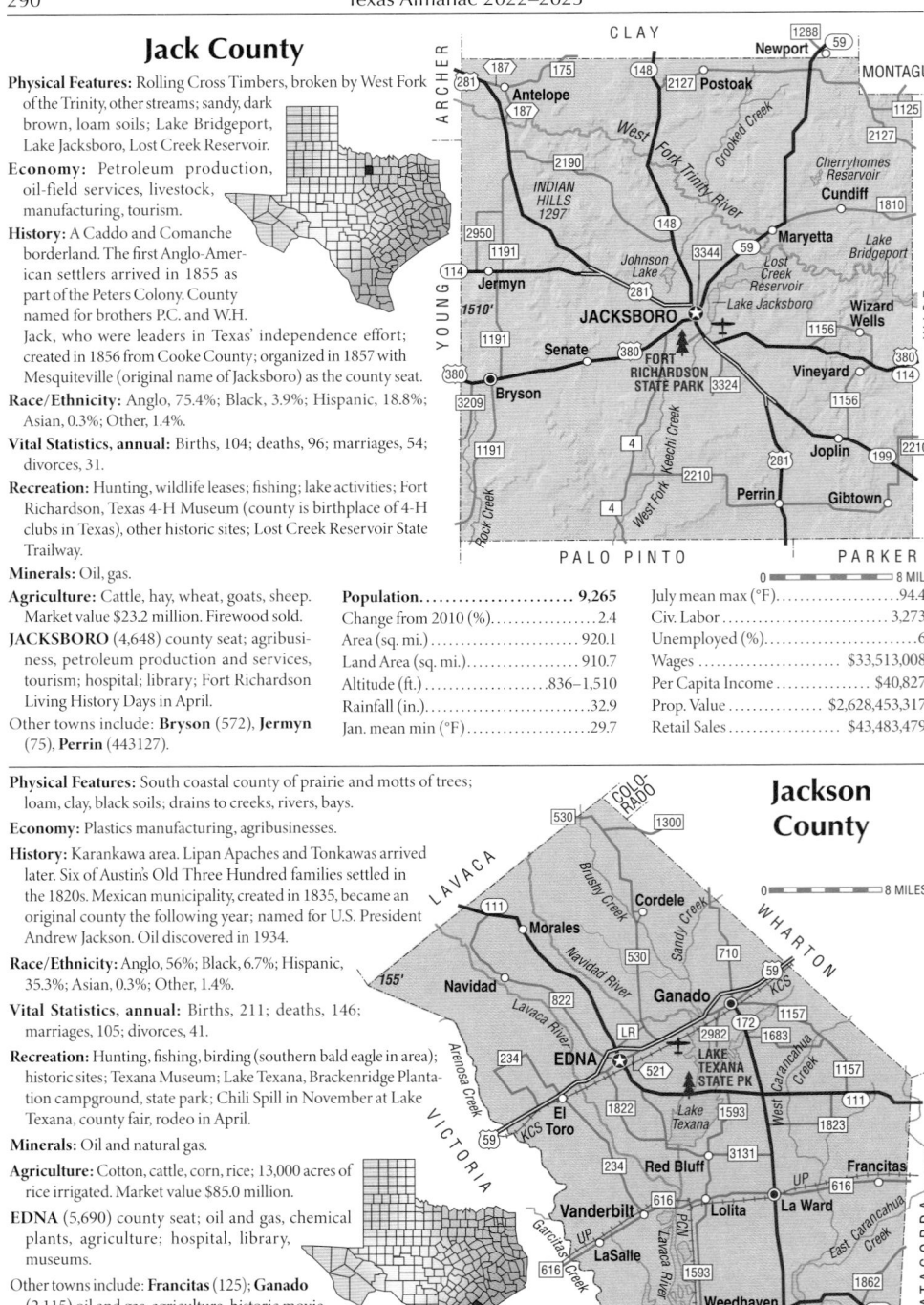

Population	**14,561**
Change from 2010 (%)	3.5
Area (sq. mi.)	856.9
Land Area (sq. mi.)	829.4
Altitude (ft.)	sea level–155
Rainfall (in.)	43.3
Jan. mean min (°F)	42.0
July mean max (°F)	94.0
Civ. Labor	7,163
Unemployed (%)	5.5
Wages	$69,559,738
Per Capita Income	$46,596
Prop. Value	$4,241,445,363
Retail Sales	$152,494,331

Jasper County

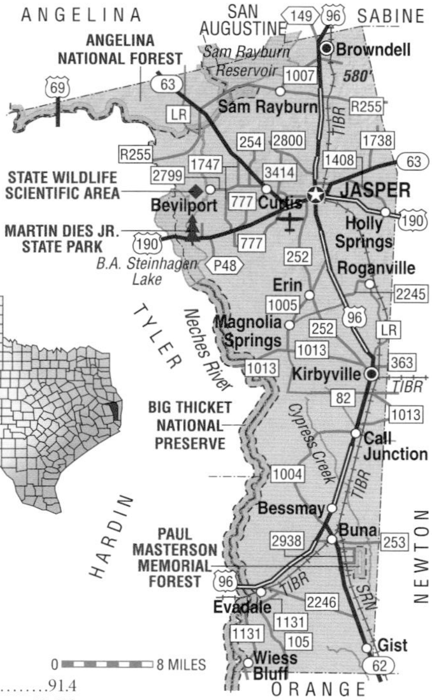

Physical Features: East Texas county; hilly to level; national forest; Sam Rayburn Reservoir, B.A. Steinhagen Lake; Neches River.

Economy: Timber industries; nature tourism, government/services.

History: Caddo and Atakapa Indian area. Land grants to John R. Bevil and Lorenzo de Zavala in 1829. County created in 1836, organized in 1837, from Mexican municipality; named for Sgt. William Jasper of American Revolution.

Race/Ethnicity: Anglo, 73.3%; Black, 16.1%; Hispanic, 7.3%; Asian, 0.6%; Other, 2.5%.

Vital Statistics, annual: Births, 472; deaths, 458; marriages, 249; divorces, 114.

Recreation: Lake activities; hunting, fishing; state park, Big Thicket; Butterfly Festival in October at Jasper.

Minerals: Oil, gas produced.

Agriculture: Cattle, plant nurseries, fruits, vegetables. Market value $9.1 million. Timber is major income producer. Hunting leases and fishing tournaments are major income producers.

JASPER (7,533) county seat; tourism, government/services, timber; hospital; Angelina College extension; museum; Azalea Festival in March.

Other towns include: **Browndell** (201); **Buna** (2,063) timber, oil, polka dot house, redbud festival in March; **Evadale** (1,545); **Kirbyville** (2,211) electric co-op, government/services, retail, commuters, Caboose museum, library, Magnolia Festival in April; **Sam Rayburn** (1,137).

Population	**35,726**	July mean max (°F)	91.4
Change from 2010 (%)	0.0	Civ. Labor	12,689
Area (sq. mi.)	969.7	Unemployed (%)	10.4
Land Area (sq. mi.)	938.9	Wages	$105,538,973
Altitude (ft.)	10–580	Per Capita Income	$40,834
Rainfall (in.)	59.8	Prop. Value	$4,175,046,833
Jan. mean min (°F)	38.7	Retail Sales	$473,013,286

For explanation of sources, symbols and abbreviations, see p. 204, and foldout map.

The building where Neri's Bistro operates in Jacksboro was built in 1939. Photo by Larry D. Moore, CC by SA 4.0/Wikimedia Commons

The Queen of Peace Shrine and Gardens in Port Arthur. Photo by Carol M. Highsmith, courtesy of The Library of Congress

Jeff Davis County

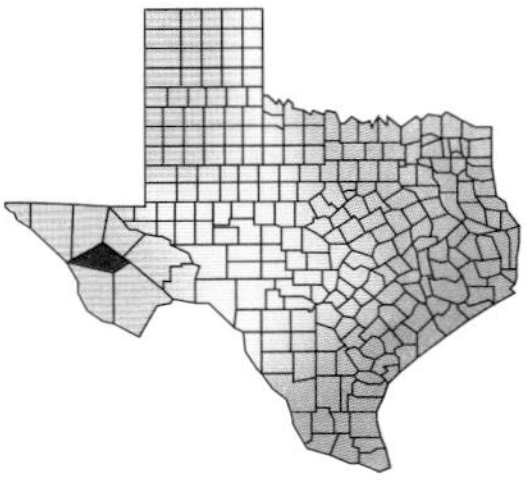

Physical Features: Highest average elevation in Texas; peaks (Mt. Livermore, 8,378 ft.), canyons, plateaus; intermountain wash, clay, loam soils; cedars, oaks in highlands.

Economy: Tourism, agriculture, McDonald Observatory.

History: Mescalero Apaches in area when Antonio de Espejo explored in 1583. U.S. Army established Fort Davis in 1854 to protect routes to west. Civilian settlers followed, including Manuel Músquiz, a political refugee from Mexico. County named for Jefferson Davis, U.S. Secretary of War, Confederate president; created 1887 from Presidio County, organized the same year.

Race/Ethnicity: Anglo, 56.2%; Black, 0.3%; Hispanic, 40.6%; Asian, 0.2%; Other, 2.3%.

Vital Statistics, annual: Births, 12; deaths, marriages, 12; divorces, 0.

Recreation: Scenic drives including loop along Limpia Creek, Mt. Livermore, Blue Mountain; hunting; Fort Davis National Historic Site; state park; McDonald Observatory on Mt. Locke; Davis Mountain Preserve; Chihuahuan Desert Research Institute; hummingbird celebration in August.

Minerals: Not significant.

Agriculture: Greenhouse tomatoes, beef cattle, horses, meat goats. Market value $29.3. Hunting leases important.

FORT DAVIS (1,162), county seat; tourism, government/services, retail; library, Overland and Old Spanish trail museums; "Coolest July 4th in Texas" celebration.

Other town: **Valentine** (123).

Population	**2,411**
Change from 2010 (%)	2.9
Area (sq. mi.)	2,264.6
Land Area (sq. mi.)	2,264.6
Altitude (ft.)	3,162–8,378
Rainfall (in.) Fort Davis	17.47
Rainfall (in.) Mt. Locke	20.37
Jan. mean min. (°F) Fort Davis	28.9
Jan. mean min. (°F) Mt. Locke	32.4
July mean max. (°F) Fort Davis	88.7
July mean max. (°F) Mt. Locke	84.5
Civ. Labor	996
Unemployed (%)	4.8
Wages	$8,283,460
Per Capita Income	$43,080
Prop. Value	$606,140,085
Retail Sales	$9,837,108

For explanation of sources, symbols and abbreviations, see p. 204, and foldout map.

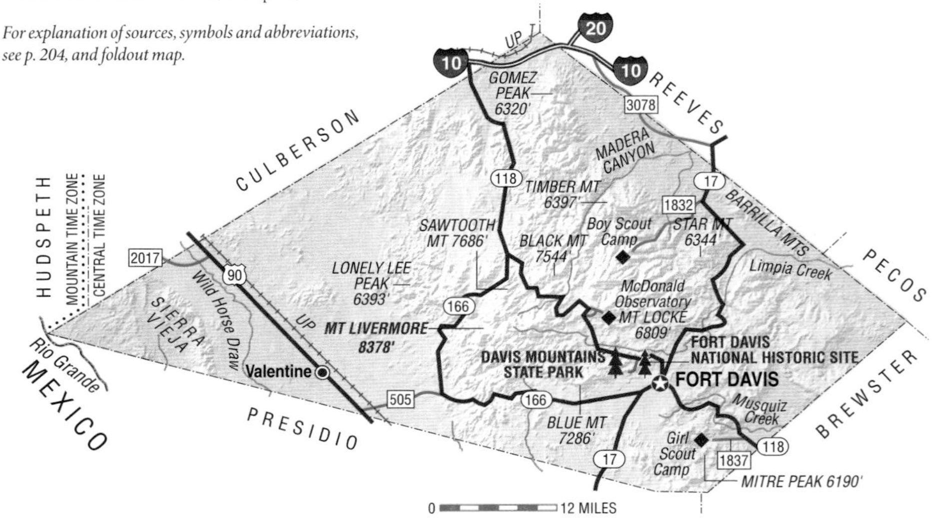

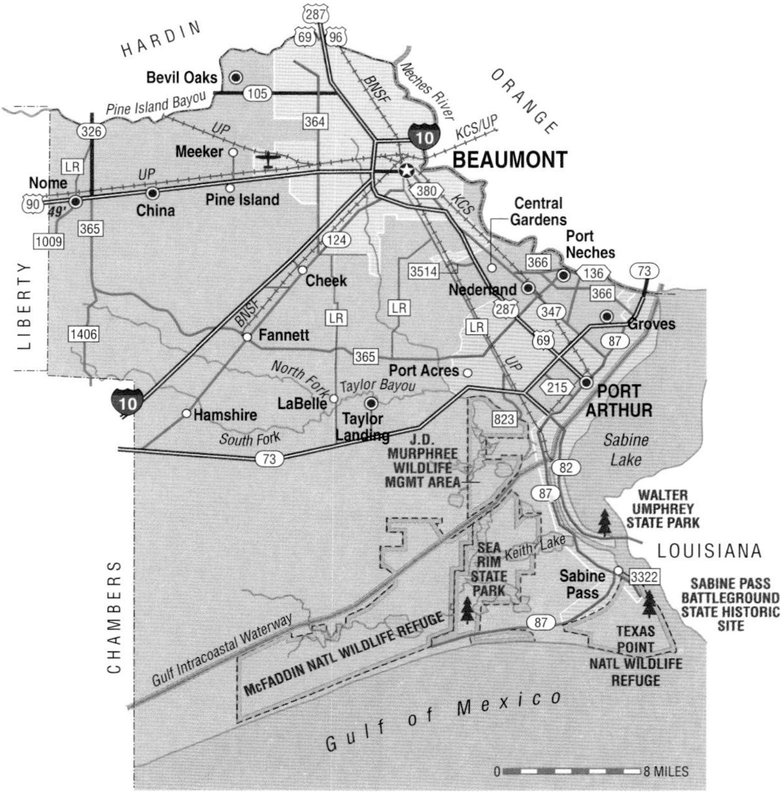

Jefferson County

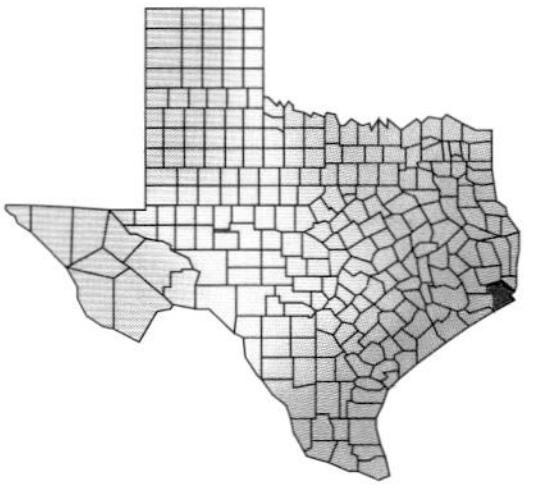

Physical Features: Gulf Coast grassy plain, with timber in northwest; beach sands, sandy loams, black clay soils; drains to Neches River, Gulf of Mexico.

Economy: Government/services, petrochemical and other chemical plants, shipbuilding, steel mill, port activity, oil-field supplies.

History: Atakapas and Orcoquizas, whose numbers were reduced by epidemics or migration before Anglo-American settlers arrived in the 1820s. Cajuns arrived in the 1840s; Europeans in the 1850s. Antebellum slaveholding area. County created in 1836 from Mexican municipality; organized in 1837; named for U.S. President Thomas Jefferson.

Race/Ethnicity: Anglo, 39.7%; Black, 33%; Hispanic, 21%; Asian, 4.1%; Other, 1.9%.

Vital Statistics, annual: Births, 3,782; deaths, 2,514; marriages, 2,045; divorces, 537.

Recreation: Beaches, fresh and saltwater fishing; duck, goose hunting; water activities; Dick Dowling Monument and Park; Spindletop site, energy, fire museums; saltwater lake; J.D. Murphree WMA, McFaddin wildlife refuge, Texas Point wildlife refuge; Lamar University events; historic sites; South Texas Fair in March-April.

Minerals: Large producer of oil, gas, sulfur, salt, sand and gravel.

Agriculture: Rice, hay, beef cattle, crawfish; considerable rice irrigated. Market value $32.3 million. Timber sales significant.

BEAUMONT (118,078) county seat; oil and gas production, government/services, engineering and industrial services, port; Lamar University, Institute of Technology; hospitals; entertainment district; Neches River Festival in April.

PORT ARTHUR (54,563) oil, chemical activities, shrimping and crawfishing, shipping, offshore marine, tourism; hospitals; museum; prison; Asian New Year Tet, Janis Joplin Birthday Bash in January. Sabine Pass and Port Acres are now within the city limits of Port Arthur.

Other towns include: **Bevil Oaks** (1,226); **Central Gardens** (4,309); **China** (1,203); **Fannett** (2,333); **Groves** (15,953) retail center, some manufacturing, government/services, tourism; hospital, pecan festival in September; **Hamshire** (759).

Also, **Nederland** (17,439) petrochemical refining, retail center, education; Windmill and French/Acadian museums; extended-care hospital; Tex Ritter memorial and park; heritage festival in March (city founded by Dutch immigrants in 1898).

Also, **Nome** (607); **Port Neches** (12,638) chemical and synthetic rubber industry, manufacturing, library, riverfront park with La Maison Beausoleil, RiverFest in May; **Taylor Landing** (238).

Population	**251,590**
Change from 2010 (%)	-0.3
Area (sq. mi.)	1,112.7
Land Area (sq. mi.)	876.3
Altitude (ft.)	sea level–49
Rainfall (in.)	60.4
Jan. mean min (°F)	41.7
July mean max (°F)	92.0
Civ. Labor	106,038
Unemployed (%)	10.6
Wages	$1,734,673,862
Per Capita Income	$44,613
Prop. Value	$34,593,396,848
Retail Sales	$4,254,144,615

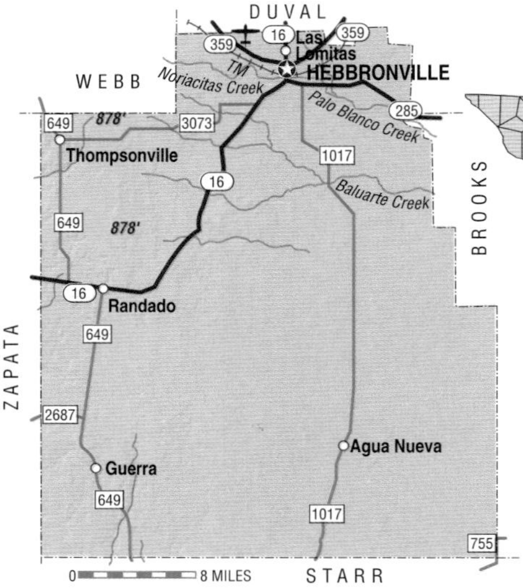

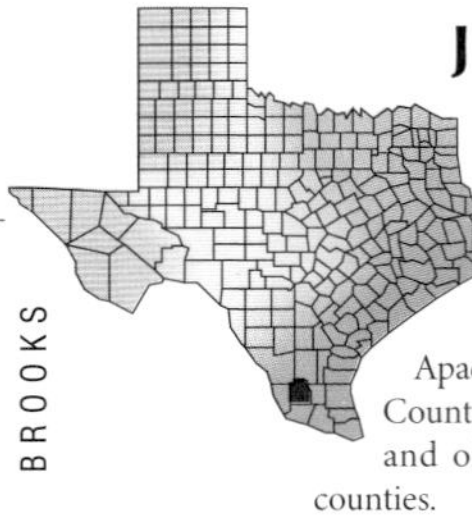

Jim Hogg County

Physical Features: South Texas county on rolling plain, with heavy brush cover; white blow sand and sandy loam; hilly, broken.

Economy: Oil, cattle operations.

History: Coahuiltecan area, then Lipan Apache. Spanish land grant in 1805 to Xavier Vela. County named for Gov. James Stephen Hogg; created and organized in 1913 from Brooks and Duval counties.

Race/Ethnicity: Anglo, 7.1%; Black, 0.3%; Hispanic, 91.2%; Asian, 0.4%; Other, 0.8%.

Vital Statistics, annual: Births, 90; deaths, 50; marriages, 32; divorces, 0.

Recreation: White-tailed deer and bobwhite hunting.

Minerals: Oil and gas.

Agriculture: Cattle, hay, milk goats; some irrigation. Market value $10.4 million.

HEBBRONVILLE (4,400) county seat; ranching, oil-field center.

Other towns include: **Guerra** (4), **Las Lomitas** (233), **South Fork Estates** (72), and **Thompsonville** (47).

Population	**5,092**	Rainfall (in.)	23.8	Wages	$18,101,367
Change from 2010 (%)	-3.9	Jan. mean min (°F)	44.8	Per Capita Income	$33,602
Area (sq. mi.)	1,136.2	July mean max (°F)	96.7	Prop. Value	$1,001,110,910
Land Area (sq. mi.)	1,136.1	Civ. Labor	1,856	Retail Sales	$36,856,203
Altitude (ft.)	230–878	Unemployed (%)	9.5		

Jim Wells County

Physical Features: South Coastal Plains; level to rolling; sandy to dark soils; grassy with mesquite brush; Lake Corpus Christi.

Economy: Oil and gas production, agriculture, nature tourism.

History: Coahuiltecans, driven out by Lipan Apaches in 1775. Tomás Sánchez established settlement in 1754. Anglo-American settlement began in 1878. County created 1911 from Nueces County; organized 1912; named for developer J.B. Wells Jr.

Race/Ethnicity: Anglo, 17.1%; Black, 0.3%; Hispanic, 81.4%; Asian, 0.3%; Other, 0.6%.

Vital Statistics, annual: Births, 639; deaths, 424; marriages, 32; divorces, 0.

Recreation: Hunting; fiestas; Tejano Roots hall of fame; South Texas museum.

Minerals: Oil, gas, caliche.

Agriculture: Cattle, sorghum, corn, cotton, dairies, goats, wheat, watermelons, sunflowers, peas, hay. Market value $121.6 million.

ALICE (18,536) county seat; oil-field service center, agribusiness, government/services; hospital; Coastal Bend College campus; Fiesta Bandana (from original name of city) in May.

Other towns include: **Alfred** (80); **Ben Bolt** (1,600); **Orange Grove** (1,301); **Pernitas Point** (274, partly in Live Oak County); **Premont** (2,537) wildflower tour in spring; **Rancho Alegre** (1,636); **Sandia** (328).

Also, part [879] of **San Diego** (4,221).

Population	**40,204**
Change from 2010 (%)	-1.6
Area (sq. mi.)	868.3
Land Area (sq. mi.)	865.0
Altitude (ft.)	50–450
Rainfall (in.)	28.4
Jan. mean min (°F)	44.9
July mean max (°F)	97.2
Civ. Labor	15,212
Unemployed (%)	11.9
Wages	$145,314,454
Per Capita Income	$42,174
Prop. Value	$2,730,431,859
Retail Sales	$455,260,398

For explanation of sources, symbols and abbreviations, see p. 204, and foldout map.

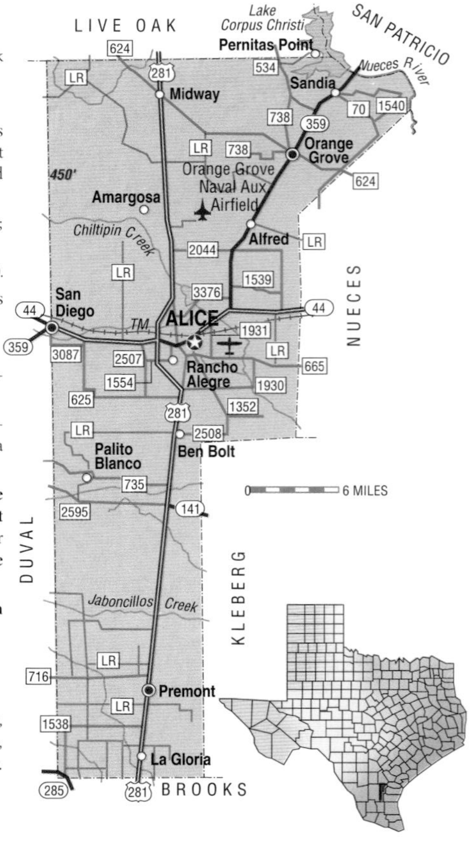

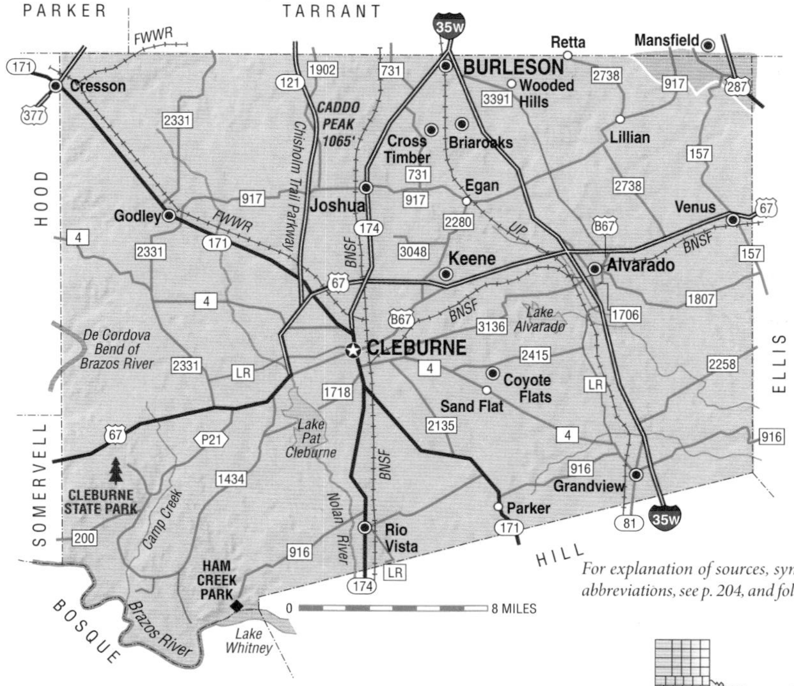

For explanation of sources, symbols and abbreviations, see p. 204, and foldout map.

Johnson County

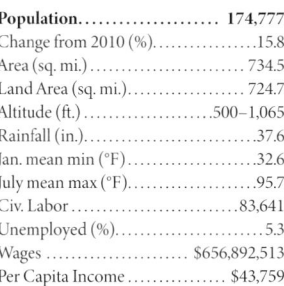

Physical Features: North central county drained by tributaries of Trinity, Brazos rivers; lakes; hilly, rolling, many soil types.

Economy: Agribusiness, railroad shops; manufacturing, distribution, lake activities, many residents employed in Fort Worth and Dallas; part of Fort Worth-Arlington metropolitan area.

History: No permanent Indian villages existed in the area. Anglo-American settlers arrived in the 1840s. County named for Col. M.T. Johnson of the Mexican War and Confederacy; created and organized in 1854. Formed from McLennan, Hill, and Navarro counties.

Race/Ethnicity: Anglo, 71.1%; Black, 3.1%; Hispanic, 22.1%; Asian, 0.5%; Other, 2.8%.

Vital Statistics, annual: Births, 2,092; deaths, 1,340; marriages, 1,228; divorces, 510.

Recreation: Bird, deer hunting; water activities on Lake Pat Cleburne, Lake Whitney; state park; sports complex; museum; Chisholm Trail; Goatneck bike ride in July.

Minerals: Limestone, sand and gravel.

Agriculture: Cattle, hay, horses, dairies, cotton, sorghum, wheat, oats, hogs. Market value $57.9 million.

CLEBURNE (33,110) county seat; manufacturing, oil and gas; hospital, library, museum; Hill College campus; Whistle Stop Christmas.

BURLESON (47,403, part in Tarrant County) agriculture, retail center; hospital.

Other towns include: **Alvarado** (4,590) County Pioneer Days; **Briaroaks** (507); **Coyote Flats** (329); **Cross Timber** (319); **Godley** (1,377); **Grandview** (1,796); **Joshua** (7,805) many residents work in Fort Worth; **Keene** (6,755) Southwestern Adventist University; **Lillian** (1,160); **Rio Vista** (1,050), and **Venus** (4,806).

Also, part of **Cresson** (1,338), and part [2,153] of **Mansfield** (72,419, mostly in Tarrant County).

Population	**174,777**
Change from 2010 (%)	15.8
Area (sq. mi.)	734.5
Land Area (sq. mi.)	724.7
Altitude (ft.)	500–1,065
Rainfall (in.)	37.6
Jan. mean min (°F)	32.6
July mean max (°F)	95.7
Civ. Labor	83,641
Unemployed (%)	5.3
Wages	$656,892,513
Per Capita Income	$43,759
Prop. Value	$19,167,879,212
Retail Sales	$2,264,786,662

An old wall in Alice. Photo by Jay Phagan, CC 2/Wikimedia Commons

Jones County

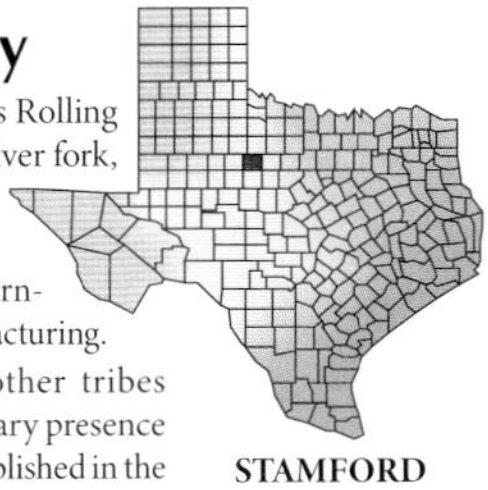

Physical Features: West Texas Rolling Plains; drained by Brazos River fork, tributaries; Lake Fort Phantom Hill.

Economy: Agribusiness; government/services; varied manufacturing.

History: Comanches and other tribes hunted in the area. U.S. military presence began in 1851. Ranching established in the 1870s. County named for the last president of the Republic, Anson Jones; created in 1858 from Bexar and Bosque counties; re-created in 1876; organized in 1881.

Race/Ethnicity: Anglo, 57.1%; Black, 11.8%; Hispanic, 28.9%; Asian, 0.4%; Other, 1.6%.

Vital Statistics, annual: Births, 147; deaths, 214; marriages, 71; divorces, 22.

Recreation: Lake activities, hunting, Fort Phantom Hill, Cowboy Reunion July 4 in Stamford.

Minerals: Oil, gas, sand and gravel, stone.

Agriculture: Cotton, wheat, sesame and peanuts; cattle. Some 3,500 acres irrigated for peanuts and hay. Market value $41.5 million.

ANSON (2,357) county seat; farming center, government/services; hospital; old courthouse, opera house, museums; Cowboys Christmas Ball in December.

STAMFORD (2,934) trade center for three counties, hospital, historic homes, cowboy museum.

HAMLIN (2,040) farm and ranching, oil and gas, electricity/steam plant using mesquite trees, hunting; hospital; museums; Runnin' the Buff 5K in December.

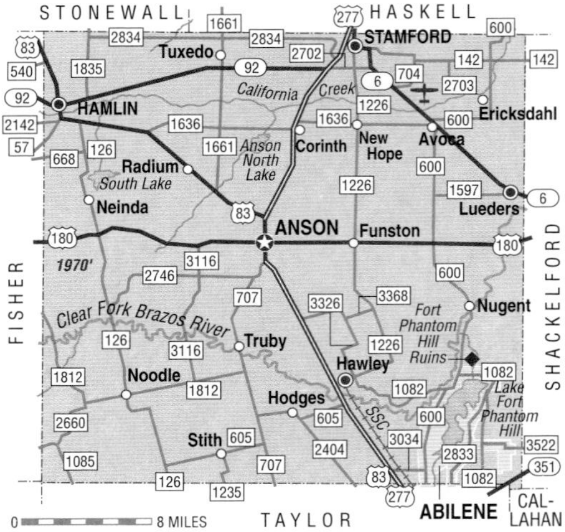

Other towns include: **Hawley** (623), **Lueders** (331) limestone quarries.

Part [5,710] of **Abilene.**

Population	**19,697**
Change from 2010 (%)	-2.5
Area (sq. mi.)	937.1
Land Area (sq. mi.)	928.6
Altitude (ft.)	1,480–1,970
Rainfall (in.)	26.1
Jan. mean min (°F)	31.1
July mean max (°F)	96.2
Civ. Labor	5,859
Unemployed (%)	6.4
Wages	$35,380,970
Per Capita Income	$32,639
Prop. Value	$1,558,116,296
Retail Sales	$232,402,280

Karnes County

Physical Features: Sandy loam, dark clay, alluvial soils in rolling terrain; traversed by San Antonio River; mesquite, oak trees.

Economy: Oil and gas, agribusiness.

History: Coahuiltecan area. Spanish ranching began around 1750. Anglo-Americans arrived in 1840s; Polish in the 1850s. County created in 1854 from Bexar, Goliad, and San Patricio counties, organized the same year; named for Texas Revolutionary figure Henry W. Karnes.

Race/Ethnicity: Anglo, 36.4%; Black, 7.2%; Hispanic, 55%; Asian, 0.2%; Other, 0.9%.

Vital Statistics, annual: Births, 180; deaths, 131; marriages, 6; divorces, 28.

Recreation: Panna Maria, nation's oldest Polish settlement, founded 1854; Old Helena restored courthouse, museum; hunting, nature tourism, guest ranches.

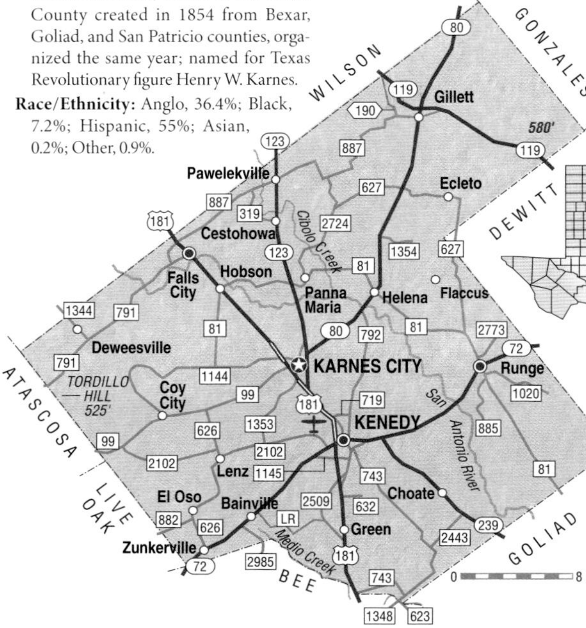

Minerals: Oil, gas, uranium.

Agriculture: Beef cattle, grain, cotton, hay. Market value $29.4 million.

KARNES CITY (3,280) county seat; oil and gas, agribusiness, tourism, processing center, oil-field servicing, manufacturing; library; Lonesome Dove Fest in September.

KENEDY (3,577) farm and oil center, library, dove/quail hunting, prison, hospital; Bluebonnet Days in April.

Other towns include: **Falls City** (686) ranching, sausage making, library, city park on river; **Gillett** (120); **Hobson** (135); **Panna Maria** (45); **Runge** (1,144) oil and gas services, farming, museum, library; cowboy breakfast in December.

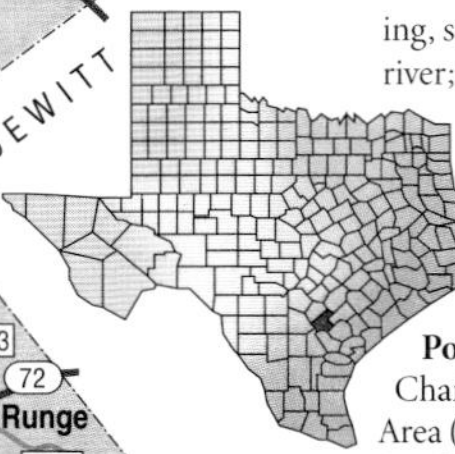

Population	**15,508**
Change from 2010 (%)	4.6
Area (sq. mi.)	753.6
Land Area (sq. mi.)	747.6
Altitude (ft.)	180–580
Rainfall (in.)	30.1
Jan. mean min (°F)	41.8
July mean max (°F)	95.1
Civ. Labor	6,829
Unemployed (%)	5.7
Wages	$92,582,206
Per Capita Income	$56,449
Prop. Value	$9,095,106,200
Retail Sales	$168,874,083

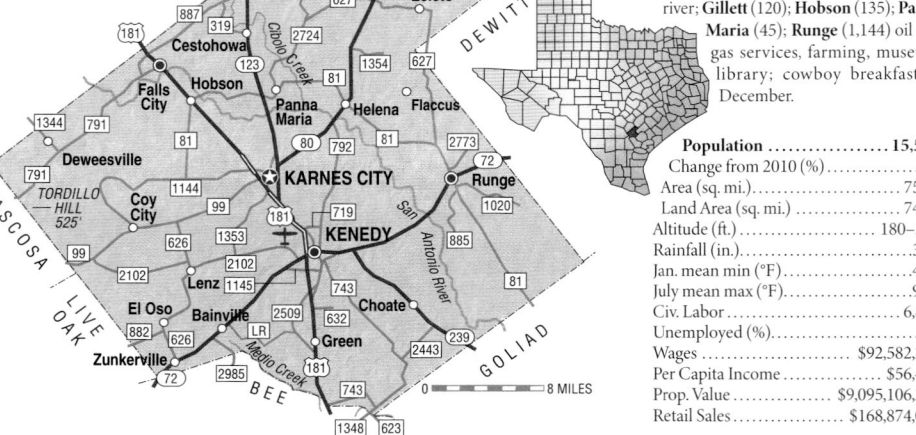

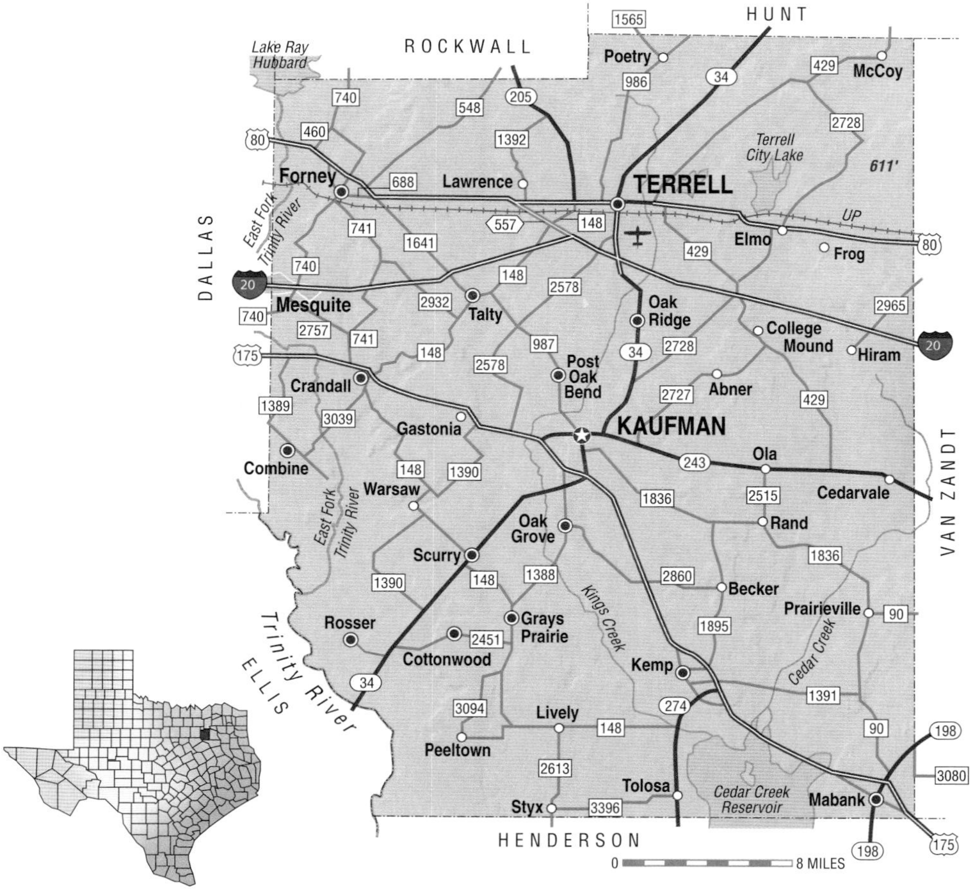

Physical Features: North Blackland prairie, draining to Trinity River; Cedar Creek Reservoir, Lake Ray Hubbard and Terrell City Lake.

Economy: Agriculture, commuting to Dallas, government/services.

History: Caddo and later Cherokee Indians in the area; removed by 1840 when Anglo-American settlement began. County created from Henderson County and organized in 1848; named for member of Texas and U.S. congresses D.S. Kaufman.

Race/Ethnicity: Anglo, 64.5%; Black, 10.6%; Hispanic, 21.6%; Asian, 0.8%; Other, 2.2%.

Vital Statistics, annual: Births, 1,539; deaths, 897; marriages, 686; divorces, 380.

Recreation: Lake activities; Porter Farm near Terrell is site of origin of U.S.-Texas Agricultural Extension program; antique centers near Forney; historic homes at Terrell.

Minerals: Gravel, sand, oil, gas.

Kaufman County

Agriculture: Beef cattle, horticulture, hay/forage, row crops, horses. Market value $57.1 million.

KAUFMAN (7,649) county seat; government/services, manufacturing and distribution, commuters to Dallas; hospital; Octoberfest.

TERRELL (19,183) agribusiness, varied manufacturing, large outlet center; private hospital, state hospital; community college, Southwestern Christian College; British flying school museum, Heritage Jubilee in April.

FORNEY (27,565) important antiques center, light industrial, commuters to Dallas, historic homes, barbecue cook-off in June.

Other towns include: **Combine** (2,270, partly in Dallas County); **Cottonwood** (212); **Crandall** (3,495) Cotton Festival in September; **Elmo** (1,049); **Grays Prairie** (379); **Kemp** (1,303); **Lawrence** (259); **Mabank** (3,423, partly in Henderson County) varied manufacturing, tourism, retail trade, Western Week in June; **Oak Grove** (686); **Oak Ridge** (699); **Post Oak Bend** (701); **Rosser** (404); **Scurry** (769); **Talty** (2,879).

Population	**135,410**
Change from 2010 (%)	31.0
Area (sq. mi.)	807.7
Land Area (sq. mi.)	780.7
Altitude (ft.)	300–611
Rainfall (in.)	39.9
Jan. mean min (°F)	33.1
July mean max (°F)	94.3
Civ. Labor	68,197
Unemployed (%)	5.5
Wages	$444,184,053
Per Capita Income	$43,972
Prop. Value	$16,980,995,978
Retail Sales	$1,728,310,428

For explanation of sources, symbols and abbreviations, see p. 204, and foldout map.

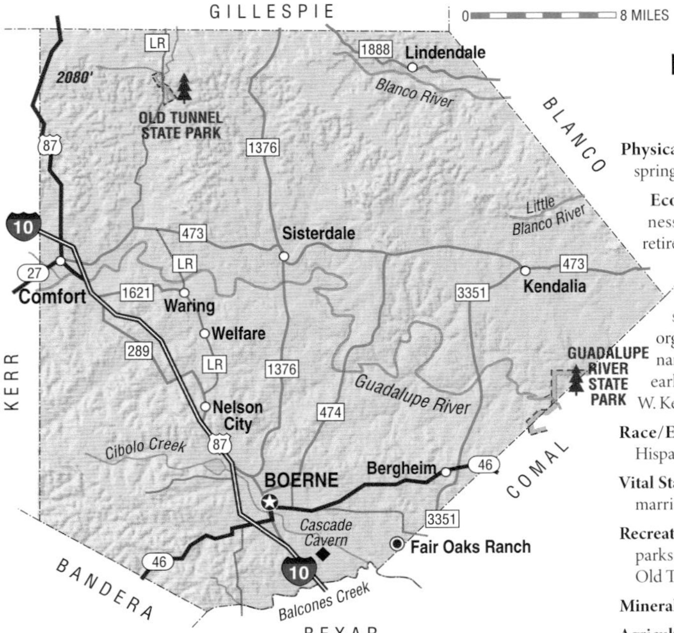

Kendall County

Physical Features: Hill Country, plateau, with spring-fed streams; caves; scenic drives.

Economy: Government/services, agribusiness, commuters to San Antonio, tourism, retirement area, some manufacturing.

History: Lipan Apaches, Kiowas and Comanches in area when German settlers arrived in 1840s. County created, organized, from Blanco, Kerr counties 1862; named for pioneer journalist-sheepman and early contributor to Texas Almanac, George W. Kendall.

Race/Ethnicity: Anglo, 72.5%; Black, 0.3%; Hispanic, 25.3%; Asian, 0.4%; Other, 1.2%.

Vital Statistics, annual: Births, 377; deaths, 377; marriages, 472; divorces, 21.

Recreation: Hunting, fishing, exotic wildlife, state parks; Cascade Cavern, Cave Without a Name, Old Tunnel; historic sites.

Minerals: Limestone rock, caliche.

Agriculture: Cattle, goats, sheep, hay. Market value $12.4 million. Cedar posts, firewood sold.

BOERNE (17,228) county seat; tourism, antiques, some manufacturing, ranching, commuting to San Antonio; library; Christmas in Comfort on Saturday after Thanksgiving.

Other towns include: **Comfort** (2,936) tourism, farming and ranching, manufacturing, Civil War monument honoring Unionists, library, museum, mountain bike trail; **Kendalia** (149); **Sisterdale** (110); **Waring** (73).

Part of **Fair Oaks Ranch** (10,042).

Population	**47,284**
Change from 2010 (%)	41.5
Area (sq. mi.)	663.0
Land Area (sq. mi.)	662.5
Altitude (ft.)	1,000–2,080
Rainfall (in.)	38.1
Jan. mean min (°F)	35.4
July mean max (°F)	92.5
Civ. Labor	22,722
Unemployed (%)	3.9
Wages	$246,675,316
Per Capita Income	$81,882
Prop. Value	$10,113,619,619
Retail Sales	$1,379,023,013

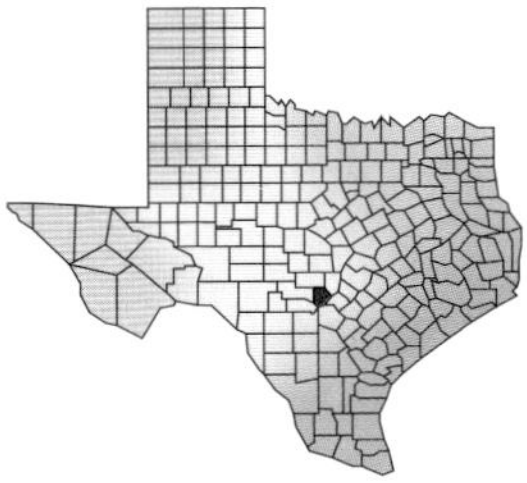

Grass returns to this ranch in Kent County, after years of brush removal and reclamation efforts. Photo by USDA NRCS Texas

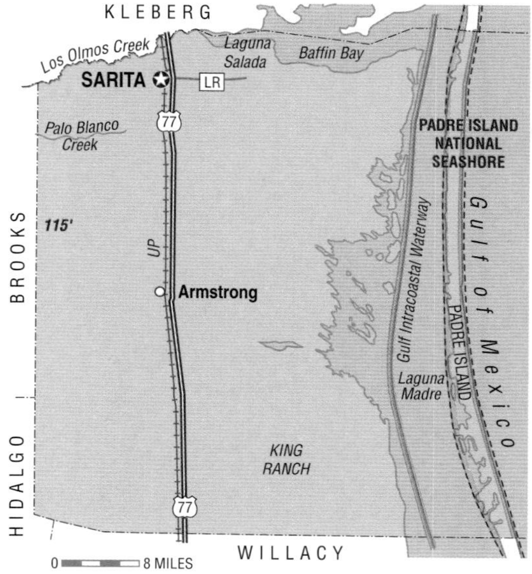

Kenedy County

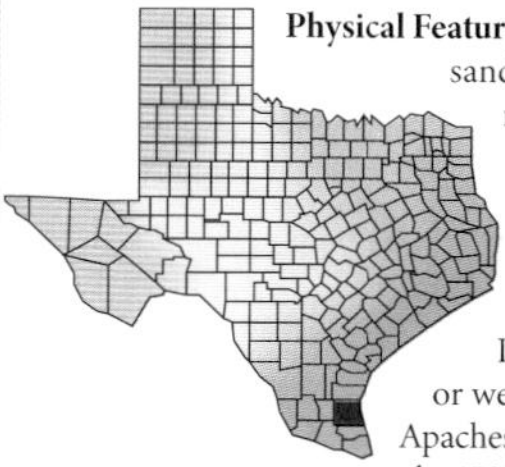

Physical Features: Gulf coastal county; flat, sandy terrain, some loam soils; motts of live oaks.

Economy: Oil, ranching, nature tourism, hunting leases, wind farm.

History: Coahuiltecan Indians who assimilated or were driven out by the Lipan Apaches. Spanish ranching began in the 1790s. Anglo-Americans arrived after the Mexican War. Among last counties created, organized, 1921 from Cameron, Hidalgo, and Willacy counties; named for pioneer steamboat operator and cattleman, Capt. Mifflin Kenedy.

Race/Ethnicity: Anglo, 21.2%; Black, 0.2%; Hispanic, 75.8%; Asian, 0.2%; Other, 2.3%.

Vital Statistics, annual: Births, 0; deaths, 3; marriages, 5; divorces, 0.

Recreation: Hunting, fishing, nature tourism.

Minerals: Oil, gas.

Agriculture: Beef cattle, horses. Market value $19.7 million. Hunting leases, nature tourism important.

SARITA (244) county seat; cattle-shipping point, ranch headquarters, gas processing; one of state's least populous counties.

Also, **Armstrong** (4).

Population	**390**	July mean max (°F)	94.6
Change from 2010 (%)	-6.3	Civ. Labor	175
Area (sq. mi.)	1,945.8	Unemployed (%)	7.4
Land Area (sq. mi.)	1,458.3	Wages	$6,388,795
Altitude (ft.)	sea level–115	Per Capita Income	$42,262
Rainfall (in.)	29.2	Prop. Value	$2,127,810,195
Jan. mean min (°F)	44.4	Retail Sales	N/A

For explanation of sources, symbols and abbreviations, see p. 204, and foldout map.

Kent County

Physical Features: Rolling, broken terrain; lake; drains to Salt and Double Mountain forks of Brazos River; sandy, loam soils.

Economy: Agribusiness, oil and gas operations, government/services, hunting leases.

History: Comanches driven out by the U.S. Army in the 1870s. Ranching developed in the 1880s. County created in 1876 from Bexar and Young territories; organized in 1892. Name honors Andrew Kent, one of 32 volunteers from Gonzales who died at the Alamo.

Race/Ethnicity: Anglo, 81.4%; Black, 0.9%; Hispanic, 15.9%; Asian, 0%; Other, 1.7%.

Vital Statistics, annual: Births, 0; deaths, 9; marriages, 4; divorces, 1.

Recreation: Hunting, fishing; scenic croton breaks and salt flat; Winterfest in December.

Minerals: Oil, gas.

Agriculture: Cattle, cotton, wheat, sorghum. Market value $9.9 million.

JAYTON (503) county seat; oil-field services, farming center; Summerfest in August.

Other towns include: **Girard** (44).

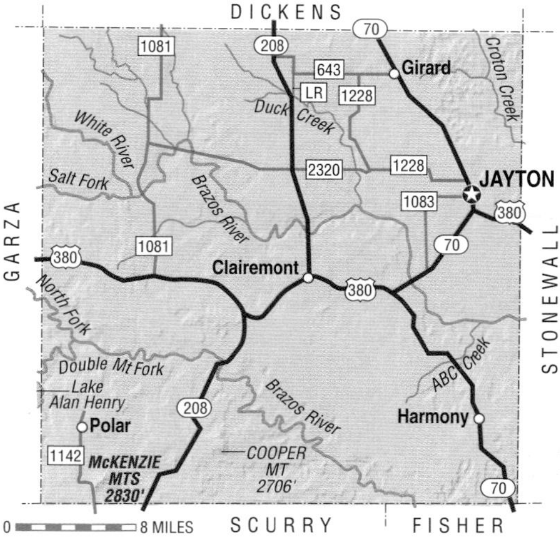

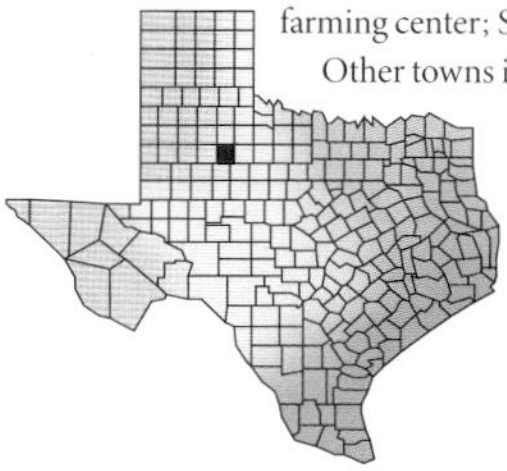

Population	**759**	July mean max (°F)	94.6
Change from 2010 (%)	-6.1	Civ. Labor	482
Area (sq. mi.)	902.9	Unemployed (%)	3.1
Land Area (sq. mi.)	902.5	Wages	$3,054,100
Altitude (ft.)	1,740–2,830	Per Capita Income	$54,630
Rainfall (in.)	23.5	Prop. Value	$861,646,559
Jan. mean min (°F)	27.2	Retail Sales	$4,857,067

Kerr County

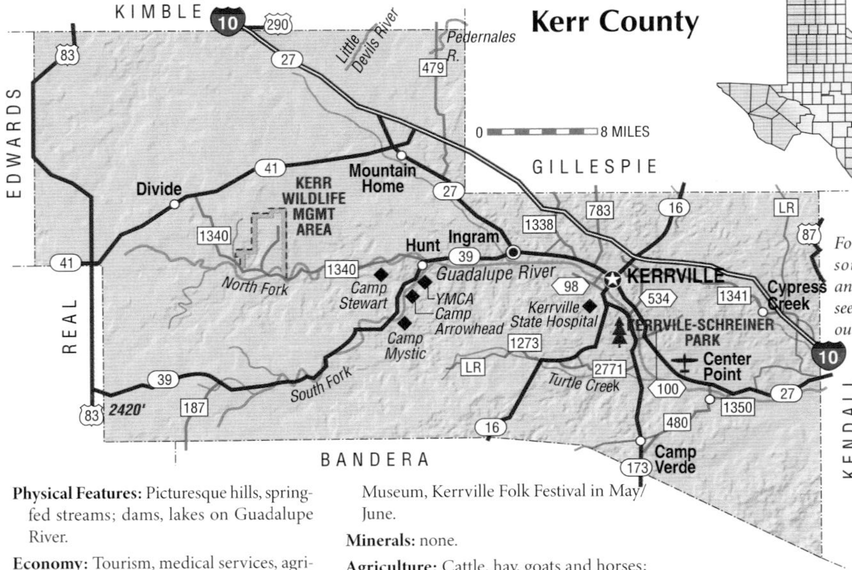

For explanation of sources, symbols and abbreviations, see p. 204, and fold-out map.

Physical Features: Picturesque hills, spring-fed streams; dams, lakes on Guadalupe River.

Economy: Tourism, medical services, agribusiness, hunting leases.

History: Lipan Apaches, Kiowas and Comanches in area. Anglo-American settlers arrived in the late 1840s. County created in 1856 from Bexar County; organized the same year; named for a member of Austin's Colony, James Kerr.

Race/Ethnicity: Anglo, 66.8%; Black, 1.5%; Hispanic, 28.9%; Asian, 0.8%; Other, 1.8%.

Vital Statistics, annual: Births, 540; deaths, 774; marriages, 334; divorces, 184.

Recreation: Youth camps, dude ranches, park, Cailloux and Point theaters, wildlife management area, Cowboy Artists Museum, Kerrville Folk Festival in May/June.

Minerals: none.

Agriculture: Cattle, hay, goats and horses; deer (second in numbers as livestock). Market value $9.3 million. Hunting leases important.

KERRVILLE (24,005) county seat; tourist center, youth camps, agribusiness, aircraft and parts, varied manufacturing; Schreiner University; state hospital, veterans hospital, private hospital; retirement center; retail trade; state arts, crafts show in May.

Other towns include: **Camp Verde** (41); **Center Point** (800); **Hunt** (708) youth camps, hospital; **Ingram** (1,855) camps, cabins; **Mountain Home** (96).

Population	**52,829**
Change from 2010 (%)	6.5
Area (sq. mi.)	1,107.3
Land Area (sq. mi.)	1,103.3
Altitude (ft.)	1,404–2,420
Rainfall (in.)	32.1
Jan. mean min (°F)	33.8
July mean max (°F)	92.2
Civ. Labor	20,988
Unemployed (%)	4.8
Wages	$230,029,844
Per Capita Income	$51,768
Prop. Value	$8,787,901,328
Retail Sales	$1,044,363,659

The Kerrville-Schreiner Park Amphitheater. Photo by Larry D. Moore, CC by SA 4.0/Wikimedia Commons

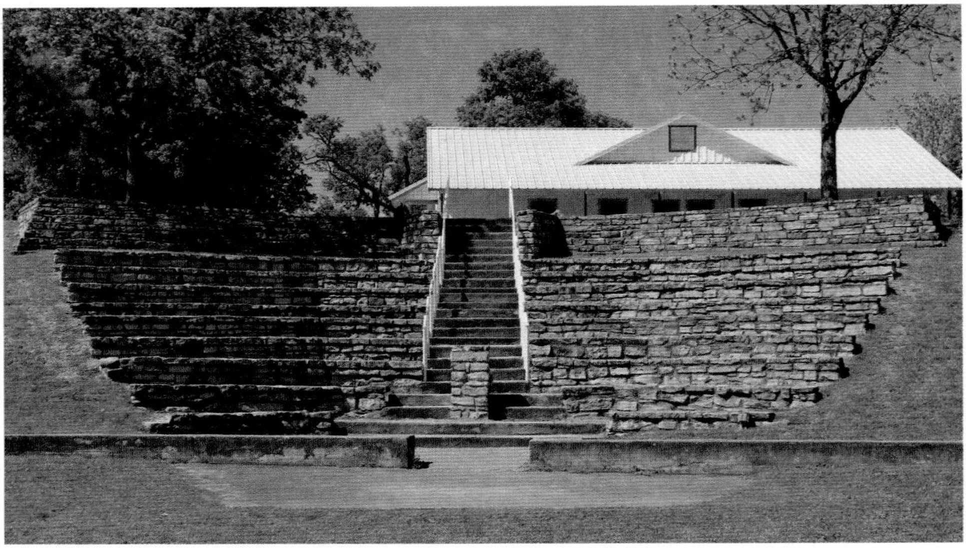

Kimble County

Population	**4,604**
Change from 2010 (%)	-0.1
Area (sq. mi.)	1,251.2
Land Area (sq. mi.)	1,251.0
Altitude (ft.)	1,476–2,460
Rainfall (in.)	27.0
Jan. mean min (°F)	27.8
July mean max (°F)	94.3
Civ. Labor	1,818
Unemployed (%)	4.5
Wages	$12,810,435
Per Capita Income	$44,371
Prop. Value	$2,928,093,841
Retail Sales	$94,121,010

Physical Features: Picturesque Edwards Plateau; rugged, broken by numerous streams; drains to Llano River; sandy, gray, chocolate loam soils.

Economy: Livestock production and market, tourism, cedar oil and wood products, metal building materials.

History: Apache, Kiowa and Comanche area until the 1870s. U.S. military outposts protected the first Anglo-American settlers in the 1850s. County created from Bexar County in 1858 and organized in 1876. Named for George C. Kimble, a Gonzales volunteer who died at the Alamo.

Race/Ethnicity: Anglo, 68.1%; Black, 0.3%; Hispanic, 30%; Asian, 0.4%; Other, 0.9%.

Vital Statistics, annual: Births, 39; deaths, 45; marriages, 24; divorces, 22.

Recreation: Hunting, fishing in spring-fed streams, nature tourism; among leading deer counties; state park; Kimble Kounty Kow Kick on Labor Day, Wild Game dinner on Thanksgiving Saturday.

Minerals: gravel.

Agriculture: Cattle, meat goats, sheep, Angora goats, pecans. Market value $10.9 million. Hunting leases important. Firewood, cedar sold.

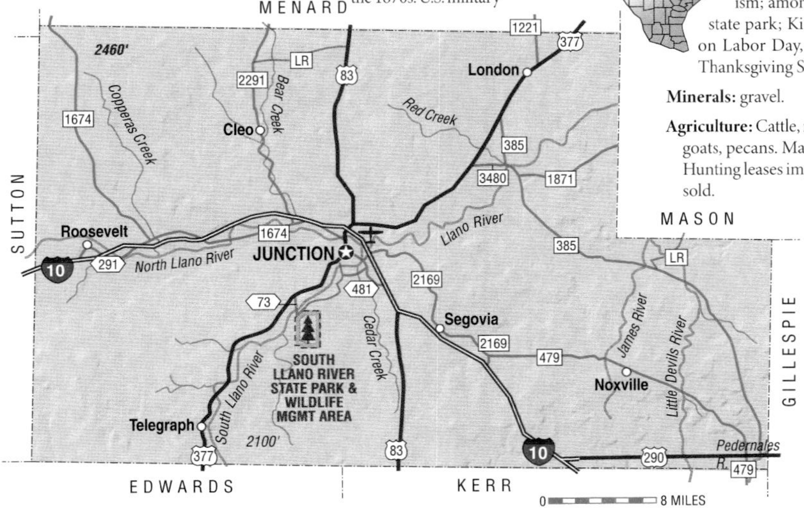

JUNCTION (2,522) county seat; tourism, varied manufacturing, livestock production; two museums; Texas Tech University center; hospital; library, airport.

Other towns include: **London** (180); **Roosevelt** (14).

King County

Physical Features: Hilly, broken by Wichita, Brazos tributaries; extensive grassland; dark loam to red soils.

Economy: Oil and gas, ranching, government/services, horse sales, hunting leases.

Population	**274**
Change from 2010 (%)	-4.2
Area (sq. mi.)	913.3
Land Area (sq. mi.)	910.9
Altitude (ft.)	1,450–2,250
Rainfall (in.)	25.5
Jan. mean min (°F)	27.0
July mean max (°F)	95.9
Civ. Labor	285
Unemployed (%)	1.4
Wages	$2,218,449
Per Capita Income	$78,849
Prop. Value	$597,162,733
Retail Sales	N/A

History: Apache area until Comanches moved in about 1700. Comanches were removed by U.S. Army in 1874-75 after which ranching began. County created in 1876 from Bexar District; organized in 1891; named for William P. King, a volunteer from Gonzales who died at the Alamo.

Race/Ethnicity: Anglo, 85.4%; Black, 0%; Hispanic, 13.5%; Asian, 0%; Other, 1%.

Vital Statistics, annual: Births, 0; deaths, 0; marriages, 5; divorces, 0.

Recreation: 6666 Ranch visits, hunting, roping and ranch horse competitions.

Minerals: Oil, gas.

Agriculture: Cattle, horses, wheat, hay, cotton. Market value $13.8 million. Hunting leases important.

GUTHRIE (188) county seat; ranch-supply center, government/services; community center complex, library; Thanksgiving community supper.

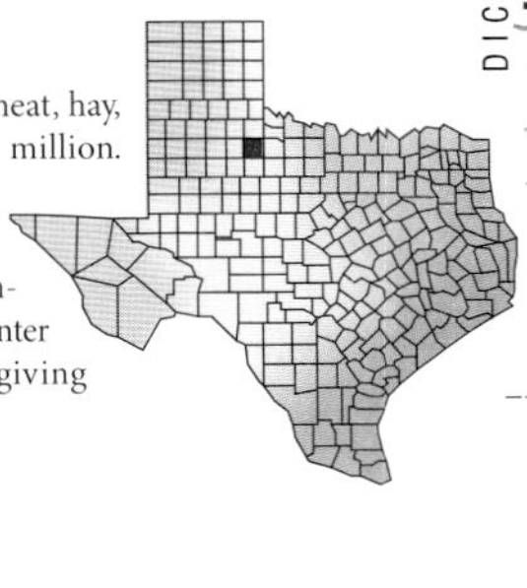

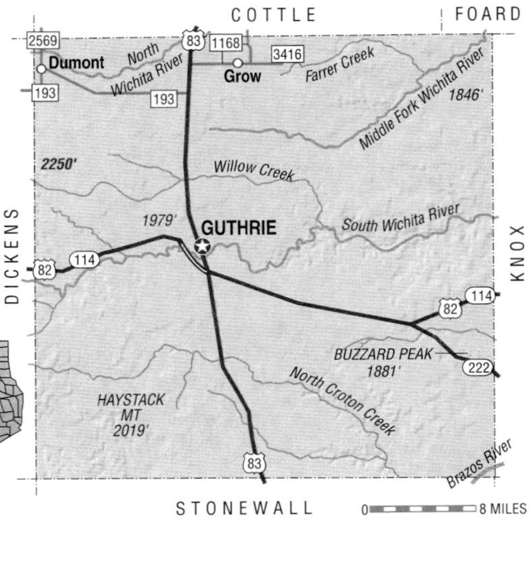

Kinney County

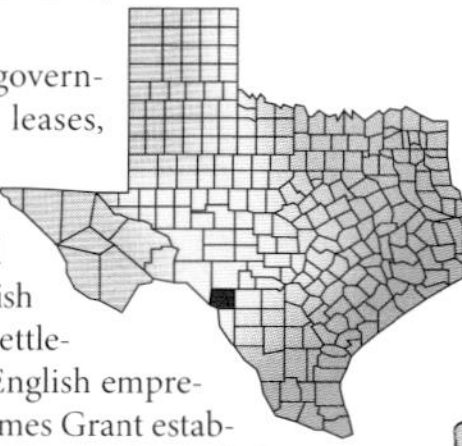

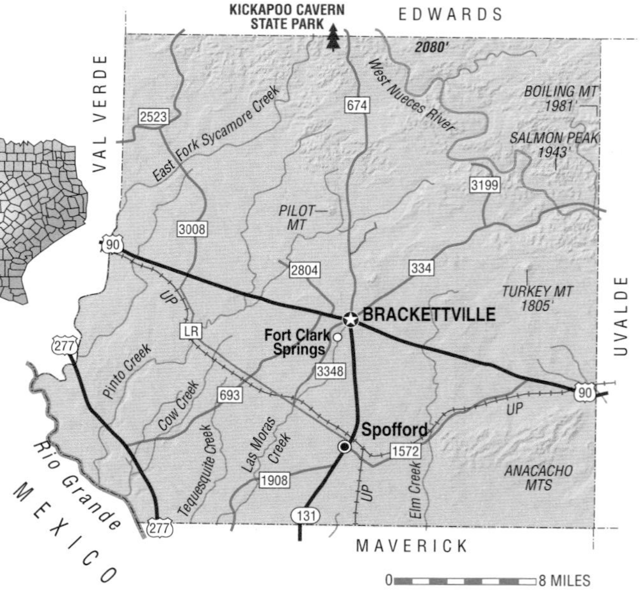

Physical Features: Hilly, broken by Rio Grande tributaries; Anacacho Mountains; Nueces Canyon.

Economy: Agribusiness, government/services, hunting leases, wind farm, gas pipelines.

History: Coahuiltecans in the area, later Apaches and Comanches arrived. Spanish Franciscans established settlement in the late 1700s. English empresarios John Beales and James Grant established English-speaking colony in 1834. Black Seminoles served as army scouts in the 1870s. County created from Bexar County in 1850; organized in 1874; named for H.L. Kinney, founder of Corpus Christi.

Race/Ethnicity: Anglo, 33.9%; Black, 1%; Hispanic, 62.8%; Asian, 0.3%; Other, 1.7%.

Vital Statistics, annual: Births, 47; deaths, 42; marriages, 8; divorces, 0.

Recreation: Hunting; old Fort Clark Springs; Kickapoo Caverns State Park; Seminole Indian cemetery; Cinco de Mayo, Juneteenth.

Minerals: Not significant.

Agriculture: Cattle, sheep, goats, hay, sorghum, cotton, corn, oats, wheat, pecans. Market value $5.0 million. Hunting important.

BRACKETTVILLE (1,692) county seat; agriculture, tourism; museum, Fort Clark Days in March.

Other towns include: **Fort Clark Springs** (1,231); **Spofford** (96).

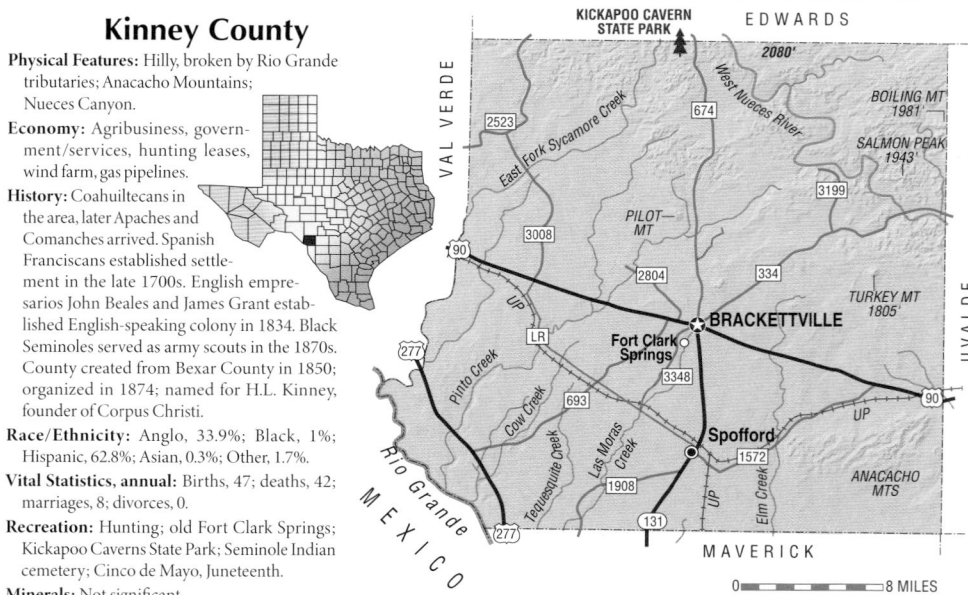

Population	**3,575**
Change from 2010 (%)	-0.6
Area (sq. mi.)	1,365.1
Land Area (sq. mi.)	1,363.1
Altitude (ft.)	790–2,080
Rainfall (in.)	23.6
Jan. mean min (°F)	38.8
July mean max (°F)	93.9
Civ. Labor	1,364
Unemployed (%)	5.1
Wages	$12,726,590
Per Capita Income	$32,219
Prop. Value	$2,101,366,618
Retail Sales	$12,375,404

Kleberg County

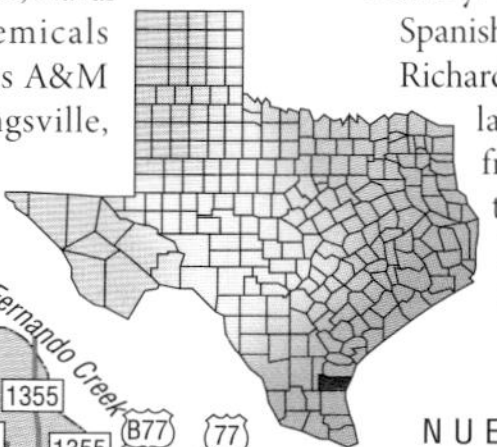

Physical Features: Coastal plain, broken by bays; sandy, loam, clay soils; tree motts.

Economy: Oil and gas, Naval air station, chemicals and plastics, Texas A&M University – Kingsville, agriculture.

History: Coahuiltecan and Karankawa area. Spanish land grants date to 1750s. In 1853 Richard King purchased Santa Gertrudis land grant. County created 1913 from Nueces County, organized the same year; named for San Jacinto veteran and rancher Robert Kleberg.

Race/Ethnicity: Anglo, 19.3%; Black, 3.8%; Hispanic, 73.3%; Asian, 2.2%; Other, 1.1%.

Vital Statistics, annual: Births, 435; deaths, 243; marriages, 224; divorces, 98.

Recreation: Fishing, hunting, water sports, park at Baffin Bay; wildlife sanctuary; winter bird watching; university events, museum; King Ranch headquarters, tours; La Posada celebration in November.

Minerals: Oil, gas.

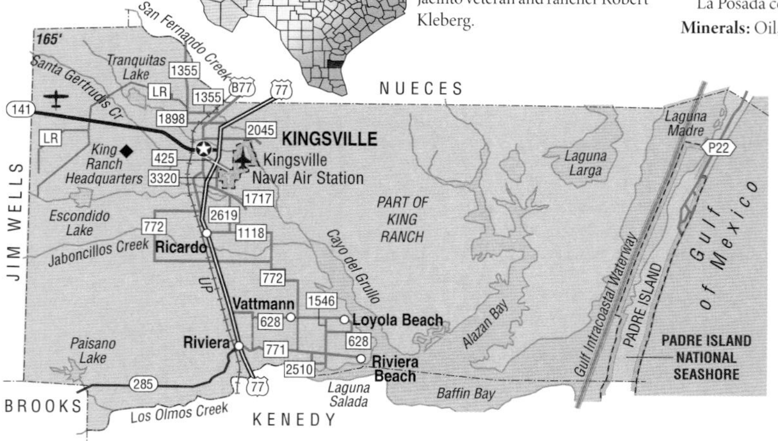

Agriculture: Cattle, grain sorghum, cotton. Market value $52.8 million. Hunting leases and ecotourism important.

KINGSVILLE (25,315) county seat; government/services, oil, gas, agribusiness, tourism, chemical plant, university, Coastal Bend College branch; hospital; ranching heritage festival in February, King Ranch Breakfast in November.

Other towns: **Ricardo** (1,090), **Riviera** (724).

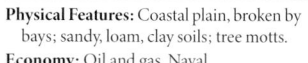

Population	**32,135**
Change from 2010 (%)	0.2
Area (sq. mi.)	1,090.2
Land Area (sq. mi.)	881.3
Altitude (ft.)	sea level–165
Rainfall (in.)	30.4
Jan. mean min (°F)	45.8
July mean max (°F)	95.1
Civ. Labor	13,295
Unemployed (%)	7.8
Wages	$131,809,844
Per Capita Income	$41,526
Prop. Value	$2,687,127,460
Retail Sales	$458,365,059

Knox County

Physical Features: Eroded breaks on West Texas Rolling Plains; Brazos, Wichita rivers; sandy, loam soils; Lake Davis, Lake Catherine, and Truscott Brine Lake.

Economy: Oil, agriculture, government/services.

History: Indian conscripts were used as labor during the Spanish period to mine copper deposits along the Brazos River. Ranching and farming developed in the 1880s. German colony settled in 1895. County created from the Bexar, Young territories in 1858; re-created in 1876; organized in 1886; named for U.S. Secretary of War Henry Knox.

Race/Ethnicity: Anglo, 57.7%; Black, 5.6%; Hispanic, 34.7%; Asian, 0.1%; Other, 1.6%.

Vital Statistics, annual: Births, 45; deaths, 61; marriages, 22; divorces, 13.

Recreation: Lake activities, fishing, hunting; Knox City seedless watermelon festival in July.

Minerals: Oil, gas.

Agriculture: Wheat, cattle, cotton. Some cotton irrigated. Market value $60.5 million.

BENJAMIN (256) county seat; ranching, farm center; veterans memorial.

MUNDAY (1,275) portable buildings, other manufacturing; A&M vegetable research station.

KNOX CITY (1,135) agribusiness, petroleum center; USDA plant materials research center; hospital.

Other towns include: **Goree** (203); **Rhineland** (120) old church established by German immigrants.

For explanation of sources, symbols and abbreviations, see p. 204, and foldout map.

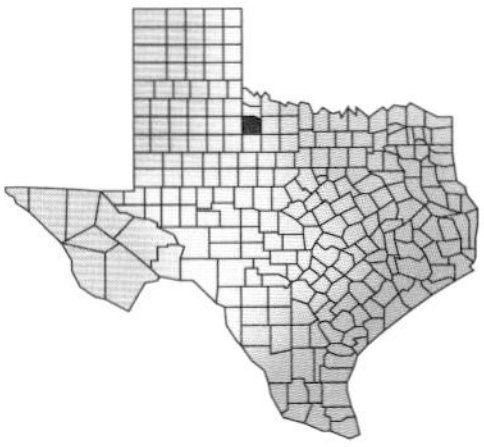

Population	**3,683**
Change from 2010 (%)	-1.0
Area (sq. mi.)	855.5
Land Area (sq. mi.)	850.6
Altitude (ft.)	1,200–1,794
Rainfall (in.)	26.4
Jan. mean min (°F)	29.1
July mean max (°F)	96.3
Civ. Labor	1,486
Unemployed (%)	4.7
Wages	$13,493,693
Per Capita Income	$39,587
Prop. Value	$900,220,430
Retail Sales	$20,296,138

The Fort Clark Historic District in Kinney County. Photo by Jerrye & Roy Klotz, MD, CC by SA 4.0/Wikimedia Commons

Lamar County

Physical Features: North Texas county on divide between Red, Sulphur rivers; soils chiefly blackland, except along Red; pines, hardwoods; Pat Mayse Lake and Lake Crook.

Economy: Varied manufacturing, agribusiness, medical, government/services.

History: Caddo Indian area. First Anglo-American settlers arrived about 1815. County created in 1840 from Red River County; organized in 1841; named for second president of Republic, Mirabeau B. Lamar.

Race/Ethnicity: Anglo, 73.7%; Black, 12.5%; Hispanic, 8.3%; Asian, 0.6%; Other, 4.7%.

Vital Statistics, annual: Births, 680; deaths, 641; marriages, 465; divorces, 254.

Recreation: Lake activities; Gambill goose refuge; hunting, fishing; state park; Trail de Paris rail-to-trail; Sam Bell Maxey Home; State Sen. A.M. Aikin Archives, other museums.

Minerals: Negligible.

Agriculture: Beef, hay, dairy, soybeans (first in acreage), wheat, corn, sorghum, cotton. Market value $73.4 million.

PARIS (25,297) county seat; varied manufacturing, food processing, government/services; hospitals; junior college; museums; Tour de Paris bicycle rally in July; archery pro-am tournament in March.

Other towns include: **Arthur City** (180), **Blossom** (1,558), **Brookston** (130), **Chicota** (150), **Cunningham** (110), **Deport** (556, partly in Red River County), **Pattonville** (180), **Petty** (130), **Powderly** (1,204), **Reno** (3,360), **Roxton** (647), **Sumner** (95), **Sun Valley** (77), **Toco** (80).

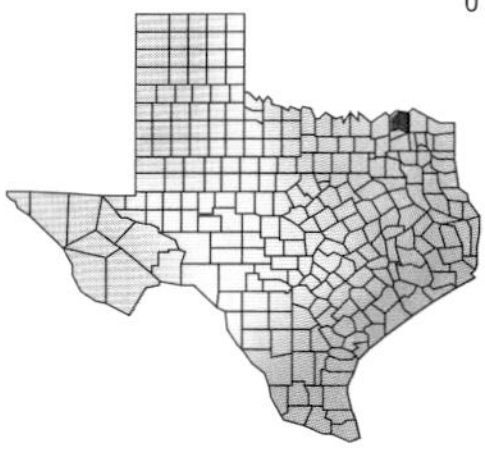

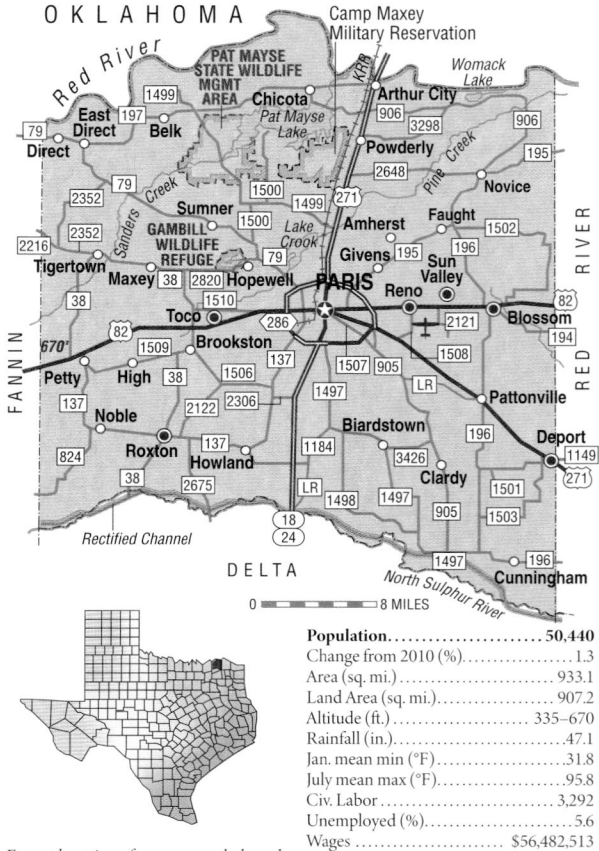

For explanation of sources, symbols and abbreviations, see p. 204, and foldout map.

Population	**50,440**
Change from 2010 (%)	1.3
Area (sq. mi.)	933.1
Land Area (sq. mi.)	907.2
Altitude (ft.)	335–670
Rainfall (in.)	47.1
Jan. mean min (°F)	31.8
July mean max (°F)	95.8
Civ. Labor	3,292
Unemployed (%)	5.6
Wages	$56,482,513
Per Capita Income	$39,913
Prop. Value	$6,132,513,667
Retail Sales	$808,949,035

Shops along Main Street in Paris. Photo by Adavyd, CC 3/Wikimedia Commons

Lamb County

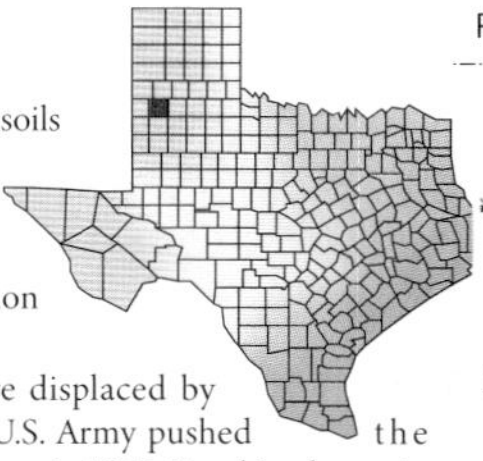

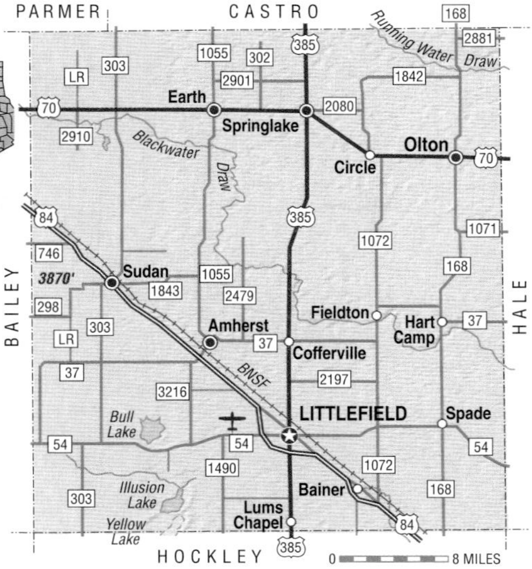

Physical Features: Rich, red, brown soils on the High Plains; some hills; drains to upper Brazos River tributaries; numerous playas.

Economy: Agribusiness; distribution center; denim textiles.

History: Apache tribes, who were displaced by Comanches around 1700. The U.S. Army pushed the Comanches into the Indian Territory in 1875. Ranching began in the 1880s; farming started after 1900. County created in 1876 from the Bexar District and organized in 1908; named for Lt. G.A. Lamb, who died in battle of San Jacinto.

Race/Ethnicity: Anglo, 37.9%; Black, 4.6%; Hispanic, 55%; Asian, 0.1%; Other, 2.1%.

Vital Statistics, annual: Births, 187; deaths, 147; marriages, 65; divorces, 3.

Recreation: Waylon Jennings Birthday Bash in June at Littlefield, museums, Earth Day in April.

Minerals: Oil, stone, gas.

Agriculture: Fed cattle; cotton, corn, wheat, grain sorghum, vegetables, soybeans, hay; sheep. 179,500 acres irrigated. Market value $575.3 million.

LITTLEFIELD (5,840) county seat; milk processing, agribusiness, manufacturing; hospital, prison, museum.

Olton (2,022) agribusiness, retail center; Sandcrawl museum; pheasant hunt in winter; Sandhills Celebration in August.

Other towns include: **Amherst** (630); **Earth** (957) farming center, dairies, feed lot; **Fieldton** (20); **Spade** (64); **Springlake** (96); **Sudan** (892) farming center, government/services, Homecoming Day in fall.

Population	**12,565**	July mean max (°F)	92.0
Change from 2010 (%)	-10.1	Civ. Labor	23,650
Area (sq. mi.)	1,017.7	Unemployed (%)	6
Land Area (sq. mi.)	1,016.2	Wages	$267,834,532
Altitude (ft.)	3,390–3,870	Per Capita Income	$43,063
Rainfall (in.)	18.9	Prop. Value	$1,564,372,299
Jan. mean min (°F)	24.5	Retail Sales	$128,952,656

Lampasas County

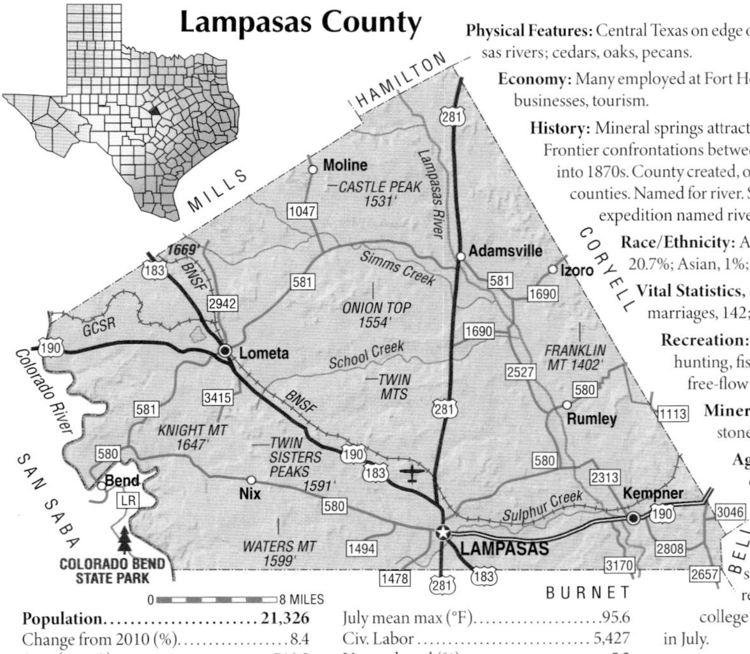

Physical Features: Central Texas on edge of Hill Country; Colorado, Lampasas rivers; cedars, oaks, pecans.

Economy: Many employed at Fort Hood, several industrial plants, agribusinesses, tourism.

History: Mineral springs attracted first Anglo-Americans in 1853. Frontier confrontations between settlers, Comanches continued into 1870s. County created, organized, in 1856 from Bell, Travis counties. Named for river. Some have speculated that an early expedition named river for city of Lampazos in Mexico.

Race/Ethnicity: Anglo, 70.9%; Black, 3%; Hispanic, 20.7%; Asian, 1%; Other, 4.1%.

Vital Statistics, annual: Births, 219; deaths, 197; marriages, 142; divorces, 79.

Recreation: Scenic drives; state park; deer hunting, fishing in streams; Hancock Springs free-flow swim area at Lampasas.

Minerals: Sand and gravel, building stone.

Agriculture: Beef cattle, hay, goats, exotic animals. Market value $18.4 million. Hunting leases, ecotourism.

LAMPASAS (7,787) county seat; manufacturing, health care, retail; historic downtown; hospital, college extensions; museum; Spring Ho in July.

Other towns include: **Bend** (115, partly in San Saba County); **Izoro** (17); **Kempner** (1,165); **Lometa** (887) market and shipping point; Diamondback Jubilee in March.

Population	**21,326**	July mean max (°F)	95.6
Change from 2010 (%)	8.4	Civ. Labor	5,427
Area (sq. mi.)	713.9	Unemployed (%)	5.2
Land Area (sq. mi.)	712.8	Wages	$49,421,250
Altitude (ft.)	800–1,669	Per Capita Income	$45,655
Rainfall (in.)	32.2	Prop. Value	$2,953,825,367
Jan. mean min (°F)	33.4	Retail Sales	$252,236,860

La Salle County

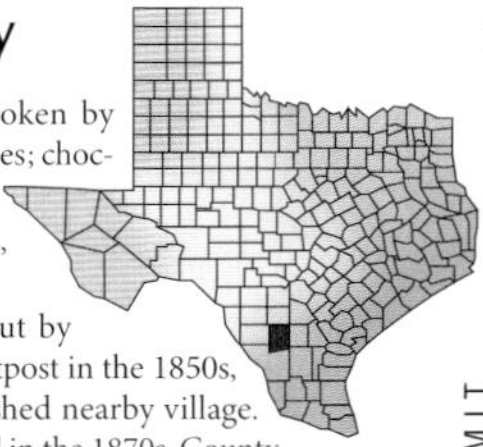

Physical Features: Brushy plain, broken by Nueces, Frio rivers and their tributaries; chocolate, dark gray, sandy loam soils.

Economy: Agribusiness, hunting leases, tourism, government services.

History: Coahuiltecans, squeezed out by migrating Apaches. U.S. military outpost in the 1850s, settlers of Mexican descent established nearby village. Anglo-American ranching developed in the 1870s. County created from Bexar District in 1858; organized in 1880; named for Robert Cavelier Sieur de La Salle, French explorer who died in Texas.

Race/Ethnicity: Anglo, 11.3%; Black, 0.2%; Hispanic, 87.5%; Asian, 0%; Other, 0.7%.

Vital Statistics, annual: Births, 104; deaths, 61; marriages, 34; divorces, 13.

Recreation: Nature trails; school where Lyndon B. Johnson taught; wildlife management area; deer, bird, javelina hunting, fishing; wild hog cookoff in March.

Minerals: Oil, gas.

Agriculture: Beef cattle, peanuts, watermelons, grain sorghum. Market value $6.3 million.

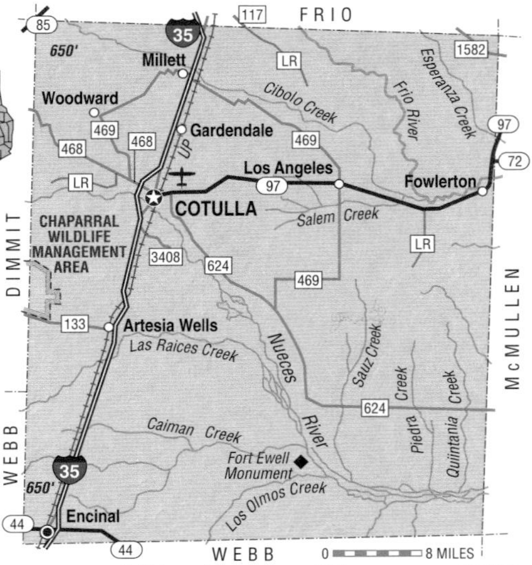

COTULLA (4,063) county seat; oil and lodging, state prison; hunting center; Brush Country museum.

Other towns include: **Encinal** (583), **Fowlerton** (48).

Population	**7,426**
Change from 2010 (%)	7.8
Area (sq. mi.)	1,494.2
Land Area (sq. mi.)	1,486.7
Altitude (ft.)	255–650
Rainfall (in.)	24.7
Jan. mean min (°F)	38.9
July mean max (°F)	9,609.0
Civ. Labor	9,222
Unemployed (%)	5.1
Wages	$48,508,877
Per Capita Income	$50,656
Prop. Value	$7,951,912,008
Retail Sales	$126,728,331

Lavaca County

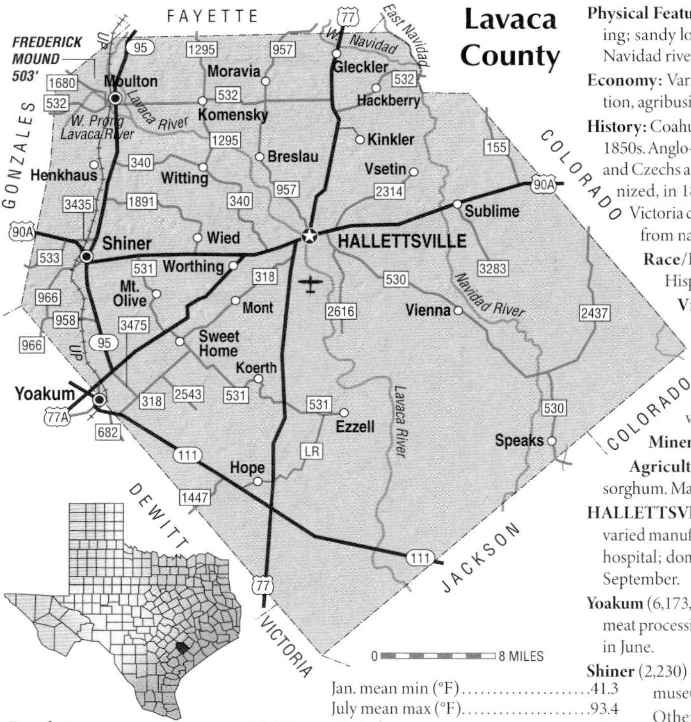

Physical Features: Coastal Plains county; north rolling; sandy loam, black waxy soils; drains to Lavaca, Navidad rivers.

Economy: Varied manufacturing, oil and gas production, agribusinesses, tourism.

History: Coahuiltecan area; later a Comanche area until 1850s. Anglo-Americans first settled in 1831. Germans and Czechs arrived 1880–1900. County created, organized, in 1846 from Colorado, Jackson, Gonzales, Victoria counties. Name is Spanish for cow, la vaca, from name of river.

Race/Ethnicity: Anglo, 71%; Black, 6.8%; Hispanic, 20.5%; Asian, 0.3%; Other, 1.3%.

Vital Statistics, annual: Births, 231; deaths, 269; marriages, 118; divorces, 31.

Recreation: Deer, other hunting, fishing; wildflower trails, historic sites, churches; Fiddlers Frolics in Hallettsville in April.

Minerals: Some oil, gas.

Agriculture: Cattle, forage, poultry, rice, corn, sorghum. Market value $50.5 million. Hunting leases.

HALLETTSVILLE (2,753) county seat; retail center; varied manufacturing; agribusiness; museum, library, hospital; domino, "42" tournaments; Kolache Fest in September.

Yoakum (6,173, partly in DeWitt County); cattle, leather, meat processing; hospital; museum; Tom Tom festival in June.

Shiner (2,230) Spoetzl brewery, varied manufacturing; museum; clinic; Half Moon Holidays in July.

Other towns include: **Moulton** (924) agribusiness, Town & Country Jamboree in July; **Sublime** (75); **Sweet Home** (360).

Population	**20,437**
Change from 2010 (%)	6.1
Area (sq. mi.)	970.4
Land Area (sq. mi.)	969.7
Altitude (ft.)	85–503
Rainfall (in.)	41.1
Jan. mean min (°F)	41.3
July mean max (°F)	93.4
Civ. Labor	8,293
Unemployed (%)	5
Wages	$60,520,037
Per Capita Income	$53,483
Prop. Value	$5,867,239,715
Retail Sales	$221,744,786

Lee County

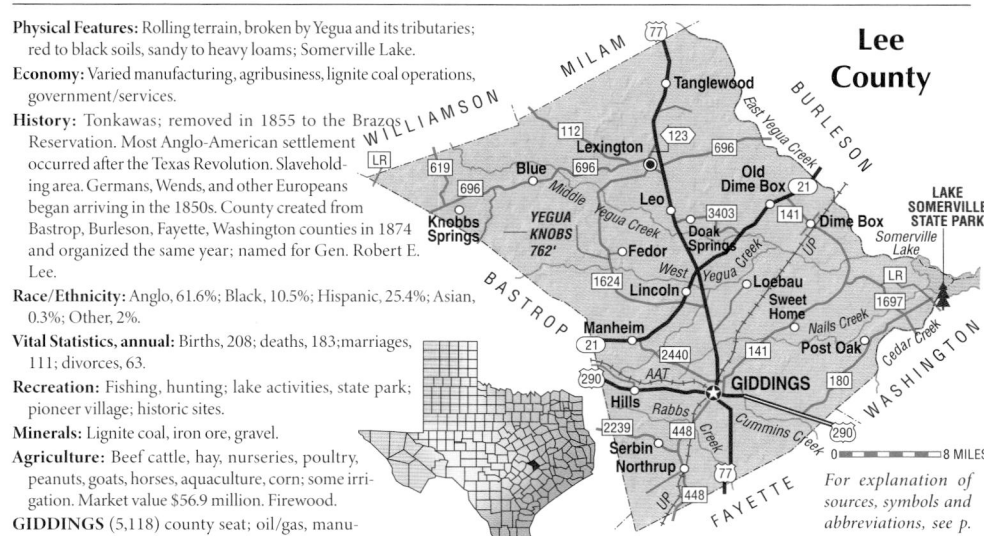

Physical Features: Rolling terrain, broken by Yegua and its tributaries; red to black soils, sandy to heavy loams; Somerville Lake.

Economy: Varied manufacturing, agribusiness, lignite coal operations, government/services.

History: Tonkawas; removed in 1855 to the Brazos Reservation. Most Anglo-American settlement occurred after the Texas Revolution. Slaveholding area. Germans, Wends, and other Europeans began arriving in the 1850s. County created from Bastrop, Burleson, Fayette, Washington counties in 1874 and organized the same year; named for Gen. Robert E. Lee.

Race/Ethnicity: Anglo, 61.6%; Black, 10.5%; Hispanic, 25.4%; Asian, 0.3%; Other, 2%.

Vital Statistics, annual: Births, 208; deaths, 183;marriages, 111; divorces, 63.

Recreation: Fishing, hunting; lake activities, state park; pioneer village; historic sites.

Minerals: Lignite coal, iron ore, gravel.

Agriculture: Beef cattle, hay, nurseries, poultry, peanuts, goats, horses, aquaculture, corn; some irrigation. Market value $56.9 million. Firewood.

GIDDINGS (5,118) county seat; oil/gas, manufacturing, agriculture; museum, old Presbyterian church (1886); rodeo in May.

Other towns include: **Dime Box** (381); **Lexington** (1,216) utility plant, livestock-marketing center, small businesses, log cabins heritage center, homecoming rodeo and barbecue cookoff in May; **Lincoln** (336); **Serbin** (109) Wendish museum.

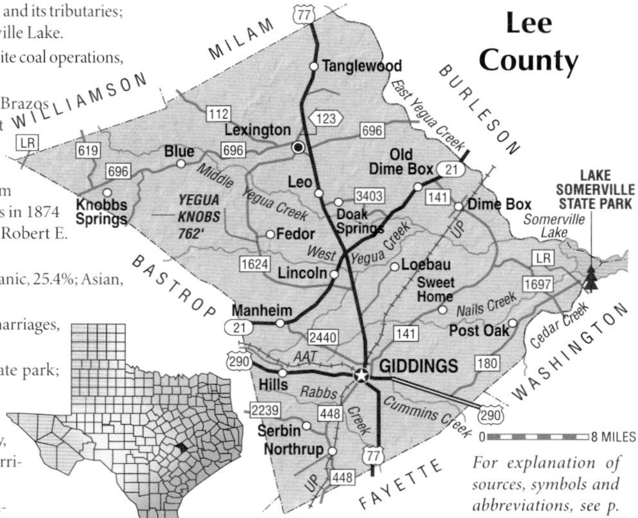

For explanation of sources, symbols and abbreviations, see p. 204, and foldout map.

Population	**17,411**
Change from 2010 (%)	4.8
Area (sq. mi.)	631.1
Land Area (sq. mi.)	629.0
Altitude (ft.)	238–762
Rainfall (in.)	36.6
Jan. mean min (°F)	37.2
July mean max (°F)	94.1
Civ. Labor	9,080
Unemployed (%)	4.4
Wages	$89,261,484
Per Capita Income	$50,665
Prop. Value	$4,070,242,167
Retail Sales	$1,040,885,721

Leon County

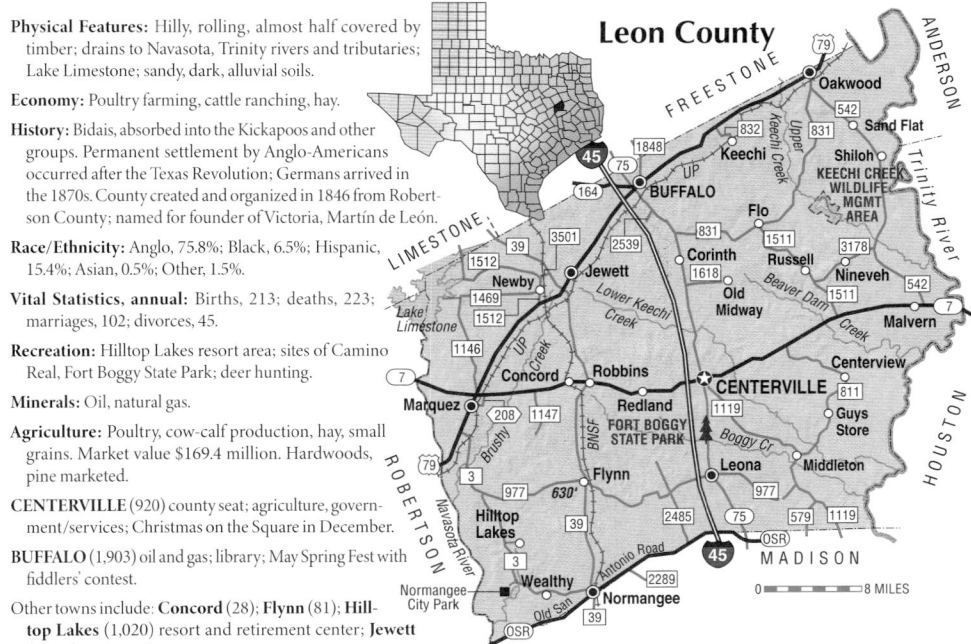

Physical Features: Hilly, rolling, almost half covered by timber; drains to Navasota, Trinity rivers and tributaries; Lake Limestone; sandy, dark, alluvial soils.

Economy: Poultry farming, cattle ranching, hay.

History: Bidais, absorbed into the Kickapoos and other groups. Permanent settlement by Anglo-Americans occurred after the Texas Revolution; Germans arrived in the 1870s. County created and organized in 1846 from Robertson County; named for founder of Victoria, Martín de León.

Race/Ethnicity: Anglo, 75.8%; Black, 6.5%; Hispanic, 15.4%; Asian, 0.5%; Other, 1.5%.

Vital Statistics, annual: Births, 213; deaths, 223; marriages, 102; divorces, 45.

Recreation: Hilltop Lakes resort area; sites of Camino Real, Fort Boggy State Park; deer hunting.

Minerals: Oil, natural gas.

Agriculture: Poultry, cow-calf production, hay, small grains. Market value $169.4 million. Hardwoods, pine marketed.

CENTERVILLE (920) county seat; agriculture, government/services; Christmas on the Square in December.

BUFFALO (1,903) oil and gas; library; May Spring Fest with fiddlers' contest.

Other towns include: **Concord** (28); **Flynn** (81); **Hilltop Lakes** (1,020) resort and retirement center; **Jewett** (1,337) steel mill, civic center, museum, library, Classic Coon Hunt in January; **Leona** (186) candle factory; **Marquez** (297); **Normangee** (731, partly in Madison County) farming and tourism; library, museum, city park; **Oakwood** (517).

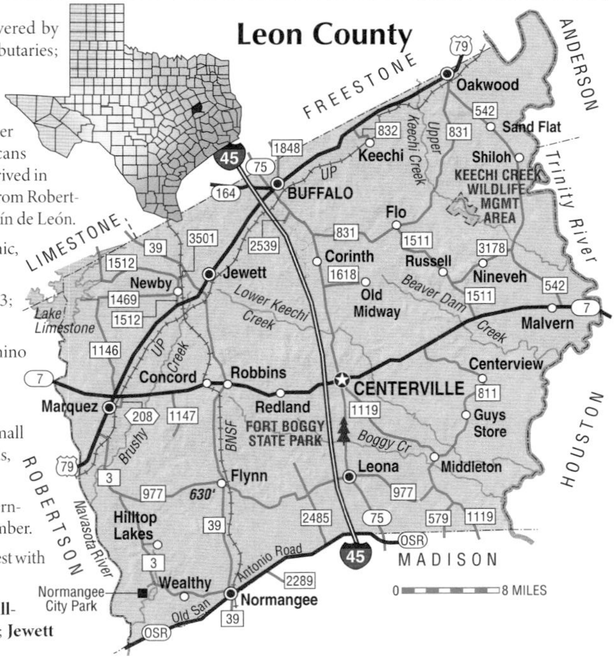

Population	**17,588**
Change from 2010 (%)	4.7
Area (sq. mi.)	1,080.6
Land Area (sq. mi.)	1,073.2
Altitude (ft.)	150–630
Rainfall (in.)	42.3
Jan. mean min (°F)	34.9
July mean max (°F)	93.2
Civ. Labor	6,123
Unemployed (%)	7.7
Wages	$67,424,128
Per Capita Income	$40,056
Prop. Value	$4,697,314,390
Retail Sales	$181,378,332

Liberty County

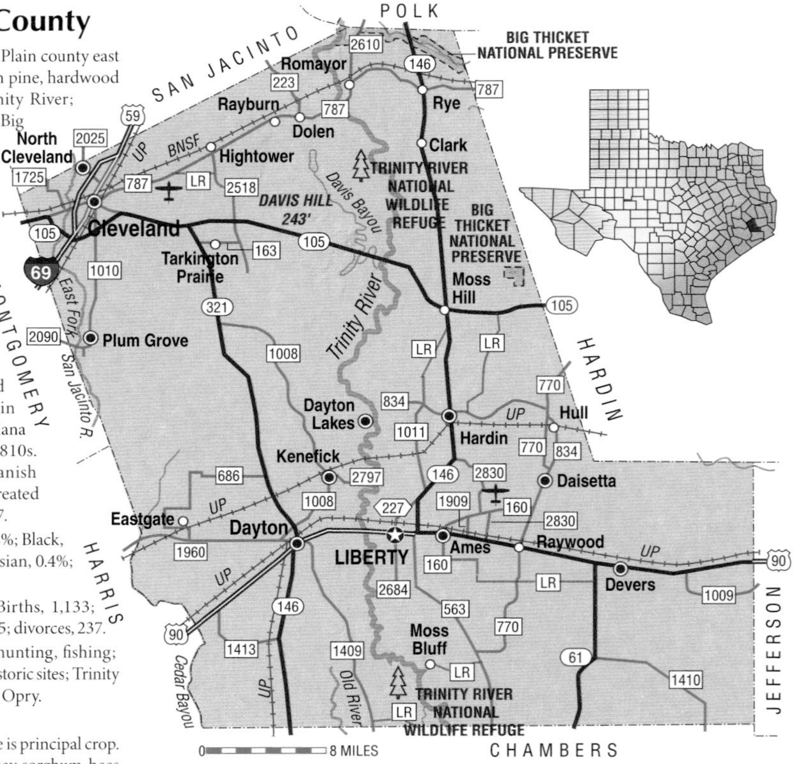

Physical Features: Coastal Plain county east of Houston; 60 percent in pine, hardwood timber; bisected by Trinity River; sandy, loam, black soils; Big Thicket.

Economy: Agribusiness; chemical plants; varied manufacturing; tourism; forest industries; prisons; many residents work in Houston; part of Houston metropolitan area.

History: Karankawa tribal area until the 1740s. Spanish established Atascosito settlement in 1756. Settlers from Louisiana began arriving in the 1810s. County named for Spanish municipality, Libertad; created in 1836, organized in 1837.

Race/Ethnicity: Anglo, 63.8%; Black, 9.3%; Hispanic, 24.3%; Asian, 0.4%; Other, 1.9%.

Vital Statistics, annual: Births, 1,133; deaths, 765; marriages, 555; divorces, 237.

Recreation: Big Thicket; hunting, fishing; national wildlife refuge; historic sites; Trinity Valley exposition; Liberty Opry.

Minerals: Oil, gas.

Agriculture: Beef cattle; rice is principal crop. Also nursery crops, corn, hay, sorghum, bees (first in number of colonies). Market value $29.9 million. Some lumbering.

LIBERTY (10,165) county seat; petroleum-related industry, agribusiness; library, museum, regional historical resource depository; Liberty Bell, Price Daniel House; hospital; Jubilee in March.

Cleveland (8,960) forest products processed, shipped; tourism; library; museum; hospital.

Dayton (9,186) rice, oil center.

Other towns include: **Ames** (1,218); **Daisetta** (1,151); **Dayton Lakes** (109); **Devers** (527); **Hardin** (979); **Hull** (803); **Kenefick** (686); **North Cleveland** (314); **Plum Grove** (717); **Raywood** (231); **Romayor** (135); **Rye** (150).

For explanation of sources, symbols and abbreviations, see p. 204, and foldout map.

Population	**91,098**	July mean max (°F)	92.1
Change from 2010 (%)	20.4	Civ. Labor	34,054
Area (sq. mi.)	1,176.3	Unemployed (%)	10.4
Land Area (sq. mi.)	1,158.4	Wages	$219,743,376
Altitude (ft.)	3–243	Per Capita Income	$37,874
Rainfall (in.)	61.3	Prop. Value	$10,414,481,576
Jan. mean min (°F)	41.2	Retail Sales	$936,024,230

A pair of white ibis wading at the Trinity River National Wildlife Refuge in Liberty County. Photo by William L. Pharr, CC by SA 4.0/Wikimedia Commons

Limestone County

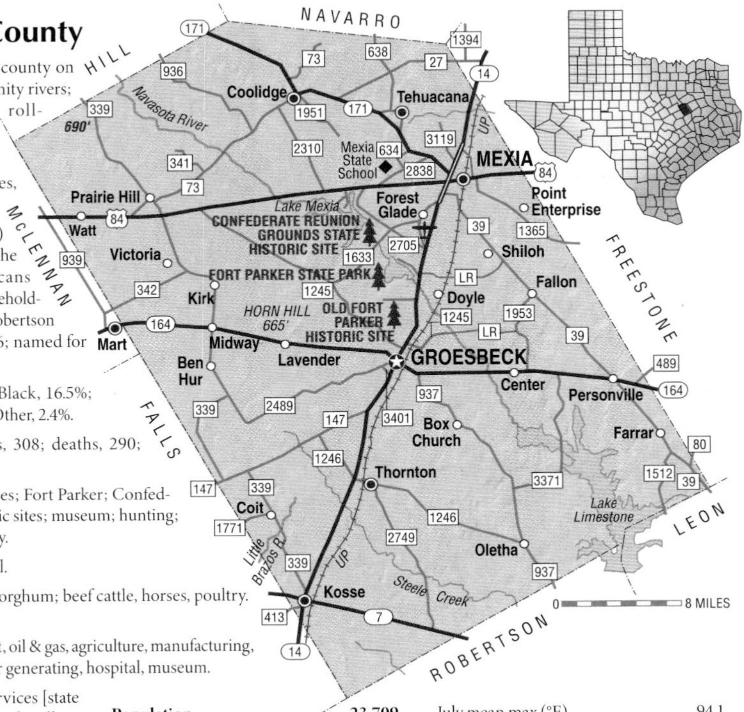

Physical Features: East central county on divide between Brazos and Trinity rivers; borders Blacklands, level to rolling; drained by Navasota and tributaries; Lake Limestone.

Economy: Government/services, electricity-generating plant.

History: Tawakoni (Tehuacana) and Waco area, later Comanche raiders. First Anglo-Americans arrived in 1833. Antebellum slaveholding area. County created from Robertson County and organized in 1846; named for indigenous rock.

Race/Ethnicity: Anglo, 57.3%; Black, 16.5%; Hispanic, 23.1%; Asian, 0.4%; Other, 2.4%.

Vital Statistics, annual: Births, 308; deaths, 290; marriages, 156; divorces, 12.

Recreation: Fishing, lake activities; Fort Parker; Confederate Reunion Grounds; historic sites; museum; hunting; Groesbeck fiddle festival in May.

Minerals: Natural gas, lignite coal.

Agriculture: Hay, corn, wheat, sorghum; beef cattle, horses, poultry. Market value $66.3 million.

GROESBECK (4,308) county seat, oil & gas, agriculture, manufacturing, hunting, mining, prison, power generating, hospital, museum.

MEXIA (7,605) government/services [state school], manufacturing; hospital, college extension campus; Boomtown History Day in April.

Other towns include: **Coolidge** (997), **Kosse** (473), **Prairie Hill** (150), **Tehuacana** (286), **Thornton** (541).

Population	**23,709**
Change from 2010 (%)	1.4
Area (sq. mi.)	933.2
Land Area (sq. mi.)	905.3
Altitude (ft.)	363–690
Rainfall (in.)	40.3
Jan. mean min (°F)	35.2
July mean max (°F)	94.1
Civ. Labor	8,211
Unemployed (%)	6.8
Wages	$85,421,058
Per Capita Income	$37,774
Prop. Value	$3,693,786,852
Retail Sales	$234,527,725

Lipscomb County

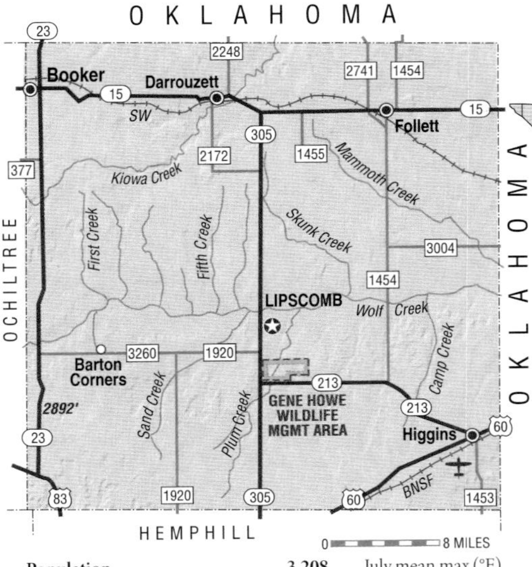

Physical Features: High Plains, broken in east; drains to tributaries of Canadian, Wolf Creek; sandy loam, black soils.

Economy: Oil and gas, agribusinesses, government/services.

History: Apaches, later Kiowas and Comanches who were driven into Indian Territory in 1875. Ranching began in late 1870s. County created in 1876 from Bexar District; organized in 1887; named for A.S. Lipscomb, Republic of Texas leader.

Race/Ethnicity: Anglo, 63.1%; Black, 0.2%; Hispanic, 34.1%; Asian, 0.4%; Other, 2%.

Vital Statistics, annual: Births, 48; deaths, 21 ;marriages, 12; divorces, 18.

Recreation: Hunting; Wolf Creek museum, prairie chicken booming grounds.

Minerals: Oil, natural gas.

Agriculture: Cattle, corn, wheat, grain sorghum, hay, sunflowers. Some 23,000 acres irrigated. Market value $79.3 million.

LIPSCOMB (28), county seat; livestock center.

BOOKER (1,487, partly in Ochiltree County) trade center, library.

Other towns include: **Darrouzett** (341) Deutsches Fest in July; **Follett** (440); **Higgins** (398) library, Will Rogers Day in August.

Population	**3,208**
Change from 2010 (%)	-2.8
Area (sq. mi.)	932.3
Land Area (sq. mi.)	932.2
Altitude (ft.)	2,220–2,892
Rainfall (in.)	22.3
Jan. mean min (°F)	18.1
July mean max (°F)	94.0
Civ. Labor	1,574
Unemployed (%)	3.8
Wages	$33,367,391
Per Capita Income	$77,810
Prop. Value	$606,600,750
Retail Sales	$19,146,598

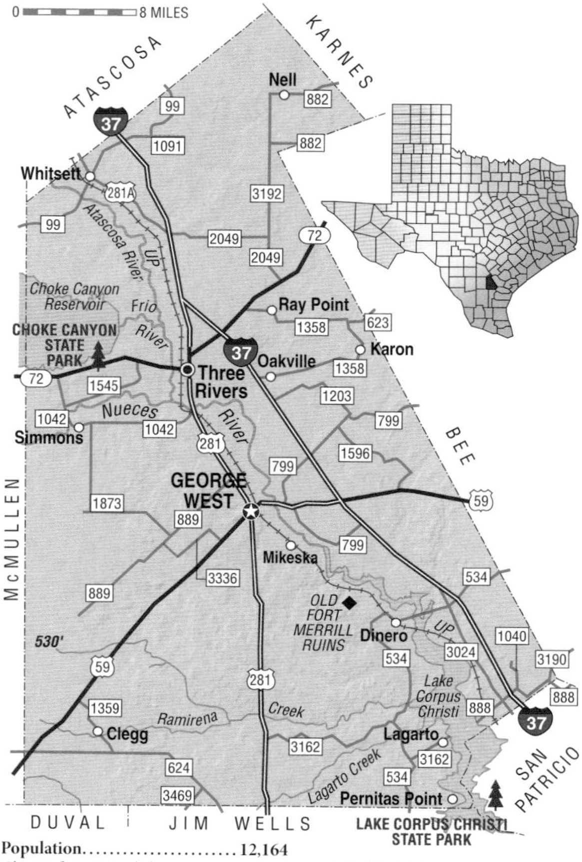

Live Oak County

Physical Features: Brushy plains between San Antonio and Corpus Christi, partly broken by Nueces and tributaries; black waxy, gray sandy, other soils; Lake Corpus Christi, Choke Canyon Reservoir.

Economy: Oil, government/services, tourism, agribusinesses.

History: Coahuiltecans squeezed out by Lipan Apaches and Spanish. Spanish ranching started in the 1810s. Settlers from Ireland arrived in 1835. County named for predominant tree; created and organized in 1856 from Nueces and San Patricio counties.

Race/Ethnicity: Anglo, 56.8%; Black, 3.8%; Hispanic, 37.4%; Asian, 0.4%; Other, 1.3%.

Vital Statistics, annual: Births, 133; deaths, 143; marriages, 56; divorces, 51.

Recreation: Lakes; water activities; state park; hunting; historic sites including Fort Merrill (1850s).

Minerals: Oil, gas, sand, gravel.

Agriculture: Cow-calf operations; hogs; corn, grain sorghum, cotton; some irrigation for hay, coastal Bermuda pastures. Market value $19.5 million.

GEORGE WEST (2,568) county seat, ranching, oil and gas operations, museums, library, Storyfest in November.

Three Rivers (2,018) oil and gas, hunting and fishing, agriculture, federal prison, salsa festival in April.

Other towns include: **Dinero** (344); **Lagarto** (735), **Pernitas Point** (274, partly in Jim Wells County), **Whitsett** (200).

Population	**12,164**			Unemployed (%)	7.5
Change from 2010 (%)	5.5	Rainfall (in.)	26.4	Wages	$53,985,817
Area (sq. mi.)	1,078.9	Jan. mean min (°F)	42.4	Per Capita Income	$37,415
Land Area (sq. mi.)	1,039.7	July mean max (°F)	95.5	Prop. Value	$5,187,276,990
Altitude (ft.)	94–530	Civ. Labor	4,865	Retail Sales	$179,305,899

A cute artisan shop in George West. Photo by Billy Hathorn, CC 3/Wikimedia Commons

Llano County

Physical Features: Central county drains to Colorado, Llano rivers; rolling to hilly; Lake Buchanan, Inks Lake, Lake Lyndon B. Johnson.

Economy: Tourism, retirement, ranch trading center, vineyards.

History: Tonkawas, later Comanches. Anglo-American and German settlers arrived in the 1840s. County name is Spanish for plains; created and organized in 1856 from Bexar District and Gillespie County.

Race/Ethnicity: Anglo, 85.8%; Black, 0.6%; Hispanic, 11.3%; Asian, 0.4%; Other, 1.7%.

Vital Statistics, annual: Births, 178; deaths, 311; marriages, 112; divorces, 73.

Recreation: Leading deer-hunting county; fishing, lake activities, major tourist area, Enchanted Rock, eagles' nest on Highway 29, bluebonnet festival, Hill Country Wine Trail in spring.

Minerals: Granite, vermiculite, llanite.

Agriculture: Beef cattle, sheep, goats. Market value $15.7 million. Deer-hunting, wildlife leases.

LLANO (3,529) county seat; agriculture, hunting, tourism; hospital; historic district; museum; Texas gold panning championship in September.

Kingsland (6,348) tourism, retirement community, recreation, vineyards; library; archaeological center; AquaBoom on July 4.

Other towns include: **Bluffton** (75); **Buchanan Dam** (1,537) hydroelectric industry, tourism, fishing, water sports; **Castell** (72); **Horseshoe Bay** (4,016, partly in Burnet County); **Sunrise Beach** (797); **Tow** (305); **Valley Spring** (50).

Population	**21,784**
Change from 2010 (%)	12.9
Area (sq. mi.)	965.9
Land Area (sq. mi.)	934.0
Altitude (ft.)	825–2,000
Rainfall (in.)	27.7
Jan. mean min (°F)	32.2
July mean max (°F)	97.7
Civ. Labor	8,324
Unemployed (%)	5.3
Wages	$51,196,308
Per Capita Income	$49,905
Prop. Value	$8,140,736,475
Retail Sales	$183,066,796

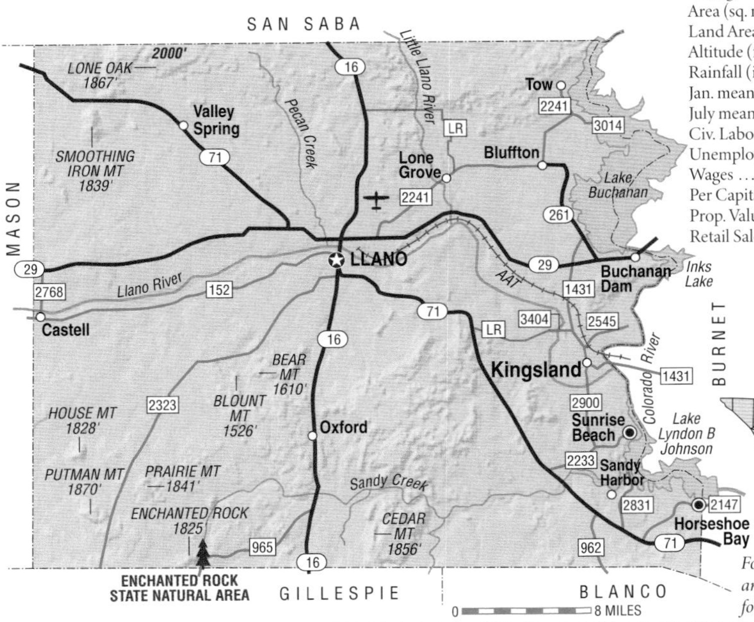

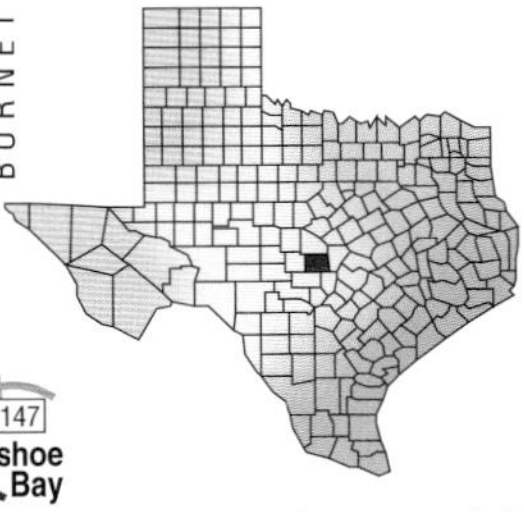

For explanation of sources, symbols and abbreviations, see p. 204, and foldout map.

Loving County

Physical Features: Flat desert terrain with a few low-rolling hills; slopes to Pecos River; Red Bluff Reservoir; sandy, loam, clay soils.

Economy: Oil and gas operations; cattle.

History: Land developers began operations in late 19th century. Oil discovered 1925. County created 1887 from Tom Green County; organized 1893, deorganized 1897, again organized 1931, the last organized. Named for Oliver Loving, trail driver. County is state's least populous.

Race/Ethnicity: Anglo, 71.8%; Black, 0%; Hispanic, 22.9%; Asian, 0%; Other, 5.2%.

Vital Statistics, annual: Births, 0; deaths, 0; marriages, 0; divorces, 0.

Recreation: Pecos River, Red Bluff Lake.

Minerals: Oil, gas.

Agriculture: Cattle ranching. Market value $912,000.

MENTONE (29) county seat, oil-field supply center; the only town.

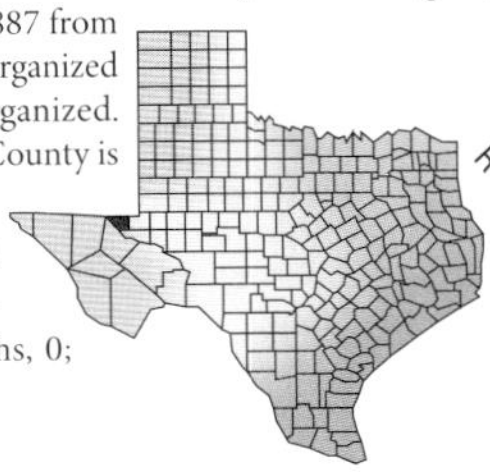

Population	**96**
Change from 2010 (%)	17.1
Area (sq. mi.)	676.7
Land Area (sq. mi.)	668.9
Altitude (ft.)	2,660–3,374
Rainfall (in.)	12.6
Jan. mean min (°F)	29.7
July mean max (°F)	99.3
Civ. Labor	307
Unemployed (%)	1.3
Wages	$2,627,180
Per Capita Income	$53,734
Prop. Value	$8,971,199,795
Retail Sales	$8,147,312

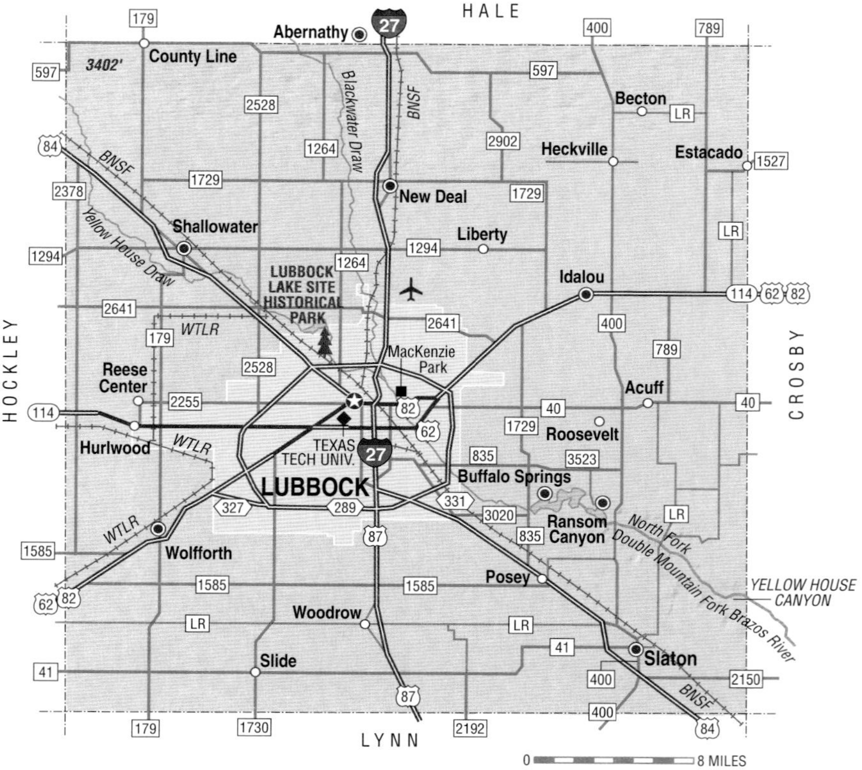

Lubbock County

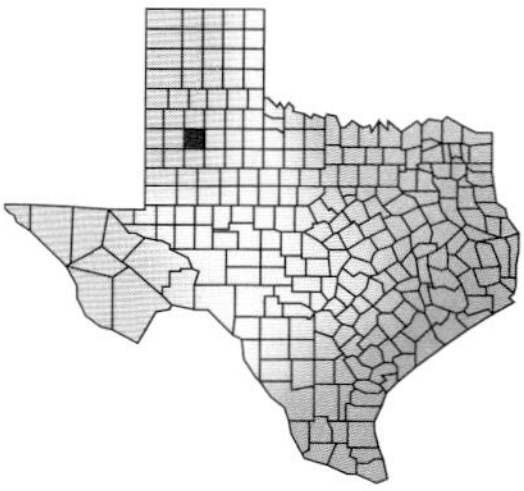

Physical Features: South Plains, broken by 1,500 playas, upper Brazos River tributaries; rich soils with underground water.

Economy: Among world's largest cottonseed processing centers, a leading agribusiness center, cattle feedlots, varied manufacturing, higher education center, medical center, government/services.

History: Evidence of human habitation for 12,000 years. In historic period, Apache Indians, followed by Comanche hunters. Sheep raisers from Midwest arrived in the late 1870s. Cotton farms brought in Mexican laborers in the 1940s-1960s. County named for Col. Tom S. Lubbock, an organizer of the Confederate Terry's Rangers; county created in 1876 from Bexar District; organized in 1891.

Race/Ethnicity: Anglo, 52.2%; Black, 7.2%; Hispanic, 36.3%; Asian, 2.2%; Other, 1.8%.

Vital Statistics, annual: Births, 4,112; deaths, 2,441; marriages, 2,163; divorces, 826.

Recreation: Lubbock Lake archaeological site; Texas Tech events; civic center; Buddy Holly statue, Walk of Fame, Lubbock Music Fest in fall; planetarium; Ranching Heritage Center; Panhandle-South Plains Fair, National Cowboy symposium in September; wine festivals; Buffalo Springs Lake.

For explanation of sources, symbols and abbreviations, see p. 204, and foldout map.

Minerals: Oil, gas, stone, sand and gravel.

Agriculture: Second in bales of cotton produced. Fed beef, cow-calf operations; poultry, eggs; hogs. Other crops, nursery, grain sorghum, wheat, sunflowers, soybeans, hay, vegetables; more than 155,000 acres irrigated, mostly cotton. Market value $219.5 million.

Education: Texas Tech University with law and medical schools; Lubbock Christian University; South Plains College branch; Wayland Baptist University off-campus center.

LUBBOCK (259,158) county seat; center for large agricultural area; manufacturing includes electronics, earth-moving equipment, food containers, fire-protection equipment, clothing, other products; distribution center for South Plains; feedlots; museum; government/services; hospitals, psychiatric hospital; wind power center.

Other towns include: **Buffalo Springs** (493); **Idalou** (2,301); **New Deal** (827); **Ransom Canyon** (1,113); **Shallowater** (2,528); **Slaton** (6,048) agriculture, government/services, Harvey House hotel, museums, sausagefest in October; **Wolfforth** (5,757) retail, government/services.

Also, part of **Abernathy** (2,706).

Population	**308,880**
Change from 2010 (%)	10.8
Area (sq. mi.)	900.7
Land Area (sq. mi.)	895.6
Altitude (ft.)	2,821–3,402
Rainfall (in.)	19.1
Jan. mean min (°F)	26.4
July mean max (°F)	92.8
Civ. Labor	158,123
Unemployed (%)	4.9
Wages	$1,800,105,667
Per Capita Income	$44,311
Prop. Value	$26,776,317,523
Retail Sales	$6,212,966,699

Lynn County

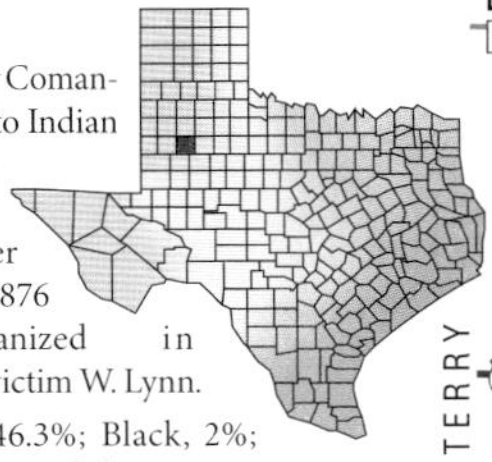

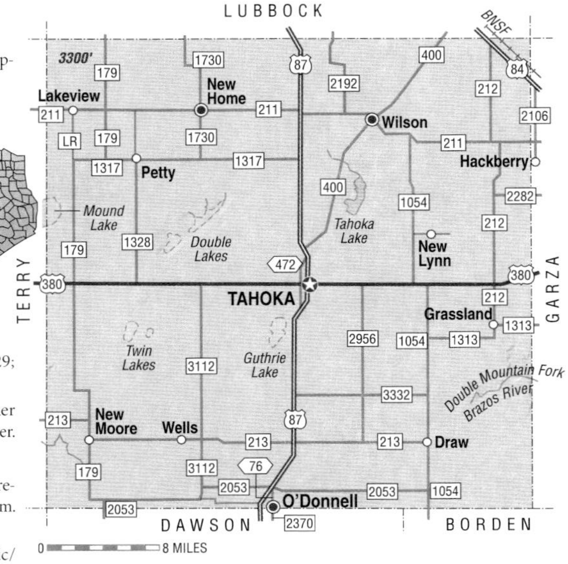

Physical Features: South Plains, broken by Caprock Escarpment, playas, draws; sandy loam, black, gray soils.

Economy: Agribusiness.

History: Apaches, ousted by Comanches who were removed to Indian Territory in 1875. Ranching began in 1880s. Farming developed after 1900. County created in 1876 from Bexar District; organized in 1903; named for Alamo victim W. Lynn.

Race/Ethnicity: Anglo, 46.3%; Black, 2%; Hispanic, 50.1%; Asian, 0.1%; Other, 1.2%.

Vital Statistics, annual: Births, 70; deaths, 51; marriages, 29; divorces, 13.

Recreation: Pioneer museum in Tahoka; Dan Blocker museum in O'Donnell; sandhill crane migration in winter.

Minerals: Oil, natural gas.

Agriculture: Cotton produces largest income (first in acreage); 72,000 acres irrigated. Also, ranching, grain sorghum. Market value $111.4 million.

TAHOKA (2,765) county seat; agricultural center, electric/telephone cooperatives; hospital; museum; Harvest Festival in the fall.

O'Donnell (840, partly in Dawson County) commercial center.

Other towns include: **New Home** (366); **Wilson** (496).

Population	**6,151**
Change from 2010 (%)	4.0
Area (sq. mi.)	893.5
Land Area (sq. mi.)	891.9
Altitude (ft.)	2,660-3,300
Rainfall (in.)	21.1
Jan. mean min (°F)	28.0
July mean max (°F)	91.9
Civ. Labor	2,746
Unemployed (%)	7.5
Wages	$21,389,152
Per Capita Income	$43,141
Prop. Value	$1,557,077,293
Retail Sales	$21,820,813

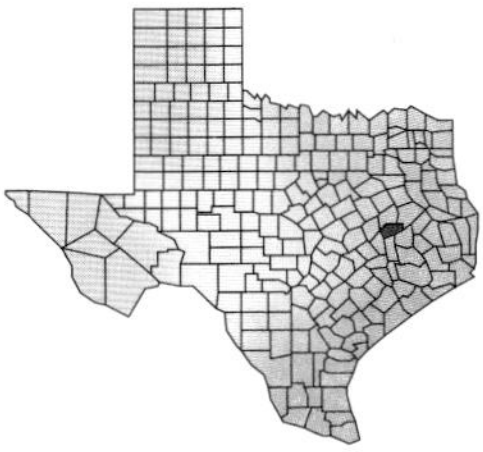

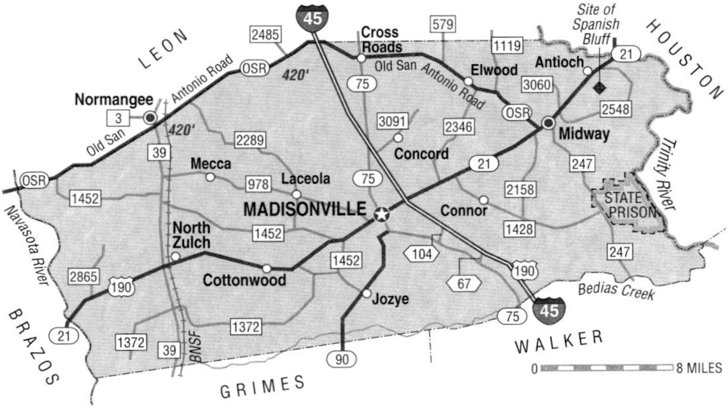

Madison County

Physical Features: Hilly, draining to Trinity, Navasota rivers, Bedias Creek; one-fifth of area timbered; alluvial, loam, sandy soils.

Economy: Prison, government/services, varied manufacturing, agribusiness, oil production.

History: Caddo, Bidai Indian area; Kickapoos migrated from the east. Spanish settlements established in 1774 and 1805. Anglo-Americans arrived in 1829. Census of 1860 showed 30 percent of population was black. County named for U.S. President James Madison; created from Grimes, Leon, and Walker counties 1853; organized 1854.

Race/Ethnicity: Anglo, 53%; Black, 19.1%; Hispanic, 24.5%; Asian, 0.5%; Other, 2.5%.

Vital Statistics, annual: Births, 145; deaths, 126; marriages, 111; divorces, 52.

Recreation: Fishing, hunting; Spanish Bluff where survivors of the Gutiérrez-Magee expedition were executed in 1813; other historic sites.

Minerals: sand, oil.

Agriculture: Nursery crops, cattle, horses, poultry raised; forage for livestock. Market value $124.1 million.

MADISONVILLE (4,734) county seat; farm-trade center, varied manufacturing; hospital, library; Spring Fling in April.

Other towns, **Midway** (229); **Normangee** (706, mostly in Leon County); **North Zulch** (600).

Population	**14,188**
Change from 2010 (%)	0.5
Area (sq. mi.)	472.4
Land Area (sq. mi.)	466.1
Altitude (ft.)	131–420
Rainfall (in.)	45.1
Jan. mean min (°F)	36.9
July mean max (°F)	94.4
Civ. Labor	4,439
Unemployed (%)	7
Wages	$47,011,455
Per Capita Income	$32,648
Prop. Value	$2,677,160,200
Retail Sales	$277,792,588

Marion County

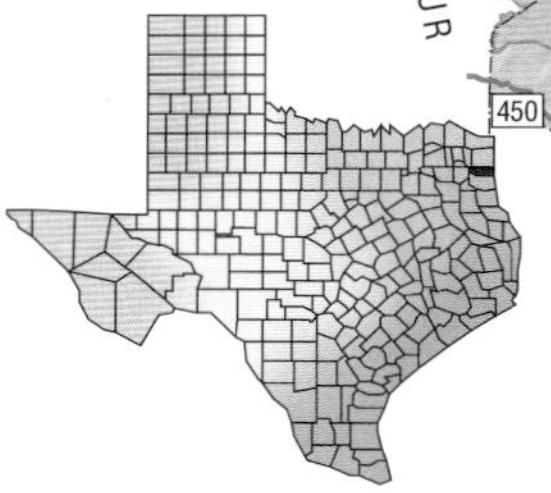

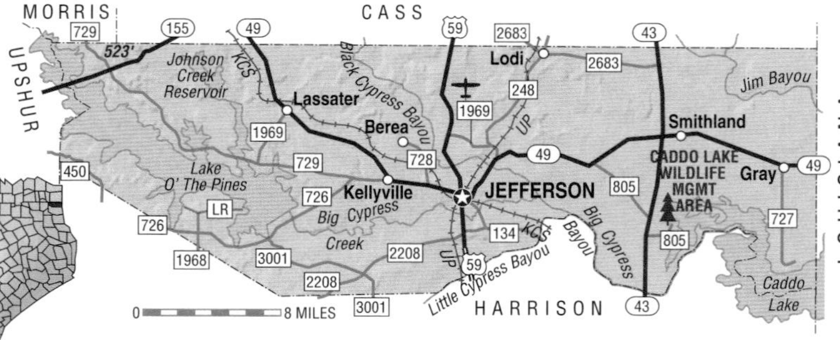

Physical Features: Northeastern county; hilly, three-quarters forested with pines, hardwoods; drains to Caddo Lake, Lake O' the Pines, Big Cypress Bayou; Johnson Creek Reservoir.

Economy: Agriculture, tourism, forestry, food processing.

History: Caddoes forced out in 1790s. Kickapoo in area when settlers arrived from Deep South around 1840. Antebellum slaveholding area. County created 1860 from Cass County, organized the same year; named for Gen. Francis Marion of American Revolution.

Race/Ethnicity: Anglo, 69.1%; Black, 22.7%; Hispanic, 3.8%; Asian, 0.6%; Other, 3.5%.

Vital Statistics, annual: Births, 104; deaths, 167; marriages, 79; divorces, 40.

Recreation: Lake activities, hunting, Excelsior Hotel, 84 medallions on historic sites including Jay Gould railroad car, museum, historical homes tour in May, Spring Festival.

Minerals: Iron ore, natural gas, oil.

Agriculture: Beef cattle, hay. Market value $5.9 million. Forestry is most important industry.

JEFFERSON (1,967) county seat; tourism, syrup works, forestry; museum, library; historical sites.

Other towns include: **Lodi** (175).

Population	**9,760**
Change from 2010 (%)	8.7
Area (sq. mi.)	420.3
Land Area (sq. mi.)	380.9
Altitude (ft.)	168–523
Rainfall (in.)	48.2
Jan. mean min (°F)	32.7
July mean max (°F)	92.6
Civ. Labor	4,202
Unemployed (%)	7.7
Wages	$20,212,989
Per Capita Income	$39,895
Prop. Value	$1,343,045,995
Retail Sales	$59,802,126

Martin County

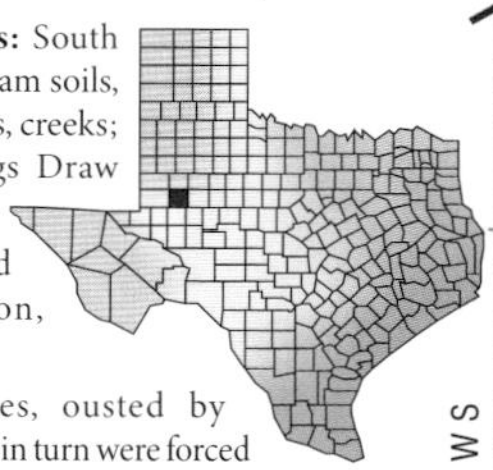

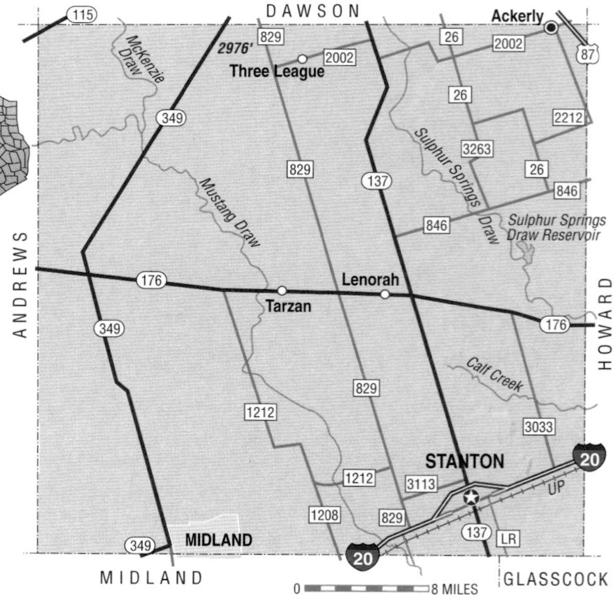

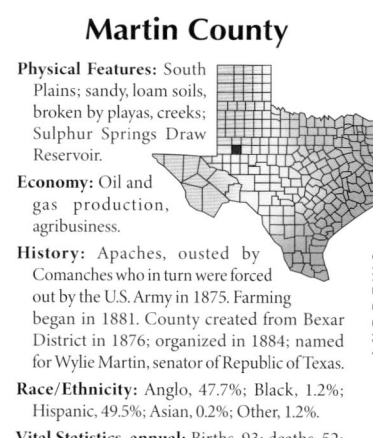

Physical Features: South Plains; sandy, loam soils, broken by playas, creeks; Sulphur Springs Draw Reservoir.

Economy: Oil and gas production, agribusiness.

History: Apaches, ousted by Comanches who in turn were forced out by the U.S. Army in 1875. Farming began in 1881. County created from Bexar District in 1876; organized in 1884; named for Wylie Martin, senator of Republic of Texas.

Race/Ethnicity: Anglo, 47.7%; Black, 1.2%; Hispanic, 49.5%; Asian, 0.2%; Other, 1.2%.

Vital Statistics, annual: Births, 93; deaths, 52; marriages, 28; divorces, 17.

Recreation: Museum, settlers reunion in July at Stanton.

Minerals: Oil, gas.

Agriculture: Cotton, beef cattle, milo, wheat, horses, meat goats. Market value $54.3 million.

STANTON (3,002) county seat; oil and gas production, agribusiness; commuting to Midland, Big Spring; hospital; museum, historic monastery, other historic buildings; Old Sorehead trade days April, June, October.

Other towns include: **Ackerly** (237, partly in Dawson County); **Lenorah** (83); **Tarzan** (30). A small part of **Midland**.

Population	**5,731**
Change from 2010 (%)	5.9
Area (sq. mi.)	915.7
Land Area (sq. mi.)	914.9
Altitude (ft.)	2,470–2,976
Rainfall (in.)	17.6
Jan. mean min (°F)	30.0
July mean max (°F)	94.0
Civ. Labor	2,548
Unemployed (%)	5.4
Wages	$29,924,455
Per Capita Income	$60,844
Prop. Value	$10,745,360,740
Retail Sales	$110,223,869

Mason County

Physical Features: Central county; hilly, draining to Llano and San Saba rivers and their tributaries; limestone, red soils; varied timber.

Economy: Sand plants, agriculture, tourism, hunting.

History: Lipan Apaches in area, driven south by Comanches around 1790. German settlers arrived in the mid-1840s, followed by Anglo-Americans. Mexican immigration increased after 1930. County created from Bexar and Gillespie counties in 1858, organized the same year; named for Mexican War victim U.S. Army Lt. G.T. Mason.

Race/Ethnicity: Anglo, 72.1%; Black, 0.4%; Hispanic, 26.3%; Asian, 0.1%; Other, 0.9%.

Vital Statistics, annual: Births, 51; deaths, 44; marriages, 23; divorces, 14.

Recreation: Hunting, fishing; kayaking, rock crawling, camping; historic homes of stone; prehistoric Indian artifacts exhibit; Fort Mason, where Robert E. Lee served; bat cave; wildflower drives in spring, Roundup rodeo in July.

Minerals: Sand, topaz, granite.

Agriculture: Beef cattle, hay, meat goats. Market value $21.7 million. Hunting leases important.

MASON (2,298) county seat; agriculture, hunting, nature tourism; museums, historical district, homes, rock fences built by German settlers; wild game dinner in November.

Other towns include: **Art** (14), **Fredonia** (55), **Pontotoc** (125).

For explanation of sources, symbols and abbreviations, see p. 204, and foldout map.

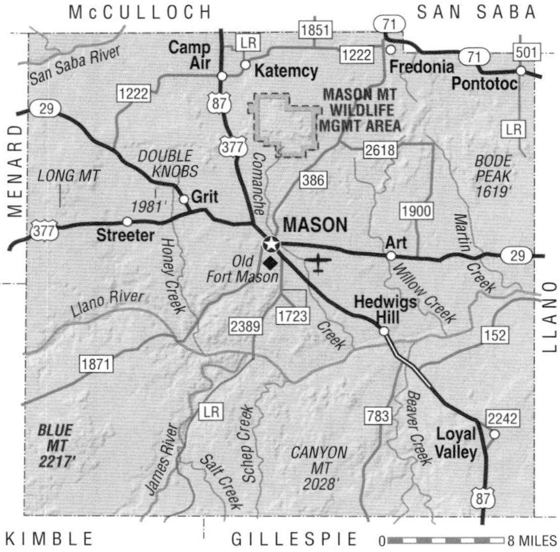

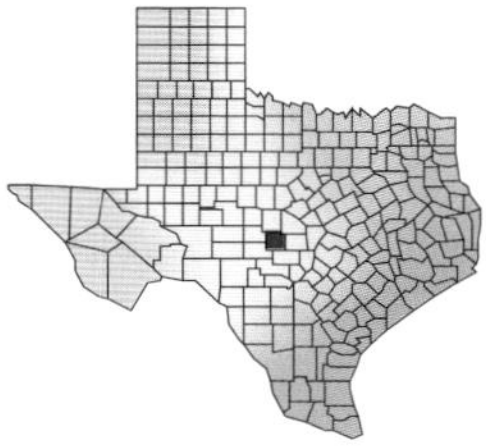

Population	**4,301**
Change from 2010 (%)	3.8
Area (sq. mi.)	932.2
Land Area (sq. mi.)	928.8
Altitude (ft.)	1,180–2,217
Rainfall (in.)	29.2
Jan. mean min (°F)	32.1
July mean max (°F)	92.3
Civ. Labor	1,755
Unemployed (%)	5
Wages	$10,153,937
Per Capita Income	$47,439
Prop. Value	$2,672,054,104
Retail Sales	$23,218,007

A view of Lake O' the Pines in Marion County. Photo by the U.S. Army Corps of Engineers

This M114 155 mm howitzer is displayed in front of the McCulloch County courthouse in Brady. Photo by Larry D. Moore, CC by SA 4.0/ Wikimedia Commons

Matagorda County

Physical Features: Gulf Coastal Plain; flat, broken by bays; many different soils; drains to Colorado River, creeks, coast; South Texas Project Reservoir.

Economy: Agribusiness, oil and gas fields, refinery.

History: Karankawa tribal area, Tonkawas in the area later. Anglo-Americans arrived in 1822. Mexican immigration increased after 1920. An original county, created in 1836 from a Spanish municipality, named for canebrake; organized in 1837; settled by Austin colonists.

Race/Ethnicity: Anglo, 43.1%; Black, 10.6%; Hispanic, 42.8%; Asian, 1.9%; Other, 1.3%.

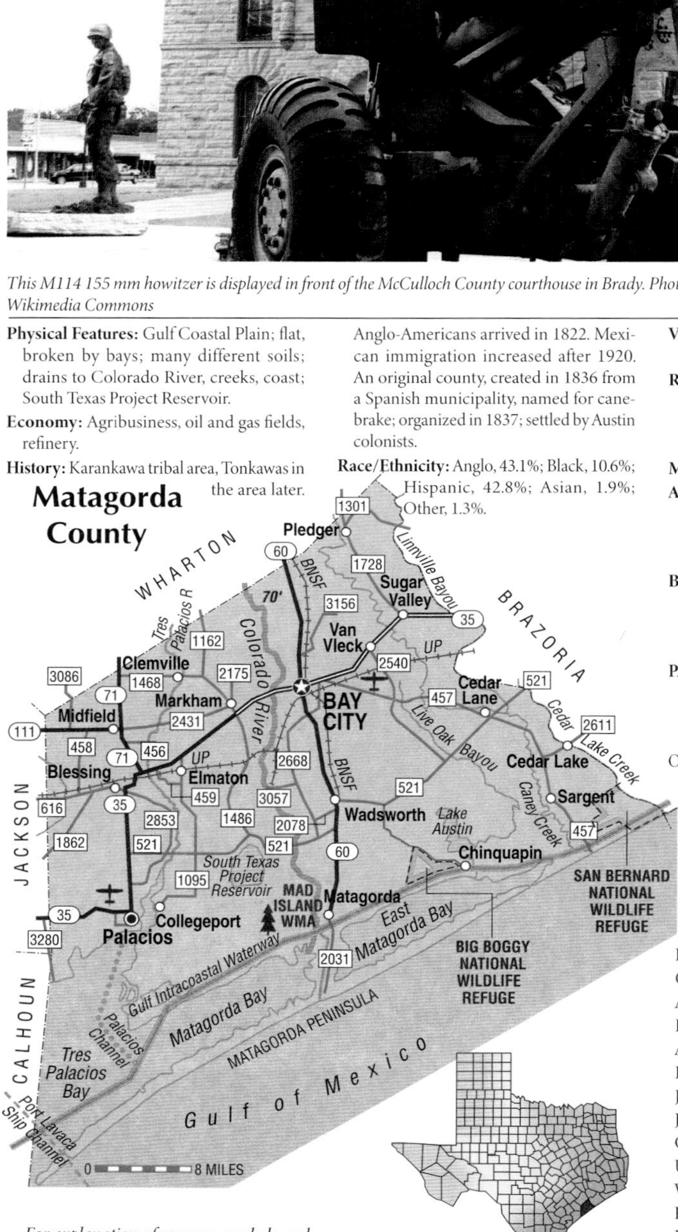

For explanation of sources, symbols and abbreviations, see p. 204, and foldout map.

Vital Statistics, annual: Births, 533; deaths, 407; marriages, 304; divorces, 89.

Recreation: Wildlife hunting and viewing, fishing (fresh and salt water), beaches, sailing, historic sites, museums; Bay City rice festival in October.

Minerals: Oil and gas.

Agriculture: Cotton, rice, soybeans, corn, grain sorghum; some 33,000 acres of crops irrigated; cattle, turf, aquaculture (first in value). Market value $124.2 million.

BAY CITY (17,431) county seat; government/services, education, nuclear power plant; petrochemicals; agribusiness; hospital, junior college branch.

PALACIOS (4,589) tourism, seafood industry; hospital; Marine Education Center; public fishing piers; Bay Festival on Labor Day.

Other towns include: **Blessing** (989) historic sites; **Cedar Lane** (300); **Collegeport** (80); **Elmaton** (160); **Markham** (1,096); **Matagorda** (465); **Midfield** (305); **Pledger** (265); **Sargent** (900) retirement community, fishing, birding, commercial fishing, barbecue cookoff in April; **Van Vleck** (2,214); **Wadsworth** (160).

Population	**36,292**
Change from 2010 (%)	-7.5
Area (sq. mi.)	1,612.5
Land Area (sq. mi.)	1,100.3
Altitude (ft.)	sea level–70
Rainfall (in.)	48.9
Jan. mean min (°F)	45.4
July mean max (°F)	91.5
Civ. Labor	16,106
Unemployed (%)	9.1
Wages	$147,337,009
Per Capita Income	$45,237
Prop. Value	$8,640,030,577
Retail Sales	$412,419,274

Maverick County

Physical Features: Southwestern county on the Rio Grande; broken, rolling surface, with dense brush; clay, sandy, alluvial soils.

Economy: Oil, government/services, agribusiness, tourism.

History: Coahuiltecan area; later Comanches arrived. Spanish ranching began in the 1760s. Anglo-Americans arrived in 1834. County named for Sam A. Maverick, whose name is now a synonym for unbranded cattle; created in 1856 from Kinney County; organized in 1871.

Race/Ethnicity: Anglo, 3.2%; Black, 0.1%; Hispanic, 95.1%; Asian, 0.2%; Other, 1.2%.

Vital Statistics, annual: Births, 1,150; deaths, 398; marriages, 594; divorces, 40.

Recreation: Tourist gateway to Mexico; white-tailed deer, bird hunting; fishing; historic sites, Fort Duncan museum.

Minerals: Oil, gas, sand, gravel.

Agriculture: Cattle feedlots; pecans, vegetables, sorghum, wheat; goats, sheep. Some irrigation from Rio Grande. Market value $43.0 million.

EAGLE PASS (28,992) county seat; government/services, retail center, tourism; hospital; junior college, Sul Ross college branch; entry point to Piedras Negras, Mex., Nacho Festival in Piedras Negras in October.

Other communities include: **Chula Vista** (3,980), **Eidson Road** (9,132), **El Indio** (169), **Las Quintas Fronterizas** (4,114), and **Rosita** (2,797), all immediately south of Eagle Pass. Also, **Elm Creek** (2,870) and **Quemado** (226).

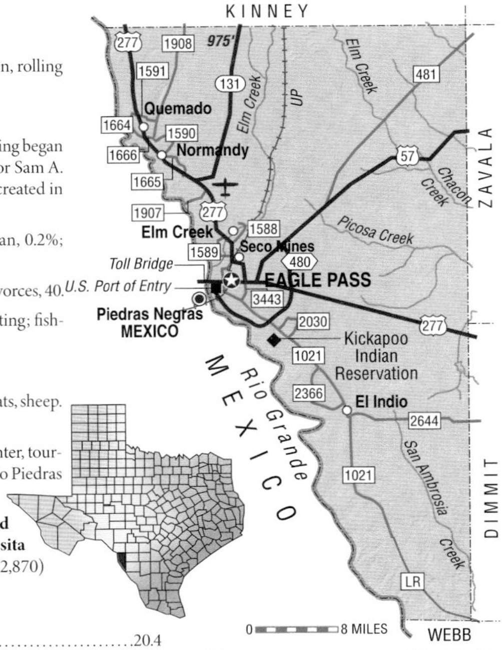

Population	**57,888**	Rainfall (in.)	20.4	Wages	$171,400,673
Change from 2010 (%)	19.4	Jan. mean min (°F)	41.5	Per Capita Income	$31,380
Area (sq. mi.)	1,291.8	July mean max (°F)	98.1	Prop. Value	$4,513,081,913
Land Area (sq. mi.)	1,279.3	Civ. Labor	23,914	Retail Sales	$641,844,151
Altitude (ft.)	550–975	Unemployed (%)	15.5		

McCulloch County

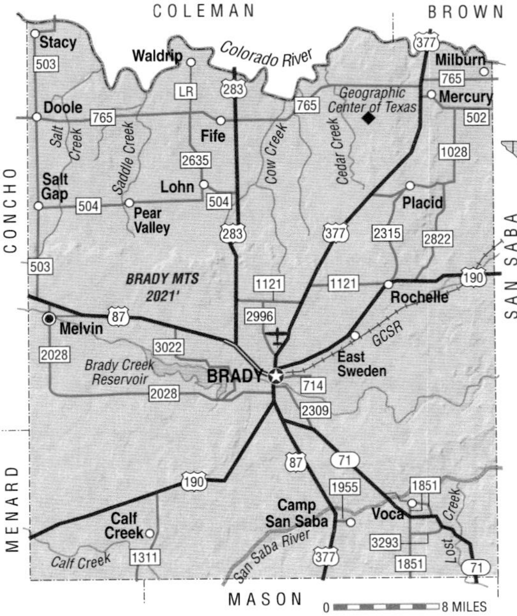

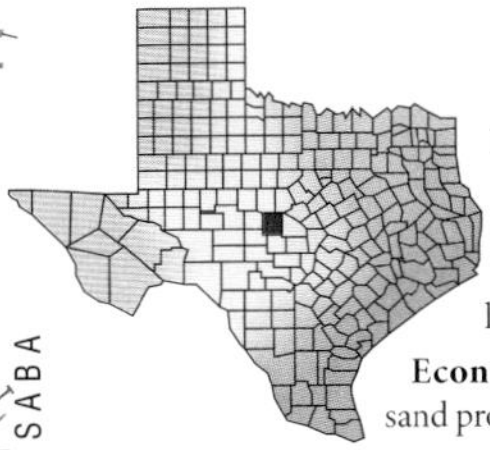

Physical Features: Hilly and rolling; drains to Colorado River, Brady Creek and Brady Creek Reservoir, San Saba River; black loams to sandy soils.

Economy: Agribusiness, industrial sand production, hunting leases.

History: Apache area. First Anglo-American settlers arrived in the late 1850s, but Comanche raids delayed further settlement until the 1870s. County created from Bexar District in 1856; organized in 1876; named for San Jacinto veteran Gen. Ben McCulloch.

Race/Ethnicity: Anglo, 63.4%; Black, 1.6%; Hispanic, 32.9%; Asian, 0.3%; Other, 1.5%.

Vital Statistics, annual: Births, 87; deaths, 117; marriages, 22; divorces, 50.

Recreation: Hunting, lake activities, museums, goat cookoff on Labor Day, Hogtoberfest in October, golf tournaments.

Minerals: Sand, oil, and gas.

Agriculture: Beef cattle and sheep; also small grains, goats, hay, cotton. Market value $22.5 million. Hunting leases.

BRADY (5,602) county seat; silica sand, oil-field equipment, ranching, tourism, other manufacturing; hospital; Heart of Texas car show in April, Cinco de Mayo.

Other towns: **Doole** (74), **Lohn** (149), **Melvin** (182), **Mercury** (166), **Rochelle** (163), and **Voca** (56).

Population	**8,323**	July mean max (°F)	94.2
Change from 2010 (%)	7.2	Civ. Labor	3,169
Area (sq. mi.)	1,073.4	Unemployed (%)	7
Land Area (sq. mi.)	165.6	Wages	$24,932,450
Altitude (ft.)	1,280–2,021	Per Capita Income	$38,895
Rainfall (in.)	27.6	Prop. Value	$1,817,827,259
Jan. mean min (°F)	32.2	Retail Sales	$99,521,939

McLennan County

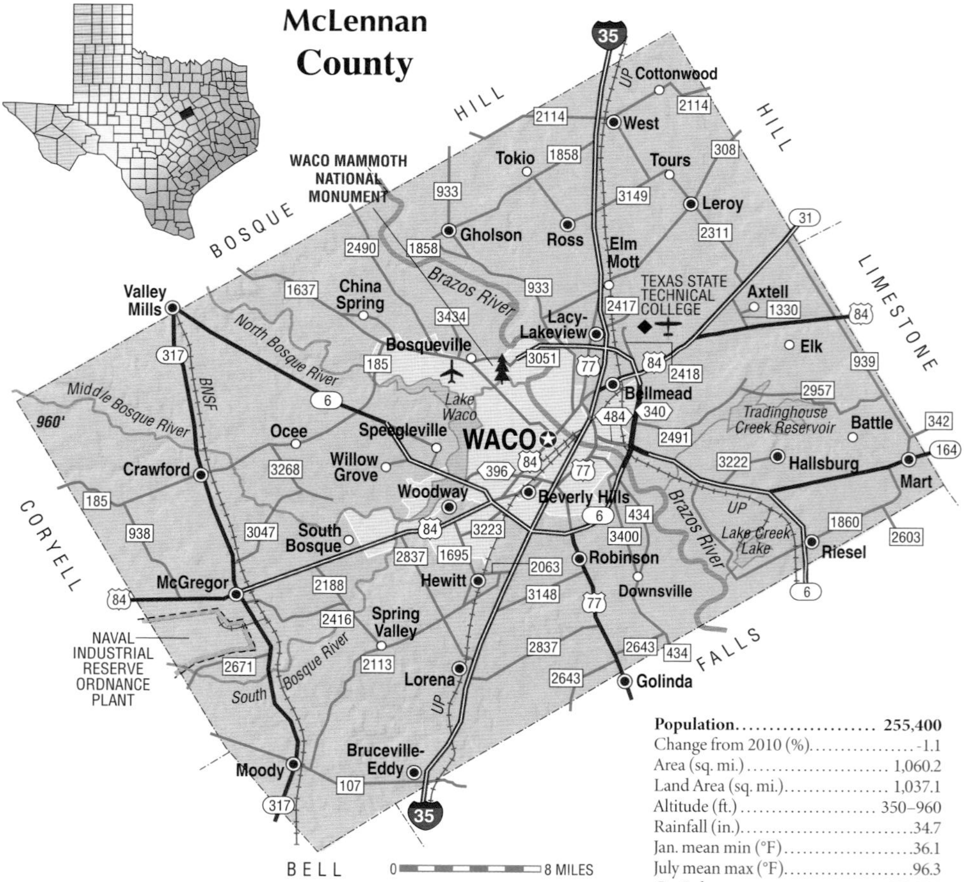

Population	**255,400**
Change from 2010 (%)	-1.1
Area (sq. mi.)	1,060.2
Land Area (sq. mi.)	1,037.1
Altitude (ft.)	350–960
Rainfall (in.)	34.7
Jan. mean min (°F)	36.1
July mean max (°F)	96.3
Civ. Labor	122,535
Unemployed (%)	5.1
Wages	$1,549,288,666
Per Capita Income	$42,159
Prop. Value	$28,490,833,687
Retail Sales	$3,841,047,862

Physical Features: Central Texas county of mostly Blackland prairie, but rolling hills in west; drains to Bosque, Brazos rivers and Lake Waco, Tradinghouse Creek Reservoir, Lake Creek Lake; heavy, loam, sandy soils.

Economy: Agribusiness, education, health services.

History: Tonkawas, Wichitas and Wacos in area. Anglo-American settlers arrived in the 1840s. Indians removed to Brazos reservations in 1854. County created from Milam County in 1850, organized the same year; named for settler, Neil McLennan Sr.

Race/Ethnicity: Anglo, 54.6%; Black, 14.4%; Hispanic, 26.9%; Asian, 1.6%; Other, 2.2%.

Vital Statistics, annual: Births, 3,528; deaths, 2,123; marriages, 1,666; divorces, 810.

Recreation: Texas Ranger Hall of Fame, museum; Texas Sports Hall of Fame; Dr Pepper Museum; Cameron Park; drag boat races April and May; zoo; historic sites, homes; museums; libraries, art center; symphony; civic theater; Baylor University events; Heart o' Texas Fair in October.

Minerals: Sand, gravel, limestone.

Agriculture: Corn, silage, wheat, beef cattle, dairies. Market value $179.7 million.

Education: Baylor University; community college; Texas State Technical College; university extensions.

WACO (138,400) county seat; manufacturing, higher education, medical services/hospital, government/services, finance; riverside park, historic suspension bridge, zoo; Magnolia Silos market; Waco Mammoth National Monument; wine festivals in April and October.

HEWITT (14,820) medical services/hospital, construction, retail; car show and concert in April.

WEST (2,939) known for Czech foods; varied manufacturing; Westfest Labor Day weekend.

Other towns include: **Axtell** (300); **Bellmead** (10,731); **Beverly Hills** (1,993); **Bruceville-Eddy** (1,857, partly in Falls County); **China Spring** (1,401); **Crawford** (765); **Elm Mott** (300); **Gholson** (1,114); **Hallsburg** (472); **Lacy-Lakeview** (6,914); **Leroy** (347); **Lorena** (1,785); **Mart** (1,971) agricultural center, some manufacturing, museum, juvenile correction facility.

Also: **McGregor** (5,264) agriculture, manufacturing, distribution; private telephone museum; Frontier Founders Day in September; **Moody** (1,415) agriculture, commuting to Waco, Temple; library; Cotton Harvest fest in September; **Riesel** (1,041); **Robinson** (11,883); **Ross** (294); **Woodway** (9,230).

Part of **Golinda** (589, mostly in Falls County) and part of **Valley Mills** (1,180, mostly in Bosque County).

For explanation of sources, symbols and abbreviations, see p. 204, and foldout map.

McMullen County

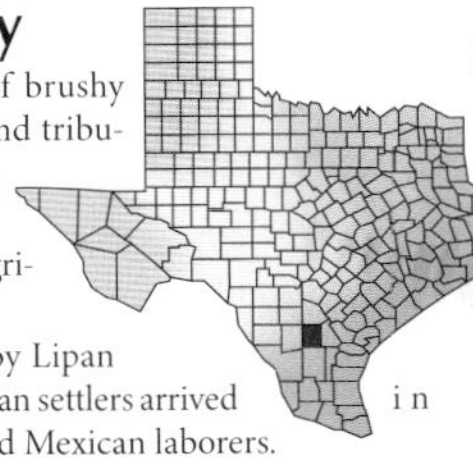

Physical Features: Southern county of brushy plain, sloping to Frio, Nueces rivers and tributaries, Choke Canyon Reservoir; saline clay soils.

Economy: Government/services, retail, agriculture, oil and gas services.

History: Coahuiltecans, squeezed out by Lipan Apaches and other tribes. Anglo-American settlers arrived in 1858. Sheep ranching of 1870s attracted Mexican laborers. County created from Atascosa, Bexar, Live Oak counties 1858; organized 1862, reorganized 1877; named for Nueces River pioneer-empresario John McMullen.

Race/Ethnicity: Anglo, 57.8%; Black, 0.4%; Hispanic, 40.8%; Asian, 0.4%; Other, 0.5%.

Vital Statistics, annual: Births, 0; deaths, 7; marriages, 11; divorces, 1.

Recreation: Hunting, wildlife viewing; lake activities, state park, wildlife management area; Labor Day rodeo.

Minerals: Gas, oil, lignite coal, caliche, kaolinite.

Agriculture: Beef cattle. Market value $8.3 million. Wildlife enterprises important.

Tilden (301), county seat; oil, gas, lignite mining, ranch center, government/services.

Other towns include: **Calliham** (100).

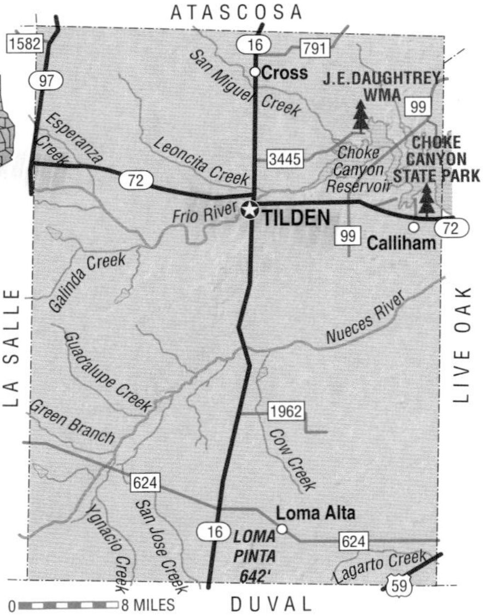

Population	**749**	Altitude (ft.)	150–642	Unemployed (%)	3
Change from 2010 (%)	6.7	Rainfall (in.)	24.0	Wages	$7,595,891
Area (sq. mi.)	1,156.8	Jan. mean min (°F)	42.6	Per Capita Income	$65,250
Land Area (sq. mi.)	1,139.4	July mean max (°F)	96.4	Prop. Value	$4,164,609,958
		Civ. Labor	673	Retail Sales	$19,354,234

Medina County

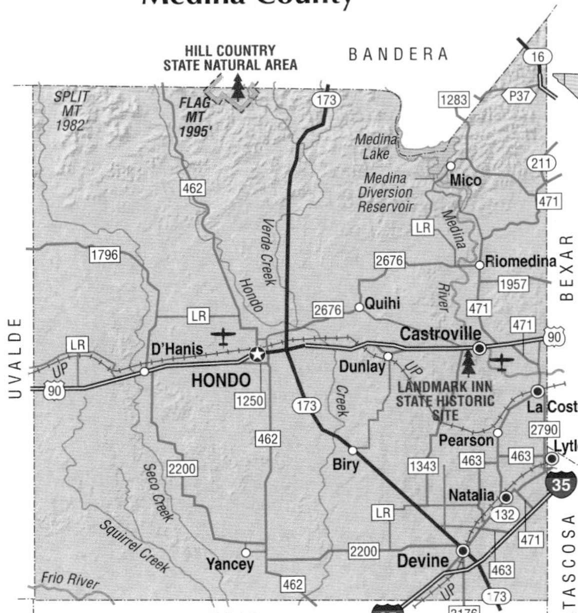

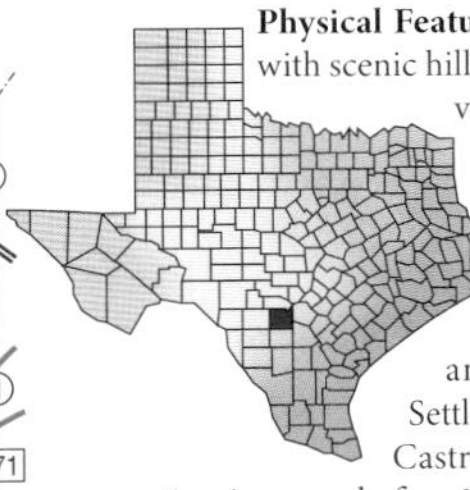

Physical Features: Southwestern county with scenic hills in north; south has fertile valleys, rolling surface; Medina River, Medina Lake.

Economy: Agribusiness, tourism, commuters to San Antonio.

History: Lipan Apaches and Comanches in area. Settled by Alsatians led by Henri Castro in 1844. Mexican immigration increased after 1900. County created and organized in 1848 from Bexar; named for river, probably for Spanish engineer Pedro Medina.

Race/Ethnicity: Anglo, 43%; Black, 1.8%; Hispanic, 53.1%; Asian, 0.5%; Other, 1.3%.

Vital Statistics, annual: Births, 585; deaths, 428; marriages, 255; divorces, 133.

Recreation: A leading deer area; scenic drives, camping, fishing, historic buildings, museum, market trail days most months.

Minerals: Oil and natural gas.

Agriculture: Cattle, corn, grains, cotton, hay, vegetables, aquaculture; 50,000 acres irrigated. Market value $93.9 million.

HONDO (9,618) county seat; flight training center, aerospace industry, agribusiness, varied manufacturing, hunting leases; hospital; prisons; wild game festival in January.

CASTROVILLE (3,114) farming; tourism; commuting to San Antonio; Landmark Inn, museum; St. Louis Day celebration in August.

DEVINE (5,001) commuters, shipping for truck crop-livestock; fall festival in October.

Other towns: **D'Hanis** (873), **La Coste** (1,293), **Natalia** (1,617), **Riomedina** (60), **Yancey** (209). Also, **Lytle** (3,066, mostly in Atascosa County).

Population	**53,794**	July mean max (°F)	94.9
Change from 2010 (%)	16.9	Civ. Labor	22,031
Area (sq. mi.)	1,334.4	Unemployed (%)	5.2
Land Area (sq. mi.)	1,325.4	Wages	$112,659,440
Altitude (ft.)	570–1,995	Per Capita Income	$41,095
Rainfall (in.)	30.3	Prop. Value	$7,064,827,834
Jan. mean min (°F)	39.1	Retail Sales	$763,427,302

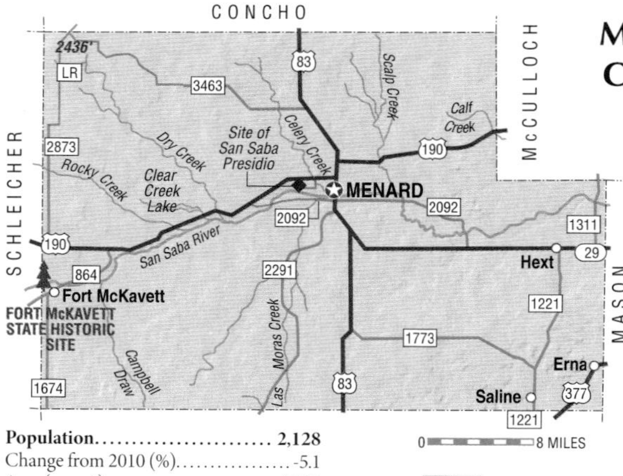

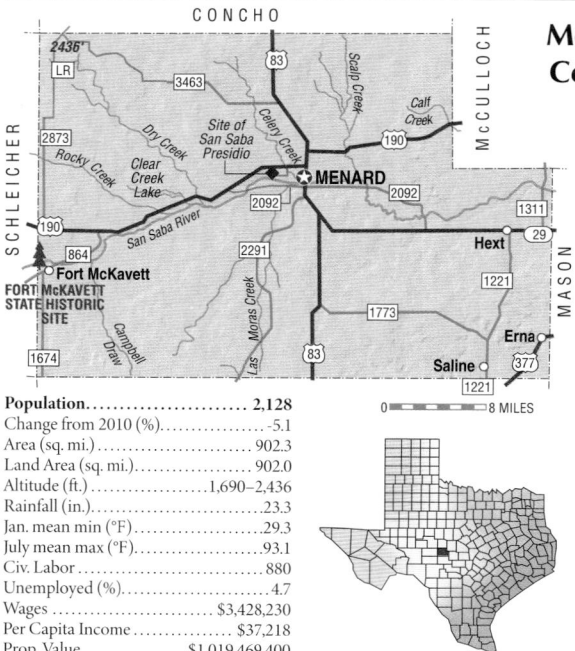

Menard County

Physical Features: West central county of rolling topography, draining to San Saba River and tributaries; limestone soils.

Economy: Agriculture, tourism, oil, gas production. History: Apaches, followed by Comanches in 18th century. Mission Santa Cruz de San Sabá established in 1757. A few Anglo-American and German settlers arrived in 1840s. County created from Bexar County 1858, organized 1871; named for Galveston's founder, Michel B. Menard.

Race/Ethnicity: Anglo, 55.8%; Black, 0.5%; Hispanic, 42.9%; Asian, 0.1%; Other, 0.5%.

Vital Statistics, annual: Births, 15; deaths, 33; marriages, 4; divorces, 7.

Recreation: Hunting, fishing; historic sites, including Spanish presidio, mission, irrigation ditches; U.S. fort; railroad museum; Jim Bowie barbecue cook-off in May.

Minerals: Oil, gas.

Agriculture: Cattle, sheep, goats, pecans, hay. Market value $9.1 million. Hunting leases, ecotourism important.

MENARD (1,378) county seat; agribusiness, government/services; hunters blowout ball in early November.

Other towns include: **Fort McKavett** (50); **Hext** (75).

Population	**2,128**
Change from 2010 (%)	-5.1
Area (sq. mi.)	902.3
Land Area (sq. mi.)	902.0
Altitude (ft.)	1,690–2,436
Rainfall (in.)	23.3
Jan. mean min (°F)	29.3
July mean max (°F)	93.1
Civ. Labor	880
Unemployed (%)	4.7
Wages	$3,428,230
Per Capita Income	$37,218
Prop. Value	$1,019,469,400
Retail Sales	$21,499,617

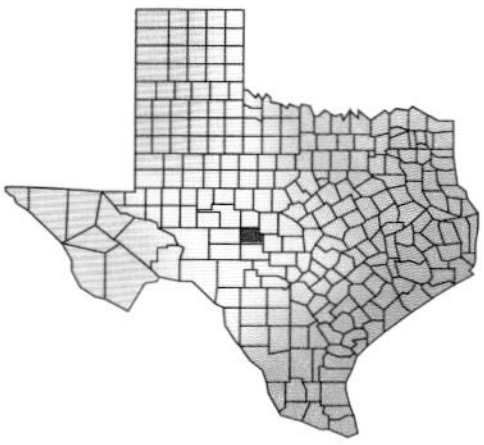

Midland County

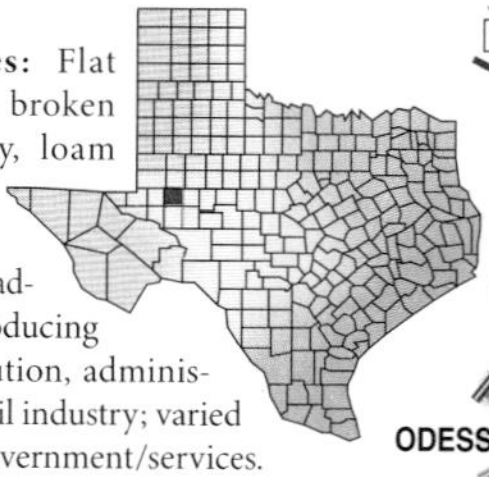

Physical Features: Flat western county, broken by draws; sandy, loam soils with native grasses.

Economy: Among leading petroleum-producing counties; distribution, administrative center for oil industry; varied manufacturing; government/services.

History: Comanches in area in 19th century. Sheep ranching developed in the 1880s. Permian Basin oil boom began in the 1920s. County created from Tom Green County in 1885 and organized the same year; name came from midway location on the railroad between El Paso and Fort Worth. The Chihuahua Trail and Emigrant Road were pioneer trails that crossed the county.

Race/Ethnicity: Anglo, 42.9%; Black, 6%; Hispanic, 47.3%; Asian, 1.8%; Other, 1.8%.

Vital Statistics, annual: Births, 3,032; deaths, 1,098; marriages, 1269; divorces, 714.

Recreation: Permian Basin Petroleum Museum, Library, Hall of Fame; Museum of Southwest; Commemorative Air Force and Museum; community theater; metropolitan events; homes of Presidents Bush.

Minerals: Oil, natural gas.

Agriculture: Beef cattle, horses, sheep and goats; cotton, hay, pecans; some 11,000 acres irrigated. Market value $16.3 million.

MIDLAND (146,701) county seat; petroleum, petrochemical center; varied manufacturing; livestock sale center; hospitals; cultural activities; community college; polo club, Texas League baseball; Celebration of the Arts in May.

Part [2,166] of **Odessa.**

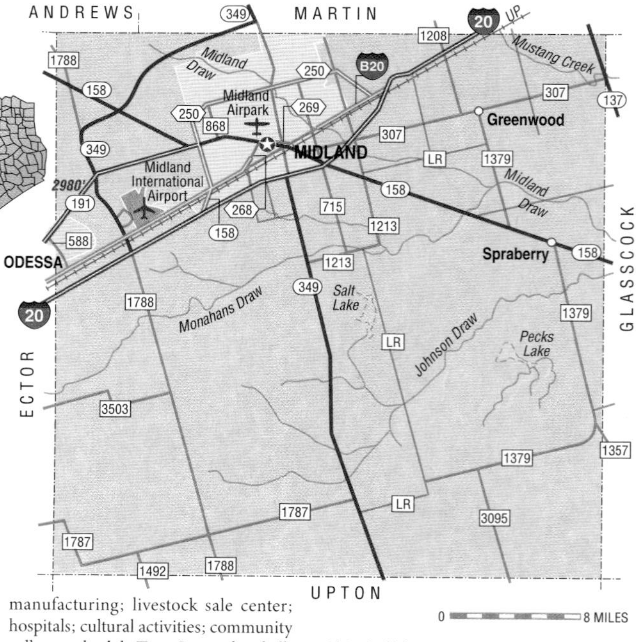

Population	**176,814**
Change from 2010 (%)	29.2
Area (sq. mi.)	902.1
Land Area (sq. mi.)	900.3
Altitude (ft.)	2,550–2,980
Rainfall (in.)	14.8
Jan. mean min (°F)	31.5
July mean max (°F)	96.2
Civ. Labor	95,625
Unemployed (%)	6.8
Wages	$1,865,556,925
Per Capita Income	$130,983
Prop. Value	$42,741,588,887
Retail Sales	$3,876,792,295

Counties of Texas

A detailed county map accompanies each of 254 county articles on pages 191–369.

Below is the legend to the symbols used on those maps:

Legend to counties

- Principal road
- Secondary road
- Local road
- Divided highway
- 10 Interstate highway
- 377 U.S. highway
- 81 State highway
- 308 Farm-to-market road
- LR Local roads
- 28 Loop
- Railway
- BNSF Railway name
- River or creek
- Lake
- Intermittent water source
- Intracoastal Waterway
- County seat
- Incorporated town
- Unincorporated town
- County boundary
- PECOS Name of neighboring county
- 400′ Elevation
- 880′ Highest point in county
- Major airport with scheduled jet service
- Municipal airport
- Military airport
- National park or wildlife management area
- Federal land
- State park or wildlife management area
- State land
- Ranger station
- Time zone line
- Boundary of prison or military installation

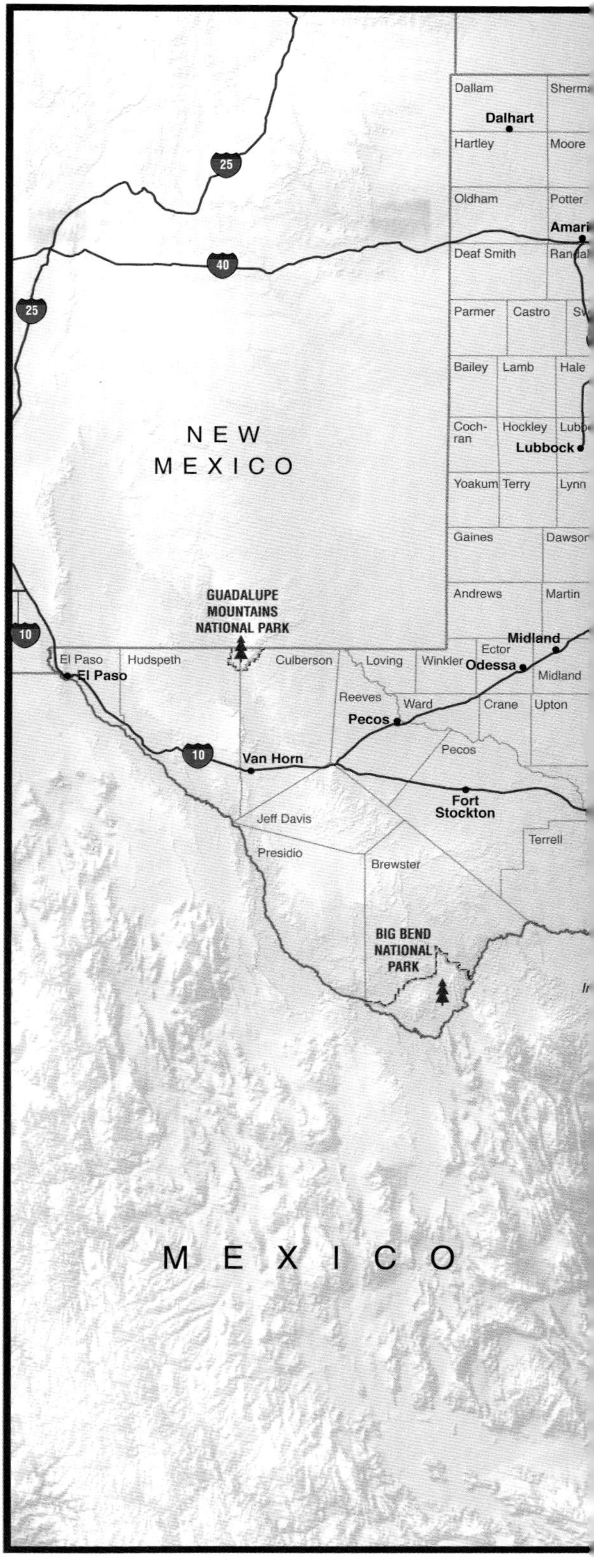

ge between Texas Cities

	Gainesville	Galveston	Houston	Huntsville	Laredo	Longview	Lubbock	Lufkin	McAllen	Odessa	Paris	Pecos	San Angelo	San Antonio	South Padre Island	Texarkana	Tyler	Van Horn	Victoria	Waco
	358																			
	307	50																		
	239	119	69																	
	180	341	311	365																
	178	253	206	151	488															
	290	560	510	466	498	447														
	238	166	119	72	429	87	490													
	551	367	345	398	143	541	618	463												
	360	538	494	458	422	472	137	491	565											
	96	342	291	224	527	102	383	184	594	447										
	434	589	545	528	417	546	203	565	560	74	521									
	275	407	363	327	321	372	183	360	444	131	352	205								
	326	241	197	217	154	334	382	285	236	336	373	363	209							
	591	387	366	428	216	570	668	484	73	622	629	630	495	286						
	188	328	283	235	572	88	475	165	624	525	92	599	430	418	648					
	59	247	197	130	456	36	419	84	508	444	101	517	336	302	540	116				
	22	654	610	594	483	633	291	642	626	161	608	88	282	428	696	686	605			
	352	154	124	186	187	328	489	242	220	447	385	476	316	114	244	407	296	542		
	151	230	180	130	334	163	345	157	401	340	194	413	209	181	441	244	128	490	202	
	84	421	371	303	490	257	208	304	572	293	178	366	230	336	621	270	232	454	399	198

US 67 from Fort Stockton to Alpine in West Texas. Photo by Jonathan Cutrer (jcutrer.com)

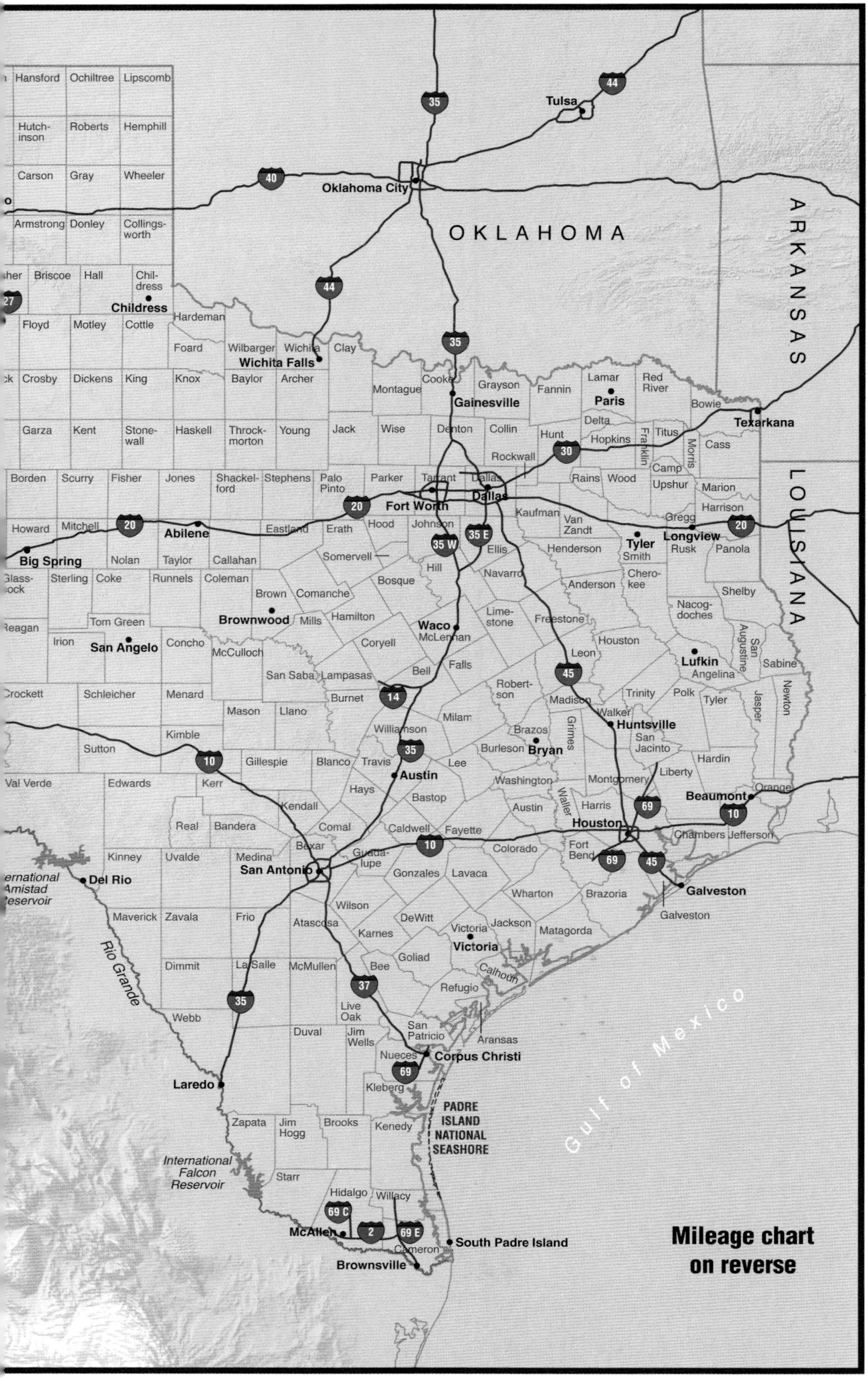

OKLAHOMA
ARKANSAS
LOUISIANA
Tulsa
Oklahoma City
Childress
Wichita Falls
Gainesville
Paris
Texarkana
Dallas
Fort Worth
Abilene
Big Spring
Longview
Tyler
Brownwood
San Angelo
Waco
Lufkin
Huntsville
Bryan
Austin
Beaumont
Houston
Galveston
San Antonio
Del Rio
International Amistad Reservoir
Rio Grande
Victoria
Corpus Christi
Laredo
International Falcon Reservoir
PADRE ISLAND NATIONAL SEASHORE
McAllen
South Padre Island
Brownsville
Gulf of Mexico
Mileage chart on reverse

Mileag

	Abilene	Amarillo	Austin	Beaumont	Big Bend	Big Spring	Brownsville	Brownwood	Bryan	Childress	Corpus Christi	Dalhart	Dallas	Del Rio	El Paso	Fort Stockton	Fort
Amarillo	266																
Austin	213	478															
Beaumont	412	637	238														
Big Bend	392	484	462	699													
Big Spring	107	222	289	519	281												
Brownsville	516	765	325	437	636	567											
Brownwood	77	342	137	350	398	174	471										
Bryan	253	503	100	158	559	360	382	191									
Childress	154	116	367	521	483	204	671	231	388								
Corpus Christi	387	636	192	288	524	438	159	329	237	542							
Dalhart	343	82	556	719	525	294	842	420	637	197	713						
Dallas	180	361	192	276	559	287	517	157	165	245	377	443					
Del Rio	246	450	232	434	253	231	378	231	318	382	268	520	388				
El Paso	439	418	573	810	329	332	801	493	660	482	691	417	617	424			
Fort Stockton	250	338	335	572	136	143	563	260	422	347	453	398	416	185	238		
Fort Worth	150	337	187	301	529	257	512	127	167	222	372	419	30	358	587	385	
Gainesville	195	309	252	345	584	301	577	185	232	193	437	391	69	416	625	439	65
Galveston	398	646	206	78	651	493	374	336	145	531	219	728	288	393	774	536	309
Houston	348	596	162	86	603	449	352	286	95	480	207	678	238	349	730	492	259
Huntsville	304	528	153	113	602	411	414	241	54	412	269	610	170	369	714	475	191
Laredo	373	609	232	396	434	406	199	330	318	528	141	686	424	179	602	364	416
Longview	305	482	256	194	649	412	557	278	177	366	411	564	125	488	742	535	155
Lubbock	162	119	368	574	360	104	655	232	415	139	526	196	322	332	344	220	292
Lufkin	336	529	219	108	675	443	470	274	121	414	325	611	168	439	761	523	199
McAllen	480	728	300	430	578	531	56	423	364	634	152	806	491	322	745	507	486
Odessa	167	255	334	567	222	60	609	219	408	263	480	315	347	247	274	83	317
Paris	281	403	294	292	665	388	615	257	234	287	470	485	103	488	717	516	131
Pecos	240	320	388	625	190	133	616	293	475	337	506	374	420	238	207	53	390
San Angelo	89	293	203	436	300	87	481	96	277	225	352	371	252	158	402	164	222
San Antonio	244	493	79	281	406	295	272	187	165	398	143	570	271	154	548	310	262
South Padre	530	779	339	451	644	251	27	473	396	684	172	856	531	392	815	577	526
Texarkana	359	495	340	256	744	466	634	335	261	379	489	576	178	566	795	594	209
Tyler	277	457	224	192	647	384	526	242	145	342	381	539	97	455	714	500	127
Van Horn	328	401	454	690	199	221	682	378	540	425	571	447	508	304	119	119	478
Victoria	334	600	122	209	522	402	230	259	152	489	85	677	292	264	661	423	287
Waco	183	423	102	242	518	290	427	123	85	307	287	504	91	334	610	372	86
Wichita Falls	141	225	283	412	513	234	608	169	270	109	474	307	136	388	552	376	112

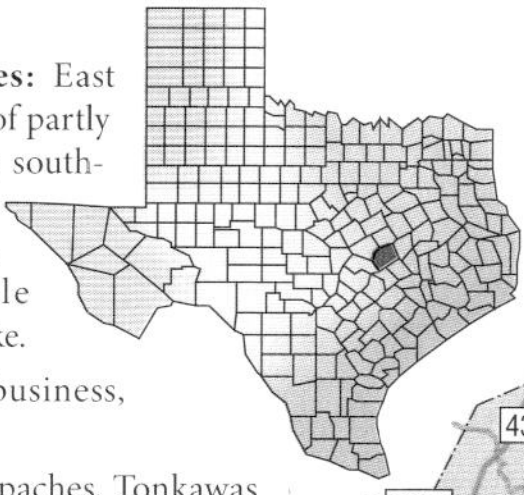

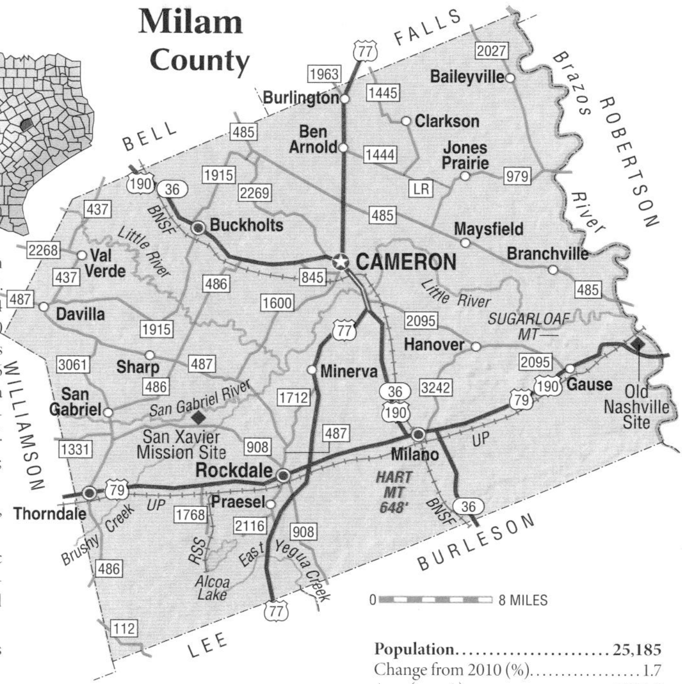

Physical Features: East central county of partly level Blackland; southeast rolling to Post Oak Belt; Brazos, Little rivers; Alcoa Lake.

Economy: Agribusiness, manufacturing.

History: Lipan Apaches, Tonkawas and Comanches in area. Mission San Francisco Xavier established 1745–1748. Anglo-American settlers arrived in 1834 and a private fort was established in 1840 at Bryant Station to help protect the settlers from Indian raids. County created in 1836 from municipality named for Ben Milam, a leader who died at the battle for San Antonio in December 1835; organized in 1837.

Race/Ethnicity: Anglo, 60%; Black, 8.8%; Hispanic, 29%; Asian, 0.4%; Other, 1.6%.

Vital Statistics, annual: Births, 320; deaths, 288; marriages, 147; divorces, 79.

Recreation: Fishing, hunting; historic sites include Fort Sullivan, Indian battlegrounds, mission sites; museum in old jail at Cameron, El Camino Real.

Minerals: Barite, limited oil and gas production.

Agriculture: Cattle, poultry (first in number of turkeys), corn. Market value $129.5 million.

CAMERON (5,619) county seat; government/services, manufacturing; hospital, library; dewberry festival in April.

ROCKDALE (5,656) government/services; hospital, juvenile detention center.

Other towns include: **Buckholts** (546); **Burlington** (100); **Davilla** (191); **Gause** (425); **Milano** (445); **Thorndale** (1,394) agribusiness, farming, ranching, antiques, barbecue cook-off in June.

For explanation of sources, symbols and abbreviations, see p. 204, and foldout map.

Population	**25,185**
Change from 2010 (%)	1.7
Area (sq. mi.)	1,021.8
Land Area (sq. mi.)	1,016.9
Altitude (ft.)	250–648
Rainfall (in.)	37.0
Jan. mean min (°F)	33.8
July mean max (°F)	88.7
Civ. Labor	9,852
Unemployed (%)	6.5
Wages	$58,430,624
Per Capita Income	$37,238
Prop. Value	$4,265,575,689
Retail Sales	$238,607,905

The historic Vaughn Building in Midland. Photo by Larry D. Moore, CC by SA 4.0

Mills County

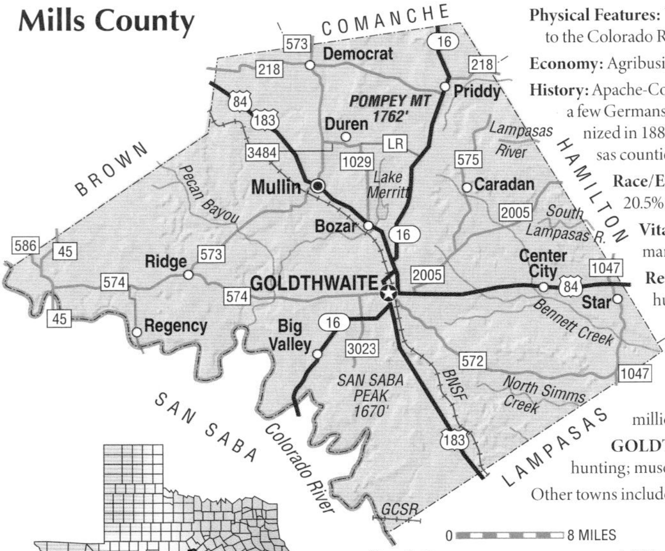

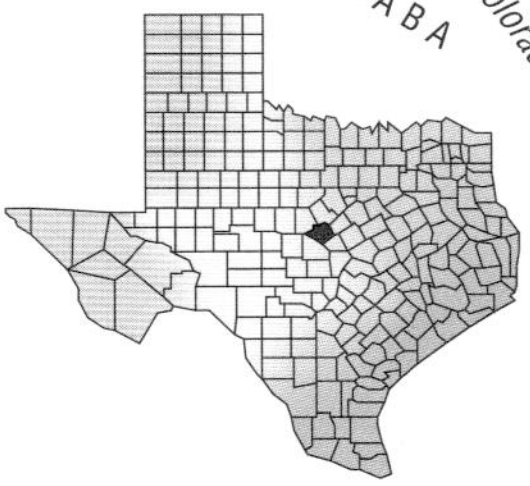

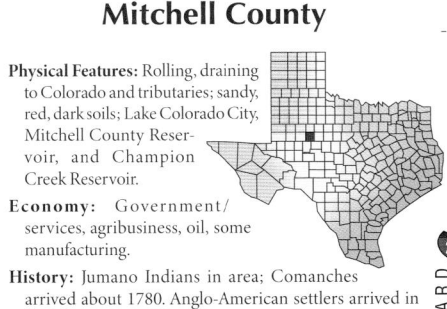

Physical Features: West central county of hills, plateau draining to the Colorado River; sandy, loam soils.

Economy: Agribusiness, hunting leases.

History: Apache-Comanche area of conflict. Anglo-Americans and a few Germans settled in the 1850s. County created and organized in 1887 from Brown, Comanche, Hamilton, Lampasas counties; named for pioneer jurist John T. Mills.

Race/Ethnicity: Anglo, 77.3%; Black, 0.5%; Hispanic, 20.5%; Asian, 0.1%; Other, 1.3%.

Vital Statistics, annual: Births, 30; deaths, 62; marriages, 27; divorces, 13.

Recreation: Fishing; deer, dove and turkey hunting; Regency suspension bridge; rangeland recreation.

Minerals: Not significant.

Agriculture: Cattle, dairies, sheep (first in numbers), goats, hay. Market value $30.9 million.

GOLDTHWAITE (1,888) county seat; agribusiness, hunting; museum; barbecue & goat cook-off in April.

Other towns include: **Mullin** (177); **Priddy** (215); **Star** (97).

Population	**4,899**	July mean max (°F)	91.5
Change from 2010 (%)	-0.7	Civ. Labor	1,937
Area (sq. mi.)	749.8	Unemployed (%)	4.3
Land Area (sq. mi.)	748.3	Wages	$13,001,014
Altitude (ft.)	1,112–1,762	Per Capita Income	$39,334
Rainfall (in.)	30.6	Prop. Value	$2,244,301,819
Jan. mean min (°F)	33.0	Retail Sales	$111,434,972

Mitchell County

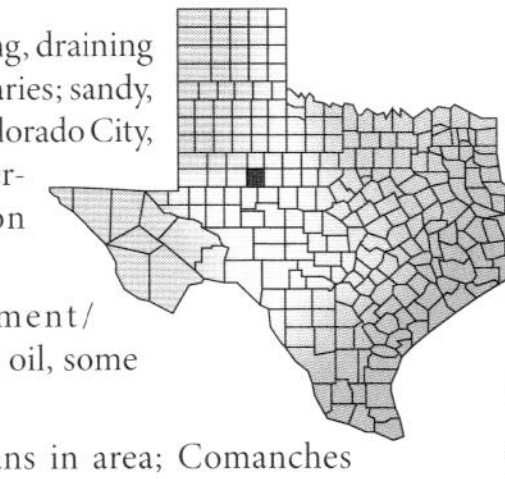

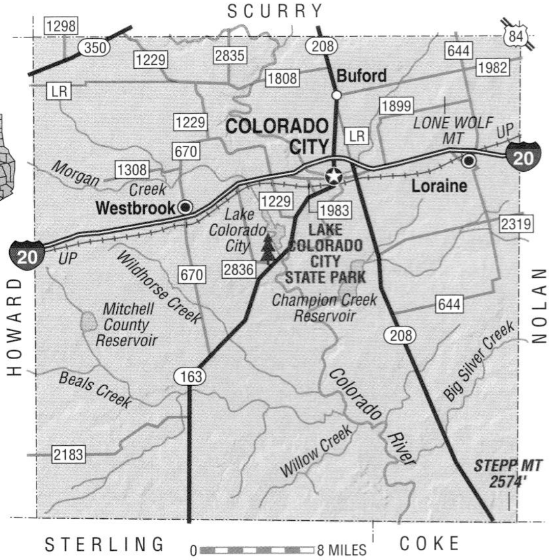

Physical Features: Rolling, draining to Colorado and tributaries; sandy, red, dark soils; Lake Colorado City, Mitchell County Reservoir, and Champion Creek Reservoir.

Economy: Government/ services, agribusiness, oil, some manufacturing.

History: Jumano Indians in area; Comanches arrived about 1780. Anglo-American settlers arrived in the late 1870s after Comanches were forced into Indian Territory. County created in 1876 from Bexar District and organized in 1881; named for pioneer brothers Asa and Eli Mitchell.

Race/Ethnicity: Anglo, 48.2%; Black, 10.6%; Hispanic, 39.5%; Asian, 0.3%; Other, 1.2%.

Vital Statistics, annual: Births, 88; deaths, 109; marriages, 50; divorces, 24.

Recreation: Lake activities, state park, museums, hunting, Colorado City playhouse.

Minerals: Oil.

Agriculture: Cotton principal crop, grains also produced. Cattle, sheep, goats, hogs raised. Market value $21.7 million.

COLORADO CITY (3,790) county seat; cotton, cattle, oil; hospital/medical services; opera house; poppy-mallow blooms at sports complex; goat cook-off in October.

Other towns include: **Loraine** (587) and **Westbrook** (256), trade centers. The community around **Lake Colorado City** (570).

For explanation of sources, symbols and abbreviations, see p. 204, and foldout map.

Population	**8,531**	July mean max (°F)	95.0
Change from 2010 (%)	-9.3	Civ. Labor	2,362
Area (sq. mi.)	915.9	Unemployed (%)	8.4
Land Area (sq. mi.)	911.1	Wages	$22,255,322
Altitude (ft.)	1,930–2,574	Per Capita Income	$33,593
Rainfall (in.)	20.4	Prop. Value	$1,524,365,779
Jan. mean min (°F)	28.3	Retail Sales	$41,751,473

Montague County

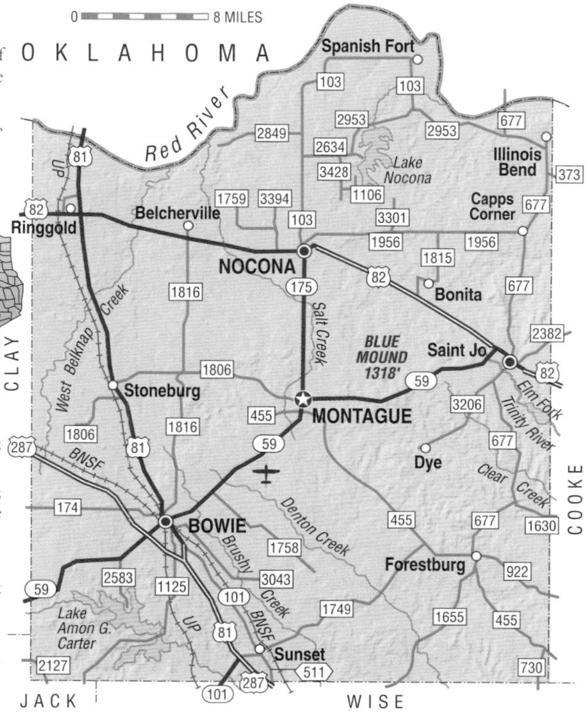

Physical Features: Rolling, draining to tributaries of Trinity, Red rivers; sandy loams, red, black soils; Lake Nocona, Lake Amon G. Carter.

Economy: Agribusiness, oil, varied manufacturing, government/services.

History: Kiowas and Wichitas who allied with Comanches. Anglo-American settlements developed in the 1850s. County created from Cooke County in 1857, organized in 1858; named for pioneer Daniel Montague.

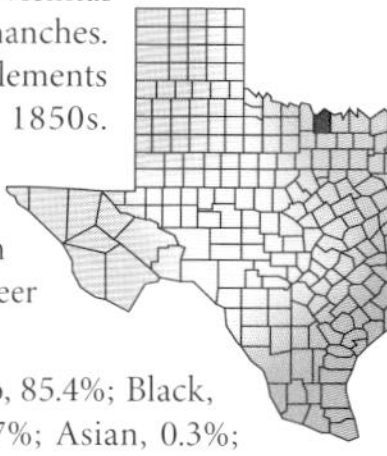

Race/Ethnicity: Anglo, 85.4%; Black, 0.3%; Hispanic, 11.7%; Asian, 0.3%; Other, 2%.

Vital Statistics, annual: Births, 237; deaths, 263; marriages, 124; divorces, 60.

Recreation: Lake activities; quail, turkey, deer hunting; scenic drives; museums; historical sites, motorcycle dirt track.

Minerals: Oil, gas, rock.

Agriculture: Beef, hay, pecans, melons, peaches. Market value $33.4 million.

MONTAGUE (299) county seat.

BOWIE (5,133) varied manufacturing, oil and gas operations; hospital, library; Jim Bowie Days in June.

NOCONA (3,027) athletic goods, boot manufacturing; hospital; art galleries, museums; Wheels & Grills barbecue cook-off and car show in September.

Other towns include: **Forestburg** (50); **Ringgold** (100); **Saint Jo** (1,074) wineries, retail center, art galleries, museums, rodeo in August; **Sunset** (579).

Population	**19,695**	July mean max (°F)	93.3
Change from 2010 (%)	-0.1	Civ. Labor	8,832
Area (sq. mi.)	938.3	Unemployed (%)	5.8
Land Area (sq. mi.)	930.9	Wages	$48,689,055
Altitude (ft.)	715–1,318	Per Capita Income	$42,230
Rainfall (in.)	35.1	Prop. Value	$3,880,218,587
Jan. mean min (°F)	29.2	Retail Sales	$222,622,731

The United Methodist Church in Montague. Photo by QuesterMark, CC 2/Wikimedia Commons

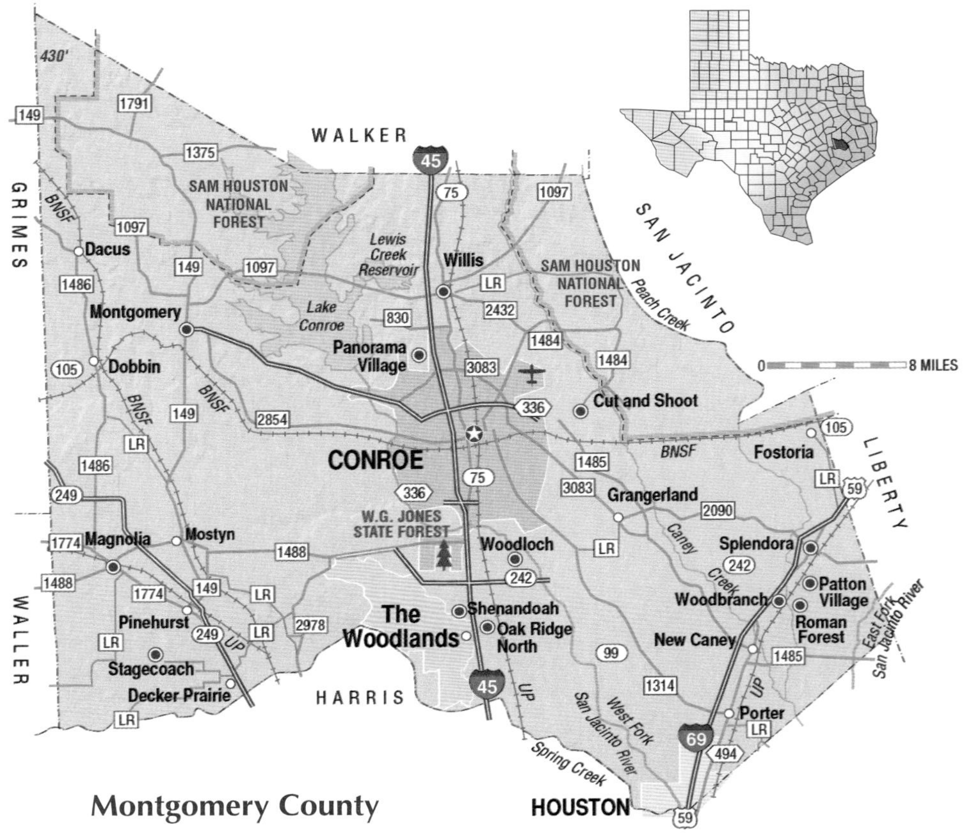

Montgomery County

Physical Features: Rolling, half timbered; Sam Houston National Forest; loam, sandy, alluvial soils; Lake Conroe and Lewis Creek Reservoir.

Economy: Varied manufacturing, oil production, medical research, government/services, many residents work in Houston.

History: Orcoquisac and Bidais tribes, removed from the area by the 1850s. Anglo-Americans arrived in the 1820s as part of Austin's colony. County created and organized in 1837 from Washington County; named for Richard Montgomery, American Revolution general.

Race/Ethnicity: Anglo, 64.8%; Black, 4.8%; Hispanic, 25.1%; Asian, 2.9%; Other, 2.2%.

Vital Statistics, annual: Births, 7,336; deaths, 3,623; marriages, 3,390; divorces, 1,809.

Recreation: Hunting, fishing; Lake Conroe activities; national and state forests; hiking, boating, horseback riding; historic sites.

Minerals: Natural gas.

Agriculture: Greenhouse crops, hay, beef cattle, horses. Market value $25.8 million. Timber important.

CONROE (90,276) county seat; government/services, hospital/medical services, commuters to Houston; new Sam Houston State University medical school; community college, museum; Cajun catfish festival in October.

The Woodlands (122,233) commuters to Houston, energy, tourism; college branches, hospitals, museums, parks, concerts, festivals at Mitchell Pavilion.

Other towns include: **Cut and Shoot** (1,409); **Dobbin** (310); **Grangerland** (300); **Magnolia** (2,118) government/services, drilling technology, construction, depot museum, Love Bug Fest in June; **Montgomery** (1,308) commuters to Houston and Conroe, antiques stores, pioneer museum, historic homes tour in April; **New Caney** (6,800); **Oak Ridge North** (3,382); **Panorama Village** (2,337); **Patton Village** (2,132).

Also: **Pinehurst** (5,448); **Porter** (4,200); **Porter Heights** (1,974); **Roman Forest** (2,061); **Shenandoah** (3,185); **Splendora** (2,240); **Stagecoach** (320); **Willis** (7,809) commuters to Conroe and Houston; **Woodbranch** (1,410); **Woodloch** (213).

Also, part [5,741] of **Houston** [Kingwood], hospital.

Population	**604,391**
Change from 2010 (%)	32.6
Area (sq. mi.)	1,076.9
Land Area (sq. mi.)	1,041.9
Altitude (ft.)	50–430
Rainfall (in.)	48.8
Jan. mean min (°F)	40.4
July mean max (°F)	93.5
Civ. Labor	285,994
Unemployed (%)	6.5
Wages	$3,017,993,587
Per Capita Income	$63,424
Prop. Value	$80,207,163,615
Retail Sales	$9,384,141,632

For explanation of sources, symbols and abbreviations, see p. 204, and foldout map.

Moore County

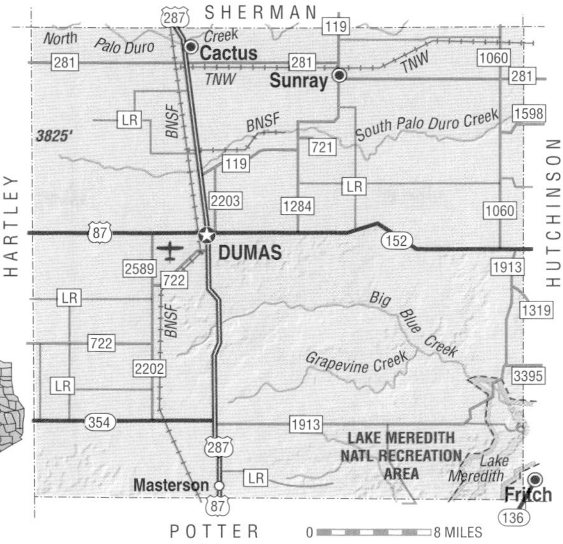

Physical Features: Flat to rolling, broken by creeks; sandy loams; Lake Meredith.

Economy: Varied agribusiness, petroleum, natural gas.

History: Comanches, removed to Indian Territory in 1874–1875; ranching began soon afterward. Farming developed after 1910. Oil boom in the 1920s. County created in 1876 from Bexar District; organized in 1892; named for Republic of Texas navy commander E.W. Moore.

Race/Ethnicity: Anglo, 31.3%; Black, 2.1%; Hispanic, 54.9%; Asian, 9.7%; Other, 1.8%.

Vital Statistics, annual: Births, 438; deaths, 164; marriages, 151; divorces, 97.

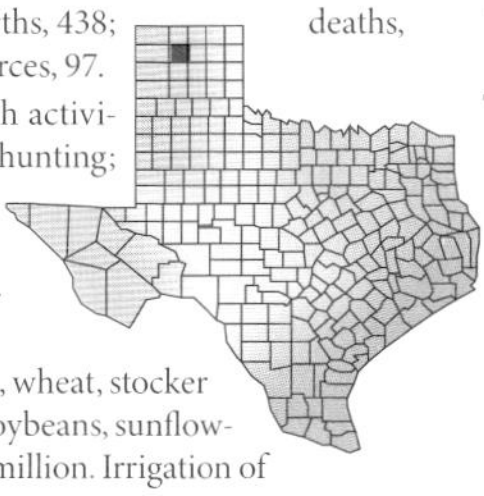

Recreation: Lake Meredith activities; pheasant, deer, quail hunting; historical museum; arts center; free overnight RV park; Dogie Days in June.

Minerals: Oil and gas.

Agriculture: Fed beef, corn, wheat, stocker cattle, sorghum, cotton, soybeans, sunflowers. Market value $478.1 million. Irrigation of 122,000 acres.

DUMAS (14,044) county seat; tourism, retail trade, varied agribusiness; hospital, hospice, retirement complex.

Other towns include: **Cactus** (3,241), **Sunray** (1,828). Small part of **Fritch**.

Population	**21,046**
Change from 2010 (%)	-3.9
Area (sq. mi.)	909.6
Land Area (sq. mi.)	899.7
Altitude (ft.)	2,915–3,825
Rainfall (in.)	18.4
Jan. mean min (°F)	22.1
July mean max (°F)	91.6
Civ. Labor	10,629
Unemployed (%)	3.6
Wages	$148,846,177
Per Capita Income	$46,108
Prop. Value	$2,787,536,775
Retail Sales	$434,958,732

Morris County

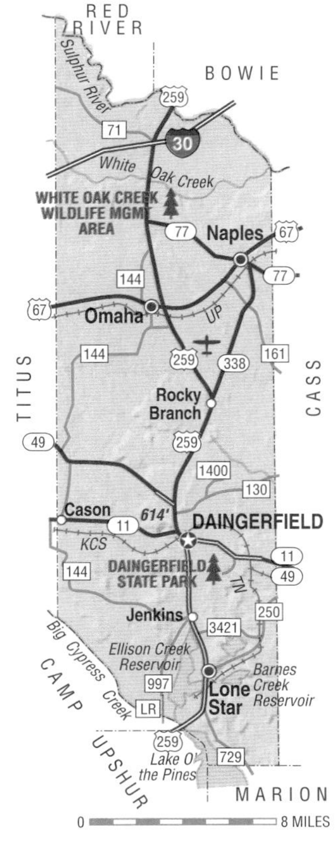

Physical Features: East Texas county of forested hills; drains to streams, Lake O' the Pines, Ellison Creek Reservoir, Barnes Creek Reservoir.

Economy: Steel manufacturing, agriculture, timber, government/services.

History: Caddo Indians until the 1790s. Kickapoo and other tribes in area 1820s-30s. Anglo-American settlement began in mid-1830s. Antebellum slaveholding area. County named for legislator-jurist W.W. Morris; created from Titus County and organized in 1875.

Race/Ethnicity: Anglo, 64.4%; Black, 21.8%; Hispanic, 9.8%; Asian, 0.3%; Other, 3.4%.

Vital Statistics, annual: Births, 161; deaths, 179; marriages, 97; divorces, 18.

Population	**12,428**
Change from 2010 (%)	-3.9
Area (sq. mi.)	258.7
Land Area (sq. mi.)	252.0
Altitude (ft.)	228–614
Rainfall (in.)	46.8
Jan. mean min (°F)	35.1
July mean max (°F)	94.1
Civ. Labor	4,652
Unemployed (%)	11.3
Wages	$46,422,016
Per Capita Income	$41,068
Prop. Value	$1,235,264,463
Retail Sales	$98,628,526

Recreation: Activities on Lake O' the Pines, small lakes; fishing, hunting; state park.

Minerals: Iron ore.

Agriculture: Beef cattle, broiler production, hay. Market value $44.2 million. Timber industry significant.

DAINGERFIELD (2,454) county seat; varied manufacturing, government/services; library, museum, city park, historic theater; Daingerfield Days in October.

Other towns include: **Cason** (173); **Lone Star** (1,508) oil-field equipment manufactured, catfish farming, Starfest in September; **Naples** (1,343) trailer manufacturing, livestock, watermelon festival in July; **Omaha** (980), retail center, government/services, commuters.

For explanation of sources, symbols and abbreviations, see p. 204, and foldout map.

Motley County

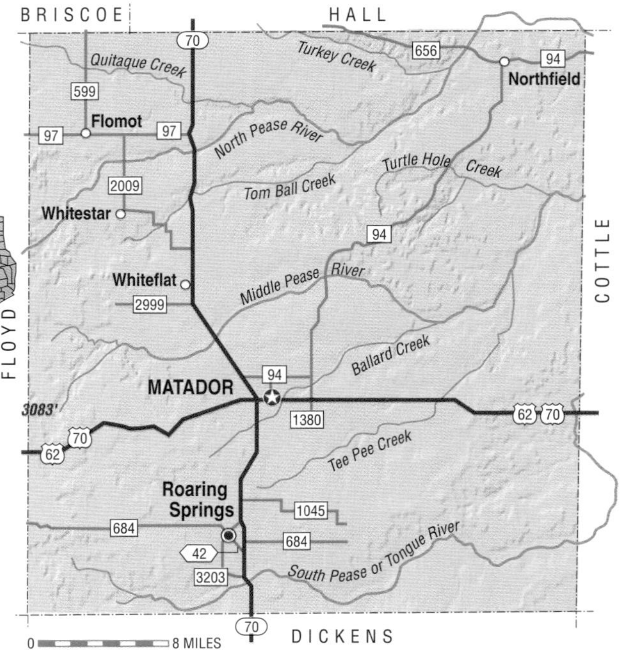

Physical Features: Western county just below Caprock; rough terrain, broken by Pease tributaries; sandy to red clay soils.

Economy: Agriculture, government/services, light manufacturing.

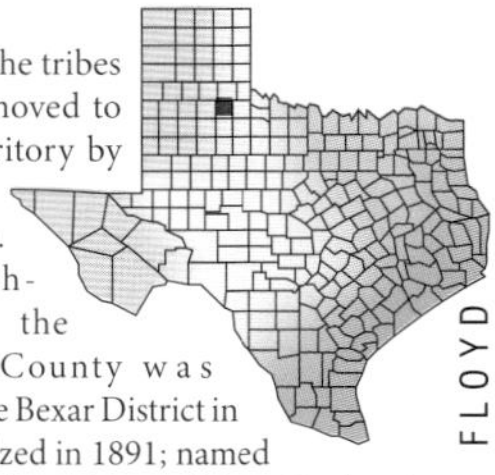

History: Comanche tribes in the area, removed to the Indian Territory by the U.S. Army in 1874–1875. Cattle ranching began in the late 1870s. County was created out of the Bexar District in 1876 and organized in 1891; named for Dr. J.W. Mottley, a signer of Texas Declaration of Independence (however, name was misspelled in legislative statute).

Race/Ethnicity: Anglo, 81.2%; Black, 2%; Hispanic, 15.8%; Asian, 0%; Other, 0.8%.

Vital Statistics, annual: Births, 0; deaths, 17; marriages, 21; divorces, 0.

Recreation: Quail, dove, turkey, deer, feral hog hunting; Matador Ranch headquarters; spring-fed pool at Roaring Springs; Motley-Dickens settlers reunion in August at Roaring Springs.

Minerals: Minimal.

Agriculture: Beef cattle, cotton, peanuts, hay, wheat. Some irrigation. Market value $15.2 million. Hunting leases important.

MATADOR (609) county seat; ranching, farming, government/services; museum, historic oil-derrick gas station; motorcycles race in April.

Other towns include: **Flomot** (181) bluegrass festival in May, and **Roaring Springs** (235).

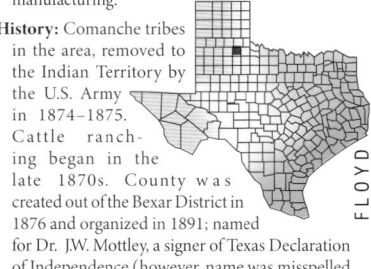

Population	**1,205**
Change from 2010 (%)	-0.4
Area (sq. mi.)	989.8
Land Area (sq. mi.)	989.6
Altitude (ft.)	1,800–3,083
Rainfall (in.)	23.4
Jan. mean min (°F)	29.6
July mean max (°F)	94.2
Civ. Labor	449
Unemployed (%)	5.1
Wages	$2,619,922
Per Capita Income	$32,988
Prop. Value	$360,305,810
Retail Sales	$6,798,587

The Pilgrim's Pride plant in Nacogdoches. Photo by Billy Hathorn, Public Domain/Wikimedia Commons

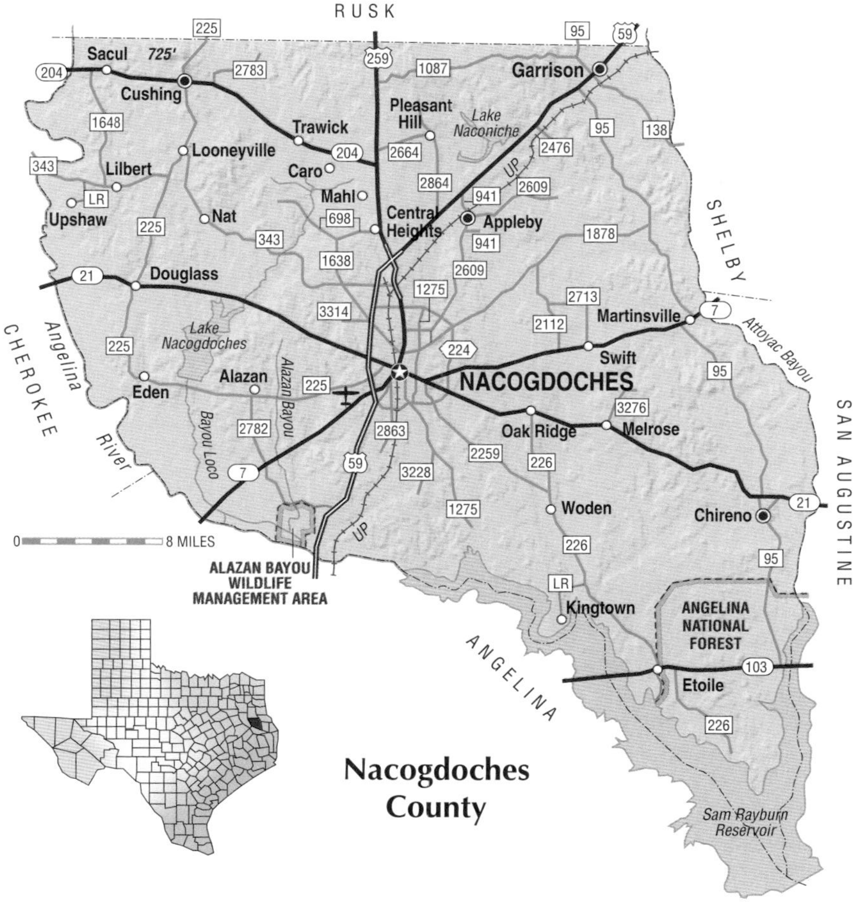

Nacogdoches County

Physical Features: East Texas county on divide between the Angelina River and Attoyac Bayou; hilly; two-thirds is forested; red, gray, sandy soils; Sam Rayburn Reservoir, Lake Nacogdoches, Lake Naconiche.

Economy: Agribusiness, timber, manufacturing, education, tourism.

History: Caddo tribes, joined by displaced Cherokees in the 1820s. Indian tribes moved west of the Brazos River by 1840. Spanish missions established in 1716. Spanish settlers arrived in the mid-1700s.

Anglo-Americans arrived in the 1820s. An original county of the Republic in 1836, organized in 1837. Name comes from Caddo tribe in the area.

Race/Ethnicity: Anglo, 59.1%; Black, 17.3%; Hispanic, 19.5%; Asian, 1.5%; Other, 2.4%.

Vital Statistics, annual: Births, 864; deaths, 605; marriages, 462; divorces, 160.

Recreation: Lake and river activities; Stephen F. Austin State University events; Angelina National Forest; historic site.

Tourist attractions include the Old Stone Fort, pioneer homes, museums, Millard's Crossing Historic Village, Piney Woods Native Plant Center; Azalea Trail in March, Blueberry Festival in June.

Minerals: First Texas oil discovered here, 1866; gas, oil, clay, and stone.

Agriculture: A leading poultry-producing county (third in number of broilers); beef cattle raised. Market value $370.7 million. Substantial timber sold.

NACOGDOCHES (33,677) county seat; varied manufacturing, lumber mills, wood products, trade center; hospitals; Stephen F. Austin State University; Nine Flags Festival in November/December.

Other towns include: **Appleby** (491), **Chireno** (386), **Cushing** (610), **Douglass** (380), **Etoile** (700), **Garrison** (881), **Martinsville** (350), **Sacul** (150), **Woden** (400).

For explanation of sources, symbols and abbreviations, see p. 204, and foldout map.

Population	**65,027**
Change from 2010 (%)	0.8
Area (sq. mi.)	981.2
Land Area (sq. mi.)	946.5
Altitude (ft.)	164–725
Rainfall (in.)	49.3
Jan. mean min (°F)	35.8
July mean max (°F)	93.2
Civ. Labor	27,901
Unemployed (%)	5.9
Wages	$244,202,306
Per Capita Income	$38,569
Prop. Value	$6,133,393,788
Retail Sales	$871,842,943

Navarro County

Physical Features: Level Blackland, some rolling; drains to creeks, Trinity River; Navarro Mills Lake, Richland-Chambers Reservoir, Lake Halbert.

Economy: Diversified manufacturing, agribusinesses, oil-field operations, distribution.

History: Kickapoo and Comanche area. Anglo-Americans settled in the late 1830s. Antebellum slaveholding area. County created in 1846 from Robertson County, organized the same year; named for Republic of Texas leader José Antonio Navarro.

Race/Ethnicity: Anglo, 56.6%; Black, 12.7%; Hispanic, 27%; Asian, 0.5%; Other, 3%.

Vital Statistics, annual: Births, 664; deaths, 568; marriages, 339; divorces, 165.

Recreation: Lake activities; Pioneer Village; historic buildings; youth exposition, Derrick Days in April.

Minerals: Longest continuous Texas oil flow; more than 200 million barrels produced since 1895; natural gas, sand and gravel also produced.

Agriculture: Beef cattle, cotton, sorghum, corn, wheat, sunflowers, herbs, horses, dairies. Market value $73.3 million.

CORSICANA (24,601) county seat; major distribution center, pecans, candy, fruitcakes; varied manufacturing; agribusiness; hospital; Navarro College; Texas Youth Commission facility.

Other towns include: **Angus** (455); **Barry** (265); **Blooming Grove** (863); **Chatfield** (40); **Dawson** (810); **Emhouse** (143); **Eureka** (318); **Frost** (653); **Goodlow** (194).

Also: **Kerens** (1,568) commuting, nature tourism, Cotton Harvest Festival in October; **Mildred** (405); **Mustang** (21); **Navarro** (221); **Oak Valley** (410); **Powell** (147); **Purdon** (133); **Retreat** (405); **Rice** (1,002); **Richland** (274).

Population	**52,013**
Change from 2010 (%)	9.0
Area (sq. mi.)	1,085.9
Land Area (sq. mi.)	1,009.6
Altitude (ft.)	250–623
Rainfall (in.)	39.8
Jan. mean min (°F)	34.7
July mean max (°F)	94.1
Civ. Labor	22,772
Unemployed (%)	5.7
Wages	$193,827,690
Per Capita Income	$39,652
Prop. Value	$6,509,663,456
Retail Sales	$678,521,365

The Mustang Bowl in Sweetwater was built by the Works Progress Administration in 1939. Photo by Larry D. Moore, CC by SA 4.0/Wikimedia Commons

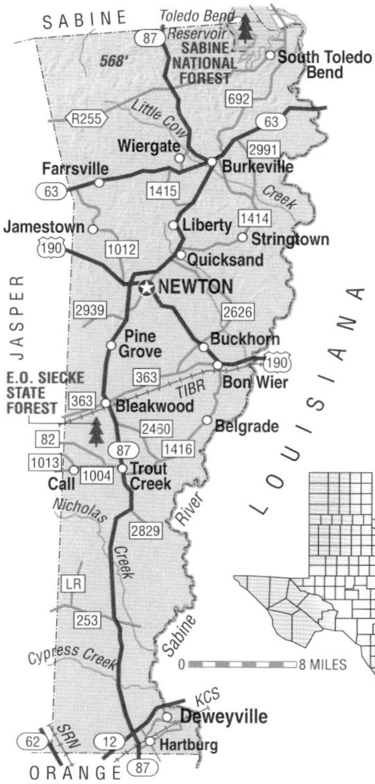

Newton County

Physical Features: Easternmost Texas county of densely forested hills, valleys; spring-fed streams; Toledo Bend Reservoir; Sabine River; mostly sandy soils.

Economy: Forestry, government/services, tourism.

History: Caddo Indian area. Displaced Coushattas moved across area from South. Anglo-American settlement established in 1830s. Antebellum slaveholding area. County created 1846 from Jasper County, organized the same year; named for American Revolutionary soldier John Newton.

Race/Ethnicity: Anglo, 73.1%; Black, 20.5%; Hispanic, 3.4%; Asian, 0.5%; Other, 2.4%.

Vital Statistics, annual: Births, 136; deaths, 168; marriages, 72; divorces, 47.

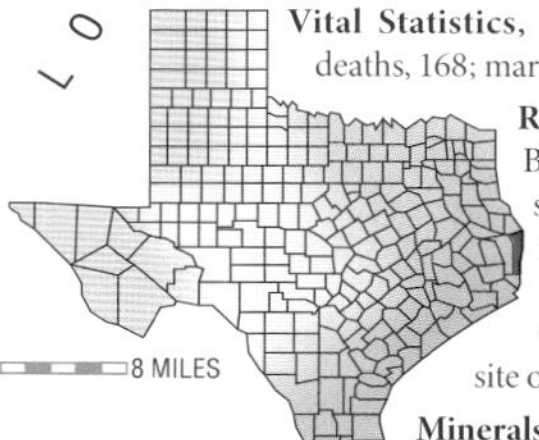

Recreation: Toledo Bend Reservoir, water sports, fishing, hunting, birding, tourism, state forest, Azalea Canyons; Belgrade, site of early town.

Minerals: Oil, gas.

Agriculture: Cattle, hay, nursery crops, vegetables, goats, hogs. Market value $1.6 million. Hunting leases. Major forestry area.

NEWTON (2,338) county seat; lumber manufacturing, plywood mill, private prison unit, tourist center; genealogical library, museum; Wild Azalea festival in March.

Deweyville (873) power plant, commercial center for forestry, farming area.

Other towns include: **Bon Wier** (375); **Burkeville** (603); **Call** (493); **South Toledo Bend** (454); **Wiergate** (350).

Population	**13,317**
Change from 2010 (%)	-7.8
Area (sq. mi.)	939.7
Land Area (sq. mi.)	933.7
Altitude (ft.)	10–568
Rainfall (in.)	54.9
Jan. mean min (°F)	36.5
July mean max (°F)	93.1
Civ. Labor	5,144
Unemployed (%)	10.7
Wages	$12,750,968
Per Capita Income	$34,265
Prop. Value	$2,582,808,227
Retail Sales	$38,910,205

For explanation of sources, symbols and abbreviations, see p. 204, and foldout map.

Nolan County

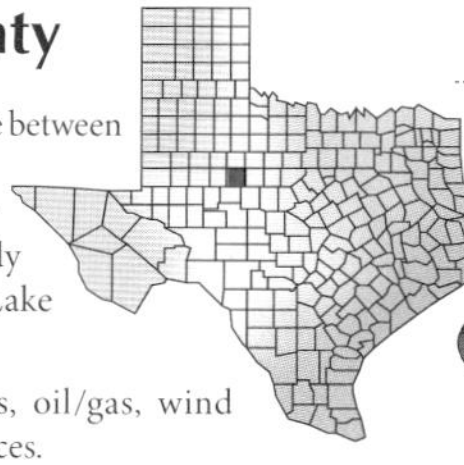

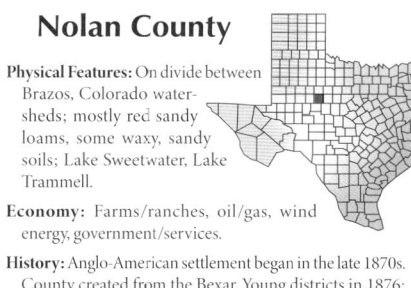

Physical Features: On divide between Brazos, Colorado watersheds; mostly red sandy loams, some waxy, sandy soils; Lake Sweetwater, Lake Trammell.

Economy: Farms/ranches, oil/gas, wind energy, government/services.

History: Anglo-American settlement began in the late 1870s. County created from the Bexar, Young districts in 1876; organized in 1881; named for adventurer Philip Nolan, who was killed near Waco.

Race/Ethnicity: Anglo, 54.7%; Black, 4.7%; Hispanic, 38.6%; Asian, 0.3%; Other, 1.4%.

Vital Statistics, annual: Births, 205; deaths, 178; marriages, 110; divorces, 35.

Recreation: Lakes, hunting, pioneer museum; rattlesnake roundup in March, Soap Box Derby in June.

Minerals: Oil, gas.

Agriculture: Beef cattle, cotton, sorghum. Market value $36.6 million. Some 3,300 acres irrigated.

SWEETWATER (10,285) county seat; wind energy, varied manufacturing, gypsum; hospital; Texas State Technical College; WWII museum.

Other towns include: **Blackwell** (286, partly in Coke County), Oak Creek Reservoir to south; **Maryneal** (50); **Nolan** (60); **Roscoe** (1,240).

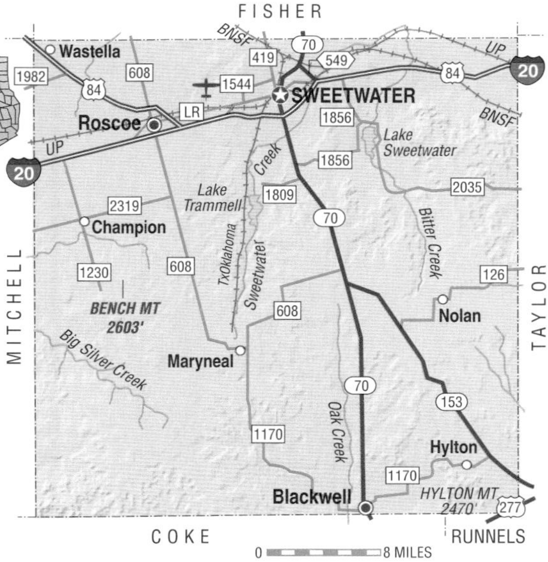

Population	**14,256**
Change from 2010 (%)	-6.3
Area (sq. mi.)	914.0
Land Area (sq. mi.)	912.0
Altitude (ft.)	1,896–2,603
Rainfall (in.)	22.4
Jan. mean min (°F)	29.0
July mean max (°F)	93.9
Civ. Labor	7,263
Unemployed (%)	4.9
Wages	$75,291,142
Per Capita Income	$46,066
Prop. Value	$3,365,596,869
Retail Sales	$263,242,827

Nueces County

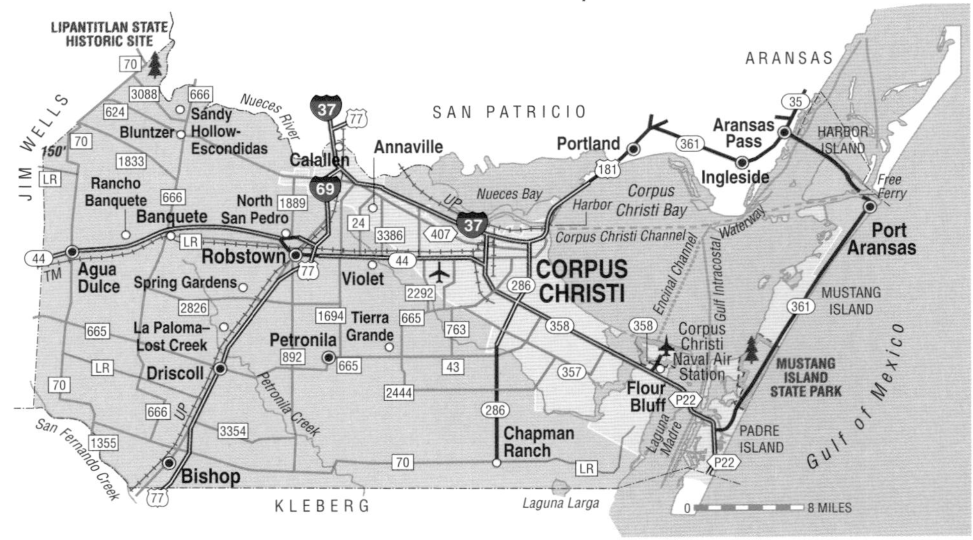

Physical Features: Southern Gulf Coast county; flat, rich soils, broken by bays, Nueces River, Petronila Creek; includes Mustang Island, north tip of Padre Island.

Economy: Petroleum processing, deepwater port facility, agriculture, tourism.

History: Coahuiltecan, Karankawa and other tribes who succumbed to disease or fled by 1840s. Spanish settlers arrived in the 1760s. Settlers from Ireland arrived around 1830. County name is Spanish for nuts; county named for river; created and organized in 1846 out of San Patricio County.

Race/Ethnicity: Anglo, 28.3%; Black, 3.6%; Hispanic, 64.4%; Asian, 2.1%; Other, 1.4%.

Vital Statistics, annual: Births, 5,054; deaths, 2,937; marriages, 2,436; divorces, 657.

Recreation: Major resort area; beaches, fishing, water sports, birding; Padre Island National Seashore, Mustang Island State Park, Lipantitlan State Historic Site; Art Museum of South Texas, Corpus Christi Museum of Science and History; Texas State Aquarium; Museum of Asian Cultures; professional baseball, hockey; greyhound race track.

Minerals: Oil, gas, sand, gravel.

Agriculture: Grain sorghum (second in acreage), cotton, cattle, wheat, hay, nurseries/turfgrass. Market value $161.0 million.

CORPUS CHRISTI (327,618) county seat; seaport, naval bases, varied manufacturing, petroleum processing, tourism; hospitals; museums; Army depot; Texas A&M University-Corpus Christi, Del Mar College; USS Lexington museum, Harbor Lights; Buccaneer Days in late April.

PORT ARANSAS (4,153) deepwater port, tourism, marine research, Coast Guard base, fishing industry; University of Texas Marine Science Institute; museum, beach; Celebration of Whooping Cranes in February; Texas Sand Fest in April.

ROBSTOWN (11,212) agriculture, transportation, tourism, petroleum processing; regional fairgrounds; Cottonfest in October, Fiesta Mexicana in March.

Other towns include: **Agua Dulce** (838); **Banquete** (795); **Bishop** (3,092) petrochemicals, agriculture, pharmaceuticals, plastics, nature trail, Old Tyme Faire in April; **Chapman Ranch** (200); **Driscoll** (744); **La Paloma-Lost Creek** (505); **North San Pedro** (868); **Petronila** (121); **Rancho Banquete** (415); **Sandy Hollow-Escondidas** (259); **Spring Gardens** (662); **Tierra Grande** (441), and **Tierra Verde** (320).

Annaville, Calallen, and Flour Bluff are now part of Corpus Christi.

Population	**363,049**
Change from 2010 (%)	6.7
Area (sq. mi.)	11,656.0
Land Area (sq. mi.)	835.5
Altitude (ft.)	sea level–150
Rainfall (in.)	32.5
Jan. mean min (°F)	46.6
July mean max (°F)	93.1
Civ. Labor	163,641
Unemployed (%)	7.6
Wages	$2,073,469,587
Per Capita Income	$44,889
Prop. Value	$46,061,562,283
Retail Sales	$5,658,049,252

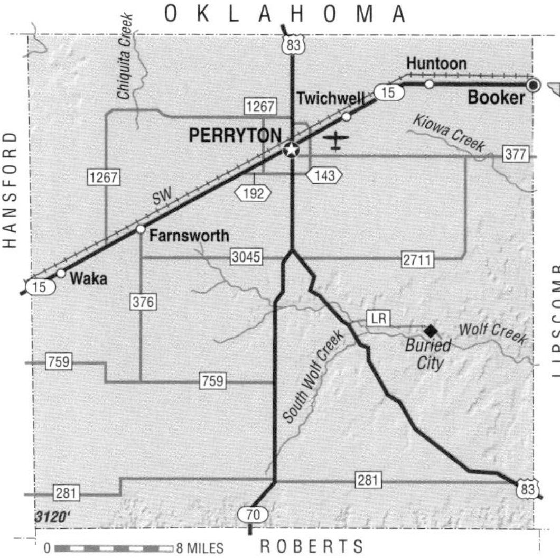

Ochiltree County

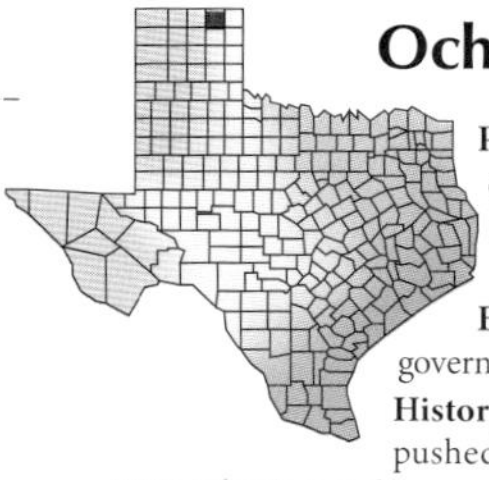

Physical Features: Panhandle county bordering Oklahoma; level, broken by creeks; deep loam, clay soils.

Economy: Agribusiness, oil/gas, government/services.

History: Apache groups, who were pushed out by Comanches in late 1700s. The Comanches were removed to the Indian Territory in 1874–1875 by U.S. Army. Ranching developed in 1880s; farming began after 1900. Created from the Bexar District in 1876, organized in 1889; named for Republic of Texas leader W.B. Ochiltree.

Race/Ethnicity: Anglo, 42.1%; Black, 0.2%; Hispanic, 56.1%; Asian, 0.2%; Other, 1.2%.

Vital Statistics, annual: Births, 184; deaths, 83; marriages, 95; divorces, 48.

Recreation: Wolf Creek park; Museum of the Plains; Prehistoric settlement site of "Buried City"; pheasant hunting, also deer and dove; Wheatheart of the Nation celebration in August.

Minerals: Oil, natural gas, caliche.

For explanation of sources, symbols and abbreviations, see p. 204, and foldout map.

Agriculture: Cattle, swine, corn, cotton, wheat (second in acreage), sorghum, hay and forages; some 50,000 acres irrigated. Market value $349.1 million.

PERRYTON (8,816) county seat; oil/gas, cattle feeding, grain center; hospital; college.

Other towns include: **Farnsworth** (130); **Waka** (65). Also, **Booker** (1,558, mostly in Lipscomb County).

Population	**10,219**
Change from 2010 (%)	0.0
Area (sq. mi.)	918.1
Land Area (sq. mi.)	917.6
Altitude (ft.)	2,550–3,120
Rainfall (in.)	22.1
Jan. mean min (°F)	19.0
July mean max (°F)	92.4
Civ. Labor	3,818
Unemployed (%)	4.9
Wages	$50,086,903
Per Capita Income	$60,862
Prop. Value	$1,783,639,637
Retail Sales	$81,303,997

Oldham County

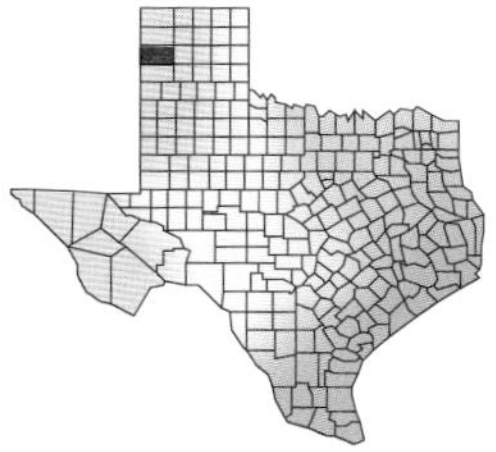

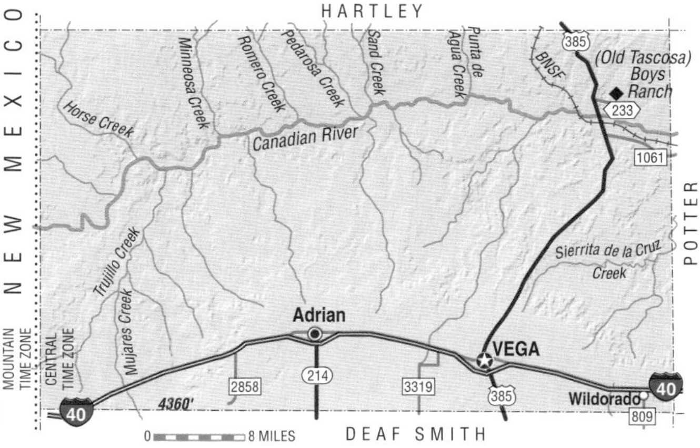

Physical Features: Northwestern Panhandle county; level, broken by Canadian River and tributaries.

Economy: Agriculture, wind energy, sand and gravel.

History: Apaches; followed later by Comanches, Kiowas. U.S. Army removed the Indians in 1875. Anglo ranchers and Spanish pastores (sheep men) from New Mexico were in the area in the 1870s. County created in 1876 from Bexar District; organized in 1880; named for editor-Confederate senator W.S. Oldham.

Race/Ethnicity: Anglo, 82.5%; Black, 2.5%; Hispanic, 12.5%; Asian, 0.7%; Other, 1.5%.

Vital Statistics, annual: Births, 23; deaths, 17; marriages, 9; divorces, 3.

Recreation: Old Tascosa, Cal Farley's Boys Ranch, Boot Hill Cemetery, museums; midway point on old Route 66; County Roundup in August, Boys Ranch rodeo Labor Day weekend.

Minerals: Sand and gravel, oil, natural gas, stone.

Agriculture: Beef cattle; crops include wheat, grain sorghum. Market value $156.0 million.

VEGA (917) county seat; farm and ranch trade center; transportation; museums.

Other towns include: **Adrian** (167); **Wildorado** (210). Also, **Cal Farley's Boys Ranch** (297).

Population	**2,126**
Change from 2010 (%)	3.6
Area (sq. mi.)	1,501.4
Land Area (sq. mi.)	1,500.5
Altitude (ft.)	3,140–4,360
Rainfall (in.)	19.2
Jan. mean min (°F)	20.7
July mean max (°F)	92.3
Civ. Labor	921
Unemployed (%)	3.5
Wages	$12,364,279
Per Capita Income	$55,479
Prop. Value	$1,390,655,307
Retail Sales	$54,080,952

Orange County

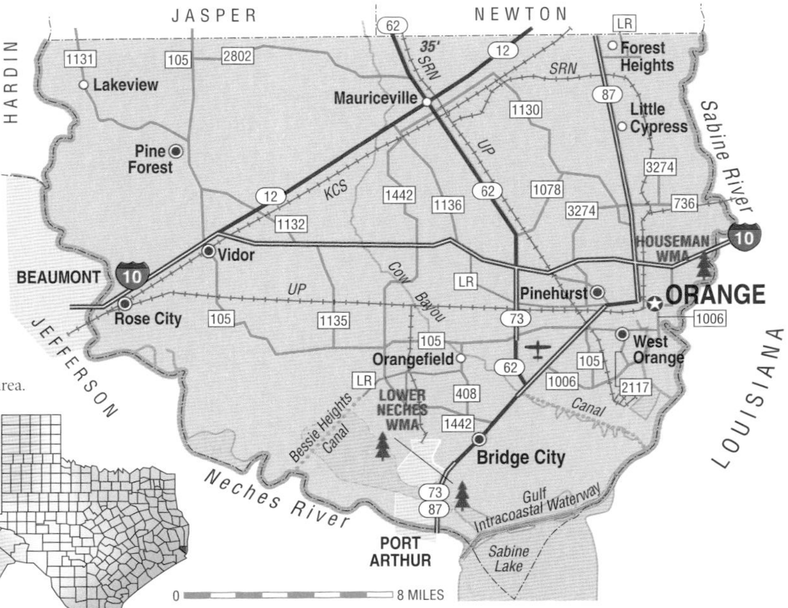

Physical Features: In southeastern corner of the state; bounded by Sabine, Neches rivers, Sabine Lake; coastal soils; two-thirds timbered.

Economy: Oil and gas production, electric power plants, commercial fishing.

History: Atakapan Indian area. French traders in area by 1720. Anglo-American settlement began in the 1820s. County created from Jefferson County in 1852, organized the same year; named for early orange grove.

Race/Ethnicity: Anglo, 80.9%; Black, 8.8%; Hispanic, 6.9%; Asian, 1%; Other, 2.1%.

Vital Statistics, annual: Births, 1,218; deaths, 947; marriages, 680; divorces, 211.

Recreation: Fishing, hunting, water sports, birding, county park, museums; historical homes, crawfish and crab festivals in spring.

Minerals: Oil and gas.

Agriculture: Beef cattle, forages, citrus, bees. Market value $5.0 million. Hunting leases. Timber important.

ORANGE (18,297) county seat; seaport, petrochemical plants, varied manufacturing, food and timber processing shipping; hospital, theater, museums; Lamar State College-Orange; Mardi Gras/gumbo festival in February.

BRIDGE CITY (7,868) varied manufacturing, ship repair yard, steel fabrication, fish farming, government/services; library; tall bridge and newer suspension bridge over Neches; stop for Monarch butterfly in fall during its migration to Mexico.

Vidor (10,570) steel processing, railroad-car refinishing; library; barbecue festival in April.

Other towns include: **Mauriceville** (3,804); **Orangefield** (725); **Pine Forest** (508); **Pinehurst** (2,077); **Rose City** (501); **West Orange** (3,181).

Population	**82,461**
Change from 2010 (%)	0.8
Area (sq. mi.)	379.5
Land Area (sq. mi.)	333.7
Altitude (ft.)	sea level–35
Rainfall (in.)	64.2
Jan. mean min (°F)	39.6
July mean max (°F)	91.2
Civ. Labor	36,235
Unemployed (%)	9.3
Wages	$315,343,215
Per Capita Income	$45,663
Prop. Value	$8,286,699,132
Retail Sales	$1,015,571,472

For explanation of sources, symbols and abbreviations, see p. 204, and foldout map.

The sign at Cal Farley's Boys Ranch in Oldham County. Photo by Nicholas Henderson, CC 2/Wikimedia Commons

Palo Pinto County

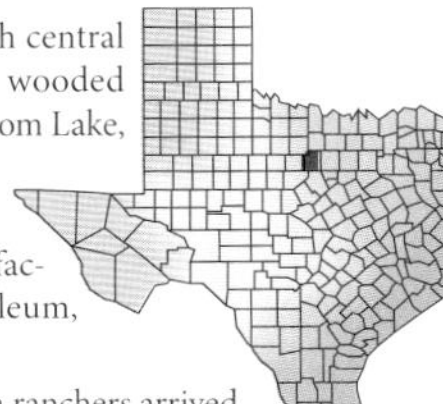

Physical Features: North central county; broken, hilly, wooded in parts; Possum Kingdom Lake, Lake Palo Pinto; sandy, gray, black soils.

Economy: Varied manufacturing, tourism, petroleum, agribusiness.

History: Anglo-American ranchers arrived in the 1850s. Conflicts between settlers and numerous Indian tribes who had sought refuge on the Brazos River resulted in Texas Rangers removing the Indians in 1856. County created in 1856 from Bosque and Navarro counties; organized in 1857; named for creek (in Spanish name means painted stick).

Race/Ethnicity: Anglo, 73.7%; Black, 2.4%; Hispanic, 21.4%; Asian, 0.5%; Other, 1.8%.

Vital Statistics, annual: Births, 353; deaths, 348; marriages, 190; divorces, 122.

Recreation: Lake activities, hunting, fishing, state parks, Rails to Trails hiking, biking, fossil park.

Minerals: Oil, gas, clays.

Agriculture: Cattle, dairy products, nursery crops, hay, wheat. Market value $43.2 million. Cedar posts marketed.

Palo Pinto (354) county seat; government center.

MINERAL WELLS (17,430, part [193] in Parker County) oil and gas, manufacturing, tourism; hospital, Weatherford College branch; art center; state park east of city in Parker County; Crazy Water Festival in October.

Other towns include: **Gordon** (488); **Graford** (620) retirement/recreation area, Possum Fest in October; **Mingus** (257); **Santo** (445), and **Strawn** (676).

Population	**29,008**
Change from 2010 (%)	3.2
Area (sq. mi.)	985.5
Land Area (sq. mi.)	951.8
Altitude (ft.)	782–1,530
Rainfall (in.)	32.1
Jan. mean min (°F)	32.2
July mean max (°F)	95.5
Civ. Labor	12,960
Unemployed (%)	6.3
Wages	$92,741,547
Per Capita Income	$41,193
Prop. Value	$5,632,372,747
Retail Sales	$369,698,342

Panola County

Physical Features: East Texas county; sixty percent forested, rolling plain; broken by Sabine, Murvaul Creek; Toledo Bend Reservoir, Lake Murvaul, Martin Creek Lake.

Economy: Gas, oil-field operations, food processing, agribusiness.

History: A Caddo tribal area. Anglo-American settlement established in 1833. Antebellum slaveholding area. County name is Indian word for cotton; created from Harrison, Shelby counties in 1846; organized the same year.

Race/Ethnicity: Anglo, 71.8%; Black, 16.2%; Hispanic, 9.6%; Asian, 0.3%; Other, 1.9%.

Vital Statistics, annual: Births, 287; deaths, 266; mmarriages, 157; divorces, 75.

Recreation: Fishing, water activities, hunting; Jim Reeves memorial, Tex Ritter museum and Texas Country Music Hall of Fame.

Minerals: Oil, gas, coal.

Agriculture: Broilers, cattle, forages. Market value $100.7 million. Timber sales significant.

CARTHAGE (6,941) county seat; petroleum processing, poultry, sawmills; hospital, junior college; Oil & Gas Blast in October.

Other towns include: **Beckville** (902), **Clayton** (125), **DeBerry** (200), **Gary** (311), **Long Branch** (150), **Panola** (305). Also, **Tatum** (1,416, mostly in Rusk County).

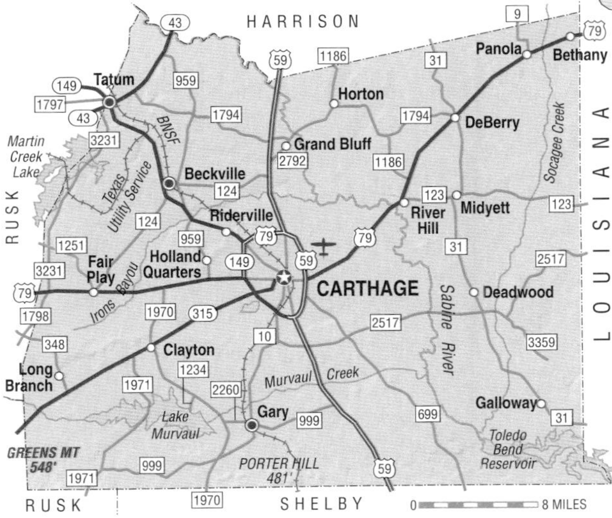

Population	**24,586**
Change from 2010 (%)	3.3
Area (sq. mi.)	821.3
Land Area (sq. mi.)	801.8
Altitude (ft.)	172–548
Rainfall (in.)	51.4
Jan. mean min (°F)	35.2
July mean max (°F)	93.0
Civ. Labor	8,879
Unemployed (%)	7.8
Wages	$96,297,706
Per Capita Income	$45,467
Prop. Value	$4,860,871,222
Retail Sales	$262,434,385

Parker County

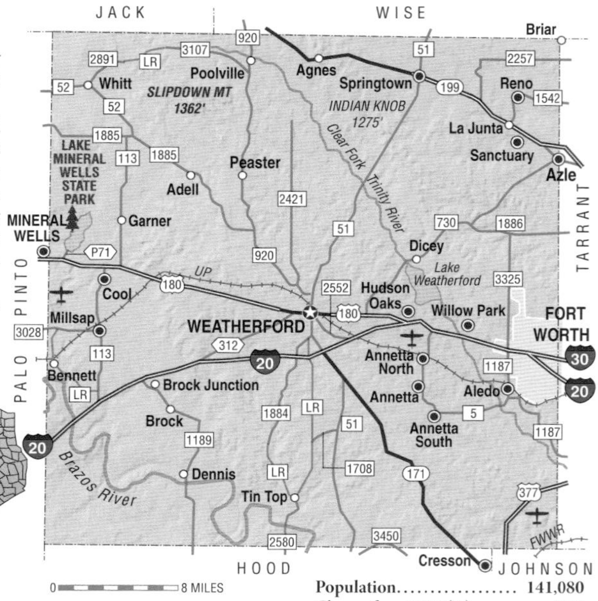

Physical Features: Hilly, broken by Brazos, Trinity tributaries, Lake Mineral Wells, Lake Weatherford; varied soils.

Economy: Agriculture, varied manufacturing, retail sales, government/services, commuting to Fort Worth; part of Dallas-Fort Worth metropolitan area.

History: Comanche and Kiowa area in the late 1840s when Anglo-American settlers arrived. County named for pioneer legislator Isaac Parker; created in 1855 from Bosque, Navarro counties, organized the same year.

Race/Ethnicity: Anglo, 83.2%; Black, 1.4%; Hispanic, 12.5%; Asian, 0.4%; Other, 2.2%.

Vital Statistics, annual: Births, 1,484; deaths, 1,066; marriages, 777; divorces, 383.

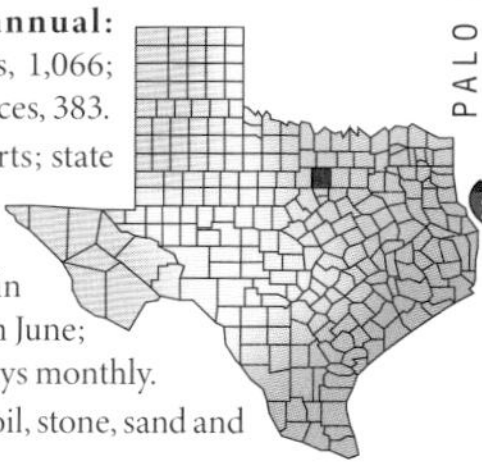

Recreation: Water sports; state park and trailway; nature trails; hunting; Peach Festival in July and rodeo days in June; first Monday trade days monthly.

Minerals: Natural gas, oil, stone, sand and gravel, clays.

Agriculture: Beef cattle, greenhouses, hay, horses (first in number), peaches, sheep and goats, vegetables, pecans, aquaculture. Market value $65.0 million.

WEATHERFORD (32,587) county seat; retail center, manufacturing, warehousing, tourism, commuting to Fort Worth, government/services, equine industry; hospital, Weatherford College; museums, public gardens, historic buildings.

Other towns include: **Aledo** (4,423); **Annetta** (3,132), **Annetta North** (581) and **Annetta South** (592); **Cool** (185); **Dennis** (953); **Hudson Oaks** (2,479); **Millsap** (474); **Peaster** (555); **Poolville** (520); **Reno** (3,146); **Sanctuary** (344); **Springtown** (3,142) commuters, government/services, Wild West Festival in September; **Whitt** (38); **Willow Park** (5,562).

Also, parts of **Azle** (13,351); **Briar** (6,116), and **Cresson** (1,338); part [193] of **Mineral Wells.** Also, a small part of **Fort Worth.**

Population	**141,080**
Change from 2010 (%)	20.7
Area (sq. mi.)	910.1
Land Area (sq. mi.)	903.5
Altitude (ft.)	700–1,362
Rainfall (in.)	35.8
Jan. mean min (°F)	30.1
July mean max (°F)	93.2
Civ. Labor	68,910
Unemployed (%)	4.8
Wages	$438,764,586
Per Capita Income	$55,811
Prop. Value	$21,511,240,430
Retail Sales	$2,800,469,549

Parmer County

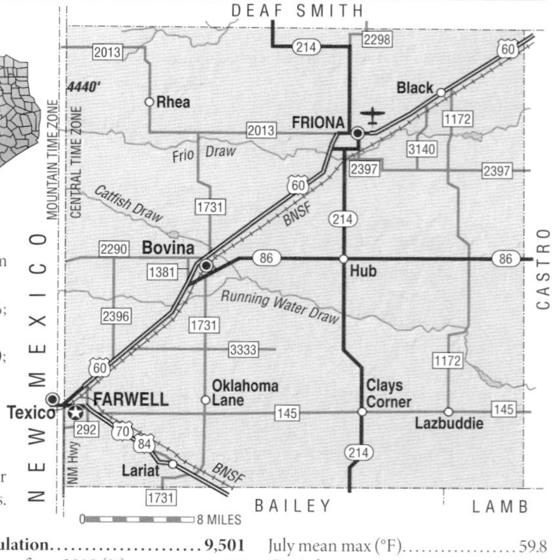

Physical Features: High Plains, broken by draws, playas; sandy, clay, loam soils.

Economy: Cattle feeding, grain elevators, meatpacking plant, other agribusiness.

History: Apaches, pushed out in late 1700s by Comanches and Kiowas. U.S. Army removed Indians in 1874–1875. Anglo-Americans arrived in 1880s. Mexican migration increased after 1950. County named for Republic figure Martin Parmer; created from Bexar District in 1876, organized in 1907.

Race/Ethnicity: Anglo, 33.3%; Black, 1.5%; Hispanic, 64.1%; Asian, 0.2%; Other, 0.6%.

Vital Statistics, annual: Births, 159; deaths, 75; marriages, 20; divorces, 17.

Recreation: Hunting, playa lake, Border Town Days in July at Farwell.

Minerals: Not significant.

Agriculture: Cattle (second in numbers), dairies (third in number of cows); wheat, corn, cotton, sorghum, alfalfa; apples, potatoes. 163,000 acres irrigated. Market value $893.3 million.

FARWELL (1,255) county seat; agribusiness, grain storage, farm equipment plants.

FRIONA (3,815) farming, feed lots, feed mill; hospital; museum; Cheeseburger Festival in July.

Other towns include: **Bovina** (1,776) farm trade center; **Lazbuddie** (248).

Population	**9,501**
Change from 2010 (%)	-7.5
Area (sq. mi.)	885.2
Land Area (sq. mi.)	880.8
Altitude (ft.)	3,785–4,440
Rainfall (in.)	20.1
Jan. mean min (°F)	22.5
July mean max (°F)	59.8
Civ. Labor	5,197
Unemployed (%)	2.6
Wages	$80,980,425
Per Capita Income	$49,541
Prop. Value	$1,727,491,539
Retail Sales	$77,556,903

Pecos County

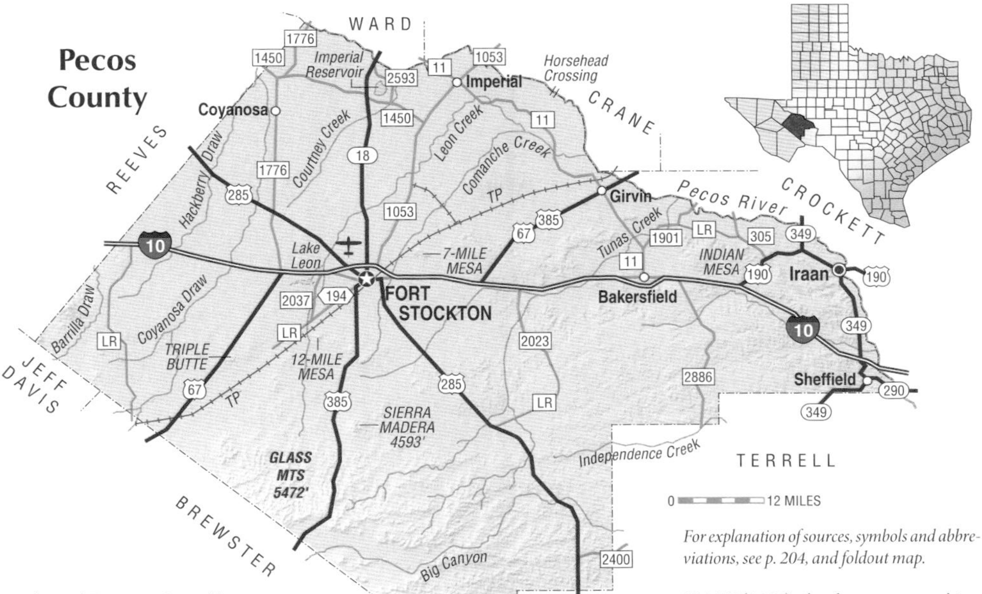

For explanation of sources, symbols and abbreviations, see p. 204, and foldout map.

Physical Features: Second largest county; high, broken plateau in West Texas; draining to Pecos and tributaries; Imperial Reservoir, Lake Leon; sandy, clay, loam soils.

Economy: Oil, gas, agriculture, government/services, wind turbines.

History: Comanches in area when military outpost established in 1859. Settlement began after the Civil War. Created from Presidio County in 1871; organized in 1872; named for Pecos River, name origin uncertain.

Race/Ethnicity: Anglo, 25.2%; Black, 3.3%; Hispanic, 69.7%; Asian, 0.5%; Other, 1%.

Vital Statistics, annual: Births, 203; deaths, 114; marriages, 84; divorces, 14.

Recreation: Old Fort Stockton, Annie Riggs Museum, stagecoach stop, scenic drives, Dinosaur Track Roadside Park, cattle-trail sites, archaeological museum with oil and ranch-heritage collections; Comanche Springs Water Carnival in summer.

Minerals: Natural gas, oil, gravel, caliche.

Agriculture: Cattle, alfalfa, pecans, sheep, goats, onions, peppers, melons. Market value $46.2 million. Aquaculture firm producing shrimp. Hunting leases.

FORT STOCKTON (8,470) county seat, distribution center for petroleum industry, government/services, agriculture, tourism, varied manufacturing, winery, prison units, spaceport launching small satellites; hospital; historical tours.

IRAAN (1,216) oil and gas center, ranching, farming; hospital, museum; Alley Oop park, county park.

Other towns include: **Coyanosa** (172); **Girvin** (20); **Imperial** (234) center for irrigated farming; **Sheffield** (322) oil, gas center.

Population	**15,052**
Change from 2010 (%)	-2.9
Area (sq. mi.)	4,764.8
Land Area (sq. mi.)	4,763.9
Altitude (ft.)	2,040–5,472
Rainfall (in.)	15.2
Jan. mean min (°F)	33.2
July mean max (°F)	94.3
Civ. Labor	6,645
Unemployed (%)	7.5
Wages	$69,515,634
Per Capita Income	$39,731
Prop. Value	$5,327,610,221
Retail Sales	$493,753,119

A view of the lake at Lake Mineral Wells State Park in Parker County. Photo by Larry D. Moore, CC by SA 4.0/Wikimedia Commons

Polk County

Physical Features: Rolling; densely forested, with Big Thicket, unique plant, animal life; Neches, Trinity rivers, tributaries; lake.

Economy: Timber, lumber production, tourism, manufacturing.

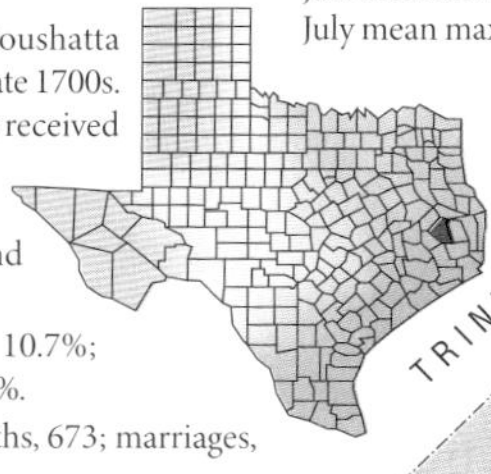

History: Caddo area; Alabama and Coushatta Indians arrived from Louisiana in the late 1700s. Anglo-American and Hispanic families received land grants in the early 1830s. County named for U.S. President James K. Polk; created from Liberty County and organized 1846.

Race/Ethnicity: Anglo, 70.5%; Black, 10.7%; Hispanic, 15%; Asian, 0.4%; Other, 3.1%.

Vital Statistics, annual: Births, 562; deaths, 673; marriages, 324; divorces, 175.

Recreation: Lake and state park, water activities, fishing, hunting, Alabama-Coushatta Reservation, museum, Big Thicket, woodland trails, champion trees, historic homes.

Minerals: Oil, gas, sand, gravel.

Agriculture: Hay and greenhouse nurseries; vegetables raised; income also from beef cattle, horses. Market value $6.8 million. Timber and hardwood.

LIVINGSTON (5,247) county seat; lumber, tourism, oil; museum, hospital; Civil War re-enactment in February.

West Livingston (9,474) includes **Blanchard**, East Tempe, Moore Hill, and Polunsky prison unit.

Other towns include: **Ace** (40); **Camden** (1,200); **Corrigan** (1,683) plywood plant; **Dallardsville** (350); **Goodrich** (317); **Leggett** (500); **Moscow** (170) historic sites; **Onalaska** (2,464); **Seven Oaks** (118).

Population	**50,293**
Change from 2010 (%)	10.7
Area (sq. mi.)	1,109.7
Land Area (sq. mi.)	1,057.1
Altitude (ft.)	68–484
Rainfall (in.)	51.5
Jan. mean min (°F)	39.6
July mean max (°F)	93.7
Civ. Labor	18,790
Unemployed (%)	8.6
Wages	$135,574,050
Per Capita Income	$39,818
Prop. Value	$5,998,481,422
Retail Sales	$554,657,489

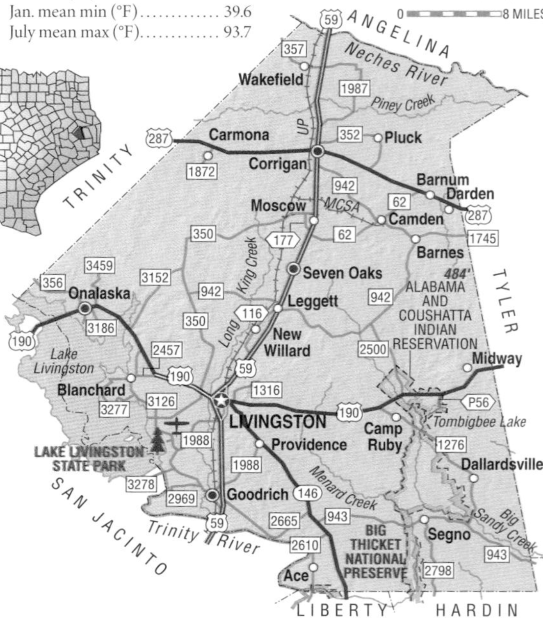

Potter County

Physical Features: Mostly level, part rolling; broken by Canadian River and tributaries; sandy, sandy loam, chocolate loam, clay soils; Lake Meredith.

Economy: Transportation and distribution hub for large area, manufacturing, agribusiness, tourism, government/services, petrochemicals, gas processing.

History: Apaches, pushed out by Comanches in the 1700s. Comanches removed to Indian Territory in 1874–1875. Ranching began in the late 1870s. Oil boom in the 1920s. County named for Robert Potter, Republic leader; created in 1876 from Bexar District; organized in 1887.

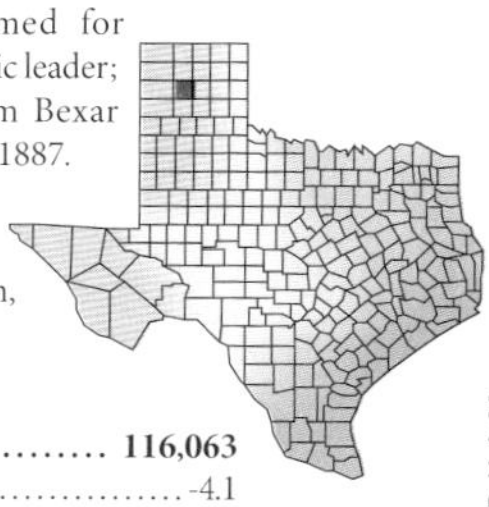

Race/Ethnicity: Anglo, 43.8%; Black, 9.3%; Hispanic, 38.7%; Asian, 5.4%; Other, 2.5%.

Vital Statistics, annual: Births, 1,944; deaths, 1,231; marriages, 1429; divorces, 415.

Recreation: Lake activities, Alibates Flint Quarries National Monument, hunting, fishing, Wildcat Bluff nature center, Cadillac Ranch car sculpture, professional sports events, Tri-State Fair in September.

Minerals: Natural gas, oil, helium.

Agriculture: Beef cattle production and processing; wheat, sorghum, cotton. Market value $24.8 million.

AMARILLO (202,314 total, part [97,022] in Randall County) county seat; hub for northern Panhandle oil and ranching, distribution and marketing center, tourism, manufacturing, food processing, prison; hospitals; Amarillo College, Texas Tech University medical, engineering, pharmacy schools; Quarter Horse Hall of Fame, museum.

Other towns include: **Bishop Hills** (173) and **Bushland** (1,485).

Population	**116,063**
Change from 2010 (%)	-4.1
Area (sq. mi.)	922.0
Land Area (sq. mi.)	908.4
Altitude (ft.)	2,915–3,910
Rainfall (in.)	20.4
Jan. mean min (°F)	23.4
July mean max (°F)	91.4
Civ. Labor	54,717
Unemployed (%)	4.5
Wages	$1,043,142,033
Per Capita Income	$46,086
Prop. Value	$10,749,076,338
Retail Sales	$2,489,644,457

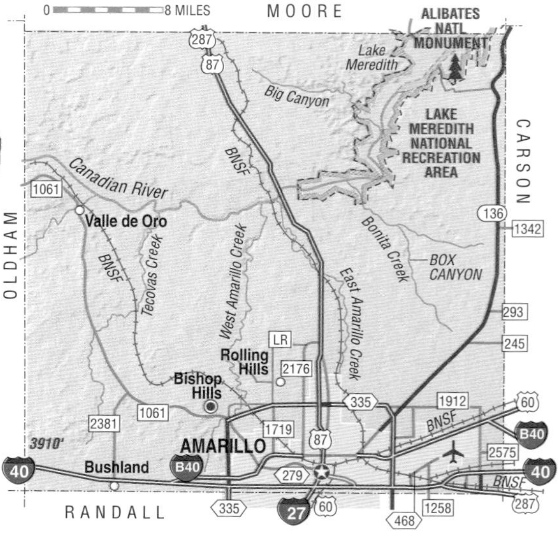

The Llano Cemetery in Amarillo. Photo by Ammodramus, CC/Wikimedia Commons

Presidio County

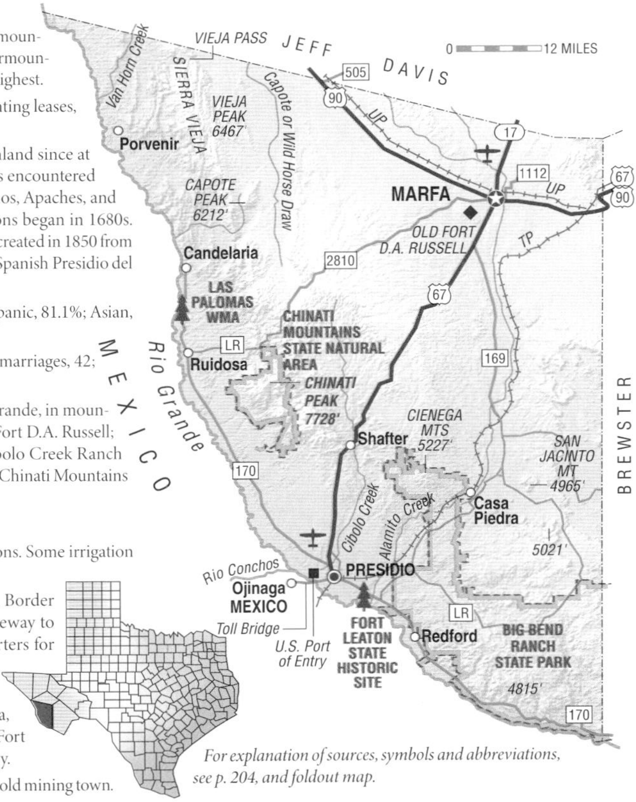

Physical Features: Rugged, some of Texas' tallest mountains; clays, loams, sandy loams on uplands; intermountain wash; timber sparse; Capote Falls, state's highest.

Economy: Government/services, ranching, hunting leases, tourism.

History: Presidio area has been cultivated farmland since at least 1200 A.D. Spanish explorers of the 1500s encountered permanent villages along Rio Grande. Jumanos, Apaches, and Comanches in the area when Spanish missions began in 1680s. Anglo-Americans arrived in the 1840s. County created in 1850 from Bexar District; organized in 1875; named for Spanish Presidio del Norte (fort of the north).

Race/Ethnicity: Anglo, 15.9%; Black, 0.5%; Hispanic, 81.1%; Asian, 1.2%; Other, 1%.

Vital Statistics, annual: Births, 108; deaths, 36; marriages, 42; divorces, 0.

Recreation: Hunting; scenic drives along Rio Grande, in mountains; ghost towns, mysterious Marfa Lights; Fort D.A. Russell; Big Bend Ranch State Park; hot springs; Cibolo Creek Ranch Resort; Chinati Foundation art festival in fall. (Chinati Mountains State Natural Area not yet open to public.)

Minerals: Sand, gravel, silver, zeolite.

Agriculture: Cattle, tomatoes, hay, onions, melons. Some irrigation near Rio Grande. Market value $48 million.

MARFA (1,650) county seat; ranching supply, Border Patrol headquarters, tourism, art center, gateway to mountainous area; Paisano Hotel, headquarters for movie Giant; Old Timers Roping on Memorial Day weekend.

PRESIDIO (3,774) international bridge to Ojinaga, Mex., gateway to Mexico's West Coast by rail; Fort Leaton historic site; asado cook-off in February.

Other towns include: **Redford** (67); **Shafter** (57) old mining town.

For explanation of sources, symbols and abbreviations, see p. 204, and foldout map.

Population	**6,535**	Rainfall (in.) Presidio	10.8	Unemployed (%)	12.7
Change from 2010 (%)	-16.4	Jan. mean min. Marfa (°F)	23.2	Wages	$25,886,010
Area (sq. mi.)	3,855.9	Jan. mean min. Presidio (°F)	34.5	Per Capita Income	$46,581
Land Area (sq. mi.)	3,855.2	July mean max. Marfa (°F)	88.5	Prop. Value	$1,375,692,183
Altitude (ft.)	2,400–7,728	July mean max. Presidio (°F)	100.8	Retail Sales	$57,801,644
Rainfall (in.) Marfa	15.4	Civ. Labor	2,869		

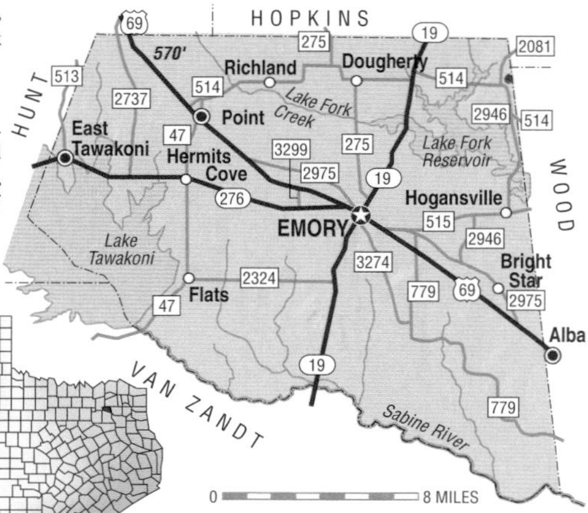

Physical Features: Northeastern county; rolling; partly Blackland, sandy loams, sandy soils; Sabine River, Lake Tawakoni, Lake Fork Reservoir.

Economy: Agribusiness, some manufacturing.

History: Caddo area. In the 1700s, Tawakoni Indians entered the area. Anglo-Americans arrived in the 1840s. County, county seat named for Emory Rains, Republic leader; created in 1870 from Hopkins, Hunt, and Wood counties, organized the same year; birthplace of National Farmers Union, 1902.

Race/Ethnicity: Anglo, 86.2%; Black, 2.2%; Hispanic, 8.7%; Asian, 0.5%; Other, 2.2%.

Vital Statistics, annual: Births, 102; deaths, 150; marriages, 84; divorces, 52.

Recreation: Lake Tawakoni and Lake Fork Reservoir activities; birding, Eagle Fest in February.

Minerals: Gas, oil.

Agriculture: Beef, forages, dairies, vegetables (second in sweet potato acreage), fruits, nurseries. Market value $22.8 million.

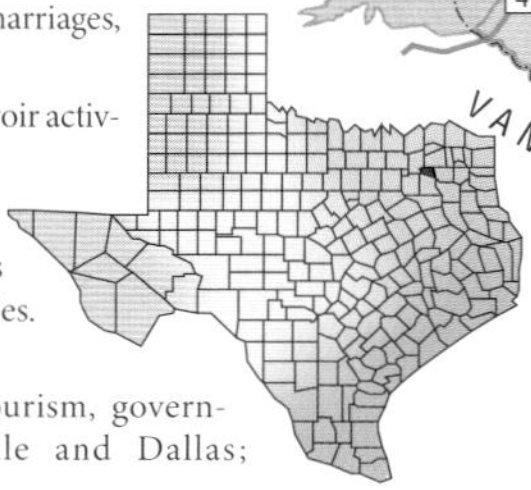

EMORY (1,451) county seat; local trade, tourism, government/services, commuting to Greenville and Dallas; African-American museum.

Other towns include: **East Tawakoni** (976) and **Point** (922), manufacturing, tourism, tamale fest on July 4. Part of **Alba** (543), mostly in Wood County.

Rains County

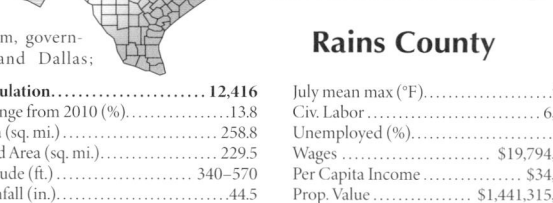

Population	**12,416**
Change from 2010 (%)	13.8
Area (sq. mi.)	258.8
Land Area (sq. mi.)	229.5
Altitude (ft.)	340–570
Rainfall (in.)	44.5
Jan. mean min (°F)	31.4
July mean max (°F)	91.4
Civ. Labor	6,230
Unemployed (%)	3.9
Wages	$19,794,190
Per Capita Income	$34,819
Prop. Value	$1,441,315,968
Retail Sales	$110,520,875

Randall County

Physical Features: Panhandle county; level, but broken by scenic Palo Duro Canyon, Buffalo Lake; Bivins Lake; silty clay, loam soils.

Economy: Agribusiness, education, tourism, part of Amarillo metropolitan area.

History: Comanche Indians removed in the mid-1870s; ranching began soon afterward. County created in 1876 from the Bexar District; organized in 1889; named for Confederate Gen. Horace Randal (name misspelled in statute).

Race/Ethnicity: Anglo, 69.3%; Black, 3%; Hispanic, 23.8%; Asian, 1.4%; Other, 2.3%.

Vital Statistics, annual: Births, 1,667; deaths, 1,050; marriages, 481; divorces, 467.

Recreation: State park, with Texas outdoor musical drama each summer; Panhandle-Plains Historical Museum; West Texas A&M University events; aoudad sheep, migratory waterfowl hunting in season; Buffalo Lake National Wildlife Refuge; cowboy breakfasts at ranches.

Minerals: Not significant.

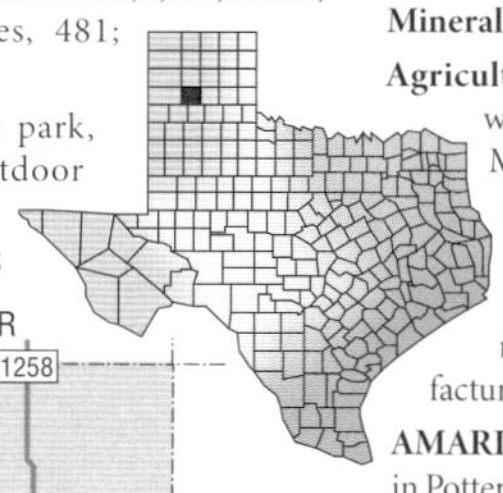

Agriculture: Grain sorghum, beef cattle, wheat, silage, cotton, dairies, hay. Market value $479.5 million.

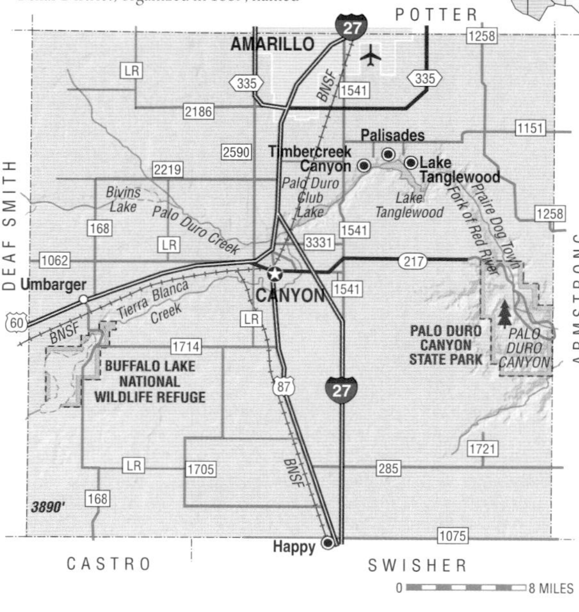

CANYON (16,179) county seat; West Texas A&M University, tourism, commuting to Amarillo, ranching, farm center, light manufacturing, gateway to state park.

AMARILLO (202,314 total, part [105,292] in Potter County) hub for northern Panhandle oil and ranching, distribution and marketing center, manufacturing; hospitals.

Other towns include: **Lake Tanglewood** (847); **Palisades** (364); **Timbercreek Canyon** (460); **Umbarger** (327) German sausage festival in November.

Part of **Happy** (651, mostly in Swisher County).

Population	**139,034**
Change from 2010 (%)	15.2
Area (sq. mi.)	922.4
Land Area (sq. mi.)	911.5
Altitude (ft.)	2,700-3,890
Rainfall (in.)	20.2
Jan. mean min (°F)	21.5
July mean max (°F)	91.7
Civ. Labor	73,278
Unemployed (%)	3.7
Wages	$417,147,039
Per Capita Income	$49,544
Prop. Value	$13,444,282,345
Retail Sales	$2,014,405,564

Reagan County

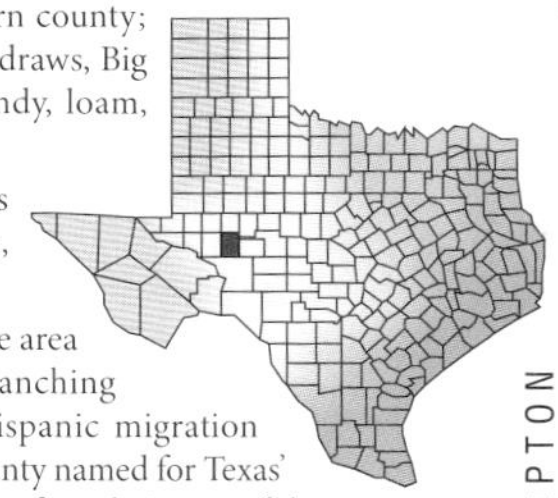

Physical Features: Western county; level to hilly, broken by draws, Big Lake (intermittent); sandy, loam, clay soils.

Economy: Oil and gas production, hunting, ranching.

History: Comanches in the area until the mid-1870s. Ranching began in the 1880s. Hispanic migration increased after 1950. County named for Texas' U.S. Sen. John H. Reagan, first chairman of the Texas Railroad Commission; county created and organized in 1903 from Tom Green County.

Race/Ethnicity: Anglo, 28.4%; Black, 1.7%; Hispanic, 69.1%; Asian, 0%; Other, 0.6%.

Vital Statistics, annual: Births, 70; deaths, 29; marriages, 25; divorces, 10.

Recreation: Site of 1923 discovery well Santa Rita No. 1 on University of Texas land.

Minerals: Gas, oil.

Agriculture: Cotton, cattle, sheep, goats. Market value $18.2 million. Hunting leases important.

BIG LAKE (3,661) county seat; center for oil activities, agriculture, government/services; hospital; Spring bluegrass festival, St. Rita festival in August.

For explanation of sources, symbols and abbreviations, see p. 204, and foldout map.

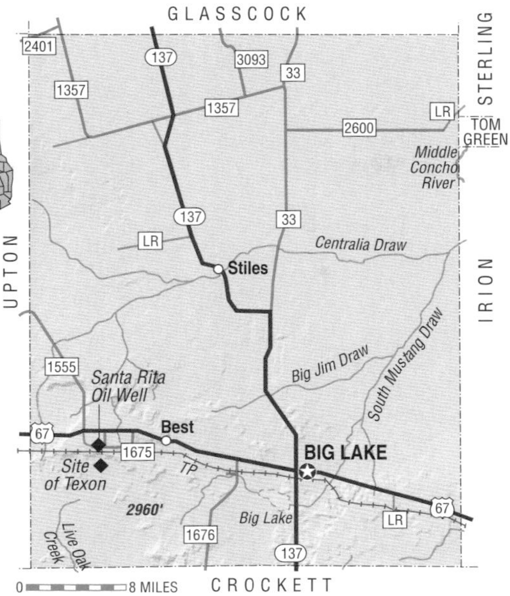

Population	**3,836**	July mean max (°F)	93.5
Change from 2010 (%)	13.9	Civ. Labor	1,726
Area (sq. mi.)	1,176.0	Unemployed (%)	8.2
Land Area (sq. mi.)	1,175.3	Wages	$31,895,262
Altitude (ft.)	2,370–2,960	Per Capita Income	$51,945
Rainfall (in.)	19.3	Prop. Value	$5,552,610,162
Jan. mean min (°F)	30.8	Retail Sales	$34,693,751

A marshy inlet of Lake Fork Reservoir in Rains County. Photo by Carol M. Highsmith, courtesy of the Library of Congress

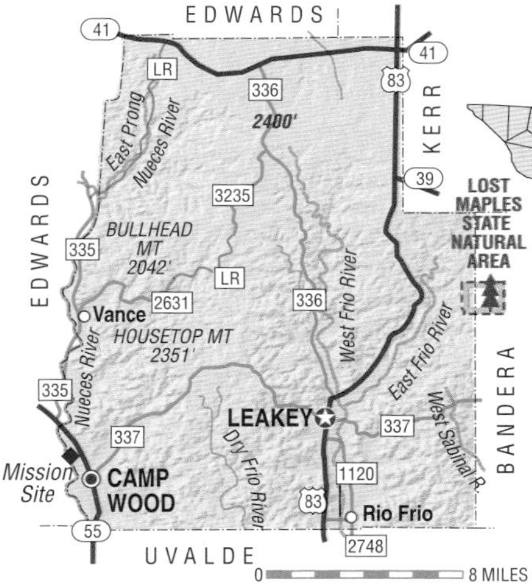

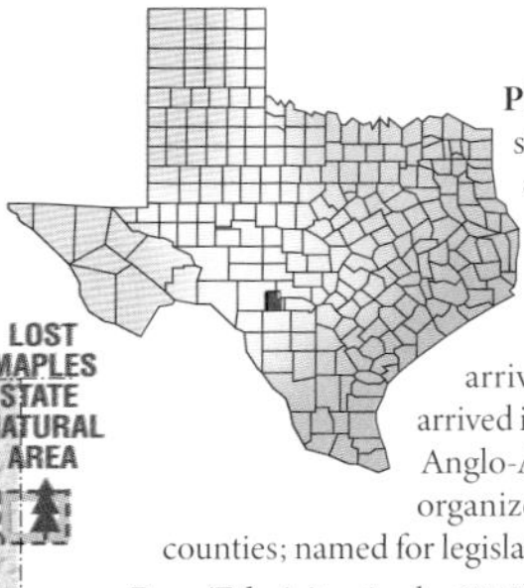

Real County

Physical Features: Hill Country, spring-fed streams, scenic canyons; Frio, Nueces rivers; cedars, pecans, walnuts, many live oaks.

Economy: Ranching, tourism, government/services, cedar cutting.

History: Tonkawa area; Lipan Apaches arrived in early 1700s; later, Comanche hunters arrived in the area. Spanish mission established in 1762. Anglo-Americans arrived in 1850s. County created, organized in 1913 from Bandera, Edwards, and Kerr counties; named for legislator-ranchman Julius Real.

Race/Ethnicity: Anglo, 69.1%; Black, 0.5%; Hispanic, 28%; Asian, 0%; Other, 2.1%.

Vital Statistics, annual: Births, 41; deaths, 38; marriages, 20; divorces, 0.

Recreation: Tourist and hunting center, birding, fishing, camping, scenic drives, state natural area.

Minerals: Not significant.

Agriculture: Goats, sheep, beef cattle produce most income. Market value $1.3 million. Cedar posts processed.

LEAKEY (464) county seat; tourism, ranching; museums; July Jubilee.

CAMP WOOD (725) tourism, hunting, ranching; medical clinic; San Lorenzo de la Santa Cruz mission site; museum; Lindbergh Park, settlers reunion in August.

Other towns include: **Rio Frio** (50).

Population	**3,499**
Change from 2010 (%)	5.7
Area (sq. mi.)	700.1
Land Area (sq. mi.)	699.2
Altitude (ft.)	1,400–2,400
Rainfall (in.)	27.4
Jan. mean min (°F)	33.6
July mean max (°F)	93.0
Civ. Labor	1,129
Unemployed (%)	6.7
Wages	$6,170,778
Per Capita Income	$36,070
Prop. Value	$1,313,608,351
Retail Sales	$32,489,826

Red River County

Physical Features: On Red-Sulphur rivers' divide; 39 different soil types; half timbered; River Crest Reservoir.

Economy: Manufacturing, government/services, agriculture.

History: Caddo Indians abandoned the area in the 1790s. One of the oldest counties; settlers were moving in from the United States in the 1810s. Kickapoo and other tribes arrived in the 1820s. Antebellum slaveholding area. County created in 1836 as original county of the Republic; organized in 1837; named for Red River, its northern boundary.

Race/Ethnicity: Anglo, 71%; Black, 17.6%; Hispanic, 7.5%; Asian, 0.2%; Other, 3.5%.

Vital Statistics, annual: Births, 115; deaths, 180; marriages, 58; divorces, 51.

Recreation: Historical sites include pioneer homes, birthplace of John Nance Garner; fall foliage; water activities; hunting of deer, turkey, duck, small game.

Minerals: Small oil flow.

Agriculture: Beef cattle, corn, soybeans, wheat, sorghum, hay. Market value $94.0 million. Timber sales substantial.

CLARKSVILLE (2,991) county seat; varied manufacturing; hospital, library; Historical Society bazaar in October.

Other towns include: **Annona** (285); **Avery** (433); **Bagwell** (150); **Bogata** (1,052); **Detroit** (675) commercial center in west. Part of **Deport** (558).

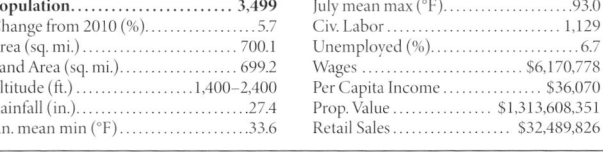

Population	**11,649**
Change from 2010 (%)	-9.4
Area (sq. mi.)	1,056.7
Land Area (sq. mi.)	1,036.6
Altitude (ft.)	260–560
Rainfall (in.)	48.8
Jan. mean min (°F)	30.8
July mean max (°F)	91.9
Civ. Labor	5,238
Unemployed (%)	6.4
Wages	$29,604,724
Per Capita Income	$43,039
Prop. Value	$2,231,223,241
Retail Sales	$54,039,790

Reeves County

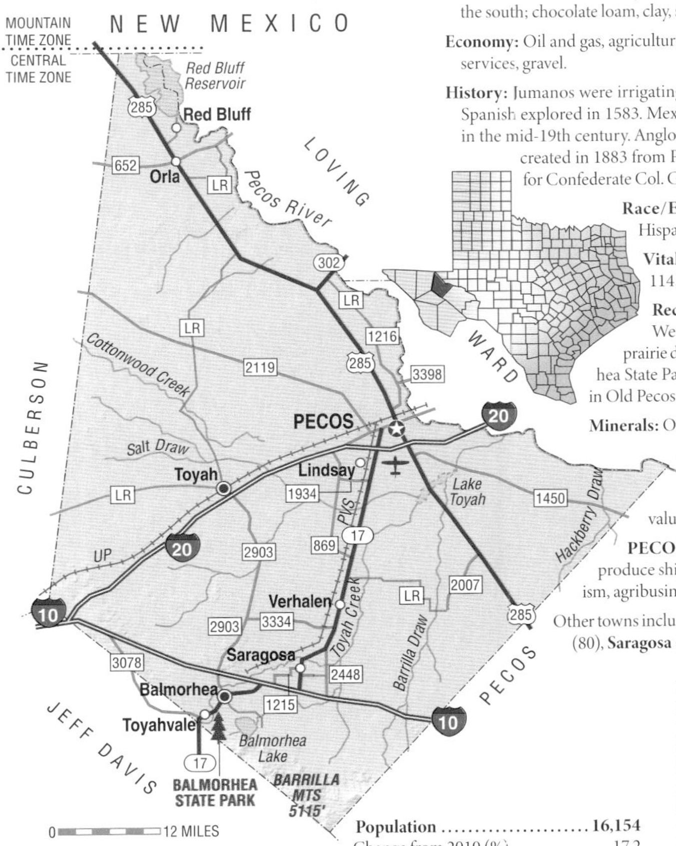

For explanation of sources, symbols and abbreviations, see p. 204, and foldout map.

Physical Features: Rolling plains, broken by many draws, Pecos River, Balmorhea Lake, Lake Toyah, Red Bluff Reservoir; Barrilla Mountains on the south; chocolate loam, clay, sandy, mountain wash soils.

Economy: Oil and gas, agriculture, tourism, food processing, government/services, gravel.

History: Jumanos were irrigating crops from springs (Balmorhea) when Spanish explored in 1583. Mexican farmers supplied nearby Fort Davis in the mid-19th century. Anglo-Americans arrived in the 1870s. County created in 1883 from Pecos County; organized in 1884; named for Confederate Col. George R. Reeves.

Race/Ethnicity: Anglo, 17.4%; Black, 4.5%; Hispanic, 76.6%; Asian, 0.8%; Other, 0.5%.

Vital Statistics, annual: Births, 206; deaths, 114; marriages, 85; divorces, 22.

Recreation: Replica of Judge Roy Bean store, West of Pecos museum; park with javelina, prairie dogs; scenic drives; water activities; Balmorhea State Park with San Solomon Springs pool; Night in Old Pecos, cantaloupe festival in July.

Minerals: Oil, gas, gravel.

Agriculture: Ranching, dairies, hay, cotton, cantaloupes, pecans, pistachios. Some 11,000 acres irrigated. Market value $10.9 million.

PECOS (10,574) county seat; food processing, produce shipping, government/services, prison, tourism, agribusiness; hospital; 16th of September fiesta.

Other towns include: **Balmorhea** (538), **Lindsay** (288), **Orla** (80), **Saragosa** (185), **Toyah** (96), **Toyahvale** (60).

Population	**16,154**
Change from 2010 (%)	17.2
Area (sq. mi.)	2,642.1
Land Area (sq. mi.)	2,635.4
Altitude (ft.)	2,460–5,115

Rainfall (in.) Pecos	11.61
Rainfall (in.) Balmorhea	13.54
Jan. mean min. Pecos (°F)	28.1
Jan. mean min. Balmorhea (°F)	30.3
July mean max. Pecos (°F)	98.5
July mean max. Balmorhea (°F)	94.4
Civ. Labor	7,910
Unemployed (%)	7.5
Wages	$98,975,585
Per Capita Income	$45,458
Prop. Value	$14,768,048,059
Retail Sales	$302,801,992

The public library in Leakey, county seat of Real County. Photo by Billy Hathorn, CC 3/Wikimedia Commons

Refugio County

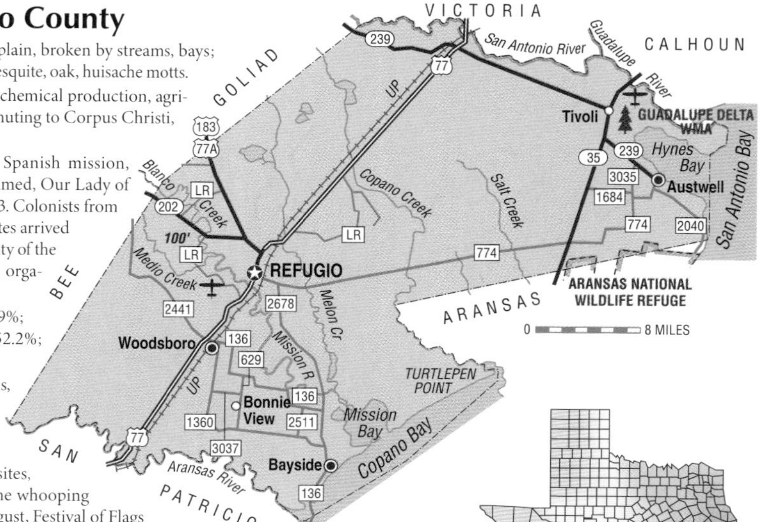

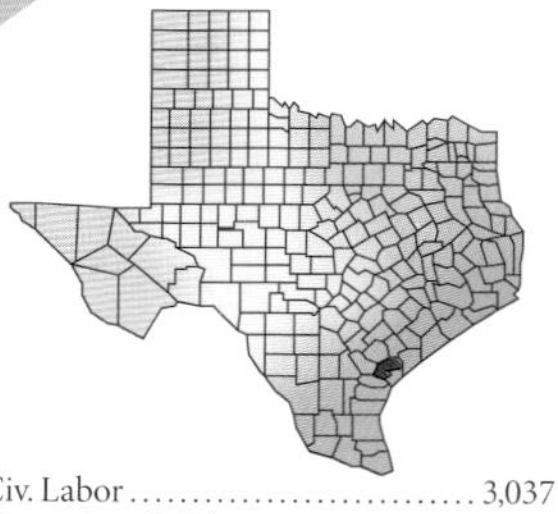

Physical Features: Coastal plain, broken by streams, bays; sandy, loam, black soils; mesquite, oak, huisache motts.

Economy: Petroleum, petrochemical production, agribusinesses, tourism, commuting to Corpus Christi, Victoria.

History: Karankawa area. Spanish mission, for which the county is named, Our Lady of Refuge, established in 1793. Colonists from Ireland and the United States arrived in the 1830s. Original county of the Republic created in 1836, organized in 1837.

Race/Ethnicity: Anglo, 39.9%; Black, 5.9%; Hispanic, 52.2%; Asian, 0.3%; Other, 1.3%.

Vital Statistics, annual: Births, 99; deaths, 108; marriages, 27; divorces, 20.

Recreation: Water activities, hunting, fishing, historic sites, wildlife refuge, home of the whooping crane; chili cook-off in August, Festival of Flags in October.

Minerals: Oil, natural gas.

Agriculture: Cotton, beef cattle, sorghum, corn, soybeans, horses. Market value $35.9 million. Hunting leases.

REFUGIO (2,695) county seat; petroleum, agribusiness center; hospital; museum, historic homes.

Other towns include: **Austwell** (144); **Bayside** (318) resorts; **Tivoli** (477); **Woodsboro** (1,447) commercial center.

Population	**6,871**
Change from 2010 (%)	-6.9
Area (sq. mi.)	818.2
Land Area (sq. mi.)	77.4
Altitude (ft.)	sea level–100
Rainfall (in.)	36.9
Jan. mean min (°F)	44.3
July mean max (°F)	92.0

Civ. Labor	3,037
Unemployed (%)	7.2
Wages	$23,044,134
Per Capita Income	$46,464
Prop. Value	$1,786,210,407
Retail Sales	$77,159,038

Roberts County

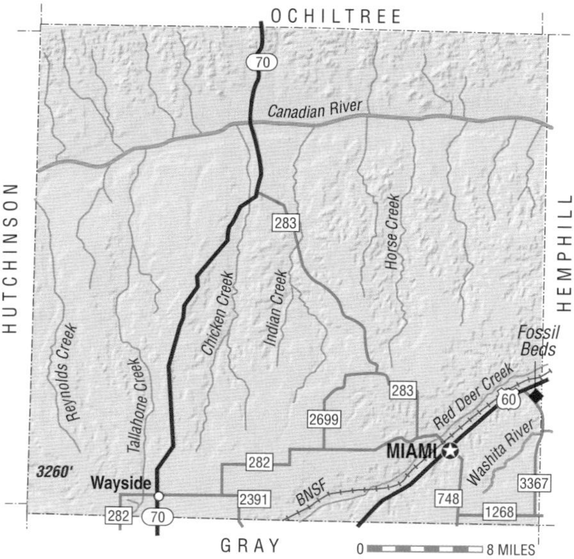

For explanation of sources, symbols and abbreviations, see p. 204, and foldout map.

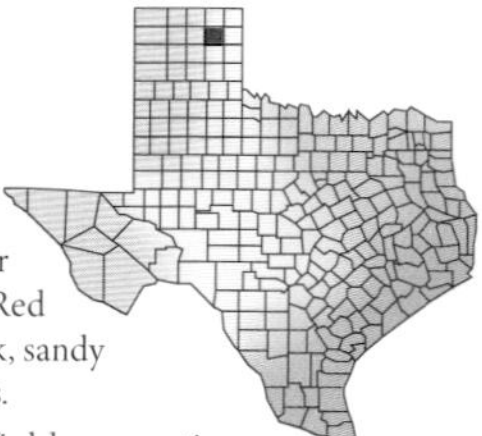

Physical Features: Rolling, broken by Canadian River and tributaries; Red Deer Creek; black, sandy loam, alluvial soils.

Economy: Oil-field operations, agribusiness.

History: Apaches; pushed out by Comanches who were removed in 1874–1875 by the U.S. Army. Ranching began in the late 1870s. County created in 1876 from Bexar District; organized in 1889; named for Texas leaders John S. Roberts and Gov. O.M. Roberts.

Race/Ethnicity: Anglo, 89.8%; Black, 0%; Hispanic, 8.5%; Asian, 0%; Other, 1.5%.

Vital Statistics, annual: Births, 0; deaths, 6; marriages, 6; divorces, 1.

Recreation: Scenic drives, hunting, museum; national cow-calling contest in June.

Minerals: Production of gas, oil.

Agriculture: Beef cattle; wheat, sorghum, corn, soybeans, hay; 6,300 acres irrigated. Market value $18.3million.

MIAMI (553) county seat; ranching, oil center, some manufacturing.

Population	**851**
Change from 2010 (%)	-8.4
Area (sq. mi.)	924.2
Land Area (sq. mi.)	924.1
Altitude (ft.)	2,380–3,260
Rainfall (in.)	24.1
Jan. mean min (°F)	22.1

July mean max (°F)	92.1
Civ. Labor	411
Unemployed (%)	4.1
Wages	$3,096,028
Per Capita Income	$48,344
Prop. Value	$551,021,753
Retail Sales	$1,529,994

Physical Features: Rolling in north and east, draining to bottoms along Brazos, Navasota rivers; sandy soils, heavy in bottoms; Lake Limestone, Twin Oaks Reservoir, Camp Creek Reservoir.

Economy: Agribusiness, government/services, oil and gas.

History: Tawakoni, Waco, Comanche, and other tribes. Anglo-Americans arrived in the 1820s. Antebellum slave-holding area. County created in 1837, organized in 1838, subdivided into many others later; named for pioneer Sterling Clack Robertson.

Race/Ethnicity: Anglo, 56.1%; Black, 19.5%; Hispanic, 22.2%; Asian, 0.6%; Other, 1.3%.

Vital Statistics, annual: Births, 211; deaths, 173; marriages, 91; divorces, 34.

Recreation: Hunting, fishing; historic sites; dogwood trails, wildlife preserves.

Minerals: Gas, oil, lignite coal.

Agriculture: Poultry, beef cattle, cotton, hay, corn; 20,000 acres of cropland irrigated. Market value $158.1 million.

FRANKLIN (1,701) county seat; oil and gas, power plants, agriculture; Carnegie library.

HEARNE (4,637) railroad center; depot museum, historic homes, World War II POW camp; October Sticks & Stones golf and dominoes (Texas 42) tournament.

Other towns include: **Bremond** (978) mining, agriculture, power utilities, library, museum, Polish Days in late June; **Calvert** (1,124) agriculture, tourism, antiques, Maypole festival, tour of homes; **Mumford** (170); **New Baden** (150); **Wheelock** (225).

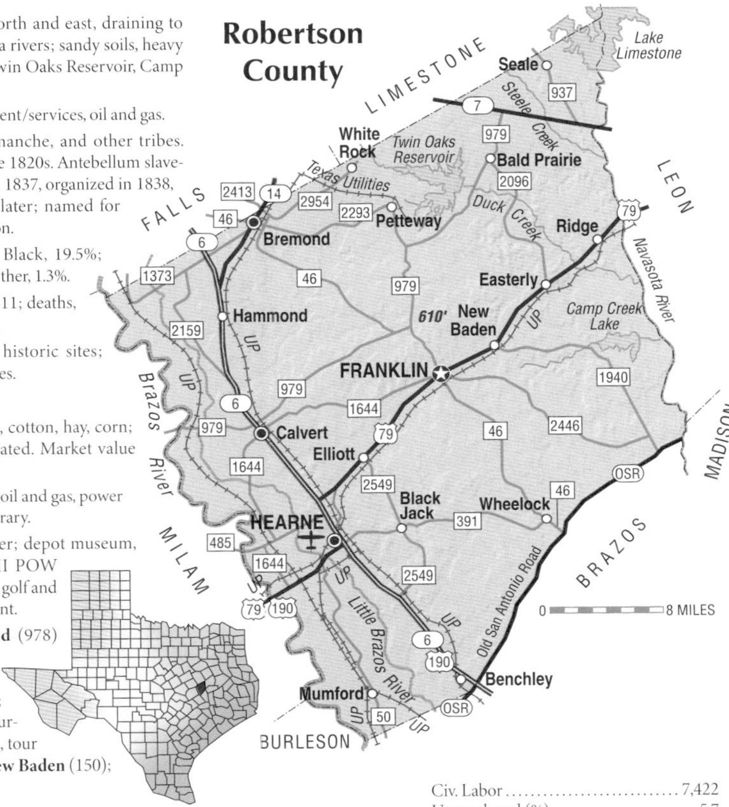

Population	**17,708**	Altitude (ft.)	230–610	Civ. Labor	7,422
Change from 2010 (%)	6.5	Rainfall (in.)	39.5	Unemployed (%)	5.7
Area (sq. mi.)	865.4	Jan. mean min (°F)	38.8	Wages	$61,268,508
Land Area (sq. mi.)	855.7	July mean max (°F)	94.9	Per Capita Income	$42,463
				Prop. Value	$5,642,636,427
				Retail Sales	$121,002,078

The Depot Museum in Hearne. Photo by Billy Hathorn, CC 3/Wikimedia Commons

Rockwall County

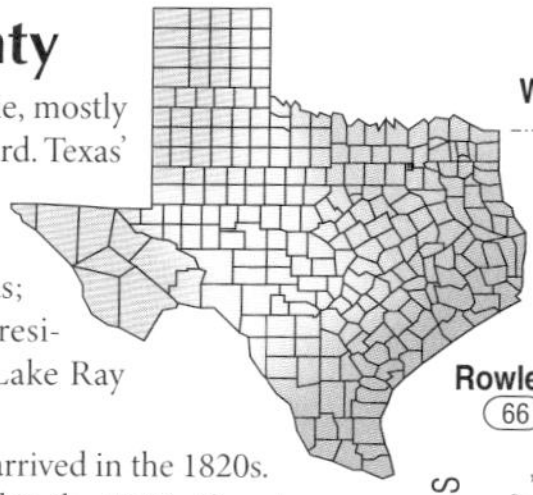

Physical Features: Rolling prairie, mostly Blackland soil; Lake Ray Hubbard. Texas' smallest county.

Economy: Industrial employment in local plants and in Dallas; in Dallas metropolitan area; residential development around Lake Ray Hubbard.

History: Caddo area. Cherokees arrived in the 1820s. Anglo-American settlers arrived in the 1840s. County created in 1873 from Kaufman, organized the same year; named for wall-like rock formation.

Race/Ethnicity: Anglo, 71%; Black, 6.1%; Hispanic, 17.9%; Asian, 2.8%; Other, 2%.

Vital Statistics, annual: Births, 1,034; deaths, 545; marriages, 1,463; divorces, 319.

Recreation: Lake activities; proximity to Dallas; unusual rock outcrop.

Minerals: Not significant.

Agriculture: Small grains, cattle, horticulture, horses. Market value $7.8 million.

ROCKWALL (45,641) county seat; commuters, varied manufacturing, government/services; hospital; harbor retail and entertainment district; Founders Day in April.

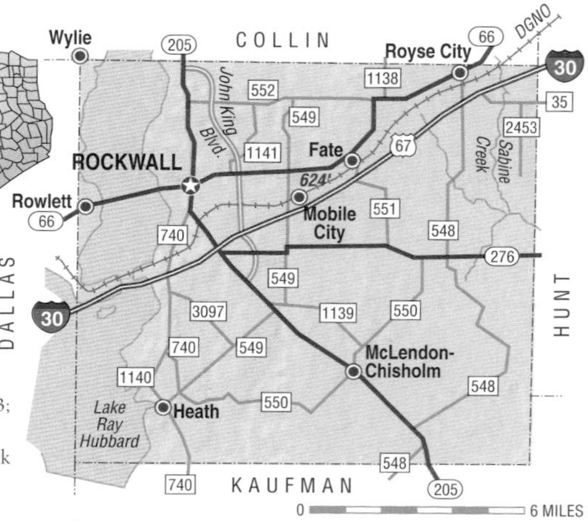

Other towns include: **Fate** (15,121); **Heath** (9,099); **McLendon-Chisholm** (3,541) chili cookoff in October; **Mobile City** (223); **Royse City** (13,191) government/services, varied manufacturing, agribusiness, museum, library, Funfest in October.

Part [8,267] of **Rowlett**, hospital, and a small part of **Wylie.**

Population	**103,363**	Rainfall (in.)	38.6	Wages	$434,940,300
Change from 2010 (%)	31.9	Jan. mean min (°F)	33.0	Per Capita Income	$62,237
Area (sq. mi.)	148.7	July mean max (°F)	96.0	Prop. Value	$15,720,293,005
Land Area (sq. mi.)	127.0	Civ. Labor	53,858	Retail Sales	$2,112,468,140
Altitude (ft.)	431–624	Unemployed (%)	4.8		

Runnels County

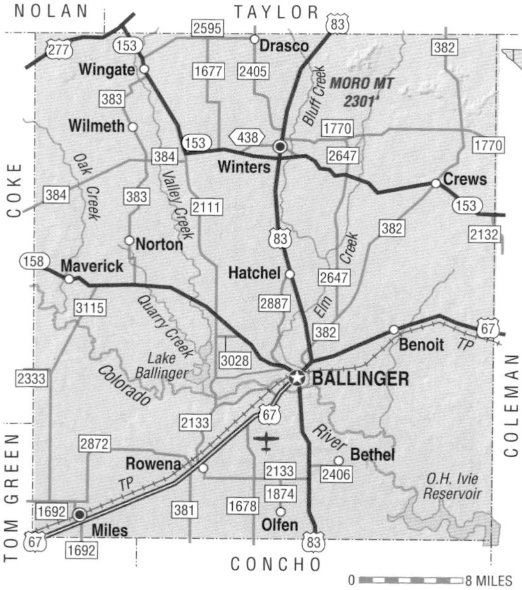

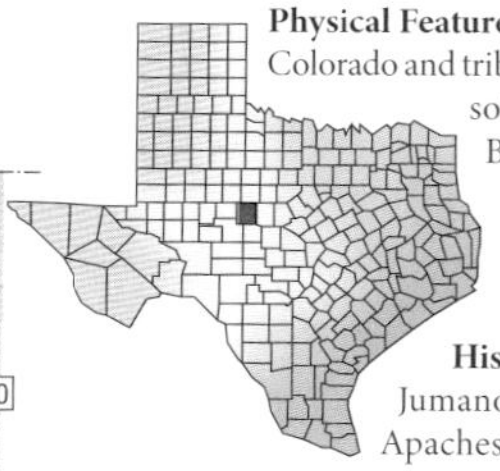

Physical Features: Level to rolling; bisected by Colorado and tributaries; sandy loam, black waxy soils; O.H. Ivie Reservoir, Lake Ballinger.

Economy: Agribusiness, oil, government/services, manufacturing.

History: Spanish explorers found Jumanos in area in the 1650s; later, Apaches and Comanches driven out in the 1870s by U.S. military. First Anglo-Americans arrived in the 1850s; Germans, Czechs around 1900. County named for planter-legislator H.G. Runnels; created in 1858 from Bexar and Travis counties; organized in 1880.

Race/Ethnicity: Anglo, 60.5%; Black, 1.5%; Hispanic, 36.2%; Asian, 0.1%; Other, 1.5%.

Vital Statistics, annual: Births, 112; deaths, 140; marriages, 53; divorces, 18.

Recreation: Deer, dove and turkey hunting; lakes; fishing; antique car museum; historical markers in county.

Minerals: Oil, gas, sand.

Agriculture: Cattle, cotton, wheat, sorghum, dairies, sheep and goats. Market value $53.4 million.

BALLINGER (3,620) county seat; varied manufacturing, meat processing; Carnegie Library, hospital, Western Texas College extension; the Cross, 100-ft. tall atop hill; city park; Festival of Ethnic Cultures in April.

Other towns include: **Miles** (849); **Norton** (50); **Rowena** (349); **Wingate** (100); **Winters** (2,427) manufacturing, museum, hospital.

Population	**10,121**	July mean max (°F)	94.4
Change from 2010 (%)	-3.6	Civ. Labor	4,531
Area (sq. mi.)	1,057.1	Unemployed (%)	3.9
Land Area (sq. mi.)	1,050.9	Wages	$30,856,175
Altitude (ft.)	1,915–2,301	Per Capita Income	$41,929
Rainfall (in.)	24.0	Prop. Value	$1,716,913,212
Jan. mean min (°F)	31.2	Retail Sales	$108,018,574

For explanation of sources, symbols and abbreviations, see p. 204, and foldout map.

Rusk County

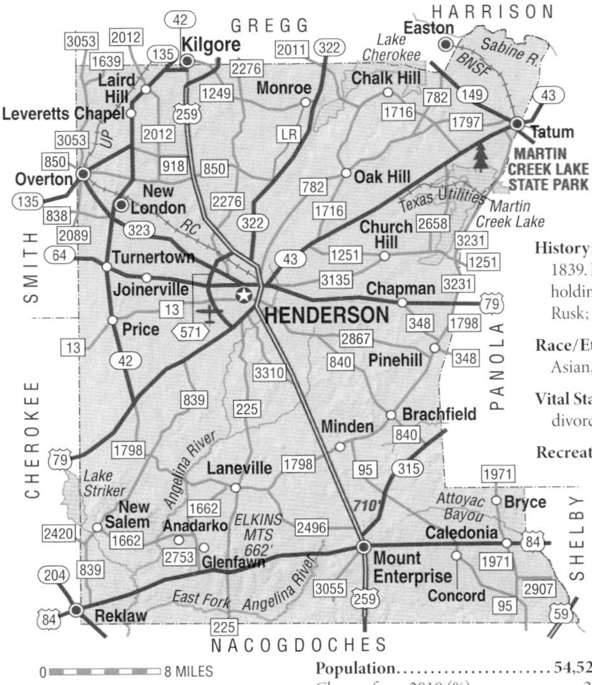

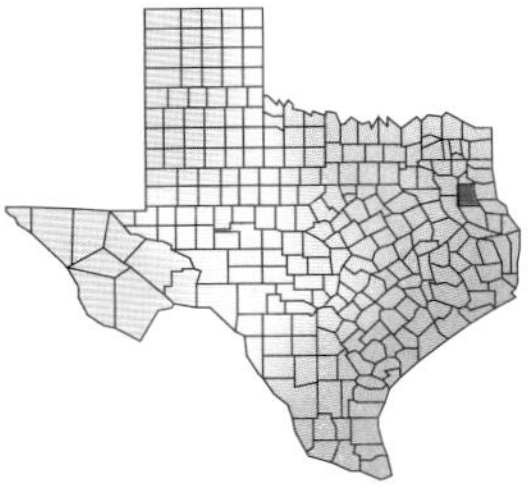

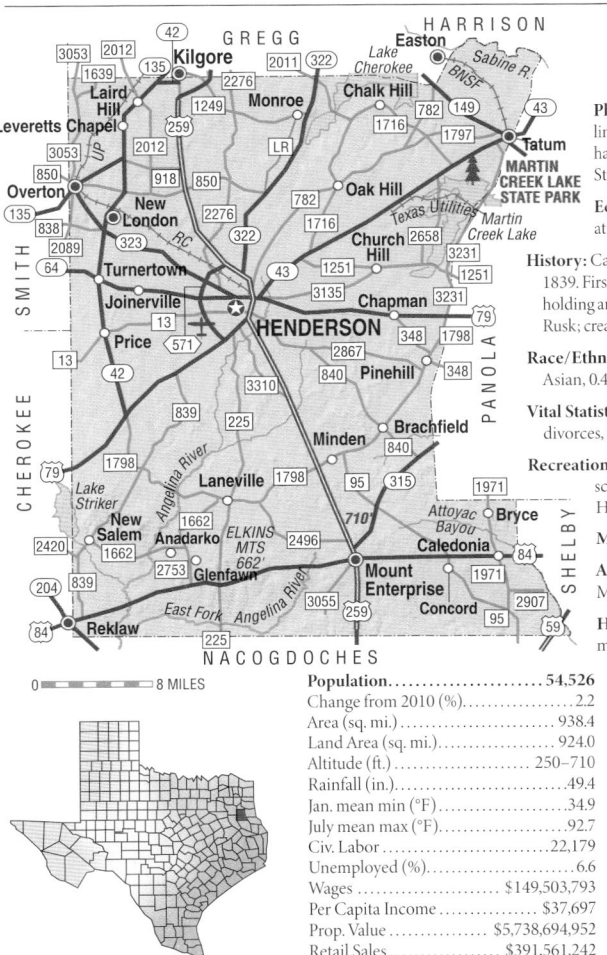

Physical Features: East Texas county on Sabine-Angelina divide; varied deep, sandy soils; over half in pines, hardwoods; Martin Creek Lake, Lake Cherokee, Lake Striker.

Economy: Oil and gas, lignite mining, electricity generation, agriculture.

History: Caddo area. Cherokees settled in the 1820s; removed in 1839. First Anglo-Americans arrived in 1829. Antebellum slave-holding area. County named for Republic, state leader Thomas J. Rusk; created and organized from Nacogdoches County in 1843.

Race/Ethnicity: Anglo, 63%; Black, 16.5%; Hispanic, 17.8%; Asian, 0.4%; Other, 2.1%.

Vital Statistics, annual: Births, 645; deaths, 544; marriages, 287; divorces, 225.

Recreation: Water sports, state park, historic homes and sites, scenic drives, site of East Texas Field discovery oil well; Henderson syrup festival in November.

Minerals: Oil, natural gas, lignite.

Agriculture: Beef cattle, forage, poultry, nursery plants. Market value $100.2 million. Timber income substantial.

HENDERSON (13,688) county seat; power plant, mining, lumber, state jails; hospital, museum.

Population	**54,526**
Change from 2010 (%)	2.2
Area (sq. mi.)	938.4
Land Area (sq. mi.)	924.0
Altitude (ft.)	250–710
Rainfall (in.)	49.4
Jan. mean min (°F)	34.9
July mean max (°F)	92.7
Civ. Labor	22,179
Unemployed (%)	6.6
Wages	$149,503,793
Per Capita Income	$37,697
Prop. Value	$5,738,694,952
Retail Sales	$391,561,242

Other towns include: **Joinerville** (140); **Laird Hill** (300); **Laneville** (169); **Minden** (150); **Mount Enterprise** (438); **New London** (1,011) site of 1937 school explosion that killed 293 students and faculty; **Overton** (2,558, partly in Smith County) oil, lumbering center, petroleum processing, prison, A&M research center, blue-grass music festival in July; **Price** (275); **Tatum** (1,419, partly in Panola County); **Turnertown-Selman City** (271).

Also: part of **Easton** (515, mostly in Gregg County), part of **Reklaw** (395, mostly in Cherokee County), and part [3,515] of **Kilgore** (14,852 total).

The post office in New London in Rusk County. Photo by Nsaum75, CC by SA 4.0/Wikimedia Commons

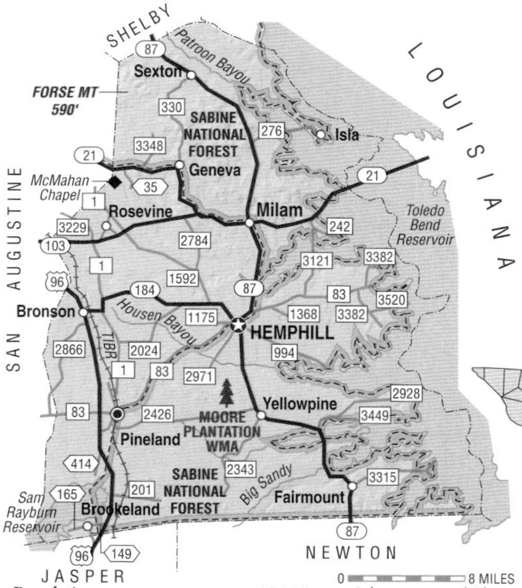

Sabine County

Physical Features: Eighty percent forested; 114,498 acres in national forest; Sabine River, Toledo Bend Reservoir on east; Sam Rayburn Reservoir on southwest.

Economy: Timber, government/services, tourism.

History: Caddo area. Spanish land grants in the 1790s brought first Spanish and Anglo settlers. An original county, created in 1836; organized in 1837. Name means cypress in Spanish.

Race/Ethnicity: Anglo, 83.3%; Black, 7.8%; Hispanic, 4.8%; Asian, 0.3%; Other, 3.5%.

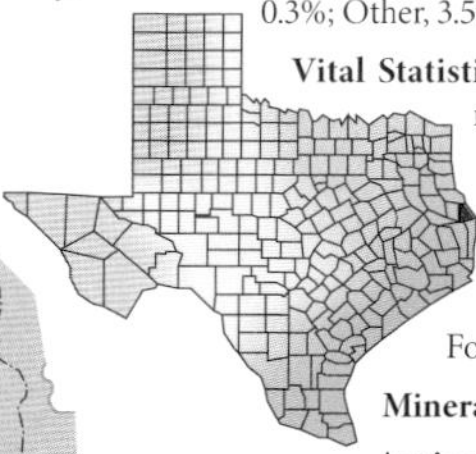

Vital Statistics, annual: Births, 111; deaths, 168; marriages, 77; divorces, 6.

Recreation: Lake activities, hunting, campsites, hiking trails, marinas, historic homes; McMahan's Chapel, pioneer Protestant church; Sabine National Forest; Lobanillo Swales historic trail.

Minerals: Glauconite, oil.

Agriculture: Beef cattle; forage, fruit raised. Market value $17.7 million. Significant timber industry.

HEMPHILL (1,233) county seat; timber, lake activities, tourism; hospital; NASA Columbia museum, library; Boo Bash at Halloween.

Other towns include: **Bronson** (377); **Brookeland** (300); **Geneva** (200); **Milam** (1,512); **Pineland** (793) timber processing.

Population	**10,917**	July mean max (°F)	92.7
Change from 2010 (%)	0.8	Civ. Labor	3,972
Area (sq. mi.)	592.3	Unemployed (%)	9.9
Land Area (sq. mi.)	530.7	Wages	$26,008,303
Altitude (ft.)	164–590	Per Capita Income	$36,627
Rainfall (in.)	51.9	Prop. Value	$1,516,636,619
Jan. mean min (°F)	35.6	Retail Sales	$81,075,344

San Augustine County

Physical Features: Hilly East Texas county, 80 percent forested with 66,799 acres in Angelina National Forest, 4,317 in Sabine National Forest; Sam Rayburn Reservoir; varied soils, sandy to black alluvial.

Economy: Timber, poultry, tourism.

History: Presence of Ais Indians attracted Spanish mission in 1717. First Anglos and Indians from U.S. southern states arrived around 1800. Antebellum slaveholding area. County created and named for Mexican municipality in 1836; an original county; organized in 1837.

Race/Ethnicity: Anglo, 67%; Black, 23.3%; Hispanic, 7.8%; Asian, 0.2%; Other, 1.4%.

Vital Statistics, annual: Births, 79; deaths, 128; marriages, 54; divorces, 4.

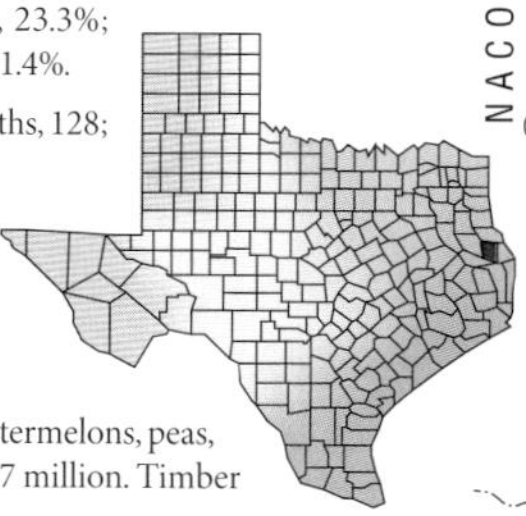

Recreation: Lake activities, historic homes, tourist facilities in national forests; sassafras festival in October.

Minerals: Small amount of oil.

Agriculture: Poultry, cattle, horses; watermelons, peas, corn, truck crops. Market value $56.7 million. Timber sales significant.

SAN AUGUSTINE (1,918) county seat; logging, poultry farms, tourism; hospital; Mission Dolores museum.

Other towns include: **Broaddus** (203).

Population	**8,458**	July mean max (°F)	92.7
Change from 2010 (%)	-4.6	Civ. Labor	2,962
Area (sq. mi.)	592.3	Unemployed (%)	9.3
Land Area (sq. mi.)	530.7	Wages	$20,029,623
Altitude (ft.)	164–590	Per Capita Income	$42,299
Rainfall (in.)	51.9	Prop. Value	$1,839,107,030
Jan. mean min (°F)	35.6	Retail Sales	$64,544,332

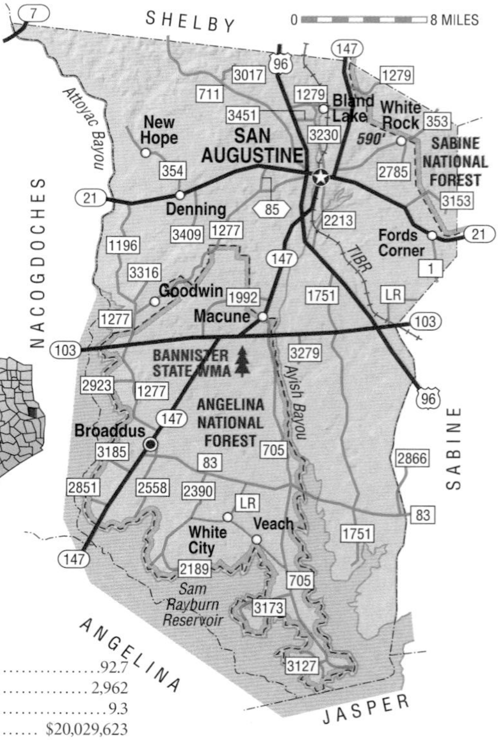

For explanation of sources, symbols and abbreviations, see p. 204, and foldout map.

San Jacinto County

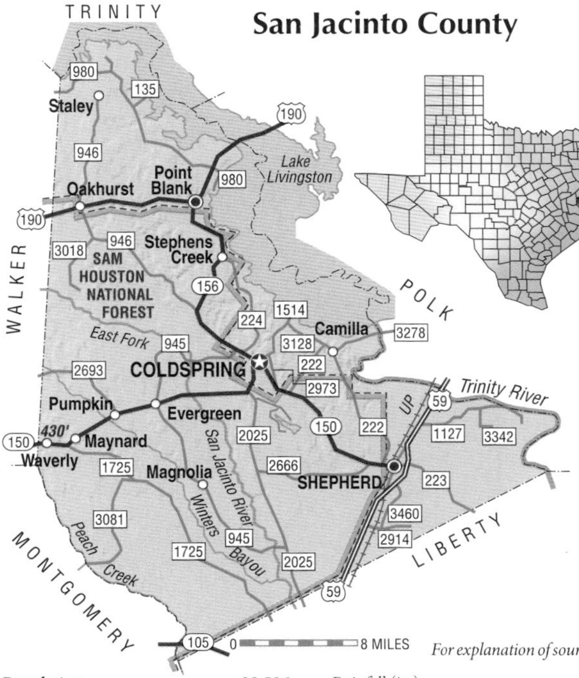

Physical Features: East Texas county north of Houston; rolling hills; eighty percent of area is forested; Sam Houston National Forest; Trinity and East Fork of San Jacinto rivers; Lake Livingston.

Economy: Timber and oil.

History: Atakapa Indian area. Anglo-Americans arrived in the 1820s. Land grants issued to Mexican families in the early 1830s. County created from Liberty, Montgomery, Polk, and Walker counties in 1869; organized in 1870; named for the battle.

Race/Ethnicity: Anglo, 72.9%; Black, 9.7%; Hispanic, 14.7%; Asian, 0.4%; Other, 2.1%.

Vital Statistics, annual: Births, 283; deaths, 313; marriages, 120; divorces, 118.

Recreation: Lake activities, hunting, old courthouse and jail; Wolf Creek car show in Coldspring in October. Approximately 60 percent of county in national forest.

Minerals: Oil, rock, gravel and iron ore.

Agriculture: Beef cattle and forages. Market value $7.2 million. Timber is a principal product.

COLDSPRING (976) county seat; lumbering, oil, farming center, tourism; historic sites.

SHEPHERD (2,649) lumbering, tourism, ranching.

Other towns include: **Oakhurst** (242); **Point Blank** (748) logging, agribusiness, construction.

For explanation of sources, symbols and abbreviations, see p. 204, and foldout map.

Population	**29,506**	Rainfall (in.)	50.7	Wages	$21,708,268
Change from 2010 (%)	11.8	Jan. mean min (°F)	38.2	Per Capita Income	$36,260
Area (sq. mi.)	627.9	July mean max (°F)	92.4	Prop. Value	$3,606,160,151
Land Area (sq. mi.)	569.2	Civ. Labor	11,897	Retail Sales	$64,673,049
Altitude (ft.)	62–430	Unemployed (%)	8		

The Sam Rayburn Reservoir can hold up to 2,857,077 acre-feet of water. Photo by Ricraider, CC 3/Wikimedia Commons

San Patricio County

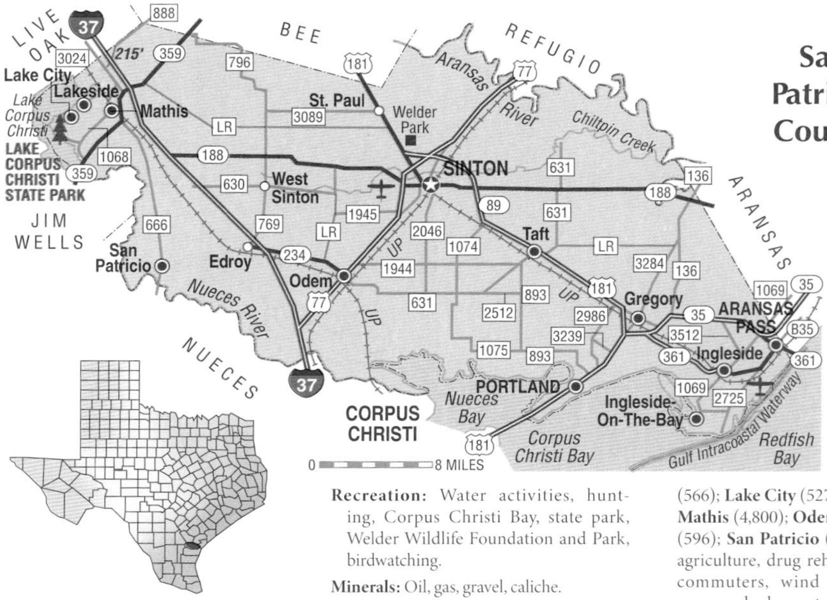

Physical Features: Grassy, coastal prairie draining to Aransas, Nueces rivers and to bays; sandy loam, clay, black loam soils; Lake Corpus Christi.

Economy: Oil, petrochemicals, agribusiness, manufacturing, tourism, in Corpus Christi metropolitan area.

History: Karankawa area. Mexican sheep herders in the area before colonization. Settled by Irish families in 1830 (name is Spanish for St. Patrick). Created, named for municipality in 1836; organized in 1837, reorganized in 1847.

Race/Ethnicity: Anglo, 37.9%; Black, 1.3%; Hispanic, 58.4%; Asian, 0.7%; Other, 1.4%.

Vital Statistics, annual: Births, 1,021; deaths, 642; marriages, 290; divorces, 243.

Recreation: Water activities, hunting, Corpus Christi Bay, state park, Welder Wildlife Foundation and Park, birdwatching.

Minerals: Oil, gas, gravel, caliche.

Agriculture: Cotton, grain sorghum, beef cattle, corn. Market value $131.3 million. Fisheries income significant.

SINTON (5,240) county seat; oil, agribusiness, tourism; Go Texan Days in October.

ARANSAS PASS (8,388, part [808] in Aransas County) deepwater port, shrimping, tourism, offshore oil-well servicing, aluminum and chemical plants; hospital; Shrimporee in May.

PORTLAND (22,115) retail center, petrochemicals, commuters to Corpus Christi; Indian Point pier; Windfest in April.

Other towns include: **Edroy** (301); **Gregory** (1,854); **Ingleside** (9,895) offshore well servicing, chemical and manufacturing plants, commuters, birding, Round Up Days in April; **Ingleside-on-the-Bay** (566); **Lake City** (527); **Lakeside** (300); **Mathis** (4,800); **Odem** (2,367); **St. Paul** (596); **San Patricio** (402); **Taft** (2,862) agriculture, drug rehabilitation center, commuters, wind farm, blackland museum, barbecue, tamale and hot sauce cook-off in December; **Taft Southwest** (1,342).

Population	**66,688**
Change from 2010 (%)	2.9
Area (sq. mi.)	707.8
Land Area (sq. mi.)	693.5
Altitude (ft.)	sea level–215
Rainfall (in.)	35.3
Jan. mean min (°F)	44.2
July mean max (°F)	93.4
Civ. Labor	29,426
Unemployed (%)	9.6
Wages	$270,186,138
Per Capita Income	$46,506
Prop. Value	$20,567,988,963
Retail Sales	$959,265,084

For explanation of sources, symbols and abbreviations, see p. 204, and foldout map.

West Texas Feed and Mercantile shop in Eldorado. Photo by Billy Hathorn, CC/Wikimedia Commons

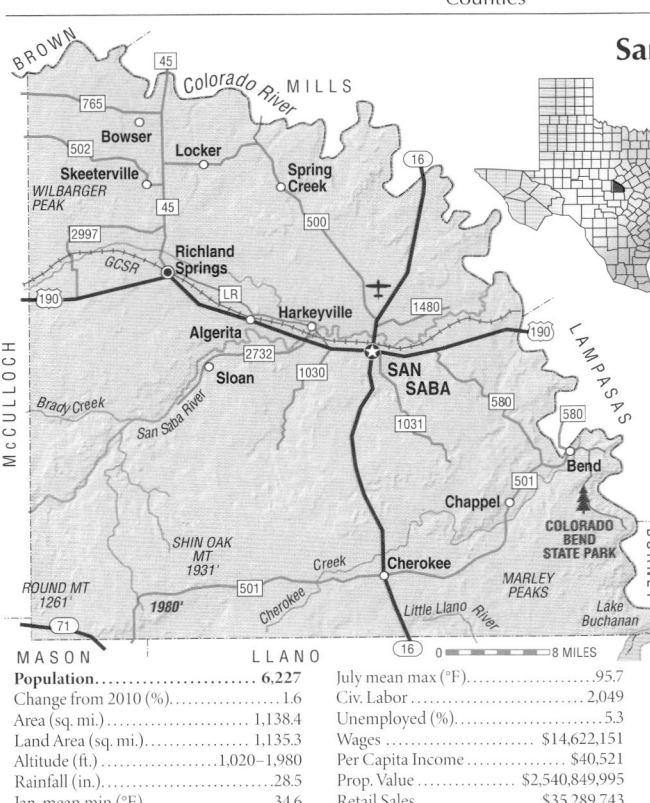

San Saba County

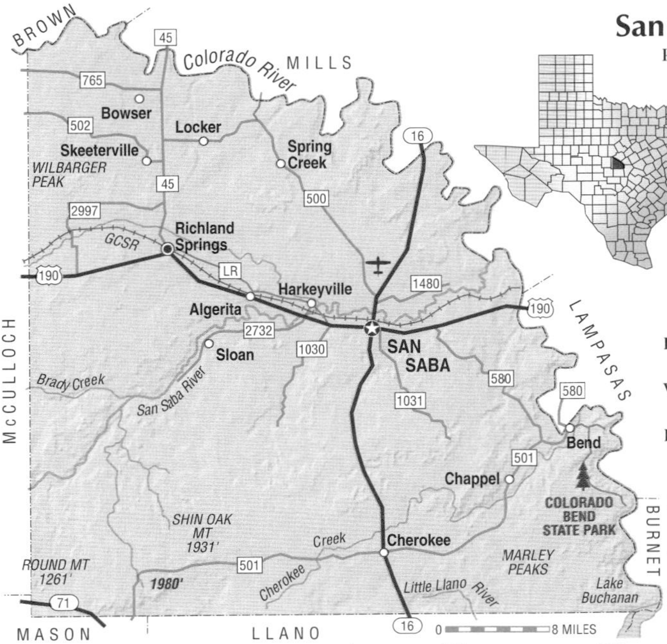

Physical Features: West central county; hilly, rolling; bisected by San Saba River; Colorado River on east; black, gray sandy loam, alluvial soils; northern tip of Lake Buchanan.

Economy: Pecan processing plants, tourism, hunting leases.

History: Apaches and Comanches in the area when Spanish explored. Anglo-American settlers arrived in 1850s. County created from Bexar District in 1856, organized the same year; named for river.

Race/Ethnicity: Anglo, 63.8%; Black, 3.2%; Hispanic, 31.3%; Asian, 0.1%; Other, 1.3%.

Vital Statistics, annual: Births, 73; deaths, 54; marriages, 13; divorces, 2.

Recreation: State park with Gorman Falls; deer hunting; historic sites; fishing; scenic drives; wildflower trail.

Minerals: Rock quarry, limestone and sand stone.

Agriculture: Cattle, pecans (second in acreage), wheat, hay, some sheep/goats. Market value $35.8 million. Hunting, wildlife leases.

SAN SABA (3,212) county seat; claims title "Pecan Capital of the World"; stone processing, varied manufacturing, prison; Cow Camp cookoff in May.

Other towns include: **Bend** (115, partly in Lampasas County); **Cherokee** (175); **Richland Springs** (330).

Population	**6,227**
Change from 2010 (%)	1.6
Area (sq. mi.)	1,138.4
Land Area (sq. mi.)	1,135.3
Altitude (ft.)	1,020–1,980
Rainfall (in.)	28.5
Jan. mean min (°F)	34.6
July mean max (°F)	95.7
Civ. Labor	2,049
Unemployed (%)	5.3
Wages	$14,622,151
Per Capita Income	$40,521
Prop. Value	$2,540,849,995
Retail Sales	$35,289,743

Schleicher County

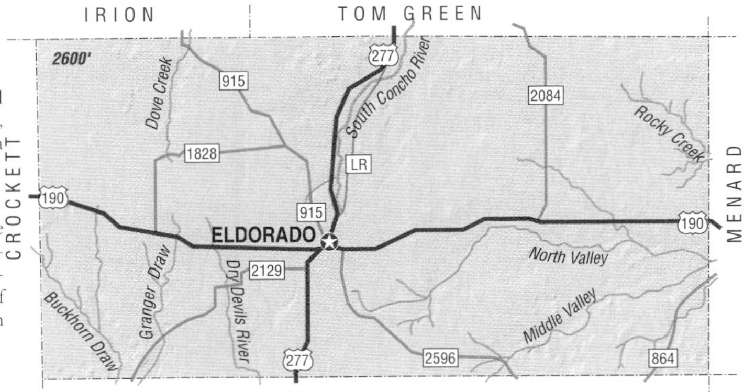

Physical Features: West central county on edge of Edwards Plateau, broken by Devils, Concho, San Saba tributaries; part hilly; black soils.

Economy: Oil, ranching, hunting.

History: Jumanos in the area in the 1630s. Later, Apaches and Comanches; removed in the 1870s. Ranching began in the 1870s. Census of 1890 showed third of population from Mexico. County named for Gustav Schleicher, founder of German colony; county created from Crockett County in 1887, organized in 1901.

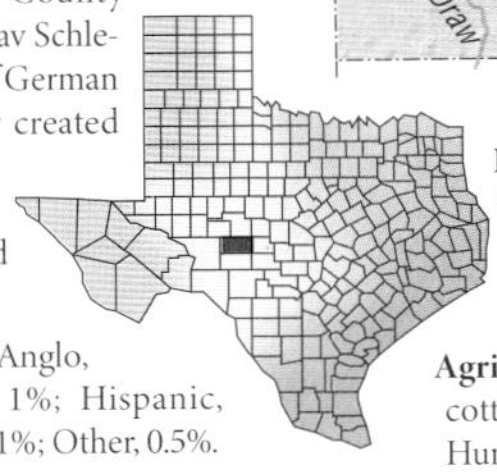

Race/Ethnicity: Anglo, 42.8%; Black, 1%; Hispanic, 55.3%; Asian, 0.1%; Other, 0.5%.

Vital Statistics, annual: Births, 23; deaths, 23; marriages, 11; divorces, 5.

For explanation of sources, symbols and abbreviations, see p. 204, and foldout map.

Recreation: Hunting, livestock show in January, youth and open rodeos, mountain bike events.

Minerals: Oil, natural gas.

Agriculture: Beef cattle, sheep, goats, and cotton, hay. Market value $17.8 million. Hunting leases important.

ELDORADO (1,584) county seat; oil activities, center for livestock, mohair marketing, woolen mill, government/services; hospital.

Population	**2,822**
Change from 2010 (%)	-18.5
Area (sq. mi.)	1,310.7
Land Area (sq. mi.)	1,310.6
Altitude (ft.)	2,070–2,600
Rainfall (in.)	23.2
Jan. mean min (°F)	31.1
July mean max (°F)	92.1
Civ. Labor	1,144
Unemployed (%)	5.9
Wages	$8,650,864
Per Capita Income	$42,255
Prop. Value	$1,362,126,357
Retail Sales	$10,018,720

Scurry County

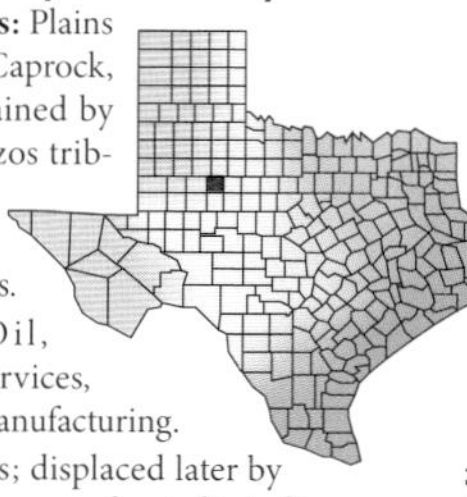

Physical Features: Plains county below Caprock, some hills; drained by Colorado, Brazos tributaries; Lake J.B. Thomas; sandy, loam soils.

Economy: Oil, government/services, agribusiness, manufacturing.

History: Apaches; displaced later by Comanches who were relocated to Indian Territory in 1875. Ranching began in the late 1870s. County created from Bexar District in 1876; organized in 1884; named for Confederate Gen. W.R. Scurry.

Race/Ethnicity: Anglo, 51%; Black, 4.2%; Hispanic, 43%; Asian, 0.3%; Other, 1.2%.

Vital Statistics, annual: Births, 230; deaths, 179; marriages, 134; divorces, 63.

Recreation: Lake J.B. Thomas water recreation; Towle Memorial Park; museums, community theater, White Buffalo Days and Bikefest in October.

Minerals: Oil, gas.

Agriculture: Cotton, wheat, cattle, hay. Market value $45.2 million.

SNYDER (11,073) county seat; oil, wind energy, agriculture; Western Texas College, hospital, museum; Western Swing days in June.

Other towns include: **Dunn** (75); **Fluvanna** (180); **Hermleigh** (308); **Ira** (250).

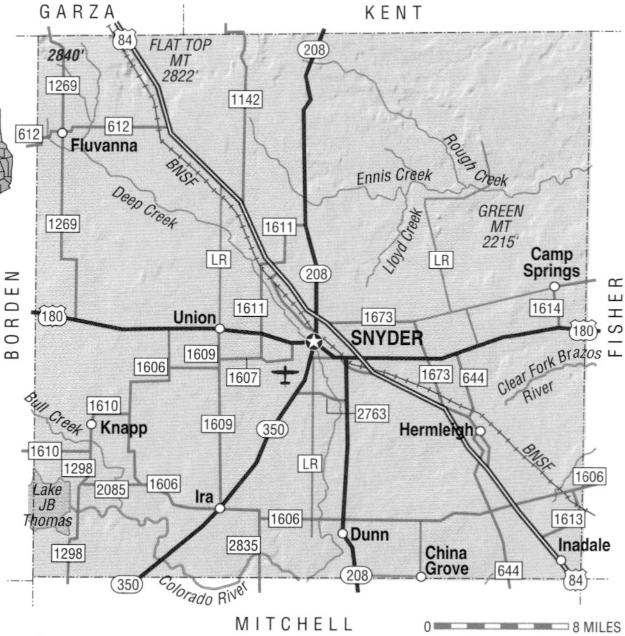

Population	**16,697**
Change from 2010 (%)	-1.3
Area (sq. mi.)	907.5
Land Area (sq. mi.)	905.4
Altitude (ft.)	1,800–2,840
Rainfall (in.)	22.7
Jan. mean min (°F)	28.2
July mean max (°F)	93.9
Civ. Labor	5,962
Unemployed (%)	7.5
Wages	$76,933,827
Per Capita Income	$42,915
Prop. Value	$3,893,433,314
Retail Sales	$257,617,903

Shackelford County

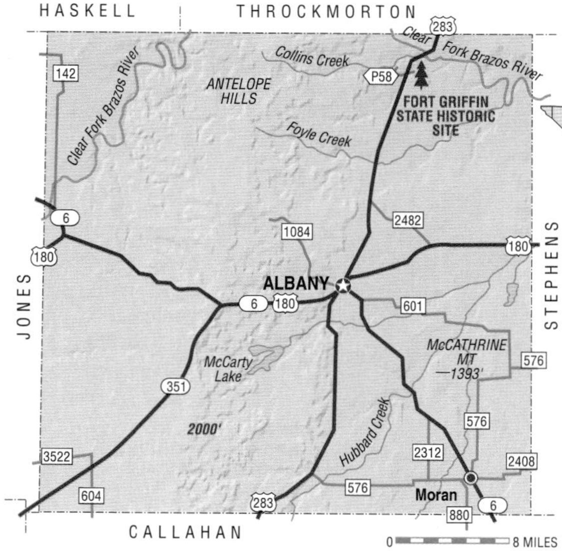

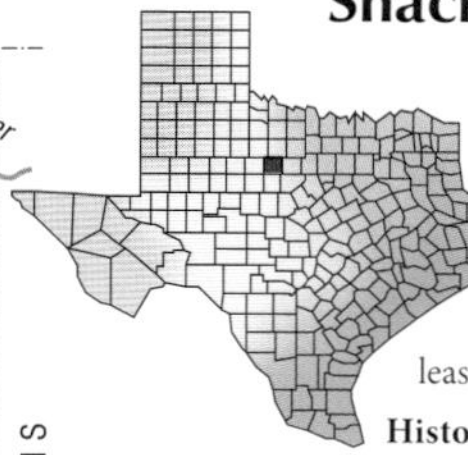

Physical Features: Rolling, hilly, drained by tributaries of Brazos; sandy and chocolate loam soils; lake.

Economy: Oil and ranching, some manufacturing, hunting leases.

History: Apaches; driven out by Comanches. First Anglo-American settlers arrived soon after establishment of military outpost in the 1850s. County created from Bosque County in 1858; organized in 1874; named for Dr. Jack Shackelford (sometimes referred to as John), Texas Revolution hero.

Race/Ethnicity: Anglo, 86.5%; Black, 0.4%; Hispanic, 11.2%; Asian, 0.3%; Other, 1.4%.

Vital Statistics, annual: Births, 43; deaths, 27; marriages, 14; divorces, 15.

Recreation: Fort Griffin historic site, courthouse historical district, hunting, lake, outdoor activities, June Fandangle musical about area history.

Minerals: Oil, natural gas.

Population	**3,382**
Change from 2010 (%)	0.1
Area (sq. mi.)	915.6
Land Area (sq. mi.)	914.3
Altitude (ft.)	1,150–2,000
Rainfall (in.)	28.4
Jan. mean min (°F)	30.2
July mean max (°F)	94.4
Civ. Labor	1,759
Unemployed (%)	4.2
Wages	$16,778,328
Per Capita Income	$113,163
Prop. Value	$1,265,455,306
Retail Sales	$19,064,302

Agriculture: Beef cattle, wheat, hay, cotton. Market value $16.6 million. Hunting leases.

ALBANY (2,037) county seat; oil, ranching, hunting; medical clinics; historical district, Old Jail art center, car museum.

Other town: **Moran** (275).

Shelby County

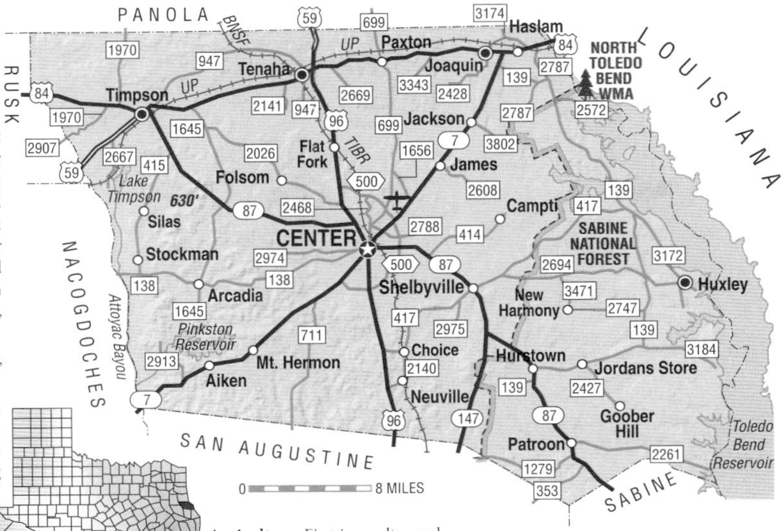

Physical Features: East Texas county; partly hills, much bottomland; well-timbered, 67,762 acres in national forest; Attoyac Bayou, other streams; Toledo Bend Reservoir, Pinkston Reservoir; sandy, clay, alluvial soils.

Economy: Poultry, timber, cattle, tourism.

History: Caddo Indian area. First Anglo-Americans settled in the 1810s. Antebellum slaveholding area. Original county of the Republic, created in 1836; organized in 1837; named for Isaac Shelby of the American Revolution.

Race/Ethnicity: Anglo, 60.9%; Black, 16.9%; Hispanic, 20.1%; Asian, 0.5%; Other, 1.3%.

Vital Statistics, annual: Births, 390; deaths, 300; marriages, 189; divorces, 60.

Recreation: Toledo Bend Reservoir activities; Sabine National Forest; hunting, fishing, camping; historic sites, restored 1885 courthouse.

Minerals: Natural gas, oil.

Agriculture: First in poultry and egg production. Beef cattle and hay. Market value $467.6 million. Timber sales significant.

CENTER (5,335) county seat; poultry, timber, oil and gas, tourism; hospital, Panola College extension, museum; What-A-Melon festival in July, poultry festival in October.

Other towns include: **Huxley** (372); **Joaquin** (795); **Shelbyville** (600); **Tenaha** (1,144); **Timpson** (1,124) livestock, timber, farming, commuters, genealogy library, Frontier Days in July.

For explanation of sources, symbols and abbreviations, see p. 204, and foldout map.

Population	**24,249**
Change from 2010 (%)	-4.7
Area (sq. mi.)	834.6
Land Area (sq. mi.)	795.6
Altitude (ft.)	174–630
Rainfall (in.)	54.2
Jan. mean min (°F)	35.1
July mean max (°F)	94.4
Civ. Labor	11,346
Unemployed (%)	6.1
Wages	$95,835,679
Per Capita Income	$41,767
Prop. Value	$2,830,567,285
Retail Sales	$297,217,790

The police station and City Hall for Timpson in Shelby County. Photo by Hourick, public domain/Wikimedia Commons

Sherman County

Physical Features: A northern Panhandle county; level, broken by creeks, playas; sandy to dark loam soils; underground water.

Economy: Agribusiness, tourism.

History: Apaches; pushed out by Comanches in the 1700s. Comanches removed to Indian Territory in 1875. Ranching began around 1880; farming after 1900. County named for Republic of Texas Gen. Sidney Sherman; created from Bexar District in 1876; organized in 1889.

Race/Ethnicity: Anglo, 51.9%; Black, 0.4%; Hispanic, 46.3%; Asian, 0.1%; Other, 1.1%.

Vital Statistics, annual: Births, 39; deaths, 34; marriages, 16; divorces, 9.

Recreation: Depot museum; pheasant, pronghorn hunting, jamboree and rodeo in July, carriage driving event in September.

Minerals: Natural gas, oil.

Agriculture: Beef and stocker cattle, wheat, corn, milo, cotton; 127,000 acres irrigated. Market value $838.1 million.

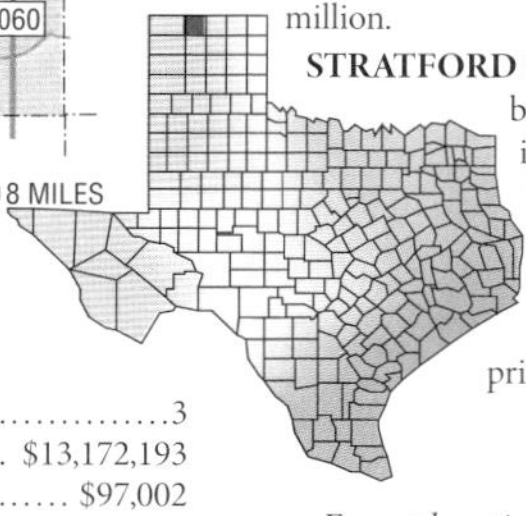

STRATFORD (2,049) county seat; agribusiness, petroleum, tourism, birdseed packaging; VA clinic; science and art museum.

Texhoma (1,142 [with 333 in Texas]) other principal town.

Population	**3,077**
Change from 2010 (%)	1.4
Area (sq. mi.)	923.2
Land Area (sq. mi.)	923.0
Altitude (ft.)	3,200–3,805
Rainfall (in.)	17.8
Jan. mean min (°F)	19.5
July mean max (°F)	91.5
Civ. Labor	1,362
Unemployed (%)	3
Wages	$13,172,193
Per Capita Income	$97,002
Prop. Value	$1,067,975,244
Retail Sales	$47,992,202

For explanation of sources, symbols and abbreviations, see p. 204, and foldout map.

Some nice old buildings across the street from Tyler City Square in Smith County. Photo by Rupak.bhattacharya, CC 3.0/Wikimedia Commons

Smith County

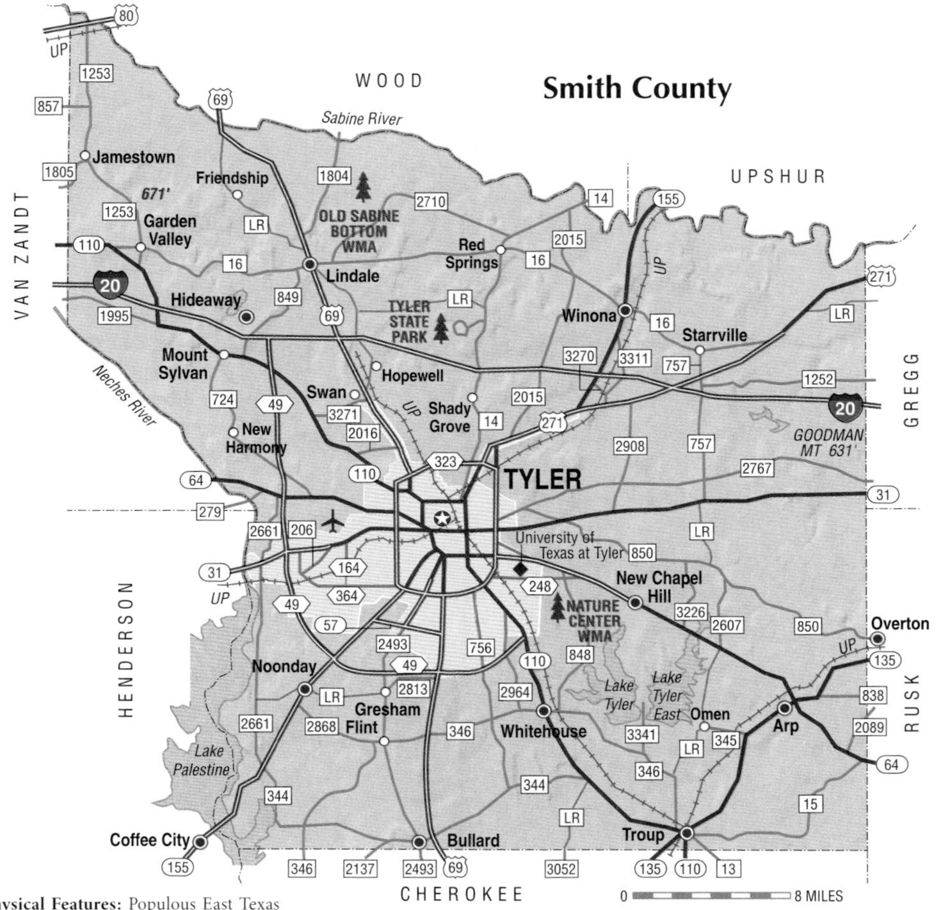

Physical Features: Populous East Texas county of rolling hills, many timbered; Sabine, Neches rivers, other streams; Lake Palestine, Lake Tyler, Lake Tyler East; alluvial, gray, sandy loam, clay soils.

Economy: Medical facilities, education, government/services, agribusiness, petroleum production, manufacturing, distribution center, tourism.

History: Caddoes of area reduced by disease and other tribes in the 1790s. Cherokees settled in the 1820s; removed in 1839. In the late 1820s, first Anglo-American settlers arrived. Antebellum slaveholding area. County named for Texas Revolution Gen. James Smith; county created and organized in 1846 from Nacogdoches County.

Race/Ethnicity: Anglo, 59%; Black, 16.9%; Hispanic, 20.1%; Asian, 1.6%; Other, 2.1%.

Vital Statistics, annual: Births, 3,109; deaths, 2,111; marriages, 1,717; divorces, 659.

Recreation: Activities on Palestine, Tyler lakes; Rose Garden; state park; Goodman Museum; Caldwell Zoo; collegiate events; Juneteenth celebration, Rose Festival in

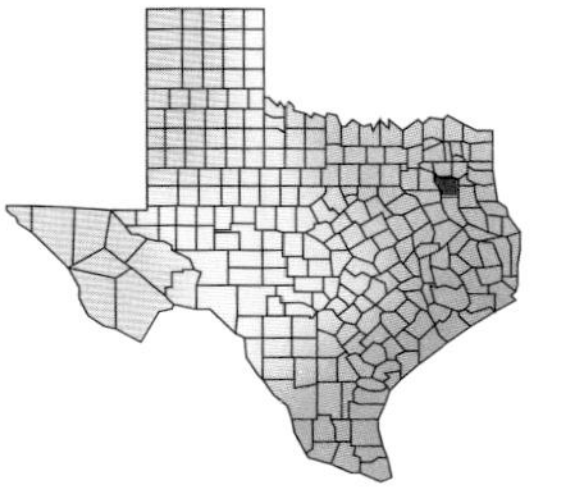

October, Azalea Trail, East Texas Fair in September/October.

Minerals: Oil, gas.

Agriculture: Horticultural crops and nurseries, beef cattle, forages, fruits and vegetables, horses, Christmas trees. Market value $53.6 million. Timber sales substantial.

TYLER (108,173) county seat; health services, education, retail center, varied manufacturing; University of Texas at Tyler, Tyler Junior College, Texas College, University of Texas Health Science Center; hospitals, nursing school; museums, Camp Ford historic park; styles itself, "City of Roses".

Other towns include: **Arp** (1,036) Strawberry Festival in April; **Bullard** (2,872, part in Cherokee County); **Flint** (2,500); **Hideaway** (3,191); **Lindale** (6,496) distribution center, foundry, varied manufacturing, Country Fest in October; **New Chapel Hill** (637); **Noonday** (811) Sweet Onion festival in June; **Troup** (1,980, part in Cherokee County) plastic manufacturing, motorcyle customization, Crawfish Boil in May; **Whitehouse** (8,899) commuters to Tyler, government/services, Yesteryear festival in June; and **Winona** (599).

Part of **Overton** (2,503, mostly in Rusk County).

Population	**231,516**
Change from 2010 (%)	10.4
Area (sq. mi.)	949.7
Land Area (sq. mi.)	921.5
Altitude (ft.)	275–671
Rainfall (in.)	46.6
Jan. mean min (°F)	36.4
July mean max (°F)	92.7
Civ. Labor	110,097
Unemployed (%)	5.6
Wages	$1,388,942,257
Per Capita Income	$56,292
Prop. Value	$25,760,133,062
Retail Sales	$4,238,328,465

Somervell County

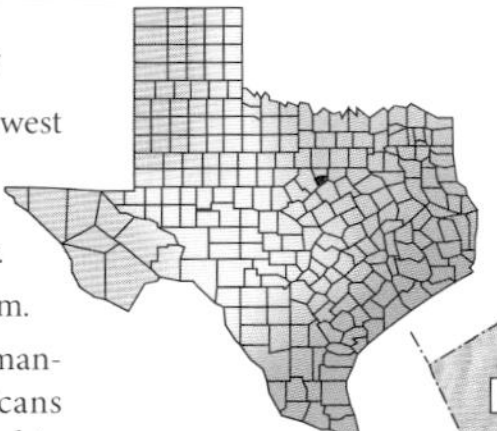

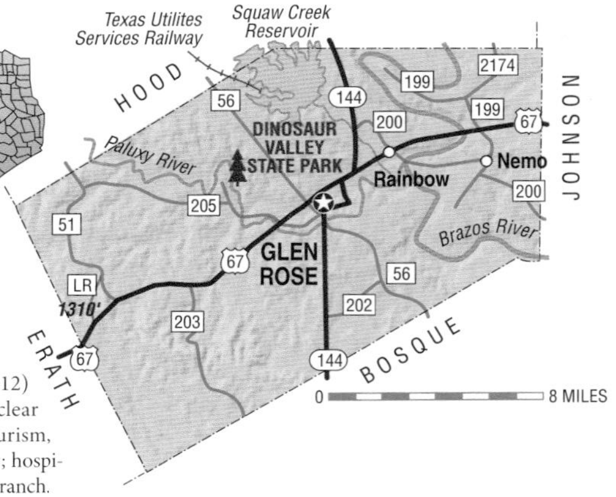

Physical Features: Hilly terrain southwest of Fort Worth; Brazos, Paluxy rivers; Squaw Creek Reservoir; gray, dark, alluvial soils; second-smallest county.

Economy: Nuclear power plant, tourism.

History: Wichita, Tonkawa area; Comanches arrived later. Anglo-Americans arrived in the 1850s. County created in 1875 as Somerville County from Hood County, organized the same year. Spelling was changed in 1876; named for Republic of Texas Gen. Alexander Somervell.

Race/Ethnicity: Anglo, 74.8%; Black, 0.6%; Hispanic, 21.8%; Asian, 0.5%; Other, 2.1%.

Vital Statistics, annual: Births, 77; deaths, 98; mmarriages, 81; divorces, 22.

Recreation: Fishing, hunting; unique geological formations; dinosaur tracks in state park; Glen Rose Big Rocks Park; Fossil Rim Wildlife Center; nature trails, museums; exposition center; Paluxy Pedal bicycle ride in October.

Minerals: Sand, gravel, silica, natural gas.

Agriculture: Cattle, hay. Market value $4.1 million. Hunting leases important.

GLEN ROSE (2,812) county seat; nuclear power plant, tourism, farm trade center; hospital; Hill College branch.

Other towns include: **Nemo** (56); **Rainbow** (121).

Population	**9,569**
Change from 2010 (%)	12.7
Area (sq. mi.)	192.0
Land Area (sq. mi.)	186.5
Altitude (ft.)	550–1,310
Rainfall (in.)	36.9
Jan. mean min (°F)	27.4
July mean max (°F)	97.0
Civ. Labor	4,385
Unemployed (%)	5.7
Wages	$57,804,184
Per Capita Income	$45,812
Prop. Value	$3,743,194,579
Retail Sales	$54,402,437

Starr County

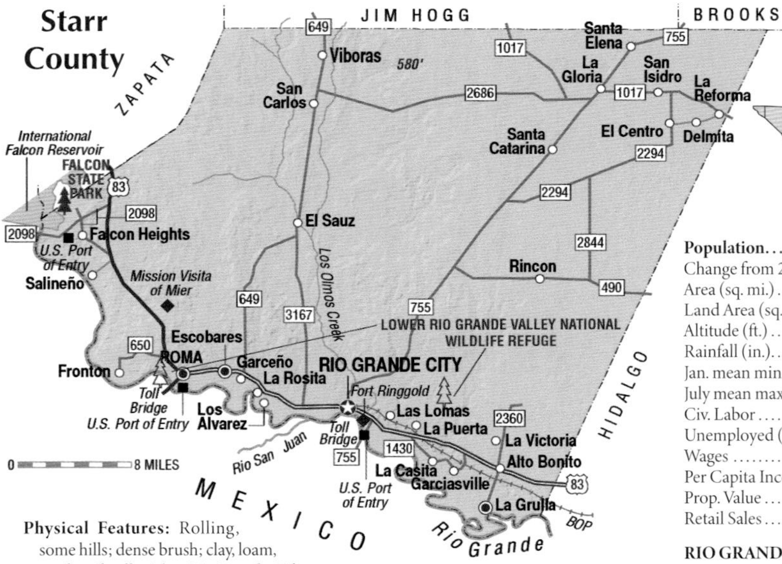

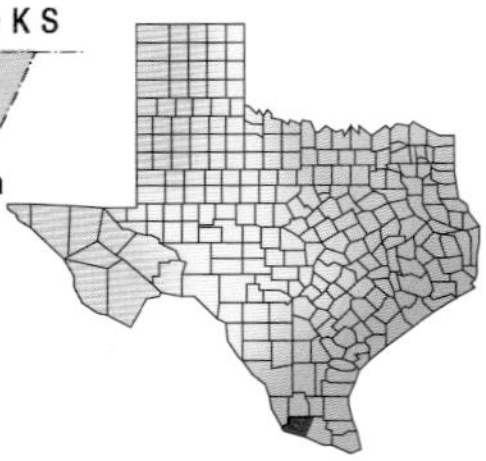

Physical Features: Rolling, some hills; dense brush; clay, loam, sandy soils, alluvial on Rio Grande; Falcon Reservoir.

Economy: Vegetable packing, other agribusiness, oil processing, tourism, government/services.

History: Coahuiltecan Indian area. Settlers from Spanish villages that were established in 1749 on south bank began to move across river soon afterward. Fort Ringgold established in 1848. County named for Dr. J.H. Starr, secretary of treasury of the Republic; county created from Nueces County and organized in 1848.

Race/Ethnicity: Anglo, 4.2%; Black, 0%; Hispanic, 95.4%; Asian, 0.1%; Other, 0.1%.

Vital Statistics, annual: Births, 1,283; deaths, 397; marriages, 409; divorces, 0.

Recreation: Falcon Reservoir activities; deer, white-wing dove hunting; access to Mexico; historic houses, Lee House at Fort Ringgold; grotto at Rio Grande City; Roma Fest in November.

Minerals: Oil, gas, sand, gravel.

Agriculture: Beef and fed cattle; vegetables, cotton, sorghum; 8,500 acres irrigated for vegetables. Market value $47.2 million.

Population	**63,690**
Change from 2010 (%)	4.5
Area (sq. mi.)	1,229.1
Land Area (sq. mi.)	1,223.2
Altitude (ft.)	125–580
Rainfall (in.)	22.7
Jan. mean min (°F)	45.9
July mean max (°F)	98.4
Civ. Labor	26,452
Unemployed (%)	17.7
Wages	$136,437,394
Per Capita Income	$27,713
Prop. Value	$3,330,907,105
Retail Sales	$521,591,939

RIO GRANDE CITY (15,074) county seat; government/services, tourism, agriculture; hospital, college branches; trolley tours; Vaquero Days in February.

ROMA-Los Saenz (11,221) agriculture center; La Purísima Concepción Visita.

Other towns include: **Delmita** (226); **Escobares** (2,837); **Falcon Heights** (56); **Fronton** (170); **Garceño** (391); **Garciasville** (59); **La Casita** (112); **La Grulla** (1,688); **La Puerta** (590); **La Rosita** (70); **Las Lomas** (3,295); **La Victoria** (156); **Los Alvarez** (286); **North Escobares** (108); **Salineño** (175); **San Isidro** (227); **Santa Elena** (35).

Stephens County

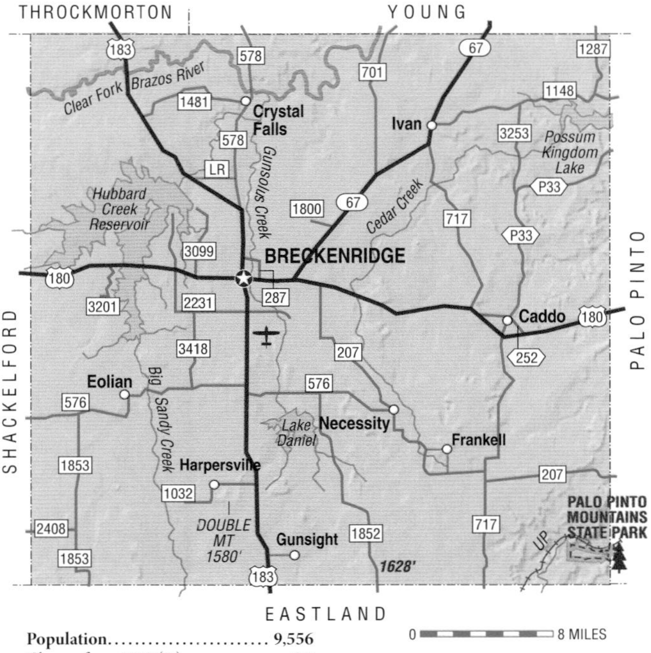

Physical Features: West central county; broken, hilly; Hubbard Creek Reservoir, Possum Kingdom Lake, Lake Daniel; Brazos River; loam, sandy soils.

Economy: Oil, agribusiness, manufacturing, recreation.

History: Comanches, Tonkawas in the area when Anglo-American settlement began in the 1850s. County created as Buchanan in 1858 from Bosque County; renamed in 1861 for Confederate Vice President Alexander H. Stephens; organized in 1876.

Race/Ethnicity: Anglo, 69.9%; Black, 2%; Hispanic, 25.8%; Asian, 0.4%; Other, 1.6%.

Vital Statistics, annual: Births, 119; deaths, 107; marriages, 61; divorces, 14.

Recreation: Lake activities, state park, hunting, campsites, historical points, Swenson Museum, Sandefer Oil Museum, aviation museum, festival and car show in fall.

Minerals: Oil, natural gas, stone.

Agriculture: Beef cattle, hogs, goats, sheep; wheat, oats, hay, peanuts, grain sorghum, cotton, pecans. Market value $10.6 million.

BRECKENRIDGE (5,684) county seat; oil, agriculture, oil-field equipment, aircraft parts; hospital, prison, Texas State Technical College branch, library.

Other towns include: **Caddo** (70) gateway to Possum Kingdom State Park.

For explanation of sources, symbols and abbreviations, see p. 204, and foldout map.

Population	**9,556**
Change from 2010 (%)	-0.8
Area (sq. mi.)	921.5
Land Area (sq. mi.)	896.7
Altitude (ft.)	995–1,628
Rainfall (in.)	30.0
Jan. mean min (°F)	30.3
July mean max (°F)	95.8
Civ. Labor	4,026
Unemployed (%)	5.4
Wages	$34,944,969
Per Capita Income	$43,971
Prop. Value	$1,571,009,951
Retail Sales	$89,794,858

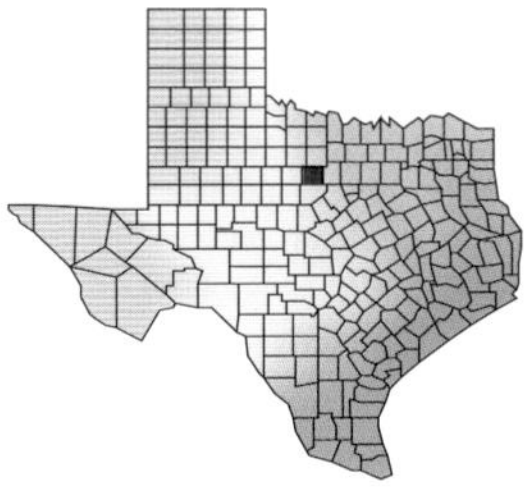

An old stone building in Rio Grande City. Photo by Carol M. Highsmith, courtesy of the Library of Congress

Sterling County

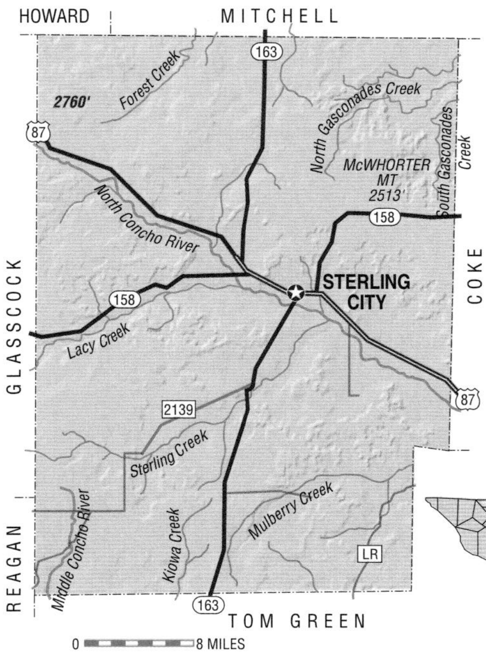

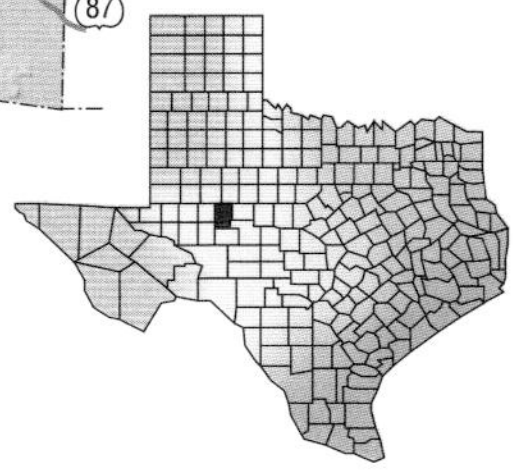

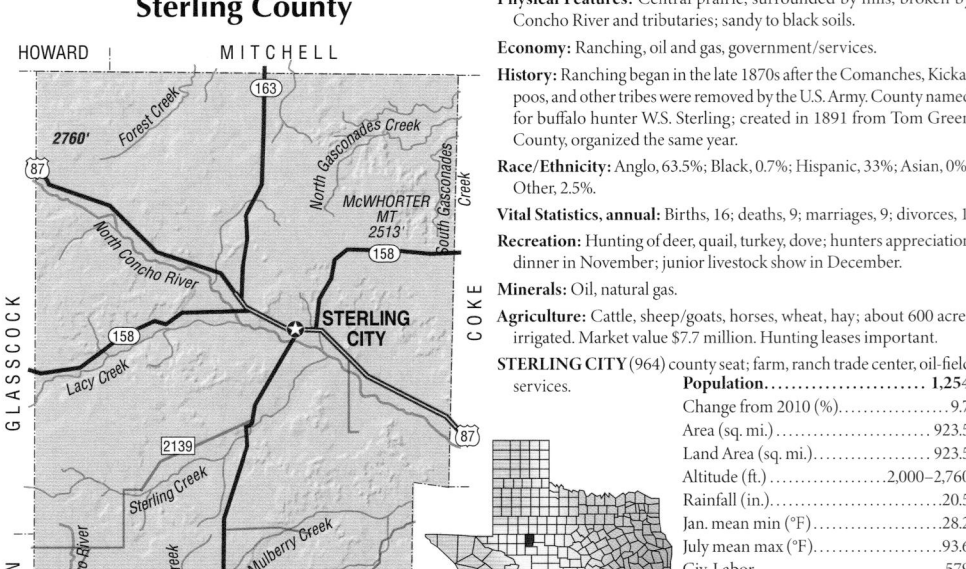

Physical Features: Central prairie, surrounded by hills, broken by Concho River and tributaries; sandy to black soils.

Economy: Ranching, oil and gas, government/services.

History: Ranching began in the late 1870s after the Comanches, Kickapoos, and other tribes were removed by the U.S. Army. County named for buffalo hunter W.S. Sterling; created in 1891 from Tom Green County, organized the same year.

Race/Ethnicity: Anglo, 63.5%; Black, 0.7%; Hispanic, 33%; Asian, 0%; Other, 2.5%.

Vital Statistics, annual: Births, 16; deaths, 9; marriages, 9; divorces, 1.

Recreation: Hunting of deer, quail, turkey, dove; hunters appreciation dinner in November; junior livestock show in December.

Minerals: Oil, natural gas.

Agriculture: Cattle, sheep/goats, horses, wheat, hay; about 600 acres irrigated. Market value $7.7 million. Hunting leases important.

STERLING CITY (964) county seat; farm, ranch trade center, oil-field services.

Population	**1,254**
Change from 2010 (%)	9.7
Area (sq. mi.)	923.5
Land Area (sq. mi.)	923.5
Altitude (ft.)	2,000–2,760
Rainfall (in.)	20.5
Jan. mean min (°F)	28.2
July mean max (°F)	93.6
Civ. Labor	579
Unemployed (%)	6.0
Wages	$6,729,972
Per Capita Income	$61,920
Prop. Value	$916,417,867
Retail Sales	$14,433,638

Stonewall County

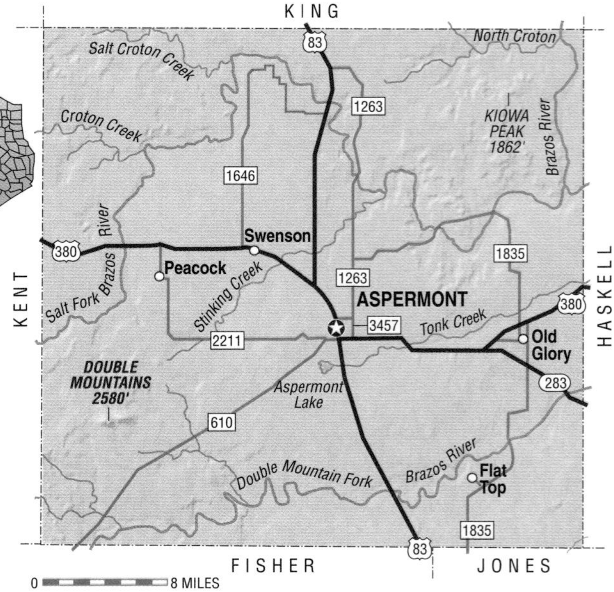

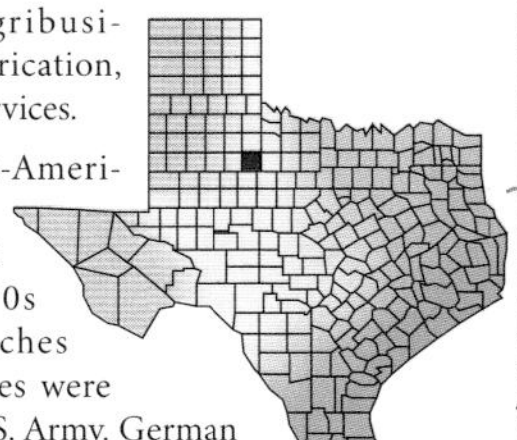

Physical Features: Western county on Rolling Plains below Caprock, bisected by Brazos forks; sandy loam, sandy, other soils; some hills.

Economy: Agribusiness, light fabrication, government/services.

History: Anglo-American ranchers arrived in the 1870s after Comanches and other tribes were removed by U.S. Army. German farmers settled after 1900. County named for Confederate Gen. T.J. (Stonewall) Jackson; created from Bexar District in 1876, organized in 1888.

Race/Ethnicity: Anglo, 78.5%; Black, 2%; Hispanic, 16.8%; Asian, 0.8%; Other, 1.5%.

Vital Statistics, annual: Births, 20; deaths, 29; marriages, 4; divorces, 3.

Recreation: Deer, quail, feral hog, turkey hunting; rodeos in June, September.

Minerals: Gypsum, gravel, oil.

Agriculture: Beef cattle, wheat, cotton, peanuts, hay. Also, grain sorghum, meat goats and swine. Market value $15.5 million.

ASPERMONT (861) county seat; oil field and ranching center, light fabrication; hospital; livestock show in February, Springfest.

Other towns include: **Old Glory** (100) farming center.

Population	**1,382**
Change from 2010 (%)	-7.2
Area (sq. mi.)	920.2
Land Area (sq. mi.)	916.3
Altitude (ft.)	1,450–2,580
Rainfall (in.)	23.8
Jan. mean min (°F)	28.5
July mean max (°F)	97.0
Civ. Labor	576
Unemployed (%)	4.0
Wages	$5,551,554
Per Capita Income	$58,541
Prop. Value	$758,272,926
Retail Sales	$23,653,596

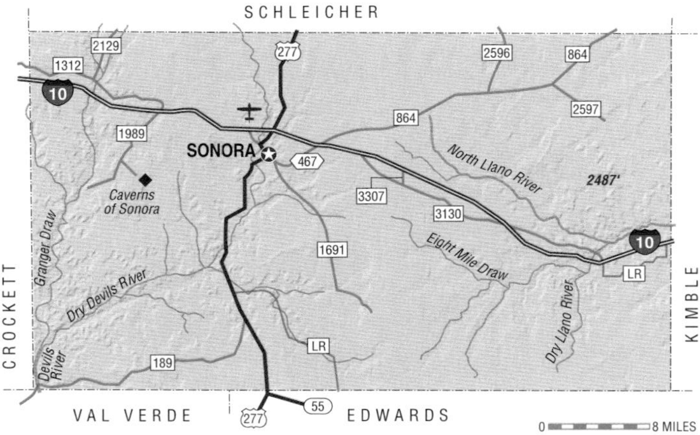

Sutton County

Physical Features: Southwestern county; level in west, rugged terrain in east, broken by tributaries of Devils, Llano rivers; black, red loam soils.

Economy: Natural gas, ranching, hunting.

History: Lipan Apaches drove out Tonkawas in 1600s. Comanches, military outpost, and disease forced Apaches south. Anglo-Americans settled in 1870s. Mexican immigration increased after 1890. County created from Crockett in 1887; organized in 1890; named for Confederate Col. John S. Sutton.

Race/Ethnicity: Anglo, 36.1%; Black, 0%; Hispanic, 63%; Asian, 0.2%; Other, 0.5%.

Vital Statistics, annual: Births, 50; deaths, 30; marriages, 25; divorces, 9.

Recreation: Hunting, Miers Museum, ranch museum, Caverns of Sonora, wildlife sanctuary, Cinco de Mayo.

Minerals: Oil, natural gas.

Agriculture: Meat goats (first in numbers), sheep, cattle, Angora goats (second in numbers). Exotic wildlife. Wheat and oats raised for grazing, hay; minor irrigation. Market value $10.4 million. Hunting leases important.

SONORA (2,967) county seat; natural gas production, ranching, tourism; Dry Devils River Music Flood in October.

Population	**3,664**
Change from 2010 (%)	-11.2
Area (sq. mi.)	1,454.4
Land Area (sq. mi.)	1,453.9
Altitude (ft.)	1,840–2,487
Rainfall (in.)	23.0
Jan. mean min (°F)	29.2
July mean max (°F)	94.4
Civ. Labor	1,158
Unemployed (%)	8.9
Wages	$19,513,451
Per Capita Income	$61,646
Prop. Value	$1,735,871,766
Retail Sales	$69,181,522

Swisher County

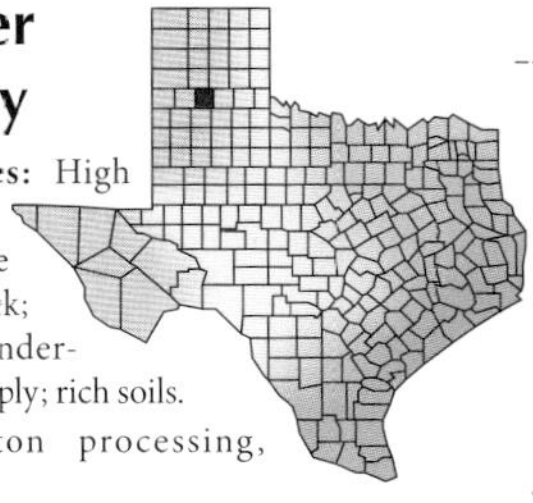

Physical Features: High Plains; level, broken by Tule Canyon and Creek; playas; large underground water supply; rich soils.

Economy: Cotton processing, manufacturing.

History: Apaches; displaced by Comanches around 1700. U.S. Army removed Comanches in 1874. Ranching began in the late 1870s. Farming developed after 1900. County named for J.G. Swisher of Texas Revolution; county created from Bexar, Young territories in 1876; organized in 1890.

Race/Ethnicity: Anglo, 45.9%; Black, 8%; Hispanic, 44%; Asian, 0%; Other, 1.8%.

Vital Statistics, annual: Births, 111; deaths, 81; marriages, 27; divorces, 4.

Recreation: Mackenzie battle site, Picnic celebration in July at Tulia.

Minerals: Not significant.

Agriculture: Cotton, cattle, wheat, corn, sorghum, cucumbers. Some 65,000 acres irrigated. Market value $623.9 million.

TULIA (4,698) county seat; agriculture, government/services, manufacturing; hospital, library, museum.

Other towns include: **Happy** (666, partly in Randall County); **Kress** (683); **Vigo Park** (36).

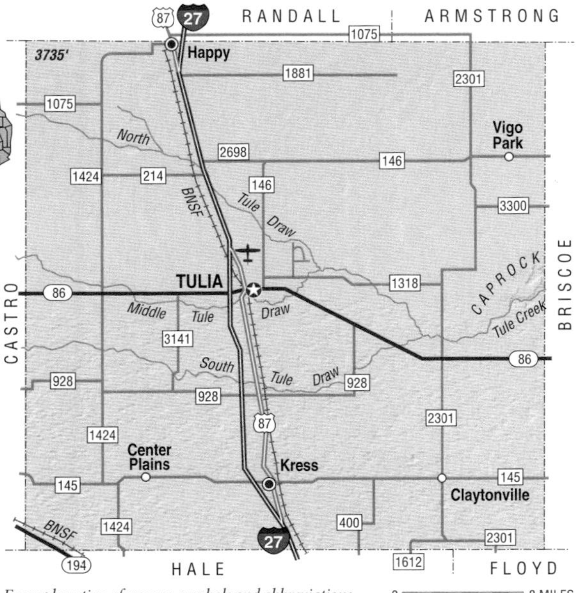

For explanation of sources, symbols and abbreviations, *see p. 204, and foldout map.*

Population	**7,439**
Change from 2010 (%)	-5.3
Area (sq. mi.)	900.7
Land Area (sq. mi.)	890.2
Altitude (ft.)	3,160–3,735
Rainfall (in.)	21.6
Jan. mean min (°F)	22.0
July mean max (°F)	91.9
Civ. Labor	2,596
Unemployed (%)	5.2
Wages	$18,972,203
Per Capita Income	$51,779
Prop. Value	$914,894,780
Retail Sales	$45,745,610

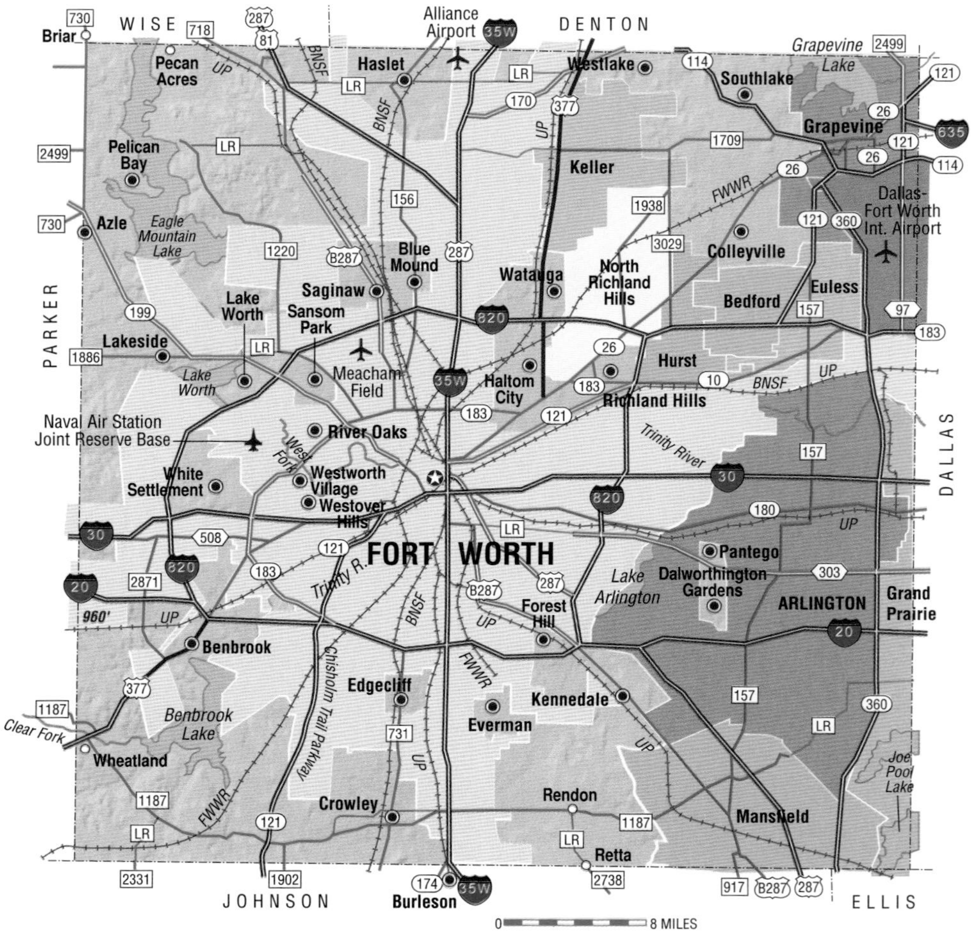

Tarrant County

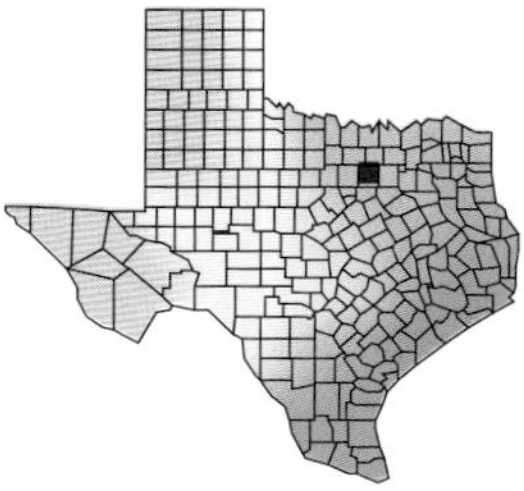

Physical Features: Part Blackland, level to rolling; drains to Trinity; Lake Worth, Grapevine Lake, Eagle Mountain Lake, Benbrook Lake, Joe Pool Lake, Lake Arlington.

Economy: Tourism, planes, helicopters, foods, mobile homes, electronic equipment, chemicals, plastics among products of more than 1,000 factories, large federal expenditure, D/FW International Airport, economy closely associated with Dallas urban area.

History: Caddoes in area. Comanches, other tribes arrived about 1700. Anglo-Americans settled in the 1840s. Named for Republic of Texas Gen. Edward H. Tarrant, who helped drive Indian tribes from area. County created in 1849 from Navarro County; organized in 1850.

Race/Ethnicity: Anglo, 46%; Black, 16.3%; Hispanic, 29%; Asian, 5.6%; Other, 2.9%.

Vital Statistics, annual: Births, 28,364; deaths, 12,277; marriages, 14,067; divorces, 7,354.

Recreation: Scott Theatre; Amon G. Carter Museum; Kimbell Art Museum; Modern Art Museum; Museum of Science and History; Casa Mañana; Botanic Gardens; Fort Worth Zoo; Log Cabin Village, all in Fort Worth.

Also, Six Flags Over Texas at Arlington; Southwestern Exposition, Stock Show; Convention Center; Stockyards Historical District; Texas Rangers and Dallas Cowboys at Arlington, other athletic events.

Minerals: Production of cement, sand, gravel, stone, gas.

Agriculture: Hay, beef cattle, wheat, horses, horticulture. Market value $29.4 million. Firewood marketed.

Education: Texas Christian University, University of Texas at Arlington, Texas Wesleyan University, Texas A&M University School of Law, University of North Texas Health Science Center, Southwestern Baptist Theological Seminary, Tarleton State University branch, and several other academic centers including a junior college system with five campuses and various centers.

FORT WORTH (895,100, small parts in Denton, Parker and Wise counties) county seat; a major mercantile, commercial and financial center; airplane, helicopter and other manufacturing plants; hospitals/health care; distribution center; oil and gas; stock show and rodeo January/February.

A cultural center with renowned art museums, Bass Performance Hall; many conventions held in downtown center; agribusiness center for wide area with grain-storage and feed-mill operations; adjacent to D/FW International Airport.

ARLINGTON (391,791) University of Texas-Arlington, General Motors plant, tourism, the Texas Rangers baseball team, AT&T Stadium, retail, hospitals, bowling museum, art museum; Scottish festival in June.

Other towns include: **Hurst** (38,479); **Euless** (56,965); **Bedford** (49,530) helicopter plant, hospital, Celtic festival in fall (these three contiguous cities are sometimes referred to as H.E.B.).

Azle (13,285, partly in Parker County) government/services, retail, medical care/hospital, commuters to Fort Worth, museum, Sting Fling festival in September; **Benbrook** (23,912) varied manufacturing, hospitals; **Blue Mound** (2,435); **Briar** (6,301, parts in Wise and Parker counties).

Also, **Colleyville** (27,091) medical services, commuters, government/services, barbecue cookoff in April; **Crowley** (15,945) varied manufacturing, government/services, hospital; **Dalworthington Gardens** (2,333); **Edgecliff** (2,979); **Everman** (6,215); **Forest Hill** (12,894).

Also, **Grapevine** (54,277) tourist center, distribution, near the D/FW International Airport, hospitals, museums, art galleries, Grapefest in September; **Haltom City** (43,003) light manufacturing, food processing, medical center; library; **Haslet** (1,928) commuters, government/services, chili fest and rodeo in May; **Keller** (46,651) Bear Creek Park, Wild West Fest.

Also, **Kennedale** (8,486) commuters, printing, manufacturing, library, drag strip, custom car show in May; **Lakeside** (1,635); **Lake Worth** (4,858) retail, tourism, museum, nature center; **Mansfield** (70,080, partly in Johnson, Ellis counties) varied manufacturing, retail, government/services, commuters, hospital, community college, library, museum, parks, Pecan festival in September; **North Richland Hills** (71,210) hospital; **Pantego** (2,462); **Pelican Bay** (1,905); **Rendon** (14,490); **Richland Hills** (7,917).

Also, **River Oaks** (7,928); **Saginaw** (24,337) manufacturing, distribution/trucking, food processing/flour mill, Train & Grain festival in October; **Sansom Park** (5,625); **Southlake** (31,613) technology, financial, retail center, hospital, parks, Oktoberfest; **Watauga** (24,402); **Westlake** (1,725); **Westover Hills** (710); **Westworth Village** (2,772).

Also, **White Settlement** (17,719) aircraft manufacturing, drilling equipment, technological services, museums including Civil War museum, parks, historic sites; industrial park; settlers day festival in fall.

Also, part [9,983] of **Burleson**; part [61,070] of **Grand Prairie**, and part of **Pecan Acres** (4,745).

Largest U.S. Media Markets

Rank	TV Homes
1. New York	7.10 million
2. Los Angeles	5.28 million
3. Chicago	3.25 million
4. Philadelphia	2.82 million
5. Dallas/Fort Worth	**2.62 million**
6. Washington, D.C.	2.48 million
7. Houston	**2.42 million**
8. San Francisco	2.41 million
9. Boston	2.36 million
10. Atlanta	2.34 million

Source: Nielsen Media Research, 2019.

Population	**2,060,239**
Change from 2010 (%)	13.9
Area (sq. mi.)	902.3
Land Area (sq. mi.)	863.6
Altitude (ft.)	420–960
Rainfall (in.)	35.5
Jan. mean min (°F)	32.4
July mean max (°F)	95.5
Civ. Labor	1,087,875
Unemployed (%)	5.9
Wages	$14,854,891,704
Per Capita Income	$53,292
Prop. Value	$269,626,851,344
Retail Sales	$35,727,101,457

For explanation of sources, symbols and abbreviations, see p. 204, and foldout map.

A bird show featuring a hyacinth macaw at the Fort Worth Zoo. Photo by Jerry Tillery, CC 2/Wikimedia Commons

Taylor County

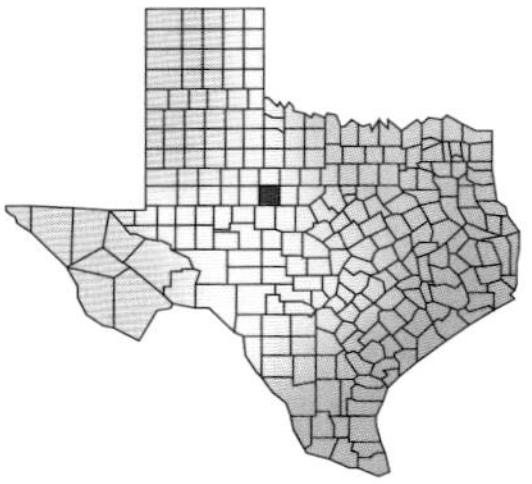

Physical Features: Prairies, with Callahan Divide, draining to Colorado River tributaries, Brazos River forks; Lake Abilene, Lake Kirby; mostly loam soils.

Economy: Agribusiness, oil and gas production, education, Dyess Air Force Base.

History: Comanches in the area about 1700. Anglo-American settlers arrived in the 1870s. Named for Alamo heroes Edward, James, and George Taylor, brothers; county created from Bexar, Travis counties in 1858 and organized in 1878.

Race/Ethnicity: Anglo, 62%; Black, 7.1%; Hispanic, 25.3%; Asian, 1.9%; Other, 3.4%.

Vital Statistics, annual: Births, 2,097; deaths, 1,378; marriages, 1285; divorces, 383.

Recreation: Abilene State Park, lake activities, Nelson Park Zoo, college events, Buffalo Gap historical tour and arts festival in April, Western Heritage ranch rodeo in May, as well as the West Texas Fair in September at Abilene.

Minerals: Oil, natural gas.

Agriculture: Beef cattle, small grains, cotton, milo. Market value $31.5 million.

Education: Abilene Christian University, Hardin-Simmons University, McMurry University, Texas Tech University pharmacy school, nursing school, and branch campus, and Cisco Junior College branch.

ABILENE (123,302, a small part in Jones County) county seat; retail center, oil and gas, military, colleges; hospitals, Abilene State School; Fort Phantom Hill (in Jones County). Wylie is now part of Abilene.

Other communities include: **Buffalo Gap** (512) historic sites; **Impact** (29); **Lawn** (315); **Merkel** (2,646) oil and wind energy, ranching, hunting, commuting, museum, health clinic, part of Bankhead Highway (early 1900s transcontinental route); classic car show in March; **Ovalo** (225); **Potosi** (3,574); **Trent** (347); **Tuscola** (753); **Tye** (1,318).

Population	**139,044**
Change from 2010 (%)	5.7
Area (sq. mi.)	919.3
Land Area (sq. mi.)	915.6
Altitude (ft.)	1,640–2,490
Rainfall (in.)	24.8
Jan. mean min (°F)	30.2
July mean max (°F)	94.2
Civ. Labor	66,701
Unemployed (%)	4.6
Wages	$790,472,878
Per Capita Income	$47,793
Prop. Value	$14,027,547,182
Retail Sales	$2,373,333,002

For explanation of sources, symbols and abbreviations, see p. 204, and foldout map.

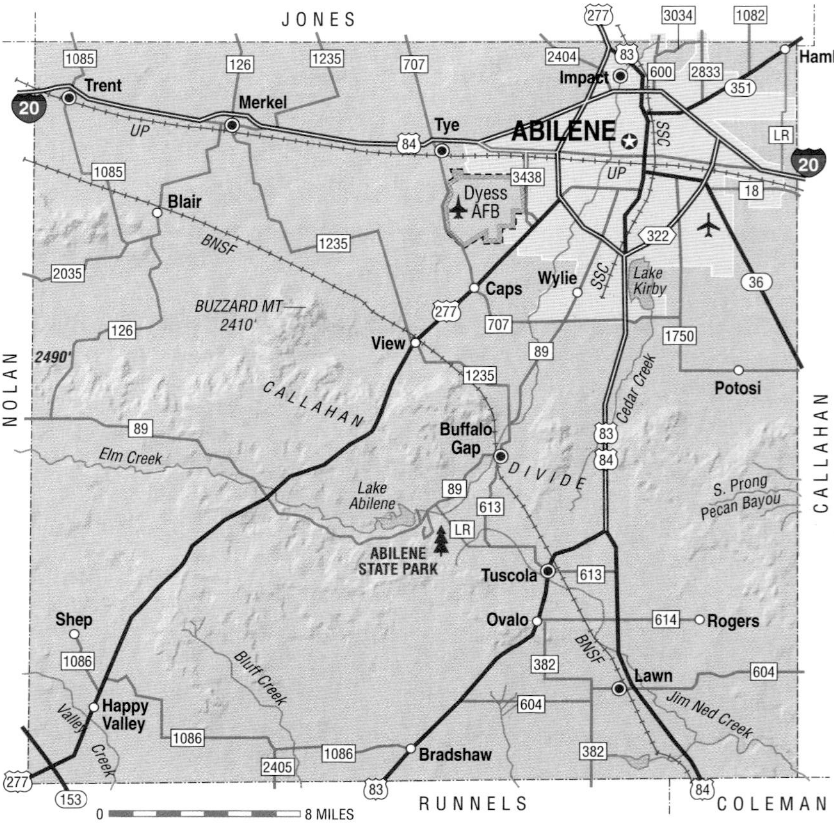

Terrell County

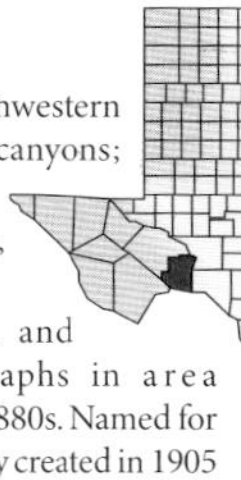

Physical Features: Trans-Pecos southwestern county; semi-mountainous, many canyons; rocky, limestone soils.

Economy: Ranching, hunting leases, oil/gas exploration, tourism.

History: Coahuiltecans, Jumanos, and other tribes left many pictographs in area caves. Sheep ranching began in the 1880s. Named for Confederate Gen. A.W. Terrell; county created in 1905 from Pecos County, organized the same year.

Race/Ethnicity: Anglo, 50%; Black, 0.6%; Hispanic, 47.8%; Asian, 0.1%; Other, 1.3%.

Vital Statistics, annual: Births, 0; deaths, 17; marriages, 6; divorces, 0.

Recreation: Nature tourism, hunting, especially white-tailed and mule deer, Rio Grande Wild and Scenic River, varied wildlife, hiking trail; Snake Days in June, Cactus Pachanga in October.

Minerals: Gas, oil, limestone.

Agriculture: Goats (meat, Angora); sheep (meat, wool); some beef cattle. Market value $4.2 million. Wildlife leases important.

Sanderson (681) county seat; ranching, hunting, tourism, government/services; museum.

Other town: **Dryden** (13).

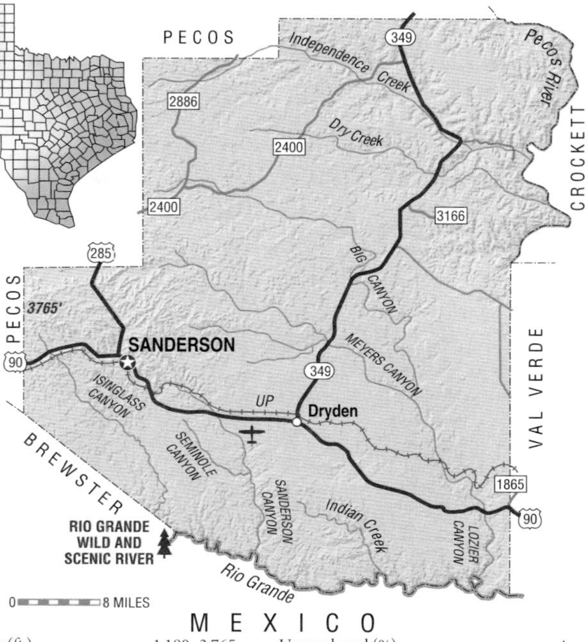

Population	**794**	Altitude (ft.)	1,180–3,765	Unemployed (%)	4
Change from 2010 (%)	-19.3	Rainfall (in.)	14.7	Wages	$3,260,909
Area (sq. mi.)	2,358.1	Jan. mean min (°F)	31.5	Per Capita Income	$49,591
Land Area (sq. mi.)	2,358.0	July mean max (°F)	92.2	Prop. Value	$599,540,811
		Civ. Labor	403	Retail Sales	$3,030,796

Terry County

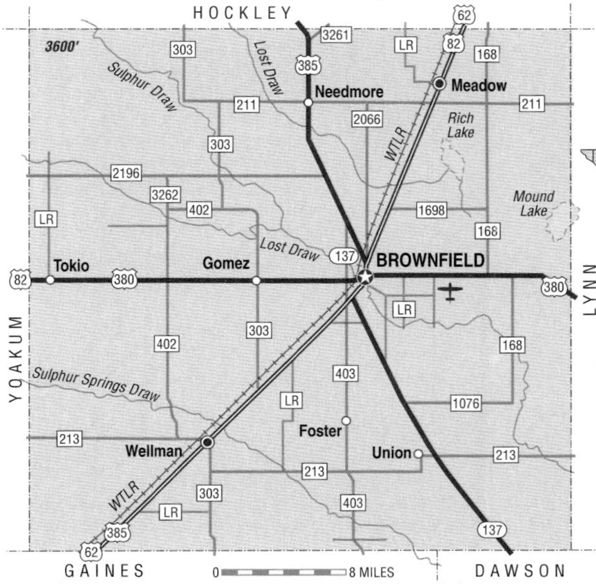

Physical Features: South Plains, broken by draws, playas; sandy, sandy loam, loam soils.

Economy: Oil-field services, agribusiness, peanut processing.

History: Comanches removed in the 1870s by U.S. Army. Ranching developed in the 1890s; farming after 1900. Oil discovered in 1940. County named for Confederate Col. B.F. Terry, head of the Eighth Texas Cavalry (Terry's Texas Rangers). Created from the Bexar District in 1876; organized in 1904.

Race/Ethnicity: Anglo, 38.9%; Black, 4.5%; Hispanic, 55.3%; Asian, 0.1%; Other, 0.9%.

Vital Statistics, annual: Births, 189; deaths, 139; marriages, 73; divorces, 43.

Recreation: Museum, aquatic center, vineyard festival in August, harvest festival in October.

Minerals: Oil, gas, salt mining.

Agriculture: Cotton is principal crop; peanuts (third in acreage), grain sorghum, guar, wheat, melons, cattle, grapes. 98,000 acres irrigated. Market value $136.9 million.

BROWNFIELD (9,707) county seat; oil-field services, government/services, vineyards, peanut processing; hospital; quilt trail displays in April.

Other towns include: **Meadow** (590); **Tokio** (6); **Wellman** (204).

Population	**12,544**	July mean max (°F)	92.4
Change from 2010 (%)	-0.8	Civ. Labor	4,853
Area (sq. mi.)	890.9	Unemployed (%)	6.7
Land Area (sq. mi.)	888.8	Wages	$35,371,729
Altitude (ft.)	3,080–3,600	Per Capita Income	$37,741
Rainfall (in.)	19.6	Prop. Value	$1,322,663,540
Jan. mean min (°F)	26.9	Retail Sales	$215,154,561

Throckmorton County

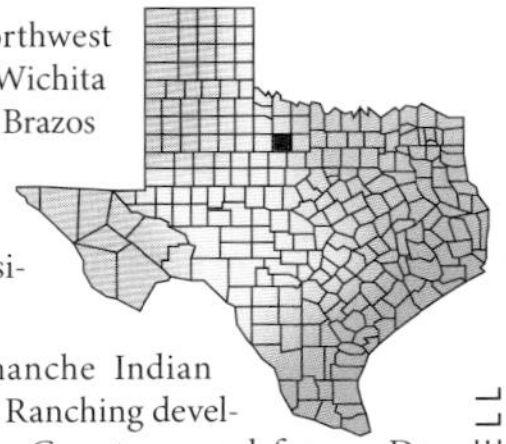

Physical Features: Northwest county southwest of Wichita Falls; rolling, between Brazos forks; red to black soils.

Economy: Oil, agribusiness, hunting.

History: Site of Comanche Indian Reservation 1854-59. Ranching developed after Civil War. County named for Dr. W.E. Throckmorton, father of Gov. J.W. Throckmorton; county created from Fannin in 1858; organized in 1879.

Race/Ethnicity: Anglo, 84.5%; Black, 0.4%; Hispanic, 13.2%; Asian, 0.4%; Other, 1.2%.

Vital Statistics, annual: Births, 10; deaths, 30; marriages, 18; divorces, 2.

Recreation: Hunting, fishing; historic sites include Camp Cooper, site of former Comanche reservation, restored ranch home; Millers Creek Reservoir; wild game dinner in January.

Minerals: Natural gas, oil.

Agriculture: Beef cattle, horses, wheat, hay. Market value $27.3 million. Mesquite firewood sold. Hunting leases important.

THROCKMORTON (735) county seat; varied manufacturing, oil-field services; hospital; Old Jail museum.

Other towns include: **Elbert** (21), **Woodson** (234).

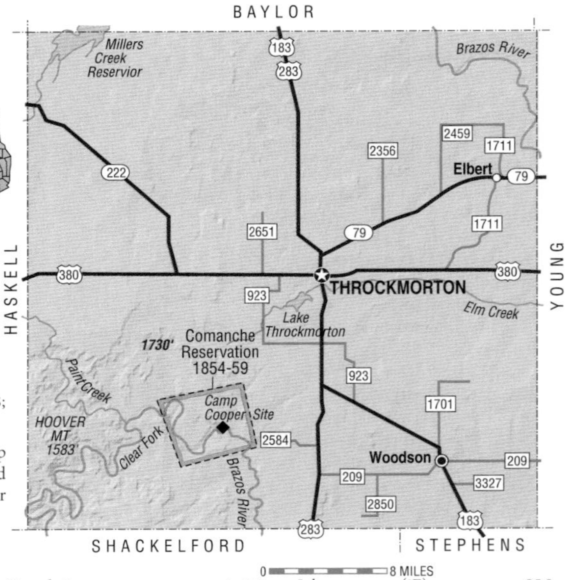

Population	**1,448**	July mean max (°F)	95.8
Change from 2010 (%)	-11.8	Civ. Labor	654
Area (sq. mi.)	915.5	Unemployed (%)	4.9
Land Area (sq. mi.)	912.6	Wages	$3,174,541
Altitude (ft.)	1,100–1,730	Per Capita Income	$41,454
Rainfall (in.)	29.8	Prop. Value	$960,145,352
Jan. mean min (°F)	29.6	Retail Sales	$8,006,418

Titus County

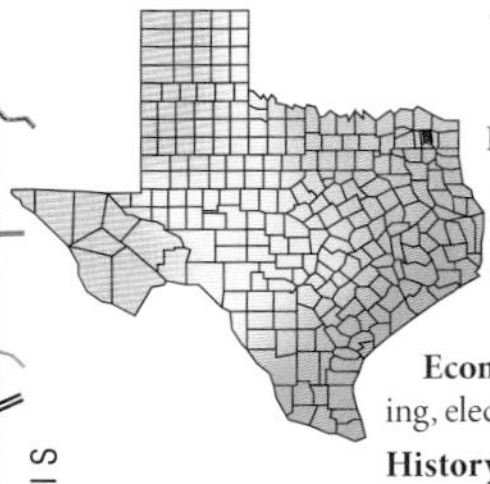

Physical Features: Northeast Texas county; hilly, timbered; drains to Big Cypress Creek, Sulphur River; Lake Bob Sandlin, Welsh Reservoir, Monticello Reservoir.

Economy: Agribusiness, varied manufacturing, electric power generation.

History: Caddo area. Cherokees and other tribes settled in the 1820s. Anglo-American settlers arrived in the 1840s. Named for pioneer settler A.J. Titus; county created from Bowie and Red River counties in 1846, organized the same year.

Race/Ethnicity: Anglo, 44%; Black, 9.7%; Hispanic, 43.6%; Asian, 0.7%; Other, 1.7%.

Vital Statistics, annual: Births, 500; deaths, 311; marriages, 237; divorces, 36.

Recreation: Fishing, hunting, lake activities, state park, rodeo, railroad museum, flower gardens.

Minerals: Lignite coal, oil, gas.

Agriculture: Poultry, beef cattle, hay, horticulture, horses. Market value $149.3 million. Timber sales significant.

MOUNT PLEASANT (17,064) county seat; tourism, varied manufacturing, food-processing plants; hospital; Northeast Texas Community College; jubilee and outhouse races in May.

Other towns include: **Cookville** (105), **Millers Cove** (161), **Talco** (499), **Winfield** (528).

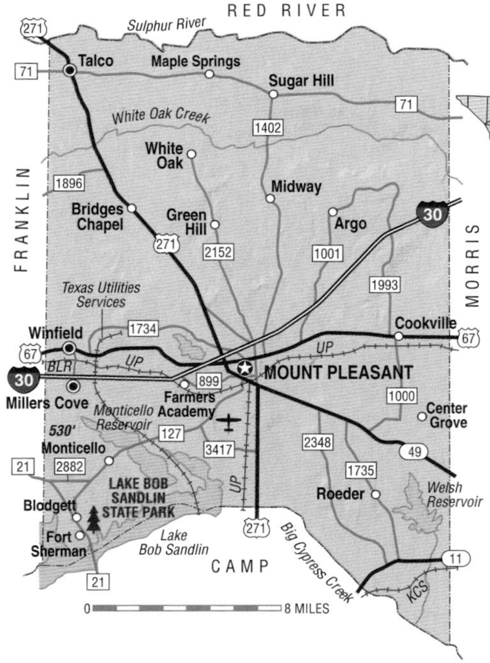

Population	**33,690**	Rainfall (in.)	47.7	Wages	$218,658,464
Change from 2010 (%)	4.2	Jan. mean min (°F)	31.1	Per Capita Income	$37,070
Area (sq. mi.)	425.6	July mean max (°F)	92.9	Prop. Value	$3,590,285,664
Land Area (sq. mi.)	406.1	Civ. Labor	13,443	Retail Sales	$861,305,538
Altitude (ft.)	250–530	Unemployed (%)	5.6		

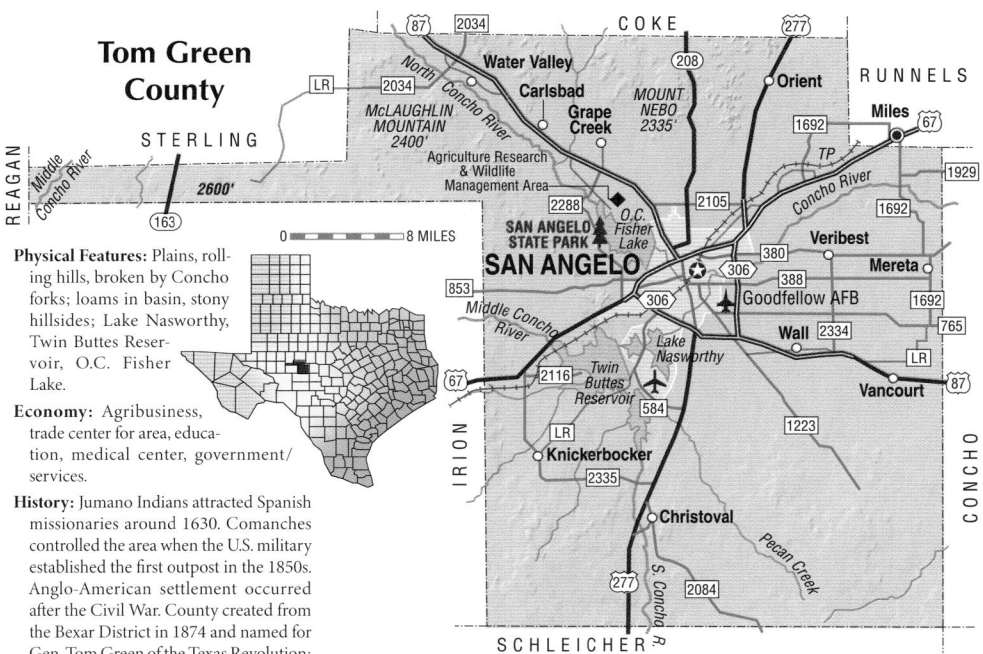

Tom Green County

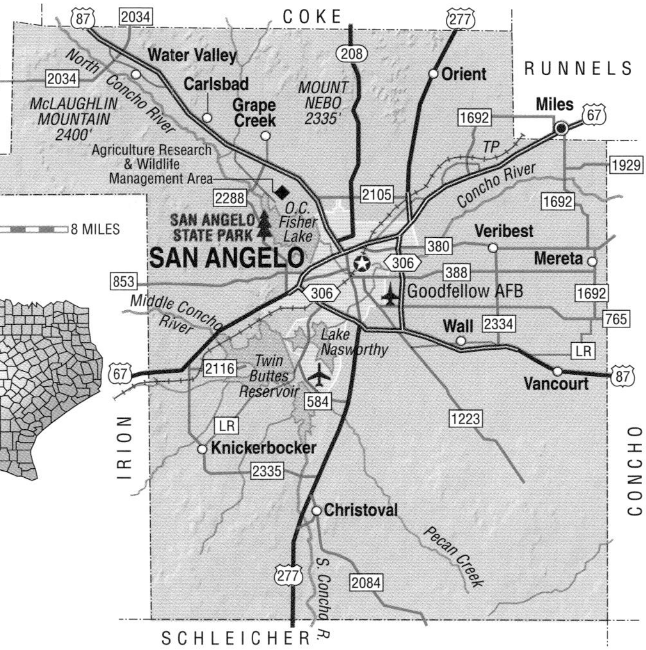

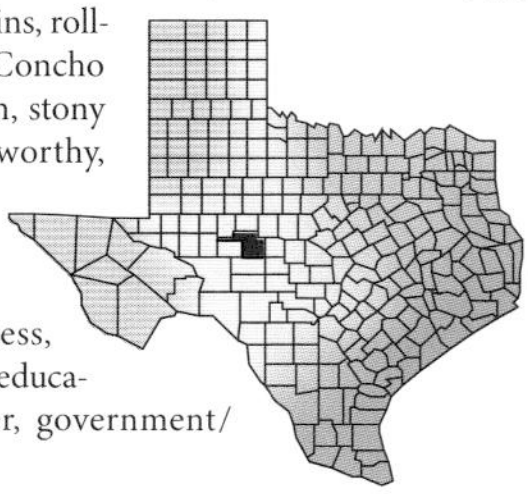

Physical Features: Plains, rolling hills, broken by Concho forks; loams in basin, stony hillsides; Lake Nasworthy, Twin Buttes Reservoir, O.C. Fisher Lake.

Economy: Agribusiness, trade center for area, education, medical center, government/services.

History: Jumano Indians attracted Spanish missionaries around 1630. Comanches controlled the area when the U.S. military established the first outpost in the 1850s. Anglo-American settlement occurred after the Civil War. County created from the Bexar District in 1874 and named for Gen. Tom Green of the Texas Revolution; organized in 1875; twelve other counties were created from the original area.

Race/Ethnicity: Anglo, 50.9%; Black, 3.7%; Hispanic, 42%; Asian, 1%; Other, 2.1%.

Vital Statistics, annual: Births, 1,721; deaths, 973; marriages, 926; divorces, 349.

Recreation: Water sports, hunting, Fort Concho museum, symphony, Christmas at Old Fort Concho, February rodeo.

Minerals: Oil, natural gas.

Agriculture: Cotton, beef cattle, goats, sheep (third in number), small grains, milo. About 30,000 acres irrigated. Market value $100.0 million.

SAN ANGELO (100,052) county seat; government/services, retail, transportation, education; hospitals, Angelo State University, Howard Junior College branch; riverwalk; Museum of Fine Arts, drag boat races in June.

Other towns include: **Carlsbad** (780); **Christoval** (576); **Grape Creek** (3,201); **Knickerbocker** (94); **Mereta** (131); **Vancourt** (131); **Veribest** (115); **Wall** (329); **Water Valley** (203).

Population	**117,613**
Change from 2010 (%)	6.7
Area (sq. mi.)	1,540.6
Land Area (sq. mi.)	1,522.0
Altitude (ft.)	1,675–2,600
Rainfall (in.)	23.0
Jan. mean min (°F)	29.6
July mean max (°F)	94.5
Civ. Labor	53,714
Unemployed (%)	5.2
Wages	$585,376,492
Per Capita Income	$48,876
Prop. Value	$10,112,719,265
Retail Sales	$2,150,771,436

For explanation of sources, symbols and abbreviations, see p. 204, and foldout map.

Farm animals spotted just outside Mount Pleasant in Titus County. Photo by Carol M. Highsmith, courtesy of the Library of Congress

Travis County

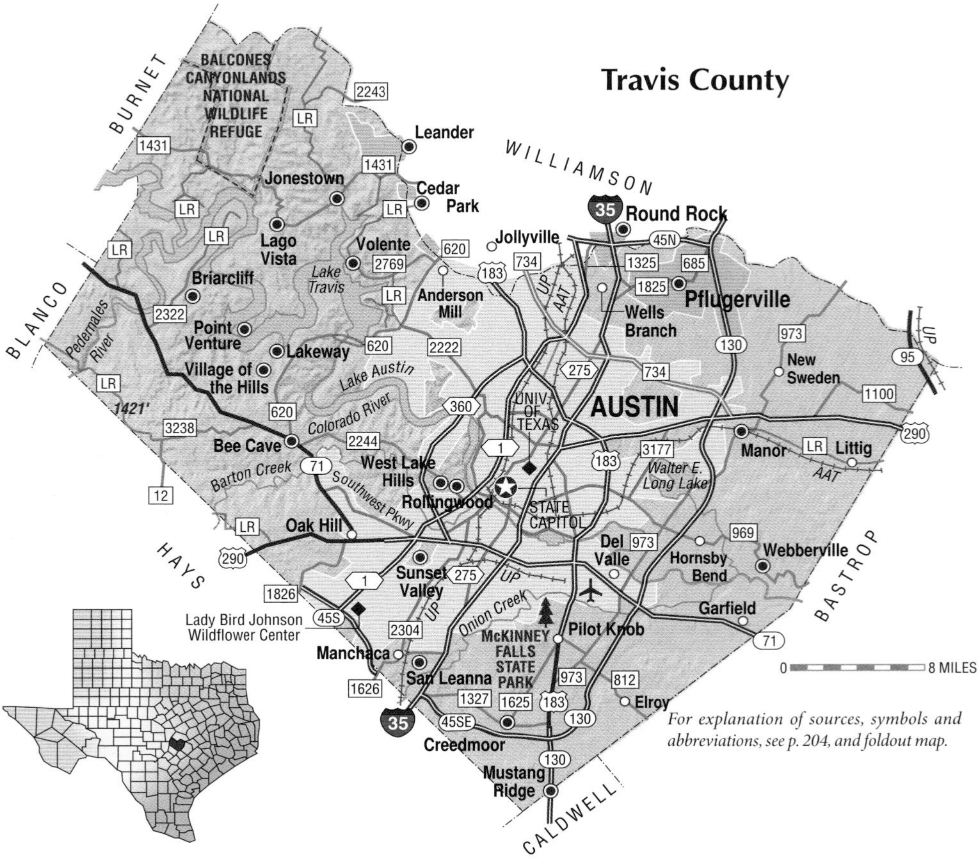

For explanation of sources, symbols and abbreviations, see p. 204, and foldout map.

Physical Features: Central county of scenic hills, broken by Colorado River; Lake Travis, Lake Austin, Lady Bird Lake, Walter E. Long Lake; cedars, pecans, other trees; diverse soils, mineral deposits.

Economy: Government/services, education, technology, research, and industry.

History: Tonkawa and Lipan Apache area; Comanches, Kiowas arrived about 1700. Spanish missions from East Texas temporarily relocated near Barton Springs in 1730 before removing to San Antonio. Anglo-Americans arrived in the early 1830s. County created in 1840, when Austin became Republic's capital, from Bastrop County; organized in 1843; named for Alamo commander Col. William B. Travis; many other counties created from its original area.

Race/Ethnicity: Anglo, 47.8%; Black, 8.1%; Hispanic, 34.7%; Asian, 6.5%; Other, 2.7%.

Vital Statistics, annual: Births, 16,297; deaths, 5,380; marriages, 9,906; divorces, 2,469.

Recreation: Colorado River lakes, hunting, fishing; McKinney Falls State Park; LBJ Presidential Library, Lady Bird Johnson Wildflower Center; collegiate, metropolitan, governmental events; official buildings and historic sites; museums, including Bullock state history museum; Sixth St. restoration area; scenic drives; many city parks; South by Southwest film, music festival in March.

Minerals: Production of lime, stone, sand, gravel, oil and gas.

Agriculture: Cattle, nursery crops, hogs; sorghum, corn, cotton, small grains, pecans. Market value $28.1 million.

Education: University of Texas, St. Edward's University, Concordia Lutheran University, Huston-Tillotson College, Austin Community College, Episcopal and Presbyterian seminaries.

AUSTIN (984,115, part [55,385] in Williamson County) county seat and state capital; state and federal payrolls, IRS center, high-tech industries, healthcare/hospitals, including state institutions for blind, deaf, mental illnesses; popular retirement area. Anderson Mill, Del Valle, and Oak Hill are now part of Austin.

Other towns include: **Bee Cave** (6,897) retail, tourism, SpringFest in April; **Briarcliff** (1,775); **Creedmoor** (222); **Garfield** (1,845); **Jonestown** (2,092) tourism, retail, commuters, Chili Pod chili cookoff in April; **Lago Vista** (7,335); **Lakeway** (15,981) residential real estate, retail, tourism, lake activities; **Manchaca** (1,233); **Manor** (13,817); **Mustang Ridge** (957, partly in Caldwell County).

Also, **Pflugerville** (67,738) high-tech industries, agriculture, government/services, Deutchenfest in May; **Point Venture** (1,043); **Rollingwood** (1,585); **San Leanna** (540); **Sunset Valley** (663); **The Hills** (2,480) residential community; **Volente** (597); **Webberville** (466); **Wells Branch** (13,772); **West Lake Hills** (3,250).

Also, part [8,447] of **Cedar Park,** part [882] of **Jollyville,** and part [1,779] of **Round Rock,** all mostly in Williamson County.

Population	**1,273,554**
Change from 2010 (%)	24.3
Area (sq. mi.)	1,023.0
Land Area (sq. mi.)	990.2
Altitude (ft.)	400–1,421
Rainfall (in.)	34.3
Jan. mean min (°F)	36.3
July mean max (°F)	95.2
Civ. Labor	755,518
Unemployed (%)	4.5
Wages	$16,225,051,190
Per Capita Income	$71,666
Prop. Value	$282,103,045,807
Retail Sales	$20,675,125,912

Trinity County

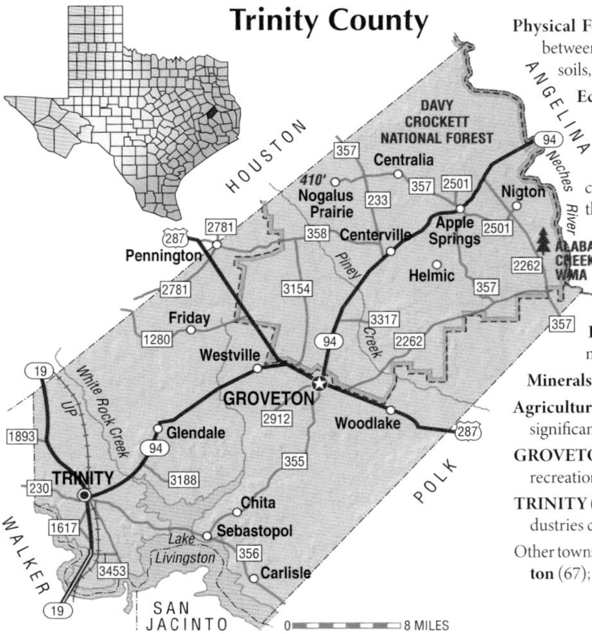

Physical Features: Heavily forested East Texas county of hills, between Neches and Trinity (Lake Livingston) rivers; rich alluvial soils, sandy upland; 67,910 acres in national forest.

Economy: Forestry, cattle, tourism, government/services.

History: Caddoes, reduced by disease in the late 1700s. Kickapoo, Alabama, and Coushatta in area when Anglo-Americans settled in the 1840s. Named for river; county created in 1850 out of Houston County, organized the same year.

Race/Ethnicity: Anglo, 78.5%; Black, 9.8%; Hispanic, 9%; Asian, 0.2%; Other, 2.1%.

Vital Statistics, annual: Births, 151; deaths, 225; marriages, 71; divorces, 40.

Recreation: Lake activities, fishing, hiking, hunting, national forest, historic site.

Minerals: Limited oil, gas, sand and gravel.

Agriculture: Beef cattle. Market value $8.2 million. Timber sales significant. Hunting leases, fishing.

GROVETON (1,055) county seat; logging, government/services, recreation; museum, library; Bear Chase marathon in April.

TRINITY (2,741) government/services, steel fabrication, forest-industries center, commuters; hospital.

Other towns include: **Apple Springs** (350); **Centralia** (190); **Pennington** (67); **Sebastopol** (300) historic town; **Woodlake** (180).

Population	**14,530**
Change from 2010 (%)	-0.4
Area (sq. mi.)	714.0
Land Area (sq. mi.)	693.6
Altitude (ft.)	131–410
Rainfall (in.)	49.3
Jan. mean min (°F)	35.1
July mean max (°F)	92.9
Civ. Labor	5,369
Unemployed (%)	7.7
Wages	$21,209,409
Per Capita Income	$36,062
Prop. Value	$2,405,853,452
Retail Sales	$82,961,027

Tyler County

Physical Features: Hilly East Texas county; densely timbered; drains to Neches River; B.A. Steinhagen Lake; Big Thicket is unique plant and animal area.

Economy: Lumbering, government/services, some manufacturing, tourism, hunting leases.

History: Caddoan area. Cherokees, Alabama, and Coushatta pushed into area from U.S. South in the 1820s. Anglo-Americans settled in the 1830s. Named for U.S. President John Tyler; county created in 1846 from Liberty County, organized the same year.

Race/Ethnicity: Anglo, 78.5%; Black, 11.5%; Hispanic, 7.4%; Asian, 0.2%; Other, 2.2%..

Vital Statistics, annual: Births, 213; deaths, 274; marriages, 138; divorces, 80.

Recreation: Big Thicket National Preserve; Heritage Village; lake activities; Allan Shivers Museum; state forest; historic sites; dogwood festival in spring; rodeo, frontier frolics in September; gospel music fest in June.

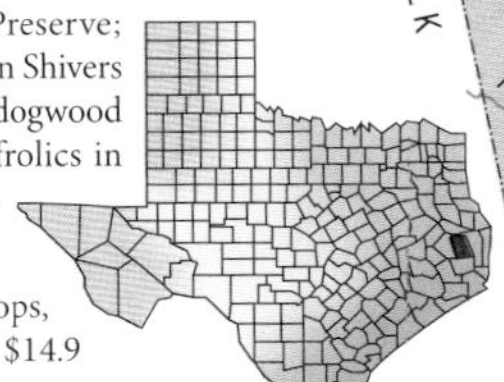

Minerals: Oil, natural gas.

Agriculture: Cattle, hay, nursery crops, blueberries, horses. Market value $14.9 million. Timber sales significant.

WOODVILLE (2,727) county seat; lumber, cattle market, varied manufacturing, tourism; hospital, prison.

Other towns include: **Chester** (324) **Colmesneil** (603), **Doucette** (160), **Fred** (300), **Hillister** (250), **Ivanhoe** (2,001), **Spurger** (590), **Warren** (882).

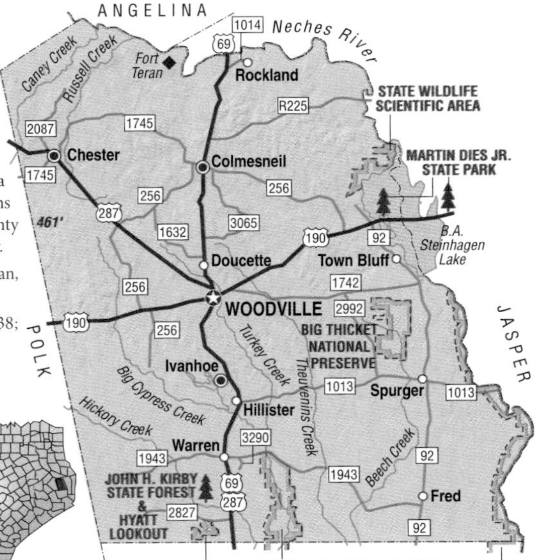

Population	**22,735**
Change from 2010 (%)	4.5
Area (sq. mi.)	935.6
Land Area (sq. mi.)	924.5
Altitude (ft.)	50–461
Rainfall (in.)	56.2
Jan. mean min (°F)	37.5
July mean max (°F)	91.8
Civ. Labor	7,456
Unemployed (%)	9.1
Wages	$41,101,968
Per Capita Income	$32,978
Prop. Value	$2,797,139,982
Retail Sales	$147,313,630

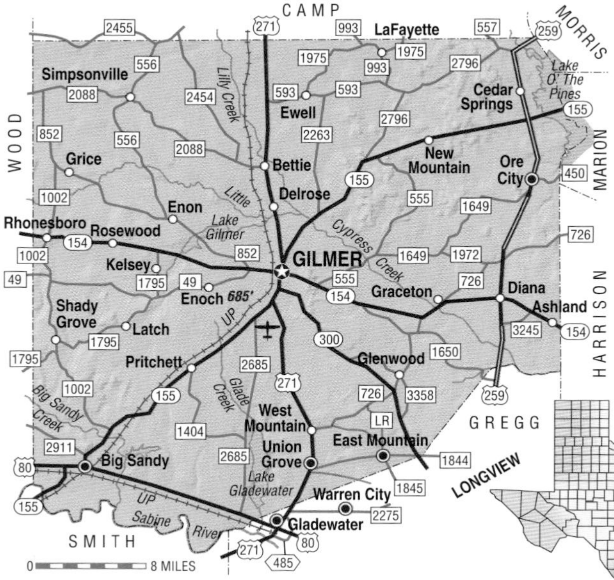

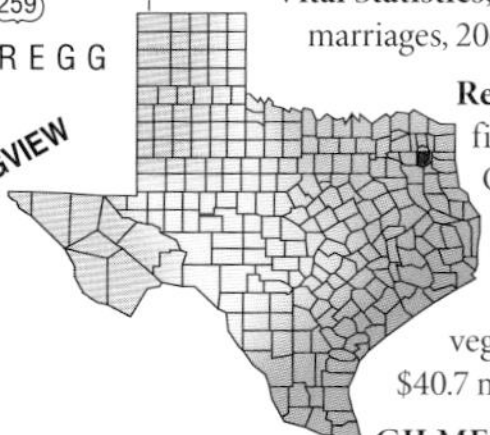

Upshur County

Physical Features: East Texas county; rolling to hilly, over half forested; drains to Sabine River, Little Cypress Creek, Lake O' the Pines, Lake Gilmer, Lake Gladewater.

Economy: Manufacturing, oil, gas, agribusiness, timber.

History: Caddoes; reduced by epidemics in the 1700s. Cherokees in area in the 1820s. Anglo-American settlement in the mid-1830s. County created from Harrison, Nacogdoches counties in 1846, organized the same year; named for U.S. Secretary of State A.P. Upshur.

Race/Ethnicity: Anglo, 78.9%; Black, 7.8%; Hispanic, 9.8%; Asian, 0.3%; Other, 2.8%.

Vital Statistics, annual: Births, 449; deaths, 471; marriages, 206; divorces, 174.

Recreation: Scenic trails, hunting, fishing, fall foliage, Yamboree in October at Gilmer.

Minerals: Oil, gas, sand, gravel.

Agriculture: Dairies, cattle, hay, vegetable crops, poultry. Market value $40.7 million. Timber a major product.

GILMER (5,085) county seat; agriculture, communications, electric power; museum; trails, parks; site of Cherokee village.

Other towns include: **Big Sandy** (1,402); **Diana** (585); **East Mountain** (851); **Ore City** (1,227); **Union Grove** (373). Part of **Gladewater** (6,341).

Population	**41,204**
Change from 2010 (%)	4.8
Area (sq. mi.)	592.6
Land Area (sq. mi.)	583.0
Altitude (ft.)	228–685
Rainfall (in.)	47.1
Jan. mean min (°F)	31.4
July mean max (°F)	93.4
Civ. Labor	17,433
Unemployed (%)	6.7
Wages	$77,438,104
Per Capita Income	$37,563
Prop. Value	$3,543,555,804
Retail Sales	$294,717,018

Upton County

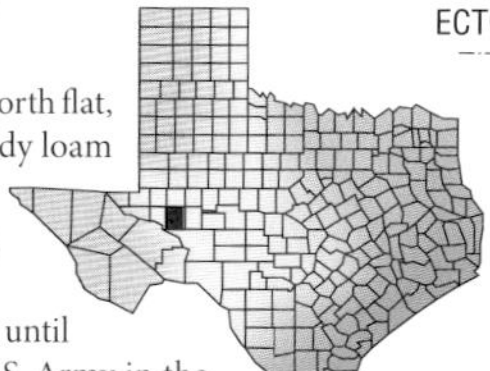

Physical Features: Western county; north flat, south rolling, hilly; limestone, sandy loam soils, drains to creeks.

Economy: Oil, wind turbines, farming, ranching.

History: Apache and Comanche area until the tribes were removed by the U.S. Army in the 1870s. Sheep and cattle ranching developed in the 1880s. Oil discovered in 1925. County created in 1887 from Tom Green County; organized in 1910; the name honors brothers John and William Upton, Confederate colonels.

Race/Ethnicity: Anglo, 40.8%; Black, 1.2%; Hispanic, 56.4%; Asian, 0%; Other, 1.4%.

Vital Statistics, annual: Births, 61; deaths, 36; marriages, 32; divorces, 17.

Recreation: Historic sites, Mendoza Trail museum, scenic areas, dinosaur tracks west of McCamey.

Minerals: Oil, natural gas.

Agriculture: Cotton, sheep, goats, cattle, watermelons, pecans. Extensive irrigation. Market value $19.1 million.

RANKIN (846) county seat, oil, ranching, farming; hospital; Barbados cookoff in May, All Kid rodeo in June.

McCAMEY (2,065) government/services, wind and solar power, oil; hospital; Wind Energy cookoff and festival in September.

Other town: **Midkiff** (182).

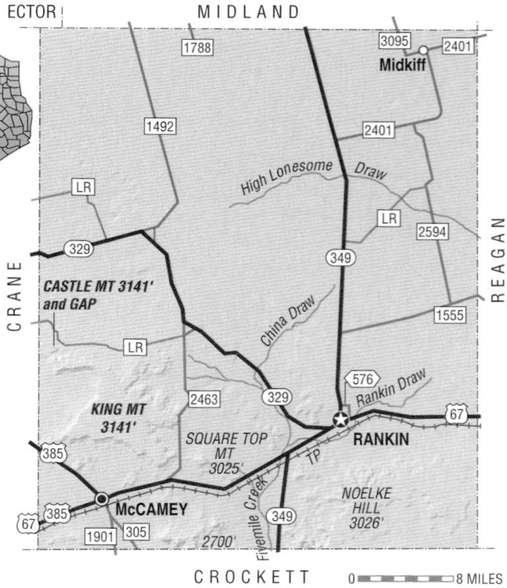

Population	**3,619**
Change from 2010 (%)	7.9
Area (sq. mi.)	1,241.5
Land Area (sq. mi.)	1,241.3
Altitude (ft.)	2,310–3,141
Rainfall (in.)	15.1
Jan. mean min (°F)	31.9
July mean max (°F)	95.3
Civ. Labor	1,931
Unemployed (%)	5.3
Wages	$38,765,943
Per Capita Income	$47,118
Prop. Value	$8,038,930,930
Retail Sales	$30,945,104

Uvalde County

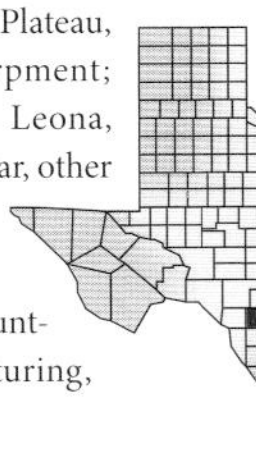

Physical Features: Edwards Plateau, rolling hills below escarpment; spring-fed Sabinal, Frio, Leona, Nueces rivers; cypress, cedar, other trees, including maple groves.

Economy: Agribusinesses, hunting leases, light manufacturing, tourism.

History: Mission Nuestra Señora de la Candelaria founded in 1762 for Lipan Apaches near present-day Montell; Comanches harassed mission. U.S. military outpost established in 1849. County created from Bexar in 1850; re-created and organized in 1856; named for 1778 governor of Coahuila, Juan de Ugalde, with name Anglicized.

Race/Ethnicity: Anglo, 25.1%; Black, 0.4%; Hispanic, 73%; Asian, 0.4%; Other, 0.9%.

Vital Statistics, annual: Births, 429; deaths, 233; marriages, 159; divorces, 14.

Recreation: Deer, turkey hunting; Garner State Park; water activities on rivers; John Nance Garner museum; Uvalde Memorial Park; scenic trails, historic sites.

Minerals: Asphalt, stone, sand, gravel.

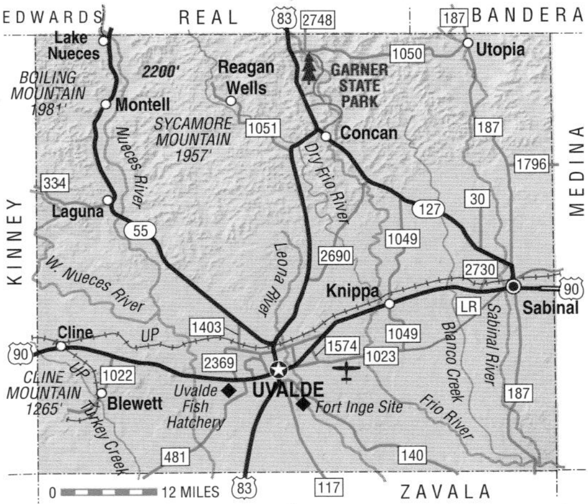

Agriculture: Cattle, vegetables, corn, cotton, sorghum, sheep, goats, hay, wheat. Substantial irrigation. Market value $87.1 million.

UVALDE (16,086) county seat; vegetable, wool, mohair processing, tourism; opera house; junior college, A&M research center; hospital; Fort Inge Day in April.

SABINAL (1,705) farm, ranch center, tourism, retirement area.

Other towns include: **Concan** (500); **Knippa** (639); **Utopia** (213) resort; **Uvalde Estates** (2,228).

Population	**26,743**
Change from 2010 (%)	1.3
Area (sq. mi.)	1,558.6
Land Area (sq. mi.)	1,552.0
Altitude (ft.)	650–2,200
Rainfall (in.)	24.6
Jan. mean min (°F)	38.6
July mean max (°F)	96.1
Civ. Labor	11,292
Unemployed (%)	6.1
Wages	$102,003,337
Per Capita Income	$41,116
Prop. Value	$4,394,155,349
Retail Sales	$399,754,064

Val Verde County

Physical Features: Southwestern county bordering Mexico, rolling, hilly; brushy; Devils, Pecos rivers, Rio Grande and Amistad Reservoir; limestone, alluvial soils.

Economy: Agribusiness, tourism, trade center, military, Border Patrol, hunting leases, fishing.

History: Apaches, Coahuiltecans, Jumanos present when Spanish came through in the late 1500s. Comanches arrived later. U.S. military outpost established in 1850s to protect settlers. Only county named for Civil War battle; Val Verde means green valley. Created in 1885 from Crockett, Kinney, Pecos counties, organized the same year.

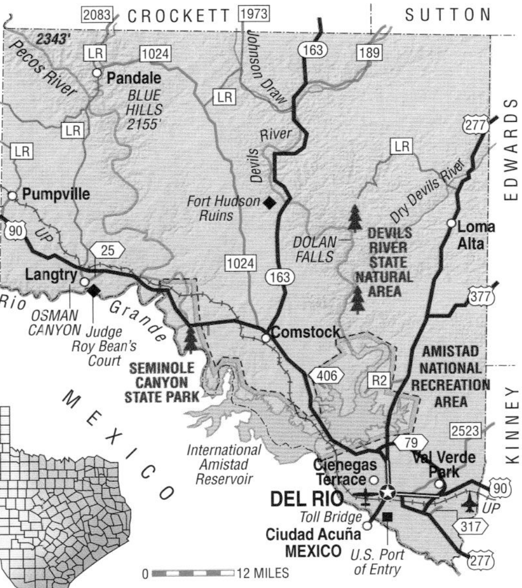

Race/Ethnicity: Anglo, 15.2%; Black, 1.2%; Hispanic, 82%; Asian, 0.4%; Other, 1%.

Vital Statistics, annual: Births, 904; deaths, 353; marriages, 478; divorces, 172.

Recreation: Gateway to Mexico; deer hunting, fishing; Amistad lake activities; two state parks; Langtry restoration of Judge Roy Bean's saloon; ancient pictographs; San Felipe Springs; winery.

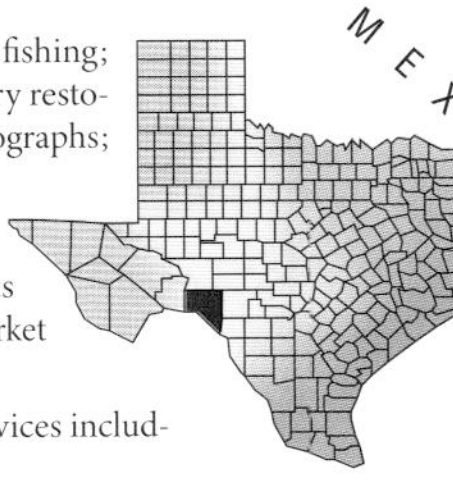

Minerals: Production sand and gravel, gas, oil.

Agriculture: Sheep, Angora goats, meat goats (second in numbers); cattle; minor irrigation. Market value $9.4 million.

DEL RIO (35,982) county seat; government/services including federal agencies/military, agribusiness, tourism; hospital, extension colleges; Fiesta de Amistad in October.

Laughlin Air Force Base (1,502).

Other towns and places include: **Cienegas Terrace** (3,804); **Comstock** (344); **Langtry** (30); **Val Verde Park** (2,648).

Population	**50,853**
Change from 2010 (%)	4.0
Area (sq. mi.)	323.7
Land Area (sq. mi.)	3,144.8
Altitude (ft.)	845–2,343
Rainfall (in.)	20.2
Jan. mean min (°F)	38.7
July mean max (°F)	96.4
Civ. Labor	21,726
Unemployed (%)	6.6
Wages	$194,649,485
Per Capita Income	$38,331
Prop. Value	$4,489,519,292
Retail Sales	$647,146,418

Van Zandt County

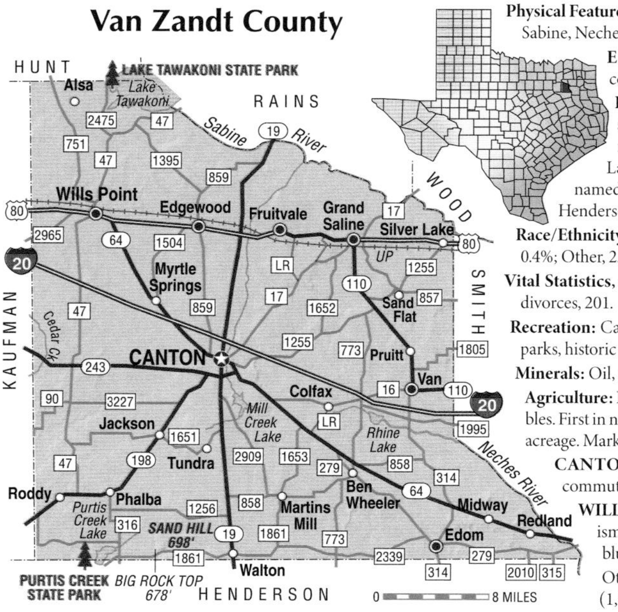

Physical Features: Eastern county in three soil belts; level to rolling; Sabine, Neches rivers; Lake Tawakoni; partly forested.

Economy: Agriculture, government/services, commuters to Dallas/Tyler.

History: Caddo tribes, reduced by epidemics before settlers arrived. Cherokees settled in the 1820s; removed in 1839 under policies of Republic President Lamar; Anglo-American settlement followed. County named for Republic leader Isaac Van Zandt; created from Henderson County in 1848, organized the same year.

Race/Ethnicity: Anglo, 83.3%; Black, 2.8%; Hispanic, 10.8%; Asian, 0.4%; Other, 2.5%.

Vital Statistics, annual: Births, 608; deaths, 621; marriages, 337; divorces, 201.

Recreation: Canton First Monday trade days, lake activities, state parks, historic sites.

Minerals: Oil, gas.

Agriculture: Nurseries, beef cattle, hay and foliage, dairies, vegetables. First in nursery stock acreage in the open and in sweet potato acreage. Market value $104.6 million.

CANTON (3,966) county seat; tourism, agribusiness, commuters; museums, bluegrass festival in June.

WILLS POINT (3,777) government/services, retail, tourism, commuters to Dallas and Tyler; depot museum, bluebird festival in April.

Other towns include: **Ben Wheeler** (504); **Edgewood** (1,554) commuters, heritage park, antiques; **Edom** (397) arts and crafts; **Fruitvale** (433); **Grand Saline** (3,311) salt plant, agriculture, medical services/hospital, Salt Palace museum, salt prairie marsh, birding, Salt Festival in June; **Van** (2,875) oil center, hay, cattle, oil festival in October.

Population	**56,376**
Change from 2010 (%)	7.2
Area (sq. mi.)	859.6
Land Area (sq. mi.)	842.6
Altitude (ft.)	330–698
Rainfall (in.)	44.2
Jan. mean min (°F)	33.7
July mean max (°F)	93.7
Civ. Labor	26,225
Unemployed (%)	5.1
Wages	$114,324,765
Per Capita Income	$39,609
Prop. Value	$6,538,106,440
Retail Sales	$561,127,502

Victoria County

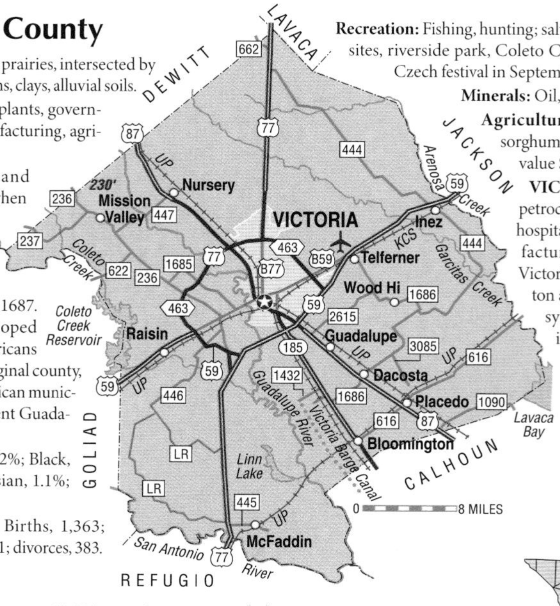

Physical Features: Rolling prairies, intersected by many streams; sandy loams, clays, alluvial soils.

Economy: Petrochemical plants, government/services, oil, manufacturing, agribusiness, tourism.

History: Karankawas and other tribes in the area when Spanish explored in 1528. Comanches, Tawakonis arrived later. La Salle's camp on Garcitas Creek 1685–1687. Spanish ranching developed in the 1750s. Anglo-Americans arrived after 1836. An original county, created in 1836 from Mexican municipality named for President Guadalupe Victoria of Mexico.

Race/Ethnicity: Anglo, 44.2%; Black, 6%; Hispanic, 46.9%; Asian, 1.1%; Other, 1.5%.

Vital Statistics, annual: Births, 1,363; deaths, 847; marriages, 621; divorces, 383.

Recreation: Fishing, hunting; saltwater activities, historic homes, sites, riverside park, Coleto Creek Reservoir and park, zoo, Czech festival in September at Victoria.

Minerals: Oil, gas, sand, gravel.

Agriculture: Corn, beef cattle, grain sorghums, cotton, rice, soybeans. Market value $58.4 million.

VICTORIA (66,891) county seat; petrochemicals, government/services, hospitals/healthcare, retail, oil, manufacturing, agribusiness, tourism; Victoria College, University of Houston at Victoria; community theater, symphony, museums; Bootfeast in October.

Other towns include: **Bloomington** (2,488), **Inez** (2,357), **Nursery** (600), **Placedo** (753), **Telferner** (700).

Population	**91,329**
Change from 2010 (%)	5.2
Area (sq. mi.)	888.8
Land Area (sq. mi.)	882.1
Altitude (ft.)	sea level–230
Rainfall (in.)	41.1
Jan. mean min (°F)	40.7
July mean max (°F)	94.1
Civ. Labor	40,682
Unemployed (%)	7
Wages	$453,788,173
Per Capita Income	$48,938
Prop. Value	$9,964,443,013
Retail Sales	$1,811,390,475

Walker County

For explanation of sources, symbols and abbreviations, see p. 204, and foldout map.

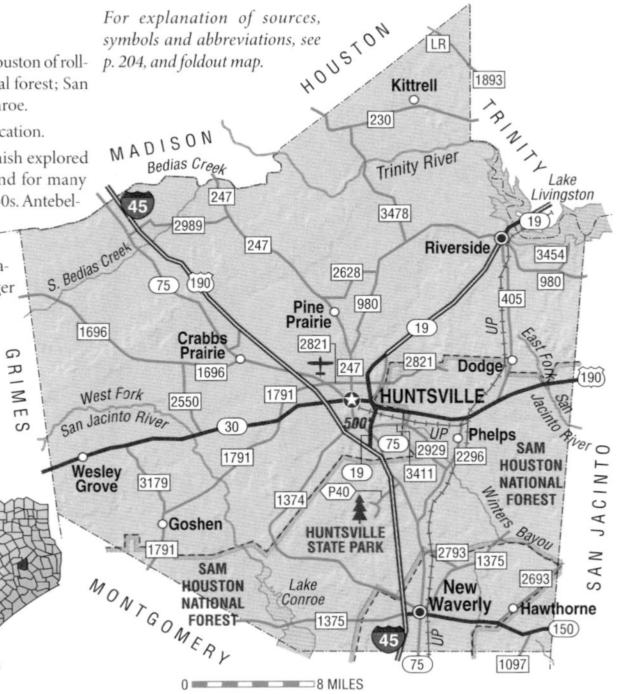

Physical Features: South central county north of Houston of rolling hills; more than 70 percent forested; national forest; San Jacinto, Trinity rivers; Lake Livingston, Lake Conroe.

Economy: State employment in prison system, education.

History: Coahuiltecans, Bidais in area when Spanish explored around 1690. Later, area became trading ground for many Indian tribes. Anglo-Americans settled in the 1830s. Antebellum slaveholding area. County created in 1846 from Montgomery County and organized the same year; first named for U.S. Secretary of the Treasury R.J. Walker; renamed 1863 for Texas Ranger Capt. S.H. Walker.

Race/Ethnicity: Anglo, 55.1%; Black, 22.6%; Hispanic, 19.2%; Asian, 1%; Other, 1.8%.

Vital Statistics, annual: Births, 667; deaths, 513; marriages, 435; divorces, 203.

Recreation: Fishing, hunting, lake activities; Sam Houston museum, homes, grave; prison museum; other historic sites, state park, Sam Houston National Forest; Sam Houston folk festival in spring.

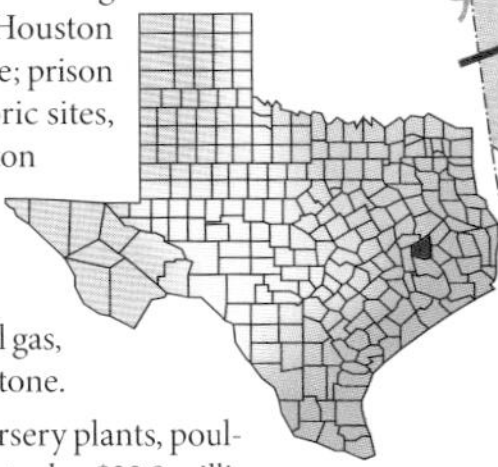

Minerals: Clays, natural gas, oil, sand and gravel, stone.

Agriculture: Cattle, nursery plants, poultry, cotton, hay. Market value $33.8 million. Timber sales substantial.

HUNTSVILLE (43,899) county seat; state prison system, Sam Houston State University, forest products, varied manufacturing; hospital; museums, arts center.

Other towns include: **Dodge** (150), **New Waverly** (1,062), **Riverside** (585).

Population	**75,949**	July mean max (°F)	93.3
Change from 2010 (%)	11.9	Civ. Labor	24,013
Area (sq. mi.)	801.5	Unemployed (%)	6.6
Land Area (sq. mi.)	784.2	Wages	$285,133,649
Altitude (ft.)	131–500	Per Capita Income	$29,838
Rainfall (in.)	49.1	Prop. Value	$7,225,783,075
Jan. mean min (°F)	39.7	Retail Sales	$821,750,519

The Victoria County Monument in Memorial Square Park was designed for the Texas Centennial in 1936. It is on the National Register of Historic Places. Photo by Larry D. Moore, CC by SA 4.0/Wikimedia Commons

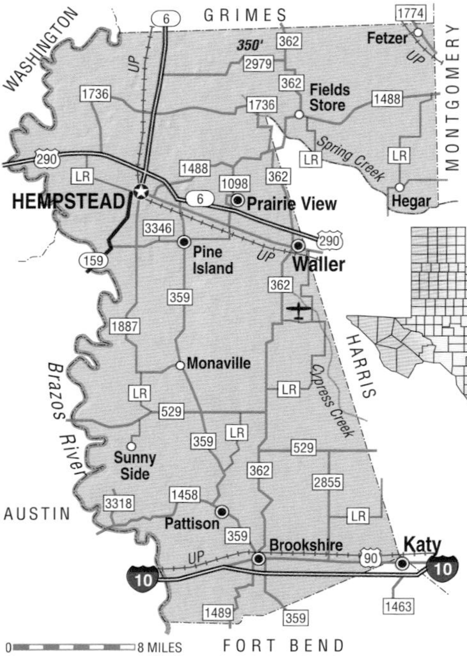

Waller County

Physical Features: South central county west of Houston on rolling prairie; drains to Brazos; alluvial soils; about 20 percent forested.

Economy: Agribusiness, education, equine-related businesses, part of Houston metropolitan area.

History: Bidais Indians reduced to about 100 when Anglo-Americans settled in 1820s. Antebellum slaveholding area. County named for Edwin Waller, Republic leader; created in 1873 from Austin, Grimes counties, organized the same year.

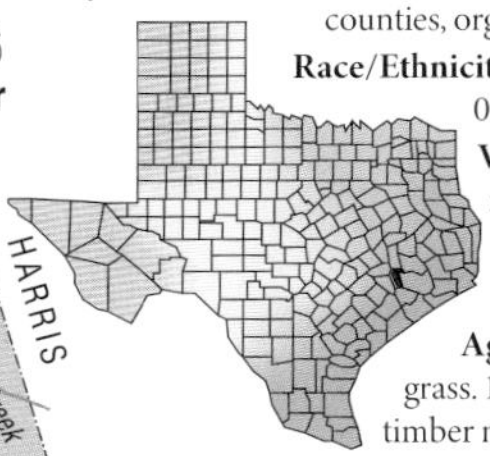

Race/Ethnicity: Anglo, 43.7%; Black, 23.4%; Hispanic, 30.7%; Asian, 0.5%; Other, 1.5%.

Vital Statistics, annual: Births, 592; deaths, 305; marriages, 321; divorces, 103.

Recreation: Fishing, hunting; historic sites; museum.

Minerals: Oil, gas.

Agriculture: Cattle, hay, rice, greenhouse nurseries, turf grass. 10,000 acres irrigated. Market value $102.4 million. Some timber marketed.

HEMPSTEAD (7,507) county seat; varied manufacturing, commuting to Houston, agribusiness center, large vegetable market; watermelon fest in July.

PRAIRIE VIEW (6,625) home of Prairie View A&M University.

Other towns include: **Brookshire** (5,937), **Pattison** (628), **Pine Island** (1,200), **Waller** (3,119, partly in Harris County) agriculture, education, construction.

Also, part [2,081] of **Katy** (21,729, mostly in Harris County) hospitals.

Population	**54,822**	Rainfall (in.)	45.5	Wages	$271,409,883
Change from 2010 (%)	26.9	Jan. mean min (°F)	38.0	Per Capita Income	$42,456
Area (sq. mi.)	517.8	July mean max (°F)	95.0	Prop. Value	$11,554,542,051
Land Area (sq. mi.)	513.4	Civ. Labor	24,052	Retail Sales	$566,535,524
Altitude (ft.)	100–350	Unemployed (%)	7		

Ward County

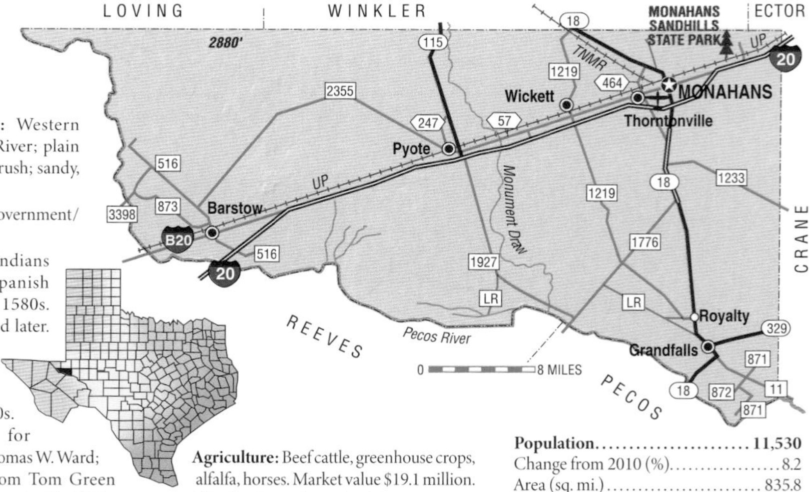

Physical Features: Western county on Pecos River; plain covered by grass, brush; sandy, loam soils.

Economy: Oil, gas, government/services.

History: Jumano Indians in area when Spanish explored in the 1580s. Comanches arrived later. Railroad stations established in the 1880s. Oil discovered in the 1920s. County named for Republic leader Thomas W. Ward; county created from Tom Green County in 1887; organized in 1892.

Race/Ethnicity: Anglo, 37.1%; Black, 4.3%; Hispanic, 56.8%; Asian, 0.3%; Other, 1.2%.

Vital Statistics, annual: Births, 198; deaths, 134; marriages, 103; divorces, 26.

Recreation: Sandhills state park, camel treks, Million Barrel museum in Monahans, county park, Butterfield stagecoach festival in July.

Minerals: Oil, gas, caliche, sand, gravel.

Agriculture: Beef cattle, greenhouse crops, alfalfa, horses. Market value $19.1 million. Hunting leases important.

MONAHANS (7,801) county seat; oil and gas, tourism, ranching; hospital, Odessa College extension.

Other towns include: **Barstow** (384); **Grandfalls** (398); **Pyote** (133) Rattlesnake bomber base museum; **Thorntonville** (543); **Wickett** (543).

Population	**11,530**
Change from 2010 (%)	8.2
Area (sq. mi.)	835.8
Land Area (sq. mi.)	835.6
Altitude (ft.)	2,400–2,880
Rainfall (in.)	13.9
Jan. mean min (°F)	30.9
July mean max (°F)	94.9
Civ. Labor	5,656
Unemployed (%)	8.8
Wages	$71,386,595
Per Capita Income	$53,870
Prop. Value	$5,449,344,564
Retail Sales	$171,353,244

Washington County

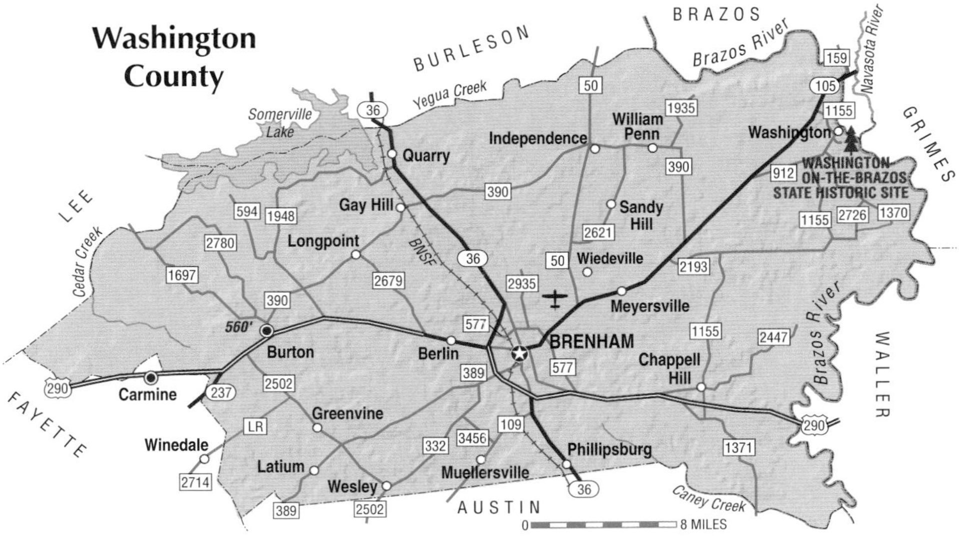

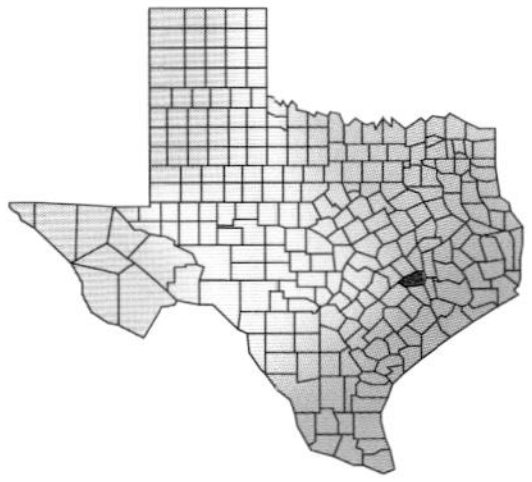

Physical Features: South central county in Brazos valley; rolling prairie of sandy loam, alluvial soils.

Economy: Agribusiness, oil, tourism, manufacturing, government/services.

History: Coahuiltecan tribes and Tonkawas in area when Anglo-American settlers arrived in 1821. Antebellum slaveholding area. Germans arrived around 1870. County named for George Washington; an original county, created in 1836, organized in 1837.

Race/Ethnicity: Anglo, 63.2%; Black, 17%; Hispanic, 17%; Asian, 1.3%; Other, 1.3%..

Vital Statistics, annual: Births, 402; deaths, 389; marriages, 221; divorces, 113.

Recreation: Many historic sites, including Washington-on-the-Brazos, Texas Baptist Historical Museum, Star of Republic Museum; wildflowers, Somerville Lake, fishing, hunting, birding; antique rose nursery; Bluebonnet festival in April.

Minerals: Oil, gas and stone.

Agriculture: Cattle, poultry, dairy products, hogs, horses; hay, corn, sorghum, cotton, small grains, nursery crops. Market value $35.6 million.

BRENHAM (17,646) county seat; Blue Bell creamery, retail, tourism; hospital; Blinn College; Maifest.

Other towns include: **Burton** (302) agriculture, tourism, national landmark cotton gin, festival in April; **Chappell Hill** (750) agriculture, industrial, tourism, museum, historic homes, Scarecrow festival in October; **Washington** (100) site of signing of Texas Declaration of Independence.

Population	**35,570**
Change from 2010 (%)	5.5
Area (sq. mi.)	621.8
Land Area (sq. mi.)	604.0
Altitude (ft.)	150–560
Rainfall (in.)	45.1
Jan. mean min (°F)	39.0
July mean max (°F)	94.2
Civ. Labor	15,180
Unemployed (%)	5.5
Wages	$180,791,155
Per Capita Income	$55,735
Prop. Value	$8,014,827,268
Retail Sales	$549,247,329

For explanation of sources, symbols and abbreviations, see p. 204, and foldout map.

Geese feeding in a fallow rice field in Waller County. Photo by Beverly Moseley, USDA NRCS Texas

Webb County

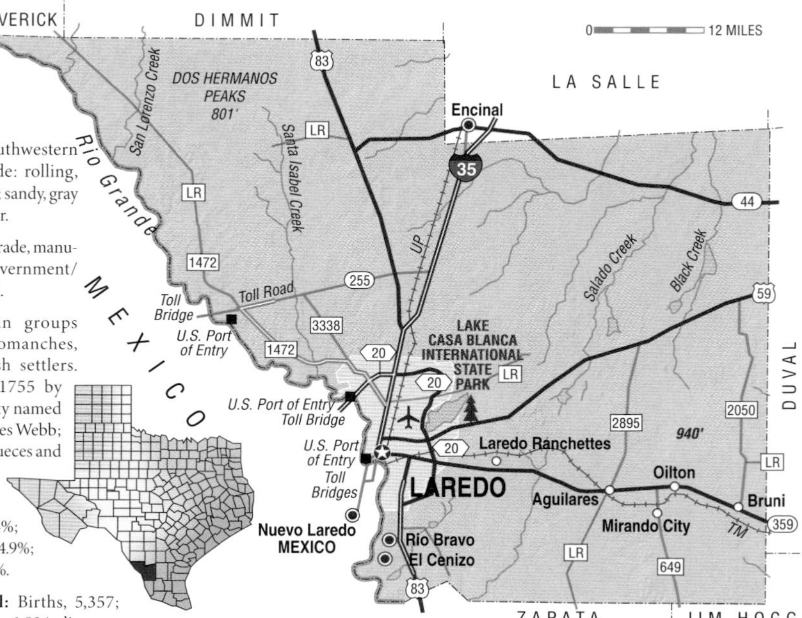

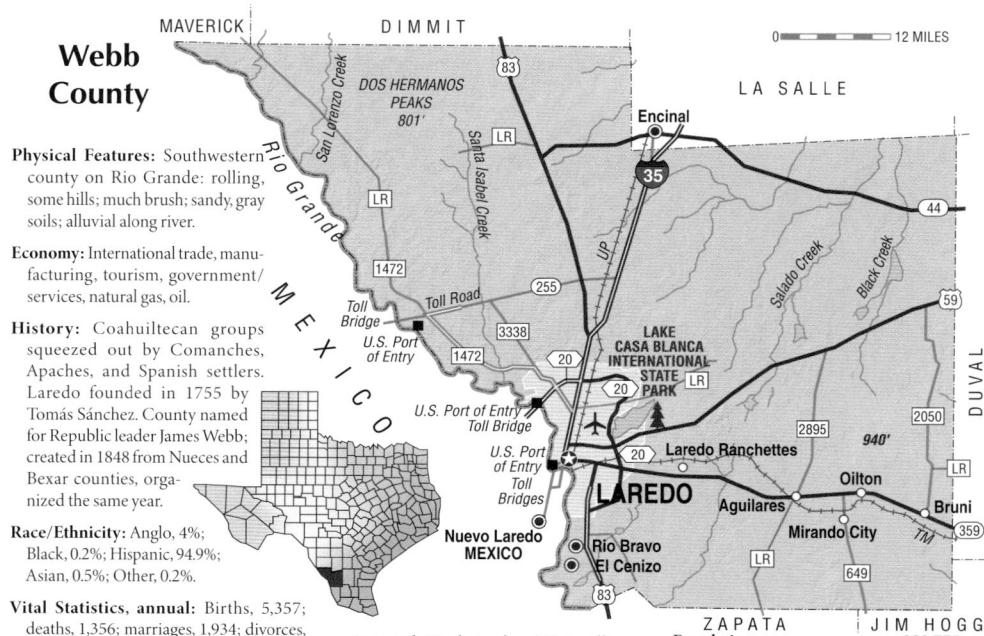

Physical Features: Southwestern county on Rio Grande: rolling, some hills; much brush; sandy, gray soils; alluvial along river.

Economy: International trade, manufacturing, tourism, government/services, natural gas, oil.

History: Coahuiltecan groups squeezed out by Comanches, Apaches, and Spanish settlers. Laredo founded in 1755 by Tomás Sánchez. County named for Republic leader James Webb; created in 1848 from Nueces and Bexar counties, organized the same year.

Race/Ethnicity: Anglo, 4%; Black, 0.2%; Hispanic, 94.9%; Asian, 0.5%; Other, 0.2%.

Vital Statistics, annual: Births, 5,357; deaths, 1,356; marriages, 1,934; divorces, 111.

Recreation: Tourist gateway to Mexico; hunting, fishing; Lake Casa Blanca park, water recreation; historic sites; Museum of Republic of the Rio Grande; Fort McIntosh; minor league baseball, hockey; Washington's Birthday celebration.

Minerals: Natural gas, oil, coal.

Agriculture: Onions, melons, nursery crops, cattle, horses, goats. About 2,500 acres irrigated. Market value $28.4 million. Mesquite sold. Hunting leases important.

LAREDO (266,898) county seat; international trade, retail center, government/services; rail, highway gateway to Mexico; junior college, Texas A&M International University, community college; hospitals; entertainment/sports arena; "El Grito" on Sept. 15; Jalapeño festival in February.

Other towns and places include: **Bruni** (389); **El Cenizo** (3,127); **Mirando City** (337); **Oilton** (368); **Rio Bravo** (4,660).

Population	**280,775**
Change from 2010 (%)	12.2
Area (sq. mi.)	3,375.6
Land Area (sq. mi.)	3,361.5
Altitude (ft.)	310–940
Rainfall (in.)	20.2
Jan. mean min (°F)	46.1
July mean max (°F)	99.3
Civ. Labor	114,651
Unemployed (%)	7
Wages	$1,056,275,660
Per Capita Income	$32,466
Prop. Value	$27,156,408,045
Retail Sales	$3,416,335,248

This bridge spanning the Colorado River in Wharton County was built in the 1930s and is no longer used by traffic. Today it is listed on the National Register of Historic Places. Photo by Larry D. Moore, CC by SA 4.0/Wikimedia Commons

Wharton County

Physical Features: Gulf prairie; bisected by the Colorado River; alluvial, black, sandy loam soils.

Economy: Oil, agribusiness, hunting, manufacturing, government/services.

History: Karankawas in area until the 1840s. Anglo-American colonists settled in 1823. Czechs, Germans arrived in 1880s. Mexican migration increased after 1950. County named for John A. and William H. Wharton, brothers active in Texas Revolution; created in 1846 from Jackson, Matagorda, Colorado counties, organized the same year.

Race/Ethnicity: Anglo, 43.4%; Black, 12.4%; Hispanic, 42.6%; Asian, 0.4%; Other, 0.9%.

Vital Statistics, annual: Births, 595; deaths, 417; marriages, 223; divorces, 97.

Recreation: Waterfowl hunting, fishing, big-game, birding; museums; river-front park at Wharton; historic sites; old Plaza Theater at Wharton.

Minerals: Oil, gas.

Agriculture: Rice (first in acreage); cotton, milo, corn, sorghum, soybeans; 72,000 acres irrigated. Also, eggs, nurseries/turf grass (first in value of sales), cattle, aquaculture. Market value $208.5 million.

WHARTON (8,653) county seat; health care, plastics, government/services; hospitals, junior college; Juneteenth, wine/arts festival in October.

EL CAMPO (11,918) agribusiness, hunting, varied manufacturing, old-field services, rice processing; hospital; Polka Expo in November.

Other towns include: **Boling** (1,133); **Danevang** (61); **East Bernard** (2,351) commuters, agribusiness, retail, klobase-kolache festival in June; **Glen Flora** (210); **Hungerford** (305); **Lane City** (111); **Louise** (1,024); **Pierce** (51).

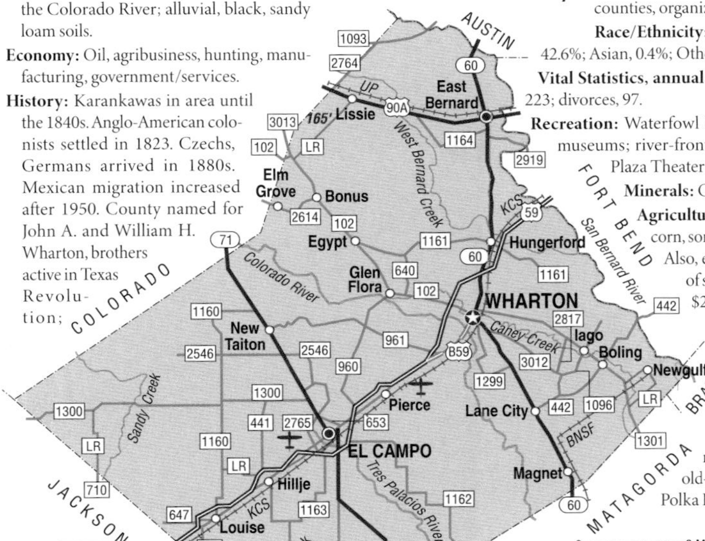

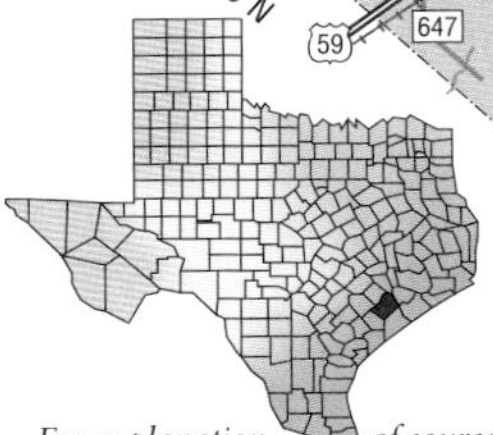

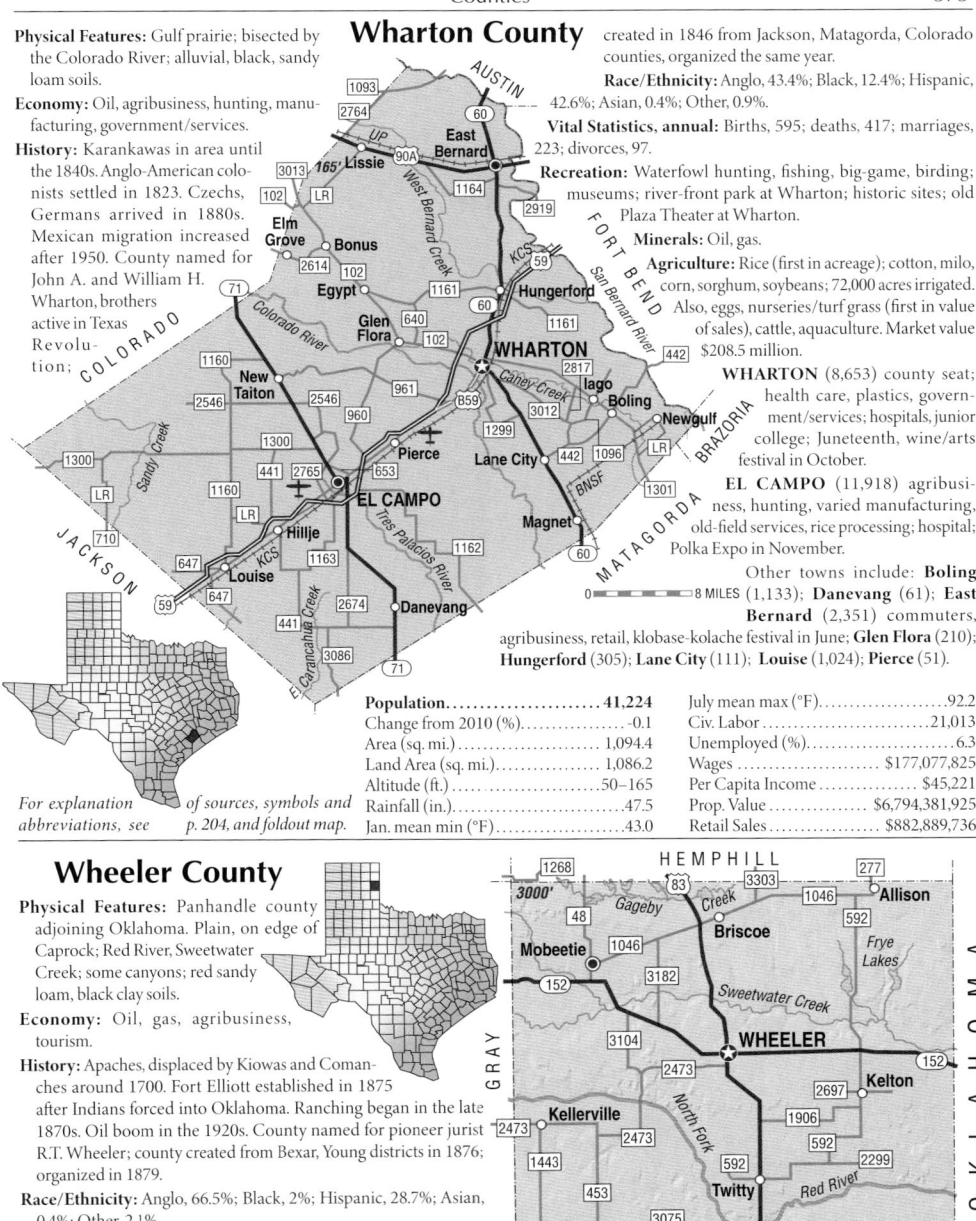

For explanation of sources, symbols and abbreviations, see p. 204, and foldout map.

Population	**41,224**	July mean max (°F)	92.2
Change from 2010 (%)	-0.1	Civ. Labor	21,013
Area (sq. mi.)	1,094.4	Unemployed (%)	6.3
Land Area (sq. mi.)	1,086.2	Wages	$177,077,825
Altitude (ft.)	50–165	Per Capita Income	$45,221
Rainfall (in.)	47.5	Prop. Value	$6,794,381,925
Jan. mean min (°F)	43.0	Retail Sales	$882,889,736

Wheeler County

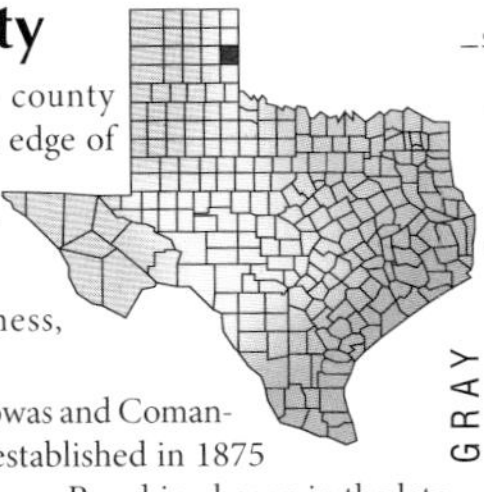

Physical Features: Panhandle county adjoining Oklahoma. Plain, on edge of Caprock; Red River, Sweetwater Creek; some canyons; red sandy loam, black clay soils.

Economy: Oil, gas, agribusiness, tourism.

History: Apaches, displaced by Kiowas and Comanches around 1700. Fort Elliott established in 1875 after Indians forced into Oklahoma. Ranching began in the late 1870s. Oil boom in the 1920s. County named for pioneer jurist R.T. Wheeler; county created from Bexar, Young districts in 1876; organized in 1879.

Race/Ethnicity: Anglo, 66.5%; Black, 2%; Hispanic, 28.7%; Asian, 0.4%; Other, 2.1%.

Vital Statistics, annual: Births, 81; deaths, 72; marriages, 67; divorces, 5.

Recreation: Pioneer West museum at Shamrock; historic sites; Old Mobeetie jail, trading post, Fort Elliott.

Minerals: Oil, natural gas.

Agriculture: Fed beef, cow-calf and stocker cattle, swine, horses; wheat, rye, grain sorghum, cotton. Market value $70.6 million.

WHEELER (1,550) county seat; oil & gas, agriculture, government/services; hospital, medical clinics, museum, library, aquatics center.

SHAMROCK (1,777) tourism, agribusiness antiques shops; hospital, library, old Route 66 sites; St. Patrick's Day event.

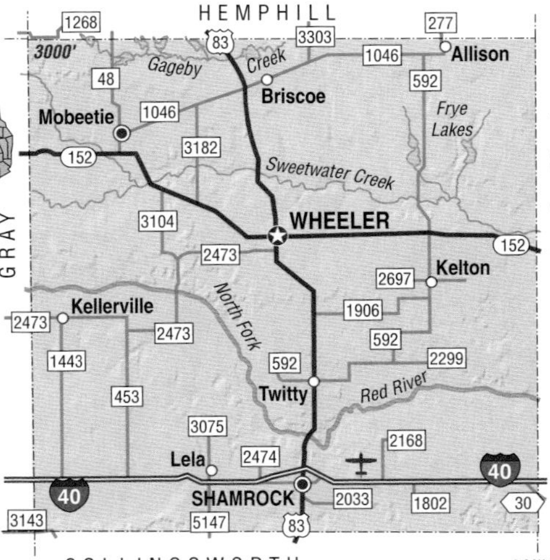

Other towns include: **Allison** (135); **Briscoe** (135); **Mobeetie** (96).

Population	**5,178**	July mean max (°F)	93.3
Change from 2010 (%)	-4.3	Civ. Labor	2,285
Area (sq. mi.)	915.5	Unemployed (%)	6.6
Land Area (sq. mi.)	914.5	Wages	$22,908,972
Altitude (ft.)	2,005–3,000	Per Capita Income	$44,309
Rainfall (in.)	25.2	Prop. Value	$2,251,296,707
Jan. mean min (°F)	24.0	Retail Sales	$60,276,183

Wichita County

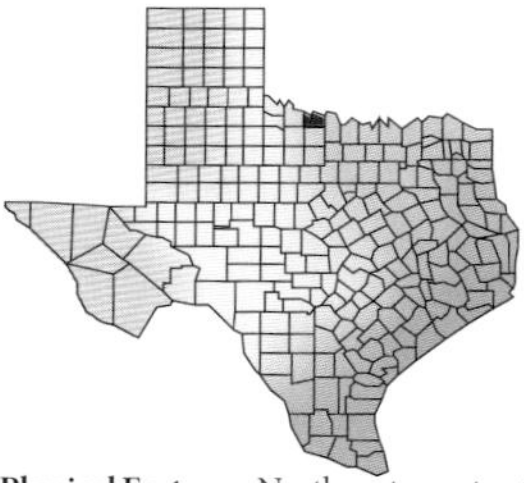

Physical Features: Northwest county in prairie bordering Oklahoma; drained by Red, Wichita rivers; North Fork Buffalo Creek Reservoir, Lake Wichita; sandy, loam soils.

Economy: Manufacturing, retail trade center, air base, government/services, agriculture.

History: Wichitas and other Caddoan tribes in the area in the 1700s; later, Comanches, Apaches also present until the 1850s. Anglo-American settlement increased after 1870. County named for tribe; created from Young Territory in 1858; organized in 1882.

Race/Ethnicity: Anglo, 64.3%; Black, 10%; Hispanic, 20.1%; Asian, 2.1%; Other, 3.2%.

Vital Statistics, annual: Births, 1,740; deaths, 1,304; marriages, 1,126; divorces, 404.

Recreation: Museums; historic sites; Texas-Oklahoma High School Oil Bowl football game; collegiate activities; water sports; Fiestas Patrias parade, Ranch Round-up in August.

Minerals: Oil.

Agriculture: Beef cattle, horticulture, wheat, hay. Seventy-five percent of hay irrigated; 10 percent of wheat/cotton. Market value $33.8 million.

WICHITA FALLS (105,754) county seat; distribution center for large area of Texas and Oklahoma, government/services, varied manufacturing, oil-field services; hospitals, including North Texas state hospital; Midwestern State University, vocational-technical training center; hiking trails; Hotter'n Hell bicycle race in August; Sheppard Air Force Base.

Other cities include: **Burkburnett** (11,194) some manufacturing, Trails and Tales of Boomtown USA display and tours; **Cashion** (355); **Electra** (2,719) oil, agriculture, manufacturing, commuters to Wichita Falls; hospital; goat barbecue in May; **Iowa Park** (6,379) manufacturing, prison, Parkfest in May; **Kamay** (640); **Pleasant Valley** (336).

Population	**132,920**
Change from 2010 (%)	1.1
Area (sq. mi.)	633.1
Land Area (sq. mi.)	627.8
Altitude (ft.)	912–1,240
Rainfall (in.)	28.9
Jan. mean min (°F)	29.8
July mean max (°F)	96.9
Civ. Labor	54,990
Unemployed (%)	5.7
Wages	$600,876,160
Per Capita Income	$44,479
Prop. Value	$10,150,475,799
Retail Sales	$1,852,390,217

An NRSC Conservationist talks to a farmer in his watermelon field in Raymondville. Photo by Ken Hammond, USDA NRCS

Wilbarger County

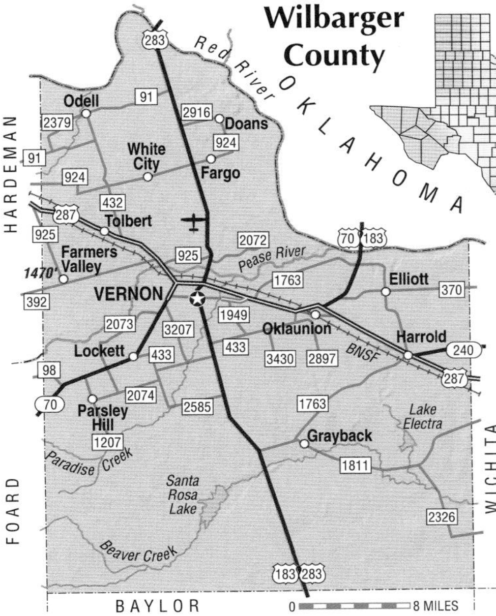

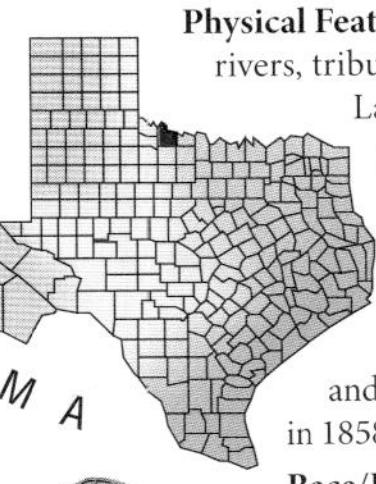

Physical Features: Gently rolling prairie draining to Red, Pease rivers, tributaries; sandy, loam, waxy soils; Santa Rosa Lake, Lake Electra.

Economy: Agribusiness, electricity generating plant, government/services.

History: Anglo-American settlement developed after removal of the Comanches into the Indian Territory in 1875. County named for pioneers Josiah and Mathias Wilbarger; created from the Bexar District in 1858 and organized in 1881.

Race/Ethnicity: Anglo, 55.9%; Black, 8.8%; Hispanic, 31.1%; Asian, 0.9%; Other, 3.1%.

Vital Statistics, annual: Births, 177; deaths, 163; marriages, 137; divorces, 25.

Recreation: Doan's Crossing, on route of cattle drives; Waggoner Ranch, other historic sites; hunting, fishing; Red River Valley Museum; Santa Rosa roundup in May.

Minerals: Oil.

Agriculture: Wheat, cattle, cotton, alfalfa, peanuts; 15,000 acres irrigated. Market value $51.9 million.

VERNON (10,307) county seat; government/services, agribusiness, manufacturing, electricity-generating plant; college; state hospital/mental health center, private hospital, prison; museums; vintage car show in August.

Other towns include: **Harrold** (200); **Lockett** (150) A&M extension center; **Odell** (100); **Oklaunion** (138).

Population	**12,465**
Change from 2010 (%)	-7.9
Area (sq. mi.)	977.9
Land Area (sq. mi.)	970.8
Altitude (ft.)	1,030–1,470
Rainfall (in.)	27.9
Jan. mean min (°F)	27.7
July mean max (°F)	96.6
Civ. Labor	5,037
Unemployed (%)	7.4
Wages	$66,261,865
Per Capita Income	$46,314
Prop. Value	$2,321,946,178
Retail Sales	$328,610,842

Willacy County

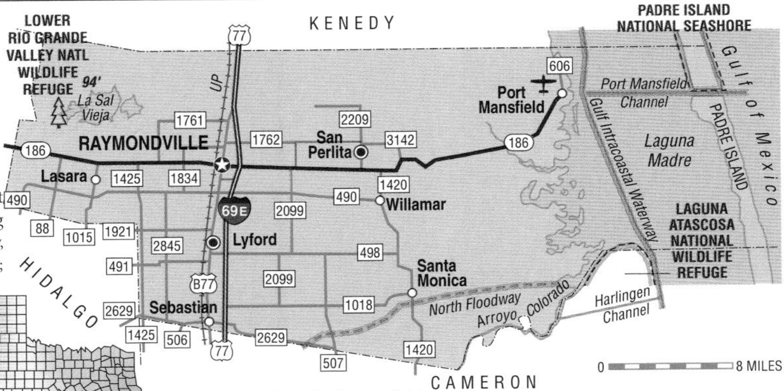

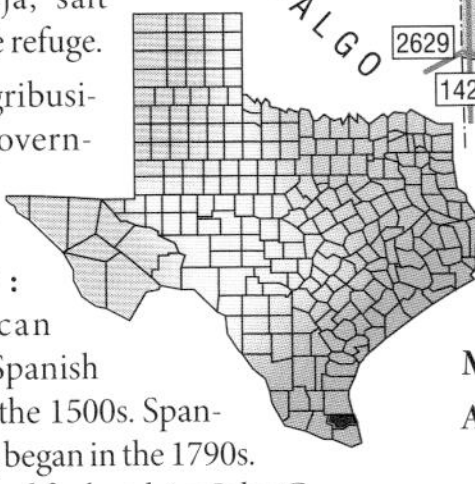

Physical Features: Flat coastal prairie sloping toward Gulf; alluvial, sandy, marshy soils; Padre Island; La Sal Vieja, salt lake; wildlife refuge.

Economy: Agribusiness, oil, government/services.

History: Coahuiltecan area when Spanish explored in the 1500s. Spanish ranching began in the 1790s. County named for legislator John G. Willacy; created in 1911 from Cameron, Hidalgo counties, organized in 1912; reorganized in 1921 after most of its territory was given over to the newly created Kenedy County.

Race/Ethnicity: Anglo, 8.7%; Black, 1.7%; Hispanic, 88.3%; Asian, 0.5%; Other, 0.4%.

Vital Statistics, annual: Births, 291; deaths, 151; marriages, 108; divorces, 50.

Recreation: Fresh and saltwater fishing, hunting of deer, turkey, dove; mild climate attracts many winter tourists.

Minerals: Oil, natural gas.

Agriculture: Cotton, sorghum, corn, vegetables, sugar cane watermelon; 20 percent of cropland irrigated. Livestock includes cattle, horses, goats, hogs. Market value $88.1 million.

RAYMONDVILLE (10,998) county seat; agribusiness, oil, food processing, tourism, enterprise zone, prison; museum; Boot Fest in October.

Other towns include: **Lasara** (924); **Lyford** (2,539); **Port Mansfield** (168) charter fishing, bait and tackle, ecotourism/birding, nature trail, fishing tournament in July; **San Perlita** (554); **Sebastian** (1,805).

Population	**21,566**
Change from 2010 (%)	-2.6
Area (sq. mi.)	784.3
Land Area (sq. mi.)	590.6
Altitude (ft.)	sea level–94
Rainfall (in.)	26.1
Jan. mean min (°F)	47.6
July mean max (°F)	96.7
Civ. Labor	6,688
Unemployed (%)	12.2
Wages	$40,118,044
Per Capita Income	$27,584
Prop. Value	$2,266,785,106
Retail Sales	$97,060,339

For explanation of sources, symbols and abbreviations, see p. 204, and foldout map.

Williamson County

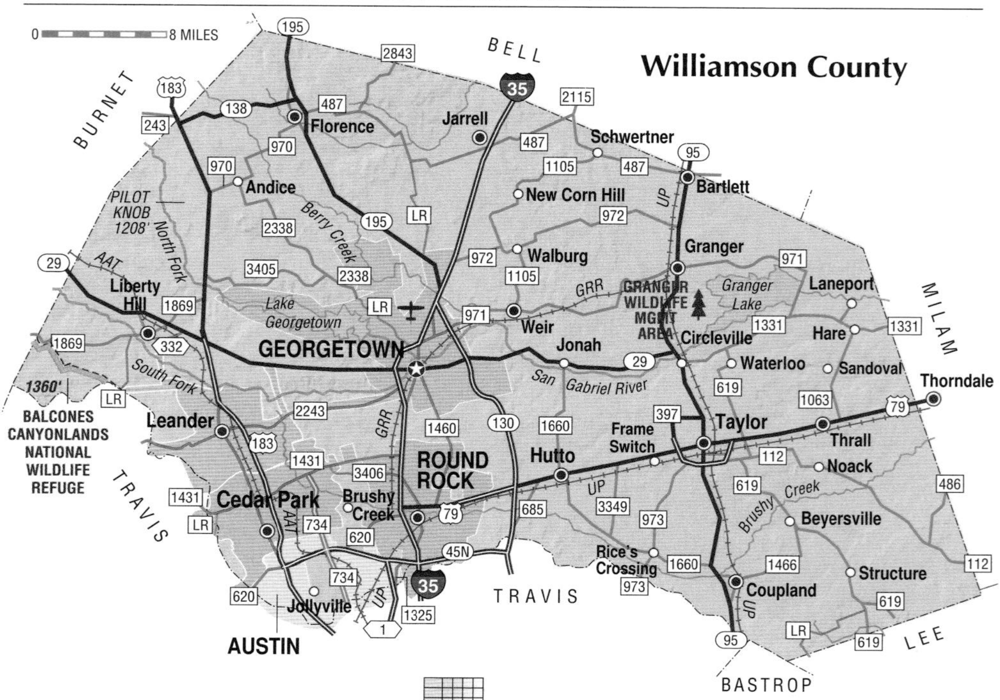

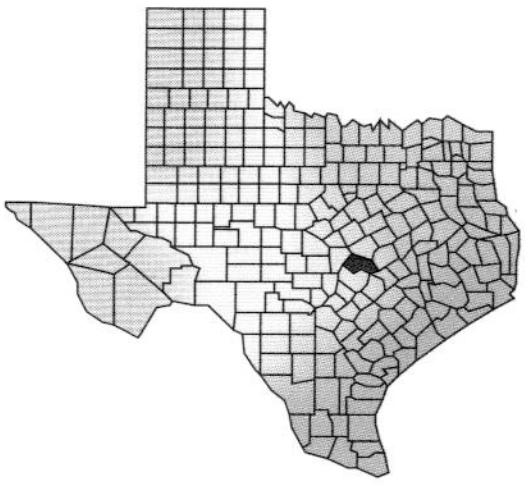

Physical Features: Central county near Austin. Level to rolling; mostly Blackland soil, some loam, sand; drained by San Gabriel River and tributaries; Granger Lake, Lake Georgetown.

Economy: Agribusinesses, varied manufacturing, education center, government/services; the county is part of Austin metropolitan area.

History: Tonkawa area; later, other tribes moved in. Comanches raided until the 1860s. Anglo-American settlement began in the late 1830s. County named for Robert M. Williamson, pioneer leader; created from Milam County and organized in 1848.

Race/Ethnicity: Anglo, 58.7%; Black, 6.3%; Hispanic, 24.8%; Asian, 6.9%; Other, 3%.

Vital Statistics, annual: Births, 6,428; deaths, 2,625; marriages, 2,646; divorces, 811.

Recreation: Lake recreation; Inner Space Cavern; historic sites; deer hunting, fishing; Gov. Dan Moody Museum at Taylor; San Gabriel Park; old settlers park; walking tours, rattlesnake sacking, barbecue cookoff, frontier days in summer; Round Rock minor league baseball; Cedar Park Center, home of Austin Spurs NBA developmental basketball team and the Texas Stars AHL hockey team.

Minerals: Building stone, sand and gravel.

Agriculture: Corn, cattle, sorghum, cotton, wheat, hay, nursery crops. Market value $114.9 million.

GEORGETOWN (75,756) county seat; education, health, government/services, manufacturing, retail; hospital; Southwestern University; Red Poppy festival in April.

ROUND ROCK (119,899, part [1,779] in Travis County) semiconductor, varied manufacturing, tourism and distribution center; hospital; Texas Baptist Children's Home.

CEDAR PARK (77,541, part [8,447] in Travis County) energy equipment manufacturing, millwork, concrete production, commuting to Austin; hospital, community college extension; steam-engine train; Cedar Fest in the spring.

TAYLOR (18,154) varied manufacturing, wholesale, transportation, government/services; hospital, college extension campuses, museum, parks; Blackland Prairie Day in May.

Other towns include: **Andice** (300); **Bartlett** (2,789, partly in Bell County) cotton, corn production, commuters, prison, first rural electrification in nation in 1933, clinic, library, Friendship Fest in September; **Brushy Creek** (27,199); **Coupland** (317); **Florence** (1,306).

Also, **Granger** (1,624); **Hutto** (26,801) agriculture, manufacturing, government/services, commuters to Austin, museum, Olde Tyme Days in October; **Jarrell** (1,870); **Jollyville** (18,409, partly in Travis County); **Leander** (59,110) varied manufacturing, government/services, community college campus, Old Town street festival in May, Leanderthal Lady prehistoric site; **Liberty Hill** (2,931) artisans center; **Schwertner** (175); **Thrall** (1,036); **Walburg** (277); **Weir** (544).

Also, part [55,385] of **Austin.**

For explanation of sources, symbols and abbreviations, see p. 204, and foldout map.

Population	**589,216**
Change from 2010 (%)	39.4
Area (sq. mi.)	1,134.4
Land Area (sq. mi.)	1,118.3
Altitude (ft.)	400–1,360
Rainfall (in.)	35.7
Jan. mean min (°F)	36.5
July mean max (°F)	94.9
Civ. Labor	325,591
Unemployed (%)	4.4
Wages	$3,203,731,758
Per Capita Income	$53,145
Prop. Value	$89,578,669,179
Retail Sales	$9,811,759,549

Physical Features: Upper Coastal Plains; mostly sandy soils, some heavier; San Antonio River, Cibolo Creek.

Economy: Agribusiness, oil and gas, commuters to San Antonio; part of San Antonio metropolitan area.

History: Coahuiltecan Indians in area when Spanish began ranching around 1750. Anglo-American settlers arrived in the 1840s. Germans, Polish settled in the 1850s. County created from Bexar, Karnes counties and organized in 1860; named for James C. Wilson, a member of the Mier Expedition.

Race/Ethnicity: Anglo, 56.8%; Black, 1.3%; Hispanic, 40.1%; Asian, 0.3%; Other, 1.3%.

Vital Statistics, annual: Births, 562; deaths, 410; marriages, 266; divorces, 157.

Recreation: Rancho de las Cabras mission ranch ruins, historic homes; the Stockdale watermelon jubilee in June; Floresville peanut festival in October.

Minerals: Oil, gas, clays.

Agriculture: Cattle, corn, sorghum, hay, cotton. Market value $68.6 million.

FLORESVILLE (8,104) county seat; government/services, distribution, retail trade; hospital; parks.

Other towns include: **La Vernia** (1,426); **Pandora** (110); **Poth** (2,344) agriculture, commuting to San Antonio; bicycle ride in September; **Stockdale** (1,702) agriculture, commuting to San Antonio, museum, nature center, watermelon jubilee in June; **Sutherland Springs** (420).

Part of **Nixon** (2,542, mostly in Gonzales County).

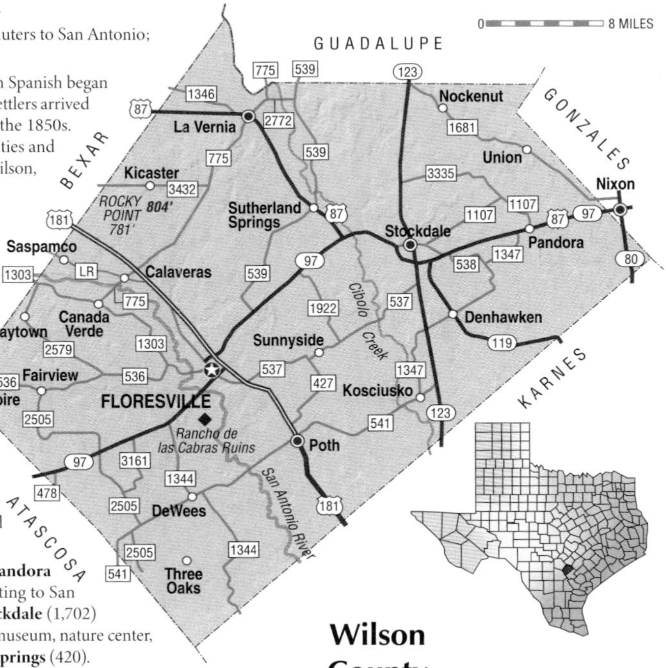

Wilson County

Population	**52,127**	Rainfall (in.)	29.1	Wages	$96,619,215
Change from 2010 (%)	21.5	Jan. mean min (°F)	32.2	Per Capita Income	$46,448
Area (sq. mi.)	808.4	July mean max (°F)	95.5	Prop. Value	$5,761,592,385
Land Area (sq. mi.)	803.7	Civ. Labor	25,055	Retail Sales	$533,777,666
Altitude (ft.)	300–804	Unemployed (%)	4.6		

Winkler County

Physical Features: Western county adjoining New Mexico on plains, partly sandy hills.

Economy: Oil and natural gas, ranching, prison, some farming.

History: Apache area until arrival of Comanches in the 1700s. Anglo-Americans began ranching in the 1880s. Oil discovered in 1926. Mexican migration increased after 1960. County named for Confederate Col. C.M. Winkler; created from Tom Green County in 1887; organized in 1910.

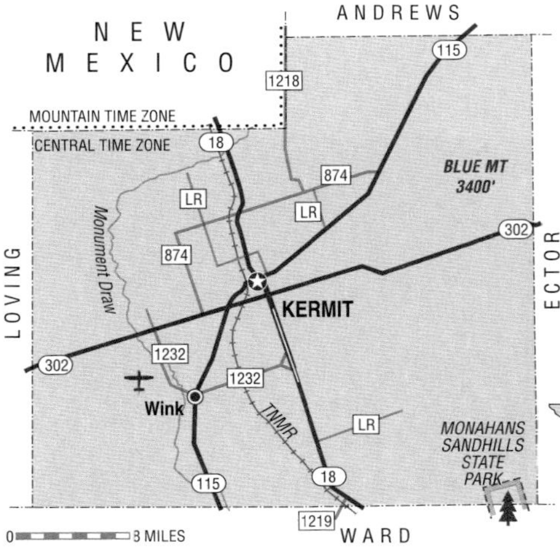

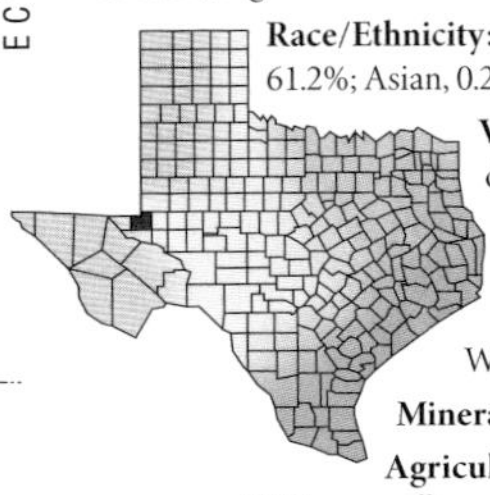

Race/Ethnicity: Anglo, 34.7%; Black, 1.8%; Hispanic, 61.2%; Asian, 0.2%; Other, 1.9%.

Vital Statistics, annual: Births, 136; deaths, 70; marriages, 32; divorces, 16.

Recreation: Part of Monahans Sandhills State Park; museum; Roy Orbison festival in June at Wink; Wink Sink, large sinkhole.

Minerals: Oil, gas.

Agriculture: Beef cattle. Market value $3.4 million.

KERMIT (6,494) county seat; oil, gas, ranching, some farming; hospital; Celebration Days in August.

WINK (1,066) oil, gas, ranching.

Population	**7,990**	July mean max (°F)	96.9
Change from 2010 (%)	12.4	Civ. Labor	3,927
Area (sq. mi.)	841.3	Unemployed (%)	8.1
Land Area (sq. mi.)	841.1	Wages	$56,534,519
Altitude (ft.)	2,665–3,400	Per Capita Income	$63,667
Rainfall (in.)	13.1	Prop. Value	$3,605,351,293
Jan. mean min (°F)	28.9	Retail Sales	$128,391,317

Wise County

Physical Features: Northwest county of rolling prairie, some oaks; clay, loam, sandy soils; Lake Bridgeport, Eagle Mountain Lake.

Economy: Petroleum, sand and gravel, agribusiness, many residents work in Fort Worth.

History: Caddo Indian groups. Delaware tribe present when Anglo-Americans arrived in the 1850s. County created in 1856 from Cooke County, organized the same year; named for Virginian, U.S. Sen. Henry A. Wise, who favored annexation of Texas.

Race/Ethnicity: Anglo, 76.5%; Black, 0.9%; Hispanic, 19.9%; Asian, 0.4%; Other, 2.1%.

Vital Statistics, annual: Births, 837; deaths, 554; mmarriages, 434; divorces, 278.

Recreation: Lake activities, hunting, exotic deer preserve, historical sites, Lyndon B. Johnson National Grassland, heritage museum; Decatur Chisholm trail days in June, Bridgeport Butterfield stage days in July.

Minerals: Gas, oil, sand, gravel.

Agriculture: Beef cattle, hay, dairies, horses, wheat, goats. Market value $46.3 million.

DECATUR (7,086) county seat; petroleum center, dairying, cattle marketing, some manufacturing; hospital.

BRIDGEPORT (7,077) trade center for lake resort, oil and gas production, manufacturing, prison release facility; time-share housing, art community.

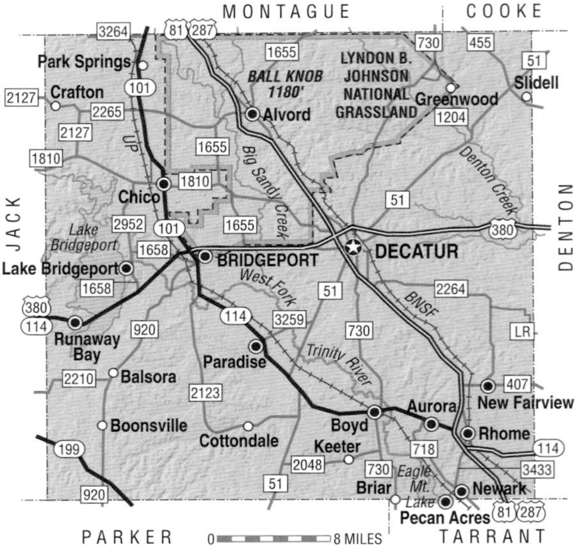

Other towns include: **Alvord** (1,576); **Aurora** (1,550) sand and gravel, manufacturing, equestrian center, "alien crash" site; **Boyd** (1,504) chili cookoff in May; **Briar** (6,116, mostly in Tarrant County); **Chico** (1,181); **Greenwood** (76); **Lake Bridgeport** (398); **Newark** (1,244); **New Fairview** (1,563); **Paradise** (560); **Pecan Acres** (4,480, partly in Tarrant County); **Rhome** (1,845); **Runaway Bay** (1,575) tourism, fishing, boating, golf club, Firecracker Scramble in July; **Slidell** (175).

For explanation of sources, symbols and abbreviations, see p. 204, and foldout map.

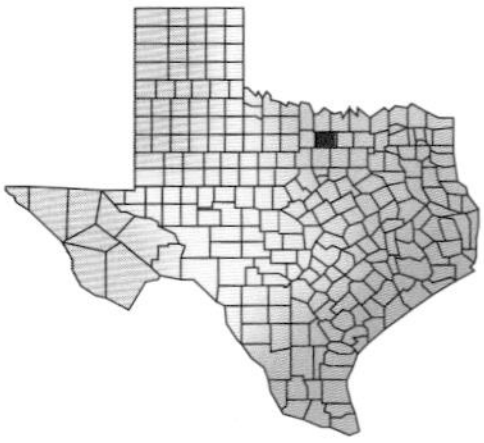

Population	**69,609**	Rainfall (in.)	34.7	Wages	$265,245,614
Change from 2010 (%)	17.7	Jan. mean min (°F)	29.7	Per Capita Income	$44,870
Area (sq. mi.)	922.6	July mean max (°F)	94.2	Prop. Value	$12,978,854,947
Land Area (sq. mi.)	904.4	Civ. Labor	32,445	Retail Sales	$840,335,495
Altitude (ft.)	649–1,180	Unemployed (%)	5.2		

The Select movie theater in Mineola. Photo by Renelibrary, CC by SA 4.0/Wikimedia Commons

Wood County

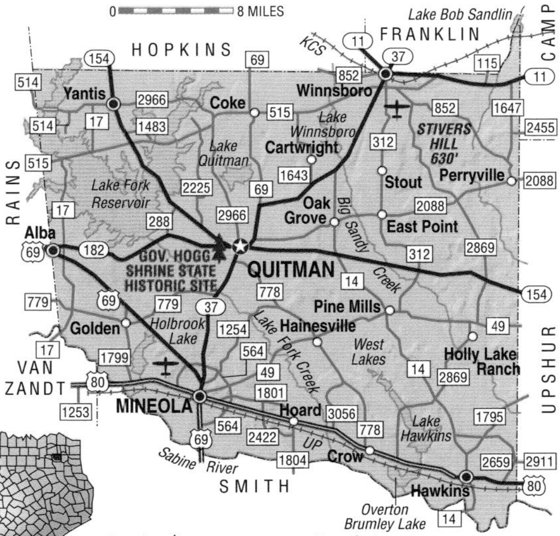

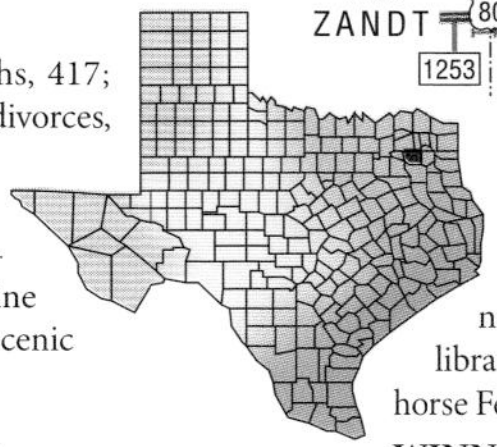

Physical Features: Hilly northeastern county almost half forested; sandy to alluvial soils; drained by Sabine and tributaries; Lake Fork Reservoir, Lake Quitman, Lake Winnsboro, Lake Hawkins, Holbrook Lake.

Economy: Agribusiness, oil, gas, tourism.

History: Caddo Indians, reduced by disease. Anglo-American settlement developed in the 1840s. County created from Van Zandt County in 1850, organized the same year; named for Gov. George T. Wood.

Race/Ethnicity: Anglo, 81.7%; Black, 5.1%; Hispanic, 10.5%; Asian, 0.4%; Other, 2%.

Vital Statistics, annual: Births, 417; deaths, 613; marriages, 238; divorces, 176.

Recreation: Autumn trails; lake activities; hunting, fishing, birding; Gov. Hogg shrine and museum; historic sites; scenic drives; Mineola depot.

Minerals: Gas, oil, sand, gravel.

Agriculture: Cattle, dairies, poultry, forages, vegetables, nurseries. Market value $127.5 million. Timber production significant.

QUITMAN (1,850) county seat; tourism, food processing, some manufacturing; hospital; botanical gardens; Dogwood Fiesta.

MINEOLA (4,777) agriculture, railroad center (Amtrak), oil and gas, heritage and nature tourism; museum, library; nature preserve; Ironhorse Festival in November.

WINNSBORO (3,399, partly in Franklin County) poultry production, dairies, distribution, prison; hospital.

Other towns include: **Alba** (562, partly in Rains County); **Golden** (398) Sweet Potato festival in October; **Hawkins** (1,354) petroleum, water bottling, Jarvis Christian College; oil festival in October; **Holly Lake Ranch** (3,031); **Yantis** (419).

Population	**45,084**
Change from 2010 (%)	7.4
Area (sq. mi.)	695.7
Land Area (sq. mi.)	645.2
Altitude (ft.)	270–630
Rainfall (in.)	43.0
Jan. mean min (°F)	32.5
July mean max (°F)	94.4
Civ. Labor	18,144
Unemployed (%)	5.8
Wages	$112,713,190
Per Capita Income	$39,803
Prop. Value	$5,666,501,904
Retail Sales	$553,227,433

Yoakum County

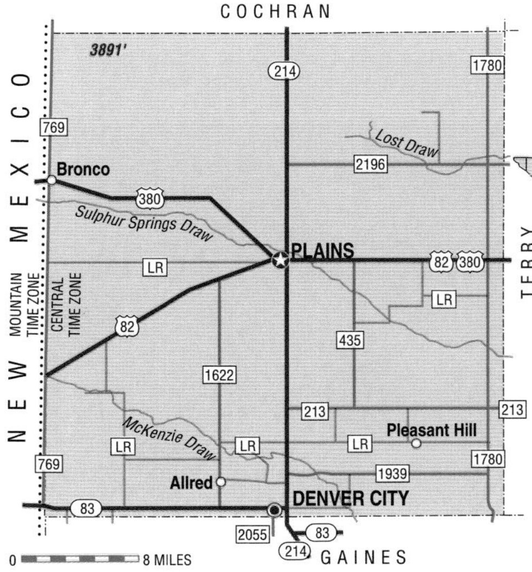

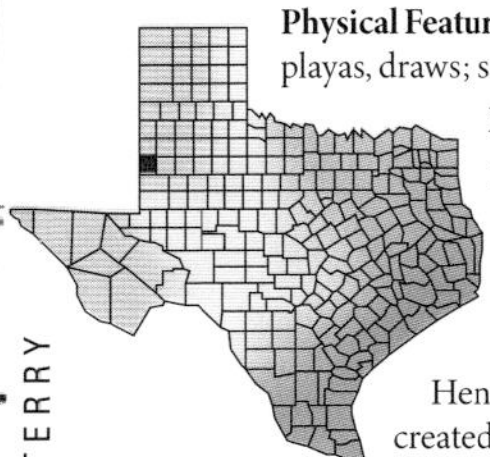

Physical Features: Western county is level to rolling; playas, draws; sandy, loam, chocolate soils.

Economy: Oil and gas, agriculture.

History: Comanche hunting area. Anglo-Americans began ranching in the 1890s. Oil discovered in 1936. Mexican migration increased in the 1950s. County named for Henderson Yoakum, pioneer historian; created from Bexar District in 1876; organized in 1907.

Race/Ethnicity: Anglo, 29.7%; Black, 0.7%; Hispanic, 68.1%; Asian, 0.2%; Other, 1.1%.

Vital Statistics, annual: Births, 162; deaths, 63; marriages, 55; divorces, 26.

Recreation: Tsa Mo Ga museum at Plains; Plains watermelon roundup on Labor Day weekend.

Minerals: Oil, natural gas.

Agriculture: Cotton, peanuts (third in acreage), sorghum, wheat, watermelons, cattle. Some 90,000 acres irrigated. Market value $100.2 million.

Population	**8,829**
Change from 2010 (%)	12.1
Area (sq. mi.)	799.7
Land Area (sq. mi.)	799.7
Altitude (ft.)	3,400–3,891
Rainfall (in.)	18.2
Jan. mean min (°F)	25.7
July mean max (°F)	91.7
Civ. Labor	3,264
Unemployed (%)	9.1
Wages	$43,242,110
Per Capita Income	$44,932
Prop. Value	$2,931,844,880
Retail Sales	$76,773,226

PLAINS (1,644) county seat; oil, agribusiness center.

DENVER CITY (5,044) center for oil, agriculture activities in two counties; hospital/medical services, library, museum; Annie Armstrong dugout shelter.

Young County

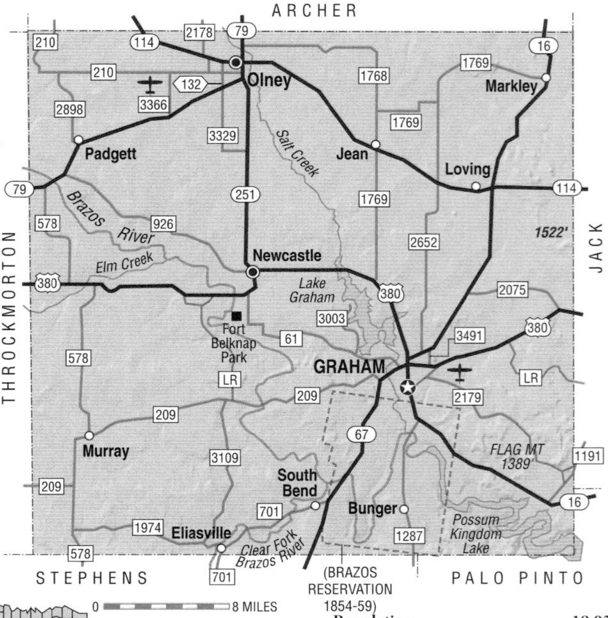

Physical Features: Hilly, broken; drained by Brazos and tributaries; Possum Kingdom Lake, Lake Graham.

Economy: Oil, agribusiness, tourism, hunting leases.

History: U.S. military outpost established in 1851. Site of Brazos Indian Reservation from 1854–1859 with Caddoes, Wacos, and other tribes. Anglo-American settlers arrived in the 1850s. County named for early Texan, Col. W.C. Young; created from Bosque and Fannin counties, and organized in 1856; reorganized in 1874.

Race/Ethnicity: Anglo, 76.1%; Black, 1.2%; Hispanic, 20.3%; Asian, 0.3%; Other, 1.9%.

Vital Statistics, annual: Births, 215; deaths, 239; marriages, 139; divorces, 82.

Recreation: Lake activities; hunting; Fort Belknap; marker at oak tree in Graham where ranchers formed forerunner of Texas and Southwestern Cattle Raisers Association.

Minerals: Oil, gas, sand, and gravel.

Agriculture: Beef cattle; wheat is the chief crop, also hay, cotton, pecans, nursery plants. Market value $21.7 million.

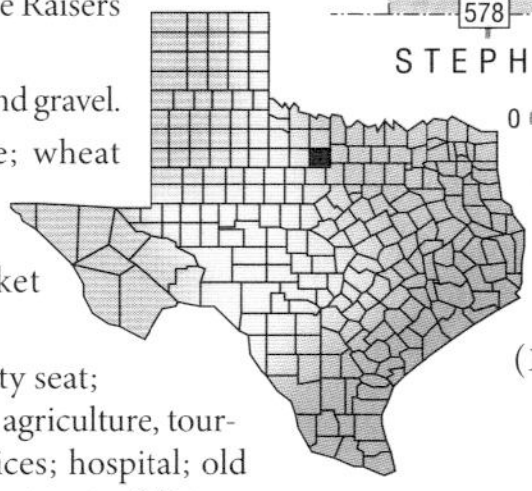

GRAHAM (9,158) county seat; oil and gas production, agriculture, tourism, government/services; hospital; old post office museum and art center; Western heritage days in September.

Other towns include: **Loving** (300); **Newcastle** (595) old coal-mining town; **Olney** (3,235) aluminum, varied manufacturing, hospital; One-Arm Dove Hunt in September; **South Bend** (100).

For explanation of sources, symbols and abbreviations, see p. 204, and foldout map.

Population	**19,029**
Change from 2010 (%)	2.6
Area (sq. mi.)	930.9
Land Area (sq. mi.)	914.5
Altitude (ft.)	995–1,522
Rainfall (in.)	31.5
Jan. mean min (°F)	28.3
July mean max (°F)	96.2
Civ. Labor	7,669
Unemployed (%)	5.4
Wages	$80,444,407
Per Capita Income	$50,732
Prop. Value	$2,533,051,623
Retail Sales	$288,056,231

The welcome sign on U.S. 83 as you enter Crystal City in Zavala County. Photo by Barbara Brannon, CC 2/Wikimedia Commons

Zapata County

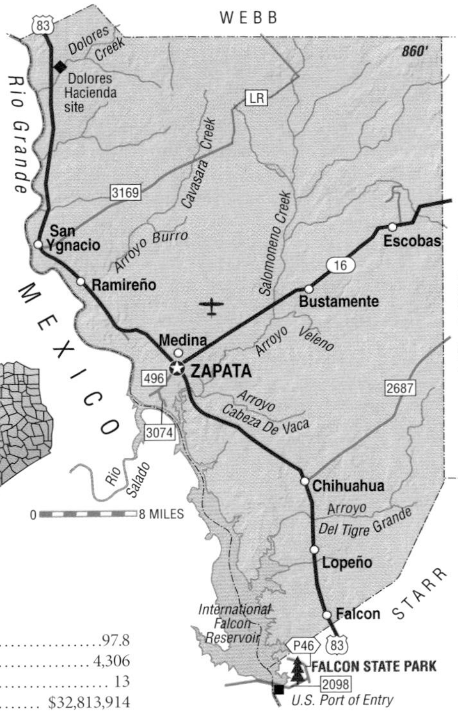

Physical Features: South Texas county of rolling, brushy topography; broken by tributaries of Rio Grande; Falcon Reservoir.

Economy: Natural gas and oil production and services, banking, tourism/Falcon Reservoir activities.

History: Coahuiltecan Indians in area when the ranch settlement of Nuestra Señora de los Dolores was established in 1750. Anglo-American migration increased after 1980. County named for Col. Antonio Zapata, pioneer rancher; created and organized in 1858 from Starr, Webb counties.

Race/Ethnicity: Anglo, 5.3%; Black, 0%; Hispanic, 94.1%; Asian, 0.2%; Other, 0.1%.

Vital Statistics, annual: Births, 270; deaths, 85; marriages, 25; divorces, 2.

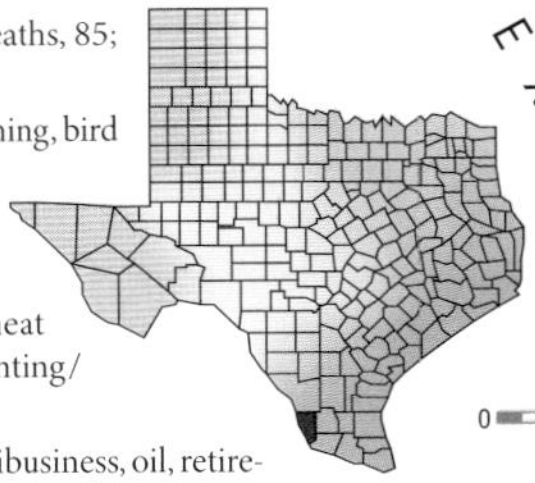

Recreation: Lake, state park, hunting, fishing, bird watching, golfing, Dolores Hacienda site, rock hunting.

Minerals: Natural gas, caliche.

Agriculture: Beef cattle, sorghum, meat goats. Market value $6.3 million. Hunting/wildlife leases important.

Zapata (4,924) county seat; tourism, agribusiness, oil, retirement center; clinic; fajita cook-off in November.

Other towns include: **Falcon** (186); **Lopeño** (185); **Medina** (4,387), and **San Ygnacio** (558) historic buildings, museum.

Population	**14,196**
Change from 2010 (%)	1.3
Area (sq. mi.)	1,058.0
Land Area (sq. mi.)	998.4
Altitude (ft.)	301–860
Rainfall (in.)	19.8
Jan. mean min (°F)	46.3
July mean max (°F)	97.8
Civ. Labor	4,306
Unemployed (%)	13
Wages	$32,813,914
Per Capita Income	$28,936
Prop. Value	$1,661,393,140
Retail Sales	$80,353,042

For explanation of sources, symbols and abbreviations, see p. 204, and foldout map.

Zavala County

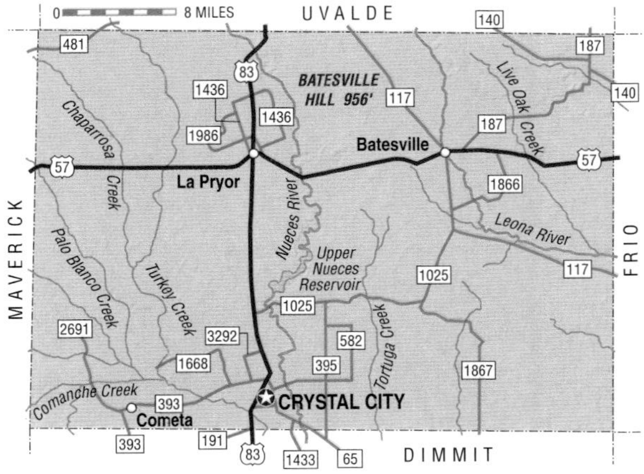

Physical Features: Southwestern county near Mexican border; rolling plains broken by much brush; Nueces, Leona, other streams; Upper Nueces Reservoir.

Economy: Agribusiness, food packaging, leading county in Winter Garden truck-farming area, government/services.

History: Coahuiltecan area; Apaches, Comanches arrived later. Ranching developed in the late 1860s. County created from Maverick and Uvalde counties in 1858; organized in 1884; named for Texas Revolutionary leader Lorenzo de Zavala.

Race/Ethnicity: Anglo, 5.3%; Black, 0.2%; Hispanic, 94%; Asian, 0%; Other, 0.2%.

Vital Statistics, annual: Births, 195; deaths, 111; marriages, 44; divorces, 0.

Recreation: Hunting, fishing; spinach festival in November.

Minerals: Oil, natural gas.

Agriculture: Cattle, grains, vegetables, cotton, pecans. About 30,000 acres irrigated. Market value $66.6 million. Hunting leases important.

CRYSTAL CITY (7,189) county seat; agribusiness, food processing, oil-field services; site of World War II detention center. Home of Popeye statue.

Other towns include: **Batesville** (1,039) and **La Pryor** (1,798).

Population	**12,116**
Change from 2010 (%)	3.8
Area (sq. mi.)	1,301.7
Land Area (sq. mi.)	1,297.4
Altitude (ft.)	540–956
Rainfall (in.)	19.6
Jan. mean min (°F)	43.6
July mean max (°F)	97.2
Civ. Labor	3,417
Unemployed (%)	13.6
Wages	$24,988,737
Per Capita Income	$30,779
Prop. Value	$2,934,815,450
Retail Sales	$59,020,478

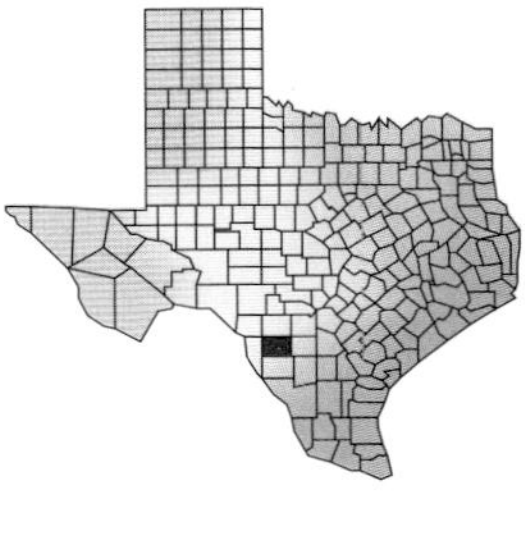

The Great Texas Land Rush

Stake your claim!

It seems unbelievable, but the **Great Texas Land Rush** has been active since 2011, and today it is stronger than ever! Funds raised through the Land Rush program are used to support the creation of each new edition of the Texas Almanac and improve our web presence at TexasAlmanac.com.

We'd like to extend a big ***Thank You!*** to our current adopters, listed below.

Ad Hall, adopted by Henry D. Hall Jr.
Alanreed, adopted by Margaret Gibson
Allen, adopted by Martinique Allen
Almeda, adopted by Margaret Gibson
Almedes, adopted by John
Alpine, adopted by Cindy Brandimarte
Amarillo, adopted by Joe & Mary Hughes
Anadarko, adopted by Ricardo Cruz
Annetta, adopted by Johnny D. Chapman
Appleby, adopted by David L Peavy
Aransas Pass, adopted by Marie Halff
Argyle, adopted by Kay Teer
Arlington, adopted by Floreen Henry & Family
Athens, adopted by Afred Smith, Marine Smith & Donald Lyles
Austin, adopted by Austin Faith LaPorte
Austin, adopted by Tommy & Sandy Hughes
Azle, adopted by Nancy Nation Jay
Bainville, adopted by Matt Mendiola
Baker, adopted by Judy G. Russell
Barnhart, adopted by Herbie R Taylor
Barton Creek, adopted by Weird Austin Productions, Inc.
Bastrop, adopted by Kevin & Debra DeWitt Jordan
Beaukiss, adopted by Karen & Connie Moss
Bee Cave, adopted by The Waldens
Bell Bottom, adopted by Tamarah Humphrey
Bells, adopted by Charming Grace Boutique
Bennett, adopted by Paula Wallace Cairns
Beth, adopted by Kimberly L
Bexar, adopted by Omega Delta Phi - Beta Theta Chapter
Blanco, adopted by Brenda Weeks Norris
Bland Lake, adopted by Kathleen Nelson
Boerne, adopted by Baby Girl
Bogata, adopted by Frank Vin Robinson
Borger, adopted by Robert & Laura Garrett
Bostick, adopted by Tina A. Griffith
Brad, adopted by Krista Fowles
Brady, adopted by Kailyn & HoneyGrove Smith
Brazosport, adopted by Carl Wolfe
Breckenridge, adopted by Herbie R Taylor
Brileytown, adopted by Jena L. Briley
Broaddus, adopted by Mayor Shirley J Parker
Brownsboro, adopted by Jacob Leon Cook
Brownsville, adopted by Felix Garza, Jr.
Brushy Creek, adopted by Round Rock Preservation
Bryans Mill, adopted by Brandy Luckey
Bryant Station, adopted by Denton Bryant KSJ
Buckner, adopted by Josh & Katie Asbill
Bunker Hill Village, adopted by Charlotte Lee
Bute, adopted by Joel Dixon
Caldwell, adopted by Kim & Doug Unerfusser
Cameron, adopted by Weird Austin Productions
Caney Head, adopted by Joe Moss
Canyon, adopted by Amanda Torrez
Carpenter, adopted by Jennifer, Eric, Andrew, Justin, & Katie
Cayote, adopted by Lloyd Tackitt
Center Point, adopted by Kate Crosby
Centerville, adopted by The Bain Family
Clear Creek, adopted by Ron & Beverly Little
Cleveland, adopted by Thomas Glenn Crawford
Clifton, adopted by = JE =
Colleyville, adopted by Andrew & Winnie Wayne
Cornelia, adopted by Chloe Cornelia Johnson
Crabapple, adopted by Peter Pehl II
Creedmoor, adopted by Peter Pehl II
Crockett, adopted by charles thompson
Cross Creek, adopted by Weird Austin Productions, Inc.
Cut & Shoot, adopted by Karen & Bob Yawn
D'Hanis, adopted by Mary Gilhooly
Dale, adopted by Emilie Jones Siarkiewicz
Dallas, adopted by Debra Polsky
Datura, adopted by Barbara Ribling
Diddy Wa Diddy, adopted by David M. Lanagan
Ding Dong, adopted by Barry Gidden
Doak Springs, adopted by Rachel Mae Cooper-Anderson
Dobbin, adopted by Ann & James Smith
Dodd City, adopted by Weird Austin Productions, Inc.
Dog Ridge, adopted by Phillip R Smith
Douglassville, adopted by Brandy Luckey
Douro, adopted by Ector County Utility District
Eagle'S Nest, adopted by Arrowhead Treazures, LLC
East Sweden, adopted by Mandie de Leon
Ecleto, adopted by Urrutia family
Edinburg, adopted by Ricardo Garza
Electra, adopted by Elaine Faucett
Elk, adopted by Charles Barton Family
Elroy, adopted by Todd Carlstrand
Ernest, adopted by Weird Austin Productions, Inc.
Erwin, adopted by Krista Fowles
Eureka Mills, adopted by The Notzon Family
Fairview, adopted by Crownover Family
Fairview, adopted by The Raymond Hall Family
Fedor, adopted by Fedor Mercantile & Gift Company
Flannagan'S Ranch, adopted by Rosemary Laverne Flanagan King
Florence, adopted by Roger & Cecelia Motzko
Fort Hood, adopted by Lane Abner Johnston
Fort Stockton, adopted by Kate Crosby
Fort Worth, adopted by Floreen Henry & Family
Fredericksburg, adopted by Liebeskind, A Children's Boutique
Frisco, adopted by Jim Whitten
Fruitvale, adopted by R&B Brand
Gainesville, adopted by Krista Fowles
Galveston, adopted by Dustin Henry
Gardendale, adopted by John N. Tyler
Garfield, adopted by Martin Legal Video
Gay Hill, adopted by Marissa Warner
George, adopted by Richard & Margaret George
Germantown, adopted by Claudia & Ford Frost
Giddings, adopted by Lone Star Back Roads, LLC
Gillespie, adopted by Friends of Gillespie County Country Schools, Inc
Gillett, adopted by Raul Degollado Serenil Sr
Glen Cove, adopted by Dennis & Bonnie Nelson
Glenrio, adopted by the Blu Turtle of Old Route 66 Association of Texas
Gonzales, adopted by Jose H Cantu
Good, adopted by personal
Grand Saline, adopted by Joel Robert Dixon
Grape Creek, adopted by Thomas J Mccarran
Grey Forest, adopted by Gus Van Steenberg & Family
Griffith, adopted by Tina A. Griffith
Guys Store, adopted by Angelica Proctor-Saddler
Hamilton Pool, adopted by Weird Austin Productions, Inc.
Harper, adopted by Mary Ann Walker
Harris, adopted by The Hughes Family
Harrold, adopted by Mindee Thweatt
Haskell, adopted by Kate Anger
Helotes, adopted by Edna Marnock Smith
Hishway, adopted by Jerald & Dee Lee
Hooleyan, adopted by Hoolyan Au Naturele Medical Cannabis Co
Houston, adopted by The Hughes Family
Houston Heights, adopted by Harley Grace LaPorte
Hughlett, adopted by Crownover Family
Hurst, adopted by Jay Ward
Independence, adopted by The Quinlan Family
Jacksboro, adopted by Jim Hawkins & Allen Hamilton
Jamaica Beach, adopted by Ron & Beverly Little
Jericho, adopted by Blair & Blanca Schaffer
Jerusalem, adopted by Amy Nelson
Johnsue, adopted by Taryn Peterson
Jot-Em-Down, adopted by Black Ranches
Jourdanton, adopted by Eye Care For Texans - Dr. Ron Mixon, OD
Judkins, adopted by Haskell Shelton Jr
Jumbo, adopted by JK Keeling Farms
Junction, adopted by Steve Palmer
Kamey, adopted by McKamey Bros
Katy, adopted by Scott & Jenny Wallace
Kelley, adopted by Kelley Miller
Keltys, adopted by Robert & John Hensley & Mary Hensley Johnson
Kennard, adopted by Paul Standley

Kerrville, adopted by Kate Crosby
Kleberg, adopted by Krista Fowles
Kolls, adopted by Adam Kolls
La Junta De Los Rios, adopted by juan
La Porte, adopted by Georgia Malone
Lake Jackson, adopted by Carl Wolfe
Laloma, adopted by ROBERT LEE MATTA
Langtry, adopted by Arrowhead Treazures, LLC
Las Islitas, adopted by Donna Dominguez-Lent Russell
Lauback, adopted by Megan Laubach
Lawrence Chapel, adopted by Jerry Moss
League City, adopted by John&Geri Paden
Leon, adopted by The Bain Family
Leon Springs, adopted by John Campbell
Lesley, adopted by Thelma L Hall Beasley
Lewisville, adopted by Kristie SS Steed
Lightner, adopted by Kelly Barker
Longview, adopted by Jim & Suzanne Bardwell
Lovelady, adopted by Mildred Brown & Donald Lyles
Loveless, adopted by Mark & Kara Bradbury
Luckenbach, adopted by Mary Hartwig
Lueders, adopted by LAURIE BEAL COOK
Lufkin, adopted by Jim Whitten
Magnet, adopted by William Loocke
Magnolia, adopted by Josey Reynolds/Helen Vandergriff
Mankins, adopted by David Pettijohn
Marfa, adopted by Cindy Brandimarte
Margaret, adopted by Margaret Gibson
Mathis, adopted by Dennis Parrish
Mcbride, adopted by Joshua McBride
Mcgregor, adopted by The Leslie Family
Medicine Mound, adopted by Bill Holcomb
Menard, adopted by Cynthia Womack
Midyett, adopted by Bob B. Midyett Jr
Miller Community, adopted by Gary S. King
Milligan, adopted by Lucy Anderson
Minden, adopted by Joe Earl Conway
Mineral Wells, adopted by Nanette & Dennis Sever
Mixon, adopted by Malachi Scott Dwaine Mixon
Mixon, adopted by Malachi Scott Dwaine Mixon
Mobeetie, adopted by Jan Hart
Mont, adopted by Irene Polansky Szwarc
Monterey, adopted by Rick Ferguson, Brooke Ferguson, Brittney Ferguson, Summer
Montgomery, adopted by Ken & Elisabeth Becker
Montgomery, adopted by Beth Blevins
Morgan'S Point, adopted by Claude Hunter
Morris, adopted by Krista Fowles
Mount Sharp, adopted by Dodie Juarez Scott
Mudville, adopted by All Things Texas@ John Mowey
Munn, adopted by Valerie Munn Hearn
Nacogdoches, adopted by Jim Whitten
New Braunfels, adopted by Gina Perryman
New Deal, adopted by Cindy Brandimarte
New York, adopted by Joel Dixon
North Waco, adopted by Michael Bauer
Nurillo, adopted by John Carlos Trevino
O'Donnell, adopted by TM
Oak Point, adopted by John Lusk
Oakalla, adopted by Wanda Williams Langford
Oakdale, adopted by HoganFarm
Odessa, adopted by Jane, Eileen & Joe Suggs, Jr.
Ogarita, adopted by Lee Webb
Orange Grove, adopted by Albert Sanchez Jr
Paradise, adopted by Camille Cobb
Pasche, adopted by Golda Marie Foster (grdaughter of John Q & Ora Ledbetter Triplett)
Pecos, adopted by Yolanda Lara Diaz
Peerless, adopted by Laura Lindley
Pelham, adopted by Michael Heiskell
Pernitas Point, adopted by Mr.&Mrs Albert (Yvette) Sanchez Jr.
Perry, adopted by Perry Barker
Perryman'S Crossing, adopted by Gina Perryman
Pflugerville, adopted by Tony Bain & Matt Burkhard
Pickett Valley, adopted by Fred Dillard
Pickton, adopted by Rose Bryant
Pilgrim, adopted by Michael & Kacie Pilgrim
Pinehill, adopted by Fred Buckner Vinson
Piney Point Village, adopted by Charlotte Lee
Pipe Creek, adopted by K. L. Backhaus
Pistol Hill, adopted by Joe Brown
Pittsburg, adopted by John R. Pitts, Jr.
Plains, adopted by Jean & Ed Callary
Pleasant Ridge, adopted by Robbie Pierce Ferguson
Pleasanton, adopted by Eye Care For Texans - Dr. Ron Mixon, OD
Pluto, adopted by PLUTO TV
Point Enterprise, adopted by Jennifer & Jack Dixon
Port Acres, adopted by the Bill & Delores Atkinson Family
Porvenir, adopted by Amanda Shields
Poteet, adopted by Eye Care for Texans - Dr. Ron Mixon, OD
Prairie View, adopted by Roy Elzie Donald Lyles Endowment College Fund
Presidio, adopted by Felix Salmeron
Presidio, adopted by CARAN DRIVER
Pringle, adopted by Mike Pringle
Quihi, adopted by John Germann
Rankin, adopted by Cynthia Rackley Cooper
Rath City, adopted by Bob Rogers, Robert Rogers & Clive Siegle
Raven Hill, adopted by Conchata Laferrel Clark
Rayner, adopted by Rick Ferguson, Brooke Ferguson, Brittney Ferguson, Summer
Redland, adopted by Airborne Excavation & Utility Jeff Tagert
Riceville, adopted by Ronny & Sheri Cortez
Richardson, adopted by FASTSIGNS of Richardson
Riesel, adopted by Sheryl Thompson
Roberts, adopted by David Fleming Bragg
Roberts, adopted by Cindy Roberts Bragg
Rockdale, adopted by JOY KORNEGAY
Rollingwood, adopted by Weird Austin Productions, Inc.
Roma (-Los Saenz), adopted by Now salinas
Rosenberg, adopted by Danny M. Diaz
Rosenfeld, adopted by Michael Rosenfeld
Round Rock, adopted by Caran Driver
Rowlett, adopted by Keep Rowlett Beautiful, Inc.
Ruidosa, adopted by Jumano Indian Nation
Salome, adopted by Eddie & Penelope Hernandez
San Antonio, adopted by His Eminence Archbishop Ray Gonia, ECLJ
San Benito, adopted by Hon. Daniel T. Robles & Linda D. Robles
San Felipe, adopted by Edith Elizabeth Pollitz
San Patricio, adopted by Mary Margaret Baldeschwiler
San Roman, adopted by Mario & Jeanette San Roman
San Ygnacio, adopted by GeorgiAnne Uribe Brochstein
Sand Branch, adopted by Thompson
Sanderson, adopted by Karen Elizabeth Balestrini (KERR)
Sandies Chapel, adopted by Melinda Clingman
Sandy Elm, adopted by Teddy & Gay Lynn Olsovsky
Sandy Hill, adopted by Mary & Joe Hughes
Sarahville De Viesca, adopted by Rancho Viesca
Savoy, adopted by Chucos Auto Repair llc
Seagoville, adopted by Krista Fowles
Shamrock, adopted by Nanette & Dennis Sever
Siloam, adopted by The Slone Family
Slaton, adopted by Jerry Kitten
Stephenville, adopted by Stephen Gilhooly
Stevenson, adopted by Caroline Brooks
Stinnett, adopted by Nanette & Dennis Sever
Study Butte, adopted by The DiBona Family
Sunset Valley, adopted by Weird Austin Productions, Inc.
Sweet Union, adopted by Glynis Riser
Swinney Switch, adopted by Paige Willett
Taylor, adopted by Lone Star Back Roads LLC
Taylors Creek, adopted by Fred Dillard Dillard Ranch
Telegraph, adopted by Chris & Beth Ann Kelm
Terlingua, adopted by The DiBona Family
Terlingua, adopted by The DiBona Family
Tevis Bluff, adopted by Sequila Tevis
Texarkana, adopted by John & Sakiko Willis
Travis, adopted by Liz, Tom & Austin Kaplan
Travis Ranch, adopted by Roy, Elzie & Donald Lyles Scholarship Fund (R)
Truby, adopted by Bill Truby
Tuff, adopted by Howard Purnell
Turkey Creek, adopted by Joel Dixon
Turlington, adopted by Lucas Garcia
Turnertown, adopted by THE CONTRACTORS BAND
Tusculum, adopted by Ben Adam
Tyler, adopted by Donald Lyles Doing Business As The Texas Telegram Telegraph (R) & The Texas Town Ta
Valentine, adopted by Dallas Love Ya
Verhalen, adopted by Michael Cate
Vreeland, adopted by Jack A. Muggli, Grandson of Jacob Martin Muggli Sr, the founder of Vreeland.
Waller, adopted by The McCaig Family
Webberville, adopted by Susan Hensley
Webster, adopted by Sue Craddock Hamm
Weisinger, adopted by the Warren Steffen family, descendants of the Dampier/Gibbs/Fultz family
Wheatland, adopted by Valerie Russell
Wheelock, adopted by Alice & Julia Hedrick
Whitewright, adopted by Molly Malinda M. Reed
Williamson Settlement, adopted by John C Poole
Wills Point, adopted by Letitia Wills-Smith
Wimberley, adopted by Margaux Vautherot
Woodward, adopted by Kaye Arnold
Zapata Ranch, adopted by Amanda Lynne Clements
Ziler, adopted by Howard County Judge Kathryn Wiseman
Zulu, adopted by TEXASZULU.COM

Population

U.S. CENSUS OF TOWNS

CENTER OF POPULATION BY DECADES

TEN LARGEST U.S. METRO AREAS

The population of Nacogdoches has grown by 13% since this photo was taken in 2002. Photo by Jeff Attaway, CC by 2.0/Flickr.

Population 2010 and 2019

Population: Numbers in parentheses are from the 2010 U.S. census. The Census Bureau counts only incorporated cities and a few unincorporated towns called Census Designated Places.

Population figures at the far right for incorporated cities and CDPs are the Texas Demographic Center estimates for July 1, 2019. (Note: The results of the 2020 U.S. Census were not yet available at press time.) Names of the incorporated cities are in capital letters, e.g., "ABBOTT".

The population figure given for other towns is an estimate received from local officials through a Texas Almanac survey.

When no 2010 census was conducted for a newly incorporated city, these places show "(nc)" for "not counted" in place of a 2010 population figure.

Location: The county in which the town is located follows the name of the town. If more than one county is listed, the town is principally in the first-named county, e.g., "ABERNATHY, Hale-Lubbock".

Businesses: For incorporated cities, the number following the county name indicates the number of businesses in the city as of January 2018 as reported by the state comptroller. For unincorporated towns, it is the number of businesses within the postal zip code as reported by the U.S. Bureau of the Census for 2016.

For example, "ABBOTT, Hill, 22" means Abbott in Hill County had 22 businesses.

Post Offices: Places with post offices, as of May 2021, are marked with an asterisk (*), e.g., "*Afton".

Town, County	Pop. 2019
A	
*ABBOTT, Hill, 22 (356)	375
*ABERNATHY, Hale, Lubbock, 95 (2,805)	2,699
*ABILENE, Taylor, Jones, 4,121 (117,463)	123,302
Ables Springs, Kaufman	20
Abner, Kaufman	75
Abram, Hidalgo (2,067)	2,461
Acala, Hudspeth	25
*Ace, Polk, 1	40
*ACKERLY, Dawson, Martin, 16 (220)	227
Acme, Hardeman	7
Acton, Hood	1,129
Acuff, Lubbock	152
Acworth, Red River	50
Adams Gardens, Cameron	350
Adams Store, Panola	12
Adamsville, Lampasas	75
Addicks, Harris	[part of Houston]
Addielou, Red River	31
*ADDISON, Dallas, 1,841 (13,056)	16,450
Adell, Parker	100
*Adkins, Bexar, 36	400
Admiral, Callahan	18
Adobes, Presidio	5
*ADRIAN, Oldham, 6 (166)	167
Advance, Parker	100
*Afton, Dickens, 4	15
Agnes, Parker	60
*AGUA DULCE, Nueces, 20 (812)	838
Agua Dulce, El Paso (3,014)	3,428
Agua Nueva, Jim Hogg	5
Aguilares, Webb (21)	23
*Aiken, Floyd, 1	52
Aiken, Shelby	150
Aikin Grove, Red River	15
Airport Heights, Starr (161)	177
Airport Road Addition, Brooks, (93)	86
Airville, Bell	65
Alabama-Coushatta, Polk	572
*ALAMO, Hidalgo, 560 (18,353)	20,208
Alamo Alto, El Paso	19
Alamo Beach, Calhoun	100
ALAMO HEIGHTS, Bexar, 333 (7,031)	8,614
Alanreed, Gray, 1	48
Alazan, Nacogdoches	100
*ALBA, Wood, Rains, 70 (504)	562
*ALBANY, Shackelford, 123 (2,034)	2,037
Albert, Gillespie	25
Albion, Red River	52
Alderbranch, Anderson	3
Aldine, Harris (15,869)	17,792
*ALEDO, Parker, 278 (2,716)	4,423
Aleman, Hamilton	50
Alexander, Erath	40
Aley, Henderson	45
Alfred, Jim Wells (91)	80
Algerita, San Saba	10
Algoa, Galveston	135
*ALICE, Jim Wells, 687 (19,104)	18,536
Alice Acres, Jim Wells (490)	466
*Alief, Harris	[part of Houston]
Allamoore, Hudspeth	10
*ALLEN, Collin, 2,916 (84,246)	105,524
Allenfarm, Brazos	35
Allenhurst, Matagorda	72
Allen's Chapel, Fannin	30
Allen's Point, Fannin	40
Allentown, Angelina	800
Alleyton, Colorado, 14	165
*Allison, Wheeler, 6	135
Allmon, Floyd	24
Allred, Yoakum	90
ALMA, Ellis, 14 (331)	402
Almira, Cass	30
*ALPINE, Brewster, 336 (5,905)	5,928
Alsa, Van Zandt	30
*Altair, Colorado, 6	30
*ALTO, Cherokee, 57 (1,225)	1,306
Alto Bonito Heights, Starr (342)	366
Altoga, Collin	137
ALTON, Hidalgo, 269 (12,298)	17,165
Alum Creek, Bastrop	70
*ALVARADO, Johnson, 224 (3,785)	4,590
*ALVIN, Brazoria, 998 (24,236)	29,391
*ALVORD, Wise, 58 (1,334)	1,576
Amada Acres, Starr (92)	82
Amargosa, Jim Wells (291)	311
*AMARILLO, Potter, Randall, 6,780 (190,695)	202,314
Amaya, Zavala (93)	87
Ambia, Lamar	16
Ambrose, Grayson	90
AMES, Liberty, 10 (1,003)	1,218
Ames, Coryell	10
*AMHERST, Lamb, 14 (721)	630
Amherst, Lamar	125
Amistad, Val Verde (53)	45
Ammannsville, Fayette	137
Amphion, Atascosa	26
Amsterdam, Brazoria	193
Anacua, Starr (12)	9
Anadarko, Rusk	30
*ANAHUAC, Chambers, 89 (2,243)	2,491

Town, County	Pop. 2019
Anchor, Brazoria	150
*ANDERSON, Grimes, 48 (222)	243
Anderson Mill, Williamson, Travis	[part of Austin]
Ander-Weser-Kilgore, Goliad	322
Andice, Williamson	300
*ANDREWS, Andrews, 518 (11,088)	14,704
*ANGLETON, Brazoria, 583 (18,862)	21,483
ANGUS, Navarro, 24 (414)	455
*ANNA, Collin, 276 (8,249)	14,708
Annaville, Nueces	[part of Corpus Christi]
ANNETTA, Parker, 70 (1,288)	3,132
ANNETTA NORTH, Parker, 11 (518)	581
ANNETTA SOUTH, Parker, 10 (526)	592
*ANNONA, Red River, 5 (315)	285
*ANSON, Jones, 102 (2,430)	2,357
Antelope, Jack	65
ANTHONY, El Paso, 133 (5,011)	5,640
Antioch, Cass	45
Antioch, Delta	10
Antioch, Madison	15
Antioch Colony, Hays	25
*ANTON, Hockley, 16 (1,126)	1,100
APPLEBY, Nacogdoches (474)	491
*Apple Springs, Trinity, 10	350
*AQUILLA, Hill, 9 (109)	114
*ARANSAS PASS, San Patricio, Aransas, 341 (8,204)	8,757
Arbala, Hopkins	41
Arcadia, Shelby	35
*ARCHER CITY, Archer, 66 (1,834)	1,920
ARCOLA, Fort Bend, 67 (1,642)	2,360
Arden, Irion	7
Argo, Titus	90
*ARGYLE, Denton, 271 (3,282)	4,555
*ARLINGTON, Tarrant, 10,904 (365,438)	391,791
Armstrong, Bell	25
Armstrong, Kenedy, 3	4
Arneckeville, DeWitt	50
Arnett, Coryell	15
Arnett, Hockley	5
*ARP, Smith, 70 (970)	1,036
Arroyo City, Cameron	600
Arroyo Colorado Estates, Cameron, (997)	1,120
Arroyo Gardens, Cameron (456)	527
*Art, Mason, 14	14
Artesia Wells, La Salle, 2	35
*Arthur City, Lamar, 6	180
Arvana, Dawson	8
Asa, McLennan	46
Ash, Houston	19
Ashby, Matagorda	60
*ASHERTON, Dimmit, 15 (1,084)	1,018
Ashland, Upshur	45
Ashtola, Donley	20
Ashwood, Matagorda	132
Asia, Polk	83
*ASPERMONT, Stonewall, 56 (919)	861
Atascocita, Harris (65,844)	78,165
*Atascosa, Bexar, 46	600
Ater, Coryell	12
*ATHENS, Henderson, 595 (12,710)	13,649
*ATLANTA, Cass, 273 (5,675)	5,610
Atlas, Lamar	28
Atoy, Cherokee	50
*AUBREY, Denton, 208 (2,595)	4,855
Augusta, Houston	40
AURORA, Wise, 28 (1,220)	1,550
*AUSTIN, Travis, Williamson, 37,458 (790,491)	984,115
Austonio, Houston	37
*AUSTWELL, Refugio, 9 (147)	144
Authon, Parker	15
*Avalon, Ellis, 3	400
*AVERY, Red River, 21 (482)	433
*AVINGER, Cass, 29 (444)	431
Avoca, Jones, 2	121
*Axtell, McLennan, 21	300
*AZLE, Tarrant, Parker, 577 (10,947)	13,285

B

Town, County	Pop. 2019
Back, Gray	6
*Bacliff, Galveston, 90 (8,619)	10,073
*Bagwell, Red River, 1	150
*BAILEY, Fannin, 10 (289)	315
BAILEY'S PRAIRIE, Brazoria, 16 (727)	789
Baileyville, Milam	32
Bainer, Lamb	10
Bainville, Karnes	8
*BAIRD, Callahan, 78 (1,496)	1,496
Baker, Floyd	28
Bakersfield, Pecos	9
*BALCH SPRINGS, Dallas, 615 (23,728)	26,426
BALCONES HEIGHTS, Bexar, 175 (2,941)	3,362
Bald Hill, Angelina	100
Bald Prairie, Robertson	40
*BALLINGER, Runnels, 202 (3,767)	3,620
*BALMORHEA, Reeves, 18 (479)	538
Balsora, Wise	50
B and E, Starr (518)	571
*BANDERA, Bandera, 286 (857)	941

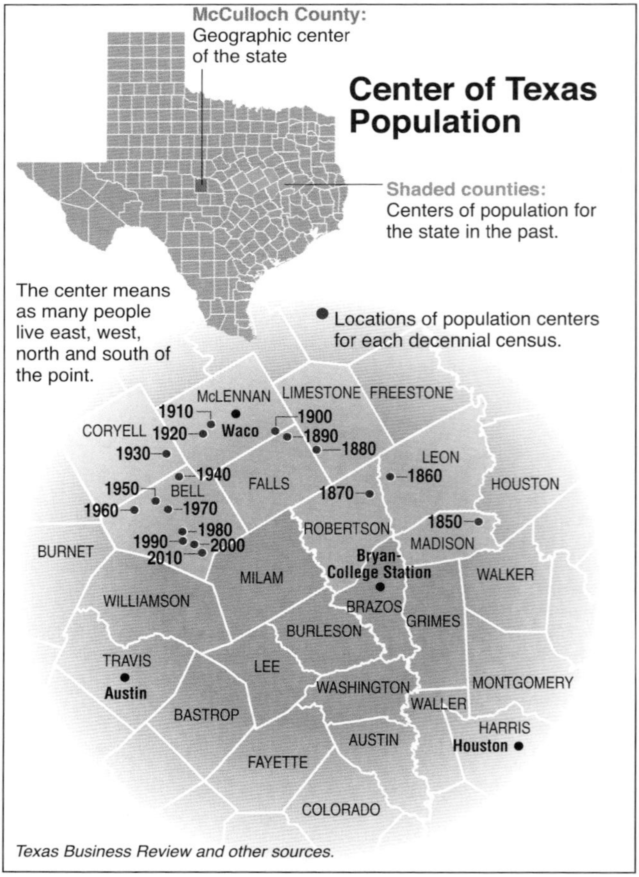

Texas Business Review and other sources.

Town, County	Pop. 2019
Bandera Falls, Bandera	90
*BANGS, Brown, 48 (1,603)	1,588
*Banquete, Nueces, 9 (726)	795
Barbarosa, Guadalupe	46
Barclay, Falls	58
*BARDWELL, Ellis, 4 (649)	726
*Barker, Harris, 11	2,500
*Barksdale, Edwards, 2	100
Barnes, Polk	75
*Barnhart, Irion, 11	110
Barnum, Polk	50
Barrera, Starr (108)	112
Barrett, Harris, 21 (3,199)	3,483
*BARRY, Navarro (242)	265
*BARSTOW, Ward, 3 (349)	384
*BARTLETT, Williamson, Bell, 61 (2,684)	2,789
Barton Corners, Lipscomb	4
Barton Creek, Travis (3,077)	3,402
BARTONVILLE, Denton, 116 (1,469)	1,814
Barwise, Floyd	16
*Basin, Brewster, 3	30
Bassett, Bowie	100
*BASTROP, Bastrop, 764 (7,218)	9,226
Bateman, Bastrop	12
*Batesville, Zavala, 10 (1,068)	1,050
Batesville, Red River	14
*Batson, Hardin, 14	140
Battle, McLennan	100
Baxter, Henderson	150
*BAY CITY, Matagorda, 547 (17,614)	17,431
Baylor Lake, Childress	50
BAYOU VISTA, Galveston, 34 (1,537)	1,645
*BAYSIDE, Refugio, 13 (325)	318
*BAYTOWN, Harris, Chambers, 1,940 (71,802)	81,725
BAYVIEW, Cameron, 12 (383)	408
Bazette, Navarro	30
BEACH CITY, Chambers (2,198)	2,856
BEAR CREEK, Hays (382)	466
*BEASLEY, Fort Bend, 22 (641)	804
Beattie, Comanche	48
*BEAUMONT, Jefferson, 3,768 (117,267)	118,078
Beaver Dam, Bowie	10
Bebe, Gonzales	42
Becker, Kaufman	300
*BECKVILLE, Panola, 21 (847)	902
Becton, Lubbock	62
*BEDFORD, Tarrant, 1,409 (46,979)	49,530
*BEDIAS, Grimes, 31 (443)	474
BEE CAVE, Travis, 493 (3,925)	6,897
Bee House, Coryell	15
*BEEVILLE, Bee, 470 (12,863)	13,554
Belcherville, Montague	25
Belfalls, Bell	30
Belgrade, Newton	20
Belk, Lamar	58
*BELLAIRE, Harris, 709 (16,855)	18,283
Bell Branch, Ellis	125
*BELLEVUE, Clay, 18 (362)	347
*BELLMEAD, McLennan, 251 (9,901)	10,731
*BELLS, Grayson, 43 (1,392)	1,542
*BELLVILLE, Austin, 290 (4,097)	4,602
Belmena, Milam	15
Belmont, Gonzales, 6	55
Belott, Houston	101
*BELTON, Bell, 838 (18,216)	22,695
Ben Arnold, Milam	100
*BENAVIDES, Duval, 21 (1,362)	1,239
*Ben Bolt, Jim Wells, 4	1,600
*BENBROOK, Tarrant, 682 (21,234)	23,912
Benchley, Robertson, Brazos	110
*Bend, San Saba, Lampasas, 1	115
*Ben Franklin, Delta, 1	60
Ben Hur, Limestone	42
*BENJAMIN, Knox, 14 (258)	256
Benjamin Perez, Starr (34)	30
Bennett, Parker	120
Benoit, Runnels	10
Bentonville, Jim Wells	15
*Ben Wheeler, Van Zandt, 70	504
*Berclair, Goliad, 3	253
Berea, Houston	41
Berea, Marion	200
Bergheim, Kendall, 17	1,213
Berlin, Washington	40
Bernardo, Colorado	155
BERRYVILLE, Henderson, 8 (975)	1,075
*BERTRAM, Burnet, Williamson, 86 (1,353)	1,576
Bessmay, Jasper	400
Best, Reagan	2
Bethany, Panola	50
Bethel, Anderson	75
Bethel, Henderson	125
Bethel, Runnels	20
Bethlehem, Upshur	75
Bettie, Upshur	110
Beulah, Limestone	12
BEVERLY HILLS, McLennan, 99 (1,995)	1,993
BEVIL OAKS, Jefferson, 29 (1,274)	1,226
Bevilport, Jasper	12
Beyersville, Williamson	80
Biardstown, Lamar	75
*Bigfoot, Frio, 10 (450)	537
Big Hill, Limestone	9
*BIG LAKE, Reagan, 146 (2,936)	3,661
*BIG SANDY, Upshur, 87 (1,343)	1,402
*BIG SPRING, Howard, 669 (27,282)	28,349
Big Thicket Estates, Liberty, Polk, (742)	882
Big Valley, Mills	35
*BIG WELLS, Dimmit, 8 (697)	694
Biloxi, Newton	75
Birch, Burleson	200
Birome, Hill	30
Birthright, Hopkins	100
Biry, Medina	24
*BISHOP, Nueces, 62 (3,134)	3,092
BISHOP HILLS, Potter (193)	173
*Bivins, Cass, 6	215
Bixby, Cameron (504)	598
Black, Parmer	100
Blackfoot, Anderson	50
Black Hill, Atascosa	60
Black Hills, Navarro	80
Black Jack, Cherokee	47
Black Jack, Robertson	45
Black Oak, Hopkins	150
*BLACKWELL, Nolan, Coke, 16 (311)	286
Blair, Taylor	25
Blanchard, Polk	500
*BLANCO, Blanco, 248 (1,739)	2,098
Blanconia, Bee, Refugio	100
Bland Lake, San Augustine	80
*BLANKET, Brown, 19 (390)	377
Blanton, Hill	5
Bleakwood, Newton	450
*Bledsoe, Cochran, 1	126
*Bleiblerville, Austin, 4	125
*Blessing, Matagorda, 22 (927)	989

Ten Largest U.S. Metro Areas

Rank	Metro Area	2019 Estimates
1.	New York	19,216,182
2.	Los Angeles	13,214,799
3.	Chicago	9,458,539
4.	**Dallas-Fort Worth**	**7,573,136**
5.	**Houston**	**7,066,141**
6.	Washington, D.C.	6,280,487
7.	Miami	6,166,488
8.	Philadephia	6,102,434
9.	Atlanta	6,020,364
10.	Phoenix	4,948,203

Source: U.S. Census.

Town, County	Pop. 2019
Blevins, Falls	36
Blewett, Uvalde	7
Blodgett, Titus	60
*BLOOMBURG, Cass, 9 (404)	406
*BLOOMING GROVE, Navarro, 19 (821)	863
*Bloomington, Victoria, 10 (2,459)	2,488
*BLOSSOM, Lamar, 59 (1,494)	1,558
Blue, Lee	75
Blueberry Hill, Bee (866)	863
*Bluegrove, Clay	135
BLUE MOUND, Tarrant, 49 (2,394)	2,435
*BLUE RIDGE, Collin, 50 (822)	957
Bluetown, Cameron (356)	351
*Bluff Dale, Erath, 24	400
*Bluffton, Llano, 5	75
*BLUM, Hill, 16 (444)	471
Bluntzer, Nueces	150
Boca Chica Village, Cameron	34
*BOERNE, Kendall, 1,419 (10,471)	17,228
*BOGATA, Red River, 52 (1,153)	1,052
Bois d'Arc, Anderson	25
Bois d'Arc, Rains	6
Bold Springs, Polk	100
Boles Home, Hunt	100
*Boling, Wharton, 32 (1,122)	1,133
Bolivar, Denton	140
Bolivar Peninsula, Galveston, (2,417)	2,800
Bomarton, Baylor	15
Bonami, Jasper	12
Bonanza, Hopkins	26
Bonanza Hills, Webb (37)	41
*BONHAM, Fannin, 353 (10,127)	10,786
Bonita, Montague	25
BONNEY, Brazoria (310)	357
Bonnie View, Refugio	97
Bonus, Wharton	44
*Bon Wier, Newton, 6	375
*BOOKER, Lipscomb, Ochiltree, 54 (1,516)	1,487
Boonsville, Wise	52
Booth, Fort Bend	50
Bootleg, Deaf Smith	10
Borden, Colorado	20
*BORGER, Hutchinson, 414 (13,251)	12,331
Bosqueville, McLennan	200
Boston, Bowie	[part of New Boston]
Botines, Webb (117)	123
*BOVINA, Parmer, 42 (1,868)	1,776
Bowers City, Gray	10
*BOWIE, Montague, 357 (5,218)	5,133
Bowman, Archer	300
Bowser, San Saba	20
Box Canyon, Val Verde (34)	27
Box Church, Limestone	45
Boxelder, Red River	100
Boxwood, Upshur	20
Boyce, Ellis	125
*BOYD, Wise, 132 (1,207)	1,504
Boyd, Fannin	105
*Boys Ranch, Oldham, 3 (282)	301
Boz-Bethel, Ellis	100
Bozar, Mills	9
Brachfield, Rusk	40
Bracken, Comal	95
*BRACKETTVILLE, Kinney, 65 (1,688)	1,692
Brad, Palo Pinto	16
Bradford, Anderson	60
Bradshaw, Taylor	61
*BRADY, McCulloch, 243 (5,528)	5,602
Branch, Collin	530
Branchville, Milam	127
*Brandon, Hill, 3	75
*Brashear, Hopkins, 15	280
*BRAZORIA, Brazoria, 214 (3,019)	3,531
Brazos, Palo Pinto	97
BRAZOS COUNTRY, Austin, 16 (469)	488
Brazos Point, Bosque	20
Brazosport, Brazoria	60,138
*BRECKENRIDGE, Stephens, 277 (5,780)	5,684
*BREMOND, Robertson, 41 (929)	978
*BRENHAM, Washington, 977 (15,716)	17,646
Breslau, Lavaca	65
Briar, Tarrant, Wise, Parker, (5,665)	6,301
BRIARCLIFF, Travis, 53 (1,438)	1,775
BRIAROAKS, Johnson, 8 (492)	507
Brice, Hall, Briscoe	20
*BRIDGE CITY, Orange, 227 (7,840)	7,868
*BRIDGEPORT, Wise, 302 (5,976)	7,077
Bridges Chapel, Titus	60
*Briggs, Burnet, 9	172
Bright Star, Rains	25
Brinker, Hopkins	100
*Briscoe, Wheeler, 2	135
Bristol, Ellis (668)	736
*BROADDUS, San Augustine, 26 (207)	203
Broadway, Lamar	25
BROCK, Parker,	967
Brock Junction, Parker	100
Bronco, Yoakum	30
*Bronson, Sabine, 7	377
*BRONTE, Coke, 43 (999)	1,025
*Brookeland, Sabine, 29	300
*Brookesmith, Brown, 1	61
Brooks, Panola	40
Brookshier, Runnels	15
*BROOKSHIRE, Waller, 194 (4,702)	5,937
BROOKSIDE VILLAGE, Brazoria, 39 (1,523)	1,632
*Brookston, Lamar, 14	130
Broom City, Anderson	20
BROWNDELL, Jasper (197)	201
*BROWNFIELD, Terry, 245 (9,657)	9,707
Browning, Smith	25
*BROWNSBORO, Henderson, 70 (1,039)	1,286
Brownsboro, Caldwell	50
*BROWNSVILLE, Cameron, 4,930 (175,023)	184,500
*BROWNWOOD, Brown, 639 (19,288)	19,556
Broyles Chapel, Anderson	60
*BRUCEVILLE-EDDY, McLennan, Falls, 27 (1,475)	1,857
Brumley, Upshur	75
Brundage, Dimmit (27)	23
*Bruni, Webb, 6 (379)	389
Brushie Prairie, Navarro	35
Brushy Creek, Williamson, (21,764)	27,199
Brushy Creek, Anderson	125
*BRYAN, Brazos, 2,485 (76,201)	86,202
Bryans Mill, Cass	150
Bryarly, Red River	3
Bryce, Rusk	15
*BRYSON, Jack, 12 (539)	572
*Buchanan Dam, Llano, 41 (1,519)	1,537
Buchanan Lake Village, Llano, (692)	766
Buchel, DeWitt	45
Buckeye, Matagorda	16
*BUCKHOLTS, Milam, 14 (515)	546
Buckhorn, Austin	50
Buckhorn, Newton	80
Buckner, Parker	10
*BUDA, Hays, 719 (7,295)	17,862
Buena Vista, Starr (102)	117
Buena Vista, Shelby	20
*BUFFALO, Leon, 154 (1,856)	1,903
*BUFFALO GAP, Taylor, 44 (464)	512
Buffalo Mop, Limestone	21
BUFFALO SPRINGS, Lubbock, (453)	493
Buffalo Springs, Clay	45
Buford, Mitchell	30
Bugscuffle, Rusk	12
Bula, Bailey	35
Bulcher, Cooke	3
*BULLARD, Smith, Cherokee, 200 (2,463)	4,183
Bull Run, Newton	90
*BULVERDE, Comal, Bexar, 428 (4,630)	5,806
*Buna, Jasper, 87 (2,142)	2,063
Buncombe, Panola	95
Bunger, Young	24
BUNKER HILL VILLAGE, Harris, 69 (3,633)	3,865
Bunyan, Erath	20
*BURKBURNETT, Wichita, 228 (10,811)	11,194
BURKE, Angelina (737)	727
*Burkett, Coleman	90
*Burkeville, Newton, 25	603
Burleigh, Austin	150
*BURLESON, Johnson, Tarrant, 1,452 (36,690)	47,403
*Burlington, Milam, 3	100

Town, County	Pop. 2019
*BURNET, Burnet, 432 (5,987)	7,025
Burns, Bowie	400
Burns City, Cooke	45
Burrantown, Houston	70
*BURTON, Washington, 81 (300)	302
*Bushland, Potter, 17	1,485
Bustamante, Zapata	10
Busterville, Hockley	6
Butler, Bastrop	40
Butler, Freestone	67
Butterfield, El Paso (114)	139
*BYERS, Clay, 14 (496)	474
*BYNUM, Hill, 9 (199)	210
Byrd, Ellis	30
Byrdtown, Lamar	22

C

Town, County	Pop. 2019
*CACTUS, Moore, 35 (3,179)	3,241
*Caddo, Stephens, 4	70
*CADDO MILLS, Hunt, 133 (1,338)	1,698
Cade Chapel, Navarro, Freestone	25
Cadiz, Bee	15
Calallen, Nueces	[part of Corpus Christi]
Calaveras, Wilson, Bexar	100
*CALDWELL, Burleson, 290 (4,104)	4,515
Caledonia, Rusk	75
Calf Creek, McCulloch	23
Calina, Limestone	10
*Call, Newton, 5	493
Callender Lake, Van Zandt, (1,039)	1,290
*Calliham, McMullen, 4	100
CALLISBURG, Cooke (353)	379
Call Junction, Jasper	50
*CALVERT, Robertson, 50 (1,192)	1,124
Camargito, Starr (388)	418
*Camden, Polk, 6	1,200
*CAMERON, Milam, 203 (5,552)	5,619
Cameron Park, Cameron, (6,963)	7,417
Camilla, San Jacinto	200
Camp Air, Mason	12
*CAMPBELL, Hunt, 45 (638)	675
*Campbellton, Atascosa, 5	350
Camp Creek Lake, Robertson	350
Campo Verde, Starr (132)	148
Camp Ruby, Polk	35
Camp San Saba, McCulloch	36
Camp Seale, Polk	53
Camp Springs, Scurry	10
Camp Swift, Bastrop (6,383)	7,908
Camp Switch, Gregg	70
Campti, Shelby	25
Camp Verde, Kerr	41
*CAMP WOOD, Real, 37 (706)	725
Canada Verde, Wilson	40
*CANADIAN, Hemphill, 146 (2,649)	2,717
Candelaria, Presidio	55
CANEY CITY, Henderson, 12 (217)	230
Cannon, Grayson	50
*CANTON, Van Zandt, 812 (3,581)	3,966
Cantu Addition, Brooks (188)	181
*Canutillo, El Paso, 197 (6,321)	7,073
*CANYON, Randall, 447 (13,303)	16,179
Canyon City, Comal	800
Canyon Creek, Hood (916)	1,070
*Canyon Lake, Comal, 288 (21,262)	27,978
Cape Royale, San Jacinto (670)	611
Caplen, Galveston	60
Capps Corner, Montague	30
Cap Rock, Crosby	6
Caps, Taylor	300
Caradan, Mills	20
Carancahua, Jackson	375
*CARBON, Eastland, 10 (272)	270
Carbondale, Bowie	10
Carey, Childress	25
Carlisle, Trinity	110
Carlos, Grimes	60
*Carlsbad, Tom Green, 10 (719)	780
CARL'S CORNER, Hill, 3 (173)	187
Carlson, Travis	20
*Carlton, Hamilton, 2	75
*CARMINE, Fayette, 51 (250)	262
Carmona, Polk	50
Caro, Nacogdoches	70
Carrizo Hill, Dimmit (582)	593
*CARRIZO SPRINGS, Dimmit, 153 (5,368)	5,567
Carroll, Smith	60
Carroll Springs, Anderson, Henderson	20
*CARROLLTON, Dallas, Denton, 5,038 (119,097)	143,325
Carson, Fannin	22
Carta Valley, Edwards	12
Carterville, Cass	39
*CARTHAGE, Panola, 365 (6,779)	6,941
Cartwright, Wood	144
Casa Blanca, Starr (54)	63
Casa Piedra, Presidio	8
Casas, Starr (39)	49
Cash, Hunt	56
CASHION, Wichita (348)	355
*Cason, Morris, 1	173
Cass, Cass	100
Cassie, Burnet	496
Cassin, Bexar	200
*Castell, Llano, 2	72
CASTLE HILLS, Bexar, 302 (4,116)	4,509
Castolon, Brewster	8
*CASTROVILLE, Medina, 194 (2,785)	3,114
Catarina, Dimmit, 13 (118)	100
*Cat Spring, Austin, 24	200
Caviness, Lamar	90
Cawthon, Brazos	75
Cayote, Bosque	75
*Cayuga, Anderson, 2	137
Cedar Bayou, Harris	1,555
*Cedar Creek, Bastrop, 143	145
*CEDAR HILL, Dallas, Ellis, 1,228 (45,028)	48,836
Cedar Hill, Floyd	24
Cedar Lake, Matagorda	160
*Cedar Lane, Matagorda, 3	300
*CEDAR PARK, Williamson, Travis, 2,495 (48,932)	77,541
Cedar Point, Polk (630)	624
Cedar Shores, Bosque	270
Cedar Springs, Falls	90
Cedar Springs, Upshur	100
Cedarvale, Kaufman	50
Cedar Valley, Bell	14
Cee Vee, Cottle	45
Cego, Falls	42
Cele, Travis	20
*CELESTE, Hunt, 34 (814)	907
*CELINA, Collin, Denton, 307 (6,028)	13,399
*CENTER, Shelby, 349 (5,193)	5,335
Center, Limestone	76
Center City, Mills, Hamilton	27
Center Grove, Houston	39
Center Grove, Titus	35
Center Hill, Houston	105
Center Plains, Swisher	20
Center Point, Camp	41
*Center Point, Kerr, 39	800
Center Point, Upshur	50
Centerview, Leon	20
*CENTERVILLE, Leon, 83 (892)	920
Centerville, Trinity	60
Central, Angelina	1,400
Central Gardens, Jefferson, (4,347)	4,309
Central Heights, Nacogdoches	300
Central High, Cherokee	30
*Centralia, Trinity	190
Cesar Chavez, Hidalgo (1,929)	2,210
Cestohowa, Karnes	110
Chalk, Cottle	17
Chalk Hill, Rusk	200
Chalk Mountain, Erath, Somervell	25
Chambliss, Collin	29
Champion, Nolan	10
Champions, Harris	21,250
Chances Store, Burleson	15
*CHANDLER, Henderson, 157 (2,734)	3,259
Chaney, Eastland	35
*Channelview, Harris, 398 (38,289)	46,373
*CHANNING, Hartley, 5 (363)	346
Chaparrito, Starr (114)	106
Chapeno, Starr (47)	51
Chapman, Rusk	20
*Chapman Ranch, Nueces	200
Chappel, San Saba	25
*Chappell Hill, Washington, 50	750
Charco, Goliad	96
Charleston, Delta, Hopkins	150
Charlie, Clay	70
*CHARLOTTE, Atascosa, 40 (1,715)	1,865
*Chatfield, Navarro, 3	40
Cheapside, Gonzales, DeWitt	5
Cheek, Jefferson	1,096
Cheneyboro, Navarro	100

Town, County	Pop. 2019
*Cherokee, San Saba, 10	175
Cherry Spring, Gillespie	75
*CHESTER, Tyler, 13 (312)	324
Chesterville, Colorado	30
*CHICO, Wise, 66 (1,002)	1,181
*Chicota, Lamar	150
Chihuahua, Zapata	77
*CHILDRESS, Childress, 177 (6,105)	6,289
*CHILLICOTHE, Hardeman, 16 (707)	665
*Chilton, Falls, 10 (911)	958
*CHINA, Jefferson, 30 (1,160)	1,203
CHINA GROVE, Bexar, 59 (1,179)	1,321
China Grove, Scurry	15
*China Spring, McLennan, 63 (1,281)	1,401
Chinati, Presidio	8
Chinquapin, Matagorda	6
*CHIRENO, Nacogdoches, 17 (386)	386
Chita, Trinity	81
Choate, Karnes	30
Chocolate Bayou, Brazoria	60
Choice, Shelby	35
*Chriesman, Burleson, 1	30
*CHRISTINE, Atascosa (390)	439
*Christoval, Tom Green, 26 (504)	576
Chula Vista, Maverick (3,818)	3,980
Chula Vista, Zavala (450)	479
Chula Vista, Cameron (288)	263
Church Hill, Rusk	20
Churchill, Brazoria	90
*CIBOLO, Guadalupe, 474 (19,580)	31,951
Cienegas Terrace, Val Verde, (3,424)	3,804
Cinco Ranch, Fort Bend, Harris, (18,274)	25,089
Cipres, Hidalgo	20
Circle, Lamb	6
Circle Back, Bailey	8
Circle D-KC Estates, Bastrop, (2,393)	2,730
Circleville, Williamson	50
*CISCO, Eastland, 159 (3,899)	3,834
Cistern, Fayette	137
Citrus City, Hidalgo (2,321)	2,883
Citrus Grove, Matagorda	30
Clairemont, Kent	12
Clairette, Erath	55
Clara, Wichita	100
Clardy, Lamar	160
*CLARENDON, Donley, 94 (2,026)	1,772
Clareville, Bee	25
Clark, Liberty	75
Clarkson, Milam	10
*CLARKSVILLE, Red River, 123 (3,285)	2,991
CLARKSVILLE CITY, Gregg, Upshur, 23 (865)	932
*CLAUDE, Armstrong, 60 (1,196)	1,210
Clauene, Hockley	10
Clawson, Angelina	1,500
Clay, Burleson	61
Clays Corner, Parmer	15
*Clayton, Panola, 2	125
Claytonville, Swisher	85
Clear Creek, Burnet	78
CLEAR LAKE SHORES, Galveston, 85 (1,063)	1,190
*CLEBURNE, Johnson, 1,126 (29,337)	33,110
Clegg, Live Oak	125
Clemville, Matagorda	25
Cleo, Kimble	3
*CLEVELAND, Liberty, 492 (7,675)	8,960
Cleveland, Austin	125
Cliffside, Potter	206
*CLIFTON, Bosque, 223 (3,442)	3,594
Climax, Collin	82
Cline, Uvalde	15
*CLINT, El Paso, 63 (926)	1,163
Clinton, Hunt	150
Close City, Garza	65
Cloverleaf, Harris (22,942)	24,256
*CLUTE, Brazoria, 355 (11,211)	11,919
*CLYDE, Callahan, 174 (3,713)	3,956
*COAHOMA, Howard, 27 (817)	948
Coble, Hockley	11
Cochran, Austin	200
COCKRELL HILL, Dallas, 92 (4,193)	4,412
COFFEE CITY, Henderson, 13 (278)	1,504
Coffeeville, Upshur	50
Cofferville, Lamb	4
Coit, Limestone	25
Coke, Wood	53
*COLDSPRING, San Jacinto, 92 (853)	976
*COLEMAN, Coleman, 207 (4,709)	4,305
Colfax, Van Zandt	94
Colita, Polk, Trinity	50
College Hill, Bowie	40
College Mound, Kaufman	500
*Collegeport, Matagorda	80

An old Santa Fe train station in Clifton. Photo by Larry D. Moore, CC by 4.0/Wikimedia Commons.

CITIES & TOWNS

Town, County	Pop. 2019
*COLLEGE STATION, Brazos, 2,576 (93,857)	118,410
*COLLEYVILLE, Tarrant, 1,145 (22,807)	27,091
*COLLINSVILLE, Grayson, 51 (1,624)	1,934
*COLMESNEIL, Tyler, 34 (596)	603
Colony, Rains	35
Colorado Acres, Webb (296)	338
*COLORADO CITY, Mitchell, 175 (4,146)	3,790
Coltharp, Houston	40
Colton, Travis	50
*COLUMBUS, Colorado, 271 (3,655)	3,868
*COMANCHE, Comanche, 218 (4,335)	4,349
*COMBES, Cameron, 45 (2,895)	3,094
COMBINE, Kaufman, Dallas, 52 (1,942)	2,270
Cometa, Zavala	10
*Comfort, Kendall, 140 (2,363)	2,936
*COMMERCE, Hunt, 237 (8,078)	9,696
*COMO, Hopkins, 30 (702)	746
*Comstock, Val Verde	344
Comyn, Comanche	30
*Concan, Uvalde, 36	500
*Concepcion, Duval (62)	57
Concord, Cherokee	50
*Concord, Leon, 1	28
Concord, Madison	50
Concord, Rusk	23
Concrete, DeWitt	46
Cone, Crosby	50
Conlen, Dallam	14
Connor, Madison	20
*CONROE, Montgomery, 3,454 (56,207)	90,276
Content, Bell	25
*CONVERSE, Bexar, 528 (18,198)	29,120
Conway, Carson	20
Cooks Point, Burleson	60
*Cookville, Titus, 10	105
COOL, Parker, 6 (157)	185
*COOLIDGE, Limestone, 13 (955)	997
*COOPER, Delta, 72 (1,969)	1,997
Cooper, Houston	27
Copano Village, Aransas	210
*Copeville, Collin, 4	243
*COPPELL, Dallas, Denton, 1,376 (38,659)	41,250
*COPPERAS COVE, Coryell, 658 (32,032)	35,270
COPPER CANYON, Denton, 37 (1,334)	1,515
Corbet, Navarro	80
Cordele, Jackson	51
CORINTH, Denton, 490 (19,935)	23,304
Corinth, Jones	10
Corinth, Leon	50
Corley, Bowie	35
Cornersville, Hopkins	200
Cornett, Cass	30
Cornudas, Hudspeth	5
*CORPUS CHRISTI, Nueces, 9,140 (305,215)	327,618
*CORRIGAN, Polk, 66 (1,595)	1,683
*CORSICANA, Navarro, 903 (23,770)	24,601
Coryell City, Coryell	70
*Cost, Gonzales, 7	84
Cotton Center, Fannin	33
*Cotton Center, Hale, 4	300
Cottondale, Wise	300
Cotton Gin, Freestone	28
Cotton Patch, DeWitt	11
COTTONWOOD, Kaufman (185)	212
Cottonwood, Madison	40
Cottonwood, McLennan	150
Cottonwood, Somervell	24
COTTONWOOD SHORES, Burnet, 51 (1,123)	1,359
*COTULLA, La Salle, 144 (3,603)	4,063
Couch, Karnes	10
Coughran, Atascosa	20
Country Acres, San Patricio (185)	179
County Line, Lubbock	59
County Line, Rains	40
*COUPLAND, Williamson, 19	317
Courtney, Grimes	60
COVE, Chambers, 22 (510)	567
Cove Springs, Cherokee	49
*COVINGTON, Hill, 19 (269)	276
Cox, Upshur	30
*Coyanosa, Pecos, 13 (163)	172
Coy City, Karnes	30
Coyote Acres, Jim Wells (508)	581
COYOTE FLATS, Johnson (312)	329
Crabbs Prairie, Walker	240
Craft, Cherokee	21
Crafton, Wise	100
*CRANDALL, Kaufman, 108 (2,858)	3,495
*CRANE, Crane, 101 (3,353)	3,582
*CRANFILLS GAP, Bosque, 16 (281)	286
*CRAWFORD, McLennan, 40 (717)	765
Creath, Houston	20
Crecy, Trinity	15
CREEDMOOR, Travis, 35 (202)	222
Crescent Heights, Henderson	180
*CRESSON, Hood, Johnson, Parker, 87 (741)	1,123
Crews, Runnels	30
Crisp, Ellis	115
*CROCKETT, Houston, 278 (6,950)	6,741
*Crosby, Harris, 388 (2,299)	2,875
*CROSBYTON, Crosby, 51 (1,741)	1,602
Cross, Grimes	53
Cross, McMullen	25
Cross Cut, Brown	22
Cross Mountain, Bexar (3,124)	3,708
*CROSS PLAINS, Callahan, 57 (982)	1,014
CROSS ROADS, Denton, 106 (1,563)	1,618
Cross Roads, Henderson	160
Cross Roads, Madison	75
Cross Roads, Milam	35
Crossroads, Cass	60
Crossroads, Delta	20
Crossroads, Harrison	100
Crossroads, Hopkins	50
CROSS TIMBER, Johnson (268)	319
Croton, Dickens	7
Crow, Wood	178
*CROWELL, Foard, 34 (948)	813
*CROWLEY, Tarrant, 352 (12,838)	15,945
Crown, Atascosa	10
Cruz Calle, Duval	12
Cryer Creek, Navarro	15
Crystal Beach, Galveston	800
*CRYSTAL CITY, Zavala, 101 (7,138)	7,189
Crystal Falls, Stephens	10
Crystal Lake, Anderson	12
Cuadrilla, El Paso	67
*CUERO, DeWitt, 320 (6,841)	7,482
Cuevitas, Hidalgo (40)	50
*CUMBY, Hopkins, 42 (777)	826
Cumings, Fort Bend (981)	1,398
Cundiff, Jack	45
*CUNEY, Cherokee, 2 (140)	140
*Cunningham, Lamar, 2	110
Currie, Navarro	25
Curtis, Jasper	150
*CUSHING, Nacogdoches, 44 (612)	610
Cusseta, Cass	30
*CUT AND SHOOT, Montgomery, 62 (1,070)	1,409
Cuthand, Red River	116
Cyclone, Bell	47
Cypress, Franklin	20
Cypress Creek, Kerr	200
*Cypress, Harris, 2,552	120,000
Cypress Mill, Blanco	200

D

Town, County	Pop. 2019
Dacosta, Victoria	89
Dacus, Montgomery	190
Daffan, Travis	500
*DAINGERFIELD, Morris, Titus, 90 (2,560)	2,454
*DAISETTA, Liberty, 20 (966)	1,151
Dalby Springs, Bowie	75
*Dale, Caldwell, 35	300
*DALHART, Dallam, Hartley, 323 (7,930)	8,097
*Dallardsville, Polk, 1	350
*DALLAS, Dallas, Collin, Denton, 41,922 (1,197,816)	1,357,986
Dalton, Cass	50
DALWORTHINGTON GARDENS, Tarrant, 153 (2,259)	2,333
*Damon, Brazoria, 25 (552)	614
*DANBURY, Brazoria, 48 (1,715)	1,883
*Danciger, Brazoria, 1	90
*Danevang, Wharton, 5	61

Town, County	Pop. 2019
Daniels, Panola	75
Danville, Gregg, Rusk	200
Darby Hill, San Jacinto	25
Darco, Harrison	10
Darden, Polk	320
*DARROUZETT, Lipscomb, 16 (350)	341
Datura, Limestone	2
*Davilla, Milam	191
Davis, Atascosa	8
Davis Prairie, Limestone	17
*Dawn, Deaf Smith	52
*DAWSON, Navarro, 23 (807)	810
*DAYTON, Liberty, 397 (7,242)	9,186
DAYTON LAKES, Liberty (93)	109
Deadwood, Panola	106
DEAN, Clay, 9 (493)	463
Dean, Hockley	20
*Deanville, Burleson, 4	130
*DeBerry, Panola, 23	200
*DECATUR, Wise, 495 (6,042)	7,086
Decker Prairie, Montgomery	2,000
DeCORDOVA, Hood (2,683)	2,998
*DEER PARK, Harris, 959 (32,010)	34,050
*DE KALB, Bowie, 66 (1,699)	1,673
*DE LEON, Comanche, 115 (2,246)	2,217
Delhi, Caldwell	150
Delia, Limestone	20
*DELL CITY, Hudspeth, 17 (365)	378
Del Mar Heights, Cameron (113)	97
*Delmita, Starr, 4 (216)	226
Delray, Panola	45
*DEL RIO, Val Verde, 882 (35,591)	35,982
Delrose, Upshur	35
Del Sol, San Patricio (239)	231
*Del Valle, Travis, 118	[part of Austin]
Delwin, Cottle	12
Demi-John, Brazoria	300
Democrat, Mills, Comanche	8
Denhawken, Wilson	52
*DENISON, Grayson, 843 (22,682)	25,402
Denning, San Augustine	100
*DENNIS, Parker, 2	953
Denson Springs, Anderson	60
*DENTON, Denton, 3,635 (113,383)	142,944
Denton, Callahan	6
*DENVER CITY, Yoakum, Gaines, 159 (4,479)	5,044
*DEPORT, Lamar, Red River, 15 (578)	556
Derby, Frio	50
*Desdemona, Eastland	180
Desert, Collin	35
*DeSOTO, Dallas, 1,079 (49,047)	52,631
*DETROIT, Red River, 36 (732)	678
*DEVERS, Liberty, 20 (447)	527
*DEVINE, Medina, 233 (4,350)	5,001
Dew, Freestone	150
DeWees, Wilson	60
Deweesville, Karnes	12
*Deweyville, Newton, 11 (1,023)	873
Dewville, Gonzales	30
Dexter, Cooke	12
*D'Hanis, Medina, 21 (847)	873
Dial, Fannin	76
Dialville, Cherokee	200
*Diana, Upshur, 39	585
*DIBOLL, Angelina, 113 (5,359)	5,279
Dicey, Parker	40
*DICKENS, Dickens, 12 (286)	253
*DICKINSON, Galveston, 541 (18,680)	21,576
*Dike, Hopkins, 6	170
*DILLEY, Frio, 86 (3,894)	4,269
Dilworth, Gonzales	18
Dilworth, Red River	25
*Dime Box, Lee, 15	381
*DIMMITT, Castro, 117 (4,393)	4,063
Dimple, Red River	60
Dinero, Live Oak, 1	344
Ding Dong, Bell	301
Direct, Lamar	85
Dirgin, Rusk	50
DISH, Denton (201)	467
Divide, Kerr	50
Divot, Frio	30
Dixie, Grayson	17
Dixon, Hunt	31
Dixon-Hopewell, Houston	10
Doak Springs, Lee	50
Doans, Wilbarger	20
*Dobbin, Montgomery, 1	310
Dobrowolski, Atascosa	10
Dodd, Castro	12
*DODD CITY, Fannin, 17 (369)	395
*Dodge, Walker, 5	150
*DODSON, Collingsworth (109)	104
Dodson Prairie, Palo Pinto	18
Doffing, Hidalgo (5,091)	5,722
Dog Ridge, Bell	215
Dogwood City, Smith	800
Dolen, Liberty	75
DOMINO, Cass, 8 (93)	100
*Donie, Freestone, 7	250
*DONNA, Hidalgo, 536 (15,798)	17,235
*Doole, McCulloch	74
Doolittle, Hidalgo (2,769)	3,033
DORCHESTER, Grayson (148)	167
Dorras, Stonewall, Fisher	20
Doss, Cass	15
*Doss, Gillespie, 7	100
Dot, Falls	17
Dotson, Panola	35
Double Bayou, Chambers	200
DOUBLE OAK, Denton, 100 (2,867)	3,234
DOUBLE HORN, Burnet	238
*Doucette, Tyler, 3	160
*Dougherty, Floyd, 2	91
Dougherty, Rains	40
*Douglass, Nacogdoches, 20	380
*DOUGLASSVILLE, Cass, 8 (229)	225
Downing, Comanche	30
Downsville, McLennan	150
Downtown Texas, Milam	34
Doyle, San Patricio (254)	243
Doyle, Limestone	50
Dozier, Collingsworth	4
Drane, Navarro	16
DRAPER, Denton (27)	33
Drasco, Runnels	15
Draw, Lynn	18
Dreka, Shelby	30
Dresden, Navarro	25
Dreyer, Gonzales	20
*Driftwood, Hays, 89 (144)	193
*DRIPPING SPRINGS, Hays, 622 (1,788)	5,918
*DRISCOLL, Nueces, 12 (739)	744
Drop, Denton	90
*Dryden, Terrell, 1	13
Dubina, Fayette	272
*DUBLIN, Erath, 156 (3,654)	3,562
Dudley, Callahan	25
Duffau, Erath	76
*DUMAS, Moore, 378 (14,691)	14,044
Dumont, King, Dickens	19
Dunbar, Rains	40
*DUNCANVILLE, Dallas, 1,139 (38,524)	39,782
Dundee, Archer	12
Dunlap, Cottle	10
Dunlap, Travis	80
Dunlay, Medina	145
Dunn, Scurry	75
Duplex, Fannin	25
Durango, Falls	54
Duren, Mills	15
Duster, Comanche	25
Dye, Montague	30

E

Town, County	Pop. 2019
Eagle, Chambers	30
*EAGLE LAKE, Colorado, 106 (3,639)	3,777
*EAGLE PASS, Maverick, 902 (26,248)	28,992
*EARLY, Brown, 183 (2,762)	3,049
*EARTH, Lamb, 23 (1,065)	957
East Afton, Dickens	13
East Alto Bonito, Starr (824)	953
*EAST BERNARD, Wharton, 113 (2,272)	2,351
East Caney, Hopkins	100
East Columbia, Brazoria	95
East Delta, Delta	60
East Direct, Lamar	48
Easter, Castro	26
Easterly, Robertson	61
Eastgate, Liberty	200
East Hamilton, Shelby	25
*EASTLAND, Eastland, 211 (3,960)	4,010
East Lopez, Starr (166)	179
EAST MOUNTAIN, Upshur, 20 (797)	851
EASTON, Gregg, Rusk, 5 (510)	639
East Point, Wood	40
East Sweden, McCulloch	40
EAST TAWAKONI, Rains, 24 (883)	976
Ebenezer, Camp	55

Town, County	Pop. 2019
Ebenezer, Jasper	50
Echo, Coleman	6
Ecleto, Karnes	22
*ECTOR, Fannin, 12 (695)	740
*EDCOUCH, Hidalgo, 46 (3,161)	3,368
*EDEN, Concho, 54 (2,766)	1,828
Eden, Nacogdoches	100
Edgar, DeWitt	8
Edge, Brazos	10
EDGECLIFF, Tarrant (2,776)	2,979
Edgewater Estates, San Patricio (72)	73
*EDGEWOOD, Van Zandt, 97 (1,441)	1,554
Edgeworth, Bell	15
Edhube, Fannin	40
*EDINBURG, Hidalgo, 1,921 (74,569)	99,454
*EDMONSON, Hale, 5 (111)	101
*EDNA, Jackson, 257 (5,499)	5,690
Edna Hill, Erath	32
EDOM, Van Zandt, 16 (375)	397
*Edroy, San Patricio, 1 (331)	301
Egan, Johnson	133
*Egypt, Wharton, 3	26
Eidson Road, Maverick (8,960)	9,132
Elam Springs, Upshur	50
Elbert, Throckmorton (30)	21
Elbow, Howard	10
El Brazil, Starr (47)	50
El Camino Angosto, Cameron, (253)	254
*EL CAMPO, Wharton, 609 (11,602)	11,918
El Castillo, Starr (188)	219
El Cenizo, Starr (249)	283
EL CENIZO, Webb, 25 (3,273)	3,127
El Centro, Starr	50
El Chaparral, Starr (464)	507
*ELDORADO, Schleicher, 67 (1,951)	1,584
Eldorado Center, Navarro	20
Eldridge, Colorado	10
*ELECTRA, Wichita, 72 (2,791)	2,719
Elevation, Milam	12
*ELGIN, Bastrop, 419 (8,135)	10,262
Elias-Fela Solis, Starr (30)	36
Eliasville, Young	100
*El Indio, Maverick, 1 (190)	169
Elk, McLennan	150
*ELKHART, Anderson, 60 (1,371)	1,299
EL LAGO, Harris, 67 (2,706)	2,680
*ELLINGER, Fayette, 9	386
Elliott, Robertson	55
Elliott, Wilbarger	50
*Elmaton, Matagorda, 3	160
Elm Creek, Maverick (2,469)	2,870
*ELMENDORF, Bexar, 71 (1,488)	2,112
El Mesquite, Starr (38)	44
Elm Grove, Cherokee	50
Elm Grove, San Saba	15
Elm Grove, Wharton	76
Elm Grove Camp, Guadalupe	88
*Elm Mott, McLennan, 70	300
*Elmo, Kaufman, 1 (768)	1,049
Elmont, Grayson	15
Elm Ridge, Milam	25
Elmwood, Anderson	15
Eloise, Falls	19
El Oso, Karnes	35
*EL PASO, El Paso, 16,474 (649,121)	686,265
El Quiote, Starr (208)	223
El Rancho Vela, Starr (274)	291
El Refugio, Starr (331)	392
Elroy, Travis	125
*ELSA, Hidalgo, 158 (5,660)	7,174
El Sauz, Starr	50
El Socio, Starr (130)	144
Elton, Dickens	4
El Toro, Jackson	136
Elwood, Fannin	31
Elwood, Madison	50
*Elysian Fields, Harrison, 7	500
Emberson, Lamar	80
Emerald Bay, Smith (1,047)	1,080
EMHOUSE, Navarro, 2 (133)	143
Emmett, Navarro	100
*EMORY, Rains, 179 (1,239)	1,451
Encantada-Ranchito El Calaboz, Cameron (2,255)	2,201
ENCHANTED OAKS, Henderson, (326)	344
*ENCINAL, La Salle, 28 (559)	583
*Encino, Brooks, 6 (143)	145
*Energy, Comanche, 2	70
Engle, Fayette	141
English, Red River	100
*Enloe, Delta, 1	90
*ENNIS, Ellis, 685 (18,513)	21,101
Enoch, Upshur	25
*Enochs, Bailey	80
Enon, Upshur	204
*Eola, Concho, 4	215
Eolian, Stephens	9
*Era, Cooke, 5	150
Ericksdahl, Jones	35
Erin, Jasper	70
Erna, Menard, Mason	27
Erwin, Grimes	52
Escobares, Starr, 44 (1,188)	2,837
Escobar I, Starr (324)	352

Humphries House in Edgewood. Photo by Renelibrary, CC by 4.0/Wikimedia Commons.

Town, County	Pop. 2019
Escobas, Zapata	2
Eskota, Fisher	32
Esperanza, Hudspeth	75
Espey, Atascosa	55
Estacado, Lubbock, Crosby	32
*ESTELLINE, Hall, 3 (145)	131
Estes, Aransas	300
Ethel, Grayson	40
*Etoile, Nacogdoches, 12	700
Eugenio Saenz, Starr (159)	170
Eula, Callahan	125
*EULESS, Tarrant, 1,423 (51,277)	56,965
Eulogy, Bosque	10
EUREKA, Navarro, 9 (307)	318
Eureka, Franklin	18
*EUSTACE, Henderson, 57 (991)	1,007
*Evadale, Jasper, 16 (1,483)	1,545
*EVANT, Coryell, Hamilton, 37 (426)	405
Evergreen, Starr (73)	79
Evergreen, San Jacinto	100
EVERMAN, Tarrant, 117 (6,108)	6,215
Ewell, Upshur	20
Ezzell, Lavaca	55

F

Town, County	Pop. 2019
*Fabens, El Paso, 67 (8,257)	8,500
Fabrica, Maverick (923)	989
FAIRCHILDS, Fort Bend (763)	1,068
*FAIRFIELD, Freestone, 223 (2,951)	2,984
Fairland, Burnet	340
Fairlie, Hunt	80
Fairmount, Sabine	1,500
Fair Oaks, Limestone	15
FAIR OAKS RANCH, Bexar, Comal, Kendall, 154 (5,986)	9,434
Fair Play, Panola	80
FAIRVIEW, Collin, 289 (7,248)	9,021
Fairview, Armstrong	10
Fairview, Cass	20
Fairview, Gaines	160
Fairview, Hockley	20
Fairview, Hood	30
Fairview, Howard	5
Fairview, Wilson	95
Fairy, Hamilton	40
New Falcon, Zapata (191)	175
Falconaire, Starr (132)	128
*Falcon Heights, Starr, 1 (53)	56
Falcon Lake Estates, Zapata, (1,036)	1,155
Falcon Mesa, Zapata (405)	342
Falcon Village, Starr (47)	43
*FALFURRIAS, Brooks, 133 (4,981)	4,916
Fallon, Limestone	100
*FALLS CITY, Karnes, 32 (611)	686
Falman, San Patricio (76)	73
Famuliner, Cochran	5
Fannett, Jefferson (2,252)	2,333
*Fannin, Goliad, 6	359
Fargo, Wilbarger	169
Farmers Academy, Titus	75
*FARMERS BRANCH, Dallas, 1,975 (28,616)	41,093
Farmers Valley, Wilbarger	30
*FARMERSVILLE, Collin, 201 (3,301)	4,534
Farmington, Grayson	40
*Farnsworth, Ochiltree, 6	130
Farrar, Limestone	51
Farrsville, Newton	152
*FARWELL, Parmer, 47 (1,363)	1,255
Fashing, Atascosa	35
*FATE, Rockwall, 261 (6,434)	15,121
Faught, Lamar	25
Faulkner, Lamar	10
Fawil, Newton	183
*FAYETTEVILLE, Fayette, 69 (258)	262
Faysville, Hidalgo (439)	500
Fedor, Lee	92
*Fentress, Caldwell, 8	380
Fernando Salinas, Starr (15)	12
*FERRIS, Ellis, 101 (2,436)	2,987
Fetzer, Waller	150
Fields Store, Waller	500
*Fieldton, Lamb, 1	20
Fife, McCulloch	32
Fifth Street, Fort Bend (2,486)	3,338
Files Valley, Hill	60
Fincastle, Henderson	75
Finney, Hale	18
*Fischer, Comal, 17	400
Fisk, Coleman	40
Five Points, Ellis	25
Flaccus, Karnes	15
Flagg, Castro	26
*Flat, Coryell, 2	210
Flat Fork, Shelby	10
*FLATONIA, Fayette, 102 (1,383)	1,507
Flat Prairie, Trinity	33
Flats, Rains	40
Flat Top, Stonewall	5
*Flint, Smith, 193	2,500
Flo, Leon	12
Flomot, Motley	181
Flora, Hopkins	20
Flor del Rio, Starr (122)	134
*FLORENCE, Williamson, 103 (1,136)	1,306
*FLORESVILLE, Wilson, 355 (6,448)	8,104
Florey, Andrews	25
Flour Bluff, Nueces	[part of Corpus Christi]
Flowella, Brooks (118)	116
Flower Hill, Colorado	20
*FLOWER MOUND, Denton, 2,290 (64,669)	79,640
Floyd, Hunt	90
*FLOYDADA, Floyd, 115 (3,038)	2,562
*Fluvanna, Scurry, 8	180
*Flynn, Leon, 4	81
Foard City, Foard	10
Fodice, Houston	49
*FOLLETT, Lipscomb, 25 (459)	440
Folsom, Shelby	30
Ford, Deaf Smith	25
Fords Corner, San Augustine	30
Fordtran, Victoria	18
Forest, Cherokee	85
*Forestburg, Montague, 14	50
Forest Chapel, Lamar	105
Forest Glade, Limestone	340
Forest Grove, Milam	60
Forest Heights, Orange	250
FOREST HILL, Tarrant, 328 (12,355)	12,894
Forest Hill, Lamar	50
Forest Hill, Wood	30
*FORNEY, Kaufman, 761 (14,661)	27,565
*Forreston, Ellis, Navarro, 2	400
*FORSAN, Howard, 9 (210)	215
Fort Bliss, El Paso (8,591)	9,137
Fort Clark Springs, Kinney, (1,228)	1,231
*Fort Davis, Jeff Davis, 59 (1,201)	1,162
*Fort Hancock, Hudspeth, 8 (1,750)	1,832
Fort Hood, Bell, Coryell, (29,589)	26,245
*Fort McKavett, Menard	50
Fort Parker, Limestone	2
Fort Parker State Park, Limestone	30
Fort Sherman, Titus	200
Fort Spunky, Hood	15
*FORT STOCKTON, Pecos, 314 (8,283)	8,470
*FORT WORTH, Tarrant, Denton, Parker, Wise, 20,779 (741,206)	895,100
Foster, Terry	6
Fostoria, Montgomery	586
Fouke, Wood	30
Four Corners, Fort Bend, (12,382)	17,948
Four Corners, Brazoria	60
Four Corners, Chambers	18
Four Corners, Montgomery	500
Four Points, Webb (18)	15
Fowlerton, La Salle, 4 (55)	48
Frame Switch, Williamson	25
*Francitas, Jackson, 2	125
Frankel City, Andrews	2
Frankell, Stephens	8
*FRANKLIN, Robertson, 83 (1,564)	1,701
*FRANKSTON, Anderson, 89 (1,229)	1,216
*Fred, Tyler, 6	300
*FREDERICKSBURG, Gillespie, 1,193 (10,530)	11,482
*Fredonia, Mason, San Saba, 2	55
Freedom, Rains	32
*FREEPORT, Brazoria, 309 (12,049)	12,990
*FREER, Duval, 91 (2,818)	2,632
Freestone, Freestone	100
Frelsburg, Colorado	75
Frenstat, Burleson	50

Town, County	Pop. 2019
*Fresno, Fort Bend, 113 (19,069)	28,243
Fresno, Collingsworth	10
Freyburg, Fayette	148
Friday, Trinity	70
Friendship, Dawson	40
Friendship, Smith	200
Friendship, Upshur	25
Friendship Village, Bowie	200
*FRIENDSWOOD, Galveston, Harris, 1,179 (35,805)	40,659
Frio Town, Frio	9
*FRIONA, Parmer, 86 (4,123)	3,815
*FRISCO, Collin, Denton, 5,120 (116,989)	190,974
*FRITCH, Hutchinson, Moore, 66 (2,117)	1,961
Frog, Kaufman	90
Fronton, Starr (180)	170
Fronton Ranchettes, Starr (113)	117
*FROST, Navarro, 21 (643)	653
Fruitland, Montague	20
*FRUITVALE, Van Zandt, 11 (408)	433
Frydek, Austin	900
Fulbright, Red River	150
*FULSHEAR, Fort Bend, 318 (1,134)	13,914
*FULTON, Aransas, 98 (1,358)	1,437
Funston, Jones	26
Furrh, Panola	40

G

Town, County	Pop. 2019
Gadston, Lamar	35
*Gail, Borden, 5 (231)	284
*GAINESVILLE, Cooke, 773 (16,002)	16,709
Galena, Smith	50
*GALENA PARK, Harris, 160 (10,887)	11,022
Galilee, Smith	150
*GALLATIN, Cherokee (419)	447
Galloway, Panola	71
*GALVESTON, Galveston, 1,887 (47,745)	50,372
*GANADO, Jackson, 112 (2,003)	2,115
Garceño, Starr (420)	391
*Garciasville, Starr, 2 (46)	59
*Garden City, Glasscock, 31 (334)	427
*Gardendale, Ector, 45 (1,574)	1,959
Gardendale, La Salle	80
GARDEN RIDGE, Comal, 116 (3,259)	4,187
Garden Valley, Smith	150
Garfield, Travis (1,698)	1,845
Garfield, DeWitt	16
*GARLAND, Dallas, 5,949 (226,876)	242,493
Garland, Bowie	45
Garner, Parker	196
Garner State Park, Uvalde	50
GARRETT, Ellis, 9 (806)	900
Garretts Bluff, Lamar	25
*GARRISON, Nacogdoches, 43 (895)	881
*Garwood, Colorado, 21	600
*GARY, Panola (311)	311
Garza-Salinas II, Starr (719)	785
Gastonia, Kaufman	100
*GATESVILLE, Coryell, 372 (15,751)	15,997
*Gause, Milam, 6	425
Gay Hill, Washington	40
Geneva, Sabine	200
Geneview, Stonewall	3
Gentry's Mill, Hamilton	20
George's Creek, Somervell, Johnson, Hood	43
*GEORGETOWN, Williamson, 2,136 (47,400)	75,756
*GEORGE WEST, Live Oak, 157 (2,445)	2,568
Georgia, Lamar	55
Germany, Houston	23
Geronimo, Guadalupe, 5 (1,032)	1,374
GHOLSON, McLennan, 21 (1,061)	1,114
Gibtown, Jack	20
*GIDDINGS, Lee, 326 (4,881)	5,118
Gilchrist, Galveston, 1	300
*Gillett, Karnes, 12	120
Gilliland, Knox	20
*GILMER, Upshur, 392 (4,905)	5,085
Gilpin, Dickens	2
Ginger, Rains	70
*Girard, Kent (50)	44
Girvin, Pecos	20
Gist, Jasper	20
Givens, Lamar	135
*GLADEWATER, Gregg, Upshur, 332 (6,441)	6,788
Glaze City, Gonzales	10
Glazier, Hemphill	48
Gleckler, Lavaca	78
Glen Cove, Coleman	40
Glendale, Trinity	175
Glenfawn, Rusk	100
*Glen Flora, Wharton, 3	210
Glenn, Dickens	4
GLENN HEIGHTS, Dallas, Ellis, 160 (11,278)	13,396
Glenrio, Deaf Smith	10
*GLEN ROSE, Somervell, 235 (2,444)	2,812
Glenwood, Upshur	150
Glidden, Colorado, 1 (661)	762
Globe, Lamar	60
Glory, Lamar	30
*Gober, Fannin, 1	146
*GODLEY, Johnson, 65 (1,009)	1,377
*Golden, Wood, 6	398
Goldfinch, Frio	35
*Goldsboro, Coleman, 1	15
*GOLDSMITH, Ector, 18 (257)	286
*GOLDTHWAITE, Mills, 82 (1,878)	1,888
*GOLIAD, Goliad, 138 (1,908)	2,089
GOLINDA, Falls, McLennan, 18 (559)	592
Golly, DeWitt	41
Gomez, Terry	6
*GONZALES, Gonzales, 360 (7,237)	7,576
Goober Hill, Shelby	30
Goodland, Bailey	10
Goodlett, Hardeman	80
GOODLOW, Navarro, 4 (200)	194
Good Neighbor, Hopkins	40
Goodnight, Armstrong	20
*GOODRICH, Polk, 32 (271)	317
Goodsprings, Rusk	40
Goodwill, Burleson	12
Goodwin, San Augustine	70
*GORDON, Palo Pinto, 30 (478)	488
*Gordonville, Grayson, 21	165
*GOREE, Knox, 8 (203)	203
*GORMAN, Eastland, 43 (1,083)	1,034
Goshen, Walker	250
Gould, Cherokee	20
*Gouldbusk, Coleman, 3	70
Graceton, Upshur	100
*GRAFORD, Palo Pinto, 30 (584)	620
*GRAHAM, Young, 515 (8,903)	9,158
Graham, Garza	60
*GRANBURY, Hood, 1,249 (7,978)	10,454
Grand Acres, Cameron (49)	43
Grand Bluff, Panola	115
*GRANDFALLS, Ward, 10 (360)	398
*GRAND PRAIRIE, Dallas, Tarrant, Ellis, 4,737 (175,396)	195,756
*GRAND SALINE, Van Zandt, 119 (3,136)	3,311
*GRANDVIEW, Johnson, 109 (1,561)	1,796
Grandview, Dawson	8
Grandview, Gray	13
*GRANGER, Williamson, 54 (1,419)	1,624
Grangerland, Montgomery	300
GRANITE SHOALS, Burnet, 90 (4,910)	5,337
GRANJENO, Hidalgo, 2 (293)	320
Grape Creek, Tom Green, (3,154)	3,201
*GRAPELAND, Houston, 87 (1,489)	1,456
*GRAPEVINE, Tarrant, 2,825 (46,334)	54,277
Grassland, Lynn	40
Gray, Marion	12
Grayback, Wilbarger	10
GRAYS PRAIRIE, Kaufman, 6 (337)	379
Graytown, Wilson, Bexar	85
Green, Karnes	50
Green Hill, Titus	80
Green Lake, Calhoun	51
Greenpond, Hopkins	150
Green's Creek, Erath	75
Green Valley, Denton	100
Green Valley Farms, Cameron, (1,272)	1,526
Greenview, Hopkins	25
*GREENVILLE, Hunt, 979 (25,557)	28,992
Greenvine, Washington	35
Greenwood, Hopkins	100
Greenwood, Midland	2,000

Town, County	Pop. 2019
Greenwood, Red River	20
*Greenwood, Wise, 3	76
*GREGORY, San Patricio, 38 (1,907)	1,854
Gresham, Smith	1,000
GREY FOREST, Bexar, 16 (483)	566
Gribble Springs, Denton	55
Grice, Upshur	20
Griffith, Cochran	12
Grigsby, Shelby	15
Grit, Mason	15
*GROESBECK, Limestone, 131 (4,328)	4,308
*GROOM, Carson, 32 (574)	542
Grosvenor, Brown	24
*GROVES, Jefferson, 316 (16,144)	15,953
*GROVETON, Trinity, 46 (1,057)	1,055
Grow, King	9
Gruenau, DeWitt	18
Gruene, Comal	[part of New Braunfels]
*GRUVER, Hansford, 41 (1,194)	1,133
Guadalupe, Victoria	70
Guadalupe-Guerra, Starr (37)	57
Guadalupe Station, Culberson	10
*Guerra, Jim Hogg (6)	4
Gum Springs, Cass	59
GUN BARREL CITY, Henderson, 322 (5,672)	6,222
Gunsight, Stephens	6
*GUNTER, Grayson, 74 (1,498)	1,660
Gus, Burleson	50
*GUSTINE, Comanche, 10 (476)	490
*Guthrie, King, 1 (160)	188
Gutierrez, Starr (79)	84
*Guy, Fort Bend, 9	239
Guys Store, Leon	20

H

Town, County	Pop. 2019
Haciendito, Presidio	10
HACKBERRY, Denton, 53 (968)	1,128
Hackberry, Cottle	30
Hackberry, Edwards	3
Hackberry, Garza	5
Hackberry, Lavaca	40
Hagansport, Franklin	40
Hagerville, Houston	70
Hail, Fannin	30
Hainesville, Wood	95
*HALE CENTER, Hale, 40 (2,252)	2,059
Halfway, Hale	165
Hall, San Saba	25
*HALLETTSVILLE, Lavaca, 213 (2,550)	2,753
Halls Bluff, Houston	67
HALLSBURG, McLennan, 12 (507)	472
*HALLSVILLE, Harrison, 123 (3,577)	4,344
*HALTOM CITY, Tarrant, 1,331 (42,409)	43,003
Hamby, Taylor	100
*HAMILTON, Hamilton, 181 (3,095)	3,108
*HAMLIN, Jones, Fisher, 70 (2,124)	2,040
Hammond, Robertson	44
Hamon, Gonzales	20
*Hamshire, Jefferson, 18	759
Hancock, Comal	1,000
Hancock, Dawson	20
*Hankamer, Chambers, 12	226
Hannibal, Erath	25
Hanover, Milam	25
*HAPPY, Swisher, Randall, 34 (678)	666
Happy Union, Hale	25
Happy Valley, Taylor	12
Harbin, Erath	21
*HARDIN, Liberty, 11 (819)	979
Hare, Williamson	60
*Hargill, Hidalgo, 3 (877)	919
*HARKER HEIGHTS, Bell, 662 (26,700)	32,665
Harkeyville, San Saba	12
*Harleton, Harrison, 22	390
*HARLINGEN, Cameron, 2,167 (64,849)	68,835
Harmon, Lamar	12
Harmony, Floyd	42
Harmony, Grimes	12
Harmony, Kent	10
Harmony, Nacogdoches	50
*Harper, Gillespie, 31 (1,192)	1,388
Harpersville, Stephens	5
Harrison, McLennan	100
Harrold, Wilbarger, 3	200
*HART, Castro, 23 (1,114)	1,014
Hartburg, Newton	893
Hart Camp, Lamb	4
*Hartley, Hartley, 19 (540)	595
Harvard, Camp	48
Harvey, Brazos	1,000
Harwell Point, Burnet	138
*Harwood, Gonzales, 12	118
*HASKELL, Haskell, 96 (3,322)	3,169
Haslam, Shelby	100
*HASLET, Tarrant, 249 (1,517)	1,928
Hasse, Comanche	50
Hatchel, Runnels	6
Hatchettville, Hopkins	20
Havana, Hidalgo (407)	393
HAWK COVE, Hunt, 3 (483)	559
*HAWKINS, Wood, 86 (1,278)	1,354
*HAWLEY, Jones, 55 (634)	623
Hawthorne, Walker	100
Haynesville, Wichita	65
HAYS, Hays, 2 (217)	263
Hazeldell, Comanche	12
H. Cuellar Estates, Starr (20)	19
*HEARNE, Robertson, 160 (4,459)	4,637
HEATH, Rockwall, Kaufman, 264 (6,921)	9,099
*Hebbronville, Jim Hogg, 84 (4,558)	4,400
HEBRON, Denton, 43 (415)	449
Heckville, Lubbock	91
*HEDLEY, Donley, 7 (329)	287
Hedwigs Hill, Mason	12
HEDWIG VILLAGE, Harris, 253 (2,557)	2,601
Hefner, Knox	3
Hegar, Waller	100
Heidelberg, Hidalgo (1,725)	1,877
*Heidenheimer, Bell, 6	224
Helena, Karnes	35
Helmic, Trinity	86
*HELOTES, Bexar, 515 (7,341)	10,297
*HEMPHILL, Sabine, 136 (1,198)	1,233
*HEMPSTEAD, Waller, 241 (5,770)	7,507
*HENDERSON, Rusk, 606 (13,712)	13,688
Henkhaus, Lavaca	88
Henly, Hays	140
*HENRIETTA, Clay, 123 (3,141)	3,104
Henry's Chapel, Cherokee	75
*HEREFORD, Deaf Smith, 395 (15,370)	15,635
Hermits Cove, Rains	40
*Hermleigh, Scurry, 16 (345)	308
Hester, Navarro	35
*HEWITT, McLennan, 398 (13,549)	14,820
*Hext, Menard, 1	75
HICKORY CREEK, Denton, 126 (3,247)	4,924
Hickory Creek, Houston	31
Hickory Creek, Hunt	40
*HICO, Hamilton, 143 (1,379)	1,428
*HIDALGO, Hidalgo, 481 (11,195)	13,984
HIDEAWAY, Smith (3,083)	3,191
Higginbotham, Gaines	21
*HIGGINS, Lipscomb, 15 (397)	398
High, Lamar	14
Highbank, Falls	20
High Hill, Fayette	176
*High Island, Galveston, 5	300
Highland, Erath	60
HIGHLAND HAVEN, Burnet, (431)	442
HIGHLAND PARK, Dallas, 457 (8,564)	8,666
*Highlands, Harris, 120 (7,522)	7,793
HIGHLAND VILLAGE, Denton, 511 (15,056)	17,300
Hightower, Liberty	225
HILL COUNTRY VILLAGE, Bexar, 98 (985)	1,102
Hillcrest, Colorado	25
HILLCREST VILLAGE, Brazoria, (730)	758
*Hillister, Tyler, 11	250
Hillje, Wharton	51
Hills, Lee	20
*HILLSBORO, Hill, 385 (8,456)	8,767
Hillside Acres, Webb (30)	49
Hilltop, Frio (287)	282
Hilltop, Starr (77)	85
*Hilltop Lakes, Leon (1,101)	1,020
HILSHIRE VILLAGE, Harris, 18 (746)	793
Hinckley, Lamar	40
Hindes, Atascosa	14

Town, County	Pop. 2019
Hinkles Ferry, Brazoria	100
Hiram, Kaufman	75
*HITCHCOCK, Galveston, 175 (6,961)	7,895
Hitchland, Hansford	15
Hix, Burleson	35
Hoard, Wood	45
Hobbs, Fisher	32
Hobson, Karnes, 11	135
Hochheim, DeWitt	70
*Hockley, Harris, 147	400
Hodges, Jones	150
Hogansville, Rains	300
Hogg, Burleson	20
Holiday Beach, Aransas (514)	507
HOLIDAY LAKES, Brazoria, 5 (1,107)	1,242
*HOLLAND, Bell, 49 (1,121)	1,170
Holland Quarters, Panola	40
*HOLLIDAY, Archer, 75 (1,758)	1,774
Holly, Houston	95
Holly Grove, Polk	20
Holly Lake Ranch, Wood (2,774)	3,031
Holly Springs, Jasper, Newton	50
HOLLYWOOD PARK, Bexar, 121 (3,062)	3,396
Holman, Fayette	101
Homer, Angelina	475
Homestead Meadows North, El Paso (5,124)	5,571
Homestead Meadows South, El Paso (7,247)	7,600
*HONDO, Medina, 276 (8,803)	9,618
*HONEY GROVE, Fannin, 63 (1,668)	1,732
Honey Island, Hardin	200
Hood, Cooke	13
Hooker Ridge, Rains	250
*HOOKS, Bowie, 50 (2,769)	2,720
Hoover, Gray	5
Hoover, Lamar	20
Hope, Lavaca	45
Hopewell, Franklin	50
Hopewell, Houston	22
Hopewell, Lamar	90
Hopewell, Red River	152
Hopewell, Smith	45
HORIZON CITY, El Paso, 268 (16,735)	19,733
Hornsby Bend, Travis (6,791)	8,332
Horseshoe Bend, Cooke (789)	971
HORSESHOE BAY, Llano, Burnet, 168 (3,418)	4,016
Hortense, Polk	20
Horton, Delta	40
Horton, Panola	200
*HOUSTON, Harris, Fort Bend, Montgomery, 87,046 (2,100,263)	2,325,298
Howard, Ellis	60
HOWARDWICK, Donley, 9 (402)	368
*HOWE, Grayson, 63 (2,600)	3,391
Howland, Lamar	65
Hoxie, Williamson	60
Hoyte, Milam	20
Hub, Parmer	25
*HUBBARD, Hill, 64 (1,423)	1,405
Hubbard, Bowie	350
Huber, Shelby	15
Huckabay, Erath	150
HUDSON, Angelina, 81 (4,731)	4,979
Hudson Bend, Travis (2,981)	3,617
HUDSON OAKS, Parker, 153 (1,662)	2,479
Huffines, Cass	140
*Huffman, Harris, 155	15,000
Hufsmith, Harris	500
*HUGHES SPRINGS, Cass, 66 (1,760)	1,733
*Hull, Liberty, 15 (669)	803
*HUMBLE, Harris, 1,834 (15,133)	15,704
*Hungerford, Wharton, 16 (347)	305
*Hunt, Kerr, 38	708
Hunter, Comal	40
HUNTERS CREEK VILLAGE, Harris, 103 (4,367)	4,738
*HUNTINGTON, Angelina, 107 (2,118)	2,149
Huntoon, Ochiltree	22
*HUNTSVILLE, Walker, 1,135 (38,548)	43,899
Hurley, Wood	30
Hurlwood, Lubbock	152
Hurnville, Clay	10
*HURST, Tarrant, 1,601 (37,337)	38,479
Hurstown, Shelby	20
Hurst Springs, Coryell	10
*HUTCHINS, Dallas, 134 (5,338)	6,240
*HUTTO, Williamson, 551 (14,698)	26,801
HUXLEY, Shelby, 5 (385)	372
*Hye, Blanco, 11	72
Hylton, Nolan	6

I

Town, County	Pop. 2019
Iago, Wharton (161)	151
Ida, Grayson	30
*IDALOU, Lubbock, 88 (2,250)	2,301
Iglesia Antigua, Cameron (413)	444
Ike, Ellis	50
Illinois Bend, Montague	40
IMPACT, Taylor, 1 (35)	29
*Imperial, Pecos, 6 (278)	234
Inadale, Scurry	12
Independence, Washington	140
India, Ellis	30
Indian Creek, Brown	28
Indian Creek, Smith	300
Indian Gap, Hamilton	35
Indian Hill, Newton	7
Indian Hills, Hidalgo (2,591)	3,079
INDIAN LAKE, Cameron (640)	833
Indianola, Calhoun	200
Indian Rock, Upshur	45
Indian Springs, Polk (785)	920
Indio, Starr (50)	66
Indio, Presidio	5
*INDUSTRY, Austin, 44 (304)	331
*Inez, Victoria, 51 (2,098)	2,357
*INGLESIDE, San Patricio, 215 (9,387)	9,895
INGLESIDE-ON-THE-BAY, San Patricio, 13 (615)	566
*INGRAM, Kerr, 174 (1,804)	1,855
*IOLA, Grimes, 11 (401)	435
IOWA COLONY, Brazoria, 26 (1,170)	6,107
*IOWA PARK, Wichita, 173 (6,355)	6,379
*Ira, Scurry, 12	250
*IRAAN, Pecos, 58 (1,229)	1,216
*IREDELL, Bosque, 19 (339)	343
Ireland, Coryell	60
*Irene, Hill	170
Ironton, Cherokee	110
*IRVING, Dallas, 6,682 (216,290)	245,941
Isla, Sabine	350
Israel, Polk	25
*ITALY, Ellis, 59 (1,863)	1,957
*ITASCA, Hill, 55 (1,644)	1,761
Ivan, Stephens	15
IVANHOE, Tyler (1,425)	2,001
*Ivanhoe, Fannin, 8	110
Izoro, Lampasas, Coryell	17

J

Town, County	Pop. 2019
JACINTO CITY, Harris, 206 (10,553)	10,499
*JACKSBORO, Jack, 188 (4,511)	4,648
Jackson, Shelby	50
Jackson, Van Zandt	25
*JACKSONVILLE, Cherokee, 708 (14,544)	15,152
Jacobia, Hunt	60
Jakes Colony, Guadalupe	95
JAMAICA BEACH, Galveston, 43 (983)	1,088
James, Shelby	75
Jamestown, Newton	196
Jamestown, Smith	75
Jardin de San Julian, Starr (22)	26
*JARRELL, Williamson, 138 (984)	1,870
*JASPER, Jasper, 409 (7,590)	7,533
*JAYTON, Kent, 21 (534)	503
Jean, Young	110
*JEFFERSON, Marion, 216 (2,106)	1,967
Jenkins, Morris	350
Jennings, Lamar	85
*Jermyn, Jack, 3	75
JERSEY VILLAGE, Harris, 262 (7,620)	7,907
*JEWETT, Leon, 67 (1,167)	1,337
JF Villarreal, Starr (104)	111
Jiba, Kaufman	50
*JOAQUIN, Shelby, 40 (824)	795
Joe Lee, Bell	8
*JOHNSON CITY, Blanco, 146 (1,656)	2,167
Johnsville, Erath	45
Johntown, Red River	175
*Joinerville, Rusk	140
Joliet, Caldwell	70

Town, County	Pop. 2019
JOLLY, Clay, 5 (172)	159
Jollyville, Williamson, Travis, (16,151)	18,409
Jonah, Williamson	60
*Jonesboro, Coryell, Hamilton, 8	125
JONES CREEK, Brazoria, 26 (2,020)	2,158
Jones Prairie, Milam	20
JONESTOWN, Travis, 89 (1,834)	2,092
*Jonesville, Harrison, 2	70
Joplin, Jack	15
Joppa, Burnet	84
Jordans Store, Shelby	20
*JOSEPHINE, Collin, 27 (812)	1,750
*JOSHUA, Johnson, 267 (5,910)	7,805
Josserand, Trinity	29
Jot-Em-Down, Delta, Hunt	8
*JOURDANTON, Atascosa, 152 (3,871)	4,522
Joy, Clay	110
Jozye, Madison	36
Juarez, Cameron (1,017)	1,169
Jud, Haskell	60
*Judson, Gregg, 9	1,057
Juliff, Fort Bend	100
Jumbo, Panola	60
*JUNCTION, Kimble, 182 (2,574)	2,522
Justiceburg, Garza, 3	45
*JUSTIN, Denton, 193 (3,246)	4,320

K

Town, County	Pop. 2019
Kalgary, Crosby	2
*Kamay, Wichita, 5	640
Kamey, Calhoun	25
Kanawha, Red River	90
*Karnack, Harrison, 22	350
*KARNES CITY, Karnes, 103 (3,042)	3,280
Karon, Live Oak	25
Katemcy, Mason	80
*KATY, Harris, Waller, Fort Bend, 2,528 (14,102)	21,912
*KAUFMAN, Kaufman, 366 (6,703)	7,649
K-Bar Ranch, Jim Wells (358)	337
Keechi, Leon	15
*KEENE, Johnson, 103 (6,106)	6,755
Keeter, Wise	250
Keith, Grimes	50
*KELLER, Tarrant, 1,437 (39,627)	46,651
Kellerville, Wheeler	15
Kellogg, Hunt	20
Kellyville, Marion	75
Kelsey, Upshur	50
Kelton, Wheeler	34
*KEMAH, Galveston, 339 (1,773)	2,006
*KEMP, Kaufman, 103 (1,154)	1,303
Kemper City, Victoria	16
*KEMPNER, Lampasas, 82 (1,089)	1,165
*Kendalia, Kendall, 12	149
*KENDLETON, Fort Bend, 3 (380)	461
*KENEDY, Karnes, 142 (3,296)	3,577
KENEFICK, Liberty, 13 (563)	686
*KENNARD, Houston, 13 (337)	329
*KENNEDALE, Tarrant, 313 (6,763)	8,486
*Kenney, Austin, 3	957
Kenser, Hunt	100
Kensing, Delta	30
Kent, Culberson	30
Kentucky Town, Grayson	20
*KERENS, Navarro, 53 (1,573)	1,568
*KERMIT, Winkler, 200 (5,708)	6,494
Kerrick, Dallam, 2	35
*KERRVILLE, Kerr, 1,389 (22,347)	24,005
Kerrville South, Kerr	6,600
Key, Dawson	10
Kiam, Polk	24
Kicaster, Wilson	190
Kickapoo Indian Reservation, Maverick	366
*Kildare, Cass	104
*KILGORE, Gregg, Rusk, 863 (12,975)	14,329
*KILLEEN, Bell, 2,548 (127,921)	151,463
King, Coryell	30
King Ranch Headquarters, Kleberg	191
*KINGSBURY, Guadalupe, 19 (782)	874
*Kingsland, Llano, 161 (6,030)	7,348
Kingston, Hunt	140
*KINGSVILLE, Kleberg, 600 (26,213)	25,315
Kingtown, Nacogdoches	300
Kingwood, Harris, Montgomery	[part of Houston]
Kinkler, Lavaca	75
Kiomatia, Red River	50
KIRBY, Bexar, 118 (8,000)	8,743
*KIRBYVILLE, Jasper, 126 (2,142)	2,211
Kirk, Limestone	10
Kirkland, Childress, Hardeman	25
Kirtley, Fayette	93
*KIRVIN, Freestone (129)	136
Kittrell, Walker	126
Klein, Harris	45,000
Klondike, Dawson	50
*Klondike, Delta, 5	175
Klump, Washington	20
Knapp, Scurry	10
*Knickerbocker, Tom Green, 1	94
*Knippa, Uvalde, 13 (689)	639
Knobbs Springs, Lee	20
KNOLLWOOD, Grayson, 4 (432)	591
*Knott, Howard, 4	200
*KNOX CITY, Knox, 43 (1,130)	1,135
Koerth, Lavaca	45
Kokomo, Eastland	25
Komensky, Lavaca	75
*Kopperl, Bosque, 9	225
Kosciusko, Wilson	390
*KOSSE, Limestone, 22 (464)	473
*KOUNTZE, Hardin, 115 (2,123)	2,217
*KRESS, Swisher, 22 (715)	683
KRUGERVILLE, Denton, 65 (1,662)	2,013
*KRUM, Denton, 179 (4,157)	5,589
*KURTEN, Brazos, 2 (398)	409
*KYLE, Hays, 923 (28,016)	47,899
Kyote, Atascosa	34

L

Town, County	Pop. 2019
LaBelle, Jefferson	40
*La Blanca, Hidalgo, 15 (2,488)	2,652
La Carla, Starr (70)	73
La Casita, Starr (128)	112
Laceola, Madison	10
La Chuparosa, Starr (49)	55
Lackland Air Force Base, Bexar, (9,918)	9,124
La Coma, Webb (48)	53
*LA COSTE, Medina, 27 (1,119)	1,293
Lacy, Trinity	44
LACY-LAKEVIEW, McLennan, 128 (6,489)	6,914
*LADONIA, Fannin, 22 (612)	632
La Escondida, Starr (153)	170
La Esperanza, Starr (229)	212
LaFayette, Upshur	80
*LA FERIA, Cameron, 194 (7,302)	7,703
La Feria North, Cameron (212)	231
Lagarto, Live Oak	735
La Gloria, Jim Wells	70
La Gloria, Starr	150
Lago, Cameron (204)	176
Lago Vista, Starr (115)	124
*LAGO VISTA, Travis, 292 (6,041)	7,335
*LA GRANGE, Fayette, 413 (4,641)	4,759
*LA GRULLA, Starr, 22 (1,622)	1,688
Laguna, Uvalde	8
Laguna Heights, Cameron, (3,488)	4,219
Laguna Park, Bosque, 4 (1,276)	1,261
Laguna Seca, Hidalgo (266)	274
LAGUNA VISTA, Cameron, 72 (3,117)	3,348
Laguna Vista, Burnet	94
La Homa, Hidalgo (11,985)	12,102
*Laird Hill, Rusk, 1	300
La Isla, El Paso	27
Lajitas, Brewster	75
*LA JOYA, Hidalgo, 75 (3,980)	4,409
La Junta, Parker	300
Lake Arrowhead, Clay	250
LAKE BRIDGEPORT, Wise, 6 (340)	398
Lake Brownwood, Brown, (1,532)	1,450
Lake Bryan, Brazos (1,728)	1,977
Lake Cherokee, Rusk (3,071)	3,198
Lake Cisco, Eastland	300
LAKE CITY, San Patricio (509)	527
Lake Colorado City, Mitchell, (588)	570

Town, County	Pop. 2019
*Lake Creek, Delta, Lamar, 2	55
*LAKE DALLAS, Denton, 240 (7,105)	8,399
Lake Dunlap, Guadalupe (1,934)	2,303
Lakehills, Bandera (5,150)	5,912
*LAKE JACKSON, Brazoria, 754 (26,849)	28,421
Lake Kiowa, Cooke (1,906)	1,809
Lake Leon, Eastland	75
Lake Medina Shores, Bandera, (1,235)	1,375
Lake Meredith Estates, Hutchinson, (437)	406
Lake Murvaul, Panola	300
Lake Nueces, Uvalde	60
LAKEPORT, Gregg, 34 (974)	1,051
Lakeshore Gardens-Hidden Acres, San Patricio (504)	456
LAKESIDE, San Patricio (312)	300
LAKESIDE, Tarrant, 64 (1,307)	1,635
LAKESIDE CITY, Archer, 24 (997)	1,047
Lakeside Village, Bosque	226
LAKE TANGLEWOOD, Randall, 10 (796)	847
Lake Victor, Burnet	265
Lake View, Val Verde (199)	210
*LAKEVIEW, Hall, 5 (107)	92
Lakeview, Floyd	39
Lakeview, Lynn	15
Lakeview, Orange	75
*LAKEWAY, Travis, 784 (11,391)	15,981
Lakewood Harbor, Bosque	250
LAKEWOOD VILLAGE, Denton, (545)	731
*LAKE WORTH, Tarrant, 324 (4,584)	4,858
La Loma de Falcon, Starr (95)	101
Lamar, Aransas, Refugio (636)	618
*LA MARQUE, Galveston, 389 (14,509)	17,326
Lamasco, Fannin	32
*LAMESA, Dawson, 319 (9,422)	8,857
La Minita, Starr (171)	176
Lamkin, Comanche	87
*LAMPASAS, Lampasas, 383 (6,681)	7,787
Lanark, Cass	30
*LANCASTER, Dallas, 699 (36,361)	39,508
*Lane City, Wharton, 4	111
Lanely, Freestone	27
Laneport, Williamson	40
*Laneville, Rusk, 5	169
*Langtry, Val Verde	30
Lanier, Cass	80
Lannius, Fannin	79
Lantana, Denton (6,874)	8,473
La Paloma, Cameron (2,903)	3,526
La Paloma Addition, San Patricio, (330)	311
La Paloma-Lost Creek, Nueces, (408)	505
La Paloma Ranchettes, Starr, (239)	258
La Parita, Atascosa	48
*LA PORTE, Harris, 948 (33,800)	34,757
La Presa, Webb (319)	291
*La Pryor, Zavala, 11 (1,643)	1,798
La Puerta, Starr (632)	590
*LAREDO, Webb, 6,909 (236,091)	266,898
Laredo Ranchettes, Webb (22)	22
La Reforma, Starr	20
Lariat, Parmer	100
La Rosita, Starr (85)	70
*Larue, Henderson, 23	250
*LaSalle, Jackson	110
Lasana, Cameron (84)	69
*Lasara, Willacy, 1 (1,039)	924
Las Escobas, Starr	5
Las Haciendas, Webb (7)	4
Las Lomas, Starr (3,147)	3,295
Las Lomitas, Jim Hogg (244)	233
Las Palmas, Zapata (67)	75
Las Palmas II, Cameron (1,605)	1,907
Las Pilas, Webb (28)	27
Las Quintas Fronterizas, Maverick, (3,290)	4,114
Lassater, Marion	60
Las Yescas, Cameron	221
Latch, Upshur	50
Latex, Harrison	75
*LATEXO, Houston, 9 (322)	338
La Tina Ranch, Cameron (618)	737
Latium, Washington	30
Laughlin Air Force Base, Val Verde, (1,569)	1,502
Laurel, Newton	357
Laureles, Cameron (3,692)	3,670

The historic commercial district in Lancaster. Photo by Renelibrary, CC by 4.0/Wikimedia Commons.

Town, County	Pop. 2019
Lavender, Limestone	30
*LA VERNIA, Wilson, 217 (1,034)	1,426
La Victoria, Starr (171)	156
*LA VILLA, Hidalgo, 17 (1,957)	2,544
*LAVON, Collin, 120 (2,219)	3,839
*LA WARD, Jackson, 5 (213)	221
*LAWN, Taylor, 10 (314)	315
Lawrence, Kaufman	259
*Lazbuddie, Parmer, 5	248
*LEAGUE CITY, Galveston, Harris, 2,813 (83,560)	108,604
Leagueville, Henderson	50
*LEAKEY, Real, 66 (425)	464
*LEANDER, Williamson, 1,135 (26,526)	59,110
LEARY, Bowie, 13 (495)	515
*Ledbetter, Fayette, Lee, 13	83
Leedale, Bell	24
*Leesburg, Camp, 11	128
*Leesville, Gonzales, 2	152
*LEFORS, Gray, 9 (497)	474
*Leggett, Polk, 5	500
Lehman, Cochran	6
Leigh, Harrison	60
Lela, Wheeler	135
*Lelia Lake, Donley, 1	70
*Leming, Atascosa, 6 (946)	1,028
*Lenorah, Martin, 6	83
Lenz, Karnes	50
Leo, Cooke	20
Leo, Lee	10
*LEONA, Leon, 8 (175)	186
*LEONARD, Fannin, 102 (1,990)	2,092
Leon Junction, Coryell	50
Leon Springs, Bexar	[part of San Antonio]
*LEON VALLEY, Bexar, 475 (10,151)	11,799
*LEROY, McLennan, 10 (337)	347
Lesley, Hall	25
*LEVELLAND, Hockley, 424 (13,542)	13,555
Leverett's Chapel, Rusk	400
Levi, McLennan	50
Levita, Coryell	70
*LEWISVILLE, Denton, 3,655 (95,290)	114,262
*LEXINGTON, Lee, 74 (1,177)	1,216
*LIBERTY, Liberty, 448 (8,397)	10,165
Liberty, Lubbock	228
Liberty, Milam	40
Liberty, Newton	128
Liberty City, Gregg (2,351)	2,624
*LIBERTY HILL, Williamson, 363 (967)	2,931
Liberty Hill, Houston	73
Liberty Hill, Milam	25
Lilbert, Nacogdoches	100
*Lillian, Johnson, 9	1,160
*Lincoln, Lee, 11	336
*LINDALE, Smith, 409 (4,818)	6,496
*LINDEN, Cass, 77 (1,988)	1,945
Lindenau, DeWitt	50
Lindendale, Kendall	70
*LINDSAY, Cooke, 38 (1,018)	1,148
Lindsay, Reeves (271)	288
*Lingleville, Erath	100
*Linn, Hidalgo, 4 (801)	749
Linn Flat, Nacogdoches	60
Linwood, Cherokee	40
*LIPAN, Hood, 44 (430)	500
*Lipscomb, Lipscomb (37)	28
*Lissie, Wharton, 5	72
Littig, Travis	35
Little Cypress, Orange	900
*LITTLE ELM, Denton, 800 (25,898)	53,126
*LITTLEFIELD, Lamb, 147 (6,372)	5,840
Little Hope, Wood	25
Little Midland, Burnet	82
Little New York, Gonzales	15
*LITTLE RIVER-ACADEMY, Bell, 36 (1,961)	2,098
Lively, Kaufman	50
LIVE OAK, Bexar, 406 (13,131)	16,451
*LIVERPOOL, Brazoria, 21 (482)	561
*LIVINGSTON, Polk, 588 (5,335)	5,247
*LLANO, Llano, 240 (3,232)	3,529
Llano Grande, Hidalgo (3,008)	2,702
Locker, San Saba	16
Lockett, Wilbarger	150
Lockettville, Hockley	20
*LOCKHART, Caldwell, 471 (12,698)	14,410
*LOCKNEY, Floyd, 46 (1,842)	1,637
Locust, Grayson	118
*Lodi, Marion, 1	175
Loebau, Lee	35
Logan, Panola	40
LOG CABIN, Henderson, 6 (714)	780
*Lohn, McCulloch, 1	149
Loire, Wilson, Atascosa	50
Lois, Cooke	10
*Lolita, Jackson, 19 (555)	606
Loma Alta, McMullen	25
Loma Alta, Val Verde	30
Loma Grande, Zavala (107)	101
Loma Linda, San Patricio (122)	123
Loma Linda East, Jim Wells (254)	267
Loma Linda East, Starr (44)	41
Loma Linda West, Starr (114)	134
Loma Vista, Starr (160)	170
Lomax, Howard	25
*LOMETA, Lampasas, 38 (856)	887
*London, Kimble, 5	180
Lone Camp, Palo Pinto	110
Lone Cedar, Ellis	18
Lone Grove, Llano	50
*LONE OAK, Hunt, 49 (598)	696
Lone Oak, Colorado	50
Lone Pine, Houston	81
*LONE STAR, Morris, 42 (1,581)	1,508
Lone Star, Cherokee	20
Lone Star, Floyd	42
Lone Star, Lamar	35
*Long Branch, Panola, 4	150
Long Lake, Anderson	30
Long Mott, Calhoun	76
Longoria, Starr (92)	100
Longpoint, Washington	30
*LONGVIEW, Gregg, Harrison, 3,509 (80,455)	83,749
Longworth, Fisher	47
Looneyville, Nacogdoches	50
*Loop, Gaines, 6 (225)	243
*Lopeño, Zapata (174)	185
Lopezville, Hidalgo (4,333)	4,197
*LORAINE, Mitchell, 15 (602)	587
*LORENA, McLennan, 150 (1,691)	1,785
*LORENZO, Crosby, 30 (1,147)	1,142
Los Altos, Webb (140)	147
Los Alvarez, Starr (303)	286
Los Angeles, La Salle	15
Los Angeles Subdivision, Willacy, (121)	143
Los Arcos, Webb (127)	134
Los Arrieros, Starr (91)	93
Los Barreras, Starr (288)	302
Los Centenarios, Webb (87)	98
Los Corralitos, Webb (35)	44
Los Ebanos, Starr (280)	302
*Los Ebanos, Hidalgo, 1 (335)	313
Los Escondidos, Burnet	80
*LOS FRESNOS, Cameron, 219 (5,542)	7,937
Los Fresnos, Webb (67)	80
Los Huisaches, Webb (17)	14
*LOS INDIOS, Cameron, 21 (1,083)	1,075
Los Lobos, Zapata (9)	7
Los Minerales, Webb (20)	17
Los Nopalitos, Webb (62)	62
Losoya, Bexar	500
Lost Creek, Travis (4,509)	4,631
Lost Prairie, Limestone	2
Los Veteranos I, Webb (24)	22
Los Veteranos II, Webb (24)	28
LOS YBANEZ, Dawson, 1 (19)	18
*LOTT, Falls, 49 (759)	773
*Louise, Wharton, 37 (995)	1,024
Lovelace, Hill	30
*LOVELADY, Houston, 33 (649)	639
*Loving, Young, 4	300
*Lowake, Concho, 1	40
LOWRY CROSSING, Collin, 57 (1,711)	1,753
Loyal Valley, Mason	52
Loyola Beach, Kleberg	185
*Lozano, Cameron (404)	430
*LUBBOCK, Lubbock, 7,871 (229,573)	259,158
LUCAS, Collin, 209 (5,166)	8,183
Luckenbach, Gillespie	25
*LUEDERS, Jones, 10 (346)	331
Luella, Grayson	639
*LUFKIN, Angelina, 1,810 (35,067)	36,423
*LULING, Caldwell, 248 (5,411)	5,835
*LUMBERTON, Hardin, 449 (11,943)	12,816
Lums Chapel, Lamb	6
Luther, Howard	3
Lutie, Collingsworth	10
Lydia, Red River	109
*LYFORD, Willacy, 44 (2,611)	2,539

Town, County	Pop. 2019
Lynn Grove, Grimes	25
*Lyons, Burleson, 3	360
*LYTLE, Atascosa, Medina, Bexar, 190 (2,492)	3,069
Lytton Springs, Caldwell	300

M

Town, County	Pop. 2019
*MABANK, Kaufman, Henderson, 222 (3,035)	4,178
Mabelle, Baylor	9
Mabry, Red River	60
*Macdona, Bexar, 4 (559)	603
Macon, Franklin	21
Macune, San Augustine	50
*MADISONVILLE, Madison, 205 (4,396)	4,734
Madras, Red River	61
Magnet, Wharton	42
*MAGNOLIA, Montgomery, 954 (1,393)	2,118
Magnolia, San Jacinto	150
Magnolia Beach, Calhoun	250
Magnolia Springs, Jasper	20
Maha, Travis	200
Mahl, Nacogdoches	150
Mahomet, Burnet	97
Majors, Franklin	13
*MALAKOFF, Henderson, 113 (2,324)	2,434
Mallard, Montague	12
*MALONE, Hill, 13 (269)	279
Malta, Bowie	350
Malvern, Leon	12
Mambrino, Hood	74
*Manchaca, Travis, 106 (1,133)	1,233
Manchester, Red River	185
Mangum, Eastland	15
Manheim, Lee	50
Mankin, Henderson	30
Mankins, Archer	10
*MANOR, Travis, 276 (5,037)	13,817
*MANSFIELD, Tarrant, Johnson, Ellis, 2,003 (56,368)	70,080
Manuel Garcia, Starr (203)	180
Manuel Garcia II, Starr (77)	72
*MANVEL, Brazoria, 342 (5,179)	12,671
Maple, Bailey	40
Maple, Red River	30
Maple Springs, Titus	25
Mapleton, Houston	32
*Marathon, Brewster, 18 (430)	399
*MARBLE FALLS, Burnet, 706 (6,077)	7,098
*MARFA, Presidio, 148 (1,981)	1,650
Margaret, Foard, Hardeman	50
Marie, Runnels	10
*MARIETTA, Cass (134)	129
*MARION, Guadalupe, 106 (1,066)	1,243
*Markham, Matagorda, 13 (1,082)	1,096
Markley, Young	25
*MARLIN, Falls, 154 (5,967)	5,577
Marlow, Milam	45
*MARQUEZ, Leon, 31 (263)	297
Mars, Van Zandt, Henderson	20
*MARSHALL, Harrison, 853 (23,523)	23,950
Marston, Polk	25
*MART, McLennan, 64 (1,897)	1,971
*MARTINDALE, Caldwell, 49 (1,116)	1,262
Martinez, Starr (69)	72
Martins Mill, Van Zandt	158
Martin Springs, Hopkins	200
*Martinsville, Nacogdoches, 2	350
Marvin, Lamar	48
Maryetta, Jack	7
*Maryneal, Nolan, 5	50
Marysville, Cooke	12
*MASON, Mason, 216 (2,114)	2,298
Massey Lake, Anderson	30
Masterson, Moore, 2	2
*MATADOR, Motley, 39 (607)	609
*Matagorda, Matagorda, 27 (503)	465
*MATHIS, San Patricio, 141 (4,942)	4,800
Matthews, Colorado	20
*MAUD, Bowie, 37 (1,056)	1,095
*Mauriceville, Orange, 14 (3,252)	3,804
Maverick, Runnels	35
Maxdale, Bell	25
Maxey, Lamar	70
*Maxwell, Caldwell, 26	500
*May, Brown, 13	270
*Maydelle, Cherokee, 1	250
Mayfield, Hale	26
Mayfield, Hill	25
Mayflower, Newton	50
Maynard, San Jacinto	90
*MAYPEARL, Ellis, 47 (934)	1,116
Maysfield, Milam	140
*McAdoo, Dickens, 2	75
*McALLEN, Hidalgo, 5,480 (129,872)	144,785
McBeth, Brazoria	20
*McCAMEY, Upton, 69 (1,887)	2,065
*McCaulley, Fisher	96
McClanahan, Falls	30
McCook, Hidalgo	50
McCoy, Atascosa	30
McCoy, Floyd	20
McCoy, Kaufman	20
McCoy, Panola	30
McCoy, Red River	175
*McDade, Bastrop, 17 (685)	746
*McFaddin, Victoria	50
McGirk, Hamilton, Mills	18
*McGREGOR, McLennan, 197 (4,987)	5,264
*McKINNEY, Collin, 4,631 (131,117)	197,391
McKinney Acres, Andrews (815)	1,079
*McLEAN, Gray, 24 (778)	747
McLENDON-CHISHOLM, Rockwall, 5 (1,373)	3,541
*McLeod, Cass, 3	600
McMahan, Caldwell	90
McMillin, San Saba	15
McNair, Harris	2,039
McNary, Hudspeth	100
McNeil, Caldwell	50
*McQueeney, Guadalupe, 41 (2,545)	2,793
*MEADOW, Terry, 16 (593)	590
Meadow Grove, Bell	22
MEADOWLAKES, Burnet, 41 (1,777)	1,816
MEADOWS PLACE, Fort Bend, 111 (4,660)	4,591
Mecca, Madison, Grimes	48
Medicine Mound, Hardeman	25
Medill, Lamar	50
Medina, Zapata (3,935)	4,387
*Medina, Bandera, 31	850
Meeker, Jefferson	2,280
Meeks, Bell	6
*MEGARGEL, Archer, 11 (203)	196
*MELISSA, Collin, 206 (4,695)	13,461
Melrose, Nacogdoches	400
*MELVIN, McCulloch, 4 (178)	182
*MEMPHIS, Hall, 74 (2,290)	2,063
*MENARD, Menard, 59 (1,471)	1,378
Mendoza, Caldwell	100
Menlow, Hill	12
*Mentone, Loving, 5 (19)	29
Mentz, Colorado	100
*MERCEDES, Hidalgo, 502 (15,570)	17,096
Mercury, McCulloch	166
*Mereta, Tom Green, 2	131
*MERIDIAN, Bosque, 78 (1,493)	1,515
*Merit, Hunt, 1	225
*MERKEL, Taylor, 92 (2,590)	2,646
Merle, Burleson	10
Merriman, Eastland	14
*MERTENS, Hill, 6 (125)	131
*MERTZON, Irion, 52 (781)	797
*MESQUITE, Dallas, Kaufman, 3,193 (139,824)	142,030
Mesquite, Starr (505)	543
Metcalf Gap, Palo Pinto	6
*MEXIA, Limestone, 260 (7,459)	7,605
*Meyersville, DeWitt, 6	110
Meyersville, Washington	15
*MIAMI, Roberts, 22 (597)	553
Mico, Medina	107
Midcity, Lamar	50
Middleton, Leon	26
*Midfield, Matagorda, 4	305
*Midkiff, Upton, 14	182
*MIDLAND, Midland, Martin, 5,000 (111,147)	146,701
*MIDLOTHIAN, Ellis, 964 (18,037)	34,164
*MIDWAY, Madison, Montgomery, 20 (228)	229
Midway, Dawson	12
Midway, Fannin	51
Midway, Jim Wells	24
Midway, Limestone	9
Midway, Polk	525
Midway, Red River	40
Midway, Titus	110
Midway, Upshur	20
Midway, Van Zandt	31
Midway North, Hidalgo (4,752)	5,011
Midway South, Hidalgo (2,239)	2,562

Town, County	Pop. 2019
Midyett, Panola	150
Miguel Barrera, Starr (128)	139
Mikes, Starr (910)	985
Mikeska, Live Oak	10
Mila Doce, Hidalgo (6,222)	6,778
*Milam, Sabine, 11 (1,480)	1,512
*MILANO, Milam, 20 (428)	445
Milburn, McCulloch	8
MILDRED, Navarro, 6 (368)	405
*MILES, Runnels, 50 (829)	849
*MILFORD, Ellis, 16 (728)	767
Mill Creek, Washington	40
Miller Grove, Hopkins	115
MILLERS COVE, Titus, 3 (149)	161
*Millersview, Concho, 5	80
Millett, La Salle	60
Millheim, Austin	170
*Millican, Brazos, 3 (240)	245
*MILLSAP, Parker, 54 (403)	474
Milo Center, Deaf Smith	5
Milton, Lamar	50
Mims, Brazoria	160
*Minden, Rusk, 4	150
*MINEOLA, Wood, 370 (4,515)	4,777
Mineral, Bee	65
*MINERAL WELLS, Palo Pinto, Parker, 591 (16,788)	17,430
Minerva, Milam	100
Mings Chapel, Upshur	50
*MINGUS, Palo Pinto, 17 (235)	257
Minter, Lamar	78
Mi Ranchito Estate, Starr (281)	257
Mirando City, Webb, 13 (375)	337
*MISSION, Hidalgo, 1,827 (77,049)	86,214
Mission Bend, Fort Bend, Harris, (36,501)	46,172
Mission Valley, Victoria	225
*MISSOURI CITY, Fort Bend, Harris, 1,911 (67,358)	80,681
Mixon, Cherokee	50
*MOBEETIE, Wheeler, 10 (101)	96
MOBILE CITY, Rockwall, 3 (188)	223
Moffat, Bell	1,406
Moffett, Angelina	100
Moline, Lampasas	32
*MONAHANS, Ward, 280 (6,953)	7,801
Monaville, Waller	180
Monkstown, Fannin	35
Monroe, Rusk	96
Monroe City, Chambers	5
Mont, Lavaca	30
*Montague, Montague, 18 (304)	299
*Montalba, Anderson, 10	110
*MONT BELVIEU, Chambers, 193 (3,835)	6,666
Monte Alto, Hidalgo (1,924)	1,976
Monte Grande, Cameron	97
Montell, Uvalde	20
*MONTGOMERY, Montgomery, 582 (621)	1,308
Monthalia, Gonzales	32
Monticello, Titus	20
*MOODY, McLennan, 74 (1,371)	1,415
*Moore, Frio, 13 (475)	441
Moore's Crossing, Travis	25
MOORE STATION, Henderson, (201)	214
Mooreville, Falls	96
Mooring, Brazos	80
Moraida, Starr (212)	241
Morales, Jackson	72
Morales-Sanchez, Zapata (84)	74
*MORAN, Shackelford, 9 (270)	275
Moravia, Lavaca	165
*MORGAN, Bosque, 15 (490)	518
Morgan Creek, Burnet	126
Morgan Farm Area, San Patricio, (463)	450
*Morgan Mill, Erath, 3	206
MORGAN'S POINT, Harris, 21 (339)	358
MORGAN'S POINT RESORT, Bell, 70 (4,170)	4,736
Morning Glory, El Paso (651)	625
*Morse, Hansford, 7 (147)	112
*MORTON, Cochran, 41 (2,006)	1,846
Morton, Harrison	75
Morton Valley, Eastland	46
*Moscow, Polk, 12	170
Mosheim, Bosque	75
Moss Bluff, Liberty	65
Moss Hill, Liberty	180
Mostyn, Montgomery	90
*MOULTON, Lavaca, 62 (886)	924
*Mound, Coryell, 2	125
Mound City, Anderson, Houston	25
MOUNTAIN CITY, Hays, 13 (648)	785
*Mountain Home, Kerr, 20	96
Mountain Peak, Ellis	300
Mountain Springs, Cooke	600
Mount Bethel, Panola	65
*MOUNT CALM, Hill, 21 (320)	336
*MOUNT ENTERPRISE, Rusk, 45 (447)	438
Mount Haven, Cherokee	30
Mount Hermon, Shelby	80
Mount Olive, Lavaca	50
*MOUNT PLEASANT, Titus, 720 (15,564)	17,064
Mount Rose, Falls	15
Mount Selman, Cherokee	325
Mount Sylvan, Smith	181
*MOUNT VERNON, Franklin, 150 (2,662)	2,789
Mount Vernon, Houston	43
Mozelle, Coleman	15
Muellersville, Washington	20
*MUENSTER, Cooke, 137 (1,544)	1,642
Mulberry, Fannin	141
Muldoon, Fayette, 9	95
*MULESHOE, Bailey, 173 (5,158)	5,159
*MULLIN, Mills, 10 (179)	177
Mullins Prairie, Fayette	107
*Mumford, Robertson, 3	170
*MUNDAY, Knox, 40 (1,300)	1,275
Munger, Limestone	5
Mungerville, Dawson	20
Muniz, Hidalgo (1,370)	1,552
*MURCHISON, Henderson, 44 (594)	618
Murillo, Hidalgo (7,344)	9,095
MURPHY, Collin, 506 (17,708)	20,595
Murray, Young	29
Murvaul, Panola	150
MUSTANG, Navarro, 1 (21)	21
Mustang, Denton	25
Mustang Mott, DeWitt	20
MUSTANG RIDGE, Travis, Caldwell, 36 (861)	957
*Myra, Cooke, 3	150
Myrtle Springs, Van Zandt (828)	850

N

Town, County	Pop. 2019
*NACOGDOCHES, Nacogdoches, 1,348 (32,996)	33,677
*Nada, Colorado, 12	165
*NAPLES, Morris, 46 (1,378)	1,343
Narciso Pena, Starr (30)	36
Naruna, Burnet	95
*NASH, Bowie, 122 (2,960)	3,825
Nash, Ellis	40
NASSAU BAY, Harris, 183 (4,002)	4,095
Nat, Nacogdoches	50
*NATALIA, Medina, 64 (1,431)	1,617
NAVARRO, Navarro (210)	221
Navarro Mills, Navarro	90
*NAVASOTA, Grimes, 351 (7,049)	7,867
Navidad, Jackson	227
*NAZARETH, Castro, 17 (311)	291
Necessity, Stephens	10
Nechanitz, Fayette	57
*Neches, Anderson, 4	175
*NEDERLAND, Jefferson, 642 (17,547)	17,439
Needmore, Bailey	20
Needmore, Terry	7
*NEEDVILLE, Fort Bend, 137 (2,823)	3,522
Negley, Red River	136
Neinda, Jones	21
Nell, Live Oak	60
Nelson City, Kendall	50
Nelsonville, Austin	200
Nelta, Hopkins	36
*Nemo, Somervell, 17	56
Nesbitt, Harrison (281)	262
Netos, Starr (31)	37
Neuville, Shelby	65
*NEVADA, Collin, 55 (822)	1,098
*NEWARK, Wise, 56 (1,005)	1,244
*New Baden, Robertson, 3	150
NEW BERLIN, Guadalupe, 11 (511)	621
New Bielau, Colorado	30
*NEW BOSTON, Bowie, 171 (4,550)	4,556
*NEW BRAUNFELS, Comal, Guadalupe, 3,376 (57,740)	87,388
New Bremen, Austin	125
Newburg, Comanche	32
Newby, Leon	40
*New Caney, Montgomery, 236	6,800

Town, County	Pop. 2019
*NEWCASTLE, Young, 20 (585)	595
NEW CHAPEL HILL, Smith, 8 (594)	637
New Colony, Bell	12
New Colony, Cass	65
New Corn Hill, Williamson	475
New Davy, DeWitt	20
*NEW DEAL, Lubbock, 27 (794)	827
NEW FAIRVIEW, Wise, 27 (1,258)	1,563
Newgulf, Wharton	10
New Harmony, Shelby	40
New Harmony, Smith	350
NEW HOME, Lynn (334)	366
NEW HOPE, Collin, 18 (614)	635
New Hope, Cherokee	50
New Hope, Jones	9
New Hope, San Augustine	75
New Hope, Smith	75
New Hope, Wood	15
Newlin, Hall	27
*NEW LONDON, Rusk, 12 (998)	1,011
New Lynn, Lynn	4
New Moore, Lynn	10
New Mountain, Upshur	20
Newport, Clay, Jack	75
New Salem, Palo Pinto	89
New Salem, Rusk	55
Newsome, Camp	113
*NEW SUMMERFIELD, Cherokee, 22 (1,111)	1,227
New Sweden, Travis	60
New Taiton, Wharton	10
*NEWTON, Newton, 57 (2,478)	2,338
*New Ulm, Austin, 41	974
*NEW WAVERLY, Walker, 93 (1,032)	1,062
New Wehdem, Austin	414
New Willard, Polk	160
New York, Henderson	60
NEYLANDVILLE, Hunt, 1 (97)	105
NIEDERWALD, Hays, Caldwell, 22 (565)	665
Nigton, Trinity	87
Nimrod, Eastland	45
Nina, Starr (141)	149
Nineveh, Leon	50
Nix, Lampasas	14
*NIXON, Gonzales, Wilson, 66 (2,385)	2,553
Noack, Williamson	70
Nobility, Fannin	100
Noble, Lamar	14
Nockernut, Wilson	20
*NOCONA, Montague, 133 (3,033)	3,027
Nocona Hills, Montague (675)	645
Nogalus Prairie, Trinity	109
*Nolan, Nolan, 1	60
*NOLANVILLE, Bell, 63 (4,259)	5,533
*NOME, Jefferson, 25 (588)	607
Noodle, Jones	40
NOONDAY, Smith, 62 (777)	811
Nopal, DeWitt, Gonzales	25
*NORDHEIM, DeWitt, 19 (307)	304
Norman, Williamson	40
Normandy, Maverick	114
*NORMANGEE, Leon, Madison, 70 (685)	713
*Normanna, Bee, 2 (113)	112
Norse, Bosque	110
North Alamo, Hidalgo (3,235)	3,926
NORTH CLEVELAND, Liberty, 5 (247)	314
North Escobares, Starr (118)	108
Northfield, Motley	15
NORTHLAKE, Denton, 56 (1,724)	3,435
North Pearsall, Frio (614)	657
*NORTH RICHLAND HILLS, Tarrant, 1,948 (63,343)	71,210
Northridge, Starr (78)	91
Northrup, Lee	86
North San Pedro, Nueces (895)	868
North Star, Archer	10
*North Zulch, Madison, 13	600
Norton, Runnels	50
*Notrees, Ector, 1	20
*NOVICE, Coleman (139)	126
Novice, Lamar	35
Noxville, Kimble	3
Nugent, Jones	50
Nunelee, Fannin	90
*Nursery, Victoria, 4	600

O

Town, County	Pop. 2019
Oakalla, Burnet	99
Oakdale, Polk	25
Oak Forest, Gonzales	24
OAK GROVE, Kaufman (603)	686
Oak Grove, Bowie	90
Oak Grove, Colorado	40
Oak Grove, Wood	140
Oak Hill, Rusk	200
Oak Hill, Travis	[part of Austin]
*Oakhurst, San Jacinto, 6 (233)	242
Oak Island, Chambers (363)	401
Oakland, Cherokee	50
Oakland, Colorado, Lavaca, 1	80
Oakland, Van Zandt	26
OAK LEAF, Ellis, 35 (1,298)	1,442
OAK POINT, Denton, 106 (2,786)	4,487
OAK RIDGE, Kaufman, 14 (495)	699
OAK RIDGE, Cooke (141)	238
Oak Ridge, Grayson	161
Oak Ridge, Nacogdoches	225
OAK RIDGE NORTH, Montgomery, 229 (3,049)	3,382
Oak Trail Shores, Hood (2,755)	3,411
OAK VALLEY, Navarro, 2 (368)	410
Oakville, Live Oak, 4	260
*OAKWOOD, Leon, 26 (510)	517
Oatmeal, Burnet	74
*O'BRIEN, Haskell, 2 (106)	101
Ocee, McLennan	84
Odds, Limestone	24
Odell, Wilbarger	100
*ODEM, San Patricio, 65 (2,389)	2,367
*ODESSA, Ector, Midland, 4,021 (99,940)	126,729
*O'DONNELL, Lynn, Dawson, 22 (831)	840
Oenaville, Bell	108
O'Farrell, Cass	20
Ogburn, Wood	10
*OGLESBY, Coryell, 19 (484)	467
*Oilton, Webb, 1 (353)	368
Oklahoma, Montgomery	800
Oklahoma Flat, Hockley	4
Oklahoma Lane, Parmer	25
*Oklaunion, Wilbarger, 4	138
Okra, Eastland	20
Ola, Kaufman	65
Old Boston, Bowie	100
Old Center, Panola	83
Old Dime Box, Lee	225
*Olden, Eastland, 3	113
Oldenburg, Fayette	92
Old Escobares, Starr (97)	106
*Old Glory, Stonewall, 2	100
Old Midway, Leon	12
*Old Ocean, Brazoria, 14	150
OLD RIVER-WINFREE, Chambers, 17 (1,245)	1,475
Old Salem, Bowie	50
Old Union, Bowie	100
Old Union, Limestone	25
Oletha, Limestone	53
Olfen, Runnels	35
Olin, Hamilton	15
Olivarez, Hidalgo (3,827)	4,822
Olivia, Calhoun	215
Olivia Lopez de Gutierrez, Starr, (93)	79
Ollie, Polk	5
*Olmito, Cameron, 65 (1,210)	1,074
Olmito and Olmito, Starr (271)	308
Olmos, Guadalupe	65
OLMOS PARK, Bexar, 108 (2,237)	2,508
*OLNEY, Young, 123 (3,285)	3,235
*OLTON, Lamb, 64 (2,215)	2,022
*OMAHA, Morris, 30 (1,021)	980
Omen, Smith	150
*ONALASKA, Polk, 127 (1,764)	2,464
Opdyke, Hockley	50
OPDYKE WEST, Hockley, 2 (174)	196
Oplin, Callahan	75
O'Quinn, Fayette	191
Oran, Palo Pinto	61
*ORANGE, Orange, 611 (18,595)	18,297
Orangedale, Bee	40
*Orangefield, Orange, 6	725
*ORANGE GROVE, Jim Wells, 109 (1,318)	1,301
Orangeville, Fannin	60
Orason, Cameron (129)	135
*ORCHARD, Fort Bend, 15 (352)	434
*ORE CITY, Upshur, 52 (1,144)	1,227
Orient, Tom Green	57
*Orla, Reeves, 14	80
Osage, Colorado	10
Osage, Coryell	30
Oscar, Bell	58
Osceola, Hill	95
Otey, Brazoria	31

Town, County	Pop. 2019
Ottine, Gonzales	80
Otto, Falls	48
*Ovalo, Taylor, 3	225
*OVERTON, Rusk, Smith, 87 (2,554)	2,558
OVILLA, Ellis, Dallas, 132 (3,492)	4,320
Owens, Brown	16
Owens, Crosby	4
Owentown, Smith	100
Owl Creek, Bell	130
Owl Ranch, Jim Wells (225)	193
Oxford, Llano	18
OYSTER CREEK, Brazoria, 34 (1,111)	1,170
*Ozona, Crockett, 125 (3,225)	2,912
P	
Pablo Pena, Starr (63)	67
Pacio, Delta	35
Padgett, Young	18
*PADUCAH, Cottle, 48 (1,186)	1,085
*Paige, Bastrop, 34	275
Paint Creek, Haskell	150
*PAINT ROCK, Concho, 12 (273)	200
Paisano Park, San Patricio (130)	130
*PALACIOS, Matagorda, 113 (4,718)	4,589
*PALESTINE, Anderson, 776 (18,712)	19,115
PALISADES, Randall (325)	364
Palito Blanco, Jim Wells	750
*PALMER, Ellis, 76 (2,000)	2,203
PALMHURST, Hidalgo, 109 (2,607)	2,737
PALM VALLEY, Cameron, 18 (1,304)	1,241
PALMVIEW, Hidalgo, 383 (5,458)	10,829
Palmview South, Hidalgo, (5,575)	6,064
Palo Blanco, Starr (204)	234
Paloduro, Armstrong	10
Paloma Creek, Denton (2,501)	3,177
Paloma Creek South, Denton, (2,753)	3,569
*Palo Pinto, Palo Pinto, 8 (333)	354
Paluxy, Hood, Erath	36
*PAMPA, Gray, 553 (17,994)	17,277
Pancake, Coryell	11
Pandale, Val Verde	25
*Pandora, Wilson, 1	110
*PANHANDLE, Carson, 80 (2,452)	2,315
*Panna Maria, Karnes, 6	45
*Panola, Panola, 1	305
PANORAMA VILLAGE, Montgomery, 31 (2,170)	2,337
*PANTEGO, Tarrant, 393 (2,394)	2,462
Panther Junction, Brewster	130
Papalote, Bee	75
*PARADISE, Wise, 81 (441)	560
*PARIS, Lamar, 1,127 (25,171)	25,297
Park, Fayette	25
PARKER, Collin, 124 (3,811)	5,216
Parker, Johnson	93
Park Springs, Wise	90
Parsley Hill, Wilbarger	25
Parvin, Denton	44
*PASADENA, Harris, 3,246 (149,043)	156,841
Patillo, Erath	10
Patman Switch, Cass	40
Patonia, Polk	15
Patricia, Dawson	50
Patroon, Shelby	25
*PATTISON, Waller, 32 (472)	628
PATTON VILLAGE, Montgomery, 17 (1,557)	2,132
Pattonfield, Upshur	20
*Pattonville, Lamar, 9	180
Pawelekville, Karnes	110
*Pawnee, Bee, 6 (166)	155
Paxton, Shelby	50
Paynes Corner, Gaines	18
PAYNE SPRINGS, Henderson, 26 (767)	807
Peach Creek, Brazos	150
Peacock, Stonewall	100
Peadenville, Palo Pinto	15
Pearl, Coryell	50
*PEARLAND, Brazoria, Harris, Fort Bend, 3,428 (91,252)	122,331
Pearl City, DeWitt	4
*PEARSALL, Frio, 234 (9,146)	10,577
Pearson, Medina	24
Pearsons Chapel, Houston	95
Pear Valley, McCulloch	37
*PEASTER, Parker, 2	555
Pecan Acres, Tarrant, Wise (4,099)	4,745
*PECAN GAP, Delta, Fannin, 7 (203)	204
Pecan Grove, Fort Bend, (15,963)	20,569
PECAN HILL, Ellis, 12 (626)	706
Pecan Plantation, Hood (5,294)	5,719
Pecan Wells, Hamilton	6
*PECOS, Reeves, 345 (8,780)	10,574
Peeltown, Kaufman	75
Peerless, Hopkins	90
Peggy, Atascosa	22
Pelham, Navarro	75
PELICAN BAY, Tarrant, 12 (1,547)	1,905
Pena, Starr (118)	127
*Pendleton, Bell, 1	369
*PENELOPE, Hill, 4 (198)	207
*PEÑITAS, Hidalgo, 98 (4,385)	4,721
*Pennington, Trinity, Houston, 7	67
*Penwell, Ector, 6	41
Peoria, Hill	105
*Pep, Hockley	30
Percilla, Houston	95
Perezville, Hidalgo (5,376)	6,022
Pernitas Point, Live Oak, Jim Wells	274
*Perrin, Jack, 14 (398)	431
Perry, Falls	76
*PERRYTON, Ochiltree, 404 (8,802)	8,816
Perryville, Wood	35
Personville, Limestone	50
Pert, Anderson	20
Peters, Austin	150
*PETERSBURG, Hale, Floyd, 23 (1,202)	1,108
Peter's Prairie, Red River	40
Petersville, DeWitt	38
*PETROLIA, Clay, 12 (686)	672
PETRONILA, Nueces, 2 (113)	121
Petteway, Robertson	25
Pettibone, Milam	25
Pettit, Hockley	30
*Pettus, Bee, 10 (558)	559
*Petty, Lamar, 5	130
Petty, Lynn	8
Peyton, Blanco	30
*PFLUGERVILLE, Travis, 1,666 (46,936)	67,738
Phalba, Van Zandt	73
*PHARR, Hidalgo, 1,751 (70,400)	81,473
Phelps, Walker	98
Phillipsburg, Washington	75
Pickens, Henderson	20
Pickett, Navarro	30
*Pickton, Hopkins, 11	300
Pidcoke, Coryell	50
Piedmont, Grimes	50
Piedmont, Upshur	20
*Pierce, Wharton, 2	51
Pike, Collin	47
Pilgrim, Gonzales	22
Pilgrim Rest, Rains	72
Pilot Grove, Grayson	48
Pilot Knob, Travis	500
*PILOT POINT, Denton, 190 (3,856)	4,590
Pine, Camp	78
Pine Branch, Red River	40
PINE FOREST, Orange, 15 (487)	508
Pine Forest, Hopkins	100
Pine Grove, Cherokee	30
Pine Grove, Newton	180
Pine Harbor, Marion (810)	790
Pinehill, Rusk	70
*Pinehurst, Montgomery, 108 (4,624)	5,448
PINEHURST, Orange, 210 (2,097)	2,077
PINE ISLAND, Waller (988)	1,200
Pine Island, Jefferson	350
*PINELAND, Sabine, 29 (850)	793
Pine Mills, Wood	75
Pine Prairie, Walker	450
Pine Springs, Culberson	20
Pine Springs, Smith	150
Pineview, Wood	10
Pinewood Estates, Hardin, (1,678)	1,698
Piney, Austin	60
PINEY POINT VILLAGE, Harris, 59 (3,125)	3,338
Pin Hook, Lamar	48
Pioneer, Eastland	20
*Pipe Creek, Bandera, 116	130
Pitner Junction, Rusk	20
*PITTSBURG, Camp, 231 (4,497)	4,760

Town, County	Pop. 2019
*Placedo, Victoria, 4 (692)	753
Placid, McCulloch	32
Plain, Houston	30
*PLAINS, Yoakum, 52 (1,481)	1,644
*PLAINVIEW, Hale, 718 (22,194)	20,124
*PLANO, Collin, Denton, 10,742 (259,841)	290,855
*PLANTERSVILLE, Grimes, 56	869
Plaska, Hall	20
PLEAK, Fort Bend, 28 (1,044)	1,517
Pleasant Farms, Ector	800
Pleasant Grove, Falls	35
Pleasant Grove, Limestone	20
Pleasant Grove, Upshur	35
Pleasant Grove, Wood	30
Pleasant Hill, Polk (522)	597
Pleasant Hill, Eastland	15
Pleasant Hill, Nacogdoches	250
Pleasant Hill, Yoakum	30
*PLEASANTON, Atascosa, 461 (8,934)	10,912
PLEASANT VALLEY, Wichita, (336)	336
Pleasant Valley, Garza	5
*Pledger, Matagorda	265
Pluck, Polk	53
*Plum, Fayette, 2	145
PLUM GROVE, Liberty, 6 (600)	717
Pluto, Ellis	30
POETRY, Hunt, Kaufman,	90
*POINT, Rains, 41 (820)	922
*POINT BLANK, San Jacinto, 17 (688)	748
*POINT COMFORT, Calhoun, 30 (737)	694
Point Enterprise, Limestone	200
POINT VENTURE, Travis, 19 (800)	1,043
Polar, Kent	15
*Pollok, Angelina, 34	400
*PONDER, Denton, 68 (1,395)	2,280
Ponta, Cherokee	50
*Pontotoc, Mason, 1	125
Poole, Rains	20
*Poolville, Parker, 28	520
Port Acres, Jefferson	[part of Port Arthur]
Port Alto, Calhoun	45
*PORT ARANSAS, Nueces, 418 (3,480)	4,153
*PORT ARTHUR, Jefferson, 1,082 (53,818)	54,563
*Port Bolivar, Galveston, 60	700
*Porter, Montgomery, 376	4,200
Porter Heights, Montgomery, (1,653)	1,974
Porter Springs, Houston	50
*PORT ISABEL, Cameron, 269 (5,006)	5,288
*PORTLAND, San Patricio, 487 (15,099)	22,115
*PORT LAVACA, Calhoun, 437 (12,248)	12,641
Port Mansfield, Willacy, 11 (226)	168
*PORT NECHES, Jefferson, 315 (13,040)	12,638
*Port O'Connor, Calhoun, 46 (1,253)	1,139
Port Sullivan, Milam, Robertson	15
Porvenir, Presidio	3
Posey, Hopkins	12
Posey, Lubbock	225
*POST, Garza, 173 (5,376)	5,138
Post Oak, Blanco	10
Post Oak, Lee	100
Postoak, Jack, Clay	20
Postoak, Lamar	65
POST OAK BEND, Kaufman, 9 (595)	701
Post Oak Point, Austin	60
*POTEET, Atascosa, 124 (3,260)	3,554
*POTH, Wilson, 48 (1,908)	2,344
Potosi, Taylor (2,991)	3,574
*POTTSBORO, Grayson, 133 (2,160)	2,479
Pottsville, Hamilton	105
*Powderly, Lamar, 40 (1,178)	1,204
*POWELL, Navarro, 9 (136)	147
*POYNOR, Henderson, 11 (305)	315
Prado Verde, El Paso (246)	266
Praesel, Milam	115
Praha, Fayette	90
Prairie Chapel, McLennan	35
Prairie Dell, Bell	34
*Prairie Hill, Limestone, 4	150
Prairie Hill, Washington	20
*Prairie Lea, Caldwell, 6	320
Prairie Point, Cooke	22
*PRAIRIE VIEW, Waller, 44 (5,576)	6,625
Prairieville, Kaufman	75
*PREMONT, Jim Wells, 57 (2,653)	2,537
*PRESIDIO, Presidio, 93 (4,426)	3,774
Preston, Grayson (2,096)	2,016
*Price, Rusk, 4	275
*Priddy, Mills, 8	215
PRIMERA, Cameron, 33 (4,070)	4,905
Primrose, Van Zandt	26
*PRINCETON, Collin, 263 (6,807)	15,222
Pringle, Hutchinson	20
Pritchett, Upshur	125
*Proctor, Comanche, 5	228
*PROGRESO, Hidalgo, 55 (5,507)	6,073
PROGRESO LAKES, Hidalgo, 9 (240)	268
Progress, Bailey	49
Prospect, Rains	40
*PROSPER, Collin, Denton, 650 (9,423)	24,579
Providence, Floyd	78
Providence, Polk	350
PROVIDENCE VILLAGE, Denton, (4,786)	6,414
Pruitt, Cass	25
Pruitt, Van Zandt	45
Pueblo Nuevo, Webb (521)	555
Puerto Rico, Hidalgo	50
Pullman, Potter	31
Pumphrey, Runnels	15
Pumpkin, San Jacinto	100
Pumpville, Val Verde	25
Punkin Center, Dawson	8
Punkin Center, Eastland	12
*Purdon, Navarro, 8	133
Purley, Franklin	100
*Purmela, Coryell, 1	50
Pursley, Navarro	40
Purves, Erath	50
*PUTNAM, Callahan, 2 (94)	96
*PYOTE, Ward, 7 (114)	133

Q

Town, County	Pop. 2019
*Quail, Collingsworth, 1 (19)	18
Quail Creek, Victoria (1,628)	1,739
*QUANAH, Hardeman, 100 (2,641)	2,480
Quarry, Washington	60
Quarterway, Hale	24
*QUEEN CITY, Cass, 74 (1,476)	1,477
*Quemado, Maverick, 9 (230)	226
Quesada, Starr (25)	34
Quicksand, Newton	50
Quihi, Medina	125
*QUINLAN, Hunt, 203 (1,394)	1,541
QUINTANA, Brazoria, 3 (56)	20
*QUITAQUE, Briscoe, Floyd, 14 (411)	392
*QUITMAN, Wood, 191 (1,809)	1,850

R

Town, County	Pop. 2019
Rabbs Prairie, Fayette	79
Raccoon Bend, Austin	775
Rachal, Brooks	36
Radar Base, Maverick (762)	917
Radium, Jones	10
Rafael Pena, Starr (17)	13
Ragtown, Lamar	30
*Rainbow, Somervell, 15	121
Raisin, Victoria	85
Raleigh, Navarro	40
*RALLS, Crosby, 50 (1,944)	1,824
Ramireno, Zapata (35)	27
Ramirez, Duval	42
Ramirez, Perez, Starr (78)	75
Ramos, Starr (116)	122
Ranchette Estates, Willacy (152)	143
Ranchitos Del Norte, Starr (112)	99
Ranchitos East, Webb (212)	231
Ranchitos Las Lomas, Webb, (266)	298
Rancho Alegre, Jim Wells (1,704)	1,636
Rancho Banquete, Nueces (424)	415
Rancho Chico, San Patricio (396)	494
Ranchos Penitas West, Webb, (573)	587
RANCHO VIEJO, Cameron, 43 (2,437)	2,531
Rancho Viejo, Starr (228)	265
Rand, Kaufman	70
Randado, Jim Hogg, Zapata	6
*Randolph, Fannin, 2	600
Randolph Air Force Base, Bexar (1,241)	1,386
*RANGER, Eastland, 83 (2,468)	2,444
RANGERVILLE, Cameron, (289)	350

Town, County	Pop. 2019
*RANKIN, Upton, 42 (778)	846
Rankin, Ellis	10
RANSOM CANYON, Lubbock, 42 (1,096)	1,113
Ratamosa, Cameron (254)	258
*Ratcliff, Houston, 2	106
Ratibor, Bell	22
Rattan, Delta	10
*RAVENNA, Fannin, 5 (209)	221
Rayburn, Liberty	60
Rayland, Foard	30
*RAYMONDVILLE, Willacy, 181 (11,284)	10,998
Ray Point, Live Oak	200
*Raywood, Liberty, 12	231
Razor, Lamar	20
*Reagan, Falls, 2	300
Reagan Wells, Uvalde	30
Reagor Springs, Ellis	250
*Realitos, Duval, 4 (184)	167
Red Bank, Bowie	125
Red Bluff, Jackson	45
Red Bluff, Reeves	40
Redfield, Nacogdoches (441)	421
Redford, Presidio (90)	67
Red Hill, Cass	28
Red Hill, Limestone	20
Red Lake, Freestone	50
Redland, Angelina (1,047)	1,118
Redland, Leon	35
Redland, Van Zandt	45
RED LICK, Bowie (1,008)	1,027
*RED OAK, Ellis, 495 (10,769)	13,648
Red Ranger, Bell	30
*Red Rock, Bastrop, 26	40
Red Springs, Baylor	42
Red Springs, Smith	350
Redtown, Anderson	30
Redtown, Angelina	500
*REDWATER, Bowie, 18 (1,057)	1,109
Redwood, Guadalupe (4,338)	5,219
Reeds Settlement, Red River	50
Reedville, Caldwell	520
Reese, Cherokee	75
Refuge, Houston	20
*REFUGIO, Refugio, 128 (2,890)	2,695
Regency, Mills	25
Regino Ramirez, Starr (85)	91
Rehburg, Washington	20
Reid Hope King, Cameron (786)	853
Reilly Springs, Hopkins	75
Rek Hill, Fayette	168
*REKLAW, Cherokee, Rusk, 8 (379)	393
Relampago, Hidalgo (132)	148
Rendon, Tarrant (12,552)	14,490
RENO, Parker, Tarrant, 34 (2,494)	3,146
RENO, Lamar, 104 (3,166)	3,360
RETREAT, Navarro (377)	405
Retreat, Grimes	25
Reynard, Houston	75
Rhea, Parmer	98
Rhineland, Knox	120
*RHOME, Wise, 106 (1,522)	1,845
Rhonesboro, Upshur	40
Ricardo, Kleberg (1,048)	1,090
*RICE, Navarro, 57 (923)	1,002
Rice's Crossing, Williamson	130
*Richards, Grimes, 19	300
*RICHARDSON, Dallas, Collin, 4,767 (99,223)	124,695
*RICHLAND, Navarro, 6 (264)	274
Richland, Rains	50
*RICHLAND HILLS, Tarrant, 376 (7,801)	7,917
*RICHLAND SPRINGS, San Saba, 8 (338)	330
*RICHMOND, Fort Bend, 997 (11,679)	13,598
RICHWOOD, Brazoria, 79 (3,510)	4,341
Riderville, Panola	50
Ridge, Mills	25
Ridge, Robertson	67
Ridgeway, Hopkins	54
Ridings, Fannin	200
*RIESEL, McLennan, 61 (1,007)	1,041
Rincon, Starr	5
Ringgold, Montague, 4	100
RIO BRAVO, Webb, 60 (4,794)	4,660
*Rio Frio, Real, 4	50
*RIO GRANDE CITY, Starr, 507 (13,834)	15,074
Rio Grande Village, Brewster	12
*RIO HONDO, Cameron, 58 (2,356)	2,729
*Riomedina, Medina, 9	60
Rios, Duval	75
*RIO VISTA, Johnson, 38 (873)	1,050
*RISING STAR, Eastland, 41 (835)	820
Rita, Burleson	50
Rivera, Starr (162)	182
Riverby, Fannin	8
River Crest Estates, Angelina	150
Rivereno, Starr (61)	61
River Hill, Panola	125
RIVER OAKS, Tarrant, 151 (7,427)	7,928
Rivers End, Brazoria	90
*RIVERSIDE, Walker, 27 (510)	585

An old post office in Robstown. Photo by Larry D. Moore, CC by SA 4.0/Wikimedia Commons.

Town, County	Pop. 2019
*Riviera, Kleberg, 27 (689)	724
Riviera Beach, Kleberg	155
Roach, Cass	50
ROAD RUNNER, Cooke	1
Roane, Navarro	120
*ROANOKE, Denton, 457 (5,962)	9,012
Roans Prairie, Grimes, 4	64
*ROARING SPRINGS, Motley, 8 (234)	235
Robbins, Leon	20
*ROBERT LEE, Coke, 49 (1,049)	1,092
Robertson, Crosby	10
ROBINSON, McLennan, 350 (10,509)	11,883
*ROBSTOWN, Nueces, 339 (11,487)	11,212
*ROBY, Fisher, 28 (643)	624
*Rochelle, McCulloch, 4	163
*ROCHESTER, Haskell, 12 (324)	310
Rock Bluff, Burnet	90
Rock Creek, Somervell	70
*ROCKDALE, Milam, 249 (5,595)	5,656
Rockett, Ellis	300
Rockford, Lamar	30
Rockhouse, Austin, Fayette	100
*Rock Island, Colorado, 3	160
Rockland, Tyler	98
Rockne, Bastrop	190
*ROCKPORT, Aransas, 685 (8,766)	10,449
*ROCKSPRINGS, Edwards, 59 (1,182)	1,149
*ROCKWALL, Rockwall, 1,952 (37,490)	45,641
*Rockwood, Coleman, 3	53
Rocky Branch, Morris	135
Rocky Creek, Blanco	20
ROCKY MOUND, Camp, 2 (75)	71
Rocky Point, Burnet	152
Roddy, Van Zandt	29
Rodney, Navarro	15
Roeder, Titus	75
Roganville, Jasper	70
*ROGERS, Bell, 41 (1,218)	1,247
Rogers, Taylor	151
Rolling Hills, Potter	1,000
Rolling Meadows, Gregg	362
ROLLINGWOOD, Travis, 124 (1,412)	1,585
Roma Creek, Starr (350)	325
*ROMA-Los Saenz, Starr, 200 (9,765)	11,221
ROMAN FOREST, Montgomery, (1,538)	2,061
*Romayor, Liberty, 2	135
*Roosevelt, Kimble, 1	14
Roosevelt, Lubbock	362
*ROPESVILLE, Hockley, 20 (434)	430
Rosalie, Red River	100
*Rosanky, Bastrop, 18	210
*ROSCOE, Nolan, 52 (1,322)	1,240
*ROSEBUD, Falls, 49 (1,412)	1,345
ROSE CITY, Orange, 34 (502)	501
Rose Hill, Harris	3,500
Rose Hill, San Jacinto	30
ROSE HILL ACRES, Hardin (441)	441
*ROSENBERG, Fort Bend, 1,139 (30,618)	37,823
Rosevine, Sabine	50
Rosewood, Upshur	100
*Rosharon, Brazoria, 169 (1,152)	1,384
Rosita, Maverick (2,704)	2,797
Rosita, Duval	25
*ROSS, McLennan, 8 (283)	294
*ROSSER, Kaufman, 6 (332)	404
*Rosston, Cooke, 2	75
Rossville, Atascosa	200
*ROTAN, Fisher, 53 (1,508)	1,470
Rough Creek, San Saba	8
Round House, Navarro	40
*ROUND MOUNTAIN, Blanco, 14 (181)	205
Round Mountain, Travis	59
Round Prairie, Navarro	40
*ROUND ROCK, Williamson, Travis, 4,166 (99,887)	119,899
Round Timber, Baylor	2
*ROUND TOP, Fayette, 75 (90)	90
Roundup, Hockley	20
Rowden, Callahan	15
*Rowena, Runnels, 10	349
*ROWLETT, Dallas, Rockwall, 1,558 (56,199)	67,818
*ROXTON, Lamar, 21 (650)	647
Royalty, Ward	27
*ROYSE CITY, Rockwall, Collin, 449 (9,349)	13,191
Rucker, Comanche	28
Rugby, Red River	24
Ruidosa, Presidio	18
*RULE, Haskell, 15 (636)	600
Rumley, Lampasas	30
RUNAWAY BAY, Wise, 32 (1,286)	1,575
*RUNGE, Karnes, 27 (1,031)	1,144
Rural Shade, Navarro	30
*RUSK, Cherokee, 163 (5,551)	5,796
Russell, Leon	27
Rutersville, Fayette	137
Ruth Springs, Henderson	120
*Rye, Liberty, 4	150

S

Town, County	Pop. 2019
Sabanno, Eastland	12
*SABINAL, Uvalde, 52 (1,695)	1,705
*Sabine Pass, Jefferson, 13	[part of Port Arthur]
SACHSE, Dallas, Collin, 655 (20,329)	26,162
*Sacul, Nacogdoches	150
*SADLER, Grayson, 16 (343)	365
Sagerton, Haskell	171
*SAGINAW, Tarrant, 527 (19,806)	24,337
St. Francis, Potter	30
*ST. HEDWIG, Bexar, 88 (2,094)	2,488
*SAINT JO, Montague, 40 (1,043)	1,074
St. John Colony, Caldwell	150
St. Lawrence, Glasscock	90
St. Mary's Colony, Bastrop	50
ST. PAUL, Collin, 38 (1,066)	1,105
St. Paul, San Patricio (584)	596
*SALADO, Bell, 309 (2,126)	2,380
Salem, Cherokee	20
Salem, Grimes	54
Salem, Newton	218
Salesville, Palo Pinto	88
Saline, Menard	70
*Salineño, Starr (201)	175
Salineño North, Starr (115)	116
Salmon, Anderson	20
Salt Flat, Hudspeth	8
Salt Gap, McCulloch	25
*Saltillo, Hopkins, 5	200
Samaria, Navarro	90
Sammy Martinez, Starr (110)	113
*Samnorwood, Collingsworth (51)	56
Sample, Gonzales	16
Sam Rayburn, Jasper (1,181)	1,137
*SAN ANGELO, Tom Green, 3,481 (93,200)	100,052
*SAN ANTONIO, Bexar, 39,746 (1,327,407)	1,548,248
San Antonio Prairie, Burleson	20
*SAN AUGUSTINE, San Augustine, 127 (2,108)	1,918
*SAN BENITO, Cameron, 581 (24,250)	24,581
San Carlos, Hidalgo (3,130)	3,486
San Carlos, Starr	10
San Carlos I, Webb (316)	338
San Carlos II, Webb (261)	283
Sanco, Coke	15
SANCTUARY, Parker, 29 (329)	344
Sand Branch, Dallas	400
*Sanderson, Terrell, 13 (837)	681
Sand Flat, Johnson	133
Sand Flat, Leon	32
Sand Flat, Rains	45
Sand Flat, Smith	100
Sand Flat, Van Zandt	25
Sand Hill, Upshur	75
Sandhill, Floyd	33
*Sandia, Jim Wells, 39 (379)	328
*SAN DIEGO, Duval, Jim Wells, 99 (4,488)	4,217
Sandlin, Stonewall	3
Sandoval, Starr (32)	39
Sandoval, Williamson	60
Sand Springs, Howard (835)	859
Sandusky, Grayson	15
Sandy, Blanco	150
Sandy, Limestone	5
SANDY OAKS, Bexar,	4,579
Sandy Harbor, Llano	85
Sandy Hill, Washington	50
Sandy Hollow-Escondidas, Nueces, (296)	259
SANDY POINT, Brazoria,	237
*SAN ELIZARIO, El Paso, 56 (13,603)	14,313
*SAN FELIPE, Austin, 33 (747)	867
San Fernando, Starr (68)	69
*SANFORD, Hutchinson, 5 (164)	151
San Gabriel, Milam, Williamson	70
*SANGER, Denton, 311 (6,916)	9,388
*San Isidro, Starr, 10 (240)	227
San Jose, Duval	15
*SAN JUAN, Hidalgo, 587 (33,856)	38,033

Town, County	Pop. 2019
San Juan, Starr (129)	137
SAN LEANNA, Travis (497)	540
San Leon, Galveston (4,970)	5,439
*SAN MARCOS, Hays, Caldwell, Guadalupe, 1,953 (44,894)	69,731
SAN PATRICIO, San Patricio (395)	402
San Pedro, Cameron (530)	457
*SAN PERLITA, Willacy (573)	554
San Roman, Starr	5
*SAN SABA, San Saba, 157 (3,099)	3,212
SANSOM PARK, Tarrant, 102 (4,686)	5,625
Santa Anna, Starr (13)	13
*SANTA ANNA, Coleman, 57 (1,099)	1,010
Santa Catarina, Starr	15
SANTA CLARA, Guadalupe, 22 (725)	725
Santa Cruz, Starr (54)	54
*Santa Elena, Starr, 2	35
*SANTA FE, Galveston, 419 (12,222)	13,654
*Santa Maria, Cameron, 2 (733)	651
Santa Monica, Willacy (83)	76
*SANTA ROSA, Cameron, 39 (2,873)	2,766
Santa Rosa, Starr (241)	242
Santel, Starr (44)	42
*Santo, Palo Pinto, 25	445
*San Ygnacio, Zapata, 4 (667)	558
*Saragosa, Reeves, 3	185
*Saratoga, Hardin, 11	1,000
Sardis, Ellis	60
Sargent, Matagorda	900
*Sarita, Kenedy, 18 (238)	244
Saron, Trinity	6
Saspamco, Wilson	300
*Satin, Falls, 2	86
Sattler, Comal	2,500
Saturn, Gonzales	15
Savannah, Denton (3,318)	4,227
*SAVOY, Fannin, 29 (831)	860
Scenic Oaks, Bexar (4,957)	5,678
Schattel, Frio	30
*SCHERTZ, Guadalupe, Comal, Bexar, 1,107 (31,506)	42,709
Schicke Point, Calhoun	70
Schroeder, Goliad	347
*SCHULENBURG, Fayette, 330 (2,852)	3,006
Schumansville, Guadalupe	678
Schwab City, Polk	120
*Schwertner, Williamson, 1	175
Scissors, Hidalgo (3,186)	3,460
*SCOTLAND, Archer, 19 (501)	512
*SCOTTSVILLE, Harrison, 20 (376)	391
Scranton, Eastland	40
Scrappin Valley, Newton	25
*Scroggins, Franklin, 17	150
*SCURRY, Kaufman, 64 (681)	769
*SEABROOK, Harris, 479 (11,952)	14,059
*SEADRIFT, Calhoun, 52 (1,364)	1,496
*SEAGOVILLE, Dallas, 486 (14,835)	17,107
*SEAGRAVES, Gaines, 47 (2,417)	2,946
Seale, Robertson	60
*SEALY, Austin, 366 (6,019)	6,805
Seaton, Bell	60
Seawillow, Caldwell	75
*Sebastian, Willacy, 10 (1,917)	1,805
Sebastopol, Trinity	300
Seco Mines, Maverick (560)	597
Security, Montgomery	200
Sedalia, Collin	24
Segno, Polk	80
Segovia, Kimble	12
*SEGUIN, Guadalupe, 1,223 (25,175)	31,884
Sejita, Duval	24
Selden, Erath	55
Selfs, Fannin	30
SELMA, Bexar, Guadalupe, Comal, 325 (5,540)	11,795
*SEMINOLE, Gaines, 376 (6,430)	7,660
Sempronius, Austin	25
Senate, Jack	20
Serbin, Lee	109
Serenada, Williamson (1,641)	1,724
Seth Ward, Hale (2,025)	1,899
SEVEN OAKS, Polk, 4 (111)	118
Seven Pines, Gregg, Upshur	50
SEVEN POINTS, Henderson, 101 (1,455)	1,558
Seven Sisters, Duval	25
Sexton, Sabine	29
*SEYMOUR, Baylor, 120 (2,740)	2,740
Shadybrook, Cherokee (1,967)	2,115
Shady Grove, Cherokee	30
Shady Grove, Houston	83
Shady Grove, Panola	45
Shady Grove, Smith	250
Shady Grove, Upshur	40
Shady Grove , Burnet	114
Shady Hollow, Travis (5,004)	5,196
Shady Oaks, Henderson	300
SHADY SHORES, Denton, 71 (2,612)	3,200
Shafter, Presidio	57
*SHALLOWATER, Lubbock, 136 (2,484)	2,528
*SHAMROCK, Wheeler, 103 (1,910)	1,777
Shangri La, Burnet	108
Shankleville, Newton	35
Shannon, Clay	20
Sharp, Milam	52
SHAVANO PARK, Bexar, 100 (3,035)	4,007
Shawnee Prairie, Angelina	20
Shaws Bend, Colorado	100
*Sheffield, Pecos, 11	322
Shelby, Austin	300
*Shelbyville, Shelby, 27	600
Sheldon, Harris (1,990)	2,157
SHENANDOAH, Montgomery, 330 (2,134)	3,185
Shep, Taylor	25
*SHEPHERD, San Jacinto, 72 (2,319)	2,649
*Sheridan, Colorado, 14	300
*SHERMAN, Grayson, 1,517 (38,315)	44,113
Sherry, Red River	15
Sherwood, Irion, Tom Green	170
Sherwood Shores, Grayson, (1,190)	1,141
Sherwood Shores, Bell	774
Sherwood Shores, Burnet	920
Shields, Coleman	8
Shiloh, Leon	30
Shiloh, Limestone	250
*SHINER, Lavaca, 146 (2,069)	2,230
Shirley, Hopkins	20
*Shiro, Grimes, 3	210
Shive, Hamilton	60
SHOREACRES, Harris, 21 (1,493)	1,580
Short, Shelby	15
Shovel Mountain, Burnet	148
*Sidney, Comanche, 3	148
Sienna Plantation, Fort Bend, (13,721)	19,403
*Sierra Blanca, Hudspeth, 12 (553)	574
Siesta Acres, Maverick (1,885)	2,011
Siesta Shores, Zapata (1,382)	1,563
Silas, Shelby	75
Siloam, Bowie	50
*SILSBEE, Hardin, 307 (6,611)	6,805
*Silver, Coke, 1	34
Silver City, Milam	25
Silver City, Navarro	100
Silver City, Red River	25
Silver Creek Village, Burnet	300
Silver Lake, Van Zandt	42
*SILVERTON, Briscoe, 35 (731)	687
Silver Valley, Coleman	15
Simmons, Live Oak	65
*Simms, Bowie, 8	300
Simms, Deaf Smith	6
*SIMONTON, Fort Bend, 49 (814)	965
Simpsonville, Matagorda	6
Simpsonville, Upshur	100
Sinclair City, Smith	50
Singleton, Grimes	45
*SINTON, San Patricio, 183 (5,665)	5,240
Sipe Springs, Comanche	70
Sisterdale, Kendall	110
Sivells Bend, Cooke	36
Six Mile, Calhoun	300
Skeeterville, San Saba	10
*SKELLYTOWN, Carson, 12 (473)	436
*Skidmore, Bee, 17 (925)	932
Slate Shoals, Lamar	10
*SLATON, Lubbock, 158 (6,121)	6,048
Slayden, Gonzales	10
Slide, Lubbock	245
*Slidell, Wise, 2	175
Sloan, San Saba	30
Slocum, Anderson	150
Smetana, Brazos	80
*SMILEY, Gonzales, 8 (549)	571
Smithland, Marion, Cass	179
Smith Point, Chambers	180
Smithson Valley, Comal	1,000

CITIES & TOWNS

Town, County	Pop. 2019
*SMITHVILLE, Bastrop, 254 (3,817)	4,461
Smithwick, Burnet	102
*SMYER, Hockley, 7 (474)	477
Smyrna, Cass	215
Smyrna, Rains	25
*SNOOK, Burleson, 21 (511)	535
Snow Hill, Collin	23
Snow Hill, Upshur	75
*SNYDER, Scurry, 520 (11,202)	11,073
*SOCORRO, El Paso, 590 (32,013)	34,740
Soldier Mound, Dickens	10
Solis, Cameron (512)	431
*SOMERSET, Bexar, 73 (1,631)	1,996
*SOMERVILLE, Burleson, 77 (1,376)	1,502
Sommer's Mill, Bell	27
*SONORA, Sutton, 133 (3,027)	2,967
*SOUR LAKE, Hardin, 103 (1,813)	1,944
South Alamo, Hidalgo (3,361)	3,589
*South Bend, Young, 2	100
South Bosque, McLennan	1,523
South Brice, Hall	19
South Fork Estates, Jim Hogg (70)	72
SOUTH FRYDEK, Austin	225
*SOUTH HOUSTON, Harris, 629 (16,983)	17,674
*SOUTHLAKE, Tarrant, Denton, 1,743 (26,575)	31,613
Southland, Garza	157
South La Paloma, Jim Wells (345)	324
*SOUTHMAYD, Grayson, 19 (992)	1,122
SOUTH MOUNTAIN, Coryell, (384)	365
*SOUTH PADRE ISLAND, Cameron, 357 (2,816)	2,766
*South Plains, Floyd	67
South Point, Cameron (1,376)	1,388
South Purmela, Coryell	10
South Shore, Bell	60
SOUTHSIDE PLACE, Harris, 61 (1,715)	1,867
South Sulphur, Hunt	60
South Toledo Bend, Newton, (524)	454
Southton, Bexar	113
*Spade, Lamb, 2 (73)	64
Spanish Fort, Montague	50
Sparenberg, Dawson	40
Sparks, El Paso (4,529)	5,501
Sparks, Bell	40
Speaks, Lavaca	60
*SPEARMAN, Hansford, 111 (3,368)	3,245
Speegleville, McLennan	1,655
*Spicewood, Burnet, 279	4,000
Spider Mountain, Burnet	92
*SPLENDORA, Montgomery, 169 (1,615)	2,240
SPOFFORD, Kinney (95)	96
Spraberry, Midland	46
*Spring, Harris, 2,188 (54,298)	68,450
*SPRING BRANCH, Comal, 380	254
Spring Creek, Hutchinson	20
Spring Creek, San Saba	20
Springdale, Cass	55
Springfield, Anderson	30
Spring Gardens, Nueces (563)	662
Spring Hill, Bowie	100
Spring Hill, Navarro	60
Spring Hill, San Jacinto	38
*SPRINGLAKE, Lamb, 9 (108)	96
*SPRINGTOWN, Parker, 306 (2,658)	3,142
SPRING VALLEY, Harris, 142 (3,715)	4,248
Spring Valley, McLennan	400
*SPUR, Dickens, 49 (1,318)	1,173
*Spurger, Tyler, 15	590
Stacy, McCulloch	20
Staff, Eastland	65
*STAFFORD, Fort Bend, Harris, 1,410 (17,693)	19,501
Stag Creek, Comanche	45
STAGECOACH, Montgomery, 11 (538)	620
Stairtown, Caldwell	35
Staley, San Jacinto	30
*STAMFORD, Jones, Haskell, 133 (3,124)	2,934
Stampede, Bell	6
Stamps, Upshur	45
*STANTON, Martin, 105 (2,492)	3,002
*Staples, Guadalupe, 5 (267)	272
*Star, Mills, 1	97
STAR HARBOR, Henderson, 13 (444)	495
Star Route, Cochran	15
Starrville, Smith	75
Startzville, Comal	7,000
Steele Hill, Dickens	4
Stephens Creek, San Jacinto	385
*STEPHENVILLE, Erath, 908 (17,123)	21,245
Sterley, Floyd	31
*STERLING CITY, Sterling, 46 (888)	964
Stewards Mill, Freestone	22
Stewart, Rusk	15
Stiles, Reagan	4
Stillwell Store, Brewster	2
*STINNETT, Hutchinson, 50 (1,881)	1,760
Stith, Jones	50
*STOCKDALE, Wilson, 80 (1,442)	1,702
Stockman, Shelby	55
STOCKTON BEND, Hood (305)	334
Stoneburg, Montague	51
Stoneham, Grimes	15
*Stonewall, Gillespie, 25 (505)	543
Stony, Denton	25
Stout, Wood	302
*Stowell, Chambers, 9 (1,756)	2,096
Stranger, Falls	12
*STRATFORD, Sherman, 65 (2,017)	2,049
Stratton, DeWitt	25
*STRAWN, Palo Pinto, 34 (653)	676
Streeter, Mason	85
*STREETMAN, Freestone, 26 (247)	259
String Prairie, Bastrop	40
Stringtown, Newton	20
Structure, Williamson	50
Stubblefield, Houston	15
Stubbs, Kaufman	50
Study Butte, Brewster, 29 (233)	247
Sturgeon, Cooke	10
Styx, Kaufman	50
Sublime, Lavaca	75
*SUDAN, Lamb, 23 (958)	892
Sugar Hill, Titus	90
*SUGAR LAND, Fort Bend, 4,317 (78,817)	131,448
Sugar Valley, Matagorda	45
*SULLIVAN CITY, Hidalgo, 67 (3,998)	4,273
*Sulphur Bluff, Hopkins, 4	280
*SULPHUR SPRINGS, Hopkins, 794 (15,449)	16,279
Summerfield, Castro, Parmer	48
Summerville, Gonzales	45
*Sumner, Lamar, 31	95
*SUNDOWN, Hockley, 41 (1,397)	1,422
Sunny Side, Waller	250
Sunnyside, Castro	64
Sunnyside, Wilson	100
SUNNYVALE, Dallas, 256 (5,130)	6,795
*SUNRAY, Moore, 45 (1,926)	1,828
Sunrise, Falls	200
*SUNRISE BEACH, Llano, 36 (713)	797
*Sunset, Montague, Wise, 15 (497)	579
Sunset, Starr (47)	50
Sunset Acres, Webb (23)	20
Sunset Oaks, Burnet	198
SUNSET VALLEY, Travis, 142 (648)	663
SUN VALLEY, Lamar, 32 (69)	77
SURFSIDE BEACH, Brazoria, 34 (482)	571
*Sutherland Springs, Wilson, 6	420
Swamp City, Gregg	8
Swan, Smith	150
*SWEENY, Brazoria, 103 (3,684)	4,047
Sweet Home, Guadalupe	294
*Sweet Home, Lavaca, 5	360
Sweet Home, Lee	30
Sweet Union, Cherokee	40
*SWEETWATER, Nolan, 373 (10,906)	10,285
Swenson, Stonewall	80
Swift, Nacogdoches	210
Swiss Alp, Fayette	17
Sylvan, Lamar	68
*Sylvester, Fisher, 1	79

T

Town, County	Pop. 2019
Tabor, Brazos	150
Tadmor, Houston	67
*TAFT, San Patricio, 61 (3,048)	2,862
Taft Southwest, San Patricio, (1,460)	1,342

Town, County	Pop. 2019
*TAHOKA, Lynn, 70 (2,673)	2,765
*TALCO, Titus, 16 (516)	499
*Talpa, Coleman, 8	127
TALTY, Kaufman, 30 (1,535)	2,879
Tamina, Montgomery	900
Tanglewood, Lee	60
Tanquecitos South Acres, Webb, (233)	240
Tanquecitos South Acres II, Webb, (50)	51
Tarkington Prairie, Liberty	300
*Tarpley, Bandera, 6	30
*Tarzan, Martin, 7	30
Tascosa Hills, Potter	90
*TATUM, Rusk, Panola, 68 (1,385)	1,419
*TAYLOR, Williamson, 549 (15,191)	18,154
TAYLOR LAKE VILLAGE, Harris, 66 (3,544)	3,594
TAYLOR LANDING, Jefferson, (228)	238
Taylorsville, Caldwell	35
Taylor Town, Lamar	40
Tazewell, Hopkins	20
*TEAGUE, Freestone, 115 (3,560)	3,495
Teaselville, Smith	150
*TEHUACANA, Limestone, 3 (283)	286
Telegraph, Kimble	3
*Telephone, Fannin, 7	210
*Telferner, Victoria, 5	700
Telico, Ellis, Navarro	115
*Tell, Childress, Cottle, Hall	20
*TEMPLE, Bell, 2,199 (66,102)	78,267
*TENAHA, Shelby, 32 (1,160)	1,144
Tenmile, Dawson	30
*Tennessee Colony, Anderson, 13	300
*Tennyson, Coke, 1	46
*Terlingua, Brewster, 2 (58)	50
*TERRELL, Kaufman, 836 (15,816)	19,183
TERRELL HILLS, Bexar, 113 (4,878)	5,344
Terry Chapel, Falls	30
Terryville, DeWitt	40
*TEXARKANA, Bowie (Miller, Ark.), 3,467 (66,035)	69,491
*TEXAS CITY, Galveston, 1,018 (45,099)	51,178
TEXHOMA, Sherman (Texas Co., Okla.), 27 (1,295)	1,142
*TEXLINE, Dallam, 26 (507)	519
Texroy, Hutchinson	50
Thalia, Foard	50
*THE COLONY, Denton, 929 (36,328)	46,686
Thedford, Smith	65
The Grove, Coryell	100
THE HILLS, Travis (2,472)	2,480
Thelma, Bexar	150
Thelma, Limestone	20
Theon, Williamson	30
Thermo, Hopkins	56
*The Woodlands, Montgomery, 766 (93,847)	122,233
*Thicket, Hardin, 2	306
*Thomaston, DeWitt	45
*THOMPSONS, Fort Bend, 6 (246)	331
Thompsonville, Jim Hogg (46)	47
Thompsonville, Gonzales	30
Thornberry, Clay	75
*THORNDALE, Milam, 75 (1,336)	1,394
*THORNTON, Limestone, 16 (526)	541
THORNTONVILLE, Ward, 11 (476)	543
Thorp Spring, Hood	222
*THRALL, Williamson, 32 (839)	1,036
Three League, Martin	20
Three Oaks, Wilson	150
*THREE RIVERS, Live Oak, 101 (1,848)	2,018
Three States, Cass	45
*THROCKMORTON, Throckmorton, 49 (828)	735
Thunderbird Bay, Brown (663)	602
Thurber, Erath	48
Tidwell, Hunt	50
Tierra Bonita, Cameron (141)	119
Tierra Dorada, Starr (28)	31
Tierra Grande, Nueces (403)	441
Tierra Verde, Nueces (277)	320
Tigertown, Lamar	400
TIKI ISLAND, Galveston, 31 (968)	1,083
*Tilden, McMullen, 42 (261)	301
Tilmon, Caldwell	60
TIMBERCREEK CANYON, Randall (418)	460
Timberwood, Bexar (13,447)	16,881
*TIMPSON, Shelby, 68 (1,155)	1,124
Tin Top, Parker	500
*TIOGA, Grayson, 44 (803)	1,018
TIRA, Hopkins (297)	316
*Tivoli, Refugio, 5 (479)	477
TOCO, Lamar, 3 (75)	80
Todd City, Anderson	10
TODD MISSION, Grimes, 93 (107)	117
Tokio, McLennan	250
Tokio, Terry	6
*TOLAR, Hood, 48 (681)	983
Tolbert, Wilbarger	15
Tolette, Lamar	40
Tolosa, Kaufman, Henderson	65
*TOMBALL, Harris, 1,459 (10,753)	11,754
*TOM BEAN, Grayson, 27 (1,045)	1,129
Tomlinson Hill, Falls	64
TOOL, Henderson, 53 (2,240)	2,374
Topsey, Coryell	35
*Tornillo, El Paso, 12 (1,568)	1,540
Tours, McLennan	130
*Tow, Llano, 6	305
Town Bluff, Tyler	429
*TOYAH, Reeves, 3 (90)	96
*Toyahvale, Reeves, 1	60
Tradewinds, San Patricio (180)	186
Travis, Falls	48
Travis Ranch, Kaufman (2,556)	3,217
Trawick, Nacogdoches	375
Treasure Island, Brazoria	152
Treasure Island, Guadalupe	172
*TRENT, Taylor, 3 (337)	347
*TRENTON, Fannin, 58 (635)	684
Trickham, Coleman	29
Trimmer, Bell	390
*TRINIDAD, Henderson, 28 (886)	882
*TRINITY, Trinity, 138 (2,697)	2,741
TROPHY CLUB, Denton, 290 (8,024)	13,947
*TROUP, Smith, Cherokee, 102 (1,869)	2,097
Trout Creek, Newton	70
*TROY, Bell, 103 (1,645)	1,982
Truby, Jones	26
Trumbull, Ellis	100
Truscott, Knox	50
Tucker, Anderson	175
*Tuleta, Bee, 12 (288)	306
*TULIA, Swisher, 128 (4,967)	4,698
Tulip, Fannin	10
Tulsita, Bee (14)	2
Tundra, Van Zandt	34
Tunis, Burleson	150
*TURKEY, Hall, 20 (421)	375
Turlington, Freestone	27
Turnersville, Coryell	125
Turnersville, Travis	90
*Turnertown-Selman City, Rusk, 3	271
Turtle Bayou, Chambers	55
*TUSCOLA, Taylor, 73 (742)	753
Tuxedo, Jones	42
Twichell, Ochiltree	22
Twitty, Wheeler	12
*TYE, Taylor, 57 (1,242)	1,318
*TYLER, Smith, 4,648 (96,901)	108,173
*Tynan, Bee, 6 (278)	283
Type, Williamson, Bastrop	40

U

Town, County	Pop. 2019
UHLAND, Hays, Caldwell, 22 (1,014)	1,355
*Umbarger, Randall, 2	327
UNCERTAIN, Harrison, 3 (94)	97
Union, Scurry	20
Union, Terry	8
Union, Wilson	52
UNION GROVE, Upshur, 2 (357)	373
Union Grove, Bell	12
Union High, Navarro	30
Union Hill, Denton	25
UNION VALLEY, Hunt (307)	425
Unity, Lamar	60
*UNIVERSAL CITY, Bexar, 579 (18,530)	21,927
UNIVERSITY PARK, Dallas, 861 (23,068)	25,017
Upper Meyersville, DeWitt	33
Upshaw, Nacogdoches	400
Upton, Bastrop	25
Urbana, San Jacinto	15
Utley, Bastrop	30

Town, County	Pop. 2019
*Utopia, Uvalde, 35 (227)	213
*UVALDE, Uvalde, 548 (15,751)	16,086
Uvalde Estates, Uvalde (2,171)	2,228

V

Town, County	Pop. 2019
Valdasta, Collin	82
*VALENTINE, Jeff Davis, 4 (134)	123
*Valera, Coleman, 2	80
Valle de Oro, Potter	250
Valle Vista, Starr (469)	512
Valley Creek, Fannin	110
*VALLEY MILLS, Bosque, McLennan, 84 (1,203)	1,253
*Valley Spring, Llano	50
*VALLEY VIEW, Cooke, 87 (757)	833
Valley View, Runnels	10
Valley View, Upshur	75
Valley View, Wichita	210
Valley Wells, Dimmit	21
Val Verde, Milam	25
Val Verde Park, Val Verde (2,384)	2,648
*VAN, Van Zandt, 137 (2,632)	2,875
*VAN ALSTYNE, Grayson, 184 (3,046)	4,449
Vance, Real	20
*Vancourt, Tom Green, 1	131
Vandalia, Red River	35
*Vanderbilt, Jackson, 7 (395)	418
*Vanderpool, Bandera, 5	20
Vandyke, Comanche	20
*VAN HORN, Culberson, 94 (2,063)	1,913
*Van Vleck, Matagorda, 27 (1,844)	2,214
Vasco, Delta	20
Vashti, Clay	70
Vattmann, Kleberg	25
Vaughan, Hill	75
Veach, San Augustine	12
Vealmoor, Howard	5
*VEGA, Oldham, 39 (884)	917
*VENUS, Johnson, 84 (2,960)	4,806
Vera, Knox	30
Verdi, Atascosa	110
Verhalen, Reeves	12
*Veribest, Tom Green, 3	115
*VERNON, Wilbarger, 322 (11,002)	10,307
Verona, Collin	34
Vessey, Red River	15
Viboras, Starr	15
Vick, Concho	20
*VICTORIA, Victoria, 2,769 (62,592)	66,891
Victoria, Limestone	25
Victoria Vera, Starr (110)	106
Victory City, Bowie	350
*VIDOR, Orange, 434 (10,579)	10,570
Vienna, Lavaca	40
View, Taylor	350
Vigo Park, Swisher	36
Villa del Sol, Cameron (175)	197
*Village Mills, Hardin, 17	200
Villa Pancho, Cameron (788)	936
Villarreal, Starr (131)	143
Villa Verde, Hidalgo (874)	875
Vincent, Howard	10
Vineyard, Jack	19
VINTON, El Paso, 78 (1,971)	2,042
Violet, Nueces	160
Vistula, Houston	21
*Voca, McCulloch, 7	56
VOLENTE, Travis, 28 (520)	597
Volga, Houston	9
*VON ORMY, Bexar, 84 (1,085)	1,320
Voss, Coleman, 2	20
*Votaw, Hardin, 1	160
Vsetin, Lavaca	45

W

Town, County	Pop. 2019
*WACO, McLennan, 4,335 (124,805)	138,400
*Wadsworth, Matagorda, 10	160
*WAELDER, Gonzales, 32 (1,065)	1,144
Wagner, Hunt	75
Waka, Ochiltree, 2	65
Wakefield, Polk	25
WAKE VILLAGE, Bowie, 108 (5,492)	5,669
*Walburg, Williamson, 4	277
Walcott, Deaf Smith	5
Waldeck, Fayette	34
Waldrip, McCulloch	15
Walhalla, Fayette	38
*Wall, Tom Green, 16	329
Wallace, Van Zandt	70
*WALLER, Waller, Harris, 264 (2,326)	3,119
*WALLIS, Austin, 54 (1,252)	1,344
*Wallisville, Chambers, 17	300
Walnut Bend, Cooke	45
Walnut Grove, Panola	125
*WALNUT SPRINGS, Bosque, 23 (827)	911
Walton, Van Zandt	60
Wamba, Bowie	430
Waneta, Houston	19
Waples, Hood	155
*Warda, Fayette, 3	121
Ward Creek, Bowie	10
*Waring, Kendall, 7	73
*Warren, Tyler, 26 (757)	882
WARREN CITY, Gregg, Upshur, 8 (298)	277
Warrenton, Fayette	186
Warsaw, Kaufman	100
Washburn, Armstrong	120
*Washington, Washington, 24	100
*WASKOM, Harrison, 86 (2,160)	2,263
Wastella, Nolan	12
*WATAUGA, Tarrant, 539 (23,497)	24,402
Waterloo, Williamson	70
Waterman, Shelby	40
*Water Valley, Tom Green, 7	203
Watson, Burnet	50
Watt, Limestone	25
Waverly, San Jacinto, Walker	200
*WAXAHACHIE, Ellis, 1,272 (29,621)	37,983
Wayne, Cass	15
Wayside, Armstrong, 2	25
Wayside, Roberts	40
Wealthy, Leon	12
*WEATHERFORD, Parker, 1,862 (25,250)	32,587
Weatherly, Hall	8
Weaver, Hopkins	35
WEBBERVILLE, Travis, 12 (392)	466
Webbville, Coleman	15
*WEBSTER, Harris, 826 (10,684)	11,989
Weches, Houston	46
Weedhaven, Jackson	35
Weeping Mary, Cherokee	85
*Weesatche, Goliad, 3	411
*WEIMAR, Colorado, 157 (2,151)	2,299
*WEINERT, Haskell, 6 (172)	161
*WEIR, Williamson, 20 (450)	544
Wiess Bluff, Jasper	60
*Welch, Dawson, 4 (222)	230
Welcome, Austin	300
Weldon, Houston	131
Welfare, Kendall	10
*Wellborn, Brazos, 7	400
*WELLINGTON, Collingsworth, 54 (2,189)	2,002
*WELLMAN, Terry, 3 (203)	204
*WELLS, Cherokee, 24 (790)	813
Wells, Lynn	10
Wells Branch, Travis (12,120)	13,772
*WESLACO, Hidalgo, 1,125 (35,670)	42,047
Wesley, Washington, Austin	65
Wesley Grove, Walker	25
*WEST, McLennan, 177 (2,807)	2,939
West Alto Bonito, Starr (696)	743
*WESTBROOK, Mitchell, 15 (253)	256
*WEST COLUMBIA, Brazoria, 168 (3,905)	4,160
Westcott, San Jacinto	55
Westdale, Jim Wells (372)	404
Western Lake, Parker (1,525)	1,698
*Westhoff, DeWitt, 8	410
WESTLAKE, Tarrant, Denton, 99 (992)	1,725
*WEST LAKE HILLS, Travis, 374 (3,063)	3,250
West Livingston, Polk (8,071)	9,474
West Mineola, Wood	20
*Westminster, Collin, 5 (861)	1,155
West Mountain, Upshur	325
West Odessa, Ector (22,707)	29,224
*WESTON, Collin, 14 (563)	580
WESTON LAKES, Fort Bend, (2,482)	4,699
WEST ORANGE, Orange, 107 (3,443)	3,181
Westover, Baylor	18
WESTOVER HILLS, Tarrant, (682)	710
Westphalia, Falls	186
West Point, Fayette, 11	213

Town, County	Pop. 2019
West Sharyland, Hidalgo (2,309)	2,207
West Sinton, San Patricio	150
WEST TAWAKONI, Hunt, 41 (1,576)	1,844
WEST UNIVERSITY PLACE, Harris, 280 (14,787)	15,699
Westville, Trinity	46
Westway, El Paso (4,188)	4,297
Westway, Deaf Smith	15
Westwood Shores, Trinity (1,162)	1,053
WESTWORTH VILLAGE, Tarrant, 67 (2,472)	2,772
*WHARTON, Wharton, 335 (8,832)	8,653
Wheatland, Tarrant, Parker	175
*WHEELER, Wheeler, 61 (1,592)	1,550
Wheeler Springs, Houston	89
*Wheelock, Robertson, 4	225
White City, San Augustine	20
White City, Wilbarger	40
*WHITE DEER, Carson, 42 (1,000)	963
*WHITEFACE, Cochran, 15 (449)	432
Whiteflat, Motley	4
White Hall, Bell	262
Whitehall, Grimes	30
*WHITEHOUSE, Smith, 315 (7,660)	8,899
*WHITE OAK, Gregg, 249 (6,469)	6,570
White Oak, Titus	60
White River Lake, Crosby	83
White Rock, Hunt	60
White Rock, Red River	90
White Rock, Robertson	80
White Rock, San Augustine	60
*WHITESBORO, Grayson, 202 (3,793)	4,075
*WHITE SETTLEMENT, Tarrant, 341 (16,116)	17,719
White Star, Motley	6
Whiteway, Hamilton	8
*WHITEWRIGHT, Grayson, Fannin, 84 (1,604)	1,721
*Whitharral, Hockley	158
Whitman, Washington	25
*WHITNEY, Hill, 184 (2,087)	2,202
Whitsett, Live Oak, 9	200
Whitson, Coryell	50
*Whitt, Parker	38
Whon, Coleman	35
*WICHITA FALLS, Wichita, 3,030 (104,553)	105,754
*WICKETT, Ward, 34 (498)	543
Wied, Lavaca	65
Wiedeville, Washington	35
*Wiergate, Newton, 1	350
Wigginsville, Montgomery	100
Wilcox, Burleson	39
Wilderville, Falls	45
*Wildorado, Oldham, 10	210
Wild Peach, Brazoria (2,452)	2,615
Wildwood, Hardin (1,235)	1,173
Wilkins, Upshur	75
William Penn, Washington	40
*WILLIS, Montgomery, 459 (5,662)	7,809
Willow City, Gillespie, 3	22
Willow Grove, McLennan	100
WILLOW PARK, Parker, 173 (3,982)	5,562
Willow Springs, Fayette	74
Willow Springs, Rains	25
*WILLS POINT, Van Zandt, 211 (3,524)	3,777
*WILMER, Dallas, 66 (3,682)	4,478
Wilmeth, Runnels	15
*WILSON, Lynn, 15 (489)	496
Wilson, Falls	42
*WIMBERLEY, Hays, 669 (2,626)	3,170
Winchell, Brown	20
Winchester, Fayette	232
WINDCREST, Bexar, 237 (5,364)	5,933
Windemere, Travis (1,037)	1,184
*WINDOM, Fannin, 14 (199)	206
*WINDTHORST, Archer, 45 (409)	395
Winedale, Fayette, Washington	67
*WINFIELD, Titus, 17 (524)	528
*Wingate, Runnels, 3	100
*WINK, Winkler, 33 (940)	1,066
Winkler, Navarro, Freestone	26
*Winnie, Chambers, 149 (3,254)	3,606
*WINNSBORO, Wood, Franklin, 281 (3,252)	3,399
*WINONA, Smith, 42 (576)	599
Winter Haven, Dimmit	123
*WINTERS, Runnels, 81 (2,562)	2,427
Witting, Lavaca	90
WIXON VALLEY, Brazos, 18 (254)	255
Wizard Wells, Jack	69
*Woden, Nacogdoches, 3	400
*WOLFE CITY, Hunt, 53 (1,412)	1,543
*WOLFFORTH, Lubbock, 188 (3,670)	5,757
Womack, Bosque	25
Woodbine, Cooke	250
WOODBRANCH, Montgomery, (1,282)	1,410
Woodbury, Hill	45
WOODCREEK, Hays, 37 (1,457)	1,755
Wooded Hills, Johnson	580
Wood Hi, Victoria	35
*Woodlake, Trinity, 1	180
Woodland, Red River	128
*Woodlawn, Harrison, 5	550
WOODLOCH, Montgomery, (207)	213
Woodrow, Fort Bend	190
Woodrow, Lubbock	2,034
Woods, Panola	65
*WOODSBORO, Refugio, 58 (1,512)	1,447
*WOODSON, Throckmorton, 13 (264)	234
Wood Springs, Smith	200
*WOODVILLE, Tyler, 177 (2,586)	2,727
Woodville, Cherokee	20
Woodward, La Salle	6
WOODWAY, McLennan, 352 (8,452)	9,230
Woosley, Rains	47
*WORTHAM, Freestone, 30 (1,073)	1,058
Worthing, Lavaca	55
Wright City, Smith	172
Wrightsboro, Gonzales	10
Wyldwood, Bastrop (2,505)	2,756
*WYLIE, Collin, Rockwall, Dallas, 1,222 (41,427)	53,514
Wylie, Taylor	[part of Abilene]

Y

Town, County	Pop. 2019
*Yancey, Medina, 14	209
*YANTIS, Wood, 64 (388)	419
Yard, Anderson	50
Yarrellton, Milam	35
Yellowpine, Sabine	97
*YOAKUM, Lavaca, DeWitt, 224 (5,815)	6,173
*YORKTOWN, DeWitt, 130 (2,092)	2,112
Youngsport, Bell	49
Yowell, Delta, Hunt	30
Ysleta del Sur Pueblo, El Paso	350
Yznaga, Cameron (91)	74

Z

Town, County	Pop. 2019
Zabcikville, Bell	76
*Zapata, Zapata, 143 (5,089)	4,924
Zapata Ranch, Willacy (108)	117
Zarate, Starr (59)	63
*ZAVALLA, Angelina, 40 (713)	730
*Zephyr, Brown, 12	201
Zimmerscheidt, Colorado	50
Zion Hill, Guadalupe	595
Zipperlandville, Falls	22
Zorn, Guadalupe	287
Zuehl, Guadalupe (376)	393
Zunkerville, Karnes	15

Elections

2020 PRESIDENTIAL ELECTION

2020 GENERAL ELECTION

2020 PRESIDENTIAL PRIMARIES

2020 PARTY PRIMARIES

Candidate placards for the 2020 General Election stand outside Collin College in McKinney, on November 1, 2020. Photo by Chris Zúniga/Flickr (CC).

2020 Presidential Election Results by County

Below are the official results by county. Listed are the leading candidates for U.S. president: Joseph Biden for the Democratic Party, Donald Trump for the Republican Party, Jo Jorgensen for the Libertarian Party, and Howie Hawkins for the Green Party.

The total number of votes counted in the presidential race, 11,315,056, was 66.73 percent of the registered voters. The voting-age population in November 2020 was estimated at 21,596,071. The statewide turnout in the previous presidential election in 2016 was 59.39 percent of the registered voters.

For historical election results, including presidential races since 1848, senator and primary races since 1906, governor races since 1845, and prohibition elections since 1854, see the "Elections" section at texasalmanac.com.

Source: Texas Secretary of State.

County	Registered Voters	Turnout %	Presidential Race							
			Trump	%	Biden	%	Jorgensen	%	Hawkins	%
Statewide	**16,955,519**	**66.73**	**5,890,347**	**52.06**	**5,259,126**	**46.48**	**126,243**	**1.12**	**33,396**	**0.30**
Anderson	29,274	65.68	15,110	78.59	3,955	20.57	134	0.70	22	0.11
Andrews	10,272	57.08	4,943	84.31	850	14.50	60	1.02	10	0.17
Angelina	53,166	65.03	25,076	72.53	9,143	26.44	274	0.79	75	0.22
Aransas	18,306	67.14	9,239	75.17	2,916	23.73	103	0.84	31	0.25
Archer	6,538	73.36	4,300	89.66	446	9.30	45	0.94	4	0.08
Armstrong	1,498	74.23	1,035	93.08	75	6.74	2	0.18	0	0.00
Atascosa	29,409	61.61	12,039	66.45	5,876	32.43	143	0.79	58	0.32
Austin	20,293	71.72	11,447	78.65	2,951	20.28	123	0.85	33	0.23
Bailey	3,539	52.56	1,434	77.10	409	21.99	14	0.75	2	0.11
Bandera	17,098	74.37	10,057	79.10	2,505	19.70	120	0.94	30	0.24
Bastrop	52,096	70.38	20,516	55.96	15,474	42.20	531	1.45	128	0.35
Baylor	2,408	70.68	1,494	87.78	183	10.75	22	1.29	1	0.06
Bee	16,033	58.75	6,006	63.76	3,288	34.90	93	0.99	27	0.29
Bell	215,974	58.98	67,893	53.30	57,014	44.76	1,980	1.55	440	0.35
Bexar	1,189,373	64.81	308,618	40.04	448,452	58.18	8,837	1.15	2,798	0.36
Blanco	9,344	79.63	5,443	73.15	1,911	25.68	72	0.97	15	0.20
Borden	499	83.37	397	95.43	16	3.85	2	0.48	1	0.24
Bosque	12,724	71.72	7,469	81.84	1,561	17.10	83	0.91	13	0.14
Bowie	61,407	62.31	27,116	70.87	10,747	28.09	300	0.78	91	0.24
Brazoria	224,256	69.11	90,433	58.35	62,228	40.15	1,860	1.20	417	0.27
Brazos	122,137	69.64	47,530	55.88	35,349	41.56	1,812	2.13	252	0.30
Brewster	7,524	64.09	2,461	51.04	2,258	46.83	89	1.85	14	0.29
Briscoe	1,025	70.73	639	88.14	78	10.76	7	0.97	1	0.14
Brooks	5,521	44.99	998	40.18	1,470	59.18	10	0.40	6	0.24
Brown	23,954	66.67	13,698	85.78	2,107	13.19	134	0.84	24	0.15
Burleson	12,440	69.20	6,743	78.33	1,788	20.77	63	0.73	15	0.17
Burnet	33,697	73.35	18,767	75.93	5,639	22.81	268	1.08	34	0.14
Caldwell	25,945	57.71	8,031	53.64	6,672	44.56	190	1.27	47	0.31
Calhoun	13,080	60.06	5,641	71.80	2,148	27.34	61	0.78	6	0.08
Callahan	9,773	69.91	6,012	88.00	734	10.74	71	1.04	15	0.22
Cameron	218,910	52.16	49,032	42.94	64,063	56.11	728	0.64	336	0.29
Camp	7,904	64.02	3,626	71.66	1,394	27.55	31	0.61	7	0.14
Carson	4,345	71.85	2,779	89.01	297	9.51	37	1.19	3	0.10
Cass	20,889	66.67	11,033	79.22	2,795	20.07	79	0.57	17	0.12
Castro	3,853	54.06	1,602	76.91	466	22.37	9	0.43	6	0.29
Chambers	30,709	70.51	17,353	80.15	3,997	18.46	250	1.15	50	0.23
Cherokee	29,166	66.89	15,101	77.41	4,210	21.58	161	0.83	36	0.18
Childress	3,658	62.30	1,943	85.26	310	13.60	18	0.79	8	0.35
Clay	7,959	72.17	5,069	88.25	614	10.69	46	0.80	12	0.21
Cochran	1,771	56.47	809	80.90	177	17.70	11	1.10	3	0.30
Coke	2,414	73.70	1,586	89.15	178	10.01	10	0.56	5	0.28
Coleman	5,960	69.19	3,641	88.29	451	10.94	23	0.56	9	0.22
Collin	648,670	75.67	252,318	51.40	230,945	47.05	6,075	1.24	1,246	0.25
Collingsworth	1,942	62.72	1,048	86.04	155	12.73	12	0.99	1	0.08
Colorado	14,378	69.38	7,472	74.91	2,420	24.26	50	0.50	19	0.19
Comal	115,876	76.71	62,740	70.58	24,826	27.93	1,106	1.24	191	0.21
Comanche	9,562	63.65	5,177	85.06	853	14.02	49	0.81	5	0.08
Concho	1,757	72.17	1,058	83.44	197	15.54	10	0.79	3	0.24
Cooke	27,268	69.66	15,596	82.10	3,210	16.90	156	0.82	26	0.14
Coryell	41,450	56.68	15,438	65.71	7,565	32.20	410	1.75	77	0.33

Presidential Vote 2020

Trump
Biden

Winning candidate for president, by county.

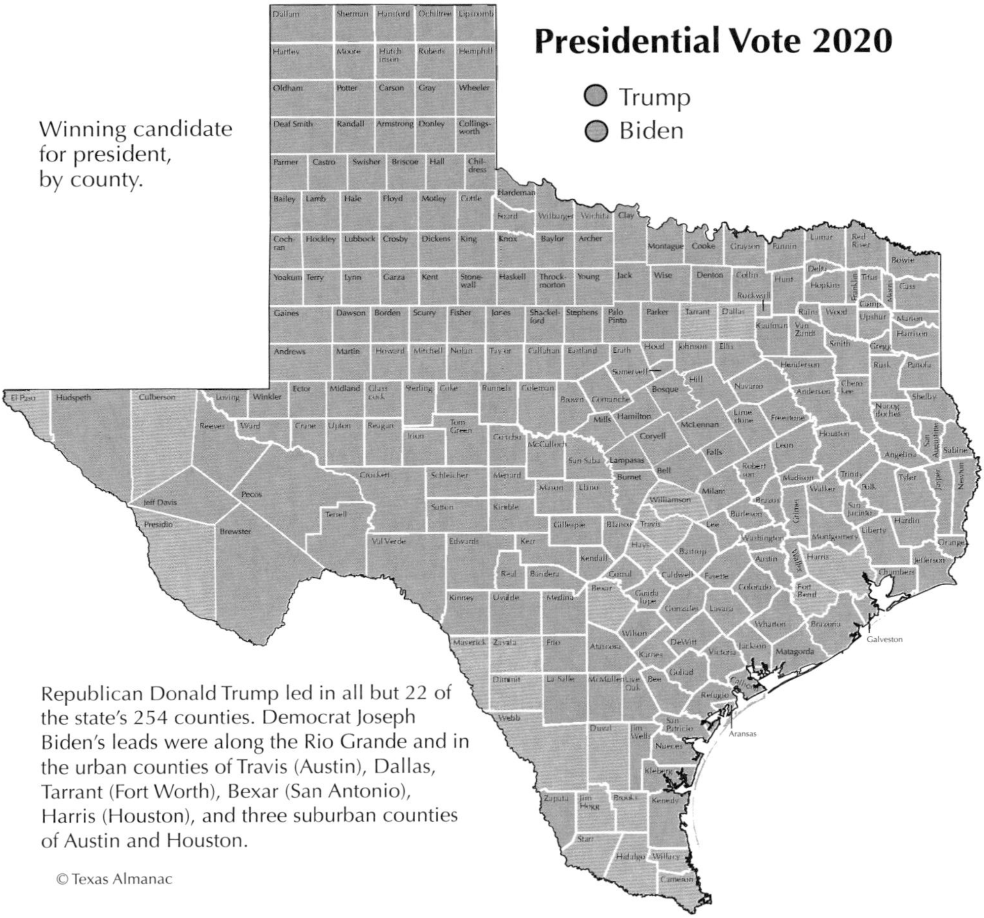

Republican Donald Trump led in all but 22 of the state's 254 counties. Democrat Joseph Biden's leads were along the Rio Grande and in the urban counties of Travis (Austin), Dallas, Tarrant (Fort Worth), Bexar (San Antonio), Harris (Houston), and three suburban counties of Austin and Houston.

County	Registered Voters	Turnout %	Presidential Race							
			Trump	%	Biden	%	Jorgensen	%	Hawkins	%
Cottle	1,041	63.59	540	81.57	113	17.07	6	0.91	3	0.45
Crane	2,663	56.44	1,247	82.97	241	16.03	10	0.67	4	0.27
Crockett	2,473	63.65	1,220	77.51	344	21.86	9	0.57	1	0.06
Crosby	3,629	53.82	1,396	71.48	527	26.98	22	1.13	8	0.41
Culberson	1,709	50.56	415	48.03	438	50.69	9	1.04	2	0.23
Dallam	3,046	52.82	1,389	86.33	197	12.24	18	1.12	5	0.31
Dallas	1,398,469	65.75	307,076	33.40	598,576	65.10	9,635	1.05	3,667	0.40
Dawson	7,104	53.34	2,951	77.88	808	21.32	25	0.66	5	0.13
Deaf Smith	8,900	51.80	3,294	71.45	1,264	27.42	35	0.76	17	0.37
Delta	3,949	65.64	2,162	83.41	403	15.55	24	0.93	3	0.12
Denton	565,089	73.96	222,480	53.23	188,695	45.15	5,421	1.30	1,092	0.26
DeWitt	12,094	67.12	6,567	80.89	1,494	18.40	46	0.57	11	0.14
Dickens	1,328	74.40	853	86.34	130	13.16	3	0.30	2	0.20
Dimmit	7,341	49.94	1,384	37.75	2,264	61.76	10	0.27	8	0.22
Donley	2,322	70.97	1,438	87.26	198	12.01	11	0.67	1	0.06
Duval	8,346	60.54	2,443	48.35	2,575	50.96	22	0.44	13	0.26
Eastland	12,230	67.81	7,237	87.27	983	11.85	60	0.72	12	0.14
Ector	80,872	55.14	32,697	73.33	11,367	25.49	428	0.96	89	0.20
Edwards	1,499	71.11	893	83.77	168	15.76	5	0.47	0	0.00
Ellis	120,188	71.13	56,717	66.34	27,565	32.24	954	1.12	220	0.26
El Paso	488,470	54.60	84,331	31.62	178,126	66.78	2,746	1.03	1,445	0.54

County	Registered Voters	Turnout %	Presidential Race							
			Trump	%	Biden	%	Jorgensen	%	Hawkins	%
Erath	23,935	70.42	13,684	81.18	2,916	17.30	218	1.29	35	0.21
Falls	10,361	59.19	4,177	68.11	1,899	30.96	44	0.72	13	0.21
Fannin	22,199	67.60	12,171	81.10	2,655	17.69	155	1.03	23	0.15
Fayette	17,398	74.38	10,171	78.60	2,661	20.56	83	0.64	26	0.20
Fisher	2,646	69.01	1,448	79.30	352	19.28	21	1.15	5	0.27
Floyd	3,850	52.96	1,584	77.69	438	21.48	15	0.74	2	0.10
Foard	884	62.33	445	80.76	99	17.97	6	1.09	1	0.18
Fort Bend	482,368	74.12	157,718	44.12	195,552	54.70	3,028	0.85	1,091	0.31
Franklin	7,061	70.94	4,161	83.07	804	16.05	36	0.72	8	0.16
Freestone	12,481	69.79	6,991	80.25	1,635	18.77	67	0.77	18	0.21
Frio	8,984	58.76	2,823	53.48	2,422	45.88	23	0.44	11	0.21
Gaines	9,701	61.81	5,355	89.31	576	9.61	54	0.90	10	0.17
Galveston	228,482	67.87	93,911	60.56	58,842	37.95	1,913	1.23	393	0.25
Garza	2,681	61.66	1,413	85.48	231	13.97	5	0.30	4	0.24
Gillespie	20,404	77.68	12,514	78.95	3,176	20.04	140	0.88	16	0.10
Glasscock	800	81.63	611	93.57	39	5.97	3	0.46	0	0.00
Goliad	5,766	69.29	3,085	77.22	877	21.95	24	0.60	2	0.05
Gonzales	12,629	60.56	5,627	73.57	1,948	25.47	57	0.75	15	0.20
Gray	12,406	62.73	6,840	87.90	829	10.65	97	1.25	16	0.21
Grayson	86,740	68.57	44,163	74.26	14,506	24.39	634	1.07	136	0.23
Gregg	72,867	65.85	32,493	67.72	14,796	30.84	551	1.15	113	0.24
Grimes	17,877	69.44	9,432	75.98	2,833	22.82	118	0.95	30	0.24
Guadalupe	111,142	69.84	47,553	61.26	28,805	37.11	1,023	1.32	211	0.27
Hale	18,997	50.46	7,177	74.87	2,279	23.77	97	1.01	31	0.32
Hall	1,926	60.70	995	85.12	168	14.37	4	0.34	1	0.09
Hamilton	5,832	74.61	3,616	83.11	641	14.73	52	1.20	40	0.92
Hansford	3,009	68.03	1,849	90.33	166	8.11	27	1.32	3	0.15
Hardeman	2,486	63.56	1,330	84.18	241	15.25	9	0.57	0	0.00
Hardin	39,952	69.17	23,858	86.33	3,474	12.57	276	1.00	27	0.10
Harris	2,480,522	66.15	700,630	42.70	918,193	55.96	16,819	1.03	5,129	0.31
Harrison	45,933	64.70	21,466	72.23	7,908	26.61	294	0.99	42	0.14
Hartley	2,909	71.43	1,868	89.89	195	9.38	14	0.67	1	0.05
Haskell	3,377	65.56	1,840	83.11	353	15.94	15	0.68	6	0.27
Hays	152,840	71.57	47,680	43.59	59,524	54.41	1,735	1.59	418	0.38
Hemphill	2,355	73.04	1,486	86.40	206	11.98	25	1.45	3	0.17
Henderson	54,663	66.44	28,911	79.61	7,060	19.44	264	0.73	75	0.21
Hidalgo	391,309	56.45	90,527	40.98	128,199	58.04	1,261	0.57	865	0.39
Hill	23,625	63.20	11,926	79.87	2,860	19.15	119	0.80	26	0.17
Hockley	13,781	58.78	6,536	80.69	1,482	18.30	61	0.75	16	0.20
Hood	44,831	72.59	26,496	81.42	5,648	17.36	319	0.98	71	0.22
Hopkins	23,954	66.55	12,719	79.79	3,046	19.11	143	0.90	31	0.19
Houston	13,444	70.20	7,060	74.80	2,314	24.52	56	0.59	7	0.07
Howard	17,526	58.43	8,054	78.64	2,069	20.20	89	0.87	28	0.27
Hudspeth	2,085	55.88	779	66.87	371	31.85	10	0.86	5	0.43
Hunt	59,367	65.01	29,163	75.56	8,906	23.07	434	1.12	71	0.18
Hutchinson	13,533	64.83	7,681	87.55	965	11.00	115	1.31	10	0.11
Irion	1,298	68.49	759	85.38	120	13.50	8	0.90	2	0.22
Jack	5,254	71.98	3,418	90.38	331	8.75	24	0.63	9	0.24
Jackson	9,482	67.00	5,231	82.34	1,033	16.26	53	0.83	23	0.36
Jasper	23,374	66.79	12,542	80.34	2,954	18.92	105	0.67	7	0.04
Jeff Davis	1,670	78.14	784	60.08	501	38.39	17	1.30	3	0.23
Jefferson	149,372	63.44	47,570	50.20	46,073	48.62	897	0.95	199	0.21
Jim Hogg	3,800	53.58	833	40.91	1,197	58.79	4	0.20	2	0.10
Jim Wells	26,636	51.32	7,453	54.52	6,119	44.77	69	0.50	28	0.20
Johnson	105,574	68.22	54,628	75.85	16,464	22.86	771	1.07	142	0.20
Jones	9,635	69.96	5,660	83.96	999	14.82	63	0.93	19	0.28
Karnes	8,359	62.83	3,968	75.55	1,234	23.50	30	0.57	17	0.32
Kaufman	81,901	69.25	37,624	66.34	18,405	32.45	528	0.93	146	0.26
Kendall	33,836	78.18	20,083	75.92	6,020	22.76	289	1.09	46	0.17
Kenedy	296	65.54	127	65.46	65	33.51	1	0.52	1	0.52
Kent	592	78.04	411	88.96	47	10.17	1	0.22	3	0.65

County	Registered Voters	Turnout %	Presidential Race							
			Trump	%	Biden	%	Jorgensen	%	Hawkins	%
Kerr	37,726	73.54	20,879	75.25	6,524	23.51	283	1.02	51	0.18
Kimble	3,113	73.63	1,987	86.69	284	12.39	17	0.74	4	0.17
King	183	86.89	151	94.97	8	5.03	0	0.00	0	0.00
Kinney	2,270	70.62	1,144	71.37	446	27.82	11	0.69	2	0.12
Kleberg	18,749	58.37	5,504	50.29	5,314	48.56	97	0.89	29	0.26
Knox	2,391	60.90	1,180	81.04	265	18.20	7	0.48	4	0.27
Lamar	32,390	66.20	16,760	78.16	4,458	20.79	172	0.80	28	0.13
Lamb	8,085	54.55	3,521	79.84	840	19.05	40	0.91	7	0.16
Lampasas	15,424	67.42	8,086	77.76	2,144	20.62	145	1.39	24	0.23
La Salle	4,426	54.36	1,335	55.49	1,052	43.72	12	0.50	7	0.29
Lavaca	13,661	74.64	8,804	86.34	1,333	13.07	46	0.45	8	0.08
Lee	11,145	72.56	6,255	77.35	1,750	21.64	65	0.80	16	0.20
Leon	11,727	73.97	7,523	86.73	1,072	12.36	57	0.66	14	0.16
Liberty	46,155	63.56	23,302	79.44	5,785	19.72	218	0.74	29	0.10
Limestone	13,963	65.14	6,789	74.65	2,213	24.33	66	0.73	27	0.30
Lipscomb	1,977	68.44	1,205	89.06	131	9.68	17	1.26	0	0.00
Live Oak	7,572	66.75	4,199	83.08	819	16.20	30	0.59	6	0.12
Llano	16,688	75.86	10,079	79.61	2,465	19.47	99	0.78	16	0.13
Loving	111	59.46	60	90.91	4	6.06	2	3.03	0	0.00
Lubbock	183,320	65.90	78,861	65.27	40,017	33.12	1,617	1.34	276	0.23
Lynn	4,028	56.93	1,853	80.81	428	18.67	10	0.44	2	0.09
Madison	5,361	64.09	2,904	84.52	490	14.26	36	1.05	6	0.17
Marion	149,461	65.48	59,543	60.84	36,688	37.49	1,297	1.33	243	0.25
Martin	706	73.09	460	89.15	53	10.27	2	0.39	1	0.19
Mason	7,822	67.73	4,169	78.69	1,088	20.54	30	0.57	10	0.19
Matagorda	7,596	64.03	3,470	71.34	1,339	27.53	47	0.97	8	0.16
Maverick	3,467	62.30	1,857	85.97	288	13.33	13	0.60	2	0.09
McCulloch	3,168	78.09	1,991	80.48	457	18.47	19	0.77	2	0.08
McLennan	22,026	62.32	9,845	71.72	3,733	27.19	115	0.84	33	0.24
McMullen	33,050	46.43	6,881	44.84	8,332	54.29	73	0.48	60	0.39
Medina	33,763	67.11	15,642	69.04	6,773	29.89	184	0.81	45	0.20
Menard	1,469	69.98	823	80.06	197	19.16	6	0.58	2	0.19
Midland	90,392	65.12	45,624	77.51	12,329	20.95	777	1.32	126	0.21
Milam	15,838	66.79	7,984	75.48	2,496	23.60	72	0.68	24	0.23
Mills	3,429	73.05	2,217	88.50	271	10.82	15	0.60	2	0.08
Mitchell	4,524	57.01	2,170	84.14	397	15.39	11	0.43	1	0.04
Montague	14,001	70.13	8,615	87.74	1,097	11.17	78	0.79	24	0.24
Montgomery	370,060	73.38	193,382	71.22	74,377	27.39	3,166	1.17	526	0.19
Moore	9,995	55.11	4,359	79.14	1,062	19.28	66	1.20	21	0.38
Morris	8,583	65.09	3,872	69.30	1,669	29.87	36	0.64	10	0.18
Motley	859	75.90	604	92.64	46	7.06	2	0.31	0	0.00
Nacogdoches	38,786	69.06	17,378	64.88	9,000	33.60	302	1.13	83	0.31
Navarro	29,959	63.83	13,800	72.16	5,101	26.67	167	0.87	53	0.28
Newton	9,400	64.83	4,882	80.11	1,173	19.25	34	0.56	5	0.08
Nolan	8,871	60.39	4,131	77.11	1,162	21.69	53	0.99	10	0.19
Nueces	211,652	60.16	64,617	50.75	60,925	47.85	1,404	1.10	368	0.29
Ochiltree	5,192	60.79	2,812	89.10	302	9.57	37	1.17	3	0.10
Oldham	1,425	70.81	917	90.88	81	8.03	10	0.99	1	0.10
Orange	54,442	66.11	29,186	81.09	6,357	17.66	376	1.04	51	0.14
Palo Pinto	18,946	65.92	10,179	81.50	2,178	17.44	101	0.81	27	0.22
Panola	16,808	68.13	9,326	81.44	2,057	17.96	57	0.50	11	0.10
Parker	103,999	73.20	62,045	81.50	13,017	17.10	880	1.16	158	0.21
Parmer	4,537	58.41	2,135	80.57	488	18.42	23	0.87	4	0.15
Pecos	8,323	56.09	3,215	68.87	1,382	29.61	50	1.07	21	0.45
Polk	40,520	59.69	18,573	76.79	5,387	22.27	171	0.71	50	0.21
Potter	57,736	57.74	22,820	68.45	9,921	29.76	454	1.36	126	0.38
Presidio	4,789	46.29	721	32.52	1,463	65.99	21	0.95	12	0.54
Rains	8,320	72.75	5,155	85.16	842	13.91	43	0.71	13	0.21
Randall	93,313	69.31	50,796	78.54	12,802	19.79	910	1.41	129	0.20
Reagan	1,879	59.82	942	83.81	172	15.30	7	0.62	3	0.27
Real	2,702	73.35	1,643	82.90	320	16.15	14	0.71	5	0.25

County	Registered Voters	Turnout %	Presidential Race							
			Trump	%	Biden	%	Jorgensen	%	Hawkins	%
Red River	8,489	68.39	4,517	77.80	1,246	21.46	36	0.62	7	0.12
Reeves	7,558	48.81	2,254	61.10	1,395	37.82	30	0.81	8	0.22
Refugio	5,007	67.23	2,210	65.66	1,108	32.92	26	0.77	21	0.62
Roberts	680	80.88	529	96.18	17	3.09	4	0.73	0	0.00
Robertson	11,844	68.38	5,646	69.71	2,374	29.31	66	0.81	13	0.16
Rockwall	71,102	75.79	36,726	68.15	16,412	30.45	611	1.13	121	0.22
Runnels	7,025	62.76	3,807	86.35	552	12.52	39	0.88	11	0.25
Rusk	32,388	66.00	16,534	77.34	4,629	21.65	155	0.73	50	0.23
Sabine	8,050	68.21	4,784	87.12	669	12.18	27	0.49	7	0.13
San Augustine	6,108	65.52	3,007	75.14	980	24.49	13	0.32	2	0.05
San Jacinto	18,969	66.64	10,161	80.39	2,337	18.49	101	0.80	39	0.31
San Patricio	43,248	59.87	16,516	63.79	8,988	34.71	291	1.12	93	0.36
San Saba	3,776	68.91	2,308	88.70	287	11.03	7	0.27	0	0.00
Schleicher	1,709	67.82	940	81.10	211	18.21	6	0.52	2	0.17
Scurry	9,489	61.86	4,983	84.89	818	13.94	53	0.90	15	0.26
Shackelford	2,320	70.17	1,484	91.15	130	7.99	10	0.61	4	0.25
Shelby	15,570	64.78	7,975	79.06	2,068	20.50	37	0.37	4	0.04
Sherman	1,520	65.26	886	89.31	91	9.17	9	0.91	5	0.50
Smith	146,149	68.48	69,080	69.02	29,615	29.59	1,126	1.12	254	0.25
Somervell	6,712	73.70	4,105	82.98	768	15.52	56	1.13	10	0.20
Starr	34,050	51.47	8,247	47.06	9,123	52.06	92	0.52	63	0.36
Stephens	5,672	67.00	3,385	89.08	397	10.45	16	0.42	2	0.05
Sterling	939	68.05	584	91.39	51	7.98	1	0.16	3	0.47
Stonewall	953	77.23	615	83.56	116	15.76	4	0.54	1	0.14
Sutton	2,449	63.58	1,222	78.48	322	20.68	9	0.58	4	0.26
Swisher	3,941	59.76	1,845	78.34	478	20.30	22	0.93	10	0.42
Tarrant	1,212,524	68.84	409,741	49.09	411,567	49.31	10,368	1.24	2,617	0.31
Taylor	83,696	65.88	39,547	71.73	14,588	26.46	827	1.50	150	0.27
Terrell	673	68.05	334	72.93	119	25.98	3	0.66	2	0.44
Terry	6,589	54.82	2,812	77.85	757	20.96	33	0.91	10	0.28
Throckmorton	1,216	73.52	806	90.16	82	9.17	5	0.56	1	0.11
Titus	17,666	59.67	7,570	71.81	2,856	27.09	94	0.89	19	0.18
Tom Green	70,086	64.51	32,313	71.47	12,239	27.07	546	1.21	96	0.21
Travis	854,577	71.21	161,337	26.51	435,860	71.62	8,905	1.46	2,094	0.34
Trinity	11,541	60.12	5,579	80.41	1,323	19.07	25	0.36	11	0.16
Tyler	14,556	66.36	8,194	84.82	1,403	14.52	52	0.54	11	0.11
Upshur	28,619	66.01	15,809	83.68	2,877	15.23	179	0.95	22	0.12
Upton	2,207	61.98	1,178	86.11	170	12.43	13	0.95	7	0.51
Uvalde	17,420	59.38	6,174	59.69	4,073	39.38	66	0.64	29	0.28
Val Verde	28,927	52.82	8,284	54.21	6,771	44.31	170	1.11	47	0.31
Van Zandt	38,965	66.80	22,270	85.56	3,516	13.51	175	0.67	33	0.13
Victoria	56,612	60.39	23,358	68.32	10,380	30.36	339	0.99	103	0.30
Walker	35,038	67.39	15,375	65.12	7,884	33.39	287	1.22	63	0.27
Waller	35,116	64.74	14,260	62.73	8,191	36.03	201	0.88	82	0.36
Ward	6,880	59.01	3,241	79.83	764	18.82	29	0.71	26	0.64
Washington	23,947	72.77	12,959	74.36	4,261	24.45	178	1.02	20	0.11
Webb	137,840	49.62	25,898	37.86	41,820	61.14	446	0.65	233	0.34
Wharton	25,697	65.23	11,926	71.15	4,694	28.01	105	0.63	36	0.21
Wheeler	3,514	66.51	2,159	92.38	168	7.19	7	0.30	3	0.13
Wichita	83,575	55.09	32,069	69.65	13,161	28.59	675	1.47	125	0.27
Wilbarger	8,196	55.20	3,524	77.90	956	21.13	33	0.73	11	0.24
Willacy	12,804	43.34	2,441	43.99	3,108	56.01	0	0.00	0	0.00
Williamson	376,672	76.87	139,729	48.26	143,795	49.66	4,998	1.73	790	0.27
Wilson	35,036	71.39	18,463	73.81	6,350	25.39	151	0.60	39	0.16
Winkler	4,013	52.98	1,753	82.46	358	16.84	14	0.66	1	0.05
Wise	45,643	70.91	27,032	83.52	4,973	15.37	310	0.96	47	0.15
Wood	32,382	70.34	19,049	83.63	3,509	15.40	175	0.77	40	0.18
Yoakum	4,407	59.70	2,174	82.63	420	15.96	31	1.18	6	0.23
Young	11,769	70.01	7,110	86.30	1,034	12.55	76	0.92	18	0.22
Zapata	8,257	46.92	2,033	52.48	1,826	47.13	11	0.28	4	0.10
Zavala	8,066	54.29	1,490	34.03	2,864	65.40	13	0.30	12	0.27

General Election, 2020

Below are the official voting results for the general election held November 3, 2020, as canvassed by the State Canvassing Board. Federal races include presidential, Senate, and House of Representatives elections. Statewide races include railroad commissioner, courts of criminal appeals, and Texas Supreme Court. District races include the state senate and state board of education.

Omitted races include the state House of Representatives, judges for the court of appeals, and district judges, as well as races with single entrants; these can be found at our website, texasalmanac.com.

Abbreviations used are (Dem.) Democrat, (Rep.) Republican, (Lib.) Libertarian, (Ind.) Independent and (W-I) Write-in.

Federal Races

President

Donald J. Trump (Rep.)	5,890,347	52.06%
Joseph R. Biden (Dem.)	5,259,126	46.48%
Jo Jorgensen (Lib.)	126,243	1.12%
Howie Hawkins (Green)	33,396	0.30%
President R. Boddie (W-I)	2,012	0.02%
Brian Carroll (W-I)	2,785	0.02%
Todd Cella (W-I)	205	0.00%
Jesse Cuellar (W-I)	49	0.00%
Tom Hoefling (W-I)	337	0.00%
Gloria La Riva (W-I)	350	0.00%
Abram Loeb (W-I)	360	0.00%
Robert Morrow (W-I)	56	0.00%
Kasey Wells (W-I)	114	0.00%
Total vote	11,315,056	

U.S. Senate

John Cornyn (Rep.)	5,962,983	53.51%
Mary "MJ" Hegar (Dem.)	4,888,764	43.87%
Kerry Douglas Mckennon (Lib.)	209,722	1.88%
David B. Collins (Green)	81,893	0.73%
Ricardo Turullols-Bonilla (W-I)	678	0.01%
Total Vote	11,144,040	

U.S. House of Representatives

(See map of districts on p. 514.)

District 1

Louie Gohmert (Rep.)	219,726	72.58%
Hank Gilbert (Dem.)	83,016	27.42%
Total Vote	302,742	

District 2

Dan Crenshaw (Rep.)	192,828	55.61%
Sima Ladjevardian (Dem.)	148,374	42.79%
Elliott Robert Scheirman (Lib.)	5,524	1.59%
Total Vote	346,726	

District 3

Van Taylor (Rep.)	230,512	55.07%
Lulu Seikaly (Dem.)	179,458	42.87%
Christopher J. Claytor (Lib.)	8,621	2.06%
Total Vote	418,591	

District 4

Pat Fallon (Rep.)	253,837	75.14%
Russell Foster (Dem)	76,326	22.59%
Lou Antonelli (Lib.)	6,334	1.88%
Tracy Jones (W-I)	1,306	0.39%
Total Vote	337,803	

District 5

Lance Gooden (Rep.)	173,836	61.99%
Carolyn Salter (Dem.)	100,743	35.93%
Kevin A. Hale (Lib.)	5,834	2.08%
Total Vote	280,413	

District 6

Ron Wright (Rep.)	179,507	52.8%
Stephen Daniel (Dem.)	149,530	43.98%
Melanie A. Black (Lib.)	10,955	3.22%
Total Vote	339,992	

District 7

Lizzie Fletcher (Dem.)	159,529	50.79%
Wesley Hunt (Rep.)	149,054	47.45%
Shawn Kelly (Lib.)	5,542	1.76%
Total Vote	314,125	

District 8

Kevin Brady (Rep.)	277,327	72.51%
Elizabeth Hernandez (Dem.)	97,409	25.47%
Chris Duncan (Lib.)	7,735	2.02%
Total Vote	382,471	

District 9

Al Green (Dem.)	172,938	75.48%
Johnny Teague (Rep.)	49,575	21.64%
Jose R. Sosa (Lib.)	6,594	2.88
Total Vote	229,107	

District 10

Michael McCaul (Rep.)	217,216	52.48%
Mike Siegel (Dem.)	187,686	45.35%
Roy Eriksen (Lib.)	8,992	2.17%
Total Vote	413,894	

District 11

August Pfluger (Rep.)	232,568	79.71%
Jon Mark Hogg (Dem.)	53,394	18.3%
Wacey Alpha Cody (Lib.)	5,811	1.99%
Total Vote	291,773	

District 12

Kay Granger (Rep.)	233,853	63.72%
Lisa Welch (Dem.)	121,250	33.04%
Trey Holcomb (Lib.)	11,918	3.25%
Total Vote	367,021	

District 13

Ronny Jackson (Rep.)	217,124	79.38%
Gus Trujillo (Dem.)	50,477	18.46%
Jack B. Westbrook (Lib.)	5,907	2.16%
Total Vote	273,508	

District 14

Randy Weber (Rep.)	190,541	61.64%
Adrienne Bell (Dem.)	118,574	38.36%
Total Vote	309,115	

District 15

Vicente Gonzalez (Dem.)	115,605	50.5%
Monica de la Cruz-Hernandez (Rep.)	109,017	47.62%
Ross Lynn Leone (Lib.)	4,295	1.88%
Total Vote	228,917	

District 16

Veronica Escobar (Dem.)	154,108	64.72%
Irene Armendariz-Jackson (Lib..)	84,006	35.28%
Total Vote	238,114	

District 17

Pete Sessions (Rep.)	171,390	55.85%
Rick Kennedy (Dem.)	125,565	40.92%
Ted Brown (Lib.)	9,918	3.23%
Total Vote	306,873	

District 18

Sheila Jackson Lee (Dem.)	180,952	73.29%
Wendell Champion (Rep.)	58,033	23.51%
Luke Spencer (Lib.)	4,514	1.83%
Vince Duncan (Ind.)	3,396	1.38%
Total Vote	246,895	

District 19

Jodey C. Arrington (Rep.)	198,198	74.78%
Tom Watson (Dem.)	60,583	22.86%
Joe Burnes (Lib.)	6,271	2.37%
Total Vote	265,052	

District 20

Joaquin Castro (Dem.)	175,078	64.67%
Mauro Garza (Rep.)	89,628	33.11%
Jeffrey Blunt (Lib.)	6,017	2.22%
Total Vote	270,723	

District 21

Chip Roy (Rep.) .... 235,740 .... 51.95%
Wendy R. Davis (Dem.) .... 205,780 .... 45.35%
Arthur DiBianca (Lib.) .... 8,666 .... 1.91%
Tommy Wakely (Green) .... 3,564 .... 0.79%
Total Vote 453,750

District 22

Troy Nehls (Rep.) .... 210,259 .... 51.53%
Sri Preston Kulkarni (Dem.) .... 181,998 .... 44.6%
Joseph LeBlanc Jr. (Lib.) .... 15,791 .... 3.87%
Total Vote 408,048

District 23

Tony Gonzales (Rep.) .... 149,395 .... 50.56%
Gina Ortiz Jones (Dem.) .... 137,693 .... 46.6%
Beto Villela (Lib.) .... 8,369 .... 2.83%
Total Vote 295,457

District 24

Beth Van Duyne (Rep.) .... 167,910 .... 48.81%
Candace Valenzuela (Dem.) .... 163,326 .... 47.48%
Darren Hamilton (Lib.) .... 5,647 .... 1.64%
Steve Kuzmich (Ind.) .... 4,229 .... 1.23%
Mark Bauer (Ind.) .... 2,909 .... 0.85%
Total Vote 344,021

District 25

Roger Williams (Rep.) .... 220,088 .... 55.93%
Julie Oliver (Dem.) .... 165,697 .... 42.11%
Bill Kelsey (Lib.) .... 7,738 .... 1.97%
Total Vote 393,523

District 26

Michael C. Burgess (Rep.) .... 261,963 .... 60.61%
Carol H. Iannuzzi (Dem.) .... 161,009 .... 37.25%
Mark Boler (Lib.) .... 9,243 .... 2.14%
Total Vote 432,215

District 27

Michael Cloud (Rep.) .... 172,305 .... 63.06%
Ricardo "Rick" de la Fuente (Dem.) .... 95,466 .... 34.94%
Phil Gray (Lib.) .... 5,482 .... 2.01%
Total Vote 273,253

District 28

Henry Cuellar (Dem.) .... 137,494 .... 58.3%
Sandra Whitten (Rep.) .... 91,925 .... 38.98%
Bekah Congdon (Lib.) .... 6,425 .... 2.72%
Total Vote 235,844

District 29

Sylvia Garcia (Dem.) .... 111,305 .... 71.13%
Jaimy Z. Blanco (Rep.) .... 42,840 .... 27.38%
Phil Kurtz (Lib.) .... 2,328 .... 1.49%
Total Vote 156,473

District 30

Eddie Bernice Johnson (Dem.) .... 204,928 .... 77.49%
Tre Pennie (Rep.) .... 48,685 .... 18.41%
Eric Williams (Ind.) .... 10,851 .... 4.1%
Total Vote 264,464

District 31

John Carter (Rep.) .... 212,695 .... 53.43%
Donna Imam (Dem.) .... 176,293 .... 44.29%
Clark Patterson (Lib.) .... 8,922 .... 2.24%
Jonathan Scott (W-I) .... 147 .... 0.04%
Total Vote 398,057

District 32

Colin Allred (Dem.) .... 178,542 .... 51.95%
Genevieve Collins (Rep.) .... 157,867 .... 45.93%
Christy Mowrey Peterson (Lib.) .... 4,946 .... 1.44%
Jason Sigmon (Ind.) .... 2,332 .... 0.68%
Total Vote 343,687

District 33

Marc Veasey (Dem.) .... 105,317 .... 66.82%
Fabian Cordova Vasquez (Rep.) .... 39,638 .... 25.15%
Carlos Quintanilla (Ind.) .... 8.071 .... 5.12%
Jason Reeves (Lib.) .... 2,586 .... 1.64%
Rene Welton (Ind.) .... 1,994 .... 1.27%
Total Vote 157,606

District 34

Filemon B. Vela (Dem.) .... 111,439 .... 55.43%
Rey Gonzalez (Rep.) .... 84,119 .... 41.84%
Anthony Cristo (Lib.) .... 3,222 .... 1.6%
Chris B. Royal (Ind.) .... 2,247 .... 1.12%
Total Vote 201,027

District 35

Lloyd Doggett (Dem.) .... 176,373 .... 65.37%
Jenny Garcia Sharon (Rep.) .... 80,795 .... 29.95%
Mark Loewe (Lib.) .... 7,393 .... 2.74%
Jason Mata Sr. (Ind.) .... 5,236 .... 1.94%
Total Vote 269,797

District 36

Brian Babin (Rep.) .... 222,712 .... 73.61%
Rashad Lewis (Dem.) .... 73,418 .... 24.27%
Chad Abbey (Lib.) .... 4,848 .... 1.6%
Hal J. Ridley Jr. (Green) .... 1,571 .... 0.52%
Total Vote 302,549

State Races

Railroad Commissioner

James "Jim" Wright (Rep.) .... 5,831,263 .... 53.01%
Chrysta Castañeda (Dem.). .... 4,792,422 .... 43.56%
Matt Sterett (Lib.) .... 247,659 .... 2.25%
Katija "Kat" Gruene (Green) .... 129,638 .... 1.18%
Total vote 11,000,982

Supreme Court

Chief Justice

Nathan Hecht (Rep.) .... 5,827,085 .... 52.98%
Amy Clark Meachum (Dem.) .... 4,893,402 .... 44.49%
Mark Ash (Lib.) .... 277,491 .... 2.52%
Total Vote 10,997,978

Justice, Place 6 — Unexpired Term

Jane Bland (Rep.) .... 6,050,534 .... 55.24%
Kathy Cheng (Dem.) .... 4,903,527 .... 44.76%
Total Vote 10,954,061

Justice, Place 7

Jeff Boyd (Rep.) .... 5,843,420 .... 53.31%
Staci Williams (Dem.) .... 4,861,649 .... 44.35%
William Bryan Strange III .... 256,742 .... 2.34%
Total Vote 10,961,811

Justice, Place 8

Brett Busby (Rep.) .... 5,847,135 .... 53.4%
Gisela D. Triana (Dem.) .... 4,826,674 .... 44.08%
Tom Oxford (Lib.) .... 274,959 .... 2.51%
Total Vote 10,948,768

Court of Criminal Appeals

Judge, Place 3

Bert Richardson (Rep.) .... 5,953,924 .... 54.53%
Elizabeth Davis Frizell (Dem.) .... 4,964,460 .... 45.47%
Total Vote 10,918,384

Judge, Place 4

Kevin Patrick Yeary (Rep.) .... 5,974,016 .... 54.82%
Tina Clinton (Dem.) .... 4,924,207 .... 45.18%
Total Vote 10,898,223

Judge, Place 9

David Newell (Rep.) .... 6,015,909 .... 55.3%
Brandon Birmingham (Dem.) .... 4,863,142 .... 44.7%
Total Vote 10,879,051

State Senate

District 1

Bryan Hughes (Rep.) .... 267,404 .... 75.26%
Audrey Spanko (Dem.) .... 87,885 .... 24.74%
Total Vote 355,289

District 4

Brandon Creighton (Rep.) .... 281,105 .... 67.35%
Jay Stittleburg (Dem.) .... 126,019 .... 30.19%
Cameron Brock (Lib.) .... 10,277 .... 2.46%
Total Vote 417,401

District 6

Carol Alvarado (Dem.)..........137,895........84.05%
Timothy Duffield (Lib.)..........26,166........15.95%
Total Vote..........164,061

District 11

Larry Taylor (Rep.)..........231,268........59.45%
Susan Criss (Dem.)..........148,225..........38.1%
Jared Wissel (Lib..)..........9,519..........2.45%
Total Vote..........389,012

District 12

Jane Nelson (Rep.)..........293,399........62.29%
Shadi Zitoon (Dem.)..........177,610........37.71%
Total Vote..........471,009

District 13

Borris L. Miles (Dem.)..........200,195........80.47%
Milinda Morris (Rep.)..........48,581........19.53%
Total Vote..........248,776

District 18

Lois W. Kolkhorst (Rep.)..........277,872........65.79%
Michael Antalan (Dem.)..........144,489........34.21%
Total Vote..........422,361

District 19

Roland Gutierrez (Dem.)..........158,726........49.85%
Peter P. "Pete" Flores (Rep.)..........148,213........46.55%
Jo-Anne Valdivia (Lib.)..........11,465..........3.6%
Total Vote..........318,404

District 20

Juan "Chuy" Hinojosa (Dem.)..........154,311........58.48%
Judy Cutright (Rep.)..........109,563........41.52%
Total Vote..........263,874

District 21

Judith Zaffirini (Dem.)..........167,672........60.14%
Frank Pomeroy (Rep.)..........111,142........39.86%
Total Vote..........278,814

District 22

Brian Birdwell (Rep.)..........257,208........68.45%
Robert Vick (Dem.)..........109,563........31.55%
Total Vote..........375,746

District 24

Dawn Buckingham (Rep.)..........264,517........69.54%
Clayton Tucker (Dem.)..........115,853........30.46%
Total Vote..........380,370

District 26

José Menéndez (Dem.)..........199,829........79.99%
Julián Villarreal (Green)..........50,004........20.01%
Total Vote..........249,833

District 27

Eddie Lucio Jr. (Dem.)..........134,035........64.81%
Vanessa Tijerina (Rep.)..........72,768........35.19%
Total Vote..........206,803

District 28

Frank Pomeroy (Rep.)..........248,025..........100%

District 29

César J. Blanco (Dem.)..........176,360........67.32%
Bethany Hatch (Rep.)..........85,619........32.68%
Total Vote..........261,979

State Board of Education

District 1

Georgina Perez (Dem.)..........287,623........55.77%
Jennifer Ivey (Rep.)..........228,140........44.23%
Total Vote..........515,763

District 5

Rebecca Bell-Metereau (Dem.)..........493,930........48.94%
Lani Popp (Rep.)..........475,824........47.15%
Stephanie Berlin (Lib.)..........39,456..........3.91%
Total Vote..........1,009,210

District 6

Will Hickman (Rep.)..........371,958........49.76%
Michelle Palmer (Dem.)..........354,179........47.38%
Whitney Bilyeu (Lib.)..........21,414..........2.86%
Total Vote..........747,551

District 8

Audrey Young (Rep.)..........567,058........73.43%
Audra Rose Berry (Lib.)..........205,187........26.57%
Total Vote..........772,245

District 9

Keven M. Ellis (Rep.)..........571,322........74.71%
Brenda Davis (Dem.)..........193,364........25.29%
Total Vote..........764,686

District 10

Tom Maynard (Rep.)..........441,700........50.84%
Marsha Burnett-Webster (Dem.)..........398,453........45.86%
Trip Seibold..........28,603..........3.29%
Total Vote..........868,756

District 14

Sue Melton-Malone (Rep.)..........582,027........67.81%
Greg Alvord (Dem.)..........276,303........32.19%
Total Vote..........858,330

District 15

Jay Johnson (Rep.)..........496,080........77.79%
John Betancourt (Dem.)..........141,675........22.21%
Total Vote..........637,755

Texas Election Turnout by Voting Age Population

Year	2020	2016	2012	2008	2004	2000	1996	1992	1988	1984	1980	1976
Major Candidates	**Trump/ Biden**	**Trump/ Clinton**	**Obama/ Romney**	**Obama/ McCain**	**Bush/Kerry**	**Bush/Gore**	**Clinton/ Dole**	**Clinton/ Bush/Perot**	**Bush/ Dukakis**	**Reagan/ Mondale**	**Reagan/ Carter**	**Carter/ Ford**
Percent of VAP that voted	52.4	46.5	43.7	45.6	46.1	44.3	41.0	47.6	44.3	47.6	45.6	46.1
Percent of registered voters that voted	66.7	58.6	59.5	56.6	51.8	53.2	72.9	66.2	68.3	68.4	64.8	66.6

The **voting age population (VAP)** refers to the total number of persons of voting age regardless of citizenship, military status, felony conviction or mental state. The Bureau of the Census is the source for the VAP estimates.

Since the National Voter Registration Act of 1993, non-voters cannot be removed from registration rolls of a county until two federal elections have been held. So, for instance, if a person moved in December 2016 from one county to another, that person could be counted as a non-voter in the previous county of residence through the general election of November 2020. These are called "suspense voters" on county rolls and have affected the statistical reports of the percentage of registered voters participating in elections.

The presidential elections have a larger voter turnout than off-year and state elections.

Sources: Federal Election Commission and the Texas Secretary of State office.

2020 Presidential Primaries: Results by County

Below are the official canvass results by county in the party primaries for president held March 3, 2020.

This table lists the principal candidates in the Democratic primary: Joseph Biden, Bernie Sanders, and Michael Bloomberg.

Source: Texas Secretary of State.

In the Republican primary, the top candidate is listed; Donald Trump received 94.13% percent of votes cast in the Republican primary.

Alongside the number of votes received by each candidate is listed the percent of the total vote received.

Republican Primary		County	Democratic Primary					
Trump	%		Biden	%	Sanders	%	Bloomberg	%
1,898,664	**94.13%**	**Statewide**	**725,562**	**34.64%**	**626,339**	**29.91%**	**300,608**	**14.35%**
7,646	96.63%	Anderson	763	47.96%	336	21.12%	300	18.86%
2,281	93.41%	Andrews	81	35.06%	84	36.36%	33	14.29%
12,166	94.97%	Angelina	1,652	50.85%	648	19.94%	466	14.34%
3,820	92.14%	Aransas	504	42.75%	222	18.83%	176	14.93%
2,455	94.86%	Archer	74	44.31%	28	16.77%	31	18.56%
676	96.99%	Armstrong	11	39.29%	10	35.71%	4	14.29%
4,220	94.05%	Atascosa	806	29.48%	741	27.10%	585	21.40%
4,662	95.55%	Austin	460	44.79%	214	20.84%	205	19.96%
832	90.73%	Bailey	47	40.17%	34	29.06%	15	12.82%
3,997	95.76%	Bandera	443	38.59%	282	24.56%	171	14.90%
7,672	94.83%	Bastrop	2,371	32.14%	2,280	30.90%	1,000	13.55%
876	95.01%	Baylor	27	41.54%	5	7.69%	19	29.23%
1,596	95.17%	Bee	493	44.25%	242	21.72%	173	15.53%
21,480	94.10%	Bell	7,851	43.06%	4,798	26.32%	2,456	13.47%
75,555	93.40%	Bexar	49,552	28.79%	57,051	33.15%	26,231	15.24%
2,232	96.00%	Blanco	376	36.08%	240	23.03%	143	13.72%
235	97.92%	Borden	2	33.33%	1	16.67%	2	33.33%
3,647	95.87%	Bosque	293	40.98%	172	24.06%	114	15.94%
12,024	94.42%	Bowie	2,066	56.00%	700	18.98%	487	13.20%
33,464	93.40%	Brazoria	8,904	40.88%	5,860	26.90%	3,138	14.41%
17,063	90.63%	Brazos	4,099	31.58%	4,749	36.59%	1,002	7.72%
934	94.73%	Brewster	354	26.90%	408	31.00%	151	11.47%
470	91.98%	Briscoe	9	26.47%	4	11.76%	5	14.71%
69	95.83%	Brooks	289	18.63%	522	33.66%	424	27.34%
5,846	96.28%	Brown	369	48.17%	184	24.02%	69	9.01%
3,346	94.87%	Burleson	383	50.59%	122	16.12%	150	19.82%
6,480	95.65%	Burnet	1,028	39.51%	579	22.25%	432	16.60%
2,969	93.69%	Caldwell	987	32.89%	958	31.92%	432	14.40%
2,131	95.43%	Calhoun	427	46.01%	191	20.58%	159	17.13%
2,382	96.09%	Callahan	120	47.43%	74	29.25%	14	5.53%
7,645	92.69%	Cameron	7,554	23.95%	10,520	33.36%	6,402	20.30%
1,874	95.37%	Camp	350	52.63%	120	18.05%	114	17.14%
1,420	97.39%	Carson	66	49.62%	25	18.80%	18	13.53%
4,381	96.54%	Cass	626	55.99%	204	18.25%	151	13.51%
661	94.43%	Castro	51	30.18%	32	18.93%	60	35.50%
7,300	94.51%	Chambers	506	40.38%	342	27.29%	185	14.76%
7,547	95.90%	Cherokee	844	51.46%	299	18.23%	270	16.46%
1,196	94.92%	Childress	52	43.33%	32	26.67%	15	12.50%
2,771	95.19%	Clay	133	49.63%	43	16.04%	34	12.69%
397	92.76%	Cochran	17	53.13%	8	25.00%	4	12.50%
818	95.45%	Coke	26	36.62%	12	16.90%	14	19.72%
2,238	94.99%	Coleman	70	42.94%	36	22.09%	16	9.82%
64,574	93.61%	Collin	30,128	35.56%	25,628	30.25%	11,277	13.31%
687	95.02%	Collingsworth	22	34.92%	11	17.46%	15	23.81%
3,578	94.86%	Colorado	432	46.15%	167	17.84%	146	15.60%
20,429	94.80%	Comal	3,643	36.19%	2,417	24.01%	1,406	13.97%
2,601	94.41%	Comanche	146	38.52%	82	21.64%	85	22.43%
709	87.42%	Concho	27	41.54%	19	29.23%	10	15.38%
8,160	93.84%	Cooke	500	40.72%	310	25.24%	230	18.73%

2020

Leading candidates by county: Joseph R. Biden, Sen. Bernie Sanders, and Michael R. Bloomberg

(Sen. Elizabeth Warren received 5 delegates.)

Presidential Primary

- Biden (113 delegates)
- Sanders (99 delegates)
- Bloomberg (11 delegates)
- Tie

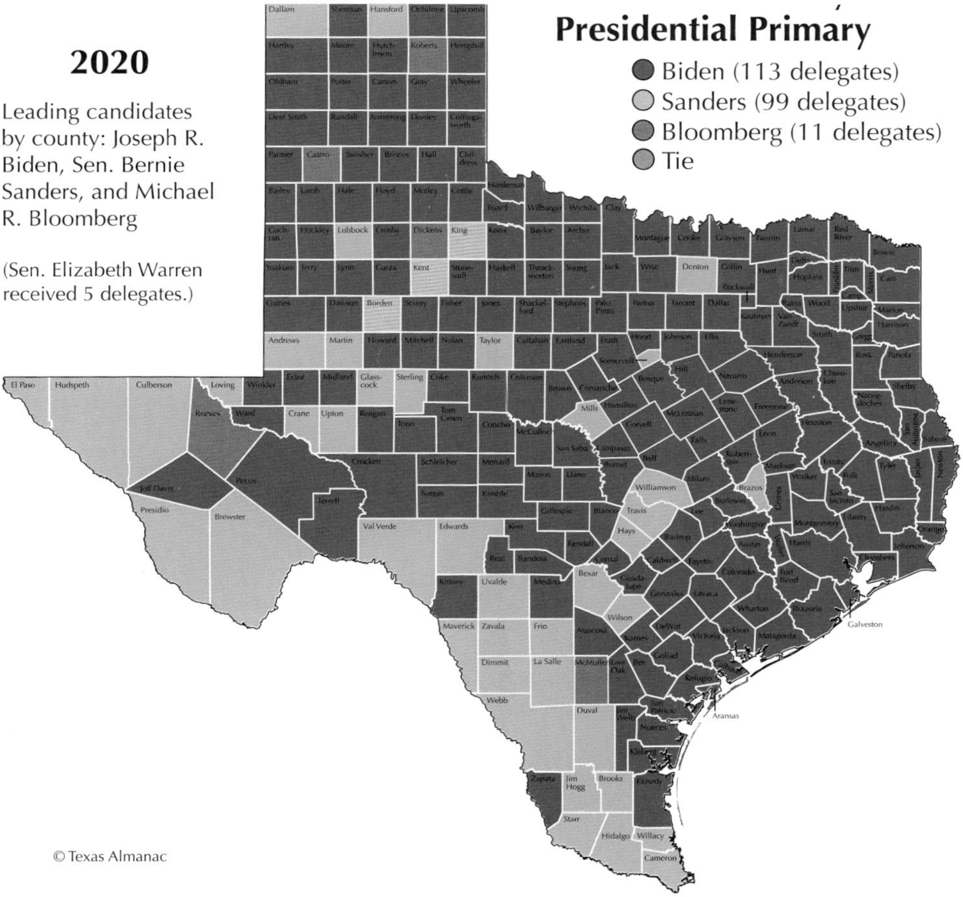

Republican Primary		County	Democratic Primary					
Trump	%		Biden	%	Sanders	%	Bloomberg	%
6,586	93.18%	Coryell	982	40.08%	702	28.65%	337	13.76%
349	93.07%	Cottle	20	32.79%	18	29.51%	8	13.11%
571	94.38%	Crane	24	32.43%	25	33.78%	12	16.22%
517	89.45%	Crockett	84	26.84%	77	24.60%	42	13.42%
742	87.60%	Crosby	83	43.23%	55	28.65%	33	17.19%
28	100.00%	Culberson	128	21.81%	188	32.03%	137	23.34%
769	94.59%	Dallam	20	29.85%	26	38.81%	9	13.43%
79,464	92.71%	Dallas	98,192	40.66%	64,842	26.85%	32,702	13.54%
1,645	91.34%	Dawson	101	30.33%	71	21.32%	90	27.03%
1,408	94.62%	Deaf Smith	133	36.44%	85	23.29%	84	23.01%
1,303	90.93%	Delta	72	48.32%	33	22.15%	23	15.44%
62,385	93.33%	Denton	22,054	32.74%	22,301	33.10%	8,166	12.12%
2,689	95.46%	DeWitt	237	45.58%	109	20.96%	89	17.12%
458	94.05%	Dickens	16	27.59%	8	13.79%	18	31.03%
73	93.59%	Dimmit	433	18.55%	688	29.48%	536	22.96%
745	95.64%	Donley	33	45.83%	15	20.83%	11	15.28%
157	91.81%	Duval	515	22.33%	821	35.60%	505	21.90%
3,667	96.40%	Eastland	152	38.78%	124	31.63%	50	12.76%
10,681	95.92%	Ector	1,173	34.23%	1,018	29.71%	577	16.84%
569	89.61%	Edwards	3	8.57%	11	31.43%	4	11.43%
21,203	94.21%	Ellis	4,480	45.96%	2,388	24.50%	1,401	14.37%

Republican Primary		County	Democratic Primary					
Trump	%		Biden	%	Sanders	%	Bloomberg	%
16,913	91.90%	El Paso	19,363	28.25%	24,851	36.26%	14,090	20.56%
7,031	93.30%	Erath	376	33.84%	325	29.25%	154	13.86%
1,671	95.92%	Falls	349	48.14%	139	19.17%	156	21.52%
5,010	94.60%	Fannin	417	42.38%	191	19.41%	180	18.29%
4,774	95.58%	Fayette	529	42.97%	229	18.60%	235	19.09%
611	95.92%	Fisher	81	50.31%	29	18.01%	18	11.18%
854	89.61%	Floyd	53	46.09%	22	19.13%	17	14.78%
308	89.53%	Foard	15	50.00%	7	23.33%	2	6.67%
53,105	92.77%	Fort Bend	29,219	41.98%	18,297	26.29%	10,468	15.04%
1,662	97.42%	Franklin	188	50.54%	58	15.59%	69	18.55%
3,304	95.91%	Freestone	333	48.33%	167	24.24%	107	15.53%
397	94.75%	Frio	515	20.30%	697	27.47%	540	21.28%
1,595	97.61%	Gaines	71	39.23%	46	25.41%	31	17.13%
27,075	94.64%	Galveston	9,278	41.46%	5,504	24.60%	2,958	13.22%
565	96.91%	Garza	40	42.11%	21	22.11%	20	21.05%
5,608	94.13%	Gillespie	617	41.63%	240	16.19%	260	17.54%
354	98.88%	Glasscock	3	23.08%	6	46.15%	4	30.77%
1,357	95.23%	Goliad	187	49.47%	63	16.67%	66	17.46%
2,990	89.55%	Gonzales	239	38.00%	129	20.51%	135	21.46%
3,667	96.25%	Gray	117	42.55%	79	28.73%	38	13.82%
13,470	95.76%	Grayson	2,381	40.06%	1,548	26.04%	1,018	17.13%
10,705	96.90%	Gregg	2,876	52.14%	1,092	19.80%	796	14.43%
3,821	95.93%	Grimes	503	45.69%	246	22.34%	177	16.08%
16,023	92.81%	Guadalupe	3,812	37.90%	2,837	28.21%	1,402	13.94%
2,463	95.72%	Hale	243	37.50%	171	26.39%	111	17.13%
483	97.58%	Hall	42	49.41%	18	21.18%	20	23.53%
2,101	94.60%	Hamilton	162	44.51%	62	17.03%	68	18.68%
1,128	94.79%	Hansford	8	34.78%	12	52.17%	0	0.00%
654	95.47%	Hardeman	59	47.97%	20	16.26%	19	15.45%
8,808	97.70%	Hardin	692	48.87%	285	20.13%	222	15.68%
181,894	93.94%	Harris	121,866	37.69%	92,158	28.50%	47,459	14.68%
8,193	96.74%	Harrison	1,675	50.01%	617	18.42%	614	18.33%
1,089	95.69%	Hartley	36	64.29%	11	19.64%	0	0.00%
764	96.46%	Haskell	104	59.77%	20	11.49%	15	8.62%
14,248	92.43%	Hays	7,092	27.93%	9,817	38.66%	2,134	8.40%
768	95.40%	Hemphill	39	52.70%	8	10.81%	14	18.92%
11,381	96.27%	Henderson	1,389	45.98%	594	19.66%	529	17.51%
11,460	92.53%	Hidalgo	15,893	26.79%	16,721	28.18%	15,118	25.48%
5,255	95.63%	Hill	559	43.77%	284	22.24%	248	19.42%
3,089	93.46%	Hockley	160	40.92%	110	28.13%	72	18.41%
12,705	94.36%	Hood	943	39.44%	508	21.25%	453	18.95%
4,727	96.79%	Hopkins	563	46.03%	271	22.16%	204	16.68%
3,899	96.70%	Houston	496	55.30%	157	17.50%	132	14.72%
3,317	93.62%	Howard	299	38.28%	166	21.25%	173	22.15%
163	95.88%	Hudspeth	89	25.07%	103	29.01%	52	14.65%
12,280	93.83%	Hunt	1,287	39.32%	1,019	31.13%	468	14.30%
4,308	95.16%	Hutchinson	130	36.72%	89	25.14%	75	21.19%
458	94.43%	Irion	22	39.29%	16	28.57%	6	10.71%
1,813	96.85%	Jack	80	45.45%	33	18.75%	35	19.89%
2,408	94.69%	Jackson	192	52.03%	60	16.26%	55	14.91%
6,035	97.42%	Jasper	669	51.23%	220	16.85%	262	20.06%
448	93.92%	Jeff Davis	119	36.06%	81	24.55%	35	10.61%
13,921	96.95%	Jefferson	9,815	48.47%	3,981	19.66%	3,800	18.77%
12	92.31%	Jim Hogg	288	23.40%	343	27.86%	299	24.29%
1,165	93.57%	Jim Wells	1,619	34.40%	1,044	22.18%	1,021	21.70%
16,756	96.38%	Johnson	2,326	37.50%	1,790	28.86%	943	15.20%
2,556	92.37%	Jones	160	46.92%	83	24.34%	43	12.61%
1,613	94.05%	Karnes	210	33.87%	147	23.71%	129	20.81%
13,790	92.13%	Kaufman	2,351	42.39%	1,485	26.78%	819	14.77%

2020

Donald Trump won every county.

Presidential Primary

Trump (117 delegates)
155 delegates were possible.

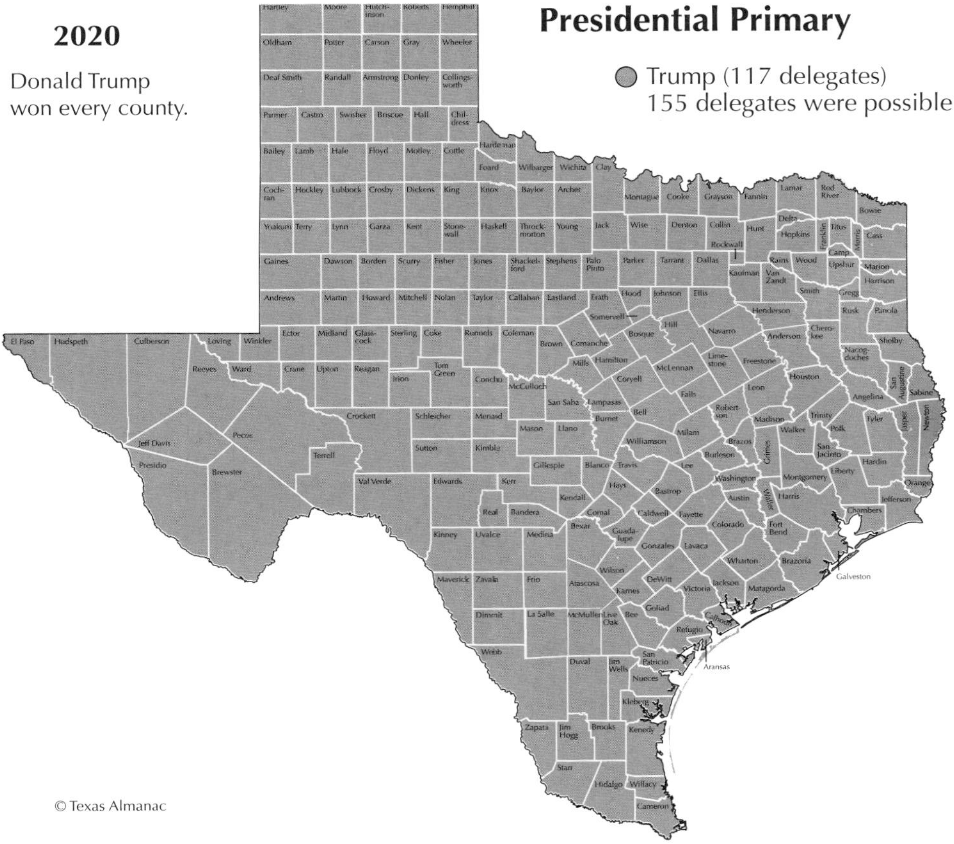

Republican Primary		County	Democratic Primary					
Trump	%		Biden	%	Sanders	%	Bloomberg	%
6,793	95.29%	Kendall	924	35.79%	554	21.46%	432	16.73%
13	86.67%	Kenedy	30	24.79%	22	18.18%	23	19.01%
189	96.92%	Kent	14	33.33%	4	9.52%	14	33.33%
9,739	93.55%	Kerr	1,054	37.55%	628	22.37%	453	16.14%
1,296	93.04%	Kimble	41	40.20%	27	26.47%	14	13.73%
111	98.23%	King	0	0.00%	1	50.00%	1	50.00%
741	85.86%	Kinney	58	40.00%	23	15.86%	29	20.00%
1,602	94.12%	Kleberg	950	38.24%	629	25.32%	454	18.28%
721	91.27%	Knox	53	63.86%	14	16.87%	6	7.23%
6,836	97.41%	Lamar	864	46.80%	389	21.07%	303	16.41%
1,610	94.93%	Lamb	117	39.80%	75	25.51%	71	24.15%
2,860	96.01%	Lampasas	359	40.61%	182	20.59%	130	14.71%
81	91.01%	La Salle	262	21.34%	291	23.70%	248	20.20%
3,899	97.16%	Lavaca	234	41.86%	103	18.43%	97	17.35%
2,833	95.04%	Lee	338	47.74%	153	21.61%	114	16.10%
3,905	96.87%	Leon	247	55.88%	67	15.16%	69	15.61%
9,482	95.20%	Liberty	804	43.70%	471	25.60%	325	17.66%
4,009	92.18%	Limestone	354	45.74%	163	21.06%	153	19.77%
768	93.43%	Lipscomb	18	36.73%	9	18.37%	7	14.29%
1,731	95.85%	Live Oak	164	51.57%	48	15.09%	57	17.92%
4,810	95.46%	Llano	544	40.57%	245	18.27%	248	18.49%
24	82.76%	Loving	1	11.11%	3	33.33%	2	22.22%
28,165	93.71%	Lubbock	4,481	30.63%	4,577	31.29%	1,801	12.31%

Republican Primary		County	Democratic Primary					
Trump	%		Biden	%	Sanders	%	Bloomberg	%
864	87.18%	Lynn	36	49.32%	14	19.18%	17	23.29%
1,817	91.81%	Madison	69	44.23%	31	19.87%	27	17.31%
22,282	92.03%	Marion	5,384	41.68%	3,086	23.89%	1,687	13.06%
247	96.48%	Martin	8	42.11%	0	0.00%	10	52.63%
2,039	95.95%	Mason	160	51.45%	79	25.40%	32	10.29%
1,482	95.98%	Matagorda	373	59.97%	106	17.04%	83	13.34%
1,002	90.03%	Maverick	16	30.77%	20	38.46%	4	7.69%
1,409	89.18%	McCulloch	86	40.95%	35	16.67%	34	16.19%
4,613	93.02%	McLennan	680	48.33%	295	20.97%	217	15.42%
358	96.50%	McMullen	1,150	14.39%	2,726	34.10%	1,419	17.75%
5,665	96.59%	Medina	881	38.09%	561	24.25%	300	12.97%
478	91.22%	Menard	26	42.62%	18	29.51%	7	11.48%
18,832	92.74%	Midland	1,507	38.50%	994	25.40%	599	15.30%
3,892	93.24%	Milam	428	40.42%	270	25.50%	179	16.90%
1,306	95.47%	Mills	30	29.41%	32	31.37%	19	18.63%
1,186	94.13%	Mitchell	69	51.49%	25	18.66%	21	15.67%
3,837	96.38%	Montague	211	43.96%	112	23.33%	77	16.04%
61,272	95.31%	Montgomery	9,995	39.02%	6,483	25.31%	3,749	14.64%
2,222	93.87%	Moore	119	41.32%	77	26.74%	38	13.19%
1,196	98.03%	Morris	328	52.99%	120	19.39%	109	17.61%
384	97.71%	Motley	8	44.44%	3	16.67%	4	22.22%
7,393	93.69%	Nacogdoches	1,370	40.38%	988	29.12%	404	11.91%
6,753	93.74%	Navarro	891	46.87%	423	22.25%	343	18.04%
2,604	91.63%	Newton	196	55.21%	62	17.46%	67	18.87%
1,954	92.83%	Nolan	171	43.62%	107	27.30%	46	11.73%
16,137	96.38%	Nueces	8,588	37.92%	5,661	24.99%	4,268	18.84%
1,717	95.76%	Ochiltree	33	38.82%	21	24.71%	14	16.47%
600	97.24%	Oldham	16	40.00%	9	22.50%	8	20.00%
13,179	95.87%	Orange	1,163	44.02%	574	21.73%	495	18.74%
4,768	93.99%	Palo Pinto	347	39.08%	205	23.09%	170	19.14%
4,116	97.77%	Panola	493	58.69%	129	15.36%	117	13.93%
23,300	95.79%	Parker	2,064	38.74%	1,348	25.30%	809	15.18%
785	95.97%	Parmer	48	42.11%	31	27.19%	19	16.67%
1,236	93.99%	Pecos	222	25.61%	218	25.14%	219	25.26%
6,912	92.39%	Polk	580	35.41%	334	20.39%	315	19.23%
8,678	95.13%	Potter	1,215	34.64%	1,055	30.07%	520	14.82%
145	96.67%	Presidio	168	16.63%	415	41.09%	137	13.56%
2,379	96.28%	Rains	176	43.35%	71	17.49%	81	19.95%
19,662	95.14%	Randall	1,591	33.62%	1,414	29.88%	623	13.16%
541	89.42%	Reagan	9	33.33%	7	25.93%	8	29.63%
822	96.48%	Real	47	34.81%	39	28.89%	15	11.11%
1,862	98.15%	Red River	273	51.22%	114	21.39%	83	15.57%
90	100.00%	Reeves	328	22.45%	313	21.42%	345	23.61%
1,159	89.22%	Refugio	158	35.35%	67	14.99%	127	28.41%
425	99.07%	Roberts	1	9.09%	0	0.00%	6	54.55%
2,704	96.40%	Robertson	479	52.70%	159	17.49%	160	17.60%
11,910	94.10%	Rockwall	2,407	40.53%	1,507	25.37%	789	13.29%
1,861	95.34%	Runnels	77	46.11%	28	16.77%	18	10.78%
8,240	95.66%	Rusk	1,016	55.25%	282	15.33%	326	17.73%
2,248	97.61%	Sabine	167	50.45%	46	13.90%	64	19.34%
1,465	97.15%	San Augustine	274	57.44%	67	14.05%	91	19.08%
4,129	96.11%	San Jacinto	456	52.66%	169	19.52%	125	14.43%
5,053	94.17%	San Patricio	1,825	43.04%	1,077	25.40%	646	15.24%
1,358	96.52%	San Saba	22	21.15%	10	9.62%	19	18.27%
489	96.07%	Schleicher	45	36.89%	29	23.77%	21	17.21%
2,474	93.43%	Scurry	98	38.28%	77	30.08%	31	12.11%
737	97.10%	Shackelford	27	50.00%	13	24.07%	3	5.56%
4,960	92.92%	Shelby	261	57.24%	80	17.54%	72	15.79%
577	95.37%	Sherman	18	42.86%	10	23.81%	5	11.90%

Republican Primary		County	Democratic Primary					
Trump	%		Biden	%	Sanders	%	Bloomberg	%
26,907	95.59%	Smith	5,378	45.92%	2,636	22.51%	1,827	15.60%
2,193	93.68%	Somervell	94	29.56%	95	29.87%	56	17.61%
46	100.00%	Starr	1,048	13.77%	3,167	41.61%	1,258	16.53%
1,751	97.44%	Stephens	69	47.59%	24	16.55%	18	12.41%
298	96.13%	Sterling	5	27.78%	7	38.89%	1	5.56%
217	98.64%	Stonewall	35	47.30%	6	8.11%	14	18.92%
682	86.77%	Sutton	28	36.36%	20	25.97%	11	14.29%
944	94.78%	Swisher	94	45.63%	24	11.65%	52	25.24%
118,494	94.64%	Tarrant	59,267	38.21%	47,506	30.63%	19,273	12.43%
14,737	92.15%	Taylor	1,939	39.92%	1,388	28.58%	384	7.91%
87	97.75%	Terrell	36	20.93%	23	13.37%	28	16.28%
1,574	86.87%	Terry	75	31.65%	63	26.58%	60	25.32%
394	97.52%	Throckmorton	18	69.23%	4	15.38%	4	15.38%
3,692	95.18%	Titus	436	46.88%	205	22.04%	166	17.85%
14,676	94.42%	Tom Green	1,769	39.28%	1,309	29.06%	559	12.41%
37,832	89.80%	Travis	53,297	23.71%	84,224	37.47%	18,759	8.35%
3,197	94.36%	Trinity	260	45.45%	101	17.66%	117	20.45%
4,147	96.33%	Tyler	300	47.77%	104	16.56%	131	20.86%
5,978	97.14%	Upshur	705	53.01%	254	19.10%	180	13.53%
597	94.02%	Upton	19	20.21%	28	29.79%	23	24.47%
2,334	94.80%	Uvalde	631	24.81%	633	24.89%	593	23.32%
2,484	90.20%	Val Verde	832	26.21%	856	26.97%	674	21.24%
10,147	96.66%	Van Zandt	725	47.70%	340	22.37%	261	17.17%
10,605	93.03%	Victoria	1,763	44.75%	974	24.72%	461	11.70%
5,328	97.16%	Walker	1,164	43.16%	692	25.66%	347	12.87%
4,891	95.04%	Waller	1,014	38.70%	869	33.17%	346	13.21%
1,340	91.28%	Ward	112	28.21%	98	24.69%	111	27.96%
4,898	97.03%	Washington	676	41.86%	323	20.00%	280	17.34%
2,642	90.17%	Webb	5,372	19.93%	9,446	35.05%	5,903	21.90%
6,602	93.00%	Wharton	612	41.32%	364	24.58%	303	20.46%
1,535	96.48%	Wheeler	31	46.27%	14	20.90%	13	19.40%
12,006	93.50%	Wichita	1,707	37.54%	1,300	28.59%	606	13.33%
2,115	90.85%	Wilbarger	120	42.40%	59	20.85%	45	15.90%
162	97.01%	Willacy	682	22.71%	903	30.07%	684	22.78%
40,954	93.08%	Williamson	18,198	29.87%	19,322	31.71%	6,852	11.25%
6,720	95.00%	Wilson	848	36.54%	587	25.29%	429	18.48%
661	93.36%	Winkler	40	46.51%	17	19.77%	13	15.12%
9,773	96.75%	Wise	645	35.19%	491	26.79%	335	18.28%
9,114	95.63%	Wood	753	51.22%	256	17.41%	218	14.83%
957	94.57%	Yoakum	33	37.50%	30	34.09%	16	18.18%
3,540	95.37%	Young	185	43.33%	82	19.20%	61	14.29%
38	100.00%	Zapata	823	26.55%	814	26.26%	677	21.84%
109	99.09%	Zavala	721	26.13%	779	28.23%	706	25.59%

Political Party Organizations

Democratic State Executive Committee

txdemocrats.org

Chairman: Gilberto Hinojosa

P.O. Box 15707, Austin 78761

Republican State Executive Committee

texasgop.org

Chairman: Allen West

P.O. Box 2206, Austin 78768

Libertarian State Executive Committee

lptexas.org

Chair: Whitney Bilyeu

100 Congress Ave., Ste. 2000, Austin 78701

Green State Executive Committee

txgreens.org

Co-Chairs: Alfred Molison and Laura Palmer

P.O. Box 271080, Houston 77277

Texas Primary Elections, 2020

Following are the official results for the contested races in the Democratic and Republican primaries held March 3, 2020. Included are selected federal, statewide, and selected district races. Runoffs were held on July 14.

Some data was omitted for space, including the Texas House of Representatives, judges in the Court of Appeals, judges in the Criminal Court of Appeals, judges in the state Supreme Court, district-level races, races in which only a single candidate was running, select races in the US House of Representatives, and some party propositions.

For full and historical election results, see texasalmanac.com.

Source: Texas Secretary of State.

Democratic Primary

Federal Races

President

Joseph Biden	725,562	34.64%
Bernie Sanders	626,339	29.91%
Michael Bloomberg	300,608	14.35%
Elizabeth Warren	239,237	11.42%
Pete Buttigieg	82,671	3.95%
Amy Klobuchar	43,291	2.07%
Julián Castro	16,688	0.8%
Tom Steyer	13,929	0.67%
Michael Bennet	10,324	0.49%
Tulsi Gabbard	8,688	0.41%
Andrew Yang	6,674	0.32%
Roque "Rocky" De La Fuente	5,469	0.26%
Cory Booker	4,941	0.24%
Marianne Williamson	3,918	0.19%
John K. Delaney	3,280	0.16%
Robby Wells	1,505	0.07%
Deval Patrick	1,304	0.06%
Total vote	2,094,428	

U.S. Senate

Mary "M.J." Hegar	417,160	22.31%
Royce West	274,074	14.66%
Cristina Tzintzun Ramirez	246,659	13.19%
Annie "Mamá" Garcia	191,900	10.27%
Amanda K. Edwards	189,624	10.14%
Chris Bell	159,751	8.55%
Sema Hernandez	137,892	7.38%
Michael Cooper	92,463	4.95%
Victor Hugo Harris	59,710	3.19%
Adrian Ocegueda	41,566	2.22%
Jack Daniel Foster Jr.	31,718	1.7%
D.R. Hunter	26,902	1.44%
Total Vote	1,869,419	

U.S. House of Representatives

District 3

Lulu Seikaly	28,250	44.55%
Sean McCaffity	27,736	43.73%
Tanner Do	7,433	11.72%
Total Vote	63,419	

District 10

Mike Siegel	35,651	43.99%
Pritesh Gandhi	26,818	33.09%
Shannon Hutcheson	18,578	22.92%
Total Vote	81,047	

District 12

Lisa Welch	36,750	81.06%
Danny Anderson	8,588	18.94%
Total Vote	45,338	

District 13

Gus Trujillo	6,998	42.09%
Greg Sagan	5,773	34.72%
Timothy W. Gassaway	3,854	23.18%
Total Vote	16,625	

District 14

Adrienne Bell	26,152	61.83%
Eddie Fisher	4,967	11.74%
Sanjanetta Barnes	4,482	10.6%
Mikal Williams	4,055	9.59%
Robert "Puga" Thomas	2,640	6.24%
Total Vote	42,296	

District 22

Sri Preston Kulkarni	34,664	53.07%
Derrick A. Reed	16,126	24.69%
Nyanza Davis Moore	9,449	14.47%
Carmine Petrillo III	5,074	7.77%
Total Vote	65,313	

District 23

Gina Ortiz Jones	41,718	66.41%
Efrain V Valdez	6,964	11.09%
Rosalinda "Rosey" Ramos Abuabara	6,896	10.98%
Ricardo R. Madrid	4,518	7.19%
Jaime Escuder	2,725	4.34%
Total Vote	62,821	

District 24

Kim Olson	24,442	41.04%
Candace Valenzuela	18,078	30.36%
Jan McDowell	5,965	10.02%
Crystal Fletcher	3,386	5.69%
Richard Fleming	3,010	5.05%
Sam Vega	2,677	4.5%
John Biggan	1,996	3.35%
Total Vote	59,554	

District 26

Carol H. Iannuzzi	31,019	55.34%
Mat Pruneda	15,701	28.01%
Neil Durrance	9,329	16.64%
Total Vote	56,049	

District 30

Eddie Bernice Johnson	58,804	70.63%
Shenita "Shae" Cleveland	11,358	13.64%
Barbara Mallory Caraway	10,452	12.55%
Hasani Burton	2,638	3.17%
Total Vote	83,252	

District 31

Christine Eady Mann	24,145	34.7%
Donna Imam	21,352	30.69%
Tammy Young	9,956	14.31%
Michael Edward Grimes	7,542	10.84%
Eric Hanke	4,117	5.92%
Dan Janjigian	2,471	3.55%
Total Vote	69,583	

Statewide Races

Railroad Commissioner

Chrysta Castañeda	598,638	33.85%
Roberto R. "Beto" Alonzo	506,748	28.65%
Kelly Stone	383,453	21.68%
Mark Watson	279,911	15.83%
Total Vote	1,768,750	

Supreme Court

Chief Justice

Amy Clark Meachum	1,434,175	80.51%
Jerry Zimmerer	347,186	19.49%
Total Vote	1,781,361	

State Senate

District 11

Susan Criss	26,155	53.01%
Margarita Ruiz Johnson	23,188	46.99%
Total Vote	49,343	

District 12

Shadi Zitoon .... 32,831 .... 57.48%
Randy Daniels .... 24,291 .... 42.52%
Total Vote 57,122

District 13

Borris L Miles .... 36,514 .... 55.43%
Melissa Morris .... 22,840 .... 34.67%
Richard R. Andrews .... 6,525 .... 9.9%
Total Vote 65,879

District 19

Xochil Peña Rodriguez .... 30,821 .... 43.92%
Roland Gutierrez .... 26,550 .... 37.83%
Freddy Ramirez .... 12,808 .... 18.25%
Total Vote 70,179

District 27

Eddie Lucio Jr .... 31,046 .... 49.76%
Sara Stapleton Barrera .... 22,221 .... 35.62%
Ruben Cortez .... 9,122 .... 14.62%
Total Vote 62,389

District Races

State Board of Education

District 5

Rebecca Bell-Metereau .... 143,351 .... 68.51%
Letti Bresnahan .... 65,885 .... 31.49%
Total Vote 209,236

District 6

Michelle Palmer .... 52,028 .... 46.8%
Kimberly Mcleod .... 38,439 .... 34.57%
Debra Kerner .... 20,712 .... 18.63%
Total Vote 111,179

District 10

Marsha Burnett-Webster .... 133,862 .... 84.5%
Stephen Wyman .... 24,549 .... 15.5%
Total Vote 158,411

Propositions

1 – Right to healthcare

In Favor .... 1,923,052 .... 94.51%
Against. .... 111,801 .... 5.49%
Total Vote 2,034,853

2 – Right to a 21st-century public education

In Favor .... 1,931,961 .... 94.98%
Against. .... 102,209 .... 5.02%
Total Vote 2,034,170

3 – Right to clean air, safe water, climate policy

In Favor .... 1,989,221 .... 97.63%
Against. .... 48,352 .... 2.37%
Total Vote 2,037,573

4 – Right to economic security

In Favor .... 1,919,677 .... 94.95%
Against. .... 102,152 .... 5.05%
Total Vote 2,021,829

Democratic Runoff

Federal Races

U.S. Senate

District 15

Mary "M.J." Hegar .... 502,516 .... 52.24%
Royce West .... 459,457 .... 47.76%
Total Vote 961,973

U.S. House of Representatives

District 3

Lulu Seikaly .... 20,617 .... 60.72%
Sean McCaffity .... 13,339 .... 39.28%
Total Vote 33,956

District 10

Mike Siegel .... 26,799 .... 54.22%
Pritesh Gandhi .... 22,629 .... 45.78%
Total Vote 49,428

District 13

Gus Trujillo .... 4,988 .... 66.36%
Greg Sagan .... 2,529 .... 33.64%
Total Vote 7,517

State Races

Railroad Commissioner

Chrysta Castañeda .... 579,698 .... 62.02%
Roberto R. "Beto" Alonzo .... 355,053 .... 37.98%
Total Vote 934,751

State Senate

District 19

Roland Gutierrez .... 16,593 .... 52.75%
Xochil Peña Rodriguez .... 14,864 .... 47.25%
Total Vote 31,457

District 27

Eddie Lucio Jr. .... 16,942 .... 53.54%
Sara Stapleton Barrera .... 14,702 .... 46.46%
Total Vote 31,644

State Board of Education

District 6

Michelle Palmer .... 39,757 .... 64.23%
Kimberly McLeod .... 22,139 .... 35.77%
Total Vote 61,896

Republican Primary

Federal Races

President

Donald J. Trump .... 1,898,664 .... 94.13%
Uncommitted .... 71,803 .... 3.56%
Bill Weld .... 15,824 .... 0.78%
Joe Walsh .... 14,772 .... 0.73%
Roque "Rocky" De La Fuente Guerra .... 7,563 .... 0.37%
Bob Ely .... 3,582 .... 0.18%
Matthew John Matern .... 3,512 .... 0.17%
Zoltan G. Istvan .... 1,447 .... 0.07%
Total vote 2,017,167

U.S. Senate

John Cornyn .... 1,470,669 .... 76.04%
Dwayne Stovall .... 231,104 .... 11.95%
Mark Yancey .... 124,864 .... 6.46%
John Anthony Castro .... 86,916 .... 4.49%
Virgil Bierschwale .... 20,494 .... 1.06%
Total Vote 1,934,047

U.S. House of Representatives

District 7

Wesley Hunt .... 28,060 .... 61%
Cindy Siegel .... 12,497 .... 27.17%
Maria Espinoza .... 2,716 .... 5.9%
Kyle Preston .... 1,363 .... 2.96%
Jim Noteware .... 937 .... 2.04%
Laique Rehman .... 424 .... 0.92%
Total Vote 45,997

District 11

August Pfluger .... 56,093 .... 52.21%
Brandon Batch .... 16,224 .... 15.1%
Wesley W. Virdell .... 7,672 .... 7.14%
Jamie Berryhill .... 7,496 .... 6.98%
J.Ross Lacy .... 4,785 .... 4.45%
J.D. Faircloth .... 4,257 .... 3.96%
Casey Gray .... 4,064 .... 3.78%
Robert Tucker .... 3,137 .... 2.92%
Ned Luscombe .... 2,066 .... 1.92%
Gene Barber .... 1,641 .... 1.53%
Total Vote 107,435

District 13

Josh Winegarner .... 39,130 .... 38.97%
Ronny Jackson .... 20,048 .... 19.96%
Chris Ekstrom .... 15,387 .... 15.32%
Elaine Hays .... 7,701 .... 7.67%
Lee Harvey .... 3,841 .... 3.82%
Vance Snider II .... 3,506 .... 3.49%

Mark Neese	2,984	2.97%
Matt McArthur	1,816	1.81%
Diane Knowlton	1,464	1.46%
Richard Herman	915	0.91%
Asusena Reséndiz	818	0.81%
Jamie Culley	779	0.78%
Monique Worthy	748	0.74%
Catherine "I Swear" Carr	707	0.7%
Jason Foglesong	579	0.58%
Total Vote	100,423	

District 16

Sam Williams	5,097	31.26%
Irene Armendariz-Jackson	4,147	25.43%
Anthony Aguero	2,184	13.39%
Jaime Arriola Jr	2,115	12.97%
Blanca Ortiz Trout	1,662	10.19%
Patrick Hernandez-Cigarruista	1,100	6.75%
Total Vote	16,305	

District 17

Pete Sessions	21,706	31.61%
Renée Swann	13,072	19.04%
George W. Hindman	12,405	18.07%
Elianor Vessali	6,286	9.15%
Scott Bland	4,947	7.2%
Trent Sutton	3,662	5.33%
Todd Kent	2,367	3.45%
Kristen Alamo Rowin	1,183	1.72%
Laurie Godfrey McReynolds	1,105	1.61%
David Saucedo	975	1.42%
Jeff Oppenheim	483	0.7%
Ahmad Adnan	477	0.69%
Total Vote	68,668	

District 22

Troy Nehls	29,583	40.45%
Kathaleen Wall	14,201	19.42%
Pierce Bush	11,281	15.43%
Greg Hill	10,315	14.1%
Dan Mathews	2,165	2.96%
Bangar Reddy	1,144	1.56%
Joe Walz	1,039	1.42%
Shandon Phan	773	1.06%
Diana Miller	771	1.05%
Jon Camarillo	718	0.98%
Douglas Haggard	398	0.54%
Howard Steele	283	0.39%
Matt Hinton	274	0.37%
Brandon T. Penko	96	0.13%
Aaron Hermes	92	0.13%
Total Vote	73,133	

District 24

Beth Van Duyne	32,067	64.33%
David Fegan	10,295	20.65%
Desi Maes	2,867	5.75%
Sunny Chaparala	2,808	5.63%
Jeron Liverman	1,809	3.63%
Total Vote	49,846	

District 31

John Carter	53,070	82.28%
Mike Williams	5,560	8.62%
Christopher Wall	3,155	4.89%
Abhiram Garapati	2,717	4.21%
Total Vote	64,502	

District 32

Genevieve Collins	22,908	52.88%
Floyd Mclendon	14,699	33.93%
Jon Hollis	1,945	4.49%
Jeff Tokar	1,892	4.37%
Mark Sackett	1,880	4.34%
Total Vote	43,324	

Statewide Race

Railroad Commissioner

James "Jim" Wright	991,593	55.29%
Ryan Sitton	801,904	44.71%
Total Vote	1,793,497	

District Races

State Senate

District 13

Milinda Morris	5,363	65.03%
William J. Booher	2,884	34.97%
Total Vote	8,247	

State Board of Education

District 5

Robert Morrow	54,460	40%
Lani Popp	46,276	33.99%
Inga Cotton	35,425	26.02%
Total Vote	136,161	

District 14

Sue Melton-Malone	108,389	61.09%
Maria Y. Berry	69,048	38.91%
Total Vote	177,437	

Propositions

1 – No restriction on prayer in public schools

In Favor	1,768,450	88.62%
Against	227,105	11.38%
Total Vote	1,995,555	

2 – No restrictions on the right to bear arms

In Favor	1,700,394	85.38%
Against	291,190	14.62%
Total Vote	1,991,584	

3 – Ban taxpayer-funded lobbying

In Favor	1,862,609	94.3%
Against	112,642	5.7%
Total Vote	1,975,251	

4 – Build wall along the southern border

In Favor	1,861,692	93.86%
Against	121,880	6.14%
Total Vote	1,983,572	

Republican Runoff

Federal Races

U.S. House of Representatives

District 13

Ronny Jackson	36,684	55.57%
Josh Winegarner	29,327	44.43%
Total Vote	66,011	

District 15

Monica De La Cruz-Hernandez	7,423	75.95%
Ryan Krause	2,350	24.05%
Total Vote	9,773	

District 16

Irene Armendariz-Jackson	5,170	65.43%
Sam Williams	2,731	34.57%
Total Vote	7,901	

District 17

Ipete Sessions	18,524	53.51%
Renée Swann	16,096	46.49%
Total Vote	34,620	

District 18

Wendell Champion	4,000	71.81%
Irobert M. Cadena	1,570	28.19%
Total Vote	5,570	

District Races

State Board of Education

District 5

Lani Popp	55,990	77.96%
Robert Morrow	15,827	22.04%
Total Vote	71,817	

Government

87TH LEGISLATURE REPORT

HISTORICAL DOCUMENTS

CHIEF OFFICIALS, 1691–2021

STATE, LOCAL, & FEDERAL GOVERNMENT

The city hall in Strawn, in Palo Pinto County.
Photo by Nicholas Henderson, CC 2/Flickr

North Richland Hills Senator Kelly Hancock (far end of the table) chairs the Senate Business and Commerce Committee. Senate Media Photo.

Report on the 87th Legislature

By Carolyn Barta

In short, the 87th session of the Texas Legislature was unlike any other, with the regular session addressing unparalleled challenges, and the aftermath casting Texas into the national spotlight.

Lawmakers convened for the biennial five-month session on January 12, 2021, under a unique set of circumstances: in the midst of a global coronavirus pandemic that created health and economic issues, and less than a week after protesters stormed the nation's Capitol over a disputed presidential election, raising security and political concerns. Add to that, social and racial unrest across the nation.

Then a brutal winter snowstorm in February left more than 4.8 million Texans without electricity and water for days during a power blackout, resulting in an estimated at least 200 deaths, billions of dollars in damage to homes, farmers and businesses, and the exposure of a vulnerable electrical grid and regulatory system.

The political backdrop clearly favored Republicans, who maintained majorities in both the Texas House (83 to 67) and Senate (18 to 13) and whose major voice was Gov. Greg Abbott, gearing up to run for a third four-year term in 2022.

After quickly moving to repair regulatory problems affecting the power grid, the GOP-controlled Legislature pursued a social-issue agenda that would appeal to the most conservative voters who dominated the 2020 electorate. President Donald Trump easily carried the state by 5.6 percentage points, and the Democrats' highly touted effort to pick up nine seats to regain a Texas House majority failed miserably. Democrats' successes were confined largely to urban county elections.

Both state chambers had Republican leaders: Lt. Gov. Dan Patrick presided again over the Senate, and Dade Phelan, a four-term Beaumont Republican, was elected speaker by House members, succeeding one-term speaker Dennis Bonnen.

Emboldened by their 2020 electoral success, Republicans pushed through permitless carry of handguns, a near-total ban on abortion, penalties for cities that cut police budgets, a proposal targeting the teaching of critical race theory and a Patrick priority to require pro sports teams with state government contracts to play the national anthem at games. Gov. Abbott called it "the most conservative session in a generation."

The session solidified Texas' position as a "mega-red" state and a bedrock of the conservative movement in the Republican Party, with former President Trump continuing to cast a long shadow over Texas lawmakers and the state's electorate.

Still, it wasn't all easy sailing for the Republicans. One of Gov. Abbott's top priorities was a "voter integrity" bill. It would ban 24-hour and drive-through voting, bar unsolicited distribution of mail-in ballots, empower partisan poll watchers, impose uniform early-voting hours statewide and prohibit polling places from opening before 1 p.m. on Sundays, which critics said targeted Black voters who participated in "souls to the polls" voter drives on Sunday mornings.

Democrats individually walked out of the House just hours before adjournment on May 31 until a quorum of 100 (two-thirds of the 150-member body) was no longer present, thus thwarting the bill's passage — only the fourth time in history that the quorum-busting tactic was used.

Gov. Abbott retaliated by vetoing a portion of the budget that would leave some 2,100 Capitol staffers unpaid for two years but could be reversed in a special session if legislators finished their work to his satisfaction.

Despite the pandemic and partisan tensions, lawmakers passed the only required bill — the state budget taking effect September 1, 2021. Cobbling together the $248.6 billion no-tax-increase budget proved less onerous than expected. Consumers returned to the marketplace as people were vaccinated against COVID-19 and the state began to open up, and financial forecasts improved during the session.

Abbott, to the delight of his base but against some opposition, lifted mask mandates and declared the state to be reopened to 100% capacity as of March 10, 2021.

Lawmakers said the budget kept 2019 promises to better fund public schools and cut taxes, though it would spend about 5% less than the previous budget. Critics called it too lean to keep up with the state's fast-growing needs, as some 700,000 new residents were expected over the next two years.

After the winter storm, everything took a back seat to fixing the power grid. Reforms included required weatherization and emergency communication, and a restructuring of the Energy Reliability Council of Texas (ERCOT) board of directors and the Public Utility Commission (PUC). New laws would create power outage alerts so Texans could prepare for looming blackouts, impose more control by elected officials over the ERCOT board and expand the PUC from three to five members.

Gov. Abbott declared that "everything that needed to be done was done to fix the power grid." However, days after the session's close, facing temperatures in the high 90s, ERCOT called on consumers to cut back on energy use to avoid summer power outages.

Media attention focused on the session's so-called "red meat" conservative bills, including:

Abortion: The "heartbeat" bill banned abortions after a fetal heartbeat is detected, which could be as early as six weeks, before a woman might know she is pregnant.

Guns: Texans 21 and older who can legally possess a handgun would no longer need a state-issued license, a background check or pass a safety course to carry a handgun, openly or concealed. Permitless carry passed despite a 2019 mass shooting targeting Hispanics in an El Paso Walmart that killed 23 persons.

Border security: The budget included more than $1 billion for border security. After the session, Gov. Abbott declared that Texas would build the border wall that Trump began and diverted $250 million from state prisons to begin funding design and construction.

Defunding the police: A ban on defunding the police in the ten largest cities was approved, over the objection of local officials who said the state overstepped into areas of local control.

Critical race theory: Teaching "critical race theory" in public schools was restricted, which opponents feared would stifle teachers from adding context to teaching racial history, social justice and current events.

Among issues that failed:

- Expansion of health insurance coverage under the Affordable Care Act. Texas ranks No. 1 in the percent of children (12.7%) who lack health insurance. Expansion of Medicaid would have brought health insurance to around a million Texans without a tax.
- Air-conditioning in state-run jails and prisons. One in five of the state's 100 lockups have no air-conditioning and nearly half are only partially cooled.
- Virtual education funding. Texas schools are funded largely based on in-person attendance, and a bill to fund remote instruction failed, leaving online instruction uncertain in many districts.

Other bills passed:

- Booze-to-go. Texans can buy beer and wine starting at 10 a.m. on Sundays, and Texas businesses can continue to sell alcohol to go, which was allowed during the pandemic.
- Broadband. A State Broadband Development Office will award grants, low-interest loans and other incentives to build out broadband access. Nearly a million Texans, approximately 3.4% of the state's population, lack broadband access at home, including 90% in rural areas.
- Criminal justice/policing: Reforms in response to George Floyd's death by Minneapolis police included banning police chokeholds and requiring police to stop colleagues from misusing deadly force.

COVID-19 affected the session in many ways, from health protocols to reduced public interaction, such as the number of Texans willing to testify in committee hearings. A bill to rein in the governor's power to restrict business operations during a pandemic died, but the Legislature responded otherwise to COVID-19: assuring families access to nursing homes during health emergencies, providing a liability shield for businesses and protecting churches from closure by public officials.

COVID-19 also delayed U.S. Census results. Detailed population numbers needed to redraw legislative and congressional districts were unavailable in the regular session, requiring a special session in the fall.

Before that, Gov. Abbott called a 30-day special session beginning July 8, 2021, to address the failed voter bill and other issues, including an overhaul of bail-setting procedures, limiting access to school sports teams for transgender students, abortion-inducing drugs, social media censorship and border security.

Democrats again stymied passage of the voter bill when 50-plus legislators bolted the state on a chartered flight for Washington, D.C., where they lobbied for passage of federal voting legislation that would supersede state law. Several tested positive for COVID-19 while there. The exodus wasn't expected to permanently kill the Texas "elections integrity" bill, but it put Texas at the center of a national struggle on voting rights following the disputed presidential election. Abbott promised to keep calling special sessions until the Democrats capitulated.

The fall redistricting session would include the addition of two congressional seats, reflecting population growth, to Texas' 36-member delegation of 23 Rs, 13 Ds. New faces were assured as a result of several GOP retirements, but Republicans were poised to grow their strength, also controlling the redrawing of legislative districts required by new census numbers.

Carolyn Barta is a former political writer for The Dallas Morning News and retired journalism professor at Southern Methodist University. ☆

Declaration of Independence of the Republic of Texas

The Declaration of Independence of the Republic of Texas was adopted in general convention at Washington-on-the-Brazos, March 2, 1836.

Richard Ellis, president of the convention, appointed a committee of five to write the declaration for submission to the convention. However, there is much evidence that George C. Childress, one of the members, wrote the document with little or no help from the other members. Childress is therefore generally accepted as the author.

The text of the declaration is followed by the names of the signers of the document. The names are presented here as the signers actually signed the document.

Our thanks to the staff of the Texas State Archives for furnishing a photocopy of the signatures.

UNANIMOUS

Declaration of Independence,

BY THE
DELEGATES OF THE PEOPLE OF TEXAS,
IN GENERAL CONVENTION,
AT THE TOWN OF WASHINGTON,
ON THE SECOND DAY OF MARCH, 1836.

WHEN A GOVERNMENT has ceased to protect the lives, liberty and property of the people from whom its legitimate powers are derived, and for the advancement of whose happiness it was instituted; and so far from being a guarantee for the enjoyment of those inestimable and inalienable rights, becomes an instrument in the hands of evil rulers for their oppression; when the Federal Republican Constitution of their country, which they have sworn to support, no longer has a substantial existence, and the whole nature of their government has been forcibly changed without their consent, from a restricted federative republic, composed of sovereign states, to a consolidated central military despotism, in which every interest is disregarded but that of the army and the priesthood — both the eternal enemies of civil liberty, and the ever-ready minions of power, and the usual instruments of tyrants; When long after the spirit of the Constitution has departed, moderation is at length, so far lost, by those in power that even the semblance of freedom is removed, and the forms, themselves, of the constitution discontinued; and so far from their petitions and remonstrances being regarded, the agents who bear them are thrown into dungeons; and mercenary armies sent forth to force a new government upon them at the point of the bayonet. When in consequence of such acts of malfeasance and abdication, on the part of the government, anarchy prevails, and civil society is dissolved into its original elements: In such a crisis, the first law of nature, the right of self-preservation — the inherent and inalienable right of the people to appeal to first principles and take their political affairs into their own hands in extreme cases — enjoins it as a right towards themselves and a sacred obligation to their posterity, to abolish such government and create another in its stead, calculated to rescue them from impending dangers, and to secure their future welfare and happiness.

Nations, as well as individuals, are amenable for their acts to the public opinion of mankind. A statement of a part of our grievances is, therefore, submitted to an impartial world, in justification of the hazardous but unavoidable step now taken of severing our political connection with the Mexican people, and assuming an independent attitude among the nations of the earth.

The Mexican government, by its colonization laws, invited and induced the Anglo-American population of Texas to colonize its wilderness under the pledged faith of a written constitution, that they should continue to enjoy that constitutional liberty and republican government to which they had been habituated in the land of their birth, the United States of America. In this expectation they have been cruelly disappointed, inasmuch as the Mexican nation has acquiesced in the late changes made in the government by General Antonio Lopez de Santa Anna, who, having overturned the constitution of his country, now offers us the cruel alternative either to abandon our homes, acquired by so many privations, or submit to the most intolerable of all tyranny, the combined despotism of the sword and the priesthood.

It has sacrificed our welfare to the state of Coahuila, by which our interests have been continually depressed, through a jealous and partial course of legislation carried on at a far distant seat of government, by a hostile majority, in an unknown tongue; and this too, notwithstanding we have petitioned in the humblest terms, for the establishment of a separate state government, and have, in accordance with the provisions of the national constitution, presented the general Congress, a republican constitution which was without just cause contemptuously rejected.

It incarcerated in a dungeon, for a long time, one of our citizens, for no other cause but a zealous endeavor to procure the acceptance of our constitution and the establishment of a state government.

It has failed and refused to secure on a firm basis, the right of trial by jury; that palladium of civil liberty, and only safe guarantee for the life, liberty, and property of the citizen.

It has failed to establish any public system of education, although possessed of almost boundless resources (the public domain) and, although, it is an axiom, in political science, that unless a people are educated and enlightened it is idle to expect the continuance of civil liberty, or the capacity for self-government.

It has suffered the military commandants stationed among us to exercise arbitrary acts of oppression and tyranny; thus trampling upon the most sacred rights of the citizen and rendering the military superior to the civil power.

It has dissolved by force of arms, the state Congress of Coahuila and Texas, and obliged our representatives to fly for their lives from the seat of government; thus depriving us of the fundamental political right of representation.

It has demanded the surrender of a number of our citizens, and ordered military detachments to seize and carry them into the Interior for trial; in contempt of the civil authorities, and in defiance of the laws and constitution.

It has made piratical attacks upon our commerce; by commissioning foreign desperadoes, and authorizing them to seize our vessels, and convey the property of our citizens to far distant ports of confiscation.

It denies us the right of worshipping the Almighty according to the dictates of our own consciences, by the support of a national religion calculated to promote the temporal interests of its human functionaries rather than the glory of the true and living God.

It has demanded us to deliver up our arms; which are essential to our defense, the rightful property of freemen, and formidable only to tyrannical governments.

It has invaded our country, both by sea and by land, with intent to lay waste our territory and drive us from our homes; and has now a large mercenary army advancing to carry on against us a war of extermination.

It has, through its emissaries, incited the merciless savage, with the tomahawk and scalping knife, to massacre the inhabitants of our defenseless frontiers.

It hath been, during the whole time of our connection with it, the contemptible sport and victim of successive military revolutions and hath continually exhibited every characteristic of a weak, corrupt and tyrannical government.

These, and other grievances, were patiently borne by the people of Texas until they reached that point at which forbearance ceases to be a virtue. We then took up arms in defense of the national constitution. We appealed to our Mexican brethren for assistance. Our appeal has been made in vain. Though months have elapsed, no sympathetic response has yet been heard from the Interior. We are, therefore, forced to the melancholy conclusion that the Mexican people have acquiesced in the destruction of their liberty, and the substitution therefor of a military government — that they are unfit to be free and incapable of self-government.

The necessity of self-preservation, therefore, now decrees our eternal political separation.

We, therefore, the delegates, with plenary powers, of the people of Texas, in solemn convention assembled, appealing to a candid world for the necessities of our condition, do hereby resolve and DECLARE *that our political connection with the Mexican nation has forever ended; and that the people of Texas do now constitute a* FREE, SOVEREIGN *and* INDEPENDENT REPUBLIC, *and are fully invested with all the rights and attributes which properly belong to the independent nations; and, conscious of the rectitude of our intentions, we fearlessly and confidently commit the issue to the decision of the Supreme Arbiter of the destinies of nations.*

RICHARD ELLIS, president of the convention and Delegate from Red River.

Charles B Stewart

Thos Barnett
John S.D. Byrom

Franco Ruiz
J. Antonio Navarro
Jesse B. Badgett
Wm D. Lacey
William Menefee
Jno Fisher
Mathew Caldwell
William Mottley
Lorenzo de Zavala
Stephen H. Everitt
Geo W Smyth

Elijah Stapp
Claiborne West

Wm B Scates

M.B. Menard
A.B. Hardin
J.W. Bunton
Thos J. Gasley
R. M. Coleman
Sterling C. Robertson
Benj Briggs Goodrich
G.W. Barnett
James G. Swisher
Jesse Grimes
S. Rhoads Fisher
John W. Moore
John W. Bower
Saml A Maverick from Bejar
Sam P. Carson
A. Briscoe
J.B. Woods
Jas Collinsworth
Edwin Waller
Asa Brigham
Geo. C. Childress
Bailey Hardeman
Rob. Potter

Thomas Jefferson Rusk
Chas. S. Taylor
John S. Roberts

Robert Hamilton
Collin McKinney
Albert H Latimer
James Power

Sam Houston
David Thomas

Edwd Conrad
Martin Parmer
Edwin O. LeGrand
Stephen W. Blount
Jas Gaines
Wm Clark, Jr
Sydney O. Penington
Wm Carrol Crawford
Jno Turner

Test. H.S. Kimble, Secretary

Documents Concerning the Annexation of Texas to the United States

For an overview of the subject, please see these discussions: The New Handbook of Texas, Texas State Historical Association, Austin, 1996; Vol. 1, pages 192–193. On the web: **https://tshaonline.org/handbook/online/articles/mga02**. Also see, the Texas State Library and Archives website: **www.tsl.state.tx.us/ref/abouttx/annexation/index.html** and the Texas Almanac website: **https://texasalmanac.com/topics/history/timeline/annexation-and-statehood**.

Joint Resolution for Annexing Texas to the United States

Resolved

by the Senate and House of Representatives of the United States of America in Congress assembled,

That Congress doth consent that the territory properly included within and rightfully belonging to the Republic of Texas, may be erected into a new State to be called the State of Texas, with a republican form of government adopted by the people of said Republic, by deputies in convention assembled, with the consent of the existing Government in order that the same may by admitted as one of the States of this Union.

2. And be it further resolved, That the foregoing consent of Congress is given upon the following conditions, to wit:

First, said state to be formed, subject to the adjustment by this government of all questions of boundary that may arise with other government,

—and the Constitution thereof, with the proper evidence of its adoption by the people of said Republic of Texas, shall be transmitted to the President of the United States, to be laid before Congress for its final action on, or before the first day of January, one thousand eight hundred and forty-six.

Second, said state when admitted into the Union, after ceding to the United States all public edifices, fortifications, barracks, ports and harbors, navy and navy yards, docks, magazines and armaments, and all other means pertaining to the public defense, belonging to the said Republic of Texas, shall retain funds, debts, taxes and dues of every kind which may belong to, or be due and owing to the said Republic;

and shall also retain all the vacant and unappropriated lands lying within its limits, to be applied to the payment of the debts and liabilities of said Republic of Texas, and the residue of said lands, after discharging said debts and liabilities, to be disposed of as said State may direct; but in no event are said debts and liabilities to become a charge upon the Government of the United States.

Third — New States of convenient size not exceeding four in number, in addition to said State of Texas and having sufficient population, may, hereafter by the consent of said State, be formed out of the territory thereof, which shall be entitled to admission under the provisions of the Federal Constitution;

and such states as may be formed out of the territory lying south of thirty-six degrees thirty minutes north latitude, commonly known as the Missouri Compromise Line, shall be admitted into the Union, with or without slavery, as the people of each State, asking admission shall desire;

and in such State or States as shall be formed out of said territory, north of said Missouri Compromise Line, slavery, or involuntary servitude (except for crime) shall be prohibited.

3. And be it further resolved, That if the President of the United States shall in his judgment and discretion deem it most advisable, instead of proceeding to submit the foregoing resolution of the Republic of Texas, as an overture on the part of the United States for admission, to negotiate with the Republic; then,

Be it resolved, That a State, to be formed out of the present Republic of Texas, with suitable extent and boundaries, and with two representatives in Congress, until the next appointment of representation, shall be admitted into the Union, by virtue of this act, on an equal footing with the existing States, as soon as the terms and conditions of such admission, and the cession of the remaining Texian territory to the United States shall be agreed upon by the governments of Texas and the United States:

And that the sum of one hundred thousand dollars be, and the same is hereby, appropriated to defray the expenses of missions and negotiations, to agree upon the terms of said admission and cession, either by treaty to be submitted to the Senate, or by articles to be submitted to the two houses of Congress, as the President may direct.

Approved, March 1, 1845.

Source: Peters, Richard, ed., The Public Statutes at Large of the United States of America, v.5, pp. 797–798, Boston, Chas. C. Little and Jas. Brown, 1850.

Twenty-Ninth Congress: Session 1 — Resolutions [No. 1.] Joint Resolution for the Admission of the State of Texas into the Union

Whereas

the Congress of the United States, by a joint resolution approved March the first, eighteen hundred and forty-five, did consent that the territory properly included within, and rightfully belonging to, the Republic of Texas, might be erected into a new State, to be called _The State of Texas,_ with a republican form of government, to be adopted by the people of said republic, by deputies in convention assembled, with the consent of the existing government, in order that the same might be admitted as one of the States of the Union;

which consent of Congress was given upon certain conditions specified in the first and second sections of said joint resolution;

and whereas the people of the said Republic of Texas, by deputies in convention assembled, with the consent of the existing government, did adopt a constitution, and erect a new State with a republican form of government, and, in the name of the people of Texas, and by their authority, did ordain and declare that they assented to and accepted the proposals, conditions, and guaranties contained in said first and second sections of said resolution:

and whereas the said constitution, with the proper evidence of its adoption by the people of the Republic of Texas, has been transmitted to the President of the United States and laid before Congress, in conformity to the provisions of said joint resolution:

Therefore—

Resolved by the Senate and House of Representatives of the United States of America in Congress assembled, That the State of Texas shall be one, and is hereby declared to be one, of the United States of America, and admitted into the Union on an equal footing with the original States in all respects whatever.

Sec. 2. And be it further resolved, That until the representatives in Congress shall be apportioned according to an actual enumeration of the inhabitants of the United States, the State of Texas shall be entitled to choose two representatives.

Approved, December 29, 1845.

Source: Minot, Geo., ed., Statutes at Large and Treaties of the United States of America from Dec. 1, 1845, to March 3, 1851, V. IX, p. 108

Constitution of Texas

The complete official text of the Constitution of Texas, including the original document, which was adopted Feb. 15, 1876, plus all amendments approved since then, is available on the State of Texas website:

statutes.capitol.texas.gov

An index and search features at that website allow exploration of the 17 Articles and subsequent Sections of the Constitution, along with other Texas Statutes.

For election information, upcoming elections, amendment or other election votes, and voter registration information, go to:

sos.state.tx.us/elections/index.shtml

According to the **Legislative Reference Library of Texas**, "The Texas Constitution is one of the longest in the nation and is still growing. As of 2019 (the 86th Legislature), the Texas Legislature has proposed a total of 690 amendments. Of these, 507 have been adopted, and 180 have been defeated by Texas voters. Thus, the Texas Constitution has been amended 507 times since its adoption in 1876."

Amending the Texas Constitution requires a two-thirds favorable vote by both the Texas House of Representatives and the Texas Senate, followed by a majority vote of approval by voters in a statewide election.

Prior to 1973, amendments to the constitution could not be submitted by a special session of the Legislature. But the constitution was amended in 1972 to allow submission of amendments if the special session was opened to the subject by the governor.

Constitutional amendments are not subject to a gubernatorial veto. Once submitted, voters have the final decision on whether to change the constitution as proposed.

The table on the next page lists the total number of amendments submitted to voters by the Texas Legislature, how many were adopted, the year in which the Legislature approved them for submission to voters; e.g., the 70th Legislature in 1987 approved 28 bills proposing amendments to be submitted to voters, of which 20 were adopted.

For more information on bills and constitutional amendments, see the Legislative Reference Library of Texas website:

lrl.texas.gov

Amendments, 2019

The following 10 amendments were submitted to voters by the 86th Legislature in an election on **Nov. 5, 2019**.

HJR 4: The constitutional amendment providing for the creation of the flood infrastructure fund to assist in the financing of drainage, flood mitigation, and flood control projects. **Adopted.**

Votes for: 1,538,726; Votes against: 437,384

HJR 12: The constitutional amendment authorizing the legislature to increase by $3 billion the maximum bond amount authorized for the Cancer Prevention and Research Institute of Texas. **Adopted.**

Votes for: 1,259,398; Votes against: 77,939

HJR 34: The constitutional amendment authorizing the legislature to provide for a temporary exemption from ad valorem taxation of a portion of the appraised value of certain property damaged by a disaster. **Adopted.**

Votes for: 1,679,049; Votes against: 294,235

HJR 38: The constitutional amendment prohibiting the imposition of an individual income tax, including a tax on an individual's share of partnership and unincorporated association income. **Adopted.**

Votes for: 1,477,373; Votes against: 509,547

HJR 72: The constitutional amendment permitting a person to hold more than one office as a municipal judge at the same time. **Defeated.**

Votes for: 685,827; Votes against: 1,298,866

HJR 95: The constitutional amendment authorizing the legislature to exempt from ad valorem taxation precious metal held in a precious metal depository located in this state. **Adopted.**

Votes for: 982,881; Votes against: 932,885

HJR 151: The constitutional amendment allowing increase distributions to the available school fund. **Adopted.**

Votes for: 1,459,578; Votes against: 509,590

SJR 24: The constitutional amendment dedicating the revenue received from the existing state sales and use taxes that are imposed on sporting goods to the Texas Parks and Wildlife Department and the Texas Historical Commission to protect Texas' natural areas, water quality, and history by acquiring, managing,and improving state and local parks and historic sites while not increasing the rate of the state sales and use taxes. **Adopted.**

Votes for: 1,745,353; Votes against: 237,656

SJR 32: The constitutional amendment to allow the transfer of a law enforcement animal to a qualified caretaker in certain circumstances. **Adopted.**

Votes for: 1,858,876; Votes against: 123,648

SJR 79: The constitutional amendment providing for the issuance of additional general obligation bonds by the Texas Water Development Board in an amount not to exceed $200 million to provide financial assistance for the development of certain projects in economically distressed areas. **Adopted.**

Votes for: 1,294,936; Votes against: 677,619

Amendments, 2021

The following 8 amendments will be submitted to voters by the 87th Legislature in an election on Nov. 2, 2021.

HJR 99: Proposing a constitutional amendment authorizing a county to finance the development or redevelopment of transportation or infrastructure in unproductive, underdeveloped, or blighted areas in the county; authorizing the issuance of bonds and notes.

HJR 125: Proposing a constitutional amendment to allow the surviving spouse of a person who is disabled to receive a limitation on the school district ad valorem taxes on the spouse's residence homestead if the spouse is 55 years of age or older at the time of the person's death.

HJR 143: Proposing a constitutional amendment authorizing the professional sports team charitable foundations of organizations sanctioned by certain professional associations to conduct charitable raffles at rodeo venues.

HJR 165: Proposing a constitutional amendment providing additional powers to the State Commission on Judicial Conduct with respect to candidates for judicial office.

SJR 19: Proposing a constitutional amendment establishing a right for residents of certain facilities to designate an essential caregiver for in-person visitation.

SJR 27: Proposing a constitutional amendment to prohibit this state or a political subdivision of this state from prohibiting or limiting religious services of religious organizations.

SJR 35: Proposing a constitutional amendment authorizing the legislature to provide for an exemption from ad valorem taxation of all or part of the market value of the residence homestead of the surviving spouse of a member of the armed services of the United States who is killed or fatally injured in the line of duty.

SJR 47: Proposing a constitutional amendment changing the eligibility requirements for certain judicial offices.

Constitutional Amendments Submitted to Voters by the Texas Legislature

(Proposed/Adopted)

Year	No.	Year	No.	Year	No.
1879	1/1	1931	9/9	1979	12/9
1881	2/0	1933	12/4	1981	10/8
1883	5/5	1935	13/10	1982	3/3
1887	6/0	1937	7/6	1983	19/16
1889	2/2	1939	4/3	1985	17/17
1891	5/5	1941	5/1	1986	1/1
1893	2/2	1943	3/3	1987	28/20
1895	2/1	1945	8/7	1989	21/19
1897	5/1	1947	9/9	1990	1/1
1899	1/0	1949	10/2	1991	15/12
1901	1/1	1951	7/3	1993	19/14
1903	3/3	1953	11/11	1995	14/11
1905	3/2	1955	9/9	1997	15/13
1907	9/1	1957	12/10	1999	17/13
1909	4/4	1959	4/4	2001	20/20
1911	5/4	1961	14/10	2003	22/22
1913	8/0	1963	7/4	2005	9/7
1915	7/0	1965	27/20	2007	17/17
1917	3/3	1967	20/13	2009	11/11
1919	13/3	1969	16/9	2011	10/7
1921	5/1	1971	18/12	2013	10/10
1923	2/1	1973	9/6	2015	7/7
1925	4/4	1975	12/6	2017	7/7
1927	8/4	1977	15/11	2019	10/9
1929	7/7	1978	1/1	2021	8/NA

Source: Legislative Reference Library of Texas

Early Leaders of Texas

The presidents of the Republic of Texas and the state's first Governor, from top left: **David G. Burnet**, provisional president; **Sam Houston**, second and fourth presidents; **Mirabeau B. Lamar**, third president; **Anson Jones**, the Republic's last president; and **J. Pinckney Henderson**, the Lone Star State's first governor.

Texas' Chief Governmental Officials

On this and the following pages are lists of the principal administrative officials who have served the Republic and State of Texas with dates of their tenures of office. In a few instances, there are disputes as to the exact dates of tenures. Dates listed here are those that appear the most authentic.

★ ★ ★ ★ ★ ★ ★

Governors and Presidents

Spanish Royal Governors

(Some authorities would include Texas under administrations of several earlier Spanish governors. The late Dr. C.E. Castañeda, Latin-American librarian of The University of Texas and authority on the history of Texas and the Southwest, would include the following four: Francisco de Garay, 1523–1526; Pánfilo de Narváez, 1526–28; Nuño de Guzmán, 1528–1530; and Hernando de Soto, 1538–1543.)

Domingo Terán de los Rios....1691–1692
Gregorio de Salinas Varona....1692–1697
Francisco Cuerbo y Valdés....1698–1702
Mathías de Aguirre....1703–1705
Martín de Alarcón....1705–1708
Simón Padilla y Córdova....1708–1712
Pedro Fermin de Echevers y Subisa....1712–1714
Juan Valdéz....1714–1716
Martín de Alarcón....1716–1719
José de Azlor y Virto de Vera, Marqués de San Miguel de Aguayo....1719–1722
Fernando Pérez de Almazán....1722–1727
Melchor de Mediavilla y Azcona....1727–1731
Juan Antonio Bustillo y Ceballos....1731–1734
Manuel de Sandoval....1734–1736
Carlos Benites Franquis de Lugo....1736–1737
Joseph Fernández de Jáuregui y Urrutia....1737–1737
Prudencio de Orobio y Basterra....1737–1741
Tomás Felipe Winthuisen (or Winthuysen)....1741–1743
Justo Boneo y Morales....1743–1744
Francisco García Larios....1744–1748
Pedro del Barrio Junco y Espriella....1748–1750
Jacinto de Barrios y Jáuregui....1751–1759
Angel de Martos y Navarrete....1759–1767
Hugo Oconór....1767–1770
Juan María Vicencio, Barón de Ripperdá....1770–1778
Domingo Cabello y Robles....1778–1786
Rafael Martínez Pacheco....1787–1790
Manuel Muñoz....1790–1799
Juan Bautista de Elguezábal....1799–1805
Antonio Cordero y Bustamante....1805–1808
Manuel María de Salcedo....1808–1813

(Mexico's War of Independence 1810–1812 created governmental instability.)

Juan Bautista de las Casas................................1811–1811
(Revolutionary governor)
Cristóbal Domínguez, Benito de Armiñan, Mariano Varela, Juan Ignacio Pérez, Manuel Pardo *(ad interim)*..........................1813–1817
Antonio María Martínez................................1817–1821

Governors Under Mexican Rule

The first two governors under Mexican rule, Trespalacios and García, were of Texas only as Texas was then constituted. Beginning with Gonzáles, 1824, the governors were for the joint State of Coahuila y Texas.

José Felix Trespalacios................................1822–1823
Luciano García................................1823–1824
Rafael Gonzáles................................1824–1826
Victor Blanco................................1826–1827
José María Viesca................................1827–1830
Ramón Eca y Músquiz................................1830–1831
José María Letona................................1831–1832
Ramón Eca y Músquiz................................1832–1832
Juan Martín de Veramendi................................1832–1833
Juan José de Vidáurri y Villasenor................................1833–1834
Juan José Elguezábal................................1834–1835
José María Cantú................................1835–1835
Agustín M. Viesca................................1835–1835
Marciel Borrego................................1835–1835
Ramón Eca y Músquiz................................1835–1835

Provisional Colonial Governor, Before Independence

Henry Smith (Impeached)..........................1835–Jan. 1836
(James W. Robinson served as acting governor after Smith was impeached.)

Presidents of the Republic of Texas

David G. Burnet..........Mar. 16, 1836–Oct. 22, 1836
(provisional)
Sam Houston..........Oct. 22, 1836–Dec. 10, 1838
Mirabeau B. Lamar..........Dec. 10, 1838–Dec. 13, 1841
Sam Houston..........Dec. 13, 1841–Dec. 9, 1844
Anson Jones..........Dec. 9, 1844–Feb. 19, 1846

Governors Since Annexation

Abbrevations: (D) Democrat, (R) Republican, (I) Independent. Many of the early Governors ran with no party affiliation.

J. Pinckney Henderson................Feb. 19, 1846–Dec. 21, 1847
(Albert C. Horton served as acting governor while Henderson was away in the Mexican War.)
George T. Wood........................Dec. 21, 1847–Dec. 21, 1849
Peter Hansbrough Bell................Dec. 21, 1849–Nov. 23, 1853
(Resigned to enter U.S. House of Representatives.)
J. W. Henderson........................Nov. 23, 1853–Dec. 21, 1853
Elisha M. Pease........................Dec. 21, 1853–Dec. 21, 1857
Hardin R. Runnels (D)................Dec. 21, 1857–Dec. 21, 1859
Sam Houston..........................Dec. 21, 1859–Mar. 16, 1861
(Resigned because of state's secession from the Union.)
Edward Clark..........................Mar. 16, 1861–Nov. 7, 1861
Francis R. Lubbock....................Nov. 7, 1861–Nov. 5, 1863
(Resigned to enter Confederate Army.)
Pendleton Murrah......................Nov. 5, 1863–June 17, 1865
(Fled to Mexico upon the fall of Confederacy. Lt. Gov. Fletcher S. Stockdale briefly acted as governor after Murrah's departure.)
Andrew J. Hamilton....................June 17, 1865–Aug. 9, 1866
(Hamilton received a commission as "military governor of Texas" from President Abraham Lincoln on Nov. 14, 1862. He appears to have served in that capacity continuously until his "reappointment" as "provisional governor" by President Andrew Johnson on June 17, 1865. Apparently Johnson used the term "reappointment" because Hamilton was already serving as military governor.)
James W. Throckmorton................Aug. 9, 1866–Aug. 8, 1867
Elisha M. Pease (R)....................Aug. 8, 1867–Sept. 30, 1869
(Appointed under martial law after Throckmorton was removed on July 30, 1867, by Gen. Philip Sheridan. Pease formally took possession of the office on Aug. 8. He resigned and vacated the office Sept. 30, 1869, but no successor was named until Jan. 8, 1870. Some historians extend Pease's term to that date, but in reality Texas was without a head of governemnt for that period.)
Edmund J. Davis (R)....................Jan. 8, 1870–Jan. 15, 1874
(Appointed provisional governor after being elected.)
Richard Coke (D)........................Jan. 15, 1874–Dec. 1, 1876
(Resigned to enter U.S. Senate.)
Richard B. Hubbard (D)................Dec. 1, 1876–Jan. 21, 1879
Oran M. Roberts (D)....................Jan. 21, 1879–Jan. 16, 1883
John Ireland (D)........................Jan. 16, 1883–Jan. 18, 1887
Lawrence Sullivan Ross (D)...........Jan. 18, 1887–Jan. 20, 1891
James Stephen Hogg (D)................Jan. 20, 1891–Jan. 15, 1895
Charles A. Culberson (D)...............Jan. 15, 1895–Jan. 17, 1899
Joseph D. Sayers (D)....................Jan. 17, 1899–Jan. 20, 1903
S. W. T. Lanham (D)....................Jan. 20, 1903–Jan. 15, 1907
Thos. Mitchell Campbell (D)...........Jan. 15, 1907–Jan. 17, 1911
Oscar Branch Colquitt (D).............Jan. 17, 1911–Jan. 19, 1915
James E. Ferguson (D)..................Jan. 19, 1915–Sept. 25, 1917
(Impeached in August 1917. Lt. Gov. Hobby served as acting governor during the impeachment proceedings. Ferguson was removed from office Sept. 25.)
William Pettus Hobby (D).............Aug. 25, 1917–Jan. 18, 1921
Pat Morris Neff (D)....................Jan. 18, 1921–Jan. 20, 1925
Miriam A. Ferguson (D)................Jan. 20, 1925–Jan. 17, 1927
Dan Moody (D)..........................Jan. 17, 1927–Jan. 20, 1931
Ross S. Sterling (D)....................Jan. 20, 1931–Jan. 17, 1933
Miriam A. Ferguson (D)................Jan. 17, 1933–Jan. 15, 1935
James V. Allred (D).....................Jan. 15, 1935–Jan. 17, 1939
W. Lee O'Daniel (D)....................Jan. 17, 1939–Aug. 4, 1941
(Resigned to enter U.S. Senate.)
Coke R. Stevenson (D)..................Aug. 4, 1941–Jan. 21, 1947
Beauford H. Jester (D).................Jan. 21, 1947–July 11, 1949
(Died in office. Succeeded by Lt. Gov. Shivers.)
Allan Shivers (D).......................July 11, 1949–Jan. 15, 1957
Price Daniel (D)........................Jan. 15, 1957–Jan. 15, 1963
John Connally (D)......................Jan. 15, 1963–Jan. 21, 1969
Preston Smith (D).......................Jan. 21, 1969–Jan. 16, 1973
Dolph Briscoe (D).......................Jan. 16, 1973–Jan. 16, 1979
(Effective in 1975, the term of office was increased from 2 to 4 years.)
William P. Clements (R)...............Jan. 16, 1979–Jan. 18, 1983
Mark White (D)..........................Jan. 18, 1983–Jan. 20, 1987
William P. Clements (R)...............Jan. 20, 1987–Jan. 15, 1991
Ann W. Richards (D)....................Jan. 15, 1991–Jan. 17, 1995
George W. Bush (R)....................Jan. 17, 1995–Dec. 21, 2000
(Resigned to become U.S. president.)
Rick Perry (R)..........................Dec. 21, 2000–Jan. 20, 2015
Greg Abbott (R)..............................Jan. 20, 2015–present

★ ★ ★ ★ ★ ★ ★

Vice Presidents and Lieutenant Governors

Vice Presidents of the Republic

Lorenzo de Zavala.....................Mar. 16, 1836–Oct, 17, 1836
(Provisional.)
Mirabeau B. Lamar....................Oct. 22, 1836–Dec.10, 1838
David G. Burnet........................Dec. 10, 1838–Dec.13, 1841
Edward Burleson........................Dec. 13, 1841–Dec. 9, 1844
Kenneth L. Anderson....................Dec. 9, 1844–July 3, 1845
(Died in office.)

Lieutenant Governors

Albert C. Horton (D) ....May 2, 1846–Dec. 21, 1847
John A. Greer (D) ....Dec. 21, 1847–Dec. 22, 1851
J. W. Henderson (D)....................Dec. 22, 1851–Nov. 23, 1853
(Briefly succeeded to governorship when Gov. Bell resigned to enter U.S. House of Representatives.)
D. C. Dickson (D).......................Dec. 21, 1853–Dec. 21, 1855
H. R. Runnels (D).......................Dec. 21, 1855–Dec. 21, 1857
F. R. Lubbock (D) ....Dec. 21, 1857–Dec. 21, 1859
Edward Clark (I).........................Dec. 21, 1859–Mar. 16, 1861
(Succeeded Gov. Sam Houston when Houston refused to take oath to Confederacy.)
John M. Crockett (D) .... Nov. 7, 1861–Nov. 5, 1863
Fletcher S. Stockdale (D)................ Nov. 7, 1863–June 17, 1865
(Fall of Confederacy.)
George W. Jones (D) ....Aug. 9, 1866–July 30, 1867
(Jones was removed by Gen. Philip Sheridan.)
J. W. Flanagan (R)... 1869
(Elected in 1869, Flanagan was appointed U.S. senator and was never inaugurated as lt. governor.)
R. B. Hubbard (D)........................Jan. 15, 1873–Dec. 1, 1876
(Succeeded Gov. Richard Coke when he resigned to become U.S. senator.)
J. D. Sayers (D)...............................Jan. 21, 1879–Jan. 18, 1881
L. J. Storey (D)...............................Jan. 18, 1881–Jan. 16, 1883
Marion Martin (D) ....Jan. 16, 1883–Jan. 20, 1885
Barnett Gibbs (D).........................Jan. 20, 1885–Jan. 19, 1887
T. B. Wheeler (D)..........................Jan. 19, 1887– Jan. 21, 1891
George C. Pendleton (D) ....Jan. 21, 1891–Jan. 17, 1893
M. M. Crane (D) ....Jan. 17, 1893–Jan. 15, 1895
George T. Jester (D).......................Jan. 15, 1895–Jan. 17, 1899
J. N. Browning (D) ....Jan. 17, 1899– Jan. 20, 1903
George D. Neal (D) ....Jan. 20, 1903–Jan. 15, 1907
A. B. Davidson (D).........................Jan. 15, 1907–Jan. 21, 1913
Will H. Mayes (D)..........................Jan. 21, 1913–Aug. 14, 1914
(resigned)
William P. Hobby (D)...................Jan. 19, 1915–Aug. 25, 1917
(Served as acting governor during the impeachment of Gov. Jim Ferguson. Took oath as governor after Ferguson was removed from office Sept. 25.)
W. A. Johnson (D)....................... Sept. 29, 1917–Jan. 18, 1921
(Selected as president of the state Senate and acting lt. governor, serving Hobby's unexpired term. He was then elected statewide to the office in 1918.)
Lynch Davidson (D) .... Jan. 18, 1921–Jan. 16, 1923
T. W. Davidson (D) ....Jan. 16, 1923–Jan. 20, 1925
Barry Miller (D)............................Jan. 20, 1925–Jan. 20, 1931
Edgar E. Witt (D) ....Jan. 20, 1931–Jan. 15, 1935
Walter Woodul (D) ....Jan. 15, 1935–Jan. 17, 1939
Coke R. Stevenson (D)...................Jan. 17, 1939–Aug. 4, 1941
(Became governor upon resignation of Gov. W. Lee O'Daniel to become U.S. senator.)
John Lee Smith (D) .... Jan. 19, 1943–Jan. 21, 1947
Allan Shivers (D)......................... Jan. 21, 1947–July 11, 1949
(Shivers succeeded to the governorship on death of Gov. Beauford H. Jester.)
Ben Ramsey (D)........................ Jan. 16, 1951–Sept. 18, 1961
(Ramsey resigned to become a member of the Texas Railroad Commission.)
Preston Smith (D)....................... Jan. 15, 1963–Jan. 21, 1969
Ben Barnes (D)........................... Jan. 21, 1969–Jan. 16, 1973
William P. Hobby Jr. (D)................ Jan. 16, 1973–Jan. 15, 1991
Robert D. Bullock (D)................... Jan. 15, 1991–Jan. 19, 1999
Rick Perry (R)............................. Jan. 19, 1999–Dec. 21, 2000
Bill Ratliff (R) ....Dec. 28, 2000–Jan. 14, 2003
(Elected by state Senate when Perry succeeded to governorship.)
David Dewhurst (R) .... Jan. 21, 2003–Jan. 20, 2015
Dan Patrick (R) ....Jan. 20, 2015–present

★ ★ ★ ★ ★ ★ ★

Secretaries of State Of the Republic

Raines Yearbook for Texas, 1901, gives the following record of Secretaries of State during the era of the Republic of Texas:

Under David G. Burnet: Samuel P. Carson, James Collingsworth, and W. H. Jack.

Under Sam Houston (first term): Stephen F. Austin, 1836. J. Pinckney Henderson and Dr. Robert A. Irion, 1837–1838.

Under Mirabeau B. Lamar: Bernard Bee appointed Dec. 16, 1838; James Webb appointed Feb. 6, 1839; D. G. Burnet appointed Acting Secretary of State, May 31, 1839; N. Amory appointed Acting Secretary of State, July 23, 1839; D. G. Burnet appointed Acting Secretary of State, Aug. 5, 1839; Abner S. Lipscomb appointed Secretary of State, Jan. 31, 1840, and resigned Jan. 22, 1841; Joseph Waples appointed Acting Secretary of State, Jan. 23, 1841, and served until Feb. 8, 1841; James S. Mayfield appointed Feb. 8, 1841; Joseph Waples appointed April 30, 1841, and served until May 25, 1841; Samuel A. Roberts appointed May 25, 1841; reappointed Sept. 7, 1841.

Under Sam Houston (second term): E. Lawrence Stickney, Acting Secretary of State until Anson Jones was appointed Dec. 13, 1841. Jones served as Secretary of State throughout this term except during the summer and part of this term of 1842, when Joseph Waples filled the position as Acting Secretary of State.

Under Anson Jones: Ebenezer Allen served from Dec. 10, 1844, until Feb. 5, 1845, when Ashbel Smith became Secretary of State. Allen was again named Acting Secretary of State, March 31, 1845, and later named Secretary of State.

In addition to the above, documents in the Texas State Archives indicate that **Joseph C. Eldredge**, Chief Clerk of the State Department during much of the Republic's existence, signed a number of documents in the absence of the office-holder in the capacity of "Acting Secretary of State."

State Secretaries of State

Charles Mariner ....Feb. 20, 1846–May 4, 1846
David G. Burnet............................May 4, 1846–Jan. 1, 1848
Washington D. Miller ....Jan. 1, 1848–Jan. 2, 1850
James Webb ....Jan. 2, 1850–Nov. 14, 1851
Thomas H. Duval.......................Nov. 14, 1851–Dec. 22, 1853
Edward Clark .... Dec. 22, 1853–Dec. 1857
T. S. Anderson..............................Dec. 1857–Dec. 27, 1859
E. W. Cave ....Dec. 27, 1859–Mar. 16, 1861
Bird Holland .... Mar. 16, 1861–Nov. 1861
Charles West ....Nov. 1861–Sept. 1862
Robert J. Townes .... Sept. 1862–May 2, 1865
Charles R. Pryor.............................May 2, 1865–Aug, 1865
James H. Bell ....Aug. 1865–Aug. 1866
John A. Green ....Aug. 1866–Aug. 1867
D. W. C. Phillips................................ Aug. 1867–Jan. 1870
J. P. Newcomb .... Jan. 1, 1870–Jan. 17, 1874
George Clark.............................. Jan. 17, 1874–Jan. 27, 1874
A. W. DeBerry............................ Jan. 27, 1874–Dec. 1, 1876
Isham G. Searcy ....Dec. 1, 1876–Jan. 23, 1879
J. D. Templeton.......................... Jan. 23, 1879–Jan. 22, 1881
T. H. Bowman........................... Jan. 22, 1881–Jan. 18, 1883

J. W. Baines .... Jan. 18, 1883–Jan. 21, 1887
John M. Moore ....Jan. 21, 1887–Jan. 22, 1891
George W. Smith.........................Jan. 22, 1891–Jan. 17, 1895
Allison Mayfield ....Jan. 17, 1895–Jan. 5, 1897
J. W. Madden ....Jan. 5, 1897–Jan. 18, 1899
D. H. Hardy.............................. Jan. 18, 1899–Jan. 19, 1901
John G. Tod ....Jan. 19, 1901–Jan., 1903
J. R. Curl ....Jan. 1903–April 1905
O. K. Shannon................................April 1905–Jan. 1907
L. T. Dashiel .... Jan. 1907–Feb. 1908
W. R. Davie .... Feb. 1908–Jan. 1909
W. B. Townsend ....Jan. 1909–Jan. 1911
C. C. McDonald................................ Jan. 1911–Dec. 1912
J. T. Bowman .... Dec. 1912–Jan. 1913
John L. Wortham .... Jan. 1913–June 1913
F. C. Weinert .... June 1913–Nov. 1914
D. A. Gregg .... Nov. 1914–Jan. 1915
John G. McKay................................. Jan. 1915–Dec. 1916
C. J. Bartlett .... Dec. 1916–Nov. 1917
George F. Howard............................ Nov. 1917–Nov. 1920
C. D. Mims ....Nov. 1920–Jan. 1921
S. L. Staples .... Jan. 1921–Aug. 1924
J. D. Strickland .... Sept. 1924–Jan. 1, 1925
Henry Hutchings .... Jan. 1, 1925–Jan. 20, 1925
Mrs. Emma G. Meharg ....Jan. 20, 1925–Jan. 1927
Mrs. Jane Y. McCallum .... Jan. 1927–Jan. 1933
W. W. Heath ....Jan. 1933–Jan. 1935
Gerald C. Mann............................ Jan. 1935–Aug. 31, 1935
R. B. Stanford............................Aug. 31, 1935–Aug. 25, 1936
B. P. Matocha........................... Aug. 25, 1936–Jan. 18, 1937
Edward Clark .... Jan. 18, 1937–Jan. 1939
Tom L. Beauchamp .... Jan. 1939–Oct. 1939
M. O. Flowers........................... Oct. 26, 1939–Feb. 25, 1941
William J. Lawson...........................Feb. 25, 1941–Jan. 1943
Sidney Latham .... Jan. 1943–Feb. 1945
Claude Isbell .... Feb. 1945–Jan. 1947
Paul H. Brown............................... Jan. 1947–Jan. 19, 1949
Ben Ramsey .... Jan. 19, 1949–Feb. 9, 1950
John Ben Shepperd......................Feb. 9, 1950–April 30, 1952
Jack Ross.................................April 30, 1952–Jan. 9, 1953
Howard A. Carney ....Jan. 9, 1953–Apr. 30, 1954
C. E. Fulgham .... May 1, 1954–Feb. 15, 1955
Al Muldrow .... Feb. 16, 1955–Nov. 1, 1955
Tom Reavley...............................Nov. 1, 1955–Jan. 16, 1957
Zollie Steakley.............................Jan. 16, 1957–Jan. 2, 1962
P. Frank Lake ....Jan. 2, 1962–Jan. 15, 1963
Crawford C. Martin ....Jan. 15, 1963–Mar. 12, 1966
John L. Hill.............................Mar. 12, 1966–Jan. 22, 1968
Roy Barrera...............................Mar. 7, 1968–Jan. 23, 1969
Martin Dies Jr. .... Jan. 23, 1969–Sept. 1, 1971
Robert D. (Bob) Bullock ....Sept. 1, 1971–Jan. 2, 1973
V. Larry Teaver Jr. ....Jan. 2, 1973–Jan. 19, 1973
Mark W. White Jr........................ Jan. 19, 1973–Oct. 27,1977
Steven C. Oaks ....Oct. 27, 1977–Jan. 16, 1979
George W. Strake Jr.......................Jan. 16, 1979–Oct. 6, 1981
David A. Dean...........................Oct. 22, 1981–Jan. 18, 1983
John Fainter .... Jan. 18, 1983–July 31, 1984
Myra A. McDaniel ....Sept. 6, 1984–Jan. 26, 1987
Jack Rains............................... Jan. 26, 1987–June 15, 1989
George Bayoud Jr.......................June 19, 1989–Jan. 15, 1991
John Hannah Jr..........................Jan. 17, 1991–Mar. 11, 1994
Ronald Kirk ....April 4, 1994–Jan. 10, 1995
Antonio O. "Tony" Garza Jr. ....Jan. 18, 1995–Dec. 2, 1997
Alberto R. Gonzales.......................Dec. 2, 1997–Jan. 10, 1999
Elton Bomer .... Jan. 11, 1999–Dec. 31, 2000
Henry Cuellar ....Jan. 2, 2001–Oct. 5, 2001
Gwyn Shea ....Jan. 2, 2002–Aug. 4, 2003
Geoff Connor ....Sept. 26, 2003–Jan. 1, 2005
J. Roger Williams...........................Jan. 1, 2005–July 1, 2007
Phil Wilson............................... July 1, 2007–July 6, 2008

The Capitals of Texas

The capitals of the six nations that have ruled Texas have been:

Spain: Valladolid (before 1551) and Madrid

France: Paris

Mexico: Mexico City, D.F.

Republic Of Texas: San Felipe de Austin, Washington-on-the-Brazos, Harrisburg, Galveston Island, Velasco, Columbia, Houston, and Austin

United States: Washington, D.C.

Confederate States Of America: Montgomery, Alabama and Richmond, Virginia

Learn more at TexasAlmanac.com

Esperanza (Hope) Andrade .... July 23, 2008–Nov. 23,2012
John T. Steen Jr.......................... Nov. 27, 2012–Jan. 7, 2014
Nandita Berry.............................Jan. 7, 2014–Jan 21, 2015
Carlos H. Cascos...........................Jan 21, 2015–Jan 5, 2017
Rolando B. Pablos.........................Jan 5, 2017–Dec. 17, 2018
David Whitley.......................... Dec. 17, 2018–May 27, 2019
(Senate refused to confirm)
Ruth Ruggero Hughs ....Aug. 19, 2019–May 31, 2021
(Resigned)
Vacant... May 31, 2021

★ ★ ★ ★ ★ ★ ★

Attorneys General of the Republic

David Thomas and Peter W. Grayson........ Mar. 2–Oct. 22, 1836
J. Pinckney Henderson, Peter W. Grayson,
John Birdsall, and A.S. Thurston..................... 1836–1838
J.C. Watrous ....Dec. 1838–June 1, 1840
Joseph Webb and F.A. Morris 1840–1841
George W. Terrell, Ebenezer Allen 1841–1844
Ebenezer Allen 1844–1846

State Attorneys General

Volney E. Howard (D) .... Feb. 21, 1846–May 7, 1846
John W. Harris (D)...................... May 7, 1846–Oct. 31, 1849
Henry P. Brewster.......................Oct. 31, 1849–Jan. 15, 1850
A. J. Hamilton ....Jan. 15, 1850–Aug. 5, 1850
(The first few attorneys general held office by appointment of the governor. The office was made elective in 1850 by constitutional amendment. Ebenezer Allen was the first elected attorney general.)
Ebenezer Allen .... Aug. 5, 1850–Aug. 2, 1852
Thomas J. Jennings .... Aug. 2, 1852–Aug. 4, 1856
James Willie.............................Aug. 4, 1856–Aug. 2, 1858
Malcolm D. Graham (D) ....Aug. 2, 1858–Aug. 6, 1860
George M. Flournoy (D)................Aug. 6, 1860–Jan. 15, 1862
N. G. Shelley (D) ....Feb. 3, 1862–Aug. 1, 1864
B. E. Tarver (D).........................Aug. 1, 1864–Dec. 11, 1865
Wm. Alexander (Unionist) ....Dec. 11, 1865–June 25, 1866
W. M. Walton (D) ....June 25, 1866–Aug. 27, 1867
Wm. Alexander (R) .... Aug. 27, 1867–Nov. 5, 1867
Ezekiel B. Turner (I).....................Nov. 5, 1867–July 11, 1870
Wm. Alexander (R) ....July 11, 1870–Jan. 27, 1874
George Clark (D)....................... Jan. 27, 1874–Apr. 25, 1876
H. H. Boone (D)........................ Apr. 25, 1876–Nov. 5, 1878
George McCormick ....Nov. 5, 1878–Nov. 2, 1880
J. H. McLeary (D) ....Nov. 2, 1880–Nov. 7, 1882
John D. Templeton (D)..................Nov. 7, 1882–Nov. 2, 1886
James S. Hogg (D).......................Nov. 2, 1886–Nov. 4, 1890
C. A. Culberson (D).....................Nov. 4, 1890–Nov. 6, 1894

M. M. Crane (D) .... Nov. 6, 1894–Nov. 8, 1898
Thomas S. Smith (D)................... Nov. 8, 1898–Mar. 15,1901
C. K. Bell (D) .... Mar. 20, 1901–Jan. 1904
R. V. Davidson (D) .... Jan. 1904–Dec. 31, 1909
Jewel P. Lightfoot (D) .... Jan. 1, 1910–Aug. 31, 1912
James D. Walthall (D)..................... Sept. 1, 1912–Jan. 1, 1913
B. F. Looney (D) .... Jan. 1, 1913–Jan., 1919
C. M. Cureton (D) .... Jan. 1919–Dec. 1921
W. A. Keeling (D)............................. Dec. 1921–Jan. 1925
Dan Moody (D)................................. Jan. 1925–Jan. 1927
Claude Pollard (D)............................ Jan. 1927–Sept. 1929
R. L. Bobbitt (D) .... Sept. 1929–Jan. 1931
(Appointed)
James V. Allred (D)............................ Jan. 1931–Jan. 1935
William McCraw (D).......................... Jan. 1935–Jan. 1939
Gerald C. Mann (D) .... Jan. 1939–Jan. 1944
(Resigned)
Grover Sellers (D).............................. Jan. 1944–Jan. 1947
Price Daniel (D)................................. Jan. 1947–Jan. 1953
John Ben Shepperd (D) .... Jan. 1953–Jan. 1, 1957
Will Wilson (D).......................... Jan. 1, 1957–Jan. 15, 1963
Waggoner Carr (D) .... Jan. 15, 1963–Jan. 1, 1967
Crawford C. Martin (D)................ Jan. 1, 1967–Dec. 29, 1972
John Hill (D) .... Jan. 1, 1973–Jan. 16, 1979
Mark White (D)......................... Jan. 16, 1979–Jan. 18, 1983
Jim Mattox (D).......................... Jan. 18, 1983–Jan. 15, 1991
Dan Morales (D)........................ Jan. 15, 1991–Jan. 13, 1999
John Cornyn (R) .... Jan. 13, 1999–Dec. 2, 2002
Greg Abbott (R)......................... Dec. 2, 2002–Jan. 20, 2015
Ken Paxton (R) .... Jan. 20, 2015–present

★ ★ ★ ★ ★ ★ ★

Treasurers of the Republic

Asa Brigham... 1838–1840
James W. Simmons...................................... 1840–1841
Asa Brigham... 1841–1844
Moses Johnson... 1844–1846

State Treasurers

James H. Raymond...................... Feb. 24, 1846–Aug. 2, 1858
C.H. Randolph .... Aug. 2, 1858–June 1865
(Randolph fled to Mexico upon collapse of Confederacy. No exact date is available for his departure from office or for Harris' succession to the post. It is believed Harris took office Oct. 2, 1865.)
Samuel Harris.......................... Oct. 2, 1865–June 25, 1866
W.M. Royston .... June 25, 1866–Sept. 1, 1867
John T. Allan .... Sept. 1, 1867–Jan. 1869
George W. Honey .... Jan. 1869–Jan. 1874
(Honey was removed from office for a short period in 1872 and B. Graham served in his place.)
B. Graham *(short term)* .... beginning May 27, 1872
A. J. Dorn .... Jan. 1874–Jan. 1879
F. R. Lubbock................................... Jan. 1879–Jan. 1891
W. B. Wortham................................. Jan. 1891–Jan. 1899
John W. Robbins .... Jan. 1899–Jan. 1907
Sam Sparks .... Jan. 1907–Jan. 1912
J. M. Edwards................................... Jan. 1912–Jan. 1919
John W. Baker .... Jan. 1919–Jan. 1921
G. N. Holton................................ July 1921–Nov. 21, 1921
C. V. Terrell............................ Nov. 21, 1921–Aug. 15, 1924
S. L. Staples .... Aug. 16, 1924–Jan. 15, 1925
W. Gregory Hatcher...................... Jan. 16, 1925–Jan. 1, 1931
Charley Lockhart .... Jan. 1, 1931–Oct. 25, 1941
Jesse James............................ Oct. 25, 1941–Sept. 29, 1977
Warren G. Harding .... Oct. 7, 1977–Jan. 3, 1983
Ann Richards............................... Jan. 3, 1983–Jan. 2, 1991
Kay Bailey Hutchison........................ Jan. 2, 1991–June 1993
Martha Whitehead........................... June 1993–Aug. 1996

The office of treasurer was eliminated by constitutional amendment in an election Nov. 7, 1995, effective the last day of August 1996.

★ ★ ★ ★ ★ ★ ★

Railroad Commissioners

After the first three names in the following list, each commissioner's name is followed by a surname in parentheses. The name in parentheses is the name of the commissioner whom that commissioner succeeded.

John H. Reagan.......................... June 10, 1891–Jan. 20, 1903
L. L. Foster............................ June 10, 1891–April 30, 1895
W. P. McLean........................... June 10, 1891–Nov. 20, 1894
L. J. Storey (McLean)................. Nov. 21, 1894–Mar. 28,1909
N. A. Stedman (Foster).................... May 1, 1895–Jan. 4, 1897
Allison Mayfield (Stedman)............. Jan. 5, 1897–Jan. 23, 1923
O. B. Colquitt (Reagan)................. Jan. 21, 1903–Jan. 17, 1911
William D. Williams (Storey) .... April 28, 1909–Oct. 1, 1916
John L. Wortham (Colquitt).............. Jan. 21, 1911–Jan. 1, 1913
Earle B. Mayfield (Wortham) .... Jan. 2, 1913–Mar. 1, 1923
Charles Hurdleston (Williams) .... Oct. 10, 1916–Dec. 31,1918
Clarence Gilmore (Hurdleston).......... Jan. 1, 1919–Jan. 1, 1929
N. A. Nabors (A. Mayfield) .... Mar. 1, 1923–Jan. 18, 1925
William Splawn (E. Mayfield)........... Mar. 1, 1923–Aug. 1, 1924
C. V. Terrell (Splawn) .... Aug. 15, 1924–Jan. 1, 1939
Lon A. Smith (Nabors) .... Jan. 29, 1925–Jan. 1, 1941
Pat M. Neff (Gilmore)...................... Jan. 1, 1929–Jan. 1, 1933
Ernest O. Thompson (Neff)............... Jan. 1, 1933–Jan. 8, 1965
G. A. (Jerry) Sadler (Terrell) .... Jan. 1, 1939–Jan. 1, 1943
Olin Culberson (Smith) .... Jan. 1, 1941–June 22, 1961
Beauford Jester (Sadler).................. Jan. 1, 1943–Jan. 21, 1947
William J. Murray Jr. (Jester) .... Jan. 21, 1947–Apr. 10, 1963
Ben Ramsey (Culberson) .... Sept. 18, 1961–Dec. 31, 1976
Jim C. Langdon (Murray) .... May 28, 1963–Dec. 31, 1977
Byron Tunnell (Thompson)........... Jan. 11, 1965–Sept. 15, 1973
Mack Wallace (Tunnell)............. Sept. 18, 1973–Sept. 22, 1987
Jon Newton (Ramsey) .... Jan. 10, 1977–Jan. 4, 1979
John H. Poerner (Langdon) .... Jan. 2, 1978–Jan. 1, 1981
James E. Nugent (Newton) .... Jan. 4, 1979–Jan. 3,1995
Buddy Temple (Poerner).................. Jan. 2, 1981–Mar. 2, 1986
Clark Jobe (Temple)........................ Mar. 3, 1986–Jan. 5, 1987
John Sharp (Jobe) .... Jan. 6, 1987–Jan. 2, 1991
Kent Hance (Wallace) .... Sept. 23, 1987–Jan. 2, 1991
Robert Krueger (Hance)................. Jan. 3, 1991–Jan. 22, 1993
(Krueger resigned when Gov. Ann Richards appointed him interim U.S. senator on the resignation of Sen. Lloyd Bentsen.)
Lena Guerrero (Sharp)................ Jan. 23, 1991–Sept. 25, 1992
James Wallace (Guerrero) .... Oct. 2, 1992–Jan. 4, 1993
Barry Williamson (Wallace)............... Jan. 5, 1993–Jan. 4, 1999
Mary Scott Nabers (Krueger) .... Feb. 9, 1993–Dec. 9, 1994
Carole K. Rylander (Nabers) .... Dec. 10, 1994–Jan. 4, 1999
Charles Matthews (Nugent).............. Jan. 3, 1995–Jan. 31, 2005
Antonio Garza (Williamson)........... Jan. 4, 1999–Nov. 18, 2002
Michael Williams (Rylander) .... Jan. 4, 1999–Mar. 31, 2011
Victor G. Carrillo (Garza) .... Feb. 19, 2003–Jan. 3, 2011
Elizabeth A. Jones (Matthews) .... Feb. 2, 2005–Feb. 28, 2012
David Porter (Carrillo) .... Jan. 5, 2011–Jan. 2, 2017
Barry T. Smitherman (Williams).......... July 8, 2011–Jan. 2, 2015
Buddy Garcia (Jones) .... April 16, 2012–Dec. 7, 2012
(Appointed by Gov. Perry.)
Ryan Sitton (Smitherman)................. Jan 5, 2015–Jan. 4, 2021
Christi Craddick (Garcia) .... Dec. 17, 2012–present
Wayne Christian (Porter)...................... Jan 9, 2017–present
Jim Wright (Sitton)............................ Jan. 4, 2021–present

★ ★ ★ ★ ★ ★ ★

Comptrollers of Public Accounts For the Republic

John H. Money....Dec. 30, 1835–Jan. 17, 1836
H. C. Hudson....Jan. 17, 1836–Oct. 22, 1836
Elisha M. Pease....June 1837–Dec. 1837
F. R. Lubbock....Dec. 1837–Jan. 1839
Jas. W. Simmons....Jan. 15, 1839–Sept. 30, 1840
Jas. B. Shaw....Sept. 30, 1840–Dec. 24, 1841
F. R. Lubbock....Dec. 24, 1841–Jan. 1, 1842
Jas. B. Shaw....Jan. 1, 1842–Jan. 1, 1846

State Comptrollers of Public Accounts

Jas. B. Shaw....Feb. 24, 1846–Aug. 2, 1858
Clement R. Johns....Aug. 2, 1858–Aug. 1, 1864
Willis L. Robards....Aug. 1, 1864–Oct. 12, 1865
Albert H. Latimer....Oct. 12, 1865–Mar. 27, 1866
Robert H. Taylor....Mar. 27, 1866–June 25, 1866
Willis L. Robards....June 25, 1866–Aug. 27, 1867
Morgan C. Hamilton....Aug. 27, 1867–Jan. 8, 1870
A. Bledsoe....Jan. 8, 1870–Jan. 20, 1874
Stephen H. Darden....Jan. 20, 1874–Nov. 2, 1880
W. M. Brown....Nov. 2, 1880–Jan. 16, 1883
W. J. Swain....Jan. 16, 1883–Jan. 18, 1887
John D. McCall....Jan. 18, 1887–Jan. 15, 1895
R. W. Finley....Jan. 15, 1895–Jan. 15, 1901
R. M. Love....Jan. 15, 1901–Jan. 1903
J. W. Stephen....Jan. 1903–Jan. 1911
W. P. Lane....Jan. 1911–Jan. 1915
H. B. Terrell....Jan. 1915–Jan. 1920
M. L. Wiginton....Jan. 1920–Jan. 1921
Lon A. Smith....Jan. 1921–Jan. 1925
S. H. Terrell....Jan. 1925–Jan. 1931
Geo. H. Sheppard....Jan., 1931–Jan. 17, 1949
Robert S. Calvert....Jan. 17, 1949–Jan., 1975
Robert D. (Bob) Bullock....Jan. 1975–Jan. 3, 1991
John Sharp....Jan. 3, 1991–Jan. 2, 1999
Carole Keeton Strayhorn....Jan. 2, 1999–Jan. 1, 2007
Susan Combs....Jan. 1, 2007–Jan. 1, 2015
Glenn Hegar....Jan. 2, 2015–present

★ ★ ★ ★ ★ ★ ★

U.S. Senators from Texas

U.S. Senators were selected by the legislatures of the states until the U.S. Constitution was amended in 1913 to require popular elections. In Texas, the first Senator chosen by the voters in a general election was Charles A. Culberson in 1916. Because of political pressures, however, the rules of the Democratic Party of Texas were changed in 1904 to require that all candidates for office stand before voters in the primary. Consequently, Texas' Senators faced voters in 1906, 1910 and 1912 before the U.S. Constitution was changed.

Following is the succession of Texas representatives in the United States Senate since the annexation of Texas to the Union in 1845:

Houston Succession

Sam Houston (I)....Feb. 21, 1846–Mar. 4, 1859
John Hemphill (D)....Mar. 4, 1859–July 11, 1861
Louis T. Wigfall and W. S. Oldham took their seats in the Confederate Senate, Nov. 16, 1861, and served until the Confederacy collapsed. After that event, the State Legislature on Aug. 21, 1866, elected David G. Burnet and Oran M. Roberts to the U.S. Senate, anticipating immediate readmission to the Union, but they were not allowed to take their seats.
Morgan C. Hamilton (R)....Feb. 22, 1870–Mar. 3, 1877
Richard Coke (D)....Mar. 4, 1877–Mar. 3, 1895
Horace Chilton (D)....Mar. 3, 1895–Mar. 3, 1901
Joseph W. Bailey (D)....Mar. 3, 1901–Jan. 8, 1913
(Resigned.)
Rienzi Melville Johnston (D)....Jan. 8, 1913–Feb. 3, 1913
(Appointed to fill vacancy.)
Morris Sheppard (D)....Feb. 13, 1913–Apr. 9, 1941
(Died in office)
Andrew J. Houston (D)....June 2–26, 1941
(Appointed to fill vacancy; died in office.)
W. Lee O'Daniel (D)....Aug. 4, 1941–Jan. 3, 1949
Lyndon B. Johnson (D)....Jan. 3, 1949–Jan. 20, 1961
(Resigned to become U.S. vice president.)
William A. Blakley (D)....Jan. 20, 1961–June 15, 1961
(Appointed to fill vacancy.)
John G. Tower (R)....June 15, 1961–Jan. 21, 1985
Phil Gramm (R)....Jan. 21, 1985–Dec. 2, 2002
John Cornyn (R)....Dec. 2, 2002–present

Rusk Succession

Thomas J. Rusk (D)....Feb 21, 1846–July 29, 1857
(Died in office.)
J. Pinckney Henderson (D)....Nov. 9, 1857–June 4, 1858
(Died in office.)
Matthias Ward (D)....Sept. 29, 1858–Dec. 5, 1859
(Appointed to fill vacancy.)
Louis T. Wigfall (D)....Dec. 5, 1859–Mar. 23, 1861
(Succession was broken by secession. See note above under Houston Succession.)
James W. Flanagan (R)....Feb. 22, 1870–Mar. 3, 1875
Samuel B. Maxey (D)....Mar. 3, 1875–Mar. 3, 1887
John H. Reagan (D)....Mar. 3, 1887–June 10, 1891
(Resigned to head Texas Railroad Commission.)
Horace Chilton (D)....Dec. 7, 1891–Mar. 30,1892
(Appointed to fill vacancy.)
Roger Q. Mills (D)....Mar. 30, 1892–Mar. 3, 1899
Charles A. Culberson (D)....Mar. 3, 1899–Mar. 4, 1923
Earle B. Mayfield (D)....Mar. 4, 1923–Mar. 4, 1929
Tom Connally (D)....Mar. 4, 1929–Jan. 3, 1953
Price Daniel (D)....Jan. 3, 1953–Jan. 15, 1957
(Resigned to become governor.)
William A. Blakley (D)....Jan. 15, 1957–Apr. 27, 1957
(Appointed to fill vacancy.)
Ralph W. Yarborough (D)....Apr. 27, 1957–Jan. 12, 1971
Lloyd Bentsen (D)....Jan. 12, 1971–Jan. 20, 1993
(Resigned to become U.S. Secretary of Treasury.)
Robert Krueger (D)....Jan. 20, 1993–June 14, 1993
(Appointed to fill vacancy.)
Kay Bailey Hutchison (R)....June 14, 1993–Jan. 20, 2013
Ted Cruz (R)....Jan. 20, 2013–present

★ ★ ★ ★ ★ ★ ★

General Land Office Commissioners For the Republic

John P. Borden....Aug. 23, 1837–Dec. 12, 1840
H. W. Raglin....Dec. 12, 1840–Jan. 4, 1841
Thomas William Ward....Jan. 4, 1841–Mar. 20, 1848
(Part of term after annexation.)

State Land Commissioners

George W. Smyth....Mar. 20, 1848–Aug. 4, 1851
Stephen Crosby....Aug. 4, 1851–Mar. 1, 1858
Francis M. White....Mar. 1, 1858–Mar. 1, 1862
Stephen Crosby....Mar. 1, 1862–Sept. 1, 1865

The Texas Capitol cupola. Photo by Justtraveling.com.

Francis M. White......Sept. 1, 1865–Aug. 7, 1866
Stephen Crosby......Aug. 7, 1866–Aug. 27, 1867
Joseph Spence......Aug. 27, 1867–Jan. 19, 1870
Jacob Kuechler......Jan. 19, 1870–Jan. 20, 1874
J. J. Groos......Jan. 20, 1874–June 15, 1878
W. C. Walsh......July 30, 1878–Jan. 10, 1887
R. M. Hall......Jan. 10, 1887–Jan. 16, 1891
W. L. McGaughey......Jan. 16, 1891–Jan. 26, 1895
A. J. Baker......Jan. 26, 1895–Jan. 16, 1899
George W. Finger......Jan. 16, 1899–May 4, 1899
Charles Rogan......May 11, 1899–Jan. 10, 1903
John J. Terrell......Jan. 10, 1903–Jan. 11, 1909
J. T. Robison......Jan, 1909–Sept. 11, 1929
J. H. Walker......Sept. 11, 1929–Jan., 1937
William H. McDonald......Jan 1937–Jan. 1939
Bascom Giles......Jan. 1939–Jan. 5, 1955
J. Earl Rudder......Jan. 5, 1955–Feb. 1, 1958
Bill Allcorn......Feb. 1, 1958–Jan. 1, 1961
Jerry Sadler......Jan. 1, 1961–Jan. 1, 1971
Bob Armstrong......Jan. 1, 1971–Jan. 1, 1983
Garry Mauro......Jan. 1, 1983–Jan. 7, 1999
David Dewhurst......Jan. 7, 1999–Jan. 3, 2003
Jerry Patterson......Jan. 3, 2003–Jan. 2, 2015
George P. Bush......Jan. 2, 2015–present

★★★★★★★

Speakers of the House For the Republic

Speaker	Term	Congress
Ira Ingram	1836–37	1st
Branch Tanner Archer	1837	2nd
Joseph Rowe	1838	2nd
John M. Hansford	1838–39	3rd
David Spangler Kaufman	1840–41	4th, 5th
Kenneth L. Anderson	1841–42	6th
Nicholas H. Darnell	1842–43	7th
Richardson A. Scurry	1843–44	8th
John M. Lewis	1844–45	9th

State Speakers of the House

Speaker, Residence	Term	Leg.
William E. Crump (D), Bellville	1846	1st
John Brown (D), Brownsboro	1846	1st
Edward T. Branch (D), Liberty	1846	1st
William H. Bourland (D), Paris	1846	1st
Stephen W. Perkins (D), Columbia	1846	1st
James W. Henderson (D), Houston	1847–48	2nd
Charles G. Keenan (D), Huntsville	1849–51	3rd
David C. Dickson (D), Anderson	1851–53	4th
Hardin R. Runnels (D), Boston	1853–55	5th
Hamilton P. Bee (D), Laredo	1855–57	6th
William S. Taylor (D), Larissa	1857–58	7th
Matt F. Locke (D), Lafayette	1858–59	7th
Marion DeKalb Taylor (D), Jefferson	1859–61	8th
Constantine W. Buckley (D), Richmond	1861	9th
Nicholas H. Darnell (D), Dallas	1861–62	9th
Constantine W. Buckley (D), Richmond	1863	9th
Marion DeKalb Taylor (D), Jefferson	1863–65	10th
Nathaniel M. Burford (Unionist), Dallas	1866	11th
(Vacant under Congressional Reconstruction and military administration, 1867-1870)		
Ira H. Evans (R), Corpus Christi	1870–71	12th
William H. Sinclair (R), Galveston	1871–73	12th
Marion DeKalb Taylor (D), Jefferson	1873–74	13th
Guy M. Bryan (D), Galveston	1874–76	14th
Thomas R. Bonner (D), Tyler	1876–79	15th
John H. Cochran (D), Dallas	1879–81	16th
George R. Reeves (D), Pottsboro	1881–83	17th
Charles R. Gibson (D), Waxahachie	1883–85	18th
Lafayette L. Foster (D), Groesbeck	1885–87	19th
George C. Pendleton (D), Belton	1887–89	20th
Frank P. Alexander (D), Greenville	1889–91	21st
Robert T. Milner (D), Henderson	1891–93	22nd
John H. Cochran (D), Dallas	1893–95	23rd
Thomas Slater Smith (D), Hillsboro	1895–97	24th

Speaker, Residence	Term	Leg.
L. Travis Dashiell (D), Jewett	1897–99	25th
J. S. Sherrill (D), Greenville	1899–1901	26th
Robert E. Prince (D), Corsicana	1901–03	27th
Pat M. Neff (D), Waco	1903–05	28th
Francis W. Seabury (D), Rio Grande City	1905–07	29th
Thomas B. Love (D), Lancaster	1907–09	30th
Austin M. Kennedy (D), Waco	1909	31st
(Resigned during 31st session)		
John W. Marshall (D), Whitesboro	1909–11	31st
Sam Rayburn (D), Bonham	1911–13	32nd
Chester H. Terrell (D), San Antonio	1913–15	33rd
John W. Woods (D), Rotan	1915–17	34th
Franklin O. Fuller (D), Coldspring	1917–19	35th
R. Ewing Thomason (D), El Paso	1919–21	36th
Charles G. Thomas (D), Lewisville	1921–23	37th
Richard E. Seagler (D), Palestine	1923–25	38th
R. Lee Satterwhite (D), Amarillo	1925–27	39th
Robert L. Bobbitt (D), Laredo	1927–29	40th
W. S. Barron (D), Bryan	1929–31	41st
Fred H. Minor (D), Denton	1931–33	42nd
Coke R. Stevenson (D), Junction	1933–37	43rd–44th
Robert W. Calvert (D), Hillsboro	1937–39	45th
R. Emmett Morse (D), Houston	1939–41	46th
Homer L. Leonard (D), McAllen	1941–43	47th
Price Daniel (D), Liberty	1943–45	48th
Claud H. Gilmer (D), Rocksprings	1945–47	49th
William O. Reed (D), Dallas	1947–49	50th
Durwood Manford (D), Smiley	1949–51	51st
Reuben Senterfitt (D), San Saba	1951–55	52nd–53rd
Jim T. Lindsey (D), Texarkana	1955–57	54th
Waggoner Carr (D), Lubbock	1957–61	55th–56th
James A. Turman (D), Gober	1961–63	57th
Byron M. Tunnell (D), Tyler	1963–65	58th
Ben Barnes (D), De Leon	1965–69	59th–60th
Gus F. Mutscher (D), Brenham	1969–72	61st–62nd
(Resigned during 62nd session)		
Rayford Price (D), Palestine	1972–73	62nd
Price Daniel Jr. (D), Liberty	1973–75	63rd
Bill Clayton (D), Springlake	1975–83	64th–67th
Gib Lewis (D), Fort Worth	1983–93	68th–72nd
Pete Laney (D), Hale Center	1993–2003	73rd–77th
Tom Craddick (R), Midland	2003–09	78th–80th
Joe Straus (R), San Antonio	2009–19	81st–85th
Dennis Bonnen (R), Angleton	2019–21	86th
Dade Phelan (R), Beaumont	2021–present	87th

★ ★ ★ ★ ★ ★ ★

Chief Justice of the Supreme Court Republic of Texas

James Collinsworth.................... Dec. 16, 1836–July 23, 1838
John Birdsall ....Nov. 19–Dec. 12, 1838
(Senate refused to confirm)
Thomas J. Rusk..........................Dec. 12, 1838–Dec. 5, 1840
John Hemphill ....Dec. 5, 1840–Dec. 29, 1845

Under Constitutions of 1845 and 1861

John Hemphill ....Mar. 2, 1846–Oct. 10, 1858
Royall T. Wheeler.........................Oct. 11, 1858–April 1864
Oran M. Roberts........................Nov. 1, 1864–June 30, 1866

Under Constitution of 1866 (Presidential Reconstruction)

George F. Moore ....Aug. 16, 1866–Sept. 10, 1867
(Removed under Congressional Reconstruction by military authorities who appointed members of the next court.)

Under Constitution of 1866 (Congressional Reconstruction)

Amos Morrill............................Sept. 10, 1867–July 5, 1870

Under Constitution of 1869

Lemuel D. Evans ....July 5, 1870–Aug. 31, 1873
Wesley Ogden...........................Aug. 31, 1873–Jan. 29, 1874
Oran M. Roberts........................ Jan. 29, 1874–Apr. 18, 1876

Under Constitution of 1876

Oran M. Roberts..........................Apr. 18, 1876–Oct. 1, 1878
George F. Moore .... Nov. 5, 1878–Nov. 1, 1881
Robert S. Gould......................... Nov. 1, 1881–Dec. 23, 1882
Asa H. Willie ....Dec. 23, 1882–Mar. 3, 1888
John W. Stayton ....Mar. 3, 1888–July 5, 1894
Reuben R. Gaines.........................July 10, 1894–Jan. 5, 1911
Thomas J. Brown......................... Jan. 7, 1911–May 26, 1915
Nelson Phillips..........................June 1, 1915–Nov. 16, 1921
C. M. Cureton.............................Dec. 2, 1921–Apr. 8, 1940
Hortense Sparks Ward..................Jan. 8, 1925–May 23, 1925
(Mrs. Ward headed a special Supreme Court to hear one case in 1925.)
W. F. Moore .... Apr. 17, 1940–Jan. 1, 1941
James P. Alexander......................... Jan. 1, 1941–Jan. 1, 1948
J. E. Hickman..............................Jan. 5, 1948–Jan. 3, 1961
Robert W. Calvert......................... Jan. 3, 1961–Oct. 4, 1972
Joe R. Greenhill .... Oct. 4, 1972–Oct. 25, 1982
Jack Pope ....Nov. 29, 1982–Jan. 5, 1985
John L. Hill Jr...............................Jan. 5, 1985–Jan. 4, 1988
Thomas R. Phillips........................Jan. 4, 1988–Sept. 3 2004
Wallace B. Jefferson.....................Sept. 14, 2004–Oct. 1, 2013
Nathan L. Hecht...............................Oct. 1, 2013–present

★ ★ ★ ★ ★ ★ ★

Presiding Judges, Court of Appeals (1876–1891) and Court of Criminal Appeals (1891–present)

Mat D. Ector............................May 6, 1876–Oct. 29, 1879
John P. White............................Nov. 9, 1879–Apr. 26, 1892
James M. Hurt..........................May 4, 1892–Dec. 31, 1898
W. L. Davidson..........................Jan. 2, 1899–June 27, 1913
A. C. Prendergast....................... June 27, 1913–Dec. 31, 1916
W. L. Davidson............................Jan. 1, 1917–Jan. 25, 1921
Wright C. Morrow.......................Feb. 8, 1921–Oct. 16, 1939
Frank Lee Hawkins .... Oct. 16, 1939–Jan. 2, 1951
Harry N. Graves.........................Jan. 2, 1951–Dec. 31, 1954
W. A. Morrison............................Jan. 1, 1955–Jan. 2, 1961
Kenneth K. Woodley....................... Jan. 3, 1961–Jan. 4, 1965
W. T. McDonald.........................Jan. 4, 1965–June 25, 1966
W. A. Morrison..........................June 25, 1966–Jan. 1, 1967
Kenneth K. Woodley....................... Jan. 1, 1967–Jan. 1, 1971

John F. Onion Jr.	Jan. 1, 1971–Jan. 1, 1989
Michael J. McCormick	Jan. 1, 1989–Jan. 1, 2001
Sharon Keller	Jan. 1, 2001–present

★ ★ ★ ★ ★ ★ ★

Administrators of Public Education, Superintendents of Public Instruction

Pryor Lea	Nov. 10, 1866–Sept. 12, 1867
Edwin M. Wheelock	Sept. 12, 1867–May 6, 1871
Jacob C. DeGress	May 6, 1871–Jan. 20, 1874
O. H. Hollingsworth	Jan. 20, 1874–May 6, 1884
B. M. Baker	May 6, 1884–Jan. 18, 1887
O. H. Cooper	Jan 18, 1887–Sept. 1, 1890
H. C. Pritchett	Sept. 1, 1890–Sept. 15, 1891
J. M. Carlisle	Sept. 15, 1891–Jan. 10, 1899
J. S. Kendall	Jan. 10, 1899–July 2, 1901
Arthur Lefevre	July 2, 1901–Jan. 12, 1905
R. B. Cousins	Jan. 12, 1905–Jan. 1, 1910
F. M. Bralley	Jan. 1, 1910–Sept. 1, 1913
W. F. Doughty	Sept. 1, 1913–Jan. 1, 1919
Annie Webb Blanton	Jan. 1, 1919–Jan. 16, 1923
S. M. N. Marrs	Jan. 16, 1923–April 28, 1932
C. N. Shaver	April 28, 1932–Oct. 1, 1932
L. W. Rogers	Oct. 1, 1932–Jan. 16, 1933
L. A. Woods	Jan. 16, 1933–1951

The office of State Superintendent of Public Instruction was abolished by the **Gilmer-Aikin Laws of 1949** and the office of Commissioner of Education was created. The Commissioner is appointed by the State Board of Education, (also created by the Gilmer-Aikin Laws) the members of which are elected by the people.

State Commissioners of Education

J. W. Edgar	May 31, 1951–June 30, 1974
Marlin L. Brockette	July 1, 1974–Sept. 1, 1979
Alton O. Bowen	Sept. 1, 1979–June 1, 1981
Raymon Bynum	June 1, 1981–Oct. 31, 1984
W. N. Kirby	April 13, 1985–July 1, 1991
Lionel R. Meno	July 1, 1991–Mar. 1, 1995
Michael A. Moses	Mar. 9, 1995–Aug. 18, 1999
Jim Nelson	Aug. 18, 1999–Mar. 25, 2002
Felipe Alanis	Mar. 25, 2002–July 31, 2003
Shirley J. Neeley	Jan. 12, 2004–July 1, 2007
Robert Scott	July 1, 2007–July 2, 2012
Michael Williams	Sept. 1, 2012–Dec. 31, 2015
Mike Morath	Jan. 4, 2016–present

★ ★ ★ ★ ★ ★ ★

State Commissioners of Agriculture

Robert Teague Milner	1907–1908
Edward Reeves Kone	1908–1914
Fred Davis	1915–1920
George B. Terrell	1921–1930
James E. McDonald	1931–1950
John C. White	1951–1977
Reagan V. Brown	1977–1982
Jim Hightower	1983–1990
Rick Perry	1991–1998
Susan Combs	1999–2006
Todd Staples	2007–2015
Sid Miller	2015–present

Cecilia Abbott.

Photo courtesy of the Office of the First Lady.

First Ladies of Texas

Martha Evans Gindratt Wood	1847–1849
Bell Administration	1849–1853
(Gov. Peter Hansbrough Bell was not married while in office.)	
Lucadia Christiana Niles Pease	1853–57; 1867–69
Runnels Administration	1857–1859
(Gov. Hardin R. Runnels never married.)	
Margaret Moffette Lea Houston	1859–1861
Martha Evans Clark	1861
Adele Barron Lubbock	1861–1863
Susie Ellen Taylor Murrah	1863–1865
Mary Jane Bowen Hamilton	1865–1866
Annie Rattan Throckmorton	1866–1867
Ann Elizabeth Britton Davis	1870–1874
Mary Home Coke	1874–1876
Janie Roberts Hubbard	1876–1879
Frances Wickliff Edwards Roberts	1879–1883
Anne Maria Penn Ireland	1883–1887
Elizabeth Dorothy Tinsley Ross	1887–1891
Sarah Stinson Hogg	1891–1895
Sally Harrison Culberson	1895–1899
Orlene Walton Sayers	1899–1903
Sarah Beona Meng Lanham	1903–1907
Fannie Brunner Campbell	1907–1911
Alice Fuller Murrell Colquitt	1911–1915
Miriam A. Wallace Ferguson	1915–1917
(Miriam A. Wallace Ferguson was Mistress of the Mansion while her husband, James E. Ferguson, was governor, 1915–1917. She served as both Governor and Mistress of the Mansion, 1925–1927 and 1933–1935.)	
Willie Cooper Hobby	1917–1921
Myrtle Mainer Neff	1921–1925
Mildred Paxton Moody	1927–1931
Maud Gage Sterling	1931–1933
Jo Betsy Miller Allred	1935–1939
Merle Estella Butcher O'Daniel	1939–1941
Fay Wright Stevenson	1941–1942
(Died in the Governor's Mansion on Jan. 3, 1942.)	
Edith Will Scott Stevenson	1942–1946
(Mother of Gov. Coke R. Stevenson and Mistress of the Mansion upon the death of the governor's wife.)	
Mabel Buchanan Jester	1946–1949
Marialice Shary Shivers	1949–1957
Jean Houston Baldwin Daniel	1957–1963
Idanell Brill Connally	1963–1969
Ima Mae Smith	1969–1973
Betty Jane Slaughter Briscoe	1973–1979
Rita Crocker Bass Clements	1979–1983
Linda Gale Thompson White	1983–1987
Rita Crocker Bass Clements	1987–1991
Richards Administration	1991–1995
(Gov. Ann Richards was not married while in office.)	
Laura Welch Bush	1995–2000
Anita Thigpen Perry	2000–2015
Cecilia Abbott	2015–present

State Government

Texas state government is divided into executive, legislative, and judicial branches under the Texas Constitution adopted in 1876.

The chief executive is the Governor, whose term is for four years. Other elected state officials with executive responsibilities include the Lieutenant Governor, Attorney General, Comptroller of Public Accounts, Commissioner of the General Land Office, and Commissioner of Agriculture. The terms of those officials are also four years.

The Secretary of State and the Commissioner of Education are appointed by the Governor.

Except for making numerous appointments and calling special sessions of the Legislature, the Governor's powers are limited in comparison with those in most states.

The Governor's office welcomes comments and concerns, which are relayed to government officials who may offer assistance. **Send a message through the webform at:**

https://gov.texas.gov/contact

Or call the **Citizen's Opinion Hotline:**

1 (800) 252-9600

State Government Income and Expenditures

Taxes are the state government's primary source of income. On this and the following pages are summaries of state income and expenditures, percent change from previous year, tax collections, tax revenue by type of tax, a summary of the state budgets for the 2018–2019 and 2020–2021 bienniums, Texas Lottery income and expenditures, and the amount of federal payments to state agencies. **Totals may not sum due to rounding.**

State Revenues by Source and Expenditures by Function

Amounts (in $ Millions) and Percent Change from Previous Year

Revenues by Source	2020	%	2019	%	2018	%	2017	%	2016	%
Tax Collections	57,380	-3.4	59,381	6.8	55,585	12	49,643	2.4	48,476	-6.2
Federal Income	58,117	38.7	41,904	5.8	39,618	3.3	38,366	-2.8	39,474	7.6
Licenses, Fees, Permits, Fines, and Penalties	6,241	-4.6	6,542	1.0	6,477	3.5	6,258	2.1	6,128	1.5
State Health Service Fees and Rebates	7,497	5.8	7,088	-6.7	7,599	13.4	6,702	201.9	8,071	32.8
Net Lottery Proceeds	2,392	-4.7	2,510	12.6	2,229	8.5	2,053	80.2	2,220	17.2
Land Income	1,809	-19.6	2,251	9.2	2,061	21.6	1,694	48.7	1,140	-26.4
Interest and Investment Income	2,529	1.0	2,504	35.4	1,849	9.3	1,691	24.1	1,362	-2.2
Settlements of Claims	624	-3.4	647	18.8	544	3.2	528	-19.1	652	20.5
Escheated Estates	715	3.2	693	9.0	636	-35	979	78.5	548	0.0
Sales of Goods and Services	255	-8.6	279	-2.2	285	-7.5	308	5.2	293	-36.1
Other Revenues	4,016	-3.0	4,142	26.2	3,282	10.4	2,973	1.9	2,918	13.2
Total Net Revenues	**141,576**	**10.7**	**127,941**	**6.5**	**120,166**	**8.1**	**111,195**	**-0.1**	**111,280**	**1.7**
Expenditures by Function	**2020**	**%**	**2019**	**%**	**2018**	**%**	**2017**	**%**	**2016**	**%**
Executive	3,165	4.2	3,038	5.4	2,883	3.6	2,783	7.1	2,599	5.5
Legislative	139	-8.0	151	8.4	139	-7.3	150	8.2	138	-2.5
Judicial	411	23	334	-7.9	362	4.8	346	3.6	333	5.0
General Government Total	3,714	5.4	3,522	4.1	3,384	3.2	3,279	6.8	3,071	5.1
Education	42,869	13.9	37,653	2.4	36,783	3.6	35,505	-1.3	35,964	3.4
Employee Benefits	4,972	0.2	4,961	4.2	4,760	0.1	4,755	5.6	4,502	11.2
Health and Human Services	57,197	10.3	51,873	2.9	50,421	2.7	49,075	-3.3	50,734	9.6
Public Safety and Corrections	4,877	-6.1	5,193	-3.4	5,375	9.1	4,928	2.0	4,829	5.8
Transportation	12,647	20.5	10,494	5.5	9,952	-3	10,261	6.8	9,608	12.9
Natural Resources/Recreational Services	3,116	10.8	2,812	2.4	2,746	34.2	2,046	-28.2	2,847	9.5
Regulatory Agencies	331	-1.5	336	7.5	312	-10.7	350	-42.8	611	26.4
Lottery Winnings Paid*	541	-20.9	684	9.0	628	12.7	557	-17.2	672	21.4
Debt Service – Interest	1,661	1.0	1,645	3.3	1,593	26.8	1,256	11.4	1,127	-4.2
Capital Outlay	1,192	40.2	851	42.1	599	-2.4	614	2.4	599	44.7
Total Net Expenditures	**133,118**	**10.9**	**120,025**	**3.0**	**116,554**	**3.5**	**112,625**	**-1.7**	**114,570**	**7.7**

* Does not include payments made by retailers.

All amounts rounded. Revenue and expenditures exclude trust funds. Fiscal years end August 31.

Source: 2020 State of Texas Annual Cash Report, Revenue and Expenditures of State Funds for the Year Ending August 31, 2021, Comptroller of Public Accounts' Office.

Governor Greg Abbott
P.O. Box 12428
Austin 78711
(512) 463-2000
gov.texas.gov/
Salary: $153,750

Lt. Governor Dan Patrick
P.O. Box 12068
Austin 78711
(512) 463-0001
www.ltgov.texas.gov/
Salary: Same as Senator when serving as President of the Senate, same as Governor when serving as Governor.

Attorney General
Ken Paxton
P.O. Box 12548
Austin 78711
(512) 463-2100
www.texasattorneygeneral.gov/
Salary: $153,750

Comptroller of Public
Accounts Glenn Hegar
P.O. Box 13528
Austin 78711
(512) 463-4600
comptroller.texas.gov/
Salary: $153,750

Texas Land Commissioner
George P. Bush
P.O. Box 12873
Austin 78711
(512) 463-5256
www.glo.texas.gov
Salary: $140,938

Agriculture Commissioner
Sidney C. Miller
P.O. Box 12847
Austin 78711
(512) 463-7476
www.texasagriculture.gov
Salary: $140,938

Secretary of State
Vacant
P.O. Box 12697
Austin 78711
(512) 463-5770
www.sos.state.tx.us
Salary: $132,924

Education Commissioner
Michael H. Morath
1701 N. Congress Ave.
Austin 78701
(512) 463-8985
tea.texas.gov/
Salary: $220,375

State Government Budget Summary, 2022–2023 Biennium

Source: Legislative Budget Board; www.lbb.state.tx.us.

The Legislative Budget Board's (LBB) baseline appropriations for state government operations for the 2022–2023 biennium total $248.5 billion from All Funds functions of state government. The funding is a $13.5 billion, or 5.2 percent, decrease from the 2020–2021 biennial level of $262.1 billion.

General Revenue Funds, including funds dedicated within the General Revenue Fund, total $116.4 billion for the 2022–2023 biennium, an increase of $6.1 billion, or 5.5 percent, from the adjusted 2020–2021 biennial spending level of $110.3 billion. The table below details the difference in spending by article.

General Revenue Funds, by Article

Article (Governmental Division)	Estimated/ Budgeted 2020–2021	2022–2023 Budget	Biennial Change	Percentage Change
Art. I: General Government	$3,977.4	$4,064.3	$86.9	2.2
Art. II: Health and Human Services	$33,629.6	$34,291.4	$661.8	2.0
Art. III: Agencies of Education	$60,402.8	$62,745.1	$2,342.3	3.9
Public Education	$44,561.5	$46,551.3	$1,989.8	4.5
Higher Education	$15,841.3	$16,193.8	$352.5	2.2
Art. IV: The Judiciary	$553.8	$551.6	–$2.3	–0.4
Art. V: Public Safety & Criminal Justice	$11,869.5	$12,055.0	$185.5	1.6
Art. VI: Natural Resources	$933.1	$1,002.1	$69.00	7.4
Art. VII: Business & Economic Dev.	$520.9	$490.1	–$30.8	–5.9
Art. VIII: Regulatory	$367.8	$301.7	–$66.1	–18.0
Art. IX: General Provisions		$456.8		
Art. X: The Legislature	$408.1	$410.2	$2.1	0.5
House Bill 2	–2,393.4			
Total, All Articles	**$110,269.6**	**$116,368.2**	**$6,098.60**	**5.5**

All figures in millions.

Source: Summary of Conference Committee Report For Senate Bill 1: Appropriations for the 2022–23 Biennium May 2021.

State Tax Collections 2002–2020

FY	State Tax Collections (in millions)	Resident Population	Per Capita Tax Collections	Taxes as % of Personal Income
2020	$57,379.8	29,293,475	$1,959	3.6
2019	$59,380.7	28,950,175	$2,051	4.1
2018	$55,584.8	28,668,600	$1,939	4.0
2017	$49,643.4	28,255,300	$1,757	3.8
2016	$48,476.2	27,845,500	$1,741	3.8
2015	$51,683.1	27,389,200	$1,887	4.0
2014	$50,992.6	26,788,600	$1,896	4.3
2013	$47,781.0	26,399,510	$1,810	4.2
2012	$44,079.1	26,005,770	$1,695	4.0
2011	$38,856.2	25,592,790	$1,518	3.8
2010	$35,368.9	25,191,450	$1,404	3.7
2009	$37,822.5	24,737,000	$1,529	4.1
2008	$41,357.9	24,250,000	$1,705	4.3
2007	$36,955.6	23,778,000	$1,554	4.3
2006	$33,544.5	23,339,000	$1,437	4.1
2005	$29,838.3	22,808,000	$1,308	4.0
2004	$27,913.0	22,409,000	$1,246	4.1
2003	$26,126.7	22,052,000	$1,185	4.1
2002	$26,279.1	21,673,000	$1,213	4.2

Sources: 2020 State of Texas Annual Cash Report; historic data collected from older reports.

Tax Revenues, 2019–2020

Type of Tax	FY 2019	% Change	FY 2020	% Change
Sales	$34,023.9	6.5	$34,099.1	0.2
Motor Vehicle Sales/Rentals*	$5,010.5	0.7	$4,815.2	-3.9
Motor Fuels	$3,743.0	1.9	$3,524.7	-5.8
Franchise	$4,217.8	14.4	$4,418.4	4.8
Oil Production	$3,886.8	14.6	$3,229.4	-16.9
Insurance	$2,599.0	3.6	$2,741.7	5.5
Cigarette & Tobacco	$1,410.3	6.8	$1,299.0	-7.9
Natural Gas Production	$1,685.7	17.8	$925.5	-45.1
Alcoholic Beverages	$1,369.4	6.0	$1,125.3	-17.8
Hotel	$636.1	5.8	$470.7	-26.0
Utility	$471.4	4.2	$478.2	1.4
Other Taxes	$326.5	3.4	$252.7	-22.6
Total	**$59,380.7**	**6.8**	**$57,379.8**	**-3.4**

All figures in millions.
*Includes tax on manufactured housing sales.

Source: 2020 State of Texas Annual Cash Report.

Federal Revenue by Agency

Texas received $58.1 billion in federal funds during fiscal 2020, an increase of $16.2 billion, or 38.7 percent from fiscal 2019. Federal funds accounted for 41.0 percent of total net revenue, the largest source of revenue in fiscal 2020.

	2017	2018	2019	2020
Health and Human Services	$24,418.8	$25,483.4	$27,279.5	$32,103.8
Governor – Fiscal	$179.7	$223.6	$310.5	$8,710.9
Texas Education Agency	$5,074.6	$5,168.8	$5,608.0	$5,226.7
Texas Dept. of Transportation	$4,250.5	$3,875.2	$4,026.4	$5,217.4
Texas Workforce Commission	$1,235.2	$1,296.9	$1,427.9	$2,384.8
General Land Office	$287.9	$341.0	$413.0	$925.8
Dept. of Agriculture	$580.6	$611.3	$638.6	$742.0
Texas Division of Emergency Management	–	–	–	$625.3
Dept. of Family and Protective Services	$447.5	$446.3	$491.7	$526.7
All other Agencies	$1,890.8	$2,171.9	$1,708.8	$1,653.4
Total	$38,365.6	$39,618.6	$41,904.5	$58,116.8

Totals may not sum due to rounding. All figures in millions.

Source: 2020 State of Texas Annual Cash Report

Texas Lottery

Source: Texas Lottery Commission; www.txlottery.org/

The State Lottery Act was passed by the Texas Legislature in July 1991. Texas voters approved a constitutional amendment authorizing a state lottery in an election on Nov. 5, 1991, by a vote of 1,326,154 to 728,994. Since the first ticket was sold on May 29, 1992, the Texas Lottery® has generated more than $115 billion in total sales and more than $33 billion in revenue for the state. More than $70 billion in prizes have been distributed to players through June 2021.

Since 1997, the Texas Lottery has contributed more than $23 billion to the Foundation School Fund, which supports public education. Before September 1997, revenues were only deposited in the General Revenue Fund.

As authorized by the state Legislature, certain Texas Lottery revenues have been earmarked to benefit state programs, including the Fund for Veterans Assistance, which is administered by the Texas Veterans Commission. Sales and unclaimed prizes from the veterans' designated scratch-off games have totaled $162.6 million since 2010.

Other Texas Lottery funds, such as unclaimed prizes, contribute to other causes and programs as authorized by the Texas Legislature.

Distribution of Texas Lottery proceeds for fiscal year 2020:

- 66.3 percent to prizes paid
- 37.4 percent to the Foundation School Fund
- 7.5 percent to retailer commissions
- 5.2 percent for lottery administration
- 0.5 percent to the Texas Veterans Commission. ☆

Texas Lottery Financial Data

Start-up to Aug. 31, 2020. All amounts in millions.

Period	Sales	Value of Prizes Won	Retailer Comm-issions	Revenue to State of Texas*
Start-up – FY 1992	$591.6	$268.9	$29.6	$250.0
FY 1993	$1,856.1	$981.7	$92.8	$656.8
FY 1994	$2,760.2	$1,528.7	$138.0	$927.7
FY 1995	$3,036.5	$1,689.3	$151.8	$1,015.0
FY 1996	$3,432.3	$1,951.1	$171.7	$1,098.3
FY 1997	$3,745.5	$2,151.7	$187.4	$1,182.8
FY 1998	$3,090.0	$1,648.1	$154.6	$1,097.8
FY 1999	$2,571.6	$1,329.0	$128.8	$953.4
FY 2000	$2,657.3	$1,508.8	$133.0	$862.8
FY 2001	$2,825.3	$1,643.2	$141.3	$864.0
FY 2002	$2,966.3	$1,715.4	$148.4	$928.9
FY 2003	$3,130.7	$1,845.2	$156.6	$949.1
FY 2004	$3,487.9	$2,068.6	$174.4	$1,051.0
FY 2005	$3,662.5	$2,228.0	$183.2	$1,070.3
FY 2006	$3,774.7	$2,310.6	$188.8	$1,090.3
FY 2007	$3,774.2	$2,315.3	$188.8	$1,093.0
FY 2008	$3,671.5	$2,281.1	$183.8	$1,034.9
FY 2009	$3,720.1	$2,299.8	$186.1	$1,062.2
FY 2010	$3,738.4	$2,300.2	$187.3	$1,063.1
FY 2011	$3,811.3	$2,387.2	$190.8	$1,023.8
FY 2012	$4,190.8	$2,632.6	$209.8	$1,155.5
FY 2013	$4,376.3	$2,767.4	$218.9	$1,214.1
FY 2014	$4,384.6	$2,741.2	$219.5	$1,220.7
FY 2015	$4,529.7	$2,858.3	$226.7	$1,242.7
FY 2016	$5,067.5	$3,186.4	$253.5	$1,392.3
FY 2017	$5,077.5	$3,257.4	$253.9	$1,334.0
FY 2018	$5,626.8	$3,666.1	$281.5	$1,450.5
FY 2019	$6,251.5	$4,056.5	$313.1	$1,636.6
FY 2020	$6,704.0	$4,442.4	$335.6	$1,683.7
Total	**$108,512.7**	**$66,060.2**	**$5,429.7**	**$31,605.3**

*Revenue to the state presented on an accrual basis.

Muenster Senator Drew Springer with Secretary of the Senate Patsy Spaw. Senate Media Photo.

Texas Legislature

The Texas Legislature has **181 members: 31 in the Senate** and **150 in the House of Representatives**. Regular sessions convene on the second Tuesday of January in odd-numbered years, but the governor may call special sessions. Article III of the Texas Constitution deals with the legislative branch. On the web: **capitol.texas.gov**

The following lists are of members of the **87th Legislature**, which convened for its Regular Session on Jan. 12, 2021, and adjourned on May 31, 2021. The **88th Legislature** is scheduled to convene on Jan. 10, 2023, and adjourn May 29, 2023.

State Senate

Thirty-one members of the State Senate are elected to four-year, overlapping terms. Salary: The salary of all members of the Legislature, both Senators and Representatives, is $7,200 per year and $124 per diem during legislative sessions; mileage allowance at same rate provided by law for state employees. The per diem payment applies during each regular and special session of the Legislature.

Senatorial Districts include one or more whole counties; some counties have more than one Senator.

The **address of Senators** is Texas Senate, P.O. Box 12068, Austin 78711-2068; phone (512) 463-0200; Fax: (512) 463-0326. On the web: senate.texas.gov.

President of the Senate: Lt. Gov. Dan Patrick; **President Pro Tempore**: Brian Birdwell (R-Granbury); **Secretary of the Senate**: Patsy Spaw; **Sergeant-at-Arms**: Rick DeLeon.

Texas State Senators

District, Member, Party-Hometown, Occupation

1. Bryan Hughes, R-Mineola; attorney.
2. Bob Hall, R-Edgewood; retired military.
3. Robert Nichols, R-Jacksonville; engineer.
4. Brandon Creighton, R-Conroe; attorney.
5. Charles Schwertner, R-Georgetown; surgeon.
6. Carol Alvarado, D-Houston; small-business owner.
7. Paul Bettencourt, R-Houston; tax advisor.
8. Angela Paxton, R-McKinney; consultant, former educator.
9. Kelly G. Hancock, R-North Richland Hills; business owner.
10. Beverly Powell, D-Burleson; education advocate.
11. Larry Taylor, R-Friendswood; insurance agent.
12. Jane Nelson, R-Flower Mound; businesswoman.
13. Borris L. Miles, D-Houston; insurance and real estate developer.
14. Sarah Eckhardt, D-Austin; attorney.
15. John Whitmire, D-Houston; attorney.
16. Nathan Johnson, D-Dallas; attorney.
17. Joan Huffman, R-Houston; attorney.
18. Lois W. Kolkhorst, R-Brenham; business owner.
19. Roland Gutierrez, D-San Antonio; attorney.
20. Juan (Chuy) Hinojosa, D-McAllen; attorney.
21. Judith Zaffirini, D-Laredo; communications specialist, former educator.
22. Brian Birdwell, R-Granbury; retired military.
23. Royce West, D-Dallas; attorney.
24. Dawn Buckingham, R-Lakeway; physician.
25. Donna Campbell, R-New Braunfels; physician.
26. José Menéndez, D-San Antonio; businessman.
27. Eddie Lucio Jr., D-Brownsville; advertising executive.
28. Charles Perry, R-Lubbock; certified public accountant.
29. César Blanco, D-El Paso; consultant.
30. Drew Springer, R-Muenster; financial services.
31. Kel Seliger, R-Amarillo; business owner.

House of Representatives

This is a list of the current members of the House of Representatives. They were elected for two-year terms from the districts shown below. Representatives and senators receive the same salary.

The **address of all Representatives** is House of Representatives, P.O. Box 2910, Austin, 78768-2910; phone: (512) 463-1000; Fax: (512) 463-5896. On the web: house.texas.gov

Speaker, Dade Phelan (R-Beaumont). **Chief Clerk**, Robert Haney. **Sergeant-at-Arms**, Michael Black.

Texas State Representatives

District, Member, Party-Hometown, Occupation

1. Gary VanDeaver, R-New Boston; educator, retired.
2. Bryan Slaton, R-Royse City; business owner.
3. Cecil Bell, Jr., R-Magnolia; contractor.
4. Keith Bell, R-Forney; electrical contractor.
5. Cole Hefner, R-Mount Pleasant; insurance agent.
6. Matt Schaefer, R-Tyler; attorney.
7. Jay Dean, R-Longview; self-employed.
8. Cody Harris, R-Palestine; ranch broker.
9. Chris Paddie, R-Marshall; general manager.
10. Vacant.
11. Travis Clardy, R-Nacogdoches; attorney.
12. Kyle Kacal, R-College Station; rancher.
13. Ben Leman, R-Anderson; business, rancher.
14. John Raney, R-College Station; bookstore owner.
15. Steve Toth, R-The Woodlands; business owner.
16. Will Metcalf, R-Conroe; banker.
17. John Cyrier, R-Lockhart; general contractor.
18. Ernest Bailes IV, R-Shepherd; self-employed.
19. James White, R-Hillister; educator, rancher.
20. Terry M. Wilson, R-Marble Falls; military, retired.
21. Dade Phelan, R-Beaumont; real estate developer.
22. Joe Deshotel, D-Beaumont; attorney, contractor.
23. Mayes Middleton, R-Wallisville; oil & gas.
24. Greg Bonnen, R-Friendswood; neurosurgeon.
25. Cody Vasut, R-Angleton; attorney.
26. Jacey Jetton, R-Sugar Land; business owner.
27. Ron Reynolds, D-Missouri City; attorney.
28. Gary Gates, R-Richmond; real estate investor.
29. Ed Thompson, R-Pearland; insurance agent.
30. Geanie W. Morrison, R-Victoria; state representative.
31. Ryan Guillen, D-Rio Grande City; investor.
32. Todd Hunter, R-Corpus Christi; attorney.
33. Justin Holland, R-Heath; real estate broker.
34. Abel Herrero, D-Robstown; attorney.
35. Oscar Longoria, D-Peñitas; attorney.
36. Sergio Muñoz, Jr., D-Palmview; attorney.
37. Alex Dominguez, D-Brownsville; attorney.
38. Eddie Lucio III, D-Brownsville; attorney.
39. Armando Martinez, D-Weslaco; attorney.
40. Terry Canales, D-Edinburg; attorney.
41. R.D. "Bobby" Guerra, D-Mission; attorney.
42. Richard Peña Raymond, D-Laredo; mediator.
43. J. M. Lozano, R-Kingsville; business.
44. John Kuempel, R-Seguin; salesman.
45. Erin Zwiener, D-Driftwood; writer.
46. Sheryl Cole, D-Austin; lawyer, CPA.
47. Vikki Goodwin, D-Austin; real estate broker.
48. Donna Howard, D-Austin; community advocate.
49. Gina Hinojosa, D-Austin; attorney.
50. Celia Israel, D-Austin; realtor.
51. Eddie Rodriguez, D-Austin; business development consultant.
52. James Talarico, D-Round Rock; nonprofit director.
53. Andrew Murr, R-Junction; attorney, rancher.
54. Brad Buckley, R-Salado; veterinarian.
55. Hugh Shine, R-Temple; financial advisor.
56. Charles "Doc" Anderson, R-Waco; veterinarian.
57. Trent Ashby, R-Lufkin; title insurance executive.
58. DeWayne Burns, R-Cleburne; investor, farmer, rancher.
59. Shelby Slawson, R-Stephenville; attorney, entrepreneur, small-business owner.
60. Glenn Rogers, R-Graford; rancher.
61. Phil King, R-Weatherford; attorney.
62. Reggie Smith, R-Van Alstyne; attorney.
63. Tan Parker, R-Flower Mound; business consultant.
64. Lynn Stucky, R-Denton; veterinarian.
65. Michelle Beckley, D-Carrollton; business owner.
66. Matt Shaheen, R-Plano; technology executive.
67. Jeff Leach, R-Plano; attorney.
68. David Spiller, R-Jacksboro; attorney.
69. James B. Frank, R-Wichita Falls; business owner.
70. Scott Sanford, R-McKinney; minister.
71. Stan Lambert, R-Abilene; banker, retired.
72. Drew Darby, R-San Angelo; attorney, business.
73. Kyle Biedermann, R-Fredericksburg; business owner.
74. Eddie Morales, D-Eagle Pass; attorney.
75. Mary González, D-Clint; consultant.
76. Claudia Ordaz Perez, D-El Paso
77. Lina Ortega, D-El Paso; attorney.
78. Joe Moody, D-El Paso; attorney.
79. Art Fierro, D-El Paso.
80. Tracy King, D-Batesville; business.
81. Brooks Landgraf, R-Odessa; attorney, rancher.
82. Tom Craddick, R-Midland; business development manager.
83. Dustin Burrows, R-Lubbock; attorney.
84. John Frullo, R-Lubbock; small-business owner.
85. Phil Stephenson, R-Wharton; CPA.

86. John Smithee, R-Amarillo; attorney.
87. Four Price, R-Amarillo; attorney.
88. Ken King, R-Canadian; oil & gas service executive.
89. Candy Noble, R-Lucas.
90. Ramón Romero, Jr., D-Fort Worth; CEO.
91. Stephanie Klick, R-Fort Worth; registered nurse.
92. Jeff Cason, R-Bedford.
93. Matt Krause, R-Fort Worth; attorney.
94. Tony Tinderholt, R-Arlington; retired.
95. Nicole Collier, D-Fort Worth; attorney.
96. David Cook, R-Mansfield; attorney.
97. Craig Goldman, R-Fort Worth; real estate, finance.
98. Giovanni Capriglione, R-Southlake; finance.
99. Charlie Geren, R-River Oaks; restaurant owner and rancher.
100. Jasmine Crockett, D-Dallas; attorney.
101. Chris Turner, D-Grand Prairie; communications.
102. Ana-Maria Ramos, D-Richardson; attorney, professor.
103. Rafael Anchía, D-Dallas; attorney.
104. Jessica González, D-Dallas; attorney.
105. Terry Meza, D-Irving; attorney.
106. Jared Patterson, R-Frisco; energy management.
107. Victoria Neave, D-Dallas; attorney.
108. Morgan Meyer, R-Dallas; attorney.
109. Carl Sherman, Sr., D-DeSoto; pastor, business.
110. Toni Rose, D-Dallas; mental health liaison.
111. Yvonne Davis, D-Dallas; small-business owner.
112. Angie Chen Button, R-Richardson; marketing.
113. Rhetta Bowers, D-Rowlett; educator.
114. John Turner, D-Dallas; attorney.
115. Julie Johnson, D-Farmers Branch; attorney.
116. Trey Martinez Fischer, D-San Antonio; contractor.
117. Philip Cortez, D-San Antonio; public relations.
118. Leo Pacheco, D-San Antonio; human resources.
119. Liz Campos, D-San Antonio; self-employed.
120. Barbara Gervin-Hawkins, D-San Antonio; education.
121. Steve Allison, R-San Antonio; attorney.
122. Lyle Larson, R-San Antonio; self-employed.
123. Diego Bernal, D-San Antonio; attorney.
124. Ina Minjarez, D-San Antonio; attorney.
125. Ray Lopez, D-San Antonio.
126. Sam Harless, R-Spring; automobile dealer.
127. Dan Huberty, R-Kingwood; finance.
128. Briscoe Cain, R-Deer Park; attorney.
129. Dennis Paul, R-Houston; engineer.
130. Tom Oliverson, R-Cypress; anesthesiologist.
131. Alma Allen, D-Houston; educational consultant.
132. Mike Schofield, R-Katy; attorney.
133. Jim Murphy, R-Houston; consultant.
134. Ann Johnson, D-Houston; attorney.
135. Jon Rosenthal, D-Houston; engineer.
136. John Bucy, III, D-Austin; education.
137. Gene Wu, D-Houston; attorney.
138. Lacy Hull, R-Houston.
139. Jarvis Johnson, D-Houston; business owner.
140. Armando Walle, D-Houston; legal assistant.
141. Senfronia Thompson, D-Houston; attorney.
142. Harold Dutton, Jr., D-Houston; attorney.
143. Ana Hernandez, D-Houston; attorney.
144. Mary Ann Perez, D-Houston; insurance agent.
145. Christina Morales, D-Houston; funeral director.
146. Shawn Thierry, D-Houston; attorney.
147. Garnet Coleman, D-Houston; business consulting.
148. Penny Morales Shaw, D-Houston; attorney.
149. Hubert Vo, D-Houston; business.
150. Valoree Swanson, R-Spring; business.☆

Texas State House of Representatives 2021–2022

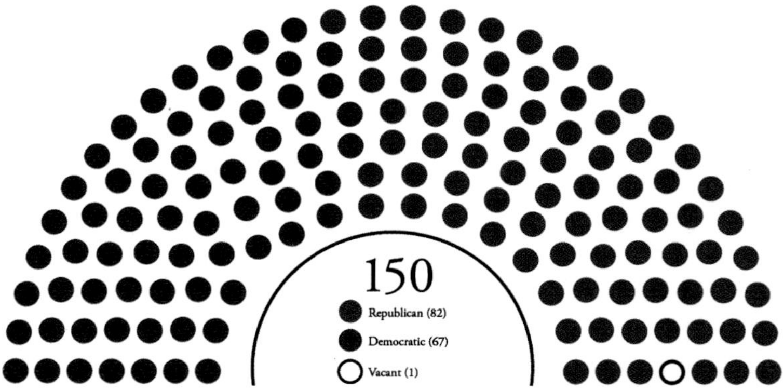

The current Supreme Court with only eight members. In the top row, left to right: Justice Rebecca Huddle, Justice J. Brett Busby, Justice John Phillip Devine, Justice James Blacklock, Justice Jane Bland. Bottom row, left to right: Justice Debra Lehrmann, Chief Justice Nathan Hecht, and Justice Jeffrey Boyd. Photo by Ostler McCarthy.

Texas State Judiciary

The judiciary of the state consists of nine justices of the Supreme Court of Texas; nine judges of the Court of Criminal Appeals; 80 justices of the 14 Courts of Appeals; 459 judges of the State District Courts; 13 judges of the Criminal District Courts; 527 County Court judges; 805 Justice Court judges; and more than 1,200 Municipal Court judges in 944 cities.

Since 1876, judges at all levels are elected by voters in partisan elections. The Judicial Campaign Fairness Act was added to the Texas Election Code in 1995 by the 74th Legislature and limits individual campaign contributions to $5,000 for a statewide judicial office and $1,000–$5,000 for other judicial offices, depending on judicial district population. The exception is law firms, for which a $50 limit is set.

In addition to its system of formal courts, the State of Texas has established 18 **Alternative Dispute Resolution Centers**. The centers are headed by a director and help ease the caseload of Texas courts by using mediation, arbitration, negotiation, and moderated settlement conferences to handle disputes.

Centers are located in Amarillo, Austin, Beaumont, Bryan–College Station, Conroe, Corpus Christi, Dallas, Denton, El Paso, Fort Worth, Houston, Kerrville, Lubbock, Paris, Richmond, San Antonio, San Marcos, and Waco.

(The list of U.S. District Courts in Texas can be found in the Federal Government section, page 519.)

State Higher Courts

The state's higher courts include the Supreme Court, the Court of Criminal Appeals, the Courts of Appeals, and District Courts. Justices of the Supreme Court, Court of Criminal Appeals, and Courts of Appeals are elected to six-year, overlapping terms. District Court judges are elected to four-year terms.

Base judicial salaries as set by the 86th Legislature are: Supreme Court and Court of Criminal Appeals chief justices, $170,500, justices, $168,000; Court of Appeals chief justices, $156,500; justices, $154,000. Court of Appeals justices also may receive additional compensation paid by counties for extra judicial service, not to exceed $9,000 per year.

District Court judges receive $140,000 from the state. They may receive additional compensation paid by counties, not to exceed $18,000 per year.

The justices listed below are current as of August 2021. Notations in parentheses are term of office expiration dates. Elsewhere in this section are lists of District Court judges by district number, district court numbers in each county, and county court judges.

Supreme Court

Chief Justice, Nathan L. Hecht (12/31/26). **Justices**: J. Brett Busby (12/31/26); Jeffrey S. Boyd (12/31/26); Debra H. Lehrmann (12/31/22); John Phillip Devine (12/31/24); James D. "Jimmy" Blacklock (12/31/24); Jane Bland (12/31/24) and Rebecca Huddle (12/31/22). The ninth seat is vacant as of press time.

Clerk of Court, Blake A. Hawthorne. Location of court, Austin. Web: **txcourts.gov/supreme.**

Court of Criminal Appeals

Presiding Judge, Sharon Keller (12/31/24). **Judges**: Bert Richardson (12/31/26); Kevin Yeary (12/31/26); David Newell (12/31/26); Jesse F. McClure III (12/31/22); Mary Lou Keel (12/31/22), Scott Walker (12/31/22); Barbara Parker Hervey (12/31/24); and Michelle Slaughter (12/31/24). State Prosecuting Attorney, Stacey M. Soule.

Clerk of Court, Deanna Williamson. Location of court, Austin. Web: **http://www.txcourts.gov/cca.**

Courts of Appeals

These courts have jurisdiction within their respective supreme judicial districts. A constitutional amendment approved in 1978 raised the number of associate justices for Courts of Appeals where needed. Judges are elected from the district for six-year terms. An amendment adopted in 1980 changed the name of the old Courts of Civil Appeals to the Courts of Appeals and changed the jurisdiction of the courts. Terms end on 12/31 of the year in parentheses.

First District, Houston:* **Chief Justice** Sherry Radack (2022). **Justices**: Gordon Goodman (2024); Sarah Beth Landau (2024); Julie Countiss (2024); Richard Hightower (2024); Peter M. Kelley (2024); Veronica Rivas-Malloy (2026); and Amparo M. Guerra (2026). **Clerk of Court**, Christopher A. Prine. **Counties in the First District:** Austin, Brazoria, Chambers, Colorado, Fort Bend, Galveston, Grimes, Harris, Waller, Washington.

Second District, Fort Worth: Chief Justice: Bonnie Sudderth (2024). **Justices**: Dana Womack (2026); Elizabeth Kerr (2022); J. Wade Birdwell (2024); Dabney Bassel (2024); Mike Wallach (2024); and Brian Walker (2026). **Clerk of Court**, Debra Spisak. **Counties in the Second District:** Archer, Clay, Cooke, Denton, Hood, Jack, Montague, Parker, Tarrant, Wichita, Wise, Young.

Third District, Austin: Chief Justice Darlene Byrne (2026). **Justices**: Edward Smith (2024); Chari L. Kelly (2024); Melissa Goodwin (2022); Thomas Baker (2024); and Gisela Triana (2024). **Clerk of Court**, Jeffrey D. Kyle. **Counties in the Third District:** Bastrop, Bell, Blanco, Burnet, Caldwell, Coke, Comal, Concho, Fayette, Hays, Irion, Lampasas, Lee, Llano, McCulloch, Milam, Mills, Runnels, San Saba, Schleicher, Sterling, Tom Green, Travis, Williamson.

Fourth District, San Antonio: Chief Justice Rebeca C. Martinez (2026). **Justices**: Beth Watkins (2024); Patricia O'Connel Alvarez (2024); Luz Elena Chapa (2024); Liza Rodriguez (2024); Irene Alarcon Rios (2020); and Lori I. Valenzuela (2026). **Clerk of Court**, Keith E. Hottle. **Counties in the Fourth District:** Atascosa, Bandera, Bexar, Brooks, Dimmit, Duval, Edwards, Frio, Gillespie, Guadalupe, Jim Hogg, Jim Wells, Karnes, Kendall, Kerr, Kimble, Kinney, La Salle, Mason, Maverick, McMullen, Medina, Menard, Real, Starr, Sutton, Uvalde, Val Verde, Webb, Wilson, Zapata, Zavala.

Fifth District, Dallas: Chief Justice Robert D. Burns, III (2024). **Justices**: Robbie Partida-Kipness (2024); Lana Myers (2022); Erin Nowell (2024); David Schenck (2022); Bill Pedersen, III (2024); Amanda Reichek (2024); Cory Carlyle (2024); Ken Molberg (2024); Leslie L. Osborne (2024); Craig Smith (2026); Bonnie Lee Goldstein (2026); and Dennise Garcia (2026). **Clerk of Court**, Lisa Matz. **Counties in the Fifth District:** Collin, Dallas, Grayson, Hunt, Kaufman, Rockwall.

Sixth District, Texarkana: Chief Justice Josh R. Morris, III (2020). **Justices**: Scott Stevens (2024) and Ralph K. Burgess (2026). **Clerk of Court**, Debbie Autrey. **Counties in the Sixth District:** Bowie, Camp, Cass, Delta, Fannin, Franklin, Gregg, Harrison, Hopkins, Hunt, Lamar, Marion, Morris, Panola, Red River, Rusk, Titus, Upshur, Wood.

Seventh District, Amarillo: Chief Justice Brian P. Quinn (2026). **Justices**: Judy Parker (2024); Patrick A. Pirtle (2024); and Larry Doss (2022). **Clerk of Court**, Bobby Ramirez. **Counties in the Seventh District:** Armstrong, Bailey, Briscoe, Carson, Castro, Childress, Cochran, Collingsworth, Cottle, Crosby, Dallam, Deaf Smith, Dickens, Donley, Floyd, Foard, Garza, Gray, Hale, Hall, Hansford, Hardeman, Hartley, Hemphill, Hockley, Hutchinson, Kent, King, Lamb, Lipscomb, Lubbock, Lynn, Moore, Motley, Ochiltree, Oldham, Parmer, Potter, Randall, Roberts, Sherman, Swisher, Terry, Wheeler, Wilbarger, Yoakum.

Eighth District, El Paso: Chief Justice Yvonne Rodriguez (2022). **Justices**: Jeff Alley (2022) and Gina Palafox (2022). **Clerk of Court**, Elizabeth G. Flores. **Counties in the Eighth District:** Andrews, Brewster, Crane, Crockett, Culberson, El Paso, Hudspeth, Jeff Davis, Loving, Pecos, Presidio, Reagan, Reeves, Terrell, Upton, Ward, Winkler.

Ninth District, Beaumont: Chief Justice Scott Golemon (2026). **Justices**: Charles Kreger (2022); Leanne Johnson (2024); and Hollis Horton (2024). **Clerk of Court**, Carol Harley. **Counties in the Ninth District:** Hardin, Jasper, Jefferson, Liberty, Montgomery, Newton, Orange, Polk, San Jacinto, Tyler.

Tenth District, Waco: Chief Justice Thomas W. Gray (2024). **Justices**: Matt Johnson (2026) and John Neill. (2024). **Clerk of Court**, Nita Whitener. **Counties in the Tenth District:** Bosque, Brazos, Burleson, Coryell, Ellis, Falls, Freestone, Hamilton, Hill, Johnson, Leon, Limestone, Madison, McLennan, Navarro, Robertson, Somervell, Walker.

Eleventh District, Eastland: Chief Justice John Bailey (2024). **Justices**: W. Stacy Trotter (2022) and Bruce Williams (2026). **Clerk of Court**, Sherry Williamson. **Counties in the Eleventh District:** Baylor, Borden, Brown, Callahan, Coleman, Comanche, Dawson, Eastland, Ector, Erath, Fisher, Gaines, Glasscock, Haskell, Howard, Jones, Knox, Martin, Midland, Mitchell, Nolan, Palo Pinto, Scurry, Shackelford, Stephens, Stonewall, Taylor, Throckmorton.

Twelfth District, Tyler: Chief Justice James T. Worthen (2026). **Justices**: Brian Hoyle (2022) and Greg Neeley (2024). **Clerk of Court**, Katrina McClenny. **Counties in the Twelfth District:** Anderson, Angelina, Cherokee, Gregg, Henderson, Houston, Nacogdoches, Rains, Rusk, Sabine, San Augustine, Shelby, Smith, Trinity, Upshur, Van Zandt, Wood.

Thirteenth District, Corpus Christi: Chief Justice Dori Contreras (2024). **Justices**: Nora Longoria (2024); Leticia Hinojosa (2022); Jaime Tijerina (2024); Gina Benavides (2024); and Clarissa Silva (2026). **Clerk of Court**, Kathy S. Mills. **Counties in the Thirteenth District:** Aransas, Bee, Calhoun, Cameron, DeWitt, Goliad, Gonzales, Hidalgo, Jackson, Kenedy, Kleberg, Lavaca, Live Oak, Matagorda, Nueces, Refugio, San Patricio, Victoria, Wharton, Willacy.

Fourteenth District, Houston†: Chief Justice Tracy E, Christopher (2026). **Justices**: Kevin Jewell (2022); Jimmy Zimmerer (2024); Charles A. Spain (2024); Frances Bourliot (2024); Meagan Hassan (2024); Randy Wilson (2022); Margaret "Meg" Poissant (2024); and Kenneth Wise (2026). **Clerk of Court**, Christopher A. Prine. **Counties in the Fourteenth District:** Austin, Brazoria, Chambers, Colorado, Fort Bend, Galveston, Grimes, Harris, Waller, Washington.☆

*The location of the First Court of Appeals was changed from Galveston to Houston by the 55th Legislature, with the provision that all cases originated in Galveston County be tried in that city and with the further provision that any case may, at the discretion of the court, be tried in either city.

†Because of the heavy workload of the Houston-area Court of Appeals, the 60th Legislature in 1967 provided for the establishment of a Fourteenth Appeals Court in Houston.

District Judges in Texas

Sources: Texas Judicial Directory and Texas State Directory.

Below are the names of all district judges in Texas, as of July 2021, listed in district court order. To determine which judges have jurisdiction in specific counties, refer to the **Texas Courts by County** table, on pages 460–461.

Dist	Judge
1	Craig M. Mixson (R)
1-A	Delinda Gibbs-Walker (R)
2	Chris Day (R)
3	Mark A. Calhoon (R)
4	J. Clay Gossett (R)
5	Bill Miller (R)
6	Wes Tidwell (R)
7	Kerry L. Russell (R)
8	Eddie Northcutt (R)
9	Phil Grant (R)
10	Kerry Neves (R)
11	Kristen B. Hawkins (D)
12	David W. Moorman (R)
13	James Lagomarsino (R)
14	Eric V. Moyé (D)
15	Jim Fallon (R)
16	Sherry Shipman (R)
17	Melody Wilkinson (R)
18	Sydney B. Hewlett (R)
19	Thomas West (R)
20	John W. Youngblood (R)
21	Carson Campbell (R)
22	Bruce Boyer (R)
23	Ben Hardin (R)
24	Jack W. Marr (R)
25	William D. Old, III (R)
25-A	Jessica R. Crawford (R)
26	Donna King (R)
27	John Gauntt (R)
28	Nanette Hasette (D)
29	Michael Moore (R)
30	Jeff McKnight (R)
31	Steven R. Emmert (R)
32	Glen N. Harrison (R)
33	Allan Garrett (R)
34	William E. Moody (D)
35	Michael L. Smith (R)
36	Starr Bauer (R)
37	Nicole Garza (D)
38	Camile G. DuBose (R)
39	Shane Hadaway (R)
40	Bob Carroll (R)
41	Anna Perez (D)
42	James Eidson (R)
43	Craig Towson (R)
44	Ashley Wysocki (R)
45	Mary Lou Alvarez (D)
46	Dan Mike Bird (R)
47	Daniel L. Schaap (R)
48	David L. Evans (R)
49	Joe Lopez (D)
50	Jennifer A. Habert (R)
51	Carmen Symes Dusek (R)
52	Trent D. Farrell (R)
53	Maria Cantu Hexel (D)
54	Susan Kelly (R)
55	Latosha L. Payne (D)
56	Lonnie Cox (R)
57	Antonia Toni Arteaga (D)
58	Kent Walston (D)
59	Larry Phillips (R)
60	Justin Sanderson (D)
61	Fredericka Phillips (D)
62	Will Biard (R)
63	Roland Andrade (R)
64	Danah Zirpoli (R)
65	Yahara Lisa Gutierrez (D)
66	A. Lee Harris (R)
67	Donald J. Cosby (R)
68	Martin Hoffman (D)
69	Ron Enns (R)
70	Denn Whalen (R)
71	Brad Morin (R)
72	Ann-Marie Carruth (R)
73	David A. Canales (D)
74	Gary Coley (R)
75	Mark Morefield (R)
76	Angela Saucier (R)
77	Patrick Simmons (R)
78	Meredith Kennedy (R)
79	Richard Terrell (D)
80	Jeralynn Manor (D)
81	Lynn Ellison (R)
82	Bryan F. Rusty
83	Robert Cadena (R)
84	Curtis W. Brancheau (R)
85	Kyle Hawthorne (R)
86	Casey Blair (R)
87	Deborah Oakes Evans (R)
88	Earl Stover, III (R)
89	Charles M. Barnard (R)
90	Stephen Bristow (R)
91	Steven R. Herod (R)
92	Luis M. Singleterry (D)
93	Fernando Mancias (D)
94	Bobby Galvan (D)
95	Monica Purdy (D)
96	Joseph Patrick Pat Gallagher (R)
97	Jack McGaughey (R)
98	Rhonda Hurley (D)
99	Phillip Hays (R)
100	Stuart Messer (R)
101	Staci Williams (D)
102	Jeff M. Addison (R)
103	Janet Leal (D)
104	Jeff Propst (R)
105	Jack W. Pulcher (R)
106	Reed Filley (R)
107	Benjamin Euresti, Jr. (D)
108	Doug Woodburn (R)
109	John L. Pool (R)
110	William P. Smith (R)
111	Monica Zapata Notzon (D)
112	Pete Gomez, Jr. (D)
113	Rabeea Collier (D)
114	Austin Reeve Jackson (R)
115	Dean Fowler (R)
116	Tonya Parker (D)
117	Sandra Watts (D)
118	Timothy Yeats (R)
119	Ben Woodward (R)
120	Maria Salas-Mendoza (D)
121	John A. Trey Didway (R)
122	John Ellisor (R)
123	LeAnn Kay Rafferty (R)
124	F. Alfonso Charles (R)
125	Kyle Carter (D)
126	Aurora Martinez Jones (D)
127	R.K. Sandill (D)
128	Courtney Arkeen (R)
129	Michael Gomez (D)
130	Denise M. Fortenberry (R)
131	Norma Gonzales (D)
132	Ernie B. Armstrong (R)
133	Jaclanel McFarland (D)
134	Dale B. Tillery (D)
135	Stephen Williams (R)
136	Baylor Wortham (D)
137	John Trey McClendon (R)
138	Gabriela Gabby Garcia (D)
139	J. R. Bobby Flores (D)
140	Douglas H. Freitag (R)
141	John P. Chupp (R)
142	David G. Rogers (R)
143	Michael Swanson (R)
144	Michael Mery (D)
145	Jeff Davis (R)
146	Jack Jones (R)
147	Clifford A. Brown (D)
148	Carlos Valdez (D)
149	Terri Tipton Holder (R)
150	Monique Diaz (D)
151	Mike Engelhart (D)
152	Robert Schaffer (D)
153	Susan McCoy (R)
154	Felix Klein (R)
155	Jeff Steinhauser (R)
156	Patrick L. Flanigan (R)
157	Tanya Garrison (D)
158	Steve Burgess (R)
159	Paul E. White (R)
160	Aiesha Redmond (D)
161	Justin Low (R)
162	Maricela Moore (D)
163	Rex Wayne Peveto (R)
164	Cheryl E. Thornton (D)
165	Ursula A. Hall (D)
166	Laura Salinas (D)
167	Dayna Blazey (D)
168	Marcos Lizarraga (D)
169	Gordon G. Adams (R)
170	Jim Meyer (R)
171	Bonnie Rangel (D)
172	Mitch Templeton (R)
173	Dan Moore (R)
174	Hazel B. Jones (D)
175	Catherine Torres-Stahl (D)
176	Nikita Harmon (D)
177	Robert Johnson (D)
178	Kelli Johnson (D)
179	Ana Martinez (D)
180	DaSean Jones (D)
181	Titiana D. Frausto (R)
182	Danilo Danny Lacayo (D)
183	Chuck Silverman (D)
184	Abigail Anastasio (D)
185	Jason Luong (D)
186	Jefferson Moore (R)
187	Stephanie R. Boyd (D)
188	Scott Novy (R)
189	Scot Dollinger (D)
190	Beau Miller (D)
191	Gena Slaughter (D)
192	Kristina Williams (R)
193	Bridgett Whitmore (D)
194	Ernest B. White III (D)
195	Hector Garza (D)
196	Andrew Bench (R)

Dist	Judge
197	Adolfo Cordova (D)
198	Melvin Rex Emerson (R)
199	Angela Tucker (R)
200	Jessica Mangrum (D)
201	Amy Clark Meachum (D)
202	John Tidwell (R)
203	Raquel Rocky Jones (D)
204	Tammy Kemp (D)
205	Francisco X. Dominguez (D)
206	Rose Guerra Reyna (D)
207	Jack H. Robison (R)
208	Greg Glass (D)
209	Brian Warren (D)
210	Alyssa G. Perez (D)
211	Brody Shanklin (R)
212	Patricia V. Grady (R)
213	Christopher R. Wolfe (R)
214	Inna Klein (R)
215	Elaine H. Palmer (D)
216	Albert D. Patillo III (R)
217	Robert K. Inselmann, Jr. (R)
218	Russell Wilson (R)
219	Jennifer Edgeworth (R)
220	Shaun Carpenter (R)
221	Lisa B. Michalk (R)
222	Roland Saul (R)
223	Phil Vanderpool (R)
224	Cathy Stryker (R)
225	Peter Sakai (D)
226	Velia J. Meza (D)
227	Kevin M. O'Connell (R)
228	Frank Aguilar (D)
229	Baldemar Balde Garza (D)
230	Chris Morton (D)
231	Jesus Jesse Nevarez Jr. (R)
232	Josh Hill (D)
233	Kenneth E. Newell (R)
234	Lauren Reeder (D)
235	Janelle M. Haverkamp (R)
236	Tom Lowe (R)
237	Les Hatch (R)
238	Elizabeth Leonard (R)
239	Patrick Sebesta (R)
240	Frank J. Fraley (D)
241	Jack M. Skeen, Jr. (R)
242	Lowell Kregg Hukill (R)
243	Selena N. Solis (D)
244	James Rush (R)
245	Tristan H. Longino (D)
246	Angela Graves-Harrington (D)
247	Janice Berg (D)
248	Hilary Unger (D)
249	Wayne Bridewell (R)
250	Karin Crump (D)
251	Ana Estevez (R)
252	Raquel West (D)
253	Chap B. Cain III (R)
254	Kim Brown (D)
255	Kim Cooks (D)
256	David Lopez (D)
257	Sandra Peake (D)
258	Travis Kitchens (R)
259	Brooks H. Hagler (D)
260	Steve Parkhurst (R)
261	Lora Livingston (D)
262	Lori C. Gray (D)
263	Amy Martin (D)
264	Paul LePak (R)
265	Jennifer Bennett (D)
266	Jason Cashon (R)

Dist	Judge
267	Robert E. Bobby Bell (R)
268	R. O'Neil Williams (D)
269	Cory Sepolio (D)
270	Dedra Davis (D)
271	Brock Smith (R)
272	John Brick (R)
273	James A. Payne Jr. (R)
274	Gary L. Steel (R)
275	Marla Cuellar (D)
276	Robert Rolston (R)
277	Stacey Mathews (R)
278	Hal R. Ridley (R)
279	Randy Shelton (D)
280	Barbara J. Stalder (D)
281	Christine Weems Harris
282	Amber Givens-Davis (D)
283	Lela D. Mays (D)
284	Kristin Bays (R)
285	Aaron Haas (D)
286	Jay M. Pat Phelan (R)
287	Gordon H. Green (D)
288	Cynthia Marie Chapa (D)
289	Carlos Quezada (D)
290	Jennifer Pe√±a (D)
291	Stephanie Mitchell (D)
292	Brandon Birmingham (D)
293	Maribel Flores (D)
294	Chris Martin (R)
295	Donna Roth (D)
296	John Roach, Jr. (R)
297	David Hagerman (R)
298	Emily G. Tobolowsky (D)
299	Karen Sage (D)
300	Randall Hufstetler (R)
301	Mary Brown (D)
302	Sandra Jackson (D)
303	Rhonda Hunter (R)
304	Andrea Martin (D)
305	Cheryl Lee Shannon (D)
306	Anne Darring (R)
307	Tim Womack (R)
308	Gloria Lopez (D)
309	Linda Marie Dunson (D)
310	Sonya Heath (D)
311	Germaine Tanner (D)
312	Clinton Chip Wells (D)
313	Natalia Oakes (D)
314	Michelle Moore (D)
315	Leah Shapiro (D)
316	James Mosley (R)
317	Larry Thorne (D)
318	David W. Lindemood (R)
319	David Stith (R)
320	Pamela C. Sirmon (R)
321	Robert Wilson (R)
322	James B. Munford (R)
323	Alex Kim (R)
324	Jerome S. Jerry Hennigan (R)
325	Judith G. Wells (R)
326	Paul Rotenberry (R)
327	Linda Chew (D)
328	Walter Armatys (R)
329	Randy M. Clapp (R)
330	Andrea Plumlee (D)
331	Chantal Melissa Eldridge (D)
332	Mario E. Ramirez, Jr. (D)
333	Brittanye Morris (D)
334	Dawn Deshea Rogers (D)
335	Reva Towslee-Corbett (R)
336	Laurine J. Blake (R)

Dist	Judge
337	Colleen Gaido (D)
338	Ramona Franklin (D)
339	Teiva Bell (D)
340	Jay Weatherby (R)
341	Beckie Palomo (D)
342	Kimberly Fitzpatrick (R)
343	Janna Whatley (R)
344	Randy McDonald (R)
345	Jan Soifer (D)
346	Paty Baca (D)
347	Missy Medary (R)
348	Megan Fahey (R)
349	Pam Foster Fletcher (R)
350	Thomas Wheeler (R)
351	Natalia Nata Cornelio (D)
352	Josh Burgess (R)
353	Madeleine Connor (D)
354	Kelli Aiken (R)
355	Bryan Bufkin (R)
356	Steven Thomas (R)
357	Juan A. Magallanes (D)
358	John F. Shrode (R)
359	Kathleen A. Hamilton (R)
360	Patricia Baca Bennett (R)
361	Steve Smith (R)
362	Bruce McFarling (R)
363	Tracy Holmes (D)
364	William B. Billy
365	Amado Abascal (D)
366	Tom Nowak (R)
367	Margaret Barnes (R)
368	Rick J. Kennon (R)
369	C. Michael Davis (R)
370	Noe Gonzalez (D)
371	Mollee Westfall (R)
372	Scott Wisch (R)
377	Eli Garza (R)
378	William D. Doug Wallace (R)
379	Ron Rangel (D)
380	Ben N. Smith (R)
381	Jose L. Garza (D)
382	Brett Hall (R)
383	Lyda Ness Garcia (D)
384	Patrick M. Garcia (D)
385	Leah G. Robertson (R)
386	Jacqueline Jackie Valdez (D)
387	Janet Buening Heppard (D)
388	Marlene Gonzalez (D)
389	Leticia Letty Lopez (D)
390	Julie H. Kocurek (D)
391	Brad Goodwin (R)
392	Scott McKee (R)
393	Doug Robison (R)
394	Roy B. Ferguson (D)
395	Ryan D. Larson (R)
396	George Gallagher (R)
397	Brian Keith Gary (R)
398	Keno Vasquez (D)
399	Frank J. Castro (D)
400	Tameika Carter (D)
401	George Flint (R)
402	J. Brad McCampbell (R)
403	Brenda Kennedy (D)
404	Ricardo M. Adobbati (D)
405	Jared Robinson (R)
406	Oscar O.J. Hale, Jr. (D)
407	Tina Torres (D)
408	Angelica Jimenez (D)
409	Sam Medrano, Jr. (D)
410	Jennifer Robin (R)

Dist	Judge
411	John Wells (R)
412	Justin R. Gilbert (R)
413	William C. Bosworth, Jr. (R)
414	Vicki Menard (R)
415	Graham Quisenberry (R)
416	Andrea Thompson (R)
417	Cynthia Wheless (R)
418	Tracy A. Gilbert (R)
419	Catherine A. Mauzy (D)
420	Edwin Allen Ed Klein (R)
421	Chris Schneider (R)
422	Shelton Gibbs IV (R)
423	Chris Duggan (D)
424	Evan Stubbs (R)
425	Betsy F. Lambeth (R)
426	Steve Duskie (R)
427	Tamara Needles (D)
428	William Bill Henry (R)
429	Jill R. Willis (R)
430	Israel Ramon (D)
431	Jim Johnson (R)
432	Ruben Gonzalez, Jr. (R)
433	Dibrell Dib Waldrip (R)
434	Christian Becerra (D)
435	Patty Maginnis (R)
436	Lisa K. Jarrett (R)

Dist	Judge
437	Melisa Skinner (R)
438	Rosie Alvarado (D)
439	David Rakow (R)
440	Grant Kinsey (R)
441	Jeff Robnett (R)
442	Tiffany Haertling (R)
443	Cindy Ermatinger (R)
444	David A. Sanchez (D)
445	Gloria M. Rincones (D)
446	Sara Kate Billingsley (R)
448	Sergio H. Enriquez (D)
449	Renee Rodriguez-Betancourt (D)
450	Brad Urrutia (D)
451	Kirsten Cohoon (R)
452	Robert Hofmann (R)
453	Sherri Tibbe (D)
454	Daniel J. Danny Kindred (R)
455	Dustin Howell (R)
456	Heather Hines Wright (R)
457	Vince Santini (R)
458	Robert L. Rolnick (D)
459	Maya Guerra Gamble (D)
460	Selena Alvarenga (D)
461	Patrick Bulanek (R)
462	Lee Ann Breading (R)
464	Joe Ramirez (D)

Dist	Judge
466	Stephanie Bascon (R)
467	Derbha Jones(R)
468	Lindsey Wynne (R)
469	Piper McCraw (R)
470	Emily Miskel (R)
471	Andrea Bouressa (R)
505	Kali Morgan (D)
506	Gary W. Chaney (R)
507	Julia Maldonado (D)

Criminal District Courts	
Dallas 1	Tina Yoo Clinton (D)
Dallas 2	Nancy Kennedy (D)
Dallas 3	Audra LaDawn Riley (D)
Dallas 4	Dominique Collins (D)
Dallas 5	Carter Thompson (D)
Dallas 6	Jeanine Howard (D)
Dallas 7	Chika Anyiam (D)
El Paso	Diane Navarette (D)
Jefferson	John B. "Johnny" Stevens (D)
Tarrant 1	Elizabeth Beach (R)
Tarrant 2	Wayne Francis Salvant (R)
Tarrant 3	Robb Catalano (R)
Tarrant 4	Mike Thomas (R)

Administrative Judicial Regions of Texas

There are 11 administrative judicial regions in the state for administrative purposes. Presiding Judges are appointed by the Governor to four-year terms. They must be active or retired region judges or active or retired appellate judges with judicial experience in a region court. They receive extra compensation of $5,000, paid by counties in the administrative region.

The Presiding Judge convenes an annual conference of judges in the administrative region to consult on business in the courts and to adopt rules for administering cases in the region.

The Presiding Judge may assign active or retired region judges residing within the administrative region to any of its region courts. The Presiding Judge of one administrative region may request the Presiding Judge of another administrative region to assign a judge from that region to sit in a region court in the requesting Judge's administrative region.

The Chief Justice of the Supreme Court of Texas convenes an annual conference of the 11 Presiding Judges to determine the need for assignment of judges and to promote the uniform administration of the assignments. The Chief Justice can assign judges of one administrative region for service in another region.

First Region: Ray Wheless, McKinney (3/2021): Collin, Dallas, Ellis, Fannin, Grayson, Kaufman, Rockwall.

Second Region: Olen Underwood, Conroe (5/2022): Angelina, Bastrop, Brazos, Burleson, Chambers, Grimes, Hardin, Jasper, Jefferson, Lee, Liberty, Madison, Montgomery, Newton, Orange, Polk, San Jacinto, Trinity, Tyler, Walker, Waller, Washington.

Third Region: Billy Ray Stubblefield, Georgetown (2/2022): Austin, Bell, Blanco, Bosque, Burnet, Caldwell, Colorado, Comal, Comanche, Coryell, Falls, Fayette, Gonzales, Guadalupe, Hamilton, Hays, Hill, Lampasas, Lavaca, Llano, McLennan, Milam, Navarro, Robertson, San Saba, Travis, Williamson.

Fourth Region: Sid L. Harle, San Antonio (12/2021): Aransas, Atascosa, Bee, Bexar, Calhoun, De Witt, Dimmit, Frio, Goliad, Jackson, Karnes, La Salle, Live Oak, Maverick, McMullen, Refugio, San Patricio, Victoria, Webb, Wilson, Zapata, Zavala.

Fifth Region: Missy Medary, Alice (11/2023): Brooks, Cameron, Duval, Hidalgo, Jim Hogg, Jim Wells, Kenedy, Kleberg, Nueces, Starr, Willacy.

Sixth Region: Stephen B. Ables, Kerrville (12/2024): Bandera, Brewster, Crockett, Culberson, Edwards, El Paso, Gillespie, Hudspeth, Jeff Davis, Kendall, Kerr, Kimble, Kinney, Mason, McCulloch, Medina, Menard, Pecos, Presidio, Reagan, Real, Sutton, Terrell, Upton, Uvalde, Val Verde.

Seventh Region: Dean Rucker, Midland (4/2023): Andrews, Borden, Brown, Callahan, Coke, Coleman, Concho, Crane, Dawson, Ector, Fisher, Gaines, Garza, Glasscock, Haskell, Howard, Irion, Jones, Kent, Loving, Lynn, Martin, Midland, Mills, Mitchell, Nolan, Reeves, Runnels, Schleicher, Scurry, Shackelford, Sterling, Stonewall, Taylor, Throckmorton, Tom Green, Ward, Winkler.

Eighth Region: David L. Evans, Fort Worth (12/2022): Archer, Clay, Cooke, Denton, Eastland, Erath, Hood, Jack, Johnson, Montague, Palo Pinto, Parker, Somervell, Stephens, Tarrant, Wichita, Wise, Young.

Ninth Region: Ana Estevez, Amarillo (2/2024): Armstrong, Bailey, Baylor, Briscoe, Carson, Castro, Childress, Cochran, Collingsworth, Cottle, Crosby, Dallam, Deaf Smith, Dickens, Donley, Floyd, Foard, Gray, Hale, Hall, Hansford, Hardeman, Hartley, Hemphill, Hockley, Hutchinson, King, Knox, Lamb, Lipscomb, Lubbock, Moore, Motley, Ochiltree, Oldham, Parmer, Potter, Randall, Roberts, Sherman, Swisher, Terry, Wheeler, Wilbarger, Yoakum.

Tenth Region: Alfonso Charles, Longview (2/2022): Anderson, Bowie, Camp, Cass. Cherokee, Delta, Franklin, Freestone, Gregg, Harrison, Henderson, Hopkins, Houston, Hunt, Lamar, Leon, Limestone, Marion, Morris, Nacogdoches, Panola, Rains, Red River, Rusk, Sabine, San Augustine, Shelby, Smith, Titus, Upshur, Van Zandt, Wood.

Eleventh Region: Susan Brown, Houston (3/2022): Brazoria, Fort Bend, Galveston, Harris, Matagorda, Wharton. ☆

Texas Courts by County

Below are listed the state district court or courts, court of appeals district, administrative judicial district, and U.S. judicial district for each county in Texas as of August 2021. For the names of the district court judges, see table by district number on page 457. Lists of other judges in the Texas court system begin on page 493.

County	State Dist. Court(s)	Ct. of Appeals Dist	Adm. Jud. Reg.	U.S. Jud. Dist.
Anderson	3, 87, 349, 369	12	10	E-Tyler
Andrews	109	8	7	W-Midland
Angelina	159, 217	12	2	E-Lufkin
Aransas	36, 156, 343	13	4	S-C.Christi
Archer	97	2	8	N-W. Falls
Armstrong	47	7	9	N-Amarillo
Atascosa	81, 218	4	4	W-San Ant.
Austin	155	1, 14	3	S-Houston
Bailey	287	7	9	N-Lubbock
Bandera	198	4	6	W-San Ant.
Bastrop	21, 335, 423	3	2	W-Austin
Baylor	50	11	9	N-W. Falls
Bee	36, 156, 343	13	4	S-C. Christi
Bell	27, 146, 169, 264, 426	3	3	W-Waco
Bexar	37, 45, 57, 73, 131, 144, 150, 166, 175, 186, 187, 224, 225, 226, 227, 285, 288, 289, 290, 379, 386, 399, 407, 408, 436, 437, 438	4	4	W-San Ant.
Blanco	33, 424	3	3	W-Austin
Borden	132	11	7	N-Lubbock
Bosque	220	10	3	W-Waco
Bowie	5, 102, 202	6	10	E-Texark
Brazoria	149, 239, 300, 412, 461	1, 14	11	S-Galves
Brazos	85, 272, 361	10	2	S-Houston
Brewster	394	8	6	W-Pecos
Briscoe	110	7	9	N-Amarillo
Brooks	79	4	5	S-C. Christi
Brown	35	11	7	N-S. Angelo
Burleson	21, 335	10	2	W-Austin
Burnet	33, 424	3	3	W-Austin
Caldwell	22, 207, 421	3	3	W-Austin
Calhoun	24, 135, 267	13	4	S-Victoria
Callahan	42	11	7	N-Abilene
Cameron	103, 107, 138, 197, 357, 404, 444, 445	13	5	S-Brownsville
Camp	76, 276	6	10	E-Marshall
Carson	100	7	9	N-Amarillo
Cass	5	6	10	E-Marshall
Castro	64, 242	7	9	N-Amarillo
Chambers	253, 344	1, 14	2	S-Galves
Cherokee	2, 369	12	10	E-Tyler
Childress	100	7	9	N-Amarillo
Clay	97	2	8	N-W. Falls
Cochran	286	7	9	N-Lubbock
Coke	51	3	7	N-S. Angelo
Coleman	42	11	7	N-S. Angelo
Collin	199, 219, 296, 366, 380, 401, 416, 417, 428, 429, 468, 469, 470, 471	5	1	E-Sherman
Collingsworth	100	7	9	N-Amarillo
Colorado	25, 25-A	1, 14	3	S-Houston
Comal	22, 207, 274, 433, 463, 466	3	3	W-San Ant.
Comanche	220	11	3	N-Ft. Worth
Concho	119	3	7	N-S. Angelo
Cooke	235	2	8	E-Sherman
Coryell	52, 440	10	3	W-Waco
Cottle	50	7	9	N-W. Falls
Crane	109	8	7	W-Midland
Crockett	112	8	6	N-S. Angelo
Crosby	72	7	9	N-Lubbock
Culberson	205, 394	8	6	W-Pecos
Dallam	69	7	9	N-Amarillo
Dallas	14, 44, 68, 95, 101, 116, 134, 160, 162, 191, 192, 193, 194, 195, 203, 204, 254, 255, 256, 265, 282, 283, 291, 292, 298, 301, 302, 303, 304, 305, 330, 363, Cr. 1, Cr. 2, Cr. 3, Cr. 4, Cr. 5, Cr. 6, Cr. 7,	5	1	N-Dallas

County	State Dist. Court(s)	Ct. of Appeals Dist	Adm. Jud. Reg.	U.S. Jud. Dist.
Dawson	106	11	7	N-Lubbock
Deaf Smith	222	7	9	N-Amarillo
Delta	8, 62	6	10	E-Sherman
Denton	16, 158, 211, 362, 367, 393, 431, 442, 462, 467	2	8	E-Sherman
DeWitt	24, 135, 267	13	4	S-Victoria
Dickens	110	7	9	N-Lubbock
Dimmit	293, 365	4	4	W-San Ant.
Donley	100	7	9	N-Amarillo
Duval	229	4	5	S-C. Christi
Eastland	91	11	8	N-Abilene
Ector	70, 161, 244, 358, 446	11	7	W-Midland
Edwards	452	4	6	W-Del Rio
Ellis	40, 378, 443	10	1	N-Dallas
El Paso	34, 41, 65, 120, 168, 171, 205, 210, 243, 327, 346, 383, 384, 388, 409, 448, Cr. 1	8	6	W-El Paso
Erath	266	11	8	N-Ft. Worth
Falls	82	10	3	W-Waco
Fannin	336	6	1	E-Sherman
Fayette	155	3	3	S-Houston
Fisher	32	11	7	N-Abilene
Floyd	110	7	9	N-Lubbock
Foard	46	7	9	N-W. Falls
Fort Bend	240, 268, 328, 387, 400, 434, 458, 505	1, 14	11	S-Houston
Franklin	8, 62	6	10	E-Texark
Freestone	77, 87	10	10	W-Waco
Frio	81, 218	4	4	W-San Ant.
Gaines	106	11	7	N-Lubbock
Galveston	10, 56, 122, 212, 306, 405	1, 14	11	S-Galves
Garza	106	7	7	N-Lubbock
Gillespie	216	4	6	W-Austin
Glasscock	118	11	7	N-S. Angelo
Goliad	24, 135, 267	13	4	S-Victoria
Gonzales	25, 25-A	13	3	W-San Ant.
Gray	31, 223	7	9	N-Amarillo
Grayson	15, 59, 397	5	1	E-Sherman
Gregg	124, 188, 307	6, 12	10	E-Tyler
Grimes	12, 506	1, 14	2	S-Houston
Guadalupe	25, 25-A, 274, 456	4	3	W-San Ant.
Hale	64, 242	7	9	N-Lubbock
Hall	100	7	9	N-Amarillo
Hamilton	220	10	3	W-Waco
Hansford	84	7	9	N-Amarillo
Hardeman	46	7	9	N-W. Falls
Hardin	88, 356	9	2	E-B'mont
Harris	11, 55, 61, 80, 113, 125,127, 129, 133, 151, 152, 157, 164, 165, 174, 176, 177, 178, 179, 180, 182, 183, 184, 185, 189, 190, 208, 209, 215, 228, 230, 232, 234, 245, 246, 247, 248, 257, 262, 263, 269, 270, 280, 281, 295, 308, 309, 310, 311, 312, 313, 314, 315, 333, 334, 337, 338, 339, 351, 507	1, 14	11	S-Houston
Harrison	71	6	10	E-Marshall
Hartley	69	7	9	N-Amarillo
Haskell	39	11	7	N-Abilene
Hays	22, 207, 274, 428, 453	3	3	W-Austin
Hemphill	31	7	9	N-Amarillo
Henderson	3, 173, 392	12	10	E-Tyler
Hidalgo	92, 93, 139, 206, 275, 332, 370, 389, 398 , 430, 449, 464	13	5	S-McAllen
Hill	66	10	3	W-Waco
Hockley	286	7	9	N-Lubbock
Hood	355	2	8	N-Ft. Worth

County	State Dist. Court(s)	Ct. of Appeals Dist	Adm. Jud. Reg.	U.S. Jud. Dist.
Hopkins	8, 62	6	10	E-Sherman
Houston	3, 349	12	10	E-Lufkin
Howard	118	11	7	N-Abilene
Hudspeth	205, 394	8	6	W-Pecos
Hunt	196, 354	5, 6	10	N-Dallas
Hutchinson	84, 316	7	9	N-Amarillo
Irion	51	3	7	N-S. Angelo
Jack	271	2	8	N-Ft. Worth
Jackson	24, 135, 267	13	4	S-Victoria
Jasper	1, 1-A	9	2	E-B'mont
Jeff Davis	394	8	6	W-Pecos
Jefferson	58, 60, 136, 172, 252, 279, 317, Cr. 1	9	2	E-B'mont
Jim Hogg	229	4	5	S-Laredo
Jim Wells	79	4	5	S-C. Christi
Johnson	18, 249, 413	10	8	N-Dallas
Jones	259	11	7	N-Abilene
Karnes	81, 218	4	4	W-San Ant.
Kaufman	86, 422	5	1	N-Dallas
Kendall	451	4	6	W-San Ant.
Kenedy	105	13	5	S-C. Christi
Kent	39	7	7	N-Lubbock
Kerr	198, 216	4	6	W-San Ant.
Kimble	452	4	6	W-Austin
King	50	7	9	N-W. Falls
Kinney	63	4	6	W-Del Rio
Kleberg	105	13	5	S-C. Christi
Knox	50	11	9	N-W. Falls
Lamar	6, 62	6	10	E-Sherman
Lamb	154	7	9	N-Lubbock
Lampasas	27	3	3	W-Austin
La Salle	81, 218	4	4	S-Laredo
Lavaca	25, 25-A	13	3	S-Victoria
Lee	21, 335	3	2	W-Austin
Leon	87, 278, 369	10	10	W-Waco
Liberty	75, 253	9	2	E-B'mont
Limestone	77, 87	10	10	W-Waco
Lipscomb	31	7	9	N-Amarillo
Live Oak	36, 156, 343	13	4	S-C. Christi
Llano	33, 424	3	3	W-Austin
Loving	143	8	7	W-Pecos
Lubbock	72, 99, 137, 140, 237, 364	7	9	N-Lubbock
Lynn	106	7	7	N-Lubbock
Madison	12, 278	10	2	S-Houston
Marion	115, 276	6	10	E-Marshall
Martin	118	11	7	W-Midland
Mason	452	4	6	W-Austin
Matagorda	23, 130	13	11	S-Galves
Maverick	293, 365	4	4	W-Del Rio
McCulloch	452	3	6	W-Austin
McLennan	19, 54, 74, 170, 414	10	3	W-Waco
McMullen	36, 156, 343	4	4	S-Laredo
Medina	454	4	6	W-San Ant.
Menard	452	4	6	N-S. Angelo
Midland	142, 238, 318, 385, 441	11	7	W-Midland
Milam	20	3	3	W-Waco
Mills	35	3	7	N-S. Angelo
Mitchell	32	11	7	N-Abilene
Montague	97	2	8	N-W. Falls
Montgomery	9, 221, 284, 359, 410, 418, 435, 457	9	2	S-Houston
Moore	69	7	9	N-Amarillo
Morris	76, 276	6	10	E-Marshall
Motley	110	7	9	N-Lubbock
Nacogdoches	145, 420	12	10	E-Lufkin
Navarro	13	10	3	N-Dallas
Newton	1, 1-A	9	2	E-B'mont
Nolan	32	11	7	N-Abilene
Nueces	28, 94, 105, 117, 148, 214, 319, 347	13	5	S-C. Christi
Ochiltree	84	7	9	N-Amarillo
Oldham	222	7	9	N-Amarillo
Orange	128, 163, 260	9	2	E-B'mont
Palo Pinto	29	11	8	N-Ft. Worth
Panola	123	6	10	E-Tyler
Parker	43, 415	2	8	N-Ft. Worth
Parmer	287	7	9	N-Amarillo

County	State Dist. Court(s)	Ct. of Appeals Dist	Adm. Jud. Reg.	U.S. Jud. Dist.
Pecos	83, 112	8	6	W-Pecos
Polk	258, 411	9	2	E-Lufkin
Potter	47, 108, 181, 251, 320	7	9	N-Amarillo
Presidio	394	8	6	W-Pecos
Rains	8, 354	12	10	E-Tyler
Randall	47, 181, 251	7	9	N-Amarillo
Reagan	112	8	6	N-S. Angelo
Real	38	4	6	W-San Ant.
Red River	6, 102	6	10	E-Texark
Reeves	143	8	7	W-Pecos
Refugio	24, 135, 267	13	4	S-Victoria
Roberts	31	7	9	N-Amarillo
Robertson	82	10	3	W-Waco
Rockwall	382, 439	5	1	N-Dallas
Runnels	119	3	7	N-S. Angelo
Rusk	4	6, 12	10	E-Tyler
Sabine	1, 273	12	10	E-Lufkin
San Augustine	1, 273	12	10	E-Lufkin
San Jacinto	258, 411	9	2	S-Houston
San Patricio	36, 156, 343	13	4	S-C. Christi
San Saba	33, 424	3	3	W-Austin
Schleicher	51	3	7	N-S. Angelo
Scurry	132	11	7	N-Lubbock
Shackelford	259	11	7	N-Abilene
Shelby	123, 273	12	10	E-Lufkin
Sherman	69	7	9	N-Amarillo
Smith	7, 114, 241, 321	12	10	E-Tyler
Somervell	18, 249	10	8	W-Waco
Starr	229, 381	4	5	S-McAllen
Stephens	90	11	8	N-Abilene
Sterling	51	3	7	N-S. Angelo
Stonewall	39	11	7	N-Abilene
Sutton	112	4	6	N-S. Angelo
Swisher	64, 242	7	9	N-Amarillo
Tarrant	17, 48, 67, 96, 141, 153, 213, 231, 233, 236, 297, 322, 323, 324, 325, 342, 348, 352, 360, 371, 372, 396, 432, Cr. 1, Cr. 2, Cr. 3, Cr. 4	2	8	N-Ft. Worth
Taylor	42, 104, 326, 350	11	7	N-Abilene
Terrell	63, 83	8	6	W-Del Rio
Terry	121	7	9	N-Lubbock
Throckmorton	39	11	7	N-Abilene
Titus	76, 276	6	10	E-Texark
Tom Green	51, 119, 340, 391	3	7	N-S. Angelo
Travis	53, 98, 126, 147, 167, 200, 201, 250, 261, 299, 331, 345, 353, 390, 403, 419, 427, 450, 455, 459, 460	3	3	W-Austin
Trinity	258, 411	12	2	E-Lufkin
Tyler	1-A, 88	9	2	E-Lufkin
Upshur	115	6, 12	10	E-Marshall
Upton	112	8	6	W-Midland
Uvalde	38	4	6	W-Del Rio
Val Verde	63, 83	4	6	W-Del Rio
Van Zandt	294	12	10	E-Tyler
Victoria	24, 135, 267, 377	13	4	S-Victoria
Walker	12, 278	10	2	S-Houston
Waller	506	1, 14	2	S-Houston
Ward	143	8	7	W-Pecos
Washington	21, 335	1, 14	2	W-Austin
Webb	49, 111, 341, 406	4	4	S-Laredo
Wharton	23, 329	13	11	S-Houston
Wheeler	31	7	9	N-Amarillo
Wichita	30, 78, 89	2	8	N-W. Falls
Wilbarger	46	7	9	N-W. Falls
Willacy	197	13	5	S-Brownsville
Williamson	26, 277, 368, 395, 425	3	3	W-Austin
Wilson	81, 218	4	4	W-San Ant.
Winkler	109	8	7	W-Pecos
Wise	271	2	8	N-Ft. Worth
Wood	402	6, 12	10	E-Tyler
Yoakum	121	7	9	N-Lubbock
Young	90	2	8	N-W. Falls
Zapata	49	4	4	S-Laredo
Zavala	293, 365	4	4	W-Del Rio

Texas State Agencies

On the following pages is information about several of the many state agencies in Texas. Information was supplied to the Texas Almanac by the agencies, their websites, and from news reports. The web address for more information about state agencies, boards, and commissions is: https://www.tsl.texas.gov/apps/lrs/agencies/index.html.

Texas Commission on Environmental Quality

Source: Texas Commission on Environmental Quality; www.tceq.texas.gov

The Texas Commission on Environmental Quality (TCEQ) is the state's leading environmental agency. The TCEQ works to protect Texas' human and natural resources in a manner consistent with sustainable economic development. The agency has about 2,700 employees; of those, about 800 work in the 16 regional offices.

One of the TCEQ's major functions is issuing permits and other authorizations for the control of air pollution, the safe operation of water and wastewater utilities, and the management of hazardous and nonhazardous waste.

The agency promotes voluntary compliance with environmental laws through pollution prevention programs, regulatory workshops, and assistance to businesses and local governments. When environmental laws are violated, the TCEQ has the authority to levy penalties as much as $25,000 a day per violation for administrative cases. In a typical year, the agency conducts more than 105,000 investigations at regulated entities for compliance with state and federal laws and receives about 4,000 complaints.

Office of Air

Texas is home to some of the largest U.S. cities, with several metropolitan populations of greater than 1 million people. With these concentrated populations, vehicular traffic and other emissions can create air quality issues among the most challenging in the country.

The state has a fast-growing population, a large industrial base concentrated along the Gulf Coast, and an oil and gas industry expanding throughout much of the state. The TCEQ conducts survey activities along with targeted and/or specialized monitoring activities to evaluate changing air quality conditions across the state.

The TCEQ measures air quality across the state for compliance with federal standards, as well as for localized compounds of concern. Texas' air toxic monitoring network is one of the most comprehensive in the country with more than 80 monitoring sites located across the state.

The TCEQ is responsible for developing a state implementation plan to bring metropolitan areas into compliance with federal air quality standards, such as the ozone standard. The leading areas of concern for ozone issues are the Houston-Galveston-Brazoria and Dallas–Fort Worth areas.

Office of Water

The TCEQ preserves and improves the quality of the state's surface waters by establishing surface water quality standards; monitoring, assessing, and reporting conditions; and implementing plans to reduce pollution and improve water quality. It protects surface water users through the water rights permitting process and the watermaster programs.

TCEQ Budget for FYE 2022 and FYE 2023	
Assessment, Planning and Permitting	$245,820,762
Safe Drinking Water	$48,087,570
Enforcement and Compliance Support	$142,708,918
Pollution Cleanup	$87,475,953
River Compact Commissions	$5,982,211
Indirect Administration	$116,937,401
Total	**$647,012,815**

Source: SB1, General Appropriations Bill, 2021.

The TCEQ is also responsible for most state and federal regulatory programs that protect groundwater, administers permits for the discharge of wastewater and stormwater, and conducts Section 401 certifications of federal permits.

The agency enforces the federal Safe Drinking Water Act, oversees the protection of the state's approximately 7,000 public water systems providing drinking water to roughly 27 million customers, and has general supervision of water districts.

Office of Waste

Waste management projects at the TCEQ include Superfund projects, pesticide collections, and permits and authorizations for municipal and industrial waste management. Another major cleanup program focuses on leaking petroleum storage tanks. In 2019, there were 55 Superfund sites in the state, and work continues at another 1,344 sites.

The TCEQ issues permits and other authorizations for municipal and industrial waste management, including landfills and storage, processing, and recycling operations. In addition, the safe recycling of both municipal and industrial waste streams is encouraged.

The TCEQ also regulates the disposal of radioactive material, with the exception of naturally occurring radioactive material (NORM) generated as a result of oil and gas exploration. This includes the regulation of the receipt, processing, storage, and disposal of by-product and low-level radioactive waste, the licensing of uranium and thorium recovery facilities, decommissioning of inactive uranium-recovery facilities, permitting for underground injection control, and legacy radioactive material disposal sites.

Help With Understanding Environmental Rules

The TCEQ offers services to anyone interested in environmental stewardship and navigating TCEQ's programs and regulatory requirements. Staff members host workshops on recycling and disposal opportunities, and on regulatory and pollution prevention topics.

The TCEQ also offers free compliance assistance to thousands of small businesses and local governments each year. Contact the TCEQ at PO Box 13087, Austin, 78711; (512) 239-1000; www.tceq.texas.gov. ☆

Health and Human Services

Source: Texas Health and Human Services, hhs.texas.gov

Texas Health and Human Services (HHS) is the oversight agency for the state's health and human services system. HHS also administers state and federal programs that provide financial, health, and social services to Texans. Executive Commissioner Cecile Erwin Young was appointed on Aug. 14, 2020.

In 2003, the 78th Texas Legislature mandated an unprecedented transformation of the state's health and human services system, blending 12 agencies into five. The system transformed again in 2017, with the goal of removing bureaucratic silos, creating clear lines of accountability, and making it easier for people to find out about services or benefits they might qualify for.

Today's HHS consists of only two agencies: Texas Health and Human Services Commission (HHSC) and the Texas Department of State Health Services (DSHS). The executive commissioner is appointed by the governor and confirmed by the Senate. The Department of Family and Protective Services is an independent agency under the HHSC umbrella.

HHS is located at4601 Guadalupe St., Austin, 78711-3247; Phone: 512-424-6500; TTY: 512-424-6597.

Health and Human Services Commission

The HHSC oversees the licensing and credentialing of facilities for long-term care, including nursing homes and assisted living; licenses child care providers; and manages daily operations at state-supported hospitals and living centers.

It also delivers benefits and services such as Medicaid, SNAP food benefits, and TANF cash assistance; services for women and people with special health needs; long-term care for the aging and those with disabilities; and behavioral health services.

Department of State Health Services

DSHS serves as the public health authority for Texas, providing vital statistics and health data to the public, leading the public-health response in times of disaster or outbreaks, and administering chronic and infectious disease prevention and testing. The department also licenses and regulates facilities on topics including youth camps and mobile food establishments. It is led by Commissioner of Public Health Dr. John Hellerstedt.

The client services DSHS previously provided were transferred to HHSC in 2016.

Department of Family and Protective Services

The Department of Family and Protective Services (DFPS) works to protect children and vulnerable adults through prevention programs, investigations, and services and referrals. DFPS has five major programs:

- Adult Protective Services
- Child Protective Services
- Investigations
- Prevention and Early Intervention
- Statewide Intake

HHS Budget for FYE 2022 and FYE 2023

Dept. of Family and Protective Services	$4,602.1
Dept. of State Health Services	$1,865.6
Health and Human Services Commission	$78,600.1
Total	**$85,067.8**

All figures in millions. Total may not sum due to rounding.
Source: SB1, General Appropriations Bill, 2021.

To report abuse, neglect, or exploitation of children, the elderly or people with disabilities, call 1-800-252-5400 or report online at www.txabusehotline.org. For emergencies call 911.

DFPS headquarters address: 701 W. 51st St., Austin, 78751; Mailing address: PO Box 149030, Austin, 78714-9030; www.dfps.state.tx.us.

Other HHSC Programs

The Family Violence program offers emergency shelter and services to victims and their children.

The Disaster Assistance program processes grant applications for victims of presidentially declared disasters, such as tornados, floods, and hurricanes.

As of 2017, the HHS no longer provides refugee resettlement services. Nonprofit agencies, including U.S. Committee for Refugees and Immigrants (USCRI),l have stepped in to provide health services for these groups.☆

Major HHS Programs at a Glance

The **Medicaid** program provides healthcare coverage for one out of every three children in Texas, pays for half of all births, and accounts for 25 percent of the state's total budget. In 2018, an average of 4 million Texans received healthcare coverage through Medicaid.

The Children's Health Insurance Program (CHIP) is designed for families who earn too much money to qualify for Medicaid yet cannot afford private insurance.

The Temporary Assistance for Needy Families (TANF) program provides basic financial assistance for needy children and the parents or caretakers with whom they live. As a condition of eligibility, caretakers must sign and abide by a personal-responsibility agreement. Time limits for benefits have been set by both state and federal welfare-reform legislation.

SNAP food benefits, formerly known as food stamps, is a federally funded program that assists low-income families, the elderly, and single adults obtain a nutritionally adequate diet.

Both SNAP and TANF benefits are delivered via the electronic benefit transfer (EBT) system, through which clients access benefits at about 12,000 retail locations statewide with the Lone Star card. Information about Medicaid, CHIP, and other health and human services programs can be found at www.211texas.org, or by calling **2-1-1**, a toll-free local resource for information on HHS programs.

The General Land Office Building in Austin was completed in 1857. Photo by Larry D. Moore, CC by 3.0/Wikimedia Commons.

The General Land Office

Source: General Land Office of Texas, glo.texas.gov

History of the General Land Office

The Texas General Land Office (GLO) is one of the oldest governmental entities in the state, dating back to the Republic of Texas. The first General Land Office was established in 1836 by the Republic's constitution, and the first Texas Congress enacted the provision into law in 1837. The GLO was established to oversee distribution of public lands, register titles, issue patents on land, and maintain records of land granted.

In the early years of statehood, beginning in 1845, Texas established the precedent of using its vast public domain for public benefit. The first use was to sell or trade land to eliminate the huge debt remaining from Texas' War for Independence and the early years of the Republic.

Texas also gave away land to settlers as homesteads; to veterans as compensation for service; for internal improvements, including building railroads, shipbuilding, and improving rivers for navigation; and to build the state Capitol.

The public domain was closed in 1898 when the Texas Supreme Court declared there was no more vacant and unappropriated land in Texas. In 1900, all remaining unappropriated land was set aside by the Legislature to benefit public schools.

Today, 13 million acres of land and minerals, owned by the Permanent School Fund, the Permanent University Fund, various other state agencies, and the Veterans Land Board, are managed by the GLO and the Commissioner of the Texas General Land Office.

This includes over 4 million acres of submerged coastal lands, which consist of bays, inlets, and the area from the Texas shoreline to the three-marine-league line (10.36 miles) in the Gulf of Mexico. It is estimated that more than 1 million acres make up the public domain of the state's riverbeds and another 1.7 million acres are excess lands belonging to the Permanent School Fund.

The GLO is the steward of the Texas Gulf Coast, serving as the premier state agency for protecting and renourishing the coast and fighting coastal erosion. In 1999, the Legislature created the Coastal Erosion Planning and Response Act and put the GLO in charge of facilitating restoration and preservation of eroding beaches, dunes, wetlands, and other bay shorelines along the Texas coast.

The Permanent School Fund owns mineral rights alone in almost 7.4 million acres covered under the Relinquishment Act, the Free Royalty Act, and the various sales acts, and it has outright ownership to about 747,522 upland acres, mostly west of the Pecos River.

Historic Distribution of the Public Lands of Texas

PURPOSE	ACRES
Settlers	**68,027,108**
Spain and Mexico	24,583,923
Spanish and Mexican Grants south of the Nueces River, recognized by Act of Feb. 10, 1852	3,741,241
Headrights	30,360,002
Republic colonies	4,494,806
Preemption land	4,847,136
Military	**9,874,262**
Bounty	5,354,250
Battle donations	1,162,240
Veterans donations	1,377,920
Confederate	1,979,852
Improvements	**37,155,714**
Road	27,716
Navigation	4,261,760
Irrigation	584,000
Ships	17,000
Manufacturing	111,360
Railroads	32,153,878
Education	**52,329,168**
University, public school, and eleemosynary institutions	52,329,168
Total of distributed lands	**167,386,252**

Texas Veterans Land Board Programs

The Veterans Land Board (VLB) was formally established by the Legislature to administer benefits for Texas Veterans in 1946, with the first loan made in 1949.

Since then, the programs have evolved to include low-interest land, housing, and home improvement loans. VLB has funded more than 220,000 loans amounting to more than $11 billion for Texas veterans, military members, and their families since its inception.

VLB strives to offer the best benefits program in the nation and works to ensure that Texas veterans are aware of these benefits.

In a joint effort with the Texas Veterans Commission, the VLB operates the Texas Veterans Call Service Center to connect veterans, military members, and their families with the benefits and services they need. For more information, contact VLB at 1-800-252-VETS (8387) or https://vlb.texas.gov/

Texas State Veterans Homes

In 1997, the 75th Legislature approved legislation authorizing the Veterans Land Board to construct and operate Texas State Veterans Homes under a cost-sharing program with the U.S. Department of Veterans Affairs (USDVA). The homes provide affordable, quality, long-term care for Texas' veterans.

Texas State Veterans Cemeteries

The VLB owns and operates several cemeteries under USDVA guidelines. The USDVA funds the design and construction of the cemeteries, but the land must be donated.

The Alamo

In 2011, the 82nd Legislature granted authority over the Alamo to the GLO. The Alamo hosts millions of visitors from around the world each year. UNESCO designated the Alamo and four other Spanish missions in San Antonio as U.S. World Heritage sites in 2015.

Plans to create a museum and visitors center to house rock legend Phil Collins' donated collection of Alamo and Texana artifacts are underway. ☆

Texas Historical Commission

The Texas Historical Commission protects and preserves the state's historic and prehistoric resources. The Texas State Legislature established the Texas State Historical Survey Committee in 1953 to identify important historic sites across the state.

The Texas Legislature changed the agency's name to the Texas Historical Commission in 1973 and increased its mission and its protective powers. Today the agency's concerns include archaeology, architecture, community heritage development, historic sites, history programs, and education. The commission:

- Works with communities and individuals to help identify important historic resources and develop a plan to preserve them.
- Provides leadership and training to county historical commissions, heritage organizations, and museums in Texas' 254 counties.
- Helps protect Texas' diverse architectural heritage, including historic county courthouses.
- Partners with communities to stimulate tourism and economic development.
- Assists Texas cities in the revitalization of their historic downtowns through the Texas Main Street Program.
- Administers the state's historical marker program, which has around 15,000 markers across the state.
- Consults with citizens and groups to nominate properties as Recorded Texas Historic Landmarks, State Archeological Landmarks, and to the National Register of Historic Places.
- Operates 20 state historic sites including house museums, military forts, and archeological sites.
- Works with property owners to save archeological sites on private land and ensures archeological sites are protected as land is developed for highways and other public construction projects.

Mailing address: PO Box 12276, Austin 78711-2276; (512) 463-6100; www.thc.texas.gov.

Railroad Commission of Texas

The Railroad Commission of Texas has primary regulatory jurisdiction over the oil and natural gas industry, pipeline transporters, the natural gas and hazardous liquid pipeline industry, natural gas utilities, the liquefied petroleum gas (LP-gas) industry, rail industry, and coal and uranium surface mining operations. It also promotes the use of LP-gas as an alternative fuel in Texas through research and education.

The commission exercises its statutory responsibilities under provisions of the Texas Constitution, the Texas Natural Resources Code, the Texas Water Code, the Texas Utilities Code, the Coal and Uranium Surface Mining and Reclamation Acts, the Pipeline Safety Acts, and the Railroad Safety Act.

The commission has regulatory and enforcement responsibilities under federal law, including the Federal Railroad Safety Act, the Local Rail Freight Assistance Act, the Surface Coal Mining Control and Reclamation Act, the Pipeline Safety Acts, the Resource Conservation Recovery Act, and the Clean Water Act.

The Railroad Commission was established by the Texas Legislature in 1891 and given jurisdiction over rates and operations of railroads, terminals, wharves, and express companies. In 1917, the legislature declared pipelines to be common carriers and gave the commission regulatory authority over them. It was also given the responsibility to administer conservation laws relating to oil and natural gas production.

The Railroad Commission exists to protect the environment, public safety, and the rights of mineral interest owners; to prevent waste of natural resources; and to assure fair and equitable utility rates in those industries over which it has authority. Mailing address: PO Box 12967, Austin 78711-2967; (512) 463-7158; www.rrc.state.tx.us.

Texas Department of Juvenile Justice

The Texas Department of Juvenile Justice was created on Dec. 1, 2011, by Senate Bill 653, 82nd Legislature. Its creation abolished both the Texas Youth Commission and the Texas Juvenile Probation Commission.

The agency's executive director is Camille Cain, and it has a 13-member commission who are appointed to six-year terms. It is chaired by Wes Ritchey of Dalhart.

The **Texas Youth Commission (TYC)** had operated correctional facilities and halfway houses for serious youth offenders. In 2007, widespread sexual and physical abuse was uncovered at many of its facilities. After a number of supervisors were dismissed, the entire TYC board resigned on March 15, 2007, and their powers were transferred to a conservator. The 80th Texas Legislature approved a bill to overhaul the troubled agency.

The **Texas Department of Juvenile Justice** is a unified state juvenile justice agency that works in partnership with local county governments, courts, and communities to promote public safety by providing services to youth from initial contact through end of supervision. Its expressed goals are to:

- Support development of county-based programs and services for youth and families that reduce the need for out-of-home placement;
- Seek alternatives to placing youthful offenders in secure state facilities, while also addressing treatment of youth and protecting the public;
- Locate facilities as geographically close as possible to workforce and other services, and support youths' connection to their families;
- Encourage regional and county collaboration;
- Enhance the continuity of care throughout the juvenile justice system; and
- Use secure facilities of a size that supports effective youth rehabilitation and public safety.

The agency is located at Braker H Complex, 11209 Metric Blvd., Austin 78758. Mailing Address: PO Box 12757, Austin 78711-2757; (512) 490-7130; https://www.tjjd.texas.gov/.

Texas Workforce Commission

The Texas Workforce Commission (TWC) is the state government agency charged with overseeing and providing workforce development services to employers and job seekers of Texas. It is led by three appointed commissioners, representing the public (Bryan Daniel), labor (Julian Alvarez III), and employers (Aaron Demerson).

For employers, TWC offers recruiting, retention, training and retraining, outplacement services, and information on labor law and labor market statistics.

For job seekers, TWC offers career development information, job search resources, training programs, and, as appropriate, unemployment benefits. While targeted populations receive intensive assistance to overcome barriers to employment, all Texans can benefit from the services offered by TWC and its network of workforce partners.

The Texas Workforce Commission is part of a local and state network dedicated to developing the workforce of Texas. The network is composed of the statewide efforts of the commission coupled with planning and service provision on a regional level by 28 local workforce boards. This network gives customers access to local workforce solutions and statewide services in a single location — Texas Workforce Centers.

Primary services of the Texas Workforce Commission and its network partners are funded by federal tax revenue and are generally free to all Texans. Mailing address: 101 E. 15th Street, Austin 78778; (512) 463-2222; www.twc.state.tx.us. ☆

Texas State Boards and Commissions

Following is a list of appointees to state boards and commissions, as well as names of other state officials, revised to **August 18, 2021**. Information includes, where available, (1) date of creation; (2) whether the position is elective or appointive; (3) length of term; (4) compensation, if any; (5) number of members; (6) names of appointees, their hometowns, and expiration of terms. In some instances the date of term expiration has passed; in such cases, no new appointment had been made by press time, and the official is continuing to fill the position until a successor is named. Most positions marked "apptv." are appointed by the Governor. Where otherwise, appointing authority is given. Most advisory boards are not listed. Salaries for commissioners and administrators are those that were authorized by the appropriations bill passed by the 85th Legislature for the 2018–2019 biennium. They are "not-to-exceed" salaries: maximum authorized salaries for the positions. Actual salaries may be less than those stated here.

Accountancy, Texas State Board of Public: (1945 with 2-yr. terms; reorganized 1959 as 9-member board with 6-yr. overlapping terms; number of members increased to 12 in 1979; increased to 15 in 1989); per diem and expenses: Presiding Officer Manuel "Manny" Cavazos IV, Manor (1/31/23); Susan I. Adams, Colleyville (1/31/27); Kelly V. Aimone, Houston (1/31/25); Olivia Espinoza-Riley, Addison (1/31/27); Renee D. Foshee, San Marcos (1/31/27); Lisa A. Friel, San Antonio (1/31/23); Ray R. Garcia, Houston (1/31/27); Jamie D. Grant, Arlington (1/31/23); Jill A. Holup, Austin (1/31/25); James D. "Jim" Ingram IV, College Station (1/31/23); Kevin J. Koch, Temple (1/31/25); Debra D. Seefeld, Montgomery (1/31/25); Debra S. Sharp, Houston (1/31/23); Jeannette P. Smith, Mission (1/31/25); Sheila M. Vallés-Pankratz, Mission (1/31/27). Exec. Dir. William Treacy ($182,875), 505 E. Huntland Dr., Ste. 380, Austin 78752-3757; (512) 305-7800.

Acupuncture Examiners, Texas State Board of: (1993); apptv.; 6-yr.; per diem; 9 members: Presiding Officer Donna S. Guthery, Bellaire (1/31/23); Elisabeth Lee "Elle" Carlson, Garland (1/31/25); Sheri J. Davidson, Houston (1/31/25); Maria M. Garcia, Plano (1/31/27); Samantha A. Gonzalez, San Antonio (1/31/27); Raymond J. Graham, El Paso (1/31/27); Mary E. Hebert, Nacogdoches (1/31/25); Grant E. Weidler, Spring (1/31/23); Rey Ximenes, Spicewood (1/31/27). Exec. Dir. Stephen "Brint" Carlton, 333 Guadalupe, Tower 3, Ste. 610, PO Box 2018, Austin 78768-2018; (512) 305-7010.

Adjutant General's Dept. (See Military Dept., Texas.)

Administrative Hearings, State Office of: Created in 1991 by 72nd Leg.; apptv.; 2-yr.; 1 member: Chief Admin. Law Judge Kristofer Monson, Driftwood (5/15/22) ($180,000), 300 W. 15th St., Ste. 504, Austin 78701; (512) 475-4993.

Aging and Disability Services Council, Department of (DADS): Est. 2003 by the 78th Legislature; later abolished by 84th Legislature (Senate Bill 200) effective 9/1/2017 and services merged into Texas Health and Human Services Commission.

Alcoholic Beverage Commission, Texas: (1935 as Liquor Control Board; name changed in 1970); apptv.; 6-yr; per diem and expenses; administrator apptd. by commission; 5 members: Chair Kevin J. Lilly, Houston (11/15/21); M. Scott Adkins, El Paso (11/15/23); Jason E. Boatright, Dallas (11/15/23); Hasan K. Mack, Austin (11/15/25); Deborah Gray Marino, San Antonio (11/15/25). Exec. Dir. Bentley Nettles ($200,000), 5806 Mesa Dr., PO Box 13127, Austin 78711; (512) 206-3333.

Alzheimer's Disease and Related Disorders, Texas Council on: (1999); apptv.; 2-yr.; 15 members (3 ex officio; 12 appointed by Gov., Lt. Gov., and House Speaker: Chair Marc Diamond, Dallas; Byron Cordes, San Antonio; Laura DeFina, Dallas; Joe A. Evans Jr., Beaumont (8/31/21); Vaunette Fay, Houston; Ana Guerrero Gore, Galveston; Char Hu, Dallas; Eddie Patton, Jr., Sugar Land (3/31/21); Mary Quiceno, Dallas; Sudha Seshadri, San Antonio; Terrence Sommers, Amarillo; Angela Turner, Normangee. Ex officio members include 1 from Texas Dept. of State Health Services and 2 from Texas Health and Human Services Commission. 1100 W. 49th St., PO Box 149347, Austin 78714-9347; (800) 242-3399.

Angelina and Neches River Authority: (1935 as Sabine-Neches Conservation Dist.; reorganized in 1950 and name changed to Neches River Conservation Dist.; changed to present name in 1977); apptv.; expenses; 6-yr.; 9 members: Pres. Jody Anderson, Lufkin (9/5/25); Kimberly M. Childs, Nacogdoches (9/5/25); Eddie Hopkins, Jasper (9/5/23); Donnie R. Kee, Diboll (9/5/23); Virginia M. "Ginger" Lymbery, Lufkin (9/5/23); Dale Morton, Nacogdoches (9/5/21); Thomas R. "Tom" Murphy, Crockett (9/5/25); Skip Ogle, Tyler (9/5/21); Francis G. Spruiell, Center (9/5/21). Gen. Mgr. Kelley Holcomb, 2901 N. John Redditt Dr., Lufkin 75904; (936) 632-7795.

Animal Health Commission, Texas: (1893 as Texas Livestock Sanitary Commission; name changed in 1959; members increased to 9 in 1973; raised to current number in 1983); apptv.; per diem and expenses; 6-yr.; 13 members: Chair Coleman Locke, Hungerford (9/6/21); Jim Eggleston, Weatherford (9/6/21); Jimmie Ruth Evans, San Antonio (9/6/25); Melanie Johnson, Houston (9/6/25); Kenneth "Ken" Jordan, San Saba (9/6/21); Barret J. Klein, Boerne (9/6/25); Wendee C. Langdon, Lubbock (9/6/23); Joe Leathers, Guthrie (9/6/25); Thomas "Tommy" Oates, Huntsville (9/6/25); Joseph G. "Joe" Osterkamp, Muleshoe (9/6/23); Keith M. Staggs, Gonzales (9/6/23); Leo Vermedahl, Dalhart (9/6/23); Michael L. Vickers, Falfurrias (9/6/21). Exec. Dir. Andy Schwartz ($155,814), 2105 Kramer Ln., PO Box 12966, Austin 78711-2966; (512) 719-0700.

Appraiser Licensing & Certification Board, Texas: (1991); 6-yr.; apptv.; per diem on duty; 9 members; 1 ex officio: Texas General Land Office; 8 apptd: Chair Sara Oates, Austin (1/31/25); Clayton Black, Stanton (1/31/23); R. Chance Bolton, Bee Cave (1/31/27); Rolando Castro, Cypress (1/31/23); Paola Escalante-Castillo, Weslaco (1/31/27); Martha Gayle Reid Lynch, El Paso (1/31/27); Stephanie Robinson, McKinney (1/31/25); Lisa Sprinkle, El Paso (1/31/25). Comm. Chelsea Buchholtz, PO Box 12188, Austin 78711-2188; (512) 936-3001.

Architectural Examiners, Texas Board of: (1937 as 3-member board; raised to 6 members in 1951 and to 9 in 1977); apptv.; 6-yr.; per diem and expenses. Chair Debra Dockery, San Antonio (1/31/23); Tim A. Bargainer, Georgetown (1/31/25); Chase Bearden, Austin (1/31/21); Darren L. James, Lewisville (1/31/25); Rosa G. Salazar, Dallas (1/31/23); Joyce J. Smith, Burnet (1/31/23); Fernando Trevino Sr., San Antonio (1/31/25); Jennifer Nicole Walker, Lampasas (1/31/21); Robert Scott "Bob" Wetmore, Austin (1/31/21). Exec. Dir. Julie Hildebrand ($151,429), 505 E. Huntland Dr., Ste. 350, PO Box 12337, Austin 78711; (512) 305-9000.

Arts, Texas Commission on the: (1965 as Texas Fine Arts Commission; name changed to Texas Commission on the Arts and Humanities in 1971; to present form in 1979); apptv.; 6-yr.; expenses; members: Chair Dale W. Brock, Fort Worth (8/31/23); Theresa W. Chang, Houston (8/31/25); Mila Gibson, Sweetwater (8/31/21); Adrian Guerra, Roma (8/31/23); Mary Ann Apap Heller, Austin (8/31/25); Patty Nuss, Corpus Christi (8/31/23); Karen Partee, Marshall (8/31/25); Sean Payton, Killeen (8/31/21); Marci Roberts, Marathon (8/31/21). Exec. Dir. Gary Gibbs

($129,927), 920 Colorado St., Ste. 501, PO Box 13406, Austin 78711-3406; (512) 463-5535.

Assistive and Rehabilitative Services, Department of (DARS): (2004) apptv.; 6-yr.; 9 members: Department was dissolved in September 2016 and programs were transferred to Texas Workforce Commission.

Athletic Trainers, Advisory Board of: (1971 as Texas Board of Athletic Trainers; name changed in 1975); expenses; 6-yr.; 5 members: Chair Britney Webb, San Marcos (1/31/27); Michael Fitch, Dallas (1/31/23); Darrell Ganus, Kilgore (1/31/21); David Schmidt, San Antonio (1/31/23); David Weir, College Station (1/31/25). PO Box 12157, Austin 78711; (512) 463-5699.

Auditor's Office, State: (1929); 2-yr.; apptd. by Legislative Audit Committee, a joint Senate-House committee: State Auditor (vacant), Robert E. Johnson Bldg., 1501 Congress Ave., P.O. Box 12067, Austin 78711-2067; (512) 936-9500.

Autism and Pervasive Developmental Disorders, Texas Council on: (1987); abolished by the 84th Legislature in 2015. Duties transferred to Texas Health and Human Services Commission.

Banking, Texas Department of: (1923); 2-yr.; apptd. by State Finance Commission; Comm. Charles G. Cooper ($242,925); 2601 N. Lamar Blvd., Austin 78705; (512) 475-1300. (See also Finance Commission of Texas.)

Bar of Texas, State: (1939 as administrative arm of Supreme Court); 46 directors, 36 elected by membership, 6 apptd by Texas Supreme Court, 4 by bar president; 3-yr. terms; also 14 ex officio members, including immediate past chair and out-of-state members; expenses paid from dues collected from membership. Chair Santos Vargas, Texas Law Center, 1414 Colorado St., Austin 78711; (512) 427-1463.

Barbering, Advisory Board on: (1929 as 3-member Texas Board of Barber Examiners; members increased in 1975; name changed in 2005 and functions transferred to Texas Dept. of Licensing & Regulation); 6-yr.; apptd. by dept. commissioners; 5 members: Presiding Officer Ron Jemison, Houston (9/29/21); James Bowens, Round Rock (9/29/19); Jenny Hatch, Alpine (9/29/21); Michelle Wasser, Austin (9/29/25); Ronald Weathers, De Soto (9/29/23). PO Box 12157, Austin 78711; (512) 463-6599.

Behavioral Health Executive Council, Texas: (2019, created by Legislature to comprise 4 existing Boards of Examiners); 6-yr. for presiding member, 2-yr. for others; 9 members: Presiding Member Gloria Canseco, San Antonio (2/1/25); John K. Bielamowicz, Waxahachie (2/1/22); Brian C. Brumley, Sumner (2/1/23); Susan Fletcher, Frisco (2/1/23); George F. Francis IV, Georgetown (2/1/23); Steven Hallbauer, Rockwall (2/1/23); Ben Morris, Cleburne (2/1/22); Jeanene L. Smith, Austin (2/1/22); Christopher S. Taylor, Dallas (2/1/22). Exec. Dir. Darrel D. Spinks, 333 Guadalupe St., Ste. 3-900, Austin 78701; (512) 305-7700.

Blind, Texas Commission for the: as of September 2016 the commission was incorporated into the Texas Workforce Commission.

Blind and Visually Impaired, Texas School for the: (1979); apptv.; 6-yr.; expenses; 9 members: Pres. Lee Sonnenberg, Lubbock (1/31/19); Mary K. Alexander, Valley View (1/31/21); Dan Brown, Pflugerville (1/31/23); Michael Hanley, Leander (1/31/23); Beth Jones, Anna (1/31/25); Brenda Lee, Brownwood (1/31/21); Joseph Muniz, Harlingen (1/31/21); Julie Prause, Columbus (1/31/23); Elaine Robertson, Katy (1/31/25). Supt. Emily Coleman ($142,159), 1100 W. 45th St., Austin 78756; (512) 454-8631.

Bond Review Board, Texas: (1987); composed of Gov., Lt. Gov., House Speaker, and Comptroller; oversees debt financing for Texas' infrastructure and other public purposes, debt issuance, and debt management functions of state and local entities, and the state's private activity bond allocation; Exec. Dir. Rob Latsha ($117,500); 300 W. 15th St., Ste. 409, PO Box 13292, Austin 78711-3292; (512) 463-1741.

Brazos River Authority: (1929 as Brazos River Conservation and Reclamation District; name changed to present form in 1953); apptv.; 6-yr; expenses; 21 members: Presiding Officer Cynthia A. Flores, Round Rock (2/1/21); Thomas Abraham, Sugar Land (2/1/25); Gary Boren, Lubbock (2/1/25); Mike Fernandez, Abilene (2/1/25); Jennifer "Jen" Henderson, Round Rock (2/1/23); Rick Huber, Granbury (2/1/21); Judy Ann Krohn, Georgetown (2/1/23); Traci Garrett LaChance, Danbury (2/1/23); Jim Lattimore Jr., Graford (2/1/25); Royce Lesley, Comanche (2/1/23); Wesley D. Lloyd, Waco (2/1/25); John H. Luton, Granbury (2/1/21); W.J. "Bill" Rankin, Brenham (2/1/21); Austin Ruiz, Harker Heights (2/1/21); Alan K. Sandersen, Sugar Land (2/1/23); David Savage, Katy (2/1/25); Jarrod D. Smith, Danbury (2/1/23); Jeffery Scott Tallas, Sugar Land (2/1/21); W. Wintford "Ford" Taylor III, Waco (2/1/21); R. Wayne Wilson, Bryan (2/1/23); 1 vacancy. Gen. Mgr. David Collinsworth, 4600 Cobbs Dr., PO Box 7555, Waco 76714; (254) 761-3100.

Canadian River Compact Commission: (1951, negotiates with New Mexico and Oklahoma regarding waters of the Canadian); apptv.; 6-yr.; Comm. Roger S. Cox (12/31/21), PO Box 1750, Amarillo 79105-1750; (806) 242-9651.

Canadian River Municipal Water Authority: (1953); 2-yr.; 17 members apptd. by member cities: Pres. Richard Ellis, Levelland; Donnie Brumley, Plainview; Jerry Carlson, Pampa; James O. Collins, Lubbock; Tyke Dipprey, Plainview; Rickey Dunn, Brownfield; Charles Gillingham, Borger, Bill Hallerberg, Amarillo; Jay House, Lubbock; Jay Dee House, Tahoka; Glendon Jett, Borger; Buddy Moore, Levelland; Cris Norris, Lamesa; Mac Smith, Pampa; Roy Urrutia, Amarillo; Charlie Vaughn, O'Donnell; Chad Wilson, Slaton. Gen. Mgr. Kent Satterwhite, 9875 Water Authority Rd., PO Box 9, Sanford 79078; (806) 865-3325.

Cancer Prevention & Research Institute of Texas: (1985 as Texas Cancer Council; name changed in 2007); apptv.; 6-yr.; expenses; 9 members, 3 each apptd. by Gov., Lt. Gov., and House Speaker: Presiding Officer Donald "Dee" Margo, El Paso (1/31/27); David A. Cummings, San Angelo (1/31/23), Ambrosio Hernandez, Pharr (1/31/25); Will Montgomery, Dallas (1/31/23); Mahendra C. Patel, San Antonio (1/31/21); Cindy Barberio Payne, Spring Branch (1/31/25); William Rice, Austin (1/31/25); Craig Rosenfeld, Dallas (1/31/17); 1 vacancy. CEO Wayne Roberts ($281,875), 1701 Congress Ave., Ste. 6-127, PO Box 12097, Austin 78711; (512) 463-3190.

Cardiovascular Disease and Stroke, Texas Council on: (1999); apptv.; 6-yr.; 14 members: 3 ex officio: 1 each from Texas Workforce Commission, Health and Human Services Commission, Texas Dept. of State Health Services; 11 apptd.: Chair Suzanne Hildebrand, Live Oak (2/1/25); Elie R. Balesh, Houston (2/1/25); Stanley Duchman, Houston (2/1/27); Janet Hewlett, Florence (2/1/23); Samantha Kersey, Dickinson (2/1/25); Sherron D. Meeks, Odessa (2/1/27); J. Neal Rutledge, Austin (2/1/23); Shilpa Shamapant, Austin (2/1/27); Harry "Kyle" Sheets, Ovalo (2/1/23); E'Loria Simon-Campbell, Houston (2/1/25); Maricella "Marcie" Gonzalez Wilson, Lakeway (2/1/27). PO Box 149347, Austin 78714-9347; (512) 776-7111.

Cemetery, Texas State: (1997); apptv.; 6-yr.; 3 members: Chair Benjamin M. Hanson, Austin (2/1/21); James L. "Jim" Bayless Jr., Austin (2/1/23); Carolyn Hodges, Houston (2/1/25). Admin. Nathan Stephens, 909 Navasota St., Austin 78702; (512) 463-6600.

Central Colorado River Authority (See Colorado River Authority, Central.)

Chemist, Office of the Texas State: (1911); ex officio, indefinite term: State Chemist Tim Herrman, 445 Agronomy Rd., PO Box 3160, College Station 77841-3160; (979) 845-1121.

Chiropractic Examiners, Texas Board of: (1949); apptv.; 6-yr.; expenses; 9 members: Pres. Mark Bronson, Fort Worth (2/1/27); Sarah Abraham, Sugar Land (2/1/27); Brandon Allen, Austin

(2/1/25); Nicholas Baucum, Corpus Christi (2/1/27); Michael P. Henry, Austin (2/1/25); Mindy Neal, Bovina (2/1/23); Ebony Todd, Fort Hood (2/1/23); Debra White, Nacogdoches (2/1/23); Scott Wofford, Abilene (2/1/25). Exec. Dir. Patrick Fortner ($100,830), 333 Guadalupe St., Ste. 3-825, Austin 78701; (512) 305-6700.

Civil Commitment Office, Texas: (2011 as Office of Violent Sex Offender Management; took present name in 2015); apptv.; 6-yr.; 5 members: Chair Christy Jack, Fort Worth (2/1/23); Jose Aliseda, Beeville (2/1/25); Roberto Dominguez, Mission (2/1/23); Rona Stratton Gouyton, Fort Worth (2/1/27); Kathryn E. "Katie" McClure, Kingwood (2/1/27). Exec. Dir. Marsha McLane, 4616 W. Howard Ln., Bldg. 2, Ste. 350, Austin 72728; (512) 341-4421.

Coastal Water Authority: (1967 as Coastal Industrial Water Authority; name changed in 1985); 2-yr.; per diem and expenses; 7 members; 4 apptd. by Houston mayor; 3 by Gov.: Pres. D. Wayne Klotz, Houston (3/31/23); Tony L. Council, Houston (3/31/23); Thomas A. Reiser, Houston (4/1/19); Jon M. "Mark" Sjolander, Dayton (4/1/22); Joseph G. Soliz, Houston (3/31/18); Douglas E. Walker, Beach City (4/1/19); Giti Zarinkelk, Houston (3/31/18). Exec. Dir. Donald R. Ripley, 1801 Main St., Ste. 800, Houston 77002; (713) 658-9020.

Colorado River Authority, Central: (1935); Abolished December 1, 2017 by 85th Legislature. All assets were transferred to Coleman County.

Colorado River Authority, Lower: (1934 as 9-member board; members increased in 1951 and 1975); apptv.; 6-yr.; per diem on duty; 15 members: Chair Timothy Timmerman, Austin (2/1/25); Michael L. "Mike" Allen, Kerrville (2/1/25); Lori A. Berger, Flatonia (2/1/21); Melissa K. Blanding, Driftwood (2/1/27); Stephen F. Cooper, El Campo (2/1/23); Joseph M. "Joe" Crane, Bay City (2/1/27); Laura D. Figueroa, Brenham (2/1/23); Carol Freeman, Llano (2/1/27); Raymond A. "Ray" Gill Jr., Horseshoe Bay (2/1/23); Thomas L. "Tom" Kelley, Eagle Lake (2/1/23); Robert "Bobby" Lewis, Elgin, (2/1/25); Thomas Michael Martine, Cypress Mill (2/1/25); Margaret D. "Meg" Voelter, Austin (2/1/25); Martha Leigh M. Whitten, San Saba (2/1/27); Nancy Eckert Yeary, Lampasas (2/1/23). Gen. Mgr. Phil Wilson, 3700 Lake Austin Blvd., PO Box 220, Austin 78767; (512) 578-3200.

Colorado River Authority, Upper: (1935 as 9-member board; reorganized in 1965); apptv.; 6-yr.; per diem and expenses; 9 members: Chair Nancy Blackwell, Ballinger (2/1/27); Reese Braswell, Bronte (2/1/27); Erica Hall, Abilene (2/1/27); Fred Hernandez Jr., San Angelo (2/1/25); Leslie Lasater, San Angelo (2/1/27); Tanner Mahan, Menard (2/1/23); Kathryn Mews, Menard (2/1/23); Hugh "Che" Stone, San Angelo (2/1/23); Mason Vaughan, Eldorado (2/1/25). Director Scott McWilliams, 512 Orient, San Angelo 76903; (325) 655-0565.

Consumer Credit Commissioner, Texas Office of: Comm. Leslie L. Pettijohn ($196,000), 2601 N. Lamar Blvd., Austin 78705; (512) 936-7600. Consumer Help Line: (800) 538-1579.

Cosmetology, Advisory Board on: (1935 as 3-member State Board of Hairdressers and Cosmetologists; name changed and members increased in 1971; changed to current name in 2005 and functions transferred to Texas Dept. of Licensing and Regulation); apptv.; per diem and expenses; 6-yr.; 10 members: Presiding Officer Aleshia Rivera, Mount Pleasant (9/29/25); Anthony Anderson, Spring Branch (9/29/25); Aurora B. Farthing, Lubbock (9/29/25); Natalie Inderman, Shallowater (9/29/25); Betty Neff, Austin (9/29/23); Mary Paschal-Lindsay, Pearland (9/29/23); Vanessa Robbins, Houston (9/29/21); Ron Robinson, Waco (12/20/21); Sam Webb, Austin (9/29/21); 1 ex officio member representing Texas Education Agency. c/o Texas Dept. of Licensing & Regulation, 920 Colorado St., PO Box 12157, Austin 78711; (512) 463-6599.

Counselors, Texas State Board of Examiners of Professional: (1981); apptv.; 6-yr.; expenses; 9 members: Chair Steven Hallbauer, Rockwall (2/1/23); Carmelia "Lia" Amuna, Killeen (2/1/27); Loretta J. Bradley, Lubbock (2/1/27); Brenda S. Compagnone, San Antonio (2/1/25); Vanessa Hall, Tomball (2/1/25); Garrett A. Narren, Dallas (2/1/25); Roy Smith, Midland (2/1/23); Carolyn Janie Stubblefield, Dallas (2/1/23); Christopher S. Taylor, Dallas (2/1/27). Admin. Cristina De Luna, 333 Guadalupe St., Ste. 2-450, Austin 78701; (512) 305-7700.

County and District Retirement System, Texas: (See Retirement System, Texas County and District.)

Court Administration, Office of: (1985); apptd. by State Supreme Court chief justice; 1 member who also serves as executive director of the Texas Judicial Council: Admin. Dir. David Slayton ($197,415), 205 W. 14th St., Ste. 600, PO Box 12066, Austin 78711-2066; (512) 463-1625.

Court Interpreter Advisory Board, Licensed: Apptv. by Texas Supreme Court; part of Judicial Branch Certification Commission; staggered terms; 6-yr., 5 members: Presiding Officer Laura Angelini, San Antonio (2/1/27); Luis Garcia, Keller (2/1/27); Robert Richter Jr., Houston (2/1/19); Melissa Wallace, San Antonio (2/1/19); Cynthia de Peña, McAllen (2/1/23). 205 W. 14th St., Ste. 600, PO Box 12066, Austin 78711-2066; (512) 463-1630.

Court Reporters Certification Advisory Board: Apptv. by Texas Supreme Court; part of Judicial Branch Certification Commission; staggered terms; 6-yr., 7 members: Presiding Officer Cathleen Stryker, San Antonio (2/1/27); Janice Eidd-Meadows, Tyler (12/31/27); Deborah K. Hamon, Rockwall (2/1/23); Shari J. Krieger, Mansfield (2/1/27); Molly Pela, Houston (2/1/19); Whitney Alden Riley, Boerne (2/1/19); Kim Tindall, San Antonio (2/1/23). 205 W. 14th St., Ste. 600, PO Box 12066, Austin 78711-2066; (512) 475-4368.

Credit Union Commission: (1949 as 3-member Credit Union Advisory Commission; name changed and members increased to 6 in 1969; increased again in 1981); apptv.; 6-yr.; expenses; 9 members: Chair Yusuf E. Farran, El Paso (2/15/21); Elizabeth L. "Liz" Bayless, Austin (2/15/25); Karyn C. Brownlee, Coppell (2/15/23); Steven "Steve" Gilman, Houston (2/15/21); Sherri Brannon Merket, Midland (2/15/23); James L. "Jim" Minge, Arlington (6/15/23); Kay Rankin-Swan, Monahans (2/15/25); David F. Shurtz, Hudson Oaks (2/15/25); Beckie Stockstill Cobb, Deer Park (2/15/21). Comm. John J. Kolhoff ($192,500), 914 E. Anderson Ln., Austin 78752; (512) 837-9236.

Crime Stoppers Council, Texas: (1981); apptv.; 4-yr.; per diem and expenses; 5 members: Chair Greg New, Waxahachie (9/1/24); Lauren Day, Austin (9/1/24); Perry Gilmore, Amarillo (9/1/21); Carlo Hernandez, Brownsville (9/1/21); Stephanie Vanskike, Beaumont (9/1/24). www.the texascrimestoppers.org.

Crime Victims' Institute: (1995 as function of attorney general's office; transferred to Sam Houston State University in 2003); apptv.; 2-yr.; 15 members: Justin Berry, Austin (1/31/23); Lee Ann Breading, Denton (1/31/23); Abigail Brookshire (1/31/23); Melissa Carter, Bryan (1/31/22); Matthew L. Ferrara, Austin (1/31/22); Libby Hamilton, Austin (1/31/23); Joan Huffman (1/31/23); Shawn Kennington, Pittsburg (1/31/22); Lindsay Kinzie, Fort Worth (1/31/22); Gene Pack, Houston (1/31/22); JD Robertson, Wimberley (1/31/22); Andrea Sparks, Austin (1/31/22); Hector Villarreal, Alice (1/31/22); James White, Hillister (1/31/23); Erleigh Wiley, Forney (1/31/23). Dir. Mary Breaux, 816 17th St., PO Box 2180, Huntsville 77341-2180; (936) 294-3100.

Criminal Justice, Texas Department of: (1989, assumed duties of former Department of Corrections, Adult Probation Commission and Board of Pardons and Paroles); apptv; 6-yr.; expenses; 9 members: Chair Patrick O'Daniel, Austin (2/1/23); Rodney Burrow, Pittsburg (2/1/27); E.F. "Mano" DeAyala, Houston (2/1/23); Molly Francis, Dallas (2/1/2025); Faith Johnson, Dallas (2/1/25); Larry Miles, Amarillo (2/1/23); Eric Nichols, Austin (2/1/27); Derrelynn Perryman, Fort Worth (2/1/27); Sichan Siv, San Antonio (2/1/25). Exec. Dir. Bryan Collier ($275,501), 209

W. 14th St., Ste. 500, PO Box 13084, Austin 78711-3084; (512) 463-9988.

Deaf, Texas School for the: (1979); apptv.; 6-yr.; expenses; 9 members: Pres. Eric Hogue, Wylie (1/31/21); Shawn P. Saladin, Edinburg (1/31/23); Angie Wolf, Dripping Springs (1/31/21); Sha Cowan, Dripping Springs (1/31/23); Ryan D. Hutchison, Austin (1/31/21); Dina Lynne Moore, Round Rock (1/31/27); Christopher Moreland, New Braunfels (1/31/23); David Saunders, Waxahachie (1/31/25); Keith Sibley, Bedford (1/31/25); Heather Withrow, Austin (1/31/25). Supt. Claire Bugen ($148,908), 1102 S. Congress Ave., Austin 78704; (512) 462-5353.

Demographic Center, Texas: (2001); created by 77th Legislature; State Demographer Lloyd B. Potter, 1700 Congress Ave., PO Box 13455, Austin 78711; (512) 463-8390.

Dental Examiners, State Board of: (1919 as 6-member board; increased to 9 members in 1971; increased to 12 in 1981; increased to 15 in 1991; sunsetted in 1994; reconstituted with 18 members in 1995; reduced to present number in 2005); apptv.; 6-yr.; per diem and expenses; 11 members: Presiding Officer David H. Yu, Austin (2/1/25); Linda Treviño Burke, Harlingen (2/1/25); Bryan Henderson II, Dallas (2/1/23); Lorie Jones, Magnolia (2/1/23); Yvonne E. Maldonado, El Paso (2/1/27); Robert G. McNeill, Dallas (2/1/27); Margo Y. Melchor, Houston (2/1/27); Lois M. Palermo, League City (2/1/25); Marquita Pride, Little Elm (2/1/27); Jorge Quirch, Missouri City (2/1/23); Kathryn Sisk, Spring Branch (2/1/23). Exec. Dir. Casey Nichols ($105,000), 333 Guadalupe, Tower 3, Ste. 800, Austin 78701-3942; (512) 463-6400.

Diabetes Council, Texas: (1983; with 5 ex officio and 6 public members serving 2-yr. terms; changed in 1987 to 3 ex officio and 8 public members; changed to present in 1991; term length changed from 4 to 6 years in 1997); 6-yr.; 16 members: 11 apptv.: Chair Feyi Obamehinti, Keller (2/1/23); Gary Francis, San Antonio (2/1/27); Felicia Fruia-Edge, Rancho Viejo (2/1/23); Dirrell Jones, Farmers Branch (2/1/25); Aida "Letty" Moreno-Brown, El Paso (2/1/27); Ninfa Peña-Purcell, College Station (2/1/27); Stephen Ponder, Belton (2/1/25); Ardis Reed, Hideaway (2/1/23); Jason Ryan, Houston (2/1/25); Maryanne Strobel, Cypress (2/1/27); Christine Wicke, McKinney (2/1/25). The 5 ex officio members include 1 each from Texas Workforce Commission, Texas Health and Human Services Commission, Texas Dept. of State Health Services, Employees Retirement System, and Teacher Retirement System. Coord. Ashley Doyle, 1100 W. 49th St., PO Box 149347, Austin 78714-9347; (512) 776-2834.

Dietitians, State Board of Examiners of: All duties transferred to the Texas Department of Licensing and Regulation transferred to the Texas Department of Licensing and Regulation. Abolished in 2015 by the 84th Legislature, S.B. 202.

Disabilities, Governor's Committee on People with: (1949 as Gov.'s Committee on Employment of the Handicapped; re-created in 1983 as Gov.'s Committee for Disabled Persons; given current name and expanded duties in 1991); apptv.; 2-yr. and at pleasure of Gov.; 12 members: Chair Aaron W. Bangor, Austin (2/1/22); Kori A. Allen, Plano (2/1/22); Ellen M. Bauman, Joshua (2/1/23); Evelyn M. Cano, Pharr (2/1/22); Elyse L. Lieberman, Victoria (2/1/23); Eric N. Lindsay, San Antonio (2/1/23); Richard Martinez, San Antonio (2/1/22); Kristie L. Orr, College Station (2/1/23); Dylan Rafaty, Plano (2/1/23); Emma F. Rudkin, Boerne (2/1/22); Amy L. Scott, Austin (2/1/22); Kristopher A.W. "Kris" Workman, Sutherland Springs (2/1/23). Exec. Dir. Ron Lucey, 1100 San Jacinto Blvd., Austin 78701; (512) 463-5739; 7-1-1 TDD.

Disabilities, Texas Council for Developmental: (1971); apptv.; 6-yr.; 27 members; 19 apptv.: Chair Mary Durheim, Spring (2/1/23); Rebecca "Hunter" Adkins, Lakeway (2/1/21); Kimberly Blackmon, Fort Worth (2/1/21); Ronald "Ronnie" Browning, Spring (2/1/23); Gladys Cortez, McAllen (2/1/23); Kristen Cox, El Paso (2/1/21); Maverick Crawford III, San Antonio (2/1/25); Andrew "Andy" Crim, Fort Worth (2/1/25); Scott McAvoy, Cedar Park (2/1/21); Michael Peace, Poteet (2/1/25); Randell Resneder, Lubbock (2/1/21); Eric Shahid, Somerville (2/1/25); Molly Spratt, Austin (2/1/21); Emmett "Toby" Summers III, San Antonio (2/1/21); Robert Schier III, Elgin (2/1/23); Lora Taylor, Houston (2/1/25); John Thomas, Weatherford (2/1/23); Kimberly Torres, Houston (2/1/25), 1 vacancy. 8 ex officio members from various state agencies. Exec. Dir. Beth Stalvey ($138,433), 6201 E. Oltorf St., Ste. 600, Austin 78741-7509; (512) 437-5432.

Disabilities, Texas Council on Purchasing from People with: Duties transfered to Texas Workforce Commission in 2015. Abolished by the legislature in 2015.

Disabilities, Texas Office for Prevention of Developmental: Abolished in 2017.

Education, State Board of: (1866; re-created in 1928 and re-formed in 1949 by Gilmer-Aikin Act to consist of 21 elective members from districts co-extensive with 21 congressional districts at that time; increased to 24 with congressional redistricting in 1971; increased to 27 with congressional redistricting in 1981; reorganized by special legislative session as 15-member apptv. board in 1984; became elective board again in 1988); expenses; 4-yr.; 15 members: Dist. 1: Georgina C. Pérez (D), El Paso (1/1/23); Dist. 2: Ruben Cortez Jr. (D), Brownsville (1/1/23); Dist. 3: Marisa B. Perez-Diaz (D), Converse (1/1/23); Dist. 4: Lawrence A. Allen Jr. (D), Houston (1/1/23); Dist. 5: Rebecca Bell-Metereau (D), San Marcos (1/1/23); Dist. 6: Will Hickman (R), Houston (1/1/23); Dist. 7: Matt Robinson (R), Dickinson (1/1/23); Dist. 8: Audrey Young (R), Nacogdoches (1/1/23); Dist. 9: Chair Keven Ellis (R), Lufkin (1/1/23); Dist. 10: Tom Maynard (R), Florence (1/1/23); Dist. 11: Patricia Hardy (R), Fort Worth (1/1/23); Dist. 12: Pam Little (R), Fairview (1/1/23); Dist. 13: Aicha Davis (D), Dallas (1/1/23); Dist. 14: Sue Melton-Malone (R), Robinson (1/1/23); Dist. 15: Jay Johnson (R), Pampa (1/1/23). c/o Texas Education Agency, 1701 Congress Ave., Austin 78701-1494; (512) 463-9007.

Education Agency, Texas: (1949, established by Gilmer-Aikin Act, replacing office led since 1866 by State Superintendent of Public Instruction); presently led by Commissioner of Education, apptd. by Gov. since 1995; 4-yr.: Comm. Mike Morath ($220,375 plus supplement), 1701 Congress Ave., Austin 78701; (512) 463-9734.

Education Board, Southern Regional: (1969); apptv.; 4-yr.; 5 members: Gov. Greg Abbott (ex officio, 1/20/23); Harrison Keller, Austin (6/30/21); Pedro Martinez, San Antonio (6/30/23); Mike Morath, Austin (6/30/22); Larry Taylor, Friendswood (6/30/24). Pres. Stephen L. Pruitt, 592 10th St. N.W., Atlanta, GA 30318-5776; (404) 875-9211.

Educator Certification, State Board for: (1995); apptv.; 6-yr.; expenses; 15 members; 4 ex officio: rep. of Comm. of Education, rep. of Comm. of Higher Education, rep. of alternative certification program, dean of a college of education; 11 apptv.: Chair John P. Kelly, Pearland (2/1/23); Robert "Bob" Brescia, Odessa (2/1/23); Rohanna Brooks-Sykes, Spring (2/1/27); Tommy L. Coleman, Livingston (2/1/25); Julia Dvorak, Pflugerville (2/1/25); Rex Gore, Austin (2/1/27); Melissa Isaacs, Jewett (2/1/27); Andrew Kim, New Braunfels (2/1/27); Courtney Boswell MacDonald, Kerrville (2/1/23); Shareefah Mason, Dallas (2/1/25); Jean Streepey, Dallas (2/1/25). 1701 Congress Ave., 5th Fl., Austin 78701-1494; (512) 936-8400.

Edwards Aquifer Authority: (1993); 4-yr.; expenses; 17 members (2 apptv. and 15 elected from single-member districts). Apptv. members: Fohn Bendele, Medina & Uvalde Cos. (12/1/24); Gary Middleton, South Central Texas Water Advisory Committee (12/1/24). Elected members: Dist. 1: Carol Patterson, Bexar Co. (12/1/22); Dist. 2: Byron Miller, Bexar Co. (12/1/24); Dist. 3: Abelardo A. "Abe" Salinas III, Bexar Co. (12/1/22); Dist. 4: Benjamin Youngblood III, Bexar Co. (12/1/24); Dist. 5: Randall Perkins, Bexar Co. (12/1/22); Dist. 6: Deborah Carington, Bexar Co. (12/1/24); Dist. 7: Enrique Valdivia, Bexar Co. (12/1/22); Dist. 8: Kathleen Krueger, Comal Co. (12/1/24); Dist. 9: Ronald J. Walton, Comal & Guadalupe Cos. (12/1/22); Dist. 10: Austin

Bodin, Hays Co. (12/1/22); Dist. 11: Rachel Allyn Sanborn, Hays & Caldwell Cos. (12/1/22); Dist. 12: Scott Yanta, Medina Co. (12/1/24); Dist. 13: Chair Luana Buckner, Medina & Atascosa Cos. (12/1/22); Dist. 14: Donald W. Baker, Uvalde Co. (12/1/24); Dist. 15: Rader Gilleland, Uvalde Co. (12/1/22). Gen. Mgr. Roland Ruiz, 900 E. Quincy St., San Antonio 78215; (210) 222-2204.

Emergency Communications, Commission on State: (1985 as 17-member Advisory Commission on State Emergency Communications; name changed and members reduced to 12 in 2000); apptv.; 4-yr.; expenses; 12 members, 3 ex officio: reps. of Dept. of State Health Services, Public Utility Comm., and Dept. of Information Resources; 9 apptd.: Presiding Officer Debbie S. "Debi" Hays, Odessa (9/1/23); James Beauchamp, Midland (9/1/25); Sue A. Brannon, Midland (9/1/23); Lucille Maes, Angleton (9/1/25); Jack D. Miller, Denton (9/1/21); Clinton Sawyer, Amherst (9/1/25); Catherine A. "Cathy" Skurow, Portland (9/1/23); Larry L. "Chip" VanSteenberg, Conroe (9/1/21); Von C. Washington Sr., El Paso (9/1/21). Exec. Dir. Kelli Merriweather ($132,835), 333 Guadalupe St., Ste. 2-212, Austin 78701; (512) 305-6911.

Emergency Management, Texas Division of: (1951 as Division of Defense and Disaster Relief; incorporated into Dept. of Public Safety in 1963; took current name in 2009; became component of Texas A&M University System in 2019.) Chief W. Nim Kidd, 1033 La Posada Dr., Ste. 300, Austin 78752; (512) 424-2208.

Emergency Services Retirement System, Texas: (See Retirement System, Texas Emergency Services.)

Engineers and Land Surveyors, Texas Board of Professional: (1937 as 6-member Texas State Board of Registration for Professional Engineers; members increased to 9 in 1981; name changed to Texas Board of Professional Engineers in 1997, took current name in 2019 when merged with Texas Board of Professional Land Surveying); apptv.; per diem and expenses; 6-yr.; 10 members, inc. 1 rep from General Land Office with unlimited term (Mark J. Neugebauer, Round Rock); 9 termed members: Chair Sina K. Nejad, Beaumont (9/26/25); Ademola Adejokun, Arlington (9/26/23); Lamberto Ballí, Boerne (9/26/21); Albert Cheng, Houston (9/26/21); Coleen M. Johnson, Leander (9/26/25); Marguerite McClinton Stoglin, Grand Prairie (9/26/25); Cathy Norwood, Midland (9/26/21); Rolando Rubiano, Harlingen (9/26/23); Kiran Shah, Richmond (9/26/23). Exec. Dir. Lance Kinney ($176,040), 1917 S. Interstate 35, Austin 78741; (512) 440-7723.

Environmental Quality, Texas Commission on: (1913 as State Board of Water Engineers; name changed in 1962 to Texas Water Commission; reorganized and name changed in 1965 to Water Rights Commission; reorganized and name changed back to Texas Water Commission in 1977 to perform judicial function for the Texas Dept. of Water Resources; name changed to Texas Natural Resource Conservation Commission in 1993; changed to present form in 2002); apptv.; 6-yr.; 3 members full-time ($201,000): Chair Jon Niermann, Austin (8/31/21); Bobby Janecka, Austin (8/31/25); Emily Lindley, Austin (8/31/23). Exec. Dir. Toby Baker ($223,277), 12100 Park 35 Circle, PO Box 13087, Austin 78711-3087; (512) 239-1000.

Ethics Commission, Texas: (1991); apptv.; 4-yr.; 8 members: 4 apptd. by Gov., 2 by Lt. Gov., 2 by House Speaker: Chair Chad M. Craycraft, Dallas (11/19/23); Randall H. Erben, Austin (11/19/21); Chris Flood, Houston (11/19/19); Mary K. "Katie" Kennedy, Houston (11/19/23); Patrick W. Mizell, Houston (11/19/21); Richard S. Schmidt, Corpus Christi (11/19/21); Joseph O. Slovacek, Houston (11/19/21); Steven D. Wolens, Dallas (11/19/19). Exec. Dir. Anne Temple Peters ($139,097), 201 E. 14th St., 10th Fl., PO Box 12070, Austin 78711-2070; (512) 463-5800. Disclosure Filing Fax: (512) 463-8808.

Facilities Commission, Texas: (2007; formerly Texas Building and Procurement Commission); apptv.; 6-yr.; 7 members: Chair Steven Alvis, Houston (1/31/23); William Allensworth, Austin (1/31/21); Brian Bailey, Austin (1/31/27); Eddy Betancourt, Mission (1/31/23); Patti C. Jones, Lubbock (1/31/21); C. Price Wagner, Dallas (1/31/25); 1 vacancy. Exec. Dir. Mike Novak ($177,982), 1711 San Jacinto Blvd., PO Box 13047, Austin 78711-3047; (512) 463-3446.

Family and Protective Services, Department of: (1991 as Dept. of Protective and Regulatory Services; reorganized to present form in 2004); apptv.; 6-yr.; 9 members: Chair Bonnie Hellums, Houston (2/1/23); Connie Almeida, Richmond (2/1/27); Omedi "Dee Dee" Cantu Arismendez, Alice (2/1/27); Liesa Hackett, Huntsville (2/1/23); Greg Hamilton, Hutto (2/1/27); Cortney Jones, Austin (2/1/25); Matt Kouri, Austin (2/1/23); Julie Krawczyk, Garland (2/1/25); Enrique Mata, El Paso (2/1/25). Comm. Jaime Masters ($215,000), 701 W. 51st St., PO Box 149030, Austin 78714-9030; (512) 438-4800. Abuse Hotline: (800) 252-5400. Ombudsman Hotline: (800) 720-7777.

Film Commission, Texas: (1971, became part of the Economic Development and Tourism Division in office of Gov. in 2015); Dir. Stephanie Whallon ($108,700), 1100 San Jacinto Blvd., Ste. 3.410, PO Box 12428, Austin 78711; (512) 463-9200.

Finance Commission of Texas: (1923 as Banking Commission; reorganized as Finance Commission in 1943 with 9 members; members increased to 12 in 1983; changed back to 9 members in 1989; increased to 11 in 2009); apptv.; 6-yr.; per diem and traveling expenses; Chair Phillip A. Holt, Bonham (2/1/22); Robin Armstrong, Friendswood (2/1/22); Robert "Bob" Borochoff, Houston (2/1/22); Hector J. Cerna, Eagle Pass (2/1/26); Larry Long, Dallas (2/1/26); William M. "Will" Lucas, Center (2/1/24); George "Cliff" McCauley, San Antonio (2/1/24); Sharon McCormick, Frisco (2/1/26); Vince E. Puente Sr., Fort Worth (2/1/24); Debbie Scanlon, Missouri City (2/1/22); Laura Nassri Warren, Palmhurst (2/1/26). Exec. Dir. Charles G. Cooper, 2601 N. Lamar Blvd., Austin 78705; (512) 936-6222. (See also Banking, Texas Department of.)

Fire Fighters' Pension Commissioner: (1937); Abolished by the 83rd Legislature, S.B. 220 in 2013. (See Retirement System, Texas Emergency Services.)

Fire Protection, Texas Commission on: (1991; formed by consolidation of Fire Dept. Emergency Board and Commission on Fire Protection Personnel Standards and Education); apptv.; 6-yr.; expenses; 13 members: Presiding Officer J.P. Steelman, Longview (2/1/23); Christopher G. Cantu, Round Rock (2/1/27); David Coatney, College Station (2/1/27); Sue De Villez, Georgetown (2/1/25); Michael Glynn, Roanoke (2/1/27); Paul Hamilton, Amarillo (2/1/25); Mike Jones, Burleson (2/1/23); Clyde Loll, Huntsville (2/1/27); Bob D. Morgan, Fort Worth (2/1/23); Mala Sharma, Houston (2/1/23); Tim Smith, Lubbock (2/1/27); Kelly Vandygriff, Abernathy (2/1/25); Rusty Wilson, Mesquite (2/1/25). Exec. Dir. Mike Wisko ($117,103), 1701 Congress, Ste. 1-105, PO Box 2286, Austin 78768-2286; (512) 936-3838.

Forensic Science Commission, Texas: (2005); apptv.: 2-yr.; 9 members: 4 apptd. by Gov., 3 by Lt. Gov., and 2 by Atty. Gen.: Presiding Officer Jeffrey J. Barnard, Dallas (9/1/21); Bruce Budowle, North Richland Hills (9/1/22); Patrick Buzzini, Spring (9/1/22); Michael Coble, Fort Worth (2/1/21); Mark Daniel, Fort Worth (9/1/21); Nancy Downing, Bryan (9/1/22); Jasmine Drake, Houston (9/1/22); Sarah Kerrigan, The Woodlands, (9/1/21); Jarvis Parsons, Bryan (9/1/2021). Coor. Kathryn Adams, 1700 Congress Ave., Ste. 445, Austin, TX 78701; (888) 296-4232.

Funeral Service Commission, Texas: (1903 as State Board of Embalming; 1935 as State Board of Funeral Directors and Embalmers; name changed to present form in 1987); apptv.; per diem and expenses; 6-yr.; 7 members: Presiding Officer Larry Allen, Mesquite (2/1/27); Timothy Brown, McAllen (2/1/27); Kevin Combest, Lubbock (2/1/25); Melanie Grammar, Whitewright (2/1/25); Dianne Hefley, Amarillo (2/1/23); Jonathan Scepanski, McAllen (2/1/25); Kristin Tips, San Antonio

(2/1/23). Exec. Dir. Glenn Bower ($99,721), 333 Guadalupe St., Ste. 2-110, Austin 78701; (512) 936-2474.

Geoscientists, Texas Board of Professional: (2001); apptv.; expenses; 3-yr.; 9 members (6 professional geoscientists, 3 public members): Chair Becky L. Johnson, Fort Worth (2/1/23); Bereket M. Derie, Georgetown (2/1/27); Margon Dillard, Richmond (2/1/25); Steven Fleming, Shavano Park (2/1/27); Edward F. Janak Jr., Fredericksburg (2/1/25); W. David Prescott II, Amarillo (2/1/25); Brandon Stowers, Austin (2/1/23); LaFawn Thompson, New Braunfels (2/1/27); Mark N. Varhaug, Dallas (2/1/23). Exec. Dir. Rene D. Truan ($109,157), 333 Guadalupe St., Ste. 1-530; PO Box 13225, Austin 78711; (512) 936-4408.

Guadalupe River Authority, Upper: (1939); apptv.; 6-yr.; 9 members: Pres. Blake W. Smith, Hunt (2/1/27); Lynda Ables, Kerrville (2/1/25); Gene Allen, Kerrville (2/1/25); Aaron C. Bulkley, Hunt (2/1/25); Austin Dickson, Kerrville (2/1/27); Mike Hughes, Ingram (2/1/23); Diane L. McMahon, Kerrville (2/1/27); William R. Rector, Kerrville (2/1/23); Maggie Snow, Kerrville (2/1/23). Gen. Mgr. Ray Buck, 125 Lehmann Dr., Ste. 100, Kerrville 78028; (830) 896-5445.

Guadalupe-Blanco River Authority: (1935); apptv.; per diem and expenses on duty; 6-yr.; 9 members: Chair Dennis L. Patillo, Victoria (2/1/27); William Carbonara, Cuero (2/1/25); Steve Ehrig, Gonzales (2/1/25); Oscar Fogle, Lockhart (2/1/23); Don B. Meador, San Marcos (2/1/25); Kenneth A. Motl, Port Lavaca (2/1/23); Sheila L. Old, Seguin (2/1/27); Andra Wisian, Boerne (2/1/27); 1 vacancy. Gen. Mgr. Kevin Patteson, 933 E. Court St., Seguin 78155; (830) 379-5822.

Guaranteed Student Loan Corporation, Texas: (1979 as nonprofit corp.); as of July 21, 2019, the organization is named Trellis Company.

Guardianship Certification Advisory Board: Apptv. by Texas Supreme Court; part of Judicial Branch Certification Commission; staggered terms; 6-yr., 5 members: Presiding Officer Jamie Maclean, Austin (2/1/27); Jason S. Armstrong, Lufkin (2/1/19); Gladys Burwell, Friendswood (2/1/19); Toni Rhodes Glover, Fort Worth (2/1/23); Chris Wilmoth, Dallas (2/1/27). 205 W. 14th St., Ste. 600, PO Box 12066, Austin 78711-2066; (512) 475-4368.

Gulf Coast Authority: (1969); apptv.; 2-yr.; per diem, expenses on duty; 9 members: 3 apptd. by Gov., 3 by County Commissioners Courts of counties in district, 3 by Mayors Councils of cities in district. Chair Franklin D. R. Jones, Jr., Harris Co. (8/31/21); Billy J. Enochs, Galveston Co. (8/31/21); Gloria Anays Millian Matt, Harris Co. (8/31/21); Lamont E. Meaux, Chambers Co. (8/31/22); W. Chris Peden, Galveston Co. (8/31/21); Mark Schultz, Chambers Co. (8/31/20); Kevin Scott, Galveston Co. (8/31/22); Rita E. Standridge, Chambers Co. (8/31/22); 1 vacancy. Gen. Mgr. Elizabeth Fazio Hale, 910 Bay Area Blvd., Houston 77058; (281) 488-4115.

Gulf States Marine Fisheries Commission: (1949 with members from Texas, Alabama, Florida, Louisiana and Mississippi); apptv.; 3-yr.; 3 Texas members: 2 ex officio: Texas Parks and Wildlife Dept. exec. dir. and 1 member of Legislature; 1 apptd. by Gov.: Douglass W. "Doug" Boyd, Boerne (3/17/23). Exec. Dir. David M. Donaldson, 2404 Government St., Ocean Springs, MS 39564; (228) 875-5912.

Health and Human Services Commission, Texas: (1939 as Dept. of Public Welfare; changed to Texas Dept. of Human Resources in 1977; changed to Texas Dept. of Human Services in 1985; changed to present name in 1992). Exec. Comm. Cecile Erwin Young ($290,258), 4601 W. Guadalupe St., PO Box 13247, Austin 78711-3247; (512) 424-6500.

Health Coordinating Council, Texas Statewide: (1977); apptv.; 6-yr.; 17 members (4 ex officio; 13 apptd. by Gov.): Chair Ayeez A. Lalji, Sugar Land (8/1/19); Dave Allen, San Antonio (8/31/23); Carol Boswell, Andrews (8/1/21); Salil V. Deshpande, Houston (8/1/19); Chelsea Elliott, Austin (8/31/23); Elva Concha LeBlanc, Fort Worth (8/1/19); Elizabeth J. "Betty" Protas, League City (8/31/23); Melinda Rodriguez, San Antonio (8/1/21); Courtney Sherman, Fort Worth (8/1/21); D. Bailey Wynne, Dallas (8/31/23); Nancy Carolyn Williams Yuill, Sugar Land (8/1/19); Shaukat Ali Zakaria, Houston (8/1/21); Yasser Zeid, Longview (8/1/21). Ex-officio members include 1 each from Texas Dept. of State Health Services and Texas Higher Education Coordinating Board, and 2 from Texas Health and Human Services Commission. Coord. Matt Turner, PO Box 149347, Austin, TX 78714-9347; (512) 776-6541.

Health Professions Council: (1993); ex officio; 12 members: 1 from Gov.'s office and 1 each from the following 11 regulating agencies: Texas Board of Chiropractic Examiners, Texas State Board of Dental Examiners, Texas Medical Board, Texas Board of Nursing, Texas Optometry Board, Texas State Board of Pharmacy, Executive Council of Physical Therapy and Occupational Therapy Examiners, Texas Behavioral Health Executive Council, Texas Board of Veterinary Medical Examiners, Texas Funeral Service Commission, Texas Health and Human Services Licensing and Certification Unit. Admin. Officer John Monk ($100,000), 333 Guadalupe St., Ste. 2-220, Austin 78701; (512) 305-8550.

Health Services, Texas Department of State: (2003, merging Texas Dept. of Health, Texas Dept. of Mental Health and Mental Retardation, Texas Health Care Information Council, Texas Comm. on Alcohol and Drug Abuse); Comm. John William Hellerstedt ($271,083), 1100 W. 49th St., PO Box 149347, Austin 78714-9347; (512) 776-7111.

Health Services Authority, Texas: (2007); apptv.; 2-yr.; expenses; 2 ex officio plus 12 apptd. members: Chair Shannon Calhoun, Goliad (6/15/21); Paula Anthony-McMann, Tyler (6/15/21); Victoria Ai Linh Bryant, Houston (6/15/21); Lourdes Cuellar, Houston (6/15/21); Salil Deshpande, Houston (6/15/21); Emily Hartmann, El Paso (6/15/21); Kenneth James, Volente (6/15/21); Jerome Lisk, Tyler (6/15/21); Leticia Rodriguez, Monahans (6/15/21); Jonathan Sandstrom Hill, Lakeway (6/15/21); Siobhan Shahan, Amarillo (6/15/21); Carlos Vital, Friendswood (6/15/21). 901 S. MoPac Blvd., Bldg. 1, Ste. 300, Austin 78746; (512) 329-2730.

Health Services Council, Texas Department of State: (1975); Abolished August 31, 2016.

Hearing Instruments, State Committee of Examiners in the Fitting and Dispensing of: (1969); Abolished by the 84th Legislature, S.B 202. As of Oct. 1, 2016, all duties transferred to the Texas Department of Licensing and Regulation.

Higher Education Coordinating Board, Texas: (1953 as temporary board; became permanent 15-member Texas Commission on Higher Education in 1955; changed to Texas College and University Systems Coordinating Board in 1965; name and membership changed to present form in 1987); apptv.; 6-yr.; expenses; 9 members, plus 1 ex officio student rep. serving 1-yr.: Chair Fred Farias III, McAllen (8/31/25); S. Javaid Anwar, Midland (8/31/21); Ricky A. Raven, Sugar Land (8/31/21); Emma W. Schwartz, El Paso (8/31/25); Matthew B. Smith, Copperas Cove (5/31/22); R. Swan Torn, Houston (8/31/25); Donna N. Williams, Arlington (8/31/23); Welcome W. Wilson Jr., Houston (8/31/23); 2 vacancies. Comm. of Higher Education Harrison Keller ($299,813), 1200 E. Anderson Ln., PO Box 12788, Austin 78711-2788; (512) 427-6101.

Higher Education Tuition Board, Texas Prepaid: (1995); apptv.; expenses; 6 members, plus 1 ex officio chair: State Comptroller; 2 apptd. by Gov. and 4 by Lt. Gov. Members: Michele Purgason, Arlington (2/1/23); Ben Streusand, Spring (2/1/13); Judy Trevino, San Antonio (2/1/27); Javier Villalobos, McAllen (2/1/23); Jarrod Winkcompleck, Austin (2/1/23); Deborah Zuloaga, El Paso (2/1/19). c/o Educational Opportunities and Investment Division, Comptroller of Public Accounts, PO Box 13528, Austin 78711-3528; (800) 445-4723.

A group tours the Landmark Inn State Historic Site, which is maintained by the Texas Historical Commission. Photo courtesy of the Texas Historical Commission

Historian, Texas State: (2005); apptv.; 2-yr.; Monte L. Monroe, Lubbock (9/30/22).

Historical Commission, Texas: (1953); apptv.; expenses; 6-yr.; 15 members: Chair John L. Nau III, Houston (2/1/27); Donna Bahorich, Houston (2/1/25); Earl Broussard, Austin (2/1/23); Jim Bruseth, Austin (2/1/25); Monica Zárate Burdette, Rockport (2/1/27); John W. Crain, Dallas (2/1/25); Garrett Donnelly, Midland (2/11/23); Renee Dutia, Dallas (2/1/25); Lilia Garcia, Raymondville (2/1/27); David Gravelle, Dallas (2/1/27); Laurie Limbacher, Austin (2/1/23); Catherine McKnight, Dallas (2/1/23); Tom Perini, Buffalo Gap (2/1/27); Gilbert E. Peterson, Alpine (2/1/25); Daisy Sloan White, College Station (2/1/23). Exec. Dir. Mark Wolfe ($156,652), 1511 Colorado St., PO Box 12276, Austin 78711; (512) 463-6100.

Holocaust and Genocide Commission, Texas: (2009); created by 81st Legislature. apptv.; 4-yr.; 15 members: Chair Lynne Aronoff, Houston (2/1/23); Jeffrey L. Beck, Dallas (2/1/23); Fran Berg, Dallas (2/1/21); Anne U. Clutterbuck, Houston (2/1/19); Laura Ehrenberg-Chesler, San Antonio (4/13/21); Ilan Emanuel, Corpus Christi (2/1/23); Jonathan Gurwitz, San Antonio (2/1/21); Lucy Taus Katz, Austin (2/1/25); Matthew A. Kornhauser, Houston (2/1/19); Sandra B. Lessig, Houston (2/1/19); Elliott Naishtat, Austin (5/10/21); David A. Patterson, Dallas (4/13/21); Gilbert Tuhabonye, Austin (2/1/21); Providence Umugwaneza, San Antonio (2/1/25); Edward B. Westermann, San Antonio (2/1/21). Exec. Dir. Joy Nathan ($85,600), PO Box 12276, Austin 78711-2276; (512) 463-5108.

Housing and Community Affairs, Texas Department of: (1979 as Texas Housing Agency; merged with Department of Community Affairs and name changed in 1991); apptv.; expenses; 6-yr.; 7 members: Chair Leo Vasquez, Houston (1/31/23); Brandon Batch, Midland (1/31/21); Paul A. Braden, Dallas (1/31/23); Kenny Marchant, Coppell (1/31/25); Ajay Thomas, Austin (1/31/25); Sharon Thomason, Wolfforth (1/31/21); 1 vacancy. Exec. Dir. Bobby Wilkinson ($192,299), 221 E. 11th St., PO Box 13941, Austin 78711-3941; (512) 475-3800.

Housing Corporation, Texas State Affordable: (1994); 6 yrs.; 5 members: Chair Bill Dietz, Waco (2/1/25); Valerie V. Cardenas, San Juan (2/1/25); Courtney Johnson Rose, Missouri City (2/1/27); Andy Williams, Fort Worth (2/1/23); Lemuel Williams, Austin (2/1/27). Pres. David Long, 6701 Shirley Ave., Austin 78752; (512) 477-3555.

Human Rights, Texas Commission on: (2004 as part of the Texas Workforce Commission's Civil Rights Division); as of September 1, 2015, the duties and authority of the commission were transferred to the Texas Workforce Commissioners.

Indigent Defense Commission, Texas: (2001 as Texas Task Force on Indigent Defense, took present name and form in 2011); 13 members: 8 ex officio: Chief Justice of Supreme Court and 3 other judges, 2 reps. from Texas Senate, 2 from House of Reps.; 5 apptd., 2-yr.: Alex Bunin, Houston (2/1/23); Valerie Covey, Georgetown (2/1/22); Richard Evans, Bandera (2/1/22); Missy Medary, Corpus Christi (2/1/22); Gonzalo Rios, San Angelo (2/1/23). Exec. Dir. Geoff Burkhart ($146,000), 209 W. 14th St., Rm. 202, Austin 78701; (512) 936-6994. Toll-free: (866) 499-0656.

Industrialized Building Code Council, Texas: (1973); apptv.; 2-yr.; 12 members: Presiding Officer Roland L. Brown, Midlothian (2/1/21); Suzanne R. Arnold, Garland (2/1/22); Janet Hoffman, Galveston (2/1/22); Otis W. Jones, Houston (2/1/21); Binoy J. Kurien, Pearland (2/1/22); Edwin O. Lofton Jr., Horseshoe Bay (2/1/22); Edward Martin Jr., Austin (2/1/21); Scott A. McDonald III, Keller (2/1/21); Marcela A. Rhoads, Dallas (2/1/22); John D. Scholl, Claude (2/1/22); Stephen Shang, Austin (2/1/21); William F. "Dubb" Smith III, Dripping Springs (2/1/22); c/o Texas Dept. of Licensing and Regulation, PO Box 12157, Austin 78711; (512) 539-5735.

Information Resources, Texas Department of: (1981 as Automated Information and Telecommunications Council; name changed to current in 1990); 6-yr.; expenses; 10 members: 3 ex officio, reps of Dept. of Criminal Justice, Texas Education Agency, and Texas Parks and Wildlife Dept.; 7 apptv.: Chair Ben Gatzke, Fort Worth (2/1/23); Mike Bell, Spring (2/1/23); Stuart A. Bernstein, Austin (2/1/21); Stacey Napier, Austin (2/1/25); Jeffrey Tayon, Houston (2/1/21); Kara Thompson, Austin (2/1/25); 1 vacancy. Exec. Dir. Amanda Crawford ($194,182), 300 W.15thSt., Ste. 1300, PO Box 13564, Austin 78711-3564; (512) 475-4700.

Injured Employee Counsel, Office of: (2005; represents the interests of workers' compensation claimants); apptv.; 2-yr.; 1 member: Public Counsel Jessica Barta ($151,048), 7551 Metro Center Dr., Ste. 100, Austin 78744; (866) 393-6432.

Insurance, Texas Dept. of: (1876 as Dept. of Insurance; changed to Dept. of Agriculture, Insurance, Statistics and History in 1887; to Dept. of Insurance and Banking in 1907; to present name in 1923); Commissioner (apptv.; 2-yr.; position vacant), 333 Guadalupe St., PO Box 12030, Austin 78711; (512) 676-6000.

Insurance Counsel, Office of Public: (See Public Insurance Counsel, Office of.)

Interstate Commission for Adult Offender Supervision: (1937 as Interstate Compact for the Supervision of Parolees and Probationers; took present name in 2000); 50 member states; apptv.: Pam Alexander-Schneider, Lubbock (2/1/27). Compact Admin. for Texas Rene Hinojosa ($165,193). Chair Jeremiah

Stromberg, 3070 Lake Crest Circle, Ste. 400-264, Lexington KY 40513; (859) 721-1050.

Interstate Mining Compact Commission: (1970); 24 member states, plus 2 associate member states; ex officio or apptv., according to gov's. choice; Texas reps. are appointed from the Texas Railroad Commission: Jim Wright. Exec. Dir. Tom Clarke, 437 Carlisle Dr., Ste. A, Herndon, VA 20170; (703) 709-8654.

Interstate Oil & Gas Compact Commission: (1935); 30 member states, plus 8 associate member states; ex officio or apptv., according to gov's. choice; per diem and expenses. Official rep. for Texas: Wayne Christian. Exec. Dir. Lori Wrotenbery, 900 NE 23rd St., Oklahoma City, OK 73105; (405) 522-8380.

Jail Standards, Texas Commission on: (1975); apptv.; 6-yr.; expenses; 9 members: Chair Bill Stoudt, Longview (1/31/25); Patricia M. Anthony, Garland (1/31/25); Raul "Pinky" Gonzales, Refugio (1/31/27); Duane Lock, Southlake (1/31/23); Monica H. McBride, Alpine (1/31/25); Ben Perry, Waco (1/31/23); Esmaeil Porsa, Parker (1/31/23); Ross Garrick Reyes, Melissa (1/31/27); Kelly Rowe, Lubbock (2/1/27). Exec. Dir. Brandon Wood ($116,740), 300 W. 15th St., Ste. 503, PO Box 12985, Austin 78711-2985; (512) 463-5505.

Judicial Branch Certification Commission: (2015); apptv.; 6-yr.; 9 members, inc. 4 apptd by Supreme Court and 5 judges: Chair Sid L. Harle, San Antonio (2/1/23); Velma Arellano, Corpus Christi (2/1/21); Mark P. Blenden, Bedford (2/1/23); Don D. Ford III, Houston (2/1/19); Glen Harrison, Sweetwater (2/1/27); Ann Murray Moore, Edinburg (2/1/21); William C. Sowder, Lubbock (2/1/25); Polly Jackson Spencer, San Antonio (2/1/19); Victor Villarreal, Laredo (2/1/25). 205 W. 14th St., Se. 600, PO Box 12066, Austin 78711-2066; (512) 475-4368.

Judicial Compensation Commission: (2007); apptv.; 6-yr.; expenses; 9 members: Chair William Strawn, Austin (2/1/21); Carlos Amaral, Plano (2/1/25); Alejandro Cestero, Houston (2/1/21); Conrith Warren Davis, Sugar Land (2/1/23); Rebeca Aizpuru Huddle, Bellaire (2/1/25); Linda W. Kinney, Comfort (2/1/23); Curt Nelson, San Antonio (2/1/25); Scott J. Salmans, McGregor (2/1/21); 1 vacancy. 205 W. 14th St., PO Box 12066, Austin 78711-2066; (512) 463-1625.

Judicial Conduct, State Commission on: (1965 as 9-member Judicial Qualifications Commission; name changed to present in 1977); expenses; 6-yr.; 13 members: 6 apptd. by Supreme Court; 2 by State Bar; 5 by Gov.: Chair David C. Hall, Sweetwater (11/19/21); Ronald E. Bunch, Waxahachie (11/19/23); Sujeeth B. Draksharam, Sugar Land (11/19/21); Valerie Ertz, Dallas (11/19/23); Janis Holt, Silsbee (11/19/25); M. Patrick Maguire, Kerrville (11/19/21); Darrick L. McGill, Georgetown (11/19/21); David Patronella, Houston (11/19/21); Clifton Roberson, Tyler (11/19/25); David Schenck, Dallas (11/19/25); Frederick Tate, Colleyville (11/19/23); 2 vacancies. Exec. Dir. Jacqueline Habersham ($128,000), 300 W. 15th St., PO Box 12265, Austin 78711; (512) 463-5533.

Judicial Council, Texas: (1929 as Texas Civil Judicial Council; name changed in 1975); 6-yr.; expenses; 22 members: 16 ex officio and 6 apptd. from general public: Chair Nathan L. Hecht, Dallas (12/31/26); Sharon Keller, Dallas (12/31/24). Legislative Members: Brandon Creighton, Conroe; Jeff Leach, Plano; Reggie Smith, Van Alstyne; Judith Zaffirini, Laredo. Judicial Members: Bill Gravell Jr., Round Rock (2/1/23); Claudia Laird, Conroe (2/1/25); Missy Medary, Corpus Christi (2/1/25); Emily Miskel, McKinney (2/1/23); Valencia Nash, Dallas (2/1/25); Kathleen Person, Temple (2/1/23); Sherry Radack, Houston (2/1/23); Maggie Sawyer, Brady (2/1/23); Edward J. Spillane, College Station (2/1/25); Ken Wise, Houston (2/1/25). Citizen Members: Kevin Bryant, Dallas (6/30/23); Sonia Clayton, Houston (6/30/25); Jon Gimble, Waco (6/30/25); Rachel Racz, Fort Worth (6/30/23); Kenneth S. Saks, San Antonio (6/30/21); Evan Young, Austin (6/30/21). Exec. Dir. David Slayton ($197,415), 205 W. 14th St., Ste. 600, PO Box 12066, Austin 78711-2066; (512) 463-1625.

Judicial Districts Board: (1985); 13 ex officio members (term in other office); 1 apptv. (4 yrs.); ex officio: Chief Justice of Texas Supreme Court; Presiding Judge, Court of Criminal Appeals; Presiding Judge of each of 11 Administrative Judicial Districts; Gov. apptee.: Thomas Phillips, West Lake Hills (12/31/22). 205 W. 14th St., Austin 78701.

Juvenile Justice Department, Texas: (2011, combining the Texas Youth Commission and Texas Juvenile Probation Commission); apptv.; 6-yr.; expenses; 13 members: Chair Wes Ritchey, Dalhart (2/1/27); Edeska Barnes Jr., Jasper (2/1/27); James Castro, Bergheim (2/1/23); Mona Lisa Chambers, Houston (2/1/25); Pama Hencerling, Victoria (2/1/23); Pat Sabala Henry, Morton (2/1/23); Lisa K. Jarrett, San Antonio (2/1/27); Ann Lattimore, Cedar Park (2/1/27); Melissa Martin, Deer Park (2/1/25); David "Scott" Matthew, Georgetown (2/1/25); Vincent Morales Jr., Rosenberg (2/1/25); Allison Palmer, San Angelo (2/1/23); James Smith, Midland (2/1/23). Exec. Dir. Camille Cain ($216,725), 11209 Metric Blvd., PO Box 12757, Austin 78711-2757; (512) 490-7130. Abuse Hotline: (866) 477-8354.

Land Board, School: (1939); 2-yr.; per diem and expenses; 5 members: 1 ex officio: Comm. of General Land Office; 4 apptd.: 1 by Atty. Gen. and 3 by Gov.; ex officio chair: George P. Bush; members: Gilbert Burciaga, Austin (8/29/21); Michael A. Neill, Athens (8/29/21); Michael Scott Rohrman, Dallas (8/29/21); Todd A. Williams, Dallas (8/29/21). c/o General Land Office, 1700 Congress Ave., Austin 78701-1495; (512) 463-5001.

Land Board, Veterans: (1949 as 3-member ex officio board; reorganized 1956); 4-yr.; per diem and expenses; 3 members: 1 ex officio chair: Comm. of General Land Office; 2 apptd.: Grant Moody, San Antonio (12/29/24); Judson Scott, Bee Cave (12/29/22). Exec. Sec. Mark Havens ($233,171), 1700 Congress Ave. PO Box 12873, Austin 78711-2873; (512) 463-5001.

Land Surveying, Texas Board of Professional: (See Engineers and Land Surveyors, Texas Board of Professional.)

Lavaca-Navidad River Authority: (1954 as 7-member Jackson County Flood Control District; reorganized as 9-member board in 1959; name changed to present form in 1969); apptv.; 6-yr.; per diem and expenses; 9 members: Pres. Ronald Kubecka, Deutschburg (5/1/21); Jerry Adelman, Palacios (5/1/23); Callaway Aimone, Edna (5/1/25); Sandra "Sandy" Johs, La Ward (5/1/21); Lee Kucera, Edna (5/1/23); Terri Parker, Ganado (5/1/23); Leonard Steffek, Edna (5/1/25); Jennifer Storz, Edna (5/1/21); Charles Taylor, Cape Carancahua (5/1/25). Gen. Mgr. Patrick Brzozowski, 4631 FM 3131, Edna 77957; (361) 782-5229.

Law Enforcement, Texas Commission on: (1965 as Texas Commission on Law Enforcement Officer Standards & Education; changed name to present form in 2014); apptv.; 6-yr.; expenses; 9 members: Presiding Officer Kim Lemaux, Arlington (8/30/21); Janna Atkins, Abilene (8/30/23); Patricia Burruss, Dallas (8/30/25); Michael Griffis, Odessa (8/30/25); Jason Hester, Lago Vista (8/30/25); Ron E. Hood, Dripping Springs (8/30/23); Jack W. Taylor, Austin (8/30/23); Sharon Breckenridge Thomas, San Antonio (8/30/21); Tim Whitaker, Richmond (8/30/21). Exec. Dir. Kim Vickers ($136,649), 6330 E. Hwy. 290, Ste. 200, Austin 78723; (512) 936-7700.

Law Examiners, Texas Board of: (1919); 9 attorneys apptd. by Supreme Court biennially for 6-year terms expiring Sept. 30 of odd-numbered years. Chair Augustin Rivera Jr., Corpus Christi (9/30/23); Barbara Ellis, Austin (9/30/25); Teresa Ereon Giltner, Dallas (9/30/23); C. Alfred Mackenzie, Waco (9/30/21); Dwaine M. Massey, Houston (9/30/23); Anna M. McKim, Lubbock (9/30/21); Harold "Al" Odom, Houston (9/30/25); Cynthia Eva Hujar Orr, San Antonio (9/30/21); Carlos R. Soltero, Austin (9/30/25). Exec. Dir. Nahdiah Hoang, 205 W. 14th St., PO Box 13486, Austin 78711-3486; (512) 463-1621.

Law Library, Texas State: (1971); ex officio; expenses; 3 members: reps. of Atty. Gen., Chief Justice of Supreme Court, Presiding Judge of Court of Criminal Appeals. Dir. Dale Propp ($97,034),

205 W. 14th St., PO Box 12367, Austin 78711-2367; (512) 463-1722.

Legislative Budget Board: (1949); 10 members; 5 ex officio: Lt. Gov.; House Speaker; Chair, Senate Finance Comm.; Chair, House Appropriations Comm.; Chair, House Ways and Means Comm.; 5 other members of Legislature. Dir. Jerry McGinty ($220,000), 1501 Congress Ave., PO Box 12666, Austin 78711; (512) 463-1200.

Legislative Council, Texas: (1949); 14 ex officio members: Lt. Gov.; House Speaker; 6 senators apptd. by Lt. Gov.; 5 representatives by Speaker; Chair, House Administration Committee. Exec. Dir. Jeff Archer ($179,826), 1501 Congress Ave., PO Box 12128, Austin 78711-2128; (512) 463-1155.

Legislative Redistricting Board: (1951); 5 ex officio members: Lt. Gov., House Speaker, Atty. Gen., Comptroller of Public Accounts, Comm. of General Land Office; PO Box 12128, Austin 78711-2128; (512) 463-1151.

Legislative Reference Library: (1909); 3 ex officio members: Lt. Gov., House Speaker, Chair of House Appropriations Comm.; 3 Legislative members; indefinite term. Dir. Mary Camp ($165,000), 1100 Congress Ave., Rm. 2N.3, Austin 78701; (512) 463-1252.

Librarian, State: (1839; present office est. 1909); apptv., indefinite term: Mark Smith ($148,197), PO Box 12927, Austin 78711-2927; (512) 463-5455.

Library and Archives Commission, Texas State: (1909 as 5-member Library and State Historical Commission; name changed to present form in 1979); apptv.; per diem and expenses on duty; 6-yr.; 7 members: Chair Martha Wong, Houston (9/28/21); David C. Garza, Brownsville (9/28/25); F. Lynwood Givens, Plano (9/28/21); Arthur T. "Art" Mann, Hillsboro (9/28/23); Bradley S. "Brad" Tegeler, Austin (9/28/25); Darryl Tocker, Austin (9/28/23); 1 vacancy. Dir. and Librarian Mark Smith ($148,197), 1201 Brazos St., PO Box 12927, Austin 78711-2927; (512) 463-5474.

Licensing and Regulation, Texas Department of: (1989); apptv.; 6-yr.; expenses; 7 members: Chair Rick Figueroa, Brenham (2/1/21); Thomas F. Butler, Deer Park (2/1/25); Gerald R. Callas, Beaumont (2/1/23); Helen Callier, Kingwood (2/1/21); Nora Castañeda, Harlingen (2/1/25); Joel Garza, Pearland (2/1/21); Gary Wesson, Richmond (2/1/23). Exec. Dir. Brian E. Francis ($185,250), 920 Colorado St., PO Box 12157, Austin 78711; (512) 463-6599.

Lottery Commission, Texas: (1993); 6-yr.; apptv.; expenses; 5 members: Chair Robert G. Rivera, Dallas (2/1/21); Cindy Lyons Fields, El Paso (2/1/23); Mark A. Franz, Austin (2/1/25); Erik C. Saenz, Houston (2/1/23); Jamey Steen, Houston (2/1/25). Exec. Dir. Gary Grief ($213,344), 611 E. 6th St., PO Box 16630, Austin 78761-6630; (512) 344-5000.

Lower Colorado River Authority (See Colorado River Authority, Lower.)

Lower Concho River Water and Soil Conservation Authority (See Concho River Water and Soil Conservation Authority, Lower.)

Lower Neches Valley Authority (See Neches Valley Authority, Lower.)

Manufactured Housing Division: (1995, part of Texas Dept. of Housing and Community Affairs); apptv.; 6-yr.; 5 members: Chair Ronnie Richards, Clear Lake Shores; Jason R. Denny, Austin (1/31/25); Joe Gonzalez, Round Rock (1/31/27); Sylvia Guzman, Spring (1/31/25); Keith C. Thompson, Lubbock (1/31/23). Exec. Dir. Joe A. Garcia, 1106 Clayton Ln., Ste. 270W, PO Box 12489, Austin 78711-2489; (512) 475-2200.

Marriage and Family Therapists, Texas State Board of Examiners of: (1991); apptv.; 6-yr.; per diem and transportation expenses; 9 members: Presiding Member Lisa V. Merchant, Clyde (2/1/23); Russell F. "Russ" Bartee, Fort Worth (2/1/25); Jodie Elder, Dallas (2/1/27); George F. Francis IV, Georgetown (2/1/23); Evelyn Husband-Thompson, Houston (2/1/27); Daniel W. Parrish, DeSoto (2/1/25); Anthony C. Scoma, Austin (2/1/27); Jeanene L. Smith, Austin (2/1/25); Richmond E. Stoglin, Arlington (2/1/23). Board Admin. Sarah Faszholz ($72,000), 333 Guadalupe St., Tower 3, Rm. 900, Austin 78701; (512) 305-7700.

Medical Board, Texas: (1907 as 11-member Texas State Board of Medical Examiners; members increased to 12 in 1931, 15 in 1981,18 in 1993 and 19 in 2003; changed to present name in 2005 by Senate Bill 419); apptv.; 6-yr.; per diem on duty; 19 members, inc. 12 doctors: Pres. Sherif Z. Zaafran, Houston (4/13/21); Devinder S. Bhatia, Houston (4/13/25); George L. De Loach, Livingston (4/13/23); James S. Distefano, College Station (4/13/25); Kandace B. Farmer, Highland Village (4/13/21); Jeffrey L. Luna, Livingston (4/13/21); Robert D. Martinez, Mission (4/13/25); Jayaram B. Naidu, Odessa (4/13/21); Satish Nayak, Andrews (4/13/25); Manuel "Manny" Quinones Jr., San Antonio (4/13/23); Jason K. Tibbels, Bridgeport (4/13/25); David G. Vanderweide, League City (4/13/23). 7 Public Members: Arun Agarwal, Dallas (4/13/25); Sharon J. Barnes, Rosharon (4/13/23); Michael E. Cokinos, Houston (4/13/21); Robert Gracia, Richmond (4/13/23); Tomeka M. Herod, Allen (4/13/25); LuAnn Morgan, Midland (4/13/21); 1 vacancy. Exec. Dir. Stephen Brint Carlton ($156,145), 333 Guadalupe St., Tower 3, Ste. 610, PO Box 2018, Austin 78768-2018; (512) 305-7010. Consumer Complaint Hotline: (800) 201-9353.

Medical Physicists, Texas Board of Licensure for Professional: (1991); abolished by the Legislature in 2015. All duties transferred to the Texas Medical Board.

Medical Radiologic Technology Board: (2015); apptv.; 6-yr.; 9 members: Presiding Officer Faraz Khan, Houston (2/1/25); Nicholas Beckmann, Houston (2/1/27); Linda Brown, Port Neches (2/1/23); Jennifer Flanagan, Fort Worth (2/1/23); Regan Landreth, Georgetown (2/1/25); Shannon Lutz, Cypress (2/1/23); Scott Morren, Anton (2/1/27); Shaila D. Parker, Dallas (2/1/27); Carol Waddell, West (2/1/25). Exec. Dir. Stephen "Brint" Carlton, 333 Guadalupe St., Tower 3, Ste. 610, Austin 78701; (512) 305-7010.

Midwestern State University Board of Regents: (1959); apptv.; 6-yr.; 9 members: Chair R. Caven Crosnoe, Wichita Falls (2/25/20); Warren T. Ayres, Wichita Falls (2/25/22); Tiffany Burks, Grand Prairie (2/25/22); Guy A. "Tony" Fidelie Jr., Wichita Falls (2/25/24); Shawn Hessing, Fort Worth (2/25/20); Nancy Marks, Wichita Falls (2/25/20); Oku Okeke, Wichita Falls (2/25/24); Karen Liu Pang, Irving (2/25/24); Shelley Sweatt, Wichita Falls (2/25/22). Pres. Suzanne Shipley, 3410 Taft Blvd., Wichita Falls 76308; (940) 397-4000.

Midwifery Board, Texas: (1999); abolished by the Legislature in 2015. All duties transferred to the Texas Department of Licensing and Regulation.

Military Dept., Texas: (1836 by Republic of Texas; Adjutant General's Dept. established 1905, renamed 2013); apptv.; commanded by Adjutant General, Maj. Gen. Tracy R. Norris, Austin (1/1/21); ($178,196); assisted by Army National Guard Maj. Gen. Gregory P. Chaney, Austin; Air National Guard Maj. Gen. Thomas M. Suelzer, Keller; State Air Guard Maj. Gen. Robert J. Bodisch, Austin. Officers serve at the pleasure of the Gov.; c/o Camp Mabry, PO Box 5218, Austin 78703; (512) 782-5001.

Military Preparedness Commission, Texas: (2003); apptv.; 6-yr.; 3 ex-officio members (1 Senator, 1 House Representative, 1 General); 13 apptv.: Chair Kevin Pottinger, Fort Worth (2/1/27); Patrick Akuna, Killeen (2/1/25); Carol Bonds, San Angelo (2/1/25); Garry Bradford, Corpus Christi (2/1/25); Darrell Coleman, Wichita Falls (2/1/25); Tom Duncavage, League City (2/1/23); Woody Gilliland, Abilene (2/1/23); Dennis Lewis, Texarkana (2/1/27); Benjamin Miranda, El Paso (2/1/23); Kenneth Sheets, Mesquite (2/1/27); Annette Sobel, Lubbock (2/1/23); Shannalea Taylor, Del Rio (2/1/27); James Whitmore,

New Braunfels (2/1/23). Dir. Keith Graf, PO Box 12428, Austin 78711; (512) 475-1475.

Motor Vehicles, Texas Department of: (2009); apptv.; 6-yr.; 9 members: Chair Charles Bacarisse, Houston (2/1/25); Christian Alvarado, Austin (2/1/27); Stacey Gillman, Houston (2/1/25); Brett Graham, Denison (2/1/23); Tammy McRae, Conroe (2/1/25); Sharla Omumu, Cypress (2/1/27); John M. Prewitt, Cypress (2/1/23); Manuel "Manny" Ramirez, Fort Worth (2/1/27); Paul R. Scott, Lubbock (2/1/23). Exec. Dir. Whitney Brewster ($202,739), 4000 Jackson Ave., Austin 78731; (888) 368-4689.

Municipal Retirement System, Texas (See Retirement System, Texas Municipal.)

Music Office, Texas: (1990, became part of the Office of Gov. in 1991); Dir. Brendon Anthony, 1100 San Jacinto Blvd., Ste. 3.418, PO Box 12428, Austin 78711; (512) 463-6666.

Neches River Municipal Water Authority, Upper: (1953 as 9-member board; members decreased to 3 in 1959); apptv.; 6-yr.; 3 members: Pres. Phil Jenkins, Palestine (2/1/23); Jay Herrington, Palestine (2/1/27); Paul Morris, Palestine (2/1/25). Gen. Mgr. Monty D. Shank, 210 FM 1892 (Frankston), PO Box 1965, Palestine 75802; (903) 876-2237.

Neches Valley Authority, Lower: (1933); apptv.; per diem and expenses on duty; 6-yr.; 9 members: Pres. Kal A. Kincaid, Beaumont (7/28/23); Lonnie B. Grissom, Woodville (7/28/21); Steve Lucas, Beaumont (7/28/25); Clint A. Mitchell, Nederland (4/28/23); Ivy Pate, Beaumont (7/28/21); James M. Scott, Beaumont (7/28/25); Charles "Caleb" Spurlock, Woodville (7/28/25); Jeanie Turk, Sour Lake (7/28/21); William D. "Bill" Voigtman, Silsbee (4/28/23). Gen. Mgr. Scott Hall, 7850 Eastex Fwy., PO Box 5117, Beaumont 77726-5117; (409) 892-4011.

Nueces River Authority: (1953 as Nueces River Conservation and Reclamation District; name changed to present form in 1971); apptv.; 6-yr.; per diem and expenses; 21 members: Pres. Dan Leyendecker, Corpus Christi (2/1/25); Alston Beinhorn, Catarina (2/1/23); Jane D. Bell, Corpus Christi (2/1/25); Allan P. Bloxsom III, Kendalia (2/1/21); Dane Bruun, Corpus Christi (2/1/25); Eric Burnett, Portland (2/1/27); Amy M. Clark, Three Rivers (2/1/21); Marshall Davidson, Ingleside (2/1/23); Chad Foster Jr., Uvalde (2/1/23); John W. Galloway, Beeville (2/1/21); Annelise Gonzalez, San Antonio (2/1/23); Lana P. Guthrie, Rocksprings (2/1/25); Debra Young Hatch, Corpus Christi (2/1/23); Karin E. Knolle, Sandia (2/1/27); Travis W. Pruski, Floresville (2/1/21); David Purser, Karnes City (2/1/25); Armandina "Dina" Ramirez, Karnes City (2/1/25); Tomas Ramirez III, Devine (2/1/21); Bill Schuchman, Jourdanton (2/1/23); Anita Shackelford, Leakey (2/1/25); Tony Wood, Corpus Christi (2/1/23). Exec. Dir. John Byrum, 539 Hwy. 83 S., Uvalde 78801; (830) 278-6810.

Nursing, Texas Board of: (1909 as 5-member Texas Board of Nurse Examiners; members increased to 6 in 1931 and to 9 in 1981; name changed to present and members increased to 13 in 2007); apptv.; per diem and expenses; 6-yr.; 13 members: Pres. Kathy Shipp, Lubbock (1/31/23); Daryl Chambers, Grand Prairie (1/31/27); Laura Disque, Edinburg (1/31/25); Carol Kay Hawkins, San Antonio (1/31/25); Mazie Mathews Jamison, Dallas (1/31/23); Kenneth D. "Ken" Johnson, San Angelo (1/31/27); Kathy Leader-Horn, Granbury (1/31/27); Allison Porter-Edwards, Bellaire (1/31/27); Tamara Rhodes, Amarillo (1/31/23); David Saucedo II, El Paso (1/31/27); Melissa Schat, Granbury (1/31/25); Rickey "Rick" Williams, Killeen (1/31/25); Kimberly "Kim" Wright, Big Spring (1/31/23). Exec. Dir. Katherine A. Thomas ($166,879), 333 Guadalupe St., Ste. 3-460, Austin 78701-3944; (512) 305-7400.

Occupational Therapy Examiners, Texas Board of: (1983 as 6-member board; increased to 9 in 1999); apptv.; 6-yr.; per diem and expenses; 9 members: Chair Stephanie Johnston, Magnolia (2/1/27); Jacob Boggus, Harlingen (2/1/27); Blanca Cardenas, Mission (2/1/23); Jennifer Clark, Iola (2/1/25); Karen Gardner, Brenham (2/1/23); DeLana Honaker, Amarillo (2/1/23); Eddie Jessie, Houston (2/1/25); Sally Harris King, Houston (2/1/27); Todd Novosad, Bee Cave, (2/1/25). Exec. Dir. Ralph Harper ($100,893), 333 Guadalupe St., Ste. 2-510, Austin 78701-3942; (512) 305-6900.

Offenders with Medical or Mental Impairments, Texas Correctional Office on: apptv.; 6-yr.; 21 members: 11 ex officio from various state agencies; 10 apptd. by Gov.: Chair Robb Catalano, Fort Worth (2/1/25); Sanjay Adhia, Sugar Land (2/1/27); Allan Cain, Carthage (2/1/23); James B. Eby, Wichita Falls (2/1/25); Matthew Faubion, San Antonio (2/1/23); Scott MacNaughton, San Antonio (2/1/23); Trenton R. Marshall, Burleson (2/1/25); Casey O'Neal, Austin (2/1/25); Denise Oncken, Houston (2/1/27); Rogelio Rodriguez, El Paso (2/1/27). Dir. April Zamora ($135,599), 4616 W. Howard Ln., Ste. 200, Austin 78728; (512) 671-2134.

One-Call Board of Texas: (1997; created by the Underground Facility Damage Prevention and Safety Act and serves as the board for the Texas Underground Facility Notification Corp.); apptv.; 3-yr.; 12 members: Chair Robert DeLeon, Corpus Christi (8/31/22); Joe Canales, Austin (8/31/22); Joseph Costa, DeSoto (8/31/23); Sandy Galvan, San Antonio (8/31/22); William Geise, Austin (8/31/23); Sam Kannappan, Houston (8/31/22); Marcela Navarrete, El Paso (8/31/21); Christopher Nowak, Houston (8/31/23); Manish Seth, Missouri City (8/31/21); George Spencer, Austin (8/31/23); Les Stephens, San Marcos (8/31/21); Richard Tesson, Houston (8/31/21). Exec. Dir. Don Ward, 9415 Burnet Rd., Ste. 311, PO Box 9764, Austin 78766; (512) 467-2850.

Optometry Board, Texas: (1921 as 6-member State Board of Examiners in Optometry; name and number of members changed to present in 1981); apptv.; per diem; 6-yr.; 9 members: Chair Mario Gutierrez, San Antonio (1/31/23); Judith Chambers, Austin (1/31/25); John Todd Cornett, Amarillo (1/31/25); Ronald L. Hopping, Friendswood (1/31/27); Carey A. Patrick, Allen (1/31/27); Rene D. Peña, El Paso (1/31/27); Meghan Schutte, (1/31/25); Ty Sheehan, San Antonio (1/31/23); Bill Thompson, Richardson (1/31/23). Exec. Dir. Kelly Parker ($95,000), 333 Guadalupe St., Ste. 2-420, Austin 78701-3942; (512) 305-8500.

Orthotics and Prosthetics, Texas Board of: abolished by the Legislature in 2013. All duties transferred to the Texas Department of Licensing and Regulation.

Pardons and Paroles, Texas Board of: (1893 as Board of Pardon Advisers; changed in 1936 to Board of Pardons and Paroles with 3 members; members increased to 6 in 1983; made a division of the Texas Dept. of Criminal Justice in 1990); apptv.; 6-yr.; 7 members (chairman, $176,300; members, $112,750 each): Chair David Gutiérrez, Gatesville (2/1/27); D'Wayne Jernigan, Huntsville (2/1/25); Carmella Jones, Angleton (2/1/25); James LaFavers, Amarillo (2/1/23); Brian Long, Palestine (2/1/23); Linda Molina, San Antonio (2/1/27); Ed Robertson, Austin (2/1/27). Parole Commissioners: Elodia Brito, Amarillo; Lee Anne Eck-Massingill, Gatesville; Ira Evans, Angleton; Mary J. Farley, Huntsville; Troy Fox, Austin; Raymond Gonzalez, Amarillo; James Paul Kiel, Palestine; Tracy Long, Huntsville; Jeffrey Marton, Amarillo; Marsha Moberley, Austin; Anthony Ramirez, San Antonio; Wanda Saliagas, Palestine; Charles Speier, San Antonio; Roel Tejeda, Gatesville. Gen. Counsel Bettie L. Wells ($125,172), 8610 Shoal Creek Blvd., PO Box 13401, Austin 78711-3401; (512) 406-5452.

Parks and Wildlife Commission, Texas: (1963 as 3-member board; members increased to 6 in 1971 and to 9 in 1983); apptv.; expenses; 6-yr.; 9 members: Chair Arch H. "Beaver" Aplin III, Lake Jackson (2/1/23); James E. Abell, Kilgore (2/1/25); Oliver J. Bell, Houston (2/1/23); Paul L. Foster, El Paso (2/1/27); Anna B. Galo, Laredo (2/1/27); Jeffery D. Hildebran, Houston (2/1/25); Robert L. "Bobby" Patton Jr., Fort Worth (2/1/25); Travis B. "Blake" Rowling, Dallas (2/1/27); Dick Scott, Wimberley (2/1/23). Exec. Dir. Carter Smith ($200,643), 4200 Smith School Rd., Austin 78744; (512) 389-4800.

Pecos River Compact Commission: (1942, negotiates with New Mexico regarding waters of the Pecos); apptv.; 6-yr.; salary and expenses. Comm. Frederic "Rick" Tate (1/23/23), PO Box 340, Marfa 79843; (432) 729-3224.

Pension Review Board, Texas: (1979); apptv.; 6-yr.; 7 members: Chair Stephanie V. Leibe, Austin (1/31/27); Keith Brainard, Georgetown (1/31/25); Marcia Dush, Austin (1/31/25); Rossy Fariña-Strauss, Austin (1/31/23); Christopher Gonzales, Cypress (1/31/27); Robert D. "Rob" Ries, Austin (1/31/23); Christopher Zook, Houston (1/31/27). Exec. Dir. Anumeha Kumar ($126,730), 300 W. 15th St., PO Box 13498, Austin 78711-3498; (512) 463-1736.

Pharmacy, Texas State Board of: (1907 as 6-member board; members increased to current number in 1981); apptv.; 6-yr.; 11 members: Pres. Julie Spier, Katy (8/31/23); Rick Fernandez, Northlake (8/31/23); Daniel Guerrero, San Marcos (8/31/23); Lori Henke, Amarillo (8/31/23); Donnie Lewis, Athens (8/31/25); Bradley A. Miller, Austin (8/31/25); Donna Montemayor, San Antonio (8/31/25); Chip Thornsburg, San Antonio (8/31/21); Suzete Tijerina, Castle Hills (8/31/21); Rick Tisch, Spring (8/31/25); Jenny Downing Yoakum, Kilgore (8/31/21). Exec. Dir. Allison Vordenbaumen Benz ($132,490), 333 Guadalupe St., Ste. 3-500, Austin 78701; (512) 305-8000. Consumer complaints: (800) 821-3205.

Physical Therapy and Occupational Therapy Examiners, Executive Council of: (1971); apptv.; 2-yr.; expenses; 5 members: Presiding Officer Manoranjan "Mano" Mahadeva, Frisco (2/1/23); Donivan Hodge, Spicewood (2/1/23); Eddie Jessie, Houston (2/1/25); Stephanie Johnston, Magnolia (2/1/21); Barbara Sanders, Austin (2/1/23). Exec. Dir. Ralph Harper ($100,893), 333 Guadalupe St., Ste. 2-510, Austin 78701-3942; (512) 305-6900.

Physical Therapy Examiners, Texas Board of: (1971); apptv.; 6-yr.; expenses; 9 members: Chair Harvey Aikman, Mission (1/31/27); Glenda Clausell, Houston (1/31/27); Jacob Delgado, Hewitt (1/31/25); Manuel "Tony" Domenech, Austin (1/31/23); Donivan Hodge, Spicewood (1/31/23); Liesl Olson, Lubbock (1/31/27); Kathryn "Kate" Roby, Temple (1/31/25); Barbara Sanders, Austin (1/31/23); Melissa Skillern, Manvel (1/31/25). Exec. Dir. Ralph Harper ($100,893), 333 Guadalupe St., Ste. 2-510, Austin 78701-3942; (512) 305-6900.

Physician Assistant Board, Texas: (1993 as Physician Assistant Advisory Council; changed to present name in 1995); apptv.; 6-yr.; 13 members: Chair Karrie Lynn Crosby, Robinson (2/1/27); Steve S. Ahmed, Big Spring (2/1/25); Clay P. Bulls, Abilene (2/1/27); Jennifer L. Clarner, Austin (2/1/23); Victor S. Ho, Houston (2/1/27); Lawrence G. "Larry" Hughes, Frisco (2/1/25); Sandra Longoria, Harlingen (2/1/25); Cameron J. McElhaney, Austin (2/1/23); Janith K. Mills, Irving (2/1/23); Melinda Ann Moore Gottschalk, Round Rock (2/1/25); Gregory Rowin, Harlingen (2/1/23); Andrew Sauer, Amarillo (2/1/27); Lali Shipley, Austin (2/1/27). Exec. Dir. Stephen Brint Carlton ($156,145), 333 Guadalupe, Tower 3, Ste. 610, TX 78768; (512) 305-7010. Consumer Complaints: (800) 201-9353.

Plumbing Examiners, Texas State Board of: (1947 as 6-member board; members increased to 9 in 1981); apptv.; expenses; 6-yr.; Chair Frank S. Denton, Conroe (9/5/25); James "Ron" Ainsworth, Midland (9/5/23); Ben Friedman, Dallas (9/5/21); Milton Gutierrez, Fort Worth (9/5/21); Robert F. Jalnos, San Antonio (9/5/21); William "Bill" Klock, Houston (9/5/23); Thomas "Justin" MacDonald, Kerrville (9/5/25); Mark Savasta, Houston (9/5/23); David "Dave" Yelovich, Friendswood (9/5/25). Exec. Dir. Lisa G. Hill ($114,239), 929 E. 41st St., PO Box 4200, Austin 78765-4200; (512) 936-5200.

Podiatric Medical Examiners Advisory Board: (1923 as 6-member State Board of Chiropody Examiners; name changed to State Board of Podiatry Examiners in 1967; made 9-member board in 1981; name changed to present in 1996; in 2017 the licensing and regulation of the practice of Podiatry transferred to the Texas Department of Licensing and Regulation); apptv.; 6-yr.; expenses; 9 members: Presiding Officer Travis A. Motley, Fort Worth (2/1/23); Cory Brown, Abilene (2/1/23); Leslie Campbell, Allen (2/1/27); Maria "Yvette" Hernandez, Rio Grande City (2/1/23); James Michael Lunsford, Austin (2/1/25); Joe E. Martin, College Station (2/1/25); Amanda S. Nobles, Longview (2/1/27); Renee Pietzsch, Georgetown (2/1/27); Cirenia Hernandez Terrazas, Austin (2/1/25). PO Box 12157, Austin 78711; (512) 463-6599.

Port Freeport Commission: (1925); apptv.; 6-yr.; 6 elected members: Chair John Hoss, Freeport (5/31/23); Dan Croft, Jones Creek (5/31/25); Rob Giesecke, Damon (5/31/27); Shane Pirtle, Brazoria (5/31/23); Rudy Santos, Angleton (5/31/27); Ravi K. Singhania, Brazosport (5/31/25). Exec. Dir. Phyllis Saathoff, 1100 Cherry St., Freeport 77541; (979) 233-2667.

Prepaid Higher Education Tuition Board, Texas (See Higher Education Tuition Board, Texas Prepaid.)

Preservation Board, State: (1983); 2-yr.; 6 members (3 ex officio: Gov., Lt. Gov., House Speaker); 3 apptv.: 1 apptd. by Gov.: Alethea Swann Bugg, San Antonio (2/1/23); 1 senator apptd. by Lt. Gov.; 1 representative by Speaker. Exec. Dir. Rod Welsh ($175,990), 201 E. 14th St., PO Box 13286, Austin 78711; (512) 463-5495.

Prison Board (See Criminal Justice, Texas Dept. of.)

Private Security Advisory Committee, Texas: (1969 as Board of Private Investigators and Private Security Agencies; reorganized in 1998 as Texas Comm. on Private Security; re-established in 2004 as a bureau of the Texas Dept. of Public Safety named Texas Private Security Board and in 2020 took its current name); apptv.; expenses; 6-yr.; 8 members (1 ex officio: Dir., Dept. of Public Safety); 7 apptd. members: Chair Patricia James, Houston (1/31/21); D. Wade Hayden, San Antonio (1/31/25); Derrick A. Howard, Universal City (1/31/23); Alan S. Trevino, Austin (1/31/23); Debbra Ulmer, Houston (1/31/25); 2 vacancies. Service Dir. Chris Sims ($128,851), 6100 Guadalupe St., PO Box 4087, Austin 78773-0001; (512) 424-7293.

Process Server Certification Advisory Board: apptv. by Texas Supreme Court; part of Judicial Branch Certification Commission; staggered terms; 6-yr., 5 members: Presiding Officer Patrick J. Dyer, Missouri City, (2/1/27); Rhonda Hughey, Kaufman (2/1/19); Eric Johnson, Rosharon (2/1/27); Melissa K. Perez, Waxahachie (2/1/23); Justiss Rasberry, El Paso (2/1/19). 205 W. 14th St., PO Box 12066, Austin 78711-2066; (512) 475-4368.

Prosecuting Attorney, State: (1923) apptd. by Court of Criminal Appeals: Stacey M. Soule ($154,000), 209 W. 14th St., Austin 78701; (512) 463-1660.

Psychologists, Texas State Board of Examiners of: (1969 as 6-member board; members increased to 9 in 1981); apptv.; 6-yr.; per diem and expenses; 9 members: Presiding Member John K. Bielamowicz, Waxahachie (10/31/21); Herman Adler, Houston (10/31/23); Jamie Becker, Plano (10/31/25); Ryan T. Bridges, Houston (10/31/23); Jeanette Deas Calhoun, Tyler (10/31/25); Susan Fletcher, Frisco (10/31/21); Ronald S. "Ron" Palomares, Denton (10/31/21); Sangeeta Singg, San Angelo (10/31/25); Andoni Zagouris, McAllen (10/31/23). Board Admin. Diane Moore ($60,000), 333 Guadalupe St., Ste. 3-900, Austin 78701; (512) 305-7700.

Public Finance Authority, Texas: (1984, assumed duties of Texas Building Authority); apptv.; per diem and expenses; 6-yr.; 7 members: Chair Billy M. Atkinson Jr., Sugar Land (2/1/23); Larry G. Holt, College Station (2/1/27); Ramon Manning, Houston (2/1/21); Shanda Perkins, Burleson (2/1/25); Jay A. Riskind, Austin (2/1/23); Brendan Scher, Austin (2/1/25); Ben Streusand, Spring (2/1/25). Exec. Dir. Lee Deviney ($151,994), 300 W. 15th St., Ste. 411, PO Box 12906 Austin 78711-2906; (512) 463-5544.

Public Insurance Counsel, Office of: (1991). Public Counsel (apptv.; 2-yr.) Melissa R. Hamilton ($149,976), (2/1/21), 333 Guadalupe St., Ste. 3-120; Austin 78701; (512) 322-4143.

The Texas Racing Commission regulates horse and grayhound racing in the state. Photo by Travis Isaac, CC by 2.0/Flickr,

Public Safety Commission: (1935 with 3 members; members increased to 5 in 2007); apptv.; expenses; 6-yr.; 5 members: Chair Steven P. Mach, Houston (1/1/22); Nelda L. Blair, Conroe (1/1/26); Steve H. Stodghill, Dallas (1/1/24); Dale Wainwright, Austin (1/1/24); 1 vacancy. Dir. of Texas Dept. of Public Safety Steven C. McCraw ($247,981), 5805 N. Lamar Blvd., PO Box 4087, Austin 78773-0001; (512) 424-2000.

Public Utility Commission: (1975); apptv.; 6-yr.; 3 members ($201,000): Chair Peter Lake, Austin (9/1/23); Lori Cobos, Austin (9/1/21); Will McAdams, Austin (9/1/25). Exec. Dir. Thomas Gleeson ($200,000), 1701 Congress Ave., 7th Fl., PO Box 13326, Austin 78711-3326; (512) 936-7000.

Public Utility Counsel, Office of: (1983); apptv.; 2-yr.; Interim Public Counsel: Chris Ekoh ($110,538), 1701 Congress Ave., Ste. 9-180, PO Box 12397, Austin 78711-2397; (512) 936-7500.

Racing Commission, Texas: (1986); apptv.; 6-yr.; per diem and expenses; 9 members; 2 ex officio: Chair, Public Safety Comm. and Comm. of Agriculture; 7 apptv.: Chair Robert C. Pate, Corpus Christi (2/1/23); Margaret Martin, Boerne (2/1/21); Connie McNabb, Montgomery (2/1/21); Michael "Mike" Moore, Fort Worth (2/1/23); Arvel "A.J." Waight Jr., Willow City (2/1/21); 2 vacancies. Exec. Dir. Chuck Trout ($90,200), 8505 Cross Park Dr., Ste. 110, PO Box 12080, Austin 78711; (512) 833-6699.

Radiation Advisory Board, Texas: (1961); apptv.; 6-yr.; 18 members: Ronal Benke, Austin (4/16/27); Charles Cavnor, Little Elm (4/16/25); John Hageman, San Antonio (4/16/23); Mark C. Harvey, Houston (4/16/27); Frank "Neal" Leavell, Lampasas (4/16/21); Lisa Masters, San Antonio (4/16/27); Darlene Metter, San Antonio (4/16/25); Sanjay Narayan, Dallas (4/16/27); William Pate, League City (4/16/25); Kenneth "Ken" Peters, Granbury (4/16/25); Doug Posey, Corpus Christi (4/16/23); Gerald T. "Tim" Powell, Bay City (4/16/27); Kevin L. Raabe, Floresville (4/16/23); Robert "Bob" Redweik, Tomball (4/16/25); Darshan J. Sachde, Austin (4/16/25); Mark Silberman, Austin (4/16/23); Lynn Slaney Silguero, Frisco (4/16/23); Simon Trubek, Austin (4/16/27). 8407 Wall St., PO Box 149347, Austin 78714-9347; (888) 899-6688.

Radioactive Waste Disposal Compact Commission, Texas Low-Level: (1993); apptv.; 6-yr.; expenses; 6 Texas members, plus 2 members from Vermont; Texas apptees.: Chair Brandon T. Hurley, Grapevine (8/31/25); Richard H. Dolgener, Andrews (8/31/21); Lisa Edwards, Granbury (8/31/23); Linda Morris, Waco (8/31/21); Jeff Munday, Austin (8/31/25); John M. Salsman, Driftwood (8/31/23). Exec. Dir. Stephen Raines, 919 Congress Ave., Ste. 830, Austin 78701; (737) 300-2154.

Railroad Commission of Texas: (1891); elective; 6-yr.; 3 members, $140,937 each: Wayne Christian (12/31/22); Christi Craddick (12/31/24); Jim Wright (12/31/26). Exec. Dir. Wei Wang ($192,600), 1701 Congress Ave., PO Box 12967, Austin 78711-2967; (512) 463-7158.

Real Estate Commission, Texas: (1949 as 6-member board; members increased to current number in 1979); apptv.; per diem and expenses; 6-yr.; 9 members: Chair R. Scott Kesner, El Paso (1/31/25); Jason Hartgraves, Frisco (1/31/25); Leslie Lerner, Houston (1/31/27); Jan Fite Miller, Kemp (1/31/23); Benjamin "Ben" Peña, Bayview (1/31/27); Barbara Russell, Denton (1/31/25); DeLora Wilkinson, Cypress (1/31/23); Micheal Williams, Colleyville (1/31/23); Mark Woodroof, Houston (1/31/27). Exec. Dir. Chelsea Buchholtz ($180,250), 1700 Congress Ave., Ste. 400, PO Box 12188, Austin 78711-2188; (512) 936-3000.

Real Estate Research Center, Texas: (1971); apptv.; 6-yr.; 10 members; 1 ex officio: rep. of Texas Real Estate Commission; 9 apptv.: Chair Russell L. Cain, Port Lavaca (1/31/23); Troy C. Alley Jr., DeSoto (1/31/23); Doug Foster, San Antonio (1/31/27); Vicki Fullerton, The Woodlands (1/31/25); Patrick Geddes, Dallas (1/31/23); W. Douglas Jennings, Fort Worth (1/31/27); Besa Martin, Boerne (1/31/27); Walter F. "Ted" Nelson, Houston (1/31/25); Rebecca "Becky" Vajdak, Temple (1/31/25). Exec. Dir. Gary Maler ($247,367), 1700 Research Pkwy., Ste. 200, Texas A&M University, 2115 TAMU, College Station 77843-2115; (979) 845-2031.

Red River Authority of Texas: (1959); apptv.; 6-yr.; per diem and expenses; 9 members: Pres. Todd W. Boykin, Amarillo (8/11/21); Mary Lou Bradley, Memphis (8/11/25); Jerry Bob Daniel, Truscott (8/11/21); Jerry Dan Davis, Wellington (8/11/23); Michael R. Sandefur, Texarkana (8/11/23); George Wilson Scaling II, Henrietta (8/11/21); Zackary K. Smith, Canyon (8/11/25); Stephen A. Thornhill, Denison (8/11/25); Joe L. Ward, Telephone (8/11/23). Gen. Mgr. Randall W. Whiteman, 3000 Hammon Rd., PO Box 240, Wichita Falls 76307; (940) 723-8697.

Red River Compact Commission: (1949, negotiates with Oklahoma, Arkansas and Louisiana regarding waters of the Red); apptv.; 6-yr.; salary and expenses. Comm. Robin Phillips (2/1/23), 300 N. Travis St., Sherman 75090; (903) 814-7273.

Redistricting Board, Legislative (See Legislative Redistricting Board.)

Rehabilitation Council of Texas: (1973); apptv.; 3-yr.; at least 15 members: Chair Michael A. Ebbeler Jr., Austin (10/29/22);

Matt Berend, Scotland (10/29/21); Amanda Bowdoin, Forney (10/29/23); Jennifer Clouse, Temple (2/25/23); Lisa Cowart, Beaumont (10/29/21); JoAnn Fluke, Abilene (10/29/21); Cheryl A. Fuller, Austin; Lindsey Geeslin, Waco (10/29/23); Gennadiy Goldenshteyn, Dallas (2/25/23); Bobbie Hodges, Fort Worth (10/29/22); Paul Hunt, Austin (10/29/21); Elizabeth Kendell, San Antonio (10/29/22); Lisa Maciejewski-West, San Angelo (10/29/22); April Pollreisz, Amarillo (10/29/21); Joe Powell, Irving (10/29/21); Emily Robinson, Pflugerville (10/29/23); Rodrick Robinson, McKinney (10/29/23); Karen Stanfill, Houston (10/29/22); Crystal Stark, College Station (10/29/21); Abdi Warsame, Wylie (2/25/23). 101 E. 15th St., Rm. 144T, Austin 78788-0001; (512) 936-3445.

Respiratory Care Board: (2015); apptv.; 6-yr.; 9 members: Presiding Officer Latana T. Jackson, Cedar Hill (2/1/23); Samuel L. Brown Jr., Marshall (2/1/25); Tim R. Chappell, Plano (2/1/27); Sam Gregory "Gregg" Marshall, Round Rock (2/1/27); Debra E. Patrick, McKinney (2/1/25); Shad J. Pellizzari, Cedar Park (2/1/23); Kandace D. "Kandi" Pool, San Angelo (2/1/27); Hammad Nasir Qureshi, Tomball (2/1/25); Sonia K. Sanderson, Beaumont (2/1/23). Exec. Dir. Stephen "Brint" Carlton, 333 Guadalupe St., Tower 3, Ste. 610, Austin 78701; (512) 305-7010.

Retirement System, Texas County & District: (1967); apptv.; 6-yr.; 9 members: Chair Mary Louise Nicholson, Fort Worth (12/31/23); Tammy Biggar, Bonham (12/31/25); Chris Davis, Alto (12/31/21); Susan Fletcher, Frisco (12/31/23); Chris Hill, McKinney (12/31/21); Deborah Hunt, Georgetown (12/31/21); Kara Sands, Corpus Christi (12/31/23); Chris Taylor, Fort Worth (12/31/25); Holly Williamson, Houston (12/31/25). Exec. Dir. Amy Bishop, 901 S. MoPac Expwy., Bldg. IV, Ste. 500, Austin 78746; (512) 328-8889.

Retirement System, Texas Emergency Services: (1977; formerly the Fire Fighters' Relief and Retirement Fund); apptv.; expenses; 6-yr.; 9 members: Chair Jenny Moore, Lake Jackson (9/1/21); Courtney Gibson Bechtol, Rockport (9/1/21); Nathan Douglas, Seabrook (9/1/25); Matthew "Matt" Glaves, Alvin (9/1/25); Edward J. Keenan, Houston (9/1/23); Pilar Rodriguez, Edinburg (9/1/21); Jerry Romero, El Paso (2/1/25); Rodney Alan Ryalls, Burkburnett (9/1/23); Stephanie Lynn Wagner, Wimberley (9/1/23). Exec. Dir. Shirley Hays ($105,000), PO Box 12577, Austin 78711; (512) 936-3372.

Retirement System, Texas Municipal: (1947); apptv.; 6-yr.; expenses; 6 members: Chair David Landis, Perryton (2/1/21); Anali Alanis, Pharr (2/1/21); Jesús A. Garza, Victoria (2/1/23); Juan Diego Huizar, Pleasanton (2/1/23); Bill Philibert, Deer Park (2/1/25); Bob Scott, Carrollton (2/1/25). Exec. Dir. David Wescoe, 1200 N. I-35, PO Box 149153, Austin 78714-9153; (512) 476-5576.

Retirement System of Texas, Employees: (1949); apptv.; 6-yr.; 6 members: 1 apptd. by Gov., 1 by Chief Justice of State Supreme Court, 1 by House Speaker; 3 elected by ERS members: Chair I. Craig Hester, Austin (8/31/22); Brian R. Barth, Austin (8/31/25); Ilesa Daniels, Houston (8/31/21); James "Jim" Kee, San Antonio (8/31/26); Catherine Melvin, Austin (8/31/23); 1 vacancy. Exec. Dir. Porter Wilson ($316,117), 200 E. 18th St., PO Box 13207, Austin 78711-3207; (877) 275-4377.

Retirement System of Texas, Teacher: (1937 as 6-member board; members increased to 9 in 1973); 6-yr.; expenses; 9 members; 2 apptd. by State Board of Education, 3 by Gov., 4 by Gov. after being nominated by popular ballot of retirement system members: Chair Jarvis V. Hollingsworth, Missouri City (8/31/23); Michael Ball, Argyle (8/31/25); David Corpus, Humble (8/31/25); John Elliott, Austin (8/31/21); Christopher Moss, Lufkin (8/31/21); James Dick Nance, Hallettsville (8/31/23); Nanette Sissney, Whitesboro (8/31/23); Robert H. Walls, San Antonio (8/31/25); 1 vacancy. Exec. Dir. Brian Guthrie ($355,141), 1000 Red River St., Austin 78701-2698; (512) 542-6400.

Rio Grande Compact Commission: (1929, negotiates with Colorado and New Mexico regarding waters of the Rio Grande); apptv.; 6-yr.; salary and expenses; Comm. Robert "Bobby" Skov, Fabens (6/9/25), 401 E. Franklin Ave. Ste. 560, El Paso 79901; (915) 764-0014.

Risk Management, State Office of: apptv.; 2-yr.; 5 members: Chair Lloyd M. Garland, Lubbock (2/1/25); Ricardo "Rick" Galindo III, San Antonio (2/1/25); Rosemary Gammon, Plano (2/1/21); Tomas Gonzalez, El Paso (2/1/23); Gerald Ladner Sr., Austin (2/1/21). Exec. Dir. Stephen Vollbrecht ($150,563), 300 W. 15th St., 6th Fl., PO Box 13777, Austin 78711-3777; (512) 475-1440.

Sabine River Authority of Texas: (1949); apptv.; per diem and expenses; 6-yr.; 9 members: Cary "Mac" Abney, Marshall (7/6/21); Thomas "Tom" Beall, Milam (7/6/23); Jeffrey D. "Jeff" Jacobs, Rockwall (7/6/25); Joshua A. "Josh" McAdams, Center (7/6/25); Jeanette Sterner, Holly Lake Ranch (7/6/21); Cliff Todd, Long Branch (7/6/23); Janie Walenta, Quitman (7/6/23); Kevin M. Williams, Orange (7/6/25); Laurie Woloszyn, Longview (7/6/21). Exec. VP David Montagne, PO Box 579, Orange 77631-0579; (409) 746-2192.

Sabine River Compact Commission: (1953, negotiates with Louisiana regarding the waters of the Sabine); apptv.; 6-yr.; salary and expenses; 2 commissioners: Jerry F. Gipson, Longview (7/12/22); Michael H. Lewis, Newton (7/12/19); c/o PO Box 13087, Austin 78711; (512) 239-4730.

San Antonio River Authority: (1937); elective; 6-yr.; 12 members: Chair Darrell T. Brownlow, Wilson Co. (11/4/25); Jim Campbell, Bexar Co. (11/2/21); Alicia L. Cowley, Goliad Co. (11/2/21); John J. Flieller, Wilson Co. (11/2/21); James Fuller, Goliad Co. (11/4/25); Lourdes Galvan, Bexar Co. (11/4/25); Jerry G. Gonzales, Bexar Co. (11/4/25); Michael W. Lackey, Bexar Co. (11/2/21); Hector R. Morales, Bexar Co. (11/7/23); Gaylon J. Oehlke, Karnes Co. (11/4/25); Deb B. Prost, Bexar Co. (11/7/23); H.B. "Trip" Ruckman III, Karnes Co. (11/2/21). Gen. Mgr. Derek Boese, 100 E. Guenther St., San Antonio 78204; (210) 227-1373.

San Jacinto River Authority: (1937); apptv.; expenses while on duty; 6-yr.; 7 members: Pres. Ronnie Anderson, Mont Belvieu (10/16/21); Ed Boulware, Montgomery (10/16/23); Stacey Buick, Montgomery (10/16/21); William "Wil" Faubel, Montgomery (10/16/25); Mark Micheletti, Kingwood (10/16/23); Ricardo "Rick" Mora, The Woodlands (10/16/25); 1 vacancy. Gen. Mgr. Jace A. Houston, 1577 Dam Site Rd., PO Box 329, Conroe 77305; (936) 588-3111.

Savings and Mortgage Lending, Department of: (1961); commissioner apptd. by State Finance Commission. Comm. Caroline C. Jones ($194,750), 2601 N. Lamar Blvd., Ste. 201, Austin 78705; (512) 475-1350.

School Land Board (See Land Board, School.)

School Safety Center, Texas: (2001); apptv.; 2-yr.; 5 ex officio members from the Texas Higher Education Coord. Board, Texas Education Agency, Health and Human Services Comm., Attorney General's office, and the Texas Juvenile Justice Dept.; 12 apptd. members: Bill Avera, Jacksonville (2/1/22); Craig Bessent, Abilene (2/1/22); Kerri Brady, Georgetown (2/1/22); Lizeth Cuellar Olivarez, Laredo (2/1/23); Edwin S. Flores, Dallas (2/1/23); Bryan Hedrick, Hereford (2/1/22); James M. Mosley, Borger (2/1/23); Teresa K. Oldham, Jarrell (2/1/22); Michael L. Slaughter, Wylie (2/1/23); Jill M.Tate, Colleyville (2/1/23); Alan Trevino, Burnet (2/1/22); Robert W. Wilson, Silsbee (2/18/23). Director Kathy Martinez-Prather, 601 University Dr., San Marcos 78666; (512) 245-8082.

Securities Board, Texas State: (1957, the outgrowth of several amendments to the Texas Securities Act, originally passed in 1913); expenses; 6-yr.; 5 members: Chair E. Wally Kinney, Comfort (1/20/25); Robert Belt, Houston (1/20/23); Kenny Koncaba, Friendswood (1/20/23); Ejike E. Okpa, Dallas (1/20/27); Melissa Tyroch, Belton (1/20/25). Comm. Travis J. Iles ($162,491), 208 E. 10th St., Austin 78701; (512) 305-8301.

Sex Offender Treatment, Council on: (1983); apptv.; expenses; 6-yr.; 7 members: Presiding Officer Aaron Paul Pierce, Temple (2/1/23); Elizabeth Perez Aliseda, Beeville (2/1/23); Ezio Leite, North Richland Hills (2/1/27); Emily Orozco-Crousen, Abilene (2/1/27); Velma "Jean" Stanley, Lufkin (2/1/25); Tiffany Strother, Godley (2/1/25); James Taylor, San Antonio (2/1/21). Exec. Dir. Pamela Adams, c/o Texas Dept. of State Health Services, PO Box 149347, Austin 78714-9347; (512) 834-4530

Skill Standards Board, Texas: (1995); abolished and its powers and duties were transferred to the Texas Workforce Investment Council on September 1, 2015.

Social Worker Examiners, Texas State Board of: (1993); apptv.; 6-yr.; per diem and travel expenses; 9 members: Presiding Member Brian C. Brumley, Sumner (2/1/27); Katie Andrade, Mount Pleasant (2/1/27); Megan Marie Graham, Houston (2/1/23); Ben W. Morris, Cleburne (2/1/27); Martha Mosier, College Station (2/1/23); Audrey Ramsbacher, San Antonio (2/1/23); Asia Rodgers, Fort Worth (2/1/25); Dolores Saenz-Davila, McAllen (2/1/25); Jennifer Swords, Fort Worth (2/1/25). Admin. Sarah Faszholz ($72,000), 333 Guadalupe St., Tower 3, Rm. 900, Austin 78701; (512) 305-7700.

Soil & Water Conservation Board, Texas State: (1939); 2-yr.; 7 members: 2 apptd. by Gov.; 5 elected by district directors: Chair Marty H. Graham, Rocksprings (5/5/22); David Basinger, Deport (5/1/22); Scott Buckles, Stratford (5/7/23); José Dodier Jr., Zapata (5/7/23); Barry Mahler, Iowa Park (5/7/23); Gov. Apptees.: Tina Y. Buford, Harlingen (2/1/22); Carl Ray Polk Jr., Lufkin (2/1/23). Exec. Dir. Rex Isom ($150,283), 1497 Country View Ln., Temple 76504; (254) 773-2250.

Special Education, Continuing Advisory Committee for: (1997); apptv.; 4-yr.; 17 members: Shemica S. Allen, Allen (2/1/23); Teresa Bronsky, Plano (2/1/23); Jana S. Burns, Saginaw (2/1/21); Elizabeth A. "Beth" Donaldson, Stowell (2/1/21); Rachel A. Dreiling, Dallas (2/1/21); Alicia Giordano, Humble (2/1/21); Amy Litzinger, Austin (2/1/21); Stephanie Martinez, Laredo (2/1/23); Jana McKelvey, Austin (2/1/23); Kristine H. Mohajer, Leander (2/1/21); Susan Nichols, Carrollton (2/1/21); Laurie Goforth Rodriguez, Dickinson (2/1/21); Jen Stratton, Austin (2/1/23); Agata K. "Agatha" Thibodeaux, Katy (2/1/21); Ray Tijerina, San Antonio (2/1/23); Laura Villarreal, Universal City (2/1/23); Jo Ann Garza Wofford, New Braunfels (2/1/21). c/o Texas Education Agency, 1701 Congress Ave., Austin 78701; (512) 463-9734; Parent Information Line: (800) 252-9668.

Speech Language Pathologists and Audiologists Advisory Board: (2015); apptv.; 6-yr.; 9 members: Presiding Officer Sherry Sancibrian, Lubbock (3/3/22); Emanuel Bodner, Houston (9/1/21); Cheval Bryant, Sugar Land (9/1/25); Tammy Camp, Shallowater (9/1/23); Kristina Kelley, Dallas (9/1/23); Cristen Plummer-Culp, Round Rock (9/1/25); Kimberly Ringer, Pflugerville (9/1/23); Elizabeth Sterling, Austin (9/1/25); 1 vacancy. PO Box 12157, Austin 78711; (512) 463-6599.

Stephen F. Austin State University Board of Regents: (1969); apptv.; expenses; 6-yr.; 9 members: Chair Karen G. Gantt, McKinney (1/31/23); David Alders, Nacogdoches (1/31/25); Robert A. Flores, Nacogdoches (1/31/27); Brigettee Carnes Henderson, Lufkin (1/31/23); M. Thomas Mason, Dallas (1/31/23); Judy Larson Olson, The Woodlands (1/31/25); Laura Rectenwald, Longview (1/31/27); Nancy C. Windham, Nacogdoches (1/31/27); Jennifer Wade Winston, Lufkin (1/31/25). Pres. Scott Gordon, 1936 North St., Nacogdoches 75962; (936) 468-3401.

Sulphur River Basin Authority: (1985); apptv.; 6-yr.; 7 members: Chair Chris Spencer, Hughes Springs (2/1/23); Gary Cheatwood, Bogata (2/1/23); Emily Glass, Sulphur Springs (2/1/27); Reeves Hayter, Paris (6/15/25); Kirby Hollingsworth, Mount Vernon (2/1/27); Wallace E. "Wally" Kraft II, Paris (2/1/25); Kelly Mitchell, Texarkana (2/1/23). Exec. Dir. Chris Hartung, 911 N. Bishop St., Ste. C104, Wake Village 75501; (903) 223-7887.

Sunset Advisory Commission: (1977); 12 members: 5 members of House of Representatives, 5 members of Senate, 1 public member apptd. by Speaker, 1 public member by Lt. Gov.; 2-yr.; expenses. Public members: Ralph Duggins, Fort Worth (9/1/21); Julie Harris-Lawrence, Surfside Beach (9/1/21). Exec. Dir. Jennifer Jones ($190,000), 1501 Congress Ave., 6th Fl., PO Box 13066, Austin 78711; (512) 463-1300.

Teacher Retirement System (See Retirement System of Texas, Teacher.)

Texas A&M University System Board of Regents: (1875); apptv.; 6-yr.; expenses; 9 members: Chair Tim Leach, Midland (2/1/23); Robert L. Albritton, Fort Worth (2/1/27); James R. "Randy" Brooks, San Angelo (2/1/27); Jay Graham, Houston (2/1/25); Michael A. "Mike" Hernandez III, Fort Worth (2/1/25); Bill Mahomes, Dallas (2/1/27); Elaine Mendoza, San Antonio (2/1/23); Michael J. Plank, Houston (2/1/25); Cliff Thomas, Victoria (2/1/23). Chancellor John Sharp, 301 Tarrow St., College Station 77840; (979) 458-7700.

Texas Southern University Board of Regents: (1947); apptv.; expenses; 6-yr.; 9 members: Chair Albert H. Myres, Sr., Houston (2/1/25); Caroline Baker Hurley, Houston (2/1/27); James M. Benham, College Station (2/1/23); Marc C. Carter, Houston (2/1/23); Pamela A. Medina, Houston (2/1/25); Stephanie D. Nellons-Paige, Houston (2/1/25); Ron J. Price, Mesquite (2/1/23); Marilyn A. Rose, Houston (2/1/27); Mary Evans Sias, Richardson (2/1/27). Pres. Lesia L. Crumpton-Young, 3100 Cleburne St., Houston 77004; (713) 313-7011.

Texas State Technical College Board of Regents: (1960 as Board of the Texas State Technical Institute; changed to present name in 1991); apptv.; expenses; 6-yr.; 9 members: Chair Curtis Cleveland, Waco (8/31/21); Tony Abad, Waco (8/31/21); John K. Hatchel, Woodway (2/1/23); Keith Honey, Longview (8/31/25); Charles "Pat" McDonald, Richmond (8/31/23); Alejandro "Alex" Meade III, Mission (8/31/21); Kathy Powell, San Angelo (8/31/25); Tiffany Tremont, New Braunfels (8/31/23); Ron Widup, Arlington (8/31/25). Chancellor Mike Reeser, 3801 Campus Dr., Waco 76705; (254) 799-3611.

Texas State University System Board of Regents: (1911 as Board of Regents of State Teachers Colleges; name changed in 1965 to Board of Regents of State Senior Colleges; changed to present form in 1975); apptv.; per diem and expenses; 6-yr.; 9 members: Chair Charlie Amato, San Antonio (2/1/25); Duke Austin, Houston (2/1/23); Garry Crain, The Hills (2/1/23); Sheila Faske, Rose City (2/1/27); Dionicio "Don" Flores, El Paso (2/1/25); Nicki Harle, Baird (2/1/23); Stephen Lee, Beaumont (2/1/27); William F. Scott, Nederland (2/1/25); Alan L. Tinsley, Madisonville (2/1/27). Chancellor Brian McCall, 601 Colorado St., Austin 78701-2904; (512) 463-1808.

Texas Tech University System Board of Regents: (1923); apptv.; expenses; 6-yr.; 9 members: Chair J. Michael Lewis, Dallas (1/31/23); Arcilia Acosta, Dallas (1/31/27); Cody Campbell, Fort Worth (1/31/27); Pat Gordon, El Paso (1/31/27); Mark Griffin, Lubbock (1/31/25); Ginger Kerrick Davis, Webster (1/31/25); John Steinmetz, Dallas (1/31/23); John Walker, Houston (1/31/23); Dusty Womble, Lubbock (1/31/25). Chancellor Tedd L. Mitchell, 1508 Knoxville Ave., Ste. 302, PO Box 42011, Lubbock 79409-2011; (806) 742-2161.

Texas Woman's University Board of Regents: (1901); apptv.; expenses; 6-yr.; 9 members: Chair Kathleen Wu, Dallas (2/1/23); Bernadette C. Coleman, Denton (2/1/23); Teresa H. Doggett, Austin (2/1/21); Bob Hyde, Irving (2/1/25); Jill Jester, Denton (2/1/23); Stacie D. McDavid, Fort Worth (2/1/25); Janelle Shepard, Weatherford (2/1/27); Mary P. Wilson, Austin (2/1/25); Crystal Wright, Houston (2/1/27). Chancellor Dr. Carine M. Feyten, 304 Administration Dr., Denton 76204; (940) 898-2000.

Transportation Commission, Texas: (1917 as State Highway Commission; merged with Mass Transportation Commission and name changed to State Board of Highways and Public

Transportation in 1975; merged with Texas Dept. of Aviation and Texas Motor Vehicle Commission and name changed to present form in 1991); governs the Texas Department of Transportation; apptv.; 6-yr.; 5 members: Chair J. Bruce Bugg Jr., San Antonio (2/1/27); Alvin New, Christoval (2/1/27); Laura Ryan, Cypress (2/1/23); Robert C. Vaughn, Dallas (2/1/25); 1 vacancy. Exec. Dir. Marc D. Williams ($344,000), 125 E. 11th St., Austin 78701; (512) 463-8588.

Trinity River Authority: (1955); apptv.; per diem and expenses; 6-yr.; 25 members: Pres. Kevin Maxwell, Crockett (3/15/21); Cathy Altman, Midlothian (3/15/23); Whitney D. Beckworth, Fort Worth (3/15/21); Henry Borbolla III, Fort Worth (3/15/25); C. Cole Camp, Arlington (3/15/25); Megan W. Deen, Fort Worth (3/15/23); Tommy G. Fordyce, Huntsville (3/15/25); Lisa A. Hembry, Dallas (3/15/23); Jerry F. House, Leona (3/15/23); John W. Jenkins, Hankamer (3/15/21); David B. Leonard, Liberty (3/15/25); Victoria K. Lucas, Terrell (3/15/23); D. Joe McCleskey, Apple Springs (3/15/23); Robert F. McFarlane, Palestine (3/15/21); Lewis H. McMahan, Dallas (3/15/25); Manny Rachal, Livingston (3/15/21); Steven L. Roberts, Coldspring (3/15/23); William O. Rodgers, Fort Worth (3/15/21); Amir A. Rupani, Dallas (3/15/25); Kathryn L. Sanders, Athens (3/15/25); C. Dwayne Somerville, Mexia (3/15/25); Frank H. Steed Jr., Kerens (3/15/21); Brenda K. Walker, Palestine (3/15/25); David G. Ward, Madisonville (3/15/23); Edward C. Williams III, Dallas (3/15/21). Gen. Mgr. Kevin Ward, 5300 S. Collins St., PO Box 60, Arlington 76004; (817) 467-4343.

Tuition Board, Texas Prepaid Higher Education (See Higher Education Tuition Board, Texas Prepaid.)

University Lands, Board for Lease of: (1929 as 3-member board; members increased to 4 in 1985); 2-yr.; 4 members: Comm. of General Land Office, 2 members of Board of Regents of The University of Texas, 1 of Board of Regents of Texas A&M University. Ex officio Chair George P. Bush; Christina Melton Crain, Dallas (2/1/25); Mike Hernandez III, Fort Worth (2/1/25); Nolan Perez, Harlingen (2/1/27). Interim CEO: Joe Quoyeser, 825 Town and Country Ln., Ste. 1100, Houston 77024; (713) 352-3808.

University of Houston System Board of Regents: (1963); apptv.; expenses; 6-yr.; 9 members: Chair Tilman J. Fertitta, Houston (8/31/21); Durga D. Agrawal, Houston (8/31/25); Doug H. Brooks, Plano (8/31/23); Alonzo Cantu, McAllen (8/31/25); Steve I. Chazen, Bellaire (8/3123); Beth Madison, Houston (8/31/21); John A. McCall Jr., Crockett (8/31/25); Gerald W. McElvy, Southlake (8/31/21); Jack B. Moore, Houston (8/31/23). Chancellor Renu Khator, 4800 Calhoun Rd., Houston 77004; (832) 842-3444.

University of North Texas System Board of Regents: (1949); apptv.; 6-yr.; expenses; 9 members: Chair Laura Wright, Dallas (5/22/21); Melisa Denis, Southlake (5/22/25); Mary Denny, Aubrey (5/22/23); Daniel Feehan, Fort Worth (5/22/25); Milton B. Lee II, San Antonio (5/22/23); A.K. Mago, Dallas (5/22/21); Carlos Munguia, University Park (5/22/23); G. Brint Ryan, Dallas (5/22/21); John Scott Jr., Keller (5/22/25). Chancellor Lesa Roe, 1901 Main St., Dallas 75201; (214) 571-4800.

University of Texas System Board of Regents: (1881); apptv.; expenses; 6-yr.; 9 members: Chair Kevin P. Eltife, Tyler (2/1/27); Christina Melton Crain, Dallas (2/1/25); R. Steven Hicks, Austin (2/1/23); Jodie Lee Jiles, Houston (2/1/25); Janiece Longoria, Houston (2/1/23); Nolan Perez, Harlingen (2/1/27); Stuart W. Stedman, Houston (2/1/27); Kelcy L. Warren, Dallas (2/1/25); James C. "Rad" Weaver, San Antonio (2/1/23). Chancellor James B. Milliken, 210 W. Seventh St., Austin 78701-2982; (512) 499-4400.

Upper Colorado River Authority (See Colorado River Authority, Upper.)

Upper Guadalupe River Authority (See Guadalupe River Authority, Upper.)

Upper Neches River Municipal Water Authority (See Neches River Municipal Water Authority, Upper.)

Utility Commission, Public (See Public Utility Commission.)

Veterans Commission, Texas: (1927 as Veterans State Service Office; reorganized as Veterans Affairs Commission in 1947 with 5 members; name changed to present form in 1985); apptv.; 6-yr.; per diem while on duty and expenses; 5 members: Chair Laura Koerner, Fair Oaks Ranch (12/31/23); Kevin Barber, Houston (12/31/21); Mary Dale, Cedar Park (12/31/25); Mike Hernandez, Abilene (12/31/25); Kimberlee Shaneyfelt, Dallas (12/31/23). Exec. Dir. Thomas P. Palladino ($151,123), PO Box 12277, Austin 78711-2277; (512) 463-6564.

Veterans Land Board (See Land Board, Veterans.)

Veterinary Medical Examiners, Texas Board of: (1911; revised 1953; made 9-member board in 1981); apptv.; expenses on duty; 6-yr.; 9 members: Pres. Jessica Quillivan, Magnolia (8/26/21); Sue Allen, Waco (8/26/25); Sandra "Lynn" Criner, Needville (8/26/21); Samantha Mixon, Boerne (8/26/23); Raquel Olivier, Houston (8/26/23); Keith Pardue, Austin (8/26/21); Randall Skaggs, Perryton (8/26/23); Michael White, Conroe (8/26/25); Victoria Whitehead, Lubbock (8/26/25). Exec. Dir. John M. Helenberg ($113,413), 333 Guadalupe St., Ste. 3-810, Austin 78701; (512) 305-7555.

Water Development Board, Texas: (1957; legislative function for the Texas Dept. of Water Resources, 1977); apptv.; per diem and expenses; 6-yr.; 3 members: Chair Brooke T. Paup, Austin (2/1/25); Kathleen Jackson, Beaumont (12/31/23); 1 vacancy. Exec. Admin. Jeff Walker ($188,285), 1700 Congress Ave., Austin 78701; (512) 463-7847.

Women, Governor's Commission for: (1967); apptv.; 2-yr; up to 15 members: Chair Karen Harris, Lakehills (12/31/21); Tina Yturria Buford, Harlingen (12/31/21); Cynthia Conroy, El Paso (12/31/21); Starr Corbin, Georgetown (12/31/21); Sasha Crane, McAllen (12/31/21); Amy Henderson, Amarillo (12/31/21); Ashlee Kleinert, Dallas (12/31/21); Karen Manning, Houston (12/31/21); Nathali Parker, Round Rock (12/31/21); Rienke Radler, Fort Worth (12/31/21); Jinous Rouhani, Austin (12/31/21); Catherine Susser, Corpus Christi (12/31/21); Patsy Wesson, Fort Worth (12/31/21); Laura Koenig Young, Tyler (12/31/21). Exec. Dir. Christina McKinney ($63,600), 1100 San Jacinto Blvd., Rm. 2.256, PO Box 12428, Austin 78711; (512) 475-2615.

Workers' Compensation, Commissioner of: (1991; functions transferred to the Texas Dept. of Insurance Division of Workers' Compensation in 2005); apptv.; 2-yr.; Comm. Cassie Brown ($169,111), Austin (2/1/23), 7551 Metro Center Dr., Ste. 100, PO Box 12050, Austin 78711; (800) 252-7031.

Workforce Commission, Texas: (1936 as Texas Employment Commission; name changed 1995); apptv.; 6-yr.; 3 members ($201,000): Chair Bryan Daniel, Georgetown (2/1/25); Julian Alvarez III, Harlingen (2/1/23); Aaron Demerson, Austin (2/1/27). Exec. Dir. Ed Serna ($182,500), 101 E. 15th St., Austin 78778-0001; (512) 463-2222.

Workforce Investment Council, Texas: (1993); apptv.; 19 members: 5 ex officio members (representing Economic Development and Tourism Office, Higher Education Coord. Board, Texas Education Agency, Texas Health and Human Services Comm., Texas Workforce Comm.); 14 apptd.: Chair Mark Dunn, Lufkin (9/1/25); Gina Aguirre Adams, Jones Creek (9/1/21); Joe Arnold, Muldoon (9/1/21); Jesse Gatewood, Corpus Christi (9/1/23); Lindsey Geeslin, Waco (9/1/21); Lauren Gore, Houston (9/1/25); Thomas Halbouty, Southlake (9/1/25); Michael Hinojosa, Dallas (9/1/23); John Martin, San Antonio (9/1/23); Wayne Oswald, Houston (9/1/21); Paul Puente, Houston (9/1/21); Richard Rhodes, Austin (9/1/25); Rick Rhodes, Austin (9/1/23); Brandon Willis, Beaumont (9/1/25). Dir. Lee Rector ($125,000), 1100 San Jacinto Blvd., Ste. 1.100, Austin 78701; (512) 936-8100. ☆

Storefronts in Denton. Photo by Nicholas Henderson, CC by 2.0/Flickr

Local Government

Texas has **254 counties**, a number that has not changed since 1931 when Loving County was organized. Loving has a population of 169, according to the July. 1, 2019, Texas Demographic Center estimate, compared with 164 in 1970 and a peak of 285 in 1940. It is the **least-populous county** in Texas. In contrast, Harris County has **the most residents** in Texas, with a 2019 population estimate of **4,713,325**.

Counties range in area from Rockwall's 148.7 square miles to the 6,192.8 square miles in Brewster, which is equal to the combined area of the states of Connecticut and Rhode Island.

The Texas Constitution makes a county a legal subdivision of the state. Each county has a **commissioners court**. It consists of four commissioners, each elected from a commissioner's precinct, and a county judge elected from the entire county. In smaller counties, the county judge retains judicial responsibilities in probate and insanity cases. **For names of county and district officials, see tables on pages 501–512.**

There are **1,223 incorporated municipalities** in Texas that range in size from 18 residents in Los Ybanez to Houston's 2,325,489, according to the July 1, 2019, Texas Demographic Center estimates. More than 80 percent of the state's population lives in cities and towns, meeting the U.S. Census Bureau definition of urban areas.

Texas had **348 incorporated towns with more than 5,000 population**, according to the 2019 Texas Demographic Center estimates. Under law, these cities may adopt their own charters (called home rule) by a majority vote. Cities of fewer than 5,000 may be chartered only under the general law.

Some home-rule cities may show fewer than 5,000 residents because population has declined since adopting home-rule charters.

Mayors and City Managers of Texas Cities

This list was compiled from online sources and phone calls. It includes the name of each city's mayor, as well as the name of the city manager, city administrator, city coordinator, or other managing executive for municipalities having that form of government. **Home-rule cities are marked in this list by a single-dagger symbol (†) after the name.**

A

Abbott . . . . Anthony R. Pustejovsky
Abernathy . . . . Ron Johnson
City Mgr., Joe Hines
Abilene (†) . . . . Anthony Williams
City Mgr., Robert Hanna
Ackerly . . . . Scott Ragle
Addison (†) . . . . Joe Chow
City Mgr., Wes Pierson
Adrian . . . . Maggie Gruhlkey
Agua Dulce . . . . John Howard
Alamo (†) . . . . Diana Martinez
City Mgr., Bobby Salinas
Alamo Heights (†) . . . . . . Bobby Rosenthal
City Mgr., Buddy Kuhn
Alba . . . . Don Heinert
Albany . . . . Susan Montgomery
City Mgr., Billy Holson
Aledo . . . . Kit Marshall
City Admin., Bill Funderburk
Alice (†) . . . . Cynthia Carrasco
City Mgr., Michael Esparza
Allen (†) . . . . Ken Fulk
City Mgr., Eric Ellwanger
Alma . . . . Ginger Gonzalez
City Mgr., Jim Benton
Alpine (†) . . . . Andres (Andy) Ramos
City Mgr., Megan Antrim, Interim
Alto . . . . Jimmy Allen

Alton (†) . . . Salvador Vela
City Mgr., Jeff Underwood

Alvarado . . . Jacob Wheat
City Mgr., Paul DeBuss

Alvin (†) . . . Paul Horn
City Mgr., Junru Roland

Alvord . . . Jim Enochs
City Admin., Clint Mercer

Amarillo (†) . . . Ginger Nelson
City Mgr., Jared Miller

Ames . . . Cornelius Gilmore

Amherst . . . Clinton Sawyer

Anahuac . . . Charlie Henry
City Admin., Kenneth Kathan

Anderson . . . Karen McDuffie

Andrews (†) . . . Flora Braly
City Mgr., Steve Eggleston

Angleton (†) . . . Jason Perez
City Mgr., Chris Whittaker

Angus . . . Julie Humphries

Anna (†) . . . Nate Pike
City Mgr., Jim Proce

Annetta . . . Sandy Roberts

Annetta North . . . Robert Schmidt

Annetta South . . . Charles Marsh

Annona . . . George English, Sr.

Anson (†) . . . Sara Alfaro
City Mgr., Sonny Campbell

Anthony . . . Benjamin Romero

Anton . . . Blake Cate
City Mgr., Mike Sea

Appleby . . . Gerald Hebert, Sr.

Aquilla . . . Justin Earl

Aransas Pass (†) . . . Ram Gomez
City Mgr., Gary Edwards

Archer City . . . Kelvin Green
City Mgr., George Huffman

Arcola . . . Fred A. Burton
City Admin., Annette Guajardo-Goldberg

Argyle . . . Bryan Livingston
Town Mgr., Richard Olson

Arlington (†) . . . Jim Ross
City Mgr., Trey Yelverton

Arp . . . Terry Lowry

Asherton . . . Alex Bustamante, Jr.

Aspermont . . . Steven Ellis
City Admin., Lorenzo Calamaco

Athens (†) . . . Toni Clay
City Mgr., Elizabeth Borstad

Atlanta (†) . . . Travis Ransom
City Mgr., David Cockrell

Aubrey . . . Chris Rich
Town Admin., Mark Kaiser

Aurora . . . Terry Solomon
City Admin., Toni Wheeler

Austin (†) . . . Steve Adler
City Mgr., Spencer Cronk

Austwell . . . Molly Grace Garcia

Avery . . . Alex Ackley

Avinger . . . Marvin Parvino

Azle (†) . . . Alan Brundrett
City Mgr., Tom Muir

B

Bailey . . . Kenneth Burks

Bailey's Prairie . . . Tammy Mutina

Baird . . . Donny Smith
City Admin., Lori Higgins

Balch Springs (†) . . . Carrie Gordon
City Mgr., Susan Cluse

Balcones Heights . . . Suzanne de Leon
City Admin., David J. Harris

Ballinger (†) . . . Dawni Seymore
City Mgr., Brian Frieda

Balmorhea . . . John L. Davis

Bandera . . . Suzanne Schauman
City Admin., Terry Byrd

Bangs . . . Eric Bishop

Bardwell . . . Jodie Odlozil

Barry . . . Charles Worsham

Barstow . . . Olga Abila

Bartlett . . . Chad Mees
City Admin., Joseph Resendez

Bartonville . . . Bill Scherer
Town Admin., Sylvia Ordeman

Bastrop (†) . . . Connie Schroeder
City Mgr., Paul A. Hofmann

Bay City (†) . . . Robert Nelson
City Mgr., Shawna Burkhart

Bayou Vista . . . Lou Wortham

Bayside . . . Donna Easton

Baytown (†) . . . Brandon Capetillo
City Mgr., Rick Davis

Bayview . . . Gary Paris

Beach City . . . Ryan Dagley

Bear Creek . . . Mark Bohm

Beasley . . . Kenneth Reid

Beaumont (†) . . . Becky Ames
City Mgr., Kyle Hayes

Beckville . . . Gene Mothershed

Bedford (†) . . . Michael Boyter
City Mgr., Jimmy Stathatos

Bedias . . . Gwen Boullion

Bee Cave (†) . . . Kara King
City Mgr., Clint Garza

Beeville (†) . . . Francisco Dominguez, Jr.
City Mgr., John Benson

Bellaire (†) . . . Andrew S. Friedberg
City Mgr., Brant Gary, Interim

Bellevue . . . Robert Ratliff

Bellmead (†) . . . Gary Moore
City Mgr., Yousry (Yost) Zakhary

Bells . . . Terry Crumby
City Admin., Beth Woodson

Bellville . . . James Harrison
City Admin., Shawn Jackson

Belton (†) . . . Wayne Carpenter
City Mgr., Sam A. Listi

Benavides . . . Sijifredo (Chacho) Flores

Benbrook (†) . . . Jerry Dittrich
City Mgr., Andy Wayman

Benjamin . . . Sylinda Meinzer

Berryville . . . Ron Hewlett

Bertram . . . Mike Dickinson

Beverly Hills . . . David Gonzales

Bevil Oaks . . . Rebecca (Becky) Ford

Big Lake . . . Phil Pool

Big Sandy . . . Rex Rozell
City Admin., Laura Rex

Big Spring (†) . . . Shannon D. Thomason
City Mgr., Todd Darden

Big Wells . . . Robert D. Juarez, Jr.

Bishop . . . Tem Miller

Bishop Hills . . . Betty Benham

Blackwell . . . Laura Rozzlle

Blanco . . . Rachel Lumpee
City Admin., Will Daves

Blanket . . . B.J. McGinnis

Bloomburg . . . Delores Simmons

Blooming Grove . . . Gary Patterson

Blossom . . . Charlotte Burge

Blue Mound . . . Darlene Copeland

Blue Ridge . . . Rhonda Williams

Blum . . . Chryle Hackler

Boerne (†) . . . Tim Handren
City Mgr., Ben Thatcher

Bogata . . . Larry Hinsley

Bonham (†) . . . H.L. Compton
City Mgr., Sean Pate

Bonney . . . Raymond Cantu

Booker . . . B.J. Alvarado

Borger (†) . . . Karen Felker
City Mgr., Garrett Spradling

Bovina . . . Frank Gonzalez, Jr.
City Mgr., Cesar Marquez

Bowie (†) . . . Gaylynn Burris
City Mgr., Bert Cunningham

Boyd . . . Rodney Holmes
City Admin., Greg Arrington

Brackettville . . . Eric J. Martinez
City Admin., Nora Y. Rivas

Brady (†) . . . Anthony Groves
City Mgr., Dennis Jobe

Brazoria . . . Roger Shugart
City Mgr., Mike Collard

Brazos Country . . . Albert Sykes

Breckenridge (†) . . . Bob Sims
City Mgr., Erika McComis

Bremond . . . Rick Swick

Brenham (†) . . . Milton Y. Tate, Jr.
City Mgr., James Fisher

Briarcliff . . . Al Hostetler
City Admin., Aaron Johnson

Briaroaks . . . Jerry D. Mabry

Bridge City (†) . . . David Rutledge
City Mgr., Jerry D. Jones

Bridgeport (†) . . . Randy Singleton
City Mgr., Chester Nolen

Broaddus . . . Shirley Parker

Brock . . . Jay Hamilton

Bronte . . . Paul Gohman

Brookshire . . . Darrell Branch

Brookside Village . . . Craig Bailey

Browndell . . . Tincy Brooks

Brownfield (†) . . . Geronimo M. Gonzales
City Mgr., Jeff Davis

Brownsboro . . . Dusty Wise

Brownsville (†) . . . Juan (Trey) Mendez, III
City Mgr., Noel Bernal

Brownwood (†) . . . Stephen E. Haynes
City Mgr., Emily Crawford

Bruceville-Eddy . . . Connally Bass
City Admin., Sonya Bishop

Bryan (†) . . . Andrew Nelson
City Mgr., Kean Register

Bryson . . . Lutitia Ford

Buckholts . . . Teresa Eaton

Buda (†) . . . Lee Urbanovsky
City Mgr., Kenneth Williams

Buffalo . . . Jerrod Jones

Buffalo Gap . . . David L. Perry

Buffalo Springs . . . Meggan Wilkes

Bullard . . . Pam Frederick
City Mgr., David Hortman

Bulverde (†) . . . Bill Krawietz
City Mgr., Danny Batts

Bunker Hill Village . . . Robert P. Lord
City Admin., Karen Glynn

Burkburnett (†) . . . Carl Law
City Mgr., Lawrence Cutrone

Burke . . . John Thomas Jones

Burleson (†) . . . Chris Fletcher
City Mgr., Bryan Langley

Burnet (†) . . . Crista Goble Bromley
City Mgr., David Vaughn

Burton . . . David Zajicek

Byers . . . Norrieca Dalton

Bynum . . . Casi D. Wood

C

Cactus . . . . Socorro Marquez
City Mgr., Aldo Gallegos
Caddo Mills . . . . Ron Olson
City Mgr., Matt McMahan
Caldwell . . . . Norris L. McManus
City Admin., Camden White
Callisburg . . . . Nathan Caldwell
Calvert . . . . Marcus D. Greaves
City Admin., Kevin O'Carroll
Cameron (†) . . . . Bill Harris
City Mgr., J. Rhett Parker
Campbell . . . . Terry Trapp
Camp Wood . . . . Josh Cox
Canadian . . . . Terrill Bartlett
City Mgr., Joe Jarosek
Caney City . . . . Lamar Matthews
Canton . . . . Lou Ann Everett
City Mgr., Lonny Cluck
Canyon (†) . . . . Gary Hinders
City Mgr., Joe Price
Carbon . . . . Corey Hull
Carl's Corner . . . . Susan Ezell
Carmine . . . . Wade Eilers
Carrizo Springs (†) . . . . Wayne Seiple
City Mgr., Ronnie J. Guest, Jr.
Carrollton (†) . . . . Kevin Falconer
City Mgr., Erin Rinehart
Carthage (†) . . . . Olin Joffrion
City Mgr., Stephen K. Williams
Cashion . . . . Debra Carr
Castle Hills . . . . JR Trevino
City Mgr., Ryan Rapelye
Castroville . . . . Darrin Schroeder
City Admin., Scott Dixon
Cedar Hill (†) . . . . Stephen Mason
City Mgr., Greg Porter
Cedar Park (†) . . . . Corbin Van Arsdale
City Mgr., Brenda Eivens
Celeste . . . . Larry Godwin
Celina (†) . . . . Sean Terry
City Mgr., Jason Laumer
Center (†) . . . . David Chadwick
City Mgr., Chad Nehring
Centerville . . . . Noal Ray Goolsby
Chandler . . . . Libby Fulgham
City Admin., John Whitsell
Channing . . . . Troy Williams
Charlotte . . . . Buddy Lee Daughtry
Chester . . . . Floyd Petri
Chico . . . . Colleen Self
Childress (†) . . . . Cary Preston
City Mgr., Kevin Hodges
Chillicothe . . . . Cathy Young
China . . . . William (Butch) Sanders
China Grove . . . . Mary Ann Hajek
City Admin., Susan Conaway
Chireno . . . . Susan Higginbotham
City Admin., Steven Spencer
Christine . . . . Jerry Flores
Cibolo (†) . . . . Stosh Boyle
City Mgr., Robert T. Herrera
Cisco (†) . . . . Tammy Douglas
City Mgr., Darwin Archer
Clarendon . . . . Sandy Skelton
City Admin., David Dockery
Clarksville . . . . Ann Rushing
City Mgr., Damien Carrasco, Interim
Clarksville City . . . . Joe B. Spears
City Mgr., Matt Maines
Claude . . . . Bill Wood
Clear Lake Shores . . . . Kurt Otten
City Admin., Brent Spier
Cleburne (†) . . . . Scott Cain
City Mgr., Steve Polasek
Cleveland (†) . . . . Richard Boyett
City Mgr., Bobby Penington
Clifton . . . . Richard Spitzer
City Admin., Pamela K. Harvey
Clint . . . . Dora H. Aguirre
Clute (†) . . . . Calvin Shiflet
City Mgr., CJ Snipes
Clyde . . . . Rodger Brown
City Admin., Christopher McGuire
Coahoma . . . . Warren Wallace
Cockrell Hill . . . . Luis D. Carrera
City Admin., Bret Haney
Coffee City . . . . Frank Serrato
Coldspring . . . . Pat Eversole
Coleman (†) . . . . Tommy Sloan
City Mgr., Diana Lopez
College Station (†) . . . . Karl Mooney
City Mgr., Bryan Woods
Colleyville (†) . . . . Richard Newton
City Mgr., Jerry Ducay
Collinsville . . . . Derek Kays
Colmesneil . . . . Don Baird
Colorado City (†) . . . . Robert Oliver
City Mgr., David Hoover
Columbus . . . . Lori An Gobert
City Mgr., Donald Warschak
Comanche . . . . Mary A. Boyd
Combes . . . . Marco Sanchez
Town Admin., Aida Gutierrez
Combine . . . . Tim Ratcliff
Commerce (†) . . . . Wyman Williams
City Mgr., Howdy Lisenbee
Como . . . . Jerry Radney
Conroe (†) . . . . Jody Czajkoski
City Admin., Paul Virgadamo, Jr.
Converse (†) . . . . Alfred (Al) Suarez
City Mgr., Le Ann Piatt
Cool . . . . Dorothy Hall
Coolidge . . . . Jesse Ashmore
Cooper . . . . Darren Braddy
Coppell (†) . . . . Wes Mays
City Mgr., Mike Land
Copperas Cove (†) . . . . Bradi Diaz
City Mgr., Ryan Haverlah
Copper Canyon . . . . Ron Robertson
Town Admin., Donna Welsh
Corinth (†) . . . . Bill Heidemann
City Mgr., Bob Hart
Corpus Christi (†) . . . Paulette M. Guajardo
City Mgr., Peter Zanoni
Corrigan . . . . Johnna Gibson
City Mgr., Darrian Hudman
Corsicana (†) . . . . Don Denbow
City Mgr., Connie Standridge
Cottonwood . . . . Karen Deloney
Cottonwood Shores . . . . Donald Orr
City Admin., J.C. Hughes
Cotulla . . . . Javier Garcia
City Admin., Larry Dovalina
Coupland . . . . Jack R. Piper
Cove . . . . Leroy Stevens
Covington . . . . George Burnett
Coyote Flats . . . . Doug Peterson
Crandall . . . . Danny Kirbie
City Mgr., Jana Shelton
Crane . . . . Kelly Nichols
City Admin., Dru Gravens
Cranfills Gap . . . . David D. Witte
Crawford . . . . Brian Porter
City Mgr., Brian Bolfing
Creedmoor . . . . Fran Klestinec
City Admin., Robert Wilhite
Cresson . . . . Teena Conway
Crockett (†) . . . . Ianthia Fisher
City Admin., John Angerstein
Crosbyton . . . . Dusty Cornelius
City Admin., Amy Wallace
Cross Plains . . . . Jerry Cassle
City Admin., Debbie Gosnell
Cross Roads . . . . T. Lynn Tompkins, Jr.
Town Admin., Kristi Gilbert
Cross Timber . . . . Patti Meier
Crowell . . . . Ronnie Allen
Crowley (†) . . . . Billy P. Davis
City Mgr., Robert Loftin
Crystal City (†) . . . . Frank Moreno, Jr.
City Mgr., Santos Camarillo
Cuero (†) . . . . Sara Post-Meyer
City Mgr., Raymie Zella
Cumby . . . . Doug Simmerman
Cuney . . . . Jessie Johnson
Cushing . . . . Robert Sides
Cut and Shoot . . . . Nyla Akin Dalhaus

D

Daingerfield (†) . . . . Lou Irvin
City Mgr., Keith Whitfield
Daisetta . . . . Kellie Taylor
Dalhart (†) . . . . Clinton Hale
City Mgr., James Stroud
Dallas (†) . . . . Eric Johnson
City Mgr., T.C. Broadnax
Dalworthington Gardens . . . Laurie Bianco
City Admin., Lola Hazel,
Danbury . . . . Melinda Strong
Darrouzett . . . . Jerry Reynolds
City Mgr., Coleen Bradley
Dawson . . . . Stephen Sanders
Dayton (†) . . . . Caroline Wadzeck
City Mgr., Theo Melancon
Dayton Lakes . . . . Justin McCormick
Dean . . . . Steve L. Sicking
Decatur (†) . . . . Mike McQuiston
City Mgr., Brett Shannon
DeCordova . . . . Dave Hanson
Deer Park (†) . . . . Jerry Mouton, Jr.
City Mgr., James Stokes
De Kalb . . . . Lowell Walker
De Leon (†) . . . . Jan Grisham
City Admin., David Denman
Dell City . . . . Pamela Dean
Del Rio (†) . . . . Bruno (Ralphy) Lozano
City Mgr., Matt Wojnowski
Denison (†) . . . . Janet Gott
City Mgr., Greg Smith
Dennis . . . . James Synowsky
Denton (†) . . . . Gerard Hudspeth
City Mgr., Sara Hensley, Interim
Denver City (†) . . . . Tommy Hicks
City Mgr., Stan David
Deport . . . . Patrick Watson
DeSoto (†) . . . . Rachel L. Proctor
City Mgr., Brandon Wright
Detroit . . . . Kenneth Snodgrass
Devers . . . . Steven Horelica
Devine . . . . Cory Thompson
City Admin., John Vidaurri
Diboll (†) . . . . Trey Wilkerson
City Mgr., Gerry Boren
Dickens . . . . David Warren
City Admin., Lillian Atkinson
Dickinson (†) . . . . Sean Skipworth
City Mgr., Theo Melancon
Dilley . . . . Gilbert Villanueva Eguia
City Admin., Juan F. Estrada

Dimmitt (†) . . . . Roger Malone
City Mgr., Daniel Jackson
Dish . . . . William Sciscoe
Dodd City . . . . Jackie Lackey
Dodson . . . . Steve Kane
Domino . . . . Moria White
Donna (†) . . . . Rick Morales
City Mgr., Carlos Yerena
Dorchester . . . . David Smith
Double Horn . . . . Cathy Sereno
Double Oak . . . . Von Beougher
Douglassville . . . . DeWitt McCall
Draper . . . . Jamie Sue Harris
Dripping Springs . . . . Bill Foulds, Jr.
City Admin., Michelle Fischer
Driscoll . . . . Mark Gonzalez
Dublin . . . . David Leatherwood
City Mgr., Bobby Mendez
Dumas (†) . . . . Bob Brinkmann
City Mgr., Arbie Taylor
Duncanville (†) . . . . Barry L. Gordon
City Mgr., Aretha R. Ferrell-Benavides

E

Eagle Lake . . . . Mary Parr
City Mgr., Melinda A. Landin
Eagle Pass (†) . . . . Rolando Salinas, Jr.
City Mgr., George Antuna
Early . . . . Robert G. Mangrum
City Admin., Tony Aaron
Earth . . . . Sawnya Bullock
East Bernard . . . . Marvin R. Holub
Eastland (†) . . . . Larry Vernon
City Mgr., JJ Oznick
East Mountain . . . . Marc Covington
Easton . . . . Walter Ward
East Tawakoni . . . . Harold Chandler
Ector . . . . Jerry M. Newell
Edcouch . . . . Virginio Gonzalez, Jr.
City Mgr., Victor Hugo de la Cruz
Eden . . . . Agapito Torres
City Admin., Laura Beeson
Edgecliff Village . . Dennis (Mickey) Rigney
City Admin., Veronica Gamboa
Edgewood . . . . Steve Steadham
Edinburg (†) . . . . Richard Molina
City Mgr., Ron Garza
Edmonson . . . . Sammy Shannon
Edna (†) . . . . Lance Smiga
City Mgr., Gary Broz
Edom . . . . Barbara Crow
El Campo (†) . . . . Chris Barbee
City Mgr., Courtney Sladek
El Cenizo . . . . Elsa Degollado
City Admin., Jaime Montes
Eldorado . . . . George Arispe
Electra (†) . . . . Lynda Lynn
City Admin., Steve Bowlin
Elgin (†) . . . . Ron Ramirez
City Mgr., Thomas Mattis
Elkhart . . . . Jennifer McCoy
El Lago . . . . Shawn Findley
Ellinger . . . . Matt Mikulenka
Elmendorf . . . . Michael J. Gonzales
City Admin., Cody D. Dailey
El Paso (†) . . . . Oscar Leeser
City Mgr., Tommy Gonzalez
Elsa (†) . . . . Alonzo Perez
City Mgr., JJ Ybarra
Emhouse . . . . Jimmy Barkley
Emory . . . . Earl Hill, III
City Admin., Mike Dunn
Enchanted Oaks . . . . Natalie Onate
Encinal . . . . Sylvano Sanchez
City Mgr., Velma Davila
Ennis (†) . . . . Angeline Juenemann
City Mgr., Marty Nelson
Escobares . . . . Lorena Cantu
Estelline . . . . Jeff Jones
Euless (†) . . . . Linda Martin
City Mgr., Loretta Getchell
Eureka . . . . Tammy Cantrell
Eustace . . . . Dustin Shelton
Evant . . . . Roger T. Kircus
Everman (†) . . . . Ray Richardson
City Mgr., Craig Spencer

F

Fairchilds . . . . Lance Bertolino
Fairfield . . . . Kenneth Hughes
City Admin., Nate Smith
Fair Oaks Ranch (†) . . . . Greg Maxton
City Mgr., Tobin Maples
Fairview (†) . . . . Henry Lessner
Town Mgr., Julie Couch
Falfurrias . . . . Justo Ramirez
City Admin., Andy Garcia
Falls City . . . . Brent Houdmann
Farmers Branch (†) . . . . Robert C. Dye
City Mgr., Charles S. Cox
Farmersville . . . . Bryon Wiebold
City Mgr., Benjamin L. White
Farwell . . . . Joe Stanton
Fate (†) . . . . David Billings
City Mgr., Michael Kovacs
Fayetteville . . . . Mike Stroup
Ferris . . . . Fred Pontley
City Admin., Gloria Perkins
Flatonia . . . . Bryan Milson
City Mgr., Sarah Novo
Florence . . . . Mary Condon
Floresville (†)
. . . . Cecelia (Cissy) Gonzalez-Dippel
City Mgr., Andy Joslin
Flower Mound (†) . . . . Derek France
Town Mgr., Debra Wallace, Interim
Floydada . . . . Bobby Gilliland
City Mgr., Darrell Gooch
Follett . . . . Lynn Blau
City Mgr., Robert Williamson
Forest Hill (†) . . . . Gerald Joubert
City Mgr., Sheyi I. Ipaye
Forney (†) . . . . Amanda Lewis
City Mgr., Charles Daniels, Interim
Forsan . . . . Steve Park
Fort Stockton . . . . Joe Chris Alexander
City Mgr., Frank Rodriguez, III
Fort Worth (†) . . . . Mattie Parker
City Mgr., David Cooke
Franklin . . . . Molly Hedrick

Bottle Plant Cafe in Glen Rose. Photo by Nicholas Henderson, CC by 2.0/Flickr

Frankston . . . . Tommy Carr
Fredericksburg (†). . . . . . . Charlie Kiehne
City Mgr., Kent Myers
Freeport (†). . . . . .Brooks Bass
City Mgr., Tim Kelty
Freer . . . . Arnold Cantu
City Mgr., Ana A. Garcia
Friendswood (†) . . . . .Mike Foreman
City Mgr., Morad Kabiri
Friona . . . . Ricky White
City Mgr., Leander (Lee) Davila
Frisco (†). . . . . Jeff Cheney
City Mgr., George Purefoy
Fritch . . . . .Richard Hein
City Mgr., Drew Brassfield
Frost . . . . .Scott Dowdle
Fruitvale . . . . Vicki Ferguson
Fulshear (†). . . . . .Aaron Groff
City Mgr., Jack Harper
Fulton . . . . Kelli Cole

G

Gainesville (†). . . . . .Tommy Moore
City Mgr., Barry Sullivan
Galena Park (†) . . . . Esmeralda Moya
Gallatin . . . . .Juanita Cotton
Galveston (†). . . . . Craig Brown
City Mgr., Brian Maxwell
Ganado . . . . Clinton Tegeler
Garden Ridge . . . . .Robb Erickson
City Admin., Nancy Cain
Garland (†) . . . . Scott LeMay
City Mgr., Bryan Bradford
Garrett . . . . Matt Newsom
Garrison . . . . .Russell Wright
Gary . . . . Mark Thornton
Gatesville (†). . . . . .Gary Chumley
City Mgr., William H. (Bill) Parry, III
Georgetown (†) . . . . .Josh Schroeder
City Mgr., David Morgan
George West (†). . . . . .Andrew Garza
City Mgr., Shirley Holm, Interim
Gholson . . . . Phillip Bagley
Giddings (†) . . . . John Dowell
City Mgr., Ricky Jorgensen
Gilmer (†) . . . . Tim Marshall
City Mgr., Greg Hutson
Gladewater (†). . . . . John (JD) Shipp
City Mgr., Ricky Tow
Glenn Heights (†) . . . . . . Harry A. Garrett
City Mgr., David A. Hall
Glen Rose . . . . .Julia Douglas
City Admin., Michael Leamons
Godley . . . . .Jan Whitegead
City Mgr., David J. Wallis
Goldsmith. . . . . .Richard Bradley
City Mgr., Bennie Cope
Goldthwaite . . . . .Mike McMahan
City Mgr., Robert E. Lindsey, III
Goliad. . . . . Brenda Moses
Golinda . . . . Joyce Farar
Gonzales (†) . . . . Connie L. Kacir
City Mgr., Tim Patek
Goodlow . . . . Nantambu Kambon
Goodrich . . . . Kelly Nelson
Gordon . . . . Jack Coleman
Goree . . . . .Randy Hibdon
Gorman (†) . . . . .David Perry
Graford. . . . . Carl S. Walston
Graham (†) . . . . .Neal Blanton
City Mgr., Brandon Anderson
Granbury (†). . . . . .Nin Hulett
City Mgr., Chris Coffman
Grandfalls. . . . . Jeff Corean
City Admin., Donna Edens
Grand Prairie (†). . . . . Ron Jensen
City Mgr., Tom Hart
Grand Saline . . . . .Jeremy Gunnels
City Admin., Tully Davidson
Grandview . . . . .Zachary Stewart
City Mgr., David D. Henley
Granger . . . . .Trevor Cheatheam
City Admin., Christy Cavness Bradshaw
Granite Shoals (†) . . . . Will Skinner
City Mgr., Jeffery D. Looney
Granjeno . . . . .Yvette Cabrera
Grapeland. . . . . .Mitchell Woody
Grapevine (†) . . . . William D. Tate
City Mgr., Bruno Rumbelow
Grays Prairie. . . . . Lorenzo Garza, Jr.
Greenville (†) . . . . .Jerry Ransom
City Mgr., Summer Spurlock
Gregory . . . . .Jeronimo B. Garcia
Grey Forest . . . . .Mitch Thornton
Groesbeck. . . . . .Ray O'Docharty
City Admin., Chris Henson
Groom .Tim Case
Groves (†) . . . . .Chris Borne
City Mgr., D.E. Sosa
Groveton. . . . . Tommy Walton
Gruver . . . . Buster Davis
City Mgr., Johnnie Williams
Gun Barrel City (†) . . . . David Skains
City Mgr., Jeff Arnswald
Gunter . . . . Mark Millar
City Mgr., Rick Chaffin
Gustine. . . . . Ken Huey

H

Hackberry. . . . . Ronald Austin
City Admin., Brenda Lewallen
Hale Center. . . . . W.H. Johnson
City Mgr., Mike Cypert
Hallettsville . . . . .Alice Jo Summers
City Admin., Grace Ward
Hallsburg . . . . .Mike Glockzin
Hallsville . . . . Jesse Casey
Haltom City (†) . . . . .An Truong
City Mgr., Rex L. Phelps
Hamilton . . . . Jim McInnis
City Admin., Ryan Polster
Hamlin . . . . Curtis Collins
City Admin., Bobby Evans
Happy. Sara Tirey
Hardin . . . . .Harry Johnson
Harker Heights (†). . . . . .Spencer H. Smith
City Mgr., David R. Mitchell
Harlingen (†). . . . . Chris Boswell
City Mgr., Dan Serna
Hart . . . . Eliazar Castillo
City Admin., Adrian Rosas
Haskell . . . . .Alberto Alvarez, Jr.
City Admin., June Ellis
Haslet . . . . Gary Hulsey
City Admin., James Quin
Hawk Cove . . . . . . .Delores (Dotty) Spence
City Admin., Rhonda McKeehan
Hawkins . . . . Stephen Lucas
Hawley . . . . Billy Richardson
Hays . . . . Larry Odom
Hearne (†). . . . . Ruben Gomez
City Mgr., John Naron
Heath (†). . . . . Kelson Elam
City Mgr., Aretha L. Adams
Hebron . . . . Kelly Clem
Hedley . . . . Carrie Butler
Hedwig Village . . . . Tom Jinks
City Admin., Kelly Johnson
Helotes . . . . .Rich Whitehead
City Admin., Marian Mendoza
Hemphill . . . . Robert Hamilton
City Mgr., Thad Smith
Hempstead (†). . . . . Dave Shelburne
Henderson (†) . . . . John (Buzz) Fullen
City Mgr., Jay Abercrombie
Henrietta . . . . Roy L. Boswell
City Admin., Kelley Bloodworth
Hereford (†) . . . . Tom Simons
City Mgr., Steve Bartels
Hewitt (†) . . . . .Steve Fortenberry
City Mgr., Bo Thomas
Hickory Creek. . . . . Lynn Clark
Town Admin., John Smith
Hico . . . . .Eddie Needham
City Admin., Adam Niolet
Hidalgo (†) . . . . Sergio Coronado
City Mgr., Julian Gonzalez
Hideaway . . . . Ray Hutcheson
Higgins . . . . Brandon L. Range
City Mgr., Kim Eggleston
Highland Haven . . . . Olan Kelley
Highland Park (†) . . . . . . Margo Goodwin
Town Admin., Bill Lindley
Highland Village (†) . . . . Charlotte Wilcox
City Mgr., Paul Stevens
Hill Country Village Gabriel Durand-Hollis
City Admin., Frank Morales
Hillcrest Village . . . . Tom Wilson
Hillsboro (†) . . . . Andrew L. Smith
City Mgr., Megan Henderson
Hilshire Village . . . . .Russell Herron
City Admin., Susan Blevins
Hitchcock (†). . . . . Chris Armacost
City Admin., Marie Gelles
Holiday Lakes . . . . Norman Schroeder
Holland . . . . .Johnny Kallus, Acting
Holliday . . . . Allen Moore
Hollywood Park . . . . . . Oscar Villareal, Jr.
Hondo (†) . . . . James W. Danner
City Mgr., Scott L. Albert
Honey Grove . . . . Claude Caffee
Hooks . . . . Alfred (Al) Turnage
Horizon City (†) . . . . Ruben Mendoza
Horseshoe Bay (†) . . . . Cynthia Clinesmith
City Mgr., Stan R. Farmer
Houston (†) . . . . .Sylvester Turner
Howardwick . . . . Tony Clemishire
Howe . . . . .Bill French
City Admin., Joe Shephard
Hubbard . . . . .Mary Alderman
City Mgr., Jason Patrick
Hudson . . . . .Robert Smith
City Admin., James Freeman
Hudson Oaks . . . . Marc Povero
City Admin., Sterling Naron
Hughes Springs . . . . James Samples
City Mgr., Stephen Barnes
Humble (†) . . . . Norman Funderburk
City Mgr., Jason Stuebe
Hunters Creek Village . . . . .Jim Pappas
City Admin., Tom Fullen,
Huntington . . . . Frank Harris
City Admin., Bill Stewart
Huntsville (†) . . . . .Andy Brauninger
City Mgr., Aron Kulhavy
Hurst (†) . . . . Henry Wilson
City Mgr., Clay Caruthers
Hutchins . . . . .Mario Vasquez
City Admin., Trudy Lewis

Hutto (†) . . . . Mike Snyder
City Mgr., Warren Hutmacher
Huxley . . . . Larry Vaughn

I

Idalou . . . . Russ Perkins
City Admin., Suzette Williams
Impact . . . . Trevor Dickson
Indian Lake . . . . James Chambers
Industry . . . . Mable Meyers
Ingleside (†) . . . . Ronnie Parker
City Mgr., Linnette Barker
Ingleside on the Bay . . . . . Jo Ann Ehmann
Ingram . . . . Kathy Rider
Iola . . . . Christina Stover
Iowa Colony . . . . . Michael Byrum-Bratsen
City Mgr., Robert Hemminger
Iowa Park (†) . . . . Ray Schultz
City Mgr., Jerry Flemming
Iraan . . . . Darren Brown
Iredell . . . . Joel Wellborn
Irving (†) . . . . Rick Stopfer
City Mgr., Chris Hillman
Italy . . . . Bryant Cockran
City Admin., Shawn Holden
Itasca . . . . James Bouldin
City Admin., CinDee Garrett
Ivanhoe . . . . Cathy Bennett

J

Jacinto City (†) . . . . Ana Diaz
City Mgr., Lon Squyres
Jacksboro . . . . Joe Mitchell
City Mgr., Michael Smith
Jacksonville (†) . . . . Randy Gorham
City Mgr., Greg Smith
Jamaica Beach . . . . Clay Morris
City Admin., Brad Heiman, Interim
Jarrell . . . . Larry Bush
City Mgr., Vanessa Shrauner
Jasper (†) . . . . Randy Sayers
City Mgr., Denise Kelley
Jayton . . . . George Chisum
Jefferson . . . . Rob Baker
Jersey Village (†) . . . . Bobby Warren
City Mgr., Austin Bleess
Jewett . . . . John Sitton
Joaquin . . . . Frank Cooper
Johnson City . . . . Rhonda Stell
Jolly . . . . D. LeAnn Skinner
Jones Creek . . . . Terry Jeffers
Jonestown . . . . Paul Johnson
City Admin., Steve Jones
Josephine . . . . Joe Holt
Joshua (†) . . . . Joe Hollarn
City Mgr., Mike Peacock
Jourdanton . . . . Robert A. Williams
City Mgr., Lamar Schulz
Junction . . . . Russell Hammonds
Justin . . . . Liz Woodall
City Mgr., Chuck Ewings

K

Karnes City . . . . Leroy T. Skloss
City Mgr., Ken Roberts
Katy (†) . . . . Bill Hastings
City Admin., Byron J. Hebert
Kaufman (†) . . . . Jeff Jordan
City Mgr., Michael T. Slye
Keene (†) . . . . Gary Heinrich
City Mgr., Bernie Parker
Keller (†) . . . . Armin Mizani
City Mgr., Mark Hafner
Kemah . . . . Carl Joiner
City Admin., Walter Gant, III
Kemp . . . . Christi Neal
City Admin., Regina Kiser
Kempner . . . . John (JW) Wilkerson
Kendleton . . . . Darryl K. Humphrey, Sr.
Kenedy . . . . Joe Baker
City Mgr., William Linn
Kenefick . . . . Martin (Marty) Wells
Kennard . . . . Jesse Stephens
City Admin., Michael Deckard
Kennedale (†) . . . . Brian Johnson
City Mgr., George Campbell
Kerens . . . . Jeffrey Saunders
Kermit (†) . . . . Jerry L. Phillips
City Mgr., Frankie Davis
Kerrville (†) . . . . Bill Blackburn
City Mgr., E.A. Hoppe
Kilgore (†) . . . . Ronnie E. Spradlin, III
City Mgr., Josh Selleck
Killeen (†) . . . . Jose L. Segarra
City Mgr., Kent Cagle
Kingsbury . . . . Shirley Nolen
Kingsville (†) . . . . Sam R. Fugate
City Mgr., Mark McLaughlin
Kirby (†) . . . . . Kimberly McGehee Aldrich
City Mgr., Monique Vernon
Kirbyville . . . . Frank George
Kirvin . . . . J.W. Walthall
Knollwood . . . . Rosalie Dunn
Knox City . . . . Kent DeVille
City Admin., Sam Watson
Kosse . . . . Brooks Valls
Kountze . . . . Fred Williams
City Admin., Roderick Hutto
Kress . . . . Amparo Becerra
Krugerville . . . . Jeff Parrent
City Admin., Jeff Parrent
Krum . . . . Ronald G. Harris, Jr.
Kurten . . . . Chris Court
Kyle (†) . . . . Travis Mitchell
City Mgr., Scott Sellers

L

La Coste . . . . Andy Keller
City Admin., George Salzman
Lacy Lakeview (†) . . . . Sharon Clark
City Mgr., Keith Bond
Ladonia . . . . Jan Cooper
La Feria (†) . . . . Olga H. Maldonado
City Mgr., Jaime S. Sandoval
Lago Vista (†) . . . . Ed Tidwell
City Mgr., Tracie Hlavinka
La Grange (†) . . . . Jan Dockery
City Mgr., Shawn Raborn
La Grulla . . . . Pedro A. Flores
City Mgr., Marlen Garza
Laguna Vista (†) . . . . Nadine Smith
City Mgr., Ed Meza
La Joya (†) . . . . Isidro Casanova
City Admin., Jacqueline Bazan
Lake Bridgeport . . . . Sherry Pewitt
Lake City . . . . Dennis Veit
Lake Dallas (†) . . . . Andi Nolan
City Mgr., Mike Wilson, Interim
Lake Jackson (†) . . . . Gerald Roznovsky
City Mgr., Modesto Mundo
Lakeport . . . . Johnny Sammons
Lakeside (San Patricio Co.) . . . . Jeff Mason
Lakeside (Tarrant Co.) . . . . Pat Jacob
Town Admin.Norman Craven,
Lakeside City . . . . Cory Glassburn
City Admin., Eric Stevens
Lake Tanglewood . . . . George Moore
Lakeview . . . . Kelly Clark
Lakeway (†) . . . . Thomas Kilgore
City Mgr., Julie Oakley
Lakewood Village . . . . Mark Vargus
Town Admin., Linda Asbell
Lake Worth (†) . . . . Walter Bowen
City Mgr., Stacey Almond
Lamesa (†) . . . . Josh Stevens
City Mgr., Wayne Chapman, Interim
Lampasas (†) . . . . TJ Monroe
City Mgr., Finley Degraffenried
Lancaster (†) . . . . Clyde C. Hairston
City Mgr., Opal Mauldin-Jones
La Porte (†) . . . . Louis R. Rigby
City Mgr., Corby Alexander
Laredo (†) . . . . Pete Saenz
City Mgr., Robert A. Eads
Latexo . . . . Robert Hernandez
La Vernia . . . . Robert W. Gregory
La Villa . . . . Alma Moron
Lavon . . . . Vicki Sanson
City Admin., Kim Dobbs
La Ward . . . . Richard Koch
Lawn . . . . Veronica Burleson
League City (†) . . . . Pat Hallisey
City Mgr., John Baumgartner
Leakey . . . . Hazel Pendley
Leander (†) . . . . Christine Sederquist
City Mgr., Rick Beverlin
Leary . . . . B.J. Martin
City Admin., Randy Mansfield
Lefors . . . . Michael Ray
Leona . . . . Ernest (Bubba) Oden
Leonard . . . . Michael Pye
City Admin., Terry McCalpin
Leon Valley (†) . . . . Chris Riley
City Mgr., Gilbert Perales
Leroy . . . . David Williams
Levelland (†) . . . . Barbra Pinner
City Mgr., Erik Rejino
Lewisville (†) . . . . Rudy Durham
City Mgr., Donna Barron
Lexington . . . . Allen Retzlaff
Liberty (†) . . . . Carl Pickett
City Mgr., Tom Warner
Liberty Hill . . . . Liz Branigan
City Admin., Lacie Hale
Lindale (†) . . . . Jeff Daugherty
City Mgr., Carolyn Caldwell
Linden . . . . Lynn Reynolds
City Admin., Lee Elliott
Lindsay . . . . Scott Neu
Lipan . . . . Mike Stowe
Little Elm (†) . . . . Curtis Cornelious
City Mgr., Matt Mueller
Littlefield (†) . . . . Eric Turpen
City Mgr., Mitch Grant
Little River-Academy . . . . . Drew Lanham
Live Oak (†) . . . . Mary M. Dennis
City Mgr., Scott Wayman
Liverpool . . . . Bill Strickland
Livingston . . . . Judy B. Cochran
City Mgr., Bill Wiggins
Llano . . . . Gail Lang
City Mgr., Scott Edmonson
Lockhart (†) . . . . Lew White
City Mgr., Steve Lewis
Lockney . . . . Michael DeLeon
City Mgr., G.A. (Buster) Poling, Jr.
Log Cabin . . . . Jennifer Williams
Lometa . . . . Stephen Brister Hicks

Lone Oak . . . . . Doug Williams
Lone Star . . . . . Randy Hodges
Longview (†) . . . . . Andy Mack
City Mgr., Keith Bonds
Loraine . . . . . Mark Overton
Lorena . . . . . Tommy Ross
City Mgr., Joseph R. Pace
Lorenzo . . . . . Tim Tiner
City Admin., Michael Chambers
Los Fresnos (†) . . . . . Alejandro Flores
City Mgr., Mark Milum
Los Indios . . . . . Jaime Gonzalez
City Admin., Jared Hockema
Los Ybanez . . . . . Mary A. Ybanez
City Mgr., John Castillo
Lott . . . . . Sue Tacker
Lovelady . . . . . William B. Shoemaker
Lowry Crossing . . . . . Derek Stephens
Lubbock (†) . . . . . Dan Pope
City Mgr., W. Jarrett Atkinson
Lucas (†) . . . . . Jim Olk
City Mgr., Joni Clarke
Lueders . . . . . Benny Jarvis
Lufkin (†) . . . . . Mark Hicks
City Mgr., Bruce Green
Luling (†) . . . . . Mike Hendricks
City Mgr., Mark Mayo
Lumberton (†) . . . . . Don Surratt
City Mgr., Steve Clark
Lyford . . . . . Rick Salinas
Lytle . . . . . Ruben Gonzalez
City Admin., Josie Campa

M

Mabank . . . . . Jeff Norman
City Mgr., Bryant Morris
Madisonville . . . . . Bill Parten
City Mgr., Camilla Viator
Magnolia . . . . . Todd Kana
City Admin., Don Doering
Malakoff . . . . . Delois Pagitt
City Admin., Ann Barker
Malone . . . . . James Lucko
Manor (†) . . . . . Larry Wallace, Jr.
City Mgr., Thomas M. Bolt
Mansfield (†) . . . . . Michael Evans
City Mgr., Joe Smolinski
Manvel (†) . . . . . Debra Marz Davison
City Mgr., Kyle J. Jung
Marble Falls (†) . . . . . Richard Westerman
City Mgr., Mike Hodge
Marfa . . . . . Manny Baeza
City Admin., Amanda Roane
Marietta . . . . . (vacant)
City Mgr., Charles Elliott
Marion . . . . . Victor Contreras
Marlin (†) . . . . . Carolyn Lofton
City Mgr., Cedric Davis, Sr.
Marquez . . . . . Stynette Clary
City Mgr., Lauren Powers
Marshall (†) . . . . . Amy Ware
City Mgr., Mark Rohr
Mart . . . . . Len Williams
Martindale . . . . . Katherine Glaze
City Admin., Jared Anable
Mason . . . . . Whitney Leifeste
City Admin., John Palacio
Matador . . . . . Pat Smith
Mathis (†) . . . . . Ciri Villarreal
City Mgr., Michael Barrera
Maud . . . . . Jimmy Clary
Maypearl . . . . . Joy Landry
McAllen (†) . . . . . Javier Villalobos
City Mgr., Roel Roy Rodriguez
McCamey . . . . . Patty Jones
McGregor (†) . . . . . James S. Hering
City Mgr., Kevin Evans
McKinney (†) . . . . . George Fuller
City Mgr., Paul Grimes
McLean . . . . . Tanner Hess
McLendon-Chisholm . . . . . Keith Short
City Admin., Lisa Palomba
Meadow . . . . . Natalie Howard
City Admin., Terri McClanahan
Meadowlakes . . . . . Mark Bentley
City Mgr., Johnnie Thompson
Meadows Place . . . . . Charles D. Jessup, IV
Megargel . . . . . Melissa Latham
Melissa (†) . . . . . Reed Greer
City Mgr., Jason Little
Melvin . . . . . Josephine Castillo
Memphis . . . . . Joe Davis
Menard . . . . . Barbara Hooten
City Admin., Don Kerns
Mercedes (†) . . . . . Oscar D, Montoya, Sr.
City Mgr., Alberto Perez
Meridian . . . . . Johnnie Hauerland
City Admin., Marie Garland
Merkel . . . . . Mary Schrampfer
City Mgr., Steve Campbell
Mertens . . . . . Don O. Dillard
Mertzon . . . . . Bill Taylor
Mesquite (†) . . . . . Bruce Archer
City Mgr., Cliff Keheley
Mexia (†) . . . . . Geary Smith
City Mgr., Eric Garretty
Miami . . . . . Chad Breeding
Midland (†) . . . . . Patrick Payton
City Mgr., Robert Patrick
Midlothian (†) . . . . . Richard Reno
City Mgr., Chris Dick
Midway . . . . . Brenda Ford
Milano . . . . . Karl Westbrook
Mildred . . . . . Bryan Roach
Miles . . . . . Travis McMillan
Milford . . . . . Bruce Perryman
Miller's Cove . . . . . Willie B. Garrett
Millsap . . . . . Jamie French
City Mgr., Mark Barnes
Mineola . . . . . Jayne Lankford
City Mgr., Mercy L. Rushing
Mineral Wells (†) . . . . . Regan Johnson
City Mgr., Randy Criswell
Mingus . . . . . Milo Moffit
Mission (†) . . . . . Armando O'Caña
City Mgr., Randy Perez
Missouri City (†) . . . . . Robin J. Elackatt
City Mgr., Bill Atkinson, Interim
Mobeetie . . . . . Bobbie Walker
Mobile City . . . . . Kenny Phillips
Monahans (†) . . . . . Adam Steen
City Mgr., Rex M. Thee
Mont Belvieu (†) . . . . . Nick Dixon
City Mgr., Nathan Watkins
Montgomery . . . . . Sara Countryman
City Admin., Richard Tramm
Moody . . . . . Charleen Dowell
City Admin., William A. Sterling
Moore Station . . . . . Charles Anderson
Moran . . . . . Steven W. Taggart
Morgan . . . . . Jonathan W. Croom, II
Morgan's Point . . . . . Michel J. Bechtel
City Admin., Brian Schneider
Morgan's Point Resort . . . . . Dennis Green
City Mgr., Dalton Rice,
Morton . . . . . Kim Silhan
City Mgr., Veronica Olguin
Moulton . . . . . Mark Zimmerman
City Admin., LuAnn D. Rogers
Mountain City . . . . . Ralph McClendon
City Admin., Tiffany Cornutt
Mount Calm . . . . . Jimmy Tucker
Mount Enterprise . . . . . Brandon Jones
Mount Pleasant (†) . . . . . Tracy Craig, Sr.
City Mgr., Ed Thatcher
Mount Vernon . . . . . Brad Hyman
City Admin., Tina Rose
Muenster . . . . . Tim Felderhoff
City Admin., Adam Deweber
Muleshoe (†) . . . . . Colt Ellis
City Mgr., Ramon Sanchez
Mullin . . . . . Bo Mackey
Munday . . . . . Robert Bowen
City Admin., Ricky Ake
Murchison . . . . . John Placyk
Murphy (†) . . . . . Scott Bradley
City Mgr., Mike Castro
Mustang Ridge . . . . . Alisandro Flores

N

Nacogdoches (†) . . . . . Jimmy Mize
City Mgr., Mario Canizares
Naples . . . . . David Betts
Nash . . . . . Robert Bunch
City Admin., Doug Bowers
Nassau Bay (†) . . . . . Bob Warters
City Mgr., Jason Reynolds
Natalia (†) . . . . . Tommy Ortiz
City Admin., Rene Hinojosa
Navarro . . . . . Vickie Lynn Farmer
Navasota (†) . . . William A. (Bert) Miller, III
City Mgr., Brad Stafford
Nazareth . . . . . Marlin Durbin
City Mgr., Lacey Farris
Nederland (†) . . . . . Don Albanese
City Mgr., Christopher Duque
Needville . . . . . Sandra Dorr
Nevada . . . . . Ben Ponce
Newark . . . . . Mark Wondolowski
New Berlin . . . . . Walter Williams
New Boston . . . . . Ronald Humphrey
City Admin., Elizabeth Lea
New Braunfels (†) . . . . . Rusty Brockman
City Mgr., Robert Camareno
Newcastle . . . . . (vacant)
New Chapel Hill . . . . . Riley Harris
New Deal . . . . . Regina Hobson
New Fairview . . . . . Nolan Schoonmaker
New Home . . . . . Steve Lisemby
New Hope . . . . . Andy Reitinger
New London . . . . . Dale McNeel
New Summerfield . . . . . Jane Barrow
Newton . . . . . Mark Bean
City Admin., Donald H. Meek
New Waverly . . . . . Nathaniel James
Neylandville . . . . . Kathy Wilson
Niederwald . . . . . Reynell Smith
Nixon . . . . . Dorothy Riojas
Nocona . . . . . Robert Fenoglio
City Mgr., Lynn Henley
Nolanville (†) . . . . . Andy Williams
City Mgr., Kara Escajeda
Nome . . . . . Kerry Abney
Noonday . . . . . Mike Turman
Nordheim . . . . . Katherine Payne
Normangee . . . . . Troy Noey
North Cleveland . . . . . Bob Bartlett

The Luther Hotel in Palacios. Photo by Larry D. Moore, CC by 4.0/Wikimedia Commons

Northlake . . . . David Rettig
Town Mgr., Drew Corn
North Richland Hills (†) . . . Oscar Trevino
City Mgr., Mark Hindman
Novice . . . . Bobby Green

O

Oak Grove . . . . Jeffrey Davis
Oak Leaf . . . . .Tom Leverentz
Oak Point . . . . Dena Meek
City Mgr., Stephen Ashley
Oak Ridge (Cooke Co.) . . . . Chad Ramsey
Oak Ridge (Kaufman Co.) . . . . . . Al Rudin
Oak Ridge North . . . . Paul Bond
City Mgr., Heather Neeley
Oak Valley . . . . Jarrett Greer
Oakwood . . . . Jacquelyn Morrow
O'Brien . . . . Chris Casillas
Odem . . . . .Virginia Garza
Odessa (†) . . . . Javier Joven
City Mgr., Michael Marrero
O'Donnell . . . . Kim Parker
Oglesby . . . . .Bruce Pomerenke
Old River-Winfree . . . . .Joe Landry
Olmos Park . . . . Ronald Hornberger
City Mgr., Celia DeLeon
Olney (†) . . . . Rue Rogers
City Admin., Neal Welch
Olton . . . . Mark McFadden
City Admin., Keeley Adams
Omaha . . . . Ernest Paul Pewitt
Onalaska . . . . B. Milton (Chip) Choate
City Admin., Angela Stutts
Opdyke West . . . . Wayne Riggins
Orange (†) . . . . Larry Spears, Jr.
City Mgr., Mike Kunst
Orange Grove . . . . Carl Srp
City Admin., Todd Wright
Orchard . . . . Rod Pavlock
Ore City . . . . Angie Edwards
Overton . . . . .C.R. Evans
City Admin., Clyde Carter, Interim
Ovilla . . . . Richard Dormier
City Mgr., Pam Woodall
Oyster Creek . . . . Justin Mills
City Admin., Toby Guenter

P

Paducah . . . . .Rodger Brannen
Paint Rock . . . . Ricky Donaldson
Palacios (†) . . . . .Linh Chau
City Mgr., David Kocurek
Palestine (†). . . . . Dana Goolsby
City Mgr., Teresa Herrera
Palisades . . . . Jerry Lane
Palm Valley . . . . George Rivera
Palmer . . . . Kenneth Bateman
City Admin., Alicia Baran
Palmhurst . . . . Ramiro J. Rodriguez, Jr.
City Mgr., Lori A. Lopez
Palmview (†) . . . . Ricardo Villareal
City Mgr., Michael Leo
Pampa (†) . . . . .Lance DeFever
City Mgr., Shane Stokes
Panhandle . . . . .Doyle Robinson
City Mgr., Terry Coffee
Panorama Village . . . . .Lynn Scott
Pantego . . . . Doug Davis
City Mgr., Joe Ashton
Paradise . . . . Roy Steel
Paris (†). . . . . Paula Portugal
City Mgr., Grayson Path
Parker . . . . Lee Pettle
City Admin., Luke Olson
Pasadena (†) . . . . Jeff A. Wagner
Pattison . . . . Joe Garcia
Patton Village . . . . Scott Anderson
Payne Springs . . . .(vacant)
Pearland (†). . . . . Kevin Cole
City Mgr., Clay Pearson
Pearsall (†) . . . . Mary Moore
City Mgr., Federico Reyes
Peaster . . . . Don Smelley
Pecan Gap . . . . .Cole Hoskison
Pecan Hill . . . . Don Schmerse
City Admin., Shelley Martinez
Pecos (†) . . . . David Flores
City Mgr., Heather Ramirez, Interim
Pelican Bay . . . . Glen Oberg
Penelope . . . . .Allen Neal
Peñitas (†) . . . . .Rodrigo (Rigo) Lopez
City Mgr., Omar Romero
Perryton . . . . Kerry Symons
City Mgr., David Landis
Petersburg . . . . .Misty Wilson
City Mgr., Mario Martinez
Petrolia . . . . Buddy Alexander
Petronila . . . . Todd Wright
Pflugerville (†) . . . . Victor Gonzales
City Mgr., Sereniah Breland
Pharr (†) . . . . Ambrosio (Amos) Hernandez
City Mgr., Edward M. Wylie, Interim
Pilot Point (†) . . . . . . Shea Dane-Patterson
City Mgr., Britt M. Lusk
Pine Forest . . . . .Cathy Nagel
Pinehurst . . . . T.W. Permenter
City Admin., Jerry Hood
Pine Island . . . . Steve Nagy
Pineland . . . . Joe Lane
Piney Point Village . . . . Mark Kobelan
City Admin., Paul Davis, Interim
Pittsburg (†) . . . . David Abernathy
City Mgr., Clint Hardeman
Plains . . . . Shane McKinzie
City Admin., Steve Vasquez
Plainview (†) . . . . Charles Starnes
City Mgr., Jeffrey Snyder
Plano (†) . . . . .John B. Muns
City Mgr., Mark D. Israelson
Plantersville . . . . Karen Hale
Pleak Village . . . . Larry Bittner
Pleasanton (†) . . . . Clinton J. Powell
City Mgr., Johnny Huizar
Pleasant Valley . . . . Jerry Gholson
Plum Grove . . . . .Barbara Norris
Poetry . . . . Tara Senkevech
Point . . . . Johnny Northcutt
Point Blank . . . . Mark T. Wood
City Mgr., Kelly Hoot
Point Comfort . . . . John Warren
City Admin., Robby Silva
Point Venture . . . . .Eric Love
Ponder . . . . Matthew Poole
Port Aransas (†). . . . . Charles R. Bujan
City Mgr., David Parsons
Port Arthur (†) . . . . Thurman (Bill) Bartie
City Mgr., Ron Burton
Port Isabel (†) . . . . . . Juan Jose (JJ) Zamora
City Mgr., Jared Hockema
Portland (†). . . . . Cathy Skurow
City Mgr., Randy L. Wright
Port Lavaca (†). . . . . .Jack Whitlow
City Mgr., Joanna P. (Jody) Weaver

Port Neches (†) . . . . Glenn Johnson
City Mgr., André Wimer
Post . . . . Marvin Self
City Mgr., J. Rhett Parker
Post Oak Bend . . . . Alison Novak
City Admin., Barbara A. Bedrick
Poteet . . . . Denise Sanchez
City Admin., Eric A. Jiminez
Poth . . . . Chrystal Eckel
Pottsboro . . . . Frank Budra
City Mgr., Kevin Farley
Powell . . . . Clay Jackson
Poynor . . . . Dannie Smith
Prairie View (†) . . . . Brian E. Rowland
Premont . . . . Priscilla Vargas
Presidio . . . . John Ferguson
City Admin., Brad Newton
Primera . . . . Jorge Ledesma
City Admin., Celina Gonzales
Princeton . . . . Brianna Chacón
City Mgr., Derek Borg
Progreso . . . . Gerardo Alanis
City Admin., Alfredo Espinosa
Progreso Lakes . . . . . . O.D. (Butch) Emery
Prosper (†) . . . . Ray Smith
Town Mgr., Harlan Jefferson
Providence Village (†) . . . . . . Linda Inman
Town Mgr., Brian Roberson
Putnam . . . . Hubert Donaway
Pyote . . . . Abigail Pritchard

Q

Quanah (†) . . . . Kathy Butler
City Admin., Paula Wilson
Queen City . . . . Harold Martin
Quinlan . . . . Jacky Goleman
City Admin., John Adel
Quintana . . . . Shari Wright
City Admin., Tammi Cimiotta
Quitaque . . . . Janice Henson
City Mgr., Maria Merrell
Quitman . . . . Randy Dunn
City Admin., Rodney D. Kieke

R

Ralls . . . . Don Hamilton
City Admin., Kim Perez
Rancho Viejo . . . . Maribel B. Guerrero
Town Admin., Fred Blanco
Ranger (†) . . . . John Casey
City Mgr., Gerald Gunstanson
Rangerville . . . . Wayne Halbert
Rankin . . . . Brandon Brown
Ransom Canyon . . . . Jana Trew
City Admin., Maria Elena Quintanilla
Ravenna . . . . Claude L. Lewis
Raymondville (†) . . . . Gilbert Gonzales
City Mgr., Eleazar Garcia, Jr.
Red Lick . . . . (vacant)
Red Oak (†) . . . . Mark Stanfill
City Mgr., Todd Fuller
Redwater . . . . Robert Lorance
Refugio . . . . Wanda Dukes
Reklaw . . . . Bob Parrott
Reno (Lamar Co.) . . . . Bart Jetton
Reno (Parker Co.) . . . . Sam White
City Admin., Scott Passmore
Retreat . . . . Janice Barfknecht
Rhome . . . . Jo Ann Wilson
City Admin., Cynthia Northrop
Rice . . . . Vickie Young
City Admin., Tonya Roberts
Richardson (†) . . . . Paul Voelker
City Mgr., Dan Johnson
Richland . . . . Kenneth Guard
Richland Hills (†) . . . . Edward Lopez
City Mgr., Candice Edmondson
Richland Springs . . . . Johnie Reeves
Richmond (†) . . . . . Rebecca (Becky) Haas
City Mgr., Terri Vela
Richwood (†) . . . . Steve Boykin
City Mgr., Eric Foerster
Riesel . . . . Kevin Hogg
Rio Bravo (†) . . . . Daisy Lee Valdez
City Admin., Jesus Olivares
Rio Grande City (†) . . . . Joel Villarreal
City Mgr., Noe Castillo
Rio Hondo . . . . . . Gustavo (Gus) Olivares
City Admin., Ben Medina
Rio Vista . . . . Jeff Faraizl
Rising Star . . . . Jimmy Carpenter
City Admin., Jan Clark
River Oaks (†) . . . . Joe Ashton
City Admin., Marvin Gregory
Riverside . . . . John LeMaire
Road Runner . . . . David Ortega, Jr.
Roanoke (†) . . . . Scooter Gierisch
City Mgr., Scott Campbell
Roaring Springs . . . . Jeff Thacker
Robert Lee . . . . Jason Moran
City Supt., Luke Sheldon
Robinson (†) . . . . Bert Echterling
City Mgr., Craig Lemin
Robstown (†) . . . . Gilbert Gomez
Roby . . . . Eli Sepeda
City Mgr., Jack W. Brown
Rochester . . . . Lonnetta Farrar
City Admin., Gail Nunn
Rockdale (†) . . . . John King
City Mgr., Barbara Holly
Rockport (†) . . . . Patrick R. (Pat) Rios
City Mgr., Kevin Carruth
Rocksprings . . . . LaWanda Goller
Rockwall (†) . . . . Kevin Fowler
City Mgr., Mary Smith
Rocky Mound . . . . Noble T. Smith
Rogers . . . . Billy Crow
City Admin., Chris Hill
Rollingwood . . . . Mike Dyson
City Admin., Amber Lewis
Roma (†) . . . . Jaime Escobar, Jr.
City Mgr., Crisanto Salinas
Roman Forest . . . . Chris Parr
City Admin., Liz Mullane
Ropesville . . . . Brenda Rabel
Roscoe . . . . Frank S. (Pete) Porter
City Mgr., Cody Thompson
Rosebud . . . . Marlene Zipperlen
City Admin., Kenny Ray Murray
Rose City . . . . Bonnie Stephenson
Rose Hill Acres . . . . David Lang
Rosenberg (†) . . . . Kevin Raines
City Mgr., John Maresh
Ross . . . . Jim Jaska
Rosser . . . . Shannon R. Corder
Rotan . . . . Pete Garcia
City Mgr., Carla Thornton
Round Mountain . . . . Alvin Gutierrez
Round Rock (†) . . . . Craig Morgan
City Mgr., Laurie Hadley
Round Top . . . . Mark Massey
Rowlett (†) . . . . Tammy Dana-Bashian
City Mgr., Brian Funderburk
Roxton . . . . Paul Helms
City Mgr., Janet Wheeler
Royse City (†) . . . . Clay Ellis
City Mgr., Carl Alsabrook
Rule . . . . Delle Watkins
Runaway Bay . . . . Herman White
City Admin., Pamela Woods
Runge . . . . Homer Lott, Jr.
Rusk (†) . . . . Ben Middlebrooks
City Mgr., Amanda Hill
Sabinal . . . . Charles D. Story

S

Sachse (†) . . . . Mike Felix
City Mgr., Gina Nash
Sadler . . . . Jackie Moss
City Admin., Jaime Vannoy
Saginaw (†) . . . . Todd Flippo
City Mgr., Gabe Reaume
Saint Hedwig . . . . Dee Grimm
Saint Jo . . . . Tom Weger
Salado . . . . Michael Coggin
Village Admin., Don Ferguson
San Angelo (†) . . . . Brenda Gunter
City Mgr., Daniel Valenzuela
San Antonio (†) . . . . Ron Nirenberg
City Mgr., Erik Walsh
San Augustine . . . . Leroy Hughes
City Mgr., John Camp
San Benito (†) . . . . . Ricardo (Rick) Guerra
City Mgr., Manuel De La Rosa
Sanctuary . . . . Megg Galloway
San Diego . . . . Ruperto Canales, III
City Dir., Issabelle N. Garcia
Sandy Oaks . . . . Micki L. Ball
Sandy Point . . . . Charles J. Waller, Jr.
San Elizario . . . . Antonio Araujo
City Admin., Maya Sanchez
San Felipe . . . . Bobby Byars
Sanford . . . . Dallis Shelton
Sanger (†) . . . . Thomas Muir
City Mgr., John Noblitt
San Juan (†) . . . . Mario Garza
City Mgr., Benjamin Arjona
San Leanna . . . . Molly Quirk
City Admin., Rebecca Howe
San Marcos (†) . . . . Jane Hughson
City Mgr., Bert Lumbreras
San Patricio . . . . Jackie Hale
San Perlita . . . . George M. Guadiana
San Saba . . . . Ken Jordan
City Mgr., Stan Weik
Sansom Park . . . . Art Minor
City Admin., Angela Winkle
Santa Anna . . . . Harold Fahrlender
Santa Clara . . . . Jeff Hunt
Santa Fe (†) . . . . Jason Tabor
City Mgr., Glen Adams
Santa Rosa . . . . Bobby de la Fuente
Savoy . . . . Rick Berube
Schertz (†) . . . . Ralph Gutierrez
City Mgr., Mark Browne
Schulenburg . . . . Elaine Kocian
City Admin., Tami Walker
Scotland . . . . Ron Hoff
Scottsville . . . . Kerry L. Cade
Scurry . . . . Johnny Blazek
Seabrook (†) . . . . Thom Kolupski
City Mgr., Gayle Cook
Seadrift . . . . Elmer DeForest
Seagoville (†) . . . . Dennis K. Childress
City Mgr., Patrick Stallings
Seagraves . . . . Rick Dollahan
Sealy (†) . . . . Carolyn Bilski
City Mgr., Warren Escovy

Seguin (†) . . . . Donna Dodgen
City Mgr., Steve Parker
Selma . . . . Tom Daly
City Admin., Johnny Casias
Seminole (†) . . . . John Belcher
City Admin., Tommy Phillips
Seven Oaks . . . . Centa Evans
Seven Points . . . . Skippy Waters
Seymour . . . . Jon Hrncirik
City Admin., Jeff Brasher
Shady Shores . . . . Cindy Aughinbaugh
Town Admin., Wendy Admin.
Shallowater . . . . Royking Potter
City Mgr., Russel Moses
Shamrock . . . . Lynn Ramsey
City Mgr., Troy Potts
Shavano Park . . . . Bob Werner
City Mgr., Bill Hill
Shenandoah . . . . Ritch Wheeler
City Admin., Kathie Reyer
Shepherd . . . . Charles Minton
Sherman (†) . . . . David Plyler
City Mgr., Robby Hefton
Shiner . . . . Fred Hilscher
Shoreacres . . . . David Jennings
City Mgr., Troy Harrison
Silsbee (†) . . . . Kevin Garner
City Mgr., DeeAnn Zimmerman
Silverton . . . . Lane B. Garvin
City Admin., Brian Barboza
Simonton . . . . Laurie Boudreaux
City Admin., Jennifer Jones Ward
Sinton (†) . . . . Edward Adams
City Mgr., John D. Hobson
Skellytown . . . . Amanda Dickerson
Slaton (†) . . . . Clifton Shaw
City Admin., Mike Lamberson
Smiley . . . . Michael K. Mills
Smithville . . . . Joanna Morgan
City Mgr., Robert Tamble
Smyer . . . . Joe Riddle
Snook . . . . John W. See, III
Snyder (†) . . . . Tony Wofford
City Mgr., Merle Taylor
Socorro (†) . . . . Ivy Avalos
City Mgr., Adriana Rodarte
Somerset . . . . Lydia P. Hernandez
City Admin., Omar H. Pachecano
Somerville . . . . Tommy Thompson
City Admin., Danny Segundo
Sonora . . . . Juanita Gomez
City Mgr., Arturo Fuentes
Sour Lake . . . . Bruce Robinson
City Mgr., Jack Provost
South Frydek . . . . Laura Meyer
South Houston . . . . Joe Soto
Southlake (†) . . . . John Huffman
City Mgr., Shana K. Yelverton
Southmayd . . . . David Turner
South Mountain . . . . Donald Smart
South Padre Island (†) . . . Patrick McNulty
City Mgr., Randy Smith
Southside Place . . . . Andy Chan
City Mgr., David Moss
Spearman . . . . Tobe Shields
City Mgr., Wade Willson
Splendora . . . . Dorothy Welch
Spofford . . . . Alex Solis
City Mgr., Sarah Terrazas
Spring Branch . . . . James Mayer
Springlake . . . . Gaylon Conner
Springtown . . . . Greg Hood
City Admin., David Miller
Spring Valley Village . . . . . . Marcus Vajdos
City Admin., Julie Robinson
Spur . . . . Louise Jones
St. Paul . . . . David Gensler
Stafford (†) . . . . Cecil Willis, Jr.
Stagecoach . . . . Galen Mansee
Stamford (†) . . . . James Decker
City Mgr., Alan Plumlee
Stanton . . . . Sally Poteet
City Admin., Jessie Montez
Staples . . . . Ronnie Clark
Star Harbor . . . . Warren Claxton
Stephenville (†) . . . . Doug Svien
City Mgr., Allen Barnes
Sterling City . . . . Lane Horwood
City Admin., Laura Arizola
Stinnett . . . . Colin Locke
City Admin., Durk Downs
Stockdale . . . . Ray Wolff
City Mgr., Banks Akin
Stockton Bend . . . . Edward Reiter
Stratford . . . . Greg Wright
City Admin., Tommy Bogart
Strawn . . . . Omer Mallory
City Admin., Danny Miller
Streetman . . . . Johnny A. Robinson
Sudan . . . . Sam Miller
Sugar Land (†) . . . . Joe R. Zimmerman
City Mgr., Mike Goodrum
Sullivan City (†) . . . . . . Leonel (Leo) Garcia
City Mgr., Ana M. Mercado
Sulphur Springs (†) . . . . John A. Sellers
City Mgr., Marc Maxwell
Sun Valley . . . . Tom Wagnon
Sundown . . . . Jonathan Strickland
City Admin., Billy Hernandez
Sunnyvale (†) . . . . Saji George
Town Mgr., Susan Guthrie
Sunray . . . . Bruce Broxson
City Mgr., K.J. Perry
Sunrise Beach Village . . . . . Tommy Martin
Sunset Valley . . . . Marc Bruner
City Admin., Sylvia Carrillo
Surfside Beach . . . . Gregg Bisso
Sweeny (†) . . . . Jeff Farley
City Mgr., Reese Cook
Sweetwater (†) . . . . Jim McKenzie
City Mgr., David A. Vela

T

Taft . . . . Pedro Lopez
City Mgr., Melissa Gonzalez
Tahoka . . . . John B. Baker
City Admin., Julie Arrington
Talco . . . . Mike Sloan
Talty . . . . Frank Garrison
City Admin., James Stroman
Tatum . . . . Clay Lassen
Taylor (†) . . . . Brandt Rydell
City Mgr., Brian Laborde
Taylor Lake Village . . . . Jon Keeney
Taylor Landing . . . . John Durkay
Teague . . . . James Monks
City Admin., Theresa Bell
Tehuacana . . . . Roy Cholopisa
Temple (†) . . . . Tim Davis
City Mgr., Brynn Myers
Tenaha . . . . Mike William Ramsey
City Mgr., Natalie Harris
Terrell (†) . . . . E. Rick Carmona
City Mgr., Mike Sims
Terrell Hills (†) . . . . John Low
City Mgr., William Foley
Texarkana (†) . . . . Bob Bruggeman
City Mgr., David Orr, Interim
Texas City (†) . . . . Dedrick Johnson, Sr.
Texhoma . . . . Missy Cartwright
Texline . . . . Jeff Finnegan
City Mgr., Marcia French
The Colony (†) . . . . Joe McCourry
City Mgr., Troy Powell
The Hills (Village of-) . . . . . Greg Wharton
City Mgr., Wendy L. Smith
Thompsons . . . . Freddie Newsome
Thorndale . . . . George Galbreath
City Admin., William Kiesling
Thornton . . . . Kenneth Capps
City Mgr., Victoria Winstead
Thorntonville . . . . David Mitchell
Thrall . . . . Troy Marx
Three Rivers . . . . Felipe Q. Martinez
City Mgr., Thomas Salazar
Throckmorton . . . . Will Carroll
Tiki Island . . . . Vernon (Goldie) Teltschick
Timbercreek Canyon . . . . Bill Young
City Mgr., Katie Paul
Timpson . . . . Debra Smith
Tioga . . . . Craig Jezek
Tira . . . . Allen Joslin
Toco . . . . John J. Waller
Todd Mission . . . . George C. Coulam
City Mgr., Neal Wendele
Tolar . . . . Terry Johnson
Tom Bean . . . . Daniel Harrison
Tomball (†) . . . . Gretchen Fagan
City Mgr., David Esquivel
Tool . . . . Tawnya Austin
City Admin., Makenzie Lyons
Toyah . . . . Bobby Creamer
Trent . . . . Leanna West
Trenton . . . . Rodney Alexander
Trinidad . . . . Larry Estes
City Admin., Terri R. Newhouse
Trinity . . . . Wayne Huffman
City Mgr., Steven Jones, Interim
Trophy Club (†) . . . . Alicia Fleury
Town Mgr., Wade Carroll
Troup . . . . Joe Carlyle
City Mgr., Gene Cottle
Troy . . . . Michael Morgan
City Admin., Jeff Straub
Tulia (†) . . . . Dusty George
City Mgr., B.J. Potts
Turkey . . . . Christy Yates
City Mgr., Larry Plumlee
Tuscola . . . . Dale Martin
Tye . . . . Bill Murphy
Tyler (†) . . . . Don Warren
City Mgr., Edward Broussard

U

Uhland . . . . Naomi Schrock
City Admin., Karen Gallaher
Uncertain . . . . Judye Patterson
Union Grove . . . . Mallory Dippold Shelton
Union Valley . . . . Craig Waskow
Universal City (†) . . . . John Williams
City Mgr., Kim Turner
University Park (†)
. . . . Thomas H. (Tommy) Stewart
City Mgr., Robbie Corder
Uvalde (†) . . . . Don McLaughlin
City Mgr., Vince DiPiazza

V

Valentine . . . . Summer Webb
Valley Mills . . . . Josh Thayer

Valley View . . . . Mike Chalke
Van . . . . .Don Smith
City Mgr., Charles West
Van Alstyne . . . . Jim Atchison
City Mgr., Lane Jones
Van Horn . . . . Becky Brewster
Vega . . . . Roudy Blasingame
Venus . . . . James Burgess
City Admin., Tonya Roberts
Vernon (†) . . . . Pam Gosline
City Mgr., Martin Mangum
Victoria (†) . . . . Jeff Bauknight
City Mgr., Jesús A. Garza
Vidor (†) . . . . Kelly Carder
City Mgr., Robbie Hood
Vinton . . . . Manuel (Manny) Leos
Village Admin., Andrea Carrillo
Volente . . . . .Dan Thost
Von Ormy . . . . .Sally Martinez

W

Waco (†) . . . . Dillon Meek
City Mgr., Bradley Ford
Waelder . . . . Roy Tovar
City Mgr., Steven McKay
Wake Village (†). . . . . .Sheryl Collum
City Admin., Jim Roberts
Waller . . . . Danny L. Marburger
Wallis . . . . .Dennis L. Diggs
Walnut Springs . . . . .Sammy Ortega
Warren City . . . . Ricky Wallace
Waskom . . . . .Jesse Moore
Watauga (†). . . . . .Arthur L. Miner
City Mgr., Andrea Gardner
Waxahachie (†) . . . . .David Hill
City Mgr., Michael Scott
Weatherford (†). . . . . Paul Paschall
City Mgr., James Hotopp
Webberville . . . . Hector Gonzales
Webster (†) . . . . Donna Rogers
City Mgr., Michael K. Ahrens
Weimar . . . . .Milton R. Koller
City Mgr., Mike Barrow
Weinert. . . . . David Caldwell
Weir . . . . Alber Walther
Wellington . . . . J.D. Hamby
City Mgr., Jon Sessions
Wellman . . . . Eddie Garza
Wells. . . . . Tony McKnight
Weslaco (†) . . . . David Suarez
City Mgr., Mike R. Perez
West . . . . .Tommy Muska
City Admin., Shelly Nors
Westbrook . . . . Lynn Gaston
West Columbia . . . . . Laurie B. Kincannon
City Mgr., Debbie Sutherland
Westlake . . . . Laura Wheat
Town Mgr., Amanda DeGan
West Lake Hills . . . . Linda Anthony
City Admin., Travis Askey
Weston . . . . .Jim Marischen
Weston Lakes . . . . .Ramona Neal
West Orange (†). . . . . Randy Branch
Westover Hills. . . . . Kelly Thompson
West Tawakoni . . . . Jim Turnipseed
City Admin., Anette Lemons
West University Place (†) . . . .Susan Sample
City Mgr., David J. Beach
Westworth Village . . . . .L. Kelly Jones
City Admin., Mike Murray
Wharton (†). . . . . Tim Barker
City Mgr., Andres Garza, Jr.
Wheeler . . . . Bob McCain
White Deer . . . . Robert Peets
Whiteface . . . . Judy Deavours
Whitehouse (†) . . . . .James Wansley
City Mgr., Leslie Black
White Oak (†) . . . . .Kyle Kutch
City Coord., Charles Smith
Whitesboro . . . . W.D. (Dee) Welch
City Admin., Michael Marter
White Settlement (†) . . . . Ronald A. White
City Mgr., Jeff James
Whitewright . . . . Tona Shiplet
Whitney . . . . Trey Jetton
City Admin., Chris Bentley
Wichita Falls (†) . . . . . .Stephen Santellana
City Mgr., Darron Leiker
Wickett . . . . .Xavier Estrada
Willis (†). . . . . Leonard Reed
City Mgr., Robert Evans
Willow Park . . . . Doyle Moss
City Admin., Bryan Grimes
Wills Point . . . . Mark Turner
City Admin., Pam Pearson
Wilmer . . . . Sheila Petta
City Admin., Rona Stringfellow
Wilson . . . . Randy Dunn
Wimberley . . . . Gina Fulkerson
City Admin., Mike Boese
Windcrest (†). . . . . .Dan Reese
City Mgr., Rafael Castillo
Windom . . . . Donny Cobb
Windthorst . . . . Greg P. Vieth
Winfield . . . . Debbie Cruitt
Wink. . . . . .Eric Hawkins
Winnsboro . . . . Andrea Newsom
City Admin., Craig Lindholm
Winona . . . . .Curtis Land
Winters .Lisa Yates
Wixon Valley . . . . James (Jim) Soefje
Wolfe City . . . . .Sharion Scott
Wolfforth . . . . Mike Wright
City Mgr., Darrell Newsom
Woodbranch Village . . . . Mike Tyson
Woodcreek . . . . Gloria Whitehead
City Mgr., Brenton B. Lewis
Woodloch . . . . Ralph Leino, Jr.
Woodsboro . . . . Kay Roach
Woodson . . . . Bobby Mathiews
Woodville . . . . Paula M. Jones
City Admin., Mandy K. Risinger
Woodway (†) . . . . .Jane Kittner
City Mgr., Shawn Oubre
Wortham . . . . Pellie Goolsby
Wylie (†) . . . . Matthew Porter
City Mgr., Chris Holsted

Y

Yantis . . . . John D. (Trey) Norris, III
Yoakum (†) . . . . .Carl O'Neill
City Mgr., Kevin Coleman
Yorktown . . . . Bill Baker
City Mgr., John Barth

Z

Zavalla . . . . Carlos Guzman

The Innovation Pipeline in Tyler. Photo by Michael Barera, CC by SA 4.0/Wikimedia Commons

Polk County Courthouse in Livingston. Photo by Jim Evans, CC by 4.0/Wikimedia Commons.

County Courts

Each Texas county has one county court created by the Texas Constitution — a constitutional county court — which is presided over by the county judge (see table beginning on page 501 for a list of county judges). In more populated counties, the Legislature has created statutory county courts, including courts at law, probate courts, juvenile courts, domestic relations courts, and criminal courts at law. Following is a list of statutory county courts and judges, as reported in the Texas Judicial Directory as of July 2021. Other courts with jurisdiction in each county can be found on pages 456–461. Other county and district officials can be found on pages 501–512.

Anderson: Court at Law, Brendan Jeffrey Doran.

Angelina: Court at Law No. 1, Joe Lee Register; No. 2, Clyde M. Herrington.

Aransas: Court at Law, Richard Bianchi.

Atascosa: Court at Law, Bob Brendel

Austin: Court at Law, Daniel W. Leedy.

Bastrop: Court at Law, M. Benton Eskew.

Bell: Court at Law No. 1, Jeanne Parker; No. 2, John Michael Mischtian; No. 3, Rebecca DePew.

Bexar: Court at Law No. 1, Helen Petry Stowe; No. 2, Grace M. Uzomba; No. 3, David J. Rodriguez; No. 4, Alfredo Ximenez; No. 5, John Amos Longoria; No. 6, Wayne A. Christian; No. 7, Michael DeLeon; No. 8, Mary D. Roman; No. 9, Gloria Saldana; No. 10, J. Frank Davis; No. 11, Carl T. Stolhandske; No. 12, Yolanda Huff; No. 13, Rosie Gonzalez; No. 14, Carlo R. Key; No. 15, Melissa Vara. **Probate Court**, No. 1, Oscar Kazen; No. 2, Veronica Vasquez.

Bosque: Court at Law, Luke A. Giesecke.

Bowie: Court at Law, Craig L. Henry.

Brazoria: Court at Law No. 1 & **Probate Court**, Courtney T. Gilbert; No. 2 & **Probate Court**, Marc W. Holder; No. 3 & **Probate Court**, Jeremy E. Warren; No. 4 & **Probate Court**, Lori L. Rickert.

Brazos: Court at Law No. 1, Amanda S. Matzke; No. 2, James White Locke.

Brown: Court at Law, Sam Clifton Moss.

Burnet: Court at Law, Linda M. Bayless.

Caldwell: Court at Law, Barbara L. Molina.

Calhoun: Court at Law, Alex R. Hernandez.

Cameron: Court at Law No. 1, Arturo A. McDonald Jr.; No. 2, Laura Betancourt; No. 3, David Gonzales III; No. 4, Sheila Garcia Bence; No. 5, Estela Chavez-Vasquez.

Cass: Court at Law, Donald W. Dowd.

Cherokee: Court at Law, Janice C. Stone.

Collin: Court at Law No. 1, Corinne Ann Mason; No. 2, Barnett Walker; No. 3, Lance S. Baxter; No. 4, David D. Rippel; No. 5, Dan K. Wilson; No. 6, Jay A. Bender; No. 7, David Waddill. **Probate Court**, Weldon S. Copeland Jr.

Comal: Court at Law No. 1, Randy C. Gray; No. 2 Charles A. Stephens II; No. 3, Deborah Wigington.

Cooke: Court at Law, John H. Morris.

Coryell: Court at Law, John R. Lee.

Dallas: Court at Law No. 1, D'Metria Benson; No. 2, Melissa Bellan; No. 3, Sally L. Montgomery; No. 4, Paula Rosales; No. 5, Mark Greenberg. County **Criminal** Court No. 1, Dan Patterson; No. 2, Julia Hayes; No. 3,

Audrey Moorhead; No. 4, Nancy Cutler Mulder; No. 5, Lisa Green; No. 6, Angela M. King; No. 7, Remeko Tranisha Edwards; No. 8, Carmen P. White; No. 9, Peggy Hoffman; No. 10, Etta J. Mullin; No. 11, Shequitta Kelly. **Probate Court** No. 1, Brenda Hull Thompson; No. 2, Ingrid Michelle Warren; No. 3, Margaret R. Jones-Johnson.

Denton: Court at Law No. 1 & **Juvenile Court**, Kimberly McCary; No. 2, Robert Ramirez. **Criminal Court at Law** No. 1, David W. Jahn; No. 2, Susan Piel; No. 3, Forrest Beadle; No. 4, Chance Oliver; No. 5, Charles (Coby) Waddill. **Probate Court**, Bonnie J. Robison.

Ector: Court at Law No. 1, Brooke Hendricks; No. 2, Christopher M. Clark.

Ellis: Court at Law No. 1, Jim Chapman; No. 2, A. Gene Calvert Jr.

El Paso: Court at Law No. 1, Ruth Reyes; No. 2, Julie Gonzalez; No. 3, Javier Alvarez; No. 4, Alejandro Gonzalez; No. 5, Jesus Rodriguez; No. 6, M. Sue Kurita; No. 7, Ruben Morales. **Criminal Court at Law** No. 1, Alma R. Trejo; No. 2, Robert S. Anchondo; No. 3, Carlos Carrasco; No. 4, Jessica Vazquez. **Probate Court** No. 1, Patricia B. Chew; No. 2, Eduardo Gamboa.

Erath: Court at Law, Blake B. Thompson.

Fannin: Court at Law, Charles Butler.

Fisher: Multicounty **Court at Law**, David C. Hall (also Mitchell and Nolan Counties)

Fort Bend: Court at Law No. 1, Christopher G. Morales; No. 2, Jeffery A. McMeans; No. 3, Juli Mathew; No. 4, Toni M. Wallace; No. 5, Teana V. Watson; No. 6, Sherman Hatton, Jr.

Galveston: Court at Law No. 1, John Grady; No. 2, Kerri M. Foley; No. 3, Jack Ewing. **Probate Court**, Kimberly A. Sullivan.

Gillespie: Court at Law, Christopher G. Nevins

Grayson: Court at Law No. 1, James C. Henderson; No. 2, Carol M. Siebman.

Gregg: Court at Law No. 1, R. Kent Phillips. No. 2, Vincent L. Dulweber.

Grimes: Court at Law, Tuck Moody McLain

Guadalupe: Court at Law No. 1, Bill Squires; No. 2, Kirsten Legore.

Harris: Civil **Court at Law** No. 1, Vacant; No. 2, Jim F. Kovach; No. 3, LaShawn A. Williams; No. 4, Lesley Briones. County **Criminal Court at Law** No. 1, Alex Salgado; No. 2, Ronnisha Bowman; No. 3, Erica Hughes; No. 4, Shannon Baldwin; No. 5, David M. Fleischer; No. 6, Kelley Andrews; No. 7, Andrew A. Wright; No. 8, Franklin Bynum; No. 9, Toria J. Finch; No. 10, Lee Harper Wilson; No. 11, Sedrick T. Walker II; No. 12, Genesis Draper; No. 13, Raul Rodriguez; No. 14, David L. Singer; No. 15, Tonya Jones; No. 16, Darrell William Jordan. **Probate Court** No. 1, Jerry W. Simoneaux; No. 2, Michael B. Newman; No. 3, Jason Cox; No. 4, James Horwitz.

Harrison: Court at Law, Joe M. Black IV.

Hays: Court at Law No. 1, Robert E. Updegrove; No. 2, Chris Johnson; No. 3, Dan O'Brien.

Henderson: Court at Law No 1, Scott S. Williams; No 2, Nancy Adams Perryman.

Hidalgo: Court at Law No. 1, Rodolfo Gonzalez; No. 2, Jaime Palacios; No. 4, Federico Garza Jr.; No. 5, Arnoldo Cantu; Jr. No. 6, Albert Garcia; No. 7, Sergio Valdez; No. 8, Omar Maldonado, No. 9, Patricia O'Caña-Oliveres; No. 10 Armando J. Marroquin. **Probate Court**, JoAnne Garcia.

Hill: Court at Law, Matthew S. Crain.

Hood: Court at Law, Vincent Messina.

Hopkins: Court at Law, Nicholas C. Harrison.

Houston: Court at Law, Sarah Tunnell Clark.

Hunt: Court at Law No. 1, Timothy S. Linden; No. 2, Joel D. Littlefield.

Jefferson: Court at Law No. 1, Gerald W. Eddins; No. 2, Terrence L. Holmes; No. 3, Clint M. Woods.

Jim Wells: Court at Law, Michael Ventura Garcia

Johnson: Court at Law No. 1, Robert B. Mayfield III; No. 2, F. Steven McClure.

Kaufman: Court at Law No. 1, Tracy Gray; No. 2, Bobby L. Rich, Jr.

Kerr: Court at Law, Susan F. Harris.

Kleberg: Court at Law, Jamie E. Carrillo.

Lamar: Court at Law, Bill H. Harris.

Liberty: Court at Law, Thomas A. Chambers; No. 2, Wesley N Hinch.

Lubbock: Court at Law No. 1, Mark J. Hocker; No. 2, Drue A. Farmer; No. 3, Benjamin Webb.

McLennan: Court at Law No. 1, Vikram Deivanayagam; No. 2, T. Bradley Cates.

Medina: Court at Law, Mark Cashion.

Midland: Court at Law No. 1, K. Kyle Peeler; No. 2, Marvin L. Moore.

Mitchell: Multicounty **Court at Law**, David C. Hall. (also Fisher and Nolan Counties)

Montgomery: Court at Law No. 1, Dennis D. Watson; No. 2, Claudia L. Laird; No. 3, Amy Tucker; No. 4, Mary Ann Turner; No. 5, Keith Mills Stewart.

Moore: Court at Law, Jerod Pingelton.

Nacogdoches: Court at Law, John A. (Jack) Sinz.

Navarro: Court at Law, Amanda D. Putman.

Nolan: Multicounty **Court at Law**, David C. Hall. (also Fisher and Mitchell Counties)

Nueces: Court at Law No. 1, Robert J. Vargas; No. 2, Lisa Elisabet Gonzales; No. 3, Deeanne Galvan; No. 4, Mark H. Woerner; No. 5, Timothy J. McCoy.

Orange: Court at Law No. 1, Mandy White-Rogers; No 2, Troy Johnson.

Panola: Court at Law, Terry D. Bailey.

Parker: Court at Law No. 1, Jerry D. Buckner; No. 2, Lynn Marie Johnson.

Polk: Court at Law, Tom Brown.

Potter: Court at Law No. 1, Walt Weaver; No. 2, Matt Hand.

Randall: Court at Law No. 1, James W. Anderson. No. 2, Matthew Martindale.

Reeves: Court at Law, Scott W. Johnson.

Rockwall: Court at Law No. 1, Brian Williams; No. 2 Stephani Woodward.

Rusk: Court at Law, Chad W. Dean.

San Patricio: Court at Law, M. Elizabeth Welborn.

Smith: Court at Law No. 1, Jason A. Ellis; No. 2, Taylor Heaton. No. 3, Floyd Thomas Getz.

Starr: Court at Law, Orlando Rodriguez.

Tarrant: Court at Law No. 1, Donald R. Pierson; No. 2, Jennifer Rymell; No. 3, Mike Hrabal. **Criminal Court at Law** No. 1, David Cook; No. 2, Carey F. Walker; No. 3, Bob McCoy; No. 4, Deborah L. Nekhom; No. 5, Jamie Cummings; No. 6, Molly S. Jones; No. 7, Cheril S. Hardy; No. 8, Charles L. Vanover; No. 9, Brent A. Carr; No. 10, Phil A. Sorrels. **Probate Court** No. 1, Christopher W. Ponder; No. 2, Brooke Ulrickson Allen.

Taylor: Court at Law No. 1, Robert Harper; No. 2, Harriett L. Haag.

Tom Green: Court at Law No. 1, Charles (Ben) Nolen; No. 2, Penny Anne Roberts.

Travis: Court at Law No. 1, J. Todd T. Wong; No. 2, Eric M. Shepperd; No. 3, John H. Lipscombe; No. 4, Dimple Malhotra; No. 5, Nancy Hohengarten; No. 6, Brandy Mueller; No. 7, Elisabeth A. Earle; No. 8, Carlos H. Barrera; No. 9, Kim Williams. **Probate Court**, Guy Herman.

Val Verde: Court at Law, Sergio J. Gonzalez.

Van Zandt: Court at Law, Joshua Wintters.

Victoria: Court at Law No. 1, Travis H. Ernst; No. 2, Daniel F. Gilliam.

Walker: Court at Law, Tracy M. Sorensen.

Waller: Court at Law, Carol A. Chaney.

Washington: Court at Law, Eric Thomas Berg.

Webb: Court at Law No. 1, Hugo D. Martinez; No. 2, Victor G. Villarreal.

Wichita: Court at Law No. 1, Gary Wayne Butler; No. 2, Greg King.

Williamson: Court at Law No. 1, Brandy Hallford; No. 2, Laura B. Barker; No. 3, Doug Arnold; No. 4, John B. McMaster.

Wise: Court at Law No. 1, Greg Lowery; No. 2, Stephen J. Wren. ☆

Regional Councils of Government

Source: Texas Association of Regional Councils; www.txregionalcouncil.org/

The concept of regional planning and cooperation, fostered by enabling legislation in 1965, has spread across Texas since organization of the **North Central Texas Council of Governments** in 1966.

Regional councils are voluntary associations of local governments that deal with problems and planning needs that cross the boundaries of individual local governments or that require regional attention.

These concerns include criminal justice, emergency communications, job-training programs, solid-waste management, transportation, and water-quality management. The councils make recommendations to member governments and may assist in implementing the plans. Financing is provided by local, state, and federal governments.

The **Texas Association of Regional Councils** is at 701 Brazos, Ste. 780, Austin 78701; (512) 478-4715. Following is a list of the 24 regional councils, member counties, executive director, and contact information:

1. **Panhandle Regional Planning Commission**: Armstrong, Briscoe, Carson, Castro, Childress, Collingsworth, Dallam, Deaf Smith, Donley, Gray, Hall, Hansford, Hartley, Hemphill, Hutchinson, Lipscomb, Moore, Ochiltree, Oldham, Parmer, Potter, Randall, Roberts, Sherman, Swisher, and Wheeler. Kyle Ingham, P.O. Box 9257, Amarillo 79105-9257; (806) 372-3381; www.theprpc.org.
2. **South Plains Association of Governments**: Bailey, Cochran, Crosby, Dickens, Floyd, Garza, Hale, Hockley, King, Lamb, Lubbock, Lynn, Motley, Terry, and Yoakum. Tim Pierce, P.O. Box 3730, Lubbock 79452-3730; (806) 762-8721; www.spag.org.
3. **Nortex Regional Planning Commission**: Archer, Baylor, Clay, Cottle, Foard, Hardeman, Jack, Montague, Wichita, Wilbarger, and Young. Dennis Wilde, P.O. Box 5144, Wichita Falls 76307-5144; (940) 322-5281; www.nortexrpc.org.
4. **North Central Texas Council of Governments**: Collin, Dallas, Denton, Ellis, Erath, Hood, Hunt, Johnson, Kaufman, Navarro, Palo Pinto, Parker, Rockwall, Somervell, Tarrant, and Wise. R. Michael Eastland, P.O. Box 5888, Arlington 76005-5888; (817) 695-9101; www.nctcog.org.
5. **Ark-Tex Council of Governments**: Bowie, Cass, Delta, Franklin, Hopkins, Lamar, Morris, Red River, and Titus. Chris Brown, 4808 Elizabeth St., Texarkana, Texas 75503; (903) 832-8636; www.atcog.org.
6. **East Texas Council of Governments**: Anderson, Camp, Cherokee, Gregg, Harrison, Henderson, Marion, Panola, Rains, Rusk, Smith, Upshur, Van Zandt, and Wood. David Cleveland, 3800 Stone Rd., Kilgore 75662-6297; (903) 984-8641; www.etcog.org.
7. **West Central Texas Council of Governments**: Brown, Callahan, Coleman, Comanche, Eastland, Fisher, Haskell, Jones, Kent, Knox, Mitchell, Nolan, Runnels, Scurry, Shackelford, Stephens, Stonewall, Taylor, and Throckmorton. Tom Smith, 3702 Loop 322, Abilene 79602-7300; (325) 672-8544; www.wctcog.org.
8. **Rio Grande Council of Governments**: Brewster, Culberson, El Paso, Hudspeth, Jeff Davis, Presidio, and Doña Ana County, N.M. Annette Gutierrez, 8037 Lockheed Dr., Ste. 100, El Paso 79925; (915) 533-0998; www.riocog.org.
9. **Permian Basin Regional Planning Commission**: Andrews, Borden, Crane, Dawson, Ector, Gaines, Glasscock, Howard, Loving, Martin, Midland, Pecos, Reeves, Terrell, Upton, Ward, and Winkler. Virginia Belew, PO Box 60660, Midland 79711-0660; (432) 563-1061; www.pbrpc.org.

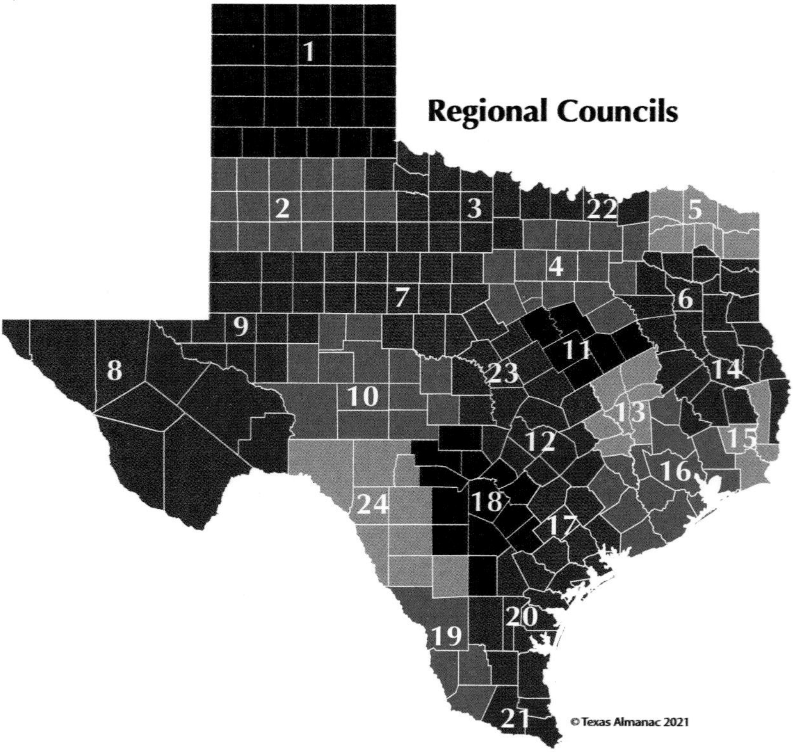

10. **Concho Valley Council of Governments**: Coke, Concho, Crockett, Irion, Kimble, Mason, McCulloch, Menard, Reagan, Schleicher, Sterling, Sutton, and Tom Green. John Austin Stokes, 2801 W. Loop 206, Ste. A, San Angelo 76904; (325) 944-9666; www.cvcog.org.

11. **Heart of Texas Council of Governments**: Bosque, Falls, Freestone, Hill, Limestone, and McLennan. Russell Devorsky, 1514 S. New Road, Waco 76711; (254) 292-1800; www.hotcog.org.

12. **Capital Area Council of Governments**: Bastrop, Blanco, Burnet, Caldwell, Fayette, Hays, Lee, Llano, Travis, and Williamson. Betty Voights, 6800 Burleson Rd., Bldg. 310, Ste. 165, Austin 78744; (512) 916-6018; www.capcog.org.

13. **Brazos Valley Council of Governments**: Brazos, Burleson, Grimes, Leon, Madison, Robertson, and Washington. Tom Wilkinson Jr., P.O. Drawer 4128, Bryan 77805-4128; (979) 595-2800; www.bvcog.org.

14. **Deep East Texas Council of Governments**: Angelina, Houston, Nacogdoches, Newton, Polk, Sabine, San Augustine, San Jacinto, Shelby, Trinity, and Tyler. Lonnie Hunt, 1405 Kurth Dr., Lufkin, 75904; (963) 634-2247; www.detcog.gov.

15. **South East Texas Regional Planning Commission**: Hardin, Jasper, Jefferson, and Orange. Shanna Burke, 2210 Eastex Fwy., Beaumont 77703; (409) 899-8444; www.setrpc.org.

16. **Houston-Galveston Area Council**: Austin, Brazoria, Chambers, Colorado, Fort Bend, Galveston, Harris, Liberty, Matagorda, Montgomery, Walker, Waller, and Wharton. Chuck Wemple, 3555 Timmons Ln., Ste. 120, Houston 77227-2777; (713) 993-4514; www.h-gac.com.

17. **Golden Crescent Regional Planning Commission**: Calhoun, DeWitt, Goliad, Gonzales, Jackson, Lavaca, and Victoria. Michael Ada, 1908 N. Laurent, Ste. 600, Victoria 77901; (361) 578-1587; www.gcrpc.org.

18. **Alamo Area Council of Governments**: Atascosa, Bandera, Bexar, Comal, Frio, Gillespie, Guadalupe, Karnes, Kendall, Kerr, McMullen, Medina, and Wilson. Diane Rath, 82700 NE Loop 410, Ste. 101, San Antonio 78217; (210) 362-5200; www.aacog.com.

19. **South Texas Development Council**: Jim Hogg, Starr, Webb, and Zapata. Robert Mediola, 1002 Dicky Lane, Laredo 78044-2187; (956) 722-3995; www.stdc.cog.tx.us.

20. **Coastal Bend Council of Governments**: Aransas, Bee, Brooks, Duval, Jim Wells, Kenedy, Kleberg, Live Oak, Nueces, Refugio, and San Patricio. John P. Buckner, 2910 Leopard St, Corpus Christi 78408; (361) 883-5743; coastalbendcog.org.

21. **Lower Rio Grande Valley Development Council**: Cameron, Hidalgo, and Willacy. Manny Cruz, 301 W. Railroad St., Weslaco 78596; (956) 682-3481; www.lrgvdc.org.

22. **Texoma Council of Governments**: Cooke, Fannin, and Grayson. Eric Bridges, 1117 Gallagher Dr., Ste. 470, Sherman 75090; (903) 813-3514; www.tcog.com.

23. **Central Texas Council of Governments**: Bell, Coryell, Hamilton, Lampasas, Milam, Mills, and San Saba. Jim Reed, P.O. Box 729, Belton 76513-0729; (254) 770-2210; www.ctcog.org.

24. **Middle Rio Grande Development Council**: Dimmit, Edwards, Kinney, La Salle, Maverick, Real, Uvalde, Val Verde, and Zavala. Nick Gallegos, 307 W. Nopal, Carrizo Springs 78834; (830) 876-3533; www.mrgdc.org. ☆

County Tax Appraisers

The following list of Chief Appraisers for Texas counties was furnished by the State Property Tax Division of the State Comptroller's office. It includes the mailing address for each appraiser and is current to August 2021.

Anderson: Adrienne Polk, P.O. Box 279, Palestine 75802

Andrews: Susan Brewer, 600 N. Main St. Andrews 79714

Angelina: Tim Chambers, P.O. Box 2357, Lufkin 75902

Aransas: Mike Soto, 11 Hwy 35 N, Rockport 78382

Archer: Kimbra York, P.O. Box 1141, Archer City 76351

Armstrong: Melissa Clement, P.O. Box 149, Claude 79019

Atascosa: Michelle L. Berdeaux, P.O. Box 600, Pleasanton 78065

Austin: Greg Cook, 906 E. Amelia St., Bellville 77418

Bailey: Jessica Rivera, 302 Main St., Muleshoe 79347

Bandera: Shawn Davis, P.O. Box 1119, Bandera 78003

Bastrop: Faun Cullens, P.O. Box 578, Bastrop 78602

Baylor: Mitzi Welch, 211 N. Washington, Seymour 76380

Bee: Patricia Davis, 401 N. Washington, Beeville 78102

Bell: Billy White, P.O. Box 390, Belton 76513

Bexar: Michael Amezquita, P.O. Box 830248, San Antonio 78283

Blanco: Candice Fry, P.O. Box 338, Johnson City 78636

Borden: Tracy Cooley, P.O. Box 298, Gail 79738

Bosque: Christopher Moser, P.O. Box 393, Meridian 76665

Bowie: Mike Brower, P.O. Box 6527, Texarkana 75505

Brazoria: Al Baird, 500 N. Chenango, Angleton 77515

Brazos: Mark Price, 4051 Pendleton Dr., Bryan 77802

Brewster: Denise Flores, 107 W. Avenue E, #2, Alpine 79830

Briscoe: Theresa Clinton, P.O. Box 728, Silverton 79257

Brooks: Daniel Garcia, P.O. Drawer A, Falfurrias 78355

Brown: Brett McKibben, 403 Fisk Ave., Brownwood 76801

Burleson: Tonya Barnes, P.O. Box 1000, Caldwell 77836

Burnet: Stan Hemphill, P.O. Box 908, Burnet 78611

Caldwell: Shanna Ramzinski, P.O. Box 900, Lockhart 78644

Calhoun: Jesse Hubbell, P.O. Box 49, Port Lavaca 77979

Callahan: Stephanie McPherson, 132 W. 4th St., Baird 79504

Cameron: Richard Molina, P.O. Box 1010, San Benito 78586

Camp: Jan Tinsley, 143 Quitman St., Pittsburg 75686

Carson: Shannon Hensley, P.O. Box 970, Panhandle 79068

Cass: Lacy Hicks, 502 N. Main St., Linden 75563

Castro: Steven Cole Pierce, 204 S.E. 3rd (Rear), Dimmitt 79027

Chambers: Mitchell McCullough, P.O. Box 1520, Anahuac 77514

Cherokee: J.L. Flowers, P.O. Box 494, Rusk 75785

Childress: Twila Butler, 1710 Ave. F NW, Childress 79201

Clay: Lisa Murphy, P.O. Box 108, Henrietta 76365

Cochran: David Greener, 109 S.E. First St., Morton 79346

Coke: Gayle Sisemore, P.O. Box 2, Robert Lee 76945

Coleman: Bill W. Jones, P.O. Box 914, Coleman 76834

Collin: Bo Daffin, 250 W. Eldorado, McKinney 75069

Collingsworth: Dwight Bowen, 800 West Ave., Box 9, Wellington, 79095

Colorado: Robert Maes., P.O. Box 10, Columbus 78934

Comal: Rufino Lozano, 900 S. Seguin Ave., New Braunfels 78130

Comanche: JoAnn Hohertz, 8 Huett Cir., Comanche 76442

Concho: D'Andra Warlick, P.O. Box 68, Paint Rock 76866

Cooke: Doug Smithson, 201 N. Dixon, Gainesville 76240

Coryell: Mitch Fast, 705 E. Main St., Gatesville 76528

Cottle: Nakia Hargrave, P.O. Box 459, Paducah 79248

Crane: Byron Bitner, 511 W. 8th St., Crane 79731

Crockett: Janet M. Thompson, P.O. Box 1569, Ozona 76943

Crosby: Gary Zeitler, P.O. Box 505, Crosbyton 79322

Culberson: Maricel Gonzalez, P.O. Box 550, Van Horn 79855

Dallam: Holly McCauley, P.O. Box 579, Dalhart 79022

Dallas: Ken Nolan, 2949 N. Stemmons Fwy., Dallas 75247

Dawson: Norma J. Brock, P.O. Box 797, Lamesa 79331

Deaf Smith: Danny Jones, P.O. Box 2298, Hereford 79045

Delta: Kim Gregory, P.O. Box 47, Cooper 75432

Denton: Hope McClure, P.O. Box 2816, Denton 76202

DeWitt: Denise Moore, 103 E. Bailey St., Cuero 77954

Dickens: Patti Abbott, P.O. Box 180, Dickens 79229

Dimmit: Norma Carrillo, 203 W. Houston St., Carrizo Springs 78834

Donley: Paula Lowrie, P.O. Box 1220, Clarendon 79226

Duval: Raul Garcia, P.O. Box 809, San Diego 78384

Eastland: Randy Clark, P.O. Box 914, Eastland 76448

Ector: Anita Campbell, 1301 E. 8th St., Odessa 79761

Edwards: Renn Rudasill Riley, P.O. Box 858, Rocksprings 78880

Ellis: Kathy Rodrigue, P.O. Box 878, Waxahachie 75168

El Paso: Dinah Kilgore, 5801 Trowbridge Dr., El Paso 79925

Erath: Jerry Lee, 1195 W. South Loop, Stephenville 76401

Falls: Andrew Hahn, 403 Craik St., Marlin 76661

Fannin: Michael Jones, 831 W. State Hwy. 56, Bonham 75418

Fayette: Richard Moring, P.O. Box 836, La Grange 78945

Fisher: Kellen Walker, P.O. Box 516, Roby 79543

Floyd: Jim Finley, P.O. Box 249, Floydada 79235

Foard: Debbie Stribling, P.O. Box 419, Crowell 79227

Fort Bend: Jordan Wise, 2801 B.F. Terry Blvd., Rosenberg 77471

Franklin: Genea Burnaman, P.O. Box 720, Mount Vernon 75457

Freestone: Bud Black, 218 N. Mount St., Fairfield 75840

Frio: Luciano R. Gonzales, P.O. Box 1129, Pearsall 78061

Gaines: Gayla Harridge, P.O. Box 490, Seminole 79360

Galveston: Tommy Watson, 9850 Emmet F Lowry Exp, Ste. A, Texas City 77591

Garza: Diane Josey, P.O. Drawer F, Post 79356

Gillespie: Scott Fair, 1159 S. Milam, Fredericksburg 78624

Glasscock: Priscilla A. Ginnetti, P.O. Box 155, Garden City 79739

Goliad: Robert Ckodre, P.O. Box 34, Goliad 77963

Gonzales: John Liford, P.O. Box 867, Gonzales 78629

Gray: Tyson Paronto, P.O. Box 836, Pampa 79066

Grayson: Shawn Coker, 515 N. Travis, Sherman 75090

Gregg: Libby Neely, 4367 W. Loop 281, Longview 75604

Grimes: Mark Boehnke, P.O. Box 489, Anderson 77830

Guadalupe: Peter Snaddon, 3000 N. Austin St., Seguin 78155
Hale: Nikki Branscum, P.O. Box 29, Plainview 79073
Hall: Gina Chavira, 512 W. Main St., Ste. 14, Memphis 79245
Hamilton: Heather Donahoo, 119 E. Henry St., Hamilton 76531
Hansford: Brandi Thompson, 709 W. 7th Ave., Spearman 79081
Hardeman: Richard Petree, P.O. Box 388, Quanah 79252
Hardin: Crystal Smith, P.O. Box 670, Kountze 77625
Harris: Roland Altinger, P.O. Box 920975, Houston 77292
Harrison: Robert Lisman, P.O. Box 818, Marshall 75671
Hartley: Juan Salazar, P.O. Box 405, Hartley 79044
Haskell: Wanda Hester, P.O. Box 467, Haskell 79521
Hays: Laura Raven, 21001 N. IH-35, Kyle 78640
Hemphill: Pam Scates, 223 Main St., Canadian 79014
Henderson: Linda Moncada, P.O. Box 430, Athens 75751
Hidalgo: Rolando Garza, P.O. Box 208, Edinburg 78540
Hill: Mike McKibben, P.O. Box 416, Hillsboro 76645
Hockley: Lorie Marquez, P.O. Box 1090, Levelland 79336
Hood: Greg Stewart, P.O. Box 819, Granbury 76048
Hopkins: Cathy Singleton, P.O. Box 753, Sulphur Springs 75483
Houston: Carey Minter, P.O. Box 112, Crockett 75835
Howard: Richard Petree, P.O. Box 1151, Big Spring 79721
Hudspeth: Adolfo Ramirez, P.O. Box 429, Sierra Blanca 79851
Hunt: Brent South, P.O. Box 1339, Greenville 75403
Hutchinson: Joe Raper, P.O. Box 5065, Borger 79008
Irion: Byron Bitner, P.O. Box 980, Mertzon 76941
Jack: Kathy Conner, P.O. Box 958, Jacksboro 76458
Jackson: Damon Moore, 404 N. Allen St., Edna 77957
Jasper: Lori Barnett, P.O. Box 1300, Jasper 75951
Jeff Davis: Lisa Reyna, P.O. Box 373, Fort Davis 79734
Jefferson: Angela Bellard, P.O. Box 21337, Beaumont 77720
Jim Hogg: Jorge Arellano, P.O. Box 459, Hebbronville 78361
Jim Wells: J. Sidney Vela, P.O. Box 607, Alice 78333
Johnson: Jim Hudspeth, 109 N. Main, Cleburne 76033
Jones: Kim McLemore, P.O. Box 348, Anson 79501
Karnes: Brian Stahl, 915 S. Panna Maria Ave., Karnes City 78118
Kaufman: Sarah Curtis, P.O. Box 819, Kaufman 75142
Kendall: Shelby Presley, 118 Market Ave., Boerne 78006
Kenedy: Thomas G. Denney, P.O. Box 39, Sarita 78385
Kent: Cindy Watson, P.O. Box 68, Jayton 79528
Kerr: Sharon Constantinides, P.O. Box 294387, Kerrville 78029
Kimble: Kenda McPherson, P.O. Box 307, Junction 76849
King: Kala Briggs, P.O. Box 117, Guthrie 79236
Kinney: Todd Tate, P.O. Box 1377, Brackettville 78832
Kleberg: Tina Flores, P.O. Box 1027, Kingsville 78364
Knox: Mitzi Welch, P.O. Box 47, Benjamin 79505
Lamar: Stephanie Lee, P.O. Box 400, Paris 75461
Lamb: Lesa Kloiber, P.O. Box 950, Littlefield 79339
Lampasas: Susan Jones, P.O. Box 175, Lampasas 76550
La Salle: Martin Villareal, P.O. Box 1530, Cotulla 78014
Lavaca: Pamela Lathrop, P.O. Box 386, Hallettsville 77964
Lee: James Orr, 898 E. Richmond, Ste. 100, Giddings 78942
Leon: Jeff Beshears, P.O. Box 536, Centerville 75833
Liberty: Lana McCarty, P.O. Box 10016, Liberty 77575
Limestone: Karen Wietzikoski, P.O. Drawer 831, Groesbeck 76642
Lipscomb: Angela Peil, P.O. Box 128, Darrouzett 79024
Live Oak: Debra Morin, P.O. Box 2370, George West 78022
Llano: Scott Dudley, 103 E. Sandstone, Llano 78643
Loving: Sherlene Burrows, P.O. Box 352, Mentone 79754
Lubbock: Tim Radloff, P.O. Box 10542, Lubbock 79408
Lynn: Rebecca Norris, P.O. Box 789, Tahoka 79373
Madison: Matt Newton, P.O. Box 1328, Madisonville 77864
Marion: Anna Lummus, 801 N. Tuttle St., Jefferson 75657
Martin: Marsha Graves, P.O. Box 1349, Stanton 79782
Mason: Liza Trevino, P.O. Box 1119, Mason 76856
Matagorda: Vince Maloney, 2225 Ave. G, Bay City 77414

The atrium at the Fayette County Courthouse. Photo by Jim Evans, CC by 4.0/Wikimedia Commons.

Maverick: Maggie Duran, P.O. Box 2628, Eagle Pass 78852

McCulloch: Zane Brandenberger, 306 W. Lockhart, Brady 76825

McLennan: Joe Don Bobbitt, 315 S. 26th St., Waco 76710

McMullen: Blaine Patterson, P.O. Box 338, Tilden 78072

Medina: Johnette Dixon, 1410 Ave. K, Hondo 78861

Menard: Kayla Wagner, P.O. Box 1008, Menard 76859

Midland: Jerry Bundick, P.O. Box 908002, Midland 79708

Milam: Leslie Sootoo, P.O. Box 769, Cameron 76520

Mills: Codi Ann McCarn, P.O. Box 565, Goldthwaite 76844

Mitchell: John Stewart, 2112 Hickory St., Colorado City 79512

Montague: Kim Haralson, P.O. Box 121, Montague 76251

Montgomery: Tony Belinoski, P.O. Box 2233, Conroe 77305

Moore: Samantha Trujillo, P.O. Box 717, Dumas 79029

Morris: Summer Golden, P.O. Box 563, Daingerfield 75638

Motley: Jim Finley, P.O. Box 249, Floydada 79235

Nacogdoches: Gary Woods, 216 W. Hospital St., Nacogdoches 75961

Navarro: Thomas Dally, P.O. Box 3118, Corsicana 75110

Newton: Margie L. Herrin, 109 Court St., Newton 75966

Nolan: Brenda Klepper, P.O. Box 1256, Sweetwater 79556

Nueces: Ronnie Canales, 201 N. Chaparral, Ste. 206, Corpus Christi 78401

Ochiltree: Donna Lee Stewart, 825 S. Main, Ste. 100, Perryton 79070

Oldham: Leann Voyles, P.O. Box 310, Vega 79092

Orange: Scott Overton, P.O. Box 457, Orange 77631

Palo Pinto: Donna E. Kozlovsky, P.O. Box 250, Palo Pinto 76484

Panola: Michael Douglas McPhail, 1736 Ballpark Dr., Carthage 75633

Parker: Rick Armstrong, 1108 Santa Fe Dr., Weatherford 76086

Parmer: Jill Timms, P.O. Box 56, Bovina 79009

Pecos: Sam Calderon III, P.O. Box 237, Fort Stockton 79735

P.O.lk: Chad Hill, 114 Matthews St., Livingston 77351

Potter: Jeff Dagley, P.O. Box 7190, Amarillo 79114

Presidio: Cynthia Ramirez, P.O. Box 879, Marfa 79843

Rains: Sherri McCall, P.O. Box 70, Emory 75440

Randall: Jeff Dagley, P.O. Box 7190, Amarillo 79114

Reagan: Jacquelyn Botello, P.O. Box 8, Big Lake 76932

Real: Juan Saucedo, P.O. Box 158, Leakey 78873

Red River: Christie Ussery, P.O. Box 461, Clarksville 75426

Reeves: John Huddleston, P.O. Box 1229, Pecos 79772

Refugio: Connie Raymond, P.O. Box 156, Refugio 78377

Roberts: Hether Williams, P.O. Box 458, Miami 79059

Robertson: Nancy Commander, P.O. Box 998, Franklin 77856

Rockwall: Kevin Passons, 841 Justin Rd., Rockwall 75087

Runnels: Paul Scott Randolph, P.O. Box 524, Ballinger 76821

Rusk: Weldon Cook, P.O. Box 7, Henderson 75653

Sabine: Cari Papania, P.O. Box 137, Hemphill 75948

San Augustine: Evelyn Watts, 122 N. Harrison St., San Augustine 75972

San Jacinto: Kelly Foxworth, P.O. Box 1170, Coldspring 77331

San Patricio: Robert Cenci, P.O. Box 938, Sinton 78387

San Saba: Jan Vanderburg, 423 E. Wallace St., San Saba 76877

Schleicher: Liza Trevino, P.O. Box 936, Eldorado 76936

Scurry: Jackie Martin, 2612 College Ave., Snyder 79549

Shackelford: Clayton Snyder, P.O. Box 2247, Albany 76430

Shelby: Robert N. Pigg, 724 Shelbyville St., Center 75935

Sherman: Teresa Edmond, P.O. Box 239, Stratford 79084

Smith: Carol Dixon, 245 South S.E. Loop 323, Tyler 75702

Somervell: Wes Rollen, 112 Allen Dr., Glen Rose 76043

Starr: Rosalva Guerra, 100 N. FM 3167, Ste. 300, Rio Grande City 78582

Stephens: Gary Zeitler, P.O. Box 351, Breckenridge 76424

Sterling: Ronnie Krejci, P.O. Box 28, Sterling City 76951

Stonewall: Debra Smith, P.O. Box 308, Aspermont 79502

Sutton: Mary Bustamante, 300 E. Oak St., Ste. 2, Sonora 76950

Swisher: Andrew Moritz, P.O. Box 8, Tulia 79088

Tarrant: Jeff Law, 2500 Handley-Ederville Rd., Fort Worth 76118

Taylor: Gary Earnest, P.O. Box 1800, Abilene 79604

Terrell: Blain Chriesman, P.O. Box 747, Sanderson 79848

Terry: Eddie Olivas, P.O. Box 426, Brownfield 79316

Throckmorton: DeDe Smith, P.O. Box 788, Throckmorton 76483

Titus: Shirley Dickerson, P.O. Box 528, Mount Pleasant 75456

Tom Green: Bill Benson, 2302 Pulliam St., San Angelo 76905

Travis: Marya Crigler, P.O. Box 149012, Austin 78714

Trinity: Greg Gallant, P.O. Box 950, Groveton 75845

Tyler: David Luther, P.O. Drawer 9, Woodville 75979

Upshur: Amanda Thibodeaux, 105 Diamond Loch, Gilmer 75644

Upton: Linda Zarate, P.O. Box 1110, McCamey 79752

Uvalde: Roberto Valdez, 209 N. High St., Uvalde 78801

Val Verde: Cherry Sheedy, 417 W. Cantu Rd., Del Rio 78842

Van Zandt: Scott Hyde, P.O. Box 926, Canton 75103

Victoria: John Haliburton, 2805 N. Navarro, Ste. 300, Victoria 77901

Walker: Raymond Kiser, P.O. Box 1798, Huntsville 77342

Waller: Becky Gurrola, P.O. Box 887, Hempstead 77445

Ward: Norma Valdez, P.O. Box 905, Monahans 79756

Washington: Dyann White, P.O. Box 681, Brenham 77834

Webb: Martin Villarreal, 3302 Clark Blvd., Laredo 78043

Wharton: Tylene Gamble, 308 E. Milam, Wharton 77488

Wheeler: Kimberly Morgan, P.O. Box 1200, Wheeler 79096

Wichita: Lisa Stephens-Musick, P.O. Box 5172, Wichita Falls 76307

Wilbarger: Sandy Burkett, P.O. Box 1519, Vernon 76385

Willacy: Agustin Lopez, 688 FM 3168, Raymondville 78580

Williamson: Alvin Lankford, 625 FM 1460, Georgetown 78626

Wilson: Jennifer Coldewey, 1611 Railroad St., Floresville 78114

Winkler: Gary Zietler, P.O. Box 1219, Kermit 79745

Wise: Michael Hand, 400 E. Business 380, Decatur 76234

Wood: Tracy Nichols, P.O. Box 1706, Quitman 75783

Yoakum: Brooks Barrett, P.O. Box 748, Plains 79355

Young: Luke Robbins, P.O. Box 337, Graham 76450

Zapata: Amada Gonzalez, 200 E. 7th Ave., Ste. 240, Zapata 78076

Zavala: Yolanda Lavenant, 323 W. Zavala, Crystal City 78839

☆

Wet-Dry Counties

Source: Texas Alcoholic Beverage Commission; www.tabc.state.tx.us

Although the laws regulating the alcoholic beverage industry are consistent statewide, the Alcoholic Beverage Code allows for local-option elections to determine the types of alcoholic beverages that may be sold and how they can be sold.

Elections can be held by counties, cities, or individual justice of the peace precincts. In the time since our last edition went to press, four counties have moved from Part Wet to Wet: Crane, Kerr, Mason, and Wilson.

As of August 2021, there were 59 completely wet counties in Texas and 5 completely dry counties.

Over time, Texas has been getting "wetter." In 2003, there were 35 completely wet counties and 51 completely dry. In 1995, there were 53 dry counties, and in 1986, there were 62 dry counties. The list below reflects the wet, part wet, and dry coding on the map.

Counties where all alcoholic beverage sales are legal everywhere (59): Aransas, Austin, Bexar, Brazos, Brewster, Brooks, Burnet, Cameron, Childress, Clay, Collingsworth, Colorado, Comal, Cottle, Crane, Crosby, Culberson, Dimmit, Donley, Duval, Ector, El Paso, Fayette, Fisher, Fort Bend, Goliad, Gonzales, Guadalupe, Hidalgo, Hudspeth, Jim Hogg, Kendall, Kenedy, Kerr, Kinney, Kleberg, La Salle, Mason, Midland, Mitchell, Nolan, Nueces, Ochiltree, Presidio, San Saba, Scurry, Sherman, Starr, Sutton, Val Verde, Victoria, Waller, Washington, Webb, Wharton, Wilbarger, Wilson, Zapata, Zavala.

Counties that are partially wet (190): Anderson, Andrews, Angelina, Archer, Armstrong, Atascosa, Bailey, Bandera, Bastrop, Baylor, Bee, Bell, Blanco, Bosque, Bowie, Brazoria, Briscoe, Brown, Burleson, Caldwell, Calhoun, Callahan, Camp, Carson, Cass, Castro, Chambers, Cherokee, Cochran, Coke, Coleman, Collin, Comanche, Concho, Cooke, Coryell, Crockett, Dallam, Dallas, Dawson, Deaf Smith, Delta, Denton, DeWitt, Dickens, Eastland, Edwards, Ellis, Erath, Falls, Fannin, Floyd, Foard, Franklin, Freestone, Frio, Gaines, Galveston, Garza, Gillespie, Glasscock, Gray, Grayson, Gregg, Grimes, Hale, Hall, Hamilton, Hansford, Hardeman, Hardin, Harris, Harrison, Hartley, Haskell, Hays, Henderson, Hill, Hockley, Hood, Hopkins, Houston, Howard, Hunt, Hutchinson, Irion, Jack, Jackson, Jasper, Jeff Davis, Jefferson, Jim Wells, Johnson, Jones, Karnes, Kaufman, Kimble, King, Knox, Lamar, Lamb, Lampasas, Lavaca, Lee, Leon, Liberty, Limestone, Lipscomb, Live Oak, Llano, Loving, Lubbock, Lynn, Madison, Marion, Martin, Matagorda, Maverick, McCulloch, McLennan, McMullen, Medina, Menard, Milam, Mills, Montague, Montgomery, Moore, Morris, Motley, Nacogdoches, Navarro, Newton, Oldham, Orange, Palo Pinto, Panola, Parker, Parmer, Pecos, Polk, Potter, Rains, Randall, Reagan, Real, Red River, Reeves, Refugio, Robertson, Rockwall, Runnels, Rusk, Sabine, San Augustine, San Jacinto, San Patricio, Schleicher, Shackelford, Shelby, Smith, Somervell, Stephens, Sterling, Stonewall, Swisher, Tarrant, Taylor, Terrell, Terry, Titus, Tom Green, Travis, Trinity, Tyler, Upshur, Upton, Uvalde, Van Zandt, Walker, Ward, Wheeler, Wichita, Willacy, Williamson, Winkler, Wise, Wood, Yoakum, Young.

Counties where no sales of alcoholic beverages are legal anywhere (5): Borden, Hemphill, Kent, Roberts, Throckmorton. ☆

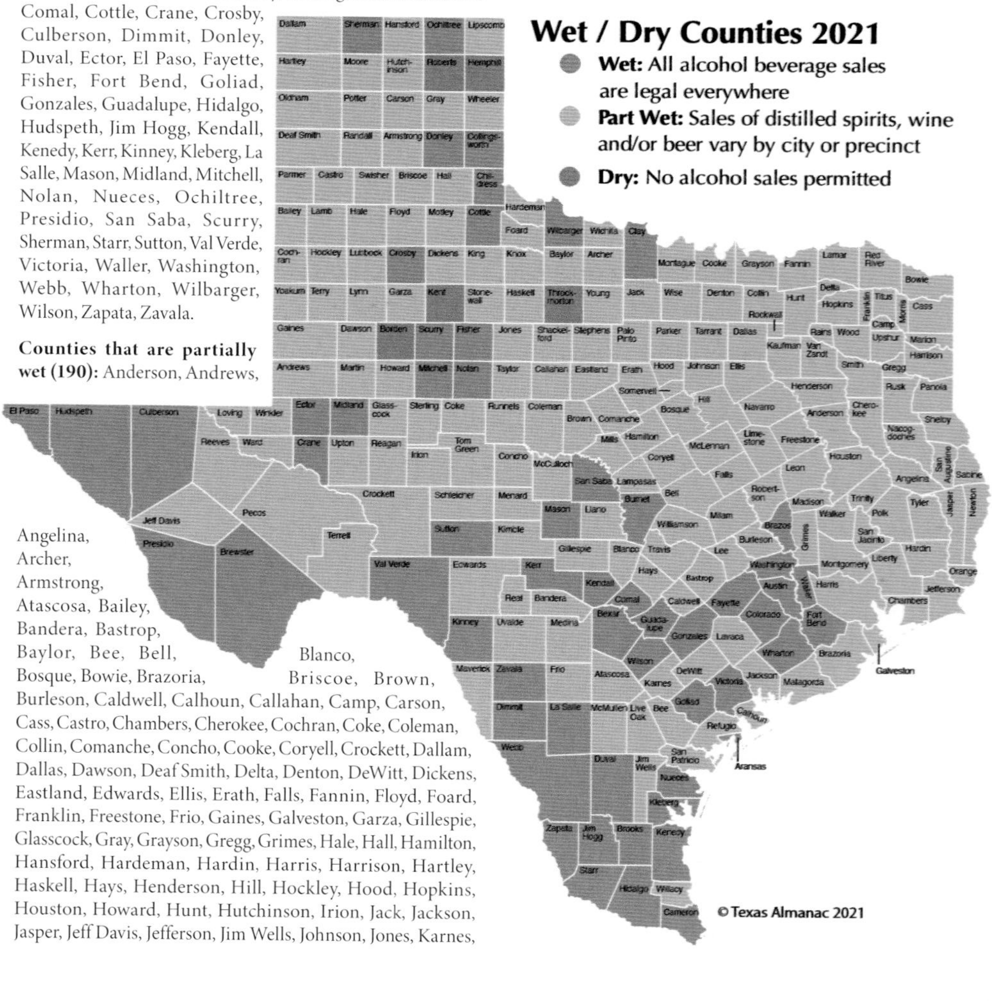
Wet / Dry Counties 2021
Wet: All alcohol beverage sales are legal everywhere
Part Wet: Sales of distilled spirits, wine and/or beer vary by city or precinct
Dry: No alcohol sales permitted
© Texas Almanac 2021

Texas County and District Officials – Table No. 1

County Seats, County Judges, County Clerks, County Attorneys, County Treasurers, Tax Assessors–Collectors, and Sheriffs

See Table No. 2 on **pages 507–512** for District Clerks, District Attorneys, and County Commissioners. Judges in county courts at law, as well as probate courts, juvenile/domestic relations courts, county criminal courts, and county criminal courts of appeal, are on **pages 493–495**. The officials listed here are elected by popular vote. If no county attorney is listed, the district attorney, whose name is listed in Table No. 2, assumes the duties of that office.

County	County Seat	County Judge	County Clerk	County Attorney	County Treasurer	Assessor–Collector	Sheriff
Anderson	Palestine	Robert D. Johnston	Mark Staples	—	Tara Holliday	Margie Grissom	W.R. Flores
Andrews	Andrews	Charlie Falcon	Vicki Scott	Sean Galloway	*Office abolished 1985.*	Robin Harper	Rusty Stewart
Angelina	Lufkin	Don Lymbery	Amy Fincher	Cary Kirby	Jill Brewer	Billie Page	Greg Sanches
Aransas	Rockport	C.H. (Burt) Mills, Jr.	Carrie Arrington	Amanda Oster	Alma Cartwright	Anna Marshall	William (Bill) Mills
Archer	Archer City	Randall C. Jackson	Karren Winter	David Levy	Patricia A. Vieth	Dawn Vieth	Jack Curd
Armstrong	Claude	Hugh Reed	Tawnee Blodgett	—	Susan Overcast McGrath	Jamie Craig	Melissa Anderson
Atascosa	Jourdanton	Robert Hurley	Diane Gonzales	Lucinda A. Vickers	Laura Pawelek	Loretta Holley	David Soward
Austin	Bellville	Tim Lapham	Carrie Gregor	—	Bryan Haevischer	Kim Rinn	Jack Brandes
Bailey	Muleshoe	Sherri Harrison	Robin Dickerson	Jackie R. Claborn, II	Shonda L. Black	Maria Gonzalez	Richard Wills
Bandera	Bandera	Richard Evans	Tandie Mansfield	Janna Lindig	Beverly Schmidt	Rebekah (Reba) Dolphus	Dan Butts
Bastrop	Bastrop	Paul Pape	Rose Pietsch	—	Jo Dawn Bomar	Ellen Owens	Maurice Cook
Baylor	Seymour	Rusty A. Stafford	Chris Jakubicek	Cynthia Ayres-Walker	Kevin Hostas	Jeanette Holub	Sam Mooney
Bee	Beeville	George (Trace) Morill, III	Nickelle Gonzales	Michael Knight	*Office abolished 1982.*	Michelle Matus	Alden E. Southmayd, III
Bell	Belton	David Blackburn	Shelley Coston	James E. Nichols	Gaylon Evans	Shay Luedeke	Eddy Lange
Bexar	San Antonio	Nelson W. Wolff	Lucy Adame-Clark	*Office abolished.*	*Office abolished 1985.*	Albert Uresti	Javier Salazar
Blanco	Johnson City	Brett Bray	Laura Walla	Deborah Earley	Camille Swift	Kristen Spies	Don Jackson
Borden	Gail	Ross D. Sharp	Jana Underwood	Marlo Holbrooks	Shawna Gass	Benny Allison	Benny Allison
Bosque	Meridian	Cindy Vanlandingham	Tab Ferguson	Natalie Koehler	Carla Sigler	Arlene Swiney	Trace Hendricks
Bowie	New Boston	Bobby Howell	Tina Petty	—	Donna Burns	Josh Davis	Jeff Neal
Brazoria	Angleton	L.M. (Matt) Sebesta, Jr.	Joyce Hudman	—	Cathy Campbell	Kristin R. Bulanek	Bo Stallman
Brazos	Bryan	Duane Peters	Karen McQueen	Earl Gray	Laura Taylor Davis	Kristeen Roe	Wayne Dicky
Brewster	Alpine	Eleazar R. Cano	Sarah Vasquez	J. Steve Houston	Julie K. Morton	Sylvia Vega	Ronny Dodson
Briscoe	Silverton	Wayne Nance	Bena Hester	Emily Teegardin	Mary Jo Brannon	Jon Etta Ziegler	Garrett Davis
Brooks	Falfurrias	Eric Ramos	Elvaray B. Silvas	David T. Garcia	Alan Hernandez	Urbino (Benny) Martinez	Urbino (Benny) Martinez
Brown	Brownwood	Paul D. Lilly	Sharon Ferguson	Shane Britton	Ann Krpoun	Christine Pentecost	Vance Hill
Burleson	Caldwell	Keith Schroeder	Anna L. Schielack	Susan Deski	Stephanie Smith	Jessica Lucero	Gene Hermes
Burnet	Burnet	James Oakley	Janet Parker	Eddie Arredondo	Karrie Crownover	Sheri Frazier	Calvin Boyd
Caldwell	Lockhart	Hoppy Haden	Teresa Rodriguez	—	Angela Meuth Rawlinson	Darla Law	Mike Lane
Calhoun	Port Lavaca	Richard Meyer	Anna Goodman	—	Rhonda Kokena	Kerri Boyd	Bobbie Vickery
Callahan	Baird	G. Scott Kniffen	Nicole Crocker	Shane Deel	Jan Windham	Tammy Walker	Eric Pechacek
Cameron	Brownsville	Eddie Treviño, Jr.	Sylvia Garza-Perez	Luis V. Saenz	David A. Betancourt	Tony Yzaguirre, Jr.	Eric Garza
Camp	Pittsburg	A.J. Mason	Elaine Young	James W. Wallace, III	Kim Pittman	Missy Huffman	John Cortelyou
Carson	Panhandle	Dan Looten	Celeste Bichsel	Scott Sherwood	Denise Salzbrenner	Jackie Moore	Tam Terry
Cass	Linden	Becky Wilbanks	Amy L. Varnell	—	Melissa Shores	Angela Young	Larry Rowe
Castro	Dimmitt	Carroll Gerber	JoAnna Blanco	Shalyn Hamlin	Elaine D. Flynt	Pam Rickert	Salvador Rivera
Chambers	Anahuac	Jimmy Sylvia	Heather Hawthorne	Ashley Cain Land	Nicole M. Whittington	Denise Hutter	Brian C. Hawthorne
Cherokee	Rusk	Chris Davis	Laverne Lusk	Dana Young	Erin Curtis	Shonda McCutcheon Potter	Brent Dickson

County	County Seat	County Judge	County Clerk	County Attorney	County Treasurer	Assessor–Collector	Sheriff
Childress	Childress	Jay Mayden	Barbara Spitzer	Greg Buckley	Brenda Overstreet	Kathy Dobbs	Michael (Mike) Pigg
Clay	Henrietta	Mike Campbell	Sasha Kelton	Seth C. Slagle	Danja Bloodworth	Maribel Longoria	Jeffrey C. Lyde
Cochran	Morton	Pat Sabala Henry	Lisa Smith	Amanda Martin	Doris Sealy	Treva Jackson	Jorge De La Cruz
Coke	Robert Lee	Hal Spain	Monica Reyes	Nicholas E. Arrott, II	Therese Emert	Josie Dean	Wayne McCutchen
Coleman	Coleman	Billy D. Bledsoe	Stacey Mendoza	Hayden J. Wise	Jerri Ann Wilson	Jamie Dodgen	Les Cogdill
Collin	McKinney	Chris Hill	Stacey Kemp	—	—	Kenneth Maun	Jim Skinner
Collingsworth	Wellington	John A. James	Jackie Johnson	Gaylon Davis	Gina Harris	Sharon Chism	Kent Riley
Colorado	Columbus	Ty Prause	Kimberly Menke	Jay E. Johannes	Joyce Guthmann	Erica Kollaja	R.H. (Curly) Wied
Comal	New Braunfels	Sherman Krause	Bobbie Koepp	—	Renee Couch	Kristen H. Hoyt	Mark Reynolds
Comanche	Comanche	Stephanie L. Davis	Ruby Lesley	Craig Willingham	Patsy Phifer	Grace Everhart	Chris Pounds
Concho	Paint Rock	David Dillard	Phyllis F. Lovell	Bryan Clayton	Jenifer Gierisch	Chad Miller	Chad Miller
Cooke	Gainesville	Steve Starnes	Pam Harrison	Edmund J. Zielinski	Patty Brennan	Brandy Ann Carr	Ray Sappington
Coryell	Gatesville	Roger A. Miller	Barbara Simpson	Brandon Belt	Randi McFarlin	Justin K. Carothers	Scott Williams
Cottle	Paducah	Karl Holloway	Vickey Wederski	Greg Buckley	Crystal Tucker	Nakia Hargrave	Mark Box
Crane	Crane	Roy Hodges	Janie Macias	Austin Rawls	Sheila Pahl	Judy Crumrine	Andrew Aguilar
Crockett	Ozona	Fred Deaton	Ninfa Preddy	Jody K. Upham	Laura Conner	Michelle M. Medley	Antonio Alejandro, III
Crosby	Crosbyton	Rusty Forbes	Tammy Marshall	Michael Sales	Debra Riley	Michele Cook	Ethan Villanueva
Culberson	Van Horn	Carlos G. Urias	Linda McDonald	Stephen Mitchell	Adrian Hinojos	Jose Morales	Oscar Carrillo
Dallam	Dalhart	Wes Ritchey	Terri Banks	Whitney Hill	Kenda McKay	Jami Parr	Shane Stevenson
Dallas	Dallas	Clay Jenkins	John F. Warren	—	Pauline Medrano	John R. Ames	Marian Brown
Dawson	Lamesa	Foy O'Brien	Clare Christy	Steven B. Payson	Terri Stahl	Sylvia Ortiz	Matt Hogg
Deaf Smith	Hereford	D.J. Wagner	Rachel Garman	—	Karen Smith	Teresa Garth	J. Dale Butler
Delta	Cooper	Jason Murray	Jane Jones	Jay Garrett	Debbie Huie	Dawn Stewart	Charla Singleton
Denton	Denton	Andy Eads	Juli Luke	—	Cindy Yeatts Brown	Michelle French	Tracy Murphree
DeWitt	Cuero	Daryl L. Fowler	Natalie Carson	A. Jay Condie	Carol Ann Martin	Ashley D. Mraz	Carl Bowen
Dickens	Dickens	Kevin Brendle	Becky Hill	Aaron Clements	Darla Thomason	Rebecca Haney	Terry Braly
Dimmit	Carrizo Springs	Francisco G. Ponce	Mario Z. Garcia	Daniel Gonzalez	Estanislado Martinez	Mary E. Sandoval	Marion Boyd
Donley	Clarendon	John C. Howard	Vicky Tunnell	Landon Lambert	Wanda Smith	Kristy Christopher	Charles (Butch) Blackburn
Duval	San Diego	Gilbert N. Saenz	Elodia M. Garza	Baldemar Gutierrez	Sylvia Lazo	Roberto Elizondo	Romeo R. Ramirez
Eastland	Eastland	Rex Fields	Cathy Jentho	—	Christina Dodrill	Andrea May	Jason Weger
Ector	Odessa	Debi Hays	Jennifer Martin	Gregory Barber	Cleopatra Anderson-Callaway	Lindy Wright	Mike Griffis
Edwards	Rocksprings	Souli Asa Shanklin	Olga Lydia Reyes	Allen Ray Moody	Lupe S. Enriquez	Lorri Garcia Ruiz	James W. Guthrie
Ellis	Waxahachie	Todd Little	Krystal Valdez	Ann Montgomery	Cheryl Chambers	Richard Rozier	Brad Norman
El Paso	El Paso	Ricardo A. Samaniego	Delia Briones	Jo Anne Bernal	*Office abolished 1989.*	Ruben P. Gonzalez	Richard Wiles
Erath	Stephenville	Alfonso Campos	Gwinda Jones	Lisa Pence	Kimberly Barrier	Jennifer Carey	Matt Coates
Falls	Marlin	Jay Elliott	Elizabeth Perez	Kathryn (Jody) Gilliam	Sheryl Pringle	Kayci Nehring	Joe Lopez
Fannin	Bonham	Randy Moore	Tammy Biggar	Richard Glaser	David E. Woodson	Gail Young	Mark Johnson
Fayette	La Grange	Joe Weber	Brenda Fietsam	Peggy Supak	*Office abolished 11-3-87.*	Sylvia Mendoza	Keith Korenek
Fisher	Roby	Ken Holt	Pat Thomson	Michael Hall	Jeanna Parks	Jonnye Lu Gibson	Randy Ford
Floyd	Floydada	Marty Lucke	Ginger Morgan	Lex Herrington	Lori Morales	Delia Suarez	Paul Raissez
Foard	Crowell	Mark Christopher	Debra Hopkins	Marshall Capps	Darcy Moore	Mike Brown	Mike Brown
Fort Bend	Richmond	KP George	Laura Richard	Bridgette Smith-Lawson	Bill Rickert	Carmen P. Turner	Eric Fagan
Franklin	Mount Vernon	Scott Lee	Betty Crane	Landon Ramsay	Betty Sue Allen	Sue Ann Harper	Ricky Jones

County	County Seat	County Judge	County Clerk	County Attorney	County Treasurer	Assessor–Collector	Sheriff
Freestone	Fairfield	Linda Grant	Linda Jarvis	Brian Evans	Jeannie Keeney	Daniel M. Ralstin	Jeremy Shipley
Frio	Pearsall	Arnulfo C. Luna	Aaron Tomas Ibarra	Joseph Sindon	Pete Jasso Martinez	Anna Alaniz	Michael (Mike) Morse
Gaines	Seminole	Tom Keyes	Terri Berry	Joe H. Nagy, Jr.	Michael Lord, Jr.	Susan Shaw	Ronny Pipkin
Galveston	Galveston	Mark Henry	Dwight D. Sullivan	—	Kevin C. Walsh	Cheryl E. Johnson	Henry Trochesset
Garza	Post	Lee Norman	Jim Plummer	Ted Weems	LuAnne Terry	Nancy Wallace	Terry Morgan
Gillespie	Fredericksburg	Mark Stroeher	Mary Lynn Rusche	Steven A. Wadsworth	Kelly Eckhardt	Vicki J. Schmidt	Buddy Mills
Glasscock	Garden City	Billy Ray Reynolds	Rebecca Batla	Hardy Wilkerson	Alan Dierschke	Tina Flores	Keith Burnett
Goliad	Goliad	Mike Bennett	Mary Ellen Flores	Rob Baiamonte	Bryan Howard	Michelle Garcia	Roy Boyd
Gonzales	Gonzales	Patrick C. Davis	Lona Ackman	Paul Watkins	Sheryl Barborak	Crystal Cedillo	Robert Ynclan
Gray	Pampa	Chris Porter	Jeanne Horton	Josh Seabourn	Scott Hahn	Gaye Whitehead	Michael Ryan
Grayson	Sherman	Bill Magers	Deana Patterson	—	Gayla Hawkins	Bruce Stidham	Tom Watt
Gregg	Longview	Bill Stoudt	Michelle Gilley	—	*Office abolished 1-1-1988.*	Kirk Shields	Maxey Cerliano
Grimes	Anderson	Joe Fauth, III	Vanessa Burzynski	Jon C. Fultz	Tom Maynard	Mary Ann Waters	Donald G. Sowell
Guadalupe	Seguin	Kyle Kutscher	Teresa Kiel	Dave Willborn	Linda Douglass	Daryl John	Arnold S. Zwicke
Hale	Plainview	David Mull	Latrice Kemp	Jim Tirey	Ida A. Tyler	Roland Nash	David Cochran
Hall	Memphis	Ray Powell	Olivia M. Fisher	Harley Caudle	Janet Bridges	Teresa Altman	Tom Heck
Hamilton	Hamilton	W. Mark Tynes	Cynthia K. Puff	Mark Henkes	Shawna Dyer	Terry Payne Short	Justin Caraway
Hansford	Spearman	Benny D. Wilson	Janet Torres	Cheryl Nelson	Lynn French	Linda Cummings	Robert Mahaffee
Hardeman	Quanah	Ronald Ingram	Ellen London	Stanley Watson	Traysha Newsom	Jan Evans	Pat Laughery
Hardin	Kountze	Wayne McDaniel	Glenda Alston	Matthew Minick	Deborah McWilliams	Shirley Cook	Mark Davis
Harris	Houston	Lina Hidalgo	Teneshia Hudspeth	Christian D. Menefee	Dylan Osborne	Ann Harris Bennett	Ed Gonzalez
Harrison	Marshall	Chad Sims	Liz James	—	Sherry Rushing	Veronica King	Brandon (BJ) Fletcher
Hartley	Channing	Ronnie Gordon	Melissa Mead	Robert Elliott	Dinkie Parman	Chanze Fowler	Chanze Fowler
Haskell	Haskell	Kenny Thompson	Belia Abila	Kris Fouts	Stacia Leach	Connie Benton	David Halliburton
Hays	San Marcos	Ruben Becerra	Elaine Cárdenas	—	Britney Bolton Richey	Jenifer O'Kane	Gary Cutler
Hemphill	Canadian	George Briant	Lisa Johnson	Kyle Miller	Kay Smallwood	Chris Jackson	Brent Clapp
Henderson	Athens	Wade McKinney	Mary Margaret Wright	Clint Davis	Michael Bynum	Peggy Goodall	Botie Hillhouse
Hidalgo	Edinburg	Richard F. Cortez	Arturo Guajardo, Jr.	—	Lita Leo	Pablo (Paul) Villarreal, Jr.	J.E. (Eddie) Guerra
Hill	Hillsboro	Justin Lewis	Nicole Tanner	David Holmes	Rhonda Burkhart	Krissi Hightower	Rodney B. Watson
Hockley	Levelland	Sharla Baldridge	Jennifer Nicole Palermo	Anna Hord	Denise Bohannon	Debra C. Bramlett	Ray Scifres
Hood	Granbury	Ron Massingill	Katie Lang	Matthew A. Mills	Leigh Ann McCoy	Andrea Ferguson	Roger Deeds
Hopkins	Sulphur Springs	Robert Newsom	Tracy Smith	Dusty Rabe	Danny Davis	Debbie Pogue Mitchell	Lewis Tatum
Houston	Crockett	Jim L. Lovell	Terri Meadows	Daphne Lynette Session	Janis Omelina	Danette Millican	Randy Hargrove
Howard	Big Spring	Kathryn Wiseman	Brent Zitterkopf	Joshua Hamby	Sharon Adams	Tiffany Sayles	Stan Parker
Hudspeth	Sierra Blanca	Thomas D. Neely	Brenda Sanchez	Mary Anne Bramblett	Blanca Santana	Patricia Rose	Arvin West
Hunt	Greenville	Bobby W. Stovall	Jennifer Lindenzweig	G. Calvin Grogan	Brittni Turner	Randy L. Wineinger	Terry Jones
Hutchinson	Stinnett	Cindy Irwin	Jan Barnes	Craig Jones	Kathy Sargent	Carrie Kimmell	Blaik Kemp
Irion	Mertzon	Molly Criner	Shirley Graham	James Ridge	Carolyn Huelster	Joyce Gray	W.A. Estes
Jack	Jacksboro	Brian Keith Umphress	Vanessa James	Michael Brad Dixon	Brad Campsey	Sharon Robinson	Thomas Spurlock
Jackson	Edna	Jill S. Sklar	Katherine R. Brooks	—	Mary Horton	Monica Foster	A.J. (Andy) Louderback
Jasper	Jasper	Mark Allen	Debbie Newman	—	Rene Kelley-Ellis	Bobby Biscamp	Mitchel Newman
Jeff Davis	Fort Davis	Curtis Evans	Jennifer Wright	Teresa L. Todd	Dawn Kitts	William (Bill) Kitts	William (Bill) Kitts
Jefferson	Beaumont	Jeff Branick	Theresa Goodness	—	Charlie Hallmark	Allison Nathan Getz	Zena Stephens
Jim Hogg	Hebbronville	Juan Carlos Guerra	Zonia G. Morales	Rodolfo Gutierrez	Gloria (Gigi) Benavides	Norma Liza S. Hinojosa	Erasmo Alarcon, Jr.

County	County Seat	County Judge	County Clerk	County Attorney	County Treasurer	Assessor–Collector	Sheriff
Jim Wells	Alice	Juan Rodriguez, Jr.	J.C. Perez, III	Michael Guerra	Mark Dominguez	Mary Lozano	Danny Bueno
Johnson	Cleburne	Roger Harmon	Becky Ivey	Bill Moore	Kathy Blackwell	Scott Porter	Adam King
Jones	Anson	Dale Spurgin	LeeAnn Jennings	Chad Cowan	Sandy Taber	Gloria Little	Danny Jimenez
Karnes	Karnes City	Wade J. Hedtke	Carol Swize	Jennifer M. Dillingham	Vi Swierc	Tammy Braudaway	Dwayne Villanueva
Kaufman	Kaufman	Hal Richards	Laura Hughes	—	Chuck Mohnkern	Brenda Samples	Bryan Beavers
Kendall	Boerne	Darrel L. Lux	Darlene Herrin	—	Sheryl D'Spain	James Hudson	Al Auxier
Kenedy	Sarita	Louis E. (Bud) Turcotte, III	Veronica Vela	Allison Strauss	Cynthia M. Salinas	Irma G. Longoria	Ramon Salinas, III
Kent	Jayton	Jim White	Craig Harrison	Katie Lackey	Christy Long	William Scogin	William Scogin
Kerr	Kerrville	Rob Kelly	Jackie (JD) Dowdy	Heather Stebbins	Tracy Soldan	Bob Reeves	Larry Leitha
Kimble	Junction	Delbert R. Roberts	Haydee Torres	Andrew James Heap	Jolene Williams	Allen Castleberry	Allen Castleberry
King	Guthrie	Duane Lee Daniel	Jammye D. Timmons	George (Trey) Poage	Maggie Oliver	Amy McCauley	Michael R. McWhirter
Kinney	Brackettville	Tully Shahan	Rick Alvarado	Brent Smith	Diana Gutierrez	Martha Peña-Padron	Brad Coe
Kleberg	Kingsville	Rudy Madrid	Stephanie G. Garza	Kira Talip Sanchez	Priscilla Alaniz Cantu	Maria Victoria Valadez	Richard Kirkpatrick
Knox	Benjamin	Stan Wojcik	Lisa Cypert	Lina Reyes Trevino	Julie Bradley	Penny Eaton	Hunter Embesi
Lamar	Paris	Brandon Bell	Ruth Sisson	Gary Young	Camey Boyer	Haskell Maroney	Scott Cass
Lamb	Littlefield	James M. DeLoach	Tonya Ritchie	Scott A. Say	Jerry Yarbrough	Brenda Goheen	Gary Maddox
Lampasas	Lampasas	Randall J. Hoyer	Connie Hartmann	John K. Greenwood	Melissa Karcher	Betty Salinas	Jesus (Jess) G. Ramos
La Salle	Cotulla	Joel Rodriguez, Jr.	Margarita Esqueda	Elizabeth Martinez	Maria Perez	Dora A. Gonzales	Anthony Zertuche
Lavaca	Hallettsville	Mark Myers	Elizabeth A. Kouba	Kyle A. Denney	Karen Bludau	Deborah A. Sevcik	Micah Harmon
Lee	Giddings	Paul E. Fischer	Sharon Blasig	Martin Placke	Melinda (Lyndy) Krause	David Matthijetz	Casey Goetz
Leon	Centerville	Byron Ryder	Christie Wakefield	Keith Cook	Brandi S. Hill	Robin Shafer	Kevin Ellis
Liberty	Liberty	Jay H. Knight	Lee Haidusek Chambers	Matthew Poston	Kim Harris	Richard Brown	Robert (Bobby) Rader
Limestone	Groesbeck	Richard Duncan	Kerrie Cobb	William Roy DeFriend	Carol Pickett	Stacy L. Hall	Murray Agnew
Lipscomb	Lipscomb	Mickey Simpson	Kim Blau	Matthew D. Bartosiewicz	Kimberly L. Long	Gailan Winegarner	John Worthington
Live Oak	George West	Jim Huff	Ida Vasquez	Dwayne McWilliams	Kitley Moffatt-Wasicek	Deanna Atkinson	Larry Busby
Llano	Llano	Ron Cunningham	Marci Hadeler	Dwain K. Rogers	Teresa Kassell	Kris Fogelberg	Bill Blackburn
Loving	Mentone	Skeet Lee Jones	Mozelle Carr	Stephen Simonsen	Regina Wilkinson	Chris H. Busse	Chris H. Busse
Lubbock	Lubbock	Curtis Parrish	Kelly Pinion	—	Chris Winn	Ronnie Keister	Kelly S. Rowe
Lynn	Tahoka	Mike Braddock	Karen Strickland	Rebekah Filley	Amy Schuknecht	Donna Willis	Wanda Mason
Madison	Madisonville	A.J. (Tony) Leago	Susanne Morris	—	Judi Delesandri	Karen M. Lane	Bobby Adams
Marion	Jefferson	Leward J. LaFleur	Vickie Smith	Angela Smoak	Terrie S. Neuville	Karen Jones	David Capps
Martin	Stanton	Bryan Cox	Linda Gonzales	James Napper	Cynthia O'Donnell	Kathy Hull	Brad Ingram
Mason	Mason	Jerry Bearden	Pam Beam	Rebekah Whitworth	Polly McMillan	Joe Lancaster	Joe Lancaster
Matagorda	Bay City	Nate McDonald	Stephanie Wurtz	Jennifer Chau	Loretta K. Griffin	Becky Cook	Frank D. Osborne
Maverick	Eagle Pass	David Saucedo	Sara Montemayor	Jaime A. Iracheta	Rito Valdez	Isamari Villarreal	Tom Schmerber
McCulloch	Brady	Frank Trull	Christine A. Jones	Mark Marshall	Mikkie Williams	Silvia Campos	Matt Andrews
McLennan	Waco	Scott Felton	Andy Harwell	—	Bill Helton	Randy H. Riggs	Parnell McNamara
McMullen	Tilden	James E. Teal	Mattie S. Sadovsky	Kimberly Kreider-Dusek	Jill Atkinson	Bessilia (Bessie) Guerrero	Emmett Shelton
Medina	Hondo	Chris Schuchart	Gina Champion	—	Debbie Southwell	Melissa Lutz	Randy Brown
Menard	Menard	Brandon Corbin	Christy Eggleston	Luke Davis	Ron Wood	Tim Powell	Buck Miller
Midland	Midland	Terry Johnson	Alison Haley	Russell Malm	Mitzi Baker	Karen Hood	David Criner
Milam	Cameron	Steve Young	Jodi Morgan	Bill Torrey	Linda Acosta	Sherry Mueck	Mike Clore
Mills	Goldthwaite	Ed Smith	Sonya Scott	Gerald Hale	Summer Campbell	Lori King	Clint Hammonds

County	County Seat	County Judge	County Clerk	County Attorney	County Treasurer	Assessor–Collector	Sheriff
Mitchell	Colorado City	Mark Merrell	Carla Kern	Sterling T. Burleson, II	Jennifer Rivera	Sylvia Clanton	Patrick Toombs
Montague	Montague	Kevin Benton	Kim Jones	Clay V. Riddle	Jennifer Fenoglio	Kathryn Phillips	Marshall Thomas
Montgomery	Conroe	Mark J. Keough	Mark Turnbull	B.D. Griffin	Melanie K. Bush	Tammy J. McRae	Rand Henderson
Moore	Dumas	Rowdy Rhoades	Brenda McKanna	Scott Higginbotham	Kara Milligan	Chris A. Rivera	Morgan W. Hightower
Morris	Daingerfield	Doug Reeder	Scott Sartain	Ricky Shelton	Molly Cummings	Kim Thomasson	Jack Martin
Motley	Matador	James B. (Jim) Meador	D'anna Russell	Tom Edwards	Misty Jones	Ronda Miller	Robert Fisk
Nacogdoches	Nacogdoches	Greg Sowell	June Clifton	John Fleming	Denise Baublet	Kim Morton	Jason Bridges
Navarro	Corsicana	H.M. Davenport, Jr.	Sherry Dowd	—	Ryan Douglas	Mike Dowd	Elmer Tanner
Newton	Newton	Kenneth Weeks	Sandra K. Duckworth	—	Ginger Sims	Melissa J. Burks	Robert Burby
Nolan	Sweetwater	Whitley May	Sharla Keith	Samantha Morrow	Jeanne Wells	Kathy Bowen	David Warren
Nueces	Corpus Christi	Barbara Canales	Kara Sands	Jenny P. Dorsey	*Office abolished 11-3-87.*	Kevin Kieschnick	J.C. Hooper
Ochiltree	Perryton	Charles E. Kelly	Jeri Ann McGarraugh	Jose N. Meraz	Britney Meraz	Linda Womble	Terry Bouchard
Oldham	Vega	Don R. Allred	Darla Lookingbill	Kent Birdsong	Sherri Johnson	Linda Brown	Brent Warden
Orange	Orange	John Gothia	Brandy Robertson	John Kimbrough	Christy Khoury	Karen Fisher	Jimmy Lane Mooney
Palo Pinto	Palo Pinto	Shane Long	Janette K. Green	Maegan Kostiha	Tanya Fallin	Stacy L. Choate	Brett E. McGuire
Panola	Carthage	LeeAnn Jones	Bobbie Davis	—	Joni Reed	Holly Gibbs	Sarah Fields
Parker	Weatherford	Pat Deen	Lila Deakle	John Forrest	Jenny Barnwell	Jenny Gentry	Russ Authier
Parmer	Farwell	Trey Ellis	Susie Spring	Jeff W. Actkinson	Sharon May	Awyna Sanchez	Randy Geries
Pecos	Fort Stockton	Joe Shuster	Liz Chapman	Frank Lacy	Sonia Murphy	Santa Acosta	TJ Perkins
Polk	Livingston	Sydney Murphy	Schelana Hock	—	Terri Williams	Leslie Jones Burks	Byron A. Lyons
Potter	Amarillo	Nancy Tanner	Julie Smith	Scott Brumley	Leann Jennings	Sherri Aylor	Brian Thomas
Presidio	Marfa	Cinderela Guevara	Flor Zubia	Rod Ponton	Frances Garcia	Natalia Williams	Danny Dominguez
Rains	Emory	Wayne Wolfe	Linda Wallace	Robert Vititow	Teresa Northcutt	Sheila Floyd	David Traylor
Randall	Canyon	Christy Dyer	Susan Allen	—	Angie Parker	Christina McMurray	Christopher Forbis
Reagan	Big Lake	Jim O'Bryan	Terri Curry	Michele Dodd	Ginna Hruska	Cynthia Aguilar	Jeff N. Garner
Real	Leakey	Bella A. Rubio	D'Ann Green	Bobby Jack Rushing	Mairi Gray	Terrie Pendley	Nathan T. Johnson
Red River	Clarksville	L.D. Williamson	Shawn Weemes	Val Varley	Sandra Embrey	Tonya R. Martin	Jimmy Caldwell
Reeves	Pecos	Leo Hung	Dianne O. Florez	Alva Alvarez	Zulema Rodriguez	Rosemary Chabarria	Arturo (Art) Granado
Refugio	Refugio	Robert Blaschke	Ida Ramirez	Deborah A. Bauer	Rita Trojcak	Ida Turner	Raul (Pinky) Gonzales
Roberts	Miami	Rick L. Tennant	Toni Rankin	William P. Weiman	Amy Tennant	Hether Williams	Bruce Skidmore
Robertson	Franklin	Charles L. Ellison	Stephanie M. Sanders	W. Coty Siegert	Melinda Turner	Michael (Duba) Brewer	Gerald Yezak
Rockwall	Rockwall	David Sweet	Jennifer Fogg	—	David Peek	Kim Sweet	Terry Garrett
Runnels	Ballinger	Barry Hilliard	Julia Miller	Ben Clayton	Ann Strube	Robin Burgess	Carl L. Squyres
Rusk	Henderson	Joel Hale	Trudy McGill	Micheal E. Jimerson	Andy Vinson	Nesha Partin	Johnwayne Valdez
Sabine	Hemphill	Daryl Melton	Jamie Clark	Robert G. Neal, Jr.	Tricia Jacks	Martha M. Stone	Thomas N. Maddox
San Augustine	San Augustine	Jeff Boyd	Margo Noble	Wesley Hoyt	Pam Smith	Regina Barthol	Robert Cartwright
San Jacinto	Coldspring	Fritz Faulkner	Dawn Wright	—	Dianna (Dee Dee) Adams	Betty Davis	Greg Capers
San Patricio	Sinton	David Krebs	Gracie Alaniz-Gonzales	Tamara Cochran-May	Denise Janak	Marcela Thormaehlen	Oscar Rivera
San Saba	San Saba	Byron Theodosis	Kim Wells	Randall Robinson	Lois VanBeck	David Jenkins	David Jenkins
Schleicher	Eldorado	Charlie Bradley	Mary Ann Gonzalez	Clint T. Griffin	Jennifer L. Henderson	Vanessa Covarrubiaz	Jason Chatham
Scurry	Snyder	Dan Hicks	Melody Appleton	Michael Hartman	Kirsta Koennecke	Jana Young	Trey Wilson
Shackelford	Albany	Robert Skelton	Cheri Hawkins	Rollin Rauschl	Tammy Brown	Edward A. Miller	Edward A. Miller
Shelby	Center	Allison Harbison	Jennifer Fountain	Gary W. Rholes	Ann Blackwell	Debora Riley	Kevin Windham
Sherman	Stratford	Terri Beth Carter	Laura Rogers	Kim Allen	Alicia Law	Valerie McAlister	Ted Allen

County	County Seat	County Judge	County Clerk	County Attorney	County Treasurer	Assessor–Collector	Sheriff
Smith	Tyler	Nathaniel Moran	Karen Phillips	—	Kelli R. White	Gary Barber	Larry Smith
Somervell	Glen Rose	Danny L. Chambers	Michelle Reynolds	Andrew Lucas	Susanne Graves	April Campos	Alan West
Starr	Rio Grande City	Eloy Vera	Humberto Gonzalez	Victor Canales, Jr.	Romeo Gonzalez	Ameida Salinas	Rene (Orta) Fuentes
Stephens	Breckenridge	Michael Roach	Jackie Ensey	Gary Trammel	Sharon Trigg	Christie Latham	Kevin Roach
Sterling	Sterling City	Deborah Horwood	Jerri McCutchen	Lilli Hensley	Rhea McGinnis	Julie McEntire	Tim A. Sanders
Stonewall	Aspermont	Ronnie Moorhead	Holly McLaury	Riley Branch	Anya Mullen	Jim B. Ward	William (Bill) Mullen
Sutton	Sonora	Rachel Chavez Duran	Pam Thorp	Dawn B. Cahill	Janell Schniers	Kathy Sanchez Marshall	Oscar Chavez
Swisher	Tulia	Harold Keeter	C.J. Chasco	J. Michael Criswell	Tricia Speed	Deborah Lemons	Jim McCaslin
Tarrant	Fort Worth	B. Glen Whitley	Mary Louise Nicholson	—	*Office abolished 4-2-83.*	Wendy Burgess	Bill E. Waybourn
Taylor	Abilene	Downing A. Bolls, Jr.	Larry Bevill	—	Lesa Hart Crosswhite	Kay Middleton	Ricky Bishop
Terrell	Sanderson	Dale Lynn Carruthers	Raeline Thompson	Kenneth D. Bellah	Rebecca Luevano	Santiago Gonzalez, Jr.	Santiago Gonzalez, Jr.
Terry	Brownfield	J.D. Wagner	Kim Carter	Jo'Shae Ferguson-Worley	Karen Grigsby	Rexann W. Furlow	Timothy Click
Throckmorton	Throckmorton	Trey Carrington	Dianna Moore	Kris Fouts	Brenda Rankin	Doc Wigington	Doc Wigington
Titus	Mount Pleasant	Brian P. Lee	Joan Newman	John Mark Cobern	Sheryl Preddy	Melissa Stevens	Tim C. Ingram
Tom Green	San Angelo	Stephen C. Floyd	Christina Ubando	Chris Taylor	Dianna Spieker	Becky Robles	J. Nick Hanna
Travis	Austin	Andy Brown	Dana DeBeauvoir	Delia Garza	Dolores Ortega Carter	Bruce Elfant	Sally Hernandez
Trinity	Groveton	Doug Page	Shasta Bergman	Colton Hay	B.L. Dockens	Nancy Shanafelt	Woody Wallace
Tyler	Woodville	Jacques L. Blanchette	Donece Gregory	—	Leann Monk	Lynnette Cruse	Bryan Weatherford
Upshur	Gilmer	Todd Tefteller	Terri Ross	—	Brandy Vick	Luana Howell	Larry Webb
Upton	Rankin	Dusty Kilgore	LaWanda McMurray	Paige Skehan	Vivian Venegas	Monica Zarate	Dan Brown
Uvalde	Uvalde	William R. Mitchell	Valerie Del Toro Romero	John Dodson	Joni Deorsam	Rita C. Verstuyft	Ruben Nolasco
Val Verde	Del Rio	Lewis Owens	Generosa Gracia-Ramon	David E. Martinez	Aaron D. Rodriguez	Elodia Garcia	Joe Frank Martinez
Van Zandt	Canton	Don Kirkpatrick	Susan Strickland	—	Kenny Edwards	Misty Stanberry	Steve Hendrix
Victoria	Victoria	Ben Zeller	Heidi Easley	—	Sean Kennedy	Ashley Hernandez	Justin Marr
Walker	Huntsville	Danny Pierce	Kari French	—	Amy Klawinsky	Diana L. McRae	Clint McRae
Waller	Hempstead	Carbett (Trey) J. Duhon, III	Debbie Hollan	Elton Mathis	Joan Sargent	Ellen C. Shelburne	Troy Guidry
Ward	Monahans	Greg M. Holly	Denise Valles	Alan Nicholas	Carleigh Ennis	Vicki Heflin	Frarin Valle
Washington	Brenham	John Durrenberger	Beth A. Rothermel	Renee Ann Mueller	Peggy Kramer	Cheryl Gaskamp	Otto H. Hanak
Webb	Laredo	Tano E. Tijerina	Margie Ramirez Ibarra	Marco A. Montemayor	Raul Reyes	Patricia Barrera	Martin Cuellar
Wharton	Wharton	Phillip Spenrath	Barbara Svatek	G.A. (Trey) Maffett	Donna Thornton	Cindy Hernandez	Shannon Srubar
Wheeler	Wheeler	Jerry Hefley	Margaret Dorman	Leslie Standerfer	Renee Warren	Cindy Brown	Johnny G. Carter
Wichita	Wichita Falls	Woodrow W. Gossom, Jr.	Lori Bohannon	—	Bob Hampton	Tommy Smyth	David Duke
Wilbarger	Vernon	Greg Tyra	Jana Kennon	Cornell Curtis	Joann Carter	Sherrie Campsey	Brian Fritze
Willacy	Raymondville	Aurelio (Keter) Guerra	Susana R. Garza	Annette C. Hinojosa	Ruben Cavazos	Elizabeth Barnhart	Joe Salazar
Williamson	Georgetown	Bill Gravell, Jr.	Nancy E. Rister	Doyle (Dee) Hobbs, Jr.	D. Scott Heselmeyer	Larry Gaddes	Mike Gleason
Wilson	Floresville	Richard L. Jackson	Eva S. Martinez	Tom Caldwell	Jan Hartl	Dawn Polasek Barnett	Jim Stewart
Winkler	Kermit	Charles M. Wolf	Pam Greene	Thomas Duckworth, Jr.	Susan Willhelm	Minerva Soltero	Darin Mitchell
Wise	Decatur	J.D. Clark	Sherry Lemon	James Stainton	Katherine Hudson	Monte Shaw	Lane Akin
Wood	Quitman	Lucy Hebron	Kelley Price	—	Becky S. Burford	Carol Taylor	Kelly Cole
Yoakum	Plains	Jim Barron	Summer Lovelace	—	Darla Welch	Jan Parrish	David Bryant
Young	Graham	John C. Bullock	Kay Hardin	Chris Baran	Ann Daily	Christy Centers	Travis Babcock
Zapata	Zapata	Joe Rathmell	Mary Jayne Villarreal-Bonoan	Said Alfonso Figueroa	Romeo Salinas	Delia Mendoza	Raymundo Del Bosque
Zavala	Crystal City	Joe Luna	Michelle Bonilla	Eduardo Serna	Elizabeth Tovar	Cindy Martinez-Rivera	Eusevio Salinas

Texas County and District Officials — Table No. 2

District Clerks, District Attorneys, and County Commissioners

See Table No. 1 on **pages 501–506** for County Seats, County Judges, County Clerks, County Attorneys, County Treasurers, Tax Assessors-Collectors, and Sheriffs. Judges in county courts at law, as well as probate courts, juvenile/domestic relations courts, county criminal courts, and county criminal courts of appeal, are on **pages 493–495**. If more than one district attorney is listed for a county, the district court number is noted in parentheses after each attorney's name. The officials listed here are elected by popular vote. If no district attorney is listed, the county attorney, whose name is listed in Table No. 1, assumes the duties of that office.

County	District Clerk	District Attorney	Comm. Precinct 1	Comm. Precinct 2	Comm. Precinct 3	Comm. Precinct 4
Anderson	Teresia Coker	Allyson Mitchell	Greg Chapin	Rashad Mims	Kenneth Dickson	Joey Hill
Andrews	Sherry Dushane	Sean Galloway	Kerry Pack	Mark Savell	Jeneane Anderegg	Jim Waldrop
Angelina	Reba Squyres	Janet Cassels	Rodney Paulette	Kermit Kennedy	Terry Pitts	Bobby Cheshire
Aransas	Pam Heard	—	Jack Chaney	Leslie (Bubba) Casterline	Pat Rousseau	Wendy Laubach
Archer	Lori Rutledge	Casey Polhemus	Wade Scarbrough	Darin Wolf	Pat Martin, III	Darryl Lightfoot
Armstrong	Tawnee Blodgett	Randall C. Sims	Adam Ensey	Dustin Sanders	Robert Harris	Mike Ollinger
Atascosa	Margaret E. Littleton	Audrey Gossett Louis	Mark Gillespie	Stuart Knowlton	Eliseo Perez	Kennard (Bubba) Riley
Austin	Sue Murphy	Travis J. Koehn	Mark Lamp	Robert (Bobby) Rinn	Leroy Cerny	Chip Reed
Bailey	Becky Espinoza	Kathryn Gurley	Gary Don Gartin	Mike Slayden	Cody Black	Jim Daniel
Bandera	Tammy Kneuper	Stephen Harpold	Bruce Eliker	Bobby Harris	Jack Moseley	Jordan (Jody) Rutherford
Bastrop	Sarah Loucks	Bryan Goertz	Mel Hamner	Clara Beckett	Mark Meuth	Donna Snowden
Baylor	Chris Jakubicek	Hunter Brooks	Rick Gillispie	Larry Elliott	Reed Slaggle	Charlie Piatt
Bee	Zenaida Silva	Jose Aliseda	Kristofer Linney	Dennis DeWitt	Sammy G. Farias	Kenneth Haggard
Bell	Joanna Staton	Henry Garza	Russell Schneider	Bobby Whitson	Bill Schumann	John Driver
Bexar	Mary Angie Garcia	Joe Gonzales	Rebeca Clay-Flores	Justin Rodriguez	Trish DeBerry	Tommy Calvert
Blanco	Debby Elsbury	Wiley B. (Sonny) McAfee	Tommy Weir	Emil Ray Uecker	Chris Liesmann	Paul Granberg
Borden	Jana Underwood	Ben R. Smith	Norman (Jibber) Herridge	Randy Adcock	Ernest Reyes	Greg Stansell
Bosque	Juanita Miller	Adam Sibley	Billy Hall	Terry Townley	Larry (Shotgun) Philipp	Ronny Liardon
Bowie	Jill Harrington	Jerry Rochelle	Sammy Stone	Tom Whitten	James Strain	Mike Carter
Brazoria	Rhonda Barchak	Tom Selleck	Donald (Dude) Payne	Ryan Cade	Stacy Adams	David Linder
Brazos	Gabriel Garcia	Jarvis Parsons	Steve Aldrich	Russ Ford	Nancy Berry	Irma Cauley
Brewster	Jo Ann Salgado	Ori White	Jim Westermann	Sara Allen Colando	Ruben Ortega	Mike Pallanez
Briscoe	Bena Hester	Wade Jackson	Ken Wood	Jack Wellman	Danny Francis	John Burson
Brooks	Lesvia Gonzales	Carlos Omar Garcia	Eduardo (Eddie) Garza	Rolando Gutierrez	Horacio Villareal, III	Ernesto (Pepe) Williams
Brown	Cheryl Jones	Micheal Murray	Gary Worley	Joel Kelton	Wayne Shaw	Larry Traweek
Burleson	Dana Fritsche	Susan Deski	Dwayne Faust	Vincent Svec, Jr.	David Hildebrand	Carol Hill
Burnet	Casie Walker	Wiley B. (Sonny) McAfee	Jim Luther, Jr.	Damon Beierle	Billy Wall	Joe Don Dockery
Caldwell	Juanita Allen	Fred Weber	B.J. Westmoreland	Barbara Shelton	Edward (Ed) Theriot	Joe Roland
Calhoun	Anna Kabela	Dan Heard	David Hall	Vern Lyssy	Joel Behrens	Gary Reese
Callahan	Sharon Owens	Shane Deel	Rick McGowen	Bryan Farmer	Tom Windham	Erwin Clark
Cameron	Laura Perez-Reyes	Luis V. Saenz	Sofia C. Benavides	Joey Lopez	David A. Garza	Gus Ruiz
Camp	Teresa Bockmon	David Colley	George French	Steve Hudnall	Perry Weeks	Steve Lindley
Carson	Celeste Bichsel	Luke M. Inman	Mike Britten	James Martin	Mike Jennings	Kevin Howell
Cass	Jamie Albertson	Courtney Shelton	Brett Fitts	Danny Joe Shaddix	Paul Cothren	Darrell Godwin
Castro	JoAnna Blanco	Shalyn Hamlin	Paul Ramirez	Tim Elliott	Michael Goolsby	Ralph Brockman
Chambers	Patti L. Henry	Cheryl Swope Lieck	Jimmy Gore	Kenneth Mark Tice	Tommy Hammond	Billy Combs
Cherokee	Alison Dotson	Elmer Beckworth	Kelly Traylor	Steven Norton	Patrick Reagan	Billy McCutcheon
Childress	Barbara Spitzer	Luke M. Inman	Jeremy Hill	Mark Ross	Kevin Hackler	Rick Elliott

County	District Clerk	District Attorney	Comm. Precinct 1	Comm. Precinct 2	Comm. Precinct 3	Comm. Precinct 4
Clay	Marianne Bowles	Casey Polhemus	Richard Lowery	Johnny Gee	Retta Collins	Chase Broussard
Cochran	Lisa Smith	Angela L. Overman	Timothy Roberts	Matt Evans	Eric Silhan	Reynaldo Morin
Coke	Monica Reyes	Allison Palmer	Donald Robertson	Paul Williams	Marshall Millican	Joe Sefcik
Coleman	Darlene Huddle-Boyd	Heath Hemphill	Matt Henderson	Jim Rice	Scotty Lawrence	Alan Davis
Collin	Lynne Finley	Greg Willis	Susan Fletcher	Cheryl Williams	Darrell Hale	Duncan Webb
Collingsworth	Jackie Johnson	Luke M. Inman	Farris Nation	James Ellis	Joel Sherwood	Kirby Campbell
Colorado	Linda Holman	Jay E. Johannes	Doug Wessels	Darrell Kubesch	Keith Neuendorff	Darrell Gertson
Comal	Heather Kellar	Jennifer Tharp	Donna Eccleston	Scott Haag	Kevin Webb	Jen Crownover
Comanche	Brenda Dickey	Adam Sibley	Gary (Corky) Underwood	Russell Gillette	Sherman Sides	Jimmy Dale Johnson
Concho	Phyllis F. Lovell	John Best	Trey Bradshaw	Ralph Willberg	Gary Gierisch	Aaron (Sonny) Browning
Cooke	Marci A. Gilbert	John Warren	Gary Hollowell	Jason Snuggs	Adam Arendt	Leon Klement
Coryell	Becky Moore	Dusty Boyd	Kyle Matthews	Daren Moore	Ryan Basham	Ray Ashby
Cottle	Vickey Wederski	Hunter Brooks	Jimmy Sweeney	Steven Beck, Jr.	Manuel Cruz	John B. Brothers
Crane	Janie Macias	Amanda Navarette	Manuella Kirkpatrick	Brian Brents	Domingo Escobedo	Cody Bob Harrelson
Crockett	Ninfa Preddy	Laurie English	Frank Tambunga	G.L. Bunger, V	Wesley Bean	Mike Medina
Crosby	Shari Smith	Michael Sales	Larry McCauley	Frank Mullins	Donald Kirksey	Kevin Langdon
Culberson	Linda McDonald	Yvonne Rosales	Javier Mendoza	Raul Rodriguez	Gilda Morales	Adrian Norman
Dallam	Terri Banks	Erin Lands	Carl McCarty	Corey Crabtree	Levi James	Floyd French
Dallas	Felicia Pitre	John Creuzot	Theresa Daniel	J.J. Koch	John Wiley Price	Elba Garcia
Dawson	Adreana Gonzalez	Philip Mack Furlow	Mark Shofner	Martha Hernandez	Nicky Goode	Russell Cox
Deaf Smith	Elaine Gerber	Chris Strowd	Chris Kahlich	Jerry O'Connor	Mike Brumley	Dale Artho
Delta	Jane Jones	Will W. Ramsay	Eric Lair	Jimmy Sweat	Bobby Asbill	Mark Brantley
Denton	David Trantham	Paul Johnson	Ryan Williams	Ron Marchant	Bobbie J. Mitchell	Dianne Edmondson
DeWitt	Esther Ruiz	Robert C. Lassmann	Curtis G. Afflerbach	James B. Pilchiek, Sr.	James Kaiser	Richard Randle
Dickens	Becky Hill	Wade Jackson	Dennis Wyatt	Mike Smith	Charles Morris	Jerry Alexander
Dimmit	Maricela G. Gonzalez	Roberto Serna	Mike Uriegas	Alonso G. Carmona	Juan Carmona	Valerie Rubalcaba
Donley	Fay Vargas	Luke M. Inman	Mark White	Daniel Ford	Neil Koetting	Dan Sawyer
Duval	Rachel S. Vela	Gocha Ramirez	Pete Guerra	Rene Perez	David Garza	Gilberto Uribe, Jr.
Eastland	Tessa K. Culverhouse	Russ Thomason	Andy Maxwell	James Crenshaw	Ronnie Wilson	Robert Rains
Ector	Clarissa Webster	Dusty Gallivan	Mike Gardner	Greg Simmons	Don Stringer	Armando S. Rodriguez
Edwards	Olga Lydia Reyes	Tonya Ahlschwede	Marty H. Graham	Lee D. Sweeten	Matt Fry	Kenneth Reed
Ellis	Melanie Reed	Ann Montgomery	Randy Stinson	Lane Grayson	Paul Perry	Kyle Butler
El Paso	Norma Favela Barceleau	Yvonne Rosales	Carlos Leon	David Stout	Iliana Holguin	Carl L. Robinson
Erath	Wanda Greer	Alan Nash	Dee Stephens	Albert Ray	Joe Brown	Jim Buck
Falls	Christy Wideman	Kathryn (Jody) Gilliam	Milton Albright	F.A. Green	Jason Willberg	Nita Wuebker
Fannin	Nancy Young	Richard Glaser	Edwina Lane	A.J. Self	Jerry Magness	Dean Lackey
Fayette	Linda Svrcek	Peggy Supak	Jason McBroom	Luke Sternadel	Harvey Berckenhoff	Drew Brossmann
Fisher	Gina Pasley	Richard Thompson	Gordon Pippin	Dexter Elrod	Preston Martin	Kevin Stuart
Floyd	Patty Davenport	Wade Jackson	Tanner R. Smith	Clint Bigham	Nathan Johnson	David Martinez
Foard	Debra Hopkins	John Staley Heatly	Rick Hammonds	Rockne Wisdom	Larry Wright	Anthony Hinsley
Fort Bend	Beverley McGrew Walker	Brian Middleton	Vincent Morales, Jr.	Grady Prestage	Andy Meyers	Ken DeMerchant
Franklin	Ellen Jaggers	Will W. Ramsay	Jerry Cooper	Larkin Jumper	Charlie Emerson	Sam Young
Freestone	Teresa Black	Brian Evans	Andy Bonner	Thomas Craig Oakes	Lloyd Lane	Clyde Ridge, Jr.

County	District Clerk	District Attorney	Comm. Precinct 1	Comm. Precinct 2	Comm. Precinct 3	Comm. Precinct 4
Frio	Ofilia M. Trevino	Audrey Gossett Louis	Joe Vela	Richard Graf	Raul Carrizales	Jose Asuncion
Gaines	Susan Murphree	Philip Mack Furlow	Brian Rosson	Craig Belt	David Murphree	Biz Houston
Galveston	John D. Kinard	Jack Roady	Darrell Apffel	Joe Giusti	Stephen D. Holmes	Ken Clark
Garza	Jim Plummer	Philip Mack Furlow	Jeff Williams	Charles Morris	Ted Brannon	Jerry Benham
Gillespie	Jan Davis	Lucy Wilke	Charles Olfers	Keith Kramer	Dennis Neffendorf	Donnie Schuch
Glasscock	Rebecca Batla	Hardy Wilkerson	Charles Gully	Mark Halfmann	Gary Jones	John Seidenberger
Goliad	Mary Ellen Flores	Rob Lassmann	Kenneth Edwards	Alonzo Morales	Kirby Brumby	David Bruns
Gonzales	Janice Sutton		K.O. (Dell) Whiddon	Donnie R. Brzozowski	Kevin T. La Fleur	Collie Boatright
Gray	Jo Mays	Franklin McDonough	Logan Hudson	Lake Arrington	John Mark Baggerman	Jeff Haley
Grayson	Kelly Ashmore	Brett Smith	Jeff Whitmire	David Whitlock	Phyllis James	Bart Lawrence
Gregg	Trey Hattaway	Tom Watson	Ronnie L. McKinney	Darryl Primo	Floyd Wingo	Shannon E. Brown
Grimes	Diane Leflore	Andria Bender	Chad Mallett	David E. Dobyanski	Barbara Walker	Phillip Cox
Guadalupe	Linda Balk		Greg Seidenberger	Drew Engelke	Michael Carpenter	Judy Cope
Hale	Carla Cannon	Wally Hatch	Harold King	Chris Daniel	Kenny Kernell	Jimmy Kelly
Hall	Olivia M. Fisher	Luke M. Inman	Ronny Wilson	Terry Lindsey	Gary Proffitt	Troy Glover
Hamilton	Sandy Layhew	Adam Sibley	Johnny Wagner	Keith Allen Curry	Lloyd Huggins	Dickie Clary
Hansford	Janet Torres	Mark Snider	Ira G. (Butch) Reed	David L. Thomas	Tim Stedje	Danny Henson
Hardeman	Ellen London	Staley Heatly	Chris Call	Haden Braziel	Barry Haynes	Rodney Foster
Hardin	Dana Hogg	Rebecca Walton	L.W. Cooper, Jr.	Chris Kirkendall	Amanda Young	Alvin Roberts
Harris	Marilyn Burgess	Kim Ogg	Rodney Ellis	Adrian Garcia	Tom S. Ramsey	R. Jack Cagle
Harrison	Sherry Griffis	Reid McCain	William D. Hatfield	Zephaniah Timmins	Phillip Mauldin	Jay Ebarb
Hartley	Melissa Mead	Erin Lands	David Vincent	David Spinhirne	Chad Hicks	Robert (Butch) Owens
Haskell	Debbie Gressett	Mike Fouts	Jerry Don Garcia	Elmer Adams	Matt Sanders	Neal Kreger
Hays	Beverly Crumley	Wes Mau	Debbie Ingalsbe	Mark Jones	Lon Shell	Walt Smith
Hemphill	Lisa Johnson	Franklin McDonough	Dawn E. Webb	Tim Alexander	Curt McPherson	Nicholas Thomas
Henderson	Betty Herriage	Jenny Palmer	Wendy Spivey	Scott Tuley	Charles (Chuck) McHam	Mark Richardson
Hidalgo	Laura Hinojosa	Ricardo Rodriguez, Jr.	David L. Fuentes	Eduardo (Eddie) Cantu	Joe M. Flores	Ellie Torres
Hill	Marchel Eubank	Mark Pratt	Andrew Montgomery	Larry Crumpton	Scotty Hawkins	Martin Lake
Hockley	Dennis Price	Angela L. Overman	Alan Wisdom	Larry Carter	Seth Graf	Tommy Clevenger
Hood	Tonna Trumble Hitt	Ryan Sinclair	Kevin Andrews	Ron Cotton	Jack Wilson	Dave Eagle
Hopkins	Cheryl Fulcher	Will W. Ramsay	Mickey Barker	Greg Anglin	Wade Bartley	Joe Price
Houston	Carolyn Rains	Donna Gordon Kaspar	Gary Lovell	Willie Kitchen	Gene Stokes	Jimmy Henderson
Howard	Joanna Gonzales	Hardy Wilkerson	Eddilisa Ray	Craig Bailey	Jimmie Long	John Cline
Hudspeth	Brenda Sanchez	Yvonne Rosales	Andrew Virdell	Sergio Quijas	Johny Sheets	Delbert (Sonny) Berry
Hunt	Susan Spradling	Noble D. Walker	Mark Hutchins	Randy Strait	Phillip Martin	Steven Harrison
Hutchinson	Robin Stroud	Mark Snider	Gary Alexander	Dwight Kirksey	Ben Bentley	Chris Prock
Irion	Shirley Graham	Allison Palmer	Tia Paxton	Jeff Davidson	John Nanny	Bill (Beaver) McManus, III
Jack	Tracie Pippin	James Stainton	Gary Oliver	Darren Francis	Henry D. Birdwell, Jr.	Terry Ward
Jackson	Sharon Mathis	Pam Guenther	Wayne Hunt	Wayne Bubela	Glenn Martin	Dennis Karl
Jasper	Rosa Norsworthy	Anne Pickle	Seth Martindale	Roy Parker	Willie Stark	Vance Moss
Jeff Davis	Jennifer Wright	Ori White	Jody Adams	Todd Jagger	John Davis	Albert W. Miller
Jefferson	Jamie Smith	Bob Wortham	Vernon Pierce	Darrell Bush	Michael Sinegal	Everette (Bo) Alfred
Jim Hogg	Zonia G. Morales	Gocha Ramirez	Humberto Martinez	Abelardo Alaniz	Sandalio Ruiz	Cynthia Guerra Betancourt
Jim Wells	R. David Guerrero	Carlos Omar Garcia	Margie H. Gonzalez	Ventura Garcia	Renee Kirchoff Chapa	Wicho Gonzalez

County	District Clerk	District Attorney	Comm. Precinct 1	Comm. Precinct 2	Comm. Precinct 3	Comm. Precinct 4
Johnson	David Lloyd	Dale Hanna	Rick Bailey	Kenny Howell	Mike White	Larry Woolley
Jones	Lacey Hansen	Joe Edd Boaz	Roy Spalding	Lonnie Vivian	Todd McWilliams	Joel Spraberry
Karnes	Denise Rodriguez	Audrey Gossett Louis	Shelby Dupnik	Benny Lyssy	James Rosales	Sharon Chesser
Kaufman	Rhonda Hughey	Erleigh Norville Wiley	Mike Hunt	Skeet Phillips	Terry Barber	Ken Cates
Kendall	Susan Jackson	Nicole S. Bishop	Christina Bergmann	Richard W. Elkins	Richard Chapman	Don Durden
Kenedy	Veronica Vela	John T. Hubert	Joe Recio	Israel Vela, Jr.	Sarita Armstrong Hixon	Cindy Gonzales
Kent	Craig Harrison	Mike Fouts	Roy W. Chisum	Don Long	Daryl Ham	Robert Graham
Kerr	Dawn Lantz	Stephen Harpold (198th); Lucy Wilke (216th)	Harley David Belew	Tom Moser	Jonathan Letz	Don Harris
Kimble	Haydee Torres	Tonya Ahlschwede	Brady Schulze	Kelly Simon	Dennis Dunagan	Kenneth Hofmann
King	Jammye D. Timmons	Hunter Brooks	Reggie Hatfield	Larry Rush	Doris Tidmore	Jay Hurt
Kinney	Rick Alvarado	Suzanne West	Mark Frerich	Joe Montalvo	Dennis Dodson	Tim Ward
Kleberg	Jennifer Whittington	John T. Hubert	David Rosse	Chuck Schultz	Jerry Martinez	Marcus Salinas
Knox	Lisa Cypert	Hunter Brooks	Johnny McCown	Dan Godsey	Ray Herring	Nathan Urbanczyk
Lamar	Shawntel Golden	Gary Young	Alan Skidmore	Lonnie Layton	Ronnie Bass	Kevin Anderson
Lamb	Debbie Long	Scott A. Say	Cory DeBerry	Kent Lewis	Danny Short	Lee Logan
Lampasas	Edith Wagner Harrison	John K. Greenwood	Bobby Carroll	Jamie Smart	Lewis Bridges	Mark Rainwater
La Salle	Margarita Esqueda	Audrey Gossett Louis	Noel Niavez	Joaquin Alba	Erasmo Ramirez, Jr.	Raul Ayala
Lavaca	Lori A. Wenske	Kyle A. Denney	Edward Pustka	Ronald Berckenhoff	Kenny Siegel	Dennis W. Kocian
Lee	Lisa Teinert	Martin Placke	Mark Matthijetz	Richard Wagner	Alan Turner	Steven Knobloch
Leon	Cassandra Noey	James (Caleb) Henson	Joey Sullivan	David Ferguson	Kyle Workman	David Grimes
Liberty	Delia Sellers	Jennifer L. Bergman	Bruce Karbowski	Greg Arthur	David S. Whitmire	Leon Wilson
Limestone	Carol Jenkins	William Roy DeFriend	Bill David Sadler	W.A. (Sonny) Baker	Stephen Friday	Bobby Forrest
Lipscomb	Kim Blau	Franklin McDonough	Juan Cantu	Merle Miller	Scotty Schilling	Dan Cockrell
Live Oak	Melanie Matkin	Jose Aliseda	Richard Lee	Donna Kopplin Mills	Mitchell Williams	Emilio Garza
Llano	Joyce Gillow	Wiley B. (Sonny) McAfee	Peter R. Jones	Linda Raschke	Mike Sandoval	Jerry Don Moss
Loving	Mozelle Carr	Randall (Randy) Reynolds	Harlan Hopper	Ysidro (Joe) Renteria	Raymond W. King	William (Bill) Wilkinson
Lubbock	Barbara Sucsy	K. Sunshine Stanek	Terence Kovar	Jason Corley	Gilbert A. Flores	Chad Seay
Lynn	Courtney Odom	Philip Mack Furlow	Mark Woodley	John Hawthorne	Don Blair	Larry Durham
Madison	Rhonda Savage	Brian Risinger	Ricky Driskell	Carl Wiseman	Carl L. Cannon	David Pohorelsky
Marion	Susan Anderson	Angela Smoak	J.R. Ashley	Jacob Pattison	Ralph Meisenheimer	Charles W. Treadwell
Martin	Linda Gonzales	Hardy Wilkerson	Kenny Stewart	Robin Barnes	Bobby Holland	Koy Blocker
Mason	Pam Beam	Tonya Spaeth Ahlschwede	Reggie Loeffler	Wil Frey	Buddy Schuessler	Stephen Mutschink
Matagorda	Janice L. Hawthorne	Steven Reis	Edward (Bubba) Cook	Kent Pollard	Troy Shimek	Charles (Bubba) Frick
Maverick	Leopoldo Vielma	Roberto Serna	Gerardo (Jerry) Morales	Rosy Cantu	Olga Ramos	Roberto Ruiz
McCulloch	Michelle Pitcox	Tonya Spaeth Ahlschwede	Carol Anderson	Randy Deans	Jason Behrens	Rick Kemp
McLennan	Jon Gimble	Barry Johnson	Jim Smith	Patricia Miller	Will Jones	Ben Perry
McMullen	Mattie S. Sadovsky	Jose Aliseda	Larry Garcia	Murray Swaim	Scotty McClaugherty	Max Quintanilla, Jr.
Medina	Cindy Fowler	Mark P. Haby	Tim Neuman	Larry Sittre	David Lynch	Jerry Beck
Menard	Christy Eggleston	Tonya Ahlschwede	Frank Davis	Jay Cunningham	Ed Keith	Larry Burch
Midland	Alex (Lex) Archuleta	Laura A. Noldolf	Scott Ramsey	Robin Donnelly	Luis D. Sánchez	Randy Prude
Milam	Karen Berry	Bill Torrey	Henry (Hub) Hubnik	Donald Shuffield	Art Neal	Jeff Muegge
Mills	Sonya Scott	Micheal Murray	Mike Wright	Jed Garren	Dale Partin	Jason Williams

County	District Clerk	District Attorney	Comm. Precinct 1	Comm. Precinct 2	Comm. Precinct 3	Comm. Precinct 4
Mitchell	Belinda Blassingame	Ricky Thompson	Dennis Jones	Jeremy Strain	Jesse Munoz	Ricky Bailey
Montague	Robin Woods	Casey Polhemus	Roy Darden	Mike Mayfield	Mark Murphey	Bob Langford
Montgomery	Melisa Miller	Brett Ligon	Robert C. Walker	Charlie Riley	James Noack	James Metts
Moore	Mayra Rivero	Erin Lands	Daniel Garcia	Miles Mixon	Dee Vaughan	Lynn Cartrite
Morris	Gwen Ashworth	Ricky Shelton	Greg Frazier	Kerry McCoy	Michael Clair	Todd Freeman
Motley	D'anna Russell	Wade Jackson	Douglas Campbell	Roegan Cruse	Franklin Jameson	Timmy Brooks
Nacogdoches	Loretta Cammack	Andrew Jones	Jerry Don Williamson	Sandy McCorvey	Robin Dawley	Mark Harkness
Navarro	Joshua B. Tackett	William Thompson	Jason Grant	Eddie Perry	Eddie Moore	James Olsen
Newton	Bree Allen	Courtney Tracy Ponthier	Danny Bentsen	Phillip A. White	Gary Fomby	Wesley (Gene) Thompson
Nolan	Jamie Clem	Richard Thompson	Terry Willman	Seth Mahaffey	Tommy White	Henry Ortega, Jr.
Nueces	Anne Lorentzen	Mark A. Gonzalez	Robert Hernandez	Joe A. (JAG) Gonzalez	John Marez	Brent Chesney
Ochiltree	Shawn Bogard	Jose N. Meraz	Duane Pshigoda	Joe Johnson	JW DeWitt	Kevin Walker
Oldham	Darla Lookingbill		Quincy Taylor	Larry Groneman	Roger Morris	Billy Don Brown
Orange	Vickie Edgerly	John Kimbrough	Johnny Trahan	Theresa Beauchamp	Kirk Roccaforte	Robert Viator
Palo Pinto	Jonna Banks	Kriste Burnett	Gary Glover	Mike Reed	Mike Pierce	Jeff Fryer
Panola	Lindsey Smith	Danny Buck Davidson	Billy Alexander	David A. Cole	Craig M. Lawless	Dale LaGrone
Parker	Sharena Gilliland	Jeff Swain	George Conley	Craig Peacock	Larry Walden	Steve Dugan
Parmer	Sandra Warren	Kathryn Gurley	Kirk Frye	Charles Wilkins	Kenny White	Casey Russell
Pecos	Gayle Henderson	Ori White (83rd); Laurie English (112th)	Tom Chapman	Robert Gonzales	Mickey Jack Perry	Santiago Cantu, Jr.
Polk	Bobbye Richards	Lee Hon	Guylene Robertson	Ronnie Vincent	Milt Purvis	C.T. (Tommy) Overstreet
Potter	Stephnie Menke	Randall Sims	H.R. Kelly	Mercy Murguia	John Coffee	Alphonso Vaughn
Presidio	Flor Zubia	Ori White	Brenda Silva Bentley	Eloy Aranda	Jose Cabezuela	Frank (Buddy) Knight
Rains	Laura Pate	Robert Vititow	Jeremy Cook	Mike Willis	Korey Young	Joe Humphrey
Randall	Joel Forbis	Robert Love	Rusty Carnes	Mark Benton	Bob Robinson	Buddy DeFord
Reagan	Terri Curry	Laurie English	Mike Vargas	Tim Sellman	Tommy Holt	Mary Loftin
Real	D'Ann Green	Christina Mitchell Busbee	Brad Hart	Shawn D. Gray	Ramon Ybarra	Charles E. Hunger
Red River	Janice Gentry	Val Varley	Donnie Gentry	David Hutson	Jeff Moore	Danny Halley
Reeves	Patricia Tarin	Randall W. Reynolds	Rojelio Alvarado	Israel Campos	Paul Hinojos	Tony Trujillo
Refugio	Sylvia M. Lopez	Robert C. Lassmann	Roy Payne	Stanley Tuttle	Gary Lee Wright	Blaine Wolfshohl
Roberts	Toni Rankin	Franklin McDonough	Cleve Wheeler	William Gill	Kelly Flowers	James F. Duvall
Robertson	Barbara W. Axtell	W. Coty Siegert	Ty Rampy	Donald Threadgill	Chuck Hairston	James Taylor
Rockwall	Lea Carlson	Kenda Culpepper	Cliff Sevier	Lee Gilbert	Dennis Bailey	Janet Nichol
Runnels	Tammy Burleson	John Best	Carl King	Ronald Presley	Brandon Poehls	Juan Ornelas
Rusk	Terri Pirtle Willard	Micheal E. Jimerson	Randy Gaut	Robert Kuykendall	Greg Gibson	Bennie Whitworth
Sabine	Lisa Pitre	J. Kevin Dutton	Brent Cox	Jimmy McDaniel	Stanley Jacks	James Lowe
San Augustine	Jeanette Bryan	J. Kevin Dutton	Tommy Pickard	Ed Wilson	Joey Holloway	Rodney Ainsworth
San Jacinto	Tammy Currie	Robert H. Trapp	Laddie McAnally	Donny Marrs	David Brandon	Mark Nettuno
San Patricio	Heather B. Marks	Samuel B. Smith	Sonia Lopez	Gary Moore	Lilly Wilkinson	Howard Gillespie
San Saba	Kim Wells	Wiley B. (Sonny) McAfee	James Lebow	Rickey Lusty	Kenley Kroll	Pat Pool
Schleicher	Mary Ann Gonzalez	Allison Palmer	Gary Gibson	Steve Nelson	Kirk Griffin	Chris Meador
Scurry	Candace Jones	Ben Smith	Terry D. Williams	Craig Merritt	Shawn McCowen	Jim Robinson
Shackelford	Cheri Hawkins	Joe Edd Boaz	Steve Riley	Ace Reames	Lanham Martin	Cody Jordan
Shelby	Lori Oliver	Karren Price	Roscoe McSwain	Jimmy Lout	Stevie Smith	Tom Bellmyer

County	District Clerk	District Attorney	Comm. Precinct 1	Comm. Precinct 2	Comm. Precinct 3	Comm. Precinct 4
Sherman	Laura Rogers	Erin Lands	Dana Buckles	Terry Mathews	Jeff Crippen	David Davis
Smith	Penny Clarkston	Jacob Putman	Neal J. Franklin	Cary Nix	Terry Lee Phillips	JoAnn Hampton
Somervell	Virginia Dixon	Dale Hanna	Jeff Harris	Dwayne Johnson	Tammy Ray	Wade Busch
Starr	Orlando Velasquez	Gocha Ramirez	Jaime Alvarez	Raul (Roy) Peña, III	Eloy Garza	Ruben D. Saenz
Stephens	Christie Coapland	Dee Hudson Peavy	David Fambro	Mark McCullough	William H. Warren	Eric O'Dell
Sterling	Jerri McCutchen	Allison Palmer	Ross Copeland	Edward Michulka, Jr.	Tommy Wright, Jr.	Reed Stewart
Stonewall	Holly McLaury	Mike Fouts	Donna McCoy	Jan Harris	Kirk Meador	Gary Myers
Sutton	Pam Thorp	Laurie K. English	Lee C. Bloodworth	Bob Brockman	Carl Teaff	Fred Perez
Swisher	C.J. Chasco	J. Michael Criswell	Lloyd Rahlfs	Danny Morgan	Joe Murrell	Larry Buske
Tarrant	Thomas A. Wilder	Sharen Wilson	Roy Charles Brooks	Devan Allen	Gary Fickes	J.D. Johnson
Taylor	Tammy Robinson	James Hicks	Randall D. Williams	Kyle Kendrick	Brad Birchum	Chuck Statler
Terrell	Raeline Thompson	Suzanne West	Adam Johnson	Mike Sanchez	Arnulfo Serna	Heather Gully
Terry	Paige Lindsey	Jo'Shae Ferguson-Worley	Mike Swain	Kirby Keesee	Martin Lefevere	Ernesto Elizardo
Throckmorton	Dianna Moore	Mike Fouts	Casey Wells	Kasey Hibbitts	Lance Sullivan	Klay Mitchell
Titus	Marcus Carlock	David Colley	Jeff Parchman	John Fitch	Dana Applewhite	Jimmy Parker
Tom Green	Anthony Joseph Monico	Allison Palmer (51st); John H. Best (119th)	Ralph Hoelscher	Sammy Farmer	Rick Bacon	Bill Ford
Travis	Velva L. Price	José Garza	Jeff Travillion	Brigid Shea	Ann Howard	Margaret Gómez
Trinity	Kristen Raiford	Benny L. Schiro	Tommy Park	Mike Loftin	Neal Smith	Steven Truss
Tyler	Pamela Reneé Crews	Lucas Babin	Joe Blacksher	Stevan Sturrock	Mike Marshall	Charles (Buck) Hudson
Upshur	Karen Bunn	Billy Byrd	Gene Dolle	Dustin Nicholson	Michael Ashley	Jay Miller
Upton	LaWanda McMurray	Laurie English	Pete Jackson	Tommy Owens	Mike Smart	Gary Wolfe
Uvalde	Christina J. Ovalle	Christina Mitchell Busbee	John Yeackle	Mariano Pargas, Jr.	Jerry W. Bates	Roland (Ronnie) Garza
Val Verde	Jo Ann Cervantes	Suzanne West	Martin Wardlaw	Juan Carlos Vazquez	Robert Beau Nettleton	Gustavo (Gus) Flores
Van Zandt	Karen L. Wilson	Tonda Curry	Chad LaPrade	Virgil Melton, Jr.	Keith Pearson	Tim West
Victoria	Kim Plummer	Constance Filley Johnson	Danny Garcia	Kevin M. Janak	Gary Burns	Clint Ives
Walker	Robyn Flowers	Will Durham	Danny Kuykendall	Ronnie White	Bill Daugette	Jimmy Henry
Waller	Liz Pirkle	Elton Mathis	John A. Amsler	Walter E. Smith	Kendric D. Jones	Justin Beckendorff
Ward	Patricia Oyerbides	Randall W. Reynolds	Tino Sanchez	Larry Hanna	Dexter Nichols	Eddie Nelms
Washington	Tammy Brauner	Julie Renken	Don Koester	Candice Bullock	Kirk Hanath	Joy Fuchs
Webb	Esther Degollado	Isidro (Chilo) Alaniz	Jesse Gonzalez	Rosaura (Wawi) Tijerina	John C. Galo	Cindy Liendo
Wharton	Kendra Charbula	Dawn Elizabeth Allison	Richard Zahn	Bud Graves	Steven Goetsch	Doug Mathews
Wheeler	Sherri Jones	Franklin McDonough	Jackie Don May, Jr.	Robert Hink	David Simpson	John Walker
Wichita	Patti Flores	John Gillespie	Mark Beauchamp	Mickey Fincannon	Barry Mahler	Jeff Watts
Wilbarger	Brenda Peterson	Staley Heatly	John Wright	Phillip Graf	Kelly Neel	Josh Patterson
Willacy	Isabel Adame	Annette C. Hinojosa	Eliberto (Beto) Guerra	(vacant)	Henry De La Paz	Eduardo (Eddy) Gonzales
Williamson	Lisa David	Shawn Dick	Terry Cook	Cynthia Long	Valerie Covey	Russ Boles
Wilson	Deborah Bryan	Audrey Gossett Louis	Gary Martin	Paul W. Pfeil	Jeffery Pierdolla	Larry A. Wiley
Winkler	Geneva Baker	Amanda Navarette	Billy J. Stevens	Robbie Wolf	Victor Berzoza	Billy Ray Thompson
Wise	Brenda Rowe	James Stainton	Biff Hayes	Kevin Burns	Danny Lambert	Gaylord Kennedy
Wood	Donna Huston	Angela Albers	Virgil Holland	Jerry Gaskill	Mike Simmons	Russell Acker
Yoakum	Sandra Roblez	Bill Helwig	Woodson W. Lindsey	Ray Marion	Tommy Box	Tim Addison
Young	Jamie Freeze Land	Dee Peavy	Stacy Creswell	Matt Pruitt	Stacey Rogers	Jimmy Wiley
Zapata	Dora Martinez Castañon	Isidro (Chilo) Alaniz	Paco Mendoza	Olga M. Elizondo	Jose A. Solis	Norberto Garza
Zavala	Rachel Ramirez	Robert Serna	Joe Cruz	Raul Gomez	Jesse Gonzales	Florencio (Flo) Melendrez

Texans in Congress

Besides the two members of the U.S. Senate allocated to each state, Texas was allocated 36 members in the U.S. House of Representatives for the 116th Congress. The term of office for members of the House is two years; the terms of all members will expire on Jan. 3, 2023. Senators serve six-year terms. Sen. John Cornyn's term will end in 2027. Sen. Ted Cruz's term will end in 2025.

Addresses and phone numbers of the lawmakers' Washington and district offices are below, as well as the committees on which they serve. Washington zip codes are 20515 for members of the House and 20510 for senators. The telephone area code for Washington is 202. On the Internet, House members can be reached through www.house.gov/writerep.

In 2018, members of Congress received a salary of $174,000. Members in leadership positions received $193,400.

U.S. SENATE

(Total members 100; Republicans 53, Democrats 45, Independents 2.)

CORNYN, John. Republican (Home: Austin); Washington Office: 517 HSOB; (202) 224-2934, Fax 228-2856. www.cornyn.senate.gov.

John Cornyn.

Texas Offices: 221 W. 6th, Ste. 1530, Austin 78701, (512) 469-6034; 5001 Spring Valley, Ste. 1125 E, Dallas 75244, (972) 239-1310; 222 E. Van Buren, Ste. 404, Harlingen 78550, (956) 423-0162; 5300 Memorial Dr., Ste. 980, Houston 77007, (713) 572-3337; 1500 Broadway, Ste. 1230, Lubbock 79401, (806) 472-7533; 600 Navarro, Ste. 210, San Antonio 78205, (210) 224-7485; 100 E. Ferguson, Ste. 1004, Tyler 75702, (903) 593-0902.

Committees: Finance, Judiciary, Select Committee on Intelligence.

CRUZ, Ted. Republican (Home: Houston); Washington Office: 404 RSOB; (202) 224-5922. www.cruz.senate.gov.

Ted Cruz.

Texas Offices: 300 E. 8th, Ste. 961, Austin 78701, (512) 916-5834; 3626 N. Hall, Ste. 410, Dallas 75219, (214) 599-8749; 1919 Smith, Ste. 9047, Houston 77002, (713) 718-3057; 200 S. 10th, Ste. 1603, McAllen 78501, (956) 686-7339; 9901 IH-10W, Ste. 950, San Antonio 78230, (210) 340-2885 305; S. Broadway, Ste. 501, Tyler 75702, (903) 593-5130.

Committees: Foreign Relations; Commerce, Science and Transportation; Judiciary; Rules and Administration; Joint Economic Committee.

U.S. HOUSE of REPRESENTATIVES

(Total districts 435; Republicans 212, Democrats 220, 3 vacant. Texas delegation of 36; 23 Republicans, 13 Democrats.)

District 1 — GOHMERT, Louie, R-Tyler; Washington Office: 2269 RHOB; (202) 225-3035, Fax 226-1230; District Offices: 1121 ESE Loop 323, Ste. 206, Tyler 75701, (903) 561-6349; 101 E. Methvin, Ste. 302, Longview 75601, (903) 236-8597; 300 E. Shepherd, Ste. 210, Lufkin 75901, (936) 632-3180; 102 W. Houston, Marshall 75670, (866) 535-6302; 101 W. Main, Ste. 160, Nacogdoches 75961, (936) 715-9514. Committees: Judiciary, Natural Resources.

District 2 — CRENSHAW, Dan, R-Kingwood; Washington Office: 413 CHOB; (202) 225-6565. District Office: 1801 Kingwood Dr., Ste. 240, Kingwood 77339. Committees: Energy and Commerce.

District 3 — TAYLOR, Van, R-Plano; Washington Office: 1404 LHOB; (202) 225-4201; District Office: 5600 Tennyson Parkway, Ste. 275, Plano 75204. Committees: Financial Services.

District 4 — FALLON, Pat, R-Sherman; Washington Office, 1118 LHOB; (202) 225-6673, Fax 225-3332: District Offices: 6531 Horizon, Ste. A, Rockwall 75032, (972) 771-0100; 100 W. Houston, Ste. 14, Sherman 75090, (903) 820-5170; 2500 N. Robison, Ste. 190, Texarkana 75599, (903) 716-7500. Committees: Armed Services, Oversight and Reform.

District 5 — GOODEN, Lance, R-Terrell; Washington Office: 1722 LHOB; (202) 225-3484. District Office: 18601 LBJ Freeway, Ste. 725, Mesquite 75150. Committee: Financial Services.

District 6 — ELLZEY, Jake, R-Midlothian; Washington Office: 428 CHOB; (202) 225-2002. Committees: Financial Services.

District 7 — FLETCHER, Lizzie Pannill, D-Houston; Washington Office: 119 CHOB; (202) 225-2571; District Office: 5599 San Felipe Rd., Ste. 950, Houston 77056. Committees: Energy and Commerce; Science, Space, and Technology.

District 8 — BRADY, Kevin, R-The Woodlands; Washington Office: 1011 LHOB; (202) 225-4901, Fax 225-5524. District Offices: 200 River Pointe, Ste. 304, Conroe 77304, (936) 441-5700; 1300 11th St., Ste 400, Huntsville 77340, (936) 439-9532. Committee: Joint Committee on Taxation, Ways and Means.

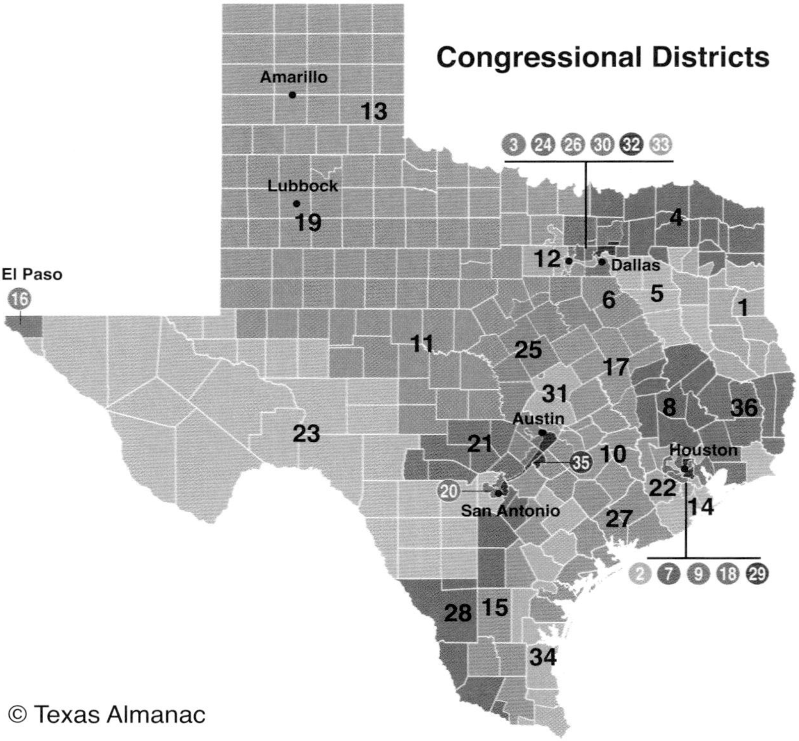

District 9 — GREEN, Al, D-Houston; Washington Office: 2347 RHOB; (202) 225-7508; District Office: 3003 South Loop West, Ste. 460, Houston 77054, (713) 383-9234. Committees: Financial Services, Homeland Security.

District 10 — McCAUL, Michael, R-West Lake Hills; Washington Office: 2001 RHOB; (202) 225-2401, Fax 225-5955. District Offices: 3301 Northland Dr., Ste. 212, Austin 78731, (512) 473-2357; 2000 S. Market, Ste. 303, Brenham 77833, (979) 830-8497; 1773 Westborough Dr., Ste. 223, Katy 77449, (281) 398-1247; 990 Village Sq., Ste. B, Tomball 77375, (281) 255-8372. Committees: Foreign Affairs, Homeland Security.

District 11— PFLUGER, August, R-San Angelo; Washington Office: 1531 LHOB; (202) 225-3605. District Offices: 6 Desta Dr., Ste. 2000, Midland 79705, (432) 687-2390; 501 Center Ave., Brownwood 76801, (325) 646-1950; 132 Houston St., Granbury 76048, (682) 936-2577; 104 W. Sandstone, Llano 78643, (325) 247-2826; 119 W. 4th, Odessa 79761, (866) 882-3811; 33 E. Twohig, Ste. 307, San Angelo 76903, (325) 659-4010. Committees: Foreign Affairs, Homeland Security.

District 12 — GRANGER, Kay, R-Fort Worth; Washington Office: 1026 LHOB; (202) 225-5071, Fax 225-5683; District Office: 1701 River Run Rd., Ste. 407, Fort Worth 76107, (817) 338-0909. Committee: Appropriations.

District 13 — JACKSON, Ronny, R-Levelland; Washington Office: 118 CHOB; (202) 225-3706, Fax 225-3486; District Offices: 620 S. Taylor, Ste. 200, Amarillo 79101, (806) 371-8844; 2525 Kell Blvd., Ste. 406, Wichita Falls 76308, (940) 692-1700. Committee: Armed Services, Foreign Affairs.

District 14 — WEBER, Randy, R-Friendswood; Washington Office: 107 CHOB; (202) 225-2831. District Offices: 505 Orleans, Ste. 103, Beaumont 77701, (409) 835-0108; 122 West Way, Ste. 301, Lake Jackson 77566, (979) 285-0231; 174 Calder Rd., Ste. 150, League City 77573, (281) 316-0231. Committees: Science, Space and Technology; Transportation and Infrastructure.

District 15 — GONZALEZ, Vicente, D-McAllen; Washington Office: 113 CHOB; (202) 225-2531. District Offices: 131 W. Main St., Benavides 78341, (888) 217-0261; 217 E. Miller, Ste. 200, Falfurrias 78355, (361) 209-3027; 1305 W. Hackberry Ave., McAllen 78501, (956) 682-5545; 404 S. Mier St., San Diego 78384, (888) 217-0261; 1243 Cardinal Ln., Seguin 78155, (830) 358-0497. Committees: Financial Services, Foreign Affairs.

District 16 — ESCOBAR, Veronica, D-El Paso; Washington Office: 1330 LHOB; (202) 225-4831. District Office; 221 N. Kansas, Ste. 1500, El Paso 79901, (915) 541-1400. Committees: Armed Services, Judiciary, Ethics.

District 17 — SESSIONS, Pete, R-Waco; Washington Office: 2440 RHOB; (202) 225-6105; District Offices: 400 Austin Ave., Ste. 302, Waco 76701, (254) 732-0748; 2700 Earl Rudder Fwy, S. Hwy. 6, Ste. 4500, College Station 77845, (979) 431-6340. Committees: Financial Services, Oversight and Reform, Science, Space, and Technology.

District 18 — JACKSON LEE, Sheila, D-Houston; Washington Office: 2426 RHOB; (202) 225-3816, Fax 225-3317; District Offices: 1919 Smith, Ste. 1180, Houston 77002, (713) 655-0050; 420 W. 19th St., Houston 77008, (713) 861-4070; 6719 W. Montgomery, Ste. 204, Houston 77091, (713) 691-4882; 4300 Lyons Ave., Houston 77020, (713) 227-7740. Committees: Budget, Homeland Security, Judiciary.

District 19 — ARRINGTON, Jodey, R-Lubbock; Washington Office: 1107 LHOB; (202) 225-4005. District Offices: 500 Chestnut St., Abilene 79602, (325) 763-1611; 1312 Texas Ave., Ste. 219, Lubbock 79401, (806) 763-1611. Committee: Ways and Means.

District 20 — CASTRO, Joaquin, D-San Antonio; Washington Office: 2241 RHOB; (202) 225-3236. District Office: 727 E. Cesar E. Chavez Blvd., Ste. B-128, San Antonio 78206, (210) 348-8216. Committees: Education and Labor; Intelligence; Foreign Affairs.

District 21 — ROY, Chip S., R-Dripping Springs; Washington Office: 1005 LHOB; (202) 225-4236. District Office: 1100 NE Interstate 410 Loop, #640, San Antonio 78209, (210) 821-5024. Committees: Judiciary; Veterans' Affairs.

District 22 — NEHLS, Troy E., R-Richmond; Washington Office: 1104 LHOB; (202) 225-5951, Fax 225-5241. District Offices: 1117 FM 359, Ste. 210, Richmond, 77406, (346) 762-6600. Committees: Transportation and Infrastructure; Veterans' Affairs.

District 23 — GONZALES, Tony, R-San Antonio; Washington Office: 1104 LHOB; (202) 225-4511, Fax 225-2237. District Offices; 6333 De Zavala, Ste A216, San Antonio 78249, (210) 806-9920 (appt. only); 712 E. Gibbs, Ste. 101., Del Rio 78840, (830) 308-6200; 103 W. Callaghan, Fort Stockton 79735, (432) 299-6200; 124 S. Houston, Socorro 79927, (915) 990-1500 (appt only). Committees: Appropriations.

District 24 — VAN DUYNE, Beth, R-Irving; Washington Office: 1337 LHOB; (202) 225-6605, Fax 225-0074. District Office: 3100 Olympus Blvd, Ste. 440, Dallas, 75019, (972) 966-5500. Committees: Transportation and Infratructure; Small Business.

District 25 — WILLIAMS, Roger, R-Austin; Washington Office: 1708 LHOB; (202) 225-9896. District Offices: 1005 Congress Ave., Ste. 925, Austin 78701, (512) 473-8910; 115 S. Main, Ste. 206, Cleburne 76033, (817) 774-2575. Committee: Financial Services; Small Business.

District 26 — BURGESS, Michael, R-Lewisville; Washington Office: 2161 RHOB; (202) 225-7772, Fax 225-2919. District Office: 2000 S. Stemmons Fwy., Ste. 200, Lake Dallas 75065, (972) 497-5031. Committees: Budget; Energy and Commerce; Rules.

District 27 — CLOUD, Michael, R-Victoria; Washington Office: 512 CHOB; (202) 225-7742. District Offices: 101 N. Shoreline Blvd., Ste. 300, Corpus Christi 78401, (361) 884-2222; 5606 N. Navarro, Ste. 203, Victoria 77904, (361) 894-6446. Committees: Agriculture; Oversight and Reform.

District 28 — CUELLAR, Henry, D-Laredo; Washington Office: 2372 RHOB; (202) 225-1640. District Offices: 602 E. Calton Rd., Laredo 78041, (956) 725-0639; 615 E. Houston, Ste. 451, San Antonio 78205, (210) 271-2851; 117 E. Tom Landry, Mission 78572, (956) 424-3942; 100 N. FM 3167, Rio Grande City 78582, (956) 487-5603. Committee: Appropriations.

District 29 — GARCIA, Sylvia, D-Houston; Washington Office: 1620 LHOB; (202) 225-1688; District Office: 11811 East Fwy., Ste. 430, Houston 77029. Committees: Financial Services, Judiciary.

District 30 — JOHNSON, Eddie Bernice, D-Dallas; Washington Office: 2306 RHOB; (202) 225-8885, Fax 225-1477; District Office: 1825 Market Center Blvd., Dallas 75207, (214) 922-8885. Committees: Science, Space, and Technology; Transportation and Infrastructure.

District 31 — CARTER, John, R-Round Rock; Washington Offices: 2208 RHOB; (202) 225-3864. District Offices: 1717 N. I-35, Ste. 303, Round Rock 78664, (512) 246-1600; 6544B S. General Bruce Dr., Temple 76502, (254) 933-1392. Committee: Appropriations.

District 32 — ALLRED, Colin, D-Dallas; Washington Office: 114 CHOB; (202) 225-2231; District Office: 12750 Merit Dr., Ste. 1434, Dallas 75251, (972) 392-0505. Committees: Foreign Affairs, Transportation and Infrastructure, Veterans' Affairs.

District 33 — VEASEY, Marc, D-Fort Worth; Washington Office: 2348 RHOB; (202) 225-9897. District Offices: 1881 Sylvan Ave., Ste 108, Dallas 75028, (214) 741-1387; 6707 Brentwood Stair Rd., Ste. 200, Fort Worth 76112, (817) 920-9086. Committees: Armed Services; Energy and Commerce.

District 34 — VELA, Filemon, D-Brownsville; Washington Office: 307 CHOB; (202) 225-9901. District Offices: 500 E. Main, Alice 78332, (361) 230-9776; 333 Ebony Ave., Brownsville 78520, (956) 544-8352; 1390 W. Expressway 83, San Benito 78586, (956) 276-4497; 301 W. Railroad, Weslaco 78596, (956) 520-8273. Committees: Agriculture, Armed Services.

District 35 — DOGGETT, Lloyd, D-Austin; Washington Office: 2307 RHOB; (202) 225-4865. District Offices: 300 E. 8th, 4th Floor, Austin 78701, (512) 916-5921; 217 W. Travis St., San Antonio 78205, (210) 704-1080. Committees: Agriculture; Armed Services.

District 36 — BABIN, Brian, R-Woodville; Washington Office: 2236 RHOB; (202) 225-1555, Fax 226-0396. District Offices: 203 Ivy Ave., Ste 600, Deer Park 77536, (832) 780-0966; 1201 Childers Rd., Orange 77630, (409) 883-8075; 100 W. Bluff Dr., Woodville 75979, (409) 331-8066. Committees: Transportation and Infrastructure; Science, Space and Technology. ☆

U.S. Tax Collections in Texas

Fiscal Year	Individual Income and Employment Taxes	Corporation Income Taxes	Estate Taxes	Gift Taxes	Excise Taxes	TOTAL U.S. Taxes Collected in Texas
(in thousands) *Information for fiscal years furnished by the Internal Revenue Service.*						
2020	$ 239,159,253	$ 14,508,511	$ 1,023,884	$ 113,036	$ 17,291,862	$ 275,485,613
2019	245,361,121	18,470,193	1,620,965	148,057	22,661,021	292,330,171
2018	240,169,156	15,756,288	1,395,067	135,733	22,592,120	280,048,364
2017	225,236,761	22,939,596	1,314,828	123,822	21,340,788	270,955,237
2016	218,950,277	19,021,716	1,318,116	140,191	21,698,393	261,138,693
2015	226,945,577	32,083,819	1,167,572	115,516	19,591,942	279,904,425
2014	211,993,178	32,585,544	1,557,068	89,865	19,110,528	265,336,183
2013	195,542,035	33,933,242	890,069	596,861	18,950,003	249,912,209
2012	171,880,127	27,984,282	796,227	180,060	18,619,137	219,459,878
2011	160,086,749	21,880,905	117,936	359,987	15,850,240	198,295,817
2010	147,748,859	24,991,374	1,210,600	287,181	14,904,099	189,142,112
2009	158,798,111	24,235,172	1,780,030	242,918	15,465,279	200,521,512
2008	178,761,539	39,971,658	1,549,767	243,043	15,150,053	235,676,058
2007	160,306,445	41,823,425	1,473,490	218,194	21,569,350	225,390,904

Federal Funds Distribution in Texas

	2019		2020
Total all	**$ 207.0 billion**		**$ 320.8 billion**
Direct payments	$ 101.3 billion	Direct payments	$ 128.8 billion
Grants	50.7 billion	Grants	62.9 billion
Contracts	51.0 billion	Contracts	80.6 billion
Other financial assistance	5.0 billion	Other financial assistance	5.5 billion
Loans	–978.0 million	Loans	43.0 million
Top 5 by program			
Social Security retirement	$ 51.7 billion	Social Security retirement	$44.71 billion
Medical assistance	24.2 billion	Paycheck Protection Program	22.15 billion
Veterans compensation	9.2 billion	Medical assistance	3.92 billion
Social Security disability	9.1 billion	Coronavirus Relief Fund	7.47 billion
Social Security survivors	6.8 billion	Veterans compensation	6.34 billion
Top 5 by agency			
Social Security Administration	$ 72.0 billion	Social Security Administration	$ 76.2 billion
Department of Defense	44.1 billion	Department of Defense	72.0 billion
Department of Health and Human Svs	38.8 billion	Small Business Administration	46.1 billion
Department of Veterans Affairs	18.9 billion	Department of Health and Human Svs	46.1 billion
Department of Agriculture	9.7 billion	Department of Veterans Affairs	19.5 billion

Information for fiscal years from USAspending.gov.

Federal Funds Distribution to States, trailing 12 months

Rank	State	Total	Per Capita	Rank	State	Total	Per Capita
1	California	$ 474.8 billion	$12,008	12	Michigan	$ 117.5 billion	$11,806
2	**Texas**	**305.2 billion**	**10,783**	13	Arizona	115.5 billion	16,464
3	New York	268.2 billion	13,513	14	South Carolina	113.4 billion	22,593
4	Florida	258.1 billion	12,300	15	North Carolina	105.7 billion	10,285
5	Pennsylvania	234.8 billion	18,332	16	Georgia	105.6 billion	10,128
6	Indiana	160.9 billion	24,129	17	Massachusetts	101.9 billion	14,857
7	Minnesota	153.3 billion	27,484	18	Wisconsin	99.4 billion	17,147
8	Illinois	141.4 billion	11,045	19	Tennessee	99.0 billion	14,761
9	Virginia	138.5 billion	16,375	20	New Jersey	92.8 billion	10,309
10	Ohio	126.7 billion	10,868				
11	Kentucky	122.4 billion	27,489				

Source: USAspending.gov.

Major Military Installations

Below are listed the major military installations in Texas in 2018. Data are taken from the U.S. Department of Defense Base Structure Report 2017 and other sources. "Civilian" refers to Department of Defense and contractor personnel. *In October 2010, Fort Sam Houston, Lackland AFB, and Randolph AFB were merged into Joint Base San Antonio under the jurisdiction of the U.S. Air Force 502nd Air Base Wing.

U.S. Navy

Naval Air Station Corpus Christi

Location: Corpus Christi (est. 1941).

Address: NAS Corpus Christi, 11001 D St., Corpus Christi 78418

Main phone number: (361) 961-2811

Personnel: 1,369 active-duty; 395 reserve; 710 civilians.

Major units: Naval Air Training Command Headquarters; Training Air Wing 4; Marine Aviation Training Support Group; Coast Guard Air Group; Corpus Christi Army Depot (est. 1961).

Naval Air Station-Joint Reserve Base Fort Worth

Location: westside Fort Worth (est. 1994)

[Carswell, est. in 1942 as Fort Worth Army Air Field, closed in 1993].

Address: NAS-JRB, 1510 Chennault Ave., Fort Worth 76113

Main phone number: (817) 782-3058

Personnel: Active-duty — 2 Army, 232 Navy, 487 Marines, 159 Air Force; Reserve — 605 Army, 2,074 Navy, 1,366 Marines, 975 Air Force, 1,709 Air National Guard; 892 civilians.

Major units: Navy Fleet Logistics Support Squadrons 59; 8th Marine Corps District; Marine Air Group 41; 14th Marine Regiment; Marine Aviation Logistics Squadron 41; Marine Fighter Attach Squadron 112; 136th Airlift Wing, Texas Air National Guard; U.S. Army 90th Aviation Support Battalion; 10th Air Force, 301st Fighter Wing, Air Force Reserve.

Naval Air Station Kingsville

Location: Kingsville (est. 1942).

Address: NAS Kingsville, Texas 78363

Main phone number: (361) 516-6136

Personnel: 363 active-duty; 159 reserve; 243 civilians.

Major units: Training Air Wing Two; Training Squadrons 21 and 22; Naval Auxiliary Landing Field Orange Grove; McMullen Target Range, Escondido Ranch.

U.S. Army

Fort Bliss

Location: El Paso (est. 1849).

Address: Fort Bliss, Texas 79916

Main phone number: (915) 568-2121

Personnel: 25,546 active-duty; 260 reserve; 5,660 civilians.

Major units: 1st Armored Division; 32nd Air and Missile Defense Command; 15th Sustainment Brigade; 5th Armored Brigade; Air Defense Artillery School; 11th Air Defense Artillery Brigades; Joint Task Force North; 204th Military Intelligence Battalion; 212th Fires Brigade; 402nd Field Artillery Brigade; Biggs Army Airfield (est. 1916).

Fort Hood

Location: Killeen (est. 1942).

Address: Fort Hood, Texas 76544

Main phone number: (254) 286-5139

Personnel: 36,391 active-duty; 805 reserve; 6,915 civilians.

Major units: III Corps, Headquarters Command; First Army Division West; 1st Cavalry Division; 13th Sustainment Command; 89th Mili-tary Police Brigade; 3rd Cavalry Regiment; 41st Fires Brigade; 504th Battlefield Surveillance Brigade; Army Operational Test Command; Darnell Army Medical Center.

Fort Sam Houston*

Location: San Antonio (est. 1878).

Address: Fort Sam Houston, Texas 78234

Main phone number: (210) 221-1211

Personnel: 10,462 active-duty; 692 reserve; 10,506 civilians.

Major units: U.S. Army North; U.S. Army South; Brooke Army Medical Center; Institute of Surgical Research; Army Medical Command; Army Medical Dept. Center and School; 5th Recruiting Brigade; 12th Brigade, Western Region (ROTC); Camp Bullis (est. 1917), training area.

Red River Army Depot

Location: 18 miles west of Texarkana (est. 1941).

Address: Red River Army Depot, Texarkana 75507

Main phone number: (903) 334-2141

Personnel: 19 active-duty; 93 reserve; 3,059 civilians.

Major unit: Defense Distribution Center; U.S. Army Tank-Automotive and Armaments Command.

U.S. Air Force

Dyess Air Force Base

Location: Abilene (est. 1942 as Tye Army Airfield, closed at end of World War II, re-established in 1956).

Address: Dyess Air Force Base, Texas 79607

Main phone number: (325) 696-3113

Personnel: 4,221 active-duty; 425 reserve; 710 civilians.

Major units: 7th Bomb Wing (Air Combat Command); 317th Airlift Group.

Goodfellow Air Force Base

Location: San Angelo (est. 1940).

Address: Goodfellow AFB, San Angelo 76908

Main phone number: (325) 654-3876

Personnel: 3,195 active-duty; 29 reserve; 635 civilians.

Major units: 17th Training Wing; 517th Training Squadron; 17th Medical Group. 17th Mission Support Group.

Lackland Air Force Base*

Location: San Antonio (est. 1942 when separated from Kelly Field).

Address: Lackland Air Force Base, Texas 78236

Main phone number: (210) 671-1110

Personnel: 21,532 active-duty; 4,224 reserve; 9,296 civilians.

Major units: 37th Training Wing; 737th Training Group; 341th, 342nd, 343rd, 344th, and 345th Training Squadrons; Defense Language Institute; Inter-American Air Force Academy; Kelly Field Annex (was Kelly Air Force Base, est. 1916).

Laughlin Air Force Base

Location: Del Rio (est. 1942).

Address: Laughlin Air Force Base, Texas 78843

Main phone number: (830) 298-3511

Personnel: 1,288 active-duty; 82 reserve; 1,108 civilians.

Major unit: 47th Flying Training Wing.

Randolph Air Force Base*

Location: San Antonio (est. 1930).

Address: Randolph Air Force Base, Texas 78150

Main phone number: (210) 652-1110

Personnel: 2,649 active-duty; 538 reserve; 5,177 civilians.

Major units: 12th Flying Training Wing; 359th Medical Group; Air Education and Training Command; 902nd Mission Support Group; Air Force Recruiting Command; Air Force Manpower Agency.

Sheppard Air Force Base

Location: Wichita Falls (est. 1941).

Address: Sheppard Air Force Base, Texas 76311

Main phone number: (940) 676-2511

Personnel: 5,973 active-duty; 131 reserve; 1,603 civilians.

Presidential Medal of Freedom

President Donald Trump bestowed a Presidential Medal of Freedom to Babe Didricksen Zaharias posthumously in 2021.

Mildred Ella "Babe" Didricksen Zaharias was born in Port Arthur in 1911 and is widely regarded as one of the greatest athletes of all time. She competed in golf, baseball, basketball, and track and field, winning 2 gold medals in track and field in the 1932 Summer Olympics. Later she became a professional golfer and won 10 LPGA championships.

Major units: 82nd Training Wing; 80th Flying Training Wing; NCO Academy.

Texas Military Forces

Camp Mabry

Location: Austin. Just west of MoPac Blvd.

Address: Box 5218, Austin, Texas 78763

Main phone number: (512) 465-5101

Web site: https://tmd.texas.gov/

Adjutant General of Texas: Maj. General Tracy R. Norris

Major units: Joint Force Headquarters, the Standing Joint Interagency Task Force, the 36th Infantry Division, the 147th Reconnaissance Wing, 149th Fighter Wing, and the 136th Airlift Wing. Texas Air National Guard.

Texas Military Forces Museum: open Wednesday–Sunday, 10 a.m. - 4 p.m.

Tracing their history to early frontier days, the Texas Military Forces are organized into the Army and Air National Guard and the Texas State Guard.

The governor is commander-in-chief of the Texas Military Forces. This command function is exercised through the adjutant general appointed by the governor and approved by federal and state legislative authority.

When not in active federal service, Camp Mabry, in west Austin, serves as the administative and storage headquarters. Camp Mabry was established in the early 1890s as a summer encampment of the Texas Volunteer Guard, a forerunner of the Texas National Guard. The name honors Woodford Haywood Mabry, adjutant general from 1891–1898.

The State Guard, an all-volunteer backup force, was created by the Legislature in 1941. It became an active element of the state military forces in 1965 with a mission of reinforcing the National Guard in emergencies, and replacing National Guard units called into federal service. The State Guard had a membership of approximately 2,200 personnel in 2018.

The Army National Guard is available for state and national emergencies and has been used extensively during natural disasters. There were 17,000 Texans serving in the Texas Army National Guard in 2018.

When the military forces were reorganized following World War II, the Texas Air National Guard was added. Its units augment major Air Force commands. Approximately 3,000 men and women currently make up the Air Guard in the state.

Since 2003, some 31,000 National Guard troops from Texas have served in Iraq and Afghanistan.

In 2018, Adjutant General Norris commanded a total of some 22,000 soldiers, airmen, and civilians.

When called into active federal service, National Guard units come within the chain of command of the Army and Air Force units. ☆

Federal Courts in Texas

Source: The following list of U.S. appeals and district court judges and officials was compiled from court websites.

Texas is divided into four federal judicial districts, each of which is comprised of several divisions. Appeal from all Texas federal courts is to the U.S. Fifth Circuit Court of Appeals in New Orleans.

U.S. Court of Appeals, Fifth Circuit

The Fifth Circuit is composed of Louisiana, Mississippi, and Texas. Sessions are held in each of the states at least once a year and may be scheduled at any location having adequate facilities. U.S. circuit judges are appointed for life and received a salary of $231,800 in 2021.

Circuit Judges:

- Chief Judge, Priscilla R. Owen, Austin.
- Catharina Haynes, James C. Ho, and Don R. Willett, Dallas.
- Edith H. Jones, Gregg J. Costa, Jennifer Walker Elrod, and Jerry E. Smith, Houston.
- James E. Graves Jr., Leslie H. Southwick, and Cory Todd Wilson, Jackson, Miss.
- Stuart Kyle Duncan, Lafayette, La.
- James L. Dennis, Kurt Damian Engelhardt, and Stephen A. Higginson, New Orleans, La.
- Andrew Stephen Oldham, San Antonio.
- Carl E. Stewart, Shreveport, La.

Senior Judges: Fortunato P. Benavides and Patrick E. Higginbotham, Austin; Carolyn Dineen King and Thomas M. Reavley, Houston; Rhesa H. Barksdale and E. Grady Jolly, Jackson, Miss.; John M. Duhé Jr., Jacques L. Wiener Jr., W. Eugene Davis, and Edith Brown Clement, New Orleans, La.

Clerk of Court: Lyle W. Cayce, New Orleans, La.

U.S. District Courts

U.S. district judges are appointed for life and received a salary in 2021 of $218,600.

Northern Texas District

www.txnd.uscourts.gov

District Judges:

- Chief Judge, Barbara M.G. Lynn, Dallas.
- Matthew J. Kacsmaryk, Amarillo.
- Jane J. Boyle, Ada Brown, David C. Godbey, Ed Kinkeade, Sam A. Lindsay, Reed O'Connor, Karen Gren Scholer, and Brantley Starr, Dallas.
- Mark T. Pittman, Fort Worth.
- James Wesley Hendrix, Lubbock.

Senior Judges: A. Joe Fish and Sidney A. Fitzwater, Dallas; John H. McBryde and Terry R. Means, Fort Worth; Sam R. Cummings, Lubbock.

Clerk of District Court: Karen Sublett Mitchell, Dallas.

U.S. Attorney: Prerak Shah.

Federal Public Defender: Jason Hawkins.

U.S. Marshal: (vacant).

Bankruptcy Judges: Chief Judge, Harlin D. Hale, Dallas. Judges, Stacey G.C. Jernigan and Michelle V. Larson, Dallas; Edward L. Morris and Mark X. Mullin, Fort Worth; Robert L. Jones, Lubbock.

Following are the divisions of the Northern District and the counties in each division:

Abilene Division

Callahan, Eastland, Fisher, Haskell, Howard, Jones, Mitchell, Nolan, Shackelford, Stephens, Stonewall, Taylor, and Throckmorton. **Magistrate:** John R. Parker, Abilene. **Courtroom Deputy:** Jennifer Chittum.

Amarillo Division

Armstrong, Briscoe, Carson, Castro, Childress, Collingsworth, Dallam, Deaf Smith, Donley, Gray, Hall, Hansford, Hartley, Hemphill, Hutchinson, Lipscomb, Moore, Ochiltree, Oldham, Parmer, Potter, Randall, Roberts, Sherman, Swisher, and Wheeler. **Magistrate:** Lee Ann Reno, Amarillo. **Deputy-in-charge:** Christopher Kordes.

Dallas Division

Dallas, Ellis, Hunt, Johnson, Kaufman, Navarro, and Rockwall. **Magistrates:** David L. Horan, Irma Carrillo Ramirez, Rebecca Rutherford, and Renee H. Toliver, Dallas. **Courtroom Deputies:** Marie Gonzales, Lavenia Price, Shakira Todd, and Mervin Wright.

Fort Worth Division

Comanche, Erath, Hood, Jack, Palo Pinto, Parker, Tarrant, and Wise. **Magistrates:** Jeffrey L. Cureton and Hal R. Ray Jr., Fort Worth. **Courtroom Deputies:** Julie Harwell and Elsherie Moore.

Lubbock Division

Bailey, Borden, Cochran, Crosby, Dawson, Dickens, Floyd, Gaines, Garza, Hale, Hockley, Kent, Lamb, Lubbock, Lynn, Motley, Scurry, Terry, and Yoakum. **Magistrate:** D. Gordon Bryant Jr., Lubbock. **Courtroom Deputy:** Zelma Medrano.

San Angelo Division

Brown, Coke, Coleman, Concho, Crockett, Glasscock, Irion, Menard, Mills, Reagan, Runnels, Schleicher, Sterling, Sutton, and Tom Green. **Division Manager:** Erik Paltrow.

Wichita Falls Division

Archer, Baylor, Clay, Cottle, Foard, Hardeman, King, Knox, Montague, Wichita, Wilbarger, and Young. **Magistrate:** Hal R. Ray Jr., Wichita Falls.

Western Texas District

www.txwd.uscourts.gov

District Judges:

- Chief Judge, Orlando L. Garcia, San Antonio.
- Robert Pitman and Lee Yeakel, Austin.
- Alia Moses, Del Rio.
- Kathleen Cardone, David C. Guaderrama, and Frank Montalvo, El Paso.
- David Counts, Midland.
- Fred Biery, Jason Pulliam, and Xavier Rodriguez, San Antonio.
- Alan Albright, Waco.

Senior Judges: James R. Nowlin and Sam Sparks, Austin; David Briones, El Paso; Robert A. Junell, Midland and Pecos; David A. Ezra, San Antonio.

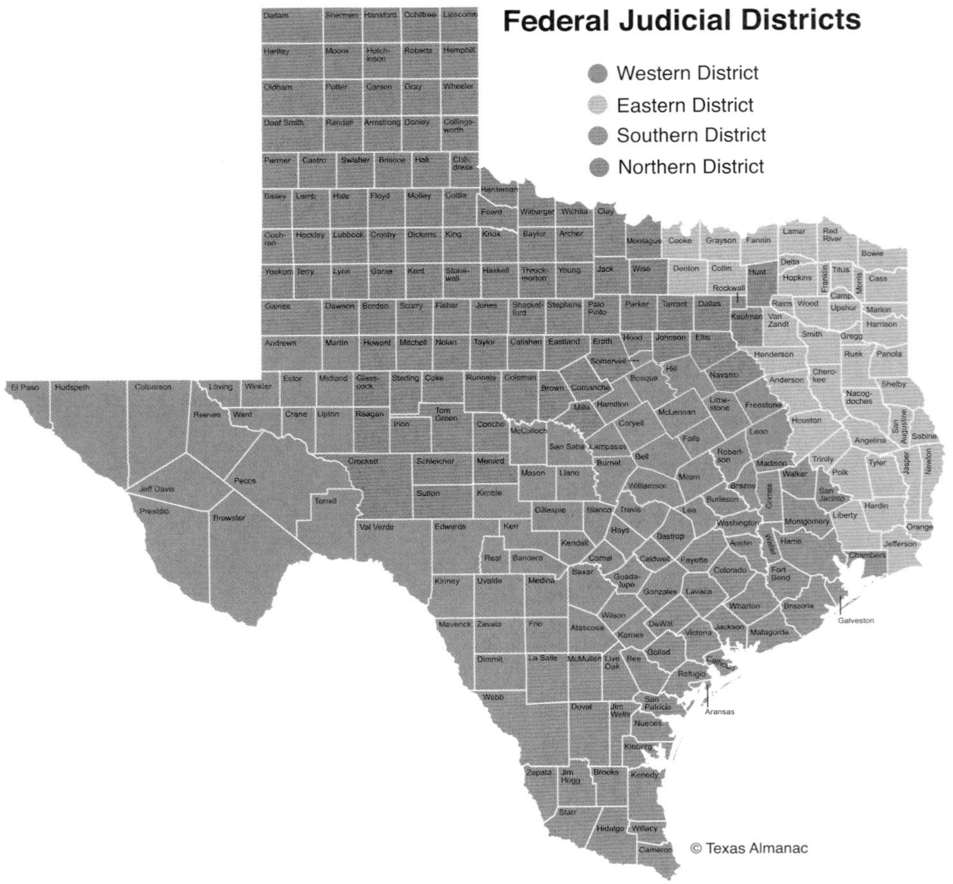

Clerk of District Court: Jeannette Clack, San Antonio.

U.S. Attorney: Ashley Hoff.

Federal Public Defender: Maureen Scott Franco.

U.S. Marshal: Susan L. Pamerleau.

Bankruptcy Judges: Chief Judge, Ronald B. King. Judges, H. Christopher Mott and Tony M. Davis, Austin; Craig A. Gargotta, San Antonio.

Following are the divisions of the Western District, and the counties in each division.

Austin Division

Bastrop, Blanco, Burleson, Burnet, Caldwell, Gillespie, Hays, Kimble, Lampasas, Lee, Llano, Mason, McCulloch, San Saba, Travis, Washington, and Williamson. **Magistrates:** Andrew W. Austin, Susan Hightower, and Mark Lane, Austin. **Courtroom Deputies:** Ka Kin "Zing" Cheng, Amanda Deichert, and James Ferrell.

Del Rio Division

Edwards, Kinney, Maverick, Terrell, Uvalde, Val Verde, and Zavala. **Magistrates:** Victor Roberto Garcia and Collis White, Del Rio. **Courtroom Deputies:** Mary Cienega and Carmen Levrie.

El Paso Division

El Paso, Hudspeth. **Magistrates**: Anne T. Berton, Robert F. Castañeda, Leon Schydlower, and Miguel A. Torres, El Paso. **Courtroom Deputies:** Veronica Medina, Veronica Montoya, Cecie Rodriguez, and Rita Velez.

Fort Hood Division

Fort Hood Military Reservation. **Courtroom Deputy:** Michelle Ortiz.

Midland-Odessa Division

Andrews, Crane, Ector, Martin, Midland, and Upton. Court for the Midland-Odessa Division is held at Midland, but may, at the discretion of the court, be held in Odessa. **Magistrate:** Ronald C. Griffin, Midland. **Courtroom Deputy:** Monica Ramirez.

Pecos Division

Brewster, Culberson, Jeff Davis, Loving, Pecos, Presidio, Reeves, Ward, and Winkler. **Magistrate:** David B. Fannin, Alpine. **Courtroom Deputy:** Yvette Lujan.

San Antonio Division

Atascosa, Bandera, Bexar, Comal, Dimmit, Frio, Gonzales, Guadalupe, Karnes, Kendall, Kerr, Medina, Real, and Wilson. **Magistrates:** Henry J. Bemporad, Elizabeth S.

"Betsy" Chestney, and Richard B. Farrer, San Antonio. **Courtroom Deputies:** Amy Jackson, Valeria Sandoval, and Crystal Sosa.

Waco Division

Bell, Bosque, Coryell, Falls, Freestone, Hamilton, Hill, Leon, Limestone, McLennan, Milam, Robertson, and Somervell. **Magistrate:** Jeffrey C. Manske, Waco. **Courtroom Deputy:** Jennifer Galindo-Beaver.

Eastern Texas District

www.txed.uscourts.gov

District Judges:

- Chief Judge, Rodney Gilstrap, Marshall.
- Ron Clark, Marcia A. Crone, Thad Heartfield, and Michael J. Truncale, Beaumont.
- Sean D. Jordan and Richard Schell, Plano.
- Amos L. Mazzant III, Sherman.
- Robert W. Schroeder III, Texarkana.
- J. Campbell Barker and Jeremy D. Kernodle, Tyler.

Clerk of District Court: David A. O'Toole.

U.S. Attorney: Nicholas J. Ganjei.

Federal Public Defender: John D. McElroy.

U.S. Marshal: John M. Garrison.

Bankruptcy Judges: Chief Judge, Brenda T. Rhoades, Plano; Joshua Searcy, Tyler.

Following are the divisions of the Eastern District and the counties in each division:

Beaumont Division

Hardin, Jasper, Jefferson, Liberty, Newton, and Orange. **Magistrates:** Keith F. Giblin and Zach Hawthorn, Beaumont. **Courtroom Deputies:** Tonya Piper and Sherre White.

Lufkin Division

Angelina, Houston, Nacogdoches, Polk, Sabine, San Augustine, Shelby, Trinity, and Tyler. **Deputy-in-charge:** Brandy Fairley.

Marshall Division

Camp, Cass, Harrison, Marion, Morris, and Upshur. **Magistrate:** Roy Payne, Marshall. **Courtroom Deputy:** Becky Andrews.

Sherman Division

Collin, Cooke, Delta, Denton, Fannin, Grayson, Hopkins, and Lamar. **Magistrates:** Christine A. Nowak, Sherman, and Kimberly C. Priest Johnson, Plano. **Courtroom Deputies:** Jane Amerson and Karen Lee.

Texarkana Division

Bowie, Franklin, Red River, and Titus. **Magistrate:** Caroline M. Craven, Texarkana. **Courtroom Deputy:** Hailey Amox.

Tyler Division

Anderson, Cherokee, Gregg, Henderson, Panola, Rains, Rusk, Smith, Van Zandt, and Wood. **Magistrates:** John D. Love and K. Nicole Mitchell, Tyler. **Courtroom Deputies:** Sharon Baum and Lisa Hardwick.

Southern Texas District

www.txs.uscourts.gov

District Judges:

- Chief Judge, Lee H. Rosenthal, Houston.
- Rolando Olvera and Fernando Rodriguez Jr., Brownsville.
- David S. Morales, Nelva Gonzales Ramos, and Drew B. Tipton, Corpus Christi.
- Jeffrey V. Brown, Galveston.
- Alfred H. Bennett, Keith P. Ellison, Charles Eskridge, Vanessa D. Gilmore, Andrew S. Hanen, George C. Hanks Jr., and Lynn N. Hughes, Houston.
- Marina Garcia Marmolejo and Diana Saldaña, Laredo.
- Micaela Alvarez, Randy Crane, and Ricardo H. Hinojosa, McAllen.

Senior Judges: Janis Graham Jack, Corpus Christi; David Hittner, Kenneth M. Hoyt, Sim Lake, Gray H. Miller, Hilda G. Tagle, and Ewing Werlein Jr., Houston; John D. Rainey, Victoria.

Clerk of Court: Nathan Ochsner, Houston.

U. S. Attorney: Jennifer Lowery, Houston.

Federal Public Defender: Marjorie A. Meyers.

U.S. Marshal: T. Michael O'Connor.

Bankruptcy Judges: Chief Judge, David Jones, Houston; Judges, Marvin Isgur, Christopher M. Lopez, and Jeffrey P. Norman, Houston; Eduardo V. Rodriguez, McAllen.

Following are the divisions of the Southern District and the counties in each division:

Brownsville Division

Cameron and Willacy. **Magistrates:** Ronald G. Morgan and Ignacio Torteya III, Brownsville. **Deputy-in-charge:** Rosy D'Venturi.

Corpus Christi Division

Aransas, Bee, Brooks, Duval, Jim Wells, Kenedy, Kleberg, Live Oak, Nueces, and San Patricio. **Magistrates:** Julie K. Hampton and Jason B. Libby, Corpus Christi. **Deputy-in-charge:** Jared Marks.

Galveston Division

Brazoria, Chambers, Galveston, and Matagorda. **Magistrate:** Andrew M. Edison, Galveston. **Deputy-in-charge:** Lucia Smith.

Houston Division

Austin, Brazos, Colorado, Fayette, Fort Bend, Grimes, Harris, Madison, Montgomery, San Jacinto, Walker, Waller, and Wharton. **Magistrates:** Peter Bray, Christina A. Bryan, Dena Hanovice Palermo, Sam S. Sheldon, and Frances H. Stacy, Houston. **Deputy-in-charge:** Darlene Hansen.

Laredo Division

Jim Hogg, La Salle, McMullen, Webb, and Zapata. **Magistrates:** Christopher A. dos Santos, John A. Kazen, and Diana Song Quiroga, Laredo. **Deputy-in-charge:** Aimee Veliz.

McAllen Division

Hidalgo and Starr. **Magistrates:** Juan F. Alanis, J. Scott Hacker, and Nadia S. Medrano, McAllen. **Deputy-in-charge:** Velma T. Barrera.

Victoria Division

Calhoun, DeWitt, Goliad, Jackson, Lavaca, Refugio, and Victoria. **Deputy-in-charge:** Lana Tesch. ☆

Law Enforcement

TEXAS CRIME HISTORY

CRIME PROFILE OF TEXAS COUNTIES

CORRECTIONAL INSTITUTIONS IN TEXAS

Texas Army National Guard soldiers were called in to support local law enforcement during a protest against police brutality in Austin, Texas on May 31, 2020. U.S. Army photo by Charles E. Spirtos/Flickr.

Crime in Texas

Source: Texas Department of Public Safety, Austin; www.dps.texas.gov

The crime statistics in this chapter are all thanks to the **Uniform Crime Reporting (UCR)** programs used by law enforcement agencies in Texas, and nationwide. The first of these programs in the United States was the Committee on Uniform Crime Records, developed by the International Association of Chiefs of Police (IACP) in the 1920s. The first IACP crime collection program, in 1930, was voluntary, and gathered information from 400 police agencies in 43 states. The FBI was authorized as the national clearinghouse for the information collected by that program.

UCR programs collect data on a summary basis, which provides reliable information about crime, but has many limitations. In 1985 a new system was outlined for **Incident Based Reporting (IBR)**, whereby crime data is collected electronically, and includes the circumstances of each incident. The national system, called NIBRS, has been slow to grow, but state programs and the FBI have worked in partnership to assist in the transition. In 2015, the Criminal Justice Information Services Division's Advisory Policy Board set a goal to **sunset summary reporting systems and adopt NIBRS by January 1, 2021.**

Texas first adopted the Uniform Crime Report in 1976, and the Department of Public Safety accepted the responsibility of collecting, validating, and tabulating reports from across the state. The Uniform Crime Reporting Section, created specifically for this purpose, is part of the Crime Records Service division of the department.

The state became certified to collect NIBRS data in 1998, and in 2015, House Bill 11 set a goal to transition all of Texas to NIBRS by September 1, 2019. About 550 agencies met that goal. Another 900 agencies pledged to transition by January 1, 2021. (We have not yet been able to confirm if this goal had been met.)

In Texas, the Department of Public Safety collects data for the national UCR program from police, sheriff's offices, and its own officers. Data are estimated for non-reporting agencies and those that did not have 12 months of data. Agencies that contributed data for the 2019 Crime in Texas report include: 76 college and university police departments, 58 independent school district and zero population police departments, 247 county sheriff's offices, and 673 city police departments.

Mass Attacks in Texas

According to the 2019 Crime in Texas report, the largest challenge facing the law enforcement community that year was mass attacks in public places. The FBI reported that Texas led the nation in active shooter events in 2019. The six that occurred in the state resulted in 36 deaths and 52 wounded. The U.S. Secret Service reported that Texas had 3 of the country's 34 mass attacks in public places that same year, resulting in the death of 33 people. Below is a summary of those three attacks.

- On May 29, 2019 a gunman shot three people in Liberty County, killing one, at a plumbing company. He fled the scene then shot and injured a sheriff's deputy during pursuit. The gunman shot and killed himself before he could be arrested.
- On August 3, 2019 a gunman killed 23 people and injured another 25 when he opened fire in a Wal-Mart in El Paso. Although the accused's trial began in 2020, it was delayed due to the COVID-19 pandemic.
- On August 31, 2019 a gunman fired at police officers before going on a shooting rampage through Midland-Odessa, killing 7 people and wounding 25. The attack ended when the gunman was shot and killed by police.

After these attacks, Governor Abbott created a task force of state legislators and subject matter experts to find ways to detect and prevent mass attacks before they happen.

Crime Summary, 2019

During 2019, there was a reported total of 805,879 index offenses in Texas. This represents a crime-volume increase of 1.1 percent when compared to 796,924 reported offenses in 2018.

In 2019, there were 2,779.3 crimes per 100,000 people, compared with 2,776.6 in 2018, according to data compiled by the Department of Public Safety's Uniform Crime Reporting (UCR) program. The 2019 crime rate is based on a population of 28,995,881.

Monthly crime variations show that, in general, crime occurrences peaked in the month of July. During 2019, Texas law enforcement officers made 698,834 arrests.

Index Crimes

Of the seven major crime categories, the UCR defines violent crime as murder, rape, robbery, and aggravated assault; property crime is defined as burglary, larceny-theft, and motor vehicle theft. The 2019 violent crime rate increased 1.6 percent from 2018, and the nonviolent, or property, crime rate increased 1.0 percent from 2018.

Texas Crime Rate* by Offense, 2019

Crime	2019	2018	% Change
Murder	4.8	4.6	4.9%
Rape	50.5	51.9	-2.6%
Robbery	99.5	98.5	1.0%
Aggravated Assault	260.7	258.4	0.9%
Violent Crime Total	**415.6**	**413.4**	**0.5%**
Burglary	387.7	409.4	-5.3%
Larceny-Theft	1,711.5	1,710.8	0.0%
Motor Vehicle Theft	264.5	242.9	8.9%
Property Crime Total	**2,363.7**	**2,363.2**	**0.0%**
Index Crime Total	**2,779.3**	**2,776.6**	**0.1%**

*Crime rate based on the 2019 Texas population of 28,995,881

Source: 2019 Crime in Texas, TDPS

The estimated value of property stolen during the commission of index crimes in 2019 was more than $2.2 billion, and about 26 percent of that property was recovered.

Arson

The reported number of arsons committed in Texas in 2019 was 2,366, a decrease of 3.0 percent from 2018. In 2019, arson victims suffered losses of $50.9 million, a 34.7-percent decrease when compared with 2018 arson losses of nearly $80 million.

Family Violence

Family violence decreased by 0.1 percent in 2019 from 2018. In 2019, there were 196,902 reported incidents of family violence involving 211,536 victims and 206,275 offenders. In 2016, there were 197,023 reported incidents of family violence involving 212,885 victims and 207,360 offenders.

DUI and Drug-Related Crimes

In 2019 there were 71,959 DUI arrests in Texas, a decrease of 2.7 percent from 2018. Of those arrests,4,448 or 6.2 percent were of persons under the age of 21.

Texas reported 128,295 drug abuse arrests in 2019, a decrease of 13.6 percent from the previous year. Sales and manufacturing arrests accounted for 19,958 of the total (about 16 percent), and the remaining 108,337 arrests (84 percent) were for possession.

In a breakdown by drug type, the arrests for sales and manufacturing were 58.6 percent synthetic narcotics, 17.3 percent opium or cocaine, 9.4 percent marijuana, and 14.6 percent other. By contrast, possession arrests were 41.7 percent marijuana, 18.8 percent opium or cocaine, 9.6 percent synthetic narcotics, and 29.9 percent other.

Hate Crimes

There were 407 hate crimes incidents reported in Texas in 2019, an increase of 7.1 percent from 2018. Incidents involved a total of 521 victims and 499 offenders.

Reporting for Hate Crime bias improved dramatically in 2019. Broken down by bias motivation, 64.5 percent of incidents were motivated by race/ethnicity/ancestry, 15.5 percent by sexual orientation, 9.8 percent by religion, 4.5 percent by disability, 1.9 percent by gender, and 1 percent by gender identity. Crimes occurred most frequently in residences, and 55.7 percent of offenders were white, 21.2 percent were black, 3.3 percent were multi-racial, and the racial group of 18.7 percent of offenders was unknown.

Law Enforcement Assaults and Deaths

Assaults on law enforcement personnel increased 4.8 percent in 2019 to 4,838. Nine law officers were killed in the line of duty in 2019, and another five died in duty-related accidents. ☆

Texas Index Crimes by Volume 2000–2019

Year	Murder	Rape*	Robbery	Assault	Violent Crime Total	Change from Prior Year	Burglary	Larceny/ Theft	Motor Vehicle Theft	Property Crime Total	Change from Prior Year
2000	1,236	7,821	30,186	73,987	**113,230**	0.7%	188,205	634,575	92,878	**915,658**	2.1%
2001	1,331	8,191	35,330	77,221	**122,073**	7.8%	204,240	669,587	102,838	**976,665**	6.7%
2002	1,305	8,541	37,599	78,713	**126,158**	3.3%	212,702	690,028	102,943	**1,005,673**	3.0%
2003	1,417	7,986	37,000	75,706	**122,109**	–3.2%	219,733	697,790	98,174	**1,015,697**	1.0%
2004	1,360	8,401	35,811	75,983	**121,555**	–0.5%	220,079	696,220	93,844	**1,010,143**	–0.5%
2005	1,405	8,505	35,781	75,409	**121,100**	–0.4%	219,733	676,022	93,471	**989,226**	–2.1%
2006	1,385	8,407	37,271	74,624	**121,687**	0.5%	215,754	648,083	95,750	**959,587**	–3.0%
2007	1,415	8,430	38,777	73,570	**122,192**	0.4%	228,325	662,481	94,026	**984,832**	2.6%
2008	1,373	8.004	37,757	76,487	**115,625**	–5.4%	230,263	654,133	85,411	**969,807**	–1.5%
2009	1,327	8,286	38,041	74,135	**121,789**	5.3%	240,193	678,340	76,617	**995,150**	2.6%
2010	1,247	7,626	32,865	71,561	**113,299**	–7.0%	229,269	654,484	68,220	**951,973**	–4.3%
2011	1,089	7,445	28,399	68,028	**104,961**	–7.4%	215,512	613,528	63,379	**892,419**	–6.3%
2012	1,145	7,692	30,375	67,050	**106,262**	1.2%	204,976	605,362	64,982	**875,320**	–1.9%
2013	1,151	7,443	31,852	65,267	**105,713**	–0.5%	190,567	604,389	65,671	**860,627**	–1.7%
2014	1,187	11,466	30,857	65,338	**108,848**	3.0%	166,429	570,385	67,741	**804,555**	–6.5%
2015	1,314	12,208	31,883	67,358	**112,763**	3.6%	152,444	555,867	67,081	**775,392**	–3.6%
2016	1,473	13,320	33,250	72,609	**120,652**	7.0%	148,073	548,941	68,523	**765,537**	–1.3%
2017	1,412	14,332	32,120	75,347	**123,211**	2.1%	133,145	518,414	67,285	**718,844**	–6.1%
2018	1,324	14,891	28,273	74,165	**118,653**	–3.7%	117,513	491,028	69,730	**678,271**	–5.6%
2019	1,403	14,656	28,854	75,595	**120,508**	1.6%	112,405	496,279	76,687	**685,371**	1.0%

* In 2014, the FBI changed the definition of rape.

Source: Annual crime reports published by TDPS.

Crime Profile of Texas Counties, 2019

	No. Agencies Reporting	Murder	Rape	Robbery	Assault	Burglary	Larceny-Theft	Auto Theft	Total Index Crimes	Crime Rate per 100,000
Anderson	3	2	23	14	99	249	511	80	978	1,696.2
Andrews	2	0	13	3	68	69	188	23	364	1,970.4
Angelina	6	2	56	40	199	503	1,587	183	2,570	2,968.8
Aransas	4	0	25	12	110	282	728	64	1,221	3,924.5
Archer	1	0	3	0	3	2	0	0	8	451.9
Armstrong	1	0	0	0	1	10	5	3	19	1,011.2
Atascosa	6	1	9	11	66	219	653	122	1,081	2,106.0
Austin	5	0	5	3	38	80	147	30	303	1,009.7
Bailey	2	0	1	0	5	20	34	2	62	889.8
Bandera	1	0	2	1	9	95	143	27	277	1,205.4
Bastrop	5	6	57	30	178	271	793	136	1,471	1,649.3
Baylor	2	0	1	0	4	6	18	4	33	930.9
Bee	2	2	3	5	39	154	332	20	555	1,709.1
Bell	13	18	232	193	569	1,384	4,939	616	7,951	2,221.2
Bexar	27	122	1,818	2,122	8,128	9,707	58,687	8,623	89,207	4,436.8
Blanco	3	0	6	1	12	23	25	12	79	670.3
Borden	1	0	1	0	0	5	4	1	11	1,705.4
Bosque	3	0	3	0	25	44	42	11	125	729.5
Bowie	8	4	65	48	294	501	1,809	130	2,851	3,034.8
Brazoria	23	10	117	132	403	986	4,750	470	6,868	1,798.2
Brazos	4	3	157	101	366	817	3,421	337	5,202	2,266.4
Brewster	3	1	2	0	16	30	15	7	71	770.9
Briscoe	1	0	0	0	0	2	0	1	3	200.9
Brooks	2	0	0	1	15	48	62	1	127	1,799.6
Brown	4	0	28	7	85	192	643	58	1,013	2,689.4
Burleson	3	1	7	3	16	44	97	4	172	933.7
Burnet	6	0	26	7	87	164	390	57	731	1,466.2
Caldwell	4	0	13	3	61	67	259	23	426	986.4
Calhoun	3	0	16	3	58	81	174	14	346	1,796.5
Callahan	3	0	0	0	8	58	55	14	135	966.5
Cameron	21	4	233	236	1,115	1,674	8,677	353	12,292	2,903.8
Camp	2	0	6	1	22	38	82	11	160	1,227.7
Carson	2	1	2	3	23	21	23	6	79	1,328.2
Cass	5	1	19	6	70	110	281	27	514	1,742.6
Castro	2	0	4	0	25	24	38	10	101	1,335.6
Chambers	3	3	9	9	83	148	533	35	820	2,104.0
Cherokee	4	0	0	0	5	23	65	5	98	1,755.6
Childress	2	0	1	0	4	14	23	4	46	632.5
Clay	1	0	8	0	8	33	49	21	119	1,149.1
Cochran	1	0	0	0	3	12	15	0	30	1,078.4
Coke	1	0	0	0	2	10	0	4	16	476.8
Coleman	2	1	3	0	20	21	15	2	62	1,153.9
Collin	17	7	266	259	635	1,458	9,713	897	13,235	1,302.4

Source: Crime in Texas 2019 report, TDPS.

Crime Profile of Texas Counties, 2019

	No. Agencies Reporting	Murder	Rape	Robbery	Assault	Burglary	Larceny-Theft	Auto Theft	Total Index Crimes	Crime Rate per 100,000
Collingsworth	1	N/A	N/A	N/A	N/A	N/A	N/A	N/A	N/A	N/A
Colorado	4	1	12	3	22	54	154	19	265	1,254.3
Comal	4	2	61	34	263	405	1,267	166	2,198	1,316.9
Comanche	3	2	2	1	13	43	143	15	219	1,634.6
Concho	1	0	0	0	11	8	0	0	19	444.8
Cooke	3	3	20	8	91	97	350	23	592	1,489.4
Coryell	3	0	22	7	127	185	735	27	1,103	1,472.3
Cottle	1	0	0	0	0	0	0	0	0	0.0
Crane	2	0	3	0	4	7	7	6	27	560.2
Crockett	1	0	0	1	1	9	5	4	20	579.2
Crosby	3	0	1	1	3	29	13	4	51	1,120.1
Culberson	1	N/A	N/A	N/A	N/A	N/A	N/A	N/A	N/A	N/A
Dallam	2	0	5	0	27	54	101	19	206	2,085.4
Dallas	33	244	1,274	5,806	8,432	13,979	52,851	15,269	97,855	3,324.8
Dawson	2	2	7	12	55	136	296	30	538	4,379.7
Deaf Smith	2	0	2	5	82	85	249	36	459	2,473.5
Delta	1	0	0	0	1	10	16	1	28	525.4
Denton	25	7	358	177	457	1,009	6,250	672	8,930	1,322.5
DeWitt	2	1	11	0	70	75	214	15	386	2,426.6
Dickens	2	0	0	0	1	5	1	2	9	406.9
Dimmit	1	1	2	0	8	39	93	7	150	1,459.1
Donley	1	2	0	0	2	12	16	2	34	1,046.2
Duval	3	0	0	0	19	27	43	41	130	1,084.4
Eastland	6	3	15	1	18	65	89	14	205	1,181.9
Ector	4	17	155	149	1,153	715	3,689	866	6,744	4,044.7
Edwards	1	0	1	0	1	1	2	2	7	366.9
Ellis	9	3	37	39	132	379	1,672	174	2,436	1,404.1
El Paso	11	41	369	363	2,029	1,293	9,594	1,004	14,693	1,748.7
Erath	4	2	32	9	60	131	405	23	662	1,547.5
Falls	2	0	2	8	19	27	25	13	94	623.8
Fannin	4	2	18	2	42	84	262	41	451	1,388.3
Fayette	4	0	17	1	38	72	183	14	325	1,285.1
Fisher	1	0	0	0	0	9	5	0	14	368.5
Floyd	2	0	2	1	26	15	37	4	85	1,482.1
Foard	2	0	0	0	0	1	2	0	3	255.1
Fort Bend	11	15	216	235	1,016	1,251	7,190	568	10,491	1,358.3
Franklin	1	0	1	1	5	10	15	2	32	319.4
Freestone	4	1	8	3	38	92	138	18	298	1,513.9
Frio	3	0	0	1	24	93	123	25	266	1,327.7
Gaines	3	2	5	2	29	56	127	19	240	1,130.8
Galveston	17	16	255	200	447	1,022	5,284	752	7,976	2,242.6
Garza	1	0	5	0	10	17	11	2	45	686.9
Gillespie	2	1	3	1	20	17	163	6	211	784.9

Source: Crime in Texas 2019 report, TDPS.

Crime Profile of Texas Counties, 2019

	No. Agencies Reporting	Murder	Rape	Robbery	Assault	Burglary	Larceny-Theft	Auto Theft	Total Index Crimes	Crime Rate per 100,000
Glasscock	1	0	0	0	1	5	16	4	26	1,857.1
Goliad	1	1	3	2	16	19	49	11	101	1,331.9
Gonzales	4	1	18	1	92	57	217	22	408	1,958.2
Gray	2	0	18	8	115	165	517	32	855	3,941.9
Grayson	14	5	71	40	222	491	1,439	214	2,482	1,870.8
Gregg	7	9	96	77	344	639	2,453	293	3,911	2,981.7
Grimes	2	0	8	4	28	100	130	30	300	1,056.1
Guadalupe	4	3	75	31	160	320	1,535	120	2,244	1,471.6
Hale	4	0	5	4	56	158	421	32	676	2,111.1
Hall	2	1	0	1	2	9	9	0	22	774.4
Hamilton	2	0	5	0	9	16	30	4	64	908.7
Hansford	2	0	0	0	4	7	6	6	23	425.0
Hardeman	2	0	0	0	5	6	11	1	23	594.3
Hardin	5	3	5	7	75	132	347	79	648	1,133.7
Harris	45	392	2,469	11,920	19,935	26,031	112,958	20,770	194,475	4,071.5
Harrison	4	6	4	20	152	352	837	112	1,483	2,300.6
Hartley	1	0	0	0	0	3	3	4	10	348.8
Haskell	2	0	1	0	8	12	21	9	51	889.4
Hays	5	9	138	58	249	474	2,545	261	3,734	1,617.2
Hemphill	1	0	0	0	2	1	12	0	15	394.0
Henderson	10	2	73	14	123	414	524	128	1,278	1,602.4
Hidalgo	21	19	433	331	1,495	2,470	15,638	750	21,136	2,449.0
Hill	4	1	12	4	40	84	431	46	618	1,771.9
Hockley	3	2	25	10	117	143	318	30	645	2,822.5
Hood	2	1	15	8	57	133	595	72	881	1,458.0
Hopkins	3	1	15	7	37	37	144	49	290	788.4
Houston	3	1	2	0	35	72	157	12	279	1,215.1
Howard	2	3	15	21	166	226	903	193	1,527	4,192.8
Hudspeth	1	0	0	0	8	3	9	2	22	442.5
Hunt	5	7	38	37	394	302	947	166	1,891	2,065.8
Hutchinson	2	0	16	4	30	100	251	25	426	2,224.0
Irion	1	0	0	0	4	2	10	0	16	1,065.2
Jack	2	0	2	2	11	25	34	11	85	969.4
Jackson	3	1	4	2	9	28	92	13	149	3,001.3
Jasper	3	3	18	2	84	239	467	78	891	2,498.7
Jeff Davis	1	0	2	0	2	4	6	1	15	673.6
Jefferson	7	29	148	428	1,202	1,476	4,569	589	8,441	3,326.8
Jim Hogg	1	0	0	0	5	10	7	3	25	479.8
Jim Wells	3	0	11	11	188	362	778	51	1,401	3,654.1
Johnson	8	1	104	38	323	434	1,496	241	2,637	1,456.6
Jones	5	0	2	1	9	46	78	8	144	1,026.2
Karnes	3	1	2	2	50	99	158	29	341	2,178.9
Kaufman	7	4	54	32	149	417	1,297	226	2,179	1,662.9

Source: Crime in Texas 2019 report, TDPS.

Crime Profile of Texas Counties, 2019

	No. Agencies Reporting	Murder	Rape	Robbery	Assault	Burglary	Larceny-Theft	Auto Theft	Total Index Crimes	Crime Rate per 100,000
Kendall	2	0	7	4	31	45	350	49	486	1,086.7
Kenedy	1	0	0	0	0	2	3	3	8	1,810.0
Kent	1	0	0	0	4	2	3	0	9	1,265.8
Kerr	3	1	29	1	71	80	413	35	630	1,201.6
Kimble	2	0	1	1	5	7	3	1	18	418.0
King	1	0	0	0	0	0	0	0	0	0.0
Kinney	1	0	0	0	0	1	0	0	1	49.8
Kleberg	3	3	30	14	100	203	592	28	970	3,147.0
Knox	3	0	2	0	1	24	14	5	46	1,270.0
Lamar	4	1	40	21	228	222	609	70	1,191	2,410.7
Lamb	4	0	9	4	30	72	134	17	266	2,050.1
Lampasas	2	1	4	1	20	40	234	13	313	1,677.7
La Salle	2	0	0	1	5	7	37	0	50	660.9
Lavaca	5	2	7	3	33	91	107	9	252	1,135.6
Lee	2	0	9	3	39	28	146	15	240	1,508.9
Leon	1	0	0	0	11	36	70	10	127	824.9
Liberty	4	2	45	16	155	376	1,023	195	1,812	2,077.5
Limestone	3	0	3	2	28	83	102	10	228	975.5
Lipscomb	1	0	0	0	0	2	2	0	4	119.6
Live Oak	2	0	1	1	3	1	9	2	17	375.2
Llano	3	1	3	0	26	41	98	16	185	993.2
Loving	1	0	0	0	1	3	14	3	21	12,804.9
Lubbock	9	11	283	471	1,909	2,557	8,946	1,312	15,489	5,056.2
Lynn	3	0	0	0	1	8	8	5	22	369.7
Madison	2	0	1	4	23	40	32	21	121	844.0
Marion	2	0	0	5	17	40	37	10	109	1,112.5
Martin	2	0	0	0	0	2	6	0	8	136.8
Mason	1	0	1	0	7	4	5	1	18	419.8
Matagorda	5	0	36	12	113	247	818	53	1,279	3,523.1
Maverick	2	1	4	7	39	270	705	73	1,099	1,874.1
McCulloch	2	0	1	0	11	37	40	8	97	1,226.8
McLennan	16	12	159	159	769	1,153	4,968	557	7,777	3,068.2
McMullen	1	0	0	0	0	1	10	1	12	1,602.1
Medina	5	2	23	8	121	135	425	97	811	1,643.0
Menard	1	0	0	1	2	1	0	0	4	189.1
Midland	3	3	37	23	277	229	1,796	379	2,744	1,573.9
Milam	4	1	4	2	32	65	192	34	330	1,318.3
Mills	1	0	1	0	14	11	9	0	35	716.6
Mitchell	2	0	0	2	12	45	96	14	169	2,125.8
Montague	3	0	7	3	54	107	131	9	311	1,686.2
Montgomery	11	14	144	161	807	1,505	5,543	770	8,944	1,495.0
Moore	3	2	11	2	32	61	222	49	379	1,780.4

Source: Crime in Texas 2019 report, TDPS.

Crime Profile of Texas Counties, 2019

	No. Agencies Reporting	Murder	Rape	Robbery	Assault	Burglary	Larceny-Theft	Auto Theft	Total Index Crimes	Crime Rate per 100,000
Morris	5	0	4	4	18	35	98	12	171	1,403.4
Motley	1	0	1	0	0	1	2	0	4	325.2
Nacogdoches	4	4	26	28	120	247	827	95	1,347	2,058.8
Navarro	5	2	66	20	156	236	713	73	1,266	2,559.2
Newton	2	0	4	1	23	64	59	13	164	1,208.1
Nolan	3	0	2	4	29	121	166	18	340	2,552.4
Nueces	8	33	276	514	2,124	2,141	9,149	942	15,179	4,183.7
Ochiltree	2	0	2	0	9	31	86	9	137	1,389.5
Oldham	1	0	0	0	0	4	2	0	6	282.0
Orange	6	1	29	27	157	369	811	159	1,553	1,876.4
Palo Pinto	2	1	7	4	20	175	308	42	557	1,923.3
Panola	2	2	13	5	45	96	317	34	512	2,258.3
Parker	6	3	48	14	116	272	1,015	147	1,615	1,170.9
Parmer	4	0	1	1	7	17	27	10	63	646.0
Pecos	2	0	3	1	24	41	103	26	198	1,269.7
Polk	4	6	42	9	56	257	670	132	1,172	2,329.1
Potter	4	15	162	248	1,051	1,484	5,559	1,014	9,533	4,418.8
Presidio	3	0	2	0	4	2	6	0	14	205.9
Rains	2	0	0	0	10	22	30	7	69	563.4
Randall	3	0	30	6	41	132	264	40	513	1,273.1
Reagan	1	0	0	0	7	11	18	3	39	1,034.8
Real	1	0	0	0	3	15	39	5	62	1,783.1
Red River	3	0	2	2	24	42	45	10	125	1,040.5
Reeves	2	3	3	3	90	48	190	57	394	2,486.6
Refugio	3	0	2	0	7	36	34	7	86	1,237.9
Roberts	1	0	0	0	0	1	1	0	2	223.5
Robertson	2	1	1	3	25	93	168	33	324	1,876.2
Rockwall	5	2	31	10	60	125	877	116	1,221	1,275.3
Runnels	4	0	0	1	13	39	36	3	92	907.7
Rusk	4	5	16	5	86	231	695	86	1,124	2,198.8
Sabine	3	0	5	0	9	42	25	10	91	867.6
San Augustine	2	0	1	0	12	34	16	7	70	863.5
San Jacinto	1	0	26	1	17	115	173	42	374	1,297.2
San Patricio	8	2	29	15	113	218	703	92	1,172	1,990.1
San Saba	2	0	1	0	11	30	39	6	87	1,448.6
Schleicher	1	0	0	0	4	6	6	1	17	605.2
Scurry	2	0	9	3	155	89	163	19	438	2,614.5
Shackelford	1	0	0	0	5	1	2	0	8	248.7
Shelby	3	1	8	4	61	110	224	45	453	1,878.2
Sherman	2	0	0	0	0	3	5	0	8	260.8
Smith	10	7	132	82	550	918	3,655	427	5,771	2,495.0
Somervell	1	0	0	0	4	11	16	3	34	376.7
Starr	6	1	17	7	120	162	398	76	781	1,209.9

Source: Crime in Texas 2019 report, TDPS.

Crime Profile of Texas Counties, 2019

	No. Agencies Reporting	Murder	Rape	Robbery	Assault	Burglary	Larceny-Theft	Auto Theft	Total Index Crimes	Crime Rate per 100,000
Stephens	2	0	1	1	13	29	83	12	139	1,486.3
Sterling	1	0	0	1	1	3	8	2	15	1,130.4
Stonewall	1	0	0	0	1	0	0	0	1	74.7
Sutton	2	0	1	0	2	3	7	5	18	486.6
Swisher	3	0	4	7	25	40	114	8	198	2,926.4
Tarrant	39	101	998	1,690	4,666	7,035	37,547	5,950	57,987	2,828.4
Taylor	6	6	101	71	344	654	2,464	221	3,861	2,697.0
Terrell	1	N/A	N/A	N/A	N/A	N/A	N/A	N/A	N/A	N/A
Terry	2	0	6	0	20	41	89	21	177	1,455.4
Throckmorton	1	0	0	2	2	2	4	2	12	804.8
Titus	2	2	29	14	95	127	457	43	767	2,331.1
Tom Green	3	6	82	33	269	601	2,608	250	3,849	3,250.4
Travis	18	35	692	1,085	3,200	5,329	33,748	3,540	47,629	3,626.5
Trinity	2	0	1	1	4	28	35	10	79	664.9
Tyler	2	5	6	1	57	122	96	39	326	1,512.6
Upshur	4	0	10	8	61	108	206	29	422	1,113.0
Upton	1	0	0	0	2	3	25	3	33	893.6
Uvalde	3	2	10	4	53	106	588	23	786	2,940.7
Val Verde	2	2	13	10	42	153	497	47	764	1,561.5
Van Zandt	5	2	11	2	37	120	281	59	512	937.8
Victoria	2	6	85	58	292	510	1,698	165	2,814	3,054.7
Walker	2	0	31	24	187	167	589	91	1,089	1,500.6
Waller	6	3	26	19	80	98	389	51	666	1,260.1
Ward	2	1	8	4	50	56	279	18	416	3,526.6
Washington	2	0	26	8	109	110	355	36	644	1,836.5
Webb	5	6	110	167	605	768	3,862	325	5,843	2,142.5
Wharton	4	0	19	25	105	177	552	60	938	2,265.7
Wheeler	1	0	0	0	5	1	7	3	16	481.2
Wichita	6	4	115	92	227	676	2,688	278	4,080	3,108.1
Wilbarger	2	0	11	4	35	46	147	11	254	2,006.8
Willacy	5	0	18	4	134	158	221	12	547	2,598.1
Williamson	14	6	167	87	320	801	4,971	322	6,674	1,234.3
Wilson	4	0	7	0	13	94	111	23	248	633.9
Winkler	3	2	3	1	26	71	125	32	260	3,352.2
Wise	5	3	24	7	81	147	457	60	779	1,127.1
Wood	6	0	41	6	46	111	246	48	498	1,083.7
Yoakum	2	0	2	0	2	33	39	9	85	984.5
Young	3	1	11	3	21	50	87	15	188	1,051.9
Zapata	1	0	1	5	46	76	105	2	235	1,665.0
Zavala	2	0	4	0	17	41	27	5	94	787.3
TOTAL	**1,060**	**1,402**	**14,645**	**28,850**	**75,498**	**112,146**	**495,814**	**76,605**	**804,958**	**2,779.3**

Source: Crime in Texas 2019 report, TDPS.

Texas Department of Criminal Justice

Source: Texas Department of Criminal Justice, www.tdcj.texas.gov

The **Texas Board of Criminal Justice** is composed of nine non-salaried members who are appointed by the governor for staggered six-year terms. The board employs the Texas Department of Criminal Justice (TDCJ) executive director, sets rules and policies that guide the agency, and considers other agency actions at its meetings.

Board members serve in a separate capacity as the Board of Trustees for the **Windham School District** by hiring a superintendent and providing similar oversight. The Windham School District is a separate entity primarily funded through the Texas Education Agency (TEA).

In addition to hiring the TDCJ executive director, the board appoints an inspector general, a director of internal audits, a director of state counsel for offenders, and a prison rape elimination act ombudsman.

The TDCJ executive director is responsible for the administration and enforcement of statutes relative to the criminal justice system.

The Correctional Institutions Division, Private Facility Contract Monitoring and Oversight Division, Parole Division, and Community Justice Assistance Division are most involved in the everyday confinement and supervision of convicted felons.

The actual supervision of probationers is the responsibility of local community supervision and corrections departments. Victim Services coordinates a central mechanism for crime victims to participate in the criminal justice process.

Operating Budget 2020

Budget Item	Total, All Funds ($ in millions)	Percent of Total
A: Provide Prison Diversions	$248.0	7.0%
B: Special Needs Offenders	$27.6	0.8%
C: Incarcerate Felons	$2,909.0	81.8%
D: Board of Pardons and Paroles	$30.0	0.8%
E: Operate Parole System	$182.6	5.1%
F: Indirect Administration	$101.7	2.9%
G: Ensure Adequate Facilities	$58.0	1.6%
TOTAL	**$3,556.9**	**100%**

Source: TDCJ Fiscal Year 2020 Operating Budget

Inmate Profile
As of Fiscal Year 2018

Sex – Ethnicity – Age	
Male: 91.6%	Hispanic: 33.5%
Black: 32.7%	Other: 0.6%
White: 33.3%	Average age: 39.4
Average Sentences	
Prison: 19.5 years	State jail: 1.1 year
Average Part Of Sentence Served	
Prison: 61.0%	State jail: 99.5%
(Based on offenders released in Fiscal Year 2018.)	
Education	
Average IQ	90.7
Percent lacking high school diploma or GED:	81.3%

Source: TDCJ Annual Review 2018

Divisions of the TDCJ

The **Correctional Institutions Division** (CID) is responsible for the confinement of adult felony and state jail offenders who are sentenced to incarceration in a secure state-operated correctional facility. More about this division on the next page.

Private Facility Contract Monitoring and Oversight Division is responsible for oversight and monitoring contracts for privately operated secure facilities, as well as community-based facilities, which include substance abuse treatment services.

The **Parole Division** supervises all offenders released on parole or mandatory supervision; conducts release and transition planning; and verifies compliance with statutory provisions of release.

In addition, this division contracts for electronic monitoring and processing responses to violations, administers programs and services through District Resource Centers and Parole Offices, and coordinates the Interstate Compact for Adult Offender Supervision.

The **Community Justice Assistance Division** (CJAD) administers community supervision, also known as adult probation in Texas. CJAD is responsible for the distribution of formula and grant funds; the development of standards, including best-practice treatment standards; approval of Community Justice Plans and budgets; conducting program and fiscal audits; and providing training and certification of community supervision officers. The remaining divisions support the overall operation of the TDCJ. These include:

- **Office of the General Counsel**
- **Administrative Review and Risk Management**
- **Business and Finance**
- **Information Technology**
- **Manufacturing, Agribusiness and Logistics**
- **Facilities**
- **Rehabilitation Programs**
- **Re-entry and Integration Programs**
- **Health Services and Human Resources**

Correctional Institutions Division

In addition to the incarceration of offenders, the CID has the following support functions, including: classification and records; counsel substitute; laundry, food and supply; offender transportation; and correctional training and staff development.

The table below lists all of the correctional institutions in the state alphabetically by county. It includes both those operated by the CID as well as privately-operated facilities, which have been overseen by the **Private Facility Contract Monitoring and Oversight Division** since June 15, 2007.

The town listed is the nearest one to the facility, although the unit may actually be in another county. For instance, the Middleton Transfer Facility is in Jones County, but the nearest city is Abilene, which is in Taylor County. ☆

On-Hand Population As of Aug. 31, 2020	
Prisoners	
Prison	117,380
State Jails	1,748
SAFP (Substance Abuse)	1,412
TOTAL	**120,540**
Parole	
Mandatory Supervision Population	111,593
Probation	
Community Supervision Placements*	84,891

*Total adults on direct, indirect, and pretrial supervision, minus transfers

Source: TDCJ Statistical Report 2020

Correctional Institutions in Texas

County	Unit	Nearest Town	Max. Capacity, Gender	Employees	Type* (Operator**)
Anderson	Beto	Tennessee Colony	3,471 Male	633	Prison (CID)
Anderson	Coffield	Tennessee Colony	4,139 Male	879	Prison (CID)
Anderson	Gurney	Tennessee Colony	2,128 Male	437	Transfer (CID)
Anderson	Michael	Tennessee Colony	3,800 Male	816	Prison (CID)
Anderson	Powledge	Palestine	1,137 Male	290	Prison (CID)
Angelina	Diboll	Diboll	518 Male	136	Private Prison (MTC)
Angelina	Duncan	Diboll	606 Male	139	Geriatric (CID)
Bee	Garza East	Beeville	2,458 Male	442	Transfer (CID)
Bee	Garza West	Beeville	2,278 Male	401	Transfer (CID)
Bee	McConnell	Beeville	2,900 Male	542	Prison (CID)
Bexar	Dominguez	San Antonio	2,276 Male	382	State Jail (CID)
Bowie	Telford	New Boston	2,872 Male	706	Prison (CID)
Brazoria	Clemens	Brazoria	1,215 Male	348	Prison (CID)
Brazoria	Darrington	Rosharon	1,931 Male	546	Prison (CID)
Brazoria	Ramsey	Rosharon	1,891 Male	429	Prison (CID)
Brazoria	Scott	Angleton	1,130 Male	307	Prison (CID)
Brazoria	Stringfellow	Rosharon	1,212 Male	313	Prison (CID)
Brazoria	Terrell, C.T.	Rosharon	1,603 Male	466	Prison (CID)
Brazos	Hamilton	Bryan	1,166 Male	256	Pre-Release (CID)
Brown	Havins	Brownwood	596 Male	181	Pre-Release (CID)
Burnet	Halbert	Burnet	612 Female	135	SAFPF (CID)
Caldwell	Lockhart	Lockhart	500 Female, 500 Male	204	Private Prison/Work Program (MTC)
Cherokee	Hodge	Rusk	989 Male	333	DDP (CID)
Cherokee	Skyview	Rusk	562 Female/Male	295	Psychiatric (CID)

* **Prison types:** SAFPF (Substance Abuse Felony Punishment Facilities); DDP (Developmentally Disabled Program)
** **Operator abbreviations:** CID (TDCJ Correctional Institutions Division); MTC (Management and Training Corporation); LaSalle (LaSalle Corrections)
[1]. Employee and capacity data includes those working and held at the nearby Baten Intermediate Sanction Facility

Source: TDCJ Unit Directory

Correctional Institutions in Texas

County	Unit	Nearest Town	Max. Capacity, Gender	Employees	Type* (Operator**)
Childress	Roach	Childress	1,384 Male	289	Prison (CID)
Coryell	Crain	Gatesville	2,115 Female	711	Prison (CID)
Coryell	Hilltop	Gatesville	553 Female	268	Prison (CID)
Coryell	Hughes	Gatesville	2,984 Male	741	Prison (CID)
Coryell	Mountain View	Gatesville	645 Female	300	Prison (CID)
Coryell	Murray	Gatesville	1,341 Female	341	Prison (CID)
Coryell	Woodman	Gatesville	900 Female	270	State Jail (CID)
Dallas	Hutchins	Dallas	2,276 Male	399	State Jail (CID)
Dawson	Smith	Lamesa	2,234 Male	408	Prison (CID)
DeWitt	Stevenson	Cuero	1,384 Male	272	Prison (CID)
Duvall	Glossbrenner	San Diego	612 Male	123	SAFPF (CID)
El Paso	Sanchez	El Paso	1,100 Male	287	State Jail (CID)
Falls	Hobby	Marlin	1,384 Female	299	Prison (CID)
Falls	Marlin	Marlin	606 Female	126	Transfer (CID)
Fannin	Cole	Bonham	900 Male	226	State Jail (CID)
Fannin	Moore, C.	Bonham	1,224 Male	245	Transfer (CID)
Fort Bend	Jester I	Richmond	323 Male	119	SAFPF (CID)
Fort Bend	Jester III	Richmond	1,131 Male	288	Prison (CID)
Fort Bend	Jester IV	Richmond	550 Male	381	Psychiatric (CID)
Fort Bend	Vance	Richmond	378 Male	116	Prison (CID)
Freestone	Boyd	Teague	1,372 Male	298	Prison (CID)
Frio	Briscoe	Dilley	1,384 Male	233	Prison (CID)
Galveston	Hospital Galveston	Galveston	365 Female/Male	496	Medical (CID)
Galveston	Young	Galveston	455 Female	302	Medical (CID)
Gray	Jordan (Baten)	Pampa	1,008 Male[1]	289[1]	Prison (CID)
Grimes	Luther	Navasota	1,316 Male	323	Prison (CID)
Grimes	Pack	Navasota	1,478 Male	334	Prison (CID)
Hale	Formby	Plainview	1,100 Male	278	State Jail (CID)
Hale	Wheeler	Plainview	576 Male	127	State Jail (CID)
Harris	Kegans	Houston	667 Male	155	State Jail (CID)
Harris	Lychner	Humble	2,276 Male	413	State Jail (CID)
Hartley	Dalhart	Dalhart	1,398 Male	237	Prison (CID)
Hays	Kyle	Kyle	520 Male	117	Private Prison (MTC)
Hidalgo	Lopez	Edinburg	1,100 Male	257	State Jail (CID)
Hidalgo	Segovia	Edinburg	1,224 Male	233	Pre-Release (CID)
Houston	Eastham	Lovelady	2,474 Male	583	Prison (CID)
Jack	Lindsey	Jacksboro	1,031 Male	202	State Jail (MTC)
Jasper	Goodman	Jasper	612 Male	155	Transfer (CID)
Jefferson	Gist	Beaumont	2,276 Male	368	State Jail (CID)
Jefferson	Leblanc	Beaumont	1,224 Male	248	Pre-Release (CID)
Jefferson	Stiles	Beaumont	2,981 Male	756	Prison (CID)
Johnson	Estes	Venus	1040 Male	191	Private Prison (MTC)

* **Prison types:** SAFPF (Substance Abuse Felony Punishment Facilities); DDP (Developmentally Disabled Program)

** **Operator abbreviations:** CID (TDCJ Correctional Institutions Division); MTC (Management and Training Corporation); LaSalle (LaSalle Corrections)

[1]. Employee and capacity data includes those working and held at the nearby Baten Intermediate Sanction Facility

Source: TDCJ Unit Directory

Correctional Institutions in Texas

County	Unit	Nearest Town	Max. Capacity, Gender	Employees	Type* (Operator**)
Jones	Middleton	Abilene	2,128 Male	504	Transfer (CID)
Jones	Robertson	Abilene	2,984 Male	683	Prison (CID)
Karnes	Connally	Kenedy	2,148 Male	602	Prison (CID)
La Salle	Cotulla	Cotulla	606 Male	99	Transfer (CID)
Liberty	Cleveland	Cleveland	520 Male	134	Private Prison (MTC)
Liberty	Henley	Dayton	576 Female	124	State Jail (CID)
Liberty	Hightower	Dayton	1,384 Male	335	Prison (CID)
Liberty	Plane	Dayton	2,291 Female	418	State Jail (CID)
Lubbock	Montford	Lubbock	1,044 Male	705	Psychiatric (CID)
Madison	Ferguson	Midway	2,421 Male	578	Prison (CID)
Medina	Ney	Hondo	576 Male	134	State Jail (CID)
Medina	Torres	Hondo	1,384 Male	298	Prison (CID)
Mitchell	Wallace	Colorado City	1,448 Male	255	Prison (CID)
Pecos	Fort Stockton	Fort Stockson	606 Male	114	Transfer (CID)
Pecos	Lynaugh	Fort Stockton	1,416 Male	289	Prison (CID)
Polk	Polunsky	Livingston	2,984 Male	691	Prison (CID)
Potter	Clements	Amarillo	3,798 Male	1,050	Prison (CID)
Potter	Neal	Amarillo	1,732 Male	383	Prison (CID)
Rusk	Bradshaw	Henderson	1,980 Male	266	State Jail (MTC)
Rusk	East Texas	Henderson	224 Female, 2,012 Male	493	Multi-Use (MTC)
Rusk	Moore, B.	Overton	500 Male	109	Private Prison (MTC)
San Saba	San Saba	San Saba	606 Female	135	Transfer (CID)
Scurry	Daniel	Snyder	1,384 Male	224	Prison (CID)
Stephens	Sayle	Breckenridge	632 Male	146	SAFPF (CID)
Swisher	Tulia	Tulia	606 Male	117	Transfer (CID)
Terry	Rudd	Brownfield	612 Male	145	Transfer (CID)
Travis	Travis County	Austin	1,161 Male	264	State Jail (CID)
Tyler	Lewis	Woodville	2,231 Male	570	Prison (CID)
Walker	Byrd	Huntsville	1,365 Male	282	Prison (CID)
Walker	Ellis	Huntsville	2,482 Male	604	Prison (CID)
Walker	Estelle	Huntsville	3,480 Male	980	Prison (CID)
Walker	Goree	Huntsville	1,321 Male	315	Prison (CID)
Walker	Holliday	Huntsville	2,128 Male	435	Transfer (CID)
Walker	Huntsville	Huntsville	1,705 Male	446	Prison (CID)
Walker	Wynne	Huntsville	2,621 Male	697	Prison (CID)
Wichita	Allred	Iowa Park	3,722 Male	939	Prison (CID)
Willacy	Willacy County	Raymondville	1,069 Male	183	State Jail (La Salle)
Wise	Bridgeport	Bridgeport	520 Male	117	Private Prison (MTC)
Wood	Johnston	Winnsboro	612 Male	160	SAFPF (CID)

* **Prison types:** SAFPF (Substance Abuse Felony Punishment Facilities); DDP (Developmentally Disabled Program)
** **Operator abbreviations:** CID (TDCJ Correctional Institutions Division); MTC (Management and Training Corporation); LaSalle (LaSalle Corrections)
[1]. Employee and capacity data includes those working and held at the nearby Baten Intermediate Sanction Facility

Source: TDCJ Unit Directory

Culture & the Arts

AFRICAN AMERICAN TEXANS

MUSEUMS, TEXAS MEDAL OF THE ARTS

TEXAS INSTITUTE OF LETTERS

STATE ARTISTS, POETS, & HISTORIANS

FILM & TELEVISION

HOLIDAYS & RELIGION

Visitors to the Dallas Museum of Art view a painting November 20, 2019.
Photo by risingthermals/Flickr (CC).

African American Texans

By Dr. Merline Pitre

African Americans have been part of the landscape of Texas as long as Europeans. Nearly spanning a period of five centuries, the African American presence began in 1528 with the arrival of an African slave, Esteban, who accompanied the first Spanish exploration of the land in the southwestern part of the United States that eventually became Texas. From this time forward, African American experience and journey included hardships and triumphs. Subjected to slavery, segregation and discrimination during this long history, African Americans have made significant contribution to the growth and development of Texas.

Spanish Texas

Esteban, one of four survivors of the Cabeza de Vaca expedition in 1528, established a pattern of Black involvement in Spanish Texas. Blacks accompanied most Spanish expeditions into Texas during the 16th and 17th centuries. By the late 18th century, the Black and mulatto inhabitants comprised more than 15% of the population. Although the Spanish introduced slavery into Texas, the majority of the Blacks living in the province were free. For example, in 1771 San Antonio listed a population of 1,779 Black males and of that number only four were slaves.

Free Blacks faced few, if any, restrictions on their freedom. They were socially accepted and followed whatever trade or profession they chose. These included teachers, shoemakers, teachers and landowners, to name a few. William Goyens is an example of a prominent Black businessman and landowner.

Slavery and Freedom

Unlike free Blacks who inhabited Spanish Texas, the majority of African Americans entered Texas as slaves. Slavery as an institution of significant impact came to Texas with Anglo Americans. The first Anglo Americans who settled in Texas came from the southern part of the United States, where slavery was a thriving institution, and, as such, brought their slaves along with them. During the time of the first Anglo settlement (1821) to the Texas Revolution (1836), slavery grew slowly. Upon gaining its independence from Mexico in 1836, the newly found Republic of Texas continued the "peculiar institution." During the Republic period, the slave population grew from 5,000 in 1836 to 30,000 in 1845, the year Texas was annexed to the United States. Slavery grew by leaps and bounds after annexation, reaching 58,161 in 1850. By the end of the Civil War, there were approximately 400,000 slaves in Texas. This increase was due in large part to the fact that many slave owners in

Above: The hat and saddle used by Fred Whitfield, a professional rodeo cowboy who specialized in tie-down roping. In his career he won eight world championships from the Professional Rodeo Cowboys Association and three National Finals Rodeo aggregate titles. The above display is from the National Multicultural Western Heritage Museum in Fort Worth. Photo by the Texas Historical Commission, www.thc.texas.gov.

other states had sent their slaves to East Texas since that area was far removed from the fighting. They came from as far away as Louisiana, Mississippi, Arkansas, and Virginia.

The overwhelming majority of the slaves were concentrated along the coast and river valleys of East Texas and labored in agricultural pursuits, primarily in cotton farming. Slaves were responsible for over 90% of the cotton grown in the state. Texans who engaged in rice farming and stock raising also depended on slave labor. So slavery was very profitable in East Texas.

The institution of slavery in Texas was similar to that of other southern states. The treatment of slaves varied from location to location, from plantation to plantation, from owner to owner. The typical slave faced a life replete with hardship. The majority of slaves were field hands who worked mostly on cotton plantations from sunup to sundown. The number of artisans, house servants and urban slaves was small, but still their work and behavior were regulated by a set of rules prescribed by the master. Living arrangements included crude cabins, inadequate clothing and only enough food for substance. Despite the restriction placed on them, the slaves showed a remarkable ability to cope with a hostile environment and to think and act in terms of survival and freedom.

The end of slavery came as a result of a bloody and costly civil war that lasted from 1861 to 1865. The collapse of the Confederacy and Robert E. Lee's surrender on April 9, 1865, meant freedom for the slaves. Although President Abraham Lincoln issued the Emancipation Proclamation on January 1, 1863, freeing slaves in the rebellion states, it was only in areas the Union troops had conquered that the slaves became freed people. For African Americans of Texas, freedom did not come until June 19, 1865 (commonly referred to as Juneteenth). On that date General Gordon Granger, the Union commander of the Department of Texas, arrived at the Port of Galveston and read General Order #3 and announced that the slaves of the state of Texas were free. Despite this reading of the official Emancipation Proclamation of Texas, not all slaves were freed. In isolated areas of the state where the army was unable to reach, the masters did not inform the slaves and, therefore, some slaves were not freed until 1868.

The immediate reaction of slaves on being set free varied. There was crying and weeping. Some slaves were confused and didn't know where to go. Others tested their freedom by walking off the plantations, only to return a short time afterward. Still others wanted the same things as their White counterparts — schooling, clothes and sufficient food. After their initial shock, African Americans had to rebuild their lives, locate family members and begin to live their lives as self-sufficient free men and women. The Freedmen's Bureau aided in the transition from slavery to freedom by providing legal assistance and helping to establish schools. But even before the Freedmen's Bureau could provide assistance, Blacks organized makeshift schools and began establishing their own religious institutions.

Yet the transition was not easy and was further complicated by the fact that the social order had changed and the racial animosity that separated Blacks and Whites still abided. The legal system was used to regulate Black behavior. A lack of land ownership and a reign of terror tied the masses of Blacks to a second form of slavery: sharecropping. Consequently, during the first year of freedom there was a mass migration of ex-slaves to urban centers such as Galveston, Houston, San Antonio, Marshall and Beaumont. Other migration occurred away from plantations in rural areas where Blacks established freedom colonies and on the outskirts of cities where they established freedmen's towns.

Reconstruction and Post Reconstruction

Reconstruction presented challenges and possibilities for White and Black Texans. In order to keep Blacks in a subservient position and to ensure that White supremacy prevailed, the 1866 Texas Constitution, drawn up and ratified by former Confederates, replaced slave codes with Black codes that denied freed people the right to vote, serve on juries or testify against Whites in court. But this denial of legal, civil and political rights did not endure. In March 1867 the United States Congress intervened through a series of Reconstruction Acts and demanded that all former Confederate states ratify the 14th amendment and grant legal and political rights to African Americans. These acts ordered southern states to summon constitutional conventions and write new constitutions denying constitutional rights to no one on account of race, color or previous condition of servitude. The result of which was that 11 African American delegates were elected to help write a new state constitution for Texas — a constitution that protected civil rights, established the state's first public education system and extended the franchise to all men.

After the ratification of the 1869 constitution and the passage of the 15th amendment, 42 men of color were elected to serve in the state legislature from 1870 to 1898 and helped to move the state toward democracy. These Black legislators' concern first and foremost was to further Black struggle for power and participation in the existing political, social and economic institutions. As members of the state legislature and constitutional conventions, Black lawmakers helped lay the foundation for public school systems of the state, make reforms in mental asylum and correctional institutions, and pass laws that granted universal suffrage and the protection of civil rights. Working along with these legislators was another Black, Norris Wright Cuney, who became the tutelary head of the state Republican Party from 1884 to 1896.

Reconstruction in Texas came to an end in 1873 when Democrats regained control of the state legislature. White Democrats then proceeded to reverse many of the democratic reforms instituted by Black and White Republicans. So from 1874 to 1900, even as Black Republicans tried to help move the state toward democracy, African Americans of Texas entered a period that some historians call the "nadir." That is, Whites suppressed Blacks politically, socially and economically. Additionally, lynching and other forms of violence were used to keep Blacks in their "place," most notably in East Texas.

The economic position of Blacks was not bright during the last half of the 19th century. The masses of Blacks were sharecroppers or tenant farmers. Of the Blacks who were not sharecroppers, 25% worked in towns and cities as restaurant workers, barbers, saloon keepers, launderers and as domestic help. Additionally, Black men worked in the lumber industry, on railroad construction and as longshoremen in towns like Galveston.

Given this economic reality, Blacks relied on education as a means of upward mobility. Still, education had its problems. The state established a segregated public-education system that underfunded African American schools and limited access to books, libraries and other educational resources. Black schools did not share equally in state money with Whites. As late as 1900, two-thirds of all Black schools met in churches or rented buildings. As for institutions of higher learning, church-affiliated institutions (Wiley, Bishop, Tillotson, Samuel Huston, Texas College and Mary Allen) along with Prairie View College carried the burden of educating Black students.

Despite the fact that Black public schools and Prairie View College were underfunded and double-taxed, between 1880 and 1900 the illiteracy rate among African Americans fell from 75.4% to 38%. This rate would continue to fall in the 20th century as the Julius Rosenwald Fund provided grants (which had to be matched by the Black community) for the construction of public schools in the rural areas of the South for African Americans. Between 1920 and 1932, Texas boasted of 527 Rosenwald schools, mostly in East and Central Texas. During the first half of the 20th century, the number of Black institutions of higher learning would increase from seven to nine.

Despite this glimmer of hope found in education, at the dawn of the 20th century the political gains that African Americans had made from 1870 to 1900 were virtually lost. The imposition of the poll tax and the purification of the ballot via the White Democratic primary that began in 1905 meant fewer African Americans would be voting. For example, there were 100,000 Black voters in 1890 compared to 5,000 in 1906. The majority of Blacks had been disenfranchised by the following methods: violence, economic coercion, literacy tests, poll taxes and the White Democratic primary. Coupled with these subterfuges, Blacks lived in a segregated world. Racial boundaries that were somewhat fluid during post-Reconstruction in Texas solidified throughout the 1880s and 1990s and culminated in the Supreme Court decision in *Plessy v Ferguson* in 1896 that declared racial segregation legal.

Segregation (Jim Crow) and Black Response

In Texas, the nadir of the African American experience extended to the 20th century as segregation and violence deepened. Segregation was not just a system of physical separation of races. It was a social and legal system that denied Blacks equal access to everything from health care and jobs to education and justice. Coupled with segregation in keeping Blacks in their place was violence found most notably in the form of lynching and White-instigated race riots. Most notable among these were the following race riots and lynchings: Waco (1916), Houston (1917), Longview (1919), Kirvin Lynching (1922) and Beaumont (1943).

Black Texans responded to this violence and discrimination in several ways. Some fought back, some endured, some left the state for the North or the West, some moved from rural areas to towns and cities within the state. Still others formed self-help and protest organizations such as the fraternal orders, benevolent societies, literary clubs, the Urban League and the NAACP. Despite their second-class status, African Americans built viable and progressive communities throughout the state. As in the 19th century, they continued to organize churches, schools and social organizations that served their needs. As sharecroppers and tenant farmers, they organized a Black cooperative to raise prices for their produce. One also saw the rise of Black newspapers in large cities of the state, including the *Houston Informer*, *San Antonio Register* and *Dallas Express*.

One of the most significant achievements of African Americans of the 20th century was their participation in the Texas Centennial of 1936. There, under the leadership of A. Maceo Smith of the Dallas Chamber of Commerce and

Right: A sharecropper's wife preparing poke salad, 1939. Photo by Russell Lee/Wikimedia Commons.

Below: The lone remaining sharecropper's house at the Potter Farm, near Terrell. Photo by Carol M. Highsmith/Library of Congress.

Samuel W. Houston of Huntsville, the Hall of Negro Life was built in Fair Park in Dallas and October 19, 1936, was designated as Negro Day.

The establishment of the Hall of Negro Life was a way of preserving the history and culture of Black Texans. Among other things that were included in the hall were two exhibits: one highlighting Historically Black Colleges and Universities (HBCUs) and one dealing with aesthetics. The aesthetic exhibit featured Samuel A. Countee, Aaron Douglas and Frank Sheinall. Later, the world-renowned artist John T. Biggers' painting, along with that of James Thibodeaux, would also be on exhibit. Over the years other artists, musicians and writers were highlighted, such as Blind Lemon Jefferson, Huddie (Leadbelly) Ledbetter, Eddie Durham, Scott Joplin, Maud Cuney Hare and J. Mason Brewer.

In addition to highlighting outstanding personalities, events and organizations, Negro Day proved to be an opportunity for African American Texans to meet and plan strategies to end Jim Crow practices and discrimination. Out of this initial meeting came the idea of establishing the Texas Conference of State Branches of the NAACP, whereby all branches would coordinate their activities to eliminate Jim Crow through the Texas Conference. Two major cases sponsored by the Conference of State Branches were *Smith v Allwright* (1944) and *Sweatt v Painter* (1951). The first case involved the NAACP's effort to have the White Democratic primary statute (a law stating that only White men should vote in the Democratic primary) declared unconstitutional. Victory came in 1944 when the Supreme Court sided with the NAACP. The second case, *Sweatt v Painter,* centered around a frontal attack on segregated professional education. In its verdict the Supreme Court ordered a Black man, Heman Sweatt, admitted to the University of Texas Law School, notwithstanding a Black law school existed at Texas Southern University. *Sweatt v Painter* set precedence for *Brown v Board of Education* by implying that "separate but equal" was unconstitutional. *Brown v Board of Education* reversed *Plessy v Ferguson* and stated in writing that separate but equal was unconstitutional.

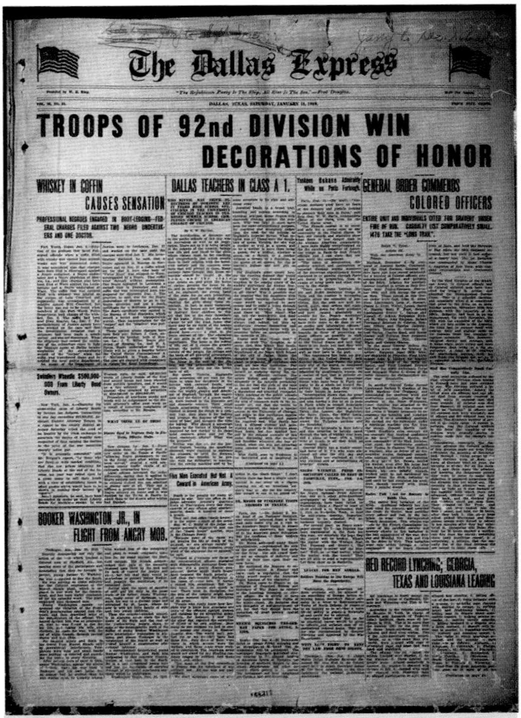
The Dallas Express

TROOPS OF 92nd DIVISION WIN DECORATIONS OF HONOR

WHISKEY IN COFFIN CAUSES SENSATION

DALLAS TEACHERS IN CLASS A 1.

GENERAL ORDER COMMENDS COLORED OFFICERS

BOOKER WASHINGTON JR., IN FLIGHT FROM ANGRY MOB.

RED RECORD LYNCHING; GEORGIA, TEXAS AND LOUISIANA LEADING

This edition of The Dallas Express was published on Jan. 11, 1919. The Dallas Express was the longest-running Black newspaper in Texas when it closed its doors in 1970. Photo found on Wikimedia Commons.

Civil Rights and Voting Rights

Viewing *Brown* as a pathway to equality and as a boost to the civil rights movement, Black activists became all the more determined to change the status quo. From 1955 to 1966, they launched a steady campaign to integrate public schools and to gain access to better jobs and public facilities. Within a decade many of the public schools in Texas had been integrated.

In the last half of the 20th century, each battle for civil rights required hard work, commitment and constant pressure on public officials. Sometimes it also required physically testing the law as many students at Texas Southern University, Wiley College, Bishop College and Prairie View University staged sit-in demonstrations in their respective cities. These sit-in demonstrations in large, as well as small, cities effectively desegregated many public facilities and helped bolster the Civil Rights Act of 1964, an act that legally assured integration in public accommodations in hotels, restaurants, swimming pools and golf courses.

Much of the civil rights activities from the mid-20th century to the present have focused on consolidating the gains made during the last century. For Texas Blacks, most of the gains have come via voting rights. One cannot exaggerate the political significance of the overthrow of the White Democratic primary. Prior to *Smith v Allwright* (1944), only 30,000 Blacks were registered voters. In 1948 that number more than tripled to 100,000. In 1964 it reached 57% of the Black voting-age population. This percentage increased even more when the 24th amendment (1964) and the Voting Rights Act of 1965 struck down the poll tax and other subterfuges for voting. Moreover, the court-mandated reapportionment in 1966 made it possible for Blacks to send three members of their race to the Texas legislature, the first since Reconstruction — Curtis Graves and Joseph Lockridge to the House and Barbara Jordan to the Senate. Afterwards, Blacks led a campaign against at-large districts.

The Supreme Court concurrence in a lawsuit filed for single-member districts in Texas enabled African Americans to win legislative seats at the local, state and national levels. The result of which was that Barbara Jordan became the first Black female from the South to be elected to Congress. Today, five Black Texans have been elected to Congress. Twenty Blacks sit in the Texas legislature compared to three in 1968. Of that number, six are female. Most of the school boards, city councils and county commissioners in the state have at least one or more Black members. Coupled with this is the number of Black mayors who are or have been elected

Barbara Jordan sat on the House Judiciary Committee during the Watergate hearings. Photo by U.S. House of Representatives Photography Office

in small and large cities. For example, in 1995 Ronald Kirk became the first African American mayor in Dallas. In 1998 Lee P. Brown became the first African American to serve as mayor in Houston, and Sylvester Turner is currently serving as mayor in Houston. Also, in 1985 John Wiley Price and El Franco Lee became the first Black county commissioners in Dallas and Houston, respectively. The judiciary, an area that had been difficult for Blacks to get elected to office, now sees a large number of Blacks elected. In fact, 19 Black women were elected as judges in Harris County in 2018.

Culture

As African Americans lived through the horrors of Jim Crow and the struggles of the civil rights movement, they continued to participate in the state's social and cultural life and to add their creative talents to the artistic development of both the state and the nation. For example, Juneteenth celebrations that started during Reconstruction have kept the memory of "first freedom" alive and are now celebrated in many other states and countries throughout the world, culminating in 2021 with its designation as an American national freedom holiday.

In keeping with the idea of preserving African American culture, there are a number of African American museums that have been established over the years. The most notable are the African American Museum of Dallas and the Buffalo Soldiers National Museum in Houston. Concomitant with preserving Black culture are the contributions of musicians, artists, writers and playwrights: Thomas Meloncon's *The Diary of Black Men* and Ntozake Shange's *For Colored Girls* made their way to Broadway. Shange's novel *Sassafrass, Cypress & Indigo* was a national best-seller. Musical icon Beyonce Knowles Carter of Houston and Erykah Badu have won Grammy and national awards for their music in the jazz, rhythm, blues and pop genres. Novelists J. California Cooper's *A Piece of Mine* and Anita Bunkley's *Emily: The Yellow Rose* also won national acclaim.

Conclusion

Without a doubt, African Americans' contribution and hard labor have made the state of Texas what it has become in the 21st century. In the latest census taken in 2020, African Americans are 12% of the state's population. Two-thirds of African Americans live in the Dallas-Fort Worth and Houston metropolitan areas. Making up a significant part of the population are cities such as Beaumont, Port Arthur, Austin and San Antonio. Yet the contribution of the African American history and culture of this state is not relegated to large or small cities, rural or urban centers, or to a geographic region. Their contribution attests to their abiding influence on Texas and American culture and institutions.

Despite the gains made by African Americans in the state of Texas, it would be premature to write the epitaph of the civil rights movement. Unfinished, the agendas abound. There are still pressing economic issues relating to employment, housing, and services. In point of fact, racial and gender income inequality is prevalent. The issue of affirmative action is still considered a divisive factor in many cities. Also, Texas has had a long history of Blacks dying at the hand of the police, and as such, one of its most current and pressing issues centers around police brutality and criminal justice reform. This issue was exacerbated when George Floyd, a Houston native, died in Minneapolis while in custody. In the aftermath of the state and nationwide protests against police brutality that erupted after Floyd's death, police reform efforts presented by state lawmakers still await a victory. There is no gainsaying that the problem of race remains in Texas. But by the same token, no one can deny that the civil rights movement in Texas changed the political landscape of the state.

Celebrations, Festivals, and Events

Juneteenth (June 19, 1865). Celebrated since its inception as the day slaves were emancipated in Texas, Juneteenth became a state holiday in Texas in 1986 and ten years later a state holiday in Oklahoma. It is now recognized in 47 other states and several countries around the world. A bill in Congress making it a national holiday was passed in 2021 and signed into law by President Biden.

Kwanzaa is a celebration of life, prosperity and good harvest. It is observed from December 26 to January 1 each year. The seven principles commemorating Kwanzaa are self-determination, purpose, creativity, unity, community responsibility, economics and faith.

Black History Month started as Negro History Week by Carter G. Woodson in 1914. Its purpose was to expose and draw awareness to the contribution African Americans have made to this country and the world. Later, Negro History

The struggle never ended: Houston police chief Art Acevedo (center) and Black Lives Matter organizer DeRay Mckesson (right) discuss racial tension and police misconduct at The Summit on Race in America in 2019. Photo by Jay Godwin, courtesy of the LBJ Library

Week became Black History Week. In 1976 it became Black History Month in recognition of the need to expose African Americans' life history and contribution to the nation's society.

Martin Luther King Jr. Day celebrates the life of Martin L. King Jr. and his work in the civil rights movement. It became a national holiday in 1997 and is celebrated on the third Monday in January, which falls near King's birthday (January 15, 1929). In Texas the celebration takes on many forms — parades, public-speaking contests, church services and as a day of providing various forms of service to the community.

Harambee Festival, held in Dallas, is the oldest and largest African American cultural event in the state. This community-based festival celebrates African American culture with musical performances and free health screenings.

African American Book Festival is an interactive community gathering and cultural celebration of African American writers and their works and is held in Austin each year. Among other things, its program includes author presentations, book discussions, pop culture and conversations with children.

The Prairie View Trail Ride is the oldest African American trail ride in the United States. This 88-mile ride from Hempstead, Texas, to the Houston rodeo is held each year in the month of March.

Further Reading

Barr, Alwyn. *Black Texans: A History of African Americans in Texas 1528-1995*. Second Editions. Norman: University of Oklahoma Press, 1996.

Beil, Gail. "Four Marshallites' Role in the Passage of the Civil Rights Act of 1964," *Southwestern Historical Quarterly* 106 (July 2002) 1-24.

Campbell, Randolph B. *An Empire for Slavery: The Peculiar Institution in Texas, 1821-1865*. Baton Rouge: Louisiana State University Press, 1989.

Carrigan, William D. *The Making of a Lynching Culture: Violence and Vigilantism in Central Texas, 1836-1916*. Urbana: University of Illinois Press, 2004

Crouch, Barry A. *The Freedmen's Bureau and Black Texans*. Austin: University of Texas Press, 1992

Glasrud, Bruce and James M Smallwood. *The African American Experience in Texas*, Lubbock: Texas Tech University Press, 2007

Glasrud, Bruce and Merline Pitre. *Black Women in Texas History*. College Station: Texas A&M University Press, 2009

Hine, Darlene Clark. *Black Victory: The Rise and Fall of the White Primary in Texas*. Columbia: University of Missouri Press, 2003

Ladino, Robyn Duff. *Desegregating Texas Schools: Eisenhower, Shivers, and the Crisis At Mansfield High*. Austin: University of Texas Press, 1990.

Pitre, Merline. *Through Many Dangers, Toils and Snares: Black Leadership in Texas, 1868-1898*. College Station: Texas A&M University, 2017.

Pitre, Merline. *In Struggle against Jim Crow: Lulu B. White and the NAACP, 1900-1957*. College Station: Texas A & M University Press, 2010.

Pitre, Merline, *Born to Serve: A History of Texas Southern*. Norman: The University of Oklahoma Press, 2018.

Reid, Debra. "Racism and Sexism in Rural Texas: The Contested Nature of Progressive Reform 1870-1910" in *Seeking Inalienable Rights: Black Texans and their Quest for Justice*. College Station: Texas A & M University Press: 37-57.

Seals, Donald. "The Wiley-Bishop Student Movement: A Case Study of the 1960 Civil Rights Sit-ins." *Southwestern Quarterly* 106 (June 2003): 419-40.

Taylor, Quintard. *In Search of the Racial Frontier: African Americans in the American West, 1528-1990*. New York: W.W. Norton, 1998.

Texas Museums of Art, Science, History

Listed below are links to the websites of Texas museums. Where required, some have indication of the area of emphasis of the exhibits.

Abilene

Frontier Texas! (history)
frontiertexas.com

Grace Museum (art, history)
thegracemuseum.org

National Center for Children's Illustrated Literature (art)
nccil.org

Addison

Cavanaugh Flight Museum
cavflight.org

Albany

Old Jail Art Center (art)
theojac.org

Alpine

Museum of the Big Bend (history)
museumofthebigbend.com

Amarillo

Amarillo Museum of Art
amarilloart.org

American Quarter Horse Hall of Fame & Museum
aqha.com/museum

Don Harrington Discovery Center (science, children's)
discoverycenteramarillo.org

Texas Pharmacy Museum
ttuhsc.edu/pharmacy/museum

Angleton

Brazoria County Historical Museum
brazoriacountytx.gov/departments/museum

Austin

Blanton Museum of Art
blantonmuseum.org

Bob Bullock Texas State History Museum
thestoryoftexas.com

Capitol Visitors Center (history)
tspb.texas.gov/prop/tcvc/cvc/cvc.html

The Contemporary Austin (art)
thecontemporaryaustin.org

Elisabet Ney Museum (art, history)
austintexas.gov/elisabetney

French Legation Museum (history)
thc.texas.gov/historic-sites/french-legation-state-historic-site

Harry Ransom Humanities Research Center (history, literature)
hrc.utexas.edu

Lady Bird Johnson Wildflower Center
wildflower.org

Lyndon B. Johnson Presidential Library
lbjlibrary.org

Mexic-Arte Museum (art)
mexic-artemuseum.org

O. Henry Museum (history)
austintexas.gov/department/o-henry-museum

Pioneer Farms
pioneerfarms.org

Texas Memorial Museum (history, natural history)
tmm.utexas.edu

Texas Military Forces Museum
texasmilitaryforcesmuseum.org

Texas Music Museum
texasmusicmuseum.org

Thinkery (children's museum)
thinkeryaustin.org

Umlauf Sculpture Garden & Museum
umlaufsculpture.org

Wild Basin Wilderness Preserve
stedwards.edu/centers-institutes/wild-basin-creative-research-center

Women and Their Work
womenandtheirwork.org

Bay City

Matagorda County Museum and Children's Museum
visitbaycity.org/arts-culture/museum

Beaumont

Art Museum of Southeast Texas
amset.org

Edison Museum (science)
edisonmuseum.org

Fire Museum of Texas
firemuseumoftexas.org

Spindletop/Gladys City Boomtown Museum (history)
lamar.edu/spindletop-gladys-city

Texas Energy Museum (history)
texasenergymuseum.org

Beeville

Beeville Art Museum
facebook.com/pages/category/Art-Museum/Beeville-Art-Museum-103515313030905

Belton

Bell County Museum
bellcountymuseum.org

Big Spring

Heritage of Big Spring
heritagebigspring.com

Bonham

Fannin County Museum of History
fannincountymuseum.org

Fort Inglish Village
visitbonham.com/things-to-see/fort-inglish-village

Sam Rayburn Library/Museum
cah.utexas.edu/museums/rayburn.php

Borger

Hutchinson County Historical Museum
borgertx.gov/264/Hutchinson-County-Historical-Museum

Brownsville

Brownsville Heritage Museum (history)
brownsvillehistory.org

Brownsville Museum of Fine Art
bmfa.us

Children's Museum of Brownsville
cmofbrownsville.org

Costumes of the Americas Museum
cotam.net

RGV Commemorative Air Force Museum
rgvcaf.org/museum.html

Stillman House Museum (history)
www.brownsvillehistory.org/stillman-house-museum.html

Brownwood

Brown County Museum of History
browncountyhistory.org/bcmoh.html

Lehnis Railroad Museum
brownwoodtexas.gov/228/Lehnis-Railroad-Museum

Bryan-College Station

Brazos Valley African American Museum
bvaam.org

Brazos Valley Museum of Natural History
brazosvalleymuseum.org

Children's Museum of the Brazos Valley
cmbv.org

George H.W. Bush Presidential Library
bush41.org

University Art Galleries
uart.tamu.edu

Buffalo Gap

Buffalo Gap Historic Village
taylorcountyhistorycenter.com

Burton

Burton Cotton Gin and Museum
cottonginmuseum.org

Canadian

The Citadelle Art Museum
thecitadelle.org

River Valley Pioneer Museum
rivervalleymuseum.org

Canyon

Panhandle-Plains Historical Museum
panhandleplains.org

Carthage

Texas Country Music Hall of Fame & Tex Ritter Museum
tcmhof.com

Clarendon

Saints' Roost Museum (history)
saintsroostmuseum.com

Clifton

Bosque Museum (history)
bosquemuseum.org

Conroe

Heritage Museum of Montgomery County
heritagemuseum.us

Corpus Christi

Art Museum of South Texas
artmuseumofsouthtexas.org

Corpus Christi Museum of Science and History
ccmuseum.com

The facade of the Ellsworth Kelly "Austin" Chapel stands at the Blanton Museum of Art on the University of Texas campus in Austin, TX, on March 7, 2020. Photo by Keith Ewing/Flickr (CC).

Texas State Aquarium
texasstateaquarium.org

Texas State Museum of Asian Cultures
texasasianculturesmuseum.org

USS Lexington Museum
usslexington.com

Corsicana

Pearce Western Art/Civil War Museum
pearcemuseum.com

Cotulla

Brush Country Historical Museum
texastropicaltrail.com/plan-your-adventure/historic-sites-and-cities/sites/brush-country-museum

Dalhart

XIT Museum (history)
xitmuseum.com

Dallas

African American Museum
aamdallas.org

Crow Museum of Asian Art
crowcollection.org

Dallas Heritage Village
dallasheritagevillage.org

Dallas Historical Society (Fair Park)
dallashistory.org

Dallas Museum of Art
dma.org

Frontiers of Flight Museum
flightmuseum.com

George W. Bush Presidential Center
georgewbushlibrary.smu.edu

Perot Museum of Nature and Science
perotmuseum.org

Nasher Sculpture Center
nashersculpturecenter.org

Meadows Museum (art)
meadowsmuseumdallas.org

The Sixth Floor Museum (history)
jfk.org

Denison

Red River Railroad Museum
redriverrailmuseum.org

Denton

Courthouse-on-the-Square Museum
dentoncounty.gov/Facilities/Facility/Details/Courthouseonthe Square-Museum-11

Denton Firefighters Museum
discoverdenton.com/listing/denton-firefighters-museum/455

University of North Texas Art Galleries
galleries.cvad.unt.edu

Dublin

Dublin Bottling Works
dublinbottlingworks.com

Dublin Rodeo Heritage Museum
rodeoheritagemuseum.org

Dumas

Window on the Plains Museum
dumasmuseumandartcenter.org

Edgewood

Edgewood Heritage Park and Historical Village
edgewoodheritagepark.org

Edinburg

Museum of South Texas History
mosthistory.org

El Campo

El Campo Museum of Natural History
elcampomuseum.org

El Paso

Centennial Museum/Chihuahuan Desert Gardens
utep.edu/centennial-museum

El Paso Museum of Archaeology
archaeology.elpasotexas.gov

El Paso Museum of Art
epma.art

El Paso Museum of History
history.elpasotexas.gov

Fort Davis

Chihuahuan Desert Research Institute
cdri.org

Fort Stockton

Annie Riggs Museum (history)
historicfortstocktontx.com/attractions-2/annie-riggs-memorial-museum

Fort Worth

Amon Carter Museum (art)
cartermuseum.org

Cattle Raisers Museum
cattleraisersmuseum.org

Fort Worth Museum of Science and History
fwmuseum.org

Kimbell Art Museum
kimbellart.org

Log Cabin Village (history)
logcabinvillage.org

Modern Art Museum of Fort Worth
themodern.org

National Cowgirl Museum and Hall of Fame
cowgirl.net

Sid Richardson Collection of Western Art
sidrichardsonmuseum.org

Texas Civil War Museum
texascivilwarmuseum.com

Fredericksburg

Gillespie County Historical Society
pioneermuseum.net

National Museum of the Pacific War
pacificwarmuseum.org

Frisco

Museum of the American Railroad
historictrains.org

National Videogame Museum
nvmusa.org

Galveston

The Bryan Museum (art, history)
thebryanmuseum.org

Galveston Children's Museum
galvestoncm.org

Moody Mansion
moodymansion.org

Offshore Energy Center/Ocean Star (science, industry)
oceanstaroec.com

Texas Seaport Museum and Tallship "Elissa"
galvestonhistory.org/sites/1877-tall-ship-elissa-at-the-galveston-historic-seaport

Gilmer

Flight of Phoenix Aviation Museum
flightofthephoenix.org

Greenville

Audie Murphy/American Cotton Museum
cottonmuseum.com

Henderson

The Depot Museum (history)
depotmuseum.com

Houston

Blaffer Art Museum, University of Houston
blafferartmuseum.org

Children's Museum of Houston
cmhouston.org

Contemporary Arts Museum
camh.org

Czech Center Museum
czechcenter.org

The Health Museum
thehealthmuseum.org

Houston Center for Contemporary Craft
crafthouston.org

Houston Center for Photography
hcponline.org

Houston Fire Museum (history)
houstonfiremuseum.org

Houston Museum of Natural Science
hmns.org

Lawndale Art Center
lawndaleartcenter.org

Lone Star Flight Museum
lonestarflight.org

The Menil Collection (art)
menil.org

Museum of Fine Arts
mfah.org

Museum of Printing History
printingmuseum.org

San Jacinto Museum of History
sanjacinto-museum.org

Space Center Houston
spacecenter.org

Huntsville

Sam Houston Memorial Museum
samhoustonmemorialmuseum.com

Texas Prison Museum
txprisonmuseum.org

Kerrville

Museum of Western Art
museumofwesternart.com

Kilgore

East Texas Oil Museum
easttexasoilmuseum.kilgore.edu

Lake Jackson

Lake Jackson Historical Museum
ljhistory.org

Laredo

Republic of the Rio Grande Museum
webbheritage.org/museums

Texas A&M International University Planetarium
tamiu.edu/planetarium

League City

Butler Longhorn Museum
butlerlonghornmuseum.com

West Bay Common School Children's Museum (history)
oneroomschoolhouse.org

Longview

Longview Museum of Fine Arts
lmfa.org

Lubbock

FiberMax Center for Discovery: Agriculture
agriculturehistory.org

Buddy Holly Center (history, music)
buddyhollycenter.org

Museum of Texas Tech University (art, humanities, science)
depts.ttu.edu/museumttu

National Ranching Heritage Center
depts.ttu.edu/nrhc

Science Spectrum
sciencespectrum.org

Lufkin

Naranjo Museum of Natural History
naranjomuseum.org

Texas Forestry Museum
treetexas.com

Marfa

The Chinati Foundation (art)
chinati.org

Marshall

Harrison County Historical Museum
harrisoncountymuseum.org

Michelson Museum of Art
michelsonmuseum.org

McAllen

International Museum of Art & Science
theimasonline.org

McKinney

Heard Natural Science Museum & Wildlife Sanctuary
heardmuseum.org

Midland

Museum of the Southwest (art, science, children's)
museumsw.org

Petroleum Museum
petroleummuseum.org

Nacogdoches

Millard's Crossing Historic Village
mchvnac.com

New Braunfels

McKenna Children's Museum
mckennakids.org

Sophienburg Museum & Archives
www.sophienburg.com

Odessa

Ellen Noel Art Museum
noelartmuseum.org

Presidential Archives and Library
shepperdinstitute.com/presidential-archives

Orange

Stark Museum of Art
starkculturalvenues.org

Panhandle

Carson County Square House Museum
squarehousemuseum.weebly.com

Perryton

Museum of the Plains
museumoftheplains.com

Plano

Heritage Farmstead Museum
heritagefarmstead.org

Port Arthur

Museum of the Gulf Coast (history)
museumofthegulfcoast.org

Port Lavaca

Calhoun County Museum (history)
calhouncountymuseum.org

Richmond

George Ranch Historical Park
georgeranch.org

Rockport

Texas Maritime Museum
texasmaritimemuseum.org

Rosenberg

The Black Cowboy Museum
blackcowboymuseum.org

Rosenberg Railroad Museum
rosenbergrrmuseum.org

Round Top

Henkel Square (history)
henkelsquareroundtop.com

Winedale Historical Complex
cah.utexas.edu/museums/winedale.php

San Angelo

Miss Hattie's Bordello Museum
misshatties.com

San Angelo Museum of Fine Arts and Children's Art Museum
samfa.org

San Antonio

The Alamo
thealamo.org

Briscoe Western Art Museum
briscoemuseum.org

Holocaust Memorial Museum
hmmsa.org

Institute of Texan Cultures
texancultures.com

Magic Lantern Castle Museum
www.magiclanterns.org

The McNay (art)
mcnayart.org

San Antonio Art League & Museum
saalm.org

San Antonio Museum of Art
samuseum.org

Witte Museum (science, history)
wittemuseum.org

San Marcos

LBJ Museum San Marcos
lbjmuseum.com

Southwestern Writers Collection and Wittliff Gallery of Southwestern & Mexican Photography
thewittliffcollections.txstate.edu

Sarita

Kenedy Ranch Museum of South Texas
kenedy.org/museum

Schulenburg

Stanzel Model Aircraft Museum
stanzelmuseum.org

Serbin

Texas Wendish Heritage Museum
texaswendish.org/museum

Sherman

Sherman Jazz Museum
shermanjazzmuseum.com

The Sherman Museum (history)
theshermanmuseum.org

Snyder

Scurry County Museum
scurrycountymuseum.org

Sulphur Springs

SouthWest Dairy Museum and Education Center
southwestdairyfarmers.com

Teague

The B-RI Railroad Museum
therailroadmuseum.com

Temple

Czech Heritage Museum
czechheritagemuseum.org

Railroad and Heritage Museum
templerrhm.org

Texarkana

Museum of Regional History
texarkanamuseum.org

The Woodlands

The Woodlands Children's Museum
woodlandschildrensmuseum.org

Thurber

W.K. Gordon Center for Industrial History of Texas
tarleton.edu/gordoncenter

Tyler

Discovery Science Place
discoveryscienceplace.org

Historic Aviation Memorial Museum
tylerhamm.com

Smith County Historical Museum
tylertexasonline.com/tyler-texas-museums.htm

Tyler Museum of Art
tylermuseum.org

Victoria

Children's Discovery Museum
cdmgoldencrescent.com

Museum of the Coastal Bend (history)
museumofthecoastalbend.org

The Nave Museum (art)
navemuseum.com

Waco

Dr Pepper Museum (history)
drpeppermuseum.com

Martin Museum of Art
baylor.edu/martinmuseum/

Mayborn Museum Complex (history, science)
baylor.edu/mayborn

Texas Ranger Hall of Fame/Museum
texasranger.org

Texas Sports Hall of Fame
tshof.org

Washington

Star of the Republic Museum (history)
starmuseum.org

Weatherford

Museum of the Americas
museumoftheamericas.com

National Vietnam War Museum
nationalvnwarmuseum.org

Wharton

20th Century Technology Museum
20thcenturytech.com

White Settlement

White Settlement Historical Museum
wsmuseum.com

Wichita Falls

Kell House Museum (history)
wichita-heritage.org

Wichita Falls Museum of Art
wfma.msutexas.edu

Museum of North Texas History
museumofnorthtexashistory.org

Professional Wrestling Hall of Fame & Museum
pro-wrestling-hall-of-fame-museum.business.site

Yoakum

Yoakum Heritage Museum
yoakumareachamber.com/visit-yoakum/experience-history☆

Public Libraries in Texas

Texas public libraries continue to strive to meet the education and information needs of Texans by providing library services of high quality with often-times-limited resources.

Each year, services provided by public libraries increase, with more visits to public libraries and higher attendance in library programs.

The challenges facing public libraries in Texas are many and varied. The costs for providing electronic and online sources, in addition to traditional services, are growing faster than budgets.

Urban libraries are trying to serve growing populations, while libraries in rural areas are trying to serve remote populations and provide distance learning where possible.

National rankings of public libraries are published by the Institute of Museum and Library Services at imls.gov/research-evaluation/data-collection/public-libraries-survey.

When comparing Texas statistics to those nationally, Texas continues to rank below most of the other states in most categories, with the exception of public use of internet terminals.

Complete statistical information on public libraries is available on the Texas State Library's website: tsl.texas.gov/landing/statistics.html. There is also a listing of libraries at: tsl.texas.gov/texshare/libsearch. ☆

Source: Library Development Division of the Texas State Library and Archives in Austin.

Texas Institute of Letters Awards

Each year since 1939, the **Texas Institute of Letters** (texasinstituteofletters.org) has honored outstanding literature and journalism that is either by Texans or about Texas subjects.

Awards have been made for fiction, nonfiction, Southwest history, general information, magazine and newspaper journalism, children's books, translation, poetry, and book design. The awards of recent years are listed below; see previous recipients at tshaonline.org.

2021

Bryan Washington: *Memorial: A Novel*

Marisol Cortez: *Luz at Midnight*

Joe Holley: *Sutherland Springs*

Chera Hammons: *Maps of Injury*

David Meischen: *Anyone's Son*

Miguel Angel González-Quiroga: *War and Peace on the Rio Grande Frontier: 1830-1880*

Darcie Little Badger: *Elatsoe*

Francisco Stork: *Illegal*

Christina Soontornvat: *A Wish in the Dark*

Jerome Pumphrey and Jarrett Pumphrey: *The Old Truck*

Mary Ann Jacob: designer of *Daddy-O's Book of Big-Ass Art,* by Bob "Daddy-O" Wade

David Meischen: "Crossing the Light," *Storylandia*

ire'ne lara silva: "A Place Before Words," *Texas Highways*

Lon Tinkle Award (for career): Benjamin Alire Sáenz

2020

Oscar Cásares: *Where We Come From*

Bryan Washington: *Lot: Stories*

Holly George-Warren: *Janis: Her Life and Music*

Ron Tyler: *The Art of Texas: 250 Years*

Naomi Shihab Nye: *The Tiny Journalist*

Lupe Mendez: *Why I Am Like Tequila* (Aquarius Press)

Sergio Troncoso: "Rosary on the Border" in *A Peculiar Kind of Immigrant's Son*

Skip Hollandsworth: "Sabika's Story," in *Texas Monthly*

Rebecca Balcárcel: *The Other Half of Happy*

Rubén Degollado: *Throw: A Novel*

José M. Hernández: *The Boy Who Touched the Stars*

Cyrus Cassells: translator of *Still Life with Children: Selected Poems of Francesc Parcerisas*

Lon Tinkle Award (for career): John Rechy

2019

Ben Fountain: *Beautiful Country Burn Again: Democracy, Rebellion, and Revolution*

Natalia Sylvester: *Everyone Knows You Go Home*

Stephen Markley: *Ohio*

Tarfia Faizullah: *Registers of Illuminated Villages*

Megan Peak: *Girldom*

Brent Nongbri: *God's Library: The Archaeology of the Earliest Christian Manuscripts*

David Bowles: *The Feathered Serpent, Dark Heart of Sky: Myths of Mexico* and *They Call Me Güero*

Varian Johnson: *The Parker Inheritance*

Chris Barton: *What Can You Do with a Voice Like That?*

Clay Reynolds: "Railroad Man," *New Madrid,* and "Autumn Moon," *New Texas*

Lon Tinkle Award (for career): Naomi Shihab Nye

2018

Jan Reid: *Sins of the Younger Sons*

Chanelle Benz: *The Man Who Shot Out My Eye is Dead*

Roger D. Hodge: *Texas Blood: Seven Generations Among the Outlaws, Ranchers, Indians, Missionaries, Soldiers, and Smugglers of the Borderlands*

Jerry D. Thompson: *Tejano Tiger: José de los Santos Benavides and the Texas-Mexico Borderlands, 1823–1891*

Sasha Pimentel: *For Want of Water: and other poems*

Vanessa Villarreal: *Beast Meridian*

Brett Anthony Johnston: "Miss McElroy," *Ecotone*

Rose Cahalan: "Ride Like a Girl," *Texas Observer*

Michael Merschel: *Revenge of the Star Survivors*

Francisco X. Stork: *Disappeared*

Xelena González and Adriana M. Garcia: *All Around Us*

Philip Boehm: translator of *Chasing the King of Hearts,* by Hanna Krall

Mary Ann Jacob: designer, *The Nueces River, Rio Escondido,* by Margie Crisp and William B. Montgomery

Lon Tinkle Award (for career): Sandra Cisneros

2017

Paulette Jiles: *News of the World*

Amy Gentry: *Good as Gone*

Skip Hollandsworth: *The Midnight Assassin*

Max Krochmal: *Blue Texas: The Making of a Multiracial Democratic Coalition in the Civil Rights Era*

Bruce Bond: *Gold Bee*

Miriam Bird Greenberg: *In the Volcano's Mouth*

Stephen Harrigan: "Off Course," *Texas Monthly*

David Meischen: "Cicada Song," *Salamander*

Kathi Appelt and Alison McGhee: *Maybe a Fox*

Phillippe Diederich: *Playing for the Devil's Fire*

Dianna Hutts Aston: *A Beetle Is Shy*

Kristie Lee: *From Tea Cakes to Tamales*

Lon Tinkle Award (for career): Pat Mora

2016

Antonio Ruiz–Camacho: *Barefoot Dogs*

Mary Helen Specht: *Migratory Animals*

Jan Jarboe Russell: *The Train to Crystal City*

Andrew Torget III: *Seeds of Empire*

Laurie Ann Guerrero: *A Crown for Gumecindo*

J. Scott Brownlee: *Requiem for Used Ignition Cap*

W.K. Stratton: "My Brother's Secret," *Texas Monthly*

Brian Van Reet: "The Chaff," *Iowa Review*

Don Tate: *The Remarkable Story of George Moses Horton: Poet*

Brian Yansky: *Utopia, Iowa*

Pat Mora: *The Remembering Day/El dia de los muertos*

Andrea Caillouet: *The Luck Archive: Exploring Belief, Superstition, and Tradition*

Marian Schwartz: translator of *Anna Karenina,* by Leo Tolstoy

Lon Tinkle Award (for career): Sarah Bird

2015

Elizabeth Crook: *Monday, Monday*

Michael Morton: *Getting Life: An Innocent Man's 25-Year Journey from Prison to Peace*

Merritt Tierce: *Love Me Back*

Lawrence T. Jones: *Lens on the Texas Frontier*

Katherine Hoerth: *Goddess Wears Cowboy Boots*

Brian Van Reet: "Eat the Spoil," in *Missouri Review*

Chloe Honum: *The Tulip-Flame*

Pamela Colloff: "The Witness," *Texas Monthly*

Bill Wittliff and Ellen McKie: *The Devil's Backbone,* written by Bill Wittliff, illustrated by Jack Unruh

Nikki Lofton: *Nightingale's Nest*

Glaudia Guadalupe Martinez: *Pig Park*

Pat Mora and Lilbby Martinez: *I Pledge Allegiance*

Lon Tinkle Award (for career): Lawrence Wright

2014

Tom Zigal: *Many Rivers to Cross*

John Talifarro: *All The Great Prizes: The Life of John Hay from Lincoln to Roosevelt*

Lawrence Wright: *Going Clear: Scientology, Hollywood, and the Prison of Belief*

Nan Cuba: *Body and Bread*

Raúl Coronado: *A World Not to Come: A History of Latino Writing and Print Culture*

Pattiann Rogers: *Holy Heathen Rhapsody*

Bret Anthony Johnston: "To a Good Home," *Virginia Quarterly Review*

Sasha West: *Failure And I Bury The Body*

John MacCormack: "Life On The Shale," *San Antonio Express-News,* series

Lindsay Starr: *Two Prospectors: The Letters of Sam Shepard and Johnny Dark*

Xavier Garza: *Maximilian and the Mystery of the Bingo Rematch*

Kathi Appelt: *The True Blue Scouts of Sugar Man Swamp*

David Bowles: *Flower, Song, Dance: Aztec and Mayan Poetry*

Lon Tinkle Award (for career): Jan Reid

2013

Ben Fountain: *Billy Lynn's Long Halftime Walk*

Margie Crisp: *River of Contrasts*

Kevin Grauke: *Shadows of Men*

Kate Sayen Kirkland: *Captain James A. Baker of Houston: 1857–1941*

Ken Fontenot: *Kingdom of Birds*

James Sanderson: "Bankers," in *Descant*

Kathleen Winter: *Nostalgia for the Criminal Past*

Mellissa Del Bosque: "The Deadliest Place in Mexico," *The Texas Observer,* February, 12, 2012

Kristina Kachele: *In the Country of Empty Crosses,* written by Arturo Madrid

Donna Rubin: *Log Cabin Kitty*

Melodie Cuate: *Journey to Plum Creek*

Lon Tinkle Award (for career): Stephen Harrigan

2012

Stephen Harrigan: *Remember Ben Clayton*

Steven Fenberg: *Unprecedented Power: Jesse Jones, Capitalism, and the Common Good*

Siobhan Fallon: *You Know When the Men Are Gone*

Christopher Long: *The Looshaus*

Jennifer Grotz: *The Needle*

Bret Anthony Johnston: "Paradeability," *American Short Fiction*

Jose Antonio Rodriguez: *The Shallow End of Sleep*

Skip Hollandsworth: "The Lost Boys," *Texas Monthly,* April 2011

Jordan Smith: "The Science of Injustice," *Austin Chronicle,* August 19, 2011

Barbara Werden and Lindsay Starr: *Lone Star Law,* written by Michael Ariens

Dave Oliphant: *After-Dinner Declarations* by Nicanor Parra

Elaine Scott: *Space, Stars and the Beginning of Time*

J.L. Powers: *This Thing Called the Future*

Lon Tinkle Award (for career): Gary Cartwright

2011[1]

Jan Reid: *Comanche Sundown*

Gary Lavergne: *Before Brown: Heman Marion Sweatt, Thurgood Marshall and the Long Road to Justice*

Neil Foley: *Quest for Equality: The Failed Promise of Black-Brown Solidarity*

Bruce Machart: *The Wake of Forgiveness*

Barbara Ras: *The Last Skin*

Elyse Fenton: *Clamor*

Pamela Colloff: "Innocence Lost," *Texas Monthly,* October 2010

C.W. Smith: "Caustic," *Southwest Review,* Summer 2010

Tim Madigan: series on the surgery of a child, *Fort Worth Star-Telegram*

Julie Savasky and DJ Stout: *The Gernsheim Collection*

Diane Gonzales Bertrand: *The Party for Papa Luis/La Fiesta Para Papa Luis*

Dotti Enderle: *Crosswire*

Lon Tinkle Award (for career): C.W. Smith

2009

Scott Blackwood: *We Agreed to Meet Just Here*

Bryan Burrough: *The Big Rich: The Rise and Fall of the Greatest Texas Oil Fortunes*

John Pipkin: *Woodsburner*

Emilio Zamoro: *Claiming Rights and Righting Wrongs in Texas: Mexican Workers and Job Politics During World War II*

William Virgil Davis: *Landscape and Journey*

John Spong: "Holding Garmsir," *Texas Monthly,* January 2009.

Gwendolyn Zepeda: *Sunflowers/Girasoles*

Marjorie Kempner: "Discovered America," *Southwest Review,* Fall 2009

Lindsay Starr: *"I Do Not Apologize for the Length of This Letter": The Mari Sandoz Letters on Native American Rights, 1940–1965*

Lon Tinkle Award (for career): Larry L. King

2008

Brendan M. Greeley Jr.: *The Two Thousand Yard Stare: Tom Lea's World War II Paintings, Drawings, and Eyewitness Accounts*

Thomas Cobb: *Shavetail*

Ann Weisgarber: *The Personal History of Rachel DuPree*

Rick Bass: "Mary Katherine's First Deer" in *Gray's Sporting Journal*

Todd Benson and Guillermo Contreras: "Texas' Deadliest Export" in the *San Antonio Express-News*

Benjamin Alire Saenz: *The Perfect Season for Dreaming*

Claudia Guadalupe Martinez: *The Smell of Old Lady Perfume*

James Allen Hall: *Now You're the Enemy*

Kerry Neville Bakken: "Indignity" in *Gettysburg Review*

James M. Smallwood: *The Feud that Wasn't: The Taylor Ring, Bill Sutton, John Wesley Hardin, and Violence in Texas*

Barbara Whitehead: *Traces of Forgotten Places*

Reginald Gibbons: translator of *Sophocles, Selected Poems: Odes and Fragments*

Lon Tinkle Award (for career): Carolyn Osborn ☆

---

1 Beginning in 2011, the award date reflects the actual date of the presentation. For instance, Larry King's 2009 award was actually presented in 2010.

State Cultural Agencies Assist the Arts

Culture in Texas, as in any market, is a mixture of activity generated by both the commercial and the nonprofit sectors.

The commercial sector encompasses Texas-based profit-making businesses, including commercial recording artists, nightclubs, record companies, private galleries, assorted boutiques that carry fine art collectibles, and private dance and music halls.

Texas also has extensive cultural resources offered by nonprofit organizations that are engaged in charitable, educational, and humanitarian activities.

The Legislature has authorized five state agencies to administer cultural services and funds for the public good. The agencies are:

Texas Commission on the Arts; Texas Film Commission; Texas Historical Commission; Texas State Library and Archives Commission; and the State Preservation Board.

Although not a state agency, another organization that provides cultural services to the citizens of Texas is Humanities Texas.

The Commission on the Arts was established in 1965 to develop a receptive climate for the arts through the conservation and advancement of Texas' rich and diverse arts and cultural industries.

The Texas Commission on the Arts' goals are:

- Provide grants for the arts and cultural industries in Texas.
- Provide the financial, human, and technical resources necessary to ensure viable arts and cultural communities.
- Promote widespread attendance at arts and cultural performances and exhibitions in Texas.
- Ensure access to arts in Texas through marketing, fund raising, and cultural tourism.
- The commission is responsible for several initiatives including:
- Arts Education: programs that serve the curricular and training needs of the state's school districts, private schools, and home schools.
- Marketing and Public Relations: marketing and fund-raising expertise to generate funds for agency operations and increase visibility of the arts in Texas.
- Cultural Tourism: programs that develop and promote tourism destinations featuring the arts.

Information on programs is available on the Texas Commission on the Arts at arts.texas.gov. ☆

Source: Principally the Texas Commission on the Arts, along with other state cultural agencies.

Dancers perform in "The Good Fight Jam" in San Antonio, TX, on October 24, 2020. Photo by Cooper Chiu/Flickr (PD).

Performing Arts Organizations: Dance, music, theater

The Texas Commission on the Arts provides a listing of performing arts companies and artists in Texas at arts.texas.gov/artroster/roster/show/all. There are links arranged by category; dance, theater, music, etc.

There is also https://www.arts.texas.gov/resources/art-in-communities, which provides more information about community arts programs, as well as swpap.org, with performing arts organizations by city.

golf082/Flickr (CC)

Anthony V. Moulay/Flickr (CC)

Dave Pinter/Flickr (CC)

Wally Gobetz/Flickr (CC)

libby rosof/Flickr (CC)

Clockwise: Jennifer Holliday sings in Northalsted, Chicago, IL, on August 7, 2010; Boz Scaggs performs at Bluesfest 2014 in LeBreton Flats, Ottawa, Canada, on April 18, 2014; Matthew McConaughey presents the Lincoln Navigator at the 2016 New York International Auto Show on March 22, 2016; a detail is shown of Trenton Doyle Hancock's "Flower Bed II: A Prelude to Damnation" from the Institute of Contemporary Art in Philadelphia, Pennsylvania, on April 24, 2008; The National September 11 Memorial & Museum, whose plaza was designed by Elaine Molinar and Craig Dykers, is shown in Battery Park City, New York, New York, on April 29, 2012.

Texas Medal of the Arts Awards

The Texas Medals of the Arts are presented to artists and arts patrons with Texas ties.

The awards are administered by the Texas Cultural Trust Council.

The council was established to raise money and awareness for the Texas Cultural Trust Fund, which was created by the Legislature in 1993 to support cultural arts in Texas (**txculturaltrust.org**).

The medals, awarded every two years, were first presented in 2001. A concurrent proclamation by the state Senate and House of Representatives honors the recipients, and the governor presents the awards in Austin.

Source: Texas Commission on the Arts.

2019

Design: Brandon Maxwell, Longview, fashion designer, photographer.
Music: Boz Scaggs, Plano, singer/songwriter.
Visual arts: Trenton Doyle Hancock, Houston and Paris, TX, artist.
Music Ensemble: Conspirare, Austin, choral ensemble.
Literary: Stephen Harrigan, Austin, Abilene, and Corpus Christi, author, journalist.
Film: Matthew McConaughey, Austin, Uvalde, and Longview, actor.
Multimedia: Mark Seliger, Amarillo and Houston, photographer.
Theater: Jennifer Holliday, Houston, singer, actor.
Arts education: Vidal M. Treviño School of Communications and Fine Arts, Laredo.
Architecture: Elaine Molinar, El Paso, and Craig Dykers, San Antonio.

2017

Lifetime Achievement Award: Kenny Rogers of Houston.
Multimedia: Kris Kristofferson, Brownsville.
Music: Yolanda Adams, Houston.
Visual arts: Leo Villareal, El Paso, artist.
Dance: Lauren Anderson, Houston.
Literary: John Phillip Santos, San Antonio.
Film: Janine Turner, Euless, actor.
Journalism: Scott Pelley, San Antonio, news broadcaster.
Television: Jaclyn Smith, Houston, actor.
Theater: Renée Elise Goldsberry, Houston.
Arts education: Dallas Black Dance Theatre.
Architecture: Frank Welch, Dallas.
Individual arts patron: Lynn Wyatt, Houston.
Corporate arts patrons: John Paul and Eloise DeJoria, Austin.
Foundation arts patron: Tobin Endowment, San Antonio.

2015

Lifetime Achievement Award: The Gatlin Brothers of Seminole, Abilene, and Odessa.
Multimedia: Emilio Nicolas Sr. of San Antonio, for work as broadcaster.
Music: T Bone Burnett of Fort Worth.
Visual arts: Rick Lowe of Houston, artist.

Dance: Kilgore Rangerettes.
Literary: Lawrence Wright, Austin and Dallas.
Film: Jamie Foxx, Terrell, actor.
Television: Dan Rather, Wharton, news broadcaster.
Television: Chandra Wilson, Houston, actor.
Theater: Robert Schenkkan, Austin.
Arts education: Booker T. Washington High School for the Performing and Visual Arts, Dallas.
Architecture: Charles Renfro, Houston.
Individual arts patron: Margaret McDermott, Dallas.
Corporate arts patron: Dr Pepper Snapple Group, Plano.
Standing Ovation Award: Ruth Altshuler of Dallas.

2013

Multimedia: Eva Longoria of Corpus Christi, for work as actress, author, and philanthropist.
Music: Steve Miller of Dallas.
Visual arts: James Surls, Splendora, artist.
Dance: Houston Ballet.
Television/Film: Ricardo Chavira, San Antonio, actor.
Theater arts: Joe Sears and Jaston Williams, Austin (Greater Tuna fame).
Arts education: Big Thought / Gigi Antoni, Dallas.
Individual arts patron: Gene Jones and Charlotte Jones Anderson, Dallas.
Foundation arts patron: Kimbell Arts Foundation, Fort Worth.
Corporate arts patron: Texas Monthly.

2011

Lifetime Achievement Award: Barbara Smith Conrad from Center Point near Pittsburg, operatic mezzo-soprano and civil rights icon.
Music: ZZ Top of Houston, legendary band that sold over 50 million albums.
Literary: Robert M. Edsel, Dallas, author and founder/president of the Monuments Men Foundation for the Preservation of Art.
Visual arts: James Drake, Lubbock, artist.
Television: Bob Schieffer, Fort Worth, CBS news anchor.
Theater arts: Alley Theatre, Houston.
Multimedia: Ray Benson, Austin, front man for Asleep at the Wheel and co-writer of the play A Ride with Bob based on the life of Bob Wills.
Film: Marcia Gay Harden, UT-Austin graduate, Oscar-winning actress.
Film: Bill Paxton, Fort Worth, four-time Golden Globe nominee.
Arts education: Tom Staley, director of the Harry Ransom Center at UT-Austin.
Individual arts patron: Ernest and Sarah Butler of Austin, major donors to Austin arts groups.
Corporate arts patron: H-E-B, grocer with a long history of supporting the arts throughout Texas.

2009

A Standing Ovation Award was presented to former First Lady Laura Bush of Midland and Dallas.
Lifetime Achievement Award: posthumously to artist Robert Rauschenberg, born in Port Arthur.
Music: Clint Black of Katy, country music singer/songwriter.
Literary: T.R. Fehrenbach of San Antonio. Mr. Fehrenbach, born in San Benito, is the author of 18 nonfiction books, including Lone Star: A History of Texas and Texans.
Visual arts: Keith Carter of Beaumont, photographer.
Theater arts: Betty Buckley of Fort Worth, Tony Award winner and film actress.
Multimedia: *Austin City Limits,* the 30-year television series.
Film: Robert Rodriguez of Austin. Mr. Rodriguez, born in San Antonio, is a film director and writer.
Architecture: David Lake of Austin and Ted Flato of Corpus Christi, both now working in San Antonio.
Arts education: Pianist James Dick of Round Top, founder of the International Festival-Institute there.
Individual arts patron: Edith O'Donnell of Dallas.
Corporate arts patron: Anheuser-Busch of St. Louis and Houston.

2007

Lifetime Achievement Award: Broadcast newsman Walter Cronkite of Houston.
Music: Ornette Coleman of Fort Worth, jazz saxophonist.
Dance: Alvin Ailey American Dance Theater. The late Alvin Ailey, born in Rogers, was a creator of African American dance works.
Literary: writer Sandra Brown of Waco.
Visual arts: Jesús Moroles of Corpus Christi/Rockport, sculptor.
Theater arts: actress Judith Ivey of El Paso.
Multimedia: Bill Wittliff of Taft and Austin, publisher, writer, photographer, director, producer.
Arts education: Paul Baker of Hereford/Waelder. Headed drama departments at Baylor and Trinity universities.
Individual arts patron: Diana and Bill Hobby of Houston.
Corporate arts patron: Neiman Marcus, Dallas.
Foundation arts patron: Sid W. Richardson Foundation of Fort Worth.

2005

Lifetime Achievement Award: singer Vikki Carr of El Paso.
Television/theater: actress Phylicia Rashad of Houston.
Music: singer/songwriter Lyle Lovett of Klein.
Dance: Ben Stevenson of Houston and Fort Worth.
Literary arts: Naomi Shihab Nye of San Antonio.
Visual arts: Jose Cisneros of El Paso.
Theater: Robert Wilson of Waco.
Arts education: Ginger Head-Gearheart of Fort Worth, advocate of arts education in public schools.
Individual arts patrons: Joe R. and Teresa Lozano Long of Austin, philanthropists.
Foundation arts patron: Nasher Foundation/Dallas.

2003

Lifetime Achievement: John Graves of Glen Rose, author of *Goodbye to A River.*
Media-film/television acting: Fess Parker of Fort Worth.
Music: country singer Charley Pride of Dallas.
Dance: Tommy Tune of Wichita Falls and Houston.
Theater: Enid Holm of Odessa, actress and former executive director of Texas Nonprofit Theatres.
Literary arts: Sandra Cisneros of San Antonio.
Visual arts: sculptor Glenna Goodacre of Dallas.
Folk arts: Tejano singer Lydia Mendoza of San Antonio.
Architecture: State Capitol Preservation Project of Austin, headed by Dealey Herndon.
Arts education: theater teacher Marca Lee Bircher, Dallas.
Individual arts patron: philanthropist Nancy B. Hamon of Dallas.
Corporate arts patron: Exxon/Mobil based in Irving.
Foundation arts patron: Houston Endowment Inc.

2001

Lifetime Achievement: Van Cliburn of Fort Worth.
Film: actor Tommy Lee Jones of San Saba.
Music: singer-songwriter Willie Nelson of Austin.
Dance: Debbie Allen of Houston, choreographer, director, actress and composer.
Theater: *Texas* musical-drama producer Neil Hess of Amarillo.
Literary arts: playwright Horton Foote of Wharton.
Visual arts: muralist John Biggers of Houston.
Folk arts: musician brothers Santiago Jimenez Jr. and Flaco Jimenez of San Antonio.
Architecture: restoration architect Wayne Bell of Austin.
Arts education: theater arts director Gilberto Zepeda Jr. of Pharr.
Individual arts patron: philanthropist Jack Blanton of Houston.
Corporate arts patron: SBC Communications Inc. of San Antonio.
Foundation arts patron: Meadows Foundation of Dallas.☆

State Artists of Texas

Since 2001, a committee of seven members appointed by the governor, lieutenant governor, and speaker of the House of Representatives selects the poet laureate, state artists, and state musician based on recommendations from the Texas Commission on the Arts. Earlier, the Legislature made the nominations.

The state historian is appointed by the governor and is recommended by both the Texas State Historical Association and the Texas Historical Commission.

Sources: Texas State Library and Archives; Texas Commission on the Arts; The Dallas Morning News.

Years	Artist, Hometown/Residence
1971-72	Joe Ruiz Grandee, Arlington
1972-73	Melvin C. Warren, Clifton
1973-74	Ronald Thomason, Weatherford A.C. Gentry Jr., Tyler, alternate
1974-75	Joe Rader Roberts, Dripping Springs Bette Lou Voorhis, Austin, alternate
1975-76	Jack White, New Braunfels
July 4, 1975 –July 4, 1976	Robert Summers, Glen Rose Bicentennial Artist
1976-77	James Boren, Clifton Kenneth Wyatt, Lubbock, alternate
1977-78	Edward "Buck" Schiwetz, DeWitt County Renne Hughes, Tarrant County, alternate
1978-79	Jack Cowan, Rockport Gary Henry, Palo Pinto County, alternate Joyce Tally, Caldwell County, alternate
1979-80	Dalhart Windberg, Travis County Grant Lathe, Canyon Lake, alternate
1980-81	Harry Ahysen, Huntsville Jim Reno, Simonton, alternate
1981-82	Jerry Newman, Beaumont Raul Guiterrez, San Antonio, alternate
1982-83	Dr. James H. Johnson, Bryan Armando Hinojosa, Laredo, alternate
1983-84	Raul Gutierrez, San Antonio James Eddleman, Lubbock, alternate
1984-85	Covelle Jones, Lubbock Ragan Gennusa, Austin, alternate
1986-87	Chuck DeHaan, Graford
1987-88	Neil Caldwell, Angleton Rey Gaytan, Austin, alternate
1988-89	George Hallmark, Walnut Springs Tony Eubanks, Grapevine, alternate

Year	Two-dimensional	Three-dimensional
1990-91	Mondel Rogers, Sweetwater	Ron Wells, Cleveland
1991-92	Woodrow Foster, Center	Kent Ullberg, Corpus Christi
	Harold Phenix, Houston, alternate	Mark Clapham, Conroe, alternate
1993-94	Roy Lee Ward, Hunt	James Eddleman, Lubbock
1994-95	Frederick Carter, El Paso	Garland A. Weeks, Wichita Falls
1998-99	Carl Rice Embrey, San Antonio	Edd Hayes, Humble
2000-02	none designated	
2003	Ralph White, Austin	Dixie Friend Gay, Houston
2004	Sam Caldwell, Houston	David Hickman, Dallas
2005	Kathy Vargas, San Antonio	Sharon Kopriva, Houston
2006	George Boutwell, Bosque County	James Surls, Athens
2007	Lee Herring, Rockwall	David Keens, Arlington
2008	Janet Eager Krueger, Encinal	Damian Priour, Austin
2009	René Alvarado, San Angelo	Eliseo Garcia, Farmers Branch
2010	Marc Burckhardt, Austin	John Bennett, Fredericksburg
2011	Melissa Miller, Austin	Jesús Moroles, Rockport
2012	Karl Umlauf, Waco	Bill FitzGibbons, San Antonio
2013	Jim Woodson, Waco, Fort Worth	Joseph Havel, Houston
2014	Julie Speed, Austin, Marfa	Ken Little, Canyon, San Antonio
2015	Vincent Valdez, San Antonio	Margo Sawyer, Houston, Elgin
2016	Dornith Doherty, Houston, Southlake	Dario Robleto, San Antonio, Houston
2017	Kermit Oliver, Refugio, Houston, Waco	Beverly Penn, San Marcos
2018	Sedrick Huckaby, Fort Worth	Beili Liu, Austin
2019	Mary McCleary, Nacogdoches	Rick Lowe, Houston
2020	Earlie Hudnall Jr., Houston	Gabriel Dawe, Dallas
2021	Annette Lawrence, Denton	Jennifer Ling Datchuk, San Antonio
2022	Celia Álvarez Muñoz, El Paso, Arlington	Jesse Lott, Houston

State Historians of Texas

Year	Historian, College
2007-09	Jesús de la Teja, Texas State Univ.
2009-12	Light Cummins, Austin College
2012-16	Bill O'Neal, Panola College
2016-18	vacant
2018-22	Monte Monroe, Texas Tech Univ.

State Musicians of Texas

Year	Artist, Hometown/Residence
2003	James Dick, Round Top
2004	Ray Benson, Austin
2005	Johnny Gimble, Tyler
2006	Billy Joe Shaver, Waco
2007	Dale Watson, Pasadena/Austin
2008	Shelley King, Austin
2009	Willie Nelson, Abbott/Austin
2010	Sara Hickman, Austin
2011	Lyle Lovett, Klein
2012	Billy Gibbons (ZZ Top), Houston
2013	Craig Hella Johnson, Austin
2014	Flaco Jiménez, San Antonio
2015	Jimmie Vaughn, Dallas/Austin
2016	Joe Ely, Lubbock, Austin
2017	George Strait, Poteet/San Antonio
2018	Marcia Ball, Orange/Austin
2019	Little Joe Hernandez, Temple/San Antonio
2020	Emily Gimble, Austin

Poets Laureate of Texas

Years	Poet, Hometown/Residence
1955-57	Pierre Bernard Hill, Hunt
1957-59	Margaret Royalty Edwards, Waco
1959-61	J.V. Chandler, Kingsville Edna Coe Majors, Colorado City, alt.
1961	Lorena Simon, Port Arthur
1962	Marvin Davis Winsett, Dallas
1963	Gwendolyn Bennett Pappas, Houston Vassar Miller, Houston, alternate
1964-65	Jenny Lind Porter, Austin Edith Rayzor Canant, Texas City, alt.
1966	Bessie Maas Rowe, Port Arthur Grace Marie Scott, Abilene, alternate
1967	William E. Bard, Dallas Bessie Maas Rowe, Port Arthur, alt.
1968	Kathryn Henry Harris, Waco Sybil Leonard Armes, El Paso, alt.
1969-70	Anne B. Marely, Austin Rose Davidson Speer, Brady, alt.
1970-71	Mrs. Robby K. Mitchell, McKinney Faye Carr Adams, Dallas, alternate
1971-72	Terry Fontenot, Port Arthur Faye Carr Adams, Dallas, alternate
1972-73	Mrs. Clark Gresham, Burkburnett Marion McDaniel, Sidney, alternate
1973-74	Violette Newton, Beaumont Stella Woodall, San Antonio, alternate
1974-75	Lila Todd O'Neil, Port Arthur C.W. Miller, San Antonio, alternate

Poets Laureate of Texas

Years	Poet, Hometown/Residence
1975-76	Ethel Osborn Hill, Port Arthur Gene Shuford, Denton, alternate
1976-77	Florice Stripling Jeffers, Burkburnett Vera L. Eckert, San Angelo, alternate
1977-78	Ruth Carruth, Vernon Joy Gresham Hagstrom, Burkburnett, alternate.
1978-79	Patsy Stodghill, Dallas Dorothy B. Elfstroman, Galveston, alt.
1979-80	Dorothy B. Elfstroman, Galveston Ruth Carruth, Vernon, alternate
1980-81	Weems S. Dykes, McCamey Mildred Crabree Speer, Amarillo, alt.
1981-82	none designated
1982-83	William D. Barney, Fort Worth Vassar Miller, Houston, alternate
1983-87	none designated
1987-88	Ruth E. Reuther, Wichita Falls
1988-89	Vassar Miller, Houston
1989-93	none designated
1993-94	Mildred Baass, Victoria
1994-99	none designated
2000	James Hoggard, Wichita Falls
2001	Walter McDonald, Lubbock
2002	none designated
2003	Jack Myers, Mesquite
2004	Cleatus Rattan, Cisco
2005	Alan Birkelbach, Plano
2006	Red Steagall, Fort Worth
2007	Steven Fromholz, Kopperl, Sugar Land
2008	Larry Thomas, Houston
2009	Paul Ruffin, Huntsville
2010	Karla K. Morton, Denton, Fort Worth
2011	David M. Parsons, Conroe
2012	Jan Seale, McAllen
2013	Rosemary Catacalos, San Antonio
2014	Dean Young, Austin
2015	Carmen Tafolla, San Antonio
2016	Laurie Ann Guerrero, San Antonio
2017	Jenny Browne, San Antonio
2018	Carol Coffee Reposa, San Antonio
2019	Carrie Fountain, Austin
2020	Emmy Pérez, McAllen
2021	Cyrus Cassells, Austin
2022	Lupe Mendez, Galveston, Houston, Rio Grande Valley

Philosophical Society of Texas Awards of Merit

The Philosophical Society of Texas established the Award of Merit in 2000.

The categories were expanded in 2012 to separate categories, one for fiction and one for nonfiction.

In 2015, an award for poetry was introduced.

The book must be about Texas or the author must have been born in or have resided within the boundaries claimed by the Republic of Texas in 1836.

2000		Gregg Cantrell, *Stephen F. Austin, Empresario*, Yale University Press, 1999.
2001		Frank D. Welch, *Philip Johnson & Texas*, University of Texas Press, 2000.
2002		Hal K. Rothman, *LBJ's Texas White House: "Our Heart's Home,"* Texas A&M University Press, 2001.
2003		James L. Haley, *Sam Houston*, University of Oklahoma Press, 2002.
2004		Randolph B. Campbell, *Gone to Texas: A History of the Lone Star State*, Oxford University Press, 2003.
2005		David La Vere, *The Texas Indians*, Texas A&M University Press, 2004.
2006		Mavis P. Kelsey Sr. and Robin Brandt Hutchinon, *Engraved Prints of Texas, 1554–1900*, Texas A&M University Press, 2005
2007		Richard B. McCaslin, *At the Heart of Texas, 100 Years of the Texas State Historical Association, 1897–1997*, Texas State Historical Association Press, 2006.
2008		Stephen Fox, *The Country Houses of John F. Staub*, Texas A&M University Press, 2007.
2009		Pekka Hämäläinen, *The Comanche Empire*, Yale University Press, 2008.
2010		Emilio Zamora, *Claiming Rights and Righting Wrongs in Texas: Mexican Workers and Job Politics During World War II*, Texas A&M University Press, 2009.
2011		Dan K. Utley and Cynthia J. Beeman, *History Ahead: Stories beyond the Texas Roadside Markers*, Texas A&M University Press, 2011.
2012	Fiction	Gerald Duff, *Blue Sabine*, Moon City Press, 2011.
	Non-fiction	Michael Berryhill, *The Trails of Eroy Brown: The Murder Case that Shook the Texas Prison System*, University of Texas Press, 2011.
2013	Fiction	Ben Rehder, *The Chicken Hanger: A Novel*, Texas Christian University Press, 2012.
	Non-fiction	Jan Reid, *Let the People In: The Life and Times of Ann Richards*, UT Press, 2012.
2014	Fiction	Thomas Zigal, *Many Rivers to Cross*, Texas Christian University Press, 2013.
	Non-fiction	Raúl Coronado, *A World Not to Come: A History of Latino Writing and Print Culture*, Harvard University Press, 2013.
2015	Fiction	Sara Bird, *Above the East China Sea*, Knopf, 2014.
	Fiction	James Magnuson, *Famous Writers I have Known: A Novel*, W.W. Norton & Company, 2014.
	Non-fiction	Katie Robinson Edwards, *Midcentury Modern Art in Texas*, University of Texas Press, 2014.
	Poetry	Christian Wiman, *Once in the West*, Farrar, Straus and Giroux, 2014.
2016	Fiction	Sanderia Faye, *Mourner's Bench*, University of Arkansas Press, 2015.
	Non-fiction	Ron J. Jackson Jr. and Lee Spencer White, *Joe: The Slave Who Became an Alamo Legend*, University of Oklahoma Press, 2015.
	Poetry	James Hoggard, *New and Selected Poems*, TCU Press, 2015.
2017	Fiction	Dominic Smith, *The Last Painting of Sara de Vos*, 2016.
	Non-fiction	Kenneth Hafertepe, *The Material Culture of German Texans*, 2016.
	Poetry	Jonathan Fink, *Barbarossa*, 2016.
2018	Fiction	Chanelle Benz, *The Man Who Shot Out My Eye Is Dead*, 2017.
	Non-fiction	Andrew Sansom and William E. Reaves, *Of Texas Rivers and Texas Art*, 2017.
	Poetry	Dan Williams, *Past Purgatory, A Distant Paradise*, 2017.
2019	Fiction	Elizabeth Crook, *The Which Way Tree*, 2018.
	Non-fiction	Andrew Saansom, Seasons at Selah: The Legacy of the Bamberger Ranch Prserve, 2018.
	Poetry	Megan Peak, *Girldom*, 2018.
2020	Fiction	Leila Meachan, *Dragonfly*, 2019.
	Non-fiction	Stephen Harrigan, *Big Wonderful Thing: A History of Texas*, 2019.
	Poetry	Edward Vidaurre, *JazzHouse*, 2019.

Recent Movies Made in Texas

Following is a partial list of recent major productions filmed in Texas in descending order by date.

The date is for the year of release of the film, while actual location shots occurred earlier.

Location information is from the Texas Film Commission and other sources.

Sources: Texas Film Commission, and online.

The totals are not comprehensive.

When only a small portion of the movie is known to have been filmed in Texas, "(part)" is listed next to the movie title. Some of the major artists who worked on the project are listed in the column at far right.

Year	Movie	Locations	Artists
2019	**Addict Named Hal**	Austin, Pflugerville	Lane Michael Stanley (director)
2019	**The Big Bend**	Study Butte, Terlingua	Brett Wagner (director)
2019	**Brother's Keeper**	Abilene	Todd Randall (director)
2019	**Caged Birds**	Dallas	Fredrick Leach (director)
2019	**The Dark and the Wicked**	Granbury	Brett Wagner
2019	**Flip Turn**	Dallas, Irving	Alin Bijan (director)
2019	**Fugitive Dreams**	Austin, Bartlett, Bastrop, Elgin, Fredericksburg, Manor	Jason Neulander (director)
2019	**The Get Together**	Austin, Blanco, Hallettsville, Pflugerville, San Antonio	Laura Perez (director)
2019	**Inbetween Girl**	Austin, Galveston	Mei Makino (director)
2019	**Marfa**	Marfa, Lockney, Plainview	Andy Stapp (director)
2019	**Miss Juneteenth**	Fort Worth	Channing Godfrey Peoples (director)
2019	**No Ordinary Love**	Fort Worth	Chyna Robinson (director)
2019	**Run Hide Fight**	Dallas, Red Oak	Kyle Rankin (director)
2019	**Twelve Mighty Orphans**	Fort Worth, Weatherford	Ty Roberts (director)
2019	**VFW**	Dallas	Joe Begos (director)
2019	**We Can Be Heroes**	Austin	Robert Rodriguez (director)
2018	**The Iron Orchard**	Big Spring, Midland, Odessa, Austin	Ty Roberts (director), Austin Nichols
2018	**1985**	Dallas	Yen Tan (director), Michael Chiklis, Virginia Madsen
2016	**Everybody Wants Some**	Austin, Bastrop, Elgin, Manor, San Marcos, Taylor, Weimar, Wimberley	Richard Linklater (director), Blake Jenner
2015	**My All American**	Austin, Dallas, Fort Worth, San Antonio, Elgin, Manor, Smithville	Angelo Pizzo (director), Aaron Eckhart, Finn Wittrock
2013	**Boyhood**	Alpine, Austin, Houston, San Marcos, Big Bend, Webster, Pedernales State Park	Ethan Hawke, Patricia Arquette, Richard Linklater (director)
2013	**Parkland**	Dallas, Austin	Billy Bob Thornton, Zac Efron
2011	**Bernie**	Carthage, Smithville, Georgetown, Bastrop, Lockhart, Austin	Jack Black, Shirley MacLaine, Matthew McConaughey, Richard Linklater (director)
2011	**The Tree of Life**	Bastrop, Austin, Dallas, Houston, La Grange, Matagorda, San Marcos, Smithville, Waco	Brad Pitt, Sean Penn
2009	**Friday the 13th**	Austin, Bastrop, La Grange, Marshall, Wimberley	Marcus Nispel (director)
2006	**No Country for Old Men (part)**	Marfa	Ethan and Joel Coen (directors), Tommy Lee Jones

Number of Production Projects in Texas by Year

	2007	2008	2009	2010	2011	2014	2015	2016	2017	2018	2019
Feature Films	36	27	60	38	16	26	14	24	19	18	21
TV Series	14	12	20	17	15	14	20	15	23	26	39
Total	**50**	**39**	**80**	**55**	**31**	**40**	**34**	**39**	**42**	**44**	**60**

Sources: Texas Film Commission and the Motion Picture Association of America (2021).

Television series that were recently produced in Texas include *Fear the Walking Dead, The Son,* Emmy-nominated *The Long Road Home, Fixer Upper, The Leftovers, American Crime,* and some syndicated programs, in addition to the long-running *Austin City Limits.*

Film and Television Work in Texas

For almost a century, Texas has been one of the nation's top filmmaking states, after California and New York. More than 1,600 films have been made in Texas since 1910, including *Wings*, the first film to win an Academy Award for Best Picture, which was made in San Antonio in 1927.

Texas' attractions to filmmakers are its diverse locations, abundant sunshine and moderate winter weather, and a variety of support services. The economic benefits of hosting on-location filming over the past decade are estimated at more than $3 billion. Besides salaries paid to locally hired technicians and actors, as well as fees paid to location owners, the production companies do business with hotels, car rental agencies, lumberyards, restaurants, grocery stores, utilities, security services, and florists.

All types of projects come to Texas besides films, including television features and news organizations, commercials, corporate films, and game videos.

Many projects made in Texas originate in California studios, but Texas is also the home of many independent filmmakers who make films outside the studio system. Some films and television shows made in Texas have become icons. *Giant*, John Wayne's *The Alamo*, and the long-running TV series *Dallas* all made their mark on the world's perception of Texas.

The Texas Film Commission, a division of the Office of the Governor, markets to Hollywood Texas' locations, support services, and workforce availablity. The legislature funded the Texas Moving Image Incentive Program with $22 million in the 2018–2019 biennium.

The commission's free services include location research, employment referrals for production assistants, red-tape-cutting, and information on weather, travel, and other topics affecting production. ☆

Source: Texas Film Commission at gov.texas.gov/film/

Production still from Fugitive Dreams *(2019). Photo courtesy of Jason Neulander.*

Regional Commissions

Amarillo Film Office
1000 S. Polk, Amarillo 79101
(800) 646-3388
visitamarillo.com/media/film

Austin Film Office
111 Congress Ave., Ste. 700
Austin 78701,
(866) 462-8784
austinfilmcommission.com

Brownsville Border Film Commission
650 Ruben M. Torres Sr. Blvd.
Brownsville 78521,
(956) 546-3721
filmbtx.com

Corpus Christi Film Commission
101 N. Shoreline Dr., Ste. 430
Corpus Christi 78401
(800) 678-6232
visitcorpuschristitx.org/media

Dallas Film Commission
325 N. St. Paul St., Ste. 700
Dallas 75201,
(214) 571-1050
dallasfilmcommission.com

El Paso Film Commission
One Civic Center Plaza
El Paso 79901,
(915) 534-0600
filmelpaso.com

Fort Worth Film Commission
111 W. 4th St., Ste. 200
Fort Worth 76102, (817) 698-7842
filmfortworth.com

Houston Film Commission
701 Avenida de las Americas,
Ste. 200 Houston 77010,
(713) 853-8959
houstonfilmcommission.com

San Antonio Film Commission
203 S. St. Mary's St., Ste. 120
San Antonio 78205, (210) 207-6730
filmsanantonio.com

South Padre Island Film Commission
sopadre.com/about/
film-on-south-padre-island/

Holidays, Anniversaries, and Festivals, 2022–2023

Below are listed the principal federal and state government holidays; Christian, Jewish, and Islamic holidays and festivals; and special recognition days for 2021 and 2022.

Technically, the United States does not observe national holidays. Each state has jurisdiction over its holidays, which are usually designated by its legislature.

This list was compiled partially from the Texas Government Code, the U.S. Office of Personnel Management, and *Astronomical Phenomena 2021* and *Astronomical Phenomena 2022*, which are published jointly by the U.S. Naval Observatory and the United Kingdom Hydrographic Office.

See the footnotes for explanations of the symbols.

2022		
New Year's Day	§	Sat., Jan. 1
Epiphany		Thurs., Jan. 6
Sam Rayburn Day	‡	Thurs., Jan. 6
Martin Luther King Jr. Day	§	Mon., Jan. 17
Confederate Heroes' Day	§	Wed., Jan. 19
Valentine's Day		Mon., Feb. 14
Presidents' Day	§	Mon., Feb. 21
Primary Election Day		Tues., March 1
Ash Wednesday		Wed., March 2
Texas Independence Day	§	Wed., March 2
Texas Flag Day	‡	Wed., March 2
César Chávez Day	§	Thurs., March 31
Ramadan, first day of		Sun., April 3
Former Prisoners of War Day	‡	Sat., April 9
Palm Sunday		Sun., April 10
Good Friday	§	Fri., April 15
Passover (Pesach), first day of		Sat., April 16
Easter Day		Sun., April 17
San Jacinto Day	§	Thurs., April 21
Mother's Day		Sun., May 8
Armed Forces Day		Sat., May 21
Ascension Day		Thurs., May 26
Memorial Day	§	Mon., May 30
Shavuot (Feast of Weeks)		Sun., June 5
Whit Sunday — Pentecost		Sun., June 5
Trinity Sunday		Sun., June 12
Flag Day (U.S.)		Tues., June 14
Emancipation Day in Texas (Juneteenth)	§	Sun., June 19
Father's Day		Sun., June 19
Independence Day	§	Mon., July 4
Islamic New Year		Fri., July 29
Lyndon Baines Johnson Day	§	Sat., Aug. 27
Labor Day	§	Mon., Sept. 5
Grandparents Day		Sun., Sept. 11
Rosh Hashanah (Jewish New Year)		Mon., Sept. 26
Yom Kippur (Day of Atonement)		Wed., Oct. 5
Sukkot (Tabernacles), first day of		Mon., Oct. 10
Columbus Day	‡	Mon., Oct. 10
Halloween		Mon., Oct. 31
Father of Texas Day	‡	Thurs., Nov. 3
General Election Day	§	Tues., Nov. 8
Veterans Day	§	Fri., Nov. 11
Thanksgiving Day	§	Thurs., Nov. 24
First Sunday in Advent		Sun., Nov. 27
Hanukkah, first day of		Mon., Dec. 19
Christmas Day	§	Sun., Dec. 25

2023		
New Year's Day	§	Sun., Jan. 1
Epiphany		Fri., Jan. 6
Sam Rayburn Day	‡	Fri., Jan. 6
Martin Luther King Jr. Day	§	Mon., Jan. 16
Confederate Heroes' Day	§	Thurs., Jan. 19
Valentine's Day		Tues., Feb. 14
Presidents' Day	§	Mon., Feb. 20
Ash Wednesday		Wed., Feb. 22
Texas Independence Day	§	Thurs., March 2
Texas Flag Day	‡	Thurs., March 2
Ramadan, first day of		Thurs., Mar 23
César Chávez Day	§	Fri., March 31
Palm Sunday		Sun., April 2
Passover (Pesach), first day of		Thurs., April 6
Good Friday	§	Fri., April 7
Easter Day		Sun., April 9
Former Prisoners of War Day	‡	Sun., April 9
San Jacinto Day	§	Fri., April 21
Mother's Day		Sun., May 14
Ascension Day		Thurs., May 18
Armed Forces Day		Sat., May 20
Shavuot (Feast of Weeks)		Fri., May 26
Whit Sunday — Pentecost		Sun., May 28
Memorial Day	§	Mon., May 29
Trinity Sunday		Sun., June 4
Flag Day (U.S.)		Wed., June 14
Father's Day		Sun., June 18
Emancipation Day in Texas (Juneteenth)	§	Mon., June 19
Independence Day	§	Tues., July 4
Islamic New Year		Wed., July 19
Lyndon Baines Johnson Day	§	Sun., Aug. 27
Labor Day	§	Mon., Sept. 4
Grandparents Day		Sun., Sept. 10
Rosh Hashanah (Jewish New Year)		Sat., Sept. 16
Yom Kippur (Day of Atonement)		Mon., Sept. 25
Sukkot (Tabernacles), first day of		Sat., Sept. 30
Columbus Day	‡	Mon., Oct. 9
Halloween		Tues., Oct. 31
Father of Texas Day	‡	Fri., Nov. 3
General Election Day	§	Tues., Nov. 7
Veterans Day	§	Sat., Nov. 11
Thanksgiving Day	§	Thurs., Nov. 23
First Sunday in Advent		Sun., Dec. 3
Hanukkah, first day of		Fri., Dec. 8
Christmas Day	§	Mon., Dec. 25

Federal legal public holidays are shown in bold. If the holiday falls on a Sunday, the following Monday may be treated as a holiday. If the holiday falls on a Saturday, the preceding Friday may be treated as a holiday.

§ **State holiday in Texas**. For state employees, the Friday after Thanksgiving Day, Dec. 24, and Dec. 26 are also holidays. **Optional holidays** are César Chávez Day, Good Friday, Rosh Hashanah, and Yom Kippur. **Partial-staffing holidays** are Confederate Heroes Day, Texas Independence Day, San Jacinto Day, Emancipation Day in Texas, and Lyndon Baines Johnson Day. State offices will be open on optional holidays and partial-staffing holidays.

‡ **State Recognition Days**, as designated by the Texas Legislature.

Notes on holidays:

- Confederate Heroes Day combines the birthdays of Robert E. Lee (Jan. 19) and Jefferson Davis (June 3).
- Presidents' Day combines the birthdays of George Washington (Feb. 22) and Abraham Lincoln (Feb. 12).
- Jewish and Islamic holidays are tabular, meaning they begin at sunset on the previous evening.
- Between 1939 and 1957, Texas observed Thanksgiving Day on the last Thursday in November. As a result, in a November having five Thursdays, Texas celebrated national Thanksgiving on the fourth Thursday and Texas Thanksgiving on the fifth Thursday. In 1957, Texas changed the state observance to coincide with the national holiday.

Religious Affiliation Change: 2000 to 2010

Texas remains one of the nation's more "religious" states, even though a smaller portion of Texans is affiliated with a congregation than ten years ago.

At the same time, the estimated number of Muslims in the state increased to 421,972, making it the fifth-largest religious group in the state and making Texas first in the nation in number of Muslims.

Texas ranks in the upper half among the states in percentage of the population belonging to a denomination. According to the *2010 U.S. Religion Census*, at least **56.0 percent** of Texans are adherents to a religion. The national average is 48.8 percent.

The census, sponsored by the Association of Statisticians of American Religious Bodies, is the only U.S. survey to report religious membership down to the county level, as well as at the state level. The census relies on self-reports from congregations for membership numbers.

But in the past, the African-American churches did not participate in the study, and in 2010 less than half of those congregations participated.

Only 345,998 black Protestants were counted in Texas in 2010. According to the U.S. Census of 2010, there were 2,782,876 blacks in Texas, which would mean 87.6 percent of black Texans, who are predominately Protestant, were designated as unaffiliated to any church. This probably leaves out some one million Texas church members.

In 1990, it was estimated that there were 815,000 black Baptists in Texas. An estimate of the membership in black Pentecostal churches was about 300,000. And an estimate for black Methodists in Texas was approximately 200,000.

According to the *2010 U.S. Religion Census*, Texas ranks:

— **First** in number of evangelical Protestants, with 6,457,044.

— **First** in number that belong to nondenominational Christian churches, with 1,546,542.

— **First** in number of Muslims, with 421,972 estimated. New York is second with 392,953 estimated.

— **Second**, behind Pennsylvania, in number of Mainline Protestants at 1,641,527.

— **Second**, behind California, in number of Hindus.

— **Third** in number of Buddhists.

— **Third** in number of Catholics.

— **Fifth** in number of Mormons.

Carrying over those estimates into 2010 and adjusting for these additions, the percentage of Texans that are adherents* of a religion would be closer to **59.8 percent** in 2010.

[In addition, the religion census includes denominations that provide numbers of congregations but who have not enumerated the numbers of adherents in each congregation. Even with factoring in an average congregation size of 100 persons for Protestant congregations (a figure used by the census study), the total percentage would vary less than one percent, to **60.7 percent.**]

Although that is higher than the 56.0 percent figure compiled from the reporting churches, still it would be down from **67.1 percent** 20 years ago, indicating a move away from religious affiliation in Texas.

However, with the total state population booming, the churches still reported an **increase of 2.17 million** members, while the total population of Texas increased by 4.29 million from 2000 to 2010.

During the same period, the number of Texans not attached to a religion rose by **2.13 million.**

Thus, according to the Texas Almanac analysis from a variety of sources, there are **10.1 million** persons in the state who are not claimed by a religious group and about 15 million who are congregation members. (The U.S. census counted **25,145,561** persons in Texas in 2010.)

Largest Religious Bodies	Adherents*	Percent of Texas Population
1. Catholic Church	4,673,500	18.59 %
2. Southern Baptist Convention	3,722,194	14.80 %
3. Non-Denominational Christian	1,546,542	6.15 %
4. United Methodist Church	1,122,736	4.46 %
5. Muslim estimate	421,972	1.68 %
6. Church of Christ	351,129	1.40 %
7. Latter-Day Saints (Mormons)	296,141	1.18 %
8. Assembly of God	275,565	1.10 %
9. Presbyterian Church (U.S.A.)	155,046	0.62 %
10. Episcopal Church	148,439	0.59 %
11. Lutheran (Missouri Synod)	132,508	0.53 %
12. Lutheran (E.L.C.A.)	111,647	0.44 %
Unclaimed by any faith	10,103,455	40.20 %

**Adherents* include all full members, their children, and others who regularly attend services. All figures used here by the Texas Almanac refer to these adherents.*

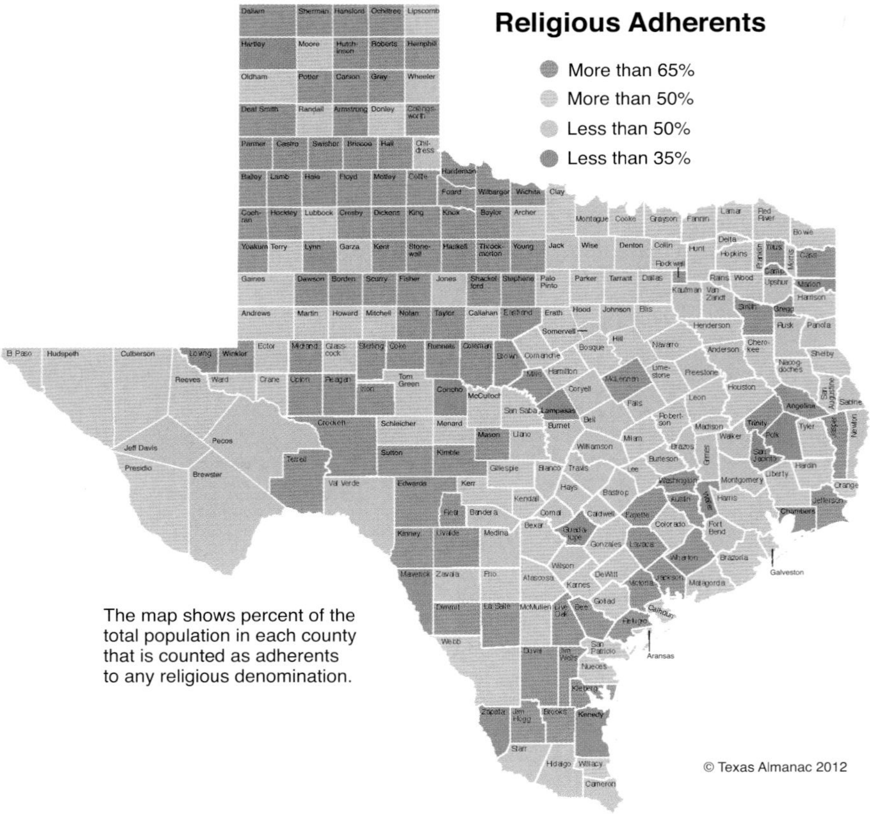
Religious Adherents
More than 65%
More than 50%
Less than 50%
Less than 35%
The map shows percent of the total population in each county that is counted as adherents to any religious denomination.
© Texas Almanac 2012

Numbers of Members Statewide by Denomination

Religious Groups in Texas	2000	Change	2010
Adventists	**46,323**	**+ 27,797**	**74,120**
Church of God (Seventh Day) (70 congregations)	—		—
Church of God General Conference	55		65
Seventh-Day Adventists	46,268		74,055
Baha'i	**10,777**	**+ 2,458**	**13,253**
Baptist	**4,537,918**	**+ 52,228**	**4,590,143**
Alliance of Baptists (9 congregations)			—
American Baptist Association	61,272		39,354
American Baptist Churches in the USA	7,057		7,172
Baptist General Conference	340		1,320
Baptist Missionary Association of America	123,198		—
Conservative Baptist Association of America (1 congregation)			—
Free Will Baptist, National Association of, Inc.	2,822		3,111
Independent Baptist Fellowship International (258 cong.)			—
Interstate & Foreign Landmark Missionary Baptists Association	93		—
Landmark Baptist, Indep. Assns. & Unaffil. Churches	964		—
National Primitive Baptist Convention, USA	4,463		—
North American Baptist Conference	1,569		1,157
Primitive Baptists Associations			—
Primitive Baptist Church — Old Line (118 congregations)			—
Progressive Primitive Baptists	197		—
Reformed Baptist Churches of America (27 congregations)			—
Regular Baptist Churches, General Assn. of (6 congregations)	684		—
Seventh Day Baptist General Conference			67

Religious Groups in Texas	2000	Change	2010
Southern Baptist Convention	3,519,459		3,722,194
Southwide Baptist Fellowship (13 congregations)			—
Two-Seed-in-the-Spirit Predestinarian Baptists	29		—
Black Baptists (Estimate)*	(815,771)*		(815,771)*
National Baptist Convention of America, Inc.			89,050
National Baptist Convention, USA, Inc.			59,529
National Missionary Bapist Convention, Inc.			34,039
Progressive National Baptist Convention, Inc.			2,683
Full Gospel Baptist Church Fellowship (52 congregations)			—
Buddhist (95 congregations)	**—**		**66,116**
Mahayana			49,874
Theravada			13,461
Vajrayana			2,781
Catholic Church	**4,368,969**	**+ 304,531**	**4,673,500**
(Christian Scientists) Church of Christ, Scientist (64 cong.)	**—**		**—**
Churches of Christ	**424,907**	**– 30,843**	**394,064**
Church of Christ	377,264		351,129
Independent Christian Churches and Churches of Christ	43,602		40,078
International Churches of Christ	4,041		2,857
(Disciples of Christ) Christian Church	**111,288**	**– 36,471**	**74,817**
Episcopal	**177,910**	**– 29,471**	**148,439**
Episcopal Church, The	177,910		148,439
Reformed Episcopal Church			—
Anglican Church in North America (111 congregations)			—
Hindu (34 congregations in 2000)	**—**		**60,725**
Indian-American HIndu Temple Assn.			36,550
Post-Renaissance			968
Renaissance			98
Traditional Temples			23,109
Holiness	**86,942**	**– 1,738**	**85,204**
Christian & Missionary Alliance, The	3,858		5,465
Church of Christ (Holiness), U.S.A. (4 congregations)			—
Church of God (Anderson, Ind.)	4,669		3,990
Churches of Christ in Christian Union (2 congregations)			—
Free Methodist Church of North America	874		1,864
Missionary Church, The	403		3,119
Nazarene, Church of the	50,528		44,836
Salvation Army	25,070		23,761
Wesleyan Church, The	1,540		2,169
Jain (6 congregations)	**—**		**—**
Jehovah's Witnesses (426 congregations)	**—**		**—**
Judaism, (estimate) *	**(128,000)***	**– 67,355**	**60,645**
Conservative			**17,889**
Orthodox			**8,410**
Reconstructionist			**356**
Reform			**33,990**
Lutheran	**301,518**	**– 29,452**	**272,066**
Church of the Lutheran Brethren of America	—		72
Church of the Lutheran Confession (4 congregations)	—		—
Evangelical Lutheran Church in America	155,019		111,647
Evangelical Lutheran Synod	—		—
Free Lutheran Congregations, The Assoc. of	368		75
Lutheran Church–Missouri Synod, The	140,106		132,508
Lutheran Congregations in Mission for Christ	—		20,936
North American Lutheran Church (26 congregations)	—		—
Wisconsin Evangelical Lutheran Synod	6,025		6,828

Religious Groups in Texas	2000	Change	2010
Mennonite/Amish	**4,930**	**– 1,330**	**3,600**
Amish, Old Order or Conservative Unaffiliated	24		309
Amish, undifferentiated	68		52
Apostolic Christian Church of America, Inc.	27		46
Beachy Amish Mennonite Churches	127		265
Brethren in Christ Church (1 congregation)			—
Church of God in Christ (Mennonite)	849		1,068
Church of the Brethren	284		118
Conservative Mennonite Conference	191		106
Evangelical Bible Churches, Fellowship of (was Ev. Menn. Bre.)			—
Eastern Pennsylvania Mennonite Church	65		—
Grace Brethren Churches, Fellowship of (3 congregations)			—
Mennonite Brethren Churches, U.S. Conference of	425		403
Mennonite, other	1,655		—
Mennonite Church USA	1,215		1,233
Messianic Judaism	**—**		**—**
Association of Messianic Congregations (1 congregation)	—		—
Union of Messianic Jewish Congregations (5 congregations)	—		—
Methodist	**1,219,533**	**+ 94,912**	**1,314,445**
Black Methodists (estimate)*	(197,191)*		(150,000)*
African Methodist Episcopal Zion	(2,191)*		1,327
African Methodist Episcopal	(150,000)*		43,839
Christian Methodist Episcopal	(45,000)*		37,986
Congregational Methodist Church	—		2,396
Evangelical Methodist Church (11 congregations)			—
Southern Methodist Church (2 congregations)			—
United Methodist Church, The	1,022,342		1,122,736
(Mormons)	**158,268**	**+ 142,323**	**300,591**
Church of Jesus Christ of Latter-day Saints, The	155,451		296,141
Community of Christ	2,817		4,450
Muslim, estimate	**114,999**	**+ 306,973**	**421,972**
Non-denominational (Evangelical Protestant)	**—**		**1,546,542**
Independent Non-Charismatic Churches	145,249		—
Independent Charismatic Churches	159,449		—
Orthodox (Eastern Christian)	**22,755**	**+ 9,695**	**32,450**
Antiochian Orthodox of North America	4,642		5,348
Armenian Apostolic Church/Cilicia	80		—
Armenian Apostolic Church/Etchmiadzin	1,275		515
Assyrian Apostolic Church			—
Coptic Orthodox Church (8 congregations)	—		3,866
Eritrean Orthodox	—		1,000
Ethiopian Orthodox (4 congregations)			—
Greek Orthodox Archdiocese of America	9,444		12,167
Greek Orthodox Archdiocese of Vasiloupulis	135		—
Malankara Archdiocese/Syrian Orthodox Church in North Amer.	825		1,260
Malankara Orthodox Syrian Church, American Diocese of the	2,675		2,433
Romanian Orthodox Archdiocese in Americas)	413		600
Orthodox Church in America (Territorial Dioceses)	2,096		2,657
Russian Orthodox Church Outside of Russia (4 congregations)	—		1,022
Serbian Orthodox Church in North America	1,110		1,372
Syrian Orthodox Church of Antioch	60		210
Pentecostal/Charismatic	**615,258**	**+ 61,825**	**677,083**
Apostolic Faith Mission of Portland, Ore.	—		135
Assemblies of God	228,098		275,565
Assemblies of God International Fellowship (3 congregations)	—		—
Black Pentecostals (estimate)*	(300,000)*		(300,000)*
Church of God in Christ (estimate)*	(300,000)*		77,545
Church of Our Lord Jesus Christ of Apostolic Faith (22 cong.)	—		—
Calvary Chapel Fellowship Churches (57 congregations)	—		—
Church of God (Cleveland, Tenn.)	38,259		47,709

Religious Groups in Texas	2000	Change	2010
Church of God of Prophecy	2,906		3,610
Church of God of the Apostolic Faith, Inc. (18 congregations)	—		—
Church of Our Lord Jesus Christ of Apostolic Faith (22 cong.)	—		—
Congregational Holiness Church	—		1,280
International Church of the Foursquare Gospel	12,501		11,047
Open Bible Standard Churches, Inc.	—		148
Pentecostal Church of God	11,592		13,486
Pentecostal Holiness Church, International	10,265		15,576
Pentecostal Church International, United (656 congregations)	—		—
Vineyard USA	11,637		8,527
Presbyterian	**204,804**	**– 21,514**	**183,290**
Associate Reformed Presbyterian Church	28		223
Cumberland Presbyterian Church	8,422		6,355
Cumberland Presbyterian Church in America (19 cong.)	—		—
Evangelical Presbyterian Church	1,449		2,883
Korean Presbyterian Church Abroad (2 congregations)	—		—
Korean Presbyterian Church in America (8 congregations)	—		—
Korean-American Presbyterian Church (4 congregations)	—		—
Orthodox Presbyterian Church, The	644		824
Presbyterian Church (USA)	180,315		155,046
Presbyterian Church in America	13,946		17,959
Reformed Presbyterian Church General Assembly (1 cong.)	—		—
Reformed Presbyterian Church Hanover Presbytery (1 cong)	—		—
Reformed Presbyterian Church in the United States (1 cong.)	—		—
(Quakers)	**1,074**	**+ 1,700**	**2,774**
Evangelical Friends Church International	—		1,845
Friends General Conference	—		929
Unaffiliated Friends Meetings (2 congregations)	—		—
Reformed/Congregational	**30,308**	**+ 2,599**	**32,907**
Communion of Reformed Evangelical Churches (5 cong.)	—		—
Christian Reformed Church in North America	1,936		1,416
Conservative Congregational Christian Conference	25		29
Evangelical Assn. of Reformed, and Congregational (5 cong.)	—		—
Evangelical Free Church of America, The	9,720		13,486
Hungarian Reformed Churches (2 congregations)	—		—
Reformed Church in America	2,040		512
United Church of Christ	16,587		17,464
Sikh (24 congregations)	**—**		**—**
Tao (1 congregation)	**—**		**—**
Unitarian Universalist Association	**6,872**	**+ 1,235**	**8,107**
Unity Churches, Association of (43 congregations)	**—**		**—**
Zoroastrian (3 congregations)	**NR**		**1,095**
OTHERS			
Christian Brethren (4 congregations)			—
Evangelical Covenant Church, The	1,022		1,393
Grace Gospel Fellowship (4 congregations)			—
Independent Fundamentalist Churches of America (1 cong.)			—
Metropolitan Community Churches, Universal Fellowship of	5,570		2,765
National Spiritualist Association of Churches (4 congregations)			—
New Apostolic Church of North America (13 congregations)			—
Polish National Catholic Church (3 congregations)	—		—
Statewide Totals**	**12,875,018**	**+ 2,167,088**	**15,042,106**
Unclaimed (not counted as adherent to religion)	7,976,802	+ 2,126,653	10,103,455

**Texas Almanac estimates. **2000 statewide totals include smaller denominations not reported in 2010 and not listed here.*

Compiled from the 2010 survey sponsored by the Association of Statisticians of American Religious Bodies, also other sources, including: Churches and Church Membership in the United States 2000, Glenmary Research Center, Nashville, Tenn., 2002. National Council of Churches of Christ in the USA, New York, Yearbook of American and Canadian Churches, annual. New Handbook of Texas, 1996, various: "Christian Methodist Episcopal Church," by Charles E. Tatum; "African-American Churches," "African Methodist Episcopal Church," and "African Methodist Episcopal Zion Church," by William E. Montgomery; "Religion," by John W. Storey.

Health & Science

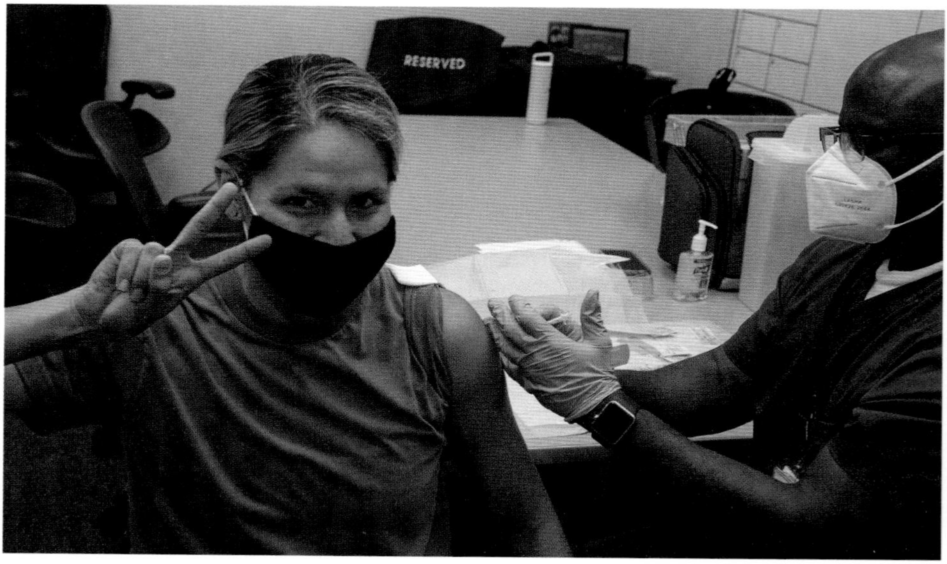

CORONAVIRUS PANDEMIC IN TEXAS

HONORED SCIENTISTS

VITAL STATISTICS

HOSPITALS

DRUG TREATMENT

MENTAL HEALTH CARE

Air Force Major Kimberly Bender recieves the first of two COVID-19 vaccine shots at Brooke Army Medical Center, Joint Base San Antonio, Fort Sam Houston. Photo by Joint Base San Antonio/Flickr.

COVID-19 art on 6th Street in Austin. Photo by Leah Rogers, CC by 4.0/Wikimedia Commons.

Coronavirus (COVID-19) Pandemic in Texas 2020–2021

by Dr. Ana Martinez-Catsam

On March 2, 2020, San Antonio city officials filed suit against the Centers for Disease Control and Prevention and other federal departments and officials, seeking to delay the release of individuals quarantined at Lackland Air Force Base. The previous month, Americans evacuated from Wuhan, China, where the novel coronavirus had been detected, arrived at Lackland AFB to undergo quarantine. In mid-February, 144 passengers from a cruise ship docked in Japan joined those already quarantined at Lackland.

By late February, San Antonio officials learned that a few released evacuees had tested positive for the novel coronavirus, referred to as COVID-19. The day the city filed suit, San Antonio Mayor Ron Nirenberg declared a public health emergency and prohibited those released from quarantine from traveling to or through San Antonio. Within days of San Antonio's actions, other Texas cities canceled events and restricted public gatherings.

On March 4, 2020, the Texas Department of State Health Services reported the state's first positive case not involving an evacuated quarantined person. On March 13, following an increase of positive cases, Governor Greg Abbott declared Texas a public health disaster, which allowed him to employ available resources, such as deploying Texas National Guard to assist health officials in addressing the crisis. Six days later, on March 19, the governor issued **Executive Order GA-08**, which prohibited gathering in groups of more than 10 and visiting nursing homes or other assisted living facilities, asked people to avoid specific businesses that required in-person congregation, and closed schools to in-person instruction.

Municipal governments experiencing an increase in positive cases issued declarations of local disaster and health emergency. The local proclamations outlined actions that either supplemented those already adopted or enhanced preventative measures.

On March 31, as the number of positive cases and deaths increased, Governor Abbott issued **Executive Order GA-14**, which would be in effect until April 30, 2020. While not referred to as a stay-at-home order, it required that services not deemed essential be conducted from home. Some counties issued "Stay Home, Work Safe" orders. Businesses, except for those exempt, were required to cease operation. Residents were encouraged to remain home except when seeking necessary services or engaging in allowable activities. Little did we know how long it would take before life would return to normal.

The Spread and Symptoms of COVID-19

It took time to discover exactly how the disease was being transmitted from person to person, but today we know. According to the Centers for Disease Control and Prevention (CDC), COVID-19 spreads through respiratory droplets or airborne transmission.

Respiratory Droplets

When individuals with COVID-19, whether symptomatic or asymptomatic, cough, talk, sneeze, and breathe, they create respiratory droplets that carry the virus. While medical experts are still learning about the virus, there is a consensus that direct contact, defined as within 6 feet, with an infected individual will increase the risk of infection and spread. When in close contact, respiratory droplets are inhaled through the nose or mouth and deposited on the mucous membranes.

Airborne Transmission

Airborne transmission occurs when droplets from people with COVID-19 remain in the air for minutes or hours. Poor ventilation in enclosed spaces allows for airborne transmission. Under such conditions, individuals who are more than 6 feet away or those who enter areas afterward can be exposed to the virus.

COVID-19

Symptoms	Recommendations to Protect Oneself and Prevent Spread	People at Greatest Risk
• Fever or chills • Cough • Shortness of breath or difficulty breathing • Fatigue • Muscle or body aches • Headache • New loss of taste or smell • Sore throat • Congestion or runny nose • Nausea or vomiting • Diarrhea	• Wear a mask over the nose and mouth • Maintain 6 feet apart • Avoid crowds • Wash hands with soap for 20 seconds or use alcohol-based hand sanitizer • Cover coughs and sneezes • Avoid touching eyes, nose, or mouth with unwashed hands • Clean and disinfect touched surfaces • Monitor health daily for symptoms • Avoid poorly ventilated spaces • Stay home when sick	• Older adults (risk increases with age 50 and older) • Adults of any age with underlying medical conditions

Counties with the Highest Confirmed Cases and Deaths (as of 6/1/2021)

County	Confirmed Cases	Fatalities
Harris County	400,436	6,442
Dallas County	260,526	4,079
Tarrant County	218,175	3,064
Bexar County	183,999	3,572
El Paso County	136,132	2,717

Peak Periods: Sample Daily Reporting Exceeding 10,000 New Cases

Date	Confirmed New Cases	New Fatalities
17-Jul-20	14,916	242
25-Nov-20	14,648	189
17-Dec-20	16,864	235
29-Dec-20	26,990	281
5-Jan-21	26,543	324
20-Jan-21	25,512	337

Daily Statewide Confirmed COVID-19 Cases

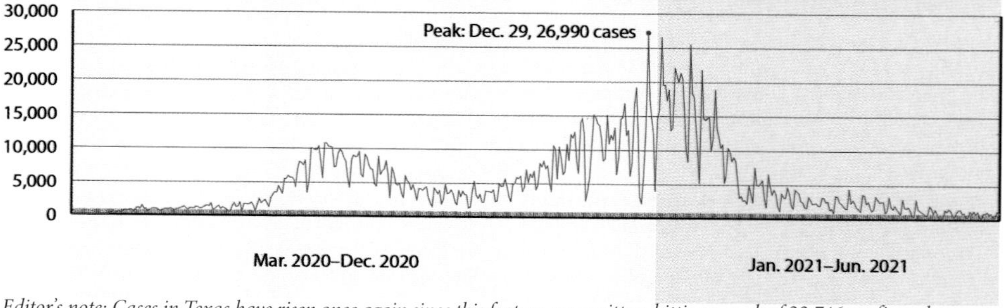

Editor's note: Cases in Texas have risen once again since this feature was written, hitting a peak of 22,746 confirmed cases on Aug. 31, 2021.

State Response Timeline: March 2020–April 2021

The table below does not provide a comprehensive list of all state government responses. Furthermore, the summaries highlight only sections of the cited proclamations or orders. You can view all of the orders online at: **https://lrl.texas.gov/legeLeaders/governors/displayDocs.cfm?govdoctypeID=5&governorID=45**

Date	Selected Summary of Action
13-Mar-20	**Governor declares a State of Disaster**
19-Mar-20	**Executive Order GA-08** Avoiding gathering in groups of more than 10 Avoiding in-person congregation in bars, eating establishments, gyms, massage parlors (drive-thru, delivery, and pickup encouraged) Shall not visit nursing, retirement, or other long-term care facilities Temporarily closes schools
24-Mar-20	**Executive Order GA-10** Requires daily reports of hospital bed capacity Requires daily reports of COVID-19 test results
26-Mar-20	**Executive Order GA-11** Mandatory self-quarantine for airline passengers making Texas their final destination and whose last point of departure or whose travel originated from certain areas A quarantine period of 14 days or until departure from Texas
31-Mar-20	**Executive Order GA-14** Requires all individuals to minimize in-person contact and social engagements except when engaging in or obtaining essential services Remote telework for services or activities not defined as essential services When engaging in essential daily activities, social distancing is recommended
17-Apr-20	**Executive Order GA-15** Requires hospitals to reserve at least 25% of their capacity for COVID-19 patients
17-Apr-20	**Executive Order GA-16 (reopening Texas)** Continual restriction on minimizing social engagement Reopened services starting April 24, 2020: retail services classified as non-essential provide service through pickup and mail or doorstep delivery Drive-thru, pickup, or delivery options for food establishments instead of dining in Visits to tattoo studies, gyms, massage parlors, and cosmetology salons discouraged Schools remain closed to in-person instruction
27-Apr-20	**Executive Order GA-18 (reopening Texas)** Continual restriction on minimizing social engagement 25% occupancy for retail stores, restaurants, theaters, shopping malls, museums, and libraries
27-Apr-20	**Executive Order GA-19** Requires hospitals to reserve at least 15% of their capacity for COVID-19 patients
27-Apr-20	**Executive Order GA-20 (reopening Texas Travel)** Rescinds executive order GA-12, which required self-quarantine for 14 days for anyone who entered Texas through Louisiana Rescinds executive order GA-11 as it applies to travelers from Louisiana only GA-11 remains in effect for travelers from other points of origin
5-May-20	**Executive Order GA-21 (reopening Texas)** 25% occupancy for listed establishments Excluded from the occupancy list: bars, massage establishments, tattoo and piercing studios, interactive amusement venues, and sexually-oriented establishments Schools remain closed to in-person instruction
3-Jun-20	**Executive Order GA-26 (reopening Texas)** 50% occupancy for business establishments

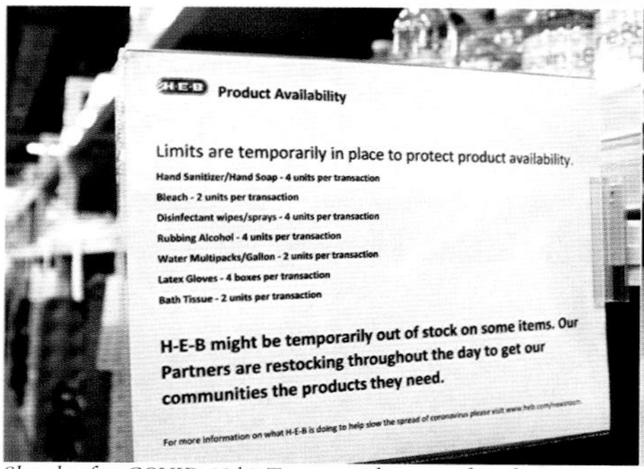

Shortly after COVID-19 hit Texas, a wide range of products were out of stock at stores all over the state. Photos by 2C2K Photography CC by 2.0/ Wikimedia Commons.

Date	Selected Summary of Action
2-Jul-20	**Executive Order GA-29** Masks covering the nose and mouth required inside commercial and public spaces when social distancing is not possible Provides exemptions to mask requirement such as: under 10 years; those with medical conditions; while eating; while in a body of water; engaged in outdoor physical activity and maintaining social distance
17-Sep-20	**Executive Order GA-30 (reopening Texas)** Up to 75% occupancy for business establishments except in areas with high COVID-19 hospitalizations No occupancy limit, with at least 6 feet social distancing, for personal care and beauty service establishments 50% occupancy for amusement parks Bars and other establishments not defined as restaurants that hold a Texas Alcoholic Beverage Commission (TABC) permit remain closed to in-person occupancy Following health protocols recommended
17-Sep-20	**Executive Order GA-31** Hospitals are to suspend surgeries not deemed medically necessary as not to deplete their ability to cope with the COVID-19 crisis Requires hospitals to reserve at least10% of their capacity for COVID-19 patients
7-Oct-20	**Executive Order GA-32 (reopening Texas)** No occupancy limit for outdoor events, establishments, areas unless restricted in other sections of the order 50% occupancy for professional, collegiate, or similar sporting events 50% on-premise occupancy for bars and similar TABC permit holding establishments if not in high hospitalization areas
2-Mar-21	**Executive Order GA-34 (reopening Texas)** Removal of occupancy limitations by the state if not in high hospitalization areas No state mandate requiring masks/face coverings, but those unable to maintain social distancing are encouraged to wear them This order does not prevent businesses or other establishments from requiring employees and customers to follow hygiene measures, including wearing face coverings
5-Apr-21	**Executive Order GA-35** No governmental entity can require individuals to receive the COVID-19 vaccine State agencies and political subdivisions can not require individuals to provide vaccination status as a condition to receive services or entering spaces Public or private entities receiving public funds can not require consumers to provide documentation regarding COVID-19 vaccination status This state order supersedes local orders
18-May-21	**Executive Order GA-36** Governmental entities or officials can not require individuals to wear face coverings

COVID-19 Impact: Economic

The coronavirus pandemic fueled a statewide economic crisis. Quarantines, capacity restrictions, and "Stay Home, Work Safe" orders adversely impacted all industries and businesses. Among the most affected by the pandemic were the leisure and hospitality industries. Restaurants, bars, retail stores, hotels/motels, amusement parks, gyms, and other such businesses saw a decline in sales revenue, experienced high unemployment rates, and closed their doors. Amid restrictions, some businesses launched or expanded online service and delivery and curbside pickup. Despite these pandemic adjustments and 2020 "reopening Texas" capacity limits ranging from 25%-75%, businesses continued to struggle. In September 2020, the Texas Restaurant Association projected that 15% of the state's restaurants would close permanently.

The lowest-paid workers, many of whom are in the service industries, suffered the most significant unemployment rate from the pandemic onset. In June 2020, the third month of a double-digit unemployment rate, the United Way of Texas conducted a statewide survey that found that workers in the hospitality and leisure industry reported the most significant impact from COVID-19. In 2019, the average wage for Texas hotel/motel housekeeping staff was $23,900, while desk clerks earned $23,300. In April 2021, The American Hotel & Lodging Association approximated that the hotel industry lost 296,387 jobs to the COVID-19 pandemic.

The United Way's survey further found that low-income households and those living below the Federal Poverty Level suffered the highest job losses. The survey revealed that 71% of the Dallas/Fort Worth metroplex, an area with high COVID-19 cases and fatalities, expressed economic concerns. Faced with economic uncertainty, Dallas/Fort Worth metroplex residents applied for unemployment (21%), applied for Supplemental Nutrition Assistance Program (SNAP) (12%), utilized food banks/pantries (17%), and relied on credit cards (22%). Thirty-four percent of those surveyed said their Coronavirus Aid, Relief, and Economic Security (CARES) Act stimulus check assisted with at most two weeks of expenses, including food and rent. As the health crisis continued, unemployment rates in Texas remained high compared to 2019.

The unemployment rate in Texas increased starting in March 2020 as the pandemic influenced state and local government response. COVID-19-related state and municipal closures and operation restrictions resulted in struggling industries and increased unemployment rates.

The highest unemployment rate occurred in April when Executive Order GA-14 and municipal "Stay Home, Work Safe" went into effect. The May rate remained in the double digits as the state enacted plans for limited reopening. Continual COVID-19 positive cases and deaths mandated continual business restrictions. While unemployment rates started declining during the fall of 2020, they were about double compared to the pre-COVID-19 rate of 3.4–3.7.

As unemployment increased, families and officials grew concerned about homelessness as many struggled to pay rents or mortgages. On September 1, 2020, a CDC order placed a moratorium on residential eviction to prevent the spread of COVID-19. The CARES Act further provided protective provisions for tenants. At the state level, the Texas Department of Housing and Community Affairs, the Supreme Court of Texas, and the Texas of Office Court Administration partnered to create the Texas Eviction Diversion Program (TEDP) to help tenants by providing property owners/landlords with alternatives to eviction. On September 25, 2020, Governor Abbott announced that over $171 million in funding from the federal CARES Act would support TEDP and other rental assistance programs. Some municipal governments, such as Dallas, Austin, San Antonio, and Houston, adopted ordinances to protect renters from eviction by providing or extending grace periods to resolve delinquencies.

Federal Poverty Level

Household (persons in the family)	2020 Poverty Guideline (income)	2021 Poverty Guideline (income)
2	$17,240	$17,420
3	$21,720	$21,960
4	$26,200	$26,500
5	$30,682	$31,040

Office of the Assistant Secretary for Planning and Evaluation: 2020 Poverty Guidelines https://aspe.hhs.gov/2020-poverty-guidelines; 2021 Poverty Guidelines https://aspe.hhs.gov/2021-poverty-guidelines

Texas Unemployment Rates, January 2019 – June 2021*

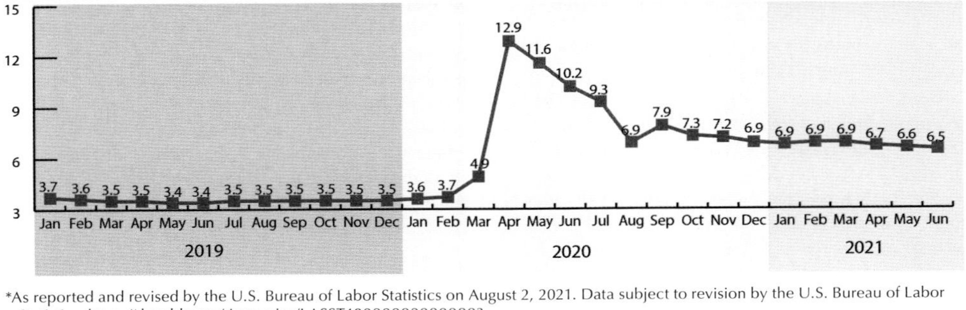

*As reported and revised by the U.S. Bureau of Labor Statistics on August 2, 2021. Data subject to revision by the U.S. Bureau of Labor Statistics: https://data.bls.gov/timeseries/LASST480000000000003

Staff from Harlandale Independent School District in San Antonio set out meal bags for families at a USDA-sponsored summer lunch program. Bagged meals of cold breakfasts and hot lunches are placed on a table for drivers to take at a safe distance. Photo by USDA/Wikimedia Commons.

Impact: Social

Homeless Population

The pandemic and associated restrictions proved challenging for the vulnerable homeless population. Capacity restrictions and social distancing measures forced homeless shelters to reduce the number of individuals they accommodated and slowed services to the unsheltered.

The limited access to shelters pushed more people to live on the streets. According to the CDC, unsheltered homeless populations were at greater risk for COVID-19 infection, especially in areas with high community spread. In response, municipalities, including San Antonio and El Paso, working with social organizations, opened auxiliary shelters and hotels to assist the homeless. Cities, among them Dallas, also allocated federal COVID-19 relief funds to address the homeless issue. Dallas designated funds toward supporting the renovation of hotels that serve as shelters.

When shelters and food pantries closed, charitable organizations and communities established resource hubs for the unsheltered that provided food, water, hygiene kits, masks, showers, and COVID-19 information. Volunteers also delivered food and water to the unsheltered. Cities relied on health department staff and volunteers to administer COVID-19 testing to the homeless.

Cities must conduct "point-in-time" counts of their homeless population every two years, with the latest slated for January 2021 to receive federal funds. The pandemic drove Texas cities to cancel or delay their counts. The South Alamo Regional Alliance for the Homeless, which usually attracts more than 400 volunteers to carry out the count in San Antonio, canceled its in-person survey. Many also requested exemptions for counting the unsheltered. While some cities decided against undertaking the count and relied on past data, others conducted the count using modified tactics to ensure the health safety of volunteers and the homeless. Houston's Coalition for the Homeless performed the survey in January 2021. Its data revealed that 15% of those surveyed had become homeless because of the pandemic. The count is far from accurate as the unsheltered can be missed in population counts. The extent of the pandemic's impact on the homeless population and how many Texans became homeless due to the health crisis are unknown.

Food Insecurity

The loss of jobs during the COVID-19 crisis further exacerbated food insecurities, especially among the working poor. In November 2020, a U.S. Census Bureau survey revealed that over 2.5 million Texas households, 66% being either Black or Hispanic, suffered from food insecurity. The same month Feeding Texas, a state network of food banks, reported that food banks assisted an average of 400,000 families weekly from March to August. Approximately half of those seeking assistance were doing so for the first time.

As more Texans experienced food insecurity, food banks lost 70% of their volunteers and 75% of their distribution partners (church pantries, Boys and Girls Clubs) due to the pandemic and associated restrictions. The Houston Food Bank, the largest in the state, usually relied on about 1,000 workers but was down to 150 in December 2020. The Texas Military Department deployed National Guard members to communities to assist food banks in distributing food to those in need. Faced with pandemic conditions, food banks employed drive-through distributions.

Food banks in highly impacted areas estimated they would be distributing millions of pounds worth of food but expected a shortfall that would outpace demand. The end of programs, such as the Farmers to Families Food Box, and the reduction of funding to the Texas Department of Agriculture, which provides fruits and vegetables to food banks, caused additional concern.

Food insecurity also led to an increase in Texans applying for Supplemental Nutrition Assistance Program (SNAP). Other federal programs available to Texans included The Child Nutrition Programs and Pandemic EBT (P-EBT). With school closures, low-income families who relied on school meals for their children were eligible for P-EBT, a one-time benefit. Despite attempts to address food insecurity amid the pandemic, the number of Texans suffering from hunger increased, with children being the most vulnerable.

Education

In June 2021, the Texas Education Agency (TEA) reported that approximately 11.3% (over 600,000) of students disengaged when schools closed at the onset of the pandemic. With school doors closed to in-person instruction, schools turned to virtual education. During the shift, schools reported losing contact with students. Moreover, the pandemic exposed inequity as many low-income families lacked access to computers or the internet to engage in online instruction. Approximately 15.5% of low-income students were not fully engaged compared to 5% of higher-income students. Hispanic and Black students had the highest percentage of disengagement. A survey of San Antonio conducted by the Urban Education Institute at the University of Texas at San Antonio further highlighted that children struggled with engagement because of hunger. The survey revealed that 22% of older students found it necessary to find employment or increase their hours to help their families, resulting in poor academic performance. For the 2020-2021 school year, teachers and school administrators were tasked with addressing the "COVID slide," an academic backslide, while developing methods of instruction that upheld social distancing requirements.

Mental Health

School closures and virtual instruction have created a sense of isolation and anxiety for many children. The stressors of the pandemic and limited access to mental health services have led to an increase in mental health-related issues among adolescents. According to the CDC, a nationwide rise in adolescent mental health-related emergency room visits began in April 2020 compared to 2019. The most significant increase at 31% was among adolescents aged 12-17 years. Hospitals also saw a 24% increase for children ages 5 to 11 years. In September 2020, Fort Worth's Cook Children's Medical Center admitted 37 adolescents after failed suicide attempts, the most significant number since they began tracking in 2015. In response, school districts, often partnering with local agencies or organizations, began offering on-campus and virtual counseling.

Adults also reported an increase in mental health issues since the onset of the pandemic. The CDC reported that during August 2020-February 2021, adults experiencing symptoms of depression or anxiety increased from 36.4% to 41.5%. The most significant increase was found among adults aged 18-29 years. According to a June 2020 CDC survey, 40% of adults in the United States struggled with mental health, with increased suicidal thoughts. According to the U.S. Office of National Drug Control Policy, substance and alcohol abuse has increased since March 2020.

Impact: Politics During a Pandemic

When the coronavirus pandemic struck the nation in the spring of 2020, the United States was experiencing a highly contentious election year. The partisan division influenced government response, further fueling the partisanship in the nation. Democrats generally supported stricter pandemic policies, including face-covering mandates and continued shutdowns, to ensure the virus slowdown. Republicans favored less stringent guidelines, opposing general mask mandates and supporting reopening by early summer 2020. A *U.S. News* report revealed that between May 1 and July 31, 2020, Democratic-led states not only implemented stricter pandemic policies but also rolled back their reopening in response to a new wave of confirmed cases. Republican-led states continued their scheduled reopening without making adjustments to the strictness of their pandemic response policies.

Tensions ran high between the Republican-dominated federal government and states, particularly those held by Democrats, over response to the health crisis. Among the criticisms levied at President Donald Trump's administration was the delayed response. By the time President Trump issued a state of emergency on March 13, 2020, several municipal and state governments had already introduced strategies to prevent the spread of COVID-19. States and municipal governments led the way in responding to the pandemic. The partisan conflict between Republican and Democratic was the most intense between Republican-led state governments and municipalities with strong Democratic-leaning leaders. In Texas, the cities (El Paso, San Antonio, Dallas-Fort Worth, Houston) with the largest populations are also Democratic pockets and reported the highest recorded COVID-19 cases and deaths. These cities criticized Governor Abbott's COVID-19 policies, which were in line with the Republican's less stringent response to the health crisis.

Face Covering

In June 2020, as COVID-19 cases increased, an ABC News/Ipsos poll found that more Americans wore a face covering when leaving home; however, mask usage has become a politically contentious issue. Democrats were more likely than Republicans to wear masks, support face-covering mandates, and comply with businesses requiring patrons to wear masks. Conservative Republicans were the least likely to wear masks or support action requiring face coverings. Republicans opposed to required mask mandates cited personal freedom or questioned the effectiveness of masks in slowing the spread of COVID-19 in spite of proven science. In response, Democrats accused those who refused to abide by health recommendations of endangering the public and possibly prolonging the pandemic and economic recovery. When Republican Governor Abbott issued Executive Order

GA-34, rescinding restrictions including mask-wearing, Democratic municipal leaders in the hardest-hit urban centers voiced their opposition. GA-34 prohibits municipal leaders from implementing local mask mandates.

The conflict over face coverings spilled over to malls, streets, and businesses. In July 2020, after Executive Order GA-29, which required masks under certain circumstances, anti-maskers rallied at the state capitol. Generally, anti-mask protests took place in larger urban centers with a higher count of confirmed COVID-19 cases. In December 2020, anti-maskers protested at North Star Mall in San Antonio. On March 2, 2021, when Abbott rescinded COVID-19 orders, including face coverings and local governments' or businesses' ability to require masks, Democratic leaders in highly impacted areas condemned the governor for acting prematurely. Having been denied the authority to implement face-covering mandates, municipal leaders encouraged Texans to continue wearing face-coverings to protect themselves and those around them.

Conflicts between Republican state and Democratic municipal leaders over face coverings, anti-mask protests, and confrontations in stores by those refusing to abide by mask requirements highlighted the pandemic's partisan divide in Texas.

Reopening Texas

Approximately one month after Governor Abbott declared a state of emergency, he issued the first executive order (GA-16) that commenced the reopening of Texas. Occupancy restrictions increased by 25% with each occupancy increase. When Texas experienced new waves of increased cases in the summer and fall, the governor's rollout plan remained in place without modification to occupancy percentages. When Governor Abbott announced on March 2, 2021, that he was rescinding COVID-19 restrictions and businesses would reopen at total capacity, Democratic leaders, such as San Antonio Mayor Ron Nirenberg, disapproved of the governor's decision. The governor reasoned that the COVID-19 vaccine and the decline in confirmed cases allowed for full reopening despite less than 50% of Texans being vaccinated in March 2021.

COVID-19 Vaccinations

Just as government response and face coverings revealed a partisan divide, so has the COVID-19 vaccine. Since the federal government began the vaccine rollout, a national trend has emerged in which a growing number of Republicans have either refused vaccination or have expressed skepticism. Opposition or hesitancy stems from multiple factors, including distrust of science, distrust of government, and mixed partisan messages since the outset of the pandemic that downplayed the severity of the virus. In February 2021, a University of Texas/Texas Tribune Poll found that approximately 59% of Texas Republicans were hesitant or refused the COVID-19 vaccine. More than 60% of white Republicans in the state rejected vaccination. Twenty-five percent of Texas Democrats polled expressed opposition to vaccination.

Public health officials have expressed concerns that vaccination rates among Blacks and Hispanics continue to be lower than among Whites despite disproportionate COVID-19 hospitalization and death. As Blacks and Hispanics have a larger young population, the vaccine rollout excluded a sizable portion of these communities. Other barriers that limited vaccine access for low-income people, a large percentage being Black and Hispanic, include language, transportation, and occupational obstacles. A University of Pittsburgh and West Health Policy Center study revealed that Blacks in some Texas communities had to travel further to a vaccine hub than white residents. Socioeconomic and race/ethnicity divides continued as data showed that neighborhoods in the poorest sections received fewer doses or faced barriers in obtaining vaccines. After more than 50% of first-dose vaccines in Dallas went to wealthier white neighborhoods, city officials developed a plan to target zip codes in lower-socioeconomic communities of color. However, state officials threatened to slash their allocation if they moved forward with the project. In February, the Federal Emergency Management Agency (FEMA) set up vaccination sites in underserved communities in Dallas-Fort Worth and Houston, areas with high confirmed cases and fatalities. As vaccinations remained low among these vulnerable populations, health officials launched informational campaigns encouraging vaccination.

As of May 30, 2021, only 44.2% (12,804,890) of Texans have received the first dose of the COVID-19 vaccine, and only 35.4% (10,272,326) have been fully vaccinated. Texas has administered 75% of the doses provided.

1918 Spanish Influenza & Coronavirus: When the coronavirus appeared, comparisons to the Spanish Influenza pandemic of 1918 began to emerge. The table provides a general comparison.

Spanish Influenza*	COVID-19
Symptoms	
• fever/chills • cough • fatigue • breathing difficulty • headache • body aches • sore throat • congestion or runny nose • Death resulted from pneumonia, the deadly complication of Spanish influenza.	• fever/chills • cough • fatigue • difficulty breathing • headache • body aches • loss of taste or smell • sore throat • congestion or runny nose • nausea or vomiting • diarrhea
Recommendations to Slow Spread	
U.S. Public Health Service (PHS) Recommendations: • Avoid contact with others • Avoid indoor and outdoor crowds • Cover coughs and sneezes • Rest and avoid excessive fatigue • Do not spit on the floor or sidewalk • Do not share utensils, cups, or other items • Get fresh air by spending time outdoors away from crowds **PHS recommendations supplemented by local health department and other medical organization requirements or recommendations:** • Wearing gauze masks • Disinfection of public transit • Quarantine	**CDC Recommendations:** • Monitor daily health • Wear a mask that covers the nose and mouth • Social distancing indoors and outdoors: 6 feet distance between individuals who are not of the same household • Avoid crowds and poorly ventilated indoor spaces • Wash hands often with soap and water or use sanitizer with at least 60% alcohol if unable to use soap and water • Cover coughs and sneezes • Clean and disinfect high-touch surfaces • Get the COVID-19 vaccine
Most Affected Populations	
Age: healthy adults 20-40; those over 60; young children	**Age**: highest cases among 20-60-year-olds with higher confirmed case percentage in 30-39 age group
Reported Confirmed Cases in Texas*	
Second Wave: September 1918: 2,515 October 1918: 8,996	2,487,480 (as of May 10, 2021)
Reported Deaths in Texas*	
Second Wave: September 1918: 129 October 1918: 6,089	49,594 (as of May 10, 2021)
Similar Pandemic State/Municipal Response	
Municipal governments, advised by health officials (city health officers), took the lead in responding to the spread of influenza. Among the actions adopted by local governments: • prohibiting public gatherings (closing venues of entertainment, schools, churches) • requiring businesses to restrict customer capacity • forbidding jury trials • recommending people remain at home • some recommending masks (San Antonio encouraged those sneezing or coughing to wear masks; Cameron required barbers to wear masks)	Among the actions adopted by state & local governments: • prohibiting public gatherings (closing venues of entertainment, schools, churches) • restricting capacity • requiring businesses to disinfect • delaying jury trials • stay-at-home orders • required mask-wearing

**Spanish Influenza cases and deaths as reported by the State Registrar of Vital Statistics are considered underreported as influenza was not a reportable disease.*

Works Sourced

Adeel, Abdul Basit, Michael Catalano, Olivia Catalano, Grant Gibson, etc. "COVID-19 Policy Response and the Rise of the Sub-National Governments." *Canadian Public Policy/Analyse de politiques* 46, Issue 4 (December 2020): 556-584.

AgriLife Today. "COVID-19 pandemic erases two decades of food security gains in Texas, U.S." Published October 14, 2020. https://agrilifetoday.tamu.edu/2020/10/14/covid-19-pandemic-erases-two-decades-of-food-security-gains-in-texas-u-s.

American Hotel & Lodging Association. "Texas: COVID-19 Impact on State's Hotel Industry."

Aratani, Lauren. "How did face masks become a political issue in America?" *The Guardian*. June 29, 2020.

Biediger, Shari. "To mask or not to mask: San Antonio reacts to new CDC guidance." San Antonio Report, May 15, 2021.

Bowen, Kacey. "Protesters gather at Texas Capitol for 'Shed the Mask' rally." FOX 7-Austin, July 4, 2020.

Cannon, Matt. "Police Break Up Face Mask Protest at Texas Mall, Arrest One Man." *Newsweek*, December 29, 2020.

Centers for Disease Control and Prevention (CDC). Accessed May 11, 2021. https://www.cdc.gov/coronavirus/2019-nCoV/index.html.

Centers for Disease Control and Prevention (CDC). "The Deadliest Flu: The Complete Story of the Discovery and Reconstruction of the 1918 Pandemic Virus."

Centers for Disease Control and Prevention (CDC). "History of 1918 Flu Pandemic."

Centers for Disease Control and Prevention. "Interim Guidance on People Experiencing Unsheltered Homelessness." Updated March 23, 2021.

Connelly, Christopher. "Report: Texas Does One of the Worst Jobs in the Nation at Caring for Kids during the Pandemic," KERA News, March 2, 2021.

Democrat and Chronicle.com. "Texas COVID-19 Vaccine Tracker." https://data.democratandchronicle.com/covid-19-vaccine-tracker/texas/48.

Diamond, Dan. "I'm still a zero: Vaccine-resistant Republicans warn that their skepticism is worsening." *The Washington Post*, April 20, 2021.

Dimmick, Iris. "San Antonio's Homeless Population Shows Surprising Trend as COVID-19 Rages in Bexar County." *San Antonio Report*, July 13, 2020.

Donald, Jessica and Spencer Grubbs. "Housing Affordability and Homelessness in Texas," FiscalNotes, March 2021.

Feeding Texas. "COVID-19 Impact: Texas Food Banking + Food Insecurity." November 2020.

Fernandez, Stacy. "230,000 Texas families filed for SNAP food assistance in March, twice as many as same month last year." *The Texas Tribune*, April 13, 2020.

Garnham, Juan Pablo. "Texas food banks may be less equipped to help hungry households in the new year." *The Texas Tribune*, December 7, 2020.

Garnham, Juan Pablo. "Texas' local officials blast Gov. Greg Abbott for 'irresponsible action' of lifting coronavirus restrictions." *The Texas Tribune*, March 2, 2021.

Gernhart, Gary, Office of PHS Historian. "A Forgotten Enemy: PHS's Fight Against the 1918 Influenza Pandemic." *Public Health Reports* 114, No. 6 (Nov.-Dec. 1999).

Harper, Karen Brooks. "Three FEMA-run vaccination sites aimed at underserved Texans to open later this month, Abbott says." *The Eagle*, February 10, 2021.

Henson, Jim and Joshua Blank. "Forget Fatigue — Political Leadership is Still Fueling COVID-19 in Texas." The Texas Politics Project, The University of Texas at Austin, December 7, 2020.

Huerta, Tiffany and Joe Herrera. "Researchers gather data to learn how COVID-19 pandemic affects teaching in San Antonio." KSAT.com, December 21, 2020.

Igielnik, Ruth. "Most Americans say they regularly wore a mask in stores in the past month; fewer see others doing it." Pew Research Center, June 20, 2020.

Influenza Encyclopedia. "The American Influenza Epidemic of 1918-1919." University of Michigan Center for the History of Medicine and Michigan Publishing.

Jaspers, Bret. "Dallas Leverages COVID-19 Pandemic to Address Long-Term Homelessness: Federal relief dollars are being used to buy and renovate hotels." *Texas Standard*, December 8, 2020.

Joy, William. "North Texas vaccines are going to mostly white, wealthy residents according to state, federal data." WFAA 8 ABC, March 14, 2021.

Leeb, Rebecca T., Rebecca H. Bitsko, Lakshmi Radhakrishnan, Pedro Martinez, Rashid Njai, and Kristin M. Holland. "Mental Health-Related Emergency Department Visits Among Children Aged <18 Years during the COVID-19 Pandemic — United States, January 1-October 17, 2020." Morbidity and Mortality Weekly Report-CDC, November 12, 2020.

Legislative Reference Library of Texas. "COVID-19 related Executive Orders by Governor Greg Abbott." https://lrl.texas.gov/legeLeaders/governors/displayDocs.cfm?govdoctypeID=5&governorID=45.

Lozano, Juan A. "Pandemic cited as cause of homelessness for some in Houston." AP News, March 24, 2021.

Luckingham, Bradford. *Epidemic in the Southwest*, 1918-1919. University of Texas-El Paso: Texas Western Press, 1984.

Luckingham, Bradford. "TO MASK OR NOT TO MASK: A Note on the 1918 Spanish Influenza Epidemic in Tucson." *The Journal of Arizona History* 25, No. 2 (Summer 1984).

Martinez, Marissa. "Texas no longer has a statewide mask mandate. But face coverings are still required in some businesses and public places." *The Texas Tribune*, March 10, 2021.

Martinez, Marissa, Juan Pablo Garnham and Mandi Cai. "COVID-19 vaccine demand drops in Texas, though less than a quarter of population is fully vaccinated." *The Texas Tribune*, April 23, 2021.

Martinez, Marissa and Sami Sparber. "As Texas expands COVID-19 vaccination eligibility, racial disparities persist among Black, Hispanic residents." *The Texas Tribune*, March 19, 2021.

Martinez-Catsam, Ana Luisa. "Desolate Streets: The Spanish Influenza in San Antonio." *The Southwestern Historical Quarterly* 116, No. 3 (January 2013).

Martinez-Catsam, Ana Luisa. "The Spanish Influenza of 1918: The Function of the *El Paso Morning Times* to a Community in Crisis." *Journal of the West* 52, No. 1 (Winter 2013).

Menchaca, Megan. "Texas cities face difficulties counting their unsheltered homeless population — at a time when their numbers matter most." *The Texas Tribune*, February 4, 2021.

Novak, Anna, Mitchell Ferman, and Mandi Cai. "10 months into pandemic, Texas' unemployment rate stays near Great Recession-level highs." *The Texas Tribune*, June 26, 2021.

Office of the Texas Governor. "Governor Abbott Announces Over $171 Million in CARES Act Funding for Rental Assistance, Texas Eviction Diversion Program." Published September 25, 2020. https://gov.texas.gov/news/post/governor-abbott-announces-over-171-million-in-cares-act-funding-for-rental-assistance-texas-eviction-diversion-program.

Office of the Texas Governor. "Governor Abbott's Proactive Response to the Coronavirus Threat."

Opdycke, Sandra. *The Flu Epidemic of 1918: America's Experience in the Global Health Crisis*. New York: Routledge Taylor & Francis Group, 2014.

Oxner, Reese. "White Republicans are refusing to get COVID-19 vaccine more than any other demographic group in Texas." *The Texas Tribune*, March 24, 2021.

Men lining up at a "spraying station" at Love Field for a preventative treatment for the influenza in November 1918. Source: U.S. National Archives and Records Administration, Public Domain

Platoff, Emma and Juan Pablo Garnham. "Dallas County axes plan to prioritize vaccinating communities of color after state threatens to slash allocation." *The Texas Tribune*, January 20, 2021.

Price, Sean. "Pandemic Pressures: COVID-19 Poses Serious Behavioral Health Challenges." Texas Medical Association, October 2020. https://www.texmed.org/TexasMedicineDetail.aspx?id=54816.

Russonello, Giovanni. "Nearly half of Republicans say they don't want a Covid vaccine, a big public health challenge." *The New York Times*, April 14, 2021.

Schneider, Andrew. "In Texas, All State Agencies Asked to Pare Budgets Due to COVID-19." NPR, August 3, 2020.

Sparber, Sami, Carrington Tatum, and Emma Platoff. "San Antonio mayor demands extension of coronavirus quarantine, bans evacuees from entering city." *The Texas Tribune*, March 2, 2020.

Stevenson, Stefan. "Texas health officials aim COVID-19 vaccine ad campaign at reluctant minority groups." *Fort Worth Star-Telegram*, April 20, 2021.

Swaby, Aliyya. "Warning of 'COVID slide,' Texas Education Agency reports 1 in 10 students have disengaged during the pandemic." *The Texas Tribune*, June 30, 2020.

Taboada, Melissa B. "As pandemic grinds on, Texas students increasingly feel alone and scared, and some are thinking about suicide." *The Texas Tribune*, December 22, 2021.

Texas Comptroller of Public Accounts Fiscal Notes. "Weathering the Pandemic: Texas Industries and COVID-19."

Texas Department of Housing and Community Affairs. "Texas Eviction Diversion Program (TEDP)." https://www.tdhca.state.tx.us/TEDP.htm.

Texas Department of State Health Services. https://txdshs.maps.arcgis.com/apps/dashboards/ed483ecd702b4298ab01e8b9cafc8b83.

United Way of Tarrant County. "COVID-19 Survey Results: Shedding Light on the Impact on Texas Communities." https://www.unitedwaytarrant.org/blog/general/covid-19-survey-results-shedding-light-on-the-impact-of-texas-communities.

University of Texas at Austin. "Protections for Texas Renters: COVID-19." https://sites.utexas.edu/covid19relief/tenant-protections.

U.S. Bureau of Labor Statistics. "Local Area Unemployment Statistics (Texas)."

U.S. Bureau of Labor Statistics. "State Employment and Unemployment Summary." Released January 26, 2021.

USA FACTS. "Texas Coronavirus Vaccination Progress." https://usafacts.org/visualizations/covid-vaccine-tracker-states/state/texas?utm_source=google&utm_medium=cpc&utm_campaign=ND-COVID-Vaccine&gclid=Cj0KCQjwna2FBhDPARIsACAEc_Wc6-uMTPXKX-Zvq0kbfF42lteVuIaWQCYsjtkP3vGQTVQnuqhywBoaAvLvEALw_wcB

Vahratian, Anjel, Stephen J. Blumberg, Emily P. Terlizzi, and Jeannine S. Schiller. "Symptoms of Anxiety or Depressive Disorder and Use of mental Health Care Among Adults during the COVID-19 Pandemic - United States, August 2020-February 2021." Morbidity and Mortality Weekly Report-CDC, April 2, 2021.

VanDusky-Allen, Julie and Olga Shvetsova. "How America's Partisan Divide over Pandemic Responses Played Out in the States," The Conversation, May 12, 2021.

Vela, Jorge A. "City of Laredo assists homeless people amid pandemic." Laredo Morning Times online, September 6, 2020.

Vela, Katie and Morjoriee White. "COVID-19 Response Prompts New Collaborations and Programs in San Antonio." Texas Homeless Network. https://www.thn.org/2020/09/11/sarah-covid-response.

Velasquez, JJ. "It's bullshit: County Judge Wolff says governor's repeal of COVID-19 measures leaves SA vulnerable." *San Antonio Report*, March 2, 2021.

Wellerman, Zak. "East Texas Food Bank receives help from Texas Army National." *Tyler Morning Telegraph*, April 15, 2020.

Zelinski, Andrea. "Why Eight Texas Republicans Broke From Their Party Over Mask Mandates." *Texas Monthly*, May 17, 2021. ☆

Death, Birth Rates Continue Trends in Texas Vital Statistics

Heart disease and cancer remained the major causes of death in 2015, the latest year for which statistical breakdowns were available from the Center for Health Statistics, Texas Department of State Health Services.

Of the 189,166 deaths, heart disease claimed 43,133 lives and cancer claimed 39,018 lives. These two diseases have been the leading causes of death in Texas and the nation since 1950. Chronic respiratory diseases (COPD) ranked third with 10,216 deaths.

These three diseases accounted for nearly half, 49 percent, of all Texas resident deaths in 2015.

The number of babies born to Texas mothers in 2015 was 403,439, an increase from 399,482 in 2014. The state's birth rate in 2015 was 14.7 per 1,000 population, down slightly from 14.8 in 2014. In 1960, the figure was 25.7.

In 2019, the number of induced abortions increased slightly to 57,929 from 2016's count of 54,507. The highest number of induced abortions was 81,591 in 2008.

Healthcare and Deaths in Texas Counties

County	2019 Physicians	2016 Hospital Beds	Total Deaths 2015	2015 Pregnancy rate*	2019 Abortions
Statewide Total	**56,765**	**78,578**	**189,166**	**79.9**	**56,620**
Anderson	67	156	655	82.3	47
Andrews	13	34	137	97.7	12
Angelina	195	446	871	75.5	77
Aransas	15	0	360	87.8	21
Archer	1	0	91	51.7	6
Armstrong	0	0	38	71.9	1
Atascosa	33	67	408	82.1	63
Austin	11	32	272	70.6	30
Bailey	2	25	50	110.5	4
Bandera	12	0	221	63.0	21
Bastrop	36	8	660	77.7	135
Baylor	8	49	61	79.1	1
Bee	22	69	271	94.3	43
Bell	899	1,005	2,274	97.5	932
Bexar	4,733	7,287	12,982	82.6	5,337
Blanco	4	0	122	64.8	14
Borden	0	0	10	103.4	1
Bosque	15	25	224	72.2	22
Bowie	278	840	1,076	75.5	8
Brazoria	396	272	2,155	81.7	634
Brazos	525	586	1,076	57.0	340
Brewster	16	25	81	68.9	12
Briscoe	0	0	20	59.6	0
Brooks	1	0	90	106.6	7
Brown	67	188	515	64.4	25
Burleson	5	25	214	78.2	18
Burnet	113	71	528	78.0	47
Caldwell	20	59	320	74.4	73
Calhoun	22	25	198	88.3	31
Callahan	3	0	179	59.4	3
Cameron	540	1,314	2,684	86.9	424
Camp	12	25	132	83.4	3
Carson	0	0	58	54.2	1
Cass	10	43	414	78.6	1
Castro	5	17	65	94.4	0
Chambers	16	39	290	76.3	43
Cherokee	66	97	557	96.5	123
Childress	12	39	75	68.2	1
Clay	5	25	131	49.7	4
Cochran	1	18	31	72.7	0
Coke	0	0	53	90.1	4
Coleman	4	25	131	58.1	2
Collin	2,673	2,384	4,005	62.4	1,631
Collings-wrth	1	13	39	54.4	0
Colorado	30	103	256	91.1	26
Comal	242	348	1,108	84.7	210
Comanche	14	25	188	88.6	10
Concho	2	16	33	87.9	3
Cooke	26	78	413	89.0	43

County	2019 Physicians	2016 Hospital Beds	Total Deaths 2015	2015 Pregnancy rate*	2019 Abortions
Coryell	39	25	526	62.3	77
Cottle	0	0	31	48.3	0
Crane	2	25	36	88.6	4
Crockett	1	0	26	94.9	2
Crosby	1	25	77	81.2	1
Culberson	23	14	14	94.8	2
Dallam	0	0	38	118.7	0
Dallas	7,103	7,807	15,727	85.5	7,595
Dawson	6	23	129	101.5	9
Deaf Smith	18	42	143	94.8	17
Delta	9	0	73	75.3	1
Denton	0	1,297	3,374	63.3	3
DeWitt	1,041	49	253	93.2	1,356
Dickens	0	0	26	98.5	2
Dimmit	8	48	109	102.6	19
Donley	1	0	51	52.3	0
Duval	0	0	149	105.3	23
Eastland	11	52	265	68.0	30
Ector	244	650	1,196	97.2	242
Edwards	1	0	33	83.3	0
Ellis	1,325	164	1,209	70.3	664
El Paso	181	2,419	5,296	82.7	693
Erath	34	98	323	54.4	68
Falls	2	36	178	66.3	23
Fannin	12	25	458	73.5	18
Fayette	27	65	326	78.9	19
Fisher	2	14	52	84.0	1
Floyd	4	25	67	74.4	2
Foard	0	0	16	61.5	2
Fort Bend	1,086	1,033	2,984	74.5	1,332
Franklin	3	0	122	73.9	7
Freestone	10	37	202	73.0	16
Frio	14	40	155	98.5	32
Gaines	9	25	128	119.8	7
Galveston	579	252	2,675	78.4	674
Garza	2	0	56	82.0	9
Gillespie	78	86	318	77.7	19
Glasscock	0	0	3	80.4	0
Goliad	1	0	87	69.6	2
Gonzales	16	33	187	106.5	28
Gray	19	115	267	92.0	2
Grayson	320	600	1,461	77.0	151
Gregg	390	738	1,274	78.2	31

Physicians – All M.D.s and D.O.s. in direct patient care. (2020.)
Hospital Beds – Beds (2016) not including military and veteran's hospitals, nor beds in hospitals that were not in compliance with state regulations.
*Abortion total statewide includes abortions performed in Texas but county of residence unknown, plus abortions obtained outside the state by Texas residents.

County	2019 Physicians	2016 Hospital Beds	Total Deaths 2015	2015 Pregnancy rate*	2019 Abortions
Grimes	14	25	279	87.1	29
Guadalupe	121	125	1,043	65.0	200
Hale	31	68	322	76.2	22
Hall	0	0	57	42.6	1
Hamilton	14	42	154	79.0	7
Hansford	5	14	53	76.4	1
Hardeman	3	45	49	93.8	4
Hardin	12	0	536	69.1	42
Harris	12,117	14,807	25,342	88.0	14,475
Harrison	34	149	677	70.1	9
Hartley	9	21	51	63.8	0
Haskell	4	25	62	74.2	1
Hays	310	322	1,007	63.6	520
Hemphill	6	26	34	105.3	0
Henderson	78	127	1,084	70.8	58
Hidalgo	1,063	2,429	4,179	91.9	1,011
Hill	16	116	455	68.7	29
Hockley	12	48	224	76.7	9
Hood	87	73	751	87.3	39
Hopkins	32	96	398	73.0	26
Houston	9	25	268	78.3	42
Howard	40	150	416	85.5	32
Hudspeth	1	0	12	76.7	0
Hunt	109	181	958	68.5	110
Hutchinson	12	25	275	78.7	1
Irion	0	0	10	52.4	0
Jack	9	17	96	79.1	2
Jackson	9	25	146	91.5	17
Jasper	23	59	458	87.8	47
Jeff Davis	1	0	16	52.2	0
Jefferson	540	1,585	2,514	88.6	520
Jim Hogg	0	0	50	106.9	6
Jim Wells	33	135	424	94.3	60
Johnson	106	137	1,340	73.8	188
Jones	6	92	214	63.8	4
Karnes	6	25	131	97.3	17
Kaufman	74	91	897	71.8	196
Kendall	81	0	377	63.2	49
Kenedy	0	0	3	41.1	0
Kent	0	0	9	74.1	0
Kerr	134	124	774	79.0	53
Kimble	3	15	45	67.4	1
King	0	0	0	23.3	1
Kinney	0	0	42	102.7	1
Kleberg	22	96	243	75.2	40
Knox	2	28	61	76.2	2
Lamar	1	393	641	78.0	9
Lamb	126	75	147	84.7	52
Lampasas	5	25	197	68.8	2
La Salle	11	0	61	106.3	22
Lavaca	21	50	269	81.5	11
Lee	5	0	183	81.5	22
Leon	4	0	223	87.1	7
Liberty	46	29	765	77.0	133
Limestone	23	78	290	86.0	23
Lipscomb	0	0	21	76.6	0
Live Oak	1	0	143	81.0	11
Llano	15	30	311	86.3	10
Loving	0	0	0	–	0
Lubbock	758	1,556	2,441	67.3	283
Lynn	6	24	51	73.4	3
Madison	9	25	126	74.3	15
Marion	1	0	167	81.1	23
Martin	4	18	52	94.9	28
Mason	2	0	44	101.1	3
Matagorda	38	75	407	91.1	217
Maverick	48	101	398	106.4	26
McCulloch	6	25	117	70.9	13
McLennan	534	522	2,123	71.4	159
McMullen	0	0	7	96.5	2
Medina	25	25	428	76.2	59
Menard	1	0	33	57.6	2
Midland	261	563	1,098	98.1	191
Milam	9	35	288	87.2	18
Mills	2	0	62	45.1	3
Mitchell	5	25	109	80.2	2
Montague	12	87	263	79.3	13
Montgom-ery	1,393	1,237	3,623	75.3	753
Moore	20	25	164	104.6	4
Morris	4	0	179	73.6	6
Motley	0	0	17	42.6	0
Nacgdoches	140	392	605	62.4	52
Navarro	51	162	568	81.3	49
Newton	3	0	164	63.6	9
Nolan	14	86	178	86.4	8
Nueces	904	2,035	2,937	78.3	596
Ochiltree	7	25	83	89.8	2
Oldham	0	0	17	62.0	0
Orange	33	0	947	88.1	100
Palo Pinto	29	74	348	77.4	19
Panola	12	42	266	70.1	139
Parker	133	129	1,066	67.4	117
Parmer	2	25	75	89.3	1
Pecos	10	39	114	85.4	15
Polk	45	66	673	88.7	39
Potter	443	1,140	1,231	85.4	15
Presidio	3	0	36	82.3	9
Rains	1	0	150	62.7	5
Randall	86	4	1,050	66.5	15
Reagan	2	21	29	109.4	2
Real	0	0	38	100.0	3
Red River	3	0	180	65.5	5
Reeves	13	25	114	98.1	21
Refugio	3	20	108	88.6	4
Roberts	0	0	6	46.7	0
Robertson	0	0	173	76.6	15
Rockwall	203	170	545	62.9	103
Runnels	12	50	140	69.1	5
Rusk	44	96	544	72.9	27
Sabine	3	25	168	81.9	10
S. Augustine	2	18	128	66.8	57
San Jacinto	4	0	313	70.9	29
San Patricio	27	75	642	92.1	83
San Saba	1	0	54	102.2	3
Schleicher	1	14	23	37.7	1
Scurry	18	25	179	81.7	10
Shackelford	1	0	27	84.2	2
Shelby	7	0	300	89.6	7
Sherman	0	0	34	71.8	1
Smith	864	1,204	2,111	76.0	242
Somervell	13	16	96	53.1	7
Starr	22	48	397	100.9	54
Stephens	8	40	107	87.2	7
Sterling	0	0	9	82.5	0

Physicians – All M.D.s and D.O.s. in direct patient care. (2020.)
Hospital Beds – Beds (2016) not including military and veteran's hospitals, nor beds in hospitals that were not in compliance with state regulations.
*Abortion total statewide includes abortions performed in Texas but county of residence unknown, plus abortions obtained outside the state by Texas residents.

County	2019 Physicians	2016 Hospital Beds	Total Deaths 2015	2015 Pregnancy rate*	2019 Abortions
Stonewall	2	12	29	96.6	0
Sutton	2	12	30	72.4	4
Swisher	4	20	81	95.0	0
Tarrant	4,530	6,284	12,277	76.6	4,672
Taylor	351	829	1,378	77.6	140
Terrell	0	0	17	91.7	1
Terry	4	45	139	97.5	6
Throck-mortn	2	0	30	51.9	1
Titus	61	174	311	79.5	26
Tom Green	298	574	973	78.7	135
Travis	3,627	2,881	5,380	70.5	3,452
Trinity	3	45	225	78.5	12
Tyler	4	49	274	76.5	19
Upshur	9	0	471	69.0	6
Upton	2	29	36	101.3	2
Uvalde	34	25	233	88.2	38
Val Verde	40	93	353	101.3	62
Van Zandt	14	52	621	71.7	26
Victoria	213	717	847	84.2	113
Walker	66	123	513	62.0	137
Waller	9	0	305	64.5	86
Ward	2	0	134	100.5	13
Washington	48	60	389	75.7	43
Webb	253	569	1,356	91.6	293
Wharton	35	208	417	89.6	61
Wheeler	6	41	72	84.2	1
Wichita	313	479	1,304	74.1	153
Wilbarger	13	47	163	85.8	8
Willacy	7	0	151	79.6	15
Williamson	1,100	833	2,625	66.6	991
Wilson	32	44	410	72.2	61
Winkler	2	19	70	99.1	7
Wise	79	148	554	76.9	63
Wood	26	50	613	72.2	16
Yoakum	6	24	63	99.2	7
Young	21	50	239	73.4	6
Zapata	1	0	85	97.8	17
Zavala	2	0	111	91.5	15

Physicians – All M.D.s and D.O.s. in direct patient care. (2020.)
Hospital Beds – Beds (2016) not including military and veteran's hospitals, nor beds in hospitals that were not in compliance with state regulations.
*Abortion total statewide includes abortions performed in Texas but county of residence unknown, plus abortions obtained outside the state by Texas residents.

Marriage and Divorce

These charts are for certain years, including 1946, when there was a significant increase in marriages after World War II as well as a significant increase in divorces. Also included are the years 1979-81 when the marriage and divorce rates reached another peak. *Source: Statistical Abstracts of the United States, National Vital Statistics System.*

Texas

Year	Total marriages	Marriage rate*	Total divorces	Divorce rate**
1940	86,500	13.5	27,500	4.3
1946	**143,092**	**20.5**	**57,112**	**8.4**
1950	89,155	11.6	37,400	4.9
1955	91,210	10.4	34,921	4.0
1960	91,700	9.6	34,732	3.6
1965	111,500	10.5	41,300	3.9
1970	139,500	12.5	51,500	4.6
1975	153,200	12.5	76,700	6.3
1979	**172,800**	**12.9**	**92,400**	**6.9**
1980	**181,800**	**12.8**	**96,800**	**6.8**
1981	**194,800**	**13.2**	**101,900**	**6.9**
1985	213,800	13.1	101,200	6.2
1990	182,800	10.5	94,000	5.5
1995	188,500	10.1	98,400	5.3
2000	196,400	9.6	85,200	4.2
2005	169,300	7.4	74,000	3.2
2010	174,171	6.9	82,098	3.3
2015	187,415	6.8	71,123	2.6
2016	n/a	7.1	n/a	2.6
2017	n/a	7.1	n/a	2.2
2018	n/a	6.1	n/a	2.6
2019	n/a	4.9	n/a	2.1

*Rate per 1,000 population.

United States

Year	Total marriages	Marriage rate*	Total divorces	Divorce rate**
1940	1,595,879	12.1	264,000	2.0
1946	**2,291,045**	**16.4**	**610,000**	**4.3**
1950	1,667,231	11.1	385,144	2.6
1955	1,531,000	9.3	377,000	2.3
1960	1,523,381	8.5	393,000	2.2
1965	1,800,200	9.3	479,000	2.5
1970	2,159,000	10.6	708,000	3.5
1975	2,152,700	10.1	1,036,000	4.9
1979	**2,331,300**	**10.6**	**1,181,000**	**5.4**
1980	**2,390,300**	**10.6**	**1,189,000**	**5.2**
1981	**2,422,100**	**10.6**	**1,213,000**	**5.3**
1985	2,425,000	10.2	1,187,000	5.0
1990	2,443,000	9.8	1,182,000	4.7
1995	2,336,000	8.9	1,169,000	4.4
2000	2,329,000	8.2	**944,000	4.0
2005	2,230,000	7.5	847,000	3.6
2010	2,096,000	6.8	872,000	3.6
2015	2,221,579	6.9	800,909	3.1
2016	2,251,411	7.0	776,288	3.0
2017	2,236,496	6.9	787,251	2.9
2018	2,132,853	6.5	782,038	2.9
2019	2,015,603	6.1	746,971	2.7

***Since 2000, the total number of divorces does not include four to six states, including California.*

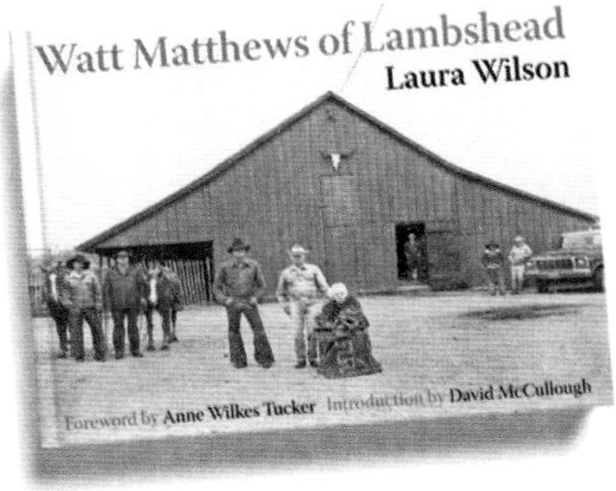
Watt Matthews of Lambshead
Laura Wilson
Foreword by Anne Wilkes Tucker Introduction by David McCullough

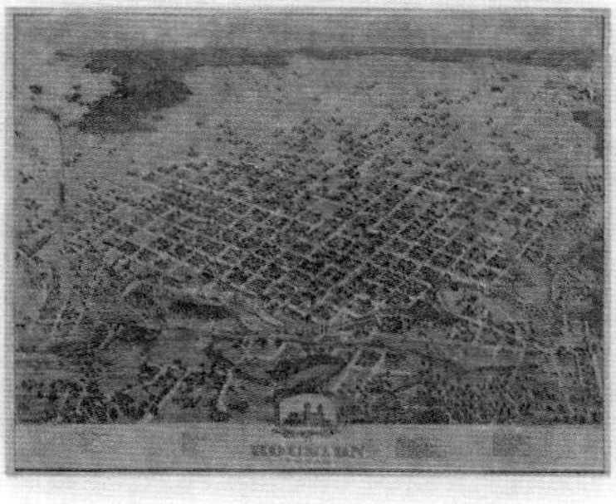

Texas
ALMANAC

Texans in the National Academy of Sciences

The National Academy of Sciences is a private organization of researchers dedicated to the furtherance of science and its use for the general welfare. A total of 136 scientists who have had positions with Texas institutions have been named members or associates.

Established by congressional acts of incorporation, which were signed by President Lincoln in 1863, the academy acts as official adviser to the federal government in matters of science and technology. Election to the academy is one of the highest honors that can be accorded a scientist. As of May 2019, the number of active members was 2,537.

Elected from Texas in 2019 was Robert C. Kennicutt, Jr., of Texas A&M University.

Three foreign associates with ties to Texas institutions have been elected to the academy: in 1970, D.H.R. Barton from Texas A&M; in 1997, Johann Deisenhofer of UTSWMC in Dallas, and, in 2002, Jan-Ake Gustafsson of the University of Houston.

In 1931, Robert Moore (UT-Austin 1920–69) and Hermann Muller (Rice 1915-18, UT-Austin 1920–32) became the first scientists from Texas institutions elected to the academy. ☆

Source: National Academy of Sciences

Academy Member	Affiliation*	Elected
Perry L. Adkisson	A&M	1979
Richard W. Aldrich	UT-Austin	2008
James P. Allison	UT-MD Anderson	1997
Abram Amsel †	UT-Austin	1992
Neal R. Amundson †	U of H	1992
Dora E. Angelaki	Baylor Medical	2014
Charles J. Arntzen	A&M	1983
David H. Auston	Rice	1991
Paul F. Barbara †	UT-Austin	2006
Allen J. Bard	UT-Austin	1982
Bonnie Bartel	Rice	2016
Frederic C. Bartter †	UTHSC-San Antonio	1979
John D. Baxter †	HMRI	2003
Arthur L. Beaudet	Baylor Medical	2011
Brian J.L. Berry	UT-Dallas	1975
Bruce Beutler	UTSWMC	2008
Lewis R. Binford	SMU	2001
R.H. Bing †	UT-Austin	1965
Harold C. Bold †	UT-Austin	1973
Norman E. Borlaug	A&M	1968
Michael S. Brown	UTSWMC	1980
James J. Bull	UT-Austin	2016
Karl W. Butzer †	UT-Austin	1996
Horace R. Byers †	A&M	1952
Luis A. Caffarelli	UT-Austin	1991
C. Thomas Caskey	Baylor Medical	1993
Joseph W. Chamberlain †	Rice	1965
Zhijian (James) Chen	UTSWMC	2014
Wah Chiu	Baylor Medical	2012
C.W. Chu	U of H	1989
Melanie H. Cobb	UTSWMC	2006
Neal G. Copeland	HMRI	2009
F. Albert Cotton †	A&M	1967
Robert F. Curl Jr.	Rice	1997
Marcetta Darensbourg	A&M	2017
Ronald A. DePinho	UT-MD Anderson	2012
Gerard H. de Vaucouleurs †	UT-Austin	1986
Ronald DeVore	A&M	2017
Bryce DeWitt †	UT-Austin	1990
Robert E. Dickinson	UT-Austin	1988
Richard A. Dixon	UNT	2007
Stephen J. Elledge	Baylor Medical	2003
Ronald W. Estabrook †	UTSWMC	1979
Mary K. Estes	Baylor Medical	2007
Karl Folkers †	UT-Austin	1948
Marye Anne Fox	UT-Austin	1994
David L. Garbers †	UTSWMC	1993
Wilson S. Geisler	UT-Austin	2008
Quentin H. Gibson	Rice	1982
Alfred G. Gilman †	UTSWMC	1985
Joseph L. Goldstein	UTSWMC	1980
John B. Goodenough	UT-Austin	2012
William E. Gordon	Rice	1968
Verne E. Grant †	UT-Austin	1968
Norman Hackerman †	Welch	1971
Namoi J. Halas	Rice	2013
Carl G. Hartman †	UT-Austin	1937

Academy Member	Affiliation*	Elected
Dudley Herschbach	A&M	1967
David M. Hillis	UT-Austin	2008
Helen H. Hobbs	UTSWMC	2007
Lora Virginia Hooper	UTSWMC	2015
A. James Hudspeth	UTSWMC	1991
Thomas J.R. Hughes	UT-Austin	2009
Nancy A. Jenkins	MHRI	2008
Robert C. Kennicutt, Jr.	A&M	2019
James L. Kinsey †	Rice	1991
Steven A. Klievwer	UTSWMC	2015
Ernst Knobil †	UTHSC-Houston	1986
Jay K. Kochi †	U of H	1982
P. Kusch †	UT-Dallas	1956
Alan M. Lambowitz	UT-Austin	2004
David M. Lee	A&M	1991
Beth Levine	UTSWMC	2013
Herbert Levine	Rice	2011
Gardner Lindzey †	UT-Austin	1989
Guillermina Lozano	UT-MD Anderson	2017
Alan G. MacDiarmid †	UT-Dallas	2002
David J. Mangelsdorf	UT-Austin	2008
John L. Margrave †	Rice	1974
Martin M. Matzuk	Baylor Medical	2014
S.M. McCann †	UTSWMC	1983
Allan H. MacDonald	UT-Austin	2010
Steven L. McKnight	UTSWMC	1992
David J. Meltzer	SMU	2009
Robert Moore †	UT-Austin	1931
Nancy A. Moran	UT-Austin	2004
Hermann Muller †	Rice, UT-Austin	1931
Hans J. Muller-Eberhard †	UTHSC-Houston	1974
Ferid Murad	UTHSC-Houston	1997
Jack Myers †	UT-Austin	1975
Kyriacos C. Nicolaou	Rice	1996
Robert N. Noyce †	Sematech/Austin	1980
David R. Nygren	UT-Arlington	2000
Eric N. Olson	UTSWMC	2000
Bert W. O'Malley	Baylor Medical	1992
Jose N. Onuchic	Rice	2006
Theophilus Shickel Painter †	UT-Austin	1938
Luis F. Parada	UTSWMC	2011
John Patterson †	UT-Austin	1941
Kenneth L. Pike †	SIL	1985
William H. Press	UT-Austin	1994
Darwin J. Prockop	A&M	1991
Lester J. Reed †	UT-Austin	1973
Peter M. Rentzepis	A&M	1978
Rebecca Richards-Kortum	Rice	2015
Peter J. Rossky	UT-Austin	2011
David W. Russell	UTSWMC	2006
Marlan O. Scully	A&M	2001
Richard E. Smalley †	Rice	1990
Esmond E. Snell †	UT-Austin	1955
Richard C. Starr †	UT-Austin	1976
Patrick Stover	A&M	2016
Thomas Südhof	UTSWMC	2002
Max D. Summers	A&M	1989

Academy Member	Affiliation*	Elected
Harry L. Swinney	UT-Austin	1992
Joseph S. Takahashi	UTSWMC	2003
John T. Tate	UT-Austin	1969
Karen K. Uhlenbeck	UT-Austin	1986
Jonathan W. Uhr	UTSWMC	1984
Roger H. Unger	UTSWMC	1986
H.S. Vandiver †	UT-Austin	1934
Moshe Y. Vardi	Rice	2015
Ellen S. Vitetta	UTSWMC	1994
Salih J. Wakil	Baylor Medical	1990
Xiaodong Wang	UTSWMC	2004
Steven Weinberg †	UT-Austin	1972
D. Fred Wendorf	SMU	1987
John Archibald Wheeler †	UT-Austin	1952
Roger J. Williams †	UT-Austin	1946
Jean D. Wilson	UTSWMC	1983
Peter G. Wolynes	Rice	1991
James E. Womack	A&M	1999
Masahi Yanagisawa	UTSWMC	2003
Clarence Zener †	A&M	1959
Huda Y. Zoghbi	Baylor Medical	2004

† Deceased

* **A&M** – Texas A&M University
Baylor Medical – Baylor College of Medicine, Houston
HMRI – Houston Methodist Research Institute
Rice – Rice University
SIL – Summer Institute of Linguistics
SMU – Southern Methodist University
U of H – University of Houston
UNT – University of North Texas
UT-Austin – The University of Texas at Austin
UT-Dallas – The University of Texas at Dallas
UTHSC – Houston—The University of Texas Health Science Center at Houston
UTHSC – The University of Texas Health Science Center at San Antonio
UT-MD – The University of Texas MD Anderson Cancer Center – Houston
UTSWMC – The University of Texas Southwestern Medical Center at Dallas
Welch – Robert A. Welch Foundation

Science Research Funding at Universities

The following chart shows funding for research and development by source at universities in Texas, in order of total R&D funding. The figures are from the National Science Foundation and are for fiscal year 2019.

(Thousands of dollars)	All R&D expenditures	Federal gov.	State/local gov.	Business	Nonprofit org.	Institutional funds
United States	$83,496,348*	$44,455,265	$4,495,452	$5,053,576	$5,683,937	$21,109,703
Texas (all colleges statewide)	**$5,967,210**	**$2,347,454**	**$854,553**	**$436,376**	**$446,322**	**$1,610,434**
1. U. Texas M.D. Anderson Ctr.	969,496	176,156	258,019	214,509	28,010	136,565
2. Texas A&M University	952,156	359,609	190,465	274,537	59,798	26,396
3. University of Texas-Austin	696,111	407,981	21,573	144,157	40,388	6,374
4. Baylor College of Medicine	651,920	309,354	32,232	193,449	85,736	0
5. U. Texas Southwestern Med. Dallas	496,697	203,544	79,363	68,457	59,096	54,920
6. U. Texas Health Sci., Houston	271,525	132,647	38,516	43,586	22,721	13,506
7. University of Houston	195,398	68,523	38,963	65,710	11,270	2,335
8. Texas Tech University	193,923	35,136	23,788	104,700	13,963	126
9. U. Texas Health Sci., San Antonio	188,483	96,502	20,807	42,551	19,715	409
10. Rice University	182,564	83,584	6,013	53,316	23,426	5,411
11. U. Texas Medical Branch	175,372	107,806	5,054	46,065	11,808	0
12. University of Texas-Dallas	126,661	48,466	12,133	38,469	22,831	0
13. University of Texas-Arlington	123,207	41,764	16,970	51,329	6,057	2,069
14. University of Texas-El Paso	106,809	41,261	17,507	33,594	4,587	8,988
15. University of Texas-San Antonio	84,326	34,588	12,247	27,509	2,408	2,181
16. University of North Texas, Denton	78,691	17,345	2,735	53,843	1,087	1,874
17. Texas State University	64,554	29,614	4,871	25,361	3,983	0
18. Uni. of Texas-Rio Grande Valley	52,016	13,629	6,309	27,496	3,996	368
19. U. North Texas, Health Science Ctr.	50,124	27,260	11,355	8,142	1,492	3
20. Texas Tech U., Health Sci. Ctr.	44,072	11,345	17,778	8,854	1,963	3,699
21. Southern Methodist University	42,562	17,869	1,092	18,220	2,034	4
22. Baylor University	33,304	6,955	1,157	19,443	2,955	1,642
23. Texas A&M U.-Corpus Christi	32,944	14,451	8,481	3,981	2,548	3,004
24. Texas A&M University-Kingsville	22,268	8,419	4,190	3,985	5,223	0
25. Prairie View A&M University	18,018	9,346	4,886	3,454	111	0
26. Uni. of Texas Health Science-Tyler	16,538	5,626	2,226	5,640	2,320	1
27. Tarleton State University	13,171	4,632	2,946	5,383	79	35
28. Texas Tech U. Health Sci., El Paso	11,883	2,279	2,544	6,306	335	56
29. St. Edward's University	9,650	6,500	1,500	700	500	300
30. Sam Houston University	9,445	3,723	183	5,310	115	61

Colleges and universities not listed received less.
*Total includes some $2.27 billion from other sources. Source: National Science Foundation.

National Health Expenditures

GDP and Expenditures ($ billion)	1970	1980	1990	2000	2010	2019
Total Health Expenditures	**$74.9**	**$255.8**	**$724.3**	**$1,377.2**	**$2,593.6**	**$3,795.4**
Percent of GDP	7.2	9.2	12.5	13.8	17.4	17.7
Per capita amount (in dollars)	$356	$1,110	$2,854	$4,878	$8,402	$11,582
Personal health care expenditure	$63.1	$217.0	$615.3	$1,161.5	$2,196.1	$9,787
Cost of private insurance	$1.4	$ 7.7	$ 29.1	$52.3	$108.5	$882
Hospital care expenditures	$27.2	$100.5	$250.4	$415.5	$822.3	$1192
Gross Domestic Product (GDP)	**$1,038**	**$2,788**	**$5,801**	**$9,952**	**$14,527**	**$21,433.2**

Source: U.S. Centers for Medicare and Medicaid Services.

Comparison of Vital Statistics

Data from 2018 with states that either border Texas or have large populations. ***Lowest and highest with number in bold.***

State/Country	Birthrate*	Death rate*	Life expectancy
Texas	13.0	7.0	78.4
Alaska	13.4	6.0	78.0
Arkansas	12.1	10.7	75.6
California	11.3	6.8	80.8
Florida	10.2	9.6	78.9
Georgia	11.9	8.1	77.2
Illinois	11.1	8.6	78.8
Louisiana	12.7	9.9	75.6
Michigan	10.8	9.9	77.7
New Mexico	10.9	9.1	77.2
New York	11.4	8.0	80.5
Ohio	11.5	10.6	76.8
Oklahoma	12.4	10.4	75.6
Utah	**14.6**	**5.8**	79.6
New Hampshire	**8.7**	9.4	79.1
West Virginia	10.1	**13.0**	74.4
United States	11.4	8.7	78.7
Japan	7.0	11.44	84.7
Brazil	13.4	6.8	75.0
Canada	10.2	8.1	83.6
Afghanistan	36.1	12.6	**53.3**
Germany	8.6	12.2	81.3
Italy	8.4	10.7	82.7
Monaco	**6.6**	10.5	**89.4**
Mexico	17.3	5.4	77.0
Angola	**42.2**	8.24	61.7
Russia	9.7	**13.4**	72.2
South Sudan	38.3	9.8	58.6
Qatar	9.4	**1.4**	79.6
United Kingdom	11.8	9.4	81.3
World	18.1	7.7	70.5

*Rates are number during 1 year per 1,000 persons.
Sources: National Vital Statistics System 2018; CIA World Factbook, 2018; Texas Vital Statistics Annual Report 2015.

Life Expectancy for Texans by Group

	All	Whites	Blacks	Hispanics
Total population	78.2	78.3	74.6	79.5
Males	75.8	75.8	71.5	76.9
Females	80.7	80.6	77.3	82.0

Source: Texas Department of State Health Services, for 2017.

Texas Births by Race/Ethnicity and Sex

	2019	2015	2000	1990
All Races	377,599	403,439	363,325	316,257
All Male	—	205,972	185,591	161,522
All Female	—	197,467	177,734	154,735
White Total	124,678	136,663	142,553	150,461
White Male	—	69,935	72,972	77,134
White Female	—	66,728	69,581	73,327
Black Total	47,326	47,515	41,180	43,342
Black Male	—	24,140	21,128	21,951
Black Female	—	23,375	20,052	21,391
Hispanic Total	179,689	191,080	166,440	115,576
Hispanic Male	—	97,469	84,750	58,846
Hispanic Female	—	93,611	81,690	56,730
Other* Total	28,181	28,181	13,152	6,687
Other Male	—	14,428	6,741	3,591
Other Female	—	13,753	6,411	3,287

**Other includes births of unknown race/ethnicity.*
Source: Texas Department of State Health Services.

Disposition of Bodies in Texas by Percent of Deaths

Year	Burial	Cremation	Donation of body	Removal from state/other
1989	83.7%	7.1%	0.7%	8.5%
1995	81.7%	11.6%	0.8%	5.8%
2001	75.5%	17.3%	0.8%	6.3%
2003	73.1%	19.7%	0.9%	6.2%
2014	52.0%	39.3%	-	-
2015	50.1%	41.2%	-	-
2016	48.2%	42.4%	1.4%	8.1%
2017	46.8%	43.9%	1.4%	7.9%

Sources: Texas DSHS (to 2003) and National Funeral Directors Association.

Nobel Prizes to Texans

John B. Goodenough received the Nobel Prize in Chemistry in 2019 for his work with others on the development of lithium-ion batteries, notably a cathode that provided a higher voltage than previously available.

Goodenough also received a doctorate in physics from the University of Chicago in 1952, and worked at the Massachusetts Institute of Technology and Oxford University in Great Britain.

Community Hospitals in Texas

– Of the 652 reporting hospitals in Texas in 2020, 528 were considered community hospitals.

(A community hospital is defined as either a nonfederal, short-term general hospital or a special hospital whose facilities and services are available to the public. A hospital may include a nursing home-type unit and still be classified as short-term, provided that the majority of its patients are admitted to units where the average length of stay is less than 30 days.)

– The 528 hospitals employed 371,350 full-time equivalent people (FTEs) with a payroll, including benefits, of more than $31.7 billion.

– These hospitals contained some 66,844 beds.

Source: The Texas Hospital Association.

– The average length of stay was 5.3 days in 2017, compared to 6.8 days in 1975. This was less than the U.S. average of 5.5 days.

– The average cost per adjusted admission in Texas was $12,357 or $2,552 per day. This was 5.8 percent less than the U.S. average of $13,126.

– There were 2.7 million admissions in Texas, which accounted for 14.5 million inpatient days.

– There were 45.1 million outpatient visits in 2017, of which 11.9 million were emergency room visits.

– Of the FTEs working in community hospitals within Texas, there were 122,050 registered nurses and 7,700 licensed vocational nurses. ☆

Shannon Medical Center Hospital is shown in San Angelo on July 13, 2020. Photo by Jonathan Cutrer/Flickr (CC).

Mental Health and Substance Abuse

Diagnosis of Adult Clients in Texas/United States: 2018–2019

Diagnosis	Texas clients	% of clients diagnosis		Employed as % of known employment
		Texas	United States	Texas
Schizophrenia	43,367	19.7	13.5	12.0
Bipolar disorder	137,410	62.4	42.0	27.0
Other psychoses	657	0.3	2.2	18.0
All other diagnoses	3,585	1.6	35.3	29.0
No diagnosis/deferred	35,017	15.9	6.9	25.9
Total	**220,036**	**100.0**	**100.0**	**23.9**

Source: U.S. Department of Health and Human Services, Center for Mental Health Services, Uniform Reporting System, 2019.

Readmission Within 180 Days of Mental Health Treatment: 2019

Age	Civil* Texas	Civil U.S.	States/Terr. reporting	Forensic* Texas	Forensic U.S.
		In percent of clients.			
0 to 12	17.6%	13.2%	11	50%	10.3%
13 to 17	12.6	15.1	19	1.4	9.6
18 to 20	13.3	15.6	34	3.3	9.3
21 to 64	18.3	18.6	51	7.9	10.9
65 to 74	9.4	13.6	34	8.1	10.5
75 and over	0	5.9	14	–	9.0
Age not available	–	66.7	1	–	–
Total	**17.4**	**17.8**	**53**	**7.5**	**10.8**

*Forensic services are mental health services provided to persons directed into treatment by the criminal justice system; others are listed as "Civil." *Source: U.S. Department of Health and Human Services, Center for Mental Health Services,* Uniform Reporting System, 2019.

Substance Abuse Treatment in Texas: 2019

Facility operation	No.	%	Clients in treatment on March 29, 2019		
			No.	%	Clients under 18
Private nonprofit	196	38.3	11,137	30.9	783
Private for-profit	257	50.2	19,331	53.7	192
Local/county/community	27	5.3	894	2.5	132
State	9	1.8	1,278	3.6	19
Federal	22	4.3	3,343	9.3	–
Tribal	1	0.2	12	0.1	–
Total	**512**	**100.0**	**35,995**	**100.0**	**1,126**
Problem treated					**. . . per 100,000 pop.**
Alcohol and drug abuse	308	80.4	12,159	34.5	54
Drug abuse only	338	88.3	18,694	53.1	84
Alcohol abuse only	274	71.5	4,368	12.4	20

Source: National Survey of Substance Abuse Treatment Services, 2019.

Estimated Use of Drugs in Texas and Bordering States: 2018–2019

State	Any illicit drug	Marijuana	Other than marijuana[1]	Cigarettes	Binge alcohol[2]	Pain reliever misuse[4]
	Current users[3] as ***percent of population, age 12+ years****. Selected states.*					
U.S. total	12.34%	10.80%	3.31%	16.91%	11.24%	3.58%
Texas	**8.75**	**7.19**	**2.93**	**16.67**	**9.43**	**3.62**
Arkansas	9.45	8.46	2.91	22.55	10.22	3.66
Louisiana	9.41	7.74	3.26	22.07	10.86	3.85
Oklahoma	12.11	10.07	3.36	23.68	10.64	3.89
New Mexico	13.89	12.43	2.89	19.30	9.48	3.71

[1]Marijuana users who have also used another drug are included. [2]Binge use is defined as drinking five or more drinks on the same occasion on at least one day in the past 30 days. [3]Used drugs at least once within month. [4]Within the last year. *Source: U.S. Substance Abuse and Mental Health Services Administration,* National Survey on Drug Use and Health, 2018-2019.

State Institutions for Mental Health Services

Mental health services were provided to some 416,338 Texans in 2019 in various institutions, including community centers.

In 2004, the Texas Department of State Health Services was created (DSHS), bringing together:

— the Texas Department of Health,

— the Texas Department of Mental Health and Mental Retardation (MHMR),

— Commission on Alcohol and Drug Abuse,

— the Texas Health Care Information Council.

In 2016, Texas Health and Human Services was created by the Legislature with two agencies: the Texas Health and Human Services Commission (HHSC) and DSHS, with many direct client services transferred from DSHS to HHSC, including mental health services.

In 2019, state mental health agency expenditure was $1,095,727,077, with $541 million for community services, according to the federal Uniform Reporting System for the states.

Following is a list of the 10 state hospitals, the year each was founded, and number of beds in 2019, totalling 2,269.

Hospitals for Persons with Mental Illness

Austin State Hospital — Austin; 1857; 263 beds.
Big Spring State Hospital — Big Spring; 1937; 180 beds.
El Paso Psychiatric Center — El Paso; 1974; 71 beds.
Kerrville State Hospital — Kerrville; 1950; 220 beds.
North Texas State Hospital — Wichita Falls (1922), 268 beds and Vernon (1969); 294 beds.
Rio Grande State Center — Harlingen; 1962; 52 beds.
Rusk State Hospital — Rusk; 1919; 288 beds.
San Antonio State Hospital — San Antonio; 1892; 268 beds.
Terrell State Hospital — Terrell; 1885; 291 beds.
Waco Center for Youth — Waco; 1979; 74 beds.

Following is a list of community mental health centers, the year each was founded, and the counties each serves.

Community Mental Health Centers

Abilene — Betty Hardwick Center; 1971; Callahan, Jones, Shackelford, Stephens, and Taylor.

Amarillo — Texas Panhandle Centers; 1968; Armstrong, Carson, Collingsworth, Dallam, Deaf Smith, Donley, Gray, Hall, Hansford, Hartley, Hemphill, Hutchinson, Lipscomb, Moore, Ochiltree, Oldham, Potter, Randall, Roberts, Sherman, and Wheeler.

Austin — Integral Care; 1967; Travis.

Beaumont — Spindletop Center; 1967; Chambers, Hardin, Jefferson, and Orange.

Big Spring — West Texas Centers; 1997; Andrews, Borden, Crane, Dawson, Fisher, Gaines, Garza, Glasscock, Howard, Kent, Loving, Martin, Mitchell, Nolan, Reeves, Runnels, Scurry, Terrell, Terry, Upton, Ward, Winkler, and Yoakum.

Brownwood — Center for Life Resources; 1969; Brown, Coleman, Comanche, Eastland, McCulloch, Mills, and San Saba.

Bryan-College Station — MHMR Authority of Brazos Valley; 1972; Brazos, Burleson, Grimes, Leon, Madison, Robertson, and Washington.

Conroe — Tri-County Behavioral Healthcare; 1983; Liberty, Montgomery, and Walker.

Corpus Christi — Nueces Center for Mental Health & Intellectual Disabilities; 1970; Nueces.

Dallas — North Texas Behavioral Health Authority (NTBHA); 1967; Dallas, Ellis, Hunt, Kaufman, Navarro, and Rockwall.

Denton — Denton County MHMR Center; 1987; Denton.

Edinburg — Tropical Texas Behavioral Health; 1967; Cameron, Hidalgo, and Willacy.

El Paso — Emergence Health Network; 1968; El Paso.

Fort Worth — MHMR of Tarrant County; 1969; Tarrant.

Galveston — Gulf Coast Center; 1969; Brazoria and Galveston.

Granbury — Pecan Valley Centers for Behavioral & Developmental HealthCare; 1977; Erath, Hood, Johnson, Palo Pinto, Parker, and Somervell.

Houston — The Harris Center for Mental Health and IDD; 1965; Harris.

Jacksonville — Anderson-Cherokee Community Enrichment Services (ACCESS); 1995; Anderson and Cherokee.

Kerrville — Hill Country Mental Health & Developmental Disabilities Centers; 1997; Bandera, Blanco, Comal, Edwards, Gillespie, Hays, Kendall, Kerr, Kimble, Kinney, Llano, Mason, Medina, Menard, Real, Schleicher, Sutton, Uvalde, and Val Verde.

Laredo — Border Region Behavioral Health Center; 1969; Jim Hogg, Starr, Webb, and Zapata.

Longview — Community Healthcore; 1970; Bowie, Cass, Gregg, Harrison, Marion, Panola, Red River, Rusk, and Upshur.

Lubbock — StarCare Specialty Health System; 1969; Cochran, Crosby, Hockley, Lubbock, and Lynn.

Lufkin — Burke Center; 1975; Angelina, Houston, Jasper, Nacogdoches, Newton, Polk, Sabine, San Augustine, San Jacinto, Shelby, Trinity, and Tyler.

Lytle — Camino Real Community Services; 1996; Atascosa, Dimmit, Frio, La Salle, Karnes, Maverick, McMullen, Wilson, and Zavala.

McKinney — LifePath Systems; 1986; Collin.

Midland — PermiaCare; 1969; Brewster, Culberson, Ector, Hudspeth, Jeff Davis, Midland, Pecos, and Presidio.

Plainview — Central Plains Center; 1969; Bailey, Briscoe, Castro, Floyd, Hale, Lamb, Motley, Parmer, and Swisher.

Portland — Coastal Plains Community Center; 1996; Aransas, Bee, Brooks, Duval, Jim Wells, Kenedy, Kleberg, Live Oak, and San Patricio.

Rosenberg — Texana Center; 1996; Austin, Colorado, Fort Bend, Matagorda, Waller and Wharton.

Round Rock — Bluebonnet Trails Community Services; 1997; Bastrop, Burnet, Caldwell, Fayette, Gonzales, Guadalupe, Lee, and Williamson.

San Angelo — MHMR Services for the Concho Valley; 1969; Coke, Concho, Crockett, Irion, Reagan, Sterling, and Tom Green.

San Antonio — The Center for Health Care Services; 1966; Bexar.

Sherman — Texoma Community Center; 1974; Cooke, Fannin, and Grayson.

Temple — Central Counties Services; 1967; Bell, Coryell, Hamilton, Lampasas, and Milam.

Terrell — Lakes Regional MHMR Center; 1996; Camp, Delta, Franklin, Hopkins, Lamar, Morris, and Titus.

Tyler — Andrews Center Behavioral Healthcare System; 1970; Henderson, Rains, Smith, Van Zandt, and Wood.

Victoria — Gulf Bend Center; 1970; Calhoun, DeWitt, Goliad, Jackson, Lavaca, Refugio, and Victoria.

Waco — Heart of Texas Region MHMR Center; 1969; Bosque, Falls, Freestone, Hill, Limestone, and McLennan.

Wichita Falls — Helen Farabee Centers; 1969; Archer, Baylor, Childress, Clay, Cottle, Dickens, Foard, Hardeman, Haskell, Jack, King, Knox, Montague, Stonewall, Throckmorton, Wichita, Wilbarger, Wise, and Young. ☆

Source: U.S. Department of Health and Human Services and the Texas Health and Human Services.

Education

PUBLIC SCHOOLS

UIL WINNING SCHOOLS

TEXAS HISTORY DAY

UNIVERSITIES AND COLLEGES

Students of the San Antonio Academy of Texas engage in Upper School Field Day on April 12, 2019. Photo by San Antonio Academy of Texas (CC).

Texas Public Schools

Sources: Reports and online directory of the Texas Education Agency, tea.texas.gov; Summary of 2020—21 Conference Committee Report for HB1; additional reporting by A.J. Smuskiewicz.

Enrollment in Texas public schools continues to rise. In the 2019-2020 school year, 5,493,940 students were enrolled. That's an increase of 1.1 percent over enrollment in the 2018–2019 school year, and a jump of 13.9 percent above enrollment from 2009-2010, according to the Texas Education Agency.

In Texas, there are 1,202 independent and common school districts and 180 charter operators. Independent school districts are administered by an elected board of trustees and deal directly with the Texas Education Agency. Common districts are supervised by elected county school superintendents and county trustees. Charter schools are discussed later in this article.

There were 20 school districts with more than 50,000 students enrolled in their various schools, and 29.2 percent of all students in Texas attend school in those large districts. By contrast, only 1.8 percent of Texas students are enrolled at the 394 smallest districts in Texas, each of which has fewer than 500 students enrolled.

5 Largest School Districts, by Enrollment (May 2021)

School District	County	Enrollment
Houston ISD	Harris	196,943
Dallas ISD	Dallas	145,113
Cypress-Fairbanks ISD	Harris	114,881
Northside ISD	Bexar	103,151
Katy ISD	Harris, Fort Bend, Waller	84,176

5 Smallest School Districts, by Enrollment (May 2021)

School District	County	Enrollment
San Vicente ISD	Brewster	14
Doss Consolidated CSD	Gillespie	18
Divide ISD	Kerr	22
Valentine ISD	Jeff Davis	35
Comquest Academy CSD	Harris	38

Brief History of Public Education In Texas

Public education was one of the primary goals of the early settlers of Texas, who listed in the Texas Declaration of Independence the failure to provide education as one of their grievances against Mexico.

As early as 1838, President Mirabeau B. Lamar's message to the Republic of Texas Congress advocated setting aside public domain for public schools. His interest caused him to be called the "Father of Education in Texas." In 1839, Congress designated three leagues of land to support public schools for each Texas county and 50 leagues for a state university. In 1840, each county was allocated one more league of land.

The Republic, however, did not establish a public school system or a university. After Texas was admitted into the Union, the 1845 Texas State Constitution advocated public education, instructing the Legislature to designate at least 10 percent of the tax revenue for schools. Further delay occurred until Gov. Elisha M. Pease, on Jan. 31, 1854, signed the bill setting up the Texas public school system.

The public school system was made possible by setting aside $2 million out of $10 million Texas received for relinquishing its claim to land north and west of its present boundaries in the Compromise of 1850.

Early Funding and Administration Changes

During 1854, legislation provided for state apportionment of funds based upon an annual census. Also, railroads receiving grants were required to survey alternate sections to be set aside for public-school financing. The first school census that year showed 65,463 students; state fund apportionment was 62 cents per student.

When adopted in 1876, the present Texas Constitution provided: "All funds, lands, and other property heretofore set apart and appropriated for the support of public schools; all the alternate sections of land reserved by the state of grants heretofore made or that may hereafter be made to railroads, or other corporations, of any nature whatsoever; one half of the public domain of the state, and all sums of money that may come to the state from the sale of any portion of the same shall constitute a perpetual public school fund."

More than 52 million acres of the Texas public domain were allotted for school purposes. (See table "Distribution of the Public Lands of Texas" on page 465.)

In 1949, the Gilmer-Aikin Laws reorganized the state system of public schools by making sweeping changes in administration and financing. The Texas Education Agency, headed by the governor-appointed Commissioner of Education, administers the public-school system.

The policy-making body for public education is the 15-member State Board of Education, which is elected from separate districts for overlapping four-year terms. Current membership of the board is listed on page 501 in the State Government chapter.

Targeting Student Performance

The 68th Legislature passed one of the most historic education-reform bills of the past 50 years when lawmakers met in special session in the summer of 1984. House Bill 72 came in response to growing concern over deteriorating literacy among Texas' schoolchildren over two decades, reflected in students' scores on standardized tests.

Provisions of HB 72 raised teachers' salaries, but tied those raises to teacher performance. It also introduced more stringent teacher certification and initiated competency testing for teachers. Lawmakers also created the 22:1 class size ratio for kindergarten through fourth-grade classes and the no-pass, no-play rule.

Sweeping Reforms

In 1995, the 74th Legislature took on a monumental task and completely rewrote all the state's public education laws.

The Public Schools Reform Act of 1995 increased local control of public schools by limiting the Texas Education Agency to recommending and reporting on educational goals; overseeing charter schools; managing the permanent, foundation, and available school funds; administering an accountability system; creating and implementing the student testing program; recommending educator appraisal and counselor evaluation instruments; and developing plans for special, bilingual, compensatory, gifted and talented, vocational, and technology education.

It also reduced the authority of the State Board of Education. The goal was to return as much authority as possible to the local level. However, each subsequent legislature has reinstated some state-level control.

Charter Schools

Charter-school legislation in Texas provides for four types of charter schools: the home-rule school district charter, the campus or campus-program charter, the open-enrollment charter and a university-sponsored charter. A charter contract is typically granted for five years and can be revoked if the school violates its charter.

Since the inception of the charter school movement in Texas, the charter contracts have been granted by the State Board of Education (SBOE). However, SB2 passed during the 2013 legislative session shifted the authority to grant a charter to the commissioner of education. The State Board of Education, however, may veto any of his selections.

There are currently 175 active charter school districts in Texas. Since 1996, 338 charters have been approved and 157 have closed (including 38 closures due to the charter being revoked). So far, no district has created a home-rule charter, although citizens in Dallas ISD discussed it. There are 123 campus charter schools, which are created by school districts and overseen by each school district's board of trustees.

The most popular form of charter schools is the open-enrollment charter. These are public schools released from some Texas education laws and regulations. Many charter schools have focused efforts on educating young people who are at risk of dropping out of school or who have dropped out and then returned to school. There were 837 open-enrollment schools, representing 336,745 students during the 2019-2020 school year.

The state also approves university-sponsored charters; 29 of such schools are active and in operation, according to a search of TEA's online directory.

During the 2019-2020 school year, about 6.1 percent of the state's public school students attended open-enrollment charter schools.

State Appropriations

For FY22–23, general revenue financing for public education totals $46.6 billion, an increase of $2.0 billion over the FY20–21 funding level. Most of the funding for public education comes through the Foundation School Program system. The 86th Legislature increased FSP funding by $11.5 billion in General Revenue funding, with the intent to increase salaries for teachers and provide school district property tax relief.

Supplemental appropriation for public education include:

- $60 million for supplemental special education services.
- Increases the state's contribution rates at the Teacher Retirement System from 7.5 percent in 2020-21 to 7.75 percent in FY 2022 and 8.0 percent in FY 2023.
- Provides 897.6 million, an increase of $39.5 million, to maintain current helath insurance premiums and benefits for retired teachers.

Permanent School Fund

The Texas public school system was established and the Permanent School Fund (PSF) set up by the Fifth Legislature, Jan. 31, 1854.

The 158-year-old PSF is managed by the State Board of Education and is the second-largest educational endowment

Permanent School Fund

Year	Fund Value* (in millions)	Funds Distributed to Schools (in millions)
2020	$46,675.6	$1,701.7
2019	$46,500.4	$1,535.8
2018	$44,067.5	$1,235.8
2017	$41,418	$1,056.4
2016	$37,263.9	$1,056.4
2015	$33,833.5	$8,38.7
2014	$34,951.2	$8,38.7
2013	$27,277	$1,020.9
2012	$25,503	$1,020.9
2011	$24,091.6	$1,092.8
2010	$22,107.8	$60.7
2009	$20,545.3	$716.5
2008	$23,142.4	$716.5
2007	$25,311.8	$843.1
2006	$22,802.7	$841.9
2005	$21,354.3	$880
2004	$19,261.8	$825.1
2003	$18,037.3	N/A
2002	$17,047.2	N/A
2001	$19,021.8	N/A
2000	$22,275.6	N/A
1999	$19,615.7	$698.5
1998	$16,296.2	$661.9
1997	$15,496.6	$690.8
1996	$12,995.8	$692.7
1995	$12,273.2	$740
1994	$11,330.6	$737
1993	$11,822.5	$737.7
1992	$10,944.9	$739.5
1991	$10,227.8	$739.2
1990	$7,328.2	$700.3
1980	$2,464.6	$3
1970	$842.2	$287.2
1960	$425.8	$164.2
1950	$161.2	$94
1940	$68.3	$34.6
1930	$38.7	$27.3
1920	$25.7	$18.4
1910	$16.8	$5.9

*Prior to 1991, the PSF reported cash, bonds at par, and stock at book value. From 1991 to the present, the PSF has reported cash, bonds and stocks at fair value.

Texas School Enrollment and Expenditures per Student

School Year	Enrollment	Spending per student
2019-2020	5,493,940	—
2018-2019	5,431,910	$12,861
2017–2018	5,399,682	$12,634
2016–2017	5,343,893	$12,264
2015–2016	5,284,306	$11,704
2014–2015	5,232,065	$10,971
2013–2014	5,151,925	$9,903
2012–2013	5,058,939	$9,969
2011–2012	4,978,120	$10,335
2010–2011	4,912,385	$11,142
2009–2010	4,824,778	$11,543
2008–2009	4,728,204	$11,567
2007–2008	4,651,516	$10,162
2006–2007	4,576,933	$9,629
2005–2006	4,505,572	$9,269

Graduates and Dropouts

School Year	Graduates	*Dropouts
2018-2019	355,615	34,477
2017-2018	347,893	33,697
2016–2017	334,424	33,050
2015–2016	324,311	33,466
2014–2015	313,397	33,437
2013–2014	303,109	35,358
2012–2013	301,418	34,696
2011–2012	292,636	36,276
2010–2011	290,581	34,363
2009–2010	280,520	33,235
2008–2009	264,275	40,923
2007–2008	252,121	45,796
2006–2007	241,193	55,306
2005–2006	240,485	51,841
2004–2005	239,716	18,290

* Grades 7–12.

in the United States. It is invested in global markets and broadly diversified.

Every year, a distribution is made from PSF to pay a portion of educational costs in each public school district. The amount distributed is subject to two constraints set in Article VII, Section 5 of the Texas Constitution:

- The SBOE may not approve a distribution rate or transfer to the Available School Fund (ASF) that exceeds 6 percent of the average market value of the fund, excluding real property.
- The total distributions over a 10-year period to the ASF may not exceed the total return on the PSF's investment assets over the same period.

The fund was first established in 1854 with $2.0 million. The funds distributed to schools that year was $40,587. By the year 1900 the fund had grown to $9.1 million. Funds distributed to schools in 1900 totalled $3.0 million. The PSF balance, as of Aug. 31, 2020, was $46.7 billion, an increase of $175.2 million from the prior year.

The PSF also provides a guarantee for bonds issued by local school districts, allowing districts to pay lower interest rates. As of Aug. 31, 2012, PSF assets guaranteed $77.7 billion in school district bonds to 844 public school districts and $1.4 billion in charter district bonds to 14 charter districts.

COVID-19 Pandemic

As the pandemic spread in early 2020, public schools throughout the United States ceased in-person learning. When a quick recovery became more unlikely, schools established online, or remote, learning for students. Many Texas public schools reopened to in-person education for the autumn term of 2020, ahead of schools in most other states. In July 2020, Governor Greg Abbott gave individual school districts the option of in-school classes. [1]

Public School Personnel and Salaries

Personnel Category	Personnel 2018—2019	Personnel 2019—2020	% Change from Previous	Average Base Salaries 2018—2019	Average Base Salaries 2019—2020	% Change from Previous
Teachers	358,445	363,098	1.30%	$54,121	$57,091	5.49%
Campus Administrators	21,812	21,960	0.68%	$78,947	$82,511	4.51%
Central Administrators	8,287	8,352	0.78%	$103,379	$108,366	4.82%
Professional Support*	73,190	74,966	2.43%	$64,063	$67,334	5.11%
Total Professionals	**461,734**	**468,376**	**1.44%**	—	—	—
Educational Aides	74,325	78,125	5.11%	$21,210	$22,067	4.04%
Auxiliary Staff	184,109	188,764	2.53%	$26,891	$28,279	5.16%
Total Staff	**720,168**	**735,265**	**2.10%**	—	—	—

*Personnel figures are full-time equivalent
** The Professional Support category includes supervisors, counselors, educational diagnosticians, librarians, nurses/physicians, therapists, and psychologists.

Source: TEA Staff Salary reports for 2018-2019 and 2019-2020

The closing and reopening of public schools generated much controversy. Some parents opposed remote learning, viewing it as substandard education, difficult for children psychologically, unhealthy for social development, and unnecessary because children and adolescents were at low risk for contracting, transmitting, or developing serious illness from COVID-19. [1] Others, including leaders of the Texas State Teachers Association, [1, 2] favored the school shutdowns for safety reasons, arguing that any in-person contact could increase the virus's spread among faculty, staff, and students.

As online learning continued and in-class learning remained nonmandatory, some students dropped out of the public school system entirely. [3] In some districts, teams of teachers visited the homes of missing students every few weeks. [3]

In May 2021, a study conducted by University of Kentucky researchers for the National Bureau of Economic Research reported that the reopening of Texas schools may have led to an acceleration in the number of COVID-19 cases in Texas. [1, 4] According to the researchers' computer model estimates, there may have been 43,000 additional cases and 800 additional deaths within two months of the autumn 2020 reopenings. However, a spokesperson for the Texas Education Agency (TEA) disputed those model estimates and maintained that allowing the option of in-class attendance was the correct decision. The spokesperson noted that only five percent of students, teachers, and staff had developed confirmed cases of COVID-19 during the 2020-21 school year. [1, 4]

Masks

In March 2021, Governor Abbott ended the state mandate ordering that face masks be worn in public settings, leaving mask policies up to individual school districts. [1, 5] However, he advised public schools to follow TEA's guidelines, which recommended wearing masks inside schools. [1, 6] Some parents and students opposed mask-wearing regulations, considering them to be unconstitutional intrusions on personal freedoms and individual decisions. [5] Others believed that masks should remain mandatory for everyone, arguing that they were needed for safety. [7]

Despite the loosening of the mask restrictions and the reopening of schools, Governor Abbott renewed the COVID-related public disaster declaration in May 2021. [8]

Vaccine

As of May 2021, about 40 percent of Texans were fully vaccinated against the coronavirus that causes COVID-19. [4] Even after vaccination became common in mid-2021, the mask-wearing recommendation continued because student and staff vaccination statuses could not be known with certainty. [1]

Enrollment

The TEA reported in January 2021 that enrollment in Texas public schools from early education through 12th grade decreased by about 157,000 students, or three percent, from October 2019 to October 2020. [9, 10] More than half of that decline occurred in the nonmandatory grade levels of early education, pre-kindergarten, and kindergarten. However, enrollment also declined for the mandatory grades (1 through 12) by about one percent. This was the first enrollment decline reported for Texas public schools since that data was first collected. The drop was likely related to students not returning to either in-class or online learning during the pandemic. [10]

Finances

During the summer of 2020, many school administrators and financial experts feared that a tight state budget, as well as the economic slowdown and school shutdowns, would have severe impacts on school-district budgets. [11]

However, according to a March 2021 report, sweeping COVID-related economic-relief legislation signed by President Joe Biden earlier that month was expected to provide local governments with financial windfalls. [11] In April 2021, state officials announced the release of $11.2 billion from the $18 billion in available federal COVID-relief funds to help public schools address pandemic-related problems, such as computer systems for remote learning and desk barriers for in-person learning. [12, 13]

Numerous school districts participated in a state-funded program in 2021 to incentivize teachers in poor communities to do extra intervention and tutoring for students during holiday and summer breaks and after-school hours. [14] The funds came from the TEA's Teacher Incentive Allotment. The districts hoped that the program, which raised some teacher salaries to more than $100,000, would help students catch up with lost learning stemming from school closures.

References

1. Martinez, Marissa. "Resuming in-person learning at Texas schools last fall accelerated spread of COVID-19, study says." *The Texas Tribune*. May 10, 2021. https://www.texastribune.org/2021/05/10/texas-schools-coronavirus-increase-study/
2. "TSTA demands the governor shut down schools for the year, take other steps to protect Texans' health" [press release]. Texas State Teachers Association, Facebook. April 1, 2020. https://www.facebook.com/texasstateteachersassociation/photos/tsta-demands-the-governor-shut-down-schools-for-the-year-take-other-steps-to-pro/10158048809838433/
3. McNeel, Bekah. "In San Antonio, teachers hit the streets in search of students disappearing from online learning." *The Texas Tribune*. March 3, 2021. https://www.texastribune.org/2021/03/03/texas-schools-missing-students/
4. Lenthang, Marlene. "Rapid school reopenings may have led to thousands of COVID cases, hundreds of deaths in Texas." ABC News. May 20, 2021. https://abcnews.go.com/Health/rapid-school-reopenings-led-thousands-covid-cases-hundreds/story?id=77778717
5. Bohra, Neelam. "Parents sue Katy ISD for keeping mask mandate after Gov. Abbott lifted statewide requirement." *The Texas Tribune*. April 2, 2021. https://www.texastribune.org/2021/04/02/texas-katy-isd-mask-lawsuit/
6. SY 20-21 public health planning guidance. Texas Education Agency. March 25, 2021. https://tea.texas.gov/sites/default/files/covid/SY-20-21-Public-Health-Guidance.pdf
7. McNeel, Bekah. "'I've never done any of this': A Texas parent reluctantly dives into a school district's battle over masks." *The Texas Tribune*. April 12, 2021. https://www.texastribune.org/2021/04/12/texas-comal-isd-masks-coronavirus/
8. "COVID-19 support: Public health orders." Texas Education Agency. 2020-2021. https://tea.texas.gov/texas-schools/health-safety-discipline/covid/covid-19-support-public-health-orders
9. Summary of Texas public schools student enrollment trends: January 2021. Texas Education Agency. March 4, 2021. https://tea.texas.gov/sites/default/files/covid/SY21-Student-Enrollment-Summary-Table.pdf
10. Mitchell, Isaiah. "Enrollment drop hits Texas public schools." *The Texan*. January 14, 2021. https://thetexan.news/enrollment-drop-hits-texas-public-schools/
11. Ramsey, Ross. "Analysis: Government budgets looked terrible when COVID-19 started. A federal windfall has flipped the outlook." *The Texas Tribune*. March 12, 2021. https://www.texastribune.org/2021/03/12/texas-budget-coronavirus/
12. McGee, Kate. "Texas releases $11 billion of $18 billion in federal stimulus money for public schools." *The Texas Tribune*. April 28, 2021. https://www.texastribune.org/2021/04/28/texas-schools-stimulus-money/
13. Ramsey, Ross. "Analysis: A $5.5 billion shift in who pays for public education in Texas." *The Texas Tribune*. April 9, 2021. https://www.texastribune.org/2021/04/09/texas-education-property-taxes/
14. McNeel, Bekah. "Pay for some Texas teachers will top $100,000 in bid to aid poorer schools devastated by COVID-19." *The Texas Tribune*. May 17, 2021. https://www.texastribune.org/2021/05/17/texas-teacher-salaries-coronavirus/

University Interscholastic League Winning Schools for the 2018–2019 and 2020–2021 School Years

Source: University Interscholastic League, uiltexas.org

The **UIL Lone Star Cup** is awarded annually to six high schools, one in each of the six UIL classifications, based on their team performance in district and state championships. The winning schools receive the UIL Lone Star Cup trophy and a $1,000 scholarship. In the school year 2019-20, the Cup was not awarded due to the COVID-19 pandemic.

YEAR	1A	2A	3A	4A	5A	6A
Lone Star Cup Champions						
2020–21	Nazareth	Shiner	Brock	Argyle	Highland Park (Dallas)	The Woodlands (Conroe)
2018–19	Nazareth	Mason	Brock	Argyle	Highland Park (Dallas)	Southlake Carroll

The schools of individuals who won state championships in the academic, music, and the arts categories are listed first, then the winners in some sports categories. For other sports results, see page 180. A dash (—) in the box means there was no competition in that conference in that category for that year. In the year 2019-20, the spring state academic competitions were canceled due to the COVID-19 pandemic.

State Champions, Academics

YEAR	1A	2A	3A	4A	5A	6A
Overall State Meet Academic Champions						
2020–21	Slidell	Sabine Pass	Holliday	Lindale	PSJA Southwest	Clements (Sugar Land)
2018–19	Borden County	Sabine Pass	Holliday	Argyle	Lovejoy (Lucas)	Cypress Woods
Accounting						
2020–21	Happy	Vega	Holliday	Andrews	Tivy (Kerrville)	Keller
2018–19	Jayton	Union Grove (Gladewater)	Idalou	Argyle	Hallsville	Cypress Woods
Calculator Applications						
2020–21	Rankin	Sabine Pass	Brock	Spring Hill (Longview)	Canyon (New Braunfels)	North Shore (Houston)
2018–19	Santa Anna	Muenster	Ponder	Argyle	Canutillo (El Paso)	North Shore (Houston)
Computer Applications						
2020–21	Happy	Sanford Fritch	Elysian Fields	Andrews	Friendswood	Flower Mound
2018–19	Springlake-Earth	Vega	Chapel Hill (Mount Pleasant)	Melissa	Waller	Cypress Woods
Computer Science						
2020–21	Aspermont	San Augustine	Fairfield	School for Talented & Gifted (Dallas)	Lovejoy (Lucas)	Cypress Woods
2018–19	Borden County	Ozona	Ponder	Giddings	Austin LBJ	Cypress Woods
Number Sense						
2020–21	Jonesboro	Woodsboro	Sabine (Gladewater)	Salado	Highland Park (Dallas)	Clements (Sugar Land)
2018–19	Bellevue	Poolville	Sabine (Gladewater)	Wichita Falls Hirschi	Highland Park (Dallas)	Clements (Sugar Land)
Mathematics						
2020–21	Knippa	Woodsboro	Idalou	Calhoun (Port Lavaca)	Highland Park (Dallas)	Clements (Sugar Land)
2018–19	Fruitvale	Muenster	Sabine (Gladewater)	Salado	Highland Park (Dallas)	Dulles (Sugar Land)
Science						
2020–21	Guthrie	Eldorado	Skidmore-Tynan	Argyle	Sharyland Pioneer (Mission)	Martin (Arlington)
2018–19	Klondike (Lamesa)	Valley View	Whitney	La Feria	Lubbock	Dulles (Sugar Land)
Social Studies						
2020–21	Knippa	Lindsay	Llano	Wimberley	Montgomery Lake Creek	Lake Ridge (Mansfield)
2018–19	Hartley	Sabine Pass	Tolar	Hereford	Hallsville	Pearland Dawson
Current Issues						
2020–21	Fruitvale	Mason	New Caney Infinity ECHS	Wimberley	Montgomery Lake Creek	Health Careers (San Antonio)
2018–19	Borden County	Sabine Pass	Holliday	Argyle	College Station	Humble Atascosita

YEAR	1A	2A	3A	4A	5A	6A
Literary Criticism						
2020–21	Graford	Mason	S&S Consolidated (Sadler)	Argyle	Sulphur Springs	Seven Lakes (Katy)
2018–19	Graford	Sabine Pass	Holliday	Argyle	Sulphur Springs	McKinney
Poetry Interpretation						
2020–21	Irion County	West Hardin (Saratoga)	Chisum (Paris)	Tuloso-Midway (Corpus Christi)	PSJA Southwest	Judson (Converse)
2018–19	Irion County	Mason	Malakoff	Little Cypress-Mauriceville	Victoria West	Judson (Converse)
Prose Interpretation						
2020–21	Aspermont	Sundown	White Oak	Tuloso-Midway (Corpus Christi)	Corsicana	Judson (Converse)
2018–19	Petersburg	West Hardin (Saratoga)	Kemp	Little Cypress-Mauriceville	Tuloso-Midway (Corpus Christi)	Plano
Ready Writing						
2020–21	Prairie Lea	Falls City	East Chambers (Winnie)	Calallen (Corpus Christi)	Highland Park (Dallas)	Martin (Arlington)
2018–19	Woodson	Shelbyville	Franklin	Bullard	College Station	Pearland Dawson
Speech Team						
2020–21	Chireno	Mason	White Oak	Salado	Lovejoy (Lucas)	Plano
2018–19	Borden County	Shelbyville	London (Corpus Christi)	North Lamar (Paris)	Lovejoy (Lucas)	Pflugerville Hendrickson
Informative Speaking						
2020–21	Nazareth	Stamford	White Oak	Lampasas	Pflugerville	Plano West
2018–19	Lometa	Leon (Jewett)	Holliday	North Lamar (Paris)	Mount Pleasant	Plano West
Persuasive Speaking						
2020–21	Chireno	Schulenburg	Lexington	Salado	A&M Conslidated (College Station)	Plano West
2018–19	Borden County	Latexo	London (Corpus Christi)	North Lamar (Paris)	Dripping Springs	Plano West
Lincoln-Douglas Debate						
2020–21	Irion County	Shelbyville	Canadian	Hereford	Medina Valley (Castroville)	Cypress Lakes (Katy)
2018–19	Guthrie	Gary	London (Corpus Christi)	Bandera	Lovejoy (Lucas)	Plano West
Spelling & Vocabulary						
2020–21	San Isidro	Forsan	Henrietta	Hudson (Lufkin)	Sherman	Vandegrift (Austin)
2018–19	Irion County	Brackettville	Holliday	Snyder	Frisco Independence	Midway (Waco)
Spelling & Vocabulary Team						
2020–21	Moulton	Forsan	Henrietta	Giddings	Denton	Allen
2018–19	Kennard	Sabine Pass	Holliday	Burnet	Lubbock	El Paso Coronado
Journalism Team						
2020–21	Nazareth	Martin's Mill	Central (Pollok)	Lindale	Lovejoy (Lucas)	United South (Laredo)
2018–19	Savoy	San Isidro	Gateway (Georgetown)	Wimberley	Leander Rouse	Sterling (Baytown)
Editorial Writing						
2020–21	Nazareth	Albany	Paradise	Lindale	Joshua	Lamar (Houston)
2018–19	Grady (Lenorah)	San Isidro	Coleman	Devine	Lovejoy (Lucas)	Beaumont West Brook
Feature Writing						
2020–21	San Isidro	Shelbyville	Central (Pollok)	Chapel Hill (Tyler)	Ryan (Denton)	Hebron (Carrollton)
2018–19	Savoy	Mason	Gateway (Georgetown)	Argyle	Lindale	Mansfield
Headline Writing						
2020–21	Nazareth	Martin's Mill	Cole (San Antonio)	Kilgore	Aledo	Cinco Ranch (Katy)
2018–19	Nazareth	Martin's Mill	Van Alstyne	Bridgeport	PSJA Memorial (Alamo)	Stevens (San Antonio)
News Writing						
2020–21	Lasara	Archer City	Central (Pollok)	Center	Liberty Hill	Willis
2018–19	Savoy	Lindsay	Whitney	Henderson	Gregory-Portland	Sterling (Baytown)

State Champions, Publications

Year	Yearbooks (Gold Awards)	Print Newspapers (Gold Awards)
2020–21	Burges (El Paso); McKinney; Texas (Texarkana); Vista Ridge (Cedar Park); Westlake (Austin)	Albany; Bowie (Austin); McCallum (Austin); Pleasant Grove (Texarkana); St. Mark's (Dallas); Texas (Texarkana)
2019–20	Haltom; Highland Park; Kealing (Austin); Legacy (Mansfield); McKinney; Pleasant Grove (Texarkana); St. Thomas Episcopal (Houston); Texas (Texarkana); Vista Ridge (Cedar Park)	Albany; Pleasant Grove (Texarkana); St. Mark's (Dallas); Texas (Texarkana)

State Champions, Music and Theater

YEAR	1A	2A	3A	4A	5A	6A
One-Act Play						
2020–21	Rankin	Christoval	Shallowater	Corpus Christi Tuloso-Midway	Pharr-San Juan-Alamo Southwest	Northside Taft
2019–20	Spring state academic championships were canceled due to COVID-19 pandemic.					
State Marching Band Contest						
2020–21	—	Ganado	—	Lake Belton	—	Harlingen
2019–20	Irion	—	Mineola	—	Cedar Park	—

State Champions, Athletics

YEAR	1A	2A	3A	4A	5A	6A
Cross Country Team, Boys						
2020–21	Miller Grove (Cumby)	Port Aransas	Presidio	San Elizario	Grapevine	Carroll (Southlake)
2019–20	Miller Grove (Cumby)	Great Hearts Monte Vista (San Antonio)	Eustace	Decatur	Eastwood (El Paso)	Carroll (Southlake)
Cross Country Individual, Boys						
2020–21	Miller Grove	Poolville	Onalaska	Melissa	Grapevine	Wylie
2019–20	Miller Grove (Cumby)	Great Hearts Monte Vista (San Antonio)	Luling	Melissa	Aledo	La Porte
Cross Country Team, Girls						
2020–21	Nazareth	Sundown	Lago Vista	Canyon	Boerne Champion	Flower Mound (Lewisville)
2019–20	Miller Grove (Cumby)	Gruver	Holliday	Canyon	Boerne	Carroll (Southlake)
Cross Country Individual, Girls						
2020–21	Earth Springlake	Wellington	Cameron Yoe	Celina	Cedar Park	Denton Guyer
2019–20	Miller Grove (Cumby)	Lindsay	Whitesboro	Salado	McKinney North	Plano
Golf Team, Boys						
2020–21	Sterling City	Normangee	Brock	Argyle	Highland Park (Dallas)	Westlake (Austin)
2019–20	UIL state spring sports were canceled due to the COVID-19 pandemic.					
Golf Individual, Boys						
2020–21	Fort Elliott (Briscoe)	Tahoka	Columbus	Wimberley	Highland (Dallas)	Keller
2019–20	UIL state spring sports were canceled due to the COVID-19 pandemic.					
Golf Team, Girls						
2020–21	Robert Lee	Normangee	Wall	Andrews	Alamo Heights (San Antonio)	Hebron (Lewisville)
2019–20	UIL state spring sports were canceled due to the COVID-19 pandemic.					
Golf Individual, Girls						
2020–21	Eula (Clyde)	Martin's Mill	Chapel Hill (Mount Pleasant)	Carrollton (Ranchview)	Granbury	San Angelo Central
2019–20	UIL state spring sports were canceled due to the COVID-19 pandemic.					
Tennis, Team						
2020–21	—	—	—	Hereford	Highland Park (Dallas)	Westwood (Round Rock)
2019–20	—	—	—	Fredericksburg	Highland Park (Dallas)	Memorial (Houston)
Tennis, Boys Singles						
2020–21	Nueces Canyon (Barksdale)	Sabine Pass	Wall	Canyon	Lebanon Trail (Frisco)	Midland
2019–20	UIL state spring sports were canceled due to the COVID-19 pandemic.					

YEAR	1A	2A	3A	4A	5A	6A
Tennis, Boys Doubles						
2020–21	Crowell	Mason	Little River Academy	Wimberley	College Station A&M Consolidated	Westwood (Round Rock)
2019–20	UIL state spring sports were canceled due to the COVID-19 pandemic.					
Tennis, Girls Singles						
2020–21	Slidell	Mason	Franklin	Devine	Heritage (Frisco)	Bowie (Austin)
2019–20	UIL state spring sports were canceled due to the COVID-19 pandemic.					
Tennis, Girls Doubles						
2020–21	Nueces Canyon (Barksdale)	Mason	Reagan (Big Lake)	Stafford	Heritage (Frisco)	Houston Memorial
2019–20	UIL state spring sports were canceled due to the COVID-19 pandemic.					
Tennis, Mixed Doubles						
2020–21	Sterling City	Mason	Groesbeck	Hereford	Amarillo	Westwood (Round Rock)
2019–20	UIL state spring sports were canceled due to the COVID-19 pandemic.					
Track & Field, Boys Team						
2020–21	Paducah	Shiner	Brock	La Vega (Waco)	Liberty (Frisco)	Summer Creek (Humble)
2019–20	UIL state spring sports were canceled due to the COVID-19 pandemic.					
Track & Field, Girls Team						
2020–21	Ackerly Sands	Panhandle	Cameron Yoe	Kennedale	Lancaster	DeSoto
2019–20	UIL state spring sports were canceled due to the COVID-19 pandemic.					

Swimming & Diving, Team

	GIRLS		BOYS	
YEAR	5A	6A	5A	6A
2020–21	Lubbock	Conroe (The Woodlands)	Wakeland (Frisco)	Conroe (The Woodlands)
2019–20	Lubbock	Southlake Carroll	Kingwood Park (Humble)	Kingwood (Humble)

Wrestling, Boys

2020–21	**TEAM: 5A** Randall (Canyon) **6A** Allen **5A Weight Class 106**: Randall (Canyon) **113**: Creekview (Carrollton) **120**: Lubbock **126**: Randall (Canyon) **132**: Dumas **138**: Dumas **145**: Randall (Canyon) **152**: Heritage (Colleyville) **160**: Centennial (Burleson) **170**: Argyle **182**: Randall (Canyon) **195**: Lovejoy (Lucas) **220**: Creekview (Carrollton) **285**: Midlothian **6A** Weight Class 106: Allen **113**: Martin (Arlington) **120**: Allen **126**: Allen **132**: Martin (Arlington) **138**: West (Plano) **145**: Martin (Arlington) **152**: Martin (Arlington) **160**: Prosper **170**: Clemens (Schertz) **182**: Woodlands College Park (Conroe) **195**: Klein **220**: Martin (Arlington) **285**: Allen
2019–20	**TEAM**: **5A** Randall (Canyon) **6A** Allen **5A Weight Class 106**: Carrollton (Creekview) **113**: East (Wylie) **120**: Lubbock **126**: Midlothian **132**:Lone Star (Frisco) **138**: Reedy (Frisco) **145**: Midlothian **152**: Dripping Springs **160**: Randall (Canyon) **170**: Randall (Canyon) **182**: New Waverly **195**: Creekview (Carrollton) **220**: Cedar Park **285**: Foster (Richmond) **6A Weight Class 106**: Ellison (Killeen) **113**: Allen **120**: Martin (Arlington) **126**: Martin (Arlington) **132**: Keller **138**: Vandegrift (Austin) **145**: Allen **152**: Vista Ridge (Cedar Park) **160**: Allen **170**: Katy **182**: Klein **195**: Allen **220**: Prosper **285**: New Braunfels

Wrestling, Girls

2020–21	**TEAM: 5A** Allen **6A** Randall (Canyon) **5A** Weight Class 95: Randall (Canyon) **102**: Randall (Canyon) **110**: Hanks (El Paso) **119**: Caprock (Amarillo) **128**: Centennial (Burleson) **138**: Kingwood Park (Humble) **148**: Friendswood **165**: The Colony (Lewisville) **185**: Hanks (El Paso) **215**: Kingwood Park (Humble) **6A** Weight Class 95: Woodlands College Park (Conroe) **102**: Allen **110**: Carroll (Southlake) **119:** Bowie (Austin) **128**: Cypress Ranch **138**: San Marcos **148**: Allen **165**: Tompkins (Katy) **185**: Woodlands College Park (Conroe) **215**: Steele (Cibolo)
2019–20	**TEAM**: **5A** Eastwood (El Paso) **6A** Trinity (Euless) **5A Weight Class 95**: Eastlake (El Paso) **102**: Lovejoy (Lucas) **110**: Eastwood (El Paso) **119**: Independence (Frisco) **128**: Eastwood (El Paso) **138**: Kingwood Park (Humble) **148**: Burges (El Paso) **165**: Kimball (Dallas) **185**: Parkland (El Paso) **215**: Donna **6A Weight Class 95**: Woodlands College Park (Conroe) **102**: Cypress Creek **110**: Martin (Arlington) **119**: Weatherford **128**: West (Plano) **138**: Morton Ranch (Katy) **148**: West (Plano) **165**: Tompkins (Katy) **185**: Woodlands College Park (Conroe) **215**: Steele (Cibolo)

State and National History Day Contests, 2020–2021

Each year thousands of students, encouraged by teachers and parents statewide, participate in the National History Day program in Texas. Texas History Day, an affiliate of NHD, is a highly regarded academic program for 6th through 12th grade students. Students that place first or second at the state contest get the chance to compete in the national contest in Washington, D.C. Learn more at **texashistoryday.com.**

State History Day Winners 2020

Theme: Breaking Barriers

	Junior	Senior
	Documentaries	
Individual	1st: *The International Space Station: A Symbol of Unity,* East Central Heritage MS (San Antonio)	1st: *"Kill the Indian, Save the Man"; How the Traumatic Shared Experience of Native American Boarding Schools Broke Intertribal Barriers and Led to the Formation of Pan-Indianism,* Livingston HS
	2nd: *Barbara Jordan: Breaking Racial and Gender Barriers. Equality for All; Privileges for None,* Santa Fe JH	2nd: *To Hell and Back,* IMPACT Early College HS (Baytown)
Group	1st: *Loving v. Virginia: Breaking Barriers in Anti-Miscegenation,* CM Rice MS (Plano)	1st: *Taking Giant Steps: Breaking Societal Barriers Through the Intellectual Growth of Jazz,* Goose Creek Memorial, Sterling HS
	2nd: *Flying the Hump,* Sartartia MS (Sugar Land)	2nd: *A Land Without Mercy: Robert Peary's Expedition to the North Pole,* Plano East SR HS
	Exhibits	
Individual	1st: *Tearing Down the Barrier Between East West: The Fall of the Berlin Wall,* Gentry JH (Baytown)	1st: *The CCC: Breaking Barriers One Park At A Time,* New Caney HS
	2nd: *Mendez v. Westminster: Breaking Barriers for a Seat In the Classroom,* Shotwell MS (Houston)	2nd: *Joan Ganz Cooney: Breaking Barriers in Educational Broadcasting,* Belton New Tech HS at Waskow
Group	1st: *His Mission, His Legacy — Dr. Hector P. Garcia, A Man of the People,* St. Matthew Catholic School (San Antonio)	1st: *'B' is for Breaking Barriers: How Sesame Street Revolutionized Children's Television and Education,* Health Careers HS (San Antonio)
	2nd: *Swinging for Equality,* Hornedo MS (El Paso)	2nd: *The Equal Rights Amendment: Campaign Success to State ERAs,* Dickinson HS
	Performances	
Individual	1st: *Madam CJ Walker,* Lewis MS (Houston)	1st: *The Catt in the Hat Breaks Barriers for the Rat,* Impact Early College HS (Baytown)
	2nd: *The BTT Shunt: Blalock's Diary,* Atlas Academy (Waco)	2nd: *little people, BIG DREAMS — A story of unwavering faith and resilience,* Liberty HS (Frisco)
Group	1st: *Mr. Rogers: Breaking Barriers,* Stillman MS (Brownsville)	1st: *King Henry VIII's Greatest Heir: Religious Freedom in America,* Highland Park HS (Dallas)
	2nd: *Penicillin: Breaking Barriers in the Health Care Field,* Sartartia MS (Sugar Land)	2nd: *Felix Tijerina: Breaking Barriers by opening doors for Latin Americans,* Veterans Memorial Early College HS (Brownsville)
	Websites	
Individual	1st: *Breaking Barriers to Universal Vaccination,* Sartartia MS (Sugar Land)	1st: *Ethel Payne: Paving The Way To Equality Through Journalism,* Granbury HS
	2nd: *Turbulence Couldn't Shake Her: Bessie Coleman, Aviatrix,* Cedar Bayou JH (Baytown)	2nd: *"Deeds, Not Words!": The Suffragettes, Women Breaking Barriers,* Belton New Tech HS at Waskow
Group	1st: *Termination, Restoration, and Beyond: How the Alabama-Coushatta Tribe of Texas Continues to Face and Break Barriers in History,* Livingston JH	1st: *The Delano Grape Strike: How a Coalition of Immigrants Ended Labor Injustice,* Plano East SR HS
	2nd: *The Wright Brothers: Making the Impossible, Possible,* Sycamore Springs MS (Dripping Springs)	2nd: *Asking For the Moon: How the Space Race Created the Digital Age,* Plano East SR HS
	Papers	
Individual	1st: *Breaking Barriers to Universal Vaccination,* Sartartia Middle School (Sugar Land)	1st: *Dr. Hector Garcia: The Driving Force Who Persuaded Lyndon Johnson to Break the Barrier of Racial Discrimination,* Sterling HS
	2nd: *The Fifth Circuit Four: The Unheralded Judges Who Helped to Break Legal Barriers in the Deep South,* Belmont Home School	2nd: *Breaking Economic Barriers: How the Woman's Commonwealth of Belton, Texas, Changed Their World,* Lorena HS

National History Day 2020

1st Place Senior Group Exhibit	1st Place Senior Individual Website	1st Place Junior Individual Paper	3rd Place Senior Group Performance
'B' is for Breaking Barriers: How Sesame Street Revolutionized Children's Television and Education, Health Careers HS (San Antonio)	*"Deeds, Not Words!": The Suffragettes, Women Breaking Barriers,* Belton New Tech HS at Waskow	*The Fifth Circuit Four: The Unheralded Judges Who Helped to Break Legal Barriers in the Deep South,* Belmont Home School	*Felix Tijerina: Breaking Barriers by opening doors for Latin Americans,* Veterans Memorial Early College HS (Brownsville)

State History Day Winners 2021

Theme: Communication in History: The Key to Understanding

	Junior	Senior
Documentaries		
Individual	1st: *Operation Rubicon: The Intelligence Coup of the Century,* Otto MS (Plano)	1st: *In the Words of Those Who Endured: How Slave Narratives are the Key to Understanding the Lives of Former Enslaved African Americans and Communicating an Accurate History of Slavery in America,* Livingston HS
	2nd: *Nikola Tesla: Lightning Fast Communication,* Lamar MS (Austin)	2nd: *Hidden on the "B" Side: Black Gospel Music of the Civil Rights Movement,* Waco HS
Group	1st: *Frances Ellen Watkins Harper: Protest Through Poetry,* Macario Garcia MS (Sugar Land)	1st: *Exposing the Lie: James Baldwin's Communication of the American Truth,* IMPACT Early College HS, Creek Memorial HS (Baytown)
	2nd: *Empowerment and Tragedy: American Propaganda During World War II,* Colleyville MS	2nd: *Music for Humanity: The Legacy of Live Aid,* Highland Park HS (Dallas)
Exhibits		
Individual	1st: *Margo Jones: A Pioneering Voice for Regional Theatre and Theatre-in-the-Round,* Livingston JH	1st: *The 1900 Storm, New Caney HS*
	2nd: *The Culper Spy Ring,* East Central Heritage MS (San Antonio)	2nd: *Glasnost: Transparency that Ended an Era,* Highland Park HS (Dallas)
Group	1st: *1st: Lewis Hine Child Labor Exposed,* Austin Peace Academy (Austin)	1st: *Jazz Diplomacy: The Cold War SWINGs in America's Favor,* Plano East Senior HS
	2nd: *Is It a Crime to Vote?,* Greenville Christian	2nd: *The Stories They Tell: Communicating the Daily Realities of Rural Americans during the Great Depression through FSA Photography,* Health Careers HS (San Antonio)
Performances		
Individual	1st: *Transformation of Songs to Hymns to Freedom,* Stovall MS (Houston)	1st: *Communication Amidst Chaos,* IMPACT Early College HS (Baytown)
	2nd: *The Importance of Communication in WWI and WWII,* Gentry JH (Baytown)	2nd: *The Unpublished Issue of the New-York Weekly Journal,* Carver HS (Houston)
Group	1st: *We Fight! We Sacrifice! We Triumph!,* Waco ATLAS Academy	1st: *Lady with the Lamp: Florence Nightingale's Mathematical Approach to Healthcare Reform,* Plano East Senior HS
	2nd: *Sacagawea: Translating Through the Heart of a New Nation,* Marathon ISD	2nd: *A Nation to Gain: Suffragettes Communicating Through Tactics,* Lorena HS
Websites		
Individual	1st: *Selling Space: The Significance of Propaganda During the Space Race,* Dripping Springs MS	1st: *There's Always Work at the Post Office: The United States Postal Service and Its Ongoing Fight for Financial Stability,* New Caney HS
	2nd: *Testing the Electoral College: The Letters that Influenced the Election of 1800,* Canyon Ridge MS (Austin)	2nd: *Cold War Propaganda: McCarthyism, the Space Race and Beyond,* Carnegie Vanguard HS (Houston)
Group	1st: *Marie Curie: Perception vs. Reality – How Bias and Miscommunication in Secondary Sources Distorts the Truth,* Sycamore Springs MS (Dripping Springs)	1st: *Won't You Be My Neighbor? The Story of Fred Rogers, a Television Program, and a Message to Millions,* Plano East Senior HS
	2nd: *Space Communication: Mission Control and the Apollo Program,* Gentry JH (Baytown)	2nd: *Bletchley Park: Cracking the 'Enigma' Codes,* El Paso HS
Papers		
Individual	1st: *Unlocking the Enemy's Secrets: How Bletchley Park Used the Communication of the Axis Powers to Aid the Allies,* Hornedo MS (El Paso)	1st: *The Stab-in-the-Back Legend: How Conspiracy-laden Communication Destroyed the Weimar Republic,* Plano East Senior HS
	2nd: *Dorothea Lange: Lens on the Great Depression,* Richards School for Young Women Leaders (Austin)	2nd: *Rosie the Housewife: Propaganda for Women to Leave the Workforce after World War II,* Lorena HS

National History Day 2021

1st Place Senior Exhibits	3rd Place Junior Individual Website
The 1900 Storm, New Caney HS	*Selling Space: The Significance of Propaganda During the Space Race,* Dripping Springs MS

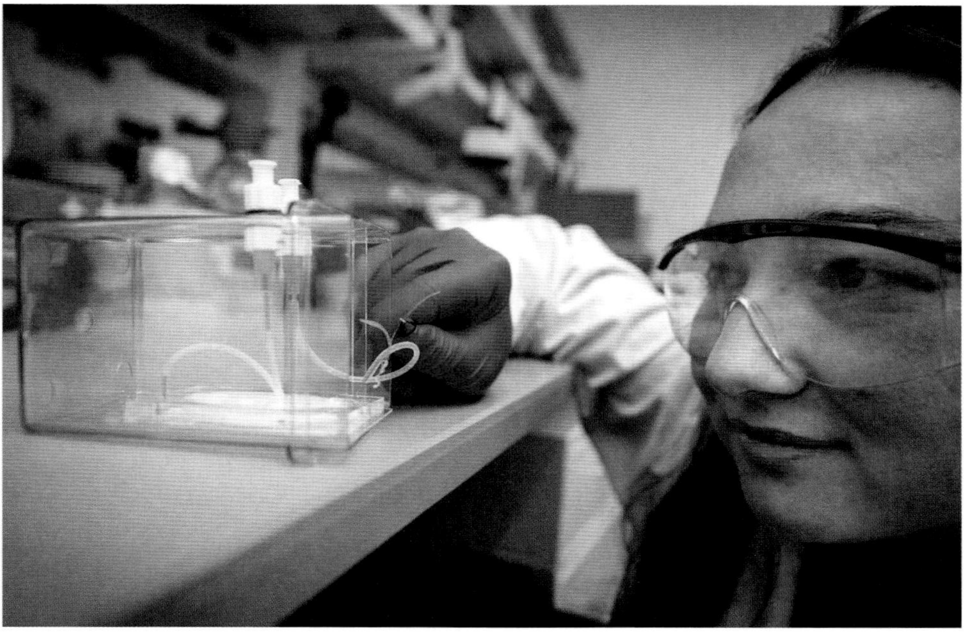

Visiting graduate student from the University of Texas at Austin, Albina Khasanova, loads a plant seedling into an EcoFAB as part of a program with the DOE Joint Genome Institute and Environmental Genomics and Systems Biology Division at Berkeley Lab on February 6, 2020. Photo by Thor Swift via US Department of Energy Joint Genome Institute/Flickr (CC).

Colleges and Universities

Sources: Texas Higher Education Coordinating Board; highered.texas.gov; Legislative Budget Board, "Summary of 2020–21 Conference Committee Report for HB1"

Enrollment in Texas public, independent, career, and private colleges and universities in fall 2019 totaled 1,575,721 students, an increase of 4,000 students, 0.3 percent, above the fall 2018 enrollment of 1,571,721.

Enrollment in fall 2019 in the 37 public universities was 657,985, a 0.04 percent decrease from 2018's enrollment of 658,219. Health-related institutions had enrollment in 2019 of 26,169, a 1.5 percent increase from fall 2018 (25,786) but a decrease of 4.3 percent from fall 2016 (27,353).

The state's public community colleges, Lamar State Colleges, and Texas State Technical College System, which offer two-year degree programs, reported fall 2019 enrollments totaling 762,083 students, an increase of 0.5 percent over enrollment of 758,133 reported in fall 2017.

Enrollments for fall 2019 at independent and career colleges and universities was 129,484 students, down slightly from the 129,583 students enrolled in fall 2018.

Cost of Public Higher Education in Texas 2020

	2-Year Schools (82)	4-Year Schools (37)
Average Tuition and Fees	$2,760	$9,502
Average Debt	$15,422	$25,374
% of Students with Debt	28.9%	57.7%

Brief History of Higher Education in Texas

The first permanent institutions of higher education established in Texas were church-supported schools, although there were some earlier efforts:

Rutersville University was established in 1840 by Methodist minister Martin Ruter in Fayette County and was the predecessor of Southwestern University in Georgetown, which was established in 1843;

Baylor University, now at Waco, was established in 1845 at Independence, Washington County, by the Texas Union Baptist Association; and

Austin College, now at Sherman, was founded in 1849 at Huntsville by the Brazos Presbytery of the Old School Presbyterian Church.

Other historic Texas schools of collegiate rank included:

Larissa College, 1848, at Larissa, Cherokee County; McKenzie College, 1841, Clarksville, Red River County; Chappell Hill Male and Female Institute, 1850, Chappell Hill, Washington County; Soule University, 1855, Chappell Hill; Johnson Institute, 1852, Driftwood, Hays County; Nacogdoches University, 1845, Nacogdoches; Salado College, 1859, Salado, Bell County.

Add-Ran College, established in 1873 at Thorp Spring, Hood County, was the predecessor of present-day Texas Christian University, Fort Worth.

Texas A&M University and The University of Texas

The Agricultural and Mechanical College of Texas (now Texas A&M University), authorized by the Legislature in 1871, opened its doors in 1876 to become the first publicly supported institution of higher education in Texas.

In 1881, Texans established The University of Texas in Austin, with a medical branch in Galveston. The Austin institution opened Sept. 15, 1883, and the Galveston school opened in 1891.

First College for Women

In 1901, the 27th Legislature established the Girls Industrial College, which began classes at its campus in Denton in 1903. A campaign to establish a state industrial college for women was led by the State Grange and Patrons of Husbandry.

A bill was signed into law on April 6, 1901, creating the college. It was charged with a dual mission, which continues to guide the university today, to provide a liberal arts education and to prepare young women with a specialized education "for the practical industries of the age."

In 1905, the name of the college was changed to the College of Industrial Arts; in 1934, it was changed to Texas State College for Women.

Since 1957, the institution, which is now the largest university principally for women in the United States, has been the Texas Woman's University.

Historic, Primarily Black Colleges

A number of Texas schools were established primarily for blacks, although collegiate racial integration has long been the status quo. Title III of the Higher Education Act of 1965 established the term Historically Black College/University (HBCU), defined as a school of higher learning that was established and accredited before the 1964 Civil Rights Act and was dedicated to educating African Americans.

Today there are ten HBCUs in Texas: state-supported Prairie View A&M University (originally established as Alta Vista Agricultural College in 1876) Prairie View; and Texas Southern University, Houston; privately supported Huston-Tillotson University, Austin; Jarvis Christian College, Hawkins; Wiley College, Marshall; Paul Quinn College, originally located in Waco, now in Dallas; and Texas College, Tyler.

Predominantly black colleges that are important in the history of higher education in Texas, but which have ceased operations, include Bishop College, established in Marshall in 1881, then moved to Dallas; Mary Allen College, established in Crockett in 1886; and Butler College, originally named the Texas Baptist Academy, in 1905 in Tyler.

Top 5 Undergrad Majors at Public Universities, 2019

1. Business, Management, Marketing, and Related Support Services (20,620 students)
2. Health Professions and Related Programs (11,559 students)
3. Multi/Interdisciplinary Studies (11,159 students)
4. Engineering (9,195 students)
5. Biological and Biomedical Sciences (7,073 students)

Source: Texas Public Higher Education Almanac 2020

Hispanic-Serving Institutions

Title V of the Higher Education Act of 2008 established grant programs for public colleges that qualify as Hispanic-Serving Institutions (HSIs). An HSI is defined as a not-for-profit institution of higher learning with a full-time equivalent undergraduate student enrollment that is at least 25 percent Hispanic.

According to the Hispanic Association of Colleges & Universities, Texas has 100 HSIs, including many community colleges, operating today.

State Appropriations

The general revenue funds for higher education totaled \$16.2 billion for FY22–23, an increase of 2.2 percent over the FY20–21 funding level. This amount represents about 14.0 percent of the total general revenue budget. Rates for all of the higher education formulas were increased over the FY22-23 rates.

The general revenue funds increase includes:

- \$8.6 billion, a \$486 million increase to the current biennium, to fund a number of higher education institutions, including \$4.1 billion to General Academic Institutions, Lamar State Colleges and Texas State Technical Colleges; \$2.6 billion to Health Related Institutions; and \$1.8 billion to Community Colleges, with a continued focus on performance-based funding.
- \$199 million for graduate medical education to maintain a 1.1 to 1.0 ratio for residency slots, and \$118.5 million for the Texas Child Mental Health Care Consortium.
- \$1.25 billion for financial aid programs, including \$866 million for TEXAS Grants program; \$178.6 million for Tuition Equalization Grants program; \$88.5 million for Texas Educational Opportunity Grants (TEOG) Public Community Colleges; \$7.5 million for TEOG State and Technical Colleges; and \$110 million for Student Financial Aid to be allocated to TEXAS Grants, Tuition Equalization Grants, TEOG Public Community Colleges and TEOG Public State and Technical Colleges.☆

Universities and Colleges

Sources: Texas Higher Education Coordinating Board (highered.texas.gov) and txhighereddata.org and individual institutions. Dates of establishment may differ from Brief History on page 595 because schools use the date when authorization was given rather than date of first classes.

Name of Institution, Location; (*type or ownership, if private sectarian institution); date of founding; president (unless otherwise noted)	Number of Faculty, 2019	Enrollment		
		Fall Term, 2019	Fall Term, 2020§	% Change
Abilene Christian University, Abilene; (3–Church of Christ); 1906 (as Childers Classical Institute; as Abilene Christian College, 1914; as university, 1976); Dr. Phil Schubert.	—	4,854	4,853	-0.02
ALAMO COLLEGES (9), Dr. Mike Flores, chancellor. 1978 (as San Antonio Community College District; 1982, as Alamo Community College District; current name, 2009). System consists of following colleges and presidents:	2,145	67,774	67,155	-0.91
Northeast Lakeview College, San Antonio; (7); 2007; Dr. Veronica Garcia.	197	6,540	6,551	0.17
Northwest Vista College, San Antonio; (7); 1995; Dr. Ric Baser.	544	18,010	18,186	0.98
Palo Alto College, San Antonio; (7); 1983; Dr. Robert Garza.	269	10,763	10,950	1.74
San Antonio College, San Antonio; (7); 1925; Dr. Robert Vela.	688	19,499	18,847	-3.34
St. Philip's College, San Antonio; (7); 1898; Dr. Adena Williams Loston.	447	12,962	12,621	-2.63
Alvin Community College, Alvin; (7); 1949; Dr. Christal Albrecht.	323	5,985	5,609	-6.28
Amarillo College, Amarillo; (7); 1929; Dr. Russell Lowery-Hart.	402	9,766	8,893	-8.94
Amberton University, Garland; (3); 1971 (as Amber University; current name, 2001); Dr. Melinda H. Reagan.	—	1,074	1,102	2.61
Angelina College, Lufkin; (7); 1968; Dr. Michael J. Simon.	265	4,564	4,067	-10.89
Angelo State University, San Angelo; Dr. Steven O'Day.	See **Texas Tech University**			
Arlington Baptist University, Arlington; (3–Baptist); 1939 (as Bible Baptist Seminary; 1965 as Arlington Baptist College; name changed to current in 2017); Dr. D. L. Moody.	—	—	—	—
Austin College, Sherman; (3–Presbyterian USA); 1849; Dr. Steven P. O'Day.	—	1,314	1,302	-0.91
Austin Community College, Austin; (7); 1972; Dr. Richard M. Rhodes.	1,886	38,730	36,898	-4.73
Baylor College of Medicine, Houston; (5); 1903 (in Dallas; moved to Houston, 1943; Baptist until 1969); Dr. Paul Klotman, M.D.	—	1,580	1,592	0.76
Baylor University, Waco; (3–Southern Baptist); 1845 (in Independence; merged with Waco University and moved to Waco, 1887); Dr. Linda A. Livingstone.	—	18,033	19,297	7.01
Blinn College, Brenham; (7); 1883 (as academy; jr. college, 1927); Dr. Mary Hensley Ed. D, chancellor.	665	19,183	17,906	-6.66
Brazosport College, Lake Jackson; (7); 1967; Dr. Millicent M. Valek.	180	4,212	3,911	-7.15
Brookhaven College, Farmers Branch	See **Dallas County Community College District**			
Cedar Valley College, Lancaster	See **Dallas County Community College District**			
Central Texas College, Killeen; (7); 1965; Dr. Jim Yeonopolus, chancellor.	582	9,492	8,091	-14.76
Cisco College, Cisco; (7); 1909 (as Cisco Junior College, a private institution; became state school in 1939; name changed to current in 2009); Dr. Thad J. Anglin, Chancellor.	179	3,539	3,226	-8.84
Clarendon College, Clarendon; (7); 1898 (as church school; became state school in 1927); Mr. Texas D. Buckhaults, Interim President.	74	1,579	1,433	-9.25
Coastal Bend College, Beeville; (7); (1966 as Bee County College, name changed in 1999); Dr. Justin Hoggard, President.	183	4,818	4,108	-14.74
College of the Mainland, Texas City; (7); 1967; Dr. Warren Nichols.	263	4,687	4,351	-7.17
Collin College, McKinney; (7); 1985 (as Collin County Community College); Dr. H. Neil Matkin, district president.	1,408	34,328	35,537	3.52
Concordia University Texas, Austin; (3–Lutheran Church–Missouri Synod); 1926 (as Concordia Lutheran College; current name, 1995); part of Concordia University System. Dr. Donald Christian.	—	2,511	2,253	-10.27
Criswell College, Dr. Barry Creamer, President.	—	—	—	—
Dallas Baptist University, Dallas; (3–Baptist); 1898 (as Decatur Baptist College; moved to Dallas, name changed to Dallas Baptist College, 1965; became university, 1985); Dr. Adam C. Wright, president.	—	4,487	4,247	-5.35
Dallas Christian College, Dallas; (3–Christian); 1950; Dr. Brian D. Smith.	—	—	—	—
DALLAS COUNTY COMMUNITY COLLEGE DISTRICT (9), Dr. Joe May, chancellor. System consists of following colleges and presidents:	2,618	82,246	69,210	-15.85
Brookhaven College, Farmers Branch; (7); 1978; Dr. Linda Braddy, president.	609	11,069	10,205	-7.81
Cedar Valley College, Lancaster; (7); 1977; Dr. Joseph Seabrooks.	285	7,646	5,943	-22.27
Eastfield College, Mesquite; (7); 1970; Dr. Eddie Tealer.	546	14,396	12,377	-14.02
El Centro College, Dallas; (7); 1966; Dr. Bradford Williams, president.	128	10,849	10,214	-5.85
Mountain View College, Dallas; (7); 1970; Dr. Beatriz Joseph, vice chancellor.	190	11,274	7,844	-30.42

*Type: (1) Public University System
(2) Public University
(3) Independent Senior College or University
(4) Public Medical School or Health Science Center
(5) Independent Medical, Dental or Chiropractic School
(6) Public Technical College System
(7) Public Community College
(8) Independent Junior College
(9) Public Community College System
(10) Public Lower-Level Institution

§ Preliminary numbers.

Name of Institution, Location; (*type or ownership, if private sectarian institution); date of founding; president (unless otherwise noted)	Number of Faculty, 2019	Enrollment Fall Term, 2019	Enrollment Fall Term, 2020§	Enrollment % Change
North Lake College, Irving; (7); 1977; Dr. Christa Slejko, president.	325	9,598	8,587	-10.53
Richland College, Dallas; (7); 1972; Dr. Kathryn K. Eggleston, president.	597	17,414	14,040	-19.38
Del Mar College, Corpus Christi; (7); 1935; Dr. Mark Escamilla.	517	12,008	10,579	-11.90
Eastfield College, Mesquite	See **Dallas County Community College District**			
East Texas Baptist University, Marshall; (3–Baptist); 1913 (as College of Marshall; as East Texas Baptist College, 1944; as university, 1984); Dr. J. Blair Blackburn.	—	1,656	1,714	3.50
El Centro College, Dallas	See **Dallas County Community College District**			
El Paso Community College, El Paso; (7); 1969; five campuses: Mission del Paso, Northwest, Rio Grande, Transmountain, and Valle Verde; Dr. William Serrata.	1,234	28,124	25,357	-9.84
Frank Phillips College, Borger; (7); 1948; includes campus in Perryton; Dr. Jud Hicks.	89	1,492	1,558	4.42
Galveston College, Galveston; (7); 1967; Dr. W. Myles Shelton.	96	2,306	2,149	-6.81
Grayson College, Denison; (7); 1963; Dr. Jeremy McMillen.	202	4,473	4,012	-10.31
Hardin-Simmons University, Abilene; (3–Southern Baptist); 1891 (as Simmons College; as Simmons University, 1925; current name, 1934); Eric I. Bruntmyer.	—	2,324	2,128	-8.43
Hill College, Hillsboro; (7); 1923 (as Hillsboro Junior College; name changed to current, 1962); Dr. Pamela Boehm.	203	4,537	4,068	-10.34
Houston Baptist University, Houston; (3–Baptist); 1960; Dr. Robert B. Sloan Jr.	—	3,741	3,963	5.93
HOUSTON COMMUNITY COLLEGE (9), Cesar Maldonado, chancellor. Houston; 1971. System consists of following colleges and presidents:	2,296	47,697	37,676	-21.01
Central College, Houston; (7); Dr. Muddassir Siddiqi.	—	—	—	—
Coleman College for Health Sciences, Houston; (7); 2004; Dr. Phil Nicotera.	—	—	—	—
Northeast College, Houston; (7); Dr. Destry Dokes (interim).	—	—	—	—
Northwest College, Houston; (7); Dr. Zachary R. Hodges.	—	—	—	—
Southeast College, Houston; (7); Dr. Melissa Gonzalez.	—	—	—	—
Southwest College, Houston; (7); Dr. Madeline Burillo-Hopkins.	—	—	—	—
Online College, (7); Dr. Margaret Ford Fisher	—	—	—	—
Howard County Junior College District (9), Dr. Cheryl T. Sparks, president. Big Spring, 1945. System consists of the following:	157	47,697	37,676	-21.01
Howard College, Big Spring; (7); 1945; (also has campuses in Lamesa and San Angelo).	140	4,303	3,728	-13.36
Southwest Collegiate Institute for the Deaf, Big Spring; (7)	17	79	48	-39.24
Howard Payne University, Brownwood; (3–Baptist); 1889; Dr. Cory Hines.	—	1,031	468	-54.61
Huston-Tillotson University, Austin; (3–United Church of Christ and United Methodist); 1952 (as Huston-Tillotson College, the merger of Tillotson College, 1875, and Samuel Huston College, 1876; current name, 2005); Dr. Colette Pierce Burnette.	—	1,121	1,070	-4.55
Jacksonville College, Jacksonville; (8–Missionary Baptist); 1899; Dr. William Michael Smith.	—	511	524	2.54
Jarvis Christian College, Hawkins; (3); 1912; Dr. Lester Newman.	—	829	637	-23.16
Kilgore College, Kilgore; (7); 1935; Dr. Brenda Kays.	256	5,305	4,954	-6.62
Kingwood College, Kingwood	See **Lone Star College System**			
Lamar University and all branches	See **Texas State University System**			
Laredo Community College, Laredo; (7); 1946; Dr. Ricardo J. Solis.	264	10,165	5,243	-48.42
Lee College, Baytown; (7); 1934; Dr. Dennis Brown.	388	7,516	4,258	-43.35
LeTourneau University, Longview; (3); 1946 (as LeTourneau Technical Institute; became 4-yr. college, 1961); Dr. Dale A. Lunsford.	—	2,932	3,125	6.58
LONE STAR COLLEGE SYSTEM (9), Dr. Stephen C. Head., chancellor. 1973; formerly North Harris Montgomery Community College District. System consists of following colleges and presidents:	3,496	78,452	70,738	-9.83
Lone Star College–Cy-Fair, Houston; (7); 2003; Dr. Seelpa Keshvala.	897	20,946	20,568	-1.80
Lone Star College–Houston North, The Woodlands; (7); Dr. Stephen C. Head, chancellor	—	2,524	1,878	-25.59
Lone Star College–Kingwood, Humble; (7); 1984; Dr. Katherine Persson.	513	10,981	10,383	-5.45
Lone Star College–Montgomery, Conroe; (7); 1995; Dr. Rebecca L. Riley.	597	13,445	13,287	-1.18
Lone Star College–North Harris, Houston; (7); 1973; Dr. Gerald F. Napoles.	651	12,054	10,121	-16.04
Lone Star College–Tomball, Tomball; (7); 1986; Dr. Lee Ann Nutt.	343	7,146	5,768	-19.28
Lone Star College–University Park, Houston; (7); 2012; Shah Ardalan.	495	11,356	8,733	-23.10
Lubbock Christian University, Lubbock; (3–Church of Christ); 1957; Dr. L. Timothy Perrin.	—	1,755	1,664	-5.19
McLennan Community College, Waco; (7); 1965; Dr. Johnette McKown.	422	8,705	7,743	-11.05
McMurry University, Abilene; (3–Methodist); 1923; Dr. Sandra S. Harper.	—	1,175	1,094	-6.89
Midland College, Midland; (7); 1972; Dr. Steve Thomas.	255	5,115	5,006	-2.13
Midwestern State University, Wichita Falls; (2); 1922; Dr. Suzane Shipley.	340	5,500	5,860	6.55
Montgomery College, Conroe	See **Lone Star College System**			

*Type: (1) Public University System
(2) Public University
(3) Independent Senior College or University
(4) Public Medical School or Health Science Center
(5) Independent Medical, Dental or Chiropractic School
(6) Public Technical College System
(7) Public Community College
(8) Independent Junior College
(9) Public Community College System
(10) Public Lower-Level Institution

§ Preliminary numbers.

Name of Institution, Location; (*type or ownership, if private sectarian institution); date of founding; president (unless otherwise noted)	Number of Faculty, 2019	Enrollment		
		Fall Term, 2019	Fall Term, 2020§	% Change
Mountain View College, Dallas	See **Dallas County Community College District**			
Navarro College, Corsicana; (7); 1946; four campuses: Corsicana, Mexia, Midlothian and Waxahachie; Dr. Kevin G. Fegan.	417	8,036	7,154	-10.98
North Central Texas College, Gainesville; (7); 1924 (as Gainesville Jr. College; Cooke County College, 1960; present name, 1994); five campuses: Bowie, Corinth, Flower Mound, Gainesville, and Graham. Dr. Brent Wallace, chancellor.	445	9,382	8,197	-12.63
Northeast Lakeview College, San Antonio	See **Alamo Colleges**			
Northeast Texas Community College, Mount Pleasant; (7); 1984; Dr. Ron Clinton.	163	2,988	2,854	-4.48
North Harris College, Houston	See **Lone Star College System**			
North Lake College, Irving	See **Dallas County Community College District**			
Northwest Vista College, San Antonio	See **Alamo Colleges**			
Odessa College, Odessa; (7); 1946; Dr. Gregory Williams.	261	6,806	6,383	-6.22
Our Lady of the Lake University of San Antonio, San Antonio; (3–Roman Catholic); 1895 (as school for girls; as senior college, 1911; as university, 1975); two campuses: San Antonio and Houston; Dr. Diane E. Melby.	—	2,974	2,797	-5.95
Palo Alto College, San Antonio	See **Alamo Colleges**			
Panola College, Carthage; (7); 1947 (as Panola Junior College; name changed, 1988); Dr. Gregory S. Powell.	141	2,611	2,531	-3.06
Paris Junior College, Paris; (7); 1924; Dr. Pamela Anglin.	178	4,858	4,385	-9.74
Parker University, Dallas; (5); 1982 as Parker College of Chiropractic; name changed to present in 2011. Dr. William E. Morgan.	—	1,717	1,557	-9.32
Paul Quinn College, Dallas; (3–African Methodist Episcopal Church); 1872 (in Waco; moved to Dallas, 1990); Dr. Michael J. Sorrell.	—	554	468	-15.52
Prairie View A&M University, Prairie View	See **Texas A&M University System**			
Ranger College, Ranger; (7); 1926; Dr. William J. Campion.	135	2,342	2,302	-1.71
Rice University, Houston; (3); chartered, 1891; opened, 1912 (as Rice Institute; as William Marsh Rice University, 1960); Dr. David W. Leebron.	—	7,231	7,437	2.85
Richland College, Dallas	See **Dallas County Community College District**			
St. Edward's University, Austin; (3–Catholic); 1885; Dr. Montserrat Fuentes.	—	3,976	3,591	-9.68
St. Mary's University of San Antonio, San Antonio; (3–Roman Catholic); 1852; Dr. Thomas J. Mengler, J.D.	—	3,485	3,458	-0.77
St. Philip's College, San Antonio	See **Alamo Colleges**			
Sam Houston State University, Huntsville	See **Texas State University System**			
San Antonio College, San Antonio	See **Alamo Colleges**			
SAN JACINTO COLLEGE DISTRICT (9), Dr. Brenda Lang Hellyer, chancellor. San Jacinto consolidated its campuses in 2020. System consists of following colleges and provosts	1,296	32,452	30,840	-4.97
Central, Pasadena; (7); Dr. Van Wigginton.	523	15,302	15,015	-1.88
North, Houston; (7); Dr. William Raffetto.	351	10,043	10,963	9.16
South, Houston; (7); Dr. Brenda Jones.	422	12,550	13,519	7.72
Schreiner University, Kerrville; (3–Presbyterian); 1923; Dr. Charlie McCormick.	—	1,342	1,244	-7.30
Southern Methodist University, Dallas; (3–Methodist); 1911; Dr. R. Gerald Turner.	—	11,824	12,373	4.64
South Plains College, Levelland; (7); 1957; Dr. Robin Satterwhite.	369	9,179	8,799	-4.14
South Texas College, McAllen; (7); NA; Dr. Shirley A. Reed.	1,119	32,478	28,502	-12.24
South Texas College of Law, Houston; (3); 1923; Michael F. Barry.	—	977	1,003	2.66
Southwest Collegiate Institute for the Deaf, Big Spring	See **Howard County Junior College District**			
Southwest Texas Junior College, Uvalde; (7); 1946; Dr. Hector Gonzales.	219	6,911	6,514	-5.74
Southwest Texas State University, San Marcos	See **Texas State University System**			
Southwestern Adventist University, Keene; (3–Seventh-Day Adventist); 1893 (as Keene Industrial Academy; as Southwestern Junior College, 1916; as Southwestern Union College, 1963; as Southwestern Adventist College,1980; as university, 1996); Dr. Ken Shaw.	—	687	772	12.37
Southwestern Assemblies of God University, Waxahachie; (3–Assemblies of God); 1927 (in Enid, Okla., as Southwestern Bible School; moved to Fort Worth and merged with South Central Bible Institute, 1941; moved to Waxahachie as Southwestern Bible Institute, 1943; as Southwestern Assemblies of God College,1963; as university, 1996); Dr. Kermit S. Bridges.	—	2,061	1,985	-3.69
Southwestern Christian College, Terrell; (3–Church of Christ); 1948 (as Southern Bible Institute in Fort Worth; moved to Terrell and changed name, 1950); Dr. Ervin D. Seamster, Jr.	—	110	80	-27.27

*Type: (1) Public University System
(2) Public University
(3) Independent Senior College or University
(4) Public Medical School or Health Science Center
(5) Independent Medical, Dental or Chiropractic School
(6) Public Technical College System
(7) Public Community College
(8) Independent Junior College
(9) Public Community College System
(10) Public Lower-Level Institution

§ Preliminary numbers.

Name of Institution, Location; (*type or ownership, if private sectarian institution); date of founding; president (unless otherwise noted)	Number of Faculty, 2019	Enrollment		
		Fall Term, 2019	Fall Term, 2020§	% Change
Southwestern University, Georgetown; (3–United Methodist); 1840 (merger of Rutersville College, 1840; McKenzie College, 1841; Wesleyan College, 1846; and Soule University, 1855; first named Texas University; current name, 1875); Dr. Edward B. Burger.	—	1,502	1,506	0.27
Stephen F. Austin State University, Nacogdoches; (2); 1921; Dr. Scott Gordon.	709	12,862	12,620	-1.88
Sul Ross State University, Alpine (See **Texas State University System**)	134	1,644	1,559	-5.17
Sul Ross State University–Rio Grande College, Uvalde (See **Texas State University System**)	43	821	916	11.57
Tarleton State University, Stephenville	See **Texas A&M University System**			
TARRANT COUNTY COLLEGE DISTRICT (9), Eugene V. Giovannini, chancellor. Fort Worth; 1965 (as Tarrant County Junior College; name changed, 1999). System consists of following colleges and presidents:	2,440	54,378	57,856	6.40
Northeast Campus, Hurst; (7); Dr. Tahita Fulkerson (interim).	504	11,800	12,249	3.81
Northwest Campus, Fort Worth; (7); Dr. Zarina Blankenbaker.	355	7,838	9,066	15.67
South Campus, Fort Worth, (7); Dr. Peter Jordan.	387	7,555	8,081	6.96
Southeast Campus, Arlington, (7); Dr. William Coppola.	409	10,972	11,345	3.40
Trinity River Campus, Fort Worth, (7); Dr. S. Sean Madison.	380	6,236	6,780	8.72
Connect Campus, (7); Carlos Morales.	405	9,977	10,335	3.59
Temple College, Temple; (7); 1926; Dr. Christy Ponce.	230	4,887	4,929	0.86
Texarkana College, Texarkana; (7); 1927; Dr. Jason Smith.	213	4,087	3,838	-6.09
TEXAS A&M UNIVERSITY SYSTEM (1), Dr. John Sharp, chancellor. System consists of following colleges and presidents:	6,706	147,758	150,341	1.75
Texas A&M University, College Station; (2); 1876 (as Agricultural and Mechanical of Texas; current name,1963); includes College of Veterinary Medicine and College of Medicine at College Station; Dr. M. Katherine Banks.	2,518	63,859	65,370	2.37
Texas A&M University at Galveston, Galveston; (2); 1962 (as Texas Maritime Academy; as 4-yr. Moody College of Marine Sciences and Maritime Resources, 1971); Col. Michael E. Fossum USAFR (Ret.), COO.	138	1,644	1,660	0.97
Prairie View A&M University, Prairie View; (2); 1876 (as Alta Vista Agricultural College; as Prairie View State Normal Institute, 1879; as Prairie View Normal and Industrial College; as Prairie View A&M College, 1947, as branch of Texas A&M University System; current name, 1973); Dr. Ruth Simmons	454	8,940	9,449	5.69
Tarleton State University, Stephenville; (2); 1899 (as John Tarleton College; as state-run John Tarleton Agricultural College,1917; as Tarleton State College, 1949; current name, 1973); includes campus in Killeen; Dr. F. Dominic Dottavio.	750	13,177	14,033	6.50
Texas A&M International University, Laredo; (2); 1970 (as Laredo State University; current name, 1993); Dr. Pablo Arenaz.	343	8,305	8,464	1.91
Texas A&M University–Corpus Christi, Corpus Christi; (2); 1973 (as upper-level Corpus Christi State University; current name, 1993; 4-year in 1994); Kelly M. Quintanilla.	420	11,452	10,820	-5.52
Texas A&M University–Kingsville, Kingsville; (2); 1925 (as South Texas Teachers College; as Texas College of Arts and Industries, 1929; as Texas A&I University, 1967; joined University of South Texas System, 1977; joined Texas A&M University System, 1993); Dr. Mark Hussey.	478	7,479	6,917	-7.51
West Texas A&M University, Canyon; (2); 1910 (as West Texas State Normal College; as West Texas State Teachers College, 1923; as West Texas State College, 1949; as West Texas State Univ., 1963; current name, 1993); Dr.Walter Wendler.	430	9,970	10,103	1.33
Texas A&M University–Commerce, Commerce; (2); 1889 (as East Texas Normal College; as East Texas State Teachers College, 1923; as East Texas State College, 1957; university status conferred and named changed to East Texas State University, 1965; transferred to Texas A&M System, 1995); includes ETSU Metroplex Commuter Facility, Mesquite; Dr. Mark J. Rudin.	570	11,725	12,245	4.43
Texas A&M University–Texarkana, Texarkana; (2); 1971 (as East Texas State University at Texarkana; transferred to Texas A&M System and name changed, 1996); Dr. Emily Fourmy Cutrer.	141	2,053	2,153	4.87
Texas A&M University–Central Texas, Killeen; (2); Dr. Marc A. Nigliazzo.	163	2,440	2,341	-4.06
Texas A&M University–San Antonio, San Antonio; (2); Dr. Cynthia Teniente-Matson.	301	6,714	6,786	1.07
Texas A&M University Health Science Center, (4); Includes Baylor College of Dentistry, College of Medicine, Graduate School of Biomedical Sciences, Institute of Biosciences and Technology, School of Rural Public Health, and HSC satellite locations; Dr. Carrie L. Byington, M.D., Vice Chancellor for Health Services.	—	2,887	3,064	6.13
Texas Christian University, Fort Worth; (3–Disciples of Christ); 1873 (as AddRan Male and Female College at Thorp Spring; moved to Waco, 1895; as AddRan Christian University, 1889; current name,1902; moved to Fort Worth, 1910); Dr. Victor J. Boschini Jr., chancellor.	—	10,979	11,328	3.18
Texas Chiropractic College, Pasadena; (5); 1908; Dr. Stephen A Foster.	—	269	255	-5.20
Texas College, Tyler; (3–C.M.E.); 1894; Dr. Dwight J. Fennell.	—	940	765	-18.62
Texas College of Osteopathic Medicine, Fort Worth	See **University of North Texas Health Science Center at Fort Worth**			

*Type: (1) Public University System
(2) Public University
(3) Independent Senior College or University
(4) Public Medical School or Health Science Center
(5) Independent Medical, Dental or Chiropractic School
(6) Public Technical College System
(7) Public Community College
(8) Independent Junior College
(9) Public Community College System
(10) Public Lower-Level Institution

§ Preliminary numbers.

Name of Institution, Location; (*type or ownership, if private sectarian institution); date of founding; president (unless otherwise noted)	Number of Faculty, 2019	Enrollment		
		Fall Term, 2019	Fall Term, 2020§	% Change
Texas Lutheran University, Seguin; (3–Evangelical Lutheran); 1891 (as Evangelical Lutheran College in Brenham; as Lutheran College of Seguin, 1912; as Texas Lutheran College,1932; as university, 1996); Dr. Debbie Cottrell.	—	1,474	1,446	-1.90
Texas Southern University, Houston; (2); 1926 (as Houston Colored Junior College; as 4-yr. Houston College for Negroes, mid-1930s; as Texas State University for Negroes, 1947; present name, 1951); Dr. Lesia L. Crumpton-Young.	588	9,034	7,016	-22.34
Texas Southmost College, Brownsville; (7); 1926 (as The Junior College of the Lower Rio Grande Valley; 1931 as Brownsville Junior College; current name, 1949); Dr. Jesús Roberto Rodriguez.	248	8,628	8,780	1.76
TEXAS STATE TECHNICAL COLLEGE SYSTEM (6), Dr. Michael L. Reeser, chancellor. System consists of following colleges and provosts:	632	11,694	15,054	28.73
Texas State Technical College–Harlingen, Harlingen; (7) 1967; Cledia Hernandez.	187	4,297	5,356	24.65
Texas State Technical College–Marshall, Marshall; (7) 1991 (as extension center; as independent college, 1999); Barton Day.	41	628	1,057	68.31
Texas State Technical College–Waco, Waco; (7) 1965 (as James Connally Technical Institute; current name, 1969); Dr. Adam Hutchinson.	240	3,977	4,923	23.79
Texas State Technical College–West Texas, Abilene, Breckenridge, Brownwood and Sweetwater; (7) 1970; Rick Denbow.	111	1,963	2,454	25.01
Texas State Technical College–North Texas, Red Oak; (7) 2014; Marcus Balch	22	248	476	91.94
Texas State Technical College–Fort Bend, Rosenberg; (7) 2016; Randall Wooten	31	581	788	35.63
TEXAS STATE UNIVERSITY SYSTEM (1), Dr. Brian McCall, chancellor. System consists of following colleges and presidents:	3,886	85,942	87,468	1.78
Lamar University, Beaumont; (2); 1923 (as South Park Junior College; as Lamar College, 1932; as Lamar State College of Technology, 1951; present name, 1971; transferred from Lamar University System, 1995); Dr. Kenneth Evans.	543	14,811	15,845	6.98
Lamar State College–Orange, Orange; (10); 1969 (transferred from Lamar University System, 1995; current name, 2000); Dr. Thomas Johnson.	112	2,395	2,382	-0.54
Lamar State College–Port Arthur, Port Arthur; (10); 1909 (as Port Arthur College; joined Lamar University System, 1975; joined TSU System, 1995; current name, 2000); Dr. Betty J. Reynard.	123	2,710	2,687	-0.85
Lamar Institute of Technology, Beaumont; (10); (joined TSU System, 1995); Dr. Lonnie L. Howard.	183	4,011	4,576	14.09
Sam Houston State University, Huntsville; (2); 1879; Dr. Dana G. Hoyt.	979	21,363	21,654	1.36
Sul Ross State University, Alpine; (2); 1917 (as Sul Ross State Normal College; as Sul Ross State Teachers College, 1923; as Sul Ross State College, 1949; current name, 1969); Dr. William (Bill) Kibler.	119	1,644	1,559	-5.17
Sul Ross State University – Rio Grande College, Uvalde, Eagle Pass, Del Rio (2); 1973 (current name, 1995); Dr. William (Bill) Kibler.	39	821	916	11.57
Texas State University, San Marcos; (2); 1903 (as Southwest Texas Normal School; as Southwest Texas State Normal College, 1918; as Southwest Texas State Teachers College, 1923; as Southwest Texas State College, 1959; as Southwest Texas State University, 1969; current name, 2003); Dr. Denise M. Trauth.	1,788	38,187	37,849	-0.89
TEXAS TECH UNIVERSITY SYSTEM (1), Tedd L. Mitchell M.D., chancellor. System consists of following colleges and presidents:	1,984	54,445	57,174	5.01
Angelo State University, San Angelo; (2); 1928 (was part of Texas State University System; joined Texas Tech system, 2007); Dr. Brian J. May.	420	10,289	10,722	4.21
Texas Tech University, Lubbock; (2); 1923 (as Texas Technological College; current name, 1969); Dr Lawrence Schovanec.	1,564	38,250	40,382	5.57
Texas Tech University Health Sciences Center, Lubbock; (4); 1972; Dr. Tedd L. Mitchell, M.D.	—	5,141	5,295	3.00
Texas Tech University Health Sciences Center, El Paso; (4); 2013; Dr. Richard Lange.	—	765	775	1.31
Texas Wesleyan University, Fort Worth; (3–United Methodist); 1891 (as college; current name, 1989); Dr. Frederick G. Slabach.	—	2,607	2,495	-4.30
Texas Woman's University, Denton; (2); 1901 (as College of Industrial Arts; as Texas State College for Women, 1934; current name, 1957); Carine M. Feyten, chancellor and president.	928	15,710	16,030	2.04
Tomball College, Tomball	See **Lone Star College System**			
Trinity University, San Antonio; (3–Presbyterian U.S.A.); 1869 (at Tehuacana; moved to Waxahachie, 1902; to San Antonio, 1942); Dr. Danny J. Anderson.	—	2,685	2,685	0.00
Trinity Valley Community College, Athens; (7); 1946 (as Henderson County Junior College); includes campus at Terrell; Dr. Jerry King.	266	6,432	5,662	-11.97
Tyler Junior College, Tyler; (7); 1926; Dr. L. Michael Metke, chancellor.	589	12,291	11,725	-4.60
University of Dallas, Irving; (3–Roman Catholic); 1956; Dr. John G. Plotts (interim).	—	2,481	2,489	0.32
UNIVERSITY OF HOUSTON SYSTEM (1), Dr. Renu Khator, chancellor. System consists of following colleges and presidents:	3,535	74,369	76,335	2.64
University of Houston, Houston; (2); 1927; Dr. Renu Khator.	2,092	46,148	47,066	1.99
University of Houston–Clear Lake, Houston; (2); 1974; Ira K. Blake.	514	9,082	9,060	-0.24
University of Houston–Downtown, Houston; (2); 1948 (as South Texas College; joined University of Houston System, 1974); Dr. Juan Sánchez Muñoz.	724	14,640	15,251	4.17

*Type: (1) Public University System
(2) Public University
(3) Independent Senior College or University
(4) Public Medical School or Health Science Center
(5) Independent Medical, Dental or Chiropractic School
(6) Public Technical College System
(7) Public Community College
(8) Independent Junior College
(9) Public Community College System
(10) Public Lower-Level Institution

§ Preliminary numbers.

Name of Institution, Location; (*type or ownership, if private sectarian institution); date of founding; president (unless otherwise noted)	Number of Faculty, 2019	Enrollment		
		Fall Term, 2019	Fall Term, 2020§	% Change
University of Houston–Victoria, Victoria; (2); 1973; Robert K. (Bob) Glenn.	205	4,499	4,958	10.20
University of the Incarnate Word, San Antonio; (3–Roman Catholic); 1881 (as Incarnate Word College; current name, 1996); Dr. Thomas M. Evans.	—	7,734	7,104	-8.15
University of Mary Hardin-Baylor, Belton; (3–Baptist); 1845; Dr. Randy O'Rear	—	3,846	3,876	0.78
UNIVERSITY OF NORTH TEXAS SYSTEM (1), Lesa B. Roe, chancellor. System consists of following colleges and presidents:	1,911	45,451	47,247	3.95
University of North Texas, Denton; (2); 1890 (as North Texas Normal College; as North Texas State Teachers College, 1923; as North Texas State College, 1949; as university, 1961; current name, 1988); Dr. Neal J. Smatresk.	1,682	39,192	40,727	3.92
University of North Texas at Dallas, Dallas; (2); (2000); Robert Mong.	229	4,040	4,190	3.71
University of North Texas Health Science Center at Fort Worth, Fort Worth; (4);1966 (as private college; part of North Texas State University, 1975; current name, 1993); Dr. Michael R. Williams.	—	2,219	2,330	5.00
University of St. Thomas, Houston; (3–Roman Catholic); 1947; Dr. Richard Ludwick.	—	3,438	3,693	7.42
THE UNIVERSITY OF TEXAS SYSTEM (1), James B. Milliken, chancellor. System consists of following colleges and presidents:	8,386	210,207	211,390	0.56
University of Texas at Austin, The, Austin; (2); 1883; Dr. Jay Hartzell.	2,798	50,894	50,287	-1.19
University of Texas at Arlington, The, Arlington; (2); 1895 (as Arlington College; as state-run Grubbs Vocational College, 1917; as North Texas Agricultural and Mechanical College, 1923; as Arlington State College, 1949; current name, 1967); Dr. Teile C. Lim (interim).	1,318	42,863	42,733	-0.30
University of Texas Rio Grande Valley, The, (2); 1973 (as branch of Pan American College; as University of Texas–Pan American at Brownsville, 1989; present name, 2015); Guy Bailey.	—	204	221	8.33
University of Texas at Dallas, The, Richardson; (2); 1961 (as Graduate Research of the Southwest; as Southwest Center for Advanced Studies, 1967; joined UT System with current name, 1969; full undergraduate program, 1975); Dr. Richard C. Benson.	1,229	29,543	28,669	-2.96
University of Texas at El Paso, The, El Paso; (2); 1913 (as Texas College of Mines and Metallurgy; as Texas Western College of UT, 1949; current name, 1967); Dr. Healther Wilson.	1,046	25,144	24,879	-1.05
University of Texas–Pan American, The, Edinburg. Merged with Brownsville campus in 2015 to form The University of Texas–Rio Grande Valley.				
University of Texas of the Permian Basin, The, Odessa; (2); 1969 (as 2-yr., upper-level institution; expanded to 4-yr., 1991); Dr. Sandra K. Woodley.	280	5,283	5,485	3.82
University of Texas at San Antonio, The, San Antonio; (2); 1969; Dr. Taylor Eighmy.	1,255	32,389	34,429	6.30
University of Texas at Tyler, The, Tyler; (2); 1971 (as Tyler State College; as Texas Eastern University, 1975; joined UT System, 1979); Dr. Michael V. Tidwell.	460	9,130	9,354	2.45
University of Texas Health Science Center at Houston, The, Houston; (4); 1972; includes Dental Branch (1905); Graduate School of Biomedical Sciences (1963); Medical School (1970); School of Allied Health Sciences (1973); School of Nursing (1972); School of Public Health (1967); Division of Continuing Education (1958); Dr. Giuseppe N. Colasurdo, M.D.	—	5,317	5,656	6.38
University of Texas Health Science Center at San Antonio, The, San Antonio; (4) 1968; includes Dental School (1970); Graduate School of Biomedical Sciences (1970); Health Science Center (1972); Medical School (1959 as South Texas Medical School of UT; present name, 1966); School of Allied Health Sciences (1976); School of Nursing (1969); Dr. William L. Henrich M.D.	—	3,383	3,464	2.39
University of Texas Health Science Center at Tyler, The, Tyler; (4); 1949 (as East Texas Tuberculosis Sanatorium; as East Texas Chest Hospital, 1971; joined UT system with current name, 1977); Dr. Kirk A. Calhoun M.D.	—	68	91	33.82
University of Texas M.D. Anderson Cancer Center, The, Houston; (4); 1941; Dr. Peter W.T. Pisters, M.D.	—	376	359	-4.52
University of Texas Medical Branch at Galveston, The, Galveston; (4) 1891; includes Graduate School of Biomedical Sciences (1952); Medical School (1891); School of Allied Health Sciences (1968); School of Nursing (1890); Vacant	—	3,314	3,464	4.53
University of Texas Southwestern Medical Center, The, Dallas; (4); 1943 (as private institution; as Southwestern Medical College of UT, 1948; as UT Southwestern Medical School at Dallas, 1967; joined UT Health Science Center at Dallas, 1972); includes Graduate School of Biomedical Sciences (1947); School of Allied Health Sciences (1968); Southwestern Medical School (1943); Dr. Daniel K. Podolsky M.D.	—	2,299	2,299	0.00
Vernon College, Vernon; (7); 1970; includes Wichita Falls campus; Dr. Dusty R. Johnston.	142	2,930	2,786	-4.91
Victoria College, Victoria; (7); 1925; Dr. David Hinds.	191	3,683	3,214	-12.73
Wayland Baptist University, Plainview; (3–Southern Baptist); 1910; Dr. Bobby Hall	—	2,948	2,539	-13.87
Weatherford College, Weatherford; (7); 1869 (as branch of Southwestern University; as denominational junior college, 1922; as municipal junior college, 1949); Dr. Tod Allen Farmer.	309	5,821	5,454	-6.30
Western Texas College, Snyder; (7); 1969; Dr. Barbara Beebe.	81	2,009	1,442	-28.22
Wharton County Junior College, Wharton; (7); 1946; Dr. Betty A. McCrohan.	289	6,904	6,097	-11.69
Wiley College, Marshall; (3–Methodist); 1873; Dr. Herman J. Felton, Jr.	—	715	615	-13.99

*Type: (1) Public University System
(2) Public University
(3) Independent Senior College or University
(4) Public Medical School or Health Science Center
(5) Independent Medical, Dental or Chiropractic School
(6) Public Technical College System
(7) Public Community College
(8) Independent Junior College
(9) Public Community College System
(10) Public Lower-Level Institution

§ Preliminary numbers.

Business

ECONOMY AND EMPLOYMENT

BANKING, INSURANCE, CONSTRUCTION

COMMERCIAL FISHING AND TOURISM

ELECTRIC GRIDS, OIL, GAS

MINERALS AND MEDIA

Many restaurants struggled to survive in 2020, but Campisi's "Egyptian" Restaurant is still serving pizza and spaghetti in Dallas. Photo by Lorie Shaull, CC 2/Flickr

COVID-19 Drains Texas Economy Through 2020

Source: Excerpted from the State of Texas Annual Cash Report 2020, *Comptroller of Public Accounts.*

Starting in August 2019, Texas nonfarm jobs stood at a total of 12,836,000. By August 2020, the Texas economy lost 616,600 nonfarm jobs, largely due to economic shocks from the COVID-19 pandemic and the recent fall in energy prices.

This decrease of 4.8 percent was the second-smallest percentage loss over this period among the ten most populous states (behind Georgia at 4.2 percent) and the sixteenth-smallest loss among all states.

Private-sector employment fell by 5.4 percent, while government employment (federal, state and local) fell by 1.4 percent.

Texas Industry Performance

Employment in the goods-producing industries decreased by 7.2 percent in fiscal 2020, while employment in the service-providing industries fell by 4.4 percent.

Employment decreased in all three of the goods-producing industries (mining and logging, manufacturing, and construction), led by a 24.6 percent fall in mining and logging. All but one of the service-providing industries also saw year-over-year declines in employment, with the largest percentage losses in the leisure and hospitality (17.7 percent) and information (6.3 percent) industries.

Financial activities was the only major industry in which employment increased over the year (by 0.4 percent, or 3,600 jobs).

Mining and Logging

Mining industry employment peaked in December 2014 at 321,900 and then declined steadily, reaching a low of 204,300 in September 2016. Industry employment then grew consistently for more than two years to reach 256,200 in January 2019. Since that time, mining employment has fallen by 27 percent.

From August 2019 to August 2020, mining employment decreased by 61,000, with most (49,600) of that loss occurring since March 2020. In addition to substantial exploration activities within the state and in the Gulf of Mexico, Texas is headquarters for many of the nation's largest oil and natural gas refining and distribution companies and has a large number of energy-related jobs in other industries.

As in the mining industry, employment in those industries and sectors has experienced significant declines over the year.

Consumer Spending

Consumer spending is a major component of the Texas economy. In fiscal 2016, for the first time since 2010, state sales tax collections fell (by 2.3 percent) from the previous year's total. The decline in state sales tax revenue was led by reduced collections from the oil- and natural gas-related exploration and production sectors, but collections from the manufacturing, retail trade, information, and real estate sectors also were down compared to 2015. Growth in sales tax collections resumed in 2017, with revenue up 2.3 percent over 2016. Sales tax revenue was up again in 2018, by 10.5 and by another 6.5 percent in 2019 to reach $34.0 billion.

Despite economic disruptions resulting from the COVID-19 virus, 2020 sales tax collections increased by a further 0.2 percent from 2019. State sales tax collections from all major sectors other than retail trade declined significantly from year ago levels, with the largest declines in the oil- and gas-related sectors.

However, collections from retail trade were up, as increased consumer spending on home improvements, home entertainment, distance learning and outdoor recreation in response to the COVID-19 pandemic spurred higher remittances from building materials, home furnishing, electronics and appliance, and sporting goods retailers.

Retail trade tax collections were also boosted by online out-of-state vendors and marketplace providers who did not have tax collection obligations a year ago. Tax remittances from the information sector were depressed, as federal law in July began prohibiting sales taxation of internet service.

The Consumer Confidence Index is a monthly measure of consumer optimism, an important factor affecting the sales of housing, automobiles and other major purchases. The index for the four-state West South Central (WSC) Region, which includes Texas, was down by 34 percent in fiscal 2020. The index for the nation as a whole was down 36 percent.

Gross Domestic Product in Current Dollars

	Millions of dollars			Percent of U.S. total			GDP* 2019	
	2018	2019	2020	2018	2019	2020	China	22,526,502
United States	**20,611,861**	**21,433,226**	**20,936,558**	**100**	**100**	**100**	United States	20,524,945
1. California	2,975,083	3,132,801	3,091,872	14.4	14.6	14.8	India	9,155,083
2. Texas	**1,795,635**	**1,843,803**	**1,759,734**	**8.7**	**8.6**	**8.4**	Japan	5,231,066
3. New York	1,705,010	1,772,261	1,699,045	8.3	8.3	8.1	Germany	4,482,448
4. Florida	1,050,298	1,106,500	1,095,888	5.1	5.2	5.2	Russia	3,968,180
5. Illinois	863,040	885,583	863,517	4.2	4.1	4.1	Indonesia	3,196,682
6. Pennsylvania	778,375	808,738	780,176	3.8	3.8	3.7	United Kingdom	3,118,396
7. Ohio	675,030	695,362	675,037	3.3	3.2	3.2	France	3,097,061
8. Georgia	602,024	625,714	619,240	2.9	2.9	3	Brazil	3,092,216
9. New Jersey	612,979	634,784	619,061	3	3	3	Italy	2,562,135
10. Washington	575,417	612,997	618,705	2.8	2.9	3	Mexico	2,525,481

Source: Bureau of Economic Analysis, U.S. Department of Commerce, 2020.

**Estimated GDP in millions of U.S. dollars, from the World Factbook of the CIA.*

Manufacturing

The Texas manufacturing industry lost 39,900 jobs over the past year, a decrease of 4.4 percent. Durable goods employment was down 32,800, with the largest losses in the fabricated metals (16,500) and machinery (10,200) manufacturing sectors. Both sectors are closely associated with oil and natural gas exploration and production, and employment in those sectors has been decreasing along with that in the mining industry.

Overall, durable goods employment decreased by 5.6 percent. Nondurable-goods manufacturing employment fell by 7,100 (2.2 percent). Total manufacturing employment in August 2020 was 869,100.

The value of Texas exports in 2014 was a record $289 billion, an increase of 3.3 percent from 2013. Those exports provided a substantial boost to manufacturing, notably for companies producing chemicals, computers and electronics, petroleum products, industrial machinery and transportation equipment. In 2015, the value of Texas exports fell sharply (to $251 billion, down 13.1 percent), hurt by falling oil prices and a stronger dollar. Texas exports continued to fall in 2016, down another 7.4 percent. However, Texas 2017 exports were up 13.5 percent from the 2016 level and increased by another 19.4 percent in 2018.

In November 2019, for the first time since October 2016, monthly Texas exports decreased on a year-over-year basis; total 2019 exports were still 4.8 percent higher than 2018 exports. However, exports have fallen sharply since March. For the period January 2020 to July 2020, the value of exports was 21.3 percent lower than that of the corresponding period of 2019.

Texas, however, remains the nation's leading exporting state, as it has been for more than a decade. Texas exports comprised 20 percent of total U.S. exports in 2019.

Construction

Construction employment decreased by 39,300 (5.0 percent) in fiscal 2020 to reach 739,800 in August 2020. Employment in the heavy and civil engineering construction sector decreased at the highest rate of any construction sector, falling by 7.9 percent (14,100).

Total housing construction activity in 2020 was up from 2019. Single-family building permits issued in the year ending in July 2020, at 130,862, were up 12.8 percent from the same period one year earlier. Building permits for multi-family units rose by 13.2 percent.

According to Multiple Listing Service data from the Texas A&M Real Estate Center, the median sales price for an existing Texas single-family home rose by 8.9 percent, from $246,000 in July 2019 to $268,000 in July 2020.

In July 2020, Texas had a 2.8-month inventory of existing homes for sale, the lowest level since at least 1990.

Professional and Business Services

Employment in the professional and business services industry fell by 23,000 jobs (1.3 percent) in fiscal 2020. Employment changes varied considerably among industry sectors, with the largest increases in accounting and bookkeeping services (6.3 percent) and architectural, engineering, and related services (4.8 percent).

The employment services sector, which includes temporary help agencies with many of its jobs in temporary and/or part-time positions, had both the largest absolute and percentage decreases in employment (28,600, 9.5 percent). Total professional and business services employment was 1,778,500 in August 2020.

Education and Health Services

The education and health services industry, composed of the educational services and health care and social assistance sectors, lost 70,200 jobs in fiscal 2020, a decrease of 4.0 percent. The relatively small educational services sector saw a decrease of 14,700 jobs (6.7 percent). Employment in the much larger health care and social assistance sector fell by 3.6 percent rate (55,500 jobs). In all, Texas education and health services employment fell to 1,675,100 in August 2020.

For more information

For a more detailed overview of population, income, jobs, wages and education trends of Texas' 12 economic regions, visit: https://comptroller.texas.gov/economy/economic-data/regions/

Financial Activities

In fiscal 2020, overall employment in the financial activities industry grew by 0.4 percent (3,600 jobs). The finance and insurance sector grew by 12,000 (2.1 percent) while the real estate and rental and leasing sector fell by 8,400 (3.7 percent). Credit intermediation (which includes financial institutions such as banks) is the industry's largest sector, employing 274,500 as of August 2020. Total Texas financial activities industry employment reached 809,700 in August 2020.

Trade, Transportation and Utilities

The trade, transportation and utilities industry, the state's largest employer with 20 percent of total nonfarm jobs in August 2020, lost 74,400 jobs (3.0 percent) over the year. Employment in all three industry sectors — retail trade, wholesale trade and transportation, warehousing and utilities — fell during fiscal 2020. Wholesale trade employment was down 6.8 percent (41,500), transportation, warehousing and utilities employment fell by 3,100 (0.5 percent), and employment in the retail trade sector decreased by 29,800 (2.3 percent). In all, the trade, transportation and utilities industry provided 2,438,400 Texas jobs in August 2020.

Information

The information industry is a collection of diverse sectors, representing established sectors of the economy (newspaper publishing, data processing, television broadcasting, and wired telephone services) as well as some newer sectors (cell phone service providers, Internet providers, and software). The publishing sector saw the largest percentage fall in employment over the year (7.0 percent, 2,700 jobs).

Total industry employment fell 6.3 percent (13,100) to reach 195,900 in August 2020.

Leisure and Hospitality

Employment in the leisure and hospitality industry decreased by 247,600 (17.7 percent) over the fiscal year. The majority of the industry's job losses occurred in the food services and drinking places sector, which lost 198,000 jobs (15.7 percent). The largest percentage loss was in the arts, entertainment, and recreation sector, which fell by 31.2 percent (49,400).

Total leisure and hospitality employment in August 2020 was 1,147,500, representing about 9 percent of total Texas employment.

Other Services

The other services industry is a varied mix of business activities including repair and maintenance services; laundry services; religious, political and civic organizations; funeral services; parking garages; beauty salons; and a wide range of personal services.

Personal and laundry services employment decreased by 15.3 percent, the highest rate among other service sectors. In all, other services industry employment fell by 23,100 to reach 423,600 in August 2020.

Government Employment

Government employment decreased by 1.4 percent (28,600) over the year. Federal government employment increased by 26,500, largely on the strength of temporary census hiring.

However, local government employment decreased by 31,100 and state government employment fell by 24,100. Total government employment in Texas was 1,954,000 in August 2020.

Texas Gross Domestic Product, 2011–2020, By Industry (in millions)

Industry	2011	2012	2013	2014	2015	2016	2017	2018	2019	2020
Agriculture, Forestry, Fishing/Hunting	$ 8,465	$ 8,218	$ 10,898	$ 10,403	$ 11,888	$ 8,709	$ 9,072	$ 10,898	$10,820	$12,460
% change*	(6.3)	(2.9)	32.6	(4.5)	14.3	(26.7)	4.2	20.1	20.5	15.2
Natural Resources and Mining	146,001	158,861	183,266	199,598	116,107	92,152	115,515	141,191	153,186	103,944
% change	19.6	8.8	15.4	8.9	(41.8)	(20.6)	25.4	22.2	-5.2	-32.1
Construction	56,842	63,588	68,103	75,385	81,424	85,386	87,540	95,486	100,869	100,421
% change	2.0	11.9	7.1	10.7	8.0	4.9	2.5	9.1	8.6	-0.4
Manufacturing	203,495	206,104	224,083	202,685	212,902	197,408	206,063	226,125	246,436	247,373
% change	15.3	1.3	8.7	(9.5)	5.0	(7.3)	4.4	9.7	3.7	0.4
Trade, Transportation, Utilities	244,618	266,982	275,782	289,279	306,115	307,889	322,390	345,636	353,621	347,552
% change	6.7	9.1	3.3	4.9	5.8	0.6	4.7	7.2	5.8	-1.7
Information	50,188	49,328	53,965	53,327	57,767	60,196	62,819	65,308	69,609	67,755
% change	0.2	(1.7)	9.4	(1.2)	8.3	4.2	4.4	4.0	5.5	-2.7
Financial Activities	178,923	192,555	202,323	221,251	234,397	249,593	254,810	265,853	293,873	292,945
% change	6.9	7.6	5.1	9.4	5.9	6.5	2.1	4.3	5.7	-0.3
Professional and Business Services	140,676	150,573	157,256	170,065	181,455	184,354	194,950	211,854	228,118	226,946
% change	6.8	7.0	4.4	8.1	6.7	1.6	5.7	8.7	7.4	-0.5
Educational and Health Services	89,109	92,472	95,613	99,694	107,190	112,839	117,308	121,979	129,974	127,535
% change	4.3	3.8	3.4	4.3	7.5	5.3	4.0	4.0	5.7	-1.9
Leisure and Hospitality Services	40,420	43,476	45,459	50,814	56,459	58,500	60,275	62,235	68,289	60,788
% change	3.8	7.6	4.6	11.8	11.1	3.6	3.0	3.3	5.3	-11
Other Private Services	25.735	27,658	28,889	31,213	32,584	32,924	33,911	35,700	38,083	37,539
% change	1.7	7.5	4.5	8.0	4.4	1.0	3.0	5.5	5.7	-1.4
Government and Schools	146,749	151,562	156,612	161,676	170,356	175,750	181,588	185,083	194,079	192,622
% change	0.6	3.3	3.3	3.2	5.4	3.2	3.3	5.5	3.9	-0.8
TOTAL	$1,331,221	$1,411,377	$1,502,249	$1,565,390	$1,568,644	$1,565,700	$1,646,211	$1,767,418	1,886,957	1,817,880
% change	7.6	6.0	6.4	4.2	0.2	(0.2)	5.1	7.4	4.7	-3.7
TOTAL (in 2009 chained dollars)**	$1,343,791	$1,411,379	$1,472,104	$1,512,351	$1,590,409	$1,594,408	$1,615,822	$1,672,640	1,788,527	1,729,047
% change	3.2	5.0	4.3	2.7	5.2	0.3	1.3	3.5	4.4	-3.3

*Percent change from the previous year. **In 1996, the U.S. Department of Commerce introduced the chained-dollar measure. The new measure is based on the average weights of goods and services in successive pairs of years. It is "chained" because the second year in each pair, with its weights, becomes the first year of the next pair. *Source: 2020 Comprehensive Annual Financial Report for the State of Texas.*

Per Capita Income by County, 2019

Below are listed data for 2019 for total personal income and per capita income by county. Total income is reported in millions of dollars. The middle column indicates the percent of change in total personal income from 2018 to 2019.

In the far right column is the county's rank in the state for per capita income. Midland County was first with $130,983. The lowest per capita income was in Hudspeth County at $23,569.

Source: Bureau of Economic Analysis, U.S. Department of Commerce, 2020.

Top Ten			Lowest Ten		
County	**Major cities**	**PCI**	**County**	**Major cities**	**PCI**
1. Midland	Midland	$130,983	**245. Childress**	Childress	$30,731
2. Shackelford	Albany	113,163	**246. Frio**	Pearsall	30,223
3. Sherman	Stratford	97,002	**247. Cameron**	Brownsville	29,928
4. Glasscock	Garden City	84,623	**248. Walker**	Huntsville	29,838
5. Kendall	Boerne	81,882	**249. Bee**	Beeville	29,792
6. Hartley	Dalhart, Channing	81,238	**250. Zapata**	Zapata	28,936
7. King	Guthrie	78,849	**251. Starr**	Rio Grande City	27,713
8. Eastland	Eastland, Cisco, Ranger	78,826	**252. Willacy**	Raymondville	27,584
9. Lipscomb	Lipscomb, Booker	77,810	**253. Hidalgo**	McAllen	27,415
10. Irion	Mertzon	72,177	**254. Hudspeth**	Fort Hancock	23,569

County	Total Income ($ mil)	% change 2018-19	Per capita income	Rank in State
United States	$18,542,262	3.9	$56,474	–
Metropolitan	16,588,018	4	58,650	–
Nonmetro	1,954,244	3.9	43,035	–
Texas	$1,531,346	4.6	$52,829	–
Metropolitan	1,399,196	4.7	54,064	–
Nonmetro	132,151	3.9	42,420	–
Anderson	2,080	4.4	36,027	223
Andrews	968	5.9	51,769	58
Angelina	3,438	1.8	39,644	189
Aransas	1,213	3.1	51,614	60
Archer	448	3.7	52,335	55
Armstrong	101	2.8	53,422	50
Atascosa	1,926	4.3	37,644	208
Austin	1,535	3.6	51,118	62
Bailey	313	2.2	44,665	117
Bandera	1,038	4.3	44,925	112
Bastrop	3,397	7	38,289	201
Baylor	164	3.6	46,615	86
Bee	970	4.1	29,792	249
Bell	15,939	5.1	43,919	134
Bexar	95,830	4	47,830	79
Blanco	654	5.6	54,814	43
Borden	40	-7.7	61,287	24
Bosque	792	3	42,366	147
Bowie	3,839	2.3	41,172	168
Brazoria	18,105	5	48,374	77
Brazos	9,478	4.6	41,348	164
Brewster	446	4.2	48,422	76
Briscoe	69	1.6	44,413	123
Brooks	259	4.2	36,558	219
Brown	1,502	1.7	39,661	187
Burleson	848	4.2	45,970	97
Burnet	2,395	4.9	49,731	69
Caldwell	1,512	5.9	34,617	230
Calhoun	984	4.7	46,208	93
Callahan	585	4.5	41,962	157
Cameron	12,664	3.7	29,928	247
Camp	486	0.1	37,111	215
Carson	288	7.7	48,571	75
Cass	1,128	2.4	37,566	210
Castro	485	8	64,427	16
Chambers	2,482	7.4	56,610	37
Cherokee	1,855	1.9	35,245	228
Childress	225	2	30,731	245
Clay	464	4.7	44,295	128
Cochran	112	-0.8	39,333	194
Coke	141	3.4	41,669	160
Coleman	349	3	42,683	144
Collin	70,852	6.3	68,474	12
Collingsworth	123	6.5	42,026	155
Colorado	1,008	4.3	46,909	85
Comal	9,381	7.5	60,056	29
Comanche	590	6.7	43,242	137
Concho	97	8.1	35,758	224
Cooke	2,181	5.2	52,875	53
Coryell	2,702	4.8	35,570	226
Cottle	84	-1.6	60,260	28
Crane	245	5.9	51,025	63
Crockett	154	6	44,458	122
Crosby	216	2.6	37,580	209
Culberson	129	7.8	59,506	32
Dallam	472	7.9	64,756	15

County	Total Income ($ mil)	% change 2018-19	Per capita income	Rank in State
Dallas	165,463	3.5	62,782	20
Dawson	511	-2.8	40,131	178
Deaf Smith	971	5.2	52,368	34
Delta	217	4.8	40,622	54
Denton	52,713	6.8	59,414	174
De Witt	1,197	2.7	59,389	33
Dickens	75	2.8	33,843	232
Dimmit	393	3.2	38,800	198
Donley	149	-3.2	45,531	104
Duval	435	3	39,029	195
Eastland	1,447	1.7	78,826	8
Ector	8,338	6.3	50,161	67
Edwards	88	11.2	45,429	107
Ellis	8,496	7	45,968	206
El Paso	31,652	4	37,715	98
Erath	1,728	5.4	40,462	176
Falls	610	1.7	35,258	227
Fannin	1,415	5.3	39,830	183
Fayette	1,383	3.5	54,552	45
Fisher	171	-9	44,630	119
Floyd	255	6.9	44,646	118
Foard	52	-6.2	44,895	113
Fort Bend	48,420	6.2	59,653	31
Franklin	443	2.1	41,307	165
Freestone	753	2.9	38,182	202
Frio	614	4.1	30,223	246
Gaines	954	11.3	44,405	124
Galveston	18,561	4.6	54,250	46
Garza	203	3.8	32,601	240
Gillespie	1,708	3.6	63,291	19
Glasscock	119	-0.2	84,623	4
Goliad	349	5.1	45,589	103
Gonzales	933	-2.1	44,789	116
Gray	966	3.1	44,127	129
Grayson	5,991	5.4	43,987	130
Gregg	5,839	3.3	47,109	84
Grimes	1,066	6.1	36,909	217
Guadalupe	7,641	5.5	45,797	100
Hale	1,190	5.5	35,633	225
Hall	98	-3.6	33,095	235
Hamilton	513	4.2	60,584	27
Hansford	353	5.7	65,330	13
Hardeman	165	0.4	42,023	156
Hardin	2,720	3.3	47,221	82
Harris	282,809	3.8	60,002	30
Harrison	2,854	3.3	42,891	143
Hartley	453	12.2	81,238	6
Haskell	226	5.9	39,899	181
Hays	10,435	8	45,332	108
Hemphill	218	2.3	57,053	36
Henderson	3,321	4.4	40,135	177
Hidalgo	23,815	3.8	27,415	253
Hill	1,511	4.1	41,240	166
Hockley	971	2.5	42,162	153
Hood	3,167	5.7	51,384	61
Hopkins	1,541	4.5	41,562	161

County	Total Income ($ mil)	% change 2018-19	Per capita income	Rank in State
Houston	910	2.7	39,609	190
Howard	1,589	2.9	43,348	136
Hudspeth	115	6.9	23,569	254
Hunt	3,835	5.3	38,892	197
Hutchinson	921	3.5	43,981	131
Irion	111	2.5	72,177	10
Jack	365	-5.1	40,827	173
Jackson	688	9.2	46,596	87
Jasper	1,451	2	40,834	172
Jeff Davis	98	4.3	43,080	139
Jefferson	11,223	1.8	44,613	120
Jim Hogg	175	4.6	33,602	233
Jim Wells	1,707	3.3	42,174	152
Johnson	7,694	6.1	43,759	135
Jones	655	6.4	32,639	239
Karnes	881	5	56,449	38
Kaufman	5,987	9.1	43,972	132
Kendall	3,884	5.5	81,882	5
Kenedy	17	0	42,262	149
Kent	42	1.1	54,630	44
Kerr	2,723	3.4	51,768	59
Kimble	192	3.1	44,371	125
King	21	-10.6	78,849	7
Kinney	118	1.4	32,219	242
Kleberg	1,274	3.1	41,526	162
Knox	145	-0.9	39,587	192
Lamar	2,147	5	43,063	180
Lamb	589	6.6	45,655	140
Lampasas	1,085	3.1	50,656	102
La Salle	300	3.3	39,913	66
Lavaca	1,078	3.5	53,483	49
Lee	873	8.8	50,665	65
Leon	697	2.3	40,056	179
Liberty	3,341	5.5	37,874	203
Limestone	885	4.2	37,774	204
Lipscomb	252	3.3	77,810	9
Live Oak	457	4.1	37,415	212
Llano	1,088	4.6	49,905	68
Loving	9	18.6	53,734	48
Lubbock	13,762	4	44,311	126
Lynn	257	9.3	43,141	138
McCulloch	311	-0.6	38,895	196
McLennan	10,819	2.8	42,159	154
McMullen	48	3.2	65,250	14
Madison	466	3.5	32,648	238
Marion	393	3.3	39,895	182
Martin	351	-4.6	60,844	26
Mason	203	2.3	47,439	81
Matagorda	1,658	6.1	45,237	109
Maverick	1,843	3.7	31,380	243
Medina	2,120	4.8	41,095	170
Menard	80	4.1	37,218	214
Midland	23,162	3.8	130,983	1
Milam	924	3.9	37,238	213
Mills	192	2.8	39,334	193
Mitchell	287	0.4	33,593	234

County	Total Income ($ mil)	% change 2018-19	Per capita income	Rank in State
Montague	837	4.2	42,230	151
Montgomery	38,523	5.8	63,424	18
Moore	966	6.4	46,108	94
Morris	509	1.3	41,068	171
Motley	40	4.5	32,988	236
Nacogdoches	2,515	1.5	38,569	199
Navarro	1,987	4.4	39,652	188
Newton	466	1.7	34,265	231
Nolan	678	4.4	46,066	96
Nueces	16,263	3.5	44,889	114
Ochiltree	599	3.4	60,862	25
Oldham	117	-0.6	55,479	42
Orange	3,808	2.1	45,663	101
Palo Pinto	1,202	4.6	41,193	167
Panola	1,055	-0.2	45,467	105
Parker	7,974	6.6	55,811	40
Parmer	476	8	49,541	72
Pecos	629	4.9	39,731	186
Polk	2,045	4.2	39,818	184
Potter	5,411	2.8	46,086	95
Presidio	312	3.1	46,581	88
Rains	436	5.6	34,819	229
Randall	6,823	4.7	49,544	71
Reagan	200	0.1	51,945	56
Real	125	2.2	36,070	221
Red River	517	3.5	43,039	141
Reeves	726	12.2	45,458	106
Refugio	323	4.4	46,464	90
Roberts	41	-5	48,344	78
Robertson	725	2	42,463	145
Rockwall	6,530	7.4	62,237	21
Runnels	430	6.8	41,929	158
Rusk	2,051	2.6	37,697	207
Sabine	386	5	36,627	218
San Augustine	348	7.1	42,299	148
San Jacinto	1,046	4.6	36,260	220
San Patricio	3,103	3.2	46,506	89
San Saba	245	0.6	40,521	175
Schleicher	118	1	42,255	150
Scurry	717	-1	42,915	142
Shackelford	369	1	113,163	2
Shelby	1,056	-1.7	41,767	159
Sherman	293	13.1	97,002	3

County	Total Income ($ mil)	% change 2018-19	Per capita income	Rank in State
Smith	13,102	3.2	56,292	39
Somervell	418	4.3	45,812	99
Starr	1,791	3.7	27,713	251
Stephens	412	1.8	43,971	133
Sterling	80	0.9	61,920	22
Stonewall	79	-3.5	58,541	35
Sutton	233	-2	61,646	23
Swisher	383	1.4	51,779	57
Tarrant	112,047	4.4	53,292	51
Taylor	6,597	5	47,793	80
Terrell	38	1.8	49,591	70
Terry	466	9	37,741	205
Throckmorton	62	8.3	41,454	163
Titus	1,214	2.7	37,070	216
Tom Green	5,826	4.1	48,876	74
Travis	91,300	6	71,666	11
Trinity	528	3.2	36,062	222
Tyler	715	3.9	32,978	237
Upshur	1,568	3.6	37,563	211
Upton	172	6.3	47,118	83
Uvalde	1,099	3	41,116	169
Val Verde	1,879	5.6	38,331	200
Van Zandt	2,241	4.5	39,609	191
Victoria	4,506	4.4	48,938	73
Walker	2,177	3.7	29,838	248
Waller	2,346	6.6	42,456	146
Ward	646	11.5	53,870	47
Washington	2,000	4.2	55,735	41
Webb	8,982	3.7	32,466	241
Wharton	1,879	4.4	45,221	110
Wheeler	224	0.3	44,309	127
Wichita	5,881	4	44,479	121
Wilbarger	591	2.2	46,314	92
Willacy	589	0	27,584	252
Williamson	31,385	9.1	53,145	52
Wilson	2,372	4.9	46,448	91
Winkler	510	10.9	63,667	17
Wise	3,140	6	44,870	115
Wood	1,813	4.5	39,803	185
Yoakum	391	6.7	44,932	111
Young	914	1.5	50,732	64
Zapata	410	1.5	28,936	250
Zavala	364	5	30,779	244

8 Largest States' Unemployment Rates

Rank	State	June 2021	July 2021	Monthly Change
1.	Florida	11.5%	5.1%	–6.4%
2.	**Texas**	**6.5%**	**6.2%**	**–0.3%**
3.	Georgia	4.0%	3.7%	–0.3%
4.	Pennsylvania	6.9%	6.6%	–0.3%
5.	New York	14.7%	7.6%	–7.1%
6.	North Carolina	8.8%	4.4%	–4.4%
7.	Michigan	9.0%	4.8%	–4.2%
8.	California	13.2%	7.6%	–5.6%

Source: Bureau of Labor Statistics. August 2021.

Average Work Hours and Earnings

The following table compares the average weekly earnings, hours worked per week, and average hourly wage in Texas for production workers in selected industries in April 2020 and April 2021. Figures are provided by the Texas Workforce Commission.

Industry	Average Weekly Earnings		Average Weekly Hours		Average Hourly Earnings	
	April 2021	April 2020	April 2021	April 2020	April 2021	April 2020
Mining and Logging	$1,277.46	$1,188.14	45.3	44.6	$28.20	$26.64
Mining (including Oil & Gas)	1,283.68	1,185.91	45.2	44.6	28.40	26.59
Manufacturing						
Durable Goods	1,145.88	1,063.42	44.5	42.3	25.75	25.14
Fabricated Metal Product Mfg.	1,026.48	869.46	47.0	43.3	21.84	20.08
Nondurable Goods	788.16	852.52	41.2	43.1	19.13	19.78
Trade, Transportation, Utilities						
Wholesale Trade	1,023.00	944.15	42.2	40.4	24.83	23.37
Machinery, Equipment, Supplies	1,048.71	1,067.24	41.5	42.1	25.27	25.35
Retail Trade						
Auto Dealers/Parts	648.49	621.33	36.7	36.7	17.67	16.93
Building Material/Garden Equip.	462.35	499.46	32.4	34.0	14.27	14.69
Food/Beverage Stores	413.62	384.62	33.6	33.1	12.31	11.62
Gasoline Stations	377.48	376.88	32.5	34.2	11.63	11.02
Clothing/Accessories Stores	278.41	256.46	21.4	20.8	13.01	12.33

Employment in Texas by Industry

Employment in Texas reached 12,624,300 in June 2021, up 654,200 jobs since June 2020. The following table shows Texas Workforce Commission estimates of the nonagricultural labor force by industry for June 2021 and the percent change during the year in the number employed. *Source: Texas Workforce Commission. Additional information available at the website twc.texas.gov.*

Industry	June 2021	Monthly Change	Annual Change	Annual % Change
Total Nonagricultural	12,624,300	55,800	654,200	5.5%
Private	10,660,300	54,100	607,600	6
Goods-Producing	1,790,600	2,600	27,200	1.5
Mining & Logging (oil, gas)	189,200	2,900	12,200	6.9
Construction	726,600	-3,300	-100	0
Manufacturing	874,800	3,000	15,100	1.8
Service-Providing	10,833,700	53,200	627,000	6.1
Trade, Transportation, Utilities	2,564,700	6,600	129,100	5.3
Information	202,300	100	11,300	5.9
Financial Activities	827,200	800	30,600	3.8
Professional & Business Services	1,855,800	13,200	151,300	8.9
Education & Health Services	1,719,800	9,500	43,400	2.6
Leisure & Hospitality	1,291,500	19,000	184,600	16.7
Other Services	408,400	2,300	30,100	8
Government	1,964,000	1,700	46,600	2.4

Help Wanted: Top Online Postings of Job Vacancies

Occupation	July 2021	June 2021	Employer	July 2021	June 2021
Registered Nurses	31,826	30,879	Baylor Scott & White Health	8,029	7,102
Sales, Wholesale	21,386	21,656	Deloitte	4,548	4,337
Sales, Retail	19,571	19,430	HCA–Healthcare Company	4,131	4,197
Customer Service	19,517	19,581	Houston Methodist	3,475	3,084
Truck Drivers	17,222	16,475	Christus Health	2,642	3,181
Software Developers	17,173	16,135	UnitedHealth Group	2,552	2,123
Computer Tech	15,877	15,328	Anthem Blue Cross	2,505	2,337

Source: Texas Workforce Commission from Conference Board Help Wanted Online Data Series.

Largest Banks Operating in Texas by Asset Size

Source: Texas Department of Banking, December 31, 2018

Abbreviations: NA, not available; N.A. National Association.

	Name	City	Class	Assets (thousands of dollars)	Loans (thousands of dollars)
1	Charles Schwab Bank SSB	Westlake	State	351,075,000	25,537,000
2	JP Morgan Chase Bank	New York NY	National	246,711,590	NA
3	Bank of America	Charlotte NC	National	165,066,597	NA
4	USAA Federal Savings Bank	San Antonio	National	121,715,724	38,358,368
5	Comerica Bank	Dallas	State	86,257,000	50,582,000
6	Wells Fargo Bank	San Francisco CA	National	81,141,105	NA
7	BBVA USA	Birmingham AL	State	44,240,950	NA
8	Frost Bank	San Antonio	State	44,092,014	17,889,863
9	Texas Capital Bank N.A.	Dallas	National	40,035,375	24,393,255
10	Prosperity Bank	El Campo	State	35,563,929	19,617,895
11	Charles Schwab Premier Bank SSB	Westlake	State	33,115,000	0
12	Independent Bank	McKinney	State	18,110,591	12,770,197
13	Citibank	Sioux Falls SD	National	14,290,000	NA
14	Plains Capital Bank	University Park	State	14,229,718	7,290,482
15	Zions Bancoporation N.A.	Salt Lake City UT	National	12,993,040	NA
16	First Financial Bank N.A.	Abilene	National	12,065,711	5,322,562
17	International Bank of Commerce	Laredo	State	10,556,686	5,709,148
18	Capital One	New Orleans LA	National	10,391,469	NA
19	Woodforest National Bank	The Woodlands	National	9,792,477	4,868,649
20	Veritex Community Bank	Dallas	State	9,232,171	6,969,847
21	NexBank	Dallas	State	9,082,950	4,484,518
22	Truist Bank	Charlotte NC	State	7,572,143	NA
23	Amarillo National Bank	Amarillo	National	7,400,429	5,158,468
24	BOKF	Tulsa OK	National	7,005,971	NA
25	Southside Bank	Tyler	State	6,994,558	3,716,598
26	Allegiance Bank	Houston	State	6,423,375	4,659,169
27	Happy State Bank	Happy	State	6,326,783	3,429,087
28	TBK Bank SSB	Dallas	State	6,082,072	5,083,712
29	Cadence Bank N.A.	Birmingham AL	National	5,899,767	NA
30	Regions Bank	Birmingham AL	State	5,401,441	NA
31	Wells Fargo Bank South Central N.A.	Houston	National	5,262,057	340,038
32	Broadway National Bank	San Antonio	National	4,874,723	2,545,097
33	American National Bank of Texas	Terrell	National	4,448,694	2,406,771
34	Bancorp South Bank	Tupelo MS	State	4,433,845	NA
35	CommunityBank of Texas N.A.	Beaumont	National	4,029,141	2,891,632
36	First National Bank Texas	Killeen	National	3,889,580	1,351,218
37	First United Bank & Trust	Durant OK	State	3,860,938	NA
38	City Bank	Lubbock	State	3,730,641	2,242,676
39	Inwood National Bank	Dallas	National	3,667,073	1,967,049
40	TIB The Independent BankersBank	Farmers Branch	National	3,585,613	1,218,169
41	Texas Bank and Trust Company	Longview	State	3,580,389	2,484,802
42	VeraBank N.A.	Henderson	National	3,193,383	1,644,130
43	Spirit of Texas Bank SSB	College Station	State	3,166,882	2,430,939
44	First Bank & Trust	Lubbock	State	2,991,053	1,516,387
45	Guaranty Bank & Trust N.A.	Mount Pleasant	National	2,891,363	1,909,755
46	Lone Star National Bank	Pharr	National	2,737,786	1,302,827
47	Texas Exchange Bank SSB	Crowley	State	2,712,587	740,867
48	American Momentum Bank	College Station	State	2,700,117	1,822,788
49	Vantage Bank Texas	San Antonio	State	2,653,253	2,034,678
50	WestStar Bank	El Paso	State	2,520,224	1,587,625

Deposits/Assets of Commercial Banks by County

Source: Federal Reserve Bank of Dallas as of Dec. 31, 2018.

(in thousands of dollars)

County	Banks	Deposits	Assets
Andrews	2	$786,813	$891,775
Angelina	1	209,518	253,557
Atascosa	2	156,141	179,741
Austin	5	2,247,370	2,640,246
Bailey	1	82,066	95,914
Bandera	2	200,559	222,443
Bastrop	2	732,743	832,163
Baylor	1	144,154	164,051
Bee	1	394,903	434,881
Bell	4	3,272,585	3,878,149
Bexar	8	35,295,268	41,739,510
Blanco	1	103,668	118,188
Bosque	2	212,576	235,388
Bowie	2	403,265	457,687
Brazoria	7	1,064,722	1,202,395
Brazos	2	1,376,265	1,702,781
Briscoe	1	48,994	58,522
Brooks	1	70,721	78,668
Brown	2	597,258	692,419
Burleson	1	518,430	585,429
Burnet	1	216,982	246,255
Caldwell	2	299,387	337,880
Calhoun	1	288,038	317,838
Callahan	1	361,301	417,210
Cameron	4	2,035,806	2,399,293
Camp	1	456,470	574,188
Carson	1	31,919	35,898
Cass	2	418,016	485,983
Castro	1	1,108,104	1,315,753
Chambers	1	107,951	121,100
Cherokee	2	1,939,996	2,323,662
Childress	1	100,825	109,158
Coke	1	35,596	41,227
Coleman	2	146,726	164,425
Collin	4	15,351,268	19,740,097
Collingsworth	1	346,069	397,725
Colorado	4	429,944	509,599
Comanche	1	84,215	92,919
Concho	2	180,945	205,992
Cooke	2	1,105,043	1,257,696
Coryell	2	628,133	702,303
Cottle	1	45,174	49,436
Crockett	1	226,569	255,317
Crosby	2	744,025	854,498
Dallas	24	98,710,887	124,594,733
Dawson	1	317,970	350,327
Deaf Smith	1	148,705	169,091
Delta	2	70,832	82,931
Denton	4	1,014,778	1,154,602
DeWitt	2	373,066	426,164
Dickens	1	40,782	45,300
Dimmit	1	65,660	75,849
Donley	1	35,155	42,941
Duval	2	95,912	108,840
Ector	2	741,013	835,144
Edwards	1	69,285	79,024
Ellis	4	1,329,849	1,514,241
El Paso	2	1,762,700	2,069,095
Erath	1	80,827	90,526
Fannin	1	86,664	99,674
Fayette	4	1,234,697	1,386,252
Fisher	1	72,316	79,543
Floyd	1	98,753	110,149
Foard	1	35,591	39,756
Franklin	1	137,570	191,004
Frio	2	651,437	747,255
Galveston	4	2,443,359	2,818,052
Gillespie	1	856,602	1,027,574
Gonzales	1	358,672	405,478
Gray	1	46,957	55,419
Grayson	3	531,304	603,838
Gregg	3	2,738,363	3,154,115
Grimes	2	286,326	329,785
Guadalupe	3	740,993	840,515
Hale	1	28,433	41,842
Hall	1	52,154	60,348
Hansford	3	383,962	442,146
Hardeman	1	54,058	59,433
Harris	17	19,229,546	22,831,273
Harrison	1	196,806	219,573
Haskell	1	61,248	69,714
Henderson	2	511,511	574,094
Hidalgo	5	2,837,932	3,245,212
Hill	1	147,021	174,653
Hockley	2	169,732	189,546
Hood	2	552,532	621,225
Hopkins	2	1,287,599	1,468,635
Houston	3	149,554	171,239
Howard	1	355,314	392,240
Hunt	1	45,217	49,406
Irion	1	413,042	443,331
Jack	1	214,449	240,334
Jackson	1	52,037	55,733
Jasper	1	224,576	257,831
Jeff Davis	1	77,685	85,847
Jefferson	1	2,811,864	3,280,197
Jim Hogg	1	77,858	93,485
Johnson	1	183,874	202,974
Jones	1	57,552	62,995
Karnes	2	742,308	820,886
Kaufman	2	2,934,672	3,243,517
Kendall	1	131,506	147,556
Kerr	1	144,894	159,550
Kimble	2	104,219	114,513
Kleberg	1	439,043	528,374
Lamar	3	503,771	598,254
Lamb	1	1,232,126	1,401,066
Lampasas	1	120,111	137,448
La Salle	1	87,693	98,237
Lavaca	2	901,613	1,014,153
Lee	1	188,031	209,953
Leon	2	904,919	1,029,838
Liberty	1	265,398	307,164
Limestone	2	263,888	305,100
Live Oak	2	473,387	541,096
Llano	2	324,676	364,865
Lubbock	9	7,202,629	8,437,114
Lynn	1	48,239	53,804
Martin	1	204,361	223,418
Mason	2	139,674	170,695
McCulloch	2	246,566	275,947
McLennan	12	3,601,061	4,121,667

No independent banks were reported in 59 counties.

Total bank assets in Dallas County were $124.6 biillion in 2018. In Harris County (Houston), assets were $22.8 billion, and in Bexar County (San Antonio), assets were $41.7 billion.
Besides the three largest cities, banks in three other counties had assets over $10 billion, Wharton, Webb (Laredo) and Collin (Plano).

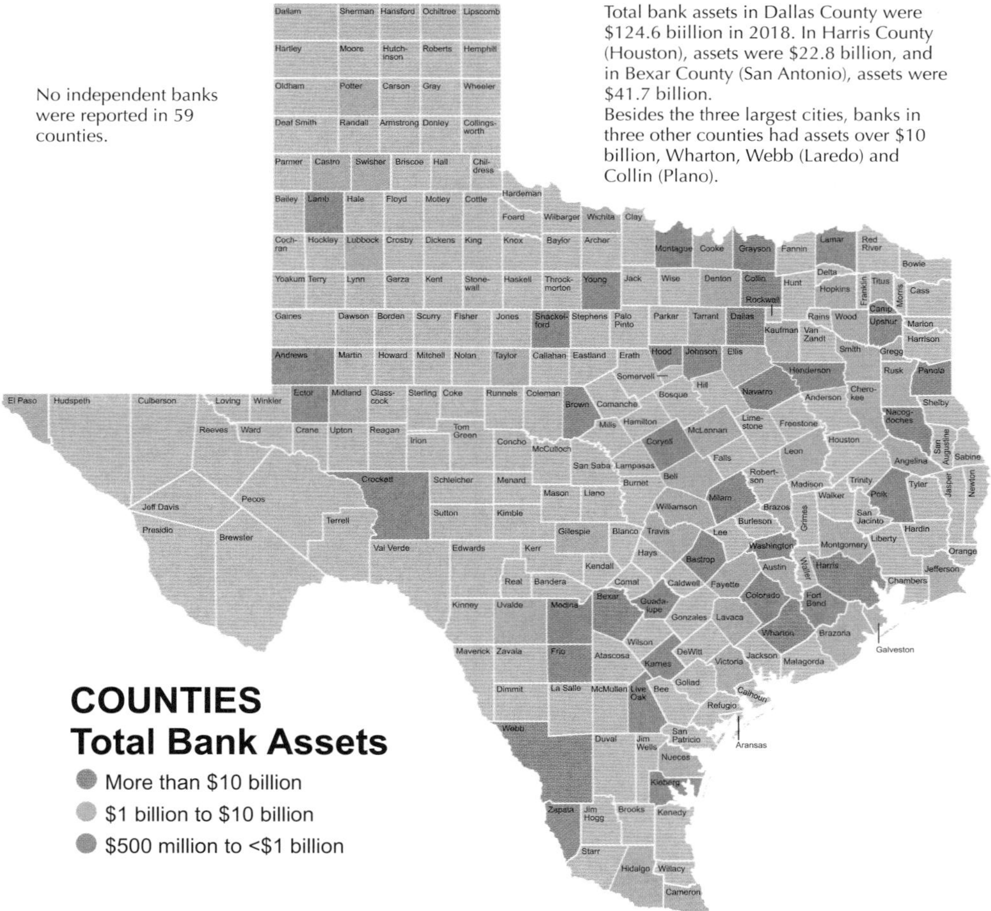

County	Banks	Deposits	Assets
Medina	3	544,978	615,950
Menard	1	31,988	36,668
Midland	5	4,546,544	5,152,536
Milam	3	753,409	865,275
Mills	1	284,812	315,242
Mitchell	1	113,904	125,272
Montague	1	600,346	694,569
Montgomery	1	5,338,201	5,923,725
Morris	2	174,566	229,772
Nacogdoches	1	649,877	727,918
Navarro	4	865,304	999,160
Nolan	2	266,816	296,100
Nueces	5	2,322,016	2,636,085
Ochiltree	1	150,362	172,423
Orange	1	190,459	208,340
Palo Pinto	1	90,435	105,391
Panola	2	473,116	603,570
Parker	2	533,691	592,673
Parmer	1	140,134	158,719
Pecos	2	352,805	388,375
Polk	3	719,847	843,224
Potter	3	4,930,457	5,774,064
Presidio	1	111,062	129,531
Randall	1	140,739	159,818

County	Banks	Deposits	Assets
Rockwall	1	56,079	62,457
Runnels	3	354,889	393,200
Rusk	2	2,463,609	2,805,100
Sabine	1	53,507	61,500
San Jacinto	2	147,118	162,736
San Patricio	1	126,919	142,889
San Saba	1	52,416	60,969
Schleicher	1	50,905	60,537
Scurry	2	217,249	246,149
Shackelford	1	516,595	592,295
Shelby	2	395,923	455,099
Sherman	1	211,463	244,798
Smith	4	5,420,176	7,478,325
Starr	1	71,385	84,166
Sterling	1	173,449	183,532
Stonewall	1	57,348	67,891
Sutton	1	340,941	423,400
Swisher	2	2,902,560	3,488,531
Tarrant	9	3,270,178	3,860,943
Taylor	3	6,407,214	7,846,262
Titus	2	1,963,071	2,367,052
Tom Green	1	235,462	270,620
Travis	3	242,106	315,275
Trinity	1	52,297	57,825

County	Banks	Deposits	Assets
Tyler	1	129,181	144,198
Upshur	2	510,368	587,879
Uvalde	1	1,589,321	1,734,034
Val Verde	1	23,455	28,288
Van Zandt	1	125,454	145,753
Walker	1	412,049	469,922
Ward	1	157,971	176,873
Washington	4	763,614	860,573
Webb	4	8,811,325	11,650,632
Wharton	3	18,334,982	23,884,829
Wheeler	1	66,550	75,402
Wichita	4	1,796,545	2,130,172
Wilbarger	1	248,340	294,284
Williamson	4	1,249,028	1,396,930
Wilson	1	41,929	51,535
Wise	2	240,164	279,433
Wood	2	1,551,311	2,052,193
Young	3	650,882	767,275
Zapata	2	378,887	513,078
Zavala	1	56,042	64,839

Texas Total Bank Resources and Deposits: 1905–2018

On Dec. 31, 2018, Texas had 409 national and state banks, the lowest number since our records began in 1905. In 1986, the number of independent banks in the state peaked at 1,972. In 2018, total assets were the highest ever at nearly $400 billion. Deposits peaked in 2018 at $328.9 billion. *Source: Federal Reserve Bank of Dallas.*

Date	National Banks			State Banks			Combined Total		
	No. Banks	Assets (in thousands)	Deposits (in thousands)	No. Banks	Assets (in thousands)	Deposits (in thousands)	No. Banks	Assets (in thousands)	Deposits (in thousands)
Sept. 30, 1905	440	$ 189,484	$ 101,285	29	$ 4,341	$ 2,213	**469**	$ 193,825	$ 103,498
Nov. 10, 1910	516	293,245	145,249	621	88,103	59,766	**1,137**	381,348	205,015
Dec. 29, 1920	556	780,246	564,135	1,031	391,127	280,429	**1,587**	1,171,373	844,564
Dec. 31, 1930	560	1,028,420	826,723	655	299,012	231,909	**1,215**	1,327,432	1,058,632
Dec. 31, 1940	446	1,695,662	1,534,702	393	227,866	179,027	**839**	1,923,528	1,713,729
Dec. 31, 1950	442	6,467,275	6,076,006	449	1,427,680	1,338,540	**891**	7,894,955	7,414,546
Dec. 31, 1960	468	10,520,690	9,560,668	532	2,997,609	2,735,726	**1,000**	13,518,299	12,296,394
Dec. 31, 1970	530	22,087,890	18,384,922	653	8,907,039	7,958,133	**1,183**	30,994,929	26,343,055
Dec. 31, 1980	641	75,540,334	58,378,669	825	35,186,113	31,055,648	**1,466**	110,726,447	89,434,317
Dec. 31, 1985	1,058	144,674,908	111,903,178	878	64,349,869	56,392,634	**1,936**	209,024,777	168,295,812
Dec. 31, 1986	1,077	141,397,037	106,973,189	895	65,989,944	57,739,091	**1,972**	207,386,981	164,712,280
Dec. 31, 1987	953	135,690,678	103,930,262	812	54,361,514	47,283,855	**1,765**	190,052,192	151,214,117
Dec. 31, 1988	802	130,310,243	106,740,461	690	40,791,310	36,655,253	**1,492**	171,101,553	143,395,714
Dec. 31, 1989	687	133,163,016	104,091,836	626	40,893,848	36,652,675	**1,313**	174,056,864	140,744,511
Dec. 31, 1990	605	125,808,263	103,573,445	578	45,021,304	40,116,662	**1,183**	170,829,567	143,690,107
Dec. 31, 1993	502	139,409,250	111,993,205	510	44,566,815	39,190,373	**1,012**	183,976,065	151,183,578
Dec. 31, 1994	481	140,374,540	111,881,041	502	47,769,694	41,522,943	**983**	188,144,234	153,403,984
Dec. 31, 1995	456	152,750,093	112,557,468	479	49,967,946	42,728,454	**935**	202,718,039	155,285,922
Dec. 31, 1996	432	152,299,695	122,242,990	445	52,868,263	45,970,674	**877**	205,167,958	168,213,664
Dec. 31, 1997	417	180,252,942	145,588,677	421	54,845,186	46,202,808	**838**	235,098,128	191,791,485
Dec. 31, 1998	402	128,609,813	106,704,893	395	50,966,996	42,277,367	**797**	179,576,809	148,982,260
Dec. 31, 1999	380	128,878,607	99,383,776	373	52,266,148	42,579,986	**753**	181,144,755	141,963,762
Dec. 31, 2000	358	112,793,856	88,591,657	351	53,561,550	43,835,525	**709**	166,355,406	132,427,182
Dec. 31, 2001	342	85,625,768	72,812,548	344	59,047,520	47,843,799	**686**	144,673,288	120,656,347
Dec. 31, 2002	332	95,308,420	79,183,418	337	62,093,220	49,715,186	**669**	157,401,640	128,898,604
Dec. 31, 2003	316	75,003,613	62,567,943	337	61,448,617	49,790,333	**653**	136,452,230	112,358,276
Dec. 31, 2004	311	82,333,800	67,977,669	328	69,127,411	54,950,601	**639**	151,461,211	122,928,270
Dec. 31, 2005	302	96,505,262	77,688,463	324	76,697,256	61,257,128	**626**	173,202,518	138,945,591
Dec. 31, 2006	286	97,936,270	79,389,737	322	83,910,356	66,132,394	**608**	181,846,626	145,522,131
Dec. 31, 2007	282	107,260,539	83,637,302	330	154,283,181	114,537,280	**612**	261,543,720	198,174,582
Dec. 31, 2008	267	108,816,852	84,802,191	327	164,658,101	115,186,285	**594**	273,474,953	199,988,476
Dec. 31, 2009	263	153,639,579	109,552,071	318	162,958,865	120,962,911	**581**	316,598,444	230,514,982
Dec. 31, 2010	253	149,498,073	120,827,780	314	162,772,458	127,925,865	**567**	312,270,531	248,753,645
Dec. 31, 2011	250	159,621,331	129,799,399	302	169,525,070	137,180,187	**552**	329,146,401	266,979,586
Dec. 31, 2012	227	156,392,247	139,945,006	293	205,788,318	169,156,089	**520**	362,180,565	302,101,095
Dec. 31, 2013	211	138,785,446	118,373,970	283	216,540,710	181,010,324	**494**	355,326,156	299,384,294
Dec. 31, 2014	203	128,134,221	108,506,074	267	235,388,932	197,078,456	**470**	363,523,153	305,584,530
Dec. 31, 2015	195	117,391,368	99,420,411	252	246,932,641	204,350,121	**477**	364,324,009	303,770,532
Dec. 31, 2016	186	122,431,838	104,027,309	244	254,560,238	208,323,981	**430**	376,992,076	312,351,290
Dec. 31, 2017	183	133,291,358	111,896,128	240	259,417,028	212,732,825	**423**	392,708,386	324,628,953
Dec. 31, 2018	176	$137,477,382	$114,245,832	233	$262,400,881	$214,562,067	**409**	$399,878,263	$328,907,699

Texas State Banks

Consolidated Statement, Foreign and Domestic Offices, as of Dec. 31, 2018

Source: Federal Reserve Bank of Dallas

Number of Banks	233
(thousands of dollars)	
Assets	
Cash and balances due from banks:	
Non-interest-bearing balances and currency and coin	$ 4,962,045
Interest-bearing balances	13,098,333
Held-to-maturity securities	13,547,370
Available-for-sale securities	47,367,624
Equity securities not held for trading	54,182
Federal funds sold in domestic offices	1,365,496
Securities purchases under agreements to resell	11,642
Loans and lease financing receivables:	
Loans and leases held for sale	1,665,108
Loans and leases held for investment	163,989,470
Less: allowance for loan and lease losses	1,811,630
Loans and leases, net	162,177,840
Trading Assets	141,420
Premises and fixed assets	3,902,016
Other real estate owned	178,289
Investments in unconsolidated subsidiaries and associated companies	49,909
Direct/indirect investments in real estate ventures	12,944
Intangible assets	6,070,415
Other assets	7,796,248
Total Assets	**$ 262,400,881**
Liabilities	
Deposits:	
In domestic offices	$ 214,164,380
Non-interest-bearing	79,784,426
Interest-bearing	134,379,960
In foreign offices, edge & agreement subsidiaries and IBFs	497,687
Non-interest-bearing	264,633
Interest-bearing balances	233,054
Federal funds purchased and securities sold under agreements to repurchase:	
funds in domestic offices	451,840
securities sold under agreement to repurchase	2,280,725
Trading liabilities	299,103
Other borrowed money (mortgages/leases)	9,615,243
Subordinated notes and debentures	580,055
Other liabilities	2,000,675
Total Liabilities	$ 229,889,708
Equity Capital	
Perpetual preferred stock	$ 4,906
Common stock	482,034
Surplus (exclude surplus related to preferred stock)	16,457,220
Retained earnings	16,645,362
Accumulated other comprehensive income	–1,077,974
Other equity capital components	–7,519
Total bank equity capital	32,504,029
Minority interest in cons. subsidiaries	7,144
Total Equity Capital	$ 32,511,173
Total liabilities, minority interest and equity capital	**$ 262,400,881**

Texas National Banks

Consolidated Statement, Foreign and Domestic Offices, as of Dec. 31, 2018

Source: Federal Reserve Bank of Dallas

Number of Banks	176
(thousands of dollars)	
Assets	
Cash and balances due from banks:	
Non-interest-bearing balances and currency and coin	$ 2,708,378
Interest-bearing balances	9,238,424
Held-to-maturity securities	2,771,738
Available-for-sale securities	21,161,149
Equity securities not held for trading	37,944
Federal funds sold in domestic offices	3,375,562
Securities purchases under agreements to resell	125,000
Loans and lease financing receivables:	
Loans and leases held for sale	5,646,116
Loans and leases held for investment	87,674,263
Less: allowance for loan and lease losses	1,005,273
Loans and leases, net of allowance	86,668,990
Trading Assets	27,594
Premises and fixed assets	1,595,444
Other real estate owned	74,985
Investments in unconsolidated subsidiaries and associated companies	29,807
Direct/indirect investments in real estate ventures	2,099
Intangible assets	847,772
Other assets	3,166,380
Total Assets	**$ 137,477,382**
Liabilities	
Deposits:	
In domestic offices	$ 114,245,638
Non-interest-bearing	30,220,646
Interest-bearing	84,024,992
In foreign offices, edge & agreement subsidiaries and IBFs	0
Non-interest-bearing	0
Interest-bearing balances	0
Federal funds purchased and securities sold under agreements to repurchase:	
funds in domestic offices	792,297
securities sold under agreement to repurchase	883,402
Trading liabilities	21,011
Other borrowed money (mortgages/leases)	5,861,778
Subordinated notes and debentures	223,153
Other liabilities	975,172
Total Liabilities	$ 123,002,451
Equity Capital	
Perpetual preferred stock	$ 160,750
Common stock	357,986
Surplus (exclude surplus related to preferred stock)	4,607,653
Retained earnings	9,621,463
Accumulated other comprehensive income	– 278,689
Other equity capital components	– 7,973
Total bank equity capital	14,461,190
Minority interest in consolidated subsidiaries	13,741
Total Equity Capital	$ 14,474,937
Total liabilities, minority interest and equity capital	**$ 137,477,382**

Savings and Loan Associations in Texas

This table includes all thrifts that are not also classified as banks under federal law: that is, it includes federal savings and loan associations and federal savings banks. *Source: Texas Department of Savings and Mortgage Lending.*

Year ending	Number of Inst.	Total Assets	Mortgage Loans	Cash/ Securities	Deposits	FHLB/ Borrowed Money	†Net Worth
				in thousands of dollars			
Dec. 31, 2018	5	$83,782,803	$6,020,272	$43,883,996	$73,570,292	$153,368	$8,284,160
Dec. 31, 2017	5	82,642,161	7,155,350	41,128,877	73,813,038	62,068	7,559,159
Dec. 31, 2016	6	80,671,509	48,621,797	29,471,795	73,504,651	349,316	7,166,859
Dec. 31, 2015	6	73,722,445	47,512,693	24,727,034	65,397,606	213,039	6,703,177
Dec. 31, 2014	8	71,253,195	45,943,853	29,164,768	62,899,043	379,957	6,470,089
Dec. 31, 2013	8	66,605,862	41,812,008	34,083,458	59,101,594	196,784	5,941,114
Dec. 31, 2012	12	64,448,340	41,967,892	20,925,955	57,004,423	579,846	5,645,916
Dec. 31, 2011	12	57,857,491	40,757,220	15,671,590	50,819,345	657,598	5,079,133
Dec. 31, 2010	19	53,980,441	17,005,657	14,230,550	46,935,007	987,211	4,840,466
Dec. 31, 2009	19	46,524,327	17,810,587	9,702,023	40,272,742	973,610	4,254,794
Dec. 31, 2008	22	87,572,855	49,816,471	31,763,898	52,606,655	27,137,730	6,582,759
Dec. 31, 2005	19	55,755,096	42,027,293	9,140,789	30,565,411	11,299,136	4,228,103
Dec. 31, 2000	25	55,709,391	43,515,610	1,512,444	28,914,234	17,093,369	4,449,097
Dec. 31, 1995	45	52,292,519	27,509,933	5,971,364	28,635,799	15,837,632	3,827,249
Dec. 31, 1994	50	50,014,102	24,148,760	6,790,416	29,394,433	15,973,056	3,447,110
Dec. 31, 1990 §	131	72,041,456	27,475,664	20,569,770	56,994,387	17,738,041	–4,566,656
Conservatorship	51	14,952,402	6,397,466	2,188,820	16,581,525	4,304,033	–6,637,882
Privately Owned	80	57,089,054	21,078,198	18,380,950	40,412,862	13,434,008	2,071,226
Dec. 31, 1989 §	196	90,606,100	37,793,043	21,218,130	70,823,464	27,158,238	–9,356,209
Conservatorship	81	22,159,752	11,793,445	2,605,080	25,381,494	7,103,657	–10,866,213
Privately Owned	115	68,446,348	25,999,598	18,613,050	45,441,970	20,054,581	1,510,004
Dec. 31, 1988	204	110,499,276	50,920,006	26,181,917	83,950,314	28,381,573	–4,088,355
Dec. 31, 1985	273	91,798,890	60,866,666	10,426,464	72,806,067	13,194,147	3,903,611
Dec. 31, 1980	318	$34,954,129	$27,717,383	$3,066,791	$28,439,210	$3,187,638	$1,711,201

Texas Savings Banks

The savings bank charter was approved by the Legislature in 1993, and the first savings bank was chartered in 1994. Savings banks operate similarly to savings and loans associations in that they are housing-oriented lenders. Under federal law, a savings bank is categorized as a commercial bank and not a thrift. Therefore savings-bank information is also reported with state and national bank information. *Source: Texas Department of Savings and Mortgage Lending.*

Year ending	Number of Inst.	Total Assets	Mortgage Loans	Cash/ Securities	Deposits	FHLB/ Borrowed Money	†Net Worth
			in thousands of dollars				
Dec. 31, 2018	24	$24,434,061	$11,003,911	$9,104,353	$17,635,204	$3,653,055	$2,877,779
Dec. 31, 2017	24	22,355,393	10,721,196	7,199,404	16,479,408	3,194,283	2,462,036
Dec. 31, 2016	28	18,715,828	13,394,235	2,937,083	14,032,907	1,813,466	2,679,435
Dec. 31, 2015	28	13,790,890	10,291,788	2,597,416	10,218,604	1,199,403	2,202,693
Dec. 31, 2014	29	11,031,064	8,211,320	2,947,322	8,257,801	659,216	1,977,443
Dec. 31, 2013	30	10,194,983	7,148,798	3,389,771	7,739,381	499,261	1,812,736
Dec. 31, 2012	30	10,142,623	6,816,212	2,630,941	7,610,074	699,816	1,674,039
Dec. 31, 2011	30	9,530,011	6,132,972	2,650,324	7,247,147	568,547	1,543,269
Dec. 31, 2010	29	8,559,443	4,568,866	4,164,611	6,720,417	332,684	1,329,943
Dec. 31, 2009	29	8,372,892	4,283,372	1,237,215	6,330,896	307,494	1,201,409
Dec. 31, 2008	28	3,988,377	1,980,651	538,162	3,119,082	411,119	434,893
Dec. 31, 2007	26	9,967,678	6,471,833	1,027,709	6,162,709	2,328,467	1,372,231
Dec. 31, 2006	22	9,393,482	6,444,178	836,821	5,721,314	2,453,757	1,138,780
Dec. 31, 2005	19	8,720,497	5,605,678	985,535	5,308,639	1,967,673	1,352,882
Dec. 31, 2004	22	12,981,650	6,035,081	1,654,978	8,377,409	3,000,318	1,482,078
Dec. 31, 2003	23	17,780,413	8,396,606	3,380,565	11,901,441	3,315,544	2,422,317
Dec. 31, 2000	25	11,315,961	9,613,164	514,818	8,644,826	1,455,497	1,059,638
Dec. 31, 1995	13	7,348,647	5,644,591	1,106,557	4,603,026	2,225,793	519,827
Dec. 31, 1994	8	$6,347,505	$2,825,012	$3,139,573	$3,227,886	$2,628,847	$352,363

† Net worth includes permanent stock and paid-in surplus general reserves, surplus and undivided profits. § In 1989 and 1990, the Office of Thrift Supervision, U.S. Department of the Treasury, separated data on savings and loans (thrifts) into two categories: those under the supervision of the Office of Thrift Supervision (Conservatorship Thrifts) and those still under private management (Privately Owned).

Credit Unions: End of 2018

	# Credit Unions	Members	Surplus Funds	Savings	Loans	Assets
Texas	454	9.0 million	$21.6 billion	$88.8 billion	$78.1 billion	$104.4 billion
U.S.	5,572	117.5 million	$350.6 billion	$1,234.8 billion	$1,058.9 billion	$1,470.8 billion

Sources: Texas Credit Union Department and Credit Union National Association.

	U.S. Credit Union History				Texas Credit Union History			
Year	**# Credit Unions**	**Members (million)**	**Savings ($ billion)**	**Loans ($ billion)**	**# Credit Unions**	**Members (million)**	**Savings ($ billion)**	**Loans ($ billion)**
2017	5,800	113.6	1,181.0	978.4	NA	8.8	86.1	73.3
2016	6,022	109.2	1,114.4	889.5	NA	8.5	81.7	68.1
2015	6,259	105.0	1.029.1	804.9	478	8.3	77.6	63.2
2014	6,513	101.5	971.2	728.9	490	8.2	73.2	NA
2013	6,795	98.4	930.0	659.4	503	8.1	70.1	55.0
2010	7,605	92.6	804.3	580.3	550	7.5	58.9	43.3
2005	9,198	87.0	591.4	474.2	625	6.8	40.2	32.7
2000	10,860	79.8	380.9	309.3	714	6.5	28.4	22.6
1995	12,230	69.3	278.8	198.4	819	5.4	20.3	14.7
1990	14,549	61.6	201.1	141.3	954	4.4	13.9	8.9
1980	21,465	43.9	61.7	48.7	1,379	3.2	4.8	3.7
1970	23,687	22.8	15.4	14.1	1,435	1.5	1.0	1.0
1960	20,094	12.0	4.8	4.4	1,159	0.7	0.3	0.3
1950	10,586	4.6	0.9	0.7	484	0.2	0.04	0.04

Source: Credit Union National Association.

Credit Unions in Texas

Source: Texas Credit Union Department, National Credit Union Administration, and Credit Union National Association.

Credit unions are chartered at federal and state levels. The National Credit Union Administration (NCUA) is the regulatory agency for the federal-chartered credit unions in Texas.

The Texas Credit Union Department is the regulatory agency for the state-chartered credit unions. It was established in 1969 as a separate agency by the 61st Legislature. In 2018, it supervised 182 active credit unions. These state-chartered credit unions served 3.9 million Texans and had approximately $41.9 billion in assets in 2018.

The department is supervised by the nine-member Texas Credit Union Commission, which is appointed by the governor to staggered terms of six years, with the terms of one-third of the members expiring Feb. 15 of each odd-numbered year.

The Texas Credit Union League was the state association for federal and state credit unions beginning in 1934. It is now called Cornerstone Credit Union League and includes Oklahoma and Arkansas. The league's address is 6801 Parkwood Blvd., Ste. 300, Plano 75024.

The address for the Texas Credit Union Department is 914 East Anderson Lane, Austin 78752. Their website is cud.texas.gov. ☆

Comparison of Texas credit unions

as of Dec. 31, 2018

	State	Federal
No. of institutions	182	272
Total assets	$41.9 billion	$62.2 billion
Asset growth	3.4%	2.0%
Avg. asset size	$230.2 million	$229.8 million
No. with <$5 mil. asset	28	40
Net Income	$363.8 million	$508.6 million

Source: Texas Credit Union Department.

Credit Outstanding by Lenders 2018

	U.S. Outstanding ($ billion)	Market share
Banks/Savings Insti.	$1,682.0	42.0%
Finance Companies	534.0	13.3%
Credit Unions	469.2	11.7%
Federal Government*	1,236.6	30.8%
Educational Institutions*	30.4	0.8%
Nonfinancial business	38.6	1.0%
Pools of Securitized Assets	18.3	0.5%
Total	$ 4,009.2	

** Includes student loans. Source: Federal Reserve Board.*

Insurance in Texas

Source: 2018 Annual Report, Texas Dept. of Insurance.

The Texas Department of Insurance reported that on Aug. 31, 2018, there were 2,819 entities licensed to handle insurance business in Texas and 641,371 agents and adjusters.

Under reforms in 1993-94, a three-member State Board of Insurance was replaced by the department, with a Commissioner of Insurance appointed by the governor for a two-year term in each odd-numbered year and confirmed by the Texas Senate.

On Sept. 1, 2005, legislation passed by the 79th Legislature took effect, transferring functions of the Texas Workers' Compensation Commission to the department and creating within it the Division of Worker's Compensation.

Also established was the office of Commissioner of Workers' Compensation, appointed by the governor, to enforce and implement the Texas Workers' Compensation Act.

Property/Casualty filings in Texas

A single-form filing submission may contain multiple policy forms and endorsements.

Type form	2017	2018	2019	2020
Personal liability	55	43	42	25
Bond/miscellaneous	363	304	197	208
Certificate of insurance	12	8	6	5
Commercial automobile	487	286	345	253
Commercial property	437	316	178	258
General liability	1,348	824	649	796
Homeowners	414	319	188	208
Inland marine	173	169	100	256
Identity theft	13	1	4	2
Commercial multi-peril	1,082	798	566	697
Personal automobile	431	256	271	512
Professional liability	512	375	288	327
Workers' compensation	103	98	109	71
Cyber risk	15	27	19	29
Total filing submissions	**5,588**	**3,930**	**3,041**	**3,763**
Actual forms received	**28,744**	**28,042**	**26,744**	**25,941**

Inspection Operations in Texas

The inspections office of the Texas Department of Insurance oversees amusement rides for building code standards as well as commercial and residential buildings for windstorm compliance.

Windstorm operations	2017	2018	2019	2020
Applications processed	33,983	50,341	30,959	42,698
Inspections completed	5,517	6,828	4,050	3,352
Certificates of compliance	32,020	41,784	29,044	28,054
Amusement ride safety	**2017**	**2018**	**2019**	**2020**
Inspection certif. approved	10,521	9,597	9,946	4,869
Injuries reported	89	77	75	19
Non-compliant operators	334	301	159	120

Agent/adjuster licensing

Licenses, certificates, and registrations.

Agents / Adjusters	2017	2018	2019	2020
Life, accident, health	236,521	240,844	251,850	271,049
Property, casualty	139,221	142,146	146,289	149,153
Adjusters	130,855	145,328	153,413	154,106
Life only	42,359	44,477	47,995	57,405
Total, including other types	**616,957**	**641,371**	**671,383**	**704,697**

Premium Rates Compared

Auto Insurance: Average for Coverage by State, 2021

The U.S. average is $1,758. Maine has the least expensive at $1,080. Most expensive states listed below:

1. Michigan $3,141
2. Louisiana $2,601
3. Nevada $2,402
4. Kentucky.............................$2,368
5. DC.....................................$2,188
6. Florida $2,162
7. California............................$2,125
8. New York $2,062
9. Rhode Island.......................$2,040
10. Connecticut $2,036

16. Texas................................$1,823

In dollars, twelve-month rates. Information not available from some states. Source: carinsurance.com.

Homeowners Insurance: Average Premiums by State, 2021

The national average rate was $1,228. Most expensive states listed below:

1. Oklahoma........................... $3,572
2. Kansas $3,174
3. **Texas.................................. $2,940**
4. Florida $2,876
5. Arkansas $2,875
6. Louisiana $2,656
7. Nebraska $2,636
8. Mississippi $2,625
9. Alabama $2,599
10. South Dakota $2,594

In dollars, twelve-month rates. $200,000 dwelling with $1,000 deductible and $100,000 liability. Source: insurance.com.

Texas Insurance Premiums, Payments			
Year	**Total Premiums**	**Claim Payments**	**Ratio**
2019	$182.3 billion	$141.3 billion	77.5
2018	$175.8 billion	$134.2 billion	76.3
2017	$160.5 billion	$134.4 billion	83.7
2016	$152.3 billion	$119.3 billion	78.3

Texas Top 5 Auto Insurers/2020		
Group	**Premiums**	**% of market**
State Farm	$3,255,666,985	14.01
Progressive	3,102,637,389	13.35
Berkshire Hathaway	3,082,237,706	13.26
Allstate	2,824,829,475	12.15
USAA	1,974,516,601	8.5
Texas Top 5 Homeowners Insurers/2020		
State Farm	$1,861,662,578	18.52
Allstate	1,347,747,828	13.41
USAA	1,017,411,403	10.12
Farmers Ins.	1,005,685,319	10.01
Liberty Mutual	646,266,603	6.43
Texas Top 5 Health Insurers/2020		
UnitedHealth	$18,032,763,135	22.67
Health Care Service Corp.	11,252,545,385	14.15
Centene	9,846,533,636	12.38
Humana	7,571,581,460	9.52
Anthem	5,667,059,885	7.13
Texas Top 5 Life Insurers/2020		
New York Life	$770,242,872	5.96
Metropolitan	734,496,097	5.69
Northwestern Mutual	693,474,568	5.37
Prudential of America	584,510,373	4.53
Lincoln National	511,452,224	3.96

Personal Auto	
Companies in state	177
Groups in state	60
Policies (liability)	19,834,608
Total Premiums	$23,241,970,616
Homeowners Insurance	
Companies in state	154
Groups in state	70
Homeowners	4,882,463
Dwelling	775,441
Tenants	1,869,824
Total Premiums	$10,049,707,575
Health Insurance	
Companies in state	476
Groups in state	189
Insured Texans	23,280,468
Texans without insurance	5,233,960
Texas estimated pop.	28,514,428
Total Premiums	$79,528,121,948
Life Insurance	
Companies in state	432
Groups in state	159
Total Premiums	$12,914,861,552

Ten-year history, number of insurance companies operating in Texas										
	2008	**2009**	**2010**	**2011**	**2012**	**2013**	**2014**	**2015**	**2016**	**2017**
Life/Health										
Texas	170	161	161	157	153	149	146	145	145	140
Non-Texas	520	514	504	499	485	483	479	477	475	474
Non-U.S.	0	0	0	0	7	6	6	6	6	6
subtotal	690	675	665	656	645	638	638	628	626	620
Property/Casualty										
Texas	250	250	243	238	236	225	224	235	245	221
Non-Texas	942	948	948	947	935	948	946	952	940	941
Non-U.S.	0	0	0	0	18	17	16	15	16	17
subtotal	1,192	1,198	1,191	1,185	1,189	1,190	1,186	1,202	1,201	1,179
Other*										
Texas	348	353	350	332	324	301	303	295	298	295
Non-Texas	486	504	515	512	487	464	467	462	480	494
Non-U.S.	0	0	0	0	7	6	6	6	6	7
subtotal	834	857	865	844	818	771	776	763	784	796
Grand Total	**2,716**	**2,730**	**2,721**	**2,685**	**2,652**	**2,599**	**2,600**	**2,593**	**2,611**	**2,595**

*_**Other**_ includes: Nonprofit legal services corporations, third-party administrators, continuing care retirement communities, and health maintenance organizations.

Source: 2017 Annual Report, Texas Department of Insurance.

Construction

Texas Non-Residential Contract Awards

The chart below shows the total value of non-residential construction contract awards in Texas by month in billions of dollars. The change over the period from January 2018 to January 2019 was an increase of 21.9 percent.

Month	Total Awards
September 2015	$ 2.572
October 2015	3.261
November 2015	2.140
December 2015	1.697
January 2016	2.410
February 2016	1.469
March 2016	2.540
April 2016	1.840
May 2016	2.147
June 2016	2.455
July 2016	2.009
August 2016	2.373
September 2016	3.090
October 2016	2.517

Month	Total Awards
November 2016	1.803
December 2016	2.312
January 2017	2.952
February 2017	2.007
March 2017	2.447
April 2017	2.938
May 2017	3.561
June 2017	2.904
July 2017	3.415
August 2017	2.469
September 2017	2.345
October 2017	4.794
November 2017	2.152
December 2017	1.822

Month	Total Awards
January 2018	2.212
February 2018	1.938
March 2018	2.194
April 2018	1.689
May 2018	2.907
June 2018	4.517
July 2018	4.595
August 2018	2.192
September 2018	1.774
October 2018	1.834
November 2018	1.998
December 2018	2.567
January 2019	$ 2.697

Source: State Comptroller, 2019.

State Expenditures for Highways

The chart below shows net expenditures (excluding trusts) for state highway construction and maintenance by fiscal year and percent change from the previous year.

Year	Net Expenditures	Percent change
2007	$ 5,359,397,359	4.4
2008	$ 5,208,591,565	– 2.8
2009	$ 4,252,879,534	– 18.3
2010	$ 3,353,467,064	– 21.1
2011	$ 3,774,008,186	12.5
2012	$ 4,186,493,637	10.9
2013	$ 4,491,601,827	7.3
2014	$ 5,305,157,884	18.1
2015	$ 5,192,484,124	– 2.1
2016	$ 6,159,245,504	18.6
2017	$ 6,748,220,204	9.6
2018	$ 6,381,670,144	– 5.4

Source: Texas Annual Cash Reports.

Federal Funds for Highways

The chart below shows fiscal 2019 dispersement of Federal Highway Administration funds for construction and maintenance in thousands of dollars. The column at right shows dollars per capita.

State	Highway Funds	
	Total	Lane-miles
U.S. Total	$ 42,355,403	8,804,092
1. California	3,963,775	394,383
2. Texas	**3,790,154**	**679,917**
3. Florida	2,046,153	274,149
4. New York	1,812,763	239,763
5. Pennsylvania	1,771,931	251,271
6. Illinois	1,535,424	306,614
7. Ohio	1,447,596	262,377
8. Georgia	1,394,444	272,017
9. Michigan	1,137,059	256,207
10. North Carolina	1,126,340	227,544
11. Virginia	1,098,983	163,648

Source: Federal Highway Administration, 2019.

Texas Single-Family Building Permits

Year	No. of Dwelling Units		Avg. Value per Unit ($)	
	Units	% change	Value	% change
1980	67,870	–	$ 51.900	–
1981	66,161	– 2.5	55,700	7.3
1982	78,714	19.0	53,800	– 3.4
1983	103,252	31.2	63,400	17.8
1984	84,565	– 18.1	68,000	7.3
1985	67,964	– 19.6	71,000	4.4
1986	59,143	– 13.0	72,200	1.7
1987	43,975	– 25.6	77,700	7.6
1988	35,908	– 18.3	83,900	8.0
1989	36,658	2.1	90,400	7.7
1990	38,233	4.3	95,500	5.6
1991	46,209	20.9	92,800	– 2.8
1992	59,543	28.9	95,400	2.8
1993	69,964	17.5	96,400	1.0
1994	70,452	0.7	99,500	3.2
1995	70,421	0.0	100,300	0.8
1996	83,132	18.1	102,100	1.8
1997	82,228	– 1.1	108,900	6.7
1998	99,912	21.5	112,800	3.6
1999	101,928	2.0	118,800	5.3
2000	108,782	6.7	127,100	7.0
2001	111,915	2.9	124,700	– 1.9
2002	122,913	9.8	126,400	1.4
2003	137,493	11.9	128,800	1.9
2004	151,384	10.1	137,600	6.8
2005	166,203	9.8	144,300	4.9
2006	163,032	– 1.9	155,100	7.5
2007	120,366	– 26.2	169,000	9.0
2008	81,107	– 32.6	174,100	3.0
2009	68,230	– 15.9	167,900	– 3.6
2010	68,170	– 0.1	179,200	6.7
2011	67,254	– 1.3	191,100	6.6
2012	81,926	21.8	192,300	0.6
2013	93,478	14.1	197,500	2.7
2014	103,045	10.2	208,900	5.8
2015	105,448	2.3	217,100	3.9
2016	106,511	1.0	220,300	1.5
2017	116,766	9.6	$ 226,100	2.6

Real Estate Center at Texas A&M University, 2019.

Commercial Fishing in Texas

Total Texas coastwide landings in 2017 were more than 93.3 million pounds, valued at more than $236.9 million. Shrimp accounted for most of the weight and value of all seafood landed (see chart at bottom).

The Coastal Fisheries Division of the Texas Parks and Wildlife Department manages the marine fishery resources of Texas' four million acres of saltwater, including the bays and estuaries and out to nine nautical miles in the Gulf of Mexico.

The division works toward sustaining fishery populations at levels that are necessary to ensure replenishable stocks of commercially and recreationally important species.

It also focuses on habitat conservation and restoration and leads the agency research on all water-related issues, including assuring adequate in-stream flows for rivers and sufficient freshwater inflows for bays and estuaries. ☆

Leading U.S. Ports in 2017

Rank	Port	Value in Dollars (in millions)
1	New Bedford, MA	$ 389.5
2	Dutch Harbor, AK	173.0
3	Naknek-King Salmon, AK	154.0
4	Kodiak, AK	152.0
5	Alaska Peninsula, AK	111.5
14	**Brownsville–Port Isabel, TX**	**62.2**

Source: National Ocean Economics Program, 2019.

Top Fishing Ports for Texas in 2017

Rank	Port	Pounds (000)	Dollars (000)
1	Brownsville–Port Isabel	23,000	$ 62,800
2	Palacios	20,200	54,500
3	Galveston	18,800	48,700
4	Port Arthur	17,100	37,100

Source: National Ocean Economics Program, 2019.

Landings by State 2017

Rank	States	Pounds (000)	Dollars (000)
	Total, U.S.	9,923,678	$ 5,428,140
1	Alaska	6,004,882	1,764,462
2	Massachusetts	242,137	605,250
3	Maine	208,677	511,315
4	Louisiana	898,425	370,222
5	Washington	215,976	277,740
6	Florida	87,818	238,855
7	**Texas**	**93,361**	**236,993**
8	Virginia	343,964	183,203

Source: National Marine Fisheries Service, 2019.

Texas Commercial Fishery Landings by Species

	2017		2015		2012	
Species	**Pounds**	**Value**	**Pounds**	**Value**	**Pounds**	**Value**
Shrimp, Brown	49,857,425	$ 115,006,107	52,552,655	$ 96,897,374	43,707,869	$ 92,254,541
Shrimp, White	28,914,208	74,195,669	16,644,175	45,591,742	24,100,143	62,970,321
Oyster, Eastern	3,503,518	20,403,679	1,582,685	8,232,088	5,817,191	21,302,111
Snapper, Red	2,212,786	9,881,455	2,151,587	9,387,187	1,122,665	4,447,884
Shrimp, marine, other	101,960	62,835	25,844	9,794	1,023,748	4,021,505
Crab, Blue	4,126,389	5,415,937	3,914,228	5,109,692	2,849,739	2,875,694
Drum, Black	1,926,052	2,457,801	1,812,617	2,003,383	1,612,023	1,485,663
Snapper, Vermilion	149.071	442.915	306,820	919,931	511,224	1,433,985
Croaker, Atlantic	87,768	766,557	90,084	745,8567	88,918	740,110
Total, including others	**93,361,097**	**$236,992,832**	**80,356,029**	**$173,418,614**	**90,557,774**	**$213,313,076**

Source: National Ocean Economics Program and National Marine Fisheries Service, 2019.

Tourism, Travel Impact Estimates by County, 2017

This analysis covers most travel in Texas including business, pleasure, shopping, to attend meetings and other destinations. **Spending** is all spending on goods and services by visitors at a destination. **Earnings** are wages and salaries of employees and income of proprietors of businesses that receive travel expenditures. Employment associated with these businesses are listed under **jobs**. **Local tax** receipts are from hotel taxes, local sales taxes, auto rental taxes, etc., as separate from state tax receipts, as well as spending by travel employees and property taxes attributable to travel businesses and employees. *Source: Office of the Governor, Economic Development and Tourism.*

County	Jobs	Spending	Earnings	Local tax
		(in thousands)		
Anderson	681	$54,813	$14,056	$1,575
Andrews	433	29,194	6,705	752
Angelina	1,530	130,608	31,166	3,140
Aransas	1,288	102,093	33,087	3,397
Archer	9	1,864	172	17
Armstrong	8	1,226	95	6
Atascosa*	740	64,047	21,762	2,178
Austin	420	42,686	10,011	847
Bailey	73	4,441	1,298	132
Bandera	734	29,633	21,615	2,178
Bastrop	1,973	155,312	69,207	6,997
Baylor	28	6,299	772	72
Bee*	393	40,094	9,350	1,009
Bell	5,352	445,138	137,258	14,207
Bexar	69,220	7,106,223	2,398,606	314,164
Blanco	194	15,969	4,366	522
Borden	1	108	12	0
Bosque	200	16,614	8,002	692
Bowie	1,874	189,350	36,794	4,247
Brazoria	4,843	372,276	111,490	11,817
Brazos	6,162	479,396	151,433	17,196
Brewster	1,583	74,300	39,438	3,489
Briscoe	8	1,271	166	10
Brooks	77	12,926	1,903	235
Brown	642	50,158	16,441	1,827
Burleson	161	14,514	4,256	342
Burnet	1,130	82,449	32,877	3,425
Caldwell	213	33,108	8,582	788
Calhoun	393	42,702	10,801	1,504
Callahan	54	3,839	1,065	74
Cameron	9,571	801,598	212,848	27,058
Camp	86	15,975	1,693	127
Carson	22	5,837	414	27
Cass	270	20,510	5,267	463
Castro	21	2,502	447	32
Chambers	248	39,120	8,064	1,630
Cherokee	449	34,960	8,793	784
Childress	188	14,453	3,241	619
Clay	44	20,575	778	56
Cochran	13	870	200	13
Coke	45	3,472	709	44
Coleman	80	6,742	1,518	154
Collin	15,658	1,500,619	645,351	66,202
Collingsworth	15	1,889	246	19

County	Jobs	Spending	Earnings	Local tax
		(in thousands)		
Colorado	507	55,988	13,652	1,195
Comal	4,690	405,262	148,845	15,611
Comanche	130	13,744	2,665	256
Concho	10	1,200	407	27
Cooke	577	60,728	16,502	1,792
Coryell	497	44,308	13,006	1,298
Cottle	10	1,677	181	12
Crane	36	3,322	626	85
Crockett	185	27,688	3,068	303
Crosby	25	1,609	442	30
Culberson	184	37,033	5,482	809
Dallam	283	14,121	6,144	618
Dallas	97,079	9,045,095	4,363,486	427,939
Dawson	210	17,710	3,443	373
Deaf Smith	178	16,175	3,605	461
Delta	14	1,515	311	21
Denton	6,806	713,091	245,921	27,936
DeWitt*	607	58,669	15,336	1,514
Dickens	7	483	137	11
Dimmit*	245	31,312	5,483	887
Donley	94	6,418	1,905	225
Duval	59	10,187	1,060	114
Eastland	245	16,171	4,416	555
Ector	2,522	425,258	86,756	14,726
Edwards	7	873	178	10
Ellis	1,256	167,432	47,721	5,452
El Paso	13,850	1,465,780	440,993	50,597
Erath	493	44,969	13,134	1,334
Falls	99	10,267	2,303	255
Fannin	119	14,966	2,640	310
Fayette	484	48,373	10,680	1,233
Fisher	7	992	167	13
Floyd	32	4,916	685	46
Foard	4	370	94	8
Fort Bend	4,998	518,759	173,847	18,545
Franklin	112	9,456	1,770	200
Freestone	380	46,148	5,662	666
Frio*	375	34,848	8,474	1,004
Gaines	166	16,778	3,689	439
Galveston	10,840	989,973	289,894	40,726
Garza	102	9,724	2,923	225
Gillespie	1,001	102,974	30,436	4,688

**Oil and gas production in recent years may affect travel impact estimates.*

Travel Impacts by Origin of Visitor, 2017

Origin	Spending ($Billions)	Earnings ($Billions)	Jobs (Thousand)	Tax Receipts ($Millions) Local	State	**Federal
Other U.S.	$28.1	$10.3	283.8	$783	$1,459	$1,754
International	$6.8	$1.9	62.6	$150	$344	$280
Texas	$29.7	$9.0	284.6	$595	$1,536	$1,414
All visitors	**$64.6**	**$21.2**	**631.0**	**$1,528**	**$3,338**	**$3,448**
Other Travel*	$10.2	$4.5	46.6	0	0	$1,106
Total Travel	**$74.7**	**$25.7**	**677.6**	**$1,528**	**$3,338**	**$4,554**

*Other Travel includes resident air travel, travel arrangement, and convention / trade shows.
**Federal includes motor vehicle fuel and airline ticket taxes, as well as income taxes attributable to travel industry income.

Source: Survey for the Office of Governor.

County	Jobs	Spending (in thousands)	Earnings	Local tax
Glasscock	3	258	44	2
Goliad	62	10,214	1,883	217
Gonzales*	217	28,781	5,255	680
Gray	537	42,017	13,062	1,246
Grayson	1,632	208,497	39,849	4,404
Gregg	2,586	219,822	60,375	6,303
Grimes	229	19,130	5,604	500
Guadalupe	2,002	165,633	70,231	6,524
Hale	703	48,242	12,610	1,382
Hall	13	2,283	311	34
Hamilton	56	6,171	1,365	160
Hansford	21	2,026	338	45
Hardeman	62	5,701	885	104
Hardin	493	43,916	10,275	1,138
Harris	109,463	12,165,938	5,247,543	594,078
Harrison	688	88,366	15,150	1,189
Hartley	12	1,053	205	15
Haskell	97	5,829	1,416	216
Hays	3,820	348,914	120,122	12,830
Hemphill	65	8,637	1,517	344
Henderson	496	110,527	21,561	1,980
Hidalgo	16,863	1,268,691	389,497	38,656
Hill	502	58,226	10,199	946
Hockley	347	24,281	6,627	548
Hood	532	63,134	17,087	1,951
Hopkins	532	66,320	13,099	1,230
Houston	237	32,484	5,913	433
Howard	862	114,305	19,329	3,079
Hudspeth	16	5,138	414	20
Hunt	826	108,037	30,989	2,747
Hutchinson	397	38,076	9,210	1,013
Irion	16	10,120	416	21
Jack	39	4,347	747	66
Jackson	102	11,836	2,443	252
Jasper	520	38,870	11,408	1,198

County	Jobs	Spending (in thousands)	Earnings	Local tax
Jeff Davis	115	8,699	4,360	188
Jefferson	6,088	548,993	128,520	16,527
Jim Hogg	55	5,015	1,251	99
Jim Wells	736	66,125	16,358	1,251
Johnson	1,155	150,770	34,509	3,954
Jones	123	8,247	2,585	175
Karnes*	446	54,288	13,195	1,434
Kaufman	825	137,285	26,809	2,798
Kendall	1,276	87,004	32,197	2,814
Kenedy	13	829	320	13
Kent	7	714	142	7
Kerr	1,543	98,360	40,388	3,936
Kimble	138	16,466	2,580	388
King	0	43	7	0
Kinney	108	5,691	2,081	115
Kleberg	524	57,610	14,091	1,539
Knox	18	2,760	375	29
La Salle*	595	37,187	14,650	1,745
Lamar	867	70,867	21,008	2,099
Lamb	101	12,804	1,905	175
Lampasas	164	15,165	3,361	402
Lavaca	143	16,967	4,178	450
Lee	207	24,239	6,297	513
Leon	247	32,534	5,156	630
Liberty	438	53,195	18,276	1,633
Limestone	132	18,430	2,810	405
Lipscomb	8	2,232	200	12
Live Oak*	261	35,765	5,181	710
Llano	2,202	106,885	47,838	4,136
Loving	1	44	7	0
Lubbock	8,672	757,603	279,900	25,832
Lynn	15	1,096	252	17
Madison	104	10,890	2,260	308
Marion	129	8,540	2,062	213

Oil and gas production in recent years may affect travel impact estimates.

County	Jobs	Spending	Earnings	Local tax
		(in thousands)		
Martin	93	17,482	1,737	101
Mason	52	3,045	738	85
Matagorda	1,045	66,052	23,286	2,808
Maverick*	657	59,383	14,697	1,830
McCulloch	156	18,494	2,546	471
McLennan	5,772	556,876	149,083	16,348
McMullen*	13	1,960	468	19
Medina	379	43,673	8,968	768
Menard	14	2,612	305	25
Midland	3,687	544,447	104,044	16,187
Milam	314	28,447	6,931	627
Mills	21	2,784	492	56
Mitchell	62	9,703	1,863	242
Montague	287	18,370	5,146	493
Montgomery	7,133	632,996	311,864	31,168
Moore	389	42,936	7,343	1,287
Morris	43	5,510	995	79
Motley	5	736	101	7
Nacgdoches	1,120	78,953	21,569	2,620
Navarro	599	50,688	12,329	1,426
Newton	32	4,796	716	57
Nolan	399	25,312	9,195	1,235
Nueces	14,895	1,140,074	385,275	49,230
Ochiltree	196	18,856	3,658	527
Oldham	53	8,595	934	87
Orange	1,099	120,943	27,933	2,940
Palo Pinto	555	71,755	13,719	1,178
Panola	194	17,446	3,559	567
Parker	855	110,602	25,987	2,631
Parmer	39	4,856	731	64
Pecos	586	62,303	9,803	2,496
Polk	795	56,603	18,565	1,490
Potter	8,312	755,558	207,026	26,748
Presidio	79	15,432	2,947	655
Rains	92	8535	2,888	204
Randall	1,260	113,680	23,831	2,411
Reagan	172	11,551	3,030	160
Real	94	7,497	2,420	181
Red River	33	4,298	1,002	70
Reeves	1,342	120,899	25,076	5,471
Refugio	108	21,609	2,531	257
Roberts	2	1,004	43	2
Robertson	246	22,106	4,572	700
Rockwall	891	97,352	27,912	3,534
Runnels	82	6,898	1,441	126
Rusk	346	36,560	7,641	786
Sabine	117	12,601	2,428	139
S.Augustne	109	7,437	1,918	131
SanJacinto	151	11,857	2,774	158
SanPatricio	1,326	140,681	37,759	4,704
San Saba	74	4,489	1,025	101
Schleicher	7	457	130	9
Scurry	572	37,976	12,099	1,176
Shackelford	84	2,288	1,533	112
Shelby	527	34,918	8,878	893
Sherman	29	5,086	453	31
Smith	3,924	354,399	104,858	10,487
Somervell	156	17,600	4,252	608
Starr	245	27,636	5,628	632
Stephens	82	7,147	1,766	192
Sterling	16	2,356	226	16
Stonewall	20	1,057	280	17
Sutton	138	7,937	2,059	326
Swisher	44	3,536	860	68
Tarrant	76,486	5,613,557	4,283,738	345,928
Taylor	3,789	422,356	100,711	12,755
Terrell	14	1,098	199	8
Terry	201	11,335	3,480	411
Throckmrton	11	3,336	202	13
Titus	518	55,034	11,298	1,326
Tom Green	3,354	218,875	77,976	6,920
Travis	56,325	5,666,532	2,009,187	267,471
Trinity	225	10,993	5,977	390
Tyler	140	10,935	2,415	235
Upshur	180	22,334	3,725	344
Upton	54	3,252	801	94
Uvalde	834	82,685	20,689	2,964
Val Verde	662	55,972	16,178	1,854
Van Zandt	485	51,397	10,934	1,004
Victoria	1,524	215,854	41,638	5,326
Walker	1,132	106,675	24,187	2,568
Waller	229	50,695	8,400	1,223
Ward	856	53,952	15,760	2,459
Washington	672	91,919	17,082	1,904
Webb*	6,103	568,444	154,510	16,024
Wharton	484	41,084	9,963	1,292
Wheeler	155	19,477	3,033	409
Wichita	3,371	219,588	56,433	6,643
Wilbarger	255	22,532	5,211	705
Willacy	162	25,687	4,199	386
Williamson	5,620	627,148	176,440	21,953
Wilson*	395	34,179	10,101	850
Winkler	93	11,658	1,667	294
Wise	898	58,350	17,172	1,668
Wood	366	26,630	8,406	566
Yoakum	73	6,360	1,435	199
Young	313	23,258	7,276	666
Zapata	181	15,747	2,947	218
Zavala	45	7,351	902	80

**Oil and gas production in recent years may affect travel impact estimates.*

Telecommunications Trends to High-Speed, Wireless

The chart below shows the move to wireless communications, and the decline in the number of telephone land lines in Texas and nationwide. The chart also shows the growth of high-speed Internet use in the state and in the United States. *Sources: Federal Communications Commission and Public Utility Commission of Texas.*

	2000	2005	2009	2011	2013	2016
Mobile Wireless Telephone Subscribers						
Texas	6,705,000	14,424,000	21,008,000	23,482,000	24,890,000	28,840,000
U.S.	90,643,000	192,053,000	261,284,000	290,304,000	310,691,000	395,900,000
Local Telephone Wirelines/Landlines						
Texas	13,657,444	12,310,000	10,500,000	9,590,000	8,840,000	8,110,000
U.S.	188,499,586	157,041,487	152,945,000	143,319,000	133,233,000	121,331,000
Internet Connections						
Texas	253,000	2,943,000	7,484,000	17,487,000	23,612,000	30,171,000
U.S.	4,107,000	42,518,000	102,043,000	206,124,000	275,608,000	369,416,000

U.S. Internet Lines by Technology (in thousands)

	aDSL	Cable Modem	Fiber	Satellite	Fixed Wireless	Mobile Wireless	Total
2013	30,657	52,760	7,250	1,623	810	190,706	284,692
2017	25,506	64,059	12,906	1,826	1,245	302,562	408,816

The chart below shows the percent of the population that in 2016 had access to advanced, high-quality voice, data, graphics, and video offerings. The chart shows that almost 28 percent of the rural population in Texas is without that access. *Source: Federal Communications Commission 2018 Broadband Progress Report.*

Percent with access to advanced telecommunications, 2016 (25 Mbps/3 Mbps)

	Population with access		Urban with access		Rural with access	
	Total	Percent	Population	Percent	Population	Percent
Texas	27,763,538	93.4 %	23,251,241	97.6 %	4,512,297	72.3 %
U.S.	313,389,000	81.2 %	226,701,000	89.7 %	27,694,000	45.7 %

A telecommunications repair employee works beside a strip mall on US I-10 and Fry Road in Katy on March 24, 2006. Photo by Bill Jacobus/Flickr (CC).

Texas Electric Grids: Demand and Capacity

- The Electric Reliability Council of Texas (**ERCOT**) operates the electric grid for 75 percent of the state.
- The Panhandle, South Plains, and a corner of Northeast Texas are under the Southwest Power Pool (**SPP**).
- El Paso and the far western corner of the Trans Pecos are under the Western Electric Coordinating Council (**WECC**).
- The southeast corner of Texas is under the **SERC** Reliability Corporation.

The councils were first formed in 1968 to ensure adequate bulk power supply.

	Actual (in megawatts)						**Estimate**		**Projected**
	2011	**2012**	**2013**	**2014**	**2015**	**2016**	**2017**	**2018**	**2019**
ERCOT demand	68,416	66,548	67,245	66,454	69,877	71,110	69,512	73,473	74,853
capacity	69,595	73,219	74,396	73,950	76,798	78,466	78,251	77,558	78,085
% margin*	1.7	9.1	9.6	10.1	9.0	9.4	11.1	9.3	7.4
SPP demand	54,991	53,177	47,647	46,076	48,894	51,883	51,577	51,687	52,422
capacity	62,044	72,802	71.897	65,302	63,426	63,350	67,780	68,714	67,618
% margin	11.4	27.0	33.8	29,4	22.9	18.1	31.4	32.9	29.0
WECC demand	117,755	130,465	132,875	127,092	131,072	139,431	136,903	136,679	136,244
capacity	147,147	147,527	167,171	162,119	164,417	165,881	160,337	164,960	163,492
% margin	20.0	11.6	20.5	21.6	20.3	15.9	14.6	17.1	16.1
SERC demand	161,995	158,041	121,810	123,866	127,742	128,985	127,575	128,851	129,811
capacity	201,103	198,140	165,171	159,822	159,279	160,896	160,253	161,117	162,434
% margin	19.4	20.2	26.3	22.5	19.8	19.8	20.4	20.3	20.1
U.S. demand	759,642	768,943	759,310	723,411	741,056	768,510	752,080	755,578	760,642
capacity	892,426	927,060	944,515	917,167	916,439	923,873	931,379	963,135	996,104
% margin	14.9	17.1	19.6	21.1	19.1	16.8	19.3	21.6	23.6

Capacity Margin is the amount of unused available capability of an electric power system at* ***summer peak* *load as a percentage of capacity resources. Source: Federal Energy Information Administration, March 2019. 2017–2019 data from ERCOT.*

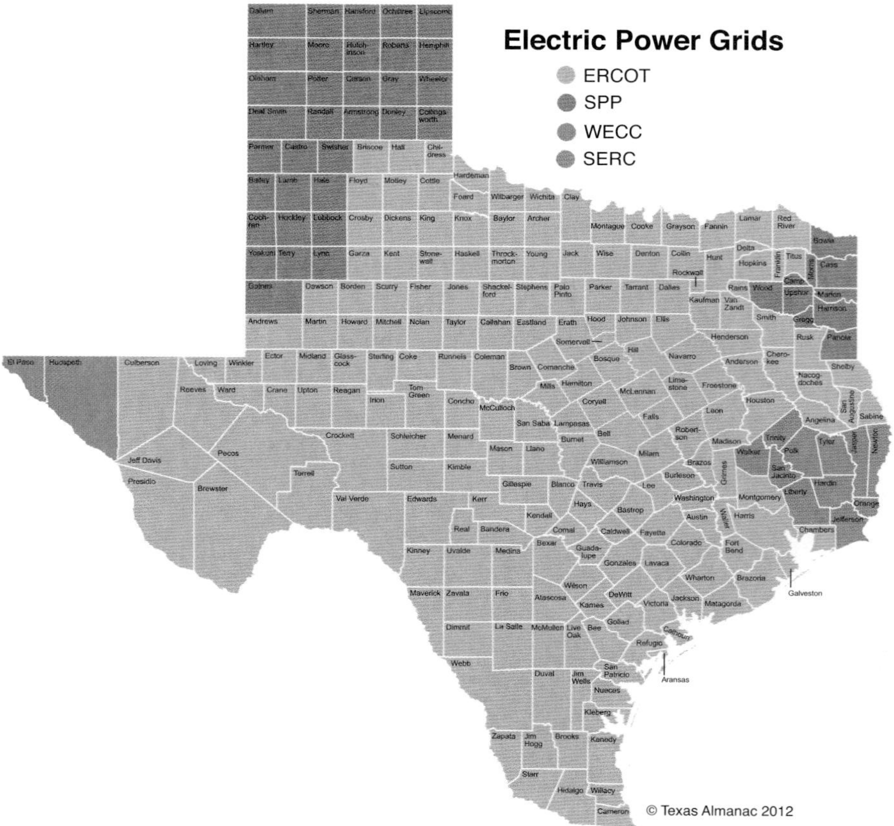

Wind turbines stand in West Texas on February 13, 2019. Photo by Jonathan Cutrer/Flickr (CC).

Wind Energy Continues Expansion in State

Sources: U.S. Energy Information Administration and the American Wind Energy Association, 2019.

Texas continues to lead the nation in installed wind capacity and generation. In the first quarter of 2019, Texas had 25 percent of the nation's installed wind capacity, reaching almost 25,000 megawatts. Iowa was second in installed wind capacity, at 8,957 megawatts.

With Texas' significant growth in turbine development, wind generation was responsible for about 16 percent of total electricity generation in the state in 2018, more than double what it was in 2011 at 6.9 percent.

The Texas plains continue to see rapid growth in wind farms, while more recently expansion has begun offshore on the Gulf Coast.

In all, Texas has five of the ten largest wind generation projects in the country. Roscoe Wind Farm, which stretches across Nolan, Mitchell, Scurry, and Fisher counties, is the largest in the state, with a capacity of 782 MW.

It is third in the nation to Alta farm in California at 1,548 MW and Shepherds Flat in Oregon at 845 MW. ☆

Installed Wind Capacity in megawatts (MW)		
YEAR	**Texas**	**U.S.**
2019 (Q1)	24,895	97,227
2018	24,899	96,487
2017	22,637	89,078
2016	20,321	82,183
2015	14,208	66,008
2014	14,098	65,879
2013	12,354	61,110
2012	10,648	49,802
2011	10,394	46,919
2010	10,089	40,267
2009	9,403	34,863
2008	7,427	24,651
2007	4,296	16,596
2005	1,995	9,149
2000	181	2,566

2018 Renewable Energy as Portion of Net Generation of Electricity

(in thousand megawatt hours.)

State	Total Electric	Total Renewable	% Renewable	Hydroelectric	Wind
1. Washington	116,763	90,734	77.7 %	81,576	7,356
2. California	197,227	84,302	42.7 %	25,898	13,650
3. Texas	474,777	82,104	17.3 %	1,433	75,753
4. Oregon	84,836	45,679	53.8 %	36,729	7,137
5. New York	134,356	38,000	28.3 %	30,911	4,383
6. Iowa	64,187	22,922	35.7 %	999	21,685
United States	4,178,000	713,000	17.1 %	292,000	275,000

Source: Energy Information Administration, 2019.

Texas Oil Production History

The table shows the year of oil or gas discovery in each county, oil production in 2019 and 2020, and total oil production from date of discovery to Jan. 1, 2021. The counties omitted have not produced oil.

The table has been compiled by the *Texas Almanac* from information provided in past years by the Texas Mid-Continent Oil & Gas Assoc., which used data from the U.S. Bureau of Mines and the Texas state comptroller. Since 1970, production figures have been compiled from records of the Railroad Commission of Texas. The figures in the final column are cumulative of all previously published figures. The change in sources, due to different techniques, may create some discrepancies in year-to-year comparisons among counties.

County	Year of Discovery	Production in Barrels*		Total Production to Jan. 1, 2021
		2019	2020	
Anderson	1928	594,778	527,888	310,561,329
Andrews	1929	39,498,552	37,946,849	3,289,958,078
Angelina	1936	0	0	1,002,699
Aransas	1936	22,664	17,812	89,412,574
Archer	1911	893,043	765,033	510,779,083
Atascosa	1917	25,162,285	19,650,637	334,091,181
Austin	1915	356,351	284,575	122,191,361
Bandera	1995	1,532	512	46,409
Bastrop	1913	97,297	69,293	18,940,681
Baylor	1924	72,503	60,849	59,643,830
Bee	1929	236,212	191,588	115,266,222
Bell	1980	0	0	446
Bexar	1889	76,499	67,986	37,509,849
Borden	1949	7,878,426	6,628,106	469,855,575
Bosque	2006	0	0	309
Bowie	1944	22,958	22,679	7,242,524
Brazoria	1902	3,133,469	2,691,952	1,316,951,552
Brazos	1942	8,001,246	8,426,069	201,943,704
Brewster	1969	0	0	56
Briscoe	1982	0	0	4,065
Brooks	1935	136,260	72,949	183,252,609
Brown	1917	77,472	67,305	55,053,365
Burleson	1938	16,272,084	15,383,341	276,536,814
Caldwell	1922	1,077,222	942,118	299,445,335
Calhoun	1935	129,117	81,311	108,735,810
Callahan	1923	106,767	98,005	88,641,029
Cameron	1944	0	0	480,603
Camp	1940	80,903	55,998	31,447,023
Carson	1921	114,242	89,603	184,187,986
Cass	1936	463,886	485,392	119,458,572
Chambers	1916	2,426,819	1,987,292	943,279,000
Cherokee	1926	194,323	152,110	76,914,561
Childress	1961	4,914	1,928	1,814,292
Clay	1917	436,011	372,915	212,707,708
Cochran	1936	2,771,917	2,627,186	556,184,024
Coke	1942	317,812	234,446	231,848,743
Coleman	1902	196,538	152,607	98,874,429
Collin	1963	0	0	53,000
Collngswrth	1936	4,905	3,700	1,303,956
Colorado	1932	142,061	130,944	48,478,581
Comanche	1918	58,433	41,725	6,634,872
Concho	1940	274,724	219,546	31,210,035
Cooke	1924	1,038,153	875,117	420,601,518
Coryell	1964	0	0	1,100
Cottle	1955	95,657	81,695	6,688,838
Crane	1926	7,664,933	6,990,103	1,883,946,084
Crockett	1925	6,254,570	5,260,862	471,729,509
Crosby	1955	919,997	663,291	38,613,028
Culberson	1953	897,535	482,202	101,433,832
Dallam	2015	0	0	116
Dallas	1986	0	0	232
Dawson	1934	3,327,123	3,124,305	440,937,183
Delta	1984	0	0	65,089
Denton	1937	21,372	11,132	11,951,483
DeWitt	1930	41,828,686	33,391,255	589,635,125
Dickens	1953	431,729	356,921	30,437,721
Dimmit	1943	41,036,494	31,896,966	541,740,208
Donley	1967	0	0	3,143
Duval	1905	882,327	772,410	603,867,578
Eastland	1917	146,574	124,332	160,530,151
Ector	1926	20,239,577	16,840,739	3,437,595,733
Edwards	1946	1,625	1,901	617,257
Ellis	1953	0	32	844,860
Erath	1917	1,267	476	2,298,570
Falls	1937	1,424	785	896,350
Fannin	1980	0	0	13,354
Fayette	1943	1,716,432	2,021,316	182,536,536
Fisher	1928	1,367,812	1,825,000	262,910,313
Floyd	1952	0	0	268,610
Foard	1929	74,338	64,062	25,524,946
Fort Bend	1919	745,937	696,511	715,398,653
Franklin	1936	398,058	284,625	184,009,930
Freestone	1916	24,202	16,925	47,299,677
Frio	1934	7,228,834	6,978,801	206,617,109
Gaines	1935	23,532,295	21,721,970	2,566,837,208
Galveston	1922	163,322	127,943	465,078,931
Garza	1926	2,196,451	1,909,215	382,013,465
Glasscock	1925	51,106,016	49,288,064	574,818,570
Goliad	1930	206,493	127,296	89,613,209
Gonzales	1902	41,688,233	36,270,882	383,273,749
Gray	1925	876,144	896,713	688,840,329
Grayson	1930	1,012,472	888,413	276,171,131
Gregg	1931	1,383,663	1,164,978	3,321,498,571
Grimes	1952	367,883	293,559	27,017,013
Guadalupe	1922	707,778	628,980	218,935,872
Hale	1946	1,131,070	979,498	206,585,490
Hamilton	1938	26	17	164,720
Hansford	1937	249,697	206,287	42,767,157
Hardeman	1944	795,020	568,807	97,232,986
Hardin	1893	913,367	760,190	464,372,711
Harris	1905	779,498	761,738	1,396,751,943

Total includes condensate production.

County	Year of Discovery	Production in Barrels*		Total Production to Jan. 1, 2021
		2019	2020	
Harrison	1928	467,050	439,117	104,907,904
Hartley	1937	222,983	187,934	11,511,391
Haskell	1929	883,984	771,130	124,448,894
Hays	1956	0	0	296
Hemphill	1955	403,516	339,804	75,363,591
Henderson	1934	434,876	349,741	184,434,355
Hidalgo	1934	49,471	30,145	136,238,874
Hill	1929	0	0	80,670
Hockley	1937	11,965,204	10,814,434	1,876,844,456
Hood	1958	0	0	2,860,142
Hopkins	1936	153,160	139,621	93,161,245
Houston	1934	506,394	360,641	79,350,048
Howard	1925	87,623,802	96,471,676	1,208,960,682
Hudspeth	2008	0	0	59
Hunt	1942	459	467	2,027,944
Hutchnson	1923	474,216	376,819	541,468,656
Irion	1928	13,061,688	9,889,670	214,805,771
Jack	1923	845,674	820,078	220,308,421
Jackson	1934	2,326,311	1,758,113	700,716,814
Jasper	1928	302,886	260,298	46,404,824
Jeff Davis	1980	0	0	20,866
Jefferson	1901	519,563	398,709	578,631,223
Jim Hogg	1921	14,755	15,032	114,403,405
Jim Wells	1931	81,647	63,631	464,670,197
Johnson	1962	0	0	556,906
Jones	1926	420,371	483,981	230,656,349
Karnes	1930	107,666,119	93,733,010	993,166,760
Kaufman	1948	57,783	43,120	25,764,445
Kenedy	1947	115,691	81,073	43,323,490
Kent	1946	3,242,442	2,637,337	631,247,258
Kerr	1982	0	0	79,044
Kimble	1939	259	292	102,621
King	1943	1,808,002	1,475,697	204,357,798
Kinney	1960	0	0	402
Kleberg	1919	92,160	52,753	342,599,871
Knox	1946	176,789	174,992	65,121,138
Lamb	1945	226,387	203,522	428,431,680
Lampasas	1985	0	0	43,890,960
La Salle	1940	60,521,023	48,048,112	108569246
Lavaca	1941	7,026,029	6,219,215	87,317,545
Lee	1939	2,291,985	2,392,393	157,408,964
Leon	1936	605,774	429,998	79,863,595
Liberty	1904	791,523	600,442	562,936,406
Limestone	1920	63,382	59,905	121,426,749
Lipscomb	1956	991,813	739,650	99,614,806
Live Oak	1930	12,554,220	9,927,934	221,046,347
Llano	1978	0	0	647
Loving	1921	83,047,027	88,548,818	532,022,988
Lubbock	1941	955,535	824,244	89,020,852
Lynn	1950	275,045	179,177	24,593,435
Madison	1946	3,018,718	2,135,717	70,088,178
Marion	1910	493,628	354,591	59,982,745
Martin	1945	134,016,957	144,970,375	966,107,872
Matagorda	1901	187,670	189,534	292,046,458
Maverick	1929	1,162,465	968,981	69,882,459
McCulloch	1938	43,345	34,238	2,695,334
McLennan	1902	744	443	351,177
McMullen	1922	30,317,698	25,309,501	410,520,930
Medina	1901	95,691	77,546	12,513,738
Menard	1946	96,541	84,049	9,474,984
Midland	1945	189,503,922	189,294,777	1,537,052,962
Milam	1921	2,460,458	1,730,926	32,019,895
Mills	1982	0	0	28,122
Mitchell	1920	2,408,655	2,087,392	277,826,071
Montague	1919	946,145	794,511	356,696,403
Montgmry	1931	837,502	805,797	790,848,796
Moore	1926	244,833	191,405	34,438,439
Morris	2004	26,124	29,455	129,624
Motley	1957	38,937	33,134	11,487,581
Nacgdches	1866	9,393	7,855	7,365,112
Navarro	1894	131,865	114,488	222,821,568
Newton	1937	523,233	523,022	74,804,177
Nolan	1939	1,133,980	1,004,301	220,115,272
Nueces	1930	165,370	127,315	574,994,320
Ochiltree	1951	4,076,815	3,156,820	224,216,313
Oldham	1957	353,709	294,439	20,757,634
Orange	1913	424,871	338,203	172,365,391
Palo Pinto	1902	102,603	74,278	28,745,288
Panola	1917	239,893	205,001	122,174,798
Parker	1942	770	459	5,634,974
Parmer	1963	0	0	144,000
Pecos	1926	35,873,489	39,166,108	1,999,296,380
Polk	1930	445,335	380,073	145,187,923
Potter	1925	698,799	401,562	15,244,541
Presidio	1980	0	0	4,641
Rains	1955	0	0	148,911
Reagan	1923	52,531,529	46,612,896	847,090,468
Real	2003	1,015	781	31,231
Red River	1951	71,879	63,461	9,464,819
Reeves	1939	116,180,451	99,701,067	661,366,162
Refugio	1920	2,158,154	1,942,609	1,371,298,287
Roberts	1945	1,476,099	906,479	77,732,568
Robertson	1944	1,988,016	1,961,127	48,323,975
Runnels	1927	337,349	267,581	154,671,193
Rusk	1930	1,375,959	1,268,634	1,868,042,243
Sabine	1981	951	294	4,993,930
S.Augustine	1947	16,745	11,426	3,504,337
S. Jacinto	1940	47,299	53,113	30,125,349
S. Patricio	1930	377,708	248,037	498,453,039
San Saba	1982	0	0	499,480
Schleicher	1934	264,885	214,069	94,782,273
Scurry	1923	15,539,814	14,736,493	2,277,236,873
Shackelford	1910	352,865	313,047	191,308,614
Shelby	1917	25,672	18,141	6,118,387
Sherman	1938	62,066	69,958	10,445,628
Smith	1931	1,282,130	1,154,798	286,426,639
Somervell	1978	0	0	95,568
Starr	1929	341,690	245,817	318,023,085
Stephens	1916	1,790,012	1,572,887	373,137,393
Sterling	1947	670,508	548,698	104,506,171
Stonewall	1938	1,776,098	1,249,718	286,991,561

Total includes condensate production.

County	Year of Discovery	Production in Barrels*		Total Production to Jan. 1, 2021
		2019	2020	
Sutton	1948	28,290	18,570	9,251,811
Swisher	1981	0	0	6
Tarrant	1969	0	0	368,843
Taylor	1929	351,957	347,958	150,999,769
Terrell	1952	29,592	21,966	10,843,539
Terry	1940	3,051,822	2,480,101	500,791,035
Thrckmrton	1925	689,937	572,084	233,210,423
Titus	1936	403,777	297,779	218,758,554
Tm Green	1940	477,033	336,014	100,079,472
Travis	1934	4,281	4,216	802,969
Trinity	1946	19,297	15,079	1,701,445
Tyler	1937	388,872	315,903	75,590,583
Upshur	1931	81,010	70,614	293,964,370
Upton	1925	74,270,073	77,466,624	1,365,581,514
Uvalde	1950	0	0	1,814
Val Verde	1935	1,306	539	161,366
Van Zandt	1929	448,849	423,875	560,231,986
Victoria	1931	1,717,604	1,004,628	266,906,405
Walker	1934	65,396	55,568	1,266,890
Waller	1934	152,145	108,605	35,716,695
Ward	1928	49,180,683	47,101,254	1,070,771,906
Washngtn	1915	311,161	822,695	40,145,551
Webb	1921	325,223	1,144,254	285,301,712
Wharton	1925	677,916	629,313	366,697,137
Wheeler	1910	1,132,290	902,639	179,596,644
Wichita	1910	1,530,086	1,310,916	858,850,699
Wilbarger	1915	738,971	615,502	275,385,532
Willacy	1936	184,967	155,180	122,127,766
Williamson	1915	7,034	7,991	9,692,643
Wilson	1941	2,158,376	2,289,898	72,687,092
Winkler	1926	22,038,249	21,505,501	1,190,423,385
Wise	1942	172,739	149,865	116,577,630
Wood	1940	3,235,836	3,153,194	1,256,185,574
Yoakum	1936	27,419,490	26,111,179	2,440,437,070
Young	1917	888,987	783,830	327,697,866
Zapata	1919	55,556	25,771	50,941,907
Zavala	1937	7,161,114	6,841,813	110,003,489

Source: Railroad Commission, 2019–20 production reports.

**Total includes condensate production.*

Rig Counts and Wells Drilled by Year

Year	Rotary rigs active*		Permits	Texas wells completed		Wells drilled**
	Texas	U.S.	Texas	Oil	Gas	Texas
1990	348	1,009	14,033	5,593	2,894	11,231
1995	251	723	11,244	4,334	3,778	9,785
1996	283	779	12,669	4,061	4,060	9,747
1997	358	945	13,933	4,482	4,594	10,778
1998	303	827	9,385	4,509	4,907	11,057
1999	226	622	8,430	2,049	3,566	6,658
2000	343	918	12,021	3,111	4,580	8,854
2001	462	1,156	12,227	3,082	5,787	10,005
2002	338	830	9,716	3,268	5,474	9,877
2003	449	1,032	12,664	3,111	6,336	10,420
2004	506	1,192	14,700	3,446	7,118	11,587
2005	614	1,381	16,914	3,454	7,197	11,154
2006	746	1,649	18,952	4,761	8,534	12,764
2007	834	1,769	19,994	5,084	8,643	13,778
2008	898	1,880	24,073	6,208	10,361	16,615
2009	432	1,086	12,212	5,860	8,706	14,585
2010	659	1,541	18,029	5,392	4,071	9,477
2011	838	1,875	22,480	5,380	3,008	8,391
2012	899	1,919	22,479	10,936	3,580	14,535
2013	835	1,761	21,471	19,249	4,917	24,166
2014	882	1,862	25,792	24,999	3,585	29,554
2015	430	977	10,549	15,578	2,787	19,503
2016	236	510	8,113	7,813	2,129	10,468
2017	430	876	12,600	5,394	1,022	6,914
2018	513	1,032	13,307	8,588	1,813	10,986
2019	463	944	9,514	6,936	1,694	8,630
2020	206	436	5,322	8,867	2,032	10,899

*Texas Railroad Commission. *Source for rig count: Baker Hughes Inc. This is an annual average from monthly reports.*

Wells drilled in years before 2019 are oil and gas well **completions and dry holes drilled/plugged. Starting in 2019, only completions are counted.

Top Oil-Producing Counties since Discovery

There are 43 counties that have produced more than 500 million barrels of oil since discovery. The counties are ranked below. The column at right lists the number of regular producing oil wells in the county in February 2021.

Rank	County	Barrels	Oil Wells
1	Ector	3,437,595,733	6,248
2	Gregg	3,321,498,571	2,824
3	Andrews	3,289,958,078	9,798
4	Gaines	2,566,837,208	3,555
5	Yoakum	2,440,437,070	3,749
6	Scurry	2,277,236,873	2,277
7	Pecos	1,999,296,380	3,272
8	Crane	1,883,946,084	3,706
9	Hockley	1,876,844,456	3,671
10	Rusk	1,868,042,243	1,749
11	Midland	1,537,052,962	6495
12	Harris	1,396,751,943	242
13	Refugio	1,371,298,287	475
14	Upton	1,365,581,514	4983
15	Brazoria	1,316,951,552	228
16	Wood	1,256,185,574	609
17	Howard	1,208,960,682	5,199
18	Winkler	1,190,423,385	1,738
19	Ward	1,070,771,906	3,370
20	Karnes	993,166,760	3097
21	Martin	966,107,872	5,818
22	Chambers	943,279,000	138
23	Wichita	858,850,699	4479
24	Reagan	847,090,468	4,296
25	Montgomery	790,848,796	111
26	Fort Bend	715,398,653	238
27	Jackson	700,716,814	266
28	Gray	688,840,329	2,210
29	Reeves	661,366,162	2576
30	Kent	631,247,258	590
31	Duval	603,867,578	557
32	De Witt	589,635,125	1188
33	Jefferson	578,631,223	187
34	Nueces	574,994,320	124
35	Glasscock	574,818,570	4,203
36	Liberty	562,936,406	456
37	Van Zandt	560,231,986	218
38	Cochran	556,184,024	1,530
39	Dimmit	541,740,208	2113
40	Hutchinson	541,468,656	1712
41	Loving	532,022,988	1554
42	Archer	510,779,083	2543
43	Terry	500,791,035	783

Source: Texas Railroad Commission.

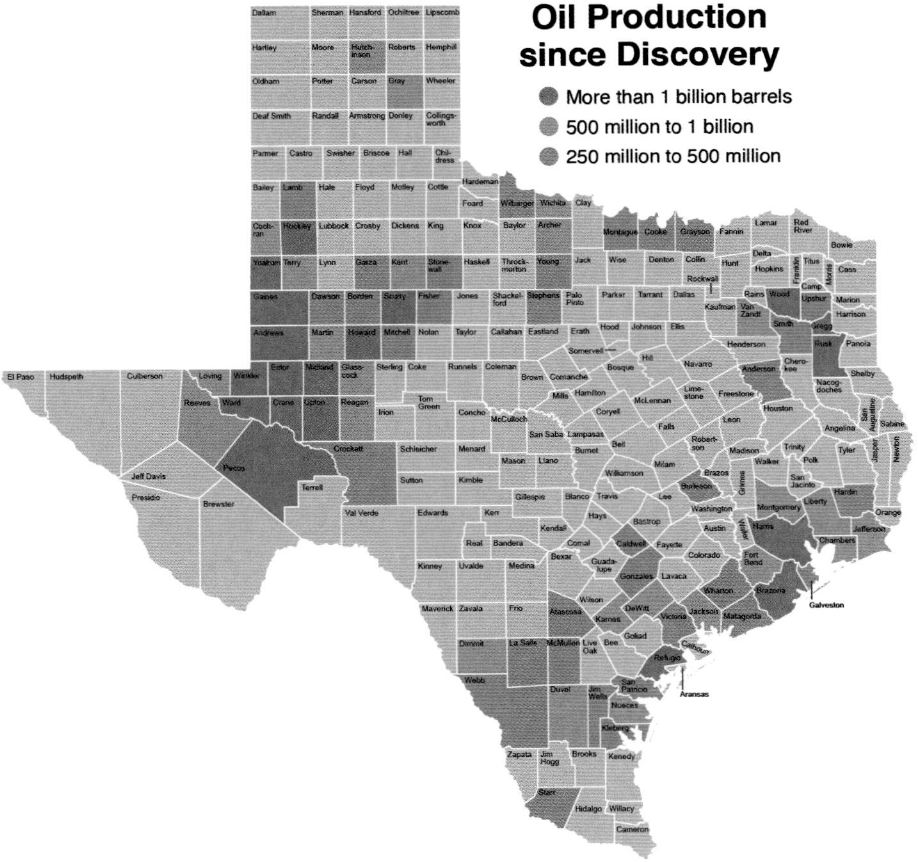

Oil and Gas Production by County, 2020

In 2020 in Texas, the total natural gas production from gas wells was 6,567,517,206 thousand cubic feet (MCF) and total crude oil production from oil wells was 1,491,652,615 barrels (BBL). Total condensate was 267,073,743 barrels. Total casinghead production was 3,899,249,800 MCF. Counties not listed in the chart below had no production in 2020. Source: Texas Railroad Commission.

County	Oil (BBL)	Casinghead (MCF)	GW Gas (MCF)	Condensate (BBL)
Anderson	527,486	725,709	1,608,489	23,355
Andrews	37,995,183	60,965,361	9,854,082	1,575,742
Angelina	0	0	82,365,736	2,687
Aransas	17,812	153,640	3,049,313	100,840
Archer	765,154	219,303	13,989	111
Atascosa	19,650,637	21,732,292	1,623,704	29,590
Austin	284,542	297,977	8,448,693	25,174
Bandera	512	0	0	0
Bastrop	69,293	47,478	26,727	4,609
Baylor	60,584	4,367	0	0
Bee	191,526	212,008	8,967,064	91,544
Bexar	68,017	18	0	0
Borden	6,628,259	7,409,839	0	0
Bowie	22,679	0	8,566	4,219
Brazoria	2,706,047	625,107	8,177,472	317,758
Brazos	8,426,069	9,032,687	1,442,516	55,445
Brooks	72,819	131,354	11,621,428	254,681
Brown	67,641	163,631	437,675	607
Burleson	15,416,834	12,280,093	1,644,681	63,732
Caldwell	942,101	34,252	0	0
Calhoun	80,817	123,771	321,588	7,293
Callahan	97,912	185,600	211,433	939
Cameron	0	0	27,759	780
Camp	55,998	0	34,373	0
Carson	89,968	380,755	7,012,129	29,447
Cass	485,545	311,528	165,093	1,243
Chambers	1,980,215	717,539	3,061,069	36,088
Cherokee	152,102	366,619	18,834,266	167,913
Childress	1,928	0	0	0
Clay	372,803	1,291,758	261,595	4,658
Cochran	2,627,186	1,809,419	57,290	140
Coke	234,436	1,237,914	242,724	2,679
Coleman	152,471	258,981	226,233	1,432
Collngswrth	3,700	39,868	746,867	92
Colorado	130,944	308,245	10,104,080	266,415
Comanche	41,715	76,964	287,799	377
Concho	215,582	128,709	185,589	398
Cooke	875,388	1,706,534	10,425,758	104,090
Cottle	81,695	8,885	1,811,884	19,818
Crane	6,988,445	33,784,540	7,756,882	66,474
Crockett	5,261,199	55,889,626	36,451,507	127,699
Crosby	663,291	6,149	0	0
Culberson	482,202	2,140,720	403,044,647	37,756,293
Dallas	0	0	6,328,446	0
Dawson	3,124,305	1,442,716	0	0
De Witt	33,224,351	95,487,693	165,265,355	20,948,511
Denton	11,132	276,008	146,476,995	189,668
Dickens	356,673	21,246	0	0
Dimmit	31,894,188	112,700,728	129,397,931	13,763,794
Donley	0	0	9,907	223
Duval	772,136	114,729	5,369,459	23,831
Eastland	124,217	315,400	1,203,461	17,173
Ector	16,540,414	39,016,330	2,291,933	4,726
Edwards	1,901	0	1,855,697	193
Ellis	32	12	2,453,483	0
Erath	496	354	1,919,748	2,201
Falls	785	0	0	0
Fayette	2,009,558	5,605,396	23,829,546	1,107,930
Fisher	1,832,056	2,397,271	7,523	70
Foard	64,083	7,663	40,029	0
Fort Bend	696,511	502,087	5,106,181	96,804
Franklin	284,625	92,075	775,072	21,415
Freestone	16,925	56,448	79,020,942	44,712
Frio	6,923,008	10,458,696	819,732	6,461
Gaines	21,710,218	20,422,598	234,767	2,862
Galveston	127,803	34,213	850,606	78,574
Garza	1,909,215	206,599	0	0
Glasscock	49,288,070	209,058,849	431,717	8,124
Goliad	127,296	80,892	4,473,048	56,928
Gonzales	36,271,501	49,156,129	200,517	7,543
Gray	896,545	1,314,455	5,364,217	9,327
Grayson	888,429	2,904,429	1,343,232	22,196
Gregg	1,165,644	1,694,069	23,126,217	112,778
Grimes	293,559	1,756,573	7,315,244	41,383
Guadalupe	628,736	40	0	0
Hale	972,809	1,121,877	0	0
Hamilton	17	0	47,357	0
Hansford	206,365	1,478,666	7,917,010	23,550
Hardeman	568,855	119,835	0	0
Hardin	760,073	537,946	3,494,977	253,402
Harris	761,738	423,013	6,409,204	100,157
Harrison	439,062	1,038,625	272,386,920	364,227
Hartley	187,888	67,514	853,689	0
Haskell	771,130	801,449	0	0
Hemphill	361,897	3,521,572	77,204,876	1,429,170
Henderson	349,642	2,755,689	6,372,836	15,248
Hidalgo	30,145	1,553	41,439,799	508,237
Hill	0	0	8,210,180	0
Hockley	10,814,410	5,805,143	17,014	1,416
Hood	0	0	29,473,527	57,299
Hopkins	139,688	73,180	30,354	3,480
Houston	360,641	417,061	2,029,755	102,064
Howard	95,159,559	183,214,383	158,166	2,384
Hunt	467	0	0	0
Hutchinson	376,733	1,626,829	3,676,762	81,385
Irion	9,884,321	138,849,017	1,067,130	12,394
Jack	817,181	7,048,482	5,858,991	63,785
Jackson	1,758,113	376,134	3,344,017	57,923
Jasper	260,298	400,951	8,622,986	472,130
Jefferson	398,494	340,713	3,271,218	208,945
Jim Hogg	15,032	524	5,050,234	71,431
Jim Wells	63,644	197,226	2,310,400	11,394
Johnson	0	0	142,844,221	6,678

Source: Texas Railroad Commission

County	Oil (BBL)	Casinghead (MCF)	GW Gas (MCF)	Condensate (BBL)
Jones	484,170	168,713	14,938	452
Karnes	93,484,371	194,692,511	127,340,680	12,808,928
Kaufman	43,120	18,889	0	0
Kenedy	81,073	113,005	26,723,482	223,845
Kent	2,637,307	5,792,360	0	0
Kimble	292	0	0	0
King	1,475,697	203,762	75,217	40
Kleberg	52,753	124,046	5,342,501	107,905
Knox	174,988	189,769	0	0
La Salle	48,131,932	100,843,434	177,519,418	3,600,408
Lamb	210,397	189,056	0	0
Lavaca	6,216,928	9,935,400	26,518,618	1,240,019
Lee	2,392,492	4,426,313	564,292	20,512
Leon	430,132	1,063,419	32,631,642	31,546
Liberty	600,474	355,644	5,765,212	160,061
Limestone	59,905	12	27,498,791	16,514
Lipscomb	761,233	8,795,319	30,808,815	996,365
Live Oak	9,927,923	31,583,122	45,018,569	3,388,741
Loving	88,448,816	194,022,172	270,215,343	45,657,468
Lubbock	824,058	70,222	0	0
Lynn	179,177	55,944	0	0
Madison	2,135,224	5,702,848	1,667,108	88,149
Marion	354,436	295,078	1,099,176	20,578
Martin	144,405,379	292,095,499	6,762	110
Matagorda	185,730	201,105	10,855,908	310,103
Maverick	968,981	2,890,739	1,239,689	31,048
McCulloch	34,238	0	0	0
McLennan	443	0	0	0
McMullen	25,286,633	40,899,348	63,756,504	3,192,894
Medina	77,546	133	8,880	0
Menard	84,049	2,304	19,489	248
Midland	187,685,246	546,663,063	3,896,451	68,561
Milam	1,730,926	1,459,911	14,039	207
Mills	0	0	4,501	0
Mitchell	2,087,392	703,042	0	0
Montague	797,161	7,597,331	38,891,424	312,960
Montgomry	805,797	1,466,855	2,140,252	37,548
Moore	191,405	1,035,117	22,629,957	4,559
Morris	29,455	20,078	0	0
Motley	33,134	3,955	0	0
Nacogdchs	7,855	33,818	109,092,030	43,467
Navarro	114,488	120,222	299,663	10,693
Newton	523,024	686,218	1,771,067	100,950
Nolan	1,004,165	1,506,956	176,005	395
Nueces	127,355	195,984	7,033,611	156,233
Ochiltree	3,160,245	16,366,840	10,441,974	195,857
Oldham	284,628	473,941	37,004	0
Orange	338,203	691,806	1,699,477	138,531
Palo Pinto	74,271	1,489,544	4,418,819	31,147
Panola	205,128	1,274,745	508,695,130	1,364,474
Parker	459	124,832	51,240,410	64,321
Pecos	38,976,089	85,385,259	41,864,165	123,397
Polk	380,073	228,602	18,184,616	446,991
Potter	401,437	3,121,249	7,645,513	70,664
Reagan	46,673,113	309,463,793	847,350	11,295
Real	781	0	0	0
Red River	63,205	0	0	0
Reeves	100,281,191	301,529,123	849,877,878	86,791,989
Refugio	1,931,069	5,963,814	1,415,282	21,543
Roberts	908,654	11,100,033	20,248,817	311,711
Robertson	1,961,127	940,544	51,782,645	3,448
Runnels	267,581	457,484	57,298	939
Rusk	1,268,753	1,715,657	96,554,264	537,400
Sabine	294	38	706,863	0
SanAugustn	11,426	197,326	214,958,585	16,289
San Jacinto	53,031	25,986	2,244,628	68,752
San Patricio	247,966	518,365	3,366,906	104,251
Schleicher	212,889	1,759,789	4,103,444	36,592
Scurry	14,647,692	40,946,476	0	0
Shackelford	313,103	413,902	746,107	9,405
Shelby	18,197	347,390	66,212,134	24,239
Sherman	73,274	76,412	13,129,374	4,682
Smith	1,154,808	1,269,363	19,618,205	260,120
Somervell	0	0	3,064,120	3,598
Starr	247,059	583,770	28,905,203	328,525
Stephens	1,572,741	1,951,212	5,698,423	36,263
Sterling	548,500	4,246,029	2,080,975	21,256
Stonewall	1,250,561	2,216,423	0	0
Sutton	18,570	33,529	19,169,476	31,089
Tarrant	0	0	356,151,886	10,901
Taylor	348,083	163,017	13,676	0
Terrell	21,908	330,693	11,532,068	57,316
Terry	2,480,003	390,628	0	0
Throckmrtn	572,076	1,934,970	105,965	3,686
Titus	297,779	1,233	0	84
Tom Green	334,825	2,263,359	307,159	6,945
Travis	4,216	0	0	0
Trinity	15,079	0	66,337	1,349
Tyler	315,903	282,509	8,298,581	921,824
Upshur	70,614	18,187	21,268,174	180,835
Upton	77,466,936	263,131,553	8,521,014	145,342
Val Verde	484	0	2,850,460	8
Van Zandt	423,875	203,311	1,641,179	2,009
Victoria	1,005,664	876,647	2,846,753	37,766
Walker	55,568	1,244,580	528,040	35,840
Waller	108,605	149	1,101,669	8,885
Ward	47,105,059	98,974,258	51,565,064	4,746,132
Washington	750,500	3,078,731	55,012,827	1,322,257
Webb	1,144,254	4,215,494	735,166,574	10,987,872
Wharton	629,125	795,732	7,635,295	129,350
Wheeler	899,289	7,571,749	72,837,978	1,645,850
Wichita	1,311,097	232,828	0	0
Wilbarger	615,492	93,466	0	0
Willacy	155,180	183,724	2,801,159	32,053
Williamson	7,991	0	0	0
Wilson	2,289,897	1,219,653	165	0
Winkler	21,588,063	42,378,962	12,560,911	867,420
Wise	149,207	3,052,471	163,145,260	313,729
Wood	3,153,194	49,177,534	4,719,366	167,309
Yoakum	26,111,179	38,646,237	40,642	0
Young	783,308	1,111,416	857,863	20,632
Zapata	25,771	51,207	65,485,719	52,891
Zavala	6,842,108	6,282,704	159,066	0

Source: Texas Railroad Commission

Top Gas-Producing Counties, 1993–2021

The top 37 natural gas-producing counties are listed in the chart below. The fourth column at the right lists the number of producing gas wells in the county in February 2021. Seventy-five counties have produced more than 500 billion cubic feet of natural gas since 1993 (see map). MCF is thousand cubic feet.

Rank	County	Gas (MCF)	Gas Wells
1	Webb	12,077,090,696	6,123
2	Panola	8,225,902,264	4,781
3	Tarrant	8,209,296,370	3,989
4	Zapata	6,505,149,450	2,661
5	Hidalgo	5,247,132,874	1,204
6	Johnson	5,106,839,554	2,843
7	Freestone	4,562,558,413	2,918
8	Wise	4,486,680,589	4,085
9	Pecos	4,194,566,316	1,200
10	Denton	3,729,452,041	2,742
11	Reeves	3,324,471,873	1,596
12	Hemphill	3,142,196,211	2,227
13	Starr	3,034,741,424	1,046
14	Harrison	2,993,972,409	2,119
15	Wheeler	2,941,751,975	1,663
16	Rusk	2,756,155,235	2,152
17	Robertson	2,670,875,707	873
18	Crockett	2,654,199,501	5,492
19	Loving	2,087,389,189	855

Rank	County	Gas (MCF)	Gas Wells
20	Nacogdoches	1,992,090,444	1,238
21	DeWitt	1,951,772,817	960
22	Dimmit	1,646,503,074	1,802
23	Culberson	1,626,443,526	656
24	Limestone	1,621,203,990	1,091
25	Sutton	1,601,547,344	5,257
26	Lavaca	1,571,944,409	429
27	La Salle	1,501,020,653	1,052
28	Terrell	1,450,695,723	638
29	San Augustine	1,449,883,612	309
30	Karnes	1,443,865,314	988
31	Parker	1,415,735,465	1,439
32	Leon	1,341,748,235	547
33	Shelby	1,328,615,245	603
34	Brooks	1,327,773,404	357
35	Gregg	1,317,820,663	782
36	Duval	1,300,852,074	323
37	Lipscomb	1,289,140,673	1,315

Source: Texas Railroad Commission.

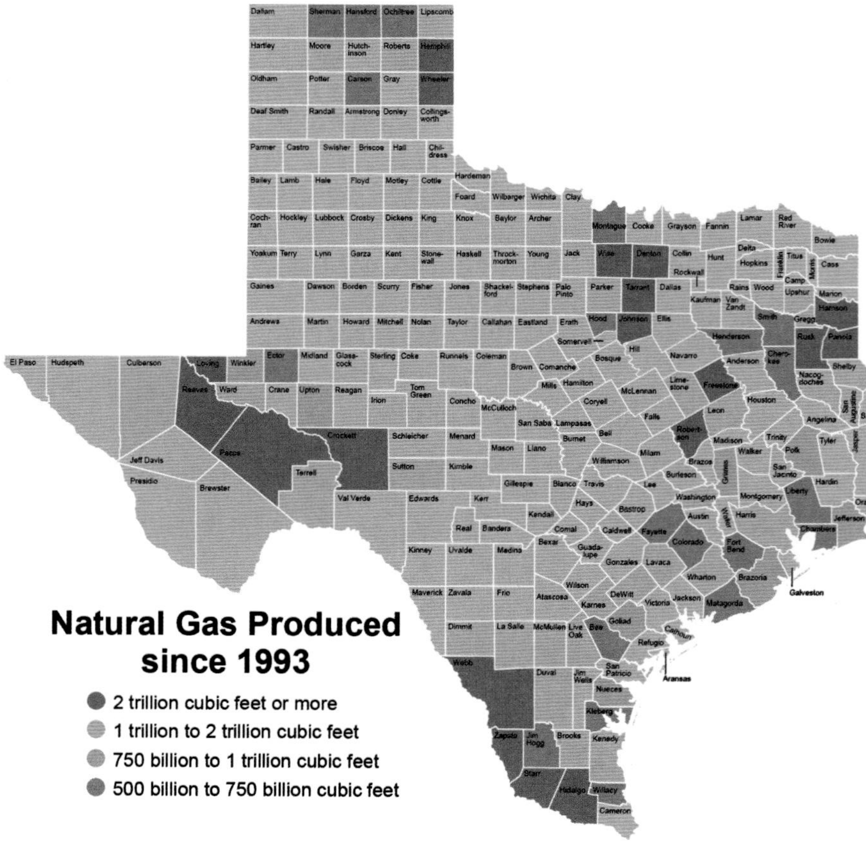

Petroleum Production and Income in Texas

Year	Crude Oil				Natural Gas		
	Production (thousand barrels)	Value (in thousands)	Average Price per barrel (nominal)	*Average price per barrel (2005 $)	Production (million cubic feet)	Value (in thousands)	Wellhead Price (cents per **Mcf)
1915	24,943	$ 13,027	$ 0 .52	NA	13,324	$ 2,594	19.5
1925	144,648	262,270	1.81	NA	134,872	7,040	5.2
1935	392,666	367,820	0.94	NA	642,366	13,233	2.1
1945	754,710	914,410	1.21	NA	1,711,401	44,839	2.6
1955	1,053,297	2,989,330	2.84	NA	4,730,798	378,464	8.0
1965	1,000,749	2,962,119	2.96	NA	6,636,555	858,396	12.9
1970	1,249,697	4,104,005	3.28	NA	8,357,716	1,203,511	14.4
1975	1,221,929	9,336,570	7.64	NA	7,485,764	3,885,112	51.9
1982	923,868	29,074,126	31.77	57.33	6,497,678	13,567,151	208.8
1983	876,205	22,947,814	29.35	50.95	5,643,183	14,672,275	225.0
1984	874,079	25,138,520	28.87	48.31	5,864,224	13,487,715	230.0
1985	860,300	23,159,286	26.80	43.52	5,805,098	12,665,114	218.0
1986	813,620	11,976,488	14.73	23.40	5,663,491	8,778,410	155.0
1987	754,213	13,221,345	17.55	27.10	5,516,224	7,612,389	138.0
1988	727,928	10,729,660	14.71	21.96	5,702,643	7,983,700	141.0
1989	679,575	12,123,624	17.81	25.62	5,595,190	8,113,026	145.0
1990	672,081	15,047,902	22.37	30.98	5,533,771	8,281,372	149.7
1991	672,810	12,836,080	19.04	25.47	5,509,990	7,713,986	143.0
1992	642,059	11,820,306	18.32	23.94	5,436,408	8,643,888	174.0
1993	572,600	9,288,800	16.19	20.70	5,606,498	7,365,800	204.0
1994	533,900	7,977,500	14.98	18.76	5,675,748	6,220,300	185.0
1995	503,200	8,177,700	16.38	20.09	5,672,105	5,305,200	155.0
1996	478,100	9,560,800	20.31	24.44	5,770,255	6,945,000	217.0
1997	464,900	8,516,800	18.66	22.07	5,814,745	8,134,200	232.0
1998	440,600	5,472,400	12.28	14.36	5,772,080	6,362,900	196.0
1999	337,100	5,855,800	17.29	19.93	5,538,929	6,789,700	219.0
2000	348,900	10,037,300	28.60	32.26	5,645,972	12,837,600	368.0
2001	325,500	7,770,500	23.41	25.82	5,668,602	13,708,700	400.0
2002	335,600	8,150,400	23.77	25.80	5,611,958	9,840,800	295.0
2003	333,300	9,708,600	29.13	30.96	5,671,689	14,797,800	488.0
2004	327,910	12,762,650	38.79	40.08	5,817,227	17,077,700	546.0
2005	327,600	12,744,600	52.61	52.61	5,700,613	16,399,400	733.0
2006	314,600	19,353,500	61.31	59.38	6,077,786	23,500,800	639.0
2007	311,830	21,341,100	68.30	64.30	6,421,375	22,968,420	625.0
2008	315,896	30,409,170	96.85	89.28	7,271,815	34,415,890	797.0
2009	349,391	18,455,530	57.40	52.31	7,573,033	12,167,800	367.0
2010	369,953	26,054,900	76.23	68.88	7,246,042	11,796,700	448.0
2011	448,903	39,420,500	91.99	81.15	7,051,594	13,646,300	395.0
2012	724,422	55,145,600	92.50	NA	7,128,775	12,959,100	266.0
2013	749,876	73,666,700	95.80	NA	7,725,119	15,358,900	373.0
2014	927,417	85,962,300	87.02	NA	8,171,230	18,034,000	428.0
2015	1,004,774	48,132,920	48.79	NA	7,871,200	8,827,180	263.0
2016	974,612	32,854,310	42.40	NA	6,996,000	20,566,930	255.0
2017	1,026,765	49,869,976	48.57	NA	6,300,292	20,664,957	328.0
2018	1,274,569	76,359,429	59.91	NA	5,742,978	19,468,695	339.0
2019	1,586,337	90,405,346	56.99	NA	6,775,942	14,907,072	220.0
2020	1,495,495	$ 58,563,584	$ 39.16	NA	6,593,494	$ 11,802,354	179.0

Revised May 2019. NA, not available.

*In chained (2005) dollars, from the U.S. Energy Information Administration (EIA).

**Mcf (thousand cubic feet)

Sources: Previously from the Texas Railroad Commission, Texas Mid-Continent Oil & Gas Association and, beginning in 1979, data are from Department of Energy. Data since 1993 are from the state comptroller and EIA and the railroad commission. Federal figures do not include gas that is vented or flared or used for pressure maintenance and repressuring, but do include non-hydrocarbon gases.

Offshore Production History – Oil and Gas

The cumulative offshore natural gas production as of Jan. 1, 2021, was 4,213,049,080 thousand cubic feet (Mcf). The cumulative offshore oil production was 42,776,352 barrels.

Production in Recent Years

Year	Crude Oil BBL	Casing-head Mcf	Gas Well Gas Mcf	Conden-sate BBL
2000	548,046	335,415	44,086,237	220,309
2005	450,378	389,301	38,589,312	451,692
2009	480,514	1,673,140	38,218,699	918,218
2010	477,303	1,160,607	28,143,515	866,959
2011	522,307	925,166	23,916,678	566,425
2012	605,389	902,900	17,011,234	435,049
2013	500,209	460,876	15,053,574	370,290
2014	424,191	574,464	12,280,841	354,585
2015	291,428	233,094	9,982,738	281,510
2016	154,005	48,816	8,337,712	231,975
2017	118,474	35,054	6,049,351	183,464
2018	129,485	59,654	4,117,566	203,940
2019	132,838	78,601	3,282,580	174,754
2020	105,514	56,486	2,477,909	126,695

2020 Production by Area

Offshore Area	Crude Oil BBL	Casing-head Mcf	Gas Well Gas Mcf	Conden-sate BBL
Brazos-LB	0	0	0	0
Brazos-SB	0	0	0	0
Galveston-LB	61,785	33,269	149,956	77,745
Galveston-SB	0	0	0	0
High Island-LB	0	0	537,149	0
High Island-SB	0	0	0	0
Matagrda Is.-LB	42,492	21,075	0	0
Matagrda Is.-SB	0	0	0	0
Mustang Is.-LB	0	0	620,239	9,647
Mustang Is.-SB	1,237	2,142	1,170,565	39,303
N. Padre Is.-LB	0	0	0	0
Sabine Pass	0	0	0	0
Total	**105,514**	**56,486**	**2,477,909**	**126,695**

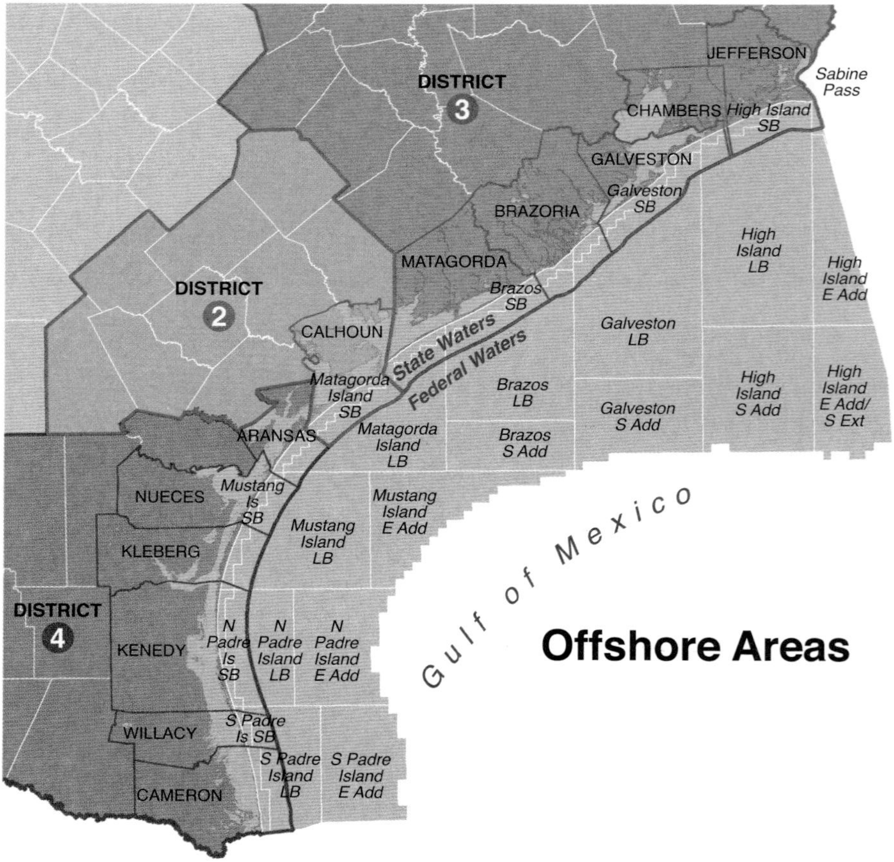

Receipts by Texas from Tidelands

The Republic of Texas had proclaimed its Gulf boundaries as three marine leagues, recognized by international law as traditional national boundaries. These boundaries were never seriously questioned when Texas joined the Union in 1845.

In 1930 a congressional resolution authorized the U.S. Attorney General to file suit to establish offshore lands as properties of the federal government. Congress returned the disputed lands to Texas in 1953, and the U.S. Supreme Court confirmed Texas' ownership in 1960.

In 1978, the federal government also granted states a "fair and equitable" share of the revenues from offshore leases within three miles of the states' outermost boundary. States did not receive any such revenue until 1986.

The table shows annual receipts from tidelands in the Gulf of Mexico by the Texas General Land Office from 1963 to Aug. 31, 2018. It does not include revenue from bays and other submerged area owned by Texas. Totals include previous years not shown in this chart.

Source: General Land Office.

From	To	Total	Bonus	Rental	Royalty	Lease
9-01-1963	8-31-1964	$ 3,656,236.75	$ 2,435,244.36	$ 525,315.00	$ 695,677.39	. . .
9-01-1964	8-31-1965	54,654,576.96	53,114,943.63	755,050.12	784,583.21	. . .
9-01-1965	8-31-1966	22,148,825.44	18,223,357.84	3,163,475.00	761,992.60	. . .
9-01-1966	8-31-1967	8,469,680.86	3,641,414.96	3,711,092.65	1,117,173.25	. . .
9-01-1967	8-31-1968	6,305,851.00	1,251,852.50	2,683,732.50	2,370,266.00	. . .
9-01-1968	8-31-1969	6,372,268.28	1,838,118.33	1,491,592.50	3,042,557.45	. . .
9-01-1969	8-31-1970	10,311,030.48	5,994,666.32	618,362.50	3,698,001.66	. . .
9-01-1970	8-31-1971	9,969,629.17	4,326,120.11	726,294.15	4,917,214.91	. . .
9-01-1971	8-31-1972	7,558,327.21	1,360,212.64	963,367.60	5,234,746.97	. . .
9-01-1972	8-31-1973	9,267,975.68	3,701,737.30	920,121.60	4,646,116.78	. . .
9-01-1973	8-31-1974	41,717,670.04	32,981,619.28	1,065,516.60	7,670,534.16	. . .
9-01-1974	8-31-1975	27,321,536.62	5,319,762.85	2,935,295.60	19,066,478.17	. . .
9-01-1975	8-31-1976	38,747,074.09	6,197,853.00	3,222,535.84	29,326,685.25	. . .
9-01-1976	8-31-1977	84,196,228.27	41,343,114.81	2,404,988.80	40,448,124.66	. . .
9-01-1977	8-31-1978	118,266,812.05	49,807,750.45	4,775,509.92	63,683,551.68	. . .
9-01-1978	8-31-1979	100,410,268.68	34,578,340.94	7,318,748.40	58,513,179.34	. . .
9-01-1979	8-31-1980	200,263,803.03	34,733,270.02	10,293,153.80	155,237,379.21	. . .
9-01-1980	8-31-1981	219,126,876.54	37,467,196.97	13,100,484.25	168,559,195.32	. . .
9-01-1981	8-31-1982	250,824,581.69	27,529,516.33	14,214,478.97	209,080,586.39	. . .
9-01-1982	8-31-1983	165,197,734.83	10,180,696.40	12,007,476.70	143,009,561.73	. . .
9-01-1983	8-31-1984	152,755,934.29	32,864,122.19	8,573,996.87	111,317,815.23	. . .
9-01-1984	8-31-1985	140,561,690.79	32,650,127.75	6,837,603.70	101,073,959.34	. . .
9-01-1985	8-31-1986	516,503,771.08	6,365,426.23	4,241,892.75	78,289,592.27	$427,606,859.83
9-01-1986	8-31-1987	60,066,571.05	4,186,561.63	1,933,752.50	44,691,907.22	9,254,349.70
9-01-1987	8-31-1988	56,875,069.22	14,195,274.28	1,817,058.90	28,068,202.53	12,794,533.51
9-01-1988	8-31-1989	61,793,380.04	12,995,892.74	1,290,984.37	35,160,568.40	12,345,934.53
9-01-1989	8-31-1990	68,701,751.51	7,708,449.54	1,289,849.87	40,331,537.06	19,371,915.04
9-01-1990	8-31-1991	90,885,856.99	3,791,832.77	1,345,711.07	70,023,601.01	15,724,712.14
9-01-1991	8-31-1992	51,154,511.34	4,450,850.00	1,123,585.54	26,776,191.35	18,803,884.45
9-01-1992	8-31-1993	60,287,712.60	3,394,230.00	904,359.58	34,853,679.68	21,135,443.34
9-01-1993	8-31-1994	57,825,043.59	3,570,657.60	694,029.30	32,244,987.95	21,315,368.74
9-01-1994	8-31-1995	62,143,227.78	8,824,722.93	674,479.79	34,691,023.35	17,951,001.71
9-01-1995	8-31-1996	68,166,645.51	13,919,246.80	1,102,591.39	32,681,315.73	20,463,491.59
9-01-1996	8-31-1997	90,614,935.93	22,007,378.46	1,319,614.78	41,605,792.50	25,682,150.19
9-01-1997	8-31-1998	104,016,006.75	36,946,312.49	2,070,802.90	38,760,320.91	26,238,570.45
9-01-1998	8-31-1999	53,565,810.30	5,402,171.00	2,471,128.47	23,346,515.93	22,345,994.90
9-01-1999	8-31-2000	55,465,763.99	3,487,564.80	2,171,636.35	24,314,241.99	25,492,320.85
9-01-2000	8-31-2001	68,226,347.58	9,963,608.68	1,830,378.11	23,244,034.74	33,188,326.05
9-01-2001	8-31-2002	30,910,283.91	9,286,015.20	1,545,583.01	13,369,771.56	6,708,914.14
9-01-2002	8-31-2003	50,881,515.90	15,152,092.40	1,071,377.60	19,648,641.39	15,009,404.51
9-01-2003	8-31-2004	54,379,791.20	14,448,555.70	1,094,201.41	25,199,635.21	13,637,398.88
9-01-2004	8-31-2005	53,594,809.87	9,148,220.20	1,624,666.50	32,406,328.78	10,415,594.39
9-01-2005	8-31-2006	60,829,271.63	22,565,845.14	1,605,090.30	23,287,994.53	13,370,341.66
9-01-2006	8-31-2007	52,513,621.85	15,879,784.44	2,022,859.80	18,785,626.55	15,825,351.06
9-01-2007	8-31-2008	86,705,980.28	4,632,175.50	1,485,080.97	68,408,943.01	12,179,780.80
9-01-2008	8-31-2009	65,835,625.76	3,896,795.20	1,020,204.33	53,166,364.50	7,752,261.73
9-01-2009	8-31-2010	49,647,832.14	3,352,431.20	603,406.00	41,901,754.81	3,790,240.13
9-01-2010	8-31-2011	50,360,843.36	4,088,819.06	546,404.80	43,602,027.62	2,123,591.88
9-01-2011	8-31-2012	37,561,595.54	2,436,420.00	217,356.00	33,327,417.09	1,580,402.45
9-01-2012	8-31-2013	32,676,026.13	1,079,400.00	339,941.00	30,353,820.49	902,864.64
9-01-2013	8-31-2014	28,103,953.40	217,000.00	193,125.00	26,665,893.97	1,027.934.53
9-01-2014	8-31-2015	17,922,043.53	969,600.00	71,894.00	16,302,558.59	577,990.94
9-01-2015	8-31-2016	7,053,383.42	0.00	112,350.00	6,819,050.31	121,983.11
9-01-2016	8-31-2017	7,422,396.66	100,800.00	48,712.00	7,172,244.48	100,640.18
9-01-2017	8-31-2018	10,237,935.90	0.00	48,000.00	5,759,255.41	4,430,680.49
Totals		$ 3,974,612.907.55	$ 774,513,049,71	$ 147,166,154.10	$ 2,213,663,471.20	$ 839,270.232.54
Inside three-mile line		$ 533,256,002.78	$ 180,838,499.91	$ 39,193,553.27	$ 313,223,949.60	0.00
Between three-mile and three marine-league line		$ 2,599,261,306.65	$ 591,022,465.41	$ 107,734,519.64	$1,900,439,521.60	0.00
Outside three marine-league line		$ 842,095,598,12	$ 2,652,084.39	$ 173,281.19	0.00	$ 839,270,232,54

Nonpetroleum Minerals

Sources: U.S. Geological Survey's mineral industry surveys, www.usgs.gov/centers/nmic/mineral-industry-surveys; Bureau of Economic Geology, The University of Texas at Austin, www.beg.utexas.edu

There are many nonpetroleum, or nonfuel, minerals found in Texas. Although they are overshadowed by production of petroleum, natural gas, and natural gas liquids, many are important to the economy.

In 2020, Texas nonfuel mineral production was valued at **$6.0 billion**, a 5.9 percent decrease from the $6.5 billion in total value for 2019, and accounted for 7.4 percent of the total U.S. nonfuel mineral production value of $82.3 billion. Among all 50 states, **Texas ranked third in nonfuel mineral production** for the sixth year in a row (since 2015), behind Arizona ($7.0 billion in 2020) and Nevada ($8.2 billion).

The nonfuel mineral commodities produced in Texas in 2020 include: barite, cement (portland), gold, gypsum, helium, lime, ammonia, salt, sand and gravel (both construction and industrial), selenium, stone (both crushed and dimension), sulfur, talc, vanadium, and zeolites (clinoptilolite).

Texas was the leader in both crushed and dimension stone production, and second to California in sand and gravel (construction).

ALUMINUM: No aluminum ores are mined in Texas, but three Texas plants process aluminum materials in one or more ways. Plants in San Patricio and Calhoun counties produce aluminum oxide (alumina) from imported raw ore (bauxite), and a plant in Milam County reduces the oxide to aluminum.

ASBESTOS: Small occurrences of amphibole-type asbestos have been found in the state. In West Texas, richterite, a white, long-fibered amphibole, is associated with some of the talc deposits northwest of Allamoore in Hudspeth County. Another type, tremolite, has been found in the Llano Uplift of Central Texas where it is associated with serpentinite in eastern Gillespie and western Blanco counties. No asbestos is mined in Texas.

ASPHALT (NATIVE): Asphalt-bearing Cretaceous limestones crop out in Burnet, Kinney, Pecos, Reeves, Uvalde, and other counties. The most significant deposit is in southwestern Uvalde County, where asphalt occurs naturally in pore spaces of the Anacacho Limestone. The material is quarried and used extensively as road-paving material. Asphalt-bearing sandstones occur in Anderson, Angelina, Cooke, Jasper, Maverick, Montague, Nacogdoches, Uvalde, Zavala, and other counties.

BARITE: Deposits of a heavy, nonmetallic mineral, barite (barium sulphate), have been found in many localities, including Baylor, Brown, Brewster, Culberson, Gillespie, Howard, Hudspeth, Jeff Davis, Kinney, Live Oak, Llano, Taylor, Val Verde, and Webb counties. During the 1960s, there was small, intermittent production in the Seven Heart Gap area of the Apache Mountains in Culberson County, where barite was mined from open pits. Most of the deposits are known to be relatively small, but the Webb County deposit has not been evaluated. Grinding plants, which prepare barite mined outside of Texas for use chiefly as a weighting agent in well-drilling muds and as a filler, are located in Brownsville, Corpus Christi, El Paso, Galena Park, Galveston, and Houston.

BASALT (TRAP ROCK): Masses of basalt, a hard, dark-colored, fine-grained igneous rock, crop out in Kinney, Travis, Uvalde, and several other counties along the Balcones Fault Zone, and also in the Trans-Pecos area of West Texas. Basalt is quarried near Knippa in Uvalde County for use as road-building material, railroad ballast, and other aggregate.

BENTONITE (see CLAYS).

BERYLLIUM: Occurrences of beryllium minerals at several Trans-Pecos localities have been recognized for several years.

BRINE (see also SALT, SODIUM SULPHATE): Many wells in Texas produce brine by solution mining of subsurface salt deposits, mostly in West Texas counties such as Andrews, Crane, Ector, Loving, Midland, Pecos, Reeves, Ward, and others. These wells in the Permian Basin dissolve salt from the Salado Formation, an enormous salt deposit that extends in the subsurface from north of the Big Bend northward to Kansas, has an east-west width of 150 to 200 miles, and may have several hundred feet of net salt thickness. The majority of the brine is used in the petroleum industry, but it also is used in water softening, the chemical industry, and other uses. Three Gulf Coast counties, Fort Bend, Duval, and Jefferson, have brine stations that produce from salt domes.

BUILDING STONE (DIMENSION STONE): Granite and limestone currently are quarried for use as dimension stone. The granite quarries are located in Burnet, Gillespie, Llano, and Mason counties; the limestone quarries are in Shackelford and Williamson counties. Past production of limestone for use as dimension stone has been reported in Burnet, Gillespie, Jones, Tarrant, Travis, and several other counties. There also has been production of sandstone in various counties for use as dimension stone.

CEMENT MATERIALS: Cement is currently manufactured in Bexar, Comal, Dallas, Ector, Ellis, Hays, McLennan, Nolan, and Potter counties. Many of these plants utilize Cretaceous limestones and shales or clays as raw materials for the cement. On the Texas High Plains, a cement plant near Amarillo uses impure caliche as the chief raw material. Iron oxide, also a constituent of cement, is available from the iron ore deposits of East Texas and from smelter slag. Gypsum, added to the cement as a retarder, is found chiefly in the North-Central, Central, and Trans-Pecos areas.

A new greenfields white cement production plant has been proposed near Brady, but it has been delayed due to local opposition. It would be the third of its kind in the U.S.

Cement Production in Texas
(metric tons)

Type	2020	2017
Portland and Blended	11,858,581	11,465,785
Masonry	297,338	304,320
Clinker	10,864,668	10,128,636

Source: Industry surveys at USGS

CHROMIUM: Chromite-bearing rock has been found in several small deposits around the margin of the Coal Creek serpentinite mass in northeastern Gillespie County and northwestern Blanco County. Exploration has not revealed significant deposits.

CLAYS: Texas has an abundance and variety of ceramic and nonceramic clays and is one of the country's leading producers of clay products.

Almost any kind of clay, ranging from common clay used to make brick and tile to clays suitable for manufacture of specialty whitewares, can be used for ceramic purposes. Fire clay suitable for use as refractories occurs chiefly in East and North-Central Texas; ball clay, a high-quality plastic ceramic clay, is found in East Texas.

Ceramic clay suitable for quality structural clay products, such as structural building brick, paving brick, and drain tile, is especially abundant in East and North-Central Texas. Common clay suitable for use in the manufacture of cement and ordinary brick is found in most counties of the state. Many of the Texas clays will expand or bloat upon rapid firing and are suitable for the manufacture of lightweight aggregate, which is used mainly in concrete blocks and highway surfacing.

Nonceramic clays are utilized without firing. They are used primarily as bleaching and absorbent clays, fillers, coaters, additives, bonding clays, drilling muds, catalysts, and potentially as sources of alumina. Most of the nonceramic clays in Texas are bentonites and fuller's earth. These occur extensively in the Coastal Plain and locally in the High Plains and Big Bend areas. Kaolin clays in parts of East Texas are potential sources of such nonceramic products as paper coaters and fillers, rubber fillers, and drilling agents. Relatively high in alumina, these clays also are a potential source of metallic aluminum.

COAL (see also LIGNITE): Bituminous coal, which occurs in North-Central, South, and West Texas, was a significant energy source in Texas prior to the large-scale development of oil and gas. During the period from 1895–1943, Texas mines produced more than 25 million tons of coal. The mines were inactive for many years, but the renewed interest in coal as a major energy source prompted a revaluation of Texas' coal deposits. In the late 1970s, bituminous coal production resumed in the state on a limited scale when mines were opened in Coleman, Erath, and Webb counties.

Much of the state's bituminous coal occurs in North-Central Texas. Deposits are found there in Pennsylvanian rocks within a large area that includes Coleman, Eastland, Erath, Jack, McCulloch, Montague, Palo Pinto, Parker, Throckmorton, Wise, Young, and other counties. Before the general availability of oil and gas, underground coal mines near Thurber, Bridgeport, Newcastle, Strawn, and other points annually produced significant coal tonnages. Preliminary evaluations indicate substantial amounts of coal may remain in the North-Central Texas area. The coal seams there are generally no more than 30 inches thick and are commonly covered by well-consolidated overburden. Ash and sulphur content are high. Beginning in 1979, two bituminous coal mine operations in North-Central Texas, one in southern Coleman County and one in northwestern Erath County, produced coal to be used as fuel by the cement industry. Neither mine is currently operating.

In South Texas, bituminous coal occurs in the **Eagle Pass district of Maverick County**, and bituminous cannel coal is present in the Santo Tomas district of Webb County. The Eagle Pass area was a leading coal-producing district in Texas during the late 1800s and early 1900s. The bituminous coal in that area, which occurs in the Upper Cretaceous Olmos Formation, has a high ash content and a moderate moisture and sulfur content. According to reports, Maverick County coal beds range from four to seven feet thick.

The cannel coals of western Webb County occur near the Rio Grande in middle Eocene strata. They were mined for more than 50 years and used primarily as a boiler fuel. Mining ceased from 1939 until 1978, when a surface mine was opened 30 miles northwest of Laredo to produce cannel coal for use as fuel in the cement industry and for export. An additional mine has since been opened in that county. Tests show that the coals of the Webb County Santo Tomas district have a high hydrogen content and yield significant amounts of gas and oil when distilled. They also have a high sulfur content. A potential use might be as a source of various petrochemical products.

Texas Coal and Lignite Production
(short tons)

Year	Total
2020	19,639,076
2019	23,306,720
2018	24,842,955
2017	35,415,535
2016	39,139,879
2015	36,277,112
2014	43,633,881
2013	42,449,594
2012	43,536,176
2011	45,587,404
2010	41,419,857
2009	37,099,067
2008	40,152,112
2007	38,403,681
2006	46,128,231
2005	47,168,916
2004	45,680,097
2003	48,179,875
2002	44,683,793
pre-2002	1,143,894,272

Source: Railroad Commission of Texas

Coal deposits in the Trans-Pecos country of West Texas include those in the Cretaceous rocks of the Terlingua area of Brewster County, the Eagle Spring area of Hudspeth County, and the San Carlos area of Presidio County. The coal deposits in these areas are believed to have relatively little potential for development as a fuel. They have been sold in the past as a soil amendment (see **LEONARDITE**).

COPPER: Copper minerals have been found in the Trans-Pecos area of West Texas, in the Llano Uplift area of Central Texas, and in redbed deposits of North Texas. No copper has been mined in Texas during recent years, and the total copper produced in the state has been relatively small. Past attempts to mine the North Texas and Llano Uplift copper deposits resulted in small shipments.

Practically all the copper production in the state has been from the Van Horn–Allamoore district of Culberson and Hudspeth counties in the Trans-Pecos area. Chief output was from the Hazel copper-silver mine of Culberson County that yielded over 1 million pounds of copper during 1891–1947. Copper ores and concentrates from outside of Texas are processed at smelters in El Paso and Amarillo.

CRUSHED STONE: Texas is among the leading states in the production of crushed stone. Most production consists of limestone; other kinds of crushed stone produced in the state include basalt (trap rock), dolomite, granite, marble, rhyolite, sandstone, and serpentinite. Large tonnages of crushed stone are used as aggregate in concrete, as road material, and in the manufacture of cement and lime. Some is used as riprap, terrazzo, roofing chips, filter material, and fillers, as well as other purposes. In 2018, Texas led the country in the production of crushed stone, followed by Pennsylvania, Florida, and North Carolina.

DIATOMITE (DIATOMACEOUS EARTH): Diatomite is a very lightweight siliceous material consisting of the remains of microscopic aquatic plants (diatoms). It is used chiefly as a filter and filler; other uses are for thermal insulation, as an abrasive, as an insecticide carrier, as a lightweight aggregate, and for other purposes. The diatomite was deposited in shallow, fresh-water lakes that were present in the High Plains during portions of the Pliocene and Pleistocene epochs. Deposits have been found in Armstrong, Crosby, Dickens, Ector, Hartley, and Lamb counties. No diatomite is mined in Texas.

DOLOMITE ROCK: Dolomite rock, which consists largely of the mineral dolomite (calcium-magnesium carbonate), commonly is associated with limestone in Texas. Areas in which dolomite rock occurs include Central Texas, the Callahan Divide, and parts of the Edwards Plateau, High Plains, and West Texas. Some of the principal deposits of dolomite rock are found in Bell, Brown, Burnet, Comanche, Edwards, El Paso, Gillespie, Lampasas, Mills, Nolan, Taylor, and Williamson counties. Dolomite rock can be used as crushed stone (although much of Texas dolomite is soft and not a good aggregate material), in the manufacture of lime, and as a source of magnesium.

FELDSPAR: Large crystals and crystal fragments of feldspar minerals occur in the Precambrian pegmatite rocks that crop out in the Llano Uplift area of Central Texas, including Blanco, Burnet, Gillespie, Llano, and Mason counties, and in the Van Horn area of Culberson and Hudspeth counties in West Texas. Feldspar has been mined in Llano County for use as roofing granules and as a ceramic material. Feldspar is currently mined in Burnet County for use as an aggregate.

FLUORSPAR: The mineral fluorite (calcium fluoride), which is known commercially as fluorspar, occurs in both Central and West Texas. In Central Texas, the deposits that have been found in Burnet, Gillespie, and Mason counties are not considered adequate to sustain mining operations. In West Texas, deposits have been

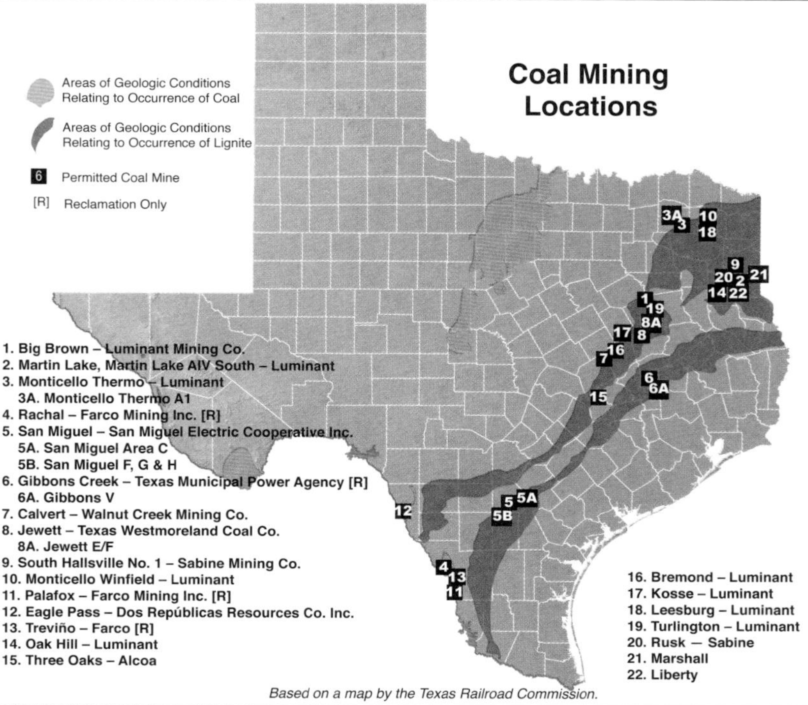

Based on a map by the Texas Railroad Commission.

Coal and Lignite Mine Production
(in short tons)

Mine	Acres Bonded	2018	2019	2020	Cumulative Total
1. Big Brown	4,363.10	0	-	-	171,155,954
2. Martin Lake	17,167.70	2,471,147	924,947	-	315,950,912
Martin Lake AIV South	2,308.00	0	-	-	6,771,850
3. Monticello-Thermo	1,876.10	0	-	-	42,849,720
Monticello-Thermo A-1	278.9	0	-	-	792,213
4. Rachal	615.9	0	-	-	963,827
5. San Miguel	10,424.10	1,981,967	700,709	655,269	90,913,367
San Miguel Area C	3,668.20	195,081	-	-	22,747,139
San Miguel F, G, & H	1,996.00	787,644	2,303,071	1,992,447	5,083,162
6. Gibbons Creek	4,976.60	0	-	-	30,431,174
Gibbons Creek V	1,796.10	0	-	-	12,547,611
7. Calvert	6,072.00	2,030,297	2,156,794	1,972,073	57,569,286
8. Jewett	9,593.20	0	-	-	173,220,612
Jewett E/F	3,917.00	0	-	-	35,937,586
9. South Hallsville No. 1	16,299.90	1,221,253	1,065,829	693,180	114,303,250
10. Monticello-Winfield	13,269.00	0	-	-	277,049,944
11. Palafox	2,575.20	0	-	-	5,355,519
12. Eagle Pass	5,848.00	2,146,219	1,638,483	250,766	8,916,057
13. Treviño	531.9	0	-	-	890,453
14. Oak Hill	18,064.90	0	-	-	129,763,914
15. Three Oaks	11,654.90	93,632	-	-	75,274,333
16. Bremond	3,370.60	0	-	-	236
17. Kosse	11,440.60	8,683,043	9,594,365	10,104,902	99,379,810
18. Leesburg	4,293.00	0	-	-	0
19. Turlington	3,614.30	0	-	-	16,504,979
20. Rusk	8,825.00	2,313,432	2,073,093	933,156	14,746,033
21. Marshall	1,101.00	185,097	185,718	83,235	1,120,462
22. Liberty	3,424.80	2,734,143	2,663,711	2,954,048	16,168,176
Statewide Total	**173,446.80**	**24,842,955**	**23,306,720**	**19,639,076**	***1,886,638,233**

* Statewide cumulative total includes the cumulative amount mined from the following "no longer permitted" mines: Little Bull Creek (428,932), Powell Bend (1,569,875), Thurber (465,984), Darco (6,798,881), and Sandow (150,966,982).

Source: Coal Production through 2020 report, Railroad Commission of Texas

found in Brewster, El Paso, Hudspeth, Jeff Davis, and Presidio counties. Fluorspar has been mined in the Christmas Mountains of Brewster County and processed in Marathon. Former West Texas mining activity in the Eagle Mountains district of Hudspeth County resulted in the production of approximately 15,000 short tons of fluorspar during the peak years of 1942–1950. No production has been reported in Hudspeth County since that period. Imported fluorspar is processed in Brownsville, Eagle Pass, El Paso, and Houston. Fluorspar is used in the steel, chemical, aluminum, magnesium, ceramics, and glass industries, and for various other purposes.

FULLER'S EARTH (see CLAYS).

GOLD: No major deposits of gold are known in Texas. Small amounts have been found in the Llano Uplift region of Central Texas and in West Texas; minor occurrences have been reported on the Edwards Plateau and the Gulf Coastal Plain of Texas. Nearly all of the gold produced in the state came as a by-product of silver and lead mining at Presidio mine, near Shafter in Presidio County. Additional small quantities were produced as a by-product of copper mining in Culberson County and from residual soils developed from gold-bearing quartz stringers in metamorphic rocks in Llano County. No gold mining has been reported in Texas since 1952. Total gold production in the state from 1889–1952 amounted to more than 8,419 troy ounces, according to U.S. Bureau of Mines figures. Most of the production, at least 73 percent and probably more, came from the Presidio mine.

GRANITE: Granites in shades of red and gray and related intrusive igneous rocks occur in the Llano Uplift of Central Texas and in the Trans-Pecos country of West Texas. Deposits are found in Blanco, Brewster, Burnet, El Paso, Gillespie, Hudspeth, Llano, McCulloch, Mason, Presidio, and other counties. Quarries in Burnet, Gillespie, Llano, and Mason counties produce Precambrian granite for a variety of uses, such as dimension stone and crushed stone.

GRAPHITE: Graphite, a soft, dark-gray mineral, is a form of very high-grade carbon. It occurs in Precambrian schist rocks of the Llano Uplift of Central Texas, notably in Burnet and Llano counties. Crystalline-flake graphite ore formerly was mined from open pits in the Clear Creek area of western Burnet County and processed at a plant near the mine. The mill now occasionally grinds imported material. Uses of natural crystalline graphite are refractories, steel production, pencil leads, lubricants, foundry facings, and crucibles, as well as other purposes.

GRINDING PEBBLES (ABRASIVE STONES): Flint pebbles, suitable for use in tube-mill grinding, are found in the Gulf Coastal Plain, where they occur in gravel deposits along rivers and in upland areas. Grinding pebbles are produced from Frio River terrace deposits near the McMullen–Live Oak county line, but the area is now part of the Choke Canyon Reservoir area.

GYPSUM: Gypsum is widely distributed in Texas. Chief deposits are bedded gypsum in the area east of the High Plains, in the Trans-Pecos country, and in Central Texas. It also occurs in salt-dome caprocks of the Gulf Coast. The massive, granular variety, which is known as rock gypsum, is the kind most commonly used by industry. Other varieties include alabaster, satin spar, and selenite.

Gypsum is one of the important industrial minerals in Texas. Bedded gypsum is produced from surface mines in Culberson, Fisher, Gillespie, Hardeman, Hudspeth, Kimble, Nolan, and Stonewall counties. Gypsum was formerly mined at Gyp Hill salt dome in Brooks County and at Hockley salt dome in Harris County. Most of the gypsum is calcined and used in the manufacture of gypsum wallboard, plaster, joint compounds, and other construction products. Crude gypsum is used chiefly as a retarder in portland cement and as a soil conditioner.

HELIUM: Helium is a very light, nonflammable, chemically inert gas. The U.S. Interior Department has ended its helium operation near Masterson in the Panhandle. The storage facility at Cliffside gas field near Amarillo and the 425-mile pipeline system will remain in operation until the government sells its remaining unrefined, crude helium. Helium is used in cryogenics, welding, pressurizing and purging, leak detection, synthetic breathing mixtures, and for other purposes. **In 2018, there were four helium extraction plants in Texas.**

IRON: Iron oxide (limonite, goethite, and hematite) and iron carbonate (siderite) deposits occur widely in East Texas, notably in Cass, Cherokee, Marion, and Morris counties, and also in Anderson, Camp, Harrison, Henderson, Nacogdoches, Smith, Upshur, and other counties. Magnetite (magnetic, black iron oxide) occurs in Central Texas, including a deposit at Iron Mountain in Llano County. Hematite occurs in the Trans-Pecos area and in the Llano Uplift of Central Texas. The extensive deposits of glauconite (a complex silicate containing iron) that occur in East Texas and the hematitic and goethitic Cambrian sandstone that crops out in the northwestern Llano Uplift region are potential sources of low-grade iron ore.

Limonite and other East Texas iron ores are mined from open pits in Cherokee and Henderson counties for use in the preparation of portland cement, as a weighting agent in well-drilling fluids, as an animal feed supplement, and for other purposes. East Texas iron ores also were mined in the past for use in the iron-steel industry.

KAOLIN (see CLAYS).

LEAD AND ZINC: The lead mineral galena (lead sulfide) commonly is associated with zinc and silver. It formerly was produced as a by-product of West Texas silver mining, chiefly from the Presidio mine at Shafter in Presidio County, although lesser amounts were obtained at several other mines and prospects. Deposits of galena also are known to occur in Blanco, Brewster, Burnet, Gillespie, and Hudspeth counties.

Zinc, primarily from the mineral sphalerite (zinc sulphide), was produced chiefly from the Bonanza and Alice Ray mines in the Quitman Mountains of Hudspeth County. In addition, small production was reported from several other areas, including the Chinati and Montezuma mines of Presidio County and the Buck Prospect in the Apache Mountains of Culberson County. Zinc mineralization also occurs in association with the lead deposits in Cambrian rocks of Central Texas.

LEONARDITE: Deposits of weathered (oxidized) low-Btu value bituminous coals, generally referred to as "leonardite," occur in Brewster County. The name leonardite is used for a mixture of chemical compounds that is high in humic acids. In the past, material from these deposits was sold as soil conditioner. Other uses of leonardite include modification of viscosity of drill fluids and as sorbants in water-treatment.

LIGHTWEIGHT AGGREGATE (see CLAYS, DIATOMITE, PERLITE, VERMICULITE).

LIGNITE: Almost all current coal production in Texas is located in the Tertiary-aged lignite belts that extend across the Texas Gulf Coastal Plain from the Rio Grande in South Texas to the Arkansas and Louisiana borders in East Texas. The Railroad Commission of Texas (RRC) reported that in 2018, Texas produced 24.8 million short tons of lignite from 12 mines. Cumulative production in 2018 was 1.8 billion short tons of lignite and coal. See the map and table opposite for more detail on coal and lignite mining.

The near-surface lignite resources, occurring at depths of less than 200 feet in seams of three feet or thicker, are estimated at 23 billion short tons. Recoverable reserves of strippable lignite, those that can be economically mined under current conditions of price and technology, are estimated by the EIA to be 722 million short tons.

Additional lignite resources of the Texas Gulf Coastal Plain occur as deep-basin deposits. Deep-basin resources, those that occur at depths of 200 to 2,000 feet in seams of five feet or thicker, are comparable in magnitude to near-surface resources. The deep-basin lignites are a potential energy resource that conceivably could be utilized by in situ (in place) recovery methods such as underground gasification.

As with bituminous coal, lignite production was significant prior to the general availability of oil and gas. Remnants of old underground mines are common throughout the area of lignite occurrence. Large reserves of strippable lignite have again attracted the attention of energy suppliers, and Texas is now the nation's sixth leading producer of coal, 99 percent of it lignite. Twelve large strip mines are now producing lignite that is burned for mine-mouth electric-power generation, and additional mines are planned. Mines are located in Atascosa, Franklin, Freestone, Harrison, Hopkins, Leon, Limestone, McMullen, Milam, Panola, Robertson, Rusk, and Titus counties.

LIME MATERIAL: Limestones, which are abundant in some areas of Texas, are heated to produce lime (calcium oxide) at a number of plants in the state. High-magnesium limestone and dolomite are used to prepare lime at a plant in Burnet County. Other lime plants are located in Bexar, Bosque, Comal, Hill, Johnson, and Travis counties. Lime production captive to the kiln's operator occurs in several Texas counties. Lime is used in soil stabilization, water purification, paper and pulp manufacture, metallurgy, sugar refining, agriculture, construction, removal of sulfur from stack gases, and for many other purposes.

LIMESTONE (see also BUILDING STONE): Texas is one of the nation's leading producers of limestone, which is quarried in more than 60 counties. Limestone occurs in nearly all areas of the state with the exception of most of the Gulf Coastal Plain and High Plains. Although some of the limestone is quarried for use as dimension stone, most of the output is crushed for uses such as bulk building materials (crushed stone, road base, concrete aggregate), chemical raw materials, fillers or extenders, lime and portland cement raw materials, agricultural limestone, and removal of sulfur from stack gases.

MAGNESITE: Small deposits of magnesite (natural magnesium carbonate) have been found in Precambrian rocks in Llano and Mason counties of Central Texas. At one time, there was small-scale mining of magnesite in the area; some of the material was used as agricultural stone and as terrazzo chips. Magnesite also can be calcined to form magnesia, which is used in metallurgical furnace refractories and other products.

MAGNESIUM: On the Texas Gulf Coast in Brazoria County, magnesium chloride is extracted from sea water at a plant in Freeport and used to produce magnesium compounds and magnesium metal. During World War II, high-magnesium Ellenburger dolomite rock from Burnet County was used as magnesium ore at a plant near Austin.

MANGANESE: Deposits of manganese minerals, such as braunite, hollandite, and pyrolusite, have been found in several areas, including Jeff Davis, Llano, Mason, Presidio, and Val Verde counties. Known deposits are not large. Small shipments have been made from Jeff Davis, Mason, and Val Verde counties, but no manganese mining has been reported in Texas since 1954.

MARBLE: Metamorphic and sedimentary marbles suitable for monument and building stone are found in the Llano Uplift and nearby areas of Central Texas and the Trans-Pecos area of West Texas. Gray, white, black, greenish black, light green, brown, and cream-colored marbles occur in Central Texas in Burnet, Gillespie, Llano, and Mason counties. West Texas metamorphic marbles include the bluish-white and the black marbles found southwest of Alpine in Brewster County and the white marble from Marble Canyon north of Van Horn in Culberson County. Marble can be used as dimension stone, terrazzo, and roofing aggregate, and for other purposes.

MERCURY (QUICKSILVER): Mercury minerals, chiefly cinnabar, occur in the Terlingua district and nearby districts of southern Brewster and southeastern Presidio counties. Mining began there about 1894, and from 1905–1935, Texas was one of the nation's leading producers of quicksilver. Following World War II, a sharp drop in demand and price, along with depletion of developed ore reserves, caused abandonment of all the Texas mercury mines.

With a rise in the price, sporadic mining took place from 1951–1960. In 1965, when the price of mercury moved to a record high, renewed interest in the Texas mercury districts resulted in the reopening of several mines and the discovery of new ore reserves. By April 1972, however, the price had declined, and the mines have reported no production since 1973.

MICA: Large crystals of flexible, transparent mica minerals in igneous pegmatite rocks and mica flakes in metamorphic schist rocks are found in the Llano Uplift area of Central Texas and the Van Horn area of West Texas. Most Central Texas deposits do not meet specifications for sheet mica, and although several attempts have been made to produce West Texas sheet mica in Culberson and Hudspeth counties, sustained production has not been achieved. A mica quarry operated for a short time in the early 1980s in the Van Horn Mountains of Culberson and Hudspeth counties to mine mica schist for use as an additive in rotary drilling fluids.

MOLYBDENUM: Small occurrences of molybdenite have been found in Burnet and Llano counties, and wulfenite, another molybdenum mineral, has been noted in rocks in the Quitman Mountains of Hudspeth County. Molybdenum minerals also occur at Cave Peak north of Van Horn in Culberson County, in the Altuda Mountain area of northwestern Brewster County, and in association with uranium ores of the Gulf Coastal Plain.

PEAT: This spongy organic substance forms in bogs from plant remains. It has been found in the Gulf Coastal Plain in several localities including Gonzales, Guadalupe, Lee, Milam, Polk, and San Jacinto counties. There has been intermittent, small-scale production of some of the peat for use as a soil conditioner.

PERLITE: Perlite, a glassy igneous rock, expands to a lightweight, porous mass when heated. It can be used as a lightweight aggregate, filter aid, horticultural aggregate, and for other purposes. Perlite occurs in Presidio County, where it has been mined in the Pinto Canyon area north of the Chinati Mountains. No perlite is currently mined in Texas, but perlite mined outside of Texas is expanded at plants in Bexar, Dallas, El Paso, Guadalupe, Harris, and Nolan counties.

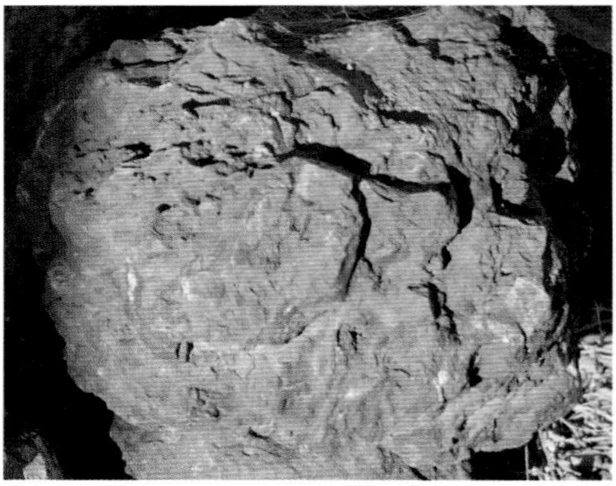

A sample of manganese ore at the Chihuahuan Desert Research Institute. Photo by Rosie Hatch

PHOSPHATE: Rock phosphate is present in Paleozoic rocks in several areas of Brewster and Presidio counties in West Texas and in Central Texas, but the known deposits are not large. In Northeast Texas, sedimentary rock phosphate occurs in thin conglomeratic lenses in Upper Cretaceous and Tertiary rock units; possibly some of these low-grade phosphorites could be processed on a small scale for local use as a fertilizer. Imported phosphate rock is processed at a plant in Brownsville.

POTASH: The potassium mineral polyhalite is widely distributed in the subsurface Permian Basin of West Texas and has been found in many wells in that area. During 1927–1931, the federal government drilled a series of potash-test wells in Crane, Crockett, Ector, Glasscock, Loving, Reagan, Upton, and Winkler counties. In addition to polyhalite, which was found in all of the counties, these wells revealed the presence of the potassium minerals carnallite and sylvite in Loving County and carnallite in Winkler County. The known Texas potash deposits are not as rich as those in the New Mexico portion of the Permian Basin and have not been developed.

PUMICITE (VOLCANIC ASH): Deposits of volcanic ash occur in Brazos, Fayette, Gonzales, Karnes, Polk, Starr, and other counties of the Texas Coastal Plain. Deposits also have been found in the Trans-Pecos area, High Plains, and in several counties east of the High Plains. Volcanic ash is used to prepare pozzolan cement, cleansing and scouring compounds, and soaps and sweeping compounds, as well as a carrier for insecticides and for other purposes. It has been mined in Dickens, Lynn, Scurry, Starr, and other counties.

QUICKSILVER (see MERCURY).

RARE-EARTH ELEMENTS AND METALS: The term "rare-earth elements" is commonly applied to elements of the lanthanide group (atomic numbers 57 through 71) plus yttrium. Yttrium, atomic number 39 and not a member of the lanthanide group, is included as a rare-earth element because it has similar properties to members of that group and usually occurs in nature with them. The metals thorium and scandium are sometimes termed "rare metals" because their occurence is often associated with the rare-earth elements.

The majority of rare-earth elements are consumed as catalysts in petroleum cracking and other chemical industries. Rare earths are widely used in the glass industry for tableware, specialty glasses, optics, and fiber optics. Cerium oxide has growing use as a polishing compound for glass, gem stones, cathode-ray tube faceplates, and other polishing. Rare earths are alloyed with various metals to produce materials used in the aeronautic, space, and electronics industries. The addition of rare-earth elements may improve resistance to metal fatigue at high temperatures, reduce potential for corrosion, and selectively increase conductivity and magnetism of the metal.

Various members of this group, including thorium, have anomalous concentrations in the rhyolitic and related igneous rocks of the Quitman Mountains and the Sierra Blanca area of Trans-Pecos, Texas.

SALT (SODIUM CHLORIDE) (see also BRINES): Salt resources of Texas are virtually inexhaustible. Enormous deposits occur in the subsurface Permian Basin of West Texas and in the salt domes of the Gulf Coastal Plain. Salt also is found in the alkali playa lakes of the High Plains, the alkali flats or salt lakes in the Salt Basin of Culberson and Hudspeth counties, and along some of the bays and lagoons of the South Texas Gulf Coast.

Texas is one of the leading salt-producing states. Rock salt is obtained from underground mines in salt domes at Grand Saline in Van Zandt County and Hockley Dome in Harris County. Salt is produced from rock salt and by solution mining as brines from wells drilled into the underground salt deposits.

SAND, INDUSTRIAL: Sands used for special purposes, due to high silica content or to unique physical properties, command higher prices than common sand. Industrial sands in Texas occur mainly in the Central Gulf Coastal Plain and in North-Central Texas. They include abrasive, blast, chemical, engine, filtration, foundry, glass, hydraulic-fracturing (proppant), molding, and pottery sands. Recent production of industrial sands has been from Atascosa, Colorado, Hardin, Harris, Liberty, Limestone, McCulloch, Newton, Smith, Somervell, and Upshur counties.

SAND AND GRAVEL (CONSTRUCTION): Sand and gravel are among the most extensively utilized resources in Texas. Principal occurrence is along the major streams and in stream terraces. Sand and gravel are important bulk construction materials, used as railroad ballast, base materials, and for other purposes. In 2018, Texas was second only to California in production of sand and gravel (construction). Arizona and Washington were the next two largest producers.

SANDSTONE: Sandstones of a variety of colors and textures are widely distributed in a number of geologic formations in Texas. Some of the sandstones have been quarried for use as dimension stone in El Paso, Parker, Terrell, Ward, and other counties. Crushed sandstone is produced in Freestone, Gaines, Jasper, McMullen, Motley, and other counties for use as road-building material, terrazzo stone, and aggregate.

SERPENTINITE: Several masses of serpentinite, which formed from the alteration of basic igneous rocks, are associated with other Precambrian metamorphic rocks of the Llano Uplift. The largest deposit is the Coal Creek serpentinite mass in northern Blanco and Gillespie counties from which terrazzo chips have been produced. Other deposits are present in Gillespie and Llano counties. (The features that are associated with surface and subsurface Cretaceous rocks in several counties in or near the Balcones Fault Zone and that are commonly known as "serpentine plugs" are not serpentine at all, but are altered igneous volcanic necks and pipes, and mounds of altered volcanic ash, palagonite, that accumulated around the former submarine volcanic pipes.)

SHELL: Oyster shells and other shells in shallow coastal waters and in deposits along the Texas Gulf Coast have been produced in the past chiefly by dredging. They were used to a limited extent as raw material in the manufacture of cement, as concrete aggregate and road base, and for other purposes. No shell has been produced in Texas since 1981.

SILVER: During the period 1885–1952, the production of silver in Texas, as reported by the U.S. Bureau of Mines, totaled about 33 million troy ounces. For about 70 years, silver was the most consistently produced metal in Texas, although always in moderate quantities. All of the production came from the Trans-Pecos country of West Texas, where the silver was mined in Brewster County (Altuda Mountain), Culberson and Hudspeth counties (Van Horn Mountains and Van Horn–Allamoore district), Hudspeth County (Quitman Mountains and Eagle Mountains), and Presidio County (Chinati Mountains area, Loma Plata mine, and Shafter district).

Chief producer was the Presidio mine in the Shafter district, which began operations in the late 1800s, and, through September 1942, produced more than 30 million ounces of silver, more than 92 percent of Texas' total silver production. Water in the lower mine levels, lean ores, and low price of silver resulted in the closing of the mine in 1942. Another important silver producer was the Hazel copper-silver mine in the Van Horn–Allamoore district in Culberson County, which accounted for more than 2 million ounces.

An increase in the price of silver in the late 1970s stimulated prospecting for new reserves, and exploration began near the old Presidio mine, near the old Plata Verde mine in the Van Horn Mountains district, at the Bonanza mine in the Quitman Mountains district, and at the old Hazel mine. A decline in the price of silver in the early 1980s, however, resulted in reduction of exploration and mine development in the region. The recent rise in the value of silver has sparked new interest in the Shafter mining district of West Texas.

SOAPSTONE (see TALC AND SOAPSTONE).

SODIUM SULFATE (SALT CAKE): Sodium sulfate minerals occur in salt beds and brines of the alkali playa lakes of the High Plains in West Texas. In some lakes, the sodium sulfate minerals are present in deposits a few feet beneath the lakebeds. Sodium sulfate also is found in underground brines in the Permian Basin. Current production is from brines and dry salt beds at alkali lakes in Gaines and Terry counties. Past production was reported in Lynn and Ward counties. Sodium sulfate is used chiefly by the detergent and paper and pulp industries. Other uses are in the preparation of glass and other products.

STONE (see BUILDING STONE and CRUSHED STONE).

STRONTIUM: Deposits of the mineral celestite (strontium sulfate) have been found in a number of places, including localities in Brown, Coke, Comanche, Fisher, Lampasas, Mills, Nolan, Real, Taylor, Travis, and Williamson counties. Most of the occurrences are very minor, and no strontium is currently produced in the state.

SULFUR: Texas is one of the world's principal sulfur-producing areas. The sulfur is mined from deposits of native sulfur, and it is extracted from sour (sulfur-bearing) natural gas and petroleum. Recovered sulfur accounted for more than 90 percent of all 2018 sulfur production in the United States. Native sulfur is found in large deposits in the caprock of some of the salt domes along the Texas Gulf Coast and in some of the surface and subsurface Permian strata of West Texas, notably in Culberson and Pecos counties.

Native sulfur obtained from the underground deposits is known as Frasch sulfur, so called because of Herman Frasch, the chemist who devised the method of drilling wells into the deposits, melting the sulfur with superheated water, and forcing the molten sulfur to the surface. Most of the production now goes to the users in molten form.

Frasch sulfur is produced from only one Gulf Coast salt dome in Wharton County and from West Texas underground Permian strata in Culberson County. Operations at several Gulf Coast domes have been closed in recent years. During the 1940s, acidic sulfur earth was produced in the Rustler Springs district in Culberson County for use as a fertilizer and soil conditioner. Sulfur is recovered from sour natural gas and petroleum at plants in numerous Texas counties.

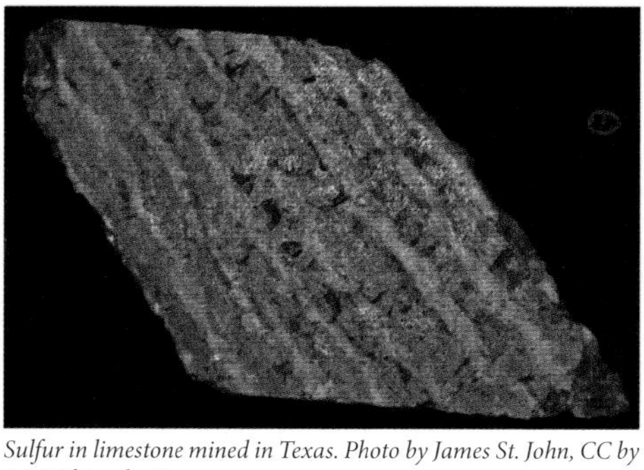

Sulfur in limestone mined in Texas. Photo by James St. John, CC by 2.0/Wikimedia Commons

Sulfur is used in the preparation of fertilizers and organic and inorganic chemicals, in petroleum refining, and for many other purposes.

TALC AND SOAPSTONE: Deposits of talc are found in the Precambrian metamorphic rocks of the Allamoore area of eastern Hudspeth and western Culberson counties. Soapstone, containing talc, occurs in the Precambrian metamorphic rocks of the Llano Uplift area, notably in Blanco, Gillespie, and Llano counties. Current production is from surface mines in the Allamoore area. Talc is used in ceramic, roofing, paint, paper, plastic, synthetic rubber, and other products.

TIN: Tin minerals have been found in El Paso and Mason counties. Small quantities were produced during the early 1900s in the Franklin Mountains north of El Paso. Cassiterite (tin dioxide) occurrences in Mason County are believed to be very minor. The only tin smelter in the United States, built at Texas City by the federal government during World War II and later sold to a private company, processes tin concentrates from ores mined outside of Texas, tin residues, and secondary tin-bearing materials.

TITANIUM: The titanium mineral rutile has been found in small amounts at the Mueller prospect in Jeff Davis County. Another titanium mineral, ilmenite, occurs in sandstones in Burleson, Fayette, Lee, Starr, and several other counties. Deposits that would be considered commercial under present conditions have not been found.

TRAP ROCK (see BASALT).

TUNGSTEN: The tungsten mineral scheelite has been found in small deposits in Gillespie and Llano counties and in the Quitman Mountains in Hudspeth County. Small deposits of other tungsten minerals have been prospected in the Cave Peak area north of Van Horn in Culberson County.

URANIUM: Uranium deposits were discovered in the Texas Coastal Plain in 1954 when abnormal radioactivity was detected in the Karnes County area. A number of uranium deposits have since been discovered within a belt of strata extending more than 250 miles from the middle Coastal Plain southwestward to the Rio Grande.

Various uranium minerals also have been found in other areas of Texas, including the Trans-Pecos, the Llano Uplift, and the High Plains. With the exception of small shipments from the High Plains during the 1950s, all the uranium production in Texas has been from the Coastal Plain. Uranium has been obtained from surface mines extending from northern Live Oak County, southeastern Atascosa County, across northern Karnes County, and into southern Gonzales County. Uranium is produced by in-situ leaching, brought to the surface through wells, and stripped from the solution at recovery operations.

In 1999, uranium mining shut down because of decreased value and demand. Production resumed in Texas in late 2004, when inventories were depleted and market prices rose to economic levels that allowed resumption of production. A total of 1.4 million pounds (606.5 tons) of eU_3O_8 was produced in South Texas in 2007.

There are no active uranium recovery operations in Texas, though as of 2017 there are 10 permits for uranium exploration in seven counties: Bee, Brooks, Duval, Goliad, Jim Hogg, Kleberg, and Live Oak.

VERMICULITE: Vermiculite, a mica-like mineral that expands when heated, occurs in Burnet, Gillespie, Llano, Mason, and other counties in the Llano Uplift region. It has been produced at a surface mine in Llano County. Vermiculite, mined outside of Texas, is exfoliated (expanded) at plants in Dallas, Houston, and San Antonio. Exfoliated vermiculite is used for lightweight concrete aggregate, horticulture, insulation, and other purposes.

VOLCANIC ASH (see PUMICITE).

ZEOLITES: The zeolite minerals clinoptilolite and analcime occur in Tertiary lavas and tuffs in Brewster, Jeff Davis, and Presidio counties in West Texas. Clinoptilolite also is found associated with Tertiary tuffs in the southern Texas Coastal Plain, including deposits in Karnes, McMullen, and Webb counties, and currently is produced in McMullen County. Zeolites, sometimes called "molecular sieves," can be used in ion-exchange processes to reduce pollution, as a catalyst in oil cracking, in obtaining high-purity oxygen and nitrogen from air, in water purification, and for many other purposes.

ZINC (see LEAD AND ZINC). ☆

Texas Newspapers, Radio, and Television Stations

Sources: 2021 Texas Newspaper Directory; FCC, https://www.fcc.gov/media/filing-systems-and-databases

Texas is rich with newspapers and broadcast media, many of which have long histories. In the following list, only printed, subscription newspapers appear, and their frequency of publication is indicated by the following codes: (D) daily or at least four days a week, (TW) triweekly, (S) semiweekly, (SM) semimonthly, (M) monthly; all others are weeklies. Radio and TV stations are those with valid operating licenses as of July 2021. Not included are those with construction permits or pending applications. ☆

—A—

Abernathy: Newspaper: *Abernathy Advocate.*

Abilene: Newspaper: *Abilene Reporter-News* (D). **Radio-AM:** KSLI, 1280 kHz; KWKC, 1340; KYYW, 1470; KZQQ, 1560. **Radio-FM:** KGNZ, 88.1 MHz; KACU, 89.5; KAGT, 90.5; KAQD, 91.3; KMWX, 92.5; KULL, 100.7; KEAN, 105.1; KKHR, 106.3; KEYJ, 107.9. TV Stations: KXVA-Ch. 15; KRBC-Ch. 29; KTAB-Ch. 30.

Agua Dulce: Radio-FM: KOUL, 107.7 MHz.

Alamo: Radio-FM: KJAV, 104.9 MHz.

Alamo Heights: Radio-AM: KDRY, 1100 kHz.

Albany: Newspaper: *Albany News.* **Radio-FM:** KQOS, 91.7 MHz.

Aledo: Newspaper: *The Community News.*

Alice: Newspaper: *Alice Echo-News Journal* (S). **Radio-AM:** KOPY, 1070 kHz. **Radio-FM:** KAWV, 88.3 MHz; KOPY, 92.1; KNDA, 102.9.

Allen: Newspaper: *Allen American.* **Radio-FM:** KESN, 103.3 MHz.

Alpine: Newspapers: *Alpine Avalanche*; *The Big Bend Gazette* (M). **Radio-AM:** KVLF, 1240 kHz. **Radio-FM:** KBAL, 90.3 MHz; KRTP, 91.7; KALP, 92.7.

Alvin: Newspaper: *Alvin Sun.* **Radio-AM:** KTEK, 1110 kHz. **Radio-FM:** KACC, 89.7 MHz. TV Station: KFTH-Ch. 36.

Amarillo: Newspaper: *Amarillo Globe-News* (D). **Radio-AM:** KGNC, 710 kHz; KIXZ, 940; KDJW, 1010; KZIP, 1310; KTNZ, 1360; KPUR, 1440. **Radio-FM:** KJRT, 88.3 MHz; KXLV, 89.1; KACV, 89.9; KAVW, 90.7; KXRI, 91.9; KQIZ, 93.1; KMXJ, 94.1; KXSS, 96.9; KGNC, 97.9; KPRF, 98.7; KBZD, 99.7; KXGL, 100.9; KATP, 101.9; KVWE, 102.9; KJJP, 105.7. TV Stations: KVII-Ch. 7; KACV-Ch. 9; KFDA-Ch. 10; KCIT-Ch. 15; KAMR-Ch. 19.

Anahuac: Newspaper: *The Progress.*

Andrews: Newspaper: *Andrews County News* (S). **Radio-AM:** KACT, 1360 kHz. **Radio-FM:** KACT, 105.5 MHz.

Anna: Newspaper: *Anna-Melissa Tribune.*

Anson: Newspaper: *Western Observer.* **Radio-FM:** KTLT, 98.1 MHz.

Aransas Pass: Newspaper: *Aransas Pass Progress.* **Radio-FM:** KKWV, 88.1 MHz.

Archer City: Newspaper: *Archer County News.* **Radio-FM:** KPMA, 91.9 MHz.

Arlington: Radio-FM: KLTY, 94.9 MHz. TV Station: KPXD-Ch. 25.

Arroyo: Radio-FM: KVJS, 88.1 MHz.

Athens: Newspaper: *Athens Daily Review* (D). **Radio-AM:** KLVQ, 1410 kHz.

Atlanta: Newspaper: *Cass County Citizen's Journal-Sun.* **Radio-AM:** KPYN, 900 kHz. **Radio-FM:** KNRB, 100.1 MHz.

Austin: Newspapers: *Austin American-Statesman* (D); *Austin Business Journal*; *West Austin News* (SM). **Radio-AM:** KLBJ, 590 kHz; KVET, 1300; KTSN, 1490. **Radio-FM:** KAZI, 88.7 MHz; KMFA, 89.5; KUT, 90.5; KVRX, 91.7; KLBJ, 93.7; KKMJ, 95.5; KVET, 98.1; KASE, 100.7; KPEZ, 102.3; KBPA, 103.5. TV Stations: KTBC-Ch. 7; KXAN-Ch. 21; KLRU-Ch. 22; KNVA-Ch. 23; KVUE-Ch. 33; KEYE-Ch. 34.

Austwell: Radio-FM: KIBQ, 105.9 MHz.

Azle: Newspaper: *The Azle News.* **Radio-FM:** KYDA,101.7 MHz.

—B—

Baird: Newspaper: *Baird Banner.* **Radio-FM:** KABW, 95.1 MHz.

Balch Springs: Radio-AM: KSKY, 660 kHz.

Ballinger: Newspaper: *Runnels County Register.* **Radio-AM:** KRUN, 1400 kHz. **Radio-FM:** KKCN, 103.1 MHz.

Bandera: Newspaper: *Bandera Bulletin.* **Radio-FM:** KEEP, 103.1 MHz.

Bangs: Radio-FM: KBNX, 97.9 MHz.

Bartlett: Newspaper: *Tribune-Progress.*

Bastrop: Newspaper: *Bastrop Advertiser* (S). **Radio-FM:** KHIB, 88.5 MHz; KLZT, 107.1.

Batesville: Radio-FM: KRZU, 90.7 MHz; KQSA, 97.9.

Bay City: Newspaper: *The Bay City Tribune* (S). **Radio-FM:** KQUE, 88.1 MHz; KZBJ, 89.5; KNTE, 101.7; KMKS, 102.5.

Baytown: Newspaper: *Baytown Sun* (D). **Radio-AM:** KWWJ, 1360. TV Station: KUBE-Ch. 31.

Beaumont: Newspaper: *The Beaumont Enterprise* (D). **Radio-AM:** KLVI, 560 kHz; KZZB, 990; KIKR, 1450. **Radio-FM:** KLBT, 88.1 MHz; KGHY, 88.5; KTXB, 89.7; KVLU, 91.3; KQXY, 94.1; KYKR, 95.1; KTCX, 102.5; KQQK, 107.9. TV Stations: KBMT-Ch. 12; KFDM-Ch. 15; KITU-Ch. 29.

Bee Cave: Radio-FM: KTXX, 104.9 MHz.

Beeville: Newspaper: *Beeville Bee-Picayune* (S). **Radio-AM:** KIBL, 1490 kHz. **Radio-FM:** KVFM, 91.3 MHz; KTKO, 105.7; KRXB, 107.1.

Bellaire: Radio-AM: KGOW, 1560 kHz.

Bellmead: Radio-FM: KBHT, 104.9 MHz.

Bells: Radio-FM: KMKT, 93.1 MHz.

Bellville: Newspaper: *The Bellville Times.* **Radio-AM:** KULF, 1090 kHz.

Belton: Newspaper: *The Belton Journal.* **Radio-FM:** KOOC, 106.3 MHz. TV Station: KNCT-Ch. 17.

Benavides: Radio-FM: KXTM, 94.3 MHz.

Benbrook: Radio-AM: KFLC, 1270 kHz. **Radio-FM:** KESS, 107.1 MHz.

Big Lake: Newspaper: *Big Lake Wildcat.*

Big Sandy: Newspaper: *Big Sandy–Hawkins Journal.* **Radio-FM:** KTAA, 90.7 MHz.

Big Spring: Newspaper: *Big Spring Herald* (D). **Radio-AM:** KBYG, 1400 kHz; KBST, 1490. **Radio-FM:** KBCX, 91.5 MHz; KBTS, 94.3; KBST, 95.7; KBUG, 100.9. TV Station: KCWO-Ch. 33.

Big Wells: Radio-FM: KHBE, 102.1 MHz.

Bishop: Radio-FM: KMZZ, 106.9 MHz.

Blanco: Newspaper: *Blanco County News.* TV Station: KNIC-Ch. 18.

Blanket: Radio-FM: KQMJ, 104.7 MHz

Bloomington: Radio-FM: KHVT, 91.5 MHz; KLUB, 106.9.

Blossom: Radio-FM: KISY, 92.7 MHz

Boerne: Newspaper: *The Boerne Star* (S). **Radio-AM:** KBRN,

1500 kHz.

Bogata: Newspaper: *Bogata News–Talco Times.*

Bonham: Newspaper: *The Fannin County Leader.* **Radio-AM:** KFYN, 1420 kHz.

Booker: Newspaper: *The Booker News.*

Borger: Newspaper: *Borger News-Herald* (D). **Radio-FM:** KWAS, 88.1 MHz; KQFX, 104.3; KQTY, 106.7. TV Station: KEYU-Ch. 31.

Bovina: Radio-FM: KKNM, 96.5 MHz.

Bowie: Newspaper: *The Bowie News* (S). **Radio-AM:** KNTX, 1410 kHz.

Brackettville: Newspaper: *Kinney County Post.* **Radio-FM:** KEDV, 90.3 MHz; KUDR, 94.7.

Brady: Newspaper: *Brady Standard-Herald.* **Radio-AM:** KNEL, 1490 kHz. **Radio-FM:** KNEL, 95.3 MHz.

Breckenridge: Newspaper: *Breckenridge American.* **Radio-AM:** KROO, 1430 kHz. **Radio-FM:** KQXB, 89.9 MHz; KLXK, 93.5.

Brenham: Newspaper: *The Banner-Press* (D). **Radio-AM:** KWHI, 1280 kHz. **Radio-FM:** KUBJ, 89.7 MHz; KLTR, 94.1; KTTX, 106.1.

Bridgeport: Radio-FM: KBOC, 98.3 MHz.

Brookshire: Radio-AM: KCHN, 1050 kHz.

Brownfield: Newspaper: *Brownfield News* (S). **Radio-AM:** KKUB, 1300 kHz. **Radio-FM:** KLTB, 89.7 MHz; KHLK, 104.3.

Brownsville: Newspapers: *The Brownsville Herald* (D); El Nuevo Heraldo (D). **Radio-AM:** KVNS, 1700 kHz. **Radio-FM:** KBNR, 88.3 MHz; KKPS, 99.5. TV: KVEO-Ch. 24.

Brownwood: Newspaper: *Brownwood Bulletin* (TW). **Radio-AM:** KXYL, 1240 kHz; KBWD, 1380. **Radio-FM:** KBUB, 90.3 MHz; KHBW, 91.7; KQBZ, 96.9; KPSM, 99.3; KOXE, 101.3.

Bryan: Newspaper: *The Eagle* (D). **Radio-AM:** KTAM, 1240 kHz; KAGC, 1510. **Radio-FM:** KORA, 98.3 MHz; KNFX, 99.5; KKYS, 104.7. TV Stations: KBTX-Ch. 16; KYLE-Ch. 29.

Buda: Radio-FM: KROX, 101.5 MHz.

Buffalo: Newspapers: *Buffalo Express.* **Radio-FM:** WTAW, 103.5 MHz.

Buffalo Gap: Radio-FM: KBGT, 93.3 MHz.

Bullard: Radio-FM: KZXM, 94.3 MHz.

Buna: Newspaper: *The Buna Beacon.*

Burkburnett: Newspaper: *Burkburnett Informer Star.* **Radio-FM:** KYYI, 104.7 MHz.

Burke: Radio-FM: KAGZ, 97.7 MHz.

Burleson: Radio-AM: KCLE, 1460 kHz.

Burnet: Newspapers: *Burnet Bulletin; Citizens Gazette.* **Radio-FM:** KMPN 95.9 MHz; KBEY, 103.9.

Bushland: Radio-FM: KTXP, 91.5 MHz.

—C—

Caldwell: Newspaper: *Burleson County Tribune.* **Radio-FM:** KALD, 91.9 MHz; KAPN, 107.3.

Callisburg: Radio-FM: KPFC, 91.9 MHz.

Cameron: Newspaper: *The Cameron Herald.* **Radio-AM:** KTON, 1330 kHz. **Radio-FM:** KMIL, 105.1 MHz.

Campbell: Radio-FM: KRVA, 107.1 MHz.

Canadian: Newspaper: *The Canadian Record.* **Radio-FM:** KHHC, 91.9 MHz.

Canton: Newspapers: *Canton Herald; Van Zandt News.* **Radio-AM:** KWJB, 1510 kHz.

Canyon: Newspaper: *The Canyon News* (S). **Radio-FM:** KWTS, 91.1 MHz; KARX, 107.1; KZRK, 107.9.

Carbon: Radio-FM: KJDE, 100.1 MHz.

Carrizo Springs: Newspaper: *The Carrizo Springs Javelin.* **Radio-AM:** KBEN, 1450 kHz. **Radio-FM:** KCZO, 92.1 MHz.

Carrollton: Newspaper: *Carrollton Leader.* **Radio-AM:** KJON, 850 kHz.

Carthage: Newspaper: *The Panola Watchman* (S). **Radio-AM:** KGAS, 1590 kHz. **Radio-FM:** KRTG, 88.3 MHz; KTUX, 98.9; KGAS, 104.3.

Cedar Lake: Radio-FM: KQVI, 89.9 MHz.

Cedar Park: Newspaper: *Hill Country News.* **Radio-FM:** KGSR, 93.3 MHz.

Celina: Newspaper: *Celina Record.*

Center: Newspaper: *The Light and Champion.* **Radio-AM:** KDET, 930 kHz. **Radio-FM:** KQBB, 100.5 MHz.

Centerville: Newspaper: *Centerville News.* **Radio-FM:** KKEE, 101.3 MHz; KUZN, 105.9.

Channing: Radio-FM: KAMT, 105.1 MHz.

Charlotte: Radio-FM: KSAQ, 102.3 MHz.

Childress: Newspaper: *The Red River Sun.* **Radio-AM:** KCTX, 1510 kHz. **Radio-FM:** KCTX, 96.1 MHz; KCHT 99.7.

Christine: Radio-FM: KWYU, 96.9 MHz.

Christoval: Radio-FM: KQTC, 99.5 MHz.

Clarendon: Newspaper: *The Clarendon Enterprise.* **Radio-FM:** KYCL, 88.9 MHz; KEFH, 99.3.

Clarksville: Newspaper: *Clarksville Times.* **Radio-AM:** KHDY, 1350 kHz. **Radio-FM:** KXQJ, 90.1 MHz; KHDY, 98.5.

Claude: Newspaper: *The Claude News.* **Radio-FM:** KPUR, 95.7 MHz.

Cleburne: Newspaper: *Cleburne Times-Review* (D). **Radio-AM:** KHFX, 1140 kHz.

Cleveland: Newspaper: *Cleveland Advocate.* **Radio-FM:** KTHT, 97.1 MHz.

Clifton: Newspaper: *The Clifton Record.* **Radio-FM:** KWOW, 104.1 MHz.

Clute: Newspaper: *The Facts* (D).

Clyde: Newspaper: *Clyde Journal.*

Coahoma: Radio-FM: KXCS, 105.5 MHz.

Cockrell Hill: Radio-AM: KRVA, 1600 kHz.

Coleman: Newspaper: *Chronicle & Democrat-Voice.* **Radio-AM:** KSTA, 1000 kHz. **Radio-FM:** KXYL, 102.3 MHz.

College Station: Radio-AM: KZNE, 1150 kHz; KWBC, 1550; WTAW, 1620. **Radio-FM:** KEOS, 89.1 MHz; KLGS, 89.9; KAMU, 90.9; KNDE, 95.1. TV Station: KAMU-Ch. 12.

Colorado City: Newspaper: *Colorado City Record.* **Radio-AM:** KVMC, 1320 kHz. **Radio-FM:** KEHM, 99.3 MHz; KAUM, 107.1

Columbus: Newspapers: *The Banner-Press Newspaper; The Colorado County Citizen.* **Radio-FM:** KULM, 98.3 MHz.

Comanche: Newspaper: *The Comanche Chief.* **Radio-AM:** KCOM, 1550 kHz. **Radio-FM:** KYOX, 94.3 MHz; KCXX 103.9.

Comfort: Newspaper: *The Comfort News.* **Radio-FM:** KMYO, 95.1 MHz.

Commerce: Radio-FM: KETR, 88.9 MHz; KYJC, 91.3.

Comstock: Radio-FM: KDER, 99.3 MHz.

Concan: Radio-FM: KHCU, 93.1 MHz.

Conroe: Newspaper: *The Courier* (D). **Radio-AM:** KJOZ, 880 kHz; KYOK, 1140. **Radio-FM:** KHPT, 106.9 MHz. TV Stations: KPXB-Ch. 32; KTBU-Ch. 33.

Converse: Radio-AM: KTMR, 1130 kHz.

Cooper: Newspaper: *Cooper Review.* **Radio-FM:** KPCO, 89.9 MHz; KIKT, 93.5.

Coppell: Newspapers: *Citizens' Advocate; Coppell Gazette.*

Copperas Cove: Newspaper: *Copperas Cove Leader-Press* (S). **Radio-FM:** KSSM, 103.1 MHz.

Corpus Christi: Newspapers: *Corpus Christi Caller-Times* (D); *Coastal Bend Daily Legal & Business News* (D). **Radio-AM:** KCTA, 1030 kHz; KCCT, 1150; KSIX, 1230; KKTX, 1360; KUNO, 1400; KEYS, 1440. **Radio-FM:** KPLV, 88.7 MHz; KEDT, 90.3; KBNJ, 91.7; KMXR, 93.9; KBSO, 94.7; KZFM, 95.5; KLTG, 96.5; KRYS, 99.1. TV Stations: KIII-Ch. 8; KZTV-Ch. 10; KRIS-Ch. 13; KSCC, Ch. 19; KEDT-Ch. 23; KORO-Ch. 27.

Corrigan: Radio-FM: KYTM, 99.3 MHz.

Corsicana: Newspaper: *Corsicana Daily Sun* (D). **Radio-AM:** KAND, 1340 kHz.

Cotulla: Radio-FM: KCOT, 96.3 MHz; KWMJ, 100.7.

Crane: Newspaper: *Crane News.* **Radio-AM:** KXOI, 810 kHz. **Radio-FM:** KMMZ, 101.3 MHz.

Creedmoor: Radio-AM: KZNX, 1530 kHz.

Crockett: Newspaper: *Houston County Courier.* **Radio-AM:** KIVY, 1290 kHz. **Radio-FM:** KCKT, 88.5 MHz; KIVY, 92.7; KBPC, 93.5.

Cross Plains: Newspaper: *Cross Plains Review.*

Crowell: Newspaper: *Foard County News.* **Radio-FM:** KTUT, 98.9 MHz.

Crystal City: Newspaper: *Zavala County Sentinel.* **Radio-FM:** KHER, 94.3 MHz.

Cuero: Newspaper: *Cuero Record.* **Radio-FM:** KTLZ, 89.9 MHz.

Cuney: Radio-FM: KVUT, 99.7 MHz.

—D—

Daingerfield: Newspaper: *The Steel Country Bee.*

Dalhart: Newspaper: *Dalhart Texan* (S). **Radio-AM:** KXIT, 1240 kHz. **Radio-FM:** KTDH, 89.3 MHz; KTDA, 91.7; KBEX 96.1.

Dallas: Newspapers: *The Dallas Morning News* (D); *Dallas Business Journal; Daily Commercial Record* (D); *Park Cities News; Texas Jewish Post.* **Radio-AM:** KLIF, 570 kHz; KGGR, 1040; KRLD, 1080; KFXR, 1190; KTCK, 1310; KNGO, 1480. **Radio-FM:** KNON, 89.3 MHz; KERA, 90.1; KCBI, 90.9; KKXT, 91.7; KZPS, 92.5; KBFB, 97.9; KLUV, 98.7; KJKK, 100.3; WRR, 101.1; KDMX, 102.9; KKDA, 104.5; KRLD, 105.3. TV Stations: WFAA-Ch. 8; KERA-Ch. 14; KDTX-Ch. 21; KDFI-Ch. 27; KDAF-Ch. 32; KDFW-Ch. 35; KXTX-Ch. 36.

Decatur: Newspaper: *Wise County Messenger* (S). **Radio-FM:** KDKR, 91.3 MHz; KRNB, 105.7. TV Station: KMPX-Ch. 30.

Deer Park: Radio-FM: KAMA, 104.9 MHz.

De Leon: Newspaper: *De Leon Free Press.*

Dell City: Newspaper: *Hudspeth County Herald.*

Del Mar Hills: Radio-AM: KVOZ, 890 kHz.

Del Rio: Newspaper: *The 830 Times.* **Radio-AM:** KDRN, 1230 kHz; KWMC, 1490. **Radio-FM:** KVFE, 88.5 MHz; KTPD, 89.3; KDLI, 89.9; KDLK, 94.1; KTDR, 96.3. TV Station: KYVV-Ch. 28.

Del Valle: Radio-AM: KIXL, 970 kHz.

Denison: Radio-FM: KYFB, 91.5 MHz.

Denton: Newspaper: *Denton Record-Chronicle* (D). **Radio-FM:** KFZO, 99.1 MHz; KHKS, 106.1. TV Station: KDTN-Ch. 29.

Denver City: Newspaper: *Denver City Press.*

Deport: Newspaper: *Deport-Blossom Times.*

DeSoto: Newspaper: *Focus Daily News* (D).

Detroit: Newspaper: *Detroit Weekly.* **Radio-FM:** KFYN, 104.3 MHz.

Devine: Newspaper: *The Devine News.* **Radio-FM:** KRPT, 92.5 MHz.

Diboll: Radio-AM: KSML, 1260 kHz. **Radio-FM:** KAFX, 95.5 MHz.

Dilley: Radio-FM: KKDL, 93.7 MHz; KVWG, 95.3; KLMO, 98.9.

Dimmitt: Newspaper: *The Castro County News.* **Radio-AM:** KDHN, 1470 kHz. **Radio-FM:** KNNK, 100.5 MHz.

Doss: Radio-FM: KGKV, 88.1 MHz.

Dripping Springs: Newspapers: *Dripping Springs Century News; News-Dispatch.* **Radio-FM:** KLLR, 91.9 MHz.

Dublin: Newspaper: *The Dublin Citizen.* **Radio-FM:** KSTV, 93.1 MHz.

Dumas: Newspaper: *Moore County News-Press* (S). **Radio-AM:** KDDD, 800 kHz. **Radio-FM:** KDDD, 95.3 MHz.

—E—

Eagle Lake: Radio-FM: KJJB, 95.3 MHz.

Eagle Pass: Radio-AM: KEPS, 1270 kHz. **Radio-FM:** KEPI, 88.7 MHz; KEPX, 89.5; KINL, 92.7. TV Station: KVAW-Ch. 18.

Early: Radio-FM: KJKB, 106.7 MHz.

East Bernard: Newspaper: *East Bernard Express.*

Eastland: Newspaper: *Eastland County Today.* **Radio-FM:** KQXE, 91.1 MHz; KATX, 97.7.

Eden: Newspaper: *Eden Echo.* **Radio-FM:** KPDE, 91.5 MHz.

Edinburg: Radio-AM: KURV, 710 kHz. **Radio-FM:** KOIR, 88.5 MHz; KBFM, 104.1; KVLY, 107.9.

Edna: Newspaper: *Jackson County Herald-Tribune.* **Radio-FM:** KIOX, 96.1 MHz.

El Campo: Newspaper: *El Campo Leader-News* (S). **Radio-AM:** KULP, 1390 kHz. **Radio-FM:** KXBJ, 96.9 MHz.

Eldorado: Newspaper: *Eldorado Success.* **Radio-FM:** KOPE, 88.9 MHz; KLDE, 104.9; KPEP, 106.5.

Electra: Newspaper: *Electra Star-News.* **Radio-FM:** KOLI, 94.9 MHz.

Elgin: Newspaper: *Elgin Courier.* **Radio-AM:** KTAE, 1260 kHz.

Elkhart: Radio-FM: KATG, 88.1 MHz.

Ellinger: Radio-FM: KTIM, 89.1 MHz.

El Paso: Newspapers: *El Paso Times* (D); West Texas County Courier. **Radio-AM:** KROD, 600 kHz; KTSM, 690; KAMA, 750; KQBU, 920; KXPL, 1060; KHRO, 1150; KVIV, 1340; KHEY, 1380; KELP, 1590; KSVE, 1650. **Radio-FM:** KTEP, 88.5 MHz; KKLY; 89.5; KVER, 91.1; KOFX, 92.3; KSII, 93.1; KINT, 93.9; KYSE, 94.7; KLAQ, 95.5; KHEY, 96.3; KBNA, 97.5; KTSM, 99.9; KPRR, 102.1. TV Stations: KCOS-Ch. 13; KFOX-Ch. 15; KTSM-Ch. 16; KVIA-Ch. 17; KDBC-Ch. 18; KTFN-Ch. 20; KSCE-Ch. 21; KINT-Ch. 25.

Emory: Newspaper: *Rains County Leader.*

Encinal: Radio-FM: KQBI, 91.7 MHz; KELT, 102.5; KZPL, 105.1.

Encino: Radio-FM: KZTX, 91.1 MHz.

Ennis: Newspaper: *The Ennis News.*

Escobares: Radio-FM: KERG, 104.7 MHz.

Estelline: Radio-FM: KZES, 91.3 MHz.

—F—

Fabens: Radio-FM: KPAS, 103.1 MHz.

Fairfield: Newspapers: *Freestone County Times; The Fairfield Recorder.* **Radio-FM:** KNES, 99.1 MHz.

Falfurrias: Newspaper: *Falfurrias Facts.* **Radio-AM:** KLDS, 1260 kHz. **Radio-FM:** KRVP, 91.5 MHz; KDFM, 103.3; KPSO, 106.3.

Fannett: Radio-FM: KZFT, 90.5 MHz.

Farmersville: Newspaper: *Farmersville Times.* **Radio-AM:** KFCD, 990 kHz. **Radio-FM:** KXEZ, 92.1 MHz.

Farwell: Newspaper: *The State Line Tribune.* **Radio-AM:**

KIJN, 1060 kHz. **Radio-FM:** KIJN, 92.3 MHz; KICA, 98.3. TV Station: KPTF-Ch. 18.

Ferris: Newspaper: *The Ellis County Press.* **Radio-AM:** KDFT, 540 kHz.

Flatonia: Newspaper: *The Flatonia Argus.*

Floresville: Newspaper: *Wilson County News.* **Radio-FM:** KJMA, 89.7 MHz; KTFM, 94.1.

Flower Mound: Radio-FM: KTCK, 96.7 MHz.

Floydada: Newspaper: *The Floyd County Hesperian-Beacon.* **Radio-AM:** KFLP, 900 kHz. **Radio-FM:** KFLP, 106.1 MHz.

Forney: Newspaper: *Forney Messenger.*

Fort Davis: Newspaper: *Jeff Davis County Mountain Dispatch.*

Fort Stockton: Newspaper: *Fort Stockton Pioneer.* **Radio-AM:** KFST, 860 kHz. **Radio-FM:** KRAF, 88.3 MHz; KFST, 94.3.

Fort Worth: Newspapers: *Fort Worth Star-Telegram* (D); *Commercial Recorder* (D); *Tarrant County Commercial Record* (S); *Fort Worth Business Press* (SM). **Radio-AM:** WBAP, 820 kHz; KFJZ, 870; KHVN, 970; KKGM, 1630. **Radio-FM:** KTCU, 88.7 MHz; KLNO, 94.1; KSCS, 96.3; KEGL, 97.1; KPLX, 99.5; KDGE, 102.1; KMVK, 107.5. TV Stations: KFWD-Ch. 9; KTXA-Ch. 18; KTVT-Ch. 19; KXAS-Ch. 24.

Franklin: Newspapers: *Franklin News Weekly; Franklin Advocate.* **Radio-FM:** KVLX, 103.9 MHz.

Frankston: Radio-FM: KOYE, 96.7 MHz.

Fredericksburg: Newspaper: *Fredericksburg Standard-Radio Post.* **Radio-AM:** KNAF, 910 kHz. **Radio-FM:** KIVM, 91.1 MHz; KBLC, 91.5; KNAF, 105.7. TV Station: KCWX-Ch. 5.

Freeport: Radio-FM: KJOJ, 103.3 MHz.

Freer: Radio-FM: KBTD, 89.1 MHz; KQCI, 91.5; KBRA, 95.9..

Friona: Newspaper: *Friona Star.* **Radio-FM:** KGRW, 94.7 MHz.

Frisco: Newspaper: *Frisco Enterprise.* **Radio-AM:** KATH, 910 kHz.

Fritch: Newspaper: *The Eagle Press.*

—G—

Gail: Newspaper: *Borden Star.*

Gainesville: Newspaper: *Gainesville Daily Register* (S). **Radio-AM:** KGAF, 1580 kHz. **Radio-FM:** KZMJ, 94.5 MHz.

Galveston: Newspaper: *The Galveston County Daily News* (D). **Radio-AM:** KGBC, 1540 kHz. **Radio-FM:** KOVE, 106.5 MHz. TV Stations: KTMD-Ch. 22; KLTJ-Ch. 23.

Gardendale: Radio-FM: KFZX, 102.1 MHz.

Garland: Radio-AM: KAAM, 770 kHz. TV Station: KUVN-Ch. 33.

Garwood: Radio-FM: KPUY, 97.3 MHz.

Gatesville: Newspaper: *Gatesville Messenger & Star-Forum* (S). **Radio-FM:** KVLW, 88.1 MHz.

Georgetown: Newspaper: *Williamson County Sun* (S). **Radio-FM:** KHFI, 96.7 MHz; KLJA, 107.7.

George West: Radio-FM: KGWT, 93.5 MHz; KXAF 97.9.

Giddings: Newspaper: *Giddings Times & News.* **Radio-FM:** KANJ, 91.1 MHz; KGID 96.3.

Gilmer: Newspaper: *Gilmer Mirror.* **Radio-FM:** KFRO, 95.3 MHz.

Ginger: Radio-FM: KYFA, 91.5 MHz.

Gladewater: Newspaper: *Gladewater Mirror.* **Radio-AM:** KEES, 1430 kHz.

Glen Rose: Newspaper: *Glen Rose Reporter.* **Radio-FM:** KTFW, 92.1 MHz.

Goldsmith: Radio-FM: KTXO, 94.7 MHz.

Goldthwaite: Newspaper: *The Goldthwaite Eagle.* **Radio-FM:** KRNR, 100.5 MHz.

Goliad: Newspaper: *Goliad Advance-Guard.* **Radio-FM:** KHMC, 95.9 MHz; KPQG 104.3.

Gonzales: Newspaper: *The Gonzales Inquirer.* **Radio-AM:** KCTI, 1450 kHz. **Radio-FM:** KCTI, 88.1 MHz; KMLR, 106.3.

Graham: Newspaper: *The Graham Leader* (S). **Radio-AM:** KSWA, 1330 kHz. **Radio-FM:** KWKQ, 94.7 MHz.

Granbury: Newspaper: *Hood County News* (S). **Radio-AM:** KPIR, 1420 kHz.

Grand Prairie: Radio-AM: KKDA, 730 kHz.

Grand Saline: Newspaper: *Grand Saline Sun.*

Granite Shoals: Radio-FM: KAJZ, 106.5 MHz.

Grape Creek: Radio-FM: KPTJ 104.5 MHz.

Grapeland: Newspaper: *The Messenger* (S).

Greenville: Newspaper: *Herald-Banner* (TW). **Radio-AM:** KGVL, 1400 kHz. **Radio-FM:** KTXG, 90.5 MHz. TV Station: KTXD-Ch. 23.

Greenwood: Radio-FM: KAGP 89.1 MHz.

Gregory: Radio-FM: KPUS, 104.5 MHz.

Groesbeck: Newspaper: *Groesbeck Journal.*

Groom: Newspaper: *The Groom News.*

Groves: Radio-FM: KCOL, 92.5 MHz.

Groveton: Radio-FM: KFON, 93.9 MHz.

Guthrie: Radio-FM: KJAG, 107.7 MHz

—H—

Hallettsville: Newspaper: *Hallettsville Tribune-Herald.* **Radio-FM:** KTXM, 99.9 MHz.

Hallsville: Radio-FM: KTLH, 107.9 MHz.

Haltom City: Radio-FM: KLIF, 93.3 MHz.

Hamilton: Newspaper: *Hamilton Herald-News.* **Radio-AM:** KCLW, 900 kHz.

Hamlin: Newspaper: *The Hamlin Herald.* **Radio-FM:** KCDD, 103.7 MHz.

Hardin: Radio-FM: KGBV, 90.7 MHz.

Harker Heights: Radio-FM: KUSJ, 105.5 MHz.

Harlingen: Newspaper: *The Valley Morning Star* (D). **Radio-AM:** KGBT, 1530 kHz. **Radio-FM:** KJJF, 88.9 MHz; KFRQ, 94.5; KBTQ, 96.1. TV Stations: KMBH-Ch. 16; KGBT-Ch. 18; KLUJ-Ch. 21.

Harper: Radio-FM: KZAH, 99.1 MHz.

Hartley: Radio-FM: KOGW, 90.5 MHz.

Haskell: Radio-FM: KVRP, 97.1 MHz.

Hawley: Radio-FM: KTJK, 101.7 MHz.

Hearne: Newspaper: *Robertson County News.* **Radio-FM:** KEDC, 88.5 MHz; KVJM, 103.1.

Hebbronville: Newspapers: *The Enterprise News; Hebbronville View* (SM). **Radio-FM:** KOTX 98.7 MHz; KEKO, 101.7; KUFA, 104.3.

Helotes: Radio-FM: KONO, 101.1 MHz.

Hemphill: Newspaper: *The Sabine County Reporter.* **Radio-FM:** KTHP, 103.9 MHz.

Hempstead: *The Waller County Express.* **Radio-FM:** KTWL, 105.3 MHz.

Henderson: Newspaper: *The Henderson News* (S). **Radio-AM:** KWRD, 1470 kHz.

Henrietta: Newspaper: *Clay County Leader.*

Hereford: Newspaper: *Hereford Brand* (S). **Radio-AM:** KPAN, 860 kHz. **Radio-FM:** KRLH, 90.9 MHz; KPAN, 106.3.

Hewitt: Radio-FM: KIXT, 106.7 MHz.

Hico: Newspaper: *The Hico News Review.* **Radio-FM:**

KCBN, 107.7.

Highland Park: Radio-AM: KBDT, 1160 kHz. **Radio-FM:** KVIL, 103.7 MHz.

Highlands: Newspaper: *Highlands Star-Crosby Courier.*

Highland Village: Radio-FM: KWRD, 100.7 MHz.

Hillsboro: Newspaper: *Hillsboro Reporter* (S). **Radio-AM:** KHBR, 1560 kHz. **Radio-FM:** KBRQ, 102.5 MHz.

Holliday: Radio-FM: KGVB, 90.9 MHz; KWFB, 100.9.

Hondo: Newspaper: *Hondo Anvil Herald.* **Radio-AM:** KCWM, 1460 kHz. **Radio-FM:** KZIC, 89.9 MHz; KAHL, 105.9.

Hooks: Radio-FM: KTRG, 94.1 MHz; KPWW, 95.9.

Hornsby: Radio-FM: KOOP, 91.7 MHz.

Houston: Newspapers: *Houston Chronicle* (D); *Daily Court Review* (D); *Houston Business Journal; Jewish Herald-Voice.* **Radio-AM:** KILT, 610 kHz; KTRH, 740; KBME, 790; KEYH, 850; KPRC, 950; KLAT, 1010; KNTH, 1070; KCOH, 1230; KXYZ, 1320; KSHJ, 1430; KMIC, 1590. **Radio-FM:** KUHF, 88.7 MHz; KPFT, 90.1; KTSU, 90.9; KXNG, 91.7; KQBT, 93.7; KTBZ, 94.5; KKHH, 95.7; KHMX, 96.5; KBXX, 97.9; KODA, 99.1; KILT, 100.3; KLOL, 101.1; KMJQ, 102.1; KLTN, 102.9; KRBE, 104.1; KHCB, 105.7. TV Stations: KUHT-Ch. 8; KHOU-Ch. 11; KTRK-Ch. 13; KTXH-Ch. 19; KZJL-Ch. 21; KETH-Ch. 24; KRIV-Ch. 26; KIAH-Ch. 34; KPRC-Ch. 35.

Howe: Radio-FM: KHYI, 95.3 MHz.

Hudson: Radio-FM: KZXL, 96.3 MHz.

Humble: Radio-AM: KGOL, 1180 kHz. **Radio-FM:** KSBJ, 89.3 MHz.

Hunt: Radio-FM: KYRT, 97.9 MHz; KLKV, 99.9.

Huntington: Radio-FM: KSML, 101.9 MHz.

Huntsville: Newspaper: *The Huntsville Item* (D). **Radio-AM:** KM2XVL, 1220 kHz; KHCH, 1410; KHVL, 1490. **Radio-FM:** KSHU, 90.5 MHz; KVST, 99.7; KSAM, 101.7.

Hurst: Radio-AM: KMNY, 1360 kHz.

Hutto: Radio-FM: KYLR, 92.1 MHz.

—I—

Idalou: Newspaper: *Idalou Beacon.* **Radio-FM:** KRBL, 105.7 MHz; KLZK, 107.7.

Ingleside: Newspaper: *The Ingleside Index.* **Radio-FM:** KAJE, 107.3 MHz.

Ingram: Newspaper: *West Kerr Current.* **Radio-FM:** KTXI, 90.1 MHz; KFXE, 96.5.

Iowa Park: Newspaper: *Iowa Park Leader.* **Radio-FM:** KXXN, 97.5 MHz.

Irving: Newspaper: *The Irving Rambler.* TV Station: KSTR-Ch. 34.

—J—

Jacksboro: Newspaper: *Jacksboro Herald-Gazette.* **Radio-FM:** KFWR, 95.9 MHz.

Jacksonville: Newspaper: *Jacksonville Progress* (S). **Radio-AM:** KEBE, 1400 kHz. **Radio-FM:** KBJS, 90.3 MHz; KEBE, 95.1; KLJT, 102.3; KOOI, 106.5. TV Station: KETK-Ch. 22.

Jasper: Newspaper: *The Jasper Newsboy.* **Radio-AM:** KCOX, 1350 kHz. **Radio-FM:** KTXJ, 102.7 MHz; KJAS, 107.3.

Jefferson: Newspaper: *Jefferson Jimplecute.* **Radio-FM:** KHCJ, 91.9 MHz; KJTX, 104.5.

Jewett: Newspaper: *Jewett Messenger.*

Johnson City: Newspaper: *Johnson City Record Courier.* **Radio-FM:** KFAN, 107.9 MHz.

Jourdanton: Radio-FM: KLEY, 95.7 MHz.

Junction: Newspaper: *Junction Eagle.* **Radio-AM:** KMBL, 1450 kHz. **Radio-FM:** KYKK, 93.5 MHz.

—K—

Karnes City: Newspaper: *The Karnes Countywide.* **Radio-FM:** KHHL, 103.1 MHz.

Katy: Newspaper: *Katy Times.* TV Station: KYAZ-Ch. 25.

Kaufman: Newspaper: *The Kaufman Herald.*

Keene: Radio-FM: KJRN, 88.3 MHz.

Kempner: Radio-FM: KOOV, 106.9 MHz.

Kenedy: Radio-AM: KAML, 990 kHz. **Radio-FM:** KCAF, 92.1 MHz.

Kerens: Radio-FM: KRVF, 106.9 MHz.

Kermit: Newspaper: *The Winkler County News.* **Radio-FM:** KDCJ, 91.5 MHz; KWXW, 93.7.

Kerrville: Newspapers: *The Kerrville Daily Times* (TW); *Hill Country Community Journal.* **Radio-AM:** KERV, 1230 kHz. **Radio-FM:** KKER, 88.7 MHz; KHKV, 91.1; KRNH, 92.3; KRVL, 94.3; KKVR, 106.1. TV Station: KMYS-Ch. 32.

Kilgore: Newspaper: *Kilgore News Herald* (S). **Radio-AM:** KDOK, 1240 kHz. **Radio-FM:** KZLO, 88.7 MHz; KKTX, 96.1.

Killeen: Newspaper: *Killeen Daily Herald* (D). **Radio-AM:** KRMY, 1050 kHz. **Radio-FM:** KNCT, 91.3 MHz; KIIZ, 92.3. TV Station: KAKW-Ch. 13.

Kingsland: Radio-FM: KHSB, 104.7 MHz.

Kingsville: Newspaper: *The Kingsville Record.* **Radio-AM:** KINE, 1330 kHz. **Radio-FM:** KTAI, 91.1 MHz; KKBA, 92.7; KFTX, 97.5.

Kirbyville: Newspaper: *Kirbyville Banner.*

Krum: Radio-FM: KNOR, 93.7 MHz.

Kurten: Radio-FM: KPWJ, 107.7 MHz.

Kyle: Newspaper: *Hays Free Press.*

—L—

La Feria: Newspaper: *La Feria News.*

La Grange: Newspaper: *The Fayette County Record* (S). **Radio-AM:** KVLG, 1570 kHz. **Radio-FM:** KBUK, 104.9 MHz.

Lake Dallas: TV Station: KAZD-Ch. 31.

Lake Jackson: Radio-FM: KYBJ, 91.1 MHz; KGLK, 107.5.

Lakeway: Newspaper: *Lake Travis View.*

Lamesa: Newspaper: *Lamesa Press Reporter* (S). **Radio-AM:** KPET, 690 kHz. **Radio-FM:** KBKN, 91.3 MHz; KTXC, 104.7.

Lampasas: Newspaper: *Lampasas Dispatch Record* (S). **Radio-AM:** KCYL, 1450 kHz.

La Porte: Newspaper: *Bay Area Observer.* **Radio-FM:** KHJK, 103.7 MHz.

Laredo: Newspaper: *Laredo Morning Times* (D). **Radio-AM:** KLAR, 1300 kHz; KLNT, 1490. **Radio-FM:** KHOY, 88.1 MHz; KBNL, 89.9; KJBZ, 92.7; KQUR, 94.9; KRRG, 98.1; KNEX, 106.1. TV Stations: KGNS-Ch. 8; KLDO-Ch. 19.

Laughlin AFB: Radio-FM: KDRX, 106.9 MHz.

La Vernia: Newspaper: *La Vernia News.*

League City: Radio-AM: KHCB, 1400 kHz.

Leander: Radio-FM: KUTX, 98.9 MHz.

Lefors: Radio-FM: KPWD, 91.7 MHz; KHNZ, 101.3.

Leonard: Newspaper: *The Leonard Graphic.*

Levelland: Newspaper: *Levelland & Hockley County News-Press* (S). **Radio-AM:** KLVT, 1230 kHz. **Radio-FM:** KJDL, 105.3 MHz.

Lewisville: Newspaper: *Lewisville Leader.* **Radio-FM:** KDXX, 107.9 MHz.

Lexington: Newspaper: *Lexington Leader.*

Liberty: Newspaper: *The Vindicator.* **Radio-FM:** KHIH, 99.9 MHz.

Liberty Hill: Newspaper: *The Liberty Hill Independent.*

Lindale: Newspaper: *Lindale News & Times.*

Lindsay: Newspaper: *Lindsay Letter.*

Little Elm: Newspaper: *Little Elm Journal.*

Littlefield: Newspaper: *The Lamb County Leader-News* (S). **Radio-AM:** KZZN, 1490 kHz.

Livingston: Newspaper: *Polk County Enterprise* (S). **Radio-AM:** KETX, 1440 kHz. **Radio-FM:** KEHH, 92.3 MHz.

Llano: Newspaper: *The Llano News.* **Radio-FM:** KVHL, 91.7 MHz; KTHE, 96.3; KITY, 102.9. TV Station: KBVO-Ch. 27.

Lockhart: Newspaper: *Lockhart Post-Register.* **Radio-AM:** KFIT, 1060 kHz.

Lometa: Radio-FM: KACQ, 101.9 MHz.

Longview: Newspaper: *Longview News-Journal* (D). **Radio-AM:** KFRO, 1370 kHz. **Radio-FM:** KYKX, 105.7 MHz. TV Stations: KFXK-Ch. 20; KCEB-Ch. 28.

Lorena: Radio-FM: KYAR, 98.3 MHz.

Lorenzo: Radio-FM: KKCL, 98.1 MHz.

Los Ybañez: Radio-FM: KJJT, 98.5 MHz.

Louise: Radio-FM: KABA, 90.3 MHz.

Lovelady: Radio-FM: KHMR, 104.3 MHz.

Lubbock: Newspaper: *Lubbock Avalanche-Journal* (D). **Radio-AM:** KRFE, 580 kHz; KFYO, 790; KJTV, 950; KKAM, 1340; KWBF, 1420; KBZO, 1460; KDAV, 1590. **Radio-FM:** KTXT, 88.1 MHz; KTTZ, 89.1; KAMY, 90.1; KKLU, 90.9; KLBB, 93.7; KFMX, 94.5; KLLL, 96.3; KQBR, 99.5; KONE, 101.1; KZII, 102.5; KXTQ, 106.5. TV Stations: KCBD-Ch. 11; KPTB-Ch. 16; KTTZ-Ch. 25; KAMC-Ch. 27; KLBK-Ch. 31; KJTV-Ch. 35.

Lufkin: Newspaper: *The Lufkin Daily News* (D). **Radio-AM:** KRBA, 1340 kHz. **Radio-FM:** KLDN, 88.9 MHz; KSWP, 90.9; KAVX, 91.9; KYBI, 100.1; KYKS, 105.1. TV Station: KTRE-Ch. 9.

Luling: Newspaper: *Luling Newsboy and Signal.* **Radio-FM:** KAMX, 94.7 MHz.

Lumberton: Radio-AM: KHTW, 1300 kHz. **Radio-FM:** KKHT, 100.7 MHz.

Lytle: Radio-FM: KZLV, 91.3 MHz.

—M—

Mabank: Newspaper: *The Monitor* (S). **Radio-AM:** KTXV, 890 kHz.

Madisonville: Newspaper: *Madisonville Meteor.* **Radio-AM:** KMVL, 1220 kHz. **Radio-FM:** KHML, 91.5 MHz; KAGG, 96.1; KMVL, 100.5.

Malakoff: Radio-FM: KCKL, 95.9 MHz.

Manor: Radio-AM: KTXW, 1120 kHz; KELG, 1440.

Marble Falls: Newspaper: *The Highlander* (S). **Radio-FM:** KBMD, 88.5 MHz.

Marathon: Radio-FM: KDKY, 91.5 MHz.

Marfa: Newspaper: *The Big Bend Sentinel.* **Radio-FM:** KRTS, 93.5 MHz.

Marion: Radio-AM: KBIB, 1000 kHz.

Markham: Radio-FM: KKHA, 92.5 MHz; KBYC, 104.5.

Marlin: Newspaper: *The Marlin Democrat.* **Radio-FM:** KRMX, 92.9 MHz.

Marshall: Newspaper: *Marshall News Messenger* (D). **Radio-AM:** KMHT, 1450 kHz. **Radio-FM:** KBWC, 91.1 MHz; KDPM, 92.3; KMHT, 103.9.

Mart: Radio-FM: KWAA, 88.9 MHz.

Mason: Newspaper: *Mason County News.* **Radio-FM:** KZZM, 101.7 MHz; KHLB, 102.5; KMSN, 104.1.

McAllen: Newspaper: *The Monitor* (D). **Radio-AM:** KRIO, 910 kHz. **Radio-FM:** KHID, 88.1 MHz; KVMV, 96.9; KGBT, 98.5. TV Station: KNVO-Ch. 17.

McCook: Radio-FM: KCAS, 91.5 MHz.

McCoy: Radio-FM: KMPI, 90.5 MHz.

McGregor: Newspaper: *The McGregor Mirror & Crawford Sun.*

McKinney: Newspapers: *Collin County Commercial Record* (S); *McKinney Courier-Gazette.* **Radio-FM:** KNTU, 88.1 MHz.

McQueeney: Radio-FM: KZAR, 97.7 MHz.

Memphis: Radio-FM: KHNZ, 101.5 MHz; KLSR, 105.3.

Menard: Newspaper: *Menard News and Messenger.* **Radio-FM:** KTCY, 105.3 MHz.

Mercedes: Newspaper: *The Mercedes Enterprise.* **Radio-FM:** KTEX, 100.3 MHz.

Meridian: Newspaper: *Meridian Tribune.* **Radio-FM:** KITT, 106.5 MHz.

Merkel: Radio-AM: KMXO, 1500 kHz. **Radio-FM:** KHXS, 102.7 MHz.

Mertzon: Radio-FM: KMEO, 91.9 MHz; KBTP, 101.1; KBJX, 103.5.

Mesquite: Newspaper: *Mesquite News.* **Radio-FM:** KEOM, 88.5 MHz.

Mexia: Newspaper: *The Mexia News* (S). **Radio-AM:** KEKR, 1590 kHz.

Meyersville: Radio-FM: KQBQ, 100.1 MHz.

Miami: Newspaper: *Miami Chief.*

Midland: Newspaper: *Midland Reporter-Telegram* (D). **Radio-AM:** KCRS, 550 kHz; KWEL, 1070; KLPF, 1180; KMND, 1510. **Radio-FM:** KVDG, 90.9 MHz; KNFM, 92.3; KZBT, 93.3; KQRX, 95.1; KCRS, 103.3; KCHX, 106.7. TV Stations: KUPB-Ch. 18; KMID-Ch. 26.

Midlothian: Newspaper: *Midlothian Mirror.*

Miles: Newspaper: *Miles Messenger.* **Radio-FM:** KMLS, 95.5 MHz.

Mineola: Newspaper: *Wood County Monitor.* **Radio-FM:** KMOO, 99.9 MHz.

Mineral Wells: Radio-AM: KVTT, 1110 kHz. **Radio-FM:** KYQX, 89.3 MHz.

Mirando City: Radio-FM: KBDR, 100.5 MHz.

Mission: Newspaper: *Progress Times.* **Radio-AM:** KIRT, 1580 kHz. **Radio-FM:** KQXX, 105.5 MHz.

Missouri City: Radio-AM: KBRZ, 1460 kHz.

Monahans: Newspaper: *The Monahans News.* **Radio-AM:** KCKM, 1330 kHz. **Radio-FM:** KMRA, 91.1 MHz; KBAT, 99.9.

Mont Belvieu: Radio-FM: KFNC, 97.5 MHz.

Moody: Radio-FM: KLTO, 99.1 MHz.

Moran: Radio-FM: KCKB, 104.1 MHz.

Morton: Radio-FM: KQOA, 91.1 MHz; KPGA, 91.9.

Moulton: Newspaper: *Moulton Eagle.*

Mountain Home: Radio-FM: KAXA, 103.7 MHz.

Mount Pleasant: Newspaper: *Mount Pleasant Tribune* (S). **Radio-AM:** KIMP, 960 kHz. **Radio-FM:** KYZQ, 88.3 MHz.

Mount Vernon: Newspaper: *Mount Vernon Optic-Herald.* **Radio-FM:** KDDM, 100.5 MHz.

Muenster: Newspaper: *Muenster Enterprise.* **Radio-FM:** KTMU, 88.7 MHz; KZZA, 106.7.

Muleshoe: Newspaper: *Muleshoe Journal.* **Radio-FM:** KVRQ, 93.3 MHz.

Munday: Newspaper: *The Knox County News-Courier.*

Murphy: Newspaper: *Murphy Monitor.*

—N—

Nacogdoches: Newspaper: *Nacogdoches Daily Sentinel* (S). **Radio-AM:** KSFA, 860 kHz. **Radio-FM:** KSAU, 90.1 MHz; KJCS, 103.3; KTBQ, 107.7. TV Station: KYTX-Ch. 15.

Naples: Newspaper: *The Monitor.*

Natalia: Radio-FM: KYRQ, 90.3 MHz.

Navasota: Newspaper: *The Navasota Examiner.* **Radio-FM:** KWUP, 92.5 MHz.

Nederland: Radio-AM: KBED, 1510 kHz.

Needville: Newspaper: *Hometown Journal.*

New Boston: Newspaper: *Bowie County Citizens Tribune.* **Radio-AM:** KLBW, 1530 kHz. **Radio-FM:** KEWL, 95.1 MHz; KZRB, 103.5; KTTY, 105.1.

New Braunfels: Newspaper: *New Braunfels Herald-Zeitung* (D). **Radio-AM:** KGNB, 1420 kHz. **Radio-FM:** KNBT, 92.1 MHz.

Newcastle: Radio-FM: KBLY, 100.5 MHz.

New Deal: Radio-FM: KTTU, 97.3 MHz.

Newton: Newspaper: *Newton County News.*

New Ulm: Newspaper: *New Ulm Enterprise.* **Radio-FM:** KNRG, 92.3 MHz.

New Waverly: Radio-FM: KNLY, 91.1 MHz.

Nocona: Newspaper: *Nocona News.*

Nolanville: Radio-FM: KLFX, 107.3 MHz.

Normangee: Newspaper: *The Normangee Star.*

—O—

Oakwood: Radio-FM: KDNT, 94.5 MHz.

O'Brien: Radio-FM: KZOB, 105.5 MHz.

Odem: Radio-FM: KXAI, 98.3 MHz.

Odessa: Newspaper: *Odessa American* (D). **Radio-AM:** KFLB, 920 kHz; KOZA, 1230. **Radio-FM:** KBMM, 89.5 MHz; KLVW, 90.5; KXWT, 91.3; KMRK, 96.1; KMCM, 96.9; KODM, 97.9; KHKX, 99.1; KQLM, 107.9. TV Stations: KOSA-Ch. 7; KWES-Ch. 9; KMLM-Ch. 15; KPEJ-Ch. 23; KPBT-Ch. 28; KWWT-Ch. 30.

O'Donnell: Newspaper: *O'Donnell Index-Press.*

Olney: Newspaper: *Olney Enterprise.*

Olton: Newspaper: *Olton Enterprise.*

Orange: Newspaper: *The Orange Leader* (S). **Radio-AM:** KOGT, 1600 kHz. **Radio-FM:** KKMY, 104.5 MHz; KIOC, 106.1.

Ore City: Radio-FM: KAZE, 106.9 MHz.

Overton: Radio-FM: KTYK, 100.7 MHz.

Ozona: Newspaper: *Ozona Stockman.* **Radio-FM:** KYXX, 94.3 MHz; KCMZ, 105.5.

—P—

Paducah: Newspaper: *Paducah Post.* **Radio-FM:** KPZX, 94.7 MHz.

Paint Rock: Newspaper: *The Concho Herald.*

Palacios: Newspaper: Palacios Beacon. **Radio-FM:** *KPAL, 91.3 MHz; KPLU, 100.7.*

Palestine: Newspaper: *Palestine Herald-Press* (TW). **Radio-AM:** KNET, 1450 kHz. **Radio-FM:** KYFP, 89.1 MHz; KYYK, 98.3.

Pampa: Newspaper: *The Pampa News* (TW). **Radio-AM:** KGRO, 1230 kHz. **Radio-FM:** KAVO, 90.9 MHz; KOMX, 100.3; KDRL, 103.3.

Panhandle: Newspaper: *Panhandle Herald & White Deer News.* **Radio-FM:** KPQP, 106.1 MHz.

Paris: Newspaper: *The Paris News* (TW). **Radio-AM:** KZHN, 1250 kHz; KPLT, 1490. **Radio-FM:** KHCP, 89.3 MHz; KQPA, 91.9; KOYN, 93.9; KBUS, 101.9; KPLT, 107.7.

Pasadena: Radio-AM: KIKK, 650 kHz; KLVL, 1480. **Radio-FM:** KFTG, 88.1 MHz; KKBQ, 92.9.

Pearland: Newspaper: *The Reporter News.*

Pearsall: Newspaper: *Frio-Nueces Current.* **Radio-AM:** KMFR, 1280 kHz. **Radio-FM:** KSAG, 103.3 MHz; KSAH, 104.1.

Pecan Grove: Radio-AM: KREH, 900 kHz.

Pecos: Newspaper: *Pecos Enterprise.* **Radio-AM:** KIUN, 1400 kHz. **Radio-FM:** KPKO, 91.3 MHz; KDNZ, 97.3; KPTX, 98.3.

Perryton: Newspaper: *Perryton Herald* (S). **Radio-AM:** KEYE, 1400 kHz. **Radio-FM:** KEYE, 93.7 MHz.

Pflugerville: Radio-AM: KOKE, 1600 kHz.

Pharr: Newspaper: *Advance News Journal.* **Radio-AM:** KVJY, 840 kHz.

Pilot Point: Newspaper: *Pilot Point Post-Signal.* **Radio-FM:** KZMP, 104.9 MHz.

Pineland: Radio-FM: KFAH, 99.1 MHz.

Pittsburg: Newspaper: *The Pittsburg Gazette.* **Radio-FM:** KGWP, 91.1 MHz; KPIT, 91.7; KSCN, 96.9; KMPA, 103.1.

Plains: Radio-FM: KPHS, 90.3 MHz.

Plainview: Newspaper: *Plainview Herald* (TW). **Radio-AM:** KVOP, 1090 kHz; KREW, 1400. **Radio-FM:** KPMB, 88.5 MHz; KBAH, 90.5; KWLD, 91.5; KRIA, 103.9; KKYN, 106.9.

Plano: Newspaper: *Plano Star Courier.* **Radio-AM:** KTNO, 620 kHz.

Pleasanton: Newspaper: *Pleasanton Express.* **Radio-AM:** KWMF, 1380 kHz.

Pleasant Valley: Radio-FM: KZAM, 98.7 MHz.

Point Comfort: Radio-FM: KJAZ, 94.1 MHz.

Port Aransas: Newspaper: *Port Aransas South Jetty.*

Port Arthur: Newspaper: *The Port Arthur News* (TW). **Radio-AM:** KDEI, 1250 kHz; KOLE, 1340. **Radio-FM:** KQBU, 93.3 MHz; KTJM, 98.5. TV Station: KBTV-Ch. 27.

Port Isabel: Newspaper: *Port Isabel-South Padre Press.* **Radio-FM:** KNVO, 101.1 MHz; KLME, 105.5.

Portland: Radio-FM: KSGR, 91.1 MHz; KLHB, 105.5.

Port Lavaca: Newspaper: *Port Lavaca Wave.* **Radio-FM:** KNAL, 93.3 MHz.

Port Neches: Radio-AM: KBPO, 1150 kHz.

Port O'Connor: Radio-FM: KHPO, 91.9 MHz.

Post: Newspaper: *The Post Dispatch.* **Radio-FM:** KSSL, 107.3 MHz.

Prairie View: Radio-FM: KPVU, 91.3 MHz.

Premont: Radio-FM: KLBD, 88.1 MHz.

Presidio: Newspaper: *The Presidio International.*

Princeton: Newspaper: *Princeton Herald.*

Prosper: Newspaper: *Prosper Press.*

—Q—

Quanah: Newspaper: *Quanah Tribune-Chief.* **Radio-AM:** KOLJ, 1150 kHz. **Radio-FM:** KQTX, 98.1 MHz.

Quemado: Radio-FM: KQMD, 88.1 MHz.

Quitaque: Newspaper: *Valley Tribune.*

—R—

Ralls: Newspaper: *Crosby County News.*

Ranchitos Las Lomas: Radio-FM: KLIT, 93.3 MHz.

Ranger: Radio-FM: KWBY, 98.5 MHz.

Rankin: Radio-FM: KXFS, 93.7 MHz.

Raymondville: Newspaper: *Raymondville Chronicle/ Willacy County News.* **Radio-AM:** KSOX, 1240 kHz. **Radio-FM:** KVHI, 88.7 MHz; KBUC, 102.1; KBIC, 105.7.

Refugio: Newspaper: *Refugio County Press.* **Radio-FM:** KRIK, 100.5 MHz; KZAI, 103.7; KXHM, 106.1.

Reno: Radio-FM: KLOW, 98.9 MHz.

Richardson: Radio-AM: KKLF, 1700 kHz.

Riesel: Newspaper: *Riesel Rustler.*

Rio Grande City: Radio-FM: KXJT, 88.3 MHz; KRGX, 95.1; KQBO, 107.5. TV Station: KTLM-Ch. 14.

Robert Lee: Newspaper: *Observer/Enterprise.* **Radio-FM:** KJVI, 105.7 MHz.

Robinson: Radio-FM: KWPW, 107.9 MHz.

Robstown: Newspaper: *Nueces County Record-Star.* **Radio-AM:** KROB, 1510 kHz. **Radio-FM:** KLUX, 89.5 MHz; KSAB, 99.9; KMIQ, 104.9.

Rockdale: Newspaper: *Rockdale Reporter.* **Radio-FM:** KRXT, 98.5 MHz.

Rockport: Newspaper: *The Rockport Pilot* (S). **Radio-FM:** KKPN, 102.3 MHz.

Rocksprings: Newspaper: *Rocksprings Record and Texas Mohair Weekly.*

Rollingwood: Newspaper: *Westlake Picayune.* **Radio-AM:** KJCE, 1370 kHz.

Roma: Radio-FM: KRIO, 97.7 MHz.

Rosebud: Newspaper: *The Rosebud News.*

Rosenberg: Newspaper: *Fort Bend Herald and Texas Coaster* (TW). **Radio-AM:** KQUE, 980 kHz. TV Station: KXLN-Ch. 30.

Rotan: Newspaper: *Double Mountain Chronicle.*

Round Rock: Newspaper: *Round Rock Leader* (S). **Radio-FM:** KNLE, 88.1 MHz; KFMK, 105.9.

Rowena: Newspaper: *The Rowena Press.*

Roxton: Newspaper: *Roxton Progress* (SM).

Royse City: Newspaper: *Royse City Herald Banner.*

Rudolph: Radio-FM: KTER, 90.7 MHz.

Rusk: Newspaper: *Cherokeean Herald.* **Radio-AM:** KTLU, 1580 kHz.

—S—

Sabinal: Radio-FM: KHAV, 107.1 MHz.

Sachse: Newspaper: *Sachse News.*

Saint Jo: Newspaper: *Saint Jo Tribune.*

Salado: Newspaper: *Salado Village Voice.*

San Angelo: Newspaper: *San Angelo Standard-Times* (D). **Radio-AM:** KGKL, 960 kHz; KKSA, 1260; KCCE, 1340. **Radio-FM:** KLRW, 88.5 MHz; KNAR, 89.3; KNCH, 90.1; KLTP, 90.9; KDCD, 92.9; KSAO, 93.9; KIXY, 94.7; KGKL, 97.5; KELI, 98.7; KCLL, 100.1; KWFR, 101.9; KMDX, 106.1; KSJT, 107.5. TV Stations: KLST-Ch. 11; KSAN-Ch. 16; KIDY-Ch. 19.

San Antonio: Newspapers: *San Antonio Express-News* (D); *San Antonio Business Journal*; *The Hart Beat.* **Radio-AM:** KTSA, 550 kHz; KSLR, 630; KKYX, 680; KTKR, 760; KONO, 860; KRDY, 1160; WOAI, 1200; KZDC, 1250; KAHL, 1310; KXTN, 1350; KCHL, 1480; KEDA, 1540. **Radio-FM:** KPAC, 88.3 MHz; KSTX, 89.1; KSYM, 90.1; KYFS, 90.9; KRTU, 91.7; KROM, 92.9; KXXM, 96.1; KAJA, 97.3; KISS, 99.5; KCYY, 100.3; KQXT, 101.9; KJXK, 102.7; KZEP, 104.5; KVBH, 107.5. TV Stations: KLRN-Ch. 9; KSAT-Ch. 12; KVDA-Ch. 15; KHCE-Ch. 16; KWEX-Ch. 24; WOAI-Ch. 28; KENS-Ch. 29; KABB-Ch. 30.

San Augustine: Newspaper: *San Augustine Tribune.* **Radio-FM:** KXXE, 92.5 MHz.

San Benito: Newspaper: *San Benito News.* **Radio-FM:** KHKZ, 106.3 MHz.

Sanderson: Radio-FM: KEVK, 105.1 MHz.

San Diego: Radio-FM: KXAM, 102.5 MHz; KUKA, 105.9.

Sanger: Radio-FM: KAWA, 89.7 MHz.

San Juan: Radio-AM: KUBR, 1210 kHz.

San Marcos: Newspaper: *San Marcos Daily Record* (D). **Radio-FM:** KTSW, 89.9 MHz.

San Saba: Newspaper: *San Saba News & Star.* **Radio-AM:** KROY, 1410 kHz. **Radio-FM:** KNUZ, 106.1 MHz.

Santa Anna: Radio-FM: KXXU, 104.3 MHz; KSZX, 105.5.

Santa Fe: Radio-FM: KJIC, 90.5 MHz.

Savoy: Radio-FM: KQDR, 107.3 MHz.

Schertz: Radio-FM: KBBT, 98.5 MHz.

Schulenburg: Newspaper: *Schulenburg Sticker.*

Scotland: Radio-FM: KTWF, 95.5 MHz.

Seabrook: Radio-FM: KROI, 92.1 MHz.

Seadrift: Radio-FM: KMAT, 105.1 MHz.

Sealy: Newspaper: *The Sealy News.* **Radio-FM:** KQLC, 90.7 MHz.

Seguin: Newspaper: *The Seguin Gazette* (S). **Radio-AM:** KWED, 1580 kHz. **Radio-FM:** KSMG, 105.3 MHz.

Seminole: Newspaper: *Seminole Sentinel* (S). **Radio-AM:** KIKZ, 1250 kHz. **Radio-FM:** KSEM, 106.3 MHz.

Seymour: Newspaper: *The Baylor County Banner.* **Radio-AM:** KSEY, 1230 kHz. **Radio-FM:** KSEY, 94.3 MHz.

Shamrock: Newspaper: *County Star-News.* **Radio-FM:** KSNZ, 92.9 MHz.

Shepherd: Newspaper: *San Jacinto News-Times.*

Shenandoah: Radio-AM: KRCM, 1380 kHz.

Sherman: Newspaper: *Herald Democrat* (D). **Radio-AM:** KJIM, 1500 kHz. TV Station: KXII-Ch. 12.

Shiner: Newspaper: *The Shiner Gazette.*

Silsbee: Newspaper: *Silsbee Bee.* **Radio-FM:** KAYD, 101.7 MHz.

Silverton: Newspaper: *The Caprock Courier.*

Sinton: Newspaper: *The News of San Patricio.* **Radio-AM:** KDAE, 1590 kHz. **Radio-FM:** KNCN, 101.3 MHz.

Slaton: Newspaper: *The Slatonite.* **Radio-FM:** KVCE, 92.7 MHz.

Smiley: Radio-FM: KSXT, 90.3 MHz; KBQQ, 103.9.

Smithville: Newspaper: *Smithville Times.*

Snyder: Newspaper: *The Snyder News* (S). **Radio-AM:** KSNY, 1450 kHz. **Radio-FM:** KGWB, 91.1 MHz; KHMZ 94.9; KLYD, 98.9; KSNY, 101.5. TV Station: KPCB-Ch. 17.

Somerset: Radio-AM: KYTY, 810 kHz.

Somerville: Radio-FM: KXBT, 88.1 MHz.

Sonora: Newspaper: *The Devil's River News.* **Radio-FM:** KHOS, 92.1 MHz.

South Padre Island: Radio-FM: KESO, 92.7 MHz; KZSP, 95.3.

Spearman: Newspaper: *Reporter-Statesman.* **Radio-FM:** KTOT, 89.5 MHz; KXDJ, 98.3.

Springtown: Newspaper: *Springtown Epigraph.* **Radio-FM:** KSQX, 89.1 MHz.

Spur: Newspaper: *Texas Spur.*

Stamford: Newspapers: *The New Stamford American*; *The Stamford Star.* **Radio-AM:** KVRP, 1400 kHz. **Radio-FM:** KLGD, 106.9 MHz.

Stanton: Newspaper: *Martin County Messenger.* **Radio-FM:** KFLB, 88.1 MHz; KTPR, 89.9; KXQT, 105.9.

Stephenville: Newspaper: *Stephenville Empire Tribune* (S). **Radio-AM:** KSTV, 1510 kHz. **Radio-FM:** KQXS, 89.1 MHz; KEQX, 89.5; KTRL, 90.5.

Sterling City: Radio-FM: KNRX, 96.5 MHz.

Stockdale: Radio-AM: KQQB, 1520 kHz.

Stratford: Newspaper: *Sherman County Gazette.* **Radio-FM:** KUHC, 91.5 MHz.

Sulphur Bluff: Radio-FM: KETE, 99.7 MHz.

Sulphur Springs: Newspaper: *Sulphur Springs News-Telegram* (S). **Radio-AM:** KSST, 1230 kHz. **Radio-FM:** KGPF, 91.1 MHz; KZRF, 91.9; KSCH, 95.9.

Sunset Valley: Radio-FM: KVLR, 92.5 MHz.

Sweetwater: Newspaper: *Sweetwater Reporter* (TW). **Radio-AM:** KXOX, 1240 kHz. **Radio-FM:** KXOX, 96.7. TV Station: KTXS-Ch. 20.

—T—

Taft: Radio-FM: KYRK, 106.5 MHz.

Tahoka: Newspaper: *Lynn County News.* **Radio-FM:** KMMX, 100.3 MHz; KAMZ, 103.5.

Tatum: Radio-FM: KZQX, 100.3 MHz.

Taylor: **Newspaper:** *Taylor Press*. **Radio-FM:** KLQB, 104.3 MHz.

Teague: **Newspaper:** *Teague Chronicle*.

Temple: **Newspaper:** *Temple Daily Telegram* (D). **Radio-AM:** KTEM, 1400 kHz. **Radio-FM:** KVLT, 88.5 MHz; KBDE, 89.9; KLTD, 101.7. TV Station: KCEN-Ch. 9.

Terrell: **Newspaper:** *The Terrell Tribune*. **Radio-AM:** KPYK, 1570 kHz.

Terrell Hills: **Radio-AM:** KLUP, 930 kHz. **Radio-FM:** KTKX, 106.7 MHz.

Texarkana: **Newspaper:** *Texarkana Gazette* (D). **Radio-AM:** KCMC, 740 kHz; KTFS, 940; KKTK, 1400. **Radio-FM:** KTXK, 91.5 MHz; KTAL, 98.1; KKYR, 102.5. TV Station: KTAL-Ch. 26.

Texas City: **Newspaper:** *The Post Newspaper* (S). **Radio-AM:** KYST, 920 kHz.

The Colony: **Newspaper:** *The Colony Courier-Leader*.

Thorndale: **Newspaper:** *Thorndale Champion*. **Radio-FM:** KOKE, 99.3 MHz.

Three Rivers: **Newspaper:** *The Progress*. **Radio-FM:** KEMA, 94.5 MHz.

Throckmorton: **Newspaper:** *Throckmorton Tribune*.

Timpson: **Newspaper:** *East Texas Press*.

Todd Mission: **Radio-FM:** KTWL, 105.3 MHz.

Tolar: **Radio-FM:** KOME, 95.5 MHz.

Tomball: **Radio-AM:** KSEV, 700 kHz.

Tom Bean: **Radio-FM:** KLAK, 97.5 MHz.

Trenton: **Newspaper:** *Trenton Tribune*.

Trinity: **Newspaper:** *Trinity County News-Standard*. **Radio-FM:** KTYR, 89.7 MHz.

Troup: **Radio-FM:** KTBB, 97.5 MHz.

Tulia: **Newspaper:** *Swisher County News*. **Radio-FM:** KBTE, 104.9 MHz.

Turkey: Newpaper: *Caprock Courier*.

Tye: **Radio-FM:** KBCY, 99.7 MHz.

Tyler: **Newspaper:** *Tyler Morning Telegraph* (D). **Radio-AM:** KTBB, 600 kHz; KGLD, 1330; KYZS, 1490. **Radio-FM:** KVNE, 89.5 MHz; KGLY, 91.3; KRWR, 92.1; KTYL, 93.1; KNUE, 101.5; KKUS, 104.1. TV Station: KLTV-Ch. 7.

—U—

Umbarger: **Radio-FM:** KRBG, 88.7 MHz.

Universal City: **Radio-AM:** KSAH, 720 kHz.

University Park: **Radio-AM:** KEXB, 1440 kHz; KZMP, 1540.

Uvalde: **Newspaper:** *Uvalde Leader-News* (S). **Radio-AM:** KGWU, 1400 kHz. **Radio-FM:** KHPS, 88.9 MHz; KBNU, 93.9; KUVA, 102.3; KVOU, 104.9. TV Station: KPXL-Ch. 26.

Uvalde Estates: **Radio-FM:** KEWP, 103.5 MHz.

—V—

Valley Mills: **Newspaper:** *Valley Mills Progress* (SM).

Valley View: **Radio-FM:** KQFZ, 89.1 MHz.

Van Alstyne: **Newspaper:** *Van Alstyne Leader*.

Van Horn: **Newspaper:** *The Van Horn Advocate*. **Radio-FM:** KVHR, 91.5 MHz.

Vega: **Newspaper:** *Vega Enterprise*.

Vernon: **Newspaper:** *Vernon Record*. **Radio-AM:** KVWC, 1490 kHz. **Radio-FM:** KVED, 88.5 MHz; KVWC, 103.1.

Victoria: **Newspaper:** *Victoria Advocate* (D). **Radio-AM:** KVNN, 1340 kHz; KITE, 1410. **Radio-FM:** KAYK, 88.5 MHz; KBRZ, 89.3; KVRT, 90.7; KQVT, 92.3; KTXN, 98.7; KBAR, 100.9; KVIC, 104.7; KIXS, 107.9. TV Stations: KVCT-Ch. 11; KAVU-Ch. 20.

Vidor: **Newspaper:** *Vidor Vidorian*.

—W—

Waco: **Newspaper:** *Waco Tribune-Herald* (D). **Radio-AM:** KBBW, 1010 kHz; KWTX, 1230; KRZI, 1660. **Radio-FM:** KWBT, 94.5; KBGO, 95.7; KWTX, 97.5; WACO, 99.9; KWBU, 103.3. TV Stations: KWTX-Ch. 10; KXXV-Ch. 26; KWKT-Ch. 28.

Wake Village: **Radio-FM:** KHTA, 92.5 MHz.

Wallis: **Newspaper:** *Wallis News-Review*.

Waskom: **Radio-FM:** KQHN, 97.3 MHz.

Waxahachie: **Newspapers:** *Waxahachie Daily Light* (S); The Waxahachie Sun. **Radio-AM:** KBEC, 1390 kHz.

Weatherford: **Newspaper:** *Weatherford Democrat* (S). **Radio-AM:** KZEE, 1220 kHz. **Radio-FM:** KMQX, 88.5 MHz.

Webster: **Newspaper:** *Bay Area Citizen*.

Weimar: **Newspaper:** *Weimar Mercury*.

Wellington: **Radio-FM:** KSIF 91.7 MHz.

Wells: **Radio-FM:** KVLL, 94.7 MHz.

Weslaco: **Radio-AM:** KRGE, 1290 kHz. TV Station: KRGV-Ch. 13.

West: **Newspaper:** *The West News*.

West Lake Hills: **Radio-AM:** KTXZ, 1560 kHz.

West Odessa: **Radio-FM:** KFRI, 88.7 MHz.

Wharton: **Newspaper:** *Wharton Journal-Spectator* (S). **Radio-AM:** KANI, 1500 kHz.

Wheeler: **Newspaper:** *The Wheeler Times*. **Radio-FM:** KPDR, 90.3 MHz; KXNZ, 98.9.

Wheelock: **Radio-FM:** KVMK 100.9 MHz.

Whitehouse: **Radio-FM:** KISX, 107.3 MHz.

White Oak: **Newspaper:** *White Oak Independent*. **Radio-FM:** KAPW, 99.3 MHz.

Whitesboro: **Newspaper:** *Whitesboro News-Record*. **Radio-FM:** KMAD, 102.5 MHz.

Whitewright: **Newspaper:** *The Whitewright Sun*.

Wichita Falls: **Newspaper:** *Times Record News* (D). **Radio-AM:** KWFS, 1290. **Radio-FM:** KMCU, 88.7 MHz; KMOC, 89.5; KZKL, 90.5; KNIN, 92.9; KLUR, 99.9; KWFS, 102.3; KQXC, 103.9; KBZS, 106.3. TV Stations: KJTL-Ch. 15; KAUZ-Ch. 22; KFDX-Ch. 28.

Willis: **Radio-FM:** KAFR, 88.3 MHz.

Wills Point: **Newspaper:** *Wills Point Chronicle*.

Wimberley: **Newspaper:** *Wimberley View*.

Winfield: **Radio-FM:** KALK, 97.7 MHz.

Winnie: **Newspapers:** *The Hometown Press*; *The Seabreeze Beacon*. **Radio-FM:** KXXF 105.3 MHz.

Winnsboro: **Newspaper:** *Winnsboro News*. **Radio-FM:** KWNS, 104.7 MHz.

Winona: **Radio-FM:** KBLZ, 102.7 MHz.

Winters: **Radio-FM:** KORQ, 96.1 MHz.

Wixon Valley: **Radio-FM:** KBXT, 101.9 MHz.

Wolfforth: **Radio-FM:** KAIQ, 95.5 MHz. TV Station: KLCW-Ch. 23.

Woodville: **Newspaper:** *Tyler County Booster*.

Wylie: **Newspaper:** *The Wylie News*. **Radio-AM:** KHSE, 700 kHz.

—Y—

Yoakum: **Newspaper:** *Yoakum Herald-Times*. **Radio-FM:** KYKM, 94.3 MHz.

Yorktown: **Newspaper:** *Yorktown News-View*. **Radio-FM:** KGGB, 96.3 MHz.

—Z—

Zapata: **Newspaper:** *Zapata County News*. **Radio-FM:** KHEM, 89.3 MHz; KQHM 102.7; KJJS, 103.9. ∎

Transportation

The Texas Star discharges light crude oil from the Tranmere North Oil Jetty, River Mersey, in Liverpool, England, on April 20, 2019. She had loaded her cargo in Houston, TX. Photo by Darren Hillman/Flickr (CC).

Freight Railroads in Texas

In Texas in 2019, there were three Class I railroad companies operating. Short line railroads made up about 14.5 percent of the state's total track mileage. In 2019, railroads in the state carried some 118 million tons of freight. The leading commodities handled are listed below. A complete list of the 55 railroads in the state is in the Counties section on page 205.

Source: Association of American Railroads.

Railroads in State	Miles Operated
Class I (3, *see list at right*)	12,585
Regional	0
Short Line Railroads (51)	2,141
Total	**14,726**
Total excluding trackage rights*	**10,460**

Railroads in State	Miles Operated
Class I	12,585
Union Pacific Railroad Co.	6,356
BNSF Railway Co.	5,300
Kansas City Southern Railway Co.	929

*Trackage rights — track provided by another railroad.
Numbers in parentheses represent the number of railroad companies in each category.

Freight Traffic in Texas by Kind – 2019

Carloads originated		Tons
Chemicals	471,000	45.0 million
Nonmetallic minerals	279,400	29.0 million
Petroleum products	166,700	13.3 million
Intermodal	737,300	10.2 million
Primary metal products	44,400	4.1 million
All Other	226,300	16.4 million
Total	1,925,100	118.0 million

Carloads terminated		Tons
Nonmetallic minerals	445,700	46.3 million
Coal	383,400	44.9 million
Chemicals	357,800	34.2 million
Farm products	159,200	16.5 million
Intermodal	1,050,100	14.5 million
All Other	694,600	51.9 million
Total	3,090,800	208.3 million

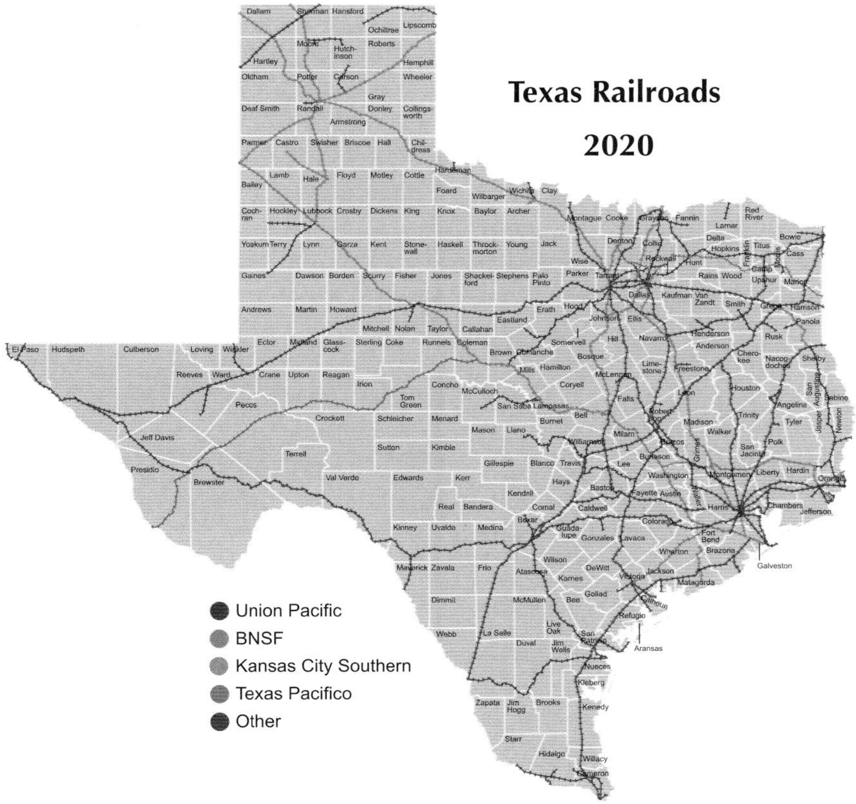

Highway Miles, Construction, Maintenance, Vehicles: 2019

Texans drove more than 24 million motor vehicles in 2019 over 315,445 miles of roadways, including city- and county-maintained roads. That driving is calculated to have included more than 575.2 million miles driven daily on the 197,865 miles of state-maintained highways alone.

The Texas Department of Transportation (TxDOT) is responsible for state highway construction and maintenance, planning for future road expansion, administering Texas tollways and toll tags, and operating the state's 12 official Texas Travel Information Centers and 76 safety rest areas.

Mileage, maintenance, and construction figures (listed by county) refer only to roads that are maintained by the state: Interstates, U.S. highways, state highways, farm-to-market roads, and some loops around urban areas. Not included are city- or county-maintained streets and roads. A lane mile is one lane for one mile; i.e., one mile of four-lane highway equals four lane miles.

Sources: Texas Department of Transportation and Department of Motor Vehicles.

County	Vehicles Registered	Lane Miles of Highway	Vehicle Miles Driven Daily	State Construction Expenditures	Combined Construction Maintenance Expenditures	Total Vehicle Registration Fees	State Net Receipts	County Net Receipts
Anderson	48,835	1,013	1,299,188	$8,085,678	$24,258,395	$3,533,581	$2,568,624	$962,741
Andrews	21,045	556	1,034,777	5,819,889	22,119,691	1,946,443	1,470,451	474,563
Angelina	80,225	956	2,191,008	80,257,605	99,265,264	6,143,364	4,795,992	1,343,520
Aransas	25,750	203	531,860	6,958,282	12,075,825	1,556,014	1,038,655	513,472
Archer	11,638	572	404,090	3,181,966	10,045,987	780,839	330,550	449,398
Armstrong	2,624	379	408,889	2,093,175	10,894,164	162,851	8,861	153,947
Atascosa	49,302	1,011	2,143,042	9,308,954	42,365,399	3,425,822	2,550,527	872,939
Austin	41,408	649	1,553,989	126,241,336	132,938,009	2,777,160	1,989,174	785,325
Bailey	6,478	491	218,310	94,044	1,391,514	507,747	110,642	396,929
Bandera	28,016	414	444,877	1,494,155	6,494,464	1,650,249	1,033,387	613,257
Bastrop	98,313	806	2,647,823	54,418,416	94,753,738	7,001,110	5,474,698	1,517,305
Baylor	4,151	531	245,130	4,853,732	14,079,989	270,289	33,070	236,778
Bee	22,776	679	638,232	4,706,100	12,552,507	1,665,221	1,064,428	599,942
Bell	307,865	1,578	8,018,655	123,405,957	178,140,973	20,745,794	16,667,895	4,058,214
Bexar	1,574,939	3,389	33,536,530	399,841,080	585,220,525	137,676,180	100,903,637	36,666,568
Blanco	19,159	463	726,425	1,870,341	5,900,090	1,420,451	956,733	461,676
Borden	1,099	344	65,419	334,519	3,692,961	52,098	3,625	48,420
Bosque	23,289	695	553,104	3,619,072	12,597,224	1,343,836	759,663	582,246
Bowie	84,973	1,212	3,134,393	11,840,352	34,756,172	5,909,673	4,569,970	1,333,805
Brazoria	319,975	1,408	6,289,357	72,042,181	93,376,963	22,660,103	18,622,786	4,013,667
Brazos	154,822	978	4,130,973	19,598,686	61,143,631	11,647,478	9,244,305	2,371,749
Brewster	9,883	606	260,438	75,452	1,549,501	594,318	254,449	336,354
Briscoe	1,905	326	58,087	328,885	2,235,285	107,896	7,315	100,471
Brooks	5,961	346	669,101	10,296,250	12,917,592	368,037	112,559	255,407
Brown	40,466	773	851,643	1,104,784	6,567,859	2,988,526	2,132,759	853,576
Burleson	23,670	542	836,871	7,783,641	13,410,954	1,625,969	1,005,392	618,762
Burnet	59,348	794	1,691,869	7,259,653	14,617,360	4,112,570	3,024,197	1,081,330
Caldwell	42,869	716	1,396,600	11,845,264	17,227,520	2,923,124	2,068,854	852,276
Calhoun	22,929	406	613,239	2,875,795	12,853,623	1,826,850	1,248,946	576,290
Callahan	16,233	744	1,069,850	3,725,942	13,805,567	1,330,285	769,285	559,718
Cameron	330,796	1,913	6,826,523	40,273,685	60,859,433	27,802,389	19,724,469	8,065,270
Camp	17,597	265	269,553	322,925	2,347,833	1,542,613	1,056,485	485,488
Carson	7,354	778	789,337	11,795,600	38,307,707	514,405	116,202	398,025
Cass	32,251	975	873,597	7,240,826	16,644,265	1,979,543	1,296,143	682,514
Castro	8,012	533	258,256	1,373,465	6,941,902	836,755	384,916	451,611
Chambers	48,766	807	2,884,385	33,794,765	48,670,367	3,340,442	2,518,207	819,186
Cherokee	47,755	1,143	1,320,855	18,331,590	43,613,037	3,123,283	2,250,274	871,358
Childress	6,224	497	434,821	1,653,724	2,962,798	375,995	63,248	312,415
Clay	12,867	756	876,146	5,844,682	17,384,484	1,010,375	484,390	524,993
Cochran	2,898	467	102,556	240,412	1,710,061	202,018	10,044	191,864
Coke	4,609	369	191,373	6,019,594	8,503,228	259,688	39,377	220,179

County	Vehicles Registered	Lane Miles of Highway	Vehicle Miles Driven Daily	State Construction Expenditures	Combined Construction Maintenance Expenditures	Total Vehicle Registration Fees	State Net Receipts	County Net Receipts
Coleman	10,626	753	407,108	$548,438	$3,325,858	$624,438	$161,930	$462,232
Collin	824,623	1,555	9,180,969	85,811,082	122,100,697	62,459,107	50,938,033	11,431,064
Collingsworth	3,263	454	90,355	311,815	2,730,116	199,295	11,684	187,457
Colorado	29,424	767	1,963,436	16,128,214	35,286,823	2,152,512	1,465,463	684,826
Comal	179,303	736	5,166,329	46,383,728	96,163,543	14,893,568	12,210,769	2,656,038
Comanche	15,587	748	471,140	2,969,224	6,787,149	1,139,816	606,904	532,469
Concho	3,492	477	317,137	3,463,845	16,112,234	187,441	10,705	176,514
Cooke	54,943	850	1,959,676	27,761,433	40,332,650	4,235,173	3,220,002	1,011,167
Coryell	59,965	768	1,226,142	10,922,173	24,022,769	3,266,864	2,351,397	911,652
Cottle	1,532	390	67,443	178,258	1,923,597	84,292	5,430	78,695
Crane	4,962	319	406,326	14,813,585	22,010,146	329,597	123,595	205,936
Crockett	5,171	783	828,658	3,715,356	10,998,081	330,732	62,499	268,095
Crosby	5,568	569	190,923	608,068	3,667,573	336,332	32,322	303,702
Culberson	2,210	754	1,013,623	19,052,609	37,145,037	133,152	7,807	125,220
Dallam	8,068	699	431,707	8,616,330	13,433,979	712,900	266,987	445,664
Dallas	2,011,951	3,374	39,863,257	791,810,562	899,499,287	162,253,871	134,286,772	27,838,993
Dawson	11,522	741	606,777	2,693,910	10,127,069	870,362	371,673	497,095
Deaf Smith	20,529	603	417,751	1,733,855	9,227,889	1,936,365	1,320,969	614,489
Delta	6,460	373	179,949	775,582	4,944,927	353,922	88,223	265,499
Denton	701,437	1,666	11,373,574	195,870,655	226,765,241	50,249,014	41,163,017	9,016,943
DeWitt	25,073	673	751,660	7,672,184	24,799,667	1,723,961	1,104,479	618,347
Dickens	2,697	469	99,378	193,045	2,139,004	155,000	8,743	146,207
Dimmit	10,530	506	678,027	9,293,450	20,583,403	926,260	561,769	364,082
Donley	3,346	469	542,508	7,132,079	16,239,652	214,164	12,546	201,430
Duval	11,268	642	427,946	2,191,760	9,851,196	734,994	296,239	438,411
Eastland	23,048	1,027	1,478,965	35,589,454	45,936,309	1,993,607	1,373,093	619,600
Ector	171,036	971	3,428,545	19,573,332	43,002,398	15,803,702	13,432,196	2,365,621
Edwards	2,957	499	137,546	512,294	6,590,435	175,006	9,898	164,992
Ellis	183,201	1,542	5,720,296	74,976,522	115,462,052	56,488,127	42,075,025	14,392,377
El Paso	670,804	1,763	12,859,357	217,982,985	249,373,521	12,102,233	9,784,752	2,305,770
Erath	41,140	843	1,220,816	12,028,383	32,790,405	2,695,656	1,915,196	776,653
Falls	17,409	746	819,018	2,988,988	15,941,006	1,213,328	649,114	563,847
Fannin	37,673	988	803,884	35,907,610	68,466,741	2,510,746	1,751,297	757,458
Fayette	35,101	1,034	1,938,096	23,172,697	39,606,061	2,222,870	1,506,193	712,283
Fisher	4,579	558	182,446	3,008,168	14,100,638	254,241	14,365	239,644
Floyd	6,663	702	165,545	1,339,360	8,204,826	468,937	94,266	374,039
Foard	1,557	298	60,177	851,055	5,547,365	90,601	4,529	86,072
Fort Bend	621,823	1,306	8,363,712	153,620,601	183,673,190	45,872,683	37,462,849	8,352,166
Franklin	12,552	342	629,295	1,228,670	9,741,862	712,150	311,316	400,044
Freestone	22,725	823	1,594,356	2,721,563	10,053,571	1,488,787	897,859	589,782
Frio	13,884	759	1,441,514	12,743,076	63,760,887	921,823	457,823	463,566
Gaines	22,864	662	776,132	1,031,711	21,179,579	1,824,579	1,222,314	601,648
Galveston	288,583	1,070	5,355,748	185,126,685	206,386,014	19,980,172	16,352,509	3,596,100
Garza	4,702	457	503,500	445,863	10,134,292	299,468	61,672	237,572
Gillespie	37,215	685	844,856	2,569,367	10,669,523	2,348,338	1,565,517	777,071
Glasscock	2,677	357	391,835	3,208,687	27,095,135	148,157	9,491	138,535
Goliad	9,444	535	350,974	13,497,240	28,589,712	514,901	139,866	374,408
Gonzales	25,272	893	1,652,341	7,228,611	31,355,304	1,821,750	1,205,410	615,191
Gray	21,530	759	626,934	4,698,945	24,419,027	1,613,627	997,010	615,318
Grayson	134,892	1,270	3,807,660	39,856,023	84,363,891	9,789,723	7,821,279	1,956,967
Gregg	126,185	822	3,124,019	8,656,043	23,726,763	10,978,206	9,163,840	1,807,627
Grimes	34,412	615	1,166,493	79,904,609	87,949,468	2,216,285	1,509,836	704,488
Guadalupe	160,821	1,014	3,831,290	18,222,281	39,001,652	11,409,807	9,041,527	2,356,266
Hale	28,277	1,059	916,566	4,944,362	25,793,244	2,049,684	1,369,348	679,117
Hall	2,958	457	247,934	1,307,422	5,547,204	182,035	10,492	171,274
Hamilton	11,308	580	375,475	2,580,704	10,811,131	710,340	240,312	469,412

County	Vehicles Registered	Lane Miles of Highway	Vehicle Miles Driven Daily	State Construction Expenditures	Combined Construction Maintenance Expenditures	Total Vehicle Registration Fees	State Net Receipts	County Net Receipts
Hansford	6,405	526	129,151	$1,843,364	$12,617,412	$494,525	$112,528	$381,775
Hardeman	3,918	465	418,334	821,909	4,009,066	245,206	13,420	231,660
Hardin	57,875	581	1,381,487	5,509,366	14,078,624	4,268,910	3,209,743	1,055,495
Harris	3,231,688	5,373	66,955,261	649,899,667	828,948,615	263,555,904	219,268,026	44,033,288
Harrison	68,424	1,181	2,679,193	10,362,154	87,855,377	4,826,523	3,608,830	1,213,890
Hartley	6,826	551	455,947	7,300,214	17,281,887	736,809	387,047	349,426
Haskell	5,700	670	236,671	871,118	3,537,804	421,933	73,905	347,654
Hays	194,733	725	6,141,995	38,999,395	67,202,440	14,204,677	11,639,114	2,540,772
Hemphill	5,468	383	148,197	1,107,220	8,269,719	360,870	82,019	278,525
Henderson	91,183	1,063	1,905,071	26,578,053	37,238,726	5,757,286	4,428,363	1,323,624
Hidalgo	644,500	2,482	12,078,002	153,824,531	226,659,930	56,305,841	41,903,225	14,382,282
Hill	43,034	1,098	2,689,023	43,437,844	69,904,424	3,144,919	2,345,353	797,237
Hockley	24,873	751	629,566	1,004,952	17,469,079	1,817,715	1,197,385	617,837
Hood	71,497	405	1,078,670	23,528,147	26,161,472	5,249,743	4,064,500	1,178,179
Hopkins	42,549	1,006	1,888,031	4,691,736	21,161,560	3,023,307	2,157,101	863,626
Houston	22,059	868	653,426	3,595,959	18,216,976	1,281,962	714,037	566,740
Howard	29,250	885	1,527,118	18,544,068	40,361,718	2,042,603	1,364,081	676,870
Hudspeth	3,833	827	1,716,004	3,156,483	13,414,280	231,502	13,012	218,380
Hunt	95,174	1,379	3,140,975	6,902,330	16,217,884	6,658,571	5,138,532	1,513,874
Hutchinson	23,255	486	332,244	1,097,617	9,396,483	1,585,242	1,026,687	557,459
Irion	3,363	246	246,621	239,479	1,841,453	261,464	70,500	190,788
Jack	10,430	583	317,565	8,850,673	13,977,436	743,382	312,090	430,729
Jackson	17,800	637	974,977	5,184,872	27,934,628	1,156,240	616,427	538,957
Jasper	38,263	774	1,045,696	2,520,462	7,633,225	2,398,179	1,640,622	756,067
Jeff Davis	2,652	468	229,055	779,055	4,256,560	157,896	31,275	126,089
Jefferson	203,259	1,128	5,311,315	65,906,574	108,126,168	14,889,410	12,180,760	2,697,365
Jim Hogg	4,397	288	163,954	805,796	9,591,615	327,912	97,528	230,245
Jim Wells	38,289	715	1,254,386	21,873,219	30,790,908	2,916,565	2,109,655	805,050
Johnson	177,966	1,003	3,625,726	16,133,571	38,252,829	14,214,594	11,486,980	2,716,275
Jones	16,718	1,005	505,341	6,648,816	27,851,877	1,390,059	824,541	563,906
Karnes	19,938	708	922,937	17,850,877	48,683,446	1,303,705	766,852	536,348
Kaufman	131,709	1,208	4,330,054	42,128,058	90,964,088	8,704,384	6,794,910	1,903,361
Kendall	65,847	453	1,300,298	29,427,054	59,097,527	6,263,612	4,857,555	1,394,098
Kenedy	699	191	471,125	5,939,951	6,976,048	31,243	2,836	28,253
Kent	1,099	323	48,832	312,309	2,607,242	51,467	4,016	47,428
Kerr	58,941	712	1,350,651	17,529,439	31,943,164	3,985,815	2,981,460	992,242
Kimble	5,556	685	769,620	7,877,524	17,203,790	321,077	57,912	262,855
King	480	229	84,963	344,602	2,441,783	22,056	1,417	20,639
Kinney	3,621	407	230,773	4,846,497	7,667,763	230,389	61,876	168,337
Kleberg	24,432	379	805,348	5,560,547	8,622,571	1,800,188	1,258,175	540,592
Knox	4,134	467	136,294	4,005,268	10,763,269	286,182	30,779	255,249
Lamar	52,432	1,011	1,284,250	8,388,250	18,107,137	3,868,232	2,890,571	975,174
Lamb	12,632	799	437,393	509,913	6,636,250	874,109	375,700	497,545
Lampasas	26,795	527	730,589	780,713	5,017,277	1,935,160	1,245,517	687,475
La Salle	7,494	648	1,378,036	5,982,270	27,985,430	586,167	251,291	334,602
Lavaca	29,083	671	706,948	1,630,359	9,733,551	1,855,132	1,221,814	631,670
Lee	25,192	522	746,374	12,682,425	26,585,461	1,742,852	1,144,005	597,659
Leon	23,379	839	1,664,263	7,188,500	22,205,963	1,525,167	951,017	572,738
Liberty	78,692	871	2,254,984	40,327,249	53,385,133	5,426,423	4,248,523	1,175,009
Limestone	24,643	770	648,661	3,117,144	16,904,731	1,528,973	914,698	612,827
Lipscomb	4,080	413	97,208	907,053	3,498,392	340,826	54,108	286,540
Live Oak	12,649	1,012	1,688,673	4,195,819	22,702,145	773,350	297,520	475,073
Llano	28,378	509	549,502	4,580,037	12,396,465	1,733,212	1,052,806	676,580
Loving	225	68	230,636	3,599,902	21,912,005	14,090	717	13,374
Lubbock	244,501	1,737	4,137,571	78,467,047	118,665,561	19,881,782	16,475,774	3,368,477
Lynn	6,392	709	470,676	960,359	5,894,530	378,945	52,739	325,182

County	Vehicles Registered	Lane Miles of Highway	Vehicle Miles Driven Daily	State Construction Expenditures	Combined Construction Maintenance Expenditures	Total Vehicle Registration Fees	State Net Receipts	County Net Receipts
Madison	13,655	585	1,162,321	$8,175,767	$27,167,939	$1,295,643	$829,234	$465,669
Marion	10,065	330	270,303	200,566	2,581,737	611,909	200,512	411,002
Martin	7,187	642	1,122,147	3,637,365	30,266,949	618,648	183,365	434,864
Mason	6,547	422	205,441	837,624	4,141,513	354,940	77,559	277,042
Matagorda	34,493	709	944,585	7,671,603	29,177,611	2,182,211	1,471,869	708,514
Maverick	49,474	502	1,060,454	5,633,609	17,727,183	3,788,248	2,902,736	883,705
McCulloch	9,517	615	333,609	1,805,752	7,934,715	625,673	185,597	439,258
McLennan	221,458	1,700	7,048,218	102,126,987	215,238,901	17,095,106	13,787,125	3,292,442
McMullen	1,892	320	309,644	6,025,715	32,591,456	96,619	5,878	90,632
Medina	56,625	765	1,421,256	2,584,950	11,914,595	4,312,708	3,258,136	1,050,868
Menard	2,860	348	175,080	888,868	4,878,755	154,000	14,072	139,686
Midland	215,289	1,078	4,548,595	43,060,417	68,728,110	19,541,922	16,870,331	2,656,305
Milam	28,876	712	808,022	14,703,135	24,607,063	1,707,432	1,061,348	644,850
Mills	6,785	462	257,702	620,681	4,349,999	412,421	76,494	335,511
Mitchell	7,034	662	814,409	1,568,298	7,238,149	391,761	65,032	326,459
Montague	26,432	856	769,052	9,232,401	27,547,141	1,746,538	1,109,017	635,798
Montgomery	551,232	1,336	11,243,112	255,724,050	281,068,853	38,805,707	32,299,994	6,450,815
Moore	23,235	487	538,532	5,925,386	9,315,779	1,769,369	1,210,699	557,619
Morris	13,334	359	534,373	391,983	3,699,969	856,925	443,665	412,910
Motley	1,679	331	49,391	4,976,875	7,746,336	95,291	5,549	89,663
Nacogdoches	56,834	981	1,849,942	35,713,555	49,903,260	4,170,490	3,119,372	1,046,950
Navarro	45,639	1,253	2,185,137	48,413,665	78,939,201	3,255,136	2,392,338	860,417
Newton	13,146	554	370,184	1,591,593	9,502,882	795,145	302,560	491,849
Nolan	14,005	689	1,282,080	3,560,211	16,446,624	976,667	471,325	504,079
Nueces	269,227	1,584	7,006,047	355,035,650	414,115,039	20,544,854	17,015,908	3,509,399
Ochiltree	11,635	432	255,999	2,144,496	11,296,055	937,449	448,179	488,709
Oldham	3,020	467	818,952	618,825	4,103,841	213,344	37,578	175,665
Orange	78,388	640	2,961,057	18,673,016	34,227,145	5,003,022	3,826,864	1,171,352
Palo Pinto	31,306	828	1,132,108	3,574,392	15,921,066	2,052,319	1,388,640	661,740
Panola	25,953	774	997,554	11,787,874	34,098,785	1,544,849	1,098,140	445,457
Parker	159,291	889	3,910,675	15,294,764	45,782,034	12,662,581	10,072,312	2,573,751
Parmer	10,098	612	396,079	16,251,850	20,120,131	764,402	293,184	471,010
Pecos	16,203	1,684	1,345,186	4,420,767	13,144,160	1,262,499	723,433	538,274
Polk	55,549	865	1,798,239	9,134,952	20,948,304	4,406,626	3,364,035	1,039,129
Potter	101,723	921	2,490,550	21,395,617	64,259,775	8,349,519	6,862,959	1,477,501
Presidio	7,728	554	228,873	5,358,469	7,764,494	517,371	184,205	332,927
Rains	15,051	268	345,428	638,087	3,462,008	923,777	478,893	443,946
Randall	137,555	891	1,570,319	40,034,715	49,701,778	11,025,868	8,822,849	2,186,497
Reagan	5,025	319	399,895	1,858,128	8,321,482	402,321	117,911	284,366
Real	4,712	295	121,381	290,637	2,063,838	289,039	69,926	218,662
Red River	13,755	754	390,419	6,284,548	18,507,590	776,680	287,322	488,903
Reeves	14,500	1,182	1,884,671	33,701,940	113,540,486	1,284,886	750,321	534,331
Refugio	7,775	464	708,489	3,784,798	14,120,404	505,917	180,265	325,120
Roberts	1,245	244	88,652	728,964	8,015,873	59,394	3,963	55,383
Robertson	20,094	660	992,969	3,592,610	22,048,651	1,283,905	707,518	575,801
Rockwall	95,452	348	2,211,676	42,993,591	56,811,999	7,701,695	6,254,527	1,436,690
Runnels	12,804	734	416,469	5,799,468	24,796,418	847,197	359,192	487,349
Rusk	50,958	1,176	1,371,140	6,103,732	31,075,521	3,386,080	2,446,049	938,040
Sabine	12,709	482	296,061	802,200	5,604,654	771,183	321,232	449,182
San Augustine	9,352	539	297,023	2,178,165	11,056,118	677,958	271,587	405,843
San Jacinto	28,409	533	846,667	8,392,120	13,901,227	1,804,717	1,127,000	675,835
San Patricio	64,469	993	2,405,508	33,526,770	59,605,514	4,568,816	3,407,611	1,156,439
San Saba	7,955	437	186,881	911,425	7,187,156	470,104	95,104	374,615
Schleicher	4,196	361	131,040	374,945	1,328,345	255,210	46,787	208,237
Scurry	19,328	687	664,363	1,170,858	5,995,602	1,875,677	1,278,578	596,407
Shackelford	4,548	355	156,871	1,793,135	9,139,964	408,157	115,826	292,060

County	Vehicles Registered	Lane Miles of Highway	Vehicle Miles Driven Daily	State Construction Expenditures	Combined Construction Maintenance Expenditures	Total Vehicle Registration Fees	State Net Receipts	County Net Receipts
Shelby	26,976	877	805,921	$3,955,682	$11,346,678	$1,959,085	$1,277,533	$680,761
Sherman	2,832	445	257,217	9,733,082	17,095,014	257,630	16,367	241,216
Smith	219,949	1,610	5,820,322	37,541,409	76,218,573	17,077,994	13,664,182	3,395,763
Somervell	11,377	199	279,365	4,010,704	12,089,045	657,727	307,784	348,790
Starr	56,313	544	1,130,297	11,403,524	16,189,524	3,886,675	2,888,004	997,459
Stephens	9,905	559	220,889	4,814,746	17,393,730	650,179	244,506	405,331
Sterling	2,449	309	271,065	1,991,412	9,128,550	129,232	27,385	101,803
Stonewall	2,021	327	73,880	475,130	3,199,348	121,119	6,166	114,821
Sutton	5,386	590	782,446	675,586	2,636,706	358,452	101,605	256,452
Swisher	6,484	805	437,653	543,509	5,053,623	403,150	62,742	339,736
Tarrant	1,666,191	3,356	32,949,988	335,903,998	467,846,369	136,862,922	115,588,771	21,087,513
Taylor	126,220	1,210	2,657,940	22,211,040	36,078,149	10,182,805	8,313,134	1,859,986
Terrell	1,249	374	81,839	64,378	873,696	57,904	4,174	53,709
Terry	10,997	628	563,270	340,309	7,826,825	844,601	348,514	495,527
Throckmorton	1,959	343	74,000	1,028,480	4,616,761	130,291	5,798	124,407
Titus	30,614	581	1,367,036	12,366,865	22,896,316	2,476,519	1,735,869	738,997
Tom Green	114,296	1,041	1,909,474	18,262,560	34,417,612	8,830,610	6,916,232	1,904,426
Travis	931,348	2,162	22,069,950	172,539,381	290,513,590	70,987,738	58,458,593	12,383,616
Trinity	15,379	443	370,129	495,016	3,803,763	916,660	431,378	484,711
Tyler	21,184	517	517,929	8,080,594	21,951,643	1,274,830	691,288	582,730
Upshur	42,937	788	1,055,075	10,972,112	22,397,543	2,591,451	1,796,078	794,062
Upton	4,771	392	383,115	1,281,812	2,868,204	372,454	126,731	245,591
Uvalde	26,960	765	757,062	3,216,193	13,040,891	1,925,563	1,335,698	588,652
Val Verde	47,887	748	626,739	10,328,469	17,286,710	3,385,697	2,528,498	854,100
Van Zandt	60,520	1,173	2,467,786	8,690,648	26,530,992	3,832,231	2,783,007	1,046,936
Victoria	87,257	925	2,309,713	17,270,495	32,183,166	6,455,345	4,986,444	1,460,691
Walker	53,858	818	2,622,782	75,895,842	96,649,688	3,795,035	2,785,510	1,005,080
Waller	54,153	591	2,177,176	39,692,559	50,602,470	3,980,812	3,025,956	952,395
Ward	15,061	668	1,389,668	4,870,529	26,597,287	1,267,531	966,553	300,381
Washington	41,879	664	1,386,699	6,202,500	18,820,181	3,065,709	2,241,467	820,497
Webb	207,040	1,224	3,628,590	43,681,379	69,302,139	20,558,728	15,813,806	4,739,433
Wharton	47,250	916	1,691,227	35,384,259	85,459,966	3,554,593	2,673,509	878,928
Wheeler	6,654	674	557,804	2,425,343	13,833,555	432,327	85,309	346,713
Wichita	106,430	1,132	2,297,543	12,582,011	33,120,979	7,464,351	5,934,263	1,523,208
Wilbarger	12,180	718	688,806	2,954,538	15,530,415	973,423	452,423	519,958
Willacy	14,312	516	490,569	10,553,461	16,034,972	864,991	374,675	489,723
Williamson	478,792	1,674	9,659,026	44,073,718	105,560,783	36,462,000	29,693,549	6,701,265
Wilson	57,729	738	1,296,810	3,028,782	16,310,801	3,634,145	2,687,821	943,084
Winkler	9,739	292	823,465	5,419,275	18,413,321	743,307	433,609	309,449
Wise	88,508	917	2,424,272	4,438,857	11,167,119	6,487,178	5,139,777	1,342,819
Wood	52,185	911	967,216	5,139,950	19,549,134	3,448,892	2,507,519	936,838
Yoakum	10,549	430	317,635	2,794,173	20,396,438	868,903	397,303	471,022
Young	22,410	703	363,656	3,542,329	11,908,407	1,565,070	965,023	598,390
Zapata	11,789	288	313,888	2,711,008	4,206,029	779,613	395,841	383,559
Zavala	8,639	541	450,618	657,084	6,017,171	591,554	243,344	348,047
Total	**24,088,245**	**197,865**	**575,222,334**	**$7,013,552,109**	**$11,419,289,607**	**$1,871,685,316**	**$1,462,282,650**	**$407,448,167**

Texas Major Toll Roads

Facilities	Authority	2019	2016	2015	2010
Roads		(**Tolls Collected** in thousands of dollars)			
Camino Colombia Toll Road	TxDOT	$20,370	$6,997	$4,079	$3,352
Central Texas Toll Facilities[1]	Central Texas Turnpike System and Regional Authority	$306,830	$239,165	$202,582	$90,006
Fort Bend Toll Roads	Fort Bend Toll Road Authority	$40,167	$29,481	$26,860	$15,675
Harris County Toll Facilities[2]	Harris County Toll Road Authority	$854,849	$759,276	$745,373	$464,269
North Texas Toll Facilities	North Texas Tollway Authority	$911,046	$671,961	$698,454	$399,054
East Texas Toll Facilities	North East Texas Regional Authority	$12,222	$8,731	$8,340	–
Total, roads		**$2,145,484**	**$1,715,611**	**$1,685,688**	**$972,356**

[1]Including U.S. 183A and Manor Expressway. [2]Including Jesse Jones Memorial Toll Bridge.
Source: Highway Statistics annual, Federal Highway Administration; and local toll authorities.

Toll Bridges

Facilities	Authority	2019	2016	2015	2010
Bridge		(**Tolls Collected** in thousands of dollars)			
Cameron County International Toll Bridge	Cameron County	$20,664	$19,412	$21,273	$22,102
Del Rio International	City of Del Rio	$8,321	$10,268	$6,558	$4,144
Eagle Pass International	City of Eagle Pass	$13,857	$14,017	$10,737	$8,106
Laredo International	City of Laredo	$68,733	$68,887	$69,215	$41,449
McAllen International	City of McAllen	$19,013	$21,096	$19,799	$11,036
Pharr International	City of Pharr	$14,736	$18,156	$13,196	$10,639
Roma International	Starr County	$2,683	$2,561	$2,988	$2,081
San Luis Pass–Vacek	Galveston County	$579	$548	$3,128	$1,265
Zaragosa	City of El Paso	$25,275	$22,252	$21,499	$16,094
TOTAL, bridges		**$173,861**	**$177,197**	**$168,393**	**$116,916**

Source: Highway Statistics annual, Federal Highway Administration.

Driver Licenses

The following list shows the number of licensed drivers by year for Texas and for all the states. Sources are the Texas Department of Public Safety (for state figures) and the Federal Highway Administration.

Year	Texas licensed drivers	Total U.S. licensed drivers
2019	17,822,760	228,679,719
2018	18,000,274	227,558,385
2017	17,675,389	225,346,257
2016	17,326,113	221,711,918
2015	16,970,365	218,084,465
2014	16,579,591	214,092,472
2013	16,230,209	212,159,728
2012	15,950,297	211,814,830
2011	16,880,877	211,874,649
2010	16,808,359	210,114,939
2009	16,602,416	209,618,386
2008	16,551,156	208,320,601

Year	Texas licensed drivers	Total U.S. licensed drivers
2007	16,330,825	205,741,845
2006	16,096,985	202,810,438
2005	15,831,852	200,548,972
2004	15,562,484	198,888,912
2003	15,091,776	196,165,666
2002	14,639,132	194,295,633
2001	14,303,799	191,275,719
2000	14,024,305	190,625,023
1995	12,369,243	176,628,482
1990	11,136,694	167,015,250
1985	10,809,078	156,868,277
1980	9,287,286	145,295,036

Motor Vehicles Crashes, Losses in Texas

Year	Number killed	†Number injured	Crashes by Kind				Vehicle Miles Traveled		Economic loss (in millions)
			Fatal	†Injury	†Non-injury	†Total	Number (in millions)	Deaths per 100 mill miles	
1960	2,254	127,980	1,842	71,100	239,300	312,242	46,353	4.9	$350
1965	3,028	186,062	2,460	103,368	365,160	470,988	* 52,163	5.8	498
1966	3,406	208,310	2,784	115,728	406,460	524,972	55,261	6.2	557
1970	3,560	223,000	2,965	124,000	886,000	1,012,965	* 68,031	5.2	1,042
1975	3,429	138,962	2,945	92,510	373,141	468,596	84,575	4.1	1,440
1980	‡ 4,424	185,964	‡ 3,863	123,577	§ 305,500	432,940	103,255	4.3	3,010
1985	3,682	231,009	3,270	151,657	300,531	452,188	143,500	2.6	3,755
1990	3,243	262,576	2,882	162,424	216,140	381,446	163,103	2.0	4,994
1991	3,079	263,430	2,690	161,470	207,288	371,448	162,780	1.9	5,604
1992	3,057	282,025	2,690	170,513	209,152	382,355	162,769	1.9	6,725
1993	3,037	298,891	2,690	178,194	209,533	390,417	167,988	1.8	11,784
1994	3,142	326,837	2,710	192,014	219,890	414,614	172,976	1.8	12,505
1995	3,172	334,259	2,790	196,093	152,190	351,073	183,103	1.7	13,005
1996	3,738	350,397	3,247	204,635	§ 90,261	298,143	187,064	2.0	7,766
1997	3,508	347,881	3,079	205,595	97,315	305,989	194,665	1.8	7,662
1998	3,576	338,661	3,160	202,223	102,732	308,115	201,989	1.8	8,780
1999	3,519	339,448	3,106	203,220	105,375	311,701	213,847	1.6	8,729
2000	3,775	341,097	3,247	205,569	110,174	318,990	210,340	1.8	9,163
2001	3,739	340,554	3,319	207,043	113,596	323,958	216,276	1.73	9,348
2002	3,826	315,061	3,544	196,211	113,089	** 324,651	215,873	1.77	21,100
2003	3,823	308,543	3,372	190,926	§ 245,607	†† 460,025	218,209	1.75	20,700
2004	3,725	288,715	3,286	180,556	245,000	447,691	229,345	1.62	19,400
2005	3,559	293,583	3,157	184,093	257,532	464,541	234,232	1.52	19,200
2006	3,523	272,779	3,120	173,861	243,970	439,027	236,852	1.49	20,400
2007	3,463	267,305	3,098	173,052	264,098	459,689	241,746	1.43	20,600
2008	3,477	243,547	3,116	159,760	257,154	438,996	234,593	1.48	22,900
2009	3,108	234,704	2,807	154,685	251,850	428,273	232,055	1.34	20,300
2010	3,050	‡‡ 217,381	2,772	141,554	233,573	391,101	234,261	1.30	22,200
2011	3,015	211,006	2,751	138,624	226,949	381,463	235,602	1.28	21,900
2012	3,417	230,957	3,037	152,301	247,679	417,707	237,831	1.44	26,000
2013	3,407	232,599	3,065	154,458	272,601	445,829	244,536	1.39	27,800
2014	3,538	237,941	3,189	158,833	297,934	476,875	242,989	1.46	38,000
2015	3,582	247,652	3,186	165,199	332,891	521,389	258,122	1.39	36,600
2016	3,794	265,077	3,404	176,381	351,153	551,971	271,263	1.40	38,800
2017	3,721	253,852	3,432	160,926	343,680	537,970	274,580	1.36	38,401
2018	3,652	249,652	3,314	167,984	350,178	521,476	282,037	1.29	39,600
2019	3,610	256,338	3,288	172,768	363,111	539,167	286,268	1.26	39,200

(Note: The highest death rate was in 1966 at 6.2.)

*Method of calculating vehicle miles traveled revised. Last changed in 1982 by TxDOT.

†In August 1967, amended estimating formula received from National Safety Council (NCS). Starting 1972, actual reported injuries are listed rather than estimates.

‡Change in counting fatalities. In 1978, counted when injury results in death within 90 days of accident. In 1983, counted when injury results in death within 30 days.

§Change in counting Non-injury accidents. For 1996–2002, only crashes having at least **one vehicle towed** were tabulated.

¶Economic loss formula changed. Last changed in 2002, when figures are calculated using NCS Average Calculable Cost on a per death basis figure for the year identified. Figures are rounded to the nearest hundred million. For 1996–2001, only property damage in crashes having at least one vehicle towed was tabulated.

**Beginning with 2002 data, the "Total" crash figure includes "Unknown Severity Crashes" which are not included on this chart. Prior to 2002 these crashes were counted in the Non-injury or Injury category.

††Beginning with 2003 crashes, only those resulting in injury or death or damage to property to the apparent extent of $1,000 are tabulated.

‡‡Beginning in 2010, number injured includes incapacitating, non-incapacitating, and possible injuries.

Source: Texas Department of Transportation (TxDOT) since 2001. Earlier statistics are from the Texas Department of Public Safety (DPS).

Foreign Consulates in Texas

In the list below, these abbreviations appear after the name of the city: (CG) Consulate General; (C) Consulate; (VC) Vice Consulate. The letter "H" before the designation indicates honorary status. Compiled from "Foreign Consular Offices in the United States," U.S. Dept. of State, June 2021; also Texas Secretary of State and individual embassies..

Angola: Houston (CG); 3040 Post Oak Blvd., Ste. 780, 77056. (713) 212-3840. angolaconsulate-tx.org

Argentina: Houston (CG); 2200 West Loop S., 77027. (713) 871-8935. chous.cancilleria.gob.ar/en

Australia: Houston (CG); 3009 Post Oak Blvd., Ste. 1310, 77056. (832) 962-8420. usa.embassy.gov.au/houston

Austria: Houston (HC); 11000 Brittmoore Park Dr., 77041. (713) 723-9979. austrianconsulatehouston.org

Bahamas: Houston (HC); 7026 Old Katy Rd., Ste. 259, 77024. (713) 980-8791. bahamasembdc.org

Barbados: Houston (HC); 3027 Sleepy Hollow Dr., Sugar Land, 77479. (832) 725-5566.

Belgium: Austin (HC); 1404 Wilson St, Ste. B, Bastrop, 76092. (512) 571-3125.
Dallas (HC); 2525 E. Southlake Blvd, Ste. B, Southlake, 76092. (817) 748-4367.
Houston (HC); 2406 Cutter Court, Seabrook, 77586. (770) 402-4988.

Belize: Houston (HC); 1120 NASA Pkwy., Ste. 220R, 77058. (832) 390-4164.
San Antonio (HC); 3510 Pinto Pony Ln., 78247. (210) 859-8234.

Bolivia: Houston (CG); 2401 Fountain View Dr., Ste. 110, 77057. (832) 916-4200. boliviatx.org

Botswana: Houston (HC); 121 N. Post Oak Ln, Apt 2601, 77024. (713) 355-8614.

Brazil: Houston (CG); 5444 Westheimer Rd., Ste. 1900, 77056. (713) 961-3063. houston.itamaraty.gov.br/en-us

Canada: Dallas (CG); 500 N. Akard St., Ste. 2900, 75201. (214) 922-9806. international.gc.ca/country-pays/us-eu/dallas.aspx
Houston (C); 5847 San Felipe St., Ste. 1700, 77057. (713) 821-1440.
Austin (HC); P.O. Box 340069, 78734. (571) 217-4377.

Chile: Houston (CG); 1300 Post Oak Blvd., Ste. 1130, 77057. (713) 963-9066

Dallas (HC); 5200 Keller Springs Rd., Ste 633. 75248

Colombia: Houston (CG); 2400 Augusta Dr., Ste. 400, 77057. (713) 979-0844. houston.consulado.gov.co

Costa Rica: Houston (CG); 3100 Wilcrest, Ste. 260, 77042. (713) 266-0484.

Cote d'Ivoire: Houston (HC); 1302 Waugh Dr., Ste. 482, 77019. (713) 410-0472.

Croatia: Houston (HC); 3610 Rice Blvd., 77005. (713) 444-1442.

Cyprus: Houston (HC); 206 Voss Rd., 77024. (281) 704-6779.

Czech Republic: Houston (HC); Czech Center Museum, 4920 San Jacinto, 77004. (254) 931-4095.

Denmark: Houston (CG); Williams Tower, 2800 Post Oak Blvd., Ste. 1910, 77056. (713) 622-9018.
Dallas (HC); 2701 Hibernia St., 75204. (214) 680-7778.

Ecuador: Houston (CG); 2603 Augusta Dr., Ste. 810, 77057. (713) 572-8731. houston.consulado.gob.ec.
Dallas (HC); 6574 Gerrard St., Frisco, 75034. (972) 712-9107.

Egypt: Houston (CG); 5718 Westheimer, Ste. 1350, 77057. (713) 961-4915. consulateofegypthouston.com

El Salvador: Dallas (CG); 7610 Stemmons Fwy., Ste. 400, 75247. (214) 637-1500.
Houston (CG); 8300 Bissonet St., Ste. 400, 77074. (346) 571-5198.
McAllen (CG); 701 S. Broadway St., 78501. (956) 800-1363.
El Paso (C); 400 W. San Antonio St., Ste. B, 79901. (915) 600-5423.
Laredo (C); 6010 McPherson Rd., Ste. 140, 78041. (956) 701-3852.

Equatorial Guinea: Houston (CG); 6401 Southwest Fwy., 77074. (713) 776-9900.

Estonia: Houston (HC); 3318 Spring Trail Dr., Sugar Land, 77479. (281) 770-3009.

Ethiopia: Houston (HC); 9301 Southwest Fwy., Ste. 250, 77074. (713) 271-7567.

Finland: Dallas (HC); 2021 McKinney Ave., Ste. 1600, 75201. (214) 999-3672.
Houston (HC); 2001 Kirby Dr., Ste. 1314, 77019. (281) 216-5132.

France: Houston (CG); 777 Post Oak Blvd., Ste. 600, 77056. (346) 272-5363. houston.consulfrance.org
Austin (HC); 3900 Petes Path, 78731.
Dallas (HC); 12720 Hillcrest, Ste. 730, 75230. (469) 438 3618.
El Paso (HC); 12270 Rojas Dr., 79936. (915) 892-1660.
San Antonio (HC); 311 Basin Dr., 78216. (210) 859-1308

Georgia: Houston (HC); 410 Pierce St., Ste. 220, 77002. (281) 766-7784.

Germany: Houston (CG); 1330 Post Oak Blvd., Ste. 1850, 77056. (713) 627-7770. houston.diplo.de
Austin (HC); 912 S. Capital of Texas Hwy., Ste. 450, 78746. (512) 852-4162.
Dallas (HC); 17130 Dallas Pkwy., Ste. 240, 75248. (972) 354-7000.

Greece: Houston (C); 2401 Fountain View Dr., Ste. 850, 77057. (713) 840-7522. mfa.gr/usa/en/consulate-in-houston

Guatemala: Houston (CG); 6300 Richmond Ave., Ste. 103, 77057. (713) 953-9531. conshouston.minex.gob.gt
Dallas (C); 4405 N. Beltwood Pkwy., Farmers Branch, 75244. (469) 886-9922.
Del Rio (C); 106 Foster Dr., 78840. (830) 422-2230. consdelrio.minex.gob.gt
McAllen (C); 705 S. Broadway St., 78501. (956) 429-3413. consmcallen.minex.gob.gt

Honduras: Dallas (CG); 3731 Briarpark Dr., Ste. 155, 77042.
Houston (CG); 3731 Briarpark Dr., Ste. 155, 77042. (346) 201-6711.
McAllen (CG); 1209 Galveston Ave., 78501. (956) 627-1210.
Irving (C); 2520 W. Irving Blvd., Ste. 400, 75061.(214) 347-4441.

Hungary: Houston (VC); 847 San Felipe St., Ste. 1700, 77057. (713) 914-1675. hungary.honoraryconsulate.network/houston

Iceland: Dallas (HC); 6827 Northwood Rd., 75225. (214) 415-2311.
Houston (HC); 777 S. Post Oak Ln., 17th floor, 77056. (713) 973-7880.

India: Houston (CG); 4300 Scotland St., 77007. (713) 626-2148. cgihouston.gov.in

Indonesia: Houston (CG); 10900 Richmond Ave., 77042. (713) 785-1691. kemlu.go.id

Ireland: Austin (CG); 515 Congress Ave., Ste. 1720, 78701. (512) 792-5500. dfa.ie/irish-consulate/austin
Houston (HC); 2630 Sutton Ct., 77027. (713) 961-3850.

Israel: Houston (CG); 24 Greenway Plz., Ste. 1500, 77046. (832) 301-3500. embassies.gov.il/houston

Italy: Houston (CG); 1330 Post Oak Blvd., Ste. 660, 77056. (713) 850-7520. conshouston.esteri.it
Dallas (HC); 8303 Elmbrook Dr., 75247. (214) 754-1832.
San Antonio (HC); 2255 W. Mistletoe Ave., 78201. (210) 735-7232.

Jamaica: Houston (HC); 6001 Savoy Dr.,Ste 509, 77036. (713) 782-8494.

Japan: Houston (CG); 2 Houston Center, 909 Fannin St., Ste. 3000, 77010. (713) 652-2977. houston.us.emb-japan.go.jp
Dallas (HC); 4524 Bentley Dr., Plano, 75093. (972) 596-5012.

Korea: Houston (CG); 1990 Post Oak Blvd., Ste. 1250, 77056.

(713) 961-0186. overseas.mofa.go.kr/us-houston-en
Dallas (C); 14001 N. Dallas Parkway, Ste. 450, 75240. (972) 701-0180. overseas.mofa.go.kr/us-dallas-en

Latvia: Houston (HC); 2120 Troon Rd., 77019. (713) 304-3831.

Lebanon: Houston (HC); 2400 Augusta Dr., Ste. 308, 77057. (713) 268-1640.

Lithuania: Houston (HC); 4030 Case St., 77005. (713) 665-4218.

Luxembourg: Austin (HC); 2700 Via Fortuna Dr., Ste. 500. (512) 413-3603.

Malawi: Wimberley (HC); (512) 569-7998.

Mali: Austin (HC); 2000 Lipanese Trail, 78733.

Malta: Dallas (HC); 7739 Southwestern Blvd., 75227. (972) 883 4785.

Mexico: Austin (CG); 5202 E. Ben White Blvd., Ste. 150, 78741. (512) 478-2866. consulmex.sre.gob.mx/austin
Dallas (CG); 1210 River Bend Dr., 75247. (214) 932-8670. consulmex.sre.gob.mx/dallas
El Paso (CG); 910 E. San Antonio Ave., 79901. (915) 747-3246. consulmex.sre.gob.mx/elpaso
Houston (CG); 10555 Richmond Ave., 77042. (713) 271-6800. consulmex.sre.gob.mx/houston
Laredo (CG); 1612 Farragut St., 78040. (956) 723-0990. consulmex.sre.gob.mx/laredo
San Antonio (CG); 127 Navarro St., 78205. (210) 227-9145. consulmex.sre.gob.mx/sanantonio
Brownsville (C); 301 Mexico Blvd., Ste. F2, 78520. (956) 542-4431. consulmex.sre.gob.mx/brownsville
Del Rio (C); 2207 N. Bedell Ave., 78840. (830) 775-2352. consulmex.sre.gob.mx/delrio
Eagle Pass (C); 2252 E. Garrison, 78852. (830) 773-9255. consulmex.sre.gob.mx/eaglepass
McAllen (C); 600 S. Broadway, 78501. (956) 686-0243. consulmex.sre.gob.mx/mcallen
Presidio (C); 319 W. De Marzo St., 79845. (432) 229-2788. consulmex.sre.gob.mx/presidio

Monaco: Dallas (HC); 11020 Tibbs St., 75230. (214) 991-2916.

Mongolia: San Antonio (HCG); P.O. Box 399, Comfort, 78013. (830) 995-5014.

Namibia: Houston (HC); 617 Caroline St., Ste. 3, 77002. (832) 242-2426.
San Antonio (HC); 106 S. St. Mary's St., Ste. 200, 78205. (210) 271-0630.

Netherlands: Dallas (HC); dallas@nlconsulate.com
Houston (HC); 10777 Westheimer Rd., Ste. 1055, 77042. (713) 783-7743.

New Zealand: Houston (HC); 3300 N. Sam Houston Pkwy. E, 77032. (713) 501-5418.

Nicaragua: Houston (CG); 6009 Richmond Ave., Ste. 100, 77057. (713) 789-2762.

Norway: Houston (CG); 3410 W. Dallas St., Ste. 100,77019. (713) 620-4200.
Dallas (HC); P.O. Box 140918, 75214. (214) 707-2213.

Pakistan: Houston (CG); 11850 Jones Rd., 77070.(281) 890-2223. pakistanconsulatehouston.org

Panama: Houston (CG); 24 Greenway Plaza, Ste. 1307, 77046. (713) 622-4451. conpahouston.com
Austin (HC); 101 Knarr St., 78734. (512) 386-1461.

Paraguay: Houston (HC); 4707 Welford Dr., Bellaire, 77401. (713) 444-9887.

Peru: Dallas (CG); 13601 Preston Rd., Ste. E650, 75240. (972) 234-0005. consulado.pe/es/Dallas
Houston (CG); 5177 Richmond Ave., Ste. 695, 77056. (713) 355-9438. consulado.pe.en/Houston

Philippines: Houston (CG); 9990 Richmond Ave., Ste. 100N, 77042. (832) 668-5139.

Poland: Houston (CG); 3040 Post Oak Blvd., Ste. 525, 77056. (713) 993-9685. houston.msz.gov.pl/pl

Portugal: Houston (HC); 721 Buckingham Dr., 77024. (713) 515-5272.

Qatar: Houston (CG); 1990 Post Oak Blvd., Ste. 900, 77056. (713) 355-8221.

Romania: Dallas (HCG); 1412 Main St., Ste. 1800, 75202. (214) 522-3799.
Houston (HC); 19927 Parsons Green Ct., Katy, 77450. (713) 629-1551.

Russia: Houston (CG); 1333 W. Loop South, Ste. 1300, 77027. (713) 337-3300. rusconhouston.mid.ru

Rwanda: Houston (HCG); 70 Terra Bella Dr., Manvel, 77578.

Saudi Arabia: Houston (CG); 5718 Westheimer Rd., Ste. 1500, 77057. (713) 785-5577.

Sierra Leone: Dallas (HC); 2301 Forest Ln., Ste. 400, Garland, 75042. (214) 552-5613.

Slovakia: Dallas (HC); 10830 N. Central Expwy., Ste. 400, 75231. (214) 251-8020.

Slovenia: Houston (HC); 11300 Kingsworthy Lane, 77024. (713) 278-1366.

South Africa: Dallas (HC); 1510 N. Hampton St., Ste. 340, DeSoto 75115. (512) 463-5887.

Spain: Houston (CG); 1800 Bering Dr., Ste. 660, 77057. (713) 783-6200. exteriores.gob.es/Consulados/HOUSTON
Austin (HC); 327 Congress Ave., Ste. 450, 78701. (512) 744-0044.
Corpus Christi (HC); P.O. Box 7589, 78467. (361) 994-7517.
Dallas (HC); 5454 La Sierra Dr., Ste. 200, 75231. (214) 373-1200.
El Paso (HC); 5130 Gateway Blvd. E., Ste. 120, 79905. (915) 274-9563.

Sri Lanka: Houston (HC); 6200 Savoy Dr., Ste. 270, 77036. (832) 287-1677.

Sweden: Houston (CG); 3730 Kirby Dr., 77098. (713) 953-1417. swedishconsulate.org
Dallas (HC); 3808 Miramar Ave., 75205. (214) 522-0148.

Switzerland: Dallas (HC); 2501 N. Harwood St., Ste. 1400, 75201. (214) 965-1025.
Houston (HC); 2000 Edwards St., 77007. (713) 467-9887.

Thailand: Houston (HCG); 3 Greenway Plaza, Ste. 800, 77046. (713) 335-3995. thaiconsulatehouston.com

Trinidad/Tobago: Houston (HC); 9 Parkside Rd., 78738. (713) 816-6477.

Tunisia: Dallas (HC); 4227 N. Capistrano Dr., 75287.(972) 267-4191.

Turkey: Houston (CG); 1990 Post Oak Blvd., Ste. 1300, 77056. (713) 622-5849. houston.cg.mfa.gov.tr

Uganda: Dallas (HC); 12801 N. Central Expwy., Ste. 750, 75243. (214) 675-7330.

Ukraine: Houston (HC); 123 N. Post Oak, Ste 410. (281) 242-6654.

United Arab Emirates: Houston (CG); 2200 Post Oak Blvd., Ste. 1500, 77056". (832) 956-6666.

United Kingdom: Houston (CG); 1301 Fannin St., Ste. 2400, 77002. (713) 210-4000.

Uruguay: Houston (HCG); 1220 Ripple Creek Dr., 77057. (713) 974-7855.
Dallas (HC); 2009 Chenault Dr., Ste. 100, Carrollton, 75006. (214) 346-2919.

Vietnam: Houston (CG); 5251 Westheimer Rd., Ste. 1100, 77056. (713) 850-1233. vietnamconsulateinhouston.org/

Foreign-Trade Zones in Texas

Foreign-trade-zone status endows a domestic site with certain customs privileges, causing it to be considered outside customs territory and therefore available for activities that might otherwise be carried on overseas.

Operated as public utilities for qualified corporations, the zones are established under grants of authority from the Foreign-Trade Zones board, which is chaired by the U.S. Secretary of Commerce. Zone facilities are available for operations involving storage, repacking, inspection, exhibition, assembly, manufacturing, and other processing.

A foreign-trade zone is especially suitable for export processing or manufacturing operations when foreign components or materials with a high U.S. duty are needed to make the end product competitive in markets abroad.

Source: U.S. Department of Commerce.

In 2021, there were 33 Foreign-Trade Zones in Texas.

Amarillo: FTZ 252
City of Amarillo
801 S. Fillmore St., Ste. 205,
Amarillo 79101

Athens: FTZ 269
Athens Economic Development Corp.
201 W. Corsicana St., Ste. 3,
Athens 75751

Austin: FTZ 183
FTZ of Central Texas Inc.
535 E. 5th St., Austin 78701

Beaumont: FTZ 115
Port Arthur: FTZ 116
Orange: FTZ 117
FTZ of Southeast Texas Inc.
P.O. Drawer 2297, Beaumont 77704

Bowie County: FTZ 258
TexAmericas Center
107 Chapel Ln., New Boston 75570

Brownsville: FTZ 062
Brownsville Navigation District
1000 Foust Rd., Brownsville 78521

Calhoun/Victoria Counties: FTZ 155
Calhoun-Victoria FTZ, Inc.
P.O. Drawer 397, Point Comfort 77978

Conroe: FTZ 265
City of Conroe
P.O. Box 3066, Conroe 77305

Corpus Christi: FTZ 122
Port of Corpus Christi Authority
222 Power St., Corpus Christi 78401

Dallas/Fort Worth: FTZ 039
D/FW International Airport Board
P.O. Box 619428, D/FW Airport 75261

Dallas/Fort Worth: FTZ 168
Metroplex International Trade Development Corp.
P.O. Box 613307, Dallas 75261

Eagle Pass: FTZ 096
City of Eagle Pass
100 S. Monroe, Eagle Pass 78853

El Paso: FTZ 068
City of El Paso
501 George Perry, Ste. I,
El Paso 79925

El Paso: FTZ 150
Westport Economic Dev. Corp.
1865 Northwestern Dr.,
El Paso 79912

Ellis County: FTZ 113
Ellis County Trade Zone Corp.
P.O. Box 788
Midlothian 76065

Fort Worth: FTZ 196
Alliance Corridor Inc.
9800 Hillwood Pkwy., Ste. 300
Fort Worth 76177

The Port of Houston is shown./Photo by Carol M. Highsmith/rawpixel (CC).

Freeport: FTZ 149
Port Freeport
1100 Cherry St., Freeport 77541

Galveston: FTZ 036
Board of Trustees of the Galveston Wharves
P.O. Box 328, Galveston 77553

Gregg County: FTZ 234
Gregg County
269 Terminal Cir., Longview 75603

Harris County: FTZ 084
Port of Houston Authority
111 East Loop North,
Houston 77029

Hidalgo County: FTZ 156
Hidalgo County Regional FTZ
100 E. Cano St., Ste. 201, Edinburg 78539

Laredo: FTZ 094
City of Laredo
5210 Bob Bullock Loop, Laredo 78041

Liberty County: FTZ 171
Liberty County Economic Development Corporation
117 Cook St., Liberty 77535

Lubbock: FTZ 260
City of Lubbock
500 Broadway St., 6th Floor,
Lubbock 79401

Lufkin: FTZ 297
City of Lufkin
P.O. Box 190, Lufkin 75902

McAllen: FTZ 012
McAllen FTZ, Inc.
6401 S. 33rd St., McAllen 78503

Midland: FTZ 165
City of Midland
P.O. Box 60305, Midland 79711

San Antonio: FTZ 080
City of San Antonio Economic Development Department
100 W. Houston St., Ste. 1900,
San Antonio 78205

Starr County: FTZ 095
Starr County Industrial Foundation
P.O. Box 502, Rio Grande City 78582

Texas City: FTZ 199
Texas City FTZ Corp.
1801 9th Avenue N., Texas City 77590

Waco: FTZ 246
City of Waco
P.O. Box 1220, Waco 76703

Annual Tonnage Handled by Major/Minor Texas Ports

Table below gives consolidated tonnage (x1,000) handled by Texas ports. All figures are in short tons (2,000 lbs.). Note that "-" indicates no commerce was reported and "0" means tonnage reported was less than 500 tons. *Source: U.S. Corps of Engineers.*

Port	2019	2015	2010	2005	2000	1995	1990
Beaumont	101,090	87,170	76,959	78,887	76,894	20,937	26,729
Brownsville	6,633	7,779	4,616	5,105	3,268	2,656	1,372
Corpus Christi	111,224	85,647	73,663	77,637	81,164	70,218	60,165
Freeport	29,844	21,133	26,676	33,602	28,966	19,662	14,526
Galveston	10,958	10,381	13,949	8,008	10,402	10,465	9,620
Houston	284,944	240,933	227,133	211,666	186,567	135,231	126,178
Matagorda Channel (Port Lavaca)	5,221	11,821	8,879	11,607	10,552	9,237	6,097
Port Arthur	33,944	35,787	30,232	26,385	20,524	49,800	30,681
Sabine Pass	22,002	418	2,494	641	910	231	631
Texas City	40,889	42,924	56,591	57,839	58,109	50,403	48,052
Victoria Channel	2,673	6,733	2,792	3,224	5,104	4,624	3,740
Anahuac	-	-	-	-	-	-	0
Aransas Pass	45	917	173	128	6	181	169
Arroyo Colorado	666	260	411	791	837	994	765
Cedar Bayou	1,811	1,271	931	1,172	1,002	473	219
Chocolate Bayou	1,103	1,171	1,005	3,537	3,488	3,480	3,463
Clear Creek	-	-	-	-	-	-	0
Colorado River	760	848	671	501	445	576	476
Dickinson	450	491	93	688	904	657	556
Double Bayou	-	-	-	257	0	-	0
Greens Bayou	6,645	6,427	5,523	3,768	0	0	0
Harbor Island (Port Aransas)	121	28	1	10	151	209	-
Liberty Channel	3	16	5	-	-	-	0
Orange	1,574	838	684	627	681	693	710
Palacios	-	-	-	-	-	-	0
Port Isabel	-	0	0	-	5	130	269
Port Mansfield	-	-	-	-	-	20	102
Rockport	-	-	-	-	-	-	644
San Bernard River	194	317	371	773	633	653	534
Other Ports	0	0	0	0	0	0	0
TOTAL*	574,061	514,012	486,658	487,100	452,991	371,021	335,312

*Excludes duplication.

Foreign/Domestic Commerce: Breakdown for 2019

Data below represent inbound and outbound tonnage for major ports. Note that "-" means no tonnage was reported. All figures in short tons x1000.

Source: U.S. Corps of Engineers

Port	Foreign		Domestic		
	Imports	Exports	Receipts	Shipments	Local
Beaumont	16,500	47,677	9,595	24,218	3,100
Brownsville	3,269	671	2,425	265	4
Corpus Christi	18,564	66,757	6,063	15,533	4,187
Freeport	7,090	18,882	20	260	0
Galveston	2,348	3,722	2,755	1,979	154
Houston	48,587	115,128	1,936	7,006	14,966
Matagorda Chl. (Port Lavaca)	484	1,719	102	434	0
Port Arthur	6,929	15,746	4,004	2,609	51
Sabine Pass	0	21,137	0	34	-
Texas City	5,879	18,757	235	4,531	225
Victoria	-	-	761	1,912	-

Gulf Intracoastal Waterway by Commodity (Texas portion)

All figures in short tons x1000.

Source: U.S. Army Corps of Engineers

Commodity	2019	2015	2010	2005	2000
Coal	365	125	93	335	121
Petroleum products	53,738	57,224	49,219	39,538	34,816
Chemicals	16,060	17,475	17,553	20,668	21,382
Raw materials	4,056	3,910	3,123	4,898	5,822
Manufactured goods	2,130	1,631	1,646	2,449	2,301
Food, farm products	399	903	574	473	960
Total	**76,748**	**81,268**	**72,917**	**69,549**	**66,440**

U.S. ports ranked by tonnage, 2019 (millions)

1. **Houston, 284.9**
2. S. Louisiana, 238
3. New York, 136.6
4. **Corpus Christi, 111.2**
5. **Beaumont, 101.1**
6. New Orleans, 92.2
7. Long Beach, 80.7
8. Baton Rouge, 73.4
9. Los Angeles, 63.0
10. Virginia, 61.7

States ranked by tonnage, 2019 (x1,000)

1. **Texas, 597,495**
2. Louisiana, 530,269
3. California, 239,154
4. New Jersey, 142,731
5. Washington, 112,267
6. Florida, 98,803
7. Kentucky, 82,081
8. Ohio, 79,117
9. Illinois, 77,616
10. Alabama, 68,431

U.S. Freight Gateways, 2019

Top gateways ranked by value of shipments, with Texas gateways highlighted. In billions of dollars ($214.8 represents $214,800,000,000).

Source: U.S. Bureau of Transportation Statistics, National Transportation Statistics, annual.

Rank	Port	Mode	Exports	Imports	Total trade	Exports as a percent of total
1	Laredo, TX	Land	$94.5	$132.3	$226.8	41.7%
2	New York, NY	Water	42.4	162.3	204.8	20.7
3	Los Angeles, CA	Water	31.0	173.6	204.6	15.1
4	John F. Kennedy Internatl. Airport, NY	Air	84.1	100.2	184.3	45.6
5	Chicago, IL	Air	49.3	134.5	183.8	26.8
6	Long Beach, CA	Water	31.9	129.7	161.5	19.7
7	Houston, TX	Water	92.3	63.1	155.4	59.4
8	Detroit, MI	Land	75.5	57.2	132.7	56.9
9	Los Angeles International Airport, CA	Air	54.0	63.1	117.1	46.1
10	Savannah, GA	Water	28.6	77.5	106.1	27.0
11	Port Huron, MI	Land	39.7	46.7	86.4	45.9
12	New Orleans, LA	Air	38.6	46.0	84.6	45.6
13	Norfolk, VA	Water	28.9	49.9	78.8	36.7
14	El Paso, TX	Land	31.6	43.4	75.0	42.2
15	Charleston, SC	Water	27.3	47.5	74.8	36.5
16	Buffalo-Niagara Falls, NY	Land	35.1	33.9	69.0	50.8
17	Cleveland, OH	Air	39.8	24.4	64.2	62.0
18	San Francisco International Airport, CA	Air	29.6	31.9	61.5	48.2
19	Atlanta, GA	Air	21.2	37.4	58.6	36.2
20	Baltimore, MD	Water	15.0	43.4	58.4	25.6
21	Dallas-Fort Worth, TX	Air	23.3	34.1	57.5	40.6
22	Miami International Airport, FL	Air	34.7	22.5	57.2	60.7
23	Tacoma, WA	Water	20.1	31.5	51.6	39.0
24	Oakland, CA	Water	15.4	35.5	50.9	30.2
25	Atlanta, GA	Air	8.0	40.2	48.2	16.5
27	Hidalgo, TX	Land	13.0	22.2	35.1	36.9
29	Corpus Christi, TX	Water	29.2	5.8	35.0	83.4
32	Eagle Pass, TX	Land	7.5	21.9	29.4	25.4
36	Beaumont, TX	Water	19.7	5.9	25.6	76.9

Border Crossings at U.S. Ports of Entry, 2020

Below are statistics for selected states as to incoming border traffic at ports of entry into the United States. Data are from the *U.S. Bureau of Transportation Statistics.*

Total in thousands. Percent of U.S. total.

Entering at border (thousands 000)	U.S. total	%	Texas	California	New York	Arizona	Michigan
Vehicle passengers	4,795.9	38.2%	1,832.6	132.6	299.1	146.9	564.8
Personal vehicles	147,481.0	38.3%	56,413.3	57,649.7	5,177.8	15,260.7	4,504.6
Pedestrians	25,046.0	38.5%	9,644.4	11,362.8	22.0	3,870.6	0.4
Trucks	11,580.7	38.0%	4,396.4	1,386.2	1,370.1	423.2	2,120.8
Containers (truck)	11,628.4	37.6%	4,368.5	1,400.1	1,390.6	422.0	2,117.7

An American Airlines flight on a Boeing 737 arrives at Dallas/Fort Worth International Airport in Grapevine on October 23, 2019. Photo by Alan Wilson/Flickr (CC).

A plane rests at Matagorda Peninsula Airport on February 24, 2019. Photo by Adam Reeder/Flickr (CC).

Public Administration

In 1945, the Texas Aeronautics Commission (TAC) was created and directed by the legislature to encourage, foster, and assist in the development of aeronautics within the state, and to encourage the establishment of airports and air navigational facilities. The Commission's first annual report of Dec. 31, 1946, stated that Texas had 592 designated airports and 7,756 civilian aircraft.

The TAC's commitment to providing air transportation was strengthened in 1989 when the TAC became the Texas Department of Aviation (TDA). And on Sept. 1, 1991, when the Texas Department of Transportation (TxDOT) was created, the TDA became the Aviation Division within the department.

The primary responsibilities of the Aviation Division include providing engineering and technical services for planning, constructing, and maintaining aeronautical facilities in the state. It is also responsible for long-range aviation facility development planning (statewide system of airports) and applying for, receiving, and disbursing federal funds.

In the Texas Airport System Plan, TxDOT has identified 289 airports and three heliports. Of the airports, 26 are commercial airports, 24 are reliever airports, and 239 are general aviation airports.

Additionally, TxDOT's Aviation Division has requested Federal Aviation Administration Reliever status for five airports. These include the privately owned Austin Executive and Houston Executive airports, as well as the publicly owned New Braunfels Municipal, Mid-Way Regional (at Midlothian), and Cleburne municipal airports.

Commercial-service airports provide scheduled passenger service. Reliever airports are a special class of general aviation airports designated by the Federal Aviation Administration (FAA). They provide alternative landing facilities in the metropolitan areas separate from the commercial-service airports and, together with the business/corporate airports, provide access for business and executive turbine-powered aircraft.

The community-service and basic-service airports provide access for single- and multi-engine, piston-powered aircraft to smaller communities throughout the state. Some community-service airports are also capable of accommodating light jets.

TxDOT is charged by the legislature with planning, programming, and implementing improvement projects at the general aviation airports. In carrying out these responsibilities, TxDOT channels the Airport Improvement Program (AIP) funds provided by the FAA for all general aviation airports in Texas.

Since 1993, TxDOT has participated in the FAA's state block grant demonstration program. Under this program, TxDOT assumes most of the FAA's responsibility for the administration of the AIP funds for airports.

The Aviation Facilities Development Program (AFDP) oversees planning and research, assists with engineering and technical services, and provides financial assistance through state grants to public bodies operating airports for the purpose of establishing, constructing, reconstructing, enlarging, or repairing airports, airstrips, or navigational facilities.

The 85th Legislature appropriated funds to TxDOT, which subsequently allocated a portion of those funds to the Aviation Division. TxDOT allocated approximately $15 million annually for the 2018-2019 biennium to the Aviation Division to help implement and administer the AFDP. These funds are in addition to the block grant funds received through the FAA's AIP.

Source: Texas Transportation Institute

Drones

The past few years have seen the advent and proliferation of unmanned aircraft systems (UASs), commonly called drones.

They have woven their way into our everyday lives as hobbyists and various professionals use them for a variety of functions that include aerial photography, real estate, construction/industrial, agriculture, emergency management/law enforcement, and insurance.

Nationwide, more than 900,000 hobbyists registered UASs as of Dec. 31, 2018, and the FAA estimates there are some 1.25 million units that can be identified as distinctly hobbyist.

Commercial UAS operator registrations number more than 277,000 since online registration began in April 2016. The commercial UAS industry is still at a very early stage and growth is expected to accelerate in the years to come. The FAA says the fleet today exceeds 835,000.

Related to UASs are the remote pilots that fly them. The FAA issues Remote Pilot Certificates under the Small UAS Rule (14 CFR Part 107), which took effect on Aug. 29, 2016. This rule also provided the regulatory structure for the operation of small UASs for commercial purposes. As of December 2018, the FAA had issued more than 116,000 Remote Pilot Certificates.

A drone hovers just outside the borders of the Guadalupe Mountains National Park on August 22, 2020. Photo by Gary Seloff/Flickr (CC).

Passenger Enplanement by Airport

Airport	2009	2011	2013	2015	2017	Percent change	2019
Abilene	81,451	80,030	78,847	88,959	86,386	-5.29%	81,813
Amarillo	404,903	399,997	373,946	347,304	334,102	5.69%	353,124
Austin	4,019,088	4,409,094	4,809,854	5,643,251	6,580,031	29.29%	8,507,410
Beaumont	22,310	14,323	26,070	35,557	24,880	16.83%	29,068
Brownsville	77,438	84,465	88,292	147,831	119,912	7.92%	129,407
College Station	73,462	70,869	84,379	91,243	74,552	12.45%	83,832
Corpus Christi	353,868	327,534	309,480	339,105	318,810	2.92%	328,109
D/FW	26,548,401	27,464,158	28,946,438	31,356,173	31,433,095	13.82%	35,778,573
Dallas/Love	3,704,594	3,841,785	3,971,077	6,495,869	7,537,325	7.21%	8,080,506
Del Rio*	13,851	9,331	6,846	-	-	-	22,439
El Paso	1,489,619	1,469,168	1,377,876	1,370,243	1,442,605	21.02%	1,745,770
Harlingen	374,232	361,494	354,717	263,423	271,086	23.72%	335,381
Houston/Bush	19,168,962	19,491,854	18,821,429	20,346,164	19,556,778	12.01%	21,905,309
Houston/Hobby	4,032,037	4,646,710	5,213,512	5,765,544	6,392,225	10.60%	7,069,614
Killeen-Ft. Hood	202,226	189,330	175,992	153,698	131,836	33.98%	176,630
Laredo	100,308	105,631	106,524	113,176	94,970	-4.13%	91,043
Longview	24,201	21,360	20,207	19,871	20,682	31.32%	27,160
Lubbock	533,635	505,381	454,661	446,081	453,680	14.66%	520,181
McAllen	360,608	335,008	332,769	390,358	339,132	24.56%	422,434
Midland	435,979	472,177	502,303	533,049	498,248	34.95%	672,382
San Angelo	60,315	55,304	60,127	64,901	60,061	10.54%	66,390
San Antonio	3,809,114	3,967,764	3,998,343	4,057,345	4,300,499	16.80%	5,022,980
Texarkana	27,530	28,626	31,214	35,469	34,574	8.44%	37,492
Tyler	73,177	73,334	81,277	77,543	49,075	21.87%	59,807
Victoria	6,113	5,115	4,204	3,129	3,259	75.94%	5,734
Waco	66,116	60,479	59,809	63,256	61,340	2.55%	62,907
Wichita Falls	43,376	38,941	43,994	45,426	39,064	3.47%	40,418
Total	**70,702,726**	**66,106,914**	**68,529,262**	**70,334,187**	**78,293,968**	**14.20%**	**91,655,913**

Percent change 2017 to 2019. *Del Rio lost commercial service in 2013 and regained service in 2018. Calendar year data.

Sources: FAA Terminal Area Forecasts and Passenger Enplanement for US Airports 2019.

Texas Air History

Passengers enplaned in Texas by scheduled carriers. (Texarkana not included.) Fiscal year data.

Source: Federal Aviation Administration.

1950.........................1,169,051
1960.........................3,113,582
1965.........................5,757,689
1970.........................10,256,691
1975.........................13,182,957
1980.........................26,216,873
1985.........................40,659,223
1990.........................49,317,029
1995.........................57,166,515
2000.........................65,090,784
2005.........................65,718,669
2008.........................69,906,579
2009.........................66,155,323
2010.........................66,850,320
2011.........................68,505,347
2012.........................69,059,805
2013.........................70,305,633
2014.........................73,714,180
2015.........................78,261,315
2016.........................80,187,617
2017.........................80,223,633
2018.........................86,428,773
2019.........................91,618,421

Leading US Airlines, 2019

Rank	Airline	Passengers
1	**Southwest**	**162.681**
2	Delta	162.494
3	**American**	**155.785**
4	United	116.256
5	JetBlue	42.836
6	SkyWest	42.329
7	Alaska	35.452
8	Spirit	33.868

In millions. Texas-based airlines in bold. *Source: U.S. Department of Transportation.*

An airplane lands at Dallas/Fort Worth International AIrport on November 21, 2019. Photo by Roman K/Flickr (CC)..

Agriculture

PRINCIPAL CROPS

VEGETABLE CROPS

FRUITS AND NUTS

LIVESTOCK AND THEIR PRODUCTS

Hay is a primary feed crop for all of the farm animals in Texas. In 2020, we harvested 9.6 million tons of hay, valued at $1.3 billion. Photo by sbmeeper1/Public Domain

Agriculture in Texas

Information was collected from Texas A&M AgriLife Extension specialists, Texas Agricultural Statistics Service, U.S. Department of Agriculture, and U.S. Department of Commerce. Caroline Gleaton, Administrative Associate V; John Robinson, Professor and Extension Specialist-Cotton Marketing; and Mark Welch, Extension Economist-Grain Marketing, Texas A&M AgriLife Extension Service compiled the information. All references are to Texas unless otherwise specified. For information on the lumber industry, see page 71 in the Environment chapter.

Agribusiness, the combined phases of food and fiber production, processing, transporting and marketing, is a leading Texas industry. Most of the following discussion is devoted to the initial phase of production on farms and ranches.

Texas agriculture is an important industry. Cash receipts from agricultural producers in 2019 were estimated at $21.2 billion, compared with $21.7 billion in 2018. Agricultural production is associated with considerable upstream and downstream economic activity. Many businesses, financial institutions, and individuals are involved in providing supplies, credit, and services to farmers and ranchers, and in processing and marketing agricultural commodities.

The potential for further growth is favorable. With the increasing demand for food and fiber throughout the world, and because of the importance of agricultural exports to thw nation's trade balance, agriculture in Texas is destined to play an important role in the future.

Major efforts of research and educational programs by the Texas A&M University System are directed toward developing the state's agricultural industry to its fullest potential. The goal is to capitalize on natural advantages that agriculture has in Texas because of the relatively warm climate, productive soils, and availability of excellent export and transportation facilities.

Texas Farms

The number and nature of farms have changed over time. The number of farms in Texas has decreased from 420,000 in 1940 to 247,000 in 2020 with an average size of 510 acres. The number of small farms is increasing — but part-time farmers and ranchers operate them.

Mechanization of farming continues as new and larger machines replace manpower and smaller equipment. Even though machinery price tags are higher than in the past, machines are technologically advanced and efficient. Tractors, mechanical harvesters, and numerous cropping machines have virtually eliminated menial tasks that for many years were traditional to farming.

Revolutionary agricultural chemicals and genetically engineered traits have appeared along with improved plants and animals. Many of the natural hazards of farming and ranching have been reduced by better use of weather information, machinery and other improvements; but rising costs, labor availability, and high-energy costs have added to concerns of farmers and ranchers.

Changes in Texas agriculture in the last 50 years include:

1. More detailed record keeping that assists in management and marketing decisions

2. More restrictions on choice or inputs/practices

3. Precision agriculture is taking on new dimensions through the use of satellites, computers, Global Positioning Systems (GPS), and other high-tech tools to help producers manage inputs such as seed, fertilizers, pesticides, and water.

Farms have become fewer, larger, specialized, and much more expensive to own and operate, but are also far more productive. Meanwhile, the number of small farms operated by part-time farmers is increasing. Land ownership is becoming more of a lifestyle used mostly for recreational purposes. Off-farm landowners are increasing.

Irrigation continues to be an important factor in crop production. Crops and livestock have made major changes in production areas, as in the concentration of cotton on the High Plains and livestock industries in Central and East Texas. Pest and disease control methods have greatly improved. Herbicides are relied upon for weed control.

Feedlot finishing, commercial broiler production, artificial insemination, improved pastures and brush control, reduced feed requirements, and other changes have greatly increased livestock and poultry efficiency. Biotechnology and genetic engineering promise new breakthroughs in reaching even higher levels of productivity. Horticultural plant and nursery businesses have expanded. Improved wildlife management has increased deer, turkey and other wildlife populations. The use of land for recreation and ecotourism is growing.

Farmers and ranchers are better educated and informed, more science- and business-oriented. Today, agriculture operates in a global, high-tech, consumer-driven environment.

Cooperation among farmers in marketing, promotion and other fields has increased. Also, agricultural producers have become increasingly dependent on off-the-farm services to supply production inputs such as feeds, chemicals, credit, and other essentials.

Agribusiness

Texas farmers and ranchers have developed considerable dependence upon agribusiness. With many producers specializing in the production of certain crops and livestock, they look beyond the farm and ranch for supplies and services. On the input side, they rely on suppliers of production needs and services and, on the output side they need assemblers, processors, and distributors.

Since 1940, the proportion of Texans whose livelihood is linked to agriculture has changed greatly. In 1940, about 23 percent of Texans were producers on farms and ranches, and about 17 percent were suppliers or were engaged in assembly, processing, and distribution of agricultural products. The agribusiness alignment in 2008 reflected less than 2 percent on farms and ranches with about 15 percent of the labor force providing production or marketing supplies and services and retailing food and fiber products.

Cash Receipts

Farm and ranch cash receipts in 2019 totaled $21.3 billion, with estimates of $1.8 billion for direct government payments. Realized gross farm income totaled $26.1 billion, with farm production expenses of $20.6 billion and net farm income totaling $5.6 billion.

Percent of Income from Products

Livestock and livestock products accounted for 67.6 percent of the $21.3 billion cash receipts from farm marketings in 2019, with the remaining 32.4 percent from crops. Receipts from livestock have trended up largely because of increased feeding operations and reduced crop acreage associated with farm programs and low prices. However, these relationships change continuously because of variations in commodity prices and volume of marketings.

Cattle and calves accounted for 39.6 percent of total cash receipts (excluding government payments) received by Texas farmers and ranchers in 2019. Milk made up 12.4 percent of receipts, poultry and eggs 12.4 percent, hogs 1.1 percent, and miscellaneous livestock 2.0 percent.

Cotton accounted for 12.1 percent of total receipts, while feed crops was 8.7 percent, food grains 2.2 percent, vegetables and melons 1.3 percent, oil crops 0.7 percent, fruits and nuts 0.8 percent, and other crops 6.7 percent.

Texas' Rank Among states

Measured by cash receipts from crops and livestock, Texas ranked fourth in 2019; California ranked first; Iowa, second; and Nebraska, third.

Texas normally leads all other states in numbers of farms and ranches and farm and ranch land, cattle slaughtered, cattle on feed, calf births, sheep and lambs, goats, cash receipts from livestock marketings, cattle and calves, beef cows, sheep and lambs, wool production, mohair production, and exports of fats, oils, and greases. Texas also usually leads in production of cotton.

Texas Agricultural Exports

The value of Texas' share of agricultural exports in fiscal year 2019 was $6.3 billion. Cotton accounted for $2.1 billion of the exports; corn and processed grain products, $295.0 million; feed and other feedgrains, $255.4; wheat, $213.9 million; vegetable oils, $12.6 million; rice, $116.5 million; hides and skins, $102.9 million; beef and veal and pork, $1.1 billion; broiler meat and other poultry products, $322.0 million; fresh fruits, $38.3 million; processed fruits and tree nuts, $105.1 million; soybeans and soybean meal, $15.1 million; fresh and processed vegetables, $82.1 million; dairy products, $386.2 million; and miscellaneous and other products, $1.2 billion.

In 2018, Texas' exports of $6.9 billion of farm and ranch products compares with $6.9 billion in 2017 and $5.8 billion in 2016.

Cash Receipts by Commodities, 2015–2019

COMMODITIES	2015	2016	2017	2018	2019	Percent of 2019
	(All values in thousands of dollars)					
All Commodities	23,162,190	20,252,874	22,242,427	21,661,381	21,249,024	**100.00%**
Animals and products	**16,719,830**	**13,171,030**	**14,437,152**	**14,268,806**	**14,355,592**	**67.56%**
Meat animals	11,681,887	8,657,563	9,095,448	8,696,035	8,666,372	40.78%
Cattle and calves	11,459,962	8,467,800	8,899,836	8,473,061	8,424,033	39.64%
Hogs	221,925	189,763	195,612	222,974	242,339	1.14%
Dairy products, milk	1,818,675	1,848,140	2,213,152	2,168,608	2,640,193	12.43%
Poultry and eggs	2,845,330	2,289,041	2,702,579	2,984,390	2,626,194	12.36%
Broilers	2,030,358	1,835,520	2,231,814	2,374,520	2,165,130	10.19%
Misc. livestock †	373,938	376,286	425,973	419,773	422,833	1.99%
Crops	**6,442,360**	**7,081,843**	**7,805,274**	**7,392,575**	**6,893,431**	**32.44%**
Food grains	590,295	422,504	348,966	500,477	473,678	2.23%
Rice	127,907	122,768	147,896	155,112	171,896	0.81%
Wheat	460,006	297,599	198,545	342,506	298,337	1.40%
Feed crops	2,026,948	2,121,556	1,742,490	1,681,655	1,841,359	8.67%
Corn	1,067,346	1,170,850	1,010,355	1,029,645	1,104,563	5.20%
Sorghum	557,781	480,609	319,035	226,114	308,847	1.45%
Hay	395,753	460,479	410,626	410,581	419,469	1.97%
Cotton	1,710,731	2,366,886	3,443,599	2,991,571	2,566,232	12.08%
Oil crops	198,370	160,357	227,383	217,182	147,356	0.69%
Vegetables and melons	373,847	398,776	438,316	440,654	281,993	1.33%
Fruits and nuts	155,646	204,673	221,729	156,682	163,350	0.77%
All other crops ‡	1,386,522	1,407,090	1,382,791	1,404,354	1,419,462	6.68%

† Includes catfish, honey, mohair, wool, chicken eggs, farm chickens, turkeys, and other animals and products.
‡ Includes miscellaneous vegetables and other field crops.
Values are rounded to the nearest thousand. Sub-categories may not sum to total because not all sub-categories are reported.

Source: USDA/ERS Farm Income and Wealth Statistics.

Hunting

The management of wildlife as an economic enterprise through leasing for hunting makes a significant contribution to the economy of many counties. Leasing the right of ingress on a farm or ranch for the purpose of hunting is the service marketed. After the leasing, the consumer—the hunter—goes onto the land to seek the harvest of the wildlife commodity. Hunting lease income to farmers and ranchers in 2020 was estimated at $718 million.

The demand for hunting opportunities is growing while the land capable of producing huntable wildlife is decreasing. As a result, farmers and ranchers are placing more emphasis on wildlife management practices to help meet requests for hunting leases.

Export Shares of Commodities

Commodity*	2016	2017	2018	2019	2019 % of U.S. Total
	(All values in millions of dollars)				
Beef and veal	845.6	965.6	1,074.4	1,029.4	12.72%
Pork	59.2	60.3	69.8	76.5	1.10%
Hides and skins	200.9	195.2	146.5	102.9	9.82%
Other livestock products [1]	143.2	189.9	189.4	211.6	6.14%
Dairy products	251.3	313.6	338.1	386.2	6.52%
Broiler meat	201.8	232.2	235.8	246.8	7.65%
Other poultry products [2]	67.2	76.9	88.8	75.2	3.83%
Vegetables, fresh	42.1	45.3	43.5	30.6	1.14%
Vegetables, processed	81.7	84.9	73.0	51.4	1.14%
Fruits, fresh	39.5	42.7	41.2	38.3	0.88%
Fruits, processed	37.3	37.3	35.2	33.2	0.88%
Tree nuts	85.4	103.3	50.1	71.9	0.79%
Rice	92.9	105.1	105.5	116.5	6.25%
Wheat	180.0	138.2	163.3	213.9	3.43%
Corn	248.1	202.1	249.2	166.2	2.17%
Feeds and other feed grains [3]	346.6	278.7	258.4	255.4	3.05%
Grain products, processed	158.8	131.5	126.5	128.9	3.22%
Soybeans	20.6	28.0	18.8	12.2	0.07%
Soybean meal	3.7	5.1	5.6	2.9	0.07%
Vegetable oils	10.5	16.4	14.5	12.6	0.46%
Other oilseeds and products[4]	128.2	143.7	153.2	126.2	6.65%
Cotton	1,708.2	2,657.7	2,601.0	2,056.4	33.45%
Tobacco	0.0	0.0	0.0	0.0	0.00%
Other plant products [5]	832.0	835.3	801.6	855.2	4.70%
Total agricultural exports	**5,784.8**	**6,889.1**	**6,883.2**	**6,300.5**	**4.63%**
Total animal products	**1,769.2**	**2,033.7**	**2,142.8**	**2,128.6**	**6.94%**
Total plant products	**4,015.6**	**4,855.3**	**4,740.5**	**4,171.8**	**3.96%**

* Totals may not add due to rounding.
1 Includes other nonpoultry meats, animal fat, live farm animals, and other animal parts.
2 Includes turkey meat, eggs, and other fowl products.
3 Includes processed feeds, fodder, barley, oats, rye, and sorghum.
4 Includes peanuts (oilstock), other oil crops, corn meal, other oilcake and meal, protein substances, bran, and residues.
5 Includes sweeteners and products, other horticulture products, planting seeds, cocoa, coffee, and other processed foods.

Data sources: USDA, Economic Research Service; USDA, Foreign Agricultural Service, Global Agricultural Trade System.

Irrigation

Agricultural irrigation in Texas peaked in 1974 at 8.6 million acres. Over the next 20 years, irrigation declined due to many factors including poor farm economics, falling water tables in certain regions, energy costs for irrigation pumping, and the movement of much of the vegetable production from South Texas to Mexico. For the past 15 years, total irrigated area has stabilized and fluctuates from year-to-year between 6 and 6.4 million acres. This puts Texas third in the nation, behind California and Nebraska in agricultural irrigation.

Although some irrigation is practiced in nearly every county of the state, about 60 percent of the total irrigated acreage is on the High Plains of Texas. Other concentrated areas of irrigation are the Upper Gulf Coast rice-producing area, the Lower Rio Grande Valley, the Winter Garden area of South Texas, and the Trans-Pecos area of West Texas.

Sprinkler irrigation is used on about 75 percent of the total irrigated acreage, with surface irrigation methods, primarily furrow and surge methods, on much of the remaining irrigated area. Texas growers are continuing the switch to center pivot irrigation machines. Texas farmers lead the nation in the adoption of efficient irrigation technologies, particularly LEPA (low energy precision application) and LESA (low elevation spray application) center pivot systems, both of which were developed by Texas A&M AgriLife Research and the Texas A&M AgriLife Extension Service.

The use of drip irrigation continues to increase and accounts for about 10 percent of the total irrigated acreage. Drip irrigation is routinely used for vegetables, vineyards and tree crops such as citrus, pecans and peaches. Some drip irrigation of cotton, forages and peanuts is being practiced in West Texas. Farmers continue to experiment with drip irrigation, but the relatively high costs and management requirements are limiting more widespread use. One exception is the Texas fast-growing wine industry, where drip irrigation is almost exclusively used for vineyards.

Agricultural irrigation uses about 58 percent of all freshwater in the state, and landscape irrigation accounts for about 40 percent of total municipal water use during the summer months. Texas is one of only a handful of states that require a state irrigator's license for the design and installation of landscape and residential irrigation systems. Cities of 20,000 persons or

This cotton harvest will be loaded into a module to be formed into a bale. Texas leads the U.S. in cotton production, and today our state's annual cotton harvest amounts to around 41.7 percent of the country's total production. Photo by USDA NRCS Texas/Flickr

larger are required to have irrigation inspectors to ensure that landscape irrigation systems meet state design and installation requirements. However, no license or certification is required for the design or installation of agricultural irrigation systems.

To meet future water demand for our rapidly growing cities and industries, several regions of the state are looking at water transfers from agriculture. The largest water transfer project is likely the San Antonio Water System Vista Ridge Pipeline, which is designed to transfer 16 billion gallons per year from the Carrizo and Simsboro aquifers in Burleson County to San Antonio. The long-term effects on water availability in Burleson County and surrounding areas are uncertain.

Texas water planning documents estimate that as much as 30 percent of future water demand could be met through agricultural irrigation conservation. However, state funding for such programs continues to decline. In about 20 percent of the irrigated area, water is delivered to farms through canals and pipelines by irrigation and other types of water districts and by river authorities. Many of these delivery networks are aging, in poor condition, and have high seepage losses. Estimates are that over 30 percent of all water diverted by irrigation districts is lost in the conveyance systems.

Approximately 80 percent of the state's irrigated acreage is supplied with water pumped from wells. Surface water sources supply the remaining area. Periods of droughts continue to plague Texas. The droughts over the last 20 years in particular have greatly impacted water availability from surface sources (rivers, reservoirs, etc.). As a result, the number of groundwater wells increased rapidly throughout South and West Texas, which could impact future water availability. Declining groundwater levels in several major aquifers is a serious problem, particularly in the Ogallala Aquifer in the Texas High Plains and the southern portion of the Carrizo-Wilcox formation.

Texas common law grants the landowner with broad rights to exploit the underlying groundwater. Laws and regulations governing groundwater use enacted in Texas over the last 50 years attempt to recognize the landowner's right to beneficially use the water, while giving water districts certain powers to manage and restrict water use. Legal battles are ongoing between these two interests. However, an increasing number of groundwater conservation districts are establishing water use limits for agricultural irrigation. The Edwards Aquifer Authority has a voluntary irrigation "opt-out" program, the first of its kind in Texas, where farmers receive payments in exchange for not irrigating during drought years.

Irrigation is an important factor in the productivity of Texas agriculture. The value of crop production from irrigated acreage is 50 to 60 percent of the total value of all crop production, although only about 30 percent of the state's total harvested cropland acreage is irrigated.

The Irrigation section was provided by Guy Fipps, Professor and Extension Agricultural Engineer, Texas A&M University.

Principal Crops

In most recent years, the value of crop production in Texas is less than 32 percent of the total value of the state's agricultural output. Cash receipts from farm sales of crops are reduced somewhat because some grain and roughage is fed to livestock on farms where produced. Drought has reduced receipts in recent years.

Receipts from all Texas crops totaled $6.9 billion in 2019, $7.4 billion in 2018, and $7.8 billion in 2017.

Cotton, corn, grain sorghum, and wheat account for a large part of the total crop receipts. In 2019, cotton contributed about 37.2 percent of the crop total; corn, 16.0 percent; and wheat, 4.3 percent. Hay, cottonseed, vegetables, peanuts, rice, soybeans, and grain sorghum are other important cash crops.

Cotton

Cotton has been a major crop in Texas for more than a century. Since 1880, Texas has led all states in cotton production in most years, and today the annual Texas cotton harvest amounts to around 41.7 percent of total production in the United States. The annual Texas cotton crop has averaged 5.7 million 480-lb. bales since 1996.

Value of upland cotton produced in Texas in 2020 was $1.4 billion. Cottonseed value in 2020 was $269.8 million — making the value of the Texas crop around $1.6 billion.

Upland cotton was harvested from 3.6 million acres in 2020 and American-Pima from 31,000 acres, for a total of 3.6 million acres. Yield for upland cotton in 2020 was 627 pounds per harvested acre, with American-Pima yielding 743 pounds per acre. Total cotton production for 2020 was 4.8 million 480 lb. bales. Upland cotton acreage harvested in 2019 totaled 5.25 million and American-Pima harvested 10,000 acres for total cotton acreage of 5.3 million acres. The yield for upland cotton was 578 pounds per acre and 816 pounds per acre for American-Pima. Total cotton production amounted to 6.3 million 480 lb. bales in 2019 and 6.9 million 480 lb. bales in 2018.

Cotton is the raw material for processing operations at gins, oil mills, compresses, and a small number of textile mills in Texas. Cotton in Texas is machine harvested. Field storage of harvested seed cotton has become common practice as gins decline in number. Most of the Texas cotton crop is exported. China, Turkey, Mexico and various Pacific Rim countries are major buyers. With the continuing development of fiber-spinning technology and the improved quality of Texas cotton, the export demand for Texas cotton has grown.

Grain Sorghum

Texas grain sorghum, in 2020, ranked number two in value of production in the U.S., with Kansas being number one. Much of the grain is exported, as well as being used in livestock and poultry feed throughout the state. Ethanol production is a more recent demand source for Texas sorghum.

Total production of grain sorghum in 2020 was 94.5 million bushels, with 63 bushels per acre yield from 1.5 million acres harvested. With an average price of $7.40 per cwt., the total value reached $391.6 million. In 2019, 1.4 million acres of grain sorghum were harvested, yielding an average of 61 bushels per acre for a total production of 85.4 million bushels. It was valued at $6.5 per cwt., for a total value of $310.4 million. In 2018, 1.4 million acres were harvested with an average of 46 bushels per acre, or

Value of Cotton & Cottonseed 1983–2020

Crop Year	Upland Cotton		Cottonseed	
	Production (Bales)	Value	Production (Tons)	Value
	(All figures in thousands)			
1983	2,380	$680,870	1,002	$162,324
1984	3,680	962,688	1,563	157,863
1985	3,910	968,429	1,635	102,156
1986	2,535	560,945	1,053	82,118
1987	4,635	1,325,981	1,915	157,971
1988	5,215	1,291,651	2,131	238,672
1989	2,870	812,784	1,189	141,491
1990	4,965	1,506,182	1,943	225,388
1991	4,710	1,211,789	1,903	134,162
1992	3,265	769,495	1,346	145,368
1993	5,095	1,308,396	2,147	255,493
1994	4,915	1,642,003	2,111	215,322
1995	4,460	1,597,037	1,828	201,080
1996	4,345	1,368,154	1,784	230,136
1997	5,140	1,482,787	1,983	226,062
1998	3,600	969,408	1,558	204,098
1999	5,050	993,840	1,987	160,947
2000	3,940	868,061	1,589	162,078
2001	4,260	580,723	1,724	159,470
2002	5,040	967,680	1,855	191,065
2003	4,330	1,199,237	1,616	202,000
2004	7,740	1,493,510	2,895	301,080
2005	8,440	1,879,757	2,869	289,739
2006	5,800	1,288,992	2,066	243,776
2007	8,250	2,391,840	2,861	443,409
2008	4,450	935,568	1,547	351,192
2009	4,620	1,328,342	1,634	254,904
2010	7,840	3,006,797	2,685	413,490
2011	3,500	1,375,920	1,228	354,892
2012	5,000	1,675,200	1,669	442,285
2013	4,170	1,493,194	1,368	347,472
2014	6,175	1,739,868	1,946	354,579
2015	5,720	1,564,992	1,844	413,056
2016	8,100	2,593,296	2,528	490,432
2017	9,270	2,950,085	2,852	393,576
2018	6,850	2,232,552	2,088	331,992
2019	6,320	1,762,522	1,902	317,634
2020	4,700	1,373,904	1,443	269,841

Source: Texas Agricultural Facts@, USDA/NASS Crop Production Annual Summary, January; and Crop Values Annual Summary, February. USDA/NASS Quick Stats data system.

Realized Gross Income* and Net Income from Farming 1982–2019

Year	**Realized Gross Farm Income	Farm Production Expenses	†Net Change In Farm Inventories	***Total Net Farm Income	***Total Net Income Per Farm
	(Values in millions of dollars)				(dollars)
1982	11,404.5	10,008.2	–127.8	1,396.3	7,197.60
1983	11,318.1	9,778.9	–590.7	1,539.2	7,933.80
1984	11,692.6	10,257.3	186.1	1,435.3	7,398.30
1985	11,375.3	9,842.8	–9.0	1,532.5	7,981.90
1986	10,450.1	9,272.8	–349.0	1,177.3	6,196.60
1987	12,296.6	10,038.7	563.2	2,257.9	12,010.10
1988	12,842.3	10,331.7	–128.4	2,510.6	13,076.20
1989	12,843.1	10,328.4	–798.6	2,514.7	12,962.10
1990	14,421.5	11,012.9	343.9	3,408.6	17,391.00
1991	14,376.4	11,270.3	150.0	3,106.1	15,767.00
1992	14,482.5	10,617.6	464.1	3,864.9	19,519.80
1993	15,817.0	11,294.6	197.0	4,522.5	20,745.40
1994	15,394.5	11,134.7	107.7	4,259.9	19,363.00
1995	15,678.9	12,537.3	243.7	3,141.6	14,151.30
1996	15,025.0	12,006.6	–290.1	3,018.4	13,475.10
1997	16,430.7	12,718.5	709.2	3,712.3	16,498.90
1998	15,506.0	12,047.4	–817.1	3,458.6	15,269.70
1999	17,469.5	12,441.9	196.0	5,027.6	22,099.30
2000	16,810.1	12,707.8	–50.2	4,102.3	17,968.90
2001	18,089.0	13,106.6	113.4	4,982.5	21,795.70
2002	16,567.9	11,372.8	436.8	5,195.1	22,686.00
2003	20,105.7	13,687.6	–137.7	6,418.1	28,026.60
2004	21,826.4	14,343.8	539.0	7,482.5	32,674.70
2005	21,928.5	15,371.6	306.7	6,556.8	28,507.90
2006	20,329.6	16,010.9	–753.8	4,318.7	18,777.00
2007	24,738.0	19,800.2	948.6	4,937.7	19,950.30
2008	22,523.4	19,674.0	–1,174.8	2,849.4	14,282.10
2009	20,648.8	18,562.9	–980.9	2,085.9	9,133.80
2010	23,474.2	18,807.4	46.6	4,666.6	22,404.40
2011	26,004.5	21,429.7	–2,494.0	4,574.7	21,811.90
2012	27,430.8	23,842.1	–1,075.4	3,588.8	NA
2013	29,303.2	24,202.8	–171.2	5,100.4	NA
2014	30,319.8	26,512.7	407.2	3,807.1	NA
2015	29,218.7	23,186.3	–416.4	6,032.4	NA
2016	24,629.3	22,105.5	–77.5	2,523.9	NA
2017	26,374.2	22,250.2	–789.1	4,124.0	NA
2018	25,707.6	21,545.2	–1,177.7	4,162.4	NA
2019	26,139.9	20,584.6	–998.9	5,555.3	NA

* Details for items may not add to totals because of rounding.
**Cash receipts from farm marketings, government payments, value of home consumption and gross rental value of farm dwellings.
***Farm income of farm operators.
† A positive value of inventory change represents current-year production not sold by December 31. A negative value is an offset to production from prior years included in current-year sales.

Source: "Economic Indicators of the Farm Sector, State Financial Summary, 1985", 1987", 1989", 1993", USDA/ERS; "Farm Business Economics Report", August 1996, "Texas Agricultural Statistics Service, October, 2010". "Farm Income and Wealth Statistics", USDA/ERS. NA = Not available

230.9 million bushels. The season's average price was $6.6 per cwt. for a total value of $230.9 million.

Although grown to some extent in all counties where crops are important, the largest concentrations are in the High Plains, Coastal Bend, and the Lower Rio Grande Valley areas.

Research to develop high-yielding hybrids resistant to diseases and insect damage continues. A history of grain sorghum appeared in the 1972–73 edition of the *Texas Almanac*.

Rice

Rice, which is grown in about 20 counties on the Coastal Prairie of Texas, ranked third in value among Texas crops for a number of years. However, in 2018, cotton, corn, hay, wheat, and grain sorghum outranked rice.

Rice farms are highly mechanized, producing rice through irrigation and using airplanes for much of the planting, fertilizing, and application of insecticides and herbicides.

Texas farmers grow long- and medium-grain rice only. The Texas rice industry, which has grown from 110 acres in 1850 to a high of 642,000 planted acres in 1954, has been marked by significant yield increases and improved varieties. Record production was in 1981, with 27.2 million cwt. harvested. Highest yield was 8,370 pounds per acre in 2012.

Several different types of rice milling procedures are in use today. The simplest and oldest method produces a product known as regular milled white rice, the most prevalent on the market today.

During this process, rice grains are subjected to additional cleaning to remove chaff, dust, foreign seed, etc., and then husks are removed from the grains. This results in a product that is the whole unpolished grain of rice with only the outer hull and a small amount of bran removed. This product is called brown rice and is sometimes sold without further treatment other than grading. It has a delightful nutlike flavor and a slightly chewy texture.

When additional layers of the bran are removed, the rice becomes white in color and begins to appear as it is normally recognized at retail level. The removal of the bran layer from the grain is performed in a number of steps using two or three types of machines. After the bran is removed, the product is ready for classification as to size. Rice is more valuable if the grains are not broken. In many cases, additional vitamins are added to the grains to produce what is called "enriched rice."

Another process may be used in rice milling to produce a product called parboiled rice. In this process, the rice is subjected to a combination of steam and pressure prior to the time it is milled in the manner described above. This process gelatinizes the starch in the grain, the treatment aiding in the retention of much of the natural vitamin and mineral content. After cooking, parboiled rice tends to be fluffy, more separate, and plump.

Still another type of rice is precooked rice, which is actually milled rice that, after milling, has been cooked. Then the moisture is removed through a dehydration process. Precooked rice requires a minimum of preparation time since it needs merely to have the moisture restored to it.

The United States produces only a small part of the world's total rice, but it is one of the leading exporters. American rice is popular abroad and is exported to more than 100 foreign countries.

Texas rice production in 2020 totaled 14.6 million cwt. from 179,000 harvested acres, with a yield of 8,150 pounds per acre. The crop value totaled $195.6 million. Rice production was 11.0 million cwt. in 2019 on 150,000 harvested acres, yielding 8,150 pounds per acre. Total value in 2019 was $141.2 million. Rice production was 15.1 million cwt. in 2018 on 189,000 harvested acres. Production in 2018 was valued at $188.3 million with a yield of 7,970 pounds per acre.

Wheat

Wheat for grain is one of the state's most valuable cash crops. In 2020, wheat was exceeded in value by cotton, corn, hay, and sorghum. Wheat pastures also provide considerable winter forage for cattle that is reflected in value of livestock produced.

Texas wheat production totaled 61.5 million bushels in 2020 as yield averaged 30.0 bushels per acre. Planted acreage totaled 4.9 million acres and 2.1 million acres were harvested. With an average price of $5.10 per bushel, the 2020 wheat value totaled $313.7 million. In 2019, Texas wheat growers planted 4.6 million acres and harvested 2.1 million acres. The yield was 34.0 bushels per acre for 2019 with total production of 71.4 million bushels at $4.44 per bushel valued at $317.0 million.

Texas wheat growers planted 4.5 million acres in 2018 and harvested grain from 1.8 million acres. The yield was 32.0 bushels per acre for a total production of 56.0 million bushels valued at $289.5 million or $5.17 per bushel.

Wheat was first grown commercially in Texas near Sherman about 1833. The acreage expanded greatly in North Central Texas after 1850 because of rapid settlement of the state and introduction of the well-adapted Mediterranean strain of wheat. A major family flour industry was developed in the Fort Worth/Dallas/Sherman area between 1875 and 1900. Now, around half of the state's acreage is planted on the High Plains and about a third of this is irrigated. Most of the Texas wheat acreage is of the hard red winter class. Because of the development of varieties with improved disease resistance and the use of wheat for winter pasture, there has been a sizable expansion of acreage in Central and South Texas.

Most all wheat harvested for grain is used in some phase of the milling industry. The better-quality hard red winter wheat is used in the production of commercial bakery flour. Lower grades and varieties of soft red winter wheat are used in family flours. By-products of milled wheat are used for feed.

Corn

Interest in corn production throughout the state has increased since the 1970's as yields improved with new varieties. Once the principal grain crop, corn acreage declined as plantings of grain sorghum increased. Only 500 thousand acres were harvested annually until the mid-1970s, when development of new hybrids occurred.

Harvested acreage was 1.8 million in 2020; 2.2 million in 2019; and 1.8 million in 2018. Yields for the corresponding years (2020-2018) were 128, 133, and 108 bushels per acre, respectively.

Most of the acreage and yield increase has occurred in Central and South Texas. In 2020, corn ranked third in value of production among the state's crops. It was valued at $1.0 billion in 2020; $1.2 billion in 2019; and $780.6 million in 2018. The grain is largely used for livestock feed, but other important uses are in ethanol and food products.

Oats

Oats are grown extensively in Texas for winter pasture, hay, silage, and greenchop feeding, and some acreage is harvested for grain.

Of the 470 thousand acres planted to oats in 2020, 60 thousand acres were harvested. The average yield was 45.0 bushels per acre. Production totaled 2.7 million bushels with a value of $11.1 million, or $4.10 per bushel. In 2019, 400 thousand acres were planted. From the plantings, 40 thousand acres were harvested, with an average yield of 50.0 bushels per acre for a total production of 2.0 million bushels. Average price per bushel was $4.26 and total production value was $8.5 million.

Texas farmers planted 450 thousand acres of oats in 2018. They harvested 50 thousand acres that averaged 50.0 bushels per acre for a total production of 2.5 million bushels at an average price of $4.82 per bushel with an estimated value of $12.1 million. Most of the acreage was used for grazing.

Almost all oat grain produced in Texas is utilized as feed for livestock within the state. A small acreage is grown exclusively for planting seed.

Sugarcane

Sugarcane is grown from seed cane planted in late summer or fall. It is harvested 12 months later and milled to produce raw sugar and molasses. Raw sugar requires additional refining before it is in final form and can be offered to consumers.

The sugarcane grinding mill operated at Santa Rosa in Cameron County is considered one of the most modern mills in the United States. Texas sugarcane-producing counties include Cameron, Hidalgo, and Willacy.

At a yield of 31.7 tons per acre, sugarcane and seed production in 2020 totaled 1.1 million tons from 35.9 thousand harvested acres. In 2019, 33.5 thousand acres were harvested for total production of 1.1 million tons valued at $20.5 million. The yield was 33.8 tons per acre. In 2018, 38.9 thousand acres were harvested, from which 1.4 million tons of sugarcane were milled. The yield averaged 36.6 tons per acre for a total value of $27.2 million.

Hay, Silage, and Other Forage Crops

A large proportion of Texas' agricultural land is devoted to forage crop production. This acreage produces much of the feed requirements for the state's large domestic livestock population as well as game animals.

A field of sunflowers near the Mexico border. Photo by Craig O'Neal, CC 2/Flickr

Approximately 87.9 million acres of pasture and rangeland, which are primarily in the western half of Texas, provide grazing for beef cattle, sheep, goats, horses, and game animals. An additional 8.3 million acres are devoted to cropland used only for pasture or grazing. The average annual acreage of forage land used for hay, silage, and other forms of machine-harvested forage is around 5 million acres.

All hay accounts for a large amount of this production with some corn and sorghum silage being produced. The most important hay crops are annual and perennial grasses and alfalfa. Production in 2020 totaled 9.6 million tons of hay from 5.0 million harvested acres at a yield of 1.9 tons per acre. Value of hay was $1.3 billion, or $147.00 per ton. In 2019, 9.2 million tons of hay were produced from 4.9 million harvested acres at a yield of 1.9 tons per acre. The value in 2019 was $1.1 billion or $130.00 per ton. In 2018, the production of hay was 8.7 million tons from 4.7 million harvested acres with a value of $1.1 billion or $143.00 per ton, at a yield of 1.8 tons per acre.

Alfalfa hay production in 2020 totaled 539,000 tons with 110,000 acres harvested and a yield of 4.9 tons per acre. At a value of $188 per ton, total value was $101.3 million. In 2019, 576,000 tons of alfalfa hay were harvested from 120,000 acres at a yield of 4.8 tons per acre. Value was $107.7 million, or $187 per ton. Alfalfa hay was harvested from 140,000 acres in 2018, producing an average of 5.6 tons per acre for total production of 784,000 tons valued at $159.9 million, or $204 per ton.

An additional sizable acreage of annual forage crops is grazed as well as much of the small grain acreage. Alfalfa, sweet corn, vetch, arrowleaf clover, grasses, and other forage plants also provide income as seed crops.

Peanuts

Well over three-fourths of the annual peanut production is from irrigated acreage. In 2020, Texas ranked fourth nationally in production of peanuts. Among Texas crops, peanuts ranked eighth in value.

Until 1973, essentially all of the Texas acreage was planted to the Spanish type, which was favored because of its earlier maturity and better drought tolerance than other types. The Spanish variety is also preferred for some uses due to its distinctive flavor. The Florunner variety, a runner market type, is now planted on a sizable proportion of the acreage where soil moisture is favorable. The variety is later maturing but better yielding than Spanish varieties under good growing conditions. Florunner peanuts have acceptable quality to compete with the Spanish variety in most products.

In 2020, peanut production totaled 490.0 million pounds from 190,000 acres planted and 175,000 harvested, yielding 2,800 pounds per acre. At 26.3 cents per pound, value of the crop was estimated at $128.9 million. In 2019, peanut production amounted to 488.0 million pounds from 165,000 acres planted and 160,000 harvested. With an average yield of 3,050 pounds per acre and average price of 28.1 cents per pound, the 2019 value of production was $137.1 million. Production in 2018 amounted to 464.0 million pounds of peanuts from 155,000 acres planted and 145,000 acres harvested, or an average of 3,200 pounds per harvested acre valued at 27.5 cents per pound for a $127.6 million value.

Soybeans

Soybean production is located in the areas of the Upper Coast, irrigated High Plains, and Red River Valley of Northeast Texas. Soybeans are adapted to the same general soil climate conditions as corn, cotton, or grain sorghum, provided moisture, disease, and insects are not limiting factors.

In low rainfall areas, yields have been too low or inconsistent for profitable production under dryland conditions. Soybeans' need for moisture in late summer minimizes economic crop possibilities in the Blacklands and Rolling Plains. In the Blacklands, cotton root rot seriously hinders soybean production. Limited moisture at critical growth stages may occasionally prevent economical yields, even in high-rainfall areas of Northeast Texas and the Coastal Prairie.

Because of day length sensitivity, soybeans should be planted in Texas during the long days of May and June to obtain sufficient vegetative growth for optimum yields.

Varieties planted during this period usually cease vegetative development and initiate reproductive processes during the hot, dry months of July and August. When moisture is insufficient during the blooming and fruiting period, yields are drastically reduced. In most areas of the state, July and August rainfall is insufficient to permit economical dryland production. The risk of dryland soybean production in the Coastal Prairie and Northeast Texas is considerably less when compared to other dryland areas because moisture is available more often during the critical fruiting period.

The 2020 soybean crop totaled 3.7 million bushels and was valued at $33.5 million, or $8.95 per bushel. Of the 120,000 acres planted, 110,000 were harvested with an average yield of 34.0 bushels per acre. In 2019, the Texas soybean crop averaged 28.0 bushels per acre from 73,000 acres harvested. Total production of 2.0 million bushels was valued at $15.7 million, or $7.70 per bushel. In 2018, the Texas soybean crop averaged 31.5 bushels per acre from 135,000 acres harvested. Total production of 4.3 million bushels was valued at $32.3 million, or $7.59 per bushel.

Sunflowers

Sunflowers constitute one of the most important annual oilseed crops in the world. The cultivated types, which are thought to be descendants of the common wild sunflower native to Texas, have been successfully grown in several countries including Russia, Argentina, Romania, Bulgaria, Uruguay, Western Canada, and portions of the northern United states. Extensive trial plantings conducted in the Cotton Belt states since 1968 showed sunflowers have considerable potential as an oilseed crop in much of this area including Texas. This crop exhibits good cold and drought tolerance, is adapted to a wide range of soil and climate conditions, and tolerates higher levels of hail, wind, and sand abrasion than other crops normally grown in the state.

In 2020, sunflower production totaled 80.0 million pounds and was harvested from 57,000 acres at a yield of 1,403 pounds per acre. With an average price of $22.90 per cwt., the crop was valued at $18.3 million. In 2019, 30,500 of the 33,000 acres planted to sunflowers were harvested with an average yield of 1,300 pounds per acre. Total production of 39.7 million pounds was valued at $7.3 million, or $18.30 per cwt.

In 2018, of 25,500 acres planted to sunflowers, 23,500 acres were harvested, yielding 1,174 pounds per acre for a total yield of 27.6 million pounds valued at $5.3 million, or $19.40 per cwt.

Reasons for growing sunflowers include the need for an additional cash crop with low water and plant nutrient requirements, the development of sunflower hybrids, and interest by food processors in Texas sunflower oil, which has high oleic acid content. Commercial users have found many advantages in this high oleic oil, including excellent cooking

Texas Crop Production, 2020

Crop	Harvested Acres (thousands)	Yield Per Acre	Unit	Total Production (thousands)	Cash Value (thousands)
Corn, grain	1,810.0	128	Bu.	231,680.0	$1,019,392.0
Corn, silage	270.0	18	Ton	4,860.0	—
Cotton, American-Pima	31.0	743	Lb : Bale	48.0	—
Cotton, Upland	3,600.0	627	Lb : Bale	4,700.0	1,373,904.0
Cottonseed	—	—	Ton	1,443.0	269,841.0
Grapefruit*	16.0	275	Box	—	68,731.0
Hay, Alfalfa	110.0	4.9	Ton	539.0	101,332.0
Hay, excluding alfalfa	4,900.0	1.85	Ton	9,065.0	1,232,840.0
Hay, All	**5,010.0**	**1.92**	**Ton**	**9,604.0**	**1,334,172.0**
Oats	60.0	45	Bu.	2,700.0	11,070.0
Onions, dry	11.0	338	Cwt.	3,718.0	73,467.0
Oranges*	7.8	172	Box	—	16,415.0
Pecans*	115.0	395	Lb.	45.4	63,365.0
Peanuts	175.0	2,800	Lb.	490,000.0	128,870.0
Potatoes	10.8	405	Cwt.	4,374.0	69,547.0
Rice	179.0	8,150	Lb : Cwt.	14,597.0	195,600.0
Sorghum, Grain	1,500.0	63	Lb : Cwt.	94,500.0	391,608.0
Sorghum, Silage	100.0	12.5	Ton	1,250.0	—
Soybeans	110.0	34	Bu.	3,740.0	33,473.0
Sugarcane for sugar & seed	35.9	31.7	Ton	1,138.0	—
Sunflowers	57.0	1,403	Lb.	79,980.0	18,329.0
Vegetables	47.9	—	Cwt.	12,841.7	215,990.0
Wheat, Winter	2,050.0	30	Bu.	61,500.0	313,650.0
Total of Listed Crops	**15,196.4**	—	—	**1,022,719.1**	**$5,597,424.0**

* Grapefruit, Texas 80-lb./box; Oranges, Texas 85-lb./box; Pecan production and value are utilized in-shell basis.

USDA/NASS, annual crop production, January; annual crop values, February.

stability, particularly for use as a deep-frying medium for potato chips, corn chips, and similar products.

Sunflower meal is a high-quality protein source free of nutritional toxins that can be included in rations for swine, poultry, and ruminants. The hulls constitute a source of roughage, which can also be included in livestock rations.

Nursery Crops

The trend to increase production of nursery crops continues to rise as transportation costs on long-distance hauling increases. This has resulted in a marked increase in the production of container-grown plants within the state. This increase is noted especially in the production of bedding plants, foliage plants, sod, and the woody landscape plants.

Plant rental services have become a multimillion-dollar business. This relatively new service provides the plants and maintains them in office buildings, shopping malls, public buildings, and even in some homes for a fee. The response has been good, as evidenced by the growth of companies providing these services.

The interest in plants for interior landscapes is confined to no specific age group as both retail nurseries and florist shops report that people of all ages are buying their plants—from the elderly in retirement homes to high school and college students in dormitory rooms and apartments.

Texas A&M AgriLife Extension specialists estimated cash receipts from nursery crops in Texas to be around $1.6 billion in 2020. Texans are creating colorful and green surroundings by improving their landscape plantings.

Vegetable Crops

Some market vegetables are produced in almost all Texas counties. In 2017, Hidalgo County was the leading Texas county in vegetable acres harvested, followed by Hartley and Frio counties. Other leading producing counties are: Terry, Guadalupe, Medina, Uvalde, Yoakum, and Waller.

Nationally, in 2020, Texas ranked eleventh in production, exceeded by California, Washington, Arizona, Florida, Oregon, Wisconsin, North Carolina, Georgia, Minnesota, and New York, respectively. Texas ranked eighth in value of fresh-market vegetables, exceeded by California, Florida, Arizona, Georgia, North Carolina, Washington, and New York, respectively.

In 2020, fresh market vegetable utilized production of 12.8 million cwt. in Texas was valued at $216.0 million. In 2019, Texas growers harvested total fresh market vegetable crops valued at $184.9 million from 47,800 acres with a utilized production of 12.6 million cwt. Texas growers harvested 15.8 million cwt. of fresh market vegetable crops from 62,000 acres, valued at $298.0 million, in 2018.

Onions

Onion production in 2020 totaled 3.7 million cwt. from 11,000 harvested acres and was valued at $73.5 million, at a yield of 338 cwt. per acre. In 2019, 3.0 million cwt. of onions were harvested from 9,000 acres and valued at $51.0 million, at a yield of 335 cwt. per acre. A total of 3.2 million cwt. of onions were produced from 11,000 harvested acres and valued at $61.3 million in 2018, yielding 300 cwt. per acre.

Carrots

Carrot production in 2018 totaled 400,000 cwt. from 1,600 harvested acres at a yield of 250 cwt. per acre. Production was valued at $3.8 million. In 2017, carrots were harvested from 1,900 acres with a value of $4.8 million. At a yield of 240 cwt. per acre, 2017 production was 456,000 cwt. Carrot production in 2016 totaled 590,000 cwt. from 2,000 harvested acres. At a yield of 295 cwt. per acre, production value was $6.6 million.

The winter carrot production from South Texas accounts for about three-fourths of total production during the winter season. *In 2019, data for carrots were discontinued.*

Vegetable Production, 2020

Crop	Harvested Acres	Yield Per Acre, Cwt.	Production, (000) Cwt.	Value (thousands of dollars)
Cabbage	6,400	290	1,856	40,832
Cucumbers	5,700	83	473	9,267
Dry Onions	11,000	338	3,718	73,467
Potatoes	10,800	405	4,374	69,547
Pumpkins	3,700	270	999	25,906
Spinach	2,100	136	286	5,485
Watermelons	19,000	290	5,510	61,033
Total	58,700	—	17,216	285,537

Numbers may not add due to rounding.

Source: USDA/NASS, Annual Vegetable Summary, February 2021; "2020 State Agriculture Overview, Texas"

All Potatoes

In 2020, all potatoes were harvested from 10,800 acres with production of 4.4 million cwt. valued at $69.5 million at a yield of 405 cwt. per acre. All potatoes were harvested from 14,800 acres with production of 7.1 million cwt. valued at $88.1 million in 2019, yielding 480 cwt. per acre. This compares with 17,500 acres harvested valued at $93.7 million in 2018 with a production of 7.4 million cwt. and a yield of 425 cwt. per acre.

Cantaloupes

Cantaloupe production in 2018 totaled 220,000 cwt. from 2,000 harvested acres and was valued at $5.1 million at a yield of 110 cwt. per acre. In 2017, cantaloupes were harvested from 2,000 acres for total production of 220,000 cwt. valued at $5.3 million, yielding 110 cwt. per acre. Of the 1,900 harvested acres in 2016, 237,500 cwt. cantaloupes were produced at a yield of 125 cwt. per acre and were valued at $5.2 million. *No data available after 2018.*

Watermelons

Watermelon production in 2020 was 5.5 million cwt. from 19,000 harvested acres with a value of $61.0 million, yielding 290 cwt. per acre. In 2019, at a yield of 290 cwt. per acre, 6.2 million cwt. watermelons were harvested from 21,500 acres and valued at $77.8 million. Watermelon production was 7.8 million cwt. from 23,000 harvested acres in 2018, with a value of $143.4 million at a yield of 340 cwt. per acre.

Cabbage

In 2020, 6,400 acres were harvested and yielded total production of 1.9 million cwt. that were valued at $40.8 million. Yield was 290 cwt. per acre. Numbers for 2019 were not reported. The 5,000 acres of cabbage harvested in Texas in 2018 brought a value of $27.4 million. At a yield of 270 cwt. per acre, total production was 1.4 million cwt.

Spinach

Spinach production is primarily concentrated in the Winter Garden area of South Texas.

The 2020 production value of spinach was estimated at $5.5 million. Production of 285,600 cwt. was harvested from 2,100 acres with a yield of 136 cwt. per acre. *In 2019, numbers were not reported for spinach.* The 2,800 acres, harvested in 2018, produced 322,000 cwt. at a yield of 115 cwt. per acre and valued at $6.1 million..

Pumpkin

Pumpkin production in 2020 was 999,000 cwt., harvested from 3,700 acres. The yield was 270 cwt. per acre and a value of $25.9 million. *Numbers for pumpkins in 2019 were not reported.* A production of 1.6 million cwt. was harvested from 4,900 acres with a yield of 330 cwt. per acre in 2018. The production value was $24.1 million.

Cucumbers

In 2020, 5,700 acres of cucumbers were harvested. Production totaled 473,100 cwt. and was valued at $9.3 million. The yield was 83 cwt. per acre. Numbers for cucumbers were not reported in 2019. At a yield of 97 cwt. per acre, the 475,300 cwt. cucumber crop in Texas during 2018 was harvested from 4,900 acres and valued at $8.7 million.

A couple picks out pumpkins at Barton Hill Farms in Bastrop. Photo courtesy of Barton Hill Farms, https://bartonhillfarms.com.

Fruits and Nuts

Texas is noted for producing a wide variety of fruits. The pecan is the only commercial nut crop in the state. The pecan is native to most of the state's river valleys and is the Texas state tree. Citrus is produced commercially in the three southernmost counties in the Lower Rio Grande Valley. Peaches represent the next most important Texas fruit crop, and there is considerable interest in growing apples.

Citrus

Texas ranks with Florida, and California as leading states in the production of citrus. Most of the Texas production is in Cameron, Hidalgo, and Willacy counties of the Lower Rio Grande Valley. In 2019/20, grapefruit utilized production was estimated at 4.4 million boxes at $11.01 per box or $68.7 million. Grapefruit production in 2018/19 was 6.1 million boxes for a total value of $65.2 million. Production in 2017/18 was 4.8 million boxes with a value of $54.1 million.

Production of oranges in 2019/20 was 1.3 million boxes for a total value of $16.4 million. In 2018/19, production was 2.5 million boxes for a total value of $24.6 million. Production was 1.9 million boxes in 2017/18 for a value of $35.5 million.

Peaches

Primary production areas are East Texas, the Hill Country, and the West Cross Timbers. Production varies substantially due to adverse weather conditions. Low-chilling varieties for early marketings are being grown in Atascosa, Frio, Webb, Karnes, and Duval counties.

The Texas peach crop's production totaled 2,420 tons in 2018. In 2017, utilized production was 2,500 tons. Value of production was $6.3 million. In 2016, utilized production was 4,200 tons that was valued at $9.2 million. *Numbers were not reported after 2018.*

Pecans

The pecan, the state tree, is one of the most widely distributed trees in Texas. It is native to over 150 counties and is grown commercially in some 30 additional counties. The pecan is also widely used as a dual-purpose yard tree. The commercial plantings of pecans have accelerated in Central and West Texas with many of the new orchards being irrigated. Many new pecan plantings are being established under trickle-irrigation systems.

In 2020, pecan orchards yielded 370 pounds per acre from 115,000 harvested acres. The utilized production was 45.4 million pounds with a value of $63.4 million or $1.52 per pound. In 2019, a yield of 335 pounds per acre was harvested from 112,000 acres. The utilized production was 37.5 million pounds with a value of $73.5 million, or $1.96 per pound. The 2018 crop totaled 33.6 million pounds from 112,000 harvested acres at a yield of 300 pounds per acre. The value was $56.1 million or $1.67 per pound.

Nationally, Texas ranked third with Georgia first and New Mexico second in utilized pecan production in 2020.

Livestock and Animal Products

Livestock and animal products accounted for about 67.6 percent of the agricultural cash receipts in Texas in 2019. The state ranks first nationally in all cattle, beef cattle, cattle on feed, sheep and lambs, wool, goats, and mohair.

Cattle and calves account for around 58.7 percent of cash receipts from marketings of livestock and animal products. Sales of livestock and animal products in 2019 totaled $14.4 billion, up from $14.3 billion in 2018.

Cattle and calves dominate livestock production in Texas, contributing around 58.7 percent of cash receipts from livestock and animal products. The January 1, 2021 inventory of all cattle and calves in Texas totaled 13.1 million head, valued at $12.7 billion, compared to 12.9 million as of January 1, 2020, valued at $12.5 billion, and 13.0 million as of January 1, 2019, valued at $12.9 billion.

On January 1, 2021, the sheep and lamb inventory stood at 730,000 head, valued at $132.9 million, compared with 735,000 head as of January 1, 2020, valued at $134.5 million. January 1, 2019 showed an inventory of 750,000 valued at $135.8 million. Sheep and lambs numbered 3.2 million on January 1, 1973, down from a high of 10.8 million in 1943. Wool production decreased from 26.4 million pounds valued at $23.2 million in 1973 to 1.4 million pounds valued at $2.4 million in 2020. Production was 1.7 million pounds in 2019 valued at $3.2 million, compared to 1.8 million pounds in 2018 and valued at $3.2 million. The price of wool per pound was 88 cents in 1973, compared to $1.80 in 2020, $1.90 in 2019, and $1.80 in 2018.

Mohair production in Texas has dropped from a 1965 high of 31.6 million pounds to 340,000 pounds in 2020. Production was valued at $2.4 million or $7.20 per pound. In 2019, production was 470,000 pounds valued at $3.8 million or $8.00 per pound. Mohair production in 2018 was 465,000 pounds valued at $3.3 million or $7.20 per pound.

Beef Cattle

Raising beef cattle is the most extensive agricultural operation in Texas. In 2019, cattle and calves were 39.6 percent of total cash receipts — $8.4 million of $21.2 million, compared with $8.5 million of $21.7 million in 2018 (39.1%) and $8.9 million of $22.2 million in 2017 (40.0%). The next leading commodity is dairy products such as milk.

Nearly all of the 254 counties in Texas derive more revenue from cattle than from any other agricultural commodity, and those that don't usually rank cattle second in importance.

Within the boundaries of Texas are 14.0 percent of all the cattle and calves in the U.S., as are 15.0 percent of the beef cows that have calved, and 13.1 percent of the calf crop as of January 1, 2021 inventory.

The number of all cattle and calves in Texas on January 1, 2021 totaled 13.1 million, compared with 12.9 million on January 1, 2020; and 13.0 million on January 1, 2019.

Calves born on Texas farms and ranches in January 1, 2021 totaled 4.6 million, compared with 4.5 million in 2020; and 4.7 million in 2019.

Dairying Product Manufacturing

The major dairy products manufactured in Texas include condensed, evaporated and dry milk, creamer, butter, and cheese. However, specifics of production and value are not available because of the small number of manufacturing plants producing these products.

Dairying

All cows' milk sold by Texas dairy farmers is marketed under the terms of Federal Marketing Orders. Most Texas dairymen are members of one of four marketing cooperatives. Associate Milk Producers, Inc. is the largest, representing the majority of the state's producers.

Texas dairy farmers received an average price for milk of $18.60 per hundred pounds in 2020, $19.10 in 2019, and $16.90 in 2018. A total of 14.8 billion pounds of milk was sold to plants and dealers in 2020, bringing in cash receipts from milk to dairy farmers of $2.8 billion. This compared with 13.8 billion pounds sold in 2019 that brought in $2.6 billion in cash receipts. In 2018, Texas dairymen sold 12.8 billion pounds of milk, which brought in cash receipts of $2.2 billion.

The annual average number of milk cows in Texas was 615,000 head as of January 1, 2021, inventory. This compared with 580,000 head as of January 1, 2020, and 545,000 as of January 1, 2019. Average milk production per cow in the state has increased steadily over the past several decades. The average milk production per cow in 2020 was 24,926 pounds. Milk per cow in 2019 was 24,513 pounds. In 2018, milk per cow was 23,948 pounds. Total milk production in Texas was 14.8 billion pounds in 2020, 13.9 billion pounds in 2019, and 12.9 billion pounds in 2018.

There were 467 farms reporting milk cows in Texas in 2017. In 2012, 985 farms reported milk cows, and in 2007, 1,293 farms reported milk cows in Texas.

Broiler hens in a chicken farm outside Luling. Photo by U.S. Department of Agriculture/Flickr

Hog Production 1974–2020				
Year	Production (1,000 Lbs.)	Average Market Weight (Lbs.)	Average Price Per Cwt. ($)	Gross Income ($1,000)
1974	350,811	253	33.3	123,277
1975	271,027	244	43.7	127,323
1976	286,053	247	41.5	117,587
1977	292,290	247	38	109,634
1978	303,135	258	43.8	135,006
1979	320,790	261	39.7	125,183
1980	315,827	259	35.9	111,700
1981	264,693	256	41.7	121,054
1982	205,656	256	49.6	112,726
1983	209,621	256	45.2	95,343
1984	189,620	262	45.5	95,657
1985	168,950	266	43.4	72,512
1986	176,660	269	47.3	82,885
1987	216,834	NA	50.6	103,983
1988	236,658	NA	41.3	100,029
1989	230,004	NA	39.9	95,482
1990	196,225	NA	48.2	92,222
1991	207,023	NA	45.1	97,398
1992	217,554	NA	36.4	79,436
1993	221,071	NA	39.9	90,571
1994	224,397	NA	35.1	78,394
1995	221,323	NA	35.5	81,509
1996	204,476	NA	45.9	94,962
1997	224,131	NA	47.4	103,050
1998	271,444	NA	30.7	86,349
1999	274,572	NA	27.5	71,604
2000	328,732	NA	36.6	115,105
2001	260,875	NA	39.1	105,217
2002	223,441	NA	28.7	67,255
2003	197,876	NA	33.6	67,998
2004	202,199	NA	44.9	90,349
2005	223,375	NA	45.4	105,989
2006	257,644	NA	40.8	108,844
2007	273,213	NA	39.7	95,581
2008	328,356	NA	40.5	143,249
2009	286,069	NA	37.6	135,077
2010	149,934	NA	50.2	96,676
2011	168,718	NA	NA	153,517
2012	414,904	NA	NA	288,652
2013	285,822	NA	NA	240,322
2014	305,146	NA	NA	248,928
2015	376,691	NA	NA	224,328
2016	365,980	NA	NA	191,892
2017	366,121	NA	NA	197,572
2018	442,476	NA	NA	225,125
2019	494,912	NA	NA	244,954
2020	505,725	NA	NA	222,327

NA = not available

Source: "1985 Texas Livestock, Dairy and Poultry Statistics", USDA, Bulletin 235, June 1986, pp. 32, 46; 1991 "Texas Livestock Statistics", USDA,; "1993 Texas Livestock Statistics", Bulletin 252, Texas Agricultural Statistics Service, August 1994; "Texas Agricultural Facts, 2009", October, 2010; "Texas Ag Facts", various years. "Meat Animals - Prod., Disp., & Income", April 2020 and April 2021; (December 1 previous year); USDA/NASS Quick Stats. Numbers from previous years revised.

Poultry and Eggs

Poultry and eggs contribute about 12.4 percent of the total cash receipts of Texas farmers in 2019. On January 1, 2020, Texas ranked sixth among the states in broilers produced and sixth in eggs produced.

In 2019, cash receipts to Texas producers from the production of poultry and eggs totaled $2.6 billion. This compares with $3.0 billion in 2018 and $2.7 in 2017.

Broiler production in 2020 totaled 702.5 million birds, compared with 675.0 million in 2019 and 653.5 million in 2018.

Swine

Texas had 1.1 million head of swine on hand, December 1, 2020 — only 1.4 percent of the U.S. swine herd.

Although the number of farms producing hogs has steadily decreased, the size of production units has increased substantially. There is favorable potential for increased production.

In 2020, 3.2 million head of hogs were marketed in Texas, producing 505.7 million pounds of pork valued at $200.5 million. In 2019, 3.2 million head of hogs were marketed, producing 494.9 million pounds of pork valued at $230.3 million. Comparable figures for 2018 were 2.7 million head marketed, and 442.5 million pounds of pork produced with a value of $200.5 million.

Sheep and Wool

Sheep and lambs in Texas numbered 730,000 head on January 1, 2021, compared to 735,000 as of 2020, and 750,000 as of January 1, 2019. All sheep were valued at $132.9 million on January 1, 2021, compared with $134.5 million as of January 1, 2020, and $135.8 million as of January 1, 2019.

Breeding ewes one year old and over numbered 445,000 as of January 1, 2021; 445,000 as of January 1, 2020; and 455,000 as of January 1, 2019. Replacement lambs less than one year old totaled 90,000 head as of January 1, 2021; 100,000 as of January 1, 2020; and 100,000 as of January 1, 2019. Sheep and lamb farms in Texas were estimated to be 14,672 as of January 1, 2017; compared to 10,674 in 2012.

Texas wool production in 2020 was 1.4 million pounds from 180,000 sheep. Value totaled $2.4 million or $1.80 per pound. This compared with 1.7 million pounds of wool from 230,000 sheep valued at $3.2 million or $1.90 per pound in 2019; and 1.8 million pounds from 240,000 sheep valued at $3.2 million or $1.80 per pound in 2018.

Most sheep and lambs in Texas are concentrated in the Edwards Plateau area of West Central Texas and nearby counties.

San Angelo has long been the largest sheep and wool market in the nation and the center for wool and mohair warehouses, scouring plants and slaughterhouses.

Goats and Mohair

All goats in Texas numbered 827,000 on January 1, 2021. This compares with 869,000 on January 1, 2020, and 842,000 on January 1, 2019.

Sheep and Wool Production 1973–2021

Year	Sheep		Wool	
	Number	Value	Production (lbs)	Value
1973	3,214,000	$64,280,000	26,352,000	$23,190,000
1974	3,090,000	80,340,000	23,900,000	15,535,000
1975	2,715,000	63,803,000	23,600,000	14,868,000
1976	2,600,000	81,900,000	22,000,000	17,380,000
1977	2,520,000	93,240,000	21,000,000	17,220,000
1978	2,460,000	111,930,000	18,500,000	15,355,000
1979	2,415,000	152,145,000	19,075,000	18,503,000
1980	2,400,000	138,000,000	18,300,000	17,751,000
1981	2,360,000	116,820,000	20,500,000	24,600,000
1982	2,400,000	100,800,000	19,300,000	16,212,000
1983	2,225,000	86,775,000	18,600,000	15,438,000
1984	1,970,000	76,830,000	17,500,000	16,100,000
1985	1,930,000	110,975,000	16,200,000	13,284,000
1986	1,850,000	107,300,000	16,400,000	13,284,000
1987	2,050,000	133,250,000	16,400,000	19,844,000
1988	2,040,000	155,040,000	18,200,000	35,854,000
1989	1,870,000	133,445,000	18,000,000	27,180,000
1990	2,090,000	133,760,000	17,400,000	19,662,000
1991	2,000,000	108,000,000	16,700,000	13,861,000
1992	2,140,000	111,280,000	17,600,000	16,896,000
1993	2,040,000	118,320,000	17,000,000	11,050,000
1994	1,895,000	106,120,000	14,840,000	15,582,000
1995	1,700,000	100,300,000	13,468,000	15,488,000
1996	1,650,000	108,900,000	9,900,000	8,316,000
1997	1,400,000	100,800,000	10,950,000	11,607,000
1998	1,530,000	122,400,000	9,230,000	5,815,000
1999	1,350,000	95,850,000	7,956,000	3,898,000
2000	1,200,000	94,800,000	7,506,000	3,678,000
2001	1,150,000	92,000,000	6,003,000	3,122,000
2002	1,130,000	88,140,000	5,950,000	4,046,000
2003	1,040,000	82,160,000	5,600,000	5,040,000
2004	1,100,000	105,600,000	5,600,000	5,712,000
2005	1,070,000	112,350,000	5,550,000	5,328,000
2006	1,070,000	124,260,000	4,900,000	4,459,000
2007	1,050,000	111,300,000	4,500,000	5,445,000
2008	960,000	97,920,000	4,200,000	4,872,000
2009	870,000	87,870,000	3,500,000	3,640,000
2010	830,000	83,000,000	3,450,000	5,451,000
2011	850,000	109,650,000	2,600,000	5,746,000
2012	670,000	102,510,000	2,100,000	3,507,000
2013	680,000	96,560,000	2,300,000	4,048,000
2014	730,000	118,990,000	2,100,000	3,297,000
2015	720,000	126,000,000	1,950,000	3,198,000
2016	725,000	131,950,000	1,800,000	3,150,000
2017	710,000	129,220,000	1,800,000	2,934,000
2018	750,000	138,750,000	1,760,000	3,168,000
2019	750,000	135,750,000	1,700,000	3,230,000
2020	735,000	134,505,000	1,350,000	2,430,000
2021	730,000	132,860,000	NA	NA

NA = not available

Source: "1985 Texas Livestock, Dairy and Poultry Statistics", USDA Bulletin 235, June 1986. "Texas Agricultural Facts" Annual Summary, Crop and Livestock Reporting Service, various years, "1993 Texas Livestock Statistics", Texas Agricultural Statistics Service, Bulletin 252, August 1994; "Texas Agricultural Statistics, 2009", October 2010, "Texas Ag Fact", February and March 2011; Texas Sheep and Wool report, January 29, 2021, Agricultural Prices, February 26, 2021, NASS/TASS Quick Stats.

Though data for the all-goat inventory is limited, the goatherd consists of Angora goats for mohair production. Angora goats totaled 61,000 as of January 1, 2021; 75,000 as of 2020; and 75,000 as of January 1, 2019.

Mohair production during 2020 totaled 340,000 pounds. This compares with 470,000 in 2019 and 465,000 pounds in 2018. Average price per pound in 2020 was $7.20 from 61,000 goats clipped for a total value of $2.4 million. In 2019, producers received $8.00 per pound from 75,000 goats clipped for a total value of $3.8 million. In 2018, producers received $7.20 per pound from 75,000 goats clipped for a total value of $3.3 million.

Over half of the world's mohair and 54 percent of the U.S. clipped are produced in Texas.

Mohair nanny with her newborn. Photo by Guy E. Connolly, courtesy of the National Wildlife Research Center/Wikimedia Commons

Horses

Nationally, Texas ranks as one of the leading states in horse numbers and is the headquarters for many national horse organizations. The largest single breed registry in America, the American Quarter Horse Association, has its headquarters in Amarillo. The National Cutting Horse Association and the American Paint Horse Association are both located in Fort Worth. In addition to these national associations, Texas also has active state associations that include Palominos, Arabians, Thoroughbreds, Appaloosas, and ponies.

Horses are still used to support the state's giant beef cattle and sheep industries. However, the largest horse numbers within the state are near urban and suburban areas where they are mostly used for recreational activities. Horses are most abundant in the heavily populated areas of the state. State participation activities consist of horse shows, trail rides, play days, rodeos, polo and horse racing. Residential subdivisions have been developed within the state to provide facilities for urban and suburban horse owners.

Goats and Mohair 1980–2021

Year	Goats		Angora Goats		Mohair	
	Number	Farm Value ($)	Number	Value ($)	Production (lbs)	Value ($)
1980	1,400,000	$64,400,000	NA	NA	8,800,000	$30,800,000
1981	1,380,000	53,130,000	NA	NA	10,100,000	35,350,000
1982	1,410,000	57,810,000	NA	NA	10,000,000	25,500,000
1983	1,420,000	53,250,000	NA	NA	10,600,000	42,930,000
1984	1,450,000	82,215,000	NA	NA	10,600,000	48,160,000
1985	1,590,000	76,797,000	NA	NA	13,300,000	45,885,000
1986	1,770,000	70,977,000	NA	NA	16,000,000	40,160,000
1987	1,780,000	82,592,000	NA	NA	16,200,000	42,606,000
1988	1,800,000	108,180,000	NA	NA	15,400,000	29,876,000
1989	1,850,000	100,270,000	NA	NA	15,400,000	24,794,000
1990	1,900,000	93,100,000	NA	NA	14,500,000	13,775,000
1991	1,830,000	73,200,000	NA	NA	14,800,000	19,388,000
1992	2,000,000	84,000,000	1,620,000	NA	14,200,000	12,354,000
1993	1,960,000	84,280,000	1,560,000	NA	13,490,000	11,197,000
1994	1,960,000	74,480,000	1,490,000	NA	11,680,000	30,602,000
1995	1,850,000	81,400,000	1,250,000	NA	11,319,000	20,940,000
1996	1,900,000	89,300,000	1,250,000	NA	7,490,000	14,606,000
1997	1,650,000	70,950,000	1,000,000	NA	6,384,000	14,556,000
1998	1,400,000	71,400,000	750,000	NA	4,650,000	12,044,000
1999	1,350,000	71,550,000	550,000	NA	2,550,000	9,384,000
2000	1,300,000	74,100,000	370,000	NA	2,346,000	10,088,000
2001	1,400,000	105,000,000	300,000	NA	1,716,000	3,775,000
2002	1,250,000	106,250,000	250,000	NA	1,944,000	3,110,400
2003	1,200,000	110,400,000	240,000	NA	1,680,000	2,856,000
2004	1,200,000	115,200,000	210,000	$13,860,000	1,620,000	3,402,000
2005	1,270,000	138,430,000	190,000	14,070,000	1,250,000	3,750,000
2006	1,310,000	137,388,000	178,000	15,200,000	1,100,000	4,400,000
2007	1,300,000	147,552,000	159,000	14,220,000	960,000	3,840,000
2008	1,185,000	120,870,000	134,000	11,250,000	820,000	3,116,000
2009	1,090,000	129,920,000	120,000	10,080,000	700,000	2,170,000
2010	1,020,000	$108,290,000	100,000	7,500,000	730,000	3,066,000
2011	980,000	NA	110,000	11,000,000	530,000	2,703,000
2012	905,000	NA	85,000	7,565,000	470,000	2,256,000
2013	872,000	NA	74,000	9,028,000	490,000	2,695,000
2014	906,000	NA	76,000	9,196,000	580,000	3,654,000
2015	908,000	NA	83,000	12,035,000	480,000	3,408,000
2016	865,000	NA	78,000	10,140,000	510,000	3,060,000
2017	892,000	NA	80,000	12,000,000	470,000	3,102,000
2018	869,000	NA	75,000	9,750,000	465,000	3,348,000
2019	842,000	NA	75,000	10,500,000	470,000	3,760,000
2020	869,000	NA	75,000	10,500,000	340,000	$2,448,000
2021	827,000	NA	61,000	$7,320,000	NA	NA

NA = Not Available

Source:"1985 Texas Livestock, Dairy and Poultry Statistics", USDA Bulletin 235, June 1986. "Texas Agricultural Facts", Crop and Livestock Reporting Service, various years; "1993 Texas Livestock Statistics", Texas Agricultural Statistics Service, Bulletin 252, August 1994; "Texas Agricultural Statistics, 2009", October 2010; "Texas Ag Facts", February and March 2011. USDA/TASS Texas Goat and Mohair, January 29, 2021; NASS Quick Stats.

Appendix

TEXAS OBITUARIES

PRONUNCIATION GUIDE

INDEX OF ENTRIES

Carol M. Highsmith and Rowdy, the mascot for the Dallas Cowboys, having fun in the endzone.
Photo by Carol M. Highsmith, courtesy of the Library of Congress/Wikimedia Commons

Obituaries: August 2019 – July 2021

Akers, Fred, 82; head coached the University of Texas at Austin football team from 1977–1986, including coaching Earl Campbell the year he won his Heisman Trophy; also coached at University of Wyoming (1975–1976) and Purdue (1987–1990) and ended his career with a record of 108–75–3; Arkansas native, moved to Horseshoe Bay in 2008; at his home in Horseshoe Bay, December 7, 2020.

Bass, Anne, 78; investor, documentary filmmaker, and philanthropist; directed *Dancing Across Borders* (2010) about a girl from Cambodia attending the School of American Ballet and becoming a professional dancer; native Hoosier rescued the Texas Ballet Theater from bankruptcy and supported the Modern Art Museum of Fort Worth and the Van Cliburn Foundation, among others; in New York City, April 1, 2020.

Benson, Cedric, 36; All-American running back for the Texas Longhorns and fourth overall pick in the NFL draft in 2005; Midland native's professional career highlights include rushing 1,000+ yards for three seasons back-to-back with the Cincinnati Bengals; ended his career after a Lisfranc injury in 2012; in Austin, August 17, 2019.

Brooks, David Owen, 65; one of a trio of men who committed what became known as the Houston Mass Murders from 1970–1973, when they abducted, tortured, raped, and murdered at least 28 young men and boys; although not the ringleader, he was found guilty and sentenced to 99 years in prison; in a hospital in Galveston, May 28, 2020.

Cochran, Cathy, 76; judge on the Texas Court of Criminal Appeals appointed by Governor Rick Perry in 2001 until retirement in 2014; earlier in her career, as Director of Criminal Justice for Governor George W. Bush, organized a committee that completely rewrote the Texas Code of Criminal Procedure; in Wimberley, February 7, 2021.

Cockrell, Lila, 97; two-time mayor of San Antonio and the second woman in the U.S. to be mayor of a major city; served four terms overall (1975-1981, 1989-1991), and inducted into the Texas Women's Hall of Fame in 1984; native of Fort Worth was denied a vote by the Texas voter ID laws in the 2019 San Antonio mayoral election when she went to the polls without the proscribed identification but was able to cast her vote two days later; in San Antonio, August 29, 2019.

Davis, Mac, 78; country music singer, songwriter, and native of Lubbock wrote several songs recorded by Elvis Presley including "A Little Less Conversation" and "In the Ghetto"; hosted the NBC television variety series *The Mac Davis Show* in the 1970s and played Will Rogers on Broadway; member of both the Nashville Songwriters Hall of Fame and the National Songwriters Hall of Fame; in Nashville, September 29, 2020.

Detmer, Hubert "Sonny," 76; legendary high school football coach amassed a record of 235-141-2 and many district titles over 35 seasons; coached his two sons, one a Heisman winner, and later his grandsons — all quarterbacks; in San Antonio, September 22, 2020.

Donley, Manuel "Cowboy," 92; pioneer of Tejano music; born in Mexico, his family moved to Austin when he was seven; played trumpet, alto saxophone, and Spanish, electric, and requinto guitars; formed Las Estrellas in 1955, which toured Texas and the Midwest for 20 years; inducted into Tejano Music Hall of Fame in 1986; in Austin, on June 28, 2020.

Edwards, David, 48; former point guard at Texas A&M, 1991-1994; native Virginian led the Aggies to first postseason tournament in the 90s in his senior year while totaling 256 assists (third best in the country); graduated as school record holder in assists (602) and steals (228); in New York, March 23, 2020.

Emmett, Andre, 37; Dallas-born professional basketball player, played four years at Texas Tech for Coach Bobby Knight; drafted in 2004 by Seattle then traded that night to the Memphis Grizzlies but played only 8 games that season; played for D-league and international teams, including the Austin Toros, Liège Basket (Belgium), and Shandong Lions (China); in Dallas, September 23, 2019.

English, Paul, 87; drummer for Willie Nelson inspired the song "Me and Paul"; described as "tough and flamboyant," the Vernon native joined the band in 1966 and also served as an unofficial bodyguard for Nelson; became a board member for Farm Aid in 1985 and held the office of treasurer for many years; on February 11, 2020.

Floyd, George Perry Jr., 46; his murder by a police officer in Minnesota sparked worldwide protests of police brutality against Blacks; his last words, "I can't breathe," became a rally for the protesters; grew up in Houston and laid to rest in Pearland; in Minneapolis, May 25, 2020.

Freeman, Dr. Thomas F., 100; lecturer and debate coach at TSU, and minister at Mount Horem Baptist Church in Houston; native Virginian coached his student debaters to multiple national and international titles; famous students included Representative Barbara Jordan and Dr. Martin Luther King, Jr.; received the Phoenix Award from the Congressional Black Caucus Foundation for "his profound influence on our nation as a legendary educator and prolific scholar"; in Houston, June 6, 2020.

George, Phyllis Ann, 70; crowned Miss Texas in 1970 and Miss America 1971 before her career as a sports reporter and news anchor for CBS; one of the first women to feature prominently in televised sports when she co-hosted live pregame shows for NFL games; later the Denton native founded the Kentucky Museum of Arts and Crafts and sold a Phyllis George Beauty line of cosmetics on HSN; in Kentucky, May 14, 2020.

Goodacre, Glenna, 80; sculptor from Lubbock, best known for designing the obverse of the Sacagawea dollar and the Vietnam

Left to right: Tejano musican Manuel "Cowboy" Donley, photo by Tom Pich, public domain; Country musician Mac Davis performing at the Alabama Music Hall of Fame 2010, photo by Carol M. Highsmith, public domain; Running back Cedric Benson playing for the Cincinnati Bengals, photo by Denverjeffrey, CC3.

Left to right: Specialist Vanessa Guillen, U.S. Army photo; Artist and musician Daniel Johnston, photo by Rich Jones, CC 2; Second baseman and broadcaster Joe Morgan , photo courtesy of the George Bush Presidential Library and Museum.

Women's Memorial; awarded the Texas Medal of Arts and inducted into the National Cowgirl Museum and Hall of Fame, both in 2003; in New Mexico, April 13, 2020.

Guillen, Vanessa, 20; U.S. Army soldier murdered in an armory at Fort Hood whose body was found buried in countryside more than two months later, focusing national attention on sexual harassment in the military; born and raised in Houston, trained as a 91F, small arms and artillery repairer; at Fort Hood, April 22, 2020.

Harris, Franklyn Allen "Tex," 81; discovered and exposed human rights abuses as a U.S. diplomat in Argentina; reported some 13,500 human rights violations at the risk of his life and career; grew up in Dallas, where he was an all-state basketball player; in Virginia, on February 23, 2020.

Holub, Emil Joseph "E.J.," 81; played center and linebacker for Texas Technical College (now Texas Tech) and professionally in the AFL and NFL; native of Schulenburg raised in Lubbock was drafted sixth overall in 1961 by the Dallas Texans (later the Kansas City Chiefs); with the AFL, was the first player to start on both offense and defense in more than one Super Bowl and the only player to start two Super Bowls at two different positions; inducted into the Kansas City Chiefs Hall of Fame (1976), the Texas Tech Hall of Fame (1977) and the National Football Foundation's College Hall of Fame (1986); in Midland, September 21, 2019.

Jalomo, Valentin, 81; Astros superfan known for his elaborately quaffed mustache and customary seat in left-center field; grew up in Taft and moved to Houston where he worked as a bilingual teacher at Houston ISD until retirement in 2002; in Houston, January 19, 2021.

Johnston, Daniel Dale, 58; cult-favorite singer-songwriter and visual artist; subject of the documentary *The Devil and Daniel Johnston* (2006) that explored his struggles with mental illness; created the famous "Hi, How Are You?" mural in Austin; at his home in Waller, September 11, 2019.

Knight, Shirley, 83; award-winning actress, including three Emmys and a Tony, never stopped working; native Kansan started in classic TV shows and nominated for Oscars for *The Dark at the Top of the Stairs* (1960) and *Sweet Bird of Youth* (1962); in later years helped build the Texas State University musical theater program to national prominence; at her daughter's San Marcos home, April 22, 2020.

Loyd, Nikki Araguz, 44; California-born author, speaker, and same-sex-marriage activist; after her husband, a sheriff's deputy and firefighter, was killed in a fire in 2010, her in-laws refused to allow her to see her stepchildren and filed two lawsuits to have the marriage annulled and to take away her firefighter's spousal benefits; a judge annulled the marriage in 2011 but she continued to fight, eventually having her marriage ruled legal in 2015; at home in Humble, November 6, 2019.

Lopez, Trinidad "Trini" III, 83; singer and guitarist, his debut album, *Trini Lopez at PJs*, sold more than a million copies and earned a gold disc; designed two guitars for Gibson in 1964 that are prized by collectors; also did some acting, including a role in *The Dirty Dozen* (1967); grew up in Dallas but started his career in Wichita Falls; in California, August 11, 2020.

Marion, Anne, 81; president of Burnett Ranches in West Texas since 1980, including the 6666 Ranch; Fort Worth native kept the Four Sixes ahead of the pack in land stewardship and breeding and has been recognized by the AQHA, the National Cowgirl Museum, and the Texas Cowboy Hall of Fame; started the Burnett Oil Company and served as chairman of the Fort Worth Chamber of Commerce; in California, February 11, 2020.

McAlester, Virginia Savage, 76; architectural historian and Dallas native, wrote *A Field Guide to American Houses*, which was named in the top ten outstanding reference books in 1984 by the American Library Association; helped found Preservation Dallas to conserve historic buildings and areas in the city; in Dallas, April 9, 2020.

McMurtry, Larry Jeff, 84; novelist and screenwriter born in Archer City, his works were mostly set in the Old West or contemporary Texas; won the Pulitzer Prize in 1985 for *Lonesome Dove*, which was adapted into a TV miniseries that won seven Emmy awards; wrote the adapted screenplay for *Brokeback Mountain* (2005) with cowriter Diana Ossana, for which they won the Academy Award for Best Adapted Screenplay; as president of the nonprofit PEN America in 1989, testified before the U.S. Congress against an immigration law that denied entry to foreign writers based on ideological differences; in Archer City, March 25, 2021.

McNally, Terrence, 81; decorated playwright with a six-decade long career; won his first Tony for *Kiss of the Spider Woman*; lived in Corpus Christi as a child, where his father owned a Schlitz distributorship; much later, wrote the controversial play *Corpus Christi*, in which Jesus and his disciples are homosexuals; in Florida, March 24, 2020.

Mobley, William Hodges, 78; former president of Texas A&M University and former chancellor of The Texas A&M University System; Ohio native promoted diversity and athletic integrity and expanded international opportunities for both

Left to right:Actress Shirley Knight, 1963 press photo; Musician Trini Lopez, photo courtesy the Dutch National Archives, CC ; Playwright Terrence McNally, Photo by ReadingRead43, CC4

students and faculty; later helped develop executive talent for corporations and academic institutions while living in Hong Kong and Shanghai; in Austin, March 25, 2020.

Moffett, Jim Bob, 82; Houston-raised oilman and philanthropist; played football at the University of Texas under coach Darrell Royal and became a major UT donor after finding success in oil; his New Orleans-based company's international operations drew intense criticism; a plan to develop land near the Barton Creek aquifer in Austin inspired activists to create the Save Our Spring Alliance and ultimately went to the U.S. Supreme Court, where the company lost; in Austin, January 8, 2021.

Morgan, Joe, 77; second baseman and member of the Big Red Machine at Cincinnati Reds; played with the Houston Colt .45s/ Houston Astros, from 1963 to 1971 and again in 1980; born in Bonham before moving with his family to California; two-time National League MVP, 10-time All Star, won the Golden Glove 5 times; voted into the Baseball Hall of Fame in 1990; after retirement he gained acclaim as a broadcaster; at home in Danville, California, October 11, 2020.

Nash, Johnny, 80; best known for 1972 hit "I Can See Clearly Now," the Houston native also sang reggae and recorded an album in Kingston, Jamaica; got his start singing covers on local television show *Matinee*; his master tapes were among those destroyed in a fire at Universal Studios in 2008; in Houston, October 6, 2020.

Neal, Frederick "Curly," 77; featured ball handler for the Harlem Globetrotters; played in more than 6,000 games in 97 countries over his 22-year career; became the fifth Globetrotter to have his jersey (22) retired in 2008; averaged 23.1 points per game as a college player in his native North Carolina; at his home in Houston, March 26, 2020.

Ohlendorf, Norbert Kurt "Dutch," 87; "Junction Boy" who survived a brutal and dangerous football camp in Bear Bryant's first year as coach at Texas A&M; enrolled from Lockhart to study mechanics and earned a walk-on spot on the football team as a sophomore in 1951; served in the Army after graduation, then became a teacher, advancing to area superintendent; continued to teach in retirement, this time as a college lecturer; in Bryan, March 11, 2020.

Pickens, Thomas "T" Boone, Jr., 91; Oklahoma-born businessman and billionaire, well-known for his oil holdings and, later, support of alternative energy sources; announced the Pickens Plan in 2008, an energy proposal that aimed to move the U.S. away from OPEC sources of energy and toward domestic sources of natural gas, and wind and solar power; at his home in Dallas, September 11, 2019.

Pride, Charley, 86; country singer and professional baseball player; a native of Mississippi, along with his brother Mack pitched for several teams in the Negro American League in the 1950s until he was drafted into the army; returned to baseball but soon became more famous for his voice; won almost every major award possible for a country musician; part-owner of the Texas Rangers and performed the national anthem at games; in Dallas, December 12, 2020.

Left to right: Country stars Charley Pride (photo by Greg Mathison, public domain) and Kenny Rogers (photo by John Mathew Smith & www.celebrity-photos.com CC 2)

Puga, Genoveva, 92; migrant farm worker who became a civil rights activist fighting citrus company Donna Fruit for worker's compensation for son's wife and child after her son, Juan Torrez, died while performing his job; after winning the case, worked to bring the same justice to other farm workers through the courts; a statute ending worker's compensation exclusion for contractors signed into law 1984; at her home in Alamo, November 22, 2020.

Reavley, Thomas, 99; served on the U.S. Court of Appeals for the Fifth Circuit from 1979 until his death in 2020; born in Quitman; drove President Franklin Roosevelt to a meeting with Winston Churchill and Joseph Stalin during Yalta Conference while serving as a lieutenant in the U.S. Navy; was Texas Secretary of State 1955-1957, state Supreme Court justice 1968-1977; in Houston, December 1, 2020.

Reid, Jan, 75; journalist and author of more than a dozen books; came to prominence writing for *Texas Monthly*, where his byline first appeared in 1973; grew up playing football and baseball in Wichita Falls; survived a shooting in 1998 and plagued by ill health; wrote both fiction and nonfiction, about history, politics, crime, sports, and occasionally music; in Austin, September 19, 2020.

Robinson, Charles P. "Charlie," 75; actor best known for playing "Mac" in the sitcom *Night Court*; native of Houston and member of the Actors Studio; performed theater in Houston before moving to Hollywood; returned to theater in 2010 and performed iconic roles including Willy Loman; in California, July 11, 2021.

Rogers, Kenneth Ray "Kenny," 81; beloved singer, songwriter, musician, and record producer born and raised in Houston; first began recording "teenage rock" in the 1950s, then became a country star; signature song "The Gambler" was a crossover hit in 1978 and won a Grammy in 1980; starred in the made-for-TV movie based on the song, as well as many other TV roles; at his home in Georgia, March 20, 2020.

Sessions, William S., 90; federal judge, appointed FBI director in 1987 by President Reagan; many associate him with the phrase "Winners Don't Use Drugs," which was included on all imported arcade games by law; the native Arkansan and Baylor graduate encouraged the FBI to develop a strong DNA program and automate the national fingerprinting process, reducing fingerprint search times from months to hours; attracted heavy criticism for the deadly

Left to right: Globetrotter Frederick "Curly" Neal, U.S Air Force photo by Airman First Class Brad Smith; Billionaire T. Boone Pickens, photo by David Shankbone, CC 3

Left to right: First baseman/outfielder Jimmy Wynn, photo by by Gary P Smith, CC 2; Artist Bob "Daddy-O" Wade, photo by Mbcoats, CC 4; Musician Billy Joe Shaver, photo by Giovanni Gallucci, www.LiveLoudTexas.com CC 2

confrontation with the Branch Davidians near Waco in 1993 and was dismissed by President Clinton later that year; in San Antonio, June 12, 2020.

Shaver, Billy Joe, 81; country music pioneer known for "Honky Tonk Heroes" and "Live Forever"; born in Corsicana where he lived with his mother and grandmother; worked as a songwriter in Nashville where he earned $50 a week; released debut album, *Old Five and Dimers Like Me*, in 1973; Willie Nelson called him the greatest living songwriter; in Waco, October 28, 2020.

Solinger, Johnny, 55; singer-songwriter and lead vocalist for Skid Row from 1999 to 2015; loved both rock and country music as a boy in the Dallas-Fort Worth area; released a solo country album in 2008; on June 26, 2021.

Solomon, Jimmie Lee, 64; attorney in Washington, D.C. hired by Major League Baseball; started in minor league relations, worked up the ladder to executive vice president of baseball development; grew up in Fort Bend County and played sports at Lamar Consolidated High School; attended Harvard Law after he was cut by the Oilers during training camp; at his home in Houston, October 8, 2020.

Stearns, Eldrewey, 89; civil rights activist, led demonstrations and sit-ins to desegregate Houston while attending law school at Texas Southern University; Galveston native won victories but no acclaim by imposing local media blackouts and once canceling a protest in exchange for integration of restaurants and theaters; in Texas City, December 23, 2020.

Villaronga, Raúl G., 82; Vietnam War veteran and first Puerto Rican mayor of Killeen for three terms (1992-1998); after serving 26 years, retired from the U.S. Army as a colonel in 1985 while stationed at Fort Hood; while mayor, negotiated an agreement with the Army to make Robert Gray Army Airfield in Fort Hood a Joint Use Airport, allowing more transportation to the area; in Killeen, March 20, 2021.

Wade, Bob "Daddy-O," 76; Austin-born artist raised in El Paso known for shaping the Texas Cosmic Cowboy counterculture in the 1970s; created outsized sculptures including the Lone Star Café Iguana, now displayed in the Fort Worth Zoo, and the World's Largest Cowboy Boots, which can be seen at the North Star Mall in San Antonio; also created hand-tinted photographs he published in two books; at home in Austin, December 23, 2019.

Walker, Jerry Jeff, 78; country and folk singer-songwriter known for "Mr. Bojangles"; born Ronald Clyde Crosby in New York state, he roamed the country playing music under stage names "Jerry Ferris" and "Jeff Walker" before adopting the current one; settled in Austin in 1970s and joined the outlaw country scene; continued writing and performing until diagnosed with throat cancer in 2017; in Austin, October 23, 2020.

Watson, Robert José "Bob," 74; professional baseball player and executive; signed by the Houston Astros in 1965 as an amateur free agent; the Californian nearly quit the game when faced with discrimination in the South while playing in the minors; played outfield and first base for the Astros from 1966-1978, then traded to the Red Sox; ended his career batting .295 with 184 home runs and 989 RBI; credited with hitting the one-millionth home run in major league history; in Houston, May 14, 2020.

White, James, 81; owner of the iconic Broken Spoke dance hall in Austin, along with his wife Annetta White and his two daughters; brought joy to patrons through food, drinks, and Texas Two-Steppin' to live bands since 1964; Austin native; in Austin, January 24, 2021.

Williams, Clayton, 88; Midland businessman who ran for Texas governor against State Treasurer Ann Richards in 1990; initially led in polls by 20 points but made ill-advised comments on the campaign trail and ultimately lost the race; continued in business, taking Clayton Williams Energy, Inc. public in 1993 and diversifying into ranching and real estate; in Midland on February 14, 2020.

Williams, Frank S., 87; retired police officer, as a patrol officer in 1963 was sent to question Lee Harvey Oswald in connection with the shooting death of fellow officer J.D. Tippit, unaware that Oswald was also wanted for the death of President John F. Kennedy the same day; later became a detective, then a sergeant before retiring from the Dallas Police Department in 1978; in Dallas, November 25, 2020.

Wilson, Pamela Francis, 65; Houston photographer and graphic designer; known for using rich lighting and saturated color in her portraits, and earned the reputation as "the Annie Leibovitz of Texas"; her work has been featured in advertising campaigns, corporate reports, and magazines; photographed six U.S. presidents and many celebrities; at home in Houston, July 18, 2020.

Wynn, Jimmy, 78; outfielder and home run-hitter for the Colt .45s and Houston Astros over 11 seasons; nicknamed "The Toy Cannon" for his short stature and long home runs; three-time All-Star, native Ohioan became the first player to hit a homer into the upper deck of the Astrodome; after retirement, returned to the Astros as a community outreach executive; in Houston, March 26, 2020.

Left to right: Musician Johnny Solinger, photo by P. Schwichtenberg, CC 3; FBI Director William S. Sessions, FBI photo

TEXAS ALMANAC PRONUNCIATION GUIDE

Texas' rich cultural diversity is reflected nowhere better than in the names of places. Standard pronunciation is used in many cases, but purely colloquial pronunciation often is used, too.

In the late 1940s, George Mitchel Stokes, a graduate student at Baylor University, developed a list of pronunciations of 2,300 place names across the state. Stokes earned his doctorate and eventually was the director of the speech division in the communications studies department at Baylor University. He retired in 1983.

In the following list based on Stokes' longer list, pronunciation is by respelling and diacritical marking. Respelling is employed as follows: "ah" as in the exclamation, ah, or the "o" in tot; "ee" as in meet; "oo" as in moot; "yoo" as in use; "ow" as in cow; "oi" as in oil; "uh" as in mud.

Note that ah, uh and the apostrophe(') are used for varying degrees of neutral vowel sounds, the apostrophe being used where the vowel is barely sounded. Diacritical markings are used as follows: bāle, băd, lĕt, rīse, rĭll, ōak, brōōd, fŏŏt.

The stressed syllable is capitalized. Secondary stress is indicated by an underline as in Atascosa — ăt uhs KŌ suh.

A

Abbott — Ă buht
Abernathy — Ă ber nă thĭ
Abilene — ĂB uh leen
Acala — uh KĀ luh
Ackerly — ĂK er lĭ
Acme — ĂK mĭ
Acton — ĂK t'n
Acuff — Ā kuhf
Adamsville — Ă d'mz vĭl
Addicks — Ă dĭks
Addielou — ă dĭ LŌŌ
Addison — A di s'n
Adkins — ĂT kĭnz
Adrian — Ā drĭ uhn
Afton — ĂF t'n
Agua Dulce — ah wuh DŌŌL sĭ
Agua Nueva — ah wuh nyōō Ā vuh
Aiken — Ā kĭn
Alamo — ĂL uh mō
Alamo Heights — ăl uh mō HĪTS
Alanreed — ĂL uhn reed
Alba — ĂL buh
Albany — AWL buh nĭ
Albert — ĂL bert
Aledo — uh LEE dō
Alexander — ĕl ĭg ZĂN der
Alfred — ĂL frĕd
Algoa — ăl GŌ uh
Alice — Ă lĭs
Alief — Ā leef
Allen — Ă lĭn
Allenfarm — ălĭn FAHRM
Alleyton — Ă lĭ t'n
Allison — ĂL uh s'n
Alma — AHL muh
Alpine — ĂL pīn
Altair — awl TĂR
Alto — ĂL tō
Altoga — ăl TŌ guh
Alvarado — ăl vuh RĀ dō
Alvin — ĂL vĭn
Alvord — ĂL vord
Amarillo — ăm uh RĬL ō
Amherst — AM herst
Ammannsville — ĂM 'nz vĭl
Anahuac — ĂN uh wăk
Anderson — ĂN der s'n
Andice — ĂN dīs
Andrews — ĂN drōōz
Angelina — ăn juh LEE nuh
Angleton — ĂNG g'l t'n
Anna — ĂN uh
Annona — ă NŌ nuh
Anson — ĂN s'n
Antelope — ĂNT uh lōp
Anton — ĂNT n
Appleby — Ă p'l bĭ
Apple Springs — ă p'l SPRĬNGZ
Aquilla — uh KWĬL uh
Aransas — uh RĂN zuhs
Aransas Pass — uh răn zuhs PĂS
Arbala — ahr BĀ luh
Arcadia — ahr KĀ dĭ uh
Archer — AHR cher
Archer City — ahr cher SĬT ĭ
Arcola — ahr KŌ luh
Argo — AHR gō
Argyle — ahr GĪL
Arlington — AHR lĭng t'n
Arneckeville — AHR nĭ kĭ vĭl
Arnett — AHR nĭt
Arp — ahrp
Artesia Wells — ahr tee zh' WĔLZ
Arthur City — ahr ther SĬT ĭ
Asherton — ĂSH er t'n
Aspermont — ĂS per mahnt
Atascosa — ăt uhs KŌ suh
Athens — Ă thĕnz
Atlanta — ăt LĂN tuh
Atlas — ĂT l's
Attoyac — AT uh yăk
Aubrey — AW brĭ
Augusta — aw GUHS tuh
Austin — AWS t'n
Austonio — aws TŌ nĭ ō
Austwell — AWS wĕl
Avalon — ĂV uhl n
Avery — Ā vuh rĭ
Avinger — Ă vĭn jer
Avoca — uh VŌ kuh
Axtell — ĂKS t'l
Azle — Ā z'l

B

Bagwell — BĂG w'l
Bailey — BĀ lĭ
Baileyboro — BĀ lĭ ber ruh
Baileyville — BĀ lĭ vĭl
Baird — bârd
Bakersfield — BĀ kers feeld
Balch Springs — bawlch or bawlk SPRĬNGZ
Ballinger — BĂL ĭn jer
Balmorhea — băl muh RĀ
Bandera — băn DĔR uh
Bangs — băngz
Banquete — băn KĔ tĭ
Barclay — BAHRK lĭ
Bardwell — BAHRD w'l
Barker — BAHR ker
Barksdale — BAHRKS dāl
Barnhart — BAHRN hahrt
Barnum — BAHR n'm
Barry — BĂ rĭ
Barstow — BAHRS tō
Bartlett — BAHRT lĭt
Bassett — BĂ sĭt
Bastrop — BĂS trahp
Batesville — BĀTS v'l
Batson — BĂT s'n
Baxter — BĂKS ter
Bay City — ba SĬT ĭ
Baylor — BĀ ler
Bayside — BĀ sīd
Baytown — BĀ town
Beasley — BEEZ lĭ
Beaukiss — bō KĬS
Beaumont — BŌ mahnt
Bebe — bee bee
Beckville — BĔK v'l
Becton — BĔK t'n
Bedias — BEE dīs
Bee — bee
Beehouse — BEE hows
Beeville — BEE vĭl
Belcherville — BĔL cher vĭl
Bell — bĕl
Bellaire — bĕl ĂR
Bellevue — BĔL vyōō

Diacritical markings are used as follows: bāle, băd, lĕt, rīse, rĭll, ōak, brōōd, fŏŏt. The stressed syllable is capitalized. Secondary stress is indicated by an underline as in Atascosa — ăt uhs KŌ suh.

A mural of local landmarks in Breckenridge. Photo by Kairos14, CC by SA 4.0/Wikimedia Commons

Bellmead — bĕl MEED
Bells — bĕlz
Bellville — BĔL vĭl
Belmont — BĔL mahnt
Belton — BĔL t'n
Ben Arnold — bĕn AHR n'ld
Benavides — bĕn uh VEE d's
Ben Bolt — bĕn BŌLT
Benbrook — BĬN bro͝ok
Benchley — BĔNCH lĭ
Bend — bĕnd
Ben Franklin — bĕn FRĂNGk lĭn
Ben Hur — bĕn HER
Benjamin — BĔN juh m'n
Bennett — BĔN ĭt
Bentonville — BĔNT n vĭl
Ben Wheeler — bĭn HWEE ler
Berclair — ber KLĂR
Bertram — BERT r'm
Bessmay — bĕs MĀ
Best — bĕst
Bettie — BĔT ĭ
Bexar — BA är or băr
Beyersville — BĪRZ vĭl
Biardstown — BĂRDZ t'n
Bigfoot — BĬG fo͝ot
Big Lake — bĭg LĀK
Big Sandy — bĭg SĂN dĭ
Big Spring — bĭg SPRĬNG
Big Wells — bĭg WĔLZ
Birdville — BERD vĭl
Birome — bī RŌM
Birthright — BERTH rīt
Bishop — BĬ sh'p
Bivins — BĬ vĭnz
Black — blăk
Blackfoot — BLĂK fo͝ot
Blackwell — BLĂK w'l
Blair — blăr
Blanchard — BLĂN cherd
Blanco — BLĂNG kō
Blanket — BLĂNG kĭt
Bleakwood — BLEEK wo͝od
Bledsoe — BLĔD sō
Blessing — BLĔ sĭng
Blewett — BLO͞O ĭt
Blooming Grove — blo͞o mĭng GRŌV
Bloomington — BLO͞OM ĭng t'n
Blossom — BLAH s'm
Blue Grove — blo͞o GRŌV
Blue Ridge — blo͞o RĬJ
Bluff Dale — BLUHF dāl
Bluffton — BLUHF t'n
Blum — bluhm
Boerne — BER nĭ
Bogata — buh GŌ duh
Boling — BŌL ĭng
Bolivar — BAH lĭ ver
Bomarton — BŌ mer t'n
Bonham — BAH n'm
Bonita — bō NEE tuh
Bonney — BAH nĭ
Bonus — BŌ n's
Bon Wier — bahn WEER
Booker — BO͝O ker
Boonsville — BO͞ONZ vĭl
Booth — bo͞oth
Borden — BAWRD n
Borger — BŌR ger
Bosque — BAHS kĭ
Boston — BAWS t'n
Bovina — bō VEE nuh
Bowie — BO͞O Ĭ
Boxelder — bahks ĔL der
Boyce — bawĭs
Boyd — boĭd
Brachfield — BRĂCH feeld
Bracken — BRĂ kĭn
Brackettville — BRĂ kĭt vĭl
Bradford — BRĂD ferd
Bradshaw — BRĂD shaw
Brady — BRĀ dĭ
Brandon — BRĂN d'n
Brashear — bruh SHĬR
Brazoria — bruh ZŌ rĭ uh
Brazos — BRĂZ uhs
Breckenridge — BRĔK uhn rĭj
Bremond — bree MAHND
Brenham — BRĔ n'm
Brewster — BRO͞O ster
Brice — brīs
Bridgeport — BRĬJ pōrt
Briggs — brĭgz
Briscoe — BRĬS kō
Britton — BRĬT n
Broaddus — BRAW d's
Brock — brahk
Bronson — BRAHN s'n
Bronte — brahnt
Brookeland — BRO͝OK l'nd
Brookesmith — BRO͝OK smith
Brooks — bro͝oks
Brookshire — BRO͝OK sher
Brookston — BRO͝OKS t'n
Brown — brown
Browndel — brown DĔL
Brownfield — BROWN feeld
Brownsboro — BROWNZ buh ruh
Brownsville — BROWNZ vĭl
Brownwood — BROWN wo͝od
Bruceville — BRO͞OS v'l
Brundage — BRUHN dĭj
Bruni — BRO͞O nĭ
Brushy Creek — bruh shĭ KREEK
Bryan — BRĪ uhn
Bryans Mill — brī 'nz MĬL

Diacritical markings are used as follows: bāle, băd, lĕt, rīse, rĭll, ōak, bro͞od, fo͝ot. The stressed syllable is capitalized. Secondary stress is indicated by an underline as in Atascosa — ăt uhs KŌ suh.

Bryarly — BRĪ er lĭ
Bryson — BRĪ s'n
Buchanan Dam — buhk hăn uhn DĂM
Buckholts — BUHK hōlts
Buckhorn — BUHK hawrn
Buda — BYO͞O duh
Buena Vista — bwā nuh VEES tuh
Buffalo — BUHF uh lō
Buffalo Gap — buhf uh lō GĂP
Buffalo Springs — buhf uh lō SPRĬNGZ
Bula — BYO͞O luh
Bullard — BO͝OL erd
Bulverde — bo͝ol VER dĭ
Buna — BYO͞O nuh
Burkburnett — berk ber NET
Burkett — BER kĭt
Burkeville — BERK vĭl
Burleson — BER luh s'n
Burlington — BER lĭng t'n
Burnet — BER nĕt
Burton — BERT n
Bushland — BO͝OSH l'nd
Bustamante — buhs tuh MAHN tĭ
Butler — BUHT ler
Byers — BĪ erz
Bynum — BĪ n'm
Byrd — berd

C

Cactus — KĂK t's
Caddo Mills — kă dō MĬLZ
Calallen — kăl ĂL ĭn
Calaveras — kăl uh VĔR's
Caldwell — KAHL wĕl
Calhoun — kăl HO͞ON
Call — kawl
Calliham — KĂL uh hăm
Callisburg — KĂ lĭs berg
Call Junction — kawl JUHNGK sh'n
Calvert — KĂL vert
Camden — KĂM dĭn
Cameron — KĂM uh r'n
Camilla — kuh MEEL yuh
Camp — kămp
Campbell — KĂM uhl
Campbellton — KĂM uhl t'n
Camp Wood — kămp WO͝OD
Canadian — kuh NĀ dĭ uhn
Candelaria — kăn duh LĔ rĭ uh
Canton — KĂNT n
Canyon — KĂN y'n
Caplen — KĂP lĭn
Caps — kăps
Caradan — KĂR uh dăn
Carbon — KAHR b'n
Carey — KĀ rĭ
Carlisle — KAHR lĭl
Carlsbad — KAHR uhlz băd
Carlton — KAHR uhl t'n
Carmine — kahr MEEN
Carmona — kahr MŌ nuh
Caro — KAH rō
Carrizo Springs — kuh ree zuh SPRĬNGZ
Carrollton — KĂR 'l t'n
Carson — KAHR s'n
Carthage — KAHR thĭj
Cash — kăsh
Cason — KĀ s'n
Cass — kăs
Castell — kăs TĔL
Castro — KĂS trō
Castroville — KĂS tro vĭl
Catarina — kăt uh REE nuh
Cat Spring — kăt SPRĬNG
Caviness — KĂ vĭ nĕs
Cayuga — kā YO͞O guh
Cedar Bayou — see der BĪ ō
Cedar Creek — see der KREEK
Cedar Hill — see der HĬL
Cedar Lake — see der LĀK
Cedar Lane — see der LĀN
Cedar Park — see der PAHRK
Cedar Valley — see der VA lĭ
Cee Vee — see VEE
Celeste — suh LĔST
Celina — suh LĪ nuh
Center — SENT er
Center City — sĕn ter SĬT ĭ
Center Point — sĕn ter POINT
Centerville — sĕn ter vĭl
Centralia — sĕn TRĀL yuh
Chalk — chawlk
Chalk Mountain — chawlk MOWNT n
Chambers — CHĀM berz
Chandler — CHĂND ler
Channelview — chăn uhl VYO͞O
Channing — CHĂN ĭng
Chapman Ranch — chăp m'n RĂNCH
Chappell Hill — chă p'l HĬL
Charco — CHAHR kō
Charleston — CHAHR uhls t'n
Charlie — CHAHR lĭ
Charlotte — SHAHR l't
Chatfield — CHĂT feeld
Cheapside — CHEEP sīd
Cheek — cheek
Cherokee — CHĔR uh kee
Chester — CHĔS ter
Chico — CHEE kō
Chicota — chĭ KŌ tuh
Childress — CHĬL drĕs
Chillicothe — chĭl ĭ KAH thĭ
Chilton — CHĬL t'n
China — CHĪ nuh
China Spring — chī nuh SPRĬNG
Chireno — sh' REE nō
Chisholm — CHĬZ uhm
Chita — CHEE tuh
Chocolate Bayou — chah kuh lĭt BĪ ō
Choice — chois
Chriesman — KRĬS m'n
Christine — krĭs TEEN
Christoval — krĭs TŌ v'l
Cibolo — SEE bō lō
Circle Back — SER k'l băk
Circleville — SER k'l vĭl
Cisco — SĬS kō
Cistern — SĬS tern
Clairemont — KLĂR mahnt
Clairette — klăr ĭ ĔT
Clarendon — KLĂR ĭn d'n
Clareville — KLĂR vĭl
Clarksville — KLAHRKS vĭl
Clarkwood — KLAHRK wo͝od
Claude — klawd
Clawson — KLAW s'n
Clay — klā
Clayton — KLĀT n
Clear Lake — KLĬR lāk
Clear Spring — klĭr SPRĬNG
Cleburne — KLEE bern
Clemville — KLĔM vĭl
Cleveland — KLEEV l'nd
Clifton — KLĬF t'n
Cline — klīn
Clint — klĭnt
Clodine — klaw DEEN
Clute — klo͞ot
Clyde — klīd
Coahoma — kuh HŌ muh
Cockrell Hill — kahk ruhl HĬL
Coke — kōk
Coldspring — KŌLD sprĭng
Coleman — KŌL m'n
Colfax — KAHL făks
Collegeport — kah lĭj PŌRT
College Station — kah lĭj STĀ sh'n
Collin — KAH lĭn
Collingsworth — KAH lĭnz werth
Collinsville — KAH lĭnz vĭl
Colmesneil — KŌL m's neel
Colorado — kahl uh RAH dō
Colorado City — kah luh rā duh or kah luh rah duh SĬT ĭ
Columbus — kuh LUHM b's
Comal — KŌ măl
Comanche — kuh MĂN chĭ
Combes — kōmz
Comfort — KUHM fert
Commerce — KAH mers
Como — KŌ mō
Comstock — KAHM stahk
Concan — KAHN kăn
Concepcion — kuhn sep sĭ ŌN
Concho — KAHN chō
Concord — KAHN kawrd
Concrete — kahn KREET
Cone — kōn
Conlen — KAHN lĭn
Conroe — KAHN rō
Converse — KAHN vers
Conway — KAHN wā
Cooke — ko͝ok
Cookville — KO͝OK vĭl
Coolidge — KO͞O lĭj
Cooper — KO͞O per
Copeville — KŌP v'l
Coppell — kahp pĕl or kuhp PĔL
Copperas Cove — kahp ruhs KŌV
Corbett — KAWR bĭt

Diacritical markings are used as follows: bāle, băd, lĕt, rīse, rĭll, ōak, bro͞od, fo͝ot. The stressed syllable is capitalized. Secondary stress is indicated by an underline as in Atascosa — ăt uhs KŌ suh. TEXAS ALMANAC ©.

Cordele — kawr DĔL
Corinth — KAH rĭnth
Corley — KAWR lĭ
Corpus Christi — kawr p's KRĬS tĭ
Corrigan — KAWR uh g'n
Corsicana — kawr sĭ KĂN uh
Coryell — kō rĭ ĔL
Cost — kawst
Cottle — KAH t'l
Cotton Center — kaht n SĔNT er
Cotton Gin — KAHT n jĭn
Cottonwood — KAHT n wo͝od
Cotulla — kuh TO͞O luh
Coupland — KŌP l'n
Courtney — KŌRT nĭ
Covington — KUHV ĭng t'n
Coy City — koi SĬT ĭ
Craft — krăft
Crafton — KRĂF t'n
Crandall — KRĂN d'l
Crane — krān
Cranfills Gap — krăn f'lz GĂP
Crawford — KRAW ferd
Creedmoor — KREED mōr
Cresson — KRĔ s'n
Crisp — krĭsp
Crockett — KRAH kĭt
Crosby — KRAWZ bĭ
Crosbyton — KRAWZ bĭ t'n
Cross — kraws
Cross Cut — KRAWS kuht
Cross Plains — kraws PLĀNZ
Cross Roads — KRAWS rōdz
Crow — krō
Crowell — KRŌ uhl
Crowley — KROW li
Crystal City — krĭs t'l SĬT ĭ
Crystal Falls — krĭs t'l FAWLZ
Cuero — KWĔR o
Culberson — KUHL ber s'n
Cumby — KUHM bĭ
Cuney — KYO͞O nĭ
Cunningham — KUHN ĭng hăm
Currie — KER rĭ
Cushing — KO͞O shĭng
Cuthand — KUHT hănd
Cyclone — SĪ klōn
Cypress — SĪ prĕs

D

Dabney — DĂB nĭ
Dacosta — duh KAHS tuh
Dacus — DĂ k's
Daingerfield — DĀN jer feeld
Daisetta — dā ZĔT uh
Dalby Springs — dĂl bĭ SPRĬNGZ
Dale — dāl
Dalhart — DĂL hahrt
Dallam — DĂL uhm
Dallas — DĂ luhs
Damon — DĀ m'n
Danbury — DĂN bĕrĭ
Danciger — DĂN sĭ ger
Danevang — DĂN uh văng
Darrouzett — dăr uh ZĔT
Davilla — duh VĬL uh
Dawn — dawn
Dawson — DAW s'n
Dayton — DĀT n
Deadwood — DĔD wo͝od
Deaf Smith — dĕf SMĬTH
Deanville — DEEN vĭl
DeBerry — duh BĔ rĭ
Decatur — dee KĀT er
Deer Park — dĭr PAHRK
De Kalb — dĭ KĂB
De Leon — da lee AHN
Del Rio — dĕl REE ō
Delta — DĔL tuh
Del Valle — dĕl VĂ lĭ
Delwin — DĔL wĭn
Denhawken — DĬN haw kĭn
Denison — DĔN uh s'n
Denning — DĔN ĭng
Dennis — DĔ nĭs
Denton — DĔNT n
Denver City — dĕn ver SĬT ĭ
Deport — DEE pōrt or dĭ PŌRT
Derby — DER bĭ
Desdemona — dĕz dĭ MŌ nuh
DeSoto — dĭ SŌ tuh
Detroit — dee TROIT
Devers — DĔ vers
Devine — duh VĪN
Dew — dyo͞o
Deweyville — DYO͞O ĭ vĭl
DeWitt — dĭ WĬT
Dewville — DYO͞O vĭl
Dexter — DĔKS ter
D'Hanis — duh HĂ nĭs
Dialville — DĪ uhl vil
Diboll — DĪ bawl
Dickens — DĬK ĭnz
Dickinson — DĬK ĭn s'n
Dike — dĭk
Dilley — DĬL i
Dilworth — DĬL werth
Dimebox — dīm BAHKS
Dimmit — DĬM ĭt
Dinero — dĭ NĔ rō
Direct — duh RĔKT
Dixon — DĬK s'n
Dobbin — DAH bĭn
Dobrowolski — dah bruh WAHL skĭ
Dodd City — dahd SĬT ĭ
Dodge — DAH j
Dodson — DAHD s'n
Donie — DŌ nĭ
Donley — DAHN lĭ
Donna — dah nuh
Doole — DOO lĭ
Dorchester — dawr CHĔS ter
Doss — daws
Doucette — DO͞O sĕt
Dougherty — DAHR tĭ
Douglass — DUHG l's
Douglassville — DUHG lĭs vĭl
Downing — DOWN ĭng
Downsville — DOWNZ vĭl
Dozier — DŌ zher
Draw — draw
Driftwood — DRĬFT wo͝od
Dripping Springs — drĭp ĭng SPRĬNGZ
Driscoll — DRĬS k'l
Dryden — DRĪD n
Dublin — DUHB lĭn
Duffau — DUHF ō
Dumas — DO͞O m's
Dumont — DYO͞O mahnt
Dundee — DUHN dĭ
Dunlap — DUHN lăp
Dunlay — DUHN lĭ
Dunn — duhn
Durango — duh RĂNG gō
Duval — DO͞O vawl

E

Eagle — EE g'l
Eagle Lake — ee g'l LĀK
Eagle Pass — ee g'l PĂS
Earth — erth
East Bernard — eest ber NAHRD
Easterly — EES ter lĭ
Eastland — EEST l'nd
Easton — EES t'n
Ector — ĔK ter
Edcouch — ĕd KOWCH
Eddy — E di
Eden — EED n
Edge — ĕj
Edgewood — ĔJ wo͝od
Edinburg — ĔD n berg
Edmonson — ĔD m'n s'n
Edna — ED nuh
Edom — EE d'm
Edroy — ĔD roi
Edwards — ĔD werdz
Egan — EE g'n
Egypt — EE juhpt
Elbert — ĔL bert
El Campo — ĕl KĂM pō
Eldorado — ĕl duh RĀ duh
Electra — ĭ LĔK truh
Elgin — ĔL gĭn
Eliasville — ee LĪ uhs vĭl
El Indio — ĕl ĪN dĭ ō
Elkhart — ĔLK hahrt
Ellinger — ĔL ĭn jer
Elliott — ĔL ĭ 't
Ellis — ĔL uhs
Elmendorf — ĔLM 'n dawrf
Elm Mott — ĕl MAHT
Elmo — ĔL mō
Eloise — ĔL o eez
El Paso — ĕl PĂS ō
Elsa — ĔL suh
Elysian Fields — uh lee zh'n FEELDZ
Emhouse — ĔM hows
Emory — ĔM uh rĭ
Encinal — ĕn suh NAHL
Encino — ĕn SEE nō
Energy — ĔN er jĭ
Engle — ĔN g'l
English — ĬNG glĭsh

Diacritical markings are used as follows: bāle, băd, lĕt, rīse, rĭll, ōak, bro͞od, fo͝ot. The stressed syllable is capitalized. Secondary stress is indicated by an underline as in Atascosa — ăt uhs KŌ suh.

Enloe — ĔN lō
Ennis — ĔN ĭs
Enochs — EE nuhks
Eola — ee Ō luh
Era — EE ruh
Erath — EE răth
Esperanza — ĕs per RĂN zuh
Estelline — ĔS tuh leen
Etoile — ĭ TOIL
Etter — ĔT er
Eula — YO͞O luh
Euless — YO͞O lĭs
Eureka — yo͞o REE kuh
Eustace — YO͞OS t's
Evadale — EE vuh dāl
Evant — EE vănt
Evergreen — Ĕ ver green
Everman — Ĕ ver m'n

F

Fabens — FĀ b'nz
Fairbanks — FĂR bangks
Fairfield — FĂR feeld
Fairlie — FĂR lee
Fair Play — făr PLĀ
Fairview — FĂR vyo͞o
Fairy — FĀ rĭ
Falfurrias — făl FYO͞O rĭ uhs
Falls — fawlz
Falls City — fawlz SĬT ĭ
Fannett — fă NĔT
Fannin — FĂN ĭn
Fargo — FAHR gō
Farmers Branch — fahr merz BRĂNCH
Farmersville — FAHRM erz vĭl
Farnsworth — FAHRNZ werth
Farrar — FĂR uh
Farrsville — FAHRZ vĭl
Farwell — FAHR w'l
Fashing — FĂ shĭng
Fate — fāt
Fayette — fā ĔT
Fayetteville — FĀ uht vĭl
Fentress — FĔN trĭs
Ferris — FĔR ĭs
Field Creek — feeld KREEK
Fieldton — FEEL t'n
Fife — fīf
Fischer — FĬ sher
Fisher — FĬSH er
Fisk — fĭsk
Flagg — flăg
Flat — flăt
Flatonia — flă TŌN yuh
Flint — flĭnt
Flomot — FLŌ maht
Florence — FLAH ruhns
Floresville — FLŌRZ vil
Florey — FLŌ ri
Floyd — floid
Floydada — floi DĀ duh
Fluvanna — flo͞o VĂN uh
Flynn — flĭn
Foard — fōrd
Foard City — fōrd SĬT ĭ
Fodice — FŌ dĭs
Follett — fah LĔT
Fordtran — fōrd TRĂN
Forest — FAW rĕst
Forestburg — FAW rĕst berg
Forney — FAWR nĭ
Forreston — FAW rĕs t'n
Forsan — FŌR săn
Fort Bend — fōrt BĔND
Fort Chadbourne — fōrt CHĂD bern
Fort Davis — fōrt DĀ vĭs
Fort Griffin — fōrt GRĬF ĭn
Fort Hancock — fōrt HĂN kahk
Fort McKavett — fōrt muh KĂ vĕt
Fort Stockton — fōrt STAHK t'n
Fort Worth — fōrt WERTH
Fowlerton — FOW ler t'n
Francitas — frăn SEE t's
Franklin — FRĂNGK lĭn
Frankston — FRĂNGS t'n
Fred — frĕd
Fredericksburg — FRĔD er rĭks berg
Fredonia — free DŌN yuh
Freeport — FREE pōrt
Freer — FREE er
Freestone — FREE stōn
Frelsburg — FRĔLZ berg
Fresno — FRĔZ nō
Friday — FRĪ dĭ
Friendswood — FRĔNZ wo͝od
Frio — FREE ō
Friona — free Ō nuh
Frisco — FRĬS kō
Fritch — frĭch
Frost — frawst
Fruitland — FRO͞OT lănd
Fruitvale — FRO͞OT vāl
Frydek — FRĪ dĕk
Fulbright — FO͝OL brīt
Fulshear — FUHL sher
Fulton — FO͝OL t'n

G

Gail — gāl
Gaines — gānz
Gainesville — GĀNZ vuhl
Galena Park — guh lee nuh PAHRK
Gallatin — GĂL uh t'n
Galveston — GĂL vĕs t'n
Ganado — guh NĀ dō
Garceno — gahr SĀ nō
Garciasville — gahr SEE uhs vĭl
Garden City — GAHRD n sĭt ĭ
Gardendale — GAHRD n dāl
Garden Valley — gahrd n VĂ lĭ
Garland — GAHR l'nd
Garner — GAHR ner
Garrett — GĂR ĭt
Garrison — GĂ rĭ s'n
Garwood — GAHR wo͝od
Gary — GĔ rĭ
Garza — GAHR zuh
Gatesville — GĀTS vil
Gause — gawz
Gay Hill — gā HĬL
Geneva — juh NEE vuh
Georgetown — JAWRJ town
George West — jawrj WĔST
Geronimo — juh RAH nĭ mō
Giddings — GĬD ĭngz
Gillespie — guh LĔS pĭ
Gillett — juh LĔT
Gilliland — GĬL ĭ l'nd
Gilmer — GĬL mer
Ginger — JĬN jer
Girard — juh RAHRD
Girvin — GER vĭn
Gladewater — GLĀD wah ter
Glasscock — GLĂS kahk
Glazier — GLĀ zher
Glen Cove — glĕn KŌV
Glendale — GLĔN dāl
Glenfawn — glĕn FAWN
Glen Flora — glĕn FLŌ ruh
Glenn — glĕn
Glen Rose — GLĔN rōz
Glidden — GLĬD n
Gober — GŌ ber
Godley — GAHD lĭ
Golden — GŌL d'n
Goldfinch — GŌLD fĭnch
Goldsboro — GŌLZ buh ruh
Goldsmith — GŌL smith
Goldthwaite — GŌLTH wāt
Goliad — GŌ lĭ ăd
Golinda — gō LĬN duh
Gonzales — guhn ZAH l's
Goodland — GO͝OD l'n
Goodlett — GO͝OD lĕt
Goodnight — GO͝OD nīt
Goodrich — GO͝OD rĭch
Gordon — GAWRD n
Gordonville — GAWRD n vĭl
Goree — GŌ ree
Gorman — GAWR m'n
Gouldbusk — GO͝OLD buhsk
Graford — GRĀ ferd
Graham — GRĀ 'm
Granbury — GRĂN bĕ rĭ
Grandfalls — grănd FAWLZ
Grand Saline — grăn suh LEEN
Grandview — GRĂN vyo͞o
Granger — GRĀN jer
Grapeland — GRĀP l'nd
Grapevine — GRĀP vīn
Grassland — GRĂS l'nd
Grassyville — GRĂ sĭ vĭl
Gray — grā
Grayburg — GRĀ berg
Grayson — GRA s'n
Green — green
Greenville — GREEN v'l
Greenwood — GREEN wo͝od
Gregg — grĕg
Gregory — GRĔG uh rĭ
Grimes — grīmz
Groesbeck — GRŌZ bĕk
Groom — gro͞om
Groveton — GRŌV t'n

Diacritical markings are used as follows: bāle, băd, lĕt, rīse, rĭll, ōak, bro͞od, fo͝ot. The stressed syllable is capitalized. Secondary stress is indicated by an underline as in Atascosa — ăt uhs KŌ suh. TEXAS ALMANAC ©.

Grow — grō
Gruene — green
Grulla — GRO͞OL yuh
Gruver — GRO͞O ver
Guadalupe — <u>gwah</u> duh LO͞O pĭ or <u>gwah</u> duh LO͞O pā
Guerra — GWĔ ruh
Gunter — GUHN ter
Gustine — GUHS <u>teen</u>
Guthrie — GUHTH rĭ
Guy — gī

H

Hackberry — HĂK bĕ rĭ
Hagansport — HĀ gĭnz pōrt
Hainesville — HĀNZ v'l
Hale — hāl
Hale Center — <u>hāl</u> SĔNT er
Hall — hawl
Hallettsville — HĂL ĕts vĭl
Hallsville — HAWLZ vĭl
Hamilton — HĂM uhl t'n
Hamlin — HĂM lĭn
Hammond — HĂM 'nd
Hamon — HĂ m'n
Hamshire — HĂM sher
Handley — HĂND lĭ
Hankamer — HĂN kăm er
Hansford — HĂNZ ferd
Happy — HĂ pĭ
Hardeman — HAHR duh m'n
Hardin — HAHRD n
Hare — hăr
Hargill — HAHR gĭl
Harleton — HAHR <u>uhl</u> t'n
Harlingen — HAHR lĭn juhn
Harper — HAHR per
Harris — HĂ rĭs
Harrison — HĂ rĭ s'n
Harrold — HĂR 'ld
Hart — hahrt
Hartburg — HAHRT berg
Hartley — HAHRT lĭ
Harwood — HAHR wo͝od
Haskell — HĂS k'l
Haslam — HĂZ l'm
Haslet — HĂS lĕt
Hasse — HĂ sĭ
Hatchell — HĂ ch'l
Hawkins — HAW kĭnz
Hawley — HAW lĭ
Hays — hāz
Hearne — hern
Heath — heeth
Hebbronville — HĔB r'n vĭl
Hebron — HEE br'n
Hedley — HĔD lĭ
Heidenheimer — HĪD n hīmer
Helena — HĔL uh nuh
Helotes — hĕl Ō tĭs
Hemphill — HĔMP hĭl
Hempstead — HĔM stĕd
Henderson — HĔN der s'n
Henly — HĔN lĭ
Henrietta — hĕn rĭ Ĕ tuh
Hereford — HER ferd
Hermleigh — HER muh lee
Hewitt — HYO͞O ĭt
Hicks — hĭks
Hico — HĪ kō
Hidalgo — hĭ DĂL gō
Higgins — HĬ gĭnz
High — hī
Highbank — HĪ băngk
High Island — hī Ī l'nd
Highlands — HĪ l'ndz
Hightower — HĪ tow er
Hill — hĭl
Hillister — HĬL ĭs ter
Hillsboro — HĬLZ buh ruh
Hindes — hīndz
Hiram — HĪ r'm
Hitchcock — HĬCH kahk
Hitchland — HĬCH l'nd
Hobson — HAHB s'n
Hochheim — HŌ hīm
Hockley — HAHK lĭ
Holland — HAHL 'nd
Holliday — HAH luh dā
Hondo — HAHN dō
Honey Grove — HUHN ĭ grōv
Honey Island — <u>huhn</u> ĭ Ī l'nd
Honey Springs — <u>huhn</u> ĭ SPRĬNGZ
Hood — ho͝od
Hooks — ho͝oks
Hopkins — HAHP kĭnz
Houston — HYO͞OS t'n or YO͞OS t'n
Howard — HOW erd
Howe — how
Howland — HOW l'nd
Hubbard — HUH berd
Huckabay — HUHK uh bĭ
Hudspeth — HUHD sp'th
Huffman — HUHF m'n
Hufsmith — HUHF smĭth
Hughes Springs — hyo͞oz SPRĬNGZ
Hull — huhl
Humble — UHM b'l
Hungerford — HUHNG ger ferd
Hunt — huhnt
Hunter — HUHNT er
Huntington — HUHNT ĭng t'n
Huntsville — HUHNTS v'l
Hurlwood — HERL wo͝od
Hutchins — HUH chĭnz
Hutchinson — HUH chĭn s'n
Hutto — HUH tō
Hye — hī
Hylton — HĬL t'n

I

Iago — ī Ā gō
Idalou — Ī duh lo͞o
Imperial — <u>ĭm</u> PĬR ĭ uhl
Inadale — Ī nuh dāl
Independence — ĭn duh PĔN d'ns
Indian Creek — ĭn dĭ uhn KREEK
Indian Gap — ĭn dĭ uhn GĂP
Industry — ĬN duhs trĭ
Inez — ī NĔZ
Ingleside — ĬNG g'l sīd
Ingram — ĬNG gr'm
Iola — ī Ō luh
Iowa Park — ī uh wuh PAHRK
Ira — Ī ruh
Iraan — ī ruh ĂN
Iredell — Ī ruh dĕl
Ireland — Ī rĭ l'nd
Irene — ī REEN
Irion — ĬR i uhn
Ironton — ĪRN t'n
Irving — ER vĭng
Italy — ĬT uh lĭ
Itasca — ī TĂS kuh
Ivan — Ī v'n
Ivanhoe — Ī v'n hō

J

Jack — jăk
Jacksboro — JĂKS buh ruh
Jackson — JĂK s'n
Jacksonville — JĂK s'n vĭl
Jamestown — JĀMZ town
Jardin — JAHRD n
Jarrell — JĂR uhl
Jasper — JĂS per
Jayton — JĀT n
Jean — jeen
Jeddo — JĔ dō
Jeff Davis — <u>jĕf</u> DA vĭs
Jefferson — JĔF er s'n
Jericho — JĔ rĭ kō
Jermyn — JER m'n
Jewett — JO͞O ĭt
Jiba — HEE buh
Jim Hogg — jĭm HAWG
Jim Wells — jĭm WĔLZ
Joaquin — waw KEEN
Johnson — JAHN s'n
Johnson City — <u>jahn</u> s'n SĬT ĭ
Johntown — JAHN town
Johnsville — JAHNZ vĭl
Joinerville — JOI ner vĭl
Jolly — JAH lĭ
Jollyville — JAH lĭ vĭl
Jonah — JŌ nuh
Jones — jōnz
Jonesboro — JŌNZ <u>buh</u> ruh
Jonesville — JŌNZ vĭl
Josephine — JŌ suh <u>feen</u>
Joshua — JAH sh' wa
Jourdanton — JERD n t'n
Joy — joi
Joyce — jawĭs
Juliff — JO͞O lĭf
Junction — JUHNGK sh'n
Juno — JO͞O nō
Justiceburg — JUHS tĭs berg
Justin — JUHS tĭn

K

Kalgary — KĂL gĕ rĭ
Kamay — KĀ ĭm ā
Kanawha — KAHN uh wah

Diacritical markings are used as follows: bāle, băd, lĕt, rīse, rĭll, ōak, bro͞od, fo͝ot. The stressed syllable is capitalized. Secondary stress is indicated by an underline as in Atascosa — <u>ăt</u> uhs KŌ suh.

State Highway 97 passes through Jourdanton in Atascosa County. Photo by Billy Hathorn, CC 3/Wikimedia Commons

Karnack — KAHR năk
Karnes — kahrnz
Karnes City — kahrnz SĬT ĭ
Katemcy — kuh TĔM sĭ
Katy — KĀ tĭ
Kaufman — KAWF m'n
Keechi — KEE chī
Keene — keen
Kellerville — KĔL er vĭl
Kemah — KEE muh
Kemp — kĕmp or kĭmp
Kemp City — kĕmp SĬT ĭ
Kempner — KĔMP ner
Kendalia — kĕn DĀL yuh
Kenedy — KĔN uh dĭ
Kennard — kuh NAHRD
Kennedale — KĔN uh dāl
Kent — kĕnt
Kerens — KER 'nz
Kermit — KER mĭt
Kerr — ker
Kerrville — KER vĭl
Kildare — KĬL dăr
Kilgore — KĬL gōr
Killeen — kuh LEEN
Kimble — KĬM b'l
King — kĭng
Kingsbury — KĬNGZ bĕ rĭ
Kingsland — KĬNGZ l'nd
Kingsmill — kĭngz MĬL
Kingston — KĬNGZ t'n
Kingsville — KĬNGZ vĭl
Kinney — KĬN ĭ
Kirby — KER bĭ
Kirbyville — KER bĭ vĭl
Kirkland — KERK l'nd
Kirvin — KER vĭn

Kleberg — KLĀ berg
Klondike — KLAHN dīk
Knickerbocker — NĬK uh bah ker
Knippa — kuh NĬP uh
Knott — naht
Knox — nahks
Knox City — nahks SĬT ĭ
Kosciusko — kuh SHOO͞S kō
Kosse — KAH sĭ
Kountze — ko͞ontz
Kress — kres
Krum — kruhm
Kurten — KER t'n
Kyle — kīl

L

La Blanca — lah BLAHN kuh
La Coste — luh KAWST
Ladonia — luh DŌN yuh
LaFayette — lah fĭ ĔT
Laferia — luh FĔ rĭ uh
Lagarto — luh GAHR tō
La Gloria — lah GLŌ rĭ uh
La Grange — luh GRĀNJ
Laguna — luh GO͞O nuh
Laird Hill — lărd HĬL
La Joya — luh HŌ yuh
Lake Creek — lāk KREEK
Lake Dallas — lāk DĂL uhs
Lake Jackson — lāk JĂK s'n
Laketon — LĀK t'n
Lake Victor — lāk VĬK ter
Lakeview — LĀK vyo͞o
Lamar — luh MAHR
La Marque — luh MAHRK
Lamasco — luh MĂS kō

Lamb — lăm
Lamesa — luh MEE suh
Lamkin — LĂM kĭn
Lampasas — lăm PĂ s's
Lancaster — LĂNG k's ter
Laneville — LĀN vĭl
Langtry — LĂNG trĭ
Lanier — luh NĬR
La Paloma — lah puh LŌ muh
La Porte — luh PŌRT
La Pryor — luh PRĪ er
Laredo — luh RĀ dō
Lariat — LĂ ri uht
Larue — luh RO͞O
La Salle — luh SĂL
Lasara — luh SĔ ruh
Lassater — LĂ sĭ ter
Latch — lĂch
Latexo — luh TĔKS ō
Lavaca — luh VĂ kuh
La Vernia — luh VER nĭ uh
La Villa — lah VĬL uh
Lavon — luh VAHN
La Ward — luh WAWRD
Lawn — lawn
Lawrence — LAH r'ns
Lazbuddie — LĂZ buh dĭ
League City — leeg SĬT ĭ
Leakey — LĀ kĭ
Leander — lee ĂN der
Leary — LĬ er ĭ
Ledbetter — LĔD bĕt er
Lee — lee
Leesburg — LEEZ berg
Leesville — LEEZ vĭl
Lefors — lĭ FŌRZ
Leggett — LĔ gĭt

Diacritical markings are used as follows: bāle, băd, lĕt, rīse, rĭll, ōak, bro͞od, fo͝ot. The stressed syllable is capitalized. Secondary stress is indicated by an underline as in Atascosa — ăt uhs KŌ suh. TEXAS ALMANAC ©.

Leigh — lee
Lela — LEE luh
Lelia Lake — leel yuh LĀK
Leming — LĔ mĭng
Lenorah — lĕ NŌ ruh
Leo — LEE ō
Leon — lee AHN
Leona — lee Ō nuh
Leonard — LĔN erd
Leon Springs — lee ahn SPRĬNGZ
Leroy — LEE roi
Levelland — LĔ v'l lănd
Levita — luh VĪ tuh
Lewisville — LO͞O ĭs vĭl
Lexington — LĔKS ĭng t'n
Liberty — LĬB er tĭ
Liberty Hill — lĭ ber tĭ HĬL
Lillian — LĬL yuhn
Limestone — LĪM stōn
Lincoln — LĬNG k'n
Lindale — LĬN dāl
Linden — LĬN d'n
Lindenau — lĭn duh NOW
Lindsay — LĬN zĭ
Lingleville — LĬNG g'l vĭl
Linn — lĭn
Lipan — lī PĂN
Lipscomb — LĬPS k'm
Lissie — LĬ sĭ
Little Elm — lĭt l ĔLM
Littlefield — LĬT uhl feeld
Little River — lĭt uhl RĬV er
Live Oak — LĬV ōk
Liverpool — LĬ ver po͞ol
Livingston — LĬV ĭngz t'n
Llano — LĂ nō
Locker — LAH ker
Lockett — LAH kĭt
Lockhart — LAHK hahrt
Lockney — LAHK nĭ
Lodi — LŌ dī
Lohn — lahn
Lolita — lō LEE tuh
Loma Alto — lō muh ĂL tō
Lometa — lō MEE tuh
London — LUHN d'n
Lone Grove — lōn GRŌV
Lone Oak — LŌN ōk
Long Branch — lawng BRĂNCH
Long Mott — lawng MAHT
Longview — LAWNG vyo͞o
Longworth — LAWNG werth
Loop — lo͞op
Lopeno — lō PEE nō
Loraine — lō RĀN
Lorena — lō REE nuh
Los Angeles — laws AN juh l's
Los Ebanos — lōs ĔB uh nōs
Los Fresnos — lōs FRĔZ nōs
Los Indios — lōs ĬN dĭ ōs
Losoya — luh SAW yuh
Lott — laht
Louise — LO͞O eez
Lovelady — LUHV lā dĭ
Loving — LUH vĭng
Lowake — lō WĀ kĭ
Lubbock — LUH buhk or LUH b'k
Lueders — LO͞O derz
Luella — lo͞o ĔL uh
Lufkin — LUHF kĭn
Luling — LO͞O lĭng
Lund — luhnd
Lutie — LO͞O tĭ
Lyford — LĪ ferd
Lynn — lĭn
Lyons — LĪ 'nz
Lytton Springs — lĭt n SPRĬNGZ

M

Mabank — MĀ băngk
Macune — muh KO͞ON
Madison — MĂ dĭ s'n
Madisonville — MĂ duh s'n vĭl
Magnolia — măg NŌL yuh
Magnolia Springs — măg nol yuh SPRINGZ
Malakoff — MĂL uh kawf
Malone — muh LŌN
Malta — MAWL tuh
Manchaca — MĂN shăk
Manchester — MĂN chĕs ter
Manheim — MĂN hīm
Mankins — MĂN kĭnz
Manor — MĀ ner
Mansfield — MĂNZ feeld
Manvel — MĂN v'l
Maple — MĀ puhl
Marathon — MĂR uh th'n
Marble Falls — mahr b'l FAWLZ
Marfa — MAHR fuh
Margaret — MAHR guh rĭt
Marietta — mĕ rĭ Ĕ tuh
Marion — MĔ rĭ uhn
Markham — MAHR k'm
Marlin — MAHR lĭn
Marquez — mahr KĀ
Marshall — MAHR sh'l
Mart — mahrt
Martin — MAHRT n
Martindale — MAHRT n dāl
Martinsville — MAHRT nz vĭl
Maryneal — mā rĭ NEEL
Marysville — MĀ rĭz vĭl
Mason — MĀ s'n
Matador — MĂT uh dōr
Matagorda — măt uh GAWR duh
Mathis — MĂ thĭs
Maud — mawd
Mauriceville — maw REES vĭl
Maverick — MĂV rĭk
Maxey — MĂKS ĭ
Maxwell — MĂKS w'l
May — mā
Maydell — MĀ dĕl
Maypearl — mā PERL
Maysfield — MĀZ feeld
McAdoo — MĂK uh do͞o
McAllen — măk ĂL ĭn
McCamey — muh KĀ mĭ
McCaulley — muh KAW lĭ
McCoy — muh KOI
McCulloch — muh KUH luhk
McFaddin — măk FĂD n
McGregor — muh GRĔ ger
McKinney — muh KĬN ĭ
McLean — muh KLĀN
McLennan — muhk LĔN uhn
McLeod — măk LOWD
McMahan — măk MĂN
McMullen — măk MUHL ĭn
McNary — măk NĂ rĭ
McNeil — măk NEEL
McQueeney — muh KWEE nĭ
Meadow — MĔ dō
Medicine Mound — mĕd uhs n MOWND
Medill — mĕ DĬL
Medina — muh DEE nuh
Megargel — muh GAHR g'l
Melissa — muh LĬS uh
Melrose — MĔL rōz
Melvin — MĔL vĭn
Memphis — MĔM fĭs
Menard — muh NAHRD
Mendoza — mĕn DŌ zuh
Mentone — mĕn TŌN
Mercedes — mer SĀ deez
Mercury — MER kyuh ri
Mereta — muh RĔT uh
Meridian — muh RĬ dĭ uhn
Merit — MĔR ĭt
Merkel — MER k'l
Mertens — mer TĔNZ
Mertzon — MERTS n
Mesquite — muhs KEET
Mexia — muh HĀ uh
Meyersville — MĪRZ vĭl
Miami — mī ĂM uh or mī ĂM ĭ
Mico — MEE kō
Middleton — MĬD uhl t'n
Midfields — MĬD feeldz
Midland — MĬD l'nd
Midlothian — mĭd LŌ thĭ n
Midway — MĬD wā
Milam — MĪ l'm
Milano — mĭ LĂ nō
Mildred — MĬL drĕd
Miles — mīlz
Milford — MĬL ferd
Miller Grove — mĭl er GRŌV
Millersview — MĬL erz vyo͞o
Millett — MĬL ĭt
Millheim — MĬL hīm
Millican — MĬL uh kuhn
Mills — mĭlz
Millsap — MĬL săp
Minden — MĬN d'n
Mineola — mĭn ĭ Ō luh
Mineral — MĬN er uhl
Mineral Wells — mĭn er uhl WĔLZ
Minerva — mĭ NER vuh
Mingus — MĬNG guhs
Minter — MĬNT er
Mirando City — mĭ răn duh SĬT ĭ
Mission — MĬSH uhn
Mission Valley — mĭsh uhn VĂ lĭ
Missouri City — muh zo͞or uh SĬT ĭ

Diacritical markings are used as follows: bāle, băd, lĕt, rīse, rĭll, ōak, bro͞od, fo͝ot. The stressed syllable is capitalized. Secondary stress is indicated by an underline as in Atascosa — ăt uhs KŌ suh.

Mitchell — MĬ ch'l
Mobeetie — mō BEE tĭ
Moline — mō LEEN
Monahans — MAH nuh hănz
Monaville — MŌ nuh vĭl
Monkstown — MUHNGKS town
Monroe — MAHN rō
Monroe City — mahn rō SĬT ĭ
Montague — mahn TĀG
Montalba — mahnt ĂL buh
Mont Belvieu — mahnt BĔL vyōō
Montell — mahn TĔL
Montgomery — mahnt GUHM er ĭ
Monthalia — mahn THĀL yuh
Moody — MŎŎ dĭ
Moore — mōr
Morales — muh RAH lĕs
Moran — mō RĂN
Morgan — MAWR g'n
Morgan Mill — mawr g'n MĬL
Morse — mawrs
Morton — MAWRT n
Moscow — MAHS kow
Mosheim — MŌ shīm
Moss Bluff — maws BLUHF
Motley — MAHT lĭ
Moulton — MŌL t'n
Mound — mownd
Mountain Home — mownt n HŌM
Mount Calm — mownt KAHM
Mount Enterprise — mownt ĔN ter prīz
Mount Pleasant — mownt PLĔ z'nt
Mount Selman — mownt SĔL m'n
Mount Sylvan — mownt SĬL v'n
Mount Vernon — mownt VER n'n
Muenster — MYŎŎNS ter
Muldoon — muhl DŎŎN
Muleshoe — MYŎŎL shōō
Mullin — MUHL ĭn
Mumford — MUHM ferd
Munday — MUHN dĭ
Murchison — MER kuh s'n
Murphy — MER fĭ
Mykawa—mĭ KAH wuh
Myra — MĪ ruh
Myrtle Springs — mert l SPRĬNGZ

N

Nacogdoches — năk uh DŌ chĭs
Nada — NĀ duh
Naples — NĀ p'lz
Nash — năsh
Natalia — nuh TĂL yuh
Navarro — nuh VĂ rō
Navasota — năv uh SŌ tuh
Nazareth — NĂZ uh r'th
Neches — NĀ chĭs
Nederland — NEE der l'nd
Needville — NEED vĭl
Nelsonville — NĔL s'n vĭl
Neuville — NYŎŎ v'l
Nevada — nuh VĀ duh
Newark — NŎŎ erk
New Baden — nyōō BĀD n
New Berlin — nyōō BER lin
New Boston — nyōō BAWS t'n
New Braunfels — nyōō BRAHN f'ls or BROWN fĕlz
Newby — NYŎŎ bĭ
New Caney — nyōō KĀ nĭ
Newcastle — NYŎŎ kăs uhl
New Gulf — nyōō GUHLF
New Home — NYŎŎ hōm
New Hope — nyōō HŌP
Newlin — NYŎŎ lĭn
New London — nyōō LUHN d'n
Newman — NYŎŎ m'n
Newport — NYŎŎ pōrt
New Salem — nyōō SĀ l'm
Newsome — NYŎŎ s'm
New Summerfield — nyōō SUHM er feeld
Newton — NYŎŎT n
New Ulm — nyōō UHLM
New Waverly — nyōō WĀ ver lĭ
New Willard — nyōō WĬL erd
Nimrod — NĬM rahd
Nineveh — NĬN uh vuh
Nixon — NĬKS uhn
Nocona — nō KŌ nuh
Nolan — NŌ l'n
Nolanville — NŌ l'n vĭl
Nome — nōm
Noonday — NŎŎN dā
Nopal — NŌ păl
Nordheim — NAWRD hīm
Normandy — NAWR m'n dĭ
Normangee — NAWR m'n jee
Normanna — nawr MĂN uh
Northrup — NAWR thr'p
North Zulch — nawrth ZŎŎLCH
Norton — NAWRT n
Novice — NAH vĭs
Nueces — nyōō Ā sĭs
Nugent — NYŎŎ j'nt
Nursery — NER suh rĭ

O

Oakalla — ō KĂL uh
Oak Grove — ōk GRŌV
Oak Hill — ōk HĬL
Oakhurst — ŌK herst
Oakland — ŌK l'nd
Oakville — ŌK vĭl
Oakwood — ŌK wŏŏd
O'Brien — ō BRĪ uhn
Ochiltree — AH k'l tree
Odell — Ō dĕl or ō DĔL
Odem — Ō d'm
Odessa — ō DĔS uh
O'Donnell — ō DAH n'l
Oenaville — ō EEN uh v'l
Oglesby — Ō g'lz bĭ
Oilton — OIL t'n
Oklaunion — ōk luh YŎŎN y'n
Olden — ŌL d'n
Oldenburg — ŌL dĭn berg
Oldham — ŌL d'm
Old Glory — ōld GLŌ rĭ
Olivia — ō LĬV ĭ uh
Olmito — awl MEE tuh
Olmos Park — ahl m's PAHRK
Olney — AHL nĭ
Olton — ŌL t'n
Omaha — Ō muh haw
Omen — Ō mĭn
Onalaska — uhn uh LĂS kuh
Oplin — AHP lĭn
Orange — AHR ĭnj
Orangefield — AHR ĭnj feeld
Orange Grove — AHR ĭnj GRŌV
Orchard — AWR cherd
Ore City — ōr SĬT ĭ
Osceola — ō sĭ Ō luh
Otey — Ō tĭ
Otis Chalk — ō tĭs CHAWLK
Ottine — ah TEEN
Otto — AH tō
Ovalo — ō VĂL uh
Overton — Ō ver t'n
Owens — Ō ĭnz
Ozona — ō ZŌ nuh

P

Paducah — puh DYŎŎ kuh
Paige — pāj
Paint Rock — pānt RAHK
Palacios — puh LĂ sh's
Palestine — PAL uhs teen
Palito Blanco — p' lee to BLAHNG kō
Palmer — PAH mer
Palo Pinto — pă lō PĬN tō
Paluxy — puh LUHK sĭ
Pampa — PĂM puh
Pandora — păn DŌR uh
Panhandle — PĂN hăn d'l
Panna Maria — păn uh muh REE uh
Papalote — pah puh LŌ tĭ
Paradise — PĂR uh dīs
Paris — PĂ rĭs
Parker — PAHR ker
Parmer — PAH mer
Parnell — pahr NĔL
Parsley Hill — pahrs lĭ HĬL
Pasadena — păs uh DEE nuh
Patricia — puh TRĬ shuh
Patroon — puh TRŎŎN
Pattison — PĂT uh s'n
Pattonville — PĂT n vĭl
Pawnee — paw NEE
Paxton — PĂKS t'n
Peacock — PEE kahk
Pearl — perl
Pearland — PĂR lănd
Pearsall — PEER sawl
Peaster — PEES ter
Pecan Gap — pĭ kahn GĂP
Pecos — PĀ k's
Penelope — puh NĔL uh pĭ
Penitas — puh NEE t's
Pennington — PĔN ĭng t'n

Diacritical markings are used as follows: bāle, băd, lĕt, rīse, rĭll, ōak, brōōd, fŏŏt. The stressed syllable is capitalized. Secondary stress is indicated by an underline as in Atascosa — ăt uhs KŌ suh. TEXAS ALMANAC ©.

Penwell — PĬN wĕl
Peoria — pee Ō rĭ uh
Percilla — per SĬL uh
Perrin — PĔR ĭn
Perry — PĔ rĭ
Perryton — PĔ rĭ t'n
Peters — PEET erz
Petersburg — PEET erz berg
Petrolia — puh TRŌL yuh
Petteway — PĔT uh wā
Pettit — PĔT ĭt
Pettus — PĔT uhs
Petty — PĔT ĭ
Pflugerville — FLO͝O ger vĭl
Pharr — fahr
Phelps — fĕlps
Phillips — FĬL uhps
Pickton — PĬK t'n
Pidcoke — PĬD kōk
Piedmont — PEED mahnt
Pierce — PĬ ers
Pilot Point — pī l't POINT
Pine Forest — pīn FAW rĕst
Pine Hill — pīn HĬL
Pinehurst — PĪN herst
Pineland — PĪN land
Pine Mills — pīn MĬLZ
Pine Springs — pīn SPRĬNGZ
Pioneer — pī uh NĬR
Pipecreek — pīp KREEK
Pittsburg — PĬTS berg
Placedo — PLĂS ĭ dō
Placid — PLĂ sĭd
Plains — plānz
Plainview — PLĀN vyōō
Plano — PLĀ nō
Plantersville — PLĂN terz vĭl
Plaska — PLĂS kuh
Plateau — plă TŌ
Pleasant Grove—plĕ z'nt GRŌV
Pleasanton — PLĔZ uhn t'n
Pledger — PLĔ jer
Plum — pluhm
Point — point
Pointblank — pint BLĂNGK
Polk — pōlk
Pollock — PAHL uhk
Ponder — PAHN der
Ponta — pahn TĀ
Pontotoc — PAHNT uh tahk
Poolville — PO͞OL vĭl
Port Aransas — pōrt uh RĂN zuhs
Port Arthur — pōrt AHR ther
Port Bolivar — pōrt BAH lĭ ver
Porter Springs — pōr ter SPRĬNGZ
Port Isabel — pōrt ĬZ uh bĕl
Portland — PŌRT l'nd
Port Lavaca — pōrt luh VĂ kuh
Port Neches — pōrt NĀ chĭs
Port O'Connor — pōrt ō KAH ner
Posey — PŌ zĭ
Post — pōst
Postoak — PŌST ōk
Poteet — pō TEET
Poth — pōth
Potosi — puh TŌ sĭ
Potter — PAHT er
Pottsboro — PAHTS buh ruh
Pottsville — PAHTS vĭl
Powderly — POW der lĭ
Powell — POW w'l
Poynor — POI ner
Prairie Dell — prĕr ĭ DĔL
Prairie Hill — prĕr ĭ HĬL
Prairie Lea — prĕr ĭ LEE
Prairie View — prĕr ĭ VYO͞O
Prairieville — PRĔR ĭ vĭl
Premont — PREE mahnt
Presidio — pruh SĬ dĭ ō
Priddy — PRĬ dĭ
Primera — pree MĔ ruh
Princeton — PRĬNS t'n
Pritchett — PRĬ chĭt
Proctor — PRAHK ter
Progreso — prō GRĔ sō
Prosper — PRAHS per
Purdon — PERD n
Purley — PER lĭ
Purmela — per MEE luh
Putnam — PUHT n'm
Pyote — PĪ ōt

Q

Quail — kwāl
Quanah — KWAH nuh
Queen City — kween SĬT ĭ
Quemado — kuh MAH dō
Quihi — KWEE hee
Quinlan — KWĬN l'n
Quintana — kwĭn TAH nuh
Quitaque — KĬT uh kwa
Quitman — KWĬT m'n

R

Rainbow — RĀN bō
Rains — rānz
Ralls — rahlz
Randall — RĂN d'l
Randolph — RĂN dahlf
Ranger — RĀN jer
Rangerville — RĀN jer vĭl
Rankin — RĂNG kĭn
Ratcliff — RĂT klĭf
Ravenna — rĭ VĔN uh
Rayburn — RĀ bern
Raymondville — RĀ m'nd vĭl
Raywood — RĀ wo͝od
Reagan — RĀ g'n
Real — REE awl
Realitos — ree uh LEE t's
Redford — RĔD ferd
Red Oak — RĔD ōk
Red River — rĕd RĬ ver
Red Rock — rĕd RAHK
Red Springs — rĕd SPRĬNGZ
Red Water — RĔD wah ter
Reeves — reevz
Refugio — rĕ FYO͞O rĭ ō
Reilly Springs — rī lĭ SPRĬNGZ
Reklaw — RĔK law
Reno — REE nō
Rhineland — RĪN l'nd
Rhome — rōm
Rhonesboro — RŌNZ buh ruh
Ricardo — rĭ KAHR dō
Rice — rīs
Richards — RĬCH erdz
Richardson — RĬCH erd s'n
Richland — RĬCH l'nd
Richland Springs — rĭch l'nd SPRĬNGZ
Richmond — RĬCH m'nd
Ridge — rĭj
Ridgeway — RĬJ wā
Riesel — REE s'l
Ringgold — RĬNG gōld
Rio Frio — ree ō FREE ō
Rio Grande City — ree ō grahn dĭ or ree ō grăn SĬT ĭ
Rio Hondo — ree ō HAHN dō
Riomedina — ree ō muh DEE nuh
Rios — REE ōs
Rio Vista — ree ō VĬS tuh
Rising Star — rī zĭng STAHR
River Oaks — rĭ ver ŌKS
Riverside — RĬ ver sīd
Riviera — ruh VĬR uh
Roane — rōn
Roanoke — RŌN ōk or RŌ uh nōk
Roans Prairie — rōnz PRĔR Ĭ
Roaring Springs — rōr ĭng SPRĬNGZ
Robert Lee — rah bert LEE
Roberts — RAH berts
Robertson — RAH bert s'n
Robinson — RAH bĭn s'n
Robstown — RAHBZ town
Roby — RŌ bĭ
Rochelle — rō SHĔL
Rochester — RAH chĕs ter
Rockdale — RAHK dāl
Rock Island — rahk Ī l'nd
Rockland — RAHK l'nd
Rockport — rahk PŌRT
Rocksprings — rahk SPRĬNGZ
Rockwall — rahk WAWL
Rockwood — RAHK wo͝od
Roganville — RŌ g'n vĭl
Rogers — RAH jerz
Roma — RŌ muh
Romayor — rō MĀ er
Roosevelt — RŌ suh v'lt or RO͞O suh v'lt
Ropesville — RŌPS vĭl
Rosanky — rō ZĂNG kĭ
Roscoe — RAHS kō
Rosebud — RŌZ b'd
Rose Hill — rōz HĬL
Rosenberg — RŌZ n berg
Rosenthal — RŌZ uhn thawl
Rosewood — RŌZ wo͝od
Rosharon — rō SHĔ r'n

Diacritical markings are used as follows: bāle, băd, lĕt, rīse, rĭll, ōak, bro͞od, fo͝ot. The stressed syllable is capitalized. Secondary stress is indicated by an underline as in Atascosa — ăt uhs KŌ suh.

Rosita — rō SEE tuh
Ross — raws
Rosser — RAW ser
Rosston — RAWS t'n
Rossville — RAWS vĭl
Roswell — RAHZ w'l
Rotan — rō TĂN
Round Rock — ROWND rahk
Round Top — ROWN tahp
Rowena — rō EE nuh
Rowlett — ROW lĭt
Roxton — RAHKS t'n
Royalty — ROI uhl tĭ
Royse City — roi SĬT ĭ
Royston — ROIS t'n
Rugby — RUHG bĭ
Ruidosa — ree uh DŌ suh
Rule — ro͞ol
Runge — RUHNG ĭ
Runnels — RUHN 'lz
Rural Shade — ro͞or uhl SHĀD
Rusk — ruhsk
Rutersville — RO͞O ter vĭl
Rye — rī

S

Sabinal — SĂB uh năl
Sabine — suh BEEN
Sabine Pass — suh been PĂS
Sabinetown — suh been TOWN
Sachse — SĂK sĭ
Sacul — SĂ k'l
Sadler — SĂD ler
Sagerton — SĀ ger t'n
Saginaw — SĂ guh naw
Saint Jo — sānt JŌ
Saint Paul — sānt PAWL
Salado — suh LĀ dō
Salesville — SĀLZ vĭl
Salineno — suh LEEN yō
Salmon — SĂL m'n
Salt Gap — sawlt GĂP
Saltillo — săl TĬL ō
Samfordyce — săm FOR dis
Sample — SĂM p'l
Samnorwood — săm NAWR wo͝od
San Angelo — săn ĂN juh lō
San Antonio — săn ăn TŌ nĭ ō
San Augustine — săn AW g's teen
San Benito — săn buh NEE tuh
Sanderson — SĂN der s'n
Sandia — săn DEE uh
San Diego — săn dĭ Ā gō
Sandy Point — săn dĭ POINT
San Elizario — săn ĕl ĭ ZAH rĭ ō
San Felipe — săn fuh LEEP
Sanford — SĂN ferd
San Gabriel — săn GĀ brĭ uhl
Sanger — SĂNG er
San Jacinto — săn juh SĬN tuh or juh SĬN tō
San Juan — săn WAHN
San Marcos — săn MAHR k's
San Patricio — săn puh TRĬSH ĭ ō
San Perlita — săn per LEE tuh
San Saba — săn SĂ buh
Santa Anna — săn tuh ĂN uh
Santa Elena — săn tuh LEE nuh
Santa Maria — săn tuh muh REE uh
Santa Rosa — săn tuh RŌ suh
Santo — SĂN tō
San Ygnacio — săn ĭg NAH sĭ ō
Saragosa — sĕ ruh GŌ suh
Saratoga — sĕ ruh TŌ guh
Sargent — SAHR juhnt
Sarita — suh REE tuh
Saspamco — suh SPĂM kō
Satin — SĂT n
Savoy — suh VOI
Schattel — SHĂT uhl
Schertz — sherts
Schleicher — SHLĪ ker
Schroeder — SHRĀ der
Schulenburg — SHO͞O lĭn berg
Schwertner — SWERT ner
Scotland — SKAHT l'nd
Scottsville — SKAHTS vĭl
Scranton — SKRĂNT n
Scurry — SKUH rĭ
Scyene — sī EEN
Seabrook — SEE bro͝ok
Seadrift — SEE drĭft
Seagoville — SEE gō vĭl
Seagraves — SEE grāvz
Seale — seel
Sealy — SEE lĭ
Sebastopol — suh BĂS tuh po͞ol
Sebastian — suh BĂS tĭ 'n
Security — sĭ KYO͞OR ĭ tĭ
Segno — SĔG nō
Segovia — sĭ GŌ vĭ uh
Seguin — sĭ GEEN
Selfs — sĕlfs
Selma — SĔL muh
Seminole — SĔM uh nōl
Seymour — SEE mōr
Shackelford — SHĂK uhl ferd
Shady Grove — shā dĭ GRŌV
Shafter — SHĂF ter
Shallowater — SHĂL uh wah ter
Shamrock — SHĂM rahk
Shannon — SHĂN uhn
Sharp — shahrp
Sheffield — SHĔ feeld
Shelby — SHĔL bĭ
Shelbyville — SHĔL bĭ vĭl
Sheldon — SHĔL d'n
Shepherd — SHĔ perd
Sheridan — SHĔ rĭ dn
Sherman — SHER m'n
Sherwood — SHER wood
Shiner — SHĪ ner
Shiro — SHĪ rō
Shive — shīv
Sidney — SĬD nĭ
Sierra Blanca — sĭer ruh BLĂNG kuh
Siloam — suh LŌM
Silsbee — SĬLZ bĭ
Silver Lake — sĭl ver LĀK
Silverton — SĬL ver t'n
Silver Valley — sĭl ver VĂ lĭ
Simms — sĭmz
Simonton — SĪ m'n t'n
Singleton — SĬNG g'l t'n
Sinton — SĬNT n
Sipe Springs — SEEP sprĭngz
Sisterdale — SĬS ter dāl
Sivells Bend — sĭ v'lz BĔND
Skellytown — SKĔ lĭ town
Skidmore — SKĬD mōr
Slaton — SLĀT n
Slayden — SLĀD n
Slidell — slī DĔL
Slocum — SLŌ k'm
Smiley — SMĪ lĭ
Smith — smĭth
Smithfield — SMĬTH feeld
Smithland — SMĬTH l'nd
Smithson Valley — smĭth s'n VĂ lĭ
Smithville — SMĬTH vĭl
Smyer — SMĪ er
Snook — sno͝ok
Snyder — SNĪ der
Somerset — SUH mer sĕt
Somervell — SUH mer vĕl
Somerville — SUH mer vĭl
Sonora — suh NŌ ruh
Sour Lake — sowr LĀK
South Bend — sowth BĔND
South Bosque — sowth BAHS kĭ
South Houston — sowth HYO͞OS t'n
Southland — SOWTH l'nd
Southmayd — sowth MĀD
South Plains — sowth PLĀNZ
Spade — spād
Spanish Fort — spă nĭsh FŌRT
Sparenberg — SPĂR ĭn berg
Speaks — speeks
Spearman — SPĬR m'n
Spicewood — SPĪS wo͝od
Splendora — splĕn DŌ ruh
Spofford — SPAH ferd
Spring — sprĭng
Springdale — SPRĬNG dāl
Springlake — sprĭng LĀK
Springtown — SPRĬNG town
Spur — sper
Spurger — SPER ger
Stacy — STĀ sĭ
Stafford — STĂ ferd
Stamford — STĂM ferd
Stanton — STĂNT n
Staples — STĀ p'lz
Starr — stahr
Stephens — STEE vĕnz
Stephenville — STEEV n vĭl
Sterley — STER lĭ
Sterling — STER lĭng
Sterling City — ster lĭng SĬT ĭ
Stiles — stīlz
Stinnett — stĭ NĔT
Stockdale — STAHK dāl
Stoneburg — STŌN berg
Stoneham — STŌN uhm
Stone Point — stōn POINT

Diacritical markings are used as follows: bāle, băd, lĕt, rīse, rĭll, ōak, bro͞od, fo͝ot. The stressed syllable is capitalized. Secondary stress is indicated by an underline as in Atascosa — <u>ăt</u> uhs KŌ suh. TEXAS ALMANAC ©.

The watertower in Tenaha in Shelby County. Photo by Hourick, Public Domain/ Wikimedia Commons

Stonewall — STŌN wawl
Stout — stowt
Stowell — STO w'l
Stranger — STRĀN jer
Stratford — STRĂT ferd
Strawn — strawn
Streeter — STREET er
Streetman — STREET m'n
Study Butte — styo͞o dĭ BYO͞OT
Sublime — s'b LĪM
Sudan — SO͞O dăn
Sugar Land — SHO͝O ger lănd
Sullivan City — suh luh v'n SĬT ĭ
Sulphur Bluff — suhl fer BLUHF
Sulphur Springs — suhl fer SPRĬNGZ
Summerfield — SUHM er feeld
Sumner — SUHM ner
Sundown — SUHN down
Suniland — SUH nĭ lănd
Sunny Side — SUH nĭ sīd
Sunray — SUHN rā
Sunset — SUHN sĕt
Sutherland Springs — suh ther l'nd SPRĬNGZ
Sutton — SUHT n
Swan — swahn
Sweeny — SWEE nĭ
Sweet Home — sweet HŌM
Sweetwater — SWEET wah ter
Swenson — SWĔN s'n
Swift — swĭft
Swisher — SWĬ sher
Sylvester — sil VES ter

T

Taft — tăft
Tahoka — tuh HŌ kuh
Talco — TĂL kō
Talpa — TĂL puh
Tanglewood — TĂNG g`l wo͝od
Tankersley — TĂNG kers lĭ
Tarrant — TAR uhnt
Tarzan — TAHR z'n
Tascosa — tăs KŌ suh
Tatum — TĀ t'm
Tavener — TĂV uh ner
Taylor — TĀ ler
Teague — teeg
Tehuacana — tuh WAW kuh nuh
Telephone — TĔL uh fōn
Telferner — TĔLF ner
Tell — tĕl
Temple — TĔM p'l
Tenaha — TĔN uh haw
Tennyson — TĔN uh s'n
Terlingua — TER lĭng guh
Terrell — TĔR uhl
Terrell Hills — ter uhl HILZ
Terry — TĔR ĭ
Texarkana — tĕks ahr KĂN uh
Texas City — tĕks ĕz SĬT ĭ
Texhoma — tĕks Ō muh
Texline — TĔKS līn
Texon — tĕks AHN
Thalia — THĀL yuh
The Grove — th' GRŌV
Thicket — THĬ kĭt
Thomaston — TAHM uhs t'n
Thompsons — TAHMP s'nz
Thorndale — THAWRN dāl
Thornton — THAWRN t'n
Thorp Spring — thawrp SPRING
Thrall — thrawl
Three Rivers — three RĬ verz
Throckmorton — THRAHK mawrt n
Thurber — THER ber
Tilden — TĬL d'n
Timpson — TĬM s'n
Tioga — tī Ō guh
Titus — TĪT uhs
Tivoli — tī VŌ luh
Tokio — TŌ kĭ ō
Tolar — TŌ ler
Tolbert — TAHL bert
Tolosa — tuh LŌ suh
Tomball — TAHM bawl
Tom Bean — tahm BEEN
Tom Green — tahm GREEN
Tool — to͞ol
Topsey — TAHP sī
Tornillo — tawr NEE yō
Tow — tow
Toyah — TOI yuh
Toyahvale — TOI yuh vāl
Trawick — TRĀ wĭk
Travis — TRĂ vĭs
Trent — trĕnt
Trenton — TRĔNT n
Trickham — TRĬK uhm
Trinidad — TRĬN uh dăd
Trinity — TRĬN ĭ tĭ
Troup — tro͞op
Troy — TRAW ĭ
Truby — TRO͞O bĭ
Trumbull — TRUHM b'l
Truscott — TRUHS k't
Tucker — TUHK er
Tuleta — to͞o LEE tuh
Tulia — TO͞OL yuh
Tulsita — tuhl SEE tuh
Tundra — TUHN druh
Tunis — TO͞O nĭs
Turkey — TER kĭ
Turlington — TER lĭng t'n

Diacritical markings are used as follows: bāle, băd, lĕt, rīse, rĭll, ōak, bro͞od, fo͝ot. The stressed syllable is capitalized. Secondary stress is indicated by an underline as in Atascosa — ăt uhs KŌ suh.

Turnersville — TER nerz vĭl
Turnertown — TER ner town
Turney — TER nĭ
Tuscola — tuhs KŌ luh
Tuxedo — TUHKS ĭ dō
Twin Sisters — twĭn SĬS terz
Twitty — TWĬ tĭ
Tye — tī
Tyler — TĪ ler
Tynan — TĪ nuhn

U

Uhland — YŎŎ l'nd
Umbarger — UHM bahr ger
Union — YŎŎN y'n
Upshur — UHP sher
Upton — UHP t'n
Urbana — er BĀ nuh
Utley — YŎŎT lĭ
Utopia — yōō TŌ pĭ uh
Uvalde — yōō VĂL dĭ

V

Valdasta — văl DĂS tuh
Valentine — VĂL uhn tīn
Valera — vuh LĬ ruh
Valley Mills — vă lĭ MĬLZ
Valley Spring — vă lĭ SPRĬNG
Valley View — vă lĭ VYŎŎ
Van — văn
Van Alstyne — văn AWLZ teen
Vancourt — VĂN kōrt
Vanderbilt — VĂN der bĭlt
Vanderpool — VĂN der pōōl
Van Horn — văn hawrn
Van Vleck — văn VLĔK
Van Zandt — văn ZĂNT
Vashti — VĂSH tī
Vaughan — vawn
Vega — VĀ guh
Velasco — vuh LĂS kō
Venus — VEE n's
Vera — VĬ ruh
Veribest — VĔR ĭ bĕst
Verhalen — ver HĂ lĭn
Vernon — VER n'n
Vickery — VĬK er ĭ
Victoria — vĭk TŌ rĭ uh
Vidor — VĪ der
Vienna — vee ĔN uh
View — vyōō
Village Mills — vĭl ĭj MĬLZ
Vincent — VĬN s'nt
Vinegarone — vĭn er guh RŌN
Vineyard — VĬN yerd
Violet — VĪ ō lĕt
Voca — VŌ kuh
Von Ormy — vahn AHR mĭ
Voss — vaws
Votaw — VŌ taw

W

Waco — WĀ kō
Wadsworth — WAHDZ werth
Waelder — WĔL der
Waka — WAH kuh
Walberg — WAWL berg
Waldeck — WAWL dĕk
Walker — WAWL ker
Wall — wawl
Waller — WAW ler
Wallis — WAH lĭs
Wallisville — WAH lĭs vĭl
Walnut Springs — wawl n't SPRĬNGZ
Walton — WAWL t'n
Warda — WAWR duh
Ward — wawrd
Waring — WĂR ĭng
Warren — WAW rĭn
Warrenton — WAW rĭn t'n
Washburn — WAHSH bern
Washington — WAHSH ĭng t'n
Waskom — WAHS k'm
Wastella — wahs TĔL uh
Watauga — wuh TAW guh
Water Valley — wah ter VĂ lĭ
Waxahachie — wawks uh HĂ chĭ
Wayland — WĀ l'nd
Weatherford — WĔ ther ferd
Weaver — WEE ver
Webb — wĕb
Webberville — WĔ ber vĭl
Webster — WĔBS ter
Weches — WEE chĭz
Weesatche — WEE săch
Weimar — WĪ mer
Weinert — WĪ nert
Weir — weer
Welch — wĕlch
Welcome — WĔL k'm
Weldon — WĔL d'n
Wellborn — WĔL bern
Wellington — WĔL ĭng t'n
Wellman — WĔL m'n
Wells — wĕlz
Weser — WEE zer
Weslaco — WĔS luh kō
West — wĕst
Westbrook — WĔST brŏŏk
Westfield — WĔST feeld
Westhoff — WĔS tawf
Westminster — wĕst MĬN ster
Weston — WĔS t'n
Westover — WĔS tō ver
Westphalia — wĕst FĀL yuh
West Point — wĕst POINT
Wharton — HWAWRT n
Wheeler — HWEE ler
Wheelock — HWEE lahk
White Deer — HWĪT Deer
Whiteface — HWĪT fās
Whiteflat — hwīt FLĂT
Whitehouse — HWĪT hows
Whitesboro — HWĪTS buh ruh
Whitewright — HWĪT rīt
Whitharral — HWĬT hăr uhl
Whitney — HWĬT nĭ
Whitsett — HWĬT sĭt
Whitson — HWĬT s'n
Whitt — hwĭt
Whon — hwahn
Wichita — WĬCH ĭ taw
Wichita Falls — wĭch ĭ taw FAWLZ
Wickett — WĬ kĭt
Wiergate — WEER gāt
Wilbarger — WĬL bahr ger
Wildorado — wĭl duh RĀ dō
Willacy — WĬL uh sĭ
Williamson — WĬL yuhm s'n
Willis — WĬ lĭs
Wills Point — wĭlz POINT
Wilmer — WĬL mer
Wilson — WĬL s'n
Wimberley — WĬM ber lĭ
Winchester — WĬN ches ter
Windom — WĬN d'm
Windthorst — WĬN thr'st
Winfield — WĬN feeld
Wingate — WĬN gāt
Winkler — WĬNGK ler
Winnie — WĬ nĭ
Winnsboro — WĬNZ buh ruh
Winona — wī NŌ nuh
Winterhaven — WĬN ter hā v'n
Winters — WĬN terz
Wise — wīz
Wizard Wells — wĭ zerd WĔLZ
Woden — WŌD n
Wolfe City — wŏŏlf SĬT ĭ
Wolfforth — WŎŎL forth
Wood — wŏŏd
Woodbine — WŎŎD bīn
Woodlake — wŏŏd LĀK
Woodland — WŎŎD l'nd
Woodlawn — wŏŏd LAWN
Woodrow — WŎŎD rō
Woodsboro — WŎŎDZ buh ruh
Woodson — WŎŎD s'n
Woodville — WŎŎD v'l
Wortham — WERTH uhm
Wright City — rīt SĬT ĭ
Wrightsboro — RĪTS buh ruh
Wylie — WĪ lĭ

Y

Yancey — YĂN sĭ
Yantis — YĂN tĭs
Yoakum — YŌ k'm
Yorktown — YAWRK town
Young — yuhng
Youngsport — YUHNGZ pōrt
Ysleta — ĭs LĔT uh

Z

Zapata — zuh PAH tuh
Zavalla — zuh VĂL uh
Zephyr — ZĔF er
Zuehl — ZEE uhl

Diacritical markings are used as follows: bāle, băd, lĕt, rīse, rĭll, ōak, brōōd, fŏŏt. The stressed syllable is capitalized. Secondary stress is indicated by an underline as in Atascosa — ăt uhs KŌ suh. TEXAS ALMANAC ©.

ADVERTISER INDEX

GENERAL INDEX

- For cities and towns not listed in the index, see lists of towns on pages 385-412. For full information about cities, see "Cities and towns" entry in this index.
- For full information about counties, also look under the cities and towns in the county, as well as the "Counties" index entry.
- Page numbers in *italics* refer to photographs and artwork and their captions.

A

B

For CITIES and TOWNS not listed in the Index, see complete list on pages 385-412.

The Point Bolivar Lighthouse at Port Bolivar near Galveston. Photo by Jim Evans, CC by SA 4.0/ Wikimedia Commons

C

For CITIES and TOWNS not listed in the Index, see complete list on pages 385-412.

For CITIES and TOWNS not listed in the Index, see complete list on pages 385-412.

Dallas El Centro is the downtown campus of Dallas Community College. It opened its doors in 1966. Photo by Michael Barera, CC by SA 4.0/Wikimedia Commons

D

E

Feral hogs can be dangerous and problematic. Photo by USDA NRCS Texas

F

G

For CITIES and TOWNS not listed in the Index, see complete list on pages 385-412.

The rolling landscape of the Texas Hill Country. Photo by Zereshk, CC 3/Wikimedia Commons

For CITIES and TOWNS not listed in the Index, see complete list on pages 385-412.

LNG tanker passing Ingleside on the Bay through a channel into the Gulf of Mexico and beyond. Photo by Rosie Hatch

I

J

K

L

For CITIES and TOWNS not listed in the Index, see complete list on pages 385-412.

M

The lightning whelk is our state seashell. Photo by James St. John, CC 2/Flickr

For CITIES and TOWNS not listed in the Index, see complete list on pages 385-412.

N

For CITIES and TOWNS not listed in the Index, see complete list on pages 385-412.

O

P

An old oil pumpjack in West Texas. Photo by Jonathan Cutrer/jcutrer.com

For CITIES and TOWNS not listed in the Index, see complete list on pages 385-412.

The Western diamondback rattlesnake can reach lengths of up to seven feet. Photo by Peter Paplanus, CC 2/Flickr

Q

R

For CITIES and TOWNS not listed in the Index, see complete list on pages 385-412.

S

For CITIES and TOWNS not listed in the Index, see complete list on pages 385-412.

A blooming agave in a West Texas sunrise. Photo by Jonathan Cutrer, jcutrer.com

T

For CITIES and TOWNS not listed in the Index, see complete list on pages 385-412.

U

V

A waterlily in the pond at the International Waterlily Collection in San Angelo. Photo by Jason Trbovich, CC2/Flickr

W

For CITIES and TOWNS not listed in the Index, see complete list on pages 385-412.

Y

Z